LIZZIE BORDEN

DID SHE ?   OR   DIDN'T SHE ?

LIZZIE BORDEN , DID SHE? OR DIDN'T SHE?
Copyright © 1992 by Historical Briefs, Inc.
All rights reserved

Developed under agreement with **Historical Briefs, Inc.**,
Box 629, Sixth Street & Madalyn Ave., Verplanck, NY
10596.

Printed by:
Monument Printers & Lithographer, Inc.
Sixth Street & Madalyn Ave., Verplanck, NY   10596

FOREWORD

On Aug. 4, 1892, Andrew Jackson Borden and his wife, Abbie, were killed with a hatchet in their cramped Fall River home on Second Street. On June 21, 1893, in New Bedford Superior Court, Andrew Borden's daughter, Lizzie Andrew Borden, was found innocent of charges of killing her father and stepmother.

That acquittal has left two unsolved mysteries in its wake.

Who, if not Lizzie, killed the Fall River banker and his wife? And why, despite a century of wars, famines, epidemics and gruesome crimes beyond count that have left millions dead has this one double homicide in a New England mill town retained its fascination? Why, 100 years later, are criminologists, novelists, playwrights, composers, choreographers, judges, lawyers, scholars, sociologists and students of the media still interested in this century-old crime?

Why has the Lizzie Borden case been made the subject of more than 100 books and hundreds of articles, of plays, films, ballet, opera, Broadway musicals...every art form except sculpture?

An English bookseller specializing in crime recently reported his most-sought-after books are those dealing with the cases of Jack the Ripper and Lizzie Borden. The Ripper murders were committed in the slums of London in August 1888 when a serial killer or killers murdered and mutilated five prostitutes. Dubbed Jack the Ripper, the killer was never identified.

As with the Borden case, a steady stream of books, non-fiction and fiction including at least one Sherlock Holmes adventure written in the manner of Sir Arthur Conan Doyle, have offered solutions to the murderer's identity. Typical of these books on the Ripper is the latest non-fiction entry, "Murder and Madness; The Secret Life of Jack the Ripper," by David Abrahamsen, M. D. Dr. Abrahamsen is a forensic psychiatrist who worked as an expert witness in the "Son of Sam" David Berkowitz case, among many others. In his new book, the psychiatrist offers an identification of the Ripper...whom, he believes, were two men working together. His solution is dramatic, startling and will not be well received by the already beleaguered British royal family.

That ongoing fascination with Jack the Ripper explains, I think, the ongoing fascination with the Borden case:

Was Lizzie in the barn behind the house at the time of the murders as she claimed?

Was Bridget Sullivan, the Bordens' overworked Irish maid, telling the truth

when she said she was asleep in her attic room at the time of her murders?

Why are 10 pages of Bridget Sullivan's testimony missing from the transcript of the inquest?

What was Lizzie's real reason for trying to buy poison at a local drug store a few days before the murders?

Did John V. Morse, brother of Andrew Borden's first wife and uncle to Lizzie, quarrel with Andrew before the killings?

If Lizzie was innocent, how could she continue to live in the house after the killings...why wasn't she afraid the unknown killer might strike again?

Why, after her acquittal, did Lizzie shower Bridget Sullivan with gifts for herself and her family in Ireland including a free trip to Ireland..and, upon Bridget's return to the Untied States, get Bridget a job in distant Montana?

Was Lizzie driven to kill by the fear her father would give his property and money to Lizzie's despised stepmother?

Was Andrew Borden guilty of child abuse or incest with Lizzie that drove her to kill him...and, if so, why did she kill her stepmother first?

Did Lizzie, known to suffer from migraine headaches, suffer from a form of epilepsy which could cause brief, temporary, but total, lapses of memory during which the victim remains unaware of the lapse or what he or she might have done during that lapse?

Did Lizzie's defense lawyers deliberately choose a jury made up of rural residents of Bristol County on the grounds these rustics would be more reluctant to condemn a woman of Lizzie's social stature to the gallows...the mandatory penalty for persons found guilty of first-degree murder?

Will these questions ever be answered?

Until they are, the case of Lizzie Borden will continue to fascinate new generations.

By John H. Ackerman, Standard-Times feature writer

The Evening Standard.

ESTABLISHED FEBRUARY, 1850.

NEW BEDFORD, THUBSDAY, AUGUST 4, 1892.

TWO CENTS.

HASKELL & TRIPP.

Half-holiday. Store closes at 1 o'clock, FRIDAY, Aug. 5th.

The usual bargain sale will be in order. *We are making things hum Friday mornings.*

Come as early as you can. Everything is here at the opening hour and usually in fair quantities; but some people are doomed to disappointment, because they seem to think "there's plenty of time, you know," and do not feel pleased when they get in about noon and find the "cream" of the bargains has been gathered.

Friday Bargain No. 1.

Seventy pairs women's kid Oxfords, sizes 2½ to 7. Opera tip, common sense heel, as good a Summer shoe as is usually sold for $1 a pair.

For this day 50c.

Friday Bargain No. 2.

Two hundred yards of Wash Pongee Silks, Figured China Silks and Brocades. Formerly 50c., 75c. and $1.

For this day 29c. a yard.

Friday Bargain No. 3.

Eighty-four women's wrappers.

Yoke back and front, fine ruffle on edge of yoke, narrow plaited and "Watteau" backs. These wrappers are made from best quality prints and some light ground momie cloth. They are the end of a manufacturer's stock at the close of his season and we bought them so low that we can offer regular $1.50 and $2 wrappers

For this day 89c. each.

Friday Bargain No. 4.

Upholstery gallery.

Balance of head rests for chair backs, covered with imitation printed silks. Regular price 25c.

For this day 12½c. each.

Friday Bargain No. 5.

Upholstery gallery.

Lot of printed flannels for draperies, 36 inches wide, usually sold at 25c. a yard.

For this day 15c. a yard.

Friday Bargain No. 6.

One hundred knife and fork baskets, strongly made, with partitions and some with handles. Our usual price is 20c. and they are cheap at that.

For this day 10c. each.

Friday Bargain No. 7.

One thousand yards of staple Ginghams of good quality, in remnants of three to six yards, will be sold.

For this day 5c. a yard.

Friday Bargain No. 8.

Some soiled stamped linen tidies that have knotted fringes at both ends and have previously sold at 25c.

For this day 10c. each.

Friday Bargain No. 9.

Lot of chamber pails, with decorative paintings. Slightly marred. Large size formerly sold at 48c.

For this day 32c. each.

HASKELL & TRIPP.

Department Stores,

Purchase and William Streets.

HORRIBLE BUTCHERY.

Fall River the Scene of a Fiendish Atrocity.

Mr. and Mrs. Andrew J. Borden Murdered.

Their Heads Beaten and Battered With a Cleaver.

Found Lying in Pools of Life Blood in Their Home.

Police Have the Place Surrounded and Mystery Prevails.

[Special Dispatch.]

FALL RIVER, August 4.—Andrew J. Borden and wife were found murdered at their home, No. 92 Second street, at 11 o'clock to-day.

Borden was found on a sofa in one of the lower rooms, with his head horribly hacked, probably with a cleaver. Up stairs, Mrs. Borden was discovered face downward, on a bed, similarly butchered.

Mr. Borden was seen on the street about one hour before. At present writing it is impossible to get particulars, as the police have put a guard about the premises and will not allow newspaper men or any others to enter. The whole affair is shrouded in mystery.

Mr. Borden was one of the largest real estate owners in the city, a man of much wealth and a director in several manufacturing and financial institutions.

THE PEOPLE ON MARS.

If There are Any Prof. Holden of Lick Observatory Says They are Esquimaux.

LICK OBSERVATORY, Cal., Aug. 4.—Edward Holden, of the Lick observatory, said last night regarding the opposition of Mars: "We have replied to many inquiries received during the present opposition of Mars. These inquiries indicate widespread interest, but in many cases they appear to be based on misapprehension of the work now being done on the planet here and elsewhere. We are simply endeavoring to obtain more accurate information regarding the planet. That is all. Future opposition in which the planet will be seen at greater altitude will be more favorable even if the planet is then more distant for it will be nearer the zenith than now.

We also wish to know how nearly Mars resembles the earth and whether it is fit to be inhabited by beings like ourselves. It has been proposed by certain astronomers to determine this question. In my opinion the time has not come to speculate on this question. My reason for saying this is that I think it very doubtful if all the observations yet made are sufficient to enable us to pronounce even the lesser points we seek. There is very little doubt that by and by science will interpret all of the phenomena now seen, and will arrive at certainties. Just now only a few things are certainly known with respect to our nearest planetary neighbor. We are giving nearly all the time of our great telescope to this work. We have found great changes in details of surface, while the main outlines have remained much the same. These changes have seemed to be so great that it is often difficult to examine by terrestrial analogies. If there are people on Mars, I think they are Esquimaux. If the red areas are land and the dark ones water, we can discover great inundations which have taken place and might mention the fact that where are now two lakes there was only one in 1877. Sometime during next Autumn we shall have finished our observations.

It is very probable that we can draw some conclusions which are certain, and it is possible that considerable new light may be thrown on this problem. I think I am justified in saying that no more could have been done than has been done. If the results are not definite then there must be extreme difficulty in the problem at hand.

Observations in Austria.

VIENNA, Aug. 4.—In an interview had by the representative of the Associated Press at the observatory in Turkenschanze, in Vienna, with Assistant Astronomer Hildebrandt, the latter said that careful observations of the planet Mars were made from the nights of July 30 to that of Aug. 2 inclusive by Herr Palisa, the chief assistant astronomer, and himself. Owing to the proximity of the planet to the southern horizon, however, the result of the observation was unsatisfactory. The progress of the planet was watched for an hour. At a point 52 degrees above the horizon snow fields could be seen distinctly extending 30 degrees from the south pole. Immediately underneath this white patch three large dark groups were observable. "Perhaps," remarked Herr Hildebrandt, "they are continents like those of our earth." The haze which enveloped the lower part of Mars, however, rendered accurate observations impossible. The north pole and the equator were observed. These observations were taken at 1 30 a. m. with the largest telescope in Central Europe.

RUSSIAN STATE PAPERS.

Publication of Secret Reports in a Newspaper at Sofia.

LONDON, Aug. 4.—The Vienna correspondent of the *Standard* says: "Count Kalnoky, the Austro-Hungarian foreign minister, has gone to Ischl to confer with Emperor Francis Joseph in regard to the Russian state papers published in the *Svaboda* of Sofia, whereof every instalment outweighs in interest the preceding one. Yesterday's instalment contained a secret report sent by M. Hitrovo, the Russian minister at Bucharest, to the chief of the Asiatic department in Russia, saying, 'Sankoff requests funds for certain persons who are ready to take an active part in a coup d' etat, and who have arranged with other persons to assassinate the Prince of Coburg. I recommend M. Sankoff's demand to your kind attention." The chief replied: 'I agree to your secret report and to the distribution of the necessary funds by M. Sankoff.' "

Another letter from Minister Hitrovo proposes the use of dynamite as the best means to bring about a rapid change in Bulgaria, and asks that cartridges be sent to Rustchuk, where a visit was expected from Prince Ferdinand.

Oil Mills Burned.

PARIS, Tex., Aug. 4.—Yesterday the National Oil Mills, machinery and three cattle cars were burned. Total loss $250,000; insurance unknown.

People's Party in Nebraska.

KEARNEY, Neb., Aug. 4.—The People's convention has nominated C. H. Van Wyck for governor.

Ocean Steamers.

Arrived—At New York, Alert, Caribien; Niagara, Havana. At Southampton, Fuerst Bismarck, New York.

ROBBERS WITH DYNAMITE BOMBS.

Four Masked Men Secure the Treasure on a California Passenger Train.

FRESNO, Cal., Aug. 4.—A passenger train, southbound, was held up by four masked robbers six miles east of Collis last night. Two of the robbers crawled over the tank to the engine cab and ordered the engineer and fireman to stop the train. They made the engineer walk ahead a quarter of a mile. They then went to the express car and ordered the messenger to open. He refused and the robbers threw six or seven dynamite bombs at the door, completely demolishing them. They then forced open the safe and took out the money. The amount is not known. They made the fireman help them carry the treasure for some distance, and then jumped on horses and galloped away. One of the messenger's ribs was broken.

Evidently Crazy.

NEW YORK, Aug. 4.—Albert Delawrens, who was impelled by hunger to write letters threatening dynamite to Baring, Magoun & Co. and to Tiffany, was arraigned at the tombs court and remanded for examination. He had all the appearance of a man who had been half starved, and is said to have eaten the prison fare ravenously. He explained that a crowbar was whirling around in his head

Approved by the President.

WASHINGTON, Aug. 4.—The president has approved the acts authorizing the appointment of receivers of national banks fixing the fees of jurors and witnesses in United States courts in certain states and territories; correcting the record of the dismissal of Quincy McNeill, major of the Thirty-ninth regiment, United States colored troops, and issuing to him an honorable discharge.

Should Have Been in Better Company.

NEW YORK, Aug. 4.—John Bowles, a Californian, was robbed of $4000 here last night, while in the company of two women in a house of ill repute. The women, Mamie Allen and Kate Joyce were arrested, and the house was raided by the police.

Treasury Figures.

WASHINGTON, Aug. 4.—The treasury department reports a net decrease of $1,124,013 in circulation during July, and a net decrease of $3,670,170 in the money and bullion in the treasury. The circulation per capita Aug. 1 was $24.41.

Ætna Again on the Rampage.

CATANIA, Aug. 4.—The eruptions at Mt. Ætna have burst forth with renewed violence. Enormous masses of lava are issuing from the southern crater, and a large stream of molten lava has appeared on the eastern side.

To Break the Deadlock.

WASHINGTON, Aug. 4.—The caucus of the Democratic members of the house yesterday afternoon decided to vote on the Durborrow bill, and, carried or defeated, let it be a settlement of the World's fair question.

Will Try the United States Market.

OTTAWA, Aug. 4.—A dispatch from the secretary of the British Columbia Sealers' association says that this season's catch will probably be sold in the United States market, instead of London, as heretofore.

Americans Will Have to Move.

ST. JOHN, N. B., Aug. 4.—Mackerel were never so plentiful as at present. Just off the harbor, American vessels are numerous. One got 300 barrels yesterday. Fishery Inspector O'Brien has notified the Ottawa authorities.

To Be Launched on the 11th.

WASHINGTON, Aug. 4.—Twin screw cruiser No. 11 will be launched at the shipyard of Harrison Loring, Boston, on the 11th inst. This vessel will probably be named Marblehead.

Deputy Doe Resigns.

BOSTON, Aug. 4.—There is one officer less on the state prison roll this morning. Nathan A. Doe, an officer with a record of twenty years' continuous service, who was suspended on Monday for alledged neglect of duty, handed in his resignation yesterday, and it was accepted.

Blue Law Regime at Lowell.

LOWELL, Mass., Aug. 4.—Channing Whitaker of Tyngsborough is threatening the druggists here with prosecution under the Sunday laws, offering as an option their signing an agreement to close their stores Sunday in future.

Mill Owners Yield.

WORCESTER, Mass., Aug. 4.—The strikes at the Packanhoag carpet mills and at the Edgeworth mill are ended, the proprietors deciding to yield to the demand of the girls who were out, and pay them sixty hours' wages for fifty-eight hours' work.

A Disgraceful Affair.

BELFAST, Me., Aug. 4.—In a drunken row in a saloon here, last night, Captain Elbridge Rolerson was scalped, had his hip broken and was otherwise injured, so that his recovery is doubtful.

Against the Iron Hall.

PHILADELPHIA, Aug. 4.—A foreign attachment was issued from the common pleas court by Otto Fleming against the supreme sitting of the Order of the Iron Hall to recover a debt of $100,000.

Lawler for Governor.

MINNEAPOLIS, Aug. 4.—The Democrats in state convention nominated Daniel Lawler for governor.

TELEGRAPHIC BREVITIES.

True Tuttle, a farmer, 62 years old, of West Pownal, Me., was struck by a Grand Trunk train, and killed.

Dudley Brown of Kensington, N. H., becoming suddenly mentally deranged, unsuccessfully attempted to shoot his wife.

Joseph Weeks, an old Norwalk (Conn.) settler, is dead. He was prominent in financial circles and a large owner of real estate.

Mrs. Michael Hartnett of Lawrence, Mass., fell down stairs. Her skull was fractured, and death resulted in a few hours.

At the regular monthly meeting of the South Shore Co-operative bank, Weymouth, Mass., $1300 was sold at a premium of 10 cents a share.

The race for the Australian cup, the great Australian turf event, was won by Queen Mab, Thalia being second and Urania third and last.

The selectmen of Braintree, Mass., have offered $200 reward for the arrest and conviction of the burglars who have been working that town of late.

Tom Graham, one of the wealthiest ranchmen in Arizona, was shot and killed by John Rhoades, as the result of a family feud in which many lives have been sacrificed.

Colonel John A. Prince, vice president of the national board of trade died at Scranton, Pa., aged 50. He was devoted to the mechanical arts, having taken out nearly 100 patents.

WEATHER INDICATIONS.

SLIGHTLY COOLER TO-MORROW.

WASHINGTON, Aug. 4.—For the 24 hours from 8 a. m. to-day: For New England, fair, except showers in northern portion to-day; slightly cooler Friday; westerly winds becoming variable.

FAIR AND COOLER.

BOSTON, Aug. 4.—Local forecast for New England until Friday night: Fair, except showers this afternoon in northern paats of Maine and Vermont; slightly cooler Friday; westerly winds.

THE NEW PARLIAMENT.

Historic Search for Gunpowder and Election of Speaker of House of Commons.

LONDON, Aug. 4.—The new parliament assembled at 2 o'clock this afternoon, the first member arriving before 8 o'clock, in order that he might secure the seat he desired to occupy.

By 1 o'clock nearly all the Opposition seats were filled. Meanwhile a number of members of the Yeomen of the Guard had reached the house, and the historic search for gunpowder in the parliamentary buildings, which has been made at the opening of every parliament since the attempt of Guy Fawkes and his plotters to blow up the king, his ministers, and the members of both houses at the opening of parliament Nov. 5, 1605, had been carried out.

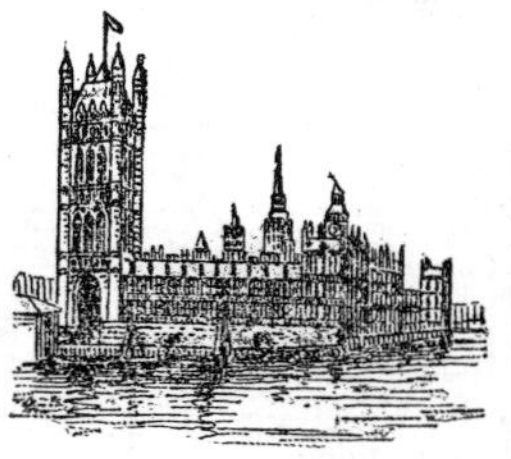

PARLIAMENT HOUSE.

When the House of Lords had assembled with the usual ceremony the Gentleman Usher of the Black Rod summoned the members of the House of Commons to hear the reading of the commission of the new parliament. Upon their return to the House of Commons the members proceeded to the election of a speaker.

The Queen's council, at which the speech from the throne is signed, will be held at Osborne to-morrow.

A MIGHTY TORRENT OF WATER

Rushes Down a Hill in St. Paul, Minn., Causing Loss of Three Lives.

ST. PAUL, Aug. 4.—It now turns out that the torrent of waters rushing down the hill last night resulted much more disastrously than at first reported. Three people were killed and several injured. The killed follow: Mrs. Adams, Mrs. J. Horn, William Krilger. Those wounded fatally are: Philip Stroehr and a five years old son; August Adams, Frederick Kreiger, Paul Kkeuk, Henry Ludwig. The accident was the result of the late rains. Upon the hillside above Page street was a deep gully, the natural outlet of the water from the country above. A year ago Paige street had been filled up across this gully, leaving a small culvert to carry off the water. This culvert had long been choked up and the recent storm had filled the deep basin to the brim, making a lake two acres wide and 45 feet deep. On Monday there appeared a crack three inches wide on the lower side of the fill, but there was no thought of immediate danger. Last night the fill let go and with a rush the vast body of water swept down upon the low land below. A general alarm of fire was sounded and all the ambulances and patrol wagons in the city were on the scene. Men, women and children were fished out and to add to the horror, the water had carried away the gas pipe and left everything in darkness. It is possible that the extent of the loss reported may be increased.

A WOMAN THE WOULD-BE ASSASSIN.

Attempt to Blow Up a Wealthy Chicagoan's Residence With Giant Powder.

CHICAGO, Aug. 4.—An attempt was made last night to blow up the residence of Charles D. Irwin, a wealthy board of trade operator, at 2300 Calumet avenue, and the police are searching high and low for the would-be assassin, who is a woman. The attempt would probably have been fatal had not persons passing frightened the woman away. The can which was left was found a few minutes later, but the finders were afraid to touch it and called for Irwin. He picked up the can and on examining its contents discovered that it was more than half filled with giant powder. In all there was 10 pounds of the deadly explosive, enough to have blown the building to atoms. The description of the woman is that she was attired in deep mourning and wore a heavy black veil.

PRIDE IN SACRED HOSPITALITY.

Government of Honduras Indignant a Approach of American Man-of-War.

PORT LIMON, Aug. 4.—The latest advices from Honduras say that the government is indignant at the ordering of an American man-of-war to the north coast. Americans and their interests have always been looked out for no matter what revolutionary upsettals were taking place. The mines and mining plants, the mills and colonies of gold and silver seekers have had no reason to even know that fighting was going on outside their districts. Bogran and his successor, Leiva, have prided themselves on their sacred hospitality to the people of the United States.

DIED OF HYDROPHOBIA.

Patrick Farrell Who Was Bitten by a Rabid Hound Expires in Lynn Hospital.

LYNN, Aug. 4.—Patrick Farrell, 52 years of age, of Swampscott, died of hydrophobia at the Lynn Hospital this morning. He was bitten by a rabid hound May 13th on the chin. The symptoms of the disease developed Monday and he then entered the hospital. Beyond light throat spasms and an aversion to water the case did not tally with those best known and described in medical works. His death was not violent. An autopsy will be held. This is the second death here from this disease since the Pranker dog ran mad and biting no less than 15 persons.

TELEGRAPHERS STRIKE.

Rumors of Possible Trouble with Union Pacific Operators.

DENVER, Col., Aug. 4.—It was rumored last night that a strike of Order of Railway Telegraphers on the Union Pacific Railroad is possible. Grand Chief Ramsay is at Omaha in conference with Manager Dickinson, who refuses to concede the revised schedule. Mr. Dickinson referred to General Manager Clarke.

Carnegie Officials Held in $10,000 Each.

PITTSBURGH, Aug. 4.—Supt. Potter, Nevin McConnell and James Dovey appeared before Judge Ewing this morning and were released on $10,000 bail each. They are all of the Carnegie company.

Sale of the Wreck of the City of Chicago.

LONDON, Aug. 4.—What remains of the wreck of the Inman Line Steamer City of Chicago, which ran ashore near the Old Head of Kinsale, has been sold privately for £420.

HOME MATTERS.

PERSONAL.—H. A. Harrington, of Hathaway, Soule & Harrington, started a few days ago for a long trip away up through Canada to somewhere in the vicinity of Hudson Bay with a party of five. They will be away a month. The Boston *News* says Mr. Harrington deserves a pleasant vacation, for he is one of the hardest working men in the shoe trade. His business success is ample evidence of this fact.

Mrs. George W. Goethals, children and nurse, and Edmund Rodman are guests of the Mansion House, Vineyard Haven.

E. N. Janson of Woonsocket, R. I., and P. S. Janson of Fall River are the guests of Joseph C. Janson.

Mrs. Perry P. Jenney is spending the Summer at Stephen C. Mendell's, near Rochester Centre.

Cornelius J. Cronin left yesterday for a visit to Rutland, Vt. He will go and return on his bicycle.

Joseph Jefferson, accompanied by his youngest son Will, arrived at Buzzards Bay yesterday afternoon upon the return from the salmon fishing trip in Canada with Gov. Russell and party.

William J. Carter, residing at No. 74 First street, who went as one of the crew of bark Progress when she sailed from this port for Chicago, has returned home. Mr. Carter was injured on the head by the windlass brake when the vessel was between Ogden and Buffalo, and was under a doctor's care at Racine. With several others he was discharged while at Racine.

At a meeting of William Logan Rodman Post 1, G. A. R., last evening, Sergt. William H. Carney was elected a member of the post.

Miss Ruth Burnett, daughter of ex-Congressman Burnett of Southboro, arrived at Buzzards Bay yesterday, to be the guest of Mrs. Cleveland. It is said that it was in honor of Miss Burnett that the Cleveland baby was named Ruth.

Robert Woolfenden and Anson Lee expect to start Monday for a vacation trip to St. Johns and Frederickton, N. B.

Thomas Jouvette and wife and Joseph Fredette and wife are spending a vacation at Rocky Point and Crescent Park.

Henry Carney, a clerk at the Monte Pio store, is spending a week's vacation at the White Mountains.

THE LAND OF SUNSHINE.—*A Unique Country where the Skies are almost Never Clouded, while the air is Cool and Bracing, like Perpetual Spring.*—As an anomalous Southern resort, by reason of the fact that there one may escape Summer heat no less than Winter cold, New Mexico is rapidly becoming famous. Averaging throughout the entire territory 5600 feet in altitude above sea-level, and characterized by dry air which, unlike a humid atmosphere, is incapable of communicating heat, the temperature in midsummer remains at a delightfully comfortable degree through the day, and at night becomes invariably brisk and bracing. The sunshine is almost constant, yet the most violent out-of-door exertion may be undertaken without fear of distressful consequences. Sunstroke or prostration are absolutely unknown there. It is an ideal land for a Summer outing. Its climate is prescribed by reputable physicians as a specific for pulmonary complaints, and the medicinal Hot Springs at Las Vegas are noted for their curative virtues. The most sumptuous hotel in the West, the Montezuma, is located at these springs. Write to Jno. J. Byrne, 723 Monadnock Block, Chicago, for "The Land of Sunshine," an entertaining and profusely illustrated book descriptive of this region, the most picturesque and romantic in the United States.

FRESH ARRIVAL.—We have just received one car-load of fresh provisions for this week, consisting of rounds, rumps and loins, roasters, fresh ribs, choice cuts of thick ribs, lamb, mutton and veal, one lot of 5-lb. boxes choice creamery, and also one large lot of fresh eggs, and we shall retail at the following low prices: Fresh eggs 22c. dozen; round steak 12c. lb.; rump steak 20c. lb.; sirloin 22c. and 24c. lb.; choice cuts thick rib corned beef 8c. lb.; other cuts 5c. and 6c. Good cuts roast beef 8c. and 10c. lb.; best cuts rib roast 15c. lb.; another car load of Christian's best Haxall Flour, such as you have all used, for the low price of 69c. bag; fine potatoes 80c. bushel; five-pound boxes choice creamery 28c. lb.; good raisins 6c. lb.; best rice four lbs. for 25c.; four lbs. common crackers 25c.; two lbs. canned corned beef 17c., regular price 25c.; rolled ox tongues, regular price 60c., now only 48c. can. Now is your chance to buy goods cheap. White Cash Store, 134 Purchase street.

TO CHICAGO AND THE WEST.—The route affording the most advantages is via the Boston & Albany, New York Central and Michigan Central roads, "The Niagara Falls Route," and the route of the "North Shore Limited," which leaves Boston at 2 p. m. daily, and arrives at Chicago at 4 30 p. m. next day. Wagner buffet sleeping cars, dining car, serving all meals en route, smoking and library car comprises the equipment of this train, and ensures to passengers all the comforts and luxuries obtainable in railway travel. Three other express trains daily. For Summer tourist folder, describing western health and pleasure resorts, address W. H. Underwood, E. P. A. Mich. Cent. R. R., Buffalo, N. Y.

ARE YOU CHAINED?—Gents' vest chains 5 and 10 year warrant from $1.25 to $3.75. Best alarm clock 95c., warranted; sale ends this month. J. S. Kelley & Son, 15 Purchase street.

COMMENCING FRIDAY MORNING at 8 o'clock we will sell muslin caps and hats and infants' cloaks at prices that will astonish you, 19 Purchase street.

SEE THE GREAT BARGAINS in hats at Nooning's for 50c. each. They are fine Milan straw, well worth $1.75.

NERVOUS PEOPLE will receive an infinite relief from Turkish and Electric Baths or Massage. 5 So. Sixth street.

CHILDREN'S MULL and Silk Hats, old prices from $1.50 to $3.50, new prices from 75c. to $1.98, 19 Purchase street.

JUST THINK! white shade hats and sailors at Nooning's for 5c. each.

PRICES SLAUGHTERED on infants' wear at the Corset Store, 19 Purchase street.

GIVE THE BABY a good start in life by feeding him with Mellin's Food.

NOTHING LIKE THEM for health. Turkish Baths, 5 So. Sixth street.

FRENCH FLOWERS at Nooning's for 25c. bunch.

GO TO WHITING & Co's. to-morrow morning, and get your share of the bargains.

LADIES' HAIR SHAMPOO, 50 cents. 5 South Sixth street.

"AYER'S HYGIENIC COFFEE" contains all the elements one's system requires.

BLUEFISH 10c. lb. Bartlett's Fish Market.

WHITING & Co's cloak room is the place to get your shirt waists.

BLUEFISH 10c. lb. Bartlett's Fish Market.

50c. for a pair of good Slippers. Devoll's.

BLUEFISH 10c. lb. Bartlett's Fish Market.

CATARRH cured by Hood's Sarsaparilla.

WE ARE DRAWING ATTENTION

TO A LINE OF

JAPANESE CARPETS!

WE HAVE A NUMBER OF VERY HANDSOME JAPANESE CARPETS

Size 9 ft. x 12 ft.

STYLES AND COLORINGS ARE FINE!

PRICES LOW!

C. F. WING,

WING BUILDING.

WHITING & CO.

SPECIAL

FRIDAY & SATURDAY SALES.

750 yards 4-4 White Ground Lawns, go on sale at 15c. per yard, very neat figures.

The balance of our 10c. Challies, will be closed out at 5c.

50 pieces White Ground Cambrics, go on sale to-morrow at 4c. per yard.

20 pieces more of those Fine Scotch Ginghams, will be sold at 15c. per yard.

We will sell you some printed Pongees at 10c. for Friday, if any left balance Saturday.

We are selling thousands of Shirt Waists, in Silk and Satine, our Satine ones are handsome as Silk.

100 pieces of Cotton Diaper, for Friday and Saturday Sales, 39c. a piece.

100 yards short lengths of Fine Drapery Silk, best $1.00 goods, go on sale Friday at 49c. per yard. You will find them at Silk Department.

TOWELS—We shall sell you to-morrow a fine Huck Towel, hemmed, at 12 1-2c. a piece, cheap at 17c.

20 Dozen Ladies' White and Cream Jersey Vests, go on sale to-morrow at 17c. a piece, match them at 25c. if you can.

This month will be a Grand Closing-Out month with us, and you will get some decided Bargains in all of our Departments.

WHITING & CO

J. V. SPARE,

Liberty Hall Building.

SPECIAL BARGAINS

—FOR—

FRIDAY.

1000 yds. short lengths Gray Mixed Domet Flannel, 32 inches wide, and very heavy, an excellent article for linings and for many other purposes will be sold for

6 1-2c.

for this sale. The width and price ought to sell them at sight.

Ladies' Outing Flannel Blouses at

35c. to Close.

Ready-made Sheets, made of Atlantic Cotton, both bleached and unbleached, well made and cheaper than you can make them yourself.

J. V. Spare.

OUTING SHIRTS!

OUTING SHIRTS!

You can never have too many

OUTING SHIRTS!

Our low prices will help you out. Quality exceptional.

Good Shirts for $1 and $1.25, laundered collars and cuffs.

Another lot of the popular blue Madras, all sizes, $1.50.

Better come at once, They're going fast.

OUTING SHIRTS!

J. & W. R. WING & CO.,

133 UNION STREET.

OUTING SHIRTS!

SECOND EDITION.

HOME MATTERS.

THE EXPORTS from New York the past week include 449 pounds whalebone.

LARCENY.—A dark coat belonging to John Carroll was stolen from the cooper shop of J. P. Kennedy in this city to-day.

DIVIDENDS.—The Border City Manufacturing Company and the American Linen Company of Fall River yesterday declared quarterly dividends of 2 per cent.

The Troy Cotton & Woollen Manufactory of Fall River has declared a dividend of $15 per share.

ANOTHER IMPORTANT LAND SALE.—F. A. F. Adams has sold to Daniel J. Wilson, jeweller, for Thomas Bennett, Jr., about 760 rods of land bounded by County, Ashland and Robeson streets. Streets are to be cut through the property and it is to be put upon the market in small lots at once. This land is finely situated and very desirable for residences.

SWEDISH SERVICE SATURDAY EVENING.—There will be a gospel meeting held in the Pleasant Street M. E. church Saturday evening at 8 o'clock. The service will be held in the interest of the Scandinavians in New Bedford conducted by Charles G. Johnson and Miss Tena Larsen, with others from Fall River, speaking in their own language. All Swedish, Danish and Norwegian are cordially invited and welcome.

REAL ESTATE SALES.—Daniel J. Ramsbottom has sold to Edward Harlow 23.76 rods of land at the northwest corner of Coggeshall and Mitchell streets.

John M. Lancaster of Fall River has sold to Timothy J. Moriarty 4.6 rods of land on the north side of contemplated Jouvert street.

Standish Bourne sold at auction yesterday mortgagees sale, house and lot on the Russell's Mills road southwest of Smith Mills knew as Phoebe Devoll farm, subject to her life support, to Walter Clifford.

T. F. Healey has sold for F. A. F. Adams lots No. 61, 63 and 65 on the Hathaway avenue plat, east of Purchase street, to Samuel Bosquet. Also, on the same plat, lots Nos. 53, 57 and 55, to Antoine Goyett.

John Whitehead has sold for George A. Briggs two lots in Fairhaven on Rogers street and Kendrick avenue, containing 54 rods, to James Gurl.

Mary Smith has sold to Margaret Banno a 200.8 rods land north side of the Belleville road.

John W. Canavan has sold to John F. Canavan 200.8 rods land north side of the Belleville road.

Shearjashub T. Viall has sold to Charles E. Cook 11.86 rods land west side of contemplated Hall street.

The Wamsutta Mills Corporation has sold to Thomas Valois 26.26 rods land north side of Austin street west of County street.

John M. Howland has sold to John J. Cotter 55.19 rods land east side of contemplated River avenue and south of the Town Farm in Fairhaven.

MATTAPOISETT.

On Thursday, July 28, a party, consisting of Mrs. Sylvester Lacy of Medford, Mr. Roderick McKay of Brockton, Miss M. J. Mahoney and Miss S. K. Bartlett of Mattapoisett, made a trip to Onset in the yacht Hector, commanded by Capt. E. C. Stetson. On Friday the same party, with the addition of Mr. Robert De Natts of Middleboro, and Miss S. B. Kinney and Mr. G. A. Barstow of Mattapoisett, started for a few days' outing at Nantucket. After leaving the moorings they were becalmed, and not being able to reach their destination that night, put into Edgartown at 5.30 p. m. Almost immediately the party took cars for Cottage City, witnessed the parade of the wheelmen on foot, and returned to the boat by the 10.30 train. The wind being favorable, the next morning Capt. Stetson again set sail and arrived at Nantucket at 11.30 where all partook of a good shore dinner. The afternoon was pleasantly spent in sight-seeing as was also the greater part of the time during Sunday and Monday. Although the passage through the sound was very rough, the return trip was pleasantly and successfully made in about six hours Tuesday morning.

Made Possible.

One of the largest successes in the way of Flavoring Extracts in the world is the **Price Flavoring Extract Company.**

Their success is attributed to the perfection of **Dr. Price's Delicious Flavoring Extracts.**

This perfection was made possible through the new processes discovered by Dr. Price for extracting from the true fruits their natural flavoring properties. Any housekeeper that will use Dr. Price's Orange, Lemon, Vanilla or any other flavor will pronounce them faultless.

The purity of Dr. Price's flavors offers the best security against the dangers which are common in the use of the ordinary flavoring extracts in the market.

BUILDING.—Andre Lesrare has petitioned for leave to erect a dwelling-house on the east side of Belleville avenue, between Sawyer and Coggeshall streets. It is to be 55 by 30 feet, 29 feet posts.

Albert Twombly desires leave to erect a building on the south side of Weld street, between Mt. Pleasant and Ashland streets. It is to be 32 by 28 feet, 15 feet posts.

Frank A. Silva asks leave to erect a building to be used as a shop on the west side of South Second street. It is to be 27 by 10 feet, 9 feet posts.

Dwelling house southwest corner of Spring and Second streets is being raised and the lower story is to be fitted for a store.

MARINE INTELLIGENCE.

ARRIVED THIS AFTERNOON.

Sch P G Thomson, Chase, New York.
Sch Hastings, Cory, New York.

SAILED.

Sch Wm A Grozier, Dunham, Provincetown.

At sea New York 3d, steamer Nacoochee, Smith, Savannah.

Passed through Hell Gate 3d, schs James B Potter, Potter, New York for Nantucket; M E Crosby, White, do for do; North Star, Coat, do for do; Elias Runyon, Eldridge, do for Taunton; Mary A Fisher, Coat, do for Fall River; L S Hatch, White, do for do.

At Philadelphia 3d, schs Ida L Hull, Gabrielson, Kennebec; Jesse Murdock, Perry, Boston; Jesse Barlow, Barlow, Atlantic City; Donna P Briggs, Guernsey, do, Old, schs Kate Markee, Perry, this port; C H Venner, Baker, Boston; Oliver Ames, Nickerson, New Haven; L A Plummer, Howes, do.

Passed Newcastle 3d, sch Thos F Pollard, hence for Philadelphia.

At Baltimore 3d, sch Hattie S Williams, Allen, Fall River. Cld, sch E J French, Kenrick, Providence.

At Georgetown, DC, 3d, sch Chas N Simmons, Babbit, Kennebec.

At Norfolk 3d, sch Jennie R Tomlinson, Fall River.

At New York 3d, schs K D Perry, New York; O A White, Boston; A M Anderson, hence. Sld, sch Eug Philip, Portsmouth.

At Richmond 3d, sch Wm H Oler, Keen, Baltimore. Sld, sch Herbert E Howes, Fall River.

SPOKEN

June 21, lat 3 N, lon 39 W, ship Francis, Stone, New York for San Francisco.

FINANCIAL.

THURSDAY, Aug. 4.

There is but very little speculation in stocks at the moment, except for specialties which have been made active by the cliques and purchases supposed to be made for the short account. Reducing of passenger rates in the West is again reported. Yesterday selling exceeded the buying, and it was noticeable that the greatest declines were in those stocks having an international market. Fears of gold exports are calculated to put a damper upon bullish ardor, inasmuch as sterling exchange is now higher than at any time during the past 25 years; still, holders of stocks are as tenacious as ever, and when the turn comes for the better, it will be found that few stocks are to be had at anything like current prices.

In the local money market there is but little demand, rates holding steady at 5 to 6 per cent.

In the Boston loan market there has been a general advance in money rates, although it does not look as though the demand was strong enough to loan money at any higher rates. Call loans 4 to 4½ per cent. Prime business paper 4½ to 5 per cent. Corporation loans 3½ to 4 per cent. The clearing house rate is 3½ to 4 per cent. New York funds sell at 12½ to 17 cents discount.

The New York money market would be called easy, call loans ranging from 1½ to 2 per cent. Prime mercantile paper 3½ to 5½ per cent.

Bar silver 85⅝c.

Sterling exchange is quiet and steady; posted rates 4.88 to 4.88½.

Government bonds dull and steady.

In Wall street stock circles this morning there was but little interest displayed. The general market suffered some reaction yesterday and indications are that they may go lower before the short interest becomes cumbersome, especially if gold goes out. London prices come ¼ to ¼ below our close of yesterday. Bank of England rate unchanged.

The New York stock market was fairly active at the opening. Atchison opened at 39¾, Chicago, Burlington & Quincy at 102¼, Delaware & Lackawanna at 138¾, Missouri Pacific at 60, Northwest at 117½, and Omaha at 52¾. As the morning advanced the market strengthened generally. Atchison advanced ¼ to 40. Omaha common advanced ¼ to 53¼; Chicago, Burlington & Quincy was an exception, declining to 101¼. Rock Island 81, St. Paul 83½, and Union Pacific 38¾. At 1 o'clc ck the market was firm and fairly active, although most of the transactions were carried on in Omaha. Atchison declined to 39¾. It was rumored that Western houses were sellers of this stock and also that Henry Villard sold 2000 shares during the early hours. Omaha advanced to 53⅝, where it held firm. London is doing very little in our market, although they sold a few hundred shares after the opening. Louisville & Nashville 71, Reading 60⅝. St. Paul 83⅜, Lake Shore 135, Dela-

---

	28⅝
Illinois Central...	
Lake Shore & Michigan Southern...	136¼
Louisville & Nashville...	71
Michigan Central...	107
Missouri Pacific...	59⅝
New Jersey Central...	137
New York & New England...	37
Northern Pacific...	21
Northern Pacific pref...	58½
North'western...	118½
New York Central & Hudson River...	114
North American...	14¼
Oregon Navigation...	
Oregon Improvement...	
Oregon Short Line...	24
Philadelphia & Reading...	60⅝
Pullman Palace Car Co...	
Chicago, Rock Island & Pacific...	81½
Chicago, St. Paul & Omaha...	52¾
Chicago, Milwaukee & St. Paul...	83½
Richmond Terminal...	8
St. Paul & Omaha...	53
St. Paul & Omaha pref...	
Union Pacific...	38⅜
Wabash, St. Louis & Pacific...	11½
Wabash, St. Louis & Pacific pref...	26½

MISCELLANEOUS

Ontario Silver...	41¼
Pacific Mail Steamship Co...	
Sugar, common...	106¼
Sugar, pref...	101¾
Western Union Telegraph...	97⅜
Silver Certificates...	85½

BOSTON, Aug. 4.

BONDS

Atchison 4s...	83½
Atchison Incomes...	60%
American Bell Telephone 7s...	
Chicago, Burlington & Northern 5s...	
Chicago & West Michigan 5s...	
Mexican Central 4s...	99

RAILROADS

Atchison, Topeka & Santa Fe...	39¾
Boston & Albany...	205½
Boston & Lowell...	*183
Boston & Maine...	250
Boston & Providence...	250
Calumet & Hecla...	
Chicago & West Michigan...	102¼
Cleveland & Canton...	5½
Cleveland & Canton pref...	19½
Flint & Pere Marquette...	18
Flint & Pere Marquette pref...	78
Mexican Central...	19⅝
New York & New England...	36¾
New York & N'w England pref...	
Old Colony...	*184
Oregon Short Line...	24
Pullman Palace Car...	
Union Pacific...	38⅜
Wisconsin Central...	
West End...	76¼
West End pref...	

MINING

Butte & Boston Mining Co...	
Calumet & Hecla Mining Co...	286
Centennial...	7¼
Franklin Mining Co...	12½
Kearsarge...	
Montana...	56⅝
Osceola Mining Co...	32½
Tamarack...	155

MISCELLANEOUS

American Bell Telephone...	204½
Erie Telephone...	47¼
Mexican Telephone...	1
New England Telephone...	59
Boston Land Co...	
New England Land Co...	18¾
San Diego Land Co...	
Topeka Land & Development Co...	*1
Lamson Store Service...	33¾
Illinois Steel Co...	72½
Thomson-Houston Electric Co...	
Am. Sugar Refineries, com...	
Am. Sugar Refineries, pref...	
Thomson-Houston...	

*Asked.

CALIFORNIA MINING STOCKS.

SAN FRANCISCO, Aug. 2.

The following are the official closing prices of mining stocks to-day:

Alta...	1 35
Best & Belcher...	1 30
Challan...	
Con. Cal. & Va...	3 35
Crown Point...	
Consolidated Imperial...	1 50
Gould & Curry...	
Hale & Norcross...	
Mexican...	1 35
Mt. Diablo...	
Ophir...	2 95
Potosi...	
Savage...	
Sierra Nevada...	1 10
Union Con...	
Yellow Jacket...	

NEW YORK PRODUCE MARKET.

NEW YORK, Aug. 4.

Flour sales 6500 packages; quiet. Wheat sales 615,000 bushels; early, ⅛ up, fell ⅝, and active. Corn sales 60,000 bushels; dull, firmer. Oats sales 45,000 bushels; quiet. Butter firm. Pork quiet. Lard dull and higher. Butter firm. Cheese firm. Sugar (raw) quiet. Petroleum quiet. Turpentine dull. Molasses quiet. Rice firm. Freights quiet. Rosin quiet. Tallow firm and quiet.

PROVISIONS AND GRAIN.

CHICAGO, Aug. 4.

Opening.

	Lard.	Wheat.	Pork.	Corn.	Sh't Ribs.
May					
June					
July					
Aug.		78¾	12.42½	50	
Sept.		80⅝	12.45		
Oct.			12.57½		
Jan.			12 o'clock.		
May					
June					
July					
Aug.		78	12.50	49½	
Sept.		80⅝	12.45		
Oct.					
Jan.			12.42½		

WEATHER INDICATIONS.

FAIR.

NEW YORK, Aug. 4.—At 8 30 a. m. the weather was cloudy, with wind south, temperature 74. *The Herald* says: In the Middle States and New England on Friday, fair weather will probably prevail, with slightly lower followed by rising temperature, and on Saturday warmer, fair weather.

ARSENIC IN THE PEPPER.

Used on the Table at the Fatal Dinner at the Cable House.

HAVERHILL, Aug. 4.—A dispatch from Newburyport states that arsenic has been found in the pepper that was used on the table at the Cable House, Salisbury Beach, on the day of the fatal dinner there.

TROUBLE FEARED AT DUQUESNE.

Whole Regiment Ordered from Homestead to Preserve the Peace.

HOMESTEAD, Aug. 4.—Trouble is anticipated at Duquesne to-day. Shortly before noon Gen. Wiley returned to camp after a consultation with Treasurer Curry and others at the Carnegie office, and at once issued orders to Col. Hulings, commander of the Sixteenth Regiment, to move his entire regiment at once to Duquesne to quell any disturbance.

When asked the cause of the difficulty at Duquesne an official said: "We had a large number of applications for work from our old men at Duquesne and many of them were returning to their old places in the mill this morning. As they were about to enter the mill they were kept back by the strikers and we had to call the militia to our aid. I do not anticipate any trouble after the militia gets there."

Democratic Campaign Managers in Session.

NEW YORK, Aug. 4.—The campaign committee of the Democratic national committee met at the headquarters on Fifth avenue this morning to form subcommittees and map out the work of the campaign. At 11 30 they went into secret session.

Trusted Town Official a Defaulter.

LINDSEY, Ont., Aug. 4.—Arthur O'Leary, general agent of this town, is missing. His defalcation is estimated at $30,000. O'Leary stood high in the esteem of the public.

The Constellation at Newport.

NEWPORT, Aug. 4.—United States ship Constellation arrived off Jamestown at 3 o'clock this afternoon and at once proceeded to anchor.

A Little Girl's Experience in a Lighthouse.

Mr. and Mrs. Loren Trescott are keepers of the Gov. Lighthouse at Sand Beach, Mich., and are blessed with a daughter, four years old. Last April she was taken down with measles, followed with a dreadful cough and turning into a fever. Doctors at home and at Detroit treated her, but in vain, she grew worse rapidly, until she was a mere "handful of bones." Then she tried Dr. King's New Discovery and after the use of two and a half bottles, was completely cured. They say Dr. King's New Discovery is worth its weight in gold, yet you may get a trial bottle free at H. A. Blackmer's drug store.

No Sir. Nothing in stock to fit you. But if you must have Shoes we can make a pair at once to fit even your wooden feet.

A prominent feature of our business is, making shoes to measure for those who cannot well be fitted with ready-made shoes.

In fact we manufacture all of our better grades of Boots and Shoes.

Come in and look at the factory connected with our stores.

76 and 78 PURCHASE STREET.

SCHULER BROTHERS.

THE BORDEN MURDER.

Portuguese Farm Employe Suspected Assassin.

Daughter of Slain Couple First Discovered the Bodies.

Threads of Evidence Picked Up by the Police.

Mr. Borden Seen on the Street Shortly Before Found Dead.

No Trace of the Implements Used in the Commission of the Crime.

[By Associated Press.]

FALL RIVER, Aug. 4.—Andrew J. Borden and his wife were found at their home, 92 Second street, at 11 o'clock this forenoon, both dead. Both had been frightfully mutilated about the head and face with an axe, cleaver or razor. Mr. Borden lay on a sofa in a room on the lower floor of the house. His head had been cut, and gashes from four to six inches long were found on his face and neck. Mrs. Borden was in her own chamber on the upper floor, and the condition of her face and head was the same as that of her husband. She lay face downward on the bed, which was a veritable pool of blood. The police were immediately notified and began an investigation. Up to the hour of writing no implements that could have been used in the commission of the crime had been found. This leads to the terrible suspicion that Mr. and Mrs. Borden were murdered. The murder and suicide theory is advanced and finds many supporters. Mr. Borden was a wealthy real estate owner and mill man, and was seen on the street half an hour before he was found dead.

There is hardly any doubt now that both were murdered. The daughter of the unfortunate couple was the first to make the discovery. She went upstairs after finding the body of her father and saw the form of her mother lying on the floor. She thought she had fallen in a swoon, but upon finding that she too was murdered, the girl fled down stairs and fainted. The police have searched in vain for any clew to the murderer. They are now after a Portuguese who runs the Borden farm at Gardner's Neck and who, it is said, was in the house a few minutes before the bodies were discovered.

It is reported that word was sent to Mrs. Borden this morning that a sick friend desired to see her to-day, but she didn't go out.

It is said that the servant, Bridget Sullivan, says she went into the room to make some inquiry of Mr. Borden about five minutes before Lizzie Borden gave the alarm. He was then sitting on the sofa reading a newspaper. Mr. Borden was on the streets and in several of the banks as late as 10 o'clock.

THE NEW HOUSE OF COMMONS.

Re-election of Sir Arthur Wellesley Peel Speaker of the Last Body.

LONDON, Aug. 4.—As Mr. Chamberlain, Mr. Balfour, and other prominent members had entered parliament they were cheered. Mr. Gladstone made his appearance in the House after 2 o'clock, and was given an enthusiastic reception. The ovation to the liberal leader lasted several minutes. When Mr. Gladstone had taken

HON. ARTHUR WELLESLEY PEEL
(Speaker of the House of commons.)

his seat he was surrounded by a crowd of members irrespective of party, all anxious to congratulate him and shake his hand. Sir M. W. Ridley, Conservative member, moved that the Hon. Arthur Wellesley Peel, who was speaker of the last house, be elected speaker of the new body. The motion was seconded by Mr. Gladstone, and carried.

TO DISBAND AT NEWPORT.

Arrival of Half a Dozen of the Smaller New Haven Yachts.

NEWPORT, R. I., Aug. 4.—The New Haven Yacht club arrived this morning consisting of but half a dozen, the smallest of the fleet. They will disband after the races, probably.

WANTS.

Advertisements under this heading 1c. a word a time. No charge less than 25c.

SITUATION—To cook, wash and iron. Apply at 375 West Middle street. aut-2t

SITUATION wanted by a girl, or to assist in housework. 75 Middle street. aut-2t

Notice.

ALL persons are hereby forbidden to harbor or trust my wife, Clara Enos, on my account, as I shall pay no bills of her contracting after this date. JOHN ENOS.
August 4, 1892. au4-3t

CONGRESS.

Republicans Ridicule the Democratic World's Fair Agreement.

WASHINGTON, Aug. 4.—In the House Mr. Catchings of Mississippi rose to a privileged report on the committee on rules. It provides that to-day it shall be in order for the Speaker to entertain motions to suspend the rules as on the first and third Mondays. This was agreed to without controversy.

Mr. Holman of Indiana immediately rose and moved to suspend the rules and pass a joint resolution extending until Aug. 10 the appropriations made by the act of last year. Agreed to.

Mr. Holman then mov'd to suspend the rules and pass a resolution that the House shall reconsider the vote by which the House receded from the World's Fair amendment; that the House instruct upon its disagreement and the bill be sent to conference. The motion was rejected.

The Republicans advanced an explanation of the agreement reached by the Democratic party yesterday and when it was read as published in the papers this morning there was an expression of feeling that it meant nothing.

Mr. Henderson of Illinois characterized it as yanking of the invitation of the spider to the fly to walk into his parlor.

Mr. Dingley of Maine voiced the general opinion of the Republicans that the Democrats had assumed the responsibility. He did not believe that any action would be taken toward passing the Durborow bill.

LATER.—The sundry civil bill has been sent to conference by a vote of yeas 141; nays 48.

Mr. Reilly of Pennsylvania moved to suspend the rules and pass a resolution providing that a vote shall be taken on the Durborrow bill at 1 o'clock to-morrow. Agreed to amid applause.

The House then proceeded to the consideration of the Durborrow and Mr. Reilly's substitute therefor.

Burglars in Newport.

NEWPORT, Aug. 4.—Burglars entered the store of Miss Tappin on Thames street, dealer in ladies' clothing, last night and stole from the safe, which they blew open, $200. Entrance was gained through the work room in the second story and down a small elevator shaft.

A Modern Penelope.

By the kitchen hearth was an American sewing machine, and a modern, careful, cheerful and healthy housewife running resinate—we passed to a weaving loom, such as Penelope might have wrought in against the day of her wedding with Odysseus. Here one of the girls tried to teach me to run the bobbin back and forth, a thread at a time, and—kept the needle going with my feet. It proved to be no more so simple as it looked, and I made awkward work of it. They showed us a skein of the pure raw yellow silk, like spun gold, and also a bolt of the most fascinating silk cloth, so delicate and fine in texture that one could see through it; but, no firm as to endure for years and with the natural yellow color of the silk.

Which we coveted the lovely fabrics we did not dare suggest a purchase, for Kyr Argites was lord of many acres and the village head; all his neighbors looked up to him; his daughters could weave, but to sell they disdained. It was like a dream to see the new Penelope weaving her robe, in a house like this in this charmingly unique household, but at length the delicate moderated a little, and for all their kind entreaties to spend the night, that they might show us how they amused themselves and dance for us, we took our lingering leave. It was a rich experience, this peep into the home life of those simple, sturdy Laconians, and one which the tourist very seldom enjoys.—Oporto Cor. Omaha Bee.

Enemies and Friends of the Farmer.

Fortunately nature has provided certain insects that destroy the tobacco worms. There is a kind of fly, very small, which punches holes in the bodies of the caterpillars, and lays its eggs in them. Little worms are hatched from their eggs and feed upon the caterpillars, finally spinning minute cocoons.

Sometimes as many as a hundred of these cocoons are found attached to a single caterpillar. Planters who know what they are about never kill the caterpillars which they find infested with these parasites, but leave them to spread the trouble among their kind. It is a curious fact that the fly parasites have other parasites that feed upon themselves, laying their eggs in the cocoons. Flocks of young turkeys are often let loose in the tobacco field in order that they may eat the caterpillars, and the planters pay their children so much for every moth they kill by striking them with pieces of shingle as they are hovering over the flowers in the twilight, which is their time for going abroad. Hornets and wasps also eat the caterpillars and so are friends of the farmers.—Washington Star.

REAL ESTATE.

STOCK AND BOND MARKETS.

Bids at the close of First Board.

NEW YORK, Aug. 4.

GOVERNMENT BONDS.

U.S. 4s, registered...	100
new 4s, registered...	116
new 4s, coupon...	116
currency 6s, 1895, (Pacifics)...	108⅜

RAILROADS

Atchison...	39¾
Clev., Cin., Chicago & St. Louis...	67¼
Chicago & Eastern Illinois...	
Chicago & Eastern Illinois pref...	
Chicago, Burlington & Quincy...	102¼
Delaware & Hudson...	139⅜
Delaware & Lackawanna...	138½

The Evening Standard.

ESTABLISHED FEBRUARY, 1856.]   NEW BEDFORD, FRIDAY, AUGUST 5, 1892.   TWO CENTS.

HASKELL & TRIPP.

Cut! Cut!! Sharp cuts in prices all over the store. Everything slow must go. Many odd lots, too small to advertise, are marked absurdly low to close out.

The bargain-seeker's opportunity is between seasons when stocks are being *simmered down* to the smallest amount possible.

Cut-price headwear.

Light-colored chip caps, formerly 45c., now 25c.

Misses' accordion plaited cashmere hats, with rosette on top, formerly 45c. Now 25c.

Cut-price parasols.

No exception. Every parasol in this store at a new, lower price to-day. All fresh goods, made this season.

Ottoman stripes, formerly $1.50. Now $1.15.

Colored Surahs, formerly $2. Now $1.50.

Changeables, formerly $2.25. Now $1.75.

Finest changeables, with border, formerly $3. Now $2.50.

Surah stripes, formerly $2.50. Now $2.

Ruffled Surahs, formerly $3.19. Now $2.50.

Cut-price flowers.

Balance of millinery flowers, all this Summer's styles, reduced to *exactly one half* the former selling prices, and they were very cheap in the first place.

Cut-price collars.

About five hundred ruffled, lace-trimmed collars for children, regular prices 25 and 37c. each. *Now all at 10c. each.*

Women's Summer shoes.

For 98c. a pair { Tan Oxfords, opera toe. Black Oxfords, opera toe, with tip. Black Oxfords, common sense, hand turn.

For $1.39 a pair { Very handsome tan-colored leather Oxfords, opera toe, all sizes.

For $2.00 a pair { Hand-sewed Oxfords of a fine and beautiful quality, and shape unexcelled.

HASKELL & TRIPP.

Department Stores,

Purchase and William Streets.

THE GOELET CUP RACE.

New York Yachts are off Over the West Island Course.

NEWPORT, R. I., Aug. 5.—The weather this morning is very bad; heavy westerly squalls denoted that Commodore Gerry's luck was a goner, and lightning and thunder beat the entries for the Goelet cups in great shape. Towards noon, however, the weather looked better and the Ituna decided to start the boats on the West Island course with westerly wind.

Entries are as follows:

Schooners—Constellation, Alcæa, Merlin, Lasca, Alert, Mayflower, Atlantic, Marguerite, Iroquois, Quickstep.

Sloops—Gracie, Ventura, Wasp, Sayonara, Harpoon, Gloriana.

The start of the race was delayed by a heavy thunder shower.

At this hour (11 30 a. m.) the yachts are leaving the harbor.

THE IDAHO MINERS' TRIAL.

John Kneebone Tells the Story of the First Shot and Subsequent Events.

BOISE CITY, Ida., Aug. 5.—In his testimony yesterday in the trial of the 25 prisoners charged with rioting at the mines, John Kneebone stated he saw the smoke of the first shot fired early on the morning of July 11, and he was positive that it was discharged by one of a party of non-union men who were hidden behind a pile of logs on the hillside. Stationed within the mouth of the tunnel were a number of 'Frisco guardsmen, but he was sure they did not fire first. The initial shot was followed by a desultory fusilade of six or seven shots and then there was a volley of 100 shots fired before the force in the mill began to reply. Kneebone said that after the abortive attempt to destroy the mill by sending the powder-laden car down the steep tramway back of the plant, he saw a man carrying a powder box toward the head of the penstock and that shortly after this the explosion occurred and the Frisco mill building collapsed. He declared he would know the men who carried the powder if he should see him. After the explosion he and his comrades determined to surrender. In a short time several hundred union miners had come down from the hills and had surrounded the mill. They compelled the Frisco men to march to the miners' union hall at Gem. At the time of the surrender he saw Thomas O'Brien, Dan Harrington, Thomas Eaton and Joseph Poynton near the Frisco mill on their way down the hill. Each one was armed with a rifle or gun. After remaining an hour or two the men were placed in box cars and taken to Wallace. Next morning Kneebone and eight others were ordered to leave town. They complied and boarded a train and went to Old Mission. That evening 15 or 20 men some on foot and some mounted, came in to that hamlet and commenced to shoot at the non-union men. Kneebone was fired at several times. He ran up the railroad track and took to the brush. He remained several hours in the timber and then went to Old Mission, but was stopped by four men, who robbed him and told him to leave the country. He missed the next steamer but caught one the next day and went to Cœur d'Elene City, thence to Spokane.

Upon cross-examination Kneebone's testimony was not shaken.

FROM THE SOUTH PACIFIC.

British and United States Coaling Stations to be put in Order.

SAN FRANCISCO, Aug. 5.—Advices from Honolulu say that H. M. S. Champion left there July 13 for Johnston Island, and anchored off the island July 18. The island was annexed the next day.

Auckland, N. Z., advices say H. M. S. Curacoa, which recently annexed Gardner, Dandier, and Nassau islands in the central Pacific, returned to Suva, Fiji, from Samoa, June 27. The Curacoa left Apia harbor June 20, and proceeded to the island of Tutgicta with the land-commissioner of Apfa, Mr. Tanzacra, who went ashore there to settle some land disputes and to select a place for a coaling station. This was formerly used by the Americans as a coaling depot but with the loss of their ships at Apia in 1889 it has been discontinued. England is to use it for the same purpose, as the commissioner has allotted land there with that design, although it may be some considerable time before the depot is ready for use. It is not understood how England can secure a coaling station at Pago Pago, the title to that harbor being given to the United States, through purchase of sites made by Harold M. Sewall while United States consul to Samoa.

The steamer Alameda, which left Auckland in July for Sydney, had on board Lieut. John H. Coffin from Mare Island, whose duty it was to put the United States coaling station at Pago Pago in order and appoint officers and men to take charge of it.

HEAVILY GUARDED TRAIN.

Shipment of Government Gold from San Francisco to Washington.

SAN FRANCISCO, Aug. 5.—A heavily armed train left here yesterday carrying fully $30,000,000 of government gold coin from the local sub-treasury to Washington. The transfer of the treasure was made with secrecy. Thirty postal and nine local coats appeared to report here. They were on hand yesterday at Fourth and Townsend streets, where a train of five baggage cars was made up. These cars were unusually strong and came from various roads. Each car has a capacity of $6,000,000 in gold coin in small boxes bearing the sub-treasury burden. Three cars of Winchester rifles were aboard for use of the guards. These precautions were taken for fear of train robbers. The train will go over the Central and Union Pacific, but as it is so heavily guarded not even the Daltons will have the courage to attack it.

The Public Health in France.

PARIS, Aug. 5.—Later reports from the suburbs of Paris show that in all but one of the outlying districts the public health has improved. The exception is Argentuil, where 100 deaths have occurred within the past week from cholera or diarrhœa and typhoid fever. Over 150 persons in the same suburb suffering from the same disease have been removed in the past two days. A majority of the sufferers are employed in the lime quarries.

Deaths from Cholera in Paris.

PARIS, Aug. 5.—A family of four persons died in the rue St. Maur, in this city, yesterday, it is said of cholera. Six other cases of death from cholera are also reported to have occurred in this city. In the suburbs of St. Ouen and St. Denis the disease is spreading.

Boston Knights Templars in Colorado.

DENVER, Col., Aug. 5.—The Boston commandery of Knights Templars comprising 79 sir knights and 43 ladies and accompanied by a band passed through Grand Junction yesterday for a trip through the State.

Shot and Killed by His Son.

EVANSVILLE, Ind., Aug. 5.—William Hudson, a freight transfer contractor, was shot and killed at noon yesterday by his eldest son Harry. The trouble grew out of a quarrel at the table. The murderer was looked up.

$5000 REWARD

For the Capture of the Assassin of the Bordens

Offered by the Two Daughters of the Murdered Couple.

Police Have their Eyes Upon Inmates of the Mansion.

No Arrests There Until After the Funeral To-morrow,

Unless Those on Whom Suspicion Rests Attempt to Leave.

[Special Dispatch.]

FALL RIVER, Aug. 5.—At almost any moment startling developments may be given to the public in the Borden murder case, and yet it is probable that no arrests will be made and the tragedy will be shrouded in mystery so far as the public is concerned until after the funeral, which will occur at 11 a. m. to-morrow. The officers in charge of the case are not disposed to create any scene at the residence where the bodies of the murdered couple lay. The city is filled with the wildest rumors of arrests, but they are without foundation. The police have the inmates of the Borden homestead under surveillance and should any one there attempt to depart it is probable an arrest would be made on suspicion. The police are particularly watchful of Mr. Morse, to whom the finger of suspicion has been pointed.

The only important announcement in connection with the case is the statement sent to all the newspaper offices by Emma and Lizzie Borden, the daughters of the murdered couple, offering a reward of $5000 for the capture of the assassin.

[By Associated Press.]

FALL RIVER, Aug. 5.—After a most thorough and persistent search no trace has been found of the murderer of Mr. and Mrs. Borden. Four policemen are on guard at the house, and have been patrolling the neighborhood since the affray was made public. A few very near relatives are allowed to enter. Those who went in to-day were a Mr. Morse of New Bedford, a cousin of the suspected man, and another close friend who gave his name as Fish. These men can give no reason why Morse should be under suspicion, other than the fact that he happened to be in this neighborhood at this time. He would not be benefited by the death of either of the parties, unless a will was made, which at this writing cannot be told. Emma, the daughter who was visiting in the vicinity of New Bedford when the murder took place, is at home to-day, and has charge of the house. Her sister Lizzie is not in much better state than yesterday, when she discovered her father's death.

This forenoon State Detective Seaver and City Marshal Hilliard had a conference, and later on visited and interrogated Miss Lizzie at the house. The results of their investigation will not be known until an arrest of some kind has been made, and that is not likely to take place until after the funeral.

The funeral will take place to-morrow morning at 11 o'clock and will be strictly private. The services will be conducted by City Missionary Buck, who was a close friend of the family, and the interment will take place at Oak Grove cemetery.

At the present time both bodies are lying in a dining-room, the windows of which a servant was washing shortly before the tragedy became known. The strict watch that has been kept over Morse was even more strictly kept to-day than ever. It appears to be the desire of the police to make no arrest until after the funeral, unless it becomes known that the murderer actually entered the house and escaped within an hour, an idea scouted by the police at the present time. The following advertisement will appear in to-night's local papers.

$5000 Reward:

The above reward will be paid to anyone who may secure the arrest and conviction of the person or persons who occasioned the death of Andrew J. Borden and his wife.

EMMA J. BORDEN,
LIZZIE A. BORDEN.

Crops Injured by Terrific Storm.

SOUTH BEND, Ind., Aug. 5.—A terrific storm visited St. Joseph county last evening. In the southwestern part it assumed the proportions of a cyclone and did great damage, especially to the growing crops. In the vicinity of North Liberty it is thought much of the corn crop is ruined. Several residences in that village were badly damaged by hail and lightning. At New Carlisle several residences were destroyed.

Salisbury and Newfoundland.

LONDON, Aug. 5.—Lord Salisbury, in view of the present political situation, declines to legislate in favor of a distress loan of £750,000 for Newfoundland, but promises to support the measure if it is introduced in Parliament. The Queen has conferred the decoration of the order of Victoria upon the maidservants of Salisbury, wife of the premier.

A Tyrolean Tragedy.

LONDON, Aug. 5.—The bodies of a clergyman and a guide, roped together, were found yesterday at the bottom of a precipice of the Solden mountain in West Tyrol.

British Miners Lose Their Lives.

LONDON, Aug. 5.—Six miners lost their lives this morning in a coal pit near Dewbury, through the pit in which they were at work becoming flooded with water.

Taken from Jail and Lynched.

WYNNE, Ark., Aug. 5.—Allen Carter (colored) who was arrested Tuesday on a charge of assaulting his 14-year-old daughter, was taken from jail last night and lynched.

Ocean Steamers.

Arrived—At New York, City of Berlin, Liverpool; Critic, Leith; Glengoil and Chitian, South America; Santiago, Cienfuegos. At Boston, Elberfeld, Hamburg. Passed Brow Head, City of Chicago, New York.

WEATHER INDICATIONS.

FAIR.

WASHINGTON, Aug. 5.—For the 24 hours from 8 a. m. to-day: For New England, clearing to-day, fair weather to-night; showers in the northern part and on the coast Saturday; slightly warmer Saturday, except on the southeast coast, where the temperature will be lower; variable winds, shifting to westerly.

COTTAGE CITY CULLINGS.

Newsy Notes About the Summer So-journers.

[Special Dispatch.]

COTTAGE CITY, Aug. 5.—A second leap year progressive whist party was given at the Wesley last evening by Miss S. Alice Fell of Cambridge, Miss Fannie Fay of Weymouth and Miss Brown of Providence. The prizes were won as follows: First prize, lady, souvenir spoon, Miss M. F. Brown of Lowell; gentleman, walking stick, Prof. Charles Jacobus of Springfield; booby prize, lady, Miss G. C. Brown of Lowell; gentleman, F. H. Wiley, Indianapolis, Ind.

The Summer meeting and school of methods of the Massachusetts Woman's Christian Temperance Union begins its session to-day. A large attendance is expected.

Schooner yachts Halcyon, Diana, sloops Corsair, Frolic and Nimbus are in Vineyard Haven.

A ball complimentary to the yachtsmen will be given in the Casino to-morrow evening.

Judge Charles Searls of Putnam, Ct., returned to that place to-day.

Mr. and Mrs. H. H. Wilder of Lowell are domiciled on Penacook avenue.

Rev. Daniel Evans and wife of East Weymouth are at Pine Highlands.

Mr. and Mrs. E. B. Rhodes of Pawtucket, R. I., are at the Aylesworth cottage.

Station 7 will be used by the yachtsmen on Saturday and Sunday.

There have been 25 applications for membership to the D. B. Club.

Edward Carter of New Bedford is here for a few days.

EAGLES BATTLED FOR A BABE.

Agonized Father Saw a Duel to the Death for Possession of His Little One.

DETROIT, Aug. 5.—Two eagles had a duel to the death for the possession of the six-months-old baby of Peter Shaw, who lives four miles north of Allis, Presque Isle island, yesterday. Mrs. Shaw had laid the baby down in the grass and returned to the house for a few moments, when an enormous eagle swooped down on the child and sank its talons into the little one's flesh and clothing. The mother heard her baby cry, but came too late to be of service, but her shrieks brought the father, who quickly comprehending the situation, mounted a horse, and armed with a rifle rode to the shore of a near by lake, where he knew there was an eagle's nest. Shaw arrived just in time to witness a terrible sight; two eagles were hovering above a craig of rock battling for possession of the baby that lay high up on the cliff. But when the father had reached the summit one of the eagles had fallen to the ground, while the other had again taken the child for another flight. The father fired and the bird and baby fell into the water. The frantic father plunged into the lake, caught up the body, but the little one was dead. He took home the body, along with those of the two eagles, one of which had been killed in the fight.

EIGHT HOUR AGREEMENT IGNORED.

Trouble Brewing Between Organized Labor and World's Fair Com.

CHICAGO, Aug. 5.—Trouble is brewing between organized labor and the World's Fair Commission. A last night's meeting of the Carpenter's Council the business agent made a report which was backed up by the signatures of numerous carpenters employed on the grounds, setting forth that the eight hour agreement and other agreements made between the Fair Directory and the labor people were being wholly ignored. It was said that not only were the contractors violating the agreement but the commission itself was working men nine hours, and a committee was appointed to visit the grounds and make a full investigation, and it was instructed to wait on the grounds' committee and ask for an adjustment. The labor men are much dissatisfied with the way matters are going and a strike of carpenters is not among the improbabilities.

THE KNIGHTS TEMPLARS CONCLAVE.

Immense Crowds Flocking to the Rocky Mountain Metropolis.

ST. LOUIS, Mo., Aug. 5.—Every one of the five roads leading from this city to Denver is having a hard time to secure transportation facilities for the immense crowds flocking to the Rocky Mountain metropolis. Special trains carrying commanderies from all sections of the South and Southeast went out last night, and each road was also compelled to put on extra trains to accommodate the travelling public which is taking advantage of the cheap rates to leave the city for a few days. Upwards of 150 extra sleepers, every one full, left this city last night.

RUINOUS TO RELIGION.

Pope Addresses a Letter Against Free Masonry to Italian Bishops.

ROME, Aug. 5.—The Pope has addressed an encyclical letter to the bishops throughout Italy, in which His Holiness declares that the actions of the Free Masons of Italy are subversive of religion.

HOME MATTERS.

LOST AT SEA.—Bark Guy C. Goss of Wareham, Capt. Mallett, at Port Townsend from New York, reports on March 18th William Steele, one of the crew, fell from the rigging and was drowned.

TIED AT MONEY.—We must vacate. Only a few weeks longer to remain. We must close out our stock. Everything must go at a discount. Wamsutta Clothing Co.

SLIGHT FIRE.—About 1 30 o'clock this morning a large oil lamp in the store of William Burke, corner of Kempton and Newton streets, exploded and a light blaze resulted. Herbert W. Nickerson discovered it, broke open the door and quenched what might have been a serious fire.

LOST HER HUSBAND.—Mr. and Mrs. Timothy Minahan of Whitentou visited friends in Fall River last week. While at the depot waiting for a homeward train they became separated. Mrs. Minahan took the train, but her husband did not, and since then she has seen nothing of him. Consequently she has asked the police to be on the lookout for him, and knows no reason for his strange disappearance. He is 45 years old, 5 feet 9 or 10 in height, erect in walking, of light complexion, and slightly bald on top. He is also known as "Joe King."

Now is THE TIME to buy your suit and save money; everything must go. Wamsutta Clothing Co.

EGG FINISH.—White's best 25c. dressing, 15c. bottle at Buchell's.

TWENTY-FIVE boys' sailor suits to be closed out at 50 cents; former price $1.00. Wamsutta Clothing Co.

TURKISH BATHS. See the price list on the second page.

TENNIS SHOES marked down to 39c. Buchell.

BEST IN THE WORLD for rheumatism; Turkish and Electric baths. 5 South Sixth street.

TENNIS SALE at Buchell's.

TAKE A BATH at No. 5 South Sixth street.

Hood's Sarsaparilla makes the weak strong.

PERSONAL.—Rev. J. W. Malcolm of Brooklyn, formerly of Pleasant Street church, arrived in this city to-day and is the guest of Mr. George L. Brownell, his father-in-law. His family have been in the city a few days. Mr. Malcolm has accepted the call to a Congregational church in Cleveland, O., and will commence his pastorate there early in September. A splendid new church edifice is in process of erection by that society, which will probably be ready for him when he assumes his duties there.

Mrs. James Hathaway of Fall River, with her daughter, Mrs. Smith of this city, and daughter, have gone on a two weeks' vacation visit to I. F. Hathaway, North Adams.

W. W. Leach and wife are spending their vacation at Vineland, N. J.

Edward P. Harrington of the Third Auditor's office of the Treasury Department, Washington, is visiting his home in this city.

Misses Mary E. and Edith Cook, and Mamie B. Stowell from this city, Louisa and Janis Bennett, and Jennie Greene from Apponeganset, are camping in Lynnewood cottage, at Cadman's Neck, for two weeks.

SIXTY MILLION BUSHELS OF WHEAT—A Bushel for Every Inhabitant of the United States. The Kansas Crop for '92.—Never in the history of Kansas has that State had such bountiful crops as this year. The farmers cannot get enough hands to harvest the great crop, and the Santa Fe railroad has made special rates from Kansas City and other Missouri river towns, to induce harvest hands to go into the State. The wheat crop of the State will be from sixty to sixty-five million bushels, and the quality is high. The grass crop is made, and is a very large one; the early potatoes, rye, barley and oat crops are made, and are all large. The weather has been propitious for corn, and it is the cleanest, best looking corn to be found in the country to-day. Cheap rates will be made from Chicago, St. Louis and all points on the Santa Fe east of the Missouri river, to all Kansas points, on August 30 and September 27, and these excursions will give a chance for Eastern farmers to see what the great Sunflower State can do. A good map of Kansas will be mailed free upon application to Jno. J. Byrne, 723 Monadnock Block, Chicago, Ill., together with reliable statistics and information about Kansas lands.

A SOUTH END EARTHQUAKE.—The South End mill district thought it had an earthquake about 9 o'clock last evening. About that hour a deep, dull report was heard from the Potomska mill yard followed by a roar that made the very earth tremble for blocks around, and continued for several minutes. A crowd of two or three hundred gathered around the mill gates expecting to learn some startling facts. Some were sure a boiler had burst, while others couldn't be dissuaded but that some one was operative with grievance had blown up the engine-room with dynamite. It finally transpired that a big "pop" safety valve on one of the boilers of mill No. 2 had given way to an excess of pressure on the boiler and blown off. No damage was done and the crowd shortly dispersed. These valves do not often blow off, but when they do the noise is something terrific.

THE HEALTH AND PLEASURE RESORTS OF MICHIGAN AND THE WEST are illustrated and described in a handsome folder, containing a fine colored map, which has just been issued by the Michigan Central "The Niagara Falls Route" and which is designed for the special use of people in the East who wish to learn something about the resorts of Michigan, Wisconsin, the Lake of Mackinac, the lakes of Minnesota, Yellowstone Park, Colorado, Utah, and the Pacific coast. Copy of folder will be sent on application to W. H. Underwood, Eastern Passenger Agent, Buffalo, N. Y.

FALL RIVER HAS A SMALL POX SCARE.—Along with other horrors in Fall River yesterday came the report that a case of small pox had been discovered on Pleasant street. The Board of Health investigated promptly and found that the story was false. One of the physicians of the Board stated that two passengers who recently landed on the steamer City of Chester had been troubled by a light rash, but neither of them was ill, and there was not the slightest occasion for alarm.

SCHOONER JANE GRAY SHIPED.—Steamer St. Paul, at San Francisco from Ounalaska, brings news of the seizure of schooner Jane Gray of San Francisco, for some unknown reason. She was a whaling vessel and had no material or outfit on board for hunting seals. She was picked up near St. Paul Island by the United States steamer Mohican and towed to Sitka.

CONSIDERED IT AN INSULT.—A Standard reporter called on Mayor Ashley this morning for a copy of the protest sent him by the W. C. T. U. of this city. The Mayor declined to give up the document, saying he considered it an insult.

WANTED.—Parents to come to our store and see what great value we can give you in children's suits. We have about 200 children's suits that are going to be sold. First come, first served. Ashley & Peirce, 72 and 74 William street.

CHILDREN'S 50 and 75c. shirt waists 35c.; boys' 50c. knee pants for 40c.; better grades at a discount from former prices. Wamsutta Clothing Co.

WE WANT YOU TO TAKE ADVANTAGE of our midsummer mark down sale of men's, youth's and children's clothing. We don't mean to carry over a single Summer suit. Ashley & Peirce.

WE HAVE JUST RECEIVED 500 pieces of those fast black hose, sizes from 9½ to 11, at 15c., two pair 25c. Ashley & Peirce.

THE CELEBRATED $2.00 and $2.50 Lamson & Hubbard hat to be closed out at $2.50. Wamsutta Clothing Co.

REGIMENTAL REUNION.—The 4th regiment, M. V. M., will hold a reunion at Camp Joe Hooker, Lakeville, late in September.

LOOK AT OUR WINDOW and see the 50c. ties in silk and satine, at 25c., and 10c. socks, 3 pairs for 25c. Wamsutta Clothing Co.

LADIES' SHAMPOO only 50 cents. No. 5 South Sixth street.

REGIMENTAL REUNION.—See advertisement 5th page.

WHALING SCHOONER BLAKELEY.—A few days ago a report was received in San Francisco from Port Townsend, by telegraph, that whaling schooner Blakeley of San Francisco had been wrecked at Middleton Island, Alaska, June 24th. W. C. Hayden, the chief officer, was said to be responsible for the published statement. Officer Hayden arrived at San Francisco 26th ult. on steamer Walla Walla, and stated that the report concerning the Blakeley was erroneous. The bark Northern Light was the vessel that went ashore at Middleton Island and she is now returning to San Francisco.

TO-MORROW (Saturday) in our children's department we commence on a large discount on suits. Wamsutta Clothing Co.

Lots of Our CUSTOMERS

WHO USE

Gas for Cooking

Have average Bills of Only

$2.00 to $3.00

PER MONTH.

Think of this and the discomfort and trouble of a large stove, costing more to run than a

GAS STOVE.

A few small ones to rent. Large ones at cost,

Only $15!

DELIVERED AND SET UP.

See our

ELECTRIC Fan Motors!

Nothing like 'em for cooling the air and driving flies. For Edison or Westinghouse current.

N. B. GAS & EDISON LIGHT CO.

COLUMBIAS

Highest grade Bicycle in the world. Perfect in material, construction and finish, fitted with the Columbia Pneumatic Tire, guaranteed against puncture, bursting or leakage.

HOYLAND SMITH,
146 Pleasant Street.
Inspection solicited. Catalogue free.

SHAPE YOUR MUSTACHE.

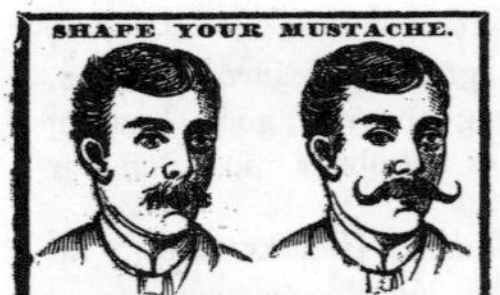

What is more disgusting than to see a man always twisting, twirling, and biting his mustache. *Avoid the bad habit* by using the instrument that will keep it always just right. Will be sent postpaid with complete outfit for 55 cents, two for one dollar. Postal note or stamps. Address the
Nason Bartlett Co., Box 2480, Boston, Mass.

BRICKS.

Lime and Hair,

FOR PLASTERING.

Cement.

Masons' Building Materials in general.

S. S. PAINE & BRO.,
Front St., just south of bridge.

ALL LIGHT WEIGHT SUMMER SUITS!

Being Closed Out at Buyers' Prices.
Don't delay another day.
A small amount will buy a big package now at

SANDERS & BARROWS',

67 and 69 William Street.

DON'T STOP ME

I know where to find the Lowest PRICES in

HARNESSES,

Carriage Lap Robes, Horse Clothing, Whips, &c., Ladies' and Gents' Riding Saddles, Trunks, Bags, Pocketbooks, Bill Books, Umbrellas and all kinds Travelling Goods.

C. F. CUSHING, - - - - Opp. City Hall,

IS THE MAN.

CUT PRICES FOR ALL Summer Clothing

ELEGANT NECKWEAR 25c. Each.

H. V. SANDERS & Co.

One Price Clothiers, OPP. CITY CLOCK, 92 Purchase St.

NEW BEDFORD BRASS FOUNDRY.

Machinists, Brass Finishers and Founders, Brass, Bronze and Composition Castings, Zinc and White Metal Pattern Castings, Phospor Bronze Castings a specialty, Lead Window Weights and High Speed Babbitt Metals, Chandelier Repairing and Brazing, Brass Finishing in all its branches. Machine Repairing promptly attended to. Lawn Mowers Sharpened and Repaired.

Foundry and Machine Shop, 108 North Water Street, foot of Elm.

WM. T. NICHOLSON, Manager, Formerly Foreman of the Armington & Sims Engine Company's Brass Foundry, Providence, R. I. je25-3m

GREAT SALE OF CARRIAGES.

—AT—

A. DAVIS ASHLEY'S,

947 Acushnet Avenue. cor. Coggeshall Street.

100 new and second-hand Carriages in endless variety; top phaeton, Stanhope, Corning and piano box buggies, Goddards, extension top surreys, canopy top surreys, buckboard changeable seats in the oak, new buckboard finished natural wood, $75.00; new open buggies $65.00 up; one $450.00 doctor's coupe nearly new, $165.00; two seated open and canopy top Ashley wagons, new and second-hand; also new and second-hand open and covered express wagons, best variety in the city; two and four seat dog carts; one new canopy top dog cart $50.00. If you want to buy or trade for any kind of a carriage that runs on wheels just look my stock over. I will guarantee the price and represent the goods just as they are; also have a fine assortment of harnesses; call early and you will get your money's worth. I also have some very desirable house lots and first-class business located lots which I will sell low for the location.

A. DAVIS ASHLEY,
947 Acushnet Ave., Cor. Coggeshall St.

TRY

39 TOBACCO!

Best in the Land for Smoking.

Be sure that the tag 39 is on every piece, and take nothing else in place of it.

Distributing Agents

Driscol, Church & Hall,
Wholesale Grocers,
NEW BEDFORD.

FINE CARRIAGES.

GEO. L. BROWNELL

OFFERS FOR SALE AT HIS

Carriage Manufactory and Repository,

Cor. Acushnet Ave. and Cannon St.,

NEW BEDFORD,............MASS.,

A FINE assortment of Carriages, namely: Landaus, Coaches, Coupe Victorias, Coupe Rockaways, Extension and Standing Top Family Carryalls, Phaetons, Goddard Box Top Buggies, Open Road and Business Wagons. Also a very large assortment of *SECOND-HAND CARRIAGES* of all descriptions, which will be sold low.

GILES G. BARKER, Supt.

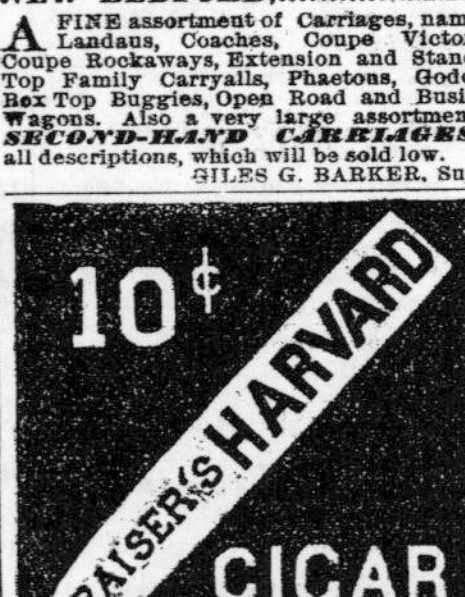

THIS CIGAR has stood the test of competition LONGER than any other popular brand, and the sales increase each year. TRY ONE and form your own opinion of its merits.

H. TRAISER & CO., Makers, Boston.

HAVE A CLEW!

Police in Pursuit of Assassin of the Bordens.

Finger of Suspicion Points to a Dartmouth Man.

Singular Stories Told by John W. Morse.

They Fail to Agree in Important Particulars.

Wonderful Self-Possession of Dead Man's Daughter.

Police Think Her Conduct is Somewhat Strange.

Unless All Signs Fail Startling Developments are at Hand.

No Trace Yet of the Axe with Which Bloody Work was Done.

A most brutal and shocking murder stirred Fall River as it has seldom been stirred yesterday morning, and no crime has ever been committed there which could compare with it in fiendishness. Andrew J. Borden, a highly respected business man, 68 years of age, and his

Andrew J. Borden,
The Murdered Man.

wife, a most estimable lady of advanced years, were literally hacked to pieces in their quiet home at No. 92 Second street, in that city, as related in the *Standard* special dispatches yesterday. The house is a two and one-half story structure, surrounded by a well kept yard and barn, and is located in a thickly settled neighborhood. The family consisted of Mr. and Mrs. Borden, an unmarried daughter, Lizzie, and a servant named Bridget Sullivan. Another unmarried daughter is away on a visit to relatives. For some days past Mr. and Mrs. Borden and Miss Lizzie had been feeling poorly, and Wednesday or the day before they suspected that their food was being tampered with, and that they were suffering from poisoning. They had determined upon an analysis, according to the servant, but as far as can be ascertained were not in possession of any definite information which would confirm their suspicions. Wednesday afternoon Mr. Borden was so unwell that he did not attend a meeting of the Massasoit Bank directors, as was his custom, and his friends inquired concerning his health.

THE ROOM WHERE MR. BORDEN WAS MURDERED.
[From a Sketch by the *Standard* Artist Yesterday.]

Yesterday morning he felt better, and between 10 and 11 o'clock went down town and transacted some business in the First National Bank. Thence he walked up North Main street and at 10 30 was seen standing on the corner of Anawan street, where he owns a handsome brick block. He gave orders to certain workmen, and then crossed the street and walked directly to his home. When he entered his house the servant was in the kitchen, and Miss Lizzie Borden, the daughter, was sleeping in her room upstairs. Just what happened afterwards is not known. At 11 15 Miss Borden awoke and descended the stairs. She passed into the front sitting room on the first floor, and there a sight met her eyes which caused her to cry out in horror. Lying on a lounge with his face toward the ceiling was the body of her father. The head was covered with wounds from half an inch to six inches in length and the wall of the skull had been crushed in. One gaping cut extended from the forehead diagonally across the face to the shoulder-blade, and had evidently been inflicted by a butcher's cleaver or broad axe. The unfortunate man's blood had flowed on the shirt front and stained the sofa pillow.

Mrs. Churchill, a neighbor, happened to be passing at the time, and noticed the agonized expression on Miss Borden's face. She hastened in and Bridget Sullivan, the servant, also ran to Miss Borden's assistance when she heard her scream.

"Where is your mother, Lizzie?" inquired Mrs. Churchill.

Miss Borden, who retained remarkable control of herself, replied that her mother had gone out. She had received a message some little time before, asking her to call on a sick friend, and the daughter supposed that she had gone on an errand of mercy. Still the door leading out to the back yard was open contrary to custom, and the young lady fearing that the conclusion regarding her mother might be incorrect, in company with Mrs. Churchill she went to her mother's room in the northwest corner on the second floor, where the poor girl's worst fears were realized.

Stretched in a sickening pool of blood was the wife and mother. The body lay between the bed and dressing case, and the skull had been battered in apparently by the same weapon which had been used on Mr. Borden, although the nature of the wounds suggested that the murderer had

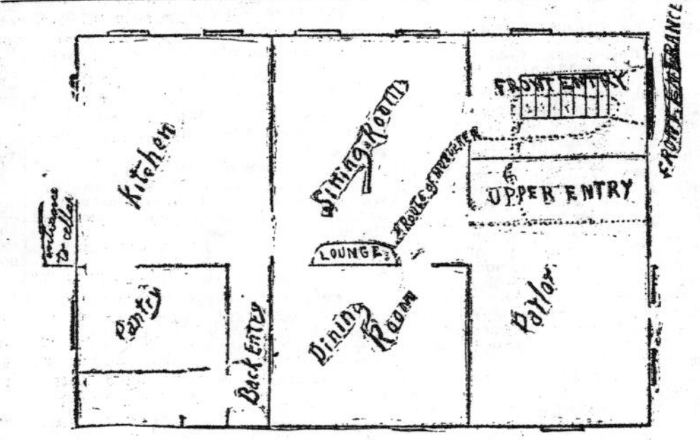

The dotted line shows the track of the murderer from the sitting room to the front entry, up stairs to the upper entry, and from there through a door into the spare bedroom on the second floor, over the parlor, where Mrs. Borden was slain.

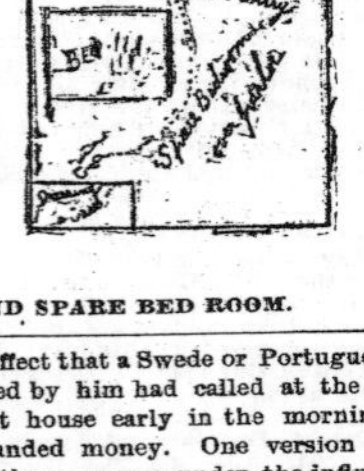

DIAGRAM OF LOWER FLOOR AND SPARE BED ROOM.

dealt his blows with the blunt edge. Miss Borden swooned and Mrs. Churchill and the servant at once raised an alarm. Unfortunately the first notice sent out was to the effect that there had been a stabbing affray on Second street, and it was said that there had been a row in a yard. A few minutes later the most intense excitement prevailed, when it became known that Andrew J. Borden had been murdered, though it was fully half an hour before the details of the awful tragedy reached the public. Business in the centre of the city was practically suspended and men in all walks of life flocked to the scene.

City Marshal Hilliard sent several officers to the house, and all quarters of the town were scoured. The first rumor that reached the police had it that Mr. Borden had been struck near the barn, and had walked back to the house and thrown himself on the lounge to die. Investigation proved, however, that the story was not true, as there was no trail of blood leading into the room where the body was found. The carpet was stained and there were no indications of a struggle.

Dr. Bowen, who resides near the murdered man, was the first to enter the house after the crime was committed. He learned the following facts: When Mr. Borden returned from the bank he removed his coat, put on a thinner garment and sat down on the sofa to read a paper. The servant, Bridget Sullivan, passed through the room on her way upstairs to wash the windows. Observing Mr. Borden and remembering that he was not as well as usual, she asked him how he was feeling. "No better or worse than yesterday," was the reply. Bridget passed Miss Borden on the stairs. The latter went out through the room in which her father was sitting and entered the barn to get a piece of iron with which she intended to mend a flower pot. She thinks that she was not absent from the house more than five minutes. She, too, noticed that her father was occupied with a newspaper, and merely nodded to him. When she returned the frightful scene which has been described met her gaze. Dr. Bowen is positive that Mrs. Borden must have entered the room where Mr. Borden sat just as the murderer finished his bloody work, and that the fiend chased her up stairs to her room, where he struck her down, as the blows were inflicted by a person who stood beside her.

Nothing was taken by the murderer, and it is conceded that he was not intent on plunder. Mr. Borden was a reserved, courteous gentleman, who amassed a fortune when a member of the firm of Borden & Almy, undertakers. He retired from business many years ago and invested largely in real estate. He was President of the Union Savings Bank, a director in the B. M. C. Durfee Safe Deposit and Trust Co., and was interested in several of the manufacturing corporations of the city. Deceased was of a retiring disposition and never figured prominently in public life. He was twice married, his second wife, who was murdered yesterday, being a daughter of the late Oliver Gray. Two unmarried daughters by his first wife survive him.

A great many people thought it incredible that a murderer could enter a house on one of the principal thoroughfares of this city, commit such a deed as startled the community yesterday, and depart without attracting attention, but when one reflects, it wasn't remarkably strange after all. If there were no outcry or commotion, not only one man, but three or four men might appear and disappear in any building that could be selected, and the chances are that they would not excite curiosity. At all events, it is certain that the fiend who struck down Mr. and Mrs. Borden was not seen about the premises by any one, and several theories have already been exploded. At noon City Marshal Hilliard and a posse of officers drove across the river and visited the property of Mr. Borden in South Swanzey. He owned two farms there, and there was a story to the effect that a Swede or Portuguese employed by him had called at the Second street house early in the morning and demanded money. One version had it that the man was under the influence of liquor, and that Mr. Borden told him he would not pay him while he was in that condition, and another, as already related, that Mr. Borden promised to go down town and get the money. It is known now that Mr. Borden had no trouble with any of his men on the farms, and that no Portuguese had been in his employ. His relations with the farm hands were of the pleasantest nature, and Marshal Hilliard and his officers found all of the latter at work.

The deed was done by somebody nearer home, but strange to relate, nobody has the slightest suspicion of who the guilty man can be. Miss Borden says that a week or two ago, a man whom she didn't know called on her father and wanted to hire a store which was vacant. The man would have used it as a saloon and Mr. Borden refused to let it. A few days ago the same man called again and was again refused. He appeared to be somewhat angry, but was certainly not provoked enough to commit the murder, and thus far there is nothing to indicate that Mr. Borden had any serious difference with anybody. He was a stern man, just to all, and demanded his rights on all occasions, but at the same time he was not quarrelsome, and treated everbody fairly and courteously.

The murderer, whoever he was, struck to kill at the first blow, and accomplished his purpose, as not a sound escaped from either of the victims. If Mr. Borden had so much as spoken, his daughter and the servant must have heard him, and the same is true of his wife. Whether she was murdered before or after her husband was cut down, is a question. The police

Borden Homestead Where the Murder was Committed.

contend that she would surely have screamed had she happened to enter the room where her husband was lying, and argue from that, that she was put out of the way first. It is not improbable, however, that she was speechless with fright and ran to her own room. It is also possible that she was in the sitting room when the murderer entered and withdrew, thinking that the latter wished to talk business with Mr. Borden. In that case, the murderer, aware that he had been observed, might have followed Mrs. Borden up stairs after he killed her husband.

State Officer Dexter arrived at the house soon after the news was made public, but confessed that he could not find the faintest clew to assist him. Two arrests which aroused the town afresh were made at about 2 o'clock. The Central Station police locked up a couple of young men for fast driving and in five minutes Court Square was packed with an excited crowd. A little later the police of the Eastern Station took into custody William Daily of Roxbury, who said that he had arrived in the city Wednesday night. There were blood stains on his clothing, which the prisoner said were two days old, and it is believed that he was telling the truth. It was as though the murderer and his clumsy but effective weapon had been swallowed up by the earth, and at last accounts yesterday afternoon the police had no clew to follow.

The Police Have a Theory.

It cannot be said that the more the police reflect on the double murder which shocked Fall River yesterday, the more they are mystified, but at midnight it was true that the more they studied the case the greater was their astonishment. State officers, as well as the men of the local force, agree that there has never been such a murder in these parts. In broad daylight, with many people within hailing distance, and at least two people within a stone's throw of the house which was the scene of the awful tragedy, two persons are cut to pieces, and there is no more commotion about the accomplishment of the foul deed than would result from slicing an apple. More than that no such killing was ever accomplished so neatly. In spite of the fact that a frightful weapon was used the blood spilled could be covered by a napkin. A pool had formed under Mr. Borden's head, and his shirt was drenched with the crimson tide, but the walls and the sofa bore no traces of the deadly work. Beyond a few spots on the shams of the pillows in the spare bedroom where Mrs. Borden's body was found, there was the evidence of the same neat handled work. There had been no bungling blows, no conflicts, the aim of the fiend who took the lives of the aged couple was true. Mrs. Borden had received no wounds as she was escaping, if she attempted to escape. She had been felled, as a butcher would fell an ox, in her tracks, and nobody, neither her daughter nor her servant, knew that she had perished.

There is somebody else who was ignorant of this pitiless attack and his name is John W. Morse. Years ago he resided in Fall River; originally he hailed from Dartmouth. He went West to seek his fortune, and his sister married Andrew J. Borden, the murdered man. Morse located in Hastings, Iowa, and it is said that

[Continued on Seventh Page.]

CHOLERA INFANTUM.

It Is Easily Avoided and May Often Be As Easily Relieved.

Cholera infantum can be prevented by proper feeding, and it can often be cured in the same way.

Mr. Horace R. Lane, of Burlington, Vt., writing to the Boston *Journal*, says:

"With this letter I send you a photograph of Bessie F. Lane, whose life, I think was saved by the use of lactated food. Her mother could not nurse the little one, and the doctor ordered one of the oldest and most widely advertised artificial foods; but Bessie refused to take it. The doctor then recommended lactated food, and the baby liked it, thrived as well as on mother's milk, and was the picture of health while living upon it. Later, when she was a little over two years old, she was taken with a severe attack of cholera infantum, and was so low that life was despaired of.

BESSIE LANE.

Lactated food was given, and all other nourishment stopped, and she soon picked up, gaining flesh rapidly, and is to-day, as the photograph shows, a picture of perfect health. I have advised many of my friends to use lactated food, and it has never yet failed to do all that is claimed for it."

Infants fed on lactated food suffer less and fewer die than those fed on any other.

Mothers should thoroughly understand what this lactated food is, how pure and nourishing and how successfully it meets nature's requirements. It is a food which contains all the nutritive properties sufficient to develop the child's bone, muscle and fat, and which is digestible from the time of birth and nourishes as long as it is eaten.

No sugar is used in it but the pure sugar of milk, and this in proportion to most closely represent mother's milk. With it is combined pure barley malt, the finest wheat gluten, and the nutritious elements of the oat, and the mixture is thoroughly cooked by high steam heat.

The little ones like it—why shouldn't they?

THE BEST

SWIFT'S SPECIFIC is the best spring medicine, because it assists nature to throw off the impurities of the blood by its prompt action on the skin, and at the same time tones up the entire organism. This is just contrary to the effect of the various potash, mercury, sarsaparilla mixtures, which bottle up the impurities in the system, thus producing much sickness and suffering. Therefore, for a

Spring Medicine

you cannot do better than to take a few bottles of S. S. S.

"As a physician, I have prescribed and used S. S. S. in my practice as a spring tonic, and for blood troubles, and have been very successful. I never used a remedy which gave such general satisfaction to myself and my patients." L. B. RITCHY, M. D.
Mackey, Ind.

Treatise on blood and skin diseases mailed free.
SWIFT SPECIFIC CO., Atlanta, Ga.

MANHOOD RESTORED.

Before & After Use.
Photographed from life.

"SANATIVO," the Wonderful Spanish Remedy, is sold with a Written Guarantee to cure all Nervous Diseases, such as Weak Memory, Loss of Brain Power, Headache, Wakefulness, Lost Manhood, Nervousness, Lassitude, all drains and loss of power of the Generative Organs in either sex, caused by over-exertion, youthful indiscretions, or the excessive use of tobacco, opium, or stimulants, which ultimately lead to Infirmity, Consumption and Insanity. Put up in convenient form to carry in the vest pocket. Price $1 a package, or 6 for $5. With every $5 order we give a written guarantee to cure or refund the money. Sent by mail to any address. Circular free in plain envelope. Mention this paper. Address,

MADRID CHEMICAL CO., Branch Office for U. S. A.
358 Dearborn Street, CHICAGO, ILL.

FOR SALE IN NEW BEDFORD, MASS., BY R. H. & H. A. Lawton, Apothecaries, Union St.

TURKISH BATHS

ARE

ALL THE RAGE.

Terms:

Single Turkish and Russian baths,	$1.00
Six Tickets for same, transferable,	5.00
Twelve Tickets for same transferable,	8.00
Plain Bath,	.50
Tub Bath,	.25
Alcohol Bath,	.50
Ladies' Head Shampoo,	.50
Massage per treatment,	2.00
Electric Bath,	2.00

YOU NEED A BATH

GO TO

No. 5 South Sixth Street.

AN INVITATION.

TO THE PUBLIC:

You are hereby invited to participate in our Grand Reduction Sale of Summer Goods, on SATURDAY, August 6th. By perusing the notes from the different departments mentioned below, you have a synopsis of *Bill of Fare* for this occasion.

MOYNAN & CO.

READ HERE.

Moynan & Co. offer for Saturday a job lot of Cambric Shirt Waists at 43c. each. Sateen Waists with ruffle on front and collar, in Navy and Red, 98c. French Chambray Waists in Blue, and Pink, with plaited back and Jabot front, $2.00.

On Saturday, we will sell all our 69c. and 75c. belts in either Leather or Silk at 45c. Lace Tidies in 3 styles, regular price 15c., for Saturday only 8c. Pretty quill fans in red, gray, pink, blue, cream and white, former price 50c., for Saturday 25c. Moynan & Co.

SILK WAISTS—China Silk Waists, lined or unlined, plaited front and back, in colors, Red, Blue or Black, former price $3.98, now $2.45. China Silk Waists, with Jabot front, in Red, Black or Blue, with polka dots, formerly $4.98, now $4.75. Surah Silk Waists, plaited fronts, collar and cuffs, plain colors, Red, Blue or Black, former price $5.50, now $4.98.

PICTURES—Special inducements in Etchings, good subjects and handsomely framed. Also Pastels, Chromos, Oleographs, Autogravures, &c., all at low prices. On Saturday all purchasers of pictures to the amount of $2.00 will be presented with a handsome *Bamboo Easel, free of charge.*

MILLINERY DEPT.—All our fine Straw Hats and Bonnets that were from $1.00 to $3.50, now 25c., 48c., and 98c.; any Trimmed Hats now on hand at one quarter regular value. Again for Saturday we offer those handsome Mull Hats in all colors, were $2.98, now $1.50. Moynan & Co.

CLOAK DEPARTMENT—Ladies' satin stripe Madras Waists, regular $1.48, now 75c. Ladies' Outing Suits (waist and skirt) were $2.29, for this sale $1.98. Ladies' Wrappers, worth $1, for this sale 79c. Ladies's Blazers in navy, black and tan, were $4 and $5, for this sale, $2.98. A few Spring Jackets were from $6 to $10, on Saturday we close them out at $1.48. Moynan & Co.

MOYNAN & Co. offer some remnants of Fancy Ribbons, former prices 25c., 39c., 50c. per yard, on Saturday they are closed out at 19c. per yard. Don't forget our Ribbon Sale, all widths and colors, at half regular prices. Come early Saturday.

BEDSPREADS, BEDSPREADS—White spreads, good, large size, worth 98c., for 65c. Lancaster spreads, 12-4 size, worth $1.25, for 98c. Imitation Marseilles spread, worth $1.75, for $1.48. Moynan & Co.

MOYNAN & Co. are showing some great values in Sample Towels, all pure linen, at 10c., 12½c, 19c., and 25c. each. Also Sample Handkerchiefs at 5c., 9c., 12½c., 15c. Come early and get a choice.

DOMET FLANNELS.—Again on Saturday you will have an opportunity of procuring a few pieces of that Domet Flannel. Summer weight and worth 10c., in lengths of from 5 to 10 yards, at 5c. per yard. Moynan & Co.

DRESS GOODS—Two Special Drives in this Dept. for Saturday. Lot No. 1 – 750 yards Fancy Wool dress goods, full 36 inches wide, sold all season at 25c., for Saturday while they last at 12½c. per yard. Lot No. 2—300 yards Plain and Fancy Dress Goods, some strictly all wool, sold freely this season at 37½c., 45c. and 50c., for Saturday only at 29c. per yard.

MOYNAN & Co. will continue for Saturday Men's fine gauze Balbriggan Shirts and Drawers, in three shades and trimmed with pearl buttons, regular 19c., for 36c. each.

LADIES' UNDERWEAR — French Balbriggan vests, silk bound and trimmed with pearl buttons, regular 35c., for Saturday only 25c. each.

FANS, FANS—All our 39c. and 50c. Paper Fans, now 25c. Also pretty Quill Fans in red, blue, cream, gray, pink and white, formerly 50c., now only 25c.

MOYNAN & Co. are headquarters for Embroideries, Ruchings, Laces, Derby Waists, Gloves, Leather and Silk Belts, Linens, Muslins, Underwear, &c. Come early Saturday and avoid the rush of afternoon and evening.

BAMBOO EASELS GIVEN AWAY FREE to all purchasers of pictures to the amount of $3. Don't omit to see our low prices on Etchings, Pastels, Chromos, &c. Moynan & Co.

The Evening Standard.

NEW BEDFORD, MASS.
FRIDAY EVENING, AUGUST 5.

THREE EDITIONS DAILY.
No. 37 Union Street.
PUBLISHED BY
E. ANTHONY & SONS,
INCORPORATED.

—TERMS—

Six Dollars a Year; Three Dollars for Six Months, in advance; Single Copies Two Cents.

FOR PRESIDENT:
BENJAMIN HARRISON
OF INDIANA.

FOR VICE-PRESIDENT:
WHITELAW REID
OF NEW YORK.

CONTENTS OF THIS EVENING'S STANDARD.

☞ As we get fuller reports of the Alabama election, it doesn't seem to have been such a great Democratic victory after all. It is now said that only a third of the white Democrats voted the regular ticket, and that the result of the election is due to negro votes. But if all the Republicans and two-thirds of the white Democrats voted for Kolb, the Alliance candidate, it is very difficult to see why he was not elected. All the majority now claimed for the regular ticket is 10,000, which is a great come down from 92,000 of two years ago. As for the methods of the election, there was a very significant telegram from one district in Alabama the day after, to the effect that the whites had made preparations to resist "negro domination," and that the other side, not wishing to make trouble, gave way. If the regular Democrats bid for the colored vote, what a humiliation for them. If they coerced or suppressed it what a comment on the freedom of elections. The whole matter of this Alabama election deserves to be probed to the bottom, and the truth made known to the country.

☞ The New York *Herald* has announced a novel plan for the present Presidential campaign. To the person who most nearly predicts the popular plurality of either Cleveland or Harrison, it will give a free trip around the world, paying all expenses; to the person making the second best prediction it will provide a trip to London, Paris and return, and the third best prediction will be rewarded by a trip to London and return. Competition is open to residents of all parts of the United States, the only conditions being that the prediction must be made on a ballot which is printed in the *Herald* every morning. Any one can make as many predictions as he has ballots.

☞ Every political organization and every candidate for office will need to become familiar with the Corrupt Practices Act with regard to elections, which is now in effect. They will have to keep a careful record of their expenditures, and be very cautious as to what they do during the campaign.

Mr. Crapo's Position.

Whenever the *Journal* speaks of Lieut.-Gov. Haile in its editorial column the utterance is accepted as coming from one having authority; and in like manner statements concerning Mr. Crapo in the *Advertiser*, occasionally enough, have a sort of ex-cathedra tone. Therefore when the *Daily Advertiser* says that "Hon. W. W. Crapo has stated definitely to his friends that he will not be a candidate for Governor, and that the office is not one which he now desires," the statement, though not particularly startling as a matter of news, is significant, inasmuch as it has the appearance of being authorized by Mr. Crapo.

Of the office which Mr. Crapo does desire the *Advertiser* has nothing to say; but let that pass. There can be no question that the *Advertiser* was a most strenuous advocate of Mr. Crapo's candidacy for the gubernatorial last year; but it is not positively certain that the support accorded by Mr. Barrett (whether Mr. Barrett's foes gave any respectable reasons for their prejudices against his lead or not) was not a powerful factor in the defeat of Mr. Crapo and the bringing of Colonel Allen to the fore. This is said in no feeling of bitterness toward the *Advertiser* or its editor, but merely to call attention to one of the curiosities of politics as developed by last year's campaign. Possibly it is because of Mr. Crapo's supposed lethal efforts in Mr. Crapo's behalf last year that Mr. Barrett is chary this year of pressing the former's claim to the United States senatorship.—*Boston Transcript.*

The *Transcript* says that the *Advertiser* "has nothing to say" "of the office Mr. Crapo does desire." That is true. Mr. Crapo has not informed us of the office which he does desire. We presume that in accordance with his loyalty to Republican principles, he will devote his time first to help achieve a victory this Fall, and not to an attempt to dictate every movement inside the party to his own ends during the next few weeks, when the party needs all its strength. That is the duty just now of every loyal Republican.—*Boston Advertiser.*

GROCERIES LOW.

Best Potatoes in the city 23c. peck.
Try our 40c. Tea; sure to please.
Yellow Eyed Beans 8c. quart.
Pea Beans 8c. quart.
Eagle Beans 8c. quart.
Red Kidney Beans 10c. quart.
Best Tapioca, 4 pounds 25c.
Good Rice, 4 pounds 25c.
Ginger Snaps, 3 pounds 25c.
Best Butter in the city 30c pound.
Choice Butter 28c. pound.
Our 35c. Coffee is a seller.
Common or Soda Crackers, 4 pounds 25c.
Quaker Rolled Oats 10c. pound.
Good Salmon, 2 cans 25c.
Best Zephyr Soda Crackers, 2 pounds 25c.
Good Shoe Blacking 5c. can.
One-half pound size Ivorene 10c. package.
Best Huckleberries 15c.
Best St. Louis Flour 66c. bag.
Choice Hanaff Flour 68c. bag.
Good Pickles 8c. bottle.

MEATS LOW.

Best Round Steak (heavy beef) 12c. pound.
Best Rump Steak 20c. pound.
Best cuts Sirloin Steak 22c. pound.
Thick Rib Corned Beef (best cuts) 8c. pound.
Shoulder Clod Corned Beef, (no bone, no fat,) solid beef, 8c. pound.
Corned Beef without bone (very choice) 6c. pound.
Good Corned Beef at 4 and 5c. pound.
All of our Corned Beef was corned by us this week, (not too salt, not too fresh,) suits every one.
Best Rib Roasts 10 to 15c. pound.
Good Roasts at 5c. pound.

ALWAYS BUY MEATS
—AT—

GRAY BROS',
288 and 294 PURCHASE ST.,
CORNER MAXFIELD,

BRANCH STORE,

FOURTH ST., Cor. THOMPSON.

HOME MATTERS.

THE THUNDER SHOWER.

House on Mill Street Struck by an Electric Bolt.

About 10.30 o'clock this morning the sky wore a most ominous aspect. Thick clouds of blackest black overhung the city and the dead calm that pervaded the atmosphere betokened an impending tempest. It came half an hour later, drops as big as cranberries, and later in a solid sheet, while poor, overtaken pedestrians sought shelter wherever they best might. Lightning flashed brilliantly, especially among clusters of wires in the centre of the city, while the thunder boomed and roared to the north, west and south of us. In fact most of the tempest seemed to pass over New Bedford, though the western part of the city got the worst of it, and nature's fireworks furnished a fine display everywhere.

One particularly heavy flash toward the close of the tempest gave every evidence of having struck near at hand, and the fire alarm sounding from box 33, corner of Kempton and Florence streets, soon afterward proved the surmise true. A house owned and occupied by Mrs. Nancy W. Hayden, situated on the south side of Mill street, just east of Florence street, had been struck by lightning, but no fire was found when the department arrived. The bolt had entered the roof near a chimney, tearing off the shingles, then passed down a wall into a sleeping room, splintering the laths and throwing plastering about, and finally shot through the outside walls and into the ground. A few clapboards were torn off. The loss will not exceed $100 and the building is insured.

During the storm a bolt of lightning struck the ground near the stone crusher on the east side of Acushnet avenue. George Murphy, a boy about 17 years of age, was thrown to the ground. It was afterwards found that his arm and legs are discolored in several places and dark spots about as large as a silver dollar in size are noticeable. Edward Murphy and Thomas Lewin, two young lads who were with him, also felt the effects of the electricity, and experienced a tingling sensation in their arms and legs. The bolt passed into the cellar of a house that is in process of construction near by, but it cannot be seen that any damage was done. The bolt evidently divided and a current passed directly through the crusher engine-house and out through an open window. William W. Sherman, the engineer, John H. Murphy and Michael Cleary, city employes, who had taken refuge there, were considerably affected and were partially stunned. After emerging from the engine-house the current passed through a tool chest. Although it was crowded full of shovels and other implements, no damage was done except to a hoe that was nearly in the centre of the chest. The blade was bent double and the handle split the entire length. The roller was within 25 feet, and evidently furnished the attraction, but it cannot be seen that it was in any way damaged.

Lightning played havoc with telephones in the north end of the city, and many of them were burned out and will require extensive repairs.

NELLIE MAY GOING TO BRAVA AGAIN.—The schooner Nellie May is again to cross the Atlantic. She has been on the dry dock at Providence, where her hull has been thoroughly calked and scraped and her sails rebent. Either next Monday or Wednesday the craft will start on her voyage to Brava. The owner of the craft, Antone Coelho, at first intended to take over a cargo of lumber and coke, but abandoned the plan and has loaded about 20 tons of ballast instead. The same captain who commanded the craft when she brought over the 48 Portuguese passengers, over whom there was so much trouble last Spring, will command her again. His name is J. J. Godinho, and he is an intelligent shipper. Brava, which is a member of the Link street Portuguese colony of Providence have got enough money together to enable them to go back to Brava to live in luxury, and as soon as they complete their arrangements for removal the Nellie May will sail.

COUNTY COMMISSIONERS' HEARING.—The county commissioners of Plymouth gave a public hearing yesterday on the petition for a highway to connect Buzzards Bay, East Wareham Neck and Onset Bay. Judge Grover of Canton appeared for Point Independence landholders. Lawyer John C. Sullivan of Middleboro for Long Neck landholders, Judge E. P. Harriman of Wellfleet for the Old Colony railroad, and the selectmen of Wareham for the town. Some 20 witnesses, all in favor of a highway, were heard and the commissioners viewed the premises. The board will send an engineer to survey a road as soon as possible. The question of crossing the Old Colony railroad at grade is the important point at issue.

PASSED EXAMINATIONS.—The following persons have passed the physician's examination for policemen: John F. Oliver, George A. Wood, Ulysses L. Clark, Patrick McDonnell, Daniel S. Considine, Robert F. Vogel, Frank E. Demers, Frank C. Kimball, Daniel Denneen, George W. Pinkham, Edward Foley, Willis C. Underwood, Frederick Hathaway, George E. Macomber, Fred M. Pease, Peter H. Topholm, James E. Eldredge, S. McKenie, Patrick J. Cox, John J. McAuliff, Albert J. Rose, Franklin C. Eldredge, Albert N. Gray, Edward Allen.

THEY WILL RAISE THE ALVA.—Mr. White, of the Boston firm of Perkins & White, which purchased the Alva, was seen yesterday afternoon. He said: "I really know nothing about the sails. Mr. Perkins has handled the matter entirely, and he is not in at present. We shall raise her if it is possible thing, and I see no reason why it would not be quite possible. Then, if she is worth it, we shall repair her and fit her all over again and sell her. If, however, she is very badly damaged she will be broken up for what she contains."

DARTMOUTH.
The Dartmouth Grange will give another of those enjoyable lawn parties Tuesday evening, Aug. 9th. The work of building the new Grange hall was begun to-day, therefore the next regular meeting will be held at the house of the Worthy Master. The committee on clambake have given the date for the bake Aug. 26th.

Miss Mason of East Warren, R. I., is visiting her friend, Miss Myra Howland.

NANTUCKET.
The 'Sconset-Nantucket ball game at 'Sconset yesterday resulted in another defeat for the visiting team, this time by the score of 9 to 1. The game was without special feature and one-sided. The batteries were: 'Sconsets, Young and Wheeler; Nantuckets, Riley and Echeveria.

The yachts to arrive yesterday were the yacht Cora of New York, the cutter Proteus of New York, and Charmer of New Bedford. The Cora belongs to John A. Morris, father-in-law of Thurlow Weed Barnes. They illuminated this evening. Judge Bisbee, with a party from Brockton, are aboard the Charmer.

For the office of register of probate and insolvency, left vacant by the death of Capt. Benjamin F. Brown, there are already two applicants, Allen Coffin, Esq., and Henry Riddell, Esq. The statutes provide that in case of vacancy in this office the Governor shall appoint some person to fill the office until the next Fall election. The Governor is at present off on a vacation and Judge Defries has designated Clerk of Courts Josiah F. Murphy to act as register of probate pending an appointment by the Governor.

FALL RIVER.
The police took 1400 people to Rocky Point yesterday.
The spinners and weavers have decided to sail to Crescent Park on Labor Day.

THE SUSPECTED MAN.

John V. Morse, a Well-to-do Western Land Owner.

He Lived in the Family of Isaac C. Davis of South Dartmouth.

Spoken of as a Man of Excellent Character.

Thirty years ago there arrived at South Dartmouth, a bright-looking young man. He had a keen eye and a manner about him which denoted that he had the making of a successful business man. This was John Vincenn Morse, whose name is unpleasantly connected with the Borden tragedy at Fall River. He asked Isaac C. Davis for work, and Mr. Davis gave it to him.

Since the finding of the mutilated bodies of Mr. and Mrs. Borden hundreds of people have looked with suspicion upon a John Morse who is known to have spent the night at Mr. Borden's house the night previous to the tragedy and there has been a great desire to learn just who he is and where he came from. Early last evening the news came from Fall River that it was John Morse of Fairhaven, later in the night it was John W. Morse of Dartmouth. The police at the Border City were certain that he was a relative of Mr. Borden, and with the intention of furnishing *Standard* readers the full particulars of this horrible crime, a representative of this paper visited Fairhaven and in a short time the story of Fairhaven's connection with this crime was entirely explained. John P. Morse, who resides there, it was learned, had not been out of town for several days and was in no way related to the unfortunate victims of this tragedy.

This morning the writer started out to learn something about John W. Morse, who at this time was located at South Dartmouth. A visit there revealed the fact that there was no such person as John W. Morse, but that John V. Morse, a relative of the murdered man, had been living for a year with Isaac C. Davis, and that he had recently left and went West. At first he settled in Illinois, buying and selling land. In this he was very successful, and is supposed to have accumulated wealth. Finally he settled in Hastings, Mills county, Iowa. About two years ago he came East with a large number of horses of his own raising, and after disposing of many of these animals at Warren, R. I., he gave a job by Mr. Borden, and was given a job. After working for Mr. Davis a few years he packed up his clothes and went West. After working for Mr. Davis a few years he packed up his clothes and went West. At first he settled in Illinois, buying and selling land. In this he was very successful, and is supposed to have accumulated wealth. Finally he settled in Hastings, Mills county, Iowa. About two years ago he came East with a large number of horses of his own raising, and after disposing of many of these animals at Warren, R. I., he made his appearance at Padanaram. There he disposed of the remainder of the horses, and about a year ago took up his residence at the house of Mr. Davis. As before stated, Mr. Davis is blind and Morse has been his adviser. His judgment in matters of business was considered good, and in nearly every particular his advice was asked.

Upon being questioned, Mr. Davis said that for several weeks he had talked of purchasing a pair of cattle of Mr. Borden, and on Thursday, after shaving Mr. Davis, he (Morse) started on foot to take the electric car for the city, intending to take the train for Fall River.

A daughter of Mr. Davis, who was present during this conversation, stated that Morse wore a light gray suit and that it was his intention of returning home last night.

Continuing, Mr. Davis said Morse was not the purchased additional cattle while away, and that he also expected to run over to Warren to see his uncle. His purchases were to have been brought home with him.

After rehearsing the above facts the scribe was questioned as to the cause for such an earnest inquiry into the particulars of Morse's character.

"Has he been hurt?" and "Has he met with an accident?" were questions asked. They had read the particulars of the Borden tragedy as printed in the third edition of the *Standard*, but never for a moment dreamed that their friend was suspected of the crime.

When told of the true situation of affairs each and every member of that household were completely surprised. The first to recover from this startling intelligence was one of the daughters. "It's nonsense," said she, "John Morse thought so much of his brother-in-law to do such a thing as that."

"You are right," replied the aged father. "He's too upright a man to harbor even such a thought. Why, sir, he thought as much of Mr. Borden as the day he married his sister who has since died, and he frequently spoke of his brother-in-law and nieces in endearing terms. No sir, John V. Morse never committed that crime. It's an awful mistake. Why, I would have trusted him with everything in the world, and would as soon think of my own son doing the deed."

It was in a like manner that the daughters spoke of Morse. Davis, and in fact every one present, gave him an excellent name, and felt confident that he would be able to clear himself from the terrible suspicion which at present is hanging over him. If it should prove that John V. Morse is in any way connected with this murder it will be as great a surprise to the members of the Davis family as was the finding of the murdered man and woman yesterday.

Morse is said to have cousins residing in this city, and he seems to be well known to the townspeople residing in Padanaram. To them he has been looked upon as a mystery, as they term it, simply because they have known nothing about him.

Morse, who is supposed to have accumulated wealth, had repeatedly talked of retiring from active business, as being a single man he had enough to live on the rest of his days.

Morse is a good looking man over six feet tall and will weigh about 200 pounds.

It is now ascertained that Miss Emma Borden, a daughter of Mr. Andrew J. Borden, one of the victims of the Fall River tragedy, was visiting the widow of Allen Brownell of Fairhaven, who resides in the east part of the town. She returned to Fall River yesterday. Miss Borden has many acquaintances in this city.

PLYMOUTH COUNTY.
The directors of the Abington & Rockland Electric Railroad Co. met Wednesday evening and voted to accept all the franchises granted by the towns along the proposed line. The company will organize at once and contracts for the construction of the road will be made as soon as possible.

The First Unitarian Society of Middleboro has extended a call to Rev. J. W. Stocks of Boston, and has also voted to purchase a $1200 organ and to enlarge their church.

The turners' strike at Leonard & Barrows' shoe factory, Middleboro, has been settled, the firm giving their old hands their places and prices.

The Middleboro fire department will hold a field day in September.

CHRISTIAN CAMP-MEETING.
CRAIGVILLE, Aug. 5.

The dull, cool weather of several days' duration yesterday gave way to clear skies and warmer air. Such a change does not altogether contribute to enlarge the attendance at the Tabernacle, because the beauties of nature become the more attractive, and lovers of the rod and the line by inland ponds and ocean fishing grounds are tempted to gratify their passion for sports. The sermon of the morning was, however, an excellent one, preached by Rev. J. P. Marvin of Rockland, R. I., from James iv, 17: "Therefore, to him that knoweth to do good, and doeth it not, to him it is sin." The danger and guilt of the neglect of positive obedience to the claims of duty by Christian people was effectively presented.

The afternoon was devoted to the annual business meeting of the association. The treasurer reported cash on hand at the beginning of the last financial year $524.05; collected from various sources, $1729.52; total, $1253.57. Cash paid, $1360.33; in hand, $13.34; total, $1253.57. The only indebtedness of the association is a balance of $300 due on the association house, now owned and run as a boarding and lodging house, and that will be paid before the present season closes.

The four members of the board of trustees whose term expired were Vice-President C. A. Tillinghast, Secretary T. S. Weeks, and Trustees H. H. Fisher of New Bedford and G. B. Merritt of Fall River, who were all re-elected to their respective positions by a unanimous vote.

An extended discussion was had in an informal way as to the future conduct of the annual series of religious meetings here, some persons advocating an arrangement of specialties for successive days, employing specialists to lead the programme for each day; others favored putting the entire series into the hands of some experienced evangelist. No formal action was taken, and the whole matter will rest as before with the trustees as to future sessions.

Resolutions of respect and sympathy relative to members of the Association deceased during the year were passed by a rising vote while prayer was offered by Rev. O. J. Wall of Fall River.

The same person was the preacher of the evening. Text Isaiah ii, 2. "The mountain of the Lord's house shall be established in the top of the mountains." The superior excellence of the Christian religion and its wonderful prevalence were presented in a very impressive manner. The sermon was followed by a social service of marked interest. This morning the preacher is Rev. I. H. Cox of New Bedford; this afternoon Rev. T. S. Weeks of Wolfborough, N. H., and this evening Rev. J. B. Weston, D. D., of Stanfordville, N. Y.

B. S. B.

FAIRHAVEN.

Some women are fixing up charges against Joshua Delano, constable, for alleged breach of civility and failure in the performance of duty. The women, it is currently reported, are very much in earnest, and have started a tyrmado which they intend shall blow Mr. Delano out of office. The wherein the constable is said to have erred was over a gate down on Fort street that some of the pin-wheel waltzers which come over to Beacon Villa from New Bedford every Tuesday and Friday night had thrown into mystery. The mistress of the mansion without a gate called to Mr. Delano when he was passing, on two occasions, and prayed that he assist her in recovering the lost property, to which the constable replied as independently and impudently (so it is said) as an ordinary citizen, that he was busy, and hadn't the time. So the ladies are canvassing for names to the above-mentioned petition, and their victim is occasionally seen on the Four Corners, humming "They're After Me." The Delano rooster would be a ripe one to pull off his nest, said a Fairhaven prophet to the reporter.

The Methodist society are in sack cloth and an other on his hard nine business recently with the Third District Court. The church people mourn her fall from grace; also the dollars that were spent in charity for her support. It seems to have been a case of casting pearls in the wrong direction, for when the woman was asked in court to hand over or go to Sherborn, she produced a bank book with about $195 on it. It is rather a sad lot for the Methodists, who wanted the prisoner poor out of temptation for a year or so, to reflect that the bail money probably came out to the church treasury and members' pockets.

The selectmen are in a muddle over a lot for a burial of a child. The child's mother is not in a condition to meet the expense, and the alleged father says he won't pay it until the courts decide that he is his man. Mattapoisett, which is the woman's settlement, is not in a mood to scrip up, and Fairhaven doesn't want to pay anything and belonging to her, and meanwhile the undertaker waits.

Handsome stables are being constructed for Miss Alice B. Train by Abner P. Pope, carpenter, of New Bedford. The plans were made by Kendall & Stevens of Boston. The size will be 46 by 26, 20 feet posts. On the ground floor will be a spacious carriage room, stalls, wash room and harness room. The building was commenced Saturday and will probably be finished this month.

Levi M. Snow started from his national vacation to Sanapee, N. H. He goes to fish, and to judge by the amount of gear he carries he intends to capture a lake full.

Tug George W. Hunt pulled off bark Gay Head from Zephyr's wars yesterday afternoon where she has been for repairs.

The Monday Club will make an excursion to Nonquitt Tuesday night by steamer Nonquitt. The club will hold a hop at the Nonquitt Hotel.

H. L. Card had a big trade last week selling about 200 gallons of ice cream.

A house is being built for Jacob Brightman on the Taber property at Oxford.

The Spray took a gay party of 30 people down the harbor last night. A supper was enjoyed on board.

EXPOSITION ECHOES.

The famed Six Nations in New York state will be well represented in the Indian exhibit at the World's fair.

In Denmark's exhibit at the World's fair will be a fine array of porcelain ware and a notable art display, including reproductions of many of the Thoswaldsen sculptures.

In Chicago during the World's fair the famed "Passion Play" will be produced exactly as it has been given for centuries, at intervals of ten years, by the people of Ober-Ammergau, Bavaria.

Several amazons of the king of Dahomey may probably be seen in the Dahomey village which will be established at the World's fair. Sixty or seventy natives and their manner of living will be shown.

W. H. Hilliard, of New York, is in San Francisco painting a picture of California scenery to hang as a representative of the Pacific slope at the World's fair. He is said to have a commission for certain work to do Californian.

One of the novel exhibits in Machinery hall at the World's fair will be a model paper mill. It will be in active operation every day and all the processes of paper making, from the pulp to the finished card, which will be in the form of a World's fair souvenir.

Just back of the New York building at the World's fair, in a depressed area, will be spread out flat an immense topographical map of that state. It will be thirty-six feet long and twenty-six wide, and will show the mountains, forests, rivers, towns and all of the great natural and artificial features of state scenery.

FINANCIAL.

SANFORD & KELLEY.

GARDNER T. SANFORD, CHARLES S. KELLEY, } **Bankers,**

Members Boston Stock Exchange,

47 North Water St., New Bedford.

STOCKS AND BONDS BOUGHT AND SOLD ON COMMISSION

At the New York and Boston Stock Boards.

CONSERVATIVE & PROFITABLE INVESTMENTS

FOR TRUST FUNDS.

New Bedford Manufacturing Stocks have a first-class record as dividend payers, and we always have some on hand to offer.

Sole Agents for the sale in this city of the 6 per cent. Guaranteed Mortgages of the Lombard Investment Co.

Auction Sale of Stocks and Bonds WEDNESDAYS AND SATURDAYS, at 10 45 A. M.

ORDERS SOLICITED.

Mass. Real Estate Co.

246 Washington St., Boston.

Dividends **7** Per Cent.

Invests in Central Real Estate in Growing Cities.

Authorized Capital - - - -	$2,000,000
Capital paid in - - - -	1,250,000
Surplus - - - - - - - -	100,000

ORGANIZED IN 1885.

Paid Dividends of 5 per cent. per annum for 4½ years. Paid Dividends of 7 per cent. per annum since July, 1890. Average Dividend since organization over 6 per cent. per annum. Surplus at close of last fiscal year, over $100,000.

Stock offered for sale at $108 per share until July 31.

Send to or call at the office for information MWF

T. E. BOWMAN & CO.,

Topeka, Kansas,

NEGOTIATORS OF

Conservative Mortgage Loans in Eastern Kansas.

$2,500,000 LOANED without loss to any investor, and have never yet had to foreclose a farm loan in these eastern counties. Write us for list of investments. s29

GEORGE LEVY, North End Pawn Broker.

Cash advanced on Real or Personal Property. All business private. au3-1m

SECOND EDITION.

HOME MATTERS.

WATER BOARD.

Important Meeting Held This Noon, When Numerous Petitions Were Granted.

A regular meeting of the New Bedford Water Board was held this noon, Mayor Ashley presiding. Present, Messrs. Kirschbaum, Kempton and Church.

Bills were presented, examined and approved amounting to $5,326.83

Weekly pay rolls for labor to the following stated amounts have been paid since the last meeting. These rolls have been certified to by the clerk and approved by the president previous to payment being made:

Date of approval.	Amounts.	
July 11th,	$539.15	
July 18th,	570.34	
July 25th,	501.42	$1,710.91
Total expenditure for the month,		$7,037.74

MAIN PIPE.

The following list of petitions for main pipe were received. Each was accompanied by a guarantee whereby petitioner agrees to provide for the payment of a rate equal in amount to 6 per cent. of placing the work indicated. Each petition received separate action as stated:

Belleville avenue, from Dean street north 250 feet, petition and guarantee signed by Barnard McQuade. Petition granted and pipe ordered laid.

Beetle street, from present terminus 96 feet east of Acushnet avenue, east 62 feet to Howard street, and thence in Howard street from Beetle street south 103 feet. Petition and guarantee signed by Robert Allen. Petition granted and pipe ordered laid.

County street from Clark street north 80 feet. Petition and guarantee signed by Lucian F. Bouchard. Petition granted and pipe ordered laid.

Robeson street from present terminus 7 feet east of Cedar street, east 133 feet. Petition and guarantee signed by Terence Clark. Petition granted and pipe ordered laid.

Acushnet avenue from terminus 353 feet south of Potomska street south 60 feet. Petition and guarantee signed by Isabella Oliveira. Petition granted and pipe ordered laid.

Independence street from present terminus 154 feet west of County street west 823 feet. Petition and guarantee signed by Joseph F. Lee and two others. Petition granted and pipe ordered laid.

Weaver street (contemplated) from Dartmouth street west 234 feet. Petition and guarantee signed by Charles E. Peirce. Petition granted and pipe ordered laid as soon as street is lowered to the proper grade.

Acushnet avenue, from present terminus 267 feet north of the Tarkiln Hill road, north 270 feet to point opposite the house of Hancock Engine Company No. 9, for their use and convenience; also that a drinking fountain be located in the vicinity. No guarantee accompanied this petition. Petition signed by Hancock Engine Company No. 9, John A. Russell captain, Allen Russell, Jr., clerk. Laid upon the table for future consideration.

Shawmut avenue, from Durfee street north 1100 feet to Grand street. Petition and guarantee signed by J. H. Woods and eight others. Petition granted and superintendent instructed to obtain the necessary pipe.

Adjourned.

REAL ESTATE SALES.—Joseph and William R. Wing and Rodolphus Beetle have sold to Charles C. Tilton and Arunah B. Crowell 44.45 rods of land on the west side of Shawmut avenue.

Martin Bartley and Robert Mitchell have sold to Callice Charet 16.70 rods of land on the east side of Rock street.

Rodolphus Beetle has sold to John Welch 628.25 rods of land at the southwest corner of Cove road and Ashley street, in Dartmouth, and Charles E. Cook has sold to Mr. Welch two additional lots on the south side of Cove road, one containing 255.68 rods and the other 260.90 rods.

Messrs. Kempton, Beetle & Tripp have sold to Mary B. Bradford the west end of "Union Wharf Store" in Fairhaven.

Rodolphus Beetle and Henry P. Jenney have sold to William A. Lowe land on the south side of Austin street, containing 17.35 rods.

Cyrus D. Hunt has sold to Levi M. Snow a lot of land on the east side of Walnut street in Fairhaven, containing 8.56 rods. Also to the same party 37.11 rods on the same street.

John Welch has sold for $2000 to Annie M. Delaney land on the east side of Acushnet avenue, containing 20 rods.

John Welch has sold to Joseph Dawson, trustee, land on the corner of the Cove road and contemplated Ashley street, Dartmouth, containing 628.25 rods.

Also to the same party, two lots in Dartmouth, containing 255.68 and 269.90 rods.

John Welch has sold to John S. Marks, land on the south side of Woodlawn avenue, New Bedford, containing 13.84 rods.

KILLED BY THE LIGHTNING.—The lightning struck and killed a mare and colt belonging to Horatio Hathaway on the Bennet place, at the Head of the River. The mare was a valuable animal for which Mr. Hathaway paid $1000.

DR. PRICE'S DELICIOUS Flavoring Extracts

NATURAL FRUIT FLAVORS.

Vanilla – Of perfect purity.
Lemon – Of great strength.
Orange – Economy in their use
Almond – Flavor as delicately
Rose etc. – and deliciously as the fresh fruit.

PROBATE COURT.

FULLER, J.

FRIDAY, Aug. 5.

[Continued from First Edition.]

Wills proved—Of Elizabeth T. Wood of New Bedford, Charles W. Clifford executor; of Hiram W. Martin of Rehoboth, Esek H. Pierce executor; of Samuel Jones of New Bedford, Louisa Jones executrix; of William C. Howland of New Bedford, Abby C. Howland and Ephraim C. Palmer executors; of Mary M. Leach of New Bedford, Benjamin Irish executor; of Ebenezer Hervey of New Bedford, James W. Hervey executor.

Administration Granted—To Pliny Mosher, on estate of Annis Mosher of Westport; to Jason N. Wheaton, on estate of Earl P. Martin of Rehoboth; to Phebe A. G. Sherman, de bonis non with the will annexed, on estate of Canaan Gifford of Westport; to Joseph I. da Terra, on estate of Jose Theodora Serpa of Boston; to William S. Simpson, on estate of Caleb H. Blake of New Bedford; to Alfred S. James, on estate of Sarah T. James of New Bedford.

Licensed to sell real estate—Executors of the will of Clarissa D. Galpin of New Bedford, to sell about three acres land to pay debts (the land adjoins that of George B. Hathaway and he has offered $130 for it); executor of the will of Russell Maxfield of New Bedford, to sell house and 15 rods land southwest corner of Maxfield and Walden streets, to pay legacies, debts, etc.; guardian of Charles J. and Albert H. Patterson of New Bedford, to sell wards' interest in real estate for maintenance.

Accounts allowed.—2d and final, of trustees under will of Matthew Luce of New Bedford; 2d and final, of guardian of Isaac N. Sherman of Dartmouth; 1st and final, of administrator estate of Justus Sherman of Westport; final, of administrator estate of Charles Howland of Dartmouth; 1st and final, of executrix will of Henry B. Jones of Providence; final of administrator with the will annexed of Edward Morse of Acushnet.

Guardians appointed—Mary A. Leahey of Margaret E., William T., Mary A., Thomas M., and Robert J. Leahey of New Bedford, minors; Ephraim C. Palmer, of Abby C., Sarah E. and Henry F. Palmer of New Bedford, minors.

Accounts rendered—Second, of executor will of Ruth E. Burroughs of New Bedford.

The estate of William A. Anthony of Fall River was declared insolvent.

Gjert Lootz was appointed a trustee under the will of Frederic W. Otto of New Bedford.

The order of distribution in the estate of Henry H. Allen of San Francisco was returned.

An allowance of $.70 was made to the widow from the personal estate of William C. N. Sanford of New Bedford.

Partition among tenants in common was decreed of real estate in Fall River in the estate of William J. Feely, late of Providence, R. I.

A petition to set aside for the benefit of William T. Ferguson $5000 of the real estate of Anna B. Ferguson of New Bedford was continued.

WAS IT MALICIOUS MISCHIEF?—There has been complaint of malicious mischief at the North End recently. This morning a calf belonging to Timothy McCrohan that was tethered in the vacant lot at the corner of Howard and Coggeshall streets was found dead with a rope wound tightly around its legs and neck. While it would be possible for the animal to have got itself into the position during the night in which it was found, there are many who think that it is a clear case of malicious mischief perpetrated by the same parties who have committed so many misdeeds in that section of late. The case has been reported to the police and will be investigated.

ALARM BUT NO FIRE.—An alarm was sounded shortly after one o'clock this afternoon from box 123, corner of Acushnet and Coffin avenues, and the firemen responded. They found a house on Brown street east of Rock street and occupied by a Portuguese family, full of smoke. Investigation proved that children had lighted a fire in a stove not connected with a chimney and the smoke filled the house. No damage was done.

NEW BEDFORD LEADS.—The following tables taken from the *Banker and Tradesman*, gives the business transacted at the office of the Registry of Deeds for the three cities in Bristol county for the week ending July 30:

	Conveyances.	Mortgages.	Attachments.	Total.
New Bedford,	48	17	7	62
Taunton,	23	18	4	45
Fall River,	25	16	2	43

THE BRISTOL MILL.—The stock of the Bristol Manufacturing Company is nearly all subscribed and the full $500,000 will probably be subscribed before the end of the present week.

Subscribers to the stock are called to meet for organization on Monday, the 15th inst.

A MUSICAL AND LITERARY ENTERTAINMENT will be given in the Bethel A. M. E. church this evening. See advertisement.

DEATHS.

In this city, 5th inst., Mary McCormick, aged 56 years.
Notice of funeral later.

The funeral of the late George Dowd will take place at his father's residence, 92 First street, Saturday, at 2 o'clock. Relatives and friends are invited to attend.

MARINE INTELLIGENCE.

The owners of sch D B Fearing, of Newport, are receiving a dividend of $12 on a 64th.

Ar at New York 4th, sch Kate Scranton, Kelley, Hyannis. Cld, sch P H Crowell, Chase, Fernandina.

Passed through Hell Gate 4th, schs H P Hallock, Tisdale, New York far Taunton; S L Thompson, Keefe, do for do; Julia Frances, Anderson, do for Fall River.

Ar at Perth Amboy 3d, sch Wm Mason, Ellis, New York.

Ar at Philadelphia 4th, schs John W Linnell, Handy, Providence; J Frank Seavey, Kelley, Kennebec. Cld, schs Allen Green, Nickerton, Weymouth; Donna T Briggs, Gurney, Plymouth; Jesse Barlow, Barlow, Wareham; Jesse Murdock, Phinney, do.

Ar at Georgetown, DC, 4th, schs Annie J Pardee, Crosby, Kennebec; Young Brothers, Thatcher, Penobscot.

Ar at Newport News 4th, sch Eagle Wing, Portsmouth.

Sld from Norfolk 4th, schs L H Brayton, this port; E F Angell, Portland; B C French, Providence.

Ar at Tamatave July 12th, bark Taria Topan, Luscomb, Boston.

It Strikes us as Remarkable

to hear of the wonderful record for curing enjoyed by Betton's Infallible Pile Salve; it cures every form of this troublesome ailmena. If not to be had at your druggist, send 50 cents to Winkelmann & Brown Drug Co., Baltimore, Md.

FINANCIAL.

Boston Money in Demand—Stock Markets Firm—Western Crop Movement — Centennial—Talk of an Increase in Chicago & Northwestern Dividend — Railroad Earnings.

FRIDAY, Aug. 5.

The probability of another heavy export shipment of gold this week is the cause of considerable realizing of floating stocks and has assisted the bears somewhat in their efforts to bring about a reaction. Short interest is much larger now than last week. Declines, however, have not been very large. Under present circumstances, favorable in many respects, unless the outflow of gold reaches dangerous proportions, a bear run would not be surprising. London is taking little interest in our market except in arbitrages. The buying yesterday was credited in many quarters to Vanderbilt interests.

The local money market continues firm at rates ranging from 5 to 6 per cent., yet there is but little renewing.

In the Boston loan market the demand for money is much better and the feeling in general is that call and time rates will remain about stationary at present figures. Call loans 4 to 4½ per cent. Prime mercantile paper 4¾ to 5 per cent. Corporation paper 4 to 5 per cent. The clearing house rate is 3½ to 4 per cent. New York funds sell at 12½ to 15 cents discount.

In New York money on call was easy, rates ranging from 1½ to 2 per cent. Prime mercantile paper 3½ to 5½ per cent.

Bar silver 85¼.

Sterling exchange is quiet and steady; posted rates $4.88 and $4.89½.

Government bonds dull and steady.

In Wall street stock circles this morning, talk was bullish for a long pull on Railroad and Industrials. Short interest in Chicago, Burlington & Quincy seems to be about as large as can be easily handled, and some inquiry by borrowers for Union Pacific, Louisville & Nashville, and Rock Island. London prices come irregular.

The New York market opened firm but not very active. Atchison opened at 39⅝, Erie 28¾, Chicago, Burlington and Quincy at 102¾, New York & New England at 36⅝, Reading at 60⅜. Rock Island 80⅞, St. Paul at 83¼ and Union Pacific at 38¼. After the opening the bears made an attempt to lower prices, but found very little stock for sale. Since then the market has hardened with the General Electric and Omaha leading. At 11 o'clock the former sold at 115 and the latter at 34¼. Atchison advanced to 39⅞, Chicago, Burlington & Quincy to 102⅝, New York and New England to 37½ and St. Paul sold at 83⅝. At the noon hour the market was generally stronger. Chicago, Burlington & Quincy was an exception, declining to 102⅜, Atchison advanced rapidly to 40, New York & New England to 37½, Erie to 29⅜, and Northwest to 118⅛. Omaha was firm at 34½. Union Pacific also held firm at 38⅛. At 1 o'clock there was not as firm a tone to the market. Chicago, Burlington & Quincy 102⅝, Atchison 39⅞, St. Paul 83¾, and Sugar 96. While the majority of the list declined fractionally Omaha on the other hand advanced to 34¼.

At 2 o'clock prices were unchanged. Atchison 40, Lake Shore 136, Delaware & Lackawanna 158, American Cotton Oil 86¼, and General Electric 114½.

At the opening of the Boston stock market prices were about as they closed. Atchison opened at 39½, C. B. & Q. at 102⅜, N. Y. & N. E. at 37⅛, Union Pacific at 38⅛, Illinois Steel at 73⅛, and Bell at 203⅛. General Electric opened at 115. Until noon the market was irregular and quite active, with trading largely in C. B. & Q., Atchison, & Mexican Central. The former declined to 102⅜, then rallied to ½. The latter advanced from 16 to 26⅛. Atchison held firm at 39⅜, N. Y. & N. E. preferred, 89, Mexican Central 15⅞, and Sugar 95. At 1 o'clock there was but little change in the general list. Mexican Central 16⅛, Union Pacific 38⅛, and Atchison 30⅞. Sales to noon, bonds $182,200, and 14,485 shares stock.

At 2 o'clock the market was steady. Boston & Montana 36¾, Atchison 39⅞, Chicago, Burlington & Quincy 103⅜, General Electric 114¾.

Union Pacific earnings are expected to show a very large increase for the month of June.

The earnings of the Mexican Central for the fourth week in July were $203,230; increase $910. For the month $651,512; increase $13,878. The line from Tula to Pachuca is included from July 1st.

The Atchison people say that instead of losing money for them the cut rates to Denver will make for them not less than $50,000 on the Knights Templars conclave alone.

Prime's Crop Bureau telegraphs as follows: Hot and dry again. All things considered, with the exception of nights being cold, weather is favorable for corn. Harvesting of oats is the order of the day this week. Central and Northern Illinois, Iowa, Wisconsin and Nebraska oat reports show general disappointment in outcome of crop; yield is varied in quantity and quality. Iowa outcome probably not over 65 per cent., if that, of last year's. Few oats have been threshed in Illinois. General condition very little different from Iowa.

The movement of Western crops has begun to be felt slightly. The first consignment of currency from New York to the West for the purpose of moving crops was made yesterday. It is said the shipments amounted to $100,000.

It is reported that No. 3 shaft of the Centennial is down about 3000 feet and there are yet no indications of profitable working ground. At present there is no copper in the bottom of the shaft while some time ago there were some streaks of pay dirt that were quite encouraging.

Unfavorable reports from the Chicago, Burlington & Northern road again. The gross decrease in June was not large, but operating expenses increased 30 per cent., thus reducing the net by one-half. Comparative figures follow:

June	1892	Increase
Gross	$152,963	*4,423
Expenses	120,496	28,339
Net	32,467	*32,762
Jan. 1 to June 30—		
Gross	971,861	4,408
Expenses	676,341	83,683
Net	295,520	*79,280

*Decrease

Latest from Chicago reads as below: "Kansas states that corn will not be over a half crop in that State, and that in Missouri it is about as bad."

The earnings of the Chicago & Northwestern Railroad for the year ending May 31st were; Gross, $31,422,272; increase, $3,628,597; net, $11,085,833; increase, $1,583,165. The total surplus of the road increased $1,094,490 over that of last year. A buying movement in the stock was noticed yesterday. Good houses say that an increase in the dividends is probable, and one broker wagered that the stock would cross 135 this year.

STOCK AND BOND MARKETS.

Bids at the close of First Board.

NEW YORK, Aug. 5.

GOVERNMENT BONDS.

U.S. 2s, registered	100
" new 4s, registered	116
" new 4s, coupons	116
" currency 6s, 1895; (Pacifics)	107

RAILROADS

Atchison	39¾
Clev., Cin., Chicago & St. Louis	—
Chicago & Eastern Illinois	—
Chicago & Eastern Illinois pre	—
Chicago, Burlington & Quincy	102½
Delaware & Hudson	139¼
Delaware & Lackawanna	158
Erie	29½
Illinois Central	103½
Lake Shore & Michigan Southern	136
Louisville & Nashville	71¼
Michigan Central	—
Missouri Pacific	60¼
New Jersey Central	—
New York & New England	37¼
Northern Pacific	21½
Northern Pacific pref	58
Chicago & Northwestern	118
New York Central & Hudson River	113¼
North American	14¼
Oregon Navigation	—
Oregon Improvement	—
Oregon Short Line	24¼
Philadelphia & Reading	60¼
Pullman Palace Car Co	195
Chicago, Rock Island & Pacific	81¼
Chicago, Milwaukee & St. Paul	83½
Chicago, Milwaukee & St. Paul pref	—
Richmond Terminal	9
St. Paul & Omaha	54
St. Paul & Omaha pref	—
Union Pacific	38¼
Wabash, St. Louis & Pacific	11½
Wabash, St. Louis & Pacific pref	25⅞

MISCELLANEOUS

Ontario Silver	41¼
Pacific Mail Steamship Co	34¾
Sugar, common	106
Sugar, pref	101¼
Western Union Telegraph	97¼
Silver Certificates	—
Gen'l Electric	115

BOSTON, Aug. 5.

BONDS

Atchison 4s	83¼
Atchison Incomes	60½
American Bell Telephone 7s	—
Chicago, Burlington & Northern 5s	—
Chicago & West Michigan 5s	—
Mexican Central 4s	—
Illinois Steel Co. 5s	*99

RAILROADS.

Atchison, Topeka & Santa Fe	39¾
Boston & Albany	205
Boston & Lowell	181
Boston & Maine	*182½
Boston & Providence	250
Chicago, Burlington & Quincy	102
Chicago & West Michigan	51
Cleveland & Canton	5¼
Cleveland & Canton pref	19½
Flint & Pere Marquette	—
Flint & Pere Marquette pref	—
Mexican Central	15½
New York & New England	36¾
New York & New England pref	87½
Old Colony	182
Oregon Short Line	—
Pullman Palace Car	—
Union Pacific	38¼
Wisconsin Central	16¾
West End	—
West End pref	—

MINING.

Butte & Boston Mining Co	—
Calumet & Hecla Mining Co	283
Centennial	7
Franklin Mining Co	12¼
Kearsarge	—
Montana	36¾
Osceola Mining Co	*32¼
Tamarack	155

MISCELLANEOUS.

American Bell Telephone	203¾
Erie Telephone	*47¼
Mexican Telephone	1.05
New England Telephone	*56¼
Newport Land	—
Boston Land Co	—
West End Land Co	18¾
San Diego Land Co	—
Topeka Land & Development Co	—
Lamson Store Service	18¼
Illinois Steel Co	—
Am. Sugar Refineries, com	—
Am. Sugar Refineries, pref	101
Thomson-Houston	—

*Asked.

CALIFORNIA MINING STOCKS.

SAN FRANCISCO, Aug. 4.

The following are the official closing prices of mining stocks to-day:

Alta	—	Mexican	1 30
Best & Belcher	1 35	Mt. Diablo	1 05
Chollar	—	Ophir	—
Con. Cal. & Va.	3 35	Potosi	—
Crown Point	—	Savage	—
Eureka Con	1 50	Sierra Nevada	1 05
Gould & Curry	—	Union Con	—
Hale & Norcross	—	Utah	—

NEW YORK PRODUCE MARKET.

NEW YORK, Aug. 5.

Flour sales 7200 packages; quiet and steady.
Wheat sales 705,000 bushels; opened steady; fell ⅛; dull.
Corn sales 200,000 bushels; moderately active.
Oats sales 50,000 bushels; dull and easier.
Beef quiet.
Pork dull.
Lard quiet.
Butter firm.
Cheese firm.
Sugar (raw) quiet.
Petroleum steady and dull.
Turpentine easy and dull.
Molasses dull.
Rice firm.
Freights active and steady.
Rosin active and easy.
Tallow firm and quiet.

PROVISIONS AND GRAIN.

CHICAGO, Aug. 5.

Opening.

	Lard.	Wheat	Pork.	Corn.	Sh't Ribs.
May	—	—	—	—	—
June	—	—	—	—	—
July	—	—	—	—	—
Aug.	—	—	—	—	—
Sept.	—	78⅝	12.52½	50⅝	—
Oct.	—	—	—	—	—
Dec.	—	81⅛	—	—	—
Jan.	—	—	13.40	—	—

12 o'clock.

	Lard.	Wheat	Pork.	Corn.	Sh't Ribs.
May	—	—	—	—	—
June	—	—	—	—	—
July	—	—	—	—	—
Aug.	—	—	—	—	—
Sept.	—	78⅛	12.55	50¼	—
Oct.	—	—	—	—	—
Dec.	—	81	—	—	—
Jan.	—	—	13.42½	—	—

LIGHTNING'S WORK.

New Barn at the Alms-House, Mattapoisett, Totally Destroyed.

[Special Dispatch.]

MATTAPOISETT, Aug. 5.—During the thunder storm this forenoon between 11 and 12 o'clock the new barn at the almshouse was struck by lightning and burned. The building, with its contents, comprising 20 of tons hay, fodder, grain, wagons, harnesses, tools and implements, was a total loss. All the live stock was saved. The loss was probably over $2000 and the insurance is $800.

The house in Marion belonging to Mrs. R. F. Hart was struck by lightning in three places to-day and badly damaged. Ten persons were in the house at the time and a Mrs. Chamberlayn had her head cut by falling glass.

THRIVING BABY FARMS.

Results of Vice Covered Up Through the Offices of the City Missionary.

HARTFORD, Ct., Aug. 5—First Selectmen Fowler to-day made a report to the board of selectmen of this town of his investigation into certain baby farms alleged to exist in Hartford and vicinity. He has found five baby farms in existence in Hartford, West Hartford and Bloomfield, where children from other towns and outside the State have been placed by Mrs. V. T. Smith, the missionary of the city mission, a charitable organization in this city. At one farm in this city 23 children had been pledged by her. Affidavits are presented from the women running the farms claiming that they were ignorant of the law and throwing the responsibility upon the city missionary for not reporting the case to the selectmen. No record of the cases had been kept; they are mostly illegitimate children. Mrs. Smith paid $2 per week for each child for their board and her son, Dr. Smith, attended them when ill. The fact was disclosed that some of the children have been adopted by persons paying from $130 to $140 to Mrs. Smith.

The report goes to show that these farms have been run in the interest of Mrs. Smith, who has received young girls from various parts of the State and placed them there during confinement, has received pay from them or their seducers or placed the babies, all under the promise of secrecy. The practice has prevailed for about eight years and probably 300 children have been boarded at these farms by Smith, mostly within four years.

Mr. Fowler's report, which is very specific, covers 33 typewritten pages and narrates among other things the attempt of a member of Mrs. Smith's family to bribe a reporter of a city paper to suppress certain facts he had unearthed.

The selectmen this morning accepted the report and authorized the publication of 100 copies. The affair creates a great sensation here, which has become notorious as a city where the results of vice can be covered up through the offices of the city missionary in the name of charity. The entire business has been conducted in defiance of the state law.

Nancy Hanks' Record Lowered.

DANVILLE, Ky., Aug. 5.—In the 3-year-old race here, Conuor, by C. F. Clay, 2:18, won with ease. He took the third heat in 2:21, breaking the world's record for 3-year-old's over a half-mile track. Nancy Hanks set the previous mark at 2:24 1-2 in 1890.

ASKED FOR POISON.

Druggist Identifies Miss Borden as the Person.

Most Important Clew Yet in the Fall River Murder.

The Young Woman Submitted to Rigorous Examination.

Antecedents of John V. Morse Being Hunted Up.

What Can Be Learned About the Murdered Man's Wealth.

[Special Dispatch.]

FALL RIVER, Aug. 5.—The Fall River *Globe* publishes a story this afternoon that at police headquarters Thursday night at 7 o'clock Capt. Desmond was posting himself on the murder by reading the papers and receiving reports. Marshal Hilliard was busy with his men, and inquiry for Assistant Marshal Fleet revealed the fact that he had gone to supper.

In a few minutes Mr. Fleet returned and then a conversation took place between him and the marshal.

Officers Harrington and Dougherty were given instructions and passed out.

Within 30 minutes after that the most important clew yet discovered was in their posession.

The two officers made their discovery on Main street.

At D. R. Smith's drug store in the city they got the first important evidence.

Then approached the clerk, Eli Bence, and from him was learned that Miss Borden had been in the store within the 36 hours past and had inquired for a certain poison.

The clerk was asked to accompany the officials and was closely questioned as to the exact facts relative to the time, the girl's mental condition and the amount and quality of the poison she had bought or called for. The officers then led the drug clerk to a residence on Second street where Miss Lizzie was stopping for the time being. The young man had not previously been well acquainted with the young woman, but told them he could identify her at sight. He did identify her and in the presence of the police officers informed them that she was in his place of business and made inquiry for a bottle of poison.

Miss Borden's reply to the accusation, as well as the exact language which was used at the the time, is known only to the two officers.

The statement above made is correct and was verified in every particular by a *Globe* reporter last night within ten minutes after it happened."

[By Associated Press.]

FALL RIVER, Aug. 5.—To-day the business men of the city have been discussing Mr. Andrew J. Borden's wealth and business methods and the discussion serves to add to the general astonishment that a crime of such a nature as yesterday's tragedy should be perpetrated within a stone's throw of city hall.

The assessors' books show that Mr. Borden was taxed for $173,650 worth of real estate most of which is situated on South Main street in the very centre of the city. His latest purchase was the Birch property for which he paid $23,000. He rarely ever owed anything. When he made a purchase he paid for it in cash or check, never caring to handle notes of any kind.

One of the largest financiers here said this morning that he doubted if a summary of his debts would show more than $1000 due. His personal estate is variously estimated as between $175,000 and $250,000. Most of it is invested in mill stocks, bank stocks and government bonds.

Late this forenoon it was reported at the police station that a young man, said to be a nephew of Mr. Borden, was being suspected of the murder. It arose from the fact that some time ago Mr. and Mrs. Borden were overheard in an angry talk with a young man over the division of some property. As the young man was parting from them at the front door he was heard to say: "By G——, you've cheated me, and I'll make you suffer."

The report was sifted and it was found that such a conversation had occurred, but it happened ten months ago and the young man has not been seen since.

The police left this clew readily and again turned their attention to the house. The antecedents of John V. Morse and his connections are being closely hunted up, and the girl Lizzie is again being subjected to a rigorous examination.

WEATHER INDICATIONS.

FAIR AND WARMER.

NEW YORK, Aug. 5.—At 8 30 a. m. the weather was clearing, wind south, temperature 74. The *Herald* says: In the Middle States and New England on Saturday warmer, clear weather will probably prevail, with southerly winds, and on Sunday fair weather, with no decided fall of temperature till evening.

GENERALLY WARMER.

BOSTON, Aug. 5.—Local forecast for New England until Saturday night: Fair, gradually warmer Saturday; variable winds.

Bad News for the President.

WASHINGTON, Aug. 5. — Telegrams received at the White House from Loon Lake announce that Mrs. Harrison's condition is not improving to the extent anticipated, and it is said they cause the president great uneasiness.

Passed the Century Mark.

PITTSBURG, Aug. 5.—William Reese, the oldest iron worker in the United States and one of the best known manufacturers here, died at Bolivar, aged 104. One of his sons is Jacob Reese, the inventor.

Abandoned at Sea.

LONDON, Aug. 5.—The bark Triade Tarabochia (Aust.) Vidulich, from Greenock May 21 for Montevideo, has been abandoned at sea on fire. The crew have arrived at Teneriffe.

Arsenic in Tea.

SALISBURY BEACH, Mass., Aug. 5.—Arsenic in tea is the generally accepted theory of the cause of the poisoning cases here.

The Ocean Steamers.

Arrived—At Boston, Galileo, Hull.

WILL REPORT AT NEXT SESSION

Conclusion Arrived at by the Homestead Congressional Committee.

WASHINGTON, Aug. 5.—The house committee on the judiciary met to consider the report of Representative Oates on the investigation made by the sub-committee into the recent disturbances at Homestead, Pa. The report was acted upon by the sub-committee, which came to the conclusion that a partial report on the matter should be made at this session; that it would be better to wait until all the testimony had been received from the Pinkertons and the Knights of Labor. Another reason advanced for the delay is that some of the members of the judiciary committee are away, and it was thought advisable to have a full attendance to consider the matter. The vote of the subcommittee resulted 3 to 2 in favor of allowing the report to go over until next session. A member of the committee expressed himself in effect that one good reason for the action of the sub-committee in delaying the report was because of the approaching elections. Another was that the Republican members objected to it on account of the subject of the tariff being incorporated in it. The full committee was busily engaged in discussing the various features of the report yesterday.

A PLAIN STATEMENT

Regarding Rights of England's "Common" People and the "Upper Ten."

LONDON, Aug. 5.—Lord Chief Justice Coleridge delivered judgment yesterday regarding right of way in an action in which the plaintiff, a workingman, sued the Duke of Rutland, because of the latter's gamekeepers stopping traffic on a highway while they were driving grouse. His lordship said that the days of high-handed interference with the rights of the people had passed. The evidence given during the trial of the suit showed that the gamekeepers knocked the plaintiff down on the highway, and that when the plaintiff complained of this treatment to the duke's son, Lord Edward Manners, the latter replied: "Go to the devil. If you are shot your life will be on your own hands." This, the lord chief justice said, could not be tolerated from any person, duke or otherwise.

Lord Manners, interposing at this point in the remarks of the lord chief justice, said that his lordship's words seemed to hold him (Lord Edward) up as a prospective murderer. To this his lordship replied: "I only said what I considered it my duty to say."

IN FREEDOM'S CAUSE.

Indications That Another Cuban Revolution is Near at Hand.

HAVANA, Aug. 5.—The secret sentiment in favor of the annexation of Cuba to the United States, long cherished by many Cubans, now begins to make itself heard in the face of the threatened expedition from Key West. A prominent Cuban says Cuba's only hope is annexation. He thinks the Cubans are unfit for self-government and that a revolutionary expedition would result only in useless bloodshed and misery.

CHICAGO, Aug. 5.—Information was received here by members of the Cuban club that another blow was about to be struck for freedom of Cuba. On July 25, it is said, a vessel bound for Cuba sailed from the vicinity of Key West, carrying a large number of men well drilled and equipped. A large supply of ammunition was also carried. The expedition is under command of General Charles Bolloff, a Pole, who rendered brilliant services to the Cuban revolution in 1868.

WORLD'S FAIR BILL PASSED.

Measure Passes Congress by a Vote of 131 to 83.

WASHINGTON, Aug. 5.—At noon the House resumed in committee of the whole the consideration of the World's Fair bill.

Mr. Cummings made a bitter speech against and Mr. Fellows of New York eloquently supported the bill. The debate continued until 1 o'clock.

Precisely at 1 o'clock the chairman of the committee of the whole stated that under the order of the House the committee must rise.

Having arisen the Durburrow bill was reported to the House. The pending amendment (the only one) was a substitute for the first section of the bill. It provides that if the World's Columbian Exposition shall deposit at a mint of the United States a sufficient quantity of silver bullion it shall be coined and delivered to the exposition in half dollar coins in amount not exceeding $5,000,000. The substitute rejected; yeas 78, nays 139.

2 04 p. m.—The World's Fair bill has been passed, 131 to 83.

Parliament.

LONDON, Aug. 5.—At noon to-day the speaker of the House of Commons took the chair. There was a small attendance many of the seats on the liberal side being unoccupied, but there was a fair number of the opposition present.

The Rebellion in Afganistan.

LONDON, Aug. 5.—A despatch to the *Times* from Simla says it is stated that four or five Russians who were captured in collisions with Afghanistan troops in the Hazarda country have been sent to Cabul, the capital.

Strength and Health.

If you are not feeling strong and healthy, try Electric Bitters. If "La Grippe" has left you weak and weary, use Electric Bitters. This remedy acts directly on liver, stomach and kidneys, gently aiding those organs to perform their functions. If you are afflicted with sick headache, you will find speedy and permanent relief by taking Electric Bitters. One trial will convince you that this is the remedy you need. Large bottles only 50 cents at H. A. Blackmer's store.

LOST.

Advertisements under this heading 1c. a word a time. No charge less than 25c.

TEN DOLLAR BILL — Between West Campbell and Allen streets, Thursday. Finder will be rewarded by leaving at 33 Allen street. au5-2t

BUNCH OF KEYS—Finder will be rewarded by returning same to 189 Purchase street. au5-tf

AMUSEMENTS.

Clambake!

OTIS A. SISSON will give a Clambake on SUNDAY, at Sylvan Grove. Open at 2 o'clock. au5-2t

ENTERTAINMENT.

There will be given in the Bethel A. M. E. Church, THIS EVENING, a Musical and Literary Entertainment for the benefit of the pastor. Admission 10 cents. Come one, come all. au5-1t

REAL ESTATE.

JOHN WHITEHEAD,

Real Estate Agent.

Several houses near Pierce Mill. Sale private. Also desirable lots on Geo. A. Briggs' estate on easy terms, and lots in all parts of the city. Desirable lots on Jas. Drown estate and Phillips and Coffin aves. au2-MWF1m

Cottage House.

Well built, good repair, in part of city growing rapidly; will make good home and *must* increase in value. Apply box 6, *Standard* office. ap25-tf

FOR SALE—In South Dartmouth, near the water, a 2½ story house with large piazza, barn, and 83 rods of land. One of the most desirable places in the village for a Summer residence. Inquire of BENJ. QUERIPEL or DANIEL H. HOWLAND, South Dartmouth. ap7-tf

AUCTION SALES.

By STANDISH BOURNE,

(Successor to Geo. A. Bourne & Son,)

Auctioneer, Commission Merchant, Real Estate Dealer and Appraiser.

Cash advanced on goods consigned for auction. Ready buyer for personal property of every description.

Office and Salesrooms 47, 49 and 51 North Second Street, near the Post Office.

Saturday's Sale.

At 10½ o'clock, at salesrooms, will be sold horses, carriages, harnesses and general merchandise, consigned during the week.

House Lot.

On SATURDAY AFTERNOON, Aug. 6, at 2½ o'clock, on the premises, will be sold the house lot containing about 18 62-100 rods, situated on the east side of Second, just north of Potomska street, lot having a frontage of 37 45-100 feet and 99½ feet.

House and Lot,

On SATURDAY, Aug. 6th, at 3½ o'clock, on the premises, will be sold the new two tenement house and lot of about 14 rods No. 406 Cedar street. The house is in excellent order and rents readily. A good chance for investors.

Valuable Real Estate.

On MONDAY, Aug. 8th, at 12½ o'clock, on the premises, will be sold the two-story house and lot of about 10 rods, situated on the northeast corner of High and Pleasant streets. The house is in perfect order, containing modern conveniences, rents readily and is in just the right spot where real estate is sure to increase in value. The house will be open on morning of sale for inspection. Lot has a frontage on Pleasant street of 43.90 ft. by 63.23 ft. on High street.

Cottage at Nonquitt.

On MONDAY, August 8th, at 3 o'clock on the premises, will be sold the three-story cottage, and lots, containing about 15,000 square feet, situated south of King Philip street, and west of Copicut street, being lots numbered 110, 111, 112, and 113, as per plan of Nonquitt.

The cottage is in first-class order in every respect, was built by Samuel M. Davis, in his usual excellent manner, and together with its desirable location is a most charming seashore resort.

Cottage will be open for inspection Tuesdays, Thursdays and Saturday from 4 to 6 P. M.

Centrally Located Real Estate by Auction.

On WEDNESDAY, Aug. 10th, at 12½ o'clock, on the premises, will be sold in the following order:

1st—The two tenement house in first-rate order, situated on the south side of Elm street, about 110 feet east of Purchase street, known as the Hallett Gifford homestead. This lot has a frontage of 27 feet by a depth of about 51½ feet.

2d—The house in rear of No. 1, formerly the homestead of Dr. Andrew Mackie, with lot containing about 8.90 rods. This has an entrance from Elm street of about 8½ feet.

3d—The right is reserved to offer the two parcels, and if a larger bid can be obtained than the sum of the separate sales, this will be the binding sale.

For plan or further particulars call at the office of the auctioneer.

To Let in Our Storage Warerooms.

We constantly have on hand first-class rooms for the storage of household goods, to be rented by the month or year.

Good dry storage room for stoves.

By JOHN B. BAYLIES,

121 and 123 Union Street,

Commission Merchant, Appraiser, and Auctioneer for the sale of Real Estate and every description of Personal Property. Furniture Bought.

H. C. HATHAWAY,

Auctioneer, Real Estate Agent and Appraiser,

Corner Acushnet Ave. and Elm St.

One of the best auction marts in the State for the sale of horses and carriages. Keeps constantly on hand carriages of every description, carriages made to order and repairing in all its branches attended to under the superintendency of J. R. Forbes. Consignments of every description solicited. Cash advanced on goods for auction. Personal property of every description bought at short notice for cash. Negotiable notes bought and sold.

Heirs' Sale of Real Estate.

On SATURDAY, Aug. 13, at 3 o'clock P. M., on the premises, will be sold without the least reserve, to wind up the estate, the house and lot of about 17 rods of land No. 75 Middle street. The house is in good condition and is situated in that part of the city where it will be sure always to rent well. Sale positive and without limit. Terms, 10 per cent. at sale. Balance on delivery of heirs' deed. au4

ALFRED WILSON,

Auctioneer and Real Estate Agent,

Room 22, Robeson Building.

Houses and land in all parts of the city for sale; tenements for rent: rents collected.

For Sale.

Two-story house on Acushnet avenue, near Walnut street; well arranged for one family; good location.

For Lease.

The Webster Block, Purchase street; 16 rooms, well adapted for a genteel boarding house, club rooms, or business purposes.

TO LET—A flat in The Winslow, corner Sixth and Union streets. Apply to A. WILSON, Robeson Building. jy14-tf

T. F. HEALEY,

Auctioneer and Real Estate Agent,

555 and 559 Purchase street, corner of Franklin street.

FOR SALE one small house, barn and 26 rods of land on North Front street. Price $1500.

Also one fine house in the west part of the city in good locality, with all the modern improvements, gas and electric lights, etc. Will be sold cheap if applied for soon.

Also a few more house lots in Fairhaven on the Howland and Briggs farms, from $15 to $17 per rod, and they are some of the choice lots.

Also one corner lot on south Belleville road for $25 per rod.

Also one lot on the corner of Sawyer and North Front streets.

Also lots on Acushnet avenue, Coggshall and Locust streets, in fact all parts of the city.

Also some desirable house lots on Hathaway avenue near Purchase street. Easy terms.

Business solicited. No charges made unless a sale, then my prices are the lowest.

BY WM. BARKER, JR., Auctioneer.

Heirs' Sale of Valuable Seashore Property at Auction.

Will be sold at auction on the premises, TUESDAY, Aug. 9, 1892, at 2 o'clock P. M., that well known point or neck of land situated at the southeasterly part of Westport, in the County of Bristol, Mass., and commonly called "Gooseberry Neck." The property comprises about 75 acres, accessible by land or water, has an extensive and valuable shore privilege furnishing an abundance of kelp, rock weed, moss and muck, excellent fishing and fowling facilities. About 12 miles southwesterly from New Bedford, in close proximity to Westport Point, Horse Neck and Westport Harbor, and one of the most desirable seaside locations on the New England coast.

For further particulars inquire of or address the subscriber at North Dartmouth, Bristol Co., Mass.

July 25, 1892. jy25-ts

REAL ESTATE.

FRANCIS W. TAPPAN,

Agent for Purchase, Sale, and Lease of REAL ESTATE.

Office, 15 North Water St., New Bedford. d&w

FRANK C. SMITH,

Real Estate Broker, Auctioneer and Appraiser,

Office - - 47 William Street,

(Opposite New Post Office.)

M. E. SMITH,

REAL ESTATE AGENT.

619 Purchase Street. Telephone 16-11.

H. A. LEONARD,

REAL ESTATE AGENT.......126 UNION STREET.

Houses and lots for sale in all parts of the city. No charges unless sale effected. je8-2m

SUMMER COTTAGE AND BARN—For sale low, situated in Acushnet; acre and one-third of high land, mostly pine grove; buildings nearly new. Inquire of A. G. ALLEY, JR., Union and Sixth streets. jy18-tf

A SPIRITED RACE.

Gloriana Beats Wasp on the Race to Newport.

New York Yachts Will Not Visit New Bedford.

Decision Reached at Fleet Meeting on the Electra.

NEWPORT, R. I., Aug. 5.—The run from New London to Newport yesterday of the New York Yacht Club fleet turned out to be interesting, and was the most spirited racing event of the club this season. The start was late and nobody saw a chance for a decent race save S. Nicholson Kane, the chairman of the regatta committee. The course was through the Race, leaving Race Rock on the port hand and the finish at the Dumplings in Narragansett Bay.

It looked glassy just at the start, but little streaks of air stirred the surface of the sea off Sarah's Ledge from about south-southeast, and the yachts drifted drearily about the line. The Wasp, Sayonara, Gloriana and Mineola were first across the line in their class, followed by the Quickstep, after which another batch of little sloops followed—the Noire, Liris and Mariquita. Next came the old schooners Gevalia, followed by the Clara and Minerva. The Iroquois was the first boat of the larger classes to get across, and then came Azalea, handicapped in the lower class; The Mayflower, Montauk, Alert, Atlantic, Shamrock and Marguerite were the next schooners across, and the Huron, Gracie, Fanny, Katrina and Athlon of the big sloops were awakened in with them. The Lasca crossed ahead of the Alcara, as did the old Merlin.

The tide was fair as the yachts started. Quickstep was the first boat to cross on the port tack, as she bore away with free sheet and gained vastly by her course, while the boats that took a starboard tack fluttered about in each other's way. The Quickstep's example was followed by many of the yachts coming behind her.

As the boats passed Race stock their order had changed, and the four sloops then leading were: Mineola, Gloriana, Wasp and Sayonara. The Quickstep was still fifth boat, but away to windward, as the boats began to get a fresher breeze, which finally settled from southwest at 1 30 p. m. The order of the other leaders at this point was: Uvira, Liris, Verena, Clara, Huron, Iroquois, Atlantic and Gevalia. Lasca was well up and Gracie led her class, with Fanny close behind and, as the wind freshened, passing through her lee as they cut the water on their 40-mile course. Marguerite was well to windward and picked up the Gloriana. On the run from Point Judith to Dumplings, Lasca ran very fast and passed the Quickstep and Wasp, blanketing the schooner in great shape. The winners in their classes are: Constellation, Lasca, Iroquois, Quickstep, Huron, Clara, Gloriana by eight seconds over Wasp and Mariquita.

The following is the official summary of the race:

FIRST-CLASS SCHOONERS.

		Elapsed	Cor.
Names.	Start. Finish.	time.	time.
	H. M. S. H. M. S.	H. M. S.	H. M. S.
Dauntless,	1 45 00	5 22 28	5 47 28
Constellation,	1 45 00	4 55 05	5 10 05
Ramona,	1 45 00	5 34 40	5 49 40
Montauk,	1 45 00	5 14 21	5 29 21

THIRD-CLASS SCHOONERS.

Alcara,	1 45 00	5 02 55	5 17 55
Merlin,	1 45 00	4 55 21	5 10 21	5 10 21
Lasca,	1 45 00	4 46 10	5 01 16
Alert,	1 45 00	5 34 46	5 54 14	5 51 03
Mayflower,	1 39 45	4 55 14	5 16 26	5 12 59
Phœbe de Lys,	1 44 48	6 26 02	6 51 34
Phantom,	1 45 00	6 01 12	6 16 12	6 11 20
Speranza,	1 45 00	6 23 27	6 48 27
Atlantic,	1 41 55	5 48 07	5 15 42	5 10 38
Comanche,	1 45 00	5 52 44	6 07 44	6 02 17

FOURTH-CLASS SCHOONERS.

Marguerite,	1 44 40	5 05 15	5 20 35	5 20 35
Iroquois,	1 36 58	4 58 12	5 21 19	5 20 57
Shamrock,	1 44 51	5 22 00	5 38 19	5 29 27

FIFTH-CLASS SCHOONERS.

Quickstep,	1 27 53	4 47 45	5 19 53	5 19 53
Peerless,	11 35 00	5 48 47	6 13 47	6 11 55
Gevalia,	1 31 15	5 22 19	5 55 59
Azalea,	11 30 00	6 08 07	6 33 07	6 25 15

THIRD-CLASS SLOOPS.

Katrina,	1 45 00	5 18 25	5 33 25	5 33 25
Gracie,	1 38 48	5 21 34	5 43 25	5 40 29
Fanny,	1 45 00	5 24 19	5 41 19
Huron,	1 38 30	5 13 09	5 34 39	5 35 19
Ventura,	1 44 48	5 48 00	6 03 12	5 48 06

| Clara, | 1 38 19 | 5 27 38 | 5 54 09 | 5 54 09 |
| Athlon, | 1 35 00 | 6 03 25 | 6 28 25 |

Wasp,	11 55 45	4 47 01	5 21 16	5 20 53
Sayonara,	1 26 35	5 08 05	5 41 30	5 40 19
Mineola,	1 27 07	4 54 51	5 27 31	5 26 23
Gloriana,	1 29 37	4 48 45	5 22 19	5 15 45
Uvira,	1 29 01	5 32 17	5 58 16	5 40 13

SEVENTH-CLASS SLOOPS.

Liris,	1 29 01	9 27 46	5 58 45	5 58 45
Minerva,	11 53 44	5 50 47	6 17 08	6 13 33
Verena,	1 30 38	5 47 56	6 18 19
Mariquita,	1 29 36	5 49 35	6 19 00	6 07 55

At the fleet meeting held aboard the Electra last night it was decided to run to Vineyard Haven Saturday if the Goelet cup races should transpire to-day. If not, the boats will race for the Goelet cups Saturday, lay at Newport Sunday, run to Vineyard Haven Monday and to Marblehead Tuesday. This vote was unanimous. If the Goelet races are decided to-day, the yachts will run to Vineyard Haven Saturday, lay there over Sunday, run to Marblehead Monday, racing for valuable cups offered by J. Pierrepont Morgan, and when they arrive there, if they ever round Cape Cod, they will race for valuable cups donated by Commodore Gerry. The Pierrepont Morgan and Gerry cups will be one each for schooners and sloops. The regatta committee of course have a guiding control of these matters, and a later fleet meeting may decide differently.

Near the finish yesterday schooner Constellation ran into schooner Idlewild and split the latter's mainsail, knocking down the owner, C. Cooper Clark and cutting his head badly. The Sayonara also carried away her jibtopsail.

Raising Queen Bees.

The breeding of queen bees for market has grown to be an important industry in this country. In every hive are developed each summer from a dozen to a score or two of queen cells, each of which is destined to produce a queen. They are bigger than the ordinary six sided cells and are of an elongated shape. The queen mother lays the same sort of eggs in them that she deposits in the other receptacles, but the worms hatched from these eggs are fed by the nurse bees with such extra rich food that the winged insects into which they are metamorphosed become queens instead of ordinary workers—that is to say, big females fully developed sexually. It is purely a matter of diet.

But inasmuch as there can be but one queen in a hive, after the old queen has gone away for good with a swarm, those of the workers left behind guard the sealed cells of the young queens that are about to emerge, only permitting one to get out at a time. If two escaped at once, as sometimes happens, they would kill each other. Perhaps one or two of the new queens fly out of the hive with swarms, but the workers which finally relinquish and allow the next queen who comes out to stab all the others to death in their cells, even helping her to perform that cruel, but necessary operation.

Thus it happens that comparatively few queens are reared. The bee-keeper, however, saves their lives by cutting off the superfluous queen cells from the combs, selling the queens produced from them for five dollars each and upward.—Cor. New Orleans Times-Democrat.

HAVE A CLEW!

[Continued from Second Page.]

he was engaged in the cattle business and prospered. Two years and a half ago he returned and has since lived in the East. On Wednesday he went to Fall River from this city on the noon train, and went to Mr. Borden's house on Second street. He remained but a short time and then drove over the river and visited Mr. Borden's farm in Swansey. At night he drove back, ate his supper in Mr. Borden's house, and slept there, occupying the spare bedroom in which his hostess was killed. He told the following stories yesterday. The word stories is used because those who listened to him say that they do not agree in certain important particulars.

John W. Morse's Stories.

He said that at about 20 minutes after 9 o'clock in the morning he left Mr. Borden's house and walked to the City Hall, where he took a car for Weybosset street. He arrived at No. 4 Weybosset street at 9 30, and called on a niece and nephew, who were visiting their named Emery. "The first I knew of this affair," said Mr. Morse yesterday noon, just after 12 o'clock, "I received a telephone message and went down town. I arrived at Mr. Borden's house at 11 40 and walked in at the gate. I picked up a couple of pears, and glancing in at the door, saw the uniforms of policemen. Bridget met me and said: 'Do you know what has happened? The folks are killed.' I went in and saw Mr. Borden's body lying on the lounge; then I went up stairs and saw Mrs. Borden's corpse."

Morse is a tall man, who looks like a farmer. He has a closely cropped beard and moustache, and his eyes are blood-shot, or have prominent veins in them. He has been on intimate terms with Mr. Borden's daughters of late, and has been driving with them frequently.

Mrs. Emery Talks.

Mrs. Emery, upon whom Mr. Morse called, was disposed to talk freely to Officer Medley, who interviewed her last evening. She said in reply to questions that she had several callers during the day, and that one of them was John Morse.

"Was Morse the name we heard?" asked the officer of a companion.

"Yes," retorted Mrs. Emery, quickly, "Morse was the man. He left here at 11 30 o'clock this morning."

"Then you noticed the time?" observed the officer.

"Oh, yes," was the reply. "I noticed the time."

"How did you fix it?" was the next question.

After some little hesitation, Mrs. Emery said, as disposed to set her family was sick, and that Dr. Bowen was her physician. "Dr. Bowen came in just as Mr. Morse left."

"Did they meet?" queried the officers.

"No, they did not," said Mrs. Emery.

At this point, the niece in question entered the room and corroborated Mrs. Emery's statements, though both women finally fixed upon 11 30 as the exact time of Mr. Morse's departure.

Mr. Morse states that he was in the Borden yard at 11 40, and it is a quick trip from Weybosset street to Second street in 10 minutes. He needed the extra 10 minutes which the women gave him. It is necessary to be accurate.

Mrs. Emery volunteered information that Mr. Morse was well-to-do, at least she supposed he was comfortably off and that he had come East to spend his money. She was not positive on this point, however. Morse's niece was asked if she had ever seen Morse before, and replied that she had. She had met him when she was five years old, and three weeks ago he had left her from the cars at Warren to the Borden farm, Swansey.

Mr. Morse's memory in regard to his niece is somewhat defective. He had said that Dr. Bowen was her physician for the first time yesterday. He was interviewed again.

"I thought that you told me, Mr. Morse," said the interviewer, "that you never saw your niece before to-day?"

"I never did," replied Mr. Morse.

"She says," was the rejoinder, "that you met her in Warren and drove her to Swansey."

"Ah! that is so. I did," said Morse.

"I saw her for just a moment."

"And I thought you told me," resumed the interviewer, "that you first learned of this affair by a telephone message calling you down town?"

"You are mistaken," said Mr. Morse. "I said no such thing."

"But you did," persisted his questioner, "and I will take my oath on it."

"You are mistaken," Morse replied once more.

Miss Lizzie Borden's Self-Possession.

Officer Harrington, who talked with Miss Lizzie Borden, says that the young woman's self-possession was wonderful. He saw her just after the murder had been committed, and said: "I suppose you are so disturbed, Miss Borden, that you don't care to say anything just now."

Miss Borden replied, "I can talk about it now as well as any other time."

"To all outward appearance she was perfectly composed.

"How long were you in the barn?" asked the officer.

"Twenty minutes."

"Are you sure about the time? Aren't you overstating it?"

"No; I am positive that I was in the barn 20 minutes."

"What happened then?"

"I came into the house and saw father lying dead on the lounge."

"What did you do?"

"I screamed for Bridget."

The police considered it singular that Miss Borden called to the servant, and it would seem that her first impulse would have led her to summon her mother. It may be that she remembered, however, that her mother had been summoned to call on a sick friend.

In the excitement that letter to Mrs. Borden, which figured prominently in the morning investigation, has been overlooked. It is now known that Bridget Sullivan, the servant, had been sent to the upper story of the house to wash windows, and that may account for the fact that she heard no unusual noise in the house. It is further learned that Mr. Borden had recently been settling up the estate of his father, Abraham Borden, of whose estate he was an executor, and that within a few days had sold some property to Abraham Borden left no will, and his estate was not large.

Three Arrests.

The first man arrested was John Joseph Maher. He was found by an officer in the outskirts, under a car on the New Boston road. He was considerably under the influence of liquor, and apparently knew so much about the murder that he was looked up. It was found that all he knew was what somebody else said about seeing a man coming down Second street and going up Pleasant street. This man had a small, dark moustache. He went up Pleasant as far as Seventh. Maher was locked up in general principles and held for drunkenness. Two suspicious peddlers of jewelry, which they were ready to exchange for old clothes, were overhauled on Bay street. One of them was a Jew. They were in a side bar top buggy and were arrested on suspicion by Officer Harrington. They told two different stories, saying at one time they had come from Brockton direct, and at another they stopped in Taunton Wednesday night and came in Thursday early yesterday morning. They were arrested about half past one, and the pair were located in the vicinity of Second street in the forenoon as early as 10 30 by the police. These were all the parties under arrest last night, but the police are vigilantly watching all avenues and chasing down every

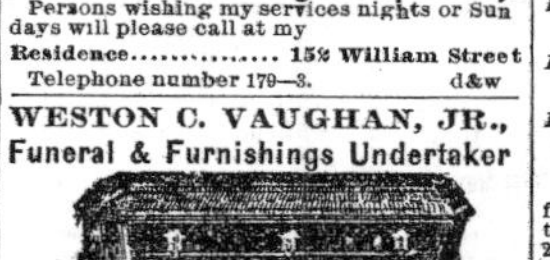

clew. Alfred Johnson had worked for Mr. Borden 12 or 14 years, and the family knew not any idea of suspicion against him.

Mr. Borden's Career.

William Cook, a cousin, stated that Andrew J. Borden was a member of the famous old Fall River Bordens. He was a cousin to Jerome and to Ludovico and others. He was a son of Abraham Borden, and years ago was the head of the old firm of Borden & Almy in the furniture business, investing his money later in real estate. Mr. Borden was about 65 years of age and a very venerable looking man. His wife was about 60. The community is deeply shocked.

Taunton Probate Records Searched.

It being learned that the police are watching Morse, the brother of the late Andrew J. Borden's first wife, an effort has been made at Taunton to obtain information relative to the condition of the property left by Abraham B. Borden, father of Andrew. It appears that Morse has been at Borden's house for the last two days, and that a settlement of the estate is in progress. It was thought that the will of Abraham Borden might have left his property in such manner as to revert to Morse in case of the death of Andrew Borden, but a search at the probate office at Taunton shows that no will was left by Abraham, and that Andrew J. was appointed administrator of the estate. Andrew J's mother left a will, but her property amounted to less than $3000, and that was all willed to her brothers and nieces.

Startling Developments Looked For.

The police have been unable to find the axe with which the bloody work was done, although they have searched carefully. They believe that it is still on the premises and admitted last night that they have a clew worth following. Unless all signs fail there will be startling developments to-day.

Scenes Never to be Forgotten.

Yesterday's scenes will never be forgotten. All day long people surged about the house where the murder had been committed, and photographers who attempted to get a snap at it were obliged to depart because of the crowds. Up to midnight groups of excited men were gathered on all the street corners eagerly discussing the details of the crime. Some of them say that they didn't dare to go home to sleep and all of them admitted that they were dumbfounded.

SECOND WEEK OF OUR
SPECIAL
Mid - Summer
SALE!

We were very much gratified with the way our bargains of last week were received, and will enumerate a few specials for this week:

All of our 50 and 75c. India Silks for this sale 39c.

All of our 25 and 37 1-2c. French Sateens for this sale 12 1-2c.

All of our 59 and 62 1-2c. all-wool Challies to close 50c.

A few pieces of 50c. Figured Mohairs we shall close at 25c.

We have just received a nice line of Belts 37 1-2c. metal Belts, shall sell this sale for 25c.

Something new, Suspender Belts, all the rage, 59c.; a regular 75c. belt.

A full line of Sizes, 32 to 40c.

Shirt Waists in the new shade of blue, sold all the season for $1; this sale 62c.

We have just received a full line of Purses and Pocketbooks—many novelties never before shown in this city and controlled by us.

We have added 1000 new pieces to our Musical Catalogue, making the largest and most complete list of music ever shown at any price, 5c. a copy or 6 copies for 25c. Ask for the new catalogue.

Kitchen Furnishing Dept.

Now is the time to buy a Hammock. We have a full line, prices ranging from 69c. to $2.69.

Croquet Sets. A regular $1.00 set for 89c., equally as good values for $1.39, $1.69, $2.29 and $3.39.

White Mountain Freezers—2 quarts, $1.25; 3 quarts, $2.09 and 4 quarts, $2.50.

Oil Stoves 1, 2 and 3 burners. Oil Stove Tea Kettles 19 to 69c.

Perry's Patent Clothes Line Hooks 7 and 10c.

Household Ammonia—pint bottles, 7c. or 4 for 25c.

Knowles & Co.

Cor. UNION & FOURTH STS.

THE TENT CATERPILLAR.

Bay State Board of Agriculture to Raid Against This Pest.

BOSTON, Aug. 5.—A committee of the Massachusetts Society for the Promotion of Agriculture held an important conference with Secretary Sessions and Professor C. H. Fernald of the state board of agriculture. The object of the conference was to provide means and make plans for the destruction of what is known as the tent caterpillar. For a number of years this pest has been increasing in great numbers in this state, and no means have been provided for its destruction. The attention of this society has been called to this fact, and it is understood that they will take hold of the matter and do all in their power to prevent the increase. The society has plenty of money, and the general opinion is that it will spend $10,000 in this work. The committee wished to get an insight into the modus operandi of the state board, and to get their suggestions as to what would be a feasible plan to adopt.

THE FARIBAULT SYSTEM.

In Opposing It Archbishop Corrigan Did Not Intend to Offend the Pope.

NEW YORK, Aug. 5.—The dispatch published from Rome, purporting to give the views of some person high in authority there, respecting the recent letter sent by Archbishop Corrigan to the pope relative to the Faribault school controversy, in which the archbishop was represented as controverting the position taken by the pope, was denied by the archbishop, who made public the letter which he had sent to the pope. The letter declares that the archbishop is always obedient to the wishes of the pope, and incidentally refers to the fact that the Catholic Sunday schools in every portion of the city make special arrangements for teaching Christian doctrine to Catholic children who attend the public schools.

A Quaker City Thief.

PHILADELPHIA, Aug. 5. — William E. Robins, attorney and conveyancer, this city, has disappeared, and it is alleged that the discrepancies in which he is involved aggregate $150,000. Robins, as accounting warden of St. Mark's church, was several thousand dollars short in his accounts with the vestry. His family is left without a penny for their support.

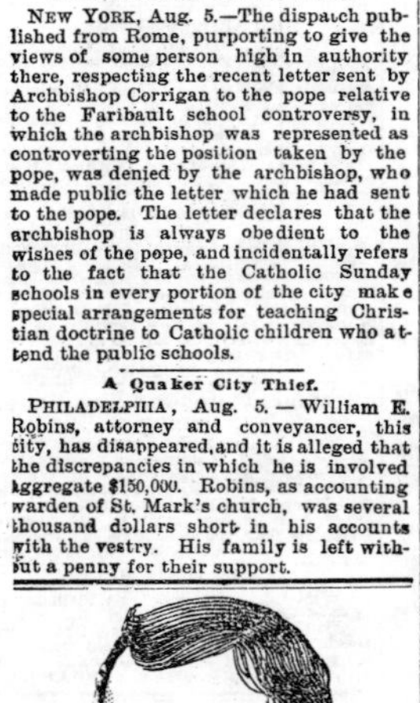
Mr. Robert W. Denvir
An Exempt Fireman of Jackson Engine Co., Long Island City, N. Y., says that at Christmas, 1890, he could only take a smell of dinner, as he was in a fearful condition from **Dyspepsia.** The next summer he went to Europe for his health, but came home uncured. In the fall he decided upon a thorough trial of

Hood's Sarsaparilla

And by Christmas had a hearty appetite, healthy digestion, and was perfectly well. His cure was due wholly to Hood's Sarsaparilla.

HOOD'S PILLS cure liver ills, constipation, biliousness, jaundice, and sick headache. Try them.

CLUBS AND STONES.

Riot at Duquesne Plant of the Carnegie Steel Co.

Foreman Seriously Assaulted While On His Way Home.

Situation Said to Portend Defeat for Homestead Strikers.

PITTSBURG, Aug. 5.—A riot occurred at the Duquesne plant of the Carnegie Steel company yesterday, resulting in the injury of about fifteen men. Foreman Milslagle and another workman were fearfully cut about the head, and about a dozen others received bruises and many were knocked kown.

The property is now in possession of the Sixteenth regiment. Colonel Hulings, who is in command, said: "Most of the Duquesne workmen having signified their intention of returning to work, a detachment of them was ordered to report for repairs yesterday. As they approached the gate the mob met and drove them back with clubs. The nine deputies in charge of the mill rushed to the spot but were powerless. The men about to enter ran for their lives, and the deputies dispatched to General Wiley who ordered the Sixteenth regiment here." Colonel Hulings reported to General Wiley that two companies would be a sufficient guard. The assailants are said to have been strikers from Homestead.

The trouble began shortly after 7 o'clock, when thirty men in the mechanical department put in an appearance. Near the entrance to the mill they were met by a crowd of nearly 300 Duquesne and Homestead strikers, the latter having gone from this place during the night. Twelve deputy sheriffs endeavored to keep back the mob in order that the thirty mechanics might pass into the works, but

They Were Soon Overpowered

and compelled to retreat. In the struggle some of the deputies had their maces taken from them. Seeing that to further resist the mob would result in bloodshed, the little band of workmen retreated.

This victory encouraged the strikers and when Foreman Milslagle came upon the scene a few minutes later, and attempted to reach the mill gate, he found himself surrounded by a howling, lawless mob, but the brave foreman, with club in hand, defied the strikers. Near the gate he found himself confronted by a dozen men. They told him that if he did not turn back he would be killed. Half a dozen of deputies then ran to his rescue. They begged of Milslagle to return to his home. Reluctantly he consented, and started for his residence, which stands on the side of a hill back of the works. He was followed by three men, one of them a Homestead steel worker. When he reached a narrow pathway running along the edge of a deep ravine, the Homesteader ran up behind him and

Dealt Him a Terrible Blow

on the top of the head. Milslagle was rendered unconscious and rolled to the bottom of the ravine. He was picked up by friends and taken to his home where he soon recovered. The assault was witnessed by the mob of strikers, who cheered when they saw Milslagle knocked down.

While they were still gloating over the victory, the strikers caught sight of Boss Carpenter Hugh Boyce hastening toward the mill gate. With a wild yell, they started for him with upraised clubs, but the deputy sheriffs promptly executed a flank movement, surrounded Boyce, and succeeded in getting him in the mill uninjured. The crowd surged about the gate, which they threatened to break down if Boyce was not brought out. Before they could carry out their threat the strikers caught sight of several companies of militia swooping down upon them in double-quick time. The sight of the bluecoats and the glistening bayonets caused the mob to scatter in all directions. In a few minutes the entire Sixteenth regiment, under command of Colonel Hulings, was in possession of the place, having arrived on a special train a few minutes after General Wiley had been apprised of the serious situation of affairs.

Colonel Hulings ordered the captains of the respective companies to place men on all streets leading to the mill, with orders to allow no one to pass without written orders. Details were also sent to Oliver and Cochran stations, while a full company took possession of the road in front of the works. Finding themselves at bay, the strikers gathered on the hill above the town, where they contented themselves with hurling vile imprecations on the heads of those below.

A Blow to Homestead Men.

Carnegie's employes have lost the strike in Duquesne, as 510 of the men have signed agreements to return to work next Monday. Fully half this number are Amalgamated men, who in order not to lose their places have deserted the organization.

This is a severe blow to the Homestead strikers who have so confidently relied upon the Duquesne men to help them out. Some of the leaders here are frank enough to admit that the desertion of so many men at this time will aid the Carnegie company in its Homestead fight. Every effort will be made to keep the Duquesne contingent from returning to work Monday morning, but the leaders acknowledge they have very little to hope for so long as the military remains.

Superintendent Potter of the Homestead mill said last night: "We have not taken back any of the old men today for the very good reason that we do not need them. We have a full complement of experienced workmen now, and by next Monday we will have every department running full time, double turn. We will board our men free of cost as long as it is necessary—that may be for a month and it may be for ten years."

CONSUL RYDER'S CASE.

European Press Evidently Making a Mountain Out of a Mole-Hill.

WASHINGTON, Aug. 5.—It is stated at the department of state that the telegrams from Europe in connection with the arrest of Consul Ryder of Copenhagen are in many respects incorrect. The American minister, Mr. Carr, has never reported to the department how Mr. Ryder was guilty of the charges, nor has he ever recommended his recall. He did report that the Danish government has made an ex-parte investigation of the charges, and had suggested that if the United States government desired to transfer Mr. Ryder to some other post, the prosecution would not be instituted in the courts.

The state department replied that the consul should be submitted to a legal trial and abide the judgment of the court. It is stated that the charges against Mr. Ryder have been greatly exaggerated in the European press, and some of them are known by the department to be unfounded. Mr. Ryder has been for many years in the consular service. He was a gallant soldier, and is suffering from a wound received in the civil war.

More Fights in Prospect.

TANGIER, Aug. 5.—Reinforcements are arriving for the troops of the sultan to enable them to renew hostilities with the rebellious Angherites. The war has caused so much injury to business that many Europeans are leaving Tangier.

Highest of all in Leavening Power.—Latest U. S. Gov't Report.

Royal Baking Powder

ABSOLUTELY PURE

CAMPAIGN CHAIRMAN.

Democrats Choose Ex-Postmaster General Dickinson for the Position.

NEW YORK, Aug. 5.—At the meeting of the Democratic national campaign committee, the first subject to come up was the selection of a chairman. The committee was in favor of Senator A. P. Gorman of Maryland for that position, but Senator Gorman persistently refused to be considered as a candidate. He declared that he did not wish to take the responsibility of conducting another campaign. On motion of E. C. Wall of Wisconsin, seconded by M. W. Ransom of North Carolina, Hon. Don M. Dickinson of Michigan was unanimously chosen permanent chairman.

DON M. DICKINSON.

On motion of Senator Gorman, B. S. Smalley of Vermont was elected permanent secretary. Chairman Harrity of the national committee was authorized to appoint the necessary sub-committees and to employ assistants and a clerical force for headquarters. He immediately appointed George F. Parker auditor and William Dufen Haynie of South Dakota superintendent of the information bureau. Frank M. Duffy of New York was appointed messenger. William C. Whitney was added to the campaign committee. The advisory committee will not be appointed for several days.

A GRAND MILITARY DISPLAY

Will Be a Feature of the Columbian Exposition Dedication Ceremonies.

WASHINGTON, Aug. 5.—Major General Schofield had an audience with the president during which the two discussed the preliminary arrangement for the military display at the dedication ceremonies incident to the opening of the World's fair in October next. On that occasion the president will review the parade, which will be composed of United States troops and civic organizations.

It is the intention, if the state of the country permits it, to have a large representation of United States troops in the parade. Arrangements have not progressed far enough to say what troops, or how many will participate, but it is the intention of the president and General Schofield to make the military part of the parade a credit to the army.

Nearly all the army posts adjacent to Chicago will be called upon to furnish troops. General Schofield is now perfecting the arrangements for their mobilization in Chicago in October.

SUED FOR $15,000.

A State Prison Official Takes Exceptions to a Newspaper's Statements.

BOSTON, Aug. 5.—Chief Engineer Gohring of the state prison has brought a suit against the Boston Herald company to recover $15,000 damages for an alleged libel contained in an article published in The Herald of Tuesday morning, Aug. 2, headed: "In through the fireroom runs the Charlestown prison underground railway."

The article alleged that Gohring was on intimate terms with certain prisoners, that he allowed them to receive dainties from outside, and after talking with the warden had repeated what the latter said to the prisoners. The article also charged the engineer with neglecting his duties. Mr. Gohring also takes exceptions to an article published in The Sunday Herald of July 31.

DIED OF HYDROPHOBIA.

Termination of the Suffering of Patrick Farrell, Bitten by a Hound.

LYNN, Mass., Aug. 5.—Patrick Farrell, 52 years of age, of Swampscott, died of hydrophobia at the Lynn hospital. Farrell was bitten on the chin by a rabid hound on May 19. The symptoms of the disease developed Monday, and he then entered the hospital. Beyond slight throat spasms and an aversion to water, the case did not tally with those best known and described in medical works. His death was not violent. An autopsy will be held. This is the second death in Lynn from this disease since the Pranker dog ran through Lynn, May 19, bitting fifteen persons.

Wouldn't Use Carnegie Material.

SOUTH BEND, Ind., Aug. 5.—The Studebaker Wagon works, the largest in the world, have been obliged to shut down, owing to 3000 men refusing to work on account of the company's using material purchased of the Carnegie Steel company.

Out of a Job.

ANNAPOLIS, Md., Aug. 5.—Sheriff Claude has dismissed James Lowman, deputy sheriff at Bay Ridge, who arrested Albert Georg, a member of the Swiss legation, on an unfounded charge of the theft of a pocketbook.

Whole Town Destroyed.

ST. PETERSBURG, Aug. 5.—The town of Rzecze, in Volhynie, was set on fire during the night, and destroyed, fourteen persons being killed, sixteen seriously injured, and 2000 rendered homeless.

The Pope's Injunction.

LONDON, Aug. 5.—A Rome dispatch says that the pope has forbidden the archbishop of Genoa to take part in receiving the King and Queen of Italy, when they visit that city to meet the naval squadron.

The Wages of Sin.

PROVIDENCE, Aug. 5.—During a drunken row in the North End, last night, Henry Monaghan, married, was seriously slashed with a razor by Mrs. Abby Smith, a loose character. The injured man is very weak from loss of blood, and is in a critical condition. The woman is under arrest.

LABOR HAS ITS INNING.

Kier Hardie and Burns Have Flattering Receptions in Parliament.

LONDON, Aug. 5.—The scenes in the vicinity of the parliament buildings yesterday were the liveliest that have been witnessed on the opening day of the session for many years. The streets and squares were crowded with a curious throng. The statues of Disraeli and other notables were utilized as coigns of vantage for the boldest of the sightseers. Cabs and carriages were eagerly scanned as they drove up, and when the idlers in the front ranks of the crowd recognized a prominent man among the occupants the word was given, and cheers went up as the notability was announced to the assemblage. The police had difficulty in keeping room open for the passage of vehicles and pedestrians, their task in restraining such a good natured crowd being perhaps more arduous than it would have been to disperse a disorderly gathering.

The rumor had spread that Mr. Gladstone was in a very feeble condition, and that, though he would insist on attending, it would be at considerable risk of a breakdown. When the aged statesman, therefore, made his appearance, giving every proof by firm step and cheerful face that he was in nearly his usual vigorous health again, the agreeable disappointment caused the crowd to break out in wild cheers for the great commoner, and he has seldom, if ever, had a more

Flattering Popular Reception.

The occasion was not without its novel feature to compensate the crowd for its coming and waiting. Kier Hardie, the labor member, made his entry upon the scene of his newly acquired functions in a theatrical fashion. He dashed up to the gates in a four-in-hand brake, covered with election posters, and filled with men and women, cheering like mad, their voices drowning the strains of a band which meanwhile played the Marseillaise. Hardie, in the garb of a workman, held the reins.

This demonstration had the desired effect of eliciting cheers from many working people in the crowd, but when, in strong contrast to this flamboyancy, John Burns walked quietly up to the entrance, the reception accorded him was as loud and apparently more general than that given to the band wagon. Another unusual sight was the advent of the noted Hindoo, Naoroji, the first native of India ever elected to parliament. He was warmly applauded, and smiled grimly as an enthusiastic admirer in the crowd called out "Three cheers for the 'Black Man,'" thus recalling at an apt moment Lord Salisbury's thoughtless and unfortunate reference years ago to Naoroji as a "black man."

Inside the Parliament Buildings

the scene was no less animated than outside. The central lobby between the house of lords and the house of commons is about a quarter as large as the rotunda of the Capitol at Washington. This small space was crowded with members and theirs friends. Almost any caller, who boldly pronounced the name of any member found the word an open sesame, and was soon button-holing the representative from his locality, seeking his influence to procure a seat from which the opening ceremonies could be witnessed. In the midst of a throng of "hayseeds," parsons, diplomats and ladies were discernable Mr. and Mrs. Henry M. Stanley, both looking very much bored. They soon made their way out of the jostling crowd.

A picturesque appearance was presented by a small party of Hindoos, in their native costumes, who had come to seek out their eminent countryman, Naoroji, and offer their congratulations.

Rt. Hon. A. W. Peel was re-elected speaker of the house of commons. Altogether, the parliament which is to witness Mr. Gladstone's fourth accession to power opened with more than usual eclat and under cheerful and gratifying auspices.

The Standard's Forecast.

The Standard understands it has been definitely settled that in the new government Mr. Gladstone will be premier, the Earl of Rosebery secretary of state for foreign affairs, Sir William Vernon Harcourt chancellor of the exchequer, and John Morley chief secretary of Ireland. The ministry will largely consist of members of Mr. Gladstone's last cabinet.

John Morley to Succeed Balfour.

LONDON, Aug. 5.—The Associated Press is authorized to state that John Morley has agreed to take the position of chief secretary for Ireland. The Liberal whips are arranging with the government for a division of the house on Tuesday. The Gladstonians will limit the number of speakers, and the McCarthyites will put up only one member, probably Thomas Sexton, to reply to Mr. Balfour. The Parnellites concur in the plan to expedite the division.

Seized by the Mohican.

SAN FRANCISCO, Aug. 5.—The steamer St. Paul, from Ounalaska, brings news of the seizure of the schooner Jane Gray, for some unknown reason. She was a whaling vessel and had no material or outfit on board for hunting seals. She was picked up near St. Paul island by the U. S. S. Mohican and towed to Sitka.

SANFORD'S
Ginger

IMPURE water, unhealthy climate, unwholesome food, malarial, epidemic and contagious influences, weakness, nervousness, and loss of sleep, that beset the traveller at this season, are nothing to those protected by SANFORD'S GINGER, greatest of health preservers.

Containing among its ingredients the purest of medicinal French brandy and the best of imported ginger, it is vastly superior to the cheap, worthless, and often dangerous gingers urged as substitutes. Ask for SANFORD'S GINGER and look for owl trademark on the wrapper. Sold everywhere.

From Yesterday's Third Edition.

TWENTY-EIGHT WHALES.

Steamer St. Paul at San Francisco Brings Late Arctic News.

Private dispatches from San Francisco report the arrival at that port of steamer St. Paul from Ounalaska. She reports the catch of the Arctic fleet as 28, two additional from last report. The Barstow has one addition and the Alice Knowles one.

BARK AT AUCTION.—Andrew H. Potter sold on Taber's wharf, at auction this afternoon, bark Maria Lila of Brava, with everything on board, to James Mackie, for $805.

WRECK OF THE ALVA SOLD.

Inquiry Into the Blame of the Sinking of Vanderbilt Yacht.

NEW YORK, Aug. 4.—The wreck of W. K. Vanderbilt's yacht Alva was to-day sold at auction to Perkins & White of Boston for $3500. The Alva's boats will be sold on Monday next.

Inquiry Into the Collision.

BOSTON, Aug. 4.—An official inquiry was begun this morning by the local board of steamboat inspectors into the sinking of the Vanderbilt yacht Alva by the H. F. Dimock.

Capt. Coleman of the Dimock exhibited his log-book, which showed that the steamer was creeping through the fog at a very low rate of speed when the collision took place. The first officer was on deck at the time, and was stationed at the bow. The witness and quartermaster were in the pilot-house and saw no signals before the collision; just before the collision saw a shadow ahead, and some one sang out "vessel right ahead," and the engines were reversed. Witness had never before seen a vessel anchored anywhere near that spot; in order to have a good safe anchorage from the track the Alva would have had to go one mile from where she was. The steamer's fog whistle was blowing constantly before the collision; the yacht lies four times her length to the eastward from where she was struck; the witness dragged her back with the Dimock, hoping to bring her up on shoal ground.

Any one representing the Alva was given an opportunity to question Capt. Copeland but no one did so.

Cornelius Bauer, first officer of the Dimock, who was on watch at the bow, testified that he first saw the Alva half a minute before the collision; heard a light bell that sounded like the bell buoy; when he heard the bell a second time the steamer was upon the Alva; had seen sailing vessels anchored in Pollock Rip sluice, but they did not make a practice of it; never saw a steamer anchored there.

Engineer Rowe of the Dimock testified to receiving order to reverse fullspeed before striking the Alva.

The hearing was then suspended, there being no more witnesses present.

It will be resumed if anyone from the Alva wishes to testify.

NEW YORK YACHTS AT NEWPORT.

A Dozen Steamers at Anchor in the Harbor Early This Afternoon.

NEWPORT, Aug. 4.—At 2 30 p. m. a dozen steam yachts of the New York Yacht Club were at anchor in the harbor, having began to arrive about half an hour before, the Electra being among the first. The white side wheeler Clermont is among those here. The schooners were just putting in an appearance by Fort Adams.

THE LANDLORD'S ADMISSION.

Insect Powder May Have Got into the Food at the Cable House.

NEWBURYPORT, Aug. 4.—Medical Examiner Snow of Newburyport, assisted by three local physicians exhumed the body of Daniel McCarthy of the Cable House this afternoon and removed the kidneys and liver which were sealed up in a jar to be forwarded to Prof. Hill at Harvard College.

Landlord Montgomery of the Cable House admits that he had a preparation of insect powder in the house, which may accidentally have got into the food. One of the employes at the Hotel states that such a preparation was kept in a pepper box in the house, and this may have got on the table by mistake.

"REMEMBER FRICK."

Warning Sent to the Head of a Quincy Granite Firm.

QUINCY, Aug. 4.—John L. Miller of the granite firm of Thomas & Miller at South Quincy has received a threatening letter signed "Remember Frick," in which the writer referred to the fact that Mr. Miller was with the strikers 15 years ago and that when he was in sympathy with them he was one of the leaders and one of the most eager to take summary vengeance on the manufacturers. The writer further states, "You are now in a position where you can use your influence to have this matter settled if you are inclined to. A keg of powder under your mansion would make it a good tomb for you."

Missing and Accounts Short.

BOSTON, Aug. 4.—Mr. Deblois, of the importing firm of Deblois & Balut, on Temple place, to-day reported to the police that Frank Middleburg, aged 18, their bookkeeper and cashier, had not been at his business since Monday and could not be found by his employers. There is said to be an unexplained shortage of from $2000 to $3000.

To Extradite "Yankee Dan."

NEW YORK, Aug. 4.—Detective Patrick Parker of Providence, who has come on to take back Daniel D. Sullivan, wanted in Providence on a charge of murder, came to police headquarters early this afternoon and consulted with Supt. Byrnes as to Sullivan's extradition. Sullivan will be arraigned in the Tombs this afternoon and later before the district attorney.

Small Pox in New Haven.

NEW HAVEN, Ct., Aug. 4.—Miss Mollie O'Brien of Winchester avenue was stricken with small pox Wednesday. Her roommate, Miss Nellie Virtue, accompanied her to the pest house. To-day Miss Virtue showed symptoms of the disease. The house where the girls resided has been isolated as an epidemic is feared.

CASES OF INSANITY
From the Effects of
"LA GRIPPE"
Are Alarmingly Prevalent.
Suicides
From the
SAME CAUSE
Are announced in every paper.
Would you be rid of the awful effects of La Grippe?
There is BUT ONE SURE REMEDY that NEVER FAILS, viz:
DANA'S SARSAPARILLA.
We Guarantee to CURE you or REFUND your money.
COULD WE DO MORE?
ISN'T IT WORTH A TRIAL?

POLICE BAFFLED.

Mystery Enshrouds Killing of Mr. and Mrs. Borden.

No Motive Known for the Foul Crime in Fall River.

Work of a Maniac Seems to be as Plausible as any.

Portuguese or Swede Farm Hand Theory is Blasted.

All the Employes Found at Work at Gardner's Neck.

Officers Still at Sea as to the Whereabouts of Murderer.

Spatters of Blood Showing a Struggle in the Sitting Room.

Bodies of the Murdered Couple Mutilated Beyond Recognition.

[Special Dispatch.]

FALL RIVER, Aug. 4.—Andrew J. Borden and his wife, both over 65 years of age, were murdered this morning at their home, No. 92 Second street in this city.

No Trace of the Murderer

has been found up to this writing, and the only suspicion falls upon

A Missing Swede,

who is said to be a farm hand; or perhaps upon some tenant with whom Mr. Borden is supposed to have quarrelled.

The first intimation that a murder had been committed was received at about 11 20 o'clock this forenoon, and the *Standard* reporter repaired to the place at once.

Scene of the Murders.

The house where the double tragedy was committed is a two and a half story residence, surrounded by trees and with a large yard and a barn in the rear of the house. On entering the house the reporter found Miss Lizzie Borden, a daughter of the murdered people, in a semi-conscious condition. In a sitting-room on the first floor, leading off the hall-way extending from the front door,

The Dead Body of Mr. Borden

was seen lying on a sofa with the head in one corner and the feet on the floor. Dr. Bowen, who had been hastily summoned to the scene, removed the sheet that had been thrown over the body and

Revealed the Horrible Sight.

The left side of the head and face, extending from the top of the skull to the neck, was cut in half a dozen places, many of the wounds being one and a half inches in depth. The skull was broken open and the brain matter was protruding from the gashes in places. The wounds had evidently been made with a heavy sharp instrument, like an axe or a cleaver.

Still Another Ghastly Find.

The officer and the others present then went upstairs to view the remains of Mrs. Borden, whom they supposed to have died from the result of a shock. Her body was found between the bed and a dressing-case in a spare room, and was lying at full length on the floor.

The physician pointed to it, and the officer and reporter pulled the bed toward the door. Blood and hair were noticed on her face, and on turning over the body, Officer Doherty drew back and exclaimed with horror,

"My God, Doctor, Her Face is Crushed in."

A closer examination of the body of Mrs. Borden showed that the unfortunate woman had been brutally murdered, the fiend probably using the blunt side of the instrument with which the husband had been killed.

Struggle Took Place in Sitting Room.

The officer ran to the station and made a detailed report to Marshal Hilliard, while the reporters commenced investigation on their own account. One of the first to look into the condition of things as found at the Borden home was a *Standard* reporter. The struggle, whatever its nature, took place in the sitting room, in Mr. Borden's case on the sofa.

The only trace was a spatter of blood on a white door. In Mrs. Borden's case there were spatters of blood on the pillow sham. Not a trace of the instrument or murderer could be found.

Great excitement prevails over the revelations of the last few hours, and everybody is at a loss to account for this strange but most

Atrocious Murder.

Who did it? and what was the motive? were questions asked at every turn. Can it be the work of a maniac? is the interrogation of those who have long known Mr. and Mrs. Borden.

All sorts of rumors are in circulation and the police at this writing are as much mystified as they were upon the discovery of the bodies. That such a crime could be successfully carried out right in the heart of the city in broad daylight, when everybody is about is a feature of the murder as full of mystery as the identity of the slayer of the unfortunate couple, who but a few hours ago were in the enjoyment of health, and who believed they were surrounded by friends loyal and true.

It is said that word was sent to Mrs. Borden early this morning saying that a sick friend desired to see her very much but for some reason she did not go. Rumor says this was done in order to get her out of the house that Mr. Borden might the easier be disposed of.

At the time the murder is supposed to have taken place, Lizzie Borden, a daughter of Mr. and Mrs. Borden, was in the barn, and made the discovery on her return to the house.

A servant girl was also engaged in washing windows near by. Shortly before she entered the sitting room where Mr. Borden sat reading, and in reply to a question concerning his health he said: "I feel as well as usual." She then went out of the room and the next that she learned

He Had Been Most Foully Butchered.

Lizzie Borden, the daughter, says that she was not aware that her father had an enemy in the world. Her father, she says, was on friendly terms with all of his tenants.

The police have sent over to Borden's farm to learn about the Swede.

As before stated, everybody is at a loss in accounting for the crime, and until some satisfactory explanation is given murder will be the town talk.

Farm Hand Theory Blasted.

The Swede or Portuguese farm hand theory has been blasted, as all the farm hands were at work. The police are still at sea as to the whereabouts of the murderer.

The Murdered Man.

Andrew J. Borden, the murdered man, was about 70 years of age. His wife, the other victim, was 62. Mr. Borden was born in Fall River Sept. 13, 1822. In 1845 he was married to Sarah A. Morse. Three children, Emma L., Alice E. and Lizzie D., were the fruit of this union. In 1865 Mr. Borden married Abby D. Gray, the other victim of this forenoon's tragedy. Mr. Borden was formerly a member of the firm of Borden & Almy, furniture dealers, and amassed a fortune. He was a heavy owner of Fall River real estate, and was allied with many of the city's business enterprises.

"NO MORE DOCTORS FOR ME!
They said I was consumptive, sent me to Florida, told me to keep quiet, no excitement, and no tennis. Just think of it. One day I found a little book called 'Guide to Health,' by Mrs. Pinkham, and in it I found out what ailed me. So I wrote to her, got a lovely reply, told me just what to do, and I am in splendid health now."

LYDIA E. PINKHAM'S Vegetable Compound

conquers all those weaknesses and ailments so prevalent with the sex, and restores perfect health.

All Druggists sell it as a standard article, or sent by mail, in form of Pills or Lozenges, on receipt of $1.00.

For the cure of Kidney Complaints, either sex, the Compound has no rival.

Mrs. Pinkham freely answers letters of inquiry. Enclose stamp for reply.

Send two 2-cent stamps for Mrs. Pinkham's beautiful 88-page illustrated book, entitled "GUIDE TO HEALTH AND ETIQUETTE." It contains a volume of valuable information. It has saved lives, and may save yours.

Lydia E. Pinkham Med. Co., Lynn, Mass.

CONGRESS.

Opposition to Junketing Trips to Chicago Developed in the Senate.

WASHINGTON, Aug. 4.—As soon as the journal was read the joint resolution extending up to and including Aug. 10th the provisions of existing law as to appropriation for the public service was received from the House and passed.

The resolution reported from committee on contingent expenses authorizing the committee on the quadro-centennial to visit the World's Fair buildings to obtain information as to the expenditures, was laid before the Senate, and Mr. Cockrell opposed it vehemently, declaring that these multitudinous arrangements for Senate committees during the recess would turn out to be disgraceful. The resolution was rejected and Mr. Pettigrew moved a reconsideration.

Pending action on that motion the Senate took a recess until 1 30.

The Senate reassembled at 1 30, and afterward a message was received from the House announcing that its speaker had signed the enrolled resolution extending the appropriations to the 10th inst. and that the House insisted on its disagreement to the Senate amendments on the sundry civil appropriation bill and agreed to a further conference. The Vice-President thereupon signed the joint resolution and, on motion of Mr. Allison, the Senate adjourned till 2 o'clock to-morrow.

BRUTAL ASSAULT

Armed Men Commit an Outrage on the Daughter of the Vicar of Bickley.

LONDON, Aug. 4.—Last evening, near Chiselhurst, as Miss Woods, daughter of the vicar of Bickley, and a niece of Rt. Hon. George J. Goshen, chancellor of the exchequer, was walking along the road in the company of a friend when they were approached by two men carrying guns. The men accosted Miss Woods and her friend. Their advances were repulsed and Miss Woods's companion fled and succeeded in escaping, but Miss Woods was not so fortunate. She was assaulted and fired upon, the shot taking effect in her face. She was rendered unconscious by the wound and was found lying on the road in that condition by a searching party which was organized as soon as the alarm had been given by her friend. Her assailants have disappeared but a vigorous search is being made for them.

ATTACKED BY AN ARMED MOB.

Three Hundred Homesteaders Assault Non-Union Men at Duquesne.

DUQUESNE, Pa., Aug. 4.—This morning a mob of three hundred from Homestead attacked a party of sixty non-union men as they were entering the steel works to make repairs. The mob was armed with clubs and stones, and in the fight foreman of the mill Stagle and another workman were seriously injured, and a dozen others were more or less hurt. Two companies will remain to guard the works. It is stated that all but 50 of the old men will return to work.

Democratic Campaign Committee.

NEW YORK, Aug. 4.—Mr. Harrity was made temporary chairman of the Democratic campaign committee and then followed a discussion which lasted over two hours. At 1 30 o'clock a recess was taken for luncheon. Mr. Whitney said the discussion was upon campaign matters, and that they had not decided as yet upon the chairman of the campaign committee. After lunch committee resumed its deliberations.

Death of ex-Senator Fulton.

HUDSON, Wis., Aug. 4. — Ex-Senator Marcus A. Fulton died to-day of apoplexy, aged 56. He was a widely known advocate of free silver coinage.

SOME oatmeals, I am told, are bitter.
H-O Hornby's Oatmeal
Is sweet.

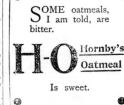

Pages 1-8.

The Evening Standard.

Pages 1-8.

ESTABLISHED FEBRUARY, 1850.

NEW BEDFORD, SATURDAY, AUGUST 6, 1892.---TWELVE PAGES. TWO CENTS.

IMPORTANT CLEW

Discovered in the Borden Murder Mystery.

Strange Man Seen at the House on Thursday.

Description Tallies With That of Westport Horse Trader.

Evidence Also of the Man Buying a Hatchet.

Corroborative Stories Told by Several Parties.

Funeral of the Victims Attended Only by Friends.

Miss Lizzie Retains Her Remarkable Composure.

Strange Incident in Search for Missing Weapon.

[Special Dispatch.]

FALL RIVER, Aug. 6.—The funeral of Mr. and Mrs. A. J. Borden occurred about 11 o'clock this forenoon and it was very quiet, there being no singing or speaking, only scriptural reading and prayer by Rev. Dr. Adams, assisted by Rev. Mr. Buck. A party of immediate friends, consisting of about 75, attended. The floral offerings were a wreath for each coffin. Three or four thousand people thronged the street, which was almost impassable. The police in strong numbers were at the house and cemetery. There were a dozen carriages in the procession and the pall-bearers were leading business men of the town. John V. Morse and Miss Lizzie Borden, against whom suspicion has been directed, attended the funeral. Lizzie showed no more emotion than she has at any other time and outwardly appeared calm and collected.

MISS LIZZIE A. BORDEN.

An Important Clew.

FALL RIVER, Aug. 6.—The *Globe* this afternoon prints the story of an important clew in connection with the Borden murder case. Last Monday, about 9 o'clock a horse and buggy entered Second street out of Spring and stopped in front of the Bordon residence. A man who is employed near by was seated in another buggy, and had ample time to study the vehicle and its occupants. The circumstance of strange men calling at the Borden residence made an impression upon the observer, and he remembered particularly the appearance of one man who got out and rang the bell. As he stood at the door the observer saw him plainly and distinctly remembers his appearance. He describes the stranger as a man of about 25 years, of sallow complexion. He wore a soft hat and dark clothes, a wide stripe running down his trousers. His feet were encased in russet or base ball shoes. The shoes he noticed particularly, for they were of peculiar make and color and laced. The man was about five feet nine inches in height.

Mr. Borden answered the door bell and the man spoke a few words and was admitted. The man who remained in the team was not so closely scrutinized and his description is not so well remembered. The man who entered remained about 10 minutes and then came out with his hat in his hand. The team was driven off in the direction of Pleasant street. This circumstance is considered of importance when the fact is known that the police have in their possession knowledge of the only person who tells of having seen a strange man at the Borden house at the time of the murder.

A boy named Kieronack, aged about 12 years, was passing the house about 11 o'clock and saw a man scale the rear fence into the back yard of Dr. Chagnon's residence. The boy went to his home and told his father. The latter was so impressed with the story that he notified Marshal Hilliard, who went to the boy and heard what he had to say. A significant thing in this connection is that the boy gave the same description of the man as did the young man who saw the stranger standing on Mr. Borden's doorstep Monday morning.

Kieronack was put to the most rigid examination by the police, and he told such a straightforward story that the marshal was convinced that it was true.

This clew was again struck yesterday in Dartmouth and Westport. Searching for information concerning Morse revealed the fact that he has recently been dealing in horses. On the way to New Bedford yesterday a Frenchman was found who told the following story: "Between 12 30 and 1 o'clock, Thursday, I was driving along in my wood wagon in front of the Merchants Mill. A strange man stopped me and climbed in. He seemed much agitated and asked me to drive him toward Westport, at the same time thrusting $4 into my hand. He took the reins and drove the horse himself. I have a wood yard on Jencks street and I told him I must stop there and get another horse, as the one we had was tired after a hard day's work. My wife was in the yard and did not like the appearance of the stranger. She positively refused to let me go to Westport with the man, so I gave him back his money and told him I could not assist him.

The description furnished by the Frenchman tallies with that given by the boy at the Pearl street station and that by the young man who saw the stranger Monday morning.

In Westport, at the head of the river, there is a camp of itinerant horse traders, who have been operating in this vicinity for some weeks. They go in and out of New Bedford continually, and Morse has been seen to associate with these people. The men came from the West, and it is thought are handling the horses reputed to be owned by Morse.

In Dartmouth it is learned that Morse reported himself to be a wealthy horse-trader. He boarded from time to time in an unpretentious cottage within a mile of the horse traders' camp.

Searchers in Westport yesterday found the traders' camp and most of its occupants. Among them is a man who fits precisely the description of the man seen by the boy Thursday noon, by the young man Monday morning and by the Frenchman Thursday afternoon.

This man appeared to be the principal of the traders, and was not to be conversed with about trifling matters or on subjects other than those pertaining to the trading. The man admitted that he was from Westport, but refused to say what part.

He is thought to have the characteristics of the Gypsies and to have led a roving life not unlike them. Two New Bedford specials worked this clew all day and found that the gang had done more or less trading in their city, and also found a hardware store where a hatchet was purchased on Wednesday by one of the men from West port. He paid $1.12 for the weapon and the clerk, who took some notice of the man, gives a description similar to those given by Fall River parties. This clew is being worked again to-day, and it is possible that the horse traders will be called upon to account for their whereabouts on Thursday.

John V. Morse.
[From a sketch from life.]

Miss Borden's Room Not Searched.

There is a good deal of excitement and interest about town in regard to a report that when the Borden house was searched for a weapon one room was not entered. This was Lizzie Borden's bedroom, and it is reported that when it was about to be searched, she forbade it being done. Up to midnight the police said at headquarters that they did not know this was fact, but officers who were at the house say it is so. The police will make further search to-day.

Hatchet Discovered.

A rumor is current that the hatchet with which the murder was committed has been discovered. It is the fourth that has been found, but this one, it is said, bears unmistakable signs of having been cleansed recently by scraping and washing. The hatchet is similar in size to a small broad ax used by carpenters, but fitted on the top of the blade with a claw like those on hammers. Just where this was found cannot be learned.

It is stated that on the hatchet, held by the teeth of the claw, was a single white hair, presumably from the head of Mr. Borden. The weapon, according to the story, had been so carefully washed and scraped that no traces of blood remained on it, the only suspicious evidence being the white hair.

A TALK WITH MR. BORDEN'S LAWYER.

A. J. Jennings Says the Murder is a Remarkable One in History.

FALL RIVER, Aug. 6.—Andrew J. Jennings was the attorney for Andrew J. Borden at the time of his death, and for many years past. Medical Examiner Dolan, by virtue of his office, has taken charge of all the personal effects of deceased, and will hold them until an administrator is appointed. The Probate Court was sitting yesterday and it was thought by relatives of the deceased that such an administrator should be appointed. In reply to Dr. Dolan in relation to this matter Mr. Jennings said: "Let the matter rest as it is."

Mr. Jennings then went to the Borden residence and had a short talk with the daughters and with Mr. Morse. He told them it was not at all necessary to appoint the administrator at the first sitting of the court following death but on the contrary it was very unusual to do so in any case before the funeral of deceased.

A newspaper man called upon Mr. Jennings at his residence on June street last evening and had a long talk with him about the case and the theories that have been advanced.

"You are familiar with Mr. Borden's affairs, Mr. Jennings?" was asked.

"I have been his law adviser for many years, and am reasonably familiar with his business affairs. They were, I believe, in perfect order."

"Do you know anything about his will?"

"I don't know that there is a will; and I may add that, if I did know, I do not think I would be at liberty to tell. That would be a matter of trust with me."

"Would there be anything in the distribution of the property to offer a motive for such a crime?"

"There certainly would not be."

"Who would profit by the death of these two people?"

"Well, no one would profit further than the natural distribution of the estate."

"Do you know this man Morse?"

"Yes, I know about him."

"Would he gain anything?"

"I do not see how he would."

"Do you know the Borden daughters?"

"Yes, I know them. I know the elder one, Emma, better than Lizzie. Emma is about my age, and I have known her almost all my life. They are quiet, modest ladies."

"Do you know anything about there being insanity in the family—about Lizzie being touched with it?"

"I do not. Never heard of it before this?"

"Have you any theory of the crime?"

"I have not. I have read many cases in the books, the newspapers and in fiction—in novels—and I never heard of a case as remarkable as is this. most outrageous, brutal crime, perpetrated in midday in an open house on a prominent thoroughfare, and absolutely motiveless—absolutely motiveless."

"The theories advanced—these quarrels about wages and about the possession of stores and that sort of thing—are simply ridiculous. They do not offer a motive. If it was shown that the thing was done during even such a quarrel, in the heat of passion, it would be different; but to suppose that for such a matter a man will lie in wait or steal upon his victim while asleep and hack him to death is preposterous. Even with revenge in his heart, the sight of his victim asleep would disarm most any man."

"Then to consider the almost miracle necessary for a man to enter, commit the deed, and escape without being discovered," suggested the reporter.

"It would be a remarkable combination of circumstances, but not a miracle," said Mr. Jennings, "impressed with it, as everybody has been. I have recalled how frequently I have entered and gone through my mother's house and out again without meeting a soul, and how I could at such times have carried off most anything without being discovered."

"And what is your notion about it being done by some member of the household?"

"Well, there were but two women of the household there and this man Morse, whose name is connected with it. He accounts so satisfactorily for every hour of that morning, showing him to be out of the house, that there seems no ground to base a reasonable suspicion. Further than that he appeared on the scene almost immediately after the discovery from the outside, and in the same clothes that he had worn in the early morning.

"Now it is almost impossible that this frightful work could have been done without the clothes of the person who did it being bespattered with blood.

"Then there is Lizzie Borden, dressed to-day in the same clothes she wore yesterday—she has not changed her clothes since. This, together with the improbability that any woman could do such a piece of work, makes the suspicion seem altogether irrational."

DOUBLE TRAGEDY IN A BALL ROOM.

Murder and Suicide at a Brilliant Society Event in Moscow.

NEW YORK, Aug. 6.—A Vienna special to the *World* says that a grand ball arranged by the officers' corps of the Czar's body Hussars last night at the casino in Moscow, Lieut. Ivan Rattovisch suddenly stepped into the middle of the room, drew a pistol and shot Prince Nicholas Sussiovitch, a brother officer. Prince Nicholas was waltzing with the lieutenant's fiancee. The prince, who received the bullet in the head, fell dead, dragging his partner with him to the floor. The assassin stepped over the body of his comrade and blew his own brains out. All this happened in less than 30 seconds. So quickly were the shots fired that interference was impossible. The young lady was with difficulty dragged from the death grip of her murdered partner. She is lying at the point of death. It was a clear case of jealousy, though there was really no grounds for suspicion on the part of the murderer.

RIOT IN A MILITARY CAMP.

Soldiers Have a Conflict with Negroes Near Springfield, Ill.

SPRINGFIELD, Ill., Aug. 6.—The town is much excited over a riot which occurred between members of the Fourth Infantry, now in camp here, and a crowd of negroes. The militiamen claim they have been annoyed by colored loafers and Thursday they tossed one of them in a blanket. Thursday night a number of soldiers were attacked at a merry-go-round and badly used up. About midnight a number of soldiers forced the guard line and came into the city, determined to punish the negroes for the attack on their comrades. They were meeting success, when the police took a hand in the row, arresting four soldiers, who were fined. The military authorities are holding their men within the camp lines and the police are watching the negroes to prevent other trouble.

PLOT TO ROB HETTY GREEN.

One of the Largest Swindles Ever Known in Chicago.

Forged Deeds Covering Half Her Land Valued at $1,000,000.

Mrs. Green's Prompt Action Protects Her Interests but Alarmed Criminals.

CHICAGO, Aug. 6.—A local paper says that one of the largest swindles ever attempted here has just been unearthed.

It appears that title deeds have been forged covering half a section of land valued at from $750,000 to $1,000,000 and the property of Hetty Green, the richest woman in the world. It is situated between 59th and 63d streets, west of Western Ave., this city.

The forged deeds are still in the hands of the forgers as far as is known. It was the attempt to borrow money on some of the property and dispose of other tracts of it in this city through forged paper that the truth became known.

Through the filing of a bill in chancery to quit a title to the property, Mrs. Green's interests have been protected. This move was made against the advice of Chief of Police McClaughoy and Chief Inspector Ross.

They fear the criminals have been warned and given a chance to escape that will prevent their capture by the detectives employed on the cases.

WEATHER INDICATIONS.

A FAIR SUNDAY.

WASHINGTON, Aug. 6.—For the 24 hours from 8 a. m. to-day: For New England, showers in northern portion and on the coast to-day, clearing to-night, fair Sunday, warmer in northern portions, southwest winds becoming variable.

Ocean Steamers.

Arrived—At New York, Umbria, Liverpool; Normania, Hamburg; Standard, Rotterdam.

HOME MATTERS.

A POSSIBLE CLEW.

Was Lizzie A. Borden in New Bedford the Day Before Her Parents' Murder?

It is rumored that Lizzie A. Borden, the daughter of Andrew J. Borden, who discovered her parents brutally murdered in Fall River last Thursday, had been in this city on a visit at the South End, and had only returned to Fall River Wednesday, the very day John V. Morse went there. The police are working on the clew.

PERSONAL.—Lieut. George H. Gooding of the U. S. Revenue Marine Service, who is stationed at Baltimore, formerly a New Bedford resident, is visiting his sister, Mrs. J. B. Wade of this city.

Mr. and Mrs. James Monarch left the city to-day for Norwich, Conn., where they will pass a two weeks' vacation.

H. M. Plummer, the mail carrier, will start Monday on a two weeks' vacation at Hanover.

Albert C. Estes, Jr., of Providence, chief draughtman for the Providence Steam & Gas Pipe Co., is spending a week in town with his uncle, Andrew L. Estes.

Allen W. Swan, who has been making a trip through the South on his bicycle, arrived in the city yesterday.

Mrs. G. A. Chambers and son, and Mrs. Minnie Damon and son, are spending the Summer at Acushnet.

Mr. William H. Safford and wife have returned from Washington and are at Woods Holl for the rest of the Summer.

Miss Mary F. Leavitt, whom the Newport school committee has elected to fill the vacancy in the corps of teachers in the Rogers High school, occasioned by the resignation of Miss Chase, is a daughter of Rev. D. P. Leavitt, formerly of this city. She received her early education in the public schools of Newport and graduated from Wellesley College. She taught two years at a large school for the blind in London, spent a Summer in travel in Europe and has been engaged three years in the high school at Clinton, Ia., resigning the last named position to go to Newport.

EXCURSION TO WASHINGTON.—William Logan Rodman Post 1, G. A. R., will make an excursion to Washington, in connection with John A. Hawes Camp, No. 35, S. of V., on Saturday, Sept. 17th, to attend the meet of the G. A. R., in that city. For arrangements of the excursion see special notice.

FIFTH MASSACHUSETTS BATTERY REUNION.—The twenty-second annual reunion of the Fifth Massachusetts Battery will be held on Tuesday. There will be a clam dinner at 2 30 at Fort Phœnix, and a supper at the Mansion House at 8 p. m. See special notice.

TIME CHEAP.—We are selling a specially good watch, stem wind, for $4.25, chain given with each watch. Lowest prices ever known on all grades. See prices in the window. Sale ends this month. J. S. Kelley & Son, 15 Purchase street.

STRUCK BY LIGHTNING.—A 16-foot cat-boat belonging to Charles Fisher of Westport was struck by lightning yesterday, damaging the mast beyond repair and otherwise injuring the craft.

THE PROTESTANT MILITARY REGIMENT meets in R. A. Peirce Post Hall next Tuesday evening, to form companies and prepare for drill. See special notice.

A BUSY PLACE yesterday was at Denison Bros. Co.'s north mill, where four schooners and one barge were unloading and loading grain and coal.

SHERIDAN GUARDS.—Members are requested to attend an important meeting to-morrow afternoon at 2 o'clock.

"AYER'S HYGIENIC COFFEE" is prepared by M. S. Ayer, of Boston, who is a vegetarian and has made diet reform a study.

TURKISH BATHS. See the price list on the second page.

REMNANTS of oil cloths and linoleums, all widths and lengths, *marked down cheap*, at Waite's, 71 William street.

BEST IN THE WORLD for rheumatism; Turkish and Electric baths. 5 South Sixth street.

FUNERAL.—Rev. W. F. Potter, of this city, officiated at the funeral of Edmund Ira Richards, at North Attleboro, on Thursday.

NO BETTER Grove for Picnics than Perry's.

LADIES' SHAMPOO only 50 cents. No. 5 South Sixth street.

No Water in any grove purer than Perry's.

SPRING HEEL BOOTS, any size, $1.50. Devoll's.

No Better aroma of the Pine than at Perry's.

TAKE A BATH at No. 5 South Sixth street.

No Better Clams than those at bake at Perry's.

HOOD'S Sarsaparilla cures kidney complaint.

ALL LIGHT WEIGHT

SUMMER SUITS!

Being Closed Out at Buyers' Prices.
Don't delay another day.
A small amount will buy a big package now at

SANDERS & BARROWS',

67 and 69 William Street.

DON'T STOP ME

I know where to find the Lowest PRICES in

HARNESSES,

Carriage Lap Robes, Horse Clothing, Whips, &c., Ladies' and Gents' Riding Saddles, Trunks, Bags, Pocketbooks, Bill Books, Umbrellas and all kinds Travelling Goods.

C. F. CUSHING, - - - - Opp. City Hall,

IS THE MAN.

CUT PRICES FOR ALL

Summer Clothing

ELEGANT NECKWEAR 25c. Each.

H. V. SANDERS & Co.

One Price Clothiers, } OPP. CITY CLOCK, 92 Purchase St.

NEW BEDFORD BRASS FOUNDRY.

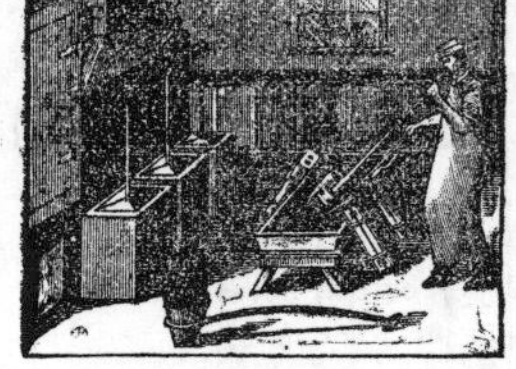

Machinists, Brass Finishers and Founders, Brass, Bronze and Composition Castings, Zinc and White Metal Pattern Castings, Phospor Bronze Castings a specialty, Lead Window Weights and High Speed Babbitt Metals, Chandelier Repairing and Brazing, Brass Finishing in all its branches. Machine Repairing promptly attended to. Lawn Mowers Sharpened and Repaired.

Foundry and Machine Shop, 108 North Water Street, foot of Elm.

WM. T. NICHOLSON, Manager, Formerly Foreman of the Armington & Sims Engine Company's Brass Foundry, Providence, R. I. je25-3m

We Use PURE PAINT. It is guaranteed to us by the manufacturer. It costs more than cheap substitutes, which are little better than whitewash. But

IT WILL WEAR. And that is what you want. The labor for putting on one is the same as the other. If you use the cheap kind

YOU SAVE 10 PER CENT. In cost and lose 75 per cent. in wear. It will pay you to have your painting done by

HART & AKIN,

No. 84 Pleasant St.,
No. 9 North Water St.,
Cor. Water and Walnut Sts.

TRY 39 TOBACCO! Best in the Land for Smoking.
Be sure that the tag 39 is on every piece, and take nothing else in place of it.
Distributing Agents
Driscol, Church & Hall,
Wholesale Grocers,
NEW BEDFORD.

VIGOR OF MEN

Easily, Quickly, Permanently Restored.
Weakness, Nervousness, Debility, and the train of evils from early errors or later excesses, the result of overwork, sickness, worry, etc. Full strength, development, and tone given to every organ and portion of the body. Simple, natural methods. Immediate improvement seen. Failure impossible. 2,000 references. Book, explanations and proofs mailed (sealed) free. Address,
ERIE MEDICAL CO., BUFFALO, N. Y.

HAY! HAY!

PRESSED HAY in small bundles, at the Stage Office, 101 North Second Street.

TURKISH BATHS

ARE

ALL THE RAGE.

Terms:

Single Turkish and Russian baths,	$1.00
Six Tickets for same, transferable,	5.00
Twelve Tickets for same transferable,	8.00
Plain Bath,	.50
Tub Bath,	.25
Alcohol Bath,	.50
Ladies' Head Shampoo,	.50
Massage per treatment,	2.00
Electric Bath,	2.00

YOU NEED A BATH

GO TO

No. 5 South Sixth Street.

FALL RIVER'S TRAGEDY.

Many Startling Stories will Bear Sifting Down.

Cruel and Unjust Rumors About Morse and Miss Borden.

True the Lady's Family Relations Have Been Strained.

Latest Developments in Poison End of the Horror.

Bereaved Family Worried by Watchful Eyes of Police.

Proceeding on the theory that a man who had a difference with Mr. Borden, one of the victims in the double murder at Fall River, entered his house Thursday morning and struck him down, it is marvellous to reflect how fortune favored him. Not once in a million times would fate have paved such a way for him. He had to deal with a family of six persons in a little two-and-a-half story house, the rooms of which are all connected, and in which it would be a difficult matter to stifle sound. He must catch Mr. Borden alone and either asleep or off his guard, and kill him with one blow. The faintest outcry would have sounded an alarm. He must also encounter Mrs. Borden alone and fell her, a heavy woman, noiselessly. To do this he must either make his way from the sitting room on the ground floor to the spare bedroom above the parlor and avoid five people in the passage, or he must conceal himself upstairs and descend under the same conditions. The murdered woman must not lisp a syllable, and her fall must not attract attention. He must then conceal the dripping axe, with which the deed was committed, and depart. In order to accomplish this he must find Emma Borden, one of the daughters, on a visit to relatives; Lizzie Borden must be in the barn and must remain there for 20 minutes—5 or 10 minutes would not do. The servant must be in an upper story. Her presence in the pantry or kitchen or any room on the first or second floors would have frustrated the fiend's designs, unless he killed her too and she died without a murmur. In making his escape there must be no stains on his clothing, for they would betray him.

And so, if the assailant of the aged couple was not familiar with the premises, his luck treated him exactly as described. He made no false move. He could not have proceeded more swiftly or surely had he lived in the modest edifice for years. At the outside he had just 20 minutes in which to complete his work. He must go in after Miss Lizzie entered the barn, and he must disappear before she returned. More than that, the sixth member of the family, John V. Morse, must vanish for two hours. He could not have been counted upon by any criminal, however shrewd, who had planned the tragedy ahead. Mr. Morse came and went at the Borden homestead. He was not engaged in business in Fall River, and there were no stated times when the wretch who did the slaughtering could depend upon his absence. He cannot loiter about the house and yard after breakfast. He must take a car for some other section of the city and he must not return until his host and hostess have been stretched lifeless. The slightest hitch in these conditions and the murderer would have been balked or arrested on the spot. Had Miss Emma remained at home she would have been a stumbling block; had Miss Lizzie left the stable a few moments earlier she would have seen all; had Bridget Sullivan, the servant, stopped work and descended to the second floor, she would have heard her mistress drop as the axe fell on her head; had John V. Morse cut short his visit on Weybosset street by so much as ten minutes the butcher would have dashed into his arms as he ran out of the gate; had Mr. Borden been on the alert he would have uttered a cry which would have brought at least three people to his assistance, and if he was not asleep, and his wife was murdered first, he would have met her slayer face to face when the latter descended the stairs.

It is a wonderful chain of circumstances which conspired to clear the coast for the wretch; so wonderful that its links baffle the understanding.

Excitement Unabated.

The excitement continues unabated, although there are no new developments. Men are gathered in knots in all of the shops and places they are accustomed to congregate in, and naturally the tragedy is the only topic of conversation.

The details of the killing are no longer commanding public attention, but every team is watched in an attempt to track the murderer or murderess. The consensus of opinion is that somebody familiar with the premises is responsible for the crime, and this conviction deepens every hour. The police are proceeding slowly, however, and no arrests have been made. Both the local force and the State officers are following the clew they struck Thursday afternoon, and the longer they pursue it the more confident they are that they are on the right track. They have the house under surveillance, and nobody is allowed on the premises without a permit.

Searching for the Weapon.

The search for the weapon with which the murders were committed has developed nothing up to date. John W. Morse, in company with D. P. Keefe, looked through the hay in the barn yesterday and made a thorough examination of the carriages and sleighs. The police hunted in a vault and an old well, but found nothing. There is a story that Dr. Dutra of Fall River happened across an axe Thursday night the blade of which had been cleaned, but no stock is taken in it. Morse was very anxious to engage Keefe, or have Keefe hire somebody to bury the blood-stained cloths and towels which were used on the victims. He said that the family wanted them put out of sight and would pay well for it. This news was communicated to Medic Examiner Dolan and he ordered that nothing on the premises should be disturbed.

The Course of the Police.

It is plain from the course which the police are pursuing that they are not looking for any farm hand or tenant who might have quarrelled with Mr. Borden, and that the persons whom they want are within a few moments' walk of the City Hall and are to all intents and purposes under arrest this moment, although the cell doors have not closed on them. In fact the officers admit this and allow that they are waiting for a couple of threads that are out to be unravelled.

Poison End of the Tragedy.

Policemen have visited all the drug stores in Fall River. In addition to the story of Miss Borden asking for poison at Levi Bence's drug store as printed in last evening's *Standard* it was found that at the apothecary shop of Stephen Brow, corner of Second and Borden streets, a man asked for corrosive sublimate a day or two ago and Mr. Borden refused to give the order. The man wanted it to cure a dog bite, he alleged, and he is known and shadowed. Last night it was learned that Miss Lizzie Borden had inquired at a drug store for hydrocyanic acid in a diluted form, saying she wished to use it on furs. Medical Examiner Dolan, who has been deeply interested in the case, said that the acid would be of little use for such purpose as it had no antiseptic qualities, but it is an exceedingly injurious acid in the human system.

Wanted Hydrocyanic Acid.

Suspicions are cruel and, if unfounded, they burn like hot iron; but in a murder mystery, where every link may strengthen the chain, they rise up at a thousand points and cannot be ignored. If a person wished to kill and avoid detection, and that person were wise, hydrocyanic acid would be first choice among all deadly drugs. It is a diluted form of prussic acid and it does its work surely. It is not necessary to use it in bulk; homœopathic doses are all-sufficient. It is absorbed by the nervous system and leaves no traces, and it produces none of the ante-mortem symptoms peculiar to most violent poisons. There is no vomiting, no spasms or convulsions, no contraction of the muscles—hydrocyanic acid simply takes hold of the heart and stops its beating. It may not have been used in this case, and the detectives do not claim that it was.

The theory that Mr. and Mrs. Borden were drugged and then murdered is not believed by the detectives, who contend that there was nothing to indicate a dose of poison heavy enough to cause death or drowsiness. Poisons do not compose people to sleep, as a rule, and if morphine had been administered there would have been traces of it in the physical appearance of the man and woman. Consequently, their theory is that a woman committed the murders. The

Blows Were a Woman's Blows,

there were many of them; cut after cut was inflicted by a sharp weapon, and no great strength would have been required to wield the axe. A man would have struck once or twice, perhaps three times, and have been contented with his work. Only a woman would make mince meat of the head of Mrs. Borden and the face of Mr. Borden. This was the view held by one of the most experienced detectives on the case yesterday afternoon. He said that he had talked it over with the other detectives, and that they agreed with him. "A breath may come, of course," he added, "and disabuse us all of this theory, but I shall not abandon it until something transpires which makes it necessary to give it up."

The stomachs of the victims have been removed and sent to Boston, where the contents will be analyzed. Until the verdict of the chemist has been rendered, no definite conclusions can be reached concerning the use of poison.

Dr. Bowen's Testimony.

Dr. Bowen's testimony, as given yesterday, bears out this idea. He said: "When I reached my home, and before I entered it, my wife said to me, 'you are wanted at the Bordens'. Something terrible has happened.' Without waiting to learn what the trouble was I hurried across the street and entered the house by the side door, which leads to the kitchen. There I was confronted by Mrs. Churchill, who lives next door to the Bordens, and by Alice Russell and Lizzie Borden. Miss Russell was sitting by Lizzie's side, rubbing her forehead and hands, and otherwise comforting her. I asked what the trouble was, and they told me that Mr. Borden had been killed. I asked how long since it had happened, and they replied that it was only a few minutes. By conservative calculation, I believe it was not over 20 minutes after they said that the fatal blows were inflicted. Alone I walked into the sitting room, and there I saw the body of Mr. Borden on a sofa. I determined to make a through investigation without delay, and proceeded. The sofa on which Mr. Borden reclined was mahogany with hair cloth covering, such as was commonly manufactured for high-class parlor furniture 40 years ago. The dead man lay partly on his right side with his coat thrown over the arm of the sofa at his head. He wore a blouse coat, and his feet rested on the carpet, as if he did not care to put his shoes on the upholstered covering. It was his custom to lie in that way.

"I was impressed at this point with the manifest absence of any sign of a struggle. Mr. Borden's hands were not clinched; no piece of furniture was overturned; there was no contraction of the muscles or indications of pain, such as we expect to find under similar circumstances. I am satisfied now, as I was then, that he was asleep when he received the first blow which was necessarily fatal. I approached the body and felt for the pulse. It had ceased to beat. Then I examined the body to note its condition and the extent of the wounds. Mr. Borden's clothing was not disarranged, and his pockets had apparently not been touched. The blows were delivered on the left side of the head, which was more exposed than the other, by reason of the dead man's position. I do not believe he moved a muscle after being struck. The blows extended from the eye and nose around the ear. In that small space there were at least 11 distinct cuts of about the same depth and general appearance. In my opinion, any one of them would have proved fatal almost instantly.

"I am inclined to think that an axe was the instrument used. The cuts were about 4 1-2 inches in length and one of them had severed the eye ball and socket. There was some blood on the floor and a spatter on the wall, but nothing to indicate the slaughter that had taken place. I calculated that nearly all the blows were delivered from behind with great rapidity. At this point, as I recall it, I returned to the kitchen and inquired for Mrs. Borden. Lizzie replied that she did not know where her mother was. She said that she (Lizzie) had been out to the barn and that the servant was on the third floor. Mrs. Churchill suggested that I go up stairs, which I did, entering the front room. I was informed that Mr. John Morse had occupied it the night before. As I passed within I was horrified to see the body of Mrs. Borden on the floor between the bed and dressing case in the northeast corner. I reached over and realized that she was dead, but at the moment I was not sure she had been murdered. I thought it might be heart disease. The sad truth was discovered too soon. Mrs. Borden had also been murdered. There were, however, no signs of a struggle in the surroundings. There was a large pool of blood under the dead woman's head as she lay face downward, with her hands under her. Her head had been literally hacked to pieces, and I easily made out 11 distinct gashes of apparently the same size as those on the husband's face. Some of these blows had been delivered from the rear and two or three from the front. One glance blow cut off nearly two square inches of flesh from the side of the head. In my judgment, the dead woman did not struggle. She was rendered unconscious by the first blow. Not a chair was displaced and not a towel disturbed on a rack near by. I next returned to the kitchen and told the women of my discovery. They were greatly shocked. I visited the dead in company with the police officers, but made no further observations. It would be impossible to determine the actual time which elapsed after the murders before I was called on to state positively who was killed first.

SCENE IN THE SPARE BED-ROOM WHERE MRS. BORDEN WAS KILLED.
[Sketched from a Photograph by the *Standard's* Artist.]

Blood Stained Clothes Buried.

Yesterday afternoon, under the direction of Officer Chace, the blood-stained clothes, which the family were anxious to dispose of, together with portions of skull which had been cut from the head of Mrs. Borden, were buried near the house. Just what Medical Examiner Dolan will say when he hears of this is not known. Earlier in the day he had forbidden any such interment.

Another matter which is attracting attention is the

Question of Time Which Elapsed

between Mr. Borden's last appearance on the streets and the first news of the murder. It is evident that there is some mistake about this time. At 11 10 on Thursday forenoon the report that there had been a stabbing affair on Second street reached a local newspaper office. The man who sent the information received it three or four minutes earlier, he thinks about five minutes after 11. At 10 30 Mr. Borden was on Main street. Probably a score of citizens can testify to that fact. He had 35 minutes in which to go to Second street, remove his coat and settle himself for a nap. He could not have reached the house before 10 45, according to those who have studied the case closely, and he is given another five minutes in which to compose [illegible] At 10 minutes of 11, then, it [illegible] he was alive on the lou[illegible] Borden passed through th[illegible] her father was sitting a[illegible] barn, and if she remained [illegible] she informed Officer Harris[illegible] death was known down town before she reached the house. It is therefore argued that she is incorrect as to the time. Allowing that Mr. Borden walked very rapidly to his home, which is not likely, as he was not feeling well, and giving a narrow leeway to the announcement of the murder, it is still evident that the job was done with a rapidity that was incomprehensible, considering its neatness. The

Unknown Villain Who Stole In

had everything in his favor, as has been plain from the start, but the police cannot understand how in the few seconds of time allotted to him he could have dispatched two persons in different parts of the house without spilling a drop of blood from his weapon or leaving behind a single trace. That weapon was as sharp as a razor. It cut clean through hair, flesh and bone. The brain that guided the arm that wielded it acted deliberately, the doctors say. The wounds prove that the blows fell with a precision that was appalling, and that they were not driven home in a wild frenzy.

And so the State officers and police refuse to accept the theory that Mr. Borden and his wife both lost their lives after the former's arrival home. They insist that

The Woman was Killed First.

The blood on the floor of the bedroom, as compared with the blood that stained the lounge, confirmed that view. It is true that the woman's body was the warmer when discovered, but that is accounted for by the fact that she was extremely fleshy, while Mr. Borden was spare and thin. If this conclusion is correct the murderer was hiding in the house, awaiting Mr. Borden's coming, and he had already completed one awful job.

Attempt to Mob Morse.

Last night a crowd of fully 1500 people surrounded the fated house, and at 7 o'clock, when John Morse and the servant appeared, the curious followed them down the street to the post office. The crowd was augmented by hundreds. There is not a bit of evidence to warrant such demonstration as was made against him last night. Some one who knew him told somebody else that he was Morse. It was like ringing an alarm of fire. People ran toward him from every direction. It was a mystery where they came from. Two police officers, appreciating his position, went to the rescue. They acted as body guards with drawn clubs. There were murderous cries of "That's the murderer," and "Lynch him!" "Lynch him!" There were enough present to do so, but no one dared to take the step. Morse did not appear in the least bit frightened, for he is a cool-nerved sort of a man. The officers escorted him to the post office and back. The incident went to show the intense excitement in this city over the affair.

Morse May Prove an Alibi.

The Fall River *News* says:

One of the most cruel incidents in connection with the murder has been the groundless suspicion that has been cast upon Mr. John V. Morse, of Iowa, who was the guest of Mr. Borden for a few hours preceding the horrible affair, and who is still stopping at the house, under the constant surveillance of the police. Mr. Morse tells a straightforward story, and his time is easily accounted for. His story, which completely relieves Mr. Morse from any connection with the affair, could have been verified by a half hour's work on the part of any one of the reporters who have spread his name broadcast over the land as the possible assassin.

Mr. Morse is a brother of the first wife of Mr. Borden and always between the two men have existed the kindest feelings of friendship and regard. Mr. Morse states that he came to Fall River from New Bedford last Wednesday on the 12 35 afternoon train. He arrived at the Borden residence about 1 30 and found Mr. Borden, his wife and daughter at home—all of them sick. He stayed until between 3 and 4 o'clock, when he went to Kirby's stable, hired a carriage and drove to Luther's Corner on business. He returned about 8 30 to 9 o'clock and sat chatting with Mr. and Mrs. Borden for some time. The former retired shortly after 9 and he and Mr. Borden a little after 10. Thursday they breakfasted about 7 o'clock, and about a quarter before 9 he walked down town to the post office, wrote a postal card and mailed it, and from there walked via. Bedford, Third and Pleasant streets to No. 4 Weybosset street to Mr. James Emery's, where Mr. Borden had informed him the night before that some relatives were visiting. These were a son and daughter, about 16 and 19 years of age, children of a brother of Mr. Morse's, residing in Minnesota, whom he had not seen for a number of years. He found that the younger relative was out, but the elder was in, though indisposed, and he spent the forenoon with her and Mrs. Emery until towards noon. They invited him to stay to dinner, but he excused himself, that he had a previous engagement, Mr. Borden's last words to him being, "John, come to dinner with us." Returning, he took a street car on which six priests were passengers, three of whom sat on the seat with him. He left the car at the corner of Pleasant and Second streets, and walked direct to Mr. Borden's residence. He did not enter the house, but went to the garden in the rear for a pear or two, and when he came back was met by the girl Bridget and a man Sawyer, who asked: "Did you know Mr. and Mrs. Borden had been murdered?" This must have been very near 12 o'clock.

It is certain that the murder was committed between 10 and 11 o'clock, and at that time, according to the testimony of Mr. Morse and the ladies whom he visited, Mr. Morse was at No. 4 Weybosset street, more than a mile away. Mrs. Emery states that Mr. Morse came to her house "not long after breakfast," and that he stayed there until about 20 minutes after 11. She invited him to dinner, but he declined, saying he had an engagement. She fixes the time by saying that he had some trouble with the lock of the door when he went out. That immediately after he had gone she went for her hat to go to the store to make a purchase for dinner. It was half-past 11. At the store she again looked at the clock there, wondering how much time she still had left to get dinner. The store clock said 11 40.

Mr. Morse's niece confirms this story, and Mrs. Horace G. Kingsley, who resides on the first floor apartment, says that she saw Mr. Morse come to the house early in the forenoon, and that she heard the trouble he had at the door and saw him as he was going away. She was getting her dinner at the time and it was after 11 o'clock, though she did not notice the exact hour.

The conductor of this car yesterday was a "spare," named Whittaker, and the *News* has been unable to find him to-day, as he would probably remember the circumstance of the six priests and Mr. Morse's riding with him. Mr. Morse's story has, however, been confirmed, so far as the priests being on a car is concerned, by Conductor Kennedy of the car going east, who says he passed the car with the priests on the hill by the Pocasset engine house, about where Mr. Morse took the car, and that he took its time and it was just 22 minutes after 11 o'clock.

Mr. Morse is a gentleman 59 years of age and of comfortable fortune. He is the uncle of the Misses Borden, his deceased sister being their mother. "I have never borrowed a dollar of Andrew Borden in my life," he said this morning, and no financial differences ever existed between us. Abraham Borden's will left me no property, and my father's will left none to Andrew Borden, the murdered man. A letter from a cashier in an Iowa bank of recent date, shows a handsome balance to Mr. Morse's credit. Mr. Morse wears a suit of light grey clothes, all he has with him since he has been in the city. There is not a spot apparent on them. "Look at me," he said, "as a man of common sense, and say if I could have committed such a horrible butchery and present the appearance I do." This last remark shows keenly the unhappy man feels the injustice that hasty suspicion has done him.

The Borden Family Nervous.

The Borden family are growing nervous under the constant watch which is being kept upon them. Lizzie Borden was only seen by two or three of her friends yesterday. She had made arrangements to go to Marion the first of next week for a short visit, and just before the tragedy wrote a letter to her friends advising them of her plans. Towards the close of the afternoon Morse also grew irritable, and had quite an altercation with David P. Keefe, who hired a man to bury the blood-stained clothes and pieces of skull for him. Keefe charged $5 for the work and Morse pronounced it robbery. Keefe said that he wouldn't do the job for $100, though under some circumstances he allowed that he might be glad to do it for nothing. Morse finally paid $3. Later, he locked the barn when a couple of Boston newspaper men were inside, and found considerable fault with the liberties people took with the premises. He was reminded that a reward of $5000 had been offered, and that everybody was intensely interested.

Miss Borden's Family Relations.

A great deal has been published concerning Lizzie Borden's relations to her father and mother, and intimates of the family, who are not numerous, by the way, agree that her life at home was not the most agreeable possible. It has been reported that her allowance was small, and that outbreaks were frequent, but it may be that some of the statements will bear modification. Last Fall the young lady made an extended tour of Europe, and some of her acquaintances say that she had everything necessary to make her comfortable. She is a devout member of the Central Congregational church, and has been prominent in the work in which the young people of the society are engaged.

Removal of the Lounge.

The day's incidents about the Borden homestead wound up with the removal of the lounge on which Mr. Borden was stretched when the axe split open his skull. It was placed in a wagon and taken to Windward's warerooms.

Miss Borden's Condition.

About midnight last night Mr. Morse summoned Dr. Bowen to attend Miss Lizzie Borden for the third time in 12 hours.

BABIES OF NEW BEDFORD.

How Many Will Escape the August Trouble.

A Physician Tells About His Tiny Patients' Health.

Boys and Girls Whose Lives Have Been Saved by Lactated Food.

Little, tender, smiling babies are plentiful in New Bedford this year.

But their saddest days of all the year are at hand. August heat results in cholera infantum and a terrible increase of infantile mortality.

It is a wise plan to prevent, rather than wait and then try to cure this dread disease. It can be done if the suggestions of Dr. Livezey, published in the *Medical Summary* are followed. Says Dr. Livezey:

"A baby born three months since was very small, lax of tissue, and had poor color. However, it seemed to thrive somewhat, for two months when its mother was subjected to a prolonged fright, after which baby began to droop, suffered with colic almost continually, and had indications of cholera infantum. Everything failed to give relief, when lactated food was substituted for mother's milk, and presto, a change was promptly effected. The colic, with everlasting screaming, subsided, cholera infantum was averted, and baby is now thriving.'

JESSE SPENCE.

W. W. Parkhurst, of Hartfield, N. Y., in a letter written this Summer, stated:

"A week ago Sunday our physician, as well as ourselves, was completely discouraged about our baby, for we knew without immediate help his stay with us would be short. We tried several kinds of food, but they did him no good. On Monday we sent 20 miles for a package of lactated food, and with less than a day's use the result was wonderful. The passages, which had been from 15 to 20 every 24 hours, in three days were reduced to three and four."

MISS PLUMMER.

F. H. Spence of Marion, Kan., writes: "Our baby, Jesse S. Spence, 16 months old, weighs 26 1-4 pounds, has used lactated food since he was two weeks old. He walks and talks and is called 'the prettiest baby in Marion.' There is nothing like lactated food, for it kept our baby strong and well, when without it he would have been sick and suffering."

GRANDMA'S PET.

"The baby I write of," says Mrs. John Sterline of Columbia Pa., "is my daughter's, Mrs. J. M. Smith. When baby was thin and sickly, and we and our neighbors thought she could not live, our family physician, Dr. S. Armor, told us to use lactated food. We got a small can, and from then to now have used twenty of the large cans.

"She is now the best and sweetest baby in the land. She sleeps from seven in the evening till seven in the morning. She goes to bed laughing and gets up laughing. I feel that lactated food has saved our baby's life."

Mrs. W. A. Chamberlain of Mattapan, Mass., writes: "When we had lost all hope, having tried a number of foods that baby could not retain, lactated food saved our boy's life, and now he is a wonder to those who know of his case. He is strong and well, due to the use of lactated food."

Mrs. William Plummer, Jr. of Epping, N. H., writes: "Before knowing of lactated food, I came very near having nervous prostration through loss of sleep and the care of a sick baby. She was near to death with cholera infantum when we got the box of lactated food. She improved right away and has never been sick since, with the exception of a slight cold. She cut her teeth without any trouble, and is so large and healthy that people think she is much older than she is."

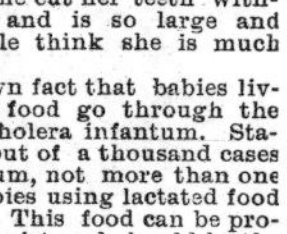

LIKES THE FOOD.

It is a well-known fact that babies living upon lactated food go through the Summer without cholera infantum. Statistics show that out of a thousand cases of cholera infantum, not more than one per cent. of the babies using lactated food have this disease. This food can be procured of any druggist and should be the diet of every little one during this dangerous season.

Brakeman Killed.

CALAIS, Me., Aug. 6.—John Burgess, a brakeman on the through mixed train on the St. Croix and Penobscot railroad, was on top of a freight car to pull a pin and allow the passenger cars to run into the station, and was thrown from the car, the rear of the train passing over both legs, killing him.

When Your Liver

is torpid and sluggish, you cannot do business successfully. Everything goes wrong. You don't feel well. Get your liver in good working order by using Dr. Hale's Household Tea, the great blood purifier and nerve tonic. It has no equal as a health restorer. For sale at Wright Drug Co.'s, 49 Purchase street.

Column 1

FINANCIAL.

SECOND EDITION.

HOME MATTERS.

PERSONAL—Ray Greene Huling delivered
the final lecture of this Summer's series before the Harvard Teachers' Association in
Weaver Hall, Harvard College, yesterday afternoon.

Arthur Chausse, son of Joseph Chausse, is
attending an educational convention at
Woonsocket, as a representative of the St.
Hyacinthe, P. Q., Seminary. He will finish
his preliminary course the present year, and
will then pursue a theological course with a
view of entering the priesthood.

J. T. Smith, of the War Department at
Washington, D. C., is visiting City Treasurer
Hathaway.

Hon. Sherman Hoar was in town last night.

Gov. Hiram A. Tuttle of New Hampshire
was registered at the Parker House last evening. He is en route to Nantucket, and is accompanied by John H. Brown of Bristol and
Frank S. Streeter of Concord, N. H.

Miss Ethel F. Evans of Assonet is spending
a vacation with relatives in this city.

REAL ESTATE SALES—John Spare has sold
to Margaret Quigley a two-story house and
3 rods of land, north side of Union street,
west of Park street.

Henry P. Jenney has sold to Edward T. Ryan 9.1 rods of land at the southeast corner of
Penniman and County streets.

George Ramsbottom has sold to Julien E.
Fortin 22.04 rods of land on the east side of
Rock street.

H. A. Leonard has sold for Ira P. Tripp to
E. Sullavou, cottage house and 20 rods land
on the west side of Park street, between
Kempton and Court streets.

John Welch has sold to a syndicate 516.56
rods of land on the Howland farm, south side
of the Cove road.

MORTUARY—The whole number of deaths
the past week is 37. Of this number 23 were
children under five years of age. There was
one stillborn. Cholera infantum claimed the
largest number of victims. Of the deaths
there were 12 from cholera infantum, five
from gastro enteritis, two each from old age,
phthisis, apoplexy and enteritis, and one
each from entero colitis, marasmus, fracture
of skull, infantile debility, cancer, gastritis,
atelectasis, pneumonia, premature birth,
convulsions, debility and cystitis.

THE STREETS—The work of widening Cove
street has been commenced by removing the
north wall between Water and County
streets. When widened this will give an
ample drive, leading from County street directly to French avenue, which is very much
used afternoons and evenings for carriage
riding.

Cottage street is now finished in macadam
from Dartmouth to Hillman streets, the last
section finished being between Morgan and
Court streets.

WHALEBONE COMING—Dispatches received
in this city yesterday afternoon from San
Francisco report the arrival there of steamer
St. Paul from Ounalaska. She brought whalebone from the fleet, and it was yesterday
shipped by rail for this city. Among the
quantities 3600 pounds Arctic and Northwest
whalebone from by F. A. Barstow and 8500
pounds do. do. from steamer Belvidere, ship
California and barks Andrew Hicks and
Horatio.

A NONAGENARIAN—Mrs. Lorinda Braley of
this city passed her 92d birthday last Thursday at the residence of her son-in-law,
Charles H. Taber, on Middle street. She entertained several friends and relatives,
among the latter there being represented
three generations of her descendants. Mrs.
Braley is remarkably well preserved, her eyesight, hearing and mental faculties being almost unimpaired by her long period of life.

THE WORK OF BOYS—Yesterday afternoon
employes of the water department had occasion to uncover the whole of the boy corner of
Logan and Front streets and found the space
filled with tin cans and other rubbish. It
was probably the work of boys.

BUILDING—George A. Brownell has petitioned for leave to erect an addition of wood
to building No. 142 Hillman street. The addition is to be 18 by 17 feet, 14 feet posts.

Column 2

Until To-Day.

It is admitted that more of the flavoring principle of the fruit is contained in

Dr. Price's Delicious Flavoring Extracts

than any other extracts with which they have been compared. Being so entirely free from the bitter and rank products of adulteration they have become the most agreeable, valuable and economical flavors known; steadily grown in popularity until to-day they are used by every intelligent housewife for truthfully reproducing the flavor of the fruit in creams, cakes, puddings, etc.

THAT CAVALRY BATTALION—Several weeks
ago it was stated in the *Standard* that a movement, having its impetus from the large staff
which participated in the 4th of July parade,
was on foot in this city for forming an independent cavalry organization. Since then
the cost of equipments and uniforms have
been ascertained, and 44 gentlemen have signified their intention of joining the organization and have expended their names to a
paper, which may be found at Church's drug
store, Union street. They are active and enthusiastic young men, and it is hoped a number
enough will be obtained to form a battalion
of two companies. Such an organization
would be drilled in regular tactics and would
be a credit to the city. Guesses are made that
such an encampment of the First Regiment,
preceding by the choice of Morgan Rotch as
major, Leopold Bartel captain of the first
company and Harry M. Church captain of the
second. There are plenty of good tacticians
in the cavalry arm in the city for instructors.

FIRST REGIMENT AT FORT WARREN—At the
annual encampment of the First Regiment,
to which Co. E of this city is attached, to be
held at Fort Warren, Boston Harbor, during
the coming week, it will be necessary in order to get within the lines to have a pass.
The only days on which visitors are allowed
are Wednesday, Thursday and Friday, and a
different pass is required for each day. On
Saturday, Aug. 13th, a dress parade and review will be tendered to His Excellency the
Governor on Boston Common, and to get
within the lines there it will also be necessary to have a pass. Honorary members or
any friends of the company desirous of visiting the camp or witnessing the review can
obtain passes at Capt. Perry's office during
the week. It will be necessary, however, to
specify the day for which the pass is desired.

ARRESTED—Charles Pugh was arrested on
a warrant this forenoon, charging him with
indecent exposure of his person in the west
part of the city.

CONTAGIOUS DISEASES—One new case of
scarlet fever has been reported at the office
of the Board of Health the past week.

MATTAPOISETT.

Rev. Wilbur Johnson and wife of Slatersville, R. I., are spending a few days in town
as the guest of Henry Barstow.

Joseph Keene and wife of New Bedford are
spending a few days with Mrs. Keene's
mother, Mrs. Martha J. Welch.

In the early part of the squall yesterday
Capt. James M. Clark's yacht broke adrift
and struck the long wharf head, which only
dented the stern a little. She swung around
and backed up into the dock into smooth
water. The undertow and swash against the
wharf kept her away so that she hardly
scratched.

The regatta of next Saturday, Aug. 13th, is
being worked up to its full extent.

DEATHS.

In Middleboro, 4th inst., Mary, widow of
James Mullins, 70.

In Carver, 1st inst., Lorenzo N. Shaw, 69.

MARINE INTELLIGENCE.

At New York 5th, steamer Richmond,
Newport News; sch J B Pace, Garfield,New
Haven; Thos C Kerswell, Rackett, Martha's
Vineyard; tug Wrestler, Boston.

Passed through Hell Gate 5th, schs Maud
Sherwood, Kelley, New York for Boston; W
D Mangam, Gifford, do for this port; Mary A
Rice, Wentworth, Fort Liberty for New London.

At Philadelphia 5th, sch D S Williams Jr,
Haselton, hence. Cld, schs Agnes Manning,
Belowar, this port; Grace Seymour, Holmes,
do; Ida F Hull, Gabrielson, Newburyport; L
C Ballard, Stone, Lynn.

Ar at Baltimore 5th, sch John A Beckerman,
Gammons, New Haven. Sld, sch W E Herriek, Kelley, Boston.

Sld from Savannah 5th, steamer City of Augusta, New York.

*Aug 4th, off Hatteras, was passed sch Agnes
I Grace.

FINANCIAL.

Rather Quiet but Firm Stocks To-day—
General Electric the Feature with Sales
at 115—Atchison Declines on London
Selling—Money Market More Active—
New York Bank Statement Shows a Big
Decrease in Reserve—Loans Expanded—
Fitchburg Earnings—Latest Crop Reports—The Advance in Mexican Central
Gossip and News Items.

SATURDAY, Aug. 6.

The markets have closed the week quiet
and steady. General Electric has been the
feature to-day as well as yesterday, talk
continuing bullish upon it with frequent predictions of 125 for it another week. The
highest up to 10 o'clock this forenoon was 115.
Other speculties have gained ground somewhat, West End common in Boston advancing ⅝. Atchison has sold off on London
selling, the income declining to 60. For the
coming week the situation may be regarded
as favorable for a rise.

The closing of the week marks little change
in the local loan market. Rates are still unchanged, between 4 and 5 per cent.

Local bank clearings for the past week
compare as below:

Week ended to-day.

	1892.	1891.	Inc.
	$541,975	$418,799	$127,176

There is no abatement in the fairly active
demand for money in the Boston market.
Bankers report that the inquiries this morning from the brokers for call money is excellent and new loans hold strong at 4 per
cent. There is some disposition to make
time loans, but lenders are not anxious to
loan on long time at present rates. At clearing loans to-day were made at 3½ to 4 per
cent. New York funds sold at 15 and 17 cents
discount per $1000.

In New York the money market closes the
week with somewhat more activity and unchanged rates.

The sterling exchange market shows little
change, commercial bills continue scarce.
There are a few spot bills, but almost no option bills.

Bonds firm.

Wall street gossip this morning said: The
Chronicle figures a loss of 4⅙ millions to
banks. London talks at trifling declines.
Talk rather favors the bulls. The experts
of specie cease and the corn crop turns out
well, prices should be higher this fall.

The New York market opened firm to-day,
but reacted immediately and continued to
sag slowly to the close. There was no special

clal features and fluctuations were all fractional. The bank statement fell flat. The
closing was quiet and steady.

The week ends in the Boston market with a
steady range of prices and no pressure to
sell stocks. Some little manifestation of interest on the part of the public was noticeable during the last few days and will likely
develop further next week if prices are sustained. To-day's market was quiet with
light trading and with stocks selling at yesterday's figures with but slight changes. The
close was firm without feature. Total sales,
bonds, $175,000 and 10,868 shares of stock.

The statement that J. B. Wheeler had withdrawn his suit against J. J. Hageman is officially confirmed. The case had become quite
celebrated, involving a large block of Mollie
Gibson stock.

General Electric stock has been the feature
of the markets to-day, sales being made at as
high a point as 115. Later sales were at 114⅜
and 114⅝.

Mexican Central has been firm to-day with
sales at 17⅜ to 17.

Mr. George R. Gibson, in an interview in
the New York *Daily Stockholder*, says:

London operators and brokers are simply
despondent. I talked with any number of
them and found distrust as prevalent as confidence was in the Summer of 1890, when
every man I met in London was looking for a
boom. Odd as it may seem, and although
Europe is now a small seller, I look for a
foreign buying movement later in the season,
notwithstanding the apparent uneasiness
over the currency question. For, as a matter of fact, London cannot enter any country
as a buyer that is not more or less committed
to the use of silver.

The gossip on General Electric is bullish in
the extreme. Once in New York J. R. Keene
is reported as putting his personal friends
into General Electric, and to be talking fabulous prices for it while in Boston. The
"boomers" are positive that it is going to
160. The advance will come 80 per cent. from
the effects of big earnings and 20 per cent.
from expert manipulation. Yesterday a Boston gentleman refused a bid of 114⅝ for the
4000 General Electric which he owns, at the
time when the stock was selling to the
market at only 114. This shows the way the
heavy holders feel towards the stock. It is
claimed that insiders are still accumulating
stock, even at these seemingly toppy prices.
The 5 per cent. bonds advanced coincident
with the stock, being taken in large blocks,
and recording a net gain of three-fourths for
the day.

To-day's New York bank statement shows
as below:

	Decrease.
Reserve,	$5,432,850
Loans,	*2,846,800
Specie,	1,075,800
Legals,	4,517,560
Deposits,	641,860
Circulation,	40,000

*Increase.

The course of the contract market on cotton shows a fall for the week of 12 to 18
points. The spot market is off ¼c. Business
in cotton is confined to the wants of the
smaller mills which buy of spot cotton from
5 to 50 bales at a time. There is nothing of
moment doing from the South. They are beginning to offer cotton of the new crop. The
lowest quotation heard is for Texas good
middling at 5c. landed. Crop prospects are
not wholly favorable; they need more rain in
Texas, and in other sections there are complaints of grassy fields. High grades of cotton are scarce and are firmly held.

The Boston News Bureau says:

We wired S. T. K. Preiss as to the truth of
the report that he estimated that corn crop
of Kansas would be over 80 per cent. of
last year's yield and receive following reply:
"Report entirely without foundation. Have
given as yet no estimates."

Missouri Pacific earnings for the fourth
week of July increased $46,000.

New York banks are now $19,118,821 in excess of legal requirements. Last year $18,-
420,875 in excess. In 1890, $1,288,000 in excess.
Early London prices to-day showed losses
of ¼ to ¾ per cent.

Silver offered to the government yesterday amounted to 994,000 ounces. Purchases
were 587,000 ounces at 85.44.

Atchison stock and incomes have been
rather heavy on London selling.

The four quarterly statements of the Fitchburg railroad mails this result for the year
ending June 30:

	1892.	1891.	Increase.
Gross,	$7,248,833	$6,851,330	$397,799
Op. Expenses,	5,112,684	4,917,538	195,146
Net,	$2,256,168	$1,933,465	$302,702
Charges,	$1,469,123	$1,380,196	$68,927
Surplus	$788,381	$553,289	$233,712

Fall River Print Cloth Market.

FALL RIVER, Aug. 6.

Cotton goods, regular and odd counts, have
been in active demand during the week and
very fair sales are reported. It is surmised
that printers find that they can dispose of the
finished product as rapidly as they can turn
it off, and it is certainly a disposition on their
part to make contracts a long distance ahead.
Inasmuch as the machinery is fully engaged
for the present, it is surmised that consumers
can more than take care of the weekly deliveries, until a scarcity of cloth is anticipated later on. Manufacturers will not
talk futures except on a 63 cent basis, though
a few goods can be obtained for shipment
next Summer for 3 7-16 cents. In a word the
situation is as strong for the factories as it
has been at any time this season, and the
outlook for dividends continues to be encouraging. It is plain that the demand of
the weavers for an advance in wages and
possible trouble in case employers refuse to
grant the raise, has nothing to do with the
inquiry, an outbreak would only cancel
contracts, and it is impossible to load up in
anticipation of a strike, for the very good
reason that there are no spots to load up on.
It is a legitimate call for goods and the market is very firm.

The following is the print cloth statement
for the week: Production 190,000 pieces, deliveries 190,000 pieces, stock not any, sales
449,000 pieces, spot 26,000 pieces, futures 423,-
000 pieces. The market is firm. Prices 3¼c
for 64x64s, 3¼ for 64x64s.

CALIFORNIA MINING STOCKS.

SAN FRANCISCO, Aug. 6.

The following are the official closing prices
of mining stocks to-day:

Alta	Mexican	1 30
Best & Belcher	1 35	Mt. Diablo	1 05
Chollar	Ophir	2 10
Con.Cal.&Va	1 55	Overman	80
Crown Point	Savage	47
Gould & Curry	1 50	Sierra Nevada	1 10
Hale & Norcross	Utah	25

Column 3

THE MURDER MYSTERY.

Mr. Morse Says He Courts the Fullest Investigation.

Immense Crowds Watch the Passing of the Funeral Cortege.

Two Axes and Two Hatchets to be Submitted to Microscopic Examination.

[By Associated Press.]

FALL RIVER, Aug. 6.—The latest developments in the murder relating particularly to the theory of poisoning has
given way in the discussion among the
people to-day to talk of the funerals,
which took place this morning. As early
as 9 o'clock the house was surrounded by
a great crowd of curiosity seekers. Reporters, artists, photographers and policemen were the only persons who were
active.

Shortly after 10 20 Mr. Morse came from
the house and talked with a group of reporters. He said it was a terrible thing
to be suspected and shadowed as he has
been, but he courts the fullest investigation as last Thursday. She did not
mingle with the family to any great extent. When Mr. Fish of Hartford, a
nephew of her stepmother, appeared, she
gave him a very cool reception.

About 11 o'clock preparations commenced for the funerals. Crowds of people, numbering between 3000 and 4000, appeared on Second street in front of the
house, and about 20 policemen stood
around and maintained a clear passageway. Rev. Dr. Adams of the First Congregational Church and City Missionary
Buck arrived and entered the house. The
bodies were laid in two plain black cloth-covered caskets in the sitting-room where
Mr. Borden was killed. An ivy wreath
was placed on Mr. Borden's bier, and a
bouquet of white roses and fern leaves,
tied with a white ribbon, was placed over
Mrs. Borden. There were 75 persons present at the services.

The services consisted of reading from
the scriptures and prayer. There was no
singing and no remarks.

The mourners who were present were
Mrs. Oliver Gray, the step-mother of the
deceased woman, G. H. Fish and wife of
Hartford, Ct., the latter a sister of Mrs.
Borden, Dr. Bowen and wife, Sourath H.
Miller and a very few of the neighbors
who had been invited to attend the services in the house. The funeral was private, that is only very few of the immediate friends were asked to accompany the
remains to the cemetery. But from 11
o'clock until 11 40 when the funeral procession of 11 hacks and two hearses started on their way, there were immense
crowds of people lining every sidewalk.

There was a detachment of police at the
cemetery and another posse accompanied
the remains on their way through Borden
and Rock streets to the northern end of
the city where the cemetery is located.

The pall-bearers for Mr. Borden were
Abraham G. Hart, cashier of the Union
Savings Bank; George W. Dean, a retired
real estate dealer; Jerome C. Borden, a
relative of deceased; Richard B. Borden,
treasurer of the Troy mills; James M.
Osborne; A. B. Borden, treasurer of the
Merchants mill. The pall-bearers for
Mrs. Borden were James C. Eddy, Henry
S. Buffinton, F. L. Almy, J. Henry Wells,
Simeon B. Chase, J. H. Boone, all of them
moving in the highest local social and
business circles.

As the procession wended its way along
North Main street many old associates of
Mr. Borden were seen to raise their hats,
and forget all knowledge of the curiosity
seekers who stood gaping beside them.
Miss Lizzie and Miss Emma Borden were
of course the principal mourners. Miss
Lizzie went out of the house first leaning
on Undertaker Winward's arm. She was
self-conscious, but her nerves were completely unstrung, as was shown by the
great trembling of her body and the manner in which she bore down on her supporter. When she reached her carriage
she felt back exhausted on the cushions.
Miss Emma, the other sister, was much
calmer and she walked quickly and took
her seat without hardly glancing at the
crowds staring at her.

Miss Lizzie Borden appeared as a very
pretty woman and quiet fresh. Her face
showed traces of the suffering she has
borne for three days. Both ladies were
without veils.

The last person to leave the house was
Mr. Morse, who went into a carriage with
Dr. Adams. During the services there
was no scene of any unusual occurrence
on such occasions and despite the very
sad circumstances surrounding the death
there were very few tears shed in public.

Two Axes and Two Hatchets.

City Marshall Hilliard has two axes and
two hatchets in his custody that were
found in the Borden cellar. A microscopic examination will be made of them
next Monday. No traces of blood can be
discovered on them with the naked eye.

WEATHER INDICATIONS.

FAIR AND SLIGHTLY WARMER.

NEW YORK, Aug. 6.—At 8 30 a. m. the
weather was clear, wind south,
temperature 73. The *Herald* says: In
the Middle States and New England on
Sunday fair, slightly warmer weather will
probably prevail; with southerly and
westerly winds, accompanied by local
rain, and on Monday warmer, fair
weather.

COOLER.

BOSTON, Aug. 6.—Local forecast for New
England until Sunday night: Fair, preceded by showers to-day on the Maine
coast. Cooler for southern sections tonight and Sunday morning; southwest to
west winds.

INDORSED BY THE PRESIDENT.

Mr. Blaine Asked the Pope to Make Archbishop Ireland a Cardinal.

CHICAGO, Aug. 6.—A special from St.
Louis to the *Herald* says some time before
the Minneapolis convention pressure was
brought to bear upon President Harrison
to get him to write a letter to the Pope
asking that Archbishop Ireland be made
cardinal. He refused. A few days before
the convention further strong pressure
resulted in a letter being written by Secretary of State Blaine, at request of President Harrison, strongly indorsing Archbishop Ireland, saying his appointment as
cardinal would not only please American
Catholics, but would be personally pleasing to Mr. Harrison. Father Phelan, editor of the *Western Watchman*.

Newport Sporting News.

NEWPORT, Aug. 6.—The Fra Diavolo,
with Senator Hill on board, had not been
sighted at Newport at 2 30.

The Wasp has returned with a broken
topmast.

Column 4

DAINTY SHOES FOR DAINTY FEET.

SCHULER BROS., - - - - 76 and 78 Purchase St.

It will pay you handsomely to
buy a pair of Misses' or Children's
shoes of our own make.

We do not have to rely on what
the manufacturer says, for we
make the shoes ourselves and
guarantee them better for the
price than you can get anywhere
else, *just* because we make them
ourselves.

If your boy or girl has never
worn Our Own make shoes, you
just try the next pair.

Store and Factory connected.

NEWPORT TO VINEYARD HAVEN.

The New York Yacht Squadron Racing to the Eastward.

NEWPORT, Aug. 6.—The morning
opened with a brisk breeze from the
southwest, which continues at noon,
though it has begun to haul west. Some of
the yachts of the New York yacht squadron left the harbor as early as 9 o'clock,
but it was half an hour later before there
began to be any great stir among the
yachts, which were obliged to carefully
pick their way out of the crowd in the
harbor. By 10 o'clock many of the steamers had up anchor and left for Brenton's
Reef light-ship, the starting point for today's race to the eastward. The departure of the steamers considerably freed the
harbor, so that the remaining white
winged craft left their anchorages and
assembled about the light-ship.

The start was made about 11 o'clock,
though several yachts had not yet come
out. A few of the yachts remain at anchor, and will stay here over Sunday in
preference to further continuing the
cruise. The wind and weather conditions
are favorable for a fine race to the Vineyard.

The Gloriana was the first boat across,
followed by the Harpoon, Wasp, Azalea,
Clara, Quickstep, Cavalier, Peerless, Verona, and Marguerite. The Constellation
was the first across of the big fellows.
She was followed by the Alert, Comanche,
Alcoea, Phantom, Dauntless, Ventura,
Fortuna, Gracie, Atlanta, Ramona, Wayward, Marguerite, and Iroquois. The
Harpoon and Wasp commenced to indulge
in a luffing match as soon as they got into
the line, and it soon became apparent that
the Boston contrebandier was outdoing
the Herreshoff boat. The Constellation is
now the leader among the schooners.

RETALIATION AGAINST CANADA.

General Manager of the Grand Trunk Expresses His Indignation.

MONTREAL, Aug. 6.—General Manager
Sargent, of the Grand Trunk Railway
Company, in an interview on the proposed
retaliation against Canada railways, said
last night that he was surprised at the
action of some of the United States Senators who were urging retaliation who
seemed to have no reason for it, unless it
was simply against this road. There, for
instance, said he, was Senator Chandler's
action in introducing a bill full of
"whereases" and suggestions against the
Grand Trunk, while that railway had
most signally benefited the State of New
Hampshire. It was nothing unless the
Grand Trunk went into it. The same
could be said of Portland. It was the
Grand Trunk that made Portland an ocean
port.

Cholera Epidemic at Teheran.

TEHERAN, Aug. 6.—The cholera has
suddenly become epidemic here. Fourteen deaths occurred on Thursday.

STOCK AND BOND MARKETS.

Bids at close of the Stock Boards to-day.

NEW YORK, Aug. 6.

GOVERNMENT BONDS.

U.S. 4s, registered	100
" new 4s, registered	.....
" new 4s, coupons	116
" currency 6s, 1895, (Pacifics)	107

RAILROADS.

Atchison	29½
Clev. Cin.,Chicago & St. Louis	.....
Chicago & Eastern Illinois	.....
Chicago & Eastern Illinois pre	.....
Chicago, Burlington & Quincy	102½
Delaware & Hudson	139
Delaware & Lackawanna	158
Erie	28⅞
Illinois Central	.....
Lake Shore & Michigan Southern	135⅜
Louisville & Nashville	71½
Michigan Central	.....
Missouri Pacific	60⅞
New Jersey Central	.....
New York & New England	37⅝
Northern Pacific	21⅜
Northern Pacific pref	56
Chicago & Northwestern	118
New York Central & Hudson River	.....
North American	.....
Oregon Navigation	.....
Oregon Improvement	.....
Oregon Short Line	.....
Philadelphia & Reading	60⅝
Pullman Palace Car Co	.....
Chicago, Rock Island & Pacific	83¼
Chicago, Milwaukee & St. Paul	80¼
Chicago, Milwaukee & St. Paul pref	.....
Richmond Terminal	.....
St. Paul & Omaha	51
St. Paul & Omaha pref	.....
Wabash, St. Louis & Pacific	38¾
Wabash, St. Louis & Pacific pref	.....

MISCELLANEOUS.

Ontario Silver	37
Pacific Mail Steamship Co	37
Sugar, common	108
Sugar, pref	101
Western Union Telegraph	97¼
Silver Certificates	87½
Gen'l Electric	115

BOSTON, Aug. 5.

BONDS.

Atchison 4s	83
Atchison Incomes	60½
American Bell Telephone 7s	114
Chicago, Burlington & Northern 5s	.....
Chicago & West Michigan 5s	.....
Mexican Central 4s	68⅝
United States Co. 6s	.....

RAILROADS.

Atchison, Topeka & Santa Fe	29½
Boston & Albany	206
Boston & Lowell	181
Boston & Maine	.....
Boston & Providence	.....
Chicago, Burlington & Quincy	102½
Chicago & West Michigan	.....
Cleveland & Canton	5½
Cleveland & Canton pref	.....
Flint & Pere Marquette	27
Flint & Pere Marquette pref	.....
Mexican Central	.....
New York & New England	37
New York & New England pref	87¼
Old Colony	182
Oregon Short Line	24
Rutland pref	.....
Union Pacific	74½
Wisconsin Central	17⅝
West End	74⅝
West End pref	.....

MINING.

Butte & Boston Mining Co	11½
Calumet & Hecla Mining Co	275
Centennial	24
Franklin Mining Co	15⅛
Kearsarge	7
Osceola Mining Co	33¼
Tamarack	150

MISCELLANEOUS.

American Bell Telephone	204
Erie Telephone	65
Mexican Telephone	.....
New England Telephone	56
Newport Land	.....
Boston Land Co	.....
West End Land & Development Co	15
San Diego Land Co	.....
Topeka Land & Investment Co	.....
Lamson Store Service	18½
Thomson-Houston Electric	72¾
Thomson-Houston	5½
Am. Sugar Refineries, com	.....
Am. Sugar Refineries, pref	.....
*Asked.	

LOST.

*—All Advertisements under this heading 1c. a
word a time. No charge less than 25c.*

LADY'S PURSE—Containing money, papers and keys; between Cummings' and
Stollard & Rushway's. Finder leave at
Standard office and get reward.   au2-4-6

WANTS.

*—All Advertisements under this heading 1c.
a word a time. No charge less than 25c.*

GIRL—For general house work, at 42 Hawthorn street.   au5-tf

Column 5

SPECIAL NOTICES.

EARTH GIVEN AWAY

At the Kempton St. School-House Lot.

☞ Send teams and have them loaded.
au6-6t

FOR RENT.

*—Advertisements one cent a word a time. No charge less than 25
cents.*

UPPER TENEMENT—Corner Kempton
and Liberty streets; two fire-rooms three
bedrooms on the floor; modern improvements.   au6-2t

REAL ESTATE.

Telephone Call......................211—4

F. A. F. ADAMS,

North Second Street
(Opposite Post Office.)

Real Estate Agency.

County Street—Fine view of harbor and
bay; desirable residence on a corner, with
75 rods of land; every improvement.

State Street—Extra lot location and neighborhood; slated roof house and stable; modern conveniences; 40 rods of land; one of the
nicest homes in the city.

Channing Cottage of 10 rooms; every improvement, lot of regret; 14 rods of land; on
a corner; sold on account of owner's ill
health; price $4150; easy terms.

Fine Residence—Corner of an orchard, on a
corner; large lot; every improvement.

Rockland Street—2½ story house and 19
rods of land; on a corner; rents well; modern
conveniences; price $4700; easy terms.

Allen Street—Near County; extra well built
cottage; new; splendid location; owner says
sell; easy terms.

Fifth Street—Cottage house, stable and 14
rods of land; great repair; price $1000.

Pleasant Street—On a corner; cottage
house; just been put in most excellent order
throughout; large lot; belongs to a widow
who says sell.

Desirable 2 1-2 Story House—Two tenements, on cottage street; new; 15 rods of
land; every improvement; rents for $40 per
month; price for such a nice house; easy
terms.

Cottage House—Stable and 113 rods of land;
finely laid out; on Orchard street; good location; valuable as an investment.

2 1-2 Story House—Two tenements; 14 rods
of land; on Fourth street; very central; best
of repair; price low; easy terms.

Nice House on Morgan street; 2½ stories;
two tenements; steam heat, &c.; rents well;
price $3500; easy terms.

Cottage of 11 Rooms, every improvement;
40 rods of land on Ashland street; location
A 1; price low as the owner moves away;
easy terms.

Cottage house, stable and 17 rods of land
on Kempton street, on a corner; price $3000;
easy terms.

Cottage of 9 rooms on a corner; steam
heat, gas, hot and cold water, set tubs, set
bowls, etc.; good neighborhood; new; just
finished; price only $3250; easy terms.

$3200 cottage, 7 rooms, every improvement and conveniences; best of repair; not
one dollar to be laid out; easy terms.

$2350—Steam heat, gas, hot and cold
water, set tubs, set bowls, etc.; splendid cottage, new; good location; a bargain; easy
terms.

Several very desirable properties in Fairhaven. Some great bargains in lots just
over the bridge from $9 to $15 per rod; easy
terms.

We have a very large list of houses, house
lots and farms that are not advertised. Call
and get a list.

F. A. F. ADAMS,

No. 38 North Second Street.

H. A. LEONARD,

REAL ESTATE AGENT,......126 UNION STREET.

Houses and lots for sale in all parts of the
city. No charges unless sale effected.   je6-2m

COURT STREET—Two story house and
barn with about 25 rods of land; all in the
very best of order; modern improvements.
This is a bargain; can be bought on easy
terms. Call and examine.

A VERY FINE two story house and 27 rods
of land; situated on high land; nice bath
room, water closet and set bowl. Will sell or
exchange for a good farm near the sea shore;
this is good investment property.

COURT STREET—Fine Bargain—Cottage
house and 12 rods of land. Can be bought for
$1350. A fine house for a party with moderate
means.

CHANCERY STREET—Very fine two story
house with 10 rods of land; fine location;
built in the best of order; can be bought for
$3000; easy terms; will rent easy for $25 per
month.

VALUABLE ESTATE FOR SALE—Comprising one cottage, one three story block
and 65 rods of land in a location where real
estate is advancing rapidly; two new mills
going up close by; owner says sell; going to
move from the city. This is the very best of
investment property.

SOME VERY FINE building lots and investment land in all parts of the city. Before
buying please call and examine my list.

FLORENCE STREET—Four new cottages
with 10 rods of land, each in the best of
neighborhoods; prices range from $1500 to
$1800, on easy terms.

ROUND STREET—New cottage with 8
rods of land, very fine view, on high land.
Can be bought for $1250. Call and examine.

PARK STREET—This is a bargain. One
and a half story cottage with 20 rods of land.
Can be bought for $1700. The land is worth
$60 per rod. Good neighborhood, one minute walk from the horse cars. This property
cannot help selling. Come early.

SUMMER STREET—New cottage house
with 12 rods of land, bath room, water closet
and furnace; in the very best of repair;
good neighborhood on the line of horse cars.
Can be bought for $2135.

A FEW MORE of those beautiful seashore
lots left at Bay View. They are selling rapidly at $3 per rod.

Two of the finest lots at Horse Neck Beach
for sale. Price $400 each.

FINE COTTAGE FOR SALE with modern
improvements, about 14 rods of land, good
stable, situated on a corner. Owner says sell.
Easy terms.

FINE GOTHIC COTTAGE for sale with 12
rods of land on a corner. Very pleasantly
situated. Finished in hard wood; with modern improvements, fine bath room and water
closet. Beautiful home for the right party.

ONE OF THE MOST desirable farms in
Southern Massachusetts for sale. Buildings
new. Beautiful view. Can be bought for
one half its original value.

PARTIES LOOKING for good investment
land or nice building lot can be accommodated by looking my list over. These lots are
situated in the west part of the city, near the
Park, and on or near the horse cars, and also
near Rockdale avenue. This is one of the
most desirable locations in the city. The
cars are sure to be continued on Union street
and through Rockdale avenue to Kempton
street, forming a belt line, which will be the
means of increasing the value of property in
this section. Now is your chance to buy.

P. DRISCOLL,

12 ROCK STREET,

Real Estate Agent.

House lots on the Briggs and Howland
farms in Fairhaven, near the Coggeshall
street bridge, are now ready for sale. Price
low. Terms easy.

Six house lots on Prospect street.

House lots on Hathaway and Howard avenues, Bakeman, Clara, Dean, River and Rock
streets.

SUMMER COTTAGE AND BARN—
House lots in the most desirable part of the
city growing rapidly; will make good home
and must increase in value. Apply box 4,
Standard office.

Column 6

AUCTION SALES.

By STANDISH BOURNE,

(Successor to Geo. A. Bourne & Son,)
Auctioneer, Commission Merchant, Real Estate Dealer and Appraiser.

Cash advanced on goods consigned for auction. Ready buyer for personal property of
every description.

Office and Salesrooms 47, 49 and 51 North Second Street, near the Post Office.

Valuable Real Estate.

☞ On MONDAY, August 8th, at 12½ o'clock,
on the premises, will be sold the two-
story house and lot of about 10 rods, situated
on the northeast corner of High and Pleasant streets. The house is in perfect order,
containing modern conveniences, rents readily and is in just the right spot for investment. A rare chance for a buyer. The house
will be open on morning of sale for inspection. Lot has a frontage of 43.90 ft. by
42.52 ft. on High street.

Cottage at Nonquitt.

☞ On MONDAY, August 8th, at 3 o'clock
on the premises, will be sold the three-
story cottage, and lots, containing about 15,-
000 square feet, situated south of King Philip
street, and west of Contest street, being lots
numbered 110, 111, 112, and 127, as per plan of
Nonquitt.

The cottage is in first-class order in every
respect, was built by Samuel M. Davis, in his
usual excellent manner, and together with its
desirable location is a most charming seaside property.

Cottage will be open for inspection Tuesdays, Thursdays and Saturday from 4 to 6 P.
M.

Centrally Located Real Estate by Auction.

☞ On WEDNESDAY, Aug. 10th, at 12½ o'clock,
on the premises, will be sold in the following order:

☞ 1st—The two tenement house in first-
rate order, situated on the south side of
Elm street, about 10 feet east of Purchase
street, known as the Hallett Gifford homestead. This lot has a frontage of 37 feet by a
depth of about 51½ feet.

☞ 2d—The house in rear of No. 1, formerly the
homestead of Dr. Andrew Mackie, with lot
containing about 8.90 rods. This has an entrance from Elm street of about 6½ feet.

☞ 3d—This right is reserved to offer the two
parcels, and if a larger bid can be obtained
than the sum of the separate sales, this will
be the binding sale.

For plan or further particulars call at the
office of the auctioneer.

Mortgagee's Sale.

By virtue of a power of sale contained in a
mortgage deed from Henry J. Riley et al. to
William D. Howland dated Dec. 24th, 1888,
and recorded Bristol County S.D., Registry
of Deeds b. 120 ps. 3, 4 and 5, and for breach
of the conditions of said mortgage, will be
sold at public auction on the premises, on
August 27th, A.D. 1892, at 3 o'clock, P. M., the
following described premises, v.z:

A certain lot of land with the buildings
thereon, situated in said New
Bedford, and bounded and described as follows, viz: beginning at the southwest corner of said lot at a stake in line of contemplated Summit street eighty (80) feet south of the
intersection of contemplated Stone[?] street
with said contemplated Summit street and at
the southwest cor of land sold to Catherine
B. Cowen; thence easterly by said
Cowen's land fifty-eight and 82-100 (58.82) feet;
thence southerly by said land of George
Howland, Jr. trustee, eighty (80) feet to a
contemplated street; thence westerly by
said contemplated street fifty-eight and 82-
100 (58.82) feet to contemplated Summit
street; thence northerly by contemplated
Summit street eighty (80) feet to the place of
beginning. Containing seventeen and 28-100
(17.28) square rods more or less. Being the
same premises conveyed to said Henry J.
Riley by George Howland, Jr., trustee by
deed dated Aug. 20th, 1886, and recorded with
Bristol County (S.D.) Deeds, B. 117 p. 264.
Terms at sale.   WM D. HOWLAND.
jy30-au5-13

To Let in Our Storage Warehouse.

We constantly have on hand first-class
rooms for the storage of household goods, to
be rented by the month or year.

Good dry storage room for stoves.

By JOHN B. BAYLIES,

121 and 123 Union Street.

Commission Merchant, Appraiser, and Auctioneer for the sale of Real Estate and
every description of Personal Property. Furniture Stored.

H. C. HATHAWAY,

Auctioneer, Real Estate Agent and Appraiser.

☞ One of the best auction marts in the
State for the sale of horses and carriages. Keep constantly on hand carriages of every
description, carriages made to order and repairing in all its branches attended to under
the superintendency of J. R. Forbes. Consignments of every description solicited.
Cash advanced on goods for auction. Personal property of every description bought
at short notice for cash. Negotiable notes
bought and sold.

Heirs' Sale of Real Estate.

☞ On SATURDAY, Aug. 13, at 3 o'clock P.
M., on the premises, will be sold without
the least reserve, to wind up the estate, the house and lot of about 17 rods of
land No. 79 Middle street. The house is in
good condition and is situated in that part of
the city where it will be sure always to rent
well. Sale positive and without limit.
Terms, 10 per cent. at sale. Balance on delivery of heirs' deed.

ALFRED WILSON,

Auctioneer and Real Estate Agent.

Room 22, - - - - Robeson Building.

☞ Houses and land in all parts of the city
for sale; tenements for rent; rents collected

For Sale.

Two-story house on Acushnet avenue, near
Walnut street; well arranged for one family;
good location.

For Lease.

The Webster Block, Purchase street; 8
rooms, well adapted for a genteel boarding
house, club rooms, or business purposes.

TO LET—A flat in The Winslow, corner
Sixth and Union streets. Apply to
WILSON, Robeson Building.   jy14-tf

T. F. HEALEY,

Auctioneer and Real Estate Agent,

555 and 559 Purchase street, corner
Franklin street.

FOR SALE one small house, barn and 2½
rods of land on North Front street. Price
$1500.

Also one fine house in the west part of the
city in good locality, with all the modern improvements, gas and electric lights, etc.
Will be sold cheap if applied for soon.

Also a few more house lots in Fairhaven on
the Howland and Briggs farms, from $15 to
$17 per rod, and they are some of the choice
lots.

Also one corner lot on south Belleville road
for $2.5 per rod.

Also one lot on the corner of Sawyer and
North Front streets.

Also lots on Acushnet avenue, Coggeshall
and Locust streets, in fact all parts of the city.
Also some desirable house lots on Hathaway avenue near Purchase street. Easy
terms.

Business solicited. No charges made
unless a sale, then my prices are the lowest.

BY WM. BARKER, Jr., Auctioneer.

Heirs' Sale of Valuable Seashore Property at Auction.

Will be sold at auction on the premises,
on MONDAY, Aug. 9, 1892, at 2 o'clock P. M.,
that well known point or neck of land situated at the southeasterly part of Westport,
in the County of Bristol, Mass., and commonly called "Gooseberry Neck." The property comprises about 75 acres, accessible by
land or water, has an extensive and valuable
shore privilege furnishing an abundance of
kelp, rock weed, moss and muck, excellent
fishing and fowling facilities. About 12
miles southwesterly from New Bedford, in
close proximity to Westport Point, Horse
Neck and Westport Harbor, and one of the
most desirable seaside locations in New
England coast.

For further particulars inquire of or address the auctioneer at North Dartmouth,
Bristol Co., Mass.

July 25, 1892.   jy25-ta

REAL ESTATE.

FRANCIS W. TAPPAN,

Agent for Purchase, Sale, and Lease of
REAL ESTATE.

Office, 15 North Water St. New Bedford. d&w

FRANK C. SMITH,

Real Estate Broker, Auctioneer and Appraiser,

Office - - 47 William Street,

(Opposite Post Office.)

M. E. SMITH,

REAL ESTATE AGENT.

619 Purchase Street.   Telephone 16-11.

FOR SALE—In South Dartmouth, near the
water, 42½ story house, with large piazza,
barn, and 83 rods of land. One of the most
desirable places in the village for a Summer
residence. Inquire of BENJ. OUERIPEL or
DANIEL H. HOWLAND, South Dartmouth. au7

SPECIAL NOTICES.

POTTER and COMPANY,
No. 137 Westminster St.,
Cor. Dorrance Street,
PROVIDENCE.

---------oooooo---------

Now arriving Fabrics for Coverings and Curtains. Fall Designs in Carpets. Antique Rugs of Special quality.

TO BATHERS.

Notice is hereby given that all persons are forbidden landing or bathing on Palmers Island under penalty of the law.
jy30-au6 WM. A. HAMMAN, Watchman.

Excursion to Washington.

The committee of arrangements for the Excursion to Washington, D. C., under the auspices of R. A. Peirce Post 190, G. A. R., have a limited number of tickets at their disposal. All persons desiring to participate are requested to apply at once. Full information can be had from any member of the committee.
F. A. WASHBURN, Chairman.
WILLIAM ALMY, Secretary.
THOMAS J. GIFFORD, Treasurer.
FRED P. MOSHER.
HENRY W. MASON.
jy30au3-6

NONQUITT HOTEL.

Now Open for the Season of 1892. Special attention given to parties, clubs, &c., &c., for dinners and suppers. Escape the heat of town and pass a cool night at Nonquitt. Boats leave New Bedford 6 45, 8 50 A. M., 1 45, 5 00 P. M. Leave Nonquitt 7 45, 9 50 A. M., 3 00, 6 00 P. M. Fine macadamized road just finished to Nonquitt.
W. H. WINGATE, Proprietor,
au3-1m Nonquitt, Mass.

PROPOSALS

For Furnishing the City of New Bedford with Wood.

NEW BEDFORD, Aug. 2, 1892.

Sealed proposals will be received at the City Clerk's office, Library building, until 12 o'clock noon, on FRIDAY, August 12th, 1892, for furnishing the city of New Bedford with 75 cords each of best quality oak and maple wood, all to be green wood. To be delivered at the city coal and wood yard, and to be subject to the measurement of the superintendent of the yard. The committee reserve the right to reject any or all bids.
For the Committee on Fuel.
CHARLES S. ASHLEY, Chairman.
au3-tau12

New Bedford Business College.

Fall term begins WEDNESDAY, Aug. 3. Applications will be received at room 30 Citizens' Bank Building, William street, on and after the above date from 9 30 A. M. to 3 30 P. M. Announcement for evening class will be made later. au2-5t

NOTICE.

Soldiers, sailors, widows, orphans, desiring to apply for pensions, back pay or bounty, can consult J. F. VINAL, from Washington, D. C., at 107 Fourth street. au2-1m

GLORIA WATER

Cures Pimples, Freckles, Black-heads and Tan, and gives a lovely complexion; price 75c. per bottle. For sale by MRS. P. W. PINKHAM, Manager of Branch Office, No. 15 Bethel street. au2-TTS1m

We have recently added the following and many other New Books, to our Circulating Library:
AULD LICHT—IDYLLS, by J. M. Barrie.
THAT DAKOTA GIRL, by Stella Gilman.
MAGIC INK, and other stories, by Wm. Black.
AUNT ANNE, by Mrs. W. K. Clifford.
THAT WILD WHEEL, by Frances Eleanor Trollope.
A LETTER OF INTRODUCTION, by W. D. Howells.
DECEMBER ROSES, by Mrs. Campbell Praed.
PRAY YOU, SIR, WHOSE DAUGHTER? by Helen W. Gardner,
YOUNG LUCRETIA, and other stories. by Mary E. Wilkins.
THE SQUIRE, by Mrs. Parr.
CYNTHIA WAKEHAM'S MONEY, by Anna Katharine Green.
THE ALPHABET OF LOVE, by Laura Jean Libby.
Terms—One Cent a day.
ROBT. W. TABER,
BOOKSELLER AND STATIONER,
No. 198 UNION STREET.

SHIRT WAISTS.

On Friday and Saturday one more lot marked down to
75 CENTS.
The most comfortable Waist one can wear these hot days. No lady should miss this Great Bargain.
LIBERTY SCARFS.
New lot received this morning.

E. C. CASE, - - - 213 UNION ST. TTS

DRESSMAKERS

Who dislike to fit dresses over ill fitting corsets, and ladies who are tired of wearing the same are invited to call and examine the
WATERHOUSE,
The best Corsets made to order in America. *Warranted all Whalebone*; and a *Perfect Fit.* Made in all colors. Prices from $2.50 to $10.00. Measures taken at
R. R. ANDREWS' CORSET ROOMS,
168 Union Street, New Bedford, Mass.
H. L. ALLEN, Sole Agent.

Buckingham's Dye for the Whiskers does its work thoroughly, coloring a uniform brown or black, which, when dry, will neither rub, wash off, nor soil linen.

Winthrop House
245 PURCHASE STREET,
Has been thoroughly renovated by Mrs. Chas. H. Wood and is open for day or regular boarders. Good rooms and well-furnished table. MWS-tf

CHARLES F. SPOONER,
Piano Tuner and Repairer.
Residence 82 Thomas street. Orders left with Briggs & Lawrence, 197 and 203 Union st. MWS

As an after-dinner pill, to strengthen the stomach, assist digestion, and correct any bilious tendencies, Ayer's Pills are considered the best. Being sugar-coated, they are as agreeable as any confection, and may be taken by the most delicate.

WILLIAM H. P. WALKER,
Counsellor at Law and Notary Public.
Room 23, over Citizens Nationa Bank. jy6-WS

During the dog-day season, the drain of nervous and vital energy may be counteracted by the use of Ayer's Sarsaparilla. In purifying the blood, it acts as a superb corrective and tonic, and enables the system to defy malarial and other climatic influences.

PARKER HOUSE CAFE.

The newly fitted Cafe connected with this hotel will be opened to the public on THURSDAY EVENING, March 21st.
HOLDER M. BROWNELL.

GEORGE PEIRCE,
ORGANS AND PIANOS
TUNED, REPAIRED AND POLISHED.
5 Dover Street.
Telephone..............................259-12

WANTED.

Crusher stone of suitable size, landed at the crusher on Acushnet avenue, north of Phillips road, for which 40 cents per ton will be paid.
A. B. DRAKE,
my6-tf Supt. of Public Works.

SPECIAL NOTICES.

HUTCHINSON'S CIRCULATING LIBRARY.
TERMS, ONE CENT A DAY.

Partial List of Books added in July:

VERBENA and other stories. Besant.
YOUNG LUCRETIA. Wilkins.
THE HEIRESS. Henry Greville.
AUNT ANNE. Clifford.
CYNTHIA WAKEHAM'S MONEY. Greene.
AULD LICHT IDYLLS. Barrie.
WHEN MAN'S SINGLE. Barrie.
THE SQUIRE. Parr.
MRS. KEATS BRADFORD. Pool.
THE NAULAHKA. Kipling.
GILBERT ELGAR'S SON. Davis.
THE WRECKER. Stevenson.
PRINCE DUSTY. Munroe.
EDELWEISS OF THE SIERRAS.
VESTY OF THE BASINS. Greene.
TESS OF D'URBERVILLES. Hardy.
COLONY OF GIRLS. Willard.
LOVE IS LORD OF ALL. Safford.
MRS. BARR'S SHORT STORIES.
TRUE DAUGHTER HARTENSTEIN.
PRATT PORTRAITS. Fuller.
ONE GOOD GUEST. Walford.
TOO SHORT A VACATION. McLaughlin.
OUT OF THE FASHION. Meade.
DAUGHTER OF THE SOUTH. Burnett.
LITTLE LADY LAGUNITAS. Savage.
NADA, THE LILY. Haggard.

HUTCHINSON'S Book Store,
194 UNION STREET.

WHEATON'S BOTTLED SODA WATER.
—IT IS—
Pure, Healthful and Delicious.

Every drop of water used is Pure Spring Water, and the juices are made from natural fruit under our own direction.
With an experience of over half a century using the most improved machinery, we are prepared to furnish the finest Bottled Soda Water in the United States.
As a drink for lunch or evening parties our GINGER ALE is unsurpassed.
CALL FOR WHEATON'S.

HIRAM WHEATON & SONS,
45 & 47 School St. Telephone 276-4.

CORSET STORE.
19 PURCHASE ST.
SPECIAL NOTICE.

We have cut prices on all of our Infants' Wear. Come quick if you are in need, and save your dollars.
10 Styles of Summer Corsets, and the largest stock in Southern Massachusetts to select from.
Agent for Domestic Paper Patterns. H. B. DIMAN, Proprietor.

7000 NEGATIVES,

Taken by Noah Gifford are in my possession. Any wishing duplicates from these negatives can obtain them by calling on *H. F. HATCH, Photographer,* opposite City Clock, or by addressing NOAH GIFFORD.

Mothers, your baby's enemy, Diphtheria, is near your door! Don't let him step over the threshold without first having a Photograph taken of baby by HATCH, who loves to take babies, and never gets out of patience. (TTS&w) New Bedford, Mass.

O'Neil
ARTIST PHOTOGRAPHER
High Class Work at Low Prices.
(Hastings Building.) TTS

TO CURE
MOTH AND FRECKLES!
Use Mme. Bush's Obliteration
The great skin remedy.
For sale by Druggists. Wholesale and retail by
Mme. B. M. BUSH, Sole Proprietor.
No. 383 Purchase St., cor. Campbell. MWS

J. H. BURGESS,
Accountant,
AND TEACHER OF
Book-keeping,
84 School St. TTS

MADAME MOREZ,
Trance Clairvoyant.
137 Middle street, first house west of Purchase street, until Aug. 30th. Ladies, 50c. Gentlemen, $1. jy2-30t

MADAME DEVOLL.
CLAIRVOYANT, DOCTRESS & BUSINESS MEDIUM.
Has moved from No. 70 Mill st., to No. 10 Bedford St. Office hours from 9 to 12 A. M., 2 to 9 P. M. jy25-12t

MADAME BRUCE,
Clairvoyant Doctor,
25 WEST CLINTON AVE., - - Cottage City, Mass.

Clairvoyant, Business and Test Medium.
Mrs. EDDY can be consulted at 128 Union street. Hours strictly from 10 to 12 A. M., and 2 to 9 P. M. Ladies 50 cts.; Gents $1.00

CHARLES E. SPARROW,
Pianos Tuned and Repaired.
Orders at Mr. Faisneau's, 14 Purchase St. Residence 292 Purchase street. TTS

CRUSHER STONE.

Fifty cents a ton will be paid for crusher stone of suitable size, delivered at the crusher on Acushnet avenue, north of Coggeshall street.
A. B. DRAKE,
je7-tf Supt. of Public Works.

REMOVAL OF NIGHT SOIL.

Persons desiring to have their vaults emptied of night soil, can leave their orders at the following places upon slates provided for that purpose:
Washburn's Grocery store, 741 Purchase st.
Central Union Grocery, 9 North Sixth street
F. C. Bliss & Son, Washington square.
ap9tf S. S. WILBUR.

TYPE-WRITING.
MRS. KENDALL, Copyist.
Room 21, ... Robeson Building.
Copying of all kinds.
Supplies for all Type-Writers.

SPECIAL NOTICES.

WALL PAPER.

If you are looking for Wall Paper, or if you think you are to want some soon, it will amply repay you to come in and buy of us. We have just put our stock in shape ready to take stock, and for the next few days we will sell

CHEAP.

To those who are finishing off houses and to contractors this is a rare chance. It is only open until we take stock and you would do well to buy as early as possible.

HENRY J. TAYLOR & SON,
Cor. William and Sixth Sts.

AGENT for the FOX and COMFORT EYEGLASS

PAT. JAN. 22. 84

The above cut represents the cemented bi focal lense in a Fox frame. I introduced both in New Bedford about 5 years ago. Since then have sold hundreds of pairs of them with the best results. This bi focal can be made up in frameless spectacles or eye glasses. Have just received a new style of eyeglass hook, neat and durable. The best out. Eyes tested by latest method. Repairing neatly done. Oculist orders correctly filled.
J. T. ALMY, - - - - - Practical Optician,
188 UNION STREET.
(Opposite Moynan & Co's) TTS

SETTLED.

SOULE PIANO AND ORGAN INVT. CO.
AT No. 147 PURCHASE STREET.

We do not keep our stock in New Bedford, Taunton, Fall River or Africa, but we *guarantee* the highest satisfaction to musical people.
We will forfeit a $500 piano if we fail to furnish a better piano than any competitor offers the public for the same price.
Our instruments are most carefully selected, by a person of very large experience. If necessary we can deliver in from 4 to 8 hours, our resources being so great.
Be sure and call upon us before selecting, as we have great bargains in second hands, as well as new instruments.

SOULE P. & O. I. CO.
Z. C. KEITH, Treas. Brockton. L. SOULE, Man. Taunton.

A NEW LOT OF FOX EYE GLASS FRAMES,
New Styles Just Received.

These frames, for which I am agent, are pleasing the public, and many have found by visiting my optical establishment, that they are far superior to the old ordinary frames.
Call and see the new spectacle attachment.
C. W. HURLL, Jr., Optician,
34 Purchase St. - - - - - - Up Stairs.
Over C. F. Wing's Carpet Store. TuThS

WHY WEAR A PLATED CHAIN
WHEN YOU CAN BUY A
SOLID GOLD CHAIN
For $10.00.

Read our guarantee, giveg with every chain sold.
We hereby guarantee the GOLD VALUE of the above chain to be $6.00, payable on return within five years.
H. B. HOWLAND. MThS

LADIES' SHIRT WAISTS,
REAL SCOTCH GINGHAM SKIRTS,
CHILDREN'S SUN HATS.
C. T. JOHNSON,
SM 7 PLEASANT STREET.

CHAS. E. WOODWORTH,
(Successor to C. W. Hurll.)
No. 27 PURCHASE ST.,
JEWELLER.
Watch, Clock and Jewelry repairing neatly done.
All work warranted. MThS

DR. H. E. MANN.
During months of July and August my office hours will be from 8 A. M. till 6 P. M.
jy27-tf

DIAMONDS, WATCHES, CLOCKS, JEWELRY, ETC.

On account of the lease of store to Moynan & Co. entire stock to be closed out regardless of cost.
J. S. KELLEY & SON,
15 Purchase Street.

MARRIED.

In this city, 5th inst., by Thomas J. Cobb, Esq., Walter W. Gammons to Lena P. Kenerson, both of this city.
In Fairhaven, 29th ult., by Rev. N. C. Alger, Benjamin Gibbs, of this city, to Miss Esther J. Allen, of Fairhaven.
In Rockland, 28th ult., Nathan A. Keene, of Rockland, to Miss Rebecca A. Chandler, of Duxbury.
In Marshfield, 31st ult., Lucius W. Osborne to Ella T. Baulding.
In Saratoga, Cal., June 29th, Lemuel J. Church, formerly of Fairhaven, to Mary L. Cunningham, of Saratoga.

DEATHS.

In this city, 5th inst., Mary McCarmack, aged 56 years.
Funeral at her late residence, 188 Middle street, Sunday, at 2 o'clock. Services at St. Lawrence Church at 2 30 o'clock. Relatives and friends are invited to attend.
In this city, 8 mo., 6th, Deborah, daughter of the late Joseph and Deborah Howland.
Notice of funeral hereafter.
In Fairhaven, 2d inst., Bertha Wright, daughter of George M. and Annie H. Waterson, aged 1 year.
In Fall River, 4th inst., Jefferson, son of Jefferson White, 14 days; Andrew J. Borden, 70; Abby D., wife of Andrew J. Borden, 67; 5th, Alice Jane, daughter of Frederick A. Spencer, 1 month; Charles Manchester, 19; Catherine, widow of Patrick Lyons, 54.
In Somerset, 4th inst., Obadiah M. Buffinton, 73.
In Taunton, (Oakland,) 5th inst., Albert, son of Ulric Ducharme, 21 days.
In Raynham, 4th inst., F. Cary Andrews, 80.
In North Easton, 4th inst., Geo. W. Andrews, 58.
In Brockton, 4th inst., Sarah J., daughter of John J. Morgan, 1; Mary, wife of Patrick Monaghan, 51; 5th, Hugh, son of Hugh McDonald, 10 months.
In Provincetown, 30th ult., Nellie, daughter of Manuel D. James, 4 months.
In Kingston, 27th ult., Thomas E. Smith, 11 months; Rose Atfield, 39; 30th, Edw. A. Merrill, 61.
In Duxbury, 30th ult., Sarah E., daughter of Elisha G. Sampson, 5 weeks; 2d inst., Mercy, widow of Otis Morton, 86
In Carver, 31st ult., Mary T. Savery, wife of Lewis Sherrett, 60.
In Charlestown, 3d inst., Capt. Phineas Leach, formerly of Plymouth, 85.
In Plymouth, 30th ult., Alice, daughter of Joseph S. Morey, 6 months.
In North Plymouth, 30th ult., Mary, daughter of Jo Frances, 3 months.
In Mansfield, 30th ult., Ellen M., wife of Isaac Aldrich, 48 years.

MINIATURE ALMANAC.

SUNDAY, AUGUST 7.
Sunrise 4 44. Sunset 6 54. Moon sets 3 14 a. m.
High water 6 49 a. m. 7 16 p. m.
Low water 12 09 a. m. 12 36 p. m.
Day of Year—220. Length of Day 14 h. 13 m.

MONDAY, AUGUST 8.
Sunrise 4 45. Sunset 6 53. Moon souths 12 00 p.m.
High water 7 42 a. m. 8 08 p. m.
Low water 1 03 a. m. 1 29 p. m.
Day of Year—221. Length of Day—14 h. 10 m.

MOON'S PHASES.
Full Moon, Monday, August 8, 6 57 p. m.
Third Quarter, Monday, August 15, 1 37 a. m.
New Moon, Monday, August 22, 5 59 a. m.
First Quarter, Tuesday, August 30, 8 29 a. m.

METEOROLOGICAL RECORD.

SATURDAY, AUGUST 6.
Barometer—7 a. m., 29.76 in. 12 m. 29.75 in.
Thermometer—7 a. m. 72 deg. 12 m. 84 deg.

For additional Ship News, Marriages and Deaths, if any, see sixth page.

MARINE INTELLIGENCE.

PORT OF NEW BEDFORD.

SATURDAY, Aug 6.
ARRIVED.
Steamer Nantucket, Bartow, Nantucket and returns.
Steamer Marthas Vineyard, Marshall, from and to the Vineyard.
Barges Bizarre and Wm H McClave, Perth Amboy, in tow of tug R H Rathburn.
SAILED.
Steamer Harry, Ricketson, Providence.
Steamer Gay Head, Daggett, Nantucket and returned.
Sch Hastings, Cory, New York.
ARRIVED YESTERDAY.
Sch Irene, St John, NB.
Barges Marvin and Anthracite, Rondout, in tow of tug Dudley Pray.

A letter from Capt Macomber, of sch Blakeley, of San Francisco, received by S Fosdick & Co, of that city, states Dec 15th, a week after leaving port, the second mate died and was buried at sea. A gale was blowing at the time and every man was needed to handle the schooner, so that it was not possible to hold religious services. The body was sewn up in canvas with a heavy weight and buried in the sea. This was the occasion of the differences between Capt Macomber and the first officer, W C Hayden, and the captain concluded that Hayden had better retire.

Sch Edw W Young, of Newport, at Providence, while on her way up the bay, morning of 22d ult, it being very foggy at the time, struck a bed of rocks off Beaver Tail. She was afterwards warped off. Her keel was knocked off, her bottom badly chafed, and she leaked badly. Her pumps were kept constantly going while she was discharging. She is now on the railway receiving new keel and other necessary repairs to her bottom, and will be ready for business in about two weeks. The damage will amount to over $1000.

Sld from Bangor 5th, sch Nellie Gray, Edgartown.
Ar at Bath 4th, schs Lavinia Campbell, Vail, Philadelphia; H L Baker, Crowell, do; James H Hoyt, Nickerson, do.
Ar at Saco 5th, sch A W Parker, New York.
Ar at Salem 5th, sch James Rothwell, Newburg.
Ar at Boston 5th, schs Richard S Spofford, Nickerson, Mobile; Elisha Gibbs, Fisher, Philadelphia; T B Garland, Crosby, South Amboy; J S Lamprey, Harding, Perth Amboy. Cld, schs S H Walker, Nicholson, Kennebec and Washington, DC; Ira Laffrinier, Crowell, Clark's Island and New York; D B Fearing, Clifford, Bangor and Washington; M E Eldridge, Kelley, Prospect, Me, and New York.
Ar at Hyannis 5th, schs H M Howes, South Amboy; N H Skinner, New York for Boston.
Passed Nobska 4th, schs Julia A Ward and John S Ames, Philadelphia for Boston.
Ar at Fall River 4th, schs Nathan Lawrence, Haskell, Norfolk; Salmon Washburn. Sld 4th, schs Mary Ellen, New York; 5th, Fanny C Bowen, Chase, Norfolk.
Sld from Providence 5th, sch Oliver Chase, Brown, Westport.
Ar at Stonington 4th, schs Josie Crowley, Clark, Greenport for this port; 5th, James Parker Sr, Anderson, New York for Somerset; Clarissa Allen, Tisdale, do for Taunton; S L Thompson, Keefe, Amboy for do; H A Deming, Hall, Port Johnson for Nantucket.
Ar at Stamford 4th, sch Golden Ball, Richmond.
Cld at New York 4th, steamer Nacoochee, Smith, Savannah; 5th, brig J H Crandon, Cape Town.
Ar at New Orleans 5th, steamer Louisiana, New York.

Sld from Port Antonio Aug 4th, steamer Ethelwold, Boston.
Ar at St Johns, PR, Aug 5th, tug Right Arm, Davis, hence via Norfolk.

For Advertisements received too late for this page see 6th page.

Smoke the New Nickel Cigar,
AMERICAN TRAMP
IT IS THE LEADER.
FOR SALE EVERYWHERE. au6-1m

ELLIS' FINE ART ROOMS,
114 WILLIAM STREET.
A NEW INVOICE OF
FRAMED PHOTOGRAPHS!
Choice for 50 Cents.
SEE THEM.

WM. PEIRCE,
Florist, Seedsman, & Landscape Gardener.
CONSERVATORIES
Cor. Elm and Cottage Sts.
Seed and Flower Store,.........232 Union St.
Connected by Telephone.

CASES OF INSANITY
From the Effects of
"LA GRIPPE"
Are Alarmingly Prevalent.
Suicides
From the
SAME CAUSE
Are announced in every paper.
Would you be rid of the awful effects of La Grippe?
There is BUT ONE SURE REMEDY that NEVER FAILS, viz:
DANA'S SARSAPARILLA.
We Guarantee to CURE you or REFUND your money.
COULD WE DO MORE?
ISN'T IT WORTH A TRIAL?
je25-tf

LATEST STYLES OF TYPE
—AT THE—
STANDARD JOB OFFICE.

SHIRTS.
T. M. Denham & Bro.
NEW BEDFORD, MASS.

The New Of Just In — PRETTIEST LOT FANCY SHIRTS MADE
YACHTING FLANNELS
CAMBRICS
OUTING FLANNELS
SEERSUCKERS
With Stiffened Collars and Cuffs.
UNLAUNDERED
From 50c. to $1.
Salesroom, 384 Acushnet Avenue.
TTS5p

WANTS.

All Advertisements under this heading 1c. a word a time. No charge less than 25c.

MALE.

GOOD MAN—$40 per month and expenses paid; to take orders; work all Winter. Address, with references, The Ontario Nurseries, Geneva, N. Y. au6-1t

MAN—With some money would like to buy an interest in good paying business (light manufacturing preferred) where he would have steady employment. Address box 14 *Standard* office. au6-1t

EXPERIENCED DRUG CLERK.—Address box 70 *Standard* office. au4-3t

FEMALE.

GOOD GIRL—To do general housework at 97 Elm street. au6-3t

RELIABLE WOMAN—For general housework. Apply at 671 Purchase st. au5-2t

ON SEASIDE FARM — Middle aged woman to assist in care of two small children and in housework. References required. P. O. box 211, South Dartmouth. au5-tf

GOOD RELIABLE WOMEN — To do housework in the country. Apply at 98 Parker street. au3-4t

LADIES—To assist me in selling the famous Gloria Water for the complexion. Terms liberal. Address MRS. P. W. TINKHAM, Manager of Branch Office, No. 15 Bethel street. au2-TTS3t

IMMEDIATELY—Girl to do general housework in small family; Centre, corner of Laurel street, Fairhaven. jy29-tf

INTELLIGENCE OFFICE — 113 North Water street. Good, reliable help. MRS. A. LETTUS. je30-tau14

EMPLOYMENT OFFICE—Good, reliable help furnished by Mrs. J. HARRINGTON, 254 Acushnet ave. f17-6m

EMPLOYMENT OFFICE—All kinds of female help from the Provinces; head cooks, waiters and general housework help. Apply at Mrs. ANNIE L. JOHN'S, 130 Purchase.

INTELLIGENCE OFFICE—34 Acushnet avenue. Good reliable help. Mrs. Wm. Atchison.

MISCELLANEOUS.

PARTNER—Either sex, light office business; money secured; references exchanged. Address box 40 *Standard* office. au2-tf

CORRESPONDING AGENTS—In every town to inform us of parties intending opening or refitting saloons, by the largest Saloon Fixture Manufacturers in the world. Good man can make $5000. The ROTHSCHILD Bar Fixture Co., 1158 Broadway, corner Twenty-seventh street, New York. jy23-TTS7t

GIRLS AND BOYS.

ON account of our extensive trade, and the popularity of our superior Teas, we have many imitators and impostors. *Beware* of them.
We Give 24, 26 and 28 inch Boys' Safeties with 35 to 50 lbs. Better wheels, 90, 100, 125 and 150 pounds. Tricycles, Velocipedes, Solid Silver Watches, Base Ball Outfits, Hammocks, Croquet Sets, and all other articles below our imitators.

AMERICAN ENTERPRISE TEA CO.,
C. Y. WILCOX,
TTS 28 Pearl St.

WE OFFER AGENTS BIG MONEY—In exclusive territory. Our new patent Safes, sell at sight in city or country. New Agents first in field actually getting rich. One agent in one day cleared $86. So can you. Catalogue free. ALPINE SAFE CO., No. 363—371, CLARK STREET, CINCINNATI, O.

$5 to $15 per day at home, selling Lightning Plater and plating jewelry, watches, tableware, &c. Plates the finest of jewelry good as new, on all kinds of metal with gold, silver or nickel. No experience. No capital. Every house has goods needing plating. H. K. DELNO & CO., Columbus, O.

FOR RENT.

All Advertisements under this heading 1c. a word a time. No charge less than 25c.

SMALL UPPER TENEMENT—On Arnold street, first house west of Atlantic. Inquire of S. D. PEIRCE, 72 and 74 William St. au5-6t

PLEASANT TENEMENT—In a good situation, in perfect order and ready to occupy at once. Rent reasonable. A. E. LUCAS, Shoeist, 163 Union st. jy30-tf

FURNISHED ROOM.—120 Middle st. Enquire in shoe shop on premises. jy29-tf

THREE PLEASANT ROOMS—180 Middle street; ring left hand bell. jy29-tf

HOUSE IN FAIRHAVEN — Pleasantly and conveniently situated. For particulars address box 80 *Standard* office. jy26-tf

LOWER TENEMENT — Corner Locust and Chestnut streets; 2 fire rooms, 3 bed rooms on floor; modern improvements. Apply at 39 Locust street. jy16-tf

THE CORNER STORE—In Parker's Block; also the east half of third story with power if desired. Inquire of GEO. R. PHILLIPS, Agent, 23 Middle street. jy6-tf

FOR SALE OR TO RENT—Two nice Organs, inquire 146 Purchase street, from 6 to 9 P. M. jy1-tf

ROOM 9 RICKETSON BLOCK—Second floor. Apply to F. B. GREENE, 38 North Water street. je23-tf

HALL—Over Turkish Bath establishment, newly fitted, suitable for lodge or club use. Inquire of A. G. ALLEY, JR., corner Union and Sixth streets. je13-tf

FINE FRONT ROOMS—80 Purchase st.; best location in the city for doctors and club room. Apply at CHEAP JOHN'S. je9-tf

COTTAGE HOUSE—10 rooms; modern improvements; 25 Chestnut street. je6-tf

TWO ROOMS—Suitable for nice offices, up one flight; also furnished rooms. Apply 188 Purchase st., Webster Block. my31-tf

SEVERAL GOOD TENEMENTS — Centrally located. Apply at 51 Fifth street. my24-tf

TWO SMALL STORES—No. 317 and 319 Acushnet avenue, very near Union street. Apply to DR. RICKETSON. my7-tf

STORE—No 12 Cheapside, formerly occupied by Pope & Wood. Apply to WM. F. CASWELL, office Crapo, Clifford & Clifford. my7-tf

HOUSE—No. 13 Pleasant street; suitable for dressmaker, milliner or dentist. Apply to F. B. GREENE, 38 North Water street. d26-tf

ROOM—In second story, over Gifford & Co's, clothiers, Union st.; 3 north windows; suitable for artists; size 16x21 ft. Apply to GIFFORD & CO. n10-tf

STALLS TO LET—At the stage stable, 191 North Second street. je8-tf

State Normal School,
BRIDGEWATER, MASS.
Entrance examination on WEDNESDAY, Sept. 7. For both sexes. For circulars address ALBERT G. BOYDEN, Principal.
jy30-S3t&w3t

Victor Bicycles

Are the best that experience, brains, skill and capital can produce.

N. E. FORD,
236 Purchase St.
AGENT FOR VICTOR AND CREDENDA BICYCLES.

39c.
Men's, Boys' and Youths' TENNIS SHOES!
Leather Trimmed. Cheap at 50c.
BUCHELL, 75 William St

LOST.

All Advertisements under this heading 1c. a word a time. No charge less than 25c.

TEN DOLLAR BILL — Between West Campbell and Allen streets, Thursday. Finder will be rewarded by leaving at 33 Allen street. au5-2t

BUNCH OF KEYS—Finder will be rewarded by returning same to 189 Purchase street. au5-tf

IF THE PERSON—Who found my pocketbook, will mail the pilot's license therein, to me at the *Standard* office, he may keep everything else. JAMES R. THOMPSON. au5-tf

POCKETBOOK—In centre of city Tuesday. Finder will be suitably rewarded by returning to *Standard* office. au4-3t

FOR SALE.

All Advertisements under this heading 1c. a word a time. No charge less than 25c.

NEW MILCH COW—In South Dartmouth; six years old, giving fourteen quarts of milk. Price $30. au6-6t C. W. POTTER.

CATBOAT LAURA — 13—6—1.5. Address F. H. MURKLAND, 55 Walnut street; telephone 235-6. au5-6t

GOOD HAY—100 tons first quality. Inquire at Union Street Railway office. au2-tf

SECOND-HAND SET TINNER'S TOOLS. In good condition. J. W. HATCH, 250 Purchase street. au1-6t

TWO SETS OF WHEELS—And Concord axles, suitable for lumber wagon, at the stage office North Second street.
jy20-tf A. RICHARDS.

ONE CUT UNDER SURREY—Lined with green cloth; pole and shafts; nearly new, being run only one season. Inquire at GEO. L. BROWNELL'S Carriage Factory, City. je14-tf

You can save money, and still get good work, by buying new Carriages and Wagons of GEO. F. COLE, No. 41 Spring Street. Fine Stock. Late Styles. Low Prices. Work guaranteed as represented. New Harnesses and stable goods. Second-hand vehicles for sale.

Second-Hand Bicycles.
FULL ASSORTMENT of all makes. HOYLAND SMITH, 146 Pleasant street. my23-tf

FURNITURE.

IF you want to buy anything in the furniture line, you can save money by buying of us, as we calculate to sell everything out at some price and close up the business by July 1st. We have some very nice Parlor Suites, Chamber Sets, Ranges, Mirrors, Wardrobes, Cheffoniers, Mattresses, Springs, odd Bedsteads, Chairs, Sofas, Crockery, Carpets, Rugs, Dining and Centre Tables, Ice Chests, Hall Stands, Sideboards, Pillows, Oil Stoves. We also have some valuable Antique furniture consisting of 1 Old Cherry Desk, 1 tall Grandfather's Clock, 1 solid Mahogany Dining Table, 1 set old English Blue Dishes, 130 pieces, in fine condition. Lot odd dishes, very old, Mahogany Stands, Bureaus, Mirrors, Hand Irons, &c., &c. Come quick if you want a bargain.
H. F. HATCH.
Photographer, opposite City Clock.

NATURAL HISTORY CAMP FOR BOYS. LAKE QUINSIGAMOND, WORCESTER, MASS.
First Term begins July 6th; second Term Aug. 3d; but campers can join at any time. Athletic Sports, Military Drill, Hunting, Fishing, Swimming, Boating, etc. A first class good time at moderate expense. For Prospectus, address W. H. RAYMENTON, Worcester, Mass. jy9-TTS1mo

FURNITURE AND PIANOS MOVED.
General Jobbing.
Goods moved in a careful manner.
Charges Moderate
Orders can be left at 61 Hill st., stable rear of 84½ Walden st., or with driver of team. F. H. SLOCUM, 2 Pease court. W&S

Notice.

ALL persons are hereby forbidden to harbor or trust my wife, CLARA ENOS, on my account, as I shall pay no bills of her contracting after this date. JOHN ENOS.
August 4, 1892. au4-3t

HARDY HITCH, JR.,
Awning, Carpet and Shade Upholsterer,
195 UNION STREET.
Telephone - - - - 153-12

POSTERS AND HAND BILLS
Printed at short notice at the
STANDARD PRINTING ROOMS.

Straw Hats!
SEE THE NEW
WIDE BRIM SAILOR
$1.00, $1.25, $1.50, $2.00.
Nobby Straws for Ladies' Wear,
Fine line Gents' Cheviot Shirts,
Yacht Shirts, Sweaters, etc.
BICYCLE AND YACHT CAPS.
Largest stock in the city. New Bedford Yacht Club Caps!
NECKWEAR.
For Summer and outing wear we show as usual the largest line in the city. Our 50c. line cannot be beat.
LADIES' BLOUSES.
Madras and French Flannel made by Brokaw, finely made and will fit.
HAMMOCKS.
Every kind, all prices. Ropes, Stretchers, Hooks.
H. H. TILLSON,
(Cummings' Block,)
43 Purchase St.

H. C. HATHAWAY'S
Sale and Exchange Stables
—AND—
REPOSITORY,
Cor. of Acushnet Ave. and Elm St.
We make a specialty of fine goods, and have on hand at all times as fine an assortment of
Horses and Carriages
as can be found in the State. A visit at the Stable, Repository and Factory will convince you of the merit of our goods.
5pmy10-tf

J. O. DOUGLASS' Sale and Exchange Stables, Mechanics' Lane, New Bedford, Mass. I keep constantly on hand and for sale or exchange a good stock of driving, family, business, and team horses. Horses bought and sold on commission. Fresh arrivals every Monday and Thursday. All horses warranted as represented.

The Evening Standard.

ESTABLISHED FEBRUARY, 1850.

NEW BEDFORD, MONDAY, AUGUST 8, 1892.

TWO CENTS.

HASKELL & TRIPP.

Unless you consider it fun, there's no excuse for making pillow cases in the face of such a price as we now offer them ready made. Is it fun to run up and hem pillow cases?

The following are 12½c. each and in most cases are less than the cloth costs:

A manufacturer of sheets, having left on his hands some remnants of bleached sheetings, has made them up for us into pillow cases, that we will now give you an opportunity to buy for 12½c. each.

Among them are the following well-known brands of cottons, and as they are much heavier grades than usually put into pillow cases you'll hardly be able to wear one out in years:

"Wamsutta."
"New Bedford."
"Pequot."
"Atlantic."
"Pepperell."
"Utica."
"Lockwood."

Dress Goods.

Cut-price sale of fine, high-grade, pure-wool suitings, reduced from 87c., 75c. and 62c. One long counter full of choice colors. *Pick for 50c. a yard.* Not for a long time, if ever, have such choice and seasonable dress fabrics been sold for half a dollar per yard.

Storm serges to suit everybody.

Every good sort, both navy and black, 50c., 75c. and $1 a yard, in narrow twills, chevron stripes, broad diagonal wale, etc. We will guarantee best values in New England on storm serges.

Three special numbers in black all-wool Henriettas:

At 85 cents. At 95 cents. At 1 dollar. } 45 inches wide, blue or jet black.

These Henriettas cannot be matched at our prices, go where you will.

More bamboo bargains are ready in the basement.

By contracting for a large quantity we are able to reduce the price on three-legged bamboo tables at 25c. apiece.

Brass mounted bamboo corner baskets with three shelves, 50c. each.

Mosquitoes kept at bay.

You may be protected from these pests at night by an expenditure of $2.22 for one of our white gauze canopies, with extra full skirt, mounted on the patent umbrella frame.

HASKELL & TRIPP.

Department Stores,

Purchase and William Streets.

WEATHER INDICATIONS.

SHOWERS ON THE COAST.

WASHINGTON, Aug. 8.—For the 24 hours from 8 a. m. to-day: For Massachusetts, Rhode Island and Connecticut, fair, probably preceded to-day by showers on the coast; warmer; southwesterly winds.

CLOUDINESS AND RAIN.

BOSTON, Aug. 8.—Local forecast for New England until Wednesday: Fair, followed by increasing cloudiness Tuesday and probably rain during the day or night; cooler Tuesday night; southwest winds becoming variable, probably shifting to easterly.

IN A WHOLESALE BREEZE.

New York Yachts on the Way from Vineyard Haven to Marblehead.

VINEYARD HAVEN, Aug. 8.—The yachts of the New York club started on their way to Marblehead this morning with a light southerly wind. After the yachts crossed the line the wind began freshening and at 7 30 a wholesale breeze blew. The racing yachts commenced getting under way long before sunrise, and shortly after Commodore Gerry and steam yacht Ituna anchored off East Chop, whence the start was made. The yachts had a strong, fair tide, which caused them to move rapidly through the water. The light air sloop yacht Wasp joined the fleet last night, having completed repairs at Newport.

The new schooner Lasca sailed for New York yesterday.

Gen. Butler accompanied the racers in his yacht America.

The 40-footer Manolia sailed westward this morning, as did several others.

But few spectators witnessed the start, probably owing to the early hour.

The order of the start was as follows:

	H.	M.	S.
Gloriana,	5	35	41
Wasp,	5	35	42
Azalea,	5	36	01
Quickstep,	5	37	27
Mariquita,	5	37	31
Harpoon,	5	38	09
Peerless,	5	42	11
Iroquois,	5	46	42
Merlin,	5	46	43
Clara,	5	47	25
Wayward,	5	47	47
Phantom,	5	47	57
Katrina,	5	48	05
Constellation,	5.	48	39
Atlantic,	5	49	52
Dantless,	5	50	23
Œnone,	5	51	41
Alcæa,	5	52	43
Ramona,	5	53	37
Miranda,	5	53	52
Mayflower,	5	54	25
Marguerite,	5	54	52
Alert,	5	55	00
Fortuna,	5	55	00

The Sayonara started to cross the line but returned.

CHATHAM, Aug. 8—10 30 a. m.—The New York yacht squadron is passing north with increasing southwest wind. They are having a fine race, carrying balloon jibs and spinnakers. If the breeze holds, they will reach Marblehead before sunset.

STABBED TO DEATH BY ITALIANS.

Party of Railroaders Assaulted on the Lehigh Valley Road Near Pittston.

WILKESBARRE, Pa., Aug. 8.—While a number of young men, said to be railroaders, were walking down the Lehigh Valley road near Pittston last evening they met a party of Italians with whom they began a quarrel. A few moments later the Italians drew knives and slashed right and left. Harry Beillette was stabbed in the head and soon dropped dead. Robert Williams was stabbed in the back and died soon afterward. John Jones escaped with several cuts about the body. His injuries are deemed serious. No arrests have yet been made.

FIRE IN NEW YORK.

Upper Stories of Two Greenwich Street Buildings Gutted.

NEW YORK, Aug. 8.—Fire broke out at 8 30 this morning on the third floor of the five story building 282 Greenwich street. The building is on the northwest corner of Warren and Greenwich streets, running from 278 to 282, and is occupied by Tarrant & Co., importers and jobbers of drugs and druggists' sundries. The fire spread rapidly and spread from 282 to 280. The three upper floors of each building were completely gutted by fire, and cellars were flooded with water. The total loss will reach $130,000, which is fully covered by insurance.

BOILER EXPLOSION IN HAVERHILL.

Fireman Dennis Brennan Had a Miraculous Escape from Death.

HAVERHILL, Aug. 8.—Just before 7 o'clock this morning a 10-horse power boiler in the engine room at the Curriers coal wharf, off Merrimac street, exploded. Fragments of the boiler were thrown in the air, and came crashing through and demolishing the roof of an adjacent shed and wrecking a coal wagon. Dennis Brennan, the fireman, was covered with ashes and mud, but escaped with a few cuts on his face. A lack of water in the boiler probably caused the explosion.

Big Fire in Baltimore.

BALTIMORE, Aug. 8.—Fire in the factory of Chatterton & Co. this morning spread very rapidly and soon gained great headway. At 8 30 the Merchants Building, Nohe Brass Works, Gree & Co's shops, R. Oppenheimer's solder factory and Chesterton Hall were all ablaze. The damage will reach $200,000.

Small Pox Scare Subsiding.

WINNEPEG, Man., Aug. 8.—The governor of North Dakota has withdrawn his proclamation placing quarantine on the Canadian Pacific, owing to the outbreak of small pox. Trains will resume running as usual today. No additional cases are reported and those who are afflicted will recover.

The Deacon Adultery Case.

PARIS, Aug. 8.—The case of Edward Parker Deacon against his wife, whom he accuses of adultery with M. Abielle, has been postponed until October. The public prosecutor has refused to intervene in the case, saying that Mr. Deacon had better lay the affair before the court himself.

$40,000 Fire in a Nebraska Town.

ALLIANCE, Neb., Aug. 8.—The post office, the Alliance *Times*, the Norton block and five other business buildings were burned yesterday. Loss $40,000; fully insured.

Notorious Robber's Fate.

JOPLIN, Mo., Aug. 8.—Geo. Hudson, the notorious robber and murderer of Grandby, was shot and killed last night in his saloon while resisting arrest.

Bowed to the Pope's Wishes.

PARIS, Aug. 8.—Don Carlos has abandoned his opposition to the republic in deference to the Pope's policy.

Duquesne Steel Works Start Up.

PITTSBURGH, Aug. 8.—The Duquesne steel works started up this morning with nearly all of the old employes at work.

Ocean Steamers.

Arrived—At Boston, Lancastrian, Liverpool.

Passed Brow Head—Cephalonia, Boston, for Liverpool.

STILL SEARCHING.

Police Resume Their Task in Borden Mansion.

Masonry About Fireplaces To-Day Taken Down.

Mayor and Medical Examiner's Visit to the Cemetery.

Prof. Wood Making All Haste to Finish His Analysis.

Police Annoyed by Employment of Private Detectives.

[Special Dispatch.]

FALL RIVER, Aug. 8.—The Borden tragedy is still as deep a mystery as ever.

There are no new developments of any importance.

The report that the police have ordered the arrest of any one leaving the building is denied by City Marshal Hilliard.

The occupants of the Borden homestead will be permitted to go in and out of the house and about the city at their pleasure, but orders have been given to cause the arrest of any of the family if they attempt to leave the city limits.

Police Search Continued.

The police to-day continued their search of the premises, overhauling every nook and corner which had not been visited on Saturday. With them was C. H. Bryant, a mason of this city, who removed portions of the fireplaces, but found they bore no traces of having been tampered with or used as a place of concealment.

Blood or Rust?

The axe with the blood or rust marks upon it has been sent to Boston to-day where microscopic examination will reveal the nature of the stains.

Dislike Private Detectives.

Mayor Coughlin and the police authorities discountenance the employment of private detectives by the family, and say that if the real purpose of these men is to ferret out the crime they should work in unison with the local police. They say there may be two views taken of the employment of these men.

An Inquest a Certainty.

There is no doubt that there will be an inquest, and it is hoped it will reveal something of importance. The authorities to-day are looking for the arrival of District Attorney Knowlton.

It is believed that Medical Examiner Dolan will spring a surprise. He has been working harder than any man interested in the case, and he has had the least to say. It is believed that he will introduce some very important evidence at the inquest.

It is probable that he will have the bloody clothes worn by the murdered people, which were buried in the yard of the Borden house, in the rear of the barn, dug up and produced in court. These clothes were buried at the request of Mr. Morse, who still remains at the house.

It is believed that when witnesses are placed upon their oath something stronger in the way of direct evidence will be brought out. The inquest will, of course, be private.

No Skirt With Blood on It.

It was reported in a Boston paper that a spot of blood, as it was believed to be, was found on a skirt in a closet of Miss Lizzie Borden's room by the police in their search of the house yesterday. This is emphatically denied and it has been stated by the police that nothing which furnished any evidence was taken from the house.

A VISIT TO THE TOMB.

Gray Hair Found on the Hatchet Matches Mrs. Borden's Locks.

[Special Dispatch.]

FALL RIVER, Aug. 8.—Perhaps the first link in the chain that must sooner or later surround the person who killed Mr. and Mrs. Borden was found yesterday afternoon, when Medical Examiner Dolan and Assistant Marshal Fleet visited the cemetery and entered the vault where the remains of the murdered couple were placed. They were there to determine, if possible, whether or not the gray hair found on the claw head of the hatchet, which the police took from the Borden house on Thursday, matched the locks of Mrs. Borden. The two men went into the vault, and both came out wearing a self-satisfied look. The hair had matched perfectly. The men got into the doctor's buggy and drove off, leaving Superintendent Morrill somewhat mystified. It may prove that the hatchet found in the cellar was the one that was used to kill Mrs. Borden, and, with this knowledge in hand, the cross-questioning of the inmates of the household before and at the inquest will probably be conducted on a plane more prolific of results than those already held.

What the Medical Examiner Says.

Dr. Dolan and Mayor Coughlin visited the cemetery yesterday and entered the vault containing the bodies of the murdered couple. Dr. Dolan said to a *Standard* reporter this forenoon that the visit was simply to see that the bodies were unmolested and to give orders that they might be properly cared for.

Prof. Wood's Analysis.

Mayor Coughlin to-day received a letter from Prof. Wood saying that he was not in Europe, as has been reported, and that he had received the packages containing the stomachs of the victims and the milk supposed to have been poisoned, and expects to find his analysis at the earliest possible moment, possibly by today or to-morrow.

THE POLICE ACTIVE.

Young Ladies Even More Gracious Than on Saturday.

[By Associated Press.]

FALL RIVER, Aug. 8.—The police are very active in their movements to-day.

Shortly after 10 o'clock Capt. Desmond, accompanied by Sergeant Edson and Officers Connors and Medley went to the house and instituted one more search.

Charles H. Bryant broke places in the old-fashioned chimney and looked in vain for any instrument that would lead to a detection of the criminal.

The officers pulled over everything in the cellar, but without obtaining anything.

The guard is still kept on the house, but the officers are under instructions not to molest the inmates nor interfere with their freedom in going about their duty.

If any attempts are made to leave the city, however, arrests will follow.

The servant girl spent yesterday and last evening with some relatives on Division street, returning to the Borden house this morning.

Mr. Morse walked over to Dr. Bowen's when the search was going on, and returned, saying that a hack was to call for him.

While the search was going on the young ladies were even more gracious to the officers than they were Saturday after the funeral.

VIEW OF THE BORDEN HOUSE AND BARN.

COTTAGE CITY NEWS.

Fireman Injured—A Woman Wields the Political Cudgel.

[Special Dispatch.]

COTTAGE CITY, Aug. 8.—John Altey, substitute fireman at the Pawnee, was badly burned yesterday morning. Dr. Bryson was summoned. Altey shoveled a lot of wet cinders into the firebox of the boiler, and a gust of flame and steam struck him full in the face, causing painful and disfiguring wounds. He will not be able to attend to his duties for some time.

The complimentary ball in the Casino Saturday night was a success from a social standpoint. The affair was not marked by large attendance, there being less than 75 couples in the march. The order contained a list of 13 dances. Sullivan's orchestra furnished acceptable music.

The street cars were severely taxed yesterday to convey the crowds to the New York Wharf.

Sloops Spray of Fairhaven and Pointer of New Bedford are in these waters. Steam yacht Indolent took out several parties yesterday.

Ladies of Grace Episcopal church will hold a fair on Wednesday next, the proceeds of which will be devoted to the rectory fund.

E. H. La Tour of Buffalo, N. Y., is at the Seaview for the season.

F. A. Marshall of Marlboro Saturday launched his new sloop. The yacht had been hauled out at Morris' landing for a general overhauling. When the craft slid down the beach Mr. Marshall grasped the bowsprit to launch with her, but he miscalculated and there were two distinct launchings.

Capt. and Mrs. W. H. Phillips are entertaining Miss Agnes Shaw of North Middleboro.

Congressman Morse spent Sunday here.

Twenty-three yachting representatives connected with Boston and New York dailies were here over Sunday.

The selectmen state that Chief Twombly is giving excellent satisfaction, reports to the contrary notwithstanding.

Mrs. Leavitt, who spoke before the W. C. T. U. Friday, was hired to tell her experiences in travelling about continental Europe as a missionary, but she digressed and took up the prohibition cudgel against the two great parties. It was a hot speech and engendered some bad feeling against the speaker and the cause she is supposed to represent.

Texas Cotton Ruined.

SALEDO, Tex., Aug. 8.—Reports of the boll worm still continue to come in. One farmer offers a hundred acres of cotton for $1 an acre. Many plantations are completely ruined.

STAFFORDS POINT, Tex., Aug. 8.—Planters in this and Fulcher sections are complaining of their cotton crops being destroyed by the boll worms.

HOME MATTERS.

WANT MORE PAY.—It is said that a petition to the City Government for an increase in pay of 25 cents per day is being quietly circulated among the policemen and being generally signed by members of the force. It is said that it will be presented at the first meeting in September.

THE HATHAWAY MILLS.—The work of excavating is nearly completed at the new Hathaway mill, and about 50 feet of the foundation in the southwest corner has been laid. About 75 men are at work, and work is being pushed rapidly. Brick-laying will commence this week.

AN EXCURSION.—The members of the New Bedford Literary associates to the number of about 150 made an excursion to Horse Neck beach yesterday in six of J. H. Pierce's barges.

READ THE TURKISH BATH advertisement.

A BIG EDITION.

The day's sales of the STANDARD Saturday were among the largest on record in Southern Massachusetts, amounting to between 9000 and 10,000 copies, before the demands of the reading public were met. The STANDARD's dispatches from Fall River cover the very latest developments in the Borden tragedy up to the hour of going to press with the different editions, and the STANDARD's readers realize that they have in their home paper more reliable and later news than can be obtained in the Boston or other dailies.

THE TITAN OF CHASMS—*A Mile Deep, 13 Miles Wide, 217 Miles Long, and Painted Like a Flower.*—The Grand Canon of the Colorado River, in Arizona, is now for the first time easily accessible to tourists. A regular stage line has been established from Flagstaff, Arizona, on the Atlantic & Pacific Railroad, making the trip from Flagstaff to the most imposing part of the canon in less than 12 hours. The stage fare for the round trip is only $20.00, and meals and comfortable lodgings are provided throughout the trip at a reasonable price. The view of the Grand Canon afforded at the terminus of the stage route is the most stupendous panorama known in nature. There is also a trail at this point leading down the canon wall, more than 6000 feet vertically, to the river below. The descent of the trail is a grander experience than climbing the Alps, for in the bottom of this terrific and sublime chasm are hundreds of mountains greater than any of the Alpine range.

A book describing the trip to the Grand Canon, illustrated by many full-page engravings from special photographs, and furnishing all needful information, may be obtained free upon application to Jno. J. Byrne, 723 Monadnock Block, Chicago, Ill.

MOVING.—The work of moving Mrs. Bridget Enos' old house from South Water street below Rivet to John street south of Butler, was commenced this morning, and in consequence horse car travel is impeded, transfer being made around the obstruction. Several electric light poles had to be temporarily moved and a few wires cut.

Workmen have commenced excavation on the open lot on the west side of South Water street above Delano, to lay a foundation for the building now on the southwest corner of Delano and South Water streets. As soon as the foundation is completed this building will be moved and work commenced on William A. Pease's new brick building on the the corner.

A REMARKABLE CASE.—A few days since a party applied to the Massachusetts Benefit Association, of which J. C. Brock is the general agent, for a policy of insurance, and he was one of 18 children, all of whom are living and all twins, there being three pairs of girls and six pairs of boys. That this one was a man of excellent judgment is evidenced by his placing his insurance with the Massachusetts Benefit, now the largest insurance company in the State, carrying as it does ninety-five million dollars insurance on twenty-eight thousand lives, and doing it at a cost of forty per cent. less than old line companies.

TO CHICAGO AND THE WEST.—The route affording the most advantages is via the Boston & Albany, New York Central and Michigan Central roads, "The Niagara Falls Route," and the route of the "North Shore Limited," which leaves Boston at 2 p. m. daily, and arrives at Chicago at 4 30 p. m. next day. Wagner buffet sleeping cars, dining car, serving all meals en route, smoking and library car comprises the equipment of this train, and ensures to passengers all the comforts and luxuries obtainable in railway travel. Three other express trains daily. For Summer tourist folder, describing western health and pleasure resorts, address W. H. Underwood, E. P. A. Mich. Cent. R. R., Buffalo, N. Y.

UNFORTUNATE.—The handsome pair of steel roans which draw Truck No. 3 are developing unfortunate traits. One of them has become almost stone blind, while the other surprised the driver this morning by making a first-class balk while exercising. The pair was thereupon hitched to the truck and for a time put through a vigorous exercising around several squares, drawing the heavy apparatus with them till the balk departed.

TENNIS AND BOATING SHOES.—Full leather, trimmed in lace piece, all sizes for men, boys and youths, worth 50 cents, our price 27 cents. These will not last long, as they are in great demand, and the price is away down. Union Shoe store.

GOT FRIGHTENED.—The liquor saloons in the city closed their doors just after 9 o'clock Saturday night. This was a mystery to a good many people, but it has leaked out that word was passed around that raids might be expected, and this caused the movement.

YOU CAN BUY THIS WEEK any straw hat we have in stock at the extreme low price of 25 cents—any hat whether $2 or any grade—they are all the same price this week, *only 25 cents each.* Gifford & Co.

THE FIFTH MASSACHUSETTS BATTERY will have its 22d annual reunion in this city tomorrow, when there will be a clam dinner at Fort Phœnix at 2 30 p. m., and supper at the Man sion House at 8. See special notice.

STREET RAILWAY.—By reference to a special notice in another column it will be seen that in pleasant weather Purchase street cars will run through to River View park every 10 minutes from 2 to 6 p. m.

C. HOWLAND ENGINE CO'S HALL will be open to the public for inspection on Wednesday evening. Those persons who assisted at the fair last Winter are especially requested to be present.

TUG NELLIE went to Woods Holl to-day to take the place of steamer City of Portsmouth, which goes on the marine railway at Vineyard Haven to repair her condenser, which is leaking.

A POCKETBOOK containing about $12 and the name Marianna Devoll, Dartmouth, was found on Saturday by Officer Wixon, who will restore it to the owner.

PROTESTANT MILITARY REGIMENT.—Officers and comrades will meet at R. A. Peirce Post Hall to-morrow evening to form companies and prepare for drill.

EXCURSION.—Over 200 persons participated in the excursion of the Robert Emmet guards to Crescent Park to-day.

IMPROVEMENT.—The Union Street Railway Company is repaving between its tracks on Purchase street at the North End.

SAND CATCHER.—A sand catcher has been put in at the northwest corner of Walnut and Fourth streets.

ONLY FIFTY CENTS.—Ladies' hair shampoo, No. 5 South Sixth street.

REGISTRARS OF VOTERS will begin the last of this month.

A TURKISH BATH will remove those pimples, No. 5 South Sixth street.

BLACK CLOTH Overgaiters 50c. Devoll's.

BLOOD diseases cured by Hood's Sarsaparilla.

WE ARE DRAWING ATTENTION

TO A LINE OF

JAPANESE CARPETS!

WE HAVE A NUMBER OF VERY HANDSOME JAPANESE CARPETS

Size 9 ft. x 12 ft.

STYLES AND COLORINGS ARE FINE!

PRICES LOW!

C. F. WING,

WING BUILDING.

WHITING & CO.

MONDAY MORNING,

—AT—

9 O'CLOCK,

We Commence a

Big Sale

—OF—

ORIENTAL

—AND—

JAPANESE RUGS!

In all Sizes,

—FOR—

PARLOR, HALL AND DINING ROOM,

AT A

GREAT DISCOUNT,

—FOR—

Three Days Only.

Our Japs are fine and prices Low. Do not wait, but come at once.

WHITING & CO.

OUTING SHIRTS!

OUTING SHIRTS!

You can never have too many

OUTING SHIRTS!

Our low prices will help you out. Quality exceptional.

Good Shirts for $1 and $1.25, laundered collars and cuffs.

Another lot of the popular blue Madras, all sizes, $1.50.

Better come at once, They're going fast.

J. & W. R. WING & CO.,

133 UNION STREET.

OUTING SHIRTS!

OUTING SHIRTS!

THE CRESCENT!

22 Purchase St.

Having removed our entire stock from the Old Stand at corner of County and High streets, we shall be pleased to see our old friends and patrons at our new quarters, 22 Purchase street, known as THE CRESCENT.

Damask Towels, knotted fringe borders in Pink, Red, Yellow, &c., only **15c.** A special bargain.

Remnants of Table Linen, good lengths, at low prices.

12 1-2c. Ginghams and Outings 10c.

Good Prints, light and dark, 5c.

SPECIAL BARGAINS

—IN—

RIBBONS.

In order to close we offer our stock of Ribbons, all styles, at greatly reduced prices, among them a good line of Moire Ribbons in Summer shades.

Chiffon Handkerchiefs, all colors, 25c.

Ruchings in fancy colors at reduced prices.

French Perfumes. 29c. an ounce.

THE CRESCENT!

22 Purchase St.

NOTHING BUT THEORIES

Search of the Borden House Avails Nothing.

Pinkerton Detective Employed by the Family.

Significant Orders of the Police Authorities Last Night.

Bottom Knocked Out of the Mysterious Stranger Story.

Murdered Couple's Pastor Preaches Upon the Tragedy.

Sunday has passed since Andrew J. Borden was found in his home on Second street, Fall River, with his face cut to ribbons, while the body of his butchered wife was stretched on the floor above, and there is still the same awful mystery, the same torturing suspicions, the same theories, with nothing to confirm or dispel them. It was a day of rest, which left people free to reflect calmly on the double tragedy and which has removed them from the rumors and discussions, bred by the fever heat and excitement of the three days preceding—days which Fall River will never forget. A few additional particulars have been gathered by those whose business it is to gather them, a thread has been picked up here and there and stray points have been investigated, but that is all. At the Borden homestead, the scene of so much turmoil and horror, all was quiet. No crowds thronged the street which runs by the residence; not that the community has lost its interest, but the authorities have determined to keep the thoroughfare clear. There is as great a desire to get at every detail on the part of the public as there was last Thursday afternoon, and that desire will be manifested until the guilty wretch has been arrested, convicted and hanged, or until the lapse of time makes it plain that this is one of the puzzles to which there is no key.

At midnight on Saturday, when the city was apparently asleep, the patrol wagon rattled into court square with a drunken unfortunate for freight, and in an instant, from nobody knows where, hundreds of people sprang from the ground and collected on Bedford street. On Saturday afternoon, and the afternoon before, and the afternoon before that, men walked slowly with papers before their faces, absorbing the news, drivers of delivery wagons allowed their horses to pick their own way and went over "the latest, all about the murder," and on every corner and in almost every doorway were groups of three, four and half a dozen, explaining and arguing, and driving home their own private convictions with their foredgiers. This illustrates the natural curiosity and the abnormal nervous tension which have taken possession of the entire town. There is nobody so poor and insignificant, nobody so rich and blase, as to be indifferent to the fate of the aged couple who were borne to their last resting places Saturday noon.

Nothing but Theories.

Unfortunately, there is nothing yet to satisfy this curiosity or to relieve the nerves of the populace from the unnatural strain, and it is a strain that is beginning to tell. They want some fresh theory, which is reasonable, and which will take them in another direction, if only for 24 hours. But at each turn the double murder puts in an appearance, to perplex and bewilder. The difficulty that overturns every opinion which has been advanced to account for the wonderful escape of the assassin is that he had not completed his task when one victim ceased to breathe. He had two to slay and must make it necessary to search for a double motive or impulse, or whatever it may be, that inspires a man to take life, and also to give him more time to glide about the house and avoid detection. "He could have slain Mr. Borden or Mrs. Borden; how could he slay them both and vanish?" people repeat to themselves over and over again.

Why Should He Have Slain Them Both?

Did he kill the woman in order to do away with a witness of his slaughter of the man? The indications are that he did not. Nothing is strange under the sun, perhaps, and certainly nothing is new, but if Mrs. Borden had interrupted him in his bloody work, and he pursued her, as some maintain, why did he wait until she entered the spare bed room? Why not strike her down on the stairs? He had no minutes to throw away. He could not tell what moment Miss Lizzie would return from the barn, or the instant the servant would leave the third floor. However, it is argued that Mr. Borden would not have fled to the spare bed room, although this is only a supposition. It is claimed that no one would have been more natural for her to have attempted to escape by the front door, or to have taken refuge in one of the lower rooms. She was a heavy woman and her weight must have told against her on the stairs. All experience accordingly contradicts this idea of a surprise and a chase. If it is correct Mrs. Borden forgot to utter a sound, although her other faculties did not entirely desert her, and she chose a course from the sitting room which was sure to hand her over to the murderer before she had taken 10 steps. That weakens the motive introduced to explain her death and makes the other theory more tenable, namely, that she perished first, and that the man who felled her struck down her husband, because the latter was not sleeping as the murderer was leaving the house. In that event the scoundrel must have loitered about the spare room after he had accomplished his purpose. Otherwise he could have escaped before the husband came back from town. If the woman fell as Mr. Borden entered the sitting room, or while he was seated on the lounge, it might have been expected that he would have heard the fall.

And so, proceeding along this line, it becomes necessary to find somebody whose hatred of Mrs. Borden was deep enough to lead to her violent ending, and also to explain the recklessness which allowed her assailant

To Remain in the House After He Had Killed Her.

If both theories are abandoned; if Mrs. Borden were not slaughtered because dead people no tales, or if Mr. Borden were not destroyed for the same reason, it remains to unearth a motive which would have inspired the same person to kill them both, and to enter the house with that intention. Small wonder that the knot tightens rather than unravels as the case is studied.

There was no special excitement at police headquarters yesterday. Medical Examiner Dolan held a long interview with Marshal Hilliard in the latter's office, and Detective Hanscom of the Pinkerton agency who has been engaged by the family, had a talk with Andrew J. Jennings in the Mellen House. The medical examiner states that the only discovery of importance made during the thorough search of the Borden house Saturday afternoon was in the spare bed room, where Mrs. Borden's body was found. Out near the window drops of blood were found, which indicated that the murdered woman had moved after the first blow was delivered. It is thought that that blow was the glancing one which has been described. The supposition is that the axe fell on the right side of the head, taking off the flesh and hair, and that the woman turned and reeled to the space between the dressing case and bureau, where the mortal wound was delivered. After that, the blows fell thick and fast. It is believed that she was approached, Mrs. Borden stood looking out of the window in the sitting room, and her blood which stained it at this point, bears out that view. Dr. Dolan says that the more he reflects on the small quantity of blood that was spilled, the more at

a loss is he to account for it. To him it seems utterly inexplicable. Ordinarily, no matter how sharp the weapon used, the rooms would have been stained a crimson hue, but such a tragedy takes place in them. Even if no external blood made its appearance, and though the wounds were inflicted after death, the veins and brain would have discharged enough fluid and gray matter to have left their mark on the furniture. But with the exception of the stains near the window and the thick pool about the head of the unfortunate man, about the head of the unfortunate man, the scene was quiet, and was as though it had been freshly washed and swept. Every time the axe fell it cut deep, but there was no gush of blood from the frightful gashes. The same condition prevails in the sitting room below, where Mr. Borden was butchered, and there was nothing to raise the suspicion that the murderer had cleaned anything, except the dripping axe. Medical Examiner Dolan made

One Other Discovery.

Yesterday he learned that Prof. Wood of Cambridge, to whose address the stomachs of the murdered couple were sent, was in Europe, and some other expert must make the analysis of their contents. Singularly, nothing has been heard regarding the delivery of the grim package in question, and Dr. Dolan will probably go to Boston to-day and make inquiries concerning it. That letter which it is alleged Mrs. Borden received on the morning of the tragedy continues to excite interest, and on this head Dr. Dolan likewise had a little information to give. He says that both Miss Lizzie Borden and the servant told him that Mrs. Borden had received such a letter, and when he asked Miss Lizzie what had become of it, she told him she had been unable to find it.

She Feared That It Had Been Burned in the kitchen stove. Nobody in the household seems to be able to give anything more than a general idea of the contents of the letter or note. It was from a friend who was ill, but if Mrs. Borden made this much known, it is curious that she did not state who the friend was or that the person with whom she was conversing did not have the curiosity to inquire.

It is expected that Detective Hanscom of the Pinkerton Agency will have a long talk with Bridget Sullivan, the servant, before many hours, and with other members of the family as well. As nearly as can be ascertained, Hanscom was not employed by the Misses Borden, who were under the instructions of Marshal Hilliard, acting under the instructions of Mayor Coughlin, but by the Misses Borden, who were advised by their counsel, Andrew J. Jennings, Esq. The friends of the ladies felt that they ought to have somebody to represent them, and Mr. Jennings was called into the case on Saturday. Detective Hanscom ought to be able to elicit considerable information from the servant.

In company with Mr. Jennings, he called at the house yesterday afternoon and remained for two hours. If, as Miss Lizzie states, she did not see her mother after 9 o'clock on the morning of the murder, it is possible that Bridget Sullivan may know something of the latter's whereabouts. It is certain that, so far as the public is concerned, the time that the occupants had not been satisfactorily accounted for. If Mrs. Borden disappeared at 9 o'clock to put shams on the pillows, and did not appear again, it is to be presumed that her stepdaughter remained down stairs while she was occupied on the second floor. At some time before Mr. Borden was killed, Bridget Sullivan went up stairs, and she may have seen her mistress on the floor. If the latter were in the habit of attending to household duties on the second floor for two hours at a time, her absence would not have attracted attention, but if she visited all parts of the house like women do, it is a little singular that nobody missed her. At all events no harm could come from ascertaining just what Miss Lizzie and the servant did with their time from the hour of rising until the murders were discovered. It might help to show the opportunities which the wretch had for entering the house and concealing himself if that was what he did. Now as to the suspicions which

Have Been Directed Against Members of the Family.

Perhaps the most intimate friend the family has had this to say yesterday noon:

When I arrived at the house on the day of the murder it was 12 o'clock or thereabouts. I found Miss Lizzie somewhat prostrated, though she did not appear to be tired out by the excitement. I went away and later on the street I heard those stories about the Portuguese. I returned to the house and told the occupants what I had heard. Instantly Miss Lizzie exclaimed:

"That isn't true at all. My father had no Portuguese in his employ. The only man of that description is a Swede in whom we have perfect confidence."

Again when it was said that a man had called and demanded money, Miss Lizzie said:

"My father owed no money. He always paid his debts."

This disproves the idea that an attempt was made to throw suspicion on some other party and divert attention from the house. When I first met Miss Lizzie and Miss Emma together, the former was the more disturbed of the two. I have known her for years. Up to date there is no evidence that points to anybody or in any direction; at least, none that has been made public. On the contrary there is everything against the theories. A good character ought to count for something. The search has been made with every means at command. They found a slight spot on Miss Lizzie's dress, I believe, which made its first appearance in Edinburgh.

An attempt was made on Saturday night to fasten the theory that Eli Bence, the drug clerk, had mistaken Miss Lizzie Borden for the woman who purchases oleomargarine and fuse lotion for State Inspector McCaffrey. This is absurd. Mr. Bence may be mistaken, of course, but State Inspector McCaffrey's partner looks about as much like Miss Borden as she does like John L. Sullivan. However, there is no great importance attached to the poison story, for when it comes to a test it was Miss Borden's word against the statement of Mr. Bence.

Pinkerton Detective's Idea.

Detective Hanscom talked at length in the Mellen House yesterday afternoon, and his ideas do not correspond with the government theory. He reviewed the case at length, but admitted that he had been at work on it too short a time to form a definite opinion. He had questioned Miss Lizzie, but found her too exhausted physically for a searching examination. The reaction had come and he did not want to weary her. He was favorably impressed with her appearance, and stated that she, like her sister, Miss Emma, appeared to be sincere and truthful. He questioned particularly the time that she spent in the barn, and she was positive that she was there 20 minutes or possibly half an hour. The murder

Looked Like the Work of a Lunatic, while Miss Lizzie appeared to be a level-headed, self-possessed woman. After a half hour in the barn half an hour, a man might have entered the house, committed both murders, and escaped by way of the basement through the door leading to the back yard. That door was found open after the murders, though it was usually closed. Detective Hanscom admitted that he had a varied experience, and usually began by breaking for the cause of death and the motive. Here the cause was apparent, but he had as yet found no motive.

A Great Explosion !

In these days of gunpowder, dynamite, giant powder, and the like, tremendous explosions are no rarity, but the greatest explosion of modern times, without doubt, that of the "old-school" idea that Consumption is incurable. Thousands of lives have been sacrificed to this mistaken notion. Modern research has established the fact that Consumption is a scrofulous disease of the lungs; and that there is a remedy which will positively eradicate it from the system—Dr. Pierce's Golden Medical Discovery. Of course, there were in the olden times many who would have pronounced modern explosives impossible and witchcraft; but there are, fortunately, few to-day who do not acknowledge that the "Golden Medical Discovery" is the one sovereign remedy for all scrofulous diseases, and Consumption is one of them.

co---t if Mr. Borden had any enemy capable of the deed. The family and Mr. Jennings could recall but one person who had a serious difference with the murdered man, and that was not of a nature to arouse suspicion in the present instance. The detective did not question Miss Borden regarding the axe found in the cellar, but had learned from another source that a flock of pigeons belonging to the Bordens had been killed in June. That might account for the blood stains on one of the axes. This axe will be sent to Boston for examination.

It looked as if at midnight very much as if Detective Hanscom had interviewed the Misses Borden for the last time. The authorities are evidently up in arms and have issued orders that nobody, not even the detective in question, is to be admitted to the house. More than that, if anybody leaves the house,

He or She Will be Promptly Arrested.

These orders were issued last night, and the public are free to interpret their true purport for themselves. Their meaning is clear enough, and it is certainly very significant.

At last accounts Miss Lizzie Borden had given way under the great strain and excitement of the last four days, and Dr. Bowen had been summoned twice last evening to attend her.

Friends from South Dartmouth.

It was expected that morbid curiosity would fill Oak Grove Cemetery with crowds of pedestrians yesterday, but for some reason or other there were fewer visitors than usual. A friend of the Borden family called during the day, and two of John Morse's acquaintances from South Dartmouth, Messrs. Davis and Howe, paid him a visit.

Rev. W. Walker Jubb's Sermon.

Mr. and Mrs. Borden were members of the Central Congregational church of Fall River, and as has already been exposed, their daughter Lizzie, was also a member. The latter has been a teacher in the mission school connected with the parish, and has always been very active in the young people's societies and the work of the church. Yesterday the Central church worshippers met with the First church congregation in the Stone church on Main street. All of the pews were filled, many being in their seats some half hour before the service began. It was supposed that the Rev. W. Walker Jubb, who occupied the pulpit, would make some allusion to the awful experiences through which one family in his charge had been compelled to pass during the week, and the supposition was correct. Mr. Jubb read for the morning lesson a portion of Matthew, containing the significant words which imply that what is concealed shall be revealed. In his prayer, Mr. Jubb evoked the divine thanks for the blessings bestowed on many, and, pausing, referred to the murder of two innocent persons. He prayed fervently that right might prevail, and that in good time the terrible mystery might be cleared away; that the people of the city might do everything in their power to assist the authorities, and asked for divine guidance for the police, that they might prosecute unflinchingly and unceasingly the search for the murderer. Mr. Jubb prayed that their hands might be strengthened, that their movements might be characterized by discretion, and that wisdom and great power of discernment might be given to them in their work. "And while we call for examination," he continued, "for the triumph of justice, let our acts be tempered with mercy. Help us to refrain from giving voice to those insinuations and innuendoes which we have no right to utter. Save us from blasting a life, innocent and blameless; keep us from taking the sweetness from a future by our ill-advised words, and let us be charitable as we remember the poor, grief stricken family and minister unto them.

The clergyman added that those who were writing of the crime might be careful of the reputations of the living, which could so easily be undermined.

For his text Mr. Jubb took the first chapter of Ecclesiastes, ninth verse: "The thing that hath been is that which shall be; and that which is done is that which shall be done; and there is no new thing under the sun." The speaker considered the monotonies of life and capitated on the causes of indifference in persons who would be nothing if not geniuses, drawing lessons from successes in humble sphere. At the end of the sermon Mr. Jubb stepped to the side of the pulpit and said slowly and impressively: "I cannot close my sermon this morning without speaking of the horrible crime that has startled our beloved city this week, ruthlessly taking from our church household two respected and esteemed members. I cannot close without referring to my pain and surprise at the atrocity of the outrage. A more brutal, cunning, daring and fiendish murder I never heard of in all my life. What must have been the person who could have been guilty of such a revolting crime? One to commit such a murder must have been without heart, without soul, a fiend incarnate, the very vilest of degraded and depraved humanity, or he must have been a maniac. The circumstances, execution and all the surroundings cover it with mystery profound. Explanations and evidence as to both perpetrator and motive are shrouded in a mystery that is almost inexplicable. That such a crime could have been committed during the busy hours of the day, right in the heart of a populous city, is passing comprehension. As we ponder, we exclaim in our perplexity, Why was the deed done? What could have induced anybody to engage in such a butchery? Where is the motive? When men resort to crime it is for plunder, for gain, from enmity, in sudden anger or for revenge. Strangely, nothing of this nature enters into this case, and again I ask—what was the motive? I believe, I am only voicing your feelings fully when I say that I hope the criminal will be speedily brought to justice. This city cannot afford to have in its midst such an influence as the murderer of Andrew J. Borden and his wife. Why, a man who could conceive and execute such a murder as that would not hesitate to burn the city.

"I trust that the police may do their duty and lose no opportunity which might lead to the capture of the criminal. I would impress upon them that they should not say too much and thus unconsciously assist in defeating the ends of justice. I also trust that the press (and I say this because I recognize its influence and power), I trust that it will use discretion in disseminating its theories and conclusions, and thus pass may be guided by consideration and charity. I would wish the papers to remember that by casting a groundless or undeserved insinuation they may blacken and blast a life forever, like a tree smitten by a bolt of lightning; a life which has always commanded respect, whose acts and motives have always been pure and holy. Let us ourselves curb our tongues and preserve a blameless life from undeserved suspicions. I think I have the right to ask for the prayers of this church and of my own congregation. The murdered husband and wife were members of this church, and a daughter now stands in the same relation to each one of you, as you, as church members, do to each other. God help and comfort her. Poor, stricken girl, may they both be comforted, and may they both obtain how fully God is their refuge."

Mysterious Stranger Story Exploded.

The mysterious stranger story told in the Standard Saturday was given credence by the police for a time, but has now been exploded. The man in question who was seen in Westport about that he was a horse dealer, but explained that at 10 o'clock Thursday morning he was in New Bedford, where he sold a horse, and another man was discovered

FINANCIAL.

SANFORD & KELLEY.

GARDNER T. SANFORD, CHARLES S. KELLEY, | Bankers,

Members Boston Stock Exchange,

47 North Water St., New Bedford.

STOCKS AND BONDS BOUGHT AND SOLD ON COMMISSION

At the New York and Boston Stock Boards.

CONSERVATIVE & PROFITABLE INVESTMENTS FOR TRUST FUNDS.

New Bedford Manufacturing Stocks have a first-class record as dividend payers, and we always have some on hand to offer.

Sole Agents for the sale in this city of the 6 per cent. Guaranteed Mortgages of the Lombard Investment Co.

Auction Sale of Stocks and Bonds

WEDNESDAYS AND SATURDAYS, at 10 45 A. M.

ORDERS SOLICITED.

Mass. Real Estate Co.

246 Washington St., Boston.

Dividends 7 Per Cent.

Invests in Central Real Estate in Growing Cities.

Authorized Capital	$2,000,000
Capital paid in	1,250,000
Surplus	100,000

ORGANIZED IN 1885.

Paid Dividends of 5 per cent. per annum for 1½ years. Paid Dividends of 7 per cent. per annum since July, 1890. Average Dividend since organization over 6 per cent. per annum. Surplus at close of last fiscal year, over $100,000.

Stock offered for sale at $108 per share until July 31.

Send to or call at the office for information MWF

T. E. BOWMAN & CO.,

Topeka, Kansas,

NEGOTIATORS OF

Conservative Mortgage Loans in Eastern Kansas.

$2,500,000 LOANED without loss to any investor, and have never yet had to foreclose a farm loan in these eastern counties. Write us for list of investments. s29

GEORGE LEVY, North End Pawn Broker.

Cash advanced on Real or Personal Property. All business private. au3-1m

SECOND EDITION.

HOME MATTERS.

RIDING SCHOOL.

Adelphi Rink to be Managed by a Stock Company.

People who are interested in horse back riding, and particularly those who supported a riding school at Adelphi Rink last Winter, are subscribing to stock for a corporation which is to be organized under the laws of the Commonwealth for the purpose of maintaining a public hall. The object is to secure Adelphi Rink, which is on leased land and continue it as a riding school. J. V. Bancroft is soliciting subscriptions and he has thus far secured over 40 shares at $100 a share. The capital stock is $5000, and among the subscribers are the most prominent people in town.

REAL ESTATE SALES.—H. A. Leonard has sold for Sanford Alger to Narcizo De Mello 15.45 rods of land on corner of Summit and Edward streets.

T. F. Healey has sold for John Thompson a farm in Rochester, comprising 75 acres land, house, barn, outbuildings, etc., to H. G. Fowler of this city for $1 and other valuable considerations.

John Whitehead has sold for George A. Briggs a lot of land containing about 20 rods, corner of River avenue and Kendrick avenue, Fairhaven, to John D. Whitehead of Providence.

John Whitehead has sold for a syndicate six house lots on Hathaway avenue, containing in all nearly 100 rods, to James Sharples, Edward Chippindale and William H. Whalley.

John Whitehead has sold for George Ramsbottom two lots of land, on Coggeshall and Mitchell streets, containing 35 rods, more or less, to Edward and Margaret Barlow.

Sanford T. Alger has sold to Marcizo C. De Mello 15.45 rods land east side of Summit street.

Standish Bourne sold at auction this afternoon house and 10 rods of land on the northeast corner of High and Pleasant streets, to Walter A. Jenney. It brought $4300 and the taxes of this year.

BUILDING.—John Hastings has petitioned for leave to erect a boiler house on the northeast corner of Prospect and Grinnell streets. It is to be 20 by 28 feet, 10 feet posts.

On the west side of North Second street, between the Germania House and Custom House, a brick building three stories in height and 27 feet wide is to be erected, extending from the line of the street until it connects with the one-story L at the rear of the north end of the Globe Building, a distance of 62 feet. The one-story L is to be raised to the height of two stories. The contractor in charge of the work is Stephen B. Wilber. The building, which will have a flat roof, is the property of George S. and Frederick A. Homer, Charles E. Hawes and William B. Macomber.

HORSES.—Charles P. Cottle of Acushnet goes to Vermont the last of the week to buy horses. Anyone wising to give their order for a pair, a horse to match another, a family or gentleman's driving horse, can do so. Satisfaction guaranteed. Call or address Chas. P. Cottle, Acushnet.

EXCURSION TO COTTAGE CITY.—The employes of the Pairpoint Manufacturing Co. will give their second annual excursion to Cottage City on Saturday by Steamer Island Home. Hill's Band will accompany the excursionists. See advertisement.

SERVING NOTICES.—The police are to-day serving notices on all owners of unlicensed dogs to attend to the matter of licensing them at once, under penalty of a wholesale slaughter of the canines.

WHALEBONE.—In this market sales have been recently made of 2950 pounds Northwest whalebone, in parcels, at a price not reported.

DEATHS.

In this city, 6th inst., Deborah, daughter of the late Joseph and Deborah Howland.

Funeral at Frien's meeting house, Spring street, thir day, (Tuesday,) 8th, at 12 o'clock. Relatives and friends are invited to attend.

MARINE INTELLIGENCE.

Sld from Bass River 7th, sch Menuncatuck, Ellis, New York.

Ar at Georgetown, DC, 6th, sch Independent, Case, Bangor.

Ar at Richmond 5th, sch J R Teel, Johnson, Washington.

Good Things Never Die.

Among the good things that help to make enjoyable our puddings, creams and pastry, which have been used by millions of housekeepers for years, is Dr. Price's Delicious Flavoring Extracts of Lemon, Orange, Vanilla, etc.

These flavors differ from all other extracts in their manner of preparation, quality of fruit used, their freedom from all injurious substances, their superior strength and delicate and agreeable taste. **One trial proves their worth.**

UNION CAMP-MEETING.

CADMAN'S NECK, Westport, Aug. 8.

This beautiful grove on the borders of the Westport river is looking its very best and sweetest after the refreshing showers Saturday. The 15th yearly meeting opens favorably. People are gathering and occupying their tents.

The religious exercises opened encouragingly under the leadership of the new president, Rev. T. F. Norris of Head of Westport. A devout and earnest spirit prevailed, and all that were present were led to expect great things from God.

The evening meeting was in charge of Pastor Donald Brown of Tiverton Corners, who will have charge of the singing during the convention.

On Sunday the Rev. G. B. Cutter of Stone church will preach at 2 p. m.

Other interesting and able speakers will be present during the week.

The committee extend a cordial invitation to the people of Westport and adjoining towns.

The weather on Sunday was all that could be wished for, and large crowds of people were present in the grove. Some doubtless were merely pleasure seekers, but many came to attend the religious services. The exercises began at 9 a. m., with a prayer meeting led by Miss Hannah Gifford. Rev. T. F. Norris, president, preached at 10 30 a. m. from Matt. i, 21: "Thou shalt call his name Jesus, for he shall save his people from their sins."

At 2 p. m. an attentive audience assembled to hear Rev. G. B. Cutter of Stone Church, Adamsville. He preached from Luke vi, 38: "Give and it shall be given unto you; good measure, pressed down, and shaken together, and running over shall men give into your bosom." A short altar service followed, at which Pastor Cutter made most affecting reference to his former life as a sailor and his conversion.

Rev. Edward Wood preached at 7 30 p. m. from I Cor. xiii, 13, on the subject of "Faith." The After Service revealed the presence of the Holy Spirit; and the believers lifted up their hearts in praise for the blessings of his grace.

One of the most enthusiastic meetings of the day was the union service of the Y. P. S. C. E. at 4 p. m., led by Mrs. Brophy, vice-president of the Pacific Union Society. Dr. Nottage, president, led the singing, which was bright and spirited.

PASTORAL RESIGNATION.—Elder William A. Burch yesterday tendered his resignation as pastor of the Foster Street Advent church, to take effect Aug. 23d. Elder Burch states that he has no plans for the future, but has felt that his work in this city has been completed.

FINANCIAL.

A Downward Movement—Atchison and B. & Q. Fall Off Considerably—General Electric Strong—Rally in Sugar at Noon—Money Markets Steady—Rates at Clearing 3 1-2 and 4 Per Cent.—Prime on the Crops—Poor Corn Reports Received To-day—Boston & Albany Statement—Flint & Pere Marquette Earnings—Other Railroad Reports—In General.

MONDAY, Aug. 8.

A reaction has been in order to-day with B. Q. and Atchison, the softest stocks. The general situation remains favorable however, the poorer crop reports causing to-day's setback. Cammack is understood to be active again, presumably on the bear side, while Keene is still operating with the bulls. S. V. White is unquestionably back of the upward move in General Electric, which touched 116 in this forenoon's trading. The money market remains dull and easy. Probably there will be no important change in rates in any of the large centres during the present month.

The local money market is unchanged.

In Boston the money market is slightly easier, though rates are not materially lower. Clearing house loans were made at 3½ and 4 per cent. New York funds sold at 15 cents discount.

In New York time loans are in light request. Call money easy.

Sterling a trifle easier in tone.

Bonds firm.

Wall street gossip this morning said: "The progress of the corn crop is now the most important influence and latest reports predict a yield under the average even with favorable weather from now on. Western brokers appear to be bearish on grangers. London about ¼ per cent. below our closing."

Atchison 39⅜ to 38⅞, Burlington & Quincy 102⅛ to 101¼, Omaha 53¼ to 53, Rock Island 80¾ to 80¼, St. Paul 83¼ to 82⅞, were the leading active stocks in New York this forenoon, course being downward. General Electric remained strong 114¾ to 116. Sugar rallied at noon to 106⅝, Western Union steady 97⅛ to 97¼. At noon the market was weak. In the early afternoon prices again fell off somewhat, but toward 1 o'clock the rally in Sugar checked the decline. General Electric continued firm.

The Boston market opened active and firm this morning. Later this strength disappeared and weakness set in. Atchison fell off to 38⅞ from 39⅜, C. B. & Q. to 101½ from 102¼, and Union Pacific declined to 38. Atchison bonds were soft; the 4s at 83, the incomes at 59⅞. Specialties were neglected except for a further rise in General Electric to 116. Tamarack copper held 158. In the early afternoon the market was quiet and weak. Sales to noon, bonds $297,000 and 20,600 shares of stock.

General Electric is reported to be earning at the rate of 16 per cent. per annum.

Silver reached the lowest price on record on Saturday, when bullion certificates sold on the stock exchange at 84. The closing price was 84¼. The commercial price of bar silver was 84⅜ cents an ounce, which made the value of the silver in a dollar a little over 65 cents. June 15 the commercial price was 89⅝ cents. The price of silver in America is based on the price in London, which is considered the silver market of the world. Primarily India sets the price, because the value of silver depends on the value of the rupee. There is $106,087,435 in silver in the treasury, which has been purchased under the Sherman act.

Deacon S. V. White has cleared off all his obligations except a little over $200,000. In six months he has paid a round $400,000. When he resumed operations after his disastrous attempt to corner corn his creditors all "signed off," and had only his word for it that he would pay them, but everybody knew that his word was as good as a bond. It will not be long before Mr. White is free from debt. His accomplishment is without parallel in Wall street. Mr. White has made his greatest gains in Western Union, Manhattan, Sugar and Cordage. He is now engineering a movement in General Electric, which promises to yield handsome profits. There is great rejoicing in the street over the successful outcome of Mr. White's affairs.

Poor's Manual says: "A controlling interest in Lackawanna was acquired in February by parties in the interest of Reading." President Sloan and Vice-President Holden are out of city, but young Mr. Holden said unofficially: "That is not a fact."

Foreign houses are buying Erie and there is a demand for calls on the stock covering three or four months' time. The talk points toward a combination by which Erie will participate more directly in the Vanderbilt, Drexel-Morgan, Reading coal alliance. It has been known for a long time that the Vanderbilts held an interest in the Erie. They are understood to have bought stock in considerable quantity around 23 about a year ago, and it is claimed that this stock has not been sold.

The Atchison's first train under the $12 round trip rate to Denver ran in four sections and carried 1443 passengers, which means $17.316 gross, said to be 50 per cent. profit.

Emery & Tucker say:

The more we study the situation, the more satisfied we become that the market is in for a rise, and it appears to be not very far off. Last week witnessed a good degree of activity throughout the whole list, in which the Vanderbilt stocks have been very prominent and the so-called "industrials" have also been active and higher. The fact that the market went off so little during the latter part of the week, in spite of determined efforts of the professional element to force a reaction, demonstrates pretty well that affairs are not all in their hands—as they have been for so long—and that there are plenty of good buyers for stocks now on the concessions.

Salt shipments of the Fint & Pere Marquette for the fourth week of July, 1892, yielded but $228.36, against $4041.60 in 1891, a decrease of $3813.24.

A 10 30 special says it is thought in the room that Cammack is bearing the market on the corn crop, while Keene is still on the bull side.

Atchison total earnings for the fourth week of July increased $53,376. For the month total increase was $137,802.

Wabash June gross increase was $65,377; net increase $44,768. For twelve months gross increase was $1,350,700; net increase $83,396.

A special meeting of the stockholders of the Butte & Boston Mining Company is called for Sept. 20th at Boston to consider the proposition to issue $2,500,000 7 per cent. mortgage bonds. Two-thirds of the shares must rate in favor of the proposition, under Montana laws, and three-quarters must be represented either in person or by proxy. The transfer books will be closed Aug. 20, reopening Sept. 21.

An exchange says:

The Bandora has seven levels all in ore, and the richness of the property is only just coming into view. Three new levels have been started on the contact, and ore of rich quality again encountered. The company is holding back the ore for a better price for silver.

Prime, the crop expert, in his weekly review of crop conditions, says:

The weather has been favorable, but corn is still from two weeks to a month late and its condition does not improve. In Illinois corn is late, the best fields are 14 days late. Many of them are tasselling out two or three feet high and great banner counties are "not in it" this year. Reports from Iowa show that the corn has not made up any of its lost time and that the crop is fully one month behind an average year. The harvest of oats is under full headway. The crop is streaked and uneven. What has been said with regard to the corn and oat crops in Illinois will apply with equal force to the situation in Ohio and Illinois. Corn reports from Kansas this week are irregular and uneven. The recent rains were light, only cooling the air and of little benefit to corn, and the crop is again in a critical condition.

Boston & Albany earnings are reported to the Massachusetts Railroad Commissioners for the June quarter, and make a highly gratifying exhibit. Comparisons follow:

QUARTER ENDED JUNE 30.

	1892.	1891.		
Gross,	$2,499,039	$2,312,448	Inc.	$186,591
Expenses,	1,492,439	1,642,595	Dec.	150,156
Net,	$1,006,600	$669,853	Inc.	336,747
Charges,	100,959	188,494	Dec.	87,535
Surplus,	905,641	481,359	Inc.	424,282

FISCAL YEAR.

Gross,	$9,821,069	$9,177,913	Inc.	643,156
Expenses,	6,803,288	6,225,242	Inc.	578,046
Net,	$3,017,781	$2,952,671	Inc.	$65,110
Charges,	1,196,961	1,330,776	Dec.	133,915
Surplus,	$1,820,820	$1,621,895	Inc.	199,025

Railroad earnings are reported as follows:

AGGREGATE EARNINGS.

Thirty-four Roads.

	1892.	1891.		
July 4th week,	$6,639,378	$6,627,160	Inc.	$12,217

Seventy-five Roads.

	1892.	1891.		
July 3d week,	$7,461,498	$7,194,839	Inc.	$266,659

Latest Flint & Pere Marquette earnings compare as follows:

Fourth week July.	1892.	1891.	Dec.
Freight.	$35,558	$42,850	$7,292
Passenger,	25,666	25,886	220
Total,	$61,224	$68,736	$7,512
Month July,	$215,102	$224,813	$9,711
Since Jan. 1,	$1,670,973	$1,666,422	*$4,549
Mileage,	625	625	

*Increase.

STOCK AND BOND MARKETS.

Bids at the close of First Board.

NEW YORK, Aug. 8.

GOVERNMENT BONDS.

U.S. 2s, registered	100
" new 4s, registered	116
" new 4s, coupons	116
" currency 6s, 1895, (Pacifics)	107

RAILROADS

Atchison	39
Clev., Cin., Chicago & St. Louis	66¾
Chicago & Eastern Illinois	—
Chicago & Eastern Illinois pre	—
Chicago, Burlington & Quincy	101¼
Delaware & Hudson	—
Delaware & Lackawanna	—
Erie	28⅞
Illinois Central	—
Lake Shore & Michigan Southern	117⅛
Louisville & Nashville	70⅞
Michigan Central	—
Missouri Pacific	59¼
New Jersey Central	—
New York & New England	36⅝
Northern Pacific	21⅞
Northern Pacific pref	57⅞
Chicago & Northwestern	117⅜
New York Central & Hudson River	—
North American	—
Oregon Navigation	—
Oregon Improvement	—
Oregon Short Line	24
Philadelphia & Reading	60
Pullman Palace Car Co	—
Chicago, Rock Island & Pacific	80¼
Chicago, Milwaukee & St. Paul	82⅞
Chicago, Milwaukee & St. Paul pref	—
Richmond Terminal	9
St. Paul & Omaha	55
St. Paul & Omaha pref	—
Union Pacific	38
Wabash, St. Louis & Pacific	10⅜
Wabash, St. Louis & Pacific pref	25⅜

MISCELLANEOUS

Ontario Silver	41
Pacific Mail Steamship Co	—
Sugar, common	105½
Sugar, pref	101⅛
Western Union Telegraph	97⅛
Silver Certificates	84½
Gen'l Electric	—

BOSTON, Aug. 8.

BONDS

Atchison 4s	83
Atchison Incomes	59⅞
American Bell Telephone 7s	114
Chicago, Burlington & Northern 5s	—
Chicago & West Michigan 5s	—
Mexican Central 4s	68½
Illinois Steel Co. 5s	*100

RAILROADS.

Atchison, Topeka & Santa Fe	39
Boston & Albany	204¾
Boston & Lowell	181
Boston & Maine	181
Boston & Providence	*183
Chicago, Burlington & Quincy	102⅛
Chicago & West Michigan	—
Cleveland & Canton	—
Cleveland & Canton pref	19½
Flint & Pere Marquette	—
Flint & Pere Marquette pref	*80
Mexican Central	15⅝
New York & New England	37
New York & New England pref	87
Old Colony	183
Oregon Short Line	*24½
Pullman Palace Car	—
Union Pacific	38
Wisconsin Central	17½
West End	—
West End pref	—

MINING.

Butte & Boston Mining Co	—
Calumet & Hecla Mining Co	280
Centennial	—
Franklin Mining Co	12⅜
Kearsarge	11
Montana	36⅜
Osceola Mining Co	*36⅜
Tamarack	158

MISCELLANEOUS.

American Bell Telephone	204
Erie Telephone	*47
Mexican Telephone	1.05
New England Telephone	56
Newport Land	—
Boston Land Co	5
West End Land Co	18⅜
San Diego Land Co	—
Topeka Land & Development Co	*1
Lamson Store Service	18⅜
Illinois Steel Co	—
Am. Sugar Refineries, com	105⅝
Am. Sugar Refineries, pref	101
Thomson-Houston	—

*Asked.

CALIFORNIA MINING STOCKS.

SAN FRANCISCO, Aug 6.

The following are the official closing prices of mining stocks to-day:

Alta	—	Mexican	1 30
Best & Belcher	1 40	Mt. Diablo	1 10
Chollar	—	Ophir	2 15
Con. Cal. & Va.	3 25	Potosi	—
Crown Point	—	Savage	—
Eureka Con.	1 50	Sierra Nevada	1 15
Gould & Curry	—	Union Con.	—
Hale & Norcross	1 00	Utah	—

NEW YORK PRODUCE MARKET.

NEW YORK, Aug. 8.

Flour sales 45,000 packages; quiet and easy.
Wheat sales 1,855,000 bushels; 1½ cents up.
Corn sales 1,175,000 bushels; active, 1¾ to 2 cents up on bad crop reports.
Oats sales 5000 bushels; dull; 1 cent up.
Beef dull and steady.
Pork quiet and firm.
Lard dull.
Butter quiet and firm.
Cheese active and very firm.
Sugar (raw) quiet and firm.
Petroleum dull.
Turpentine dull and weak.
Molasses dull.
Rice quiet and firm.
Freights quiet.
Rosin dull.
Tallow quiet and firm.

PROVISIONS AND GRAIN.

CHICAGO, Aug. 8.

Opening.

	Lard.	Wheat.	Pork.	Corn.	Sh't Ribs.
May	—	—	—	—	—
June	—	—	—	—	—
July	—	—	—	—	—
Aug.	—	—	—	—	—
Sept.	—	78½	13.50	52¾	—
Oct.	—	—	—	—	—
Dec.	—	81⅛	—	—	—
Jan.	—	—	13.90	—	—
12 o'clock.					
May	—	—	—	—	—
June	—	—	—	—	—
July	—	—	—	—	—
Aug.	—	—	—	—	—
Sept.	—	79¼	13.32½	53¼	—
Oct.	—	—	—	—	—
Dec.	—	81⅞	—	—	—
Jan.	—	—	14.00	—	—

WEATHER INDICATIONS.

WARMER.

NEW YORK, Aug. 8.—At 8 30 a. m. the weather was clear, wind west, temperature 73. The *Herald* says: In the Middle States and New England on Tuesday warmer, fair weather is likely to prevail, and on Wednesday similar conditions.

THIRTY MILLIONS IN GOLD.

Precious Cargo on Its Way from San Francisco to Washington.

OMAHA, Neb., Aug. 8.—Just before 6 last night a train of a Pullman car and six coaches besides the engine pulled into the Union depot from the West and pulled out again over the bridge. It was an ordinary appearing train except from the fact that not a sign of life was visible and the windows were tightly closed, the platforms were deserted and apparently the cars were closed and empty. Probably not one of the half-hundred men who noticed the appearance of the train suspected that behind the curtained windows was gold enough to make 30 men millionnaires, and that the barred doors shut in a company of United States soldiers armed to the teeth and on duty night and day to defend the precious cargo. But such was the case. The train was a Union Pacific special from the mint at San Francisco. It was "wild" over the road and everything else had to get out of the way. The gold was in coin and $30,000,000 worth of it was piled on the floors of the cars. A squad of 40 men of the regular army were on duty as guard. At Council Bluffs the train remained 40 minutes for lunch. As soon as the train stopped a guard appeared on the platform of each car, where no one was allowed to approach them. Even the conductor and train men were compelled to keep their positions until the train was ready to start. The captain of the troops left the train as soon as it came to a standstill and went up town. He did not return until time to start and would not talk concerning the treasure that was under his care.

British Torpedo Boat Sunk.

LONDON, Aug. 8.—Two torpedo boats attached to the British blue squadron, while manoeuvering near Portsmouth today, came into collision. One of them was so badly damaged that she sank a few minutes after the accident. The other rescued everybody on the sinking vessel.

Admiral Gherhardi at Bar Harbor.

BAR HARBOR, Me., Aug. 8.—United State flagships Philadelphia, with Admiral Gherhardi on board, and cruisers Concord and Vesuvius, arrived at daylight this morning.

The Ocean Steamers.

Arrived—At Bremerhaven, (7th,) Darmstadt, New York.

IT IS A BURNING SHAME for people to set on fire the membranes of throat and stomach, and poison the blood by indulging in fire water, the true name of most of the liquors. Try the G. O. Taylor Old Bourbon or Pure Rye Whiskeys and be agreeably surprised at their smoothness, mellowness and tonic qualities. They are the purest and best whiskeys in the world. C. H. GRAVES & SONS, Sole Proprietors, Boston, Mass., sell them only in sealed bottles.

Are You In It?

If not, why not? Why don't you always keep on hand a bottle of Dr. Hale's Household Cough Cure to allay the first irritation caused by a sudden cold? This is the finest remedy in the world for every kind of cough. You feel the good effect of the first dose, and by thorough using your cough is soon cured, 25 and 50c. bottles at Wright Drug Co.'s, 49 Purchase street.

DAINTY SHOES FOR DAINTY FEET.

It will pay you handsomely to buy a pair of Misses' or Children's shoes of our own make.

We do not have to rely on what the manufacturer says, for we make the shoes ourselves and guarantee them better for the price than you can get anywhere else, *just* because we make them ourselves.

If your boy or girl has never worn Our Own make shoes, you just try the next pair.

Store and Factory connected.

SCHULER BROS., - - - - - 76 and 78 Purchase St.

THE BORDEN BUTCHERY.

Wonder Continues to Grow as the Mystery Deepens.

[By Associated Press.]

FALL RIVER, Aug. 8.—One of the searching party who came from the Borden house alone states that Miss Emma Borden looked a person in the eye during conversation, but Miss Lizzie invariably turned her head when questioned closely.

Marshal Hilliard and Medical Examiner Dolan had a short consultation this morning, and decided to send the suspicious axe to Boston for examination as to the character of the spots on the handle.

The Medical Examiner also had a short talk with Judge Blaisdell regarding an inquest, but he made no formal report, and the date was not fixed.

Public interest in the crime is not lagging any. It is still the sole conversation, and the wonder continues to grow as the mystery deepens.

Medical Examiner Dolan said at noon that the stomachs of the victims were now being analyzed in Boston, but he was not putting much hope in any developments that may be made.

FIGHTING IN SPANISH HONDURAS.

Government Troops Drive the Insurgents into the Forests.

NEW ORLEANS, Aug. 8.—The steamer City of Dallas arrived yesterday with the latest news of the revolution in Spanish Honduras. It appears that the government has again the upper hand, that Leiva and his Cabinet will remain in control. He has chartered the steamship Spazsetti, a New Orleans vessel, and converted it into a war ship, loading her with troops. It departed from Puerto Cortez recently to attack Ceiba. It is reported that the pitched battle was fought at Ceiba between the resident revolutionists and the government troops. The latter were victorious. The vessel is said to have contributed materially to the result. The bombardment dislodged the rebels and they fled into the forests. The government is reported to have been reinforced by the addition of a band of insurgents who deserted Nuilla and marched into Puerto Cortez. The revolutionists intended to secretly march into Cawayuaga Aug. 4 and capture the city. In the event of success they would bombard and destroy all the public buildings and residences in addition to emptying the coffers of the treasury, and burn all papers they could lay hands on. Spies were in communication with Leiva daily and the plan was well laid, and would have overthrown the government had it not been frustrated. The news was dispatched to Leiva and others and a large force is now guarding the capital.

A VICTORY FOR CARNEGIE.

Stampede of the Men at Duquesne to Secure Their Old Places.

HOMESTEAD, Aug. 8.—The strikers at Duquesne went to work this morning and the Carnegie Steel Company has scored one victory. On Saturday night Superintendent Morrison posted a notice that all men who had applied for their old jobs would report at the mill at 7 o'clock this morning, as the mills would resume at that hour. Long before the time set, however, workers with dinner pails stole up unfrequented streets and along the railroad tracks, entered the mill unobserved by their fellow strikers. As 7 o'clock approached the number of men who had entered the mill yard through this means were 400. About 60 men who were leaders in the sympathy strike movement, gathered on the road near the gate and watched in moody silence the men going to work. Hearing the whistle blow for 7 o'clock an Irishman exclaimed in a loud voice, "The jig is up; we had better hustle for our places." This was the signal for a panic, and the entire crowd ran toward the gate. A freight train was backing in but the men did not wait for it but scrambled over and under in their frantic haste to get inside the mill before the whistle stopped blowing. It was a complete stampede. The effect of this break cannot but prove harmful to the men at Homestead, although the leaders will not give it up. At Duquesne steel billets can be manufactured and sent to Homestead to be rolled by the non-union, so that the firm will be in better condition to fill contracts and prosecute this fight here.

CAMPAIGN AGAINST MEXICO.

Refugees in Texas Trying to Work Up a Revolutionary Movement.

RIO GRANDE, Tex., Aug. 8.—The Mexican refugees on this side are again on the warpath, and are endeavoring to work up a revolutionary movement against Mexico. Gen. Lorenzo Garcia, who commands the northern military zone of Mexico, received word that a band of revolutionists had opened a recruiting station at the Jabaline ranch below this city. General Garcia at once telegraphed this to Gen. Frank Wheaton, commanding the military of Texas, and he ordered Second Lieutenant George L. Langhorne, of the third cavalry to proceed with a detachment of troops immediately to the scene. The troops left here two days ago and nothing has since been heard from them. It looks as though the Mexican revolutionists along the Rio Grande have entered upon another campaign against Mexico.

Held for Bigamy.

LYNN, Aug. 8.—John Francis Vaduai, alias Philip Weyys of Boston, under arrest for bigamy, was before the police court and ordered in $500 for Saturday. From the consulate at Buda Pesth, Hungary, the police have received a full history of Vaduai, showing his marriages to Emma Berger of Buda Pesth and to an actress, Nagy, the daughter of a hackney coach driver. Vaduai was bailed by Hyman Cohen of Boston.

The Tennis Championship.

LONDON, Aug. 8.—The *Pall Mall Gazette* says that O. S. Campbell, the American tennis player, has written to the United States to defend his title of champion. Commenting on his performances in this country the paper says there is no doubt that he possesses considerable ability at lawn tennis, but he did not justify the prediction of the press. He did not defeat a single English player of the first rank.

A Safe Investment

Is one which is guaranteed to bring you satisfactory results, or in case of failure a return of purchase price. On this safe plan you can buy from our advertised Druggist a bottle of Dr. King's New Discovery for Consumption. It is guaranteed to bring relief in every case, when used for any affection of Throat, Lungs or Chest, such as Consumption, Inflammation of Lungs, Bronchitis, Asthma, Whooping Cough, Croup, etc., etc. It is pleasant and agreeable to taste, perfectly safe, and can always be depended upon. Trial bottles free at H. A. Blackmer's Drug Store.

Lincoln's Foster Mother.

Abraham Lincoln was seven or eight years old when his father, Thomas Lincoln, removed from Kentucky to Indiana, where in a year or two his wife died. The year following her death Mr. Lincoln returned to Elizabethtown to search out, if possible, a former neighbor and friend, Mrs. Sally Johnston, whom, upon inquiry, he found still a widow, and to whom he at once made a proposal of marriage.

On entering Mrs. Johnston's humble dwelling Mr. Lincoln asked if she remembered him.

"Yes," replied she, "I remember you very well, Tommy Lincoln. What has brought you back to old Kentucky?"

"Well," said he, in answer, "my wife Nancy is dead."

"Why, you don't say so!"

"Yes," said Mr. Lincoln, "she died more than a year ago, and I have come back to Kentucky to look for another wife. Do you like me, Mrs. Johnston?"

"Yes," replied Mrs. Johnston, "I like you, Tommy Lincoln,"

"Do you like me well enough to marry me?"

"Yes," she answered, "I like you, Tommy Lincoln, and I like you well enough to marry you, but I can't marry you now."

"Why not?" said he.

"Because I am in debt, and I could never think of burdening the man I marry with debt; it would not be right."

"What are those debts?" said he.

She told him of the sums, "which," said she, "I have all down here in my account book."

On looking it over, he saw that her debts ranged from fifty cents to a dollar and a quarter, and amounted in the gross to something less than twelve dollars—not a very startling sum even in those days of small things.

He succeeded in putting the little book into his coat pocket without attracting her attention and went out, looked up the various parties and paid off all the little sums according to the memorandum and returned in the afternoon with the acknowledgments of payments in full. On his returning the account book to her, she exclaimed, "Why, Tommy Lincoln, have you gone and paid off all my debts?"

"Yes," he said, "and will you marry me now?"

"Yes," said she, and they were married the next morning at 9 o'clock.—Mr. Haycraft in Christian Union.

LOST.

Advertisements under this heading 1c. a word a time. No charge less than 25c.

LARGE AMETHYST RING—Sunday, between County street and French Cemetery on Robeson and Franklin streets. Suitable reward will be paid by leaving at *Standard* office. au8-3t

GOLD WATCH AND CHAIN—Sunday forenoon, near corner County and Linden streets. Finder please leave at house of French Priest, on Ashland street and be rewarded. au8-1t

WANTS.

All Advertisements under this heading 1c. a word a time. No charge less than 25c.

GIRL—For general housework. Apply at 195 Elm street. au8-3t

SITUATION—By a young lady with reference to work by the day or week. Inquire 4 Warwick street. au8-3t

MEN TO MAKE CASKET SHELLS—Apply at once at WILSON & KNAPP MFG. CO'S, 135 South Water street. au8-3t

AMUSEMENTS.

SECOND ANNUAL EXCURSION

—OF—

EMPLOYES PAIRPOINT MFG. CO.

—TO—

COTTAGE CITY, Saturday, August 13,

ON STEAMER ISLAND HOME.

Music by Hill's Full Band.

FARE, Round Trip.......75 CENTS.

Boat leaves wharf at 8 A. M. Return leaves Oak Bluffs at 5 P. M. au8-5t

AUCTION SALES.

By J. O. DOUGLASS.

REGULAR AUCTION SALE,

Thursday, Aug. 11th, 1892, at 10 15 A. M.

OF 25 horses, consisting of family, driving, express, team, farm, grocery and general business horses, in matched pairs and single. In this lot are some very good horses, two matched pairs one of them a coach or family team, closely matched, stand 16 hands high, good actors and fine drivers. Also several acclimated horses, been used in and about the city. Also harnesses, foot mats, &c. One two-horse tip-cart in good repair.

REAL ESTATE.

FRANCIS W. TAPPAN,

Agent for Purchase, Sale, and Lease of REAL ESTATE.

Office, 15 North Water St., New Bedford. d&w

FRANK C. SMITH,

Real Estate Broker, Auctioneer and Appraiser,

Office - - 47 William Street,

(Opposite New Post Office.)

M. E. SMITH,

REAL ESTATE AGENT,

619 Purchase Street. Telephone 16-11.

H. A. LEONARD,

REAL ESTATE AGENT.......126 UNION STREET.

Houses and lots for sale in all parts of the city. No charges unless sale effected.

FOR SALE—In South Dartmouth, near the water, a 2½ story house with large piazza, barn, and 83 rods of land. One of the most desirable places in the village for a Summer residence. Inquire of BENJ. QUERIPEL or DANIEL H. HOWLAND, South Dartmouth. ap7-tf

AUCTION SALES.

By STANDISH BOURNE,

(Successor to Geo. A. Bourne & Son,)

Auctioneer, Commission Merchant, Real Estate Dealer and Appraiser.

Cash advanced on goods consigned for auction. Ready buyer for personal property of every description.

Office and Salesrooms 47, 49 and 51 North Second Street, near the Post Office.

Centrally Located Real Estate by Auction.

On WEDNESDAY, Aug. 10th, at 12¾ o'clock, on the premises, will be sold in the following order:

1st—The two tenement house in first-rate order, situated on the south side of Elm street, about 110 feet east of Purchase street, known as the Hallett Gifford homestead. This lot has a frontage of 27 feet by a depth of about 51¾ feet.

2d—The house in rear of No. 1, formerly the homestead of Dr. Andrew Mackie, with lot containing about 8.90 rods. This has an entrance from Elm street of about 8¾ feet.

3d—The right is reserved to offer the two parcels, and if a larger bid can be obtained than the sum of the separate sales, this will be the binding sale.

For plan or further particulars call at the office of the auctioneer.

To Let in Our Storage Warerooms.

We constantly have on hand first-class rooms for the storage of household goods, to be rented by the month or year.

Good dry storage room for stoves.

By JOHN B. BAYLIES,

121 and 123 Union Street,

Commission Merchant, Appraiser, and Auctioneer for the sale of Real Estate and every description of Personal Property. Furniture Bought.

H. C. HATHAWAY,

Auctioneer, Real Estate Agent and Appraiser,

Corner Acushnet Ave. and Elm St.

One of the best auction marts in the State for the sale of horses and carriages. Keeps constantly on hand carriages of every description, carriages made to order and repairing in all its branches attended to under the superintendency of J. R. Forbes. Consignaments of every description solicited. Cash advanced on goods for auction. Personal property of every description bought at short notice for cash. Negotiable notes bought and sold.

Heirs' Sale of Real Estate.

On SATURDAY, Aug. 13, at 3 o'clock P. M., on the premises, will be sold wthout the least reserve, to wind up the estate, the house and lot of about 17 rods of land No. 75 Middle street. The house is in good condition and is situated in that part of the city where it will be sure always to rent well. Sale positive and without limit. Terms, 10 per cent. at sale. Balance on delivery of heirs' deed. au4

Mortgagee's Sale.

By virtue of a power of sale contained in a certain mortgage deed given by Abisha B. Bean to Alban C. Snow, dated June 30, 1888, and recorded with the Bristol County S. D. land records in book 128, at pages 348, 349 and 350, and for breach of the condition thereof, will be sold at public auction upon the premises on SATURDAY, the 3d day of September, 1892, at three o'clock in the afternoon, all and singular the premises convey by said deed, viz.: A certain lot of land with the buildings thereon, standing, situated in New Bedford, in said County of Bristol, bounded and described as follows: Beginning at the northeast corner thereof in the south line of Walnut street, at land now or formerly of Sarah Corey; thence westerly in said south line of Walnut street, twenty-nine (29) feet to land formerly of Edward Seabury; thence southerly in said Seabury's line to the north line of land now of William Rafferty seventy-six (76) feet; thence easterly in said Rafferty's line about twenty-nine (29) feet to said Rafferty's west line, and thence northerly in said Rafferty's line and in line of land of said Sarah Corey seventy-six (76) feet to the point of beginning; containing eight (8) rods, more or less. Being the same premises conveyed to Ann C. Brodhead by Nathan S. Ellis, by deed, dated October 30, 1858, and recorded in book 37, pages 340 and 341. Terms 10 per cent. at time of the sale, remainder on delivery of mortgagee's deed within ten days. Estate of Benjamin Almy, Assignee. au8-15-22-29 SOPHIA ALMY, Executrix.

ALFRED WILSON,

Auctioneer and Real Estate Agent,

Room 22, - - - Robeson Building.

Houses and land in all parts of the city for sale; tenements for rent: rents collected

For Sale.

Two-story house on Acushnet avenue, near Walnut street; well arranged for one family; good location.

For Lease.

The Webster Block, Purchase street; 16 rooms, well adapted for a genteel boarding house, club rooms, or business purposes.

TO LET—A flat in The Winslow, corner Sixth and Union streets. Apply to A. WILSON, Robeson Building. jy14-tf

T. F. HEALEY,

Auctioneer and Real Estate Agent,

555 and 559 Purchase street, corner of Franklin street.

FOR SALE one small house, barn and 20 rods of land on North Front street. Price $1500.

Also one fine house in the west part of the city in good locality, with all the modern improvements, gas and electric lights, etc. Will be sold cheap if applied for soon.

Also a few more house lots in Fairhaven on the Howland and Briggs farms, from $15 to $17 per rod, and they are some of the choice lots.

Also one corner lot on south Belleville road for $25 per rod.

Also one lot on the corner of Sawyer and North Front streets.

Also lots on Acushnet avenue, Coggshall and Locust streets, in fact all parts of the city.

Also some desirable house lots on Hathaway avenue near Purchase street. Easy terms.

Business solicited. No charges made unless a sale, then my prices are the lowest.

BY WM. BARKER, JR., Auctioneer.

Heirs' Sale of Valuable Seashore Property at Auction.

Will be sold at auction on the premises, TUESDAY, Aug. 9, 1892, at 2 o'clock P. M., that well known point or neck of land situated at the southeasterly part of Westport, in the County of Bristol, Mass., and commonly called "Gooseberry Neck." The property comprises about 75 acres, accessible by land or water, has an extensive and valuable shore privilege furnishing an abundance of kelp, rock weed, moss and muck, excellent fishing and fowling facilities. About 12 miles southwesterly from New Bedford, in close proximity to Westport Point, Horse Neck and Westport Harbor, and one of the most desirable seaside locations on the New England coast.

For further particulars inquire of or address the subscriber at North Dartmouth, Bristol Co., Mass.

July 25, 1892. jy25-ts

GEO. H. TABER, Auctioneer.

Administratrix' Sale.

By virtue of a license granted to me on the third day of June last, by the Probate Court for the County of Bristol. I shall sell at public auction on the premises hereinafter described, on THURSDAY, the 18th day of August, instant, at 11 o'clock in the forenoon, a lot of land, situated in Fairhaven, Massachusetts, and thus bounded; On the north by Bridge street, on the east by land now or formerly of Noah Spooner, on the south by land formerly of said Spooner, and on the west by Mulberry street, containing thirty-five square rods more or less. Being the premises conveyed to Elnathan E. Delano by deeds recorded in the Bristol (New Bedford District) Registry of Deeds, book 24, page 316 and book 47, page 340. Together with all the buildings thereon standing.

Said property is within five minutes' walk from the horse cars, and has thereon a large commodious house in good repair. A good well and cistern and would be convenient for two families. Terms at sale.

PHEBE S. DELANO, Administratrix of the estate of Elnathan E. Delano.

Fairhaven, Aug. 4, 1892. au4-8-15-16-17

REAL ESTATE.

JOHN WHITEHEAD,

Real Estate Agent.

Several houses near Pierce Mill. Sale private. Also desirable lots on Geo. A. Briggs' estate on easy terms, and lots in all parts of the city. Desirable lots on Jas. Drown estate and Phillips and Coffin aves. au2-MWF1m

Cottage House.

Well built, good repair, in part of city growing rapidly; will make good home and *must* increase in value. Apply box 8, *Standard* office. ap25-tf

SUMMMER COTTAGE AND BARN—For sale low, situated in Acushnet; acre and one-third of high land, mostly pine grove; buildings nearly new. Inquire of A. G. ALLEY, JR., Union and Sixth streets. jy18-tf

Kansas Corn Crop Will Be Short.

KANSAS CITY, Aug. 8.—The cool winds that are sweeping over the southwest will not save the corn of Kansas. It will probably keep the corn from burning up any further, but at the best the crop cannot well exceed half the average yield.

A Bishop Murdered.

ROME, Aug. 8.—On the arrival of the train at Florence from Foligno yesterday, the bishop of Foligno was found lying dead in one of the carriages, with several wounds on his head. The police have arrested the suspected murderer.

In Brief.

Joseph Bean of East Berlin, Conn., aged 38, dropped dead while on his way to work.

John Flaherty, aged 4, died at Waterbury, Conn., from burns received at a bonfire.

Mayor Sargent of New Haven has withdrawn from the cong ressional contest in the Second district.

John P. Russell of Walpole, N. H., 72 years of age, hung himself in the barn of Josiah Graves, with whom he resided.

George A. Comeau, who pulled a woman's teeth with fatal results, was arrested at North Adams, Mass., for manslaughter.

Mrs. Ellen S. Tolman of Lawrence, Mass., thinks the Woman's Relief Corps has been discourteous to the Army Nurses' association regarding pension bills.

Frank L. Avery, a prominent restaurant keeper of Hartford, sold out his place in New London, and local creditors attached the property, claiming the sale was a fake.

The colored waiters at the Tremont House, New Haven, struck Saturday because they learned that girls were to replace them. At breakfast time there were no waiters, but at noon girls had been secured.

William R. Russell of Hartford was discovered in a semi-unconscious condition on the steps of Centre church, New Haven. On the face was a handkerchief saturated with chloroform. His attempt to commit suicide was frustrated by the police.

THE LAND OFFICE.

Commissioner Carter's Report of the Past Year's Operations.

WASHINGTON, Aug. 8.—Commissioner Carter's annual report of the operations of the general land office for the year ended June 30, says that the liberal and just policy toward settlers upon the public domain adopted by Secretary Noble at the beginning of this administration has been productive of very satisfactory and beneficent results. The business of the bureau was brought up abreast with current work by the end of the fiscal year.

The report critisices as unjust and as causing delay, the policy that controlled the business of the office under the last administration, from 1885 to 1889, when many entries were suspended because of alleged frauds on the part of settlers. The report makes these comparisons: Total number of agricultural patents issued from 1885 to 1888, 162,754; acreage, 26,040,640; total number of agricultural patents issued from 1888 to 1892, 398,128; acreage, 63,700,480; total number of mineral patents issued from 1885 to 1888, 3700; coal patents, 211; total number of mineral patents issued from 1888 to 1892, 7354; coal patents, 685.

The report states that from 1889 to 1892, 8,425,398 acres of public lands were surveyed, against 2,715,302 during the preceding four years. During the last fiscal year the cash sales aggregated 1,571,478 acres. The homestead entries amounted to 7,716,062 acres, and the railroad selections to 2,765,443 acres. Indianapolis disposed of aggregate 97,456. The total acreage disposed of was 13,664,019. The vacant public lands in the United States aggregate 567,586,783 acres.

The commissioner recommends a liberal policy in reference to surveys of the public lands, and says a general law on the subject of public forests is demanded, which shall make adequate provision in respect to forest reservations, and the cutting and removal of timber to supply public necessities.

THE MONETARY CONFERENCE.

Names of Those Who Will Deliberate in the Name of Uncle Same.

WASHINGTON, Aug. 8.—The names of the five commissioners who are to represent the United States at the coming international monetary conference are officially announced. They are Senator William B. Allison of Iowa, Senator John P. Jones of Nevada, Congressman James B. McGreary of Kentucky, ex-Comptroller Henry W. Cannon of New York and General Francis A. Walker of Massachusetts.

Senator Allison has seen nearly thirty years' service in the United States senate and was for eight years a member of the house before his election to the senate. He is chairman of the committee on appropriations, a leading member of the committee on finance and a recognized leader in financial matters. He voted against the Stewart free coinage bill when it passed the senate in July last.

Senator Jones has been an earnest advocate of free silver. He has not spoken often in the senate, but whenever he has spoken on finance in that body his remarks have always commanded close and earnest attention. He is also a member of the senate committee on finance.

Mr. McCreary succeeded Perry Belmont as chairman of the committee on foreign affairs in the house of representatives and has devoted considerable attention to international questions. He introduced the bill which called out the pan-American conference in Washington, and also the house bill for the present monetary conference. He voted in favor of free silver. Mr. McCreary is serving his fourth term in congress. He is a Democrat in politics.

Mr. Cannon succeeded John Jay Knox as United States comptroller of the currency, and resigned to accept the presidency of the Chase National bank of New York. He is classed as opposed to free coinage of silver under existing conditions.

General Walker is a well-known writer on economic questions. He was superintendent of the tenth census and was a member of the international monetary conference held at Paris in 1878. He is president of the Massachusetts Institute of Technology, president of the American Statistical society, and honorary fellow of the Royal Statistical society of London.

MUST BECOME CITIZENS.

Interesting Decision Concerning Officers of American Boats.

WASHINGTON, Aug. 8.—An interesting question has been presented to the treasury department in regard to the steamships City of New York and City of Paris, the owners of which are preparing to have them documented as American vessels in accordance with the provisions of a special act of congress granting them that privilege under certain conditions. The steamship company is anxious to retain the present officers of those vessels, most of whom are of foreign nationality, and in order to bring them within the law requiring vessels of the United States to be officered exclusively by citizens of the United States, the company took steps to secure their speedy naturalization. The officers have taken out their first papers, but must serve out the full prohibitory period before they become full-fledged citizens.

As a test case, application was made to the treasury department for the retention of Captain Watkins as master of the City of Paris during his probational period of naturalization. The commissioners of navigation, to whom the matter was referred, has replied that the law is obligatory as to the citizenship of masters of United States vessels, and that such citizenship in the case of an alien is not established until he shall have fulfilled all the requirements of the naturalization laws.

PREACHED CHRISTIANITY.

A Polish Jew Roughly Handled by Unconverted Countrymen.

ST. PAUL, Aug. 8.—When the synagogue of the Sons of Jacob was filled with worshippers a strange rabbi, for such he was taken to be, arose and began to preach in the Hebrew tongue. He was clever and the audience was much taken with him. Suddenly he began to preach Christ crucified. Instantly the congregation was on its feet demanding that the man be put out of the house. The man continued to preach Christ, and a moment later everybody made a rush for him. He was knocked down, and after his head was thumped on the floor, he was dragged and thrown out of the synagogue. The stranger proved to be a converted Polish Jew named Nathaniel Friedman. He claims that he was invited there by a prominent member of the Sons of Jacob. Friedman threatens to bring suit against the Sons of Jacob to recover damages for his injuries. He was not seriously hurt.

Mrs. Harrison Very Sick.

LOON LAKE, N. Y., Aug. 8.—President Harrison is again with his wife at his summer residence. Mrs. Harrison is still a very sick woman. That she has improved to a wonderful degree is also certain.

New Race Course.

CHICAGO, Aug. 8.—A charter was issued to the Indiana Racing association at Chicago with a capital stock of $500,000. Work will probably be begun on a tract of land procured at Robst, Ind.

PRAISED THE MAYOR.

Dr. Bacon Speaks of the Many Evils Which Beset Norwich.

NORWICH, Conn., Aug. 8.—Rev. L. W. Bacon, D. D., of the Second Congregational church, preached yesterday in support of Mayor Harwood's policy suppressing the houses of ill-fame. He selected his text from Matthew xiii, 7. He said: "The bold and courageous movement of Mayor Harwood against organized vice in this city is the only movement for the suppression of crime which has been made in Norwich for fifteen years; that his predecessors, by their positive or negative attitude toward the criminal classes, were either tolerators, sanctioners or protectors of vice." Dr. Bacon paid his respects to the bar of the Buckingham House and to the gambling features of the fairs of the New London Agricultural society, whic has received, he said, police protection.

He complimented Mayor Harwood for his manly and aggressive policy, and charged the police of the city with being on friendly terms with brothels and gamblers, and the predecessors of Mayor Harwood for fifteen years with having countenanced and winked at vice. Dr. Bacon inquired of them how they expected to escape the indictment of the fiftieth psalm: "When thou sawest a thief, then thou consentedst with him, and hast been partakers with adulterers." Summarizing the opposition to the movement, he said, it is composed of those who said, first, "You can't;" second, "Oh, you can't," and third, "Yes, but you can't."

To these who declared man cannot be made moral by law, he replied that is true; but the law can be used to break up this infamous business as a profession and as an organized business. The law cannot make men moral, for those who are unrighteous will be unrighteous still, and those who are filthy will be filthy still. It can be used to interfere with the agencies of crime; it can arrest the agencies who sneak from place to place in the interest of vice, and who even attempt to operate upon the schoolchildren of this city.

Dr. Bacon urged all citizens who were in sympathy with the movement to stand together for its support as endorsers of Mayor Harwood's administration, and as supporters of it at the polls if necessary.

LOOKED AS IF ASLEEP.

A Dead Man's Body Lies for Many Days Beside a Railroad Track.

WORCESTER, Mass., Aug. 8.—Brakemen on the Boston and Albany railroad have noticed for a few days past a man lying under a tree in an open field about 1 1-2 miles west from Rochdale, and at first supposed that the man was only a tramp who found this place a comfortable bed. As the days passed, however, and the man's position remained unchanged, it was thought that he might be dead.

Saturday the dispatcher here was notified, and Medical Examiner P. H. Keefe of this city visited the spot yesterday. The man lay under an oak tree. He was dead. Dr. Keefe said he thought the body had been lying there about three days. The man lay on his back, with his right hand thrust in his pocket and his left hand loosely lying against his leg.

There were marks of lightning down the center of the tree, and Dr. Keefe inclines to the opinion that death resulted from lightning. It is supposed that the man was walking on the railroad Thursday evening and sought shelter under the tree from the heavy shower which passed over the town Thursday night. It seems probable that he was instantly killed.

An examination of the remains was made and a pocketbook found containing a small sum of money. A small notebook was also discovered, in which was written the name "Martis J. Downey, Monson, Mass."

The man weighed about 160 pounds. His beard and hair are reddish, and he was dressed in a black cutaway coat and vest and black and white diagonal trousers. His shoes were worn badly.

RUMOR AND DENIAL.

Concerning the Movements of "Little Napoleon" Ferdinand Ward.

HARTFORD, Aug. 8.—The reported elopement of Ferdinand Ward and a daughter of C. A. Pelton of Middletown is denied by members of Miss Pelton's family. All the members of Mr. Pelton's family are at home except the eldest daughter, who is visiting a lady friend in Massachusetts.

NEW YORK, Aug. 8.—A special from Middletown, Conn., to The Morning Advertiser says: Miss Frances Pelton, the young woman whom Ferdinand Ward is said to love, has disappeared. Ward is also gone from his summer place in Thompson. Now it is declared that the two have gone together. It was alleged at first that the two had gone to Newburyport, Mass., but a message sent from this city late last night did not serve to discover them.

MORE TROUBLE BREWING.

A Band of 700,000 Will Back Homestead Workers in Their Fight.

HOMESTEAD, Pa., Aug. 8.—Samuel Gompers, president of the American Federation of Labor, was in Homestead yesterday. He was in consultation with the leaders of the Homestead strike for several hours, at the conclusion of which he departed for New York. He refused to talk for publication, but it is understood he assured the officers of the local lodge of the Amalgamated association that the 700,000 members of the federation were in line and that the full power of the organization will be brought to bear on behalf of the Homestead steel workers, and that every member will contribute to a fund for the benefit of the strikers. The federation, according to Mr. Gompers, will also insist in carrying out the boycott on all material manufactured by the Carnegie Steel company. The Knights of Labor, too, have fallen into line and the men here feel greatly encouraged.

Vice Chairman Crawford of the advisory committee stated last night that applications for machinists are coming in from all parts of the United States and that quite a number of mechanics who came out on strike have thus found employment in union mills elsewhere. Fully 200 members of the National Guard were sent home last evening. Battery B will go home today, while the Fifth regiment will, in all probability, depart for home tomorrow.

Chaplain Adams of the Sixteenth regiment conducted religious services inside the mill yesterday.

An attempt will be made to start the Duquesne plant today. Master Mechanic Miller stated that 60 per cent. of the old men had returned to work in the mechanical department already, and he expected at least 300 men today. Vice President Carney of the Amalgamated association says he is confident that not one will go back.

The residents of Duquesne fear that if any of the men attempt to go into the mill, an effort will be made by strikers to prevent them doing so. In that event a collision with the troops is probable.

Sunday proved uneventful both at Duquesne and here.

The advisory committee last night gave out that a roller had received a letter from Manager Potter, informing him that if he would return to work a charge of murder against him would be withdrawn.

Outwardly, the strikers are as firm as ever, but many privately express a desire to return to work, and say they are only deterred by the influence of the majority. The company now has fully 1200 men in the mill.

Waiting for a Settlement.

ASHLAND, Wis., Aug. 8.—All the mines under the control of the Wisconsin Central Railroad company on the Gogebic range, save the Ashland mine, were closed Saturday night and 2000 men thrown out of work. The shut-down is indirectly due to the Homestead strike. No ore from any of these mines, except the Ashland, will be shipped until the Homestead matter is settled.

Terrible Revenge.

WYANDOTTE, Mich., Aug. 8.—Angered by a long series of insults from his fellow workmen, Herbert Gault, a laborer in a rolling mill, sought revenge on John Langstone, the chief of his persecutors, by pouring a dipper of boiling hot metal over his limbs, burning them frightfully and causing fatal injuries. Gault has a deformity of his left leg that causes him to walk with a limp. His fellow workmen have lately made him the butt of their jokes, owing to his deformity.

Sultan's Troops Defeated.

TANGIER, Aug. 8.—Fifteen hundred of the sultan's troops, with two field pieces and 500 tribesmen advanced yesterday afternoon to the Angherna hills, where they were repulsed by the rebels. They then retreated to within three miles of Tangiers. A detachment of cavalry, which attempted to charge the rebels, were also repulsed. The whole force retreated to camp in the evening, having lost fifteen, killed and wounded.

Eight-Hour Law a Factor.

DAVENPORT, Ia., Aug. 8.—The bids of two of the principal contractors for work on the Illinois and Mississippi canal (the Hennepin) have been rejected by the government because the estimates were not based on the eight-hour day as required by the new law. The effect of this will be to prevent much work on the canal this season.

Bolivian Troubles.

WASHINGTON, Aug. 8.—The department of state is in receipt of information that a serious revolutionary conspiracy has been discovered in Bolivia. A large number of prominent men, including many members of congress, have been sent beyond the frontier, and martial law has been proclaimed throughout the republic.

From Saturday's Third Edition.

ANOTHER IMPORTANT FACT.

Mr. Borden Was Making an Inventory of His Property

With the Expectation of Having His Will Drawn Up.

Police Making a Rigid Search of the House where Crime was Committed.

[Special Dispatch.]

FALL RIVER, Aug. 6.—Up to 4 o'clock this afternoon no arrests had been made in the Borden murder case.

District Attorney's Investigation.

Advices from Marion, where District Attorney Knowlton is staying at his Summer residence, say that he will probably be in Fall River Monday or Tuesday, when an investigation will be held at the Borden residence.

Mr. Borden Left No Will.

One piece of information came to the knowledge of the police this afternoon which, in light of recent events, has a peculiar significance. It is stated that Mr. Borden left no will, but for the week previous to his death he had been making an inventory of his property, preparatory to having an instrument drawn.

Police Ransack the House.

This afternoon at 3 o'clock City Marshal Hilliard, Assistant Marshal Fleet and Capt. Desmond of the police force arrived at the Borden house on Second street. They went to the front door. Mr. Hilliard asked for Miss Emma and she came to the door.

"We have come to search the house," said the Chief. "Have you any objection?"

"No sir," replied Miss Borden. "None at all. I am only too willing to have the search made, and will help you all I can. I wish you would be careful and not tear up the things any more than is necessary."

Then the police entered the doors, which were closed after them. Dr. Dolan, medical examiner, and Andrew J. Jennings, the Borden family's attorney, accompanied the officers.

Guards were posted about the building and strict orders were given to see that no one was allowed to enter or leave the residence.

The police intend to ransack the structure from cellar to attic, and go through every room, in hope of securing some bit of tangible evidence which has so far escaped their vigilance. They have commenced at the top of the house, and it is expected will devote the entire afternoon to the search.

All the members of the family, Emma, Lizzie, Mr. Morse, and the servant, are within and will not be permitted to leave until the search is concluded.

THE YACHTS AT VINEYARD HAVEN.

Racers of the Squadron Arriving on the Run from Newport.

VINEYARD HAVEN, Aug. 6.—The racers of the New York yacht squadron are beginning to arrive here on their run from Newport, with a fresh southwest wind. Flagship Electra, judges' boat Ituna and the press boat Vamoose took up their stations off West Chop at 2 45 p. m., where the time will be taken.

VENEZUELAN INSURGENTS TRIUMPH.

Gen. Crespo Takes Possession of Caracas by Force of Arms.

NEW YORK, Aug. 6.—The *Herald* publishes the following: "Gen. Crespo has entered Caracas by force of arms," was the cable from an officer of the Venezuelan insurgents yesterday to the Venezuelan junta in New York. Later came the information that Crespo had grown tired of the dilly-dallying method of the peace commissioners and of the unfilled promises of citizens' committees who pretended that they desired to effect a quiet surrender of the capital and arrange for the entrance of the insurgent forces into the city without bloodshed. He had wearied of these delaying schemes and had taken the bull by the horns; had adopted heroic measures which precipitated a sanguinary battle at the city's gates, and which had terminated in the utter defeat of the government troops and resulted in the triumphant entry of the entire revolutionary army, 25,000, with Generals Guerrers, Quintana, Vegas and others at its head. The intelligence which came yesterday, also announced the defeat and rout of Lucien Mendoza, the last general of the Villegas government at La Victoria and the capture of Gen. N. Battali and his army. It announces also that the taking of Caracas by assault was done in fulfilment of a promise given by Gen. Crespo to his wife that he should be in possession by Aug. 5 if it took all his fighting force to get there. The further information came that the insurgents had driven Rangel from the field at a point between Valencia and La Victoria, had badly whipped Gen. Juan Tovar at San Joaquin, capturing from him guns and men, and had probably recaptured 600 rifles.

President on His Way to Loon Lake.

NEW YORK, Aug. 6.—The special train carrying President Harrison to Loon Lake arrived at Jersey City at 4 34 this morning, was switched to the West Shore road and the trip was resumed. The President is accompanied by Mr. Tibbetts and a servant. He will reach Loon Lake at 1 o'clock.

Fast Transatlantic Voyage.

NEW YORK, Aug. 6.—The Steamship Umbria of the Cunard was signalled off Sandy Hook this morning thus completing her transatlantic voyage in 5 days 22 hours and 5 minutes.

THE W. C. T. U. PROTEST.—The following is the full text of the protest sent to Mayor Ashley by the W. C. T. U. and which His Honor told a *Standard* man he considered an insult:

In view of the fact that our citizens by a decisive vote have expressed the wish that no liquor saloons shall be tolerated in this city, we, the Women's Christian Temperance Union, are moved to enter a protest against the non-enforcement of the law by the officials whose duty it is to carry out the wishes of the people expressed at the polls. We are sure that at present the law is disgracefully set aside and ignored, and that the officers who solemnly took oath to do all in their power to carry into effect the wishes of the majority of the people are shamefully derelict in their duty. The following admonition was given to the judges in olden time: "Take heed what ye do; for ye judge not for man but for the Lord, who is with you in the judgment. Wherefore now let the fear of the Lord be upon you; take heed and do it; for there is no iniquity with the Lord our God nor respect of persons, nor taking of gifts." II Chron. xix, 6-7. On behalf of the

W. C. T. U.

SERIOUS ACCIDENT IN TAUNTON.—Thompson Newbury, treasurer of the Taunton Oil Cloth Works, and a well-known wealthy citizen of that city, was knocked down by his horse and very seriously injured about the head this noon.

REAL ESTATE SALES.—Standish Bourne sold at auction this afternoon lot of land on the east side of Second street, north of Potomska street, containing 13.62 rods, to J. F. Cummings for $45 per rod.

Standish Bourne sold at auction this afternoon house and lot No. 406 Cedar street to John Granger for $2560.

ARRESTED.—A. Renson, a Russian Jew living at the South End, was arrested this afternoon for assault and battery.

OPENING OF THE CAMPAIGN.

First Great Republican Gathering in Ohio.

Secretary of the Treasury Foster's Speech at Vermilion.

Wisdom of Legislators Resulting in Prosperity of the Country.

VERMILION, O., Aug. 6.—An immense throng of people cheered themselves hoarse this afternoon at Linwood Grove. It was virtually the opening of the national campaign of 1892 in Ohio for the Republicans, and the enthusiasm of those present found vent when at 1 30 p. m. the orator of the day was introduced—Charles Foster, Secretary of the Treasury.

Secretary Foster gave a historical account of American currency from the time of the colonies to the present day. Of the panics of 1814, 1837 and 1857, and the disastrous results that followed each he said: "The derangement of the paper currency was the important factor in each of the three revulsions. The trouble was always preceded by a period of great prosperity. The people were growing rich. They desired to grow rich faster. To this end they substituted for legitimate enterprise wild speculation in which they were aided, and indeed often led, by such of the banks as were untrammelled by restraining laws. Had the banks confined their issues of paper money to the proper needs of trade and industry, the

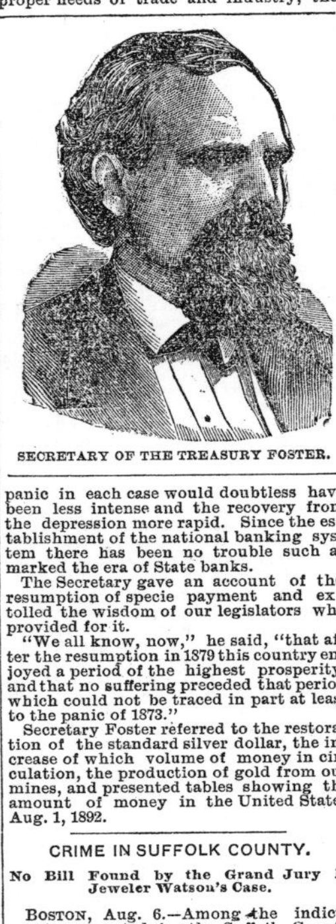

SECRETARY OF THE TREASURY FOSTER.

panic in each case would doubtless have been less intense and the recovery from the depression more rapid. Since the establishment of the national banking system there has been no trouble such as marked the era of State banks.

The Secretary gave an account of the resumption of specie payment and extolled the wisdom of our legislators who provided for it.

"We all know, now," he said, "that after the resumption in 1879 this country enjoyed a period of the highest prosperity, and that no suffering preceded that period which could not be traced in part at least to the panic of 1873."

Secretary Foster referred to the restoration of the standard silver dollar, the increase of which volume of money in circulation, the production of gold from our mines, and presented tables showing the amount of money in the United States Aug. 1, 1892.

CRIME IN SUFFOLK COUNTY.

No Bill Found by the Grand Jury in Jeweler Watson's Case.

BOSTON, Aug. 6.—Among the indictments presented by the Suffolk County grand jury was one against Massimino Repucci who killed Arnold Delorfarno several weeks ago, and one against "Dr." Sophia C. Thompson for malpractice in causing the death of a young woman.

The most interesting case on the "No bill" list was that of Edward F. Wilson the jeweller. He, after his departure from this city, returned voluntarily and was subsequently arrested at his home upon a complaint made by New York creditors. He was bailed by his friends. At the time he went away stories were afloat that he takes a large sum with him. It appears that he was found by one of his creditors penniless, without food, wandering about London. The creditor advised him to get home. In the meantime his wife had supported herself and children by working in a dry goods store.

THE PRESIDENT AT LOON LAKE.

All Reports of Mrs. Harrison's Precarious Condition Utterly False.

LOON LAKE, N. Y., Aug. 6.—The President arrived this afternoon. The meeting between husband and wife after six weeks' separation was very affectionate. There was great enthusiasm among the tourists.

All reports as to the precarious condition of Mrs. Harrison's health are utterly false. She is rapidly improving in health. Last evening she was out riding for nearly an hour.

Brakeman Killed by the Train.

WOONSOCKET, Aug. 6.—James Dean of Boston, aged 35 and unmarried, brakeman on the night freight between Pascoag and Boston, over the N. Y. & N. E. Railroad, fell under his train this morning and was run over and so badly injured that he lived but a short time after being taken to the Woonsocket hospital. He had placed his lantern on a deadwood and was running beside the car. He saw the lantern was falling, and grasped for it and fell in front of the wheels with the result given above. Dean was a conductor on the Fitchburg Railroad for many years.

Boston Newspaper Men Change.

BOSTON, Aug. 6.—J. H. Russell, city editor of the *Journal*, has resigned to accept a position with the New York *Sun*. He will be succeeded by F. A. Nichols of the reportorial staff.

The Ocean Steamers.

Arrived—At New York, LaFlandre, Antwerp. Off the Lizard, Noordland, New York for Antwerp.

THE CHARM OF BOOKS

HOW LIBRARIES ARE REGARDED BY ALL KINDS OF PEOPLE.

Most People, Educated or Ignorant, Have a Remarkable Respect for Great Collections of Books—Some Remarks About Private Libraries.

The average Briton has a respect for libraries in themselves which, considering how little he reads, how reluctant he is to spend any measurable proportion of his income on books and how absolutely he refuses to pay librarians even decent salaries, is one of the most inexplicable features of his complex character. The impressiveness of a library is felt by classes far outside the one which passes its life in using books. The ordinary population of an ordinary town, though it will not always vote the cost of a free library, is proud to believe that the town library is a good one, regards its increase as something to be recorded with triumph and enters the rooms in which it is kept with a kind of awe.

It is considered a mark of caste to possess a good library, and a house will sell better because there is a room in it which has been devoted to the keeping of books and that to men who would regard a day spent among books, even in that most enjoyable of all amusements, book sipping, as intolerably tedious.

We have been told on good evidence, though we cannot ourselves vouch for the fact, that this feeling extends to those who cannot read—a class now dying out—and it is undoubtedly true that servants, though they will neglect a library to any extent, and apparently believe that dust on bookshelves is matter in the right place, will take some trouble not to injure books if they are accumulated in any numbers. They respect them, and will, if left in sole charge, leave them to molder away in more peace and honor than they will leave furniture.

We suppose the true reason is that, as all men respect knowledge, and especially knowledge of which they only dimly perceive the use, they regard a library as a deposit of bottled wisdom, by which they can hardly profit indeed, but which they had rather not injure or disperse. That undoubtedly is the feeling of that extraordinary class, the born librarians, the men who become by a sort of voluntary selection attendants in libraries—usually the worst paid for the work involved of all varieties of clerkship—and who, although they rarely read, and are still more rarely litterateurs, have a sort of worship of books to which they will occasionally confess. They are seldom seen in London except occasionally in secondhand bookshops, but they are frequently to be met with in country towns, sometimes, though not often, with an extraordinary knowledge of and interest in bibliography. They do not know books, but they know about books; they handle them reverently and they grow irritated by the ill usage of any book to the shaking off of all conventional reticence of language.

Indeed, we are not sure whether the same feeling of respect for books as books has not a great influence with the cultivated also. They know of course, or would know if they thought about it, where the charm of a great collection of books lies namely, its power, if well consulted, of transforming the student's relation to any given subject. He becomes when he has read up a topic—really read it up, that is—with an open mind and a keen attention as regards that topic a new man, bigger, wiser and more of a superior than he was before, and this sometimes to a degree which is startling in his own eyes. The depository or containing casket of power like that is sure of respect from the man who knows of its existence.

It is a fact which every owner of a library will confirm that the reluctance to weed one is the greatest of all obstacles to its collection. A private man who loves books, unless exceptionally rich, is always, as he advances in life, tormented by the difficulty of finding room for them. They grow and grow, and the wall space does not grow and the shelves do not grow either; and unless he resorts to the unspeakably detestable expedient of reduplicating the books on each shelf—a device which not only destroys the back rows, but imperils their owner's chance of heaven, the book wanted being invariably lost for the time being, with results in evil wishes and language—there comes a time when he is at his wit's end.

Not one room in ten will allow of shelves being set at right angles to the walls instead of along them, though that quadruples book space, and the collector, with weary sighs, either heaps books above each other or leaves them in packing cases, or in desperate emergencies puts them on the floor. All this while if he would only weed them there would be plenty of room, and the opportunity of weeding is almost limitless.

We venture to say there are not five men in England possessed of 3,000 books apiece who not know perfectly well that half their volumes are lumber, books which they will never read or consult or open for any purpose whatsoever. They are the books of forgotten periods of life, the books of whim, the books of abandoned studies, or, more numerous than all, the books about which their owner's only thought is a wonder how the devil they ever got there; books he can no more account for than he could account for the foolishness of early day dreams or for the morsels of absolutely useless knowledge packed away in his memory.

He knows perfectly well the lumber ought to go the auctioneer, but he never sends it, unless indeed he changes his house; nor, if he is rich enough to keep a "librarian" or library clerk, will that invaluable person send it; he is indeed insulted or made lachrymose by the very suggestion. Master and servant have both contracted a feeling which they would never defend, a feeling of respect for the library as a library, and independent somehow of what is in it.—London Spectator.

John Had Explained.

It appears that it occasionally happens that a couple who have been content to be married at a registry office are some time afterward seized with a desire to be married again, as the law allows, in church. The "working parson" having one day got such a couple on the steps of the altar, he was rather nonplussed by the answer he got to the question, "John, wilt thou have this woman to thy wedded wife?" "Why, sir," replied the bridegroom, "I told you we was married two years ago."—Cornhill Magazine.

British Holdings in America.

The aggregate of land in the United States owned by members of the house of lords and British syndicates is 20,941,666 acres, a greater area than all of Ireland, 2,000,000 more than Scotland, and over half as much as England and Wales.—London Tit-Bits.

German scientists are now making an explosive equal to dynamite out of common jute. It is called nitrojute, and is prepared by treating jute with a mixture of nitric and sulphuric acids.

The most unstable compound known to chemistry, and therefore the most explosive substance so far discovered, is chloride of nitrogen, which probably consists of three parts of chloride united with one of nitrogen.

The Evening Standard.

ESTABLISHED FEBRUARY, 1850.]   NEW BEDFORD, TUESDAY, AUGUST 9, 1892.   TWO CENTS.

HASKELL & TRIPP.

Unless you consider it fun, there's no excuse for making pillow cases in the face of such a price as we now offer them ready made. Is it fun to run up and hem pillow cases?

The following are 12½c. each and in most cases are less than the cloth costs:

A manufacturer of sheets, having left on his hands some remnants of bleached sheetings, has made them up for us into pillow cases, that we will now give you an opportunity to buy for 12½c. each.

Among them are the following well-known brands of cottons, and as they are much heavier grades than usually put into pillow cases you'll hardly be able to wear one out in years:

"Wamsutta."
"New Bedford."
"Pequot."
"Atlantic."
"Pepperell."
"Utica."
"Lockwood."
Dress Goods.

Cut-price sale of fine, high-grade, pure-wool suitings, reduced from 87c., 75c. and 62c. One long counter full of choice colors. *Pick for 50c. a yard.* Not for a long time, if ever, have such choice and seasonable dress fabrics been sold for half a dollar per yard.

Storm serges to suit everybody.

Every good sort, both navy and black, 50c., 75c. and $1 a yard, in narrow twills, chevron stripes, broad diagonal wale, etc. We will guarantee best values in New England on storm serges.

Three special numbers in black all-wool Henriettas:

At 85 cents.
At 95 cents.
At 1 dollar.
} 45 inches wide, blue or jet black.

These Henriettas cannot be matched at our prices, go where you will.

More bamboo bargains are ready in the basement.

By contracting for a large quantity we are able to reduce the price on three-legged bamboo tables at 25c. apiece.

Brass mounted bamboo corner baskets with three shelves, 50c. each.

Mosquitoes kept at bay. You may be protected from these pests at night by an expenditure of $2.22 for one of our white gauze canopies, with extra full skirt, mounted on the patent umbrella frame.

HASKELL & TRIPP.

Department Stores,

Purchase and William Streets.

WEATHER INDICATIONS.

FAIR, SOUTHWESTERLY WINDS.

WASHINGTON, Aug. 9.—For the 24 hours from 8 a. m. to-day: For Massachusetts, Rhode Island and Connecticut, fair, southwesterly winds.

THUNDER STORMS.

BOSTON, Aug. 9.—Local forecast for New England until Wednesday night: Fair, except local showers of thunderstorms, probably during the afternoon; no decided change in temperature; winds generally southwesterly.

EXPELLED FOR IMMORALITY.

De Cobain, the ex-M. P., Conducts a Methodist Revival in Brooklyn.

NEW YORK, Aug. 9.—A morning paper says that Edward De Cobain, who was expelled from the British Parliament for failure to answer to the bar on charges of immorality, addressed a Methodist revival last evening in South Brooklyn, where many people were greatly astonished by his stirring eloquence.

After leaving England he fled to the continent, claiming he was a victim of a police conspiracy that he could not withstand, and that they had been forged so strong a case that his innocence could not have been proved. Nothing was heard from him for a long time. It is said that he was in Spain. The offence of which he was accused was a misdemeanor and he could not be extradited. He had always been known as a man who took interest in church matters, and it is said he was conducting revival meetings on the continent.

Mr. De Cobain is living in New York. He has addressed several meetings of Methodists in this city, but he had appeared here in Brooklyn until last evening, when he walked into the tent. A sort of camp and revival meeting is conducted there, under the auspices of the Fourth Avenue M. E. church. The ex-member of Parliament had never been in the church.

A member of the church met him at a gathering of Methodists last week, liked his style of oratory and invited him over to the tent. On entering he sat down at the organ and announced a hymn, which he sang in a deep voice by himself, the audience not having got warmed up sufficiently to join. A little later they would have done anything at his bidding, so great was the result of his exhortation. He, as the Conservative member, was known all over England. In eloquent language he took the side of the working-man. When the train was leaving Winslow station a shot was fired and yet he is known as a Democrat-Conservative.

The police force of Ireland never liked him, and after the riots of 1876 he dubbed them murderers and proved, as he fully believed, that they had been guilty of assassination, so much so that coroners' juries in Belfast returned verdicts of wilful murder against them. This, he says, earned for him the undying enmity of the force, and a warrant was sworn for his arrest, based on the affidavit of a young man and backed up by the evidence of others, which he says was purchased; he was convinced that the whole thing was what some people in this country would call "a put up job."

To a reporter he said: "It is an awful thing to feel oneself 3000 miles away from home with such a charge hanging over him. I swear before my Maker that I am innocent of the crimes for which I am charged. I am preparing papers to prove my case and I think I can absolutely demonstrate my innocence. The Irish police are the tools of the ministry in power. My position in Parliament was wanted by a rich man who thought he would like prestige. I have a letter from him offering to pay my expenses if I would retire in his favor. The aristocracy of Belfast did not like my independence. Out of this and the enmity of the police force grew the most devilish plot ever concocted. After my retirement I went to France and Spain. I did not hold many meetings there. I came to America last May."

"Do you intend to return to prove your innocence?" "Not yet. I am working with my friends and lawyer and I am taking their advice. Copies of declarations have been sent to London and we hope to reopen the case in Parliament. One of the most distinguished New York lawyers with whom I have consulted says he feels like putting all the papers in his gripsack and going to England to make a fight and he thinks he can show that the whole thing was a plot. He is away in the country and I am awaiting his return."

Mr. De Cobain is a most entertaining talker with a remarkable flow of language. He said that he made no effort to conceal his presence in this country and none to announce it.

BRITISH POLITICS.

McCarthy and Redmond's Demands Foreshadow Trouble for Gladstone.

LONDON, Aug. 9.—The *Times* and *Standard* both comment on the demands of Messrs. McCarthy and Redmond in behalf of evicted tenants and dynamiters as foreshadowing trouble for Mr. Gladstone.

The Welsh members met yesterday and decided to support the home rule bill.

The bi-metallist members, under the presidency of Hucks Gibbs, decided to postpone bringing the bi-metallic question to the notice of parliament until the next session.

FLOUR MILLING COMBINE.

Corporation with Ten Mills, Capital Formed in California.

SAN FRANCISCO, Aug. 9.—Articles of incorporation were filed yesterday at Sacramento for a flour milling combine with a capital of $10,000,000, paid in capital $500,000. The combine is called the Sperry Flour Co. and practically includes all the flour milling interests of California. The mills have an output of 60,000 barrels of flour per day. Horace Davis is president.

Hot Weather Good for the Crops.

INDEPENDENCE, Ia., Aug. 9.—The intensely hot weather of the last few weeks insures an average corn crop. It has been growing at a rapid rate, in some cases a growth of seven inches in a single night but the cold Spring has effectually ruined all prospects of a large crop.

OMAHA, Neb., Aug. 9.—A hot wind has been blowing in eastern Nebraska and the thermometer has remained near the hundred point for some days. If the present hot winds continue the corn crop will be much damaged.

KANSAS CITY, Mo., Aug. 9.—Hot winds have prevailed in western Missouri for the past two days and reports of damage to corn crop are coming in.

Condition of the Cotton Crop.

GALVESTON, Tex., Aug. 9.—A prominent firm of cotton factors here has issued a second report on cotton. The first, issued in May, indicated a reduction in acreage of cotton of 15 per cent. This figure is fully confirmed by the present report. The condition of the crop compared with this time a year ago shows cotton to be eight days later and its condition 4 per cent. worse. The estimated acreage of cotton over last year is 14 per cent. more and its condition 2 per cent. better.

A Catholic Chautauqua.

BUFFALO, N. Y., Aug. 9.—At the meeting of the advisory committee having in hand the site for the Catholic chautauqua, the Buffalo members will urge the selection of Point Chautauqua, the abandoned Baptist resort on Chautauqua Lake which has been offered for a reasonable figure. The site will doubtless be in New York State.

Ocean Steamers.

Arrived—At Boston, Stockholm City, London.

THE CRISIS REACHED.

Action in Borden Tragedy to be Taken at Once.

Bridget Sullivan Locked in with the Authorities.

Thorough Examination as to Her Knowledge of the Crime.

[By Associated Press.]

FALL RIVER, Aug. 9.—This morning the servant girl, Bridget Sullivan, was summoned to the central police station. She walked down in company with Officer Doherty and talked quite freely on the way. She looked very much worried and was quite pale as compared with her appearance last Thursday morning when seen first by a reporter. She told the officer that it was hard to be watched so closely and to have one's private affairs torn to pieces. She was willing, however, to have the police or any one else examine her every action since the time she arose Thursday until she was asked to go to the police station with the officer. She did not care to talk very much about the details of the family relations. She allowed that she wanted to leave two or three times, but she was urged to remain by Mrs. Borden, of whom she spoke very kindly.

She was taken at once into the city marshal's presence and also into the presence of District Attorney Knowlton and Medical Examiner Dolan. These gentlemen, who, with Judge Blaisdell and the two detectives, are now handling the case, do not care to be quoted as having given any opinion on the merits of the present status of it, but they all agree that affairs are at a critical point and action may be taken at once.

Miss Sullivan was brought before the gentlemen to undergo a thorough examination as to the facts before and after the murder as far as she knew them.

While the servant was in the district court room, locked up with the authorities, Mr. Morse was walking along through Main street, and down to the banks, closely followed by Officer Devine.

Another Clew and Discovery.

Still another clew is advanced, and there is a discovery which may and may not belong with it. The residence of Dr. Chagnon on Third street is situated close to the Borden property, being divided by a fence seven feet high. Mrs. Chagnon and her daughter Martha say that Wednesday night about 11 o'clock they distinctly saw a man jump over the fence into the Borden yard, and subsequently they heard a slight noise in the barn. Miss Collet stayed at the house to answer telephone calls. She was absent for an hour from 10:45 to 11:45 on Thursday morning.

With the statement of the midnight intruder going over the fence and subsequent noise in the barn comes another story. Shortly after the intruder was discovered a great crowd surged in the yard, and some more adventurous and inquisitive than others went into the barn. Upstairs in the hay, according to two men, the hay in the loft lay in such a condition as to plainly reveal the fact that some one had laid in it. It has been suggested that the man who came over the fence was the murderer; that he slept in the barn over night, and accomplished his hellish purpose when the opportunity offered in the morning.

But, if this be so, it is remarkable that no one saw him leave the barn or enter or come from the house. That he could have escaped, provided he committed the murder between 10:55 and 11:20, is hardly believed. It has been shown why and how he could be discovered, no matter which direction he took after leaving the place, and yet circumstances may have so favored him that with everything seemingly pointing to detection—the time, the place and the surroundings—he might have gotten away.

This is another theory the police are thinking over.

THE AMEER ALARMED.

Revolt of Hazara Tribes in Afghanistan Becoming More Serious.

SIMLA, Aug. 9.—The revolt of the Hazara tribes in Afghanistan becomes more serious daily and many of the great tribes have now combined their forces against the ameer, who is collecting all his resources to put down the rebellion. It is reported here that the ameer is anxious to meet Gen. Roberts, who with a large detachment of troops has been dispatched by the Italian government to meet the ameer. This mission is accompanied by a political agent and its object is to arrange plans with the ameer against feuds and against the advance of Russia in Afghanistan, which is the road to India. It is also reported that in view of the dispatch of Gen. Roberts, the ameer will publish generally throughout Afghanistan that a large force of India has sent him together with a large force of British troops to his aid.

THE AMERICAN WHEAT SUPPLY.

British Association Discusses Competition in Agriculture.

LONDON, Aug. 9.—The British Association yesterday discussed the question of a competition in agriculture. Edward Atkinson of Boston read a paper on American wheat supply and the decreased cost of production which enabled farmers in the West to reap the same profits from decreased prices. Prof. Wallace of Edinburgh denied that America was becoming played out as a wheat producing country. He held that on the contrary, she was on the threshold of an immense wheat supply trade with Europe, while the extent of her resources in raising cattle was almost illimitable.

PEOPLE'S PARTY CAMPAIGN.

National Executive Committee Plans a Vigorous Fight.

ST. LOUIS, Aug. 9.—The People's party national executive committee met here yesterday. A resolution was passed calling on Messrs. Washburn of Massachusetts and McFarlan of New York to call a meeting of the national committee men of the Eastern States to arrange for a vigorous campaign. "This meeting is called," said Dr. Brolgton, national committeeman, "because most of the old Greenbackers, who have been affiliated with the Democrats, are inclined to support the ticket and we want to arrange a plan of campaign that will assure of success in those States."

Prussian Minister of Interior Resigns.

BERLIN, Aug. 8.—The resignation of Herr Ernst Ludwig Herrfurth, Prussian minister of the interior, was presented to Emperor William to-day.

The Gold Train in New York City.

BUFFALO, N. Y., Aug. 9.—The specie train, carrying $20,000,000 from the San Francisco mint, reached here over the Lake Shore road at 1 o'clock this morning. It pulled in for a short stop.

SEIZED FOR SMUGGLING.

Captain of Schooner Belle Bartlett of Provincetown in Trouble.

HALIFAX, N. S., Aug. 9.—The American fishing schooner Belle Bartlett of Provincetown was seized yesterday by Collector Bourinot of Port Hawkesbury. She is charged with smuggling two years ago at Shippagan. Capt. Smith is accused of selling salt, flour and tobacco without entrance. The vessel, it is alleged, had no license.

TRAIN ROBBERS BALKED.

Attempt of Armed Men to Hold Up a Texas & St. Louis Express.

PARIS, Tex., Aug. 9.—As the south bound Texas & St. Louis express approached Winslow tunnel on the Frisco Road last night it was flagged by the watchman who said that 10 or 12 armed men had visited a residence near there and made inquiries concerning the train. They proceeded to Winslow station and as the train started again three armed men who got aboard at Winslow jumped off and disappeared in the dark. The superintendent at Fort Smith was notified and a strong force of deputy marshals were sent to guard the train. When the train was leaving Winslow station a shot was fired on the mountain side near by. This was intended for a signal to the gang at the west end that the train was coming. It was found they had prepared for the hold-up at a high trestle near the west end of the tunnel.

Disastrous Fire in Texas.

McKINNEY, Tex., Aug. 9.—Fire last night destroyed Coffey Bros.' livery stable, Hollander's shoe store, the McKinney Bank, Cole's saloon, and half a dozen grocers' and dry goods stores, besides several smaller concerns. Loss $60,000. Origin unknown.

Chinese Troops Withdraw.

ST. PETERSBURG, Aug. 9.—Advices say that Chinese troops who recently occupied various posts in the Pamirs withdrew on the first summons from the Russians.

Death of a Prominent Hudson Man.

HUDSON, Aug. 9.—George Cotting, a prominent and wealthy citizen, died last night of paralysis.

HOME MATTERS.

PERSONAL.—Capt. George F. Brightman and wife are spending their vacation at North Conway, N. H.

Capt. William Sanders and wife will go to Littleton, N. H., next week.

William C. Parker and wife, William H. Pitman, Mrs. Augustus A. Greene and Miss Jane E. Gilmore are at Bethlehem, N. H.

Mrs. B. Taber, Jr., and daughter Annie of Fairhaven, yesterday left for a short visit at Onset, and then will go to the White Mountains, as Mrs. Taber is to spend the summer.

Mr. S. Francis Richmond and wife of Taunton and Mrs. Emily Walker of Dighton, who have been occupying one of the cottages at Pease's point, returned to their homes to-day.

Squire A. Gifford, who was formerly driver of Truck 3, has been permanently assigned as driver of Onward Engine No. 1, and John Donnaghy has received a permanent appointment as driver of Truck 3.

LABOR DAY.—The joint committee on the Labor Day celebration will hold a meeting to-night, when the responses to the invitations to out-of-town organizations to participate in the exercises of the day will be read. It is proposed to observe the day on a grand scale. The committee on sports has been instructed to secure the Cove street grounds, and a ball game between two local teams for a purse of $50 will probably be arranged. Various sports for which suitable prizes will be offered are also to be made a feature.

DECLINED TO PROSECUTE.—Fred Lambert, while in an intoxicated condition, early this morning, entered house No. 11 Margin street and helped himself to a quantity of clothing, which he carried away. He was arrested shortly after in the entry of house No. 6 Margin street by Officer Eldridge, the clothing recovered, and the man taken to the station. The owners of the garments declined to prosecute, and Lambert was arraigned for drunkenness.

WILL DISCUSS ANOTHER LOCATION.—To-day Chairman S. A. Brownell issued notices to the city property committee and to members of the Board of Health to meet on Thursday evening for the purpose of considering the proposition to change the location of the small pox hospital, which is at present located on the alms-house property on West French avenue.

HORSES.—Charles P. Cottle of Acushnet goes to Vermont the last of the week to buy horses. Anyone wising to give their order for a pair, a horse to match another, a family or gentleman's driving horse, can do so. Satisfaction guaranteed. Call or address Chas. P. Cottle, Acushnet.

BROKEN PULLEY.—A broken pulley in the weave room in No. 4 Wamsutta mill is the cause of several of the weavers being out to-day. When it broke John Isherwood, a weaver, had a narrow escape from instant death.

TO BE CLOSED.—C. S. & B. Cummings' store will be closed at 10 a. m., Aug. 10th, for the remainder of the day. All the groceries and markets are to close at 10 a. m. on the 10th for that day.

THE MONDAY CLUB of Fairhaven has a dance at the hotel at Nonquitt this evening. The party will go down by steamer at 7:30 o'clock and return at 12.

DOG KILLED.—A dangerous dog which had bitten a woman was killed to-day on Coffin avenue near Orchard street by Officer Wixon at the request of the owner.

THE STAR OF PROMISE will hold its monthly temperance meeting in the Cannonville chapel on Tuesday evening. There will be a lecture by Dr. Prescott.

BICYCLE RIDERS.—If you want a bargain, look at the shoes we are selling for $2. High lace and low, formerly sold for $3. See advertisement page 5. Union Shoe Store.

BREAK-DOWN.—One of I. C. Sherman's wagons came to grief this morning on Second street, near the post office. The accident was caused by a wheel breaking.

RISE IN GRAIN.—The price in corn has risen four cents per bushel and oats two cents per bushel in this market.

WILL AUDIT BILLS.—The City Council committee on audit will meet this evening for the purpose of auditing bills.

A BIG TURTLE.—James Flood caught a mud turtle weighing 20 pounds in a lot near Allen street this forenoon.

SCHOONER NELLIE MAY, which is to sail from Providence for Brava, will not get away till next week.

Go WITH THE CLERKS on their annual outing Wednesday. Fare for round trip 85 cents, including admission to the Casino.

GOOD WATERMELONS 20 cents. G. Bros.

DONE WITH THEORIES.

District Attorney Knowlton Consults with Police.

Authorities Now Consider Nothing but Facts.

Reasons for the Government's Action from the First.

Policeman's Startling Discovery in Loft of the Barn.

They Have Knowledge that Has Not Been Given to the Public.

Yesterday was the first day since the fiendish murder in Fall River, whose morning hours developed nothing of importance so far as the public was concerned. Speculation regarding the various theories advanced went on just as it has gone on since last Thursday forenoon at 11 o'clock, but it brought nothing to the surface worth a line. As nearly as can be ascertained, it is a mistake to assume that sentiment has shifted in respect to the suspected persons. Sentiment is fickle enough, it is true, and when a community is wrought up to a tremendous pitch of excitement and stands ready to pivot as that community stands, it might be expected that the consensus of opinion would veer with every breath, but in this case it hasn't. It should be borne in mind that the friends of the Borden family have rallied to their support and that their influence is naturally making itself felt in certain quarters, but they have not yet disarmed the frightful suspicion which was originally raised, cruel and groundless though it may be. But one change has taken place so far as the city as a whole is concerned, and that is a change of opinion as to the final outcome.

It is a change which might have been anticipated Saturday afternoon when, after the funeral of the murdered couple, no arrests took place, though for hours there had been reports, which led to the belief that a number of persons would be taken into custody. People are becoming confirmed in the view that there will never be a conviction and sentence. Four days and a half have passed and nothing but circumstantial evidence, pure and simple, had been gathered. The only conclusion possible was that there was no evidence of any other nature. It was an unpleasant conclusion to reach, and men didn't arrive at it cheerfully, but they were forced to accept it. They saw but one bright spot and that was a tiny one. The government might

Sooner or Later Strike a Clew

which would put them on the track of the assassin, and he might break down and confess. But if he had no confederates and he kept his own counsel, he was safe. Such was the course of reasoning pursued yesterday, and it appeared to be logical. There was no occasion to modify it unless the police and detectives and the State officers had a secret of their own. It is only fair to observe, right here, that the police have been terribly in earnest, that they are terribly in earnest, and that they have worked efficiently and effectively. They have been criticised as they undoubtedly expected to be, but perhaps they have been criticised unjustly. At the start they were caught at a disadvantage; they were the victims of circumstances which could entangle them but one day in 365, and they made a mistake. They did not take sole and immediate possession of the premises, house, barn and yard, and mount a guard in every room. It may have been a fatal mistake, but that is a matter that no human being can pronounce upon. It might be well to bear in mind, too, that they had to deal with a horror calculated to stagger any force in the world, whatever its training or experience. Not an unparalleled horror, it may be, but one with very few equals, and the false step taken during the first hour of commotion attendant on the discovery was not surprising. They recovered their self-possession, however, and have since left no stone unturned and no clew undisturbed which could help them to break the silence in which the mystery is shrouded. It is safe to assume that

They Have Threads in Their Possession

Which have not appeared in print, not many, because the papers have been close on the heels of every new turn and twist which the case has made, but one or two.

The police probably can tell the story of Miss Lizzie Borden's movements from 9 o'clock until 11 o'clock on the morning of the tragedy; that would be interesting reading, but the press representatives have only accounted for 20 minutes of that time. The police also must be aware of Bridget Sullivan's doings on that morning. She has undoubtedly informed them when she prepared the breakfast and washed the dishes and climbed the stairs to the third story which hid her from sight and shut the sound of her falling mistress from her ears. There are many details in a case like this, and not one of them is unimportant. The public hasn't been told when the servant last saw Mrs. Borden, and it has no inkling of her observations on the second floor as she passed up to clean the window under the roof. And so the police may be in possession of several points which throw light on the slaughter for them.

Their activity yesterday was in marked contrast to their apparent apathy of the day before. The word apparent is used because in all probability they did not rest, although there was less bustle at headquarters than usual. Yesterday, however, all hands were on the alert. Besides the guard at the house, officers in citizens' dress hurried in and out of the station in Court square, other officers, also in citizens' dress, drove in various directions, returned and drove off again; the State officers were busy, Marshal Hilliard was giving directions when he was not in consultation with his subordinates and assistants. Andrew J. Jennings, counsel for the Borden family, called and failed to find the marshal in his office, and every now and then a deputy sheriff would appear on the scene. Through it all one thing was apparent, and it was significant. Neither the marshal, nor the State officers, nor the patrolmen, nor detectives were following clews which led them outside of the city limits. It was plain to all in touch with the situation that the

Combined Energies of the Government Were Directed to One Spot

and that they were bringing every resource to bear on one point. As stated, no detail is too unimportant to be dismissed without study. The police had read the theory to the effect that Mrs. Borden was not killed by the first blow and that her murderer escaped by the basement door, which is usually locked, and which was found open after the tragedy. They consulted physicians and then they settled back into the belief which has been theirs since last Friday morning. One of the officers, who admitted that he was in a position to represent the views of all who were in command of the forces, said yesterday noon:

"Our minds are made up and for the present we are done with theories. We may not be able to convince the public, but we have established to our own satisfaction the fact, as we look at it, that Mrs. Borden was killed first; that she was killed some little time before her husband and that she was instantly killed. We are as positive as we can be of anything that the murderer then waited until Mr. Borden returned and that he killed him instantly. The assassin then escaped by way of the rear door. He did not go into the cellar. No door led from the basement which would have afforded him a protection he could not find in the first floor door.

It is Well to Trust to Reason Occasionally.

Experts entertain different views, of course, but we have questioned a number of the profession since the new idea concerning Mrs. Borden's injuries was published, and their arguments confirm us in our first opinion. It is a point that will bear the closest study and it demands attention. If the latest theory is correct it upsets the whole structure on which we have been building. Unless Mrs. Borden's life was blotted out the instant the axe fell on her head a great many things happened which we have insisted all along could not have happened. She turned and uttered a cry; if she did not scream, she put up her hands to ward off the second blow. There was a second blow and blow after blow on top of it. Every person, man, woman and child, will instinctively raise their hands when attacked as Mrs. Borden was attacked if the first stroke did not kill. She would either have placed her arms above her head or she would have covered her face with her hands. Had she been stunned and fallen before the second blow was delivered we would have found at least one of the arms under the body. If she did not fall

The Axe Would Have Cut Her Hands or Arms.

Now what happened? She was standing near the window, perhaps, and we must account for the blood stains on the wall in the corner. The first blow penetrated the brain, and the heart beat for the last time. It was a frightful wound. I saw a physician sink his fingers into it up to the knuckles; a hideous wound. It was not on the back of the head, but the blade had been brought up and over and down. The murderer struck a full arm blow. As a result the blood flowed out and there was but one direction it could take; that was a direction forward, and it carried it to the wall. If the blow had fallen behind the ear or on the back of the head and the veins had been severed, the blood would have spurted backward. The woman fell and her assailant stooped over her and delivered blow after blow deliberately. For a time the eye was clear and the aim was true, but the work told. The last blow glanced and took off a piece of the scalp. No blood flowed from that last wound. The heart had ceased to beat some seconds before. I examined all the gashes and observed the last one particularly. It was the only one which did not lead into the brain, and it would not have stunned the woman. If it had been delivered first, Mrs. Borden would have screamed, and it is probable that there would have been no double murder; but it wasn't.

The First Blow Killed,

and the body crashed down to the floor, just as you may have seen an ox felled. It was a limp, motionless body. The arms swung from it like pendulums, and the impetus they received as the corpse pitched forward took them out straight. Her head lay between them when we found her. This is grim talk, but no grimmer than most of the talk for the last four days. Here is one more surprising feature of the astounding case. Nobody in the house, and there surely was one person in the house, heard that fall. It was a frame house, 48 years old. Mrs. Borden might have screamed and nobody heard her, but a fall will, nine times out of ten, arrest the attention sooner than a call, unless it is a piercing cry for aid. If this is doubted, let any person go into the second story of a house, raise a water pitcher weighing 20 pounds and drop it. Do you know that

Everybody Down Stairs Will Hear It.

Not only that, but everybody who hears it will start and will exclaim 'What's that?' Ninety-nine times out of a hundred that is the exclamation. On one occasion that I can recall, eight persons were seated at a table, when a person tripped and fell on the floor above, and the eight ejaculated 'What's that?' in chorus. But here was a body weighing more than 200 pounds, falling without anything to obstruct it, and no noise was heard. If the corpse had fallen on a bed or chair and rolled off it might be possible to explain it. But it fell with full force and must have jarred the whole house. Mr. Borden's death was noiseless. His head rested on a pillow and gave with the blows of the axe. One thing we would like to establish, is the condition of the window in the spare bed room. Was that open or shut when Dr. Bowen first entered? If it was closed, that is a singular circumstance, though it might prove nothing. Every little helps, however. It was a warm, close morning, and the room had been made up. It would have been natural for the person who put it in order to have raised the window, but Dr. Bowen doesn't remember whether the window was raised or lowered. I don't wonder. His mind was occupied with something besides windows."

The above interview is important because it represents the opinions of the entire corps of police officials. Until there is conclusive evidence to the contrary, they assert that they will feel convinced that

Mrs. Borden was Murdered First,

that her slayer closed the door on her, stole down stairs and killed her husband, escaping through the rear door and the gate.

Rev. W. Walker Jubb of the Central Congregational church and Mrs. Charles J. Holmes, a member of the congregation, called at the Borden house yesterday to console with the family. Detective Hanscom did not visit the house, and as far as could be learned, Mr. Jennings, counsel for the Misses Borden and John Morse, did not call.

In the afternoon the clothing which Mr. and Mrs. Borden wore when they were butchered was taken out of the house and buried near the barn by men under the direction of Officer Chace. Officers Devine, Linnehan, Hyde and Chace guarded the house all day. At noon Mr. Morse left the house and walked down to Pleasant street. He was shadowed by Officer Devine.

At 5 o'clock in the afternoon Mr. Morse came down town again and mailed a letter at the post office. He was obliged to wait some time at the stamp window, but he attracted no attention and few people knew that he had left the house. As usual an officer shadowed him at a distance. He returned to the house without stopping on the way, and for a wonder nobody, not even a newspaper man, attempted to address him.

The search of the house yesterday was concluded with a visit to the barn, when the police ripped up the floors of that structure and turned the barn inside out. After that Capt. Desmond on his way to the marshal's office refused to make any statement regarding the results of the search, and it has been observed that all the men on the case are becoming reticent. It is difficult to get an opinion from the superior officers bearing on the work which they have on hand, but they will talk freely on any supposed case that is put to them. One of them was asked yesterday afternoon if he considered it possible that the murderer could have left the house with his clothes stained with blood and the axe which the authorities want so badly concealed under his coat. He is an officer who has had a long and varied experience, and his views ought to be valuable. He said: "I should attach no great importance to the hour of the day in which such a deed was accomplished, or to the demeanor of any person after the discovery was made. A good deal is said sometimes about crimes which are committed in broad daylight. That is the best time to commit certain kinds of crimes. Unless the alarm is given too soon, a man may walk slowly away from a building in a populous section in the morning or afternoon and escape observation. I mean by observation close scrutiny. The more populous the neighborhood, the better his chances. A man who comes from a doorway or yard after sundown is scanned much more keenly, provided he is seen at all. His only advantage is that there are fewer to see him."

Late in the afternoon, during the trial of a civil case in the District Court, Medical Examiner Dolan submitted his official report of the murder to Judge Blaisdell. The latter took the papers, promising to read them over at the earliest moment and set a date when the inquest can be held.

At 2 o'clock in the afternoon there were indications that the police were going to move in some direction or other and either

Relieve the Suspense or Add to it.

Everybody was on the qui vive, and it was expected that a sensation might occur at any moment. But the moments dragged along into hours and nothing happened. It was known that City Marshal Hilliard and his allies had reached the point where they needed legal advice and that the marshal had sent for District Attorney Hosea M. Knowlton. Shortly after 5 o'clock the district attorney arrived. He held a brief consultation with Marshal Hilliard, a long talk with Medical Examiner Dolan, and again it looked as if a move was about to be made. Timothy Harrington, a conductor for the Globe Street Railway Co., who saw Mr. Borden on the morning of the murder and could fix the time accurately, appeared at the station house; so did Officer Harrington with a book on his arm. It closely resembled the book which druggists use for keeping a record of prescriptions and the names of persons purchasing drugs. District Attorney Knowlton went out to the Mellen House to supper. At 8 o'clock Marshal Hilliard and State Officer Seaver left the Central station and walked to the Mellen House. They met the medical examiner, and with the district attorney reviewed the case from beginning to end. No details, however slight, were omitted, and at 10 o'clock the four men were still talking.

State Officer Seaver said last evening that they had definitely fixed the time that Mr. Borden

Was Last Seen Alone on the Street

at from eight to ten minutes of 11 o'clock. A man who had been talking with him on the sidewalk opposite the Borden house saw him enter the door. This man consulted his watch and is positive of what he says. At 11 13 o'clock the news of the murder was out.

More or less time is wasted in exploding clews which amount to nothing, but that is to be expected. In addition to the alleged man whom the French boy asserted he saw jump the fence, another story regarding a man whom it was said was seen picking pears in the yard about the time of the tragedy has been circulated and run down by the police. Mrs. Nathan Chace declared she saw this man, and Detective Seaver started a search for him yesterday. It was found that he was Patrick McGowan, a mason's helper, employed by John Crowe. Mr. Crowe occupied the barn and yard on Third street, in the rear of Dr. Kelley's house, which is just south of the Borden homestead.

District Attorney Not Ready to Talk.

At 12 30 this morning the district attorney and the marshal, State Officer Seaver and Medical Examiner Dolan were still in consultation. Mayor Coughlin was with them. At a late hour all left the room in the Mellen House except District Attorney Knowlton. Five press representatives made a dash for him. He said: "Gentlemen, I have nothing to tell you. I read my newspaper in the morning, and I want all the news, but I can't help you now. When I get ready to talk I will talk with all of you, and treat you all alike."

The marshal took all the evidence which he had collected in the shape of notes, papers, etc., together with other documents, bearing on the case, into the room where the five men were closeted and they commenced at the beginning. At the close of the conference held earlier in the afternoon, the district attorney advised the officers to proceed with the utmost caution, and was extremely conservative in the conclusions which he found. At that time he had not been made acquainted with all the details. Last night the same caution was observed. The quintet were working on one of the most

Remarkable Criminal Records in History,

and were obliged to proceed slowly. The marshal began at the beginning and continued to the end. He was assisted in his explanation by the mayor and medical examiner. Mr. Seaver listened. There were details almost without end, and all of them were picked to pieces and viewed in every conceivable light. Considerable new evidence was introduced, and then the testimony of officers not present was submitted, which showed that Miss Lizzie Borden might have been mistaken in one important particular. The marshal informed the district attorney that the murder had occurred between 10 minutes of 11 o'clock and 13 minutes after 11 on Thursday morning. The time was as accurate as they could get it, and they had spared no pains to fix it.

The alarm had been given by Miss Lizzie Borden, the daughter of the murdered man, when she returned from the barn. At the moment of the discovery she did not know that her stepmother was also dead, though she explained afterwards that she thought her mother had left the house. It was but a short distance from the barn to the house. Nobody had been found who had seen anybody leaving the yard of the Borden house or entering it, although a number of people, who were named, were sitting by their windows close by. It was also true that nobody had seen Miss Borden enter or leave the barn. She had explained that she went to the stable to procure some lead for a fish line, which she was going to use at Marion. Here

There Was a Stumbling Block

which puzzled the district attorney and his assistants. On the day of the murder Miss Lizzie had explained that she went to the loft of the barn for the lead and an officer who was examining the premises also went to the loft. It was covered with dust and there were no tracks to prove that any person had been there for weeks. He took particular notice of the fact and reported back that he had walked about on the dust-covered floor on purpose to discover whether or not his own feet left any tracks. He said that they did and thought it singular anybody could have visited the floor a short time before him and make no impression on the dust. The lower floor of the stable told no such tale as it was evident that it had been used more frequently and the dust had not accumulated there. The conclusion reached was that in the excitement incident to the awful discovery, Miss Borden had forgotten just where she went for the lead. When she found her father lying on the lounge, she ran to the stairs and ascended three or four steps to call Maggie. Maggie is the name by which Bridget Sullivan was called by members of the family. She did not call for her stepmother, because, as she stated afterward, she did not think she was in. Then came the

History of the Mysterious Letter.

Miss Lizzie had said that on the morning of the tragedy her step-mother received a letter asking her to visit a sick friend. She knew that at about 9 o'clock her stepmother went upstairs to put shams on the pillows, and she did not see her again. It was that letter which led her to believe that her step-mother had gone out. Here was stumbling block number two. The officers had searched all over the house for that letter, the marshal said, but had failed to find any trace of it. Miss Lizzie had feared that it had been burned in the kitchen stove.

The marshal's men had found other letters and fragments of letters in the waste paper basket and had put them together piece by piece. The one letter that was wanted had not been found. It was considered singular that with all the furor that has been raised over this note, the woman who wrote it has not come forward before this and cleared up the mystery. It is also strange that the boy who delivered the note has not made himself known. It is believed that every boy in town old enough to do an errand

INFANT FEEDING.

Its Influence Upon Life During August.

Causes and Prevention of the Fearful Cholera Infantum.

Nearly Eighty Per Cent. of Babies Dying From Faulty Nutrition.

No Summer in a long while has seen so many deaths from cholera infantum in this and other states.

Fresh air funds and excursions by the score do not seem to mitigate the evil.

It is the little children and the babies, in city and country, whom this hot weather carries off so suddenly.

In New York city the number of deaths of little children for the last several weeks has equalled the number of births. In one week the Bureau of Vital Statistics in that city recorded 1336 deaths, an increase of more than a third over the average number, and 900 were of children under five years. From other cities and the towns where mortality returns are kept there come similar reports.

And it is all because mothers, through ignorance or carelessness, or both, do not keep the little weaklings properly fed.

Out of 1117 deaths investigated in New York State, 79 per cent. occurred in children affected with disease arising from defective or faulty nutrition!

It was found that children who got sufficient and healthful breast milk, or, failing in that, were fed upon lactated food, which is the best known substitute for pure mother's milk—it was found that instances of cholera infantum in these cases were so extremely rare that it could be emphatically said that improper feeding was principally the direct and partly the co-operative cause of the great mortality.

Lactated food is beyond question the safest and the most nourishing food for infants next to pure mother's milk, and should be used whenever the mother begins to bring up her child "by hand." It contains the same ingredeints as mother's milk, and is as pure and healthful as the air among the Vermont hills, where it is made. It may be bought of any reliable druggist, and is as economical as it is good. For 25 cents a package may be bought sufficient to make 10 pints of nourishing food, and a package that sells for a dollar contains enough for 150 meals.

The greatest care should be taken with the baby this month, and the infant's food calls for the most attention.

has visited the house since the tragedy, but the particular boy has kept in the background.

It is presumed that Mrs. Borden's correspondent feared the notoriety which would come to her, if she disclosed her identity, but it is unfortunate that she should allow any such scruples to overcome what ought to be a desire to assist in every way possible in unravelling the knot.

The marshal, medical examiner and mayor then carefully rehearsed, step by step, the summoning of Dr. Bowen, who was not at home when the murder was committed, and his

Ghastly Discovery on the Second Floor.

No theory other than that Mrs. Borden was murdered first was entertained, and Mayor Coughlin was positive that the murderer had shut the door after the deed had been accomplished. Miss Lizzie Borden's demeanor during the many interviews which the police have had with her was described at length, and the story of John W. Morse's whereabouts was retold.

When the marshal and others left the district attorney they went to the central station. On their return they had another bundle of papers, said to have been warrants, but on that point nobody was positive, as the authorities refused to state what their grand had been.

No One Jumped the Fence.

Another clew has been effectually disposed of. The case of the mysterious stranger who, it was alleged, was seen by the French boy to jump over the fence in the rear of the Borden place about the hour of the tragedy has received thorough investigation and has now been effectually disproved. Adjoining the yard of the Borden place is the house occupied by Dr. Chagnon. On the evening in question the physician was unexpectedly summoned away and asked Dr. Collet, as a favor, he would allow the latter's little son to attend to the telephone during Dr. Chagnon's absence. The boy was absent, but found Dr. Collet sent his daughter to Dr. Chagnon's residence, but upon her arrival the doctor had departed and the office was locked. The little girl decided to await the arrival of some one and sat down in the yard for that purpose. The little girl remained in the yard adjoining the Borden place. She was there at the time it was alleged the unknown man jumped the fence, and she declares that she saw no one attempt anything of the kind. The fact that there was a considerable extent of barbed wire along the top of the fence substantiates the girl's story.

Cruel and Unmanly.

The Boston *Record* says:

The *Record* wishes most earnestly to protest against one feature of this terrible mystery in Fall River, and that is the treatment accorded to the daughters of Mr. and Mrs. Borden. It is cruel, unmanly, almost passing beyond the bounds of law. Grant what you will, the uttermost measure regarding the murder, and there is not one thing affecting either daughter save the black mists of eager suspicion.

Until there is at least one piece of direct evidence connecting them with the crime, it should be the part of man and woman alike to avoid all innuendo—to insist that to treat them in any way as accused of crime is brutal, nothing short of it. Step into the place for a moment, if your imagination can compass the task—if any one who has suddenly found father and mother butchered in cold blood, at midday, and a few hours later a whole city morbidly discussing the dreadful crime in every light. The answering flow of feeling is plea enough for the shielding of the daughters of the Borden household at this time.

We say this more plainly now because we seem to find even officials in Fall River talking of the case in such false tones and looking at it in such a false light. It is not difficult to see how the thoughtless crowd of morbid neighbors and bystanders might allow themselves to be led gradually to look upon the household as practically accused of the crime. But it is strange to hear the head of the municipal government talking as he is reported in to-day's *Journal*:

"But, Mr. Mayor, what sticks me is this," said the *Journal* reporter. "How could a woman commit such a horrible deed as this, strike these blows with a brutality amounting to frenzy, with all this blood before her, and yet show no change in her ordinary demeanor, and move around as calmly as the most innocent person in the world? I can't reconcile that with guilt."

"Well, Lizzie Borden is not an emotional girl," replied the mayor. "She is not an excitable one. That, unquestionably, is her nature. She does not tell what she thinks, she does not show what she feels. Her manner is cold, at times absolutely frigid."

When the mayor of the city takes the lead in regarding a woman guilty until proved innocent, instead of holding the public quietly and sternly at arm's length, insisting her innocent until proved guilty, it is not strange that the tide of sentiment in the hearts and minds of many another should be set against her. In the name of all that is decent and civilized and womanly this daughter of a murdered father should be accorded treatment due to her place in her own family and in the world.

Analysis of Stomachs.

Prof. Woods was seen at the Harvard Medical School by a Boston *Journal* reporter yesterday, and he stated emphatically, when approached on the subject of the analysis of the stomachs submitted by the Fall River police, that he had nothing to say, and would say nothing regarding the analysis in question. But from a remark dropped, it is inferred that the professor has not finished his analysis, but that the work will be completed by Wednesday evening.

PLYMOUTH & MIDDLEBORO RAILROAD INSPECTED—The county commissioners and selectmen of Plymouth, Carver and Middleboro, accompanied by President Shumway and directors and stockholders of the Plymouth & Middleboro Railroad, made their official viewing of that road yesterday. The party left Plymouth at 11.35 a. m. on an observation car, and the run was made to Middleboro in an hour, some stops being made. On its return trip the party made a careful inspection of all bridges and changes in highways caused by avoidance of grade crossings. The inspection was continued through to Plymouth, and the train was the first one over the road to run into Plymouth station. Division Superintendent E. G. Allen of the Old Colony Railroad accompanied the party to Middleboro, returning to Boston from that point.

The road is not entirely ballasted yet, and considerable work in that direction remains to be done before it is opened for traffic.

THEY SAW THE WHALE.—The Erie (Pa.) *Herald* of Aug. 3 says of the visit of Sir Knights Bradford L. Church and William H. Heap to that city:

Among the Knights Templars on their way to Denver who passed through Erie lately were two from New Bedford, Mass., which is an old whaling town. They wore little gold whales on their badges, which they proudly showed to the brethren whose hospitality they enjoyed here. Finally they were asked whether they had ever seen a real whale, and although hailing from a whaling town had to confess that they never saw one of those sea monsters. Mr. W. C. Shaw promptly took the visitors that delight. Erie wasn't a whaling city, we had a whale in our midst. The Erie brethren took the New Bedford brethren to the Public Dock, where the whale was on exhibition, and what the Knights Templars from the old Bay State saw and smelled there for 10 cents apiece they will never forget or forgive.

PASSED THE EXAMINATION—The following passed the civil service examination for clerkships: Nellie B. Crapo, Agnes G. Reilly, Percy E. S. Birley, Mary E. Holden, Lydia M. Hunt, Charles A. Coombs, Annie W. Ellis, Mary J. Raymond, Frederick G. Bowman and Gertie E. Tripp.

COMPLAINTS have been made to the Old Colony officials that newsboys on the trains have charged more than the regular price for papers. Action has been taken on the grievance and it is not likely that the travelling public will have cause to find fault on that score in the future.

BOARD OF PUBLIC WORKS.

Mayor Ashley Wishes to Open the North End Park on Labor Day.

The Board of Public Works held its regular meeting last evening. Mayor Ashley presided and the full board was present. Superintendent Drake was elected clerk pro tem.

Abbott P. Smith appeared before the board with a proposition with relation to building over a mile of sewers. Mr. Smith represents the purchasers of the large tract of land south of Cove street and west of East French avenue, including the Ashley farm and Salisbury and Viall estate. Through this property seven 50-foot streets have been extended running south from Cove street to a street which will run westerly from East French avenue. Mr. Smith proposes to build sewers throughout the length of these streets, a distance of about 5600 feet, and he offers to pay the cost of laying them an average depth of seven feet. Mr. Smith said that 75 dwelling-houses would be built here within a year. This depth would be sufficient for his purposes, but the board could build them lower if it chose to pay the additional cost.

Superintendent Drake said that an average depth of about eight feet would be all that would ever be required. He estimated the digging at about 40 cents a linear foot for a sewer seven feet deep. Mr. Smith said he could get it done for 30 cents.

It was finally decided to instruct Mr. Drake to get the necessary levels and a decision would be reached later. The Board seemed disposed to accept the proposition.

The matter of fixing the Summer street car tracks was discussed, and Mr. Smith said that it was his judgment that after Oct. 1 the company would be willing to drop its tracks if such a grade as might be decided upon by the Board.

James M. Murkland appeared asking leave to obstruct the sidewalk on all four sides of the new Kempton street school-house, and he asked for a part of the street on Kempton and High streets.

It was finally decided that Mr. Murkland might obstruct the sidewalk and four feet of the street on Kempton street and the sidewalk on Foster and High streets, but the entire sidewalk on Pleasant street must be kept clear.

Mayor Ashley said there must be no fences, and this was the understanding.

Mr. Rotch said the Board should prohibit advertising on fences on the sidewalks, but where the fences were allowed, and Mr. Tripp said he understood that this was to be the rule in the future.

A petition of Leonard Keene, Jr., and seven others for a concrete sidewalk, paved gutters and curbing on Chestnut street between Parker and Pope streets, was placed on the visiting list.

A petition of Manuel Enos and two others asking that a curbing be laid on the south side of Allen street, between Borden and Ward streets, was referred to the visiting list.

A communication was received from C. Mialloux, calling the attention of the Board to the dangerous condition of the street in front of his house on the south side of Nelson street. It was decided to grade the street.

An application of the New Bedford Gas & Edison Light Co. for a location for poles on County street, one at the foot of Parker street and one at the southwest corner of Linden, was granted.

A communication was received from Mrs. M. E. Chase of Chicago and Mrs. I. B. Jenney declaring a tree on the east side of North Oak street a nuisance and a great detriment to the Jenney house, causing the chimney of the latter "to smoke to such an extent that some days no fire can be sustained for cooking purposes."

It was stated that North Oak street had never been accepted, and the city has nothing to do with it. The shutters can remove the trees if they choose.

Applications of F. B. Hathaway for leave to move a dwelling house 13 by 16 feet with 12 feet posts from the west side of Crapo street, through Rivet and Dartmouth streets, to the town of Dartmouth, and also for leave to move the pavilion at the Cove to the north side of Cove road, 100 feet west of County street, were granted.

Applications of George F. Bartlett for leave to move a dwelling house 39 by 31 feet with 20 feet posts from the east to the west side of Howard street, and a barn 30 by 30 feet with 20 feet feet posts from the east to the west side of Belleville avenue, were granted.

An application of Henry B. Worth for leave to maintain a hitching post at 55 Washington street was granted.

Applications of the Boston Beef Co. and W. H. Lefort to maintain signs were received. The latter application was granted.

The former request was for leave to maintain a canvas sign. It was decided to request a more specific description of the style of sign.

The labor pay roll for week ending July 30 was approved as follows:

Street department,	$2155.17
Grape street sewer extension,	954.94
North Front street sewer,	256.95
Coggeshall street sewer,	189.64
Public works permanent improvements,	98.44
General sewers,	86.56
Engineering department,	55.58
Beetle and Howard street sewer,	91.30
Parks and squares,	34.00
New Bedford & Fairhaven bridge,	21.29
Cove road sewer,	1.22
Total,	$3899.63

With relation to the Butler street widening Superintendent Drake said that Messrs. Thornton, Chace and Leonard were willing to give the five feet, but the others objected. It was decided to do nothing further about it, the members of the Board feeling that the widening would be of more benefit to the abutters than the city as there will be no lack of 50-foot streets in this locality.

It was voted to move the walls belonging to James B. Hamblin, in the line of Belleville road, on to his lot.

Superintendent Drake said that he thought a hoisting engine to remove rock from the extension of the Grape street sewer, would pay for itself on this piece of work alone. The trenches are 27 feet in depth at some points and about 20 feet in depth for a distance of 700 or 800 feet. The rock runs from six to 17 feet in thickness and a dozen men are required on the banks to hoist the stone. The cost of the hoisting engine is about $1000 and one man can run it. It was voted to buy a hoisting engine and charge it to the Grape street sewer account.

The repairing of Park Place came up. It was stated that the street was a private way and the matter was laid on the table.

It was decided to pave the brow to the police stable, if it is desired.

It was voted to give a hearing next Monday evening on the question of building sewers in First street, from Blackmer to Delano and in Cove street, from Water to Margin street.

Hearings on the layout of an extension of Division street, from Division to Cove street and on the layout of Jouvett street, from County to Crapo street were granted for Monday, Aug. 22, at 3.30 and 3.45 p. m., respectively.

Curbing was ordered as follows: West side of Crapo street, from Rockland street southerly about 200 feet; west side of Liberty street, from Court to Kempton; east side of Chestnut street, from Willis to Parker; east side of State street, from Austin to Linden; east side of County street, from Linden to Cedar; east side of Weld street, from Reynolds to Linden; west side of State street, from Linden to Weld; both sides of Clark street, from Purchase to State; south side of Cedar Grove street, from Purchase to County. The subject of ordering additional curbing was then discussed.

Mayor Ashley suggested that a fitting day

---

in his mind for formally opening the North End park was on Labor Day, which occurs on Sept. 5th. He asked the board to take the suggestion into consideration.

A. P. Smith, who was present, remarked that, if it was a matter which the board considered important, it might be taken into consideration that the street railway company would be unable to run cars to the park on this day in numbers sufficient to accommodate the crowds. The throng of people who ride on Labor Day is so great that they can scarcely be accommodated on the regular lines.

Action will be taken next Monday evening.

THE MORGAN CUPS.

Constellation and Katrina Winners in the Run to Marblehead.

MARBLEHEAD, Aug. 9.—Five years ago the New York Yacht Club made Marblehead the terminus of its annual cruise, and that experience was decidedly unpleasant, but the success of this run yesterday makes a Marblehead run and terminus more likely to be a fixture. The run was a very successful one. As the boats are series of buoys which indent the eastern shore of Massachusetts, they struck surges which severely tested all weak points in their rigging as they sped along with scuppers under. The Constellation's speed was wonderful, and the steam yacht which overtook her might well feel proud of her performance, which breaks the record of the old New York sloop Fleet Wing for the 103-mile run to Marblehead from Vineyard Haven by two hours and 13 minutes.

The Clara protested the Merlin for crossing her and putting her out of the course at the start, and Wasp has protested Katrina for fouling her with her spinnaker boom. These protests do not affect winners, however, of the Morgan cups, which are the Constellation and Katrina. For the squadron run cups the winners are Constellation, Merlin, Iroquois, Quickstep, Katrina, Clara, Walkover, Wasp. The keel schooner special cup was won by the old schooner Dauntless.

The Vamoose, press boat, left Cottage City after the fleet at 8.23 a. m., arriving at 3.15 p. m. Her performance is a capper for the Norwood's people to consider, and the steam yachtsmen of the New York Yacht Club who favored Marblehead's ability to get to Marblehead, can now appreciate her seaworthy ability. She will return Thursday to Newport, making the run in one day.

The races to-morrow for cups offered by Commodore Gerry will be sailed off Marblehead, without the time limit, under the racing rules and time allowance of the New York Yacht Club. Owners of yachts of the New York and Eastern Yacht Clubs which have not hauled out to clean since the commencement of the cruise. The preparatory signal will be made at 10.45 a. m., wind and weather permitting. The Ituna will be the committee boat, and the start and finish will be between the Ituna and the beacon at Halfway rock. Should the race be postponed, it will be sailed on the following day if possible.

New Bedford Mills.

[From the Fall River *Herald*.]

The *Herald* proposes to keep standing a line to the effect that "another new mill is to be built in New Bedford." Nearly every week lately the announcement has appeared of additions to the manufacturing interests of the Whaling City. In diversity it is far in advance of Fall River, and the breach is widening. If the rate of progression continues, although considerably in the rear just now, it will not be long before the pre-eminence of this city in the cotton manufacturing world is shared with or resigned to New Bedford. A great deal of the money is contributed by outsiders, so that the dividends will not be disbursed where they are declared. One suggestive feature of the New Bedford enterprise is the avoidance of print cloths. Just now, through some providential happening, the call for that fabric is unusually brisk, but generally the market is so unstable as to be in a congested state most of the time. It is an unwise business policy which causes mill men to produce goods for which there is little or no demand, and it is a mark of foresight to turn looms to the production of textiles of more popular makes than print cloths have proved to be of late years. If the New Bedford manufacturers would not adjust wages by the print cloth standard, which is as justly applicable to factories engaged in fancies as it is to silk establishments, there would not be as much concern felt by the workers over the prices of print cloths in this city. The same unjust system operates here, print cloths serving as the trade barometer and all classes of weavers suffering as well as those who have a direct interest in whether the contracts are large or small at remunerative prices. We suppose it will be just as useless to tell capitalists who have projects in hand or in contemplation in New Bedford, as it was in Fall River, that a cow will not always give milk.

ASSONET.

The gun shop of N. R. Davis & Sons will shut down on the 13th for two weeks' vacation.

A horse owned by Assonet parties was run to death by a farm hand, dying a few moments after arriving home from Taunton.

A Harrison and Reid flag was flung to the breeze on the 6th by George B. Cudworth, chairman of the Republican committee.

N. R. Davis has just finished his new side lock gun and forwarded 100 to St. Louis to parties for inspection. It is a great improvement on the hammerless.

TIVERTON.

This afternoon and evening the ladies of the Central Baptist church of Tiverton are to hold a lawn party and fair on the grounds of Mrs. Philip S. Grinnell. Music will be furnished by the Tiverton National band.

The event of the week will be the grand illumination next Thursday evening. It is expected that a large number will go down from Fall River to witness the display.

Miss Canning was surprised at her home in North Tiverton Friday night and presented with a gold locket and chain.

Medical Testimony.

W. Thornton Parker, M. D., Recorder, Associate Acting Assistant Surgeons of the U. S. Army, writes:

"SALEM, Mass., March 22, 1891.

"When at Stuttgart, Germany, during the winter of 1881-82; I was suffering from a severe attack of bronchitis, which seemed to threaten pneumonia. I met, at the Hotel Marquardt, Commander Beardslee, of the United States Navy, in speaking of my sickness, he remarked: 'Doctor, you can cure that chest trouble of yours by using an ALLCOCK'S POROUS PLASTER.' 'That may be true,' I answered, 'but where can I get the plaster?' 'Anywhere in the civilized world, and surely here in Stuttgart. Whenever I have a cold, I always use one and find relief.' I sent to the drug store for the plaster, and it did all that my friend had promised. Ever since then I have used it whenever suffering from a cold, and I have many times prescribed it for patients.

"The ALLCOCK'S PLASTER is the best to be had, and has saved many from severe illness, and undoubtedly, if used promptly, will save many valuable lives. Whenever one has a severe cold they should put on an ALLCOCK'S PLASTER as soon as possible. It should be placed across the chest, the upper margin just below the neck; some hot beef tea, or milk, will aid in the treatment.

"This is not a patent remedy in the ordinary sense of that term, but a standard preparation of value. The government supplies for the United States army and Indian Hospital Stores contain ALLCOCK'S PLASTERS, and the medical profession throughout the world are well aware of their reliability and excellence. I shall always recommend it, not only to break up colds, but as useful in allaying pains in the chest and in the back. It is a preparation worthy of general confidence."

COPYRIGHT 1892.

INTO A COCKED HAT.

That is just what has happened to the prices of our Spring Suits; they have been knocked into a Cocked Hat. Every time there is a big tumble something is damaged; in this case it is the price not the goods—they are just as superior in quality as they were before the tumble.

It is ridiculously easy to let good things escape you; it is not ridiculously easy to coax them back again.

THE MID-SUMMER SALE

is the buyer's opportunity. The early bird catches the worm, the wide-awake and early buyer catches the cream. Every day lessens the material for choice; just now about your choice yo can be particularly choice.

M. C. SWIFT & SON,

153, 157 and 159 Union Street,

NEW BEDFORD, - - - MASS.

ESTABLISHED 1884.

NEW BEDFORD STEAM CARPET BEATING WORKS.

Cor. North Water and North Sts.

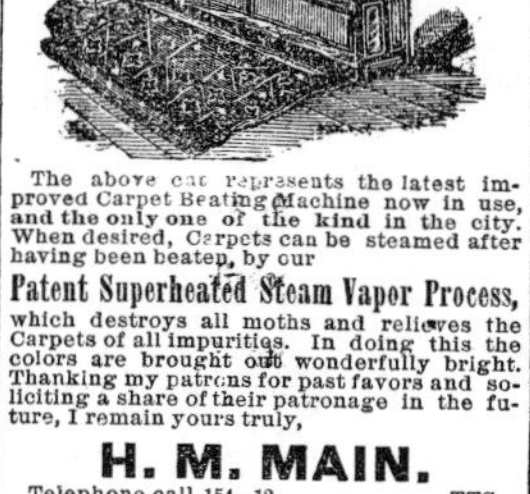

The above cut represents the latest improved Carpet Beating Machine now in use, and the only one of the kind in the city. When desired, Carpets can be steamed after having been beaten, by our

Patent Superheated Steam Vapor Process,

which destroys all moths and relieves the Carpets of all impurities. In doing this the colors are brought out wonderfully bright. Thanking my patrons for past favors and soliciting a share of their patronage in the future, I remain yours truly,

H. M. MAIN.

Telephone call 154—18. TTS

GEORGE C. BLISS,

FLORIST.

34 Arnold Street,

CORNER COTTAGE.

TELEPHONE, DAY OR NIGHT.

LINEN PAPER AND ENVELOPES.
Large Variety and Low Prices
—AT THE—
STANDARD OFFICE.

C. W. HASKINS,

Having replenished his stock by liberal purchases of new goods, offers a choice selection of Diamonds, Watches, Fine Jewelry, Optical Goods, &c. The display of Sterling Silver Table Ware and Novelties is very attractive.

Attention is invited to a large collection of Souvenir Spoons, especially some in fine Enamel and Gold from various European countries.

Fine Watch and Clock Repairing done by competent and careful workmen and fully warranted

—AT—

C. W. HASKINS',

No. 20 Purchase Street.

NATURAL HISTORY CAMP FOR BOYS. LAKE QUINSIGAMOND, WORCESTER, MASS.
First Term begins July 6th; second Term Aug. 3d; but campers can join at any time. Athletic Sports, Military Drill, Hunting, Fishing, Swimming, Boating, etc. A first class good time at moderate expense. For Prospectus, address W. H. RAYMENTON, Worcester, Mass. jy9-TTSimo

SEE NEW STYLES OF
Ball & Dance Cards
—AT THE—
STANDARD JOB ROOMS.

FINANCIAL.

SANFORD & KELLEY.

GARDNER T. SANFORD, } **Bankers.**
CHARLES S. KELLEY,

Members Boston Stock Exchange.

47 North Water St., New Bedford.

STOCKS AND BONDS BOUGHT AND SOLD ON COMMISSION

At the New York and Boston Stock Boards.

CONSERVATIVE & PROFITABLE INVESTMENTS FOR TRUST FUNDS.

New Bedford Manufacturing Stocks have a first-class record as dividend payers, and we always have some on hand to offer.

Sole Agents for the sale in this city of the 6 per cent. Guaranteed Mortgages of the Lombard Investment Co.

Auction Sale of Stocks and Bonds WEDNESDAYS and SATURDAYS, at 10 45 A. M.

ORDERS SOLICITED.

SMITH, HOYT & CO.,

Bankers and Stock Brokers,

25 Congress St., Boston, Mass.

STOCKS, Bonds, Grain and Oil bought and sold for cash or carried on moderate margin. Some new ideas will be found in our circular, which are greatly to the advantage of our customers. Buying and selling the same stock is one of them. Inquiries given careful attention. Send for circular. TT&8-1m

---

T. E. BOWMAN & CO.,

Topeka, Kansas,

NEGOTIATORS OF

Conservative Mortgage Loans in Eastern Kansas.

$2,500,000 LOANED without loss to any investor, and have never yet had to foreclose a farm loan in these cotton counties. Write us for list of investments. s29

MONEY TO LOAN!

IN large or small amounts at low rates and easy terms on Real Estate, Pianos, Organs, Horses, Carriages, &c., which can remain in possession of the owners. Loans taken from 30 days to 5 years. All business strictly confidential. Office Hours 8 to 12 A. M., and 1 to 6. 34 North Second St., (up one flight) opposite Post Office. H. F. DAMON, sep17-TT86ptf

GEORGE LEVY, North End Pawn Broker.

Cash advanced on Real or Personal Property. All business private. au13-1m

---

SECOND EDITION.

HOME MATTERS.

REAL ESTATE SALES.—Standish Bourne sold at auction yesterday afternoon the three story cottage and 15,000 square feet of land situated south of King Philip street and west of Copicut street to Charles W. Clifford of this city for $7000.

M. E. Smith has sold for Albert Cassidy to a syndicate of well-known New Bedford capitalists a tract of land on the corner of Winterville street and Rockdale avenue, containing 1799.17 rods. The terms were strictly private, but a well-informed real estate agent says that at the price paid a profit of at least $20,000 ought to be realized within the next 18 months.

M. E. Smith has sold for a syndicate three lots of land on the north side of Perry street containing 55.8 rods to Isaac Greenup.

H. A. Leonard has sold for Stephen A. Brownell to Jabez A. Gorham 9.32 rods of land on the west side of Brownell street, south of Union street. Also 18.64 rods on the east side of Sisson street, south of Union street.

T. F. Healey has sold for Andrew J. Nichols to John Crompton a tract of land, containing 384 rods, on the north side of Durfee street, west of Shawmut avenue.

Cyrille F. Lussier has sold to Francisca M. Pereira, a lot of land on the south side of Butler street.

Sarah Donaghy has sold to Francisco Manoel Terziera a lot of land on Bethel street.

Albert Cassidy has sold to Frederick S. Fuller, trustee, 1739.07 rods of land on Rockdale avenue. The price is said to have been $4400.

Sarah L. Gardiner and George A. Gardiner of Fall River have sold to Daniel and Ann Donnelly of Tiverton, 40 rods of land, with buildings, being lot No. 2 of section H on the Indian Grove plan, so-called. Annie B. Taylor and J. Taylor of Taunton have quitclaimed to Richard Robinson a house lot near the station.

Stephen A. Brownell has sold to Jabez A. Gorham 9.32 rods land west side of Brownell street.

Bethuel Penniman and others have sold to Mary E. Donovan two lots of land, one containing 21.58 and the other 49.32 rods, south side of Clark street; 46.37 rods land east side of Reynolds street; 26.45 rods land east side of Myrtle street.

Gilbert Allen has sold to John Whitehead 13.355 rods land corner of Belleville avenue and contemplated Sylvia street.

Frank W. Dean has sold to John Whitehead 10.54 rods land north side of Dean street near Belleville avenue.

James Brown has sold to John Whitehead 14½ rods land north side of Phillips avenue.

James Brown has sold to John B. Whitehead 30.78 rods land corner of Phillips and Belleville avenue.

George G. Gifford has sold to Edwin Jones 55.36 rods land west side of the Middle Point road and 27.68 rods of land south side of Woodlawn avenue.

BUILDING NOTES.—A three-story house, 52 by 2 feet in area, is building on the west side of Belleville avenue, opposite the Pierce mill, for Ezra Therrien. The carpenter work is done by Peter Drants, and Joe Trudds is the mason.

On the east side of Belleville avenue, north of the Pierce mill, a two and a half story house is building for Owen McQuade. It is 17 by 40 feet in area. Mr. Cilibar is the mason and Joe Legree the carpenter. On the next lot north a house of the same size is building for Barney McQuade, father of Owen.

On the north side of Dean street a two and a half story house is building for Thomas Cuddy. Manuel Sylvia is the contractor.

On Front street, north of Dean, a two-story house is building for Thomas Whitton. Frederick Hazard is the carpenter and Timothy Crowe the mason.

Eliza Cogan has petitioned for leave to erect an addition to house on the southeast corner of North and Hill streets. It is to be 12 by 19 feet, 20 feet posts.

MARRIED.

In Craigville, 7th inst., Wm. A. Parker, of North Harwich, to Mamie T. Holway, of West Barnstable.

In Chatham, 4th inst., Henry Percy Jones, of Cleveland, to Miss Mamie Judson Rogers, of Chatham.

DEATHS.

In Eastham, 25th ult., Irwin Brewer, 22.

MARINE INTELLIGENCE.

Ar at New York 8th, sch B L Sherman, Hallett, Ambor for Boston.

Passed through Hell Gate 8th, schs Mary B Wellington, Crosby, Rondout for Boston; Oliver Ames, Nickerson, Philadelphia for New Haven.

Ar at Philadelphia 8th, schs Lizzie H Patrick, Meyers, hence; Wm R Huston,Coleman, Fall River. Cld, sch Thos F Pollard, Jarman, this port.

Cld at Baltimore 8th,sch Benj F Poole,Ross, Providence.

Ar at Newport News 8th, schs Job H Jackson, Allyn's Point; W H Oler, Richmond. Sld, sch C A White, Boston.

Cld at Savannah 8th,steamer City of Macon, Lewis,Boston.

FINANCIAL.

Weak Opening Followed by a Rally—Atchison Sells Up to 39, Burlington & Quincy to 101 1-2—Sugar Active and Strong— Money Steady—Loans at Clearing This Morning All at 4 Per Cent.—Seven Months' Products of the Ontario and Daly Mines—Latest News on the Crops— C. B. & Q. to Expend Large Sums in Making Improvements, &c.—Railroad Reports—Gossip of the Day.

TUESDAY, Aug. 9.

Stocks to-day have been both weak and strong, at noon the strength being the most prominent. Chief fluctuations have been in Atchison and in C. B. & Q. Sugar and General Electric have been well supported. The crop reports have been more favorable to-day.

The local money market holds its own without change. Rates 5 to 6 per cent.

The Boston money market is again dull. Wool people are borrowing largely and except from this source there is no important demand. At clearing this morning loans were all made at 4 per cent. $19,098.50 funds sold at 15 and 17 cents discount.

Money holds quiet and easy in New York to-day.

Sterling exchange rates $4.87½ and 4.89.

Bonds steady.

Wall street gossip this morning said: "The bears are selling the market on corn crop prospects. They will probably bring about lower figures, although thus far little long stock has been forced out and short interest is already considerable. Foreigners appear unable or unwilling to help us bull the market. London 1½ to ½ below us.

The New York market opened ¾ lower in sympathy with London, and for the first hour prices continued to decline. Then a rally started in C. B. & Q., which carried the price up to 101½. Omaha was active and firm at 54½. In the early afternoon the market was dull and steady. Atchison 39, C. B. & Q. 101½, St. Paul 82½.

The market at 2 o'clock was firm. B. & Q. 101½.

Atchison and C. B. & Q. monopolized the trading in the Boston market this morning. Atchison opened at 38½ and touched 39. C. B. & Q. opened at 101, and gained ¾. Boston & Maine sold at 181, advanced to 182, and reacted to 181 again. Sugar was active at 107½. Tamarack 185. Calumet 280. In the early afternoon the market was steady, with prices firm.

At 2 o'clock the market was strong except for Boston & Maine which declined to 180½. Sales to noon in Boston to-day were, bonds $68,500 and 11,790 shares of stock.

Electric has sold to-day at 114½ to 115½, a slight reaction from yesterday.

The Boston bank statement shows a decrease in reserve of $578,200.

The bull movement in General Electric securities continues, and all the good things which the situation suggests as a possibility are being said in their favor. For the moment the fight to convert the bonds into stock at 120 is being heralded as a new and important discovery, and the possibility that this privilege may not apply to the next issue of bonds is being used to boom the present issue.

Eastbound shipments last week 72,745 tons, against 44,614 same week last year.

Silver offered to the government yesterday amounted to 918,000 ounces. The amount purchased was 581,000 ounces at $4.48.

Grain cars received in Chicago yesterday were 701 cars wheat, 429 cars corn, 277 cars oats.

It is stated from Chicago that the C. B. & Q. intends to spend from $10,000,000 to $12,000,000 on extensions and equipments this year in preparation for expected increase of business. A new bridge and enlarged terminal facilities at St. Louis will cost $1,600,000; other new bridges of iron are building, the Chicago freight house is to be enlarged at an expense of $100,000 and important extensions are building in Wyoming. The contract for the new building includes 50 locomotives and 2314 cars of various kinds.

A prominent New York banking house writes:

We are in receipt of a telegram from a friend in ours, a reliable and experienced man, saying that all reports about damage to crops along the Atchison lines are absolutely false. Crops are, on the contrary, in superb condition and Atchison is, from present outlook, about to have a great year.

A Kansas City special also says:

The corn crop along the Atchison's line between Chicago and Kansas City is looking finely. It is well advanced and in good shape every way. People here well informed say that the corn crop of Kansas and Nebraska is now likely to be considerably ahead of last year's, especially in the eastern and middle counties. The farmers are all enthusiastic over the outlook and say that all the bad reports sent east originate in Chicago and are intended wholly for the effect on the market.

Tamarack product for July was 920 tons, a decrease of 15 tons. Osceola product for the same time was 356 tons, an increase of $1 ton.

The Ontario product for the past seven months has been as follows:

	Silver, ozs.	Ore Value.
January	69,885.55	$85,734.88
February	64,112.61	44,531.00
March	77,850.84	10,364.86
April	76,635.50	24,794.54
May	63,551.71	43,456.51
June	66,963.66	51,070.66
July	33,048.00	55,234.80
Totals	2,669,605.07	$2,683,045.00

The usual dividend was paid at the close of each month of 50 cents per share, or $75,000 monthly, being $525,000 for 1892 thus far. The dividend paid July 30th was dividend No. 194, and it brought the total amount of dividends paid July 30th to this amount of $12,950,000. Atchison earnings move in detail than we were able to give them yesterday follow:

	TOTAL ALL LINES.		
	1892.	1891.	Inc.
Fourth July,	1,365,522	$1,521,964	$43,258
July,	3,989,479	3,827,447	143,023
Mileage,	9,344	9,328	16
*Decrease.			

Flint & Pere Marquette's June statement of gross and net earnings follows:

	1892.	1891.	Inc.
June.			
Earnings,	$213,069	$209,074	$8,996
Expenses,	151,990	161,401	*9,411
Net,	$60,079	$57,672	$2,497
Charges,	49,818	48,456	1,362
Surplus,	$10,230	$9,216	$1,044
Since Jan. 1.			
Earnings,	$1,467,001	$1,461,083	$5,912
Expenses,	1,049,036	1,083,042	*39,945
Net,	$417,964	$372,043	$45,858
Charges,	297,344	282,743	14,600
Surplus,	$120,560	$89,302	$31,258
*Decrease.			

Profit and loss from July, 1892, $1,324,788.

	1892.	1891.	Inc.
July, gross,	$215,101	$224,812	*$9,711
Since Jan. 1,	1,582,102	1,635,900	*3,798
Mileage,	630	627	3
*Decrease.			

The product of the Ontario for the week was in bullion, 33,186.40 ounces; ore sold, $35,- 932.53.

The output of the Daly for the seven months of 1892 has been as follows:

Month.	Sulphides.	Bullion, ozs.	Ore, val.
January.			$28,887.48
February,		51,146	27,250.33
March,	$67,588.47	47,689	27,874.88
April,		47,150	20,907.13
May,		48,157	20,415.60
June,		57,035	24,664.06
July,	28,663.94	33,459	30,955.83
Totals,	$96,252.41	264,506	$178,974.31
*Including $19,097.15 in ore sold, $19,098.50.			

The Daly paid its regular dividend at the close of each month, 25 cents per share, $37,- 500 monthly, or $262,500 for the seven months. The July dividend was No. 65, and brought the total of Daly dividends paid to $2,475,- 000.

The Daly output for the week was in bullion, 9238.92 ounces; ore sold, $19,098.50.

Copper remains dull at $44⅝ for spot and £45⅝ for futures in London. The New York market is heavy at 11.65c. sales and asked, with casting brand at about 10.85c. The Engineering Journal says these figures are to be considered nominal, as prices are too high for home or export sales. It understands that some of the mining companies are accumulating copper, but the effect is not yet felt in the market. The visible supply of copper abroad increased 806 tons the last half of July, when a decrease had been looked for. The increase for the first half was 3270 tons, making 3070 tons for the month, and carrying the total to 59,674 tons Aug. 1. With no imports from this country the past week, the tendency to increase should be checked at least temporarily.

STOCK AND BOND MARKETS.

Bids at the close of First Board.

NEW YORK, Aug. 9.

GOVERNMENT BONDS.	
U.S. 2s, registered	100
" new 4s, registered	116
" new 4s, coupons	116
" currency 6s, 1895, (Pacifics)	*10411

RAILROADS.	
Atchison	39
Clev., Cin., Chicago & St. Louis	66¼
Chicago & Eastern Illinois	
Chicago & Eastern Illinois pref.	
Chicago, Burlington & Quincy	101¾
Delaware & Hudson	135
Delaware & Lackawanna	157¼
Erie	28⅝
Illinois Central	
Lake Shore & Michigan Southern	134¼
Louisville & Nashville	70¾
Michigan Central	
Missouri Pacific	58
New Jersey Central	137
New York Central	113¾
New York & New England	38¼
Northern Pacific	20½
Northern Pacific pref.	58¾
Chicago & Northwestern	117¾
New York Central & Hudson River	114¼
North American	
Oregon Navigation	
Oregon Improvement	
Oregon Short Line	
Philadelphia & Reading	60½
Pullman Palace Car Co.	
Chicago, Rock Island & Pacific	85½
Chicago, Milwaukee & St. Paul	82½
Chicago, Milwaukee & St. Paul pref.	
Richmond Terminal	
St. Paul & Omaha	38½
St. Paul & Omaha pref.	
Union Pacific	38½
Wabash, St. Louis & Pacific	13½
Wabash, St. Louis & Pacific pref.	25

MISCELLANEOUS.	
Ontario Silver	41
Pacific Mail Steamship Co.	
Sugar, common	107¾
Sugar, pref.	
Western Union Telegraph	97⅝
Silver Certificates	

BONDS.	BOSTON, Aug. 9.
Atchison 4s	85
Atchison Incomes	60
American Bell Telephone 7s	114
Chicago, Burlington & Northern 5s	
Chicago & West Michigan 5s	
Eastern Railroad 6s	
Illinois Steel Co. 5s	

RAILROADS.	
Atchison, Topeka & Santa Fe	38¾
Boston & Albany	205½
Boston & Lowell	182
Boston & Maine	181
Boston & Providence	
Chicago, Burlington & Quincy	101¾
Chicago & West Michigan	
Cleveland, Akron & Columbus	
Cleveland & Canton	
Flint & Pere Marquette	*79
Flint & Pere Marquette pref.	
Mexican Central	26
New York & New England	38½
New York & New England pref.	85
Old Colony	173¾
Oregon Short Line	*24¾
Pullman Palace Car	
Union Pacific	

Wisconsin Central stock list

		Last
Wisconsin Central	17¼	
West End	73	
West End pref.	*88	

MINING.	
Butte & Boston Mining Co.	8⅜
Calumet & Hecla Mining Co.	280
Centennial	12
Franklin Mining Co.	12¼
Kearsarge	12½
Napeaug	36 ⅛
Osceola Mining Co.	157
Tamarack	

MISCELLANEOUS.	
American Bell Telephone	204
Erie Telephone	58½
Mexican Telephone	1.00
New England Telephone	56½
Newport Land	
Boston Land Co.	6¼
West End Land Co.	13¾
San Diego Land Co.	
Topeka Land & Development Co.	*1
Lamson Store Service	10
Illinois Steel Co.	83½
Am. Sugar Refineries, com	107¾
Am. Sugar Refineries, pref.	115¼
Gen'l Electric	115¾
*Asked.	

FALL RIVER STOCK QUOTATIONS.

The following are the quotations of Fall River stocks to-day as reported by Sanford & Kelley, bankers and brokers and stock auctioneers:

	Par.	Bid.	Asked.	Last Sale.
American Linen Co.	$103	115	116	116
Barnaby Mfg. Co.	100	99	99	
Barnard Mfg. Co.	100	99	99	
Border City Mfg. Co.	100	149	149	137½
Bourne Mills	100	150		
Chace Mills	100	112	110	
Cornell Mills	100		87⅛	86
Crescent Mills	100		82½	80
C. Spring Bleachery	100			31
Davol Mills	100	*97	100	99
Edison Illuminating	100			118
Fall River Bleachery	100	110		
Flint Mills	100	121	122	110
Globe St. Railway Co.	100		120	
Globe Yarn Mills	100		123½	122
Granite Mills	100	34½	242½	
Hargraves Mills	100		100	100
King Philip Mills	100	123¼	125	123½
Kerr Thread Co.	100		105	103
Laurel Lake Mills	100		110	110
Massasoit Nat'l Bank	100		103	
Mechanics' Mills	100		98	98
Merchants' Mfg. Co.	100	123	125	124
Metacomet Mills	100		94	93½
Metacomet National				
National Union Bank	100		100	104½
Narragansett Mills	100		105	105
Osborn Mills	100	108½		109
Pocasset Mfg. Co.	100		104½	104½
Pocasset Nat'l Bank	100		120	
Richard Borden Mfg.	100		164	163
Robeson Mills	100	124		*121
Sagamore Mfg. Co.	100	104½	105	104½
Seaconnet Mills	100		116	116
Shove Mills	100		113	112
Slade Mills	56	58		58
Stafford Mills	100	113	114	113
Tecumseh Mills	100		112	112
Troy C. & W. Manufac-		1025	1000	
turing				
Union Mfg. Co.	100	220	220	
Wampanoag Mills	100	104	105	100
Weetamoe Mills	100	55	56	55

CALIFORNIA MINING STOCKS.

SAN FRANCISCO, Aug. 8.

The following are the official closing prices of mining stocks to-day:

Alta	1 45	Kentuck	1 45
Best & Belcher	1 45	Mexican	1 45
Chollar		Ophir	2 25
Con. Cal. & Va.	3 50	Potosi	
Crown Point		Savage	
Eureka Con.		Sierra Nevada	1 30
Gould & Curry	1 00	Union Con.	
Hale & Norcross	1 00	Utah	

NEW YORK PRODUCE MARKET.

NEW YORK, Aug. 9.

Flour sales 8500 packages; firmer and more active.

Wheat sales 915,000 bushels; large receipts and increase in amount on passage, at noon ¼ to ½ cents up and steady.

Corn sales 265,000 bushels; off early 1 cent with the West, longs realizing, better weather and increase in amount on passage. Oats sales 10,000 bushels; dull, lower and weak.

Beef dull and steady.

Pork dull.

Pork firm.

Lard quiet and lower.

Butter firm.

Cheese firmer.

Sugar (raw) firm.

Petroleum steady and dull.

Turpentine dull and easy.

Molasses dull.

Rice firm and quiet.

Freights steady and dull.

Rosin steady and dull.

Tallow firm.

PROVISIONS AND GRAIN.

CHICAGO, Aug. 9.

	Opening.	
	Lard. Wheat. Pork.	Corn. Sh't Ribs.
May		
June	79⅝	54½
July		
Aug.		
Sept.	12 12½	54½
Oct.		
Dec.	12 o'clock.	
Jan.	82	
	Closing.	
	Lard. Wheat. Pork.	Corn. Sh't Ribs.
May		
June	78¾	53½
July		
Aug.	13.10	
Sept.		
Oct.		
Dec.		
Jan.		

WEATHER INDICATIONS.

VERY SULTRY.

NEW YORK, Aug. 9.—At 8 30 a. m. the weather was cloudy, wind south, temperature 81. The Herald says: In the Middle States and New England on Wednesday fair to partly cloudy, very sultry weather will probably prevail, with slight temperature changes and local rain, and on Thursday slightly cooler, fair weather, followed by rising temperature.

LIZZIE SUMMONED.

Miss Borden Must Appear at the Inquest Before Judge Blaisdell.

[Special Dispatch.]

FALL RIVER, Aug. 9.—At 1 25 o'clock this afternoon a hand drove up to the Central Station and Marshal Hilliard and Officer Harrington entered and drove to the Borden residence on Second street. The marshal had in his possession a summons for Miss Lizzie A. Borden to appear at the inquest which is being held in the District Court room. The marshal served the summons and the hack waited at 1 50 o'clock. Lizzie, leaning on the arm of Mrs. George Brigham, appeared and got into the hack which was driven rapidly away. Several thousand persons lined the streets or chased the hack, under the impression that the young lady had been arrested. At the station house the party got out and Miss Borden was escorted to the court-room, the doors of which were immediately closed and barred.

Fought Over a Game of Cards.

NORWICH, Ct., Aug. 9.—In a fight over a game of cards in the Portuguese lodging house formerly known as the Thames Hotel, this morning, Manuel Rose shot Manuel Pochero three times—one under the eye, once in the side and once in the shoulder. Rose is locked up awaiting the issue of the results of the shooting, which are probably fatal.

The Gold Train in New York.

NEW YORK, Aug. 9.—The treasure train from San Francisco with $20,000,000 arrived here at 10 50 with everything as safe as when it started on its voyage. Along those who went to the depot was J. Lowry Bell, second assistant postmaster-general. It was said that the first delivery would be made to-morrow to the sub-treasury and bonded for the.

Baron Hirsch's Colonists Return.

BERLIN, Aug. 9.—One hundred and eighty Jewish families have returned to Bremerhaven from the Argentine Republic in a pitiable condition.

Merit Wins.

We desire to say to our citizens, that for years we have been selling Dr. King's New Discovery for Consumption, Dr. King's New Life Pills, Bucklen's Arnica Salve and Electric Bitters, and have never handled remedies that sell as well, or that have given such universal satisfaction. We do not hesitate to guarantee them every time, and we stand ready to refund the purchase price, if satisfactory results do not follow their use. These remedies have won their great popularity purely on their merits. H. A. Blachmer, druggist.

THE CHAIN OF EVIDENCE

Forged by the Police Against Borden Murderer.

Full Report of Conference With District Attorney.

All the Facts in Possession of Authorities

Laid Before the Public by the Evening Standard.

Startling Disclosures Now Made for the First Time.

[Special Dispatch.]

FALL RIVER, Aug. 9.—The statement published in the Boston Herald this morning that warrants were issued yesterday afternoon for the supposed Borden murderers is utterly without foundation.

The gravity of the situation is such that in the near future official action may be taken, and that perhaps to-day; but up to 9 o'clock this morning no warrants had been issued, and there will be none drawn until the first day's session of the inquest is over.

The above has been authentically learned and is written to refute a story that has given the police annoyance, deceived the public, and prematurely reflected upon the parties involved.

As was announced this morning, the conference between the police and District Attorney Knowlton at the Mellen House last night lasted from 7 30 until after 1 o'clock.

The purpose of the meeting was to acquaint Mr. Knowlton with the evidence in the possession of the marshal's forces, and to familiarize him with the outside conditions in the case, that he would be obliged to overcome at the inquest, if the best interests of the Commonwealth were served. State Officer George Seaver, Marshal Hilliard and Mr. Knowlton were closeted alone for the first two hours of the evening in parlor B. When Mr. Knowlton had gathered the main facts of the tragedy in a general way he called for writing materials and began to formulate the evidence. He first desired to fix the time of the tragedy. The evidence in the marshal's possession bearing upon this point was exhaustive. It was shown that Mr. Borden, the victim, reached home after his morning trip down town between 10 45 and 10 50 o'clock. This was shown both by the testimony of men who met him on the way and by the first admissions of the Borden household after the tragedy.

It was further shown by the statements of the family that Miss Lizzie left the house to go out to the barn not later than eight minutes of 11. From the same original source of information it appears that she returned from the barn and discovered her father dead between 11 03 and 11 05 o'clock.

It was shown by substantial evidence that as early as 11 10 o'clock the first news of the murder was upon the street. At 11 15 the tidings were conveyed to the police, and before 11 20 o'clock a number of people were on their way to the Borden house. Dr. Bowen, who fixes the time of his arrival about 11 30, was present when the first officers from the Central Station put in an appearance. A strong array of testimony bearing upon the above was shown to be in the government's possession, a fact that gratified Mr. Knowlton exceedingly.

The evidence to a moral certainty fixes the commission of the murder between 10 52 and 11 05 o'clock. This allowance of 13 minutes is made upon the most liberal calculations possible from the evidence and is of great significance in the case.

The second important topic discussed was the story of Lizzie Borden, who is the last person known to have seen her father alive. What she said she did for him after he entered the house prior to adjusting his pillow, at which time she left him lying on the sofa in the position he was found when dead, proves in itself the probable accuracy of the time given.

Miss Borden, the district attorney learned, has made three radical changes in her story since the original was told. One discrepancy pertains to her whereabouts at the time of the murder. She first said she was at the water closet in the barn. Then that she was in the loft searching for lead; then that she was in both places.

The second change in her story referred to time. Originally she made the statement above credited to her. She lengthened the period of her absence from the house to 20 minutes, and latterly she has called it 30 minutes.

The third inconsistency in the narrative is a denial that she solicited the purchase of prussic acid at Smith's drug store, a fact that the police have proven to their satisfaction by competent witnesses.

Miss Lizzie's own statements show that she did not call for Mrs. Borden, after the discovery of her father dead or go to her room. That she did not search for the note her stepmother is alleged to have received, so that if absent from the house, she might send to acquaint her with the terrible news. All that she did was to notify Bridget to go out and get a doctor. Miss Borden does not account for the manner in which she spent her time while the girl was gone. Whether she remained in the room with the body or not is a question. She said there was a fire in the kitchen stove and that Mrs. Borden may have gone out and burned the note.

The remainder of Miss Borden's statements that bear upon the case pertain to the time of Mr. Morse's departure in the morning and the hour of his return. Likewise to the relations existing between her family and herself prior to the tragedy.

The district attorney then listened to the marshal's narration of the officers' work in tracing down every rumor obtained, and not finding a single clew worthy of consideration. Distances between the scene of the tragedy and the adjoining houses were specified to show that no great noise or violence could possibly have escaped the neighbors' hearing nor that of Bridget Sullivan or Miss Lizzie if she was in the barn.

Tending to destroy the value of her story of being in the barn at the place described, the evidence of one of the police officers was considered. At an early hour in the forenoon on the day of the tragedy he opened the door in the barn chamber and carefully examined the floor by aid of the stronger light. He saw no tracks in the heavy layer of dust upon the floor except those made by his own shoes. This officer, Mr. Medley, is a sound reliable investigator and his evidence has great weight.

At this point a knock at the door interrupted the proceedings and the cards of Medical Examiner Dolan and His Honor, Mayor Coughlin, were received. They were immediately requested to come up stairs, and then the medical end of the case was taken up.

It was shown that in all moral probability Mrs. Borden was the first victim. Her death might have occurred as early as 9 o'clock in the morning, and surely did occur an hour that was not much later.

Dr. Dolan's information indicated the settlement of one very important fact. There is manifestly a greater space of time between the moment of Mrs. Borden's death and that of her husband's that can be accounted for on the theory than both murders took place during the period that Miss Lizzie says she was in the barn.

Therefore the theory is negatively proved that Miss Borden, who says she was not away from home the entire morning prior to the murder, must have been in the house—under the same roof with her step-mother and the assassin—when the first murder took place.

How the fall of such a heavy woman as Mrs. Borden, who weighed over two hundred, could escape being heard in a frame house the size of the Borden residence, was unaccountable in the opinion of the authorities.

The final decision of the conference was to do nothing until morning, when the fact would be positively decided whether an inquest need be commenced or not.

It was the firm opinion of all that prior to such action being taken Bridget Sullivan ought to be given a vigorous examination.

It was stated by the marshal that she was in a very nervous state, a condition resulting from a cause yet to be fully determined.

He said that on Monday morning, after her return, she made hasty preparations to leave the house, and an officer on guard saw her packing up her effects. He asked her what she was going to do, and she replied to get out.

The marshal said the officer immediately informed him of the circumstances, and he instructed the guard to tell her she must not go on penalty of arrest.

Then Mr. Hilliard told how he called on the girl in the afternoon, and found her a physical and mental wreck.

She cried and said she could not sleep nights and was afraid to remain longer in the house.

He had reasoned with her and assured her that no harm could possibly come to her, but that availed nothing.

Bridget was not to be consoled. He left her to endure a season of mental unrest, and suggested that by this morning she might be in a ripe condition to effectually interview.

This plan was endorsed thoroughly.

While the marshal was not without some evidence of a safe character to warrant action, the desirability of adding Bridget Sullivan's important story to the general fund of information already possessed was apparent.

Then the conference adjourned.

The district attorney retired to bed at the Mellen House and the others to the Wilbur House, where for another hour the mayor and officers discussed the situation.

The mayor, who has used the press with the greatest consideration, both in his official and social capacity, has finally decided to stop talking to reporters.

His experience in being misquoted in serious ways by men who ought to know better has injured the chance of other well-meaning correspondents, and has done him a great injustice.

Postal Telegraph Boys' Strike.

Boston, Aug. 9.—Between 50 and 60 boys employed to answer messenger call boxes of the Postal Telegraph Company struck this morning. They have been receiving a commission of 40 cents on each dollar's worth of business they brought in, and now want 50 per cent.

SECOND WEEK OF OUR SPECIAL Mid-Summer SALE!

We were very much gratified with the way our bargains of last week were received, and will enumerate a few specials for this week:

All of our 50 and 75c. India Silks for this sale 39c.

All of our 25 and 37 1-2c. French Sateens for this sale 12 1-2c.

All of our 59 and 62 1-2c. all-wool Challies to close 50c.

A few pieces of 50c. Figured Mohairs we shall close at 25c.

We have just received a nice line of Belts 37 1-2c. metal Belts, shall sell this sale for 25c.

Something new, Suspender Belts, all the rage, 59c.; a regular 75c. belt.

A full line of Sizes, 32 to 40c.

Shirt Waists in the new shade of blue, sold all the season for $1; this sale 62c.

We have just received a full line of Purses and Pocketbooks—many novelties never before shown in this city and controlled by us.

We have added 1000 new pieces to our Musical Catalogue, making the largest and most complete list of music ever shown at any price, 5c. a copy or 6 copies for 25c. Ask for the new catalogue.

Kitchen Furnishing Dept.

Now is the time to buy a Hammock. We have a full line, prices ranging from 69c. to $2.69.

Croquet Sets. A regular $1.00 set for 89c., equally as good values for $1.39, $1.69, $2.29 and $3.39.

White Mountain Freezers—2 quarts, $1.25; 3 quarts, $2.09 and 4 quarts, $2.50.

Oil Stoves 1, 2 and 3 burners. Oil Stove Tea Kettles 19 to 69c.

Perry's Patent Clothes Line Hooks 7 and 10c.

Household Ammonia—pint bottles, 7c. or 4 for 25c.

Knowles & Co.

Cor. UNION & FOURTH STS.

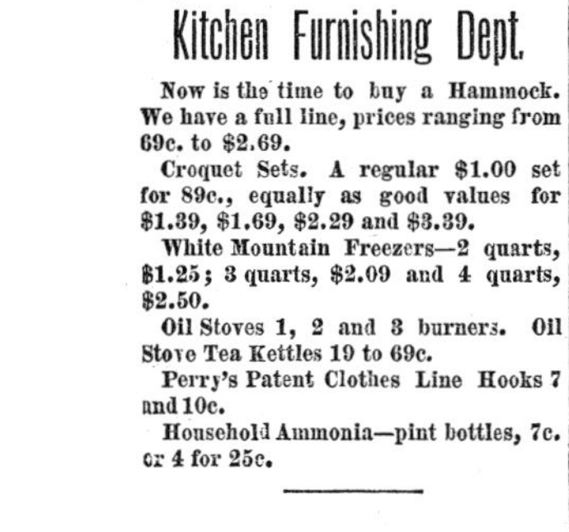

A DANGEROUS POCKET-PIECE.

Anthony Duffy's Close Acquaintance with a Dynamite Cartridge.

SCRANTON, Pa., Aug. 9.—Anthony Duffy, with his little child in his arms, accompanied by Miss Kate Coultry, were walking together in the street at Archbald when a sudden explosion threw them to the sidewalk. The young woman's arm was badly cut and mangled, and Duffy received a severe wound in the abdomen, which it is feared will have a serious effect. The child was not injured. An examination revealed part of an exploded dynamite cartridge in Duffy's vest pocket, which the heat from a pipe he had been smoking and which he placed in his vest pocket had ignited. In another pocket was also found a similar cartridge. Duffy claims ignorance of ever owning such dangerous articles and thinks that he can pick out an enemy who wanted to remove him. Duffy is a widower.

An Indiana Murder Mystery.

JEFFERSONVILLE, Ind., Aug. 9.—With an incision of a hatchet in her left temple, an unknown woman was found in the refuse of the falls. She was evidently murdered, and, to hide the crime, was thrown in the river. She was dressed in black alpaca, with faultless linen, and had a beautiful face.

SANFORD'S Ginger

IS SO RICH in health-preserving properties in the midst of summer dangers that it is almost criminal to be without it. No other ginger is so pure, so speedy and safe. For the stomach, bowels and nerves, for colds, chills and touches of rheumatism, it is a panacea without an equal.

Containing among its ingredients the purest of medicinal French brandy and the best of imported ginger, it is vastly superior to the cheap, worthless, and often dangerous gingers urged as substitutes. Ask for SANFORD'S GINGER and look for owl trade-mark on the wrapper. Sold everywhere.

A DESPERATE CAMPAIGN.

Interesting Points on the Coming Congressional Fight.

WASHINGTON, Aug. 9.—The first session of the Fifty-second congress having at last succumbed, there will now begin one of the most determined and desperate struggles for party control that has taken place in the history of congresses since the foundation of the government. From this time until the elections in November there will be kept up a vigorous campaign in every contestible district.

At no time has there been such a long list of representatives who hold their seats by narrow majorities, and therefore never has there been such an extensive field for congressional campaign work. Out of the 332 districts represented in the present congress there are fifty-seven members—forty-two Democrats and fifteen Republicans—who have been elected by majorities of less than 1000, and of this number twenty-eight were chosen by less than 500 majority.

Upon these districts, especially, the congressional committees on both sides will bestow their best efforts. Both these committees are already organized with experienced chairmen and an efficient staff, and campaign literature and speakers will be sent into the field of political battle.

The New Congress

will have, under the new apportionment, 356 representatives, an increase of twenty-four over the present. The relation of parties as the house now stands is: Democrats, 235; Republicans, 87; Alliance, 10. In many of the states there has been no redistricting, as in Pennsylvania, which will leave the district lines as they now stand, with the increase elected at large.

Some idea of the extent of the congressional contest of 1892, and what must be overcome by the Republicans, may be formed from the fact that the present Democratic and Alliance control in the house is 155 majority, and adding the twenty-four new districts will make 179 representative districts in which Republican congressional campaign managers must devote their energies. It would require a gain of about ninety to make their majority certain in the next house.

Slender Majorities.

In the following districts a change of from 10 to 500 votes would turn them into the Republican column:

State.	Dist.	Sitting Representative.	Maj.
Arkansas	1	Cato	603
"	2	Breckinridge	975
California	1	Geary	181
"	2	Cammetti	159
Connecticut	1	Sperry	602
"	4	De Forest	908
Delaware	..	Causey	668
Illinois	4	Newberry	662
"	8	Stewart	102
"	9	Snow	947
"	15	Busey	582
"	16	Fithian	516
Indiana	1	Parrett	855
Iowa	5	Hamilton	293
"	6	White	520
Maryland	6	McKay	165
Massachusetts	8	Stevens	454
"	9	Williams	131
"	11	Coolidge	150
"	12	Crosby	282
Michigan	6	Stout	683
"	8	Youmans	45
"	9	Wheeler	60
Montana	..	Dixon	283
New Hampshire	2	Daniel	839
New York	3	Coombs	18
"	23	Bently	516
"	24	Van Horn	108
"	28	Rockwell	89
"	30	Greenleaf	234
North Carolina	8	Cowles	793
Ohio	8	Hare	194
"	16	Warwick	304
"	17	Pearson	704
Pennsylvania	7	Hallowell	187
"	11	Ammerman	304
"	24	Craig, deceased	..
		Stewart, unseated	123
South Carolina	7	Elliott	477
Tennessee	2	Snodgrass	523
Virginia	2	Lawson	725
West Virginia	1	Pendleton	618
Wisconsin	..	Babbitt	313

There are about thirty other districts in which the Democratic majority in the tidal-wave campaign did not exceed 1500.

The Republicans who hold their seats by slender majorities, which

Might Be Overturned

by a change of less than 500 votes, are—

Illinois	1	Taylor	439
"	6	Hitt	511
"	10	Post	618
Iowa	3	Henderson	198
"	8	Flick	118
"	11	Perkins	907
Massachusetts	10	Walker	700
Michigan	4	Burrows	304
Minnesota	2	Lind	482
Nevada	..	Bartine	874
Pennsylvania	16	Hopkins	151
"	18	Atkinson	607
"	20	Scull	526
"	26	Griswold	868

CITIZENS DOING THEIR SHARE.

Thousands of Knights Templars to Attend the Conclave at Denver.

DENVER, Aug. 9.—The population of this city was increased nearly 85,000 yesterday and still the rush continues. Probably one quarter of the arrivals were knights, the rest being visitors attracted by the conclave. In many of the trains numbers of passengers had stood for hundreds of miles. They were packed to the doors. The depot yards and the streets here were filled with the strains of music and marching knights all day. Prairie schooners, containing families of ranchmen, occasonally passed through the streets. These people have put up hundreds of tents in the outskirts, where they will live during the conclave.

Grand Master Gobin of the grand commandery was received with a salute of twenty-one guns. He was escorted to the temple, where Grand Commander Carr of Colorado made a speech of welcome. General Gobin responded. When he learned that a prize competitive drill had been arranged, he expressed his disapproval, and Commander Carr countermanded the order for the drill. It is estimated that 25,000 swords will be in line in today's parade. Last night there were receptions at the various clubs and headquarters to the visitors. The streets were lighted up for miles by many colored stringers, fancy emblems of Masonry, colossal search lights and brilliantly decorated arches. Private residences, hotels and clubs were one blaze of brilliancy.

CANADA'S COMPROMISE

May Save the President the Necessity of Issuing a Proclamation.

WASHINGTON, Aug. 9.—Official information of the action of the Canadian authorities in withdrawing rebate from vessels arriving at Montreal from the lakes by way of the St. Lawrence river, has not yet been received at the state department. Consequently no official expression of opinion as to the subject can be had, although it is quietly intimated that the Canadian action, if such as reported, will doubtless be regarded by the president as removing all source of complaint on the score of discrimination, and so relieving him from the necessity of issuing a retaliatory proclamation.

All are Rich Men.

NEW YORK, Aug. 9.—The advisory committee of the Republican national committee is said to have been practically decided upon. Among those selected, it is said, are: B. F. Jones, Pittsburg; Hamilton Diston, Philadelphia; Nelson W. Aldrich, Rhode Island; Philetus Sawyer, Wisconsin, and George M. Pullman, Illinois. All five men are immensely wealthy.

Charges of Bigamy.

WASHINGTON, Aug. 9.—Charges have been filed at the treasury department against George Cake, appointed on Saturday by secretary Foster as immigrant inspector. The charge preferred is that he has wives in Pittsburg and New York. Acting Secretary Nettleton has instituted an inquiry as to its authenticity.

Highest of all in Leavening Power.—Latest U. S. Gov't Report.

Royal Baking Powder

ABSOLUTELY PURE

THE STRIKE BROKEN.

Five Hundred Employes Resume Work at the Duquesne Mills.

HOMESTEAD, Pa., Aug. 9.—The strikers at Duquesne went to work yesterday and the Carnegie Steel company has scored one victory. On Saturday night Superintendent Morrison posted a notice that all men who had applied for their old jobs would report at the mill at 7 o'clock in the morning, as the mill would resume at that hour. As 7 o'clock approached, the number of men whohad entered the mill yard reached 400. About sixty men, who were leaders in the sympathy strike movement, gathered on the road near the mill gate and watched in moody silence the men going in to work.

The effect of the break at Duquesne cannot but prove harmful to the men at Homestead, although the leaders will not believe it. Yet at Duquesne steel billets can be manufactured and sent to Homestead to be rolled into plates by the non-union men, so that the firm will be in far better condition to fill its contracts and prosecute its fight here.

PITTSBURG, Aug. 9.—The Duquesne rioters had a hearing before Alderman Reilly yesterday afternoon. Quite a crowd of Duquesne workmen were present to hear the cases. Squire Reilly finally held Ursie, Essler, Bukie, Bennett, Kennedy, Hogan, Nolan, Haas and Coates for court and fixed bail at $1000. Snyder and McLean were released on parole to appear for a further hearing. All of the men got bail except Ursie, who went to jail.

SHEEHAN ELECTED CHAIRMAN.

Campaign Affairs of Empire State Democrats Placed in His Hands.

SARATOGA, Aug. 9. — The Democratic state campaign committee elected Lieutenant Governor Sheehan as permanent chairman.

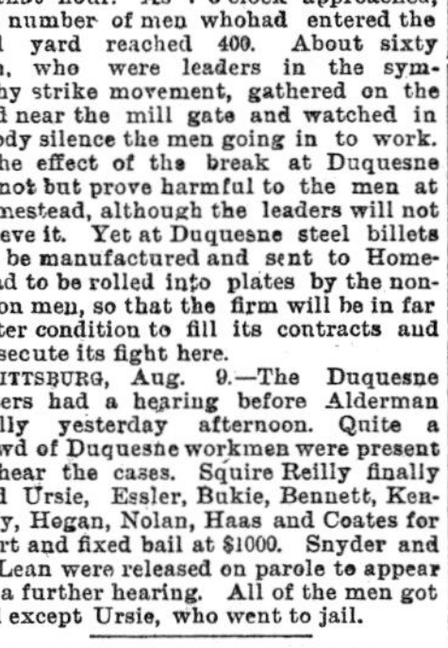

WILLIAM F. SHEEHAN.

Mr. Sheehan congratulated the committee on the excellent prospects of the party in this state, and pledged his most earnest efforts to make success this fall a certainty.

TEN THOUSAND LOOKED ON.

Three Scientific Exhibitions by Disciples of the Pugilistic Arena.

NEW YORK, Aug. 9.—Three bouts were fought last night at the Coney Island Athletic club before about 10,000 spectators. The first bout was between Billy Plimmer of England, champion 110-pound man of the world, and Jerry Barnett of New York. It resulted in favor of Plimmer, who clearly outclassed his opponent. Barnett made a game fight, however, and lasted the stipulated eight rounds. The men fought Marquis of Queensberry rules at 115 pounds.

The second bout was an eight-round contest, at 154 pounds, between Charley Kammer and Jim Sullivan, both of New York. It was a slugging match and anybody's fight up to the end of the fifth round. In the sixth Sullivan was weakened somewhat, but soon recovered and had the best of both the sixth and seventh rounds. In the eighth round honors were even. Both men displayed science. The referee declared the fight a draw.

The third bout was the fight of the night. It was to be at least a twenty-round contest at 120 pounds between George Siddons of New Orleans and Eddie Pierce of New York. Al Smith was referee. After forty-one rounds both sides agreed to call the fight a draw.

Blaine May Make a Speech.

NEW YORK, Aug. 9.—Senator Fessenden, Governor Bulkeley and three other Connecticut representatives had a conference with Chairman Carter, Secretary McComas and General Clarkson at Republican national headquarters in regard to the situation in the Nutmeg state. The Republicans intend to put some of their best campaign speakers in the New England states. It was intimated that Mr. Blaine will make at least one campaign speech in this city.

DEFIANT LABOR LEADER.

Workingman M. P. Insists on Wearing His Cap in House of Commons.

LONDON, Aug. 9.—The scenes around the houses of parliament yesterday were almost a repetition of those witnessed on the opening day. The streets were crowded with people curious to see the new members as they arrived, and the lobbies were full of persons having business, or pretending to have, with the legislators.

The galleries, not very spacious, were crowded. Among the notabilities to be seen were Prince Christian, Minister Lincoln, and numerous European diplomats. Keir Hardie, the bumptious labor member, showed his thick-skinned defiance of public opinion by again wearing his cap, which would not be so offensive in the eyes of his fellow members if it had at least the merit of cleaniness. Hardie did not remove the cap even while the mace was passing. This was more than one of the members standing near by could endure, and with a sweep of his hand he knocked the objectionable covering off Hardie's head.

Hardie turned angrily to resent the insult, and the member who had unhatted him made a gesture as if to imply that the action was unintentional, but offered no apology. It looked as if blows would result, but the other members stepped between the two disputants and the matter was dropped. Hardie picked up his cap and began strutting about with it on his ill-shaped head as if proud of the very cheap notoriety he was obtaining.

Serious Rumors Are Again Afloat

in regard to Mr. Gladstone's health. It is positively stated that he has had fainting fits three times within the past week. It is also declared that Sunday he was seized with a choleraic attack, and that it was only by the timely arrival of his physician that the ailment was gotten under such control, after three hours work, that the patient was able to receive callers.

Yesterday, though presenting a brave appearance, he showed evidence of weakness. His friends were alarmed at the lack of color in his face, and at his listlessness, except when aroused by some pressing need of action. It is argued, however, by those who claim that Mr. Gladstone is able to stand the fatigues of office, that there is no cause for fear on account of his having a bad day now and then. At his age nothing else could be expected, and it is not, they declare, at all necessary for a man to be in fighting condition every minute in order to carry on a government successfully.

Nevertheless, the Liberals are anxious to have the announcement of the cabinet made, and the other necessary business got out of the way speedily so there will be no excuse for an autumn session, and Mr. Gladstone can retire to Hawarden and recuperate until next February.

A BIG CUT-DOWN.

Sundry Civil Bill Will Cause Many Fat Posts to Be Vacated.

WASHINGTON, Aug. 9.—There will be a very considerable shaking up among the highly salaried officers of the bureau of geological survey after today, as the reductions imposed by the sundry civil bill will be carried into effect. Nearly forty members of the present force will be asked to resign, two-thirds of them being scientists employed on special work. The list includes three $4000 geologists, one $3000 geologist, two $2900 geologists, one $2000 geologist, one $2000 chemist, two $2500 geographers, one $2000 topographer and one $3000 officer, classed as a "general assistant."

These are dropped altogether. The salary of the paleontologist is cut down from $4000 to $2000, and twenty-six other employes will also have to submit to a reduction of pay.

Major Powell, chief director of the bureau, says that six of the geologists, thus summarily disposed of, have volunteered to stay and complete the work they are engaged upon with the present compensation.

Many Victims of Dynamite.

ROME, Aug. 9.—A mortar charged with dynamite was exploded Sunday, near St. Alfonso's church, during a religious fete. Eleven persons were killed and thirty-two others were injured. The victims included a number of women and children.

Ghastly War Trophies.

TANGIER, Aug. 9.—The sultan's troops brought here three prisoners captured Sunday in an engagement with the rebels. The heads of the three rebels who were slain in battle were sent to the sultan. The prisoners will be beheaded.

India's Choice.

LONDON, Aug. 9.—The Indian government has selected Richard Strachey, ex-member of the council, and G. H. Murray of the treasury as delegates to the international monetary conference.

SON. "Mother, do you never weary with all your correspondence?"

LYDIA PINKHAM. "No, my son, these letters of confidence bring to me the joy that a mother feels, whose daughter throws her arms around her neck and cries, 'Oh, mother, help me!' The women of the world are my daughters, dear."

SON. "Yes, mother, and they love you."

Lydia Pinkham's private letters from ladies in all parts of the world average **one hundred per day**, and truly has she been a **mother to the race.** Suffering women ever seek her in their extremity, and find both a helper and a friend. Correspondents will receive prompt and conscientious answers, **and the sympathy of a mother.**

LYDIA E. PINKHAM'S VEGETABLE COMPOUND

Is the only **Positive Cure and Legitimate Remedy** for the peculiar weaknesses and ailments of women.

It cures the worst forms of Female Complaints, that Bearing-down Feeling, Weak Back, Falling and Displacement of the Womb, Inflammation, Ovarian Troubles, and all Organic Diseases of the Uterus or Womb, and is invaluable to the Change of Life. Dissolves and expels Tumors from the Uterus at an early stage, and checks any tendency to Cancerous Humor. Subdues Faintness, Excitability, Nervous Prostration, Exhaustion, and strengthens and tones the Stomach. Cures Headache, General Debility, Indigestion, etc., and invigorates the whole system. For the cure of Kidney Complaints of either sex, **the Compound has no rival.**

All Druggists sell it as a **standard article**, or sent by mail, in form of Pills or Lozenges, on receipt of **$1.00.** LYDIA E. PINKHAM MED. CO., LYNN, MASS.

An Illustrated book, entitled "Guide to Health and Etiquette," by Lydia E. Pinkham, is of great value to ladies. We will present a copy to anyone addressing us with two 2-cent stamps.

From Yesterday's Third Edition.

A HIRED ASSASSIN.

Belief of Murdered Mrs. Borden's Brother-in-Law.

He Thinks Lizzie and Morse Concocted the Plot.

Gives His' Reasons for His Direct Accusation.

[By Associated Press.]

HARTFORD, Ct., Aug. 8.—George B. Fish of this city, whose wife is the sister of the murdered Mrs. Borden of Fall River, in a published interview says that he believes Lizzie Borden and J. V. Morse concocted the deed and hired some one to do it.

Lizzie and Emma are step-daughters of the murdered woman and have never been on good terms with her owing to trouble over the division of property left by the girls' mother to Mr. Borden who gave it to the second wife instead of the girls.

When asked what Lizzie's object would have been in doing this, Mr. Fish replied: "Simply to get them out of the way. No one made any money out of it, nor could they in any way by murdering the couple."

Mr. Morse was asked what he had to say in regard to this interview.

"Nothing at all. Mr. Jennings, our counsel, has advised me to have nothing to say for publication," he replied.

"But that directly implicates you and Miss Borden. Have you nothing to say to that?"

"You know as well as I do what grounds there are for such an absurd charge as that. It is entirely unreasonable; that is all I will say."

THE DANDY FIRST AT FORT WARREN.

How New Bedford Soldiers Began the Week's Tour of Duty.

[Special Dispatch.]

FORT WARREN, Boston, Aug. 8.—There were nine companies of the First in camp when the Cape contingent arrived, consisting of the right and left battalions and one of the centre battalion. Co. E left New Bedford on the 7 25 a. m. train, arriving in Boston one hour late. The boys then took the line of march for the Nantasket steamer through Tremont, Winter, Washington, Franklin and Broad streets to Rowe's wharf, where they embarked on steamer Gen. Lincoln, leaving Boston at 10 45, arriving at the Fort at 11 20, after which they commenced to fix quarter's for the week's tour of duty. Dinner was sounded at 12 30, and it was a welcome sound to all. At 3 p. m. divine service was held in the mess tent in charge of Rev. M. J. Savage, the regiment's chaplain. At 5 15 p. m. the adjutant's call for parade was sounded.

The formation was rather crowded for the first time, but that was remedied at to-day's parade. Capt. Braley is officer of the day and Lieut. Munroe officer of the guard. The Cape battalion performs guard duty. A fine concert was given by the First Regiment Band in front of Col. Matthews' quarters, which was very much enjoyed by the men. The strength of the cape companies are:

M, 3 officers, — men.
F, 2 officers, 47 men.
E, 3 officers, 52 men.
I, 3 officers, 52 men.

Last night was a beautiful moonlight night, and a nice cool breeze blowing over the fort, which made it delightful for all. Lieut. Munroe of Company M was acting as adjutant and Sergt. Baudoin of Company E as sergeant major.

One of the most laughable incidents of camp life occurred last night, when Co. F had a mosquito guard on of three men, one of them being detailed to carry a lantern on his beat with the moon shining brightly.

Our boys were very quiet until about 2 a. m., when they seemed to wake up as if by magic, and all were out in the street like bees.

The targets for big gun practice were set yesterday at the east side of the fort.

H. S. S.

THE SPEECH FROM THE THRONE.

Formal Opening of the Session of the Twenty-Fifth Parliament.

LONDON, Aug. 8.—When the House of Commons met this morning the members were summoned to the House of Lords, where the speech from the throne opening the session of the 25th Parliament was read. The speech announced that by command of Her Majesty, the present Parliament has been called in obedience to the terms of Her Majesty's proclamation of June 28, by which the late Parliament was dissolved. Previous to that dissolution, the speech added, the business of the session was completed. There was no necessity to continue the session for any great length of time for the transaction of financial and legislative business. Her Majesty expressed the hope that when Parliament meets again, at the customary season, it will again direct attention to measures of social and domestic improvement and that it will continue to advance in the path of usefulness and beneficent legislation which has been so judicially followed at previous sessions.

At 4 o'clock the House of Commons reassembled. Nearly all the members were present and the galleries were crowded. The Queen's speech was again read to the members. When the last portion was reached it was greeted with groans by the Liberals.

Capital Deserted by Cabinet Officials.

WASHINGTON, Aug. 8.—Officially this city is practically deserted. Secretary of State Foster is the only representative of the Cabinet here. At the War Department Assistant Secretary Grant presides as the head of the department, Secretary Elkins having gone to Deer Park. The affairs of the navy are looked after by Assistant Secretary Schley, in the absence of Secretary Tracy, while Attorney General Miller and Postmaster General Wanamaker are away, as is also Secretary Rusk.

Cricketers in Boston.

BOSTON, Aug. 8.—The Philadelphia cricketers arrived this morning from Halifax, N. S., where they have for the second time captured the championship. They play the all-Boston team to-day and to-morrow for the championship.

Killed by a Flying Timber.

LYNN, Aug. 8.—Morris Rich, 50 years old, was instantly killed this afternoon at L. C. Marshall's planing mill by a timber which he was dividing on a circular saw flying back and striking him in the pit of the stomach.

Cruiser No. 11.

WASHINGTON, Aug. 8.—Cruiser No. 11 was to-day named Marblehead and will be launched at the yard of Harrison at Boston Thursday at 1 o'clock.

RHODE ISLAND YACHT CLUB.—Five yachts comprising the Rhode Island Club squadron arrived this afternoon.

There were quite a number of other yachts arrived this afternoon.

ARRESTED.—Robert Brierly was arrested this afternoon on a warrant charging him with an assault on James Marshall.

FIRE INSURANCE FRAUDS.

Companies Doing Business Without a Dollar's Worth of Capital.

NEW YORK, Aug. 8.—The *Herald* says: A remarkable association of fire insurance companies has come to town in the last five months utterly worthless in every particular and fostered by men in many instances who are on a par with the companies which they control. They make an interesting chapter in the history of fire insurance permissible only by reason of a still existing and almost incomprehensibly bad law which it has pleased a number of individuals to take advantage of. In a certain measure it becomes modified, on Oct. 1. The companies referred to are the World Cooperative Fire Insurance Co., with a main office in Broadway. The New York County Cooperative Fire Insurance Co, No. 28 Broadway; The Metropolitan Cooperative Fire Insurance Co., No. 62 Bowery; the Manufacturers' and Traders' Cooperative Fire Insurance Co., Nos. 58 and 62 Broadway; the National Cooperative Fire Insurance Co., No. 50 Broadway; the Standard Cooperative Fire Insurance Co., No. 415 Broadway; the New York Home Cooperative Fire Insurance Company, Park row; the Equitable Fire Insurance Company, No. 161 Broadway. "Here," continues the *Herald*, "is a list of companies possessing not one dollar's worth of capital and in many known cases without the moral backing which corporators of this character should possess, soliciting business from the poorest and least sophisticated citizens of the city."

MILLIONNAIRE IN THE PRIZE RING.

Fight for Blood and Honor of Men in "Upper Ten" Circles at Saratoga.

SARATOGA, Aug. 8.—A prize fight in upper ten circles took place on the fair grounds at Ballston Spa at 11 30 o'clock. The principals were Daniel W. Shea of Boston, a Harvard Student and a member of the Harvard crew and football team, and Sidney Smith of Ballston, son of a wealthy and prominent family. The men are fine boxers and the match was the result of jealousy as to their respective merits. The party left Saratoga in two tally-ho coaches at 10 a. m. and drove to Ballston. "Billy" Edwards was referee and Jimmy Larkin of New York seconded Shea. The fight was a hard one and for blood. Smith won the second round. Shea was badly punished, and a dispute as to time of the second round nearly precipitated a general fight among the friends of the contestants. Smith weighs 158 pounds, and Shea 178. Time of first round, two minutes; second round, one minute fifty-four seconds. It was with London ring rules. The fighting was furious from the start. The battle was entirely for blood and honor. About 25 friends of the contestants were present. Smith is a millionnaire. Shea is prominent in Boston society.

"THE STRIKE IS BROKEN."

So Says Supt. Potter of the Carnegie Works at Homestead.

HOMESTEAD, Aug. 8.—There were about ten non-union men at Amalgamated headquarters this morning. They left the mill as it was too much like a prison. One mechanic said 13 men in his crew quit this morning and others would come out soon. He asserted that 150 men went to Pittsburgh Saturday and only 75 returned to work. He asserted that he had to sleep in his trousers to prevent them being stolen. The locked out men are encouraged by this turn in their favor.

"We received 30 applications from old men to-day," says Supt. Potter at the steel works this morning. "Several of the men were accepted and went to work. The strike is broken, we believe, but we should like to get as many of our old men back as possible. The more we get the better it will be for Homestead in the future."

POPULACE EXCITED TO FRENZY.

Cossacks Sent into Persia to Protect Russian Subjects.

ST. PETERSBURG, Aug. 8.—A dispatch from Astrabad, Persia, says that the mollahs, or priests, whose influence with the populace is very powerful, have preached that the outbreak of cholera is due to the sale of alcoholic liquors. Their language excited the populace to frenzy. Raids were forthwith made upon the dram shops, which were plundered. The mob destoyed the goods of a number of Armenian traders who are Russian subjects. The Russian consul, fearing that the trouble would grow and that he might be attacked, telegraphed to St. Petersburg for aid. The government at once gave orders for the dispatch of 25 Cossacks, who have arrived at Astrabad, where they are guarding the consulate. A Russian gunboat is now announced off the place.

VESSELS CRASHED TOGETHER.

Two Men in a Small Boat Between Lost Their Lives.

PORTSMOUTH, N. H., Aug. 8.—While the schooner Charlotte was getting under way this morning she drifted across the bow of a coaler. Two of the Charlotte's crew, Charles Bushnell of Cohasset and William J. Carroll of Boston, went into a small boat between the vessels to keep them from fouling. The vessels came together with force, smashing the boat and crushing Carroll to death. Bushnell was forced under the water and drowned.

The Strike of the Building Trades.

NEW YORK, Aug. 8.—It is expected that the strike of the building trades which had brought building to a standstill during the past few weeks will come to an end to-day. The German framers, in accordance with a resolution, returned to work this morning and the board of walking delegates of the building trades is expected to order the strike off this afternoon. The housesmiths first struck and other trades joined out of sympathy.

Small Pox in New York.

NEW YORK, Aug. 8.—Three cases of small pox were reported yesterday. They were John Edwards, 28 years old, who walked into Gouveneur Hospital last night with the disease; William Geigers, a 13-months-old child of 968 East 161st street; and Mrs. Savanon, aged 23, of 71 Thompson street. They were all sent to the reception hospital, where Mrs. Savanon died two hours later.

His Home Burned to the Ground.

PUTNAM, Ct., Aug. 8.—August Daniel's house at South Woodstock was burned to the ground Sunday. Loss $1500. Cause unknown.

CASES OF INSANITY

From the Effects of

"LA GRIPPE"

Are Alarmingly Prevalent.

Suicides

From the

SAME CAUSE

Are announced in every paper.

Would you be rid of the awful effects of La Grippe?

There is BUT ONE SURE REMEDY that NEVER FAILS, viz:

DANA'S SARSAPARILLA.

We Guarantee to CURE you or REFUND your money.

COULD WE DO MORE?

ISN'T IT WORTH A TRIAL?

je25-tf

WRIGHT Drug Company.

PUREST DRUGS

—AND—

FINEST CHEMICALS

—AT—

Lowest Prices.

WRIGHT DRUG CO.

KNIGHTS TEMPLARS IN DENVER.

Boston Commandery Greeted With Cheers Along the Streets.

DENVER, Col., Aug. 8.—The city awoke bright and early this morning and found itself in possession of the Knights Templars. They were everywhere—in cars, in carriages, and thronged the many points of interest in the city. Nearly 4000 arrived up to an early hour, and less than half of the number of trains to arrive before noon got in. Every structure in the business portion is decorated and the various entertainment clubs kept open house to-day. The famous Boston commandery, which arrived last night, paraded the streets this morning. It made a magnificent appearance and was cheered all along the street. Eminent Sir Eugene Holton led the men. The commandery was made up of six divisions. They were Berkshire, No. 2; Holden, No. 3; Thoria, No. 4; Deerfield, No. 5; Servia, No. 6, and Mascotte. Their headquarters are at the Glen Arm Hotel.

SENATOR HILL IN NEW YORK.

Will Leave This Afternoon for Normandy-by-the-Sea.

NEW HAVEN, Conn., Aug. 8.—Senator David B. Hill, who spent Sunday at the Pequot club-house here, left for New York at 7 30 on board the Fra Diavolo.

NEW YORK, Aug. 8.—Senator Hill and party landed at the foot of 26th street, East River, this afternoon, from the yacht Fra Diavolo. They went at once to the Hoffman House, and will leave this afternoon for Normandy-by-the-Sea.

Saratoga Races.

SARATOGA, Aug. 8.—First race, purse $600, for two-year-olds, six furlongs—Nick won, False Ahrens second, Woodban third; time 1 16.

Second race, purse $800, handicap, one mile—Mabel Glenn won, Badge second, Stone Mason third; time 1 42.

Third race, purse $600, five furlongs—Dr. Hasbrouk won, Gladiator second, Salonica third; time 1 01 1-2.

Fourth race, the U. S. Hotel stakes, 1 1-16 miles—Copyright won, Lady Superior second; time 1 56 1-2.

Fifth Race—Purse $500; 6 1-2 furlongs. Watterson first; Inferno second. Time, 1 20 3-4.

Wife Dead, Daughter Lost to Him.

HARTFORD, Conn., Aug. 8.—Joseph L. Parker has returned to Niantic, Conn., to find his wife dead and daughter lost to him. He went to California in 1848, ceased communication with his family after a few years, and now, having accumulated a fortune, has come here to find his daughter.

The Gold Train at Chicago.

CHICAGO, Aug. 8.—The "gold train" from San Francisco passed through here this morning. The cars bristled with muskets and no one was allowed within smelling distance of the precious freight. The train will reach Washington to-morrow morning.

Murderer's Suicide in Prison.

CONCORD, N. H., Aug. 8.—John Donnelly, who was sentenced to 30 years' imprisonment last November for killing a citizen of Berlin Falls, to-day committed suicide at the prison by cutting his throat with a case knife.

Saw Mill Burned.

MONTPELIER, Vt., Aug. 8.—Lanes' saw mill at Lanesboro, 20 miles from here, was burned yesterday with the depot and six freight cars. A quantity of lumber and a woodshed were also burned. Loss about $10,000.

Financial Crisis in India.

CALCUTTA, Aug. 8.—The continued fall in the price of silver threatens to involve India in a financial crisis. Discussion is rife as to the means to be adopted to check any further decline and to insure a recovery in value.

Death of Gideon Haynes.

NANTASKET, Aug. 8. — Hon. Gideon Haynes, at one time warden of the State prison, died this morning, of Bright's disease.

The Evening Standard.

ESTABLISHED FEBRUARY, 1850.

NEW BEDFORD, WEDNESDAY, AUGUST 10, 1892.

TWO CENTS.

LIZZIE ON THE RACK.

Sensational Statements from Her Expected.

She was Not Pressed Hard Yesterday Officials Say.

Strong Feeling of Police Against Mr. Jennings and Hanscom.

They are Accused of Attempting to Build Back Fires.

Mysterious Stranger Story Revived with New Evidence.

FALL RIVER, Aug. 10.—To-day the interest in the Borden murder cases is centreing around the police station where the inquest is still going on.

Miss Borden was driven to the station in a closed carriage accompanied by her friend, Mrs. Brigham, and City Marshal Hilliard.

She looked much brighter than she has at any time since the day following the tragedy.

She walked firmly across the guard room and her face was without emotion.

She was not as closely followed to-day as yesterday by the crowds.

Prof. Wood, the analyst, reached the station early in company with Medical Examiner Dolan.

Shortly after the inquest was resumed the two men were admitted and were behind closed doors about 20 minutes.

When they reappeared they were followen by a couple of policemen carrying a trunk containing bloody clothing and other evidences of the crime.

The trunks were placed on a carriage.

Prof. Wood shook hands with the medical examiner and jumped into the coupe, directing the driver to go to Bowenville station.

There he took the train for Boston, and the trunk was checked for the same place.

It is now allowed that a great deal of hope is being placed in the accuracy of the analysis and the examination of the blood on the clothing.

A few days ago this was not the case, the poison theory and other clews being talked of as of secondary importance.

The servant girl did not leave her friends last night nor this morning.

An officer who visited her found her in a much happier and more contented frame of mind than yesterday, when she was prostrated with nervousness and grief.

She talks in the most affectionate manner of deceased woman, the stepmother of the girls.

There is a strong feeling current in police circles against Inspector Hanscom and Mr. Jennings' course for the family.

It is alleged that the former is endeavoring to build back fires to destroy the theories of the police and that they are inspiring clews that will tend to blind the actual facts before and succeeding the murders.

Miss Borden will be put on the rack today, and sensational statements are looked for.

Yesterday she was not pressed hard, according to an official statement, and hinted at last night.

The police have become active in the search after evidence, and one or two details in regard to the missing letter said to have been received by Mrs. Borden are again being sought.

District Attorney Knowlton is working under the direction of Attorney-General Pillsbury, and it is said that the form of complaint and probably all warrants will be submitted to him.

Much credit is being given in police circles to the work of Dr. Dolan, who has practically neglected a remunerative practice since he was called on to act officially.

The only complaint against him is that his tongue will not wag to other than official inquisitions.

The Mysterious Stranger Again,

That the *Standard's* mysterious stranger has an existence, and that, too, in the close vicinity of the Borden homestead as late as half-hast ten, moving with apparent intent, on Thursday morning, the 4th of August, within less than ten minutes of the time old Mr. Borden reached home, straight toward the Borden residence, was amply established yesterday afternoon by a fresh witness of unquestioned standing and reputation in the community. Dr. Handy, who resides on Rock street says that about 10 a. m. on Thursday he saw a man standing on Second street a little south of the Borden residence, the man having such a terribly unusual appearance as to attract his attention. The stranger was ghastly white and seemed very much agitated. His eyes were particularly wild. He wore a small black mustache. The doctor could certainly identify the man he observed, as he was so struck by his desperate-looking character that he turned around in his carriage and gazed at him for a considerable time. Late last evening the police began to put some credence in this rumor, as it was said that a man answering this description was seen by Officer Hyde about the same time.

Dr. Handy was asked in connection with his statement:

Trusts Mr. Knowlton.

"Do you think they will go so far as to arrest Lizzie Borden?"

"I cannot say about that, but I trust a good deal to District Attorney Knowlton. He is a man of strong common sense. He will not move until he feels sure that he is sustained by the evidence."

"Well, now, doctor, does it seem probable or reasonable to you as a medical man that either a woman like Lizzie Borden, or an old man of the evident characteristics of Mr. Morse, could possibly commit a double murder like this, and yet maintain their composure and show no mental disturbance whatever within less than 30 minutes after such a horror as that had been committed?"

"No, sir, that would be impossible."

"The after effect of all that blood; all the horror of those wounds, the paroxysms which led to such a frenzy must show itself under all physical laws in some way on the condition of the perpetrator, however strong the effort to control?"

He replied, "It certainly would. There would be the inevitable reaction."

"I know Lizzie Borden," said the doctor; "I know the family well."

"It was not a family at swords' points? There was not cherished resentment through 27 years against the stepmother; no skeleton in the closet that would furnish a motive?"

"No, I do not think there was. There was the perfectly natural feeling toward the stepmother. Emma called her Mrs. Borden, but Lizzie, I think, might have called her mother sometimes. You see Mr. Borden was exactly what you have termed him, a puritan; he was not as affectionate a man in his manner as some. He was a hard man, perhaps, in money dealings. I used to ride with him a good deal and suggest to him to get a pair of horses for the girls to go riding. He was a just man and the home was a happy one."

"There was no indication that there would be any serious trouble over a little money?"

"I don't think the girls would take that much to heart."

"Now, as to that fence, doctor. What do you think about the impossibility to get over it in a hurry?"

"Well, I think if I had two such murders as those on my conscience I would go over it easily. Why, it isn't so high as that one there (pointing to his own back fence,) and I could go over that. Then, again, talk about no tracks in the dust in the barn. What does that prove? Nothing, nothing at all. Why, my wife will sweep a room in the house so clean that there isn't a speck of dust in it, and I'll bet you in an hour it will be covered. Marshal Hilliard talks about no tracks in the dust in the barn chamber. Why, there was plenty of time between the time he searched it and when Lizzie went up there."

Rear of Borden's House.

Showing cellar door by means of which assassin may have escaped.

"Did you ever know Lizzie Borden to show any indications of insanity?"

"No, sir."

"Nor of mental hysteria common to women?"

"Not a bit of it; there was nothing of the kind. Lizzie was not that sort of a girl. Although hysteria is common to the sex, she never showed any signs of it."

Significance of It.

Now here are two reliable persons, Officer Hyde and Dr. Handy, both of whom saw this strange man, not counting the Kirouach boy's story, to which he has persistently adhered. There was a man around that house that morning, a man whose singular appearance and pallor indicated just such a nervous temperament as might be wrought to homicidal frenzy at any moment, and then there is Mrs. Joseph F. Durfee. True, the circumstances she narrates happened several months ago, but she saw a young man, a slim man of 25, certainly not 30, on Mr. Borden's steps in the evening. He had a gray suit. "What I called pepper and salt," said Mrs. Durfee, "and he threatened Mr. Borden." "You have cheated me; I'll be even with you yet; I'll fix you yet," were the words she heard. Revenge has been cherished longer than eight or nine months by such individuals as this man's type indicates. All four of these witnesses furnish a complete link in a clew which has not yet been successfully followed, but simply set aside in the attempt to convict some member of the family.

Still Further.

And, again, very early that Thursday afternoon a Frenchman picked up a man a few miles out in the country. The man's face presented such a strange, wild expression that it scared the Canadian. He jumped into the carriage, and, jamming a dollar bill into his hands, demanded that the Frenchman drive him through the woods to a neighboring town. His unwilling driver took him as far as his own house, and there the Frenchman's wife took such a mistrust of his singular passenger that he returned his dollar and refused to go further with him. The man jumped out and pushed on afoot. This man was very white and pale and so nervous that he could not remain still. It seems a remarkable chain, and it sets people thinking. Nobody can gainsay Dr. Handy's reputation.

COTTAGE CITY NEWS.

Hotels Make Unusual Preparations for Excursionists.

[Special Dispatch.]

COTTAGE CITY, Aug. 10.—The session of the Summer Institute will close in a few days. More than 600 pupils are in attendance.

The New York schooner yacht Social is anchored off the Bluffs and the following named gentlemen of her party registered at the club: Clifford Smith, G. Douglas Petrie, Oscar B. Smith, C. A. Northrup, T. J. Mitchels, J. H. Tiffitt, O. D. Burger.

Excursion steamer Mt. Hope of Fall River will bring 1000 people here to-day. The hotels have made unusual preparations for the entertainment of these excursionists.

The famous racing yacht Pixie called here yesterday, bound west.

Henry Oliver, president of the Colorado National Bank, Tacoma, Wash., is here for a rest.

Dr. Raymond's catboat, stolen from her moorings in Vineyard Haven two weeks ago, has not been recovered.

Postmaster Scranton has purchased the Scranton homestead at Eastville. Price paid was $1500.

Moonlight sailing parties are now in order. Last night the following named young people went to Vineyard Haven in yacht Christie, Capt. Nickerson: Mr. and Mrs. Halley, Mrs. Jones, Misses Fell, Swan, Brown, Martin, Nichols, Ruviere, Holmes, Morrill, Messrs. Frisbee, Marshall, Bowman, Sawyer, Harry Frisbee.

A lady who is a guest at one of the leading hotels was Sunday a member of a yachting party in the vicinity of Chatham, when near Pollock Rip she noticed a peculiar object in the water. It proved to be an elegant waste paper basket, gay with blue ribbon, that had floated out of the Alva. The lady thinks she has a beautiful souvenir.

EARTHQUAKE IN GERMANY.

Wild Rush of Panic-Stricken School Children in Nieder Lahnstein.

BERLIN, Aug. 10.—At 8 30 this morning an earthquake was felt at Ems, Coblenz, Nassau and Nieder Lahnstein. The movement lasted for ten seconds. At Nieder Lahnstein the shock was so severe that a number of chimneys were thrown down and the people were in great fear for their lives. The school-house was damaged, and the scholars were panic-stricken. Wild rushes were made for the doors and windows, and some of the smaller children were hurt in the scramble to escape from the building, which it was thought would fall.

WEATHER INDICATIONS.

FAIR AND COOLER.

WASHINGTON, Aug. 10.—For the 24 hours from 8 a. m. to-day: For Massachusetts, Rhode Island and Connecticut, fair, southwesterly winds, cooler.

THUNDER STORMS.

BOSTON, Aug. 10.—Local forecast for New England until Thursday night: Fair weather, except thunder storms and local showers are likely this afternoon; stationary temperature, followed by slightly cooler Thursday night.

GLADSTONE'S EFFORT.

Acting on His Physicians Advice He Goes to the Country.

LONDON, Aug. 10.—Soon after Mr. Gladstone had delivered his speech yesterday it was learned that he was still feeling the effects of his illness. He had been advised by his physician not to wait the developments of the bill but to return to the country. Before he began to speak he took a drink of his customary stimulant, sherry flip, and during the delivery of his speech he had occasional recourse to the same drink. As soon as he had concluded he left for Mr. Stuart Rendel's country seat, Hatchlands, where he will remain until Thursday.

Both sides admitted the dexterity of his speech and admired the unfaltering power which poured out of neatly turned sentences.

In gleaning the opinion of the lobby the Associated Press found that the McCarthyites concurred in the opinion that the declarations were satisfactory. They could hardly express any other opinion as Mr. Balfour's reference to the party as "being squared" had obtained the credence of the whole house.

The Parnellites were not so satisfied. They were especially discontented with Mr. Gladstone for refraining from giving a pledge to release the dynamiters. Part of their discontent arises from the studied neglect of the liberal leaders to take them into their confidence. In spite of this the Parnellites are sure to vote with Mr. Gladstone on Thursday.

Mr. Balfour's reply was not the great effort that was expected. The conservative papers had led the public to believe he was preparing a strong vindication of the government policy. It seldom roused enthusiasm. It is evident his followers have agreed to shirk all legislation till they get into office. It is impossible to suppose Mr. Gladstone guilty of deliberate discourtesy in quitting the House directly after Mr. Balfour began to speak. We are forced to the conclusion that questions of health made it imperative. How then will he be able to endure the ceaseless and exhaustive labors of the treasury bench?

The *Chronicle* says: We doubt whether the oration delivered by Mr. Gladstone will be ranked among his finest efforts. It is only when started at bay that his oratorical genius soars to the highest flights. Yet it was a masterpiece of adroit allusiveness. Everybody knew that while he dealt laboriously with the speeches of Mr. Goschen and Mr. Mc Carthy it was only Mr. Redmond's demands that troubled him; and he solved the problem with consummate skill and dexterity. Nobody can say that he ignored Mr. Redmond, yet nobody can say that he even once recognized his face.

DON'T WANT A RECEIVER.

Fort Payne Stockholders Will Fight the Proposition.

BOSTON, Aug. 10.—The contention between the bondholders and the stockholders of the Fort Payne Coal & Iron Company is becoming of absorbing interest in financial circles, and at present the end appears to be a long way off.

The appointment of a receiver is not to the liking of the stockholders, who believe that tha bondholders are instituting a big scheme to freeze them out.

It will be remembered that on the 15th of last July at a meeting of the stockholders there was appointed a committee of fifteen to assist the present directors of the corporation in carrying out the plan of reorganization, and to select a board of management after the reorganization was effected.

The following members of this committee met at the Quincy House yesterday to further consider the various phases which the contest has now assumed: Hon. J. L. H. Cobb, Lewiston, Me.; Hon. Fred E. Smith, Montpelier, Vt.; Hon. Adna Brown, Springfield, Vt.; W. O. Burden, Millville; A. E. Himphill, Holyoke; George F. Pinkham, Wollaston; Hon. M. T. B. Chase, Augusta, Me.; Dr. Clarence Howe, Hanover; J. C. Leach, Bridgewater; Mr. Hawkes, Shelburne Falls.

Hon. J. L. H. Cobb presided. It was the unanimous opinion of those at the meeting that the appointment of a receiver would be most damaging in its results to the corporation, and it was decided to fight the proposition making this action permanent with all the force that the stockholders can command.

Seven of the nine directors reside in Fort Payne, and they will secure counsel to defend their interests and those of the stockholders.

Of course, nothing can be done for the present in the way of reorganization. This matter will have to remain in abeyance until the receivership question is out of the way.

There is every prospect that the property is going to be tied up for a long time, and during the interim the crossfire will be rapid and vigorous on both sides.

It is very likely that this fight will tend to depreciate the value of the property; at least, that is the belief of the committee on reorganization.

It should be understood that all the directors of the corporation are strongly in favor of the proposed plan of reorganization, and that at the meeting of the stockholders already referred to it was unanimously voted to sustain the proposition.

The stockholders have until Sept. 5th to defend the matter. The meeting adjourned, subject to the call of the chairman.

The outcome of the affair is awaited with considerable interest, even by those who are not directly connected with the company.

Republican Nominee Ineligible.

OMAHA, Neb., Aug. 10.—It has been discovered that Rev. J. G. Tate, the Republican nominee for Lieutenant-Governor, is ineligible. Tate is an Englishman and he failed to take out his papers until a year ago. The constitution requires that the Governor and Lieutenant-Governor shall have been citizens for two years prior to their election. The State committee will be called upon to fill the vacancy.

Wedding of Circus Freaks.

BOLIVAR, Mo., Aug. 10.—Extremes met in this city yesterday when the Texas giant, Col. Torvel, 7 feet 8 inches high, married Henrietta Merity, the midget, who is just 23 inches high. The couple have been the chief attraction with a circus in this section for some weeks.

Consul Ryder Confesses His Guilt.

COPENHAGEN, Aug. 10.—Henry B. Ryder, the United States consul here, who is under arrest charged with having misappropriated the sum of 200,000 kroners, has confessed that he is guilty of embezzlement and forgery.

Boston & Maine Dividend.

BOSTON, Aug. 10.—The Boston & Maine railroad has declared a $3 preferred stock dividend, payable Sept. 1st.

The Ocean Steamers.

Arrived at New York—Wisconsin, Liverpool; Sparndam, Rotterdam; Bellingham, Mediterranean ports; Spree, Bremen.

THE LEADING NEWSPAPER.

THE EVENING STANDARD has long been recognized as the leading newspaper of Southeastern Massachusetts. Every day the distance between the *Standard* and its neighbors in circulation is widening. It is of interest to advertisers to learn that the *Standard's* edition yesterday was exactly **8809**. In the amount, quality and accuracy of its news matter the *Standard* is far ahead of all other papers in this section.

HOME MATTERS.

THE SALVATION ARMY extended an invitation to the Mayor, Aldermen and Common Councilmen to its meeting last evening, and it was announced that the enforcement of the liquor law was to be the subject of discussion. When the time for holding the meeting came it was seen that none of those invited were present and the usual audience was but little augmented. The services were of the usual character, singing, prayer and exhortation. In his remarks John Mellor wished the Mayor and members of the Council were Christians and said if he knows it in future he will vote for no man who is not a true Christian. Prayer was also offered in behalf of the Mayor and he was alluded to vaguely in other testimonies, but to a person looking for a sensation there was little of interest in the meeting.

A ROOT BEER SENSATION.—The town of Rockland has been very animated for more than a week discussing the merits and evils of root beer. This started at a union temperance meeting held in the Baptist church at that place at which one of the local ministers made a vigorous tirade against a root beer manufacturing company of Hartford which had established a branch in Rockland. The town has been famed for its temperance principles, and it is stated that to purchase intoxicants of any kind within its borders was an impossibility. Rev. S. E. Ellis, a young pastor of the Centre Methodist church in Rockland, has been a most zealous temperance worker, and it was he who denounced the beverage on the ground that it might lead young men to drink intoxicants. The Hartford company have sold large quantities of their root beer extract and from their sampling store have given away bucketsful. The people of the town are divided concerning Mr. Ellis's action. The ministerial fraternity, with one exception, support him; this exception is a Congregational pastor who has been one of the imbibers. At the present time the root beer company is doing a big business and Mr. Ellis is attending the Yarmouth camp-meeting.

SIXTY MILLION BUSHELS OF WHEAT—*A Bushel for Every Inhabitant of the United States. The Kansas Crop for '92.*—Never in the history of Kansas has that State had such bountiful crops as this year. The farmers cannot get enough hands to harvest the great crop, and the Santa Fe railroad has made special rates from Kansas City and other Missouri river towns, to induce harvest hands to go into the State. The wheat crop of the State will be from sixty to sixty-five million bushels, and the quality is high. The grass crop is made, and is a very large one; the early potatoes, rye, barley and oat crops are made, and are all large. The weather has been propitious for corn, and it is the cleanest, best looking corn to be found in the country to-day. Cheap rates will be made from Chicago, St. Louis and all points on the Santa Fe east of the Missouri river, to all Kansas points, on August 30 and September 27, and these excursions will give a chance for Eastern farmers to see what the great Sunflower State can do. A good map of Kansas will be mailed free upon application to Jno. J. Byrne, 723 Monadnock Block, Chicago, Ill., together with reliable statistics and information about Kansas lands.

TO CHICAGO AND THE WEST.—The route affording the most advantages is via the Boston & Albany, New York Central and Michigan Central roads, "The Niagara Falls Route," and the route of the "North Shore Limited," which leaves Boston at 2 p. m. daily, and arrives at Chicago at 4 30 p. m. next day. Wagner buffet sleeping cars, dining car, serving all meals en route, smoking and library car comprises the equipment of this train, and ensures to passengers all the comforts and luxuries obtainable in railway travel. Three other express trains daily. For Summer tourist folder, describing western health and pleasure resorts, address W. H. Underwood, E. P. A. Mich. Cent. R. R., Buffalo, N. Y.

LARGE HAUL OF BLUEFISH.—Menhaden steamer Alaska, of Tiverton, Capt. Wilcox, made a great haul of bluefish near New London. The catch was pulled on board the steamer, but not before a portion of the net, in which it was estimated there were 2000 fish, had broken in two, allowing the fish to escape. Immediately after the haul was made the vessel turned about and went into port, having on board about 6000 bluefish, averaging four pounds each.

ICE AT THE NORTH.—Letters brought to San Francisco from Ounalaska by steamer St. Paul, from the Northern whaling fleet, were received in this city last evening, but they contain no additional particulars. One letter states that some of the vessels were in the ice northeast of Cape Thaddeus 44 days.

WILL SELL FOR A SONG!—Short lengths of carpetings, remnants of oil cloths, linoleums and straw mattings. We place no particular value on them, but we must close them out to be in condition for by and by. If you can use them you can buy them cheap. B. H. Waite & Co., 71 William street.

COME EARLY and secure the Bargains the Wamsutta Clothing Co. are offering. Our time is limited and everything must go. Wamsutta Clothing Co.

PATENTS have been granted to John B. Tarr of this city for a tobacco shaver, and to William Wadsworth of Fall River machine for punching leather loom pickers.

SEVENTY-FIVE Pairs Men's and Youths' Black Worsted Pants. Former price $4, $5 and $6, to be closed out this week at $3 per pair. Wamsutta Clothing Co.

TENDER FEET.—If there is a man with tender feet that wants to be comfortable let him see the bicycle shoe that we are selling for $2.00. Former price $3.00. Union Shoe Store.

ALL OF OUR $3.00 Hats to be closed out at $2.00. Makers, Lamson & Hubbard, Grenoble & Co. and other manufacturers. Wamsutta Clothing Co.

THE DEDICATION of the newly-furnished hall of O. Howland Engine Co., No. 4, occurs this evening.

CHILDREN'S SUITS and Knee Pants at a great reduction. Men's Suits, Youths' Suits, Boys' long pants Suits at cut prices. Wamsutta Clothing Co.

THINK OF IT.—Men's, Boys' and Youths' Tennis Shoes, leather trimmed, 27c. Union Shoe Store.

LOOK IN at our north window and see the 50c. Ties we are selling at 25c. Socks, three pairs for 25c. Wamsutta Clothing Co.

CHILDREN'S STIFF ANKLE SHOES. Devoll's.

HOOD'S Sarsaparilla is pleasant to take.

INSURANCE.

FIRE & LIGHTNING,
TORNADO,
PLATE GLASS and ACCIDENT
INSURANCE.

No. 48 North Water Street.

Ætna Ins. Co. .... Hartford
Hartford Fire Ins. Co. .... "
Connecticut Fire Ins. Co. .... "
Merchants Ins. Co .... Providence
Equitable F. & M. Ins. Co. .... "
Springfield F. & M. Ins. Co. .... Springfield
Ins. Co. of North America .... Philadelphia
Ins. Co. of State of Penn .... "
Fire Association .... "
Home Ins. Co. .... New York
Continental Ins. Co. .... "
German Am. Ins. Co. .... "
Niagara Fire Ins. Co. .... "
Williamsburgh City Fire Ins. Co. .... "
Hanover Fire Ins. Co .... "
Phœnix Assurance Co. .... London
Guardian Assurance Co. .... "
No. British & Mer. Ins. Co. .... "
Imperial Fire Ins. Co. .... "
Fitchburg Mut. Fire Ins. Co. .... Fitchburg
Dorchester Mut. Fire Ins. Co. .... Neponset
New York Plate Glass Ins. Co. .... New York
U. S. Mutual Accident Asso. .... "

GEO. N. ALDEN.
(Successor to Tillinghast & Alden.)
d&w

SAMUEL H. COOK,
Marine & Fire Insurance
AGENT AND BROKER,
No. 37 North Water Street.
(In National Bank of Commerce Building.)
Whaling Risks and their Catchings a Specialty at This Agency.

The following First Class Fire Insurance Companies are represented, viz.:
Hingham Mutual Fire Ins. Co. .... Hingham
Phœnix Ins. Co. .... Hartford
National Fire Ins. Co. .... "
Phenix Ins. Co. .... New York
Westchester Fire Ins. Co .... "
Commerce Ins. Co. .... Albany
Pennsylvania Fire Ins. Co. .... Philadelphia
American Fire Ins. Co. .... "
Queen Ins. Co. .... London
London Assurance Corp. .... "
London & Lancashire Ins. Co. .... "
Norwich Union F. Ins. Soc'y .... "
Northern Assurance Co. .... "
Firemen's Fire Ins. Co. .... Boston
The Metropolitan Plate Glass Ins. Co. .... New York
Hartford Steam Boiler Inspection and Ins. Co. .... Hartford

EDWIN EMERY. JOHN H. PEDRO
LAWRENCE GRINNELL & CO.,
Fire and Marine, Life and Plate Glass
Insurance
80 No. Water St., foot of William.
(Over Mechanics' National Bank.)

Liverpool & London & Globe Ins. Co., ... Liverpool
American Fire Ins. Co .... New York
Royal Ins. Co .... Liverpool
Prov. Washington Ins. Co .... Providence
Commercial Union Assurance Co .... London
Merchants' Ins. Co .... Newark
Boylston Ins. Co .... Boston
United States Inc. Co .... New York
Caledonian Ins. Co .... Scotland
Hamburg-Bremen Fire Ins. Co .... Bremen
American Ins. Co .... Boston
Spring Garden Ins. Co .... Philadelphia
Lowell Mutual Fire Ins. Co .... Lowell
Wachusett Mutual Fire Ins. Co .... Fitchburg
Mutual Life Ins. Co .... New York
Lloyd's Plate Glass Ins. Co .... New York

HIRAM VAN CAMPEN. JOHN W. PAUL.
HIRAM VAN CAMPEN & CO.,
FIRE, LIFE AND ACCIDENT
Insurance Agency,
No. 15 North Water Street.
Telephone Call .... 241-2.
(Established A. D. 1852.)
The following First Class Companies are represented:
Sun Fire Office .... London, Eng.
Organized A. D. 1710.
Lancashire Ins. Co .... Manchester, Eng.
The Reliance Ins. Co .... Philadelphia
Girard Fire & Marine Ins. Co. .... "
United Firemen's Ins. Co .... "
Michigan Fire & Marine Ins. Co .... Detroit, Mich.
Security Ins. Co .... New Haven, Ct.
People's Fire Ins. Co .... Manchester, N.H.
Firemen's Ins. Co .... Newark, N. J.
Newark Fire Ins. Co .... "
First National Fire Ins. Co .... Worcester, Mass.
Quincy Mut. Fire Ins. Co .... Quincy, Mass.
Holyoke Mut. Fire Ins. Co .... Salem, Mass.
Traders' & Mechanics' Ins. Co. .... Lowell, Mass.
Dorchester Mut. Fire Ins. Co. .... Boston
Cambridge Mut. Fire Ins. Co. .... Cambridgeport, Mass.
Travellers' Ins. Co., Hartford, Life & Accident.
All losses equitably adjusted and promptly paid.
New Bedford, April, 1890.

IVORY S. CORNISH. CLIFTON H. CORNISH
I. S. CORNISH & SON.
LIFE, FIRE, ACCIDENT and PLATE GLASS
—INSURANCE—
Agents and Brokers. 50 North Second St.
NEW BEDFORD, MASS.
Represent the following First-Class Companies:
Ætna Life Ins. Co. .... Hartford, Conn
Travelers Accident Ins. Co. .... Hartford, Conn
Merchants and Farmers Mutual Fire Ins. Co., ... Worcester, Mass
Citizens Mutual Ins. Co. .... Boston, Mass
Mass. Mutual Fire Ins. Co. .... Boston, Mass
Abington Mutual Fire Ins. Co. .... Abington, Mass
Salem Mutual Fire Ins. Co. .... Salem, Mass
Essex Mutual Fire Ins. Co. .... Salem, Mass
Merrimac Mutual Fire Ins. Co. .... Andover, Mass
Franklin Mutual Fire Ins. Co. .... Greenfield, Mass
Milford Mutual Fire Ins. Co. .... Milford, Mass
Glens Falls Ins. Co. .... Glens Falls, N. Y
Union Ins. Co. .... Philadelphia, Penn
New Hampshire Fire Ins. Co. .... Manchester, N.H
Peoples Fire Ins. Co. .... Manchester, N. H
Delaware Ins. Co. .... Philadelphia, Penn
Metropolitan Plate Glass Ins. Co. .... New York, N. Y
Losses promptly adjusted and paid.
Business solicited.

Bristol County Mutual Fire Ins. Co.
INCORPORATED 1829.
Insures Against Loss and Damage by
FIRE and LIGHTNING.
Insures only buildings, principally dwellings.
CASH PREMIUMS SMALL.
For reliable information call at the office,
NO. 48 NORTH WATER ST.
JAMES TAYLOR .... President
GEO. N. ALDEN .... Secretary and Treasurer
DIRECTORS:
James Taylor, Oliver P. Brightman,
Geo. F. Kingman, Isaac H. Coe,
Thos. H. Knowles, William R. Wing,
Samuel C. Hart.
Telephone Call 11—4. MWF&w

GOOD
COAL
ALWAYS

DENISON BROS. CO.,
Yard---Foot of Hillman Street.
Offices---Cor. School and South Water Sts., and Cor. Hillman and North Water Sts.

At this Season of the Year

We have a great many broken lots of Suits. One or two or three of a lot. These suits will be sold at less than the price of the goods to manufacture, in order to close them.

SANDERS & BARROWS,
67 and 69 William Street.

DON'T STOP ME
I know where to find
the Lowest
PRICES
in

HARNESSES,
Carriage Lap Robes, Horse Clothing, Whips, &c., Ladies' and Gents' Riding Saddles, Trunks, Bags, Pocketbooks, Bill Books, Umbrellas and all kinds Travelling Goods.
C. F. CUSHING, - - - - Opp. City Hall,
IS THE MAN.

CUT PRICES FOR ALL
Summer Clothing
ELEGANT NECKWEAR 25c. Each.
H. V. SANDERS & Co.
One Price Clothiers, } OPP. CITY CLOCK, 92 Purchase St.

NEW BEDFORD BRASS FOUNDRY.

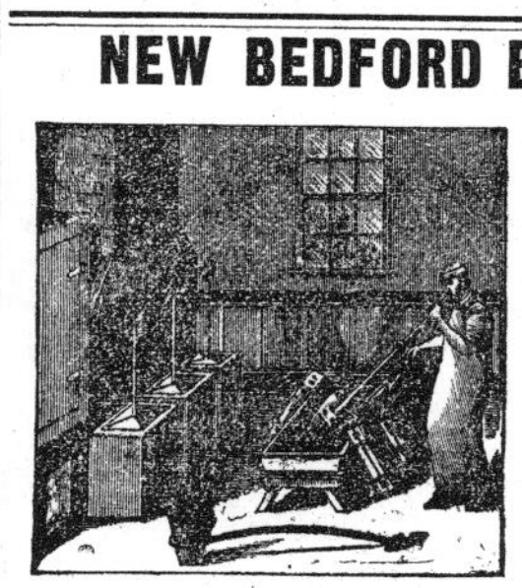

Machinists, Brass Finishers and Founders, Brass, Bronze and Composition Castings, Zinc and White Metal Pattern Castings, Phospor Bronze Castings a specialty, Lead Window Weights and High Speed Babbitt Metals, Chandelier Repairing and Brazing, Brass Finishing in all its branches. Machine Repairing promptly attended to. Lawn Mowers Sharpened and Repaired.

Foundry and Machine Shop, 108 North Water Street, foot of Elm.
WM. T. NICHOLSON, Manager, Formerly Foreman of the Armington & Sims Engine Company's Brass Foundry, Providence, R. I. je25-3m

We Use PURE PAINT. It is guaranteed to us by the manufacturer. It costs more than cheap substitutes, which are little better than whitewash. But

IT WILL WEAR. And that is what you want. The labor for putting on one is the same as the other. If you use the cheap kind

YOU SAVE 10 PER CENT. In cost and lose 75 per cent. in wear. It will pay you to have your painting done by

HART & AKIN,
No. 84 Pleasant St.,
No. 9 North Water St.,
Cor. Water and Walnut Sts.

TRY
39 TOBACCO!
Best in the Land for Smoking.
Be sure that the tag 39 is on every piece, and take nothing else in place of it.
Distributing Agents
Driscol, Church & Hall,
Wholesale Grocers,
NEW BEDFORD.

FINE CARRIAGES.

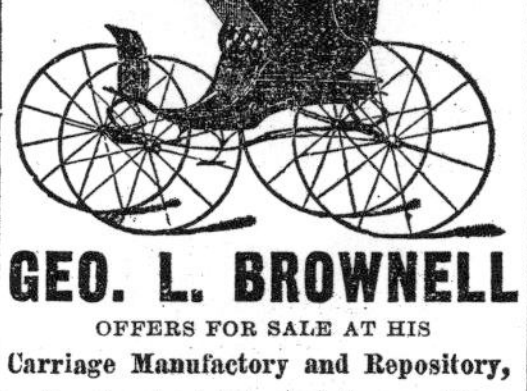

GEO. L. BROWNELL
OFFERS FOR SALE AT HIS
Carriage Manufactory and Repository,
Cor. Acushnet Ave. and Cannon St.,
NEW BEDFORD, ... MASS.,
A FINE assortment of Carriages, namely: Landaus, Coaches, Coupe Victorias, Coupe Rockaways, Extension and Standing Top Family Carryalls, Phaetons, Goddard Box Top Buggies, Open Road and Business Wagons. Also a very large assortment of SECOND-HAND CARRIAGES of all descriptions, which will be sold low.
GILES G. BARKER, Supt.

BRICKS.
Lime and Hair,
FOR PLASTERING.
Cement.
Masons' Building Materials in general.
S. S. PAINE & BRO.,
Front St., just south of bridge.

Smoke the New Nickel Cigar,

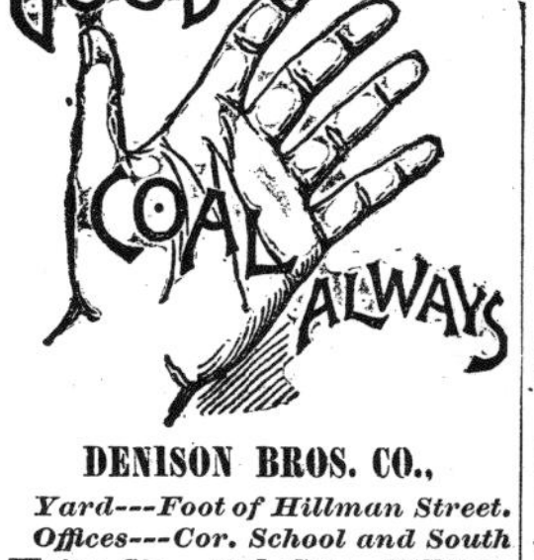
AMERICAN TRAMP

IT IS THE LEADER.
FOR SALE EVERYWHERE. au6-1m

RELEASED FROM CUSTODY.

The Police Place Confidence in Bridget Sullivan.

Nervous but Straightforward Witness at Inquest.

Miss Borden's Lawyer Refused Permission to be Present.

Attorney-General Intimates He Has a Strong Case.

"Police Officers Do Not Tell All They Know," He Says.

Instead of subsiding, the excitement in Fall River increases hourly. Yesterday it was at fever heat. In the afternoon, when the carriage was sent to the Borden homestead to convey Miss Lizzie and her friend to the station house, the news that the police had started on such an errand leaked out instantly. Business was suspended in the centre of the town, as it had been suspended on Thursday noon when the story of the tragedy was made known for the first time. What was there to see? A hack drawn by two horses, with two ladies on the back seat, and two officers in citizens' dress on the front seat, but that appeared to be sufficient. Men on wagons saw the vehicle coming, and drove like mad for the entrance to the station. Men, women and children joined in a hasty scramble for the narrow alleyway, and once more Court square was choked in a twinkling.

It isn't singular that the tension tightens. The community has reached a point where it feels that it must clear up the mystery or go insane. Men are again complaining that they go to bed with the murder on their brain, and that the same grim problem presents itself for solution the moment they open their eyes. It is the pace that kills, and for five days the pace has been furious.

Government's Lips Sealed.

It looked all day yesterday as it looked the day before, namely, as if the end was approaching. The lips of the government are sealed, but the public knows that every thread has been wound up; that there are no loose ends hanging, and that a decision must be reached within 48 hours. Will the conclusions of the officials and the prosecuting attorney of the district warrant an arrest? Have they evidence enough in their possession to make them reasonably sure of a conviction in case they do arrest the suspected. They have reviewed and re-reviewed every detail; they have examined Bridget Sullivan for hours, and every word that she has uttered has been caught by a stenographer. They have prepared to interrogate Miss Lizzie Borden and to put her replies and statements on paper. As the situation now stands these witnesses are the only two people on the face of the earth who can assist them. Others have told all that they knew, and it amounted to nothing. If the servant and Miss Borden have been equally frank, the verdict must soon be rendered. The fact that the district attorney was summoned on Monday and that Mr. Pillsbury, the attorney-general of the State, was called from Boston yesterday proved that the authorities have abandoned all hope of making further progress along the line they were pursuing. Their conference with Mr. Knowlton proved that there was

Nothing New

In the nature of their evidence. It was purely circumstantial. If it were not strong enough to hold, suspicion must be lifted from the household where it had rested, the guards on the premises must be called in and the detectives and local force must find a fresh trail. There is no fresh trail, however. The government admits that it has had but one theory from the beginning, and that if that theory is incorrect, or if they cannot confirm it, whether it is correct or incorrect, they have none to take its place.

INTERIOR VIEW OF HAY LOFT WHERE LIZZIE BORDEN SAYS SHE REMAINED AT THE TIME OF THE TRAGEDY.

Theories galore have been suggested, of course, and many of them have been tested, but none, with the exception of the one on which they have been proceeding, has been accepted. At 5 o'clock yesterday afternoon it was known that nothing of a startling nature had been developed by the inquest, so far as the examination of the servant was concerned. The girl was cool and collected, and told the story which she related when she was questioned concerning her whereabouts on the morning of the murder, and her experiences bearing on the discovery of the two bodies. She did not halt or hesitate, and the cross-examination failed to shake her. The discrepencies in her testimony as given before the district attorney and to the police officers who have interviewed her from time to time were too trifling to be noticed. If Miss Borden is as successful under fire as Bridget Sullivan has been,

The Inquest Will Not Figure Prominently in the Case.

The former was not placed on the stand yesterday afternoon. attorney-general Pillsbury arrived at the Mellen House before he was expected, and the District Attorney, City Marshal and others who were conducting the examination, left the court house immediately and engaged in a consultation with him. It is safe to state, however, that all the evidence, so far as the police are concerned, was in on Monday afternoon, and that they did not hope to add to their case by means of the more formal proceedings which were to follow.

It was given out at 430 that there would be no arrest last night, but that announcement caused no surprise. The inquest had not been finished and it was known that the government wished the attorney-general to pass on the case. He had not had time to hear all the evidence or to weigh it carefully, and while there were reports to the effect that several arrests would be made before midnight, they were not generally credited. There is one able detective who seems to have dropped out of the case entirely for the past two days, and he is Mr. Hanscom of the Pinkerton Agency. He gave an opinion on Sunday, was credited with having incurred the hostility of the local force and out-of-town officers who arrived earlier on the scene, and disappeared from the newspapers. It would be interesting to learn just what his relations to the government were and what course he advised. A great deal is sometimes taken for granted, and

Mr. Hanscom's Summing Up the Situation,

coupled with the orders issued Sunday night relative to visitors to the Borden house, led to the conclusion, and possibly a hasty conclusion, that the local force did not intend to lend him any assistance. The other officers and officials were fully occupied yesterday. When they were not in attendance at the inquest they travelled in pairs. The city marshal had State Officer Seaver for a constant companion. Medical Examiner Dolan and State Officer Rhodes hurried about in a coupe, and all four were grouped every now and then about attorney-general Pillsbury and District Attorney Knowlton.

None of the quintet cared to talk for publication. The Attorney-General left the city at 3 40 and the inquest was resumed. Mr. Pillsbury was a trifle sarcastic. He said, just before he left, that he did not think the case was so mysterious as had been reported, and joked with the press representatives concerning their clews. He was informed that the murder was mysterious enough to baffle the police, and that five days had elapsed and there had been no arrest. Somebody took the pains to further inform him that the evidence was entirely circumstantial. "You newspaper men know, or ought to know," said Mr. Pillsbury, "that you may not be in a position to pronounce on the case. There may be some things that you have not heard of and which may have an important bearing." The reply was to the effect that the head men who had been working on the murder had allowed at noon that they had no other evidence and that they ought to be pretty good authority.

"Police Officers Do Not Always Tell All They Know,"

was the parting shot of the attorney general. After Mr. Pillsbury's departure the examination in the court-house was conducted until 6 o'clock. Last evening District Attorney Knowlton issued the following brief bulletin—he was told it would grow before morning: "Inquest opened at 10 a. m. this morning before Judge Blaisdell. District attorney resepnt conducting. Inquest adjourned to Wednesday at 10 a. m."

At 5 o'clock Bridget Sullivan left the police station in company with Officer Doherty and passed down Court square. She was dressed in a green gown with hat to match and appeared to be nervous and excited. Nobody knew her, however, and she attracted no attention whatever. She went to the Borden house for a bundle and, still accompanied by Officer Doherty walked to No. 95 Division street, where her cousin, Patrick Harrington, lives, and where she passed the night. She was allowed to go on her own recognizance and seemed to be much relieved to get away from the Borden house. The government impressed her with the necessity of saying nothing about the proceedings at the inquest and she was warned not to talk with anybody about her testimony. Bridget Sullivan is one of 14 children. She came to this country six years ago. For three years she worked for a number of families in Fall River, and the police say that she bears an excellent reputation. For the last three years she has lived with the Borden family, and for some time past has been threatening to return to Ireland. She says that

Mrs. Borden Was a Very Kind Mistress

and that she was much attached to her. Mrs. Borden used to talk to her about going home to Ireland, and used to tell her that she would be lonely without her. Accordingly, the girl says that she did not have the heart to leave, but she never expected to be in an awful predicament like this. She had been terrified ever since the tragedy, she said.

Prof. Wood of Cambridge arrived on the 4 o'clock train yesterday afternoon, but was not called on to testify at the inquest yesterday. He was questioned regarding the nature of his visit, and stated that he had come to this city to see what there was for him to do.

"Have you examined any axe, Professor?" was asked.

Prof. Wood hesitated a moment, and said: "I have seen an axe."

"Will you make an examination down here?" was the next question.

"I do not expect to," was the reply. "I could not very well bring down my laboratory."

At 6 o'clock Miss Lizzie Borden, accompanied by her friend, Mrs. George Brigham, and Marshal Hilliard, entered a carriage and drove to Miss Borden's home. The excitement was not over for the day, but the district attorney's bulletin made it plain that the authorities would make no further move last night. When the inquest adjourned the situation in a nutshell was this: The authorities were evidently convinced that they could rely on Bridget Sullivan, and she was released from custody, for she has been in custody since Thursday noon. Miss Lizzie Borden has been partially examined, and the police had completed their work on the case, so far as the collection of evidence is concerned.

The Mystery About the Inquest.

There was almost as much mystery about the scenes incidental to the inquest yesterday as there was about the murder. In the first place the authorities seemed to want it understood that there was no inquest. Some of them intimated that the government was simply conducting an informal examination with a view to drawing from the witnesses their last stories and making a comparison of them. In fact, that was the impression which prevailed in town up to noon, and it was reported that the oath was not administered. Nevertheless the great pains which all connected with the proceedings took to keep information from the police made it plain that the officials were winding up the case.

The District Court room, which is usually open to all who care to visit it, and which is usually visited by the idle element, was guarded as jealously as the Borden house on Second street. During the morning an officer sat at the head of the stairs leading from the guard room, and in the afternoon two patrolmen were on duty, one at the top of the stair case and one at the foot, and warned off those who attempted to approach, and of course all those who went in or came out refused to utter a syllable.

Neither the servant nor Miss Borden was represented by counsel, and that fact occasioned some little comment. It is known that A. J. Jennings, Esq., called at the city marshal's office and applied for permission to look after the interests of the witnesses, but it was refused. It is stated that Mr. Jennings, who can protest on occasions, argued at length against being excluded, but the government would not yield, and he was obliged to withdraw. Consequently it was doubted last night if he were any better informed than the public regarding the nature of the testimony. He had a short talk on Main street with Detective Hanscom, and went home early.

It was whispered in police circles during the evening that

There was Something Very Significant

in the fact that Bridget Sullivan, the only government witness, with the exception of Miss Lizzie Borden, and a person on whom the prosecution must rely to explain certain occurrences before and after the tragedy, was allowed to go on her own recognizances, and at 6 o'clock the bearing of the officials who have worked up the case indicated that they were in possession of information which they considered as very valuable, and which they had hitherto been unable to secure.

The servant, who is intelligent and well informed, must be more intimately acquainted with the conditions of things in the Borden household than anybody outside of the family. She had worked there three years, and, as a rule, servants are observant. A friend of hers said yesterday afternoon that she knew that Bridget Sullivan wanted to tell the truth and that she had nothing to conceal. The government dismissed her solely on her promise to return in case she was wanted, and this is taken to mean that the theory which has been entertained all along is to be abandoned, or that the servant's testimony, as taken by Miss White the stenographer, contains all the information the police can possibly get from her. This was mere supposition, however, and nobody felt any too sure concerning his conclusion.

The following brief conversation took place when the servant went to the Borden house for a bundle at 5 o'clock. Miss Lizzie had not returned from the police station and her sister was keeping house:

"Are you coming back to-night, Maggie?" asked Miss Emma.

"Not to-night, Miss Emma," was the reply.

"Are you coming back to-morrow night?"

"Not to-morrow night, Miss Emma," said the servant again.

"I just wanted to know," said Miss Borden, as she bade the servant good night.

Yesterday the public looked for some action by the police as the outcome of District Attorney Knowlton's arrival Monday and conference with the city marshal, medical examiner and the State officials. The rumor that either one or two warrants had been prepared Monday evening and lacked only the signature of the city marshal to warrant their execution also impressed the public. What actually happened, however, was not in the nature of

A Decisive Movement by the Authorities.

They only proceeded to further investigation, being led to this action by a desire on the part of District Attorney Knowlton to secure better grounds for suspecting the family than have yet been discovered. The conference Monday night was not attended, it is to be noted, by any member of the family or representative of the Borden girls, who have two of the ablest friends they could possibly have on their side—Mr. A. J. Jennings, their lawyer, and detective Hanscom; nor was there any attendance of their friends or advisers at the inquiry yesterday forenoon. This remarkable feature of the case, of course, deepens the distinct impression which has been prevalent since the day of the crime was discovered, that the authorities are unfriendly to the family, or at least, find reasons to make them strongly suspect that the

Misses Borden Know More or Less About the Case.

It is very seldom that when a murder is committed in a family, the family is not taken into the confidence of the police, and much more seldom that a family has to prepare to fight the law officers of a whole city and county.

The Inquest Begun.

At 9 30 o'clock a. m. yesterday Bridget Sullivan was notified that her presence was required at police headquarters and she went to the Central Station under escort of Officer Dougherty. Awaiting her presence were District Attorney Knowlton, State Officer Seaver, Marshal Hilliard and Medical Examiner Dolan, and soon after they were joined by Mayor Coughlin. A report that an inquest was under way quickly spread, but received prompt denial by the marshal. When asked the meaning of the gathering he said it was an inquiry and the officers were searching for information. The domestic was in the presence of the officials for several hours and was subject to a searching

Horsford's
ACID PHOSPHATE.
An agreeable preparation of the phosphates, for Indigestion, Nervousness, Mental and Physical Exhaustion.
Recommended and prescribed by Physicians of all schools.
Trial bottle mailed on receipt of 25 cents in stamps. Rumford Chemical Works, Providence, R. I.

MANHOOD RESTORED.

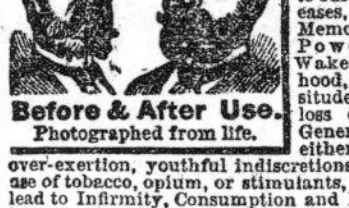

Before & After Use.
Photographed from life.

"SANATIVO," the Wonderful Spanish Remedy, is sold with a Written Guarantee to cure all Nervous Diseases, such as Weak Memory, Loss of Brain Power, Headache, Wakefulness, Lost Manhood, Nervousness, Lassitude, all drains and loss of power of the Generative Organs in either sex, caused by over-exertion, youthful indiscretions, or the excessive use of tobacco, opium, or stimulants, which ultimately lead to Infirmity, Consumption and Insanity. Put up in convenient form to carry in the vest pocket. Price $1 a package, or 6 for $5. With every $5 order we give a written guarantee to cure or refund the money. Sent by mail to any address. Circular free in plain envelope. Mention this paper. Address,
MADRID CHEMICAL CO., Branch Office for U. S. A.
358 Dearborn Street, CHICAGO, ILL.
FOR SALE IN NEW BEDFORD, MASS., BY S. H. & H. A. Lawton, Apothecaries, Union St.

A HEALTHY SKIN
Is the best safeguard to the bodily health of a human being that he can possibly have, and physicians unite in pronouncing
TURKISH BATHS
the best agent for securing it.
YOU NEED A BATH!
No. 5 South Sixth Street,

DRANK TWO GALLONS A DAY.

They Gave Him Up and He Went to the Hospital.

Smith of Providence Couldn't Walk, but Now He Can Race.

And His House Becomes a Mecca for the Folks Who Wear Crutches.

PROVIDENCE, R. I., Aug. 9.—Frank Smith has had a hard time. Not very long ago he was the owner of a prosperous business in one of the suburbs of Boston.

Now he resides at 165 Richmond street, in this city, and he is forced to work for a bare livelihood.

This change of fortune was due primarily to the breaking down of his health and consequent inability to attend to business.

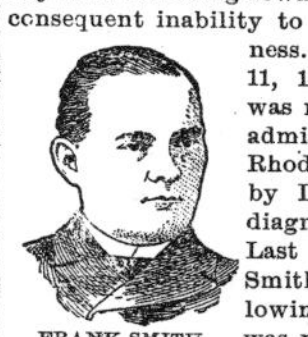

FRANK SMITH.

On December 11, 1890, Mr. Smith was recommended for admission to the Rhode Island Hospital by Dr. Terry. The diagnosis was diabetes. Last September, Mr. Smith wrote the following letter, which was published in the Providence papers: "When I was admitted to the Rhode Island Hospital, I had a stiffness and pain in my legs and staggered like an old man of 90. I drank at least two gallons of water a day. It was then that I began to lose my sight, and the five doctors that I had told me that I was afflicted with diabetes.

"I tried several medicines that were recommended, but found they did me no good. Seven weeks ago I began using Paine's celery compound, and to-day I can run as well as any man of fifty in this state. For two years I had a tingling in my fingers and toes like lightning that comes from the heart, but Paine's celery compound has got the better of that. May the Lord pour his choicest blessings on the man that discovered this boon. Every man that I see that has an ache or a pain, I tell about this compound. It cures them all.

"There is one old man who lives near me who has been on crutches for a long while. I got him a bottle of the compound and he has already thrown away his crutches.

"Every word of this is true, and I am willing to swear to it before any judge in the world. All my friends wonder how I have picked up and ask me what doctor I have had. I tell them that Paine's celery compound has done all this for me."

In an interview to-day with Mr. Smith, he stated: "The publication of this statement brought so many to see me that my house looked like a hospital. They come limping along with canes, thirty or forty a day, and I tell every one of them that Paine's celery compound will make them well. I know of a great many who have taken my advice and the compound did just what I said it would."

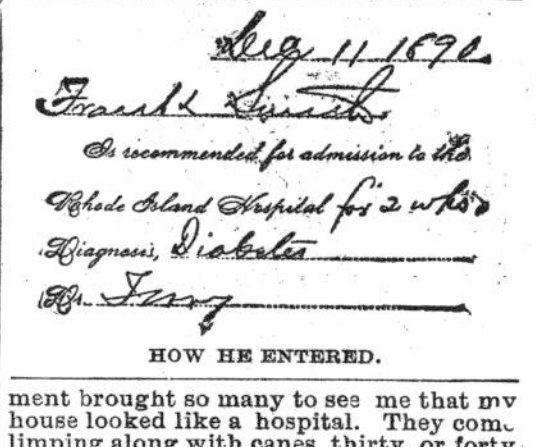
Is recommended for admission to the
Rhode Island Hospital for 2 wks
Diagnosis, Diabetes

HOW HE ENTERED.

Inquiry among Mr. Smith's friends shows that he states nothing but facts in regard to his case. Many other instances of the kind are widely talked of here in Providence, where Paine's celery compound has effected cures after physicians had given up hope. Local physicians who have been interviewed agree that it is undoubtedly the most reliable means known for curing rheumatism, diseases of the nervous system, kidney troubles.

Physicians in this city prescribe the compound freely, as they are acquainted with its formula and know that it is not a patent medicine. It gives health and strength to the weak and suffering and has the endorsement of the best people in the community.

cross-examination, every detail of the tragedy being gone over exhaustively.

Upon the arrival of the Sullivan woman at the Second District Court, which adjoins the police station, the officers were all in readiness, and a swarm of newspaper men sought admittance to the room. They were hurried out and the door closed. But Fall River is a leaky place, and at 12 30 o'clock, after the hearing adjourned for dinner, the proceedings were revealed. There were present Judge Blaisdell, District Attorney Knowlton, City Marshal Hilliard, District Officers Seaver and Rhodes, Medical Examiner Dolan, the district attorney's stenographer, Miss Annie Read, and a couple of police officials, who were among the first called to the house of the Bordens last Thursday. Bridget Sullivan

Was in Deep Distress,

and, if she had not already cried her eyes out, would probably have been very much agitated. On the contrary, while tremulous in voice and now and then crying a little, she was calm enough to receive the interrogatories without exhibiting much emotion and answered them comprehensively. The first question put to her was in regard to her whereabouts all through the morning of Thursday up to the time of the murder. She answered that she had been doing her regular work in the kitchen on the first floor. She had washed the breakfast dishes. She saw Miss Lizzie pass through the kitchen after breakfast time and the young lady might have passed through again. Bridget continued that she had finished up her work down stairs and resumed window washing on the third floor, which had been begun the preceding day. She might have seen Mrs. Borden as she went upstairs; she could hardly remember. Mr. Borden had already left the house.

The witness went up into the third floor, and while washing windows talked down to the sidewalk with a friend. She went on with the windows and might have made considerable noise as she raised and lowered them. She heard no noise inside the house in the meantime. By-and-by she heard Miss Lizzie Borden call her. She answered at once and went down stairs. She answered at once and went down stairs. Miss Borden didn't tell her what the matter was when she called her. Bridget said she went down stairs to the first floor, not thinking of looking about on the second floor, where Mrs. Borden was found dead shortly afterwards, because there was nothing to make her look around as she obeyed Miss Lizzie's call. She found Mr. Borden dead and Lizzie at the door of the room.

MEDICAL EXAMINER W. A. DOLAN.

The last point touched yesterday was the letter sent to Mrs. Borden warning her that she might be poisoned. Bridget said she knew nothing about this matter at all. Judge Blaisdell dines at 12 o'clock with great punctuality, but he waited considerably later to get as far as possible with the Sullivan woman's testimony. The poor girl begged to go home when the hearing was adjourned, but she was not allowed to.

About 1 o'clock p. m. yesterday the city, already excited and expecting a development in the Borden case, somehow found out that the authorities were going to

Bring Miss Borden to Police Headquarters.

The city marshal and Officer Harrington drove to the house in a hack at 1 40 o'clock. Apparently the entire business portion of Fall River expected the arrival of the hack at the Borden house. People gathered on all corners by which the carriage was to proceed in going to and from the house, and lined Second street sidewalks, while a long string of horses and wagons, some containing people who were out driving, were ranged in the street in front of the house.

City Marshal Hilliard does not ordinarily serve subpœnas, but he served one on this occasion. It was a regular summons to appear as a witness at an inquest. He found Mrs. George S. Brigham, an old friend of the Borden girls, in the house with the ladies. Just after the marshal entered the house Mrs. Brigham left the house and crossed the street to the office of Dr. Bowen opposite. The crowd were much excited by this, for they supposed it betokened the illness of one of the inmates of the house, and this, following upon the visit of the city marshal, looked as if the marshal had announced that it was his duty to arrest one or more of the inmates of the house. But a moment later Mrs. Brigham left the doctor's office and re-entered the Borden residence.

The city marshal served his paper, which summoned Miss Borden to the inquest, and soon after that young lady, Mrs. Brigham, the city marshal and Officer Harrington drove away from the house. They arrived at the police station at 2 o'clock. A large crowd was waiting to see who was in the carriage. Miss Borden, who was dressed in black, but not deep mourning, got out of the hack last. She was pallid and bit her nether lip as she went through the crowd, but she stepped lightly and entered the door without assistance.

What transpired after the inquest entered the Second District Court room cannot be known at present. The doors were locked, and no one but the county and city officials who are conducting the inquest was allowed within. The hearing must have been an extended one, for Miss Borden did not leave the court room till o'clock. She was then driven back to her home in a carriage, Mrs. Brigham and the city marshal with her.

A Hypothetical Solution.

The Lowell Times says:

Has this possibility been before suggested? May not the assassin have concealed himself in the house the night before and shadowed the members of the household? This question may be answered by another: Why then did he not do his murderous work and escape in the night? Possibly because his purpose was only to kill Mr. Borden, and so he waited to catch him alone. While shadowing his intended victim, may he not have been discovered by Mrs. Borden and killed her to escape detection? May not the absence of Miss Lizzie from the house and that of the servant from the lower floor have given him the very opportunity which he awaited?

As an hypothesis this is tolerable, whether we believe the murderer to have been in collusion with certain members of the household or not. At least it is certainly tenable if we are to believe that there was such collusion. It may be said that the felon could not have escaped by daylight. Yet to the best of our knowledge and belief the assassin did escape by daylight. Indeed, we are forced to accept this or the conclusion that Lizzie Borden or the servant girl did the deed. Morse was not there, be it remembered. All that we claim for our supposition is that it gets the murderer into the house under the cover of darkness, and thus disposes of the great difficulty. How he got out unobserved is another matter, but, we repeat, he did get out unless one of the two women did the butchery. That the actual killing was done by a woman of

[Continued on Seventh Page.]

PROSPEROUS VOTERS.

They Are Enjoying the Blessings of Protection.

Business and Politics in the Western Counties.

Democrats Doubtful of New York—Second Place---Gossip.

[Special Correspondence of the Standard.]
BOSTON, Aug. 9.

Having just returned from a business trip into Franklin, Berkshire, Hampden and Hampshire counties, your correspondent would report a very favorable state of business in all those sections. In the manufacturing centers extensive additions to existing "plants," are being made, or wholly new ones are being put in. All this does not indicate that the manufacturers of those lines of goods are being so terribly ground down by the McKinley bill. But more than that; not only are the manufacturers, their employes and merchants depending on them quite well satisfied with the present appearance of business matters, but the farmers are blessed with generous crops, and with a "home market" right at their doors, they seem to have no excuse for voting in support of a line of policy that will narrow their market or reduce their prices. When Gov. Russell makes his annual cattleshow pilgrimage over the state, and especially to the western part, he will have very few who will believe any statements made as to the "blight of protection." Intelligent men know the McKinley system of protection has not blighted, but stimulated and helped all kinds of business all through that section.

Of course your correspondent improved the opportunity to make some political inquiries, for it is almost time to begin shaking the tree of politics. The fruit is very unripe as yet, but it is well "set;" and a few lively caucuses will fill it out in a hurry. But there is no mistaking the fact that the Republicans in that part of the state expect and desire that the nomination for Governor go to Mr. Haile. For the second place on the ticket they will cordially support any man from the eastern part of the state. Local politics up there have hardly begun to shape themselves. Councillor Morgan of Springfield will doubtless be renominated by the Republicans; and it is hinted that Senator Kimball of Northampton will be his Democratic opponent. The latter does not deny the soft impeachment. Mr. Morgan had 19,628 votes, last year, to 18,565 for the Democratic candidate and 2286 for the Prohibition nominee. Senator Hickox from the Berkshire district will doubtless be retained, while both parties will have to choose new men in the Berkshire-Hampshire district. Capt. W. R. Kimball of Enfield is now most prominently mentioned as Republican candidate for senator in the Hampshire-Worcester district. He has already served in the House, and is a Grand Army member. Yet there is threatened opposition on account of the Congressional "unpleasantness" of two years ago. Down in the Hampden districts, the Republicans expect to carry at least one, if not both, of them, instead of being represented by two Democrats, as this year.

There is a very sharp, but perfectly good tempered, rivalry between Senator S. P. Smith of Athol and Representatives F. H. Gillett of Springfield for the Republican Second district congressional nomination. This district is strongly Republican, and either of these gentlemen is unusually well equipped to represent his constituents. They were both members of the class of 1874 of Amherst college, and are personal friends. Mr. Smith has had a little longer experience in politics, having served in the House and two years in the Senate, while Mr. Gillett has only had two years in the House. But in his last year, 1892, he was chairman of the House judiciary committee, regarded as the highest position in that body.

Up in the First district, the Democrats will undoubtedly nominate Congressman Crosby of Pittsfield, and the gossip now talked of to run against him is Lawyer N. H. Brooks of Holyoke who has won an excellent reputation in the Paper City, and has served it as city solicitor. He is a "hustler," has a host of friends who would take off their coats for him, and would lead Mr. Crosby a very hot race even if he did not come in ahead.

While one sees all kinds of talk for effect in the papers, yet once in a while we get an honest opinion. A gentleman from Troy, N. Y., who has been a candidate for high office in the Republican party, told me, the other day, that leading Democrats of that state admit to him privately that in their opinion the result there will be very close. Publicly, of course, they "claim everything;" but they know better all the time. In the opinion of this gentleman, the Republicans have an excellent show for carrying the state. The Bill men are not taking hold for Cleveland, no matter what is said by some very desirable home lots and some to the contrary, while the Republicans

are united, harmonious, active and zealous.

The talk over nomination for second place in the State ticket seems about as vague as ever. This may depend considerable upon the congressional contests, especially if it is conceded that Mr. Haile is to go to the head of the ticket. The new allotment of the districts, last year, had necessitated a new arrangement of political bed fellows, and there is considerable scrambling to get under cover before the cold caucus nights come on when many a candidate will find that he has been "left." On the protection issue properly presented as the main stake in the national contest, the Republicans should carry ten or eleven of the thirteen districts. The Republicans have all the facts on their side, while the Democrats must depend very largely on theory.

Bits of Gossip.

The Democratic state central committee will conduct a "literary bureau," taking space in papers at advertising rates for campaign matter.

The Boston Advertiser notes that the drift of the country today is away from the Democrats.

The Western Massachusetts Republicans are much pleased at having the assistance of the Morning Union, and the Union has a good strong support already assured.

The Democrats are talking up Carroll of Springfield as candidate for lieutenant governor. A. M. B.

STOP HOWLING CALAMITY.

A Wonderful Showing Made by a Democratic Journal.

(From New York Herald, July 17.)

The business of the country is in a provokingly healthy and flourishing condition. Imports during the fiscal year ending June 30 were greater than those of any former year, amounting to eight hundred and thirty-three million dollars, while exports also exceeded the highest record, and reached the enormous aggregate of one billion twenty-seven million dollars. Railroad earnings for the first six months of the year are greater than those for any similar period in history, and the output of manufactures has been greater than ever before. Business failures for the first half of the present year have been one thousand fewer in number and forty million dollars less in gross liabilities than they were during the corresponding period of 1891. New enterprises for manufacturing iron, cotton, and woolen fabrics are going into operation in various sections; and while the margin of profits is small, business is on a solid foundation, and the outlook in every direction is hopeful and encouraging. The grain crop is promising, money is abundant, and collections are easy. In the face of such a condition of things, the calamity howler must remain silent.

HE WANTS HARRISON AGAIN.

Why a Man From Saxony Would Remove His Mills to New Hampshire.

(From Manchester, N. H., Union.)

Among last week's visitors to New Hampshire from abroad was a gentleman from Saxony, who was in search of a site for a hosiery mill which he could buy upon certain conditions. This man has been, and is, engaged in the manufacture of hosiery in his own country, and before the passage of the McKinley bill employed 600 hands, who worked sixty-three hours and a half hours a week for an average of three dollars, or fifty cents a day. He marketed his goods largely in the United States, and was able to sell at satisfactory prices all he could make, but when the McKinley bill went into effect it closed the doors of the American market against him, and his mill is now running only a portion of the time because there is no sale for his goods. Therefore, he has come over the ocean to look into the situation here, and having concluded to build a factory in New England and move his business here. He wants, however, to buy upon condition that President Harrison is re-elected, for if Cleveland is elected and we have free trade, he prefers of course to remain in Saxony, where he can hire his help for one-half what he must pay here, or less.

A STRAIGHT CHALLENGE.

Democratic Editors Given a Challenge to Put Up or Shut Up.

(From American Economist.)

There is not a Democratic editor in the land from Cape Cod to San Francisco, from Lake Itasca to Key West, who is not today buying the very paper on which he prints his McKinley prices falsehoods for less money than he paid before the McKinley bill was passed. We know of our own personal knowledge that it is true of the New York free-trade dailies—one of them is saving $60,000 a year in the fall of the price of its paper below the price actually paid for it before the new tariff was enacted.

The American Protective Tariff League will pay $1,000 to that Democratic editor who will show that paper of the quality and kind used by him to publish his McKinley prices falsehoods cannot be purchased in the open market from five to forty per cent cheaper than it cost under the old tariff.

PROTECTION FOR OUR FARMERS.

From Gov. McKinley's Speech at Beatrice, Neb.

We constitute less than 5 per cent of the world's population, and yet we consume 20 per cent of the sugar of the world, 30 per cent of the coffee of the world, 33 per cent of the iron of the world, 33 per cent of the steel of the world, 33 per cent of the copper of the world, 33 per cent of the lead, 35 per cent of the cotton, 32 per cent of the wool, 40 per cent of the coal, and 50 per cent of the tin of the world. Yet there are those who would adopt an economic policy that would give to the other nations this matched market. We would

---

PITHY PRACTICAL POINTERS.

Some Solid, Satisfying Statistics Suggesting Simple Solution.

American Economist:—The year ending with June ranks as the greatest in the history of our country in manufactures, exports, domestic trades and railway earnings, while the number of failures reported are the least in five years.

Boston Journal:—The census statistics show that, between 1880 and 1890, wages in the woolen industries of this country increased 19 1-4 per cent, in the cotton industries 23 3-4 per cent, and in the manufacture of silk goods 32 per cent. And this under the "blight" of a protective tariff.

Home Market Bulletin:—On petition of 28,000 tailors, the Democratic House, in face and eyes of the mugwumps, ran in defiance of its own party platform, has passed a bill to limit the free importation of wearing apparel to $100. The dudes are distracted.

Home Market Bulletin:—The Idaho miners struck for a uniform wage of $3.50 a day. Last spring nearly 100,000 English miners struck for $1.25 a day.

Philadelphia Press:—So the Republicans have four chances of re-electing Harrison without New York and three without New York or Indiana. But the Democrats are not so well situated. There is no reasonable combination of electoral votes that can be made which will elect a Democratic President without the vote of New York. Classing West Virginia as doubtful and the reasonably sure Democratic electoral vote is 167, including four votes from Michigan.

In Australia there are caterpillars from six inches to a foot long, and when a young lady has one of them drop on her back hair she says something in a seven octave voice, with a calliope attachment rung onto it.

In 1888, at the siege of Herat by the Persians, Mahmoud Shah had a heavy bronze gun which he loaded, and when the siege was raised the gun was saved to pieces and taken back to Teheran.

The longest canal in the world is claimed to be the one which extends from the frontier of China to St. Petersburg. It measures in all 4,472 miles.

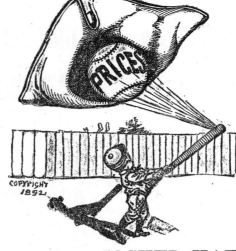

COPYRIGHT 1892.

THEY STRONGLY SUPPORT THE TAIL OF THE TICKET.
From Judge.

INTO A COCKED HAT.

That is just what has happened to the prices of our Spring Suits; they have been knocked into a Cocked Hat. Every time there is a big tumble something is damaged; in this case it is the price not the goods—they are just as superior in quality as they were before the tumble.

It is ridiculously easy to let good things escape you; it is not ridiculously easy to coax them back again.

THE MID-SUMMER SALE

is the buyer's opportunity. The early bird catches the worm, the wide-awake and early buyer catches the cream. Every day lessens the material for choice; just now about your choice you can be particularly choice.

M. C. SWIFT & SON,

153, 157 and 159 Union Street,

NEW BEDFORD,   -   -   -   MASS.

FINANCIAL.

SANFORD & KELLEY.

GARDNER T. SANFORD, CHARLES S. KELLEY, } Bankers,
Members Boston Stock Exchange,
47 North Water St., New Bedford.

STOCKS AND BONDS BOUGHT AND SOLD ON COMMISSION
At the New York and Boston Stock Boards.
CONSERVATIVE & PROFITABLE INVESTMENTS
FOR TRUST FUNDS.

New Bedford Manufacturing Stocks have a first-class record as dividend payers, and we always have some on hand to offer.

Sole Agents for the sale in this city of the 6 per cent. Guaranteed Mortgages of the Lombard Investment Co.

Auction Sale of Stocks and Bonds
WEDNESDAYS AND SATURDAYS, at 10 45 A. M.

ORDERS SOLICITED.

Mass. Real Estate Co.

246 Washington St., Boston.

Dividends 7 Per Cent.

Invests in Central Real Estate in Growing Cities.

Authorized Capital - - -	$2,000,000
Capital paid in - - -	1,250,000
Surplus - - - - - - -	100,000

ORGANIZED IN 1885.

Paid Dividends of 5 per cent. per annum for 4½ years. Paid Dividends of 7 per cent. per annum since July, 1890. Averago Dividend since organization over 6 per cent. per annum. Surplus at close of last fiscal year, over $100,000.

Stock offered for sale at $108 per share until July 31.

Send to or call at the office for information MWF

T. E. BOWMAN & CO.,

Topeka, Kansas,
NEGOTIATORS OF
Conservative Mortgage Loans in Eastern Kansas.

$2,500,000 LOANED without loss to any investor, and have never yet had to foreclose a farm loan in these eastern counties. Write us for list of investments. s29

GEORGE LEVY, North End Pawn Broker.
Cash advanced on Real or Personal Property. All business private. au3-1m

Inestimable Value.

The discovery by Dr. Price of a new process for extracting from the true fruits their natural flavor will be of inestimable value and benefit to the consumers of flavoring extracts. By this process the flavoring principle of the fruit employed is brought out so perfectly that when used to flavor cakes, creams, etc., it imparts the delicate and delicious taste of the fruit itself.

Thousands of pounds of the costly Mexican Vanilla Bean are annually consumed in the manufacture of

Dr. Price's Delicious Extract of Vanilla.

Ladies, try Dr. Price's flavors if you wish nice desserts. You will never be disappointed in their use.

SECOND EDITION.

OBITUARY.

Death of One of New Bedford's Best Known and Most Respected Citizens.

Capt. Henry Taber, who died at his residence on Orchard street in this city shortly after 2 p. m. to-day, comes from good old New England stock, his ancestors having settled in old Dartmouth in 1684. They were members of the Society of Friends, and the first recorded who took the "oath of fidelity" was Thomas Taber. Capt. Henry Taber was the son of Benjamin and Rhobe (Aikin) Taber, and he first saw the light in the town of New Bedford on March 29, 1795. He remained at home and assisted his father until he was 14 years old, receiving the limited education possible to be obtained in a country village early in this century. When he reached the age of 14 he went to sea on his first voyage as cabin boy with his uncle, John Wood, master of the ship George & Susan. The trip was to a port in Virginia, whence a cargo of tobacco was taken on board and carried to Liverpool, Eng., where it was disposed of. Young Taber's second voyage was from this country to Glasgow, Scotland, and his third to Hamburg, and at that time he was second mate of the ship, rising to the position by sheer pluck and activity thus early in life. His last trip across the Atlantic about this time was after the second war with Great Britain in 1812-15, when he was on brig Nancy, Capt. Packard, from New York to Dublin. After that Capt. Taber was chief mate for a year on a vessel commanded by Capt. John Wood, running between this port and New York, and for the 15 subsequent years he commanded the Orbit, Boston, Experiment and Helen, running between the same ports, and he owned a quarter interest in the last two

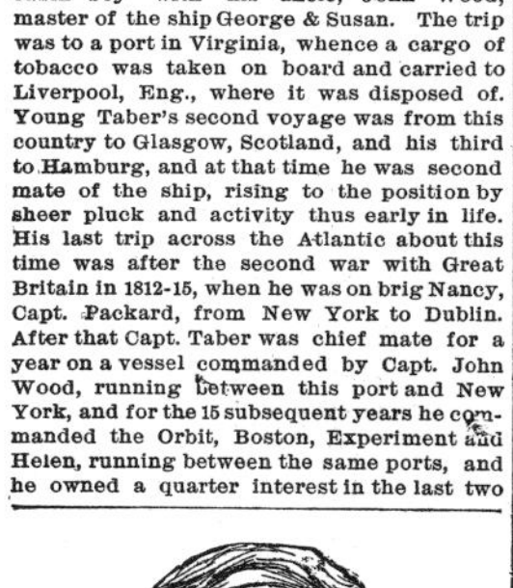

CAPT. HENRY TABER.

vessels. In those primitive days the mails were not very regular nor frequent, and on the Experiment a box was kept in which merchants at either port would deposit letters, and they were collected by the parties to whom they were dispatched on arrival. The box of the Experiment is carefully preserved by Capt. Taber's son, William G. Taber, of this city. In 1832 Capt. Taber engaged in the grocery and ship-chandlery business on Centre street in this city with David Sherman, under the firm name of Taber & Sherman, but the latter soon removed to Poughkeepsie, N. Y., to look after whaling business there in which he was interested. Two or three years later Capt. Taber formed a copartnership with his son William G. Taber, and his son-in-law John Hunt, under the name of Henry Taber & Co., and they became largely interested in the course of time in what was then New Bedford's chief industry, the whaling business. The firm remained in existence till March 1, 1866, when Capt. Taber retired, and then the firm name was changed to Taber, Gordon & Co., which it bears at the present time. Although retiring from active business life at this time, Capt. Taber was by no means shelved. His active habits and perfect health caused him to retain his share in the vital interests of his native place, and he has since been for many years one of our most industrious men. He was president of the Mutual Marine Insurance Company, now wound up, and was for years a director of the National Bank of Commerce and a stockholder in three others. He has been twice married, to Nabby, daughter of William and Nabby Gordon, in 1819, and to Sally, sister of his first wife, in 1832. The issue of these marriages were three sons and one daughter. By his industry, integrity and strict attention to business Capt. Taber acquired a fortune, which he long lived to enjoy. In politics he was always a Whig or Republican, and with the exception of two years he was a member of the State Legislature from 1838 to 1844. His manly qualities and sterling worth won him many and strong friends, who relied on him for the counsel and advice which his good sense enabled him to give wisely and well. In a life filled with usefulness he was spared far beyond the scriptural time to be an honor to his native place, a trusted counsellor to his associates and a guide for probity and truth to the rising generation. Of him it may be truly said, He rests from his labors, but his works they do follow him.

TO BE PUSHED.

Mayor Ashley Says Pleasant Street Should be Widened This Fall.

There has been considerable talk of late to the effect that Pleasant street, between Union and William streets, would be widened this Fall. This morning, after witnessing a collision of two carriages directly in front of C. F. Cushing's place of business, the writer called on Mayor Ashley to learn what truth there was in the statement as made above. The Mayor said he did not intend to let the matter drop. On the contrary, as soon as Bates & Kirby get over their rush in the Summer's business, he should bring the subject up again. He says the street should be widened, and that it ought to be widened this Fall. He proposes, if the authorities agree with him and a price cannot be agreed upon, to leave the value of property to be taken to three gentlemen who have a knowledge of the worth of real estate in this city, and then if an agreement cannot be arrived at to let the matter take the course which it naturally would. From the conversation of Mayor Ashley, it is evident that he is a strong advocate of this measure, which he says will receive his hearty support.

REAL ESTATE SALES.—Phineas F. Drew has sold to Amelia Peckham 80 rods of land on the north side of Topham street.

Mary A. Taber of Fairhaven has sold for $3000 to Jacob Brightman 200.38 rods of land at the northeast corner of North Main and North streets.

Thomas B. Tripp has sold to John Green two acres land in this city on the road from Plainville to Acushnet.

Standish Bourne sold at auction to-day to F. A. F. Adams two-tenement house and lot south side of Elm street, east of Purchase, known as the Hallett Gifford house, with the Mackie homestead and land in rear, for $4980.

PERSONAL.—William M. Worsley has resigned from the Mt. Pleasant Orchestra.

Walter Allen, William E. Hatch and E. Hill of this city registered at the New York *Herald's* bureau in Paris yesterday.

Rev. S. Wright Butler and family are the guests of ex-Alderman John Wing at his residence at Mt. Pleasant.

THE COTTON ROPE MANUFACTORY.—It is said there is a drawback to establishing a manufactory for cotton rope in this city. The machinery used in the manufacture is all of English make, and as yet parties in this country have been unable to procure it. It is said that English parties are not willing to dispose of the machinery to come to this country.

ACCIDENT.—This forenoon Arthur Renaud, a boy employed at the Bennett Mills, while playing with another boy, received a cut from a knife in the right arm, which severed the radial artery and caused him to lose much blood. He was taken to the office of Dr. E. W. Dehn, who took up the artery and rendered other necessary surgical aid.

SCHOONER JANE GRAY RELEASED.—A telegram from San Francisco gives intelligence from Ounalaska to the effect that whaling schooner Jane Gray, which was seized and towed into that port, on suspicion of taking seal in forbidden waters was released after a thorough search.

BUILDING.—Herbert Atwood is building for T. F. Healey on the east side of Acushnet avenue, north of Nye street, a three-story dwelling house 40 by 26 feet, with 24½ feet posts.

MATTAPOISETT.

Rev. C. H. Phelps is spending his vacation at East Smithfield, Pa.

Rev. Edward P. Goodwin of Chicago supplied for Mr. Phelps last Sunday.

Mrs. T. C. Keller has returned to her home in Chicago.

Mr. F. L. Keith of Worcester is visiting his grandmother, Mrs. Warren Aiken, on Cannon street.

Mrs. Andrew S. Briggs of Taunton is visiting Mrs. Edmund Bourne.

Oscar H. Ordway and wife of South Framingham arrived in town on Thursday. Mr. Ordway has returned home on his wheel, but Mrs. Ordway will visit her parents, Mr. and Mrs. Job Bolles.

Theodore Ames is with relatives in Myrick.

Schooner Menuncatuck, Ellis, is in for cargo of wood from Dennis Mahoney for New York.

Schooner yacht Ruth, which has been on a cruise westward, has returned here. She is chartered by S. D. Warren, Esq.

Walton E. Clark and wife leave town today for their home in Lima, O.

Capt. Chase of Fall River put in here last night in his catboat on his way home from Onset.

William Sweat of Portland, Me., will spend two weeks with his mother, Mrs, Sarah L. Sweat.

The regatta of the season comes off next Saturday in our harbor.

DEATHS.

In this city, 10th inst., Patrick Sullivan. Notice of funeral later.

In this city, 10th inst., John, son of John and Mary DeCosta, aged 1 year 6 months.

MARINE INTELLIGENCE.

Sld from Bath 9th, sch Jonathan Bourne, Philadelphia.

Ar at Newburyport 9th, sch J J Little, Matthews, New York.

Ar at New Haven 9th, sch Oliver Ames, Nickerson, Philadelphia.

Ar at New York 9th, schs Laura Robinson, Robbins, Boston; Hattie Paige, Crocker, do; Joseph Hay, Fisher, Cape Ann; Ira B Ellems, Marston, Edgartown.

Ar at Delaware Breakwater 9th, sch Jennie R Tomlinson, Fall River, and sld seaward.

Cld at Philadelphia 9th, sch Gov J Y Smith, Blake, Fall River.

Sld from Norfolk 9th, sch John Twohy, Boston.

FINANCIAL.

Strong Stocks—No Wide Movement, But a Slight Rally on Shorts Covering—General Electric 116—Money Firmer—Clearing House Loans To-day at 5 Per Cent.—Chicago & West Michigan Earnings—Dividend Declared—West End Gross and Net for June—Pacific Mail Rumors—Big Increase in St. Paul Earnings—Gossip.

WEDNESDAY, Aug. 10.

Bad crop reports have affected the situation to some extent but there seems no ground for fears that the general condition of the crops is critical. In stocks the market has naturally given way somewhat to these reports but the undertone is firm, and in spite of the dulness prices seem to advance readily. The ease of money continues though the demand is more brisk.

Old Colony holds well in Boston with sales this forenoon at 183¾.

In the local loan market rates remain at 5 and 6 per cent.

The prevailing rates for call money in Boston is 4 and 4½ per cent. One bank late yesterday marked up a number of call loans to 5 per cent., but this action was not generally followed. The demand from the brokers for both time and call loans is good. At clearing to-day loans were all at 5 per cent. money being in sharp demand. New York funds sold at 15 and 17 cents discount.

In New York call money loans at 1½ per cent. Time rates steady.

Sterling exchange is easier in tone, but there is no freer offering of bills.

Bonds steady.

Gossip from Wall street this morning said: "Much interest is felt in the government crop report to be published this afternoon. The bears are aggressive, but find it difficult to force out long stock. Short interest in Burlington & Quincy increased yesterday. London prices up about ¼ per cent.

The New York stock market opened quiet and steady this morning. Atchison at 39¼, Burlington & Quincy 101⅞, St. Paul 83, Rock Island 81, Omaha 54⅝, Wabash 25⅝, General Electric 115⅞, and Erie 29. Prices did not change materially during the forenoon and at noon the range was practically the same as that at the opening. In the early afternoon more evidences of strength were apparent and better figures were recorded in many cases.

Sugar was the feature at 2 o'clock, advancing to 108⅛.

The Boston market opened dull this forenoon and continued so during the first hour. Atchison held 39⅛, and later gained ¼ more, C. B. & Q. was firm at 102. Boston & Albany sold at 205. Union Pacific was out at 38⅝. West End Common sold at 74, and General Electric at 116. Copper shares were dull and neglected. In the second hour the strength of Atchison and C. B. & Q. was the feature. C. B. & Q. gained ⅛. Old Colony lost ¼. After 12 o'clock the market continued dull and steady.

At 2 o'clock the market was strong, sugar selling up to 108¼.

Sales to noon in Boston to-day were: Bonds $48,000, and 13,515 shares of stock.

It is stated on the highest authority that Dr. W. Seward Webb's Adirondack & St. Lawrence railroad will be acquired by the New York Central & Hudson River road within 30 or 60 days. No papers have been signed as yet, but the details of the transfer have been arranged, and the close connection between the two interests involved give assurance that there will be no break in the negotiations.

At 11 o'clock special says: "Market strong and shorts appear to be frightened, especially Atchison.

St. Paul earnings the first week of August increased $112,291.

A Chicago dispatch says Pacific Mail steamship subsidy of $850,000 a year has probably been paid for the last time. Members of the Transcontinental Association declare it benefits Southern Pacific alone, and most all of them will decline to pay their share after next meeting. The result will be a disorganization of the association. C. P. Huntington says there is nothing in report to effect that Pacific Mail subsidy will be discontinued.

A prominent firm of cotton factors reports the condition of the crop compared with this time last year, to be eight days later, condition 4 per cent. worse, estimated acreage of corn over last year is 14 per cent. more and condition 9 per cent. better.

Chicago & West Michigan directors have declared a dividend of 1½ per cent., payable August 15th to stock of record August 3d. Transfer books closed August 4th, will reopen August 17th.

Prime's Crop Bureau telegraphs as follows: "The week opens hot and dry. Reports from Eastern Kansas say rain is needed very badly. Corn tasseled out two or three weeks late. Had moderately hot winds three days last week and the corn crop is, to say the least, in a very critical stage in this portion of the State. That some damage has been done to the crop recently does not seem to be in any doubt now."

Editor Meany of *Poor's Manual* in regard to his item about Lackawanna being purchased by Reading says: The item was given to the Reading for approval. Not getting answer I wrote asking why proof had not been returned, and received a reply that Reading officials were examining the proof. As we heard nothing further about it I inferred that the item was all right. Mr. Meaney did not know what steps would be made for correction and modification.

A director of Edison General Co. says that the company is earning a good deal more money than its dividends show. It is paying 8 per cent. a year, is in good condition with a promising outlook. These are sufficient reasons for an advance in the stock.

The monthly report of the superintendent of the Quincy mine shows a large amount of surface and underground work performed in July, the stopes varying from poor to rich. No. 4 and No. 5 stamps were almost ready to start when the report was written. The large new engine is running smoothly at the mill. Another connection with the Pewabic mine underground has been made. Quincy will have no apparent need to purchase the Franklin mine in order to work the Pewabic property.

Latest New York Central earnings follow:

	1892.	1891.	Inc.
July gross,	$3,793,039	$3,713,429	$79,603
Jan 1 to July 1,	25,176,848	23,823,874	1,352,974

Chicago & West Michigan earnings compare as below:

Jan. 1 to June 30.	1892.	1891.	Dec.
Earnings,	$917,023	$797,447	*$119,576
Expenses,	672,616	553,922	*118,694
Net,	$244,407	$243,525	*$882
Other income,	†4,441	5,990	10,431
Total net,	$239,966	$249,515	$9,549
Charges,	138,927	144,085	5,158
Balance,	$101,039	$105,430	$4,391
Dividends,	99,573	99,573	*
Surplus,	$1,466	$5,857	$4,391
Construction,	3,399		

*Increase. †Paid out.

West End Street Railway earnings for June are given by the Advertiser thus:

Gross,	$354,300	$246.149	$600,450
Expenses,	197,107	171,308	368,416
Net,	$157,193	$74,841	$232,034
Operating percentage,	55.58	69.67	

LOCAL STOCK QUOTATIONS.

The following are the quotations of local stocks to-day as reported by Sanford & Kelley, bankers and brokers and stock auctioneers:

Banks.	Par.	Bid.	Ask'd.	Last Sale.
Citizens	$100	—	—	130
Commerce	100	—	100	98
Fairhaven	80	—	83	81
First National	100	—	—	142¼
Mechanics	100	—	—	175¼
Merchants	100	—	—	193¾
N. B. Safe Deposit & Trust Co.	100	—	—	95⅞
Manufacturing.				
Acushnet Mill	100	160	—	162¾
Bennett Mills	100	—	—	118⅝
City Mfg. Co.	100	—	*130	131⅞
Grinnell Mfg. Co.	100	170	—	175
Hathaway Mfg. Co.	100	115	—	—
Howland Mill Cor.	100	—	—	132
Morse Twist Drill	50	—	—	176½
Mt. Wash. Glass Co.	100	—	—	81
N. B. Copper Co.	100	80	—	75
N. B. Gas and Edison Light	100	—	—	124⅝
N. B. Mfg. Co.	100	150	—	152
Oneko Woolen Mill	100	40	—	—
Potomska Mills	100	—	—	*108⅛
Pairpoint Mf'g Co.	100	75	—	—
People's Gas Co.	—	—	2½	—
Pierce Mill Sub.	—	—	—	1½
Triumph Heat & Light Co.	10	—	—	3
Wamsutta Mills	100	—	110	110
Weeden Mfg Co.	100	—	—	20¼
Miscellaneous.				
Acushnet Cooperative Association	25	—	—	62
Am. Carrier Rocket	100	—	—	45
Applegate B.&S.Lasting Co.	.10	—	.05	⅛c.
Central Union Ass'n	—	—	—	126¾
Monte Pio Cooperative Ass'n	10	—	—	.37
N. B. Casket Co.	100	—	—	45
N. B. Journal Pub. Co.	100	—	—	—
N. B. Steam Coasting Co.	100	100	—	100½
N. B. Vin. & Nan. Steamboat Co.	100	—	—	—
N. B. Real Estate Association	100	—	—	105
Odd Fellows' Building Association	—	—	—	21
Union Boot & Shoe Co.	—	—	—	104¼
Union St. Railway Co.	100	—	—	140
Union St. R'y 5s	—	—	—	103
Wamsutta Club 5s	—	—	—	93¾
Wright Drug Co.	100	—	—	70

*Ex-dividend.

STOCK AND BOND MARKETS.

Bids at the close of First Board.

NEW YORK, Aug. 10.

GOVERNMENT BONDS.	
U.S. 2s, registered	100
" new 4s, registered	116
" new 4s, coupons	116
" currency 6s, 1895, (Pacifics)	107
RAILROADS.	
Atchison	39⅝
Clev., Cin., Chicago & St. Louis	66¼
Chicago & Eastern Illinois	—
Chicago & Eastern Illinois pre	—
Chicago, Burlington & Quincy	102
Delaware & Hudson	138⅞
Delaware & Lackawanna	157⅞
Erie	29
Illinois Central	—
Lake Shore & Michigan Southern	135½
Louisville & Nashville	70⅞
Michigan Central	—
Missouri Pacific	59½
New Jersey Central	—
New York & New England	—
Northern Pacific	—
Northern Pacific pref	57¾
Chicago & Northwestern	—
New York Central & Hudson River	113⅜
North American	14½
Oregon Navigation	—
Oregon Improvement	—
Oregon Short Line	—
Philadelphia & Reading	60¾
Pullman Palace Car Co.	—
Chicago, Rock Island & Pacific	80⅞
Chicago, Milwaukee & St. Paul	83¼
Chicago, Milwaukee & St. Paul pref	—
Richmond Terminal	9
St. Paul & Omaha	—
St. Paul & Omaha pref	—
Union Pacific	38¾
Wabash, St. Louis & Pacific	—
Wabash, St. Louis & Pacific pref	25⅞
MISCELLANEOUS	
Ontario Silver	41
Pacific Mail Steamship Co.	34¾
Sugar, common	107½
Sugar, pref	—
Western Union Telegraph	97⅞
Silver Certificates	—

BOSTON, Aug. 10.

BONDS	
Atchison 4s	82⅞
Atchison Incomes	59½
American Bell Telephone 7s	114
Chicago, Burlington & Northern 5s	—
Chicago & West Michigan 5s	—
Mexican Central 4s	68¼
Illinois Steel Co. 5s	—
RAILROADS.	
Atchison, Topeka & Santa Fe	39⅞
Boston & Albany	204½
Boston & Lowell	181½
Boston & Maine	180
Boston & Providence	250
Chicago, Burlington & Quincy	102
Chicago & West Michigan	50
Cleveland & Canton	5½
Cleveland & Canton pref	19¾
Flint & Pere Marquette	—
Flint & Pere Marquette pref	*79
Mexican Central	*17
New York & New England	36⅜
New York & New England pref	88
Old Colony	*183¼
Oregon Short Line	23½
Pullman Palace Car	*197
Union Pacific	38⅜
Wisconsin Central	17
West End	74
West End pref	*88
MINING.	
Butte & Boston Mining Co.	—
Calumet & Hecla Mining Co.	275
Centennial	7
Franklin Mining Co.	12⅞
Kearsarge	—
Montana	36
Osceola Mining Co.	32
Tamarack	156
MISCELLANEOUS.	
American Bell Telephone	204
Erie Telephone	*47
Mexican Telephone	1.05
New England Telephone	56
Newport Land	—
Boston Land Co.	5
West End Land Co.	18
San Diego Land Co.	*16
Topeka Land & Development Co.	*1
Lamson Store Service	18
Illinois Steel Co.	*74
Am. Sugar Refineries, com	107½
Am. Sugar Refineries, pref	101½
Gen'l Electric	115½
Gen'l Electric	11)

*Asked.

PROVISIONS AND GRAIN.

CHICAGO, Aug. 10.

Opening.	Lard.	Wheat.	Pork.	Corn.	Sh't Ribs.
May	—	—	—	—	—
June	—	—	—	—	—
July	—	—	—	—	—
Aug.	—	—	—	—	—
Sept.	—	78	12.80	52	—
Oct.	—	—	—	—	—
Dec.	—	80¾	—	—	—
Jan.	—	—	13.70	—	—
12 o'clock.					
May	—	—	—	—	—
June	—	—	—	—	—
July	—	—	—	—	—
Aug.	—	—	—	—	—
Sept.	—	78⅞	12.87½	52⅝	—
Oct.	—	—	—	—	—
Dec.	—	81⅛	—	—	—
Jan.	—	—	13.75	—	—

For Other Markets See Seventh Page.

Bucklen's Arnica Salve.

The best salve in the world for cuts, bruises, sores, ulcers, salt rheum, fever sores, tetter, chapped hands, chilblains, corns, and all skin eruptions, and positively cures piles, or no pay required. It is guaranteed to give perfect satisfaction, or money refunded. Price 25 cents per box. For sale by H. A. Blackmer.

SEARCHING FOR THE WEAPON.

Police and a Carpenter at Work in Borden House.

Still Believe a Clew is to be Found Within its Walls.

Miss Borden Gives Way to Tears in Her Strict Examination.

[Special Dispatch.]

FALL RIVER, Aug. 10.—It is still widely believed that the police will yet find some new clew to the Borden murder fiend inside the unfortunate couple's late home.

About 1 o'clock this afternoon City Marshal Hilliard and Officer Harrington were seen to accompany a carpenter named Morris Daley into the Borden homestead on Second street. The carpenter took with him his entire kit of tools. The entrance was made by the front door, which was carefully locked after them.

Although the house has previously been searched three times, and no evidence bearing on the case been found, it is surmised that at the inquest some evidence was put in that the weapon with which the terrible crime was committed is still within the four walls of the Borden house, and that in accordance with such evidence a thorough search is to be made with the assistance of the carpenter. A brick mason was in the house yesterday and tore out fire-places, and it may be that repairs are to be made though it is hardly probable that a carpenter would do masons' work.

This last movement of the police is looked upon significantly, and its result is awaited anxiously.

The inquest has been going steadily on since 10 o'clock this morning behind closed doors and with the greatest secrecy preserved. The witnesses listened to were John V. Morse and Lizzie Borden. The inquest is still in session.

[By Associated Press.]

FALL RIVER, Aug. 10.—There was an intermission in the proceedings at the inquest at 11 15 o'clock.

A few minutes later Marshal Hilliard drove to the Borden homestead and returned with John V. Morse.

Miss Lizzie Borden was taken into the matron's room.

Mr. Morse was taken into the court room, but it is said that he was not subjected to an examination.

At 12 50 o'clock the inquiry was postponed until after dinner.

Miss Borden, Mrs. Brigham, Mr. Morse and the city marshal were driven to the house in a close carriage.

Miss Borden was asked some nerve shaking questions, and when she came from the matron's room she was tear-stained and very much upset.

There was a great difference between her appearance before and after the examination.

The servant girl is kept under the eye of a policeman at her brother-in-law's house on Division street, and she was not allowed to go free as was intimated last night by detectives.

The Wreck on the Santa Fe.

DENVER, Col., Aug. 10.—The wreck yesterday on the Santa Fe, ten miles from here, proves to have injured more persons than was at first reported. The number has been increased to 18, of whom Mrs. Robers and Mrs. Edington may die. The others are not dangerously injured. The train was a vestibule from Chicago, and the wreck was caused by the spreading of the rails while the train was running at the rate of 40 miles an hour.

Death of a Well Known Newspaper Man.

NEW YORK, Aug. 10.—George A. Leach, well known in newspaper circles, died at his residence in Harlem this morning, of Bright's disease. Mr. Leach was for many years connected with the Associated Press in this city in various positions, the last being that of assistant general manager. Since retiring some years ago he has been engaged in various kinds of newspaper work in this city.

Cholera Increasing in Virulence.

ST. PETERSBURG, Aug. 10. — Advices from Teheran, the capital of Persia, show that the cholera is increasing in virulence there. The deaths in the city now average 60 daily. An official report shows that on Sunda there were reported from all the cholera infected districts of Russia 214 new cases. On the same day 2177 persons died of cholera.

Miners Threaten to Strike.

ALTOONA, Pa., Aug. 10.—At a mass meeting held in Phillipsburg last night the report of 3000 miners in the Clearfield district declared they would strike on Sept. 1st, unless an advance was made in the price of low grade coal mining, and a change made in the check weighman system.

NEW YORK PRODUCE MARKET.

NEW YORK, Aug. 10.

Flour sales 7500 packages; quiet.
Wheat sales 640,000 bushels; declined ⅛ to ⅝ of a cent on rains in Kansas; weak cables and expected favorable crop reports; advanced ¼ to ⅜ of a cent; firm and quiet.
Corn sales 100,000 bushels; sold off ¾ of a cent to 1 cent on rains West; weak cables advanced ¼ to ½ of a cent on local trade; dull.
Oats sales 50,000 bushels; steady and dull.
Beef quiet and easy.
Pork firm.
Lard dull.
Butter firm.
Cheese firm.
Sugar (raw) firm.
Petroleum firm and active.
Turpentine dull and weak.
Molasses quiet and firm.
Freights more doing and steady.
Rosin not quoted.
Tallow quiet.

G.O. TAYLOR WHISKIES

Guaranteed PURE. Uniform in QUALITY.
MEDICINALLY VALUABLE and without a trace of Fusel Oil.
NOT sold in bulk or by measure. Always in Sealed bottles. Beware of imitations and refilled bottles.
SOLD generally by Druggists, Grocers, Wine Merchants and Hotels.
LOOK for proprietors' firm name signature.
CHESTER H. GRAVES & SONS, Boston.
REFUSE SUBSTITUTES.

LOST.

Advertisements under this heading 1c. a word a time. No charge less than 25c.

JERSEY COW—Color, yellow and white. Please return same to L. A. TRIPP, Rockdale avenue and Allen street. *au10-3t

WANTS.

All Advertisements under this heading 1c. a word a time. No charge less than 25c.

YOUNG WOMAN — Who understands plain cooking and washing; references required. Address box 12 *Standard* office. au10-tf

FOR THE GERRY CUPS.

Fair Weather and a Good Southwest Sailing Breeze.

Race of New York and Eastern Yachts Off Marblehead.

Gloriana and Iroquois Off First in Their Respective Classes.

MARBLEHEAD NECK, Aug. 10. — Fair weather and a light wind from the northeast, which soon changed to a good sailing breeze from the southwest, were the conditions which confronted the New York Yacht and the Eastern Clubs this morning as they began preparations for the race for the cups offered by Commodore Gerry, open to yachts of each class which have not hauled out to clean since the commencement of the cruise.

Sails were set early on most of the racers. Shortly after 8 o'clock the Lasca and Œnone sailed away, showing they would not be in the race. Mainsails were soon set on the schooners and with the 46-footers, with their clubtopsails aloft, the fleet moved to the starting point.

The Mayflower has a new foretopmast.

The wind had settled into a fair topsail breeze from the south southwest when the Ituna, the regatta committee's boat, took her place off Half Way rock at 10 15.

At 10 45 the preparatory gun was fired and course signals hoisted showing that the boats would beat to Harding's Ledge, then have a reach to the mark 12 miles off shore and run home to finish 36 miles.

At 10 55 the starting gun for sloops was fired and four 46-footers crossed the line as follows:

	H.	M.	S.
Gloriana,	10	57	30
Barbara,	10	57	50
Wasp,	10	58	00
Harpoon,	11	00	00

At once the Gloriana tacked inshore while the Barbara held a long board to the southeast. The Wasp and Harpoon got well to windward of the Gloriana's wake, then tacked to port and stood toward Tinker's island.

At 11 o'clock the gun was fired for the schooners. Six boats got away in this order:

	H.	M.	S.
Iroquois,	11	01	40
Merlin,	11	02	20
Constellation,	11	02	50
Marguerite,	11	03	10
Alcæa,	11	03	30
Mayflower,	11	05	45

The Iroquois held off shore for a while and the Merlin and Constellation followed closely. But they took the tack inshore before the Iroquois, though the latter held the lead.

WEATHER INDICATIONS.

SLIGHTLY WARMER.

NEW YORK, Aug. 10.—At 8 30 a. m. the weather was clear, wind south, temperature 80. The *Herald* says: In the Middle States and New England on Thursday, slightly warmer, more sultry weather and southerly winds will probably prevail, with local rains near the lakes, and on Friday warmer, more sultry weather.

AUCTION SALES.

By JAMES R. DENHAM.

On SATURDAY, Aug. 13th, at 3 o'clock P. M., on the premises, will be sold house and lot of about 27 9-10 rods of land, No. 31 Allen street. Terms, 10 per cent. at sale. Balance on delivery of deed. au10-3t

REAL ESTATE.

FRANCIS W. TAPPAN,
Agent for Purchase, Sale, and Lease of REAL ESTATE.
Office, 15 North Water St., New Bedford. d&w

FRANK C. SMITH,
Real Estate Broker, Auctioneer and Appraiser,
Office - - 47 William Street,
(Opposite New Post Office.)

M. E. SMITH,
REAL ESTATE AGENT,
619 Purchase Street. Telephone 16-11.

H. A. LEONARD,
REAL ESTATE AGENT.......126 UNION STREET.
Houses and lots for sale in all parts of the city. No charges unless sale effected.

COURT STREET—Two story house and barn with about 35 rods of land; all in the very best of order; modern improvements. This is a bargain; can be bought on easy terms. Call and examine.

A VERY FINE two story house and 27 rods of land; situated on high land; nice bath room, water closet and set bowl. Will sell or exchange for a good farm near the sea shore; this is good investment property.

COURT STREET—Fine Bargain—Cottage house and 12 rods of land. Can be bought for $1350. A fine house for a party with moderate means.

CHANCERY STREET—Very fine two story house with 10 rods of land; fine location; built in the best of order; can be bought for $3000; easy terms; will rent easy for $26 per month.

VALUABLE ESTATE FOR SALE—Comprising one cottage, one three story block and 63 rods of land in a location where real estate is advancing rapidly; two new mills going up close by; owner says sell; going to move from the city. This is the very best of investment property.

SOME VERY FINE building lots and investment land in all parts of the city. Before buying please call and examine my list.

FLORENCE STREET—Four new cottages with 10 rods of land, each in the best of neighborhoods. Prices range from $1500 to $1800, on easy terms.

ROUND STREET—New cottage with 8 rods of land, very fine view, on high land. Can be bought for $1250. Call and examine.

ROUND STREET—New cottage with 8 rods of land, modern improvements. Can be bought for $2500. A nice home.

PARK STREET—This is a bargain. One and a half story cottage with 20 rods of land. Can be bought for $1700. The land is worth $60 per rod. Good neighborhood, one minute walk from the horse cars. This property cannot help selling. Come early.

SUMMER STREET—Very nice cottage with 12 rods of land, bath room, water closet and furnace; in the very best of repair; good neighborhood on the line of horse cars. Can be bought on easy terms.

A FEW MORE of those beautiful seashore lots left at Bay View. They are selling rapidly at $5 per rod.

Two of the finest lots at Horse Neck Beach for sale. Price $300 each.

FINE COTTAGE FOR SALE with modern improvements, about 14 rods of land, good stable, situated on a corner. Owner says sell. Price $3200.

FINE GOTHIC COTTAGE for sale with 12 rods of land on a corner. Very pleasantly situated. Finished in hard wood, with modern improvements, fine bath room and water closet. Beautiful home for the right party.

ONE OF THE MOST desirable farms in Southern Massachusetts for sale. Buildings new. Beautiful view. Can be bought for one half its original value.

PARTIES LOOKING for good investment land or nice building lot can be accommodated by looking my list over. These lots are situated in the west part of the city, near the Park, and on or near the horse cars, and also near Rockdale avenue. This is one of the most desirable locations in the city. The cars are sure to be continued up Union street and through Rockdale avenue to Kempton street, forming a belt line, which will be the means of increasing the value of property in this section. Now is your chance.

JOHN WHITEHEAD,
Real Estate Agent.

Several houses near Pierce Mill. Sale private. Also desirable lots on Geo. A. Briggs' estate on easy terms, and lots in all parts of the city. Desirable lots on Jas. Drown estate and Phillips and Coffin aves. au2-MWF1m

Cottage House.

Well built, good repair, in part of city growing rapidly; will make good home and *must* increase in value. Apply box 6, *Standard* office. ap25-tf

SUMMMER COTTAGE AND BARN—For sale low, situated in Acushnet; acre and one-third of high land, mostly pine grove; buildings nearly new. Inquire of A. G. ALLEY, JR., Union and Sixth streets. jy18-tf

FOR SALE—In South Dartmouth, near the water, a 2½ story house with large piazza, barn, and 83 rods of land. One of the most desirable places in the village for a Summer residence. Inquire of BENJ. QUERIPEL or DANIEL H. HOWLAND, South Dartmouth. ap7-tf

AUCTION SALES.

By STANDISH BOURNE,
(Successor to Geo. A. Bourne & Son,),
Auctioneer, Commission Merchant, Real Estate Dealer and Appraiser.

Cash advanced on goods consigned for auction. Ready buyer for personal property of every description.
Office and Salesrooms 47, 49 and 51 North Second Street, near the Post Office.

Nearly New Household Furniture and Rugs.

On MONDAY, Aug. 15th, at 2½ o'clock, at the cottage of Miss Courtis, Nonquitt, will be sold the entire household furnishings consisting in part of 10 Brass Mounted Bedsteads, Woven Wire Springs, Pillows and Mattresses for same, Ash Chamber suits, Willow sofa and chairs, several desirable pieces of old-fashioned furniture, together with the general assortment of Housekeepers' Articles, such as Odd Bedsteads, Tables, Extension Tables, Chairs, Crockery, Glassware &c. Also several Imported Rugs, Mattings &c.

To Let in Our Storage Warerooms.

We constantly have on hand first-class rooms for the storage of household goods, to be rented by the month or year.
Good dry storage room for stoves.

By JOHN B. BAYLIES,
121 and 123 Union Street,
Commission Merchant, Appraiser, and Auctioneer for the sale of Real Estate and every description of Personal Property. Furniture Bought.

H. C. HATHAWAY,
Auctioneer, Real Estate Agent and Appraiser,
Corner Acushnet Ave. and Elm St.

One of the best auction marts in the State for the sale of horses and carriages. Keeps constantly on hand carriages of every description, carriages made to order and repairing in all its branches attended to under the superintendency of J. R. Forbes. Consignments of every description solicited. Cash advanced on goods for auction. Personal property of every description bought at short notice for cash. Negotiable notes bought and sold.

Horses at Auction.

Will arrive THURSDAY MORNING, at our Salesroom, and will be sold at auction SATURDAY MORNING, at 10 o'clock, one car load of extra nice horses adapted for general purposes. If you are in want of a good family, road or work horse be sure to attend this sale. Also several good second-hand horses that have been used around the city.

Also a very nice Scippio mare, 5 years old, from the state of Maine. She is A1 in every respect and is counted in the 30 list. au9

Heirs' Sale of Real Estate.

On SATURDAY, Aug. 13, at 3 o'clock P. M., on the premises, will be sold wthout the least reserve, to wind up the estate, the house and lot of about 17 rods of land No. 75 Middle street. The house is in good condition and is situated in that part of the city where it will be sure always to rent well. Sale positive and without limit. Terms, 10 per cent. at sale. Balance on delivery of heirs' deed. au4

ALFRED WILSON,
Auctioneer and Real Estate Agent,
Room 22, - - - Robeson Building.

Houses and land in all parts of the city for sale; tenements for rent; rents collected.

For Sale.

Two-story house on Acushnet avenue, near Walnut street; well arranged for one family; good location.

For Lease.

The Webster Block, Purchase street; rooms, well adapted for a genteel boarding house, club rooms, or business purposes.

TO LET—A flat in The Winslow, corner Sixth and Union streets. Apply to A. WILSON, Robeson Building. jy14-tf

T. F. HEALEY,
Auctioneer and Real Estate Agent,
555 and 559 Purchase street, corner of Franklin street.

FOR SALE CHEAP—One farm in Rochester of 70 acres; house, barn, outbuildings, etc.; 2 good orchards on place; cut 20 tons of hay. Price $1800.

Also two cottages in Fairhaven; nearly new; fine view of river and harbor; will sell one or both; situated on Main street; will sell to the right parties on easy terms.

Also one fine house in the west part of the city in good locality, with all the modern improvements, gas and electric lights, etc. Will be sold cheap if applied for soon.

Also lots on Acushnet avenue, Coggshall and Locust streets, in fact all parts of the city.

Business solicited. No charges made unless a sale, then my prices are the lowest.

By J. O. DOUGLASS.

REGULAR AUCTION SALE,
Thursday, Aug. 11th, 1892, at 10 15 A. M.

OF 25 horses, consisting of family, driving, express, team, farm, grocery and general business horses, in matched pairs and single. In this lot are some very good horses, two matched pairs one of them a coach or family team, closely matched, stand 16 hands high, good actors and fine drivers. Also several acclimated horses, been used in and about the city. Also harnesses, foot mats, &c. One two-horse tip-cart in good repair.

REAL ESTATE.

Telephone Call.............................241—4

F. A. F. ADAMS,
North Second Street (Opposite Post office,)
Real Estate Agency.

County Street—Fine view of harbor and bay; desirable residence on a corner, with 76 rods of land; every improvement.

State Street—Excellent location and neighborhood; slated roof house and stable; modern conveniences; 40 rods of land; one of the nicest houses in the city.

Channing Cottage of 10 rooms; every improvement, best of repair; 14 rods of land; on a corner; sold on account of owner's ill health; price $4150; easy terms.

Fine Residence on Orchard street, on a corner; large lot; every improvement.

Rockland Street—2½ story house and 19 rods of land; on a corner; rents well; modern conveniences; price $4750; easy terms.

Allen Street—Near County; extra well built cottage; new; splendid location; owner says sell; easy terms.

Fifth Street—Cottage house, stable and 14 rods of land; good repair; price $4000.

Pleasant Street — On a corner; cottage house; just been put in most excellent order throughout; large lot; belongs to a widow, who says sell.

Desirable 2 1-2 Story House—Two tenements, on Cottage street; new; 15 rods of land; every improvement; rents for $60 per month; price low for such a nice house; easy terms.

Cottage House—Stable and 113 rods of land; finely laid out; on Orchard street; good location; valuable as an investment.

2 1-2 Story House—Two tenements; 14 rods of land; on Fourth street; very central; best of repair; price low; easy terms.

Nice House on Morgan street; 2½ stories; two tenements; steam heat, &c.; rents well; price $5500; easy terms.

Cottage of 11 Rooms, every improvement; 40 rods of land on Ashland street; location A1; price low as the owner moves away; easy terms.

Cottage house, stable and 17 rods of land on Kempton street, on a corner; price $3000; easy terms.

Cottage of 9 rooms on a corner; steam heat, gas, hot and cold water, set tubs, set bowls, etc.; good neighborhood; new; just finished; price only $2600; easy terms.

$2300 cottage, 9 rooms, every improvement and convenience; best of repair; not one dollar to be laid out; easy terms.

$3350—Steam heat, gas, hot and cold water, set tubs, set bowls, etc.; splendid cottage, new; good location; a bargain; easy terms.

Several very desirable properties in Fairhaven. Some great bargains in lots just over the bridge from $9 to $15 per rod; easy terms.

We Have a very large list of houses, house lots and farms that are not advertised. Call and get a list.

F. A. F. ADAMS,
No. 38 North Second Street.

RELEASED FROM CUSTODY.

[Continued from Third Page.]

the 19th century, and particularly by a
refined and cultivated woman, we hold to
be clearly impossible. As to complicity
nothing can be said at this time.

A Singular Coincidence.

A singular coincidence in connection
with the Borden murder is that the calendar pointer on the old fashioned clock, at
the residence on Second street, stopped
on the fourth, the date of the murder,
and still points to that date. The other
works of the clock are not impaired, but
tick off the minutes and the hours with
usual regularity.

Tried by Newspaper.

It is a serious matter to accuse a person
of having taken the life of a fellow being.
The gravity of the charge is augmented
when the homicide must, of necessity,
have been deliberate and premeditated,
with every circumstance of cold-blooded-
ness and precaution to add to its atrocity.
How much more care and circumspection
of judgment must therefore be exercised
in laying the full accusation of murder at
the doors of a woman and a daughter, the
accusation of murder in its most hideous
form, of parricide, and double parricide at
that! When the suspected person enjoys
an unblemished reputation, the possession
of all the Christian and social virtues and
holds a recognized place in society, every
canon of mercy, justice and common
sense demands that no word shall be
breathed against her character, no suspicion entertained that is not based on
unimpeachable evidence. That is not
what certain newspapers are doing with
regard to the Borden tragedy in Fall
River. In the absence of fundamental
facts, they intimate by innuendo and direct
assumption that Miss Lizzie Borden, the
daughter of the murdered pair, with her
own hands committed the frightful
deed. There is no evidence in support
of such an assumption. Miss Borden is
connected with the affair by reason of her
being one of the two persons in the house
at the time and the one by whom the
alarm was given. There is nothing whatever to show that her hands are red with
the blood of her father and step-mother.
A motive is conspicuous by its absence.
The theory of insanity has fallen to the
ground. It is by no means certain that
she will be financially bettered by her
father's death. By the law of the land
she should be held innocent until proved
guilty, if ever, but the newspapers aforesaid have tried her and found her guilty
on these slender grounds. Is is unfair
and uncharitable. Let every honorable
man and reputable newspaper suspend
judgment until assisted by the evidence
one way or another.

Intrinsically Improbable.

The Boston *Journal* says: The theory
on which the Fall River police appear to
be working in the Borden murder case is
so monstrous and so intrinsically improbable that every day which passes without
the discovery of evidence increases the
public impatience with it.

BASEBALL.

WASHINGTON, Aug. 9.—Luck and good
ball playing on the part of the Washing-
tons gave them a victory over the Bostons,
who went to pieces in the seventh inning.

(box scores follow)

The Local Diamond.

The New Bedfords are in hard luck. Sexton was injured Saturday afternoon while
playing at Troy, N. H., and is under a physician's care. Murphy will be unable to play
for several days, as he is suffering from water on the knee, the result of a recent accident.

...

BIBLE LESSON, SABBATH, AUG. 14, '92.

ANANIAS AND SAPPHIRA.

Of the thousands of Christian believers at
Jerusalem, after the day of Pentecost, were
—ny of the poor, and of those from distant
comes who, by their prolonged stay, had exhausted what they had provided for their
journey and support. We find therefore
those who owned property ready to dispose
of it for the needs of their brethren; and that
this unity in Christian life and practical religion won the popular favor. Particular
mention is made by the writer of the book of
the Acts of the Apostles, of one Joseph,
called Barnabas, of the island of Cyprus,
afterwards a missionary with St. Paul, who
sold land he owned, probably in Palestine,
and committed all the proceeds to the disposal of the Apostles. In contrast with this
conspicuous instance, record is made of a
notable case of hypocrisy which cast the first
shade upon the bright face of the early
church. This is the subject of the Bible
lesson for August 14, selected from the Acts
of the Apostles, chapter v, i-11. GOLDEN text:
"Be not deceived; God is not mocked; for
whatsoever a man soweth, that shall he also
reap." (Gal. vi, 7.)

Their Sin.

Verse 1. But a certain man named Ananias,
with Sapphira his wife, sold a possession...

The Evening Standard.

ESTABLISHED FEBRUARY, 1850.

NEW BEDFORD, THURSDAY, AUGUST 11, 1892.

TWO CENTS.

HASKELL & TRIPP.

FRIDAY, Aug. 12.

Another short day.

Store closes at 1 o'clock p. m.

Early Friday morning our store is thronged with bargain seekers; and they are well pleased with the *great values* we give them. Remember—these goods are ready at store opening and that we do not give samples nor send goods out "on approval." Also that every article is sold without the usual privilege of exchange.

SPECIALTY No. 1.

A fair quantity of women's cambric shirt waists, with plaited front and back, high shoulders, sizes 32 to 42.

For Friday, 25c. each.

SPECIALTY No. 2.

200 yards cream Irish linen table damask, 56 inches wide, as good quality as is usually sold for 39c. a yard.

For Friday, 25c. a yard.

SPECIALTY No. 3.

Three hundred bleached German linen damask towels, sizes 18x40 inches, with knotted fringes and pretty, fancy colored borders, absolutely worth 21c.

For Friday, 12½c. each.

SPECIALTY No. 4.

Twenty-one dozen aprons, made of thin white lawn, ample size, nearly a yard long, have two-inch Hamburg trimming with four broad tucks above and sash strings, considered very cheap at 25c.

For Friday, 12½c. each.

SPECIALTY No. 5.

Six pieces of handsome Bedford cords, as follows:

Two pieces light ecru, 36 inches wide.

Four pieces two-toned Fall colorings, 40 inches wide.

Both the above are regular half-dollar dress goods.

For Friday, 29c. a yard.

SPECIALTY No. 6.

Marvellous shoe bargain.

Broken lots of women's fine dongola button and lace boots, about 75 pairs in all, actually worth $2.50 per pair.

For Friday, $1 a pair.

SPECIALTY No. 7.

Three dozen boys' jockey hats, assorted styles, worth 50c. each.

For Friday, 10c. each.

SPECIALTY No. 8.

Three hundred manufacturers' sample strips of good ingrain carpetings, in pieces of one yard square.

For Friday, 17c. apiece.

SPECIALTY No. 9.

Lot of "diamond" market baskets, almost given away.

These baskets are 18 inches long, 12 inches wide, 7 inches deep and have a strong bail.

For Friday, 5c. each.

SPECIALTY No. 10.

Lot of blown-glass tumblers, with engraved initials, but as the assortment of letters is not complete we will reduce the price from $1.25 per dozen.

For Friday, 89c. a dozen.

HASKELL & TRIPP.

Department Stores,

Purchase and William Streets.

HE PROVED AN ALIBI.

Man on New Bedford Train Thought to be an Assassin.

Fall River Police Are Working on a Number of Clews.

Suspicion May be Entirely Diverted from Borden Family.

FALL RIVER, Aug. 11.—The Borden inquest was resumed this morning.

Charles Sawyer, who guarded the doors of the house while Officer Allen ran to the Central station, was the first witness.

He testified that he ran to the house when he saw Mrs. Russell running, and that he was with Officer Doherty and an Associated Press reporter when Dr. Bowen discovered that Mrs. Borden did not die of heart disease.

Officer George Allen was called, and he testified to having seen Mr. Borden lying on the sofa stabbed as he supposed.

Mrs. Perry Gifford was being examined at 12 o'clock.

Last night Officer Harrington went to Boston with Dr. Handy to identify a suspect answering the description of a "wild-looking" man seen last Thursday morning by the doctor as he was driving by the Borden house.

The supect was not the man.

The police have also run down a suspect who boarded the New Bedford train at Mt. Pleasant and rode into the city.

He proved an alibi easily.

Marshal Hilliard this morning submitted to another interview.

In answer to a question as to whether

Bridget Sullivan,
The Servant in the Borden Family.

or not the police had given up all hopes of locating a murderer inside of the Borden family he said the question was nonsensical, but he would answer by saying that three clews were already being run down and none of them would in any way implicate a member of the household.

He said he had not been stinted in money because of political complications.

He was not hunting clews personally, because the district attorney required his presence at the inquest, but the detectives worked most of the night, and reported to him, and he was willing to say that close medical examinations and their results would be a feature of the case, and that it might turn out that suspicions would be directed from the Borden family.

It has been proven that the suspected poisonous milk drank by the Borden family was all right when it was taken from the Borden farm and brought to this city.

Members of the family in charge of the farm drank it and they were affected in no noticeable way.

FRENCH CONSUL IMPRISONED.

Warship Demands His Release of Venezuelan Authorities.

NEW YORK, Aug. 11.—A Trinidad, W. I., special to the *Herald* says: News has been received here that the French vice-consul at Campano, Venezuela, has been seized by the Venezuelan authorities, but for what reason is unknown. A French warship was at once ordered there and demands the release of the imprisoned official. There is considerable excitement over this trouble.

It is thought the Venezuelan authorities will release the imprisoned consul and make whatever reparation which may be demanded.

A schooner laden with 10,000 rifles consigned to Colon was seized here yesterday, the government believing they were for the use of the Legalists in Venezuela. They were soon released, no evidence being produced to warrant the seizure. A claim for damages will be filed against the government.

FREIGHT TRAIN'S FATAL FALL.

Brakeman Killed and Many Train Hands Injured.

UVALDE, Tex., Aug. 11.—Last night, as the Southern Pacific fast freight was going through a deep cut near the bridge which spans the Saline river, the caboose left the track. Recent rains had swollen the river until it overflowed and filled the cut with water.

Several cars were pulled from the track by the caboose and knocked down one span of the bridge over the river. Frank Leonard, brakeman, was killed and the following injured: William Raymond, concussion of brain; E. Waldo, internally; J. F. Crawford, sprained ankle and internally injured; John Morgan, body bruised; George Quick and John Manyan received slight bruises.

The dead and wounded are all railroad men. The caboose containing the men fell 40 feet to the river and shattered into fragments. It is thought three of the wounded men will die.

Minister Carr Ordered to Denmark.

GALESBURG, Ill., Aug. 11.—It is stated Hon. Clark Carr, United States minister to Denmark, has received instructions to proceed to Denmark without delay, unless it would cause too great an inconvenience. His leave was for two months and will not expire for some time. It is said that he will leave this week, if possible. It is thought that the order results from the trouble in which the United States consul in Copenhagen is implicated.

Damaged by Lightning.

DEXTER, Me., Aug. 11.—Dr. Fitzgerald's $20,000 unoccupied house was damaged $2000 by fire that was caused by lightning this morning.

Died from Being Run Over.

CONCORD, N. H., Aug. 11. — James Burchey, freight brakeman, was run over in the Northern railroad yard last night [illegible] this morning.

WHALING NEWS.

Reports from the Atlantic Fleet Received at Provincetown.

PROVINCETOWN, Aug. 11.—Letters from whaling schooner Carrie D. Knowles reports her Aug. 7th lon. 74, lat. 36 20, with 430 barrels sperm oil. The Gage H. Phillips had 420, Rising Sun 290, Alcyone 300, Baltic 320 (1040 all told,) D. A. Small 140 (417 all told,) Golden City 200, Antarctic 300, Star King 100, E. B. Conwell 190.

WEATHER INDICATIONS.

THUNDER SHOWERS.

WASHINGTON, Aug. 11.—For the 24 hours from 8 a. m. to-day: For Massachusetts, Rhode Island and Connecticut, thunder showers to-day, clearing to-night, fair Friday, cooler Friday morning, westerly winds.

LOCAL SHOWERS.

BOSTON, Aug. 11.—Local forecast for New England until Friday night: Continued fair weather, except thunder storms, and local showers are probable this afternoon or evening; slightly cooler with less moisture; westerly winds.

CRESPO'S VICTORIES.

Revolutionists Determined to Occupy the Capital Before an Election.

NEW YORK, Aug. 11.—A special from La Guayra, Venezuela, to the *Herald*, says: Gen. Crespo is now at Los Teques with his cavalry and 4000 infantrymen. Gens. Quintana and Vega are cooperating against what is left of Mendoza's army, which is at Cua.

Crespo on Aug. 1 fought and whipped Mendoza's army between Victoria and Villa De Cura, and moved his own forces toward Caracas. On Aug. 3 his outpost, which had been for several days at Parapara reoccupied El Guayaraba.

The diplomacy of Rojas Paul has proved unavailing in bringing about a settlement of the condition of affairs. His proposed compromises have been misconstrued and his peaceful efforts have been fruitless.

The revolutionary majority is firm in its determination to prevent a presidential election until Crespo's army occupies the capital, and they refuse to participate in the sittings of the congress, thus preventing a quorum of either the senate or house.

Rojas Paul, in the senate a few days ago, said that the revolutionists having scored a moral triumph Gen. Crespo has no grounds for a continuation of hostilities. He urged congress to take steps to enforce a quorum and to proceed to the election of a president.

Dr. Bustamente created a sensation by his reply. He said there could be no compromise; the revolution must be triumphant before a president could be elected. He desired to say that no intrigues with the heirs to the dictatorship would be countenanced in or out of the country. This was greeted with loud and long continued cheering by the lobby.

SEVEN PERSONS KILLED.

Fight Over the Enforcement of Regulations to Prevent Cholera.

CONSTANTINOPLE, Aug. 11.—A dispatch received here from Trebizond says that on Aug. 5th a serious disturbance occurred at Platana, seven miles west of Trebizond. The trouble arose from the enforcement of sanitary regulations adopted by the Turkish officials to prevent the spread of cholera.

Nearly 1500 persons were detained at the lazaretto that has been established at Platana, and they attempted to break through the sanitary cordon about the lazaretto. As the local authorities were powerless to handle the crowd, a battalion of troops was summoned to quell the disturbance. The soldiers promptly responded and orders were given for the crowd to disperse. They refused to do so and the commonder ordered his men to fire.

At the first volley seven persons were killed and a large number wounded. The people were terror stricken and fled back to the lazaretto.

Iron Hall Official Denies Charges.

HARTFORD, Aug. 11.—F. Wilson Rogers, whose books as accountant of the local branch of the Order of the Iron Hall of this city, are being examined, a deficiency of $1000 having already been discovered, denies that he has misappropriated any money. He demands a trial of George P. Sturtevant, the chief justice of the branch.

Congressional Bee in His Bonnet.

NEW HAVEN, Aug. 11.—H. Holton Wood of Birmingham, a manufacturer, and president of the Derby street railway, a well-known Democrat, announces himself a candidate for the congressional nomination in the Second congressional district. He will use, he says, every honorable means to secure the nomination.

Healthful Effect of the Sweating Law.

BOSTON, Aug. 11.—It is stated by Chief Wade, in the department of the district police, that a very marked difference can now be observed in the tenements where clothing is manufactured, as compared with the unhealthful condition of things before the subject was taken up by the legislature.

A Boom for New Haven.

NEW HAVEN, Aug. 11.—The Robert S. Gould company of New York city, the largest drapery fixture and light brass goods manufactures in the United States, have decided to move their factory to this city. The company will increase their present plant and will give employment to 150 persons.

Riggin's Remains at Philadelphia.

PHILADELPHIA, Aug. 11.—The body of Charles W. Riggin, the boatswain's mate of the U. S. S Baltimore, who was killed by a Chilian mob, arrived here and was taken to an undertaker's, where it will await the public demonstration arranged for Saturday and Sunday next.

Wanted in Boston, Too.

PORTLAND, Me., Aug. 11.—Charles Dorsey, arrested here for assault and robbery two weeks ago, proves to be Charles Douney, wanted by the Boston police for robbing John Lyons of that city of $150. He will be tried for his offense here and Boston officers will arrest him as soon as the Portland officers are through with him.

Seven Soldiers Drowned.

BERLIN, Aug. 11.—Seven soldiers were drowned at Neisse, Prussian Silesia, while practicing in the military swimming school. They were ordered to go into the water beyond their depths, the proprietors supposing them to be sufficiently practiced to be able to swim.

Lightweights Fight a Fifty-Round Draw.

SAN FRANCISCO, Aug. 11.—Jim Burge of Australia and Billy Lavigne of Saginaw, Mich., lightweights, engaged in a fight to a finish for a $1200 purse at the Pacific Club last night. The referee declared it a draw at the end of the 50th round.

Big Increase in the Mackerel Catch.

OTTAWA, Aug. 11. — The fisheries department has received advices to the effect that the mackerel catch of the New England fishing fleet to date is 22,000, barrels as against 11,000 last year and 3000 in 1890.

The Ocean Steamers.

Arrived — At New York, P. Caland, Amsterdam; City of Washington, Havana; Charlois, Amsterdam. Passed Scilly, Augusta Victoria, New York. Passed Kinsale, Germanic, New York. Arrived—At Boston, British Empire, London.

THE DEACON CASE.

Authorities Offer Freedom Conditional on Withdrawal from France.

PARIS, Aug. 11.—It is stated that Edward Parker Deacon was offered release from prison on condition that he would leave France forthwith, never to return. Mr. Deacon wrote to the prefect of Nice refusing to accept the offer. The French authorities, it is said, are much disappointed at the refusal as their object was to prevent, if possible, the trial of Deacon's suit against his wife for divorce and the exposure to the world of the additional evidence going to show her guilty of misconduct with M. Abeille. Mr. Deacon's suit for divorce will come up on Sept. 23.

HOME MATTERS.

BREAK-DOWN.—A wagon loaded with produce came to grief this morning by one of the wheels breaking while at the turnout on Pope's island.

FATAL KICK OF A HORSE.—A man named Peterson, employed in a stable at the corner of Seventh and Bank streets, in Fall River, was kicked by a horse and killed this morning.

WATER MAIN.—A water main 1100 feet in length is being laid in Shawmut avenue, north of Durfee street. People in that section have endeavored to have water pipes laid in the street for years, but not until recently was the work ordered, as some of the abutters on the street hated to do away with their wells. But the improvement was started yesterday afternoon.

COLLISION.—A light wagon, loaded with spring beds, wringers and rugs, belonging to W. S. Hann of Providence, was standing on School street, between First and Water streets, this noon while another wagon was standing across the street. A horse attached to a carriage in which was a lady named Swan attempted to pass between when her carriage collided with Mr. Hann's wagon and his nigh hind wheel was broken.

CONTRACT SIGNED.—The contract for building the new police station and polling place at the corner of Blackmer and Water streets, has been signed, and this morning Bryant & Slade of Fall River, the contractors, commenced excavating for the cellar. This is the firm that has just completed the stack and set up the boilers for the Rotch Spinning Co., and if they do as good a job on the station as they have in building the Rotch mill stack, the city will have no reason to complain.

PERSONAL.—Hon. E. L. Barney is taking a ten days' vacation at the Barney homestead in Barneyville, near Swanzey.

District Attorney Knowlton came over from Fall River last evening.

William Whitehead of Coggeshall street sailed for England yesterday.

Secretary W. E. Lougee of the Y. M. C. A. arrived home from Yarmouth, N. S., yesterday.

Manuel E. Lemos has been elected agent of Meyrelle's Band.

THE TITAN OF CHASMS—*A Mile Deep, 13 Miles Wide, 217 Miles Long, and Painted Like a Flower.*—The Grand Canon of the Colorado River, in Arizona, is now for the first time easily accessible to tourists. A regular stage line has been established from Flagstaff, Arizona, on the Atlantic & Pacific Railroad, making the trip from Flagstaff to the most imposing part of the canon in less than 12 hours. The stage fare for the round trip is only $20.00, and meals and comfortable lodgings are provided throughout the trip at a reasonable price. The view of the Grand Canon afforded at the terminus of the stage route is the most stupendous panorama known in nature. There is also a trail at this point leading down the canon wall, more than 6000 feet vertically, to the river below. The descent of the trail is a grander experience than climbing the Alps, for in the bottom of this terrific and sublime chasm are hundreds of mountains greater than any of the Alpine range.

A book describing the trip to the Grand Canon, illustrated by many full-page engravings from special photographs, and furnishing all needful information, may be obtained free upon application to Jno. J. Byrne, 723 Monadnock Block, Chicago, Ill.

ARRIVING HOME.—People are beginning to arrive from their Summer homes, while business begins to boom. We wish to say we have received another carload of all kinds of provisions for this week, consisting of rounds, rumps and loins, fine roasts, thick rib corned beef, fancy chickens and fowl, fresh legs of mutton, fine lambs and veal, fresh butter and eggs, berries, Summer squashes, sweet potatoes, shell beans, string beans, green corn, cucumbers, melons and everything else to make up a first class dinner. In our grocery department we are making some special low prices. Our constantly large trade makes our goods always fresh. White Cash Store, 134 Purchase street.

THE HEALTH AND PLEASURE RESORTS OF MICHIGAN AND THE WEST are illustrated and described in a handsome folder, containing a fine colored map, which has just been issued by the Michigan Central "The Niagara Falls Route" and which is designed for the special use of people in the East who wish to learn something about the resorts of Michigan, Wisconsin, the Isle of Mackinac, the lakes or Minnesota, Yellowstone Park, Colorado, Utah, and the Pacific coast.

Copy of folder will be sent on application to W. H. Underwood, Eastern Passenger Agent, Buffalo, N. Y.

SAVE YOUR MONEY.—For this month only, bargains in diamonds, watches, clocks, jewelry, etc., at the closing-out sale of J. S. Kelley & Son, 15 Purchase street.

STAKING IT OUT.—Surveyors were at work this morning staking out the lines for the new police station and polling place in Precinct 11.

THAT IS A CHEERFUL HOME where Mellin's Food is used, for the baby is always bright and happy.

R. A. PEIRCE POST 190.—Comrades are referred to special notice of a call to assemble at headquarters Friday evening.

TURKISH, Russian, electric, or plain baths. 5 South Sixth street.

GO TO WHITING & CO's to-morrow and get a shirt waist.

WE OFFER YOU our $1.50 trimmed sailors for 98c. Nooning's is the place.

A MASSAGE will knock that rheumatism sky high. Try one at 5 South Sixth street.

"AYER'S HYGIENIC COFFEE" will agree with you when no other drink will. Try it.

GO TO WHITING & CO's and purchase a ladies' gingham, lawn or cambric wrapper.

NOW IS YOUR CHANCE to get bargains in flowers at Nooning's for 15c., 25c., 49c. bunch.

YOU NEED A BATH. Get one at No. 5 South Sixth street.

GREAT BARGAINS in towels at Whiting & Co's Friday morning.

CALL AT NOONING'S and see their $3 mull hats marked down to $2.25.

HAND-SEWED Oxford Ties $2.00. Devoll's.

AFTER diphtheria, take Hood's Sarsaparilla.

SHOCKING FATALITY.

Two Children Burned to a Crisp This Noon.

Mother Frightfully Injured in Attempts to Save Them.

Grandmother's Life Sacrificed in Her Efforts at Rescue.

Cedar Grove Street Tenement Scene of the Horror.

Property Loss by the Fire Not Very Considerable.

One of the worst fires, if not the worst in the annals of the city, in point of fatality to humanity, occurred on Cedar Grove street this morning. As a result, two young children of Louis Dupuis are dead, burned to a crisp; his wife, Emedina, is severely burned, and her mother, Mrs. Emedina Levecque, is so horribly burned that she cannot live.

The fire was in the two-and-a-half story house No. 288 Cedar Grove street, occupied by three families. The lower floor is occupied by William Bonin and his family of a wife and four children, the second floor by Theodore Levecque, his wife and two children, while in the third or attic story dwells Louis Dupuis, his wife (a daughter of Mr. and Mrs. Levecque) and their two children.

At the time of the fire there were nine people in the house, Mrs. Bonin and her four children, Mrs. Levecque and Mrs. Dupuis and her two children.

Mrs. Levecque was in her tenement at work at an oil stove, when without warning it shot into a sheet of flame. She seized it in both hands, and screaming lustily, ran with it to the back staircase to take it out of doors. On the stairs she was overcome with the flames and heat and fell to the bottom, where she landed on top of the stove. In a twinkling her clothing was a mass of flame, which communicated to the paper and woodwork, and ran rapidly up stairs.

Mrs. Dupuis ran to her mother's assistance, leaving her two babies in their beds in the attic. She was met on the first landing by a sheet of flame, which scorched her face and drove her back to save her children. The fire, however, was too fast for her and she found herself surrounded and unable to reach them. In desperation she jumped from a second story window and landed in the back yard.

Mrs. Levecque's 12-year-old daughter, Theodora, who had been to a store on an errand, arrived at this moment and was driven back by the flames.

She raised the alarm, and Charles Fourniere rang in the alarm from box 125, corner of Weld and Bowditch streets.

Oliver St. Onge ran across lots from his planing mill and succeeded in dragging Mrs. Levecque into Mrs. Bonin's kitchen near the door. Patrick O'Leary assisted him, and the unconscious and blazing woman was stripped and borne to the back yard of a house across the street. Officers Wixon, Bumpus and Sweeney guarded her and Drs. Potter and Normandin were quickly on the scene. They found her frightfully burned, the flesh literally hanging in shreds from her body. Great cracks in the flesh lay open gaping wounds, while very little hair remained unsinged on the sufferer's head. Her groans were sickening, while the terrible smell of burned flesh was nauseating in the extreme. Mrs. Levecque was placed on a door and in Benjamin Dawson's express wagon taken to several houses before a place could be found to admit her. She was finally taken into the home of Tom Lloyd and laid on the kitchen table, where the physicians attended her.

Mrs. Dupuis was tenderly raised from the ground and carried to the house of Louis Rosseau, No. 300 Cedar Grove street. She was found to be burned on the face, hands and arms, but not fatally.

Rev. Frs. Payan, Fauteaux and Fortin had early been sent for and administered the last rite of the church to the unfortunate women.

The firemen had meantime entered the house and found the south end of it in a fierce blaze. As they finally managed to reach the head of the stairs on the third floor they found the remains of Mrs. Dupris' two children, burned to a crisp. Their names were Eva, 17 months old, and Berta, 4 months old. The firemen tenderly laid them on a bed and covered them with rubber blankets.

Word was sent at once to Medical Examiner Hough, who responded promptly. He found Mrs. Levecque in a frightful condition, her flesh badly burned and apparently having inhaled a large quantity of the fire. He declared that she would probably die before night.

Mrs. Dupuis was badly burned but inhaled no fire. She was in pain from injuries received in her jump from the window and may be injured internally. Her principal thought was of her children but the awful fact of their fate was carefully kept from her. By Dr. Hough's orders the bodies of the children were removed to the undertaking rooms of John B. Jean and there viewed.

Theodora Levecque, the daughter of the horribly burned woman, had her hair singed but was not burned much of any. She was much overcome at the frightful fate of her mother, and her cries were pitiful.

Mrs. Levecque is the mother of six children, most of whom are married. Her age is 54.

Mrs. Dupuis' age is 24, and she had only the two children who met such a shocking death.

Both bereaved men were much wrought up over the unfortunate occurrence, but held up with remarkable self-control.

When the firemen arrived at the scene they at once saw that considerable damage had already been done and went to work on the fire with a will. The flames spread through the kitchen and back entryway, and it appeared as if the structure would be burned to the ground. The fire spread rapidly through the second story and worked its way through the partitions and up the rear stairway into the garret, and the whole upper part of the house was soon a seething mass of flames. The firemen to whom the circumstance of the two children's being in the upper story had been made known used every effort to stay the progress of the blaze and soon had it under subjection. Time and again efforts were made to force an entrance into the room where the fated children lay, but the dense smoke and terrible heat drove them back and it was not until it was known that the children must have perished that they were able to make their way to where the bodies lay.

The damage to the house will probably reach $1200, which is covered by an insurance of $2000. There was no insurance on any of the furniture that was in the house, and each family probably lost $400.

DIVIDED!
BROKEN IN TWO!
CUT IN HALVES!

The above is what has happened to the prices on our

Summer Furniture.

We have about 50 pieces consisting of

PIAZZA CHAIRS, SETTEES, ROCKERS, ARM and EASY CHAIRS,

which we propose to close out at once. We mention a few styles and prices to illustrate:

Small Splint Chairs $1.00, Now 50c.
Lawn Seats $1.50, Now 75c.
Common Rockers $2.75, Now $1.37.
Patent Rockers $5.50, Now $2.25.
Piazza Settees $6.50, Now $3.25.
Piazza Settees $5.50, Now $2.25.

This is an opportunity to add a few pieces to your cottage or piazza furniture at a very small cost.

C. F. WING,

34 to 40 Purchase St.

WHITING & CO.

Friday & Saturday SALES!

The balance of our $1.25 and $1.50 Laundered and Unlaundered light colored Ladies' Shirt Waists go on sale at 50c. apiece.

Fne Ladies' and Misses' Flannel Blouses, $1.75 and $2.00 will be closed out at $1.00 apiece.

Mill Remnants of 4-4 fine Bleached Cotton, 9c. quality, go on sale at 6c. per yard.

Mill Remnants of 4-4 fine Unbleached Cotton go on sale at 6c. per yard.

30 pieces of fine White Domet Flannel go on sale at 5c. per yard.

200 Ladies' Colored border, hemstitched Handkerchiefs to be closed out at 4c. apiece.

For Friday only, the balance of our French Organdie Muslins, 37 1-2c. quality, go on sale at 20c. per yard.

Remnants of drapery Satines, 25c. goods, go on sale at 14c. per yard.

50 pairs of White Blankets go on sale at 49c. per pair.

WHITING & CO.

J. V. SPARE

Liberty Hall Building.

FRIDAY MORNING

Specialties.

Balance of Stock of Challies to be closed out at 3c. a yard.

Printed Flannelette, been selling at 12 1-2, now 6c. yard.

Pacific Chambray, regular 10c. goods at 6 1-2c. a yard.

Outing Flannels in short lengths at 5 1-2c. a yard.

More of those White Crochet Spreads at 59c. each.

Gray Blankets, damaged, 55c. pair.

Remnants of Ribbons, different widths, at 8c., 10c., 12 1-2c. yard.

J. V. Spare,

LIBERTY HALL BUILDING.

OUTING SHIRTS!

OUTING SHIRTS!

You can never have too many

OUTING SHIRTS!

Our low prices will help you out. Quality exceptional.

Good Shirts for $1 and $1.25, laundered collars and cuffs.

Another lot of the popular blue Madras, all sizes, $1.50.

Better come at once, They're going fast.

OUTING SHIRTS!

J. & W. R. WING & CO.,

133 UNION STREET.

OUTING SHIRTS!

she was on the south side she was close to another door.

Nobody Entered or Left the House
while she was washing these windows. Just as she had completed her work, she saw Mr. Borden coming across the street and she hurried across the lower floor to let him in. The government has fixed the time at which he entered. The servant that attended to one or two other matters in the kitchen and went up stairs. As she passed through the sitting room she saw Mr. Borden on the lounge, and Miss Lizzie was ironing, according to her testimony. Bridget Sullivan went to the third story where her room was situated to lie down a few moments, as her back ached. The next that she knew Miss Lizzie called her and she went down to gaze on the awful scene which had startled the young woman who had summoned her. John Morse was not in the house. Medical Examiner Dolan has testified that Mrs. Borden was slaughtered some time before Mr. Borden came in. She might have been dead half or three-quarters of an hour. Accordingly, the man who was concealed in the house came in before 9 30, when the servant started to clean the windows on the outside. He did not leave before 10 30, and he could not leave the side door for some minutes after that, as Bridget Sullivan did not go upstairs to her room until after 10 30. In other words, the servant was practically on guard her room until after 10 30. In other words, the servant was practically on guard over the house. The man who did the deed must have killed both Mr. and Mrs. Borden after he returned from town, or he must have concealed himself in the house at an early hour and waited.

Prof. Wood has testified that the marks discovered on one of the axes in the possession of the police are blood marks, and he will soon determine

Whether it is Human Blood or Not.
If they are, he can make comparisons which it is thought will be conclusive evidence that this was the weapon used in the double tragedy. No information of importance has been elicited from Miss Lizzie Borden on the witness stand. She tells the same story she told in the first place, and she does not vary it in the telling. She was ironing during the morning, she says, and was in the barn 20 minutes. Much has been made of the dust which covered the top floor of the stable in which an officer's feet left tracks, but which showed no marks before he examined it. Miss Lizzie has stated that she went to the top floor, but, as has been reported, it is believed that she is his-taken.

A Significant Remark.
The remark of one of the officials, who is conversant with all the details of the government work, is significant. He informed an intimate friend Tuesday night that the government work seemed likely to be brought to a satisfactory termination.

It is becoming more and more difficult to obtain any information whatever from the police, and occasionally it is noticed that misleading statements are allowed to leak out apparently without contradiction from those authorities who are conducting the investigation. It is said there is an object in all this, and circumstances connected with the departure of the domestic, Bridget Sullivan, from the District Court room Tuesday would seem to confirm this. It was announced and apparently not without authority, that this woman had been allowed to go upon her own recognizance with the understanding that she was to appear when wanted. As a matter of fact, it was learned yesterday that this is not true, and that with her departure she was placed under a guard. This guard watched the house of her cousin on Division street all night and is still there. The Sullivan woman desired to go to church, but Marshal Hilliard dissuaded her from doing so, and apparently she was very willing to carry out the wishes of the police in this direction. The reason for the story that the domestic was free to go where she pleased without surveillance is unknown, but the fact of its falsity is good evidence that the suspicions of the authorities have not been lulled.

An Expert Opinion.
The criticism of the Fall River police for not acting with greater shrewdness and the condition of the case itself at this moment, makes the opinion of experienced criminal detectives who know something about the murder of Mr. and Mrs. Borden of importance. Benjamin Buffington, deputy sheriff and formerly district officer, and at one time tax assessor of Fall River, was one of the first persons at the Borden house last Thursday, made an examination of the premises, talked with Bridget Sullivan and Miss Lizzie Borden and made inquiries in the house surrounding the Borden residence concerning what their inmates had seen or heard. Mr. Buffington said yesterday morning:

"I made my examination of the place of the crime about 3 o'clock last Thursday, and I came away with a theory of the cause of it. The theory I am not going to state, but I will say that this is a crime unlike any other crime.

The Motive Was Not Robbery, Revenge or Spite.
It was the removal of somebody out of the way. I did not go into the house or think it was necessary. I went into the barn, looked about the fences and went over into the yard surrounding the house. There is nobody who could have told from the condition of the barn that anybody had or had not been in there. There wasn't enough dust on the floor for anybody's footsteps to have left marks in it, so whether Lizzie Borden went there or not can't be said for certain. The ground on both sides of the fences showed no signs of any person having jumped the fence, although a person might have jumped the highest fence even with a cleaver concealed about him, without much trouble. According to what one of the oldest doctors tells me, Mrs. Borden must have been killed about 9 30 o'clock. The weapon it was done with must have been thin edged, something like a cleaver. If it had been an axe or hatchet, the thickness of the blade just above would have caused wounds that opened wider, and blood would have been spattered. Mr. Borden's death I place at between five minutes of 11 and five minutes past. Bridget Sullivan told me that she heard the clock strike 11 just before Miss Lizzie called her down stairs. Now you have heard people talk about the inactivity of the police. Let me tell you that

The Police Can't Go Ahead When They Haven't Evidence to Convict.
I had a case of murder up between here and Boston, where I was State officer, which illustrates. A companion of the man I suspected told me all about it under a promise that I would not use it unless I got other testimony. As hard as I tried I could not get other evidence to convict, and I had to give it up. I had promised, and only got my information by the promise, and I never broke my word. I couldn't ask the companion to turn State's evidence. The man who committed the crime is now in jail. We pushed him on hard enough on other cases to shut him up. In this Borden case they may have been running up against an equally great difficulty in getting evidence. It is hard to break some people down. What can the police do when they cannot get evidence? They can't do anything in this case unless they get somebody to give a fairly plain clew. But I believe

This Case is Coming to Light
just as sure as fate. It will come inside of 24 hours. There is somebody who can tell you what actually transpired in that house, whether it was a man's or a woman's hand which killed Mr. and Mrs. Borden, whether the weapon is in the house now or has been taken away, and whether the person that did it had on gloves and apron and then burned them up." Mr. Buffington would not say any more at this time, but said that in the future, if any arrest was made, he would be ready to give his theory and a sketch of the family.

Detective Hanscom Still Active.
Though Pinkerton detective Hanscom has received but little newspaper attention during the past few days, that active individual is very much in the case, and from his position views with apparent equanimity the efforts of the officers of the Government. Mr. Hanscom declines to be interviewed regarding his work here, and as far as can be learned limits his consultations to numerous visits to Andrew J. Jennings, the legal ad-

---

viser of the Borden family and apparently there is some curiosity at police headquarters as to the exact nature of the labors which are being performed by Mr. Hanscom, the general presumption, being, of course, that he is here for the personal protection of Miss Lizzie Borden. Mr. Hanscom says he has no new theory to advance in the case, nothing in fact beyond what he has already said. He says the ferreting out of the mystery is in very capable hands, and that the police, under Marshal Hilliard, are doing good work. Mr. Hanscom smiles when he says this, for he knows that the local police authorities do not like his presence here in the employ of the Borden family, and have expressed themselves in very strong terms regarding the doubts which the Pinkerton man has cast upon a portion of their accumulated wisdom.

He did speak a few sentences yesterday when a *Journal* representative asked him if there was any truth in the story advanced by one of the Government officers to the effect that Detective Hanscom had two assistants here whose sole duty it was

To Shadow Officer Seaver and Marshal Hilliard,
and ascertain the clews upon which they were working, and Mr. Hanscom's reply to this was that there were some stories the absurdity of which showed that they required no answer. He said he was in Fall River not to ascertain what other people were doing, but to attend to his own affairs.

Talk of Possible Arrest.
The talk of the possible arrest of Lizzie A. Borden is again renewed. It is learned that City Marshal Hilliard will be all ready to act at once whenever the district attorney gives the word. It is Mr. Knowlton, however, who holds the reins, and none who know him believe that he will act without great deliberation and careful forethought. Bristol county is fortunate in this hour of popular excitement in the possession of an officer of such level-headedness and sound common sense. He alone stands between Lizzie A. Borden and the popular clamor, and on both sides there appears the most implicit confidence in Mr. Knowlton that he will see that justice is done. There will be no arrest unless he says so. The talk about an arrest within 24 hours and the wagers made upon it throughout the day rest entirely on his action. The general belief now is that the arrest will come Friday, or not at all for some time to come.

MATTAPOISETT.
Besides the regular preaching services at 10 45 a. m. and 7 30 p. m. Sundays, there will be a "Young People's Christian Union" meeting at 6 o'clock in the Universalist church. Weekly prayer meeting upon Friday at 7 30 p. m.; subject, "Praise;" leader, Miss Mc Coughtry. Everyone is invited to attend these meetings.

Last Sunday the largest number present at Sunday School for many months was recorded.

The Universalist Society holds its annual picnic next Wednesday, August 17th, at Mr. John Dexter's grove, Pine Island. As the Marion society has been invited to join with them it is hoped that the social bond between these two parishes will be strengthened. The ladies of the church are talking of a "Conundrum Supper" in the near future.

TISBURY.
Calvin Tilton, assisted by Mr. Sweet of New Bedford, holds Salvation meetings every Sabbath afternoon, at the hours of 2 and 5, in a grove near Indian Hill.

Rev. C. L. Rotch, who has been visiting relatives and friends in various parts of the island, soon leaves for his mission in Dakota.

Mrs. A. D. Holmes and Mrs. A. F. Ingles, of Redwing, Minn., are visiting friends at North Tisbury.

William B. Parazina of Boston made a very generous donation to the West Tisbury Library of a handsome wall clock.

Mrs. A. Weeks and daughter Agnes, of Sheboygan, Wis., are visiting family relatives in North Tisbury.

There will be no services in the Baptist churches next Sabbath and the Sabbath following.

Rev. H. A. Dickerson preached in the Congregational church last Sabbath and will supply the pulpit next Sabbath.

YARMOUTH CAMP-MEETING.
Annual Election of Officers of the Association.

YARMOUTH, Aug. 10.
The 8 o'clock meetings were largely attended and full of interest.

At 10 15 a. m. Rev. J. N. Geisler of Nantucket preached, taking for his text Psalm cx, 3. Rev. Messrs. L. H. Massey, M. B. Wilson and C. H. Walters conducted the opening exercises. The sermon held the close attention of the congregation. It was strong and finely delivered. Rev. R. M. Wilkins of West Dennis exhorted. At the close of the sermon the usual altar service was held.

Rev. Messrs. R. E. Smith of Bryantville, E. F. Clark and J. Simpson of Taunton, J. S. Fish of South Truro and G. N. Anderson of Providence arrived on the noon train.

At 1 p. m. a children's meeting was held in the Provincetown tent. Addresses were conducted by Rev. G. E. Brightman of Plymouth and Rev. G. W. Elmer of Chatham.

In the Chatham tent, at the same hour, an Epworth League meeting of thrilling interest was conducted by Rev. C. S. Davis.

At the afternoon service in the tabernacle Rev. E. F. Clark of Taunton preached one of the most effective sermons of the meeting. The campers are favored with charming weather. Everything conspires to make this gathering a delightful one. The indications point to a highly successful meeting. The singing is inspiring, the prayer meetings are crowded and enthusiastic, while the preaching thus far has been unusually fine. Larger congregations greet every preacher than in any recent years.

At 1 o'clock the annual camp-meeting association was held and the following officers were elected:
President—Rev. Walter Ela.
First Vice-President — Rev. George E. Brightman.
Second Vice-President—R. S. Douglass.
Secretary—E. O. Snow.
Treasurer—D. B. Lovell.
Directors—Rev. Messrs. George E. Dunbar, O. A. Farley, Messrs. C. C. Nickerson, Rufus Smith, Nathan Young, A. F. Sherman, Dr. Henry Shortle, and Rev. W. F. Davis.

LETTERS FROM A WHALEMAN.—Mrs. Polly Bodfish of Vineyard Haven received yesterday several letters from her son, Hartson Bodfish, who is first officer of the steamer Mary D. Hume. The letters were dated April 5 and 8, and reported having taken 28 whales during two seasons, besides having this coming season before them. All were well aboard the steamer, save one man, who was sick at the time of writing, but nothing serious, and one man died some time before. They were all comfortable and expected to reach home during the coming November.

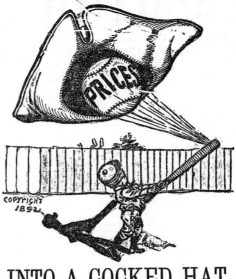

INTO A COCKED HAT.

That is just what has happened to the prices of our Spring Suits; they have been knocked into a Cocked Hat. Every time there is a big tumble something is damaged; in this case it is the price not the goods—they are just as superior in quality as they were before the tumble.

It is ridiculously easy to let good things escape you; it is not ridiculously easy to coax them back again.

THE MID-SUMMER SALE
is the buyer's opportunity. The early bird catches the worm, the wide-awake and early buyer catches the cream. Every day lessens the material for choice; just now about your choice yo can be particularly choice.

M. C. SWIFT & SON,

153, 157 and 159 Union Street,

NEW BEDFORD, - - - MASS.

To our Patrons:

C. W. HASKINS,

Having replenished his stock by liberal purchases of new goods, offers a choice selection of Diamonds, Watches, Fine Jewelry, Optical Goods, &c. The display of Sterling Silver Table Ware and Novelties is very attractive.

Attention is invited to a large collection of Souvenir Spoons, especially some in fine Enamel and Gold from various European countries.

Fine Watch and Clock Repairing done by competent and careful workmen and fully warranted

—AT—

C. W. HASKINS'

No. 20 Purchase Street.

SUMMER FLOWERS.
Pink and White Pond Lilies, Sweet Peas, Carnations, Candytuft, and various other flowers at

HATHAWAY'S Flower Store,
220 Union Street.

HAY! HAY!
PRESSED HAY in small bundles, at the Stage Office, 101 North Second Street.

TAGS constantly on hand or furnished in any quantity at short notice at STANDARD JOB ROOMS.

SEE NEW STYLES OF
Ball & Dance Cards
—AT THE—
STANDARD JOB ROOMS.

The Evening Standard.

ESTABLISHED FEBRUARY, 1850.

NEW BEDFORD, FRIDAY, AUGUST 12, 1892.

TWO CENTS.

HASKELL & TRIPP.

Hot weather hints.

Men's light ecru sateen sun umbrellas, $1.25 each.

Our parasols are selling at cut prices. We make no exceptions; *every one* marked down. You'll never need one more than you do this year.

Satin palm fans, and flat Jap fans, 3c. each. Folding fans, 5c. to 50c.; choice styles. Pocket fans of favorite sorts.

Drinking tumbler in leather case for 25c., or a nickled drinking cup that folds up to carry in your pocket for 25c.

Bay Rum in sprinkler top bottles (finest imported), 35c.

Florida water, 25c. up.

German Farina Cologne in long green bottles.

Made by Crown Perfumery Co., London. { Celebrated "Lavender Salts" and "Crab Apple Blossom."

Atomizers, 25c., 50c. and up to $1.25.

Sponges, 10c., 25c., 50c.

Rubber sponge bags, 20c., 25c.

Every good sort of toilet soap.

Celluloid soap box, 25c.

Remarkable bag bargain. 50 cents is the price.

The bag is of the new flat shape, leather on one side, with small change pocket, having oxidized clasp. The top is of cloth, with a drawing string, and there are double leather handles. We are selling immense quantities of them.

Pound package of good writing paper, 10c. (120 sheets.)

Pound package of "seconds," slightly, *very* slightly, imperfect writing paper of a high grade, 17c. a package.

Light literature.

Paper Covered novels, by famous writers of fiction, 10c. each, or three for 25c.

Sheet music, 5c., or six for 25c. More than 1000 titles. Catalogues free.

Sun bonnets, sun hats, cambric and gingham dresses for little children; at remarkably little prices.

HASKELL & TRIPP.

Department Stores,

Purchase and William Streets.

SAID NOT GUILTY!

Miss Borden Twice Answered Charge of Murder.

Continuance Granted to Monday, Aug. 22.

Morse and Bridget Sullivan Held as Witnesses.

Prisoner Calm and Dignified in the Court Room.

Her Counsel's Objections to Judge Blaisdell Overruled.

Exceptions Immediately Taken by the Astute Lawyer.

Claims Proceedings are Contrary to All Law and Justice.

Warm Words Exchanged with District Attorney Knowlton.

FALL RIVER, Aug. 12.—Lizzie A. Borden was arraigned in the Second District Court before Judge Blaisdell this morning on charges of homicide arising from the killing of her father and stepmother.

The court-room was crowded to suffocation by a motley crowd of curious people in no way directly interested, and Miss Borden's friends at court were very few in number.

Mr. Morse, Bridget Sullivan, Miss Emma Borden and City Missionary Buck were present.

Miss Borden, the prisoner, was represented by Andrew J. Jennings.

The Prisoner's Appearance.

Miss Borden was dressed in a dark blue tailor-made gown and wore a black lace hat adorned with a few red berries.

Andrew J. Jennings.
Counsel for the Prisoner.

She looked in much better condition than she was in last night just before her arrest.

She entered the court-room leaning on Missionary Buck's arm.

She was somewhat nervous, but did not show feeling by either tears or trembling.

She was given a seat beside her counsel and her sister Emma and Mr. Buck occupied a seat in front of the prisoner's dock.

Objections to Opening the Trial.

The trial was commenced by the entering of a plea signed and sworn to by the prisoner.

It recited that the prisoner objected to the opening of a trial before a justice who was already sitting at an inquest held to determine who committed the crime charged against her.

This plea was overruled for the time being and the judge asked for the reading of the complaint.

The reading was waived, and Mr. Jennings said he would enter a plea of not guilty.

District Attorney Knowlton, who was conducting the government's case, insisted that Miss Borden plead herself.

"Not Guilty."

Augustus B. Leonard, clerk of the court, asked her to stand up, which she did firmly and without assistance.

She was then asked to plead to charges of homicide, and did so in a very weak voice at first, saying "Not guilty."

Rufus B. Hilliard.

The clerk did not hear her and she raised her voice and said in quite a loud voice, "not guilty," putting strong emphasis on the first word.

Mr. Jennings then began to argue for the acceptance of his plea that his client should not be examined before the court where she had already been examined at an inquest.

Contrary to Law and Justice.

The proceeding was contrary to all law and justice. He as attorney for Lizzie Borden had been refused permission to enter and guide his client while an inquiry was being made.

It was not to be expected of human nature that the same judge could act at an inquest and at a trial and decide fairly in both cases. The proceeding was wholly unprecedented.

District Attorney's Demurrer.

District Attorney Knowlton entered a demurrer against the plea. He said he knew more than twenty cases in his own career where similar proceedings were

State Officer George F. Seaver.

gone through with, and they failed to attract attention because the crimes were not attended by such extraordinary circumstances as those which preceded this arraignment.

The matters of an inquest and the matters of a trial were entirely distinct, and it was not complimentary to His Honor's judgment to say that he could not act fairly in both cases.

Sparring Between Counsel.

There was warm sparring between the representatives of the government and the prisoner, Mr. Jennings displaying his pugnacious powers to excellent advantage.

Government Sustained.

The government's demurrer was finally sustained, and Mr. Jennings filed an objection. He moved for a trial at once.

District Attorney Knowlton objected on the ground that an inquest was still going on.

Continued to Monday, Aug. 22.

He asked for a continuance until Monday, Aug. 22d, and it was granted.

Mr. Morse and Bridget Sullivan were then held as witnesses in the sums of $500 each.

Committed Without Bail.

Miss Borden was asked to stand up and was committed without bail. She left the court room leaning on Mr. Buck's arm and was followed by Mr. Hilliard, who again placed her in charge of the matron.

She will probably remain in charge of the matron until one week from Monday.

At that time it is expected that a preliminary trial will be commenced by Judge Blaisdell.

SEVERE ELECTRICAL STORMS.

Buildings in New England and Other States Struck by Lightning.

HAVERHILL, Aug. 12. — During last night's thunder shower a house on Prospect street, West Newbury, was struck by lightning. The bolt entered the chimney, passed out, damaging nearly every room in the building. The house was owned by H. T. Bailey, and is occupied by Martin Hogan and John Regan, the members of whose families, ten in number, were all in bed and not injured.

MIDDLETOWN, N. Y., Aug. 12.—Orange and the adjoining counties were visited by severe electrical storms yesterday. At Beaver Dam the house of John Edwards was struck by lightning, and his daughter and grandchild and Harvey Edwards were killed. The other inmates received severe shocks.

ABBOTT, Tex., Aug. 12.—Lightning yesterday struck the house of J. H. Williams, shocking the whole family in a horrible manner. A six-year-old boy was instantly killed and another boy and girl were so badly burned that they cannot recover.

NORWALK, Conn., Aug. 12.—Walter Merwin's mills at Greenfield Hill, known as Gould's mills, were struck by lightning Wednesday and burned. Loss $4500.

A $30,000 FREIGHT WRECK.

Bad Smashup on the Boston & Maine at Haverhill.

HAVERHILL, Aug. 12.—The Portland express freight train No. 117 on the Boston & Maine, consisting of 35 cars which left Boston at 7 o'clock Thursday evening, drawn by engine "Exeter" was wrecked just beyond Winter street crossing here at 9 30 p. m. At this point some freight cars were standing on a side track, the rear car of which stood so near the switch as to be in the way of the cars passing on the main track. This car was struck by the engine of the freight train with the tender and half dozen of the cars derailed, all the rest badly damaged. The wrecked cars were completely demolished, one or two being reduced to splinters. A number of empty cars standing on the side track were also wrecked. The engineer and fireman of the freight train kept their places and escaped injury, as also did the conductor and others. A wrecking train from Lawrence reached the scene at an early hour this morning and the work of clearing the track was begun. The west track was not blocked, so that early trains will run as usual. The loss will reach $30,000 or more. The engine was not much damaged.

KILLED BY HOSTILE ARABS.

Tribes on the Western Bank of the Upper Congo in Insurrection.

BRUSSELS, Aug. 12.—The *Independeanci Belge* says that 20 agents of the Katanga company have been killed or captured by Arabs on the Upper Congo river. The steamer Beernaert, which was taking goods up the river, was seized, and the factories were razed. Whole tribes on the western bank of the river are in insurrection. The Arabs northwest of Nyangwe have gone down the Lualaba river and captured the station at Ribariba, killing the whites employed there. The stations on the Upper Lomassy have also been destroyed. The Arabs at Stanley Falls and Isangi, who have hitherto been loyal, are showing hostility. The Congo state authorities are sending re-enforcements to the various points threatened by the Arabs.

Washington Republican Nominees.

OLYMPIA, Wash., Aug. 12.—The Republican state committee last night nominated John H. McGraw for Governor, F. H. Luce for Lieutenant-Governor, and John L. Wilson and W. H. Doolittle for Congress.

The Ocean Steamers.

Arrived—At New York, Britannic, Liverpool; Bergma, Barbadoes. Passed Kinsale—Roman, Boston.

LIGHTNING'S VICTIMS.

Deadly Thunder Storm at Monument Beach.

Well-Known Brockton Society Lady Instantly Killed.

Another Woman Struck Dead While at Work in a Cellar.

[Special Dispatch.]

MONUMENT BEACH, August 12.—The thunder-storm here this morning was very severe. A bolt of lightning passed through two houses and killed a woman in each building.

The buildings struck were the Keith and Dunbar cottage and a house a few feet away.

The cottage was occupied by George Alden, a well known shoe manufacturer of Brockton, with his wife and two children. Mr. and Mrs. Alden had dressed and were dressing the children when the bolt entered. Mrs. Alden was instantly killed. She was 28 years of age and was well known in Brockton society circles.

The second house struck was occupied by Rev. S. S. Seward of New York. The bolt entered the lower floor and went directly into the cellar, instantly killing the cook, Ellen Eagan of Greenpoint, L. I., who was cutting kindling wood.

A son of Mr. Seward was in the tower, but other than a severe shock the other occupant was not injured.

The interior of both houses was damaged.

WILD SCENE IN HOUSE OF COMMONS.

Opinions on the Vote of "No Confidence" in Salisbury.

LONDON, Aug. 12.—The *Telegraph*, describing the scene at the House of Commons, says the ministers and their supporters did not seem unhappy.

Mr. Chamberlain's speech was probably the best he ever delivered. The Gladstonians sat tongue-tied as the merciless logic of facts was forced upon them. The Irish knew better in this instance than to try their favorite device of coughing down their opponents.

Ranking almost as high was Sir Henry James's important deliverance. Never before did he let go as he did the hour preceding the memorable discussion.

After numerous orations by Gladstonians the Conservatives made a joke of the business and ironically applauded no less a person than Maurice Healy. The tellers had to fight their way through the crowd. Mr. Trevellyan was nearly knocked down.

In its editorial the *Telegraph* says: The Gladstonians' silence in the debate is an unblushing confession that their alliance with the Irish is a sham, an imposture. The sole basis of the agreement is a desire to oust the government. They accept without a word of protest the charge of having concocted a bogus majority merely to upset the government and reconsent to climb into power without wasting a single sophism in their own defence. We should pronounce it incredible did not the unromantic parliament report prove that it occurred.

The *Times* says: "It is a party victory, won on party grounds and to be employed for party objects. No government that has remained in office for six years has enjoyed the same measure of success as the government just defeated. Blunders and disasters there are none to lay to the charge of the Unionist ministry. It is impossible to assume that a vote of "no confidence" in Salisbury is equivalent to a declaration of confidence in Gladstone. When the government meets Parliament it may turn out on the first trial of strength that Gladstone never had a real majority. They have the fear of the malady of disintegration, against which the Unionists are sure."

The *News* says: It is noticeable that the whole of Mr. Chamberlain's remarks were addressed to the Liberals. That does not look as if he thought the Tories had any future or he had anything to gain by going over to them.

The *Chronicle*, Liberal, says: The single effective point that Mr. Chamberlain made in his speech was that Mr. Gladstone will hold office for six months without defining his policy. Had an early session been conceded as we advised, Mr. Chamberlain must have cut his speech of all its most damaging passages. Until the new ministry meets no man dare say it is seated firmly enough to govern the country with authority and vigor. Until Mr. Gladstone brings his home rule measure forward it will be idle to ignore the fact that his majority is heterogeneous.

DUBLIN, Aug. 12.—The *Freeman's Journal*, after remarking that the majority against the Salisbury government is 10 more than that which rejected home rule, says: "It is more than a reversal of the decision which handed Ireland over to the rule of the Unionists. No obstruction from the peers, no ventilation of constitutional conundrums, can ever destroy the moral effect of the condemnation of the union by the Parliament which set the act of union up. Mr. Chamberlain's argument against the creation of a home rule ministry was solely an argument for Mr. Redmond. The Irish people were not deluded into the pursuit of will-o'-the-wisp schemes by Mr. Parnell, and will withstand the much less magnetic witchery of Mr. Redmond. They have shown how they can face a foe, and will now show how they can back the friends of home rule. The government shall have fair play."

The *Pall Mall Gazette* (Liberal) says: Mr. Gladstone's triumph is Mr. Parnell's also. Twenty years ago Mr. Parnell had not even entered Parliament. Before he died he converted nine of ten Irishmen against revolutionary methods. The effect of the division is irrevocable.

The *St. James Gazette* under the heading of "Leaping into Darkness," says the government was elected by a majority simply going it blind for the Grand Old Man and a half understood idea. If the disaster results in increased taxation, malignant bickerings will force a disgraceful retreat from Egypt, an open breach with Russia in Central Asia, and renewed outrages and rioting in Ireland, the country has itself to thank.

The members of the cabinet met at noon and formally agreed to resign. Most of the ministers will leave town to-day.

Mgr. Stoner to be the English Cardinal.

LONDON, Aug. 12.—A special dispatch to the *Chronicle* from Paris says that Mgr. Stoner will also be made a Cardinal at the coming papal consistory. Mgr. Stoner is an uncle of Lord Camoys and has long been a representative of the English aristocracy at Rome. After Cardinal Manning's death it was thought by many that Mgr. Stoner would succeed him, but in this they were disappointed. Mgr. Stoner is persona grata with the Prince of Wales and royalty generally and has great social influence.

The Pope and the World's Fair.

CHICAGO, Aug. 12.—Pope Leo has written another letter concerning the World's Fair. It pertains to the Catholic educational exhibit and is earnest for the great interest which His Holiness has in the success of the fair and particularly in the representation of the church and her educational methods during the progress of the great exposition.

WEATHER INDICATIONS.

FAIR AND COOLER TO-MORROW.

WASHINGTON, Aug. 12.—For the 24 hours from 8 a. m. to-day: For Massachusetts, Rhode Island and Connecticut, showers to-day; clearing to-night; fair and cooler Saturday; brisk northerly winds.

HOME MATTERS.

THE LAND OF SUNSHINE.—*A Unique Country where the Skies are almost Never Clouded, while the air is Cool and Bracing, like Perpetual Spring.*—As an anomalous Southern resort, by reason of the fact that there one may escape Summer heat no less than Winter cold, New Mexico is rapidly becoming famous. Averaging throughout the entire territory 5600 feet in altitude above sea-level, and characterized by dry air which, unlike a humid atmosphere, is incapable of communicating heat, the temperature in midsummer remains at a delightfully comfortable degree through the day, and at night becomes invariably brisk and bracing. The sunshine is almost constant, yet the most violent out-of-door exertion may be undertaken without fear of distressful consequences. Sunstroke or prostration are absolutely unknown there. It is an ideal land for a Summer outing. Its climate is prescribed by reputable physicians as a specific for pulmonary complaints, and the medicinal Hot Springs at Las Vegas are noted for their curative virtues. The most sumptuous hotel in the West, the Montezuma, is located at these springs. Write to Jno. J. Byrne, 723 Monadnock Block, Chicago, for "The Land of Sunshine," an entertaining and profusely illustrated book descriptive of this region, the most picturesque and romantic in the United States.

A MODEL MARKET.—A glance even into the market of George S. Taber, No. 9 North Sixth street, shows it to possess that most attractive of all things to costumers—neatness. The interior white paint is as clean as soap and water can make it, the brasswork around the handle to the door of the ice chest brightly polished, the meat blocks and benches have no unsightly scraps of meat or bone about them, and this is true also of the floor, which is carefully cleaned and kept covered by fresh sawdust. Over the meat blocks constantly revolve electrically propelled fans, which keep away all flies and keep up a good circulation of air. Meat scraps and all refuse pass down spouts to the cellar, canned goods are kept covered by gauze, fruits and vegetables are nice and fresh, and it is no wonder that customers in large numbers resort to a place where everything looks and is so clean and wholesome.

TO CHICAGO AND THE WEST.—The route affording the most advantages is via the Boston & Albany, New York Central and Michigan Central roads, "The Niagara Falls Route," and the route of the "North Shore Limited," which leaves Boston at 2 p. m. daily, and arrives at Chicago at 4 30 p. m. next day. Wagner buffet sleeping cars, dining car, serving all meals en route, smoking and library car comprises the equipment of this train, and ensures to passengers all the comforts and luxuries obtainable in railway travel. Three other express trains daily. For Summer tourist folder, describing western health and pleasure resorts, address W. H. Underwood, E. P. A. Mich. Cent. R. R., Buffalo, N. Y.

SPECIAL SALE FOR SATURDAY.—We shall offer some elegant bargains in ladies' shoes on Saturday morning at 9 o'clock. These are in two lots. First—Ladies' fine *enamel* button boots, sold for $4, for this sale $2. Second—100 pairs of ladies' fine dongola button, sizes 2½, 3, 3½, widths B, C, D and E, never sold for less than $2 50; while they last $1.25. A great chance to fit out the younger girls with fine shoes for little money. We have another word for you on page 5. Union Shoe Store.

H. C. HATHAWAY will sell at auction tomorrow morning at 9 o'clock, at salesroom, furniture, ranges, &c. At 10 o'clock, at mart, 20 horses adapted for general purposes; 1 pacer, safe for a lady to drive and can show a 2 30 clip. Also, several horses that have been used about the city. Also, carriages, harnesses, whips. At 3 o'clock p. m., heirs' sale of real estate at No. 75 Middle street.

PARDONED.—William A. Brightman, committed from this city to the House of Correction for drunkenness, was conditionally pardoned by the County Commissioners to-day, on the recommendation of Probation Officer Coe.

DON'T MISS THIS OPPORTUNITY to clothe yourself and children at our midsummer mark down sale. Wonderful bargains at Ashley & Peirce's, 72 and 74 William street.

G A. R., ATTENTION.—Comrades of Richard A. Peirce Post 190, G. A. R., are requested to assemble at headquarters this evening at 7 o'clock. See special notice.

HAVE YOU SEEN THEM?—That beautiful Neckwear which has been sold all the season at 50 and 75, now marked down to 37½ cents each. Ashley & Peirce.

WEAVERS' WAGES.—The Fall River Weavers' Association voted last night to drop the wage discussion for one month.

BIG DRIVES in Men's, Youths' and Children's Suits. Now is the time for you to make money. Every suit must be sold if low prices will do it. Ashley & Peirce.

FOR CADMAN'S NECK.—A barge will leave City Hall Square at 8 a. m. Sunday. See special notice.

JUST ARRIVED 75 dozen black Derby Hats in the latest styles for Fall and Winter, ranging in price from $1.00 to $3.00. Ashley & Peirce.

HEAVY RAINFALL.—The rainfall last night in this city, as gauged at the water works pump-house, was 1.13 inches.

MONITOR MIANTONOMAH was the government vessel reported in the bay in our third editon of yesterday.

COMRADES of Wm. Logan Rodman Post 1, G. A. R., are requested to meet this evening at hall. See special notice.

TURKISH, Russian, electric, or plain baths. 5 South Sixth street.

WE OFFER YOU our $1.50 trimmed sailors for 98c. Nooning's is the place.

MISS PARLOA'S COMPLETE COOK-BOOK for 10 cents at Hutchinson's Book Store.

A MASSAGE will knock that rheumatism sky high. Try one at 5 South Sixth street.

FLOWERS? You will find them at O'Neill's very cheap, some of them only 10 cents.

NOW IS YOUR CHANCE to get bargains in flowers at Nooning's for 15c., 25c., 49c. bunch.

MISS PARLOA'S Appledore Cook Books only 10 cents at Hutchinson's Book Store.

YOU NEED A BATH. Get one at No. 5 South Sixth street.

DON'T FORGET the bargains at O'Neill's Millinery Parlors.

CALL AT NOONING'S and see their $3 mull hats marked down to $2.25.

TRIMMED HATS from 98c. to $3 at O'Neill's.

HAND-SEWED House Gaiters $1. Devoll's.

BLOOD poison cured by Hood's Sarsaparilla.

DIVIDED!

BROKEN IN TWO!

CUT IN HALVES!

The above is what has happened to the prices on our

Summer Furniture.

We have about 50 pieces consisting of

PIAZZA CHAIRS, SETTEES, ROCKERS, ARM and EASY CHAIRS,

which we propose to close out at once. We mention a few styles and prices to illustrate:

Lawn Seats $1.50, Now 75c.

Common Rockers $2.75, Now $1.37.

Patent Rockers $5.50, Now $2.25.

Piazza Settees $6.50, Now $3.25.

Piazza Settees $5.50, Now $2.25.

This is an opportunity to add a few pieces to your cottage or piazza furniture at a very small cost.

C. F. WING,

34 to 40 Purchase St.

WHITING & CO.

Friday & Saturday SALES!

The balance of our $1.25 and $1.50 Laundered and Unlaundered light colored Ladies' Shirt Waists go on sale at 50c. apiece.

Fne Ladies' and Misses' Flannel Blouses, $1.75 and $2.00 will be closed out at $1.00 apiece.

Mill Remnants of 4-4 fine Bleached Cotton, 9c. quality, go on sale at 6c. per yard.

Mill Remnants of 4-4 fine Unbleached Cotton go on sale at 6c. per yard.

30 pieces of fine White Domet Flannel go on sale at 5c. per yard.

200 Ladies' Colored border, hemstitched Handkerchiefs to be closed out at 4c. apiece.

For Friday only, the balance of our French Organdie Muslins, 37 1-2c. quality, go on sale at 20c. per yard.

Remnants of drapery Satines, 25c. goods, go on sale at 14c. per yard.

50 pairs of White Blankets go on sale at 49c. per pair.

WHITING & CO.

OUTING SHIRTS!

OUTING SHIRTS!

You can never have too many

OUTING SHIRTS!

Our low prices will help you out. Quality exceptional.

Good Shirts for $1 and $1.25, laundered collars and cuffs.

Another lot of the popular blue Madras, all sizes, $1.50.

Better come at once, They're going fast.

J. & W. R. WING & CO.,

133 UNION STREET.

OUTING SHIRTS!

OUTING SHIRTS!

THE CRESCENT!

22 Purchase St.

Damask Towels 15c. Going, going, gone, unless you purchase immediately.

Towels, 4 for 25c., still on sale.

O, how light and airy. Chiffon Handkerchiefs, for the button-hole. Beauties,

Only 25 cents.

RIBBONS.

We don't *begin* to tell you *how much* we have *marked down* our line of Ribbons, but come and see for yourself.

We will close out our Gingham Dresses for children *at cost.* Sizes from 4 to 10 years of age.

Gloves, 15, 25, 37, 50c.

Corsets, a good corset for 39c.

An X-L-ent Corset for 50c.

A very nice Summer Corset, C-B a la Spirite, price $1.25.

Corsets at all prices.

Having removed our entire stock from the Old Stand at corner of County and High streets, we shall be pleased to see our old friends and patrons at our new quarters, 22 Purchase street, known as THE CRESCENT.

INSURANCE.

FIRE & LIGHTNING, TORNADO, PLATE GLASS and ACCIDENT INSURANCE.

No. 48 North Water Street.

Ætna Ins. Co.......... Hartford
Hartford Fire Ins. Co.......... "
Connecticut Fire Ins. Co.......... "
Merchants Ins. Co .... Providence
Equitable F. & M. Ins. Co.......... "
Springfield F. & M. Ins. Co.......... Springfield
Ins. Co. of North America.......... Philadelphia
Ins. Co. of State of Penn.......... "
Fire Association.......... "
Home Ins. Co.......... New York
Continental Ins. Co.......... "
German Am. Ins. Co.......... "
Niagara Fire Ins. Co.......... "
Williamsburgh City Fire Ins. Co. "
Hanover Fire Ins. Co.......... "
Phœnix Assurance Co.......... London
Guardian Assurance Co.......... "
No. British & Mer. Ins. Co.. "
Imperial Fire Ins. Co.......... "
Fitchburg Mut. Fire Ins. Co.... Fitchburg
Dorchester Mut. Fire Ins. Co..... Neponset
New York Plate Glass Ins. Co.... New York
U. S. Mutual Accident Asso...... "

GEO. N. ALDEN.
(Successor to Tillinghast & Alden.)
d&w

SAMUEL H. COOK,
Marine & Fire Insurance
AGENT AND BROKER,
No. 37 North Water Street.
(In National Bank of Commerce Building.)
Whaling Risks and their Catchings a Specialty at This Agency.
The following First Class Fire Insurance Companies are represented, viz.:
Hingham Mutual Fire Ins. Co.. Hingham
Phœnix Ins. Co.......... Hartford
National Fire Ins. Co.......... "
Phenix Ins. Co.......... New York
Westchester Fire Ins. Co.......... "
Commerce Ins. Co.......... Albany
Pennsylvania Fire Ins. Co...... Philadelphia
American Fire Ins. Co.......... "
Queen Ins. Co.......... London
London Assurance Corp.......... "
London & Lancashire Ins. Co.. "
Norwich Union F. Ins. Soc'y... "
Northern Assurance Co.......... "
Firemen's Fire Ins. Co.......... Boston
The Metropolitan Plate Glass Ins. Co.......... New York
Hartford Steam Boiler Inspection and Ins. Co.......... Hartford

EDWIN EMERY. JOHN H. PEDRO

LAWRENCE GRINNELL & CO.,
Fire and Marine, Life and Plate Glass
Insurance
60 No. Water St., foot of William.
(Over Mechanics' National Bank.)
Liverpool & London & Globe Ins. Co., Liverpool
American Fire Ins. Co.......... New York
Royal Ins. Co.......... Liverpool
Prov. Washington Ins. Co.......... Providence
Commercial Union Assurance Co..... London
Merchants' Ins. Co.......... Newark
Boylston Ins. Co.......... Boston
United States Inc. Co.......... New York
Caledonian Ins. Co.......... Scotland
Hamburg-Bremen Fire Ins. Co....... Bremen
American Ins. Co.......... Boston
Spring Garden Ins. Co.......... Philadelphia
Lowell Mutual Fire Ins. Co.......... Lowell
Wachusett Mutual Fire Ins. Co..... Fitchburg
Mutual Life Ins. Co.......... New York
Lloyd's Plate Glass Ins. Co.......... New York

HIRAM VAN CAMPEN. JOHN W. PAUL.

HIRAM VAN CAMPEN & CO.,
FIRE, LIFE AND ACCIDENT Insurance Agency,
No. 15 North Water Street.
Telephone Call .... 241-2.
(Established A. D. 1852.)
The following First Class Companies are represented:
Sun Fire Office.......... London, Eng.
Organized A. D. 1710.
Lancashire Ins. Co.......... Manchester, Eng.
The Reliance Ins. Co.......... Philadelphia
Girard Fire & Marine Ins. Co. "
United Firemen's Ins. Co.. "
Michigan Fire & Marine Ins. Co.......... Detroit, Mich.
Security Ins. Co.......... New Haven, Ct.
People's Fire Ins. Co.......... Manchester, N.H.
Firemen's Ins. Co.......... Newark, N. J.
Newark Fire Ins. Co.......... "
First National Fire Ins. Co.. Worcester, Mass.
Quincy Mut. Fire Ins. Co... Quincy, Mass.
Holyoke Mut. Fire Ins. Co.. Salem, Mass.
Traders & Mechanics' Ins. Co. Lowell, Mass.
Dorchester Mut. Fire Ins. Co. Boston
Cambridge Mut. Fire Ins. Co. Cambridgeport, Mass.
Travellers' Ins. Co., Hartford, Life & Accident.
All losses equitably adjusted and promptly paid.
New Bedford, April, 1890.

IVORY S. CORNISH. CLIFTON H. CORNISH

I. S. CORNISH & SON.
LIFE, FIRE, ACCIDENT and PLATE GLASS —INSURANCE—
Agents and Brokers. 50 North Second St.
NEW BEDFORD, MASS.
Represent the following First-Class Companies:
Ætna Life Ins. Co. Hartford, Conn
Travelers Accident Ins. Co. Hartford, Conn
Merchants and Farmers Mutual Fire Ins. Co., Worcester, Mass
Citizens Mutual Ins. Co. Boston, Mass
Mass. Mutual Fire Ins. Co. Boston, Mass
Abington Mutual Fire Ins. Co. Abington, Mass
Salem Mutual Fire Ins. Co. Salem, Mass
Essex Mutual Fire Ins. Co. Salem, Mass
Merrimac Mutual Fire Ins. Co. Andover, Mass
Franklin Mutual Fire Ins. Co. Greenfield, Mass
Milford Mutual Fire Ins. Co. Milford, Mass
Glens Falls Ins. Co. Glens Falls, N. Y
Union Ins. Co. Philadelphia, Penn
New Hampshire Fire Ins. Co. Manchester, N.H
Peoples Fire Ins. Co. Manchester, N. H
Delaware Ins. Co. Philadelphia, Penn
Metropolitan Plate Glass Ins. Co. New York, N. Y
Losses promptly adjusted and paid.
Business solicited.

Bristol County Mutual Fire Ins. Co.
INCORPORATED 1829.
Insures Against Loss and Damage by FIRE and LIGHTNING.
Insures only buildings, principally dwellings.
CASH PREMIUMS SMALL.
For reliable information call at the office,
NO. 48 NORTH WATER ST.
JAMES TAYLOR.......... President
GEO. N. ALDEN....Secretary and Treasurer
DIRECTORS:
James Taylor, Oliver P. Brightman,
Geo. F. Kingman, Isaac H. Coe,
Thos. H. Knowles, William R. Wing,
Samuel C. Hart.
Telephone Call 11—4. MWF&w

GEORGE C. BLISS, FLORIST.
34 Arnold Street,
CORNER COTTAGE.
TELEPHONE, DAY OR NIGHT.

Smoke the New Nickel Cigar,

IT IS THE LEADER.
FOR SALE EVERYWHERE. au6-1m

At this Season of the Year

We have a great many broken lots of Suits. One or two or three of a lot. These suits will be sold at less than the price of the goods to manufacture, in order to close them.

SANDERS & BARROWS,
67 and 69 William Street.

DON'T STOP ME
I know where to find the Lowest PRICES in
HARNESSES,
Carriage Lap Robes, Horse Clothing, Whips, &c., Ladies' and Gents' Riding Saddles, Trunks, Bags, Pocketbooks, Bill Books, Umbrellas and all kinds Travelling Goods.
C. F. CUSHING, - - - - Opp. City Hall,
IS THE MAN.

CUT PRICES FOR ALL Summer Clothing
ELEGANT NECKWEAR 25c. Each.
H. V. SANDERS & Co.
One Price Clothiers, OPP. CITY CLOCK, 92 Purchase St.

NEW BEDFORD BRASS FOUNDRY.

Machinists, Brass Finishers and Founders, Brass, Bronze and Composition Castings, Zinc and White Metal Pattern Castings, Phospor Bronze Castings a specialty, Lead Window Weights and High Speed Babbitt Metals, Chandelier Repairing and Brazing, Brass Finishing in all its branches. Machine Repairing promptly attended to. Lawn Mowers Sharpened and Repaired.

Foundry and Machine Shop, 108 North Water Street, foot of Elm.
WM. T. NICHOLSON, Manager, Formerly Foreman of the Armington & Sims Engine Company's Brass Foundry, Providence, R. I. je25-3m

We Use PURE PAINT. It is guaranteed to us by the manufacturer. It costs more than cheap substitutes, which are little better than whitewash. But

IT WILL WEAR. And that is what you want. The labor for putting on one is the same as the other. If you use the cheap kind

YOU SAVE 10 PER CENT. In cost and lose 75 per cent. in wear. It will pay you to have your painting done by

HART & AKIN,
No. 84 Pleasant St.,
No. 9 North Water St.,
Cor. Water and Walnut Sts.

TRY **39 TOBACCO!**
Best in the Land for Smoking.
Be sure that the tag 39 is on every piece, and take nothing else in place of it.
Distributing Agents
Driscol, Church & Hall,
Wholesale Grocers, NEW BEDFORD.

FINE CARRIAGES.

GEO. L. BROWNELL
OFFERS FOR SALE AT HIS
Carriage Manufactory and Repository,
Cor. Acushnet Ave. and Cannon St.,
NEW BEDFORD,..........MASS.,
A FINE assortment of Carriages, namely: Landaus, Coaches, Coupe Victorias, Coupe Rockaways, Extension and Standing Top Family Carryalls, Phaetons, Goddard Box Top Buggies, Open Road and Business Wagons. Also a very large assortment of *SECOND-HAND CARRIAGES* of all descriptions, which will be sold low.
GILES G. BARKER, Supt.

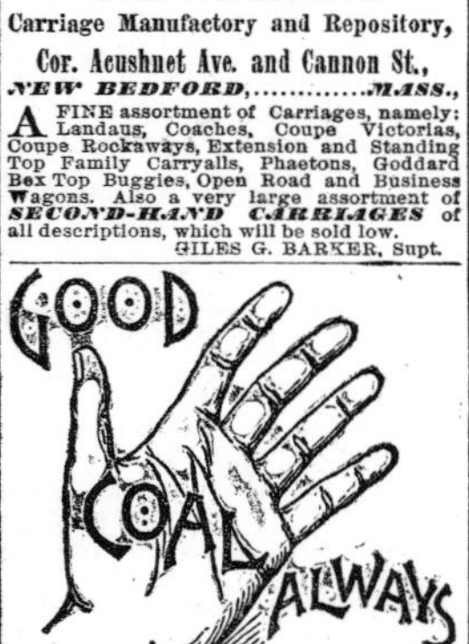

DENISON BROS. CO.,
Yard---Foot of Hillman Street. Offices---Cor. School and South Water Sts., and Cor. Hillman and North Water Sts.

ARRESTED AT LAST.

Lizzie Borden Charged With the Double Murder.

"I Knew it Was Coming" Was All She Had to Say.

Went Through the Ordeal With Remarkable Coolness.

Taken Violently Ill Soon After Being Locked Up.

Police Confident of Conviction, But Public Sentiment Divided.

What has been expected for several days in the Borden murder case has at last happened. Miss Lizzie Borden was arrested by the Fall River police, at the instance of District Attorney Knowlton, for the murder of her father and stepmother. The unfortunate young woman spent last night in the Central police station at Fall River, and will probably be transferred to New Bedford to-day. The offence is not bailable.

The inquest has not been finished and the police have not yet given up their surveillance of the other persons whom they have had practically under guard since the day of the murder.

It was intimated late last night that the police do not consider Miss Lizzie Borden to have been alone implicated in the crime.

Before the Arrest

It was growing tiresome in Fall River. The reaction had set in, and yesterday afternoon the community lost its patience. For two days it had been informed that the end was near and that the die was about to be cast; but at 3 o'clock the bulletin boards announced that no action had been taken and no verdict had been rendered, and the crowds muttered and grumbled. They wanted something done; their interest in clews and theories and suspicious characters had about died out. More than that, they were no longer satisfied with reports of the proceedings at the inquest retailed step by step. They demanded the grand finale which would bring the drama to a close or ring the curtain up on a new scene; but it seemed as if the grand finale had been indefinitely postponed. The hours dragged along and the gray walls of the court-house in the square kept their secrets, if they had any to keep. It was the same story over and over again. Witnesses known to be connected with the case appeared and disappeared; officers were sent hither and thither and various rumors were afloat regarding the probable outcome.

At 5 30 o'clock a big crowd had assembled about the police station. A number of women took up their position under an awning and remained until 7 o'clock. The officers did not interfere with them. A little news leaked out from the granite walls. It was announced that the inquest was over, the evidence was all in, and that everything depended on the decision of the district attorney. Then a little more news filtered through the masonry. There was an iron safe in the Borden house and a Boston expert was trying to unlock it. Down at the corner of Court square and Bedford street this report was supplemented by the information that the expert had encountered difficulties in his work, but was expected to strike the combination every moment.

There was more impatience. "What had the safe to do with the inquest? Could anything found in that release from the dreadful suspicion which had fastened itself on Lizzie Borden? If anything in that iron box could confirm this suspicion, why had it not been blown open before?" These and a hundred other questions were asked as fast as thought could frame them.

The clock on the City Hall struck 7 and still the small gatherings lingered. They pinned their faith to the newspapers and they had been told that the end must come before many hours. Either Miss Lizzie Borden would enter the closed carriage a free woman or she would remain in custody for many a day. If this conclusion was correct the public was aware that it could at last judge of the result for itself, and it continued to gaze at the unattractive station house.

A few moments passed and a small group of newspaper men standing in the centre of the square knew that

District Attorney Knowlton Had Made Up His Mind,

and Miss Lizzie Borden was a prisoner. The news spread and in an instant the town knew that the curtain had fallen on one terrible act. In the same instant the

Populace Took Sides,

and those sides will remain arrayed against one another for many a weary month. Men who had been wavering and tossing between this and that theory for six days, were suddenly possessed of convictions clean cut and positive. Miss Borden's supporters were astounded.

They had hoped, cheerfully and bravely, from the first to the last, that she had been unjustly accused; that the suspicion which rested on her was as unjust as it seemed atrociously cruel. They still so hope, and so they will hope to the end, but the iron entered their souls when the arrest was made public. Those who have shaken their heads whenever innocence was suggested, were quicker to believe the grim news. They had contended all along that this would be the end; in a measure the verdict of the district attorney had vindicated them.

The scenes of the earlier days of the tragedy were re-enacted on the sidewalks in the main thoroughfares, in office doorways and back shops, only now the topic of conversation was this last significant move; then it was the murdered and the probable murderer. On the one hand, there had been the feeling that the police might strike, to save their own reputations, tempered by the reflection that District Attorney Knowlton, cool, level-headed, not easily stirred, would checkmate them if they erred.

On the other hand, the impression had prevailed that the government had not been strongly fortified in its position by the inquest, and that it was too timid to move. That evidence, circumstantial though it was, which might have answered 72 hours ago, had been weakened in that it had not been reinforced during the three days of the preliminary hearing. Perhaps the most general conclusion reached on all sides was this—there were developments at the inquest of which the community has known nothing, developments which

Tightened the Chain of Circumstantial Evidence

around Lizzie Borden. The police had explained their case to District Attorney Knowlton in a parlor of the Mellen House; in the Second District Court room they had put in that case fully and exhaustively, and last night the district attorney and his associates passed upon it. They concluded that the testimony to which they had listened warranted them in holding Miss Lizzie Borden. In spite of her social standing, her spotless character, the influence brought to bear by friends and acquaintances, the effect upon the community and the many difficulties the mind encounters in comprehending the full import of such a conclusion, the government said calmly and deliberately, "We cannot release Miss Lizzie Borden from custody. An arrest is not a conviction, however, far from it.

She May be as Innocent

as she was a week ago Wednesday morning and a victim to more terrible circumstances than those which surrounded her father and step-mother when they were struck down in their home."

The case, which is sure to take its place in history with other famous cases, would not admit of hasty action. The evidence was not of a nature to warrant hasty conclusions. It has been necessary from the start to go minutely into what might seem to be the most insignificant details, and all this takes time. Nobody, outside of the small circle of police officials and State officers appreciates the influence which has been brought to bear to persuade them to abandon the theory which has kept them penned in the district court room four days. They have been forced against their better judgment to pursue every clew and demonstrate the absurdity of almost every hobby. Had they refused they would have been condemned in the event of a failure to fasten the crime upon anybody, of neglecting their duty, and every theorist and amateur detective in the town would have been positive to the end of time that his view was unassailable, or that he had seen the assassin. Consequently, theories had to be exploded and bubbles had to be pricked.

It isn't particularly easy to account for the secretiveness of the officers during the last two days. There are many matters connected with the case on which they were expected to be dumb, but it is equally true that there was news of a general nature which they might have disseminated without prejudice to their cause. They had but one line to pursue, and they had collected all their evidence along that line. No witness or suspect could escape them, and they might have prescribed to the suspense which existed and have lost nothing by it.

Details of the Arrest.

From the time that the carriage rolled up to the entrance to the Central Police Station at 4 30 o'clock yesterday afternoon and Lizzie Borden, Emma Borden and Mrs. George Brigham dismounted under the watchful eye of Marshal Hilliard, people commenced to congregate about the streets contiguous to the station house. By that intuitive perception by which the general public becomes aware of all important proceedings looking towards the capture or apprehension of criminals in noted cases, it was recognized that the most important movements of the long investigation had been entered upon, and that their passing was fraught with the greatest import to all directly concerned in the case as well as the public, restless under the week's delay in clearing the way for the arrest of the murderer. There was nothing remarkable in the appearance of the party, Miss Emma Borden being evidently the most agitated. Already in the court room were Bridget Sullivan, District Attorney Knowlton and State officer Seaver. Soon after Dr. Dolan arrived, and then an officer dashed out of the room and hurried to D. R. Smith's drug store. With him upon his return was the clerk of whom it has been alleged Lizzie Borden endeavored to purchase a deadly poison. The

Excitement Grew as the Hour Passed

and there was no movement from the court room. In the meanwhile information arrived that an expert safe opener had arrived from Boston, and had been driven hurriedly to the Borden house on Second street. Investigation showed the truth of this story and the further fact that he had commenced work upon the safe in which Andrew J. Borden kept his books and papers. This safe was found locked at the time of the tragedy and the secret of the combination died with the murdered man. The expert believed he could easily open the safe, but found the combination most intricate and he worked away without apparent result.

At 5 o'clock Marshal Hilliard and District Attorney Knowlton came from the court-room and entered a carriage. Soon the marshal returned, but the district attorney was absent for nearly an hour, and it was reported that he had visited the Second street house and had learned that the safe opener had not then completed his labors. Outside the court-room the stalwart officers kept guard and at the foot of the stairs in the station house the large force of newspaper representatives were on guard. The subordinate officers who have been working upon the case expressed their convictions that the

Long Delayed Arrest was about to be Made,

and that Lizzie Borden would not depart from the station with the remaining members of the household. Soon Bridget Sullivan emerged, and escorted by a police officer walked slowly down the street. The gravity of the situation was apparent, for the natural sternness of some of the officers, including the marshal, was increased to such an extent as to warrant the inference that something of importance in connection with the case was about to happen. Soon the inquisition was apparently ended, and then Lizzie Borden, her sister and Mrs. Brigham were escorted across the entry from the court room to the matron's room, which is situated upon the same floor. An officer came out and soon returned with supper for the party. Miss Lizzie Borden threw herself upon the lounge in the room, and the repast was disturbed but little.

Across the hall there was grave work, and the decision of the authorities to arrest Lizzie Borden was arrived at after a consultation lasting but 10 minutes. The services of Clerk Arnold were called into requisition. The warrant was quickly drawn, and the result of the long examinations and the week's work of the government was in the hands of the police force of Fall River. At this time the news was among the reporters, but none were certain enough of the fact to dispatch the intelligence to the journals they represented. The excitement became general, and men, women and children stood about the street and waited.

Soon Marshal Hilliard came out accompanied by Mr. Knowlton, and as they entered a carriage a telephone message informed Andrew J. Jennings, attorney for the family, that the two men were about to pay him a visit at his residence. This information obtained but little publicity, and not a few in the assembled crowds believed that Mr. Knowlton was being driven to the Boston train. The marshal and the district attorney proceeded to Mr. Jennings' residence and informed that gentleman that the government had

Decided Upon the Arrest of Lizzie Borden,

and, recognizing that his presence at the station would be desirable, had deemed it wise to notify him of the decision arrived at and the contemplated action. Mr. Jennings was not apparently greatly surprised, and at once made preparations to visit his client. The officials returned to the court room and were followed in a few moments by the attorney. George Brigham also came to the station and entered the presence of the women in the matron's quarters.

There was a moment's preparation, and then Lizzie Borden was notified that she was held by the Government on the charge of having murdered her father and mother. Marshal Hilliard stepped from the court room across the short entry and entered the matron's room. Lizzie Borden lay upon the lounge and the marshal walked to that part of the room.

"I have a warrant for you," he said. The young woman made no answer, but remained in the lying position, staring at the officer and undergoing a most severe mental strain. The information had a most depressing effect upon all the others present, particularly upon Miss Emma Borden, who was greatly affected. Upon the face of the prisoner there was a pallor, and while her eyes were moist with tears there was little evidence of emotion in the almost stolid countenance.

The marshal still held the warrant in his hand.

"We will waive the reading of that," said Mr. Jennings, and he looked interrogatively towards Lizzie Borden. She nodded her acquiescence, but it was clearly an effort for her to even thus express herself.

The remaining members of the party then prepared to depart, and the effects of the arrest became apparent upon the prisoner. She still displayed all the characteristics of her peculiarly unemotional nature, and though almost prostrated, she did not shed a tear. A carriage was ordered and Miss Emma Borden and Mr. and Mrs. Brigham prepared to leave. As they emerged from the station into the view of the curious crowds, the women, particularly Miss Emma, looked about with almost a pathetic glance. The people crowded forward and the police pushed them back. Miss Borden appeared to be suffering intensely, and all the external evidences of agitation were visible upon her countenance. Mrs. Brigham was more composed, but was evidently deeply concerned. The party entered the carriage and were driven rapidly towards Second street.

Government's Case.

The presentment of the police against Miss Lizzie A. Borden now is founded almost solely on Bridget Sullivan's evidence, with the other corroborative testimony on the case. From this the officers require Lizzie to account for her time for one hour, from 9 30 to 10 30, or thereabouts, when she was entirely alone in the house with her stepmother, Mrs. Borden, she having sent Bridget out of doors to wash the windows, and also for nine minutes, from about five minutes of 11 to three or four minutes past, when she was likewise alone down stairs in the sitting room with her father. The theory of the government all depends on Prof. Wood's analysis of the contents of the stomachs and the difference in time which may be down in the arrest of their functions and digestion of the food later that morning at breakfast.

The Mayor, Mr. Coughlin, believes Mrs. Borden was killed first; if so, the post mortem digestion ought to indicate the fact. Her body was said to be comparatively cold when found, while Mr. Borden's was warm and without symptoms of rigor mortis. The analysis of Mr. Borden's stomach will prove whether or not digestion ceased after it had terminated in Mrs. Borden.

Uncle John V. Morse started out at about quarter of 9; Mr. Borden went down town at 9 15; Bridget Sullivan was sent out to wash the windows all around the house, by Miss Lizzie, at about 9 30. It took her nearly an hour. There were 11 windows. She began on the north side and worked along round by the back end of the house to the south side. In doing this she commanded a view of the side of the door and steps, and saw that nobody entered there during that time. When she got round the south side of the house, working toward the street, she was out of sight of the yard. She was also out of hearing of any heavy sound of a fall in the spare chamber in the extreme northwest front of the house. As she came out to the street she came in view of the front door; she saw old Mr. Borden coming up the street, and ran round to the front door to let him in. This was about 10 40, and all the time Lizzie Borden was alone in the house with Mrs. Borden. Bridget went up to her room at about five minutes of 11. She left Lizzie smoothing the pillows for her father's nap on the lounge. She threw herself on the bed after attending to little things, but in less than five minutes Lizzie called her. She descended to find Mr. Borden dead.

Officer Medley found the lead in the barn that Lizzie was after to make sinkers. There was about twenty pounds of leaf lead in a little jug to the left of the door at which she entered, and two feet six inches from it there was a lot of pipe lead in plain sight four feet eight inches from the door. There was no lead in the barn chamber, and Lizzie says she was out there 20 minutes. That, in brief outline, is the government's theory against Lizzie A. Borden, and the points she will have to meet, if called upon.

It is very generally conceded that the government must have very much more positive evidence than it has at present to secure a conviction.

"Their only hope," said an old official, "is to break down Lizzie Borden. Their whole case depends upon that. If she holds her tongue she can never be convicted in this world in my judgment." On the contrary great stress is laid on the fact that Lizzie has an hour alone with her mother and 10 minutes alone with her father to explain.

"Judge Not."

The Fall River *News* publishes a long article appealing to the citizens "to judge not." Mr. John C. Milne of that paper says that from his own knowledge of the case Bridget Sullivan was not acting under Miss Borden's orders at all, as the police have it, but was asked to go out and wash the windows by Mrs. Borden herself, the murdered woman, before Lizzie came down from her room for breakfast. He charges some of the extended reports of what goes on at the hearing, which is so secretly conducted that even the court officer is excluded, as being made to conform to the different theories that the different reporters have already advanced and published and emphasizes this evidence in regard to Bridget as only one instance of how many small but most important points there are upon which the authorities have information, but of which the reporters and the public are in ignorance. He says:

"Again we urge that minds be left unbiased as far as possible. Suspicions are not facts or convincing testimony in court. If they were at least two arrests would have been made days ago. Another point on which the formation of opinion is prejudiced by some is the bearing of Lizzie Borden during this trying ordeal. Some construe it as calm and dignified and believe in her innocence on this account. Others look upon it as indifferent, cold and heartless, entirely unnatural and indicating a personality capable of performing such crimes as police suspicion has attributed to her. To these we say: Judge not. Undertaker Winward could tell scenes of grief that would eliminate charges of lack of feeling; friends who have been with her during these seven awful days can describe yearnings for sympathy, appealing and childlike in their simplicity, that would bring tears to many eyes. We speak whereof we know. Miss Borden has been all that Christian womanhood could ask, outside of the inquest room of which we know nothing."

Mr. Milne alluded to the frankness of Miss Borden's statements to reporters and police, made with no regard as to how they might be construed, and says there has been nothing in her deportment which justifies suspicion and belief that she is guilty.

"We ask not for sympathy on behalf of this unfortunate young woman, but justice. Simply that opinions be not formed, or if formed, that they be not expressed until further facts can be obtained."

An Editorial Opinion.

The Boston *Herald* says the arrest of Lizzie A. Borden for the double murder

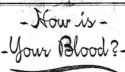

MISS LIZZIE A. BORDEN.

Of Interest to New Bedford Physicians

That every physician and nurse may have an opportunity of testing lactated food, we offer to send, free of all charges, enough for a thorough trial. Lactated food is not a secret preparation, its composition being given on each package. Physicians prescribe it for infants, invalids, the aged, and all who need a strengthening and easily digested food.
Wells, Richardson & Co., Burlington, Vt.

-How is- -Your Blood?-

I had a malignant breaking out on my leg below the knee, and was cured sound and well with two and a half bottles of S.S.S. Other blood medicines had failed to do me any good.
WILL C. BEATY, Yorkville, S. C.

TRADE S.S.S. MARK

'I was troubled from childhood with an aggravated case of Tetter, and three bottles of S.S.S. cured me permanently.
WALLACE MANN, Mannville, I. T.

Our book on Blood and Skin Diseases mailed free. SWIFT SPECIFIC CO., Atlanta, Ga.

MANHOOD RESTORED.

Before & After Use. Photographed from life.

"SANATIVO," the Wonderful Spanish Remedy, is sold with a Written Guarantee to cure all Nervous Diseases, such as Weak Memory, Loss of Brain Power, Headache, Wakefulness, Lost Manhood, Nervousness, Lassitude, all drains and loss of power of the Generative Organs in either sex, caused by over-exertion, youthful indiscretions, or the excessive use of tobacco, opium, or stimulants, which ultimately lead to Infirmity, Consumption and Insanity. Put up in convenient form to carry in the vest pocket. Price $1 a package, or 6 for $5. With every $5 order we give a written guarantee to cure or refund the money. Sent by mail to any address. Circular free in plain envelope. Mention this paper. Address,
MADRID CHEMICAL CO., Branch Office for U. S. A.
358 Dearborn Street, CHICAGO, ILL.
FOR SALE IN NEW BEDFORD, MASS., BY R. H. & H. A. Lawton, Apothecaries, Union St.

TURKISH BATHS.

LADIES.
Mrs. B. A. Morrison, Manager.
TUESDAYS and THURSDAYS till 8 P. M.
SATURDAYS till 6 P. M.

GENTLEMEN.
G. A. Cavanaugh, Manager.
Mondays, Wednesdays and Fridays till 8 P. M.
Also Saturday Nights

No. 5 South Sixth Street,

FINANCIAL.

SANFORD & KELLEY.

GARDNER T. SANFORD, CHARLES S. KELLEY, } **Bankers,**
Members Boston Stock Exchange,
47 North Water St., New Bedford.

STOCKS AND BONDS BOUGHT AND SOLD
ON COMMISSION
At the New York and Boston Stock Boards.

CONSERVATIVE & PROFITABLE INVESTMENTS
FOR TRUST FUNDS.

New Bedford Manufacturing Stocks have a first-class record as dividend payers, and we always have some on hand to offer.

Sole Agents for the sale in this city of the 6 per cent. Guaranteed Mortgages of the Lombard Investment Co.

Auction Sale of Stocks and Bonds
WEDNESDAYS AND SATURDAYS, at 10 45 A. M.

ORDERS SOLICITED.

Will be sold at auction SATURDAY, Aug. 13th, 1892, at 10 45 A. M., at office—
35 shares Wamsutta Mills.
10 shares Howland Mill Corp.
5 shares National Bank of Commerce.
10 shares City Manufacturing Corp.
20 shares Howland Mills Corp.
20 shares Potomska Mills.
1 share Odd Fellows' Building Association.

Mass. Real Estate Co.
246 Washington St., Boston.

Dividends 7 Per Cent.

Invests in Central Real Estate in Growing Cities.
Authorized Capital - - - - $2,000,000
Capital paid in - - - - 1,250,000
Surplus - - - - - - - 100,000
ORGANIZED IN 1885.
Paid Dividends of 5 per cent. per annum for 4½ years. Paid Dividends of 7 per cent. per annum since July, 1890. Average Dividend since organization over 6 per cent. per annum. Surplus at close of last fiscal year, over $100,000.
Stock offered for sale at $108 per share until July 31.
Send to or call at the office for information MWF

T. E. BOWMAN & CO.,
Topeka, Kansas,
NEGOTIATORS OF
Conservative Mortgage Loans in Eastern Kansas.

$2,500,000 LOANED without loss to any investor, and have never yet had to foreclose a farm loan in these eastern counties. Write us for list of investments. s29

GEORGE LEVY, North End Pawn Broker.
Cash advanced on Real or Personal Property. All business private. au3-1m

SECOND EDITION.

HOME MATTERS.

WHALEBONE.—There have been shipped from this city to New York within a day or two 1200 pounds Northwest whalebone.

BIG SHARK.—Edwin Lucy, when fishing in the river this forenoon between Atlas Tack Company wharf and Palmers Island, for bluefish, caught a shark five feet long weighing 40 pounds.

REAL ESTATE SALES.—M. E. Smith has sold for a syndicate four lots of land on the north side of Perry avenue, containing 73.44 rods to Elmtine Peleetie.

Charles B. Lewis has sold to James T. Mosher 20.49 rods land south side of Allen street.

DEATH OF A VETERAN.—John Wooley, a veteran of the civil war, a former resident of this city and a member of William Logan Rodman Post 1, G. A. R., who for a number of years past has been living in Rhode Island, is dead, and a meeting of the post is called for this evening to take action in regard to the funeral.

REPUBLICAN CONGRESSIONAL CONVENTION.—The Republicans of the 13th congressional district are requested to send delegates to a convention to be held in Odd Fellows' Hall in this city, Sept. 10th, at 12 o'clock m., to nominate a candidate for the 53d Congress, to choose a congressional district committee, and to recommend to the State convention a candidate for presidential elector. See special notice.

BUILDING NOTES.—Frank B. Sistare petitions for leave to move for Edward Boland, a building 25 by 38 feet, with 22 feet posts, from No. 8 Reynolds street north 16 feet.

Joseph Lague petitions for leave to build for Pierre Regnard, a dwelling-house 40 by 50 feet, with 29 feet posts, northeast corner of Front and Rivet streets.

Bryant & Slade of Fall River petition for leave to build a brick police station south east corner of Water and Blackmer streets, the walls to be 22 feet high and 15 inches thick.

MARION.

The rate of taxation is $7 per $1000. The following is a list of those who pay a tax of $25 or more:

H. D. Allen,	30	Miss M. E. Allen,	48
George D. Allen,	45	Mrs. L. M. R. Allen,	38
John H. Briggs,	30	George H. Brown,	26
R. P. Cushing,	25	Lucius Campbell,	26
Henry C. Dreyer,	30	James DeKay,	47
Mrs. A. F. Gurney,	29	A. S. Gurney,	62
J.K.Hathaway heirs,	31	A. Hathaway heirs,	38
Hadley & Handy,	26	A. J. Hadley,	61
Jos. E. Hadley,	60	W. W. Handy heirs,	30
A. A. Harwood est.,	26	Hartt boys, G. A. Nickerson, guardian,	2383
Arthur W. Hartt, Dudley H. and Jno. Philip, A.W. Nickerson and G. A. Nickerson, trus.,	2045	R. F. Hart heirs,	30
		Robert B. Hiller,	34
		B. Holmes,	53
E. Holmes,	46	C. P. Howland,	36
George L. Luce,	68	A. Nickerson,	1284
E. S. Parlow,	48	W. H. H. Ryder,	30

Non-Residents.

James W. Austin, Boston,	$45.85
Percy Brown, Boston,	29.40
John C. Brooks, Springfield,	24.92
C. A. Coolidge, Boston,	35.14
Mrs. Abby L. Delano, Rochester,	118.65
Judah Hathaway, Rochester,	51.66
Miss Marion Hovey, Boston,	119.91
George H. Lyman, Jr., Boston,	28.00
W. G. Preston, Boston,	38.71
Charles W. Ripley, New Bedford,	60.76
Mrs. John R. Shepley, St. Louis,	28.98

DEATHS.

In South Boston, 9th inst., Mary, daughter of John and the late Rose Goulding, aged 7 months 5 days.

MARINE INTELLIGENCE.

Passed through Hell Gate 11th, schs A M Dickinson, Hart, New York for Rockland.
Cld at Philadelphia 11th, schs Wm H Swan, Davidson, this port.
Cld at Baltimore 11th, sch Hattie S Williams, Allen, Fall River.
Cld at Norfolk 11th, sch Stella B Kaplan, Providence.

SPOKEN

Aug 9th, off Shinnecock, sch P J Woodruff, supposed for Philadelphia.

Spain Flooded.

MADRID, Aug. 12.—Heavy storms are sweeping over Spain and doing great damage. The rain is falling in torrents and is destroying the grape and olive crops. Much damage has been done by rivers overflowing their banks, and in some places the low country resembles huge lakes. In Huesca the flood has already carried away thirty houses, and it is feared further damage will be done.

DR. PRICE'S DELICIOUS Flavoring Extracts

NATURAL FRUIT FLAVORS.

Vanilla - Of perfect purity.
Lemon - Of great strength.
Orange - Economy in their use
Almond - Flavor as delicately
Rose etc. - and deliciously as the fresh fruit.

FINANCIAL.

Stocks Still Soft—Atchison and Burlington & Quincy Decline while General Electric Also Receives a Set-Back—Silver Weak—Money a Bit Easier—Some Loans at Clearing House To-day Made at 4 per cent—Atchison's Business—Favorable Reports Thereon from the West—Delaware & Lackawanna Earnings—Corn Crop Conditions Improved—Burlington & Quincy Makes Regular Dividend—Gossip of the Day.

FRIDAY, Aug. 12.

Crop news is more favorable to-day, but prices have nevertheless fallen off somewhat. The declaration of the B. Q. dividend did not affect values materially. Money has eased slightly.

Local loans are unchanged, generally near 5 per cent.

The recent advance in money rates in Boston has caused those who have money in New York to draw on it, and although the rates are unchanged the conditions are easier. The effect of the weather is plainly seen in business affairs, and no activity in the money market is expected until Fall. Rates in Boston, however, are better maintained than in any other part of the country. This fact has been considerably discussed of late. A prominent bank president says the banks in Boston have overloaned themselves. The recent low rates for money and the allowing of interest on deposits has caused them to loan all available funds and consequently the majority of the banks are now short. At clearing to-day loans were made at 4 and 5 per cent. New York funds sold at 17 and 20 cents discount.

Time money in New York continues abundant in supply, while the demand does not increase. Rates, therefore, are unchanged. Mercantile paper is in fair demand. Purchasers are standing a little firmer on rates, but the supply of paper is not sufficiently large for this fact to make any material change in prices.

The sterling exchange market is steady and unchanged for rates. There are no features to the market.

Bonds dull.

Wall street gossip this morning said: "Exchange houses report no bills offering and not likely that much gold will go out tomorrow in addition to the half million already engaged. Bears actively at work on the market and it looks as if prices would slip off further before bulls become aggressive again."

A weak list of stocks was the most prominent feature about the New York market this forenoon. The chief losses were in Atchison 38⅜ to 38, Burlington & Quincy 101½ to 101⅛, Reading 59¾ to 59⅛, Rock Island 80¼ to 79⅞, St. Paul 82½ to 82, and Sugar 107⅜ to 103⅞. General Electric fell back to 115 from 115¾. New England lost ¼. After 12 o'clock the market displayed no new feature. Chicago, Burlington & Quincy held steady at 101¼, after the announcement of the dividend.

The market at 2 o'clock was stronger. Reading moved up to 60.

Atchison at 38⅜ to 38 and General Electric 116 to 114⅜ monopolized trading in the Boston market this forenoon. Other shares were more or less neglected. B. & Q. held 101⅜. Boston & Maine sold at 180 and Osceola at 32¼ to 32¾. West End Railway Co. held 74. In the early afternoon the market was dull and weak.

At 2 o'clock the market was a fraction better. Sales to noon: Bonds $70,000, and 12,400 shares of stock.

Silver sold at 82¾ this morning.

The dividend of $1 per share which the directors of the Osceola Mining Co. declared yesterday, making the second payment of that amount in the current year, and calls for the distribution of $50,000, or $100,000 for both payments, representing 1892 dividend results.

A noon special says:

"C. B. & Q. has just declared the regular quarterly dividend of 1¼ per cent., payable Sept. 15."

A Lake Superior dispatch says: Shipments of iron ore are very large and season promises to be a good one in spite of dulness in iron trade.

Ontario Silver Mining Co. sold at 41 in New York yesterday.

John Bloodgood is quoted as saying that he believes fully 100,000 shares of St. Paul held in foreign names are really owned by the Vanderbilts and that the same following have been buyers of Manhattan.

The *Iron Age* reports the number of furnaces in blast Aug. 1 as 238, a decrease of 16 furnaces.

Reports of general rains throughout the corn belt during the past 24 hours have improved the condition of the corn crop. The Cincinnati *Price Current* says that indications point to 1,600,000,000 bushels.

The Delaware, Lackawanna & Western railroad's leased lines report the following operations for the quarter ended June 30:

Quarter June 30.	1892.	1891.	Inc.
Earnings,	$2,099,603	$2,012,323	$87,280
Expenses,	1,175,600	1,078,544	97,056
Net,	$924,003	$933,779	*$9,776
Charges,	598,915	581,249	17,218
Surplus,	$325,088	$352,530	*$27,442

*Decrease.

The Wagner Palace Car Company reports for the June quarter:

Gross earnings,	$904,384
Expenses and new cars,	1,158,398
Deficit,	$254,014

The above figures are from the tape, and whether there is an error in transmission is not known.

One reason for the still further decline in the price of silver yesterday to 82¾, or below the heretofore lowest price ever known, so that it is now selling at a trifle over two-thirds of the price at which it sold last year, is an opposition from an unexpected quarter. The banks in India are now so thoroughly adjusted to monometallism that they have been opposed to any change. Their dealings are based upon silver entirely as a currency for India and a single gold basis in their trading with London, and they see a great deal more difficulty than in continuing the present basis of exchange, which seems to be satisfactory all around. Their motive may be selfish in this because they are large purchasers of silver and not at all producers, and while they profit in selling if silver is higher in London, they profit in another way if their circulating medium can be furnished at a lower rate. The steady decline in the price does not promise much for the International monetary conference which is to meet in Paris in the coming Fall. The great difficulty is that the United States is a large producer of silver as well as of almost everything else, and has practically ceased to be a debtor nation, while all the other silver-producing countries are already upon a silver basis. The question of adjustment of values between the two metals seems almost impossible of solution, except by the discovery of some new gold fields such as upset the ratio between the two metals in 1850. The steady increase in the production of silver in our own country keeping pace with the growth of population, while the production of gold remains about the same, really seems an insuperable obstacle to very much of an advance in the price.

Total shipments of anthracite coal for week ending Aug. 6, 740,977 tons, against 729,654 last year, an increase of 11,323 tons. Total for year to date, 23,739,859 tons, against 22,565,654 last year, an increase of 1,174,205 tons.

A representative of the Boston News Bureau travelling through the West writes from Colorado Springs as follows:

An official of the Colorado Midland says that business has of late been showing a very satisfactory gain. The company is about to build two short branches, one to Cripple Creek, where there is quite a gold fever. When these are completed he looks for a further material gain in traffic. The enormous passenger business which the Atchison is doing on its cut rates to Denver from Chicago and Kansas City is bound to show in the earnings for August. The Atchison, Union Pacific and Rock Island run regular trains in four or five sections, and Atchison for several days has been obliged to side track all freight trains in order to give clear road for passenger traffic. Farmers all through middle and western Kansas say the set back to corn early in the Spring has been more than overcome by the recent hot weather, and the crop is looking excellent. The wool growers and cattle raisers of eastern and northern Colorado are pleased with the condition of their flocks and herds. Weather is good and grazing better than usual. Large shipments of cattle are made daily over the Union Pacific and Chicago, Burlington & Quincy.

STOCK AND BOND MARKETS.

Bids at the close of First Board.

NEW YORK, Aug. 12.

GOVERNMENT BONDS.

U.S. 2s, registered	100
" new 4s, registered	115¾
" new 4s, coupons	115¾
" currency 6s, 1895, (Pacifics)	107

RAILROADS.

Atchison	38⅛
Clev., Cin., Chicago & St. Louis	68⅛
Chicago & Eastern Illinois	—
Chicago & Eastern Illinois pre.	—
Chicago, Burlington & Quincy	101¾
Delaware & Hudson	—
Delaware & Lackawanna	155⅛
Erie	27⅞
Illinois Central	100
Lake Shore & Michigan Southern	132½
Louisville & Nashville	69¾
Michigan Central	—
Missouri Pacific	58⅞
New Jersey Central	134¾
New York & New England	36⅞
Northern Pacific	21
Northern Pacific pref	55⅞
Chicago & Northwestern	117½
New York Central & Hudson River	113⅛
North American	—
Oregon Navigation	—
Oregon Improvement	—
Oregon Short Line	—
Philadelphia & Reading	59¾
Pullman Palace Car Co	—
Chicago, Rock Island & Pacific	80
Chicago, Milwaukee & St. Paul	82½
Chicago, Milwaukee & St. Paul pref	—
Richmond Terminal	8⅜
St. Paul & Omaha	52⅜
St. Paul & Omaha pref	—
Union Pacific	33¼
Wabash, St. Louis & Pacific	11¼
Wabash, St. Louis & Pacific pref	25

MISCELLANEOUS

Ontario Silver	41
Pacific Mail Steamship Co	33½
Sugar, common	107⅞
Sugar, pref	—
Western Union Telegraph	97¾
Silver Certificates	—

BOSTON, Aug. 12.

BONDS

Atchison 4s	82⅝
Atchison Incomes	59⅛
American Bell Telephone 7s	114
Chicago, Burlington & Northern 5s	—
Chicago & West Michigan 5s	—
Mexican Central 4s	68¼
Illinois Steel Co. 5s	*100

RAILROADS.

Atchison, Topeka & Santa Fe	38¼
Boston & Albany	205
Boston & Lowell	181½
Boston & Maine	*180
Boston & Providence	250
Chicago, Burlington & Quincy	101½
Chicago & West Michigan	—
Cleveland & Canton	5½
Cleveland & Canton pref	19¾
Flint & Pere Marquette	—
Flint & Pere Marquette pref	*79
Mexican Central	—
New York & New England	*37¾
New York & New England pref	—
Old Colony	182
Oregon Short Line	23¾
Pullman Palace Car	—
Union Pacific	33¾
Wisconsin Central	—
West End	—
West End pref	—

MINING.

Butte & Boston Mining Co	—
Calumet & Hecla Mining Co	282
Centennial	7⅛
Franklin Mining Co	12½
Kearsarge	11
Montana	37
Osceola Mining Co	32
Tamarack	158

MISCELLANEOUS.

American Bell Telephone	*204½
Erie Telephone	36
Mexican Telephone	1.05
New England Telephone	56
Newport Land	—
Boston Land Co	—
West End Land Co	18
San Diego Land Co	*16
Topeka Land & Development Co	*1
Lamson Store Service	—
Illinois Steel Co	—
Am. Sugar Refineries, com	107
Am. Sugar Refineries, pref	—
Gen'l Electric	114⅜
Gen'l Electric	—

*Asked.

NEW YORK PRODUCE MARKET.

NEW YORK, Aug. 12.

Flour sales 5700 packages; quiet and easy.
Wheat sales 590,000 bushels; weak west; free receipt; advanced ⅛ on local trading, steady.
Corn sales 90,000 bushels; dull and steady, opening ⅜ down, advanced ⅛.
Oats sales 25,000 bushels; dull, lower and weak.
Beef steady.
Pork firm.
Lard dull and easy.
Butter quiet and easy.
Cheese easy and dull.
Sugar (raw) strong.
Petroleum firm.
Turpentine dull and steady.
Molasses quiet.
Rice firm.
Freights quiet.
Tallow steady.

PROVISIONS AND GRAIN.

CHICAGO, Aug. 11.

Opening.

	Lard.	Wheat.	Pork.	Corn.	Sh't Ribs.
May	—	—	—	—	—
June	—	—	—	—	—
July	—	—	—	—	—
Aug.	—	—	—	—	—
Sept.	—	78	12.75	53¼	—
Oct.	—	—	—	—	—
Dec.	—	80½	—	—	—
Jan.	—	—	13.50	—	—

12 o'clock.

	Lard.	Wheat.	Pork.	Corn.	Sh't Ribs.
May	—	—	—	—	—
June	—	—	—	—	—
July	—	—	—	—	—
Aug.	—	—	—	—	—
Sept.	—	77⅝	12.67½	52¾	—
Oct.	—	—	—	—	—
Dec.	—	80	—	—	—
Jan.	—	—	13.50	—	—

Growing Old Gracefully.

"What a lovely old lady," I heard a man remark, at the opera, lately. "She's quite as beautiful as any girl in the house. Such color and complexion is rarely seen in a woman past forty."

Indeed, the woman of whom he spoke *was* lovely. Her face was clear and smooth, her cheeks fresh and rosy, her eyes bright with perfect health and the enjoyment of life. She had passed the critical "change of life" without falling into "the sere and yellow leaf," as most American women do. How had she succeeded in doing this? Simply by using Dr. Pierce's Favorite Prescription at a time when nature stood in need of some assistance. She had taken it at the right time. In doing this she was wise. Wiser than most women who "trust to luck" in getting through the critical and trying period safely. This standard remedy is just what is needed at such a time. It is, from girlhood to old age, woman's best friend. In all diseases peculiar to the sex it accomplishes what no other remedy does—a cure. Take it, woman, when life's Autumn begins, and "grow old gracefully." Your money back if it doesn't help you.

THE BORDEN SAFE OPENED

By an Expert Operator Under Police Surveillance.

Supposition is that Something Incriminating was Found.

Miss Borden to be Taken to Taunton Jail to Await Trial.

[Special Dispatch.]

FALL RIVER, Aug. 12.—The expert safe operator that the police brought here to open the combination on the safe at the Borden house succeeded in accomplishing his task at 11 o'clock this morning.

The work was done in the presence of police officers, and upon its conclusion word was sent to the Central police station.

City Marshal Hilliard, District Attorney Knowlton and Mr. Jennings, the counsel for the family, at once went to the house and took possession of the contents of the safe.

There was quite a sum of money and many valuable papers found. All were taken to the B. M. C. Durfee Safe Deposit Company and locked up in a private compartment.

If anything of an incriminating nature was discovered in the safe, the police decline to acknowledge the fact. It is generally thought something of that nature was found.

[By Associated Press.]

The Borden safe was opened this morning, after John A. Maier of Boston had been at work on it about eight hours. The contents will not be given for publication. They consisted of a large amount of cash and some few papers. They were bundled and tied with a strong cord, and after Attorney Jennings and Officer Harrington had affixed their signatures on the outside the bundle was taken to the B. M. C. Durfee Safe Deposit & Trust Company and deposited.

The guard has been taken from the neighborhood of the house with the exception of one officer and John V. Morse is again at liberty.

Text of the Complaint.

The text of the complaint in the cases is as follows:

COMMONWEALTH OF MASSACHUSETTS.

Bristol ss.

Rufus B. Hilliard, City Marshal of Fall River, in said county, in behalf of said Commonwealth, on oath complains that Lizzie A. Borden of Fall River, in the County of Bristol at Fall River aforesaid, in the county aforesaid on the 4th day of August in the year of our Lord 1892, in and upon one Andrew J. Borden, feloniously, wilfully and of her malice aforethought, did make an assault, and that the said Lizzie A. Borden then and there with a certain weapon, to wit, a hatchet, the said Andrew J. Borden, in and upon the head of the said Andrew J. Borden, then and there feloniously, wilfully and of her malice aforethought did strike, giving unto the said Andrew J. Borden, then and there with the hatchet aforesaid by the stroke aforesaid in manner aforesaid, in and upon the head of the said Andrew J. Borden one mortal wound of which said mortal wound the said Andrew J. Borden then and there instantly died.

And so the complainant aforesaid upon his oath aforesaid further complains and says the said Lizzie A. Borden the said Andrew J. Borden in manner and form aforesaid, then and there feloniously and wilfully and of malice aforethought did kill and murder. R. B. HILLIARD.

If Miss Borden is able to be removed she will be taken to Taunton jail this afternoon on the mid-afternoon train.

SULLIVAN'S SPECIAL TRAIN.

John L. Will Travel in Style to New Orleans to Fight Corbett.

CANOE PLACE INN, L. I., Aug. 12.—John L. Sullivan's trainers have let up on him a little now that he is down to the stipulated weight of 210 pounds.

"Jimmy" Wakely was here yesterday to see the pugilist and make arrangements for his trip to New Orleans. In addition to a stateroom car there will be a baggage car on the train, which will be fitted up as a gymnasium, so that Sullivan can indulge in light exercises on the trip down. There will also be several other cars attached to the train for the accommodation of Sullivan's many admirers who are going to see the battle.

It has been arranged to leave the West Shore depot at Weehawken at 3 o'clock on the afternoon of September 1. The route over which the train will travel is the West Shore Railroad to Buffalo, Bee line road to Cincinnati and Queen and Crescent to New Orleans, the same as when Sullivan travelled South to whip Kilrain. Four hundred people will be allowed to go on the train.

To take Workingmen to World's Fair.

NEW YORK, Aug. 12.—To-day's *Mail & Express* contains a leading editorial proposing a railroad fare of $1 to Chicago during the World's Fair for all workingmen in the United States living within 1500 miles of Chicago, and says the railroads can carry the business with a margin of profit.

Attempted Suicide

PEABODY, Aug. 12.—John Larrabee of West Peabody attempted to commit suicide to-day by cutting his throat. His wife discovered him in the act. His wounds will not probably be fatal. Family troubles are said to be the cause of the act.

Good News for Glass Workers.

PITTSBURG, Aug. 12.—The window glass manufacturers and workers having amicably settled the wage question upon the basis of last year's scale, operations will be resumed at once. The resumption will give employment to 5500 men.

Eight Miners Killed.

PARIS, Aug. 12.—At Besseges a cable attached to the cage in a shaft broke and eight miners were dashed to the bottom and killed.

More Smallpox in Gotham.

NEW YORK, Aug. 12.—Three additional cases of smallpox were reported to the bureau of contagious diseases yesterday afternoon.

Salisbury's Ministry at an End.

LONDON, Aug. 12.—The vote of "no confidence" was passed in the house at midnight by 350 to 310.

France Gains More Territory.

PARIS, Aug. 12.—The French have occupied the Gloriosa island, situated north of Madagascar.

Lord Salisbury on His Way to Resign.

LONDON, Aug. 12.—At 1 o'clock this afternoon Lord Salisbury left London for Osborne House, where he will tender to the Queen the resignation of the Conservative ministry.

Merit Wins.

We desire to say to our citizens, that for years we have been selling Dr. King's New Discovery for Consumption, Dr. King's New Life Pills, Bucklen's Arnica Salve and Electric Bitters, and have never handled remedies that sell as well, or that have given such universal satisfaction. We do not hesitate to guarantee them every time, and we stand ready to refund the purchase price, if satisfactory results do not follow their use. These remedies have won their great popularity purely on their merits. H. A. Blackmer, druggist.

WEATHER INDICATIONS.

FAIR AND COOLER.

BOSTON, Aug. 12.—Local forecast for New England until Sunday morning: Fair, preceded to-day on the coast and southern sections by showers; cooler to-night and Saturday; westerly to northerly winds; also fair Sunday.

CLEAR.

NEW YORK, Aug. 12.—At 8 30 a. m, the weather was cloudy, wind south, temperature 75. The *Herald* says: In the Middle States and New England on Saturday, clear weather will prevail, with rising temperature and light westerly winds, becoming mostly southerly; and on Sunday warmer, fair weather.

TENNIS AT NAHANT.

Brilliant Playing of the Most Famous Wielders of the Racquet.

NAHANT, Aug. 12.—At 9 o'clock, after the heavy rain, very few people expected that there would be any morning play in the Nahant tennis tournament and it is greatly to the credit of Dr. Haven's well-drained court that by 10 o'clock it was sufficiently dry to permit of the commencement of the play.

This morning finds four of the contestants, Hovey, Malcolm Chace, Hobart and Hall all tied for first place, and as one more defeat to either of these men means the loss of his chances, each is playing his level best and working hard for each and every point.

E. L. Hall played this morning as if he felt reasonably sure of getting some sort of a prize. His net play helped him to place his opponent, S. T. Chase, on the defensive, and Hall won the first set 6—1 on good play, but nothing of particular note.

The rallies on the second set were interesting, Chace doing better than upon the previous one. Hall's victory at 6—3 gave him the match, his opponent still having only a big zero to his credit, and Sears will play Chace this afternoon for the last place in the tournament, and the match will undoubtedly interest their many friends.

Malcolm Chace, the brilliant young expert who gained so much glory yesterday, found no trouble in beating Quincy A. Shaw, Jr., twelve straight games, two love sets, thus placing another match to his most creditable score.

The conclusion of this contest brought on the expected match between Hobart and Hovey. It is much to be regretted that Hovey was ill this morning and in very poor condition, but he pluckily consented to play and not disappoint the expectant spectators upon the express stipulation that he should not default any games.

Hobart won the first two sets.

The third went to Hovey on the New Yorker's wild hits and the interest increased. The champion did not appear very sick when he won the next game on his good serves. Score, 3—1. Hovey leads.

In the fifth game Hobart passed Hovey twice, and after deuce had been scored put the game to his credit. The play on the following game was fast and furious, Hovey being at the net and his opponent at the base line. Loud applause greeted Hobart's tieing of the score at three games each, after deuce had been scored twice. It was now that the New York player's forehand drives become most accurate and swift, and he gained several much needed points by the skilful use of his stroke. Two such serve games went to this credit and announced "games are five to three, Hobart leads."

Hovey saved the ninth game on good smashes, but Hobart took the tenth on brilliant passes, thus winning the set 6—4 by the narrow margin of two points, 35 to 33.

This was pretty close playing between the two leading players in America and if Hovey felt sick he was successfully concealing it. He won the first game, second set, against Hobart's own service, but lost his own to pay for it. Each man seemed winning on the other's serve, a rather unusual occurrence in his case.

The winning of the third game by the Harvard player gave him a lead which slightly disconcerted his opponent, and Hobart's hits into the net increased Hovey's lead to 3-1 after very close play on this fourth game.

"This is great tennis," ejaculated many of the onlookers as Hovey won the next game on his cat-like play at the net, thus making the count 4—1 in his favor.

A beautiful long drive away past his opponent gave Hobart a game, while Hovey's errors in the net gave the New Yorker another. Score 4—3, Hovey leads, but he could not keep this lead long. Hobart kept his eye on the ball and his feet on the ground and won the next game in great style, tieing the score at four games all.

Deuce was scored twice on the ninth game before Hobart could win by hard hits, which Hovey had to knock into the net. With the score at 5-4 against him, love-40 in Hobart's favor on the next, one single point would have given Hobart the match but the Harvard player with great nerve won five straight points, pulled out the game and saved the set amidst rounds of applause.

Fire in Old Jed Prouty's Home.

BUCKSPORT, Me., Aug. 12.—The stores of Mrs. John W. Buck and H. W. White in Orland were burned last night. Mrs. Buck's loss is $500, insured; White's loss $3800, insurance $1800. A building containing grain was damaged $500.

The Vice-President at Bar Harbor.

BAR HARBOR, Me., Aug. 12.—Vice-President Morton arrived here this morning.

The Higher Education of Women.

The conservative University of Virginia has partially fallen into line in the matter of the higher education of women, who will hereafter be admitted to the academical department under certain conditions. The conditions include a testimonial of good character and evidence of adequate preparation, either by certificate or examination. The female students, however, will not be allowed to attend the regular lectures of the schools, and must obtain their instruction from the professors in charge in the form of suggestions as to the text books to read and explanations of difficult passages, etc. Examinations of the women will be held from time to time on the same subjects as are included in the curriculum of the men, and to successful candidates certificates will be given. The names of the female students are to be entered on the books of the university and the privileges of study may be withdrawn at the option of the faculty.

SPECIAL NOTICES.

Thirteenth District Congressional Convention.

The Republicans of the 13th Congressional District are requested to send delegates to a convention to be held in Odd Fellows' Hall, in the city of New Bedford, on SATURDAY, Sept. 10th, in the year of our Lord, A. D., 1892, at 12 o'clock M., for the purpose of nominating a candidate for the 53d Congress, to choose a Congressional District Committee and to recommend to the State Convention a candidate for Presidential Elector. Basis of representation will be a delegate for each 150 votes and for every fraction thereof as large as 75 cast for Republican Presidential Election in 1883 in each town and ward of a city, but every town and ward of a city is entitled to at least one delegate. For the Committee.

WALTER CLIFFORD, Chairman.

Republican papers of the District please copy and send bill to Chairman.

au12-13-17-24-sep7-9

FOUND.

All Advertisements under this heading 1c. a word a time. No charge less than 25c.

SMALL, WHITE SHARPIE BOAT—In Priests Cove. H. W. ALLEN, Fairhaven. au12-3t

LATEST STYLES OF TYPE
—AT THE—
STANDARD JOB OFFICE.

ELECTRIC SPARKS.

Electric lighting by wind engine power is reported by the London Engineer to be in operation in an English flour mill.

Electric cars are run from Ninth and Penn streets, Reading, Pa., to Klapperthat park, a distance of eleven miles, every twenty minutes at a speed of fifteen miles an hour.

The new subtreasury building at San Francisco has an electric burglar alarm installed between the rows of bricks, so that any interference with the cement or bricks will complete an electric circuit and sound an alarm.

The total average efficiency of the Frankfort-Lauffen plant which transmitted 150-horse power of electrical energy a distance of 109 miles is stated in the official reports just published to have been about 75 per cent.

It is proposed, as the science of electricity has no name of its own, to call it "electrics." The two words "electrics" and electrician would thus be in analogy with optics and optician, mechanics and mechanician, mathematics and mathematician and many others.

An ingenious lock has been invented by which doors, etc., may be locked from a distance electrically. It is specially applicable for doors in private and business houses and offices, where absolute privacy is needed or desired. The lock is operated by simply turning a switch.

A St. Louis man has taken out a patent for an electric jail. He runs wires through channels in all the bars and gratings, and between the stones or plates of the walls, ceilings and floors of his prison. By connecting their ends to a suitable alarm mechanism and keeping a current flowing through them any disturbance or attempt at escape transmits a signal.

WHIP AND SPUR.

Two oddly named horses are Wooloomooloo and Rululu.

August Belmont has named his colt by Mr. Pickwick-Henlopen, Pecksniff.

Prince Menshikoff, a wealthy Russian, recently purchased the mare Alectra for $7,000.

Sanders thinks Frou Frou (2:25¼) can wipe out all 2-year-old records save Arion's (2:10¾).

The Lorillard stakes were worth $17,790 to Tammany, $2,000 to The Pepper and $1,000 to Azra.

One of the highest prices ever paid for a weanling in Kentucky was $1,050 for a full brother to Prince Karl, 2:34.

At a meeting of the owners and lovers of horses held in London it was unanimously resolved that of all the materials for paving roads asphalt is the worst for horses.

The sum of $100,000 is being expended in improvements on the Twin City race course. The $75,000 grand stand will, when completed, compare favorably with any in the country.

Common horses sell in Australia for fourteen dollars per dozen. In New South Wales they are so numerous that property owners have them shot. Within two years between 60,000 and 70,000 head were destroyed.

"Snapper" Garrison says: "Many races are thrown away by inexperienced boys. In three races out of five where the field is large the jockey wins the race. Old Man Hayward, Taral and McLaughlin are worth ten pounds any day."

PEN, PENCIL AND BRUSH.

Rudyard Kipling believes in ghosts.

Wilhelm Busch, the German caricaturist, has made a million dollars from the sale of his funny books.

Landseer's famous and most popular painting, "The Monarch of the Glen," was recently sold for $36,225.

Count Leo Tolstoi, the Russian poet and novelist, can handle farm implements as well as the pen, and is withal a skillful shoemaker.

It is pretty certain that Corot, the French artist, did not paint more than 700 sketches, and yet there have been 12,000 examples of his work palmed upon a picture buying public.

El Tesoro del Hogar (Fireside Treasure) is a weekly published in Guayaquil, Ecuador, by Senora Dona Lasteni a Larriva de Llona, a Peruvian woman who has won some fame in South America as a poet.

Carl Rosa, a landscape painter whose works failed to secure a prize at the Paris Salon, went to the exhibition and with a pocket knife cut one of his pictures out of the frame, rolled it up and carried it away with him. The jury of award had ignored it, and this was cut for cut.

TABLE ETIQUETTE.

Hold the knife by the handle and never let the fingers reach up to the blade.

The old method of eating cheese with a knife has been given up, a fork being used in its place.

Olives, celery, radishes, strawberries with stems, and asparagus are all eaten from the fingers.

The use of many small dishes for vegetables is not good taste; indeed many vegetables should not be served at one time.

Glasses with handles are held by them. A goblet should be caught by the stem, the fingers not entwining the bowl part.

Whenever it is possible a fork must be used in place of a spoon, and that same spoon, by the bye, must never be left in a coffee or tea cup, but politely and securely laid to rest in the saucer.

Don't butter a large piece of bread and take bites from it; instead, break your bread in small pieces, one at a time, and butter it—that is, if you are eating butter—and convey it to your mouth by your fingers.—Ladies' Home Journal.

CROWN AND SCEPTER.

King Oscar of Sweden is a man of tall and spare figure, with white hair and beard.

Henry VIII during his reign put to death 71,000 persons, most of them virtuous or unoffending.

Otto, the insane king of Bavaria, is at times so violent that it is necessary for his attendants to strap him to his bed.

The sultan is coming under the suspicion of being a consumptive. His mother died of it, and he showed symptoms when he was twenty-two.

Ex-King Milan lives in some style in a fine house on the fashionable Avenue du Bois de Boulogne, in Paris. He is known in his exile as the Count de Takova.

Although the possessor of some of the finest jewels in the world, Queen Victoria is by no means fond of jewelry. Except on occasions of state ceremonials she rarely wears ornaments, with the exception of two enamel bracelets.

PHILOSOPHICAL COGITATIONS.

So many silly sheep go to wolves for protection.

The man who amounts to the most took the least time to hope.

Every man's definition of happiness is a description of the life of his neighbor.

No one will take advice, but every one who makes a mistake complains because none was given him.

AUCTION SALES.

By STANDISH BOURNE,
(Successor to Geo. A. Bourne & Son,)
Auctioneer, Commission Merchant, Real Estate Dealer and Appraiser.

Cash advanced on goods consigned for auction. Ready buyer for personal property of every description.
Office and Salesrooms 47, 49 and 51 North Second Street, near the Post Office.

Teas and Grocer's Stock.

To-morrow, SATURDAY FORENOON at *10 o'clock*, at salesrooms, will be sold a small lot of fresh canned goods and groceries. Together with a good assortment of teas and spices. Also 1 coffee mill, two pairs of extra counter scales, small lot of furniture, counters, shelving, stoves, &c.

At 10½ o'clock, horses, carriages, harnesses, and the general assortment of merchandise consigned for our regular Saturday morning sales.

Nearly New Household Furniture and Rugs.

On MONDAY, Aug. 15th, at 2½ o'clock, at the cottage of Miss Courtis, Nonquitt, will be sold the entire household furnishings consisting in part of 10 Brass Mounted Bedsteads, Woven Wire Springs, Pillows and Mattresses for same, Ash Chamber suits, Willow sofa and chairs, several desirable pieces of old-fashioned furniture, together with the general assortment of Housekeepers' Articles, such as Odd Bedsteads, Tables, Extension Tables, Chairs, Crockery, Glassware &c. Also several Imported Rugs, Mattings &c.

To Let in Our Storage Warerooms.

We constantly have on hand first-class rooms for the storage of household goods, to be rented by the month or year.
Good dry storage room for stoves.

By JOHN B. BAYLIES,
121 and 123 Union Street,
Commission Merchant, Appraiser, and Auctioneer for the sale of Real Estate and every description of Personal Property. Furniture Bought.

H. C. HATHAWAY,
Auctioneer, Real Estate Agent and Appraiser,
Corner Acushnet Ave. and Elm St.

One of the best auction marts in the State for the sale of horses and carriages. Keeps constantly on hand carriages of every description, carriages made to order and repairing in all its branches attended to under the superintendency of J. R. Forbes. Consignments of every description solicited. Cash advanced on goods for auction. Personal property of every description bought at short notice for cash. Negotiable notes bought and sold.

Horses at Auction.

Will arrive THURSDAY MORNING, at our Salesroom, and will be sold at auction SATURDAY MORNING, at 10 o'clock, one car load of extra nice horses adapted for general purposes. If you are in want of a good family, road or work horse be sure to attend this sale. Also several good second-hand horses that have been used around the city.

Also a very nice Scippio mare, 5 years old, from the state of Maine. She is A1 in every respect and is counted in the 30 list. au9

Heirs' Sale of Real Estate.

On SATURDAY, Aug. 13, at 3 o'clock P. M., on the premises, will be sold without the least reserve, to wind up the estate, the house and lot of about 17 rods of land No. 75 Middle street. The house is in good condition and is situated in that part of the city where it will be sure always to rent well. Sale positive and without limit. Terms, 10 per cent. at sale. Balance on delivery of heirs' deed. au

ALFRED WILSON,
Auctioneer and Real Estate Agent,
Room 32, - - - Robeson Building.

Houses and land in all parts of the city for sale; tenements for rent: rents collected.

For Sale.

Two-story house on Acushnet avenue, near Walnut street; well arranged for one family; good location.

For Lease.

The Webster Block, Purchase street; 16 rooms, well adapted for a genteel boarding house, club rooms, or business purposes.

TO LET—A flat in The Winslow, corner Sixth and Union streets. Apply to A. WILSON, Robeson Building. jy14-tf

T. F. HEALEY,
Auctioneer and Real Estate Agent,
555 and 559 Purchase street, corner of Franklin street.

FOR SALE CHEAP—One farm in Rochester of 70 acres; house, barn, outbuildings, etc.; 2 good orchards on place; cut 20 tons of hay. Price $1800.

Also two cottages in Fairhaven; nearly new; fine view of river and harbor; will sell one or both; situated on Main street; will sell to the right parties on easy terms.

Also one fine house in the west part of the city in good locality, with all the modern improvements, gas and electric lights, etc. Will be sold cheap if applied for soon.

Also lots on Acushnet avenue, Coggshall and Locust streets, in fact all parts of the city.

Business solicited. No charges made unless a sale, then my prices are the lowest.

By JAMES R. DENHAM.

On SATURDAY, Aug. 13th, at 3 o'clock P. M., on the premises, will be sold house and lot of about 27 9-10 rods of land, No. 31 Allen street. Terms, 10 per cent. at sale. Balance on delivery of deed. au10-3t

REAL ESTATE.

FRANCIS W. TAPPAN,
Agent for Purchase, Sale, and Lease of REAL ESTATE.
Office, 15 North Water St., New Bedford. d&w

FRANK C. SMITH,
Real Estate Broker, Auctioneer and Appraiser,
Office - - 47 William Street,
(Opposite New Post Office.)

M. E. SMITH,
REAL ESTATE AGENT,
619 Purchase Street. Telephone 16-11.

H. A. LEONARD,
REAL ESTATE AGENT.......126 UNION STREET.
Houses and lots for sale in all parts of the city. No charges unless sale effected.

JOHN WHITEHEAD,
Real Estate Agent.

Several houses near Pierce Mill. Sale private. Also desirable lots on Geo. A. Briggs' estate on easy terms, and lots in all parts of the city. Desirable lots on Jas. Drown estate and Phillips and Coffin aves. au2-MWF1m

Cottage House.

Well built, good repair, in part of city growing rapidly; will make good home and *must* increase in value. Apply box 6, *Standard* office. ap25-tf

SUMMER COTTAGE AND BARN—For sale low, situated in Acushnet; acre and one-third of high land, mostly pine grove; buildings nearly new. Inquire of A. G. ALLEY, JR., Union and Sixth streets. jy18-tf

FOR SALE—In South Dartmouth, near the water, a 2½ story house with large piazza, barn, and 83 rods of land. One of the most desirable places in the village for a Summer residence. Inquire of BENJ. QUERIPEL or DANIEL H. HOWLAND, South Dartmouth. ap7-tf

LARGE STOCK OF PAPER.

The Largest Stock and Greatest Variety of

PAPER, CARDBOARD and ENVELOPES

Carried by Any Printing Establishmer Southern Massachusetts is

—AT THE—

STANDARD C

In fact we are told by th paper manufacturers t printing offices in New great variety of stock commodate the la of our job department needed in short order, an hands our prices are alw

SECOND WEEK OF OUR
SPECIAL
Mid-Summer
SALE!

We were very much gratified with the way our bargains of last week were received, and will enumerate a few specials for this week:

All of our 50 and 75c. India Silks for this sale 39c.

All of our 25 and 37 1-2c. French Sateens for this sale 12 1-2c.

All of our 59 and 62 1-2c. all-wool Challies to close 50c.

A few pieces of 50c. Figured Mohairs we shall close at 25c.

We have just received a nice line of Belts 37 1-2c. metal Belts, shall sell this sale for 25c.

Something new, Suspender Belts, all the rage, 59c.; a regular 75c. belt.

A full line of Sizes, 32 to 40c.

Shirt Waists in the new shade of blue, sold all the season for $1; this sale 62c.

We have just received a full line of Purses and Pocketbooks—many novelties never before shown in this city and controlled by us.

We have added 1000 new pieces to our Musical Catalogue, making the largest and most complete line of music ever shown at any price, 5c. a copy or 6 copies for 25c. Ask for the new catalogue.

Kitchen Furnishing Dept.

Now is the time to buy a Hammock. We have a full line, prices ranging from 69c. to $2.69.

Croquet Sets. A regular $1.00 set for 89c., equally as good values for $1.39, $1.69, $2.29 and $3.39.

White Mountain Freezers—2 quarts, $1.25; 3 quarts, $2.09 and 4 quarts, $2.50.

Oil Stoves 1, 2 and 3 burners. Oil Stove Tea Kettles 19 to 69c.

Perry's Patent Clothes Line Hooks 7 and 10c.

Household Ammonia—pint bottles, 7c. or 4 for 25c.

Knowles & Co.
Cor. UNION & FOURTH STS.

RYDER IN DISGRACE.
Confesses That He is Guilty of Forgery and Embezzlement.

WASHINGTON, Aug. 12.—In view of the arrest of Henry B. Ryder, the United States consul at Copenhagen, the secretary of state has directed Hon. Clarke Carr, the United States minister to Denmark, to proceed at once to Copenhagen and resume charge of affairs there. Mr. Carr is now at his home in Galesburg, Ills., on leave of absence. His presence in Denmark is necessary because Mr. Ryder was the only representative of the government there, with the exception of a vice consul.

The Danish minister in Washington yesterday informed the state department that he has been notified by his government that Ryder had confessed to embezzlement and forgery. The department has not decided what course to pursue in the matter until a report of an official nature is made.

HUGH M'CURDY GRAND MASTER.
Election of Knights Templars at Denver—Next Conclave at Boston.

DENVER, Aug. 12.—Hon. Hugh McCurdy of Corunda, Mich., was elected grand master of the Knights Templars of the United States. Dr. McCurdy acknowledged the compliment in an address in which he modestly denied his own merit and eulogized the men who had preceded him in that exalted position.

Rev. H. W. Rugg of Providence was appointed grand junior warden by the grand encampment, and H. Wales Lines of Meriden, Conn., was re-elected grand treasurer. It was decided to hold the twenty-sixth triennial conclave in Boston. Ninety-six votes were cast for Boston and 78 for Cincinnati.

Gladstone is All Right.

LONDON, Aug. 12.—Herbert Gladstone says that the reports that his father is on the verge of collapse are "the merest rubbish." He intimates that the reports were spread by the Tories for a purpose.

Five Men Crushed to Death.

HARTFORD CITY, Ind., Aug. 12.—A heavy stone wall in the tank room of the Hartford City glass works caved in, killing five men and badly injuring two others.

Mr. J. G. Anderson

Of Scottdale, Pa., a veteran of the 11th Penn. Vols., says, as a result of war service he

Suffered Every Minute

From liver and kidney troubles, catarrh in the head, rheumatism and distress in his stomach. Everything he ate seemed like lead. Sleep was restless, and in the morning he seemed more tired than when he went to bed. He says:

Hood's Sarsaparilla

and Hood's Pills did me more good than everything else put together. All my disagreeable symptoms have gone." Be sure to get Hood's.

"HOOD'S PILLS are the best after-dinner Pills. They assist digestion and cure headache.

THE CABLE HOUSE POISONING.
Officials are Alert and Investigation May Lead to Arrests.

NEWBURYPORT, Mass., Aug. 12.—The examination of the remains of McCarthy and Smith, two of the victims of the poisoning at the Cable House, will probably not be made until some day next week. Medical Examiner Snow of Newburyport so stated last night, and until then the authorities have nothing to divulge as to the results of their investigations.

In the expectation that the report from Professor Hills will name arsenic as the agency of death the energies of Officers Batchelder and Shaw have been exerted to locate some person or persons, who would have a motive in doing personal injury to any of the guests of the Cable house.

While they refuse to make any statements because they do not wish to alarm any one needlessly and perhaps do a gross injustice in the absence of the cause of death being definitely determined, it is known that at least three people have been watched and their whereabouts and movements on the day of and the days preceding the murder investigated.

THE TITLE GAME.
A Cambridge Woman Swindled to the Amount of $5000.

CAMBRIDGE, Mass., Aug. 12.—Miss Caroline D. Fales of this city has been swindled out of $5000 in much the same manner that the Conveyancers' Insurance company was last Saturday. Joshua N. Briggs, the alleged principal in this case, is 71 years of age and lives in Chelsea. He was arrested yesterday on a charge of having obtained $5000 by falsely pretending that he owned the estate 277 Shawmut avenue.

Briggs claims that he is innocent of wrong intentions and that he was persuaded to lend himself to the scheme by Charles W. Bingham, now under arrest in the Charles street jail, with Austin R. Smith, charged with defrauding the Conveyancers' Title Insurance company.

It is believed by the police that in March last Bingham went to Briggs and stated that certain men of property living in Dorchester wanted to raise some ready money, and in order to do so were willing to give a deed of some property in the city proper. With this deed it was suggested they would obtain ready money from some wealthy woman who was unacquainted with the methods of transferring property.

After that, in accordance with the police theory, Briggs and Bingham appeared at a certain broker's office in Boston with a mortgage deed and note transferring the estate, 277 Shawmut avenue, owned by John L. Barry of Dorchester, to Briggs for $5000.

They then learned of Miss Fales, and met her in a Court street law office, where the deed and note were examined and pronounced correct. They seemed to be properly signed by Mr. Barry, and the transfer of the property was duly recorded in the registry of deeds.

Miss Fales accepted the deed and note, and it was not until late in May that the forgery of Barry's name was discovered. The police are now trying to find out who forged Barry's name.

BISHOP O'REILLY'S SUCCESSOR.
The Honor Falls Upon Rev. Dr. Beaven, a Native of New England.

SPRINGFIELD, Mass., Aug. 12.—A cable dispatch to Rev. Dr. Thomas D. Beaven, of the church of the Holy Rosary, Holyoke, informs him that he has been appointed bishop of the Springfield diocese to succeed the late Bishop O'Reilly. Dr. Beaven is 51 years old, being born in Springfield in 1841. He was educated in the public schools and was graduated with high honors from Holy Cross college in 1870. For two years he was professor in Loyola college, Baltimore. In 1875 he was ordained to the priesthood, and in 1878 he was appointed by Bishop O'Reilly as assistant to Rev. Julius Cosson of Spencer, to whose pastorate he succeeded in 1879.

In 1884 he was called to the pastorate of the Church of the Rosary in Holyoke, where he has labored with much earnestness and success. His departure was much felt at Spencer, where he had been instrumental in building a fine new church. He is ranked among the foremost pulpit orators of New England. He is thoroughly educated. The degree of doctor of divinity was bestowed upon him by Georgetown university in 1886. He had been for several years one of the consultors of the Springfield diocese.

Mad Dog Runs Amuck.

NORWALK, Conn., Aug. 12.—A large bird dog foaming at the mouth, with blood dripping from its nostrils, passed through the city snapping at everything within reach. Several dogs were severely bitten. It was in Darien yesterday, where it attacked several dogs and created considerable alarm about that village. It was finally driven into an alley and shot.

Decided Against the Widow.

WORCESTER, Mass., Aug. 12.—Constable David T. O'Reilly of Millville was before Judge Putnam at Uxbridge, charged with bastardy, the complainant being Mrs. Rose Doyle of Millville, a widow. After a long hearing the judge declared O'Reilly not guilty and ordered his discharge.

Robbed of Her Jewelry.

NEW HAVEN, Aug. 12.—Mrs. Mary Welsh, wife of a well-known local merchant, went in bathing at Savin Rock. While she was in the water, the bath house where she had left her clothes was broken into by thieves, who made away with $500 worth of jewelry.

Rum and a Knife.

NEW HAVEN, Aug. 12.—James T. Wynne, aged 45, was stabbed and probably fatally wounded by Edward Keefe at Savin Rock, West Haven, last night. The affair grew out of a drunken quarrel. The men are proprietors of the Converse restaurant at Railroad grove.

Killed by an Electric.

BOSTON, Aug. 12.—A little colored boy named Robert Small was killed by an electric car on Shawmut avenue yesterday afternoon. He was run over by an Egleston square electric car, inward bound, and the body was horribly mangled in the accident.

Maverick Investigation Near.

BOSTON, Aug. 12.—A dispatch from Washington states that Senator Chandler, who is chairman of the failed bank committee, expects to enter upon an investigation of the affairs of the Maverick bank in Boston next week, probably on Tuesday.

Killed by His Horse.

DEXTER, Me., Aug. 12.—While Timothy Daggett, a wealthy farmer, aged about 60 years, was harvesting grain, his horse became frightened and threw him down, killing him instantly.

Worcester's Tax Rate.

WORCESTER, Mass., Aug. 12.—The assessors have announced the tax rate as $14.60 on $1000, which is the same as last year.

Will Contest Healy's Seat.

LONDON, Aug. 12.—P. Callan (Parnellite) who was defeated in the northern division of Louth by Timothy Healy (anti-Parnellite), has lodged a petition against the election of Mr. Healy on the ground that voters were intimidated by the priests.

Highest of all in Leavening Power.—Latest U. S. Gov't Report.

Royal Baking Powder
ABSOLUTELY PURE

GRESHAM WILL TAKE THE STUMP.
The People's Party Expect to Win Half a Million Converts Thereby.

ST. LOUIS, Aug. 12.—The National People's party headquarters was alive with enthusiastic workers, all of whom were very jubilant over a telegram received and its contents verified by a letter to the effect that Judge Gresham had concluded to take the stump in the interest of the People's party and would make his opening speech at Indianapolis the latter part of this month. Chairman Taubeneck received this intelligence from the chairman of the state committee of Indiana, to whom Judge Gresham had written declaring his intentions and setting forth his reasons for making a campaign in the interest of General Weaver. In his report to the national headquarters the chairman of the state committee of Indiana states that Judge Gresham, in apprising him of his intentions, informed him by letter that he did not refuse the presidential nomination because he was not in sympathy with the party, but for a reason that was entirely personal and not political.

THE SITUATION AT HOMESTEAD.
Leaders in Doubt as to the Outcome of Affairs.

HOMESTEAD, Pa., Aug. 12.—The settlement of the strike in the Pittsburg district is viewed with varying emotions here. There are many who think that it may lead to reopening of the conference with the firm on which a settlement might be based. Others, however, place little confidence in this supposition and declare that there will be no conference unless the men can force the Carnegie Steel company to it.

The cooks' strike at the mill only caused momentary annoyance.

The prospective visit of the directory of the American Federation of Labor causes much speculation here. No one seems to know exactly why Messrs. Gompers and Maguire are coming unless it be to make a personal investigation into the prospects for winning the fight, and also what should be best done to assist in the fight. It is understood that the Federation leaders were made thoroughly acquainted with the causes leading to the struggle by Hugh O'Donnell during his eastern trip.

THE RIOT OF JULY 6.
"Watchman" Lelar Wants the Pinkertons to Pay for Deceiving Him.

PHILADELPHIA, Aug. 12.—The first suit in the local courts growing out of the riot at Homestead on July 6 was begun yesterday in common pleas court No. 4 by M. W. Collet and W. W. Carr, attorneys for William R. Lelar, against Robert Pinkerton and William A. Pinkerton, trading as Pinkerton's national detective agency.

In his statement Lelar says he was employed by the Pinkertons as a watchman at certain buildings in the state of New York, to which the defendants "then and there falsely and deceitfully pretended to be conducting the plaintiff, but of the precise location of which the plaintiff was not informed by the Pinkertons."

Then follows the accounts of the Pinkertons' famous fight with the rioters from the barges at Homestead on July 6. Lelar says that he fell into the hands of the mob, was kicked and beaten with clubs, sticks and stones and seriously injured. As the result of Lelar being forced to run the gauntlet through the mob, one of his vital organs was permanently injured, and he will be prevented from permanently undertaking the severe manual labor to which he has been accustomed, and for which he is only fitted as a means of a livelihood. The amount claimed is $80,000.

Another Plot Against Frick.

PITTSBURG, Aug. 12.—The post states that the police have discovered an anarchistic plot to assassinate H. C. Frick, chairman of the Carnegie Steel company. The intended assassin is the anarchist Aaronstamm of New York, a close friend of Bergman and Emma Goldman. The police are looking for Aaronstamm.

O'Donnell Endorsed.

HOMESTEAD, Pa., Aug. 12.—Hugh O'Donnell has returned here. The advisory committee met last night. Mr. O'Donnell made a report which was received with enthusiasm. A resolution endorsing O'Donnell was adopted.

MARQUIS DE MORES STYLE.
Dr. Carver Seeks Satisfaction from an Editor for Alleged Insult.

DENVER, Aug. 12.—Dr. W. F. Carver, the crack shot and a band of Indians, have been giving a wild west show here. Each night steers have been roped and dragged about the ring, and The Republican, of which Colonel Stapleton is editor, has criticized the performance very severely. Carver has sent the following letter to The Republican office:

"To request and unjustified attacks of the libellous Republican in the columns of that antiquated and ineffective sheet, compel me to state that during the past few years the Carver company has appeared in the leading cities of North America, Australia and Europe, without once having been accused of cruelty to animals. I have the distinction of being an honorary member of the Society for the Prevention of Cruelty to Animals, and I was the first marksman to introduce the inanimate target, thereby avoiding the cruelty of pigeon shooting, and I was always kept my corrals open to the officers of the Humane society. I do not edit a queer newspaper in which to repay to this apology of a man, but I will be at his service at the Windsor Hotel every day this week from 9 to 12. Allow me to subscribe myself, Dr. W. F. CARVER.

Carver said he had followed the challenge of Marquis de Mores to Editor Mcdillochgo as a model. Mr. Stapleton has not thus far deigned to notice the matter.

AN INVESTIGATION BEGUN.
Will Probably Show Reckless Extravagance by Iron Hall Officials.

INDIANAPOLIS, Aug. 12.—The supreme council of the Order of the Iron Hall has begun its investigation of the condition of that organization. The meeting was called to order by Supreme Chief Somerby. When the sitting adjourned the members were asked what had been done, but they refused to make anything public, except the fact that a committee of three had been appointed to investigate the books of the order and would begin its labors at once. While the supreme council was in session a dozen attorneys were before Judge Taylor arguing the application for a receiver made last week. Neither the plaintiffs nor the defendants were in court.

Attorney Hawkins, representing the plaintiffs, made the opening statement. He said that it would be shown that the supreme officers had conducted the affairs with the utmost extravagance. At Omaha, in 1889, the four days' session of the supreme council, which was composed of only forty members, cost the organization $150,000. The council had given a champagne supper to the board of trade and the council of that city, and had presented the mayor with an expensive silver service. It had also voted $3000 to Somerby as a gift. Other similar incidents were related by the attorney. The trial will last a week.

THE PRESIDENT'S VACATION.
Likely to Remain at Loon Lake Throughout August—Mrs. Harrison Improving.

TROY, N. Y., Aug. 12.—President Harrison is leading a quiet life at Loon Lake in the Adirondacks. He takes daily drives, walks in the woods and joins fishing excursions. He has taken a large room at the Loon Lake House for an office. The president expects to spend August at the lake with Mrs. Harrison and then go to his cottage at Cape May. The time for the departure, though, will depend largely on the condition of Mrs. Harrison's health. Mrs. Harrison is greatly improved since the president's arrival, and her regaining of strength is made manifest by the increased length of her daily drives.

Flyers at Grand Rapids.

GRAND RAPIDS, Mich., Aug. 12.—Hal Pointer defeated Direct at the races here. The betting was $25 to $6 in favor of Pointer, who won every heat. In the 2:19 trot, Steve Whipple won the first heat and the added purse of $5000; 2:14 1-2. Nancy Hanks, driven by Budd Doble, made a race against time. She kept up to her record and made the mile in 2:09.

Leaned Toward the Third Party.

ATLANTA, Aug. 12.—The Republican state convention was in session all day but refused to put out any state ticket. Debates showed a strong feeling in favor of the People's party ticket, at the head of which stands Colonel Peek. An electoral ticket, however, was agreed upon, after which the convention adjourned.

Peculiar Drowning Accident.

MONTREAL, Aug. 12.—The tug Paul was engaged in the Lachine canal and everything appeared all right when the men on board retired. During the night a leak occurred in some unaccountable manner, and the tug sank. There were four men asleep in their berths at the time, and three of them were drowned.

Proposed Railroad Consolidation.

CHICAGO, Aug. 12.—It is announced that the management of the Northern Pacific and Wisconsin Central railway will shortly be consolidated, the latter road becoming a part of the Northern Pacific. The ratification of the consolidation will take place in New York within the next two weeks.

WALTER Q. GRESHAM.

"How do you like that for a piece of news?" said Mr. Taubeneck. "It means that one speech from Gresham, no matter whether he makes more than one in our favor, setting forth the object of our intentions and endorsing our platform, means over 500,000 votes for the People's party that we would have been unable to control otherwise. With a flattering prospect now in Indiana, the encouraging reports received from the south and with the silver states behind us we have good cause to feel hopeful."

From Yesterday's Third Edition.

FATAL RESULT.
Mrs. Theodore Levecque Dies After Several Hours' Suffering.

Mrs. Theodore Levecque, who was so horribly burned this morning in the Cedar Grove street fire, died this afternoon.

BURNING ACCIDENT.—This morning Thomas Donogan, employed at the New Bedford Iron Foundry, met with a painful injury accident, caused by melted iron. His left leg up to the knee was badly burned. Dr. Bullard dressed the burn.

A GOVERNMENT BOAT.—There arrived in the lower harbor this afternoon a United States steamer of the monitor design. She is anchored about half way between Round Hills and Clarks Point.

WASP AND MARGUERITE.
Constellation First, But Other Schooner Probably Wins on Allowance.

MARBLEHEAD, Aug. 11.—3:15 p.m.—The Wasp leads in sloops and Mayflower in schooners with Constellation second. Marguerite probably wins on allowance.

MURDER MOST FOUL AND BRUTAL.
Litchfield (Conn.) Woman Killed by Her Drunken Husband.

NEW HAVEN, Aug. 11.—A special to the Leader says: Murder most foul and brutal has been committed in Litchfield. Nicholas O'Brien, who lives in a dilapidated farm house on the road to Milton, returned home late Tuesday night from attending a funeral. He was intoxicated and while in a drunken frenzy pulled his wife out of bed by the hair, dragged her out of doors into the street and toward Litchfield, a distance of several rods where he kicked and pounded her for several minutes. As a final impulse of his drunken rage, he lifted her up by the hair, and clutching her throat with one hand choked her until she was almost insensible. He then gave her a push into the weeds by the roadside and returned to the house, where he threw himself upon the bed and was soon in a drunken sleep. Mrs. O'Brien was found two hours later and died soon afterward. O'Brien was arrested and yesterday bound over on a charge of murder.

LAUNCHING OF THE MARBLEHEAD.
Cruiser No. 11 Plunges Into the Sea at the South Boston Shipyard.

BOSTON, Aug. 11.—Before 1 o'clock, the hour set for the launching of United States cruiser No. 11, the immense shipyard of Harrison Loring at South Boston was a lively place, with its busy shipwrights hurrying to and fro under the towering mass of steel putting on the finishing touches of lubricating to insure a perfect launch. Added to this scene of busy work was that of the gay holiday-makers who had come by invitation of the contractors to see the ship meet the water. There were hundreds of them dressed in gay attire. Assistant Secretary of the Navy J. Russell Soley represented the government at Washington and Governor Russell and a number of members of the Legislature represented Massachusetts. The city of Boston was well represented by the aldermen and council.

At the appointed hour the signal was given to knock away the shores and amid the cheers of the spectators cruiser 11 slipped slowly down the ways into the water as the Marblehead. Mr. C. F. Allen broke the bottle of wine over the ship's bows as she plunged into the sea.

August Yacht Races at Newport.

BUFFALO, Aug. 12.—The stockholders of the Brush Electric Light company of Buffalo voted unanimously in favor of consolidating with the Thomson-Houston company of Buffalo and the Edison company of New York. The stockholders of the Thomson-Houston company are also unanimously in favor of consolidation.

The Change of Life.

The sole aim of women nearing this critical period should be to keep well, strong, and cheerful.

Lydia E. Pinkham's Vegetable Compound

is peculiarly adapted to this condition. Girls about to enter womanhood find its assistance invaluable.

Overcomes among its ingredients the flatulence, Weak Back, Leucorrhœa, Falling and Displacement of the Womb, Inflammation and Ulceration, Irregularities, Flooding, and all Organic Diseases of the Uterus or Womb, Bloating, Sense of Loss of Life.

Dissolves and expels Tumors from the Uterus at an early stage, and checks any tendency to Cancerous Humors. Subdues Faintness, Excitability, Nervous Prostration, Exhaustion, Kidney Complaints and tones the Stomach.

It acts in harmony with the laws that govern the female system, and is as harmless as water.

It removes Faintness, Flatulency, destroys all craving for stimulants, and relieves Weakness of the Stomach. It cures Bloating, Headaches, Nervous Prostration, General Debility, Sleeplessness, Depression and Indigestion. That feeling of bearing down, causing pain, weight and backache, is always permanently cured by its use.

Sold by all Druggists. Price $1.00 per bottle, six for $5.00, or sent by mail, in form of Pills or Lozenges, on receipt of price, $1.00 per box for either. Liver Pills, 25c.

Correspondence freely answered. Address in confidence.
LYDIA E. PINKHAM MED. CO., LYNN, MASS.

BIRD'S EYE VIEW OF THE VICINITY OF THE FALL RIVER MURDERS.

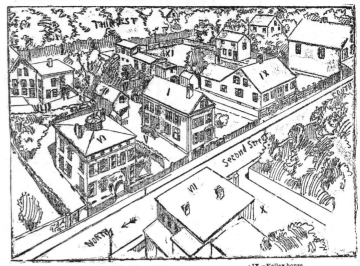

I.—Borden house.
II.—Borden barn.
III.—The well.
IV.—Fence with barbed wire on top
V.—Side entrance.
VI.—Churchill residence.
VII.—Dr. Bowen's house.
VIII.—Dr. Chagnon's house.
IX.—Kelley house.
X.—Yard where officers watch Borden house.
XI.—Kelley's Barn.
XII.—Kelley's house.
XII.—Pear orchard.

WILD RUMORS OF ARREST.
The Two Borden Girls Ushered into the Police Station.

Miss Lizzie Confronted by Eli Bence, the Drug Clerk.

Scene of Excitement About Court Square, Fall River.

[Special Dispatch.]

FALL RIVER, Aug. 11.—At 3:30 o'clock this afternoon there was a wild and exciting scene in Court Square.

A hack drove up followed by a large crowd which had run after it from the Borden residence in the belief that arrests had been made.

As soon as an entrance way to the station could be cleared, City Marshal Hilliard alighted and he was immediately followed by Miss Lizzie Borden, her sister Emma and Mrs. George Brigham, who has been Lizzie's constant companion since the tragedy.

The party was at once ushered up stairs and once more the hack was dashing wildly away with Officer Doherty its only occupant. Soon after the carriage returned and the policeman escorted into the station Eli Bence, the clerk in Smith's drug store, of whom Lizzie is said to have purchased or attempted to purchase poison.

Although the police declined to state exactly the nature of the proceedings, it is believed Bence has been summoned to make his statements when confronted by Miss Borden, and for purposes of identification.

[By Associated Press.]

FALL RIVER, Aug. 11.—A second autopsy was held in the ladies' waiting room at Oak Grove cemetery this morning. Mrs. Borden's body was examined first. The new fact discovered was a bruise on the back near the left shoulder, about the width of an axe and shaped like the head of an axe. It gives another clew to the exact position held by Mrs. Borden when the deed was committed. At 2:05 o'clock the examining physicians were at work on Mr. Borden's body. The physicians at work are Dr. Draper of Boston, and Medical Examiner Dolan, Drs. Leary and Cone of this city.

Misses Emma and Lizzie Borden, Mrs. Brigham and Miss Sullivan were brought to the police station this afternoon. They were not under arrest.

A locksmith is now trying to get into Mr. Borden's safe at the house to determine whether or not a will was made.

TENNIS AT NAHANT.
Excitement and Interest Increasing on the Third Day.

NAHANT, Aug. 11.—A gentle sea breeze tempered the atmosphere this morning and favored the tennis players who were continuing the Nahant competition. It was the third day of the meeting and as the contest narrows down the interest and excitement increases.

The scheduled match of the day was the one postponed from yesterday between Malcolm Chase of Providence and S. T. Chase of Chicago.

At one set each yesterday afternoon, they had agreed to play the match at once again this morning. The first set found the Providence boy entirely recovered from his accident of yesterday caused by collision with the stop net. He played in great form. The Western crack had thus far met with three defeats and he did not propose to add a fourth to the number if he could help it. Unusual accuracy to the lines gave the Providence Chase the lead at this start which he retained to the score of five games each.

The vantage game also went to the inter-collegiate champion on pretty passes to the far corners. With the score 5-5 against him S. T. Chase proceeded to get the count of 40-15 on his service, and on that point would have given him the game, thus tieing the score at six games all. But the boy wonder proved equal to the occasion, showed great nerve, and pulled out the game and set, 7-5. Then the champion began the second set by winning three games. But Chase was not out of this set yet, not by a considerable sight, and by a good upbrill brace he, in his turn won three straight games, tieing the count.

The seventh game was important and both men fought hard for the lead. Long rallies were played on almost every point, but by superior steadiness the Westerner won the game. Up to this time the play had alternated most exactly, as it had yesterdson, and it began to look as if a third set would be necessary. It was now or never with the Providence lad and he played with remarkable steadiness, taking three straight games, thereby winning the set and match. S. T. Chase's hard luck still pursues him and a big zero marks the number of his victories.

In the second match of the day, Clarence Hobart was pitted against C. F. Hubbard of California, represented by C. F. Hubbard. The latter's graceful, dashing style of play is too well known to be further described. This morning he adopted new and most intelligent tactics in his effort to beat the famous New Yorker. Hubbard's plan was to get to the net at every opportunity, trusting to his effectiveness as a volleyer and to Hobart's possible liability to put the ball out of court.

As the first set progressed it became apparent that the Californian's ability had previously been underestimated. Hubbard has been steadily winning a slight nervousness at this his first meeting with the best eastern cracks.

The opening game went to Hubbard, who followed up his advantage by increasing his score to 3-1 upon his good net play, aided by Hobart's hits out of court.

Hobart now won three games by the skilful execution of his famous "Lawford" stroke, and his opponent at promptly evened the court at four games all. The Californian had seemingly sure grip on the ninth game, a 40-love in his favor, but Hobart was aware of the importance of the game at this critical juncture and worked hard for every stroke, finally winning the game and taking the lead at 5-4.

From now on until the close of the set the play was as close as has been seen here this season, Hubbard surprising everybody by the persistency with which he played his noted opponent. Hubbard eventually won the set at 8-6, 48 points to 45, the Pacific player being evidently on the upgrade, by his active efforts at the net. Score 8-6. Hobart wins, and the large number of spectators enthusiastics "ly applauded the close play.

Hobart won the first game of the second set by a pretty pass beyond his opponent.

The next four successive games were taken in hand by Hobart, who won the first on a terrific smash, this, second on Hubbard's nets, third on his own hard drives and the fourth on steady play at last causing his opponent to hit the ball out of court. The Californian took the sixth game upon a series of cross-court drives past Hobart, but this was as far as he got, the latter taking the next two games, the set 6-2, and the match.

F. H. Hovey of Harvard and Quincy A. Shaw, Jr., of Jamaica Plain were the next pair of contestants in the last match of the morning.

Dr. James Dwight, the noted tennis authority, now appeared upon the scene and was promptly induced to act as referee and scorer.

The match began with Hovey having the service and he won the opening game as usual, Shaw not getting a single point. The second game went to Shaw, his left-handed service being as effective as that of his opponent. Again the intercollegiate champion's serving stood him in good stead and he obtained the lead only to lose it very soon at the announcement of "Four games to two. Mr. Shaw leads." To-day was Shaw's good day, as yesterday was his bad one, and his left-handed drives in this first set were as swift shots as ever passed over a tennis net.

The following games alternated, the eighth one being really the decisive one of the set. Back and forth went that while sphere many times, deuce being scored three times before Shaw could get the call in the position he wanted to make a left hand drive. Finally he made the winning stroke and from this lead of 5-3 he took the set 6-4 on Hovey's outs in the tenth game. Hovey's service once more stood by him in the first game of the second set but he was obliged to yield the lead on the superior net playing of Shaw in the following two games.

The Harvard player should begin to play winning ball, and whether it was time to improve the pace of his returns or the poorer play of his opponent, at any rate Hovey won three successive games on general superiority and no especially brilliant play on either side. Shaw was not beaten yet by any means, and he won the next game by good side line playing, and volleying gave Hovey the next two games and the set, 6-2. Score, one set each.

The third and deciding set commenced amidst great excitement, Hovey winning the first two games having good luck in getting the ball twice just where wanted it for his overhand smashes. The play was being done in streaks and in spite of Hovey's increased efforts Shaw won the two following games, principally upon a few more of his left-handed drives either down the side lines or out of the court. Games five and six went to Hovey, who was playing the net very effectively, and after losing the eighth game to Shaw, the intercollegiate champion ran out the set 6-3, thus winning the match.

Following are the full scores of the morning play:

Summary—Third Day's Play.

Malcolm Chase, Providence, beat S. T. Chase, Chicago, 7-5, 6-4.

Clarence Hobart, New York, beat C. P. Hubbard, of California, 8-6, 6-2.

F. H. Hovey beat Quincy A. Shaw, Jr., 4-6, 6-3, 6-3.

KNIGHTS TEMPLARS.
Hon. Hugh McCurdy of Michigan Chosen Grand Master.

DENVER, Aug. 11.—The Hon. Hugh McCurdy of Corunna, Mich., was this forenoon elected grand master of the Knights Templars of the United States.

Pages 1-8.

The Evening Standard.

Pages 1-8.

ESTABLISHED FEBRUARY, 1850.

NEW BEDFORD, SATURDAY, AUGUST 13, 1892.---TWELVE PAGES.

TWO CENTS.

HASKELL & TRIPP.

Hot weather hints.

Men's light ecru sateen sun umbrellas, $1.25 each.

Our parasols are selling at cut prices. We make no exceptions; *every one* marked down. You'll never need one more than you do this year.

Satin palm fans, and flat Jap fans, 3c. each. Folding fans, 5c. to 50c.; choice styles. Pocket fans of favorite sorts.

Drinking tumbler in leather case for 25c., or a nickled drinking cup that folds up to carry in your pocket for 25c.

Bay Rum in sprinkler top bottles (finest imported), 35c.

Florida water, 25c. up.

German Farina Cologne in long green bottles.

Made by Crown Perfumery Co., London. — Celebrated "Lavender Salts" and "Crab Apple Blossom."

Atomizers, 25c , 50c. and up to $1.25.

Sponges, 10c., 25c., 50c.

Rubber sponge bags, 20c., 25c.

Every good sort of toilet soap.

Celluloid soap box, 25c.

Remarkable bag bargain.

50 cents is the price.

The bag is of the new flat shape, leather on one side, with small change pocket, having oxidized clasp. The top is of cloth, with a drawing string, and there are double leather handles. We are selling immense quantities of them.

Pound package of good writing paper, 10c. (120 sheets.)

Pound package of "seconds," slightly, *very* slightly, imperfect writing paper of a high grade, 17c. a package.

Light literature.

Paper Covered novels, by famous writers of fiction, 10c. each, or three for 25c.

Sheet music, 5c., or six for 25c. More than 1000 titles. Catalogues free.

Sun bonnets, sun hats, cambric and gingham dresses for little children; at remarkably little prices.

HASKELL & TRIPP.

Department Stores,

Purchase and William Streets.

WEATHER INDICATIONS.

SHOWERS.

WASHINGTON, Aug. 13.—For the 24 hours from 8 a. m. to-day: For New England, showers, clearing by Sunday; northerly winds.

CONTINUED COOLER.

BOSTON, Aug. 13.—Local forecast for New England until Sunday night: Fair, except showers to-day for coast sections; continued cool; variable winds.

GRESHAM AND THE THIRD PARTY.

Secretary Taubeneck Declines to Give His Letter to the Public.

ST. LOUIS, Aug. 13.—An effort was made yesterday to secure from Chairman Taubeneck of the People's Party National Committee a copy of the letter received by him from Secretary Stoll of the Indiana State Committee, which states that Judge W. Q. Gresham will enter the coming campaign as a speaker for the Third Party. Mr. Taubeneck refused again to give out anything further, saying that the letter contained only extracts from the original Gresham letter. He said, "I will tell you what I know about the matter and it can be relied upon as correct. I know how Gresham stood two years ago, while he was recognized as a Republican leader, yet from letters in our possession we know he was in sympathy with our party and favored our principles. Knowing this to be a fact he was urged to accept the presidential nomination of the party at the Omaha convention, but declined for personal reasons and not political. When Gen. Weaver was tendered the nomination Judge Gresham wrote him a friendly letter, the contents of which I am not at liberty to make public, but I will state that he wished the General success and intimated that at the proper time he could expect more encouragement than the receipt of a personal letter. I presume that that time is at hand, judging from the letter that Judge Gresham wrote to Mr. Stoll asking him to consult the committee in regard to a suitable date for him to make a speech at Indianapolis in behalf of the party. I know this to be a fact, as I am in receipt of a letter from Mr. Stoll conveying this information to headquarters, and in his letter he quotes a portion of the contents of Judge Gresham's letter, which at this time I refuse to make public without the consent of Judge Gresham.

BOLIVAR FALLS.

City in the Hands of the Legalistas After a Bloody Battle.

NEW YORK, Aug. 13.—A special from Trinidad to the *Herald* says: News has reached here that the city of Bolivar has fallen into the hands of Legalistas after a bloody battle. The Legalistas, some 4000 men strong, were under command of Gens. Hernandez and Gil. They appeared before the city early this (Friday) morning and demanded of the commander of the government forces that he surrender. The reply was a prompt refusal. This precipitated the engagement. Hernandez and Gil at the head of their forces advanced on the position of the government troops and attacked in the face of a murderous fire. The attack was made with courage and was resisted with equal violence. For a time the decision was in the balance, but numbers told, and the governmentals gave way, contesting every inch of the ground. It was not until Gen. Laudalta and another officer had been killed at the head of their troops that the government troops retired from the field in disorder, leaving nearly 500 dead. The Legalistas, while they lost no officers, suffered fully as much as the government, losing 500 men.

MISTAKEN FOR A SEAL POACHER.

Steamer Polar Bear Fired Upon by a Detachment from the Yorktown.

PORT TOWNSEND, Wash., Aug. 13.—News has been received per steamer Bertha from Ounalaska, stating that a detachment of marines from the United States steamer Yorktown fired several volleys of rifle balls into the pilot-house of the Polar Bear, seriously wounding the chief engineer. The steamer Polar Bear is used as a tender for the canneries at Bristol Bay, and she was returning to Astoria after season's work. While passing through False Pass, Aug. 1, she ran ashore. A crowd of men armed with long range rifles appeared from behind the bluffs and without warning fired on the steamer. She got away finally, however, and left for Ounalaska, and reported the affair to the United States steamer Adams, who said the commander of the Yorktown left a detachment of marines at False Pass with instructions to allow no vessels to pass by, and it was probable that the marines mistook the Polar Bear for a British poaching steamer. The affair has created great excitement.

RUSSIAN TROOPS MOVING.

Pretenders to the Afghan Throne Being Handsomely Supported.

LONDON, Aug. 13.—A dispatch to the *News* from Odessa says Russian troops are being rapidly moved from Turkestan to the Afghan frontier.

The *Chronicle's* Odessa correspondent says: "Ishak Khan and his son Ishmail, pretenders to the Afghan throne, have taken refuge at Samarkand, with 200 adherents. All are receiving a handsome allowance from the Russian treasury and are actively intriguing against the present ruler of Afghanistan."

Better Anti-English Feeling.

The Simla correspondent of the *Times* says: "A sign of the anti-English feeling in Russia is that all Hindoos have been ordered to quit Turkestan within six months. Many bankers and traders who have settled for generations in Bokara, Samarkand, have thus been ruined. Fresh centres of disturbances have appeared in Afghan Turkey, due to emissaries of the Russian government."

LOUD TALK OF LYNCHING.

Armed Whites and Negroes Make a Race War Imminent in a Kansas Town.

LEAVENWORTH, Kan., Aug. 13.—During the past two days great excitement has prevailed at Tonganoxy, a village 20 miles west of here, and there is immense danger of a race war. Noah Ashby, a negro, was taken from jail on Wednesday to have a hearing before a justice on charge of assault upon Ada Waymer, a young white girl. The evidence was very strong, and Thursday the indignation of white people became so great that there was loud talk of lynching. The negroes did not accept the theory that Ashby was guilty and 1000 of them, well-armed, gathered to protect him. A large number of the whites also armed themselves. The mayor issued a proclamation ordering the crowd to disperse, but no attention was paid to it and fully 300 armed negroes remained about town last night and a good number of them came with the prisoner to the jail.

BITTEN BY A MAD WOLF.

Twenty Adults, Ten Children and Many Animals Raving in a Polish Town.

LONDON, Aug. 13.—Twenty adults, 10 children and numerous animals were recently bitten by a mad wolf at Lodz, Poland, and all are raving mad and beyond recovery.

Ceased to be Disturbed Districts.

LONDON, Aug. 13.—The Dublin *Gazette* announces that Mayo, Leitrim, West Meath and portions of Tipperary have ceased to be disturbed districts and that the extra police have been withdrawn. The *News*, commenting on this, asks how it is that this decision coincides with the fall of the government. "The Conservatives," it suggests, "may desire to bequeath a little trouble to their successors; else why were the police not removed earlier."

VOWED VENGEANCE.

Motive Found for Murder of Andrew J. Borden.

He Once Caused Conviction of Sailors for Mutiny.

Men Who Suffered Recently in Fall River.

Police Think Lizzie Will be Held for Grand Jury.

Eyes of the Authorities Still on Bridget Sullivan and Morse.

LYNN, Aug. 13.—The Lynn *Item* will to-day publish a story stating that Andrew J. Borden of Fall River gave the principal testimony that convicted the ringleaders in the mutiny on the ship Richard J. Borden while on the voyage from a foreign port to this country; that he and his wife were on the vessel; that his testimony in the courts was declared by the sailors to be false and exaggerated, and that the men who suffered by it vowed vengeance against him. Most, if not all, of them have been released, and it is submitted that several of them were in Fall River at the time of the murder.

[The vessel referred to by the *Item* is undoubtedly the schooner Jefferson Borden.]

FALL RIVER, Aug. 13.—The reaction in the Borden cases has set in and to-day the popular feeling is noticeably quiet.

There is very little violent discussion going on in the streets and what cases were seen were the outgrowth of expressions against the imprisoned girl.

Three days ago it was the peculiar cry that Miss Lizzie was a criminal and should be placed behind prison bars.

To-day although the district attorney and judge have given their opinions on the evidence there are many thoughtful and influential men who believe that the trial will substantiate Miss Borden's protestations of innocence.

There is now but one policeman at the Borden homestead and he is doing patrol duty in the street to prevent curious people from annoying the family.

The police have recommenced their regular patrol duty, and only three men are hunting up further evidence of the murder.

The city marshal said this morning that he was confident that the evidence to be submitted at the hearing of the 22d inst. would be strong enough to warrant the holding of Miss Borden for the grand jury.

That body will not convene until November, and the time of the special session of the Superior Court that must be held will be decided on afterward.

While direct police surveillance has been removed from Mr. Morse and Miss Sullivan, their whole connection with the case will be gone over by the police again within the next few days, and they will not be far away should the police need them.

There will not be a great many witnesses summoned for the preliminary hearing unless the present plans are changed.

The proceedings will be open to reporters.

The marshal again denies the statements made editorially and otherwise in many Boston papers to the effect that no search was made until after the funeral.

A search was made three times during the afternoon of the day of the murder, and Miss Lizzie's room was searched thoroughly and other portions of the buildings.

Police inquiry is being made again into the details of a mysterious robbery which took place at the Borden homestead about a year ago.

A ladies' watch and several articles of jewelry were taken from a dressing case in one of the upper rooms, and to this day the police have been unable to trace the thief.

Footprints in the Barn.

"Before saying anything about what I saw in the Borden house, I wish to call attention to a point that seems not to have reached the inquest," said mason Charles H. Bryant.

John Donnelly, the hackman, was among the first to enter the barn, and walked all over the loft. Then up goes Officer Medley and takes a walk around and goes before the coroner with the highly important information that he examined the dust-covered floor of the barn very carefully and could find no tracks, although he said he could easily distinguish his own.

"Now, if he could distinguish his own so easily, why didn't he find John Donnelly's, and if he couldn't find John Donnelly's heavy prints, how could he expect to find Lizzie Borden's? The air is full of theories. I'd like to hear a few people explain that."

Bryant was engaged to break open the chimneys of the Borden house in search of a concealed weapon, was sitting in the Wilbur House soon after noon, and was easily led into telling what he saw and heard and the conclusions he reached.

"I was engaged as an expert," said Bryant, "and carried out the instructions of the authorities. I do not know Lizzie nor Emma Borden, one from the other, but both were in the house and gave me every assistance. Indeed, if anything, I thought they were over anxious that I should make a complete examination.

Nothing in the Chimneys.

"So far as the chimneys were concerned I saw at a glance that it was useless to tear them open, for I could see through every flue in the house, and I told them so, but still the district attorney told me to go ahead, and I dug into them.

"That finished, I asked Miss Borden if there were any flues in the garret, such as might have been put in for a stove at some time, and she said she did not know, but I had better look. I made a careful examination, but found nothing.

"Then we made inquiries about an alleged cistern said to be in the cellar and the girls said there had been at some time, but it was an old wooden affair, which had doubtless been filled up—at any rate she had not seen it for a long time. They told us what part of the cellar it had been in, and we pried around there for some time with a crowbar and found nothing.

"During the whole time the girls, as I say, were at our service and expressed every willingness to show us through the house, giving us the keys to all the rooms.

I was in every room of the house except the front entry and observed things closely all the while. I may say that the house is furnished very plainly—notably so. The ordinary American mechanic with an ordinary salary has his house furnished as well. There was nothing in the house to indicate the wealth of the people who lived there."

"Did you know Andrew J. Borden?"

Anecdote of Andrew J. Borden.

"Not intimately, but I know he was a close-fisted business man. Here's an incident: As one of a committee of the Knights of Pythias I called upon him to see about leasing his lot on Main and Anawan streets where his big block now stands. He said he could call at the lodge rooms the next night and did so, and without any ado went straight to the business. He said he would lease the lot for a term of 20 or 50 years on a sliding scale of its assessed valuation, asking nothing but 6 per cent. on that amount. That struck us as very favorable; then he added as the condition that we build a structure costing not less than $65,000. That was all right. Then he added that at the end of the lease the building should belong to the estate.

"That knocked the whole thing. But you see how careful he was on behalf of his heirs, for he must have been dead at the expiration of the lease by thirty years at least, living his allotted time. We wanted him to provide for the sale to the estate at a figure to be fixed by judges, but he had said his say and would hear to nothing else. This is an incident fairly illustrative of Andrew J. Borden's character. He is well known to have been a hard business man, but I do not know that his treatment of his daughters was such as to furnish a possible motive for such a deed as this."

Charged With Only One Murder.

Lizzie Borden is charged with murder, but not with the murder of her stepmother. Nearly every newspaper which printed an account of the arrest of the young woman made the mistake of charging her with two murders, whereas the prosecution accuses her of committing but one.

LIZZIE BORDEN DEPARTING FOR TAUNTON JAIL.
[Sketched from a Photograph by the *Standard's* Artist.]

WHERE BRIDGET SULLIVAN IS STAYING.

A HOST OF READERS.

The EVENING STANDARD's daily increase in circulation is of remarkable interest to advertisers and its readers. Friday's edition of the STANDARD was a record breaker, the exact number of copies printed and sold being **9506.** As is it fairly estimated that every newspaper printed is read by five persons, the STANDARD's readers yesterday numbered 47,530 people.

HOME MATTERS.

PERSONAL.—At a meeting of the trustees of the Union Savings Bank of Fall River, Jerome C. Borden was elected president and member of the board of investment, to fill the vacancy occasioned by the decease of Andrew J. Borden.

Hon. Alanson Borden, justice of the Third District Court, will leave this afternoon on a 10 days' vacation at Seaconnet Point. The bench will be filled by Associate Justices Tappan and Milliken.

Gov. Tuttle of New Hampshire has been visiting 'Sconset, Nantucket.

J. H. McDermott, first officer of the steamer Nantucket, has resigned to accept a berth with the anchor Line Steamship Company running out of Buffalo, N. Y.

Robert F. Raymond, Esq., of this city is announced to speak at a prohibitory rally in Tremont Temple, Boston, on the evening of Sept. 15.

Miss Evangeline Hathaway, for two years principal of Hanover, (Mass.,) Academy, has been elected principal of the High school at Somerset. Miss Hathaway is the first woman to occupy the position. She is a graduate of Wellesley, class of '90, and belongs in Woodfords, Me., near Portland.

Rev. J. I. Bartholomew and family are at Lake Winnepesaukee, N. H., where they will remain until September.

Mrs. Mary A. Cameron is spending her vacation in New Hampshire.

Prof. Israel Smith will attend the 15th session of the American Society of Professors of Dancing, which will be held at New York from Sept. 6th to 9th.

Charles M. Dedrick and wife of this city are occupying their cottage in Fairhaven for a few weeks.

SIXTY MILLION BUSHELS OF WHEAT — *A Bushel for Every Inhabitant of the United States. The Kansas Crop for '92.*—Never in the history of Kansas has that State had such bountiful crops as this year. The farmers cannot get enough hands to harvest the great crop, and the Santa Fe railroad has made special rates from Kansas City and other Missouri river towns, to induce harvest hands to go into the State. The wheat crop of the State will be from sixty to sixty-five million bushels, and the quality is high. The grass crop is made, and is a very large one; the early potatoes, rye, barley and oat crops are made, and are all large. The weather has been propitious for corn, and it is the cleanest, best looking corn to be found in the country to-day. Cheap rates will be made from Chicago, St. Louis and all points on the Santa Fe east of the Missouri river, to all Kansas points, on August 30 and September 27, and these excursions will give a chance for Eastern farmers to see what the great Sunflower State can do. A good map of Kansas will be mailed free upon application to Jno. J. Byrne, 723 Monadnock Block, Chicago, Ill., together with reliable statistics and information about Kansas lands.

THE HEALTH AND PLEASURE RESORTS OF MICHIGAN AND THE WEST are illustrated and described in a handsome folder, containing a fine colored map, which has just been issued by the Michigan Central "The Niagara Falls Route" and which is designed for the special use of people in the East who wish to learn something about the resorts of Michigan, Wisconsin, the Isle of Mackinac, the lakes or Minnesota, Yellowstone Park, Colorado, Utah, and the Pacific coast.

Copy of folder will be sent on application to W. H. Underwood, Eastern Passenger Agent, Buffalo, N. Y.

THE APPLEDORE COOK BOOK.—We have received from Mr. Hutchinson a copy of Miss Parloa's Appledore Cook Book, a special edition having been published for his circulation. For the small sum of 10 cents every housekeeper can secure this fine collection of varied and useful recipes.

FOWLS KILLED.—Some fowls belonging to Rev. Father Fauteaux, one of the French priests in this city, were killed by a dog last night.

"AYER'S HYGIENIC COFFEE" is prepared by M. S. Ayer of Boston, who is a vegetarian, and has made diet reform a study.

YACHTING.—Schooner yacht Halcyon arrived to-day from Marion, towed by steam yacht Harold.

SECOND BAPTIST CHURCH.—Attention is called to the special notice for a meeting next Thursday evening.

MISS PARLOA'S Complete Cook Book for 10c. at Hutchinson's Book Store.

TURKISH, Russian, electric, or plain baths. 5 South Sixth street.

MISS PARLOA'S Appledore Cook Books only 10c. at Hutchinson's Book Store.

A MASSAGE will knock that rheumatism sky high. Try one at 5 South Sixth street.

AN ORIGINAL PENSION has been granted to Charles M. Dedrick of this city.

YOU NEED A BATH. Get one at No. 5 South Sixth street.

BEST ROUND STEAK 10c. Gray Bros.

CLAMBAKE, Sileh Hamer Grove, to-morrow.

SWEET POTATOES 23c. a peck. Gray Bros.

SPRING HEEL BOOTS, any size, $1.50. Devoll's.

LARGE BRIGHT BANANAS 20c. doz. Gray Bros.

CLAMBAKE, Sileh Hamer Grove, to-morrow.

MEATS LOWEST at Gray Bros.

THAT tired feeling—take Hood's Sarsaparilla.

DIVIDED!

BROKEN IN TWO!

CUT IN HALVES!

The above is what has happened to the prices on our

Summer Furniture.

We have about 50 pieces consisting of

PIAZZA CHAIRS, SETTEES, ROCKERS, ARM and EASY CHAIRS,

which we propose to close out at once. We mention a few styles and prices to illustrate:

Lawn Seats $1.50, Now 75c.

Common Rockers $2.75, Now $1.37.

Patent Rockers $5.50, Now $2.25.

Piazza Settees $6.50, Now $3.25.

Piazza Settees $5.50, Now $2.25.

This is an opportunity to add a few pieces to your cottage or piazza furniture at a very small cost.

C. F. WING,

34 to 40 Purchase St.

WHITING & CO.

GREAT BARGAINS

—IN—

Ladies'

Cotton Underwear

20 doz. more of those fine Night Dresses, at 50c. apiece.

25 doz. of elegant Night Dresses from 75c. to $2.87 apiece.

10 doz. Ladies' White Cotton Skirts from 50c. to $2.50 apiece.

100 doz. of Ladies' Cotton and Cambric Corset Covers, at 25, 37, 42, 50, 75c. and $1 apiece, all fine and nicely made, try them.

We are selling Infants' Long and Short Dresses, very cheap, get our prices.

If you want Infants' Slips we can suit you on prices and quality.

See our Corset stock, as we have all of the popular makes sold.

WHITING & CO.

J. V. SPARE,

Liberty Hall Building.

Balance of Stock of Challies to be closed out at 3c. a yard.

Printed Flannelette, been selling at 12 1-2, now 6c. yard.

Pacific Chambray, regular 10c. goods at 6 1-2c. a yard.

Outing Flannels in short lengths at 5 1-2c. a yard.

More of those White Crochet Spreads at 59c. each.

Gray Blankets, damaged, 55c. pair.

Remnants of Ribbons, different widths, at 8c., 10c., 12 1-2c. yard.

J. V. Spare,

LIBERTY HALL BUILDING.

OUTING SHIRTS!

OUTING SHIRTS!

You can never have too many

OUTING SHIRTS!

Our low prices will help you out. Quality exceptional.

Good Shirts for $1 and $1.25, laundered collars and cuffs.

Another lot of the popular blue Madras, all sizes, $1.50.

Better come at once, They're going fast.

J. & W. R. WING & CO.,

133 UNION STREET.

OUTING SHIRTS!

OUTING SHIRTS!

At this Season of the Year

We have a great many broken lots of Suits. One or two or three of a lot. These suits will be sold at less than the price of the goods to manufacture, in order to close them.

SANDERS & BARROWS,

67 and 69 William Street.

DON'T STOP ME

I know where to find the Lowest PRICES in

HARNESSES,

Carriage Lap Robes, Horse Clothing, Whips, &c., Ladies' and Gents' Riding Saddles, Trunks, Bags, Pocketbooks, Bill Books, Umbrellas and all kinds Travelling Goods.

C. F. CUSHING, - - - - Opp. City Hall,

IS THE MAN.

EARLY FALL STYLE HATS RECEIVED.

We always sell all Best Hats at Cut Prices. Fifty cents saved on any Hat bought of

H. V. SANDERS & CO.

One Price Clothiers, } OPP. CITY CLOCK, 92 Purchase St.

NEW BEDFORD BRASS FOUNDRY.

Machinists, Brass Finishers and Founders, Brass, Bronze and Composition Castings, Zinc and White Metal Pattern Castings, Phospor Bronze Castings a specialty, Lead Window Weights and High Speed Babbitt Metals, Chandelier Repairing and Brazing, Brass Finishing in all its branches. Machine Repairing promptly attended to. Lawn Mowers Sharpened and Repaired.

Foundry and Machine Shop, 108 North Water Street, foot of Elm.

WM. T. NICHOLSON, Manager, Formerly Foreman of the Armington & Sims Engine Company's Brass Foundry, Providence, R. I. je25-3m

TRY 39 TOBACCO! Best in the Land for Smoking.

Be sure that the tag 39 is on every piece, and take nothing else in place of it.

Distributing Agents

Driscol, Church & Hall, Wholesale Grocers, NEW BEDFORD.

TURKISH BATHS.

LADIES.	GENTLEMEN.
Mrs. B. A. Morrison, Manager.	G. A. Cavanaugh, Manager.
TUESDAYS and THURSDAYS till 8 P. M.	Mondays, Wednesdays and Fridays till 8 P. M.
SATURDAYS till 6 P. M.	Also Saturday Nights

No. 5 South Sixth Street.

LODGED IN JAIL.

Sheriff Wright's Wife Moved to Tears.

Recognized in Lizzie Borden Her Daughter's Friend.

Prisoner Still Displays Her Outward Indifference.

Inquest Will Not Be Reopened Before Monday.

Government Busy in Trying to Disentangle Threads.

In spite of all that has been said or written about the Fall River tragedy very little is known regarding the nature of the inquiry which has been going on in the police court room in that city for 48 hours. It is true that Miss Lizzie Borden was suspected as early as a week ago this morning, and that she has been under suspicion ever since, but it should also be borne in mind that she was not accused until last Thursday night.

In partnership with her sister, Miss Emma Borden, she had offered a reward of $5000 for the conviction of the murderer of her father and stepmother, and had secured the services of a detective to track the butcher. On the Government side, it was fair and natural to presume, that she, above any person on the face of the earth, desired to bring the wretch

TAUNTON JAIL, WHERE LIZZIE BORDEN IS A PRISONER.

who had committed the deed to the gallows. The very fact that she was suspected, was of itself sufficient to warrant such a conclusion, all other considerations aside. The only surmise possible, therefore, was that she would assist the authorities to the best of her ability in unraveling the mystery and in freeing herself from the chain of circumstances, weak or strong, which she knew surrounded her. It was to be supposed that she would not only answer every question cheerfully, but that she would volunteer every particle of information in her possession, and that the more searching the examination, the better she would be satisfied. She had everything to gain and nothing to lose by a full revelation of the truth.

Anybody in his sober senses would be slow to hint that District Attorney Knowlton, or any other prosecuting officer, was eager to convict the innocent, to embarrass witnesses, or to impose any hardship on them. At the inquest every person examined was a government witness; there was no defendant, and, of course, no witnesses for the defence. Whether Miss Borden did assist the court and the district attorney in the endeavor to clear up the grim problem which confronted them is not known. As stated, nothing that transpired at the inquest which would justify the forming of an opinion has been made public. Again, it is hardly charitable to insinuate that the government at last has a prisoner because it had to have a prisoner, irrespective of the consequences. That, too, is an accusation that few would care to bring, except in the heat of passion. If the government is possessed of ordinary intelligence, it is aware that it is a terrible thing to swear out a warrant for the arrest of a young lady charged with killing her father. If, as is openly alleged, the government has done that, because it jumped at conclusions, or because it did not appreciate the full significance of such a charge, it must be admitted that its conduct has been more extraordinary and inexplicable than any feature of the crime itself. The government knew that, once that warrant had been issued, Miss Borden's character, which had always been irreproachable, was blotted forever; it must have known that even if she left the Superior Court room next November acquitted, nothing that it could do could lift the blight from her life. The government sealed the prisoner's fate when it held her in the matron's room in the Central Police Station last Thursday night.

The Latest Clew,

and this incident illustrates the willingness of the police to still follow clews, was run to earth yesterday afternoon. For some time past a man has haunted the Central Station with a story about another man. The other man had been seen diving in and out of the swamp land near the Chace mills. Smoke was seen rising from this same swamp land, and the conclusion arrived at was that the man should be captured and the fire which made the smoke stamped out. Accordingly, Officers Harrington and Doherty went over the Chace mill district yesterday and came back as wise as they went.

Nothing in the Nature of a Will.

City Marshal Hilliard found nothing in the Borden safe that would be of moment to the government in the prosecution of its case, and nothing in the nature of a will. The guards are still on duty at the house, but their duties are of a different character from what they have been, and their labors now are solely devoted to prevent the persons of the house from being subjected to any annoyance by the curious throngs who still find something interesting in standing upon the street and staring at the place.

The Important Witnesses.

Messrs. Almy and Milne, proprietors of the Fall River *Daily News*, went bail for Mr. Morse and Bridget Sullivan. Bridget returned to her friend's residence on Division street. The police say that the most important testimony in the case will be that to be given by Bridget Sullivan, and but three men know what this testimony is. They are Judge Blaisdell, Marshal Hilliard and District Attorney Knowlton, even State Detective Seaver having been requested to retire at the time that the domestic was relating her story. It is not regarded as likely that the Sullivan woman will be put upon the witness stand at the preliminary hearing.

Lodged in Jail.

Lizzie A. Borden now occupies a small cell in the women's department of the county jail at Taunton. Of all the trying scenes through which the young woman has passed, this parting from her relatives and departure from the city of her home under the charge of police officers, to mix with low criminals of both sexes, might well be supposed to be the most severe; but beyond an evident loss of strength as she entered the train at Fall River there was no evidence of anything approaching physical prostration, and her step as she alighted from the carriage at the entrance to the Taunton jail was firmer than at any time during the journey.

"She is a remarkable woman," said Marshal Hilliard, "and is possessed of wonderful power of fortitude."

"She still retains the same Christian spirit of resignation as at the outset," remarked Rev. E. A. Buck, her pastor, "and her calmness is the calmness of innocence."

Whichever view is correct, this prisoner is certainly

A Remarkable Woman.

Her demeanor is going far to cause a retention of the interest in this case, which the people do not appear at all inclined to drop, even though the government authorities express themselves satisfied that the murderer of Mr. and Mrs. Borden is now in custody. Viewed by hundreds of people in Fall River and Taunton (the crowd awaiting her arrival in the latter city being enormous), the only evidence of agitation upon her countenance was a slight flush, and even the loud remarks of the mill girls as they pointed her out to each other apparently failed to disturb her equanimity. Certainly in Lizzie Borden some of the weaknesses of her sex are conspicuously absent.

The route taken by the carriage containing Lizzie Borden, Marshal Hilliard, Officer Seaver, and Rev. Mr. Buck toward the Fall River railroad depot was most peculiar. It is a direct road from the Central Station to the depot. Along the main thoroughfare were people eager to catch a glimpse of the prisoner, and the marshal, considerate of his charge, decided to disappoint the curiosity seekers. Accordingly the journey was up hill and down dale, through side streets, and along thoroughfares skirting the river.

Following the carriage were others containing the representatives of the leading newspapers of the East, and these latter drew up at the depot a few seconds in advance of the official vehicle. A squad of officers was on duty there, and as the crowd surged they pushed them back. The train for Taunton was a few minutes late, and until its arrival Lizzie Borden and Mr. Buck remained in the carriage. As the clang of the engine bell was heard the marshal pulled up the carriage curtains and assisted Lizzie Borden to alight.

She was prettily dressed and appeared quite prepossessing. She wore a blue dress of new design, and wore a short blue veil. At the realization that the moment for departure had arrived she seemed overcome by momentary weakness and almost tottered. She was at once supported by the marshal and Mr. Buck, and leaning upon the arms of these two she walked through the ladies' waiting room and out towards the cars. The eager crowd pushed and stared and gossiped as the party entered the rear car of the train. Rev. Mr. Buck carried a box containing a number of religious and other papers and magazines, and also some books. A telescope bag containing Miss Borden's apparel was placed in the cars. The prisoner sat near the window in a seat with Mr. Buck, and behind them was Mr. Hilliard. The blinds were drawn in order to prevent annoyance to Miss Borden by curious persons. Her glance was vacant and her thoughts were manifestly removed from her present surroundings. Not a word was exchanged between the members of the party, and the prisoner still remained in the same position, staring at nothing. In some manner the information that Miss Borden was upon the train spread, and at the few stations at which it stopped small knots of inquisitive people were gathered.

There was an incident at Somerset. Upon the platform of the station were a dozen young women, evidently mill employes, and the rear car of the train stopped directly in front of them. In the seat opposite the prisoner sat two newspaper men and as their window was raised the young women could look across and see the form of the prisoner.

"Oh, there she is!" called out one, "that's the murderess!" Then they all scampered toward the window and peered in.

Miss Borden must have heard the careless remark. But the trim figure in blue never stirred a muscle, but still retained the same attitude.

Taunton was reached at 4 20 o'clock. Awaiting her arrival was a gathering of hundreds, and they crowded about every car. Officer Seaver in order to attract their attention, hurried to the north end of the station and the throng hurried in that direction. At this time Mr. Hilliard and Mr. Buck escorted the prisoner from the south end of the station and into a carriage. Mr. Seaver joined them and the crowd found itself disappointed. After the vehicle rolled the cabs of the newspaper men.

Taunton Jail is not far removed from the centre of the city and is a picturesque looking stone structure. There is the main building and the keeper's residence, which is attached. On the outside of the structure ivy grows in profusion and the building does not resemble, except in the material of its construction, the generally accepted appearance of a place of confinement. It has accommodations for 65 prisoners, and the women's department is on the southeast side. In this portion of the building there are but nine cells, and before the arrival of Lizzie Borden but five of these were occupied. These were confined for offences of a minor nature, as it is not customary for the officials of Bristol county to send many women to Taunton, the majority being committed to the jail in this city, where there is employment for them. The matron is Mrs. Wright, wife of Sheriff Andrew J. Wright, keeper of the jail, and her personal attention is given to the female prisoners.

The officers had been notified of the coming of Miss Borden, and her arrival was unattended by any unusual ceremony inside the jail. Her step was firmer than ever as, unassisted, she walked up the three steps and into the office of the keeper. From there she was directed to the corridor which runs along the cells of the women's department, and here Mr. Hilliard left her. Returning to the office he handed the committing mittimus to Sheriff Wright, who examined and found it correct.

In the meanwhile Lizzie Borden was alone with the clergyman. He spoke words of cheer to her and left her in the care of the matron. Mr. Buck said she was not shocked at the sight of the cells, and, knowing that she was innocent, accepted the situation with a calm resignation. He said her friends would call upon her from time to timt, this being allowed by the institution.

The Cell

in which Lizzie Borden is confined is 9 1-2 feet high and 7 1-2 feet wide. Across the corridor, looking through the iron bars, her gaze will rest upon whitewashed walls. The furniture of the cell consists of a bedstead, chair and washbowl, and she will spend her time in reading. All the papers regularly subscribed for by her father will be forwarded to her, but they do not include the daily newspapers. At her personal request she has seen none of these and will not do so. Consequently she is not familiar with the comments of the papers regarding the case. Taken in charge by the matron, Lizzie Borden was escorted to the cell, and the iron doors clanged behind her.

Perhaps no person in Taunton experienced a greater surprise and shock at the arrival of Lizzie Borden than Mrs. Wright, the matron, in whose care the prisoner is. Sheriff Wright was for years a resident of Fall River, and at one time held the position of marshal of the city police, the place now occupied by Mr. Hilliard. Mr. and Mrs. Wright were well acquainted with the Borden family, but the first names of their acquaintances had slipped from their memory, and the sheriff and his wife did not connect the Borden they formerly knew with the prominent actors in this tragedy. When Lizzie Borden entered the presence of the matron the latter noticed something familiar in the countenance of the young woman, and after the retirement of Rev. Mr. Buck commenced to question her. Finally, after a number of questions, Mrs. Wright asked, "Are you not the Lizzie Borden who used as a child to play with my daughter Isabel?" The answer was an affirmative one, and the information touched Mrs. Wright to the quick. When she appeared in the keeper's office a few moments later her eyes were moist with tears.

With Noble Spirit.

Rev. Edwin A. Buck was asked by a *Standard* reporter how Lizzie bore herself, and his reply was:

"With the same noble spirit and Christian calmness in her innocence, as I believe, that she has shown from the first."

He had brought Lizzie some books for her reading, as well as some church weeklies. When asked what reading she would have, Mr. Buck hesitated somewhat. He was about to state, but finally said that he guessed he would not state, because it would go broadcast all over the country and he had marked a passage especially for her reading.

Mr. Carrier stated that it was not essential Lizzie should wear a prison dress. It was not customary with persons simply awaiting trial. The pastor, with the marshal and Officer Seaver, left the jail at 5 o'clock and the reporters soon followed.

Current Comment.

Lizzie Borden is a presumably innocent person in the eyes of the law until proved otherwise, yet from the talk on the train, in the railroad stations and in Taunton and Fall River one might readily believe nothing stood between her and the gallows. The strongest evidence against Miss Lizzie she is understood to have introduced herself. One of the officials who was present stated that as she proceeded with her story the case against her grew blacker and blacker. The most important parts of her testimony were tested. On the point of time that she remained in the loft great stress was brought to bear. It was held that the loft on a hot day was like an oven and it was considered impossible, to say the least, that a refined and cultured lady, unaccustomed to hardship, would remain in such a place for 20 minutes unless something imperative demanded it, when she could have remained quietly in a cool room within doors and waited until a cooler part of the day before making her search for the lead or whatever else she was after. She was forced to repeat her story time after time, and the prospect ahead looked darker as her examination proceeded. Although the impression cannot be fully confirmed, it is growing that Miss Lizzie was the strongest witness against herself. Inconsistencies did not necessarily have great weight, but parts of her story were regarded as improbable.

That is just the difficulty; just what Mr. Jennings complained of yesterday at the arraignment that it was possible that inadmissible questions under the rules of

Cell in which Miss Borden was Placed.

evidence had been put to Lizzie at the inquest and that she had unhesitatingly answered them.

Every Trail Should be Followed.

Mr. John C. Milne says: "Every trail should be relentlessly followed. But every one which leads away from the Borden homestead ought to be most welcome and ought to be pursued to the utmost, notwithstanding and even because of the strength of the counter-chain of evidence. The public desire the truth, much more eagerly than they desire a conviction, and they would far rather have no conviction than the condemnation of one not guilty; still, the truth, wherever it leads."

Gideon Manchester, drawtender at Stone Bridge, also saw Dr. Handy's strange man, or a man his exact counterpart, on Thursday, Aug. 4, at about noon. His brother George, who lives in Newton, R. I., was hired to drive a strangely excited man to Newport. This man gave him a full account of the murder, and was so little anxious to talk about it that Mr. Manchester began to draw him out. The first mention of murder was made accidentally and the man seemed vexed after he had talked about it. This man was very nervous. His face twitched under strong excitement. He did not think any more about it until he saw Dr. Handy's statement. The man he saw had the peculiarly white face, dark hair, eyes, and moustache. He was about 5 feet 4 inches high, and wore dark clothes. Mr. Manchester is now convinced that the man knew more about the murder than he told.

Bridget Sullivan.

Bridget Sullivan has been talking with her friends since she appeared at the inquest and was allowed to leave the Borden house. She solemnly asserts that she told all she knew about the murders, and that was nothing. She knew nothing about the murders themselves and knew of nothing that could possibly have led up to them. She strongly insisted on her belief that Miss Lizzie was not guilty. Medical Examiner Dolan has but little faith in the poison theory. As the *Standard* has stated, the only evidence that he expects from the return of the analysis of the stomachs and their contents is as to the time of the murders. The arrest yesterday was not the result of any return from Prof. Wood, as he has made none. No word is expected from him concerning the analysis for a week and possibly nothing will be heard for two weeks. It is stated on authority from the same source that there was testimony at that inquest which the public never even suspected.

The Inquest to be Reopened Monday.

The inquest, Judge Blaisdell decided last night, would not be reopened before Monday. The delay is to give the police time to work out some points they are in possession of, because all the authorities are tired out.

The Assassin's Weapon.

The hatchet supposed to have been used by the assassin is in the possession of the police. It is a peculiar weapon. It was this hatchet which was marked with what were supposed to be blood stains, and a white hair was said to have been found in the claws. There are few hatchets like it in existence; in fact, most of the doctors who examined it closely had never seen one like it. The top of this hatchet just fits into a number of the wounds on the murdered persons' heads, while the blade is just the length of several cuts. This implement may be an old-fashioned planking hatchet which years ago was discarded and had been thrown into the Borden cellar to rust away. The blade is about five inches in length at the edge, and is almost triangular in shape, the narrow part coming at the handle. The upper portion is shaped exactly like a claw hammer, but is horizontal to the handle instead of vertical. This part is about 4 1-2 inches in length from the end to the edge of the claws, which are particularly large and were evidently intended to be used in drawing spikes from floor timbers. The blade was sharp and perpendicularly thin up to about one inch from the edge, at which point it becomes thicker. Its general shape is like that of a headsman's axe, except that the claw destroys the uniformity of the contour. The handle is about 2 1-2 feet long, and the implement weighs in the vicinity of five pounds. It is an ugly looking affair, and would be an almost irresistible weapon in the hands of an infuriated person. When the two axes and the two hatchets were found in the cellar they were all examined together. Three were stained with rust, and the other was spotted with something that looked a little different from the others. It was more closely looked at, and in between the claws, firmly caught in the narrow steel, were two gray hairs. It looked convincing, but the doctors were not then satisfied. They made a microscopic examination of the stains. They were caused by blood, evidently from a human being.

Then the hairs were taken to the receiving tomb, and, under a microscope, were compared to those of the dead man. They were apparently identical in size and texture, and were certainly the same in color.

There was one more test. The blade was then compared with the cuts, and the top of the tool was measured with the indentations. Both fitted. So well were the doctors satisfied with the tests that they unhesitatingly pronounced the hatchet identical with the one that caused the wounds, and expressed it as their opinion that it was the same.

Property in the Family.

There has been an absence of suggestion concerning the motive for the two deaths in the Borden family. The police found a motive early in their researches. They have been looking for the murderer by the light of that motive. It is needless to say that they considered the love of money the motive. A. J. Borden possessed real estate valued at $173,000, according to the tax assessors of Fall River, personal property worth at a moderate appraisal, $30,000 more. His wife had about $5000 in her own name. The two girls owned personally property, principally mill stocks, valued at about $10,000 each. The family was better off than several families of the Fall River Bordens who live in grand style. Mr. Borden, it is said, early set his heart on accumulating wealth for its own sake, so he never spent it freely. It is alleged now that Mrs. Borden, who was a second wife, on more than one occasion spoke of having a large part of the property when her husband died. She may have meant that her husband was going to leave her property in his will, or that she expected to have large property from her dower rights in case her husband died intestate. About the first suggestion one can say nothing definite. Mr. A. J. Jennings is perhaps the only man who can state whether Mr. Borden was making an inventory of his property, preliminary to writing his will and whether Mr. Borden intended to divide his estate unequally between his wife and his daughters. If Mrs. Borden anticipated having a large estate in fee left her by the death of her husband, she was mistaken. The law in the case is confusing, but a statement of its application to the Borden case is easily made. Had Mr. Borden alone died and died intestate, Mrs. Borden would have received in the discretion of the Court of Probate not exceeding $5000 in real estate in fee, one half of all the real estate for use during her lifetime, with reference back to the children at her death, and such a fraction of the personal estate as the Court of Probate in its discretion allowed, this also for use during lifetime only. In a word, Mrs. Borden could have hoped to secure only rights to property which would depart from her control at the end of her life. In case Mr. Borden wished he could have entirely disinherited his children.

COTTAGE CITY NEWS.

Probability of the Erection of a New Sea View Hotel Structure.

[Special Dispatch.]

COTTAGE CITY, Aug. 13.—The owners of the Sea View property are in consultation with a Boston engineer to see if it is practicable to remove the building across the avenue to the site now occupied by the Casino. The engineer expresses an opinion that the hotel can be placed on its proposed location with considerable difficulty and that the job will be undertaken for $10,000. The hotel managers wish to enlarge the hostelry and Capt. Hart thinks a new building on the site of the present hotel, connecting with the old one, will be the most feasible plan. The Casino will be torn down or removed to a position west of that it now occupies and will be refitted for a dining room and kitchen. The Casino is a large building, but a large sum of money, say $5000, will be required to transform its interior into 24 sleeping rooms.

The Sea View hotel structure is 300 feet long, 75 feet high, and the main building is 60 feet wide. To remove it will require time and plenty of mechanical appliances. Capt. Hart prefers to build the proposed hotel where the old one is located, because the centre of the building or office rooms will be near the wharf.

Rev. Jabez Fox of Washington, D. C., will speak at Union chapel on Sunday evening next on "The Divine Language," in which the word of God is written. There will be a service of song and solo by Mrs. Milliken.

The catboat race in Vineyard Haven harbor, which was to have been sailed yesterday, was postponed because of lack of wind. There were seven entries from Edgartown.

Louis Pease's boat Ella and Eddie has a new mainsail.

Capt. J. B. Knox gave his lecture on "The Signal Service in the War of the Rebellion" in Union Chapel last evening for the benefit of the local G. A. R. post. The lecturer was assisted by Maj. A. H. Johnson, drummer.

Congressman Morse is a familiar figure about the Sea View. He is intensely interested in matters that pertain to the welfare of Cottage City.

The tennis tournament for the Tufts cup, which was to have begun yesterday, was postponed because of foul weather.

Steamer Nantucket yesterday passed a drifting whaleboat off Cape Pogue.

To-morrow, in the Baptist Temple, the programme will be as follows: 10 30 a. m., Rev. A. S. Gumbart, Boston; 3 p. m., Rev. Frank Rector, Fitchburg; 7 30 p. m., "A Business Man's View of the Gospel," by Elijah A. Morse of Canton.

Yesterday and to-day are being observed by the Baptists as Sunday school and young people's day. The speakers include Rev. O. P. Gifford, Chicago; Rev. W. H. Geistweit, Minneapolis; Rev. C. R. Blackall, Philadelphia; Rev. C. H. Spalding, Boston; Boston W. Smith, "Uncle Boston," Minneapolis; N. S. Greet, "chalk talker," Somerville; Rev. A. S. Gumbart, Boston; Abram T. Eddy, New Bedford; John H. Chapman, Chicago.

Rails have arrived to complete the street car line to the Lagoon.

Prof. Frisbee of New York is a splendid fisherman, but he got very wet in yesterday's rain squalls.

Postmaster Scranton says his business is far ahead of that of last year.

Many compliments are paid the *Standard* because of its full and reliable reports of the Borden tragedy developments.

MOTHERS RESPONSIBLE.

Simple Causes of so Much Cholera Infantum.

The Dangers of Stale Milk and the Milk of Unhealthy Cows.

Reason for Sorrow That Cold Mortality Figures Cannot Measure.

A child in the house is a wellspring of pleasure.

It enlivens all, and twining itself around the hearts of even the sterner sex, it is loved by everyone.

But it is the mother who enjoys most the delights of sweet friendship with the little one.

Children are what the mothers are,
No fondest father's fondest care
Can fashion so the infant's heart.

It is to her alone uprise
Its wakening arms; to her those eyes
Open with joy and not surprise.

It is the mother who is responsible for the health of the babe. It is she who sees the first shadow of illness. It is, unfortunately, too often her fault that the child is ill.

There is so much illness among children this Summer that half a dozen of the leading medical journals of the country have found it necessary to get out special editions upon the subjects of cholera infantum and the similar complaints of indigestion which have made such fearful mortality among infants.

Their pages overrun with the oft-told warning, that it is the children who receive insufficient nourishment from

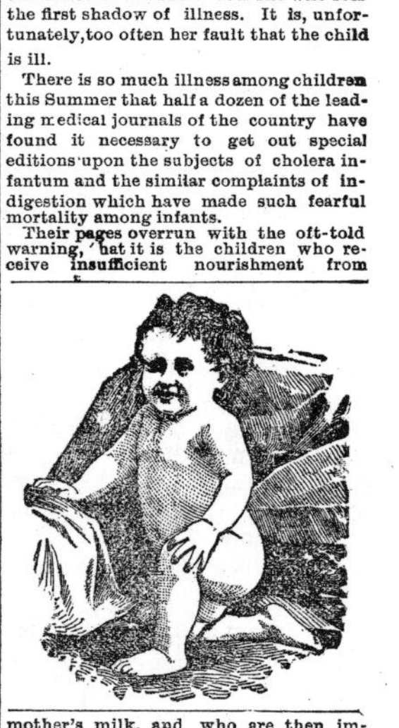

mother's milk, and who are then improperly "hand-fed," who have caused the sorrow that cannot be measured by the cold figures of mortality statistics. The advice to such mothers is:

Don't take any chances with secret preparations that are put upon the market in the guise of infant foods.

Beware of the dangers of stale milk, and milk from sick cows.

The milk-can on your door-step is one of the most fertile causes of Summer illness. To state the case mildly, it is hard in August to procure good milk.

If anything but breast milk must be given the child, use lactated food.

Lactated food is the most perfect substitute there is for mother's milk. Like nature's food, its basis is the purest sugar of milk. With it is combined the nutritious elements of the great cereals, wheat, barley, and oats, so prepared as to be readily digested and assimilated. The addition of the salts found in mother's milk makes it a perfect substitute. With the increase of cholera infantum, there has come from physicians and nurses an extraordinary demand for it.

Experience has proven that pure food and pure air are the only panaceas for the illness of infancy.

Thousands of mothers have found that nothing but lactated food will agree with their children. Mrs. August Spuhler, 59 Merrimac street, Haverhill, Mass., writes: "We have used lactated food for our little girl, and it furnished her nourishment when everything else failed. I send two photographs of her, one when she was nine months old, the other when 13 months old. [The latter appears above.] We began the use of the food when she was seven months old, at a time when she was very ill. She was quite backward in cutting teeth. Our family physician stated that she received no nourishment from my milk and recommended lactated food, which our friends also recommended. I am satisfied that to it she owes life and health."

NAMES FOR THE PARKS.

As several names have been offered for the lands lately purchased by our city for parks it is important that they should have a significance, and one as appropriate to their locality as possible. I would therefore suggest such as would most readily come to mind. For the estate purchased of Mr. H. E. Herman, "North Park;" for that granted by the United States government at Clarks Point, "South Park," and for that at the head of Court street, "West Park" or "Central." As to the naming from any former proprietor, the change of ownership since the original purchase by the Plymouth company of the old sachems of the Wampanoags, would make it impracticable. For instance, a local historical authority states that Clarks Point was owned by a Russell (Joseph, 1st,) before the Howland family, and subsequently by the Allens. Then the land lately owned by "the Greenes" was the western portion of the estate of Joseph Russell, the founder of the whale fishery here, and from whom our city received its name. The land bought of Mr. Herman was originally owned, in part, at least, by a Ward of Rhode Island, after by the Wrightingtons, then by the Perrys—subsequently by Gooding, Wilbur, Swift, Ricketson and Borden; from the latter of whom the last proprietor made his purchase. So, it will be seen, that the public would be better represented by such names as have no personal or family preference. In the case of a bequest, the name of the donor would properly be perpetuated.

DANIEL RICKETSON.

Aug. 11, 1892.

DRUGGISTS and grocers keep them. Chemists pronounce them first class. Physicians prescribe them for their patients. Connoisseurs have them on their sideboards. Once tried, always used, the G. O. Taylor Old Bourbon and Pure Rye Whiskeys. C. H. GRAVES & SONS, Sole Proprietors, Boston, Mass. Sold only in sealed bottles.

A Cook in the Time of Louis XVIII.

Louis XV had a genuine passion for horticulture. He did not content himself with perfecting a system of hothouses and of heating apparatuses for all his chateaux, but he gave impulsion also to the growing of grain of all kinds, of vegetables, and especially of new varieties of trees, for which so many royal nurseries were at that moment established.

But he was most at ease before a cooking furnace, now overseeing his ceufs a la fanatique, browned to a turn over a red hot fire, now preparing in accordance with established rules a beverage called coffee, just then coming into fashion, or concocting one of those pies which he sent, carefully wrapped up, to M. de Buffon in return for a quarter of venison received from that famous naturalist. At the same time as his father-in-law, Stanislas, Louis XV invented tables which came in without being touched by human hands to offer their contents to surfeited palates; but those of the king of France came up from under the floor, while those of the king of Poland descended from the ceiling.

One can almost imagine a monograph on monarchs who were gourmands, and we do recall Careme's witticism, "Is not the science which nourishes the equal of the one that kills?" a profound and sensible thought from a chef of whom Louis XVIII did not hesitate to take lessons. That king, who died afflicted with the gout for having indulged too freely in the pleasures of the table, merited one day the praises of the celebrated chef whose counsels he followed with docility.

A great lover of mussels, he gave Talleyrand the recipe for a sauce which added greatly to the taste of that dish; and as Talleyrand communicated to the king the reflections of his head cook, the monarch replied, "Careme is right, but I very much fear it will be a long time before I shall be able to create a minister of the public cuisine."—Paris Intermediaire.

The French flag was adopted during the revolution. The republic first took green, but gave it up and blended the Bourbon white with the red and blue, the colors of the city of Paris.

Playing cards were invented for the amusement of the crazy king, Charles VI, of France, in 1380.

The Evening Standard.

ESTABLISHED FEBRUARY, 1850.

NEW BEDFORD, MONDAY, AUGUST 15, 1892.

TWO CENTS.

HASKELL & TRIPP.

Hot weather hints.

Men's light ecru sateen sun umbrellas, $1.25 each.

Our parasols are selling at cut prices. We make no exceptions; *every one* marked down. You'll never need one more than you do this year.

Satin palm fans, and flat Jap fans, 3c. each. Folding fans, 5c. to 50c.; choice styles. Pocket fans of favorite sorts.

Drinking tumbler in leather case for 25c., or a nickled drinking cup that folds up to carry in your pocket for 25c.

Bay Rum in sprinkler top bottles (finest imported), 35c.

Florida water, 25c. up.

German Farina Cologne in long green bottles.

Made by Crown Perfumery Co., London. { Celebrated "Lavender Salts" and "Crab Apple Blossom."

Atomizers, 25c, 50c. and up to $1.25.

Sponges, 10c., 25c., 50c.

Rubber sponge bags, 20c., 25c.

Every good sort of toilet soap.

Celluloid soap box, 25c.

Remarkable bag bargain. 50 cents is the price.

The bag is of the new flat shape, leather on one side, with small change pocket, having oxidized clasp. The top is of cloth, with a drawing string, and there are double leather handles. We are selling immense quantities of them.

Pound package of good writing paper, 10c. (120 sheets.)

Pound package of "seconds," slightly, *very* slightly, imperfect writing paper of a high grade, 17c. a package.

Light literature.

Paper Covered novels, by famous writers of fiction, 10c. each, or three for 25c.

Sheet music, 5c., or six for 25c. More than 1000 titles. Catalogues free.

Sun bonnets, sun hats, cambric and gingham dresses for little children; at remarkably little prices.

HASKELL & TRIPP.

Department Stores,

Purchase and William Streets.

WEATHER INDICATIONS.

FAIR.

WASHINGTON, Aug. 15.—For the 24 hours from 8 a. m. to-day: For New England, fair, westerly winds.

GRADUALLY WARMER.

BOSTON, Aug. 15.—Local forecast for New England until Tuesday night: Continued fair, slight changes in temperature, followed by gradually warmer during Tuesday, variable winds.

CALLED PUBLIC SCHOOLS GODLESS

A Presbyterian Clergyman's Interview with Archbishop Ireland.

ST. PAUL, Minn., Aug. 15.—The Rev. L. H. Morey, a Presbyterian clergyman of Stillwater, gives the following account of an interview had between Archbishop Ireland and himself: "The archbishop charged the public schools with being Godless and professed a desire to introduce religious elements into them. I suggested that when I went to school we recited the Lord's prayer and read the Scriptures. I also suggested that committees of all religious denominations meet and formulate a ritual to be used as a textbook containing religious instructions that would not be obnoxious to any sect and which no persons of good morals could object to. He objected on the ground that I would not confess to the Catholic idea, admitting that what the Catholics wanted was the teaching of the Catholic religion in the schools. He cited an instance in which the State legislated in a matter of religion, requiring the observance of the Sabbath, and said that the State could not do that for the sake of religion, but to require the Sabbath observance of Sunday as a day of rest. He then said, 'Why not legislate in that way in the matter of public schools?' claiming that by such a plan the State would arrange religion. I objected to the Sabbath as not being a parallel, the Sabbath being common to both Catholics and Protestants, but that the Catholic religion, which he was advancing in his plans, was not common to both Catholics and Protestants. The Archbishop frankly admitted that the Protestant's conscience had good reason to be offended when Sisters of Charity were introduced into the central public schools and placed over Protestant children. I asked if I might infer from that that the garb of Sisters of Charity had a teaching force. This he practically admitted. The archbishop is an astute and plausible talker. But as I said to him, his plan involved the impossible condition of putting religious institutions by the State in the school, which is contrary to the laws and conditions of the State. I suggested that this plan was one that could stand only on its merits, and in the eye of the law this religious element robbed it of all merit. He seemed confident that some compromise would be reached by which the difficulties would be met."

YARD MEN MAY STRIKE.

Dissatisfied Men in the Employ of the Lehigh Valley and Erie Roads.

NEW YORK, Aug. 15.—The *Herald* says that the strike of switchmen and trainhands on the Lehigh Valley and Erie roads at Buffalo may extend to the yards of the various roads in Jersey City. The men in these yards received the same pay and are worked just as many hours as the switchmen in Buffalo. It was said in the Lehigh Valley yards yesterday that there would be a meeting some day this week of the members of the Switchmen's Mutual Society of North America in Jersey City to consider the question of ordering a strike in all the yards in the vicinity of Jersey City. This organization is made of conductors, switchmen and helpers. The men complain that they are required to work from 12 to 15 hours a day. They want to be paid extra for every hour they work over ten hours a day. They also want an advance in wages of from two to four cents an hour. There are 700 men employed in the Erie, 600 in the Jersey Central, 700 in the Pennsylvania, 300 in the Lehigh Valley, 500 in the Delaware & Lackawanna yards. They will all go out if a strike is ordered.

BROTHERS FIGHT A DUEL.

Rivals for the Hand of a Young Woman Resort to Deadly Weapons.

ATLANTIC CITY, N. J., Aug. 15.—It is said that a duel was fought yesterday at Woodstown, Salem county, between John Graves and William Graves, his brother, over a young women with whom both were in love. The Graves boys it is said have kept away from each other for some time. Yesterday, however, they met suddenly at Woodstown and after a few hot words decided to settle the quarrel between them by fighting a duel. The weapons used were pistols. Both men are said to have been wounded.

TELEGRAPHIC BREVITIES.

Ex-President Cleveland is strongly urged to visit the south.

Gould said to be planning a new transcontinental railroad line.

General N. G. Dunn of New York committed suicide at Denver.

W. K. Vanderbilt is to have two new steam yachts next season.

Classmate, Billy Bird and Leo won the closing races at Mystic park.

There was a fine display of fruits, flowers and vegetables at the Horticultural society's exhibition in Boston.

An Italian was probably fatally cut by a fellow-countryman at New Haven.

Satisfactory assurances has reached Berlin regarding Mr. Gladstone's foreign policy.

Free miners at Tracy City, Tenn., hustle convict laborers out of town and set fire to the stockade.

Judge Gresham says he is bound to no party and will make no political speeches this campaign.

Ex-Mayor Viall of Keene, N. H., is pleased with the outlook of his gubernatorial candidacy.

The returning Knights Templars from Denver met with a serious railroad accident near Clinton, Ia.

A demand has been made upon the Nicaraguan government for $25,000 for alleged indignities offered Dr. Meyer.

The Windsor and Tremont Houses, Marlboro, Mass., were raided, liquor being seized at both places.

Hon. S. S. Brown is the Democratic nominee for representative to the legislature at Waterville, Me.

Captain A. C. Fowler, Second artillery, United States army, is at Concord, N. H., to establish a recruiting station for his command.

A brakeman named Corliss of Woodsville, Mass., fell from a car at Groveland Junction, N. H., Saturday, and was instantly killed.

At Ridgefield, Conn., Friday, a hunting dog owned by George J. Jerome of New York, went mad and bit several dogs and two horses before being shot.

At Holden Haseltine's dairy farm, Moretown, Vt., five cows have died from anthax, and six others have been ordered slaughtered by the state inspector.

The loss to the town of Stowe, Vt., by the recent heavy rains will amount to thousands of dollars. Many bridges and roads were washed away, and the farmers will suffer.

Gustave Reider of Clinton, Mass., who shot his wife July 29 and attempted suicide, was arraigned at Clinton, pleaded not guilty, waved examination, and in default of $2000 bonds was taken to jail at ...burg.

BRIDGET SULLIVAN TALKS.

Important Statement Bearing on the Poison Theory in Fall River.

TAUNTON, Aug. 15.—A Taunton *Gazette* reporter learned from Bridget Sullivan on Sunday that the reason she laid down on the day of the Borden murders was because she was troubled with nausea that morning and vomited several times while washing windows. Previous statements from the police have been to the effect that she laid down because she was tired with the work. It is probable that this statement was held back, if made known at the inquest, as bearing upon the theory that the victims may have been dosed.

NEW STEAMSHIP FOUNDERED.

Large Vessel Just Built at Glasgow Went Down with All on Board.

LONDON, Aug. 15.—A large steamer named the Thracian, the building of which has just been completed at Glasgow and which was being towed to Liverpool, has been lost off the Isle of Man. Her crew of 17 men went down with the steamer. Everything went well until last night, when the wind freshened and in a short time was blowing a gale. The vessel was of course flying light, and as the sea increased she pitched and rolled heavily. The strain on the towing hawsers was tremendous and finally they parted. By this time the sea was so high that it was impossible to get other lines from the towboats to the steamer, and it was equally impossible for any attempt to be made to rescue those on board. The gale increased in violence and the towboats were compelled to heave to or ride out the storm. Then it was so dark that it could not be seen what happened aboard the steamer. The supposition is, however, that being perfectly helpless, she swung off into the trough of the sea and capsized. Those on the towboats saw her lights for some time after she went adrift, but the steamer went to leeward so rapidly that they were soon left. When daylight broke no traces of the steamer could be found, and the towboats made for port, where they reported that she had foundered.

CHILEAN ADVICES.

Favorable Legislation in Regard to the United States' Claims.

NEW YORK, Aug. 15.—A Valparaiso special to the *Herald* says that the protocol between the United States and Chile in regard to the establishment of a claims commission has been considered by the Council of State, and has passed for the approbation of Congress. It is thought that six months will be sufficient to make a full examination of the validity of the claims for the arbitrators.

The Trans-Andine Railroad Company has failed. It is probable that the Chilean government will invite tenders to complete the Chilean section of the road. There is a 6 per cent. guarantee on the investment. Argentine will probably follow Chile's lead with a view to the completion of the work, which is highly important.

The *Herald's* correspondent at Cuayaba, Mattogrosso, telegraphs that the government troops near Ponce had joined those under Eubauk and restored order in the province. There is no flour there, and provisions of all sorts are scarce, owing to the low water in the river. The revolutionary party committed many outrages, flogging some women for carrying cartridges to troops at Ponce.

FREIGHT CARS IN FLAMES.

Dastardly Work on the Erie Railroad Tracks at Buffalo.

BUFFALO, Aug. 15. — More dastardly work, which is attributed to the strikers, has been reported.

Word was received at 2 o'clock that a train of 42 cars on the Erie railroad, filled with fine merchandise, a mile east of William street, was burning fiercely with no protection. The switch lights on the Erie between Smith street and the Western New York & Pennsylvania target were stolen.

At 2 45 o'clock the passengers on the two trains on the Lehigh and Erie roads which had been ditched at William street, near the city line, were brought to the station by a special train. Nobody was injured, but the delay of four hours had been a dreadful experience.

Superintendent Brunn reported at 4 15 that the fire was still burning in the cars of merchandise at Cheektowaga, and says the sheriff seemed powerless to protect the property.

STRUCK AN UNKNOWN ROCK.

Damage to British Warship Warspite More Extensive than Supposed.

VICTORIA, B. C., Aug. 15.—A close examination of the British warship Warspite shows that the vessel's injuries are much more extensive than was at first supposed. A considerable length of her false bottom and steel plates have been torn away, and in three places bad indentations have been made in the actual bottom. She struck while steaming at the rate of 14 knots an hour and immediately listed to the starboard, having been hit by a rock about midships on the port side. Coming back with a plunge she again struck and though the engines were reversed she went ahead with acquired momentum. The chart issued by the British admiralty shows 30 fathoms where the rock was discovered. By a survey made by the officers of the ship it was ascertained that there was only three fathoms of water, while the Warspite was drawing 24 feet.

Seamen Kidnapped and Shipped Away.

VICTORIA, B. C., Aug. 15.—H. Sanson and five other members of the crew of the schooner Robert Lewis, have laid formal complaint before United States Consul Meyers that they were kidnapped by force by the Sailors' Union, while the schooner was lying at Port Gable, and shipped to this city. The consul will institute an inquiry.

Colorado Village Destroyed by Fire.

OURAY, COL., Aug. 15.—The entire town of Red Mountain, comprising about 60 buildings, was destroyed by fire early yesterday. The loss is about $275,000; insurance $150,000. Many people are homeless and aid is being sent them from adjoining towns. The fire was of incendiary origin.

Rumors of Rebellion in Costa Rica.

CITY OF MEXICO, Aug. 15.—San Jose, Costa Rica, advices state that rumors of rebellion are rife and that an outbreak might occur at any moment. The Conservatives deemed that their rights were being infringed upon and it was stated that they were buying arms in the United States.

Fatal Shots at a Negro Dance.

NASHVILLE, Tenn., Aug. 15.—At a negro dance in Donovan & Daly's construction camp near Marion, John Bowie (colored) fatally shot James Elliott and Samuel Hayes (white) and seriously wounded another negro laborer. He then made his escape.

Cholera's Deadly Ravages.

TEHERAN, Aug. 15.—The mortality at Tabriz is estimated at 3000. The cholera is raging with great severity. The governor and the wealthiest inhabitants have fled, and the town is almost deserted. The mortality in Teheran is about 150 a day.

The Ocean Steamers.

Arrived—At New York, Greece, London; Finance, South America. At Boston, Austrian, Glasgow.

DESERTED WIFE AND CREDITORS.

Further Developments in the Norridgewock (Me.) Scandal.

NORRIDGEWOCK, Me., Aug. 15. — The scandal which has kept this town in a state of excitement for the past week was about dying out when the sheriff's sale of the Knowlton shoe store brought to light two things: First, that Knowlton's letters to his wife, stating that he had left her abundantly provided for, are false, and further, that instead of there being any funds, there are bills pouring in from every side, and Mrs. Knowlton is left without a cent. For some ten years Knowlton has resided here, keeping a shoe store, and for a long time had a fine trade, making a host of friends and having the respect of the community. This continued until about a year ago, when there moved into the town a family by the name of Patty, consisting of a man, his wife and a bright little boy of 5 years.

The man secured work in Brackett's grocery store. The wife went about but a very little, and after a short time it was noticed that Knowlton had become quite intimate with the family, going to the house a good deal, which caused some talk. One week ago Knowlton left the town, taking the Patty woman with him. and sending by mail letters to his wife, stating that he would never return to her, as there were reasons which would make it impossible, adding that he had left money invested which would abundantly support her. The poor wife was prostrated over the affair, which was made doubly worse by the thought that there might be more in his leaving than the letters signified, which was verified only too quickly by the rumors about town and the positive statements made by those who said they saw the pair depart.

Saturday Knowlton's creditors caused the sheriff to dispose of the stock of goods. The sheriff, upon opening up the store and examining the stock, found that a large inroad had been made into it, and it is said several bills of goods which had been received lately had been run off at ruinous prices, to obtain money wherewith to skip. Mrs. Knowlton is as fine a woman as there is in town, being a general favorite with those of her acquaintance, but somewhat of an invalid. The Patty woman was plain in appearance and not fascinating. Consequently much surprise has been manifested at the state of affairs.

A DAY OF DISASTERS.

Many Pleasure Seekers Find Watery Graves on Sunday.

LYNN, Mass., Aug. 15.—A sad drowning accident took place in the surf on Nahant beach, near Hotel Nahant, yesterday afternoon at 3 o'clock, the unfortunate being George T. McLaughton of 58 Lincoln street, Malden. Mr. McLaughton went to the beach to bathe with his brother, Martin B., and when they entered the water quite a number of others were enjoying the sport. A short time after two little girls, Katherine Fitzgerald and Lillian Whitmore, felt something strike their feet, and to their horror discovered that the object beneath the surface was the body of a man.

The crowd at once notified Officer Gaffney, who with assistance got the man out and sent him to the undertaking rooms of Haven & McGovern on Central avenue, Lynn, as it was found that he had drowned before being discovered. At the undertaking rooms the remains were identified as those of George T. McLaughton by his brother Martin, who was nearly prostrated by the shock. Mr. McLaughton was an assistant professor in the Institute of Technology, Boston, was 25 years of age, unmarried, and highly respected by all. His mother died about two weeks ago, and his father, who is an elderly man, is in Newport, R. I., for his health. Medical Examiner Pinkham reviewed the remains and stated that it was accidental drowning. It is believed that McLaughton was taken with cramps, which bore him down before he could have time to call for assistance.

Four Lives Lost at Warren, R. I.

WARREN, R. I., Aug. 15.—David Murray, wife and daughter and a child, named Forbes, were all drowned in Palmer's river yesterday afternoon by the upsetting of a boat. The father of the child, Freemen Forbes, and wife and another occupant were saved. The party was returning from a clam bake, when one of the party stood up in the boat which was overloaded and upset it. All the bodies, excepting the child's, were recovered.

The Crowd Saw Him Drown.

PROVIDENCE, Aug. 16.—Patrick Hessen, aged 35, a weaver at the Riverside mills in Olneyville, was drowned while bathing in Benedict pond on the outskirts of this city yesterday. Hessan swan out into the middle of the pond, intending to swim across, but sank in the presence of a crowd along the shore, who could render no assistance. Hessan came from Amesbury, Mass., where he has two sisters. The body was recovered.

Caused by Liquor.

PROVIDENCE, Aug. 15.—Charles Marshall of Woonsocket, while laboring under a delusion that he was being pursued by policemen, jumped into the Blackstone river Saturday night, and was drowned. The body was recovered Sunday morning. The deceased had been drinking. He was about 23 years old, a moulder by trade and leaves a widow.

Other Drowning Accidents.

Robert E. Howe of Yale college, a waiter at the Irving House, Block Island, R. I., was drowned in the surf at the island. His home was at Vernon Centre, Conn.

Frank Reynolds, a son of George S. Reynolds of Plainfield, N. J., was drowned at Hammer's grove, Lake Cobboseecontee, near Agusta, Me.

Albert, the 8 1-2-year-old son of Henry B. Fairbanks, the auctioneer, of Manchester, N. H., was drowned while rowing on Lake Massabesic.

Found Dead in His Cell.

PROVIDENCE, Aug. 15.—William Baxter, 40 years of age, belonging at Woonsocket, was arrested Saturday night for drunkenness. Yesterday he was found on the floor of the cell at the central station dead, having died from concussion of the brain. It is thought that the man rolled from the bench, causing the fatal injury.

Released from Jail.

SALEM, Mass., Aug. 15.—Thomas D. Brown died in Salem jail yesterday of consumption, aged 28 years. He belonged in Gloucester and at the January, 1892, term of the superior criminal court was convicted and sentenced to three years for breaking and entering.

Big Increase Over Last Year.

SAN FRANCISCO, Aug. 15.—During last week 3818 tons of green fruit were shipped east from California. So far this season 6,500,000 pounds more fruit has been shipped than last year.

THE LIBERAL CABINET.

Mr. Gladstone Off for Osborne House to Inform Her Majesty.

LONDON, Aug. 15.—Mr. Gladstone, accompanied by Sir Algernon Edward West, left Carlton Gardens at noon today for Osborne House to lay before Her Majesty the names of those who will comprise his cabinet and to carry out the old custom which obtains of the statesman who is summoned to form a government of kissing the hand of the Queen. Notwithstanding persisted rumors as to his physical condition Mr. Gladstone looked remarkably sprightly. Instead of the journey being looked upon in the light of a severe task, his every appearance indicated it was a pleasure jaunt for him. The Liberal leader appeared fresh and smiling and was the recipient of hearty cheers as he left the doorway of the house in Carlton Gardens. Mr. Gladstone took his seat in a first class saloon car. Here he extracted a tube rose from a small box and carefully pinned it in the buttonhole of his coat. As the train pulled out the crowd cheered Mr. Gladstone, who responded by lifting his hat and bowing.

RECEIVER WILL BE APPOINTED

On Account of Loose Management, Although the Iron Hall is Solvent.

INDIANAPOLIS, Ind., Aug. 15.—The scene of activity in the Iron Hall trouble has been transferred to Philadelphia. Supreme Justice Somerby, Supreme Cashier Davis, a number of supreme trustees and the attorneys of both sides have left for that city. It develops that at the conference of attorneys with Judge Taylor it was agreed that the mutual bank should be taken from the control of its officers and placed in the hands of some person agreed upon, so that the funds of the order might be protected before the receivership suits proceed further. It is regarded as certain that a receiver will be appointed, though it is solvent, on account of the loose management developed by Somerby's testimony in court.

ENORMOUS DEATH RATE.

Fifty Per Cent. of the Cholera Cases in Russia Prove Fatal.

ST. PETERSBURG, Aug. 15.—The cholera outlook has become more favorable and hopes are expressed that further spread may have been checked by the stringent sanitary regulations enforced by the authorities. Yesterday only 12 deaths from cholera were reported.

The report shows that throughout the infected districts of Russia the daily average is 8601 new cases and 4288 deaths from the disease. It will be seen that the death percentage is enormous, being nearly 50 per cent. of those who are attacked.

HOME MATTERS.

PERSONAL.—Mrs. S. S. Briggs and Miss Estelle C. Bolles leave the city to-day for a three weeks' trip to Bar Harbor and Palermo, Me.

Mrs. Capt. McInniss of bark Josephine has arrived down from Ounalaska in steamer St. Paul and is on her way home to this city from San Francisco.

Fred S. Fuller and J. H. Hathaway of this city are registered at the Oak Hill House, Littleton, N. H.

J. G. Child and wife have started on a trip by carriage, going to Middleboro for a time, and from there to the Cape.

Capt. A. F. Rosa, of the well known steamship Vega, sailing from New York to the Azores, Portugal and Spain, was in the city to-day, visiting his uncle, Mr. P. J. Maciel, on Park street.

RETURN OF THE GUARDS.—The tour of duty of the First Infantry at Fort Warren, Boston Harbor, was completed on Saturday, and the regiment broke camp and boarded a steamer which cast off and steamed for Boston after cheers were interchanged by the men and garrison. On reaching the city a review was had before Gov. Russell and staff, Adjutant General Dalton, and other military officers, followed by dress parade. The regiment was then dismissed, and Co. E boarded the cars and arrived in this city on the 6 40 train. On reaching the armory, Capt. Perry expressed his thanks to the men for their promptness and general good order during the tour of duty. The men are much more pleased with the camp than they expected to be. The best of relations were established with the garrison, and regulars and militia fraternized like brothers.

WHALER SEIZED.—Whaling bark Lydia, Montgomery, of San Francisco, was intercepted by U. S. Steamer Rush in Bering Sea, while taking newly-killed seals from on board whaling bark Northern Light, Simmons, of San Francisco. A prize crew was placed on board the Lydia, and she was sent to Sitka.

CHANGE OF STEAMERS.—Steamer City of Fall River arrived at this port yesterday morning, discharged, and sailed at noon for Newport, where she is to be overhauled, and the City of Brockton, which takes her place on the line, will arrive to-day, and sail for New York to-night.

A LITTLE BRUSH.—Ben Slocum's catboat Minnie B., which was beaten in the Mattapoisett regatta Saturday by John Welch's Daisy, had a race home after the regatta and beat the Daisy by nearly 10 minutes.

GIVEN A CHARTER.—The Rockland & Abington Street Railway, on certificate of exigency from the railway commission, has been given a charter at the office of the Secretary of the Commonwealth. Capital $60,000.

A FEW PAIRS LEFT of those fine dongola button boots at the low price of $1.25 a pair. Remember the sizes are 2½, 3, 3½; widths, B, C, D, E. Just the thing for girls wearing ladies' sizes. Union Shoe Store.

ALL OF OUR LIGHT COLORED pants must be closed out this month at a great reduction. Men's and youths' suits in light weights and colors must be closed out. Wamsutta Clothing Co.

VACCINATED. — The crew of whaling schooner Antarctic, which arrived in port yesterday afternoon, was vaccinated by Dr. William C. Sheehy, acting port physician.

INSANE.—Matthew T. Rowe has been adjudged insane, and will be taken to the asylum at Taunton to-day by Officer Wing.

DOMESTIC FASHION REVIEW for Autumn has arrived, price 10c., at the Corset Store, 19 Purchase street.

FIFTY CENT TIES for 25c.; socks, three pair for 25c.; $3 hats to be closed out for $2, from best manufacturers. Wamsutta Clothing Co.

TAKE ONE of those marine or field glasses with you on your vacation that J. S. Kelley & Son are closing out at $6.50, at 15 Purchase st.

FALL STYLES in Domestic Paper Patterns have arrived at 19 Purchase street.

HEALTH is secured by an absolutely fair, open pore skin.

MISS PARLOA'S Complete Cook Book for 10c. at Hutchinson's Book Store.

RHEUMATISM cured. 5 South Sixth street.

BLACK CLOTH Overgaiters 50c. Devoll's.

TUB BATH—25 cents. 5 South Sixth street.

HOOD'S Sarsaparilla is purely vegetable.

DIVIDED!

BROKEN IN TWO!

CUT IN HALVES!

The above is what has happened to the prices on our

Summer Furniture.

We have about 50 pieces consisting of

PIAZZA CHAIRS, SETTEES, ROCKERS, ARM and EASY CHAIRS,

which we propose to close out at once. We mention a few styles and prices to illustrate:

Lawn Seats $1.50, Now 75c.

Common Rockers $2.75, Now $1.37.

Patent Rockers $5.50, Now $2.25.

Piazza Settees $6.50, Now $3.25.

Piazza Settees $5.50, Now $2.25.

This is an opportunity to add a few pieces to your cottage or piazza furniture at a very small cost.

C. F. WING,

34 to 40 Purchase St.

WHITING & CO.

GREAT BARGAINS

—IN—

Ladies'

Cotton Underwear

20 doz. more of those fine Night Dresses, at 50c. apiece.

25 doz. of elegant Night Dresses from 75c. to $2.87 apiece.

10 doz. Ladies' White Cotton Skirts from 50c. to $2.50 apiece.

100 doz. of Ladies' Cotton and Cambric Corset Covers, at 25, 37, 42, 50, 75c. and $1 apiece, all fine and nicely made, try them.

We are selling Infants' Long and Short Dresses, very cheap, get our prices.

If you want Infants' Slips we can suit you on prices and quality.

See our Corset stock, as we have all of the popular makes sold.

WHITING & CO.

OUTING SHIRTS!

OUTING SHIRTS! OUTING SHIRTS!

You can never have too many

OUTING SHIRTS!

Our low prices will help you out. Quality exceptional.

Good Shirts for $1 and $1.25, laundered collars and cuffs.

Another lot of the popular blue Madras, all sizes, $1.50.

Better come at once, They're going fast.

J. & W. R. WING & CO.,

133 UNION STREET.

OUTING SHIRTS!

THE CRESCENT!

22 Purchase St.

Damask Towels 15c. Going, going, gone, unless you purchase immediately.

Towels, 4 for 25c., still on sale.

O, how light and airy. Chiffon Handkerchiefs, for the button-hole. Beauties,

Only 25 cents.

RIBBONS.

We don't *begin* to tell you *how much* we have *marked down* our line of Ribbons, but come and see for yourself.

We will close out our Gingham Dresses for children at *cost*. Sizes from 4 to 10 years of age.

Gloves, 15, 25, 37, 50c.

Corsets, a good corset for 39c.

An X-L-ent Corset for 50c.

A very nice Summer Corset, C-B a la Spirite, price $1.25.

Corsets at all prices.

Having removed our entire stock from the Old Stand at corner of County and High streets, we sha[ll] be pleased to see our old fri[ends] and patrons at our new qu[arters] 22 Purchase street,

THE CRESCENT

THE BORDEN TRAGEDY.

Police Tirelessly Sifting Possible Clews to the Murder.

Statements by Lizzie A. Borden to Matron Russell.

Additional Comforts Placed in the Imprisoned Woman's Cell.

Interest in Fall River's double tragedy continues unabated, and every morsel of intelligence, whether clews followed by the police, actions of Lizzie A. Borden, or her reputed sayings, how she passes the time in jail, and what the government or defence proposes to do is eagerly sought and devoured with avidity. Although Miss Borden is under arrest the police are by no means idle, and they are following with untiring energy everything that promises to throw light on the great tragedy.

Clews.

Clews, or alleged ones, relating to the Borden murders continue to be sifted by the Fall River police. Among others was one of a suspicious person reported by a farmer as having ridden with him on the road toward Newport on Friday morning succeeding the day of the murder and who seemed to know a good deal about the tragedy. Officers Harrington and Doherty Saturday drove along through the villages of Stonebridge, New Portsmouth, Bristol Ferry, Bliss Four Corners, Tiverton, R. I., tracing this man who corresponded with the description given by Dr. Handy of a man he claimed to have seen on the morning of the murder near the Borden house. He was found to be a tramp who had been working on a farm near Fall River during the Summer, having got through there the day of the murder. He started Friday morning for Newport and entertained the farmers who gave him rides with accounts of the murder. He was found to be all right.

Another report of a suspicious party came from this city Saturday and Officer Medley looked into it. The story rested upon the fact of a tired and hungry man going into a drug store there and buying five sticks of candy.

Officers Linehan and Harrington scoured the woods over beyond the Chase mill for a man said to have been seen near the Borden house on the day of the murder. Mr. Ogswell denied the statement and said he had not been near the Borden house, as he was directing a gang of laborers at Forest Hills.

A Clew Not Before Reported.

A clew has been reported that is of such a remarkable character as to warrant investigation. The Boston *Globe* says a gentleman employed in Boston had occasion on Friday last to visit Nonquit. He was unable to transact his business in season to return by boat and therefore, after completing his business, hired a team at the livery stable in Nonquit to be driven to New Bedford. The driver, an employe of the livery stable keeper, was a bright New Bedford young man of perhaps 24 years. When the buggy in which the pair were seated were approaching at right angles a road running from Fall River to New Bedford, near a long, old-fashioned country bridge, the driver narrated to the *Globe's* informant how, on the afternoon of the murder he was driving over this same road, when he came across a man from 5 feet 7 inches to 5 feet 9 inches in height, wearing a dark felt hat and making extraordinary time in the direction of New Bedford from Fall River. He was not an every day pedestrian that attracted the attention of the driver. His general appearance was peculiar and the driver says he can swear to the man if he should see him again, as can also several other near by residents. The driver thought the pedestrian was an Italian or a Portuguese. As the team passed him the driver said he saw that the hands of the man were covered with blood, not bespattered, but literally soaked, the blood being caked in between the man's fingers.

The driver describing him said: "I thought the man had been killing hogs." Another thing which the driver noticed was the bundle which the latter carried. It was about as large as a couple of shirts or a pair of overalls and jumper, but it was soaked with blood, as the driver remarked, and looked as if dipped in a bucket of blood. Other than the blood on the man's hands and his bundle, the driver did not see any blood, none being noticed on his clothes.

In presenting this clew the gentleman says:

"Now, it is evident that whoever committed the crime in Fall River covered their tracks as but few have done before. What would have been an easier way of committing the crime than for the man about to do it to dress himself for the occasion, as would a butcher about to work at his trade? It was in the afternoon of the fatal day that the driver says he saw this pedestrian en route towards New Bedford. Others are known who saw the man. As I don't believe Lizzie is guilty I think the matter ought to be looked up. Of course, the clew is several miles away, but in justice to the girl it ought to be investigated."

Borden Mutiny Clew Exploded.

The dispatch from Lynn published in the *Standard* on Saturday afternoon connecting the imprisoned mutineers of the schooner Jefferson Borden with the murder of Andrew J. Borden and his wife on the score of revenge for their alleged testimony against them caused much excitement in Fall River for a time until it was ascertained that neither Mr. or Mrs. Borden were aboard the schooner on that voyage.

The story, however, is effectually refuted by a personal dispatch from the Warden of the State Prison at Thomaston, Me., in which he states that both George Miller and William Clark, the ringleaders in the Jefferson Borden mutiny, are still in custody there.

The Lynn dispatch was shown to Mr. Walter of Walter, Friend & Co., who are Boston ship brokers. Mr. Walter said: "Yes, I remember the trial. It was away back in '76. Capt. Patterson had killed two of his sailors and the rest of the crew were up for an attempt to murder. Two were discharged and the others got life sentences and are still in jail at Thomaston. Their friends tried to have them released some time ago, but Capt. Patterson got up a petition to keep them in and it was granted. They're still at Thomaston. But you'd better see Mr. Kinsman around on Doane street.

Mr. Kinsman, commission merchant at 19 Doane street, said: "Yes, I do know all about the matter. Capt. Patterson claimed that the men rose against him and murdered the second mate and one other, and tried to kill him and his wife and three children.

"Andrew J. Borden wasn't on the vessel at all. The only people in her cabin were Capt. Patterson and his wife, two mates and the steward."

Why the Pinkerton Man Left.

In an interview with Robert Pinkerton at New York in regard to the Borden murders he said, in reply to a question whether Lizzie Borden's arrest was justified by the facts, that he thought it was, but that such action did not necessarily imply that she was guilty. It would be quite possible for a person to enter the house by stealth and commit the crime without being seen, and to prove the point Mr. Pinkerton mentioned several cases where large sums of money had been stolen by expert sneak thieves in broad daylight.

When asked if he thought the murderer an insane person, he said:

"Judging from what I have read about the case, it seems to me that the person who killed Mr. and Mrs. Borden must have been insane, but I would not care to be quoted as advancing an insanity theory.

Continuing, he said: It seems strange that there are no more conclusive clews to be followed if the reports of blood-stained walls and ceiling are true. If they are in such a condition the murderers must have gone away with blood stains on his clothing. Now, where are these bloody clothes? The more fact that Miss Borden has told conflicting stories is more in her favor than if she had unhesitatingly stuck to the same tale, as an innocent person is more likely to make conflicting statements than is a guilty one."

Concerning the Pinkerton detective who was placed on the case and who was severely criticised by the Fall River authorities, he said:

"The authorities seem to have thought that our detective was brought into the case for the purpose of protecting Lizzie Borden from them. Such was not the case. He was hired by the family to follow any clews that might lead to the detection of the criminal. He has been removed from the case at my suggestion, as I thought it unwise to have a private on the case until the authorities had reached some decision."

The lawyer who has charge of Miss Borden's interests Mr. Pinkerton considers a very clever man, and thinks her interests will not suffer while under his care.

Comforts for Lizzie Borden's Cell.

Lizzie Borden's cell has been made more comfortable by Mrs. Andrew R. Wright giving her one of her own big feather pillows to replace the hard one that goes with prison cells, and a rocking chair from her own cosey home in an adjoining wing of the jail. The white counterpane and pillow slip of the cot bed, the browns which she had on Friday and fruit that Emma brought when she came Saturday, served to relieve further the badity of her narrow quarters, though the Taunton

---

Ferry, Bliss Four Corners, Tiverton, R. I. [continued above]

Statements by Lizzie A. Borden to Matron Russell.

cells are larger than in some jails, and they are absolutely clean, painted white, as are the stone corridors, relieved with a very light green.

Lizzie's Turn to Come By and By.

Mrs. Russell, the matron in whose charge to all River Lizzie A. Borden passed the hours from the time of her arrest Thursday until she was taken to Taunton Friday, was much impressed by her composure and entire absence of nervousness. The prisoner impressed her as being a woman of considerable deliberation of one who was bound to have her own way. Mrs. Russell thinks eventually Miss Borden will break down, although she thinks she will maintain her composure until her trial. She was not a troublesome charge. During all the hours Mrs. Russell was with Lizzie she never alluded to the crime but once, and that was just before her departure for Taunton.

"So they are going to take me to Taunton, are they?" asked Lizzie.

"I believe they are," replied Mrs. Russell.

"Well," continued Lizzie, "they seem to do about as they please with me. They were up to my house and brought me down here to the inquest twice, and then they brought me here for a rest and I did not know what it all meant. Now they are going to take me to jail. They are having their own way with me now, but I will have mine by and by."

The Coming Examination.

The government is it stated will be ready to proceed with the examination upon the day appointed for the hearing, 23d inst. There is no probability of the defendant waiving an examination and consenting to being held for the grand jury, as Mr. Jennings, her counsel, prefers to have the evidence against his client put in and contest the case in the lower court.

Press Comment on the Tragedy.

The Boston *Herald* editorially says: It was a pathetic scene that a Boston reporter witnessed at Taunton when Lizzie Borden entered the jail with her aged pastor by her side, and met for the first time in many years the matron of the prison, who had been a neighbor in Fall River when she was a child, who used often to receive visits from her as a child, and who had lost sight of her in the interval of years, but had not forgotten her name or the promise that her childhood gave. The scene was too much for this old neighbor who was now to have her in charge. "Oh, Lizzie, Lizzie," was the cry of the matron as she met the child, now grown to be a woman, accused of a terrible crime. It was one of those meetings where all the defences of life are torn asunder and people speak out of the anguish of their hearts. Every great disaster or crime has its pathetic side, and it is only in the chasms that open up us that we realize the meaning and the mystery of our existence. This little incident at the Taunton jail, contrasting the innocent childhood of a little girl with her accusation as a mature woman of complicity in a terrible tragedy, is one of those contrasts, awful beyond expression, which seems to search down to the very depth of one's soul.

Mr. Jennings' Plea in Bar.

The point raised by Andrew J. Jennings, counsel for Lizzie A. Borden, regarding the disqualification of Judge Blaisdell to sit in judgment upon Miss Borden, and to pass upon the question of probable cause to hold her, attracts to him more than an ordinary share of interest on the part of his brother attorneys. He holds that it would be "almost beyond the bounds of human nature" for Judge Blaisdell not to pre-judge this case by the evidence which he has already heard in this secret inquest against the defendant, whom the police had suspected from the first, which testimony was not open to her. Eminent counsel of Fall River say that the State constitution and the law throw a protection around those accused of murder, which is entirely destroyed by this method of secret "star chamber" inquests. It is proposed to take this matter up to the Supreme Court for its decision, and if it shall establish a construction upon the statute involved it will be a matter of very great interest to both bench and bar in future cases.

Pathetic Reference to the Unfortunate Family from the Pulpit.

FALL RIVER, Mass., Aug. 15.—Rev. Dr. Mason of the Bordoin College church, Brunswick, Me., supplied the pulpit at the Centre Congregational church yesterday, where union services were held by the parish of Rev. W. W. Jubb and Rev. Dr. Adams. In opening the services Rev. Mr. Mason prayed tenderly and sympathetically that the Lord would be with the stricken Miss Borden in her present misery; that he would give her strength to bear up under the terrible load that is oppressing her.

Dr. Mason took the simple and appropriate words "Our Father" for the text of his sermon, and during his discourse made the following reference to the Borden murder: "A dark cloud has settled down upon one of our families. But God is in that cloud. He is with that poor, tried tempest-tossed girl; he will give her strength and peace; he will make her glad. It is impossible for a wrong to be done in this world that eternity will not undo. Good is coming; good out of evil; light out of darkness. The father is over all. He will vindicate, and raise and glorify."

ANHUNGERED AND ATHIRST.

Fairhaven Experiences a Revival of the Enforcement of Sunday Laws.

One grand sweep of piety seems to have taken possession of Fairhaven yesterday, and accordingly the visitor in search of a cooling draught of "Ginger" ale or a few morsels of the succulent clam was forced to turn away anhungered and unappeased.

Grimshaw, who had extensively advertised a clambake at Fort Phœnix, was obliged to smother his claims and fires, while the cheerful smile of Snow's soda fountain was hushed and dumb.

This unwonted quiet state of affairs in accordance with action taken at a meeting of the Selectmen held Saturday afternoon, when a petition signed by many officials of the Improvement Association was taken up. It protested against allowing the venders at the fort to keep open on Sundays, on the alleged ground that it drew to the fair village a class of people from this city who are not wanted over there. Whether this be true or not, the Selectmen in their wisdom decided to prohibit the bakes.

Then up rose Selectman Peck, who, incidentally happens to be an uncle of Mr. Grimshaw, and said if Sunday piety is to affect the caterer, it should likewise fall upon the druggist with his soda apparatus. His oratory carried the day and later Constable Delano, chief of the Fairhaven police, was given orders to close each and every place of business in the town.

When notified that he could not sell cigars and soda, Mr. Snow's clerk, B. A. Wells, in the absence of the proprietor on a vacation, in charge of affairs, decided the rest of his Sunday trade about worthless, and locking the doors, hung up a sign "Gone to campmeeting." Mr. Card, who has an ice cream wagon at the Fort also suspended business.

Hundreds of horse car excursionists returned to this city happy and mad, while from the tone of their remarks, one would not be led to infer that in their enforcement of the Sunday laws to the very letter, they have struck a popular chord.

REUNION OF VETERANS.

The Independent Battalion, Massachusetts Cavalry Association, will have its reunion in this city July 24th and

A Mother Saved Her Boy's Life.

"I believe lactated food saved our little boy's life," says Mrs. Jennie Bashford of Quinter, Kansas. "He was poor and puny, and cried all the time, until we commenced feeding him the food. He is now several months old, fat and hearty, and he owes it all to lactated food."

COTTAGE CITY.

The Season is High and a Great Crowd Present.

[Special Dispatch.]

COTTAGE CITY, Aug. 15.

Yesterday was the greatest day of the season. The hotels could not provide food for the visitors. At the Pawnee the demand for entertainment was so great that a line of people in waiting for dinner seats extended to the sidewalk.

The famous steam yacht Vamoose called here yesterday, and the guests aboard visited the club.

Dr. Sullivan of Providence, R. I., was the guest of T. F. McCormick in the club cottage on Saturday. The doctor has just returned from a cruise to the eastward in his yacht Wilful of Providence, R. I.

Cottage City money freely changed hands on the catboat race at Vineyard Haven yesterday.

Following is an analysis of the water furnished by the water company: Turbidity, slight; sediment, slight; color, none; residue on evaporation, 3.70; chlorina, .02; hardness, .6; nitrogen, .0000.

The new residence of William M. Clarke at Lagoon Heights is rapidly assuming proportions.

Mr. Frank Brewer of New York will build at the Heights this Fall.

Funeral services over the remains of Mrs. Lucy Van Derlip were held yesterday at the Episcopal church. The interment will take place at Mt. Auburn.

Rev. Jabez Fox of Washington, D. C., conducted the Union chapel service last evening.

A Mr. Raymond of Boston found the diamond ring recently lost on the beach. The stones were discovered by using a sand sifter from the Wahan park croquet courts.

Miss Susie Rand, daughter of William H. Rand, is entertaining Miss Mary Powell of Chicago.

Members of a Taunton church choir are domiciled in the Clarpe cottage.

Robin Damon, founder of the Salem *Evening News*, is a guest at the Pawnee.

Leon Parker, a Hartford, Ct., cyclist, is sojourning here.

Mrs. Eliza Sparrow of Mattapoisett is at the Wesleyan avenue cottage.

Mrs. F. H. Eaves is entertaining Mrs. G. G. Bampton of Boston.

The Katama clambakes are well patronized.

Schooner yacht Brentwood of Portland, Me., is off the bluffs.

Chief Justice Calvin E. Pratt of Brooklyn, N. Y., is a guest of Dr. H. A. Tucker.

Mr. and Mrs. Dwight Wilcox of Meriden, Ct., are sojourning at Cluster Village.

At the Baptist Temple, yesterday, the speakers were Rev. A. E. Gumbart of Boston, Rev. Frank Rector of Plettsburg, and Elijah A. Morse, M. C., of Canton. Mr. Abram T. Eddy, president of the association, led the morning prayer meeting. The Chapel Hill cottage, Narragansett avenue, is undergoing extensive alterations.

Rev. T. S. Grimes of Stoneham is here for a few days.

Miss Lolie Williams of West Bridgewater is at No. 2 Cottage Park.

The Sunday school rally at the Baptist temple closed Saturday evening. A quarterly review was conducted by Rev. W. H. Gelstwert, A. T. Eddy, Rev. A. E. Gumbart and Miss Gambart. "Uncle Boston" spoke upon "The King's Favorites" and John H. Chapman of Chicago, Ill., president of the Baptist Young People's Union of America, on "Our Young People." At the illustrated lecture in the evening addresses were delivered by Rev. A. S. Gumbart and Rev. O. O. Fletcher, D. D., assisted by an Indian.

Elijah A. Morse of Canton last evening addressed a large audience in the Baptist temple on "A Business Man's View of the Gospel." It was interesting and instructive.

FALL RIVER.

Alfred Baxinet of Bedford street has received a communication from his son Joseph, who disappeared from his home 12 years ago without leaving any trace behind him as to his whereabouts. The letter was written in California and contained a check for $500, and Joseph said that he had made money in stocks in New Orleans and had removed to California, where he is now at the head of a promising mining enterprise.

There are 41,797 books in the Fall River Free Public Library.

PLYMOUTH COUNTY.

George W. Hathaway of Rochester has some chickens, a cross between white Leghorn and white Sherwoods, that are without feathers except a few on the tips of the wings and legs.

John Foster of Hanson and others, who were awarded $1350 by the county commissioners, with interest from 1856, for damages occasioned by the taking of Big Sandy pond by Abington and Rockland for a water supply, are not satisfied with the award and have brought suit against both towns. The writ is returnable in September.

BARNSTABLE COUNTY.

At a regular session of the Probate Court, held at Barnstable, 9th inst., the following business was transacted:

Wills proved—Of Benjamin P. Sears of Dennis, Olive Sears executrix; Freeman Rogers of Dennis, Charles G. Baker executor; Isaiah Crowell of Barnstable, Eliza B. Crowell executrix.

Administrations granted—On estate of Pauline Kendrick of Harwich, Isaac B. Eldridge administrator of the bonds now with will annexed; Jabez Davis of Falmouth, Walter O. Luscombe administrator de bonis non with will annexed; Christina C. T. Human, W. T. Chapin, administrator; Theophilus B. Snow, Harwich, Albert O. Long, administrator; Augustus A. Parker, Dennis, Warren Parker, administrator; George F. Buckley, Barnstable, Elizabeth J. Buckley, administratrix; Raymond Killington, Provincetown, J. H. Hopkins, administrator de bonis non.

Guardians appointed—Warren Parker, guardian of Carrie O. Parker of Dennis, minor; Edwin A. Rich, of Clarence A. Rich of Provincetown, minor; Susan R. Perkins of Winifred R. C. Perkins of Barnstable, minor; Watson B. Kelley of Braston E. Allen of Harwich, insane; Watson B. Kelley, of Samuel J. Allen of Harwich, insane; George B. Bassett, of Mehitable Bassett of Chatham, insane; Warren B. Hamblin of Stephen Hamblin of Falmouth, insane.

Licenses to sell real estate granted—To Abizall Fanney administrator of estate of Isaac Brickett of Mashpee; Emeline Wixon administratrix of estate of William Wixon, Dennis; Mary C. Crowell, guardian of Sarah A. Robbins, et als, Barnstable; Mary F. Leonard, of Jonathan Leonard, Sandwich; John Kendrick, administrator of estate of Frederick Kendrick of Orleans; Christine J. Mott, administratrix of estate of Jesse Mott, Barnstable; William J. Davis, administrator of Maria W. Howes, Barnstable; Thomas F. Kendrick, guardian of Thomas Kendrick, Harwich.

A 65 pound codfish was recently taken at Provincetown.

LABOR DAY CELEBRATION.—The trades committee on the observance of Labor day in this city at a meeting made progress in the proposed celebration. Walter N. Caswell and Benjamin Glidden of the Typographical Union were present.

A committee on sports, including Mr. Caswell, chairman, and James R. Savage and Michael Rowan, was selected.

It was decided that at 9 o'clock in the morning a procession shall form at the Cove street grounds and march to River View Park, where a basket lunch will be served. The afternoon procession will form at City Hall at 2 o'clock and march to the Cove street grounds, where the sports, under the auspices of the committee, will begin at 2:30 o'clock and continue until 6 o'clock. A charge of 15 cents will be made for admission to the grounds. In the evening there will be a dance at the Cove street grounds.

It Strikes us as Remarkable to hear of the wonderful record for curing enjoyed by Bettoa's Infallible Pile Salve; it cures every form of this troublesome malady. It cost to be had at your druggist's, or send 50 cents to Winkelmann & Brown Drug Co., Baltimore, Md.

FINANCIAL.

SECOND EDITION.

HOME MATTERS.

BRISTOL MANUFACTURING CORP.

Meeting of Stockholders for Organization To-Day.

A meeting of the stockholders of the Bristol Manufacturing Corporation for the purpose of organization was held at the office of Sanford & Kelley this forenoon. A constitution and by-laws were adopted and the following were elected directors:

Cyrenus W. Haskins, New Bedford; Thomas H. Knowles, New Bedford; Edward Kilburn, New Bedford; John P. Knowles, Jr., New Bedford; William H. Parker, Lowell; Rufus A. Soule, New Bedford; Thomas B. Wilcox, New Bedford; Benjamin Wilcox, New Bedford.

Benjamin Wilcox was elected clerk and treasurer.

The capital of the corporation will be $500,000, the full amount having been subscribed. The first payment will be 10 per cent. September 1st. The annual meeting of the corporation will be held on the third Thursday of July.

At a meeting of the directors subsequent to meeting of the stockholders, Thomas H. Knowles was elected president.

REAL ESTATE SALES.—T. F. Healey has sold for Rodolphus Beetle and others a lot of land at the corner of Coffin avenue and Bowditch street, containing 40 rods, to Daniel McAuliffe.

M. E. Smith has sold for a syndicate to John T. Champion a lot of land on the north side of Perry street, containing 13.36 rods.

Mary Enos de Terra, administratrix of the estate of Joseph Enos de Terra, has sold to Antonio Ignacio da Rosa, buildings and a lot of land west side of Second street, south of Blackmer street.

Rodolphus Beetle and others have sold to John F. and Alice A. Riley, 11.33 rods of land west side of Howard avenue.

Joseph Jackson has sold to Mary E. Smith, a tract of land in Westport at the south end of the road dividing Dartmouth and Westport.

BUILDING NOTES—Gideon Polsson petitions for leave to build for Joseph Poisson an addition 45½ by 12½ feet with 10 feet posts and flat roof in rear of building northwest corner of Water and Delano streets, to be used for business purposes.

Bernard O'Brien petitions for leave to move a building 29 by 19 feet with 12 feet posts from No. 60 Rivet street to the rear.

Edward Boland petitions for leave to erect a dwelling-house from its present location on Reynolds street to a location in rear of same lot.

Edward J. Boland desires leave to erect a dwelling-house on the east side of Reynolds street, north of Linden street. It is to be 24 by 40 feet, 22 feet posts.

DID NOT BEAT HER—We are requested to state that catboat Minnie B, Capt. Slocum, did not beat John Welch's boat Daisy at the Mattapoisett regatta on Saturday, as reported in a morning paper. Mr. Welch states that he did not race with the Minnie B. on the way from Mattapoisett to this port, as stated. He also states that if Mr. Slocum wants to race the Minnie B. against the Daisy he is ready at any time to accommodate him.

PERSCENA—Smith Marshal and wife returned this morning from a two months' trip through England.

Miss Emma J. Moore is spending her vacation at St. John, N. B.

HELD FOR ATTEMPTED RAPE—Charles Crank (colored) was held in bonds of $2000 in Fall River to-day on a charge of attempted rape on a six-year-old girl named Jennie B. Merkle.

DIVIDEND.—The Southern Massachusetts Telephone Co. has declared a dividend of $2 per share, payable to-day.

DEATHS.

In this city, 14th inst., Sarah, widow of Joseph B. Howland, aged 70 years. Funeral at the residence of Charles W. Ricketson, 17 Allen street, Tuesday, at 3 o'clock. Relatives and friends are invited to attend.

In Fairhaven, 14th inst., Phebe T., widow of John Shaw, aged 84 years 4 months.

Funeral at the residence of George F. Richard, corner of Summer and Rodman streets, Wednesday, at 1.30 o'clock. Relatives and friends are invited to attend.

In Mattapoisett, 13th inst., Nancy Boodry, aged 77 years 7 months 25 days.

Combination
Perfect

The predominating qualities of Flavoring Extracts should be absolute purity, excellent flavor and superior strength.

All of these elements are combined in a perfect degree in **Dr. Price's Delicious Flavors;** therefore if the housewife wants a complete cake, pudding or cream, she should make use of them.

Those who want the very best flavorings are never disappointed in purchasing Dr. Price's Vanilla, Lemon, Orange, etc., which are as natural as the fruit from which they are extracted.

MARINE INTELLIGENCE.

ARRIVED THIS AFTERNOON.

Sch W H Swan, Davidson, Philadelphia.

Sld from Stonington 14th, sch S L Thompson, Keefe, Taunton for New York.

Ar at New York 14th, steamer Nacoochee, Smith, Savannah; sch Oliver Ames, Nickerson, New Haven.

Passed through Hell Gate 14th, schs Wm A Morrill, Bacwell, New York for this port; W D Hervel, O'Keefe, Hoboken for Boston.

Ar at Philadelphia 14th, schs Mount Hope, Crowley, hence; Henry Lippitt, Coombs, Boston; D M Anthony, Berry, Kennebec; Julien Nelson, Kelley, Washington; 15th, Warren B Potter, Andrews, Nantucket.

Ar at Baltimore 14th, sch Independent, Case, Georgetown, D C. Cld, 13th, sch W C Tanner, Johnson, this port.

FINANCIAL.

MONDAY, Aug. 15.

Many good railroad reports have held railroad stocks steady to-day. The industrials, not being effected by these statements, have enjoyed a small boom of their own, backed by such energetic leaders as "Deacon" White and "Jim" Keene. Sugar during the forenoon touched 108½. Western Union has also been strong, selling at 99½.

The situation of the local market for money is unchanged.

The Boston money market is easier to-day. At the clearing house all the loans were made at 4 per cent. New York funds sold at 12½, 15 and 17 cents discount.

Time money in New York, says the *Financial Chronicle,* is freely offered from all quarters, but the business is light, the lenders desiring to make short contracts while the borrowers seek for long engagements. Rates are 2 per cent. for 30 days; 3½ per cent. for 60 to 90 days; 3 per cent. for four to five months, and 3½ for six to seven months on good mixed collateral. Commercial paper is only in fair demand, the banks confining their purchases to really first class names; yet the supply does not accumulate. There is no change in the sterling exchange market.

Bonds steady.

Wall street gossip this morning said: "Crop gossip was not so favorable as it was a week ago, but the Cammack party and some of the Western brokers are working hard on the bear side of the Grangers. Bull talk continues in Western Union, Industrials and Trunk lines. The decline in silver causes apprehension in England and India. London perceptibly better.

Stocks opened active and firm in New York to-day. Atchison 37½, B. Q. 101½, Erie 27½, St. Paul 82½, Reading 59½ and Western Union 99½. Sugar sold at 107½ at the start. At 11 o'clock the market was strong, Sugar leading at 108½, Western Union 99½ to 99½, St. Paul 82¾. At noon prices were off fractionally, Atchison 38, Reading 59, Sugar 108½, General Electric 115½, Rock Island 80. In the early afternoon the market was dull but prices were well sustained. At 1 o'clock Union Pacific was leading on a rally to 38½, probably on some favorable earnings report. Reading reacted to 58⅜.

The market at 3 o'clock was steady. Union Pacific strong at 38½.

Calumet & Hecla was the feature of the Boston market this morning, when one sale at 300, earlier sales being made at 290 and 295. The general market was fairly active, with Atchison 38¼ and Union Pacific 38⅞. In the early afternoon the market was dull and prices firm.

At 2 o'clock the market was strong except for West End common off ¼ to 78½.

Sales to noon in Boston to-day were, bonds $69,300 and 916 shares of stock.

Union Pacific, whole system, June gross increased $395,672; net increase, $535,896.

A 10.30 Wall street special says: "St. Paul story is confirmed in crowd on exchange."

Among the industrials National Cordage has been taken largely for Boston account up to 127½ for the common and 117¾ for the preferred, both the best figures ever reached. It is claimed the common will touch 130 before next Saturday.

Prime, in his last week's crop review, says the country has enjoyed a good week for harvesting and maturing backward crops. Corn has suffered some in Kansas, but elsewhere has done fairly well.

Dow, Jones & Co. say at 10.40 this morning: "Union Pacific earnings for June are expected to-day, and it is said both gross and net will show large increases."

A Chicago dispatch say: "We hear that notices will be sent to stockholders of record of the St. Paul road asking them to vote on making the dividend 2½ per cent. on common. This is to give the directors an indication of stockholders' wishes at the forthcoming meeting."

Atchison earnings for first week of August increased $48,363; Frisco increase $31,105; total increase $79,438.

The recent depreciation in silver is largely the result of manipulation and bear attack for the purpose of producing an effect upon values, products as well as stocks, says that shrewd observer, Mr. Henry Clews. It serves no good purpose, therefore, for silver to be dealt in on the New York Stock Exchange at the present time, especially when such results are aimed at and are so easy of accomplishment. During the war gold was originally dealt in on the New York Stock Exchange, and it was moved up and down most erratically for speculative purposes. The effect was seen to be injurious, and from a spirit of patriotism it was stricken from the list and the dealings prohibited. The same should be done with silver, for the white metal now occupies the same position at the exchange in its dealings as did gold during the war period.

Guaranteed Cure.

We authorize our advertised druggist to sell Dr. King's New Discovery for consumption, coughs and colds, upon this condition. If you are afflicted with a cough, cold or any lung, throat or chest trouble, and will use this remedy as directed, giving it a fair trial, and experience no benefit, you may return the bottle and have your money refunded. We could not make this offer did we not know that Dr. King's New Discovery could be relied on. It never disappoints. Trial bottles free at E. A. Blackmer's drug store. Large size 50 cents and $1.00.

Why Don't You Stop

coughing before the entire mucous membrane lining the air passages leading to the lungs becomes irritated, and your health from a cough neglected? There is but one remedy that gives instant relief and cures quickly. Dr. Hale's Household Cough Cure cures every kind of cough from a simple cold to incipient consumption. 25c. and 50c. bottles at Wright Drug Co., 49 Purchase street.

The silver question is daily becoming more prominent as an influence in the market. The present weakness of the bullion is believed to be the effect, in part at least, of manipulation. It is said that a combination of rich Jews in London have been short of silver and rupees ever since they were held at much higher prices. They are selling silver in New York in small lots, but enough to break the price and make quotations which astonish the world and enable them to cover their shorts. The weakness of silver tends to restrain London from buying our stocks as well as to frighten holders here. The situation at present has lent additional prominence to the proposed silver conference.

Mr. J. B. Colgate, the bullion dealer and an eminent authority, takes a gloomy view of the situation, and declares that if matters continue as they are going it will "eventually result in a bankruptcy over the world such as has never been witnessed before," and that any one can see how the intimate relations of England with all silver-paying countries will result most disastrously to her trade and bring about results far more pernicious to her than the failure of the Baring Bros.

Emery & Tucker think that there will probably be something to trade on in the coppers by Sept. 1, but there is not now. Meanwhile the market for the metal in New York continues listless and uncomfortable, owing to the absence of any demand. During the next few weeks the market is liable to remain inactive, manufacturers having had all their needs supplied for that period. Casting copper is a trifle lower at 10½, with Arizona pig unchanged. In London no change is recorded for S.M.B. at £44 10s to £44 12s 6d.

Aggregate earnings of 36 railroads for first week of August were $5,052,946, an increase of $258,877.

Chicago & West Michigan earnings first week of August increased $258,877.

The shipments of iron ore from Lake Superior ports continue much in excess of those of last year. The arrivals last week aggregated 200,000 tons. Last year the movement did not commence until August owing to ore handlers' strike at Lake Erie ports. The shipments are an excellent source of revenue for the Duluth & South Shore, Chicago & Northwest, St. Paul and Wisconsin Central. It is estimated that shipments thus far this year have aggregated 4,500,000 tons.

The *Financial and Mining Record* reports $1,447,625 paid in mining dividends in July, and $9,202,215 in seven months of this year.

The *Beacon* says: "The pool that is holding sugar common is composed of 'Jim' Keene and 'Deacon' White of New York and four or five Boston men. The aggregate wealth of this crowd is $15,000,000 or $16,000,000. They are in the pool for business, and their purpose is, if it is in the power of man, to put the price to a very high figure. That they aim at putting it to 125 there is no reason to doubt."

The gross approximate earnings of the Cleveland, Canton & Southern railroad in July were:

Period.	1892.	1891.	Inc.
July.	$89,600	$75,672	$13,827

This is against $41,666 in June, and the increase of $13,327 over July, 1891, follows an increase in that month of $24,623 over July, 1890.

Flint & Pere Marquette's earnings for the first week of August compare as below with the same week of 1891:

First week August.	1892.	1891.	Dec.
Freight.	$45,165	$61,321	$13,156
Passenger.	29,180	29,745	10,565
Total,	$46,165	$61,321	$13,156
Since Jan. 1,	$1,719,138	$1,727,745	$8,607
Mileage,	625	625	

Salt shipments for the first week of August netted the Flint & Pere Marquette $307.44, as against $387.06 the corresponding week in 1891, a decrease of $3560.62.

In the statement of the Flint & Pere Marquette for the first week of August the unusual earnings for the first week of August, 1891, are accounted for by the national encampment of the G. A. R., which was held in Detroit. Passenger earnings in the corresponding week of 1890 were but $486.

NEW YORK PRODUCE MARKET.

NEW YORK, Aug. 15.

Flour sales 5100 packages; quiet and steady. Wheat sales 210,000 bushels; dull, steady; local trade, no features. Corn sales 90,000 bushels; firmer, dull; west, higher. Oats sales 5,000 bushels; dull and firmer. Beef dull, lower. Pork quiet, easy. Lard dull, weaker. Butter quiet, easy. Cheese quiet, easy. Sugar (raw) firm. Petroleum firm and quiet. Turpentine quiet. Molasses quiet. Rice good demand. Freights quiet. Rosin quiet. Tallow quiet.

PROVISIONS AND GRAIN.

CHICAGO, Aug. 15.

	Opening.			
	Lard.	Wheat.	Pork.	Sh't Ribs.
May		85⅛		
June				
July				
Aug.				
Sept.		78	12.40	52½
Oct.				
Nov.		79½		51½
Dec.			13.47½	
Jan.				

	Closing.			
May				
June				
July				
Aug.		78	12.40	52½
Sept.				
Oct.				
Nov.				
Dec.				
Jan.		13.30		51½

LIZZIE BORDEN'S ARREST.

Marshal Hilliard Replies to Criticisms on His Actions.

District Attorney Has Evidence Not Known to the Public.

Borden Family Honor Will Not Defeat Purpose of Justice.

FALL RIVER, Aug. 15.—City Marshal Hilliard was this morning shown about 50 editorials clipped from various papers published in New England during the past few days. Most of them reflect a belief in Miss Lizzie Borden's entire innocence of the crime charged against her, and assail the Fall River police for prolonged delay in the case and for directing their efforts wholly toward proving Miss Borden guilty.

Marshal Hilliard read most of the editorials carefully and flushed once or twice when his actions were criticised pointedly. He spoke warmly as follows, and said it was about time out of town people suspended judgment in Lizzie Borden and her arrest by the Fall River police. "I started on an outside clew within a half-hour of the discovery of the tragedy on information furnished by members of the family. I have chased down more than 100 outside clews within ten days. My officers were as sceptical as I was about who committed these crimes, and it was not until all the evidence was in that action was taken. You and every other citizen must remember that the newspapers have not given anything near the facts disclosed at the inquest. This case will depend on circumstantial evidence wholly, and the people's interest cannot be subserved by throwing the evidence into the hands of the defence until a hearing or trial takes place. You and the public may rest assured of that fact.

The district attorney and myself are satisfied that the public authorities have ample cause for holding this girl, and she has not been imprisoned in haste nor without a full understanding of what her arrest means."

A great deal has been said in out-of-town papers about the cruelty of detaining a finely bred and sensitive woman as Miss Borden is. One of the greatest complaints that has been made against the police administration of police affairs has been that he was too easily moved by his feelings, too sentimental to be a police officer. That he has a very kind heart and a courteous manner is acknowledged by all the members of the Borden family, and they do not blame the authorities for the harshness of the arrest.

A great deal of nonsense is being published in connection with the case about the Borden family honor.

On this point the most important member of the "Royal" Borden family said for publication this morning: "The honor of the Bordens, whose name is so closely allied with the prosperity of the town, is not to be affected by a police suspicion perhaps resting justly on Miss Lizzie Borden. No true Borden has ever placed a stumbling block in the way of the law and no member of my family will in any way hamper the police in their investigations. Andrew J. Borden was highly respected by them, but the statement that $15,000,000 of Borden money will be used in balking the authorities is untrue and ill-advised."

The Fall River *Globe* will say editorially to-night:

There is a strong disposition on the part of a great many people to condemn the district attorney for having ordered the arrest of Lizzie Borden on the questionable assumption that he lacked sufficient evidence upon which to base a presumption of guilt. This criticism is based largely on the strength of what has beengiven by the press as a full account of the evidence elicited at the inquest. It is hardly necessary to say that the published stories of the proceedings are very incomplete and fragmentary, perhaps some of them mythical, and a great deal may have been colored according to the fancy or imagination of the reporter who had found himself forced to supply links in the scattered and disjointed accounts he has gathered of what transpired at the inquest to make a complete whole.

At all events the accounts are incomplete and, it is needless to add, not authoritative. No statement of what transpired at that inquest bearing the indorsement of anybody connected with the management of the government side of the case has been published. The latter have persistently refrained from discussing the subject and have refused to be led into the admission or denial of the correctness of what has been published. Taking such evidence therefore as has been printed as a basis on which to insist on the guilt of or to condemn the action taken by the district-attorney is manifestly unjust.

It is an instance of whether a little knowledge is a dangerous thing, and in view of all this, hasty conclusions are to be deprecated. No new facts have transpired since the arrest to indicate any change in the situation, and unless some should we can only repeat what we have already advised, that there should be a suspension of judgment until the government has submitted its case before a judicial tribunal, after which the public will be able to discuss the matter intelligently. In the advance of that is it difficult to understand what value can be put upon any opinion which individuals may form.

Stabbed by an Italian Tramp.

WAYLAND, Aug. 15—William Gilfoil, station agent of the Boston & Maine road at Tower Hill, was seriously stabbed in the right side this morning by an Italian tramp whom he found sleeping in the station. The assailant fled into the woods.

Business Troubles.

LONDON, Aug. 15.—On petition of the creditors of the financial house of C. De Mottzi & Co., Limited, of No. 7 Adams court, Old Broad street, a receiving order in bankruptcy was made to-day against the company.

When Baby was sick, we gave her Castoria.
When she was a Child, she cried for Castoria.
When she became Miss, she clung to Castoria.
When she had Children, she gave them Castoria.

LEFT THE PORTUGUESE BEHIND.

Vega's Passengers Detained by Obstinacy of Steamboat Line.

NEW YORK, Aug. 15.—Two hundred and fifty Portuguese who were landed at Ellis Island from the steamship Vega from Mediterranean ports on Saturday were still on Ellis Island yesterday, and Assistant Immigration Commissioner O'Beirne said their detention was due solely to the obstinacy of two steamship companies.

Half of the entire party were booked to go by the Norwich line to Connecticut, and the rest had tickets over the Fall River line to Boston. They were sent in two parties to the North River piers of the lines mentioned on Saturday afternoon; but both companies refused to take the passengers on the ground that there was not time before sailing time to handle the immigrants' baggage. So they were bundled back to Ellis Island, to the deep disgust of the assistant commissioner. He wrote a letter to each line yesterday instructing them, it is said, that if they refused immigrants in the future the immigrants would be sent to boarding houses, and their expenses charged to the steamboat company so refusing.

Neither steamboat line will, it is declared, pay any attention to the assistant commissioner's letter. It was declared impossible to send the passengers on when they reached the piers.

THE FREIGHT CAR FIRES.

Firemen at Buffalo Impeded in Their Work by Lawlessness.

BUFFALO, Aug. 15.—The police commissioners were busy to-day swearing in special policemen on account of the strike. The sheriff was also busy swearing in special deputies for duty in the yards. The sheriff will not call upon the militia except as a last resort. The fire department complain that the work of the men at the freight car fires was much impeded by the cutting of hose by unknown parties. Twelve lengths of hose were cut and rendered useless during the night. The number of Erie and Lehigh Valley freight cars destroyed is variously estimated from 100 to 200.

Grand Master Sweeney emphatically condemns the acts of lawlessness, and states that he has assurances from the men on strike that they were not responsible for what was done, but it was the work of irresponsible individuals.

STOCK AND BOND MARKETS.

Bids at the close of First Board.

NEW YORK, Aug. 15.

GOVERNMENT BONDS.

US 2s, registered	100
new 4s, registered	115½
new 4s, coupons	115½
currency 6s, 1895, (Pacifics)	107

RAILROADS

Atchison	37⅞
Clev., Cin., Chicago & St. Louis	66⅜
Chicago & Eastern Illinois	
Chicago & Eastern Illinois pre.	
Chicago, Burlington & Quincy	101½
Delaware & Hudson	133
Delaware & Lackawanna	155½
Erie	27⅜
Illinois Central	
Lake Shore & Michigan southern	134½
Louisville & Nashville	69¾
Michigan Central	
Missouri Pacific	
New Jersey Central	136
New York & New England	38½
Northern Pacific	20
Northern Pacific pref.	55½
Chicago & Northwestern	116½
New York Central & Hudson River	113½
North American	
Oregon Navigation	
Oregon Improvement	
Oregon Short Line	
Philadelphia & Reading	59
Pullman Palace Car Co.	
Chicago, Rock Island & Pacific	80½
Chicago, Milwaukee & St. Paul	82¾
Chicago, Milwaukee & St. Paul pref.	
Richmond Terminal	
St. Paul & Omaha	53
St. Paul & Omaha pref.	
Union Pacific	38½
Wabash, St. Louis & Pacific	11½
Wabash, St. Louis & Pacific pref.	24½

MISCELLANEOUS

Ontario Silver	41
Pacific Mail Steamship Co.	34
Sugar, common	108½
Sugar, pref.	101½
Western Union Telegraph	99½
Silver Certificates	

BOSTON, Aug. 15.

BONDS

Atchison 4s	81¾
Atchison Incomes	37¾
American Bell Telephone 7s	114
Chicago, Burlington & Northern 5s	
Chicago & West Michigan 5s	
Mexican Central 4s	68
Illinois Steel Co. 5s	

RAILROADS

Atchison, Topeka & Santa Fe	38½
Boston & Albany	
Boston & Lowell	191
Boston & Maine	181
Boston & Providence	250
Chicago, Burlington & Quincy	101½
Chicago & West Michigan	
Cleveland & Canton	5½
Cleveland & Canton pref.	19½
Flint & Pere Marquette	
Flint & Pere Marquette pref.	
Mexican Central	
New York & New England	38½
New York & New England pref.	90
Old Colony	182½
Oregon Short Line	38½
Pullman Palace Car	198
Union Pacific	38⅜
Wisconsin Central	
West End	74
West End pref.	87½

MINING

Butte & Boston Mining Co.	20½
Calumet & Hecla Mining Co.	290
Catalpa	1½
Centennial	25
Franklin Mining Co.	12½
Kearsarge	12½
Montana	
Osceola Mining Co.	37
Tamarack	153

MISCELLANEOUS

American Bell Telephone	203¼
Erie Telephone	62
Mexican Telephone	52
New England Telephone	90
Boston Land Co.	5½
Boston Land Co. pref.	
San Diego Land Co.	
Topeka Land & Development Co.	16
Lamson Store Service	25
Thomson-Houston Electric	90½
Illinois Steel Co.	105
Am. Sugar Refineries, com.	108½
Am. Sugar Refineries, pref.	101½
Gen'l Electric	115
*Asked.	

WANTS.

All Advertisements under this heading to 30 a word a time. No charge less than 25c.

FIRST-CLASS BLACKSMITH HELPER for carriage work. Apply to GEO. L. BROWNELL. aus-1t

ROOM TABLE AND TWO LAUNDRY GIRLS wanted. Apply at 5 Fifth street. aus-1t

GIRL—For general housework; no washing. Apply at 46 Fifth street. aus-1t

---

DAINTY SHOES FOR DAINTY FEET.

SCHULER BROS., - - - - 76 and 78 Purchase St.

WEATHER INDICATIONS.

MORE SULTRY.

NEW YORK, Aug. 15.—At 8.30 a. m. the weather was clear, wind west, temperature 72. The *Herald* says: In the Middle States and New England to-day, considerably warmer. On Tuesday, warmer, more sultry and fair to partly cloudy weather will probably prevail, the same conditions lasting through most of Wednesday.

Named for Her.

A pretty story of the way in which a new name was added to those in common use by Dr. Coan, one of the early Protestant ministers on that group. When the missionaries reduced Hawaiian to a written language, it was found that all the sounds could be represented by five vowels and seven consonants; in foreign words there were no allied to them.

Thus, to the native eye and ear K represents the sounds of D, G, J, Q, S, T and Z; L stands for R, and B and F are written P. All syllables must end in a vowel.

One day Dr. Coan was called upon to baptize a child and to give it the name of Maikia. Although he was well acquainted with the native language he had never heard the name before. Accordingly, after the parents and the baby had left the house, he proceeded to search his books for the name, but failed to find it.

He sent for the father of the child and asked:

"What does Maikia mean?"

"Aole ike au" (I don't know), replied the father.

"Where did you get it?"

"From you. We named the boy after your wife."

"But my wife's name is not Maikia."

"That is what you call her all the time."

The good minister was perplexed, but presently a light broke in upon him. He was in the habit of addressing his wife as "my dear," and the Hawaiian had spelled the supposed name as it sounded to him. By putting K in the place of D, and taking away the R at the end, the novel Hawaiian name had been formed from the doctor's "my dear."—Youth's Companion.

Where Nature Beats Science.

A method of treating mother of pearl shells consists in drawing upon them with a brush and wax varnish any designs desired, after which they are placed in a bath of weak muriatic acid. The latter eats away the outer coat wherever it is not protected by the varnish, the result being a lovely cameo with raised figures in white on a pearly ground. Nature, however, beats art hollow at this sort of work.

In the cretaceous epoch, hundreds of thousands of years ago, there lived certain cephalopods, since extinct, which science calls "ammonites." The pearl they produced was of wonderful beauty, and many fossil ammonites dug up today have been so operated upon by the process of decay as to form elaborate patterns on the shells in pearl and white.—English Mechanic.

Taking Treasure from the Sea.

A scientist of Christiania proposes to immortalize himself by proving the feasibility of reclaiming the gold and silver in sea water by electrolytic action. He suggests that a channel about sixty meters wide should be selected for experiment. The place should be well sheltered from sea and wind, and there should be a current of about four meters per minute.

Across this channel sixty plates of galvanized iron, each two meters by three meters, should be fixed at an angle of 30 degs. with the stream, and an electric current be passed through the plates to precipitate the precious metals. Herr Munster, to whom the credit of this conception is due, has hit on a very fascinating idea.—Pittsburg Dispatch.

Makes Some Difference.

Boutton—I didn't meet Jack Goodheart at the restaurant today.

Upton—No; Jack is a married man now, and it's three days since pay day.—New York Weekly.

The exact physical center of the United States is the stone at Fort Riley, Kan., which marks the grave of Major Ogden, who died of cholera in 1855.

SECOND WEEK OF OUR
SPECIAL
Mid-Summer
SALE!

We were very much gratified with the way our bargains of last week were received, and will enumerate a few specials for this week:

All of our 50 and 75c. India Silks for this sale 39c.

All of our 25 and 37 1-2c. French Sateens for this sale 12 1-2c.

All of our 59 and 62 1-2c. all-wool Challies to close 50c.

A few pieces of 50c. Figured Mohairs we shall close at 25c.

We have just received a nice line of Belts 37 1-2c. metal Belts, shall sell this sale for 25c.

Something new, Suspender Belts, all the rage, 59c.; a regular 75c. belt.

A full line of Sizes, 32 to 40c.

Shirt Waists in the new shade of blue, sold all the season for $1; this sale 62c.

We have just received a full line of Purses and Pocketbooks—many novelties never before shown in this city and controlled by us.

We have added 1000 new pieces to our Musical Catalogue, making the largest and most complete list of music ever shown at any price, 5c. a copy or 6 copies for 25c. Ask for the new catalogue.

Kitchen Furnishing Dept.

Now is the time to buy a Hammock. We have a full line, prices ranging from 69c. to $2.69.

Croquet Sets. A regular $1.00 set for 89c., equally as good values for $1.39, $1.69, $2.29 and $3.39.

White Mountain Freezers—2 quarts, $1.25; 3 quarts, $2.09 and 4 quarts, $2.50.

Oil Stoves 1, 2 and 3 burners. Oil Stove Tea Kettles 19 to 69c.

Perry's Patent Clothes Line Hooks 7 and 10c.

Household Ammonia—pint bottles, 7c. or 4 for 25c.

Knowles & Co.
Cor. UNION & FOURTH STS.

SHERMAN'S
IS THE
Coolest Billiard Room
IN TOWN.
62 Purchase Street.
jy19-8pMWS

BANQUET TO JUSTICE FULLER.

Will Be Entertained at the Arcadian House by the Knox County Bar.

CAMDEN, Me., Aug. 15.—Definite arrangements have been made for the reception and banquet to be given Chief Justice Melville W. Fuller of the United States supreme court, now spening the summer Camden. The Knox County Bar association will take the steamer Governor Bodwell, Wednesday morning next, at Rockland, calling at Camden for Judge Fuller, and proceed up the Penobscot bay to Castine, where dinner will be had at the Arcadian House.

The full bench of Maine has been invited, and it is also expected that Judges Webb and Putnam of the United States circuit court, Portland, will join the excursion, and John J. Herrick, Esq., of Chicago, a friend of Judge Fuller, also spending the summer at Camden. It is designed to be a pleasant and informal occasion, the guests returning home in the afternoon.

One Tough Citizen Less.

LEON, Ia., Aug. 15.—E. W. Curry, a member of the Democratic state committee, shot and killed William F. Ellis, a tough citizen who has repeatedly threatened Curry's life. Ellis hunted up Curry with the avowed intention of killing the latter. Ellis made a motion to draw a revolver, and Curry fired. Public sympathy justifies the killing.

Mr. Chas. N. Hauer

Of Frederick, Md., suffered terribly for over ten years with abscesses and running sores on his left leg. He wasted away, grew weak and thin, and was obliged to use a cane and crutch. Everything which could be thought of was done without good result, until he began taking

Hood's Sarsaparilla

which effected a perfect cure. Mr. Hauer is now in the best of health. Full particulars of his case will be sent all who address

C. I. HOOD & Co., Lowell, Mass.

HOOD'S PILLS are the best after-dinner Pills, assist digestion, cure headache and biliousness.

CHURCH STATISTICS.

Interesting Address by Superintendent Robert P. Porter.

WASHINGTON, Aug. 15.—Superintendent Robert P. Porter in his address delivered at Asbury Park yesterday made public the preliminary figures of the church statistics of the eleventh census. There are shown to be in the United States nearly 150 separate and distinct church organizations holding to widely different creeds, varying greatly in practise, and representing all possible variations of church policy. Some of the denominations were never numbered before, and it required the utmost powers of persuasion to induce them to submit to the process. Sects have been found who claim less than 100 communicants. There are seven sects which altogether number only about 4000 members and yet own church edifices worth $70,000, viz: Shakers, Amenanites, Menonite, Harmony, Separatists, New Icarian and Altruists. The Icarian and Altruists are not religious, but are organized to apply a social principle.

After the seven great denominations, Congregational, Lutheran, Methodist, Presbyterian, Roman Catholic, Baptist and Episcopal have been accounted for the other 134 religious associations represent less than 10 per cent. of the church edifices and less than 11 per cent. of the aggregate value of church property. The total number of churches of all denominations in 1890 was 142,256, against 38,183 in 1850. The total value of church property was $641,221,303, as compared with $87,446,371 in 1850. In point of number the Methodists stood first in 1850, and still retain the position; nearly one-third of all the church edifices belong to the Methodist church, while the Baptists can lay claim to more than one quarter.

Relatively speaking, the Episcopal church retains about the same position to the other denominations as it did in 1850. On the other hand, the Roman Catholic church has advanced considerable, from a trifle over 3 per cent of the total number to over 6 per cent. in point of value; however, the Catholic church has made still greater strides, from an ownership of 10 1-2 per cent. of the church property to an ownership of 18 3-4 per cent. In this respect the Catholic church now ranks second in importance, being exceeded only by the Methodist church, which returns a trifle over 20 1-2 per cent of the total value.

In 1850 the value of church property of four denomination—Methodist, Presbyterian, Baptists and Episcopal—outranked the Catholic church in this respect. According to returns of eleventh census the number of communicants in five principal religious denominations are: Congregational, 512,571; Lutheran, 1,199,514; Methodist, 4,255,377; Presbyterian, 1,276,815; Roman Catholic, 6,250,459. Total 13,496,522. The communicants of the Baptist and Episcopal, with those of other denominations, will bring the aggregate up to about 20,000,000 in all. The statistics of the colored denominations likewise show great progress. They have a total membership of 2,379,100, and own church property valued at $13,403,000.

CONGRESSMAN WARWICK DEAD.

Was Serving His First Term as Successor of Major McKinley.

WASHINGTON, Aug. 15.—John G. Warwick, representative in congress from the Sixteenth district of Ohio, died here last night. He was serving his first term in congress as the successor of Major McKinley, whom he defeated after a bitterly contested campaign. Mr. Warwick was nearly 62 years of age, and was born in Ireland. He came to America in 1850. He was interested in mercantile pursuits, milling, and farming, and was elected lieutenant governor of Ohio as a Democrat in 1883. The remains were taken to Massillon, O., his late home, over the the Pennsylvania road, arriving at Massillon at 11:45 p. m. today. Funeral services will be held Tuesday at Massillon. The following committee has been selected to accompany the body: Senators Brice of Ohio and Hill of New York, Congressman Hare and Donovan of Ohio, Caruth of Kentucky, Catchings of Mississippi, Heard of Missouri, and Bynum of Indiana.

HARRISON WON'T STUMP.

His Time Taken Up Too Much by Affairs of State.

LOON LAKE, N. Y., Aug. 15.—President Harrison, when asked whether the report was true that he intended to take to the stump this fall, giving his attention especially to the northwest, said: "I have no such plans. The affairs of public moment are such that I will not find time for campaign purposes."

"When will you write your letter accepting the nomination?"

"I have already commenced the letter, but I don't know just when it will be ready."

The improvement in Mrs. Harrison's condition continues.

Rusk Don't Want to Be Governor.

MILWAUKEE, Aug. 15.—Secretary Rusk was interviewed at his home at Viroqua as to the possibility of his being a candidate for governor. In reply to the question would he accept a nomination, the secretary said: "I have served my time in that position and I am only grateful to the people of this commonwealth for their continued confidence and favor. The mention of my name in that connection at this time is without my consent and against my wishes. I have repeatedly told my friends that this thing must stop, that I will not accept the nomination."

Trouble on an Electric Road.

NEW HAVEN, Aug. 15.—Trouble is expected on the West Haven Electric road. A set of rules for motormen and conductors recently put in force requires, the men declare, increased hours of labor without increased compensation. The men have placed the matter before the company, but without result. The men held a secret meeting last night, but its result has not been learned. Forty men are concerned.

Cold Blooded Murder by Negroes.

MEMPHIS, Aug. 15.—J. D. Tolbert, a plantation superintendent, was attacked by a gang of drunken negroes near the Second street bridge and fatally slashed with razors. The murder was without provocation. The affair has created great excitement, and a large posse followed the murderers into the country, whither they fled.

Also Wanted for Wire-Tapping.

CINCINNATI, Aug. 15.—John Green, alias George Chevlin, who is in jail at Buffalo for bigamy, will have a hard time escaping. The Western Union Telegraph company is after him for wire-tapping and has an excellent case against him. He was the ring-leader in the Redbank and other wire-tapping affairs, by all of which the pool rooms were heavy losers.

Industrial Reformatory Fired.

HUNTINGTON, Pa., Aug. 15.—A fire last night on the grounds of the Pennsylvania industrial reformatory caused $50,000 damages. The origin of the fire is attributed to incendiarism. The Consolidated Manufacturing company of Philadelphia are the heaviest losers.

Dr. Peter Brice Dead.

BIRMINGHAM, Ala., Aug. 15.—Dr. Peter Brice, superintendent of the state lunatic asylum at Tua Paloosa, and one of the most distinguished men and authorities in the south, died yesterday of Bright's disease.

Highest of all in Leavening Power.—Latest U. S. Gov't Report.
Royal Baking Powder
ABSOLUTELY PURE

CORBETT AFTER McCAFFREY.

The Californian Makes Some Interesting Offers to Dominick.

ASBURY PARK, N. J., Aug. 15.—"Sporting" Jim Corbett had an easy time of it yesterday. All day long a stream of visitors poured across Deal lake bridge to the pretty cottage occupied by the big fighter. Among the most interesting visitors was Phil Dwyer, one of his heaviest backers. The big Californian is in the pink of condition. He is fearful of being trained down to fine, and for this reason will do no more training at all for several days. Corbett seemed to be somewhat amused when his attention was called to some statements made by Dominick McCaffrey in a morning paper. After reading the article, he said: "I have all I can attend to now getting ready for my fight with Sullivan. McCaffrey says I won all my fights by scratches, catching my opponents when they were in poor condition. Now I will make this proposition to him: Whether I win or lose the fight with Sullivan, I shall be glad to go to the Manhattan Athletic club, where McCaffrey is boxing instructor, and stop him in four rounds in the presence of his friends and pupils, or I will give him $1000 if he will stand before me for four rounds in the Madison Square Garden, or if that is not satisfactory, I will give him $250 for every round he survives. As McCaffrey had ample time to prepare, this will effect prove that my victory over him was not a 'scratch' as he calls it."

A WELL-EXECUTED PLOT.

Three Distinct Fires Started in the Lehigh Valley Freight Yard.

BUFFALO, Aug. 15.—Yesterday morning somebody, supposed to be the strikers, started three fires simultaneously in different parts of the Lehigh Valley freight yards at East Buffalo. An alarm was sounded and the fire department and the reserve force were quickly dispatched to the scene. It was a well planned, well-executed plot, as the fires were started where the cars were thickest, no hydrants from which water could be obtained, and at a time when the yards were deserted. Eighteen freight cars, loaded with merchandise, and two passenger coaches, together with two office buildings were completely destroyed. A train of fifteen coal cars which was standing on a coal trestle was started down the incline and crashed into an engine at the bottom, wrecking it and a water crane. Four freight trains were also derailed and eight cars were wrecked on the Erie. The damage by the fire will reach $75,000. The whole police reserve has been ordered on duty and the situation is hourly growing worse.

SEIZURES IN THE BEHRING SEA.

The United States Men-of-War Doing Good Service.

PORT TOWNSEND, Wash., Aug. 15.—The steamer Bertha, from Unalaska, brings advices of seizures made by United States men-of-war in Behring sea. The British schooner Mountain Chief of Victoria, seized by the Adams for killing seals and violating the modus vivendi, delivered in charge of a British man-of-war; whaling bark Lydia intercepted by the Richard Rush while taking newly killed seals from aboard the whaling bark Northern Light into Behring sea; a prize crew was placed aboard and it was sent to Sitka; the whaling schooner Jane Gray, seized by the Mohican, for not leaving Behring sea after having been warned; the British schooner Wilfred of Victoria, one of the vessels which transferred its cargo of sealskins to the British steamer Coquitlan at Port Leches was seized by the Rush with fresh killed seals aboard.

MYSTERIOUS DISAPPEARANCE.

Dr. A. Newton's Absence Leads to a Suspicion of Suicide.

NEW HAVEN, Aug. 15.—Dr. A. Newton, a Meriden dentist, has disappeared and grave doubts are entertained as to whether he has not committed suicide. He is between 70 and 75 years old, and has been in business in Hartford for thirty or forty years before coming to this place. His wife and daughter are in Providence at present. He has a brother in Windsor Locks, but none of them have heard of the missing man since his disappearance. Dr. Newton had been heard to remark that when his money was gone, he would commit suicide as the world had no further use for him. He always carried a pistol, which an examination of the Meriden house failed to locate among his other effects. Last February Dr. Newton was known to have $3000. He was not an extravagant man.

Opposition Fizzles Out.

BOSTON, Aug. 15.—The Printers' anti-Reid club meeting that was to have taken place yesterday afternoon was a veritable fizzle, only six persons being present and they all "leaders." No. 6 (New York) is not pleased with the opposition manifested by sister unions to Mr. Reid.

THE LAST SAD RITES.

Imposing Ceremonies at the Obsequies of C. W. Riggin.

PHILADELPHIA, Aug. 15.—All that is mortal of Boatswains Mate Charles W. Riggin now rests in Woodland cemetery. The interment was made yesterday afternoon, and the civic and military demonstration in connection with the funeral was one of the most imposing given in this city for some time, 5000 men being in line. At 2 o'clock the body was taken from Independence hall where it layed in state, and under the chief marshalship of R. M. J. Reed, the procession formed in this order:

Detail of reserves, under command of Captain Malin.
Chief marshal and staff.
Band.
Military escort.
National Guard of Pennsylvania.
National Guard of New Jersey and Hartranft Light battery.
Grand Army division, Marshal G. L. Warren and staff.
Division of Sons of Veterans, Marshal H. L. Bertu and staff.
Division of Patriotic Order Sons of America, Marshal C. G. Mindleton and staff.
Junior Order United American Mechanics, Marshal Joseph M. Leipsett and staff.
Division of fraternal organizations, Marshal George S. Kyle and staff.
Naval veterans on foot, Marshal I. K. Archor.
Naval Post 400, Grand Army, Commander H. R. Devitt.
Admiral John A. Dahlgren Garrison, Lieutenant Thomas F. Kelly, and Farragut garrison Naval Veterans, Commander James E. Boyle.
United States Marine Guard.
Hearse and guard of honor.
United States sailors and ex-sailors and former shipmates of Riggin, all under the command of U. S. Naval officers.
Carriages containing clergyman, orators, distinguished guests.
Naval Veteran Legion.
Members of joint committee and civic societies.
Carriages containing floral offerings.

The streets were lined five deep, and the route up Chestnut street to Broad, Broad to Market, Market to Thirty-ninth and thence to the cemetery. The large cemetery was crowded, and upon arriving there the right of the line was halted on the main avenue directly opposite the Riggin plot, ranks were opened, and the hearses with a guard from the United States navy yard, proceeded through the line, the usual honors being paid. The body was met at the grave by Riggin's relatives and friends. The services opened with prayer by Rev. Samuel H. Royer, an Episcopalian, at whose church Riggin was an attendant. The rector spoke feelingly of the dead sailor, and alluded to his life for his country and his flag. Captain W. W. Kerr next delivered an oration and read the sworn testimony of each of the witnesses of the Valparaiso affair.

The choir of Centennial Baptist church, under the direction of Professor Leo Lucens, sang "My Country 'Tis of Thee," the assemblage joining in the chorus. Rev. Dr. Duncan McGregor spoke on behalf the of naval veterans. Afterwards, Dr. McGregor delivered the burial sermon. A last salute was then fired by a party of marines from the League island navy yard. It was nearly 7 o'clock when the services were concluded. The grave was lined with evergreens, and at the head was an elegant floral offering representing a broken column, with the inscription "Only a boatswain's mate." The metallic casket was incased in a plain oak casket, upon which was inscribed "Charles W. Riggin, 1892."

Close Race with Atlantic Greyhounds.

NEW YORK, Aug. 15.—The steamships Aurania and Alaska of the Cunard and Union lines respectively, steamed into port yesterday one minute's time apart. They had a thrilling race from Fastnet rock and were within hailing distance of each other the whole way across. The Aurania crossed the finish line at Sandy Hook just one minute ahead of her big rival. The Alaska left Queenstown fifty-four minutes earlier than the Aurania, the former covering the distance in 6 days 20 hours and 38 minutes, and the latter in 6 days 19 hours and 43 minutes.

Diamond Swindler Arrested.

NEW YORK, Aug. 15.—Deburgh, alias T. Burke, 45 years of age, was arrested just as he was leaving the steamer Aurania, which arrived from Liverpool yesterday. He is charged with swindling a London jeweller out of $200,000 worth of diamonds by passing worthless checks. He claims to be a resident of Buffalo and was very indignant at his arrest. The jewelry was found in his possession and then turned over to the customs authorities.

Two Midgets Wed.

NEW YORK, Aug. 15.—Miss Lottie Swartwood, a midget, was married yesterday afternoon to Leopold Kahn, better known as Admiral Dot. Rev. Dr. Wise of Temple Rudolph Sholomon performed the ceremony in accordance with the Jewish rite. The bride is 23 years of age, and the bridegroom 29. She stands 49in. in height he 48.

BRIGGS & LAWRENCE,
197 and 203 Union Street,
ARE THE ONLY LOCAL AGENTS FOR THE
OLD RELIABLE
Eddy Refrigerator,
ALSO THE
DIAMOND,
WHICH IS MUCH CHEAPER.

From Saturday's Third Edition.

MATTAPOISETT MARINES

Sail out in the Bay, With White Gleaming Sails

In a Sunshiny Day. Thirty-two Boats Sail the Annual Regatta,

While Crowds of Spectators From the Shore Scan the Water.

[Special Dispatch.]

MATTAPOISETT, Aug. 13.—The prospect for a race of the yachts this afternoon looked decidedly dubious at 9 o'clock this morning. Scarcely a breath of wind was stirring and what there was of the northeast breeze was not sufficient to move the flyers from New Bedford, Falmouth, and the head of the bay in time to reach this point for the start.

The regatta committee met at the hour named and decided to postpone the race unless there was a change in the conditions that should warrant a start. They were desirous of making this midsummer regatta the crowning event of the season and were bent on giving all a fair show.

Fortunately at 11 o'clock the wind hauled around into the southwest and by noon a whole-sail breeze was blowing, while at the same time, numerous sails were sighted below. Then it was decided that the race should take place and by 12 30 o'clock, at least 20 boats were ready for the contest, which gives promise of being the most interesting ever given by the Summer residents of this resort. The largest amount of money ever raised for a regatta in this port has been contributed for the events of this afternoon, and as a consequence of the liberal prizes offered, boats from far and near have planned to be in it with the boatmen from Mattapoisett.

The start was postponed till 2 o'clock to allow the strangers to enter.

Capt. John Welch with the Daisy from New Bedford, and the Minnie B., Capt. Benjamin Slocum, of the same port, reached here about 12 45 o'clock. They are here for business. When it soon became noised about that the ex-alderman's boat was a prize winner she came in for an examination from the critical yachtsmen at the head of the bay.

The wharves are lined with spectators, while the number of pleasure craft which are out for the afternoon's sport is very large.

The start was made from an imaginary line between Abram Paine's sloop Annie, anchored off Long wharf, and buoy No. 6.

The course for the larger boats is from the judge's boat to Angelica Point; thence to Nye's Ledge; thence to Cormorant Rocks; thence to the can buoy off West Island; thence to Nye's Ledge and back to the judge's boat, a distance in all of 14 miles. The smaller boats sailed over a shorter course and some portion of the races was in sight of the spectators the whole time. The start was as follows:

NAME.	H.	M.	S.
Sloops.			
Fin	2	05	35
Chapoquoit	2	06	16
Lorita	2	07	19
First Class Cats.			
Surprise	2	10	01
Hector	2	11	27
Flight	2	13	13
Second Class Cats.			
Success,	2	15	38
Mist,	2	15	53
Defiance,	2	16	09
Daisy,	2	16	50
Gymnote,	2	17	18
Minnie B.	2	17	45
Gwendolyn,	2	18	06
Third Class Cats.			
Algol,	2	20	18
Sippican,	2	21	01
Hermione,	2	22	08
Hera,	2	22	20
Aucoot,	2	22	30
Eina,	2	23	15
Doris,	2	23	21
Tycoon,	2	24	00
Fourth Class Cats.			
Cat,	2	25	10
Edith,	2	25	42
Marianna,	2	25	58
Ramona,	2	26	00
Frolic,	2	26	23
Hermia,	2	26	27
Annie and Susie,	2	26	50
Fifth Class Cats.			
Rena,	2	30	22
Iola,	2	31	06
Lady May,	2	31	34
Konungo,	2	32	06

The Konungo is sailed by three ladies, Miss Alice Stackpole being in command of the craft.

The Squall, which was entered in the fourth class, was disabled just before the start and did not compete.

The Fin, of the sloop class, is a peculiarly shaped boat from Wareham, and is attracting much attention. She made an excellent start, leading all the other sloops by several lengths on the first leg for Angelica point.

THE TURF.

Some Excellent Time Made at the Saratoga Races.

SARATOGA, Aug. 13.—In the first race, purse $600, 6 furlongs, Copyright won; Cottonade second; Brown Beauty third. Time—1 19 1-2.

In the second race, purse $700, 1 1-8 miles, Strathmeath won; King Crab second; Homer third. Time—2 10.

In the third race, the Watkins Glen stakes, 5 furlongs, One won; Elizabeth L. second, Bertha B. third. Time—1 04 1-2.

In the fourth race, purse $500, 7 furlongs, Tactician won; National second; Khaftan third. Time—1 35.

RAILROAD MEN STRIKE.

Higher Wages and Shorter Hours Involved in the Movement.

BUFFALO, N. Y., Aug. 13.—The switchmen employed on the New York, Lake Erie & Western, the Lehigh Valley, and Buffalo Creek roads struck at midnight last night. Their object is to obtain higher wages, although the question of ten hours is involved. The strike was fully sanctioned by Grand Master Sweeney of the Switchmen's Mutual Aid Association. About 200 men thus far are out.

AN UNSUCCESSFUL ATTEMPT

By the Amalgamated Men to Get a Strike at Duquesne.

HOMESTEAD, Aug. 13.—The effort of 40 Amalgamated men to strike the Duquesne steel works again seems to have proved a failure. This morning 700 went to work as usual.

FUNERAL.—The funeral of Capt. Henry Taber took place at his late residence on Orchard street this afternoon at 4 o'clock, and was largely attended by friends and hosts of associates in business. The services were conducted by Rev. William J. Potter of the Unitarian church, Rev. E. Williams of the New Bedford Port Society, for the Moral Improvement of Seamen, and Mrs. Ruth S. Murray of the Friends Meeting. The interment took place at Rural cemetery later, the bearers being Hon. William W. Crapo, Hon. Morgan Rotch, Hon. Andrew G. Pierce, Charles W. Clifford, Edward S. Taber and Samuel H. Cook.

REAL ESTATE SALES.—Henry C. Hathaway sold at auction this afternoon house and about 17 rods land at No. 75 Middle street to E. C. Palmer for $1815 and the taxes of 1892.

J. R. Denham sold at auction this afternoon to Phebe A. G. Sherman, house and land, No. 31 Allen street, for $2500.

VERY DOUBTFUL.

The Lynn Story About Motive for Murdering Mr. Borden

Is Scouted by Well-Known Citizens of Fall River.

Sheriff Wright Puts His Foot Down About Interviewing.

[Special Dispatch.]

FALL RIVER, Aug. 13.—Since the publication of the sensational dispatch from Lynn concerning a motive for the murder of Andrew J. Borden having been found in his giving evidence against mutinous sailors of schooner Jefferson Borden, which led to their conviction and imprisonment, diligent inquiry has been made to ascertain the truth or falsity of the statement. As a result of that inquiry it is safe to say that the story, as published in the Lynn *Item*, is a "fake." Old business men, who have known Andrew J. Borden all his life, do not hesitate to say that he not only never sailed on the Jefferson Borden, but in all probability never saw the vessel. Mr. Borden was a man who at all times stayed at home and attended to business, and his relations were such that never, at least at the period of the mutiny on the Borden, was he absent from Fall River.

TAUNTON, Aug. 13.—Sheriff Wright declines to ask or have Lizzie Borden asked, or her sister Emma, (who is visiting her at the jail,) whether their parents were on schooner Jefferson Borden, or whether either of them knew anything about the Lynn *Item* story. He lays down the law—no questions to be asked of parties in jail, whether visitors or not.

JUDGE GRESHAM INTERVIEWED.

He Will Not Take the Stump for the Third Party.

THOMPSON, Conn., Aug. 13.—Judge Walter Q. Gresham and wife have been the guests of J. W. Doane of Thompson, Conn., since last Wednesday. This afternoon Judge Gresham was interviewed by a representative of the Woonsocket *Reporter*, and stated that he would deliver no speeches during this campaign. He was questioned concerning the statement given the press recently by Chairman Taubeneck of the People's party at St. Louis to the effect that Judge Gresham had concluded to take the stump in the interest of the third party and would make the opening speech at Indianapolis, the latter part of this month, Taubeneck claiming to have received this information of G. C. Stoll, chairman of the state central committee of Indiana, to which it was alleged Judge Gresham had written.

Judge Gresham said the statement was made without authority; that he should make no political speeches during the campaign.

The judge was asked to give his views on the political outlook, but answered that he did not wish to discuss the subject. When asked concerning the truth of the Indianapolis special to the Boston *Herald*, in which Chairman George C. Stoll claimed that the judge would take the stump, Judge Gresham replied that he had not known Mr. Stoll and had had no communication or correspondence with him, and that his first answer covered his reply as to the contents of the Indianapolis dispatch. He declined to discuss the platform of the People's party.

When asked what he had to say as to the reasons given by the Indianapolis Republicans why he could not antagonize the Republican party, he replied that, as an American citizen he considered it his duty to vote according to his convictions and that he owed no slavish obedience to any party.

The Judge said he intended to return to Chicago in a day or two, and closed the interview.

TIRED OF LIFE.

An Old Soldier Ends His Trouble by a Pistol Shot.

DENVER, Col., Aug. 13.—Gen. N. G. Dunn, of New York city was found in a dying condition in his room in Stow street last night, the result of a pistol shot fired by himself with suicidal intent. He died soon after. Gen. Dunn in 1873 was engineer-in-chief on the staff of Gov. Dix. He served during the war, afterward practicing law. He came here about five years ago, since when he has been connected with different insurance companies. Various reasons are assigned for his act, lack of funds and insanity among them.

STEAMER INJURED.

She Lands Her Passengers Safely and is Then Beached.

CONEY ISLAND, L. I., Aug. 13.—While on her way to the iron pier on her last trip last night, the steamer Cepheus of the Iron Steamboat Co. struck some obstacle in the bay. There were but few persons on board and there was no panic. The boat continued on her way and landed her passengers at her pier. She had begun to list badly and it was necessary to beach her. It was found that two of her compartments were full of water. It is not known what the object was that the steamer struck.

Another Idol Shattered.

One by one the cherished idols are being dragged from the high pedestals upon which sentiment has placed them and humbled and discredited in the galling dust of repudiation. The last to tumble was "Jessie of Lucknow," the highland lassie who, in the sorely besieged city during the Indian mutiny, heard the pibroch of her clan afar off above the din of battle and long before any others could be made to hear it, and who cheered her companions just on the point of surrender to renewed exertions by her thrilling exclamation: "The Campbells are comin! Oh, dinna ye hear it; dinna ye hear it?" She is proved by the Scots themselves to be simply a pleasant myth. The matter has been thoroughly investigated and testimony from many of the survivors of the famous siege has been taken.

It is proved that there was no such person as Jessie Brown in the Residency, and that anyway it was impossible to hear the bagpipes at the distance declared. Nothing but the roaring of guns could be heard anywhere in the city, and the pipes of the highlanders were only heard long after the city was practically relieved and when the pipers were nearing the Bailey guard gate. More than this, says the New York Sun, the story has been traced to its origin in a little romance written by a French governess at Jersey for the use of her pupils, and followed through its journeyings until it reached the London Times on Dec. 12, 1857. It is sad and a shame, but Jessie has been sent to join William Tell and the other dethroned gods and goddesses, and the Scots gave her up finally and publicly a few weeks ago.

English judges of courts of assizes and nisi prius get $37.50 per day for their services—time only being counted while they are on circuit.

Forty-four families in Junction City, Kan., have all their food prepared by a co-operative cooking club. The club has been two years in existence.

The block which probably has the largest population of any in the world is in New York, bounded by Avenues B and C, Second and Third streets. It has a population of 3,500, or at the surprising rate of 1,000,000 to the square mile.

"QUITE A LOAD TO CARRY."

Little cat so dear,
Greatly do I fear,
With you I cannot tarry,
You're quite a load to carry.

WE HAVE A LOAD,
AN
OVERLOAD
OF
CHAMBER SUITS.
100
of which (about 40 different patterns) we offer you this week at
20 PER CENT.
Discount. Discount. Discount.

☞ All goods are marked in plain figures, so you can figure the discount yourself.

O O O O O O

F. R. SLOCUM,
354 to 362 Acushnet Avenue.
CASH OR INSTALMENT
HOUSEFURNISHERS

A Cure for Baldness.

Is the human race in the near future to be entirely bald on the top of its head, where the hair ought to grow? is a question agitating tonsorial circles and the manly victims thereof. Some people are born bald, some achieve baldness and others have it thrust upon them, and it is with the latter class that the distressing consequences of modern living have the most to do. As everybody is cognizant, the glory of man as well as woman is his hair. Baldness is venerable, but it is not always venerated, and then it is frightfully inconvenient. In a woman art supplies nature, but unlucky man has no such remedy that cannot be detected, and however indifferent to appearances he made be, it is not in his disposition to meekly submit to the trouble it entails.

A wise parent afflicted by a loss of hair should take a lesson in hirsute development from the lower classes in Europe and give his offspring the benefit. Whoever saw a bald workingman or shopkeeper in France? Whoever found among the peasants of Europe shining pates? The reason for this natural thatching is a most simple one; these people live outdoors, unbonneted, and it is only when man becomes reckless and superrefined in his living that the hair falls. So much for civilization.

But having discovered that civilization, not to say dissipation, is at the root of fin de siecle's hair falling, why not counteract this difficulty by starting the little chaps aright, not merely in the paths of virtue, but by taking away their hats and caps and making them go bareheaded until they are fully grown? One of these days the wisdom of some of the Old World customs will strike home in America, and it need not be called anglomania either.—Boston Herald.

Physicians Centuries Ago.

In some countries, where physicians did not thrive, sick people were placed on the roadside, that travelers who had suffered with like maladies might suggest remedies.

Such crude efforts were supplanted at Rome by shops in which various drugs and medicines were sold. Then, as now, quacks abounded, and the government, for the protection of the people, ordered that all remedies should bear a label declaring the character of the medicine, the name of its inventor, the sickness for which it was prepared, with a list of its ingredients and full directions as to the way in which it should be taken.

For disorders of the stomach a favorite prescription was to the effect that the sufferer should read aloud in a clear, distinct tone some book or speech and then take moderate exercise.

Physicians were divided, as now, into various classes of specialists—doctors for the eye, for the throat, etc. Even in those old days women practiced medicine, although they did not reach prominence in the profession.

Surgeons used various instruments, resembling in some measure those of today. They had ear probes, syringes, instruments for cutting bones, and the like. In very early times dentists came into notice, and an ancient author refers to "gold fillings."—Professor A. P. Montague in Youth's Companion.

The Eye of the Hedgehog.

Shakespeare, who seems to have been a most excellent out of doors naturalist—a minute observer of life, indeed, in all shapes—noticed the hedgehog and wrote, "The hedgehog whines at night." If any one of our readers possesses a tame hedgehog, let him examine the eye of the creature, if he has not already done so. If the eye is the index to the mind, as I firmly believe it to be, the hedgehog knows a great deal and only uses his knowledge for his own special benefit.—Blackwood's Magazine.

HASKELL & TRIPP.

Do you sew?

Here's an opportunity to buy silk or cotton very low. Brooks' famous English spool cotton—black, white or colors—2c. a spool, 24c. a dozen. As good sewing cotton as is made.

A big factory has sold to us 8000 boxes of waste sewing silk, mostly black, a few mixed colors. Price 5c. per box.

See our window display of above and secure what you may need for the next six months, at least. Such a chance *is not an every-day occurrence.*

Bamboo goods.

Special offering in basement this week.

Bamboo tables, 25c. each.

Bamboo corner basket, three shelves, brass mounted, 50c. each.

Bamboo easels, brass mounted, 5 feet high, 89c.

White Mountain ice cream freezers.

Preserving kettles.

Mason's fruit jars.

An apron bargain.

New large white aprons of hemstitched lawn with striped border and sash strings, 25c. each. Entirely unlike any aprons we have ever sold, and we think you'll agree they are better than ever before offered for 25c.

Storm serges continue the leading article in the dress goods stock. We have a great variety at 50c., 75c. and $1 per yard in navy and black. Some new armure and broad diagonal weaves are particularly stylish.

Plain colors and light mixtures in French and German suitings are all at much lower prices than early in the season. For half a dollar a yard you may now choose from a great many handsome fabrics that have been marked down from 75c. and 87c. a yard.

Strangers enjoying Summer holidays welcome at all times.

Mail orders from seashore resorts in this vicinity receive careful attention. Goods shipped same day.

HASKELL & TRIPP.

Department Stores,

Purchase and William Streets.

BELIEVES LIZZIE GUILTY.

State Detective Seaver Tells as much as He Dares.

Inquest in the Borden Murder Case Further Postponed.

Importance Attached to the Blood Spot Found on the Prisoner's Skirt.

[Special Dispatch.]

TAUNTON, Aug. 16.—State Detective Seaver had the appearance of a marble statue as he sat in a deep study in the City Hotel last night.

I understand that Jennings is going to call lawyer Howe of New York into the Borden murder case if it comes to trial, said the Standard man to him.

The last part of the sentence aroused him, as was expected. If it comes to trial, he repeated; well, it is coming to trial, and don't you make any mistake about that. Mr. Jennings can bring all the New York criminal lawyers into the case that he can find and it would not make any difference to our little man down in New Bedford. He is a match for the sharpest of them, and besides the defence won't have many legs to stand on when the case does go on.

Why, you haven't any evidence yet, and it doesn't look as though you were going to have much other than that which is purely circumstantial. You cannot thus far connect Lizzie with the case directly; there was not even a sign of blood about her clothes save that little spot on her skirt.

No? Well, her dress has gone to Boston, for upon that were spots resembling blood very much, and the blood on the skirt came from the outside somewhere. That could be easily seen with the naked eye, for the clot was heavier outside than in. How came it there, and what were those spots on the dress? Time will tell that. We expected to have the postponed inquest to-day, but it has been further put off, and I understand now that Prof. Wood cannot get around to-morrow, so it will probably be Wednesday and perhaps later before the inquest is taken up again.

You cannot say that there is anything outside of those blood spots, if they are blood spots, to connect Lizzie with the crime?

Think not? Just get into your head the fact that Lizzie never went near that barn. She had to account for her time in some way, and so she very conveniently went to the barn in her mind. But during all that time she was attending to something else and that hot fire in the kitchen occupied a part of her attention. Lizzie ironing, was she? Well, it wouldn't take my wife or yours all the morning to iron a few handkerchiefs. What do you make out of Lizzie's subsequent conduct, of her persistent coolness under what may be considered highly disadvantageous circumstances. It is the coolness of an exceedingly cunning brain and determined mind; it may be the coolness of insanity, but I question it. The amount of this story is, that this affair was not a hasty act. It was an act born of long and deep study, dwelt upon until it became as a matter of course to her, and that Sullivan girl isn't any chicken either. She knows more than she has yet told, and you mind that before long she will say things that will startle some folks. Mind you, I do not intend to convey the idea that Lizzie deliberately took her into her confidence; she is too sharp for all that, but you cannot make me believe that Bridget Sullivan is as innocent of all knowledge of that affair as she has tried to make out.

What has been done about Dr. Handy's man?

That clew is being worked for all it is worth, but in my opinion it is not worth much. How does it happen that Dr. Handy did not go right to police headquarters with his story the moment he got a chance? Now, I know the doctor is a worthy man and entitled to the utmost confidence, but I cannot ignore the facts that he is a firm friend of the family, that it was to his house Lizzie was going, and also that his information got along in a freight train when it should have come by express.

How about the man who was seen down New Bedford way with his hands "caked with blood"?

That is the silliest yarn yet, and is not worth considering a moment. It belongs to that class in which the Canadian medium takes front rank, and along with several other gauzy stories.

Then you really believe Lizzie is the guilty party?

I firmly believe she is one of the guilty parties, not only from what I know thus far of the case but from the actions of the District Attorney. He is a man who never makes errors in a case of this magnitude.

Might not his work have been the result almost wholly of what you and the other officers on the case told him?

The evidence at the inquest was what decided the matter, and no officers testified there, only the members of the family and those who were in the immediate neighborhood at the time of the murder.

It is hinted strongly that the Borden money will be spent freely to assist Lizzie in her defence. It wont be necessary to go outside the family money, will it?

It ought not since all the property now is to be divided between these two girls, and naturally enough they would use it freely to accomplish the desired result. It may not be so pleasant to invest in legal matters as in real estate but under the existing circumstances the net returns will be more satisfactory.

What do you think about Bridget's story of going upstairs and lying down because she was sick?

That is one of the things I had in mind when I said that girl knew more than she would tell. She may not have been poisoned and it would not be at all wonderful that a sight of something uncanny or any way strange and out of the common order should make her sick. But that girl Lizzie is a puzzle to me. At the house that day when outsiders

were moved to tears there was not a sign of giving way on her part. Not a bit of moisture could be noticed about her eyelids, and when she was taken through that crowd at Fall River I watched her sharply for signs of breaking down but they did not show. She is a conundrum that I will give up for the present anyhow. You will make no mistake in watching for the testimony at the hearing next week, and in expecting to hear something drop. In my opinion evidence will be produced there which will entirely change the feeling of those who doubt. But wait patiently until then and get something tangible.

Why, have you been working off a fake on me?

No, I do not mean that. I have given you my opinion so far as I dare, based upon what, to all appearance, is the true condition of affairs. I may be wrong, I sincerely hope I am for the girl's sake, but—well, time will tell.

BELIEVES LIZZIE INNOCENT.

Rev. Mr. Jubb Denounces Star Chamber Proceedings and Judge Blaisdell.

FALL RIVER, Aug. 16.—Rev. J. Walker Jubb, pastor of the Central Congregational church, of which Miss Lizzie Borden is a member, acknowledges the correctness of an interview published in a morning paper and granted a few moments after he had left the prisoner at Taunton jail yesterday afternoon.

He characterizes Judge Blaisdell's action in sitting on the bench after the inquest as indecent, outrageous, and not to be tolerated in any court of the community. He proposes to see Attorney Jennings this morning, and will do everything possible to have another justice on the bench at the preliminary hearing.

"Believe in Lizzie's innocence?" said Mr. Jubb. "Indeed I do, and I don't think her incarceration at the hands of the trial justice a travesty on justice. I would think that common decency would have caused Judge Blaisdell to step aside, after having once given judgment so far as to order the issuing of a warrant.

"The star chamber proceeding by which they secured this evidence which they claim to have is a relic of barbarism. The thing cannot be put too strongly in condemnation. They say it was merely to secure her statement uninfluenced by a lawyer's checks and restraints.

"How many questions do you suppose were asked her in that time which should not have been asked her at all under the law—questions improper in kind and form. And every word was taken down, of course, and twisted no doubt to be used against her in the trial for her life. I tell you it is an outrage. They have not enough evidence in to hold anyone for twenty-four hours, but because they can find no other explanation of the murder they suspect her and say so, and bend their energies to substantiate the statement.

Mr. Jubb says that Lizzie is looking well and bearing up in a manner that surprises him. She does not read the papers and knows only what these friends see fit to tell her. Emma took a copy of the Metropolitan, a paper which she thought gave a very fair statement of the case, but Mr. Jubb advised her against reading it, and she followed the advice.

Lizzie is supplied with sewing and reading matter sufficient to occupy her fully when she is alone. Lizzie will not be taken to Fall River to attend the inquest to-morrow, but that proceeding will probably interfere with Emma's visit to her here, as the latter's presence will possibly be required.

Unfortunate John Beattie.

John Beattie, Jr., president of the board of aldermen, has become the sorry victim of circumstances and has had stinging editorials written of him, and extended notoriety given to his name and position. A few days ago at City Hall he coincided with views expressed by friends of Bridget Sullivan, to the effect that she should have been isolated from the Borden house and placed under the direction and care of the police, but for use as the most important government witness. This remark was taken up by the beak and talons of Mr. Rumor and found their way into print in this way: "Alderman Beattie says Bridget Sullivan should have been arrested before Lizzie Borden was brought in." The Globe swooped down on the alderman in a savage editorial and a Boston paper has learned that the "Irish-American element" is threatening vengeance against him. This morning the alderman proved beyond a doubt that he never even hinted at the arrest of the servant and never traduced his position by insulting any class or creed.

Winward, the undertaker, drove into Court square this forenoon with the sofa upon which Andrew J. Borden was murdered. It had been reupholstered, and Mr. Winward wanted to know what to do with it. After consulting with Assistant Marshal Fleet it was taken to the Borden homestead on Second street. It was covered with coarse matting and none of the upholstering was in evidence.

INCENDIARY FIRE.

One of the Oldest Residences in the Town of Bourne Destroyed Last Night.

MIDDLEBORO, Aug. 16.—The residence of Mrs. Mary Bourne, one of the oldest houses in the town of Bourne, was destroyed by an incendiary fire about midnight. Loss about $1300. Nothing was saved, the family barely escaping alive.

A BETTER TIME COMING.

Adlai Stevenson Addresses Hibernians at Bloomington, Ill., at a Picnic.

BLOOMINGTON, Ill., Aug. 16.—The annual picnic of the Ancient Order of Hibernians of Bloomington was held at the fair grounds yesterday. Gen. Adlai Stevenson was one of the speakers. Among other things he said: "I believe that a better time is coming for the land from which you and your ancestors came. The time is in the near future when under the leadership of Gladstone, the people of Ireland will enjoy the same freedom and liberty that we have here in blessed America to-day. When that day comes not only will there be rejoicing in the hearts of the Irish people in America, but in that rejoicing all America will take part."

RECEIVED "PROTECTION" MONEY.

Chief of Police of Atlantic City Suspended to Await Investigation.

ATLANTIC CITY, N. J., Aug. 16.—The city council last night suspended Harry C. Eldridge, chief of police, pending investigation of charges brought against him by the police commissioner of receiving money from proprietors of a number of notorious houses for "protection." It is said that he went to the houses and demanded sums from $50 to $300.

Ocean Steamers.

Arrived—At New York, Tauric, Liverpool; Rotterdam, Amsterdam; Neptune, Montego Bay. At Bremerhaven, Elbe, from New York.

TROOPS CALLED OUT.

Strike of Switchmen Assuming a Serious Phase.

Idle Men Resort to Destruction of Valuable Property.

President McLeod of the Reading Road Talks on the Matter.

BUFFALO, Aug. 16.—The Sixty-fifth regiment has just been sent to Cheektowaga to guard the Lehigh Valley and the Erie yards.

The Seventy-fourth regiment has been called out to protect the Central and West Shore property, it being feared that switchmen on these roads may go out.

There were no sensational developments in the switchmen's strike during the night, and the situation has improved. With the two regiments of guards in the field and police reinforced by specials, the feeling is more reassuring than yesterday. The calling out of the military is generally commended, especially as the sheriff's deputies proved worthless, and many of them deserted at the first show of opposition. The police claim to be able to handle the strike inside the city limits, but in the town of Cheektowaga, where the militia were sent, the situation is different.

During the progress of the military preparations Gen. Doyle said: "You can say that the National Guard is never ordered out at midnight to put down a riot armed with blank cartridges. Every man that leaves this arsenal to-night will carry 35 rounds of ball cartridges, prepared to shoot. If there is any necessity for shooting you may depend upon it there will be hot work.

I am going through with the First Battalion, and I am going clear through the lines. We are not going out for fun."

Col. Welch arrived at William street station, outside the city line, at 1 o'clock. His orders apparently are for the keeping the people in general away and to protect the big trestle, over which there was considerable uneasiness.

OSWEGO, N. Y., Aug. 16.—Capt. Hall of the 48th regiment National Guards received orders this morning to have his company in readiness for service at Buffalo.

Waiting for the Word.

CHICAGO, Aug. 16.—It was rumored late last night that the Switchmen on the Erie in Chicago, which is the old Chicago and Atlantic, had been ordered on strike. To a reporter who called at the depot of the road a representative of the Switchmen said: "We are waiting to hear the word from Grand Master Sweeney. He is now in Buffalo. As soon as he speaks we quit, and so do all switchmen on lines running into Chicago. Strike may not reach Chicago for a week yet, but unless the demands of the strikers in the east are granted all the great railway lines will be tied up within ten days."

Grand Master Wilkinson's Statement.

Grand Master Wilkinson yesterday said his organization would not interfere with the striking switchmen unless the switchmen could show that the recent strike was a move authorized by the national officers of the Switchmen's Union. "When we had a strike some time ago," said Wilkinson, "I told Grand Master Sweeny of the switchmen, that the strike was authorized. In this case I have received no word from him or any other officer of his organization regarding the present troubles in Buffalo. If I hear nothing from them I must conclude that the strike is not authorized by the Switchmen's Union, and we will follow the tactics we pursued in the Chicago & Northwestern strike. The trainmen cannot allow an irresponsible band of strikers to throw them out of work in this way. Wilkinson left this morning for Buffalo. The conductor of the Order of Railway Conductors was closeted for three hours with Wilkinson last night at the Sherman House. The conductor refused to discuss with reporters the situation, nor would Wilkinson give any idea of the nature of the conference. Whatever its nature, it is evident the conductors are in negotiations with the trainmen, who say they will support the switchmen if the strike is authorized.

Train Fired by Strikers.

BUFFALO, Aug. 16.—An Erie train consisting of forty-two cars lying on the main tracks was set on fire at midnight, and up to 1 o'clock fifteen cars were burned. At 1 o'clock a message from the operator at the William street station says that the fire had broken out at three different places in the yards. Nothing could be done by the engines attached to the trains, as the crews were driven from the engines. The fire department was unable to do anything on account of the absence of hydrants.

At 2 o'clock in the morning a train of coal cars on the Lehigh Valley caught fire at each end and burned fiercely. Here and there at intervals of a few minutes fire broke out all along the line, and as many as a dozen different blazes were seen at one time and the sky was lurid with the reflections of the flames. Just about this time the switch lights on the Erie, between Smith station and the Western New York and Pennsylvania, were stolen and the switches left in darkness.

The fire department complains that the work of the men at the freight car fires was much impeded by the cutting of hose by unknown parties. Twelve lengths of hose were cut and rendered useless during the night. The number of Erie and Lehigh Valley freight cars destroyed by fire is variously estimated at from 100 to 200.

Police on the Alert.

At every point where the trouble is likely to occur, police are stationed. The reserves from all the precincts in the city are at East Buffalo ready for duty. When Lehigh Valley train No 32 arrived, it had a car of switchmen who had been picked up along the line of the road. The train was an hour late. Before the train had reached Williams street a number of the strikers jumped on the platform, but the guard soon drove them off the way through the yards and until the train pulled into the Erie station the passengers in the cars were constantly expecting an attack would be made upon the train.

Reliable reports received from East Buffalo and Cheektowaga showed that the Lehigh Valley had lost seventy-two cars by the fire and the Erie fourteen. All the railroad men profess to be utterly unable at present to fix an estimate of the loss. They are acting very cautiously on this point for the reason that a claim will be

[Continued on Fourth Page.]

WEATHER INDICATIONS.

FAIR.

WASHINGTON, Aug. 16.—For the 24 hours from 8 a. m. to-day: For New England, fair; northwesterly winds.

HOME MATTERS.

PERSONAL.—At the National Congregational Council, to be held at the Plymouth church, Minneapolis, Oct. 12 to 18, Massachusetts will be represented by Rev. Alonzo H. Quint, General Association; Rev. M. C. Julien of this city, Old Colony Conference; Willis E. Lougee, Pilgrim Conference; Rev. Samuel V. Cole and Deacon J. B. Parsons, Taunton Conference; Rev. Daniel W. Clark and John E. Pratt, M. D., Barnstable Conference, and many others.

Benoni Irwin, one of the best known portrait painters in the country, who is visiting at Nonquitt, was in this city yesterday calling on some of his old friends.

Thomas F. Glennon has been promoted to be superintendent of the New Bedford Manufacturing Co. John H. Hines, the former superintendent, has been appointed superintendent of the Howland Mills Corporation.

Representative Frank W. Francis and family and Miss Mabel Bliss of this city are spending a few weeks at Mrs. Cory's cottage, Westport Point.

Dr. Henry A. Kelley of Portland, Me., is in the city on a two weeks' vacation.

James E. Moore, bookkeeper for David Duff & Son, has gone on a trip to Saratoga, Montreal and other places.

Henry H. Lannigan, a well-known all-around athlete of Fall River, an ex-member of the Y. M. P. T. & B. Society and Y. M. C. A., and also an ex-member of the Fall River Caledonians, has been appointed Professor of Physical Culture at Cornell University, Ithaca, N. Y.

The Misses Lizzie and Annie Corey of Providence are visiting relatives in this city.

Miss Maria L. Hackett is spending her vacation at Central Falls, R. I.

Miss Annie F. Mosher is spending her vacation at Westport Point.

Mr. E. H. Hodgson of Georgia, accompanied by his son, Lieut. F. G. Hodgson, adjutant of the Sixth U. S. Cavalry, stationed at Fort Niobrara, Neb., are visiting Charles Strahan at Haven Side, Vineyard Haven.

Col. Tripp, of the State Board of Charities, is in the city to-day.

VETERANS OF THE THIRTY-THIRD.—The annual reunion of the Thirty-third Regiment Association was held at the Pacific House, Nantasket, yesterday. It was the thirtieth anniversary of the departure of the regiment for the seat of war. At 1 o'clock the annual business meeting was held in the hotel parlor, President Samuel Canning presiding. The following-named officers were elected on recommendation of the nominating committee:

President—William J. Hargraves.
Vice-President—C. F. Bryant.
Secretary and Treasurer—A. C. Stacy.

Remarks were made by the new president. A vote of thanks was tendered to the retiring president; also the secretary. After-dinner speeches were made by Samuel Canning, Quartermaster Richardson, A. C. Stacy, J. B. Smith, G. B. Sewell, John Barrows, C. F. Bryant and Lieut. Peabody.

THE HEALTH AND PLEASURE RESORTS OF MICHIGAN AND THE WEST are illustrated and described in a handsome folder, containing a fine colored map, which has just been issued by the Michigan Central "The Niagara Falls Route" and which is designed for the special use of people in the East who wish to learn something about the resorts of Michigan, Wisconsin, the Isle of Mackinac, the lakes or Minnesota, Yellowstone Park, Colorado, Utah, and the Pacific coast.

Copy of folder will be sent on application to W. H. Underwood, Eastern Passenger Agent, Buffalo, N. Y.

CANOE MATTERS.—The canoeists who occupy J. S. Wright's canoe house on Pope's Island are arranging for a series of races Friday evening. A neat flag of white with a large red crab has been adopted by Mr. Wright and his associates as a club flag, and the first one designed from an idea suggested by Mr. Wright was seen on the river last evening on the handsome little canoe of Arnold J. Wright. It is thought that the canoeists associated with Mr. Wright will soon form a club or association.

A REVISED EDITION of "The Care and Feeding of Infants" has just been published by the Doliber-Goodale Co., Boston, Mass. Any mother can obtain a copy, without charge, by sending them her address.

NATURALIZATION.—Iver A. Jensen filed a primary declaration in the clerk's office of the Third District Court this morning. T. A. Codd for petitioner.

DOES IT STRIKE YOU?—Large Eight Day Striking Mantel Clock, only $2.62. Best Alarm Clocks, warranted, only 95 cents. J. S. Kelley & Son, 15 Purchase street.

LINCOLN GUARDS.—Members of this organization will find it of interest to read the special notice on fourth page. Drill to-night.

W. C. T. U.—There will be a meeting of the W. C. T. U. in the Woman's Parlors, 190 Purchase street, Wednesday at 3 p. m.

GREEN GOODS.—The "green goods" swindlers are still flooding this vicinity with their circulars.

DANCING AT BEACON VILLA this evening. See special notice.

HEALTH is secured by an absolutely fair, open pore skin.

MISS PARLOA'S Appledore Cook Books only 10c. each at Hutchinson's Book Store.

RHEUMATISM cured. 5 South Sixth street.

FRENCH KID Oxford Ties $2.00. Devoll's.

TUB BATH—25 cents. 5 South Sixth street.

HOOD'S Sarsaparilla is sold by all Druggists.

THE WORK OF THE POLICE.

Difference of Opinion as to the Fall River Tragedy.

Unfavorable Criticisms and Unqualified Indorsements.

Expressions of Sympathy for the Prisoner and Recent Developments.

The terrible topic of conversation in Fall River, which for more than a week has kept the city in a turmoil, has not been changed as yet, but interest in it is beginning to lag, says the Providence Journal. The community is as anxious as ever to learn the whole truth, but it realizes at last that the information which the authorities possess is likely to be locked up for months, and it is becoming resigned to the situation, and a little indifferent regarding some of the mysteries on which the brain has been at work so incessantly. Men still discuss the murder, but they have drifted from the details of the killing to matters somewhat remote. They want to know whether a condemned person can will away property, how District Attorney Knowlton will proceed at the preliminary hearing, and a thousand and one other things which bear more directly on the future than on the past. Up to date there has been but very little veering in public opinion, always providing that it is possible to get at public opinion and weigh it correctly. But from remarks dropped here, there, and everywhere, it is gathered that people continue to cling to their original ideas concerning the butchery.

Many admit that they would be glad to abandon them if their minds would give consent, and these are the supporters of the police. Others more fortunate in their convictions contend, as they have contended from the first, that a frightful mistake has been made, and some of them are so vehement that the effect of their arguments is to be plainly seen. Their opponents are much more conservative in expressing their views and avoid, if possible, being drawn into a controversy. They do not care to have their fellows know what they think, and wisely refrain from talking. All things considered, that is the safest course to pursue, because, as has been explained over and over again, nobody has any reliable authority on which to base assertions. It is speculation pure and simple, and while it may be as judicious to speculate on one side as the other, nothing that is at all convincing can come of it. Judge Blaisdell, District Attorney Knowlton and City Marshall Hilliard probably have a secret which, if revealed, would throw much light on places which are now dark, but they are the only persons in possession of the evidence, with the exception of the official stenographer, and thus far they have carefully guarded it. Anybody is free to approach them, perhaps, but it is certain that nobody has approached them with satisfactory results.

Nevertheless, men will assume to be profoundly wise and men will talk. Some of the talk leads to disputes but when the average is over it has produced no effect on sentiment. A great deal is said about a free country which would not be said were Miss Lizzie Borden free, and considerable is heard regarding the false steps which lawyers have taken. But for the most part it comes from people of mature years, who have just taken up the study of law, and who have devoted the greater part of their lives to manufacturing cloth and buying and selling stocks. Accordingly, it is surmised that there are certain points which they have overlooked, as the curriculum which they are pursuing is but four days old with them. Still, this is only a suspicion. When the law doesn't pan out exactly as expected, these same people fall back on justice. Everybody seems to be particularly strong on justice just now. Occasionally a man will admit that his law is a trifle ragged, but he knows justice as far as he can see it, and he is positive that there has been no justice in this case; not so much as a respectable counterfeit.

Yesterday City Marshal Hilliard had something to say about the criticisms which certain newspapers were making. He said that those newspapers had not printed the information which was in the possession of the government for the very good reason that they didn't have it to print. They were basing their editorial comments on such opinions as they were able to form from their news columns, and were thus attempting to influence public sentiment and prove that the police had blundered. The government, if it had the welfare of the community at heart, could not consistently give away its case, and nothing but the peculiar circumstances which surrounded this murder and distinguished it from other murders prompted people to demand that a full expose should be made on the spot. It was manifestly unfair, he continued, to assume that because everything had not been revealed there was nothing to reveal. The police had all along been influenced in Lizzie Borden's favor. It was natural to be so influenced, and every theory that could be advanced to divert suspicion from her had been followed to a legitimate conclusion. But before the inquest had been concluded and before a preliminary hearing had been held, some of the papers were claiming that a foul injustice had been done. When all the facts were fully known, it would be in order to bring in a verdict and condemn or exonerate the government, but until the facts were known it was both idle and wrong to pronounce on the case.

There are many who entertain this view, and it seems to be a simple one. In the entire absence of the particulars of the developments brought out by the inquest, it is widely conceded that judgment should be suspended. The government can be denounced later on; it cannot escape the severest censure if it has erred, but until it can be demonstrated beyond a doubt that it had no good grounds for ordering an arrest and wrecking the reputation of an innocent person, it is as reckless a proceeding to arraign the authorities as it is to insist that the prisoner is guilty. All that is positively known is that while the inquest was in progress, before all the testimony was in, District Attorney Knowlton ordered an arrest. It may be argued that he believed that he was doing his duty, or that he had nothing to warrant such a belief. In the latter event, his mistake was almost as fatal to his own reputation as to that of the suspected woman, and nobody has ever heard that District Attorney Knowlton needed a guardian.

The Inquest.

The inquest will be resumed this afternoon at 2 o'clock. There are three or four witnesses to be examined (the marshal says that he cannot state the exact number) and after that it is not thought that there will be any more in the case until next Monday. The government is preparing its evidence and working up material for the preliminary hearing, when the prisoner will either be discharged, or held until the case can be presented to the grand jury.

Now that there is time to study every aspect of the tragedy, the amount of the bail required for Bridget Sullivan, the servant, and John V. Morse, is exciting comment. It is considered strange that the two persons who have been regarded as the most important witnesses for the government should have been placed under nominal bonds. If either of these witnesses dreaded the proceedings which are very sure to follow the arrest which has been made, either because they objected to further publicity, or for any other reason, there is nothing to detain them in Fall River, unless, as has been hinted, they are still under police surveillance. While the present feeling prevails, more than one person can be found who would gladly pay twice the bond demanded to embarrass the police; at least people so express themselves, and they talk as if they were in earnest. But, like other criticism, these comments may not rest on facts. Possibly the testimony of neither of the witnesses mentioned is so vital to the case as is generally supposed, and the government may have arranged to lay its hands on them at any moment. Furthermore, if there were any real object in spiriting them away, it would take considerable more security to hold them than is usually demanded. Until the end comes, therefore, it is as well to take it for granted that the government knows what it is doing, as to assume that it is insane, and from now on the less effort expended in concocting puzzles and in deftaking to unravel them the better for all concerned.

The crank letters continue to pour in, but, for the most part, they are silly effusions without point or meaning. They serve to illustrate how a horror of this kind stirs to unusual activity every unbalanced mind in the country, and to furnish awful examples of alleged spelling.

Topics of Discussion.

The only phase of the murder proper with which the public concerned itself yesterday related to Bridget Sullivan's movements on the morning of the tragedy. If Mr. Morse has been reported correctly, he expected to dine at the Borden homestead that noon, but some little time after 11 o'clock the servant goes upstairs and rests. The dinner hour is approaching, but as far as can be learned nobody was preparing the midday meal, though it is said the family usually sat down to the table on time. Mrs. Borden was upstairs attending to her household duties and it was not considered that she was not in the kitchen. Miss Lizzie was ironing and

ESTABLISHED 1884.

preparing to go away and the servant was lying down in her own room.

There are many things which the community does not understand in connection with the case, and this is one of them. Another is the statement of the young ladies who have been stopping at Marion regarding Miss Borden's contemplated visit. They are reported as follows: "As for Lizzie and her father, they were, without being demonstrative, very fond of each other." "We arrived on Friday, the 22d of July, and the Sunday before that would be the 17th," said one. "I saw her at church and urged her to come when we did, but she said she did not think she ought to. Her father and mother were going across the river, where they had a farm, as they have always done in the Summer, and Lizzie said her father, who would be in town every day and get his dinner at home, would be left alone if she went away. She felt as if she ought to stay at home, at least part of the time, to see that everything went all right. Still she was urged to go over to Marion with the party and told that her father could get his dinners at a restaurant or at the hotel, but Lizzie said there were other little things about his business in the way of writing that she could help him on."

It is known that Miss Borden wrote a letter, which her father mailed on the day he was murdered, advising her friends that she would join them on Monday, the 8th. On Thursday, the 4th, neither her father nor mother had gone across the river to the farmhouse in question, and there was nothing to indicate that Mr. Borden was intending to move that day. If he went on Friday he would have but one day in which to visit there and be at his home before his daughter's departure, and, consequently, she could not be of much assistance to him. It is possible, however, that her friends misunderstood Miss Borden, or that her father and mother changed their plans, thus enabling her to fit upon an earlier date for her visit. The inquest undoubtedly settled all these points yesterday.

Mr. Morse was not at the Borden house when the newspaper men called, and the latter were informed that he had gone to look for a tenement on Winter street. There is an inference nowadays from every statement made, and the inference here was that the family intended to move from the homestead where associations must be anything but pleasant. It is a curious coincidence that District Attorney Knowlton is related by marriage to the family of the late William Almy, Andrew Borden's partner in the undertaking business.

To Leave the House of Horrors.

It was given out on good authority last night that Mr. Morse and Emma were desirous of leaving their present residence as soon as possible. They do not want to stay in the house of horrors any longer, and it was confidently asserted that they are seeking to find a tenement into which to move.

The Ashes in the Cellar Story.

A story was printed yesterday to the effect that some ashes of rags had been found in the cellar of the Borden house, and that they were probably the remains of a bloody dress worn by the murderess. Marshal Hilliard said that he had heard of no such finding, and did not believe that the yarn was true.

Faith in Lizzie Unshaken.

A special meeting of the Young Woman's Christian Temperance Union and the Woman's Christian Temperance Union was held last night in the hall of the latter organization in the block that was owned by the prisoner's father. Mrs. P. S. Ayaleidts of the Woman's Union presided, and Mrs. E. F. Stafford, president of the Young Woman's Union, occupied a place on the platform.

There were no speeches; none seemed to be necessary. All present knew the purpose for which they had assembled, and there was a respectful silence when Mrs. Stafford arose and presented the following resolution:

We offer our profound sympathy to Miss Lizzie A. Borden in the sad and painful bereavement which has befallen her in the recent tragic deaths of her parents. We would also declare our unshaken faith in her as a fellow-worker and sister tenderly beloved, and would assure her of our constant and earnest prayers that she may be supported under the unprecedented trials and sorrows now resting upon her.

The resolution was unanimously adopted by a rising vote.

After the meeting the members gathered in groups and discussed the misfortune of their sister worker, but their conversation was of much the same tenor as the resolutions they had passed.

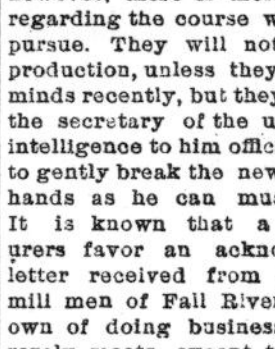

This avowal of confidence, taken in connection with the declaration of the Christian Endeavor Society, printed in yesterday's Standard, shows how Miss Borden is regarded by her society associates, people who have had a chance to see her in a fight strongly contrasting to the one which her arrest has thrown about her.

What Are the Facts?

The Boston Post says:

The city marshal of Fall River defends himself against newspaper criticism of his conduct in the Borden case by saying that if the newspapers had all the facts they would see that he is justified in his acts.

But what are the facts? The star-chamber character of the proceedings is this case is the subject of the complaint which the whole intelligent community makes, and the newspapers only echo this popular complaint.

The public wants to see fair play, and there is by no means a certainty that Lizzie Borden has received it. The conduct of her examination by the same judge who presided at the inquest does not look like it.

Much of this doubt might be dispelled if the proceeding in the inquest had been public. At least, in that case there would have been no such cause for complaint as that which now agitates the city marshal.

But it is not too late to remedy this mistake. Let the proceedings at the inquest be published; they were carefully taken down and are in the possession of the authorities, and then the public and the newspapers can form their judgment without that bias against the officials, which is now unavoidable.

More Criticism of the Police.

The Boston Herald:

The latest verdict of the Fall River police, that if Lizzie Borden committed the murder she is insane, illustrates how fond the average detective is of theorizing. Perhaps this branch of the business had better be left to experts on mental diseases when the time comes.

Should Suspend Judgment.

The Providence Journal says: It is quite true that in the case of an accused person innocence is to be presumed until guilt is proved; but that obvious fact seems to have misled some journals and some people into denouncing the arrest of Miss Borden as persecution and the legal proceedings which led to it as tyrannical. That the human mind should resist to the last the belief that such a woman could commit such a crime is entirely natural and creditable. But, as we have hitherto pointed out, it is taking too much for granted to say that the authorities, who have been investigating the Fall River murder apparently with the greatest care and patience, would venture to accuse Miss Borden without strong evidence against her; nor is the withholding of this evidence for the present any indication that it is insufficient. An extra-legal trial is just as objectionable when it seeks to establish innocence as when it seeks to prove guilt. It is no worse for Miss Borden to be charged with the crime than to be suspected of it. The public should suspend judgment in this juncture, but it cannot properly acquit her until the facts are all

FINANCIAL.

Dividend Notice.

OFFICE OF F. E. BELDEN MICA MINING CO., 128 School street, Boston, Mass. August 8th, 1892.

THE regular monthly dividend will be paid August 22d, to stockholders of record August 19th. F. EUGENE BELDEN, Treasurer. au11-13-16

SECOND EDITION.

HOME MATTERS.

TOWN BARN TO BE REBUILT.

Mattapoisett Citizens Take Action at a Meeting This Afternoon.

A special town meeting at Mattapoisett was held in Purrington Hall this afternoon at 2 o'clock to see whether the town would authorize its board of overseers of the poor to build a barn at the alms-house to replace the one recently burned by lightning, and second to see whether the town would authorize the treasurer to borrow money and issue notes of the town to pay for the same. Just 24 citizens were present.

Town Clerk W. B. Nelson called the meeting to order and read the warrant.

After two ballots Joseph L. Meigs was chosen moderator, and qualified before Justice of the Peace W. B. Nelson.

The first article of the warrant was then taken up. Selectman Noah Hammond said it was self-evident to those at the fire that the town had lost its barn and that it was equally self-evident that it should be replaced, if not this Fall, surely by Spring. A large quantity of hay and considerable stock are on the farm without proper accommodations, the remaining portions of the farm not being large enough to hold them. The insurance of $600 can be applied to the building of the new barn. The old one cost $1000. He believed there would be money enough in the treasury in addition to this sum to rebuild.

James B. Ransom said the sooner it is done the better. He advocated that the work be done by day, as there are plenty of honest carpenters in the town anxious for the job. Contract work is likely to be unsatisfactory.

It was voted 18 to 0 to authorize the overseers of the poor to build a barn at once.

William L. Hubbard moved that the town appropriate $500 in addition to the insurance, that specifications be drawn up and that the contract be awarded to the lowest bidder, subject to the approval of the selectmen.

P. A. Allen did not believe in building a barn by day work. He thought it was better to know definitely the cost before proceeding.

Mr. Hubbard's motion was put to vote and carried, 18 to 0.

On motion of Mr. Hammond it was voted to authorize the town treasurer to raise the money by notes of the town if necessary.

The meeting then adjourned after twenty minutes.

BUILDING.—A. G. Alley, Jr., has petitioned for leave to erect an addition to the rear of building No. 5 South Sixth street, which is used as a bath-house. The addition is to be 17 by 21 feet, 10 feet posts, and is for the purpose of maintaining a swimming tank.

Charles J. Francis requests permission to erect a three-tenement dwelling house on the south side of Coffin avenue, third lot east of Rock street. It is to be 27 by 40 feet, 24 feet posts.

REAL ESTATE SALES.—H. A. Leonard has sold for Stephen A. Brownell to Benj. P. Sisson of Westport, house, barn and 30 rods of land, north side of Court street, west of Florence.

Thomas D. Cannon has sold to Emma L. Phillips, 45.75 rods of land at the corner of Plainville road and Shawmut avenue.

THE CALEDONIANS have received an invitation from the Providence organization to attend the annual festivities of that society to-morrow at Rocky Point. A number of members of the local organization will attend.

PERSONAL.—F. H. Pasell and Noah Gifford left the city Sunday to attend a florists' meeting in Washington, D. C.

Officer Medley of Fall River is in the city to-day, supposed to be on business connected with the Borden murder case.

THE CITY PROPERTY COMMITTEE will hold a meeting this evening to consider the subject of building a new fire station on Hillman street, at the corner of County street.

FUNERAL NOTICE.

The funeral of Henry J., infant son of Joseph F. and Frances Whalen will take place at his father's residence, 86 Bonney street, to-morrow, at 2 30 o'clock. Relatives and friends are invited to attend.

MARINE INTELLIGENCE.

Sld from Boothbay 15th, sch S C Tyron, Richmond.

Ar at New York 15th, steamer Louisianna, Gager, New Orleans; ship Frederick Billings, Williams, San Francisco; scht S L Thompson, Keefe, Taunton; L S Hatch, White, do. Cld, steamer Richmond, Jenney, Newport News.

Ar at Perth Amboy 13th, sch Emma Knowlton, Hudson, Richmond.

Ar at Philadelphia 15th, sch Gardiner B Reynolds, Raynor, Norwick. Cld, schs Harriet S Brooks, Bullock, this port; Rhode Island, Soule, Providence.

Cld at Baltimore 15th, sch John A Beckerman, Gammons, New Haven. Sld, sch A B Sherman, New York.

Ar at Norfolk 12th, sch Horatio, hence.

Sld from Newport News 15th, schs W H Oler, Boston; J H Jackson, Allyn's Point.

FINANCIAL.

Dull but Steady Stocks—Silver Advances and Mexican Central Stiffens in Sympathy—Calumet Continues at 300 Asked—Money Markets Unchanged—Bull Talk on Calumet & Hecla—Said Intrinsic Value is 600 Rather than 300—Union Pacific Earnings—Complete June Statement Showing Operations in Detail—Westinghouse Business—Copper Exports and a Listless Copper Market—Gossip.

TUESDAY, Aug. 16.

The present market is dependent, as usual to this season of the year, upon the manipulations of the more prominent operators, who, with the public absent in the trading, are enabled to turn the market fluctuations up or down at will. The current leaders to-day are Cammack, White and Keene, followed by a host of minor room traders. The first named is proverbially a bear, the others are always to be found in bull ranks. Cammack devotes his attention to pounding the grangers on every possible excuse. White and Keene are each busy booming their especial favorites, the former Western Union and General Electric, the latter Sugar and Cordage. For the near future the situation promises to depend upon the exertions of these men.

The local money market shows few changes to-day. Demand fairly good. Rates easy.

The Boston money market is quiet and steady. The supply of paper offering is not abundant. At clearing this morning loans were all at 4 per cent. New York funds 12½ and 15 cents discount per $1000.

In New York the market for call money ranges near 2 per cent. Time rates unaltered.

Sterling dull and strong.

Bonds quiet.

Wall street gossip this morning said: Continued shipments of gold and the somewhat serious turn the strikers at Buffalo have taken, and the reported rate cutting throughout the country, are some of the influences favoring the bears. The market, however, is irregular and constantly showing strength in new spots. Just now Western Union, Manhattan and the industrials are favorites. No decided tendency to the market is indicated at the moment. Silver somewhat stronger. London lower ¼ to ⅜ per cent.

New York stocks were dull this morning. Atchison held steady at 39, however, and B. Q. was strong at 102⅜, Rock Island gained ⅜ and St. Paul ¼. Sugar broke ¾ to 109⅛. In the early afternoon there was little further change. Cordage sold at 127½, do. preferred 121. Western Union touched 100, later 100⅛. Silver moved up to 84⅛.

At 2 o'clock the market was strong.

Mexican Central jumped up ⅜ in the Boston market this morning, following the rise in silver. Other stocks were featureless. Calumet remained at 300 asked. Atchison 39, B. & Q. 102⅜, Old Colony 183. In the early afternoon the market continued dull and steady. West End 74, Boston & Maine 179⅜, up 1⅜ from closing.

The Boston News Bureau will say to-night: "Calumet at 300 may look high but copper mining experts declare the intrinsic value of the stock nearer to 600 than 300 per share. We are informed by people with good sources of such information that it is in contemplation to pay $30 per share to Calumet stockholders next year."

At 2 o'clock the market was irregular. General Electric strong at 116½, Bell 204.

Sales to noon in Boston to-day were: Bonds $38,000, and 9328 shares of stock.

Some of the bullion dealers believe that while silver may not have seen its lowest, a manipulated rally is at hand. Mr. S. V. White, who some weeks ago made a sharp and successful upward movement in certificates, is rumored to be interested in the deal, and if London does not spoil things that operator may put the price up several points.

A 10 45 special says: "The grangers appear to be strengthening. Not very much business, but the market is showing a firmer undertone. The talk among traders is that the shorts are beginning to feel uneasy."

The product of the Ontario Silver Mining Co. last week was in ore sales $21,340.

The Daly mine output last week was 14,482 ounces bullion.

Gould interests are reported as heavy sellers on every advance.

This week's Boston bank statement shows a reserve increase of $380,143.

The copper market is listless and uncomfortable, owing to the absence of any demand. During the next few weeks the market is liable to remain inactive, manufacturers having all their needs supplied for that period. Casting copper is a trifle lower at 10⅞. Arizona pig unchanged.

Atchison loans at 5 per cent. in the loan crowd, C. B. & Q. 2 per cent., Sugar 4 per cent., Union Pacific 4 per cent., New England 3 per cent.

East-bound shipments last week were 47,366 tons, against 47,675 tons the same week last year.

The Rock Island officials are exuberant over the prospects for the coming year. All parts of the road did well enough in the last fiscal year, but now they are doing far better, and it is believed that the present fiscal year will be the best in the history of the company. It is now certain that the extension of the company west of the Missouri river will earn the full interest charges this year, a result that was not expected for five years yet, as it was thought it would require until then to put the extensions on a paying basis.

Yesterday's grain car receipts at Chicago were: Wheat, 839 cars; corn, 468 cars; oats, 331 cars; total, 1638.

Heidelbach & Ickleheimer will ship $1,000,000 gold to-day. These gold exports are due to sales of American securities for European account.

The exports of copper from New York last week and since Jan. 1st and the value of the same are summarized below. There were for the week no exports of fine copper, it being all matte. The previous week there were no exports of either:

Copper.	Week Aug. 12.	Since Jan. 1.
Matte, pounds,	1,074,112	26,977,191
Fine equivalent at 55 per cent.,	590,816	14,837,454
Fine copper, pounds,		14,808,603
Total fine,	590,816	29,646,057
Value.		
Matte,	$62,423	$1,846,926
Fine copper,		1,545,552
Totals,	$62,423	$3,392,478

To-day's *Advertiser* says:

Western Union, or "Telegraph" as it is familiarly called by the boys on the street, did not touch par, but it sold and closed at 99⅞. As would be natural there was considerable of the stock offering at the $100 market, but it is more than an even chance that the first sale to-day will be at that price. The deacon told us a long time ago that it would cross 100 before Sept. 1.

To-day's Boston *Herald* says:

No explanation was heard of the great rise in Calumet & Hecla to 300 yesterday, and none is needed. When wanted there is not much of the stock to be had. When there is much to sell, which rarely happens, the market is apt to be small. An order to buy or sell "at the market" will sometimes bring wide fluctuations. It is over two years since this stock sold at 300 per share.

The June statement of the Union Pacific follows:

Grand Total Union Pacific system.

June.	1892.	1891.	Inc.
Earnings,	$3,920,413	$3,524,741	$395,671
Expenses,	2,256,194	2,396,419	*140,224
Surplus,	$1,664,218	$1,128,321	$535,896
Mileage,	8,147	8,143	4
Six months.			
Earnings,	$19,978,273	$19,437,363	$540,909
Expenses,	13,494,504	13,653,943	*159,438
Surplus,	$6,483,768	$5,783,420	$700,348

*Decrease.

Latest Atchison earnings in detail follows;

Total All Lines.

	1892.	1891.	Inc.
First August,	$950,280	$868,338	$81,942
Since July 1,	4,930,750	4,705,784	224,966
Mileage,	9,344	9,332	12

Mr. George Westinghouse is reported as saying that his company is doing a business of between $1,800,000 and $2,000,000 net for the year. Net earnings of $2,000,000 would pay all fixed charges, 7 per cent. on the preferred, 7 per cent. on the common, and leave a balance of $1,261,000. The lowest estimates are that the company is earning 15 per cent. on its entire capital.

STOCK AND BOND MARKETS.

Bids at the close of the Second Board.

NEW YORK, Aug. 16.

GOVERNMENT BONDS.

U.S. 2s, registered	100
" new 4s, registered	115½
" new 4s, coupons	115½
" currency 6s, 1895, (Pacifics)	107

RAILROADS

Atchison	38⅞
Clev., Cin., Chicago & St. Louis	—
Chicago & Eastern Illinois	—
Chicago & Eastern Illinois pref	—
Chicago, Burlington & Quincy	102¼
Delaware & Hudson	136
Delaware & Lackawanna	—
Erie	27¾
Illinois Central	100⅜
Lake Shore & Michigan Southern	135¼
Louisville & Nashville	69½
Michigan Central	—
Missouri Pacific	59⅞
New Jersey Central	134
New York & New England	36¾
Northern Pacific	20⅞
Northern Pacific pref	55⅞
Chicago & Northwestern	117⅞
New York Central & Hudson River	113¾
North American	13⅞
Oregon Navigation	—
Oregon Improvement	—
Oregon Short Line	—
Philadelphia & Reading	59¼
Pullman Palace Car Co	—
Chicago, Rock Island & Pacific	81¼
Chicago, Milwaukee & St. Paul	82⅜
Chicago, Milwaukee & St. Paul pref	—
Richmond Terminal	—
St. Paul & Omaha	53
St. Paul & Omaha pref	—
Union Pacific	38⅞
Wabash, St. Louis & Pacific	—
Wabash, St. Louis & Pacific pref	—

MISCELLANEOUS

Ontario Silver	41
Pacific Mail Steamship Co	34
Sugar, common	108⅛
Sugar, pref	—
Western Union Telegraph	100⅛
Silver Certificates	—

BOSTON, Aug. 16.

BONDS

Atchison 4s	82¾
Atchison Incomes	59⅛
American Bell Telephone 7s	114
Chicago, Burlington & Northern 5s	—
Chicago & West Michigan 5s	—
Mexican Central 4s	68½
Illinois Steel Co. 5s	100

RAILROADS.

Atchison, Topeka & Santa Fe	38⅞
Boston & Albany	205
Boston & Lowell	*182
Boston & Maine	180
Boston & Providence	250
Chicago, Burlington & Quincy	102⅜
Chicago & West Michigan	—
Cleveland & Canton	5¼
Cleveland & Canton pref	19¾
Flint & Pere Marquette	—
Flint & Pere Marquette pref	*78½
Mexican Central	16
New York & New England	36⅝
New York & New England pref	*89
Old Colony	*183
Oregon Short Line	23½
Pullman Palace Car	196
Union Pacific	39
Wisconsin Central	17
West End	73½
West End pref	*87¾

MINING.

Butte & Boston Mining Co	—
Calumet & Hecla Mining Co	*300
Centennial	7¾
Franklin Mining Co	12½
Kearsarge	—
Montana	37
Osceola Mining Co	31
Tamarack	*168

MISCELLANEOUS.

American Bell Telephone	203½
Erie Telephone	—
Mexican Telephone	1.02½
New England Telephone	53
Newport Land	*1½
Boston Land Co	—
West End Land Co	18¼
San Diego Land Co	—
Topeka Land & Development Co	*1
Lamson Store Service	18
Illinois Steel Co	—
Am. Sugar Refineries, com	108
Am. Sugar Refineries, pref	101½
Gen'l Electric	—
Gen'l Electric	—

*Asked.

FALL RIVER STOCK QUOTATIONS.

The following are the quotations of Fall River stocks to-day as reported by Sanford & Kelley, bankers and brokers and stock auctioneers:

	Par.	Bid.	Asked.	Last Sale.
American Linen Co	$100	—	114	114
Barnaby Mfg. Co	100	130	150	130
Barnard Mfg. Co	100	—	99	99
Border City Mfg. Co	100	—	140	137½
Bourne Mills	100	150	—	150
Chace Mills	100	—	112	111
Cornell Mills	100	87	—	87½
Crescent Mills	100	—	32½	30
C. Spring Bleachery	100	—	—	31
Davol Mills	100	97½	100	99
Edison Illuminating	100	—	—	—
Fall River Bleachery	100	—	100	—
Flint Mills	100	110	112	110
Globe St. Railway Co	100	—	—	—
Globe Yarn Mills	100	—	122½	120
Granite Mills	100	—	245	242½
Hargraves Mills	100	100	102	100
King Philip Mills	100	123¼	125	123¾
Kerr Thread Co	100	—	105	105
Laurel Lake Mills	100	—	110	110
Massasoit Nat'l Bank	100	—	—	185
Mechanics' Mills	100	—	98	98
Merchants' Mfg. Co	100	—	125	124
Metacomet Mills	100	—		64
Metacomet National Bank	100	—	—	130
National Union Bank	100	—	—	104½
Narragansett Mills	100	—	105	105
Osborn Mills	100	108½	—	110
Pocasset Mfg. Co	100	—	110	110
Pocasset Nat'l Bank	100	—	—	—
Richard Borden Mfg	100	103	105	103½
Robeson Mill	100	—	80	78
Sanford Spinning Co	100	—	100	—
Sagamore Mfg. Co	100	—	122½	*121
Seaconnet Mills	100	115	116	115½
Shove Mills	100	—	113	112½
Slade Mills	100	56	58	58
Stafford Mills	100	123	125	124
Tecumseh Mills	100	—	113	112½
Troy C. & W. Manufactory	500	—	1025	1000
Union Mfg. Co	100	—	220	220
Wampanoag Mills	100	—	106	103
Weetamoe Mills	100	—	56	55

*Dividend on.

CALIFORNIA MINING STOCKS.

SAN FRANCISCO, Aug. 15.

The following are the official closing prices of mining stocks to-day:

Alta	—	Mexican	1 30
Best & Belcher	1 30	Mt. Diablo	—
Chollar	—	Ophir	2 25
Con. Cal. & Va.	3 40	Potosi	—
Crown Point	—	Savage	—
Eureka Con	1 50	Sierra Nevada	1 15
Gould & Curry	—	Union Con	—
Hale & Norcross	—	Utah	—

NEW YORK PRODUCE MARKET.

NEW YORK, Aug. 16.

Flour sales 4800 packages; quiet.
Wheat sales 855,000 bushels; ⅛ to ¼c. lower; longs selling; large receipts.
Corn sales 95,000 bushels; dull and weak.
Oats sales 40,000 bushels; dull and easier.
Beef dull.
Pork firm and quiet.
Butter firm.
Cheese quiet.
Sugar (raw) firm and quiet.
Turpentine quiet.
Molasses dull and steady.
Rice firm.
Freights quiet.
Rosin steady.
Tallow firm and quiet.

PROVISIONS AND GRAIN.

CHICAGO, Aug. 16.

Opening.

	Lard.	Wheat.	Pork.	Corn.	Sh't Ribs.
May	—	85	—	53⅛	—
June	—	—	—	—	—
July	—	—	—	—	—
Aug.	—	—	—	—	—
Sept.	—	77¼	12.40	52⅜	—
Oct.	—	—	—	52¼	—
Dec.	—	79⅞	—	50⅞	—
Jan.	—	—	13.40	—	—
12 o'clock.					
May	—	85	—	53⅛	—
June	—	—	—	—	—
July	—	—	—	—	—
Aug.	—	—	—	—	—
Sept.	—	77¼	12.37½	52⅛	—
Oct.	—	—	—	52⅛	—
Dec.	—	79⅞	—	50⅞	—
Jan.	—	—	13.40	—	—

ANOTHER POSSIBLE CLEW.

Police Looking for a Man Seen Near the Borden House on Two Occasions.

FALL RIVER, Aug. 16.—The inquest in the Borden murders will not be resumed this afternoon, contrary to all expectations. The district attorney has not put in an appearance, and Marshal Hilliard went to Boston this morning.

The police have decided that 13 minutes elapsed from the time Bridget Sullivan asked Mr. Borden how he was until she was called down stairs by Miss Lizzie to give an alarm about the murder of her father.

The sofa on which Mr. Borden was murdered was brought to the Central police station this morning and will be kept there until after the trial.

The police are hunting for a man of whom the following description is given: Height five feet two inches, complexion very white, wore light gray business suit, brown derby hat, lawn tennis shoes. His only beard was a short red moustache. He was seen twice in the neighborhood of the Borden house August 1st and August 4th.

Sympathy and Justice.

NEW YORK, Aug. 16.—The *Herald* says:

It seems that about fifty editorials clipped from various New England papers were handed to City Marshal Hilliard of Fall River, yesterday, as a protest against the arrest of Lizzie Borden.

The popular sympathy for this unfortunate woman, based on belief in her innocence, is natural and creditable. At the same time it cannot properly or safely be allowed to interfere with the course of justice.

When a heinous crime has been committed and is shrouded in mystery it is the first and highest duty of the public authorities to unravel the mystery and discover the criminal. Of course no attempt to throw suspicion or fix guilt upon any innocent person is to be countenanced. But every clew and scrap of evidence are to be followed, no matter to whom it may all point or lead as the guilty one.

The Fall River authorities are in possession of much evidence that has been withheld from the public. It is on this that they have proceeded, and on this the probable innocence or guilt of the accused can alone be judged at the present time.

WEATHER INDICATIONS.

CONTINUED FAIR.

BOSTON, Aug. 16.—Local forecast for New England until Thursday night: Continued fair weather; no decided changes in temperature; variable winds, mostly westerly.

WARMER.

NEW YORK, Aug. 16.—At 8 30 a. m. the weather was clear, wind west, temperature 71. The *Herald* says: In the Middle States and New England on Wednesday, warmer, fair weather and southerly winds will probably prevail, followed by an increase of sultriness, and similar conditions on Thursday.

AN IRON HALL SENSATION.

Assignment of the Safe Deposit Company in Charge of the Order's Funds.

PHILADELPHIA, Aug. 6.—The Mutual Banking, Surety Trust & Safe Deposit Company, in which Iron Hall funds are deposited, assigned to-day.

GLADSTONE'S DEPARTURE.

Enthusiastic Farewell Extended as He Embarked on Yacht Alberta.

LONDON, Aug. 16.—Mr. Gladstone left Osborne House at 9 30 this morning on his way back to London. As he drove to East Cowes, where the royal yacht Alberta was awaiting him to convey him across the river Solent, the road was lined with people who had gathered to bid him farewell. He was cheered along the entire route. A heavy rain was falling but this in no way dampened the enthusiasm of the crowd.

Twenty minutes after leaving Osborne House he was on board the Alberta, the lines were cast off and she was steaming across the Solent. A choppy sea was running and the yacht rolled and pitched heavily, making the passage one of discomfort. Mr. Gladstone was taken to Southampton, where he took the 11 12 train for Waterloo station, London. Everywhere he was surrounded by a good natured crowd, who heartily cheered him and greeted him with cries of "Bravo, William."

THE SWITCHMEN'S STRIKE.

New York Central Officials Demand Protection for their Property.

BUFFALO, Aug. 16.—Other companies of troops arrived at William street and took up position near the 65th. Other detachments of the second regiments also followed. The soldiers will not be used for patrol duty, but held to put down disturbances.

Shortly after dark fire broke out in a box car opposite the Lackawanna Hotel. It was believed to be of incendiary origin. Battalion Chief Petzing and his men put out the fire.

Attorney D. H. McMillen and several of the New York Central officials called on Sheriff Beck at 1 this morning and demanded protection for the property of that road. Although their men had not struck the company had received intimations that they might do so, and trouble was feared. This forenoon there was no indication of a strike on the Central.

The Ocean Steamers.

Passed the Lizard—Wieland, New York.

FUNERAL.

To the Editor of the Standard:

The funeral of Sadie Meigs Purrington was held Sunday at her late residence. A large number of friends and relatives assembled to pay their last tribute of respect to their deceased friend. Twelve of her young associates occupied the room that she has so long been confined in. Rev. C. R. Tenney of Dorchester, her former pastor, read comforting passages of scripture: "The Lord is my Shepherd, I shall not want," &c., touching sacredly on the life and character from her girlhood up to the life when she ceased to be. A quartet choir from Acushnet, of which the sister presides as organist, sung the hymn, "Oh for the peace that floweth like a river," "Lead kindly light," "It is well with my soul."

The body was arrayed in white muslin and laces, with delicate trailing ferns around her, a selection from her father and mother, while she reposed in a most beautiful casket of white polished wood.

The flowers were magnificent and in abundance, there being 32 pieces. Seldom is seen such a beautiful display, all gifts from friends who esteemed her so highly, for she was really a person of rare worth. At the head of the casket stood a standard cross of greens and white flowers, from the church and Sabbath school; pink gladioli, from Sadie Crosby and Frank Spooner; a cross of white carnations, from Jennie Atsatt, Sarah Shurtleff and May Morse; pillow, from J. Hammond; family basket, from Mrs. Heman Holmes; asters, from May Lee Hiller; asters, from Mrs. Dennis; pink pond lilies with pads, attached with pink ribbon, from Mrs. Annie Edwards of California, a dear friend; basket, with motto attached, "He giveth his beloved sleep," from the writer; wreath of roses and maiden-hair ferns, from Mrs. Sarah Sweat and son William of Portland; bouquet of tea roses and ferns, with long loops of white satin ribbon, from Mr. and Mrs. Will Foster of Boston; crescent from Ellis and Madie Mendell and Annie Almy; carnations and ferns, from Mr. and Mrs. Charles Mendell; three bunches of white asters from three cousins; carnations from Mamie Briggs and Olivia Jenney; basket from Mrs. Horace Nye and Mrs. Nellie Williams of Fairhaven; white pond lilies, Mrs. Thomas Cannon, Bridgewater; potted palm, Miss Kate Jones; sweet peas, Annie Purrington, New Bedford; cut flowers from Ella Johnson, as well as others. The burial will be at the convenience of the family.

Crown her with flowers
So lovely and fair;
Holy and pure
As the bright angels are.

Weep not for her,
So happy and blest
Gone to her Savior
Sweetly to rest.

Angels will guard her
Free from all care,
Sorrow and sadness
Can ne'er enter there.

Happy and pure
Is her bright spirit now
God's holy seal
Rest on brow.

Fold her hands meekly
Across her pure breast,
Angels will lovingly
Bear her to rest.

Bear her to mansions
Of peace and of joy,
Where sin cannot enter
Nor sickness destroy.

Where parting and grief
Will no more be known;
All be united,
'Round God's holy throne.

Mattapoisett. P. H. R.

Fall River's "Boom."

To those who have followed the trend of manufacturing affairs at Fall River during the past months, the published report of the present condition of the various print mills will occasion little surprise. To others, however, who think of our greatest cotton manufacturing centre as a huge conglomeration of spindles, looms and auxiliary machinery, worked by a population whose treadmill duty is circumscribed by the morning and evening bell, and whose product, like some other commodities, is subject continually to that sharp competition which characterizes manufactured goods generally, it will give a new conception regarding the print cloth business.

While Fall River manufacturers have had some pretty uncomfortable experiences in the past, it must be admitted that at present print cloth has to contend with few of the vicissitudes of ordinary manufactures, and instead of prints being sent out in quest of consumers, the buyers are scrambling for recognition in the making of contracts for future delivery. And in this connection it is interesting to note that not only are the legitimate traders bidding on the prospective stock, but speculators as well are reported as buying in considerable quantities in the hope of gain when the accumulated contracts will be even more out of proportion to the supply than they are at present.

The rise in prices has been by easy stages, so that, at present quotations, there is conceded to be a good profit to the mills. In fact, this is so far true that the earnings of the present quarter allow of the distribution by 46 of the mills of dividends amounting to $356,880 on a capital of $18,123,000, or an average for the quarter of nearly 2 per cent.; and in addition to this there has been added as much more to their surplus or reserve funds.

Whether this showing of what is the most prosperous season in cotton manufacture ever experienced is due to the present protective tariff or not, it is a fact which goes a good way toward furnishing an argument in favor of our present policy that the gratifying conditions noted exist contemporaneously with it, and after it had been on trial long enough to affect for good or ill any industry that came directly under its influence.—*Boston Advertiser.*

LOST.

Advertisements under this heading 1c. a word a time. No charge less than 25c.

GORDON SETTER DOG—10 months old. Return to GEO. F. FLETCHER, 43 Elm street and be suitably rewarded. au16-2t

REAL ESTATE.

Cottage House.

Well built, good repair, in part of city growing rapidly; will make good home and *must* increase in value. Apply box 6, *Standard* office. ap25-tf

FOR SALE—In South Dartmouth, near the water, a 2½ story house with large piazza, barn, and 83 rods of land. One of the most desirable places in the village for a Summer residence. Inquire of BENJ. QUERIPEL or DANIEL H. HOWLAND, South Dartmouth. ap7-tf

TROUT AND FLIES

SUPERSTITIONS THAT ANGLERS INVARIABLY FOLLOW.

An Angler Discourses on the Taboos of the Sacred Fish—There Seems to Be No Reason Why Other Bait Than Flies May Not Be Used in Hooking Trout.

Angling on the Itchen, the Test and all other fashionable trout streams is governed by a rigid law that the fly is the only permissible lure. No sportsman questions the tradition, which indeed is so thoroughly established that the very poacher in the dead of night would blush at the thought of using anything grosser than an alder.

Nearly all etiquettes, howsoever difficult it may be to perceive what originally gave rise to them, are rational at bottom; but this one seems an exception. There is no obvious reason why worm or gentles or the Alexandra fly or even minnow should be tabooed. At least there is none that we can see.

Perhaps if one were venturesome enough to ask a Hampshire fisherman in what respect a minnow is offensive, we should be told that it falls into the water with a shocking splash. The splash is undeniable; but surely it is an inadequate explanation of the taboo. A minnow is not the only thing that splashes. We have seen the lightest dry fly splash abominably, to the obvious terror of the trout; and the Hampshire fisherman himself splashes, for he invariably wades, and in that act disturbs the water in half an hour more than all the minnows in the tackle shops could possibly do in a day.

It is equally impossible to think that the objectionable characteristic of the minnow is that it is too killing. The minnow is not killing at all. He who could do any good with a minnow in the pellucid waters of a chalk stream would be an artist of incomparable skill. The trout usually flee an angler's minnow in a perturbation compared with which the author of "Salome's" displeasure with the lord chamberlain is equanimity. Can it be, then, that in tabooing the minnow our fishermen are making a virtue of a necessity, and not countenancing it merely because it is useless? We might incline to this conjecture, if it were not that the best managed dry fly is usually useless too. Why are our modern fishermen so fastidious as to the means by which they achieve failure?

Rumination on the gentle makes the subject darker than ever. Indeed gentles, which may be defined as maggots, wasp grubs, caddis or any other white creeping things, are treated according to a code of angling morals which is quite inexplicably arbitrary. You must not use a gentle when it is a "stone bait;" but you do a highly meritorious action when, ten minutes afterward, he has taken to himself the wings of the greendrake and you seize him to adorn a tail. You must not use a maggot from the butchers; but you are at liberty to put a bit of white leather on a fly hook, and that oddly enough is sometimes a lure more deadly than the gentle, of which it is intended to be an imitation. You must not use an Alexandra, but nobody will hinder you from working with a 2-inch Jock Scott if you are fool enough to prefer that means of failure.

There is, however, a reason for this particular taboo. It is founded upon a wisdom akin to that of Theophile Gautier's cat, which, hearing a parrot speak, remarked reflectively: "This is not a bird. This is a gentleman. Listen to his conversation!" In the estimate of the conscientious fisherman, the Alexandra fly is not a fly. It is a minnow. Its dressing of feathers looks like wings; but there are three hooks underneath, and when the thing is in the water it has the appearance of a green minnow.

Thus far the philosophy of the taboo is unimpeachable; but we can go no further. The Alexandra's resemblance to a minnow is no closer than that of a brown hackle to a spider, which is so little close that we have the audacity to doubt whether the trout feels himself to be rising at a spider when we feel that it is a spider we are offering him. What cause indeed have we to believe that fish take our lures in the spirit in which they are given? Is it not pretty well ascertained that there is no fly, no shrimp, no prawn which has any likeness to the blue devils, the thunder-and-lightnings and other engines on which salmon willingly impale themselves? What can a trout be thinking of when it snaps at a parr tail? Let us hope that anglers will not allow this so called Nineteenth century to pass away with the premises of their science unrevised. It is high time they were considering the possibility that fish take some lures merely for the fun of the thing, or by way of resenting an insult, and not because the lures seem something good to eat.

Having gone so far in heresy, we may as well say a word for the worm. Any one caught in the act of fishing in Hampshire with a worm would be promptly expelled by his club. As he would have broken the rules, that would serve the rascal right; but really the taboo of the worm is, like crimes' acts in the eyes of the Liberal party when it is the other party which has passed them, a means of turning innocence into wrong.

The worm in itself is inoffensive. Very often, especially on a bright summer day, it would be less of a failure than a fly usually is, but that should not be accounted to its discredit. The streams on which it is forbidden are so well stocked that no harm would be done, although all the fishermen on them tried worm now and then, and succeeded as often and as abundantly as their skill permitted. Successful worm fishing in a clear stream is no mean art. It might be rated higher than success with the dry fly, for while it is true that the trout as a rule prefer a worm to an insect, it is also true that to cast a worm so as to attract the fish is much more difficult than to "place" a dry fly neatly.—London Saturday Review.

What He Was Afraid Of.

In a certain case which occurred not long ago, the ordinary rule about letting horses was not applied by a stable keeper. A young man of rather feeble appearance called for a saddle horse for a ride through the park. The horse was saddled, and the stable keeper said:

"I shall have to ask you to pay in advance."

"What?" said the surprised young man. "Do you think I would not come back with the horse?"

"Not exactly that," said the stableman. "I'm afraid the horse might come back without you!"—London Tit-Bits.

The standard coins on the continent are, in France, the franc; in Spain, the peseta; in Italy, the lira; in Holland and Austria, the florin; in Germany, the mark; in Russia, the ruble.

The first lighthouse on the American coast was built at St. Augustine, Fla., by the Spaniards.

AUCTION SALES.

By STANDISH BOURNE,

(Successor to Geo. A. Bourne & Son,) Auctioneer, Commission Merchant, Real Estate Dealer and Appraiser.

Cash advanced on goods consigned for auction. Ready buyer for personal property of every description. Office and Salesrooms 47, 49 and 51 North Second Street, near the Post Office.

Mortgagee's Sale.

On SATURDAY, Aug. 20th, at 3 o'clock, on the premises, will be sold by order of the mortgagee the cottage house, together with lot of 17.28 rods, situated on Summit st., just south of Stowell street. For legal adv. see *Evening Standard* of July 30, Aug. 6 and 13.

Mortgagee's Sale.

By virtue of a power of sale contained in a mortgage deed from Harriet E. Howland to Standish Bourne, trustee, dated June 4th, 1886, and recorded with the Bristol County (S. D.) deeds, Book 118, Pages 19 and 20, and assigned to Susan M. Hathaway Aug. 8th, 1892, and for breach of the condition contained therein, will be sold at public auction on the premises on SATURDAY, Sep. 3d, 1892, at 12½ o'clock, P. M., the following described property, viz.:

A certain tract or parcel of land with the buildings thereon standing, situated in New Bedford, in the County of Bristol, and bounded as follows: Beginning at the northeast corner of said lot at a stone monument placed in the south line of North street; thence southerly in line of land of J. R. Carson ninety-five and ninety-two one hundredths (95.92) feet to the land of Gideon Sherman, thence westerly in line of said Sherman's land thirty-one and forty-two one-hundredths (31.42) feet to land of said Sherman; thence northerly in line of said Sherman's land eleven and fifty one-hundredths (11.50) feet; thence westerly in line of said Sherman's land thirty-one and twenty-five one-hundredths (31.25) feet to land now or formerly of David B. Kempton; thence northerly in line of said Kempton land eighty-four and fifty one-hundredths (84.50) feet to a monument in the south line of North street; thence easterly in line of North street, sixty-four and ninety-one one-hundredths (64.91) feet to the point of beginning, containing twenty one and thirty-eight one-hundredths (21.38) rods, more or less, and being the same premises conveyed to said Harriet E. Howland by Standish Bourne, trustee, by mortgagee's deed, dated June 4, 1886, and recorded in Bristol county Registry of Deeds (S.D.) book 118, page 15. SUSAN M. HATHAWAY, Assignee of said Mortgage. aug9-16-23

To Let in Our Storage Warerooms.

We constantly have on hand first-class rooms for the storage of household goods, to be rented by the month of year. Good dry storage room for stoves.

By JOHN B. BAYLIES,

121 and 123 Union Street,

Commission Merchant, Appraiser, and Auctioneer for the sale of Real Estate and every description of Personal Property. Furniture Bought.

H. C. HATHAWAY,

Auctioneer, Real Estate Agent and Appraiser, Corner Acushnet Ave. and Elm St.

One of the best auction marts in the State for the sale of horses and carriages. Keeps constantly on hand carriages of every description, carriages made to order and repairing in all its branches attended to under the superintendence of J. R. Forbes. Consignments of every description solicited. Cash advanced on goods for auction. Personal property of every description bought at short notice for cash. Negotiable notes bought and sold.

ALFRED WILSON,

Auctioneer and Real Estate Agent, Room 22, - - - Robeson Building.

Houses and land in all parts of the city for sale; tenements for rent: rents collected.

For Sale.

Two-story house on Acushnet avenue, near Walnut street; well arranged for one family; good location.

For Lease.

The Webster Block, Purchase street; 16 rooms, well adapted for a genteel boarding house, club rooms, or business purposes.

TO LET—A flat in The Winslow, corner Sixth and Union streets. Apply to A. WILSON, Robeson Building. jy14-tf.

T. F. HEALEY,

Auctioneer and Real Estate Agent, 555 and 559 Purchase street, corner of Franklin street.

FOR SALE CHEAP—One farm in Rochester of 70 acres; house, barn, outbuildings, etc.; 2 good orchards on place; cut 20 tons of hay. Price $1800.

Also two cottages in Fairhaven; nearly new; fine view of river and harbor; will sell one or both; situated on Main street; will sell to the right parties on easy terms.

Also one fine house in the west part of the city in good locality, with all the modern improvements, gas and electric lights, etc. Will be sold cheap if applied for soon.

Also lots on Acushnet avenue, Coggshall and Locust streets, in fact all parts of the city.

Business solicited. No charges made unless a sale, then my prices are the lowest.

By J. O. DOUGLASS.

REGULAR AUCTION SALE,

Thursday, Aug. 18th, 1892, at 10 15 A. M.

OF 25 horses, consisting of family, driving, express, team, farm, grocery and general business horses, in matched pairs and single. In this lot are some very good horses, two matched pairs, one of them a coach or family team, closely matched, stand 16 hands high, good actors and fine drivers. Also several acclimated horses, been used in and about the city. Also harnesses, foot mats, &c. One two-horse tip cart in good repair. au16-2t

GEO. H. TABER, Auctioneer.

Administratrix' Sale.

By virtue of a license granted to me on the third day of June last, by the Probate Court for the County of Bristol, I shall sell at public auction on the premises hereinafter described, on THURSDAY, the 18th day of August, instant, at 11 o'clock in the forenoon, a lot of land, situated in Fairhaven, Massachusetts, and thus bounded; On the north by Bridge street, on the east by land now or formerly of Noah Spooner, on the south by land formerly of said Spooner, and on the west by Mulberry street, containing thirty-five square rods more or less. Being the premises conveyed to Elnathan E. Delano by deeds recorded in the Bristol (New Bedford District) Registry of Deeds, book 24, page 316 and book 47, page 340. Together with all the buildings thereon standing.

Said property is within five minutes' walk from the horse cars, and has thereon a large commodious house in good repair. A good well and cistern and will be convenient for two families. Terms at sale.

PHEBE S. DELANO, Administratrix of the estate of Elnathan E. Delano. Fairhaven, Aug. 4, 1892. au4-8-15-16-17

BY WM. BARKER, JR., Auctioneer.

Administrator's Sale of Household Furniture, Farming Tools, Carryall, &c., at Auction.

Will be sold at the late residence of Leander Potter, at Russell's Mills village, Dartmouth, WEDNESDAY, Aug. 24, 1892, at 10 o'clock A. M., a general assortment of household furniture, consisting of parlor and chamber sets, beds, tables, chairs, stoves, crockery, carpets, iron, tin and wooden ware, and other articles. The furniture is of excellent quality, in good condition, and includes several articles of ancient style. Also one good carryall; lot of farming tools and fixtures of tailor's shop and other articles. EDWIN L. POTTER, Administrator. Aug. 15, 1892. au15-7t

Pages 1-8.

The Evening Standard.

Pages 1-8.

ESTABLISHED FEBRUARY, 1850.] NEW BEDFORD, WEDNESDAY, AUGUST 17, 1892.---TEN PAGES. TWO CENTS.

HASKELL & TRIPP.

Do you sew?

Here's an opportunity to buy silk or cotton very low.

Brooks' famous English spool cotton—black, white or colors—2c. a spool, 24c. a dozen. As good sewing cotton as is made.

A big factory has sold to us 8000 boxes of waste sewing silk, mostly black, a few mixed colors. Price 5c. per box.

See our window display of above and secure what you may need for the next six months, at least. Such a chance *is not an every-day occurrence.*

Bamboo goods.

Special offering in basement this week.

Bamboo tables, 25c. each.

Bamboo corner basket, three shelves, brass mounted, 50c. each.

Bamboo easels, brass mounted, 5 feet high, 89c.

White Mountain ice cream freezers.

Preserving kettles.

Mason's fruit jars.

An apron bargain.

New large white aprons of hemstitched lawn with striped border and sash strings, 25c. each. Entirely unlike any aprons we have ever sold, and we think you'll agree they are better than ever before offered for 25c.

Storm serges continue the leading article in the dress goods stock. We have a great variety at 50c., 75c. and $1 per yard in navy and black. Some new armure and broad diagonal weaves are particularly stylish.

Plain colors and light mixtures in French and German suitings are all at much lower prices than early in the season. For half a dollar a yard you may now choose from a great many handsome fabrics that have been marked down from 75c. and 87c. a yard.

Strangers enjoying Summer holidays welcome at all times.

Mail orders from seashore resorts in this vicinity receive careful attention. Goods shipped same day.

HASKELL & TRIPP.

Department Stores,

Purchase and William Streets.

THE GREAT TRAGEDY.

Burial of the Victims in the Borden Family Lot.

Rumors of Eminent Lawyers Being Engaged for Defence.

Miss Borden's Counsel Active in His Efforts in Her Behalf.

[Special Dispatch.]

FALL RIVER, Aug. 17.—The bodies of Andrew J. Borden and his wife, which have been in the receiving tomb at Oak Grove cemetery since the funeral, were buried in the family lot this morning at 8 o'clock. Supt. Morrill and his men did the work, placing Mr. Borden's body between those of his two wives. There was no crowd and no one present to witless the last sad rites performed by the grave-diggers. With the burial of the bodies closes the second chapter of this great tragedy.

Under instructions from Medical Examiner Dolan, Civil Engineer Kieran made a new and complete plan of the Borden house yesterday. All the rooms were measured and will be written up with special regard to distances. The bloody lounge was placed in the position it had when it held the dead body of Mr. Borden, and the exact length of the sofa to the nearest door and to the bloodstains on the woodwork was secured. Then the distance from the window of the sitting-room to the north window of Dr. Kelley's house was taken, and the exact number of feet from the house to the barn and back again to Mrs. Churchill's kitchen window was determined most accurately.

This shows that the government is preparing its case with the utmost care, in order to be able to answer any question in regard to distances that may arise.

Now He Denies It.

State Detective Seaver of Taunton is in Fall River to-day. The interview with him printed in the *Standard* last evening attracted widespread attention here, and the statements therein have been severely censured by Miss Borden's friends. Mr. Seaver this noon requested a *Standard* man to say that he "denied the interview."

Eminent Counsel for Defence.

It is said Mr. Jennings will have associated with him in his defence some of the most eminent counsel in the country. Among those mentioned are Howe & Hummel and Bourke Cockran of New York city. The former are, perhaps, the most expert criminal lawyers in the country, and many is the man they have saved from the gallows. It takes a good-sized fortune to retain them alone, for they are in such great demand that nothing short of $10,000 will interest them.

A. H. Hummel,
Whose Name is Being Associated With the Borden Murder Case.

Bourke Cockran is the Tammany leader and congressman. He is one of the most eloquent lawyers in the country. He it was who played such a figure in the Democratic national convention at Chicago. This begins to look as though the story that the Bordens would not do anything to preserve the family honor was a misleading one. If true, the Borden millions are concentrated in the defence of their pride, family name and Lizzie.

A lawyer in this city commenting on the objection made by Andrew J. Jennings to having Judge Blaisdell preside at the arraignment of Lizzie A. Borden on Monday next, says: "Judge Blaisdell hears the case, and we will assume that he holds Lizze Borden for the grand jury, committing her to jail to await their action. The grand jury does not convene until next November, and as a consequence Lizzie would have to remain in confinement until that time.

Mr. Jennings knew as well as any one who knows Judge Blaisdell knows that he would not step down to allow another justice to hear the case. His Honor believes implicitly in his ability to hear and decide cases without bias, and he does not think he could be prejudiced in his trials. Without saying whether he is or is not prejudiced, Mr. Jennings knew, as every other lawyer does, that the judge, with the objection overruled, would sit on the case, if only to substantiate that he could not be effected by prejudice.

Mr. Jennings makes his point of objection and so establishes a record of having gone through an examination under protest. Then, when his client is held for the grand jury, as of course she undoubtedly will be, on probable cause, if nothing else, he can use this point with possible effect.

He can then go before the Supreme Court of the State on an application for a writ of habeas corpus and argue for the release of the defendant on the ground that she is illegally detained in jail. He appears more consistently before that body with his record of a protest in the lower court than if he had assented to the conduct of the hearing and then entered his protest afterward.

If he is upheld by the Supreme Court, then Miss Borden will be released and can remain out of jail until the session of the grand jury is finished and an indictment is found against her. If an indictment is found, of course she will then be arrested on a capias and confined till her acquittal. If she were discharged by the lower court this same process would be gone through with, and probably she would also be free until next November, when the grand jury meets."

Continuing, the lawyer said: "In this case I do not see why Mr. Jennings can't use an effective argument in an application for a writ of habeas corpus should Miss Borden be held for the grand jury. In any event, a decision on this point would be interesting, as it would establish a precedent."

STRIKE EXTENDING.

Switchmen on the New York Central Called Out.

Militia's Presence Enables a Few Trains to be Run.

Strikers Doing Their Best to Prevent Much Business Being Done.

BUFFALO, Aug. 17.—Early this morning the New York Central switchmen abandoned all work in the freight yards. This is what has been feared. The presence here of H. Walter Webb shows that the Central officers expected their men would go out. Switch tenders in the Central passenger yards and train house are included in the strike.

The switchmen on the Delaware, Lackawanna and Western have just been called out.

Central Switchmen Quit Work.

The situation this morning is not encouraging. The central switchmen having joined the strike makes it more formidable, and the central yards this morning were under picket guard. It is feared the strike will spread to the other Vanderbilt lines—the West Shore and Lake Shore roads.

Brigadier General Doyle's orders will result in concentrating the entire force of the brigade here to-day and they will all be needed, as the strike covers several miles of territory. The bulk of the soldiery are in the big Cheektowaga yards outside the city limit. The companies ordered to Buffalo by Gen. Doyle are: First separate company of Rochester, 70 men; Second separate company of Auburn, 90 men; Eighth separate company of Rochester, 85 men; Thirteenth separate company of Jamestown, 100 men; Twenty-eighth separate company of Tonawanda, 90 men; Twenty-sixth separate company of Elmira, 80 men; Thirtieth separate company of Elmira, 75 men; Thirty-fourth separate company of Geneva, 65 men; Fourty-first separate company of Syracuse; Forty-third separate company of Olean, 90 men; Forty-fifth separate company of Cortland, 70 men; Forty-eighth separate company of Oswego 100 men; Fifth battery of Syracuse, 75 men. The Sixty-fifth and Seventy-fourth regiments, now on duty, number about 700 men.

The State board of arbitration are here and will make efforts with the railroad companies and the men for a settlement of the strike.

Central Men Want More Pay.

General Superintendent Voorhees of the Central road, in a talk with an Associated Press correspondent, said there were about 150 of the Central men out and that the strike was for increased pay. The pretension of the men that they want fewer hours is all humbug, said he. They have worked in the past 11 hours a day, actual work, and they expect to continue that way, but they want the hourly compensation increased by an amount which is practically 10 per cent. The men never had objection to the number of hours.

"They have made a formal demand for it?"

"Yes, the night force came to us on Tuesday at noon and made the same demand as has been made on other roads. They belong to the Switchmen's Union, and I suppose they made up their minds to do as the other union men did. Their demand was refused. The men employed on this road have been receiving more pay than other men performing the same work on other roads in the State of New York, and we decided not to grant their request."

"Do you anticipate much trouble as a result?"

"No. There has been no demonstrations, no delay of trains. If we are given protection by the authorities we can soon fill the strikers' places."

Asked whether the fact that the West Shore has been carrying freight transfer for the Erie had anything to do with the present prompting the Central's men to go out, Mr. Voorhees said he did not think it had. "We are obliged to handle whatever freight is brought to us," said he.

The New York Central yards here passed through a strike two years ago. The company defeated the men, filling the yards with non-union workmen. It was not believed that the union could again get a strong hold in the yards, but committees have been at work for months preparing for a strike.

Troops Ready to Move.

SYRACUSE, N. Y., Aug. 17.—The 41st separate company, 60 men, Capt. John G. Butler, left for Buffalo on a special train at 1 o'clock this forenoon. The Fifth Battery will be under arms in less than an hour if further orders are received. The men are in readiness to assemble, the cannon have been oiled, and there is plenty of powder and ball on hand.

Trainmen's Grievances.

CHICAGO, Aug. 17.—The general grievance committee of the Trainmen's Union on the Northwestern railroad is holding secret sessions in this city. It is stated that a list of grievances is being prepared and that they will be presented next week.

Grand Master Sweeney Talks.

Grand Master Frank Sweeney, in an interview this morning, said he had just received a message from headquarters of the Chicago Switchmen's Union, informing him that an attempt would be made to employ switchmen in Chicago to take the places of the men, but the company had not yet succeeded in inducing any to accept their offer. "It is not likely that men who receive 27 to 29 cents an hour in Chicago will come to Buffalo to accept positions for from three to five cents an hour less wages," said Mr. Sweeney.

Questioned as to the chances of the strike becoming general, he said: "No man can predict where this thing will end. It may spread like wildfire. Certain it is that men have done everything that man with self-respect could do to avoid forcing the issues to a strike. The Lehigh men asked for a reform in prices June 11th last. The company's officers refused to listen. They have the idea that they can drive the men and frighten them into submission, but they are mistaken. There is no question of justice in their demands."

The newspapers, even the companies, admit that a man should be paid for all hours he works and entitled to a decent, respectful hearing if he finds that he is being abused. These men ask that they be paid by the hour and that they be given time to eat their dinner. They ask that when their committee go to the officers to call the attention of the officers to the abuse, that the committee be accorded common civility. The committee that waited on Supt. Burrows of the Central were insulted by him and were at once discharged. They reported to the order and as a result of Mr. Burrows' brutal treatment the men are out.

I cannot say what will be done to-day. There will be no lawlessness that the men can prevent. Every means in the law will be used to prevent other men from taking the places of the strikers, but these measures will be within the law. We are right in our demand. There was no way to obtain our rights but to strike. We ought to win if there is any justice in public opinion."

Mr. Sweeny declined to say whether he would order the Chicago men out. Any road that showed a disposition to be fair would not have any trouble.

Ordered to Buffalo.

OLEAN, N. Y., Aug. 17.—The Forty-third separate company has just been ordered out to go to Buffalo.

ROCHESTER, N. Y., Aug. 17.—Seventy-six members of Eighth separate company left this city early this morning on a special train for Buffalo, having been ordered to that place.

The West Shore men will go out today. The Buffalo, Rochester and Pittsburg men have already gone out, although their terms were acceded to. The firemen are housing the engines in the round houses and all hands are idle in the yard. There is no disturbance. Strikers say this does not measure the possible extent of the strike.

At 9 o'clock last night the Erie road started two sections of a train east with forty cars of perishable freight. The trains proceeded unmolested until reaching Alden station, where the cars were boarded by strikers who applied the brakes and pulled the pins, completely disabling both sections.

Depredations by Strikers.

Three Erie trains are now stalled at the Seneca street crossing. The strikers had tampered with the switches. No accidents are reported.

A train on its way from Black Rock to Alden with coupling apparatus was derailed by the strikers before reaching its destination. The road will be blocked for some time. A wrecking train has been sent from Buffalo.

The Lehigh Valley people say they got four trains out of the yard yesterday, and think they will have no difficulty in moving freight hereafter. Just before noon, a long train of cars was started. A gang of non-union men, evidently very green about the yards, were marched down to do it. The coupling pins had all been pulled, and the first thing to be done was to replace them. Captain Fogarty with company C, Sixty-fifth regiment, accompanied the gang. Lieutenant Lambrecht with one platoon marched along one side of the train, while Captain Fogarty with the other platoon kept guard on the other. Thus protected, the men replaced the pins and the train was started.

The Military Aspect

of affairs at Cheektowaga is of a very pronounced character. Brigadier General Doyle has pitched his headquarters at the William street station, just outside the city line, and from there issues his commands to the men. Squads of men march up and down with muskets on their shoulders and bayonets glistening in the sun. All the cars and buildings of the Erie and Lehigh Valley railroads in the vicinity are being guarded. The military lines extend from the city limits to the Lackawanna coal trestle in Cheektowaga, a distance of about a mile and a half.

Quiet at Waverly.

ELMIRA, N. Y., Aug. 17.—The situation at Waverly and Sayre yesterday was very quiet, no effort being made by the company to move any trains except passenger and milk trains, which the strikers do not interfere with. Sheriff Powell was not on the scene and the strikers had everything their own way. General union meetings were held by the different organizations.

IRON HALL'S MISFORTUNE.

Belief that Depositors will Receive but 50 Per Cent. of Their Funds.

PHILADELPHIA, Aug. 17.—The Mutual Banking, Surety Trust and Safe Deposit company, in which Iron Hall funds are deposited, has assigned.

Assignee Stockwell was asked the reasons given for the assignment. He replied by referring to the recent suit for a receivership instituted against the Iron Hall at Indianapolis, and the fact that $430,000 of the order's money is deposited in the bank. "The lawyers on both sides of the receivership suit," he continued, "with the consent and approval of Judge Taylor, came here to take away the cash and securities of the bank and remove them to Indianapolis. Mr. Krumbhaar, state superintendent of banking, has been working with the plaintiffs with the undoubted intention of wrecking this institution and the Iron Hall. It was for the purpose of protecting its creditors and keeping its assets within this jurisdiction that the assignment was made.

"The bank, in my opinion, is perfectly solvent," said the assignee, "and is able to pay dollar for dollar all around. The directors, however, cannot permit their assets and securities to go out of this jurisdiction, and thus compel their depositors to go to Indianapolis for their rights."

Mr. Stockwell declared that it was impossible at this time for him to make any statement of the assets and liabilities of the institution. The demand for the Iron Hall funds, he said, was made Monday during the joint meeting of the bank directors and officers of the order which lasted all day. The directors resisted the demand, and there was nothing left to do but to make an assignment.

It is claimed by applicants for the receivership at Indianapolis that $720,000 of the Iron Hall's funds are locked up in the institution and that the Mutual company is also surety for the Iron Hall officers

To the Extent of $1,000,000.

The amount on deposit is believed to include $170,000, said to have been advanced by the supreme justice of the order to make good an impairment of the bank's capital, which the state bank examiners discovered last spring. At that time the examiner claimed that the bank was insolvent and applied for a receiver. Among its assets set forth in the cashier's affidavit of defense was the "good will of the corporation, valued at $170,000." This item was thrown out by the court and the bank was ordered to make good the impairment, which it succeeded in doing, but has always refused to reveal whence the necessary $170,000 was obtained.

In his testimony at Indianapolis the other day, Chief Justice Somerby finally admitted that the $170,000 had been given the bank by the officers of the Iron Hall in order to save it from going into the hands of a receiver.

In addition to the Iron Hall's fund on deposit in the institution, there is also locked up $40,000 belonging to the Advance Beneficial Order, one of the short term organizations, which went down in the general crash of such schemes about a year ago. The Advance Order also made an assignment to A. E. Stockwell, who deposited the funds of the Advance Order in the bank of which he was counsel and now assignee. A few weeks ago pressure was brought on Stockwell to remove the funds of the defunct beneficial society from the Mutual bank, but he refused, declaring the institution was perfectly solvent. Stockwell was on Aug. 3 elected a trustee of the Iron Hall Building company.

Fifty Cents on the Dollar.

PHILADELPHIA, Aug. 17.—It was developed last night that the attorneys representing both plaintiff and defendant in the application for a receiver for the order of the Iron Hall made a proposition to the directors of the Mutual Bank at the meeting preceding the assignment, which if accepted would have placed the local depositors on a perfectly safe basis, as they would have obtained every cent of their deposits, amounting to only $30,000 or $35,000.

It was proposed that the directors pay each call depositor the amount due them and give bonds for payment of each time deposit, such as the funds of the Iron Hall branches as they fell due. This would have left a surplus in bank on which to continue business.

The Indianapolis people claimed that there should be in money and securities $713,000 of the order's funds in the bank, while the directors say that only $450,000 is the amount. Notwithstanding this difference the attorneys were willing that the difference should not effect the proposed agreement at this time, but should stand as an open account for future adjustment. However, the proposition was rejected and the assignment made.

Now the opinion prevails among those best posted outside the directors that the depositors will be very fortunate if they receive 50 cents on the dollar, as it is argued that if the institution was solvent as claimed there would be no need of making an assignment. Lawyers Hawkins and Smith of Indianapolis, representing both sides in the Iron Hall receivership suit, expressed the opinion last night that the receivership is now inevitable. This belief is also shared by Supreme Cashier Davis. The trio will leave for Indianapolis on the Chicago limited express to-day.

WEATHER INDICATIONS.

FAIR.

WASHINGTON, Aug. 17.—For the 24 hours from 8 a. m. to-day: For Massachusetts, Rhode Island and Connecticut fair, winds shifting to southerly.

FAIR AND WARMER.

BOSTON, Aug. 17.—Local forecast for New England until Friday night: Continued fair, slightly warmer during Thursday, generally southerly and westerly winds.

AMERICAN LABOR TROUBLES.

London Post Comments on the Crisis Through which the U. S. is Passing.

LONDON, Aug. 17.—*Post* says: "It is impossible to read the accounts of labor troubles in America without feeling the gravity of the crisis through which the great American republic is passing. The moral should be laid to heart in England, where the new unionism seems disposed to go to extreme lengths if a favorable opportunity presents itself.

Ocean Steamers.

Arrived—At New York, Majestic, Liverpool; Buffalo, London; Fulwell, Sunderland. Passed Brow Head, Teutonic, from New York.

HOME MATTERS.

PERSONAL.—Mr. and Mrs. H. V. Sanders and Miss Ella Holmes of New Bedford are guests of Oak Hill House, Littleton, N. H.

Mrs. A. B. Crapo and Mrs. P. H. Nye leave the city to-morrow for Cottage City, where they will be guests at the Island House.

At the solicitation of friends, Peter C. Keith of this city will enter for the Highland fling and sword dances in the carnival of Scottish sports under the auspices of the Caledonians of Providence at Rocky Point to-day.

Misses Mary and Rose Smith left this morning for a three weeks' visit to Kingston and other points in Canada and northern New York.

Pemberton H. Nye and Fred Hadley left the city to-day for a ten days' trip to Philadelphia.

Mrs. Capt. Elihu Gifford and her two children have arrived home from San Francisco.

Dr. E. V. McLeod and wife left the city today for Brandon, Vt., where they will spend several weeks.

Mr. and Mrs. John B. Wilson of Rome, N. Y., are visiting Mr. Wilson's brother, at 67 Fourth street.

Henry A. Brown, proprietor of Hotel Westport, has been seriously ill with nervous fever for the past two week. His friends will be glad to know he is rapidly recovering.

The *Yellowstone Journal* says:

Mr. Charles H. Barstow, who has for a period almost coeval with the memory of man been chief clerk at the Crow Indian Agency, Montana, has resigned his position with the intention of taking up his residence in Tacoma, Washington, where his little daughter is at present with her grandparents. During his long term of office Mr. Barstow has been an invaluable aid and assistance to the many agents who have in turn directed the affairs of the Crow nation; the highest tribute that could perhaps be paid him, being that despite of changes of administration and agents, he has been retained, primarily as indispensable, and secondarily, as thoroughly acceptable to each of the succeeding agents. His record is one to be proud of. Mr. Barstow is now on his way for a short visit to his Eastern friends.

THE LAND OF SUNSHINE.—*A Unique Country where the Skies are almost Never Clouded, while the air is Cool and Bracing, like Perpetual Spring.*—As an anomalous Southern resort, by reason of the fact that there one may escape Summer heat no less than Winter cold, New Mexico is rapidly becoming famous. Averaging throughout the entire territory 5600 feet in altitude above sea-level, and characterized by dry air which, unlike a humid atmosphère, is incapable of communicating heat, the temperature in midsummer remains at a delightfully comfortable degree through the day, and at night becomes invariably brisk and bracing. The sunshine is almost constant, yet the most violent out-of-door exertion may be undertaken without fear of distressful consequences. Sunstroke or prostration are absolutely unknown there. It is an ideal land for a Summer outing. Its climate is prescribed by reputable physicians as a specific for pulmonary complaints, and the medicinal Hot Springs at Las Vegas are noted for their curative virtues. The most sumptuous hotel in the West, the Montezuma, is located at these springs. Write to Jno. J. Byrne, 723 Monadnock Block, Chicago, for "The Land of Sunshine," an entertaining and profusely illustrated book descriptive of this region, the most picturesque and romantic in the United States.

POLITICAL.—H. A. Monk of Brockton is a Republican candidate for the nomination as Senator in the Second Plymouth District.

David F. Slade, Esq., of Fall River, will be a Republican candidate for Representative to the State Legislature this fall.

ANCIENT ORDER OF FORESTERS.—Several certificates of this order, given to James Brown, William Donley, Thomas Boott, David Pentleton, by Court Royal Oak No. 6448 of this city, have been appropriately framed, and are on exhibition in Ellis's window, 114 William street.

NATURALIZATION.—Martin Ryan was admitted to citizenship in the Third District Court this morning. R. F. Carroll, Esq., for petitioner.

PHYSICIANS RECOMMEND Turkish baths for invalids.

EXCURSION TO WASHINGTON.—Attention is called to the special notice of R. A. Peirce Post's excursion to Washington, which offers almost unheard of inducements.

A FAIR SKIN for the ladies. Best secured by a Turkish bath No. 5 South Sixth street.

THERE'S A BIG DROP in prices at Waite's Carpet Hall, 71 William street.

HALF A DOLLAR secures a hair shampoo, ladies, 5 South Sixth street.

CHILDREN'S STIFF ANKLE SHOES. Devoll's.

HOOD'S SARSAPARILLA purifies the blood.

GOOD NEWS

Friday Morning, Aug. 19,

We shall sell solid Antique Oak Tables, with top 16 inches square, and ample shelf underneath, all finely finished, strong, serviceable and sightly, for

89c. each.

The sale will continue through Saturday if the stock is not sooner exhausted. These are the Tables on which we created such a furore last Summer. We can take no orders before

FRIDAY MORNING,

But at that time mail or telephone orders will receive careful attention.

☞ Remember the date, FRIDAY MORNING, Aug. 19, and SATURDAY if the stock holds out.

C. F. WING,

34 to 40 Purchase st.

WHITING & CO.

GREAT BARGAINS

—IN—

Ladies'

Cotton Underwear

20 doz. more of those fine Night Dresses, at 50c. apiece.

25 doz. of elegant Night Dresses from 75c. to $2.87 apiece.

10 doz. Ladies' White Cotton Skirts from 50c. to $2.50 apiece.

100 doz. of Ladies' Cotton and Cambric Corset Covers, at 25, 37, 42, 50, 75c. and $1 apiece, all fine and nice ly made, try them.

We are selling Infants' Long and Short Dresses, very cheap, get our prices.

If you want Infants' Slips we can suit you on prices and quality.

See our Corset stock, as we have all of the popular makes sold.

WHITING & CO.

OUTING SHIRTS!

OUTING SHIRTS!

You can never have too many

OUTING SHIRTS!

Our low prices will help you out. Quality exceptional.

Good Shirts for $1 and $1.25, laundered collars and cuffs.

Another lot of the popular blue Madras, all sizes, $1.50.

Better come at once, They're going fast.

J. & W. R. WING & CO.,

133 UNION STREET.

OUTING SHIRTS!

OUTING SHIRTS!

THE CRESCENT!

22 Purchase St.

Damask Towels 15c. Going, going, gone, unless you purchase immediately.

Towels, 4 for 25c., still on sale.

O, how light and airy. Chiffon Handkerchiefs, for the button-hole. Beauties,

Only 25 cents.

RIBBONS.

We don't *begin* to tell you *how much* we have *marked down* our line of Ribbons, but come and see for yourself.

We will close out our Gingham Dresses for children at *cost.* Sizes from 4 to 10 years of age.

Gloves, 15, 25, 37, 50c.

Corsets, a good corset for 39c.

An X-L-ent Corset for 50c.

A very nice Summer Corset, C-B a la Spirite, price $1.25.

Corsets at all prices.

Having removed our entire stock from the Old Stand at corner of County and High streets, we shall be pleased to see our old friends and patrons at our new quarters, 22 Purchase street, known as THE CRESCENT.

MEAGRE DETAILS.

Fall River Seeking More Facts About the Murder.

Agitation Against Judge Blaisdell Presiding at the Inquiry.

One Form of Newspaper Ignorance Exposed by the Justice of the Court.

Yesterday, according to the Providence Journal, the Borden murder case stood thus: The prisoner who is locked up for killing her father is as innocent as the unborn, and there was no sense and reason in her arrest. The prisoner may be innocent, but the government was justified in preferring its charges against her, and she is entitled to just as much consideration as other prisoners suspected of guilt, and no more. People who will express their views, at all are beginning to express them sharply. They no longer mince their words.

The inquest set for 2 o'clock yesterday afternoon was not held. District Attorney Knowlton telegraphed that he could not be in attendance, and City Marshal Hilliard went to Boston. The lounge on which Andrew J. Borden reclined when his head was cut to pieces was wheeled into the guard room of the central police station and taken up to the district court room. It was covered with burlap, and made quite a journey before it found a resting place. It was carted from Woodward's undertaking rooms to the Borden house and thence to Court square. The report is that it is to be put in as evidence when the inquest is resumed and at the preliminary hearing. There are formalities still to be observed, and it will be necessary to prove that a butchery took place on Aug. 4. So much has been said and done that a few people are a trifle sceptical as to whether a crime has been committed. It is the most comfortable kind of scepticism introduced since the days of the first agnostic, and if it could take more general possession of the community, a great and unfamiliar peace would rest on the city.

The preliminary hearing continues to provoke discussion, which is not always entirely friendly. It is conceded that many who argue that Judge Blaisdell should not sit on the case, are prompted by a desire to see justice done, but there are many more who are anxious to appease their curiosity. They want all the facts that they can possibly collect, in order to relieve their minds. They have followed the links in the chain as far as they can go, and have found that a number of them are missing. They want them all. There are big links and little links, but none are so small that it would not be studied with interest. It is understood that the time when Andrew J. Borden entered his home, the time that Miss Lizzie spent in the barn, the time when the servant saw him sitting on the sofa, as she passed up stairs because her back ached or she was ill, and the time when the discovery of the horror was announced, is to figure very prominently in a state's case. The curious desire to inform themselves as to these various minutes and to compare them with their own minutes, jotted down from personal observation and inquiry. If, at the outside, but 13 minutes elapsed after Bridget Sullivan recognized her master, and was called to view his remains, a mistake has been made in certain calculations.

Perhaps it is a slight, unimportant mistake and perhaps it isn't; that is something that people want to know, as all mistakes are pretty sure to be given their due weight. And so it isn't difficult to explain the influence which is being brought to bear from several quarters to persuade Judge Blaisdell to step down and out. The public is quick to pick up a point, and it argues that if a judge presides who is unacquainted with the details developed at the inquest he will insist on a more thorough presentation of the government's case, and fuller particulars will be published. There is a feeling that if Judge Blaisdell, who has heard all of the testimony, should conduct proceedings, he will be satisfied with very little evidence, and that the town will but little wiser after he has rendered a verdict.

As stated, however, this line of reasoning does not apply to all. Miss Borden has friends who honestly believe that a mockery will be made of justice unless another judge is called in. They contend that Judge Blaisdell, knowing the line of thought which District Attorney Knowlton must have pursued when he ordered the arrest, did not differ with him in the conclusions reached. The presumption is that he will not differ with him next Monday. It has been explained that the result will not be different whoever occupies the bench. At least, this is the opinion advanced by competent lawyers. It would be a most unusual proceedings to discharge a prisoner held at the instance of the attorney-general or the district attorney, unless the government broke down altogether. Still, there seems to be some ground for this claim of the supporters of the accused, though it is believed that everything will depend upon custom. In the eyes of the law, a murder is a murder, and no distinction is made betwixt the different methods by which it is accomplished, or the social standing or sex of the defendant, which will change the ordinary course of procedure.

There is one noticeable feature of this case which has not been touched upon as yet. The reticence of the authorities has been freely criticized, the thick veil which has been woven about the doings at the inquest has led to more or less unfavorable comment, and the police have been arraigned for suspecting without evidence, for plaiting the ground for their suspicion. Yet nobody has called attention to the fact that not one of Miss Borden's acquaintances has taken up the story of the butchery in detail and given an exhaustive account of just what transpired in that household on Second street between the hours of breakfast and 11 o'clock on Thursday forenoon. Her friends have expressed their faith in her innocence, and a number of societies, of which the young woman was a member, have passed resolutions of condolence, but beyond the bare statement that Miss Lizzie last saw her stepmother at 9 o'clock, that she ironed until her father returned from his trip down town, and that she spent 20 minutes in the barn, they have been as dumb as District Attorney Knowlton. It is nearly a fortnight since Mr. and Mrs. Borden were slaughtered, and many conflicting tales have been belated, but few of them have been confirmed or denied by the supporters of the family. Two widely different accounts of Bridget Sullivan's whereabouts have been published, and allowed to stand. There is a nice question of time involved, but no endeavor has been made to pick to pieces the government's ideas in regard to it, or to overthrow its conclusions at any point.

Detective Hanscom has appeared on the scene and has vanished without advancing any new theory, and counsel for defence has kept his thoughts to himself and has not dissected the evidence of the police or any portion of it that has found its way into print. It is possible, of course, in view of the fragmentary nature of the evidence, that it was decided to offer no contradiction, and to await the development of the events, and it may not be strange that the prisoner cannot recall her movements on the morning of the tragedy, and go into particulars and time minutely. It would be singular, however, if any stone had been left unturned in the effort to quicken the memory and draw from her the entire history of herself prior to the murder.

Clews and Suspects.

As for clews and suspects and the like, the police have not yet captured "the" wild-eyed man, with the white, scared face, who attracted attention on Second street a week ago last Thursday morning, though they have run down several wild-eyed men. At least they were wild-eyed men when the officers came up with them. The public will excuse the police if they decline to start off on certain trails which are daily mapped out for them, though thus far they have been exceedingly credulous and willing to act on the most hare-brained suggestion. It is not absolutely necessary to dispense with reason altogether, even though a double murder has been committed, and there is a point at which the line can safely be drawn. The stranger who accosted the Frenchman, who who appeared to be in such a hurry to leave the town, had at least a few moments to spare, for he proposed a drink and he was citizen enough of the city to be aware where he could quench his thirst, as he mentioned Joe Saxton's saloon as a convenient stopping place. If every hint is seriously accepted, however, there will not be a patrolman in town for the next two years. The clairvoyants will invite them to take the 7 27 of South Webster, travel due north, double on their trail and draw forth the blood-stained axe, with a note from the assassin tied to the handle. They have followed enough blind paths, and the time is rapidly approaching when they can afford to ignore some of their half-witted advisers.

The Form of Complaint

Judge Blaisdell, who states that he doesn't mean to be frightened from his place as presiding officer at the preliminary hearing, is a man of advanced years and remarkable vitality. He is not at all disturbed over the reports which reach him regarding writs of habeas corpus, appeals and other efforts which are to be made to dethrone him. He has served in both branches of the Legislature, has been mayor of the city, and last as judge of the Second District Court since its establishment. He says that proceedings thus far have been regular, and he sees no reason why he should deviate from precedent to accommodate anybody. As a sample of the mistakes which are being made, Judge Blaisdell was shown an editorial yesterday in which the city marshal was denounced for drawing up a harsh complaint, not calculated to soothe and comfort the accused. The judge said that he did not know before that such ignorance existed. The form of the complaint was decided upon 150 years before the city marshal was born, and was adapted to fit capital crimes. The English is vigorous, but the judge thought that was not the city marshal's fault. Such a criticism illustrates the straits to which a dearth of fresh news in the case has reduced some papers.

Prayer for Miss Borden.

At a meeting of the Women's Auxiliary of the Y. M. C. A. held yesterday afternoon, Mrs. Hezekiah A. Brayton offered prayer for Miss Lizzie Borden.

That Mile of Sewers.—Abbott P. Smith, who recently petitioned the Board of Public Works to lay for him a mile of sewers on his recently acquired plat south of Cove street, between East and West French avenues, has decided to lay the sewers himself. Mr. Smith originally offered to pay 50 cents per foot toward the sewers, which he wanted laid 7 feet deep. Supt. Drake thought the sewers ought to be deeper, and also estimated that Mr. Smith's estimates for expenses were far too low. The Board listened to Mr. Smith and then took the matter under advisement. Last Monday night it was referred to Messrs. Tripp and Rotch, and yesterday these gentlemen decided that Mr. Smith ought to pay three-fourths of the expense, and that the sewers must be at the depth the Board wants them.

On hearing this decision Mr. Smith withdrew all offers, declined the Board's proposition, and will at once commence to lay the sewers on his own plans. Many think the Board has lost a golden opportunity to lay sewers at a low cost, where eventually it must lay them and assess the cost of one-half on the abutters.

Runaway Captured.—Hugh Curry of Fall River and Frederick Jones of this city, who escaped from the Union truant school at Walpole about a week ago, were captured in Fall River yesterday and were taken back to Walpole.

A New Bedford Man

Who has suffered for months with terrible pains in his shoulder, which was injured by a fall, found

HIS FIRST RELIEF

Recently in the Turkish Bath House, with a Massage by Manager Cavanaugh. Follow his example.

YOU NEED A BATH.

No. 5 South Sixth Street.

LABOR DAY PREPARATIONS.

Business Transacted at Meetings of Spinners and Weavers.

The Mule Spinners' Association held a meeting last evening, when a new system of collecting was discussed and adopted. The members of the executive committee have always done the collecting every two weeks. The new mills and the consequent increase in size of the association, have made the work of the executive committee too irksome, and after considerable discussion it was decided to have a board of collection, and that hereafter the collection be made weekly, instead of every two weeks as has been the custom. The financial report was read and accepted, and showed $323.79 for the past month.

It was voted to turn out in a body on Labor Day, and it was voted to give four prizes for the best turnout by mills. The prizes will be $10, $5, $3 and $2.

The emblems of the National Cotton Mule Spinners' Association of America were distributed among the members. It was designed in Chicago. The emblem is in the form of a monument 22 by 28 inches in size. At its base is a beehive, upon which is the word "Industry." Upon the face of the base is a striking representation of a lake, with several Fall River mills in the background. Just above, on the face of the monument proper, is an engraving of a pair of spinning mules in motion, with a spinner at work. A wreath with "Justice is all we require; we expect nothing less," is below the engraving, and just under the wreath is the word "Unity." Upon both sides of the monument just above the engraving, are two pinnacles. Upon the face of one pinnacle is the bust of Crompton, and upon the other the bust of Arkwright. Upon the apex of one pinnacle stands a spinner in overalls, with a cop in his hand, while upon the other stands a backboy holding in his hands a broom. Between these two pinnacles the monument runs upward almost to a point, upon which is a large globe, across it being clasped hands. Standing upon the globe is a statue of a woman representing Liberty. At the foot of the statue and upon the globe is a spread eagle holding a ribbon in his mouth, upon which are the words, "Defence, not Defiance." Above the whole emblem in large letters are the words, "National Cotton Mule Spinners' Association of America."

A special meeting of the New Bedford Cotton Weavers' Protective Association was held in Neptune Hall last evening. The most important business done was a vote to purchase a big banner for the association, to be ready for the Labor Day parade. The banner will be 45 by 60 inches, and will be blue on the front side and red on the reverse side. The lettering will be in gold, and on the front will be a picture of a loom with a weaver in front looking away. On the reverse side will be clasped hands, with the words "Justice is all we ask," and possibly other sentences. Secretary Hart went to Boston to-day to order the banner.

The amendment to the constitution which permits slasher tenders and cloth room help coming into the association was adopted.

John Barrett was chosen marshal of the weavers for the Labor Day parade. Some 800 badges will be ordered for the members for that day.

The Union Street Railway will pay for Meyrelles' Band on Labor Day and after the parade the band will give a concert at Fort Phœnix. The Musical Exchange Band has been hired also.

A New Cattle Pest.—The State Board of Agriculture reports that farmers in Wareham and Blandford complain of a new pest in the shape of a little black fly, which is proving a source of great annoyance to cattle. This is its first appearance in Massachusetts, but it was very troublesome in New Jersey in 1889. It is there known as the horn fly, from the fact that it settles in swarms about the roots of the cattle's horns, and such is the tenacity with which it clings that the animals are unable to shake it off and cannot reach it with the tail to switch it off. The board mentions a number of remedies, among which is tobacco dust, pyrethrum of insect powder, and a preparation known as X. O. dust. These remedies are recommended by entomologists.

Missing from Home.—Lester Gurney of Hanson, employed in the box mill of John Foster, has disappeared from his home under circumstances which lead his family to think he has either met with foul play or has killed himself. Gurney received his pay as usual at the mill on Thursday night, and since that time has not been seen or heard of. He has recently appeared to act as if in danger of becoming insane. His wife has traced him to Whitman and thence to Brockton, but none of his friends in that city saw him later than Thursday evening.

Fall River's Naval Battalion.—The new company of the naval reserve, to be located in Fall River, will consist of 44 privates, eight commissioned officers, and five "non-coms", a total of 57. An armory will be furnished, equipped with all naval appurtenances. Regular drills will be held one night each week during the Winter. Mr. Hall, the organizer, has been at work but one day, and has already recruited half of his company. No person under 18 years is eligible.

Trouble in Dartmouth Schools.—A Fall River exchange says: Supt. Crocker of the Westport and Dartmouth schools is reorganizing the schools of those towns for the coming year. In doing this he desires to drop a number of the old teachers. This has created a serious trouble which appears to be increasing.

WESTPORT HARBOR.

Arthur C. Macomber, the expressman to and from Fall River has appeared in a serviceable express wagon. The body is painted red and the running gear brown.

Miss E. Louise Brownell and sister, Lena, of New Bedford are at their uncle's, George W. Kirby's.

No service was held in the chapel Sunday on account of the camp-meeting at Cadman's Neck.

The rain of the recent storm did much good. The only damage by lightning was the striking of a tree.

An extensive addition has given Admiral Grinnell's house an improved appearance. Blinds have also been added.

The party who have been camping across the river broke camp Sunday.

Visitors to the Pleasant Hour Camping Club's headquarters, from Fall River, were numerous Sunday.

Stephen R. Howland took a party to the church at Little Compton, last Wednesday.

The Smith Mills Sunday school and society of North Dartmouth picnicked at the Horse Neck Saturday.

George W. Kirby has recently purchased a new horse—a beautiful dark brown—of Douglass, New Bedford.

CUTTYHUNK.

Capt. Vernal Clifford carried a party of ladies on a trip to Nashawena on Monday. The excursion was much enjoyed by all.

Mr. and Mrs. Stephen Davis and Miss Hattie Davis are visiting Mr. and Mrs. Clinton Davis of Nashawena.

Miss Kittie Lewis of New Bedford is visiting friends at Cuttyhunk.

Miss Lizzie Keeney has returned to Cuttyhunk from a visit to New London.

Miss Eva Akin of New Bedford has been visiting Miss Mabel Clifford at the island.

Charles Frost has been visiting Albert Jamieson at Gosnold cottage.

Mark Jamieson has returned home from a trip to South America.

FALL RIVER.

Holder Tripp, while travelling with his refrigerator wagon to Swansey Village Monday, accidentally drove into an open draw near Gray's corner, and his wagon was wrecked.

Six thousand more people travelled easterly on the Fall River line boats during last July than last year.

Leon Lemaitre of Orange street, aged nine, while walking to the top of a high fence behind his residence, fell and dislocated his jaw.

The new King Philip weave shed will hold 2900 looms, but as room will be made for 3 cloth room 950 looms will be placed in the upper room and 980 in the lower.

There was the largest trades procession in Fall River last night that has been seen for 6 many years. It was an advertisement for the excursion of the Butchers' and Grocers' Association, to be held Thursday. There were bands in line, and the procession required two hours to pass. The features were antiques and horribles, 50 open hacks containing children from the various orphans' homes of the city, and the immense potato pie made by J. H. Greaves inclosed in a glass case, built upon a low gear drawn by six horses. The pie was opened in Music Hall, and was eaten by those who participated in the parade.

SOMERSET.

The oyster privilege of Somerset will be sold next Saturday. It was sold five years ago to John W. Pettis of Providence at $1012 per year. Mr. Pettis has since died and it is owned by his heirs. A man well posted in the oyster business said recently that the beds were not worth what was paid for them, and they will not be likely to bring more than $900 this time.

LITTLE COMPTON.

At a meeting of the Town Council and Court of Probate, the following business was transacted:

Will of George S. Pierce proved and ordered recorded. Report of commissioners of insolvency presented, and notice ordered for a meeting at the next court on the estate of the late William T. David. Notice ordered on appointment of Sarah E. Brigham as administrator on the estate of Beriah W. Brigham. Account of Charles Brightman, executor on the estate of Thomas Brightman, postponed to next court. Frank B. Gifford and William O. Snell appointed truant officers at a salary of 25 cents an hour for time employed under the direction of the school committee. Pardon Brownell appointed a committee to pull up wild carrots in the cemetery and on the town lot. Bills allowed and orders for payment given: George T. Howard, surveyor, $11; Messrs. Crosby and Dyer, moving cemetery, $30; C. E. Brayton, legal services on the Second Railroad case, $25.

Y. M. C. A. Lecture Course.—The date for the lectures of the Y. M. C. A. course have all been fixed except one, and are as follows: Thursday, Oct. 20—Rev. T. DeWitt Talmage. Thursday, Nov. 17—Past Du Chaillu. Tuesday, Dec. 6—Hon. John J. Ingalls. Thursday, Feb. 2—Hon. George R. Wendling. Monday, Feb. 13—Rev. Russell H. Conwell.

The date of Congressman Breckenridge's lecture has not been arranged. It will probably be given in January. Tickets for the course amounting to $1100 have been sold, insuring a small profit to the association.

At a meeting of the lecture committee last evening it was voted to give a popular course of five entertainments, commencing on the evening of Friday, Oct. 14, with Walter Emerson, the celebrated cornetist, and a fine company. The two other attractions decided upon are Prof. J. W. Churchill, the reader, and Prof. Samuel E. Kelley's Tableaux d'Art, an entertainment which has been extremely popular wherever it has been presented.

Yachting.— Schooner yacht Atlantic of New York arrived in port yesterday and sailed to-day. Sloop yacht Saona arrived yesterday.

The Evening Standard.

ESTABLISHED FEBRUARY, 1850. NEW BEDFORD, THURSDAY, AUGUST 18, 1892. TWO CENTS.

HASKELL & TRIPP.

To-morrow, Friday, Aug. 19, the usual half-holiday.

Store opens at 8 o'clock; closes at 1 o'clock.

Shrewd shoppers recognize the Friday half-holidays as seasons of *rare bargain opportunities.*

The following will be ready at 8 o'clock:

1st Bargain Opportunity—Basement.

A lot of stone China cups, saucers and plates, in sets of three pieces, assorted in fancy colored decorations of neat patterns.

13c. for the set.

2d Bargain Opportunity—Basement.

A lot of rattan carpet-beaters reduced to close

At 12½c. each.

3d Bargain Opportunity—Main Floor, East Aisle.

About 200 fine corset covers, assorted sizes and styles, formerly 39 and 50c.

To close at 25c. each.

4th Bargain Opportunity—William St. Annex.

The balance of a manufacturer's stock of wrappers, waists and skirts, fancy basques and children's dresses (small sizes), made from lawns, ginghams, cambrics and zephyrs. Some are slightly soiled and tumbled. Among the lot are wrappers and waists worth $1.50, $2 and $2.50.

You may choose for 50c. each.

5th Bargain Opportunity—West Gallery.

A lot of handsome ruffle edge pillows, 20 inches square, filled with downoline and covered with pretty styles cotton pongees in these colors: yellow, shrimp, orange, old rose, mahogany, cream and blue. Just the thing for your hammock or piazza chair.

Take your pick for 39c. each.

6th Bargain Opportunity—Main Floor, South Middle Aisle.

About 500 yds. best quality standard prints, this season's styles, a little tumbled from handling.

4c. a yard.

7th Bargain Opportunity—Main Floor, South Aisle.

Here's a lot of silks that ought to call out every maker of fancy work.

We have culled from our silk department every remnant, soiled length, or anything in any way undesirable, in surahs, printed pongees, fancy satins, wash silks, brocades, in lengths from three-quarters of a yard to 2 yards, and without regard to former prices. Have marked the entire collection

25c. for each remnant.

Every sale final.

We can't send these goods out on approval.

We can't cut samples.

You'll best serve your own interests by being on hand promptly at 8 o'clock.

HASKELL & TRIPP.

Department Stores,

Purchase and William Streets.

WANTS TO BE HUNG.

Westport Farmer Boldly Declares Himself the Murderer.

Says He Chopped Andrew J. Borden and Wife to Pieces.

Could Not See Lizzie Suffer for His Own Horrible Crime.

Strange Story Told Fall River Police by C. H. Peckham.

The Man's Mind Probably Affected by Reading of the Tragedy.

[Special Dispatch.]

FALL RIVER, Aug. 18.—The police met with their strangest experience in the Borden murders this morning, about 10 30, when a farmer from Westport, named Charles H. Peckham, about 60 years of age, five feet and six inches in height, weighing probably 150 pounds, walked into the Central Station. He wore light pants and vest and dark coat and a straw hat, and immediately upon entering the station approached Assistant Marshal Fleet, who was in charge. He was perspiring freely and appeared to be very excited and this is what is said:

"I murdered Andrew J. Borden and his wife and I want to be strung up for it as soon as possible."

The astonished officer said: "Why did you do that?"

"I don't know why I did it. There wasn't any money to be made, but I did it any way and my conscience is bothering me so that I cannot keep still and see poor Lizzie Borden suffer."

The officer said to him: "You are quite a noble sort of a fellow and nobody would think you were a murderer. Step into the office and tell me all about it."

Peckham followed the officer into the marshal's room, where he told the following story:

"The day that I committed the murder I came in from Westport. I walked in from my home about two miles from Central Village. When I got there I took a walk up Third street and walked into Dr. Chagnon's yard, jumped over fence into Mr. Borden's yard. I then went in by the back cellar door, and on my way found a hatchet. Then I stepped upstairs, killed Mrs. Borden and hung around the place until Mr. Borden came in. After Lizzie stepped out of the room where her father was I went to the old man and chopped him to pieces. Then I started back into the cellar and put the hatchet back where I found it. Then I went into the yard, jumped over the fence back onto Third street and cleared for my farm in Westport. Now I have made a clean breast of the whole story, and I want to be locked up and hung as soon as possible."

"What did you do with the clothes you wore at that time?" asked the officer.

"I have them on now," he replied, "but there isn't any blood on them. The Bordens' blood did not splash around because it was stagnated from the effect of poison they had taken. I do not want you to be doubtful about this story, Mr. Policeman. I know my business and I think you ought to know yours."

"How did you get over the fence?"

"Jumped over, I told you."

Here Peckham illustrated his words by jumping over the rail in the marshal's office, showing that he was capable of doing that much anyway in connection with he murder.

"So without a motive and with a hatchet you killed the Borden people and give yourself up now to the police?"

"Yes sir. I know what I am doing and I know what I did do. I am all straight in the head and know everything I am saying and I can explain it too to your satisfaction."

The marshal searched the man and found on his person a pocket-book containing $5 in cash and some papers which identified him as Charles H. Peckham. He also had on his person several clippings from the New Bedford *Standard* about the murder. He was at once locked up.

Information from Westport shows that Peckham lives there on the Davis farm which he hires from a man named Cook. Deputy Sheriff Kirby says that he know the man very well and says that he has always borne a reputation there of a rather eccentric man. It is believed in this city that his mind has become unbalanced by reading and talking much of the tragedy.

[By Associated Press.]

FALL RIVER, Aug. 18.—Charles H. Peckham of Central Village, Westport, Mass., walked to the Central police station this morning and asked for the city marshal. The latter had gone to the northern part of the city with a squad of officers to hunt down a suspect, and Assistant Marshal Fleet answered his inquiry.

"Well, Mr. Marshal," said the man, "I killed Mr. and Mrs. Andrew J. Borden, and I have come from home to give myself up. I went over the back fence and through the rear door of the Borden house two weeks ago to-day, and I killed both of those people out of pure love for blood. I went out the rear door and over the back fence and walked over the New Bedford road home. I'm the murderer and I want to be locked up."

The marshal took him to the cell room and searched him. He found a pocket book with a few receipts in it, and also unearthed some official communications from the Russian bureau at Washington. Peckham is 62 years of age, about five feet six inches tall, and has thin gray beard. He says he leases a farm from Edmund Davis. The police have started to hunt up his relatives or friends.

Peckham as Known to His Neighbors.

A *Standard* reporter made inquiries in this city this morning of parties well acquainted in Westport as to the character of Peckham, who proclaims himself the murderer of Mr. and Mrs. Borden.

It was learned that Peckham is an eccentric person. For years he has been known to do all sorts of odd things. He formerly lived on the John Mosher place, but about three years ago leased the Edmund Davis farm, about two miles north of the western part of Central Village. He is 62 years of age, married, and has several children. His wife is an Englishwoman.

Last Spring the heirs of Edmund Davis decided to sell the farm, their tenant not having satisfied them, it is said, with his payments of rent. Peckham also decided to sell out, advertised A. C. Kirby to auctioneer off his goods, set the date and then a few days before the sale, rode bareback early one morning to see if Mr. Kirby would do it. This is said to be a sample of Mr. Peckham's eccentricities. His oddities are reported to have grown worse of late, and the people asked about him think he is a crank.

WEATHER INDICATIONS.

FAIR AND COOLER.

WASHINGTON, Aug. 18.—For the 24 hours from 8 a. m. to-day: For Massachusetts, Rhode Island and Connecticut fair, cooler by Friday night, southerly winds.

COTTAGE CITY NEWS.

Complimentary Concert of the Pupils and Teachers of Villa Bristhall.

[Special Dispatch.]

COTTAGE CITY, Aug. 18.—A colony of musical people delighted a select audience at the Casino last evening. The occasion was a complimentary concert by the teachers and pupils of "Villa Bristhall" to Frederick J. Hart and guests. The following named artists appeared: Mrs. Mary Bogle, the operatic artist; Miss Maud Ulmer, the popular soprano; Miss Grace Reals of Toledo, O., formerly with "The Bostonians;" Miss Hattie Lewis of Denver, Col.; Miss Cora Barnabee, niece of H. C. Barnabee of the "Bostonians;" Miss Josephine Jennings of Minneapolis, Minn.; Miss Bertha Lincoln of Washington, D. C.; soprano of the Fifth Avenue Baptist church, New York; Miss Emma Potts, contralto of the Church of the Divine Paternity, New York; Miss Laura Graves of Hatfield; Miss Emma Muller, contralto of the Fifth Avenue Baptist church, New York; J. Jerome Hayes, tenor of the Church of the Divine Paternity, New York; William A. Howland of New York, who has signed an engagement with the "Bostonians" as leading baritone; Arthur Friedlander of New York; pianists, Mrs. F. H. Mills, Mr. and Mrs. Walter J. Hall, Mr. and Mrs. E. A. Parsons, Mr. Elmer Joyce, Richard T. Percy.

Miss Ullmer's rendition of "Sing, Smile and Slumber" was received with continued applause, and Mrs. Bogle's waltz song from the "Red Hussar" gave evidence of splendid vocal cultivation. Each of the 20 numbers on the programme was applauded, and the singers held the audience till after 10 o'clock.

Yacht Sea Fox of New Bedford will sail Saturday for a week's cruise in Buzzards Bay. Capt. H. C. Cook will be a guest, and Capt. F. H. Cook will be assisted in the management of the yacht by First Officer William E. Searle of New Bedford, Steward Harry S. Golden of Worcester, and Cabin Boy Walter Wade of New Bedford.

At the Baptist Temple to-day, Rev. A. E. Dickinson, D. D., of Richmond, Va., will deliver an address on "The Bible and the Baptists," which will be followed by five-minute speeches. In the evening Rev. H. M. Wharton, D. D., of Baltimore, Md., will preach a sermon.

Frank C. Tripp of this place was severely injured yesterday in a bicycle accident.

The annual ball of the Marthas Vineyard Association will be held Saturday evening.

Capt. and Mrs. W. H. Phillips are entertaining Miss Emily G. Shaw of Middleboro, Miss Dora Hathaway, Miss Alvirah Shaw and Capt. John N. Phillips of Taunton.

John F. Hatch and family of New Bedford have registered at the Park cottage.

Capt. Joseph T. Enos of ship Greyhound is a guest of Samuel Huxford.

Edward Fabian, the humorist, gave an entertainment last evening for the benefit of the Epworth League connected with Trinity M. E. Church.

BIG CATBOAT REGATTA

Open to All New England Being Talked About at Vineyard Haven.

[Special Dispatch.]

VINEYARD HAVEN, Aug. 18.—The yacht owners of this port have in view a regatta for next Summer that shall eclipse anything of that nature yet seen in these waters.

Messrs. Castello, Norton, Davis, Arnoux and others are already at work on the scheme. It is proposed to offer prizes aggregating $1000 for all catboats owned in New England. Four catboats have already beeu ordered and they will come well up to the first-class limit. The new boat club members are very enthusiastic over the recent regatta. To-morrow catboats Pastime and Kapawick will race in the harbor for money.

BOGRAN IS LIVING.

He is on His Way to Europe and Knows of No Revolution in Honduras.

SAN FRANCISCO, Aug. 18.—The report sent from New Orleans, Louisiana, that ex-President Bogran of Honduras had been killed is not correct. He is registered at a hotel in this city and has been interviewed by the newspapers here. He says he is on his way to Europe and knows nothing about a revolution in Honduras.

The Cholera Epidemic in Russia.

ST. PETERSBURG, Aug. 18.—There were 8458 new cases of cholera and 3207 deaths reported from the infected districts yesterday. This is an increase over Tuesday's figures of 649 new cases and 535 deaths. The disease is rapidly increasing in the town of Poltava, in South Russia.

Was Discouraged.

SAVANNAH, Aug. 18.—William R. Cole shot his wife and child and then attempted suicide, without success. Despondency at his failure to get employment is thought to be the cause which led to the tragedy.

Behring Sea Arbitrators Appointed.

ROME, Aug. 18.—The Italia announces that Senator Saredo and Deputy Danieli have been appointed Italian representatives of the Behring sea arbitration commission.

A Cool Reception.

PARIS, Aug. 18.—The new British cabinet met with a cool reception on account of the presence of Lord Rosebery.

A Clincher.

INDIANAPOLIS, Aug. 18.—By order of Judge Taylor drafts on the Order of the Iron Hall have gone to protest.

Ocean Steamers.

Arrived at New York—Mississippi, London; Slavonia and Zanzibar, Hamburg. At Southampton, Normannia, New York. At Bremerhaven (last night) Lahn, New York.

TENNESSEE WAR.

The Entire State Militia Ordered to the Front.

Troops Are Outnumbered by the Reenforced Miners.

Threats of Lynching Governor Buchanan Are Freely Made.

NASHVILLE, Aug. 18.—Governor Buchanan has ordered out the entire state militia under General Sam T. Carnes. They will move to the front at once. The sheriffs of the counties of Knox, Shelby, Hamilton and Davidson were ordered to summon 1000 men each and go on a special train to the scene. The governor claims to be able to have 8000 men on the ground by this noon. Some fears were expressed that the twenty-eight men who left here last night would be attacked at Soddy, a small mining town, en route. A special just received says they just passed that place in safety.

A dispatch from Knoxville says that Tuesday night's fight at Oliver Springs was a desperate affair. Seventeen hundred miners attacked the stockade. The troops there had been reinforced by the military company from Chatanooga, and offered a stubborn resistance. According to the best information obtainable, twelve men were killed and twenty wounded in the engagement. Atfer an hour's fighting, the military, being greatly outnumbered, surrendered. They were placed under guard, and, with the convicts, were marched toward Knoxville. Nothing has been heard thus far, as the wires are cut and communication is unreliable.

A Mass Meeting of Miners

was held at Cold Creek, at which it was resolved to attack the stockade at that point and drive off the convicts and soldiers. The Knoxville companies of militia are stationed at Harriman and will await reinforcements before attempting to do anything.

A dispatch from Chattanooga says that 3000 men have volunteered as militia and will go to Coal Creek. Threats of lynching Governor Buchanan if he ventures into this section are freely made. The governor is waiting for developments.

Troops Captured by Miners.

CHATTANOOGA, Aug. 18.—A special to The News from Harriman says: Major Chandler of the Knoxville troops has just arrived from Oliver Springs and reports that guards and soldiers have been captured by 1800 miners. An attack was made in which the state forces were completely overpowered. No lives were lost.

KNOXVILLE, Tenn., Aug. 18.—The convicts and soldiers from Oliver Springs have arrived here under a heavy guard of miners. They were at once placed in box cars and started for Chattanooga.

Decidedly Warlike.

KNOXVILLE, Tenn., Aug. 18.—Over 1500 miners are massed at Coal Creek, all heavily armed. When the proposed assault on Camp Anderson is made they will force the captive soldiers, in uniform, to march at the head of the column, and have sent word to the officers in command of their intention. They believe that the officers of the camp will refuse to fire on them as long as the soldiers are in front. The miners held a meeting and several warlike speeches were made. Those in a position to know say that Camp Anderson will be defended to the last man.

Miners Reinforced.

KNOXVILLE, Tenn., Aug. 18.—At midnight the miners at Cow Creek received large reinforcements from Kentucky. Up to that hour, however, there had been no attack. Rumor says Governor Buchanan has ordered Gen. Anderson to withdraw his troops and come to Knoxville. It is also rumored that he telegraphed the miners he would withdraw the troops. There is no way of telling how the reports got out or what foundation there is for them.

NASHVILLE, Tenn., Aug. 18.—This morning a special train with 100 troops and civilians left for East Tennessee in response to the Governor's call for assistance. News from Gov. Buchanan's residence elicits the information that the Governor is confined to his bed but in no danger.

Violation of Lease Charged.

The board of prison inspectors met yesterday and considered the opinion of their attorneys, to the effect that the lessees of the convicts have violated the terms of the lease. They will give them formal notice to-day. The lessees claim they have not violated their contract.

All the Militia Ordered Out.

Late last night, after consultation with Adjt.-Gen. Normal and his attorneys, Gov. Buchanan ordered all the organized militia in the State to the scene of the trouble in the mining district.

All the troops will mass at Chattanooga this morning and will proceed to Knoxville, thence to Coal Creek.

The posses armed themselves with all sorts of pistols and guns. Co. C with 40 men, Co. F with 35, and Battery A with 32 men, a three-inch cannon, and two Gatling guns, composed the Nashville troops.

A Knoxville special says: The wires are in order along the railroad to Jelico, but no messages can be received or sent except on railroad business. The miners have a committee at every office, with an operator of their own, who reports everything to the leaders that pass along.

HOME MATTERS.

GRANITE CROSSWALKS are being laid at the corners of Washington and Bonney streets.

WHALEBONE.—About 500 pounds Northwest whalebone were shipped from this city to New York yesterday.

HANDSOME STONE.—A sidewalk is being laid on Purchase street in front of the new Five Cents Savings Bank of handsome flag.

A CONCRETE SIDEWALK is being laid on the southeast corner of Blackmer and County streets.

PROGRESSING.—Work on the tool-house on the City Stable lot is progressing. The foundations are in and the underpinning is being laid to-day.

PARK SEATS.—The Herman place on Acushnet avenue is now supplied with 30 park seats, that number having arrived yesterday and been placed on those grounds.

POLITICAL.—Republican caucuses to elect delegates to the State, Councillor and Congressional Conventions will be held in Fall River on Friday evening of this week.

WEDDING.—J. Fernley and Sarah J. Longdin were united in marriage by Rev. N. W. Mathews at the bride's home on Pleasant street yesterday in the presence of a number of friends, many of whom were from Fall River.

GRAPE STREET SEWER.—About 100 feet of the Grape street sewer extension are completed, and bottom brick laid 15 feet further west

PERSONAL.—Rev. T. G. Spencer of Fall River is in this city as Rev. N. W. Matthew's guest. Mr. Spencer is to preach in this city Sept. 4, at the Primitive Methodist Sunday School's third anniversary, when the occasion will be celebrated by a varied programme.

Miss Annie W. Ellis, an applicant for a clerkship under the civil service rules, has been selected for the position of assistant clerk at the office of the Board of Public Works. She assumes her new duties Aug. 29.

Miss Mary Barton of Providence is visiting friends in this city.

Mrs. John R. Baker and Miss Maggie Kane of Little Falls, N.Y., are visiting their brother, M. F. Kane.

Miss Lulu Crapo left the city yesterday with a party of friends for a two weeks' vacation at Stone Bridge, R. I.

G. William Needham has been engaged as organist at the church of St. John the Baptist.

H. Lester Trafford and Everett A. Dunham of Providence are in the city to-day. They were for five years very successful State agents for Massachusetts and Rhode Island of the Equitable Life Assurance Co., but resigned in order to organize the Columbia Mutual Life Assurance Co. of Providence. They will begin to write policies about Sept. 1st, and have already over $500,000 pledged.

Capt. H. M. Kenyon, T. F. Desmond, Esq., John Bertram, O.A. Sisson and John Welch are on a three days' fishing trip to Gay Head on Mr. Welch's catboat Daisy.

Isaac Magnant is to start to-morrow on a month's trip to Quebec and Montreal.

Justin McCarthy and children of Washington, D. C., have been visiting in this city this week. Mr. McCarthy is the contractor of the new post office building.

Sarah E. Gaffney and Hannah M. Leister of Springfield, Mass., are visiting friends in this city.

Miss Ella F. Bucklin, clerk of the Board of Overseers of the Poor, is enjoying her vacation at Brant Rock.

SIXTY MILLION BUSHELS OF WHEAT—*A Bushel for Every Inhabitant of the United States. The Kansas Crop for '92.*—Never in the history of Kansas has that State had such bountiful crops as this year. The farmers cannot get enough hands to harvest the great crop, and the Santa Fe railroad has made special rates from Kansas City and other Missouri river towns, to induce harvest hands to go into the State. The wheat crop of the State will be from sixty to sixty-five million bushels, and the quality is high. The grass crop is made, and is a very large one; the early potatoes, rye, barley and oat crops are made, and are all large. The weather has been propitious for corn, and it is the cleanest, best looking corn to be found in the country to-day. Cheap rates will be made from Chicago, St. Louis and all points on the Santa Fe east of the Missouri river, to all Kansas points, on August 30 and September 27, and these excursions will give a chance for Eastern farmers to see what the great Sunflower State can do. A good map of Kansas will be mailed free upon application to Jno. J. Byrne, 723 Monadnock Block, Chicago, Ill., together with reliable statistics and information about Kansas lands.

HOW TO LIVE WELL.—A great many people think because they are not rich they cannot afford to live as well as some of their rich neighbors do. Now this is a mistake; there are some store keepers in this city that deal with a class of people that think if goods do not cost a high price they cannot be good, and so for that reason high-toned dealers get high-toned prices; that is right too. We wish to say that we want the public trade, and we claim our goods are just the same if not better than some you buy from your high-priced dealer. Please read the following low prices, which will convince you: Pure Java coffee 28c. lb., worth 38c.; 5 lb. best butter 28c. lb., worth 32c.; fine tea 38c. lb., worth 50c.; good corned beef 4c. and 5c. lb., worth 8c.; best cut thick rib 8c. lb., worth 12c.; best Haxall flour, Christian's triple extra, 69c. a bag, worth 75c.; 8 lb. sweet potatoes 25c.; fresh eggs 28c. dozen, 4 dozen for $1. White Cash Store, 134 Purchase street.

RUNAWAY.—A horse belonging to David Warren, attached to a two-seated vehicle, ran away on Maxfield street this morning. The horse fell down at the corner of Purchase and Maxfield streets and broke a shaft. He again started and ran into the railroad fence at the foot of the street and was considerably cut. The occupants of the carriage escaped injury.

FRIDAY MORNING, Aug. 19, from 8 o'clock a. m. to 1 o'clock p. m. only, we'll sell China silks at twenty-nine cents (29 cents) a yard. Be on hand at the above time if in want. Also at same time 3500 yards twilled cottons in 10 and 20 yard lengths at 5 and 6 cents a yard. Knowles & Co.

A BUSY PLACE.—The busiest place at the South End during the noon hour and evenings is Grove Park, which is crowded with humanity. The settees recently placed on the park are in great demand.

CLAMBAKE AT PALMERS ISLAND.—The ladies of the First Congregational Society of Fairhaven are to hold their annual excursion and clambake at Palmers Island next Tuesday. Read the special notice.

INSANE.—Asenath, wife of John Ashley of Lakeville, who has been visiting at Acushnet, has become insane, and was to-day committed to the asylum at Taunton by Constable Pratt.

"THERE'S A GOOD TIME coming for us all." It came for the babies 20 years ago when Gustav Mellin devised his food for them and so banished colic and indigestion.

BARGAINS not only Friday morning, but all the time in Watches, Clocks, Jewelry, etc., at the closing-out sale of J. S. Kelley & Son, 15 Purchase street.

CATCH BASINS.—A catch basin has been put in at the northwest corner of Madison and Sixth streets, and another at the northwest corner of Madison and Fifth streets.

POLICE STATION.—The work of laying the foundation walls for the police station in ward six has been commenced.

THE ROAD ROLLER is engaged in rolling macadam on Fifth street, between Bedford and Wing streets.

DOES YOUR HEAD TROUBLE YOU?—Stop drinking coffee and use "Ayer's Hygienic Coffee." Grocers sell it.

THE SWAIN FREE SCHOOL.—New circulars are ready and copies will be sent free to any address.

GREAT SHIRT WAIST sale at Whiting & Co's Friday and Saturday.

PHYSICIANS RECOMMEND Turkish baths for invalids.

LOOK OUT for the great silk sale at Whiting & Co's.

A FAIR SKIN for the ladies. Best secured by a Turkish bath No. 5 South Sixth street.

LOOK OUT for the great silk sale at Whiting & Co's.

HALF A DOLLAR secures a hair shampoo, ladies, 5 South Sixth street.

HAND-SEWED Oxford Ties $2.00. Devoll's.

Three Peculiarities in Hood's Sarsaparilla.

GOOD NEWS

Friday Morning, Aug. 19,

We shall sell solid Antique Oak Tables, with top 16 inches square, and ample shelf underneath, all finely finished, strong, serviceable and sightly, for

89c. each.

The sale will continue through Saturday if the stock is not sooner exhausted. These are the Tables on which we created such a furore last Summer. We can take no orders before

FRIDAY MORNING,

But at that time mail or telephone orders will receive careful attention.

☞ Remember the date, FRIDAY MORNING, Aug. 19, and SATURDAY if the stock holds out.

C. F. WING,

34 to 40 Purchase st.

WHITING & CO.

Friday and Saturday

BARGAIN DAYS.

We place on sale a small lot of Real French all wool Challies at 28c. per yard. Come quick if you want any.

30 pieces of 50c. double-fold Dress Goods, suitable for Fall wear for Ladies and Children, will go on sale at 29c. per yard.

A few pieces all wool Homespun Suitings; go on sale at 39c. per yard, 50c. Sept. 1.

The balance of our 10c. Challies at 4c. per yard.

We shall sell you Friday some Fall colors in 12 1-2c. Ginghams at 6c. per yard.

One lot of 15c. Pongees will be sold at 10c.

White ground Chintz colored Cambrics, 4-4 wide, 12 1-2c. goods, go on sale at 8c. per yard.

20 dozen more of those 25c. Ladies' Jersey Ribbed Vests will go on sale at 17c. apiece.

10 dozen Gents' colored Balbriggan Vests and Pants, best 50c. ones 39c. a piece for Friday and Saturday.

See the Cream Table Damasks for Friday and Saturday at 39c. per yard.

Towels, Table Linens, Napkins and Housekeeping Goods, all at reduced prices in this sale.

WHITING & CO.

J. V. SPARE,

Liberty Hall Building.

Friday Morning

SPECIALTIES.

Bargain in White Goods, neat check and stripe; go on sale at 8c. yard, regular 12 1-2 and 15c. quality.

Balance of our 50c. Shirt Waists, 39c. buys them.

Chambrays, double-faced universal price 10c., our price 6 1-2c.

Another lot of those Outings at 5 1-2c.; be quick or you will lose them.

Last, but not least, Black waste sewing Silk in boxes, 5c. box; comments unnecessary.

J. V. Spare,

LIBERTY HALL BUILDING.

OUTING SHIRTS!

OUTING SHIRTS! OUTING SHIRTS!

You can never have too many

OUTING SHIRTS!

Our low prices will help you out. Quality exceptional.

Good Shirts for $1 and $1.25, laundered collars and cuffs.

Another lot of the popular blue Madras, all sizes, $1.50.

Better come at once, They're going fast.

J. & W. R. WING & CO.,

133 UNION STREET.

OUTING SHIRTS!

INSURANCE.

FIRE & LIGHTNING, TORNADO, PLATE GLASS and ACCIDENT INSURANCE.

No. 48 North Water Street.

Ætna Ins. Co.	Hartford
Hartford Fire Ins. Co.	"
Connecticut Fire Ins. Co.	"
Merchants Ins. Co	Providence
Equitable F. & M. Ins. Co.	"
Springfield F. & M. Ins. Co.	Springfield
Ins. Co. of North America	Philadelphia
Ins. Co. of State of Penn	"
Fire Association	"
Home Ins. Co.	New York
Continental Ins. Co.	"
German Am. Ins. Co.	"
Niagara Fire Ins. Co.	"
Williamsburgh City Fire Ins. Co.	"
Hanover Fire Ins. Co.	"
Phœnix Assurance Co.	London
Guardian Assurance Co.	"
No. British & Mer. Ins. Co.	"
Imperial Fire Ins. Co.	"
Fitchburg Mut. Fire Ins. Co.	Fitchburg
Dorchester Mut. Fire Ins. Co.	Neponset
New York Plate Glass Ins. Co.	New York
U. S. Mutual Accident Asso.	"

GEO. N. ALDEN.

(Successor to Tillinghast & Alden.) d&w

SAMUEL H. COOK, Marine & Fire Insurance

AGENT AND BROKER,

No. 37 North Water Street.
(In National Bank of Commerce Building.)

Whaling Risks and their Catchings a Specialty at This Agency.

The following First Class Fire Insurance Companies are represented, viz.:

Hingham Mutual Fire Ins. Co.	Hingham
Phœnix Ins. Co.	Hartford
National Fire Ins. Co.	"
Phenix Ins. Co.	New York
Westchester Fire Ins. Co	"
Commerce Ins. Co.	Albany
Pennsylvania Fire Ins. Co.	Philadelphia
American Fire Ins. Co.	"
Queen Ins. Co.	London
London Assurance Corp.	"
London & Lancashire Ins. Co.	"
Norwich Union F. Ins. Soc'y	"
Northern Assurance Co.	"
Firemen's Fire Ins. Co.	Boston
The Metropolitan Plate Glass Ins. Co.	New York
Hartford Steam Boiler Inspection and Ins. Co.	Hartford

EDWIN EMERY. JOHN H. PEDRO

LAWRENCE GRINNELL & CO.,

Fire and Marine, Life and Plate Glass

Insurance

60 No. Water St., foot of William.
(Over Mechanics' National Bank.)

Liverpool & London & Globe Ins. Co.,	Liverpool
American Fire Ins. Co	New York
Prov. Washington Ins. Co.	Providence
Commercial Union Assurance Co	London
Merchants' Ins. Co	Newark
Boylston Ins. Co	Boston
United States Inc. Co	New York
Caledonian Ins. Co	Scotland
Hamburg-Bremen Fire Ins. Co	Bremen
American Ins. Co.	Boston
Spring Garden Ins. Co	Philadelphia
Lowell Mutual Fire Ins. Co	Lowell
Wachusett Mutual Fire Ins. Co	Fitchburg
Mutual Life Ins. Co	New York
Lloyd's Plate Glass Ins. Co	New York

HIRAM VAN CAMPEN. JOHN W. PAUL.

HIRAM VAN CAMPEN & CO., FIRE, LIFE AND ACCIDENT Insurance Agency,

No. 15 North Water Street.
Telephone Call .... 241-2.
(Established A. D. 1852.)

The following First Class Companies are represented:

Sun Fire Office (Organized A. D. 1710.)	London, Eng.
Lancashire Ins. Co.	Manchester, Eng.
The Reliance Ins. Co.	Philadelphia
Girard Fire & Marine Ins. Co.	"
United Firemen's Ins. Co.	"
Michigan Fire & Marine Ins. Co.	Detroit, Mich.
Security Ins. Co.	New Haven, Ct.
People's Fire Ins. Co.	Manchester, N.H.
Firemen's Ins. Co.	Newark, N. J.
Newark Fire Ins. Co.	"
First National Fire Ins. Co.	Worcester, Mass.
Quincy Mut. Fire Ins. Co.	Quincy, Mass.
Holyoke Mut. Fire Ins. Co.	Salem, Mass.
Traders & Mechanics' Ins. Co.	Lowell, Mass.
Dorchester Mut. Fire Ins. Co.	Boston
Cambridge Mut. Fire Ins. Co.	Cambridgeport, Mass.
Travellers' Ins. Co., Hartford, Life & Accident.	

All losses equitably adjusted and promptly paid.
New Bedford, April, 1890.

IVORY S. CORNISH. CLIFTON H. CORNISH

I. S. CORNISH & SON.

LIFE, FIRE, ACCIDENT and PLATE GLASS
—INSURANCE—
Agents and Brokers. 50 North Second St.
NEW BEDFORD, MASS.

Represent the following First-Class Companies:

Ætna Life Ins. Co.	Hartford, Conn
Travelers Accident Ins. Co.	Hartford, Conn
Merchants and Farmers Mutual Fire Ins. Co.,	Worcester, Mass
Citizens Mutual Ins. Co.	Boston, Mass
Mass. Mutual Fire Ins. Co.	Boston, Mass
Abington Mutual Fire Ins. Co.	Abington, Mass
Salem Mutual Fire Ins. Co.	Salem, Mass
Essex Mutual Fire Ins. Co.	Salem, Mass
Merrimac Mutual Fire Ins. Co.	Andover, Mass
Franklin Mutual Fire Ins. Co.	Greenfield, Mass
Milford Mutual Fire Ins. Co.	Milford, Mass
Glens Falls Ins. Co.	Glens Falls, N. Y
Union Ins. Co.	Philadelphia, Penn
NewHampshire Fire Ins. Co.	Manchester, N.H
Peoples Fire Ins. Co.	Manchester, N. H
Delaware Ins. Co.	Philadelphia, Penn
Metropolitan Plate Glass Ins. Co.	New York, N. Y

Losses promptly adjusted and paid.
Business solicited.

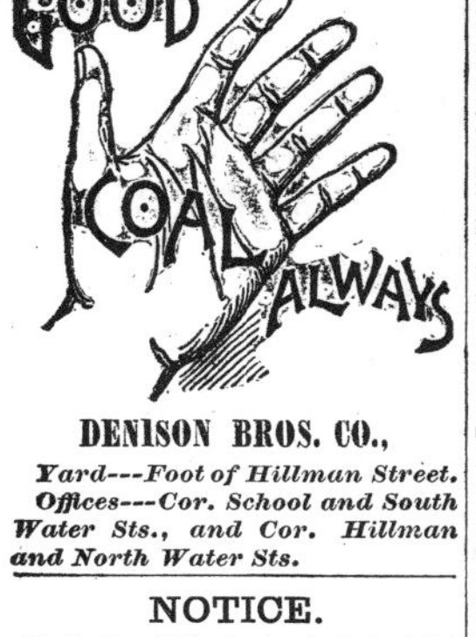

DENISON BROS. CO.,

Yard---Foot of Hillman Street. Offices---Cor. School and South Water Sts., and Cor. Hillman and North Water Sts.

NOTICE.

Having bought the bankrupt stock of the large harness factory of

GRANT & AMES,

Of SOUTH FRAMINGHAM, we can sell you a Full, Genuine Rubber-trimmed Harness at one-half the cost to make.

TRUNKS AND BAGS at the LOWEST PRICES in the city.

WILLIAM CRONIN & CO.,
Corner Elm and Pleasant Sts.

BUSINESS CARDS.

E. T. WILSON, Undertaker & Embalmer,

80 PLEASANT STREET.
(Odd Fellows' Building.)

CASKETS, Coffins, Robes, and Flowers furnished at short notice. All orders in or out of the city will receive prompt personal attention day or night.

Arterial Embalming a Specialty.

Persons wishing my services nights or Sundays will please call at my
Residence............... 15½ William Street
Telephone number 179—3. d&w

WESTON C. VAUGHAN, JR., Funeral & Furnishings Undertaker

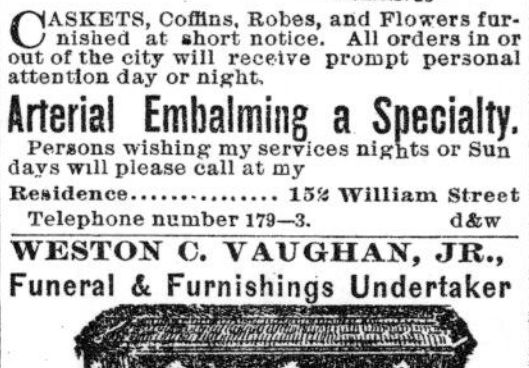

CASKETS, Coffins, Robes, and Flowers furnished at short notice; funerals attended in or out of the city; carriages furnished when desired. All orders from neighboring towns, by express or otherwise, will be promptly attended to. Telephone connection. 138 Purchase Street. Residence 142½ Purchase st. Night bell promptly answered.

BOWKER & TRIPP,

Cor. North Water and North Sts.

MACHINISTS,
Steam Heating Engineers and Contractors.

Complete Outfits of Motive Power, Steam Heating, Hot Water Heating, and General Steam Fitting. A full line of Steam Fitting and Engineers' Supplies.

Mill and heavy work a specialty. With our large machine shop, blacksmith shop and foundry attached, we have every facility for doing first-class work at moderate prices.

D. W. WILSON,
Steam Piping & General Machine Work
PIPE AND FITTINGS
Constantly on Hand.
21 Commercial Street, New Bedford, Mass.
All orders promptly attended to. Satisfaction guaranteed.
Telephone No. 344—3. ap24-tf

To our Patrons:

The proprietors of the paper have kindly allowed us this space, in order to inform the people of New Bedford and all this part of Bristol County that there is no better place on earth to buy goods in the Kitchen Furnishing Line. Our line of Barstow's Bay State Ranges have a world-wide reputation. We have a full line of Kitchen Furnishings in stock and are ready to attend to all orders for Plumbing, Tinsmithing, Tinroofing and General Jobbing in our line of business. We propose to supply the wants of our customers to the best of our ability. We intend to call special attention to the various lines of our business as often as our time will permit. You are cordially invited to visit

HAYDEN'S
KITCHEN FURNISHING HOUSE;
Cor. Acushnet Ave. and Bedford St.

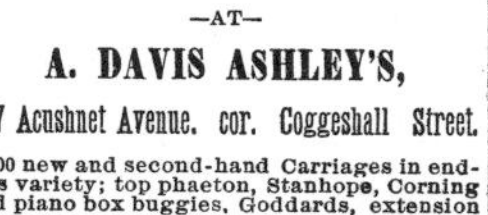

GREAT SALE OF CARRIAGES.

—AT—

A. DAVIS ASHLEY'S,
947 Acushnet Avenue. cor. Coggeshall Street.

100 new and second-hand Carriages in endless variety; top phaeton, Stanhope, Corning and piano box buggies, Goddards, extension top surreys, canopy top surreys, buckboard changeable seats in the oak, new buckboard finished natural wood, $75.00; new open buggies $65.00 up; one $450.00 doctor's coupe nearly new, $165.00; two seated open and canopy top Ashley wagons, new and second-hand; also new and second-hand open and covered express wagons, best variety in the city; two and four seat dog carts; one new canopy top dog cart $50.00. If you want to buy or trade for any kind of a carriage that runs on wheels just look my stock over. I will guarantee the price and represent the goods just as they are; also have a fine assortment of harnesses; call early and you will get your money's worth. I also have some very desirable house lots and first-class business located lots which I will sell low for the location.

A. DAVIS ASHLEY,
947 Acushnet Ave., Cor. Coggeshall St.

GEORGE C. BLISS, FLORIST.

34 Arnold Street,
CORNER COTTAGE.
TELEPHONE, DAY OR NIGHT.

POSTERS AND HAND BILLS
Printed at short notice at the
STANDARD PRINTING ROOMS.

PARENTS WHOSE CHILDREN

Are hard on their clothes, will find at our store about 200 Short Pant Suits, which they can buy at less than cost to manufacture. They are of medium weight and suitable for the next three months' wear. You can get almost two suits for the former price of one, if you come before they are gone.

SANDERS & BARROWS,

67 and 69 William Street.

DON'T STOP ME
I know where to find the Lowest PRICES in

HARNESSES,

Carriage Lap Robes, Horse Clothing, Whips, &c., Ladies' and Gents' Riding Saddles, Trunks, Bags, Pocketbooks, Bill Books, Umbrellas and all kinds Travelling Goods.

C. F. CUSHING, - - - - Opp. City Hall,
IS THE MAN.

EARLY FALL STYLE HATS RECEIVED.

We always sell all Best Hats at Cut Prices. Fifty cents saved on any Hat bought of

H. V. SANDERS & Co.

One Price Clothiers, OPP. CITY CLOCK, 82 Purchase St.

NEW BEDFORD BRASS FOUNDRY.

Machinists, Brass Finishers and Founders, Brass, Bronze and Composition Castings, Zinc and White Metal Pattern Castings, Phospor Bronze Castings a specialty, Lead Window Weights and High Speed Babbitt Metals, Chandelier Repairing and Brazing, Brass Finishing in all its branches. Machine Repairing promptly attended to. Lawn Mowers Sharpened and Repaired.

Foundry and Machine Shop, 108 North Water Street, foot of Elm.
WM. T. NICHOLSON, Manager, Formerly Foreman of the Armington & Sims Engine Company's Brass Foundry, Providence, R. I. je25-3m

THE PUBLIC IS INFORMED THAT THE

NEW BEDFORD BUSINESS COLLEGE

Has Been Purchased by the

BOSTON COMMERCIAL COLLEGE

And will hereafter be run under the management of that institution, in the same manner and following the same methods which have made the Boston Commercial College noted for its success in imparting a thorough knowledge of the branches of a business education, including short-hand and type-writing.

THE COURSE OF STUDY COMPRISES

Bookkeeping, Short-Hand, Type-Writing, Elementary and Commercial Arithmetic, Penmanship, Commercial Law, Grammar, Correspondence, English Composition, &c., &c.

The above studies can be taken separately or combined.
Persons desiring to enter can make application to the Principal at the Rooms of the

College in the Citizens' Bank Building, William St., Opposite Post Office.

For further information apply at College as above or address the
BOSTON COMMERCIAL COLLEGE, No. 1 Beacon St., Boston.

SHAPE YOUR MUSTACHE.

What is more disgusting than to see a man always twisting, twirling, and biting his mustache. Avoid the bad habit by using the instrument that will keep it always just right. Will be sent postpaid with complete outfit for 55 cents, two for one dollar. Postal note or stamps. Address the Nason Bartlett Co., Box 2480, Boston, Mass.

TRY 39 TOBACCO! Best in the Land for Smoking.
Be sure that the tag 39 is on every piece, and take nothing else in place of it.
Distributing Agents
Driscol, Church & Hall, Wholesale Grocers, NEW BEDFORD.

FINE CARRIAGES.

GEO. L. BROWNELL
OFFERS FOR SALE AT HIS
Carriage Manufactory and Repository,
Cor. Acushnet Ave. and Cannon St.,
NEW BEDFORD, ...MASS.

A FINE assortment of Carriages, namely: Landaus, Coaches, Coupe Victorias, Coupe Rockaways, Extension and Standing Top Family Carryalls, Phaetons, Goddard Box Top Buggies, Open Road and Business Wagons. Also a very large assortment of *SECOND-HAND CARRIAGES* of all descriptions, which will be sold low.
GILES G. BARKER, Supt.

A MOTIVE FOR THE MURDER.

New Bedford Police Officers Have Been at Work.

Preliminary Hearing Will Occupy About Four Days.

Authenticity of the Standard's Interview With Detective Seaver.

The discussion which the Fall River massacre has bred silll centres in the preliminary hearing, because that is the next step in the horror, but it is a discussion that amounts to little or nothing. The community learned yesterday that Judge Blaisdell, who has been under fire, had nothing to do with Miss Lizzie Borden's arrest. He simply presided at the inquest, as he was compelled to do. When District Attorney Knowlton had concluded his examination of a certain witness on the day the inquest come to a close, Miss Borden was in the matron's room. The district attorney went to the marshal's private office to compare some portions of the testimony given by the servant with the story which Miss Borden had told. Judge Blaisdell left the building for a few moments, and returned, as he supposed, to resume the inquiry. He was met by the district attorney, who said: "Judge, I propose to arrest Lizzie Borden."

At that point Judge Blaisdell's connection with the case ceased. He will pick up the threads at the beginning again next Monday morning. The district attorney ordered the arrest and attended to the writing and serving of the warrant which has seemed to certain delicate constitutions to be a very brutal instrument. It was supposed that all that transpired after Miss Borden left her home for the last time was understood, but the drift of comment since the presiding justice at the examination has been the topic for debate, indicates that a great many people are under the impression that Judge Blaisdell has already rendered a verdict.

Yesterday afternoon local interest centred in the news regarding the will which appeared in the *Standard*. It is known that along with the theory which the State has been pursuing, there is a motive which prompted the killing, and that that motive will probably be made to play an important part at the final trial. The government has already said that it had good grounds for believing that the butchery was the work of some member of the Borden family, and it has pointed out that member. It has, of course, its views as to the motive which inspired the prisoner to commit the deed. If it were to secure a fortune, the fortune is at hand; if it were to satisfy a mad impulse, there is evidence bearing on that point. The estate involved was a large one, and everything connected with its disposal is of the utmost consequence; on the one hand, to prove that it could not have disturbed the brain of the murderer, and, on the other hand, to prove that it could and probably did.

In considering this subject it is necessary to be conservative. People who are regarded as the best authorities are not infallible; they are liable to err in their conclusions. Furthermore, at this stage it is extremely difficult to obtain accurate information. Nearly everything comes indirectly, and a great deal of allowance must be made for that fact. The judge, district attorney and marshal may or may not know that Andrew J. Borden was about to make a will when his life was taken, and that there was a debate in the family over it. All that the newspapers can fairly tell their readers is that they have heard such a story from a source which they regard as reliable. If there is no foundation for it, speculation along this line is worthless; if there is ground for it, its importance cannot be overestimated. In the latter event, members of the family in Fall River and elsewhere will be able to recall a great deal that was said about the will and the feeling in regard to it. Money arrests the attention, and impresses itself on the mind sometimes, when a sermon will not.

Mr. Borden may never have referred to a will in the presence of his wife and daughters, but it is not unreasonable to suppose that he did, and it is not unreasonable to suppose that the matter interested them. In the absence of undeniable facts, it is easier to believe that there was a controversy over this subject than it is to pin one's faith to the wild-eyed, white-faced man, or the stranger seen by Manchester's dead brother on a country road. If the family relations were not pleasant a quarrel would not have been improbable. If there is any one thing that can create greater estrangement and a more enduring bitterness in the most harmonious households than dollars and cents, it has not been discovered up to date. If Miss Lizzie were not fond of her step-mother, it would not be unnatural for her to protest that Mrs. Borden should not enjoy more than her legal share in the property. It would not be unnatural for relatives, near and remote, to take sides on the question. Were such a discussion once launched, it might be expected that certain relatives would plead for the daughters, and others for the wife.

In other words, there is nothing far-fetched or impossible in all this, provided, as stated, the subject was ever broached. A sane being can hardly conceive, it must be admitted, how such a dispute, however passionate, could end in a double murder, but history contains some strange chapters. A sane being finds it difficult to comprehend that a double murder could have been committed at all, whatever the pretext or motive. The mind is only partially satisfied when it reasons that the deed was the work of a maniac, with the strength of an ox, and the arrest and surrounding circumstances will not allow it to reason long in that channel.

However, Miss Emma Borden, and perhaps Bridget Sullivan, can throw light on the theory of a will, and the former can readily explain her absence from home on the day of the tragedy, while John Morse will be able to state whether or not he attempted to interfere in behalf of the daughters, in case Mr. Borden's fortune and its disposition ever entered his head. It is safe to assume that all three have already given every scrap of information they possessed. It may or may not have covered the ground outlined above. It is hinted that it did, but it is only a hint.

An out-of-town official, who has been working on the case, had this to say yesterday regarding the subject of a will:

"Soon after the murders were committed it was learned that Mr. Borden said to Charles C. Cook, an insurance agent, who occasionally transacted business for him, 'I must make a will. I am getting to be an old man and I have put it off too long already.' This statement was made by Mr. Borden about three weeks before he was killed, and the city marshal heard of it soon after he began his work. Early in the case, too, the Government employed Officers John C. Parker and Frank Hathaway of this city, who have been busy on the Dartmouth end of the case, and are still engaged on it. They have held frequent interviews with occupants of the William Davis cottage on the Smith Mills road, and have supplied many missing links. John V. Morse visited at the cottage, and I am informed that both Miss Emma and Miss Lizzie had been there, and consulted their uncle on business, though I haven't talked with Parker or Hathaway recently and don't know just what discoveries they made. The assumption on which the State has been proceeding, however, is that the daughters Miss Emma and Miss Lizzie learned of their father's intention through their uncle. It is presumed that the latter was on very intimate terms with Mr. Borden, at least certain members of the family convey that impression, and it was understood that the will would give the girls $25,000 apiece, and that the residue of the estate would go to Mrs. Borden. Mr. Borden knew of course that the daughters and particularly Miss Lizzie, were not on the best of terms with his wife, and their relations were not becoming any more pleasant as time went on.

At this point I have got to put a case. Suppose Mr. Borden had concluded that the sum above mentioned would support his daughters comfortably, and that his wife deserved and ought to have a large share of his estate, as she had helped him to save it. If he came to such a determination, and I do not say that he did, it would be next to impossible to shake him in it. The daughters would naturally object to such a division, and Miss Lizzie might contend that her own mother had worked hard and had been economical during her life, and that her rights in the estate ought to be considered. Mr. Morse had always been interested in his nieces, and he might be expected to work in their behalf and to endeavor to persuade Mr. Borden to deal more generously with them. He is said to have had a long and confidential talk with Mr. Borden the evening before the tragedy, but what the nature of it was I do not know; I do know, however, that just before Mr. Borden was killed there were frequent journeys between the Dartmouth cottage and the Borden house on Second street, and it looked as if considerable business was being transacted. I am also pretty positive that more or less of the motive theory has come."

It is believed that the preliminary hearing will occupy three or four days, and one of the government officials intimated last night that District Attorney Knowlton might not be averse to putting in a good deal of his case. So far as the government is concerned, it does not care who presides at the inquest. At least one of the officers states that he is perfectly willing to have the defence import a judge, or manufacture one, so long as he can rule intelligently on ordinary points. He said it would not affect the result. Mr. Jennings was working on the defence yesterday, and his clerk was inquiring for people who were conspicuous on the premises soon after the butchery was announced.

The Interview with Mr. Seaver.

The *Standard's* interview with State Officer Seaver attracted such widespread attention and was so generally copied that the officer's denial of its authenticity, which has been given publicity in these columns at his request, is not allowed to go unchallenged. The following statement from the *Standard's* representative in Taunton is interesting in this connection:

The "general denial" from Mr. Seaver in the *Standard* yesterday via the telephone relative to the interview printed in the *Standard* the night before amounts to nothing. The interview was substantially as was given by Mr. Seaver, the only difference being in the phraseology. Mr. Seaver labored under a disadvantage at the time because he evidently had not the slightest idea that he was being interviewed, but every statement made in the *Standard* and attributed to him is substantially as he stated. No notes were taken at the time and therefore Mr. Seaver undoubtedly felt that he was perfectly safe in saying what he did.

W. F. GREENOUGH.

The *Mercury* says:

State Officer Seaver now thinks he didn't say so. All the same, we advise him not to do it again.

Blood on the Ceilings.

It is stated that Lawyer Andrew J. Jennings is a more successful blood hunter than the police were. Five tiny spots have been given out as the sum total of the amount found in the three active searches made by the police and all those were on the door casing or base boards.

A day or two ago Mr. Jennings made a search and discovered several good sized spots on the ceilings over the places where the bodies lay in the rooms. Mr. Jennings would neither deny nor confirm this statement last night, but it comes from an authoritative source and is generally credited.

If true, it marks an important point for the defence, because the theory of the police that no blood spurted from the wounds would be rather weakened. Still, it is by no means improbable that the spots came from the same source as those found on the boards, casings and pillow sham did; that is, were thrown from the hatchet as it swept through the air on its merciless errand of destruction, when blow after blow was administered. Still, it is a fact that the police found no blood spots on the ceiling, and if nothing more comes of it Lawyer Jennings will have the reputation of being sharp eyed as well as sharp witted.

MANHOOD RESTORED.

Before & After Use. Photographed from life.

"SANATIVO," the Wonderful Spanish Remedy, is sold with a Written Guarantee to cure all Nervous Diseases, such as Weak Memory, Loss of Brain Power, Headache, Wakefulness, Lost Manhood, Nervousness, Lassitude, all drains and loss of power of the Generative Organs in either sex, caused by over-exertion, youthful indiscretions, or the excessive use of tobacco, opium, or stimulants, which ultimately lead to Infirmity, Consumption and Insanity. Put up in convenient form to carry in the vest pocket. Price $1 a package, or 6 for $5. With every $5 order we give a written guarantee to cure or refund the money. Sent by mail to any address. Circular free in plain envelope. Mention this paper. Address,

MADRID CHEMICAL CO., Branch Office for U. S. A.
358 Dearborn Street, CHICAGO, ILL.

FOR SALE IN NEW BEDFORD, MASS., BY R. H. & H. A. Lawton, Apothecaries, Union St.

A New Bedford Man

Who has suffered for months with terrible pains in his shoulder, which was injured by a fall, found

HIS FIRST RELIEF

Recently in the Turkish Bath House, with a Massage by Manager Cavanaugh. Follow his example.

YOU NEED A BATH.

No. 5 South Sixth Street.

HILLIARD'S OPINION.

City Marshal Talks Upon Certain Phases of the Case.

FALL RIVER, Mass., Aug. 18.—"I think if you were to publish tomorrow the solid facts in the case, and all of them, you would find that before night a great many people would suddenly change their minds."

These words coming from Marshal Hilliard last night, as he sat at headquarters toying with a cigar, are ominous. There was no accent of doubt in the words.

District Attorney Knowlton and the oft-repeated assertions of those who know him, are ominous as well.

It looks to me," said the city marshal, "as though this hearing would be long. I believe it will last three or four days, though, of course, I cannot say positively."

"Would it embarrass you, marshal, if the defense should summon and cross-question some of your witnesses whom you did not find it necessary to call at this hearing."

"I think," he replied, "that all our evidence will be put in. That is what I would advise if I were asked, though, of course, I cannot say what the district attorney will do. I do think, however, that

More Evidence Will Be Put In

than otherwise would have been advanced just to satisfy the public mind as to the action taken. We wish to show that we have nothing to keep back or hide away."

"Now, marshal, the statement has gone abroad that Bridget, after Mr. Borden left the house in the morning, heard Lizzie go down cellar, and subsequently saw what she thought was a hatchet half-hidden in the parlor."

"That may have come from some party who knows," the chief replied. "I have not heard of it."

"I have devoted attention to many stories that were foolish, just because of the enormity of the crime, and in order that I might leave no stone unturned to solve it. If I had not been in this office; if I had been brought up in the same circle with her and known her as some of these people have, it is quite probable that I would have done as they are doing now.

"I will say, though, that it is strange that some of those who are looked up to for guidance by the people in their everyday life should say things that have been said from the pulpit, when they are really not in

A Position to Judge the Case

because they do not know what we do and why we acted.

"I have received today a letter from a man representing a Christian society in this city, and which I would like to give you if I could, for it seems to me to be a fair statement of the case."

The marshal then read a few extracts from the letter. The writer, whose language was somewhat biblical in form, exhorted him to proceed earnestly in the course adopted, saying that the most important matter was that the terrible crime should be brought home to the guilty party, and that when that were done, and only then, the public would be assured that justice had been done. If the prisoner was innocent, the writer said, it would be most unlikely that she would receive any but just treatment at the trial. Justice demanded that the marshal do all he could to ferret out the crime. The conviction or acquittal of the prisoner would then be reached in the natural course of events. This, the marshal thought, was only a

Fair Statement of the Case.

The letter was very different in tone from the majority of those he had received.

The chief, Detective Seaver, and Detective McHenry came home from Boston yesterday. They had been in consultation with the district attorney and Attorney General Pillsbury. Mr. McHenry has succeeded in running down sometning, but no one would say what.

Had nothing come of it, the police say they might have given it to the public, but now secrecy is necessary.

When he left here Detective McHenry went to his home in Providence. There he struck a clue that took him to Boston. From Boston it led him over into Connecticut. He visited Milford, Waterbury and Hartford in that state, and returned to Boston, where he met the marshal and Mr. Seaver. Whatever this clue may be, it has led the officers further away from home than any other clue, as far as known, that has been picked up since the investigation began.

And now the question is what it is that takes the police so far away from Andrew Borden's walls, when they have already decided upon the guilty party?

No Money Can Buy This Boy.

Mrs. William May Smith, of Provincetown, Mass., a portrait of whose little son is given here, writes:

MASTER SMITH.

"My baby was a frail little thing when he was born. He was nursed at the breast until he was four months old, when the doctors said he and his mother would both die if he was not weaned. We tried cow's milk, which was not adapted to his needs, so we used lactated food, following the directions exactly. Since then he has gained a pound a month, has had very little sickness and seems strong and bright. One friend says of him: 'I would not have given two cents for him when he was two weeks old, but now, if he was mine, no money could buy him.' And I am sure his father and mother agree with the last clause of that statement."

FELL FROM A TREE.—During the progress of yesterday's game of base ball on the Y. M. C. A. grounds, Edward Tripp, a young man about 18 years of age, who was a spectator from a tree on Union street, fell to the ground below, a distance of about 30 feet. He struck on the left side of his head, badly wrenching his neck, and when his comrades went to his assistance it was thought he was dead. He was removed to his boarding place at the corner of West Elm street and Chancery street, where in about an hour he recovered consciousness. Young Tripp was removed to the home of a relative in the evening. He complains of severe pains internally. Another youngster fell from the same perch with Tripp, but did not reach the ground, as his fall was broken and he was hustled back to a limb of safety by others in the tree. It's about time that these youngsters were prevented from making use of that special tree on the corner for the purpose named. At times there are upwards of 30 among its branches, and unless a check is put to this sort of proceeding more serious accidents will result.

YACHTING.—Schooner yachts Republic and Mohican arrived in port yesterday afternoon.

Worth Knowing.

That ALLCOCK'S POROUS PLASTERS are the highest result of medical science and skill, and in ingredients and method have never been equalled.

That they are the original and genuine porous plasters, upon whose reputation imitators trade.

That ALLCOCK'S POROUS PLASTERS never fail to perform their remedial work quickly and effectually.

That this fact is attested by thousands of voluntary and unimpeachable testimonials from grateful patients.

That for rheumatism, weak back, sciatica, lung trouble, kidney disease, dyspepsia, malaria and all local pains they are invaluable.

That when you buy ALLCOCK'S POROUS PLASTERS you absolutely obtain the best plasters made

SECOND EDITION.

HOME MATTERS.

OIL MARKET.—In this market sales have
been made of 350 barrels sperm oil, import of
schooner Antarctic, for manufacture on private terms.

BUILDING.—The syndicate which recently
purchased the property south of Cove street,
has in process of construction two dwelling-
houses. Three buildings are being staked
out, and it is said that 50 dwellings will be
erected this Fall.

THE WORK WILL GO ON.—The difficulty in
relation to connecting the dry closets with
the sewer in Cedar Grove street has been
amicably adjusted. Yesterday afternoon the
inspector of plumbing visited the premises,
and the city property committee has agreed
to use iron pipe instead of cement as required
by the Board of Health.

APPRECIATED.—A gentleman, a former resident of Mattapoisett, residing in California,
sends us seven years' subscription to the Republican Standard. He writes that not having received the paper for some weeks he
was reminded that his subscription had expired and does not wish it to happen again.
He wishes home news and knows how to get
it.

STRAIGHTENED AT LAST.—Yesterday afternoon Master Mechanic Daniel D. Briggs and
his assistant made repairs to the weather
vane on the Harrington Memorial school
building. For several months the vane has
been the source of considerable uneasiness
to many people, especially to one base ball
crank, who never let an opportunity slip of
asking Cook, the catcher, to straighten it out
by a long hit over right field fence.

THE TURF.—There was a large attendance
at the Manchester Driving Park yesterday
afternoon, when bay gelding Johnny Knott,
after losing the first heat, won the race in the
next three heats. The best time was 2 24⅞;
the exhibition was the finest ever seen on
that track and the gelding from this city reduced the record of that association's
grounds. Races sold heavily on Johnny
Knott. The judge announced the time of
the second heat as 2 24⅝, but a number of
gentlemen who held timers declare that the
heat was trotted in 2 23½, and the announced
time has been protested by J. Middleby,
driver of the animal which finished second.

THE CALEDONIANS.—The New Bedford
lodge of Caledonians, 18 members, in regalia,
with Chief William T. Moncrieff in command,
participated in the 22d annual excursion of the
Providence Caledonian Society at Rocky Point
yesterday. A great many visiting Scotsmen
were present, either as individuals or in societies, but of the latter it is said that the
New Bedford lodge made the best turnout. In
the sports several members of the I. A. Club
of this city were entered and made a good
showing, while Peter C. Keith of this city
danced in the Highland Fling and Broad-
sword dance.

REAL ESTATE SALES.—Asa J. Sherman and
others have quitclaimed to George F. Howland 150 acres of land in Dartmouth, lying
between the Tucker road and Paskamanset
river.

William A Read has sold to Lillie F. Hathaway $0.34 rods of land on the south side of
Willis street.

George H. Taber has sold for Phebe S.
Delano Snow and 35 rods of land on the corner of Bridge and Mulberry streets in Fairhaven to Z. H. Thompson for $1550.

M. E. Smith has sold for Valentine Parker
two lots of land, containing about 50 rods, on
the south side of Howard avenue to George
Gifford.

Pierre Dandurand has sold to Margaret
Kerns $3.60 rods land east side of the Bolton
road in Dartmouth.

The Rowland Mills Corporation has sold to
Anchine Desjardins 9.84 rods land north side
of Independence street.

The Rowland Mills Corporation has sold to
Thomas J. Meaney 9.84 rods land north side
of Independence street.

George F. Howland has sold for $5800 to
Jose Antonio Mariano buildings and 150 acres
and on the Tucker road in Dartmouth.

WHAT IS IT?

In point of fact it is the freedom from poisonous
and spurious ingredients, the excellence in flavor
which gives to **Dr. Price's Delicious Flavoring Extracts** of Vanilla, Orange, Lemon, etc.,
their wide popularity and increasing sale.

The retail grocers are learning that quality rather than
price, is necessary to retain the confidence of customers
and make a successful business.

FINANCIAL.

**Special Appropriations Made by the City
Council This Year.**

Just at this time, when people are looking
anxiously for their tax bills, there is more or
less said concerning the special appropriations voted by the City Government. This is
a subject which is always interesting to tax
payers, and to-day the Standard prints the
various sums appropriated up to Aug. 1. It
will be seen that thus far $201,140.81 have been
appropriated against $219,985.83 for the year
1891. Of the amount appropriated this year
over $2,000 will be collected by the authori-
ties as assessments for the construction of
sewers and placed to the credit of unappropriated funds. This practically reduces the
special appropriations to about $180,000. As
a rule the work of the year is completed by
September, but this year several special appropriations will be necessary to make up
deficiencies in general appropriations in several of the departments. There is also talk
of a special appropriation for the Hillman
street fire station. The following items may
be read with interest, being the several
amounts voted as special appropriations during the present year.

Board of Health,	$21,003
Cedar Grove Street school-house,	2,000
Cemeteries,	2,000
City stable tool-house,	7,150
Incidentals,	7,990.30
Fourth of July,	3,050
Kempton Street school-house,	46,960
Police station, ward room and lot,	5,000
Schools—Repairs of building,	5,000
High street armory,	650
Fire department workshop,	700

                $124,490.30

Sewers.

General account,	$14,200
Beetle and Howard streets,	1,200
Bellville avenue No. 2,	3,000
Coggeshall street No. 2,	800
Cottage street No. 4,	800
Cove road,	400
Delano street No. 2,	1,000
Emerson street,	198.16
Fair street,	500
Grape street extension,	500
Janney street,	1,500
Maxfield street No. 4,	1,500
Nelson street,	2,000
North Front street No. 2,	1,500
Orchard street No. 4,	6,000
Peckham street,	2,600
Sawyer street,	15,000
Shawmut avenue No. 3,	1,277.25
South First street No. 2,	300
South Front street No. 5,	1,200
Spruce street,	300
Weld street No. 3,	2,000
West French avenue,	675

         $76,650.51
        124,490.30

       $201,140.81

The following are the expenditures in the
various departments of the city for the week
ending Aug. 13:

Board of Health,	$746.52
Cemeteries,	169.72
Engineering Department,	59.36
Fire Department,	483.73
Free Public Library—Dog Fund,	10.29
Highways and Streets,	1,968.72
Incidentals,	148.87
N. B. & F. Bridge,	21.20
N. B. Water Works,	751.73
Parks and Squares,	51.15
Police Department,	1,188.65
Public Schools—Incidentals,	296.61
Public Schools—Pay of Teachers,	4.20
Public Works—Permanent Improve-	
ments,	81.42
Sewers—General account,	105.87
" Beetle and Howard streets,	353.34
" Grape street extension,	706.97

     Total, $7,156.07

THE CALEDONIANS of this city captured the
honors at the Caledonian celebration at
Rocky Point, yesterday. Sixteen members
of the local society wore plaids, and it was
the consensus of opinion that they made
the finest appearance of any society present.

NEW SIGN.—T. J. Murphy exhibits a neat
new sign announcing his steamboat and
railroad ticket agency, and it is a beauty.
Frank E. Linton did the lettering and Charles
E. Lawrence painted the steamship and
train upon it.

Pensions have been granted as follows:
Original—William McHale, H. W. Childs,
R. B. N. Cheney, Theodore Dutra, H. C. Bai-
ley; Hugh Smith (deceased), David Larkin,
J. E. Lyons, C. M. Surbonk, A. J. Heresy
Widows, etc.—Jane A. Borden, Ida Harden.

FALL RIVER ELECTRIC CARS.—The trial trip
of the electric cars came off in Fall River
yesterday afternoon and was successful.

THE EXPORTS from New York the past week
include 118 pounds whalebone.

MARION.

A boat race was sailed yesterday, the
Flight, owned by Isaac Hiller, winning in the
first class. The result in the third class is in
dispute between the Tycoon and the Sippican, both claiming to be the winner. In the
fourth class the Edith, owned by S. G. Van
Rensselaer, was the winner.

The Masonic clambake at Oakdale on
Wednesday was a perfect success. About
200 were present. Cigars were furnished by
Bro. N. P. Hayes of New Bedford.

DEATHS.

In this city, 17th inst., Patrick, son of William and Ellen Moore, aged 2 years and 3
months.

Funeral at his father's residence, 13 Borden
street, Friday, at 2 o'clock. Relatives and
friends are invited to attend.

MARINE INTELLIGENCE.

At at New York 17th, sch Salmon Washburn,
Perth Amboy for Taunton; Hattie M Howes,
Handy, Hyannis.

Passed through Hell Gate 17th, sch Hattie
Paige, Crocker, Hoboken for Boston.

At at Philadelphia 17th, schs Jesse Murdock,
Perry, Wareham; Grace Seymour, Holmes,
hence; Joe Eaton Jr, Fisher, Boston and sld
for Medford.

At at Norfolk 15th, schs J R Teel, Portland; Alice B Phillips, Tiverton.

At at Newport News 17th, sch Massasoit,
Boston.

FINANCIAL.

Money Easy—Stock Markets Firm—Louisville & Nashville Statement—Calumet &
Hecla—Currency Shipments—Copper
Situation—Crop Reports—Bullion Shipment—Anthracite Coal Shipment—Railroad Earnings.

     THURSDAY, Aug. 18.

Yesterday's stock market was a trifle irregular, but at the close of the day prices went
flying on rumor of gold taken for shipment.
A decided decline heavily. This fall in valu-
ations yesterday was of a discouraging nature to the bulls, although there are strong
indications of an improvement in the immediate future, which aggravates to see
prices go the opposite way. Still as yet very
little long stock has been forced out and the
open question is, how long will this fight con-

tinue? News from the strike is anything but
encouraging. This fact alone would have a
tendency to depress prices. Commission houses are said to be quite
heavy buyers. For the first time in
a month they report that their orders are increasing. This argues well for a more active market and its natural concomitant
higher prices. Good judges of the market
say Atchison, Union Pacific, Rock Island, and
New England are going higher. In view of
the complications at Buffalo it might be well
to take profits on bulges.

The local market money is in fair demand at rates ranging from 5 to 6 per cent.

The Boston loan market is somewhat easier, and continues very quiet. Call loans 4½
to 6 per cent. Prime mercantile paper 4½ to
5½ per cent. Corporation paper 4½ to 5½ per
cent.

The clearing-house rate is 4 per cent.

The New York money market has been
easy. Call loans 1½ to 2 per cent.
Prime mercantile paper 3½ to 5½ per cent.
Sterling exchange is quiet and steady;
posted rates are 4.87½ to 4.89.

Government bonds are dull and steady.
In Wall street stock circles this morning
the subject of discussion was the situation at
Buffalo. The governor gave orders during
the night to call out the National Guards.
Mr. Cammack is said to have returned to
town. London has been a seller. Lower
prices looked for.

In the New York stock market, at the
opening, prices were firm. Atchison opened
at 38⅝, Chicago, Burlington & Quincy at 102⅞,
Erie at 27, Missouri Pacific at 52⅜, Reading at
58⅝, Rock Island at 80⅞ and Sugar at 109¾.
At 11 o'clock the market was quite active
and stronger. Atchison advanced to 38⅝,
Chicago, Burlington & Quincy to 102⅝, Erie
to 27⅜, Missouri Pacific to 59¾, Rock Island
to 80¾, St. Paul to 82¾ and Union Pacific to
38⅜. Western Union sold at 99½ At noon
prices were hardly as high. The
feature during the morning was spent in industrials worked by insiders. This had a
depressing effect on the general list and tone,
Chicago, Burlington & Quincy was evidently
held up by short interest in the stock. Atchison 38⅜, St. Paul 82⅝, Northwest 117, Delaware & Lackawanna 156¼, and Sugar 110. At 1
o'clock the market was steady, with the exception of Sugar, which jumped to 111. Reading 58⅜, Western Union 99½, and General
Electric 118½.

The Boston stock market opened dull and
steady. Atchison opened at 38⅝, C. B. & Q.
at 102⅞, Mexican Central at 15⅜, Union Pacific
at 38⅜, Calumet & Hecla at 299½ and Sugar at
109¼. At 11 o'clock there was but little difference in the tone of the market, prices
holding steady. Atchison 38½, Boston & Albany 205, N. E. 36 and Mexican Central 15⅛,
Sugar was the exception to the general rule,
advancing rapidly to 110½. Until 1 o'clock
the market was irregular and fairly active.
Atchison 38⅜, Chicago, Burlington & Quincy
102⅝, Boston & Maine 178½, old Colony 183,
Atchison incomes 59¼ and Calumet & Hecla
298. Sugar 110½. Sales to noon: Bonds $71,-
600, and 15,460 shares of stock.

Missouri Pacific earnings for the second
week in August increased $192,000.

The lead trust is said to have $1,500,000 in
bank in New York, and to be earning a dividend on the common stock. When it will
pay the dividend, and how much it raises
against the cash on deposit, is not stated.
Good things only are told to help along the
advances in the stock.

Prime says the weather is a little cooler.
Central Illinois reports corn 30 per cent.
poorer than last year and three weeks behind
the average season. The earliest grown will
not be safe from frost before Sept. 20. The
yield of oats is 40 to 45 per cent. of last year
and poor quality. New Madison, O., looks
for not over half a corn crop. Rain is needed
badly. Oats there are threshing well. North
Dakota reports wheat filled poorly; tops of
heads empty; none cut yet; oats and barley
crops increased and wheat crop diminished.
The Calumet Conglomerate has made an
inspection of the openings of No. 1 shaft,
Tamarack, Junior. On the fourth level south
the drift is in about 465 feet and the breast is
very rich. The vein is seven or eight feet
wide, carrying copper all through. There are
several stopes on this level, and in the one
above are very rich. The breast of the drift
in the third level south is very fine also. At
No. 2 they have drifted about 50 feet each
way from the cross-cut, and they are finding
a small seam of very heavy copper-bearing
rock in a six or seven foot healthy-looking
vein. Some of the rock that comes up is very
rich and full of heavy, sprangly horns of copper, besides much fine copper.

Traffic Manager Mellen of the N. Y. & N. E.
is still economizing in operations and the
current earnings are said to reflect the
economy. The Washington express
and the Norwich boat line train will hereafter be run to Putnam as one train and the
same returning. This will be a saving of one
train 123 miles, equivalent to about $75 a day.

Total shipments of anthracite coal for
month of June 3,654,424 tons, against 3,571,339
last year, a decrease of 186,915 tons. Total for
year to date 23,967,863 tons, against 21,756,453
last year, an increase of 1,301,230 tons. The
anthracite coal companies are operating
their mines three days of eight hours each
per week. Companies outside of the combination are said to adhere as strictly and
agreeably to this schedule as those in it.
Even on this basis there is more coal mined
than is wanted. The West takes the over-
flow, leaving the tidewater markets with only
such stock as is demanded.

Deposits at the sub-treasury on account of
shipments of currency began last year early
in July and by the middle of August amounted to $6,695,000. This year deposits did not
begin until Aug. 3, and to date they aggregate
$2,085,000.

The copper situation is in a peculiar condition. From all reports lake copper is in
good demand, and the companies are all
sold up. Should the demand continue or increase, an advance in lake copper would
seem certain. It is said that a number of
producers are contending in electrical apparatus
specialty that only lake copper shall be used.
This may be one of the reasons why lake copper is so strong.

The bull pool in Rock Island is not making
much headway. Manager St. John says that
the earnings are larger than they were at
this time last year.

A dispatch from Topeka, Kansas, says late
rains have insured two-thirds of a corn crop.
Late railroad earnings have been reported
as follows:

NORTHERN PACIFIC.

Week.	1892.	Increase.
Second Aug.,	$512,382	$82,469
Since July 1,	2,992,671	162,855
Mileage,	4,379	127

WISCONSIN CENTRAL LINES.

Second Aug.,	$122,557	$19,632
Since July 1,	754,350	51,433
Mileage,	867	

ST. PAUL.

Second Aug.,	$586,698	$94,801
Since July 1,	16,459,095	3,037,338
Mileage,	6,721	3

The official figures showing the operations
of the Louisville & Nashville Railroad for
the fiscal year ended June 30 are as follows:

Year June 30.	1891-92.	Increase.
Earnings,	$21,233,721	$2,014,922
Expenses,	13,792,122	1,733,077

Net,	$7,443,599	$281,315
Other income,	533,293	*184,581

Total net,	$7,976,892	$96,724
Charges,	5,374,063	755,624

Balance,	$2,602,892	*$658,890
Division leases,	251,636	47,900

Surplus,	2,350,133	$700,092
Dividends,	2,376,000	*24,000

Deficit,	$25,867	$652,092

*Decrease.

The annual meeting of the stockholders of
the Calumet & Hecla Mining Co. of Michigan
was held yesterday. The auditor's report
made the accounts $4,193,839.71, and liabilities
$1,557,869.81. President Agassiz, in his report,
said that the large expenditures for construction heretofore planned are drawing to
a close, and by the end of the fiscal year
coming, without demands now unforseen,
will see the construction account greatly
reduced.

STOCK AND BOND MARKETS.

Bids at the close of First Board.
     NEW YORK, Aug. 18.

GOVERNMENT BONDS.

U.S. 2s, registered,	100
" new 4s, registered,	115¼
" new 4s, coupons,	116
" currency 6s, 1895, (Pacifics),	

RAILROADS.

Atchison,	38⅜
Clev., Cin., Chicago & St. Louis,	66
Chicago & Eastern Illinois,	
Chicago & Eastern Illinois pre.,	
Chicago, Burlington & Quincy,	102⅝
Delaware & Hudson,	134¼
Delaware & Lackawanna,	156¼
Erie,	27
Illinois Central,	
Lake Shore & Michigan southern,	124½
Louisville & Nashville,	69
Michigan Central,	
Missouri Pacific,	53¾
New York Central,	114¾
New York & New England,	36⅝
Northern Pacific,	21
Northern Pacific pref.,	55½
New York & New England pref.,	117½
New York Central & Hudson River,	112¼
North American,	13¼
Oregon Navigation,	
Oregon Improvement,	
Oregon Short Line,	
Philadelphia & Reading,	58¾
Pullman Palace Car Co.,	196
Chicago, Rock Island & Pacific,	80¾
Chicago, Milwaukee & St. Paul,	82¾
Chicago, Milwaukee & St. Paul pref.,	
Richmond Terminal,	12
St. Paul & Omaha,	53
St. Paul & Omaha pref.,	
Union Pacific,	38⅜
Wabash, St. Louis & Pacific,	14
Wabash, St. Louis & Pacific pref.,	29½

MISCELLANEOUS.

Ontario Silver,	41¾
Pacific Mail Steamship Co.,	33
Quicksilver,	5½
Quicksilver pref.,	
Sugar, common,	110½
Sugar pref.,	
Western Union Telegraph,	99½
Silver Certificates,	92½

BONDS.

Atchison 4s,	82½
Atchison incomes,	59¼
American Bell Telephone 7s,	
Chicago, Burlington & Northern 5s,	
Chicago & West Michigan 5s,	
Mexican Central 4s,	
Illinois Steel Co.	

RAILROADS.

Atchison, Topeka & Santa Fe,	38⅜
Boston & Albany,	205
Boston & Maine,	178
Boston & Providence,	250
Chicago, Burlington & Quincy,	102⅝
Chicago & West Michigan,	44½
Cleveland & Canton,	6
Cleveland & Canton pref.,	17
Fitchburg pref.,	
Flint & Pere Marquette,	77
Flint & Pere Marquette pref.,	15¼
Mexican Central,	15⅛
New York & New England,	36⅝
New York & New England pref.,	117½
Old Colony,	183
Oregon Short Line,	23⅜
Pullman Palace Car,	196
Union Pacific,	38¼
Wisconsin Central,	17
West End,	90½
West End pref.,	

MINING.

Butte & Boston Mining Co.,	*10
Calumet & Hecla Mining Co.,	298
Centennial,	17½
Franklin Mining Co.,	13¾
Kearsarge,	11¼
Montana,	11
Osceola Mining Co.,	24½
Tamarack,	140

MISCELLANEOUS.

American Bell Telephone,	203¼
Erie Telephone,	45
Mexican Telephone,	1¾
New England Telephone,	63
Newport Land,	
Boston Land Co.,	
West End Land Co.,	18½
San Diego Land Co.,	16½
Topeka Land & Development Co.,	16½
Lamson Store Service,	16
Illinois Steel Co.,	101
Am. Sugar Refineries, com.,	109⅞
Am. Sugar Refineries, pref.,	
Gen'l Electric,	
Gen'l Electric pref.,	

NEW YORK PRODUCE MARKET.

     NEW YORK, Aug. 18.

Flour sales 6100 packages; quiet.
Wheat sales 440,000 bushels; quiet; ⅛c up; firm
and quiet.
Corn sales 410,000 bushels; stronger.
Oats sales 140,000 bushels; firmer.
Beef dull and easy.
Pork quiet and weak.
Lard steady and quiet
Butter quiet.
Cheese no rose.
Sugar (raw) firm.
Petroleum quiet.
Turpentine quiet.
Molasses dull.
Rice firm and quiet.
Freights quiet and weak.
Rosin not quoted.
Tallow quiet.

PROVISIONS AND GRAIN.

     CHICAGO, Aug. 18.

	Lard.	Pork.	Corn.	Sh't Ribs.
Opening.				
May	84⅝		52⅜	
June				
July				
Aug.				
Sept.	77	11 22½	51	
Oct.				
Jan.	79¾		51	

May	84⅝		52¼	
June				
July				
Aug.				
Sept.	77	11 25	50¾	
Oct.				
Jan.	79¾	12 92½	51	

WEATHER INDICATIONS.

FAIR AND COOLER.

BOSTON, Aug. 18.—Local forecast for New
England until Friday night: Fair, except showers are probable in parts of
Maine and Vermont Friday afternoon or
evening, cooler Friday night in all sections, variable winds, mostly southerly to
westerly.

WARMER.

NEW YORK, Aug. 18.—At 8 30 a. m. the
weather was clear, with south, temperature 70. The Herald says to-
day: The New England on
Friday fair to partly cloudy, warmer and
more sultry weather will prevail; cloudy reflections,
followed by severe thunder storms in and
southeast of the lake region; and on Saturday cooler, fair to partly cloudy weather,
followed by rain.

Mr. Reid Passes Through Chicago.

CHICAGO, Aug. 18.—Mr. Whitelaw Reid
and party arrived here at 11 25 o'clock and
party arrived here at 11 25 o'clock and
this time last year.

DOUBTLESS A LUNATIC.

**Self-Accused Murderer of the
Bordens is Not Sane.**

**Steep Brook Excited Over the
Stories of a Strange Man.**

**No Credence Placed in the Report
About a Will Being Made.**

[Special Dispatch.]

FALL RIVER, Aug. 18.—A squad of six
policemen left the Central Station this
forenoon to scour the woods in the vicinity of Steep Brook in pursuit of another suspect in connection with the
Borden murders. Last night a man,
named Lsmai, called at the station and
said he saw hanging around the vicinity of
Steep Brook, with clothes dusty and
travel-stained and shirt apparently blood-
stained. The man had an axe in his possession and Lsmai said he noticed him
dodging in and out of the woods. Marshal Hilliard puts little faith in the story,
but nevertheless is thoroughly hunting
down this as every other clew, and is now
at his office awaiting the return of the
squad.

[By Associated Press.]

FALL RIVER, Aug. 18.—The man Peckham who gave himself up at the station
this morning is crazy beyond any doubt.
He was allowed to go into the guard-room
after a short confinement in a cell, and
begged several uniformed officers to hang
him. Assistant Marshal Fleet told him
to follow him and he would accommodate
him. He was taken to the cell-room and
locked up again. Alderman Beattie went
into the cell-room and had a long talk
with him. He says he has had some
trouble with his family. His home originally was at Middletown, Conn.

The six officers sent to hunt up the
stranger at Steep Brook have not returned
very far. The man was complained of by a
Frenchman named LeMai, who said he
saw him carrying an axe, and acting very
strange. The Steep Brook people are
much excited and the police are searching
more to allay popular clamor than to
prove the man's connection with the Borden murder. Marshal Hilliard read another batch of crank letters to the reporters this morning. They were of about
the same character as those given out a
few days ago.

The defence in the Borden case put no
credence whatever in the stories of an inventory or a will said to have been made
by Mr. Borden. All knowledge of the
affair was kept from Mr. Borden's counsel, whom he saw.almost daily, and this
fact is in itself a very unusual thing in
the minds of Miss Borden's friends.

Nelson Reed of Westport states that he
knows the suspect very well and says that
he has been crazy for some time.

Charles C. Cook denies all knowledge of
a will or of Mr. Borden having spoken of
making one, or of Borden's having ever
hinted at making an inventory of his
property.

Mr. Cook was out of town yesterday
and until noon to-day. He has been an
agent of a portion of the Borden estate for
two and a half years.

RAIDING WHALERS OFF ALASKA.

**Sealskins Found on Other than Strictly
Sealing Vessels in Behring Sea.**

SAN FRANCISCO, Cal., Aug. 18.—Mail
advices from Dutch Bay, Alaska, on the
squadron which is now paying especial attention to the whaling fleet. Every whaler found on the sea is overhauled and
thoroughly searched, the packages in the
store rooms being broken open. The reason is that nearly every whaler has a number of sealskins aboard. On July 28 the
cutter Rush overhauled the whaler Lydia
in Dutch Bay, but found no skins.

The Lydia was sent to transfer something during the night to the Northern
Light, another whaler, and the next
morning the latter was overhauled as she
was sailing for Frisco. A cask of sealskins was found, and the captain of the
Lydia admitting the transfer, his vessel
was seized and he was sent as a prisoner
to Sitka.

British Columbia sealer Mountain Chief
was seized on July 28 by United States
steamer Adams. Those sealers which
went to the Japan coast early in the season will doubtless get a warm reception,
as it is learned that Russia has sent three
steel cruisers to protect her sealing
grounds.

Surgeon Coredo of the Adams has succeeding in ascending the volcano Mount
Makushim, after three days of climbing.

THE CHICAI REVOLT.

India will Send a Political Officer to Check
the Trouble.

SIMLA, Aug. 18.—Acting upon a suggestion made by the ameer of Afghanistan, the government of India will, in October, send a political officer to the Kur-
um valley to check the Chicai revolt. This
agent will be accompanied by a military
escort. The action of the Indian government is probably due to the fact that it is
believed to be essential that both India
and Afghanistan should be free to devote themselves to the dangers that threat-
en the panic from Russia. With the native tribes in revolt the ameer has his
hands full in trying to suppress them, and
for this reason it is to India's interest to
endeavor to restore order among the
tribes so that the ameer can devote himself to the questions affecting the frontier
of his country.

ANNUAL MEETING.

Officers Chosen for the Redwood Library
and Atheneum at Newport.

NEWPORT, Aug. 18.—At the 145th annual
meeting of the Redwood Library and
Atheneum, one of the oldest institutions
of its kind in the country and maintained
by Summer residents, the following officers were elected for the year ensuing:
President, Leroy King; vice-presidents,
Henry H. Fay; secretary, W. P. Sheffield,
Jr.; treasurer, Thomas P. Peckham; directors of the library, J. Hermon, Daniel B. Fearing, Theodore K. Gibbs, William Gilpin,
David King, George Gordon King, George
C. Mason, Henry G. Marquand, W. P.
Sheffield, W. P. Sheffield, Jr., B. B. Tompkins, Frederick W. Tilton, A. A. Tucker-
man, Mrs. Henry E. Turner.

More Militia Ordered Out.

ALBANY, N. Y., Aug. 18.—Gov. Flower
has ordered out 3200 additional militia to
Buffalo, making 8000 in all.

Duke of Manchester Dead.

LONDON, Aug. 18.—The Duke of Manchester died this morning.

Watching the Hourglass.

As a miser counts his gold, night and day,
So I count the minutes told in the glass;
My eye is dim, my hair is thin and gray,
And I know I'm growing old as they pass.
When we approach the "other side" we hope
to make leaf" of our days, we are prone to look back
regretfully. A clear conscience and sound
health will lighten our gloomy reflections.
Health is the greatest blessing.—Dr. Pierce's
Golden Medical Discovery the greatest remedy for it. For all diseases that spring from
scrofulous diseases and otuer consumptive,
or lung-scrofula, it takes no time. It is the
king of liver invigorators and blood-purifi-
ers, and a powerful tonic, building up the
debilitated patient to perfect health. Contains no alcohol.

RUSSIAN FIRE HORROR.

**Government Will Have to Keep 2500 Suf-
ferers from Starving.**

ST. PETERSBURG, Aug. 18.—Last night a
fire started at Serdovsk, and before it was
extinguished, or rather before it had
burned itself out, it had destroyed 300
houses. Terrible excitement prevailed
while the conflagration was raging and
many were the appeals made to the icons,
or sacred pictures, for intervention to stay
the flames.

The attempts made to fight the fire
were only half-hearted and the destruction would probably have been greater
had not the fire in its onward progress
burned itself to a large open space across
which the flames could not leap. It is
estimated that at least 2500 persons were
rendered homeless. Few of them saved
anything beyond a few effects. The government will be compelled to aid them to
keep them from starving.

EARTHQUAKE IN WALES.

**Heavy Shocks Shook Furniture Out of
Place This Morning.**

LONDON, Aug. 18.—A severe shock of
earthquake was felt at 12 25 o'clock this
morning at Milford Haven, Wales. The
movement lasted 12 seconds. At 1 40
another shock was felt which lasted five
seconds. The latter shock resembled
an explosion. The shocks were so severe
that heavy furniture was thrown out of
place and it was remarkable that some old
houses were not torn down.

HIGH LIVING CAUSED HIS DOWNFALL.

Paymaster of the Upson Nut Co. Confesses
He is an Embezzler.

CLEVELAND, O., Aug. 18.—Stanley A.
Austin, the paymaster of the Upson Nut
Co., was arrested last night for embezzlement. He is charged with falsifying the
pay-roll. He confessed he had taken $20,-
000, but the real amount is probably
greater. High living brought about his
downfall.

TROOPS SURRENDER.

Latest Report from the Scene of the
Tennessee Mining Troubles.

CHATTANOOGA, Aug. 18.—A special to the
Times just received says: Troops at
Camp Anderson, Coal Creek, surrendered
this morning. Soldiers and sheriffs at
Clinton are enroute for home. Report
has not yet been confirmed.

Steamer Dimock Repaired.

BOSTON, Aug. 18.—Steamer H. F. Dimock, which collided with and sunk the
Vanderbilt steam yacht Alva, was towed
from the Atlantic Works, East Boston,
where she has been repairing, this morning to her dock in Boston. She will resume her trips between this city and New
York, commencing Aug. 24.

A Reformer Who Needs Reforming.

BERLIN, Aug. 18.—Socialistic papers
throughout Germany are bewailing the
blow that has been given to the cause by
the downfall of Herr Hansler, editor of
the Mannheim Volkstimme, who has embezzled funds in his trust amounting to
73,000 marks. Hansler was one of the
loudest shouters for reform, and seems to
have been a most despicable hypocrite.

Highway Robbery in Springfield.

SPRINGFIELD, Mass., Aug. 18.—E. E
Baxter of Westfield was robbed of his
watch and $80 by two highwaymen on
Liberty street, while walking toward the
train for home. The men threw him down
on the walk, and after going through his
pockets kicked him in the face and then
escaped.

A $5,000,000 Food Trust.

TRENTON, Aug. 18.—Articles of incorporation of a buckwheat trust were
filed with the secretary of state here. The
company will have a capital of $5,000,000.
The business, which is to purchase mills
and deal in other articles of food, will be
done all over the world.

The Revolt Ended.

TANGIER, Aug. 18.—The troubles with
the Anghera tribesmen have been settled
and the revolt is now ended. The settlement arrived at includes the retirement
of the governor, whose exactions led the
Anghera's into armed opposition.

The Height of Meanness.

LONDON, Aug. 18.—A dispatch from
Paris states that the sum of 70,000 francs
which has been raised at the Tuilleries
fetes in aid of the French poor and the
cholera sufferers in Russia, has been embezzled.

Dakota Millers Form a Trust.

FARGO, N.D., Aug. 18.—The North Dakota millers met here and perfected the
organization of the North Dakota Millers'
trust. John M. Turner was elected manager, with a salary of $6000 per annum.

TELEGRAPHIC BREVITIES.

North Carolina's People's party nominated Dr. W. P. Exum for governor.

A fire destroyed four blocks in the business portion of Kendrick, Ida.; loss $83,-
000.

The Missouri, Kansas and Texas will
want to increase its stock by $13,-
000,000.

Philip Clark, the 8-year-old son of
Henry Clark, fell out of a boat at Machias,
Me., and was drowned.

Ex-United States Senator Spooner has
been nominated for governor by the Wisconsin
Republican convention.

Fire at Piqua, O., destroyed the Opera
House and two other blocks. Four more
blocks were damaged.

A coal train of twenty cars ran into the
rear end of a regular freight train at Con-
tococook, N. H., smashing five cars.

The town of Chelsea, Vt., has voted
$15,000 to aid the Chelsea, Tunbridge and
South Royalton Railroad company.

John Thomas Wilson, aged 12, fell from
a wagon at Cauaan, Conn., and was
killed by the wheels passing over him.

Senator Quay and ex-Senator Thomas
C Platt have announced their intention
of actively aiding the Harrison campaign.

Edgar A. Brown, 51 years old, formerly
an assistant appraiser in the New York
custom house, died suddenly at Stamford,
Conn., of heart failure.

It is thought that depositors in the Mutual bank of Philadelphia in which were
funds of the Iron Hall, will not realize 50
cents on the dollar.

Count Guilio Valensin, owner of the
celebrated stock farm at Pleasanton.
Cal., died in Cleveland. He was well
known all over the country.

The stables of the Haverhill (Mass.) Ice
company were burned. There were nineteen horses in the stalls, and only one was
rescued. Five tons of hay and the tools
in the building were also burned. Loss
about $12,000.

Guaranteed Cure.

We authorize our advertised druggist to
sell Dr. King's New Discovery for consumption, coughs and colds, upon this condition.
If you are afflicted with a cough, cold or any
lung, throat or chest trouble, and will use
this remedy as directed, giving it a fair trial,
and experience no benefit, you may return
the bottle and have your money refunded.
We could not make this offer did we not
know that Dr. King's New Discovery could
be relied on. It never disappoints. Trial
bottles free at E. A. Blackmer's drug store.
Large size 50 cents and $1.00.

WANTS.

All Advertisements under this heading is
a word a time. No charge less than 25c.

GIRL.—To assist in general housework.
One that can cook. 439 Purchase street,
corner Pearl.   au18-2t*

REAL ESTATE.

The Evening Standard.

ESTABLISHED FEBRUARY, 1850.

NEW BEDFORD, FRIDAY, AUGUST 19, 1892.

TWO CENTS.

HASKELL & TRIPP.

Do you know what a fully equipped Kitchen-Furnishing Department we have in our light, spacious basement?

Do you know that we keep in that department *only such articles as have merit*, and sell them at the very lowest prices in the market?

The following list is necessarily very limited, but may serve to give you some idea of how we run this important stock:

Made of wood.

Step chairs that fold up, $1.25.

Pine foot stools, 19c.

Ladders,	3 step	5 step
	69c.	94c.

Wash benches, 79c. Ironing tables, $1.32.

Plain skirt boards, 37c., 48c., 57c., 69c. Cloth covered 69c. to $1.50.

Clothes horses.	3 ft.	3½ ft.	4 ft.
	67c.	72c.	79c.

Wash tubs, 60c. up. Washboards, 23c., 25c., 29c.

Wringers, $2 to $3.25.

Flour pails, 23c., 37c., 69c.

Fibre pails, 48c.

Commodes, $3.83 and $4.73.

Made of tin.

Cake boxes, 28c., 45c., 59c.

Water pots.	1qt.	2qt.	4qt.	6qt.	8qt.
	21c.	28c.	32c.	39c.	50c.

Bread raisers, 67c., 98c.

Lunch boxes, 24c. Cash boxes, 67c., 75c., 83c.

Dust pans, 5c., 9c., 12c.

Coal hods, 25c., 29c., 33c.

Foot bath tubs, 42c., 50c.

Infants' bath tubs, painted, 96c. to $1.73; many sizes.

Dinner pails, 19c. Dinner kettles, 30c., 69c.

Buffed tea kettle steamer, 42c. Oil stove tea kettle, 25c.

Milk cans.	1qt.	2qts.	3qts.	4qts.
	10c.	17c.	21c.	29c.

Egg poachers.	3 ring	6 ring
	23c.	45c.

14-quart rinsing pans, 27c.

Tea pots, 29c., 33c., 35c.

Coffee pots, 30c., 33c., 37c.

Refrigerator pans, 35c.

"Puritan" rice boilers, 87c. and $1.

Tea kettle with porcelain bowl, may be used for either boiling water or cooking cereals, 94c., $1.25, $1.83.

Preserve kettles, 12c. to 18c., according to size.

Made of iron.

Preserve kettles, best goods made:

6 qt.	8 qt.	10 qt.	12 qt.	14 qt.
42c.	48c.	53c.	57c.	65c.

Scotch bowls, tinned inside, $1.12, $1.28, $1.50.

Economy roasters, made of Russian iron, cooks tough meats so they become tender, 68c. to $1.75; five sizes.

Odorless cookers keep all steam from the room. Three sizes, $1.17, $1.31, $1.47.

"Granite" ironware, best quality, *every piece fully warranted.* Full lines of kettles, tea and coffee pots, pans, boilers, ladles. Absolutely lowest prices.

Handy hardware.

For home use all the various useful tools at prices that'll surprise you, unless you've been buying here.

Fruit jars.

Mason's jars, *first* quality, all sizes at proper prices.

A thousand other things. Come and see for yourself.

HASKELL & TRIPP.

Department Stores,

Purchase and William Streets.

THE FALL RIVER MURDERS.

Marshal Hilliard Confers with the District Attorney.

History of John V. Morse Learned in Hastings, Ia.

People There Say He is Wealthy But Very Penurious.

FALL RIVER, Aug. 19.—There are no new developments in the Borden tragedy this forenoon. City Marshal Hilliard is in New Bedford on business connected with the case, and has been in consultation with District Attorney Knowlton.

HASTINGS, Ia., Aug. 19.—This place was for about 25 years, and, in a sense, is yet, the home of John V. Morse, upon whom some suspicion of complicity in the mysterious murder of the Bordens at Fall River has fallen. A Boston *Post* man has elicited the following information here:

While Morse has succeeded in establishing a very fair alibi, it seems that Lizzie Borden, who is now under arrest for the murder, is anxious to know something of his past record. She has accordingly sent Detective Hanscom out here to investigate. The people of Hastings, and particularly John Davidson, Morse's brother-in-law, are awaiting the arrival of the detective with much interest. There really appears to be very little in Morse's record that will go to strengthen the theory that he was the slayer of Andrew Borden and his wife.

Morse came here in 1869 from Illinois, where he had been a farmer, with the exception of two or three years, during which, when a young man, he learned the butcher's trade. Morse has been a farmer ever since.

Morse's Life in Illinois.

While in Illinois Morse rented a farm. During this period he saved up something less than $1000, and then came here and bought land. He now owns two farms, 220 acres in all, of the finest land in Mills county. Both of these farms lie directly south of Hastings, only a mile and a half from the town. One of them has a fine house on it, a large barn, and is otherwise as well improved as any farm in the county.

Morse has never married, but it is the theory of those who know him best that he at one time contemplated marriage, and that he improved his farm with a view to marrying some day and occupying the place as his home.

He was always regarded by his neighbors as a very eccentric and peculiar individual. He never, apparently, formed any close friendships, always maintaining an austere reserve that with most people checked the slightest approach to intimacy. In all his dealings he was close, almost to the point of penuriousness, but he was always strictly honest. There is probably not a man in Mills county who could accuse him of dishonesty, and certainly during the quarter of a century spent here he was never guilty of a crime.

Frugal and Self-Denying.

The years Morse spent here were years of the strictest frugality, self-denial that amounted almost to greed, and no doubt all this made its impress on a character which was probably none too lovable at best.

Even after Morse became comparatively well off there was no laxation in his frugal practices. He would drive to town in an old rattletrap lumber wagon, using a pine board for a seat, when he could just as well have afforded a buggy. He would wear the same suit of clothes everywhere, and on all occasions, and one suit usually lasted him two or three years. Indeed, it is pretty certain that the suit he is now wearing at Fall River is the same one he wore when he left here two years ago.

Only once during the long period of his residence here did he show any inclination to take any comfort in life as he went along. One Winter he electrified everybody who knew him by purchasing a nice new buggy and a new suit of clothes. He suddenly showed a disposition to go into society, and all that Winter he attended parties and such other social gatherings as country and village life afforded.

Looking for a Wife.

It was evident that he was looking for a wife, but no girl seemed to take kindly to the long, lanky, awkward, hard-featured fellow, who dressed like a scarecrow and ate like a cormorant. This was no doubt the reason why when the Winter was over he sold his buggy, laid aside his store clothes and gave up his dream of connubial joy.

Among Morse's neighbors there were of course several who were devout church members, and these held the opinion that Morse's morals were decidedly below par. Not that they thought him guilty of breaking the commandments oftener than is common with the average man, but he occasionally expressed in very forcible language his contempt for preachers and church members, all of whom he classed together as canting hypocrites.

Morse Cynical and Morose.

It became a habit with him to say cynical things when he condescended to speak at all, but generally he was silent, morose and gloomy. A year or so before he went East some little talk was occasioned by his engaging an old woman from Council Bluffs to keep house for him. Some of the people professed to be considerably scandalized by this, but on the whole the prevailing opinion seems to be that as he needed a housekeeper, and as this woman was well qualified for the position, his employing her was after all the business of no one but himself.

Those who know him best, however, agree that he was never anything more than eccentric. He was selfish, close, hard-fisted, almost avaricious, but scrupulously honest. On one occasion, in making a settlement with a brother of L. G. Gerung, who lives here, Morse recalled and paid for items and services which Gerung had entirely forgotten, and it is only fair to add that most of those who heard of it thought this something of an eccentricity, too.

It is somewhat singular that in the discussion of the probability of Morse's connection with the Borden murder, Morse's brother-in-law, John Davidson, whose farm adjoins that of Morse and who has known Morse since 1857, manifested almost no feeling. In fact, his extreme reticence and the little he does say might cause one to think that Davidson suspects Morse of complicity in the murder.

At Odds With His Relatives

Some years ago, however, Morse lived with the Davidsons, and the result of this was a coolness amounting almost to an estrangement, which has continued up to the present. And yet Davidson says he thinks Morse perfectly honest, although rather close in business transactions. Mrs. Davidson, who is Morse's half-sister, seems to hold an opinion of Morse which is hardly as favorable as that of her husband. She says Morse was a man who, when crossed, would never forgive, and, in fact, she describes this as a characteristic of him, and one in which she herself shares. In speaking of the arrest of Lizzie Borden she became very indignant, and exclaimed that it is most preposterous to suppose that Lizzie could have murdered her parents.

Some effort has been made to connect Morse with the horse traders who are at present hanging about Fall River. Morse was never a horse trader, but he raised a good many horses on the farm, and when he had a surplus he sold them. Two years ago, when he went East, he took with him a carload of horses. None of the animals were blooded, and there are people here who wondered at histaking such ordinary stock East.

But however peculiar, eccentric and disagreeable he may have been, he prospered, and to-day he is considered quite well off for a farmer. Besides his farms he owns stock in the Botna Valley State Bank of Hastings. He has not been in need of money recently, for a short time ago he quite willingly gave one of his tenants who pays cash rent an extension of time.

Summing it all up it appears that for about twenty-five years John V. Morse has been a very hard working farmer. He has prospered and now seems to be taking life easily.

WEATHER INDICATIONS.

COOLER WITH SHOWERS.

WASHINGTON, Aug. 19.—For the 24 hours from 8 a. m. to-day: For Massachusetts, Rhode Island and Connecticut increasing cloudiness and showers; cooler; southwesterly winds.

COOLER.

BOSTON, Aug. 19.—Local forecast for New England until Saturday night: Fair, except showers may occur in northern sections to-night, cooler during the night and Saturday, variable winds, becoming westerly and northerly.

IDAHO REPUBLICANS.

Platform Adopted by State Convention Favors Free Coinage of Silver.

MOSCOW, Idaho, Aug. 19.—The Republican convention yesterday adopted a platform favoring free and unlimited silver coinage, protecting American industries, as set forth in the National platform, and strongly indorsing President Harrison's administration, and renominated Willis Sweet for Congress by acclamation. The convention also nominated W. J. McConnell for governor on the second ballot.

W. J. McConnell,
Idaho Republicans' Choice for Governor.

GREAT FIRE IN SWITZERLAND.

Tourists at Grindelwald Hotels Join Villagers in Fighting the Flames.

BERNE, Aug. 19.—It is estimated that 50 buildings were destroyed by fire at Grindelwald. Embers from the burning structures were carried a long distance from the village, and a number of chalets miles away from Grindelwald were set on fire. Full particulars have not yet been received from the surrounding country, and for that reason it is impossible to state the exact number of buildings burned.

When the fire first broke out the tourists stopping at the Hotel Baer devoted themselves to saving their luggage and valuables. When their property was secured they joined the villagers and the guests of other hotels, and together they fought the fire. A picket line was formed and water was passed along as rapidly as possible, but the flames had gained too much headway to be subdued by this means.

PARIS GREEN FOUND.

Prof. Hills Makes His Report in the Salisbury Beach Poisoning Case.

NEWBURYPORT, Aug. 19.—Medical Examiner Snow received a report on the result of the examination of the organs of the victims of the Salisbury Beach case from Prof. Hills of Harvard. The report states that the deaths were caused by Paris green. The question now to be determined is—Was the poison administered with intent to kill? One of the theories had been from the first that there was Paris green in the string beans, which were eaten for dinner on the day of the poisoning. The case is in the hands of the State police. No arrests have yet been made. Prof. Hills will make a more detailed report later. To-day's report has been sent to the district attorney at Haverhill.

THREATS OF SHOOTING.

A Tennessee Judge and Attorney-General Warned to be Careful.

CHATTANOOGA, Tenn., Aug. 19.—A special to the *Times* from Jasper says that threats have been made by unknown men who visited the village judge and Attorney-General Brown, that they had better be careful or bullets would be put through their heads. This threat was made because the officials named are using every means to bring the members of the Inman mob to justice.

IDAHO MINES WILL CLOSE.

Union Men Must Appear at Cœur d' Alene City for Trial.

WARDNER, Id., Aug. 19.—Orders have been issued from Gen. Curtis' headquarters directing that the Poorman & Tiger mines shut down Aug. 20, because most of the employes are union men and will have to appear at Cœur d' Alene City for trial. One hundred and thirty prisoners will be taken there on the 21st or 22d inst.

Rape Fiend Held in $5000.

EASTPORT, Me., Aug. 19.—Matthew Farris, formerly of Milltown, was arraigned to-day before Justice McLarren, charged with attempt to rape the 6-years-old daughter of William Brown, and was held in $5000 for the October term of the court at Machias. The case was a most aggravated one, and the people are much incensed against Farris. Had it not been for the prompt measures taken for his safety by the police the people would have shown him little mercy.

Trades Statistics.

PARIS, Aug. 19.—Trade statistics for the first seven months of 1892 show that France during that time exported to the United States goods valued at 142,738,000 francs and imported goods valued at 466,522,000 francs.

Death of a Railroad Superintendent.

CONCORD, N. H., Aug. 19.—Hon. Edward F. Mann, superintendent of the Concord & Montreal railroad, died this morning in his 47th year.

Destructive Fire in Geneva, O.

CLEVELAND, O, Aug. 19.—The business portion of Geneva, O., 45 miles east, was destroyed by fire this morning. Loss estimated at $165,000.

Ocean Steamers.

Arrived—At New York, Haugesund and Bratten, Baracoa; Cienfuegos, St. Jago; Prins Mauritz, Port au Prince.

WAS IT A THREAT?

Andrew J. Borden Once Moved to Tears.

His Daughter Hoped He Would Come Home a Corpse.

She Said That He Probably Would Before Long.

Important Statement Made to Capt. Orrick Smalley.

Information in His Possession Awaits the District Attorney.

If all stories are true the family relations were strained between Andrew J. Borden and his daughter Lizzie, who is now held by the authorities on the charge of having murdered her father. Much has been printed concerning the relationship which had existed of late between the two, and no doubt a great deal has been printed which is no more nor less than hearsay. But to-day the *Standard* prints a statement, which, coming as it does from Capt. Orrick Smalley, chairman of the Overseers of the Poor, causes one to give more than usual credence to the story. The captain was at first disinclined to relate the circumstances of this new chapter in the mystery, and not until after being informed that his story was in possession of other newspapers out of town, would he consent to talk. Said he: "It was my intention to have acquainted District Attorney Knowlton with the circumstance before this, and I am surprised that the gentleman to whom I related the story on Wednesday has so soon repeated it."

The captain further remarked that he accidentally let it out in an argument on the possibility of Lizzie Borden having accomplished the horrible crime. And as it has leaked out here it is:

Capt. Smalley was enjoying his vacation at Craigville during the Borden murder, and the next day after the crime, while he sat on the piazza of Hotel Palmer with others discussing the terrible news from Fall River, he gave utterance to the remark that it was impossible for the daughter to carry out such a horrible deed.

There were those on that piazza, said Capt. Smalley, who did not agree with me. A stranger, to whom Capt. Smalley addressed most of his conversation, was the one who related a conversation with Andrew J. Borden, which has since opened the eyes of those who have heard it.

This gentleman said that not long since, while he was out to one of Mr. Borden's farms the old gentleman, with whom he was acquainted, came out very much disturbed. Upon being questioned he remarked that he didn't take much comfort at home with Lizzie; that she wouldn't eat at the same table with him, and that only that morning when he accidentally went into the room where she was eating she got up from the table and left the room.

This gentleman also said that Mr. Borden told him this with tears in his eyes, and further remarked that when he left the house Lizzie told him she hoped he would come home a corpse; probably you will before long.

Capt. Smalley in relating this to a *Standard* reporter said he was thunderstruck, and not being acquainted with the gentleman who had related the circumstance he made inquiries concerning him. The captain learned ed that the gentleman was a reliable person residing in Fall River. His business is that of a traveller, and he is prominently connected with one of the Fall River churches.

When asked for his name Capt. Smalley replied, "no, I decline to give his name to any other than the authorities in charge of this case. I am satisfied from what I have learned of the gentleman who made the utterances that he is a reliable man."

Capt. Smalley said the gentleman made the statements unsolicited, volunteering information which he apparently felt was not generally known.

WARM WEATHER BARGAINS.—We have some shoes that have sold slowly this Summer, and rather than carry them over to another season, have put prices on them that are sure to sell them. These are not fancy goods, but good solid shoes for men, women, and children. The low shoe for men that we have marked $2 is a great bargain for any man that works for a living. See ad. page 5. Union Shoe Store.

BIRTHDAY PARTY.—Mrs. Mary Fitchcroft celebrated her birthday anniversary at her home on Myrtle street last evening, when about 50 friends called to pay their respects. The evening was pleasantly spent in social intercourse and listening to excellent vocal and instrumental music. A fine collation was served.

LARCENY.—A young lady named Loraine, who resides in one of the Wamsutta blocks on Front street, reported to the police this morning that un unknown young man stole $7 out of her pocket and jumped out of the window and ran away. The case is being investigated.

THE FUNERAL of the late Edward Jackson occurred at Fall River yesterday and was largely attended. The New Bedford Loom Fixers' Union was represented, by a committee. John Harrison, Joseph Clifton, Job Seal and Walter Whittaker acted as pall bearers.

SOON FOUND.—A telephone message from Fall River, received by the police yesterday afternoon, that James Sunderland's gray horse and express-wagon had been stolen in that city, was soon followed by another message that the turnout had been found two squares away.

EXCURSION TO QUEBEC.—About 75 people from this city are to participate in the excursion which leaves New Bedford and Fall River Sunday for Quebec, The French Zouaves have decided not to make the trip as an organization.

THE FRANCS TIREURS have voted to make an excursion to Gay Head on Labor day.

GREAT REDUCTION in trimmed hats at Nooning's.

A PURE SKIN makes a healthy body. Try a Turkish.

LOOK OUT for the great silk sale at Whiting & Co's.

STYLISH SAILORS at Nooning's for 25 and 50 c.

HAND-SEWED House Gaiters $1. Devoll's.

ONLY A DOLLAR for a Turkish bath.

100 doses $1; true of only Hood's Sarsaparilla.

PERSONAL.—Augustus Wood, Ph. D., arrived home this morning, after three years' absence in Germany. He has been appointed by the Japanese government Professor of the English Language and Literature in the Imperial University of Tokio. Mr. Wood leaves this city next week for Japan via Vancouver.

Charles A. Paull of this city, a Harvard College medical student, is passing two weeks of his vacation at the White Mountains.

Mrs. Minnie Clymont and daughter Florence and Miss Grace Green are at the Sparrow cottage, Mattapoisett, for a few days.

Engineer Coppinger, of steamer G. W. Hunt, resigned his position yesterday.

J. C. Patnaude is to leave this city, Sunday, for a week's trip to Quebec.

Thomas B. Norris of Detroit, Mich., is at home on a visit.

William M. Worsley and George W. T. Case are engaged to play with Gifford & Graves' orchestra this coming season.

THE TITAN OF CHASMS—*A Mile Deep, 13 Miles Wide, 217 Miles Long, and Painted Like a Flower.*—The Grand Canon of the Colorado River, in Arizona, is now for the first time easily accessible to tourists. A regular stage line has been established from Flagstaff, Arizona, on the Atlantic & Pacific Railroad, making the trip from Flagstaff to the most imposing part of the canon in less than 12 hours. The stage fare for the round trip is only $20.00, and meals and comfortable lodgings are provided throughout the trip at a reasonable price. The view of the Grand Canon afforded at the terminus of the stage route is the most stupendous panorama known in nature. There is also a trail at this point leading down the canon wall, more than 6000 feet vertically, to the river below. The descent of the trail is a grander experience than climbing the Alps, for in the bottom of this terrific and sublime chasm are hundreds of mountains greater than any of the Alpine range.

A book describing the trip to the Grand Canon, illustrated by many full-page engravings from special photographs, and furnishing all needful information, may be obtained free upon application to Jno. J. Byrne, 723 Monadnock Block, Chicago, Ill.

IT COSTS NOTHING TO READ THIS, in fact it may be the means of saving you $15 or $20. F. R. Slocum has about 90 chamber suits which he offers at 80 cents on the dollar. Does it mean anything to you if you can buy, say a $60 chamber suit for $48, a $100 suit for $80? These chances don't come often. The price of every suit is marked in plain figures, so you can deduct 20 per cent. and get the net price you will have to pay. This discount is given strictly for cash, but terms will be made to accommodate instalment customers. Now is the time any of these goods can be selected for future delivery. F. R. Slocum, house furnisher, 354 to 362 Acushnet avenue.

HORSES, CARRIAGES, HARNESSES.—In addition to the horses advertised on page 6 I will sell to-morrow morning at auction the trotter Dexter. Dexter is a very promising young horse, very handsome, not afraid of electric cars, safe for ladies to drive, and a splendid saddler. Will also sell a nice pair of acclimated Michigan horses; this is a great road team and safe for ladies to drive. I think this is as fine a family team as is in the city. We have also several other horses not specified.

Also mortgagee's sale of horse, express wagon, canopy top surrey and harnesses.

PENSIONS have been granted as follows:

Original—E. J. Adams, G. S. Dohn, W. H. Warren, John Walsh, David Thompson, W. F. White, A. M. Newell, B. F. Miner.

Additional—K. Rogers, Azro Dustin, O. H. Bryant, H. L. Brown, G. I. Herrick, Thomas Hayes, George Dean.

Re-issue—Samuel Knowles.

Widows, etc.—Abbie L. Metcalf, Mary B. Campbell, Minerva Joslyn, Shirley Harmon (father,) S. L. Hallett, Polly A. D. Hoag, Margaret Hickey, Catherine J. Warren, Mary D. Griffith, minors of J. E. Crosson, Adeline D. Lyon, Charlotte McCart, Ellen Dempsey, Hannah E. Doe, Flora E. Andrews, Louisa J. Thompson, Elizabeth M. Evans, Joanna Dustin, Maria A. Brown.

JUST RECEIVED from the manufacturers 25 cases of stiff hats for Fall and Winter wear. We shall offer to-morrow, "Saturday," 15 dozen black stiff hats, as good as you ever bought at $2, our price on these hats $1.50. Just come in and see them at Ashley & Peirce's, 72 and 74 William street.

NANCY HANKS.—Charles Taber & Co. have just published a portrait of Nancy Hanks, the mare which has just broken the world's trotting record, making a mile in 2 07¼. They will be for sale by L. B. Ellis.

SPECIAL SALE of neckwear this week. We are offering special bargains in fine neckwear made in Ascots, puffs, four-in-hands, and like these goods are actually worth 50c. and 75c. We are offering them this week at 37½c. Ashley & Peirce.

CONTAGIOUS DISEASES.—One new case of typhoid fever, one new case of scarlet fever and one new case of diphtheria have been reported at the office of the Board of Health.

SPECIAL SALE of Human Hair Goods. Large stock gray hair. Curling tongs 10 cents. H. B. Coffin, 52 Purchase street.

NEVER SAW anything like the sale we are having on black hose, sold over 3000 dozen the past season. Come in and see them at 15c., two pairs 25c., at Ashley & Peirce's.

PROFITS.—The net receipts from the excursion of the St. James parish to Falmouth Heights was $308.

WE CAN SUPPLY you with a stylish sailor in any color at a low price. Nooning's is the place.

NOT GUILTY for selling those Children's Sailors for more than 15c. Grand rush at La Mode.

THE RAILS of the Union Street Railway in Purchase street, between William and Union streets, are being raised.

BE SURE and visit the mid-Summer mark down sale of men's, youths' and children's suits at Ashley & Peirce's.

CONVICTED.—By the ladies and misses for selling those sailor hats at 15c., La Mode. See our windows for bargains, unapproachable.

NEW STYLES Black Sailors 19 cents. Union Milan Sailors 35 cents Saturday only. Coffin's, 52 Purchase street.

GREAT SHIRT WAIST sale at Whiting & Co's Friday and Saturday.

CLEANLINESS IS NEXT TO GODLINESS—No. 5 South Sixth street.

PAVING on Union street, between First and Second streets, is being repaired.

LOOK OUT for the great silk sale at Whiting & Co's.

Chauncey Depew at Homburg.

HOMBURG, Aug. 19.—Mr. Chauncey M. Depew is taking the water here. All efforts to induce him to discuss the railroad troubles at Buffalo have proved futile.

The Clark Convention.

HOUSTON, Tex., Aug. 19.—The Clark convention last evening completed its ticket. George Clark was nominated for Governor, C. W. Rogers for Lieut.-Governor.

GOOD NEWS

Friday Morning, Aug. 19,

We shall sell solid Antique Oak Tables, with top 16 inches square, and ample shelf underneath, all finely finished, strong, serviceable and sightly, for

89c. each.

The sale will continue through Saturday if the stock is not sooner exhausted. These are the Tables on which we created such a furore last Summer. We can take no orders before

FRIDAY MORNING,

But at that time mail or telephone orders will receive careful attention.

☞ Remember the date, FRIDAY MORNING, Aug. 19, and SATURDAY if the stock holds out

C. F. WING,

34 to 40 Purchase st.

WHITING & CO.

Friday and Saturday

BARGAIN DAYS.

We place on sale a small lot of Real French all wool Challies at 28c. per yard. Come quick if you want any.

30 pieces of 50c. double-fold Dress Goods, suitable for Fall wear for Ladies and Children, will go on sale at 29c. per yard.

A few pieces all wool Homespun Suitings; go on sale at 39c. per yard, 50c. Sept. 1.

The balance of our 10c. Challies at 4c. per yard.

We shall sell you Friday some Fall colors in 12 1-2c. Ginghams at 6c. per yard.

One lot of 15c. Pongees will be sold at 10c.

White ground Chintz colored Cambrics, 4-4 wide, 12 1-2c. goods, go on sale at 8c. per yard.

20 dozen more of those 25c. Ladies' Jersey Ribbed Vests will go on sale at 17c. apiece.

10 dozen Gents' colored Balbriggan Vests and Pants, best 50c. ones 39c. a piece for Friday and Saturday.

See the Cream Table Damasks for Friday and Saturday at 39c. per yard.

Towels, Table Linens, Napkins and Housekeeping Goods, all at reduced prices in this sale.

WHITING & CO.

OUTING SHIRTS!

OUTING SHIRTS!

You can never have too many

OUTING SHIRTS!

Our low prices will help you out. Quality exceptional.

Good Shirts for $1 and $1.25, laundered collars and cuffs.

Another lot of the popular blue Madras, all sizes, $1.50.

Better come at once, They're going fast.

J. & W. R. WING & CO.,

133 UNION STREET.

OUTING SHIRTS!

OUTING SHIRTS!

THE CRESCENT!

22 Purchase St.

SILK GLOVES MARKDOWN.

Black and Colors, 19c.

Gents' Hose.

Fashionable shades, 25 cents. Hermsdorf stainless black, spliced heel and toe, 25c.

An excellent variety of 5c. Handkerchiefs both white and fancy borders.

A new lot of Wrappers in medium shades, also Indigo Blue $1.00 each. Good night dress 50c.

RIBBONS.

We don't *begin* to tell you *how much* we have *marked down* our line of Ribbons, but come and see for yourself.

We will close out our Gingham Dresses for children at *cost*. Sizes from 4 to 10 years of age.

Gloves, 15, 25, 37, 50c.

Corsets, a good corset for 39c.

An X-L-ent Corset for 50c.

A very nice Summer Corset, C-B a la Spirite, price $1.25.

Corsets at all prices.

Having removed our entire stock from the Old Stand at corner of County and High streets, we shall be pleased to see our old friends and patrons at our new quarters, 22 Purchase street, known as THE CRESCENT.

GOOD COAL ALWAYS

DENISON BROS. CO.,
Yard—Foot of Hillman Street.
Offices—Cor. School and South
Water Sts., and Cor. Hillman
and North Water Sts.

THE SELF-ACCUSED.

Peckham Recovers from His
Hallucination.

"I Never Did It," He Said, When
Told of His Confession.

He Was in Westport at the Time of
the Tragedy.

Bundled Into a Wagon and Tak-
en Home by His Wife.

More Facts About the Accuracy of the
Standard's Seaver Interview.

The murder has completely turned the
head of Charles H. Peckham, the man
who surrendered himself at police headquarters in Fall River yesterday, says the
Providence Journal. People who knew
him called him eccentric before the
tragedy, and now they call him stark
mad. If he had known how the activi-
ties were going to treat him, he would
not have come to town. He could not
understand the delay in hanging him, and
it is feared that he will never understand
it. He had waived a preliminary hearing
and a trial, and it seemed to him that it
ought to be an easy matter for some of
the officers to procure a rope and string
him up. That would have ended
the entire mystery, and saved the
government much trouble and expense. They could hang him in the
cell room, Peckham said, and make no
ado about it. At noon he bared his arm
to show his muscle and prove how little
exertion it was for him to kill, when the
fire alarm gong in the guard room struck
the half hour. Peckham jumped anywhere from six to ten feet and shivered.
Then he recovered himself and explained
that the gong hadn't frightened him, and
that he was still game. The police do not
dare to allow him to depart, as it is suspected that in his present state of mind
he may injure himself or somebody else,
and are holding him until his relatives,
who live on the island, can take him off
their hands.

Peckham was not the first to make a
confession, though he leads the cranks of
the country in surrendering. Several
have written from distant points to the
effect that they butchered Mr. and Mrs.
Borden, and have described the manner
in which the slaying was done most minutely. Their letters, along with a hundred or more other letters bearing in one
way or another on the murder, are in the
marshal's desk. Marshal Hilliard says
that those epistles which are not silly are
interesting, because they illustrate how
unsettled brains work, and how generally
stirred up they are when a great crime is
committed. He admits that he has ordered his men to follow a great many
blind and foolish clews just to satisfy
people and if possible allay their fears. A
squad of officers started on a wild goose
chase yesterday. A man who can neither
understand nor speak English had heard
other people who do speak English talking about a mysterious character at Steep
Brook. That was all the foundation
the story had, but nevertheless, the
people in that locality became alarmed
and wanted the authorities to investigate. Accordingly officers Perron, Harrington, Doherty, Chase and Edson drove
out to search the woods in the vicinity
of Riverview Gardens, with orders to
arrest a man covered with blood and
dust and wearing a crimson hatchet.
At last accounts they had not come up
with him.

The theory regarding the proposed will
continues to command attention, and is
variously received. As was anticipated,
nobody can be found who ever heard Mr.
Borden mention this subject, though one
of the men who professes ignorance is
pretty sure to be summoned at the hearing or the trial which will follow. Everybody who in any way can be connected
with the case is denying all knowledge of
it, in a desire to avoid publicity and escape the terrors which the witness stand
possesses for the majority. Those who
talked freely and tried to be of some assistance to the authorities when the
murders were first discovered feel that
they made a mistake, and naturally are
doing their best to forget everything that
they said. Even opinions are scarcer than
they were a couple of days ago, which is a
blessing. At one period during the excitement it was possible to fill three or
four hundred columns daily with these
same opinions, which amounted to absolutely nothing after they were expressed.
One man had one view regarding the injustice of the arrest, another some notion
as to alleged defects in the law of the
land, and so on without end, but it made
no difference and produced no effect. The
land moved. Neither was changed by calling it bad names.

There are some singular features about
the will story, but they are not particularly striking in a case which is full of
singular features. For instance, it was
not like Andrew J. Borden to take anybody into his confidence or to discuss
his own personal affairs. Even if he were
very intimate with John Morse, there
seems to be no good reason why he should
inform him of his intentions regarding a
will. It would be characteristic of the
man to go to his lawyer, have the instrument drawn, lock it up in his safe and
say nothing. He knew that there was
no love lost between his daughters and
their step-mother, and he was probably
aware that a dispute over his property
would strain their relations still further.
However, this fact, coupled with the
other fact that nobody can be found
who will acknowledge that Mr. Borden
ever mentioned a will, doesn't prove conclusively that he did not broach the subject and discuss it in his home. "Business" was transacted in the Dartmouth
cottage and in the house on Second street,
and it was business which sooner or later
will come to the surface.

The attempt to create a sentiment in
favor of Miss Lizzie Borden is reacting, as
it was sure to react. It is in the air and
there is no getting away from it. Men
who were bitter partisans 48 hours ago
are beginning to hedge and to express
themselves in more conservative terms.
It is right and proper for Miss Borden's
friends to stand up for her to the last,
but there is a right and proper way in
which to support her, and denunciation
of the government and attacks on public
officials, who have done what they believed to be their duty, were in poor
taste. At least, so many admit who were
fierce in their condemnation of the arrest,
and it is plain that if they had continued
in the course they were pursuing they
would have injured rather than helped
the prisoner's cause.

Peckham Released.
Charles H. Peckham, the unfortunate
man who thought he murdered the Bordens, was fed and given all possible attention by the Fall River police. Gradually his hallucination began to leave him.
He grew calmer and towards night no
longer spoke of the terrible crime of
which he had accused himself but a few
hours before. He seemed in fact to have
forgotten it entirely, and spoke in a
wandering way about the haying at home,
and wondered why he was in custody.

The terrible picture which had formed
gradually in his excited imagination had
been wiped away and more natural impressions were replacing it.

Mrs. Peckham, his wife, who was found
on the farm near Central Village, was
frantic with anxiety. She was told the
story of her husband's wanderings. She
said that he had suffered from temporary
insanity about five years ago. The attack
was succeeded by a semi-comatose state
after which the mind would become clear
again.

She was anxious that he should be released at once and said she was quite able
to care for him. She asserted positively
that he had not been out of her sight for
an hour since a day long before the murder, except when he visited Fall River a
week ago yesterday. He was an inoffensive man and would harm no one.

A neighbor said Peckham was about
the farm on the morning of the murder.
Mrs. Peckham sent a neighbor to Fall
River to bring her husband home. The
police had no wish to detain him when
once sure that there was no danger that
he would do violence to himself or others.

The man had simply been reading and
thinking incessantly about the murder
and his mind gave way temporarily beneath the strain. Suddenly the conviction that he himself was guilty fastened
itself upon him. The newspapers, and
his abnormal imagination, supplied the
necessary details. Instantly he set off for
Fall River. The heat was intense, and
that, with the usual exertion of fast walking, increased his mania. Hence his hurried confession and intense desire to be
hanged at once and have done with it.

The Old Man at Liberty.
At 8.45 last night Mrs. Peckham and Constable Grinnell drove up to headquarters
and said they had come for Peckham.
Captain Desmond went to the man's
cell to see if he was in a fit condition to
be set at large.

The "self-accused" was sleeping
soundly. He was awakened, and after a
glance at the suggestive surroundings he
said: "What am I doing here?" and not
"Where am I at?" as is reported in some
quarters. He was told that he had confessed to the murder of The Bordens.

"It's not so," he said. "I never did it."
After a few further questions he was
taken to the guard room.

"Do you know this man, Peckham?"
Capt. Desmond asked, pointing to Grinnell.

The old man scratched his head pen-
sively for a moment and then said heartily: "Hello, Grinnell." That was all, Mrs.
Peckham bundled him into the old country carriage, the constable whipped up the horse,
the trio were lost in the night, and
Charles Peckham's career as a murderer
was at an end. It was in truth an odd
book, and its name was "Imaginary Murder."

A Crank with Glass in His Hair.
Into the central station in Providence
yesterday wandered a well dressed, intelligent, appearing man, who said he came
from Fall River. He spoke to Lieut.
O'Neil, who was sitting behind the desk,
and said, "I've come for that $5000 re-
ward for the capture of the murderer of
Mr. and Mrs. Andrew J. Borden."
"Is that so?" said the lieutenant.
"Yes," replied the Fall River crank,
"I had him caged this morning, and he
made a clean breast of everything, and I
can lay my hands on him at any time.
Where'll I go for the reward, sir?"

Lieut. O'Neil took not throw away much
time generally in listening to cranks, but
this fellow did not show the slightest sign
of being "off" when he entered the station and so the officer got into conversation with him. During the interview he
sent to City Hall, where he
braced up beside Chief Child and began
to spin off a great tale about the murder.
Officer Feeley was there, and as the crank
removed his hat the light so struck the
man's head as to make it appear as though
his hair was filled with small electric
lights. It wasn't though, but in it must
have been a good half pint of broken glass
scattered all about over the scalp, making
it look much the same as the spangled
costume of a bare-back horse rider in a
circus.

Chief Child told the fellow he had better get down to Fall River by the first
train and get the money. The man, muttering to himself, made a double quick
step through the corridor and was soon out
of sight.

Seaver's Statements.
The Evening Standard's interview with
State Detective Seaver was the most frequently heard topic of conversation in
the murder case until the appearance of
Peckham yesterday. The Standard's resident correspondent in Taunton is a member of the staff of the Gazette of that city,
and in the Taunton paper gives the following account of how he interviewed
Mr. Seaver:

Detective Seaver is quite busy now making energetic denials of statements attributed to him in several papers, but so far
as has developed yet he has not been heard
of directly at the Gazette office.

Now it happens that there were two
newspaper men interested in Mr. Seaver
on the evening when he talked. One was
a Boston Post man and the other a Gazette
man. The Post man's interview with Mr.
Seaver is thus described this morning by
a disinterested but reputable listener:

The Post man approached him and began to argue the case, and Mr. Seaver replied at first in a non-committal sort of a
way "Perhaps," "That may be so," "Can't
tell," etc., until in some manner he became piqued at a question put of a suggestion made, and then all the Post man
had to do for about fifteen minutes was
to fold his hands, open his ears, and keep
his thinking and memorizing apparatus
hard at work. Then he went into the
Western Union and told his story. When
the Gazette man happened along a few
moments after Mr. Seaver was sitting in a
chair outside the City Hotel door.

The question was put to him about the
Borden matter and a suggestion made
that the affair might never come to trial.
Mr. Seaver had not the slightest idea that
he was being interviewed, because
the Gazette man was too old a hand to go
around with a note-book and pencil in
his hand. He knew about what he
wanted to ask, and the questions were all
formulated in his mind. When he first
spoke to Mr. Seaver the latter at once
scouted the idea of the case not coming
to trial, and as there was room for two
to sit down comfortably in the Western
Union office both went there, within plain
sight of the operator, who was sending the
Post matter in, and there Mr. Seaver and
the Gazette man sat and kept on talking
about the matter for half an hour. The
theme of inquiry was not about the blood
stains on the skirts, but the direct assertion was made that there was no evidence
about the blood except in regard to that
on the skirt, and then Mr. Seaver enlarged
upon the fact, alleged that the blood
showed plainly with the naked eye, and
that indications pointed strongly to the
fact that it went on from the outside.
Then, to draw him out still further, the
Gazette man said : "Well, that in itself
doesn't amount to much," or words to
that effect, and Mr. Seaver at once volunteered the information that one of
Lizzie's dresses with spots on it had been
sent to Prof. Wood and he was going to
see if they were blood spots or not.

Up to that time the Gazette man could
not have told whether Lizzie's dress had
been put under the microscope or not.
It remains to be seen later on whether
Prof. Wood has that dress or not.

Mr. Seaver says he did not say anything about Miss Borden being insane
and in the next breath he asks, "Does the
crime look like the work of a woman in
her sober senses or not?"

There wasn't anything in that interview of which any one need to be
ashamed, but in all things excepting
slight changes in the phraseology the interview was correct to a dot. It was also
said that the "retirement of detective
Hanscom was a big bluff."

Other papers may have put words in the
detective's mouth that he did not say, but

THAT STORY

About the Roman Boy who
to grace one of Caesar's tri-
umphals was covered with gold
leaf, and then died next day,
is familiar to every Latin student. The reason was that the
pores of his body were stopped
in their attempt to perspire off
the body's impurities. The
same condition exists with you,
no matter how clean you may
think you are. A Turkish
Bath will open your pores and
make you feel like a new being.

YOU NEED A BATH.
No. 5 South Sixth Street.

LUCKY VACATIONERS.

Many Go Away for a Rest, More
Stay at Home.

What is Often Even Better Than a
Change of Air and Scene.

Something Needed to Invigorate the
Tired Body and Mind.

Two friends, who had not seen each
other for more than a month, met upon
the street.

"How badly you look," exclaimed one
as he gazed into the haggard face of his
friend. "My dear fellow, you need a vacation."

"Vacation," cried the other, "why, I
have just come back from a month's vacation."

Too many people who go upon a vacation with the expectation of securing
health, come back jagged out, weary, and
in a worse condition than when they left.
Change is not everything. Vacations may
be pleasing, but it is often better, whether
one goes away or stays at home, to feed
the nerves and brain, the sources from
which life itself comes, with something
that can restore the wasted energy, build
the vitality, and add greatly to the
strength.

In the whole range of modern discoveries, whether in chemistry or medicine,
the one made by Professor Phelps of
Dartmouth College, known as Paine's
celery compound, stands pre-eminent.
He has so compounded the powerful
qualities of German celery seed with other
valuable brain and nerve nourishers,
as to make a remedy that has done
and is doing what was never accomplished
before, a remedy makes people
well. There are men who, long ago, faced
the possibility of having to dispose of
their business and take a long rest in order to save their lives, who are now working constantly and are kept in strength,
vitality, and good spirits by this wonderful discovery. There are women who
were weak, dragged out, miserable, who
are now fresh, rosy and happy, entirely as
a result of using this great compound.

No one can afford to neglect an opportunity to increase one's vitality, preserving one's health, and lengthening
one's life. That a preparation has been
found that will do this is acknowledged
by the most eminent physicians, and by
those who have used it, always with highly satisfactory results.

The Gazette did not. Mr. Seaver's remarks
were interesting and to the point, so they
were given to the public which doubtless
appreciated them.

A Denial from Abraham G. Hart.
The Fall River News prints the following:

The report has repeatedly reached me
that the late Andrew J. Borden stated to
me that he was about making his will,
and had made an inventory of his property for that purpose, while the fact is, that
in his almost daily conversations, sometimes for a half-hour, in which he spoke
freely on financial and business matters,
with local history and the values of real
estate thirty to forty years ago, and at the
present time, he was completely reserved,
and kept his own counsel on all family
matters, and never at any time spoke of
making a will or inventory of his estate.
Respectfully,
ABRAHAM G. HART.

Miss Borden's Goodness.
The Brockton Enterprise:
In the murder mystery at Fall River a
number of well-meaning people appear to
be making a great point of the fact that
Lizzie Borden has always lived a "good"
life, and has been active in church work
and in deeds generally that have for their
object the uplifting of the race. From
these premises they advance the theory
that, because of this previous apparent
excellence of character, it is a wild and
insulting piece of folly to accuse her of
the crime for which she is held.

This is carrying the theory that the outwardly good man do no wrong to unwise
lengths, it seems to us. Miss Borden may
not be guilty, and in fact the evidence
thus far presented to the public seems not
inconsistent with a theory of her absolute
innocence. But this woman's previous
good character, while it is a strong point
in her favor, is nothing that necessarily
absolves her totally from even the
suspicion of guilt. Defaulting bank officials are generally good till found out.
Members of churches are seldom suspected
of crime till the revelation is made some
day with the vivid suddenness of a lightning flash. And Miss Borden, if she is
proved to be guilty, will be merely another example of viciousness that has
long been cloaked and concealed under an
outward covering of purity, goodness and
truth.

Don't believe everybody guilty merely
because they are accused. And on the
other hand don't be carried away by the
theory that evil is impossible where apparent goodness has previously had its
habitation.

Mistakes in Murder Cases.
The New York Sun:
In the night of June 11, 1879, Mrs. Jane
DeForrest Hull was smothered to death at
her home in this city. She was found
in the morning with her limbs and arms
tied and with bandages on her eyes and
cloth stuffed in her mouth, and a dress twisted
around her neck. In the room there were
some evidences that plunder had been
the object of the murderer; and her
watch and chain and a number of articles
of jewelry were missing.

The detectives failed to discover anything pointing toward the guilt of the
person who turned out to be the culprit.
This person was a negro named Chastine
Cox, who went to Boston after the homicide, and who was found with the watch
and most of the jewelry in his possession
at the time of his arrest in that city. For
a considerable period, however, before the

The Evening Standard.

ESTABLISHED FEBRUARY, 1850. | NEW BEDFORD, MONDAY, AUGUST 22, 1892. | TWO CENTS.

HASKELL & TRIPP.

Do you know what a fully equipped Kitchen-Furnishing Department we have in our light, spacious basement?

Do you know that we keep in that department *only such articles as have merit*, and sell them at the very lowest prices in the market?

The following list is necessarily very limited, but may serve to give you some idea of how we run this important stock:

Made of wood.

Step chairs that fold up, $1.25.

Pine foot stools, 19c.

Ladders, 3 step 69c. 5 step 94c.

Wash benches, 79c. Ironing tables, $1.32.

Plain skirt boards, 37c., 48c., 57c., 69c. Cloth covered 69c. to $1.50.

Clothes horses. 3 ft. 67c. 3½ ft. 72c. 4 ft. 79c.

Wash tubs, 60c. up. Washboards, 23c., 25c., 29c.

Wringers, $2 to $3.25.

Flour pails, 23c., 37c., 69c.

Fibre pails, 48c.

Commodes, $3.83 and $4.73.

Made of tin.

Cake boxes, 28c., 45c., 59c.

Water pots. 1qt. 21c. 2qt. 28c. 4qt. 32c. 6qt. 39c. 8qt. 50c.

Bread raisers, 67c., 98c.

Lunch boxes, 24c. Cash boxes, 67c., 75c., 83c.

Dust pans, 5c., 9c., 12c.

Coal hods, 25c., 29c., 33c.

Foot bath tubs, 42c., 50c.

Infants' bath tubs, painted, 96c. to $1.73; many sizes.

Dinner pails, 19c. Dinner kettles, 30c., 69c.

Buffed tea kettle steamer, 42c. Oil stove tea kettle, 25c.

Milk cans. 1qt. 10c. 2qts. 17c. 3qts. 21c. 4qts. 29c.

Egg poachers. 3 ring 23c. 6 ring 45c.

14-quart rinsing pans, 27c.

Tea pots, 29c., 33c., 35c.

Coffee pots, 30c., 33c., 37c.

Refrigerator pans, 35c.

"Puritan" rice boilers, 87c. and $1.

Tea kettle with porcelain bowl, may be used for either boiling water or cooking cereals, 94c., $1.25, $1.83.

Preserve kettles, 12c. to 18c., according to size.

Made of iron.

Preserve kettles, best goods made:

6 qt. 42c. 8 qt. 48c. 10 qt. 53c. 12 qt. 57c. 14 qt. 65c.

Scotch bowls, tinned inside, $1.12, $1.28, $1.50.

Economy roasters, made of Russian iron, cooks tough meats so they become tender, 68c. to $1.75; five sizes.

Odorless cookers keep all steam from the room. Three sizes, $1.17, $1.31, $1.47.

"Granite" ironware, best quality, *every piece fully warranted*. Full lines of kettles, tea and coffee pots, pans, boilers, ladles. Absolutely lowest prices.

Handy hardware.

For home use all the various useful tools at prices that'll surprise you, unless you've been buying here.

Fruit jars.

Mason's jars, *first* quality, all sizes at proper prices.

A thousand other things. Come and see for yourself.

HASKELL & TRIPP.

Department Stores,

Purchase and William Streets.

THE DISTRICT COURT-ROOM IN FALL RIVER,
Where the Borden Murder Inquiry is Being Held This Afternoon.

READY FOR THE ORDEAL.

Lizzie Borden Arrives in Fall River This Morning.

Hearing in the Murder Case Resumed at 2 O'Clock.

Prisoner Dsplays the Same Wonderful Nerve.

Capt. Smalley Maintains What He Said is the Truth.

Prof. Wood Unable to Tell Which of the Victims Died First.

[Special Dispatch.]

FALL RIVER, Aug. 22.—Miss Lizzie Borden arrived here from Taunton on the 10 55 o'clock train at the Fall River station. Her departure from the jail at Taunton was a quiet one, as it was not expected that she would be taken to this city until later in the day. On the way down she talked with the officers on every day topics, but said nothing about the murder. On the arrival of the train in this city Detective Seaver alighted first, and was followed by Rev. Mr. Buck. Then came Miss Lizzie, closely followed by City Marshal Hilliard.

The prisoner still retains her wonderful nerve. She leaned heavily on the minister's arm, and a few steps from the train Marshal Hilliard put his arm through hers and walked with her to the door where a hack with closed blinds was standing. There was not a trace of suffering on her face, not even a tear stain. She was dressed in the same blue cloth suit she wore when taken to Taunton a week ago and her face was covered by a thin blue veil. There was a great deal of interest taken in her by the crowds about the station but there was nothing in the character of a demonstration.

Officers Doherty, Harrington, Perron, Chace, and Medley kept a clear passageway. The reporters did not pay Lizzie the same attentions by gazing as they did one week ago. When she was seated in the hack with the minister and detective the city marshal gave directions to the driver to go to the Central Station by a circuitous route. The directions were followed. Ten minutes after three or four hack-loads of reporters were landed at the Central Station. The prisoner's carriage drove down Granite street through Rock, and hauled up at the north door.

Officers Davis and McAdams cleared the passageway to the matron's room, and Mrr. Russell followed the party up stairs to again resume her duties as Miss Borden's keeper.

When the prisoner arrived at the matron's room her counsel were there awaiting her arrival, also her sister Emma and Mr. Morse.

It is currently reported that Mr. Jennings is now in possession of all Miss Borden's right in the property of her father and that he has been instructed not to spare a dollar in preparing and continuing the work of defence, even though Lizzie should be penniless at the conclusion of the trial. Therefore it is probable that the trial will be a lengthy and protracted one.

In the court-room no accommodations were made for the reporters, and they were obliged to apply to furniture stores to secure tables for their own use. As early as 11 o'clock people began to arrive in the court-room, among whom were a number of women who occupied seats where they could obtain a good view of the proceedings. They brought their knitting work with them and lunch baskets were numerous. At the head of the stairs was an officer who would only admit a few at a time and during the proceedings it is stated that only enough spectators will be allowed in the room to fill the seats.

The Prisoner's Counsel.

Col. Melvin O. Adams of Boston will assist Mr. Jennings for the defence at this hearing. When the trial comes, if the case reaches an indictment, eminent counsel from New York or Chicago, it is expected, will be called into the case.

Who Died First?

It is understood that Prof. Wood cannot definitely determine from the stomachs of Mr. and Mrs. Borden whether the latter was killed first, and, therefore, he cannot say how long before Mr. Borden was murdered she had been dead. This is a very important point to the defence and materially affects the government's theory, maintained from the first, that Mrs. Borden died, at least, an hour before her husband. It is now said that the family had been sick the night before from the milk, and that Mrs. Borden did not eat breakfast. On the contrary, there is positive evidence that she did eat breakfast with Uncle John V. Morse and Mr. Borden. It is hinted that Dr. Wood could not find the evidence as to the priority of death of Mrs. Borden, because such evidence from the digestive organs is lacking 24 hours after death has occurred. The fact is pretty evident that the element of weakness is already introduced into this part of the Commonwealth's case.

"WHAT I HAVE SAID IS TRUE."

Mr. Hathaway Denies and Capt. Smalley Reiterates His Statement.

FALL RIVER, Aug. 22.—The publication of Capt. Smalley's story ranked next to the confession of Charles H. Peckham that he was the murderer as the most prominent incident of the past week in connection with the Borden case. George W. Hathaway, who told the story to Capt. Smalley, is a travelling agent for firms dealing in stove furnishings, and his route takes in the smaller towns and villages on the Cape and in the eastern and central parts of the State. Mr. Hathaway was found at his home by a *Standard* reporter, and he says this story he told was not concerning Andrew J. Borden's family. The circumstance, he repeated, happened in the family of a friend of his in a distant part of the country, and Capt. Smalley misinterpreted it when he understood it as occurring in the Borden family. Mr. Hathaway had no personal acquaintance with Andrew J. Borden.

At the police station yesterday one of the earliest visitors of the day was Mr. Hathaway. He seemed particularly anxious to disavow the statement of Capt. Smalley and have the marshal and the public understand that he was citing the case of another family. As for himself, he said, he believes Miss Lizzie Borden innocent, and was not flattered at all over the notoriety he had obtained in the past few days.

It isn't at all improbable, however, that Mr. Hathaway will be summoned as a witness in the case.

Capt. Smalley Reiterates His Statement.

Capt. Smalley was seen at the office of the Board of Overseers of the Poor this morning by a *Standard* reporter in relation to Mr. Hathaway's statement.

"What I have said I have said, and what I have said is true," said Capt. Smalley, "that is, if this Mr. Hathaway is the same person with whom I talked."

Visiting New Bedford Druggists.

A short time previous to the Borden murder, Lizzie Borden spent several days in this city, as has been told. It was decided to make an investigation, to see if she sought to buy prussic acid here. Inspectors Hathaway and Parker with City Marshal Hilliard of Fall River have visited all the drug stores in the city, and the registering of sales of poison at the various stores has been carefully examined. No prussic acid sales on the dates investigated were found, although one druggist had a recollection that it was called for and refused. No tangible evidence resulted.

THE SILVER QUESTION IN INDIA.

Opinion that the Government Should Close the Mint.

LONDON, Aug. 22.—The *Times* correspondent at Calcutta says: "The apparent supineness of the government on the silver question is causing dissatisfaction. A difference of opinion exists in regard to the adoption of a gold standard, but the conviction is growing that the time has arrived for the government to take the public into its confidence and prevent a further fall of the rupee by closing the mints.

Sheriff Brito Assassinated.

BROWNSVILLE, Tex., Aug. 22.—S. A. Brito, the sheriff, was assassinated while returning from a fandango just outside the city yesterday, on his way home. He was well known on the frontier as a terror to evil-doers, and as such made many enemies among the criminal classes. There is no clew to the murderers.

Fire in a Furniture House.

OMAHA, Aug. 22.—Fire in Shine, Ricks & Co's furniture house last night did $100,000 damage.

WEATHER INDICATIONS.

FAIR TILL WEDNESDAY.

WASHINGTON, Aug. 22.—For the 24 hours from 8 a. m. to-day: For New England fair till Wednesday, slight changes in temperature, northerly winds, becoming variable.

CONTINUED FAIR.

BOSTON, Aug. 22.—Local forecast for New England until Wednesday: Continued fair weather, variable winds, slight changes in temperature.

LAUNCH OF THE ROANOKE.

Largest Wooden Sailing Ship in the World Now Afloat.

[Special Dispatch.]

BATH, Me., Aug. 22.—The Roanoke, the largest wooden sailing ship in the world, was successfully launched this noon, in the presence of several thousand spectators. The Roanoke was built by the firm of A. Sewall & Co., who have built nearly 100 vessels. The Roanoke is built for the 'Frisco trade, and in the con struction the best material obtainable was used. She is a model craft, one that will fly the United States flag, and be an honor to the country.

The official measurements are: Registered length, 311.2ft.; registered breadth, 49.2ft.; registered depth, 20.2ft.; height under spar deck, 9ft.; tonnage length, 304ft.; length over all, 330ft.; gross tonnage, 3539.03; net tonnage, 3400.43.

THE ROANOKE.

She has a white oak keel, 16x15, two-tier. The frame and ceiling are of yellow pine. There are two streaks of timber on each side, under both decks, running the whole length and locked in. On the middle deck they are 8x14; under the middle deck they are 6x12.

The decks are of yellow pine. The planking is yellow pine 5 inches thick; the garboard is 8 inches thick. She is square fastened; over 100,000 tree nails were used in fastening. The butt bolting is all composition. She has three sets of knees.

The ship is fitted with

All the Latest Improvements,

and has Bath iron works hoisting engine, windlass and capstan.

The rigging is wire and will spread 15,000 yards of canvas.

The cabin is finished with quartered oak, veneered, and furnished like a mansion.

The masts are all in. The lower masts are 38 inches in diameter. The foremast is 91 feet in length, main 92, mizzen 92 and the spanker 98 feet. The fore, main and mizzen topmasts are 56 feet long, 21 inches in diameter. The lower yards are 95 feet long and 22 inches in diameter. She has a steel bowsprit and carries two $200-pound anchors.

The carrying capacity is about 5400 tons. She will be ready for sea about the 10th of September and will go to New York and load for 'Frisco. When ready for sea she will cost $175,000.

Captain Joseph Hamilton of New York, formerly of the ship Undaunted, is going in command. He has been commander for twenty-six years, and he is of the opinion that he has, in the Roanoke, the finest sailing ship afloat. The crew will number forty men.

She is owned by A. Sewall & Co. and parties in New York and San Francisco. A. Sewall & Co. are managing owners. Miles M. Merry was the master builder.

TWO DEAD AND ONE WILL DIE.

Three Men Shot by Constable During a Riot at Limestone, Ind.

BEDFORD, Ind., Aug. 22.—A riot occurred yesterday at Limestone, three miles northwest, in which three men were fatally shot. A wagon load of women and men were returning to their homes and stopped in the principal street. The men got out of the wagon and created a disturbance. Constable Shultz arrived and attempted to arrest some of them, and they resisted. A general fight took place. Stones, knives, clubs and revolvers were used, three of the men being shot by the constable. The people in the wagon all belonged to one family, their names being Lentz. Two of the men who were shot are dead and another will die.

RADICALS WILL PROTEST.

Labouchere Informs His Constituents the Queen Opposes His Nomination.

LONDON, Aug. 22.—In consequence of a letter from Henry Labouchere, stating that the Queen had opposed his nomination as a member of the new ministry, the Liberal-Radical Association of Northampton, which constituency Mr. Labouchere represents in the House of Commons, has issued summonses to other Radical associations in the country to join with it in an indignation protest.

EIGHT MILES OF STANDARDS.

Eight miles of paper were run through the STANDARD'S big perfecting press, Saturday, before the entire edition was printed. The demand for Saturday's STANDARD was heavy all day, and another large edition was the result.

HOME MATTERS.

WEDDED AT THE HOTEL.

Young Couple Who Missed the Train Helped Out of Their Predicament.

Last evening there arrived on the boat from Cottage City a young couple, who after looking about for a certain train suddenly came to the realization that the train which they had intended to have taken had left the wharf. They were well dressed and appeared to be very much "gone on each other." The young man wore several diamonds and to all appearances was the son of a well-to-do gentleman. He was about 25 years of age. The young lady was stylishly dressed, and looked to be his junior some six years. Their train missed, they proceeded to the Parker House, where he registered, and to the clerk he told his tale of woe. He said they were on their way to Providence to get married and had missed the train, and he asked concerning the possibility of securing a marriage license. He gave his name as George F. Matthews of Providence, and the lady's name as Hattie L. Crowell of Providence.

After some telephoning word reached Mrs. Ruth S. Sherman, assistant at the City Clerk's office. She made out a marriage license for the young couple. The young man started for the hotel a happy man and showed his lady love the valuable document which would make them man and wife. Then he commenced to inquire about ministers, and learning that there was one stopping at the hotel he repeated his story to him. This divine happened to be Rev. Dr. Charles Arey of Boston, an uncle of Mrs. Holder M. Brownell, and he cheerfully assisted the young couple out of their difficulty by tying the knot, which was accomplished in the parlors of the hotel in the presence of several guests of the house. This forenoon, after securing his marriage certificate, Mr. and Mrs. Matthews went on their way to Providence in a happier frame of mind than last evening upon the arrival here. Immediately after the ceremony had been performed Mr. Matthews added "and wife" to his name on the register.

PERSONAL.—John L. Coggeshall of this city is one of the eight new members of the board of officers of the Massachusetts Division, L. A. W., who have just been appointed by Chief Consul George A. Perkins.

Ex-President and Mrs. Cleveland Saturday entertained Editor R. W. Gilder of the *Century* and family at Gray Gables.

Edward Kilburn, L. LeB. Holmes and wife, Mrs. Andrew H. Potter, Miss Alice E. Adams of this city, arrived home from a European trip Saturday night. They visited England, Scotland, France, Belgium and Holland and arrived in New York on Friday on steamer Fuerst Bismarck.

William A. Gibbs, clerk of engine company No. 4, and family left the city yesterday for a week at Lakeville.

Horace Carpenter is cycling through northeastern Massachusetts.

Among the graduates of the Falmouth Summer Institute this year are the following from this city: Virtue R. Bowerman, James T. Bowman, M. F. Burks, Martha Butler, Ina T. Cahoon, Stephen Cahoon, Annie L. Carr, Lillie E. Carr, and Miss H. L. Channing.

Mrs. Charles McKee of New York and Mrs. Charles Taylor of Providence are visiting this city, the guests of Mrs. Lewis Bryan and Mrs. Washington.

M. Mathews and Miss Aiken of this city registered Saturday at the New York *Herald* bureau in Paris.

Hon. William S. Greene of Fall River is in town to-day, presumably for the purpose of advancing his congressional interests.

George T. Macomber and family have taken a cottage at Onset for the season.

SIXTY MILLION BUSHELS OF WHEAT —*A Bushel for Every Inhabitant of the United States. The Kansas Crop for '92.*—Never in the history of Kansas has that State had such bountiful crops as this year. The farmers cannot get enough hands to harvest the great crop, and the Santa Fe railroad has made special rates from Kansas City and other Missouri river towns, to induce harvest hands to go into the State. The wheat crop of the State will be from sixty to sixty-five million bushels, and the quality is high. The grass crop is made, and is a very large one; the early potatoes, rye, barley and oat crops are made, and are all large. The weather has been propitious for corn, and it is the cleanest, best looking corn to be found in the country to-day. Cheap rates will be made from Chicago, St. Louis and all points on the Santa Fe east of the Missouri river, to all Kansas points, on August 30 and September 27, and these excursions will give a chance for Eastern farmers to see what the great Sunflower State can do. A good map of Kansas will be mailed free upon application to Jno. J. Byrne, 723 Monadnock Block, Chicago, Ill., together with reliable statistics and information about Kansas lands.

SISSON'S BAKE.—The weather yesterday was first class for clambakes, and as it was impossible to procure these bivalves across the river many availed themselves of an opportunity to secure them at other resorts. At Sylvan grove Otis A. Sisson fed about 200 people, and everybody said the bake was excellent.

ANOTHER BIG BARGAIN FOR THIS WEEK.—All the remaining stock of fine flannel and silk and wool shirts that have been sold for $2.00, $2.50, $3.00, and $3.50 we shall sell at the extremely low price of $1.50 each, a trade, if you need a shirt. Gifford & Co., 139 Union street.

THE DARTMOUTH GRANGE CLAMBAKE will occur at Howland's Grove, Russell's Mills, Dartmouth, on next Thursday. The bake is open to the public. Caswell's excursion wagon will leave City Hall square at 11 o'clock. See advertisement.

IF YOU WANT an enjoyable pleasure trip cheap read Hatch & Abbott's special notice of White Mountain excursion.

NOW OR NEVER for bargains. Watches, clocks and jewelry at cut prices for only 10 days more. J. S. Kelley & Son, 15 Purchase st.

SCARLET FEVER.—One new case of scarlet fever has been reported at the office of the Board of Health since Saturday.

POSTAL or telephone 158-12 and John McCullough will send for iron, metals, paper stock, rubbers, bottles, etc.

LADIES' SHAMPOO 50 cents, No. 5 South Sixth street.

A SUCCESS—Palm leaf for filling beds. John McCullough.

PURIFY THE BLOOD—No. 5 South Sixth st.

BLACK CLOTH Overgaiters 50c. Devoll's.

TUB BATH only a quarter, 5 South Sixth st.

HOOD'S Sarsaparilla tones the system.

COLD FACTS!

There are Times

WHEN MONEY EXPENDED IS MONEY SAVED.

In no greater degree can this be realized than in the outlay of a few dollars in our

WALL PAPER DEPT.

Here we have beautiful goods in abundance, but because carried over from a previous season, we sell them at a price which is only nominal.

TRY US AND SEE.

C. F. WING,

34 to 40 Purchase st.

OUTING SHIRTS !

OUTING SHIRTS!

You can never have too many OUTING SHIRTS !

Our low prices will help you out. Quality exceptional.

Good Shirts for $1 and $1.25, laundered collars and cuffs.

Another lot of the popular blue Madras, all sizes, $1.50.

Better come at once, They're going fast.

OUTING SHIRTS!

J. & W. R. WING & CO.,

133 UNION STREET.

OUTING SHIRTS !

WHITING & CO.

Great Special Sale

—OF—

SILK REMNANTS,

Direct from the mill, commences WEDNESDAY morning, the 24th, at 9 o'clock.

We have purchased from the largest silk mill in the United States their entire accumulations of PRINTED SILK REMNANTS. 5000 yards to be sold.

Lot 1 will be sold first. Pieces made up in packages for dresses, skirts and Waists.

Lot 2, after first lot is sold, will be from 4 yards to 1-2 yard remnants, and all to be sold at one price, just 39 CENTS PER YARD, and all new styles this season, and never sold at less than $1 per yard; and that is the price to-day from the piece, but these are the short lengths called remnants. We have matched up dress patterns, skirts and waists; the balance for dress trimmings and fancy work.

Our store will not open that day until half past 8 o'clock. Be on hand, as you all know how quick they have been sold in former years. At this low price the sale will be for Cash.

THE CRESCENT!

22 Purchase St.

SILK GLOVES MARKDOWN.

Black and Colors, 19c.

Gents' Hose.

Fashionable shades, 25 cents. Hermsdorf stainless black, spliced heel and toe, 25c.

An excellent variety of 5c. Handkerchiefs both white and fancy borders.

A new lot of Wrappers in medium shades, also Indigo Blue $1.00 each. Good night dress 50c.

RIBBONS.

We don't *begin* to tell you *how much* we have *marked down* our line of Ribbons, but come and see for yourself.

We will close out our Gingham Dresses for children at *cost*. Sizes from 4 to 10 years of age.

Gloves, 15, 25, 37, 50c.

Corsets, a good corset for 39c.

An X-L-ent Corset for 50c.

A very nice Summer Corset, C-B a la Spirite, price $1.25.

Corsets at all prices.

Having removed our entire stock from the Old Stand at corner of County and High streets, we shall be pleased to see our old friends and patrons at our new quarters, 22 Purchase street, known as THE CRESCENT.

SOUTH DARTMOUTH.

Some of the female population of Summer isitors at Ricketson's Point have been considerably agitated the past few days over he appearance in that locality of an old nan, who walked along the shore and seemed o be studying what the wild waves were nurmuring. When first seen it was noticed hat he carried something in his hand, and jt was thought that he might be the Fall River murderer and had the hatchet so much sought after, but closer inspection revealed it to be nothing but a cane. When approached by some of the more daring of the male population, he would turn and walk away, without answering their questions. The ladies said he slept under the salt works and begged food in the village. Constable Howland was notified, but he didn't seem to be alarmed, and only "winked the other eye." It was learned yesterday that the man lives in the village, where he owns property, and although being eccentric is as harmless as a lamb.

FALL RIVER.

The Collinses, the Quins, the O'Haras and others were locked up yesterday for gambling on the Lord's day. The prisoners black boots and do odd jobs for a living, and were in the middle of a quiet game at No. 16 Brady street when the police called. The stakes were not large, but it was poker for money.

There was a slight fire in one of the tenement houses belonging to the Osborn Mills yesterday. The damage was trifling.

A detective mistook Organist Brodkorb of St. Mary's church, this city, for Dalton on Friday last, and insisted on arresting him. Fishermen rescued the musician.

The I. A. Guards will parade in Taunton on Labor Day.

The Amalgamated Trades Unions of the city have leased Riverview Gardens for Labor Day and have hired three bands.

The Butchers' and Grocers' Association will realize almost $2000 from its excursion.

The tenement at 80 South Main street, occupied by Mrs. Elizabeth Lawrence, was broken into Saturday morning while the family was away. Two or three trunks were forced open and their contents scattered over the floor. One of the trunks belonged to Sarah Campbell, a boarder. Fifty dollars which she had in the trunk were stolen.

The American Linen Company will add to the southerly end of its mill on Ferry street a five story structure 50 feet in length, in the first story of which will be placed two compound engines, and in the other additional machinery.

TAUNTON.

Walter Newman, a painter who has been in the employ of F. W. Hayman, has left the city and his young wife is mourning for him. He went away Saturday, 13th, saying he was going to Boston to look for work. On Thursday following his wife received a letter dated New York, in which he stated that he was going to California and she could look out for herself hereafter. Mrs. Newman is left without a cent.

PLYMOUTH COUNTY.

Special Officer A. D. Bettridge of Brockton arrested Morris Welch for illegal transportation of liquor Friday afternoon in a field off Spring avenue. Welch had a jug with him. He made a kick and the officer downed him. Then three men and Mrs. Maria Owens of 44 Spring avenue, 56 years old, assailed the officer. Mrs. Owens used vigorous language and a large, stout club. Between Welch's struggles, the attack of the men and the club of Mrs. Owens, Bettridge lost his prisoner and the jug. Mrs. Owens was later arrested.

A man walked into police headquarters at Brockton Friday afternoon and gave himself up for burglary. He said he visited the grocery store of Herbert Waterman, near the East Bridgewater railroad station, broke out a pane of glass in the door, entered and stole three new revolvers. He described himself as Charles' Coy, 23 years of age, a laborer, of Providence. He was locked up. In court Coy was held in $500 for the grand jury.

The demonstration of the several labor organizations on Labor Day promises to be the greatest in Brockton. Every union will take part, and several bands have been engaged. There will be a parade at 8 o'clock, in which the Lasters' Protective Union, elastic web weavers, bakers, blacksmiths, journeymen barbers, carpenters, bricklayers, hand sewed workmen, tailors, printers, painters and decorators, cutters and treers, city laborers, building laborers, Rockland elastic web weavers, Holbrook union boot and shoe workers and others will take part. The right of line has been given to the Boot and Shoe Workers' International Union, and George Antell will be president of the day. The procession will also include local trades, and after the parade the several organizations will go to Highland Park, where the exercises of the day will take place.

Archibald Wilcox, manager of the Bridgewater Creamery, has left town. He was in debt to the Creamery Company for a large amount. His wife, whom he cruelly beat just before going away, is left in destitute circumstances, but declares she will earn and pay every cent her husband owes.

The Plymouth Foundry Company will extend its premises by building a heavy sea wall 150 feet southward from its present premises and filling in behind it. The wall requires 1000 tons of stone.

All lands at Manomet Point excepting those owned by the United States Government, on which the Life Saving Station is located and a few private cottage lots, have been sold to Thomas and William B. Arnold of Abington.

LARGEST IN THE WORLD.—The Union Belt Company of Fall River has just completed and delivered to the Fall River Iron Works Company, as part of an order for an entire equipment of belting for their No. 2 mill, four of the largest main driving belts ever made to run on one pulley. The face of the pulley measures 15 feet across. The belts are to run side by side, and less than two inches apart, at a speed of upwards of 5000 feet (nearly one mile) per minute, and are to transmit the power from a pair of Corliss triple expansion engines estimated at 2400 horse power. These belts are all triple, and their dimensions are, respectively, 180 feet, 14 inches wide; 195 feet, 14 inches wide; 210 feet, 14 inches wide; 195 feet, 50 inches wide. The hides from 800 head of cattle were used in their manufacture, and the weight of the belts is four tons.

FOOTBALL.—The executive committee of the American Football Association held a meeting in the Wilbur House, Fall River, yesterday. The committee is composed of a delegate from each State represented in the organization. At the last meeting the Eastern clubs succeeded in taking the cup trophies from the New York elevens, but the latter were not then prepared to transfer the property of the association, and it was decided to adjourn until the 21st. Arrangements for the approaching season were made yesterday, and it is the intention to commence the match games in time to finish them before the base ball players take the field.

"I BELIEVE HER INNOCENT."

Anna Katharine Greene Speaks in Behalf of Lizzie Borden.

Interesting Opinion of the Famous Writer of Detective Stories.

Another Novelist Compares the Murder With the Leavenworth Case.

[From the New York Worm.]

As a professed writer of stories in which guilt and its detection play a prominent part, I have been asked by the New York World to state my impressions concerning the very remarkable murder which has lately taken place in Fall River, and the probable culpability of the young woman upon whom the suspicions of the police have mainly fallen.

This is a strange request, and that it should be made to one who is as far removed from any practical knowledge of the workings of crime and its detection by the police as any woman of domestic tendencies can be is proof perhaps of the effect which this inexplicable affair has had upon the public mind. It is regarded as a problem, and the conjectures roused by it are similar in nature to those awakened by romances in which the evidences of crime are worked up to point with unerring certainty towards the culpability of some person presumably innocent.

ANNA KATHARINE GREEN.

But, alas! The Borden mystery, though possessing the features of romance, is fact, and dreadful fact, and the person suspected is no heroine of the imagination with whom conjecture can rightfully amuse itself, but a living woman with a heart to feel her fearful position, and a life to be degraded if not endangered by the suspicions raised against her. Therefore it is with no keen intellectual enjoyment of the analysis involved that I approach this subject, but with a serious sense of the responsibility which one assumes in venturing to give an opinion upon a topic so associated with the actualities of life and death.

Lizzie Borden was at odds with her father, a man of means. Lizzie Borden was within hearing distance when his murder took place yet heard nothing and was conscious of no alarm, but did she commit the astounding double crime which many have laid to her charge? Surely it is not for me to answer, or for anyone to answer, before she has even been committed for trial or any evidence upon oath been submitted to the public. Yet I have been urged to say what I think of the affair, and to say it just at this stage of the proceedings, so I yield to importunities which possibly may be more pressing than wise, merely promising that it is an impression only which I have to give, and that, too, one formed from the story told in the newspapers of the present date and not from any special knowledge or study of the case.

Crime, as crime, is not interesting to me. I shun horrors and rarely read the long list of assaults and murders which come with every morning's news. I did not even read the account of the Borden murder when it first appeared. Not till my attention was specially drawn to the matter did I peruse the columns devoted to this affair, so rarely is there any feeling, save repulsion, produced in me by details of this nature.

But this crime is not of the ordinary type. Indeed, it is not sufficient to class it among those of an extraordinary nature. It is unique, sole, the crime of the generation as regards mystery and the shock it gives to all natural and human probabilities. When I began to read its story I found myself startled, and before I had finished the astonishing tale I was positively aghast. These circumstances—the finding of the body of an elderly man lying slain in his own home, with no evidences of struggle or surprise visible in his countenance; a servant near, his daughter within hearing distance, yet no cry heard, no sound of a fall noticed, his watch in its place, his money intact in his pockets, thus robbing the gruesome affair at the first blush of the usual motive of theft, but supplying later certain facts which bespoke a still more subtle motive in the cupidity of the daughter anxious for the fortunes she saw slipping from her hands —all this was not new to me, all this had been gone over in my mind years and years ago with creatures of my imagination, even down to the last startling detail of the proposed will he was prevented from making by his sudden death. That there were two victims here instead of one; that the time of murder was in broad daylight, when doors and windows are supposed to be open, and any unusual sound in so light a structure as the frame house inhabited by the Bordens would be likely to attract attention, and that the most brutal of all weapons, the axe, had beep preceded by poison, are the touches whereby reality transcends romance and human nature proved to be more vindictive in its hatred and more reckless in its methods than any writer dares to make his characters in fiction.

A case of circumstantial evidence was before me calculated to arouse any one's interest and doubly so mine, but it did not carry with it supreme conviction. As in the imaginary romance to which I have alluded, stress was laid upon one fact, which, in the judgment of Gryce, the detective, so weakened the chain of events otherwise leading direct to the guilt of the suspected party, that he hesitated to arrest her; so in this actual case of horrible crime, there was one fact recorded which deterred me from condemning without fuller evidence the young woman upon whom the shadow of suspicion has so darkly fallen. This is the unnecessary brutality, even fiendishness, displayed in the slaying of this elderly couple. Mr. and Mrs. Borden were not only killed, but hacked, and this not because of resistance or from a desire to escape an alarm, but in face of non-resistance and an undoubted physical powerlessness, their energies having been previously paralyzed by poison if not utterly destroyed by the first blow they received. A man will strike and strike and strike again, even after death has set in, the object of his hatred, and there must have been hatred seemingly of a deeply rooted and prolonged nature at the bottom of this crime. A woman will strike and strike and strike again, perhaps with more unreasoning and unrelenting frenzy than a man, when her victim is a rival who has aroused her jealousy, or the man who has outraged her affections or robbed her of her children.

But for a girl of any education or training to bring down an axe again and again upon the unresisting form of a father, who, whatever his severity had been towards her, could have aroused in her no fury of antagonism which would not have been satisfied by his mere death, is not consistent with what we know of female nature, and makes one pause when the cry goes up too loudly against her. Cruelty and the shedding of blood for blood's sake are a man's prerogative, or if they are ever found developed in a woman the cases are so rare that we may well afford to give Lizzie Borden the benefit of the doubt. I believe her innocent. To slay an aged father—even an aged mother—from motives of anger or cupidity is possible to a woman even in this day and generation, as our papers frequently show, but to needlessly hack and hew them! What weight of rage could have been strong enough to carry Lizzie Borden through that? Revenge for wrongs withheld, tastes crossed or desires unsatisfied, I cannot think so.

ANNA KATHARINE GREEN.

Another Novelist Talks.

BELLPORT, L. I., Aug. 21.—The remarkably close analogy between the Borden murder and Anna Katharine Green's story, "The Leavenworth Case," has been commented upon by every reader of that popular novel. No one was more prompt to see the resemblance than the authoress herself. No outsider, perhaps, is better qualified to suggest a plausible solution of the great mystery than this keen, analytic writer of detective tales.

Anna Katharine Green does not believe that Lizzie Borden is guilty of the crime with which she is charged. She has reasons, and apparently good ones, for her opinion. Some of these she expressed to the reporter in an interview on the Borden case and afterwards wrote out for publication at the World's request. She talked freely and unreservedly.

To those who know her in private life the novelist is Mrs. Charles Rohlfs. With her husband and three pretty babies she is Summering at Bellport, L. I. She is a woman of slight figure, with blue eyes, a placid face and a matronly air.

"I am extremely averse," she said, "to be considered in the light of presuming to take up the duties of the police in theorizing upon a case of this character, a matter of life and death. Not that my views would have any particular weight in shaping the course of procedure in ferreting out the criminal, but motives might be attributed to me that are entirely foreign to my nature.

"The Leavenworth Case' has frequently been criticised as utterly improbable, yet when I read the story of the Borden murder I remarked to my husband, 'What a remarkable resemblance to The Leavenworth case!'

"In the first place, the victims of the Fall River murder and the Leavenworth case had no enemies; they were wealthy; they were both on the point of changing their wills; there were two to benefit or suffer by this action; to all appearances they were perfectly secure; both crimes were committed in a remarkably short space of time, with the regular inmates of the house within call at the time.

"The discovery of both crimes was by accident—and both were committed noiselessly.

"The pistol shot in the Leavenworth case was not heard by the inmates of the house; nor was Mrs. Borden's fall, though she weighed over 200 pounds, and from the position in which she lay when discovered must have fallen heavily.

"The mysterious man who was hired to say on the stoop, 'He has deeply wronged me,' bears a remarkably close analogy to Clavering in the Leavenworth case.

"Then the circumstantial evidence, such as it is, in the Borden case has many parallels in the Leavenworth case. The servant-girl, Hannah, in my story had left the house just about the way Bridget Sullivan did, thus drawing suspicion upon herself. Then, too, there was the contradictory theories of the detectives and their effort after they had singled out the most probably guilty one to bolster up by such evidence as came most readily to hand.

"Afterwards came all the impenetrable mystery.

"In the Leavenworth case the first one to announce the crime was Truman Harwell, the real culprit, who at times could seem to have no possible motive for its commission."

"Her character, as I have construed it from the published reports, is thoroughly womanly, and there is no doubt in my mind as to her thorough sanity. I do not see how the circumstantial evidence that has been brought forward justifies the conclusions reached.

"But while it is reasonable to suppose that Lizzie Borden is innocent, both directly or as an accomplice, yet she might have inferential or indirect knowledge of the crime sufficient to cause at least a suspicion in her mind as to who might be implicated. That would readily account for her seemingly contradictory evidence on the stand.

"The resemblance between my fiction and this deplorable fact is heightened by the possibility of some unknown

---

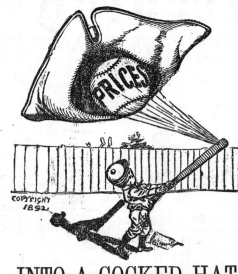

COPYRIGHT 1892.

INTO A COCKED HAT.

That is just what has happened to the prices of our Spring Suits; they have been knocked into a Cocked Hat. Every time there is a big tumble something is damaged; in this case it is the price not the goods—they are just as superior in quality as they were before the tumble.

It is ridiculously easy to let good things escape you; it is not ridiculously easy to coax them back again.

THE MID-SUMMER SALE

is the buyer's opportunity. The early bird catches the worm the wide-awake and early buyer catches the cream. Every day lessens the material for choice; just now about your choice yo can be particularly choice.

M. C. SWIFT & SON,

153, 157 and 159 Union Street,

NEW BEDFORD, - - - MASS.

Lawn Sprinklers,
Rubber Hose,
Poultry Netting,
Screen Doors,

Our Sale on
DOLLAR PAINT
is larger this season than ever before.

F. L. SOWLE & CO., 90 Purchase Street,
Hardware and Specialties. Opp City Clock.

C. W. HASKINS,

Having replenished his stock by liberal purchases of new goods, offers a choice selection of Diamonds, Watches, Fine Jewelry, Optical Goods, &c. The display of Sterling Silver Table Ware and Novelties is very attractive.

Attention is invited to a large collection of Souvenir Spoons, especially some in fine Enamel and Gold from various European countries.

Fine Watch and Clock Repairing done by competent and careful workmen and fully warranted

—AT—

C. W. HASKINS',

No. 20 Purchase Street.

PROBABLY A CRANK.

A Man Who Says He Can Find the Murderer of the Bordens.

BOSTON, Aug. 22.—"Lizzie Borden is innocent of the crime with which she is charged," said a man who called at the Boston police headquarters yesterday, and who gave his name as George A. Collier, and his residence at Quincy. He introduced himself to Lieutenant Daley, who was in charge, and informed that official that he had called to solve the Fall River mystery, if he could obtain leave to work upon the case. After stating his business he asked the Lieutenant if he could so work on the case.

"Certainly," said the Lieutenant, who from the outset perceived that he had a crank to deal with.

Collier, if that be his name, says that the crime was committed by a Frenchman, and he confidently declared he could ferret the murderer out. He said he had formerly been a police officer in Fall River, and that an ex-captain of that place had visited him soon after the crime was committed and asked him to work on the case. This business would not permit it then, but he gave his attention to it. Lieutenant Daley gave him permission to work on the case and he left for Fall River last evening.

Decidedly Inhuman.

VENICE, Aug. 22.—An infantry regiment marching from Mouselico yesterday suffered dreadfully from the heat. Over 100 exhausted soldiers were left lying by the roadside and twenty were put in hospitals in Dolo.

Davitt Pleads for Morley.

NEWCASTLE, Aug. 22.—Michael Davitt, in a speech here, said that he could not answer for the Irish votes on labor questions if John Morley should be rejected in the coming election.

Knowles & Co.

BARGAINS IN DRESS GOODS.

Lot of all-wool double fold dress goods, in Stripes, Plaids, and Mixtures, just the thing for early Fall and misses' school wear, now 39c., fully worth 50c.

Very good assortment of Pongee and corded Taffetas, 12 1-2c.

Elegant assortment of Ginghams, at 10c. and 12 1-2c.

New lot of Storm Serges.

Blue, 40-inch wide, 50c.

46-inch wide, special value, 75c.

50-inch wide, $1.

Misses' Jersey Vests, 8c. apiece.

Ladies' Jersey Vests, 12 1-2c. apiece.

Ladies' Extra Nice Jersey Vests, 25c. apiece.

Gents' Balbriggan Shirts and Drawers, 25c. and 50c.

The Best Fast Black Stockings, full regular finished seams, for Ladies', Misses' and Men's wear, to be found in the city at 25c.

Ladies' Silk Taffeta and Lisle Gloves, all prices, from 25c. up.

Ladies' and Misses' cotton underwear, in Corset Covers, Skirts, Night Gowns, best values, and largest assortment to select from. See them before buying.

Stamped Linens in Trays, Splashers, Tidies and Pillow Shams, lowest prices.

Toilet Articles, Combs, Brushes, Powders, Soaps, Perfumes, Bay Rum.

Shoe Department.

Now is the time to give you bargains. All our low shoes will be closed out at almost your own price, to make room for the largest line of Fall Goods to be found in this city. Also our Tennis Shoes must go, as we do not want to carry them over. Remember we are headquarters for these goods, and will not be undersold for the same quality goods.

We sell the celebrated CORSET SHOES, for children with weak ankles, which are the finest shoes in the world for that purpose. Come and see them. We also have "Curandier," which is a preparation for cleaning white canvas Oxfords. It is excellent.

Knowles & Co.

Cor. UNION & FOURTH STS.

OHIO'S VOTE.

McKinley Says Harrison Will Have a Greater Majority Than in 1888.

NEW YORK, Aug. 23.—Governor McKinley has left for Seabright, N. J., for a few days' rest. On Aug. 30 he will speak in Vermont and on Sept. 5 and 6 he will make two speeches in Maine. Governor McKinley said that the majority for Harrison in Ohio would be much greater, in his opinion, than that given for the Republican national ticket in 1888. "The main question with us in Ohio," he said, "is the tariff. Our people accept the Democratic national platform as a demand for free trade, pure and simple. In Ohio we are not prepared for free trade; our people don't want it and won't have it."

Something New.

WASHINGTON, Aug. 23.—A new feature has been introduced into the grand encampment of the Grand Army next September by the proposition to open the various churches of the city from 8 to 9 a. m. each day of the encampment week for a series of camp fires, to be addressed in short talks by chaplains and others, with the accompaniment of patriotic music, etc.

"Kick" Was Groundless.

WASHINGTON, Aug. 23.—In reply to the complaint made to the department of justice by the Knights of Labor that the imprisoned miners at Wallace, Ida., were not being properly treated, the attorney-general has received a telegram from Examiner Crostwaite saying he finds absolutely no grounds for the charges.

Wholesale Forgery.

CLEVELAND, Aug. 23.—There is now no doubt that the $500,000 of suspected paper issued by Paige, Carey & Co. of New York is fraudulent. John Huntingdon, the Cleveland millionaire, has sent his sworn statement from Europe declaring the use of his name upon the notes, in endorsement, to be forgery.

Presidential Appointments.

WASHINGTON, Aug. 23.—The following consular appointments have been made by the president: W. Hanley Hollis, at Mozambique, Africa; B. S. Rairden, at Batavia; William Heunke, at Chihuahua, Mex., formerly vice-consul at the same place, and J. Alexander Forbes, at Guaymas, Mex.

Brigands Got What They Wanted.

ROME, Aug. 23.—Brigands captured Baron Spitaleri and his son near Catania, Sicily, a few days ago. Countess Gianpialo offered £200 ransom. The brigands demanded more and ransacked her residence, taking £6000, after which they released their captives.

An Ill-Fated City.

TEHERAN, Aug. 23.—The ravages of cholera here are frightful. Sanitary regulations are almost unknown, and the fatalistic tendencies of the people make it almost impossible to combat the disease. Eight hundred people died yesterday.

SYSTEM OF BRIBERY

Employed by the Iron Hall to Accomplish its Purposes.

Piles of Cash Went Out to Influence Legislative Proceedings.

Detroit Branches Bring Suit and a Kick Comes from Baltimore.

INDIANAPOLIS, Aug. 23.—At the Iron Hall investigation in court yesterday a letter written by Supreme Justice Somerby to Supreme Accountant Walker related how the chief executive of the order had gone to Maine to work the legislature. "It is expensive business," the latter stated, "but it pays in the long run." The latter also stated that the supreme officer had "fixed" the New Hampshire body of legislators.

Supreme Accountant Walker testified that Somerby had drawn over $20,000 for "legal and legislative" expenses in the states of Maine, New Hampshire, Massachusetts, Connecticut, Rhode Island, New York, Deleware, Pennsylvania and Nebraska. Over $10,000 was used in the New England states to procure the passage of favorable legislation and to prevent the passage of unsatisfactory laws. The attorneys for the plaintiffs say they are ready to submit the case without argument or further evidence, but the defendants will not consent.

WANT THEIR MONEY BACK.

Members of Detroit Branches Bring Suits Against the Order.

DETROIT, Aug. 23.—The fight against the existence of the Order of the Iron Hall has extended to this city. It consists of two suits against the order, brought by former members of branches No. 1 and No. 315, both of this city. It is asserted that the supreme sitting of the order has placed in a Philadelphia bank, now insolvent, the sum of $720,000, and that this amount is liable to be lost to the organization. Branch 1, it is declared, has $12,000 to $18,000 in cash and securities deposited in Detroit banks, while branch 315 has $1859. The complainants say that the members generally desire that these funds be returned to them in just proportions. Each bill asks the court to appoint a receiver for the branch concerned. Judge Brevoort has issued an injunction to restrain the disbursements of any funds and the transfer of securities until after a hearing can be had.

Baltimore Folks Want a Receiver.

BALTIMORE, Aug. 23.—Charles J. Wiener, attorney-at-law, has filed seventeen attachments on original process in the city court against the Iron Hall and its local branches, and then, with ex-Governor Whyte, filed a bill for a receiver against them in the city court. The branches here embrace over 5000 members. The attachments were brought on matured claims ranging from $300 to $1000. Judge Dennis signed an order requiring the Iron Hall to show cause by Aug. 31 why a receiver should not be appointed.

From Yesterday's Third Edition.

ANNUAL MEETING.—At the annual meeting of the Onset Bay Grove Association to-day the following were elected to continue on the board of directors until the next annual meeting, which has been changed to the second week in January at Onset:

President—H. B. Storer, Boston.
Vice-President—William F. Nye, New Bedford.
Clerk—Charles F. Howard, Foxboro.
Directors—Nelson Huckins, Onset; John Q. A. Whittimore, Boston; Mrs. H. R. Bullock, Onset; O. A. Miller, Brockton; and Miss Helen Derry of Philadelphia.

Miss Derry was elected to fill the vacancy caused by the death of George Robbins. The others were reelected.

RELEASED.—Cornelia Allen, of this city, committed to the House of Correction Dec. 28 for keeping a disorderly house, was released by the County Commissioners to day, upon the recommendation of the probation officer, concurred in by the justice of the Third District Court.

John Lundy, of this city, committed Dec. 26 for drunkenness, was also released by the County Commissioners to-day.

HEAVY TRAVEL.—Owing to the heavy travel the passenger train that is due here at 1 45 did not arrive until nearly 2 20, about 35 minutes late. The train that left here at 1 30 passed it at Myricks.

Negro Rape Fiend Lynched.

GUERDON, Ark., Aug. 22.—A negro named Bowles, who recently outraged 16-year-old Nellie Wilkes, has been summarily dealt with by a mob. He fled after the crime, but a mob, at once organized, kept hot on his trail, and finally captured him in a farm house where he was, by force, obtaining food. He was taken to the scene of the deed, where he acknowledged his crime. He was strung up to a tree and shots fired into his body.

R. I. Yacht Club Regatta.

PROVIDENCE, Aug. 22.—Fair skies and a good breeze augurs well for the 6th annual opening regatta of the Rhode Island yacht club this morning. There are an unusually large number of entries, many being outside of the State.

Engravers Will Fight a Year.

LOWELL, Aug. 22.—A striking print cloth engraver denies the report that the engravers admit that they are beaten and says they have money enough to fight a year and intend to do so.

Killed by the Cars.

PITTSBURGH, Aug. 22.—Edward Shewell and his companion, Ella Stuffer, were killed by the cars near here yesterday while walking on the railroad track.

The First Frost.

CONCORD, N. H., Aug. 22.—The first frost of the season prevailed in this vicinity this morning.

CASES OF INSANITY

From the Effects of

"LA GRIPPE"

Are Alarmingly Prevalent.

Suicides

From the

SAME CAUSE

Are announced in every paper.

Would you be rid of the awful effects of La Grippe?

There is BUT ONE SURE REMEDY that NEVER FAILS, viz:

DANA'S SARSAPARILLA.

We Guarantee to CURE you or REFUND your money.

COULD WE DO MORE?

ISN'T IT WORTH A TRIAL?

je25-tf

Highest of all in Leavening Power.—Latest U. S. Gov't Report.

Royal Baking Powder

ABSOLUTELY PURE

SOUTH AMERICAN NEWS.

An Offensive Protocol May Make Trouble Between Peru and Chile.

NEW YORK, Aug. 22.—The *Herald's* Valparaiso correspondent telegraphs: There is a possibility of trouble between Peru and Chile arising from the protocol between France and Chile. The offensive tone of the Peruvian press and the hostile talk in the Peruvian congress have caused much comment here. If it is true, as is freely rumored, that a secret treaty against Chile has been entered into between Argentine and Peru, these countries are perfectly ready to meet them. While not seeking trouble, Chile will not brook any insults.

Minister of Foreign Affairs Errazuriz has telegraphed to the Chilean minister to state the terms of the offensive protocol to the government of that country and assure it that nothing is intended in the document to reflect in any way on the dignity and sovereignty of Peru.

A banquet was given last night by a number of Balmacedists. After it was over some of the banqueters came into collision with a number of young men who were opposed to their views. There was a lively fight, the Balmacedists retreating to the office of *La Republica*, the doors of which they closed. The office was attacked, and there was an interchange of shots. One man was wounded. Intendente Carlos Liera took immediate steps to quell the trouble and prevent further difficulty. Twenty of the participants were arrested, and there will be an investigation to-morrow.

Despite the denial of government officials, private letters received here confirm the news from Rio Grande in regard to the trouble there. Gen. Tavares now announces his intention to retire to private life at Artiges, thus removing one of the principal factors in the disturbance.

The *Herald* correspondent at Buenos Ayres says, in the Chamber of Deputies yesterday a question was asked relative to the navy supplies. The Minister of the Navy refused to reply, and subsequently President Pelligrini sent a message on the question which was deemed offensive. The message created a tumult in the chamber, many of the deputies favoring the initiation of a proceeding against Pelligrini for his insulting language.

WOULD NOT OBJECT.

Postmaster Hart Interviewed Relative to His Nomination for Governor.

BOSTON, Aug. 22.—Postmaster Hart, when asked to-day if he was a candidate for Governor, as was suggested by a morning paper item from Cottage City, said: "There are no candidates until after the convention, are there?" The reporter suggested that there were sometimes candidates for a nomination, to which Mr. Hart replied; "I don't know who is a candidate yet. The convention will settle that. But if the convention should get into trouble and nominate me I do not think I should run away. I should not pack my trunk anyway."

And with that, Mr. Hart, who had been standing in one of the corridors of the post office building, walked away.

STRIKE PRACTICALLY ENDED.

General Freight Agent of the Reading Notified to Receive Freight from all Points.

NEW YORK, Aug. 22.—A significant feature of the local railroad situation relative to the switchmen's strike was a dispatch received this morning by General Freight Agent Krase of the Reading, from the general freight agent at Philadelphia, notifying him hereafter to receive freight of Erie and from all points. Orders to receive all freight have been issued from the headquarters. At their offices it was said that the strike was a thing of the past.

HOMESTEAD DESERTED.

Strikers Securing Work Elsewhere—Soldiers Waiting to be Sent Home.

HOMESTEAD, Aug. 22.—Homestead is daily becoming more deserted, many of the strikers securing work elsewhere. The relief committee find their work much easier. The soldiers here are looking forward to Sept. 1, when they expect to be relieved. The soldiers generally are of the opinion from their constant association with the strikers that it would not be wise to remove the guard entirely for a month at any rate.

Hills Family Reunion.

FRANKLIN, Aug. 22.—The descendants of Joseph Hills, who settled in Walden in 1638, held their second annual family reunion at the Capt. Joseph Hills homestead here to-day. Dinner was served under the elms at 1 p. m. and was followed by an address of welcome. Secretary Edwin M. Hills of Taunton made a brief report and E. H. Hills, Esq., of Washington gave an interesting address.

Fatal Boiler Explosion.

MEMPHIS, Aug. 22.—A locomotive boiler exploded here yesterday and Engineer James Blunderfield was thrown into the air 100 feet and killed, Fireman Robert Pratter was torn to a mass, and the engine was demolished and the track torn up.

Death of a Centenarian.

DANBURY, Ct., Aug. 22.—Ethel Wheeler, formerly of New Fairfield, died at the home of his son here to-day, aged 100 years. He had been a well-to-do farmer and possessed considerable property.

MRS. LESLIE-WILDE HERE.

She Returns to New York from Europe Without Her Spouse.

NEW YORK, Aug. 22.—Mrs. Frank Leslie-Wilde returned to this country yesterday on the French line steamer La Bretagne after a three months' sojourn abroad.

When seen last evening Mrs. Leslie-Wilde, or Mrs. Leslie, as her many acquaintances still persist in calling her, looked exceedingly well.

"I have had a delightful trip on the Continent," she said, "but a most miserable return voyage—much rain and fog, and when not that the ship tossed and pitched frightfully.

"I was very quiet. I did not wear my diamonds once. That, you know, for a woman is synonymous with retirement."

"Your husband," the reporter ventured to ask, "does not he accompany you upon your return?"

"No," she replied, "he does not. I am forced to return for business reasons. I always return in August, and the climate here does not agree with Mr. Wilde."

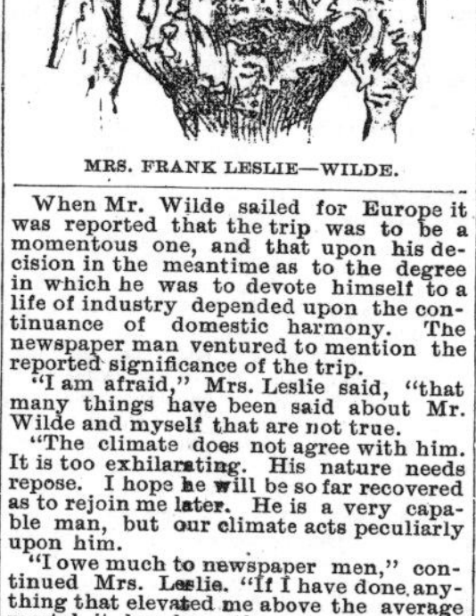

MRS. FRANK LESLIE—WILDE.

When Mr. Wilde sailed for Europe it was reported that the trip was to be a momentous one, and that upon his decision in the meantime as to the degree in which he was to devote himself to a life of industry depended upon the continuance of domestic harmony. The newspaper man ventured to mention the reported significance of the trip.

"I am afraid," Mrs. Leslie said, "that many things have been said about Mr. Wilde and myself that are not true.

"The climate does not agree with him. It is too exhilarating. His nature needs repose. I hope he will be so far recovered as to rejoin me later. He is a very capable man, but our climate acts peculiarly upon him.

"I owe much to newspaper men," continued Mrs. Leslie. "If I have done anything that elevated me above the average mortal it has been the newspaper men who have called attention to it. I might say they have made me and I hope they will continue to treat me kindly.

"If I have made a happy marriage," she added sadly, "certainly many unkind and untruthful things have been said about me. If, on the contrary, I have made an unhappy marriage, why, then, the newspapers should remember that I am a woman and am entitled to sympathy, not censure."

EFFECTS OF THE TERRIBLE HEAT.

Two Soldiers Die During the Manœuvres of the Tours Garrison.

LONDON, Aug. 22.—A Vienna correspondent says the heat has caused numerous forest fires and has injured crops, but the vintage prospects are fine.

A Paris correspondent says the hot weather has had a splendid effect on the harvest.

PARIS, Aug. 22.—During the manœuvres of the Tours Garrison two soldiers died from the effects of the heat.

VIENNA, Aug. 22.—Owing to the intense heat the Emperor has countermanded the order for the military manœuvres fixed for Aug. 29.

Confessed He Set the Fire.

BOSTON, Aug. 22.—David J. Corwin, treasurer of the Hub Blankbook & Stationery Co., to-day confessed to setting a fire in the premises occupied by the company on Cornhill on the night of Aug. 15. The firm had only moved in on Aug. 1, and the police say the stock was over insured. Mr. Corwin said to the fire marshal this morning that a sudden impulse came over him that he could not control, and under that influence he set the fire. He is in custody. Corwin is 37 years old and belongs in Newburg, N. Y. He was formerly employed in the auditor's office of the N. Y. & N. E. railroad, and was at one time chief clerk in the office of the superintendent of the Newburg & Connecticut River railroad.

The Saratoga Races.

SARATOGA, Aug. 22.—First race, 6 1-2 furlongs, Nick won, Elk Knight 2d, Pat Malloy, Jr., 3d. Time, 1 23.

Second race, seven furlongs, Saunterer won, Fenelon 2d, Louden 3d. Time, 1 27 3-4.

Third race, 1 1-8 miles, Lowlander won, Charade 2d, Badge 3d. Time, 1 53.

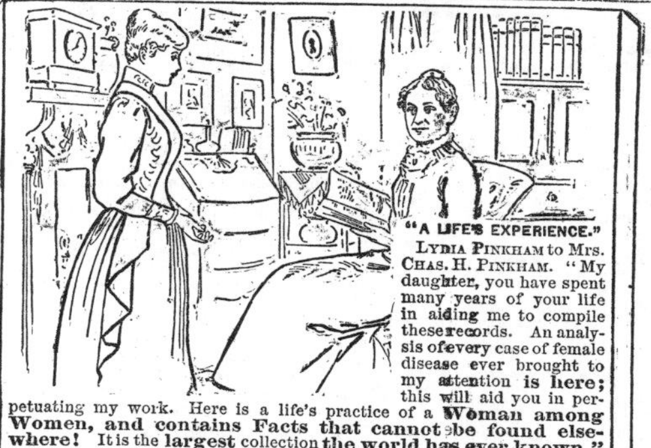

"A LIFE'S EXPERIENCE."

LYDIA PINKHAM to Mrs. CHAS. H. PINKHAM. "My daughter, you have spent many years of your life in aiding me to compile these records. An analysis of every case of female disease ever brought to my attention is here; this will aid you in perpetuating my work. Here is a life's practice of a **Woman among Women, and contains Facts that cannot be found elsewhere!** It is the **largest** collection **the world has ever known.**"

NOTE. These Records are available to the **Women of the world.** Personal attention is given to confidential letters, and correspondence is solicited from suffering women.

LYDIA E. PINKHAM'S VEGETABLE COMPOUND

Is the only **Positive Cure and Legitimate Remedy** for the peculiar weaknesses and ailments of women.

It cures the worst forms of Female Complaints, that Bearing-down Feeling, Weak Back, Falling and Displacement of the Womb, Inflammation, Ovarian Troubles, and all Organic Diseases of the Uterus or Womb, and is invaluable to the Change of Life. Dissolves and expels Tumors from the Uterus at an early stage, and checks any tendency to Cancerous Humor. Subdues Faintness, Excitability, Nervous Prostration, Exhaustion, and strengthens and tones the Stomach. Cures Headache, General Debility, Indigestion, etc., and invigorates the whole system. For the cure of Kidney Complaints of either sex, **the Compound has no rival.**

All Druggists sell it as a **standard article,** or sent by mail, in form of Pills or Lozenges, on receipt of **$1.00.** LYDIA E. PINKHAM MED. CO., LYNN, MASS.

An illustrated book, entitled "Guide to Health and Etiquette," by Lydia E. Pinkham, is of great value to ladies. We will present a copy to anyone addressing us with two 2-cent stamps.

KNOWLTON NOT READY.

Counsel for Defence Consents to a Postponement.

No Evidence Presented in the Borden Murder Trial.

Hearing Adjourned Until Thursday of This Week.

Prisoner Not Required to Enter the Court-Room.

Crowds of Curious Spectators Turned Away Disappointed.

[Special Dispatch.]

FALL RIVER, August 22.—The second district court room in this city was a continuous buzz of excited conversation in the period just preceding the trial of Lizzie Borden this afternoon. Inside the rail the entire space was filled with tables and chairs for the counsel, and newspaper men, about 35 of the latter being present. Several newspaper artists were also on hand. Among the spectators was a large predominence of ladies, doubtless due to the susceptibility of the guardian of the law at the outer portal.

When the time for the court session to commence arrived not a seat was to be had in the room, and quantities of spectators were standing. At precisely 2

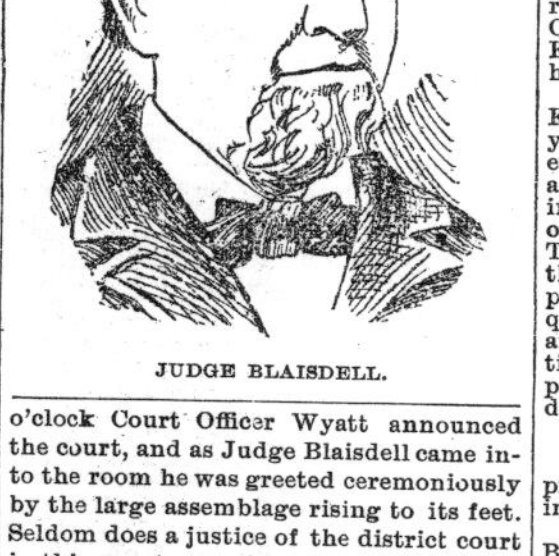

JUDGE BLAISDELL.

o'clock Court Officer Wyatt announced the court, and as Judge Blaisdell came into the room he was greeted ceremoniously by the large assemblage rising to its feet. Seldom does a justice of the district court in this county receive this mark of distinction from such an assemblage.

As the justice took his place on the bench a hush fell on the room and all eyes and ears anxiously riveted their attention on the entrance to the room in eager expectancy of some sign of the arrival of the much talked of prisoner and defendant. She was preceded several minutes by her counsel, Andrew J. Jennings of Fall River and Melvin O. Adams of Boston, who through weeks, perhaps, to come will put forth all their efforts to save a member of the Fall River elite from a convict's fate.

Their patience was in vain for she did not appear. Instead at 2 50 o'clock the bulky form of District Attorney Knowlton emerged from the judge's room. A hush at that moment fell on the officers and spectators.

Mr. Knowlton addressed Judge Blaisdell, while all the people present craned forward and listened. He said a number of things had been taken from the Borden house which needed to be examined by experts, who were not ready at the present time to render their report. On this account he asked that the examination be postponed till Thursday next.

The Judge said it did not seem to him that the demand was unreasonable, and he therefore ordered a continuance till Thursday morning at 10 o'clock.

Among those who were present in the court room was Bridget Sullivan, who was attired in a suit of blue with hat of same color, trimmed on the front with a bow of blue ribbon. She seemed at peace with herself and all the world; had a good color and was apparently not haunted by any sad thought.

John V. Morse sat a little distance at her left, and to the ordinary observer he displayed no emotion. He sat calm and unmoved and apparently was the most indifferent of spectators.

Lizzie's sister Emma, who has been with her at all times when she could since her arrest, was in Matron Russell's room from the time her sister arrived this morning, was a comforter to the girl, rendering every assistance in her power. Neither Lizzie or Emma was in the court room during the afternoon, but counsel for defence, A. J. Jennings of Fall River and M. O. Adams of Boston, were on hand, although they did not find any need to make any remarks or offer any objection to the course pursued by the government.

One of the most interesting events of the tedious wait preceding District Attorney Knowlton's announcement was furnished by a citizen, who announced himself as a taxpayer and a man who was entitled to sit down, getting a seat in a reporter's place and endeavoring to enforce his position, but who abandoned it when Officer Wyatt put in an appearance.

A conversation with the District Attorney this afternoon by a *Standard* reporter resulted in gaining not much information. He said he knew little more of the proceedings than the various outsiders. When questioned in regard to the witnesses and the order of their precedence, he said that Dr. Dolan, the medical examiner, would be the first one called by the government, but beyond that he could say nothing.

[By Associated Press.]

FALL RIVER, Aug. 22.—The court room was crowded inside the rails at 2 o'clock. Back of the rail, where the strange crowd of rough faces is usually seen, there were ladies in plenty and all were arrayed in fine clothes. Among the many who were present were Aldermen Beattie, Brady and McLaughlin, Rev. John Brown, Michael Burnham, P. W. Lyman, Drs. Leary, Dwelly, William Collins of Haverhill, St. Germain, Judge Carter of Haverhill, James T. Cummin, Mr. William Durfee, Mayor Coughlin and Benjamin Cook. There were 32 newspaper workers within the rail. Three of them were ladies. Among the men were five artists who were engaged in sketching everything from the carpet to the ceiling.

Bridget Sullivan and Mrs. Russell were on the scene early. District Attorney Knowlton appeared at 1 54 o'clock and went into the judge's private room. The judge followed shortly afterward.

Bridget Sullivan has grown very pale since the day she was first seen by the Associated Press representative. She was dressed in a suit of blue trimmed with lace and she remained for some time in conversation with Lawyer James Cummings.

The heat in the room began to make itself felt early in the proceedings and gave evidence of weary hours to come.

City Marshal Hilliard was present in a handsome new uniform with fine shoulder straps.

Dr. Dolan, Dr. Bowen, Superintendent Connell, Justice Lovatt, and crowds of female witnesses began to file in until standing-room was hardly obtainable.

The city hall bell had hardly ceased ringing the hour of two when Judge Blaisdell entered from his room and went up to the bench. As he walked along each of the 300 persons in the room arose and remained standing until he bowed and sat on a seat so filled with fate.

The rising was an innovation and an unexpected honor in the district court.

John V. Morse entered the room after the judge was seated, and ex-Congressman Robert T. Davis followed him. Attorney Phillips was the first lawyer to appear at the table set apart for the defence. City Physician Kelly and his wife were shown seats occupied by other witnesses, seats usually occupied by prisoners.

As one looked around the court-room, filled as it never was before, it was noticed that the large proportion of the guests were women. Some were old, some young, but all were curious to the last degree. They strained their necks and looked nervously at each person connected with the case as they appeared.

Mrs. Dr. Bowen and Mrs. Churchill sat in the witness seats and both were crying bitterly.

Attorney Jennings appeared at 2 18 and he was scowling, as though indignant at the curious that bent their eyes toward him.

There was a warm discussion going on in the clerk's room between District Attorney Knowlton, Attorneys Jennings and Adams regarding the admission of certain evidence to give the defendants an insight into the government's case. There was a long wait of the prisoner's appearance. She was delayed in the matron's room where her attorney and her intimate friends engaged her in conversation.

William Kennedy of Broadway created a scene during the long wait. He had taken the seat of a New Bedford *Standard* reporter and talked loudly, when Court Officer Wyatt appeared. He moved Kennedy outside the rail and directed him to a seat on the floor.

At ten minutes of 3 District Attorney Knowlton arose and said: "If it please your honor, there are some things used as evidence in this case which are wanting at the present time. They are the clothing and various parts of the furnishings of the rooms where the murder occurred. They are in the hands of the experts and they will be here to-morrow or next day probably, or the day following. Consequently we have agreed with the defendant's counsel to adjourn this hearing until Thursday, if it meets your honor's approval." An adjournment until Thursday was then ordered.

Publicity a Safeguard of Liberty.

NEW YORK, Aug. 22.—The *Herald* printed the following editorial this morning:

The formal hearing in the case of Lizzie Borden will begin at Fall River to-day to determine whether the accused shall be held to await the action of the grand jury.

It is understood that the hearing is to be public. By all means it should be so. Secret inquisitions and star chamber proceedings are foreign to American institutions and American sentiment. Especially in the case of a person accused of the highest crime known to our law should the proceedings be public in order that there may be no ground for popular suspicion as to the justice and regularity of the step taken by the public authorities.

If this course is now pursued in the case of Lizzie Borden, the chain of circumstantial evidence wrought against her will be given to the world and an intelligent public opinion may be formed as to whether she is justly accused and properly held. Such publicity is an essential safeguard of personal liberty.

TRIED TO ESCAPE.

Two Convicts at Sing Sing Shot by the Keepers in a Struggle.

SING SING, N. Y., Aug. 22.—Charles Vincent and Thomas Welsh, two convicts, attempted to escape from the prison this morning, and a desperate fight ensued between them and a number of the keepers, during which Vincent was shot and instantly killed and Welsh seriously wounded.

STEAMSHIP ROMA LOST.

Wrecked Near Algoa Bay, and Everybody on Board Drowned.

CAPE TOWN, Aug. 22.—The British steamer Roma, from London for Brisbane, has been wrecked near Algoa Bay. It is said that everybody on board was drowned.

Had a High Old Time and was Drowned.

HARTFORD, Ct., Aug. 22.—On Saturday morning Amos Johnson, James Hurlburt and Gideon Hubbard of Middletown and Wilnor D. Griswold of Portland started down the Connecticut river for a yacht sail out on the Sound. The party were having a high old time when Johnson got scared below Goodspeed's and disembarked for home. Yesterday Hubbard was found clinging to the overturned yacht at Marromas and was rescued. Hurlburt and Griswold were drowned.

Ate Liver Pills and Died.

DANBURY, Ct., Aug. 22.—Harry, the 8 years old son of John McLean of Hulls Hill, ate some "liver" pills yesterday afternoon and died 30 minutes later in spasms. The pills are said to contain strychnine, but are marked "harmless." Coroner Dolan has been summoned.

Child Drowned.

BANGOR, Aug. 22.—Fred, the eight years old son of Patrick Ford, was drowned today while playing around the lumber docks.

SANFORD'S Ginger

MOST GRATEFUL and comforting of warming stomachics, it quenches thirst, warms and strengthens weak stomachs, promotes digestion, prevents chills, destroys disease germs in water drunk, eradicates a craving for intoxicants, and protects the system from contagious influences.

Containing among its ingredients the purest of medicinal French brandy and the best of imported ginger, it is vastly superior to the cheap, worthless, and often dangerous gingers urged as substitutes. Ask for SANFORD'S GINGER and look for owl trademark on the wrapper. Sold everywhere.

WRIGHT Drug Company.

PUREST DRUGS

— AND —

FINEST CHEMICALS

— AT —

Lowest Prices.

WRIGHT DRUG CO.

RAILROAD TRAFFIC INCREASING.

The Great Switchmen's Strike Now Practically Over.

BUFFALO, Aug. 22.—Mr. Sargent, being interviewed, said: "You can deny that the firemen are going into this strike, except as part of a column composed of all the railway orders. I do not say that they will not strike, but the impression that they are to be forced to the front in this matter is absolutely incorrect.

"We have a clause in our constitution fixing a penalty of expulsion in the case of a strike without authority. The strike must be a general one. We have never yet struck out of sympathy for others, but often adjusted differences and thus avoided strikes."

Mr. Sargent could not say exactly who would take part in the deliberations, but intimated that it would be Chief Arthur of the Brotherhood of Engineers, Grand Master Wilkinson of the trainmen, Grand Master Clarke of the conductors, Grand Master Sweeney of the switchmen and himself.

"We must consider carefully," he continued, "whether the companies, did they defeat the switchmen in this struggle, would single out our orders one after another for annihilation and attempt to destroy organized labor. In a contention we might conclude that now is the time to join hands and make a fight against capital for recognition of organized labor. If this is the case a general strike may follow. But as I said, I have not come here to order a strike of the firemen unless the other orders join forces."

Mr. Sargent sent a note to Mr. Sweeney. The leaders will undoubtedly discuss the situation. The coming of the other leaders will develop later.

CHOLERINE INCREASING.

U. S. Officials Should Keep An Eye on Emigrants from Germany.

HAMBURG, Aug. 22.—It will behoove the United States emigration commissioners to keep a close watch on emigrants who arrive in that country from Hamburg to prevent the introduction of the disease euphoniously known as cholerine. Yesterday there were 27 cases of this disease reported in this city, and to-day the number is larger. It is denied that the disease is Asiatic cholera, but it is undeniable that those who die of it die in a very short time after they are attacked. The fresh cases are becoming so plentiful that the number of ambulances to convey the victims to the hospital has been increased.

MYSTERIOUS DISAPPEARANCE.

Superintendent of the Marblehead Water Works Leaves Home Never to Return.

LYNN, Aug. 22.—Kendall Pollard, superintendent of the Marblehead Water Company's works at Swampscott, is missing from his home. He went away Saturday evening telling his wife he would return in a couple of hours. Instead he sent a note, saying he would never return. The affairs of the company he turned over to his engineer, advising him to notify the officers. No further trace of him has been discovered. He was injured by an accident a few years ago and his wife fears that his disappearance is somehow due to this.

The Order Drawn Up.

WASHINGTON, Aug. 22.—It will devolve upon the treasury department to carry out the provisions of the President's proclamation, levying a duty of 20 cents a ton on vessels passing through the St. Mary Flat canals in retaliation for the duty imposed by the Canadian government on vessels passing through the Welland canal. Anticipating the action of the State Department, the officers of the Treasury Department have drawn up an order to carry out the terms of the proclamation, and this will be issued to the proper customs officers during the day.

Strike Practically Over.

BUFFALO, Aug. 22.—The railroad traffic on all the roads here has increased so decidedly that the strike is practically over. At noon Grand Master Sweeney of the switchmen was seen. "Have you seen Mr. Sargent?" he was asked. "I have, but I have nothing to say about it," was all he would say.

Pages 1-8.

The Evening Standard.

Pages 1-8.

ESTABLISHED FEBRUARY, 1850.

NEW BEDFORD, WEDNESDAY, AUGUST 24, 1892.--TEN PAGES.

TWO CENTS.

HASKELL & TRIPP.

Do you know what a fully equipped Kitchen-Furnishing Department we have in our light, spacious basement?

Do you know that we keep in that department *only such articles as have merit*, and sell them at the very lowest prices in the market?

The following list is necessarily very limited, but may serve to give you some idea of how we run this important stock:

Made of wood.

Step chairs that fold up, $1.25.

Pine foot stools, 19c.

Ladders,	3 step	5 step
	69c.	94c.

Wash benches, 79c. Ironing tables, $1.32.

Plain skirt boards, 37c., 48c., 57c., 69c. Cloth covered 69c. to $1.50.

Clothes horses.	3 ft.	3½ ft.	4 ft.
	67c.	72c.	79c.

Wash tubs, 60c. up. Washboards, 23c., 25c., 29c.

Wringers, $2 to $3.25.

Flour pails, 23c., 37c., 69c.

Fibre pails, 48c.

Commodes, $3.83 and $4.73.

Made of tin.

Cake boxes, 28c., 45c., 59c.

Water pots.	1qt.	2qt.	4qt.	6qt.	8qt.
	21c.	28c.	32c.	39c.	50c.

Bread raisers, 67c., 98c.

Lunch boxes, 24c. Cash boxes, 67c., 75c., 83c.

Dust pans, 5c., 9c., 12c.

Coal hods, 25c., 29c., 33c.

Foot bath tubs, 42c., 50c.

Infants' bath tubs, painted, 96c. to $1.73; many sizes.

Dinner pails, 19c. Dinner kettles, 30c., 69c.

Buffed tea kettle steamer, 42c. Oil stove tea kettle, 25c.

Milk cans.	1qt.	2qts.	3qts.	4qts.
	10c.	17c.	21c.	29c.

Egg poachers.	3 ring	6 ring
	25c.	45c.

14-quart rinsing pans, 27c.

Tea pots, 29c., 33c., 35c.

Coffee pots, 30c., 33c., 37c.

Refrigerator pans, 35c.

"Puritan" rice boilers, 87c. and $1.

Tea kettle with porcelain bowl, may be used for either boiling water or cooking cereals, 94c., $1.25, $1.83.

Preserve kettles, 12c. to 18c., according to size.

Made of iron.

Preserve kettles, best goods made:

6 qt.	8 qt.	10 qt.	12 qt.	14 qt.
42c.	48c.	53c.	57c.	65c.

Scotch bowls, tinned inside, $1.12, $1.28, $1.50.

Economy roasters, made of Russian iron, cooks tough meats so they become tender, 68c. to $1.75; five sizes.

Odorless cookers keep all steam from the room. Three sizes, $1.17, $1.31, $1.47.

"Granite" ironware, best quality, *every piece fully warranted.* Full lines of kettles, tea and coffee pots, pans, boilers, ladles. Absolutely lowest prices.

Handy hardware.

For home use all the various useful tools at prices that'll surprise you, unless you've been buying here.

Fruit jars.

Mason's jars, *first* quality, all sizes at proper prices.

A thousand other things. Come and see for yourself.

HASKELL & TRIPP.

Department Stores,

Purchase and Willi.

LIZZIE'S LETTER.

She Wrote Emma About Seeing a Suspicious Character.

Watched Him From an Upper Window on Monday Night.

Friends Who Read the Letter Will Testify to Its Contents.

Drug-Clerk of This City Taken to Taunton by the Police.

Paced the Jail Corridor, but Could Not See Lizzie's Face.

[Special Dispatch.]

FALL RIVER, Aug. 24.—It transpires that at the coming trial of Lizzie Borden, her letter-writing will form a feature of the evidence both for the State and the defence. The prisoner has told an intimate friend since her arrest the story of a letter which she wrote to her sister Emma, who was at the time visiting in Fairhaven. The letter was mailed two days before, and reached its destination one day before the murder. It contained a description of a singular experience which Lizzie said she had the Monday night before the murder. She was on her way to the house, according to the letter, at about 8 o'clock in the evening, and upon entering the side gate she saw a suspicious character in the back yard. The man ran at sight of her, and this action of his created much uneasiness in Lizzie's mind. She could not rest without making further inquiry into the matter, so she watched the yard from the upper window of her room, and saw what she concluded was the same man walking through the yard. It was dark and she could not give a good description of him. From other things she saw, Lizzie concluded that the house was being shadowed.

The circumstances as above related were told in the letter which Lizzie wrote the next morning and mailed to Emma at Fairhaven. Emma thought the matter rather strange and she showed the letter to several persons there who read it and who, it is said, are willing to testify to its contents. Emma then destroyed the letter.

This matter first came out at the inquest when the district attorney asked Lizzie if she had seen any suspicious characters about the house. To this question Lizzie replied that she had not on the day of the murder, but that she had on Monday night. Then she told the story of the letter which has since been investigated by the police and proven to be in the main correct.

During Lizzie Borden's incarceration at Taunton jail a New Bedford drug clerk was taken there by the police, and shown the cell in which she was locked. He paced up and down the corridor several times in an attempt to see Lizzie's face, but each time she was sitting with her back to the door. It was the intention of the New Bedford man to see if she was the same woman who had called at his store and bought, or attempted to buy, prussic acid. Whatever the reason of it, he remained in Taunton a half-day, but finally left without having seen Lizzie. It appears from this incident that the State has not given up the poison theory.

However the controversy between Capt. Orrick Smalley of this city and George W. Hathaway of Fall River may end regarding the conversation which took place on the piazza of the Craigville Hotel, it leaked out yesterday that some little time before his death A. J. Borden had spoken to a prominent business man of Fall River concerning his family relations. It is also known that he conveyed the impression that these relations were not pleasant. Mr. Borden said what he had to say on that occasion in a very few words. He did not go into particulars and the gentleman with whom he was talking did not ask any questions.

This is not an important matter of itself, but it throws more of a cloud about the excuse which Miss Lizzie Borden made when invited to visit Marion. The young woman whom she was to join at that resort stated that Miss Borden could not leave her home because her sister was away and she would be needed to take care of her father in case he went across the river to his farm. The government may be able to show that he did not intend to visit the farm, and that having made up his mind on that point he said as much to a gentleman in whom he was not in the habit of confiding.

If Miss Borden was anxious to go to Marion and remained behind her friends because she thought her father might visit his farm, it is singular that he did not inform her of his plans. This proves nothing as it stands, of course, but it certainly doesn't weaken the links in the chain of circumstantial evidence.

Another matter which is commanding attention is the second letter in the case. The first letter was addressed to Mrs. Borden, and if Miss Lizzie has been correctly reported she has stated that it was probably burned. The second letter was mailed by Mr. Borden on the morning he was butchered. Miss Lizzie wrote it and it is addressed to one of her friends at Marion. If the police can secure this letter it may throw some light on the prisoner's plans and be very valuable. Its contents have not been made public except in a general way, and nothing has been heard concerning it since the early days of the murder. If the defence has not secured possession of this letter the government may put it in at the preliminary hearing, though just what use would be made of it if the district attorney could secure it is not known, of course

The government has evidence which goes to show the woodwork in the rooms where the murders were committed was washed after the tragedy. The photos taken soon after the killing plainly show blood stains on certain portions of the rooms, which carpenters have sawed off, and which are now clean. It is rumored that photography will play an important part at either the hearing or the trial, and that the government will exhibit some ghastly pictures, showing the nature of the wounds which were inflicted.

The attempt which has been made by the supporters of the prisoner to discredit the story that the daughters of the murdered people were unhappy in their home life, is beginning to be regarded as unwise. In fact, a number of believers in Miss Borden's innocence are asserting that a mistake has been made by their allies. This mistake lies in the fact that there has been too great an anxiety to explain away every thing which points suspiciously towards Miss Borden. For instance, it has been said that the prisoner was on almost affectionate terms with her father and stepmother, while the government makes no bones of insisting that it has abundant evidence to prove that exactly the contrary is true.

In the effort to give Miss Borden the benefit of every doubt some people have gone too far, and have thus created doubts which did not extist until they undertook their defence.

At 7 o'clock last night an old man with lumbering tread, a basket in his hands and a dozen gamins at his heels walked into Court square from the direction of Borden street. He did not notice the boys; he is too much accustomed to notoriety to be annoyed at trifles now. He entered the guard-room wearledly and waited. It was John V. Morse. He had brought Lizzie's supper. He expected to visit his niece, the marshal having allowed him to do so earlier in the day. The captain of the night watch took the basket without a word. The old man didn't care to argue the question. He simply sat down in the guard-room to await the return of the basket.

In the interval he talked horse with a friend, but was inclined to give murder topics a wide berth. He hoped—incidentally—that the perpetrator of the crime would eventually be brought to justice, and said—mechanically—that it was a lamentable affair. He wondered if the police had ever found the right key which Andrew Borden always carried, and added that he had changed the lock on the door of the Borden house, not caring to sleep in a house to which so many keys were afloat. He had been in New Bedford all day, and was tired—very tired.

He had begun to speculate on the effect of the advance in electrical science on horse flesh when Capt. Desmond arrived with the lunch basket. The old man took it, lumbered out of the guard-room and started on the back trail with the street arabs in his wake.

A citizen watched the old man disappear across the square with no small show of interest.

"Andrew Borden," he said, thoughtfully, "was a man who talked little, unless the subject was of deep interest to him. You did all the talking. He did the listening.

"Let's see now! Mr. Morse went over to the farm that day after eggs, didn't he? The day of the murder, I mean. Did you ever know that when Andrew Borden wanted eggs or anything else from the farm he used to tie a note to the empty milkcan which the Swede used to call for? No? Well, that's the case. It's odd that he should have asked Mr. Morse to get the eggs on that particular day, isn't it? Rather lucky for that Swede and the foreman at the farm that they didn't happen to be at the house that particular morning, too; don't you think? They'd have been strung up to the nearest lamp-post.

"Did you know that the man used to come to the Borden house in the mornings about 11 o'clock? No? Well, that's the case. Didn't come that morning. Lucky for him. Wasn't it?

"Ever notice how long a minute is? No? Well, just look here a moment," and the citizen took out his watch and gazed at the second-hand until it had crept around the minute circle.

"There! Quite a long time, isn't it? Thirteen minutes! Why, man, a great deal can be done in 13 minutes.

"Know Cunningham, the newsdealer? Well, when he went into the paint shop at the corner of Borden street to give the alarm, he noticed that the clock there told ten minutes of 11. The work had been done then. It was 11 15 before Officer Allen got there. That's a good twenty-five minutes, isn't it? Clock may have been wrong? That's true. Let's go up and look at that clock."

We went up and looked at the clock. It was two minutes fast.

"Forget to wind it sometimes," the owner said, "but it's never more than five minutes out of the way."

"Well," the citizen resumed, "I'm only pointing out a few of the strange things about the case. There are some. There are a great many others."

This is only new evidence of the ceaseless thinking Fall River people direct toward the tragedy and its many inexplicable features. The citizen, "Circumstances," and all others, for that matter, trouble John V. Morse little. He accounted for his time to the minute, almost. The police paid an eloquent tribute to the strength of his alibi when they placed him under $500 bonds and called off the shadows in citizen's clothes which dogged his footsteps previous to the arrest.

A man named Barrett is the latest crank who is worried over being the Bordens' murderer. He came to police headquarters in Fall River yesterday afternoon and said he had been staying at the Richardson House and the people there had accused him of the crime. He pointed to a vacant place on the pavement, and said it was crowded with his pursuers. The man's brain was evidently wild with drink, and he was locked up.

WEATHER INDICATIONS.

SHOWERS AND FOG.

WASHINGTON, Aug. 24.—For the 24 hours from 8 a. m. to-day: For Massachusetts, Rhode Island and Connecticut, showers Thursday; showers in western Massachusetts to-day or to-night; fog on the coast Thursday morning; southeasterly winds.

BODY FOUND IN MILL RIVER

Identified as John Hobbs, who Strayed from the Taunton Insane Asylum.

TAUNTON, Aug. 24.—The body of a man about 50 years old was found in Mill river last night. It was identified as that of John Hobbs, a patient of the lunatic hospital, who strayed away a week ago and could not be found.

HOME MATTERS.

PERSONAL.—Andrew Ingraham of this city and Messrs. T. A. Taber and Lucius F. Alden of Brockton have been appointed by the Third Regiment Association to compile resolutions and engross the records of the dead members. Reports will be rendered annually.

George E. Dunn has resigned his place in the choir of the Unitarian church, his work in Fall River demanding all his attention.

Steve Cory of this city has received a flattering offer to play with the "Pay Train" Co. the coming season.

DON'T FORGET the Congressional caucuses to-night and vote for Randall delegates.

WEDDING ANNIVERSARY.—Mr. and Mrs. J. W. Robertson celebrated their fifteenth wedding anniversary at their residence 69½ Allen street, last evening. They were the recipients of many costly presents. A collation was served, after which the guests enjoyed themselves until a late hour.

VOTE FOR Randall delegates at the caucuses at 7 30 this evening.

LUNATIC LOCATED.—William Seymour, one of the men who escaped from the Taunton asylum, is enjoying a peaceful sojourn at Tiverton.

DON'T FORGET the Congressional caucuses to-night and vote for Randall delegates.

MURDEROUS ASSAULT.

Methodist Minister at East Harwich Struck with a Rock.

Blow on the Head Rendered Victim Unconscious for Hours.

Life of Rev. David Chambers Threatened by Anonymous Letters.

The little village of East Harwich is again stirred to the utmost depths of excitement by a deperate attempt to murder the popular pastor of the little old fashioned church known as "the old sounding board," Rev. David Chambers. It will be remembered that about two years ago there was a great sensation in the place, caused by the reported intimacy between Deacon Jonathan Buck and the young and attractive wife of Deacon Smalley. Also, that the latter was reported to have made a will in her favor, and was soon after taken suddenly and dangerously ill, and that the church members took the matter up and preferred charges against Deacon Buck which resulted in his dismissal from the church of which he had for years been organist and chorister.

His being expelled from the church created a deal of bad feeling, and his adherents have persistently refused to attend divine service there since. It is said that Deacon Buck has never become reconciled to the verdict of dismissal, and that he has vowed vengeance upon the church and openly expressed an intention of destroying its peace and prosperity, "even if it should have to be done in ashes."

Not long ago the Methodist conference settled Rev. David Chambers over this parish, in connection with the parish at North Harwich. He is a rather young man of considerable ability, and is doing a good work in harmonizing the differences between the church members, and by kind words and judicious acts is winning back into the fold many friends of the former deacon. On July 5 there came in his mail an envelope bearing the postmark of "Fremont, Neb., July 3, 8 30 a. m." It was unsealed and had a 1-cent stamp on it. He supposed it was a circular and carelessly opened it. He was astounded to find it a threatening and slanderous epistle. ordering him to leave town on penalty of forfeiting his life if he remained. It also stated that the house where he boarded was a house of assignation, and that his wife would be classed as an inmate if she remained there.

It was such a scurrilous letter that he destroyed it and did not mention the matter to any one, but he kept the envelope, bearing the postmark as above, and also on the back the postmark of the East Harwich office as received July 5. He did not seriously mind the affair till about a week ago, when he received another letter in the same kind of an envelope, unsealed, and again postmarked "Fremont, Nebraska," and addressed as before, "The Rev. David Chambers, East Harwich, Mass.," and evidently written in a disguised hand as before. This letter gave him 24 hours' notice to leave town, and said, "If you don't get out you will be helped out."

He destroyed both envelope and letter, but mentioned the affair to some intimate friends cautioning them not to make it public, as he did not wish to arouse any feeling over the matter.

Monday evening, as he took his seat at the supper table his mail was handed him, and it contained a sealed letter postmarked "Harwich, Mass., Aug 22," and directed as the others were, and in the same disguised handwriting. It made him a little nervous as he looked at the Harwich postmark and found that the anonymous writer was getting nearer home. He became still more uneasy after opening it and reading as follows:

CHAMBERS—If you have received a previous letter of warning you must be guided by it or take the consequences. This is final.

He showed it to Mrs. Chase, the lady with whom he boarded, and soon after started for the post office to mail some letters. He was met on the way by a daughter of Isaac Kendrick and invited to spend the evening at her house in company with several other guests. He consented to let his mail wait until morning and returned with Miss Kendrick to her father's house.

While they were walking along the path between the two houses, past the garden, Miss Kendrick was frightened by the sudden appearance of what seemed to be the form of a man among the corn, close beside her. Mr. Chambers is a little hard of hearing and did not notice the noise and she did not speak to him of it. About 9 30 some young men going down the street noticed a man skulking among the corn. Mr. Chambers, after accompanying some ladies home to the next house, crossed the street to his boarding place at about 9 45, and, passing in by the front of the house, went around to the side door. It was dark under the trees, and as he reached out to grasp the knob he heard footsteps close behind him and partly turned his head toward the street. Suddenly he felt something strike him in the back of his neck, and that was the last he knew for hours.

Mrs. Zebina Chase, with whom Rev. Mr. Chambers boards, says she was sitting in the sitting-room at 9 55 that night, when she heard Mr. Chambers' step outside, and as he took hold of the knob it seemed to shake and partly unlatch. She started to go to the door when it opened toward her, being pushed violently inward by the full weight of Mr. Chambers falling against it. He fell into her arms, and her daughter came to her assistance, and together they pulled him into a chair.

She ran to the front door and shouted across the street: "Mr. Isaac and Willie, come over here, quick; somebody has killed the minister."

Mr. Kendrick and his son hurried to Mrs. Chase's house and found Mr. Chambers had been struck a terrific blow on the back of the neck with a stone, just at the base of the brain, knocking him senseless.

Dr. Patterson of Harwich was sent for and he arrived in about an hour. The unfortunate man then began to regain consciousness, and his first words were:

"It's too bad that I should suffer for what other people have done."

He hardly spoke again till morning.

Mr. Kendrick went outside with a lantern and searched for the missile which had been used, and soon found it near the platform. It was a flat stone weighing just three pounds, and the man who hurled it evidently stood close behind his victim, and struck him a tremendous glancing blow, as there is a large dent in the door casing where it struck as it fell, and it also knocked the paint off the threshhold when it dropped to the ground.

Dr. Ball of Boston, who is summering on Cape Cod, said: "The pastor narrowly escaped concussion of the brain, which would have been the result if it had struck him an inch higher. He thinks Mr. Chambers will recover. Who did the villain enclose his letters to in Fremont, Neb., to act as a confederate by remailing them to East Harwich? is a question that agitates many minds. The handwriting is the same on the envelope mailed at Fremont as on the one mailed at Harwich, and the final threat is in the same hand. It very strongly resembles the writing on a postal card received from an irate man in Harwich by a Boston reporter during the excitement occasioned by the full account printed of the scenes and incidents connected with the Deacon Smalley's wife affair of two years ago. No arrests have been made as yet, but the excitement is at fever heat and there is no telling what the outcome may be. There is talk of tarring and feathering and riding on a rail.

SPONTANEOUS COMBUSTION

Causes a Blaze at F. A. Sowle's Residence This Morning.

An alarm from box 23 at about 7 30 o'clock this morning called the district fire department to the residence of Frederick A. Sowle, No. 11 Florence street. The arrival of the apparatus was timely, as the fire which originated in a pile of split wood and kindlings in the southwest corner of the cellar, had gained considerable headway and had communicated to the floor timbers overhead. The fire did not break through the floor, although it worked its way through the partitions into the back entryway and china closet. All the furniture and the piano which were on the lower floor were removed before the arrival of the department by the crowd which had gathered and was but slightly injured, the only damage being by handling. The only plausible theory of the origin of the blaze is spontaneous combustion. The loss will probably not exceed $500 or $600 and is covered by insurance placed through the agency of the late Charles Almy.

DON'T NEGLECT to attend the caucuses this evening. Vote for the renomination of Congressman Randall.

THE LAND OF SUNSHINE.—*A Unique Country where the Skies are almost Never Clouded, while the air is Cool and Bracing, like Perpetual Spring.*—As an anomalous Southern resort, by reason of the fact that there one may escape Summer heat no less than Winter cold, New Mexico is rapidly becoming famous. Averaging throughout the entire territory 5600 feet in altitude above sea-level, and characterized by dry air which, unlike a humid atmosphere, is incapable of communicating heat, the temperature in midsummer remains at a delightfully comfortable degree through the day, and at night becomes invariably brisk and bracing. The sunshine is almost constant, yet the most violent out-of-door exertion may be undertaken without fear of distressful consequences. Sunstroke or prostration are absolutely unknown there. It is an ideal land for a Summer outing. Its climate is prescribed by reputable physicians as a specific for pulmonary complaints, and the medicinal Hot Springs at Las Vegas are noted for their curative virtues. The most sumptuous hotel in the West, the Montezuma, is located at these springs. Write to Jno. J. Byrne, 723 Monadnock Block, Chicago, for "The Land of Sunshine," an entertaining and profusely illustrated book descriptive of this region, the most picturesque and romantic in the United States.

READ THE CALL for Congressional caucuses to-night. Attend and vote for Randall delegates.

PATENTS have been granted to Adolphus F. Wyman of this city for pneumatic tire; William A. G. Ashley, assignor of two-thirds to J. M. Lawton, Jr., and A. T. Howland of this city, knob attachment; Peter Frazer, Plymouth, assignor to Atlas Tack Corporation of Massachusetts, machine for making spiral springs.

DON'T NEGLECT to attend the caucuses this evening. Vote for the renomination of Congressman Randall.

THE FIRE ALARM on the Harrington Memorial School building struck wrong this morning when box 23 was pulled in. The same thing occurred a few days ago when an alarm was pulled in from box 125.

READ THE CALL for Congressional caucuses to-night. Attend and vote for Randall delegates.

FRIENDS' ACADEMY.—The Fall term of the Friends' Academy opens Sept. 22, and catalogues are now ready. The courses of study embrace primary, advanced and college preparatory work. See special notice.

DON'T NEGLECT to attend the caucuses this evening. Vote for the renomination of Congressman Randall.

OUR STOCK of furnishing goods is going fast at prices we sell for; $3 hats for $2, Lamson & Hubbard, Greenoble & Co. and other manufacturers. Wamsutta Clothing Co.

READ THE CALL for Congressional caucuses to-night. Attend and vote for Randall delegates.

NO CLEW.—Competition as well as ladies who wear good shoes have no clew as to how Buchell can sell a Vici kid, hand-sewed Oxford, for 98c. Read ad., 5th page.

READ THE CALL for Congressional caucuses to-night. Attend and vote for Randall delegates.

JOURNEYMAN PLUMBERS will hold a meeting in Neptune Hall, Market and Pleasant streets, this evening. A large attendance is requested.

VOTE FOR Randall delegates at the caucuses at 7 30 this evening.

HELP US MOVE.--How? By buying infants' wear, ladies' furnishings, &c., at the lowest prices ever offered. H. B. Diman, proprietor, 19 Purchase street.

DON'T FORGET the Congressional caucuses to-night, and vote for Randall delegates.

FINANCIAL SUCCESS.—Our mark-down sale has already proved a financial success to the crowds who are carrying away the bargains. Buchell's ad., 5th page.

VOTE for Randall delegates at the caucuses at 7 30 this evening.

ALL OF OUR children's suits to be closed out at a great discount. Children's pants, waists and caps to be closed out regardless of cost. Wamsutta Clothing Co.

DON'T FORGET the Congressional caucuses to-night, and vote for Randall delegates.

BARGAIN DAY.—A small army of women took possession of the sidewalk in front of Whiting & Co's store this morning waiting for admission to the silk remnant sale.

VOTE for Randall delegates at the caucuses at 7 30 this evening.

OUR LEASE EXPIRES Oct. 1, we must close out our stock, everything must be sold at once. Wamsutta Clothing Co.

READ THE CALL for Congressional caucuses to-night. Attend and vote for Randall delegates.

DOWN THEY GO.—Waltham watches $4.95. Five-year chains $1.25. Last week of closing sale. J. S. Kelley & Son, 15 Purchase street.

DON'T NEGLECT to attend the caucuses this evening. Vote for the renomination of Congressman Randall.

ONE OF THE UNFORTUNATES have got to move; stock to be closed at ridiculous prices. 19 Purchase street.

DON'T FORGET the Congressional caucuses to-night, and vote for Randall delegates.

NOW IS THE TIME to invest in suits and Fall overcoats. We must close them out regardless of cost. Wamsutta Clothing Co.

DON'T NEGLECT to attend the caucuses this evening. Vote for the renomination of Congressman Randall.

HAND-SEWED Oxford Ties $2.00. Devoll's.

VOTE FOR Randall delegates at the caucuses at 7 30 this evening.

WEARINESS overcome by Hood's Sarsaparilla.

COLD FACTS!

There are Times

WHEN MONEY EXPENDED IS MONEY SAVED.

In no greater degree can this be realized than in the outlay of a few dollars in our

WALL PAPER DEPT.

Here we have beautiful goods in abundance, but because carried over from a previous season, we sell them at a price which is only nominal.

TRY US AND SEE.

C. F. WING,

34 to 40 Purchase st.

WHITING & CO.

Great Special Sale

—OF—

SILK REMNANTS,

Direct from the mill, commences WEDNESDAY morning, the 24th, at 9 o'clock.

We have purchased from the largest silk mill in the United States their entire accumulations of PRINTED SILK REMNANTS. 5000 yards to be sold.

Lot 1 will be sold first. Pieces made up in packages for dresses, skirts and Waists.

Lot 2, after first lot is sold, will be from 4 yards to 1-2 yard remnants, and all to be sold at one price, just 39 CENTS PER YARD, and all new styles this season, and never sold at less than $1 per yard; and that is the price to-day from the piece, but these are the short lengths called remnants. We have matched up dress patterns, skirts and waists; the balance for dress trimmings and fancy work.

Our store will not open that day until half past 8 o'clock. Be on hand, as you all know how quick they have been sold in former years. At this low price the sale will be for Cash.

OUTING SHIRTS!

OUTING SHIRTS!

You can never have too many OUTING SHIRTS!

Our low prices will help you out. Quality exceptional.

Good Shirts for $1 and $1.25, laundered collars and cuffs.

Another lot of the popular blue Madras, all sizes, $1.50.

Better come at once, They're going fast.

OUTING SHIRTS!

J. & W. R. WING & CO.,

133 UNION STREET.

OUTING SHIRTS!

THE CRESCENT!

22 Purchase St.

SILK GLOVES MARKDOWN.

Black and Colors, 19c.

Gents' Hose.

Fashionable shades, 25 cents. Hermsdorf stainless black, spliced heel and toe, 25c.

An excellent variety of 5c. Handkerchiefs both white and fancy borders.

A new lot of Wrappers in medium shades, also Indigo Blue $1.00 each. Good night dress 50c.

RIBBONS.

We don't *begin* to tell you *how much* we have *marked down* our line of Ribbons, but come and see for yourself.

We will close out our Gingham Dresses for children at *cost.* Sizes from 4 to 10 years of age.

Gloves, 15, 25, 37, 50c.

Corsets, a good corset for 39c.

An X-L-ent Corset for 50c.

A very nice Summer Corset, C-B a la Spirite, price $1.25.

Corsets at all prices.

Having removed our entire stock from the Old Stand at corner of County and High streets, we shall be pleased to see our old friends and patrons at our new quarters, 22 Purchase street, known as THE CRESCENT.

The Evening Standard.

ESTABLISHED FEBRUARY, 1850.

NEW BEDFORD, THURSDAY, AUGUST 25, 1892.

TWO CENTS.

HASKELL & TRIPP.

To-morrow, FRIDAY, Aug. 26th, store opens at 8 o'clock, closes at 1 o'clock.

The last of the Friday half-holidays.

That you've appreciated these Friday sales is proven by the steadily-increasing business. Our books showed more money taken last Friday, than at any previous sale. But we're ambitious. To-morrow must show even better results, and to that end we shall offer a most remarkable collection of bargain attractions.

1st attraction: Cotton Dress Goods.

We shall close out all cotton dress goods after this manner: Challies, formerly 5c., for 3c. Suez cloths and printed Bedford cords, formerly 10c., for 5c.

Elegant styles, finest quality Canton Pongees, formerly 12½c., for 6¼c.

2d attraction: Straw Hats.

Every straw hat must go. A collection of women's black and navy shade hats shall go at 10c. each. Every other straw hat at exactly *one half former price.*

3d attraction: Parasols.

Any parasol may be taken at *one half former price.* Stop and think; this means that the richest creation of the parasol maker can be bought at the price of ordinary goods. This offer should be appreciated to the extent that not a parasol would remain unsold by noon.

4th attraction: Boys' Clothing.

Your boy needs a suit when school opens; here's your chance. We have 54 suits in assorted patterns and sizes from 4 to 14 years, made from strictly all wool cloths; these formerly sold for $3.69, $4.50; $5.00, $6.00. Bring the boy and fit him from this lot *at $2.89 the suit.*

5th attraction: Boilers.

A small lot copper wash boilers, worth $2.50, to close at $1.59.

6th attraction: Flowers.

A lot of millinery flowers and wreaths, some of which are slightly tumbled, formerly 25c. and 37c, now go at 5c. each.

7th attraction: Jackets.

All remaining Spring Jackets and Blazers have received marching orders. Among them can be found a good line of sizes for Ladies and Misses, all well made from good cloths, in tans, blacks and navys, and formerly sold for $5.00, $7.50, $10.00. Many of them are just right for Fall wear, but our winter stock is daily arriving: we must have room. Take your pick at $1.50 each.

8th attraction: Silk Vests.

What are left of our printed pongee and fancy china silk vests, formerly $1.00, $1.25, $1.50, shall go at 25c. each.

Don't be disappointed if you come here at 9 o'clock and find some of these attractions gone. They will be ready at 8 o'clock, and you must be prompt, if you desire the best choice.

As usual at these sales:

Every sale final.

No goods to be brought back or exchanged.

No goods sent out on approval.

HASKELL & TRIPP.

Department Stores,

Purchase and William Streets.

A DRUNKEN CHIEF OF POLICE.

Head of the Nantucket Force Suspended from Duty.

Jamaica Ginger for Sickness the Excuse He Offers.

Friends Among the Officials in Favor of His Reinstatement.

[Special Dispatch.]

NANTUCKET, Aug. 25.—John Roberts, for three years chief of the Nantucket police, has probably reached the end of his career as head guardian of the town's peace. Four or five days ago he began to get drunk, and by Sunday he had so far succeeded that the patrolmen over whom he has watched for the last 24 months had to watch over him to prevent his becoming "too noisy." Sunday forenoon he ordered Officer Hamblin to tell every member of the police force to report to their chief at once. When the men assembled in response to this unusual summons they found Mr. Roberts in a hilarious condition and the estimation of his official anthority greatly increased as the result of his morning's spree. He delivered an oration to his men in which he declared that he was going to institute then and there a grand raid on all the hotels and prevent Sunday selling. He assigned one man to each of the public houses and said that he himself would go to the Surf Side Hotel and make the bar of that establishment a useless institution.

The officers asked him if he had consulted the police committee, and he informed them that the board of selectmen and police committee were not in it, and when asked for the necessary search wareants he became indignant, said that he was running the business alone and that they must simply raid and say nothing. Naturally every man refused to obey orders and were told by Roberts that the town would have no further use for them. Then he told them to stay about the station and report to him every 30 minutes. This they did until he became sober enough to ask them what they meant by bothering him in reporting so often. At night he was drunk again, and in this condition was found at the station when he should have been on duty. Monday he was suspended and last evening there was an investigation of the matter by the board of selectmen.

At the investigation the testimony of five patrolmen was taken, as well as the statement by the Chief himself. The sum and substance of all the testimony was that Chief of Police John Roberts had been on Sunday last so drunk that he was not fit to be seen on the streets.

In answer to the charges, Roberts says that on the day and evening in question he was sick and obliged to drink Jamaica ginger, and that was all. Then he took his oath that he had not touched liquor for 12 months. This is, however, his sixth offence of drunkenness since he became chief three years ago. But that makes no difference to several members of the board, who were so anxious to defend and reinstate the chief that they forgot their duty as investigators at times, and acted more as counsel for the defence. This spirit showed itself more after the testimony had been taken and the board had gone into executive session.

The Board is about evenly divided upon the question as to whether to reinstate or discharge Roberts. The action of Chairman of Police Committee Henry Riddell in suspending Roberts is looked upon as being very commendable, but his brother members of the board, who are on the defence, even went so far as to denounce Mr. Riddell for suspending the man at all. But it is not law for the man that causes these selectmen to defend Roberts, and pity is not the strongest motive in the case of them all at any rate.

Nothing was decided last night and the question was continued until Monday night when it is thought the board will agree as to whether Roberts should be allowed to retain his present position, be set back to the office of patrolman, or discharged from the force altogether. His suspension will continue until the board settles the case. That he was not bounced then and there at the investigation is a subject of much comment and no reason or excuse can be given for a continuance of the case until Monday night.

WEATHER INDICATIONS.

THUNDER STORMS.

WASHINGTON, Aug. 25.—For the 24 hours from 8 a. m. to-day: For Massachusetts, Rhode Island and Connecticut, thunder storms to-day; clearing Friday; cooler in the interior; fresh to brisk southeasterly wind to-day shifting to northwesterly Friday.

RAIN.

BOSTON, Aug. 25.—Local forecast for New England until Friday night: Rain, probably thunder storms during the evening or night; fair Friday afternoon or night; slight changes in temperature, wind easterly to southerly.

TO PREVENT CHOLERA'S SPREAD.

Illinois Board of Health Wires Authorities at Washington.

SPRINGFIELD, Ill., Aug. 25.—The state board of health has wired to Dr. Wyman at Washington as follows: "In view of the westward spread of cholera in Europe the Illinois state board of health request that you extend the scope of your order of the 18th instant so as to include all arrivals from European ports, England included. It is also urged that the order be made operative forthwith. The services of this board are at your disposal in any manner you may indicate.

PARIS, Aug. 25.—The condition of many of the Jewish emigrants who pass through this city is such that should cholera break out among them it would find a fertile field. Within a month 1000 Jews, refugees from Russia have passed through Paris, mostly bound to the United States.

ST. PETERSBURG, Aug. 25.—The official cholera report shows yesterday 5679 new cases and 2743 deaths. The disease is spreading in this city, but the people show little concern about it. Though the number of new cases reported is large, the death rate is smaller. The doctors say the disease is less virulent, and that in addition to this the number of deaths has been lessened by the better treatment of the patients.

Shocking State of Filth and Overcrowding.

LONDON, Aug. 25.—The *Standard's* dispatch from Vienna says: "A recent inspection of the lower quarters of this city revealed a shocking state of filth and overcrowding. Tons and tons of rotten meat, sausages and fruit in provision stores and markets was seized. The law dealing with these offences is too lenient. Should cholera reach Austria-Hungary the number of victims will run into tens of thousands."

Oldest Printer in the West.

BURLINGTON, Ia., Aug. 25.—Enoch May, the oldest printer in the West, died here yesterday aged 91. He was born in Boston in 1801 and was connected with the early journalism of that city. He came here in 1840.

LIZZIE ON TRIAL.

Preliminary Proceedings of Borden Murder Case.

Court Room Was Thronged by an Eager Audience.

Examination of Witnesses Begun by District Attorney.

Medical Examiner Dolan the First to Testify.

The Story of the Autopsy of the Murdered Couple.

Most Ghastly Sight He Ever Saw in His Experience.

Minute Description of Blood Spots on the Wall.

Surveyor Kieran Instructed to Make Additions to His Plans.

[Special Dispatch.]

FALL RIVER, Aug. 25.—It is almost inconceivable to an outsider that so much interest should be manifested in the preliminary proceedings of the examination of Lizzie A. Borden for the murder of her father.

The Central police station was surrounded before 8 o'clock by men, women and children anxious to gain admittance to the Second District Court room. The mob besieged each door and begged the officer to let them in, but only in case of privileged persons were their prayers listened to. The seats in the court-room were nearly all filled early, and if one-fiftieth of the crowd outside had been let in, the seats and standing-room would have been overflowed.

Just before 9 o'clock a hack with drawn curtains drove up to the public entrance to the court room. The spectators lining each sidewalk made a frantic rush to the door and for a moment or two they overcame the resistance of the officers and filled the doorway as well as sidewalk and made locomotion impossible. Marshal Hilliard appeared in the door, waved his arms and the police charged and pushed the crowd on the run back to the north sidewalk or east and west. The door of the carriage was opened and Emma Borden, the loving and faithful sister, got out, went up stairs. The officer in the corridor on the second floor respectfully drew back and permitted her to enter Matron Russell's room, where she found Lizzie sitting in a rocking chair by one of the north windows. Emma went up at once and stooped over to kiss her sister, but met with no answering response. Lizzie greeted her with a cordial hand grasp and at once commenced talking on matters probably of mutual interest, but having no bearing, however remote, on the double tragedy. Lizzie was calm and collected, and in this she presented a marked contrast to her tearful sister. After a short personal conversation the talk became general, others present joining in till the time came for the summons to the court room.

The court-room, even during the transaction of minor business, was crowded to repletion. Fully half of the audience was composed of young ladies from 16 to 23 years of age, and they sat there an hour listening to the proceedings and taking their initiatory degree in district court matters. On the north side of the room Bridget Sullivan, soberly attired in dark clothes, occupied a seat next to Inspector Desmond.

At 10 03 the court took a recess until 10 20, and almost immediately after the crowd deepened in the room, while the court officers had hard work to keep the necessary space clear. Lizzie Borden came into the court room with her intimate friends and occupied a seat close to her counsel. She was dressed in the same suit of blue she wore on Monday and did not seem abashed at the large crowd present.

District Attorney Knowlton at 10 30, without any preliminaries, proceeded to the examination. Dr. William P. Dolan of Fall River, medical examiner, was the first witness. He said: I have had a good deal of experience in autopsies; I examined the body of Andrew J. Borden about 20 minutes of 12 on the forenoon of Aug. 4. It was on the sofa on the north side of the sitting room. The head of the sofa was to the west. A Prince Albert coat was folded up and placed on the afghan, and on the top of that was the sofa pillow. The body was lying on the right side with the face toward the kitchen door. I examined the body. Later in the day I removed the stomach and sealed it in a tight jar. I saw the body of Mrs. Borden in a room up stairs at the same time I saw Mr. Borden's. Her body was lying on the floor, face down. She was dressed in a calico dress; a silk handkerchief was lying on the floor near by, such a handkerchief as is used when a person is dusting. I cannot say if the handkerchief was cut. There was blood on the handkerchief.

Robert C. Kieran testified to the correctness of a plan which was drawn by him of the Borden house. It was on the scale of a quarter of an inch to the foot. He gave measurements taken of the yard and fence on the Borden premises. Blood spots on the floor west of the sofa in the sitting-room were described, and witness said there were blood spots on a picture five feet four inches from the sofa. On the same wall as the picture 18 inches away were blood spots. From the house to the fence on the north side of the Borden premises the distance is 15 feet 4 inches. From the house to the nearest end of the barn is 14 feet 3 inches.

Witness was cross-examined by Andrew J. Jennings, who with Melvin O. Adams of Boston represents defence. He said: The sofa was not in the sitting room when I got to the Borden house. It was brought in by Dr. Dolan's orders. There was a blood spot on the architrave of the door in the sitting room which leads to the kitchen. I did not notice that this spot indicated any direction when it struck the door. The spot was within six inches of the jamb of the door. The blood on the picture was called to my attention by Dr. Dolan, who wanted me to measure it. I noticed no other spot on the picture. The spot I found was difficult to see until I turned the picture to the light. This spot was an elongated one. I do not know if the elongation was upward or not. From the appearance of the spot I thought it had been thrown from the sitting room.

Here counsel called for the sketch of the piece of wood with the blood spot upon it. After looking it over carefully he continued the cross-examination of the witness. The witness said: The spot was on the side of the door frame nearest the parlor and about three inches from the end of the door frame.

The witness continued: There was a large pile of boards in the yard at the Borden residence up against the east fence that I did not put upon the plan simply because I forgot it.

The witness was asked if from anything he observed there was anything to prevent an ordinary man from going up on the pile and right over the fence.

The question was promptly objected to by the district attorney and was ruled out.

In answer to other questions witness said that the pile of boards was an ordinary one, regularly placed and laid up against the fence.

The witness was instructed during the noon recess to make a plan of the kitchen and measure the height of the ceiling and locate the pile of boards and place them upon the plan.

Dr. Dolan was then recalled, and he testified as follows: When I removed the sheet from Mr. Borden's body it was the most ghastly sight I have ever seen. There were ten wounds upon the left side of the head and face. The largest one was 4 1-2 inches in length, and the other wounds were of various sizes, running down to 1 1-2 inches in length. The largest one was one which commenced on the left side of the head and ran down to the lower jaw. It had cut through the left side of the skull, taking out a large piece, had cut the eye ball in half and also the cheek bone. Above the left ear there was a crushing wound which carried the skull with it into the brain. When I uncovered the body all these wounds were apparent. Some of them were flesh wounds, and some had penetrated deeply into the bones. Some of them made indentations only, and some went right through the bone. A week later I made an examination of the vital organs, and saw and found nothing that would have occasioned death.

He thought death was due to a shock, and he used the word in a medical sense.

When I first went to the house, continued the witness, one side of Mr. Borden's face was resting on the sofa, which was an old-fashioned one. It was 11 45 in the morning when I went to the house. None of the blood about the body was clotted, and blood was oozing from the wounds. There was but little blood on the clothing. The principal flow of blood was through the lounge on to the floor. Blood was dropping through, but not in great quantities. Mr. Borden had probably been dead not over half an hour.

There were 86 clots of blood on the walls in the room where Mr. Borden lay. The highest ones were 3 feet 7 inches from the floor.

At this point the district attorney presented the plans which had been prepared by Mr. Kieran to the witness, and the attention of the court and Mr. Jennings.

Witness resumed. The blood spots described an arc of a circle, beginning no more than 3 1-4 inches from Mr. Borden's head on the wall paper. On the paper above the lounge the highest spot was 6 feet 1 3-4 inches above the floor. The lowest spot was 6 feet and 1-2 inch. On the picture there were 58 spots which shot directly upward toward the east. On the moulding behind the lounge were spots, one 7 1-4 inches above the mop-board. On the carpet at the head of the lounge were two pools of blood. On the parlor door at the head of the lounge were two spots of blood. I saw two spots on the ceiling above the lounge, but do not think they were caused by human blood.

The wounds on Borden's face were made by a sharp instrument. I should say the wounds were caused by a hatchet or sharp axe. The crushing of the skull was done with some instrument which would give a leverage. I do not believe the thickness of the skull at the point where Mr. Borden's wounds were made was over 1-12 of an inch.

Mr. Knowlton asked witness the relative amount of force necessary to be used to crush the skull at the point where the blows on Borden's head were found.

Mr. Jennings objected, but the objection was overruled.

Witness said an ordinary healthy person might deliver a blow which would fracture the skull of another.

Mr. Adams objected that the question was not answered by witness.

Witness then said: An ordinarily healthy person with a four or five-pound hatchet could fracture a skull with a moderate blow.

Witness resumed. Mr. Borden was in excellent physical condition. Mrs. Borden was lying on her face on the floor. As the body was lying we could see there were wounds, and closer examination showed seven

[Continued in Later Edition. Fourth Page.]

HOME MATTERS.

WEDDING AT WAQUOIT.

Dr. Charles Warren White of Fairhaven Married to Miss Eliza W. Childs.

The home of Mrs. William Childs of Waquoit was the scene of a brilliant wedding on Aug. 23d, when her daughter Eliza Weston was married to Dr. Charles Warren White of Fairhaven.

At 1 30 Miss Childs, leaning on the arm of her brother, William Childs of this city, entered the room. They were preceded by little Winthrop Sargent, nephew of the bride, as page, and Misses Etta L. Chapman and Sarah Bailey as bridesmaids. Four young ladies holding white ribbons formed an aisle from the entrance to the bower of ferns where the bridal couple were to stand. Dr. White was attended by Joseph K. Nye of Fairhaven as best man.

The Episcopal marriage service was read by Rev. Thomas Bell of South Dartmouth. The bride was dressed in a charming gown of cream crepe de chine trimmed with Brussels point caught up with sprays of stephanotis. The bridesmaids wore dotted muslin with pink ribbons and carried bouquets of Catherine mermet roses and maiden-hair fern. Master Sargent was dressed in black velvet and pink carrying the bride's bouquet of bride roses and ferns. The young ladies holding the white ribbon were prettily dressed in delicate colors. The sisters of the bride, Mrs. Ignatius Sargent amd Miss Alice Childs, with Mr. Hiram Baker, received. Mrs. Sargent wore black India silk trimmed with green silk and lace, and Miss Childs black India silk trimmed with rich lace and carried yellow roses.

The rooms were beautifully decorated with potted plants and cut flowers. The parlor was a bower of ferns, pinks and sweet peas. The skill of the florist and decorator was manifest in the arrangement of every variety of begonia in the room containing the wedding gifts. These were of silver, cut glass, fine table linen and dainty china.

A breakfast followed the ceremony. The bride's cake rested on a small table draped with flowers at one side.

At 4 33 the bridal couple left for a wedding trip, accompanied by showers of rice, and the best wishes of their many friends.

PERSONAL.—Capt. Oliveira of the Rapoza do Mar, which arrived in port yesterday from Brava, C. V. I., in ballast, with three cabin and three steerage passengers aboard, reports that the U. S. consul to the Cape Verd Islands, Henry Pease, intended to have taken passage with him for this city, but was unable to sail because of sickness.

W. L. Chadwick of this city, accompanied by his wife, is spending his vacation at Newport, R. I.

Rev. L. F. Shepardson of Norton has accepted an invitation to become pastor of the Baptist church in Chesham, N. H., and will commence there Aug. 28.

Rev. H. N. Jeter, pastor of the Shiloh Baptist church, Newport, has been requested by the executive board of the Virginia Seminary, located at Lynchburg, to accept the financial agency of that institution. Should Mr. Jeter accept he will resign his pastorate in Newport.

Misses Saxon and Saxley leave this city today on a vacation trip. They will visit North Conway, Fabyans and Intervale, N. H.

John Thuman of this city will go out in bark Gay Head as mate.

A. P. L[illegible]re, chief engineer of the Springfield fire department, is in the city to-day, the guest of Councilman Wilber.

SIXTY MILLION BUSHELS OF WHEAT — *A Bushel for Every Inhabitant of the United States. The Kansas Crop for '92.*—Never in the history of Kansas has that State had such bountiful crops as this year. The farmers cannot get enough hands to harvest the great crop, and the Santa Fe railroad has made special rates from Kansas City and other Missouri river towns, to induce harvest hands to go into the State. The wheat crop of the State will be from sixty to sixty-five million bushels, and the quality is high. The grass crop is made, and is a very large one; the early potatoes, rye, barley and oat crops are made, and are all large. The weather has been propitious for corn, and it is the cleanest, best looking corn to be found in the country to-day. Cheap rates will be made from Chicago, St. Louis and all points on the Santa Fe east of the Missouri river, to all Kansas points, on August 30 and September 27, and these excursions will give a chance for Eastern farmers to see what the great Sunflower State can do. A good map of Kansas will be mailed free upon application to Jno. J. Byrne, 723 Monadnock Block, Chicago, Ill., together with reliable statistics and information about Kansas lands.

KEEP YOUR EYE ON THE DATES.—Friday and Saturday, we shall open up another lot of those teas that we sold a short time ago for 27c. a pound. These teas are never sold less than 50c. a pound regular. We also wish to say that the price of Java coffee is also advancing, and some retailers are selling for 38c. and 40c. a pound; we shall continue the price of this coffee at 28c., or four pounds for $1. You all know what this tea and coffee is, as nearly every family in this city has used it. We have also just received another lot of those bottle pickles that are never sold at less than 10c., now only 6c. per bottle. White Cash Store, 134 Purchase street.

NO DOUBT IT IS GENUINE.—Connoisseurs from all parts of the country have examined the Stradivarius violin owned by E. T. Ryan and described in the *Standard* some time ago, and all unhesitatingly pronounce it a work of the old master. The instrument has been examined by Theodore Thomas, who is certain of its origin. An offer of $3000 has been refused for it.

JOURNEYMAN PLUMBERS will meet this evening at Neptune Hall. All are requested to be present. The meeting will be called at 8 o'clock sharp.

NATURALIZATION.—Michael Sheerin was admitted to citizenship in the Third District Court.

SANDCATCHER.—A sandcatcher has been put in at the northwest corner of Larch and Juniper streets.

"AYER'S HYGIENIC COFFEE" is prepared by M. S. Ayer of Boston, who is a vegetarian, and has made diet reform a study.

THE REGISTRARS OF VOTERS will begin their labors next week.

CALL AT NOONING'S and purchase a sailor at a price below any one in the city.

READ KNOWLES & Co's advertisement on the eighth page.

IT IS ASTONISHING the low price we are offering you on flowers at Nooning's.

METROPOLITAN CATALOGUE, Fall and Winter, now ready at Hutchinson's book store.

HOW THE BABY LAUGHS when he sees his Mellin's Food; he knows what is good.

FIVE-CENT HATS at Nooning's.

HAND-SEWED House Gaiters $1. Devoll's.

HOOD'S Sarsaparilla cures sick headache.

COLD FACTS!

There are Times

WHEN MONEY EXPENDED IS MONEY SAVED.

In no greater degree can this be realized than in the outlay of a few dollars in our

WALL PAPER DEPT.

Here we have beautiful goods in abundance, but because carried over from a previous season, we sell them at a price which is only nominal.

TRY US AND SEE.

C. F. WING,

34 to 40 Purchase st.

WHITING & CO.

THE Last Half Holiday CLOSES THIS WEEK FRIDAY.

We shall give our customers Friday Morning some Extra Bargains.

We have taken a big lot of our $1.00 French Dress Goods, in plain, mixed, stripes and plaids, and made one price on all at 50c. per yard.

A few pieces of all wool Challies, will be sold at 28c. per yard.

The balance of our Black French Satines, Brocaded, and figured, will be closed out at 25c. per yard.

23 more Children's Gingham dresses, go on sale at $1.00 and $1.25, regular $2.00 and $2.50 goods.

Ladies' Black and White shirt waists, fine ones, will be sold at 50c. a piece.

300 Ladies' colored bordered hemstitched handkerchiefs will be sold Friday, at 4c. a piece, cheap at 5c.

A few pair of $3.50 White Blankets, soiled, will be closed out at $2.50 per pair.

We have about 800 yards of those remnant silks left at 39c. per yard, we had such a rush for.

We shall continue the same low prices on Saturday on all our goods.

WHITING & CO.

J. V. SPARE,

Liberty Hall Building.

Wonderful bargains in 36 inch Unbleached Cotton at 5 1-2c. a yard.

Cottons never were lower than at present, and it is good policy to buy now.

Also a very good cotton at 5c. yard, full yard wide, and better than any cotton ever sold at this price,

5 CENTS A YARD.

Cleaning up a lot of Fancy Ginghams, Plaids and Stripes, fast colors, goods that have been selling at 10c., now 6 1-2c. yard.

Bleached Twilled Crash, regular 5c. goods, for a short time 4c. yard, or 3 3-4c. by the piece.

Waste Silk, 5c. box.

Job lot of Shell Hair Pins, at 37c. dozen. Some pins in the lot worth 10c. each.

J. V. Spare,

LIBERTY HALL BUILDING.

OUTING SHIRTS!

OUTING SHIRTS!

You can never have too many

OUTING SHIRTS!

Our low prices will help you out. Quality exceptional.

Good Shirts for $1 and $1.25, laundered collars and cuffs.

Another lot of the popular blue Madras, all sizes, $1.50.

Better come at once, They're going fast.

J. & W. R. WING & CO.,

133 UNION STREET.

OUTING SHIRTS!

OUTING SHIRTS!

The Evening Standard.

NEW BEDFORD, MASS.

THURSDAY EVENING, AUGUST 25.

THREE EDITIONS DAILY.

No. 87 Union Street.

PUBLISHED BY

E. ANTHONY & SONS.

INCORPORATED.

—TERMS—

Six Dollars a Year; Three Dollars for Six Months, in advance; Single Copies Two Cents.

FOR PRESIDENT:

BENJAMIN HARRISON

OF INDIANA.

FOR VICE-PRESIDENT:

WHITELAW REID

OF NEW YORK.

THE REPUBLICAN STANDARD,

☞ Issued this morning, contains all the local and general news of the past week, including fullest particulars of the Fall River tragedy as far as is known, embracing the action of Charles Peckham of Westport, who gives himself up to the Fall River authorities, acknowledging himself as the murderer of the Bordens and wants to be hanged immediately, his hallucination subsequently passes off and he is passed over to his friends, the hearing in the case resumed on Monday, Lizzie Borden arrives in Fall River and displays the same wonderful nerve, no evidence presented in the case, the hearing postponed until Thursday, the goverment not being ready; Anna Katharine Green, a writer of detective stories, believes Lizzie Borden innocent, and speaks in her behalf; lively town meeting in Fairhaven, which decided to sell its farm land, and where street improvements were considered; one command of the State navy will probably be located here; story of a jaunt along the picturesque shores of Long Pond; news from the Arctic, schooner Jane Gray released by the authorities and gone North, reported seizure of schooner Blakeley for seal poaching; taxation in Dartmouth, list of heavy tax-payers; meeting of the Board of Public Works, which talks of Mr. Smith's sewers, orders sewers laid in Cove and South First streets, and decides to extend South Second street southerly to Cove street; an interesting article on Marion's Celebrities, the Summer home of Rebecca Harding Davis and Mrs. M. G. Van Rensselaer; special meeting of the City Council, committee authorized to procure estimates for a new building for No. 5 Engine Company, and for alterations, with other minor business; letters from Gospel Grove Camp-Meeting at Cadman's Neck; letter from Cottage City, impressive services at the opening of the Methodist Camp-Meeting; letters from Onset Bay Grove Camp-Meeting, big Sunday and interesting speeches; complications over the sale of the Wyoming Mills, Fall River, straightened out; Farm, Garden and Home; Bible Lesson for next Sunday; District Court reports; correspondence; with editorials, ship news, markets, miscellaneous reading, etc.

For sale by all newsdealers in this city, and at our counters, in wrappers ready for mailing, at 4 cents per copy.

CONTENTS OF THIS EVENING'S STANDARD.

☞ The result of the Congressional caucuses last evening is not surprising. It was to be expected that Mr. Randall would receive the handsome vote he deserved and that he would have a solid delegation, but it is a matter of congratulation that after all the work and boasts of Mr. Greene's lieutenants the Fall River candidate made such a weak showing. The doings of the caucuses are fully reported in the *Standard's* news columns, and our readers will not be gratified to learn of the disorderly tactics resorted to by a hopeless minority in Ward One. New Bedford caucuses have been remarkably free from rowdyism and can dispense with it in the future. The good work for Mr. Randall commenced in this city last evening should be carried on in the Cape and island towns, and there is no doubt his friends will rally and see that Mr. Randall will go into the convention with an overwhelming majority.

☞ The special committee appointed by the last legislature to consider the expediency of revising the judicial system of the Commonwealth, so far as it relates to courts inferior to the superior court and courts of probate and insolvency, will meet at the State-House to-day and organize. This committee consists of Senators Fernald, McDonald, and Butler, and Messrs. Powers of Hyde Park, Ferren of Stoneham, Presho of Boston, Parker of Boston, Kidduff of Holyoke, O'Brien of Marlboro, Ruggles of Franklin, and Barney of New Bedford, of the house of Representatives. Senator McDonald, having been appointed by Gov. Russell on the gas commission, will be unable to serve, and his successor will probably be appointed by President Pinkerton at the meeting.

☞ It is thought that the widow of Gen. John A. Logan will be chosen President of the Woman's Relief Corps at the meeting in Washington next month. She has consented to the use of her name for this purpose.

☞ Terence V. Powderly's explanations in *The Knights of Labor Journal* respecting the Homestead troubles effectually disposes of the Democratic argument that increased Protection in the steel industry was at the bottom of the controversy between the Carnegies and their workmen. This is Mr. Powderly's refutation of Democratic claptrap:

Partisan papers are endeavoring to make political capital out of the terrible scenes which took place at Homestead the other day. The Democratic papers are vehement in their denunciation of the Republican party for enacting a Tariff law under which Protection was afforded to manufacturers. There is no love for workmen in the hearts of these editors; a desire to serve party interests alone actuates them. The McKinley bill reduced the duty on the articles manufactured at Homestead, and the Democratic papers, in asserting that the trouble at that point is due to the McKinley bill, are but condemning the very thing that they themselves advocate, and on which they base their claim to power—a reduction of the tariff.

☞ The friends of Samuel C. Darling, who are advocating his candidacy for the Lieutenant-Governorship, held a meeting last evening. It was decided to issue an address to Republicans of the State, asking their support for Mr. Darling. A committee of 25 was appointed to carry out this idea.

HOME MATTERS.

SUMMER HOUSE.—R. F. Raymond, Esq., of this city is soon to commence the erection of a cottage on Pine Island in Lake Winnepesaukee.

THE CITY PROPERTY COMMITTEE hold a meeting this evening to consider the sale of the dwelling house on Foster street and to advertise for bids for the construction of the new fire station.

NAVAL RESERVE.—At a meeting interested in the formation of a company of the Naval Reserves to be held in the Y. M. C. A. building this evening, definite action will probably be taken with regard to organization.

GRAY GABLES STATION.—The new station at Gray Gables, erected by the Old Colony, has been completed as regards its exterior. The station will be a great convenience to those calling on the Cleveland household.

THE NEW POST OFFICE.—The hard oil finish on the carved and panelled oak work in the new post office is completed, and workmen are to-day putting in the plate glass windows. The tiling of the corridors will be laid next week.

HIGHWAY ORDERED LAID OUT.—It is reported that the Plymouth county commissioners, in executive session, have ordered the layout of a highway across Long Neck to connect the Cohasset Narrows bridge at Buzzards Bay with the Point Independence bridge.

THE STREETS.—The squares at the corner of Middle and Cottage streets, at the corner of North and Cottage streets and at the corner of Sycamore and Cottage streets are being repaved.

Butler street is being macadamized.

Crosswalks on the square at the corner of Washington and Bonney streets have been put in.

DOUBTFUL IF THE ALVA REACHES PORT.—Lighter Elliott and pontoons have left Vineyard Haven for Pollock Rip, where an effort will be made to raise the Alva. Divers say it will be impossible to get the hull into a port, because the rivets have started. There are indications of heavy weather, and it is probable that work on the yacht will have to be abandoned for the present.

POLITICAL.—The first Plymouth senatorial nominating convention of the prohibition party will be held in Banquet Hall, Whitman, on Friday, Sept. 2, at 10 30 o'clock a. m. At 2 p. m. at the same place, the county and town committees will hold a conference and develop plans for the fall campaign. In the evening there will be a meeting to be addressed by several speakers in the interests of the party.

IN JUSTICE TO DRUGGISTS.—We are requested to say in justice to the local druggists that in whatever instances there are of their having gotten into trouble by the watchfulness of State Inspector McCaffrey, the compounds sold have been goods bought in marketable packages, and the composition of the contents have been unknown to the unfortunate dealers who sold them. The violation of the law thereby was unknown and entirely unintentional.

RUNAWAY.—Early this morning Henry Wall and wife of North Dartmouth were driving along Austin street, when at the corner of Cedar street the horse became frightened at electric car No. 72, about three lengths distant, and ran away. In turning sharply into Cedar street, the wagon was upset, Mr. and Mrs. Wall were thrown out and badly bruised. The seat, dasher, one wheel and the harness of the turnout were smashed, but the horse was captured unharmed.

CARDERS ON LABOR DAY.—At the special meeting of the Card and Picker Room Association, held Tuesday evening, it was decided to participate in the Labor Day parade, carriages to be provided for the women of the association. The board of officers and the collectors were chosen a committee to make the necessary arrangements. Arod B. Holloway, president of the Bricklayers' and Masons' Union and chairman of the Labor Day committee, has given President Connolly of the Card Room Association orders for as many badges as the association may require for the parade.

THE CONNOLLY LIQUOR CASE.—In the Fourth District Court, before Judge George D. Alden at Middleboro, yesterday, was heard the warmly contested liquor nuisance case from the Onset Bay Grove Spiritualists' camp ground. This is the case of Edward Connelly, or Galvin, who was arrested by the Wareham officers for conducting a liquor nuisance at the Central House on Central avenue, Onset Grove. At the time of his arrest he resisted the officers and succeeded in diverting their attention for a considerable time from the several illegal liquor sellers at different points about the grove, whereby the latter were allowed to find their way to the water front, embark in a catboat, sail away down the bay, and remain, up to the present time, unheard from. The hearing was continued.

FUNERAL.—The funeral of Katie Morrisey occurred this morning at St. Lawrence church and was largely attended by relatives and friends. Rev. Fr. Mahon officiated. The floral tributes were numerous and very beautiful. Among the offerings were the following: Pillow, inscribed Katie, father and mother; lyre, inscribed Sister, Brother Dave; cross and mound, Sister Lizzie; basket, Brother Will; wreath, Brother Frank; basket, Sister Annie; basket, Brother John; basket, Brother Harry; bouquet, baby; pillow, inscribed Rest in Peace, C. S. Irish; gates ajar, inscribed Our Shopmate, employes of Hathaway, Soule & Harrington; bouquet, Mrs. Helen Wilcox; crescent, Miss Nellie Cronin; basket, Mr. and Mrs. Clarke Greene; star, Rose, Lottie and Lillie Greene; cross, Max W. Sherman; bouquet, Andrew Hamilton; wreath, Aunt Rebecca; basket, Miss Minnie Morrison; basket, E. Edward Enos and Philip S. Briggs.

Steve Corey, Anthony Senna, Bartholomew Fury, Joseph Fagan, William J. Frawley and Harry McConville acted as pall bearers. Interment was in the family lot at St. Mary's cemetery, to which place the remains were followed by a long and imposing procession.

MR. CHAMBERS RECOVERING.

Chatham Authorities Have the Assault Case in Hand, and Will Act.

The village of East Harwich is wild over the attempt on the life of Pastor Chambers. There was quite a discussion in the neighborhood yesterday over the question as to whether the town officers of Harwich or of Chatham should be notified to take official action on the affair. The road just here is the dividing line between East Harwich and South Chatham, and the house in which Mr. Chambers resides is in the town of Chatham. It was finally decided to notify Charles Bassett, Esq., chairman of the board of selectmen of Chatham, of the occurrence, which was done.

Mr. Bassett has gone to Barnstable to confer with Judge Harriman, and will probably be guided by his advice in taking steps to run down the would-be assassin.

The wounded minister's condition is somewhat improved. He is partially regaining the use of his right arm, side and leg, which have been nearly paralyzed since he was struck, and he hopes before long to be able to resume his duties. He was to go on a vacation in September, but will have to forego that privilege. Mr. Chambers thinks the man stepped close up to him and intended to kill him. "It was a terrific blow," he said, "and if I had not at that instant stepped up on the upper step, thus elevating my head a little, he would have hit me a few inches higher, and that would have finished me."

Mr. Chambers was a member of the Quarry Street M. E. church when living in Fall River, and his family, consisting of a wife and three children, reside on the corner of Eastern avenue and Pleasant street in that city. He had a local license to preach for three years or more, and at the April conference was assigned to the East and North Harwich churches. His wife said yesterday that her husband was not in the best of health. He had been drawn around a shaft in a Providence mill some years ago, and had never entirely recovered from his injuries. One of his sons, aged 16, works in a factory and another helps his mother in a little store which the family owns. The daughter is with her father at Harwich. Rev. Mr. Brooks of the Quarry Street church, broke the news of the assault to Mrs. Chambers yesterday. She had just received a letter from her husband in which he seemed to be elated over the success of last Sunday's meeting and of his good prospects in the district. Mrs. Chambers left for Harwich yesterday afternoon.

There will be no further developments in the case till the authorities get to work.

ACCIDENT.—Last evening John A. Crapo and wife were returning from Evergreen park in a buggy, and were driving down County street racing with other returning trotter owners. Mrs. Crapo was driving and when near Middle street attempted to pass a carriage ahead of them. At once the driver cramped in, and forced Mrs. Crapo against the curbing. She tried to stop the horse, but was unable and the carriage struck an unharnessed horse which was being led north by a boy. The shock threw Mr. and Mrs. Crapo out, shaking both up badly, and cutting a painful and ragged wound on Mr. Crapo's forehead over his left eye, besides otherwise bruising and scraping him. Mrs. Crapo was not much hurt. The horse that was being led was scraped and bruised, and Mr. Crapo's wagon sustained some injuries.

NONQUITT.

The first round of a tennis tournament, which is to be continued during the week, was played on the Rotch court at Nonquitt yesterday. The contestants are young girls. Last week the boys had a tournament and Charles Morgan Rotch won the first prize, a handsome silver cup. The games yesterday proved very interesting and were witnessed by many friends of the players. Two games will be played to-day and the finals come off Saturday. Several prizes will be given. The first will probably be a cup like the one taken by Master Rotch. Following is yesterday's summary:

Miss Edith Rotch-Miss Jessie Gifford. 6—0, 6—0.
Miss E. Meddaugh-Miss Julia Shewell. 6—0, 6—0.
Miss Patty Ritchie-Miss Clara Rotch. 6—0, 6—0.
Miss Margaret Putnam-Miss H. Bates. 6—0, 7—5.
Miss E. Bates-Miss Clara Leete. 6—0, 6—0.

The Nonquitt nine will play the New Bedford Y. M. C. A's on Saturday afternoon on the hotel grounds.

One of the best social events of the season will be the Mother Goose Carnival, which is announced for next Saturday evening at the hotel. The costumes now being prepared are unique and in many cases elaborate. H. A. Gray will furnish music for dancing.

WESTPORT POINT.

The second regatta of the season at this place was sailed on Monday last. There were many cat-boats from Westport Point, with a good show of harbor boats. The start was from the harbor, the course being nearly circular and repeat in order to give a fair view of the points of sailing. The entire distance was said to be 15 miles. The first prize for first class was won by James Manchester in his cat-boat, the Mary P.; the second prize in the first class was won by the Yvonne, owned by Hawes Brothers. The first prize in the second class was won by the Wood, owned by William Woods. Capt. Hammond's schooner, the Gracie Phillips, took a large number of Hotel Westport guests and others to see the race, and the Point rocks were well covered with Westport Point visitors, who sat patiently in a broiling sun for several hours watching this, the most interesting regatta of the season.

Hotel Westport will be closed about the 1st of September, owing to other engagements of the management. The season has been very satisfactory and the hotel has added largely to its popularity, already well established. There will be improved facilities for reaching Hotel Westport another season, by which it is proposed to reduce the cost and shorten the time of transit both from New Bedford and Fall River, Mr. Brown having become convinced that the stage facilities are entirely inadequate and that no improvement can be expected in that direction, has decided to take the matter in hand and provide for the wants of the hosts of people who now make Westport Point their resting place during the Summer solstice.

Several boarding-houses at the Point have been well patronized the present season, and it is rumored that others will be opened next season. As usual when a place becomes popular, there is a rise in prices of board contemplated by the older houses. The prices at Hotel Westport are fixed at the lowest rates consistent with the high character of the hotel, but arrangements will be made for adding new features of interest to guests for their entertainment without any addition of cost to guests of the hotel.

Several cottage lots have been sold this season on Horse Neck, near the road leading to Brown's landing, and negotiations are in progress for others. VISITOR.

BARNSTABLE COUNTY.

At a town meeting at Chatham Saturday, 13th, to see what the town would do with the $4000 railroad bonds maturing Sept. 1, 1892, it was voted to issue new bonds at 4½ per cent., to run for 20 years.

At the annual meeting of the Chatham Railroad Company the following gentlemen were elected as a board of directors: Marcellus Eldredge, H. Fisher Eldridge, Osborn Nickerson, S. E. Hallett and C. A. Freeman. At a subsequent meeting of the directors Marcellus Eldredge was elected president and Charles Bassett clerk and treasurer for the ensuing year.

Daniel H. Nickerson has found his pocket book, containing a check for over $100, which he lost on Yarmouth camp-ground.

DRUGGISTS SUMMONED INTO COURT.

Three Local Pharmacists Charged With Compounding Without Registration.

Clinton P. Vose of Lawrence, agent of the Board of Registration in Pharmacy, has been in the city several days visiting the druggists, with a view to ascertaining whether they were complying with chapter 313 of the acts of 1885, which created the board and defined its duties. As a result of his investigations, Walter B. Peck, doing business on South County street, James W. Hayden, clerk for Dr. Bailey, Kempton street, and Joseph Prue and Clement N. Lussier, clerks for Dr. Normandin at his stores in the north part of the city, have been summoned to appear before the District Court to-morrow morning to answer to complaints sworn out under section 9 of chapter 313 Acts of 1885. These complainants charge that the defendants retailed, compounded for sale and sold drugs, medicines, chemicals and poisons, they not being registered pharmacists or apprentices or assistants under the personal supervision of a registered pharmacist at the time of retailing, compounding for sale and selling the drugs, medicines, chemicals and poisons.

EVACUATED TO-DAY.

The Small Pox Hospital Once More Free from Patients.

The small pox hospital was to-day evacuated by the last remaining patient confined there, and after several months the hospital is once more free from patients. The nurse in charge will at once begin cleaning up about the premises.

The members of the Board of Health are to be congratulated that no new cases have arisen either from the dwellings which were infected or from discharged patients. These facts show conclusively that the health officials handled the contagion in a manner which has proven to be a wise one. It has taken time but the result has been accomplished — the disease was not allowed to spread.

GOSPEL GROVE CAMP-MEETING.

GOSPEL GROVE, Cadman's Neck, Aug. 25.

The meeting of yesterday morning was led by Herbert A. Skinner from the 5th of St. John's gospel: "The healing of the impotent man at the pool of Bethesda. Christ the great healer and purifier of our souls, the great work wrought in us by faith on our part."

The afternoon meeting was led by Rev. A. H. Nazarian from Matt. v, 48: "No need of living in blind houses when we can be filled with the light of heaven." I thank God there is such a thing as a perfect Christian, perfect love in Christ, perfect in heart made perfect by the blood of Christ. Perfect love fills your heart that we have a supreme love for God only all the way along this life journey.

THIRD DISTRICT COURT.

BORDEN, J.

THURSDAY, Aug. 25.

The only business before the court this morning was the continued case against Antone Rogers charged with the larceny on the 31st of July last of a barometer valued at $10, the property of Joseph Roderiques. E. A. Douglass, Esq., appeared for the defendant.

After hearing the testimony it was evident that the barometer was not the property of Joseph Roderiques, but was in the custody and possession of Antone F. Frates, the mate at the time of the larceny, and a new warrant was made.

Mr. Douglass insisted upon a continuance as his witnesses were all down the bay fishing, and it was finally arranged that the case be continued until Sept. 1st next with the understanding that the testimony given by the government witnesses need not be gone over again under the new complaint.

Loring Braley and his clerk, Walter Hathaway, and Edward R. Hathaway, clerk for William B. Wood, testified that Rogers tried on two or three different occasions to either sell or pawn the barometer at their places of business, and William R. Sherman said Rogers came to the store and asked him its value and wanted him to buy it.

Capt. Dayton and Inspector Parker said Rogers told them he bought it of an Irishman on Propeller wharf.

Antone F. Frates testified to its loss and what it cost

Mr. Douglass said he could prove an "alibi" easily if the case was continued.

MATTAPOISETT.

Miss Anna M. Burbank of Attleboro is the guest of her uncle, James S. Burbank of Boston, who with wife and daughter are spending the Summer here.

Mr. and Mrs. John Washburn and Miss Flora Peirce have returned from Cottage City, where they have been for an outing of a few weeks.

Aunt Keziah Randall, the centenarian, is lying dangerously ill at her residence at East Mattapoisett.

Mr. and Mrs. Albert W. Howe of Danvers and Miss Mary Stratton also brother and family of Hudson are outing at Pease's Point.

MARION.

George E. Ashley was badly injured on Wednesday while at work on the salt meadow on Charles Neck. His horse took fright and ran, dragging Mr. Ashley several hundred feet by the reins over rocks and stones. Dr. Sparrow was called, and on examination found three ribs broken on the left side. Mr. Ashley's head was badly cut and his body was badly bruised.

Col. H. A. Blake of New York is stopping at Blake's Point.

The following ladies from Fall River are also stopping at the Point: Mrs. James F. Jackson, Miss Edith Jackson, Miss Jennie Stowell, Miss Anna C. Holmes, Miss Mary L. Holmes, Miss Mabel C. Remington, Miss Louise Remington, Miss Alice Buck, Miss Isabel J. Tracy, Miss Louise H. Handy, Miss Elizabeth M. Johnson and Miss Annie C. Bush. Miss Lizzie A. Borden was originally one of the party, and was a favorite with all.

The public schools in Marion commence Sept. 19.

S. D. Hadley of Northampton and John F. Delano of Dayton, O., both formerly of Marion, are visiting friends in town.

The amount of property assessed in Marion has been increased from $900,000 to $1,400,000 since last year, and little or no change has been made in the valuation.

SWANZEY.

A serious runaway accident occurred near Lee's river bridge Tuesday afternoon. William F. Worcester, of Swanzey, was driving with an express wagon toward home when his horse began kicking; he landed Mr. Worcester on the ground and proceeded to drag him. The team of the Swanzey Bleaching and Dyeing Company came along, and the three horses sheered instantly, but the runaway ran into them, plunging the shafts of the team into the side of the leader. The injured horse soon bled to death. The driver of the bleachery team was not injured. Mr. Worcester is badly cut and bruised.

BRITISH STEAMER CAPSIZED.

Fifteen of the Crew of the Angelia Missing and Probably Drowned.

CALCUTTA, Aug. 25.—The British steamer Angelia, bound hence for England capsized in the Hooghly river. Thirty-two of her crew were saved, but 15 are missing. It has not yet been ascertained how the accident occurred.

Ocean Steamers.

Steamers arrived—Passed Brow Head, Britannic, New York. Passed Scilly, Columbia, New York. Arrived at New York—Argonaut, St. Ann's Bay; Parthian, St. Johns, P. R.; Jesmond, Cardenas; Niagara, Sagua, and Havana; At Bremerhaven, Spree, New York.

THOUGHTFUL LETTER-CARRIERS

Cherish the Memory of Their Life-Long Friend, Sunset Cox.

INDIANAPOLIS, Aug. 25.—The National Association of Letter-Carriers in convention has provided for an annual appropriation of $100 with which to decorate the grave of "Sunset" Cox in Greenwood cemetery, Brooklyn. The committee on legislation reported the receipt of a large number of letters from members of congress giving assurance of the passing at the next session of congress of the bill for the equalization of salaries of letter-carriers.

It was ordered that a protest be forwarded to the postmaster general against the practice of numerous postmasters—notably the postmaster at Boston—of employing sub-letter-carriers at 25 cents an hour when there are vacancies on the regular force of carriers. The convention elected officers and an executive board and last night was banquetted by the local branch.

Bogus Bankers Arrested.

NEW YORK, Aug. 25.—William H. Roberts and Neil McCallum, the president and secretary respectively of a bogus banking house known as the Finance Trading company, 16 Wall street, were arrested, charged with swindling a number of firms with whom they did business. These parties all ran a bogus branch of the New York house at Marion, N. C.

Big Promises by a Syndicate.

LOUISVILLE, Aug. 25.—A special from Cincinnati says the great Latonia race track has been sold by its Cincinnati and Covington stockholders to a Chicago syndicate for $500,000. It is said the Chicago owners propose to bring to the track the best horses in the world, so great will be the inducements they will hold out.

Not for Poor People.

NEW HAVEN, Aug. 25.—Backed by members of New York's "four hundred," a line of post coaches is to be established to run between New York city and Newport next summer. The coaches will be run three times a week, and this city is designated as one of the relay stations. The line will not be established as a money-making affair, but simply for the pleasure of those interested.

Granite Strikers Weakening.

NEW HAVEN, Aug. 25.—This week a large number of the strikers have returned to work in the quarries of John Peattie at Leete's island, and also in those of the Norcross Bros. and the Red Granite company at Stony Creek. The employers think that in another week all the quarries will be running full blast.

Costly Fooling.

WORCESTER, Mass., Aug. 25.—Frederick Lavin, 15 years old, was cleaning his clothes with gasolene, and another boy playfully threw a lighted match at him. The gasolene ignited and Laven was badly burned. He was taken to the city hospital, where he died.

Policeman Held for Assault.

LAWRENCE, Mass., Aug. 25.—Police Officer Hinman of North Andover, charged with assault upon Patrick Keegan, was held in $500 bonds for the grand jury. He has been suspended by the selectmen of the town.

Taylor Outdone by Berlo.

SPRINGFIELD, Mass., Aug. 25.—P. J. Berlo rode two miles in Hampden park in 4:48 2-5, breaking the world's record of 4:48 4-5, made by Taylor last fall.

Big Pot for Nightingale.

HARTFORD, Aug. 25.—Nightingale won Charter Oak park's $10,000 trot, with Globe second, Belle Vara third.

Was Hired to Kill His Chief.

NEW ORLEANS, Aug. 25.—Investigation made in Washington parish, where Captain Eugene Bunch, the noted outlaw, was killed, reveal facts tending to show that Hapgood, the accomplice of Bunch, did the killing and that he was hired by those interested in the apprehension of the outlaw to commit the deed. He was promised immunity from prosecution.

Green Goods Swindler Captured.

NEW YORK, Aug. 25.—A man giving the address of W. E. Graham, 172 Hudson street, has been sending circulars through the postoffices of Boston and vicinity offering counterfeit money for sale. Yesterday he was arrested in a cigar store and locked up. He gave the name of John Lannon, and said he was a Newark (N. J.) horseshoer.

Cake Won't Get the Job.

WASHINGTON, Aug. 25.—Secretary of the Treasury Foster, after reviewing the testimony taken in the case of George T. Cake, who was recently appointed an immigrant inspector, but whose appointment was held up subject to an investigation into a charge of bigamy, has decided not to make the appointment.

Davis is a Fighter.

GRAND JUNCTION, Colo., Aug. 25.—News has been received of a fight near East Water, U. T., between W. E. Davis and the "Brock gang" of thieves. Davis killed three of the gang and fatally wounded Brock, the leader. Davis escaped unharmed.

Smallpox from the South.

NEW YORK, Aug. 25.—The steamer Iroquois, from Jacksonville and Charleston, is detained at quarantine owing to a case of smallpox among the steerage passengers.

Welsh Clergymen Meet.

UTICA, N. Y., Aug. 25.—The triennial session of the general assembly of the Welsh Calvanistic church of the United States has begun here. The attendance is large, clergymen from England and Wales, as well as from the different states, being present. The proceedings are conducted entirely in the Welsh tongue.

Peace at Homestead.

HOMESTEAD, Pa., Aug. 25.—Everything in Homestead is quiet. The two men who were arrested by the militia for creating a disturbance on the street were given a hearing by Provost Marshal Mechling. After a severe reprimand by Colonel Mechling, they were discharged with a warning.

Atkinson Squelched.

LONDON, Aug. 25.—In the election at Derby, consequent upon Sir William Harcourt's entering the cabinet, Sir William was elected over Farmer Atkinson, his erratic Conservative opponent, by a vote of 6508 to 1619. The result was a foregone conclusion.

Bombarded by French Troops.

PARIS, Aug. 25.—A dispatch from Porto Novo, the French settlement on the slave coast, says that a force of 1200 French troops entered Dahomeyan territory on Aug. 17 and bombarded the town of Yakon en route.

What Next?

NASHVILLE, Aug. 25.—The board of prison inspectors have decided to return the convicts to the mines at once.

COAL CREEK, Tenn., Aug. 25.—Everything is very quiet here. Twelve more miners have been arrested.

For Congress.

CINCINNATI, Aug. 25.—Bellamy Storrer and John A. Caldwell were renominated for congress by the Republicans of the First and Second districts.

LIZZIE ON TRIAL.

[Continued from First Page.]

or eight cuts clear through the skull. All but four of the wounds were on the right side of the head. There were 18 cuts in all. The wounds were from the left and went backward and downward to the right. The ends of the wounds started from the front. None of the wounds on the left went through the skull. On the bridge of Mrs. Borden's nose was a contusion and there were also contusions over the right eye. These were such as might be made in falling. Afterwards we discovered a wound on the back of Mrs. Borden. It was 2 1-2 inches long and two inches deep, but did not reach the bone. Mrs. Borden was lying in a pool of clotted blood, which was not in a fluid condition like that of Mr. Borden's. There were three spots of blood on the pillow shams and others on the rail of the bed in the room where she was found. Can't say how long Mrs. Borden had been dead, probably from one to one and a half hours. The body was warm. Saw Mrs. Borden's body after I saw that of Mr. Borden.

Mr. Knowlton asked, "Was there anything inconsistent, in your opinion, as to her having been dead two hours?"

An objection was raised, but it was overruled.

Without answering the question witness said Mrs. Borden was 53 years old. She was 5 feet 4 inches in height and weighed from 215 to 235 pounds. Her death was caused by the shock from the blows. The wounds on her body commenced more posterially than those on Mr. Borden, but wound up the same. I took her stomach from the body that afternoon, put it in an air-tight jar, and sent it to an assayer. I saw a hatchet downstairs. It had a claw on the back. There were three axes downstairs I did not take the axes or the hatchet. I examined the hatchet with a claw and one of the axes. The hatchet had what looked like scratches on the blade. There was an appearance of blood on it. It had a cutting surface of four or five inches, and weighed perhaps three or four pounds. The city marshal took it. I examined it with a glass; there were two or three hairs on it, and what I took to be blood on the blade and handle. There appeared to be blood on the axes. I delivered the hatchet to Prof. Wood. I took some clothing—that of a female—but not that of a dead person—and sent it to Prof. Wood.

At this point the court took a recess till 2 30 p. m.

THE HAWAIIAN ISLANDS.

Annexation of Johnston as a Territory of Great Britain Not Likely to be Made.

HONOLULU, Aug. 25.—With regard to the annexation of Johnston Island as a territory of Great Britain, by Her Majesty's ship Champion, the minister of foreign affairs states that the cabinet has not been officially informed of the occupation of the island, but it is the impression of Her Majesty's government that Johnston and Kaluna Islands are still a portion of the Hawaiian government. Not having any official notification of the seizures, the Hawaiian government deemed it unadvisable to enter a protest, believing that Great Britain, on learning the fact, will withdraw without the necessity of a formal protest.

The minister of foreign affairs, replying to the question: "Is the government doing anything towards selling or leasing Pearl Harbor to the United States?" said that the Hawaiian government has never suggested a transfer of any portion of Pearl Harbor or any portion of the Hawaiian dominions to any foreign power.

In debate on the passage of the section in the Hawaiian postal savings bank bill the ministry were charged with the present stringency of affairs. Minister Parker said that the present condition of distress was due to the McKinley bill.

SWEENEY'S HEAD PUNCHED.

Grand Master Workman of the Switchmen Assaulted in Buffalo.

BUFFALO, Aug. 25.—The head of the Switchmen's Order at midnight last night officially declared the recent strike had been a failure. To-day the men are trying to get back into their old places. Some of them will do so. These efforts and their results and the movement or non-movement of the troops are to be the features of to-day's developments. Mr. Sweeney will be examined by the State arbitration board. At 10 minutes of 11 o'clock, at the corner of Swan and Main streets, a crowd of switchmen surrounded Master Workman Sweeney, demanding that he declare a strike from New York to Chicago.

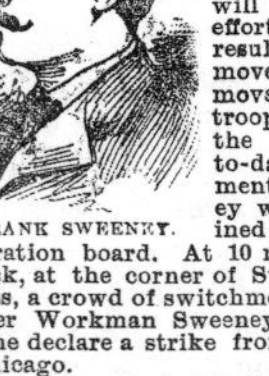

FRANK SWEENEY.

Words ensued, and Switchman Quinn of the Nickel Plate yards struck Master Workman Sweeney a terrific blow, knocking him down. Blood flowed in a stream from Sweeney's nose. Quinn got his leader's head against a telegraph pole and punched and pounded him until pulled away.

Troops Will be Withdrawn.

ALBANY, Aug. 25.—Gov. Flower says that now that the strike at Buffalo has been declared off the troops will be withdrawn prudently.

CANAL TOLLS.

Belief that the President Will Not Act at Once in the Matter.

MONTREAL, Aug. 25.—In regard to the action of President Harrison in the matter of canal tolls, it is believed by those who appear to be well informed that the government will allow the status quo to continue, as there are only six weeks of navigation remaining at the farthest. Shippers will be reimbursed the 20 cent toll by the government, and it is expected by the time next season's crop will have to be moved Canada will be independent of the American canal at St. Mary's Falls, as the canal on the Canadian side will then be fit for traffic.

WITH OPIUM AND CHINESE.

Famous Smuggling Schooner Halcyone Sails from Victoria.

PORT TOWNSEND, Wash., Aug. 26.—The famous smuggling schooner Halcyone sailed from Victoria last night with 2500 pounds of opium and 60 Chinese. Orders have been issued by the Treasury Department notifying the revenue officers on the Pacific coast to be on the lookout to intercept the vessel. The crew is supplied with firearms and ammunition, and the supposed destination of the vessel is Oregon or California.

SPECIAL NOTICES.

FINANCIAL.

SANFORD & KELLEY.

GARDNER T. SANFORD, CHARLES S. KELLEY, } **Bankers,**
Members Boston Stock Exchange,
47 North Water St., New Bedford.

STOCKS AND BONDS BOUGHT AND SOLD ON COMMISSION
At the New York and Boston Stock Boards.

CONSERVATIVE & PROFITABLE INVESTMENTS FOR TRUST FUNDS.

New Bedford Manufacturing Stocks have a first-class record as dividend payers, and we always have some on hand to offer.

Sole Agents for the sale in this city of the 6 per cent. Guaranteed Mortgages of the Lombard Investment Co.

Auction Sale of Stocks and Bonds WEDNESDAYS AND SATURDAYS, at 10 45 A. M.

ORDERS SOLICITED.

SMITH, HOYT & CO.,

Bankers and Stock Brokers,

25 Congress St., Boston, Mass.

STOCKS, Bonds, Grain and Oil bought and sold for cash or carried on moderate margin. Some new ideas will be found in our circular, which are greatly to the advantage of our customers. Buying and selling the same stock is one of them. Inquiries given careful attention. Send for circular. TT&S-1m

T. E. BOWMAN & CO.,

Topeka, Kansas,

NEGOTIATORS OF

Conservative Mortgage Loans in Eastern Kansas.

$2,500,000 LOANED without loss to any investor, and have never yet had to foreclose a farm loan in these eastern counties. Write us for list of investments. s29

MONEY TO LOAN!

IN large or small amounts at low rates and easy terms on Real Estate, Pianos, Organs, Horses, Carriages, &c., which can remain in possession of the owners. Loans taken from 30 days to 5 years. All business strictly confidential. Office Hours 8 to 12 A. M., and 1 to 6 P. M. H. F. DAMON, 34 North Second St., (up one flight) opposite Post Office. sep17-TTS6ptf

GEORGE LEVY, North End Pawn Broker. Cash advanced on Real or Personal Property. All business private. au3-1m

SECOND EDITION.

HOME MATTERS.

THE EXPORTS from New York the past week include 1019 gallons sperm oil and 558 pounds whalebone.

REAL ESTATE SALE.—H. A. Leonard has sold for A. W. Macy to G. Alberto, 16.4 rods of land north side of Dudley street, between Middle Point road and West French avenue.

THE COLUMBIA MILL.—The tract of land on the north side of Coggeshall street, south of the Bennett mill, has been purchased for a site for the new Columbia mill. The mill will run north and south.

RETURNED HOME.—The young woman who North End stories have alleged to have eloped with Eli Porter returned to the city this morning from Providence, indignantly denying the story. She says she has been visiting relatives in Providence.

BUILDING.—George E. Briggs is building for himself six three-tenement houses 28 by 38 feet in size, 27 feet posts, and three stories high, on both sides of Hemlock street.

John M. McLeod has petitioned for leave to raise building southeast corner of Seneca street and Acushnet avenue five feet.

POLITICAL.—The Republicans of Gosnold held a caucus at Cuttyhunk last evening. Timothy Akin, Sr., was chosen Congressional convention delegate, Alonzo B. Veeder delegate to the State convention, Ensign E. Howes as Senatorial delegate. The Congressional delegate is of course pledged for Mr. Randall.

PENSIONS have been granted as follows:
Original—Daniel Varey, Francis A. Hanford, George Doble, H. W. Horton, C. H. Bridges (deceased,) F. W. Hatch, G. H. Hixon.
Additional—W. B. Edwards, Patrick Fenton, E. H. Hall, J. A. Plympton, Thomas Scotchburn, Joseph Loveland, H. O. Berry, M. G. Smith, G. W. Washburn.
Increase—D. W. Graves.
Original, widows, etc.—Rosaltha A. Isbell, Cara R. B. Nelson, Mary McManus, Sarah E. Brown, Susan Hammond, Mary A. Bridges, Susan M. Smith, Martha Webley, Louisa Washburn, Sarah A. Kingman, Maria Purington (mother,) Susan Dodsworth.

NO OFFER MADE.—A report was published on Saturday last, to the effect that one Mr. Slack, member of a syndicate in control of the Wyoming Mills, Fall River, had offered the property to John Estes & Son for $50,000, an advance of $10,000 on the figure the estate brought at the auction sale. At that time it was thought that Estes had secured a bargain, but subsequent developments showed that the proceedings had been irregular, owing to an injunction which was granted, and the mills passed into the hands of Augustus J. Chace and others. Mr. Chace stated yesterday that there was no truth in the story that the plant had been offered to Estes by Slack, and said further that Slack was not connected with the syndicate, and had nothing to do with the property. The plans of the present owners are not known, but it is understood that they may operate the machinery at an early day.

MARINE INTELLIGENCE.

Ar at New York 25th, sch Caroline Knight, hence. Cld, sch George & Albert, Powers, Portland.
Passed through Hell Gate 25th, schs Warren B Potter, Andrews, Philadelphia for this port; Francis Goodnow, Coleman, Amboy for Boston.
Ar at Philadelphia 24th, sch Golden Ball, Gibbs, Staten Island; Wm F Collins, Higgins, Hyannis; Fortuna, Pierce, Kennebec; Thos H Lawrence, Kelley, do. Cld, schs Jesse Murdock, Perry, Wareham; Willie H Higgins, Jones, this port.
Cld at Baltimore 24th, sch Arthur McArdle, McGee, this port.
Cld at Georgetown, 24th, DC, sch Wm P Hood, Charlton, Baltimore.
Ar at Norfolk 23d, sch Star King, Foster, from east of Hatteras.
Sld from Norfolk 24th, schs S S Thorp, this port; Gov J Y Smith, Tiverton.
Sld from San Francisco 24th, ship Tam O'Shanter, New York.

SPOKEN.

Aug 22d, 5 miles east of Barnegat, sch Baltic, bound to this port, full of oil, all well.

Sickness Among Children,

Especially infants, is prevalent at all times, but is largely avoided by giving proper nourishment and wholesome food. The most successful and reliable is the Gail Borden "Eagle" Brand Condensed Milk. Your grocer and druggist keep it.

Made Possible.

One of the largest successes in the way of Flavoring Extracts in the world is the **Price Flavoring Extract Company.**

Their success is attributed to the perfection of **Dr. Price's Delicious Flavoring Extracts.**

This perfection was made possible through the new processes discovered by Dr. Price for extracting from the true fruits their natural flavoring properties. Any housekeeper that will use Dr. Price's Orange, Lemon, Vanilla or any other flavor will pronounce them faultless.

The purity of Dr. Price's flavors offers the best security against the dangers which are common in the use of the ordinary flavoring extracts in the market.

VALUATION AND TAXES.

Substantial Increase of Taxable Property in New Bedford.

An Increase of 700 in the Number of Assessed Polls.

Rate of Taxation One Dollar in Excess of Last Year.

Some of the Causes Which Have Produced This Change.

The assessors have so far completed their work as to furnish the following facts in relation to the assessment for the current year.

The number of polls as compared with last year is as follows:

Precinct.	1891.	1892.	Gain.	Loss.
1	1402	1553	151	
2	1567	1665	98	
3	750	765	15	
4	660	677	17	
5	612	584		28
6	786	790	4	
7	1098	1123	25	
8	742	802	60	
9	655	719	64	
10	1503	1602	99	
11	1385	1580	195	
Total,	11,160	11,860	728	28

Precinct 5 is the only one showing a loss, and the net gain is 700 polls.

The valuation of taxable property is as follows:

Precinct.	Real.	Personal.	Total.
1,	$1,974,500	$812,500	$2,787,000
2,	2,476,500	2,382,700	4,859,200
3,	1,333,800	250,300	1,584,100
4,	937,600	144,500	1,082,100
5,	1,476,500	779,510	2,256,000
6,	817,900	68,500	886,400
7,	3,681,100	5,122,813	8,803,913
8,	1,715,000	1,210,600	2,925,600
9,	3,192,900	4,113,200	7,306,100
10,	2,503,200	2,629,500	5,132,700
11,	1,983,200	665,600	2,648,800
	$22,092,200	$18,179,713	$40,271,913
In 1891,	20,953,900	17,556,943	38,510,843
Increase,	$1,138,300	$622,770	$1,761,070

The following shows the increase of personal property by precincts:

Precinct	1891.	1892.	Inc.	Dec.
1	$551,500	$812,500	$261,000	
2	2,223,200	2,382,700	159,500	
3	256,800	250,300		$6,500
4	159,500	144,500		15,000
5	789,700	779,500		10,200
6	53,300	68,500	15,200	
7	4,926,143	5,122,813	196,670	
8	1,184,900	1,210,600	25,700	
9	4,507,800	4,113,200		394,600
10	2,240,300	2,629,500	389,200	
11	663,800	665,600	1,800	
	$17,556,943	$18,179,713	$950,070	$426,300

The net increase on personal is $622,770.

The following, showing the increase in real estate by precincts, is not so accurate as the above, for the reason that real estate, wherever situated, is taxed to the owner in the precinct where he resides.

Precinct.	1891.	1892.	Increase.
1	$1,668,500	$1,974,500	$306,000
2	2,418,300	2,476,500	58,200
3	1,294,200	1,333,808	39,600
4	898,600	937,600	39,000
5	1,460,700	1,476,500	15,800
6	797,300	817,900	20,600
7	3,555,400	3,681,100	125,700
8	1,639,700	1,715,000	75,300
9	3,077,200	3,192,900	115,700
10	2,332,800	2,503,200	170,400
11	1,811,200	1,983,200	172,000
	$20,953,900	$22,092,200	$1,138,300

The taxes assessed on shares of stock in national banks located in this city, and owned by residents thereof, are paid by the banks, and the value of the same is included in the figures given for personal property of Precinct Seven. They are as follows:

First National Bank,	$588,278
Mechanics National Bank,	541,414
Merchants National Bank,	793,865
Citizens National Bank,	309,204
National Bank of Commerce,	435,252
	$2,668,013

In accordance with a decision of the Supreme Court the banks are taxed this year according to sales in open market, nearest the first day of May.

As usual polls are taxed $2 each, and the rate of taxation on property is $17.30, an increase of $1 per thousand over 1891. The are several causes which render this increase in rate unavoidable. Among them may be mentioned the distribution of several large estates, taking a very great amount of taxable personal property out of the city. The decrease in Precinct 9 is due to this cause. A glance at the table below will reveal another cause, the increase in the amount which the assessors are obliged to raise on the several accounts:

	1891.	1892.
State tax,	$26,025	$31,377.50
County tax,	47,819.40	54,410.26
City tax,	550,200	606,700
Overlay,	26,134.37	27,936.33
	$650,178.77	$720,424.09

The list of taxes will be committed to the collector on Thursday, Sept. 15th, and the tax bills will be distributed as soon thereafter as practicable. Those against non-residents who have no agents in the city, will be forwarded by mail.

A discount of 5 per cent. will be made on all taxes paid on or before Saturday, October 15th.

FINANCIAL.

THURSDAY, Aug. 25.

The market shows a decided tendency to advance and is only held in check by the desperate efforts of the bears, who are trying to save their necks by the most desperate efforts. With the strikes out of the way prices should advance at once upon the official announcement that they are off—barring unforseen occurrences in the meantime.

There was a shrinkage in the volume of business yesterday. Speculation being held in check by conflicting news regarding the switchmen's strike.

The West End street railway is now operating 1,000,000 electric car miles per month. In June the revenue electric car mileage was 846,987, in July it was 971,862, and for August it is understood it will exceed 1,000,000 miles. The result of this larger electrical mileage is seen in a decreased cost of electrical maintenance and motive power per car mile. The July statement of the road shows an increase in gross earnings of $40,676 and in net of $40,155.

At the meeting of the directors of the Grinnell Manufacturing Corporation to-day, a dividend of 3 per cent. on the capital stock of the company was declared, payable to stockholders of record at the close of business this day, payable. Sept. 1.

The local money market is fairly active at rates ranging from 5 to 6 per cent.

The Boston loan market is now beginning to feel the recent large selling of securities to New York or Boston, and there has been a general reduction in rates. Call loans 4 to 6 per cent. Prime mercantile paper 4¾ to 5½ per cent. Corporation paper 4½ to 5½ per cent. The clearing-house rate is 3½ per cent. New York funds sell at 12 to 15 cents discount.

The New York money market continues easy. Call loans 2 to 2½ per cent. Prime mercantile paper 4 to 5½ per cent.

Sterling exchange is quiet and steady; posted rates are 4.87½ and 4.89.

Government bonds have been dull and steady.

In Wall street stock circles this morning gossip was not very interesting. Exchange is tending lower and the Gould party seem to be working for higher prices On the other hand the cholera scare, disposition of Europe to take gold, the narrow character of speculation are elements in favor of bears. As the country is prosperous and progressive the bull side should be the favorite. London comes a fraction off. Bank of England unchanged.

In New York the stock market opened firm all around and during the morning, or up to 1 o'clock, showed more strength than for the last three or four days, and moderate activity.

The Boston stock market from the opening of the day until 1 o'clock was moderately active and firm in tone.

Reported earnings of railroads show figures as below:

Week.	1892.	Increase.
ST. PAUL.		
Third Aug.,	$602,615	$95,662
Since Jan. 1,	19,261,710	3,132,870
Mileage,	5,721	2
WISCONSIN CENTRAL LINES.		
Third Aug.,	$121,339	$1,297
Since Jan. 1,	3,515,180	365,573
Mileage,	867	
NORTHERN PACIFIC.		
Third Aug.,	$496,104	$48,681
Since Jan. 1,	13,903,320	*158,050
Mileage,	4,379	127
RIO GRANDE WESTERN.		
Third Aug.,	$60,700	$6,800
Since Jan. 1,	1,597,390	61,213
Mileage,	512	66

*Decrease.

One million of gold has been engaged for shipment to Austria to-morrow, and a half million more with destination unknown. The free coin and bullion, so called, in the treasury has increased $1,234,230 this month to $111,678,621. This is exclusive of the $100,000,000 greenback redemption fund, which the treasury claims the right to trench upon, but evidently does not wish to do.

Press dispatches report heavy rains in Iowa, Nebraska, Missouri and Kansas. They are much needed and will help corn fill.

Bullion shipments at Park City for week ending August 15 were nine bars weighing 9731 ounces.

The Bell Telephone Company makes the following instrument statement for the month ended Aug. 20 and eight months;

Month Aug. 20	1892.	Increase.
Shipments	7,316	1,543
Returned	5,806	1,497
Net output	1,510	46
Since Dec. 20.		
Shipments	65,219	17,453
Returned	37,482	9,774
Net output	27,737	7,679
Instruments in use Aug. 20.	538,847	37,063

Received sampler for week ending August 20, 545,000 pounds Ontario ore; 222,110 pounds Daly ore.

William H. Shockley, superintendent of the Mount Diablo Mill & Mining Company, writes us under date of the 14th inst. as follows: We have only one man working on the winze on the 6th east. There is some low grade ore here, but it does not amount to very much at present. The formation is favorable for obtaining ore here. The main stope in the intermediate between the 5th and 6th levels is giving considerable $40 ore. The north crosscut from this intermediate is in 19 feet, and cut several seams of ore assaying $20 to $40, and there is a little ore showing in the face. The east drift on the 5th level is 41 feet and is in ledge matter. We will start a north crosscut here in a short time. The stope above the 4th east shows two feet of $40 ore. There is not so much quartz showing near the No. 2 winze as we had last week. The stope above the 3d west shows 18 inches of $50 ore. We are getting a small amount of ore from the intermediate above the 3d east. The south cross-cut on the 2d east is in 155 feet, and is in very hard ground. The stope above the 2d east shows three feet of $60 ore. We are taking out a small quantity of $40 ore from the stope above the 2d west. The stope above the 1st east shows a slight improvement; we have found here 18 inches of $40 ore in the foot of the stope we have been working that looks promising. The mill has been running steadily during the week, and is crushing ore very well indeed and doing good work. Total wages, $1176.45; shipments to date, $9153.17; average assay value, $36.35; ore crushed, 249 tons 1630 pounds.

CALIFORNIA MINING STOCKS.

SAN FRANCISCO, Aug. 24.

The following are the official closing prices of mining stocks to-day:

Alta	—	Mexican	1 00
Best & Belcher	1 05	Mt. Diablo	—
Chollar	—	Ophir	2 00
Con. Cal. & Va.	3 00	Potosi	—
Crown Point	—	Savage	—
Eureka Con.	—	Sierra Nevada	—
Gould & Curry	—	Union Con.	—
Hale & Norcross	—	Utah	—

PROVISIONS AND GRAIN.

CHICAGO, Aug. 25.

Opening.

	Lard.	Wheat.	Pork.	Corn.	Sh't Ribs
May	—	—	—	—	—
June	—	—	—	—	—
July	—	—	—	—	—
Aug.	—	—	—	—	—
Sept.	—	75⅝	10.90	51⅝	—
Oct.	—	—	11.00	50½	—
Dec.	—	78⅜	—	52¾	—
Jan.	—	—	12.40	—	—

12 o'clock.

	Lard.	Wheat.	Pork.	Corn.	Sh't Ribs
May	—	—	—	—	—
June	—	—	—	—	—
July	—	—	—	—	—
Aug.	—	—	—	—	—
Sept.	—	75	10.50	51⅛	—
Oct.	—	—	11.00	50⅛	—
Dec.	—	77⅞	—	52¾	—
Jan.	—	—	12.15	—	—

BLOODY WAYFARER

Jewish Peddler Met Him on New Bedford Road.

Helped Him Clean His Clothing and Gave Him Food.

Stranger Said He Had Fought with a Farmer.

Asked Many Times Over if He Looked All Right.

Bought Blacking to Cover up Gore on His Shoes.

Peddler Could Pick out His Man Among Ten Thousand.

Startling Statements in a Letter to Emma Borden.

Mayor of Waltham's Reply to Inquiries About Samuel Robinsky.

[Special Dispatch.]

FALL RIVER, Aug. 25.—The following letter, which was mailed Aug. 18 and received at Fall River at 4 30 p. m. same day, was given out by the defence after the adjournment of the court at noon today:

Waltham, Mass., Aug. 17, 1892.

Miss Emma Borden.

Dear Madam—You must excuse that I take the liberty in sending you these few lines. I ought to have written you before this, but I was unable to do so as I was travelling every day. My name is Samuel Robinsky. I am a Jewish peddler. When the fatal murder in Fall River occurred I was only a few miles from Fall River that day. While sitting on the roadside towards New Bedford, I met a man who was covered with blood. He told me that he worked on a farm and that he never could get his wages, so he had a fight with the farmer. He said he had run away and not got any money after all. All he had was a $5 bill. He bought from me four handkerchiefs, one looking glass, one necktie, a collar and some shoe blacking. His boots were covered with blood and he put lots of blacking on them. I helped him to fix up again and get cleaned. But at this time did not know anything about the murder. I felt sorry for him and thought only that he gave the farmer a good licking.

I advised him to travel at night, which he said he would do, as he feared arrest during the day. I gave him my lunch and he gave me a quarter and told me not to say anything that I had met him. He asked me what time the train left for Boston after 8 o'clock in the evening, and I told him.

He also had a bundle with him, which was about two feet thick or big. When I am peddling I do not read any papers, only Sundays, as I am studying the English language.

When I was in Boston last Sunday, a friend of mine told me about the Fall River murder. I told him that I was in Fall River and around the neighborhood. I told him about my stranger and my friend said:

But why did you not report it to the police?

I told him I was afraid, as they would lock me up as a witness, and another thing, I did not have any license, so I was afraid. I told my friend that I would write to you and Mr. Jennings. I read Last Sunday's Boston *Globe* and thought that I might have seen the murderer. If I should see him here in Boston, I am sure, yes, dead sure, I should know him.

He is of medium height, with dark brown hair and reddish whiskers or moustache, weighing about 135 pounds. He wore a gray suit and a Derby hat. His shoes were what you call russia leather, no blacking, or so called Summer shoes. He put my blacking on to make them look black and people could not see the blood.

It was about 4 o'clock (noon) that day. I only heard about the murder at 6 or 7 o'clock that night. I kept quiet, as I had no license, and feared to be arrested. My stranger was very much afraid. He asked me a million times if he looked all right again, and I brushed him off with my shoe brush. I told him to wait till dark. If I go again to Fall River next week I shall call on you if you think it is necessary, but all I can swear to is the stranger which I have seen that afternoon. This is all, but if this man was the murderer I cannot say, but I shall find him out of a hundred thousand. I will close now. Will go to Fitchburg to-morrow morning and return to Boston Saturday night.

Please do not say anything to the police for I would be arrested. If I had known about the murder about the time I met my stranger it would have been different as I would have followed him up and perhaps got a reward. I thought it was a poor farm hand and so took pity on him as I know as a rule farmers seldom pay their hands during the Summer. Hoping that my information will be of some use to you, I remain

Very Respectfully,
SAMUEL ROBINSKY.

P. S. Please excuse paper and mistakes as I am a foreigner.

The following papers were appended to the letter:

Fall River, Aug. 19, 1892.

To George L. Mayberry, Mayor, Waltham, Mass.

Does Samuel Robinsky, a Jewish peddler, live in Waltham?

ANDREW J. JENNINGS.

Waltham, Aug. 20, 1892.

To Andrew J. Jennings, Fall River.

Cannot find that he lives here. Am told that a peddler of that name living in Boston sometimes comes out here.

G. L. MAYBERRY.

THE LATEST DEVELOPMENTS

In the Shoe Business.

We have just put in facilities for making a Special Grade of Ladies' and Gents' Shoes, especially adapted to New Bedford.

We shall give them a name also well adapted to New Bedford, and we will make them better for the money than anything you have hitherto bought.

We have some of those Shoes ready for you now.

We will have a greater assortment hereafter.

SCHULER BROS.,

76 and 78 Purchase Street.

SUICIDE BY SHOOTING.

Lawton Coggeshall Takes His Life at His Home in Newport.

NEWPORT, R. I., Aug. 25.—Lawton Coggeshall, brother of ex-Mayor Coggeshall, committed suicide early this morning by shooting. He had an attack of grip last Winter which affected his mind, and last Spring attempted to take his life. To the knowledge of his wife there was not a revolver in the house, but at 6 30 she heard a report, and upon entering his room found one on the floor and a bullet wound in his head. Deceased was prominently known in marine circles and was wreck commissioner of this district.

WEATHER INDICATIONS.

WARMER.

NEW YORK, Aug. 25.—At 8 30 a. m. the weather was cloudy and threatening, wind east temperature 79. The *Herald* says: In Middle States and New England on Friday partly cloudy, warmer, sultry weather will probably prevail, preceded by rain, with fresh to brisk southerly winds, becoming variable, and followed by clearing, and on Saturday warm, fair weather.

TELEGRAPHIC BREVITIES.

Fire in Freeport, Me., caused $6000 damage.

Crop prospects in County Cork, Ire., are gloomy.

The continued drought has injured corn in Illinois.

Steps are being taken to increase the water supply of Malden, Mass.

Fifty warships are to take part in the Columbus celebration at Genoa.

Nine new cardinals are to be appointed at the papal consistory.

C. T. Gregory has been appointed postmaster at Cannon, Conn.

The pope will refrain from interfering in our presidential election.

The station agent at Nowata, I. T., was robbed by members of the Dalton gang.

A nephew of William E. Gladstone, the British premier, is stranded in Chicago.

M. Belloc, a Paris banker, has absconded, leaving liabilities of 1,000,000 francs.

French generals have been retired for ordering military maneuvers during the extremely hot period.

The Thirty-second Maine regiment held its annual reunion at Lewiston with an attendance of about 100.

Veterans of the Fiftieth Massachusetts regiment and the Fourth battery held a reunion near Lowell, Mass.

Col. E. C. Smeed of Omaha, chief engineer of the Union Pacific railroad company, died at Philadelphia.

Twenty one dead and many wounded miners are said to have been seen in a cave near Coal Creek, Tenn.

Lieutenant Drake, U. S. N., will soon be detached from the torpedo station and ordered to join the U. S. S. New York.

The survivors of the Twenty-second Maine infantry held their annual reunion at Newport, Me., nearly 100 being present.

George William Curtis is improving in health very rapidly. He is still under the care of his physicians at his home on Staten island.

Anxiety is felt about the condition of Sir Richard Owen, K. C. B., the venerable anatomist. Sir Richard was 88 years of age last month.

James T. Leighton of New Haven who was connected with the Consolidated Car Heating company, died at Portland, Me., suddenly of heart disease. His age was about 60 years.

United States Senator Gallinger, who has been seriously ill both at Washington and at Winthrop Highlands, Mass., has so far recovered as to be able to reach his home at Concord, N. H.

The engagement is announced of Miss Helen Gammell, daughter of the late Professor William Gammell of Brown University, Providence, and Arthur Herbert of the British legation at Washington

The crisis in the Argentine Republic continues and it is said President Pellegrini must resign.

Every precaution is being taken to exclude the cholera from England.

The Russians declare they were attacked first by the Afghans in the recent fight and the Afghans declare the Russians were the aggressors.

PEN, CHISEL AND BRUSH.

W. Clark Noble, the sculptor, has completed a statue of William Ellery Channing for the city of Newport.

Walt Whitman's old house is to be moved to the outskirts of Camden, N. J., and made a memorial of the poet.

"Oliver Optic" Adams is writing another story, notwithstanding that he is seventy and has turned out over 100 books.

An inventory of the effects of the poet Racine, which has just been discovered, reveals the singular fact that at his death he did not possess a single copy of his own works.

Robert Gordon Hardie has been commissioned to paint Senator Proctor's portrait for the war department. He is a native of Vermont and married a daughter of Senator Cullom.

Tenniel, the cartoonist of Punch, is seventy-two years old, elastic of foot, supple of fingers and bright eyed as in his youth. He has but one eye, since a friend's foil maimed him in a fencing bout fifty years ago.

Mr. Gunter, the author of "Mr. Barnes of New York," "Mr. Potter of Texas" and various other successful transatlantic novels, is just on the right side of forty. He was for many years a railway clerk before he made his great success.

EDUCATIONAL NOTES.

The University of Oxford has transferred its extension work to a separate delegacy of its own.

Thirty-seven years ago the first teachers' agency in the world was established in New York city. There are now about fifty scattered through the country.

There is an excellent rule at Harvard university which prohibits any student from participating in athletic sports unless he maintains a certain standing in his studies.

The Massachusetts Society for the Prevention of Cruelty to Animals has offered several prizes for the best dialogue embodying the teachings of "Black Beauty." The dialogue thus obtained is intended for use in the public schools.

STOCK AND BOND MARKETS.

Bids at the close of First Board.

NEW YORK, Aug. 25.

GOVERNMENT BONDS.	
U.S. 2s, registered	100
" new 4s, registered	115½
" new 4s, coupons	115½
" currency 6s, 1895, (Pacifics)	—
RAILROADS	
Atchison	39⅛
Clev., Cin., Chicago & St. Louis	66½
Chicago & Eastern Illinois	—
Chicago & Eastern Illinois pref	—
Chicago, Burlington & Quincy	101¼
Delaware & Hudson	133¾
Delaware & Lackawanna	158½
Erie	27⅞
Illinois Central	—
Lake Shore & Michigan Southern	135
Louisville & Nashville	68¾
Michigan Central	—
Missouri Pacific	62⅞
New Jersey Central	135
New York & New England	31
Northern Pacific	20⅞
Northern Pacific pref	56⅛
Chicago & Northwestern	117¼
New York Central & Hudson River	112¾
North American	13⅞
Oregon Navigation	—
Oregon Improvement	—
Oregon Short Line	—
Philadelphia & Reading	59⅛
Pullman Palace Car Co	—
Chicago, Rock Island & Pacific	82⅝
Chicago, Milwaukee & St. Paul	82⅞
Chicago, Milwaukee & St. Paul pref	—
Richmond Terminal	8¼
St. Paul & Omaha	53½
St. Paul & Omaha pref	—
Union Pacific	39⅝
Wabash, St. Louis & Pacific	11½
Wabash, St. Louis & Pacific pref	25
MISCELLANEOUS	
Ontario Silver	41
Pacific Mail Steamship Co	—
Sugar, common	114⅞
Sugar, pref	106¾
Western Union Telegraph	99
Silver Certificates	83

BOSTON, Aug. 25.

BONDS	
Atchison 4s	82½
Atchison Incomes	60⅞
American Bell Telephone 7s	—
Chicago, Burlington & Northern 5s	—
Chicago & West Michigan 5s	—
Mexican Central 4s	68
Illinois Steel Co. 5s	—
RAILROADS.	
Atchison, Topeka & Santa Fe	40
Boston & Albany	205
Boston & Lowell	181
Boston & Maine	—
Boston & Providence	250
Chicago, Burlington & Quincy	102
Chicago & West Michigan	48¾
Cleveland & Canton	5⅝
Cleveland & Canton pref	19½
Flint & Pere Marquette	*20
Flint & Pere Marquette pref	*79
Mexican Central	15¾
New York & New England	31¾
New York & New England pref	83
Old Colony	182½
Oregon Short Line	25
Pullman Palace Car	—
Union Pacific	40
Wisconsin Central	17
West End	—
West End pref	—
MINING.	
Butte & Boston Mining Co	9
Calumet & Hecla Mining Co	295
Centennial	7¼
Franklin Mining Co	12⅛
Kearsarge	—
Montana	36
Osceola Mining Co.	31
Tamarack	160
MISCELLANEOUS.	
American Bell Telephone	207
Erie Telephone	45
Mexican Telephone	1.00
New England Telephone	56½
Newport Land	—
Boston Land Co	5
West End Land Co	18¼
San Diego Land Co	16½
Topeka Land & Development Co	—
Lamson Store Service	17¼
Illinois Steel Co	74
Am. Sugar Refineries, com	115
Am. Sugar Refineries, pref	—
Gen'l Electric	—
Gen'l Electric	—

*Asked.

Around the World in Eighty Days.

Did Jules Verne ever think that his imaginary Phileas Fogg would be eclipsed by an American girl, who once made the circuit in less than seventy-three days? But Phileas had to take "second money." The fame of Dr. Pierce's Golden Medical Discovery has gone around the world long ago, and left its record everywhere as a precious boon to every nation. In the whole world of medicine, nothing equals it for the cure of scrofula of the lungs (which is Consumption.) Coughs and bronchial troubles succumb to this remedy, and the blood is purified by it, until all unsightly skin blotches are driven away. Don't be sceptical, as this medicine is guaranteed to every purchaser. You only pay for the good you get.

SPECIAL NOTICES.

HEARING.

CITY OF NEW BEDFORD, CLERK'S OFFICE, Aug. 25th, 1892.

Notice is hereby given that the Mayor and Aldermen will give a hearing in their chamber, City Hall Building, on THURSDAY, Sept. 8, 1892, at 7½ o'clock P. M., to all persons interested in the petition of T. A. Tripp, for a license to set up and maintain two (2) steam engines and boilers of fifty (50) horse power, at his place of business northeast corner of Prospect and Grinnell streets.

DANIEL B. LEONARD, City Clerk.
(Mercury copy.) au25-tsep8

TUXEDO WASHING POWDER

Every package contains one pound of *the best powder made* and

A VALUABLE TICKET,

Both of which are sold for one sum of money. Ask for TUXEDO Washing Powder.

The highest quality of all in the world.

Sold by all Grocers.

TUXEDO WASHING POWDER

LINEN PAPER AND ENVELOPES.
Large Variety and Low Prices
—AT THE—
STANDARD OFFICE.

AUCTION SALES.

By STANDISH BOURNE,

(Successor to Geo. A. Bourne & Son,)
Auctioneer, Commission Merchant, Real Estate Dealer and Appraiser.

Cash advanced on goods consigned for auction. Ready buyer for personal property of every description.
Office and Salesrooms 47, 49 and 51 North Second Street, near the Post Office.

Assignee's Sale.
On SATURDAY, Aug. 27th, at 10¼ o clock, at salesrooms, will be sold, by order of the assignee, a small lot of groceries, scales, meat blocks, tools, &c., &c. Also one bay horse, one nearly new covered express wagon, harnesses, &c., &c.

Carriages, Harnesses, &c.
On SATURDAY, Aug. 27, at 10½ o'clock, at salesroom, will be sold a variety of new and second-hand carriages, harnesses, general merchandise, &c. Also 1 pony, kind and gentle, safe for ladies or children; weighs about 800 lbs.

Restaurant Stock and Fixtures.
On TUESDAY, Aug. 30, at 2 o'clock, at the store of W. D. Moor, No. 70 William street, will be sold the entire stock and fixtures pertaining to the restaurant business.

Paine Farm on Sconticut Neck.
On WEDNESDAY, Aug. 31, at 3 o'clock, on the premises, will be sold in the following manner, the above named farm;
1st.—Lot situated on the east side of the road on the north end of the farm, containing about 25 acres, more or less.
2d.—Lot joining No. 1 on the south, containing about 25 acres, more or less.
3d.—Farm house, barn, out-buildings and about 20 acres, more or less.
4th.—Lot joining No. 3 on the south, containing 15 acres, more or less.
5th.—We reserve the right to put these parcels up in one sale and if a larger bid can be obtained than the sum of the separate sales, that bid will be the binding sale.
Plenty of time before the sale to get your clam dinner held for the benefit of the Union Chapel at Dunn's Grove.

Mortgagee's Sale.
On SATURDAY, Sept. 3, at 12¾ o'clock, on the premises, will be sold by order of the mortgagee, the nearly new 2½ story house and lot containing about 21.38 rods, situated on the south side of North street; numbered 162. For legal advertisement see *Evening Standard* of August 9, 16, 23.

To Let in Our Storage Warerooms.
We constantly have on hand first-class rooms for the storage of household goods, to be rented by the month or year.
Good dry storage room for stoves.

By JOHN B. BAYLIES,

121 and 123 Union Street,
Commission Merchant, Appraiser, and Auctioneer for the sale of Real Estate and every description of Personal Property. Furniture Bought.

H. C. HATHAWAY,

Auctioneer, Real Estate Agent and Appraiser,
Corner Acushnet Ave. and Elm St.

One of the best auction marts in the State for the sale of horses and carriages. Keeps constantly on hand carriages of every description, carriages made to order and repairing in all its branches attended to under the superintendency of J. R. Forbes. Consignments of every description solicited. Cash advanced on goods for auction. Personal property of every description bought at short notice for cash. Negotiable notes bought and sold.

Saturday's Sale.
On SATURDAY, Aug. 27th, 1892, at 9 A. M., at salesroom, will be sold a lot of household goods, ranges, tapestry carpets, &c., &c.
1 billiard and pool table.
1 upright piano. au24

Horses, Carriages, Harnesses, &c.
Will arrive Thursday a car load of fine horses from Vermont, Maine and New Hampshire. In the lot are some very fine drivers. They will be offered at private sale until SATURDAY, Aug. 27th, when the balance will be sold at auction. Will also sell several second-hand horses, new and second-hand carriages, harnesses, &c., &c. Also mortgagee's sale of one heavy furniture wagon, with pole. au24

ALFRED WILSON,

Auctioneer and Real Estate Agent,
Room 22, - - - Robeson Building.

Houses and land in all parts of the city for sale; tenements for rent; rents collected

For Sale.
Two-story house on Acushnet avenue, near Walnut street; well arranged for one family; good location.

For Lease.
The Webster Block, Purchase street; 10 rooms, well adapted for a genteel boarding house, club rooms, or business purposes.

TO LET—A flat in The Winslow, corr Sixth and Union streets. Apply to WILSON, Robeson Building. jy14-tf

T. F. HEALEY,

Auctioneer and Real Estate Agent,
555 and 559 Purchase street, corner of Franklin street.

FOR SALE CHEAP—One farm in Rochester of 70 acres; house, barn, outbuildings, etc.; 2 good orchards on place; cut 20 tons of hay. Price $1800.
Also two cottages in Fairhaven; nearly new; fine view of river and harbor; will sell one or both; situated on Main street; will sell to the right parties on easy terms.
Also one fine house in the west part of the city in good locality, with all the modern improvements, gas and electric lights, etc. Will be sold cheap if applied for soon.
Also lots on Acushnet avenue, Coggshall and Locust streets, in fact all parts of the city.
Business solicited. No charges made unless a sale, then my prices are the lowest.

By WM. BARKER, Jr.

Valuable Real Estate, Engine, Machinery, Horses, Wagons, &c., at Auction.

WILL be sold on the premises, SATURDAY, Sept. 3d, 1892, at 1 o'clock P. M., that desirable property well known as the Crapo Wood Yard, on Court street, in this city, consisting of 40 rods of land with buildings, engine, boiler, shafting and other machinery. Also, two one-horse lumber wagons, two express wagons, two horses (one a superior animal,) two express harnesses, and various other articles.
Aug. 22, 1892. au22-ts

REAL ESTATE.

FRANCIS W. TAPPAN,

Agent for Purchase, Sale, and Lease of REAL ESTATE.
Office, 15 North Water St., New Bedford. d&w

Desirable Cottage, For Sale.
On Washington street, near Dartmouth, cottage house, nearly new, eight rooms, good neighbors, 11 rods of land. Price $3200. Apply on the premises, or at Tappan's real estate agency, 15 North Water street. au19tf

FRANK C. SMITH,

Real Estate Broker, Auctioneer and Appraiser,
Office - - 47 William Street,
(Opposite New Post Office.)

M. E. SMITH,

REAL ESTATE AGENT.
619 Purchase Street. Telephone 16-11.

H. A. LEONARD, REAL ESTATE AGENT,

126 UNION STREET.

Houses and house lots in all parts of the city for sale. Three fine residences. Good bargains. Call and examine tenements to let.

EDWIN JONES,

REAL ESTATE AGENT.......884 PURCHASE ST.

FOR SALE.—Lots in all parts of the city; some bargains. Also a good 2½ story house, nearly new, well arranged, convenient to mills at North End, now rents for $250 a year; cheap.
BUSINESS SOLICITED. au24-6t

Very Desirable House Lots.
Near Bliss Corner, $3 a rod and upwards. Good chance for speculators. DANIEL SWEENEY, Cove Road. au22-12t

COTTAGE HOUSE—53 Chestnut street, with 18½ rods of land; house is fitted with modern conveniences. Can be seen afternoons and evenings. V. F. HATCH, 31 North Water street. au23-tf

Cottage House.
Well built, good repair, in part of city growing rapidly; will make good home and *must* increase in value. Apply box 6, *Standard* office. ap25-tf

FOR SALE—In South Dartmouth, near the water, a 2½ story house with large piazza, barn, and 83 rods of land. One of the most desirable places in the village for a Summer residence. Inquire of BENJ. QUERIPEL or DANIEL H. HOWLAND, South Dartmouth. ap7-tf

Knowles & Co.

LAST HALF-HOLIDAY FOR THE SEASON.

BARGAINS FRIDAY MORNING.

China Silks, last chance, 29c., for Friday only.

Stamped Linen Tidies, Trays and Splashers, 9c., worth 15c., for Friday only.

French Satine Corsets, for Friday only, 39c.

Summer Ventilated Corsets, for Friday only, 39c.

Lot Cotton Dress Novelties, worth fully 12 1-2c., for Friday only 6c.

Another lot of 3500 yards Twilled Cottons, 10 to 20 yard pieces, 5 and 6c.

Best 100 yard Spool Sewing Silk, all colors and black, 6c. a spool for Friday only.

White Mull Ties for Misses and Children, worth 35 and 50c., for Friday only 19c.

Lot of Men's White Unlaundered Shirts, a little soiled and tumbled, as good a shirt as ever sold for 50c., for Friday only 39c.

Ladies' full regular finished seam, fast black Hose. Best hose made for 25c., for Friday only 19c.

Linen Napkins, all linen, worth 75c., for Friday morning only 39c.

Friday only: 1 qt. Milk cans, 6c. Howell's Household Ammonia, full pint bottles, 4c. Painted Chamber Pails, 19c. 1 lb. Japanese Tea Canisters, 5c.

BOOTS & SHOES. Friday Only.

LOT 1—A Lady's Kid Button Boot, Hand Turned, Common Sense and Opera lasts, $3.00 Boots for $2.00.

LOT 2—Is a Lady's French Kid Finish Oxford Tie, Common Sense last, for $1.50. This is a shoe we have sold for two years at $2.00 a pair.

LOT 3—Is a Misses' Russ. Oxford, Spring Heel, Russ. Tip, at 75c. a pair.

TIN PLATE STATISTICS.

A Report Which May Furnish Material for Campaign Orators.

WASHINGTON, Aug. 25.—The special report of Ira Ayer, special agent of the treasury department, deputed to examine into the question of the production of American tin and terne plate, is made public. The total production of tin and terne plates proper for the year, was 13,646,719 pounds. The production of American sheet iron or steel, made into articles or wares, tinned or terne coated, during the year, as shown by the sworn statements of manufacturers, was 4,828,228 pounds.

As these manufacturers constitute tin and terne plates within the meaning of the law, it now seems probable that when full returns of the same are received, the total production for the year, inclusive of such manufactures, will not fall much short of 20,000,000 pounds. A careful estimate shows that the quantity of black plates produced in the United States, and which entered into the manufacture of tin and terne plates during the year, was 9,296,553 pounds; add black plates sold to stamping companies to be made into articles and wares, and tinned or terned coated as per returns to date, 4,828,228 pounds, it makes the aggregate 14,124,781 pounds.

In other words, the production of tin and terne plates proper for the year was over 68 per cent., and of the total production over 70 per cent. was made from American black plates.

During the first quarter of the fiscal year five firms were engaged in the manufacture of tin and terne plates, eleven during the second, twenty during the third and twenty-six during the fourth. The probability is that at least eight new names will be added to the list of manufacturers at the end of the present quarter.

THE IRON HALL:

Action Taken by Members of the Order in Various Cities.

INDIANAPOLIS, Aug. 25.—James F. Failey, receiver for the Iron Hall, had his bond for $1,000,000 approved and property valued at $500,000 was turned over to him by Supreme Cashier Davis.

Judge Taylor issued an order making it compulsory upon all members to pay their last two assessments if they desire to participate in the final distribution of the funds of the order. At a meeting of a local branch here last night it was decided to commence a criminal prosecution of all the supreme officers of the order.

NEW HAVEN, Aug. 25.—The local lodge of the Order of the Iron Hall has practically withdrawn from the general body. There are 166 members, and at a meeting just held it was decided not to remit $3700 of assessments now due. The money in the treasury will be divided pro rata among the members in good standing.

DETROIT, Aug. 25.—Henry M. Cheever has begun eight more suits against local branches of the Iron Hall. The bill in each case asks for the appointment of a receiver. Mr. Cheever says he will begin suits against four other Detroit branches, and when this is done all the branches will have been served alike.

PHILADELPHIA, Aug. 25.—Five foreign attachments were issued against the supreme sitting of the Order of the Iron Hall. The attachments are for $1000 each, and are issued upon the petition of five members, whose certificates have matured.

Murdered for Money.

DENISON, Tex., Aug. 25.—A hunting party of four young men was found murdered on the bank of Caney creek, in the Indian Territory. Papers found on one of them indicated that his name was Cherrie, and that he traveled for the Willimantic (Conn.) Thread company. There was nothing to indicate who committed the deed, but the purpose evidently was robbery.

"YOU GAVE ME AWAY, EMMA."

Singular Utterances of Lizzie Borden to Her Sister.

Daughters of Murdered Couple Quarrelled in Police Station.

Prisoner Overcome by Emotion After Her Angry Denunciation.

[Special Dispatch.]

FALL RIVER, Mass., Aug. 24.—"You gave me away, Emma, did you not?"

"No, Lizzie, I only told Mr. Jennings what he ought to know for your defense."

"That is false. You have given me away and I know it; but remember! I will not give in one inch, never! never? That is all I have to say to you."

In a voice embittered with suppressed passion, Lizzie A. Borden this afternoon, in the presence of her attendant, Mrs. Reagan, the police matron, thus addressed her nearest and dearest relative, as with a violent wave of the hand she turned her back upon her sister, with whom the conversation just narrated had taken place.

With tears in her eyes and voice choked with sobs, Miss Emma left the room, and then the accused, overcome with emotion, fell prostrate on her bed. Another chapter in the Borden tragedy was ended.

Cast off by the sister to whom she had come with words of comfort and hope, Emma Borden returned to her home, on Second street, with Lizzie's denunciation ringing in her ears.

Mrs. Reagan, speechless and horrified, watched the prisoner intently.

The Significance of the Scene

she had witnessed was fully realized, but the compromising words of the suspected murderess, her unstrung nerves and wretched condition were a revelation. Previously she had been stoical and reserved, even in disposition, and self controlled. But in one brief minute, as Emma Borden was entering the room, a transformation had taken place and passion reigned within her where indifference had before been.

The above information that The Globe has secured comes from a source that is thoroughly reliable.

It is Not Exaggerated

and is published entirely as secured by the writer from a person in authority, who, while not himself present in the matron's room during the interview, had positive assurance from Mrs. Reagan that such occurrences took place.

In an interview with the writer, a member of the police department said: "Yes, Mrs. Reagan saw and heard all that she has been credited with. She is very reliable and truthful. She is likewise discreet, and you may depend that she will say nothing to newspaper men. If approached I have no doubt she would absolutely refuse to talk and, perhaps, in self-protection, would deny the story. But it is true. She reported it to the city marshal almost immediately after Emma's departure, and he in turn told Mr. Hilliard. The marshal was very much surprised.

"If Miss Lizzie were innocent of the murder of Mr. and Mrs. Borden, how would it be possible in any manner for Miss Emma to 'give her away?' Unless Lizzie had confided something to Emma that the latter had repeated to Mr. Jennings, there would have been no cause or reason for that conversation.

"That there has taken place

Some Violation of Confidence,

or some revelation or fact that Emma was cognizant of, is apparent to the most devoted believer in Miss Borden's innocence. That so-called betrayal was great enough to cause anger on Miss Lizzie's part and make her turn back on her sister and wholly ignore her.

"It was important enough, if Mrs. Reagan speaks the truth, for Lizzie to say she 'would not give in a single inch,' and as Mrs. Reagan says, to emphasize her words, with a gesture in which she designated a portion of her little finger as being less than she would admit. I think this is the most important development in the Borden case since the arrest was made.

"I also think it may be possible after Bridget Sullivan gives her testimony on the stand for the state to proceed in other directions. It is understood among the subordinates in the police department that Bridget has said she

Saw Lizzie in the Cellar

of the Borden house at the place where the axes were kept just prior to the murders. There are other important things that she will tell about, notably the girl's relations with the old folks. She tells a story of domestic discord among the Bordens, the like of which has not been printed in the newspapers as yet."

LABOUCHERE'S "EYE-OPENER"

Furnishes Food for Gossip in London's Leading Newspapers.

LONDON, Aug. 25.—The St. James Gazette (Tory) says that Mr. Gladstone has dished the Radicals, but has failed to muzzle their leader. When questions of foreign policy arise the government may require to be kept in office by Unionist votes.

The Chronicle (Labor and Liberal) says: Mr. Labouchere's pungent, caustic criticisms of the new ministry is having considerable constitutional importance. Perhaps it is better that Mr. Labouchere is not an administrator, but a Radical intransigent applying good and exquisite raillery to a government that is obviously tempted to go slow.

The Star (Radical) says: Mr. Labouchere's eye-opening paragraphs give as much of the truth about the appointments as we may expect to get. A positive statement concerning Mr. Labouchere's exclusion from the cabinet can only come from Mr. Gladstone or the queen.

Mr. Gladstone has sent a letter to Mr. Labouchere saying that he alone is responsible for not presenting Mr. Labouchere's name to the queen, and that his reasons for not appointing Mr. Labouchere in nowise reflects upon Mr. Labouchere's public character and services.

DYNAMITE OUTRAGE.

Carnegie Property in Pittsburg Blown Up by Unknown Parties.

PITTSBURG, Aug. 25.—A car loaded with steel ingots consigned to the Carnegie firm at Thirty-third street was blown up with dynamite or some other high explosive on a side track of the Allegheny Valley road. This is the first attempt at destruction of property around the Carnegie city mills and caused great excitement both inside and outside of the works. The body of the car was badly shattered and the contents scattered in all directions. So far as can be ascertained, no one was injured. A reserve force of police was summoned and quickly surrounded the place, but no one was captured and no clew to the perpetrators was found.

What the Pythians are Doing.

KANSAS CITY, Aug. 25.—The drilling for prizes by the different companies of the Knights of Pythias began yesterday and will continue all the week. The awards will be made on the last day of the encampment. The supreme lodge of the order is in session behind closed doors.

Highest of all in Leavening Power.—Latest U. S. Gov't Report.

Royal Baking Powder

ABSOLUTELY PURE

A RAP AT CANADA.

Senator Morgan of Alabama Says She is a bad Neighbor.

WASHINGTON, Aug. 25.—Senator Morgan of Alabama, who is a leading member af the senate committee on foreign relations, speaking of the Canadian retaliation proclamation, says:

"The fact is that Canada has always been a bad neighbor since the establishment of this government. After the revolution a lot of our Tories went to Canada, and they have transmitted through their descendants an ugly feeling toward the United States. They have made themselves offensive at every opportunity. From the seal fisheries in Alaska, to the fisheries off the eastern coast they have disregarded our rights and done all they could to injure and annoy our people.

"The recommendation of Mr. Cleveland with relation to the shipment of goods across our territory in bond should have been followed. I think President Harrison might have, with propriety and justice, gone further than he did in his proclamation, and have cut off the privilege of shipping Canadian goods through this country. The facts are that we extend every sort of proper courtesy to Canada, and her conduct in return for our friendly treatment is unbearable.

"The Canadians would not be able to feed themselves certain seasons of the year were it not for us. We get no favors from them in any way proportioned to those we grant."

"These people have been acting in such a manner as to make it necessary that we should show our resentment. A vigorous and manly course is demanded of us. I presume Canada will not cease her unneighborly conduct, but we must let it be understood by the British government that we do not intend to tolerate it."

The attention of Secretary Foster of the state department being called by a United Press reporter to the statement that the Canadian authorities proposed to make good to Canadian shippers the tolls levied by the United States in St. Mary's falls canal, he replied significantly that there would probably be some further correspondence on this subject to be made public in a few days.

MINISTERS ASKED TO EXPLAIN.

A Canadian Newspaper's Timely Editorial on the Canal Tolls Question.

TORONTO, Aug. 25.—The Globe, in an editorial on the canal tolls question, says: It is time our ministers at Ottawa broke the silence upon the question whether they promised that rebates would not be granted during the present season. It is expressly charged that such a promise was made, and our ministers owe it to themselves and to the country to give the charge an explicit denial if that can be truthfully done. If our representatives have deliberately broken a pledge, the whole country has been placed in a false position. We sincerely trust that our ministers will be able to clear themselves from so injurious an imputation.

HOWLING DERVISHES

Who Came to Convert Bad Americans, but Were Made Freaks of Instead.

NEW YORK, Aug. 25.—The immigration authorities at this port expect to have a band of howling dervishes on their hands for care and return passage to Europe before the week is out, and they are already making preparations for their reception at Ellis island. The dervishes landed here some weeks ago for the ostensible purpose of converting the American people. It was mysteriously whispered by their manager that they were going to the World's fair, and were living in hope that they would bring back with them to their homes hundreds of converts. Money was no object to them, it was said. But it seems that money was just what they wanted, and it is because they could get none that they are going to appeal to the immigration authorities for return passage.

The dervishes, who are said not to be dervishes at all, are claiming that they are here in the city hungry, friendless and penniless, deserted by the man who brought them here. He promised them great success in their religious werk. Now they say he invited them here only to make money out of their religious performances. It is against their religious tenets to give stage performances, and when they began their exhibition, they expected, they declare, that the entire performance was to be given by them as missionaries.

But when Mr. Paine began to shoot off his fireworks, they began to realize that they were on exhibition as freaks, and they raised a howl that put their every day performances to shame. When they came to New York they refused to carry out their manager's plans. There are twenty-nine men in the party that came here, and they are now living in one room in a house on Twenty-sixth street, near Fourth avenue.

Was a Doctor, Lawyer and Writer.

RONDOUT, N. Y., Aug. 25.—O. H. Mildeberger of New York, who has been summering at Pine Hill, in the Catskills, died suddenly of heart disease while engaged in a friendly game of cards. Mr. Mildeberger was about 70 years of age and was born in New York city. The deceased was possessed of considerable wealth. In early life he studied law and was admitted to practice. Mr. Mildeberger was a writer of considerable note. He also studied medicine and passed some time at leading European hospitals.

Tit for Tat.

HAMILTON, Ont., Aug. 25.—The St. George society, which has heretofore engaged Patrick S. Gilmore and his band for its winter festivities, has notified Bandmaster Gilmore that the society will not make a contract this year, in view of the action of the customs officers at Detroit preventing a Canadian band from filling an engagement in that city.

Politics Going Into Court.

INDIANAPOLIS, Aug. 25.—Prominent members of the Republican party have been in conference with the state committee for several days on the subject of testing the constitutionality of the legislative apportionment law passed by the Democrats two years ago, and it has been decided to institute the suit.

Publishers Robbed.

NEW YORK, Aug. 25.—A defalcation which it is said will reach $20,000, has been discovered in the office of Street & Smith, publishers of the New York Weekly. Alfred J. Price, the firm's bookkeeper and cashier, was arrested and committed in default of $5000 bail.

From Yesterday's Third Edition.

LIZZIE BORDEN'S LETTER.

Emma's Friends in Fairhaven Seen This Afternoon.

Mrs. Allen Brownell No Recollection of the Circumstance Related.

The Missive May Have Been Shown to Her Daughter.

Immediately upon the receipt of news from the *Standard's* special correspondent in Fall River in relation to the singular experience of Lizzie Borden as related by her at the inquest, given on the first page, a *Standard* reporter called at the residence of Mrs. Allen Brownell on Green street in Fairhaven, where Emma Borden was on a visit to Miss Helen Brownell, a daughter of Mrs. Brownell above named. Unfortunately Miss Brownell was not in town, and when the newspaper man stated that he had called for the purpose of ascertaining as to the truth of the alleged statement of Miss Borden that she had shown such a letter to her friends in Fairhaven, Mrs. Brownell said she could not say whether she had or not. She certainly had not shown such a letter to her, and she could not say whether Emma had shown such a letter to her daughter or not. She remembered that Miss Borden had had several letters during her visit, but could not remember whether she received one the day previous to the murder or not.

When asked if her daughter would not have been likely to have mentioned the fact if such a letter had been shown, Mrs. Brownell replied, "Yes, I think she would."

In speaking of the tragedy, Mrs. Brownell did not hesitate to speak strongly in support of Lizzie's innocence. She said that both of the girls always spoke in endearing terms of their father. Emma, she stated, had intended to remain in Fairhaven all Summer.

Hon. H. M. Knowlton, District Attorney, is in Boston to-day in consultation with Attorney-General Pillsbury in relation to the examination of Lizzie A. Borden of Fall River for the murder of her father and stepmother. It is also said that Mr. Knowlton is to consult in Boston Prof. Wood, who has made an analysis of clothing, the hatchet and other articles connected with the murder.

Mr. Knowlton is not expected to be in the city again until Saturday evening, a fact which indicates that the examination will last all the week.

THE TOPHAM CASE.—The latest chapter in the disputed accounts of the executors of the will of Robert C. Topham has developed in what means an action against Mrs. Mary Dugan, who claimed that the estate owed her money for groceries. The executors also claimed that Mrs. Dugan was indebted to the estate, but when the matter came up in the Superior Court Mrs. Dugan obtained judgment, and to satisfy her claim, house and lot No. 89 South Second street were sold at auction, she being the purchaser.

Now H. Wilder Emerson, through his attorney, Maj. Austin S. Cushman, has brought a petition in the Supreme Court, asking that a writ of review may be granted for the rehearing and retrial of Mrs. Mary Dugan's suit in the Superior Court; that the petitioner may be admitted as a defendant therein; that the judgment and sale may be set aside as void; and that the plaintiff, Mrs. Dugan, may be stayed from taking proceedings under the judgment, exception and sale. The petition alleges, among other things, that the sale of the property was not properly advertised or made: that there was no satisfaction of the execution; and that property assessed on a valuation of $2000 should not have been sold for $489.

The petition was presented to Judge Morton of the Supreme Bench in Boston on July 28, and on that day he ordered a hearing at the court-house in Boston for Monday, Sept. 5, at 10 a. m., at which time Mrs. Dugan must be present and show cause why the petition should not be granted. The court also ordered that in the meantime Mrs. Dugan be restrained from disposing of or conveying away the property at 89 Second street, and the papers have been duly served.

PASSENGERS ARRIVED.—This afternoon bark Rapoza do Mar, Capt. Olivier of Brava, C. V. I., arrived in port from Cape Verd Islands, with passengers on board.

PRESENTATION TO A PASTOR.—At the Foster Street Advent Church last evening a purse of money was presented Elder Burch the retiring pastor.

CAPE COD PROHIBITIONISTS.

Rev. Cyrus A. Bradley Nominated for Senator at To-day's Convention.

BUZZARDS BAY, Aug. 24.—The Prohibitionists of Barnstable, Dukes and Nantucket counties in convention this morning nominated Rev. Cyrus A. Bradley of Brewster for Senator in the Cape district; Daniel F. Chessman of Sandwich was elected a member of the State committee. A district committee was elected consisting of Dr. Moses Brown of Vineyard Haven, Rev. R. J. Kellogg of Sandwich and W. F. Sears of Harwich.

The following candidates were named for nomination papers in Barnstable county: Sheriff, Peter T. Brown of Sandwich; commissioner, W. F. Sears of Harwich; special commissioners, N. P. Baker of Falmouth, John S. Smith of Sandwich; commissioners of insolvency, W. M. Hubbard of Falmouth, J. M. Smith of Orleans, Sylvanus Coville of Dennis.

For representatives first Barnstable district, Rev. A. S. Davis of Bourne, Fred Hallett of Yarmouthport. The remaining districts are to be filled by their own conventions.

ANOTHER FIRE AT CALLAO.

Valuable Records in the American Consulate Saved with Difficulty.

CALLAO, Peru, Aug. 24.—Another fire broke out in the Hotel Itala, which is opposite the American consulate. After the firemen had been at work for some little time the water gave out, owing to the cutting of the hose at several points. The building of the Chilean and English Steamship Company caught fire and was totally destroyed, as were several other stores and business places. The valuable records in the American consulate were carried over the roofs of buildings to a place of safety. A favorable wind saved the consulate building, with but slight damage.

The loss is estimated at about 250 souls, and is divided between about 25 firms.

Gladstone Reelected.

LONDON, Aug. 24.—Mr. Gladstone has been reelected in Midlothian.

THE SITUATION IN TENNESSEE.

Coal, Iron and Railroad Co. Files an Answer as Lessee of Convicts.

NASHVILLE, Tenn., Aug. 24.—The Tennessee Coal, Iron & Railroad Company yesterday filed its answer as lessee to the notice served by the board of prison inspectors, indicating a purpose on the part of the board to declare the lease of the convicts forfeited because of insufficient bond and certain alleged defaults on the part of the lessee.

The lessee says it will make its bond good, and in view of an order of the board recently issued requiring it to remove the convicts from the main prison who were brought in on account of the troubles, it agrees to do so provided the State will agree and consent not to determine the alleged grounds of forfeiture, but will submit them to the determination of the courts, a suit having already been brought substantially covering all the grounds of complaint, and arising out of the troubles last year at Briceville.

If this agreement is made without prejudice to the rights of either the State or the lessee, the lessee says it will accept and work said convicts at said branch prisons, or such others as they may determine on, and will pay promptly to the State all future installments accruing on the lease after retaining for the time being the items above specified to be retained, all questions being reserved as to the ultimate liability of the lessee or of the State, for any and all of said items, as well as in regard to the expenses of lodging and feeding the convicts so sent back to the main prison as above stated.

The lessee asks that the convicts who were at Tracy City, Inman and Oliver Springs be returned to those places. "If you prefer the convicts shall not be worked in our mines, and think it to the interest and advantage of the state that the lease we now have may be terminated, it may be done. The company will agree to an immediate cancellation upon the fairest and most equitable terms."

The board yesterday discussed the proposition and it is understood that three members of the board at to-day's meeting will vote to make the proposed agreement and it will be ratified.

The latest news from Coal Creek is that quiet prevails. No demonstrations were made yesterday. Supplies and clothing are being rushed forward from this city to the soldiers, as their stay is indefinite, especially since the indications are that the convicts will be returned to the mines in a few days. Gen. Carnes in the examination of the dispatches in the telegraph office at Coal Creek has found many dispatches of an incriminating nature and which throw much light upon the conspiracy.

The fourth regiment of volunteers was organized here last night.

Miners' Hospital in the Mountains.

MEMPHIS, Tenn., Aug. 24.—A special to the *Commercial* from Coal Creek says a mountaineer arrived there last evening, bringing information of the discovery of a hospital in the mountains a few miles from Coal Creek, which the miners have improvised in a cave. He says he saw dead bodies there and a large number of wounded.

DRUNKEN EXCURSIONISTS.

Steamer Bay Queen Arrives at New Haven After a Riotous Trip.

NEW HAVEN, Conn., Aug. 24.—The steamer Bay Queen, regarding whose safety some fear was entertained last night in this city and New York, arrived this morning at 3 o'clock. The boat's officers said that they made a landing at 25th street, New York, at 4 30 yesterday afternoon and left New York at 9 o'clock last night. The return trip was made as quickly as the big load would permit.

Capt. Ryan of the steamer is quoted as saying that the reason that the boat was behind time was that many of the passengars were so drunk, fighting and riotous that the engineer was afraid to run faster. The passengers rushed from one side of the boat to the other, he said, and so overbalanced her that half the time only one baddle wheel was in the water and anything like speed with safety was out of the question.

The excursion party on board the Bay Queen was from New Britain and the affair was under the auspices of the New Britain Athletic club. Steamboat men here declare that the boat carried more passengers than her United States license permitted. The United States revenue authorities may look into the matter.

SCHOONER ROSA MULLER.

Ballast Will be Thrown Overboard and the Crew Fumigated.

PORTLAND, Me., Aug. 24.—The board of health and Dr. Banks of the Marine Hospital visited the schooner Rosa Muller, which is supposed to have yellow fever on board, this morning. Her captain reports four days out from Santos, one of the crew died of yellow fever. Two weeks ago the mate was taken sick and put off at Vineyard Haven. Two men were sick on the vessel here, but had no contagious disease. They were suffering from the effects of a long voyage. They were taken to the Marine Hospital. The board of health has ordered the ballast thrown overboard, and the vessel and crew will be fumigated before landing.

National Tennis Tournament.

NEWPORT, R. I., Aug. 24.—Conditions for the second day of the National tennis tournament were almost precisely similar to those of yesterday. The summary: First round—Post beat Green 6—1, 6—0, 6—1; second round—Stevens beat McCormick 6—0, 4—6, 6—1; Ames beat Nichols 4—6, 8—6, 6—4, 6—1; Chase beat Shaw 6—4, 6—0, 6—4; Larned beat Slocum 6—1, 6—3, 3—6, 6—4; Hovey beat Codman 6—3, 6—1, 6—3; Smith beat Floyd 6—2, 6—1, 7—5; Gyorth beat Barnes 6—3, 6—4, 6—1; Winslow beat A. B. Emmons 6—1, 6—3. 6—2; Hobart beat Hubbard 6—1, 6—1, 6—2. Championship doubles, Campbell and Huntington beat Hall and Hall 6—4, 6—2, 4—6, 6—3.

Warships at Gloucester.

GLOUCESTER, Aug. 24.—The warships Philadelphia, Concord and Miantonomah have arrived.

Ocean Steamers.

Arrived—At New York, City of Paris, Liverpool; Claribel, Baracoa; Strabo, Santos; at Boston, Ottoman, Liverpool.

TELEGRAPHIC BREVITIES.

The American Bar Association convened to-day at Saratoga.

John Vadua was held in $600 for the Essex County Superior Court at Lynn today for bigamy.

The Granite Cutters' Union has issued a circular calling upon members of the order to stand firm.

James S. Wilson, a railroad agent, was held up by robbers at Nowat, I. T., and $1500 in cash taken.

Extensive forest fires are ranging in valuable lands in the South Mountains within 10 miles of Carlisle, Penn.

Francis E. Gladstone, claiming to be a nephew of the "Grand Old Man" is stranded in Detroit and has asked for assistance to go to Chicago, where he expects a remittance from England.

The Sultan has given orders to the commander of the troops to be sent against the Angira tribesmen to raze every village and to exterminate the rebels.

The Louisville, New Orleans and Texas railroad wharf at Southport, La., caved in yesterday destroying a large warehouse and its contents of cotton.

A terrific rain storm has occurred in Rosalia, Lower California, the seat of the great French copper mines, destroying $100,000 worth of property.

Colored men of Chicago have organized the Northwestern Immigrant Association for the purpose of aiding and assisting the colored people to leave the Southern States and find them homes in the North.

A story comes from Trinidad that Gen. Urdanetta's fleet has sailed into Laguayra, and taken possession of the port without opposition, and has sent a peremptory demand to Carracas for Villegas' resignation.

The ship S. D. Carlton which arrived at San Francisco yesterday from Philadelphia has been 150 days on the passage. She left Philadelphia March 24, the same day the Shenandoah left New York. The latter ship arrived there June 15.

THE SWITCHMEN'S STRIKE.

East Rochester Men Go Out, but Return in a Short Time.

State Arbitration Board Commences Its Hearing.

Grievance Committees Recite Details of Demands on the Companies.

BUFFALO, N. Y., Aug. 24.—The day opens with one feature in sight, the opening of the hearing by the State arbitration board as to the cause and circumstances of the recent strike of switchmen in the railway yards here. In advance there is very little general interest in the hearing. Expectancy as to the arrival of the executive heads of labor orders, and speculation as to what will be done at the conference constitutes all there is of interest to the general public in this situation this morning. No tidings of extraordinary happenings came out of the camps this morning.

Chief Arthur of the engineers has indicated to Mr. Sweeney of the Switchmen's Order that it will be impossible for him to be present here at the proposed conference. This is construed to mean that the Engineers' Order will have nothing to do with the switchmen's difficulties and that the Engineers' Order will not colaborate in a strike.

From this it may be inferred that Mr. Sargent will not take out his men.

These facts leave the conductors, and the trainmen and telegraphers as the field in which Mr. Sweeney must search for aid in his difficulties. The conductors and telegraphers, it is believed, have little in common with the switchmen, and the trainmen are more closely associated with other orders than with the switchmen. Mr. Sargent announced yesterday that he would leave the city this afternoon for home.

Capt. Kirby, in command of troops in the Central yards, hopes that he may start home to Auburn with his second separate company this afternoon. Central traffic is going forward without guard, and the road now practically drops out of consideration as to the effects of the recent strike on business. The same is nearly true of the Lake Shore & Erie and the other lines involved.

Messrs. Sweeney and Sargent expected Chiefs Clark and Wilkinson of the conductors and trainmen respectively early this morning, but up to 11 o'clock they had not appeared and there is a growing impatience over the delay. There is a suggestion made that Clark and Wilkinson may have dropped off at Cleveland to consult with Chief Arthur of the Engineers.

Arbitration Board in Session.

The State arbitration board met this morning. Councillor Hynes, for the strikers, asked that a copy of the recent 10-hour law be placed in evidence, and the board consented.

John McMahon, a switchman recently employed by the Erie, and chairman of the grievance committee, read a copy of the well known demands made upon the Erie and other roads before the strike. Then followed a detail of the grievance committee's demands upon Superintendent Brunn and General Manager Walters of the Erie and the final refusal of the latter to accede to the demands. The polling of the 110 switchmen in the Erie yards was rehearsed as the total number voting to strike. He said he had worked over ten hours without pay since the passage of the ten hour law. The Erie officials had not said they refused to obey the ten hour law.

Grievance Chairman Bass of the Lehigh and men of the other roads recently involved were sworn, and recited the details of their demands of their companies and the steaps leading up to the strike on August 11.

East Rochester Switchmen Out.

ROCHESTER, N. Y., Aug. 24.—The switchmen employed in the Central Hudson yards at East Rochester went on strike this morning. They have no grievances, and their action is prompted by sympathy for the Buffalo switchmen. About 30 men are out.

LATER—It seems now that only 22 switchmen struck, and that the cause was a slight grievance in that they did not get pay for Sunday work, as was the custom in Buffalo. The grievance was adjusted and the men returned to work. The strike did not cause any excitement at other points.

It is learned that a number of switchtenders and yardmen also struck with the switchmen, making 50 in all. All are now at work, but may go out again this afternoon.

The Gould System.

ST. LOUIS, Mo., Aug. 24.—The local grievance committees of the different organizations of the transportation department of the Gould system will meet at the Leclede Hotel to-day. The brotherhood of engineers, the order of railway conductors, the order of railway trainmen, and possibly the switchmen and train dispatchers' organizations will be represented.

Chairman Richards of the conductors' committees says that the conference had been called for the adjustment of matters on the Gould system, but would not give the details. The Buffalo strike, he said, had given great impetus to the project for a federation of railroad labor organizations.

BODY FOUND AT WELLFLEET.

Possibly that of the Captain of the British Schooner L. P.

PROVINCETOWN, Aug. 24.—The body of an unknown man was picked up on the beach at Newcombs Hollow, Wellfleet, yesterday. The head and one arm were missing. The body had evidently been in the water a long time. It is thought it may be the body of the captain of the British schooner L. P. of St. John, wrecked off that point last May.

Irish Cricketers Coming to America.

DUBLIN, Aug. 24.—Twelve Irish cricketers under the captaincy of J. Meldon and D. Rutledge, to-day sailed from Queenstown for New York on the steamer Gallia. They are to play a series of six matches with the Germantown (Penn.) cricket club.

Gold Coin for Europe.

NEW YORK, Aug. 24.—One million dollars gold coin was taken to-day for shipment to Europe to-morrow.

CASES OF INSANITY

From the Effects of

"LA GRIPPE"

Are Alarmingly Prevalent.

Suicides

From the

SAME CAUSE

Are announced in every paper.

Would you be rid of the awful effects of La Grippe?

There is BUT ONE SURE REMEDY that NEVER FAILS, viz:

DANA'S SARSAPARILLA.

We Guarantee to CURE you or REFUND your money.

COULD WE DO MORE?

ISN'T IT WORTH A TRIAL?

je25-tf

WRIGHT Drug Company.

PUREST DRUGS

—AND—

FINEST CHEMICALS

—AT—

Lowest Prices.

WRIGHT DRUG CO.

ON THE WATCH FOR CHOLERA.

Rags from Infected Districts to Be Fumigated Before Being Landed.

BOSTON, Aug. 25.—In view of the rapid spread of cholera in Europe, the custom house authorities of Boston have issued an order that no rags shall be landed from any European port until examinations are made in each case, in order to be assured that they did not come from any cholera infected district, until they are thoroughly fumigated in a manner prescribed by the department. It will be easy enough to guard against rags being shipped here from infected districts; but the authorities say that it will not be so easy to tell from what localities the rags have been gathered before they arrive at the shipping port. A great deal, they say, will depend on the United States consuls at the various ports, as they will expected to use the greatest vigilance in ascertaining the localities from which the rags have been gathered.

OLD GLOUCESTER'S FETE.

The Quarto-Millenium Celebration in Full Swing in the Quaint Town.

GLOUCESTER, Mass., Aug. 25.—The large crowd of visitors in town has been greatly augmented and the streets are filled with sight-seers. The firemen's parade was witnessed by thousands of people. The procession was probably the longest ever seen in Essex county.

It is estimated that fully 25,000 strangers are in the city. The visitors are from all parts of the country and Canada. All precaution has been taken by the local authorities to protect the welfare of every one and guard against accidents.

The literary exercises of the anniversary were held in a mammoth tent at Stage Fort. The exercises opened with music by Baldwin's Boston Cadet orchestra, followed by prayer, offered by Rev. James C. Parsons, and then by the singing of Keller's American hymn by a large chorus. The introductory address was delivered by Hon. Asa G. Andrews, mayor of Gloucester. An original ode, "Wake, Fair City," by James Davis, was then sung by the chorus to the tune of "Hail Columbia."

The choice of Rev. J. L. R. Trask, D. D., of Springfield to deliver the oration on such an occasion as the 250th anniversary of the incorporation of Gloucester was indeed a happy one, and the orator did his subject full justice. Rev. Mr. Trask dwelt at some length on the early career of the town, rehearsing the struggles of the earlier settlers and continuing down in her history to the present.

The other literary exercises included a poem by Hiram Rich and an original ode, "The Granite Shores of Cape Ann," by Henry C. L. Haskell, with music by Osborne W. Lane.

A grand banquet at city hall marked the close of the first day of Gloucester's memorable celebration, and the whole proceedings were a marked success.

CONDITION OF CROPS

As Reported by Correspondents of The New England Homestead.

SPRINGFIELD, Mass., Aug. 25.—Special reports to The New England Homestead reveal a general shortage in the onion crop. The crop of cucumbers for pickles has an increased area and a fair crop of celery is promised. Early cabbage will not make over three-fourths of the usual supply. The great crop of beans last year caused a reduced acreage this season, on which plants are not in the best condition owing to rust. An enormous falling off in acreage and yield of lima beans is reported from California. The supply of tomatoes will not be as great as last year. Winter squashes will be in light supply, but turnips, beets and parsnips promise the usual production and range of values. The first returns on the potato crop show the acreage to be somewhat less than last year.

The Evening Standard.

ESTABLISHED FEBRUARY, 1850.

NEW BEDFORD, FRIDAY, AUGUST 26, 1892.

TWO CENTS.

HASKELL & TRIPP.

Special announcement.

On account of the bad weather this morning, these two Friday attractions will be continued through Saturday or until sold:

1st. Rich parasols at *one half* former selling prices.

2d. Boys' suits, formerly $3.69, $4.50, $5.00, now $2.89. Bring the boy and fit him here; we don't send the suits out on approval.

"Home made."

We have the exclusive sale for this city of the highest grade "home made" cotton underclothing for women and misses.

Finest materials.

Perfect fit.

Careful work.

Nothing equal to these goods is being offered *at any price.*

Those of you who have hitherto been compelled to have undergarments made up at home, simply because you couldn't buy ready made that were good enough, will have no need of further trouble on that score.

Our *"home made"* underwear has been produced to fit just such cases as yours. The cloth, the trimming, the sewing, the button holes, the fine, thick, pearl buttons—all just such as you would choose for your own work.

To be sure you must pay us more than for the ordinary sorts—some of you are willing to. We have plenty of other kinds for those who wish to pay less.

Equipoise waists.

The corset substitute—stylish, comfortable, hygienic.

A perfect supporter from the shoulders, distributing the clothing strain and weight.

Three garments in one—corset, waist and cover.

Women's, $1.75 }
Misses', $1.75 } Equipoise.
Children's, 60c. }
Infants', 75c. }

One of the most complete stocks of *desirable* corsets in this state. Prices always lowest.

White goods.

2000 yards mill remnants of beautiful plaided, striped, and lace openwork Lawns and Nainsooks, worth at wholesale 15 to 18c. *Take your pick for 12 1-2c. a yard.*

HASKELL & TRIPP.

Department Stores,

Purchase and William Streets.

HID HER FACE.

Lizzie Shudders at the Grewsome Evidence.

Medical Examiner Tells of Preparing the Skulls.

Headless Bodies of the Murdered Couple Buried.

Dr. Dolan's Cross-Examination of Deep Interest.

Defence Grants Mr. Borden Died Without a Will.

Evidence Showing His Movements Before the Tragedy.

Strain of the Situation Telling Heavily on Emma.

Lawyer Jennings Has Confidence in the Robinsky Story.

[Special Dispatch.]

FALL RIVER, Aug. 26.—The cross-examination of Dr. Dolan, Medical Examiner, dragged its weary length after the close of the report sent for the last edition of the *Standard* yesterday afternoon. Melvin O. Adams was close and searching in his questions, but he did not seem to have any particular object in view, and threw out a sort of drag-net in the seeming hope that something worth while might come into its meshes.

The talk in court circles yesterday afternoon was that the examination will last at least six days.

The cross-examination in the later stages was devoted largely to the blood spots found on the wall near the sofa where Mr. Borden was lying, and to the location, size and depth of the cuts seen on him.

The court room was hotter than Tophet all the afternoon, and while Dr. Dolan thought the temperature might reach the height of 80 degrees, the crowd of reporters in the centre of the room would readily affirm that the mercury would reach 180 degrees.

Before the court adjourned the cross-examination reached the point of the search of the Borden house on the Saturday after the murder. Witness said he took a dress skirt, an underskirt and a blouse waist belonging to Lizzie. On the skirt was a spot of blood about the size of a good sized pin-head. On the dress skirt was a smooch near the pocket. The dress skirt was examined under a glass in the house. These garments were delivered to Prof. Wood. Witness said he was afforded every facility to examine everything in the house. The city marshal had given to him the shoes and stockings said to have been worn by Lizzie on the day of the murder. There was blood on the bottom of the shoes about the shank. The shoes and stockings were delivered to Prof. Wood.

In answer to a question, which took into consideration the spots of blood on walls and door, witness said he should think the assailant of Mr. Borden stood behind him when he was struck. In all probability the assailant would have been spattered with blood. Witness could not see how spots of blood of any consequence could have gone below the waist of Mr. Borden's assailant.

At 5 30 o'clock the court decided to suspend the examination until 10 o'clock this morning.

District Attorney Knowlton said his appearance in the case is purely voluntary, and if he does not put in an appearance at the opening of the court the cross-examination of Dr. Dolan can proceed. The district attorney said he has three or four witnesses to put on in the morning to testify to Mr. Borden's movements out of doors on the morning he was murdered.

Second Day of the Trial.

The forenoon opened with cloud and rain, and as Lizzie Borden leaned against the window-casement in the warden's room in the gloomy Central Station she seemed to have a realizing sense of her condition, if one could judge by her dejected countenance of her inward state of feeling. Even the bouquets of asters which enlivened the window seemed not to be able to quell her sad thoughts. In spite of the rain, as the hour drew near for opening the court crowds on the sidewalks around the station were large, although for the first time the sterner sex predominated in numbers. Rev. E. A. Buck, the steadfast friend of Lizzie, was early on hand, and gave her in the matron's room that degree of spiritual consolation which he was able to impart.

The Strain Telling on Emma.

Emma did not arrive at the station today until a later hour than yesterday. The strain of the situation is telling on her in a stronger measure than on her unfortunate sister, and she grows perceptibly paler and thinner day by day.

Story of a Quarrel Denied.

The story of a quarrel between Emma and Lizzie, sent out yesterday, was this forenoon denied, at least by Andrew J. Jennings, senior counsel for defence. He said he has questioned both of the ladies in regard to the affair, and they say, not only is the story untrue, but there is not a shadow of veracity in it.

Mr. Jennings Interviewed.

Mr. Jennings was questioned by a *Standard* reporter concerning Samuel Robinsky's story of meeting a man on the road to New Bedford. Mr. Jennings said he has received letters innumerable from persons who are undoubtedly cranks, but the letter defence gave out bore apparently the writer's name and was the most plausible in theory and story of any received, and therefore was given for publication.

Mr. Jennings asked the newspaper representative what impression, so far as the writer's observation went, has been created in the public mind by the story of Mr. Robinsky.

The writer was unable to answer the question, owing to the shortness of time which has elapsed since the story was published.

Dr. Dolan Again on the Stand.

The court came in promptly at 10 a. m., and Lizzie Borden, Emma and their intimate friends were present. The cross-examination of Dr. Dolan, medical examiner, was resumed by M. O. Adams of Boston, counsel for defence. He said: I think the instrument with which the blows were struck on Mrs. Borden would weigh from three to five pounds. The blows were struck from behind, and the person inflicting them stood at the height of her hips when she was prostrate. Blood from her must have spattered on the lower part of the assailant's clothes. There was on the window in the room where Mrs. Borden's body was found what I at first took to be blood. I gave no one permission to wash blood from the paint in the sitting or living room. I am prepared to say someone wilfully removed spots from the parlor door the day after the murder. I counted the spots on the parlor door on the day of the murder. There were eight on the door and jamb. No other spots were removed in the sitting room that I am aware of. I do not know how many people handled the hatchet found in the house on the day of the murder. I gave the instrument to the police. I do not recall people rubbing the hatchet or axes to see if spots were rust or blood. I caused Mr. Borden's body to be searched when it was found. Keys, money loose and in a pocketbook, and a memorandum book were found. They are now in the safe at my office. I will produce them.

I Removed the Skulls

from the bodies of Mr. and Mrs. Borden on the day of the autopsy at Oak Grove Cemetery. I did so because of instructions, I think, but am not positive, from the Attorney-General. The heads were cleaned. I mean to say that the bodies were buried without the heads. I do not know if it has been said to any member of the family that such a course had been pursued.

When the announcement of removing the heads from the bodies was made by Dr. Dolan

A Shudder Ran Through the Audience.

Emma placed her hand before her eyes and bowed her head, while Lizzie sunk her face behind the black fan which she has carried every day, but almost immediately lowered it so that it covered her mouth, while she looked busily in front.

Mr. Adams then produced photographs taken in the house of the bodies immediately after the tragedy, and Lizzie looked up eagerly. The pictures were not shown however.

The cross-examination was then resumed. The witness said: I was not present at the opening of the safe; I understand that no will was found.

Mr. Adams said he is prepared to

Admit That No Will Was Made,

and that Mr. Borden was a man of means sufficient to live upon. This will save calling a number of witnesses.

In answer to further questions Dr. Dolan said: No effort has ever been made to fit the hatchet or axes to the wounds on Mr. and Mrs. Borden. I would not fix the time of the death of Mrs. Borden from 11 to 11 15 o'clock in the forenoon. I should judge she died an hour or an hour and a half before Mr. Borden, basing this opinion on the condition of the blood around her head. The Brussels carpet under Mrs. Borden's head would assist in the drying of the blood. The blood coagulated because exposed to the air, and because it was outside the living tissue. I do not think the texture of the carpet had anything to do with the blood. I base my belief that Mrs. Borden was killed an hour or an hour and a half before Mr. Borden from the firmness and coagulation of her blood. I formed my opinion the first time I saw Mrs. Borden as to the time she had been dead. No one stepped in the blood at the Borden house while I was there that I am aware of.

Treasurer Hart.

Abraham G. Hart of Fall River was the next government witness. He said: I am treasurer of the Union Savings Bank. I knew Andrew J. Borden for 40 years. He had been president of the bank all the time I had been treasurer. He was in the bank about half past nine the morning of the murder. It was his custom to go daily to the bank. On the morning of the murder I had a fancy that he was not looking well.

Cashier Burrill.

John T. Burrill, cashier of the National Union Bank of Fall River said: "Mr. Borden was a stockholder. He was in the bank between 9 15 and 9 45 on the morning of the murder."

Cashier Fuller.

Everett Fuller, cashier of the First National Bank of Fall River said: "Mr. Borden was a director of the bank. On the morning of the 4th of August he came into the bank about 9 45 and went out about five minutes of 10. I noticed him, as I was not very busy at the time."

Talked About His Will.

Charles C. Cook testified: My business is insurance. I had charge of Mr. Borden's block corner of Anawan and South Main streets. I did not see him the day of the murder. I saw him on Tuesday forenoon before the murder. I had a talk with him before the murder, three weeks perhaps, about a will. He told me he had made no will and said nothing about making one. I said nothing to Mr. Borden about it. I remember talking with Mr. Medley in my office. I remember Mr. Medley asked me a great many questions. I did not say to him that Mr. Borden said to me that (making a will) was something he had not done but must do.

Mrs. Caroline Kelley testified: "I live next to Mr. Borden on the side looking to his sitting-room. I saw him on the

[Continued on Fourth Page.]

MINING HORROR IN WALES.

Mouth of Pit Closed by a Most Frightful Explosion.

Not a Single Man of the 150 Below Made His Escape.

Scene of the Disaster at Bridgend in Glamorganshire.

LONDON, Aug. 26.—A fearful mining accident occurred this morning at the Lark Slip coal pit, near Bridgend, a mining town in Glamorganshire, Wales. The day shift of miners had not been long in the mine before a most terrible explosion was heard. The ground trembled with the force of the explosion, and the people in the vicinity knew that an accident had occurred.

The day shift composed 150 men and their relatives rushed to the pit mouth to learn the extent of the disaster. The explosion had caused the earth and rock to fall and the mouth of the pit was closed. Not a single man of the 150 in the mine had made his escape.

Hundreds of the miners in the vicinity have volunteered their services and the work of clearing the pit mouth is being pushed as rapidly as possible.

THE CHOLERA IN ENGLAND.

Anxiety Caused by Its Introduction by a Hamburg Steamer.

LONDON, Aug. 26.—There is no doubt that cholera has at last entered England. The disease was brought here by the steamer Gemma, which arrived at Gravesend yesterday from Hamburg. It was reported that the steamer was infected, but the authorities, after examining the passengers, allowed them to land. A few hours after, two aliens who had arrived on the Gemma were taken sick. They went to the hospital, where the doctors pronounced their malady cholera. In spite of everything that was done for them they died shortly after they were admitted. This has caused considerable anxiety, but there is no panicky feeling.

BERLIN, Aug. 26.—A most welcome thunder storm has passed over this city. The air has been cleared and the weather is much cooler.

The *Vossische Zeitung* asserts that before Prof. Koch left Hamburg he telegraphed to the sanitary board that the cholera there, despite every effort of the authorities to check it, is increasing. Over 800 cases he says have been recorded—nearly 300 fatal.

ANTWERP, Aug. 26.—No new cholera cases have been reported since yesterday morning.

ST. PETERSBURG, Aug. 26.—Yesterday there were 2323 new cases as compared with 5679 Wednesday and 2977 deaths, as against 2743 for the previous day. In St. Petersburg there were 103 new cases and 24 deaths.

THE IRON HALL'S AFFAIRS.

Chief Delano of Illinois Divulges What Somerby is Trying to Do.

CHICAGO, Aug. 26.—W. R. Delano, chief of the Order of the Iron Hall, in Illinois, divulged at a secret meeting held last night just what Somerby is trying to accomplish. The meeting was called by Somerby himself, but he did not remain to attend it. There were present delegates from every lodge of the order here. Speech after speech was made denouncing Somerby in the severest terms. When Delano rose to make his speech in behalf of Somerby he was overwhelmed with hisses. He finally managed to calm the delegates and ask for a receiver. He said it was Somerby's desire that a receiver should be appointed in every State where the order existed. In this way it would be easier to straighten out the affairs. Mr. Somerby had gone to Baltimore because he thought Maryland was the best State in which to carry on his work. Delano talked for an hour, and when he sat down had the delegates with him. A committee was appointed to select a man to be appointed receiver. They had not selected a man at midnight, but a name would be presented to the courts to-day.

BRIDGES GONE.

Terrible Rain Storm and Cloud-Burst in New York State.

JAMESTOWN, N. Y., Aug. 26.—A terrible rain storm passed over here early yesterday. Bridges were washed away at Asheville and other places. Portions of land were washed out into the lake, and now a number of islands dot the surface. A number of bridges on the Chautauqua lake are washed away and traffic will be delayed two days. A washout occurred on the Erie road near Grant station, delaying traffic several hours.

SHERMAN, N. Y., Aug. 26.—Last evening a cloud-burst occurred, raising the water to the highest point ever known here. An iron bridge at Dewey place was carried away. One of the abutments of the large iron bridge of the Western N. Y. & Pennsylvania railroad was wrecked, and the bridge dropped into the stream 60 feet below. A large milldam went out with Myrick's ice-house and also the iron bridge spanning French Creek at this place. People were obliged to wade to their armpits to rescue horses from the barns. Small bridges and sluices all over the city have gone.

REVOLUTION IN VENEZUELA.

Urdanetta Declares Himself Dictator and Forms a Cabinet.

NEW YORK, Aug. 26.—A Trinidad, W. I., special to the *Herald* says: "Startling news comes here from Venezuela which puts a new phase on the revolution there. Urdanetta has declared himself dictator and has formed a cabinet with Casanas as minister of the interior. Congress has been dissolved and several senators have been arrested. The banks in Caracas are all closed and the inhabitants of the city are in a state of great excitment.

STRUCK ON DEVIL'S BACK.

Tug William S. Slater of Boston Sunk Last Night.

BOSTON, Aug. 26.—Tug William S. Slater, Boston for Fort Point, Me., struck on Devil's Back at 8 o'clock last night and sank. The captain and crew of eight men rowed to this city in their boat. A dispatch from Hull this morning says the Slater's pilot house has drifted on the Spit.

All Quiet at Coal Creek.

NASHVILLE, Tenn., Aug. 26.—All remains quiet at Coal Creek. In this city there are no further developments and no stir about the executive office. Superintendent of Prisons Wade is busily engaged in securing escorts to accompany the released convicts to the mines and it is expected they will be sent next week.

Mexican Newspapermen Imprisoned.

MEXICO, Aug. 26.—Senores Garcia and Torreses, the proprietor and editor respectively of the *Monitor Republican*, have been arrested and thrown into prison. The charge against them is that of trying to incite revolution by incendiary speeches.

Great Britain Will Send Warships.

LONDON, Aug. 26.—Great Britain has accepted an invitation from the United States to take part in the naval parade in April next in connection with the Chicago Exposition, and will send a number of warships to participate.

WEATHER INDICATIONS.

FAIR AND WARMER TO-MORROW.

WASHINGTON, Aug. 26.—For the 24 hours from 8 a. m. to-day: For Massachusetts, Rhode Island and Connecticut, clearing to-day or to-night; fair Saturday; warmer Saturday, fresh northerly winds.

CLEARING.

BOSTON, Aug. 26.—Local forecast for New England until Saturday night: Clearing during the evening; fair Saturday; slight change in temperature; winds generally northerly; Sunday probably fair and warmer.

Heavy Rains and Floods in Mexico.

NEW ORLEANS, Aug. 26.—The *Times-Democrat's* El Paso (Texas) special says: The drought of several years in northern Mexico has broken with a vengeance. Unprecedented rains have prevailed for the past three days and the country is flooded. At a point 60 miles below the city of Chihuahua 20 miles of the Mexican Central tracks have been washed away. Traffic is completely suspended and it is estimated that no trains can pass for a week.

Damage by the Storm at Newburyport.

NEWBURYPORT, Aug. 26.—Last night's storm carried away the piling under the large coal shed recently erected by the Philadelphia & Reading Coal Co. and several hundred tons of coal fell into the river. Loss about $5000.

Tug-boat Sunk and One Man Lost.

NEW YORK, Aug. 26.—The tug-boat Quickstep sank at the foot of Third street, East river, this morning. The captain and two deck hands were saved, but it is reported that one life was lost.

HOME MATTERS.

PERSONAL.—Mayor Ashley and City Solicitor Desmond left the city last evening for New York where they will confer with the officers of the Gamewell Co. in relation to the threatened suit instituted by the Municipal Signal Co. of Boston.

Miss Nora H. Fairbrother is visiting New York and Brooklyn.

The following were among the 86 new members admitted to the Republican club of Massachusetts yesterday: Daniel W. Deane of Fairhaven, S. A. Holton and George W. Jones of Falmouth, Josiah Freeman and Almon T. Mowry of Nantucket, Emulous Small of Harwichport, Cyrenius A. Lovell of Osterville, William E. Marchant and C. G. M. Dunham of Edgartown, Horatio C. Sampson of Pembroke and Burrett Porter, Jr., of North Attleborough.

THE TITAN OF CHASMS—*A Mile Deep, 13 Miles Wide, 217 Miles Long, and Painted Like a Flower.*—The Grand Canon of the Colorado River, in Arizona, is now for the first time easily accessible to tourists. A regular stage line has been established from Flagstaff, Arizona, on the Atlantic & Pacific Railroad, making the trip from Flagstaff to the most imposing part of the canon in less than 12 hours. The stage fare for the round trip is only $20.00, and meals and comfortable lodgings are provided throughout the trip at a reasonable price. The view of the Grand Canon afforded at the terminus of the stage route is the most stupendous panorama known in nature. There is also a trail at this point leading down the canon wall, more than 6000 feet vertically, to the river below. The descent of the trail is a grander experience than climbing the Alps, for in the bottom of this terrific and sublime chasm are hundreds of mountains greater than any of the Alpine range.

A book describing the trip to the Grand Canon, illustrated by many full-page engravings from special photographs, and furnishing all needful information, may be obtained free upon application to Jno. J. Byrne, 723 Monadnock Block, Chicago, Ill.

H. C. HATHAWAY will sell at auction tomorrow morning, at 9 o'clock, at sales room, household furniture, ranges, one billiard and pool table, one upright piano; at 10 o'clock, at mart, a fine lot of horses adapted for general purposes, several second hand that have been used around the city; also carriages, harnesses, &c.; also mortgagee's sale of furniture wagon with pole.

TO-MORROW, Saturday, we shall offer 25 doz. black stiff hats at $1.50 each. These goods are bought direct from the manufacturer, who wanted money, and you will find them the same quality as other dealers charge you $2 and $2.25 for. They are all new hats and latest Fall and Winter styles. Ashley & Peirce.

SATURDAY, Sept. 24, is the last day we will be open for business. Everything must be sold. To-morrow we commence our Slaughter Sale. Children's suits at a large discount. Children's knee-pants, shirt waists and blouse waists must be closed out. Wamsutta Clothing Co.

SPECIAL SALE FOR TO-MORROW, Saturday, of children's suits. We are going to almost give away 200 children's suits to-morrow. Remember, school begins in about a week, and you can't afford to miss this opportunity to have the children enter school clothed in a new suit for little money. Ashley & Peirce.

SPECIAL CUT PRICES.—For Saturday we shall offer watches, clocks, jewelry, etc., at prices that will astonish you. Good clocks for 93 cents; good watches for $3.75, etc. J. S. Kelley & Son, 15 Purchase street.

REVERSIBLE COLLARS 20 cents per box. 4-ply linen collars, 10 cents each. 50 cent ties 25 c. Everything in our furnishing goods must be cleared at once. Wamsutta Clothing Co.

H. C. HATHAWAY, 37 Elm street, has received at large stock of fine cigars, regular 10c. goods, which I shall sell at 5c. each; also a large line of plug tobacco.

EVERY STYLISHLY DRESSED MAN wears a Lamson & Hubbard hat. Sold by all leading hatters. Best hat made.

DON'T MISS the special sale of children's suits, commencing Saturday morning, at Ashley & Peirce's, 72 and 74 William street.

WE HAVE A FEW Mackintosh Coats that we are closing out at a great discount. Wamsutta Clothing Co.

DISAPPOINTED ONES will find a few of those small silver chatelaine watches at $4.50, at J. S. Kelley & Son's, 15 Purchase street.

JUST ONE WEEK, and for that time *lower prices for carpetings*, in medium lengths, at Waite's, 71 William street. Better see them.

SPECIAL FOR TO-MORROW.—Read Buchell's ad., 5th page.

CALL AT NOONING'S and purchase a sailor at a price below any one in the city.

DON'T MISS the special sale of children's suits to-morrow at Ashley & Peirce's.

MEN'S RUSSIA LACE SHOES at half price tomorrow. Read Buchell's ad., 5th page.

IT IS ASTONISHING the low price we are offering you on flowers at Nooning's.

SPECIAL SALE of black stiff hats, new Fall shapes, at $1.50 each. Ashley & Peirce.

LINOLEUM, new patterns, 2 and 4 yds. wide, just in at Waite's, 71 William street.

METROPOLITAN CATALOGUE, Fall and Winter, now ready at Hutchinson's book store.

FIVE-CENT HATS at Nooning's.

SPRING HEEL BOOTS, any size, $1.50. Devoll's.

SALT RHEUM cured by Hood's Sarsaparilla.

A SUMMER BARGAIN!

Brussels and Tapestry Mats,

1 1-2 Yards Long, 3-4 Yard Wide,

HANDSOMELY FRINGED

Only 97 Cents Each!

Regular Price $1.25,

And Well Worth $2.

"A Word to the Wise Sufficient."

C. F. WING,

34 to 40 Purchase st.

OUTING SHIRTS!

OUTING SHIRTS!

You can never have too many OUTING SHIRTS!

Our low prices will help you out. Quality exceptional.

Good Shirts for $1 and $1.25, laundered collars and cuffs.

Another lot of the popular blue Madras, all sizes, $1.50.

Better come at once, They're going fast.

OUTING SHIRTS!

J. & W. R. WING & CO.,

133 UNION STREET.

OUTING SHIRTS!

WHITING & CO.

THE Last Half Holiday CLOSES THIS WEEK FRIDAY.

We shall give our customers Friday Morning some Extra Bargains.

We have taken a big lot of our $1.00 French Dress Goods, in plain, mixed, stripes and plaids, and made one price on all at 50c. per yard.

A few pieces of all wool Challies, will be sold at 28c. per yard.

The balance of our Black French Satines, Brocaded, and figured, will be closed out at 25c. per yard.

23 more Children's Gingham dresses, go on sale at $1.00 and $1.25, regular $2.00 and $2.50 goods.

Ladies' Black and White shirt waists, fine ones, will be sold at 50c. a piece.

300 Ladies' colored bordered hemstitched handkerchiefs will be sold Friday, at 4c. a piece, cheap at 5c.

A few pair of $3.50 White Blankets, soiled, will be closed out at $2.50 per pair.

We have about 800 yards of those remnant silks left at 39c. per yard, we had such a rush for.

We shall continue the same low prices on Saturday on all our goods.

WHITING & CO.

THE CRESCENT!

22 Purchase St.

SILK GLOVES MARKDOWN.

Black and Colors, 19c.

Gents' Hose.

Fashionable shades, 25 cents. Hermsdorf stainless black, spliced heel and toe, 25c.

An excellent variety of 5c. Handkerchiefs both white and fancy borders.

A new lot of Wrappers in medium shades, also Indigo Blue $1.00 each. Good night dress 50c.

RIBBONS.

We don't *begin* to tell you *how much* we have *marked down* our line of Ribbons, but come and see for yourself.

We will close out our Gingham Dresses for children at *cost.* Sizes from 4 to 10 years of age.

Gloves, 15, 25, 37, 50c.

Corsets, a good corset for 39c.

An X-L-ent Corset for 50c.

A very nice Summer Corset, C-B a la Spirite, price $1.25.

Corsets at all prices.

Having removed our entire stock from the Old Stand at corner of County and High streets, we shall be pleased to see our old friends and patrons at our new quarters, 22 Purchase street, known as THE CRESCENT.

INSURANCE.

FIRE & LIGHTNING,
TORNADO,
PLATE GLASS and ACCIDENT
INSURANCE.

No. 48 North Water Street.

Ætna Ins. Co. .... Hartford
Hartford Fire Ins. Co. .... "
Connecticut Fire Ins. Co. .... "
Merchants Ins. Co. .... Providence
Equitable F. & M. Ins. Co. .... "
Springfield F. & M. Ins. Co. .... Springfield
Ins. Co. of North America .... Philadelphia
Ins. Co. of State of Penn .... "
Fire Association .... "
Home Ins. Co. .... New York
Continental Ins. Co. .... "
German Am. Ins. Co. .... "
Niagara Fire Ins. Co. .... "
Williamsburgh City Fire Ins. Co. .... "
Hanover Fire Ins. Co. .... "
Phœnix Assurance Co. .... London
Guardian Assurance Co. .... "
No. British & Mer. Ins. Co. .... "
Imperial Fire Ins. Co. .... "
Fitchburg Mut. Fire Ins. Co. .... Fitchburg
Dorchester Mut. Fire Ins. Co. .... Neponset
New York Plate Glass Ins. Co. .... New York
U. S. Mutual Accident Asso. .... "

GEO. N. ALDEN.
(Successor to Tillinghast & Alden.)
d&w

SAMUEL H. COOK,
Marine & Fire Insurance
AGENT AND BROKER,
No. 37 North Water Street.
(In National Bank of Commerce Building.)
Whaling Risks and their Catchings a Specialty at This Agency.
The following First Class Fire Insurance Companies are represented, viz.:

Hingham Mutual Fire Ins. Co. .... Hingham
Phœnix Ins. Co. .... Hartford
National Fire Ins. Co. .... "
Phenix Ins. Co. .... New York
Westchester Fire Ins. Co. .... "
Commerce Ins. Co. .... Albany
Pennsylvania Fire Ins. Co. .... Philadelphia
American Fire Ins. Co. .... "
Queen Ins. Co. .... London
London Assurance Corp. .... "
London & Lancashire Ins. Co. .... "
Norwich Union F. Ins. Soc'y .... "
Northern Assurance Co. .... "
Firemen's Fire Ins. Co. .... Boston
The Metropolitan Plate Glass Ins. Co. .... New York
Hartford Steam Boiler Inspection and Ins. Co. .... Hartford

EDWIN EMERY. JOHN H. PEDRO
LAWRENCE GRINNELL & CO.,
Fire and Marine, Life and Plate Glass
Insurance
60 No. Water St., foot of William.
(Over Mechanics' National Bank.)

Liverpool & London & Globe Ins. Co., ... Liverpool
American Fire Ins. Co. .... New York
Prov. Washington Ins. Co. .... Providence
Commercial Union Assurance Co. .... London
Merchants' Ins. Co. .... Newark
Boylston Ins. Co. .... Boston
United States Inc. Co. .... New York
Caledonian Ins. Co. .... Scotland
Hamburg-Bremen Fire Ins. Co. .... Bremen
American Ins. Co. .... Boston
Spring Garden Ins. Co. .... Philadelphia
Lowell Mutual Fire Ins. Co. .... Lowell
Wachusett Mutual Fire Ins. Co. .... Fitchburg
Mutual Life Ins. Co. .... New York
Lloyd's Plate Glass Ins. Co. .... New York

HIRAM VAN CAMPEN. JOHN W. PAUL.
HIRAM VAN CAMPEN & CO.,
FIRE, LIFE AND ACCIDENT
Insurance Agency,
No. 15 North Water Street.
Telephone Call .... 241-2.
(Established A. D. 1852.)
The following First Class Companies are represented:

Sun Fire Office .... London, Eng.
Organized A. D. 1710.
Lancashire Ins. Co. .... Manchester, Eng.
The Reliance Ins. Co. .... Philadelphia
Girard Fire & Marine Ins. Co. .... "
United Firemen's Ins. Co. .... "
Michigan Fire & Marine Ins. Co. .... Detroit, Mich.
Security Ins. Co. .... New Haven, Ct.
People's Fire Ins. Co. .... Manchester, N.H.
Firemen's Ins. Co. .... Newark, N. J.
Newark Fire Ins. Co. .... "
First National Fire Ins. Co. .... Worcester, Mass.
Quincy Mut. Fire Ins. Co. .... Quincy, Mass.
Holyoke Mut. Fire Ins. Co. .... Salem, Mass.
Traders' & Mechanics' Ins. Co. .... Lowell, Mass.
Dorchester Mut. Fire Ins. Co. .... Boston
Cambridge Mut. Fire Ins. Co. .... Cambridgeport, Mass.
Travellers' Ins. Co., Hartford, Life & Accident.
All losses equitably adjusted and promptly paid.
New Bedford, April, 1890.

IVORY S. CORNISH. CLIFTON H. CORNISH
I. S. CORNISH & SON.
LIFE, FIRE, ACCIDENT and PLATE GLASS
—INSURANCE—
Agents and Brokers. 50 North Second St.
NEW BEDFORD, MASS.
Represent the following First-Class Companies:

Ætna Life Ins. Co. — Hartford, Conn
Travelers Accident Ins. Co. — Hartford, Conn
Merchants and Farmers Mutual Fire Ins. Co., — Worcester, Mass
Citizens Mutual Ins. Co. — Boston, Mass
Mass. Mutual Fire Ins. Co. — Boston, Mass
Abington Mutual Fire Ins. Co. — Abington, Mass
Salem Mutual Fire Ins. Co. — Salem, Mass
Essex Mutual Fire Ins. Co. — Salem, Mass
Merrimac Mutual Fire Ins. Co. — Andover, Mass
Franklin Mutual Fire Ins. Co. — Greenfield, Mass
Milford Mutual Fire Ins. Co. — Milford, Mass
Glens Falls Ins. Co. — Glens Falls, N. Y
Union Ins. Co. — Philadelphia, Penn
NewHampshire Fire Ins. Co. — Manchester, N.H
Peoples Fire Ins. Co. — Manchester, N. H
Delaware Ins. Co. — Philadelphia, Penn
Metropolitan Plate Glass Ins. Co. — New York, N. Y

Losses promptly adjusted and paid.
Business solicited.

Bristol County Mutual Fire Ins. Co.
INCORPORATED 1829.
Insures Against Loss and Damage by
FIRE and LIGHTNING.
Insures only buildings, principally dwellings.
CASH PREMIUMS SMALL.
For reliable information call at the office,
NO. 48 NORTH WATER ST.
JAMES TAYLOR .... President
GEO. N. ALDEN .... Secretary and Treasurer
DIRECTORS:
James Taylor, Oliver P. Brightman,
Geo. F. Kingman, Isaac H. Coe,
Thos. H. Knowles, William R. Wing,
Samuel C. Hart.
Telephone Call 11—4. MWF&w

Blacksmith's Helper.

A capable Carriage-smith's Helper wanted.

Brownell, Ashley & Co.,
24 to 38 FOURTH ST.

BOYS'
SHIRT WAISTS
—AND—
BLOUSES!
AT Popular Price Runs.

SANDERS & BARROWS,
67 and 69 William Street.

CLOSING OUT SALE
Of Summer Carriage Lap Robes, Horse Blankets, etc. Lowest Prices in the city for Harnesses, Ladies' and Gents' Riding Saddles, Bridles and Whips.

TRUNKS —AND— BAGS!

TRUNKS —AND— BAGS!

Pocketbooks and Purses, Bill Books, Umbrellas and all kinds of Travelling Goods, at
C. F. CUSHING'S,
HARNESS, TRUNK AND BAG EMPORIUM,
Opp. City Hall, and Branch Store 571 to 575 Purchase Street.

Our popular low prices keep our stock moving and we constantly show new FRESH GOODS. We never advertise mistatements but always back up in stock what we say in print.

EARLY FALL STYLE HATS RECEIVED.
All Best Shapes at CUT PRICES.

H. V. SANDERS & Co.
One Price Clothiers, OPP. CITY CLOCK, 92 Purchase St.

NEW BEDFORD BRASS FOUNDRY.

Machinists, Brass Finishers and Founders, Brass, Bronze and Composition Castings, Zinc and White Metal Pattern Castings, Phospor Bronze Castings a specialty, Lead Window Weights and High Speed Babbitt Metals, Chandelier Repairing and Brazing, Brass Finishing in all its branches. Machine Repairing promptly attended to. Lawn Mowers Sharpened and Repaired.

Foundry and Machine Shop, 108 North Water Street, foot of Elm.
WM. T. NICHOLSON, Manager, Formerly Foreman of the Armington & Sims Engine Company's Brass Foundry, Providence, R. I. je25-3m

SHAPE YOUR MUSTACHE.

What is more disgusting than to see a man always twisting, twirling, and biting his mustache. Avoid the bad habit by using the instrument that will keep it always just right. Will be sent postpaid with complete outfit for 35 cents, two for one dollar. Postal note or stamps. Address the Nason Bartlett Co., Box 2480, Boston, Mass.

FINE CARRIAGES.

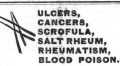

GEO. L. BROWNELL
OFFERS FOR SALE AT HIS
Carriage Manufactory and Repository,
Cor. Acushnet Ave. and Cannon St.,
NEW BEDFORD, ... MASS.,
A FINE assortment of Carriages, namely: Landaus, Coaches, Coupe Victorias, Coupe Rockaways, Extension and Standing Top Family Carryalls, Phaetons, Goddard Box Top Buggies, Open Road and Business Wagons. Also a very large assortment of SECOND-HAND CARRIAGES of all descriptions, which will be sold low.
GILES G. BARKER, Supt.

TRY
39 TOBACCO!
Best in the Land for Smoking.
Be sure that the tag 39 is on every piece, and take nothing else in place of it.
Distributing Agents
Driscol, Church & Hall,
Wholesale Grocers, NEW BEDFORD.

HATCH & COMPANY'S
EXPRESS,
No. 5 Ricketson Block, New Bedford,
DAILY,
By Passenger Trains, to all Points on the Old Colony Railroad and its Connections.

A. B. HATHAWAY,
FLORIST.
Store 220 Union Street.
Greenhouses, Court Street.

GEORGE C. BLISS,
FLORIST.
34 Arnold Street,
CORNER COTTAGE.
TELEPHONE, DAY OR NIGHT.

Smoke the New Nickel Cigar,

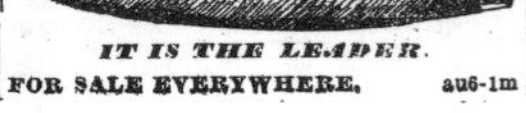

IT IS THE LEADER.
FOR SALE EVERYWHERE. au6-1m

COURT-ROOM SCENES.

Maids and Matrons on the Spectators' Bench.

Lizzie Was Calm, But She Covered Her Face Once.

Dr. Dolan Makes a Debonnaire Appearance on the Stand.

The proceedings at the District Court room in Fall River yesterday have quieted the popular exc itement over the Borden tragedy. The intense interest felt in that locality had reached a crisis where only court room scenes or some other open demonstration would satisfy the people. The hearing seemed to be the first act in the grand finale, and it stilled the storm without creating any sensations or startling disclosures.

You, readers of the *Standard*, who follow the story of the day from the vantage ground of your favorite easy chairs, imagine a court room which the cloudy sky had made unusually gloomy, crowded to the doors with gaping men and women, the only sound an ominous whispering, and every eye nervously travelling from one door to another to catch the first glimpse of the suspected murderer. This was the appearance of the court room at the intermission which followed the session of the criminal term of the Second District Court in Fall River yesterday morning. The moments of waiting were moments of suppressed excitement; even the court officer was affected. So was the most blase reporter. He had sharpened two bunches of pencils and arranged several quires of paper to suit his taste, but still he was fidgety.

Though the hearing had been announced to occur at 10 o'clock the spectators' seats began to fill at 8 30. Outside the square was not so closely packed as on the day of the adjourned meeting. It may be the people began to realize that they labored to get admittance from the police in the face of sure defeat, and didn't care to swelter in the redolent alleyway. But requests for admittance, however, were numerous enough, especially from women. Children with bare legs, bespattered with Fall River mire, ran after the officer, begging for "tickets."

It required considerable diplomacy for the best kind of people to pass the line of officers stationed all the way from the entrance to the bar. Credentials were presented with red tape, or nobody would have gone in.

The funereal court clock had tolled nine strokes when Judge Blaisdell mounted the bench to go through the daily routine of the criminal court. By that hour the room was crowded. The clerk of the court, famous in history as "George," whose other name, were he ever addressed by it, is Wyatt, was disposing of his "passengers." He was "hustling" Christian Endeavorers and young dudes—of which there were many in court—out of seats intended for the prisoners. With an indiscriminate tap on the shoulder of each, he admonished them to "Clear out of these seats or we'll have you in the dock. These belong to the prisoners." The officer was not gingerly inclined to the Christian Endeavorers and he sometimes dictates even to Judge Blaisdell.

There were only a few of the Christian Endeavor Society in the room and their interest in their unfortunate sister seems to be "petering out." But there were "women, women by the dozen." The men were largely in the minority on the seats in the rear. Occasionally a glimpse of a few hen-pecked specimens of the sex were seen hidden behind large hats trimmed in the latest style.

The tone of the dress on the women's seats indicated that in society the occupants ranked from reigning belles to washerwomen. They each and severally appeared to take great interest in the proceedings of the morning, and craned their necks to the farthest capacity to see everything. Some of them were amused at the novel appearance of the prisoners at the first session, and laughed so audibly that His Honor had to tap loudly for order.

Bridget Sullivan arrived at an early hour. As has often been stated, Bridget is a good-looking and well-dressed young woman. Yesterday she wore a dark blue serge and a trim little bonnet with a poke in front, but the most noticeable thing about Bridget was the poke in her upper lip. She looked half frightened to death and disgusted with the whole world. She gave her entire attention to her fan during the day, scarcely venturing to turn her eyes.

When the witnesses entered the court room John V. Morse trudged in the rear of the procession. So much has been written about "Uncle" Morse's seedy clothes that it was rather disappointing to find him attired in a good looking suit of black broadcloth and ministerial tie. He had, however, a sunburned hat in his hand that appeared to have been long in the service.

When District Attorney Knowlton blustered into the court room the ladies seated themselves for what they evidently thought would be a continuous feast of sensations. The room was full. Every seat was taken, that is every seat but one long settee behind Lawyers Adams and Jennings, counsel for the defence. This was to be occupied by Miss Lizzie and her friends and everyone in the court room knew it. All eyes were fixed on this and on the north door. The prisoner made her usual unceremonious entry. She was accompanied by her sister Emma, the faithful pastor Buck, Mrs. Brigham, Charles J. Holmes and Mrs. Holmes. The six comfortably filled the seat.

People in the court room who saw Lizzie Borden shortly after the murder, remarked at once on the very great change in her appearance. It is true that she has grown thin and worn, but she looked by far in better spirits than her friends. The most careful observer would fail to find much that was haggard, worn or sorrowful in her face. Not a really artistic prisoner surely, but quite as interesting in another way.

She wore the blue serge, which has now become famous, and a small black lace toque trimmed with ribbons, also black kid gloves. During both sessions Miss Lizzie sat without turning her head any farther than the witness stand, which was but slightly to her left.

It is not to be questioned that whether the prisoner is guilty or not of the crime with which she is charged that she has most remarkable powers of endurance and a robust nerve force. She is not what she has so frequently been represented—a "girl." Her sister and herself make an excellent pair of typical New England old maids. There are very few mature women, however, who could carry out a plan of conduct under such trying circumst ances as well as she.

The prisoner's face was at all times expressive of intelligence, but not for a moment of feeling. She gave a courteous attention to all the proceedings, but scanned the faces of witnesses with much the same expression that one would wear when looking over a menu. Once during the day while a discussion of her personal wardrobe between Mr. Adams and Dr. Dolan took place she colored slightly. She also gave the only signs of mental pain which she has ever been known to give. It was during the first part of the medical examiner's testimony. He was describing the awful sight which met his eyes as he removed the sheet from Andrew J. Borden's body. Miss Lizzie closed her eyes with a look of real sadness, and placed a small palm-leaf fan which she had in her hand over her face. The reporters all around her were nudging each other to look at Lizzie, but before they all had an opportunity to see the prisoner's grief the fan was lowered and Lizzie was back to her old mood. There were no tears.

Miss Emma Borden is a very slight woman, and in appearance must be of a highly nervous temperament. The descriptions of the cuts affected her far differently. She buried her head in a fan of garnet-colored satin, edged with feathers, and did not remove it for some time. Her eyes were heavy, and the only times she raised them from the floor was to cast weary glances to the members of the Borden counsel. There is a difference of only eight years in the ages of the two sisters, but the difference is much greater than that in appearance.

The elder sister was dressed in a rather prim fashion, in a black cloth gown and bonnet trimmed with gilt braid. Lizzie and Emma did not converse once with each other during the day.

Rev. Mr. Buck, in whose care they were placed, was the most attentive listener. Pastor Buck is a trifle deaf and his left hand was held up to his left ear all day long.

Medical Examiner Dolan was the observed of all observers for the day, as he occupied the witness stand most of the time. He stepped up to take his oath looking as fresh as a daisy. He wore a light gray suit and an æsthetic blue tie. The Medical Examiner of Fall River is of spacious proportions, and he very nearly filled the witness box. The moment upon entering he leaned forward and rested on his arms, and in that position continued through his entire examination. The only times he stood erect was when shifting his balance from one arm to another. He twirled his fingers when he thought and played with a fan that bore a picture of some scantily clothed nymphs swinging a pressed ham in some festoons of ribbon. He also used the fan to make drawings to illustrate his answers to some of Mr. Adams' questions. During the intervals the Doctor learned over and chatted with the court stenographer, Miss White, who occupied the desk of the clerk. Altogether he made a very debonair witness, and was himself engaging enough to counterbalance the tiresome details of his testimony.

Among the people who were given special seats inside the rail was William Henry Johnson Esq., of this city. Father Giquere of Fall River was seated among the reporters. His reverence was so well entertained that he said he should have to bring some clerical friends before the case was over.

The crowd of newspaper men were scribbling and sweating all day, and at some of the tables that would only furnish elbow room for four were crowded seven or eight men and some of them heavy weights at that. About the brightest face in the group was that of Henry G. Trickey, the murder reporter of the Boston *Globe*, who became well known from his work on the Sawtell case. Among the number were several women, but they did not create any great sensation there were so many of the sex outside the rail. They were not the sweet girl graduates of the shorthand colleges out for exercise either, but practical newspaper workers. Mrs. Percy of the New York *Herald* occupied a table with the Boston *Globe's* crack stenographer, Mrs. Barker.

The Fall River police officials, who were in the room, were a remarkably handsome set of men, but they looked woefully sleepy. City Marshal Hilliard looked a counterpart of the flattering pictures of the Prince of Wales. He had on his new uniform, which has only been worn on a few state occasions. At his elbow was Assistant Marshal Fleet and both paid the greatest attention to proceedings.

The judge and the district attorney, Dr. Dolan and Mr. Adams gave an interesting exhibition of the various ways in which the word "wound" can be pronounced. The judge being a gentleman of the old school gave it the old time roll, and the doctor the more rythmical modern interpretation. The other two gentlemen took first one pronunciation and then another.

The cross-examination in the afternoon was rather tiresome, and it told on the nerves of the district attorney. He made frequent visits to the judge's pitcher and sat on top of his table dangling his feet. Some of the Christian Endeavor women went to sleep. The sketch artists made funny pictures, and the reporters talked caucus politics and wrote Sunday school lessons to each other.

A sigh of relief went around when "George" called court adjourned.

ULCERS,
CANCERS,
SCROFULA,
SALT RHEUM,
RHEUMATISM,
BLOOD POISON.

these and every kindred disease arising from impure blood successfully treated by that never-failing and best of all tonics and medicines,

SWIFT'S SPECIFIC SSS

Books on Blood and Skin Diseases free.
Printed testimonials sent on application. Address
The Swift Specific Co.,
ATLANTA, GA.

Moderate in Price,
Excellent Quality,
—AND—
DESIRABLE FOR YOUR TABLE!

The new drink, Cocoa Coffee, 35c. for handsome can containing a pound.

The new Relish, California White Grape Mustard, large bottle for 15c.

A can of very nice Peaches for 18c.

A box of Fresh Boneless Herring for 15c.

SOMETHING NEW EVERY DAY
—AT—
ALLEY'S.

THE CRIMSON-DYED MAN.

Samuel Robinsky and His Very "English" Letter to Miss Borden.

The hearing in as far as it has proceeded, says the Providence *Journal*, developed the fact that the defence is still working on the theory that Mr. and Mrs. Borden were butchered by some man, sane or insane, who was not intimately connected with them. The tragedy has taken place, and it is necessary to find somebody who was responsible for it and to point at him, still at large and a menace to any community in which he may happen to be lurking. In other words, a singular attempt has been made to revive the impression that some type of the wild-eyed, white-faced man is not a myth, but a reality. A singular attempt because the letter which counsel for the prisoner has given to the press contains some wonderful points, worthy of study. It is written by an ignorant Jewish peddler who is "studying english," and who fears arrest. Such is his dread of detention in a cell that he refers to it several times, and to avoid attracting the attention of the authorities to himself he pens an epistle to Miss Borden and mentions her lawyer by name. His "english" is nothing to boast of in the beginning, but it improves rapidly, and he closes with a grace that a Chesterfield might envy. For instance, here are two sentences: * * * * "after all he had was a 5 doll bill he bought from me four handkerchiefs 1 looking glass, 1 necktie collar and shoe blacking his boots was covered with blood and he puts lots of blacking on it." "Hoping that my information will be of some use to you I remain very respectfully," etc.

Perhaps this Jewish peddler realized that his "English" could be amended to advantage, and called in a friend who had enjoyed wider advantages to assist him in bringing his effusion to a close. He forgets nothing, not even the postscript. His description of "his stranger" is perfect; no police inspector could add to it. He has taken accurate measures of the suspect's height, hair, weight, and dress, and he can pick him out in a crowd of 100,000 men.

The peddler does a very fair business with this stranger, and when the latter has purchased liberally of the wares offered, unloads his lunch on the fellow for a quarter. The murderer, provided he is the murderer, is as queer as the peddler. He has killed two people on a street which was choked with pedestrians and wagons, has escaped the notice of Miss Lizzie Borden and Bridget Sullivan and has passed through the city covered with the blood of his victims. He has betrayed the most astounding nerve and daring, and yet when he purchases a disguise of the first man he meets he gives away his hand, admits that he is a fugitive and that he has been fighting with a farmer. He is on the road to New Bedford and he inquires for Boston trains; even his shoes are covered with gore. To return to the peddler, an acquaintance tells him about the murder in Boston on the Sunday following the hearing and he is informed regarding it seven or eight hours after it occurred. Furthermore, he is as elusive as "his stranger" or the fiend who tore down the middle of one of the principal streets shortly after the slaughter, or the Steep Brook hermit who has again been seen with the red axe, which he has been carrying for three weeks. In short, he cannot be found, and it is suspected that he has been trifling with counsel for defence on a very serious subject. The mind dwells a few seconds on this Jewish peddler, who, by the way, has just the articles the crimson man needs, handkerchiefs, collars, neckties and blacking, and then it reverts to the Borden barn on Second street, the guest chamber where Mrs. Borden's corpse was found and the sitting room in which Mr. Borden was done to death.

The early efforts of the counsel for the defence to lead the public away from the homestead have not been altogether successful, because those efforts are directed along the channel which had been followed from its source, to its outlet, and because counsel's mysterious man is a little more improbable than the majority of his predecessors. Samuel Robinsky may be writing the truth, but if he is writing a falsehood he is not clever. His villain is too deeply dyed, too outspoken and too heavily laden. He was in a hurry and he did not throw away his fat bundle. If Robinsky had been peddling dusters aud matches on Aug. 4 "his stranger" could not have blacked his tell-tale shoes.

WHO IS SAMUEL ROBINSKY?

A Volunteer Witness Whom the Police Believe to be a Myth.

Samuel Robinsky is a Jewish peddler, according to the letter which he wrote Emma Borden, and is also a fellow whom Lizzie's attorneys, Mr. Adams and Mr. Jennings, would give a little to find just now.

As detailed in yesterday afternoon's *Standard* he sent Emma Borden a letter, in which he stated that about 4 o'clock on the day of the murder he was sitting by the road leading from Fall River to this city, when a man whose clothes and shoes were blood-bespattered came along, bought some goods from him, told him how he had had a fight with a farmer for whom he had been working and then went away.

Sam did not know of the murder at that time, but when he heard of it he sent Emma Borden a letter containing this information. This missive was dated at Waltham and was quite a well executed document, coming from one who was just learning English, he wrote.

When Lawyer Jennings was shown the letter he recognized the importance of Samuel as a witness, and sent a telegram to Mayor Mayberry of Waltham, who instituted inquiries, but was unable to find Samuel in his borough. He wired Mr. Jennings to that end, and added that he was informed that a peddler by that name was in the habit of coming from Boston occasionally.

A *Standard* reporter visited Waltham yesterday and found a few Hebrew residents, but none of them knew of Robinsky, although they would be likely to have known him if he lived there.

The peddlers' supply houses at the North End, Boston, were also visited, with no better results. No one knew Samuel, and, so far as could be ascertained, no one of that name had bought any handkerchiefs, looking glasses or shoe blacking down that way of late.

If Samuel is a flesh and blood figure he is clearly a person of no wide acquaintance among the people of his race at the North end, as a Jewish resident of Boston who had been hired by the government to find him, was unable to discover any trace of him.

The Boston police have taken the matter in hand, however, and Capt. Cain has detailed Officer Wolf to locate him, if possible. The police are inclined to believe that no such man exists.

MOTHERS SOUND ITS PRAISES.

Physicians Advise The General Use of the Purest and Best of Foods for Little Folks.

Ignorance on the part of the parents has caused the death of more infants in Massachusetts towns this Summer than all other causes combined. Said a local physician yesterday:

"Many a household might have been saved the sorrow of a lost child if the little one had only been properly fed, if the parents had followed the advice of those who know best about such things and heeded the experience of many of their neighbors.

"Lactated food given instead of the poor substances that have caused such fatal indigestion as has prevailed, would have saved many young lives."

ELEANOR.

The beautiful child of Mr. and Mrs. Richard M. Broderick of Penacook, N. H., owes her life to this food. Mrs. Broderick writes:

"Our baby commenced using lactated food when she was about two months old. Before then we had a hard time with her every night. She suffered terribly with griping pains that were the result of indigestion, and we could do nothing to ease her. Her bowels were in a terrible state, and she seemed to be fading away.

"Fortunately I heard of lactated food. I weaned the baby and tried it, and I know that it saved Eleanor's life. If mothers want to keep their children free from pain and build up a sound foundation to form the coming man or woman, they should feed the little ones on lactated food. We have used a dollar's worth of this food every month since we commenced, and she loves the sight of a food-can so much that the only way we could get her quiet for a picture was to give her a can to hold."

Lactated food is no secret whatever. It is so good and pure that even the most cautious physicians, like the eminent Drs. Agnew and Guernsey, have always advised its use.

The safe plan for this month and for the Summer months to come is to feed infants upon lactated food. It will keep them well and strong.

PHOTOGRAPHERS' PART.

Skulls of Victims Pictured for Presentation at the Inquiry.

There are not lacking evidences that the statements previously made that the work of the photographers will play an important part in the Lizzie Borden hearing have very good foundation. In addition to the photographs of the rooms in which the murdered couple were found, of the blood-stained furniture and of the bodies, it has just been developed that likenesses even more gory will probably be introduced before the hearing is closed. Photographer Walsh has performed most of the labor in his line upon this case, and among the collection of pictures which he has taken for the authorities, are two representing the skulls of Mr. and Mrs. Borden. After it was learned that such photographs were in existence, a search was commenced to discover the location of the originals, and it was ascertained that after the postmortem in Oak Grove Cemetery the heads of the victims of the double murder were removed from the bodies and taken in charge by Medical Examiner Dolan. The flesh has been removed from them and they are now in the possession of the doctor, although it is expected that the photographs will meet every purpose. It is regarded as not altogether improbable that the introduction of the skulls themselves into the court-room may follow. The photographs are life-size, and, as may be imagined, present a ghastly sight.

The "Partial" Report.

Copy of the findings of the inquest as presented to presiding Justice Blaisdell:

Bristol S. S., to J. C. Blaisdell, Justice of the Second District Court of the County of Bristol.

In conformity with section 9 of chapter 200 of the acts of the year 1877, I return herewith a copy of my record of an autopsy of the body of Mrs. Andrew J. Borden, aged 67 years, found lying in Fall River and supposed to have come to death by violence. The said autopsy was made by authority of Mayor Coughlin at 3 o'clock in the afternoon of Thursday, the 4th day of August, A. D. 1892, in the presence of W. T. Learned, residing at Fall River, and J. Q. A. Tourtellot, residing at Fall River, who were required by me to attend the same as witnesses thereof, viz.: The body was found lying upon Second street. Before proceeding with the autopsy I called the attention of the witnesses summoned by me to the appearance and position of the body, and caused them carefully to observe the same. The autopsy then proceeded as follows: On the left side of the head over the ear was a wound two and a half inches long by one and a quarter wide. On the right side of her head was a number of cuts penetrating the brain and so intermingled as to be practically impossible to count, and I further declare it to be my opinion that the said Mrs. A. J. Borden came to her death from shock, the result of blows from an axe or a large hatchet.

Dated at Fall River, in the county of Bristol, this 8th day of August, A. D., 1892.

W. A. DOLAN, Medical Examiner.

The other autopsy was in the presence of the witnesses, and was on the body of Andrew J. Borden. It states: "The autopsy then proceeded as follows: The left side of the face and head was cut and smashed in by no less than 12 distinct blows of an axe or large hatchet." In other respects, it does not differ from the above copy of the report of the autopsy on Mrs. Borden.

PROBABLY INSANE.

Dr. Albert R. Moulton so Regards Miss Lizzie Borden.

The question as to Miss Lizzie Borden's sanity is greatly interesting physicians generally, and experts in mental diseases in particular.

Dr. Albert R. Moulton, ex-State superintendent of institutions for the insane, who was in Boston yesterday, expressed his opinion on the subject to a *Globe* reporter.

The doctor, who is now settled in one of the Middle States, said he had nothing on which to base his conclusions save the reports in his own local newspapers, but from what he had read he was firmly convinced that if Miss Lizzie committed the murder she was and is insane. Most of his friends, he said, shared this opinion.

"Her disposition and temperament, as I have found them described," said he, "indicate a certain form of mental derangement, which has no particular name, perhaps, but might be called incipient mania.

"I should judge that she has been afflicted with it for years. It appears in her spells of irritability and aversion to society, often followed by extreme exhilaration, as shown in joviality or geniality. The fact that her friends or relatives have never suspected such an affliction does not in the least affect the likelihood of her insanity.

"Her actions since the tragedy also point to insanity, and are inconsistent

READ!

READ!

READ!

MOYNAN'S

Saturday Bargain List.

MOYNAN & Co. offer for Saturday Ladies' Fine Cambric Wrappers that were $1.25 and $1.50 for 98c. Also a lot of red figured waists that were 50c., for Saturday's sale only 39c.

Don't miss visiting Housefurnishing Department.

IN MILLINERY DEPARTMENT.—On Saturday we will close out all our children's sun hats at *less than half price.* Also all our ladies' straw hats in every style and color, were from $1 to $2.50; without any reserve your choice now $25c. Millinery flowers and wreaths all go at less than quarter old prices. Moynan & Co.

Great Reduction in all kinds of silk waists, newest styles.

WASH GOODS.—On Saturday you can have the remainder of our Domestic Challies (only about 500 yards) regular 5c., for this day 3c. Shantong Pongees, regular 12½c. quality, all choice patterns of this season's productions and perfectly fast colors; your choice for this sale 8½c. per yard. Only a few short lengths of those wool challies that have sold at 21c. Early comers can procure them on Saturday at 12½c. yard. Moynan & Co.

See our new stock of Kid Gloves.

DRESS GOODS.—A strictly all-wool serge, 36 inches wide, and in all the desirable colorings, staple 50c. quality; we offer while they last at 39c. Don't miss getting one of those handsome dress lengths which we are selling at about ⅓ *less* than regular value. Moynan & Co.

Parasols at prices you want to pay. Must go at once.

SATURDAY IN HOUSEFURNISHINGS.—24-inch Japanned Tea Tray regular 49c. now only 29c. 26-inch Trays regularly sold at 59c. on Saturday 39c. 28-inch Trays regular price 71c. on Saturday only 49c. Black wood handle ladles regular price 8c. for Saturday only 5c. Thin engraved tumblers regular price 89c. dozen for this sale 57c. dozen. Window screens only a few remaining, your choice *from any size* 28c.

See our new styles in Ruchings, Laces and Embroideries.

IN CLOAK DEPARTMENT.—All our Ladies' Blazer Jackets in Tans and Blues, that were $5.00 and $5.98 must go on Saturday at $2.98. Ladies' Jersey suits were $4.00 and $4.90 at $1.98. Ladies' Kado cloth capes, suitable for early Fall wear, these are a new lot just in and are worth $12.00, but will be opened for Saturday's sale at $8.98. Suits in cotton, also cotton and wool at $1.98. Moynan & Co.

See our $4.50 China Silk Waists, in Red, Blue and Black for Saturday only, $3.48.

EMBROIDERIES.—On Saturday we will sell remainder of our Embroidered, also Embroidered and Hemstitched Flouncings; some very handsome styles are included in this lot, and are worth from 50c. to 75c. all go in on Saturday at 49c. per yard. See our cheap prices on all kinds of Laces, Ruchings, Veilings, etc., etc. Moynan & Co.

Don't miss the Ribbon Sale, remember just half usual prices.

ON SATURDAY we will sell an extra size Marseilles Spread worth $1.75 for $1.48. Huck and Damask Towels worth from 21 to 25c. for this day 17c. 18 inch all linen Crash worth 8c. for 5c. per yard. Moynan & Co.

Don't miss these Japanese Silk Handkerchiefs for 29c. each.

MOYNAN & Co. offer for Saturday's Sale a lot of *Quill Fans* in all colors, worth at least 50c., for this Sale only 25c. each. *Surely see them.* Big bargain in Japanese Silk Handkerchiefs, worth from 50c. to 75c. for 29c.

For Cheap Underwear, Gents are invited to go to Moynan & Co's, on Saturday.

Come to Moynan's on Saturday for Ruchings, Veilings, Laces, Embroideries, Perfumery, &c., &c. Our prices are low and our assortments largest to be found in the city.

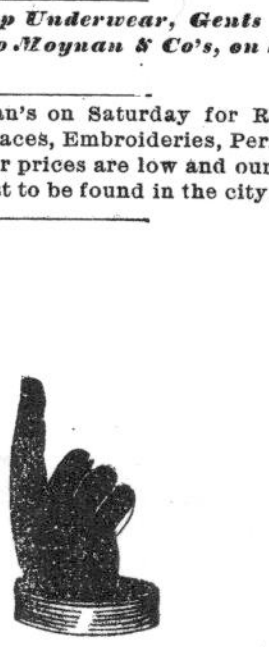

The Evening Standard.

NEW BEDFORD, MASS.

FRIDAY EVENING, AUGUST 26.

THREE EDITIONS DAILY.

No. 87 Union Street.

PUBLISHED BY

E. ANTHONY & SONS,

INCORPORATED.

—TERMS—

Six Dollars a Year; Three Dollars for Six Months, in advance; Single Copies Two Cents.

TELEPHONE CALLS.

Counting Room, - - - - 308—2
Editorial Room, - - - - 308—3

FOR PRESIDENT:

BENJAMIN HARRISON

OF INDIANA.

FOR VICE-PRESIDENT:

WHITELAW REID

OF NEW YORK.

CONTENTS OF THIS EVENING'S STANDARD.

Page 1.

Second day of the great murder trial in Fall River.
Sinking of tug William S. Slater of Boston.
One hundred and fifty lives lost by a mining explosion in Glamorganshire, Wales.
The Iron Hall's affairs.
Home matters.
Late telegraphic news.

Page 2.

Court-room scenes at the Borden hearing.
Who is Samuel Robinsky?
The story of the crimson-dyed man.

Page 3.

Lieut. Totten again predicts the end of the world.
The canal tolls dispute.
Unusual precautions to prevent introduction of cholera into Boston.
Nantucket men rescued at sea.
Meeting to consider joining the Naval Reserve.
City property committee further discusses the engine-house plans.
Early telegraphic dispatches.
Home Matters.
Suburban news.

Page 4.

Sudden death of Edmund Grinnell.
Dredging Lake Anthony.
Third District Court.
Editorials.
Home Matters.
Telegraphic dispatches.

Page 5.

Marine intelligence.
Marriages and deaths.

Page 6.

Financial news.
Second Edition — Telegraphic and local news.

Page 7.

Methods of Japanese firemen.
Joe Goddard had the best of his fight with Smith.
Yesterday's ball games.
Amusement and sporting news.

Page 8.

The tobacco crop.
Gloucester's grand parade.
Congressional candidates.
People's Party meeting in New York.
Lively scenes at a British political meeting.
Gen. Bidwell's letter accepting the Presidential nomination.
Third Edition—Telegraphic and local news.

☞ The Cleveland *Leader* thinks some one ought to save Grover Cleveland's letters and publish them in book form. They would make a queer collection. A few days since he wrote to a club of independent voters commending the spirit which put "the welfare of the country above partisan considerations." A few days later, writing to a Georgia Democrat who had decided to support the Chicago nominees, though they were distasteful to him, Cleveland said that it is "the duty of one opposed to shut his mind and heart to any feeling of irritation or resentment that might be allowed to grow out of opposition, based upon honest judgment and a conscientious desire for party success." Could two sentiments be more diametrically opposed to each other than these?

GROCERIES

—AND—

MEATS.

Choice Wine Crackers, 12c. lb.
Best Zephyr Crackers 13c., 2 lbs. 25c.
8 bars of Good Soap 25c.
4 lbs. Soda Crackers for 25c.
Good Pickles 6c. a bottle.
Yellow-eyed Beans 8c.
Pea Beans 8c. Eagle Beans 8c.
Red Kidney Beans 10c. qt.
Large Fancy Eating Pears 8c., 4 qts. 25c.
Good Watermelons 10 to 25c. each. Don't pay more as these are extra cheap.
Corned Beef good at 3c. a lb.
Our 5c. Corned Beef is fine.
Best Corned Beef in the city 8c. lb.
We corn our own Beef always and guarantee it to please everyone.
Evergreen Corn 15c. a dozen.
Tomatoes 6 lbs. for 10c.
Early Rose Potatoes 23c. a pk.

ROASTS.

We are selling lots of roasts and our prices are very low.

MEATS. **Always buy your meats of us, and you will get the best at the lowest prices**

—AT—

GRAY BROS',

288 and 294 PURCHASE ST.,

CORNER MAXFIELD,

BRANCH STORE,

FOURTH ST., Cor. THOMPSON.

☞ A Philadelphia physician who has just returned from a trip to England says: "I stopped with a gentleman in Liverpool who is making a fortune out of one of the most curious applications of the drop-a-penny-in-the-slot idea that I have ever seen. In England, by the way, they use it for a dozen things that we know nothing of in this country. The use for it to which I allude, however, is the furnishing of illuminating gas to small consumers. A small device is fastened to any ordinary gas meter, and each time a copper penny is dropped into the slot a certain amount of gas is let into the meter, and thence into the pipe leading to the burner. A little dial shows how much gas is admitted to the meter, and a dozen or more pennies can be dropped in in succession if the purchaser so desires. Over 4000 of these are now in use in Liverpool, and the demand for them in that and other big cities is so great that the company owning the patent cannot at present begin to make them fast enough to supply it."

☞ Allen W. Thurman, son of the "Old Roman," created depression in Democratic circles yesterday by deriding all pretensions of Democratic hopes in Ohio in the coming campaign. "Ohio is almost hopelessly Republican," said he. "It will probably be carried by the high tariff party, by as big a majority as McKinley received. The Democrats will not make any great efforts in the State this year. I would be in favor of closing up the campaign headquarters and taking things easy, because when we make an aggressive fight the Republicans get scared and get out every voter. If we keep still the enemy might be indifferent and not get out their vote."

☞ The president of the Summit (N. J.) Silk Manufacturing Campany, in giving the reasons why his company has established mills in that village, says that he and his associates would never have put their money into the enterprise but for the McKinley tariff bill and their faith in the reelection of President Harrison, "which faith is based on our confidence in the sound common sense of the American people.

HOME MATTERS.

THE UNION STREET RAILWAY COMPANY will occupy their new office in the Five Cents Savings Bank building Next week.

SCANDINAVIAN MEETING. — A converted Swedish royal opera singer, with Henry Carlsen of Fall River, will hold a Scandinavian gospel meeting next Saturday evening at Pleasant Street M. E. church.

BOWLING.—F. A. Abbott of the Y. M. C. A. has just completed 50 strings in the Y. M. C. A. bowling alleys and his average for the 50 strings is 162½. His highest score was 213 while his lowest score was 116.

IT DID STRIKE.—Superintendent of Fire Alarm D. D. Briggs wishes us to state that the fire alarm bell on the Harrington School did strike the alarm for the Florence street fire Wednesday, all reports to the contrary notwithstanding.

BRAKEMAN INJURED.—The forward brakeman of the old road freight from Fall River to Boston on the Old Colony had a finger and a thumb badly crushed while coupling cars at Myrick Wednesday. He was taken to Morton Hospital, Taunton.

BICYCLE RECOVERED.—On Wednesday forenoon a boy's safety bicycle was stolen from T. H. Mills' store on Purchase street. This morning the bicycle was found in a boarding-house on South Water street by Officer Cannavan, in company with Mr. Mills, who identified it as his. The boy who had stolen it is at present out of town, but immediate steps will be taken for his arrest.

OFF THE TRACK.—Engine No. 160 of the Old Colony, drawing a gravel train of New Bedford men, which has been away the past three months, arrived in this city last night. This morning while proceeding to Fall River, the engine and tender left the track just south of Weld street, tearing up the roadbed and breaking the jaws of the truck on the engine. It was taken to the local repair shop.

CLEVELAND AFTER BLUEFISH.—Ex-President Cleveland took a sail down the bay yesterday on the Ruth, having as guest Joe Jefferson. The party trolled for bluefish. The newspapers every day announce that Mr. Cleveland will speak within the next two months in different parts of the country The fact is that, instead of accepting any such invitations he has declined them all, and does not expect to make any political trips during the campaign.

ACCIDENT.—About 10 o'clock this morning William Driscoll's horse, left standing in front of the Parker House, became frightened and started to run. He succeeded in running only a few feet when he brought up against Cornelius Murphy's hack, damaging it somewhat. Willie Coleman, a little boy sitting on the seat of Driscoll's wagon, was thrown off and the horse accidentally kicked him in the chest, bruising him badly, but it is not thought broke any bones.

CHAMBERS WILL NOT LEAVE HIS POST.—Rev. David Chambers, the pastor of the Methodist church at East Harwich who was assaulted with a large stone, and who had been warned in an anonymous note to leave town, says he sees no reason for any personal attack upon him. He has endeavored to bring the two factions of the church together and thought he was succeeding. "I hope and expect," he said, "that the law will have in its grasp the person who assaulted me, but if it fails and I know the would-be assassin is abroad, it will not drive me out of town. I am here to do good and I shall remain."

NANTUCKET.

Yesterday's ball game at the Fair Grounds, between Nantucket and 'Sconset, was won by the latter team, score 11 to 5. Booth of New Bedford pitched again for Nantucket, but his support was poor.

Most of the 200 excursionists who came on the Island Home from Cottage City went to 'Sconset, and their return trip to town was made interesting by a break down and derailment just beyond Surfside, about four miles from town. News of the accident was immediately sent to all the livery stables at Nantucket and every available team was sent out to bring the stranded passengers to the boat. The captain of the steamer delayed his departure long enough for all to arrive, and the excursionists went away none the worse for their mishap and with a new experience to relate and exaggerate when they get home. The cause of the accident was a broken fish-plate under the engine. The cars were got on the rails again in time to run the night boat train according to schedule.

The Ocean House girls gave their annual complimentary dance to their Nantucket friends last evening, in Smith's Hall.

John Morley's Handsome Vote.

LONDON, Aug. 26.—The election in New-Castle-on-Tyne resulted in the return of Rt. Hon. John Morley, chief secretary for Ireland, by 2078 more votes than he received in the general election.

OBITUARY.

Sudden Death of a Well-Known Business Man This Morning.

The business men of this community were shocked this morning to learn that Edmund Grinnell, at the head of the New Bedford Iron Foundry, had died suddenly, and since this information was imparted to them his death has been the principal topic for discussion. Mr. Grinnell was about as usual yesterday, and those who had met him then could hardly account for the truth of the report, which was in circulation down town shortly after 8 o'clock.

It seems that deceased went home last evening feeling no worse than he had been for several weeks past, and this morning was found dead in the bath room with the electric light turned on. He was partially dressed. As he had previously had a severe attack of kidney trouble, it is thought this complaint, together with over-work, hurried his death, which otherwise might not have occurred for years.

Mrs. Allen, who had acted as housekeeper for Mr. Grinnell during the absence of his family, found deceased as described.

Physicians who were summoned this forenoon state that death resulted from hemorrhage into the brain.

Mr. Grinnell was the oldest son of Lydia R. and the late Joseph G. Grinnell, and was born in this city about 42 years ago. He attended the Friends' Academy, where he graduated, and while fitting for Harvard College with others in his class, his father died. This caused him to change his plans. Instead he took up his father's business, and with the assitance of Samuel Ivers carried on the New Bedford Iron Foundry, which at that time was located on North Front street. Afterwards the business was transferred to the stone building on South Water street, where it has since been conducted. After an acquaintance with business affairs he assumed control himself, Mr. Ivers retiring, and since that time Mr. Grinnell had been at the head of the New Bedford Iron Foundry, which is doing a large business, having much work, especially from many large concerns out of town. Deceased was an indefatigable worker and not infrequently was seen at his office as early as 4 o'clock in the morning. He was one of the original movers for a telephone service in this city, and secured the privilege for this section. He was also president of the Clarks Cove Guano Co. for several years, and while in this capacity conceived the idea of forming a trust of all companies engaged in the manufacture of fertilizers. Every company in the United States went into this deal, but two or three of the leading men withdrew from the scheme at the very last, and this act greatly crippled the local corporation. However, about this time Mr. Grinnell started several similar companies in the South, which have since proved profitable ventures. In the trust alluded to Mr. Grinnell was one of the three appointed to carry its plans into execution. He was also the first active president of the New Bedford Manufacturing Co., and for several years a director in the First National Bank. At the time of his death he was a prominent member of the Boston Master Builders' Association.

Mr. Grinnell married Jennie, daughter of Humphrey H. Swift of New York, formerly of this city. He leaves a widow and four children, all of whom were at Petersham, N. H. This sad intelligence was communicated to the bereaved family just before noon to-day.

Mr. Grinnell carried a large life insurance.

He was for many years a member of the New Bedford Protecting Society.

THIRD DISTRICT COURT.

BORDEN, J.

FRIDAY, Aug. 26.

Arthur H. Jennings pleaded guilty of being a tramp. He was found by Officer Gifford asleep in Gray Brothers' barn, and has had no steady employment for a long time, and has been loafing around livery stables. He has no father or mother, and is only 19 years of age. Several officers spoke a good word for Jennings, and his case was continued to Sept. 3d to enable him to get a job and go to work.

Mary Furber is a terror to the good people on West Durfee street and Wednesday morning, about 4 o'clock, while drunk, disturbed the whole neighborhood. A warrant was made for her arrest and when Officer Fay went out to arrest her yesterday he found both Mary and her husband drunk, and the house in great confusion. Mary was sent up for 60 days for the disturbance of the peace and three months for drunkenness. Her husband upon recommendation of the officers was put on probation.

One other case of drunkenness was put on probation.

Ernest Newton pleaded guilty of being drunk yesterday and was sentenced to three months in the House of Correction. He appealed and was ordered to recognize in $300.

Clement N. Lussier and Joseph Prue pleaded not guilty of violating Section 9 of Chapter 313 of the Acts of 1885, relating to registered pharmacists. F. A. Milliken, Esq., appeared for the defence, and the cases were continued to Sept. 1st next.

James W. Hayden pleaded not guilty of a violation of the same law.

Robert F. Vogel testified to having a prescription put up by Mr. Hayden at Dr. Bailey's store on Kempton street on the 24th inst. Dr. Bailey was not present at the time.

Clinton P. Vose, the agent of the Board of Pharmacy, testified to Dr. Bailey's being at his store on Water street at the time the prescription was put up for Mr. Vogel, and that Mr. Hayden was not a registered pharmacist.

Dr. Bailey took the stand and said he was short of help at present, and thought as he was registered it was not necessary for Mr. Hayden to be registered.

Judge Borden told the doctor that if his view of the law was correct one man being registered might run all the drug stores in the city with unregistered clerks. He did not think that was the spirit or intent of the law. An unregistered clerk under a registered pharmacist's personal supervision could put up prescriptions, as he understood the law, but in no other way.

The doctor allowed he should be obliged to close one of his stores if that was the law, as he could not find a registered pharmacist easily. To which the court replied that he did not make the law.

Walter B. Pack pleaded guilty of a similar offence. He said he had made application for an examination to be registered, but had not yet been examined. He was registered in Rhode Island, but was aware that did not protect him in this State.

The court read the law to the defendants and stated his views of it and what he regarded its intent, and then fined each $15, which was paid.

GOSPEL GROVE CAMP-MEETING.

GOSPEL GROVE, Cadman's Neck, Aug. 24.

At the evening service there was preaching by Rev. T. F. Norris of Westport from Acts xvii, 30: "Now God commandeth all men everywhere to repent." An earnest plea for the unsaved to come, seek and receive this great blessing of salvation, coming not only as an invitation from God, but as a command.

The meetings have increased in numbers and also a manifest increase in spiritual strength. The blessing of entire sanctification and conversions of the unsaved follow at the close of nearly every meeting.

Bro. I. T. Johnson returned home last evening on account of the illness of his wife. Rev. H. N. Brown is expected to-day and will probably lead the remainder of the meetings.

H. A. S.

CONCRETE SIDEWALK.—A concrete sidewalk has been laid on the west side of Cottage street, between Elm and Morgan streets.

HID HER FACE.

[Continued from First Page.]

morning of Aug. 4. Saw him going up the steps. He apparently tried to fix his door. I was going down street. The front door steps of Mr. Borden's house can be reached without going out of the yard. Mr. Borden had a white package in his hand. The time I saw him was about 27 minutes to 11. I was going to a dentist's office, and was late, and so remember the time. I did not see Mr. Borden before that day.

Cross examined. When I first saw Mr. Borden he was coming from his front door. I do not know how he got into the house.

Dr. Dolan Recalled.

Dr. Dolan was recalled, and at the request of the district attorney produced the keys to the Borden house.

In answering questions he said: I do do not know whether Mr. Borden used tobacco or not. The keys on the ring are arranged so far as I know just as they were when they were handed to me.

In answer to a question from the district attorney, witness said that the photographs which had been presented to the court were those taken by his directions. He also said that the only evidence he found of blood spurting from the cutting of an artery was in the case of the 86 spots he had previously mentioned, which described an arc of a circle, and that the other spots in his opinion must have been from some other cause than the spurting of the blood from a broken artery.

Mr. Borden's watch was found upon his person. The bed was all made up in the spare room when witness first saw it at 11 45, and the pillow-shams were in their proper place.

In cross examination by Mr. Adams witness said that the direction that the blood was thrown depended upon the way in which the artery was severed. He continued: I do know something about a yardstick having been found in the room. After I had made the examination I heard something about a yardstick. There was a kind of a camp-chair between the body of Mrs. Borden and the bed. I remember that a work-basket was in front of the chair.

Jonathan Clegg was the next witness. He is a dealer in hats and gentlemen's furnishing goods at No. 6 Main street. He first saw Mr. Borden in front of his store at 10 20 a. m. on the day of the murder. When Mr. Borden left his store at 10 29 a. m. he went south.

In cross-examination he said that he fixed the time at 10 29 when Mr. Borden left the store, because he had an appointment with him that morning, and that he had in his mind that his clerk must have his dinner hour. Mr. Borden was in witness' store about eight or nine minutes. Mr. Borden had been in the store of the witness on Tuesday before the murder because he was talking about witness renting a store of him.

John Cunningham, a newsdealer, was the next witness. He said that he was on Second street on the day of the murder and he heard of the murder that morning while he was passing the house from four or five men who were standing on the west side of the street. He at that time stood on the side-walk for a few moments engaged in conversation with those who had heard about the murder.

Francis H. Wixon, deputy sheriff, said: On the day of the murder I was down stairs with Marshal Hilliard. A message came by telephone to me about 10 or 15 minutes past 11. Before that I was on Second street and saw people in large numbers going along. On the receipt of the telephone message I went to Mr. Borden's house; saw no one there but Dr. Bowen; there were but few people in the street at that time.

Witness then described the scenes which occurred in the house, and said that he took the watch from Mr. Borden's pocket at the request of Dr. Dolan.

The witness was subjected to a sharp cross examination and said that he saw men in a yard adjoining Mr. Borden's house. He got over the fence and attempted to interview them, but as the one he spoke to could only speak French he got no satisfactory results.

This was the last witness before adjournment, and at 12 20 Lizzie A. Borden left the room, leaning on the arm of City Missionary Buck. After he had satisfactorily disposed of Lizzie he returned, and performed the gallant act for Emma.

At 12 30 a recess was taken until 2 o'clock.

GALE AT GLOUCESTER.

Easterly Storm Interferes With Events of the Celebration.

GLOUCESTER, Aug. 26.—The easterly storm that began yesterday increased with considerable energy during the night and three fishing schooners, Lizzie M. Stanwood, Mascot and M. A. Baston, dragged their anchors and went ashore on Rocky Neck, where they lie in bad positions. The Stanwood and Mascot will probably bilge.

The high winds blew the bunting on the buildings in all directions and the beautiful decorations of yesterday now present a bedraggled and dilapidated appearance.

The events scheduled for to-day, the concluding ones in the celebration, are the fishermen's race and grand open regatta. The harbor is full of yachts for the latter race, but it is thought it may have to be postponed owing to the rugged weather.

TELEGRAPHIC BREVITIES.

Washington Democrats favor free silver.

Prisoners escaped from jail at Lima, O.

A counterfeiters' cave was discovered at Brazil, Ind.

Gladstone denies the rumor that he is to retire in the spring.

Dirty Jewish emigrants furnish a cholera danger to Paris.

John Dillon thinks an autumn session of parliament undesirable.

Baltimore and Ohio railroad telegraphers in Baltimore have asked for more pay.

Bumper men in the Carnegie mills have struck against the employment of non-union men.

Rev. Dr. Melancthon Wooley Stryker of Chicago was elected president of Hamilton college.

The Russian finance ministry will shortly issue 25,000,000 credit roubles secured by gold.

The lost Stewart placer mines are said to have been found about twenty miles from Spar City, Colo.

The Ameer of Afghanistan has appealed to India for aid against Russian aggression in the Pamir country.

A broken journal wrecked a freight train on the Central Massachusetts road, near Barre, Mass., blocking the track several hours.

At Great Falls, N. H., an 18-year-old French girl, named Mary Ducette, jumped into the canal and was drowned. She was prob bly insay

DREDGING LAKE ANTHONY.

The Proposition to Make it a Harbor for Yachts at Cottage City.

[Special Dispatch.]

COTTAGE CITY, Aug. 26.—The proposed dredging of Lake Anthony for a harbor for small craft, as discussed at the taxpayers' meeting on Wednesday, has been productive of considerable comment. The resolutions, as offered by the committee of 20, recommended that the Sunset Lake improvement be done at a cost not exceeding $5000; if any of that amount shall be left intact after improving the pond the balance to be expended in making a suitable drive or walk. Some people who are old enough to be wiser assert that a harbor can be made of Lake Anthony for less than $5000. These men seem to see a way to dig out the pond at a very small expense and one or two gentlemen have contributed to a fund for the purpose. Some time ago an engineer examined the inlet with a view to furnishing an estimate as to the probable cost of bulkheading the entrance through the sand beach, and excavating a channel so that yachts could enter. This engineer said that $5000 would furnish a bulkhead that would withstand the forces of nature for 10 years, but he didn't mention the cost of building a sea wall several hundred yards long and jetties to match to prevent the entrance from filling up with sand. The expense that would be entailed to properly dredge Lake Anthony would be considerable. It is a well known fact that improvements of a character like those contemplated must be substantial; weak bulkheads and sea walls are simply equivalent to sinking good money into the sea.

A gentleman who has been interested in enterprises of this kind told a *Standard* reporter that a good small craft harbor can be made out of Lake Anthony for something less than $500,000. The sea wall must be solid and many men and vessels would have employment in working out stone and transporting it to the locality. Jetties must be formed of stone or the work will never endure. According to this gentleman's theory a bulkhead will define the inlet more clearly, but a channel after being dredged will immediately fill up.

A grand benefit concert will be given at the Casino this evening to Capt. John Orlando of West Falmouth, who runs a sailboat on the Lagoon, by the teachers and pupils of Villa Bristhall. Capt. Orlando has for 17 years made a scanty living by taking out sailing parties. He is a paralytic, having lost the use of his lower limbs in the exposure he suffered during a shipwreck a score of years ago.

The Republican rally and flag-raising set down for last evening was postponed to Tuesday evening next, so as not to disturb the Methodist meetings.

The annual meeting of the Marthas Vineyard Association will be held at the residence of Dr. Tucker to-morrow.

The band will not play on Ocean Park to-morrow evening.

AN INJUNCTION GRANTED.

Chancellor McGill Tightens the Rope on the Reading Coal Combine.

TRENTON, Aug. 26. — Chancellor McGill's decision in the case of the state against the railroads forming the Reading coal combine has been filed. The state's contention that the lease of the Central to the Port Reading is illegal, that the agreement is in violation of law, and the combine is a gainst the policy of the state, because it tends to the monopoly of a public necessity, are all upheld, and the preliminary injunction prayed for is granted.

Pythians Elect Officers.

KANSAS CITY, Aug. 26.—The supreme lodge, Knights of Pythias, elected the following officers: Supreme chancellor, W. W. Blackwell, Kentucky; supreme vice chancellor, Walter B. Ritchie, Ohio; supreme prelate, E. T. Blackmer, California; supreme master of the exchequer, F. J. Wiley, Delaware; supreme keeper of the records and seals, R. L. C. White, Tennessee.

The Way of the Trangessor.

JEFFERSON CITY, Mo., Aug. 26.—George A. Vincent, who in 1872 forged and negotiated nearly $500,000 of New York Central and Erie bonds, and who afterward escaped from Sing Sing, will be released from the state prison here tomorrow, his term of ten years having expired. Officers will take him to Sing Sing to serve out his unexpired term there.

Has a Good Bank Account.

HARTFORD, Aug. 26.—Jimmy Lyons, the noted crook and burglar, who surrendered himself two years ago, after being a fugitive from justice for twenty-two years, has just have released from the state prison. He immediately took the first train for Boston, where his relatives reside. He is now over 50 years of age and broken in health. He is said to be worth $50,000.

Trains Collide at Providence.

PROVIDENCE, Aug. 26.—A collision between an accommodation to this city and a freight train occurred on the New York and New England road near the Brayton avenue crossing. Both locomotives were derailed and considerably smashed up. Nearly all of the passenger coaches remained on the rails, although the windows were shattered. Passengers escaped with a shaking up.

London on the Watch.

LONDON, Aug. 26.—The steamship Gemma, from Hamburg, arrived at Gravesend with sixty aliens, some of whom are Russian Hebrews. Three of them were reported ill and, upon examination by health officers, were found to have symptoms of the cholera. The steamship was quarantined.

Actor Daboll's Funeral.

HOLLISTON, Mass., Aug. 26.—The funeral of the late W. S. Daboll occured at the residence of G. W. Slocum yesterday, Rev. J. B. Cook reading scripture selections and offering a consoling prayer. The body was exceedingly life-like in appearance. There were many floral tributes.

Accidentally Drowned.

NEW HAVEN, Aug. 26.—Charles Gardner, a 'longshoreman, aged 50 years, was employed by the Long Wharf Fish company, and was leading a small boat when he slipped and fell overboard. An effort was made to rescue him, but it was of no avail.

Flying from the French.

PARIS, Aug. 26.—An official dispatch from Porto Novo states that Colonel Dodds advanced against Sakele. The Dahomeyans, not only in Sakele, but in all the neighboring country, evacuated the district and fled northward, with the French in pursuit.

Female Balloonist Killed.

DETROIT, Aug. 26.—Gertie Carmo, the balloonist, who had been making ascensions at the Exposition grounds here, was killed by falling from a great height. Her parachute would not work.

Farmhouse and Buildings Gone.

THOMASTON, Me., Aug. 26.—The farmhouse and buildings of Daniel Mayo were destroyed by fire, including a barn full of hay, implements and grain.

Asiatic Cholera in Berlin.

LONDON, Aug. 26.—The Berlin correspondent of the *Telegraph* mentions a report, which is believed to be fabulous, that 65 persons have died of Asiatic cholera in Berlin.

From the Cholera Infected City.

BOSTON, Aug. 26.—German steamer Kehrwader from Hamburg passed Hull at 10 this forenoon. She will be quarantined.

THE GRAND ARMY PARADE.

The committee having in charge the arrangements for the great parade of the Grand Army encampment in Washington Sept. 20th have finished their work and a circular of instructions has been sent to each Grand Army post in the country. The procession will be formed on the streets radiating from the capitol grounds. The head of the column will move at 9 30 a. m. from the corner of First and B streets, southwest on B street south, and will continue the march on First street east to B street north, and thence on B street north, turning into Pennsylvania avenue on the north side of the Peace monument. Thence it will continue the march to Fifteenth street, and by a right wheel into Fifteenth street, and then by left wheel into Pennsylvania avenue, and thence past the reviewing-stands to Washington circle. The order of the procession will be as follows:

Citizens' committee, escort of commander-in-chief, old guard of Washington, Grand Army battalion of Albany, commander-in-chief, junior vice-commander-in-chief, senior vice-commander-in-chief, official staff of commander-in-chief, aid-de-camp to commander-in-chief, escort to Grand Army, first defenders, 6th Massachusetts, United States veteran signal association, departments of the Grand Army in the order of seniority, naval veterans' association.

Mrs. Gen. Logan has arranged for a reception to be held Monday evening, Sept. 19, in the rotunda of the capitol, to which will be invited the Grand Army, the Union Veterans' Union, the Woman's Relief Corps, the Ladies of the Grand Army and other patriotic organizations. Mrs. Logan will also give a reception at her home, Calumet place, to the John A. Logan posts of the United States and the woman's relief corps of Illinois Sept. 20, from 8 30 to 11 30 p. m.

Commander Yoder of the Union Veterans' Union has informed Chairman Edson that instead of 3000 he fully expected that 5000 members of the organization would attend the encampment. He asked that provision be made for that number, and quarters were assigned them in the barracks. Although Chairman Edson has in course of erection buildings which will accommodate 25,000 men, and he has already provided quarters for 20,000 men free of cost in the various school buildings, yet he is somewhat apprehensive that a greater number will come here than has been provided for. Some 20,000 have secured quarters which they will pay for, making a total of some 65,000 old soldiers who have made arrangements to attend the encampment.

THE JEWEL CASKET.

Pie knives have etched landscapes.

Asparagus servers increase in breadth.

There are several new dress lifters in the market.

New ring stands have a circular procession of hooks.

The little medicine cups have proved a great success.

In the present fashion of woman's gowns the stick pin has a great opportunity.

Although the queen chain is so nearly superseded by the chatelaine pin, some new designs still appear.

Black enamel chatelaine pins as bowknots with diamonds for polka dots are a touch of subdued elegance.

A new silver bracelet is a heavy log chain like that of gold bracelets, and closely fringed with tiny coins.

An inlaid cribbage board with mosaics of different marbles and stones and mounted in silver is a recent production.

Very elegant plates and platters of silver gilt are prepared for various purposes. They have plain centers and borders rich in perforated ornament.

Some new large silver brooches are very Japanesque. They assume natural forms. Leaves or branches of flowers are copied minutely and have the invading bug or worm.

Sponge drainers are a new article in the market. They are of glass with perforated silver platelike covers. The wet sponge is laid on the silver and the water escapes through the perforations.

SPECIAL NOTICES.

ATTENTION, WHEELMEN.

☞ Union Run and Clambake at Otis A. Sisson's, SUNDAY, Aug. 28th. All are invited. Start will be made from Crescent Club Rooms, at 10 30 A. M. au26-2t

HEARING.

CITY OF NEW BEDFORD,
CLERK'S OFFICE, Aug. 25th, 1892.

☞ Notice is hereby given that the Mayor and Aldermen will give a hearing in their chamber, City Hall Building, on THURSDAY, Sept. 8, 1892, at 7½ o'clock P. M., to all persons interested in the petition of T. A. Tripp, for a license to set up and maintain two (2) steam engines and boilers of fifty (50) horse power, at his place of business northeast corner of Prospect and Grinnell streets.

DANIEL B. LEONARD, City Clerk.

(Mercury copy.) au25-tsep8

MILL EXCURSION.

☞ Persons going on the excursion given by the Howland Mill and the New Bedford Manufacturing Co., SATURDAY, August 27th will please take notice that the train leaves this city at 7 30 A. M. au25-2t

CADMAN'S NECK.

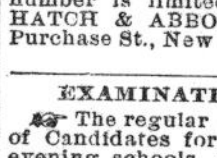

Barge City of New Bedford will leave City Square at 8 o'clock SUNDAY MORNING, for Cadman's Neck Camp-meeting, by the way of Cannonville and Smith Mills.

au25-2t A. R. CASWELL.

EXCURSION TO WHITE MOUNTAINS.

☞ Messrs. Hatch & Abbott will run an excursion to Fabyans, starting Sept. 5th, returning Sept. 10th. From New Bedford, by rail to Boston, moonlight sail to Portland, and rail to Fabyans. Three days' board at first class hotel, with meals en route both ways, and all this for only $20. Persons desiring to join will send in names at once, as number is limited. Address or apply to HATCH & ABBOTT, at either 92½ or 796 Purchase St., New Bedford. au22-tf&wtf

EXAMINATION OF TEACHERS.

☞ The regular semi-annual examination of Candidates for positions in the day or evening schools, and for positions as pupil teachers in the Training School, will be held at the School Committee Rooms, William street, on TUESDAY, WEDNESDAY and THURSDAY, Aug. 30, 31, and Sept. 1. The examination will begin promptly at 9 o'clock, Tuesday morning. Any further information which may be desired on the subject can be obtained by application at the office of the Superintendent of Schools.

For the Committee on Examination of Teachers, WM. E. HATCH, Secretary.

New Bedford, Mass., Aug. 16, 1892. au16-2w

ARCHITECTS

☞ Are invited to submit to the Committee on City Property, sketch plans for a new City Hall to be located on the present City Hall lot; with such suggestions as they may deem expedient. To be submitted on or before Sept. 1.

S. A. BROWNELL,

au12-tsep1 Chairman.

REMOVAL OF NIGHT SOIL.

☞ Persons desiring to have their vaults emptied of night soil, can leave their orders at the following places upon slates provided for that purpose:

Washburn's Grocery store, 741 Purchase st.
Central Union Grocery, 9 North Sixth street
F. C. Bliss & Son, Washington square.

ap9tf S. S. WILBUR.

NONQUITT HOTEL.

Now Open for the Season of 1892.

Special attention given to parties, clubs, &c., &c., for dinners and suppers. Escape the heat of town and pass a cool night at Nonquitt. Boats leave New Bedford 6 45, 8 50 A. M., 1 45, 5 00 P. M. Leave Nonquitt 7 45, 9 50 A. M., 3 00, 6 00 P. M. Fine macadamized road just finished to Nonquitt.

W. H. WINGATE, Proprietor,

au3-1m Nonquitt, Mass.

PARKER HOUSE CAFE.

☞ The newly fitted Cafe connected with this hotel will be opened to the public on THURSDAY EVENING, March 21st.

HOLDER M. BROWNELL.

SECOND EDITION.

HOME MATTERS.

REAL ESTATE SALES.—John Whitehead has sold for George A. Briggs two house lots in Fairhaven on Beach street, containing 36 rods, to Mary A. and Thomas Broughton.

M. E. Smith has sold to J. B. Sullivan for George Homer, 68 rods of land on Cottage, Locust and Spruce streets.

Benjamin Lawton, et al., of this city, has sold to Mary M. Freeborn, wife of Thomas M. Freeborn, for $2425, a lot of land with the dwelling house and other improvements in Newport bounded northerly on Bridge street, easterly on land of the heirs of Charles Green, southerly on land now or late of William E. Crandall and of Charles H. Albro, and westerly on land of the devisees of Job. F. Eldred.

The estate of Elnathan E. Delano has sold to Zebulon H. Thompson for $1550, 35.8 rods of land at the corner of Bridge and Mulberry streets in Fairhaven.

Oliver E. Brunell has sold to Henry K. Snow, trustee, 27.68 rods of land on the south side of contemplated Woodlawn avenue.

John M. Howland has sold to Rodolphus Beetle, trustee, 168.77 rods of land on the east side of contemplated Oak street, Fairhaven.

Willard Nye, Jr., and others have sold to Bridget Farrell 41.89 rods of land at the southeast corner of Belleville avenue and Davis street.

George A. Briggs has sold to Rodolphus Beetle, trustee, 73.557 rods of land on the south side of Kendrick avenue in Fairhaven.

Willard Nye, Jr., and others have sold to Francis H. Dowd 14.55 rods of land on the south side of a contemplated 40-foot street on the Nye place, Acushnet avenue.

REAL ESTATE SALE AT THE VINEYARD.—John F. Newton, Jr., has bought of the Wilbur Brothers of Taunton a lot of about 32,000 square feet of land on Atlantic avenue, Vineyard Highlands. It has a water frontage of 160 feet and borders on Atlantic avenue for 210 feet. Plans for a Summer cottage of ten rooms to be built on the site are now being prepared. A Mr. Jennings of Deep River, Conn., has bought the Raymond estate, consisting of a handsome house and lot of land measuring 90x100 feet on the Atlantic drive, for $6000. The Daggett lot, with a frontage of 150 feet on the drive and an area of about 30,000 square feet, has also been sold to Connecticut purchasers for $1200.

SPECIAL POLICE.—A number of the recently appointed special police were qualified today by City Clerk Leonard.

BUILDING.—George England desires leave to raise a building from its foundations on South Second street.

George E. Briggs is building for himself six three-tenement houses, 28 by 38 feet in size, 27 feet posts, and three stories high, on both sides of Hemlock street.

On the east side of Belleville avenue, south of Sawyer street, Manuel Sylvia, contractor, is building a 2½-story house, 25 by 40 feet in area, for Manuel Sousa.

On the west side of Howard street, Frederick Hazard, contractor, is building a six-tenement block, three stories high and 27 by 45 feet in area, for John Counsell.

On the southeast corner of Sawyer street and Acushnet avenue a two-story building is being constructed for Adolph Flarent, grocer, on the north side of Lincoln street, east of State.

A two-story house is building on the east side of North Front street for Richard Shaw, loomfixer.

A three-story six-tenement house, 27 by 45 feet in area, has been built by William Watling, contractor, on North Front street, south of Coggeshall, for James Hargraves. The same contractor is building a two-story house, 23 by 34 feet in area, west side of Howard street, for Robert Allen.

PIERCE AND ROTCH MILLS.—The walls and roof of the Pierce Mill are completed, and the gravelling of the roof was finished yesterday. The staging around the building is being removed and the bricks are being cleaned of all spots which they may have received while being laid. The red mortar in which the bricks were laid now shows to fine advantage. One story of the weaving mill is up and the floor for the second story has been laid. This building is to be but two stories high. The drawing frames have arrived and as other machinery arrives it is stored in the spinning mill.

The machinery for the Rotch Spinning Corporation has all arrived and the work of setting it up is in progress. The shafting is all in position, as are also the pickers and most of the cards. The work of laying the floors and painting is completed. A waste house 20 by 50 feet in area and 12 feet high and a fire pump-house 14 by 23 feet in area and 10 feet high are now in process of building.

CLAMBAKE.—The annual clambake of the First M. E. Church of Acushnet was held last Thursday, the 25th. The day was cloudy and it was feared that rain might interfere with the plans that had been made, but such was not the case. This bake only adds another to the many successes this society has made in furnishing a good clam dinner. It was superintended by Mr. Peckham, and this of course guaranteed success before the fire was started. Full justice was done the dinner by a large and good-humored company, among whom were noticed persons from Philadelphia, Brooklyn, New York, Boston, Taunton and Brockton. This bake will soon have a wide reputation. Many words of praise were heard, both for the dinner and the serving.

OBITUARY.—Mrs. Mehitable E. Howland, widow of the late Abraham H. Howland, died this forenoon at her residence on County street after an illness of several weeks.

PERSONAL.—Charles E. Smith and H. T. Soule have gone to Centre Sandwich, N. H., for a week of fishing.

DEATHS.

In this city, 26th inst., Mehitable Earl Russell, widow of Abraham H. Howland.

In Middleboro, 19th inst., Otis Bent, 76; Edna Florence Mary, daughter of Herman A. Bryant, 2 months; 21st, Ralph O., son of Herbert E. Godfrey, 3 months.

MARINE INTELLIGENCE.

Launched at Newburyport 26th inst, sch Frank Rudd, 625 tons, from the yard of Geo E Currier. She will hail from Newport, and be commanded by Capt Crandall.

Sld from Belfast 25th, sch Mary E Crosby, White, Deer Isle for New York.

Ar at New York 25th, schs Flyaway, Thomas, Hallowell; A McNichol, Sanborn, Fall River; Julia Frances, Anderson, do; Mopang, Clark, do; D K Akin, Fuller, Yarmouth; C H Trickey, Kelley, Boothbay.

Ar at Philadelphia 25th, schs Wm L Walker, Chase, Fall River; Cox & Green, Thompson, Kennebec. Cld, schs Colin C Baker, Baker, Salem; Wm F Collins, Higgins, Hyannis; Oliver Ames, Nickerson, New Haven.

Ar at West Washington 25th, schs Samuel H Walker, Nickerson, Kennebec; Wm L Roberts, Bray, do.

Ar at Baltimore 25th, schs Thos B Garland, Crosby, Long Cove, Me; R & T Hargraves, Allen, Tampa. Cld, sch Wm O Snow, Paine, Fall River.

Cld at Norfolk 25th, sch B C French, Providence.

Sld from Savannah 25th, steamer City of Macon, Boston.

Passed Tatoosh 19th, bark Carrollton, Lewis, San Francisco for Nanaimo.

FINANCIAL.

Money Easy—N. Y. & N. E. Recovers Partially from its Depression—Lake Shore Statement—Anthracite Coal Production—Railroad Earnings.

FRIDAY, Aug. 26.

In spite of continued exports of gold, the stock market is broad with a decided upward tendency, particularly in the industrials and the Gould stocks. Yesterday the cholera scare overtopped all other reports, and the markets were soft in consequence. Even the calling off of the strike failed to have any concerted effect upon prices. The undertone, however, is very strong, and stocks should be a good purchase every time they are sold down. The manipulation downward is for the purpose of gathering in stocks.

In our local market money rates have shown no special changes at 5 to 6 per cent.

The Boston loan market is not very active and rates for money are reduced somewhat. Call loans 3½ to 4½ per cent. Prime mercantile paper 4½ to 5½ per cent. Corporation paper 4½ to 5½ per cent. The clearing-house rate is 3 per cent. New York funds sell at 12 to 15 cents discount.

Money in New York is easy. Call loans 2 to 2½ per cent. Prime mercantile paper 4 to 5½ per cent.

Sterling exchange is quiet and heavy; posted rates are 4.87½ and 4.89.

Government bonds have been dull and easier.

In Wall street stock circles this morning interest was mostly centred in the decision against Reading, and although this decision was discounted by insiders yesterday, it will be likely to have an unfavorable influence on the market. London prices come fractionally lower.

The New York stock market to-day was moderately active and irregular. Atchison held firm at the opening figures—39⅜. New York & New England opened at 31½ and advanced 2⅛ per cent. to 33⅝; Reading declined from 59⅛ to 57⅞, then recovered a fraction to 58. Sugar was weak, declining from 113⅛ to 111⅛, and then advanced to 112. Missouri Pacific sold at 62 and Rock Island at 82½.

The Boston stock market was quite active to-day, especially Sugar trust, although this stock was weak, declining from 113⅞, its opening, to 111⅝, then rallied to 112, its price at 1 o'clock. Atchison was firm at between 39 and 39⅜. New York & New England rallied from its depression of the last few days, opening at 32, an advance of ½ from last night's closing, then rapidly advancing to 33⅞, this last figure about 1 o'clock. Chicago, Burlington & Quincy 101½, and Bell Telephone 206. Westinghouse Electric sold at 38⅞. Sales to noon; Bonds $75,500, and 11,050 shares of stock.

It is stated that a Northern Pacific meeting has been called for Oct. 20, although nothing is said about a dividend. But if earnings keep up a semi-annual dividend of 2 per cent. may be expected in January.

Railroad earnings are reported as below:

Mexican Central.

	1892.	Increase.
Week.		$23,361
Third Aug.,	$160,710	[illegible]093
Since Jan. 1,	4,897,249	[illegible]
Mileage,	1,847	44

Missouri Pacific.

Third Aug.,	$579,000	$65,000
Since Jan. 1,	1,611,000	1,219,000
Mileage,	5,372	141

The operations of the Lake Shore railroad for the June quarter are reported below:

Quarter June 30.	1892.	Increase.
Earnings,	$5,150,594	$351,180
Expenses,	3,227,625	82,691
Net,	$1,922,969	$268,489
Other income,	119,022	26,587
Total net,	$2,041,991	*$295,076
Charges,	1,083,522	27,041
Surplus,	$958,469	$268,035
Cash on hand,	1,286,644	*706,049

*Decrease.

The production of anthracite coal last week and for the season was:

Period.	1892. Tons.	1891. Tons.	Inc. Tons.
Week Aug. 20,	767,089	714,771	52,318
Since Jan. 1,	25,352,428	24,005,165	1,347,263

STOCK AND BOND MARKETS.

Bids at the close of First Board.

NEW YORK, Aug. 26.

GOVERNMENT BONDS.	
U.S. 2s, registered	100
" new 4s, registered	115
" new 4s, coupons	115
" currency 6s, 1895, (Pacifics)	107
RAILROADS	
Atchison	39⅞
Clev., Cin., Chicago & St. Louis	66
Chicago & Eastern Illinois	—
Chicago & Eastern Illinois pref.	—
Chicago, Burlington & Quincy	101½
Delaware & Hudson	—
Delaware & Lackawanna	157
Erie	27
Illinois Central	—
Lake Shore & Michigan Southern	—
Louisville & Nashville	68⅞
Michigan Central	—
Missouri Pacific	62⅛
New Jersey Central	135¼
New York & New England	33⅛
Northern Pacific	20⅜
Northern Pacific pref	55¾
Chicago & Northwestern	117
New York Central & Hudson River	112¾
North American	—
Oregon Navigation	—
Oregon Improvement	—
Oregon Short Line	—
Philadelphia & Reading	59
Pullman Palace Car Co	197⅛
Chicago, Rock Island & Pacific	82½
Chicago, Milwaukee & St. Paul	82⅛
Chicago, Milwaukee & St. Paul pref	—
Richmond Terminal	8½
St. Paul & Omaha	—
St. Paul & Omaha pref	—
Union Pacific	39¼
Wabash, St. Louis & Pacific	11¼
Wabash, St. Louis & Pacific pref	25⅞
MISCELLANEOUS	
Ontario Silver	—
Pacific Mail Steamship Co	—
Sugar, common	113
Sugar, pref	105
Western Union Telegraph	98⅝
Silver Certificates	—

BOSTON, Aug. 26.

BONDS	
Atchison 4s	82½
Atchison Incomes	60⅝
American Bell Telephone 7s	—
Chicago, Burlington & Northern 5s	—
Chicago & West Michigan 5s	—
Mexican Central 4s	69½
Illinois Steel Co. 5s	—
RAILROADS.	
Atchison, Topeka & Santa Fe	39
Boston & Albany	205
Boston & Lowell	*182
Boston & Maine	*178¼
Boston & Providence	250½
Chicago, Burlington & Quincy	101½
Chicago & West Michigan	—
Cleveland & Canton	5¾
Cleveland & Canton pref	19½
Flint & Pere Marquette	*20
Flint & Pere Marquette pref	75
Mexican Central	15¼
New York & New England	32
New York & New England pref	83
Old Colony	182½
Oregon Short Line	24½
Pullman Palace Car	—
Union Pacific	39¼
Wisconsin Central	16½
West End	—
West End pref	—
MINING.	
Butte & Boston Mining Co	9¼
Calumet & Hecla Mining Co	*295
Centennial	7½
Franklin Mining Co	12⅜
Kearsarge	—
Montana	36
Osceola Mining Co.	31
Tamarack	165
MISCELLANEOUS.	
American Bell Telephone	206
Erie Telephone	45
Mexican Telephone	1.10
New England Telephone	56½
Newport Land	—
Boston Land Co	5
West End Land Co	18¼
San Diego Land Co	*16½
Topeka Land & Development Co	—
Lamson Store Service	17
Illinois Steel Co	—
Am. Sugar Refineries, com	113⅞
Am. Sugar Refineries, pref	—
Gen'l Electric	—
Gen'l Electric	—

*Asked.

NEW YORK PRODUCE MARKET.

NEW YORK, Aug. 26.

Flour sales 4200 packages; weak and dull.

Wheat sales 410,000 bushels; ¾ of a cent lower and dull.

Corn sales 100,000 bushels; dull, lower and weak.

Oats sales 30,000 bushels; dull and easier.

Beef dull.
Pork quiet,
Lard quiet and easy.
Butter quiet.
Cheese quiet and weak.
Sugar (raw) firm.
Petroleum quiet.
Turpentine quiet.
Molasses quiet.
Rice firm.
Freights dull.
Rosin easy.
Tallow quiet and firm.

PROVISIONS AND GRAIN.

CHICAGO, Aug. 26.

Opening.

	Lard.	Wheat.	Pork.	Corn.	Sh't Ribs
May	—	—	—	—	—
June	—	—	—	—	—
July	—	—	—	—	—
Aug.	—	—	—	—	—
Sept.	—	75⅛	10.35	51¾	—
Oct.	—	—	10.42½	50⅜	—
Dec.	—	78	—	52¾	—
Jan.	—	—	12.10	—	—
12 o'clock.					
May	—	—	—	—	—
June	—	—	—	—	—
July	—	—	—	—	—
Aug.	—	—	—	—	—
Sept.	—	75½	10.45	51⅜	—
Oct.	—	—	10.55	50¾	—
Dec.	—	78¼	—	52⅜	—
Jan.	—	—	12.20	—	—

WEATHER INDICATIONS.

CLEAR.

NEW YORK, Aug. 26.—At 8 30 a. m. the weather was cloudy and threatening, wind east temperature 68. The *Herald* says: In Middle States and New England on Saturday, clear, slightly cooler weather will probably prevail, with light westerly winds, followed by rising temperature, and on Sunday, clear, warmer weather.

Cargo of Lime on Fire.

BOSTON, Aug. 26.—British schooner Adelaide from St. John, N. B., with lumber and lime for this port, has arrived with her lime on fire.

THE TWO SISTERS

Quarrelled in Fall River Police Station.

Matron Reagan Corroborates Story Printed in Standard.

Lizzie Walked Up and Down Like a Crazy Woman.

Newspapermen Ready to Take Oath to Statement.

Interesting Incidents of the Second Day of the Hearing.

[Special Dispatch.]

FALL RIVER, Aug. [illegible]—The Fall River *Globe* this afternoon will publish the following matter of interest connected with the Borden case:

On Wednesday afternoon a reporter of the *Globe* learned that Matron Reagan had heard Lizzie Borden quarrel with Emma, and accuse the latter of giving her away. The reporter went to Mrs. Reagan to have the story corroborated.

This question was put to the matron: "How is Miss Lizzie conducting herself now?"

The reply was: "She is very much agitated, and has been since her sister called to-day. She is wringing her hands and walking up and down the room like a crazy woman."

The reporter then asked what transpired when Emma called and the story which as related the reporter had already heard from other sources was corroborated by the matron in detail.

The remarks Matron Reagan corroborated were reproduced as accurately as possible in the *Globe* yesterday. No attempt was made to add to them or detract from them.

Matron Reagan told this story to other persons. It created a sensation, stirred up the counsel for defence, and left a good many newspapers in the cold outside the breastworks. Naturally it was denied. Everything is denied just now, and it is somewhat doubtful if a murder has been committed. People are apt to forget that a denial is no more than an assertion.

This morning the *Globe's* representative, who first heard the corroboration from Mrs. Reagan's lips, called on her. She stood at the head of the stairs, and was talking with a police officer.

The *Globe* man said:

"Excuse me, please, can I speak to you a moment, Mrs. Reagan?"

She replied: "No, sir, you cannot," and walked to the court-room door.

The *Globe* has only this to say as to the account of the incident which Mrs. Reagan corroborated. That corroboration may be true or false but it was given, and given by Mrs. Reagan. Moreover there are other persons to whom was given precisely such an account of the quarrel between the sisters as has appeared in print. The *Globe's* representative will make affidavit that Mrs. Reagan corroborated this account and another newspaper correspondent will also take his oath that a person in a position to know whereof he spoke told me the same story, and told me that it came directly from Mrs. Reagan. It is now in order for the sceptics to put in their evidence.

INCIDENTS OF THE TRIAL.

How the Lawyers Diverted Prisoner's Attention from Ghastly Topic.

FALL RIVER, Aug. 26.—When the of the effects announcement of the decapitation of their parents' bodies on the Borden girls was noticed in court this morning, and the photographs taken after the murder were produced, by a clever ruse the lawyers diverted the attention of the prisoner and her friends. The counsel for defence and the government followed Dr. Dolan's testimony with a discussion on the pronunciation of the word photographer, the question being on which syllable accent should be placed. The discussion visibly relieved the mind of the prisoner and her sister.

A Lively Spat.

There was a lively spat between Dr. Dolan and the prisoner's counsel growing out of confining questions relating to the degree of dampness in a cellar where the axes were found, the witness telling the lawyer that he was expected to answer a sensible question. Witness would not say that the axes were bone dry.

TENNIS IN THE RAIN.

Cracks at Newport Have a Hard Time in Slippery Courts.

NEWPORT, Aug. 26.—There was but a poor prospect of tennis play this morning. It rained long and hard during the night and had not ceased at 8 o'clock. Though the skies hung thickly no rain fell, and there were, at times faint indications of clearing weather. Though the Casino grounds under such circumstances can boast the driest piece of turf in the city, being remarkably well drained. They were nevertheless soft and with little elasticity. The baby steam roller was brought into use and the courts were coaxed into a fair condition.

The matches were delayed minute after minute in hopes of better weather, but the hope was vain, and at 11 30 the play was commenced in heavy drizzling rain, which had begun some time before.

The game between Chase and Hall, whose match was assigned to the court near the grand stand. The number of spectators was of course small though surprisingly good for such a day. For added to the wet rain was a decidedly cold wind, which swept across the courts with such force as to make the raising of umbrellas a dangerous luxury, while straw hats frequently took to themselves wings. Most of the spectators crowed the upper gallery above the dressing rooms.

The play had not been in progress five minutes before it was apparent that the conditions greatly handicapped the players. The turf was soft, giving the balls little life and rebound; that the ball soon became heavy and almost impossible to handle or judge with accuracy, while the players slid about upon the slippery courts and tore holes in its smooth surface with almost every step. The high winds, too, made lobbying a thing to be avoided and kept the balls close to the net.

In the first set Chase started in by showing surprising strong tennis in view of the prevailing conditions and his record in previous matches this year. His victory over Smith yesterday was a decided surprise and it was not thought that he had much chance against so strong a man as Hall. He exceeded in every point of play, and put up a strong, careful, winning game. He was favored somewhat by luck and took the set on his superior work, Hall being able to get but one game, and that after the scores had gone to 5—1. Hall, who in the first set had clearly been playing far below his standard, began to brace in the second, while Chase fell off a little.

Hall won the first two games, then carried the score to 4—2, 5—3 and then went out, doing good work through the set, though hardly reaching his form in the match with Hobart. During this set the rain stopped, and it looked like clearing for awhile. It continued terribly cold, however.

Summary: Fourth round—E. L. Hall beat S. T. Chase 1—6, 6—3, 4—6, 6—2, 6—3. Larned beat E. G. Hall 6—4, 6—3, 6—4.

Wadell's Experience with a Burglar.

"I had a queer experience with a burglar in a Minneapolis hotel during the Republican convention," said Ferd E. Wadell. "When I retired I turned the key, but without having the door quite closed, and as a result the bolt did not enter the lock. About 2 o'clock I was awakened by a slight noise. A street light shone into the room, and I could plainly see a man rifling my pockets. I had both watch and purse under my pillow, but was unarmed. I at first thought I would not take chances on getting hurt by molesting the fellow, but when I saw him coolly appropriating a scarfpin that my wife had given me, I changed my mind and said to him very quietly, 'I guess you don't need that.'

"He started toward the door, but a spirit of recklessness had seized me and I ordered him to stop. Evidently thinking me armed, he did so. He stood near an open window and held a small revolver in his hand. I told him to throw it into the street, and he did so. I then made him turn on the light, and he looked surprised and relieved to find that I was not pointing a pistol at him. He was a rather good looking young fellow and did not at all resemble a criminal. He admitted that this was not his first offense, however. He was a clerk in a Minneapolis dry goods house, and had got into a way of living which his salary would not support. He sat down on the foot of the bed and talked it all over with me.

"He was very pale and his chin quivered a little, but he did not do the baby act. He said he supposed that he would get a couple of years at Stillwater and that he deserved it. I sat up in bed and read him a lecture, then told him to go and sin no more. My words appeared to touch him. He shook my hand, thanked me for my forbearance and left me. I slept with a clear conscience until 8 o'clock. Then I awoke to find that watch, purse and scarfpin were all gone."—St. Louis Globe-Democrat.

Plymouth and the Pilgrims.

Plymouth is a busy factory village. We are sent for landmarks of the past to Plymouth Rock, the cemetery on Burial hill and the museum in Pilgrim hall. No spot is quite so famous as Plymouth Rock. The stranger is surprised to find it so small, but it is a veritable rock, where rocks are not plentiful. It is protected by a stone inclosure with iron gates, through which we pass and step on the granite of dark gray color. The hardness of the stone makes it almost impossible for relic hunters to carry off pieces, but a French traveler said he saw bits of Plymouth Rock in many states of the Union. One large fragment is built into the wall of the Church of the Pilgrims in Brooklyn.

The original rock is in two halves, each about four feet in diameter, the under part somewhat larger than the upper. At the time of the Revolution it was taken up to be carried to the center of the town to make a rallying point for patriots. The rock was broken in two halves. The lower part was left in its original place, while the other half was carried to the town square.

In 1834 the rock took another journey to the lawn in front of Pilgrim hall, and was inclosed by an iron railing, on which are inscribed the names of forty-one who signed the compact on board the Mayflower. A third journey, however, has restored it to its original position.—Peterson's Magazine.

A Story That Varies.

There is a story, more or less diffused, of a young bride on her wedding day playing the game of hide and seek, and concealing herself in one of those ancient carved chests of large size. After she had got in the lid closed and she found herself unable to raise it again, or it fastened with a spring and she was shut in. Search was made for her in every quarter but the right one, and great perplexity and dismay were caused by her disappearance. It was not till years after when chance led to the opening of the chest that the body of the young bride was discovered and the mystery of her disappearance solved.

The story is found in so many places that it may be questioned whether it is true of any one of them. Rogers tells it of a palace in Modena. The chest in which the poor bride was found is shown at Bramshill, in Hampshire, the residence of Sir John Cope. Another similar chest, with precisely the same story attached to it, was long shown at Marwell Old Hall, between Winchester and Bishop's Waltham.

The folk tale of Catskin or Peau d'Ane represents the girl flying with her bridal dresses from a marriage that is repugnant to her, and as this tale is found all over Europe, it may have metamorphosed itself into that of the bride who got into a chest and died there.—Cornhill Magazine.

Running Errands for Whole Towns.

Every one of the suburbs of New York maintains at least one errand man. Some of the larger towns keep two or three men. These men call themselves the town messengers. If a customer asks at a store for anything that is not in stock, the tradesman, if he is enterprising, says he will have it next day. He means that when the local messenger comes around he will tell him to go to a certain store in New York and get the article.

Such a messenger makes a round of all the stores in one of these little towns every night, and in the morning takes the cars or steamboat to the city and goes the rounds of the wholesale houses for the storeman, the grocer, the jeweler, the dentist, the dry goods man and all the rest. If he is smart he works the railroad for a pass on the ground that he feeds it with freight. If not, he buys a yearly commutation ticket, such as now gives a man rates as low as twenty cents for fifty miles and back.

These messengers are paid so much for each errand they run, and often make four or five dollars a day.—New York Sun.

An Artist's Privations.

Lough, an English sculptor, had an imaginative enthusiasm so vivid that he once said timidly to a friend, as if fearing ridicule:

"I fancy myself in the Acropolis sometimes and hear a roaring noise like the tide."

The sculptor's early privations were terrible. Says a writer:

"During Lough's first year in London, when engaged on his 'Milo,' he went without meat for three months, had only one bushel and a half of coal during the whole winter, tore up his shirts to make rags in which to keep his clay figure moist and slept beside it—when the cold would allow him to sleep—on the ground."—Youth's Companion.

DECLINE OF THE BOOTJACK.

It Tells a Dream of Peace and Contentment Now Faded Into Dust.

The decline of the bootjack is a song that has never yet been sung.

"I went into one of your swell New York hotels the other day," said the old timer. "and after I had wandered aimlessly around the lobby for awhile I gazed on the splendors of the ivory and gold frescoing, on the paintings and the statuary, and all the rest of it, and then I let my eye range over the office help, all sitting up like soldiers, wearing uniforms, diamonds, and carrying handkerchiefs that exhaled perfume—it was a sight that instinctively raised in my mind its contrast, way back in the days of 1847, when I used to keep a tavern on the Albany turnpike, and all we had was a good square old room, a big blazing grate fire, a couple of negroes for help and two or three black bottles for the bar. Then I thought of the old coaches, and how they would drive up with a hurrah and a yell, bringing the old time guest, with his simplicity of manners, his quaint baggage and his royal welcome to the best in the house, that merry inn on the public highway."

"Yes?"

"It made me feel that I had outlived my time. All this splendor, all this dazzle, what good was it? Then I went to my room. Stranger, if I ever did feel homesick it was when I sat down in that splendid blue and gold room on the silken chair and just reached down to pull off my boots, looking in the corner for the bootjack of my youth."

"And the bootjack?"

"Ah, the bootjack was gone. I searched under the bed, in the closet, beside the hearth, but all in vain. The bootjack of the other days had vanished."

He did not speak again for a moment or two. He seemed wrapped in deep thought. By and by he was saying slowly:

"The decline of the bootjack tells all the old timers like myself that we have about outlived our generation. When we were young everybody wore boots. There were the cowhides of the worker, the polished boots of the gentleman; the royal, spangled boots of the officer, the top boots of the horseman and the glittering boots of the swell of fashion. Every man wore his boots and owned his bootjack. There was no rush or hurry in those days. There was time then for the interchange of those graceful commonplaces of life that made existence a charm and a joy.

"Yes, those were the days in which we lived. With the decline of the bootjack a newer and a different race of people has come to us. With them all is splendor, all is show, all is hurry, bustle, business, energy, ceaseless and deathless ambition to be rich. The men of today do not even seem to have time to pull off their boots, for in the mad rush the friend of my youth has been entirely overthrown. It seems to me that the time of my own flight is not long distant."

"Yes," said the hearer slowly, "that is true; the decline of the bootjack marks an epoch in our history."

"It does, indeed. It has been said, and rightly, too, that Americans know the price of everything and the value of nothing. That is the reason why they have suffered themselves to be allured by the mad ambitions that have in the end destroyed all vestiges of the oldtime spirit of ease and contentment, as found in the inn, when as yet every gentleman wore boots and owned his own bootjack. The glass is nearly run, and the old men of that simple generation will soon be gone."—New York Recorder.

Impurities in Distilled Water.

Ice manufactured from distilled water should, it would seem, be germ free. In fact, however, it is extremely difficult to prepare absolutely germ free water on a large scale, and almost impossible to keep it so if once prepared, because every exposure to the air or contact with utensils in common use brings to it varying and often large numbers of germs which can live and grow in water. But these small numbers of common bacteria are not of the slightest importance to the salubrity of the water.

In most of the ice manufactories the distilled water is filtered through charcoal before it is run into the freezing cans, for the purpose of removing certain organic compounds which have come in the process of distillation. But these charcoal beds afford breeding places for such germs as may have escaped the ordeal of the heat. The writer has repeatedly found that while the distilled water before passing on to the filter beds was very nearly germ free, the number was increased a thousandfold on leaving them.—T. Mitchell Prudden in Harper's.

Contagious Diseases Among Plants.

All the fungus diseases of plants, such as mildew, scab, blight, rust, rot, etc., are contagious. The contagion is carried from year to year in the diseased parts, be it leaf, fruit or branch. The presence of any of this diseased material in the orchard or vineyard increases the chance of the appearance and spread of the disease another year. Nothing is so destructive to the fungus spores as fire, and all affected plants, or parts of plants, should be cut out and burned.—Chicago Herald.

One Sure Way.

Beaver—What is your idea in having your collar and cuffs attached to your shirt?

Melton—So my laundryman will bring them back with it.—Clothier and Furnisher.

Woman and a Secret.

Oil and water—woman and a secret—are hostile properties.—Bulwer Lytton.

Knowles & Co.

Cor. UNION & FOURTH STS.

Bargains in All-Wool Dress Goods, 40-inch all-wool goods, suitable for early Fall wear, 39c. Cheap at 50c.

Storm Serges in Black and Navy, all-wool, 40-inch, 50c.; 46-inch 75c.; 46-inch extra value, $1.00.

Black All-Wool Henriettas, 46-inch, 75c.; extra fine and heavy, $1.00 and $1.25; 46-inch, All-Wool, India Twill, 75c. and $1.00.

Beautiful styles in Ginghams at 10 and 12 1-2c. Large assortment to select from.

Ladies' full regular finished, Fast Black Hose, the best hose in the market for 25c. Also Ladies' Fast Black Hose, worth 50c. Three pairs in a box $1.00.

Ladies' Summer weight merino vests and pants 50c. each.

Gentlemen's Summer weight merino shirts and drawers 50c.

Gentlemen's unlaundered shirts, reinforced linen fronts and cuffs, double backs, good cotton, best shirt in the market, 50c.

Ladies' corset covers at 12 1-2, 25, 37 1-2 and 50c., in high, low, square and V shaped necks, handsomely trimmed, and decided bargains.

Ladies' and misses' night gowns, made of good materials and elegantly trimmed, at 50, 65, and 88c., $1, $1.25 and up.

Ladies' corsets, in all the popular makes, at from 49c. up to the very finest goods.

Best Germantown yarns, large full skeins, in 150 shades and colors, at only 12 1-2c. a skein.

Stamped Linens, Trays, Tidies, Splashers, Pillow Shams, Scarfs, all at popular low prices.

All kinds of embroidery and fancy working silk cheap. Knitting silk of best quality, large assortment of colors and shades at 30c. a ball. Best sewing silk in black and colors, 8c.

Table Linens, Brown and Bleached at 45c. worth 59c. Napkins at 50 and 75c, $1.00, $1.25, $1.50 and $2.00 per dozen. Towels at 12 1-2c., 19c., 25c., 37c., and 50c. up.

Lot of standard white ground prints, 5c. a yard. When out shopping don't fail to visit our store for we have just what you are looking for, and at lowest possible prices.

Knowles & Co.

HOW-THEY DO IT IN ENGLAND.

Lively Scenes at a Political Meeting Called in Behalf of Labouchere.

LONDON, Aug. 26.—A meeting of Mr. Labouchere's constituents was held in Northampton to discuss his exclusion from Mr. Gladstone's cabinet. The mayor of Northampton presided, and stated that men who had chosen Mr. Labouchere to represent them in parliament would protest against the queen's interference with the naming of Mr. Gladstone's colleagues in the cabinet. This statement elicited the fact that the meeting had been packed partially with Tory howlers. While cheered and applauded by the majority of those present, about 300 men at the sides and rear of the hall shouted derisively, and called upon the mayor to sit down. Another speaker said that the queen's prerogative extended merely to the choice of a prime minister and not to the choice of the cabinet. This remark was the signal for another riotous demonstration, at the end of which several fights were started by thugs sent to the meeting by Tories.

The resolution of regret that Mr. Labouchere had been excluded was read, but could hardly be heard amid the hisses, groans and stamping, on the outskirts of the audience. When the chairman tried to put the motion, bedlam broke loose. Vegetables were thrown, forty or fifty fights were started, and the hooting and cheering was so great that the mayor's voice was lost. Men in the back of the hall smashed chairs and fought each other with the pieces. Several heads were broken, and three men were carried out unconscious by their friends. Eventually the mayor took advantage of a temporary lull, shouted the question with all the power of his lungs, and the resolution was carried by a large majority. The disturbance then broke out afresh. The mayor left the chair, and, amid riotous scenes, the meeting dispersed.

One Vote Settled It.

WINNIPEG, Man., Aug. 26.—In the northwest legislature a want of confidence vote was carried against the government by one vote. Premier Paullain will thus be compelled to retire and a new government formed.

Will Be a Grand Sight.

NEW YORK, Aug. 26.—Twenty-five thousand school children have volunteered to march in the parade at the Columbus celebration in October.

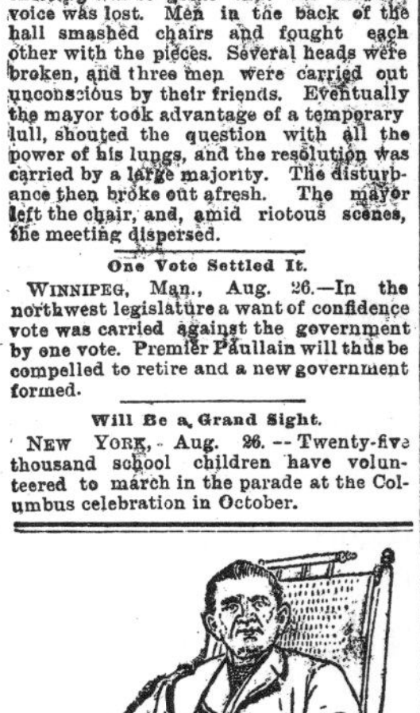

Mr. L. B. Hamlen,

Of Augusta, Me., says: "I do not remember when I began to take Hood's Sarsaparilla; it was several years ago, and I have found it does me a great deal of good in my declining years.

I am 91 Years

2 months and 26 days old, and my health is perfectly good. I have no aches or pains about me.

Hood's Sarsaparilla

regulates my bowels, stimulates my appetite, and **helps me to sleep well.** I doubt if a preparation ever was made so well suited to the wants of **old people.**" L. B. HAMLEN, Elm Street, Augusta, Me., Sept. 26, 1891.

HOOD'S PILLS are a mild, gentle, painless, safe and efficient cathartic. Always reliable.

TS aroma stimulates digestion.

H-O Hornby's Oatmeal

Enduring strength comes of its use.

BIDWELL'S ACCEPTANCE.

He Urges Immediate Emancipation of Women.

Capital and Labor Wars Receive Due Attention.

The Tariff, Public Schools and Immigration Touched Upon.

INDIANAPOLIS, Aug. 26.—The letter of acceptance of General John Bidwell of California, nominee of the Prohibition party for President of the United States, has been given out for publication in the Prohibition press today. The letter is long and discusses the principles of the party as enunciated in the Cincinnati platform. On the basis principle of absolute prohibition, General Bidwell says that the danger of monopolistic tendencies menacing the government is not so great as that of the destructive results sure to come from the liquor traffic. It is the constant menace of labor which creates the wealth of the nation, and the traffic is now sapping and impoverishing the very foundation of the national fabric.

Passing to the question of woman suffrage he urges immediate emancipation of women. The nation that first gives women equal rights with men, he says, will earn a crown of imperishable glory. He fears England will lead.

On the Question of Finance

he says the position of the party that the money should be gold, silver and paper, issued only by the government, is fair and broad. He also advocates the legal regulation of the rates of interest in all the states, believing that it will do much to check the tendency to centralization of the money power.

On the question of labor he says:

In order to relieve the labor of the country of its abnormal and often congested condition, there should be the earliest possible revision and restriction of the immigration and naturalization laws of the United States. These laws, so inimical to American labor and the best interests of all, if not purposely enacted, have doubtlessly been kept in force for partisan considerations for fear of detriment to partisan interests, till our country has become the almost daily scene of riots, lawlessness and bloodshed, and not infrequently on such a scale as to portend, if permitted to go unchecked, the possible subversion of all authority. The discord between capital and labor cannot safely be allowed to continue. No matter what the cause, it is imperative to remove it. If it is necessary to have organizations as a defense against capital or competing labor, such organizations should be authorized and be regulated by law.

On the Tariff.

We must concede that all nations have the right to levy tariffs. As Americans we are in favor of protecting all American interests. The tariff proposed by the Democratic party and that of the Republican party differ only in degree; both are sufficiently high to be termed protective. To the objection that tariffs bear unequally—that is to say, that under them the rich pay comparatively nothing and the masses nearly all the revenue so derived to support the national government—must be added the further objection that they are blinding and deceptive. The establishment of a system of income taxation could work no hardship and do no harm. When the Union needed money most during the rebellion the income tax was imposed and worked like a charm.

It helped them to save the Union and will help to save the nation now in another rebellion—the masses against the classes. One of its beneficial results would be the equal distribution of wealth, which would go far toward healing the discord between capital and labor.

He advocates the general control, and, if necessary, the government ownership of railroads. On the question of

Public Schools,

made prominent in the platform, he says:

The teachings of the American public schools should be in accord with American ideas, and with American civilization, which, of course, is a Christian civilization; but they must be strictly and absolutely non-sectarian. The standard of morality must accord with our civilization and pervade all the books and teachings of the public school, which must not in any phase be a school of immorality.

On the question of immigration he says:

The doors must be closed in self-defense. We do not want to war against foreigners. We do not ask foreigners coming to this land of freedom to change their faith; we do not propose to Protestantize or Romanize or in any way sectarize them. But we do insist that they shall not destroy our liberties by any attempt to foreignize or anarchize our government; that they should appreciate our liberties and privileges that are a condition of citizenship, they should learn to speak our national language and to read and write it fairly well.

General Bidwell closes his letter with a resume, adding that there should be taught in the public schools the principles of the freedom of the ballot and the settlement of differences between men by arbitration.

Boston Coal Rates.

BOSTON, Aug. 26.—At the regular monthly meeting of the Coal club of Boston and vicinity, held yesterday afternoon, it was unanimously voted that the prices of coal be advanced 25 cents a ton, to take effect today. The new prices are: Furnace $5.75 a ton delivered, egg $6, stove $6.25, chestnut $6.25, Shamokin $6.50, Franklin $7.50.

Seeking Congressional Honors.

Representative Charles T. O'Farrell was renominated by acclamation by the Democratic convention of the Seventh Virginia district.

Representative George T. Kribbs of Clarion was renominated for congress by the Democrats of the Twenty-eighth Pennsylvania district.

The Tenth district Wisconsin Republicans nominated Nelse P. Haugen for congress.

The Democrats of the Fourth Wisconsin district nominated Walter H. Butler for congress. The Republicans of the same district nominated Thomas Updegraff.

The Democrats of the Fourth Missouri district nominated D. D. Burns for congress.

Representative C. B. Kilgore has been renominated by the Third district Democrats of Texas.

The Fourth Missouri district People's party convention nominated Frank Burkitt for congress.

The Seventh Georgia district Democrats have chosen John W. Maddox for congress.

Thomas G. Lawson was renominated for congress by the Eighth district Democrats of Georgia.

The Democrats of the Fifth Virginia Congressional district nominated Claude A. Swanson.

THE TOBACCO CROP

Turns Out to be the Finest Harvested in Years.

SPRINGFIELD, Mass., Aug. 26.—A great boom has struck the market for the 1892 crop of cigar leaf tobacco in the Connecticut and Housatonic valleys, according to special reports published in The New England Homestead. Fully half the crop will be harvested by tomorrow. The yield per acre was never better, while the quality at harvest is almost perfect. The season has been remarkably favorable, with an almost total absence of wind, hail, frost or insect injury. In most sections the July drouth was just enough to develop the fineness of texture and light colors now so fashionable in wrappers.

Up to Tuesday night of this week probably one-fifth of the crop had been contracted for at, prices ranging from 17 to 35 cents a pound for leaf to be delivered in the bundle unassorted, after curing. The lowest prices, 17 to 24 cents, have been paid in the Housatonic valley, but in the Connecticut valley 23 cents is the lowest so far accepted, while sales have been made as high as 35 cents, and most of the business has been at from 25 to 32 cents, with active competition among buyers. These prices are for the domestic Havana seedleaf, no sales of Connecticut broad seed leaf having yet been made.

The 1891 Crop

is practically out of the growers' hands at from 15 to 30 cents, averaging probably about 24 cents, or 2 1-2 times the average prices of previous years. The Homestead intimates that the world's shortage in cigar wrappers warrants the expectation that the 1892 Connecticut and Housatonic valley crops will be moved at an average of 30 cents a pound. The acreage is very largely increased over last year, but every effort has been made to secure an even better quality. The 1891 crop is coming out of the sweat in splendid shape, and cigar manufacturers are making a rush for it at fancy prices.

The Homestead's report indicate that New York state, Pennsylvania and Wisconsin tobacco is somewhat late, better in quality than last year in New York, but greatly curtailed in area and probably in quality on Wisconsin plantations owing to wet spring and summer drouth.

The Homestead pronounces the present prices the highest growers have received since the halcyon days of this crop during war times, and intimates that Connecticut and Housatonic valley farmers may receive upwards of $3,000,000 more for this year's tobacco than on the average of previous years, if frost holds off and the cure is satisfactory.

THE PEOPLE'S PARTY

Representatives Meet and Outline Plans for the Coming Campaign.

NEW YORK, Aug. 26.—The eastern members of the national committee of the People's party met at the Astor House and perfected an organization for the campaign this fall. George F. Washburn, eastern member of the national executive committee, was chosen chairman of the new committee, and Dr. A. S. Houghton of Connecticut, secretary. Eastern headquarters will be established at 465 Washington street, Boston. Branch headquarters will be rapidly opened in other cities.

A full state ticket will be put up in Maine, New Hampshire, Rhode Island, Connecticut, New York, New Jersey, Pennsylvania and Maryland, which states were represented at the meeting. Plans for an aggressive campaign in each of these states were mapped out. Delaware and Vermont were not represented at the meeting.

Guests Fled in Their Night-Clothes.

ASHEVILLE, N. C., Aug. 26.—At 11:45 p. m., fire started in the laundry room of the Hotel Belmont, made its way to the elevator shaft and spread to the upper stories. With the exception of half a dozen the 175 guests got out safely. The remaining few had narrow escapes from death. Several sustained severe injuries. Many of the guests escaped with only their night-clothes. The hotel was destroyed.

Made a Sure Job of It.

NEW HAVEN, Aug. 26.—Herman Kantz, a German carriage-maker, about 28 years of age, made two desperate attempts to end his life shortly before noon, and his combined efforts were successful. He first diluted an ounce of arsenic in a pint of water and drank the mixture. He then slashed his throat from ear to ear, completely severing his windpipe.

Maine Team Won't Go.

AUGUSTA, Me., Aug. 26.—The Maine State Rifle team is not going to New Jersey to participate in the interstate shoot. General Sprague did not feel like appropriating the $500 needed without the indorsement of the council, and the chairman of the committee on militia would not consent.

Disaster Overtakes Miners.

LONDON, Aug. 26.—At Swansea, ten men employed in a coal pit were descending in the cage when part of the pit roof fell in. The men were caught under the falling earth and rock, and seven of them were crushed to death. The other three were rescued, but are fatally injured.

Somerby Off for Baltimore.

CHICAGO, Aug. 26.—Supreme Chief Justice Somerby of the Order of the Iron Hall has left Chicago for Baltimore, where he intends to begin the regeneration of his organization.

Another Rise in Coal.

NEW YORK, Aug. 26.—The eastern coal agents have advanced the prices of egg 30 cents, broken 10 cents, and stove and chestnut 25 cents.

Fell from a Bridge.

CONCORD, N. H., Aug. 26.—A workman named Kennedy fell from a bridge at Sewall's Falls and was killed. He belonged in Maine.

SANFORD'S Ginger

MOST GRATEFUL and comforting of warming stomachics, it quenches thirst, warms and strengthens weak stomachs, promotes digestion, prevents chills, destroys disease germs in water drunk, eradicates a craving for intoxicants, and protects the system from contagious influences.

Containing among its ingredients the purest of medicinal French brandy and the best of imported ginger, it is vastly superior to the cheap, worthless, and often dangerous gingers urged as substitutes. Ask for SANFORD'S GINGER and look for owl trademark on the wrapper. Sold everywhere.

Highest of all in Leavening Power.—Latest U. S. Gov't Report.

Royal Baking Powder

ABSOLUTELY PURE

From Yesterday's Third Edition.

DEBT STATEMENT.

A Few Figures Computed Up to Oct. 1, 1892.

The following figures, furnished by City Treasurer Hathaway, will undoubtedly be read with interest by all who are concerned in the finances of the city, showing as they do the debt of the city up to Oct. 1st, after assessments of taxes have been made, computation having been made on the basis of the three previous years:

Valuation.

Tax value 1890,		$36,871,154
" " 1891,		38,518,943
" " 1892,		40,271,913
Gross valuation for three years,		$115,662,010
Taxes remitted 1890 on $33,400.		
" " 1891 on 33,800.		
" " 1892 on 37,000.		107,200
Gross valuation less remittance,		$115,554,810.00
Net average valuation for three years,		38,518,270.00
2½ per cent. on above—the debt limit,		962,956.75

Debt.—

Water bonds 7s,	$100,000.00	
" " 6s,	240,000.00	
" " 5s,	100,000.00	
" " 4s,	120,000.00	
" trust funds,	100,000.00	$660,000.00
Park loan,		100,000.00
Sewer and improvement bonds,		926,000.00
Trust funds,		15,100.00
		$1,701,100.00
Less water debt,	660,000.00	
" park loan,	100,000.00	
" sinking fund,	203,017.23	
" amount due from State,	19,600.00	982,617,23
Net debt Oct. 1, 1892,		$718,482.77
Debt limit,	$962,956.75	
Less net debt,	718,482.77	
Short of limit,	$244,473.98	

WEDDING.—St. Joseph's rectory, Providence, was the scene of a very pretty wedding Thursday afternoon, Aug. 18. The contracting parties were Miss Margaret W. O'Connor of Providence, formerly organist of St. Joseph's church in that city, but more recently similarly engaged at the Church of St. John the Baptist in this city, and Michael Augustus Hickey of this city. Miss Katie O'Connor and Mr. Dominick Wall, sister and cousin of the bride, respectively officiated as bridesmaid and groomsman. The costume of the bride was a marvel of good taste and skilful execution. Mr. and Mrs. Hickey were the recipients of many handsome and costly presents from friends. At the conclusion of the ceremony the happy pair started on a brief wedding tour in New York city and vicinity. Mr. and Mrs. Hickey have returned to this city where they will make their permanent residence on Rockland street.

REAL ESTATE SALES.—Ruth Ashley and others have sold to Charles E. Cook and Abbott P. Smith, 1943.24 rods of land on the south side of Cove street.

Gilbert Allen has sold to Charles H. Greene 10.78 rods of land on the east side of Paige street.

Victorino Sylvia has sold to Jacinto da Silva land and building on the west side of Prospect street.

Charles R. White has sold to Gilbert Allen, trustee, the point of land in Westport, known as Gooseberry Neck.

Harriett M. Mendell has sold to William H. Reed 10.10 rods of land on the south side of River street.

Abial W. Nelson and others have sold to James Brown land and buildings on the east side of Acushnet avenue near the Nye place.

Tennis at Newport.

NEWPORT, Aug. 25.—It looked like different sort of weather early this morning for the third day's play in the national tournament from that of either of the preceding days. Instead of clear sky and gentle breezes thick clouds completely overcast the heavens and a stiff north wind blew across the courts. A summary of the morning games follows: Third round—Wrenn beat Budlong 8—6, 6—4, 6—1. Stevens beat Ames 6—1, 6—1, 6—2. Hovey beat Post 6—2, 6—4, 6—0. E. L. Hall beat Hobart 8—6, 4—6, 4—6, 6—2, 6—4.

Gloucester's Big Celebration.

GLOUCESTER, Aug. 25.—The forenoon feature of the programme in the celebration of the anniversary of the incorporation of the town was a procession two miles long of civic and military bodies, trades and tableaux. The city is packed with people and the harbor is filled with craft. Gov. Russell, Gen. Butler and officers of the United States warships had places in the procession, as did also 350 sailors and marines from Admiral Gherhardi's fleet.

Ocean Flyers Will Not Run to Hamburg.

LONDON, Aug. 25.—The Hamburg-American Packet Co. has decided, owing to the cholera in Hamburg, to entirely withdraw its fast steamers Augusta Victoria, Bismarck, Normania and Columbia from the Hamburg service for the present. They will make Southampton their port of departure and arrival; other steamers of the line will sail from Hamburg conveying emigrants. To have fast steamers obliged to quarantine at New York would be an expensive procedure.

THE MURDER TRIAL.

Afternoon Session of the Court in Fall River.

Medical Examiner Dolan Still on the Stand.

Subjected to Rigid Cross-Examination by Mr. Adams.

Important Statements About the Blood-stained Hatchet.

Instrument Was Sharp, and Appeared to Have Been Scraped.

[Special Dispatch.]

FALL RIVER, Aug. 25.—When the court came in at 2 o'clock the court room was crowded almost to suffocation. Many who had secured seats in the morning brought their lunches and clung tenaciously to the settees. Crowds flocked the street on either side of the courthouse, and the services of more than a dozen policemen in addition to the regular force on duty were required to preserve order and restrain the crowd.

The examination of Dr. Dolan was at once resumed. Witness said that any one of the blows that had been described would be a fatal one. The heart would at once stop beating and there would be no spurting of blood. The stopping of the action of the heart would not stop the flowing of the blood, but it would stop the spurting. The doctor had a talk with Lizzie Borden some time between quarter and half-past 1 on the day of the murder.

MEDICAL EXAMINER DOLAN.

He asked her if her mother had received a note and she said yes. He asked her what her mother did with the note and she said she did not know but thought she put it in the kitchen stove.

This closed the direct examination and cross-examination by Mr. Adams, which was thorough and rigid. Witness said that in his experience as a medical examiner he had had one case of homicide previous to this. When he first learned of the murder he was in his carriage in front of the Borden house, and in consequence of what he had noticed and questions he asked he went into the house and into the kitchen, where he found Dr. Bowen and Bridget Sullivan. In the sitting room at the time of his arrival were two police officers. After he had made a casual examination of Mr. Borden's body he asked where Mrs. Borden was and was told that she was upstairs. He at once went upstairs into the guest chamber, which is directly over the parlor and a room, he thought, of the same size. Dr. Bowen gave him the first information that he received regarding the murder of Mrs. Borden. When the doctor went upstairs he found Mrs. Borden lying on the floor face downward, her head about four feet from the wall and about five feet from the bed.

When the engineer who made the plans came to the house the doctor pointed out everything to him that he regarded of interest, and intended to have all measurements taken as accurately as possible.

In answer to questions by Mr. Adams, the witness said that he should say that the district attorney and Mrs. Borden were about of one build, although Mrs. Borden was a great deal the heavier of the two.

Witness said that he put his hands into the wounds on the body of Mr. Borden, but is confident that no blood dropped from his hands onto the floor. He got a small amount of blood on his clothes, but would not swear that no blood dropped on the floor.

More blood will escape from wounds if a body is suspended in a perpendicular position than when it is lying in a recumbent position on a sofa. I made an autopsy, said witness, on the 11th day of August and made a report on the 15th. A report of the autopsy was filed with the justice of this court, but he did not take it. Notes were taken at the time of the autopsy, but I cannot say what has become of them. I looked for my notes of the original autopsy, but did not find them. I wanted to see if these notes compared with the notes of the perfect autopsy on Aug. 11. This report has been filed with the District Court.

The record of what Dr. Dolan called a partial autopsy on Aug. 8 was produced, and Mr. Adams asked witness wherein it said that this autopsy was a partial one.

Witness said it did not say the autopsy was a partial one, but it is so nevertheless. The autopsy on the 11th was held at Oak Grove Cemetery, a few minutes after 11 o'clock. I cannot say whether this was made on the authority of the attorney-general or the district attorney. After the autopsy at the Borden house Aug. 8 witness assisted the officers in searching the house. While the first floor was being searched I do not know where Lizzie was, but I think she was in her room. She came from the dining room and went up stairs. I viewed the body of Mrs. Borden up stairs. I think Lizzie was in her room at that time. I do not know the time the search of the house was finished. It was as late as 12 30 or 12 45 before the search was completed. Mrs. Borden had on a light colored calico dress. Her head was four or five feet from the wall where the head of the bed was placed. The wounds went diagonally from the right toward the left side of the head to the rear. I cannot tell whether after the incised wounds were given crushing blows were made by a blunt instrument on her skull. The edge of an instrument would cut out pieces of bone and the next blow would crush the edge of the skull.

At this point a recess was taken, and counsel for defence introduced dolls to show the position of the wounds upon the head and the position in which the bodies were found.

The recess continued for five minutes or more and some friends gathered about and spoke to Emma and Lizzie Borden. The latter was grave nearly all the time, but once or twice when M. O. Adams spoke to her her face lighted up and once a faint smile stole across her countenance.

When the court came in again the cross-examination of Dr. Dolan was resumed. A doll with movable arms, legs and head was used to illustrate the position of Mrs. Borden when found and the places of the wounds on her head. Witness said: In my opinion she received the blows from behind. The wounds that were found on her back at the Oak Grove Cemetery autopsy went diagonally toward the left shoulder. The wound was about 2 1-2 inches deep when seen. It was originally two inches deep. I have no idea whether this or the wounds on the head was given first. The wound on the back was not fatal. I think the glancing scalp wound on the left side of Mrs. Borden's head may have been given while she was standing up. This was not a fatal wound. The hinge to the flap of flesh on this wound was at the rear. All the other wounds in my opinion were given while she was lying down. The blows in nearly all instances cut the hair on the woman's head. After I had got through with Mr. Borden down stairs I washed my hands at the kitchen sink. I do not think any of the officers disturbed Mr. or Mrs. Borden's bodies, at least they did not in my presence. After I had washed my hands I think I handled a hatchet and an axe down stairs. A hatchet with a claw or an axe could have fractured Mrs. Borden's skull over the left ear. The fracture could not have been done with a stone on account of the shape.

In answer to a question witness said the hatchet is now in possession of Prof. Wood.

District Attorney Knowlton said Prof. Wood will be here to-morrow or next day. He is a very busy man.

The cross-examination of Mr. Dolan was resumed. He said: Mr. Borden's skull was thick. The skull grows thin as we grow old in some places. I sent the three axes and the hatchet which were found at the Borden house to Prof. Wood. Blood spots were found by me on one of the tools—the hatchet. This looked as if it had been scraped, and it appeared to have been recently ground. It appeared to be a comparatively new one. It had some rust on the edge. I saw what I think was blood on the cutting edge and on both sides. There were some seven or eight spots in all, each about twice as large as a pin head. Such blood spots as these would dry in half an hour. I found ten or fifteen spots on the blade of one of the axes, and fully as many spots on its helve. There was a small knot in the handle that looked as if it was full of dried blood. I discovered blood upon the hatchet the day following the murder, but first saw the blood upon the axe in the city marshal's office. The axes and the hatchet were handed to me in the laundry of the house by an officer. The hatchet in my opinion would furnish adequate cause for the incise wounds in both cases, and I think the same instrument was used in both cases. The hatchet was sharp and I think it could have been used to cut through a human skull 25 or 30 times without dulling it any more than it appeared to be dulled.

The cross-examination of Dr. Dolan was not completed at the time of going to press.

"I AM NOT WELL ENOUGH TO WORK."

This is a daily event in mills, shops, factories, etc. It is the point where **Nature can endure no more,** and demands a **rest.** Then the poor sufferer, worn with toil, and broken in health, stands aside to make room for another. "Quick consumption" they called it.

To this class of women and girls we proffer both sympathy and aid. When those distressing weaknesses and derangements assail you, **remember that there is a Remedy** for all of them. We have on record thousands of such cases, that have been restored to vigorous health and lives of usefulness.

LYDIA E. PINKHAM'S VEGETABLE COMPOUND

Is the only **Positive Cure and Legitimate Remedy** for the peculiar weaknesses and ailments of women.

It cures the worst forms of Female Complaints, that Bearing-down Feeling, Weak Back, Falling and Displacement of the Womb, Inflammation, Ovarian Troubles, and all Organic Diseases of the Uterus or Womb, and is invaluable to the Change of Life. Dissolves and expels Tumors from the Uterus at an early stage, and checks any tendency to Cancerous Humor. Subdues Faintness, Excitability, Nervous Prostration, Exhaustion, and strengthens and tones the Stomach. Cures Headache, General Debility, Indigestion, etc., and invigorates the whole system. For the cure of Kidney Complaints of either sex, **the Compound has no rival.**

All Druggists sell it as a **standard article,** or sent by mail, in form of Pills or Lozenges, on receipt of **$1.00.** LYDIA E. PINKHAM MED. CO., LYNN, MASS.

An Illustrated book, entitled "Guide to Health and Etiquette," by Lydia E. Pinkham, is of great value to ladies. We will present a copy to anyone addressing us with two 2-cent stamps.

IT COSTS NOTHING

—TO—

Read This:

In fact, it may be the means of saving you $15 or $20. Does it mean anything to you if you can buy say a $60 Chamber Suit for $48? Or a $100 Suit for $80? These chances don't come often. The price of Every Suit is marked in plain figures, so you can deduct 20 per cent. and get the net price you will have to pay. This discount is given strictly for cash, but terms will be made to accommodate instalment customers. While they last (about 90 patterns,) for 80 cents on the dollar at

F. R. SLOCUM,

Housefurnisher,

354 & 362 Acushnet Av.

TROOPS LEAVING BUFFALO.

Late Strikers Think They Were Betrayed by Their Leader.

BUFFALO, Aug. 25.—After Mr. Sweeney had his wounds dressed he went to the Genesee Hotel under police escort. A bitter feeling against Sweeney has developed among the late strikers, who believe they have been duped and betrayed by him.

Troops Going Home.

About 1500 of the troops will be sent home this afternoon or evening. More will probably leave to-morrow.

Shot Down by a Soldier.

A boy named Michael Broderick, aged 17, was throwing stones at some of the soldiers of the 22d regiment. He was ordered to stop, but disobeying, some of the soldiers started to capture him. He ran and failing to halt when ordered to so do, one of the soldiers shot him through the stomach, causing a fatal wound. The soldiers claim the shooting was justified.

Deaths from the Cholera.

WASHINGTON, Aug. 25.—The vice consul general at Teheran telegraphs that the estimated deaths from cholera are 35,000; 5000 in Mehed, 12,000 in Tabriz, 8000 in Teheran and 10,000 in other places.

Charter Oak Races Postponed.

HARTFORD, Aug. 25.—Charter Oak races postponed until 12 30 to-morrow on account of rain.

Stevenson at Home.

BLOOMINGTON, Ill., Aug. 25.—Hon. Adlai Stevenson reached home last night from New York.

Women as Doctors in England.

Woman is rapidly emancipating herself from the restrictions with which she has been so long hedged about, especially in America and England. The British Medical association recently passed a resolution admitting women doctors to membership. The vote was on a motion to expunge an article in the constitution providing that "no female shall be eligible for election as a member of the association." The mover of the resolution, Dr. Galton, said times had changed in the past twenty years, and where in 1878, when the article was adopted, there were only eight women doctors in Great Britain, there are now 135. He said the battle against women in the medical profession was over, and they should extend the hand of fellowship to the women. The resolution was carried by a large majority.

CASES OF INSANITY

From the Effects of

"LA GRIPPE"

Are Alarmingly Prevalent.

Suicides

From the

SAME CAUSE

Are announced in every paper.

Would you be rid of the awful effects of La Grippe?

There is BUT ONE SURE REMEDY that NEVER FAILS, viz:

DANA'S SARSAPARILLA.

We Guarantee to CURE you or REFUND your money.

COULD WE DO MORE?

ISN'T IT WORTH A TRIAL?

je25-tf

Pages 1-8.

The Evening Standard.

Pages 1-8.

ESTABLISHED FEBRUARY, 1850.

NEW BEDFORD, SATURDAY, AUGUST 27, 1892.---TWELVE PAGES.

TWO CENTS.

BELIEF IN GUILT

Founded on the Evidence of Bridget Sullivan.

So Says a High Officialin Government Councils.

The Servant's Examination Finished This Morning.

Nothing Sensational in Her Straightforward Story.

Adjournment Taken at Noon Until Monday.

Probably at Least Three More Days of the Hearing.

Government Has Twenty Witnesses to be Heard.

Persistent Denial of Story of the Sisters' Quarrel.

[Special Dispatch.]

FALL RIVER, Aug. 27.—Since the adjournment of the court last night public opinion has been at fever heat in this city, and while a large number of people loudly proclaim their belief. in the entire innocence of Lizzie Borden, the majority either say they think she is guilty or else that they are reluctantly held to the belief that her cause is badly damaged by Bridget Sullivan's testimony.

Marshal Hilliard was in New Bedford last night and returned on the early train this morning. He said his visit to Whaleopolis was entirely of a private nature connected with the taking up of a note.

Belief That Lizzie is Guilty.

An official who stands high in the government councils was asked by a *Standard* representative this morning his opinion concerning the guilt or innocence of Lizzie Borden. He said in substance: I have no hesitation in saying that I believe her guilty of the crime.

Being pressed for the grounds on which his judgment is based, the official said it was largely composed on the evidence of Bridget Sullivan at the examination yesterday afternoon, although the developments at the private examination which resulted in Lizzie's arrest were strongly condemnatory. The official said the crime must have been committed by some one who was familiar with the arrangements of the house, and with the movements of Mr. and Mrs. Borden and Lizzie on the day of the murder. The appearance of Lizzie at the back door when Bridget Sullivan went into the back yard in the morning,and her inquiry of the servant, were suspicious circumstances against her. After this inquiry Lizzie disappeared from sight and sound. While Bridget was washing the outside windows of the house she was not seen by Bridget again around the rear, and this would give time for the murder of Mrs. Borden to have been committed. The noise made by Bridget in washing the windows would have deadened to her ears any sound which came from the upper rooms of the house. The departure of Bridget to the upper room soon after placed her out of the way while the murder of Mr. Borden was accomplished.

It is now thought that the examination will occupy at least three days next week. The government has about 20 more witnesses to put upon the stand, but whether the whole of them will be used or not will depend largely upon the length of time occupied by defence in cross-examination.

Government's Course Condemned.

The evidence given by Dr. Dolan yesterday in regard to the cutting off of the heads of Mr. and Mrs. Borden, and boiling them to remove the flesh and then preserving the skulls, although the order came from the high authority of the Attorney-General of the Commonwealth,has led to a strong feeling of opposition to the course of the government on the part of many people in this city. Those arguing the question are disposed to dispute the authority of the prosecution to perform such a ghastly act and the indignation excited has permeated circles above those composed of the most illiterate. Men (and in some cases women) who by birth and education should be capable of judging calmly and fairly, declaim if not loudly, at least strongly against what they are pleased to term a not only cruel but barbarous act of the government authorities, and this judgment formed they have allowed passion to sway them more than reason, for they ought to remember that a horrible crime has been committed and every agency, however revolting in the ordinary sense, should and must be employed to secure evidence to bring the guilty parties to justice. While there must be a shock to the sensibilities of the friends of the murdered couple at the mutilation of human remains, the cool and unimpassioned movement of justice cannot be impaired or clogged by any sentimental consideration. If there is any chance that the nature of the blows dealt on the heads of the murdered couple can be ascertained from a view of the naked skull, then these poor remains of mortality must be exhibited to the public gaze and serve the ends for which they are intended, and from this end toward which the prosecution has started its steps there is no backward movement.

Opening to To-Day's Session.

After minor proceedings in the Second District Court this morning, the government resumed its examination of Lizzie A. Borden, charged with the murder of her father. The spectators' seats were almost entirely filled by men who got the best of the big would-be congregation of women by earlier arrival and strength of push.

Lizzie and Emma Borden, dressed as in other days, except that Lizzie had a bright colored Paisley shawl over her shoulders, were escorted to seats by Pastor Buck.

Bridget Resumes the Stand.

Bridget Sullivan was called to the stand, and her direct examination was resumed by District Attorney Knowlton. She said: Mr. and Mrs. Borden complained on Wednesday that they were sick. I have not seen Lizzie go to the barn much since horses were kept by Mr. Borden a year or a year and a half ago. I have had no talk with Lizzie other than I have stated. I did not hear Lizzie say anything about hearing from Mrs. Borden.

Calling your attention to hearing Lizzie say anything about hearing Mrs. Borden, did you say anything?

I did hear her.

Did you see Lizzie crying during the day of the murder?

I did not.

Cross-examined. I came to this country six years ago; I am 25 years old;I have been told I came first to South Bethlehem, Pa.; I was in Newport a year before coming to Fall River; I was in the Perry House at Newport; I have told my story before the inquest, on Tuesday after the murder;Mr. Knowlton, Dr. Dolan and the city marshal were here then;Mr.Knowlton asked me questions then. Since I left the court-room last night my testimony has not been read to me. I talked with Mr. Knowlton in the City Marshal's office downstairs. Mr. Knowlton read a little to me from a printed paper, about a dozen words. It was about what I had testified during the day. I cannot remember what was on the paper read. I got home last night in time for supper. No other person talked with me. What the District Attorney said to me was nothing about the groans or the laugh upstairs. On the day of the murder

I Was Sent Upstairs

in the rear, overlooking the back yard. The back stairs were carpeted. I am in the habit of going out nights. I have visitors, not people from Fall River. I have not sat down with men in the back yard at Mr. Borden's. I have done so with girls. I was out the night before the murder. I got home about 10 o'clock and locked the back door when I went home. On Wednesday morning Lizzie complained that she had been sick the night before. They had for supper the night before toast, fish, tea and bread, baker's bread. I went for the bread because I had not enough for supper. I did not eat any of the baker's bread, but ate my own. I cannot say that Lizzie went out of the house on Wednesday. She went out of my sight. On Thursday morning I came down and built the fire. We had for breakfast cold mutton soup, johnny cakes, coffee and bananas. Lizzie might have hung a rough and ready felt hat in the back entry at times. There was a clothes closet in the sitting-room. Mrs. Borden kept out of doors clothing there. Mr. Borden kept a coat in this closet. Mr. Morse went out of the house on Thursday before 9 o'clock. I think Mrs. Borden was in the sitting-room at this time. She told me to wash the windows outside and inside. Lizzie was in the kitchen at this time. She had her breakfast there. I cannot tell what time Lizzie came down stairs, but it was between 8 30 and 9. There were *Harper's Magazines* in the kitchen. I have seen Lizzie reading these books, not often. I did not see her read these books Thursday morning. Lizzie came into the kitchen from the sitting-room. It was about an hour after Lizzie came down that she came to the screen door and had the talk with me when I was in the yard. I did not eat any bread Thursday morning, but I drank milk and ate some mutton soup and was sick afterwards. When I came back into the kitchen after being sick Lizzie was not there. She had had her breakfast. I do not know where she was at this time. I finished washing the dishes at that time. Mr. Morse had gone, I think, when I came in from the back yard. I did not see Mr. Borden when he went out of the house that morning. Mrs. Borden told me to wash the windows after I had finished washing the dishes. She was dusting in the dining room when she told me to wash the windows. I had the talk with Lizzie about the the screen door when I went out to wash the windows. I do not know where she came from when she spoke. I did not go into the house but once, then after a dipper after I began washing the windows. I washed the windows of the parlor, sitting-room and kitchen. I went after the dipper when I had washed the outside of the windows. I cannot tell to-day if I heard the door bell ring while I was washing windows. I had a coal fire in the kitchen. I had two ironing boards. One was used by me and the other at times by Mrs. Borden and the girls. I washed on Monday that week and ironed on Wednesday. I laid the clothes out and Mrs. Borden took one pile and Lizzie another on Thursday morning. I laid the pile for Mrs. Borden and Emma on the table in the kitchen. When I came into the kitchen after the dipper I did not see Lizzie then. I would not swear she was not in the room. Lizzie was ironing that morning (Thursday) in the dining room. When I let Mr. Borden into the house I could not at first get the door open. I said "O, pshaw!" Lizzie laughed. I don't know where she was at that time. Lizzie came into the sitting-room. She and her father had some talk. I did not notice what they said, but Lizzie spoke slowly. I went out washing the windows. Since I have been at Mr. Borden's, a year last July, Mr. Borden's house was broken into and a gold watch and money taken. It was not found out who did it. The burglary was committed in broad daylight. The barn has been broken into since. Mr. Borden, after the talk with Lizzie, took a key and went up stairs. Lizzie brought her ironing. I told her I was going out into the yard. She asked me what for, and then spoke about Mrs. Borden having a note to go out and see a sick person. I said I was sick. Soon afterwards a few minutes of 11 o'clock I went up stairs and laid down on the bed in my room. I heard the clock strike 11. It was 10 or 15 minutes past 11 when I heard Lizzie shout. When I got down stairs Lizzie was standing up against the door. She did not have her hand up to her face, nor was she wringing her hands. Lizzie sent me after Dr. Bowen and to Mrs. Russell's house. I afterwards went to Dr. Bowen's house again. I did not tell Mrs. Churchill about the note calling Mrs. Borden away. I went to Mrs. Bowen's house the second time after I went up stairs at Mr. Borden's house. I went down stairs with the officers on the day of the tragedy. We found some axes in a box in the furnace room. I saw Lizzie at the foot of the stairs when she gave the alarm. I cannot tell what dress she had on or what dress she wore on that morning. I saw no blood on her dress. The room that was burglarized previously at Mr. Borden's house led out from Mrs. Borden's room. You had to go up the back stairs and through her room. I do not know what dress Mrs. Borden had on the day of the tragedy. I had on a calico dress. It is at the house where I am stopping. I emptied no pails at the Borden house the day after the tragedy. I saw several people washing their hands at the house, Dr. Coughlin for one. I saw no one washing their hands upstairs.

At this point Mr. Adams, who had conducted the cross-examination, said: "I have nothing more to ask the witness." Mr. Knowlton said: "I would like to read a note."

A pause ensued, and Mr. Knowlton then said he guessed he would not do so at this time.

Mr. Adams asked if the examination of this witness was completed, and Mr.

[Continued on Fourth Page.]

BIG FIRE IN NEW YORK.

Metropolitan Opera House Enveloped in Flames.

Splendid Structure Gutted and a Total Loss.

Fifteen Firemen Reported Killed by Falling Walls.

Flames are Spreading to the Gedney House.

Another Conflagration in Progress on Another Street.

NEW YORK, Aug. 27, 9 30 a. m.—Four alarms have been rung in for a fire in the Metropolitan Opera House, Third avenue. The fire started in the rear part of the opera house and that part of it will probably be a total loss. It is hoped that the front part of the structure will be saved. A call for an ambulance was sent out from the scene of the fire.

Structure a Total Loss.

It is now learned that the fire started near the stage on the Seventh avenue side, and quickly spread through the whole building. The structure was completely gutted and is a total loss. The fire is spreading to the Gedney House.

There is another large fire in a clock manufacturing establishment on Green street.

Fifteen Firemen Killed.

Fifteen firemen are reported killed by the falling of a wall at the fire at 122 Worster street. The report is not (at 11 a. m.) confirmed.

Report Not True.

The reported killing of 15 men at the Wooster street fire is not true.

THE GREAT LETTER WRITER.

Another Missive from the Summer Resident of Buzzards Bay.

CHATTANOOGA, Tenn., Aug. 27.—A Republican here reasserted that "during Cleveland's administration he (Cleveland) permitted Land Commissioner Sparks to turn out 20,000 families from their homes in Minnesota and other Northwestern States." Mr. Shelley addressed a letter to Mr. Cleveland on the matter and received the following reply:

(Personal.)

Gray Gables, Buzzards Bay, Mass., Aug. 22.

Mr. Shelley, Chattanooga.

My Dear Sir—Your letter of the 12th inst. is at hand. In reply I have to say that I have not the least idea what "Your worthy friend" meant when he declared that I had been the medium through which 20,000 families were made homeless and had lost their all, fighting for their rights." I am perfectly well aware that I have been the means of saving some homes to my countrymen and have tried hard to make the burden of their lives easier. I am amazed at receiving from the southern country letters like that which you bring to my attention. I am surprised, first at the ingenuity necessary for their construction without the least semblance of foundation. I am more amazed that with my record before the people of this country such baseless lies should be deemed sufficient argument to prejudice me and the cause which I, for the time being, represent in the minds of the southern people. Yours very truly,

GROVER CLEVELAND.

FIFTEEN SAVED.

Rescuers in the Welch Mine Deliver a Few Workmen Still Alive.

LONDON, Aug. 27.—All night long the volunteer rescuing party kept up their work at the park slip pit, the scene of the explosion at Bridgend, Wales, yesterday. They worked with a will and removed an enormous quantity of debris from the mine. At 6 this morning they had penetrated 900 yards into the main shaft. Here and there the body of a miner was found, its attitude showing how suddenly death had come to them. Some of the men had died in the very act of using their picks. Ten bodies were recovered of men who did not have a second's warning of the fate hanging over them.

At about 8 o'clock while a band of rescuers was working its way further into the pit a sound was heard that caused the workmen to suddenly suspend operations. Eagerly listening they awaited a repetition of the noise. Soon it came, low and weak, but in sufficient volume to make the rescuers know that somebody behind the fallen rock and earth was alive. With a hearty cheer the rescuers again bent to their task with renewed energy. At last the separating bank of rock and earth fell inward and the rescuers entered an open space in which were huddled a number of miners who had been imprisoned since yesterday morning. It was as if the grave had given up its dead, and the grimy, toil-hardened miners cried like children when the rescuers spoke to them.

The rescuers found that most of their comrades had been badly injured and burned. So serious indeed is their condition that special arrangements will have to be made to get them from the pit. It is said the rescuers found 19 men in the recess, but it is not yet known who they are. Gusts of dangerous gases are coming from the mouth of the pit and the officials will allow no one to go down.

THE CHOLERA IN EUROPE.

Asiatic Type of the Disease Taken to Holland from Hamburg.

BERLIN, Aug. 27.—The officials deny that the Asiatic cholera is here. They say that the merchant's wife who it was supposed Thursday died of cholera was a victim of cholerine. Several suspicious cases were removed to the hospital yesterday. The physicians state they find that the patients were only suffering from diarrhœa accompanied by vomiting. At a meeting of the municipal sanitary commission last evening Herr Schrefer, the chairman, declared that up to 7 p. m. not a case of cholera had occurred in the capital.

ROTTERDAM, Aug. 27.—The steamer Jason, from Hamburg, which yesterday arrived at Maasluis, ten miles west of this city, had several cases of Asiatic cholera on board, and was put into quarantine. Six of the crew were ill with the disease and two were dead.

BRUSSELS, Aug. 27.—A woman has died of cholera here.

BREMEN, Aug. 27.—The North German Lloyd Steamship Company has announced that its vessels will carry no steerage passengers who come from Russia, during the cholera epidemic.

LIVERPOOL, Aug. 27.—The Liverpool steamship companies have instructed their agents on the continent to cease booking emigrants from cholera infected districts.

WEATHER INDICATIONS.

SHOWERS.

WASHINGTON, Aug. 27.—For the 24 hours from 8 a. m. to-day: For Massachusetts, Rhode Island and Connecticut, showers to-day, clearing to-night or Sunday morning; northerly winds.

FAIR SUNDAY.

BOSTON, Aug. 27.—Local forecast for New England until Sunday night: Cloudy, threatening, rain along the coast; clearing to-night for southern sections; generally fair Sunday; continued cool; northerly to easterly winds.

Committed for Contempt.

MONTREAL, Aug. 27.—C. M. Armstrong, president of the Montreal & Sorel Railway Co., was committed to jail for contempt by the royal commission investigating the disposition of the subsidy granted to the road, for refusing to produce the Company's books. He took out a writ of habeas corpus on the ground that the commission had no right to commit for contempt.

HOME MATTERS.

PERSONAL.—J. T. Tillinghast and wife leave to-day for Hartford, Conn., to attend the 75th anniversary of the Deaf Mute Institute there, also the 18th convention of the N. E. Gallandett Association. Eight hundred mutes from all parts of New England have already engaged accommodations.

J. J. Toomey has resigned as foreman of E. F. Dhill's shoe shop, and Victor Pilon of Quebec has been engaged as his successor.

Mayor Ashley and City Solicitor Desmond have returned home from New York. They are satisfied with the city's position in the threatened lawsuit to be instituted by the Municipal Signal Co. of Boston.

City Marshal Hilliard of Fall River came to New Bedford with District Attorney Knowlton on the late train last evening.

Capt. Franklyn Howland will supply the pulpit of the Bourne M. E. church to-morrow in the absence of the pastor, C. S. Davis, who is on his Summer vacation.

D. J. McDonald, who left this city Monday night to join the Uncle Hiram Company, will appear with that aggregation in this city on Friday evening.

Dr. George H. Earl, of Wareham, has been appointed instructor in obstetrics in the Boston University School of Medicine.

THE LAND OF SUNSHINE.—*A Unique Country where the Skies are almost Never Clouded, while the air is Cool and Bracing, like Perpetual Spring.*—As an anomalous Southern resort, by reason of the fact that there one may escape Summer heat no less than Winter cold, New Mexico is rapidly becoming famous. Averaging throughout the entire territory 5600 feet in altitude above sea-level, and characterized by dry air which, unlike a humid atmosphere, is incapable of communicating heat, the temperature in midsummer remains at a delightfully comfortable degree through the day, and at night becomes invariably brisk and bracing. The sunshine is almost constant, yet the most violent out-of-door exertion may be undertaken without fear of distressful consequences. Sunstroke or prostration are absolutely unknown there. It is an ideal land for a Summer outing. Its climate is prescribed by reputable physicians as a specific for pulmonary complaints, and the medicinal Hot Springs at Las Vegas are noted for their curative virtues. The most sumptuous hotel in the West, the Montezuma, is located at these springs. Write to Jno. J. Byrne, 723 Monadnock Block, Chicago, for "The Land of Sunshine," an entertaining and profusely illustrated book descriptive of this region, the most picturesque and romantic in the United States.

A MODEL BUSINESS SCHOOL.—Comer's Commercial College has recently issued a very attractive prospectus for '92-'93, crowded with valuable information for young men and women desirous to fit for a business life The school offers thorough and practical instruction in bookkeeping, commercial arithmetic, commercial law, penmanship, banking, expert commercial calculations, shorthand and typewriting, the English branches and every department of study useful to a knowledge of business. The book concisely treats of practical education, and is full of of excellent advice to young men and women. During the Summer it has been remodelled and about one-third added to the previous capacity. The corps of teachers has also been increased. The prospectus may be had on application. See advertisement on ninth page.

MORUARY.—The whole number of deaths the past week is 14, nine of which were children under five years of age. There was one stillborn. Of the deaths there were three from infantile debility, two from gastro enteritis, and one each from burns, enteritis, phthisis, drowned, typhoid dysentery, paralysis, heart disease. convulsions and premature birth.

PIANOS are polished by rubbing the hard surface of the varnish, thus bringing out the mirror-like brilliancy of the surface. We do this work either at your house or our shop. Please call for prices or testimonials at the old Robeson house, 5 Dover street, or telephone 259-12. It's no trouble to call and examine instruments.

OAK GROVE CEMETERY.—The wall in Oak Grove cemetery running along the east side from the Robeson street entrance for a distance of 200 feet, was completed yesterday.

The ground in that section is being cleared up preparatory to being sold as lots.

IS HE CRAZY?—Yesterday afternoon Constable Delano of Westport brought to the Central Station in this city a middle-aged man belonging at Horse Neck beach, who is thought to be crazy.

SPECIAL CUT PRICES.—For Saturday we shall offer watches, clocks, jewelry, etc., at prices that will astonish you. Good clocks for 93 cents; good watches for $3.75, etc. J. S. Kelley & Son, 15 Purchase street.

NICKEL CLOCK 90 CENTS, eight-day $2.45, small silver watches $4.25, nickel $3, solid gold $10 to $75. Dexter's, 183 Purchase street, corner mill.

LOOM FIXERS.—The next regular meeting of the loom fixers will be held Monday evening, Aug. 29. See special notice.

REGULAR MEETING R. A. Peirce Post, G. A. R., Monday evening, at headquarters. See special notice.

THE LAMSON & HUBBARD HAT has caught on and all the reputable leaders report big sales Call and see one. That means you'll buy one.

DISAPPOINTED ONES will find a few of those small silver chatelaine watches at $4.50, at J. S. Kelley & Son's, 15 Purchase street.

POSTAL or telephone 158-12 and John McCullough will send for iron, metals, paper stock, rubbers, bottles, etc.

THE STREETS.—Clinton street, between Cottage and Ash streets, is being graded.

FINE CONCERT at Cheap John's this evening from 8 to 9.

OVER TEN THOUSAND FAMILIES are using "Ayer's Hygienic Coffee" in Providence.

A SUCCESS—Palm leaf for filling beds. John McCullough.

BLACK CLOTH Overgaiters 50c. Devoll's.

HOOD'S Sarsaparilla gives new life and vigor.

BRIDGET'S STORY.

Servant One of the Most Important Witnesses.

Miss Lizzie's Movements on the Morning of the Tragedy.

Almost a Riot Over the Story of the Sisters' Quarrel.

Exciting Scenes following the Adjournment of Court.

Defence Prepared an Elaborate Denial, but Matron Didn't Sign It.

Previous to the opening of the court yesterday morning, the reporters were speculating on the reason for the absence of women. Opinions were divided as to whether it might be the unpleasant weather or a disgust on the part of the fair over the tameness of proceedings. A crowd of hangers-on about the Central Police Station occupied most of the rear seats. The women who have vowed to see the thing through were on hand as usual. They are middle-aged for the most part and appear to have a fad for murders and other interesting events that come up in the courts.

On the south side of the room sat a wild-eyed looking girl, her head shrouded in navy blue lace and set off with a jaunty blue and white sailor, tipped a little on one side. She had a very stylish figure and wore a blue flannel gown, trimmed with white braid. Every once in a few moments her eyes drooped and she sighed an ominous sigh. She sat between a good-looking young fellow and a jolly-faced girl in a big hat. The girl in blue told Clerk George, to whom she had been plying questions all day, that she was going to write a novel about the murder case. George said, "All right."

This lady was the mysterious Miss Greene, gifted with second sight and capable of seeing from afar, who gave to the police a spirited story of a dream which proved in her mind, and she thought should in other peoples' that Lizzie Borden was a murderess. It is rather odd that Miss Greene did not dispose of herself in comfortable hotel quarters and conjure up the court-room events, and so spare herself the trouble of attending at all.

Miss Lizzie Borden gave very evident signs of being exceedingly sleepy. She yawned frequently and twisted about as though very tired of sitting. The medical examiner's ghastly story affected her, but only for a brief moment. She was more indifferent than on Thursday and looked almost impertinently at some of the witnesses. All the morning she sat absolutely nothing to any one. Messrs. Adams and Jennings take excellent care of their prisoner, but during the first session she scarcely recognized their attentions or courtesies. Even to Miss Emma, who looked like a shadow, the [...] ly exhausted. Her head was resting on her hand and her eyes were closed nearly all day. Mrs. Brigham, Lizzie's bosom friend, has an animated face and snapping eyes. She wore a contented and very pleasant expression, as she took her seat, which expression continued all day. Part of the time in the morning she was occupied in reading a novel, but she was not so interested but she appreciated the district attorney's pleasantries and laughed heartily. Mrs. Holmes looked as though the burden of the whole case was resting upon her slender shoulders. She closely followed the words of the witnesses and nodded and shook her head as she thought them right or wrong.

Mrs. Catharine Kelley, wife of Dr. Kelley, made quite an impressive picture when she mounted the witness-stand. At first tears shone in her eyes, and she could hardly find words to speak, but the soothing accents of the judge reassured her more than anything else, and she finished bravely.

The District Attorney, with the courtesy which always characterizes his treatment of women, jumped to his feet when the lady took the stand, and remained erect until her examination was over. The manner in which he spoke of the prisoner was at all times most courteous-ly considerate. When he had occasion to use her name he called her Miss Lizzie. This is the habit also of Mr. Adams, but Mr. Jennings finds it to his convenience to say simply Lizzie.

As the court officer had the crowd well in hand he was not so busy as on Thursday. Most of his leisure was devoted to giving the New York reporters points on reporting. When the Angular figure of John V. Morse Took the Stand a fresh wave of interest swept over the court room and every eye was turned toward the witness, and Mr. Morse made an impressive appearance. He wore an iron-gray suit and had a beard of the same color. His eyes were dark and restless and deeply set under a straight projecting forehead. When looking straight into the face Mr. Morse has a shrewd but weird expression.

The old man had to be asked several times to raise his voice. He looked a farmer down to the ground and had the speech characteristics of that class. He said that Mrs. Borden was "tolerably comfortable," and also that Lizzie "shet" her door, and made hosts of other old-fashioned remarks, but there was something impressive in the man's manner, and even the women that are left forgot to laugh.

At an afternoon intermission the prisoner and her friends held quite a family party. Lizzie was inclined to be talkative then and chatted with her lawyers and whispered constantly with Emma. She laughed and talked with Mrs. Holmes and Mrs. Brigham, and leaned forward with her chin resting on her hands and her elbows on her knees. In this position she rolled her eyes curiously about the room, in an air of total indifference, and in spite of facts it was hard to imagine the woman a prisoner charged with murder.

A dashing young man has a advantage on the right steps of the judge's stand. He has occupied the position, which is a prominent one, most of the time since the court opened. The gentleman is Special Police Officer Harrington, who is said to have worked up more clews in the case than any one else. He is placing himself to good advantage by taking so elevated a stand, and during the female members of the court an innumerable favor. Mr. Harrington is one of the handsomest men in Fall River and perhaps his most popular policeman. He has fetching blue eyes and curling hair and an exceedingly pleasant face. Many were the admiring glances sent him from the back seats.

Another prominent figure is that of Lawyer James T. Cummings. He has no permanent seat but is usually standing about the doors. Mr. Cummings being prisoner did not speak during the morning session.

She has contracted a peculiar habit of twisting her lips with one hand or toying with her nose, and she chewed the end of a lead pencil to a fringe, though she used the pencil for nothing else.

Minister Buck and the ladies have now had so much practice in entering court that they perform that little act very gracefully. The city marshal had that pleasure at the opening, but it was Minister Buck who had no end of palms for the very effective manner in which he escorted them to dinner. He performs these functions with a deep and venerable courtliness. Lizzie is apparently too listless to care greatly for her appearance. Miss Emma looked and acted thoroughly [...]

Mr. Knowlton requested her to call for a chair whenever she became weary. He addressed her as Miss Sullivan. The court room was very still during her testimony, except for the "hurrying pens" of the scribes. Even Lizzie paid attention to the words of the witness, and Emma looked from behind her fan.

The cloudiness necessitated the lighting of the gas, which is the only means of illumination in the court room. One of the bright young men of the Fall River Globe wrote until he couldn't see the end of his pen. He was taking Bridget Sullivan's words and frantically reached for the daisy burner above him. No use, he was too short. He lighted a second match, mounted the settee and tried again. That time he got a blaze as large as a little twinkling star. He lit up again and coaxed a second forked tongue on the same burner, the most sickly suggestive gas blaze that ever had existence. A representative of a rival paper tried the second burner on the same chandelier. From that spouted a volume of flame which almost singed the wall. Some New York men endeavored to get a light from two healthy appearing burners. "George" said that the screw was out of whack on one and the other gave a half candle power light. The only burner in the room that would burn was over the Judge's desk.

Early in the afternoon's proceedings the trim figure of Mayor Coughlin appeared in the room. He took a seat at one side of the witness stand, leaned back lazily in his chair, in very much the same fashion as he would settle down to enjoy a good play. His Honor remained during the session. He appeared quite as interested in the sights about the court room as in the proceedings of the court.

BRIDGET SULLIVAN'S EVIDENCE.

Movements of Members of Borden Household on the Fatal Morning.

Interest centred in the testimony of Bridget Sullivan at the afternoon session. The proceedings were resumed, after a recess, at 4.20 o'clock, and Bridget was summoned and began to testify as printed in Friday's five o'clock edition of the Standard. She said: "My name is Bridget Sullivan, and I was known by the name of Maggie at the Borden house. I was employed there for two years and nine months. I swept the front hall every other week and had no duties in the bed rooms. At the time of the tragedy Miss Emma was not at home. She had been out of town for a week, and when she was gone the family consisted of Mr. and Mrs. Borden and Miss Lizzie. Miss Lizzie went with Miss Emma when she went away, but came back. I first saw Mr. Morse between 1 30 and 2 o'clock on the day he arrived. I saw him again walking out in the afternoon and going on the railroad. I did not see him when he arrived home that night. I got up at 6 15 o'clock Thursday morning, and it was 10 o'clock the night before when I retired. I locked the screen door and the back wooden door before I went to bed. When I came down in the morning I found the doors exactly as I had left them and I opened them. I went out for milk, and afterwards hooked up the screen door. The back door remained open. Nobody Else Came In or Out that I can remember, except members of the house. I did not go out of the house again until Mr. Borden went out. Nobody was up when I came down, and the first one I saw was Mrs. Borden. I saw her in the kitchen and on the back stairs at half-past 6.

Bridget Sullivan continued testifying, Mr. Knowlton asking her questions in a very simple form, with great kindliness of tone: Never knew anybody to go up the back way to the front part, or the front way to the back part; Mr. Borden came down about two minutes after Mrs. Borden; he went out doors before breakfast; he went into the barn and got some water; he emptied a pail from the house and came back; I was in the kitchen all the time; after Mr. Borden came in with his pail he washed up; he put his dressing coat on after washing up; think he put his necktie and collar on after breakfast; we had for breakfast cold mutton, soup, johnnycakes and coffee; breakfast, as nearly as I can recollect, was at 7 15; after breakfast they came in the sitting-room; Mr. Morse had come down to breakfast; he went out at quarter of 9, I should judge; Mr. Borden let him out; Mrs. Borden, I expect, was in the sitting room when Mr. Morse went; I saw Mr. Borden there about 9; don't know where Mr. Morse went; after Morse went, Mr. Borden went up the back stairs; did not see him when he came down or went out; don't know if he went out the front or back door; I went out in the back yard awhile; I was sick at my stomach and vomited; did not see Mrs. Borden when I came back; was out in the yard four or five minutes, and came back into the kitchen and washed dishes.

Mrs. Borden told me she wanted the windows washed inside and outside all around the house. I did not see Mrs. Borden after that. She went into the kitchen.

The Next Time I Saw Her She Was Dead. Lizzie was then through with her breakfast. She came down stairs before I went outside. She was then in the kitchen. When I came back I don't know where she was. I asked Lizzie what she wanted for breakfast and she said she didn't feel like eating anything. When I saw Mrs. Borden she had a dusting cloth and was dusting the dining room. I didn't know where Lizzie was. That was after both men had gone. I don't know whether or not I locked the screen door after I came in from vomiting. I then cleaned up the kitchen and straightened up and commenced to prepare to wash the windows. I went down cellar and got a pail, got a brush from the closet and went out to the barn to get a stick. Miss Lizzie then came into the back entry and asked where I was going. I told her I was going to wash windows and that she need not look the door.

I told her I'd get the water in the barn, and she said all right. The door was then hooked and I had to unhook it. I was down in the cellar earlier in the morning to get coal and wood. The next time I went down was when I got the pail. I got the water in the barn. It was half an hour after Mrs. Borden told me to wash the windows before I commenced. During that time I Did Not See Miss Lizzie except when she came to the screen door. Where she was I don't know. I had not been doing any work in the spare room; Lizzie Borden never did work in the spare room when her friends had occupied it. After I went out to wash the windows I saw Lizzie; she had asked me as I went out if I was going to wash the windows; I told her yes, and that if she wanted to close the windows I would get water in the barn; five windows I had to wash; I shut three before I went out, and two others were already shut. I went in after a dipper after a time. I did not see Miss Lizzie after I got out, when I had got the dipper; I had not seen anybody while I was in the barn after the dipper. When I went down stairs after the pail I went down the kitchen stairs. We wash on Monday, and iron Tuesday, and on Monday and Tuesday the cellar door was open. I opened the door the day I hung my clothes out and don't know if anybody else went in or out of it that week before the murder.

I Shut and Locked the Door Tuesday Myself.

I got through washing the windows at 20 minutes past 10, I think. Don't know how many pails of water I used. Washed the sitting room side first and then the parlor and last the dining room. The windows were shut up stairs. I then went inside at the screen door, hooked it and getting a hand basin washed the sitting room windows inside. Did not see Lizzie or Mr. Borden in the house while I was washing the sitting room windows. Didn't see anybody outside or in the house while I was washing windows. I heard Mr. Borden try to get in at the front door. Afterwards went to the front door and Found the Bolt Lock Turned. Miss Lizzie was up stairs at that time. She might have been in the hall, for I heard her laugh up stairs as I let Mr. Borden in. I went to open the door and it was locked, and I made some exclamation when she laughed aloud. I did not see her until five or ten minutes afterwards. I was in the sitting room. Mr. Borden came in and sat down at the head of the lounge in the dining room. He was reading and I was in the sitting room washing the sitting room windows. I did not see her when I let Mr. Borden in. I heard her tell her father that Mrs. Borden got a note and went out.

Lizzie Spoke Very Low.

I don't know where Lizzie went then, and I don't know whether or not she stayed in her room. After I finished in the sitting room, Mr. Borden took the key from the sitting room shelf and started up stairs the back way. When he came down I was just going into the dining room. I did not see Miss Lizzie then. She was not in the dining room, sitting room or kitchen. Then Mr. Borden sat down near the window in the sitting room, with a book or paper in his hand. He brought the key back and put it on the shelf. He sat in an easy chair, and I had started to wash the first window in the dining room. I did not see Miss Lizzie, and only saw her when she came into the dining room, and then to the kitchen, and then back again to the dining room with an ironing board. She placed the ironing board on the dining room table.

Where She Came From I Do Not Know. She put the ironing board on a corner of the table. It was about two feet long. She always ironed the handkerchiefs. I was just finishing the dining-room. [...] the door, as "I may be out," and Mrs. Borden had got a note and gone out. I then went upstairs to my room, and Miss Lizzie was downstairs working at the ironing board. I don't know but there was a sale of dry goods at Dustin's. If Mr. Borden changed his position to the sofa, I didn't know it. Soon after [...]

BRIDGET SULLIVAN.

striking resemblance to Paderewski, only he looks a shade more rational.

Bridget Sullivan silenced the room when she stepped into the dock.

Bridget was Looking a Trifle Worried, but very pretty. There was considerable style to her robust figure, which was well set off in a bottle green serge trimmed with an effective arrangement of clusters of smoked pearl buttons. Her hands were encased in gray gloves and she wore the chic looking poked toque of yesterday. Bridget is a comely-looking miss with fine waving hair and a complexion in blush roses.

She proved an excellent witness, and after she was well started on her testimony and was fairly under the district attorney's spell, she forgot her situation.

Nervousness.

HORSFORD'S Acid Phosphate.

An agreeable and beneficial tonic and food for the nerves and brain. A remedy of the highest value in Mental and Nervous Exhaustion.

Trial bottle mailed on receipt of 25 cents in stamps. Rumford Chemical Works, Providence, R. I.

SHAPE YOUR MUSTACHE.

What is more disgusting than to see a man always twisting, twirling, and biting his mustache. Stop it. You can do so by using the instrument that will keep it always just right. Will be sent postpaid with complete outfit for 35 cents, two for one dollar. Postal note or stamps. Address the Mason Bartlett Co., Box 2480, Boston, Mass.

Moderate in Price,
Excellent Quality,
—AND—
DESIRABLE FOR YOUR TABLE!

The new drink, Cocoa Coffee, 35c. for handsome can containing a pound.

The new Relish, California White Grape Mustard, large bottle for 15c.

A can of very nice Peaches for 18c.

A box of Fresh Boneless Herring for 15c.

SOMETHING NEW EVERY DAY
—AT—
ALLEY'S.

stairs, it struck 11 o'clock. I was then lying in bed, but I didn't take my clothes off. I thought I had time enough to get dinner at half-past 11. I always went up stairs before dinner, if I had time. Didn't look at the fire before I went up stairs. The dinner was to be soup to warm over and cold mutton. Had not put the soup on, and the potatoes were in the soup. A coal fire was started in the morning. I was going down stairs at 11 30. Had not gone out of the screen door again after I commenced to wash the windows inside. I next heard something, when Lizzie called me. It might have been 10 or 15 minutes after I went up stairs. She hollered at me. I knew from the way she hollered something was the matter. She Hollered Loud; She Said Her Father Was Dead.

She told me to run after Dr. Bowen. I wanted to run in ahead and see, but she told me to run quick and tell the doctor. I went and told Mrs. Bowen about it. Mrs. Bowen told me to tell Mrs. Russell about it, and I went back and told Miss Lizzie. She told me to go after Mrs. Russell. When I got back from the Bowens' Miss Lizzie was still at the door. When I got back from Mrs. Russell's Dr. Bowen had just got out of his wagon, and I think Mrs. Churchill was there. Miss Lizzie was then in the kitchen. We talked, and Miss Lizzie said she'd like us to search for Mrs. Borden. I said I'd go up stairs, and Mrs. Churchill said she'd go with me. I went up and saw Mrs. Borden before I went in. When the house was searched that day a box of hatchets was behind the furnace. I don't know if the cellar door was open when the officers were searching the house the day of the murder. I asked Lizzie where she was, and she said she was out in the back yard.

"When was it she said that?"

"After I got back from Mrs. Russell's."

"Do you know what dress she had on?"

"I don't know."

"Had Mrs. Borden said anything to you about going out?"

"No, sir."

"Was it her habit to notify you when she went out?"

Mr. Adams promptly objected to this question and the court excluded the question.

"Then the only thing you know about her going out was what Lizzie told you?"

Mr. Jennings objected to this question and said that while he did not object to the district attorney asking leading questions on unimportant matters, this was altogether too serious a point to allow such queries. District Attorney Knowlton declined to take this view of the matter, and a discussion commenced, pending which an adjournment for the day was taken.

A REMARKABLE SCENE.

Almost a Riot Over the Story Printed About the Sisters' Quarrel.

At the close of yesterday's hearing, just after the court adjourned, a scene of great excitement followed the discussion of the story published in a special dispatch to the Standard some days ago, which story detailed an alleged occurrence in the matron's room, during which it was stated that Lizzie Borden accused her sister Emma of having "given her away," and that the prisoner added that she would never give in an inch.

At the close of the hearing two or three correspondents approached Mr. Jennings, stated that their papers had instructed them to fully investigate the story in the interest of fair play, and asked liberty to question the defendant on the point in question.

Mr. Jennings grew indignant and asked if he was supposed to accord such privileges on account of every sensational article sprung by the press.

…veral reporters, whose papers had repeatedly denied the story in toto, objected to any general denunciation of the press on this account, and demanded that the blame be placed where it belonged.

As a result of this, and the statement oft repeated that Matron Reagan had entirely repudiated the words ascribed to her in describing the alleged scene between the Borden sisters, it was decided by the prisoner's friends that an affidavit re-affirming her denial should be submitted to Mrs. Reagan for her signature.

The following was prepared:

"This is to certify that my attention has been called to a report said to have been made by me in regard to a quarrel between Lizzie and her sister Emma in which Lizzie said to Emma, 'you gave me away,' etc., and that I expressly and positively deny that any such conversation took place or that I ever reported that such conversation took place; and I further deny that I ever heard anything that could be construed as a quarrel between the two sisters."

Although Mrs. Reagan's denial had been wired throughout the country, it was felt that this would settle the matter beyond question.

In this opinion all concurred, not however until after there had been much excited discussion concerning the matter generally and much unqualified denunciation of the writer of such an article at a time when its publication would injure the cause of a woman whose case is sub judice.

The Rev. Mr. Buck offered to carry the paper to Mrs. Reagan. He did so. Detective McHenry followed him into the matron's room.

The Rev. Mr. Buck explained his mission.

While Mrs. Reagan was thinking about it the detective interfered.

"Sign nothing until you have seen the marshal," he said.

The matron then said she must first consult Marshal Hilliard.

"I will go with you," said the Rev. Mr. Buck, and together they went to the marshal's room below.

When Mr. Buck returned he said to the party assembled:

"Marshal Hilliard has refused to let her sign it."

Mr. Jennings, who was excited and angry, said: "I said to the marshal that if he had refused to let Mrs. Reagan sign this paper it was the meanest thing I ever heard of."

A scene of intense excitement followed. The babel gradually shifted to the foot of the stairs. While it was being discussed there, and the air was full of denunciation of the chief's action, a reporter in the employ of the Fall River *Globe* reached the scene and excitedly demanded audience. Police had crowded about the group and words ran high.

Finally the reporter was heard.

"If you want affidavits," he said, "you'd better take mine. I know what Mrs. Reagan told me, and I am willing to swear to it."

Meantime the Rev. Mr. Buck returned from a second visit to the prisoner's room. I questioned him in the presence of John C. Milne and other citizens.

"I asked Mrs. Reagan in the presence of Mrs. Holmes, Lizzie and Emma," he said, "if she would have been willing to sign this affidavit if the marshal had not forbidden it. She replied, 'I would.'"

The minister was awfully in earnest, and made his statement clearly and carefully.

A newspaper man—Mr. Caldwell of the *Recorder*—then stated that he entered the marshal's office after Mrs. Reagan. He said: "I heard the marshal say to her, 'If you sign this you do it against my order.'"

"Then he turned around and saw me, and nearly had a fit. 'This is a private office!' he shouted. 'There is nothing here to indicate that it is such,' I replied. 'It is my private office,' he retorted, 'get out of it, sir.'"

Other witnesses added that the marshal told Mrs. Reagan that if she had anything to say the witness stand was the place to say it.

Several correspondents, the Rev. Mr. Buck, Mr. Jennings and others stated positively that Mrs. Reagan had denied the truth of the story in which it was said that she described Lizzie's denunciation of Emma and said Emma had given her away.

"The man that wrote it should be driven out of town!" "If it is true no one will believe she is innocent!" These and similar phrases were used frequently by reputable friends of the accused during the discussion of the matter.

After the excited group had dispersed I found the man who first gave the story to the *World*. He positively affirmed the correctness of the language which his paper—the Fall River *Globe*—had ascribed to Mrs. Reagan, said she quoted Lizzie as saying, angrily, "Emma, you gave me away, didn't you?" and announced that he was ready to swear to the story. "If Mrs. Reagan makes affidavit that it is untrue," he said, "I will make affidavit that it is true—every word of it, and I will produce three good men who are ready to go on the stand and swear that the matron told them the same story."

On the other hand, it is known that Mrs. Reagan has positively denied the story to several reputable persons.

At one point a riot seemed likely to result from the excited discussion of the case, and it was talked of with unabated interest last night.

Mayor Coughlin, talking with a *Standard* reporter last evening, said that he was satisfied that the first intimation of any conversation between the sisters, as reported, did not reach the ear of Marshal Hilliard until some time after it had been in the possession of the press representatives. The mayor had much confidence in the reporters who told the story of the occurrence, and are now willing to make affidavit that the matron, Mrs. Reagan, was quoted with honesty and substantial accuracy. The action of Marshal Hilliard in telling Mrs, Reagan that it was best for her to make no further comments upon the matter except on the witness-stand under oath, commended itself to his judgment. The story had been in circulation some time before it came to his ears. When he first heard it he was anxious to verify it and hastened at once to the central police station to get as much information as possible. There seemed to be no one there who was in possession of the facts except in a vague sort of way. From what he heard later and from personal inquiries, knowing personally the men who promulgated the story, he had no doubt of the accuracy of the report.

Ladies.

Are you suffering from weakness? Is your complexion sallow? Do you have a constant back-ache? Are you constipated? Do you feel all tired out? If you have any of these feelings, begin at once to use Dr. Hale's Household Tea. It will give you a clear complexion, will restore you to health and strength and will make you feel like a new person. Get it to-day at Wright Drug Co's, 9 Purchase street.

SAMUEL ROBINSKY.

There Are Three Jewish Peddlers of That Name Hailing from Boston.

It is very much like the proverbial search after the needle in the haystack—this trying to find Samuel Robinsky, the writer of the mysterious letter from Waltham to Miss Emma Borden, concerning the Borden murders.

A reporter learned last night that there are three Jewish peddlers named Samuel Robinsky living at the North End, Boston. They are all now on the road, however, and so could not be seen last night. It is expected that one, at least, and possibly all three, may arrive in town today or Sunday.

One of these Robinskys lives on Cross street. He peddles his wares in Fall River, Brockton and vicinity, and is also said to be known in Waltham. This man is one of the customers of D. Yavner, who keeps a meat market at 21 Fleet street. "No, I don't think Robinsky has got back yet from the road," said one of the clerks at this store last evening. "He usually comes in here and buys something Friday night, but as he hasn't been in I don't think he has come in."

Another of these three peddlers lives on Salem street and the third on Prince street. Several peddlers were seen last night who knew them slightly and had met them on the road. They both visited Fall River in their peddling expeditions, but it was not thought that they had ever been in Waltham. The reporter was unable to find out at what store they bought their goods, also.

"I think that they will both be in town Saturday night," said one man who knew them. "But they won't be back to-night. They usually make long trips at this time of the year."

Officer Wolf of Police Division 1 has become very much interested in the search for Robinsky, although he is rather sceptical about his having written the letter in question; he has read the letter signed by Robinsky, which was sent Miss Emma Borden, several times, and says he doesn't think it could have been written by a Jew.

"Perhaps he may have got some one to write it for him," said he, "but I don't believe that any Jew peddler that claims to be studying English could write so good a letter."

The route of Officer Wolf is through the district where the Jewish population is to be found at the North End. He can speak Hebrew, which is about the only language heard in the locality, as well as the best of them, and also understands Russian and German.

"If it is a possible thing," said he, "I am going to find that fellow." He has made inquiries of every one likely to know such a person at the North End, but thus far without any success."

A storekeeper on Salem street said last evening that he did not take any stock in the letter. One of his reasons was that Robinsky says he sold a collar to the man covered with blood. "Now there is not a Jewish peddler going out of Boston that sells collars," said he. "I believe the letter was written by somebody whose name was not Robinsky."

The Prisoner's Counsel.

The Boston *Journal* says:

Lizzie Borden's lawyers have already done such work in court as to make it clear that her case will not suffer in their hands. Messrs. Jennings and Adams are both young men just turned forty, and each has already made more than a local reputation. The two together form as strong a combination as an accused person could desire. When Col. Adams was Assistant District Attorney in Suffolk county the queer but complimentary criticism was often passed upon him that he ought not to be retained in the office because his skill and eloquence often procured convictions when the facts were probably in favor of the prisoner. Adams is a Dartmouth man, and Jennings was graduated from Brown University. By the way, Jennings was captain of the base ball nine, the first university nine that ever beat Harvard; and the sweetness of the victory was not lessened by the circumstance that six of the men who played on the nine were at the head of their class.

SENATOR DAWES TO RETIRE.

He Publicly Notifies His Constituents in a Letter of Thanks.

SPRINGFIELD, Mass., Aug. 27.—The Republican this morning publishes the following letter from Senator Dawes, dated Pittsfield, Aug. 20:

To my fellow citizens of Massachusetts:

I deem it proper that I should at an early day make public my determination not to be a

HENRY L. DAWES.

candidate for re-election to the office of United States senator. I cannot thus lay down the commission with which I have been so long intrusted without expressing my profound gratitude to my native state for the opportunity to serve her in the most honorable position in her gift, and for that uninterrupted confidence and support which have sustained my every endeavor in the public service. I shall take with me into retirement an unabated interest and abiding faith in the political principles which have contributed so largely to the prosperity and good name of our commonwealth.

OUR REPRESENTATIVE.

A Few Words for Charles S. Randall and Other Matters of Public Interest.

I am no politician, and though interested in most of our reforms, I would lend what little influence I may have in favor of the renomination and reelection of our fellow-townsman, Charles S. Randall, as our Representative, believing with William J. Rotch in his eminent qualifications, from his extensive acquaintance with the interests of our congressional district, and his unremitting labor herein during his term of service; whose successful experience will render him of far more value to our people throughout the district than a new candidate however respectable, or in other respects well qualified in those matters our immediate interests require. Let us stand by our old and well-tried citizens, not only in our national, but in our State and municipal governments. We who can look back to the days of our commercial prosperity, remember how careful we were in the choice of our public servants, have too often to regret that political partisanship has so greatly taken the place of a better qualification in our public affairs. Revolutions surely come, and it is high time that a deeper attention should be paid to our moral as well as financial interests

DANIEL RICKETSON.

A FAVORED NATION.

Beauties of Our Country Set Forth by the President.

Peace and Prosperity Have Settled Over the United States.

Stevenson's Views Expounded at the Opening of Illinois Campaign.

LOON LAKE, N. Y., Aug. 27.—The citizens of Malone received the president. An informal luncheon and a reception in the park completed the program. The president was introduced to the several thousand people there by Hon. F. D. Kilburn, and spoke as follows:

Ladies and Gentlemen, and Comrades of the Grand Army of the Republic: I very sincerely appreciate the friendly invitation extended in your behalf, which has given me the privilege of standing for a few moments among you and exchanging greetings as friends and American citizens. These non-partisan assemblages, in which we gather to express a common interest in the institutions of the civil government under which we live, a common respect for public authority and a common love for the flag, are full, I am sure, not only of interest, but of benefit to those who participate in them.

We shall presently, in the political campaign which is opening, have our separations in operation emphasized, and our separate assemblages to advocate these principles. We are here today, however, as citizens, not as partisans, to give expression to those common interests which, fortunately for us as a nation, in every time of great exigency and stress, in every time of danger to the flag, obliterate all party divisions and make us one people in its defense. We are a favored nation in that great isolation we enjoy. We are free from the dangers of close contact with any of the great military powers of the world.

Our Neighbors in the North.

The Dominion of Canada neither threatens us nor we her. We desire for her the most abundant prosperity, the fullest development of which her resources are capable, and constant peace.

But it must not be supposed that this separation which we enjoy from close contact with the great powers that are forever standing on the threatening edge of war has left us without duties or responsibilities. We have always, in our diplomacy, exercised the patience, reserve of strength and the consciousness of a right cause. I fancy that we are entering now, as a people, upon a career when our external influence in commerce is to be larger than ever before. We have, in large part, completed our great works of internal improvement.

The forests have fallen before the axes of our pioneers, and the plow now turns the soil of all that region which was once styled the "far, great west." We have accumulated prodigious wealth as a people, and I see no reason why the United States should not from this day forward step into a position of power and influence among the great commercial nations of the world, such as she has never enjoyed. From causes, as to which we differ, we have come to a condition recognized by all. We have been deprived of our once proud participation in the ocean carrying trade of the world, I think we should now resume it. The wise and timely inauguration of a new navy has demonstrated the capacity of our American shipyards to prodnce the best ships in the world.

The government, having pioneered in this work of shipbuilding, by the encouragement it has given our constructors and to our artisans, have paved the way now fo-

Building Great Ships of Commerce.

I take great delight in the contemplation of the fact, which, I believe, is now assured, that before another year has rolled around, one of the swiftest, and best of all the great lines of steamships that go out of the port of New York, will bear the American flag at the fore.

The tribute we have paid to foreign nations in the way of freight charges, I believe, will speedily, in a large measure, be abrogated forever. These great stores of agricultural products which we pour from our granaries to feed the nations of Europe, should, and, I believe, speedily will, be delivered at the port of Liverpool in American bottoms.

We will avail ourselves of all these natural resources, of all this vast capacity, inventive and constructive, which God has bestowed upon us in the belief that it has been given to us primarily; that here, in this land that so long waited the foundation of a free republic, that republic and its people might attain the highest devolopment in wealth, intelligence and morality among the nations of the world.

We Have Had a Great Struggle

within ourselves. I believe that we have seen the last serious outbreak against our laws. The one cause that could divide our people—human slavery—has, under the favor of God and by the Union army, been abolished forever, and Lincoln's proclamation has now the assent of the south itself. The law and the constitution, as the object of every American citizen's veneration and his willing obedience, is the one faith and the only safety of our people. No cause can be advanced in this country upon the lines of lawlessness. Intelligence and morality among our people, the church, the school and the home—these great rocks upon which our institutions and our safety rest—we will cherish and preserve.

And now, comrades of the Grand Army, surviving veterans of that gallant band that from mountains and valleys went out to defend the flag, I give you a comrade's greeting today. God bless you, every one. God forgive that American in this bright day of prosperity and unity, who can begrudge to any one of you the just dues of your hard service.

LONG TALK ON TARIFF.

Democratic Vice-Presidential Candidate Speaks in His Own Home.

BLOOMINGTON, Ills., Aug. 27.—[Special.]—Adlai E. Stevenson, Democratic candidate for vice president, opened the cam paign for 1892 in this city today. So far as his speech relates to the tariff question it will be his definite utterances for the whole campaign.

General Stevenson opened his address by impressing upon his hearers that grave public questions were at issue. He argued that the four years administration of President Cleveland was confessedly an honest administration, and said that those who predicted evil from Mr. Cleveland's election proved false prophets. He claimed that "the bankruptcy which now threatens the treasury" is the result, first, of the enactment of the McKinley tariff law, and, secondly, of the lavish appropriations of the Fifty-first congress. He paid his respects to the "billion dollar congress," and then went on to speak of

The Tariff.

The tariff is the all-important issue of the campaign upon which we have now entered. Shall there be a revision of our tariff laws, and, as a consequence of such legislation, a reduction of taxation; or shall it become the policy of our government to maintain, permanently, high protection? The position of the two leading political parties upon that question cannot be misunderstood. The Republican party, as illustrated by its recent enactment of the McKinley law, stands for a high protective—in other words, a prohibitory tariff. The Democratic party, as emphasized by its utterances and acts, is the advocate of tariff reform. The issue is squarely presented. Upon one side are the advocates of a high protective or prohibitory policy—a policy which enriches the few at the expense of the many. On the other, the advocates of such reduction of tariff duties as will give to our manufacturers the benefit of cheap raw material, and lessen to the consumer the cost of the necessaries of life.

The Low Tariff Law of 1846,

of which Robert J. Walker, the Democratic secretary of the treasury, was the author, provided in substance, first, that no more money should be collected than is necessary for the wants of the government, economically administered; second, that no duty be imposed upon any articles above the lowest rate that will yield the greatest amount of revenue; third, that the maximum tax shall be imposed upon luxuries; fourth, that the lowest tax should be upon the necessaries of life; fifth, that the duties should be so inposed as

[Continued on Seventh Page.]

People Who are Short

Of money must be very short indeed, if they can't afford to invest $10.00 in our store. Perhaps you will be astonished to be told that the worse off you are, the better you can afford to make this investment. Isn't it true that the less you have the more sharp-sighted you must be about your purchases, and the more you must get for what you spend. Those who have handsome balances at the bank can stand the strain of handsome prices without any difficulty whatever; those who haven't, must try to make one dollar do the work of two. Is that your situation? If it is, we've got what you want and you want what we've got.

COME AND SEE US.

M. C. SWIFT & SON,

153, 157 and 159 Union Street,

NEW BEDFORD, - - - MASS.

Lawn Sprinklers,
Rubber Hose,
Poultry Netting,
Screen Doors.

F. L. SOWLE & CO.,
Hardware and Specialties.

Our Sale on

DOLLAR PAINT

is larger this season than ever before.

90 Purchase Street,
Opp City Clock.

C. W. HASKINS,

Having replenished his stock by liberal purchases of new goods, offers a choice selection of Diamonds, Watches, Fine Jewelry, Optical Goods, &c. The display of Sterling Silver Table Ware and Novelties is very attractive.

Attention is invited to a large collection of Souvenir Spoons, especially some in fine Enamel and Gold from various European countries.

Fine Watch and Clock Repairing done by competent and careful workmen and fully warranted

—AT—

C. W. HASKINS',

No. 20 Purchase Street.

HATCH & COMPANY'S EXPRESS,

No. 5 Ricketson Block, New Bedford,

DAILY,

By Passenger Trains, to all Points on the Old Colony Railroad and its Connections.

JAHN BROS., Florists,
CLARKS POINT.
ROSES AND CARNATIONS,
A SPECIALTY.

lyr-tf

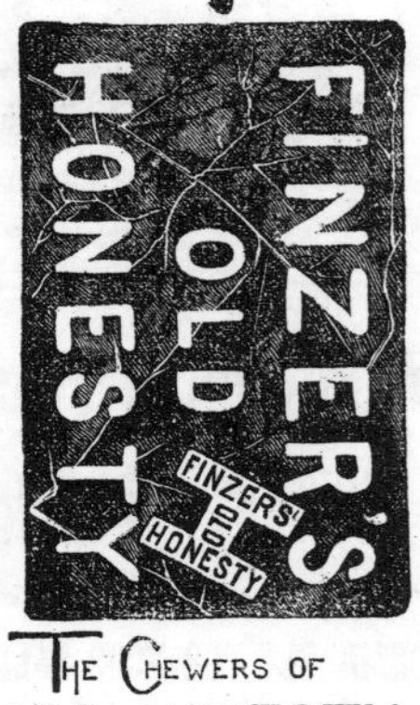

THE CHEWERS OF
OLD HONESTY
TOBACCO
WILL SOON FIND THAT IT LASTS LONGER, TASTES SWEETER THAN OTHER TOBACCOS, AND WILL PLEASE YOU. ASK YOUR DEALER FOR IT, AND INSIST ON GETTING IT.
EVERY PLUG STAMPED LIKE ABOVE CUT.
JNO. FINZER & BROS., Louisville, Ky.

SUMMER BARGAINS!

Are Now in Full Force With Us.

A lot of Remnants and short lengths of Carpets at about half price.

13 Parlor Suites cut in price from $5 to $25 per suite.

20 Chamber Sets to close, from $5 to $20 under price.

25 Baby Carriages to close at som price.

SUMMER FURNITURE!

IN GREAT VARIETY.

Refrigerators of all sizes, at rock bottom prices.

This is our annual clearing up of odds and ends, and if there is a want of anything in housekeeping, look now for it at a bargain.

CASH OR CREDIT,

CASH OR CREDIT,

CASH OR CREDIT.

PEIRCE FURNISHING CO.,

Cor. Purchase and Kempton Sts.,

THE LEADERS OF LOW PRICES IN THE HOUSE FURNISHING BUSINESS.

READ!
READ!
READ!

MOYNAN'S
Saturday Bargain List.

MOYNAN & Co. offer for Saturday Ladies' Fine Cambric Wrappers that were $1.25 and $1.50 for 98c. Also a lot of red figured waists that were 50c., for Saturday's sale only 39c.

☞ *Don't miss visiting Housefurnishing Department.*

IN MILLINERY DEPARTMENT.—On Saturday we will close out all our children's sun hats at *less than half price*. Also all our ladies' straw hats in every style and color, were from $1 to $2.50; without any reserve your choice now $25c. Millinery flowers and wreaths all go at less than quarter old prices. Moynan & Co.

☞ *Great Reduction in all kinds of silk waists, newest styles.*

WASH GOODS.—On Saturday you can have the remainder of our Domestic Challies (only about 500 yards) regular 6c., for this day 3c. Shantong Pongees, regular 12½c. quality, all choice patterns of this season's productions and perfectly fast colors; your choice for this sale 85c. per yard. Only a few short lengths of those wool challies that have sold at 21c. Early comers can procure them on Saturday at 12½c. yard. Moynan & Co.

☞ *See our new stock of Kid Gloves.*

DRESS GOODS.—A strictly all-wool serge, 36 inches wide, and in all the desirable colorings, staple 50c. quality; we offer while they last at 39c. Don't miss getting one of those handsome dress lengths which we are selling at about ⅓ less than regular value. Moynan & Co.

☞ *Parasols at prices you want to pay. Must go at once.*

SATURDAY IN HOUSEFURNISHINGS.—24-inch Japanned Tea Tray regular 49c. now only 29c. 26-inch Trays regularly sold at 59c. on Saturday 39c. 28-inch Trays regular price 71c. on Saturday 49c. These would be the ladies regular price for. for Saturday only 5c. Thin engraved tumblers regular price 89c. dozen for this sale 57c. dozen. Window screens only a few remaining, your choice *from any size 28c.*

☞ *See our new styles in Ruchings, Laces and Embroideries.*

IN CLOAK DEPARTMENT.—All our Ladies' Blazer Jackets in Tans and Blues, that were $5.00 and $5.98 must go on Saturday at $2.98. Ladies'Jersey suits were $4.00 and $4.90 at $1.98. Ladies' Kado cloth capes, suitable for early Fall wear, these are a new lot just in and are worth $12.00, but will be opened for Saturday's sale at $8.98. Suits in cotton, also cotton and wool at $1.98. Moynan & Co.

☞ *See our $4.50 China Silk Waists, in Red, Blue and Black for Saturday only, $3.48.*

EMBROIDERIES.—On Saturday we will sell remainder of our Embroidered, also Embroidered and Hemstitched Flouncings; some very handsome styles are included in this lot, and are worth from 50c. to 75c. all go in on Saturday at 29c. per yard. See our cheap prices on all kinds of Laces, Ruchings, Veilings, etc., etc. Moynan & Co.

☞ *Don't miss the Ribbon Sale, remember just half usual prices.*

☞ ON SATURDAY we will sell an extra size Marseilles Spread worth $1.75 for $1.48. Huck and Damask Towels worth from 12 to 25c. for this day 17c. 18 inch all linen Crash worth 8c. for 5c. per yard. Moynan & Co.

☞ *Don't miss those Japanese Silk Handkerchiefs for 29c. each.*

MOYNAN & Co. offer for Saturday's Sale a lot of Quill Fans in all colors, worth at least 50c., for this sale only 25c. each. *Surely see them.* Big bargain in Japanese Silk Handkerchiefs, worth from 50c. to 75c. for 29c.

☞ *For Cheap Underwear, Gents are invited to go to Moynan & Co's, on Saturday.*

Come to Moynan's on Saturday for Ruchings, Veilings, Laces, Embroideries, Perfumery, &c., &c. Our prices are low and our assortments largest to be found in the city.

The Evening Standard.

NEW BEDFORD, MASS.

SATURDAY EVENING, AUGUST 27.

THREE EDITIONS DAILY.

No. 87 Union Street.

PUBLISHED BY

E. ANTHONY & SONS,
INCORPORATED.

—TERMS:—

Six Dollars a Year; Three Dollars for Six Months, in advance; Single Copies Two Cents.

TELEPHONE CALLS.

Counting Room, - - - - 305-2
Editorial Room, - - - - 305-3

FOR PRESIDENT:

BENJAMIN HARRISON
OF INDIANA.

FOR VICE-PRESIDENT:

WHITELAW REID
OF NEW YORK.

TWELVE PAGES.

This Evening's Issue Consists of Twelve Pages and Every Patron is Entitled to that Number.

CONTENTS OF THIS EVENING'S STANDARD.

Page 1.
Conclusion of Bridget Sullivan's examination and adjournment of Borden hearing until Monday.
Metropolitan Opera House in New York in flames.
Home matters.
Late telegraphic news.
Page 2.
Scenes at the Borden murder trial.
Full report of Bridget Sullivan's evidence yesterday afternoon.
Almost a riot after adjournment of court over the story of the sisters' quarrel.
Page 3.
Senator Dawes announces his decision to retire.
Daniel Ricketson writes in behalf of Congressman Randall.
President Harrison's speech to-day at Loon Lake, N. Y.
Adlai Stevenson opens the Democratic campaign in Illinois.
Page 4.
The congressional contest.
Accident at the Wamsutta mills.
Mrs. Eliza Luther celebrates her one hundredth birthday.
Third District Court.
Editorials.
Home Matters.
Telegraphic dispatches.
Page 5.
Marine intelligence.
Marriages and deaths.
Page 6.
Financial news.
Second Edition – Telegraphic and local news.
Page 7.
Regimental reunion.
Guards' rifle practice.
Sunday notices.
Yesterday's ball games.
Amusement and sporting news.
Page 8.
Theophilus C. Ball heard from.
Third Edition—Telegraphic and local news.
Early telegraphic dispatches.
Page 9.
Interesting stories of impecunious statesmen.
Josiah Quincy's part in the Democratic campaign.
Farm, Garden and Home.
Miscellaneous reading.
Page 10.
Edgar L. Wakeman writes on London costermongers.
Olive Harper's fashion letter.
Evolution of the buckboard.
Page 11.
An old water route connecting with Lake Ontario.
Opie Read discovers a new and dreadful malady.
Mammoth trees from California to be exhibited at the World's fair.
Wisconsin's Republican leader.
Prince Bismarck's favorite son.
Miscellaneous reading.
Page 12.
On ocean steamers are imperilled by icebergs.
Bible Lesson.
Miscellaneous reading.

☞ The frantic efforts of the New York *World* and other Democratic papers to raise money to debauch the elections in the West is succeeding admirably in convincing the honest voter of the country that the Democracy is not very confident of landing Mr. Cleveland in the White House.

☞ The depression in English cotton manufactures is in somewhat startling contrast to the prosperity of our own. The losses of England are due partly to the decline in exports, owing to the increased competition of American cotton in Latin America, partly to the drop in silver (which has cut down the American exports to China) and the competition of the Bombay mills.

☞ In another column will be found a letter from Senator Dawes declining to be a candidate for re-election. His retirement is caused by the infirmities of advancing years. The State will lose an able Senator, whose long career in Congress has been an honorable and useful one. We have, however, in our midst a gentleman of experience and ability who should be selected by the Republicans of the State to succeed Mr. Dawes, and we present for their consideration the name of Hon. William W. Crapo.

☞ The new State highway commission has commenced its work, and circulars sent out by them have been received by the authorities of this city and the neighboring towns.
This commission is the result of the earnest efforts of the Massachusetts division of the League of American Wheelmen in behalf of better roads. For two years they have endeavored to get a bill through the Legislature authorizing the appointment of such a commission for the purpose of giving advice to the different town and city authorities in the Commonwealth. At the last session a compromise was effected and a bill passed under which this board was appointed. Its duties are to study the subject and to report to the next term of the General Court the best course to be pursued in the future.

HOME MATTERS.

CONTAGIOUS DISEASES.—But one new case of scarlet fever has been reported at the office of the Board of Health the past week.

IN OPERATION.—The hoisting engine recently purchased by the Public Works Department is in operation at the Grape street sewer excavation.

THE CITY HAS THE DEEDS.—This morning the City Treasurer paid the representatives of the E. Whittemore estate $3500 for land at Chepachet, and now the city has the deeds of that property.

DARTMOUTH ALL DAY'S MEETING.—The next All Day's Meeting will be held in the Christian church, Smith Mills, Dartmouth, Thursday, Sept. 1. The order of exercises will be as follows: 10:30 a. m., subject of discourse, "Having a Purpose," by Charles H. Brownell of New Bedford; 12 m., intermission for refreshments. Tea and coffee furnished; 2 p. m., preaching service; 6 p. m., praise service; 7 p. m., service, conducted by Elizabeth Manchester of New Bedford. Bible Songs of Joy and Gladness.

THE CONGRESSIONAL CONTEST.

Mr. Randall Denies He Has Entered Into Any Agreement.

The Boston *Record* last evening printed the following:

NEW BEDFORD, Aug. 26.—The success of Congressman Randall in carrying all the caucuses in this city will help him in his fight for renomination. It is given out here that he has secured the support of the Cape by agreeing to withdraw in 1894 in favor of John Simpkins.

A *Standard* reporter showed the above to Mr. Randall this forenoon.

"This statement," said the Congressman, "is entirely false. No such proposal has ever been made to me by any party, and I have made none myself. I have believed ever since Mr. Greene was announced as a candidate that I would have in the convention at least 65 out of the 98 delegates, and I think so now. I naturally feel that the Cape is entitled to name my successor."

POLITICAL.—A Republican caucus was held in Provincetown last evening, when three Randall delegates were undoubtedly elected, although the wires are down, and no news has been received. The situation up to the present time is as follows:

	Randall.	Greene.
New Bedford	22	
Eastham	1	
Provincetown	3	
Wareham	1	2
Fall River		27
	27	27

This afternoon the Republicans of Harwich will hold a caucus, and this evening caucuses will be held at Somerset and Chatham.

Next Saturday evening, Sept. 3, Dartmouth will hold Republican caucuses.

At a Republican caucus held in Wareham last evening, Capt. Benjamin F. Gibbs was chosen chairman, and William L. Chipman, Esq., secretary.

The following delegates were elected:
State—Hiram W. Barrows.
Congressional—Capt. Alden Besse.
Councillor—John M. Savery.
Senatorial—Harvey Crocker, Edward F. Handy, Frank A. Besse.
County—Adolphus Savery, Noble W. Everett, Horace M. Sprout.
Representative—Capt. B. F. Gibbs, Charles L. Kinney, Capt. Alden Besse, Robert C. Randall, Frederick C. Briggs.
Town Committee—Alden Besse, Edgar Robinson, Edward F. Handy, Henry W. Boyd, William L. Chipman, Noble W. Everett, Benjamin F. Gibbs, Charles L. Kinney, Joseph Jessup, Stephen C. Burgess, Thomas B. Griffith, George W. Bowlock, Frank A. Besse, Harvey Crocker, Hiram W. Barrows, John M. Savery, Eugene G. Stevens.
Executive Committee—B. F. Gibbs, W. L. Chipman, H. W. Boyd, C. L. Kinney, E. Robinson, H. Crocker.

The sentiment of the caucus was unanimous in favor of the renomination of Hon. Charles S. Randall for Congress.

THE NEW CITY DIRECTORY.—The City Directory for 1892 is just out and is more accurate and complete than ever before. Messrs. W. A. Greenough & Co., the publishers, have spared no pains to make the volume one that shall commend itself to every business house, office or to the home, and it should find a place near at hand to everyone in New Bedford. Despite the marvelous increase in New Bedford's population, the collectors have succeeded in compiling a very full list of residents, business concerns, secret societies and localities. The organization of the city departments and social organizations is notably more accurate than in former years.
The most notable new feature of the book is the addition of a Fairhaven directory, both of residents, business concerns and social organizations. This is something hitherto unpublished and will be of great value. Another addition this year is the publication of a list of all persons over 18 years of age who have died within the past year.
The volume is neatly printed and bound, and mechanically is a creditable job. Incidental to the Fairhaven directory are printed pictures of the Rogers School, Public Library and Town Hall.
The new directory is on sale for $2 at the store of H. S. Hutchinson & Co.

MARRIED IN CHURCH'S.—Yes, married in Church's, and it happened in this way: Yesterday afternoon a young couple who were very desirous of being married by Leopold Bartel, Esq., called at that gentleman's house only to find that he was not at home. They had made preparations to leave the city on the 5:50 train and hadn't much time to spare. Learning that Mr. Bartel was on duty at City Hall square, they at once proceeded there when they found the genial officer. To him they related the object of their visit at his house and the arrangement they had made, whereupon it was suggested that the trio adjourn to a neighboring apothecary establishment. It happened to be C. H. Church's, corner of Pleasant and Union streets. There the knot was tied as firmly as though the ceremony had been performed in a church, and the couple departed evidently as happy as though wedding bells had announced their nuptials to a host of friends. Witnesses for the occasion were picked up on the spot.

OBITUARY.—Mrs. Jefferson Borden, widow of one who was foremost in the establishment of manufacturing interests in Fall River, died yesterday from paralysis. Mrs. Borden was 80 years old in May last. She was the mother of nine children, four of whom survive her: Mrs. Walter Paine of Montreal, Mrs. George W. Dean, Messrs. Jefferson and Spencer Borden of Fall River, and three of whom, Mrs. E. Corinna Keene of Philadelphia, Norman E. Borden and Mrs. Eliza O. Durfee, wife of George B. Durfee, died in mature life, the latter within a few weeks. Mrs. Borden was, before marriage, Miss Susan Easton,and was a native of Rhode Island. She was a lady of great activity of temperament, and was an excellent wife and mother, strong in conviction and earnest in everything she undertook. For many years she was one of the most earnest members of the First Baptist church.

DENY THE STORY.—Capt. A. Lewis and Mate George Reece of Nantucket schooner Mary Ellen, deny the statement that the captain and crew of three men were under the influence of liquor last Tuesday when the vessel was anchored off Stone Horse ledge, Nantucket shoals. They also deny the story that two of his crew were picked up in the water by schooner Alaska. The mate, while in a boat trying to pick up a floating spar with a gaff attached, was upset in the water by the tide, and was rescued by the Alaska.

HAD TO STAY INDOORS.—Owing to the bad weather, ex-President Cleveland has had to stay indoors. He has had a few callers, none of whom, however, on political missions or bearing political messages. Mr. Benedict's yacht, the Oneida, on which its owner and party of friends came Thursday to see Mr. Cleveland, is still at Buzzards Bay. A short cruise, in which the Jeffersons and the Clevelands were to take part, had been talked of for yesterday, but the fog and the rain upset all plans.

ENLARGED STORE.—The eating saloon in James Greenwood's building on William street is to be discontinued after to-morrow, and E. T. Chapman, who occupies the next store east, has secured a refusal of the place with a view of enlarging his cigar store. Should he decide to take it the partition dividing the stores will be removed, and it is proposed to fit up the establishment as a pool and billiard room.

NEW BICYCLE CLUB.—At a meeting of Brockton bicyclists Thursday evening a club was organized, to be known as the Shoe City Wheelmen. Forty-five bicyclists agreed to join, and black and red were decided on as the club colors, every member to be provided with a black cap with a piece of red felt in the shape of a shoe stitched on the crown.

A LIVELY OLD LADY.

Mrs. Eliza Luther Celebrates Her Hundredth Birthday.

Mrs. Eliza Luther of Berkley participated to-day, along with a couple of hundred of relatives and friends, in a somewhat singular and, to her, unique affair. It was her hundredth birthday and the old lady was as gay as a lark, comparatively speaking. Of course she wasn't exactly in condition to dance "in the barn," nor could she strike as high a note as when she sang in the village choir some few years ago, but nevertheless she was chipper and glad to be there. Her picture shows the face of a remarkably well preserved old lady, and her eyes are as bright, her intellect as keen as they have been for a number of years, and she can tell the story of her life as glibly and intelligently as one would care to have her do.

She was born in Exeter, R. I., Aug. 28, 1792, so that her celebration actually comes one day ahead of time, because Sunday is not a reasonable day for observing anniversaries of this sort. Her parents, Ezekiel and Martha Austin, were of the poor but honest kind with a penchant for increasing the population of Little Rhody as rapidly as possible and for keeping the children out of idleness, for there were 15 of them, and all clung to life with singular tenacity. The last survivor before Mrs. Luther departed this life at Berkley, Oct. 11, 1891, on her 97th birthday.
Mrs. Luther points with pride to the fact that she at one time, when she was very small and very young, was employed in the

MRS. ELIZA LUTHER.
One Hundred Years Old To-day.

first cotton mill erected in this country. Its centennial was fittingly observed only a few months since, it will be remembered, and all Pawtucket was interested in the affair. She managed by dint of long hours and hard work to earn $1.25 a week—not in a day—in that mill, and she paid $1 for her board and lodgings. Before she went into the mill and while she was going to school, she was obliged to spin seven knots of tow before going to school and the same number on her return, and she was so small that her father was obliged to build a platform so she could properly hand her wheel. In fact, her young life was in no respect different from that of many other girls of that period, and the only remarkable feature about it now is that Mrs. Luther is able to tell of it so clearly and cleverly.

Up to within two years she has always made her own clothes, and since the death of her husband she has looked out for herself, working at housekeeping when there wasn't any particular need of it, simply to keep busy. Think of it, taking full charge of a house at the age of 93! And yet that is just what she did. A week ago she said she made her own bed, dressed and undressed herself, and had an almost abnormal appetite.
Her grandson, Daniel L. White, of the White-Smith Music Company, arranged for a big clambake on the premises to-day, with orchestral accompaniments under the direction of Harrie A. Peck of Taunton, a relative, and there was dancing and a general good time.

THIRD DISTRICT COURT.

BORDEN, J.

NEW BEDFORD, Aug. 27.

John Martin and John Magiue pleaded not guilty of the larceny of two hens, valued at $2, and half a peck of potatoes, valued at 10 cents, the property of some person to the complainant unknown. These parties were arrested early this morning by Lieut. Bryant and Officer A. H. Jones, with the above property in a bag in the possession of Martin.
Seth E. Bryant found these parties on the railroad track about 3:30 this morning in the vicinity of Logan street, walking toward the city. Martin had a bag with two hens and about half a peck of potatoes in it. The hens' necks were wrung and the feathers were not picked off them.
Officer A. H. Jones said that the men told him they bought the hens and potatoes of a farmer near Acushnet, whither they had stopped most of the night in a shed near the ice-houses on "Nash road." They told Mr. Jones where they boarded in the city and upon investigation no such place could be found.
John Martin, one of the defendants, said they sold disinfectants called "moth balls." Magiue and he started out in the country Thursday to peddle and stayed the first night in a farmer's barn. The farmer allowed them to stay in the barn and called them in the morning. The next day they sold 60 cents' worth of balls and with this money bought two hens. The price was $1 and he made up the difference with balls. He bought them of a farmer about three-quarters of a mile above Acushnet Village. The farmer gave him the potatoes. Magiue was not with him when he bought the hens. He was peddling on the other side of the road ahead of him. He did not know the farmer's name, as he had seen him once before on the bridge fishing.
Martin told the court his name was John Moore. He gave the officers the name of Martin as he did not want his friends to know he was arrested. He did tell the officers last night he boarded on Scheel street, but this morning he told them he had made a mistake, it was 213 South Water street, where he boarded with a man named Clarke. He did not know where Magiue boarded. He had only known him a week. Last night he met Magiue by appointment at River View and then as it was the nearest way to the city they went up Nash road to a shed which they went into out of the rain and then down the railroad track to the city.
These cases were suspended and the continued case of Elizabeth Ripley, charged with a single sale of liquor to Frederick Lambert on the 8th of August instant, was taken up. Hon. E. L. Barney for the defence.
Napoleon Marquis was called by the Commonwealth. He said he knew nothing about the case. He never saw Mrs. Ripley either sell or give away any liquor.
Israel Lambert said he had seen Mrs. Ripley sell liquor It was about 4 weeks ago. Napoleon Marquis, Victor Hall and himself had three glasses of lager in Mrs. Ripley's and paid 30 cents for them. It was delivered to them by Mrs. Ripley About three weeks ago he went to Mrs. Ripley's with Ardulla Carrette and had two bottles of lager and paid 20 cents for it.
Ardulle Carrette was the next witness and said he was with Israel Lambert the day before his brother Fred was arrested and they had two bottles of lager and Lambert paid for it.
Rosalie Lambert said she and her mother had bought lager of Mrs. Ripley about five or six weeks ago and paid her for it. No one was present except Mrs. Ripley, her mother and a child. It was on a Tuesday about 2 o'clock in the afternoon. I was there again with Peter Carrette and his wife. We each drank lager and paid for it. It was the same week I was there before.
Mary Carrette said she had bought lager and whiskey of Mrs. Ripley. She owed her now 30 cents—25 for the whiskey and 25 for three bottles of lager. This witness was examined through an interpreter and the court and Mr. Barney endeavored to get her to tell what she said to Mrs. Ripley in English when she got the liquor. Mrs. Ripley not understanding French, but they were unsuccessful. Mrs. Carrette said she was at Mrs. Ripley's one week ago last Thursday and tried to borrow $3 from her. Mrs. Ripley said she would pay up if she wanted to go away, and I told her if she would let me have it I would not be here when the court came off. She knew I had had liquor of her, and the first time this case was tried she came and asked me if I was going to court An officer came last night and told me to come to court this morning. Lambert is not re-lated to me. He did not ask me to come to court.
Mrs. Lambert, the mother, next testified. Knew Mrs. Ripley; bought whiskey of her three times. It was three or four weeks ago. Can't give the date. Was alone the first time. Had some lager with Peter Carretta and his wife at Mrs. Ripley's. It was paid for by them. There was a lady with a sore eye the first two times I bought the whiskey. Bought 15 cents' worth of whiskey the last time and paid Mrs. Ripley for it. About three weeks ago I bought lager of her and owe her for it. Her son Fred started for Fall River about three weeks ago to work in the mill. She was not asked to come to the court at the last trial.
Mr Barney claimed that the testimony introduced to-day was of a new nature and not in rebuttal of any evidence given at the last hearing; that the government attorney had stopped most of the night in a shed and that testimony that was to be heard to-day was to ascertain if possible which party had committed perjury.
James Hall was then called for the defence. He said he knew Mrs. Ripley and Fred Lambert. Lambert came where he was and had a half pint bottle with him which he said he got of Mrs. Ripley. Never saw any liquor sold by Mrs. Ripley. Have hired boats at her shop. Never saw Lambert buy any liquor of Mrs. Ripley. Lambert wanted me to say I got a quart at rum of Mrs. Ripley, he thought I got it there, but I got it at the drug store the Saturday night before. The father brought some liquor to a house where I was and I got a drink out of it. I don't know where he bought it.
Mr. Ripley said he never was present at any time when Israel Lambert bought liquor of his wife.
Mrs. Ripley said she never sold any liquor at all to any one and never kept any liquor at her store. The daughter Rosie bought occasant cakes of her, but never any lager. Mrs. Carrette came to her and wanted $2. She said Mr. Lambert had given her name in as a witness and she did not want to go, and if I would give her $2 she would go away out of town. Mrs. Ripley said Special Officer Stevens was in her store most every night and he told her he would testify for her.
Michael Stevens was called and said he was a special on duty south from half-past six to half-past nine. He never suspected her of selling liquor. He stopped in most every night for three or four minutes, say three or four evenings a week, he was in the store. Peter Carretta said he lived on the street where the horse cars run. He knew Mrs. Ripley; was at her store once with the women and had lager beer. He paid five cents a glass for it. It was three or four weeks ago. Never was in but once and saw her sell liquor. This closed the testimony.
After argument by counsel and a review of the case by the court, Mrs. Ripley was adjudged guilty. Judge Borden said his sympathies were with Mrs. Ripley and he had rather not convict her than to do so, particularly when it was in everybody's mouth that the liquor law was being violated every day and hour of the day in this city. That parties were selling gallons where this woman was only selling a small quantity, and whatever his sentence might be in this case he did not want it to be regarded as a precedent if any larger fish in the business were brought before him He did not wish to reflect on the officers in this case, for the evidence that was disclosed at the trial of Lambert when arrested for drunkenness compelled the issuing of the warrant. He should fine her $50, the smallest he could do under the statute. Mrs. Ripley appealed, and was ordered to recognize in $300.
Martin was again put on the stand and told by the court that if he could get any one to go surety for him he would be allowed to go and look up the man he bought the fowl of and he would now allow him to go in charge of an officer and point out his boarding place or Water street, but this he declined te do.
Each was adjudged guilty and sentenced to the House of Correction for three months. Wilfred Briar, for unlawfully selling intoxicating liquor to Joseph Tetreault on the 6th of August last at a dance at North Union Hall, was fined $50 and settled. Hon. E. L. Barney for defendant.
The larceny cases against John Martin and John Magiue have thus resumed. This witness was examined through an interpreter the court and Mr. Barney endeavored. Joseph Tetreault retracted his plea of not guilty to a complaint against him for drunkenness and pleaded guilty. He was placed on probation until Sept. 30th next.

[Continued on Sixth Page, Second Edition.]

BELIEF IN GUILT

[Continued from First Page.]

Knowlton answered affirmatively, and the court announced that the examination stands adjourned until Monday at 10:45.

Persistent Denials.

After the adjournment of the court Attorney Jennings had a long conversation with Emma Borden in the Judge's room, and after this Attorney Adams was called in.

When Mr. Jennings came out he was asked if the sisters persisted in denying the statement of a quarrel. He said, "I have not asked them. I got from them yesterday that the statement was unqualifiedly false. If you want further confirmation you can go to Rev. Mr. Buck or Mr. and Mrs. Charles J. Holmes who will make affidavit that the statement of a quarrel is false. If City Marshal Hilliard had not interfered, Mrs. Reagan would have signed the affidavit."

John C. Milne's Opinion.

John C. Milne of the Fall River *News* said the reporter who gave to the public Mrs. Reagan's statement that Emma went home and threw herself on the bed after the talk with Lizzie told what he could have no means of knowing to be true. The backman who carried Emma home states that she was very cheerful. This statement, said Mr. Milne, is one that affects Lizzie gravely and ought not to have been published, if the writer knew it to be true.

A PISTON BROKE.

Accident to the "Big Elephant" Engine at Wamsutta Mills.

Day before yesterday the west half of the big engine that runs Wamsutta Mill No. 5 broke down, and as a result only about two-thirds of the mill is running. The card and spinning rooms are partly stopped, but the weaving is all running.
The engine in question is the famous "Big Elephant" Corliss walking-beam engine of 2500 horse power that was built on the same patterns as the noted Centennial engine. Engineer Rhodes was just starting up when he heard a crash in the west cylinder and promptly shut down. It was found that the piston rod had worked loose in the piston, and when the load was brought to bear the piston rod punched a hole in the piston. It is remarkable that it did not punch through the cylinder head. The west half of the engine was uncoupled and the east half was kept running, though its load is pretty heavy.

FAIRHAVEN.

A clambake was held about a mile east of the village on Sunday last and several complaints have reached the constable. The "kickers" charge him with being partial. The bake was a private one, given by a young men's club however, and for that reason was allowable.
The building of the sidewalk about the library is being delayed by the strike of the granite workers. As the strike does not appear to be approaching a settlement, it is impossible to say when work will be resumed. About 6300 books are now numbered and ready for the library. The masons at the town hall have not been working since Friday noon on account of the storm.
Constable Delano has been hunting up dog owners during the week and reminding them that licenses are due.
Selectman Aiken swept the town office this morning for the first time since Spring cleaning.
The following additions have been made to the subscription list for the fort guns: Henry H. Rogers, $50; Mrs. N. J. Lawton, $2; cash, $10, making a total of $224.

COTTAGE CITY.

Yesterday's northeast storm was quite severe. Vineyard Haven was crowded with vessels, and at 5 o'clock many of them were making bad weather of it. With two anchors out and riding on a long scope of chain, schooners pitched flying-jib boom into the rollers. One schooner dragged and set a signal for assistance which was answered by tug Elsie.
The Gay Head did not land at the Bluffs, but discharged at the New York wharf, proceeding to Woods Holl for the night.
The Martha Vineyard also docked at the New York wharf, but in the morning came around to the Sea View wharf.
There was no boat to Nantucket in the afternoon, and passengers for that port remained at Cottage City.
The waves last night broke under the Casino embankment, and in spite of precautions in the way of sand-boxes along the high tide mark, considerable washing out was the result.
It was impossible for the late train over the Edgartown railroad to reach Cottage City, and section hands were this morning repairing damages.
Mrs. A. A. Hill's fruit and tobacco store on Circuit avenue was raided yesterday and about three plats of whiskey confiscated. The complaint was made by the selectmen and the search warrant obtained the names of Mrs. A. A. Hill and Henry Mansfield. Both parties were taken before Justice Eldridge and held in $100 bonds to appear for trial on Monday next. This store was raided early in the season, a big haul made, and the man in charge left town and has not been seen since.
The benefit concert to be given Capt. John Orlando last evening has been postponed to Monday evening.
Lewis Bartlett, superintendent of the gas works, yesterday caught a 17-pound striped bass at the railroad bridge.
The annual meeting of the Marthas Vineyard Association was held this morning at the residence of Dr. H. A. Tucker.
Sloop Pointer, Dr. Whitney of New Bedford, rode out yesterday's gale in Woods Holl harbor.
Yesterday was laymen's day at the Methodist Tabernacle.
The annual ball of the Marthas Vineyard Association will be held this evening in the Casino.

VINEYARD HAVEN.

The northeaster of yesterday abated during last night. The wind attained a velocity of 40 miles an hour and nearly an inch of rainfall occurred. Sloop yacht Naida of New Bedford was anchored near the steamboat wharf and all the occupants and all the contents were thoroughly drenched. Three-masted schooner William H. Davenport, Capt. Stacey, from an eastern coal port for Dover, N. H., with cargo of coal, dragged from the middle of the harbor to shoal water on the west side of the harbor, and struck bottom, but was quickly towed to deeper water by tug Elsie. A large fleet of tugs, barges and coasters rode out the gale in safety.
The City of Portsmouth did not return from Woods Holl on her last trip.

FALL RIVER.

John Mayman, better known as "Steeple Jack," climbed the 135-foot chimney of the Laurel Lake mill, Thursday, in one hour and 45 minutes without the aid of staging. He found the top in such condition that two feet of it were condemned, and orders have been given to rebuild it. He will also repoint the chimney for about 85 feet from the top.
Samuel Levy, 14 Seventh street, went to the ice-chest Thursday to get a bottle of soda, and while she held the bottle in her hand it burst. One piece flew into one of Mrs. Levy's eyes, completely destroying the sight.
A case of cruelty to animals seldom heard of happened Thursday morning on Easter avenue, near the lake, where two youths owned by a horse car. The animal was shot by a horse car. The animal was shot up in an enclosure high enough to allow the boys to have a good view of the holocaust. They and then set fire to the straw inside.

SECOND EDITION.

HOME MATTERS.

A NEW ENGINE.

Another Corliss Engine to be Put Into the Wamsutta Mills.

It is unfortunate that the accident to the Wamsutta Mills engine, reported in the *Standard's* first edition, happened just at this time. Had the engine held out about six weeks longer the accident would not have been of any consequence. For several weeks workmen have been engaged in build-ing a new engine-house for the present one, to receive the new engine, which the *Standard* announced as projected several months ago. The big engine has for some time been showing signs of weakness, and the mill management has been pushing things forward toward setting up the new one. The building is completed and the beds are all in, and yesterday the pillow blocks and bed plates of the new engine arrived in this city. They will be put in position at once, and it is hoped to have the new engine running in two months.

It will be a Corliss cross-compound, with a nominal horse power of 1500. The high pres-sure cylinder is 30 inches in diameter and the low pressure 56 inches, while the stroke is 72 inches. The big fly-wheel will be 30 feet in diameter, with a face of 108 inches, and is de-signed to run two belts.

When this engine is in place and running, the big walking-beam engine will be demol-ished, as it cannot be moved out. It has been in use over 20 years, but has ceased to be economical from a modern standpoint.

THIRD DISTRICT COURT.

[Continued from fourth page.]

A. C. McIntyre, alias Albert C. McIntyre, pleaded not guilty of the larceny of a suit of clothes, valued at $30, the property of Benja-min P. Higgins, from the boarding house of Lucy A. Brightman on School street, on the second day of June, 1891. U. T. St. Germain for defendant.

Benjamin F. Higgins testified to boarding at Mrs. Brightman's at that time and to hav-ing a suit of clothes in a clothes press in the front hall. The suit cost $32. Mc-Intyre boarded with Mrs. Bright-man at the time. He left on the first of June, Wednesday, and shortly after he had gone the same day he found his pants and vest had gone.

Mrs. Brightman said McIntyre boarded with her last year. He was to come "Memo-rial Day," but did not come until the next day. He brought his wife with him. He said she was his wife.

They staid at her house until Tuesday. She ordered them to leave on Monday. She had no other boarder but Mr. Higgins. Mc-Intyre had to pass the clothes press where the suit of clothes was when he came down stairs. She saw the clothes in the press, Monday afternoon about 5 o'clock. She missed a watch and two chains and a razor at the same time.

One o'clock having arrived court took a re-cess until half past two.

REAL ESTATE SALES.—Albert S. Orswell of Tiverton has sold to David Hambly about 17 acres of meadow and pasture land, with buildings, situated in the east part of the town, and David Hambly has sold the same to Dillie M. Orswell.

REAL ESTATE SALES.—Wm. H. Angell, $165.45; G. M. Austin &
Sons, 172.91; Geo. M. Babbitt, $46.02; Bessom
Bros., 102.67; Chas. H. Billings, 110.39; John
Birkinhead, 295.01; Jacob Bragg, 101.38; F. L.
Cady, 110.16; S. W. Card, 168.13; S. W. Card &
Co., 194.90; Chilton Fur. Co., 504.50; Elton O.
Cobb, 185.65; Cemey & Co., 398.00; Elijah
Copeland, 178.26; Chase Elevator Co., 225.60;
Alfred B. Day, 104.22; Lucy M. Dinsmore,
196.00; Evans, Cobb & Co., 130.68; Eliza O.
George, 347.00; Wm. Graves, 179.21; Mass.
Water Supply Dist., 156.56; Chas. L.Hallet,300.81;
Marigen H. Hallet, 133.66; A. C. Hardon, 172.67;
H. M. Gilbreth, 726.22; George S. Hodges,
125.72; James L. Hodges, 162.32; V. B. Brackett,
102.72; A. King, 111.30; L. R. King, 138.92; H.
W. Kingman, 139.11; Walter W. Leonard,
126.89; H. M. Lillibridge, 130.76; S. C. Lovell,
377.73; Elizabeth F. Noble, 156.42; Fred Paine,
231.08; E. Reed, 109.82; G. A. Robinson,
138.21; John W. Rogers, 229.76; A. V. Rogers-
son, 203.56; Rogerson Bros., 309.55; S. E.
Scholes, 114.11; D. S. Spaulding, 554.38; W. L.
Stearns, 140.99; George Ware, 127.71; J. A.
Wheeler, 181.26; J. W. White, 131.68; estate of
C. P. Williams, 377.73; Susan L. Wilson, 100.
Non-residents—E. B. Watson, 595.88; B.& P.
R. R. Co., 476.88; O. C. R. R. Co., 513.72; O'Brien
Bros., 172.25; E. J. Green, 107.16; John F.
Comey, 207.96; Samuel G. Tripp, 118 80.

It Strikes us as Remarkable to hear of the wonderful record for curing enjoyed by Beton's Infallible Itch Salve; it cures every form of this troublesome ail-ment. If not to be had at your druggist's send 50 cents to Winkelmann & Brown Drug Co., Baltimore, Md.

Until To-Day.

It is admitted that more of the flavoring principle of the fruit is contained in

Dr. Price's Delicious Flavoring Extracts

than any other extracts with which they have been compared. Being so entirely free from the bitter and rank products of adulteration they have become the most agreeable, valuable and economical flavors known; steadily grown in popularity until to-day they are used by every intelligent housewife for truthfully reproducing the flavor of the fruit in creams, cakes, puddings, etc.

WILL IT BE ANOTHER MILL?

A Movement for Another Cotton Factory Temporarily Suspended.

There have been rumors afloat recently pointing to the establishment of still an-other mill for this city. A *Standard* reporter has searched the rumor and learned that a well known mill man of this city started out some time ago to organize another cotton mill corporation. As interested several gen-tlemen in the enterprise, but just as the move took definite form, instigators of another new mill, it is said, persuaded him to with-draw his attempts and have the movement was temporarily suspended. Those who know say it may yet be revived and the sixth mill of this season erected.

GOSPEL GROVE CAMP-MEETING.

GOSPEL GROVE, Cadman's Neck, Aug. 26. The morning meeting was led by Rev. A. H. Nazanin from Ephesians ii, 19, "Now, there-fore, ye are no more strangers and foreign-ers, but fellow citizens with the saints and of the household of God." The speaker, a na-tive Armenian, related his experience in be-coming an adopted citizen of this nation and how, on his return to his native land, he was arrested on suspicion of plotting against the government there. A passport signed by James G. Blaine was a full protection from the Turkish police. We can have a glorious citizenship in heaven, Jesus Christ is our passport and through him comes deliverance from every enemy, and in the end eternal life.

In the afternoon service Rev. H. F. Hallett read a portion of the 18th chapter of Matthew and preached from the text: "Be not de-ceived; God is not mocked, for whatsoever a man soweth that shall he also reap." We never deceive God. He sees our heart, knows and understands the motive of every heart not saved by divine grace. We may deceive our fellow men, may even deceive those in our own homes, deceive our own selves by thinking we are something, mingling freely with God's people, but God will not be mocked even in this. What seed are you sowing, to the flesh or the spirit? We always get a harvest of the seed sown.

The evening meeting was led by E. T. Larkin, from the conversation of Christ with the rich man asking what he might do to inherit eternal life. The man answered wisely, yet stood outside of the kingdom. How many now understand the way and stand on the very threshold of the kingdom and yet be lost because they do not turn to God! he was kept out rather than part with his possessions. How many now fail of sal-vation rather than sacrifice their riches! She exhorted her hearers earnestly to seek and find God precious to their souls at any sacrifice.　　H. A. S.

POLITICAL.—Since the first edition of the *Standard* went to press it has been learned that Providence last evening elected three Randall delegates by acclamation. This, in-cluding also delegates elected in this city, Bareham, Wareham and Gosnold, gives Mr. Randall 28, while the Fall River candidate has 27.

Something of a contest is looked for when caucuses are held in Westport and Free-town.

GRAND ARMY FUNERAL—Post Commander B. E. Savery, Surgeon G. W. Packard, Ad-jutant J. R. Reach and Comrade Levi R. Cole, of Fletcher Webster Post No. 13, of Brock-ton, arrived in the city this morning accom-panying the remains of Arthur Washburn of Brockton formerly of this city. The detail proceeded to Rural Cemetery where the re-mains were buried with ritualistic burial ser-vice.

PRIMITIVE METHODISTS.—Sunday, Sept. 4, is the third anniversary of the formation of the Sunday School of the First Primitive Meth-odist church in this city, and the event will be celebrated by opening the new audience room for the first time. Rev. T. G. Spencer of Fall River will preach the anniversary sermon in the forenoon, and in the afternoon and evening there will be exercise by the children.

A NEW SWITCH SYSTEM. — To-morrow morning a big gang of workmen will com-mence putting in a new interlocking switch system in the Old Colony railroad between the Weld and Logan street crossings. Two switch stands have been in, and the new system will replace four old style switches and two moveable frogs. The work will be completed before night, if hustling can do it.

PERSONAL.—S. Borden of Fall River regis-tered at the New York *Herald's* bureau in Paris yesterday.

Capt. Abraham J. Slocum has resigned as master of schooner Horatio of this port, and starts for Philadelphia to-night to take com-mand of schooner Elisha Gibbs.

DRAMATIC.— The New Bedford Dramatic Co. has been engaged to present The Lan-cashire Lass under the auspices of William Logan Rodman Women's Relief Corps, No. 53, about Sept. 9th.

MANSFIELD.

The following are the heaviest tax-payers in Mansfield, with the amount they are taxed:

FINANCIAL.

Money Markets Continue Easy—Dull and Featureless Stock Markets — Cleveland, Cincinnati, Chicago & St. Louis Statement —New York Bank Statement Unfavor-able—Local Stock Sales at Auction.

SATURDAY, Aug. 27.

This week in the stock market has been an uneventful one and has consisted for the most part of a series of petty skirmishes be-tween the bull and bear forces. Industrials continue to show their marvellous strength, and while they drooped a little during the temporary absence of their chief supporters, Deacon S. V. White, they upon his return, took on fresh life and in the case of Sugar and Cordage attained the highest prices of the year. Yesterday's market was dull nearly all day and traders raided the market on re-port of cholera having struck somewhere around Chesapeake Bay. Thus support by the various pools was practically withdrawn and the result was an active and weak clos-ing.

In our local market, money is in fair de-mand at rates ranging from 5 to 6 per cent. Local clearings for this week amounted to $352,177, against $305,242 for the correspond-ing week last year.

In the Boston loan market the conditions continue easy. Call loans 3½ to 4½ per cent. Prime mercantile paper 4½ to 5¼ per cent. Corporation paper 4½ to 5¼ per cent. The clearing-house rate is 3 per cent. New York funds sell at 10 to 15 cents discount.

The New York money market has been easy. Call loans 1½ to 2½ per cent. Prime mercantile paper 4½ to 5½ per cent. Post-ed rates at 4.87 and 4.88½.

Government bonds have been dull and steady.

In Wall street stock circles this morning gossip was mixed. Bears seem to be out of ammunition and are thawing out. Traders are largely in majority as a large part of ex-change members are out of the city. The *Chronicle* figures a big loss to the banks.

The New York stock market was dull and heavy in the first hour.

Sugar was especially weak. N. E. was again the strongest, but transactions were small. Prices rallied in the last half-hour on the publication of the Bank Statement. Closing was steady and generally higher. Atchison was firm at 39. Delaware & Lackawanna ad-vanced firm, the opening 157¼ to 157½. Read-ing firm, 57½ to 57¾, and Western Union held firm at 98.

The Boston stock market during the two hours of business was dull and featureless. Atchison 39. Boston & Albany 205½. Union Pacific was moderately active and firm, opening at 38½, then advancing to 39¾. Sugar opened at 111½ and advanced to 112½. Westinghouse Electric sold at 37¼. Total sales—bonds $16,000 and 5210 shares of stock.

The New York bank statement is not very favorable. Figures show as follows:

Reserve decrease,	$2,491,000
Loans decrease,	1,386,600
Specie decrease,	4,335,000
Legals increase,	1,980
Deposit decrease,	7,320,800
Circulation decrease,	112,400

Banks now hold $922,082 in excess of legal requirements, against an excess last year of $12,768,346, and a deficit of $536,675 in 1890.

Henry Clews & Co. in their weekly market letter say:

The stock market did not disappoint ex-pectations. Prices have experienced a good advance, and indications are still favorable. As already maintained in these columns, the basis of the present advance is the confi-dence of the big holders of stocks in the future development and resources of the country. Our commercial and industrial in-terests are now enjoying a very fair share of prosperity. Business is not only on a larger scale than ever before, as demonstrated by clearing-house returns and railroad earn-ings; but it is also in exceptionally sound condition.

There is an impression around that when the next interest period arrives the Santa Fe Mining Company bondholders will foreclose. The bonds have not paid interest since their issue, and their holders probably are tired of carrying on the mine.

Another Chicago report is that Chicago, Burlington & Quincy earnings this month will amount nearly to $4,000,000, the largest in the history of the road.

A Chicago dispatch says that Atchison claims to have realized $116,000 from the sale of cut-rate Denver tickets, and earnings of the Colorado Midland road for the past two weeks have increased 400 per cent.

It is said that the Illinois Steel Company has signed the Amalgamated Association's scale for their North mills.

The Boston & Montana Mining Company has retired $46,000 bonds of the $598 issue from the sinking fund.

The operations of the Cleveland, Cincin-nati, Chicago & St. Louis railroad for June and 12 months makes the following com-parison with 1891:

1892.		Increase.
June,	$1,320,315	$169,461
Expenses,	841,522	158,566
Net,	$388,683	$10,899
Charges,	220,380	*6,032
Surplus,	$168,333	$16,931
Fiscal year.	1891-92.	
Earnings,	$13,818,115	$683,677
Expenses,	9,838,542	644,550
Net,	$3,979,573	$39,127
Charges,	2,570,174	*22,532
Surplus,	$1,409,399	$61,663

*Decrease.

LOCAL STOCK SALES AT AUCTION TO-DAY.

The following stocks were sold at auction to-day by Sanford & Kelley:

1 Union Boot & Shoe Store.		105%
1 Potomska Mills		105¼
6 Wamsutta Mills		110%

Fall River Print Cloth Market.

FALL RIVER, Aug. 27.

The following is the print cloth statement for the week: Production 190,000 pieces, de-liveries 186,000 pieces, stock on hand 400 pieces, sales 250,000 pieces, spots 28,000 pieces, futures 222,000 pieces. Market firm. Prices 3¼ cents for 60x56s, 3½ cents for 64x64s.

WEATHER INDICATIONS.

FAIR AND WARMER.

NEW YORK, Aug. 27.—At 8 30 a. m. the weather was cloudy, wind east, tem-perature 63. The *Herald* says: In the Middle States and New England on Sunday warmer, fair weather will gen-erally prevail, with fresh and light variable winds, and on Monday warmer, fair weather.

INSUFFICIENT EVIDENCE

Ground on Which Defence Will Rest.

Insanity Plea Will Not Be Used, Says Mr. Adams.

He is Confident of Acquittal of Miss Lizzie Borden.

Government is Equally Sure of Proving Its Case.

Prof. Wood Expected to Testify All Day Monday.

[Special Dispatch.]

FALL RIVER, Aug. 27.—With the ad-journment of the examination of Lizzie Borden, charged with the murder of her father, tongues are wagging and people are inquiring what will be the next move. Among inquiries made this afternoon is the one, "Why did not either the govern-ment or defence question Bridget Sullivan concerning the domestic relations of the Bordens?" The question is a hard one to answer but the failure to do so is promi-nent. It is said by the government advocates that there is no necessity to do so, while the friends of the defend-ant say their side did not press this home because they would not have received truthful answers even if they had done so. The friends of the defendant seem to be in a bitter humor regarding Bridget, but this is most unjust for the girl has been anything but a swift witness. It has been apparent from the first that she testified with the utmost reluctancy.

The prosecuting officers are confident in the light of Bridget's evidence that they have a strong enough case to present to the grand jury and they look forward with the utmost confidence to such a re-sult of the examination. They say that the time which elapsed after Lizzie was last seen with her father on the lower floor until she called the girl downstairs from the attic, gave Lizzie ample time to which to dispose of her father, while they lay strewn on the fact that Bridget, at work in the attic at windows overlooking the back yard, saw nothing of Lizzie either in go-ing to or from the barn. Then again, they say that after Lizzie was last seen by Bridget at the screen door she had ample time to kill her mother and get down stairs before her father returned.

Attorney Adams of the defence grant-ed the press representatives this after-noon a short interview. He made an analysis of what he termed the leading points in the government's case and said there is nothing in the results so far obtained to cause defence any uneasiness. He said defendant's counsel proposed to contest the government in every step and will place witnesses on their side on the stand even at this hearing.

It is now thought that Prof. Wood will give his evidence on Monday, and it is expected that the whole day will be taken up with his direct evidence and cross-ex-amination.

The defence it is said, even if the pris-oner is sent to the grand jury, will not attempt to avail itself of the insanity the-ory, but will make their fight in the up-per court entirely on the grounds of the insufficiency of the government to estab-lish the position it has taken.

At 1 o'clock this afternoon Attorney Jennings entered the matron's room at the Central station, where Lizzie Borden will remain until Monday, and had a long interview with the prisoner. The nature of their talk he declined to state, but as he did not wear a beaming cast of countenance it is safe to predict that he was not over-joyed with the result.

The interest in the case continues un-abated here, and from 12 o'clock until long after 2 p. m. women and girls besieged the station house doors in an endeavor to gain admittance to the court-room, and they went away looking dejected when they found the court would not again come in this afternoon.

THE STORY OF THE QUARREL.

Marshal Hilliard Tells Why He In-structed Matron Reagan.

[By Associated Press.]

FALL RIVER, Aug. 27.—The *Globe* will publish the following about the Matron Reagan affair to-night:

"In view of the excitement and sensa-tional happenings of yesterday afternoon, which resulted through the publication of an interview which a *Globe* reporter had with Police Matron Reagan on last Monday afternoon, the reporter called upon Marshal Hilliard this morning and talked with him concerning the matter. The marshal wanted to know how the morning papers had reported his conduct and words which followed the attempt of John C. Milne, Attorney Jennings and Rev. Mr. Buck to secure Matron Reagan's signature to the documents which they had prepared. He had not found time to read for himself.

The reporter read two or three re-ports and the marshal was informed that these papers which had criticised his ac-tions from the beginning were still pursu-ing out upon him their wrath, while the papers which have sought to give the news regardless of anybody and regard-less of anything except the truth were standing him in the position which he had taken in advising Matron Reagan to refrain from signing any document rela-tive to this case until she had given her evidence before the court.

Then the marshal was asked if he had a statement to give the public concerning this matter. He had none in particular, but he spoke further about his position. He said in substance that aside from the fact that Matron Reagan is a government witness he would not allow her to sign that paper, because she had admitted to him that she had spoken about the scene which she had witnessed between Emma and Lizzie Borden, and in signing that paper she would have compromised her-self.

The talk which Matron Reagan had had with the city marshal was contrary and in direct opposition to the spirit and in-tent of the contents of the document which the lawyer for the defence had pre-pared and had asked Matron Reagan to sign.

Matron Reagan told the marshal the story as she remembered it of the talk which she had concerning the scene above referred to, and if she had signed that document she would probably have sub-scribed to a false statement. And this statement could not have been corrected, for her name would have been attached to a written statement. This ought to be emphatic enough.

Got 82 Per Cent. of Their Investment.

WALTHAM, Mass., Aug. 27.—The Wal-tham branch of the American Endow-ment league met in the old district court room, and after settling up the affairs of the order, disbanded. The members re-ceived 82 per cent. of what they had paid in.

Swept by a Flood.

VIENNA, Aug 27.—A disastrous flood occurred at Gratz. Many buildings, in-cluding three mills, two factories and sev-eral dwellings, were swept away, and a dozen persons lost their lives.

THE LATEST DEVELOPMENTS

In the Shoe Business.

We have just put in facilities for making a Special Grade of 'Ladies' and Gents' Shoes, especially adapted to New Bedford.

We shall give them a name also well adapted to New Bedford, and we will make them better for the money than anything you have hitherto bought.

We have some of those Shoes ready for you now.

We will have a greater assortment hereafter.

SCHULER BROS.,

76 and 78 Purchase Street.

SATISFIED WITH MORLEY.

Nationalists Believe They Will Have a Genuine Irish Administration.

LONDON, Aug. 27.—Mr. Morley's short visit to Dublin has confirmed the nation-alist confidence in him. It soon became known that he had selected as private adviser and probably under-secretary for Ireland George Fottrell, a man whose veiled influence in Irish affairs has long been recognized by both English and Irish leaders. Mr. Fottrell is a close friend and inspirer of Mr. Morley. His was adviser to Sir Robert Hamilton who was under-secretary during the critical time succeeding the Phenix Park murders, and stands so well with the nationalists that his reported appointment as under-secretary was hailed with general delight as the advent of a genuine Irish adminis-tration sealing the end of the obnoxious castle denomination.

A HEARTLESS FAKE.

Story of Wreck of Yacht Wapiti and Loss of Life a Canard.

SAGINAW, Mich., Aug. 27.—The steam yacht Wapita, having on board H. W. Sibley, his wife, daughter and son, two young ladies of Rochester, N. Y., and a crew of four men, was reported lost at sea, not Georgian bay. The cook and one other person were the only ones saved.

ROCHESTER, N. Y., Aug. 27.—A special to the *Union and Advertiser* states that the story of the wrecking of the yacht Wapita is a canard; that the whole party is safe and will join the yacht on Monday. A telegram received from Mr. Sibley says he is safe.

Died of Exposure in the Alps.

LONDON, Aug. 27.—A dispatch from Chamouni announces that Prof. Nettle-ship died of cold and exposure on the Don Du Goûter, while attempting to ascend Mt. Blanc. He started on Tues-day, accompanied by two guides, and was overtaken on the way by a blinding snow storm. He wandered about on the moun-tain for a day and night before he suc-cumbed.

DEATHS.

In this city, 26th inst., Edmund Grinnell, in the 62d year of his age.

Funeral services at his late residence, cor. Second and Hawthorn streets, Monday, 29th inst., at 12 o'clock.

In this city, 27th inst., Helen R., daughter of Stephen R. and Lizzie F. Tripp, aged 18 days.

Funeral at her father's residence, 231 North street, Monday, 29th inst., at 1 o'clock.

In Middleboro, Sylvia, widow of Wm. F. Pratt, 69.

MARINE INTELLIGENCE.

ARRIVED THIS AFTERNOON.

Sch Hastings, Cory, New York.

At Bass River 26th, sch Maud Sherwood, Kelley, Amboy for Portland; M F Sprague, Fisher, Georgetown for Boston.

At at Stonington 26th, sch Donna T Briggs, Garney, Plymouth for New York.

At at New Haven 26th, sch A J Beckerman, Gammons, Baltimore.

At at New York 26th, steamer Richmond, Jersey, Norfolk. Cld, steamer Nacoochee, Smith, Savannah.

Passed through Hell Gate 26th, sch Kate Scranton, Kelley, New York for Providence.

At at Philadelphia 26th, schs Julia A Ward, Wakins, Kennebec; R B Nickerson, Nicker-son, do. Cld, schs Jesse Barlow, Harlow; Maryann; Jacob Reed, Dickerson, Brunswick; Luis, Nickerson, Providence; Narragansett, Chase, this port; Phebe J Woodruff, Watts, Boston; Jennie C Bowen, Chase, do.

Cld at Baltimore 26th, sch Henry L Peck-ham, Harding, Portsmouth.

At at Newport News 26th, schs King Philip, Portsmouth; J H Jackson Jr, New York; W H Bailey, do. Sld, sch B S Spofford, Galves-ton.

Sld from Savannah 26th, steamer City of Augusta, New York.

Old at Jacksonville 26th, sch Julia A Warr, New York.

STOCK AND BOND MARKETS.

Bids at close of the Stock Boards to-day.

NEW YORK, Aug. 27.

GOVERNMENT BONDS.

U.S. 2s, registered,	100
" new 4s, registered,	115%
" new 4s, coupons,	117%
" currency 6s, 1895, (Pacific)	107

RAILROADS.

Atchison,	39¼
Clev. Cin., Chicago & St. Louis,	65½
Chicago & Eastern Illinois	
Chicago & Eastern Illinois pfd	
Chicago, Burlington & Quincy,	101½
Delaware & Hudson,	137%
Delaware & Lackawanna,	157½
Erie,	27½
Illinois Central,	
Lake Shore & Michigan Southern,	133%
Louisville & Nashville,	73¾
Michigan Central,	
Missouri Pacific,	61½
New Jersey Central,	133%
New York & New England,	33½
Northern Pacific,	
Northern Pacific pfd,	117
Chicago & Northwestern,	
New York Central & Hudson River,	113%
North American,	13½
Oregon Navigation,	
Oregon Improvement,	
Oregon Short Line,	
Philadelphia & Reading,	57¼
Pullman Palace Car,	
Rock Island,	84½
Chicago, Milwaukee & St. Paul,	80%
Richmond Terminal,	8½
St. Paul & Omaha,	52½
St. Paul & Omaha pfd,	
Union Pacific,	39¾
Wabash, St. Louis & Pacific,	
Wabash, St. Louis & Pacific pfd,	

MISCELLANEOUS.

Ontario Silver,	41
Pacific Mail Steamship Co.,	33
Sugar, common,	112½
Sugar, pref.,	104½
Western Union Telegraph,	97½
Silver Certificates,	84%

BOSTON, Aug. 27.

BONDS.

Atchison 4s,	78½
Atchison Incomes,	60%
Boston & Montana,	
Bell Telephone 1s,	
Chicago, Burlington & Northern 5s,	
Chicago & West Michigan 5s,	
Wisconsin Central,	68¼

RAILROADS.

Atchison, Topeka & Santa Fe,	39
Boston & Albany,	205½
Boston & Lowell,	
Boston & Maine,	177
Boston & Providence,	
Chicago, Burlington & Quincy,	101½
Chicago & West Michigan,	
Cleveland & Canton,	
Cleveland & Canton pref,	
Flint & Pere Marquette,	24
Flint & Pere Marquette pref,	74
Mexican Central,	
New York & New England,	*34
New York & New England pref,	
Old Colony,	172½
Oregon Short Line,	
Pullman Palace Car,	204%
Union Pacific,	39%
Wisconsin Central,	
West End,	*17
West End pref,	72½

MISCELLANEOUS.

Butte & Boston Mining Co.,	
Calumet & Hecla Mining Co.,	291
Franklin Mining Co.,	13
Kearsarge,	12½
Osceola Mining Co.,	31
Tamarack,	160

MISCELLANEOUS.

American Bell Telephone,	205
Erie Telephone,	45
Mexican Telephone,	1.10
New England Telephone,	56½
Newport Land,	1¼
Boston Land Co.,	½
West End Land Co.,	15½
San Diego Land Co.,	
Topeka Land & Development Co.,	
Lamson Store Service,	
Illinois Steel Co.,	
Am. Sugar Refineries, com.,	112½
Am. Sugar Refineries, pref.,	
Gen'l Electric,	
Gen'l Electric	

*Asked.

Knowles &Co.

Cor. UNION & FOURTH STS.

Bargains in All-Wool Dress Goods, 40-inch all-wool goods, suitable for early Fall wear, 39c. Cheap at 50c.

Storm Serges in Black and Navy, all-wool, 40-inch, 50c.; 46-inch 75c.; 46-inch extra value, $1.00.

Black All-Wool Henriettas, 46-inch, 75c.; extra fine and heavy, $1.00 and $1.25; 46-inch, All-Wool, India Twill, 75c. and $1.00.

Beautiful styles in Ginghams at 10 and 12 1-2c. Large assortment to select from.

Ladies' full regular finished, Fast Black Hose, the best hose in the market for 25c. Also Ladies' Fast Black Hose, worth 50c. Three pairs in a box $1.00.

Ladies' Summer weight merino vests and pants 50c. each.

Gentlemen's Summer weight merino shirts and drawers 50c.

Gentlemen's unlaundered shirts, reinforced linen fronts and cuffs, double backs, good cotton, best shirt in the market, 50c.

Ladies' corset covers at 12 1-2, 25, 37 1-2 and 50c., in high, low, square and V shaped necks, handsomely trimmed, and decided bargains.

Ladies' and misses' night gowns, made of good materials and elegantly trimmed, at 50, 65, and 88c., $1, $1.25 and up.

Ladies' corsets, in all the popular makes, at from 49c. up to the very finest goods.

Best Germantown yarns, large full skeins, in 150 shades and colors, at only 12 1-2c. a skein.

Stamped Linens, Trays, Tidies, Splashers, Pillow Shams, Scarfs, all at popular low prices.

All kinds of embroidery and fancy working silk cheap. Knitting silk of best quality, large assortment of colors and shades at 30c. a ball. Best sewing silk in black and colors, 8c.

Table Linens, Brown and Bleached at 45c. worth 59c. Napkins at 50 and 75c, $1.00, $1.25, $1.50 and $2.00 per dozen. Towels at 12 1-2c., 19c., 25c., 37c., and 50c. up.

Lot of standard white ground prints, 5c. a yard. When out shopping don't fail to visit our store for we have just what you are looking for, and at lowest possible prices.

Knowles &Co.

FINE CIGARS

—AND—

Tobacco.

Cigars by the Box a Specialty

—AT—

E. B. SHERMAN'S,

62 Purchase St.

jy19-8pMWS

TROOPS LEAVE BUFFALO.

Some People Fear Lawlessness, but It is Not Likely to Occur.

BUFFALO, Aug. 27.—A slight feeling of uneasiness pervades Buffalo because of the departure of the National guard, but it is not probable that there will be any more violence of lawlessness of any kind.

Before 3 o'clock yesterday afternoon all the troops except the two regiments of Buffalo and a few separate companies, which make up the rest of the Fourth brigade, were on their way home by way of half a dozen railroads.

The banged and bruised Sweeney left town about 1 o'clock bound for the Windy City. He was unhappy. He was even prepared to swear off being a labor leader and become a newspaper reporter.

McKinley in Vermont.

BRATTLEBORO, Vt., Aug. 27.—Governor McKinley arrived here and joined Mrs. McKinley, and they went at once to Oak Ridge farm, Dummerston, eight miles from here, and are the guests of Police Commissioner Osborne of Boston, who is a cousin. Senator Proctor is also here. The governor will stay there until Tuesday, when he goes to Burlington, where he speaks in the evening at the Republican rally. Governor McKinley will stay in town nearly all of September.

A Disappointment.

GLOUCESTER, Mass., Aug. 27.—Intended illuminations last evening as a part of the 250th anniversary celebration were badly interfered with by the weather.

Mrs. Annie W. Jordan

Of 165 Tremont St., Boston, was in very poor health, from bad circulation of the blood, having rush of blood to the head, numb spells, and chills, and the physician said the veins were almost bursting all over her body. A collision with a double runner brought on neuralgia of the liver, causing great suffering. She could not take the doctor's medicine, so took

Hood's Sarsaparilla

and soon fully recovered, and now enjoys perfect health. She says she could praise Hood's Sarsaparilla all day and then not say enough.

HOOD'S PILLS are hand made, and are perfect in composition, proportion and appearance.

From Yesterday's Third Edition.

MORSE TESTIFIES.

Important Government Witness on the Stand.

Did Not See Lizzie Until After the Murder.

Learned of the Tragedy From Bridget Sullivan.

Mr. Borden and His Wife Spoke of Being Poisoned.

Said They and Lizzie Were Ill on the Tuesday Previous.

Now Famous Servant Follows Him on the Stand.

Great Hush as Bridget Opens Her Testimony.

Her Story Under Oath of the Morning of the Murder.

[Special Dispatch.]

FALL RIVER, Aug. 26.—Previous to the opening of the court this afternoon the corridors were thronged with people seeking admission, among them being a large number of well dressed women, who early sought and obtained good seats where they could listen to the proceedings of the afternoon.

At precisely 2 o'clock the court was announced. Lizzie entered the room leaning upon the arm of City Missionary Buck. She looked deeply concerned and did not walk with that firm, elastic step and unconcerned manner that characterized her bearing yesterday.

Joseph Shortsleeves was the first witness called. Mr. Borden was in my place of business on the day of the murder. It was between 10 30 and 11 o'clock when I saw him.

The cross-examination failed to elicit any additional facts.

Joseph Mather was the next witness. He talked with Mr. Borden in front of Shortsleeves' store on the day of the murder. After Mr. Borden left the store he turned south. Witness last saw him just a little one side of Spring street. He left the store about 20 minutes to 11 o'clock.

In cross-examination witness said that he was on the outside of the store at the time, while Mr. Shortsleeves was on the inside. The way he fixes the time is that he usually takes his lunch at 10 30, and he thought that morning that it was about time for him to take his lunch, and shortly after he saw Mr. Borden he looked at the City Hall clock. When the officers called he was not so precise about the time, but directly after his interview with the police the time occurred to him, and he spoke to Mr. Shortsleeves about it. He said that Mr. Borden owned several stores on the same street as the store of Mr. Shortsleeves was located on, but did not know whether Mr. Borden went into any of them on the morning of the murder or not.

A ripple of excitement passed around the room as John V. Morse was the next witness called. He said that he was 59 years of age and that his present residence was Fall River. During last year

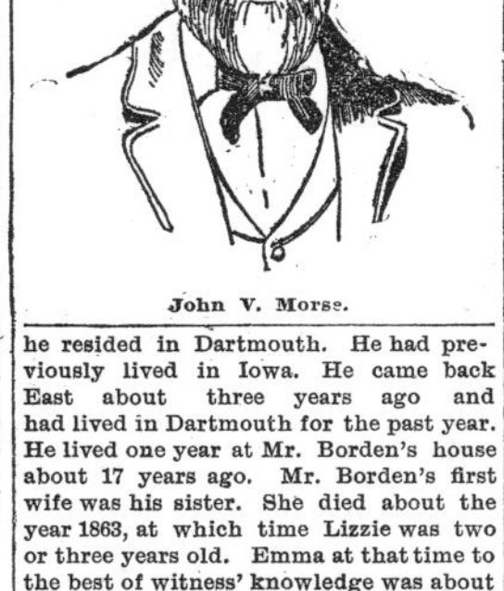

John V. Morse.

he resided in Dartmouth. He had previously lived in Iowa. He came back East about three years ago and had lived in Dartmouth for the past year. He lived one year at Mr. Borden's house about 17 years ago. Mr. Borden's first wife was his sister. She died about the year 1863, at which time Lizzie was two or three years old. Emma at that time to the best of witness' knowledge was about 8 or 9 years of age. He first heard that Mr. Borden was married to the second Mrs. Borden in 1864 or 5. Mr. Borden had lived in the same house for about twenty years. During the last year he has called at the Borden house several times, probably once a month or two months. He came to the house Aug. 3. He left New Bedford on Aug. 3 on the 12 35 train on the Fall River branch and arrived at about 1 o'clock. He at once went to the house and saw Mr. and Mrs. Borden, but did not see Lizzie or Emma, He did not eat dinner with any of the family, but dinner was spread expressly for him. He stayed at the house until a little after 3 o'clock, when he went to Swanzey. Mr. Borden did not keep a team, so he went to Swanzey in a hitch that he hired. He had some business in Swanzey of his own to transact and also did some business relating to a farm that Mr. Borden owned in that place. When he arrived at the house Mr. Borden was lying on the lounge and he was also lying there when he went away. He arrived back from Swanzey at about half-past 8 or quarter of 9. A little later he retired and heard what he supposed was Lizzie come into the house at a little after 9 o'clock. He occupied the spare chamber over the parlor. That night the door which led to the back entrance to the house was locked. Lizzie's room connected with the spare room and also with the front entrance. He was very sure that it was a little after 9 when Lizzie came in.

Highest of all in Leavening Power.—Latest U. S. Gov't Report.

Royal Baking Powder

ABSOLUTELY PURE

Mrs. Borden went to bed the night before the tragedy at a little after 9 o'clock. Witness got up next morning soon after six and when he came down stairs the first person of the household he saw was Mr. Borden. I do not remember what we had for breakfast that morning but there were bananas on the table. After breakfast Mrs. Borden was in and out. Do not remember that she had anything on her head. Did not see her go upstairs. Thtnk I went away about quarter of 9. I have no knowledge of Lizzie coming down before I went away. I saw the servant when I went out. The day before when I came from over the river Mrs. Borden let me in. I came in the back door. There was a screen door there at that time. When I went out that morning Mr. Borden let me out. There was a lock on the door. After breakfast we sat half an hour or an hour in the sitting-room. When I came out I went to the post office, down Third street to Pleasant street, and to Weybosset street, where I called on some nieces. I left their house about a quarter or 20 minutes after 11 o'clock. Mrs. Borden went into the front hall about a quarter of an hour before I went out. I do not know if she had a feather duster in her hand. The usual dinner hour at Mr. Borden's was about 12 o'clock. I came back from my nieces' house in a car to Pleasant street. Bridget Sullivan told me what had happened. I think it was about quarter to 12 when I got back to Mr. Borden's house. I found Dr. Bowen and two policemen in the house. I saw Lizzie on the lounge and I saw Mr. Borden on the lounge. Went part of the way up stairs and saw Mrs. Borden on the floor. I had previously been to the Bordens' house about the middle of July. I was on corresponding terms with Mr. Borden and Emma. I never wrote to Lizzie in my life.

Cross-examined: Soon after I got to Mr. Borden's house on the first day I had some talk with Mr. and Mrs. Borden about their health. They said something about poison, that he and she and Miss Lizzie were sick on Tuesday night. On Wednesday (the day of the talk) Mrs. Borden said Lizzie was sick upstairs. Mrs. Borden said she did not know what caused the sickness unless it might be baker's bread. I did not see Lizzie that day (Wednesday). I noticed no difference in the position of the bed in the spare room after the murder from what it occupied previous to the murder. While eating breakfast on the morning of the murder Mrs. Borden asked Bridget Sullivan what she had to do. Bridget said only common work. Then Mrs. Borden told her she had better wash the windows, and she said she would do it. Bridget was in the kitchen when I went out. I heard no sounds from Lizzie's room before I went out. I did not know whether she had got up or not. The front door had a common lock and bolt as well as a spring lock. Since the murder I have noticed the front door can be opened without springing the spring lock. The side door was usually kept hooked. When I went out the day of the murder Mr. Borden hooked it after me. I did not see Dr. Dolan when I went to the house after the murder. I went through the sitting room, glanced at Mr. Borden, went up stairs until I could see Mrs. Borden lying on the floor. Then I came down stairs and saw Lizzie lying on the lounge in the dining room. Some women were with her. I do not know who they were. I was nervous. I went out through the kitchen into the yard. Quite a number of people were there. When I went back to the house from the yard I think the cellar door was open. I think the barn door was also open. I never at any time made an examination of the barn. Some of the boards of the pile in Mr. Borden's yard were against Dr. Chagnon's fence. There were two piles of boards in Mr. Borden's yard. The highest pile was about 4 1-2 feet high. Dr. Chagnon's fence was about six feet high. There were quite a number of blood spots on the sitting-room door which opened into the parlor before they were washed out. They were from the knob down. I should say there were not less than 40 blood spots on this door. The largest were near phe bottom. I do not recollect any blood spots on the door leading from the sitting room to the dining room. I saw one blood spot on a picture above the sofa. The paper there was all covered with spots.

Mr. Jennings asked witness if he had formed an opinion if the wounds on Mr. Borden were made by a right-handed or a left-handed person.

Witness said he has formed an opinion. Counsel asked what the opinion was.

The district attorney objected and the question was ruled out.

The examination was resumed, and witness said the axes or hatches were removed from Mr. Borden's house two or three days after the murder. A policeman put them in a sack.

Redirect—I heard no one go out or in the front door on the morning of the murder. The door is usually locked all night and bolted, besides having a spring lock. I had not been to Swanzey the week of the murder and not at any time during this visit to Fall River. Mr. Borden never said anything to me about proposing to make a will nor about legacies or bequests. I think within a year while walking on Main street Mr. Borden said he might make some public bequests. Some time in May, while riding over his farm, Mr. Borden spoke of the Old Ladies' Home, and said he would give them some land there if it would do any good. I have mentioned to some one, I think before, about the cellar door being open the day of the murder. I never mentioned the fact to an officer or to anyone connected with the police department about its being shut. I have told you that the door was shut. The blood spots on the door were washed off by Miss Emma.

Cross-examination was resumed and Mr. Jennings asked, "Allow me to recall to you, did you not tell Mr. Charles J. Holmes that the cellar door was open?"

Mr. Knowlton objected, but the question was admitted. Witness said he could not remember if he had told Mr. Holmes the door was open.

Thomas Kieran was then recalled and presented remodelled plans in which the woodpile in the Borden yard appeared. The ceiling in the sitting room in the Borden house is 8 feet 10 inches above the floor.

At this point a recess of ten minutes was taken.

The next witness called was Bridget Sullivan, and a great hush fell on the audience as she mounted the witness-stand. She said: I am called Maggie. I was employed at Mr. Borden's. I had been there two years and nine months. I swept the hall every two weeks. I had no care of the beds at the time of the tragedy. Emma had been away I think about two weeks. When she was gone the family consisted of Mr. and Mrs. Borden and Lizzie. The night before the tragedy (Wednesday) Mr. and Mrs. Borden and Lizzie were at supper. I went to bed Wednesday about 10 o'clock. I locked the back door. When I came down the next morning the back door was locked. I opened both the wooden and screen doors. I left the wooden door open. The screen door was hooked. I unfastened it to let in the iceman before Mr. Borden went out. No one else went out but myself. It was about 6 15 in the morning, when I came down stairs. No one was up then. Mrs. Borden was the next one to come down. Lizzie never used the back stairs to go to her room. Mrs. Borden went into the sitting room when she went down. Mr. Borden was the next to come down. He went out before breakfast and into the barn after water. He emptied slops in the yard.

When he came in from the barn he washed up and went to breakfast. I saw Mr. Morse when I put breakfast on the table. We had cold mutton and johnny-cake. All three sat down to breakfast.

This was about quarter past seven. I saw Mr. Morse go out about a quarter of nine. Mr. Borden let him out. I did not see Mr. Morse when he went out. Don't know where I was then.

After Mr. Borden let Mr. Morse out he went into the sitting room. Then he came into the kitchen and went up stairs and soon came down.

Miss Sullivan was testifying when the last edition of the *Standard* went to press.

An Ohio Murder and Suicide.

EAST LIVERPOOL, O., Aug. 26.—A man named Unger, living seven miles from here, shot and killed his brother-in-law last night and then killed himself. Unger's wife had left him and taken refuge with her brother, who defended her from the husband, and this led to the shooting.

Quarrymen Abandon the Fight.

MILFORD, Aug. 26.—The Milford branch of the Quarrymen's Union last night voted to abandon the strike, and to advise members to secure employment where they may. This does not effect the Granite Cutters' Union, which is still holding out.

Powder Magazine Blown Up.

GAINESVILLE, Tex., Aug. 26.—Three powder magazines blew up here yesterday. The contained 600 kegs of powder. Houses near by were badly shattered and a number of persons were injured. The explosion was caused by lightning.

Troops Leaving Buffalo.

BUFFALO, Aug. 26.—All the soldiers will leave to-day except the members of the 4th brigade, which numbers 2000 men.

You Can't Keep Cool

while you're rubbing away over a tub of steaming clothes. If you want to keep comfortable and save your health (think of inhaling that fetid steam) and strength, stop the rubbing—and the steaming. Pearline does it. Pearline; cold water; no boiling; little work; that is the programme for hot-weather washing.

This taking away of the rubbing is more than a matter of saving work. It's a saving of needless and ruinous wear and tear to all your summer clothing.

Direction for this easy, safe and economical washing, on every package of Pearline.

Beware Peddlers and some unscrupulous grocers will tell you, "this is as good as" or "the same as Pearline." IT'S FALSE—Pearline is never peddled, if your grocer sends you an imitation, be honest *send it back.* 353 JAMES PYLE, New York.

T. C. BALL IS FOUND!

Missing Bennett Mill Overseer Turns Up in Albany.

His Son Leaves Woonsocket in Quest of His Parent.

Mystery Surrounding His Disappearance Will Soon be Solved.

[Special Dispatch.]

WOONSOCKET, R. I., Aug. 26.—Trustworthy information was received here last Wednesday evening by his family to the effect that Theophilus C. Ball, the New Bedford, Mass., overseer of spinning, who disappeared from Providence last

Theophilus C. Ball,
Missing Man Found in Albany, N. Y.

April, and whose family had lost all trace of him, had been located in Albany, N. Y, Thursday his son, William E. Ball, started in quest of his parent, and the mystery will probably be cleared in a few days.

RECEIVER FOR IRON HALL.

Papers to be Presented to Supreme Court of This State.

BOSTON, Aug. 26.—An application is to be made in the Supreme Judicial Court for a receiver for the Order of the Iron Hall, or that part of the order which is in the jurisdiction of the Massachusetts court. It is probable that the papers will be presented in behalf of the members of the Hyde Park branch by Lawyer Wilbur H. Powers next week. The petition will contain a clause enabling any other branch in the State to come in and be joined as a party and save the expense of bringing additional petitions. The precise ground on which the application for a receiver is made is not yet settled, but one of the most important is an allegation of fraud on the part of the supreme officers.

There is the hands of the officers of the Massachusetts branches from $200,000 to $3,000,000. The appointment of a receiver by the Indiana court has no effect on the branches here and the orders of a receiver to send him funds from this State need not be complied with.

Receiver for Pennsylvania.

PHILADELPHIA, August 26.—District Attorney George S. Graham was to-day appointed receiver of the Iron Hall for Pennsylvania.

HOPE TO DIVIDE FUNDS.

Lawrence Branch of Iron Hall Will Not Pay the Receiver.

LAWRENCE, Aug. 26.—Local Branch 185, Iron Hall, has decided not to send its funds to the receiver at Indianapolis. The branch has engaged counsel to defend their action in retaining possession of the reserve fund, which amounts to $6600. It is hoped to divide this sum among the 160 members here.

TO PREVENT CHOLERA.

Precautions Taken by the Health Officers of New York.

NEW YORK, Aug. 26.—Health Officer Jenkins this morning telegraphed from quarantine: "Steamers will be inspected most carefully. Any steamer having suspected cases or having had deaths on board will be held until a bacteriological examination can be made, and if cholera is found all persons on board will be held seven days. The sick will be removed and placed in hospital. All baggage and the vessel will be treated with steam, all parts of the vessel not subjected to steam will be washed with a solution of bichloride of mercury. I recommend that all immigrants undergo a most thorough inspection on board vessels, with detention of those from infected ports for at least five days that they be bathed and luggage be disinfected by steam; that a certificate of such cleansing, signed by the consul, be given to the ship's surgeon for presentation to the health office at the port of entry.

(Signed) WILLIAM T. JENKINS.

A SAD SNAKE STORY.

Three Children Fall Victims of a Deadly Rattler in Georgia.

ATHENS, Ga., Aug. 26.—A farmer named Wilson, living in Madison county, started from home yesterday and went to mill, leaving his wife and four children at home. Two hours later he returned to find his wife lying on the floor insensible, with four dead children about her. When the mother was restored to consciousness she said she had taken the baby to the spring, leaving the others at home. Hearing their cries, she put the baby down and hurried back to the house, where she found two dead and the others dying. The living one said they had been poking their fingers through a crack in the floor and a hen had been pecking at them. The mother went back to the spring for her baby and found it had fallen into the spring and drowned. The third child was dead when she got back to the house, and the mother swooned. Investigation showed that the supposed hen was a rattlesnake.

THE LOSS OF TUG SLATER.

Sunken Vessel Rapidly Breaking Up in the Heavy Surf.

BOSTON, Aug. 26.—The tug Slater, which sank last night, was a two-masted iron tug owned by the Boston Towboat Co. and was en route to take barges from Fort Point, Me., to New York. It was low water when she struck and she soon filled. The men saved the effects and rowed to Fort Independence, where they were cared for. The company's wreckers were unable to get near the tug, which is breaking up, on account of the heavy surf. Her mainmast and smokestack are already gone. Her value was $25,000 and the insurance $16,000.

The tug slid off Devil's Back into deeper water, and all hopes of saving her have been given up.

Hamburg Steamer at Boston.

BOSTON, Aug. 26.—The steamer Kehrweider, from Hamburg, was boarded by the port physician when she reached quarantine. She had 70 passengers, all of whom with their baggage were transferred to Galloupe's Island, where the passengers will be cleaned. The captain of the steamer reported that there has been no sickness on board and she was allowed to proceed to her wharf.

Sweeney Leaves Buffalo.

BUFFALO, Aug. 26.—Grand Master Sweeney started for Chicago this morning. He was accompanied to the Central

ITCHING AND BURNING

Sores All Over Her Body. Suffering Endless. Doctor Useless. Cured in Four Weeks by Cuticura.

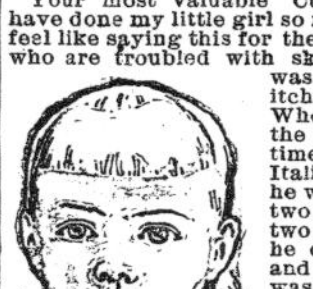

Your most valuable Cuticura Remedies have done my little girl so much good that I feel like saying this for the benefit of those who are troubled with skin diseases. She was troubled with itching, burning sores. When I took her to the doctor the first time, he called it the Italian itch, and said he would cure her in two weeks. When the two weeks were up, he called it eczema, and in that time she was worse than before. He doctored her for three months, and she was so bad that we did not know what to do. He did not do her any good. I saw the advertisement of Cuticura Remedies in the paper, and I said to my wife, "I am going to try them." Mind what I say, she was was so thick with sores that we had to soak her clothes to take them off. Itch! there was no end to it. She had it all over her body, back, legs, arms, in between her fingers. She did not have it on her head. But after taking your Cuticura Remedies for two weeks the itch stopped, and in four weeks the sores were all gone. I enclose her portrait. I am more than pleased with your Cuticura Remedies, as they speedily cured my daughter, and if anybody asks me about your remedies, I will uphold them wherever I go. CHARLES M. GRONEL, Conshohocken, Montgomery County, Pa.

Why Suffer One Moment

From torturing and disfiguring skin diseases, when a single application of the Cuticura Remedies will, in the great majority of cases, afford instant relief in the most agonizing of itching, burning, scaly, crusted, pimply and blotchy skin, scalp and blood diseases, with loss of hair, and point to a speedy, permanent, and economical cure.

Sold everywhere. Price, Cuticura, 50c.; Soap, 25c.; Resolvent, $1. Prepared by the POTTER DRUG AND CHEMICAL CORPORATION, Boston.

Send for "How to Cure Skin Diseases," 64 pages, 50 illustrations and 100 testimonials; mailed free.

BABY'S Skin and Scalp purified and beautified by Cuticura Soap. Absolutely pure.

PAINS AND WEAKNESSES

Of females instantly relieved by that new, elegant, and infallible Antidote to Pain, Inflammation and Weakness, the Cuticura Anti-Pain Plaster.

HAS STOOD THE TEST 17 YEARS.

SEAL OF HAVANA 5¢ Londres Cigar.

No Other Cigar Equals it in Quality.

SWETT, SANBORN & CO., SOLE AGENTS, 55 Union Street, Boston.

FOR SALE BY ALL Druggists and First Class Dealrs.

au6-SW8p

Charter Oak Races.

HARTFORD, Ct., Aug. 26.—The track is heavy to-day, and there is a mist falling, but the attempt to have the races will be made. The first heat of the unfinished pacing race was won by Henry H. Time, 2 22. No other races will be started to-day, but an attempt will be made to finish the pacing race.

TOO WET.—About 150 ball cranks gathered on the Y. M. C. A. grounds this afternoon to witness a game between the New Bedfords and Woonsockets, but the inclement weather proved a hindrance, and the exhibition was postponed. Preparations had been made for a good game, and Lovett was expected to pitch for the home team.

THE POLITICAL STUMP.

Men Who Will Work for Republicans in Maine and Vermont.

NEW YORK, Aug. 27.—William H. Hahn, who has charge of the speakers' bureau at Republican headquarters, has completed his schedule of speakers for Maine and Vermont. General Grosvenor of Ohio and J. Sloat Fassett are going to Maine. Robert Kennedy and General Gibson, together with General Hastings of Pennsylvania, Fairchild of Wisconsin and Geere of Iowa, will also go into the Pine Tree State. Mr. Tomsley, Mr. Griffiths and other speakers of national repute, will divide the time between Maine and Vermont.

The estate of 10,000 acres on which George Vanderbilt is erecting a baronial castle in North Carolina represents forty farms which were bouhgt up from the mountaineers at a cost of fully $500,000.

WRIGHT Drug Company.

PUREST DRUGS

—AND—

FINEST CHEMICALS

—AT—

Lowest Prices.

WRIGHT DRUG CO.

JAY GOULD'S METHODS.

Wants to Oust Certain Directors That Don't Agree to His Schemes.

NEW YORK, Aug. 27.—The attempt of Jay Gould to secure enough proxies on Wabash stock to vote at the forthcoming annual meeting of that company is explained by a gentleman in possession of the facts to be due to a desire to oust certain directors whom he cannot compel to do as he wishes in respect to the management of the road. Mr. Gould at present controls two-fifths of the directors, and wishes to control the majority of them.

The gentlemen he wishes to depose from the board include C. J. Laurence, General Hubbard, H. K. McHarg and O. D. Ashley, the present president of the company. One of these gentlemen told Mr. Sage the other day that he was determined to do what he thought right and best for the interest of the road, regardless of whether it suited Mr. Gould and Mr. Sage's interests or not. That director was Mr. McHarg. He is a large holder of the bonds of the road. It is understood that at present Mr. Ashley holds proxies on a majority of the stock.

Boy Killed by Machinery.

MONTPELIER, Vt., Aug. 27.—Harry, the 16-year-old son of John Anderson, employed at the Lane Manufacturing company's works here, was caught by a set screw in some shafting connected with a turbine wheel and instantly killed.

MELLIN'S FOOD

FOR INFANTS AND INVALIDS.

TRADE MARK.

THE ONLY *Perfect Substitute for Mother's Milk.*

INVALUABLE IN CHOLERA INFANTUM AND TEETHING.

A Quickly Assimilated Food FOR DYSPEPTICS, CONSUMPTIVES, CONVALESCENTS.

A PERFECT NUTRIENT IN ALL WASTING DISEASES.

REQUIRES NO COOKING. KEEPS IN ALL CLIMATES.

SEND for our book, "THE CARE AND FEEDING OF INFANTS," mailed *free* to any address.

Doliber-Goodale Co., BOSTON, MASS.

We Have Quite a Number of

REMNANTS

In all Grades of

CARPETING AND MATTINGS!

On which we have made

Special Low Prices

DURING AUGUST.

BRIGGS & LAWRENCE,

197 and 203 Union Street.

The Evening Standard.

ESTABLISHED FEBRUARY, 1850.

NEW BEDFORD, MONDAY, AUGUST 29, 1892.

TWO CENTS.

HASKELL & TRIPP.

"Home made."

We have the exclusive sale for this city of the highest grade "home made" cotton underclothing for women and misses.

Finest materials.

Perfect fit.

Careful work.

Nothing equal to these goods is being offered *at any price.*

Those of you who have hitherto been compelled to have undergarments made up at home, simply because you couldn't buy ready made that were good enough, will have no need of further trouble on that score.

Our *"home made"* underwear has been produced to fit just such cases as yours. The cloth, the trimming, the sewing, the button holes, the fine, thick, pearl buttons—all just such as you would choose for your own work.

To be sure you must pay us more than for the ordinary sorts—some of you are willing to. We have plenty of other kinds for those who wish to pay less.

Equipoise waists.

The corset substitute—stylish, comfortable, hygienic.

A perfect supporter from the shoulders, distributing the clothing strain and weight.

Three garments in one—corset, waist and cover.

Women's, $1.75
Misses', $1.75
Children's, 60c.
Infants', 75c.
} Equipoise.

One of the most complete stocks of *desirable* corsets in this state. Prices always lowest.

White goods.

2000 yards mill remnants of beautiful plaided, striped, and lace openwork Lawns and Nainsooks, worth at wholesale 15 to 18c. *Take your pick for 12 1-2c. a yard.*

HASKELL & TRIPP.

Department Stores,

Purchase and William Streets.

THE BORDEN INQUIRY.

Mrs. Churchill's Story of Morning of the Murder.

Prisoner's Conduct After Discovery of Tragedy.

Her Excited Condition Dwelt Upon in Cross-Examination.

Conflicting Statements of Her Visit to the Barn.

Other Important Witnesses Who Were About the Scene.

[Special Dispatch.]

FALL RIVER, Aug. 29.—The fifth day in the examination of Lizzie A. Borden, charged with the murder of her father, opened with people gathered in the vicinity of the Central police station, even in larger numbers than on other days. They gathered to-day before 8 o'clock and besieged all three of the doors. The ladies had the advantage, for the police were gallant and let them in the front door and up stairs in sufficient numbers to fill the seats before even the regular session of the District Court began.

The police grist to-day was light, and it is accounted for by a local newspaper man, who says the people have not nerve enough to get drunk since the great tragedy, but put in all their time discussing the phases of the case.

A Freetown man, one of the Pittsleys from Braley's Four Corners, who struck town on Saturday, got into an argument on Main street about the murder, and having expressed the opinion that he could beat all the detectives which Fall River can boast in the work of discovering the murderer, became involved in a quarrel which resulted in a knock-down, and in the dock he looked like a Pinkerton man just returned from Homestead. After his argument was completed, he got involved with Officer Martin and was gathered in, and this morning was fined $25 and expenses.

Emma Borden came over to the station this morning, and had an interview with her sister, entirely cordial, so far as could be learned, and remained with and accompanied Lizzie to the court-room.

Opening of the Court.

The court came in this morning promptly at 10 45. At this time attorneys Adams and Jennings, counsel for defence, were present, but government's counsel had not arrived. Defendant and her friends had not taken their seats, but in three minutes they came in and took the old familiar seats on the settee. At this time the court room was packed. District Attorney Knowlton opened promptly for the government. The first witness was Mrs. Adelaide Churchill. She said: I live next door to the Borden house. On the day of the tragedy I saw Bridget Sullivan go up the street. I saw Lizzie Borden by the screen door. She said "Oh! Mrs. Churchill, come over!" I went. Lizzie met me. She said her father had been murdered, that she came out of the barn and found him gasping in the sitting room.

Witness described a walk she had taken to a market on Main street before the tragedy, and then she said that Lizzie told her her mother had a note to go down street but did not know if she went. Lizzie also said she must have a doctor, Dr. Bowen was not at home. No one outside of the family was present in the house at this time. I found Thomas Boulds for Lizzie. He was on Second street. Lizzie got him to go for the doctor. Lizzie, Bridget and I went to the dining room. We did not see Mr. Borden then. Dr. Bowen called for a sheet to cover Mr. Borden and Bridget brought one. Soon after Mrs. Russell came in and then I went up stairs to a point where

I Could See Mrs. Borden Lying Prostrate on the Floor

in the spare room. I had seen Mr. Borden that morning in the yard about 9 o'clock. He was alone then. I saw him last headed towards the street. I saw Bridget rinsing the parlor windows. She was throwing the water from a dipper. At this time I was in the bed room. I cannot tell what time this was nor how long before Mr. Borden went away. I was in the kitchen when Mr. Borden went away. I saw no one else about the Borden premises before I left home. I went directly to the market and back. I do not remember looking into the Borden yard at any other time than when I saw Mr. Borden and Bridget. When Dr. Bowen came Lizzie said (while I was in the kitchen,) "I will have to go to the cemetery." I replied "O, no, the undertaker will look out for that." Lizzie also said her mother did not tell her where she was going that morning, although she usually did. Lizzie when I saw her had on a dress of blue and white with darker shades. The material was calico.

Mrs. Churchill Cross-examined.

The cross-examination here commenced by Andrew J. Jennings. Mrs. Churchill said: The time after I saw Mr. Borden by the east side of the steps until I saw Bridget Sullivan rinsing the windows I cannot exactly tell. I was making beds I think in the meantime. There were seven beds to be made, two beds were down stairs and the others up stairs. I made them all up I think after I saw Mr. Borden out of doors. Some of the beds up-stairs were directly opposite Mrs. Borden's spare room. I did not notice that the windows of this room were open. It was near 11 o'clock when I went to the market. I cannot say exactly the time. It took me ten or fifteen minutes to go and return. On my return I saw Bridget crossing the street from Dr. Bowen's house to the Borden house. As I put my things down in my own house I saw Lizzie inside the screen door at her house. She appeared to me to be frightened and was pale. She said to me:

"Mrs. Churchill, come over quick, somebody has killed father."

Lizzie did not say "Come over Addie." I went into the front room of my house and told my mother something had happened over at the Borden house and then went over. I saw no one out of doors as I was going over. Lizzie was alone when I reached the screen door. I said to her, "Where is your father?"

She said, "In the sitting room."

I said, "Where was you when your father was killed?"

She said, "In the barn after a piece of iron."

I said, "Where is your mother?"

Lizzie said, "She had a note to go and see a woman who was sick, but I do not know but what she is killed too. I wish some one would go and look out for her."

Lizzie was then sitting on the second step of the stairs. Lizzie said Dr. Bowen was not at home and she wanted a doctor, any one. I went and got Mr. Boulds on Second street. Soon after I got back Bridget came in and soon afterwards Mrs. Russell came. Lizzie said at this time that she wanted some one to see where her mother was. I went up the front stairs with Bridget Sullivan. At this time we went through the dining and sitting rooms to the front hall. Mr. Borden was then covered with a sheet which Bridget had put over him. I went up the front stairs behind Bridget until I could see Mrs. Borden on the floor. I left Bridget up stairs. When I got down stairs I threw up my arms and said:

"I think there must be another one."

While Lizzie was on the stairs when I first came in she said:

"Father must have an enemy. We were all sick last night. We think the milk was poisoned."

Lizzie said she did not think the Portuguese had poisoned the milk. He had been in the employ of the family many years and was not over from the farm.

Lizzie had no blood on her dress, hands or face. Her hair was done up. There was no appearance of anything wet about her. I did not notice what shoes she had on at the time.

Bridget Sullivan said to me after she got home she did not know where Mrs. Borden had gone. She usually told her when she went out. I testified at the inquest.

Witness then told who were present on that occasion and said Mr. Knowlton asked the question at that time. There was no consultation between parties present at the inquest.

Miss Alice E. Russell was the next witness. I live on Main street near Second. I have known Lizzie Borden for some considerable time. I first heard of this affair about 11 15 o'clock on the day of the murder. I went to the Borden house and hurried to get there. I saw Lizzie standing at the front door. I went in, but do not remember whether I said anything to Lizzie or not. I do not remember anything I did or how Lizzie was dressed. and do not remember anything that took place. I do not remember any conversation in regard to the matter since. I do remember Lizzie said she had come from the barn when she discovered the murder. She said she had gone out for a piece of tin or iron to fix a window. I do not know how many people were at the house when I arrived. I do know that they were coming and going all the time. I have been in the habit of going there frequently. Have usually seen the girls in a guest room used as a sitting room.

Cross-examined. When I went into the house I did not notice any blood anywhere upon Lizzie. I saw no blood on her face or hands or hair, which was done up in her usual custom. She went into the dining room shortly after my arrival and lay down on the lounge. I noticed not the first thing unusual about her dress or appearance. I recollect that I did not go upstairs before the officers came. I do know the officers went upstairs. Do not remember when they did go upstairs. Remember that they pulled open the door of Miss Lizzie's room when they went upstairs. Two searches were made after the murder, one partial and one thorough. After the first search it seemed to me that the officers were coming all day. Miss Lizzie answered all of their inquiries freely. I remember the search the day after the funeral. An extended search was made on that day through the building from the top to the bottom of the house.

I do not know whether at the time of the first search the officers made a thorough search or not. Do not know whether it was on Saturday or not. I was not at the house on Monday.

Lucy Collett was the next witness. I live on Borden street. I was at Dr. Chagnon's house the day of the murder and answered the telephone.

From where I was I could see all the Borden yard. I did not see anything unusual or anybody going in or out of it or in fact I did not see anybody there.

In cross-examination witness said I think I should have seen anybody who came over Dr. Chagnon's fence and down the carriage drive, but I might not have

[Continued on Fourth Page.]

Emma. Mr. Jennings. Lizzie. M. O. Adams.

MR. ADAMS CROSS-EXAMINING FOR THE DEFENCE.

FEARS A CHOLERA EPIDEMIC.

Dr. Abbott Thinks Everything Points in that Direction.

Fall River Physician's Warning to the People of Chicago.

Progress of the Eastern Scourge in European Countries.

CHICAGO, Aug. 29.—"Notwithstanding the statements to the contrary I fear we shall have a cholera epidemic in this country," said Dr. John H. Abbott of Fall River, Mass., who is in this city. "Everything points in that direction. It is more or less nonsensical to talk of perfect quarantine protection. Such a thing is not likely to be obtained. In England, where the regulations are much stricter than they are here, two cases have already crept in. Do we expect to be more fortunate?

Apart from this question of quarantine you must recollect that there are means of carrying the dread disease to our shores other than those which attach to passenger vessels entering our ports. If you were absolutely to cut off all personal contact with the countries where the scourge prevails there would still be danger of its reaching this land. The germ travels by sea and land. It may come to us through the mails and through the thousand and one other ways which are the result of our commercial dealings with nations. Therefore the most reasonable thing to do is to hope cholera will not attack us and at the same time prepare to resist the attack.

With reference to these preparations, a word will not be out of season. Food and drink are perhaps the two things to which each should attend. Let every one avoid above all things fruit about which there is a suspicion of taint. The street vender should be shunned and canned fruits are not safe. After fruit come vegetables. I remember about six or seven years ago reading a lengthy discussion among the medical authorities of France as to the cholera-producing qualities of a certain class of green peas, and it was admitted that green peas were a source of considerable danger in their character.

Among the other things to be eschewed, however hard it may seem, are ice cream and iced articles of every kind. As to intoxicants you must bear in mind the fact they have a tendency to depress the system and anything which brings about that result is bad. In addition to the hints which I have thrown out, every one should give full appreciation to the advice of the German philosopher, 'Keep your head cool and your feet warm.' He might have said also keep your bowels and stomach open.

Dr. John H. Abbott

Fears a cholera epidemic in this country.

Cholera in England.

LONDON, Aug. 29.—What with the assertions and denials made regarding the prevalence of cholera in England, it would be hard to decide whether the cholerine cases that have occurred have been true Asiatic cholera or not. In some quarters it is asserted that there is no doubt true cholera has effected an entrance into the country, while on the other hand it is positively asserted that the disease is nothing but simple cholerine, and no danger is to be apprehended.

Dr. Whitcomb, the sanitary officer at Gravesend, who inspected the steamer Gemma, which arrived from Hamburg on Thursday, and three of whose passengers subsequently died from what was said to be Asiatic cholera, emphatically denies that the disease was the dreaded eastern scourge. He attedned all three victims in the hospital, and says that they died of cholerine. He further says that the emigrants on the Gemma were not of the poorest classes, but were greatly superior to the general run of foreign Jews who arrive here.

In some quarters it is said it is nonsense for the officials to act on the supposition that it is only the poorest class of passengers who can convey the contagion. It is said that even first class passengers from cholera infected ports are just as likely to convey the germs of the disease as those who travel in the steerage, and that the disease is not generated on the steamer but in the cities from which they come, and there is no way of telling whether some of the first class passengers may not have only recently left a house in which some person has fallen a victim to the disease. The people who argue in this way claim that there should be no partiality shown as to what passengers should be landed from a steamer that is quarantined and all should be detained.

It is declared that the sickness on the Laura was due to acute diarrhœa, and not to cholera. The Laura is the vessel that arrived at Lynn Friday with two suspicious cases of sickness on board. The health officials would allow none of the passengers to land, but ordered the Laura to put back to sea.

Notwithstanding the denials made of the presence of cholera in the country, the residents of Gravesend were thrown into a state of excitement by the arrival of two steamers, one of which was from Hamburg, while the other it was subsequently learned was bound for Hamburg. The steamer from Hamburg was the Portia. She was subjected to a rigid examination, and all passengers were mustered for examination. The steamer's physician reported the death of a baby on the voyage, and the news of this spread among the townspeople and occasioned much alarm, the universal opinion being that it was another case of cholera. Later it was found that the child had died from infantile complaint. As the vessel and her 40 passengers were found to be free from infection, all the emigrants were allowed to land at Tilbury, opposite Gravesend. They all belonged to the poorer classes of passengers.

The *News* has reopened the agitation against the entry of pauper aliens. It demands that the government issue an order to prevent the entry of imports or immigrants from cholera-infected ports. It adds that several of the immigrants from the Portia have gone to the end of London, where they will probably develop the cholera epidemic in the next few days and become centres from which death will spread throughout the city.

The Disease at Paris.

PARIS, Aug. 29.—Twenty persons suffering with choleraic disorders were admitted to the hospital yesterday. Prof. Peters, the head physician of one of the hospitals, declares there has been cases of Asiatic cholera here and that the disease originated in the Natere poor-house.

Health Condition of Berlin Made Public

BERLIN, Aug. 29.—Dr. Harris Graham, an American physician, who has had wide experience with the cholera in Syra, is organizing the American medical students here into a body to act as assistants and nurses in the event of cholera becoming epidemic in this city. In connection with the policy decided upon, to make public the health condition of Berlin, concealing nothing from the residents, the police this morning posted a notice throughout the city announcing that a woman who had just arrived from Hamburg had died of Asiatic cholera. Appended to the notice are full instructions for the treatment of cholera.

Asiatic Cholera in Bremen.

BREMEN, Aug. 29.—Thirteen cholera patients have been admitted to the hospital here. Five of the cases were certified to as Asiatic cholera. One of the patients has died.

Danger of Infection at Southampton.

SOUTHAMPTON, Aug. 29.—Many complaints are made that in view of the danger of infection to the trans-Atlantic and other steamers, as well as the port, the authorities are not taking adequate precautions to guard against cholera. Fishing vessels arriving from infected ports, such as Havre, enter Southampton without inspection being made.

WEATHER INDICATIONS.

SLIGHT CHANGES IN TEMPERATURE.

WASHINGTON, Aug. 29.—For the 24 hours from 8 a. m. to-day: For New England, slight changes in temperature, variable winds, shifting to easterly.

UNSETTLED.

BOSTON, Aug. 29.—Local forecast for New England until Tuesday night: Fair, followed by unsettled, probably rain by Tuesday night; stationary, followed by slightly higher temperature, easterly winds, becoming variable.

HOME MATTERS.

PERSONAL.—Capt. W. H. Bixby is expected in the city Thursday afternoon and will visit the United States government property in company with the Park Commissioners.

Miss Alice M. Abrams is spending her vacation at Cambridgeport and the Highlands.

Rev. John Wild, pastor of the Second Congregational church, Plymouth, was admitted a member of the Plymouth County Association of Congregational Ministers at their quarterly meeting recently.

Rev. J. A. MacColl arrived home this morning from his European trip.

William M. Higham, senior clerk at E. Bunker's drug store, accompanied by his wife and two children, is spending his annual vacation at the residence of his wife's father, Howard Sabins, in Harwich.

Miss Lois M. Soule, of this city, was a passenger on steamer Augusta Victoria which arrived at New York Saturday afternoon from Hamburg.

SIXTY MILLION BUSHELS OF WHEAT—*A Bushel for Every Inhabitant of the United States. The Kansas Crop for '92.*—Never in the history of Kansas has that State had such bountiful crops as this year. The farmers cannot get enough hands to harvest the great crop, and the Santa Fe railroad has made special rates from Kansas City and other Missouri river towns, to induce harvest hands to go into the State. The wheat crop of the State will be from sixty to sixty-five million bushels, and the quality is high. The grass crop is made, and is a very large one; the early potatoes, rye, barley and oat crops are made, and are all large. The weather has been propitious for corn, and it is the cleanest, best looking corn to be found in the country to-day. Cheap rates will be made from Chicago, St. Louis and all points on the Santa Fe east of the Missouri river, to all Kansas points, on August 30 and September 27, and these excursions will give a chance for Eastern farmers to see what the great Sunflower State can do. A good map of Kansas will be mailed free upon application to Jno. J. Byrne, 723 Monadnock Block, Chicago, Ill., together with reliable statistics and information about Kansas lands.

THE MOSES B. TOWER SOLD.—Barkentine Moses B. Tower, late in the packet service between this port and the Azores, has been sold by Loum Snow & Son to Capt. M. J. Freitas of New York. Capt. Freitas took possession this morning and expects to sail for New York this week. The bark will still hail from New Bedford, but will be engaged in the merchant service between New York and Rio Janeiro. It is reported the price paid was $10,000.

PIANOS are polished by rubbing the hard surface of the varnish, thus bringing out the mirror-like brilliancy of the surface. We do this work either at your house or our shop. Please call for prices or testimonials at the old Robeson house, 5 Dover street, or telephone 259-12. It's no trouble to call and examine instruments.

WHALING BARK'S FINE.—Advices from Sitka, Alaska, by the steamship Mexico, state that the whaling bark Lydia has been seized in Bering sea while transferring sealskins to the bark Northern Light. She was fined $100 and released.

ON THURSDAY we place on our counter men's, youths', boys' and children's Winter overcoats, that will be sold at a great reduction. Wamsutta Clothing Co.

STYLE IS INDISPENSABLE to any man of good social standing, and nothing gives it so quickly as a Lamson & Hubbard hat. All dealers.

OUR STOCK MUST BE CLOSED OUT; only a few weeks longer to remain; lease expires Oct. 1st. We close for business Saturday night, Sept. 24th. Wamsutta Clothing Co.

RIPE WATERMELONS, every one guaranteed good and sweet, 15c. each, two for 25c., at C. S. & B. Cummings'.

YOUR MONEY'S WORTH.—If a man wants his money's worth, it will pay him to see our ad. on page 5. Union Shoe Store.

VETERAN FIREMEN will hold an adjourned meeting to-morrow evening. See special notice.

WE ARE MAKING A BIG DISCOUNT on our children's suits. They must be closed out at once. Wamsutta Clothing Co.

SEE HATHAWAY, SOULE & HARRINGTON'S recommend on page 5. Union Shoe Store.

RIPE WATERMELONS 15c. each, two for a quarter, at C. S. & B. Cummings'.

HAVE YOU HAD one of those 10c. cook books at Hutchinson's Book Store?

R. A. PEIRCE POST MEMBERS should read the special notice on the 4th page.

WATERMELONS, a great bargain, 15c. apiece, at C. S. & B. Cummings'.

PARTIES INDEBTED to the Wamsutta Clothing Co., will please call and settle.

FRENCH KID Oxford Ties $2.00. Devoll's.

HOOD'S Sarsaparilla—100 Doses One Dollar.

THE UPS AND DOWNS OF YOUR WINDOW SHADES.

Do they Please You?

Why Not See Us About Them?

Making and Hanging Shades a Specialty with Us.

OIL OPAQUE SHADES,

Decorated or Plain.

The plain shades are handsomely furnished, mounted on a warranted roller, with a fine nickel pull; are 36 inches wide and 2 yards long.

READY-MADE SHADES,

By their convenience and low prices seem to have filled a real want. We have made up a pleasing variety of curtains in both Holland and Opaque, in the most approved colorings, using a high grade roller, which we believe at the very reasonable prices will meet the requirements of the majority of curtain buyers.

SPECIAL ORDER SHADES, FOR CUSTOM CURTAINS.

We take great pleasure in referring to our *SUNFAST ROCKSONIA HOLLAND*, which we GUARANTEE to be STRICTLY FADELESS. Can we do more? In addition to this quality, it is the best fabric we have ever seen for nice curtains. If you will drop us a postal card we will send samples and give an estimate of cost free of charge.

C. F. WING,

34 to 40 Purchase st.

WHITING & CO.,

Will Continue the

Remnant Silk SALE,

Monday and Tuesday,

the 29th and 30th,

Being the last days of the sale.

On same days we shall sell a few Remnants of

DRAPERY SILKS,

Best $1.00 Goods, at

49c.

All new patterns this season.

WHITING & CO.

Fall Hats.

Buy Your New Hat Of J. & W. R. WING & CO.

Correct Qualities.

Correct Shapes.

Correct Prices.

Now Ready.

THE CRESCENT!

22 Purchase St.

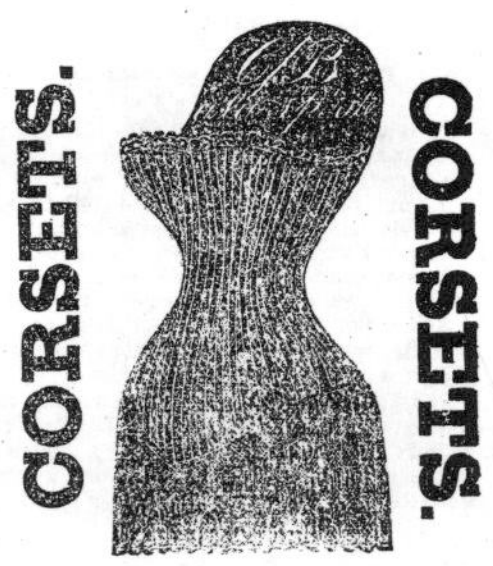

We haven't begun to tell you all about our Corsets. It is

CORSETS,

and CORSETS,

and CORSETS.

A fresh stock coming in constantly. Don't forget we have a large line of Thomson's Glove-fitting Corsets. Prices at $1, $1.25, $1.50, $1.75, $2.25; satin $5. And we give you a new pair if the steels break.

Kalamazoo Corset Waists, very similar in style to the Jackson Waist, marked down from $1 to 75c. A very few Kabo Corsets left, drab only, for 75c.; regular price $1.

Hoisery and Hose Supporters. Good Dress Shields only 10c. *Gingham Aprons* of best quality and with two full widths only 25c. If you examine the make of them you will be satisfied. They sell *every time.*

ONSET BAY.

Remarkably Successful Camp-Meeting Brought to Close.

Disagreeable Weather Has Turned the Tide of Travel Homeward.

Extensive Improvements and Additions Predicted for Next Year.

ONSET BAY, Aug. 28.

The annual camp-meeting closed with today's services and considering the inclement weather there was a large attendance. The delightful weather of the early part of the week brought in visitors in large numbers but the disagreeable northeaster of the last three days and the fact that the daily services were drawing to a close turned the trend of travel homeward. Bluefish have struck in and one boat reports a catch of 71 handsome specimens one day the last week. This will assist materially in prolonging the season and many predict that it will extend well up to the first of October. While the daily meetings have ended, services are to be held for the next three Sundays and perhaps longer. The present camp-meeting has been a remarkable one and the most successful in the history of Onset. There has been unusual harmony, the only breeze that arose being over the subject of materialization, and then the officers quieted the disturbance by declining to stand as sponsors for any of the mediums and notifying everybody that they must behold and judge for themselves. During the storm the meetings were held in the tent. To-day's services were held in the Temple and attracted large audiences both morning and afternoon.

Mrs. Cora L. V. Richmond, one of the most popular of all the speakers who come to Onset, was the speaker at both meetings. The morning service opened with a concert by the Bay State Band which was followed by vocal and instrumental music by Professors Maynard and Coffin. Mrs. Richmond who spoke under inspiration first answered the following question to the utmost satisfaction of her auditors. "Will the control inform us of the different processes of materialization; transfiguration; etherealization; personification; dematerialization and also of independent slate writing. Her exposition was described as little less than marvellous. She next took up the subject "Homes and occupations in the spirit life."

From 1 to 2 o'clock the Bay State Band gave a concert in the Temple that attracted a large and appreciative audience.

The afternoon service opened with a vocal selection by Prof. Maynard. Mrs. Richmond followed in a fervent invocation. Prof. Coffin rendered a cornet solo very finely. Mrs. Richmond before proceeding to the consideration of her subject, which was announced as "To what degree do spirits and angels influence, direct and guide human attainment?" answered several questions propounded by persons in the audience in a way that evoked loud applause.

At the close of her address Mrs. Richmond recited an excellent impromptu poem upon "The offering of flowers." This subject suggested itself because of quite an elaborate floral decoration of the platform. At the close of the poem a unanimous rising vote of thanks was tendered to her for the valuable services rendered during her stay at Onset. Joseph D. Stiles, with his spirit brave, Swift Arrow, followed with a public test seance that was said to be remarkably successful.

To-night a benefit concert was given at the Temple by Professors Maynard and Coffin that drew an audience that filled every seat. To-day the Bay State Band finished its contract. Music last Sunday is to be furnished by Carter's Band of Middleboro and the following Sunday by Ferguson's Band of Bridgewater.

W. J Colville, who is always welcome at Onset, will occupy the platform next Sunday.

M. Tribou has sold for William F. Nye a cottage site on Fourth street to Mrs. Johnson of Whitman.

There is no doubt that many notable improvements will be made the coming season. It is found that the fair given by the ladies for the benefit of the improvement fund was fully as successful as was at first reported, and that the net proceeds were nearly $1000. It is said that the project of a regular side wheel steamer to run from this place to a "sure go" for next season, as the parties backing the scheme have plenty of capital and confidence that it will prove a profitable venture.

Considerable complaint is heard about the increased tax rate which is $15 this year. In many instances complaints are heard of an increase in valuation. The assessors say that they have yet to find the person who wants to sell for the assessed value.

There is talk of a regatta on a large scale Labor Day. Owners of some of the fastest sloops and cats along the coast as far as Providence are anxious to enter if a race is sailed. If the officers of the association will offer sufficient financial encouragement it can be made the most successful race of the season.

The arrangements for the annual harvest festival are going forward rapidly.

A benefit was extended Axie Paine one evening the past week, which netted about $35.

Owing to the disagreeable weather, the attendance at the dance last evening was somewhat smaller than usual. However, it was a very enjoyable occasion, and the net receipts were about $62.

The event of the week was the annual parade and ball of the Industry Hook & Ladder Company on Thursday. It was equally enjoyed by all who attended, and the exchequer of the company was increased about $40.

A Baptist chapel is one of the new buildings projected on Point Independence. A clambake is to be given some day the coming week in aid of the building fund. Maj. T. B. Griffith is to start for Washington soon, where he will remain until after the annual encampment of the G. A. R.

Steam yacht Grace is chartered for a trip around Cape Cod to Boston.

Much satisfaction is expressed on all hands at the order of the County Commissioners this week that a public highway shall be laid out from the Cohasset Narrows bridge to the Point Independence bridge on the other side of Long Neck. It will greatly enhance the value of considerable property.

A committee of the town of Bourne, comprising Capt. Edwin Burgess of Monument Beach; Landlord Davis of Cataumet's Hotel Jacinth; and William R. Gibbs of Sagamore, have been out and traversed the country and report upon a feasible route for a highway and bridge over Monument river to connect Tudor Haven, Monument Neck, Monument Beach, Wenaumet and Cataumet direct from Buzzards Bay Village, Long Neck, Point Independent, Onset Bay, East Wareham, Wareham, Marion and Mattapoisett.

Editor Henry H. Sylvester of the New York World returned to his duties yesterday after a two weeks' sojourn at Straffin cottage.

About 50 Spiritualists visited Hog Island Thursday and enjoyed a picnic and clambake.

A party of 25 or more came up from Falmouth Friday on the steam yacht Nashawena.

Real estate agents report that there never has been a time in the history of Onset when the market was as active as at present, and there is every indication that a large number of new cottages will be erected this Fall and next Spring.

CONTRACTS AWARDED.

Bids Opened for Furniture and Gas Fittings for Our New Post-Office.

The Treasury Department, at Washington, has received bids on furniture and gas fixtures for our new post-office, and opened them last week.

The contract for furniture was awarded to the Middletown Furniture Manufacturing Company of Middletown, Pa., for $2028. The other bids were as follows:

Otto, Duker & Co., Baltimore $2293.00
K. H. Revell & Co., Chicago 2241.00
J. W. Mason & Co., New York 2328.00
Fiege, Slinbee & Co., East Saginaw, Mich. 2770.52
Jackson & Sharpe Co., Wilmington, Del. 2053.00
Robert Mitchell Furniture Co. 2686.55
Ketcham Furniture Co., Toledo, O. ... 2577.60
Yale & Towne Mfg. Co., Stamford, Ct. 4993.75
Union School Furniture Co., Battle Creek, Mich. 3141.80

The contract to furnish combination gas and electric fixtures was awarded to the Cassidy & Son Mfg. Co. of New York, whose bid was $694.35. The other bidders were:

General Fixture Co., New York $960.50
W. C Vosberg Mfg. Co., Brooklyn 776.25
Horn, Brannen & Forsyth Mfg. Co., Philadelphia 837.75
Schultz Gas Fixture & Art Metal Co., Baltimore 825.90
George W Walther & Co., Baltimore .. $16.95
R. Hollings & Co., Boston 735.00

The contract for approaches has been awarded to Edmund O'Keefe, who is superintendent in the construction of the building.

The sidewalks, 10 feet wide, will be of artificial stone, a composition of concrete, cement and gravel, to be laid soft and allowed to harden till hard as rock, and marked off into blocks 3 feet 6 inches by 5 feet. The curb will be 8 inches broad, of granite. It has been decided to also complete the driveways around the building at once, and Mr. O'Keefe has the contract.

FALL RIVER.

The Mellen House proprietor gave a complimentary dinner last evening to the representatives of the local and out of town newspapers.

There were 33 deaths in the city last week. The poor children of the city were given a sail Friday afternoon on steamer Thomas A. Morgan by the Continental Steamboat Co. of Providence.

SOMERSET.

Squeteagues have struck into the river, and several of the beauties have been caught. Andrew S. Marble is high line, having caught six fish, 24th, which weighed 26 pounds, and five more, 25th, of about the same weight. A blue fish which weighed over five pounds was captured by Nathan Staples, 25th. This is a rare fish for these waters.

TAUNTON.

Charles L. Handford, who has been a bookkeeper in an office in Taunton for the past six years, is no longer in the company's employ. A short time ago it was discovered that there was a slight discrepancy in the accounts. This was apparently satisfactorily explained, but there was a careful watch kept from that time out, and the books were thoroughly examined until it was found the shortage amounted to several thousands of dollars. Eventually all the shortage was made up and the company will not prosecute.

RAYNHAM.

Horace Case has gone into the tomato culture quite extensively, having nearly 3000 plants. Also, has 5000 cauliflower plants and 700 pepper plants and 1500 celery plan s.

REHOBOTH.

The annual reunion of the Goff family took place on the 25th at the Rehoboth homestead. There were 125 present. Organization was perfected with the choice of the following officers:

President—Bradford G. Goff.
First Vice-President—J. M. Goff.
Second Vice-President—Miss Maria Goff.
Secretary—Oscar A. Carleton.
Treasurer—J. M. Goff.
Trustees—for three years, Henry Pervear; for two years, Fra' D. Goff; for one year, Rufus H. Goff.

A fund was started as a permanent investment, to be devoted to current expenses, and the sum of $47 was raised. Ira Winsor Carpenter, Peleg Francis, and Simeon K. Goff were appointed a committee to arrange for the annual gathering in 1893, and they subsequently reported that the reunion would be held at the residence of Winsor Carpenter in Rehoboth. Three of the older members of the family have died during the past year, Isaiah Goff, aged 79, Shubael Goff, aged 83, and Mary T., wife of Gilbert Wheeler, aged 69. The two latter named both died on Dec. 26, and were buried on the same day.

PLYMOUTH COUNTY.

The town of Plymouth has purchased of the Berlin Iron Bridge Company of East Berlin, Conn., fifty-four rods of a new style, to be placed along the highways.

John Hatch of Whitman recently picked over 32 quarts of huckleberries in 3¼ hours.

The assessors of Rockland announce the valuation of the town as follows: Real estate, $2,243,857; personal estate, $597,377; total valuation, $2,841,134; number of polls assessed, 1665; tax rate, $19.50 on $1000.

Duxbury's rate of taxation, which has lately been found by the assessors, will be $14.90 on $1000 this year. It is an increase of ten cents over the rate of last year.

The fund for the Plymouth Agricultural Hall was increased last week by a subscription of $500 from Mrs. William Dyer of Weymouth, daughter of John Lane who was formerly president of the society.

The house of Peleg S. Bradford at Bridgewater was entered by burglars 26th, and a sum of money and a gold watch stolen.

LITTLE COMPTON.

An effort is being made by several citizens to arouse an interest in the history and character of the aboriginal inhabitants of the locality, the Sogkonate Indians. It is proposed that some of the highways of the town should bear the names of noted Indians whose homes were here, and already several signboards have been placed, bearing the tribal name, its queen's and that of Sassamon, and having reference to their places of residence and to famous historical incidents.

LIZZIE BORDEN'S CASE.

Government will Present Several More Witnesses.

Prof. Wood's Testimony will Play an Important Part.

Scrupulous Restrictions Placed Upon Matron Reagan.

FALL RIVER, Mass., Aug. 29.—The evening train from Boston brought with it the regiment of newspaper men and artists who took flight on Saturday evening after the close of the hearing on the Lizzie Borden case. There remain to be heard of the government's case two or three witnesses, Professor Wood and the drug clerk who sold Lizzie the poison being the chief. If the testimony of Professor Wood falls as far short of connecting Lizzie Borden with the case as that of Bridget Sullivan, then it would seem as if the case of the government must fail. Bridget Sullivan, who was thought to know so much, has told her story. The doubt is expressed that she has told it all; that the district attorney is withholding the real important features in the belief that he has drawn out enough to hold the prisoner for trial.

What he has shown is that Lizzie was in the house and had the opportunity to commit the deed—nothing more. She has told what was generally known before—nothing more. She has contradicted two or three points claimed by the officers, the principal of which is that she sat by the window, and would have seen Lizzie go to the barn if she did go; and that she, Lizzie, told her, Bridget, to wash the windows, the inference being that if she did so order the girl it was for the purpose of getting her out of the way for the time.

Lizzie's story stands therefore uncontradicted by anything Bridget has said. She has said nothing that directly connects the prisoner with the trouble. The most important witness of the government has strengthened the defense in two material points. That Lizzie told Bridget of the bargain sale of dress goods, suggesting that she go out and get herself a dress, is referred to as showing this supposed desire to be alone with the victim—that on that day's bloody work, but that is a point that will require a great deal of corroborative evidence.

If Professor Wood finds that the hatchet found in the cellar of the Borden house that had the appearance of having been recently washed up had still some spots of blood and hair, as alleged, that compare with that of Mr. and Mrs. Borden, then the presumption is that some one in the house committed the murder. If he does not so find, then the case against the defendant remains as it is, and the question will remain, why is Lizzie Borden held?

THE SISTERS' THEORY.

Think Mr. and Mrs. Borden Were Killed by Some Strange Man.

FALL RIVER, Mass., Aug. 29.—Miss Emma and Miss Lizzie Borden have a theory in regard to the murder of their parents. It is a very unsatisfactory one, but it is, nevertheless, a theory. Lizzie and Emma and Mr. Morse are absolutely certain that Lizzie did not commit the crime. They think that some strange man killed Mr. and Mrs. Borden.

They state that Mr. Borden always received his business callers between 11 and 12 o'clock in the morning. He always answered the door bell between then they say. They think that the assassin entered the house between 9 and 10 o'clock, probably, and that he came in search of Mr. Borden.

This man may have wandered through the rooms down stairs in search of his intended victim, and, not finding him, have gone to the upper story by the front way. Then, hearing a noise that disturbed him, he sought a hiding place in the clothes closet at the head of the stairs, just opposite the entrance to Lizzie's room and near the door leading into the spare room. This is as far as the family theory goes. The members of the household do not attempt to explain how or when Mrs. Borden was killed; neither can they offer any reason why Mr. Borden was murdered. They say, however, that they think the assassin could have got out of the house by the front door and escaped without detection.

Restrictions on the Matron.

FALL RIVER, Mass., Aug. 29.—Since the publication of the quarrel episode between Lizzie Borden and her sister Emma, scrupulous restrictions have been placed upon the matron, Mrs. Regan, and no one is allowed near the room where Lizzie Borden is incarcerated. The approaches are guarded, and none save her immediate friends can get near enough to see which way she grain runs on the locked door.

The Jewish Peddler's Man Again.

Like the historical ghost, the phantom of Samuel Robinsky, the Jewish peddler with an ability for writing composite letters, bobs up now and then. The latest mention of his name is in connection with a pawnbroker in Brockton, who says he was visited on the day after the Borden tragedy by a man and woman, both of whom presented an appearance of considerable agitation. They had a pair of shoes which they wished to pawn, and the broker, upon examining them, found some dark, red spots upon them. The couple departed without obtaining the desired loan, and the proprietor of the place thought nothing more about the matter until the letter alleged to have been written by Samuel Robinsky, appeared in print. Then it occurred to him that the description of the man who was seen by the peddler corresponded exactly with the appearance of the man who tried to pawn the shoes. The story appears to be a pretty one, but unfortunately for its strength, the fact is recalled that Samuel Robinsky relates with remarkable distinctiveness how he assisted the man whom he saw fleeing from Fall River to daub blacking all over his russet shoes. Certainly this

Lizzie and Bridget Agree.

Lizzie's Visitors.

Emma visited Lizzie early in the morning, bringing the prisoner's breakfast. The sisters remained together in a conversation until noon, when Uncle John V. Morse arrived with the usual basket containing Lizzie's dinner. Rev. Mr. Buck came too, but the only noticeable feature of his visit was that he did not carry his usual floral offering. Charles J. Holmes and Miss Holmes visited the prison during the day. The prisoner is as usual.

COPYRIGHT 1892.

READY FOR THE FRAY.

There may be no question whatever about your courage, but we'll undertake to say that, though you are as brave as a lion, you won't want to have anything to do with that kind of a fray. Trousers and tatters don't make just the kind of a combination you are hankering after, do they? Purchasers of our $12.00 Suits are bothered with nothing of the sort. They are just as safe from it as though they had a paid up policy of insurance against any such unpleasantness. If this suit gives you any hankering at all, it will give you an ungovernable hankering for an—other one just like it.

OUR FALL STYLE HATS

Now ready for inspection. All the leading styles, such as YEAMAN, MILLER, HARRINGTON, BOSTON DERBY and LAMSON & HUBBARD, in all grades from

$1.50 to $3.00.

M. C. SWIFT & SON,

153, 157 and 159 Union Street,

NEW BEDFORD, - - - MASS.

Lawn Sprinklers,
Rubber Hose,
Poultry Netting,
Screen Doors.

Our Sale on

DOLLAR PAINT

is larger this season than ever before.

F. L. SOWLE & CO., 90 Purchase Street,

Hardware and Specialties.   Opp City Clock.

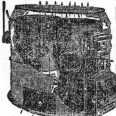

would be a distinguishing characteristic that could not fail of notice, yet the pawn broker did not see the blood-stained shoes covered with blacking and only noticed one or two dark red spots upon them. This will not be the last appearance of Robinsky for having been jumped into notice, he must of necessity attract the attention of all the letter-writing cranks in this section of the country. But if he fails to create any more excitement than upon his initial appearance this alleged Jewish peddler will never cut but the most insignificant of all the insignificant figures in this case.

Lumber Factory Destroyed.

PETOSKEY, Mich., Aug. 29.—Fire broke out in the lath room of the Northern Michigan Lumber company's factory at Panderge, near Oden, seven miles north of Petoskey. In spite of all efforts to control the fire, the flames spread with great rapidity until the immense plant was in flames. R. G. Peters is the principal stockholder in the concern, who employs over 100 men in the manufacture of lumber and hard-wood articles. The loss will be between $100,000 and $300,000, with a comparatively small amount of insurance.

Freight Trains Collide.

WASHINGTON, Mo., Aug. 29.—Two freight trains on the Missouri Pacific road collided here owing to a confounding of the orders by the train dispatcher. John Siebold, fireman of the eastbound train, was killed. Engineer Cordon and Brakemen Roper and Goodwin were seriously injured. Fifty-six cars were wrecked. The company's loss is $40,000. The train dispatcher is said to have disappeared.

They Shook the Hand of Sullivan.

CANOE PLACE INN, L. I., Aug. 29.—John L. Sullivan went to church at Southampton yesterday, accompanied by Phil Casey and other friends. He exercised twice in the afternoon, 300 men and women being present. Afterward he shook hands with 500 persons and bade them farewell. His actual weight at this time is 207 pounds.

James Mahoney Was Drowned.

NEW HAVEN, Aug. 29.—The coroner has decided that James Mahoney, whose body was found in the water near East Rock park, Friday morning, was drowned. The cuts and bruises on the face, the coroner finds, were caused by a fall. All rumors of foul play have been proven groundless.

Horses Burned to Death.

NEW YORK, Aug. 29.—A fire in West Fifty-first street destroyed twenty-five horses and a $4000 orchestrion in a beer saloon. Loss about $15,000.

Tin Plate Works Closed.

LONDON, Aug. 29.—Several Welch tin plate manufacturers closed their works on Saturday. Sixty works are now closed and 10,000 hands are idle. Many sailed on Saturday to find employment in America.

MOYNAN & CO.

IMPORTING RETAILERS.

UNION ST.   PURCHASE ST.

EMBROIDERED
Silk Handkerchiefs !

IMPORTER'S SAMPLES.

We have now on our counters at Handkerchief Department a large lot of Elegant Japanese Silk Handkerchiefs in white, black and colored, hemstitched and embroidered edges, at about half usual prices. It will pay you to come and see this lot if you anticipate buying now or at any time in the near future.

Lot 1—29c., worth 50c.
Lot 2—39c., worth 69c.
Lot 3—59c., worth 85c.
Lot 4—75c., worth $1.25.

A DRESS GOODS BARGAIN.

We shall offer while they last this special lot of 36-inch All-Wool Serges, in Black, Navy, Olive, Garnet, Brown, Green, &c., &c., a regular 50c. quality, now only **39 cents.**

Still a few of those imported Robes and Dress lengths left. Don't miss such a chance—just think of buying a

$12.50 Dress for $4.59.
$15.00 Dress for $5.98.
$22.00 Dress for $7.98.

Call and see for yourself.

PARASOLS.

We have only a few left, and they must go within the next few days. Some of them are the nicest goods and latest styles. All go at

Less than 1-2 Marked Price,

and although the season is far advanced it will pay you to buy now and keep it over for another season.

SILK WAISTS,
SATIN WAISTS,
CAMBRIC WAISTS.

All marked down to *must go* prices. Come in and see them; if you can get suited in the goods, there will be no difficulty about prices.

In Housefurnishing Dept.

Every kitchen necessary can be found here. Such as
Dish Strainers.
Knife Boxes.
Flour Sieves.
Kettles in Tin or Agate Ware.
Roasting Pans.
Chopping Trays.
Dish Pans,
and all the other hundred and one useful things required in kitchen work. Also here you find all kinds Glassware.
Fancy Vases and Ornaments in Japanese Ware.
Fancy Baskets.
Parlor and Banquet Lamps.
Pictures of all descriptions, &c., &c.

REMEMBER OUR SPECIAL SALE OF BLANKETS AT LOW PRICES.

MOYNAN & CO.,

185 and 187 Union St.

9 and 11 Purchase St.

The Evening Standard.

NEW BEDFORD, MASS.

MONDAY EVENING, AUGUST 29.

THREE EDITIONS DAILY.

No. 87 Union Street.

PUBLISHED BY

E. ANTHONY & SONS,

INCORPORATED.

—TERMS—

Six Dollars a Year; Three Dollars for Six Months, in advance: Single Copies Two Cents.

The Best Family Newspaper in Southern Massachusetts is the REPUBLICAN STANDARD.

Our Weekly Edition—a large twelve-page paper of 84 columns, containing more reading matter than any other weekly paper in Southern Massachusetts. It is published Thursday mornings. Subscription price only $1.50 a year, in advance.

FOR PRESIDENT:

BENJAMIN HARRISON

OF INDIANA.

FOR VICE-PRESIDENT:

WHITELAW REID

OF NEW YORK.

CONTENTS OF THIS EVENING'S STANDARD.

Four States have already held their general State elections of 1892—Oregon in June, Louisiana and Rhode Island in April and Alabama this month. In each the results showed Republican gains over the previous election. Oregon went Republican by an increase of 792, Rhode Island 3301, and in Alabama the Democratic loss was 101,203.

The next general election will be held in Arkansas on Monday, Sept. 5, when a governor will be elected.

On Tuesday, Sept. 4, Vermont will elect a governor. The Democrats are making strenuous efforts to reduce the Republican majority in that stronghold of Republicanism.

Maine will follow on Monday, Sept. 12. The leading orators of both parties will speak in the State in the meantime, and the result for governor and Congressmen will be watched with keen interest.

Georgia is the only October State this year. Her State election will take place on Wednesday, Oct. 5, and the Farmers' Alliance will contest Democratic supremacy.

The other States will all hold their State elections on Tuesday, Nov. 8, the day of the Presidential election.

Hon. Charles Theodore Russell of Cambridge, father of the Governor, was chosen to preside over the Democratic State Convention at the meeting of the Democratic State Committee held at headquarters Saturday. The convention will be held in Tremont Temple on Tuesday, Sept. 27, at 11 a. m. Hon. John J. Donovan, ex-mayor of Lowell, was elected chairman of the committee on resolutions, his associates to be chosen by the executive committee. The following motions were presented and passed: That all congressional caucuses be held not earlier than Sept. 17 and not later than Sept. 24; that each congressional district convention be requested to report to the State convention the name of one candidate for Presidential elector; that all such candidates be formally chosen by the State convention; that caucuses outside of Boston for the selection of delegates to all conventions be held before Sept. 13.

Labor Day occurs a week from to-day—Sept. 5—and it will probably be more generally observed than heretofore. It will be made the occasion of general demonstrations by the working people of the land, and in New York and Brooklyn where great preparations are making for a parade it is asserted that 100,000 workingmen will be in line. In this city arrangements are perfected for a fine demonstration. The day is a legal holiday in seventeen States—Colorado, Connecticut, Illinois, Indiana, Iowa, Kansas, Maine, Massachusetts, Montana, Nebraska, New Hampshire, New Jersey, New York, Ohio, Pennsylvania, South Dakota and Washington.

The Democratic calamity predictors who insisted that the McKinley tariff would prove a curse to the entire country should read *The Tradesman*, published at Chattanooga, Tenn., which gives a list of 51 new industries established or incorporated in the Southern States during the week ending Aug. 6th, together with 11 enlargements of manufactories and 17 important new buildings. Such facts, all over the country refute the Democratic arguments that the tariff is a burthen. They plainly show to the most common mind that the Republican policy puts life into business and promotes general prosperity.

It is said that the outcome of the variations, legal and otherwise, of the American Bobbin, Spool & Shuttle Company is, as now indicated, that the combination as such is a thing of the past and that the several plants will fall back by way of lease into the hands of the original owners, aided in some cases by outside capital.

HOME MATTERS.

CIVIL SERVICE LIST.—There are 81 persons eligible for employment by the city in the street department

UNION CLAMBAKE.—Cyclists from Brockton, Taunton, Fall River and this city enjoyed a union clambake yesterday at Silver Grove. The party numbered about 125, and social members of the Crescent Club of this city, under whose auspices the bake was held, went out in Caswell's excursion wagon.

THE NORTH ATLANTIC SQUADRON, Rear Admiral Bancroft Gherardi, passed the Vineyard at 5 p. m. yesterday, from Gloucester to New London, Ct. The following vessels comprise the squadron: Flagship Philadelphia, Commander Robert L. Barker; Concord, Commander Edwin White; Dolphin, Commander W. H. Bronson.

RUN OVER.—Yesterday afternoon a 9-year-old son of James Wiley, while playing on Linden street, corner of State, ran over by a passing buggy and bruised considerably. The driver of the buggy did not stop after the accident, but continued without regard to the child's injuries

HORSE CAR ACCOMMODATIONS.—As there has been considerable said about horse car accommodations to Fairhaven at the conclusion of entertainments at the Opera House, we are authorized to state that arrangements have been made with Manager Cross to advertise in his regular space in amusement column whenever a car is to run to Fairhaven.

INFANT'S HOPE IN THE LAKE.—The body of a well developed infant, weighing about 10 pounds, with good head of hair, was found in Sunset Lake, near Rainbow bridge, at Cottage City yesterday. Medical Examiner Leach viewed the body and ordered it buried. At a meeting of the officers of the Martha's Vineyard Campmeeting Association it was voted to request the medical examiner to make a thorough examination of the case.

KNIGHTS OF PYTHIAS.—The Knights of Pythias in Fall River are happy. The only prize that came east among those distributed among the Uniform Rank, Knights of Pythias, which broke camp at Kansas City Saturday, was the sixteenth, a prize of $400, offered for the full division traveling the longest distance to the encampment, and that was awarded to Abbott Division, No. 12, of this city.

THEY HOPE FOR BETTER LUCK.—The last clambake of the Scuttlecut Neck people was a financial failure for two unavoidable causes. The clams furnished by a dealer of this city were unfit for use, and they had to dig another supply of twelve bushels, both lots at their expense; then the day was so unpleasant the attendance was small. They will try it again next Wednesday, as will be seen by an advertisement in another column, and the bake deserves liberal patronage. The proceeds go towards canceling the chapel debt

VESSELS LIBELLED.—Bark Gay Head was during the past week attached by Sidney W. Knowles on account of an unpaid note of hand made by her owners for $6500. It has been removed, however, and the bark was allowed to sail.

The Portuguese schooner Forest Fairy has been libelled by James Robertson of Boston, because of a debt of $50 for supplies purchased by libellee in Boston. The matter was adjusted this morning and the libel was dismissed.

OBITUARY.—Capt. William Cook, a retired sea captain and a prominent citizen of Vineyard Haven, died suddenly at Grace Episcopal church yesterday morning of heart disease. Capt. Cook had walked from his home to the church and had just arrived when he dropped to the floor, expiring immediately. The congregation was dismissed. Capt. Cook was born in Baltimore, Md., about 71 years ago. His father was a seafaring man and moved his family to Vineyard Haven when he (William) was but eight years of age. He at a very young age followed the footsteps of his father and chose the sea for a livelihood. He was later appointed as vice-consul at Glasgow, Scotland, which position he filled for a number of years, when he finally returned to the sea, and for a number of years sailed out of New York in the foreign merchant service, and retired about ten years ago and since then has lived in Vineyard Haven. He leaves a widow and a son. Dr. Ansel G. Cook of Hartford, Ct. The funeral will probably be held on Tuesday from the Grace Episcopal church.

NONQUITT.

Despite the miserable weather the usual Saturday evening dance at the hotel was a great success. There was quite an innovation, introduced in the direction of George R. Bartlett of Concord, Mass., assisted by Miss Anna Ricketson of Nonquitt, the affair took the form of a Mother Goose Carnival. Forty-eight couples participated in the grand march. The costumes were picturesque and striking, and many were very elaborate. The affair was the social event of the season.

NORTHERN LIGHT'S CRUISE.

Capt. Healy Spills the Whalers' Whiskey

Whaling bark Northern Light arrived at San Francisco Aug. 22d, having been sent home as unseaworthy by a court of inquiry composed of officers of the Yorktown. Capt. Simonds disagreed with their judgment, but the major portion of his crew was in a state of mutiny, and he obeyed the order to come home. Only about half the crew that left on the Light returned on her, the remainder either deserting or being allowed to ship on other vessels. Capt. Simonds says he dates the failure of the cruise from April 9th, when the bark bumped on a reef off Middleton island. She commenced to leak badly, making as much as 24 inches an hour. At Ounalaska some rough repairs were made, and when the leak was reduced to eight inches an hour Capt. Simonds started his whale hunt afresh. Most of the crew fought against going on account of the bark's leak, but Simonds put to sea anyhow, and when the disgruntled sailors refused duty he put twenty-six of them in irons. Then came the order to return, provoked by complaint of the men, and of course that settled it.

Capt. Simonds reports that Wright & Bowne's whaler Sylvia, seized for having skins in possession in Bering Sea, has been sent to Sitka. The skins were only 14 in number, and the defence will be that they were taken outside the sea. The last the Northern Light heard of the Kodiak fleet the Bounding Billow had four whales, the Josephine four, the Andrew Hicks four, Wanderer one and the J.Allen two. Capt. Healy of the revenue cutter Bear aroused the indignation of the whalers by searching them and throwing their liquor overboard. Most of the blubber hunters laid in a supply of rum at Honolulu for trading purposes, and it was this stuff that the Bear search parties spilled into the sea. The whalers' crop of skins and curios will consequently be light this Fall.

The Northern Light was run on the Oakland creek mud flats 23d inst., and she will go on the dry dock. Part of her false keel is gone and it is believed the main keelson is split. Although about 40 years old up to the time of the accident, she was one of the staunchest whalers afloat.

THE COUNTY ROAD.

Some of the Abutters Encroach on the Original Lay-out.

When the County road from Lund's Corner to Taunton was laid out 50 feet wide, but there are portions of that highway which to-day are not more than 40 feet wide, made so because some of the abutters have encroached on the original lay-out, and the authorities are now considering the advisability of removing the intruders, or to speak more correctly, of cutting off such portions of land which is being used by abutters. Capt. Simonds' Corner the highway has not been encroached upon, but north of Davis' Corner to the city limit, where land is occupied on the west side, at least 10 feet have been gobbled up by the abutters.

This find was made last week when the board stones on the east side of the road was found, and after investigation it was learned that the original lay-out was 50 feet wide instead of 40 as everybody has thought of late. The subject has been called to the attention of the City Solicitor, who says the city has a right to avail itself of the original lay-out, and two of the abutters on the highway are much aggrieved because they are liable to lose 10 feet of land which they have had the use of these many years.

THIRD DISTRICT COURT.

BORDEN, J.

MONDAY, Aug. 29.

John Dunn and Thomas F. Fagan pleaded guilty of being drunk yesterday, and were each sentenced to the House of Correction for three months. They appealed and recognized in $200 each

Joseph Fournier, George E. Macomber and Frederick Ellsworth each pleaded guilty of being drunk, and went up for three months. One case of drunkenness was put on probation until Sept. 20th next.

James Varley and his wife Annie have not got along very well together for some time past, and on Wednesday last James assaulted her. She made complaint against him, and he was arrested, Saturday. Since that time all the past has been forgiven, and in court this morning their appearance was that of a recently married couple. James pleaded guilty, and was fined $5. He appealed, but afterwards withdraw his appeal. Annie raised the money and paid the fine.

Bids should be addressed to the Committee on City Property, and left with the City Clerk, Library Building, on or before THURSDAY, September 8th, at 12 o'clock noon.

A. S. BROWNELL, Chairman Committee.

SOLDIERS FIRED UPON.

Bullets of a Sharpshooter Whizzed by During Religious Service at Coal Creek.

NASHVILLE, Tenn., Aug. 29.—A special from Coal Creek gives the following account of the firing of a sharpshooter of the miners upon the soldiers while engaged in religious services Sunday: While the boys in blue were gathered upon a grassy hillside beneath some trees, listening to a sermon by Rev. Dr. Ramsey, chaplain of the First Regiment, the services were broken in upon by the whiz of several bullets as they passed close to the heads of the crowd.

As all eyes were turned toward the direction whence came the bullets, a sharpshooter was seen a moment, and then the man disappeared behind the rocks. Capt. Roach of the regiment hurried up the mountain side, soon sighted the man, but he was fast escaping, and the shots fired at him failed to bring him down.

The appearance of the scout of the militia may have a great deal of significance, for there are rumors of large numbers of miners hidden away in the mountain fastnesses.

TUMULT IN BUENOS AYRES.

Radicals Interrupt a Political Meeting and a Riot Ensues.

NEW YORK, Aug. 29.—A Buenos Ayres dispatch to the *Herald* says that city is in a state of wild excitement. Meetings were held yesterday in honor of President-elect Saenz Pena. There were 2000 Radicals present. They interrupted the meeting by shouting for Alem and Irgoyen, interspersed with cries "Down with Pena." A tumult arose and there were several collisions.

The police attempted to disperse the Radicals and there was a riotous demonstration which almost resulted in the dignity of a battle in the plaza florida. The Radicals slowly retreated to the plaza San Marten, where they made another stand and there were more fighting. The whole city is stirred up and in all probability the troops will have to be called out to preserve order.

THE FIRE RECORD.

Catholic Church Destroyed and Oil Sheds and Lake Shore Cars Burned.

FORESTVILLE, Mich., Aug. 29.—A Roman Catholic church in this place was burned to the ground yesterday and three people burned, one fatally. Fire was discovered while services were being held, and a wild panic ensued among the members of the congregation. Women and children were trampled upon and many of them were badly bruised

CLEVELAND, O., Aus. 29.—A row of oil sheds and cars belonging to the Lake Shore Railroad Company was burned last night. Loss $26,000.

NEW YORK ELEVATED ROADS.

Street Railway Syndicate Secures Jay Gould's Manhattan.

NEW YORK, Aug. 28.—The *World* says it was reported last night that the Elkins-Wildner-Yerkes syndicate has got possession of Jay Gould's holdings in the Manhattan Elevated Railway Co., and that the triumvirate of street railway men will demand three seats in the company's directorate. It was also reported that the entire control of this city's elevated roads will pass into the hands of the syndicate, and that the new management will signalize the event by immediate preparations to extend the lines beyond the Harlem.

WINNIPEG WILL RECONSIDER.

May Send Delegates to Reciprocity Convention After All.

DULUTH, Minn., Aug. 29.—Dispatches say to the effect that Winnipeg would reconsider her action of refusing to send delegates to the Grand Forks reciprocity convention, owing to strong protests from prominent Winnipeg merchants, who are anxious for reciprocity between the United States and the Dominion.

BALL PLAYER KILLED.

Struck in the Ear by an In-Curve Whizz of the Bat.

HAZLETON, Pa., Aug. 29.—At Lansford Thomas Donnelly, while batting for the Locustdale club was struck in the ear by a strong in-curve pitched by German of the Lansford team and knocked down. He was hastily carried off the field and a physician summoned, but before the latter arrived the man died.

THE BORDEN INQUIRY.

[Continued from First Page.]

done so. I got a telephone message at my father's drug store at about 10 45. I live on Borden street, between Second and Third. I was on the south piazza about an hour looking into the south yard. It would be possible for a man to have passed down the carriage way while I was there. I saw no one pass. My back was turned a part of the time.

At this point the court took a recess until 2 p. m.

[By Associated Press.]

FALL RIVER, Aug. 29.—Court came in this morning at 10 45 sharp, but at 8 o'clock the dingy court room was thronged, and the uninteresting details of the District Court were listened to by those assembled. Those proceedings were short, and for nearly one hour and a half hours the people in the benches perspired and fretted awaiting the coming of the principals in the great Fall River tragedy.

Lizzie Borden passed a fairly restful night, and at an early hour this morning was visited by her sister Emma, who stayed with her until the hour for court arrived. Among those who were present was Mrs. Fish, of Hartford, a sister of the murdered woman. Miss Lizzie entered the room after Judge Blaisdell had taken his seat, and greeted her counsel with a smile.

Mrs. Churchill Testifies.

Mrs. Adelaide B. Churchill was the first witness called, who said she lived near the Bordens on the north side of the street and she remembered well the day of the tragedy. The first she remembered of her attention being called to the affair was when she saw Bridget going for Dr. Bowen. About the same time she saw Lizzie standing against the side of the side door, apparently distressed. I opened the window and asked her what was the matter and she said: "Oh, Mrs. Churchill, somebody has killed father." I went over and asked her where her father was and she replied: "In the sitting room." Asked her where she was when it happened and she said she "was in the barn looking for something for sinkers."

Witness said that so far as she knew she was the first one outside of the family who was called to the house. The time as near as witness could recollect was about 11 o'clock. Witness asked Lizzie where her mother was, and she said her mother had a note to go somewhere, but she didn't know but what she had been killed too; she wished somebody would go and try to find her for she thought she had come in since. She said her father must have an enemy, for every one in the house had been sick. After the neighbors had commenced to come in Lizzie said again that she wished some one would go and try to find Mrs. Borden, for she was sure she had heard her come in, and here witness described finding Mrs. Borden.

Witness had seen Mr. Borden that morning about 9 o'clock; he was apparently going down town. Witness remembered seeing Bridget washing the windows, but could not give the exact time. Witness said she heard Lizzie ask Dr. Bowen to telegraph to her sister Emma, but to be careful and not say the worst as the lady with whom she was stopping was old and it might affect her. Witness described the dress which Lizzie wore on that day as a dark blue cotton cloth dress.

Mr. Jennings subjected Mrs. Churchill to a severe cross-examination, dwelling particularly on the excited condition of Lizzie when witness was first called to the scene.

[Continued on Sixth Page, Second Edition.]

FINANCIAL.

SANFORD & KELLEY.

GARDNER T. SANFORD, CHARLES S. KELLEY. } **Bankers,**

Members Boston Stock Exchange,

47 North Water St., New Bedford.

STOCKS AND BONDS BOUGHT AND SOLD ON COMMISSION

At the New York and Boston Stock Boards.

CONSERVATIVE & PROFITABLE INVESTMENTS

FOR TRUST FUNDS.

New Bedford Manufacturing Stocks have a first-class record as dividend payers, and we always have some on hand to offer.

Sole Agents for the sale in this city of the 6 per cent. Guaranteed Mortgages of the Lombard Investment Co.

Auction Sale of Stocks and Bonds WEDNESDAYS AND SATURDAYS, at 10 45 A. M.

ORDERS SOLICITED.

AMERICAN BUILDING COMPANY,

81 Westminster St., Providence, R. I.

ABSOLUTELY SAFE. NO CHANCE FOR LOSS. CONSERVATIVE MANAGEMENT. SEMI-ANNUAL DIVIDENDS.

This Company is managed by Rhode Island Bank Directors; men whom you can inquire about and become acquainted with. Investigation solicited. Our books are always open to inspection of Stockholders.

AUTHORIZED CAPITAL, - - $500,000
CAPITAL PAID IN, - - - 200,000

The third issue of $100,000 is now offered to investors in either small or large amounts, at par (100) and accrued interest at six per cent. from July 1st, 1892.

The capital of this company is invested in the very choicest business property in growing cities, largely in Providence, all rented for stores and offices. Consistent with the natural growth in population these properties are continually increasing in value, the rents are advanced from time to time, affording opportunity for larger dividends, and the price of stocks will be raised accordingly. Don't send your money a long distance to be managed by persons of unknown integrity. Invest right here at home; you will be richer in the end.

Write for list of officers and ask for any other particulars you desire to have.

Address

AMERICAN BUILDING CO.,
Box 205. PROVIDENCE, R. I.
au17MWF-2mo

Mass. Real Estate Co.

246 Washington St., Boston.

Dividends 7 Per Cent.

Invests in Central Real Estate in Growing Cities.

Authorized Capital - - $2,000,000
Capital paid in - - 1,250,000
Surplus - - - 100,000

ORGANIZED IN 1885.

Paid Dividends of 5 per cent. per annum for 4½ years. Paid Dividends of 7 per cent. per annum since July, 1890. Average Dividend since organization over 6 per cent. per annum. Surplus at close of last fiscal year, over $100,000.

Stock offered for sale at $108 per share until July 31.

Send to or call at the office for information MWF

T. E. BOWMAN & CO.,

Topeka, Kansas,

NEGOTIATORS OF

Conservative Mortgage Loans in Eastern Kansas.

$2,500,000 LOANED without loss to any investor, and have never yet had to foreclose a farm loan in these eastern counties. Write us for list of investments. s29

GEORGE LEVY, North End Pawn Broker.

Cash advanced on Real or Personal Property. All business private. au3-1m

SECOND EDITION.

HOME MATTERS.

OIL MARKET.—The 475 barrels sperm oil imported by schooner Gage H. Phillips of Provincetown have been purchased by parties here for manufacture. No price is given.

WHALEBONE.—There has been sold in this market 4000 pounds Arctic and Northwest bone, for manufacture, on private terms. The bone sold is a portion of the lot which arrived last week.

COOPERATIVE BANK.—At a regular meeting of the Acushnet Cooperative Bank held Saturday night sales were made as follows: $1150 at 6.18 per cent., $400 at 6.12 per cent., $1160 at 6.06 per cent.

BUILDING.—Herbert M. Atwood has taken the contract to build for William H. and Mary J. Read two houses 25 by 38 feet, with 23 feet posts, on the south side of River street, east of Acushnet avenue.

Mr. Frank J Gildea has petitioned for leave to move a building from its present location on the east side of Wilkinson street to a location on the east side of Howard street, north of Coggeshall street.

FUNERAL.—The funeral of the late Edmund Grinnell took place at his late residence, corner of Hawthorn and Orchard streets at 12 o'clock to-day. Relatives and friends, particularly business connections of deceased, among them many prominent business and professional men, attended in large numbers and the floral designs were elaborate and elegant. Messrs. W. A. Robinson, Arthur E. Perry, and Hon. Walter Clifford were in charge of the exercises, and Rev. William J. Potter officiated as clergyman. The choir of the Unitarian Church rendered music. The burial occurred in Rural Cemetery later, the bearers being Hon. Walter Clifford, Horace G. Howland, Franklin Woodward, and Dr. John T. Bullard of this city, Louis Robeson of Fall River, and Secretary Sayward of the Master Builders' Association of Boston, of which deceased was a member.

All for a Barley Corn.

LaFontaine, in one of his fables, tells of a barnyard fowl that scratched up a gem, while scratching for corn. Not knowing its value he gave it to a stone-cutter for a barley corn. Thus do many persons throw away the priceless pearl of health. A "trifling" cough is neglected, then comes Consumption, then death. Stay the cough, or look out for a coffin. Dr. Pierce's Golden Medical Discovery will cure catarrh in the head, bronchial or throat affections, or lung-scrofula (commonly known as the consumption of the lungs.) If taken in time and given a fair trial, it will cure, or the money paid for it will be refunded. It is the only *guaranteed* cure.

Good Things Never Die.

Among the good things that help to make enjoyable our puddings, creams and pastry, which have been used by millions of housekeepers for years, is Dr. Price's Delicious Flavoring Extracts of Lemon, Orange, Vanilla, etc.

These flavors differ from all other extracts in their manner of preparation, quality of fruit used, their freedom from all injurious substances, their superior strength and delicate and agreeable taste. **One trial proves their worth.**

ONE FARE.

Laboring Classes to Get the Benefit at Certain Hours.

On and after Sept. 1, but one fare is to be charged to the Head of the River during certain hours of the day on the Purchase street line of horse cars. This departure is for the benefit of the laboring classes.

Up to 8 a.m. but one fare will be charged on the line, the car leaving the Head of the River at 8 o'clock being the last one on which such fare can be paid. In the afternoon between 6 and 8 p.m. the same arrangement will be in force for those desiring to reach the Head of the River, the car leaving Coffin avenue at 8 p.m. being the last car on which such fares will be collected.

REAL ESTATE SALES.—Thomas J. Meaney has sold to Pierre Dandurand, 3.67 rods of land on the south side of Welcome street.

Willard Nye, Jr., has sold to Dominique Isabell, 28.80 rods of land on the northwest corner of contemplated Holly street and Belleville avenue.

Charles B. Lewis has sold to Charles B. Blankinship for $2500 land and buildings on the new Dartmouth road to Phebe A. G. Sherman.

DRIFTED AWAY.—Some time last night catboat Daisy, owned by John Welch, parted her moorings off Hastings' wharf and early this morning was seen adrift in the lower harbor just off Beetle's boat building shop, when she was secured by a son of Frank Smith, who took care of her until her owner arrived.

RELEASED.—Alanson Wallace, committed to the House of Correction from this city Dec. 28, 1891, for one year, for keeping a disorderly house, was released to-day by the County Commissioners on recommendation of the probation officer, concurred in by the justice of the Third District Court.

POLITICAL.—Brewster has elected a Randall delegate to the Congressional convention.

MARRIED.

In this city, 20th inst., by Rev. W. A. Burch, Ernest A. Caswell to Mamie G. Andrews, both of this city.

MARINE INTELLIGENCE.

Ar at Baltimore 28th, sch Rose Esterbrook, Hammett, Ashepoo, SC.

Ar at Nanaimo Aug 20th, bark Carrollton, Lewis, San Francisco.

FINANCIAL.

Dull But Steady Stocks—Chicago, Burlington & Quincy Softens But Recovers—Sugar and St. Paul Strong, Atchison Steady — Money Rates Generally Unchanged—Clearing House Loans at 3 per Cent.—Latest Flint & Pere Marquette Earnings—Disappointing Statement for the Third Week of August—Deacon White Talks on Sugar—Mollie Gibson Declares Her Regular Dividend for September—A Dull Bond Business—General Matters.

MONDAY, Aug. 29.

Prices have not changed particularly today. The bears are still in control of the boards, owing to the absence of the prominent bulls, but to-day they have not been very active and dulness has been the chief characteristic in consequence. The cholera scare is still being used as a club to knock prices. The poor statement of the Flint & Pere Marquette has caused rather a depressing feeling regarding that security, but it is hoped that later statements will show improvement. Money holds steady, with indications of coming firmness.

Local money affairs are dull and steady. The Boston money market is little changed this morning, but it is good opinion that conditions are shaping towards a decidedly firmer feeling this Fall. The larger banks are reporting that the increasing demand for money outside of Boston is very significant. At clearing this morning loans were made at 3 per cent. New York funds sold at 5, 8 and 10 cents discount.

Time money is active in New York, the demand being good. The supply continues sufficient to meet any demand as yet developed, but it seems to come from sources other than banks in the city. Mercantile paper market is quiet. Hardly any paper is now being sold to city banks, and the out-of-town demand is diminishing, owing to the requirements of depositors both in New York and in manufacturing centres, for use in paying maturing bills.

The sterling exchange market is dull and easy. Rates $4.87 to $4.88½.

Bonds dull and featureless.

Wall street gossip this morning said stocks are well held and confidence is expressed in the extent and profit of the next six months' general business. The weakness of silver, prospects of higher money and increase of imports, however, are against the market, besides the example of an aggressive and powerful bear party. London is a fraction above our closing.

Stocks in New York this morning developed few new features. Sugar remained strong at 112½ to 112¾, and St. Paul moved up to 83. Other grangers were dull and steady. B. & Q. sold off, but recovered. Western Union 97¾. After 12 o'clock and up to 1 o'clock the market was dull and featureless.

The Boston market opened dull and fairly steady this morning. Later a weak spot developed in C. B. & Q., price declining to 100⅞. Atchison held 39, do. 4s 83. In coppers, Calumet at 295, was the only feature. Among specialties Sugar sold at 112, West End 73¾, do. preferred 88, General Electric 116¼ and 116. In the early afternoon the market was dull without change. C. B. & Q. reacted a fraction to 101. Steel 74 bid.

Sales to noon in Boston to-day were bonds $21,000 and 9800 shares of stock.

Westinghouse common is quoted to-day at 38 to 38¼, sales, and ditto preferred at 51¾, sales.

The strength of General Electric continues. Sales to-day at 116¼ and 116.

Prime's crop report says the indications are that the outlook for corn has improved. There is greater danger of an early frost in the Northwest this season than last. The fact is becoming more and more apparent that the reserves of corn have not been as large as reported. Bradstreet's says the crop will be over 500,000,000 bushels of wheat and that the United Kingdom, India and Russia crops will be better than anticipated.

A mining man sums up the silver situation thus:

"The low price of silver is causing silver mines to close every day, and the amount of silver produced as a by product is not sufficient to offset the loss in price. In cases where the product of silver is large the silver is of more importance than the baser metal, and the profit in mining the baser metal will not offset the loss on the silver. On the 58,330,000 fine ounces of silver produced from the mines in the United States in 1891, 28,625,000 ounces were obtained from quartz and milling ores—strictly silver ores—while 23,707,000 ounces were obtained from lead ores and only 5,998,000 ounces from copper ores. Of the 23,707,000 ounces of silver obtained in 1891 from lead ores, 10,122,000 ounces came from Colorado, while the total silver product of the State was 21,160,000 ounces. The lead product of Colorado was 41,094 tons, and the value was $3,697,106. The silver product of the State, more than half of which was from lead ores, was valued at $27,295,093, so that in Colorado at least silver cannot be considered altogether as a by product, and the low price will tend to curtail the output of silver lead ores as well as of pure silver ores."

The September dividend list at Boston looks rather lean by comparison with that of March last, the total being $5,310,494, against $6,950,759 then. A year ago they were also considerably larger, $6,760,549. This shows a net falling off in dividends of over 20 per cent. in the Boston list.

It is said the Atchison company has sold a block of its St. Louis & San Francisco bonds to wipe out the floating indebtedness due from Frisco to Atchison.

Missouri Pacific is assessed for $10,500,000 in Arkansas.

A special meeting of Fort Payne stockholders has been called for Aug. 31st.

The Mollie Gibson Consolidated Mining & Milling Co. has declared its regular monthly dividend for September, payable Sept. 15 to stock of record Sept. 8th. The transfer books close Sept. 8th and reopen Sept. 16th. The dividend is the usual 15 cents per share and calls for $150,000. This dividend is the 26th paid by the Mollie Gibson Co.

The Illinois Steel Company has signed the Amalgamated Association's scale for its North Chicago mills.

The Boston *Transcript* says:

Bond houses tell us that they have had the dullest month in the year. Last August there were a number of desirable issues of municipal, street railway, and similar bonds in market, generally offered at prices which induced good demand for investors. This month the bond houses seem to have few issues of this character. The high range of prices engendered by the great bond demand of the early months of the year restricted purchasers this Summer and the reality has not come yet, although the autumn is expected to see a fair volume of business in these securities. The movement in the industrial shares has attracted attention of investors to some extent—more so than is supposed generally—and Boston investors have realized a very substantial profit in Sugar this Summer, as well as in electric and some other shares outside of the railway group. Boston is not doing so much in railway shares or in land booms as it did once. It has learned from experience and is making up losses in other directions.

A meeting of the stockholders of the Philadelphia, Reading & New England Railroad Co. will be held in New York on Sept. 28 for the purpose of acting upon the lease of the Dutchess County road to the company. The bonds of the Philadelphia, Reading & New England Co. are expected to be ready by Oct. 1.

Aggregate earnings of 36 railroads for the third week of August were $5,583,366, an increase of $488,535.

A sale of Cleveland & Canton at 19½ was made in the Boston market this morning.

Disappointment is felt over the way Western Union moves in the market.

Deacon S. V. White passed through Boston Saturday, and in talking with a Boston gentleman said as follows:

"I see that the Boston papers say that Henry Allen & Co. sold some Sugar for me yesterday. They have never sold any Sugar for me. I traded openly in the morning, buying and selling, but my trading on Friday resulted in a net accumulation of stock. I am going down to Rockland now to bring my family up, and will arrive in New York Tuesday morning. I do not pretend to predict the fluctuations of the market, but I have always found that a market manipulated by such lies as seem to have been given out yesterday has a speedy reaction to normal conditions, and I know that the normal condition of Sugar in this market will advance it to higher prices.

Flint & Pere Marquette's latest earnings report compare as below:

Third. week August.	1892.	1891.	Dec.
Freight,	$28,767	$32,349	$3,582
Passenger,	20,468	20,696	228
Total,	$49,235	$53,045	$3,810
Since Jan. 1,	$1,815,765	$1,831,280	$15,525
Mileage,	625	625	

Salt earnings of the Flint & Pere Marquette in the third week of August, 1891, were $4161.49. Nothing was received from this source this year.

CALIFORNIA MINING STOCKS.

SAN FRANCISCO, Aug. 27.

The following are the official closing prices of mining stocks to-day:

Alta	—	Mexican	1 20
Best & Belcher	1 25	Mt. Diablo	—
Chollar	—	Ophir	2 20
Con. Cal. & Va.	3 30	Potosi	—
Crown Point	—	Savage	—
Eureka Con	—	Sierra Nevada	1 30
Gould & Curry	—	Union Con	1 10
Hale & Norcross	1 20	Utah	—

Pronounced Hopeless, Yet Saved.

From a letter written by Mrs. Ada E. Hurd, of Groton, S. D., we quote: "Was taken with a bad cold, which settled on my lungs, cough set in and finally terminated in consumption. Four doctors gave me up, saying I could live but a short time. I gave myself up to my Saviour, determined if I could not stay with my friends on earth, I would meet my absent ones above. My husband was advised to get Dr. King's New Discovery for consumption, coughs and colds. I gave it a trial, took in all eight bottles; it has cured me and thank God I am now a well and hearty woman." Trial bottles free at H. A. Blackmer's drug store, regular size, 50 cents and $1.00.

EVEN CHILDREN KNOW THAT DR. HOUGH'S COUGH AND LUNG BALSAM,
IS THE BEST FOR
Coughs, Colds, Croup or Whooping Cough.
PRICE, 35 CENTS.
Sold by all druggists and medicine dealers.

THE BORDEN INQUIRY.

[Continued from Fourth Page.]

Witness said that when she got inside the house Lizzie was so much agitated that she fanned her fearing she would faint.

Witness stated that when they went up stairs to look for Mrs. Borden they found the door of Mrs. Borden's room was open. After they saw the body they left Bridget in the room and have no knowledge of what she did there, if anything. Witness could not remember that there was the least sign of blood on her dress, hands or face at the time she first saw her; her hair was "done up" and appeared not to be disarranged in the slightest.

Mrs. Churchill said she testified at the inquest and said that during the examination there was no suspension for consultation.

Miss Alice E. Russell, the next witness, said she had known Lizzie Borden 11 years. She thought on the day of the murder that it was 11 15 when she first heard of the affair, but she didn't know why she thought so. At any rate she went to the house and found Lizzie leaning against the door and she thinks she prevailed upon Lizzie to sit down. Witness could not remember how Lizzie was dressed, but did remember Lizzie telling her in answer to a question that she went into the barn to get a piece of iron or tin to fix a window with. [Sensation.]

Witness could not tell which window she wanted to fix. Witness was a frequent visitor at the Borden house and was received in the guest room; I sometimes went two or three times a week, and I never remember seeing Mrs. Borden in that room. It was when Lizzie was sitting on the stairs that Lizzie said her father must have an enemy. It was when a policeman suggested that some of the farm hands had done the deed that Lizzie said it could not be so for one man was sick, and the other had to stay on the farm; furthermore she would not suspect either of them in connection with this case.

Witness was sure she went upstairs before Lizzie did, so far as her knowledge of what was done after she got there went. She remembered that Lizzie answered all questions freely.

On the day of the funeral witness recollected of an extended search being made of the house. Witness could not recollect whether the first search was made as thoroughly as the last search.

It was quite evident that the evidence of Miss Russell had made considerable of an impression on the defence, and when she had finished her direct examination Lizzie's counsel put their heads together and allowed the witness to sit down for a moment.

On cross-examination, Miss Russell said she bathed Lizzie's face after she went in, and saw no signs of blood on it, nor did she see any on any of her clothing. It was witness who persuaded Lizzie to go into the dining-room and lie down, but she didn't notice what kind of shoes she had on, or what kind she usually wore in the morning. She could see no signs of any undue exertion about Lizzie, nor was she panting as though exhausted. Witness was positive that Lizzie did not go up stairs before the officers, because she remembered the officers asking her questions. She remembered the officers going up to Lizzie's room and finding it locked; of their pulling the door open and of her requesting to be allowed to look in first, because she did not know what condition it was in; she looked in and finding it all right let them in.

Miss Lucy Collet was stopping at Dr. Chagnon's house on the day of the murder to take care of the telephone; she went at 11 10 and stayed until 12 o'clock noon. She sat on the piazza all the time because she could not get into the house; from where she sat she said she could see all the yard of the Bordens. During the time she was there she saw no one passing in the yard.

On cross-examination it took just 15 minutes for witness and Mr. Jennings to come to an understanding as to where the fence was located between the Chagnon and Borden residences and then witness admitted that she was where she could not see the whole of the Borden yard, but she was sure that if anybody had entered the yard, she would have heard them.

AFTERNOON SESSION.

Government Begins to Develop the Prussic Acid Theory.

Court came in at 2 p. m., and Miss Collet was recalled and on redirect examination said that she was sitting on a bench on the piazza of Dr. Chagnon's house and about two feet from the part nearest the street.

Eli Bence, drug clerk, corner South Main and Columbia streets, two streets on the left from Second street. Remember the day of the tragedy and was acquainted with Lizzie Borden. He saw her in his store the day before, and she asked him for ten cents worth of Prussic acid to put on a sealskin sack or cape. but I told her we could not sell it without a physician's prescription. My attention was called to the fact that she was in the store on Thursday, and soon after that again, or about 6 o'clock.

My attention was called to the fact that she was the daughter of Andrew Borden.

Cross-examined. She had on a dark dress, but it wasn't blue. Witness couldn't say anything about the dress, other than that it was a dark one, and he couldn't tell whether she wore a veil or had gloves on, or what kind of a hat she wore, and he could not tell whether there was any other woman there to whom he said anything, but to his sister, and he was not sure of having sold her anything.

In fact he could remember but little outside of that particular fact. He thought he sold something to Lizzie about 6 years ago, and he knew her by sight quite well because she had been pointed out to him several times.

There were three other people in the store at the time she came in, Mr. Kilroy. Mr. Harland and another.

Witness never had said to anybody that he couldn't swear that it was Lizzie Borden; had never talked about it with George Gray; had told three persons of her being there.

WEATHER INDICATIONS.

FAIR TO PARTLY CLOUDY.

NEW YORK, Aug. 29.—At 8 30 a. m. the weather was clear, wind west, temperature 70. The *Herald* says: In the Middle States and New England on Tuesday fair to partly cloudy weather will prevail, with slight temperature changes, but much sultriness and fresh southerly winds, followed by thunder storms, and on Wednesday fair, cooler weather, preceded by rain.

G. O. TAYLOR WHISKIES

Guaranteed PURE. Uniform in QUALITY.

MEDICINALLY VALUABLE and without a trace of Fusel Oil.

NOT sold in bulk or by measure. Always in Sealed bottles. Beware of Imitations and refilled bottles. SOLD generally by Druggists, Grocers, Wine Merchants and Hotels.

LOOK for Proprietors' firm name signature.

CHESTER H. GRAVES & SONS, Boston.

REFUSE SUBSTITUTES.

A MODEL SHOE.

SCHULER BROS.

PARENTS !!

SCHOOL SHOES ! ! !

You are again about to buy your Boys' and Girls' School Shoes. We have made and are selling a Boys' and Girls' calf Shoe that for wear and perfect fit we guarantee above all other kinds made. They are solid for the tough little boy and pretty for the nice little girl. They are right in kind and right in price. We make them ourselves, therefore there is no doubt about them.

Look in our windows,

76 and 78 PURCHASE ST.,

AFFAIRS IN AFGHANISTAN.

Ameer Called Upon to Withdraw His Troops from the Indian Border.

LONDON, Aug. 29.—A dispatch to the *Times* from Simla says: "The government has replied to the Ameer of Afghanistan expressing the hope that affairs will settle down and enable him to receive the Roberts mission. The government also calls upon him to withdraw his troops from Wana, west of Waziristan, where they have a disturbing effect on the Indian border. Unless this is done Gen. Roberts will not proceed to Jellallabad."

A Calcutta dispatch to the *Times* says that rumors come from various sources that the Ameer has suffered another reverse at the hands of the Hazaras.

BARK NEWFIELD WRECKED.

Eleven of Her Crew Drowned Near Port Campbell, Victoria.

MELBOURNE, Aug. 29. — The British bark Newfield, from Sharpness, May 28, for Brisbane, has been wrecked near Port Campbell, Victoria. Eleven of her crew were drowned.

Was Despondent from Sickness.

WICHITA, Kan., Aug. 29.—Thomas Drew, a young business man at the West Side, committed suicide. He lived with his parents within a short distance of the Missouri Pacific, and when he heard the noon train he bade his mother good-bye, walked deliberately to the roadbed and placed his neck across the rail. His head was cut off as cleanly as though by a guillotine. Despondency from long sickness was the cause.

Abandoned Schooner Picked Up.

BOSTON, Aug. 29. — British schooner Speedwell, for this port, with a cargo of shingles, was picked up in the bay yesterday abandoned and towed here. She is full of water, her cargo keeping her afloat. She was riding with both anchors out and had signals of distress flying in the rigging. The Speedwell was commanded by Capt. Ellis and had a crew of four men. Their fate is unknown.

STOCK AND BOND MARKETS.

Bids at the close of First Board.

NEW YORK, Aug. 29.

GOVERNMENT BONDS.	
U.S. 2s, registered	100
" new 4s, registered	115½
" new 4s, coupons	115½
" currency 6s, 1895, (Pacifics)	107
RAILROADS	
Atchison	38⅞
Clev., Cin., Chicago & St. Louis	66
Chicago & Eastern Illinois	—
Chicago & Eastern Illinois pref	—
Chicago, Burlington & Quincy	101
Delaware & Hudson	—
Delaware & Lackawanna	—
Erie	27⅛
Illinois Central	—
Lake Shore & Michigan Southern	—
Louisville & Nashville	68½
Michigan Central	—
Missouri Pacific	60½
New Jersey Central	134
New York & New England	33¼
Northern Pacific	—
Northern Pacific pref	58
Chicago & Northwestern	117¼
New York Central & Hudson River	112¼
North American	13⅜
Oregon Navigation	—
Oregon Improvement	—
Oregon Short Line	—
Philadelphia & Reading	57
Pullman Palace Car Co	198
Chicago, Rock Island & Pacific	81⅝
Chicago, Milwaukee & St. Paul	82⅝
Chicago, Milwaukee & St. Paul pref	—
Richmond Terminal	8¾
St. Paul & Omaha	52
St. Paul & Omaha pref	—
Union Pacific	38¾
Wabash, St. Louis & Pacific	—
Wabash, St. Louis & Pacific pref	—
MISCELLANEOUS	
Ontario Silver	—
Pacific Mail Steamship Co	—
Sugar, common	112⅛
Sugar, pref	104
Western Union Telegraph	97⅛
Silver Certificates	—

BOSTON, Aug. 29.

BONDS	
Atchison 4s	82⅝
Atchison Incomes	60⅛
American Bell Telephone 7s	*114
Chicago, Burlington & Northern 5s	204
Chicago & West Michigan 5s	**8
Mexican Central 4s	*68¼
Illinois Steel Co. 5s	—
RAILROADS.	
Atchison, Topeka & Santa Fe	39
Boston & Albany	205½
Boston & Lowell	—
Boston & Maine	177
Boston & Providence	250½
Chicago, Burlington & Quincy	101⅜
Chicago & West Michigan	—
Cleveland & Canton	5⅝
Cleveland & Canton pref	19⅜
Flint & Pere Marquette	—
Flint & Pere Marquette pref	74
Mexican Central	15
New York & New England	—
New York & New England pref	—
Old Colony	182½
Oregon Short Line	23½
Pullman Palace Car	197
Union Pacific	39
Wisconsin Central	*17
West End	73¾
West End pref	88
MINING.	
Butte & Boston Mining Co	9¼
Calumet & Hecla Mining Co	290
Centennial	—
Franklin Mining Co	12¼
Kearsarge	11½
Montana	36
Osceola Mining Co	31
Tamarack	160
MISCELLANEOUS.	
American Bell Telephone	*207
Erie Telephone	45¼
Mexican Telephone	1.10
New England Telephone	57
Newport Land	*1⅛
Boston Land Co	5
West End Land Co	18⅛
San Diego Land Co	—
Topeka Land & Development Co	—
Lamson Store Service	17
Illinois Steel Co	74
Am. Sugar Refineries, com	112⅛
Am. Sugar Refineries, pref	104
Gen'l Electric	116¼
Gen'l Electric	—

*Asked.

NEW YORK PRODUCE MARKET.

NEW YORK, Aug. 29.

Flour sales 4200 barrels; dull and steady.

Wheat sales 860,000; bushels; advanced ⅞ to 1c. on wet weather abroad and damage to shipping.

Corn sales 85,000 bushels; firmer and very dull.

Oats sales 25,000 bushels; dull and firmer.

Beef dull and weak.

Pork not quoted.

Lard steadier and quiet.

Butter steady and in moderate demand.

Cheese dull and weak.

Sugar (raw) quiet and firm.

Petroleum quiet.

Turpentine dull and steady.

Molasses quiet.

Rice quiet and firm.

Freights easy and dull.

Tallow quiet and firm.

It Strikes us as Remarkable

to hear of the wonderful record for curing enjoyed by Betton's Infallible Pile Salve; it cures every form of this troublesome ailment. If not to be had at your druggist,s send 50 cents to Winkelmann & Brown Drug Co., Baltimore, Md.

WANTS.

All Advertisements under this heading 1c. a word a time. No charge less than 25c.

FIRST CLASS WAITER GIRL—At Mrs. ROSEFIELD'S Dining Rooms, 315 Acushnet avenue. au29-3t

PROVISIONS AND GRAIN.

CHICAGO, Aug. 29.

	Lard.	Wheat.	Pork.	Corn.	Sh't Ribs
Opening.					
May	—	—	—	—	—
June	—	—	—	—	—
July	—	—	—	—	—
Aug.	—	—	—	—	—
Sept.	—	76	10.65	51¼	—
Oct.	—	—	—	—	—
Dec.	—	79⅛	—	50⅞	—
Jan.	—	—	12.40	—	—
12 o'clock.					
May	—	—	—	—	—
June	—	—	—	—	—
July	—	—	—	—	—
Aug.	—	—	—	—	—
Sept.	—	76½	10.65	51	—
Oct.	—	—	—	—	—
Dec.	—	79¼	—	50⅞	—
Jan.	—	—	10.40	—	—

Horsford's ACID PHOSPHATE.

An agreeable preparation of the phosphates, for Indigestion, Nervousness, Mental and Physical Exhaustion.

Recommended and prescribed by Physicians of all schools.

Trial bottle mailed on receipt of 25 cents in stamps. Rumford Chemical Works, Providence, R. I.

"A HEALING WONDER."

Comfort Powder

Is the Best "Baby Powder" in the World.

MRS. F. EDLESTEEN, 34th St., N. Y. City, says: "I have used Comfort Powder on all my four little ones. They all like it. It relieves chafing, soreness, itching instantly, and prevents contagion."

EDNA T. ROBBINS, Chelsea, Vt., says: "After having measles, I had burning, itching blotches come. A few applications of Comfort Powder completely removed them."

ALL DRUGGISTS SELL IT.
SEND POSTAL FOR FREE SAMPLE.
COMFORT POWDER CO., Hartford, Conn.
E. S. SYKES, SECRETARY.

REAL ESTATE.

FRANCIS W. TAPPAN,
Agent for Purchase, Sale, and Lease of REAL ESTATE.
Office, 15 North Water St., New Bedford. d&w

FRANK C. SMITH,
Real Estate Broker, Auctioneer and Appraiser,
Office - - 47 William Street,
(Opposite New Post Office.)

M. E. SMITH,
REAL ESTATE AGENCY.

Houses and House Lots for sale in all parts of the city on easy terms.

Good Chance for Speculators—An estate of about 950 rods of land has been placed in my hands to be sold at the very low price of

$8.50 PER ROD.

Fifteen minutes' walk from the Pierce Mill; near horse cars; Acushnet water; electric lights, &c. Will sell well cut up in house lots. Terms, $2700 cash; balance in 3 years at 6 per cent. interest.

M. E. SMITH,
619 Purchase Street. Telephone 16-11.

H. A. LEONARD, REAL ESTATE AGENT,
126 UNION STREET.

Houses and house lots in all parts of the city for sale. Three fine residences. Good bargains. Call and examine tenements to let.

JOHN WHITEHEAD,
Coggeshall, corner of Rock Street.
Real Estate Agent.

Several houses near Pierce Mill. Sale private. Also desirable lots on Geo. A. Briggs' estate on easy terms, and lots in all parts of the city. Desirable lots on Jas. Drown estate and Phillips and Coffin aves. au2-MWF1m

John Whitehead,
COGGESHALL ST., - - - - COR. ROCK.

Has for sale 12 two-tenement houses near the mills, which pay 10 per cent. interest. Easy terms. au26-18t

Very Desirable House Lots.

Near Bliss Corner, $3 a rod and upwards. Good chance for speculators. DANIEL SWEENEY, Cove Road. au22-12t

EDWIN JONES,
REAL ESTATE AGENT.......884 PURCHASE ST.

FOR SALE.—Lots in all parts of the city; some bargains. Also a good 2½ story house, nearly new, well arranged, convenient to mills at North End, now rents for $260 a year; cheap.

BUSINESS SOLICITED. au24-6t

COTTAGE HOUSE—53 Chestnut street, with 18¼ rods of land; house is fitted with modern conveniences. Can be seen afternoons and evenings. V. F. HATCH, 31 North Water street. au23-tf

Cottage House.

Well built, good repair, in part of city growing rapidly; will make good home and *must* increase in value. Apply box 6, *Standard* office. ap25-tf

FOR SALE—In South Dartmouth, near the water, a 2½ story house with large piazza, barn, and 83 rods of land. One of the most desirable places in the village for a Summer residence. Inquire of BENJ. QUERIPEL or DANIEL H. HOWLAND, South Dartmouth. ap7-tf

AUCTION SALES.

By STANDISH BOURNE,
(Successor to Geo. A. Bourne & Son,)
Auctioneer, Commission Merchant, Real Estate Dealer and Appraiser.

Cash advanced on goods consigned for auction. Ready buyer for personal property of every description.

Office and Salesrooms 47, 49 and 51 North Second Street, near the Post Office.

Restaurant Stock and Fixtures.

On TUESDAY, Aug. 30, at 2 o'clock, at the store of W. D. Moor, No. 70 William street, will be sold the entire stock and fixtures pertaining to the restaurant business.

Paine Farm on Sconticut Neck.

On WEDNESDAY, Aug. 31, at 3 o'clock, on the premises, will be sold in the following manner, the above named farm;

1st.—Lot situated on the east side of the road on the north end of the farm, containing about 25 acres, more or less.

2d.—Lot joining No. 1 on the south, containing about 25 acres, more or less.

3d.—Farm house, barn, out-buildings and about 20 acres, more or less.

4th.—Lot joining No. 3 on the south, containing 15 acres, more or less.

5th.—We reserve the right to put these parcels up in one sale and if a larger bid can be obtained than the sum of the separate sales, that bid will be the binding sale.

Plenty of time before the sale to get your clam dinner held for the benefit of the Union Chapel at Dunn's Grove.

Mortgagee's Sale.

On SATURDAY, Sept. 3, at 12¾ o'clock, on the premises, will be sold by order of the mortgagee, the nearly new 2½ story house and lot containing about 21.38 rods, situated on the south side of North street, numbered 162. For legal advertisement see *Evening Standard* of August 9, 16, 23.

Executor's Sale of Real Estate.

On WEDNESDAY, Sept. 21, at 3 o'clock in the afternoon, on the premises, will be sold by order of the executor under the will of the late Russell Maxfield the homestead of said Maxfield, situated on the southwest corner of Maxfield and Walden streets.

The house is first-class built, in good repair, with lot of about 14½ rods, having a frontage of 49½ feet on Maxfield street by 81 feet on Walden street.

IVORY S. CORNISH, Executor.
au27-s3-10

To Let in Our Storage Warerooms.

We constantly have on hand first-class rooms for the storage of household goods, to be rented by the month or year.

Good dry storage room for stoves.

By JOHN B. BAYLIES,
121 and 123 Union Street,
Commission Merchant, Appraiser, and Auctioneer for the sale of Real Estate and every description of Personal Property. Furniture Bought.

H. C. HATHAWAY,
Auctioneer, Real Estate Agent and Appraiser,
Corner Acushnet Ave. and Elm St.

One of the best auction marts in the State for the sale of horses and carriages. Keeps constantly on hand carriages of every description, carriages made to order and repairing in all its branches attended to under the superintendency of J. R. Forbes. Consignments of every description solicited. Cash advanced on goods for auction. Personal property of every description bought at short notice for cash. Negotiable notes bought and sold.

2 1-2 Story House and Lot.

On SATURDAY, Sept. 3d, at 12¾ o'clock, P. M., on the premises will be sold at public auction, the 2½ story house on Foster street together with the lot which will be described at the sale. Said house was moved from the Kempton street schoolhouse lot and fitted in good order, being fitted for two families and is situated on Foster street, just south of the building used by the Veteran Firemen's Association. The property is sold by order of the Committee on Public Property.

STEPHEN A. BROWNELL, Chairman.

Terms 10 per cent. at sale balance on delivery of deed. aug29

Mortgagee's Sale.

By virtue of a power of sale contained in a certain mortgage deed given by Abisha B. Bean to Alban C. Snow, dated June 30, 1888, and recorded with the Bristol County S. D. land records in book 128, at pages 348, 349 and 350, and for breach of the condition thereof, will be sold at public auction upon the premises on SATURDAY, the 3d day of September, 1892, at three o'clock in the afternoon, all and singular the premises convey by said deed, viz.: A certain lot of land with the buildings thereon, standing, situated in New Bedford, in said County of Bristol, bounded and described as follows: Beginning at the northeast corner thereof in the south line of Walnut street, at land now or formerly of Sarah Corey; thence westerly in said south line of Walnut street, twenty-nine (29) feet to land formerly of Edward Seabury, thence southerly in said Seabury's line to the north line of land now of William Rafferty, seventy-six (76) feet; thence easterly in said Rafferty's line about twenty-nine (29) feet to said Rafferty's west line, and thence northerly in said Rafferty's line and in line of land of said Sarah Corey seventy-six (76) feet to the point of beginning; containing eight (8) rods, more or less. Being the same premises conveyed to Ann C. Brodhead by Nathan S. Ellis, by deed, dated October 30, 1858, and recorded in book 37, pages 340 and 341. Terms 10 per cent. at time of the sale, remainder on delivery of mortgagee's deed within ten days. Estate of Benjamin Almy, Assignee.

au8-15-22-29 SOPHIA ALMY, Executrix.

ALFRED WILSON,
Auctioneer and Real Estate Agent,
Room 22, - - - Robeson Building.

Houses and land in all parts of the city for sale; tenements for rent: rents collected

For Sale.

Two-story house on Acushnet avenue, near Walnut street; well arranged for one family; good location.

For Lease.

The Webster Block, Purchase street; 16 rooms, well adapted for a genteel boarding house, club rooms, or business purposes.

TO LET—A flat in The Winslow, corner Sixth and Union streets. Apply to A. WILSON, Robeson Building. jy14-tf

T. F. HEALEY,
Auctioneer and Real Estate Agent,
555 and 559 Purchase street, corner of Franklin street.

FOR SALE CHEAP—One farm in Rochester of 70 acres; house, barn, outbuildings, etc.; 2 good orchards on place; cut 20 tons of hay. Price $1800.

Also two cottages in Fairhaven; nearly new; fine view of river and harbor; will sell one or both; situated on Main street; will sell to the right parties on easy terms.

Also one fine house in the west part of the city in good locality, with all the modern improvements, gas and electric lights, etc. Will be sold cheap if applied for soon.

Also lots on Acushnet avenue, Coggshall and Locust streets, in fact all parts of the city.

Business solicited. No charges made unless a sale, then my prices are the lowest.

By WM. BARKER, Jr.

Valuable Real Estate, Engine, Machinery, Horses, Wagons, &c., at Auction.

WILL be sold on the premises, SATURDAY, Sept. 3d, 1892, at 1 o'clock P. M., that desirable property well known as the Crapo Wood Yard, on Court street, in this city, consisting of 40 rods of land with buildings, engine, boiler, shafting and other machinery. Also, two one-horse lumber wagons, two express wagons, two horses (one a superior animal,) two express harnesses, and various other articles.

Aug. 22, 1892. au22-ts

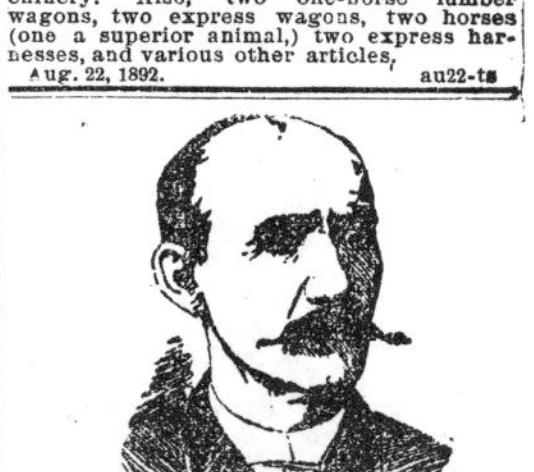

By J. O. DOUGLASS.

REGULAR AUCTION SALE,

Thursday, Sept. 1st, 1892, at 10 15 A. M.

OF 25 horses from Indiana and Canada; all young, fresh stock consisting of family, driving, farm and general business horses; weighing 1000 to 1200 lbs.; well broken to single and double harness. In this lot are some extra driving horses, some that can show good speed. Also a number of acclimated horses; been used in and about the city. Harnesses, whips, foot mats, etc.

Knowles & Co.

Cor. UNION & FOURTH STS.

Bargains in All-Wool Dress Goods, 40-inch all-wool goods, suitable for early Fall wear, 39c. Cheap at 50c.

Storm Serges in Black and Navy, all-wool, 40-inch, 50c.; 46-inch 75c.; 46-inch extra value, $1.00.

Black All-Wool Henriettas, 46-inch, 75c.; extra fine and heavy, $1.00 and $1.25; 46-inch, All-Wool, India Twill, 75c. and $1.00.

Beautiful styles in Ginghams at 10 and 12 1-2c. Large assortment to select from.

Ladies' full regular finished, Fast Black Hose, the best hose in the market for 25c. Also Ladies' Fast Black Hose, worth 50c. Three pairs in a box $1.00.

Ladies' Summer weight merino vests and pants 50c. each.

Gentlemen's Summer weight merino shirts and drawers 50c.

Gentlemen's unlaundered shirts, reinforced linen fronts and cuffs, double backs, good cotton, best shirt in the market, 50c.

Ladies' corset covers at 12 1-2, 25, 37 1-2 and 50c., in high, low, square and V shaped necks, handsomely trimmed, and decided bargains.

Ladies' and misses' night gowns, made of good materials and elegantly trimmed, at 50, 65, and 88c., $1, $1.25 and up.

Ladies' corsets, in all the popular makes, at from 49c. up to the very finest goods.

Best Germantown yarns, large full skeins, in 150 shades and colors, at only 12 1-2c. a skein.

Stamped Linens, Trays, Tidies, Splashers, Pillow Shams, Scarfs, all at popular low prices.

All kinds of embroidery and fancy working silk cheap. Knitting silk of best quality, large assortment of colors and shades at 30c. a ball. Best sewing silk in black and colors, 8c.

Table Linens, Brown and Bleached at 45c. worth 59c. Napkins at 50 and 75c, $1.00, $1.25, $1.50 and $2.00 per dozen. Towels at 12 1-2c., 19c., 25c., 37c., and 50c. up.

Lot of standard white ground prints, 5c. a yard. When out shopping don't fail to visit our store for we have just what you are looking for, and at lowest possible prices

Knowles & Co.

FINE CIGARS

—AND—

Tobacco.

Cigars by the Box a Specialty

—AT—

E. B. SHERMAN'S,

62 Purchase St.

jy19-8pMWS

STABBED TO DEATH.

Serious Result of a Quarrel Caused by Rum and Politics.

VANDALIA, Wis., Aug. 29.—A sickening tragedy occurred in Avena, in this county, in which John D. Frailey was stabbed to death by Charles Chandler, his brother-in-law. Both are well-to-do farmers. They came to Vandalia accompanied by Mrs. Chandler, mother of the murderer. Frailey was a Republican and Chandler a Democrat. Both men had been drinking and they quarreled along the road over politics. Chandler finally got out of the wagon and said he would walk. Frailey declared he should ride, and climbed out and began plying the whip to Chandler. Chandler drew his knife and stabbed Frailey once in the back and twice in the left side. During the altercation the horses became frightened and started to run. Frailey called to Chandler to stop cutting him, and to catch the horses. Frailey got up and started with Chandler after the horses, when he complained of feeling sick and sank down by the roadside and expired in the presence of Chandler and his mother.

Instantly Killed.

RUTLAND, Vt., Aug. 29.—The boiler in the electric light station at Brandon, a town six miles north of here, exploded. Adolphus Germond, 50 years old, was instantly killed, and his son Joseph Germond, the engineer, and Charles Hayles, the assistant engineer, were very badly injured.

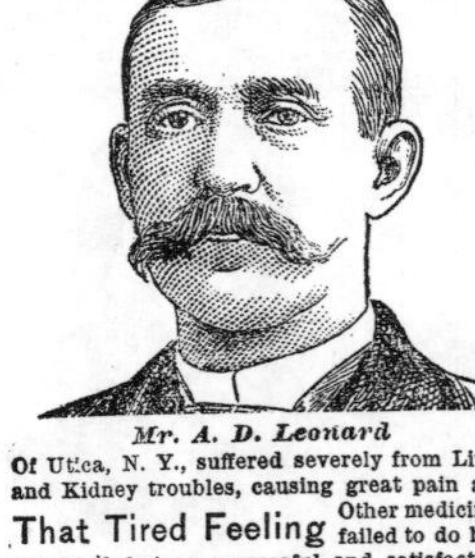

Mr. A. D. Leonard

Of Utica, N. Y., suffered severely from Liver and Kidney troubles, causing great pain and That Tired Feeling. Other medicines failed to do him any good, but so successful and satisfactory was Hood's Sarsaparilla that he has taken no other medicine and is now well. The best known **kidney and liver** remedies are so happily combined with tonics and alteratives in

Hood's Sarsaparilla

that it is an unequalled remedy for all troubles with these important organs, overcomes That Tired Feeling and **makes the weak strong.**

HOOD'S PILLS cure Habitual Constipation by restoring peristaltic action of the alimentary canal.

SENATOR DAWES.

Why He is Not a Candidate for Re-election.

Tired of Public Life After Long Career in Congress.

Sketch of Important Events in His Eventful Life.

PITTSFIELD, Mass., Aug. 29.—Senator Dawes was found by a press representative in his library at his home on Elm street, Pittsfield. He received the reporter cordially, and was free to talk about his letter, announcing that he would withdraw from a renomination to the United States senate.

Mr. Dawes said: "I have for some time been considering this step, and when I had fully made up my mind to withdraw from the senate, I thought it a duty I owed the commonwealth, and especially to the Republican party, to write the letter that I have, emphatically announcing that I was not a candidate for re-election. I have taken time to consider the matter, and I think when my term of service expires next March that I should be relieved from any further public duties. I shall have been in congress at the time my term expires thirty-six years—eighteen years in the house and eighteen years in the senate. I think this is about as long a time as any man could be expected to serve continuously. I wish to spend the remainder of my days quietly at my home here. Of course I shall practice law more or less as long as my health remains as good as it is now."

"Do you take this step, Mr. Dawes, on account of your health?"

"No, not at all. My health is as good now as it was six years ago, and even better. In fact, during the last five or six years I have been in good health, and I am perfectly well now."

Talks of His Record.

The reporter asked Mr. Dawes what he considered the most important part of his career in congress. He said: "That is a hard question to answer, but I should say as important a place as I ever filled was that of chairman of the ways and means committee in the house. I was chairman of the committee for four years. During that time three of the most important tariff bills that have ever passed went through both branches of congress and are now on the statute books."

Mr. Dawes also spoke of the tariff measure of 1868, when John A. Bingham of Ohio represented the wool growers and Mr. Dawes the wool manufacturers of the country. The bill that passed congress at that time was one of the most important ones in the history of the country, and has been on the statute books ever since. It has been the foundation of the tariff legislation in congress from that time to this, and history shows that it is an exceedingly important measure. The senior senator also spoke of the excitement which existed in Washington the winter before the war, at the time that Floyd ordered the removal of the guns to the south. He also spoke of the remarkable career of Stanton from that time on through the war. Mr. Dawes said that this was the most exciting time that he has ever experienced in the thirty-six years that he has been in congress. It was not known one day what the next would bring forth. Mr. Dawes was one of the secret committee to ascertain what was being done in the president's cabinet at that time. He said that he and two or three other men

Acted as Private Detectives,

and they were able day after day to inform the members of congress what was going on in the secret sessions of the cabinet. They had a friend in the cabinet who gave them the information, leaving notes at the roots of a certain tree in Washington, which Mr. Dawes and another member of the secret committee got and revealed the contents to the members of the house next day. This important work gave the clue to what was going on, and was an exceedingly important measure in view of the impending war. These facts have never been printed.

When the senator was asked about his career in the senate, he said that he had enjoyed his years in the senate quite as much as in the house. His work there had been more exciting, and had occupied a great deal of time, especially the committee work. He spoke particularly of the chairmanship of the committee on Indian affairs, and said: "I have visited nearly every Indian agency in this country, even going to Alaska during the time I have been chairman of this committee. I felt it necessary to make myself perfecely familiar with Indian affairs, and found that I could not do so unless I visited them at their homes. I have visited agencies in Indian territory, Dakota, California and other places many times, and last year I made the trip to Alaska. What I have accomplished for the Indians is a matter of history, and does not need repetition, I do not say that I have accomplished all this, but I do say that the committee on Indian affairs has always worked in harmony, and has been able to carry measures through congress to the advantage of the red men. While we have done our duty by the Indians, we have also been able to show to the world that the American people are disposed to be humane toward them."

Mr. Dawes has always taken an active part in the discussions of the senate as he did in the house. His opposition to authorizing the coinage of silver dollars, his work on the committee on appropriations, of which he is still a member, and other matters which have come up in the senate during his career there, do not need repetition.

His Early Days.

The early career of Senator Dawes is well known to his Berkshire constituency and pretty well known throughout the state.

He was born in Cummington in 1816, graduated from Yale college in 1830 and taught school in Windsor and other towns on the east borders of Berkshire for several years, during the whole time using his spare moments to study law. When he was admitted to the bar he commenced practice in North Adams and had his office in a little stone building which occupied the site where Boland's block now stands on Main street.

"I have lived economically all the while I have been in congress," said the senator, "and find that I come out with about the same amount of money that I went in with. I own my home here in Pittsfield, but I have not got rich out of my long career as a public servant."

Funeral of Jacob Wirth.

BOSTON, Aug. 29.—The remains of Jacob Wirth were buried at Forest Hill cemetery yesterday afternoon. Mr. Wirth died at Reichenhall, Bavaria, on Aug 10, of heart failure. The body was embalmed and brought to Boston by his widow, who had accompanied him to Europe.

Suicide with a Halter.

MANCHESTER, N. H., Aug. 29.—David P. Campbell, a well-known citizen of Bedford, aged 55, committed suicide by hanging himself with a halter to a pine tree. Despondency was assigned as the cause. A daughter and two brothers survive him.

Highest of all in Leavening Power.—Latest U. S. Gov't Report.

Royal Baking Powder

ABSOLUTELY PURE

DELUDED HEBREWS.

Lured to Ziontown Under Promise of Work and Left Destitute.

PHILADELPHIA, Aug. 29.—A number of the Hebrew section of the Federation of Labor from New York spent yesterday at Ziontown, N. J., a Hebrew settlement, investigating the charges that people had been induced to go there and invest their money in homes under promise of work and were left destitute and actually starving by Jacob Zion, a New York manufacturer, who owns all the property of the settlement.

The condition of affairs was found to be serious. Instances of two or three families being saved from starvation only by eating green fruit and with what little food they could beg in the neighborhood were discovered. The settlement consists of about thirty Hebrew families, most of whom came directly from Castle Garden and have every cent they own invested either in lots or half finished houses. For six weeks they have had no work.

HIS LABORS ENDED.

Death of Rev. William Ware After Fifty Years of Missionary Life.

SPRINGFIELD, Mass., Aug. 29.—A cable message announces the death on Friday, in Jaffna, Ceylon, of Rev. William Ware Howland, for nearly fifty years missionary of she American board on that island.

Mr. Howland was born at West Brookfield in 1817, graduated from Amherst college in 1841, and was ordained for the work in 1845, after completing a course in the Union Theological seminary. Four of his children became missionaries, the oldest, Rev. William S. Howland, was at Madura, India, and died while in this country in 1887. The second, Rev. Samuel W. Howard, is president of Jaffna college, Jaffna, Ceylon. The only daughter, Miss Susan R. Howland, is principal of a young woman's seminary in Jaffna, while Rev. John Howland is missionary of the American board in Mexico. Mr. Howland had not visited his native country since 1861.

Creditors by the Hundred.

JACKSON, Mich., Aug. 29.—The W. F. Cowham failure has developed into the most complicated and serious wreck that has occurred in this city. Creditors are still arriving from various parts of the country and there are now representatives of over a hundred of them in the city. Their claims will reach the first estimate of $250,000. The creditors have made every effort to get their account of goods, but in every instance a large share of stock has been disposed of. The books show that many of the goods have been shipped by the company, and the creditors have secured Wilson & Cobb, attorneys, and some twenty suits have been begun. They believe they will be able to show fraud and propose to push the cases to the end.

A Noted Culprit Jailed.

ST. LOUIS, Aug. 29.—A man who is said to have served in the French, English and Egyptian armies has been arrested on the charge of procuring money in Boston by means of a bogus check. This noted culprit calls himself E. C. G. Byron Dumas, and claims to be a cousin of the celebrated French novelist of that name. The charge is that while teaching the art of fencing and languages in Boston, he forged the signature of the John P. Lovell Arms company to a check for $650, cashed it and fled. Traced to Chicago he locked a detective in a hotel room and fled to St. Louis.

Socialist Labor Party Convention.

NEW YORK, Aug. 29.—The Socialist Labor party held its national convention here yesterday. Delegates from New York, Pennsylvania, Massachusetts, New Jersey and Connecticut were present. David Taylor of Boston presided and Henry Glynn of New York was elected secretary. It was unanimously resolved to nominate a presidential ticket, and the following candidates were put up: President, Simon Wing of Boston; vice-president, Charles H. Matchett of Brooklyn. Mr. Wing is a tailor and Mr. Matchett a carpenter.

Sealing Vessels Seized.

PORT TOWNSEND, Wash., Aug. 29.—Advices from Sitka, Alaska, per steamship Mexico, state that the whaling bark Lydia was seized in Behring sea while transferring sealskins to the bark Northern Light. She was fined $100, and released. Captain Hanson of the schooner Winifred, seized in Behring sea for illegal sealing, waived examination and was released on $500 bonds, on a charge of violation of the revenue laws.

Luttberg Downs McFadden.

ST. LOUIS, Aug. 29.—Five hundred people saw Max Luttberg defeat Barnie McFadden in a wrestling match at the Grand Opera house for the American welterweight championship and a purse of $1000. Both falls, catch-as-catch-can, were won by Luttberg, the first in 51 1-2 minutes and the second in 1 hour and 4 minutes.

INTERESTING FIGURES

Gleaned by New York State's Commissioner of Labor.

ALBANY, Aug. 29.—Charles F. Peck, commissioner of labor for New York state, has issued his annual report. A large portion is devoted to figures of interest in relation to the tariff. In order to prove whether "protection" as advocated by one political party or "tariff for revenue only" would prove of advantage, statistics have been gathered to show in every industry in the state the increase or decrease of production and comparative increase or decrease in wages.

The period covered by investigation includes the year immediately prior to the enactment of what is termed the "McKinley bill" and the year immediately following its becoming a law. That is, the data upon which the report has been made for the year commencing Sept. 1, 1889, up to and including Aug. 31, 1890, and the year commencing Sept. 1, 1890, up to and including Aug. 31, 1891.

Wages, Production and Industries.

It appears that there was a net increase in wages of $6,377,025.09 in the year 1891, as compared with 1890, and a net increase of production of $31,315,130.68 in the year 1891 over that of 1890. A simple analysis of this further demonstrates the interesting fact that of the 67 industries covered, 77 per cent. of them show an increase either of the wages or product, or both, and that there were no less than 89,717 instances of individual increase of wages during the same year.

While the "industries" are but 67 in number, the total "trades" represented amount to 1121, and give employment to 285,000 workingmen and women. Of the 67 industries included, 75 per cent. of them show an increase average yearly earning in the year 1891, while the total average increase of the 285,000 employes was $23.11. The average increase of yearly earnings of the employes in the 51 trades showing an increase was $43.96 in 1891, as compared with 1890.

The Total Number of Strikes

reported for the year 1891 was 4519, as against 6258 occurring in the year 1890, a decrease of 1739. Of the total number—4519—2375, or 53 per cent. of them, were in the building trades, a fact that seems to follow in natural sequence the results obtained in the special investigation of the "effect of the tariff on labor and wages."

A PRETTY ROMANCE.

Son of a Chicago Lumber Dealer Secretly Weds a Chambermaid.

LOUISVILLE, Aug. 29.—J. R. Bancroft and Mary Ridge were secretly married at Jeffersonville, Ind., last week. The particulars have just been divulged, and reveal a pretty romance. Bancroft is the son of a lumber dealer in Chicago and his bride was a chambermaid at French Lyck Spring at the time of the marriage. Four weeks ago Bancroft visited the Springs, intending to spend a few days. The first day of his visit he met the girl. The following day he fell and broke his hip, necessitating his staying at the hotel for some time. While confined to his room the girl was tireless in her attention to him, and last Saturday when he recovered he proposed to her that they go to Jeffersonville and get married. Miss Ridge consented and the ceremony was performed. The bride's parents reside at Jeffersonville, but as they are Catholics she refrained from telling them of her marriage. She pretended to them to have been in Jeffersonville on a visit. The facts leaked out and the parents have determined that the ceremony be performed by a priest.

The Iron Hall Muddle.

INDIANAPOLIS, Ind., Aug. 29.—The determination of the visiting members of the Iron Hall to call a meeting of representatives of all the branches throughout the country for Sept. 12 and endeavor to resurrect the order is causing great activity among the local members, and they generally agree that something in the way of order may be brought about out of the chaos of affairs. There are 1200 local branches of the order, and these have reserve funds aggregating $1,300,000. If this sum can be utilized by the new order it is believed it will be maintained.

Died of Smallpox.

NEW YORK, Aug. 29.—Tomaso Lombardo, an Italian, 8 months old, died of smallpox in a crowded tenement in this city. The health board was notified and the house disinfected. The child became ill a week ago, and no physician was summoned until Saturday night. Two other children in the Lombardi family have had the disease.

Suicide of a Veteran.

WORCESTER, Mass., Aug. 29.—Levi S. Bigelow, a veteran of the Fifty-first regiment, committed suicide by drowning in Lake Quinsigamond. Ill health was the cause. He was 66 years old.

We Have Quite a Number of

REMNANTS

In all Grades of

CARPETING AND MATTINGS!

On which we have made

Special Low Prices

DURING AUGUST.

BRIGGS & LAWRENCE,

197 and 203 Union Street.

From Saturday's Third Edition.

NO WOMAN IN THE CASE.

Denial of Scandal in the Ball Disappearance.

New Bedford Mill Overseer's Family Reunited.

He Has Been Working as House Painter in Albany.

Was Completely Mentally Unbalanced When He Fled.

Few Unexplained Features in Connection with the Case.

[Special Dispatch.]

WOONSOCKET, Aug. 27.—Theophilus C. Ball, the New Bedford mill overseer who disappeared June 5 last from Providence, arrived in this city, where his family now are, last evening.

Despite all the efforts of the family and the police of several cities nothing authentic seems to have been known of his whereabouts until last Wednesday when he wrote his wife here from Albany, N. Y., that he was coming home.

His son, William E. Ball of this city, immediately went to Albany, returning with his father as above stated.

Notwithstanding that Ball is at home evidently in good health, and it is said in his right mind, the element of mystery promises not to be cleared.

A *Reporter* representative called at his home to-day and found the gentleman and his family very reticent as to the cause of his flight and long silence.

They insisted that the public's interest in the matter could not be considered.

It was evident to the reporter that the husband and father had been warmly welcomed and the happiness of a family reunion was visible in the faces of those present, although Mrs. Ball suffered most poignantly during the past two months of doubt and anxiety.

The son above alluded to was asked about rumors concerning the moral side of the disappearance and said that he had himself investigated in Albany and disproved the existence of "the woman in the case."

The reporter was able to add to this assurance his own investigations into a bit of scandal afloat some time ago in connection with the case which he had run down by locating the woman in a near town, to which, purely by coincidence he had removed at the time of the disappearance.

Ball has been working as a house painter in Albany and living very quietly in a boarding house there.

In the next house to his boarding-house lived relatives of his, and the fact that they did not reveal his whereabouts is another unexplained feature of the case.

The son says his father was, at the time of his disappearance, suffering mentally from business troubles, the after effects of la grippe and the excessive use of quinine, so that he was almost if not completely unbalanced at that time.

EVERY CASK FILLED.

Whaling Schooner Baltic at Vineyard Haven from Hatteras Grounds.

VINEYARD HAVEN, Aug. 27.—Whaling schooner Baltic, Dyer, from Hatteras Grounds for Provincetown, every cask full of sperm oil, arrived here to-day.

THIRD DISTRICT COURT.

BORDEN, J.

SATURDAY AFTERNOON, Aug. 27.

The court came in at half-past two, and Elizabeth Ripley, who appealed this morning from a sentence of $50 for unlawfully keeping intoxicating liquor, withdrew her appeal and paid the fine.

The case against Albert C. McIntyre, charged with larceny of a suit of clothes from the boarding-house of Lucy A. Brightman was resumed. Mrs. Brightman, said she came to the central station as soon as she missed the clothes and swore out a complaint; that it was the next day after McIntyre went away. The police could not find him and did not until they found him in the House of Correction where he was serving a sentence for a similar offense.

Inspector Hathaway said when the warrant was issued he looked for but could not find McIntyre. He found him in the House of Correction in this city. McIntyre said when he left the city the day the officers were looking for him he took the train at Acushnet Station. He said he was serving sentence for the larceny of clothes at Taunton. He was arrested in Worcester and if it had not been for a woman and liquor he should not have got into the Taunton scrape.

McIntyre took the stand and denied all knowledge of the affair and said he only stayed at Mrs. Brightman's two nights. He came out of jail this morning where he had been serving a sentence of four months for the larceny of a vest at Taunton. Up to two years ago he made his home in Worcester, previous to that at St. Johnsbury, Vt. He came here to work for the Singer Sewing Machine Company.

Mr. St. Germain argued that there was no evidence to make out the charge, and asked for his client's discharge. The evidence was purely circumstantial, if there was any at all.

McIntyre was adjudged guilty and was sentenced to the House of Correction for four months, and appealed. He was ordered to recognize in $300.

Joaquim Lomba was brought into court this afternoon by Officer Cannavan on a warrant charging him with the larceny of a bicycle valued at $30, the property of Thomas H. Mills, on the 24th inst. Mr. Cannavan arrested him at East Wareham this morning. He was working for a Mr. Nickerson on a cranberry bog. He pleaded not guilty and the case was continued to Wednesday next.

Seventy-eight applications for naturalization, for which the fees amounted to $131, were filed in court this afternoon.

IRON HALL FUNDS ATTACHED.—Charles S. Calhoon of Local Branch No. 195 of the Iron Hall has attached the reserve fund of the order deposited in the Five Cents Savings Bank and the New Bedford Institution for Savings for a final benefit claim of $1000, which matured May 20th.

NATURALIZATION.—Mathias Offenwanger filed a primary declaration in the Third District Court this afternoon. J. I. da Terra, Esq., for petitioner.

Imprisoned Miners Rescued.

LONDON, Aug. 27.—At 1 30 o'clock it was stated that 39 of the imprisoned miners had been rescued and brought to the pit head. It is doubted that any of the others are alive.

DAY OF CONFLAGRATIONS.

Metropolitan Opera House, New York, in Ruins.

Many Persons Injured in a Fire in a Big Brick Block.

Baptist Church and Other Buildings Burned in Petersham.

NEW YORK, Aug. 27.—The Metropolitan Opera House, one of the most magnificent and expensive of modern playhouses, occupying the entire block bounded by Broadway, Seventh avenue, Thirty-ninth and Fortieth street in the short space of an hour this morning was ruined by fire. The Broadway front was saved by the firemen but fully three-quarters of the square was destroyed by the flames.

Just where the fire started is as yet unknown, but it must have been in the vicinity of the stage which backs Seventh avenue. How the flames got under such a headway is a mystery. The special building signal was rung at about 9 30, and in less than 20 minutes engine No. 27, quartered at 37th street near Seventh avenue, was at the Opera House. Then the entire interior of the theatre was a mass of fire.

As it was apparent that the block would be consumed help was called without delay. Over a dozen steamers responded, and as it was clear that there was no saving of the theatre the efforts were exerted to save the Broadway front, in which are the Bank of New Amsterdam and Zancheries Gazza's restaurant. The former covers the Thirty-ninth street corner and the latter the Fortieth street corner. This they succeeded in doing with the assistance of the wind, which was blowing strongly from the east, and swept the flames back towards Seventh avenue.

The offices in six stories of the front were not touched by the fire, but those of the opera house company which were on the Thirty-ninth street side near Seventh avenue were partly gutted and deluged with water. There was an expensive library in this portion which was also more or less ruined. Only one person is known to have been injured. His name is Cornelius Maus and he was employed by Alfred Oport, the scenic artist, who was using a part of the opera house temporarily as his studio.

Oport arrived at the theatre just as the fire was discovered and had the mortification of seeing the work of art burn upon which he had spent much of his time and had travelled over the world to sketch. Most of the pictures which he was engaged on were for use at the World's Fair and Columbian celebration. These were all ruined, together with scenery for new plays to be produced in a few days at various theatres.

Shortly before 10 o'clock the roof had been burned through and the flames shot high into the air. This rent assisted the firemen materially in saving the Broadway front. Half an hour later the flames, having in the meantime eaten up everything, had literally burned themselves out and the fire was then under control. The interior of the theatre had been overhauled and thoroughly fitted for the season, which would have taken place in a short time. When the flames had been subdued to permit of entrance to the building it was seen that the stage and everything in the proscenium arch to the rear wall on Seventh avenue had been entirely swept away, excepting the bare walls.

In the auditorium, the five tiers that rose above the arches still remained, but all the trappings of the boxes, the upholsterings of the chairs, the frescoes of the walls and dome had vanished. The flames burned fiercely, but they did not make their way through the roof, and that remained. Further than the entrance doors to the auditorium the flames had not succeeded in making their way. No trace of the flames were seen in that part of the building fronting on the corner. On Broadway it rises to a height of seven stories. This portion of the building was not even injured by water, nor did the occupants find it necessary to leave. The loss is estimated at $400,000, and is covered by insurance.

Brick Block in Ruins.

A disastrous fire broke out in the large five story brick building Nos. 120 and 126 Wooster street, which extends through to Nos. 120 and 122 Prince street. Over 100 persons were in the building at the time and many were injured in escaping. Many are missing. The fire originated in the basement of the building, occupied by the United States Frame and Picture Company, and spread with great rapidity.

The inmates fled from all available exits but many were injured in their efforts to escape. The following injured are reported: Mary E. Hanley, Catharine street, seriously burned, will die; Mary Guinseo, 219 Thompson street, body burned; Danny Stack, engineer, frightfully injured by falling walls; Jacob Langwasser, engineer, 33, injured by falling walls. The injured were removed to St. Vincent's Hospital.

The total damage has not been estimated, but it will be very heavy.

WORCESTER, Aug. 27.—The Baptist church, three residences and a boarding stable in the town of Petersham were burned last night. Origin supposed to be incendiary. The insurance is $10,000. The stable was owned by James Brooks and residences by Mr. Foster, Capt. Mudge and George Marsh.

AUGUSTA, Ga., Aug. 27.—The *Chronicle* building and property in the vicinity to the value of $300,000 were burned this morning.

NO GAMES TO-DAY.

Tennis Cranks Unable to Play on the Slippery Courts at Newport.

NEWPORT, Aug. 27.—It was wretched tennis weather again to-day, or more properly speaking, no tennis weather at all. More rain fell during the night than the night before, and consequently the courts were in even worse condition than yesterday. Not even the steam roller could render their soft and sloppy surface hard and firm enough to play on.

But the wind blew a small cyclone across the lawn, trees swayed in the gale almost to the point of breaking, while spectators and players alike sought shelter under the balconies from the biting blasts; for it was cold, bitterly cold, cold enough to be unseasonable almost, in October. Yesterday's weather, which was itself in league with rheumatism and pneumonia, was not a circumstance to the piercing chill.

Early in the morning it was hoped that play might be called under no more unfavorable conditions than on Friday, but as the morning wore on, it became apparent that there could be no comfort or safety for either players or spectators and the announcement was posted "No games to-day." A few thought the conditions no worse than on Friday, but they were only a few, and, if the truth were told, the weather yesterday was really unfit for play.

SOME oatmeals, I am told, are bitter.

H-O

Hornby's Oatmeal

Is sweet.

IT COSTS NOTHING

—TO—

Read This:

In fact, it may be the means of saving you $15 or $20. Does it mean anything to you if you can buy say a $60 Chamber Suit for $48? Or a $100 Suit for $80? These chances don't come often. The price of Every Suit is marked in plain figures, so you can deduct 20 per cent. and get the net price you will have to pay. This discount is given strictly for cash, but terms will be made to accommodate instalment customers. While they last (about 90 patterns,) for 80 cents on the dollar at

F. R. SLOCUM,

Housefurnisher,

354 & 362 Acushnet Av.

THE IRON HALL.

Petition for a Receiver for the Order in This State.

BOSTON, Aug. 27.—Joshua B. Stearn of Lynn, and other members of the Iron Hall have petitioned the court for an injunction restraining the officers of the order from transacting any further business in this State, and have asked for a receiver. The petitioners claim that the order has become wholly insolvent and unable to meet its obligations.

Creditors' Meeting.

BOSTON, Aug. 27.—At a meeting of the creditors of Gilman, Cheney & Co., the assignee gave liabilities as $75,000 and the assets $7700 and insolvency. His recommendation was adopted.

The Douglas Fir.

Seven-eighths of the forest growth of the state of Washington consists of Douglas fir, so often in California miscalled Oregon pine, because when the first mill was established in what is now Washington, immediately under the bluff on which the present statehouse now stands at Olympia, Oregon and Washington were one territory under the name of the former. Its economic value can hardly be overestimated. It is not only of immense growth, but under every variety of test has been found to possess the greatest strength of any timber grown in the United States. Some of these tests have been made by railway men and government experts, and the results have been most remarkable.—San Francisco Chronicle.

HOUSEHOLD HINTS.

An oil painting constantly hung in a dark place loses some of its vividness and therefore depreciates in value.

Never allow people to kiss a child on its mouth. Disease is so easily carried in that way that you must take the ounce of precaution.

Old pots and kettles that have become stained or have an odor may be immersed in cold suds and boiled, when they will come out as good as new.

Good for dysentery—eggs. Take an egg, beat it up lightly, swallow it at a gulp; repeat the dose every three hours during the day and you will be cured.

Paper is a good and cheap material to clean utensils. Knives rubbed with it preserve their brightness; stoves rubbed hard with it every morning will remain clean and bright and polish will be saved.

Never urge a child to stand up on its feet. Nature is a true friend and keeps such matters in her own hands. Your persistence to the contrary will weaken its ankles and bend the tender bones of the legs.

ALL ABOUT MARS.

The diameter of Mars is 4,400 miles.

The spectroscope shows air and water on Mars.

Sir W. Herschel discovered the polar ice caps of Mars.

Mars was so bright in 1719 as to be mistaken for a new star.

A year on Mars is two years and 49¼ days long, earth time.

The length of a day on Mars is twenty-four hours and thirty-seven minutes.

Mars is five times as bright now as he will be when on the far side of the sun.

There is a Beer sea on Mars, which must be a heavenly abode indeed for thirsty folks.

The moons of Mars are named Deimos and Phobos—after the warhorses of the Greek god.

The little moons of Mars are only from five to ten miles in diameter. The smaller of the two is the brighter.—New York Advertiser.

The Evening Standard.

ESTABLISHED FEBRUARY, 1850.

NEW BEDFORD, TUESDAY, AUGUST 30, 1892.

TWO CENTS.

HASKELL & TRIPP.

"Home made."

We have the exclusive sale for this city of the highest grade "home made" cotton underclothing for women and misses.

Finest materials.

Perfect fit.

Careful work.

Nothing equal to these goods is being offered *at any price.*

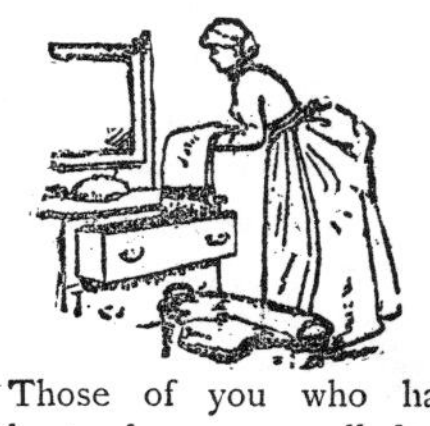

Those of you who have hitherto been compelled to have undergarments made up at home, simply because you couldn't buy ready made that were good enough, will have no need of further trouble on that score.

Our *"home made"* underwear has been produced to fit just such cases as yours. The cloth, the trimming, the sewing, the button holes, the fine, thick, pearl buttons—all just such as you would choose for your own work.

To be sure you must pay us more than for the ordinary sorts—some of you are willing to. We have plenty of other kinds for those who wish to pay less.

Equipoise waists.

The corset substitute—stylish, comfortable, hygienic.

A perfect supporter from the shoulders, distributing the clothing strain and weight.

Three garments in one—corset, waist and cover.

Women's, $1.75 }
Misses', $1.75 } Equipoise.
Children's, 60c. }
Infants', 75c. }

One of the most complete stocks of *desirable* corsets in this state. Prices always lowest.

White goods.

2000 yards mill remnants of beautiful plaided, striped, and lace openwork Lawns and Nainsooks, worth at wholesale 15 to 18c. *Take your pick for 12 1-2c. a yard.*

HASKELL & TRIPP.

Department Stores,

Purchase and William Streets.

NO BLOOD!

Not One Drop on Axes in Borden House.

Hair on the Hatchets Was Not Human Hair.

Prof. Wood's Examination of the Clothing.

No Trace of Prussic Acid in Stomachs.

Results of Analysis All in Favor of Prisoner.

Defence Strengthened by the Chemist's Testimony.

Quarrel of Lawyers Over a Piece of Plaster.

Most Important Developments Since Opening of Trial.

[Special Dispatch.]

FALL RIVER, Aug. 30.—The old, old story is not exactly told again at 5 o'clock in the morning, but it was not more than two hours later when people to-day gathered about the Central police station and waited for a chance to enter. Ladies, as on yesterday, were admitted by the front door and occupied nearly all the spectators' seats at their disposal, and here they remained all through the weary hours which occurred before the opening of the Borden case. The weather was warm this morning, and the reporters were hoping that something less forceful than an earthquake might happen to keep down the numbers. They were disappointed, however, and were forced to go into the room and sweat and swear all the morning hours, as they were crowded out of their elbow room and found, if in a moment of absent-mindedness they left their seats, some one was occupying them on their return.

It is now said that the examination will not be concluded before Thursday afternoon, provided the defence puts in its expected work, and the reporters while rejoicing at the prospect of having a good lot of copy are considerably discouraged at the outlook.

Prof. Wood Called.

The court this morning came in as per adjournment, and the room was filled with people. The most encouraging testimony which has been given for defence since the opening of the cross-examination was that of Prof. Edward S. Wood, who made an analysis of clothing, axes, hatchet and other articles sent to him.

He was the first witness called, and said: I am professor of chemistry. On Aug. 6th I received a box containing four jars. The first two were labelled "Jars of milk," and the third and fourth were labelled stomachs of "Andrew J. Borden" and "Mrs. Andrew J. Borden." The stomachs were in normal condition and healthy in appearance. I analyzed the contents. That of Mrs. Borden contained about 11 ounces of solid food. The food was partially digested, and showed wheat starch and meat. The contents contained chiefly meat and there were vegetable pulp cells which might be bread or apples. Digestion had proceeded for a period of 2 1-2 hours before death. In his opinion there was

No Appearance of Prussic Acid

in the contents of the stomach.

In Mr. Borden's stomach was found but little solid food. Digestion in his stomach I should think had advanced from 3 1-2 to four hours.

In answer to a question by Mr. Knowlton Prof. Wood reiterated that the digestion in Mrs. Borden's stomach had advanced about 2 1-2 hours and in that of Mr. Borden from 3 1-2 to four hours.

The search for prussic acid in the stomachs of both Mr. and Mrs. Borden showed no evidence of that poison contained in them.

On the 10th of August I received from Dr. Dolan a hatchet, two axes, a blue dress-skirt, dress waist, white starched skirt, lounge cover, and three small envelopes in which were hair taken from Mr. and Mrs. Borden, and hair taken from the hatchet. On Aug. 16 witness received a pair of black stockings.

There Was No Evidence of Blood

on the hatchet. The smooch on the dress skirt showed no blood stain. The white skirt showed one spot of blood. It was directly in front, about six inches from the bottom. In the hair which was sent to him marked that of A. J. Borden there were exhibits of blood. In the package marked "Mrs. Borden" there was also blood. The hair marked as

Taken from the Hatchet Was Not Human

hair. It was white, and might have been that taken from a cow or some other animal. I examined the shoes and stockings which were sent to me, but there was no sign of blood upon them. The spot on the right shoe was not blood, and there was no blood on either shoe. There was

Nothing on the Two Axes.

Near the edge of the hatchet were spots which seemed to be blood, but were found not to be. "There was a spatter on the blade, but it was not blood, and there was a spot on the side of the head of the hatchet which looked to me like blood, and I thought they were," said witness, "but they were not."

Lizzie Examines the Hatchet.

The hatchet was produced and Lizzie examined it with as much interest as did her counsel. One paper was produced by witness on which was written "hair" placed here at—time mentioned—but no hair was there.

In cross-examination Prof. Wood said the spot looked larger on the outside of the skirt than on the inside. The size of the spot was about the size of a pinhead.

Question. This you say was human blood?

Answer. I don't know; I didn't say so; I haven't examined it.

Question. Could you tell in what direction this blood came when it struck the skirt?

Answer. I could not.

Witness said it was difficult to tell the difference in blood, its source, etc., the grade was not so great as before science had progressed.

Witness said that he knew of no difference in digestion in a stout person or a lean one. The amount of gastric juice assists digestion always. The stomachs showed no appearances of irritation.

AS LIZZIE APPEARS LISTENING TO THE EVIDENCE.

The witness said he had been in the Borden house and made a cursory examination, taking no notes.

Q. If one were struck by some sharp instrument, would there be any spurting of blood?

A. Yes, if an artery was cut.

Q. And there was an artery cut?

A. There was one in the line.

Q. In what direction would the blood spurt?

A. I don't think the cutting of an artery would make any great difference. An artery never spurts over three feet.

Q. What artery could be cut by such a blow, one from the top of the head down?

A. I couldn't say; my anatomy is rather old.

Q.—You mean your knowledge of anatomy, professor, as your anatomy appears to be all right.

A. Yes, (with a laugh) that's what I mean. Those spots seen at a distance must have come from a spattering and not from an artery; came the same as from throwing a stone into a mud puddle.

Witness said that if a person stood behind the person assaulted, the blood striking the wall paper would be more or less elongated and away from the wound or the point which it had left, and the heaviest part of the stain would be farthest away; it might be the little end of the spot, but it would contain the largest amount of blood.

Witness measured the hatchet and found the handle measured 14 inches. The fibrine which blood contains causes the coagulation; witness was uncertain in regard to the exact time a person could be said to have been killed from the appearance of the blood. In regard to the position of the murderer, witness said that it appeared to him that the person stood in the dining-room when the first blow was given; this because of the spot found on the frame of the dining-room door.

Prof. Wood left the stand to examine a spot on a piece of the door taken from the dining room of the house by direction of the officers. He went into a side room to examine it, and returned and said the stain did not look to him like blood, but it might be a tobacco stain.

He Was Shown Another Hatchet,

and said upon a rough examination he did not see anything but rust upon it. However, he had been as much as six hours upon the other hatchet, and no matter what this one showed it was not to be expected that he would see anything upon a casual glance.

He continued: I looked at the spots upon the sofa. I know of nothing to conflict with the theory that the assailant stood between the door and Mr. Borden. I should say it was impossible for the assailant not to receive blood upon his

[Continued on Fourth Page.]

CHIEF ROBERTS REINSTATED.

Chairman of Nantucket Police Committee Immediately Resigns.

NANTUCKET, Aug. 30.—The selectmen voted last night to reinstate Chief of Police John Roberts, suspended last Monday for drunkenness. The vote stood 4 to 3. The chairman of the police committee, Henry Riddell, one of the three who voted according to the wishes of the people and against Roberts, immediately resigned from the committee.

The vote on reinstatement stood as follows: For reinstatement, A. H. Gardner, chairman of the board; John Harps, secretary; Joseph Brock and Hiram Folger. For expulsion, Henry Riddell, R. E. Burgess and D. C. Brayton.

It has been the talk on the street that it was almost a foregone conclusion that the vote would stand as it did. After the hearing last Wednesday and the manifest feeling of the majority of the board it was not difficult to prophesy that Roberts would again appear on the streets in full capacity of the position as chief of police. The amusing part of the business is that reinstatement is not in order until September 1, until which time the suspension shall remain in effect. The public asks, "if Roberts was not guilty of the charge of drunkenness, why should his suspension continue for two more days?"

The whole matter was decided with doors closed to the public. A *Standard* representative was allowed to remain during the transaction of routine business, but at the first mention of police, it was moved that the board should go into executive session. Mr. Riddell objected on the very reasonable ground that it was a matter of public interest, one which the public should have full knowledge of. Whereupon Chairman Gardner said that he did not propose to cater to sensation mongers. He thought he could talk more freely if none but members of the board were present, and he wanted to treat the affair as he would a family trouble and not have published broadcast any sensational exaggerations.

It was voted by a vote of 5 to 2 to go into executive session.

There may be good reasons for the board's reinstatement which have not been made public, and it is hoped that there were, and if Roberts has been unjustly censured it is hoped the facts will be brought out.

THE CHOLERA EPIDEMIC.

Rate of Mortality and Reports of Progress of Disease.

LONDON, Aug. 30.—The Berlin correspondent of the *Times* says: "Since Friday the names of all travellers bound hither from infected places have been telegraphed here in advance to facilitate the work of inspection on their arrival. Traffic from here to Hamburg is extraordinarily small, but from Hamburg here it is very heavy."

Epidemic Not a Mild One.

The *Times'* St. Petersburg correspondent says: "The average daily cholera record here is 100 new cases and 20 deaths. It is the greatest mistake to say that the epidemic is a mild one. The best authorities affirm the contrary. In some cases the victims succumb in two or three hours, often without the least vomiting or diarrhœa. The bodies of the victims frequently exhibit strong muscular movements an hour after death, thus proving the severity of the attack."

An Infected Vessel.

The schooner Helen E., said to be destined for America, and which had been detained at Dover, is now being towed to Gravesend with a yellow flag flying from her mast.

Later—Upon the Helen's arrival she was boarded by the health officers, who found she had two cases of cholera on board.

Lodging-House Inspection.

The sanitary authorities have in no wise relaxed their vigilance. Every day the lodging-houses are subjected to a rigid inspection, and it is said that they were never in a better sanitary condition. The inspection will be kept up as long as there is any danger from cholera. As it is known that over ripe fruit is a dangerous source of cholera, there is a sharp watch kept to see that all fruit is in prime condition.

Deaths Increasing.

ST. PETERSBURG, Aug. 30.—The official returns show in this city yesterday there were reported 156 new cases of cholera and 38 deaths. This is an increase of 31 new cases and 16 deaths.

Thirty New Cases.

PARIS, Aug. 30.—Thirty new cases of cholerine were reported yesterday. There were four deaths from the disease, including that of a hospital attendant.

PANAMA, Aug. 30.—It is reported that the Asiatic cholera exists in Venezuela. Yellow fever is still epidemic in that republic. The mortality among the troops is very great.

NEW YORK, Aug. 30.—A cable dispatch from Havana, received yesterday, denied the story from Mexico that cholera had broken out in Cuba.

FIRE IN MILWAUKEE.

Two Thousand Barrels of Beer and 140,000 Bushels of Malt Destroyed.

MILWAUKEE, Aug. 30.—Fire, which broke out at 3 o'clock this morning, in the Falk, Jung & Borchert brewery, on the south side, destroyed the brew house, elevator and boiler house. The elevator contained 140,000 bushels of malt and the brew house contained 2000 barrels of beer. The total loss will aggregate $250,000. Insurance not known.

Weather-Crop Report.

RALEIGH, N. C., Aug. 30.—The State weather-crop report for the week ending last night says the drought has been broken by copious rains almost everywhere, which though rather unevenly distributed have been very beneficial to some crops though too late for others.

TELEGRAPHIC BREVITIES.

The strike at Buffalo is at an end.

A fatal railroad accident happened near Brussels.

Three smuggled Chinamen were captured in Detroit.

An abandoned schooner was picked up off Scituate, Mass.

A sharpshooter fired upon the soldiers at Coal Creek, Tenn.

The Grand Army is to secure the Andersonville prison property.

A baseball player was killed at Lansford, Pa., by a pitched ball.

Hartford's $10,000 colt race was taken by Belle Flower in four heats.

President Greenhut of the whisky trust is to be arrested on his return from Europe.

Four Massachusetts cities have applied for federal supervisors at the presidential election.

The Elkins-Widner-Yerkes syndicate is said to have secured control of the Jay Gould buildings in New York Manhattan Elevated.

A committee of Northampton, Mass., citizens asked Governor Russell to withdraw the nomination of Savings Bank Commissioner Scates.

Immense damage to wheat stacks has been done in the Northwest by the rain. A frost is almost certain.

Gen. Miles yesterday received orders from Washington to take the necessary steps for the removal of 100,000 cattle now said to be on the Cherokee strip.

WEATHER INDICATIONS.

SOUTHEASTERLY WINDS.

WASHINGTON, Aug. 30.—For the 24 hours from 8 a. m. to-day: For Massachusetts, Rhode Island and Connecticut, fair, warmer; Wednesday cooler; Thursday southeasterly winds.

RAIN.

BOSTON, Aug. 30.—Local forecast for New England until Thursday: Unsettled, rain, probably beginning during the evening or night; slightly warmer, easterly winds. Thursday probably fair and cooler.

THE QUEEN SALUTED.

Journey of Her Majesty Victoria from Osborne House to Balmoral.

LONDON, Aug. 30.—The Queen started from Osborne House last evening for Balmoral, crossing to Portsmouth. The old custom of saluting, which had been dispensed with since the death of the prince consort, was revived on this occasion. All the warships lying at Portsmouth and the guard ship at Cowes saluted the Queen by firing 21 guns each. The yards of the different men-of-war were manned and their bands played the national airs.

THE BRIDGEND MINING DISASTER.

Water Flooding the Galleries Will Prevent Recovery of Bodies.

LONDON, Aug. 30.—A despatch from Bridgend, Wales, says the water is flooding some of the galleries in the Park Slip pit, the scene of the disaster on Friday. This will, it is said, probably prevent the recovery of the bodies still in the mine.

Fallen Into the Hands of Rebels.

NEW YORK, Aug. 30.—A Curacoa, W. I., dispatch to the *Herald* says: "Maracaibo, on the northwest, has fallen into the hands of the Venezuelan rebels under the leadership of Gen. Crespo. This news reached here this (Monday) evening from Caracas, and with it came the sensational news that Mendoza has declared himself dictator of Venezuela, thus seeking to oust Gen. Urdanetta.

The Ocean Steamers.

Arrived—At New York, Neptune, Montego Bay; Naronic, Liverpool; Muriel, West Indies; Veendam, Rotterdam.

HOME MATTERS.

PERSONAL.—J. E. Chandler, a Boston architect, was in the city yesterday afternoon and this forenoon on business pertaining to the drawing of plans for a new public building.

Mr. and Mrs. S. Hamblin, Mr. W. F. Hamblin and Miss Annie Shurtleff leave to-night on the Puritan for New York. Their outing will consist of a tour of New York city, Long Island and the upper Hudson, occupying about three or four weeks.

Elmer E. Tolman, well-known violinist, comes here this week to assume charge of the Opera House Orchestra. He will take pupils in violin instruction, and his many friends will be pleased to learn of his return to this city.

William E. Hatch and Walter S. Allen of this city have arrived at home from their European tour.

William H. Mathews is in the city.

Among the Clouds, published on the summit of Mt. Washington, says a mock trial was held by guests of the Central Villa last week, when Rowland Sherman of Newport, R. I., was convicted of robbing a hen roost. Capt. Brightman of New Bedford, acted as judge. The prisoner was sentenced to three years of hard labor.

Designer Herreshoff, of Bristol, R. I., with his wife and two daughters made a visit to this port this morning, in one of his fast yachts.

T. E. Bowman, of the firm of T. E. Bowman & Co., Topeka, is in the city for a day or two. His stay is so short that he will not be able to see all of his firm's investors, of whom they have about fifty in New Bedford and vicinity. He will, however, call upon any person who may express desire by addressing him through the post office, care of Robert G. Bennett, 47 Chestnut street.

Carl Zerrahn, as usual, will conduct the Worcester Musical Festival this season and Franz Kneisel will be associate.

THE TITAN OF CHASMS—*A Mile Deep, 13 Miles Wide, 217 Miles Long, and Painted Like a Flower.*—The Grand Canon of the Colorado River, in Arizona, is now for the first time easily accessible to tourists. A regular stage line has been established from Flagstaff, Arizona, on the Atlantic & Pacific Railroad, making the trip from Flagstaff to the most imposing part of the canon in less than 12 hours. The stage fare for the round trip is only $20.00, and meals and comfortable lodgings are provided throughout the trip at a reasonable price. The view of the Grand Canon afforded at the terminus of the stage route is the most stupendous panorama known in nature. There is also a trail at this point leading down the canon wall, more than 6000 feet vertically, to the river below. The descent of the trail is a grander experience than climbing the Alps, for in the bottom of this terrific and sublime chasm are hundreds of mountains greater than any of the Alpine range.

A book describing the trip to the Grand Canon, illustrated by many full-page engravings from special photographs, and furnishing all needful information, may be obtained free upon application to Jno. J. Byrne, 723 Monadnock Block, Chicago, Ill.

SO VERY CHEAP.—This week we will sell any laundered cheviot or madras shirt in our stock for one dollar each. This includes the $1.50, $2.00, and $2.50 grades, at Gifford & Cos., No. 139 Union street.

POSTPONED. — The Dartmouth All Day's Meeting, the programme of which we have heretofore published, has been postponed a week, until Thursday, Sept. 1st.

UNION STREET RAILWAY.—On and after Sept. 1 on pleasant afternoons the City Hall cars of the Fairhaven line will start at 1 30 p. m. and run as late as the travel demands.

THE PETITION of John B. Baylies and 1050 others, asking that no liquor be sold in any of the public parks, will be brought up at the next meeting of the Park Commissioners.

LABOR DAY.—The union cigar makers in town have accepted the invitation of the committee having in charge the celebration of Labor day to participate in the festivities.

REPAIRING.—The turnout of the electric road on Bedford street is being relaid and tamped up to level.

W. C. T. U.—There will be a meeting of the W. C. T. U. in the Woman's Parlors, 190 Purchase street, Wednesday at 3 p. m.

HATHAWAY, SOULE & HARRINGTON have something to say to you on page 5. Look it up.

EVERY MOTHER WISHES to give her baby the best food, and the best food is Mellin's.

PARLOA COOK BOOKS only 10 cents each at Hutchinson's Book Store.

HOW DO WE DO IT?—Buy for *cash*, sell for *cash*. See ad. on page 5. Union Shoe Store.

"AYER'S HYGIENIC COFFEE" fills a long felt want. Try it and be convinced.

HAND-SEWED Oxford Ties $2.00. Devoll's.

PURIFY your blood; Hood's Sarsaparilla.

THE UPS AND DOWNS OF YOUR WINDOW SHADES.

Do they Please You?

Why Not See Us About Them?

Making and Hanging Shades a Specialty with Us.

OIL OPAQUE SHADES,

Decorated or Plain.

The plain shades are handsomely furnished, mounted on a warranted roller, with a fine nickel pull; are 36 inches wide and 2 yards long.

READY-MADE SHADES,

By their convenience and low prices seem to have filled a real want. We have made up a pleasing variety of curtains in both Holland and Opaque, in the most approved colorings, using a high grade roller, which we believe at the very reasonable prices will meet the requirements of the majority of curtain buyers.

SPECIAL ORDER SHADES, FOR CUSTOM CURTAINS.

We take great pleasure in referring to our *SUNFAST ROCKSONIA HOLLAND*, which we GUARANTEE to be STRICTLY FADELESS. Can we do more? In addition to this quality, it is the best fabric we have ever seen for nice curtains. If you will drop us a postal card we will send samples and give an estimate of cost free of charge.

C. F. WING,

34 to 40 Purchase st.

WHITING & CO.,

Will Continue the

Remnant Silk

SALE,

Monday and Tuesday,

the 29th and 30th,

Being the last days of the sale.

On same days we shall sell a few Remnants of

DRAPERY SILKS,

Best $1.00 Goods, at

49c.

All new patterns this season.

WHITING & CO

J. V. SPARE,

Liberty Hall Building.

Wonderful bargains in 36 inch Unbleached Cotton at 5 1-2c. a yard.

Cottons never were lower than at present, and it is good policy to buy now.

Also a very good cotton at 5c. yard, full yard wide, and better than any cotton ever sold at this price,

5 CENTS A YARD.

Cleaning up a lot of Fancy Ginghams, Plaids and Stripes, fast colors, goods that have been selling at 10c., now 6 1-2c. yard.

Bleached Twilled Crash, regular 5c. goods, for a short time 4c. yard, or 3 3-4c. by the piece.

Waste Silk, 5c. box.

Job lot of Shell Hair Pins at 37c. dozen. Some pins in the lot worth 10c. each.

J. V. Spare,

LIBERTY HALL BUILDING.

Fall Hats.

Buy

Your

New

Hat

Of

J. & W. R.

WING & CO.

Correct

Qualities.

Correct

Shapes.

Correct

Prices.

Now Ready.

INSURANCE.

FIRE & LIGHTNING, TORNADO, PLATE GLASS and ACCIDENT INSURANCE.

No. 48 North Water Street.

Ætna Ins. Co........................ Hartford
Hartford Fire Ins. Co........... "
Connecticut Fire Ins. Co...... "
Merchants Ins. Co .... Providence
Equitable F. & M. Ins. Co...... "
Springfield F. & M. Ins. Co..... Springfield
Ins. Co. of North America........Philadelphia
Ins. Co. of State of Penn........ "
Fire Association.............. "
Home Ins. Co.. .... New York
Continental Ins. Co.......... "
German Am. Ins. Co.......... "
Niagara Fire Ins. Co............ "
Williamsburgh City Fire Ins. Co. "
Hanover Fire Ins. Co............ "
Phœnix Assurance Co........... London
Guardian Assurance Co..... "
No. British & Mer. Ins. Co.. "
Imperial Fire Ins. Co......... "
Fitchburg Mut. Fire Ins. Co.... Fitchburg
Dorchester Mut. Fire Ins. Co..... Neponset
New York Plate Glass Ins. Co.... New York
U. S. Mutual Accident Asso...... "

GEO. N. ALDEN.

(Successor to Tillinghast & Alden.) d&w

SAMUEL H. COOK,

Marine & Fire Insurance

AGENT AND BROKER,

No. 37 North Water Street.
(In National Bank of Commerce Building.)
Whaling Risks and their Catchings a Specialty at This Agency.

The following First Class Fire Insurance Companies are represented, viz.:

Hingham Mutual Fire Ins. Co.. Hingham
Phœnix Ins. Co.................. Hartford
National Fire Ins. Co....... .. "
Phenix Ins. Co... .... New York
Westchester Fire Ins. Co ...... "
Commerce Ins. Co.............. Albany
Pennsylvania Fire Ins. Co...... Philadelphia
American Fire Ins. Co.......... "
Queen Ins. Co.................. London
London Assurance Corp........ "
London & Lancashire Ins. Co.. "
Norwich Union F. Ins. Soc'y... "
Northern Assurance Co......... "
Firemen's Fire Ins. Co.......... Boston
The Metropolitan Plate Glass Ins. Co......... New York
Hartford Steam Boiler Inspection and Ins. Co............... Hartford

EDWIN EMERY. JOHN H. PEDRO

LAWRENCE GRINNELL & CO.,

Fire and Marine, Life and Plate Glass

Insurance

60 No. Water St., foot of William.
(Over Mechanics' National Bank.)

Liverpool & London & Globe Ins. Co., Liverpool
American Fire Ins. Co.............. New York
Prov. Washington Ins. Co... .....Providence
Commercial Union Assurance Co.....London
Merchants' Ins. Co.................... Newark
Boylston Ins. Co..........................Boston
United States Inc. Co...............New York
Caledonian Ins. Co....................Scotland
Hamburg-Bremen Fire Ins. Co.......Bremen
American Ins. Co.. ....Boston
Spring Garden Ins. Co........... Philadelphia
Lowell Mutual Fire Ins. Co.............Lowell
Wachusett Mutual Fire Ins. Co..... Fitchburg
Mutual Life Ins. Co..................New York
Lloyd's Plate Glass Ins. Co.........New York

HIRAM VAN CAMPEN. JOHN W. PAUL.

HIRAM VAN CAMPEN & CO., FIRE, LIFE AND ACCIDENT Insurance Agency,

No. 15 North Water Street.
Telephone Call ....241-2.
(Established A. D. 1852.)

The following First Class Companies are represented:

Sun Fire Office............... London, Eng.
Organized A. D. 1710.
Lancashire Ins. Co........ ..Manchester, Eng.
The Reliance Ins. Co......... Philadelphia
Girard Fire & Marine Ins. Co. "
United Firemen's Ins. Co.. "
Michigan Fire & Marine Ins. Co........................... Detroit, Mich.
Security Ins. Co............ New Haven, Ct.
People's Fire Ins. Co........Manchester, N.H.
Firemen's Ins. Co............ Newark, N. J.
Newark Fire Ins. Co....... "
First National Fire Ins. Co.. Worcester, Mass.
Quincy Mut. Fire Ins. Co... Quincy, Mass.
Holyoke Mut. Fire Ins. Co.. Salem, Mass.
Traders' & Mechanics' Ins. Co. Lowell, Mass.
Dorchester Mut. Fire Ins. Co. Boston
Cambridge Mut. Fire Ins. Co. Cambridgeport, Mass.
Travellers' Ins. Co., Hartford, Life & Accident.

All losses equitably adjusted and promptly paid.

New Bedford, April. 1890.

IVORY S. CORNISH. CLIFTON H. CORNISH

I. S. CORNISH & SON.

LIFE, FIRE, ACCIDENT and PLATE GLASS

—INSURANCE—

Agents and Brokers. 50 North Second St.
NEW BEDFORD, MASS.

Represent the following First-Class Companies:

Ætna Life Ins. Co. Hartford, Conn
Travelers Accident Ins. Co. Hartford, Conn
Merchants and Farmers Mutual Fire Ins. Co., Worcester, Mass
Citizens Mutual Ins. Co. Boston, Mass
Mass. Mutual Fire Ins. Co. Boston, Mass
Abington Mutual Fire Ins. Co. Abington, Mass
Salem Mutual Fire Ins. Co. Salem, Mass
Essex Mutual Fire Ins. Co. Salem, Mass
Merrimac Mutual Fire Ins. Co. Andover, Mass
Franklin Mutual Fire Ins. Co. Greenfield, Mass
Milford Mutual Fire Ins. Co. Milford, Mass
Glens Falls Ins. Co. Glens Falls, N. Y
Union Ins. Co. Philadelphia, Penn
New Hampshire Fire Ins. Co. Manchester, N.H
Peoples Fire Ins. Co. Manchester, N. H
Delaware Ins. Co. Philadelphia, Penn
Metropolitan Plate Glass Ins. Co. New York, N. Y

Losses promptly adjusted and paid.
Business solicited.

COAL

—OF—

All Kinds and the Best Quality

—FOR—

DOMESTIC AND FACTORY USE

CONSTANTLY IN STOCK.

HAVING purchased the business and good will of Bates & Howard am prepared to fill orders at either my old office at yard or new office, No. 224 Purchase street.

YARD, ATLANTIC WHARF, FOOT OF CANNON STREET.

ALBERT W. HOLMES.

TELEPHONES:
YARD OFFICE, 92—3.
PURCHASE STREET OFFICE, 92—2.

DR. S. F. STOWE'S Improved

Dyspepsia Lozenges

HAVE been before the public for the past seven years, and their success has established the high reputation they sustain in the cure of all Stomach Troubles. If you are subject to Heartburn, Sour Stomach, Distress after eating, Water Brash, Wind on Stomach, or Faintness and Sickness at Stomach, they are a certain remedy. For Hoarseness and Tickling Sensation of the Throat they stand unrivalled. Sold by all druggists and dealers in medicines at 10 cents per package or 3 packages for 25 cents. Observe my initials on each Lozenge, as none others are genuine, thus S. F. S.

MANUFACTORY. 555 HIGH STREET, PROVIDENCE R. I.
TTS

A Word About

GAS STOVES

The Gas Company has a few two-hole GAS STOVES with which it would like to advertise and makes the following offer:

It will install RENT FREE for 2 Months, to the first six of its gas consumers who have never used a Gas Stove, who apply, a regular Goodwin gas stove in first-class order.

This is to enable parties to prove the truth of our statement that there is "NOTHING SO CONVENIENT AS A GAS STOVE."

At the end of the two months if the customer does not conclude to purchase the stove it will be removed without cost.

NEW BEDFORD Gas & Edison Light Co.

ESTABLISHED 1884.

NEW BEDFORD

STEAM CARPET BEATING WORKS.

Cor. North Water and North Sts.

The above cut represents the latest improved Carpet Beating Machine now in use, and the only one of the kind in the city. When desired, Carpets can be steamed after having been beaten, by our

Patent Superheated Steam Vapor Process,

which destroys all moths and relieves the Carpets of all impurities. In doing this the colors are brought out wonderfully bright. Thanking my patrons for past favors and soliciting a share of their patronage in the future, I remain yours truly,

H. M. MAIN.

Telephone call 154—12. TTS

Blacksmith's Helper.

A capable Carriage-smith's Helper wanted.

Brownell, Ashley & Co.,

24 to 38 FOURTH ST.

GEORGE C. BLISS, FLORIST.

34 Arnold Street,

CORNER COTTAGE.

TELEPHONE, DAY OR NIGHT.

PURITAN SPRING WATER.

This is perfectly pure, clear, crystal water, boiling from the sand at a very low temperature. This water will be delivered fresh from the Spring daily at any place in the city.

Call at the office and test it free, then leave your order. The price is very moderate and within the reach of all.

PURITAN SPRING WATER CO.,

21 Purchase Street.

SCHOOL BEGINS TUESDAY, SEPT. 6.

The boys have been hard on clothes through vacation. They want a new suit for school.

We can fit your boy out complete with a

STRONG, SERVICEABLE SUIT

for very little money.

HEADQUARTERS

—FOR—

BOYS' CLOTHING.

SANDERS & BARROWS,

67 & 69 WILLIAM STREET.

CLOSING OUT SALE

Of Summer Carriage Lap Robes, Horse Blankets, etc. Lowest Prices in the city for Harnesses, Ladies' and Gents' Riding Saddles, Bridles and Whips.

TRUNKS —AND— BAGS!

TRUNKS —AND— BAGS!

Pocketbooks and Purses, Bill Books, Umbrellas and all kinds of Travelling Goods, at

C. F. CUSHING'S,

HARNESS, TRUNK AND BAG EMPORIUM,

Opp. City Hall, and Branch Store 571 to 575 Purchase Street.

Our popular low prices keep our stock moving and we constantly show new FRESH GOODS. We never advertise mistatements but always back up in stock what we say in print.

EARLY FALL STYLE HATS RECEIVED. All Best Shapes at CUT PRICES.

H. V. SANDERS & Co.

One Price Clothiers, OPP. CITY CLOCK, 92 Purchase St.

NEW BEDFORD BRASS FOUNDRY.

Machinists, Brass Finishers and Founders, Brass, Bronze and Composition Castings, Zinc and White Metal Pattern Castings, Phospor Bronze Castings a specialty, Lead Window Weights and High Speed Babbitt Metals, Chandelier Repairing and Brazing, Brass Finishing in all its branches. Machine Repairing promptly attended to. Lawn Mowers Sharpened and Repaired.

Foundry and Machine Shop, 108 North Water Street, foot of Elm.

WM. T. NICHOLSON, Manager, Formerly Foreman of the Armington & Sims Engine Company's Brass Foundry, Providence, R. I. je25-3m

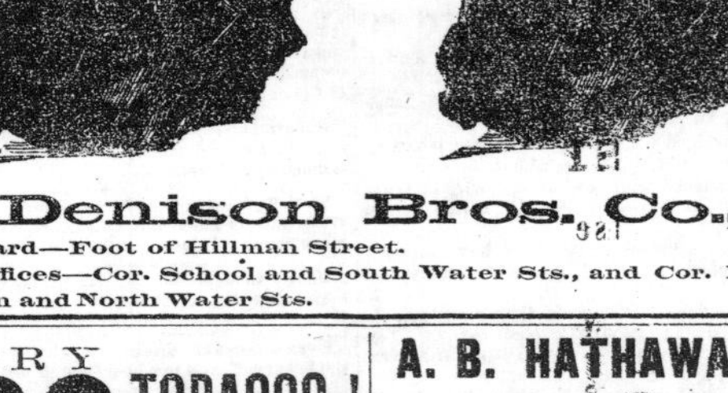

Denison Bros. Co.,

Yard—Foot of Hillman Street.
Offices—Cor. School and South Water Sts., and Cor. Hillman and North Water Sts.

TRY 39 TOBACCO! Best in the Land for Smoking.

Be sure that the tag 39 is on every piece, and take nothing else in place of it.

Distributing Agents

Driscol, Church & Hall,
Wholesale Grocers, NEW BEDFORD. au16-12t

A. B. HATHAWAY, FLORIST.

Store 220 Union Street.
Greenhouses, Court Street.

LATEST STYLES OF TYPE —AT THE— STANDARD JOB OFFICE.

AN EVENTFUL DAY.

Scenes and Incidents of the Fourth of the Trial.

Miss Lizzie Does Not Flinch Under Trying Evidence.

Indications of a Change in the Prisoner's Condition.

Steady at Most Times, but Giving Way Now and Then.

Dramatic Incident Caused by Assistant Marshal Fleet.

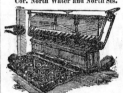

The Fall River District Court room, which still continues to be the centre of interest, was close, hot, and generally uncomfortable when the adjourned hearing in Lizzie Borden's case was opened yesterday morning.

The seats were all filled two hours before the opening, and the crowd had consumed all the good ozone which had collected since Saturday. The women have commenced coming again in unbroken ranks, and so long as they continue the seats will be filled early.

It was another curious mob from that which came at first, and they were on the whole quieter and much better dressed. Many who were in court last week still continue their visits and for what reason it is hard to tell. With all their questioning and scrutinizing (and it sometimes seemed as if they would tie their necks into knots in looking around each other's bonnets) they are, for the most part, ignorant of proceedings, and in many instances of the principal characters concerned.

There was, for instance, an intelligent-appearing, middle-aged woman, who had a front seat yesterday. It was her second day in court. Late in the afternoon she leaned over to a reporter and, without any embarrassment over her question, desired to know where and which Miss Borden was. In her two days' experience she had not discovered the identity of the prisoner.

Yesterday the friends who have accompanied Miss Borden previously were present except Mrs. Holmes. The vacancy on the seat occasioned by her absence was much of the time occupied by the substantial figure of Milton Reed. Mrs. Brigham was there as before to silently testify of her love for Lizzie, and, of course, the gallant chevalier, Minister Buck, with much taste and courtesy, performed escort duty.

There had been quite a change in the appearance of the court room it was noticed since Saturday. It was observed that Judge Blaisdell's whiskers had been trimmed in the interval. His Honor had bushy chin whiskers when he opened the case, but they had been clipped nearly to the skin.

A few new faces were seen in the newspaper pen, and some of distinction outside the bar. A very stout gentleman created much interest. He arrived early, accompanied by a lady, and upon his advent the whisper "There's Bob Ingersoll" went among the reporters.

The gentleman was William M. Hill, ex-mayor and ex-city marshal of Salem and ex-State detective. He is the stoutest man that has been seen in Fall River for some time.

Tony Pastor, who played in that city last night, was an interested spectator at both sessions of the day. Members of his company, among them Maggie Cline, were also present.

The prisoner on entering appeared refreshed with her Sunday rest, and the heretofore pale face of Emma showed faint signs of color. Lizzie walked with a haughty and firm step to her place. In addition to her usual attire she had on a stylish black tailor reefer, embellished with braid. On being seated she entered into an animated conversation with her sister, during which she smiled and looked entirely contented. She fanned vigorously during the morning session, using one of the ham advertisement fans that have been circulated about the court room.

Frequent remarks are made daily complimentary to the Borden "girls'" hair. Upon neither of them has Dame Nature lavished her gifts, but both are favored with beautiful and abundant hair. Miss Lizzie's is invariably worn high on the head. It is a medium brown in color, fine and exceptionally glossy and always carefully curled in front and shows a slight suggestion of waviness at the back. The hair of the other is darker and heavier, and truly may be termed "as soft as silk."

It was woman's day at the witness stand, and the low voices of Mrs. Churchill, Miss Russell and Miss Lucy Collet, a pretty French girl, kept the reporters' ears strained to the utmost. The court officer concerning whose interesting personality volumes might be written, wandered from one desk to another, put on his glasses and read all manuscript that came under his notice, and gave the newspaper men well received criticisms. Next to the judge and police officials they are on his mind, and he takes occasion to do them many little favors in the way of bringing ice water and hurrying messenger boys. A well known reporter said to him: "I say George, the care of all these people must be a fearful tax on you."

"Oh, I sleep well yet," was the rejoinder, "and eat three good meals a day. You just ask me up to dinner."

On no day before has the examination called such pointed reference to Lizzie Borden. The district attorney and the lawyers for the defence made frequent reference to the gown and hat which she wore as a means to identify her attire at other times. They frequently pointed at and in Mr. Adams' case touched the ornament on the little black hat, but these little personalities did not seem to annoy Lizzie.

During Eli Bence's cross-examination, which to an ordinary prisoner must have been very trying, she did not for a moment flinch. She looked the drug clerk squarely in the eye with by no means a pleasant expression.

She laughed carelessly whenever anything came up to excite her risibles, but the laugh was repressed apparently as soon as she thought about it. When, for instance, Lawyer Adams, in attempting to refresh the memory of Bence on the sound of Lizzie's voice six years ago, said in a sentimental tone, "There are accents that linger a good many years, you know," the prisoner smiled broadly, but quickly smothered it with her black gloved hand.

She gave some evidence of sadness as well as laughter. When Officer Pat Doherty was on the stand he gave a most effective recital of what he saw at the Borden house on the morning of the tragedy. He described the mutilated head of Mr. Borden, the ugly gashes and the eye hanging by a membrane, and the thick, black pool of blood around the body of Mrs. Borden in an almost dramatic manner. Even then Lizzie did not make such a show of feeling as did some of the women in the room, but she pressed her lips tightly together, closed her eyes and partially covered her face. It was only a momentary sadness however.

But these changes of moods or feeling, slight though they are, indicate a change in the prisoner's condition. They occurred less frequently in the first days of the hearing. Then she displayed a sphinx-like indifference to everything. Now she is moved to smiles or sighs and a constant shaking of her foot and chewing of her glove tips are evidence of nervousness. From these things it might be inferred that the prisoner is gradually losing hold of her fine powers of endurance, and indeed guilty or not, her ordeal in court is enough to break the strongest will.

Officer Doherty is a man of a John L. Sullivan build. His testimony was very concisely and moderately given. Officer Doherty and his colleague, Officer Harrington, occupy the same relative position to the Fall River police force that Inspectors Hathaway and Parker do to the New Bedford force. They have been among the principal workers on the case.

Mr. Doherty made himself amusing by his honest attempts to describe Lizzie Borden's attire on the morning of the murder. On first thoughts, he said, her gown was calico—a loose wrapper. After a moment of thought he announced with a blush of pride at his knowledge of dress goods that it was of challie. This was not specific enough for Mr. Adams, who wanted to know the figure upon it. That was a stickler for even Mr. Doherty, and he owned that he couldn't describe it. but might point out something like it. His eye travelled over the array of shirt waists in the room, and he finally pointed to a bashful little stenographer in a corner and said Lizzie's gown was a cross between her waist and the pepper and salt plaid combination portrayed in Mr. Jenning's pantaloons. He thought the wrapper had a starched bosom, but not a word was said about suspenders. That was leaving a chance for the defence to exercise their ingenuity in fancying a dress pattern, but after such an effort Mr. Adams did not have the heart to push questions on that subject any further.

The discussion of such personalities appear to be very annoying to Miss Emma. The airing of the cold mutton and warmed over soup story by Bridget Sullivan, which amounted practically to an expose of the style of living by the Borden household, was a source of much blushing to Emma but not to the prisoner. Should the latter hear the expression of public opinion in regard to the mutton she might think there was no reason to regret her confinement. It was the favorite topic of discussion in Fall River yesterday, and was aired under the open window of the room at the central police station, where Miss Lizzie is staying. In its recital it was embellished until it was given out that the mystery had been solved and Andrew J. Borden died from mutton.

There was more levity allowed by the court yesterday than at any previous time. The judge himself was in excellent humor and many a time was seen to indulge in a broad laugh. If there are any sounds of merriment over any matter directly connected with the case, the judge's warning tap is heard, and if this does not silence the room the court officer's echoing pound a few minutes later is sure to.

Augustus B. Leonard, the clerk of the court, is perhaps the most dignified and impressive figure in the judicial group. His admirable calmness and the long

The Clerk of the Court.

white beard suggest him as a good model for a Moses. With the constant change of witnesses at the present stage of the hearing, he had considerable business during the session yesterday. The exceeding good style in which he delivers the oaths would be applauded, no doubt, if such a thing were allowable in court. He rarely resorts to any of the indulgencies which the lawyers are entitled to and the gravest judge sometimes makes use of; such indulgencies for instance as sitting on the desk with the feet hanging over and eating apples in court. But such is the length of the sessions and the frequent dryness of the examination that even the clerk at times has been uneasy, and on different occasions has been caught with his feet on the desk and his hands over his head. He has been seen also to leave his place and pace a very short stretch of vacant carpet on one side of the judge's bench. These are only occasional breaches of dignity on Mr. Leonard's part.

The afternoon sessions especially the long cross examinations are very tiresome and any diversion is welcomed.

When Joseph Desrosier, a comely Frenchman with a fastidious moustache, was put on the witness stand yesterday and said a good, plain "No, Sir" in re-

The Interpreter and Desrosier.

sponse to Mr. Knowlton's question "Do you speak English?" a feeling of gladness swept over the court room that something out of the ordinary was about to come off. Monsieur was quite chic and not at all bashful. He talked through the interpretation of Officer Perron and those present were given an exhibition of very graceful and correct French, although that did not enter much into the consideration as they were looking for diversion and not science.

Mayor Coughlin was present. He sat near Dr. Dolan and the two carried on an uninterrupted conversation which apparently was of considerable interest. His Honor's eyes were twinkling and Dr. Dolan looked exceedingly pleased. They sat in a corner which was further ornamented by T. M. Desmond, Esq., and E. E. Wright of this city.

The only unusual disturbance in court so far was occasioned by the fainting of the wife of Dr. Bowen. She was taken from the room by Deputy Sheriff Wixon and Mayor Coughlin. The news of the severe illness of her mother was the cause.

A DRAMATIC SCENE

Caused by the Evidence of Deputy Marshal John Fleet.

Deputy Marshal John Fleet was the last witness yesterday afternoon. He testified that he first heard of the affair at a quarter of 12 Thursday. I was home when the news came from the marshal, who had sent word to me by a man in a team. I drove down to the Borden house and arrived at about 10 minutes to 12. I saw Officer Allen and Mr. Manning at the front door. Mr. Sawyer was at the rear door. Inside I found Bridget, Mr. Morse, Dr. Dolan, Dr. Bowen and Miss Lizzie. I went into the sitting room and saw Dr. Dolan standing over Mr. Borden. Then I went up stairs and saw Mrs. Borden. Soon after I went into Miss Lizzie's room and had a conversation with her. She was sitting in the room with Rev. Mr. Buck. I asked her if she knew anything about the man who killed her father and mother? She said it was not her mother, but her stepmother. Her mother was dead, I asked her if she had seen any one around the premises, and she said she had not. Then she said she heard a man talking to her father at 9 or half-past 9, and she thought they were talking about some store. I asked her if this man would do her father any injury, and she said no. I asked her if she knew this man, and she said no. She said

She Did Not Know That Any One Had Threatened Her Father.

or would do him harm.

Continuing, Deputy Fleet said: "At this point Miss Russell said: 'Lizzie, tell him all about that man.' Then Lizzie said that two weeks ago a man had come to the front door and had held a long coversation with her father. The man seemed to be angry, and was talking about a store he wanted her father to let. She said she heard Mr. Borden say he wouldn't let it for that purpose. She said she thought the man was a stranger in Fall River. I asked her if Bridget was in the house during the morning, and she said she had been washing windows and came in after her father came, and then went up stairs. She said she didn't think Bridget had anything to do with it. Lizzie said that when Bridget went up stairs she went up in the barn. 'Up in the barn?' I said, and she said 'Yes.' 'What do you mean by up?' I asked. 'Up stairs,' she said. I asked her how long she remained in the barn and she said half an hour. She said her father was lying upon a lounge in the sitting room when she went out, and that when she came back

She Found Him All Cut Up,

lying in the same position as she had left him. She also said John V. Morse had been there, and I asked her if Morse had anything to do with it. She said it was impossible, for he went away at 9 o'clock in the morning and didn't come back. She didn't tell me what she was doing in the yard. Rev. Mr. Buck and Mrs. Russell were present during the conversation. I then started to search all the rooms I could go into."

At this point some confusion was created by the fainting of Mrs. Bowen, wife of the physician. Mrs. Bowen has been a regular visitor at the court room during the hearing, and is credited with being a firm believer in the innocence of Lizzie Borden. The heat in the court room, combined with the nervous strain of the affair, caused her momentary weakness yesterday afternoon. She was carried into an adjoining room and the hearing proceeded.

The Scene at This Time Was Very Dramatic.

Every eye was directed towards the deputy marshal, and every person was bending eagerly forward to catch every word of the slowly uttered sentences. Lizzie herself bit her lips constantly, and her sister's hands were nervously moving up and down a fan which lay in her lap. At this time the gas was lighted, and this brightened the effect of the situation.

"What did you find down in the cellar?"

"Found Mr. Mullaley, with a number of axes on the floor of the wash-room. We reached the cellar, and found nothing other than the two axes and two hatchets. The two axes were dusty, or covered with ashes, and so was the little hatchet. The large hatchet was clean, with the exception of a small rust spot. It was about four inches long from the head, to the edge six inches, and it had a claw handle."

Mr. Knowlton—It was then a claw-hammer?

Witness—Yes. We looked at the hatchets a little more and then left them there, the edges on the floor. I took one of them, the big hatchet, away, and put it in the adjoining cellar.

Mr. Knowlton—Was anybody near the hatchets when you first saw them in the cellar?

Witness. They were on the cellar floor, and others present were examining them.

Mr. Knowlton. What then?

Witness. I tried the cellar door, and then went out to the barn. I satisfied myself there was nobody there to do this deed. Then I went into the house again and consulted with two of my officers and State Officer Dexter. I made another search and saw Lizzie again in the presence of two officers and Dr. Bowen was holding the door. I told him

I Wanted to Search the Room.

He said something to her. He went in. He came out and asked me if I must search the room. I said I must examine the room to make my report. He let me in then. When I got in, Miss Borden

Why the Baby Stopped Crying.

"My baby was cross and fretful and cried a great deal," writes Mrs. J. E. Churchill of Lawrence, Mass., "but when I fed him lactated food, he grew quiet and happy, and sleeps a great deal. My little girl, now five years old, was reared on the food, which is the best thing a baby can have."

Tutt's Tiny Pills

stimulate the torpid liver, strengthen the digestive organs, regulate the bowels, and are unequaled as an anti-bilious medicine. Dose small. Price, 25c. Office, 39 & 41 Park Place, N. Y.

Moderate in Price, Excellent Quality,

—AND—

DESIRABLE FOR YOUR TABLE!

The new drink, Cocoa Coffee, 35c. for handsome can containing a pound.

The new Relish, California White Grape Mustard, large bottle for 15c.

A can of very nice Peaches for 18c.

A box of Fresh Boneless Herring for 15c.

SOMETHING NEW EVERY DAY

—AT—

ALLEY'S

It Strikes us as Remarkable

to hear of the wonderful record for curing enjoyed by Betton's Infallible Pile Salve; it cures every form of this troublesome ailment. If not to be had at your druggist, send 50 cents to Winkelmann & Brown Drug Co., Baltimore.

MOYNAN & CO

IMPORTING RETAILERS.

UNION ST. PURCHASE ST.

EMBROIDERED Silk Handkerchiefs!

IMPORTER'S SAMPLES.

We have now on our counters at Handkerchief Department a large lot of Elegant Japanese Silk Handkerchiefs in white, black and colored, hemstitched and embroidered edges, at about half usual prices. It will pay you to come and see this lot if you anticipate buying now or at any time in the near future.

Lot 1—29c., worth 50c.
Lot 2—59c., worth 69c.
Lot 3—59c., worth 85c.
Lot 4—75c., worth $1.25.

A DRESS GOODS BARGAIN.

We shall offer while they last that special lot of 36-inch All-Wool Serges, in Black, Navy, Olive, Garnet, Brown, Green, &c., &c., a regular 50c. quality, now only **39 cents.**

Still a few of those imported Robes and Dress lengths left. Don't miss such a chance—just think of buying a

$12.50 Dress for $4.59.
$15.00 Dress for $5.98.
$22.00 Dress for $7.98.

Call and see for yourself.

PARASOLS.

We have only a few left, and they must go within the next few days. Some of them are the nicest goods and latest styles. All go at

Less than 1-2 Marked Price,

and although the season is far advanced it will pay you to buy now and keep it over for another season.

SILK WAISTS, SATIN WAISTS, CAMBRIC WAISTS.

All marked down to *must go prices.* Come in and see them; if you can get suited in the goods, there will be no difficulty about prices.

In Housefurnishing Dept.

Every kitchen necessary can be found here. Such as
Dish Strainers.
Knife Boxes.
Flour Sieves.
Kettles in Tin or Agate Ware.
Roasting Pans.
Chopping Trays.
Dish Pans,
and all the other hundred and one useful things required in kitchen work. Also here you find all kinds Glassware.
Fancy Vases and Ornaments in Japanese Ware.
Fancy Baskets.
Parlor and Banquet Lamps.
Pictures of all descriptions, &c., &c.

REMEMBER OUR SPECIAL SALE OF BLANKETS AT LOW PRICES.

MOYNAN & CO.,

185 and 187 Union St.
9 and 11 Purchase St.

The Evening Standard.

NEW BEDFORD, MASS.
TUESDAY EVENING, AUGUST 30.

THREE EDITIONS DAILY.
No. 87 Union Street.
PUBLISHED BY
E. ANTHONY & SONS,
INCORPORATED.
—TERMS—
Six Dollars a Year; Three Dollars for Six Months, in advance; Single Copies Two Cents.

FOR PRESIDENT:
BENJAMIN HARRISON
OF INDIANA.

FOR VICE-PRESIDENT:
WHITELAW REID
OF NEW YORK.

CONTENTS OF THIS EVENING'S STANDARD.

☞ Col. John A. Cockerill writes to the New York *Herald* that as far as his observation extends there is a steady growth of confidence all along the Republican lines. The belief of the party in its ability to reelect Mr. Harrison rests largely upon the theory that the recall of the Democratic party to any share in the administration of federal affairs would mean turmoil and disturbance. The Cleveland platform is a menace to the tariff and the wise, safe and useful national banking system. Importers, merchants and manufacturers have adjusted themselves to the existing tariff law, and while it is true that a Republican Senate stands as a barrier between the country and any revolutionary legislation for the next four years, the business interests of the country must naturally array themselves against a party which appeals in a season of prosperity and peace for a restoration upon a promise to "rip things." The business man who recalls the days of wildcat banking will not readily vote to destroy a system which gives every State all the banking facilities it requires and makes every bank note in circulation as good as gold both at home and abroad. The foolish longing and desire upon the part of the wild and irresponsible horde of financiers behind Mr. Cleveland to return to the old wildcat State banking system betrays the retrogressive character of the Democratic party. This alone serves to alarm the friends of progress, and is a sufficient notice served upon the solid business interests of the country to keep the Democratic party in the state of exile which befits it under its present leadership.

☞ We noticed yesterday the action of the street railway company in charging but one fare to the Head of the River at certain hours. This is a very good movement, but why not apply it also to the Fairhaven, and south and west end routes, as well as the north end? And since most of the laboring people leave off work at 5 o'clock, would it not be better to make the afternoon hours from 5 to 7?

We approve heartily the action of the Board of Public Works last evening in ordering the removal of all unused gas and electric poles throughout the city. There is a considerable number of these, which are a nuisance and an obstruction. We hope the order will be carried out without delay.

☞ The report of the Labor Commissioner of New York, showing the prosperity of the Empire State under the present tariff, is the severest blow the calamity howlers and the promulgators of the unconstitutionality of protection have yet received. When wages and production are increasing there is no use in telling people they are being ruined by the tariff. Perhaps David B. Hill is pleased at this showing, but the Cleveland Democrats cannot be. The great issue of the campaign is shown in a manner to be very gratifying to the Republicans.

☞ The Springfield *Morning Union* claims that at the end of two months its circulation is nearly if not quite equal to that of the *Republican*, while the circulation of the evening edition has not diminished. We are glad to see that the people of Western Massachusetts appreciate a good and sound Republican paper.

NORTH ROCHESTER.

The Sniptuit Cranberry Association are building a cranberry house to house cranberries. They have already begun to harvest their crop which is very good for a new bog.

The North Rochester Sunday School took their annual "outing" last week, Monday, at Blake's Point, Marion. It was an enjoyable time for all, particularly the little ones.

Mr. Frank L. Blake's family from Jamaica Plain are at their place on Sniptuit Hill.

Mr. H. E. Waldron's family are here for a few weeks.

Mrs. Horatio Leonard and family of Malden are at their cottage at Still Water.

The Ladies' Social had a lawn party two weeks ago at Mrs. Blake's with such success that another is to be held at Mrs. Lornin's Thursday evening. Cake and ice cream will be for sale.

The rain of last week was gladly welcomed. Although long delayed, it will do much good to the late crops. Many with dry wells would like its duplicate this week.

HOME MATTERS.

CITY HALL NOTE.—There will be a meeting of the City Council committee on city property, Thursday evening.

NATURALIZATION.—Henry Ch. Lindner was admitted to citizenship in the Third District Court this morning. F. A. Milliken, Esq., for petitioner.

SEA TURTLE.—Benjamin Quiripel caught a sea turtle weighing about 80 pounds in his trap at Ricketson's point, South Dartmouth, yesterday.

SUPERIOR COURT.—The September sitting of the Superior Court will open this year on the second, not the first, Monday of the month as heretofore.

OBITUARY.—James Loveland, a well-known East Boston painter, died suddenly at his Summer residence in South Harwich, Sunday. The interment will probably take place at Woodlawn.

BASE BALL.—C. W. Smith, the newly elected physical director of the Y. M. C. A., is expected to arrive in the city to-morro w, and will play as catcher on the Y. M. C. A. team in its game with the Nonquitts.

EXAMINATION OF TEACHERS.—The regular semi-annual examination of candidates for positions as teachers in the day or evening schools, and for positions as pupil teachers in the training school, was commenced to-day in the rooms of the school board. Twelve candidates are taking the examinations.

INSANE.—Owen Preston, who has been at the Central Police Station for several days, was removed to Taunton Insane Asylum today. He belongs in Westport, where one day last week he acted very strangely, patrolling the beach 12 hours at a time and sleeping on the marsh.

PENSIONS have been granted as follows:
Original—H. O. Nelson, Edwin Fairbanks, E. W. Deane, Eugene D. Sanborn, Robert Kirkland, C. H. Fisher, Joseph Randall, Franklin Thatcher, D. S. Quinn, J. H. Smith, W. R. Tibbetts.
Additional—H. C. Shurtleff.
Renewal and increase—W. A. Bradley.
Increase—O. G. Grinnell.
Original, widows—Caroline Freeman.

LIBERTY THEATRE will be reopened Monday (Labor Day) with two performances, afternoon and evening, by the New York All-Star Combination, one of the strongest specialty shows on the boards. Manager Weeden has been receiving communications asking for dates from a number of the most popular comedy and vaudeville companies travelling. On Monday afternoon a matinee will be given.

THE LOOM FIXERS.—The Loom Fixers' Union met last evening and completed arrangements for the Labor day parade. The committee on that celebration reported to the full association, and this action was ratified. The loom fixers will occupy the third position in the line. It was voted to offer a prize of $5 to the mill furnishing the biggest turnout of loom fixers in the parade as other unions have done.

An offer of the Y. M. P. T. & B. Society of an elegant silk banner to the society which shall receive the largest number of votes in that society's coming fair, was accepted, and it was voted to enter the competition.

OLD COLONY NOTES.—Work will commence on the double track between Acushnet and Howland's about Sept. 15.

Engine No. 85 has just received repairs at the Taunton shop. She is one of the oldest engines in service on the road, having been built at the Taunton Locomotive Works in 1866, and is one of the smallest ones now in use. It has done good work in its days of service and has a record of a mile a minute, which was made about ten years ago from Taunton to Middleboro. It made the time in eleven minutes with the Taunton firemen, called to the almshouse fire at Titicut. She had two cars to haul, and Engineer James Manion had charge of her. He received a handsome gold necktie-pin of a locomotive from the Taunton department for his quick work.

THE 27TH ANNUAL CLAMBAKE of the First Christian Church and Society occurred on the 24th inst. at Assonet, and passed off much as usual, with the exception of abundant dust. Above 1000 sat down to dinner, and with one accord acknowledged the excellence of the viands set before them. This day is one looked forward to by the inhabitants expectantly, as a time when not only the cravings of nature can be satisfied, but when friends from the country round about will meet and rejoice in each other's good fortune, or lament over one another's reverses. A social spirit pervades the day; haughty reserve is laid one side, and for the time being all seem to enjoy the full measurement of the democratic principle of equality. The Hon. Ciphax Jones seeks to enhance his political prospects and possibilities by a general hand shaking. Capt. Wayback tells his best story, and prim old maids melt into the sentimentality of long ago under the genial influence of the occasion. A bright genial lady, with an air of worldly prosperity, meets a tall melancholy person, with a pensive expression, in whom she recognizes a friend of long ago. The recognition is mutual and the rush for the "best holt" follows:

First Individual. "Why my dear Lucretia, I am delighted. How you have changed. Are your family here? I suppose they have grown to men and women."

Second Individual, (readjusting her bonnet discovers at that moment her oldest daughter passing,) calls, "Abicinthia, come here a moment." (Obedient daughter enters.) "This is my daughter."

First Individual. "You don't say so! How she has grown. Is she married?"

Second Individual. "Oh, yes. She married Napoleon Bonaparte Crocker, Olivia's oldest boy.

First Individual. "Have they any children? No? How sad. We have 10. (*Curtain.*)

Next enters loving couple from the city; She, (discovering the cash box at the cake table.) "Oh, Chollie, here is one of those nickel-in-the-slot machines. Let's drop one and hear it play a tune.

He, (suiting the action to the word,) drops a coin, but no tune. "Say," (addressing the cashier,) "wind her up will yer. Put in a register with an extract from the Pirates of Penzance. Don't-cher-know?"

Cashier. "Why, my friend, that is only a cash box."

Chollie. "That's one on us. You're welcome to all I've put in."

Loving couple retire.

The inevitable dance at the town hall follows in the evening; not under the auspices of the church, however, but under the management of some one who has an eye to worldly gain. This is also much enjoyed by the younger portion; the Sabbath school children silencing conscience with the fact that the good Book teaches that there is a time to dance, and that this is probably the time.

FREETOWN.

Valuation of real estate, $652,602; valuation of personal estate, $158,405; total, $811,007. Raised by taxation, $5000; raised under chapter 133, Acts of 1882, $450; State tax, $717.50; county tax, $1244.18; overlay, $271.88; total tax, $7683.56. Number of polls, 395. Rate of taxation $8.50 per $1000.

WESTPORT.

Edward A. Howland has been drawn as juror for the September term of the Superior Court.

PORTSMOUTH, R. I.

The public schools began the Fall term on Monday, and in district No. 1 the scholars are to christen new seats and desks.

SCATHING REMARKS.

Police Ought to Wince Under Judge Borden's Criticism.

Another Small Fry Liquor Case Brought Before Him.

His Honor Thinks It as Easy to Convict the Larger Dealers.

In the Third District Court to-day Judge Borden presided during the trial of several important cases.

Laura M. Hodge pleaded guilty of being drunk, and was sent up for one year.

Mary Morse, for a similar offence, got 30 days.

One case of drunkenness was put on probation until Sept. 30th next, and one was released by the officers.

The case against Julia Lamarine for keeping a common nuisance, continued from yesterday, was next taken up. Hon. E. L. Barney appeared for the defence.

The first witness was Officer Joseph B. Wing, who said he knew Mrs. Lamarine. Had known her for over a year. Keeps house No. 95 South Second street. Lives in lower part. Have seen her once since Jan. 1st last. It was last Sunday. Had a warrant to search house. Searched and found half apint of whiskey in rear room—kitchen. It was on a shelf on the south side. Found tumblers and a salver. Mrs. Lamarine was in the kitchen with two boys. Saw two girls and two men in another room. All the family were in the yard when we got to the house, and Mrs. Lamarine started and ran and got to the whiskey as soon as I did. Two dozen empty lager bottles were in a case marked Smith Brothers in the entry. They were wet as if recently used. Mrs. Lamarine lives in what is known as the Sturtevant house. When Mrs. Lamarine ran I ran after her and we got to the whiskey about the same time. I told her I had a warrant and she pointed to a young man and said, "him, him." He did not claim the whiskey. He did not speak to me.

Officer Cannavan said he went Sunday last to search the house. He saw the case of empty beer bottles; there were 24 in all and they had a little in each, as if recently used. Found in the kitchen a quart bottle with a "grain of whiskey in it." Four weeks ago yesterday my attention was called to the place. A carriage drove up on Cannon street and four men got out and went around into Mrs. Lamarine's house. They had the appearance of men who had been drinking. I stayed about the place for 20 minutes and they did not come out. Officer Wixon found a bottle that smelled of liquor in the middle room. It was not dusty. The bottle I found was wrapped in newspaper.

Officer Wixon said he was with the other officers. Went into the front door. Saw in the front entry a box containing 24 bottles. The box was marked Smith Brothers. Examined the bottles and found lager had been in them. Found a bottle in the middle room that had a little whiskey in it. The front door was locked and was opened for me by a young woman.

John Hernon said he knew Mrs. Lamarine since she had lived at No. 95 South Second street. He had seen people go into the house sober and come out drunk, and seen them go in drunk. Both colored and white visited the house. Saturday nights and Sundays were the worst. The people were noisy and used vulgar language and danced and sang. He had been to the station several times to see if he could not get a warrant for Deacon Sturtevant, who owns the place, for letting it to such people. I went into the place once. I was called in by a woman that lives upstairs. I have heard fiddling and seen dancing on Sundays and reported it to the officers and to the chief. Complaint had been made to Deacon Sturtevant, and Mr. Wilber on the avenue wrote him a letter about it.

William Generous lives at No. 96 South Second street. He had seen men go in sober and come out drunk. Had seen young women sitting in men's laps and had seen drinking in the house. Saw five men go in drunk last Saturday night. About 11 o'clock saw another party go into the house. The men that went into the house staggered and talked loud. There were lights in the house at the time. One week ago last Saturday night I saw others go into the place; they were under the influence of liquor. I have not complained to the Chief. I was summoned to come here as a witness.

Frederick Allen lives opposite Mrs. Lamarine's. Her house is noisy Saturday nights and Sundays. Have heard fiddling Sundays and noisy talk and singing at midnight. Have been awakened from my sleep. Have lived opposite several years. She has lived at No. 95 over a month. Have seen crowds of young men at her house and young ladies. It is a disorderly house. My attention has been attracted to the house more than once by loud talk, slang, profanity and general disorder. I have complained to my neighbors.

Francis C. Allen lives opposite. Had heard dancing tunes Sundays and noise that awoke her in the night. It was ridiculous, the actions at this house. Had seen lots of different girls at the house and had seen lots of people drinking in the house. Could not say what they drank. Had seen lots of men about the house. Had heard noise at the house late at night. At one time heard a girl swearing in the house.

Officer Gendron said last Saturday evening he was detailed to watch the house. About 10 15 a man came out of the house drunk, stayed a short time and then went in again. Shortly after saw five men go into the yard and up the back steps. In a short time two more men went into the yard. Mrs. Lamarine came out of the house and after looking up and down stooped over and picked up something. I heard noise inside as of the opening of a bottle of lager and the noise of pouring out the contents of a bottle. Heard the handling of bottles in the kitchen as if taking out or putting bottles into a beer case. Heard a noise as if some parties were wrestling inside. It rattled the windows and attracted the attention of people on the opposite side of the street. I saw 11 men go into the yard and upon the back steps while I was at the house. I left the house at 11 30 and none of the 11 men I had seen go in had come out up to that time.

Officer Stephen J. Weston said he had heard noise at the house, singing and dancing. Had seen considerable going in and coming out of the house. Had been to the house once to stop the noise.

Mary Generous lives at No. 96 South Second street. She knew Mrs. Lamarine by sight. Seen men go into her house that looked sober and came out drunk. Heard vile language and swearing in the house. Seen men go into the house most every day. Can't say how many I have seen in the house at one time. Saw Mrs Lamarine call into the house a man that was playing music on the street and she and he were fooling together. Have seen tumblers and drinking in the house. My windows and Mrs. Lamarine's were open. I have no feeling against Mrs. Lamarine only I don't like to have such scandal in the neighborhood and such talk before my children. I have seen drunken men go into and come out of her house and sober men go in and come out drunk. This closed the government testimony.

For the defence Mrs. Lamarine took the stand. She said her name was Adaline Lamarine and had lived at No. 95 South Second street for 2½ months. She never sold any liquor—the witnesses were not telling the truth. The liquor the officers found belonged to her son-in-law. Her son-in-law bought the quart of liquor Saturday night and brought it home. It had been used and the officers found the empty bottle wrapped in a paper. She has three boarders beside her family. The case of beer was bought by me for family use. Sometimes my three children that work in the mill have no appetite and want a glass of beer. I bought the beer Tuesday morning. I and my children use beer. I get a case a week and pay $1 for it. We do not use beer Sundays as we do not have to work in the mill on that day. There never was any noise in my house. All my children sing; they do not swear. Perhaps they swear when I am not around but not before me. Eleven men did not come to my house Saturday night; they might have gone up stairs. I bought the beer Tuesday morning about 9 o'clock and finished it up Saturday afternoon. My whole family drank the beer. We all drank some of the quart of liquor my son-in-law brought in Saturday night and he treated his friends—he has a great many—and what Mr. Wing found was what was left of it. The bottle found by Mr. Wixon was brought to the house by a boarder and she found the bottle in his room.

Joseph Tatro is a lather and son-in-law of Mrs. Lamarine. He lives with her at No. 95. He said the whiskey found by Mr. Wing was his. He bought a quart Saturday. It was drank by the family and his friends. The lager beer was for family use. He drank eggs and lager for his breakfast. The girls drank lager. He never saw Mrs. Lamarine sell any liquor. He had seen her give it away, but never saw her take any money for it. Two of his friends, the Coron boys, called on him last Saturday night and stayed about three-quarters of an hour. A number of men came into the house—five or six—after 10 o'clock. They were sitting around. I do not know who they were. I went to bed and left them in the kitchen. I drank with the Coron boys about half-past seven, and put what was left in a small bottle and put it in the cupboard. No beer was brought to the house Saturday night. I don't know the name of the man I bought the quart of whiskey of. It was on Water street. I paid 50 cents for it.

Mrs. Generous was recalled by the government, and said she saw two cases of beer carried to the house last Saturday night. It was about 7 o'clock. Two men that drive a beer team carried them into the house.

This closed the evidence.

Mr. Barney reviewed the case and in conclusion said he did not think the evidence sustained the complaint.

Judge Borden said he could not agree with him and in his opinion the evidence fully sustained the complaint. There were several things that were not explained as to the liquor bought, and used in the house from Saturday night to Sunday morning. The men the son-in-law left in the house when he went to bed and his statement that he did not know who they were is unexplained and taking the evidence all together he could not do otherwise than adjudge her guilty.

Judge Borden said he did not wish to say anything more about the policy of prosecuting such offenders as Mrs. Lamarine and letting the greater offenders alone. It was in the air what the reason is that the greater offenders are let alone. If the officers were to make the same efforts to convict the greater offenders that they had made in this case there would be no trouble about procuring evidence against these greater offenders. She was ordered to pay a fine of $60.

Mary Morse, sentenced to three months for drunkenness, appealed and recognized in $200.

Abraham Sampson of New York pleaded guilty of peddling eye glasses and spectacles in Fairhaven yesterday without a license. The arrest was made by Deputy Sheriff Butman. Sampson said he was a poor man and had been unfortunate in business and asked the clemency of the court. He was sentenced to pay a fine of $5.

LONG PLAIN.

Capt. Isaac Braley and family and Charles F. Leonard and family have been at Charles Neck, Marion, for a week.

The Republican caucus will be held on Saturday next at 2 p. m. at school-house hall, Long Plain, to choose delegates to all the conventions.

Walter R. Spooner and family are occupying a cottage at Marion for a few weeks.

Thomas B. Geggatt entertained a party of friends at a lawn party at his home Wednesday evening.

Miss Bertha Ashley of New Bedford is at Mrs. J. E. Borden's.

Rev. Brown E. Smith of the Baptist church preached on Sunday at the William Street Baptist church, New Bedford.

The Baptist Society have a shore party on Wednesday at Mosher's Grove, Mattapoisett.

Master Tom Martin, who has been spending his vacation at C. L. Spooner's, returned on Sunday to New Bedford.

FALL RIVER.

Katie Ross, a three-year-old child of Hugh M. Ross, residing at 6 Van Buren street, died Saturday evening from the effects of convulsions, preceded by a fall upon her head from a fence in her father's yard Thursday evening.

The assessors have estimated the valuation of property and the tax rate for this year. The valuation is $56,090,520, an increase of $1,718,590 over that of last year. The tax rate is $17.40, an increase of 20 cents per $1000 over that of last year.

Four young ladies took the veil yesterday afternoon at the Convent of the Dominican Sisters at 521 South Main street. Bishop Harkins officiated, and was assisted by Rev. Father Sauval of St. Anne's church.

SPECIAL NOTICES.

LILY OF THE VALLEY TEMPLE.
☞ Will have an excursion THURSDAY, Sept. 1, to Nonquitt. Barges leave hall at 1 30 P. M. Children 15c., adults 25c. for round trip. If stormy, it will be Saturday, Sept. 3d, if pleasant. au30-1t

NOTICE.
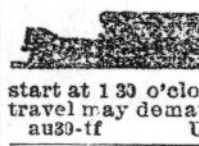
On and after September 1, 1892, on pleasant afternoons, the City Hall cars of the Fairhaven line will start at 1 30 o'clock and run as late as the travel may demand.
au30-tf UNION ST. RAILWAY CO.

SCHOOL BOOKS! SCHOOL SUPPLIES!

Prices as Low as the Lowest.

ROBERT W. TABER,
Bookseller and Stationer,
198 Union St.

WANTED TO HIRE
Furnished house by a small family without children, for the Winter season.
☞ Address box 30 *Standard* office. a29-6t

ELMER E. TOLMAN, Violinist.
Leader at the Opera House, will be ready to receive pupils after Sept. 5th, 1892.
☞ Apply at Box Office Opera House. au27-tf

INSTRUCTION IN GERMAN LANGUAGE.
☞ Perfect pronunciation. In short time to read, write and speak. Address
ROBT. LEUCHSENRING, 53 Cottage st. au23-TTS1m

NO BLOOD!

[Continued from First Page.]

person, and that it would be almost all over him. In the case of Mrs. Borden I should say that the person delivering the blows stood over the body, and that he would be

Blood Stained from Head to Foot

and more covered than in the case of Mr. Borden. There was nothing in the appearance of the stomachs to indicate anything abnormal or irregular.

Wrangle Over a Piece of Plaster.

Some controversy arose over a piece of plaster on which a spot of blood was; the plaster was handed over to Prof. Wood for examination, but Mr. Jennings objected, saying that he would not allow it to go out of his possession unless he could be assured that the blood stain would be left where it was; he was willing to admit it was human blood and to leave the plaster in the possession of the court.

The district attorney said this was the most absurdly impudent proceeding he ever heard of in his professional career; here was a man who said he was determined to take possession of his own evidence, and he requested Marshal Hilliard, since it appeared to have come to a matter of physical force, to remove the piece of wood shown on which were blood stains

Miss Lucy Collet.

before they were taken away, and the marshal removed them. Then Mr. Jennings asked the court if he could have the assurance that it would be returned in the custody of the court, and the court refused to give that assurance.

Then Mr. Jennings

Quietly Put the Plaster in his Pocket,

and said he proposed to keep it there.

The court ordered him to produce it, and after a while he did so, but said he should file a motion for a hearing on the matter, and was told that it would be kept by the court until the motion was heard.

Undertaker Winward's Evidence.

James Winward, undertaker, said that in searching Mr. Borden he found $78 in bills, watch and chain, keys and some loose change. All the money was in bills. He turned the property over to Dr. Dolan. Witness did not examine the clothes of Mrs. Borden.

In cross-examination witness said all the keys were on the ring; none of them were loose.

Witness, when asked about the wounds on Mr. Borden's face, said he thought they had been given from behind; they began on the left side of the nose and extended down through the chin; they were very close together. The bodies were delivered to him by Dr. Dolan for burial, he presumed; said he asked Dr. Dolan if he was through with the bodies, and he said, "Yes you may take them now." That was 5 30 p. m., Aug. 4. On the morning of the funeral, about 9 30, witness was notified not to bury the bodies.

John Dennie on the Stand.

John Dennie, stone cutter, was employed in the yard of Mr. Crowe on the day of the tragedy all day; was in the east end of the yard on the Third street side of it; was nearest the south fence, and could not see the Chagnon yard, nor the Borden yard, unless I stepped out. Could see all of the Crowe yard, but saw nothing but the people who worked there.

On cross-examination: There was a barn in the way of seeing the back part of the Crowe yard and in the Borden yard; saw Wixon there but don't know how he got in to the Crowe yard.

Officer Philip Harrington.

testified. His attention was first called to the matter at noon of the day; he was at home at dinner, and going down to the house made an examination of the premises. In one room he found Miss Lizzie and Miss Alice Russell; Lizzie was cool and collected, but would not or could not tell witness anything at all about the matter. She said she was in the barn twenty minutes at the time the murder was committed.

Witness asked her if it might not be half an hour.

"No," she said, "it was 20 minutes."

Then witness said "perhaps it was but 15 minutes."

"No," said Lizzie, "it was just 20 minutes."

Then witness cautioned her about what she might say, as there was considerable excitement and she must be careful. Then witness asked her about the place in the barn where she was and what, if anything, she heard, and Lizzie answered that she

Drug Clerk Eli Bence.

had heard nothing at all, nor had she seen anybody around. The story of the man who wanted to hire a store of Mr. Borden was told again, but nothing new was elicited.

Witness said he looked in the stove as he was in the kitchen, and there was

Something in the Fire Box Which Looked Like Burned Paper.

The fire was low. Witness then described his examination of the barn. Upstairs and down stairs he found nothing different from what has previously been described; the barn was simply used as a storeroom.

Witness was interrogated particularly as to what Lizzie had told him about the man who had come to see her father about the store which he wanted to hire; he was sure that Lizzie told him that her father, although refusing the man, had told him to call again, and that she did not say he said he would come again.

Adjourned to 2 p. m.

Only a Love Affair.

The Boston *Herald* prints a story that the words, "Emma, you gave me away," were really uttered by Lizzie, and thus explains it:

Lizzie had a love affair. It was a simple one. The young man, perhaps he was over 35, was met on the Cape by the accused, and he paid some attention to her, and she felt highly complimented. So, last Wednesday morning, when he called at the Borden house to express his sympathy for Lizzie, and his belief in her innocence, he met and talked to Miss Emma Borden, and the pleasant times on the Cape were contrasted with the present sad state of affairs. In some way Miss Emma Borden intimated that her sister liked him very much, and the young man departed, not thinking that his visit would be made to play such an important part in this now famous case.

Emma visited Lizzie in the afternoon at the matron's room, and, anxious to talk to her sister of matters that would be likely to make her forget, even for a moment, the awful position circumstances have placed her in, spoke of the visitor of the morning.

Lizzie heard with great interest and pleasure of the young man's sympathy and his belief in her innocence, and had begun to say how very grateful she felt for his kind thoughts and words. Then Emma, in a joking way, told Lizzie of the intimation she had given the young man regarding Lizzie's interest in him. A gleam shot from Lizzie's eyes and she straightened herself up. Her womanly nature was hurt; a confidence broken.

Then she said: "Emma, you gave me away. I'll never speak to you again."

Emma knew her sister's manner, and she made no reply to the indignant outburst. She simply sat back in a chair, and watched her sister with a smile she could not well repress. Lizzie sat still for a few minutes, then, realizing how foolish her outburst had been, regained her good temper, and began to laugh with Emma. Then the sisters embraced with a fervor that the matron has never yet seen exhibited. They kissed each other most affectionately when they parted. Yet what a vastly different construction has been placed on the words of the prisoner.

Suspect Under Surveillance.

New and important evidence for the defence, in a measure corroborating Dr. Handy's peculiar stranger, and locating him in front of the Borden house within an hour of the tragedy, has been obtained. The witnesses are perfectly reliable. The man is said to have been located in a city not far from Fall River, and he will be kept under close surveillance until wanted.

New Clew to the Mystery.

NEW YORK, Aug. 30.—A man who gave his name as William Morgan Davis and said that he was a locomotive engineer from Columbus, called at Jersey City police headquarters yesterday and told Supt. Smith that he had overheard two men who spoke in a suspicious manner about the Borden murders.

"I was in the Pennsylvania railroad yard," said Davis, at about 6 o'clock Sunday evening, and went into a car to sleep. I was reclining on one of the seats and had been there about half an hour when two men came in. One of them had a smooth-shaven face and the other wore a mustache. The smooth-faced man said to the other:

"Did you get my letters?" The other answered: "I got one, but not the other."

"'Tell me about that murder in Fall River. Do you think John did it?' asked the first speaker. 'You know he did,' was the reply. 'I left him in Boston about 10 days before the murder. He was to go to Fall River. I told him where he could find me in New York. He showed up at the time he said he would, and told me that he committed the murders. He showed me spots of blood on his pants, and said he tried to wash them out. He told me he was going to Chicago, and would write to me, but I have not heard from him."

"John is the luckiest man I ever heard of," said the other man. "I would have been hung 20 years ago if I had done what he has."

"The men then caught sight of me," continued Davis, "and hurried out of the car. I went to the station master and told him what I had heard. I also told two or three brakemen. They advised me to notify a policeman. I found Detectives Walton and Morris, and they searched around the depot and yard, but could not find the men. Two men answering their description, were seen going out of the upper end of the depot. The men were well dressed, and seemed to be about 30 or 35 years old."

Supt. Smith cross-questioned the engineer, but he stuck to his story. He said he had been out of work for some time and was here in search of employment. The superintendent has sent the man's statement to Lizzie Borden's lawyer.

SPECIAL NOTICES.

FARMERS, ATTENTION!

Important Addition to the Autumn Fair of the South Bristol Farmers' Club.

EXHIBITION OF DRESSED POULTRY.

☞ On FRIDAY, September 23d, the Club will provide space for, and give their attention to, an exhibition of dressed poultry.
All producers are cordially invited to contribute something towards this new and interesting feature of the Club's Autumn Fair.
All poultry to be dressed undrawn with heads on.
Premiums will be awarded by an impartial judge.
All exhibits may be sold at the pleasure of the owner, but must remain on exhibition until the closing of the fair Friday evening.
No exhibits, for competition, will be received after 1 o'clock P. M. Friday.
All exhibits should be plainly marked with the owner's name, breed of fowl, and class.
Thoroughbred and first-crossed stock alone accepted for exhibition.

CLASSES.
New York Broilers—To weigh not less than 2½ pounds nor more than 4 pounds per pair. To be exhibited only in pairs.
Chickens—To weigh under 4 lbs. apiece.
Chickens—To weigh over 4 lbs. apiece.
Fowl—To weigh over 5 lbs. apiece.
Green Ducks—Hatched in 1892, exhibited only in pairs.
Green Geese—Hatched in 1892.
Philadelphia Capons—Any weight.
For further information address,
HENRY M. PLUMMER,
Chairman Dressed Poultry Committee,
South Dartmouth, Mass.
au30-3t&w1t

AN OPPORTUNITY OF A LIFETIME.

☞ Never again will the people of this country have an opportunity to witness a parade of Grand Army Veterans equal to the one that will be in Washington September 20th, 1892.
Sixty thousand Veterans will march on Pennsylvania avenue in Grand Column, the same as they passed in review before Gen. Grant at the close of the war, in '65.
R. A. Peirce Post, 190, has arranged with the Pennsylvania Railroad Company one of the finest trips that can be had for ease and comfort in travelling. They will leave New Bedford Sept. 18th, at 3 P. M., on a special limited train of Pullman Sleeping Cars, that will arrive in Washington the next morning at 7 A. M., without any change whatever, giving all an opportunity of a good night's rest. The same cars will be for the exclusive use and the home of the Post and their guests during their stay in Washington, and will be located at a very central point, making them easy of access at all times.
This Post will remain in Washington until Friday evening, Sept. 23d, at 9 P. M., arriving in New Bedford the following Saturday at 12 30 P. M.
Post 190 are fortunate in procuring such excellent accommodations, as they avoid all change of cars, boats, ferries and enormous crowds that will be moving at that time, which cause delays and often times serious accidents.
The expense of this special train, for the round trip, including sleeping accommodation for the seven days, is $19.65, which secures better quarters, and at a cheaper rate, than can be otherwise obtained.
The Post have a limited number of tickets at their disposal for those who desire to participate in this beautiful excursion, and all information desired can be obtained of the Committee in charge.
Tickets will be good to return on any train until Oct. 16th, allowing stop overs at any point on the route.
F. A. WASHBURN,
HENRY W. MASON,
FRED'K. P. MOSHER, } Committee.
THOS. J. GIFFORD,
WILLIAM ALMY.
aug17-20-22-24-27-30-sep1

Umbrellas Covered.
☞ Re-covering frames saves one-third original cost.
UMBRELLAS, (Silk and Wool,) light, silky appearance, warranted not to split
J. S. WRIGHT, Umbrella Maker,
78 William Street. TuF

PENSIONS.
☞ Soldiers, sailors, widows, orphans, desiring to apply for pensions, back pay or bounty, can consult J. F. VINAL, from Washington, D. C., at 107 Fourth street. au2-1m

said: "How long will it take you?" I said I didn't know, but that I had to search the room. She said: "I do hope you will get through soon; this is making me sick." I searched the room.

Mr. Knowlton. Did you say anything more to Miss Borden?

Assistant Marshal Fleet. Yes, I said: "You say, Miss Borden, that you went out to the barn, and that you were out there half an hour, while your father and mother were killed. You still say that?" She said: "I do not. I say I was in the barn 20 minutes to half an hour." Said I, "You told me this morning that you were out there half an hour." "I don't say so now," she said, "It was 20 minutes to half an hour." "What makes you say 20 minutes to half an hour?" I asked her. "Which is it now, 20 minutes or half an hour?" She said, "It was 20 minutes to half an hour."

Mr. Knowlton. Did you search the premises then? Did you have any more talk with her then?

Marshal Fleet. I searched the room and bureau and then went behind Lizzie's door to another door. It was locked. I asked her what room that was.

She Said: "That is Father's Room."

"Is there another way to get into it?" I asked. She said there was, by going by way of the back stairs; that the door from her room was always locked. I started to go around, as there was no other way. When I got into the entry I asked her what was in the clothes press. She asked me if I must search that. I told her I must. She said she had the key and would open it. She produced the key and opened it.

Mr. Knowlton. Describe the room.

Marshal Fleet. It was about 5 by 8; there was a window in it, but it had not been opened in some time. We took nothing, and then we searched the rest of the house. I tried the door of Mrs. Borden's room from Miss Lizzie's room. It was fastened by a bolt, I think, on the other side.

Mr. Knowlton. Did you go in there? What else did you say to Miss Borden?

Marshal Fleet. When I went into Miss Borden's room Miss Lizzie said there was no use going there, that she always locked her door, and there was no possible way for anybody to get into it. I asked her when she saw her mother last. She said about 9 o'clock, when she was going down stairs. Her mother was in the room where she was found murdered. Miss Lizzie also said that

Mrs. Borden Had Received a Note or Letter

from some one that morning. She thought it was from somebody of the house.

Mr. Knowlton. What was the appearance of Lizzie at this time? Was she cool and calm?

Mr. Adams. I object.

Mr. Knowlton asked the reason for the objection, and Mr. Adams said, after a few seconds: "Well, it is of no use. I don't object."

Mr. Knowlton. Was Lizzie in tears while in her room?

Marshal Fleet. No.

Mr. Knowlton. That is all.

Mr. Adams proceeded to cross-examine the witness.

Mr. Adams. Were you aware when you asked to look into the clothes press at the head of the stairs, that Officer Doherty had already been there?

Marshal Fleet. I was not.

Mr. Adams. Do you say this was the first search?

Marshal Fleet. No; I don't. I thought it was.

"When you went to the barn, who went with you?"

"Officers Monahan and Wilson."

"Did you go up stairs?"

"Yes."

"See a work bench?"

"I didn't notice any."

"Didn't you see a bench of some kind there?"

"Yes; I did."

"Did you go to the windows?"

"No."

"Couldn't you have gone there?"

"There is a partition at one window."

"Does that prevent your getting out of this window?"

"No. I haven't said so. I didn't go to the window. I think if I had wanted to get to the windows I could have done so. The hay was piled up on the north side of the barn. I searched all around down stairs and the two officers went up stairs with me."

"This young woman

Has Been Asked Questions by the Officers

and was subsequently asked questions by you in her chamber, was she not?"

"Yes, sir."

"Do you think she said there was any talk between her father and this man who wanted to hire the store on the day of the tragedy?"

"No, not that day."

"When you went upstairs and had the second talk with her, Dr. Bowen was there as her physician, was he not?"

"Well, as friend and physician, yes."

"When you opened that closet it was full of women's clothing, was it not?"

"Yes; there were a dozen or eighteen dresses there. I examined the closet again on the Saturday following. I looked at some of the clothing the first time. There was a cloth over the dresses."

"Were you looking to see if you could find any bloody clothing?"

"Yes, I was. I was not looking very closely."

"You went through this closet and looked at each garment?"

"Yes, I did."

"That was after you had seen the axes and hatchet?"

"Yes, sir."

"Who took the hatchet you laid aside?"

"Officer Edson."

"When?"

"The following morning. He went there by order of the marshal."

"What were the other axes brought in?"

"I don't know."

"Have you heard anything about a sack or bag?"

"No, sir."

"Now this particular hatchet you laid aside, was it damp?"

"Yes; it looked to me as if it had been wiped with a damp cloth."

"See any hairs on it?"

"On no part of it."

"You examined all those hatchets to see if there was any indication of blood upon them?"

"Yes, I did."

"You made the search on Saturday?"

"Yes."

"Was it after the funeral?"

"Yes, after the procession left the house. Mr. Seaver, Marshal Hilliard, Dr. Dolan, Mr. Jennings and myself were present."

"You were given every facility to go through the house, were you not?"

"Yes, sir."

"And you searched this closet again?"

"Yes, sir."

"You went through band-boxes and barrels on Saturday, did you not?"

"Yes, sir, we went through everything."

"That's all, sir, concluded Mr. Adams, and the session was then adjourned for the day."

A Convenience for Grover.

Form of Buzzards Bay blank No. 39:

GRAY GABLES, 1892.

My Dear —— ——:

Your package of kindly sent to me per came safely to hand to-day. Permit me to return my hearty thanks and to express the hope that the grand old State of in which you reside will roll up an old-fashioned majority of this Fall in support of the time-honored Democratic principles of and

With great respect, your obt. servt.,
GROVER CLEVELAND.

—*Chicago Tribune.*

Only Right to Tell.

The Rev. Mark Guy Pearse, the eminent English Divine, writes:

"BEDFORD PLACE, RUSSELL SQUARE, LONDON, Dec. 10, 1888.

"I think it only right that I should tell you of how much use I find ALLCOCK'S POROUS PLASTERS in my family and among those to whom I have recommended them. I find them a very breastplate against colds and coughs."

BOARD OF PUBLIC WORKS.

Business of Importance Transacted at a Regular Meeting.

A regular meeting of the Board of Public Works was held last evening with Mayor Ashley in the chair and A. B. Drake clerk pro tem. Mr. Rotch was absent.

A hearing was given to those persons interested in the Coffin avenue sewer. J. B. Jean and two others objected.

Henry Leaming said that several new houses would be built if a sewer was put in. Most of the abutters want a sewer. Those who own houses in particular want sewers, while those who have not yet put up buildings appear to be the remonstrants.

It was voted to proceed with the work and to call for an appropriation.

The next business taken up was that of a sewer in Court street from County to Park street. A hearing was also given on this matter.

William Doran said he had no use for a sewer and objected, while A. B. Hathaway, florist, said it was immaterial to him. He didn't care for a sewer for his own use.

William Sanders, in a communication, acting for the County Commissioners, objected to the construction of the proposed sewer, while A. E. Lucas in a like manner put in a protest, claiming to have already good and sufficient drainage. B. S. Batchelor, who had no objection to the sewer himself, in a communication, notified the Board that the Davis Chemical Works were well drained and that the heirs of Henry V. Davis would undoubtedly protest.

F. E. Sawin said he entered the Morgan street sewer and had to cross another person's property, and the owner of this property objected to his running his drain across the land any longer. Several of his neighbors were in the same fix and it was a question of a sewer in Court street or a cesspool.

It was stated that Mrs. E. T. Chapman and Mr. Graham objected to the sewer.

George L. Brownell stated he favored the sewer. So did Joseph F. Lewis.

After some discussion it was voted to lay the matter on the table.

A communication was received from Valentine Parker offering to give the city, for the widening of Howard avenue, 60 feet wide, from Belleville avenue to Acushnet avenue, a strip of land on the southeast corner of Belleville and Howard avenues containing about 32 rods, on condition that a fence be put up on his north line and no betterments be charged him on account of the widening of said street, it being understood said avenue shall be accepted and made passable this Fall; and he waived a notice of a hearing for the layout and acceptance of said avenue.

Samuel C. France appeared to state he would not stand in the way of the improvement, but he thought that as about 60 rods of his land was to be taken that the Board might fill in a little pond that would be left on his land after the road had been widened. This, with 25 rods of land offered him by Mr. Bartlett, would be all he would expect.

Mr. Drake was asked to make an estimate of how much filling would be required, and the matter was laid over.

Isaac B. Tompkins, Jr., appeared to remonstrate against the gas company placing a pole in front of Driscol, Church & Hall's building on Union street. A hearing was ordered for next Monday evening.

It was ordered that the Board buy 10,000 feet of curbing.

Ordered, That all lamp posts and poles belonging to the New Bedford Gas & Edison Light Co. which are not in actual use be removed from the streets.

The Superintendent was ordered to send the Gas Co. notice of the above vote which goes into effect at once.

The matter of the County road was taken up, and it was decided to get the City Solicitor's opinion about taking back the land owned by the city. The road was laid out in 1828 50 feet wide, but abutters have encroached upon the road so it is now but 40 feet wide.

A communication was received from Alfred Thornton, Albert A. Chace, and Daniel B. Leonard, stating that in their opinion the widening of Butler street to 50 feet wide would be a great improvement, and hoped it would be the pleasure of the board to do the same at an early date under the provisions of law authorizing the assessment of betterments. The gentlemen thought that if the work was not done at present that the board will see the necessity of taking in for street purposes all land included in the layout of the street of 40 feet in width, that the street may be regular and the walks of a proper width. If left as at present it will be very irregular in its lines and an eyesore to all passing through it. The communication rehearsed the history of the street, and said that as long as no claims were made at the time of the laying out of the street, no legal reason could prevent the Board from taking all land lying within the street lines, and the abutters are in duty bound to properly wall or fence in their estates. The gentlemen stated they hoped the Board would see the necessity of at least widening the street to its legitimate width, 40 feet, and thereby save possible expense for damages in the future to persons using the same, by reason of irregular street lines, etc. The communication was placed on file.

The petition of the New Bedford Gas & Edison Light Co. for a location of seven poles in Madison, Water and First streets was placed on the visiting list.

The petition of the same for permission to remove two small trees on First street, near the corner of Madison, was placed on the visiting list.

The petition of W. D. Cotter and four others for a curbing on the north side of Cedar Grove street to North Front street, also on the west side of North Front street from Cedar Grove street to Coggeshall street was placed on the visiting list.

The petition of Thomas J. Gifford and eight others that some definite action be taken in regard to macadamizing Austin street between Cedar and Ashland streets was received and placed on file.

Louis Dame in a communication called attention to the condition of the street in front of his house, corner of Delano and Second streets. The street is filled with water in stormy weather. The matter was placed on visiting list.

The pay roll for week ending August 20th was approved as follows:

Street department,	$2,364.31
Grape street sewer extension,	740.19
Beetle and Howard street sewers,	378.70
General sewers,	118.33
Public works—Improvement,	83.26
Engineering department,	55.58
N. B. & F. H. bridge,	21.29
Parks and squares,	19.83
Total,	$3,781.49

The petition of Roger H. Hervey to be appointed keeper of the north park was placed on file.

The petition of the New Bedford Gas & Edison Light Company for a location of poles on Second street, west from Spring street, and one on the west side of Acushnet avenue, was placed on the visiting list.

The petition of Joab Claudino and four others for curbing on the south side of Rockland street, between Crapo and Bonney streets, and a crossing and sand-catcher on the southwest corner of Rockland and Crapo streets, was placed on the visiting list.

The petition of Andrew Springer and Ellen M. Handy for a concrete walk on the north side of Kempton street, in front of the building at the corner of Chestnut street, was placed on the visiting list.

The petition of Frank S. Gildea for permission to move a wooden building, 25 by 20 feet, from the west side of Wilkinson street through Coggeshall street to the west side of Howard street, was granted.

The petition of William Ingham, for permission to move a wooden building, 25 by 21 feet, from Coggeshall street to the southwest corner of North Front and Holly street, was granted.

The petition of Michael Englesbee for permission to move a wooden building, 25 by 21 feet, from Coggeshall street to the west side of Garfield street was granted.

A communication was received from Frank J. Gurney and 28 others stating they refused to draw any more crusher stone for less than 50 cents a ton. The communication was placed on file.

SCHOOL COMMITTEE.

Four Teachers' Resignations Accepted and Routine Business Transacted.

The adjourned meeting of the School Committee was held last evening, Vice-Chairman Pitman presiding in the absence of the Mayor. Absent—Mrs. Borden, Miss Winslow, Messrs. Hewins, Channing and Brownell.

In the absence of Secretary William E. Hatch, Isaac B. Tompkins, Jr., was chosen clerk pro tem.

Mr. Tompkins, for the committee on grammar schools, presented the resignation of Miss Mary M. Robinson as a teacher in the Middle Street school. The resignation was accepted, and the vacancy was referred to the committee on grammar schools.

Mr. Shepherd, of the committee on primary schools, presented the resignations of Miss Susie P. Diman, Helen C. Allen and Miss Gertrude M. Robinson as teachers, and moved that they be accepted and that the vacancies be referred to the committee on primary schools. The resignations were accepted and the vacancies were so referred.

Dr. Dunbar stated that Charles R. Allen, teacher of chemistry in the High School, desires the purchase of Remsen's Introduction to Chemistry to replace won-out copies of Shepherd's Chemistry, and moved that the request be granted. The motion was carried ordering the change.

Miss Sarah H. Cranston was granted a leave of absence of nine weeks on recommendation of the committee on grammar schools.

Mr. Howland, of the committee on Howland fund, presented a recommendation for the following expenditures from the income of that fund:

Parker Street Grammar School—1 Gray's Botany; 1 Holmes' Poems, Household Ed.; 1 Lowell's Poems, Household Ed.; 1 Scott's Poems, Household Ed.; 1 Tennyson's Poems, Household Ed.; 2 Montgomery's History of the United States; 12 Our World, Part I, revised edition; 1 International Dictionary. $20.72.

Fourth Street Primary School—20 Mrs. Monroe's Primer; 70 Normal Music First Reader; 1 First Series Music Chart—$29.50.

High School—15 Allen's Laboratory, Students' edition—$36.

The expenditure was ordered by 12 votes.

A communication was received, signed by Allen Russell, Jr., and 25 other residents of the Head of the River, asking that Nathan C. Briggs be appointed janitor of the Acushnet school. The communication was referred to the committee on expenditures.

On motion of Mr. Tompkins, the matter of fitting up additional rooms outside of school buildings was referred to the committee on expenditures, with power.

Mr. Sayer, of the committee on manual training, presented the resignation of Miss Florence Cleaves as teacher of drawing, presented May 26th, but on which, at that time, action was deferred. The resignation was accepted, and the vacancy was referred to the committee on High School.

On motion of Mr. Shepherd of the committee on primary schools that committee was authorized to assign assistants to the several schools and report at the next meeting.

Mr. Tompkins referred to several instances of teachers who desire transfers from one school to another and wanted the committee on such schools authorized to make the transfers.

The various members opposed this at length, as they deemed it a detriment to the efficiency of the schools. Besides they considered the reasons presented as trivial and not of sufficient moment to warrant the transfers. No action was taken.

Dr. Kennedy called attention to the necessity of soon calling another meeting on account of the evening schools.

The meeting then adjourned. A special meeting will be called Thursday evening, Sept. 8th.

COTTAGE CITY NEWS.

Defendants in Liquor Cases Released Owing to Defective Warrants.

[Special Dispatch.]

COTTAGE CITY, Aug. 30.—Mrs. A. A. Hill of the Narragansett Hotel yesterday appeared before Special Justice E. G. Eldridge to prove, if she could, that she was not guilty of a violation of the liquor law. Henry A. Mansfield, who acts in the capacity of clerk in the store where liquor was found on a recent raid by the police, was also on hand.

Mrs. Hill and Mr. Mansfield were held for this trial in the sum of $100 each, which matter of being obliged to furnish bail has caused comment.

The trial yesterday went by default, the seal had been omitted from the warrant and defendants' counsel agreed that it was illegal. Mrs. Hill and Mr. Mansfield will be rearrested and will appear in court on Thursday next.

The finding of a dead male infant in Sunset Lake on Sunday was quite a shock to the neighbors. Chief of police Twombly doesn't want to say much about the case, but he left the island on yesterday afternoon's boat with a big bag, and Deputy Sheriff Dexter and Patrolman Leighton acted so suspiciously that onlookers concluded the bag was filled with evidence.

About 700 people attended the benefit concert tendered Capt. John Orlando of West Falmouth in the Casino last evening by the teachers and pupils of "Villa Bristhall."

There were about 30 arrivals by the New York boat this morning.

There is a prospect that there may be an illumination after all. A canvass of the business men and heavy residents is making.

Mr. Richards, than whom a truer sportsman never drew bead on darting quail, is at Capt. Dunham's, Tuckernuck, shooting plover.

Business during the season now drawing to a close, has been uniformly good. Many rentals for next year have been made and the prospects for new dwellings is very good.

The bathing floats, broken adrift during last week's storm, have not been replaced.

The line of march to be taken by the children on Friday afternoon next will be as follows: From Tabernacle, through Commonwealth square, through County Park, through Arcade, down Circuit avenue to Narragansett to Sea View, turning at the club-house, round Ocean avenue to Casino. There will be refreshments at the Casino and fireworks on the park.

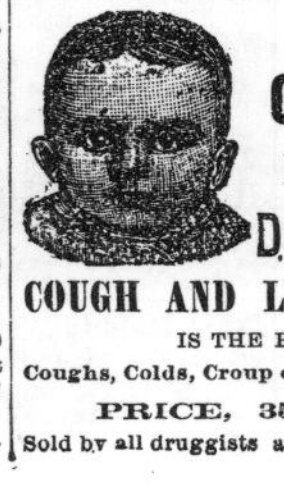

EVEN CHILDREN KNOW THAT DR. HOUGH'S COUGH AND LUNG BALSAM, IS THE BEST FOR Coughs, Colds, Croup or Whooping Cough. PRICE, 35 CENTS. Sold by all druggists and medicine dealers.

COPYRIGHT 1892

READY FOR THE FRAY.

There may be no question whatever about your courage, but we'll undertake to say that, though you are as brave as a lion, you won't want to have anything to do with that kind of a fray. Trousers and tatters don't make just the kind of a combination you are hankering after, do they? Purchasers of our $12.00 Suits are bothered with nothing of the sort. They are just as safe from it as though they had a paid up policy of insurance against any such unpleasantness. If this suit gives you any hankering at all, it will give you an ungovernable hankering for another one just like it.

OUR FALL STYLE HATS

Now ready for inspection. All the leading styles, such as YEAMAN, MILLER, HARRINGTON, BOSTON DERBY and LAMSON & HUBBARD, in all grades from

$1.50 to $3.00.

M. C. SWIFT & SON,

153, 157 and 159 Union Street,

NEW BEDFORD, - - - MASS.

JOHNSON'S ANODYNE LINIMENT Established 1810.

Originated by an Old Family Physician,

For INTERNAL as much as EXTERNAL Use.

NORTH WATERFORD, ME., Jan. 14, 1891.

I. S. JOHNSON, ESQ. My Dear Sir:—Fifty years ago this month your father, Dr. Johnson, called at my store and left with me some Johnson's Anodyne Liniment on sale. I remember him distinctly to-day, and could tell you just how he was dressed on that day fifty years ago. I have sold Johnson's Anodyne Liniment ever since and I can most truly say that it has maintained its high standard and popularity from that time to this. No medicine to-day possesses the confidence of the public to a greater extent than Johnson's Anodyne Liniment. It is doubtful if you have many customers who remember the good old Doctor who first compounded this medicine, and received it direct from his hand fifty years ago. Extending my kind wishes, I remain, JOHN B. RAND.

FOR PURELY HOUSEHOLD USE, ALMOST A CENTURY.

Generation after Generation have Known and Blessed It.

All who order direct from us, and request it, shall receive a certificate that the money shall be refunded if not abundantly satisfied. Retail price, 35 cents, Six $2.00, express prepaid, if you can't get it near home. Ask first. Sold by druggists. Full information sent free. I. S. JOHNSON & CO., 22 Custom House Street, Boston, Mass.

BEFORE AND AFTER USING.

MANHOOD RESTORED "Nerve Seeds," the wonderful remedy is sold with a written guarantee to cure all nervous diseases, such as Weak Memory, Loss of Brain Power, Headache, Wakefulness, Lost Manhood, Nightly Emissions, Quickness, Evil Dreams, Lack of Confidence, Nervousness, Lassitude, all drains and loss of power of the Generative Organs in either sex caused by over exertion, youthful errors, or excessive use of tobacco, opium or stimulants which soon lead to Infirmity, Consumption and Insanity. Put up convenient to carry in vest pocket. Sent by mail in plain package to any address for $1, or 6 for $5. (With every $5 order we give a written guarantee to cure or refund the money.) CIRCULAR FREE. Address NERVE SEED CO., Chicago, Ill.

For sale by Wright Drug Co., New Bedford, Mass. TTS

C. W. HASKINS,

Having replenished his stock by liberal purchases of new goods, offers a choice selection of Diamonds, Watches, Fine Jewelry, Optical Goods, &c. The display of Sterling Silver Table Ware and Novelties is very attractive.

Attention is invited to a large collection of Souvenir Spoons, especially some in fine Enamel and Gold from various European countries.

Fine Watch and Clock Repairing done by competent and careful workmen and fully warranted

—AT—

C. W. HASKINS',

No. 20 Purchase Street.

Smoke the New Nickel Cigar,

AMERICAN TRAMP

IT IS THE LEADER.

FOR SALE EVERYWHERE. aug-1m

Baggage Tags

ALWAYS IN STOCK AT

STANDARD OFFICE.

To our Patrons:

The proprietors of the paper have kindly allowed us this space, in order to inform the people of New Bedford and all this part of Bristol County that there is no better place on earth to buy goods in the Kitchen Furnishing Line. Our line of Barstow's Bay State Ranges have a world-wide reputation. We have a full line of Kitchen Furnishings in stock and are ready to attend to all orders for Plumbing, Tinsmithing, Tinroofing and General Jobbing in our line of business. We propose to supply the wants of our customers to the best of our ability. We intend to call special attention to the various lines of our business as often as our time will permit. You are cordially invited to visit

HAYDEN'S

KITCHEN FURNISHING HOUSE; Cor. Acushnet Ave. and Bedford St.

JAHN BROS., Florists,

CLARKS POINT.

ROSES AND CARNATIONS, A SPECIALTY.

171-M

SUMMER BARGAINS!

Are Now in Full Force With Us.

A lot of Remnants and short lengths of Carpets at about half price.

13 Parlor Suites cut in price from $5 to $25 per suite.

20 Chamber Sets to close, from $5 to $20 under price.

25 Baby Carriages to close at some price.

SUMMER FURNITURE!

IN GREAT VARIETY.

Refrigerators of all sizes, at rock bottom prices.

This is our annual clearing up of odds and ends, and if there is a want of anything in housekeeping, look now for it at a bargain.

CASH OR CREDIT.

CASH OR CREDIT,

CASH OR CREDIT.

PEIRCE FURNISHING CO.,

Cor. Purchase and Kempton Sts.,

THE LEADERS OF LOW PRICES IN THE HOUSE FURNISHING BUSINESS.

FINANCIAL.

SANFORD & KELLEY.

GARDNER T. SANFORD, CHARLES S. KELLEY, } Bankers,

Members Boston Stock Exchange,

47 North Water St., New Bedford.

STOCKS AND BONDS BOUGHT AND SOLD ON COMMISSION

At the New York and Boston Stock Boards.

CONSERVATIVE & PROFITABLE INVESTMENTS FOR TRUST FUNDS.

New Bedford Manufacturing Stocks have a first-class record as dividend payers, and we always have some on hand to offer.

Sole Agents for the sale in this city of the 6 per cent. Guaranteed Mortgages of the Lombard Investment Co.

Auction Sale of Stocks and Bonds WEDNESDAYS AND SATURDAYS, at 10 45 A. M.

ORDERS SOLICITED.

SMITH, HOYT & CO.,

Bankers and Stock Brokers,

25 Congress St., Boston, Mass.

STOCKS, Bonds, Grain and Oil bought and sold for cash or carried on moderate margin. Some new ideas will be found in our circular, which are greatly to the advantage of our customers. Buying and selling the same stock is one of them. Inquiries given careful attention. Send for circular. TT&S-1m

T. E. BOWMAN & CO.,

Topeka, Kansas,

NEGOTIATORS OF

Conservative Mortgage Loans in Eastern Kansas.

$2,500,000 LOANED without loss to any investor, and have never yet had to foreclose a farm loan in these eastern counties. Write us for list of investments. s29

MONEY TO LOAN!

IN large or small amounts at low rates and easy terms on Real Estate, Pianos, Organs, Horses, Carriages, &c., which can remain in possession of the owners. Loans taken from 30 days to 5 years. ☞ All business strictly confidential. Office Hours 8 to 12 A. M., and 1 to 6 P. M. H. F. DAMON, 34 North Second St., (up one flight) opposite Post Office. sep17-TTS6ptf

GEORGE LEVY, North End Pawn Broker.

Cash advanced on Real or Personal Property. All business private. au3-1m

SECOND EDITION.

HOME MATTERS.

REAL ESTATE SALES.—M. E. Smith has sold for Isaac Greenup two lots of land on the north side of Belleville road containing 22.46 rods to Louis E. Brightman.

T. F. Healey has sold for S. C. Hunt to Michael Englysbee two lots of land on contemplated Granfield street, running north from Coggeshall street; also for H. H. Crapo, trustee, to Clara A. Gifford lot No. 27 on Hathaway avenue, containing 16.16 rods; also to C. H. Gifford lots No. 29 and 31 on same avenue, containing 33 rods; also for a syndicate to W. Sowle two lots on contemplated Holly street, containing 36 rods.

John Whitehead has sold for George A. Briggs two house lots on River avenue, Fairhaven, about 36 rods, to John W. Dixon.

Stephen A. Brownell and John W. Bannister have sold to Bernard McGurk, 22 rods of land on the west side of McGurk street.

BUILDING.—The sills of the Enos building on South Water street are all laid, and the frame will probably be raised this week.

The new police station on South Water street has all the foundations in, including the row of basement cells of the lock-up.

William Inghen has petitioned for leave to move a dwelling house from its present location on Coggeshall street to a location at the southwest corner of North Front and Holly streets.

Michael Englesbee asks permission to move a dwelling house from its location on Coggeshall street to a location on Garfield street.

A NEW MILL SCHEME.—It is rumored that Fall River parties have recently been in consultation with E. G. Turner of Turner's Mills, with a view of purchasing a mill site on his pond and erecting a cotton mill to be run by water power. Mr. Turner at first declined to sell, but it is stated has since changed his mind and it is not altogether improbable that a cotton waste mill may be erected there.

ROCHESTER.

Miss Lillie Shirley of New Bedford is at Mrs. George H. Welds.

Mrs. John M. Hathaway of Fairhaven has been visiting at John F. Hatch's for a few days.

Picking will begin on the Freeman bog this week.

Repairs are in progress on the belfry of the Centre Church, getting it in condition for the new bell.

John F. Hatch has had a large addition built to his barn.

James A. Hartley is having a new road built so he can drive around his mill.

PLYMOUTH COUNTY.

Charles A. Eaton, ex-chief of the Brockton fire department, has leased the factory on Belmont street recently vacated by Houghton, Coolidge & Co., for the manufacture of shoes.

Saturday officers discovered in the Old Colony freight house at Campello 11 cases of beer marked "Brooks." Addison Brooks is a driver for Expressman Dennie. The officers seized the beer. The drug store of Parker & Geary, corner of Main and Ward treets, Brockton, was visited by the officers, where they seized six gallons of whiskey, a like quantity of wine and an eighth of a gallon of brandy. The house of Maurice Callahan, 310 Court street, and his store adjoining, were also raided. In the store 40 gallons of cider were seized.

Somebody entered the Public Library quarters in Satucket block, Brockton, probably on Sunday morning, by raising a window from a shed in the rear of the block, but no damage or loss of property is reported.

MARINE INTELLIGENCE.

Cld at New York 29th, steamer Richmond, Jenney, Norfolk.

Passed through Hell Gate 29th, sch Grace P Willard, Gardiner, New York for Nantucket.

Sld from Perth Amboy 29th, sch J S Lamprey, Harding, Boston.

Ar at Philadelphia 29th, schs George Twoby, Farrow, Kennebec; W S Jordan, Studley, do; B B Church, Allen, do; Ida L Hull, Gabrielson, do; John S Ames, Olsen, Boston. Cld, schs Fortuna, Pierce, Boston; Henry Lippitt, Howes, do; James H Hoyt, Nickerson, do; Kate Markee, Perry, do.

Ar at West Washington 29th, schs Maria O Teel, Johnston, Bangor; Daniel B Fearing, Clifford, do.

Sld from Norfolk 29th, schs Bertha Dean, Boston; Charles A Briggs, this port.

Sld from Savannah 29th, steamer Kansas City, New York.

DR PRICE'S DELICIOUS Flavoring Extracts

NATURAL FRUIT FLAVORS.

Vanilla - Of perfect purity.
Lemon - Of great strength.
Orange - Economy in their use
Almond -
Rose etc. - Flavor as delicately

and deliciously as the fresh fruit.

FINANCIAL.

Dull Stock Boards—Atchison Strengthens and Chicago, Burlington & Quincy Also Holds Firm—Money Easy, With Rates Unaltered—Rumors Prevalent To-day of Gold Exportations—Old Colony Earnings for Last Quarter—Statement for Year Appended—Chicago, Burlington & Quincy July Net Decreases $49,204—Splendid Atchison Statement Showing an Enormous Gain in Gross and Net—Copper Exports—In General.

TUESDAY, Aug. 30.

Selling of Reading, rumors of gold exports, and an excellent Atchison statement represent the more important happenings and gossip of to-day's financial circles. All the coalers are being talked lower on the belief that already the price of coal has been put too high and must drop. Regarding the gold export, rumors may be possible that some small exportations will be made this week. The Atchison statement is indeed a fine one and has caused a strengthening movement to set in in the stock, which has carried the price to 39, and may another week call 40 for it.

The local money market continues dull and generally easy.

Boston money is unchanged to-day. At clearing house this morning loans were again made at 3 per cent. New York funds sold at 9 cents discount.

New York advices indicate a heavier demand for money in that centre.

Sterling $4.87 and $4.88½.

Bonds dull.

Wall street gossip this morning said: "Generally thought bear brokers were using the market to sell long stock in Reading yesterday. Talk rather bearish on coalers on belief price of coal has been advanced too rapidly. Some trouble between Pacific Mail and Panama railroad. Their present arrangements expire next April. St Paul is stronger on good earnings and belief in a dividend. London not much of a feature, but still inclined to sell. To-day's prices from there irregular.

Reading was heavily sold this forenoon and the price dropped off to 56⅜. Later a rally set in, however, and at noon the price was back to 57¼, and the market for it indicated many signs of strength. Other stocks were dull. Atchison 38⅝, Burlington & Quincy 101, Erie 27, St. Paul 83⅜, Sugar 112, and Western Union 98, Union Pacific held 38⅝, General Electric 116⅛. After 12 o'clock the market continued dull, but prices were fractionally better under the influences of the advance in Reading.

At 2 o'clock the market was firm and more active.

The Boston market was intensely dull this morning, and traders attempted but little business. West End sold at 73⅝, do. preferred 87⅞. General Electric 116, and Sugar 112½. Atchison improved to 39, and B. & Q. to 101⅛. In the early afternoon the market continued dull and without feature. Sales to noon were: Bonds $96,800 and 8550 shares of stock.

The market was active and strong at 2 o'clock. New England was the feature at 34⅜, against an opening of 33⅛.

The C. B. & Q. July statement came out this noon. Net decrease during the month, $49,203.99. Since Jan. 1st, earnings have gained $509,021.71 net.

Exports of one million gold between now and Thursday are rumored.

A 11 o'clock special: London and Cammack brokers were rather sellers after opening. Traders bought the general list. Market now quiet, with Reading heavy again. We hear rumors that gold is likely to be taken to-day, but can't confirm as yet.

Boston bank statement shows an increase in reserve of $475,572.

Morosini says Gould is a bull on his properties.

It is said that C. B. & Q.'s August earnings will be the largest in the history of the company. July earnings are expected at any time now.

Boston *Post* financial says to-day:

Cleveland & Canton preferred sold at 19⅛. The business of this road is increasing every day, and I am told the stock is very cheap at present prices.

The silver question seems to be cutting quite a figure in financial circles. Matthew Marshall says of Prof. Adolph Soetber's scheme for increasing the use of silver by substituting coins of that metal of ratio of 20 to 1, or 24 to 1, in place of all gold coins now in circulation below 5.8 grammes. Prof. Soetber calculates that his scheme if adopted would add $400,000,000 gold to the bank reserves of the commercial world. Matthew Marshall believes this would only temporarily arrest the decline of silver, would not satisfy the silver men, and would not be worth the immense trouble required.

Pacific Mail stock broke in New York yesterday on rumors that the subsidy would be greatly reduced, or not paid at all, after the four months fixed by the recent meeting. Also that the Panama company would not renew its contract with the Pacific Mail Company, but was about to make an issue of bonds to build steamers of its own.

Jay Gould says he has sold no Manhattan stock and adds that he has none for sale at any price.

East-bound shipments from Chicago last week were 54,948 tons, against 45,111 tons the same week last year.

President Parsons of the New York & New England says:

The reports that the breaking up of New England Terminal Company will be an injury to New England Railroad Company are not true—on the contrary, the New England has got rid of the most expensive leech ever fastened upon it. The New England Terminal Company was a joint adventure of the Housatonic and New England Railroad companies and was a great burden to both roads.

Erie's balance for month of July decreased $92,153.

Atchison July total gross increase $184,604; net increase $187,520.

Northern Pacific June statement shows a surplus of $35,438, as compared with a surplus of $289,446 the same month last year.

Copper is reported as quiet and condition unchanged. Lake copper is quoted at 11.60 to 11.65c., though nominally 11⅝.

The product of the Ontario for the past week was, in ore sales, $5863.48; bullion, 18,445.44 ounces.

The Daly output for the past week was, in ore sales, $12,633.32; bullion, 17,090.82 ounces.

It is expected that the gross earnings of the West End Street Railway for August will aggregate between $550,000 and $560,000.

A private dispatch from New York quotes a director of Western Union as saying that he is confident Western Union dividend will be increased.

The exports of copper from New York last week and since Jan. 1, and the value of the same, are summarized below:

Copper.	Week Aug. 26.	Since Jan. 1.
Matte, pounds,	497,956	27,922,808
Matte, 55 per cent. fine,	273,875	15,357,542
Fine copper, pounds,	335,460	15,570,313
Total fine,	609,335	30,927,855
Value.		
Matte,	$25,000	$1,894,426
Fine copper,	34,700	1,628,542
Totals,	$59,700	$3,522,968

The St. Paul July statement follows:

	1892.	1891.	Inc.
July gross,	$2,716,998	$2,309,551	$407,446
Op. ex.,	1,855,648	1,584,240	271,408
Net,	861,350	725,311	136,038

The Old Colony Railroad reports its operations for the June quarter to-day, and but for the large falling off in other income the report would have compared favorably with a year ago. In 1891 this income was brought up by the sale of stock at auction for which $123,625 premium was realized. As it is, the balance above charges amounts to $203,123, a decrease of $164,752 from a year ago. Below will be found the operations for the quarter and fiscal year:

Quarter June 30, 1892.		1891.	Increase.
Earnings,	$2,295,326	$2,098,878	$196,448
Expenses,	1,732,456	1,578,614	153,842
Net,	$562,870	$520,264	$42,606
Other inc.	72,457	280,107	*207,650
Total net,	$635,327	$800,371	*$165,044
Charges,	432,205	432,496	*291
Balance,	$203,123	367,875	*$164,752
Cash,	343,575		
P.&L. surp.,	$732,888		
Fiscal year.	1891-92	1890-91	
Earnings,	$8,738,811	$8,370,448	$368,363
Expenses,	6,620,601	6,138,576	482,025
Net,	$2,118,210	$2,231,872	*$113,662
Other inc.,	557,891	372,682	185,119
Total net,	$2,676,011	$2,604,554	$71,457
Charges,	1,740,930	1,714,962	25,968
Balance,	$935,081	$889,592	$45,489

* Decrease.

STOCK AND BOND MARKETS.

Bids at the close of First Board.

NEW YORK, Aug. 30.

GOVERNMENT BONDS.

U.S. 2s, registered	100
" new 4s, registered	115½
" new 4s, coupons	115½
" currency 6s, 1895, (Pacifics)	107

RAILROADS

Atchison	38⅝
Clev., Cin., Chicago & St. Louis	66
Chicago & Eastern Illinois	—
Chicago & Eastern Illinois pre	—
Chicago, Burlington & Quincy	101⅛
Delaware & Hudson	136
Delaware & Lackawanna	156½
Erie	27⅛
Illinois Central	—
Lake Shore & Michigan Southern	134
Louisville & Nashville	68⅝
Michigan Central	—
Missouri Pacific	59¾
New Jersey Central	133
New York & New England	33⅛
Northern Pacific	20⅜
Northern Pacific pref	55⅞
Chicago & Northwestern	116⅞
New York Central & Hudson River	112½
North American	13⅝
Oregon Navigation	—
Oregon Improvement	—
Oregon Short Line	—
Philadelphia & Reading	57
Pullman Palace Car Co	198
Chicago, Rock Island & Pacific	82
Chicago, Milwaukee & St. Paul	83⅛
Chicago, Milwaukee & St. Paul pref	—
Richmond Terminal	8⅛
St. Paul & Omaha	52⅛
St. Paul & Omaha pref	—
Union Pacific	38¾
Wabash, St. Louis & Pacific	—
Wabash, St. Louis & Pacific pref	—

MISCELLANEOUS

Ontario Silver	41
Pacific Mail Steamship Co	31
Sugar, common	112⅛
Sugar, pref	—
Western Union Telegraph	98⅛
Silver Certificates	—

BOSTON, Aug. 30.

BONDS

Atchison 4s	82⅝
Atchison Incomes	60⅝
American Bell Telephone 7s	*114
Chicago, Burlington & Northern 5s	104
Chicago & West Michigan 5s	**8
Mexican Central 4s	67½
Illinois Steel Co. 5s	—

RAILROADS.

Atchison, Topeka & Santa Fe	39
Boston & Albany	205½
Boston & Lowell	—
Boston & Maine	177
Boston & Providence	250½
Chicago, Burlington & Quincy	101
Chicago & West Michigan	—
Cleveland & Canton	5⅝
Cleveland & Canton pref	19⅞
Flint & Pere Marquette	—
Flint & Pere Marquette pref	70
Mexican Central	15⅛
New York & New England	—
New York & New England pref	84⅜
Old Colony	182½
Oregon Short Line	—
Pullman Palace Car	197
Union Pacific	38⅛
Wisconsin Central	16
West End	73⅝
West End pref	87¾

MINING.

Butte & Boston Mining Co	9¼
Calumet & Hecla Mining Co	290
Centennial	—
Franklin Mining Co	12⅛
Kearsarge	11¼
Montana	36
Osceola Mining Co	31⅛
Tamarack	160

MISCELLANEOUS.

American Bell Telephone	205
Erie Telephone	—
Mexican Telephone	1.07⅛
New England Telephone	—
Newport Land	*1¼
Boston Land Co	5
West End Land Co	18⅛
San Diego Land Co	*16
Topeka Land & Development Co	—
Lamson Store Service	17
Illinois Steel Co	74
Am. Sugar Refineries, com	112
Am. Sugar Refineries, pref	104½
Gen'l Electric	116
Gen'l Electric	119

*Asked.

FALL RIVER STOCK QUOTATIONS.

The following are the quotations of Fall River stocks to-day as reported by Sanford & Kelley, bankers and brokers and stock auctioneers:

	Par.	Bid.	Asked.	Last Sale.
American Linen Co	$100	114	115	114
Barnaby Mfg. Co	100	130	—	—
Barnard Mfg. Co	100	—	99	99
Border City Mfg. Co	100	138	140	140
Bourne Mills	100	150	170	150
Chace Mills	100	110	112	111
Cornell Mills	100	88	89	87½
Crescent Mills	100	—	32½	30
C. Spring Bleachery	100	—	—	31
Davol Mills	100	—	100	99
Edison Illuminating	100	—	—	—
Fall River Bleachery	100	—	100	—
Flint Mills	100	110	112	112
Globe St. Railway Co	100	—	—	—
Globe Yarn Mills	100	118	—	120
Granite Mills	100	—	245	240
Hargraves Mills	100	100	101	100
King Philip Mills	100	121	125	124½
Kerr Thread Co	100	—	105	105
Laurel Lake Mills	100	—	110	110
Massasoit Nat'l Bank	100	—	—	185
Mechanics' Mills	100	—	99	98
Merchants' Mfg. Co	100	124	125	125
Metacomet Mills	100	—	—	64
Metacomet National Bank	100	—	—	130
National Union Bank	100	—	—	104½
Narragansett Mills	100	105	105	105
Osborn Mills	100	110	115	110
Pocasset Mfg. Co	100	—	110	110
Pocasset Nat'l Bank	100	—	—	—
Richard Borden Mfg	100	105	106	105
Robeson Mill	100	—	—	78
Sanford Spinning Co	100	—	100	—
Sagamore Mfg. Co	100	122	124	122½
Seaconnet Mills	100	—	120	118
Shove Mills	100	—	113	112½
Slade Mills	100	—	58½	58
Stafford Mills	100	123	125	124
Tecumseh Mills	100	112	113	112½
Troy C. & W. Manufactory	500	950	1025	1000
Union Mfg. Co	100	—	219	220
Wampanoag Mills	100	104	108	105½
Weetamoe Mills	100	—	55	55

PROVISIONS AND GRAIN.

CHICAGO, Aug. 29.

Opening.

	Lard.	Wheat.	Pork.	Corn.	Sh't Ribs
May	—	81¾	—	53⅝	—
June	—	—	—	—	—
July	—	—	—	—	—
Aug.	—	—	—	—	—
Sept.	—	76¼	10.65	51⅞	—
Oct.	—	—	—	—	—
Dec.	—	79⅜	—	51⅜	—
Jan.	—	—	12.50	—	—

12 o'clock.

	Lard.	Wheat.	Pork.	Corn.	Sh't Ribs
May	—	74¾	—	53⅜	—
June	—	—	—	—	—
July	—	—	—	—	—
Aug.	—	—	—	—	—
Sept.	—	75⅝	10.45	50½	—
Oct.	—	—	—	—	—
Dec.	—	78⅜	—	51	—
Jan.	—	—	12.40	—	—

AGAINST LIZZIE.

The Weight of Evidence of Prof. Wood.

His Opinions on Time of Death Most Damaging.

Prisoner Must Have Been With Her Parents

About the Time Each Met With Their End.

Stenographic Notes of Inquest Offered as Evidence.

FALL RIVER, Aug. 30.—The greatest crowd of the trial was on hand this afternoon an hour before the court opened, the corridors, aisles and every passage way being filled, and back of the settees were dozens of wall flowers. It was almost impossible for the officials to get around. On the strike of the hour of 2 the judge took his seat and the business proceeded.

Two Things Have Been Demonstrated

by the evidence of this morning, one that Lizzie was in her stepmother's room at 9 30, and that was about the time of the murder, and that she was in her father's room about the time of his death.

It is understood that while the general public thought the testimony of Prof. Wood was favorable to Lizzie because it appeared to be demonstrated that there was no blood stains on the clothes or hatchet, that

It was Really Against Her

because of his evidence in regard to the time of death.

It has already been established by the government that Lizzie was about the rooms at the times referred to above, and the times and nearly the exact time of death are nearly identical. If the testimony of Mrs. Reagan is put in relative to a

Quarrel Between the Sisters,

and it proves to be as has been stated, then the government will feel quite certain that there is no flaw in its chain.

Although the court came in promptly the district attorney did not, and it was fully fifteen minutes before he was ready for b usiness.

The first witness was Annie M. White, court stenographer, who said she was present at the inquest and took notes of the whole examination. Her notes as written out were offered in evidence.

Cross-examined, she said that when Miss Borden was examined there were others present, but she couldn't tell who were there then especially; there was then there one stranger who whom she did not know. The statements of Miss Borden were taken down by her when all the people present she knew were the judge, district attorney, Mr. Seaver, Marshal Hilliard and Dr. Dolan. The examination of Miss Borden was suspended at one time because other witnesses were examined between.

During the time examination was suspended, witness said Miss Borden, Mrs. Brigham, Officer Harrington, and she were left alone in the court room while the others went out of the room; thought Mr. Knowlton went into the judge's room.

A STUPID AND BRUTAL JOKE.

Drunken Bum Dyed Red and Placed Before the Borden House.

[Special Dispatch.]

FALL RIVER, Aug. 30.—About 1 o'clock this afternoon an incident of an intensely dramatic nature occurred. Thomas Coggeshall, a well-known bum about saloons, was caught by a crowd in a central resort. One of his hands and arms, his face, and what ought to have been the bosom of his shirt were covered with a dye substance, intensely fiery red, by some would-be joker. He was then steered out upon the street, piloted to the front of the Borden house, where he flourished his arm and promenaded up and down. A crowd of about five hundred people collected to gaze at him with horror, surprise, and a good measure of indignation. In the midst of his war dance Thomas was arrested for disturbing the peace, marched to and locked up in the Central Police Station, where he will have time to meditate upon the foolishness of his course. It was a stupid joke, and the only thing to be regretted about it is that the pains and penalties do not fall in equal measure upon the perpetrators as well as the victim.

WEATHER INDICATIONS.

FAIR AND SLIGHTLY WARMER.

NEW YORK, Aug. 30.—At 8 30 a. m. the weather was clear, wind east, temperature 74. The *Herald* says: In the Middle States and New England on Wednesday fair, slightly warmer and more sultry weather will probably prevail, followed by thunder storms and considerable rainfall, and on Thursday cooler, partly cloudy weather and rain, followed by clearing.

The New Philadelphia Mint.

WASHINGTON, Aug. 30.—Secretary Foster and Director of the Mint Leech having both returned from their outings, will shortly hold a conference as to what shall be done toward the purchase of a site and the construction of the new building for the mint at Philadelphia. Representative Bingham, as the father of the bill passed by the last congress, providing for this new $2,000,000 mint, will probably be invited to attend the conference.

Moses Pearson Dead.

PORTLAND, Me., Aug. 30.—Moses Pearson, a native of Haverhill, Mass., but who for forty-two years was a business man here, died last evening.

Strike Submitted to Arbitration.

LOWELL, Aug. 30.—The striking granite-cutters at Andover & Wheeler's works have agreed to submit the matter to arbitration, and returned to work this afternoon.

CALIFORNIA MINING STOCKS.

SAN FRANCISCO, Aug. 29.

The following are the official closing prices of mining stocks to-day:

Alta	—	Mexican	1 25
Best & Belcher	1 35	Mt. Diablo	—
Chollar	—	Ophir	2 25
Con. Cal. & Va.	3 35	Potosi	—
Crown Point	—	Savage	—
Eureka Con	—	Sierra Nevada	1 45
Gould & Curry	—	Union Con	1 25
Hale & Norcross	—	Utah	—

DEATH FROM CHOLERA.

Stringent Sanitary Regulations of British Government.

LONDON, Aug. 30.—If all the deaths that are being reported from Asiatic cholera are true, there is no doubt of Great Britain's having a visitation of the dreaded scourge. From Gravesend, Swansea, Glasgow and Dundee, towns in England, Scotland and Wales, reports come of deaths from the disease, showing that the efforts of the health officials to keep it out of the country have proved fruitless. And now comes a report that a person has died from Asiatic cholera at Bolton, the large manufacturing town which lies twelve miles northwest of Manchester.

The permission given by the health officials at Middlesborough for the landing of the crew of the steamer Gerona from Hamburg promises to have most serious results. As previously announced the vessel was placed in quarantine after one of the crew had been attacked by cholera, but in the meantime a number of the ship's company had departed for their homes. Six of them went to Dundee, where they reside, while another of the crew went to Ab. een. Among those who went to Dundee was Mr. Walker, the engineer of the Gerona. Shortly after his arrival there he was taken sick and died in a few hours. The physician who attended him says there is no doubt that his death was due to cholera.

A sailor arrived at Swansea from Cork. He was found to be suffering with cholera and was immediately removed to the cholera hospital. A steamer belonging to the same company as the Portia has been in quarantine at Cuxhaven on the Elbe, fifty-eight miles northwest of Hamburg, for a week, owing to deaths from cholera having occurred on board of her. This steamer is expected at Gravesend with a large number of poor immigrants. The inhabitants of Gravesend are awaiting her arrival with much apprehension. Gravesend is only twenty miles from London.

The local government board has issued regulations requiring shipowners, under heavy penalties, to retain aboard ship all foreign immigrants who are unable to inform the port medical officer of their destination and address to enable the local authorities to watch them until all danger of cholera is passed. No immigrant in a dirty condition will be allowed to land until all the sanitary regulations regarding bathing, etc., are complied with. The order will be rigidly executed. It will be the cause of considerable expense and annoyance to shipowners and will probably result in the cessation of the immigration of destitute aliens, at whom the order is evidently aimed. It will not interfere with emigrants in transit across England en route for America.

AT HAMBURG.

The Disease Thought to Be Abating in Several Quarters of the City.

HAMBURG, Aug. 30.—The official cholera statistics place the number of new cases of the disease reported on Saturday at 435, and the number of deaths at 145. On Sunday and up to noon yesterday 148 new cases and 72 deaths were reported.

The disease appears to be abating in several quarters of the city. There was much less demand for ambulances during the night.

In Altona 77 cases of cholera and 33 deaths from the disease were reported from noon Saturday up to noon yesterday. Owing to the outbreak of the disease in the prison, minor offenders to the number of 150 have been released. The decrease of the disease in Hamburg and Altona has been most noticeable since Sunday night. olated cases have been reported from Schiffbeck, Bergedorf, Harburg, Elmshorn and Uetersen, suburbs of Hamburg. At Wansbeck, three miles northeast of Hamburg, a favorite summer resort of the merchants of the city, there were 9 cases of the disease and 5 deaths up to Saturday evening.

Panic Prevailing.

ST. PETERSBURG, Aug. 30.—Cholera has reached Merv, in Turkestan, and a panic prevails among the inhabitants. The Armenian merchants wanted to close their shops immediately, but the governor objected to this course and threatened to expel the merchants from the country if they did not continue business. Should the Armenians be allowed to close their shops it would cause great distress. A dispatch from Vladikavkas, capital of the government of Terek, says that every town and village in the government is affected with cholera.

Precautions in the United States.

NEW YORK, Aug. 30.—The following order is about to be issued by Health Officer Jenkins: All vessels from cholera infected ports or carrying steerage passengers from infected localities will be subjected to quarantine of detention from two to five days. Passengers and their baggage will be transferred to Hoffman island, where they will receive a bath while baggage and clothing are disinfected by steam. Immediately after such transfer, steerage and cargo will be disinfected. The passengers will then return to the ship, which, in the absence of any development of any suspicious cases, will be allowed to proceed to her dock.

HARTFORD, Aug. 30.—A special meeting of the state board of health was held yesterday because a telegram was received from the Illinois board asking them to request the president to issue an order stopping all immigration from the cholera districts. The board did not think the president had the power to issue such an order, but sent word to the Illinois board that they would do all that was possible to suppress cholera if it appeared here.

WASHINGTON, Aug. 30.—Acting Secretary of the Treasury Spaulding said he believed every precautionary measure that could be taken to prevent the admission of cholera into the United States had been taken.

New Steamship Proposed.

NEW YORK, Aug. 30.—The contract between the Pacific Mail Steamship company and the Panama railroad expires Feb. 1 next, and the Panama railroad threatens that if a new contract is not signed by Thursday it will establish its own steamship service between New York and San Francisco. The Pacific Mail company has had exclusive rights over the Panama railroad under a fifteen-year contract, paying $55,000 monthly to the Panama railroad for transporting its coastwise business.

Heavy Mortgages Filed.

PORT HURON, Mich., Aug. 30.—Anderson & Co. of this city, manufacturers and dealers in carriages and agricultural implements, have filed chattel mortgages aggregating $230,000, to secure creditors. The company was involved in the failure of Cowham at Jackson. The liabilities and assets are unknown at present, but it is said the latter will far exceed the former, and if the firm is given time it will pay everyone in full.

Good Looks.

Good looks are more than skin deep, depending upon a healthy condition of all the vital organs. If the liver be inactive, you have a bilious look, if your stomach be disordered you have a dyspeptic look and if your kidneys be affected you have a pinched look. Secure good health and you will have good looks. Electric Bitters is the great alterative and tonic acts directly on these vital organs. Cures pimples, blotches, boils and gives a good complexion. Sold at H. A. Blackmer's drug store, 50 cents per bottle.

CHAMPION CIGARETTE SMOKER.

Joe Gibbs Puffs Away at One Hundred in Eight Hours.

PATERSON, N. J., Aug. 30.—Joseph Gibbs, a cigar maker, is just recovering from the remarkable performance of having smoked 100 cigarettes in eight hours. There are dark rings under his eyes, blisters on his lips, a pimple on his nose and a tinge of indigestion over his features as a result of what he did.

Gibbs was chatting the other day with Samuel Lustig, a painter, and the latter began to talk with admiration of a man he had read of in a London paper who had smoked 86 cigarettes in 11 hours and still lived. Lustig thought that a fellow who could do that must be a pretty fine kind of a fellow and remarked that he would like to see him.

"That's nothing," said Gibbs, "I could smoke a hundred of 'em in eight hours."

"Bah!" exclaimed Lustig; "I'll bet you $20 you can't."

"And you find the cigarettes?"

"Yes," exclaimed Lustig contemptuously, "I'll find the cigarettes and the coffin, too."

"I once chewed a bucket full of tobacco in four days," said Gibbs, "and I guess if there's any coffin wanted it'll be when you drop dead because you have to pay the bet."

The cigarette smoking was billed to begin at a cigar store in Main street on Sunday morning at 10 o'clock. Gibbs sat on a sort of throne built of tobacco boxes and the spectators bestowed themselves around him in attitudes of rapt admiration. A custodian of the cigarette stumps was appointed from among those present, and it was his duty to see that each cigarette was smoked to the bitter end, an umpire handing the cigarettes to the champion and "keeping tab" on them. In the first hour Gibbs smoked 31. When the score was announced a young man rose solemnly, shook him by the hand. This so encouraged Gibbs that he smoked 24 more in the next hour.

From noon until one o'clock Gibbs devoted himself to refreshment. He ate three slices of pie and drank two cups of coffee. Amid intense excitement he started on the second lap, and by three o'clock had made away with twenty-five more. In the last hour he won the wager by finishing the one hundredth.

When some one asked Gibbs if he felt the effects of his feat in his brain, he explained that he felt as well as usual in that part of his person which is contained in his skull. He declared that he considered himself the champion smoker of the century. Some of his admirers want to have a play built around him, or at any rate to bill him as a dime museum feature.

MR. SCATES NOT A CANDIDATE.

Gov. Russell's Latest Nominee for Savings Bank Commissioner Withdraws.

BOSTON, Aug. 30.—It is stated that David Scates of Northampton, Gov. Russell's latest nominee for savings bank commissioner has requested the Governor to withdraw his nomination in the interest of party harmony.

Worn and Wan and Weak and Weary.

Ho! ye women, worn and weary, with wan faces and so indescribably weak. Those distressing, dragging-down pains, and that constant weakness and wornness and weariness can be cured. For all such sufferers, Dr. Pierce's Favorite Prescription is a panacea of inestimable value. As an invigorating tonic, it imparts strength to the whole system. For "overworked," "worn-out," debilitated teachers, dress-makers, seamstresses, "shop-girls," house keepers, nursing mothers, and feeble women generally, Dr. Pierce's Favorite Prescription is the greatest earthly boon, being unequalled as an appetizing cordial and restorative tonic. As a soothing and strengthening nervine, "Favorite Prescription" is unequalled and invaluable in allaying and subduing nervous excitability, exhaustion, prostration, hysteria, spasms and other distressing, nervous symptoms, commonly attendant upon functional and organic disease. It induces refreshing sleep and relieves mental anxiety and despondency.

WANTS.

☞ *All Advertisements under this heading 1c. a word a time. No charge less than 25c.*

MAN TO SAW WOOD—21 Griffin street. au30-3t

REAL ESTATE.

FRANCIS W. TAPPAN,
Agent for Purchase, Sale, and Lease of
REAL ESTATE.
Office, 15 North Water St., New Bedford. d&w

FRANK C. SMITH,
Real Estate Broker, Auctioneer and Appraiser,
Office - - 47 William Street,
(Opposite New Post Office.)

M. E. SMITH,

REAL ESTATE AGENCY.

Houses and House Lots for sale in all parts of the city on easy terms.

Good Chance for Speculators—An estate of about 950 rods of land has been placed in my hands to be sold at the very low price of

$8.50 PER ROD.

Fifteen minutes' walk from the Pierce Mill; near horse cars; Acushnet water; electric lights, &c. Will sell well cut up in house lots. Terms, $2700 cash; balance in 3 years at 6 per cent. interest.

M. E. SMITH,
619 Purchase Street. Telephone 16-11.

FOR SALE—In South Dartmouth, near the water, a 2½ story house with large piazza, barn, and 83 rods of land. One of the most desirable places in the village for a Summer residence. Inquire of BENJ. QUERIPEL or DANIEL H. HOWLAND, South Dartmouth. ap7-tf

JAS. E. BLAKE,

Has received direct from the grower a lot of

PURE PURPLE TOP FRENCH TURNIP SEED.

They are fine grained, smooth skinned, and are considered the very best of the Turnip family.

Also German Sweet, Cowhorn and Yellow Swede, and many other varieties.

JAS. E. BLAKE,
98 North Second Street.
TTS&w

Shorthand,
Type-Writing,
Book-Keeping,
Penmanship,
Arithmetic,
English Grammar,
Business Correspondence,
&c., &c.,
—AT THE—
New Bedford Business College.

Call or send for circular to Room 31, Citizens' Bank Building, William Street.

Evening Session begins WEDNESDAY, August 24th.

TAGS Constantly on hand or furnished in any quantity at short notice at STANDARD JOB ROOMS.

AUCTION SALES.

By STANDISH BOURNE,
(Successor to Geo. A. Bourne & Son,)
Auctioneer, Commission Merchant, Real Estate Dealer and Appraiser.

Cash advanced on goods consigned for auction. Ready buyer for personal property of every description.

Office and Salesrooms 47, 49 and 51 North Second Street, near the Post Office.

Paine Farm on Sconticut Neck.

On WEDNESDAY, Aug. 31, at 3 o'clock, on the premises, will be sold in the following manner, the above named farm:

1st.—Lot situated on the east side of the road on the north end of the farm, containing about 25 acres, more or less.

2d.—Lot joining No. 1 on the south, containing about 25 acres, more or less.

3d.—Farm house, barn, out-buildings and about 20 acres, more or less.

4th.—Lot joining No. 3 on the south, containing 15 acres, more or less.

5th.—We reserve the right to put these parcels up in one sale and if a larger bid can be obtained than the sum of the separate sales, that bid will be the binding sale.

Plenty of time before the sale to get your clam dinner held for the benefit of the Union Chapel at Dunn's Grove.

Mortgagee's Sale.

On SATURDAY, Sept. 3, at 12¼ o'clock, on the premises, will be sold by order of the mortgagee, the nearly new 2½ story house and lot containing about 21.38 rods, situated on the south side of North street, numbered 162. For legal advertisement see *Evening Standard* of August 9, 16, 23.

Executor's Sale of Real Estate.

On WEDNESDAY, Sept. 21, at 3 o'clock in the afternoon, on the premises, will be sold by order of the executor under the will of the late Russell Maxfield the homestead of said Maxfield, situated on the southwest corner of Maxfield and Walden streets.

The house is first-class built, in good repair, with lot of about 14½ rods, having a frontage of 49½ feet on Maxfield street by 81 feet on Walden street.

IVORY S. CORNISH, Executor.
au27-s3-10

To Let in Our Storage Warerooms.

We constantly have on hand first-class rooms for the storage of household goods, to be rented by the month or year.

Good dry storage room for stoves.

By JOHN B. BAYLIES,
121 and 123 Union Street,
Commission Merchant, Appraiser, and Auctioneer for the sale of Real Estate and every description of Personal Property. Furniture Bought.

H. C. HATHAWAY,
Auctioneer, Real Estate Agent and Appraiser,
Corner Acushnet Ave. and Elm St.

☞ One of the best auction marts in the State for the sale of horses and carriages. Keeps constantly on hand carriages of every description, carriages made to order and repairing in all its branches attended to under the superintendency of J. R. Forbes. Consignments of every description solicited. Cash advanced on goods for auction. Personal property of every description bought at short notice for cash. Negotiable notes bought and sold.

2 1-2 Story House and Lot.

On SATURDAY, Sept. 3d, at 12¼ o'clock, P. M., on the premises will be sold at public auction, the 2½ story house on Foster street together with the lot which will be described at the sale. Said house was moved from the Kempton street schoolhouse lot and fitted in good order, being fitted for two families and is situated on Foster street, just south of the building used by the Veteran Firemen's Association. The property is sold by order of the Committee on Public Property.

STEPHEN A. BROWNELL, Chairman.

Terms 10 per cent. at sale balance on delivery of deed. aug29

ALFRED WILSON,
Auctioneer and Real Estate Agent,
Room 22, - - - Robeson Building.

☞ Houses and land in all parts of the city for sale; tenements for rent; rents collected.

For Sale.

Two-story house on Acushnet avenue, near Walnut street; well arranged for one family; good location.

For Lease.

The Webster Block, Purchase street; 16 rooms, well adapted for a genteel boarding house, club rooms, or business purposes.

TO LET—A flat in The Winslow, corner Sixth and Union streets. Apply to A. WILSON, Robeson Building. jy14-tf

T. F. HEALEY,

Auctioneer and Real Estate Agent,
555 and 559 Purchase street, corner of Franklin street.

HOUSE LOTS for sale on Coffin, Acushnet and Hathaway avenues, and in fact all parts of the city, on easy terms.

Also two cottages in Fairhaven; nearly new; fine view of river and harbor; will sell one or both; situated on Main street; will sell to the right parties on easy terms.

Business solicited. No charges made unless a sale, then my prices are the lowest.

By J. O. DOUGLASS.

REGULAR AUCTION SALE,
Thursday, Sept. 1st, 1892, at 10 15 A. M.

OF 25 horses from Indiana and Canada; all young, fresh stock consisting of family, driving, farm and general business horses, weighing 1000 to 1250 lbs.; well broken to single and double harness. In this lot are some extra driving horses, some that can show good gaits. Also a number of acclimated horses; been used in and about the city. Harnesses, whips, foot mats, etc.

By WM. BARKER, Jr.

Valuable Real Estate, Engine, Machinery, Horses, Wagons, &c., at Auction.

WILL be sold on the premises, SATURDAY, Sept. 3d, 1892, at 1 o'clock P. M., that desirable property well known as the Crapo Wood Yard, on Court street, in this city, consisting of 40 rods of land with buildings, engine, boiler, shafting and other machinery. Also, two one-horse lumber wagons, two express wagons, two horses (one a superior animal,) two express harnesses, and various other articles.

Aug. 22, 1892. au22-ts

REAL ESTATE.

H. A. LEONARD, REAL ESTATE AGENT,

126 UNION STREET.

Houses and house lots in all parts of the city for sale. Three fine residences. Good bargains. Call and examine tenements to let.

John Whitehead,

COGGESHALL ST., - - - - COR. ROCK.

Has for sale 12 two-tenement houses near the mills, which pay 10 per cent. interest. Easy terms. au26-18t

Very Desirable House Lots.

Near Bliss Corner, $3 a rod and upwards. Good chance for speculators. DANIEL SWEENEY, Cove Road. au22-12t

EDWIN JONES,

REAL ESTATE AGENT.......884 PURCHASE ST.

FOR SALE.—Lots in all parts of the city; some bargains. Also a good 2½ story house, nearly new, well arranged, convenient to mills at North End, now rents for $250 a year; cheap.

BUSINESS SOLICITED. au24-6t

COTTAGE HOUSE—53 Chestnut street, with 18¾ rods of land; house is fitted with modern conveniences. Can be seen afternoons and evenings. V. F. HATCH, 31 North Water street. au23-tf

Cottage House.

Well built, good repair, in part of city growing rapidly; will make good home and *must* increase in value. Apply box 6 *Standard* office. ap25-tf

DYNAMITE SUSPECTS

Placed Under Arrests by Detectives at Montreal—Traced from Paris.

MONTREAL, Aug. 30.—The recent dynamite outrages in France led to sensational results yesterday in Montreal. Photographs and descriptions were received here of those suspected of being implicated in the explosions, and strict watch for them was kept up for some time, but without result. Sunday the police were notified by the French officials to search the city for the suspects. After a long search detectives arrested in a house in Commission street two men, a woman and two children on suspicion of being dynamiters. The woman is the wife of one of the men and is the mother of both children. Two trunks and all the baggage around in the place were seized.

The woman and children were put in the detective's office, and the men were brought before Judge Dugas. A representative of the French government was present. The two suspects said they were not guilty of the charge against them. They came to Montreal two weeks ago on the steamer Parisian. It is suspected that they went to England from Paris, and hid until they got a ship for Montreal. The detectives refuse to give the names of the prisoners.

Gigantic Frauds Unearthed.

NEW YORK, Aug. 30.—The customs authorities have unearthed another case of gigantic frauds in the weighing department of the surveyor's office. The frauds consisted in the underweighing of sugar during the eight months between Aug. 1, 1891, and March 1, 1892, when the free sugar law went into effect. The amount of duties lost to the government by this systematic underweighing is estimated at $65,000 to $75,000. The results of the investigation have involved, so far, eight importers of sugar and a number of employes in the weighing department. The matter has been presented to the attention of the United States district attorney.

Merrimac Waters Rising.

HAVERHILL, Mass., Aug. 30.—The waters of the Merrimac have continued to rise during the day, and are now nearly as high as in any spring freshet. The river has risen about five feet, and trees and wreckage have floated by, indicating that damage has been done above this city. The water commenced to rise early last Saturday. Nearly all the yachts have been dragged from their moorings, but only four cases of damage have been reported.

SULLIVAN'S ADMIRERS.

Tender the Champion a Rousing Reception at Brooklyn.

BROOKLYN, Aug. 30.—A great seething, howling crowd crushed its way into the Clermont Avenue rink last night to witness the reception tendered John L. Sullivan. The crowd was composed of all classes. In the center of the rink was pitched a twenty-four-foot ring, and around it the multitude surged. There were a half-dozen bouts at the beginning, in which some local pugilists showed themselves, but, although these afforded some amusement, the crowd was impatient to see the only John L. About 8:30 o'clock the champion drove up to the rink door with Phil Casey, his trainer, and his sparring partner, Jack Ashton of Providence. A large crowd in the street gave him a great reception. The crowd surged to and fro and wildly cheered the champion, who bowed and smiled and was then escorted inside the rink. While the opening bouts were going on, Sullivan sat in his dressing room surrounded by his most intimate friends. Shortly before 10 o'clock the man of the evening appeared. As he emerged from the dressing room the audience

Stood Up and Yelled.

As Sullivan walked toward the ring there was pandemonium. Cheer upon cheer went up from 4000 throats. Jack Ashton followed the champion. Then a great floral harp, on which was inscribed: "John L. Sullivan, champion of the world," was handed into the ring. As Sullivan turned and bowed to the audience the howling grew louder. There were cries of "speech, speech!" and the big fellow said: "I thank you for the hearty applause and appreciation. I believe I have the good will of all the people here this evening, on my last appearance before my last fight. That fight will

JOHN L. SULLIVAN.

decide whether I am the John L. Sullivan of old or the John L. Sullivan who has passed by. I am not going to speak disparagingly of Mr. Corbett. All I will say is that I am most glad to appear here. I have deceived you once, but let by-gones be by-gones. I am going to stop speaking now, and you will next hear from me Sept. 7." Sullivan's words were punctuated by the wildest yelling. Then there were shouts for Phil Casey, and he was dragged into the ring, but he would make no speech.

His Appearance.

There appeared to be a good deal of flesh on Sullivan as he sat in his corner. His eyes were bright and flashing and his face was hardened and tanned. His shoulders are in splendid condition and his muscles show excellently. There appeared, however, to be lots of fat over his stomach and his back. It will be strange if he does not weigh in the vicinity of 220 pounds. He perspires very freely.

Ashton met the champion in three rounds. Sullivan showed the agility of a cat as he went around the ring. His actions were like lightning. He wore a confident, hardened air that could not be mistaken. He went at Ashton very hard, tapping him at short intervals, twice with the left and once with the right. Although he only touched his companion on the neck and shoulders, he had been very tired at the end of each round. It was remarked that Sullivan puffed a good deal after the finish of the rounds. The wrinkle of fat over his waistband heaved in and out to no small degree. The perspiration came freely. His Japanese valet mopped him with a cloth.

Still his admirers feel that he is in prime condition. His flesh is well colored and his striking force is as marvellous as ever. His legs are in the best of form and he is active on his feet as any one can expect. The effect of his training is very evident. He has undergone very hard work, and has in everyway the appearance of a man fit to win at New Orleans.

"GENTLEMAN JIM."

Pugilist Corbett Receives an Ovation at Madison Square Garden.

NEW YORK, Aug. 30.—Pugilist James J. Corbett was given an enthusiastic reception by 5000 admirers at the Madison Square Garden last evening. After a number of other bouts had taken place there was a pretty exhibition of boxing between Corbett and John McVeigh of Philadelphia. McVeigh, however, was too beefy and altogether too slow for Corbett. Things livened up more in the bout between Corbett and his boxing partner, Jem Daly. Though Daly is not heavy enough for Corbett, there was some pretty quick fighting and Corbett had a chance to show his nimbleness.

He is remarkably quick and his clean science urged the spectators up to a shouting point. There is no doubt that despite his somewhat disappointing development, Corbett made a host of friends by his clean methods and his evident splendid condition.

Manitoba Farmers Fear a Frost.

WINNIPEG, Man., Aug. 30.—The weather here has been constantly growing colder during the past twenty-four hours, and the farmers fear they will have a frost. Early yesterday morning the mercury had fallen to 42 degrees. The weather is cold, with a strong north wind blowing. The wheat harvesting is about three-fourths over. It is expected that harvesting will be over this week. About 30,000,000 bushels of wheat, it is calculated, will be available for export. This tallies with the immense yield of last year.

Social Science Association.

SARATOGA, Aug. 30.—The American Social Science association's five days' convention begun last evening. The opening address was given by Rev. Dr. H. L. Wayland of Philadelphia, the president; subject, "Has the State Abdicated?" An address was also made by Rev. Dr. J. M. Bulkeley of New York on "Mental and Moral Contagion."

Bicycle Record Lowered.

KINGSTON, Ont, Aug. 30.—At the bicycle meet here Wells of Toronto clipped one second from the Canadian quarter-mile dash record, lowering it to 35 seconds.

Harrison to Visit New York.

NEW YORK, Aug. 30.—It is announced at Republican national headquarters that President Harrison will be in New York on Wednesday night.

THEIR RANKS UNBROKEN.

Strikers at Homestead Still Confident of Ultimate Victory.

HOMESTEAD, Pa., Aug. 30.—There is much expectancy and subdued excitement in Homestead over a search for the guns of the captured Pinkertons, which has been ordered. Much of the reluctance in giving up the arms lies in the fact that the possession would fix upon the Homesteaders complicity in the riots and that this evidence will be used in bringing suits. Two months ago the great steel works here shut down, and so far as the men are concerned there is no weakening, nor do the majority express any doubt of victory. They are really conducting a surprisingly strong fight, considering the number of men and the mixture of races and trades. All are being held in line and show much enthusiasm. The firm naturally insists that so far as it is concerned the strike is over.

It has been learned that the Pinkerton agency some time ago sent forty men into the mill as non-union workmen. These men deserted in small squads and were taken into the strikers' ranks. They gained the confidence of the Amalgamated leaders, and have, it is said, gathered considerable evidence against participants in the riot of July 6, against whom they will make informations. It is also said that they have discovered the hiding place of the captured rifles and will proceed against those who have possession of them.

The following arrests were made last night: William Oeffener and M. J. Connelly, strikers, on warrants sworn out by Pinkerton detectives, charging them with riot and aggravated assault; Thomas J. Crawford, acting chairman of the advisory committee; William H. Gatcher, George Ryland, Burgess McLuckie and John Edwards. The first four are charged with conspiracy and riot, while Edwards' offense is described as aggravated riot. All but Edwards have been released on bail.

A RECEIVER WANTED.

Certificate Holders in the Order of the Helping Hand Dissatisfied.

LYNN, Mass., Aug. 30.—The report is current here that the Order of the Helping Hand, a five-year endowment organization, is on the verge of disintegration, and that dissatisfied certificate holders have appointed a committee to institute proceedings for a receiver and an injunction. No charge of fraud is preferred.

Elmer F. Robinson, secretary of the order, says: "The order is sound and strong, and can be perpetuated, though no one can say what will result from this wave of disaster following on the wrecking of the Iron Hall. So far no bill has been drawn against us for an injunction and receiver. These receiverships are fat plums for the receivers. It is safe to say that the Iron Hall receiver will make $100,000 out of his job. There are lawyers in plenty who will undertake injunction and receiver cases free of charge in view of the returns to be realized when they have secured the appointment for one of their friends."

Where is Captain Tineman?

NEW ORLEANS, Aug. 30.—Captain K. P. Tineman of the steamer Hispania, of which J. L. Phipps & Co. are agents, left on a leave of absence on July 22, to visit his brother, J. S. Rineman, living on Prince hill, Cincinnati. He never reached his destination, and on Aug. 17 his friends grew solicitous about him, and applied to Chief of Police Gaster of this city for information as to his whereabouts. The chief of the Cincinnati police was communicated with, and it was discovered a few days ago that he had been at the Emery Hotel, Cincinnati, from July 23 to 29. Nothing further has been heard of him. He had $1500 in his pockets when he left here, and foul play is suspected.

Somerby Visits Providence.

PROVIDENCE, Aug. 30.—F. D. Somerby, supreme chief justice of the order of Iron Hall, was in attendance at Branch No. 475, in this city, last evening. He told the members that he was a much-abused man; that the reports against him were unfounded, and that he believed that the order could be again placed on a sound basis. The opinion of the branch was about equally divided between going on and dividing up what was in the treasury. Mr. Somerby told the members that the receiver had no jurisdiction over the reserve fund—between $7000 and $8000—in its possession. Mr. Somerby left for Boston in the morning.

Costly Paintings Destroyed.

MT. VERNON, N. Y., Aug. 59.—The residence of S. M. Sissons on Chester Hill, in East Chester, has been destroyed by fire. Some costly paintings and considerable fine furniture were burned. The loss is not known. There is an insurance of $10,000.

MUTES IN CONVENTION.

Eighteenth Biennial Meeting of the New England Gallaudet Association.

HARTFORD, Aug. 30.—The eighteenth biennial meeting of the New England Gallaudet association opened in the chapel of the American Asylum for the Deaf and Dumb. About 300 members were present. After the opening prayer by Rev. Job Turner of Philipsburg, Pa., an address of welcome was made by Mayor W. W. Hyde, followed by the president's address by E. W. Frisbie of Everett, Mass.

The business meeting opened with a motion to make all those present, but not members of the association, honorary members for the time of the convention only. It was passed after much discussion and appeals to the constitution, and about twenty honorary members were thereupon elected. The minutes of the last meeting were read by G. C. Sawer, the secretary, and were approved. The treasurer's report was read and approved and a recess was taken. Among the members who have arrived is Mrs. George W. Lamb of Norwich, formerly Maria Bailey, the oldest living graduate of the school. She is 95 years old. One of her sons fought bravely through the war. She entered the school in 1817, being then 20 years old. With her at that time was her sister, Harriet Bailey, who is still living at the age of 93, and is the second oldest graduate.

At the afternoon session Mr. Tillinghast, treasurer of the Morrison fund, made his report, and announced that after serving as treasurer for sixteen years he desired to retire. There was a strong protest, but he insisted, and was then asked to present later the name of some one whom he would recommend for the nomination. Various speeches were then made before further business was taken up. The most important was by Rev. Thomas Gallaudet, D. D., of New York, who dwelt on the value of the sign language. In the evening there was a large reception, and in the evening a debate on woman suffrage attracted a good many members.

MUTINOUS SAILORS.

Captain of Brig Mary C. Mariner Attacked and Seriously Wounded.

KEY WEST, Fla., Aug. 30.—The American brig Mary C. Mariner, Captain Foss, dropped anchor in the harbor here leaking badly. She is from the port of Savacanamar. Last Saturday night a part of the crew mutinied and attacked the captain. He is seriously wounded in the head and neck and is in a very critical condition. Warrants are in the hands of the United States marshal for the arrest of the mutineers, but he is powerless to execute them because the vessel is detained at quarantine by order of the deputy state health officer at this port, and the marshal is not allowed to go aboard of the brig. It is feared the mutineers will escape in boats. The consignee has telegraphed the state health officer for permission to make the arrests.

Knights of Pythias Encampment.

KANSAS CITY, Aug. 30.—The next biennial session of the supreme lodge and encampment of the Knights of Pythias will be held in Washington. So the supreme lodge decided yesterday afternoon after a sharp contest between Louisville and Washington. Washington received 62 votes, while Louisville followed with 50. Minneapolis was not in the contest after the preliminary skirmishing, and the fight narrowed down to Louisville and Washington. The proposed changes in the constitution, which may mean a change in the management of the endowment rank, were made a special order for Wednesday. Aside from locating the next encampment routine business was only considered.

Trial for Manslaughter Begun.

PARIS, Aug. 30.—The trial of the Marquis de Mores for manslaughter for killing in a duel on June 23 last Captain Mayer of the engineer corps and a professor in the Ecole Polytechnique began yesterday. Count Lamasse and M. Guerin, the marquis' seconds, Captain Panjade and M. Delorme, Captain Mayer's seconds were also arraigned, charged with complicity in the crime. After the proceedings had commenced the Marquis de Mores harangued the court for half an hour on his meat speculations in the United States and his colonizing enterprises in Tonquin.

Husband and Wife Suicide.

NEW YORK, Aug. 30.—John Obeymeyer, a German barber, and his wife Margaret, both 68 years old, were found dead in bed at their home in this city. Both had committed suicide by taking chloroform during the night. They were in destitute circumstances and despondent at their inability to obtain work.

Had a Rough Passage.

HALIFAX, Aug. 30.—The steamer Olivette arrived here at noon yesterday from Boston, after a rough passage. She anchored below Boston from Saturday till 6 o'clock Sunday morning. Some anxiety was felt, as this was the only long passage the Olivette has had while in the service.

From Yesterday's Third Edition.

POISON THEORY.

Strong Government Evidence in Support.

Lizzie Borden Tried to Buy Prussic Acid.

Drug Clerk Bence's Positive Identification.

Two Other Witnesses Give Corroborative Testimony.

No Stranger Could Have Approached Borden House.

Witnesses Who Were in the Vicinity Saw No One.

[Special Dispatch.]

FALL RIVER, Aug. 29.—When the court came in this afternoon every seat was filled and the room was crowded to the utmost. Among the very first to arrive was the counsel for the defence, while District Attorney Knowlton was but little behind. Lizzie entered leaning upon the arm of the faithful City Missionary Buck with a firm and determined step that gave little or no evidence that the course of the proceedings was weighing upon her in the least.

The examination of Lucy Collett was resumed, and after a few questions she was allowed to retire, and Eli Bence was next called.

Drug Clerk Identifies Lizzie.

He said he was a druggist doing business on Columbia street. He saw Lizzie in the drug store the day before the tragedy. At this time she asked for ten cents' worth of prussic acid. He told her he did not sell it without a doctor's prescription. When his attention was called to Lizzie, he said the defendant was the woman who asked for the prussic acid. There were several persons in the store at the time. His attention was called to the fact on Thursday after the tragedy soon after 6 o'clock.

Under cross-examination he said: I am a drug clerk in Smith's drug store and have been for three years. Was in the front part of the store when Lizzie came in. She had on a dark dress. I cannot describe what the dress was, but I know it was not blue.

He could not say whether it was of a solid color or mixed. I cannot say if it was like the one defendant has on today, but it was dark. I cannot say what sort of a hat she had on and cannot describe it, but I know it did not have anything like a feather sticking up. I cannot say anything about any other lady that was in the store the same morning to buy goods but know that there were some in there. I was not in the front shop but a little time. I do not remember refusing to sell any lady anything that day but Lizzie. Have no recollection of selling any lady anything on that day. I have seen Lizzie Borden on the street many times and know her. I think I have sold the lady drugs before while I worked in another drug store as a clerk, about six years ago. At the time Lizzie came in the other clerks were in various parts of the store. I gave testimony at the inquest. I have never signed any statement given at the inquest. Two officers came to me on Thursday, the 4th of the present month, in regard to this matter. As I remember it the lady did not have any wrap on or any purse in her hand when she came into the store that morning. I never made a statement to anybody that I thought it was Lizzie Borden. I know George Gray, who lives on Whipple street. I never talked with him about it.

Mr. Knowlton. Is prussic acid a substance ever called for before in your store?

The question was objected to by Mr. Adams.

Objection overruled.

Witness said: Never knew it to be called for.

Mr. Knowlton. Have you heard the voice of that lady since?

Witness. Yes, sir, I have.

Mr. Knowlton. Do you recognize it as that of Lizzie Borden?

Witness. Yes, I do.

To Mr. Adams witness said he had heard Lizzie Borden talk at her house on the evening after the tragedy. Her voice was the same as that of the woman with whom he traded at his store. There was a tremor in her voice.

Mr. Adams asked if the voice was the same as that of the person with whom he had traded six years ago and said if so he must have a good memory.

Witness denied that he remembered the woman's voice so long. The voice of Lizzie Borden was the same as that of the woman with whom he talked in his store. It was not only tremulous but low.

Kilroy Identifies Miss Borden.

Frank H. Kilroy said he was in the store with Mr. Bence the day before the tragedy. It was before dinner. He knows Lizzie Borden. The lady came in and spoke to Mr. Bence. I heard her say prussic acid. Mr. Bence said: "I cannot sell that without a prescription." The lady also spoke about a sealskin cape.

"Is this the lady?" asked Mr. Knowlton, pointing to Lizzie Borden.

"It is," answered Mr. Kilroy.

In cross-examination witness said he was three or four feet away from the lady when she went into the store.

"Are you engaged in business?" asked Mr. Adams.

"No, sir," was the reply.

"In expectation of business?" said Mr. Adams.

"Yes, sir," replied the witness, as the laugh went round the room.

To Mr. Knowlton witness said: "The fact of Lizzie Borden being in the store on Wednesday (befor the murder) was discussed by Messrs. Hart and Bence and myself. We had the discussion when she went out of the store.

Another Drug Clerk Testifies.

Frederick D. Hart, a clerk in Smith's drug store at the time the woman (stated to be Lizzie Borden) called, said she called on the day before the murder for prussic acid. He never saw her before that day so far as he can now remember.

Cross-examination. The first time I saw the woman after she was in the store was in the corridor leading to the court room here a week after the tragedy. The district attorney called my attention to her at that time. She was with the marshal. I think she was dressed in black.

During the cross-examination Mr. Adams was testing the recollection of witness in regard to Lizzie's dress and hat on the day in which he saw her previously in the court room, and passed his hands over the lady's (Lizzie's) hat, pressed down the small feather in front and jammed the hat away over her eyes. She did not resist or shrink but looked pleasantly into the eyes of counsel.

Joseph Desrosier testified through an interpreter: I was sawing wood at the time of the tragedy. I did not see any one go over the fence while I was chopping and sawing the wood, although I was in a position to do so if any one had done so. The only men I saw that morning was an Irishman cutting stone and two Frenchmen teaming. I did not see anyone get over the fence.

Officer Doherty on the Stand.

Patrick Doherty testified. I am a police officer in Fall River. I was down stairs in the Central Police Office when the word of the tragedy was received. I ran when I first heard of the affair. I found a reporter sitting on the steps when I got there. Dr. Bowen let me in. Bridget was in a corner on the lower floor when I went in. Dr. Bowen removed the sheet from the body.

Witness described the wounds of Mr. Borden.

He continued: They led the way and I went up stairs, where I saw Mrs. Borden. I saw three or four blood stains on the pillow shams and some on the bed. I wanted to examine the body of the woman, but there was not room between the head of the bed and the body. I pulled the bed away and got a good view of the body. I talked with Dr. Bowen. Mrs. Borden's head was about one foot away from the wall before the bed was moved away. The space was not more than two feet between that and the dressing case. I notified the marshal of the condition of affairs right away. When I notified him it was by telephone. I had to go out of the house to telephone, and when I came back from telephoning there was a large crowd about the house and several officers present. When I arrived at the house Dr. Dolan was there. When I first came into the house that morning I did not see Miss Lizzie. I went into the attic first, to the servant girl's room. I searched the upper rooms first and then all the rest of the house except Miss Lizzie's room. I first saw Mr. Morse in the room when I got back from the telephone. I was present when the officers found the hatchet. I just looked over a man's shoulder and saw the hatchet and cannot describe it. I saw Lizzie and said: "Where were you when your father was killed?" I asked her who worked for her father, and she said Mr. Johnson and Mr. Eddy, but they could not have killed him, she said. She did not know if any one else who had worked for her father had done it.

The witness continued: South of the Chagnon house is an orchard, and it is about 60 feet long. A lane and an orchard are back of the house, and at the rear is a high board fence. On one side of the Chagnon fence leading to the rear is a driveway. On the Borden lot in the rear is a pile of boards against the fence at the southeast corner.

At this point a recess of ten minutes was taken.

A Color Blind Witness.

Policeman Doherty continued his story in cross-examination about the search of the Borden house after the tragedy. His statements were not of much importance as a whole. He said: The hatchet was found I think on a shelf near the furnace. I saw no axe. Officer Mullaley was conducting this search. The handle of this hatchet was not over 28 inches long. When I came up from the cellar Officer Medley was in the back hall talking with the girl Bridget. The pile of lumber in the Borden yard which was against Dr. Chagnon's fence was within a foot or a foot and a half from the top. The fall is not a great one into the Chagnon yard. Dr. Chagnon's house fronts on Third street. The piazza to this house is on the south side. When I saw Lizzie at the house when I was there on the day of the tragedy I have a faint recollection that the color of her dress was light blue. The bosom was starched. The dress I think was what might be called figured challie.

At this point the laugh went round the court room as witness had previously said the dress was print. He was asked to look around the room and see if he could tell any color looking like the dress. He took an observation, and then lighted on Mr. Spear's (of the New York *Sun*) necktie, and said it was like it.

Mr. Spear said he had on a white tie, and then it was more apparent that the witness was color blind.

Officer Mullaley testified he was called to the case Aug. 4. He arrived at 11 40 in the morning. Officer Allen was there. I saw Miss Russell, Dr. Bowen, Bridget Sullivan, and Lizzie Borden there. Miss Borden was in the dining room. After talking with Mrs. Churchill I went in to see Lizzie. I told her I was there to get a report. She said she had been out of doors, and when she came in her father was dead. I asked her what property her father had on his person. She told me about her father wearing a watch and chain and carrying a pocketbook. Officer Doherty, at my request, looked over Mr. Borden and reported what he found on his person. I inquired of Lizzie if she knew of an axe on the premises. Lizzie said, Yes and Bridget Sullivan would show me when I went out and up the stairs. I saw Mrs. Borden on the floor. We looked all around up stairs, and we made a good search. We were looking for the murderer or the weapon with which the deed was committed. We afterwards came down stairs and looked around. We found first two hatchets and afterwards two axes. One of the hatchets had a rust spot on it. I left one of the axes on the floor of the wash-room in the cellar.

Witness detailed at length the proceedings of the search but nothing of importance was elicited.

LEAKING BADLY.

Vineyard Haven Bound Schooner Towed Into Gloucester.

GLOUCESTER, Aug. 29.—The British schooner Cygnet, Capt. Dalton, St. John for Vineyard Haven for orders, was towed in by tug Emma Bradford, leaking badly. The captain reports encountered a severe gale last Friday. Schooner has 6 feet of water in the hold.

LOOKED LIKE A FIGHT ON THE SPOT.

Jim Corbett Threatened to Throw Mc Caffrey Out of the Window.

NEW YORK, Aug. 29.—There was a hot time in the private office of the Madison Square Garden this morning when James J. Corbett and his manager, William A. Brady, met there to arrange with Dominick McCaffrey, the boxing instructor of the Manhattan Athletic Club, for a match. Mr. Corbett became so much enraged at the remarks of the Manhattan man that he stated in emphatic language and menacing mein that if his would-be antagonist did not stop talking he would throw him from the window. McCaffrey replied that he had better try it. The scene was very dramatic, and it looked for a time as if the four round "go" might be fought on the spot. The upshot of it all was that no match was arranged.

SAYS IT IS BOSH.

Denial of the Insinuation that Iron Hall Bribed Maine Legislators.

BIDDEFORD, Me., Aug. 29.—State Assessor Benjamin F. Chadbourne, who was a Democratic member of the judiciary committee of the last Legislature was seen to-day in reference to the insinuation that Somerby and his confederates bribed the Maine Legislature to pass a bill removing the restrictions adopted at the previous session to keep the Iron Hall out of this State. "The insinuation that bribery was used is all bosh," said Assessor Chadbourne. "Were any attempt made to bribe, it would of necessity have been made in the judiciary committee, but I am willing to take oath that no money was used to influence the Legislature."

CHARTER OAK RACES.

Trevian Takes the First Heat in the $10,000 Colt Race.

HARTFORD, Ct., Aug. 29.—Charter Oak Park, Trevian wins first heat in the $10,000 colt race; time 2 18 3-4.

Old Colony Railroad's Surplus.

BOSTON, Aug. 29.—The report of the Old Colony railroad made to the Massachusetts commissioners for the quarter ending June 30th shows a surplus of $203,121, against $367,875 for the corresponding period last year.

Tennis at Newport.

NEWPORT, Aug. 29.—The play in the lawn tennis tournament began at 11 o'clock this morning, with games between Hovey and Wrenn. The largest crowd of the season was present and the weather was nearly perfect. The summary of games follow. Fifth round, Hovey beat Wrenn 6—4, 7—5, 6—3; Larned beat E. L. Hall 2—6, 6—0, 6—4, 1—6, 8—6.

Australian Bankers Fail.

LONDON, Aug. 29.—The failure was announced to-day of the firm of Redfern, Alexander & Co., Australian and New Zealand merchants and bankers, of No. 3 Great Winchester street. Liabilities, £250,000.

Died of His Injuries.

SALEM, Aug. 29.—Engineer Edward James died this morning of injuries received in the Boston & Maine smashup two weeks ago. James was in charge of the train and was blamed for the accident.

No Good.

"Is that a good dog?"

"I used to think so, but I have my doubts now."

"Why?"

"I've had him a month and nobody has tried to steal him."—Washington Star.

Pages 1-8.

The Evening Standard.

Pages 1-8.

ESTABLISHED FEBRUARY, 1850.

NEW BEDFORD, WEDNESDAY, AUGUST 31, 1892.---TEN PAGES.

TWO CENTS.

HASKELL & TRIPP.

"Home made."

We have the exclusive sale for this city of the highest grade "home made" cotton underclothing for women and misses.

Finest materials.

Perfect fit.

Careful work.

Nothing equal to these goods is being offered *at any price.*

Those of you who have hitherto been compelled to have undergarments made up at home, simply because you couldn't buy ready made that were good enough, will have no need of further trouble on that score.

Our *"home made"* underwear has been produced to fit just such cases as yours. The cloth, the trimming, the sewing, the button holes, the fine, thick, pearl buttons—all just such as you would choose for your own work.

To be sure you must pay us more than for the ordinary sorts—some of you are willing to. We have plenty of other kinds for those who wish to pay less.

Equipoise waists.

The corset substitute—stylish, comfortable, hygienic.

A perfect supporter from the shoulders, distributing the clothing strain and weight.

Three garments in one—corset, waist and cover.

Women's, $1.75 }
Misses', $1.75 } Equipoise.
Children's, 60c. }
Infants', 75c. }

One of the most complete stocks of *desirable* corsets in this state. Prices always lowest.

White goods.

2000 yards mill remnants of beautiful plaided, striped, and lace openwork Lawns and Nainsooks, worth at wholesale 15 to 18c. *Take your pick for 12 1-2c. a yard.*

HASKELL & TRIPP.

Department Stores,

Purchase and William Streets.

IN DEFENCE.

Counsel for Lizzie Borden Putting in Evidence.

Marshal Hilliard Tells of the Search at the House.

Dress Pattern Purchased by Lizzie Was Not Found.

Mr. Knowlton Calls upon Attorney Jennings to Produce it.

Detective Seaver and Other Witnesses on the Stand.

Wounds on Mr. Borden Described by Dr. F. W. Draper.

It is Decided that Prisoner Will Not Testify at the Hearing.

Defendant's Side of the Case Nearing Completion.

[Special Dispatch.]

FALL RIVER, Aug. 31.—Party lines in this city were never more strongly defined than at the present time. When I say party lines I do not mean political ones, such as Republican, Democratic, People's, or even Prohibition, but lines which are drawn from household to household, and even have their closer ones drawn inside households themselves. Fall River is now one huge camp of people divided keenly and sharply on the questions of belief and non-belief in the innocence or guilt of Lizzie A. Borden for murdering her father. Those who, during the opening days of the examination thoroughly believed in her guilt, to-day are groping and hesitating. They are tenacious in

Dr. Bowen.

retaining first impressions, but they have got a cross-counter from Prof. Wood's testimony from which it is hard for them to recover promptly. Believers in Lizzie's innocence say the evidence of Prof. Wood of no blood being found on hatchet or axes is conclusive, and they do not fail to make it public that in their point of view

The Chief Prop Has Fallen

from under the structure the government has erected.

District Attorney Knowlton states that he was cognizant a week or so ago of the substance of Prof. Wood's testimony and he does not seem at all discouraged at the answers which the professor gave or the general tenor of his evidence. The

District Attorney is Very Buoyant

by nature, and whether he has met with a decided rebuff or not is impossible for the average person to judge from looking at his countenance, naturally so ruddy and not necessarily marked by any sudden change.

The question was asked the district attorney this morning how long he thought defence would occupy in the presentation of its case and he said he has not any idea, but he would be glad to know. In fact he has become so wearied from the long continuance of the examination that he had no hesitancy in saying that he wished the train on which he was going over to Fall River was bound to Chicago.

Mr. Knowlton was also asked this morning if he thought Lizzie Borden would be put on the stand. He did not know but he thought it was unlikely after the government had put in the statement she had made at the inquest. Mr. Knowlton did not say that he

Had Taken the Wind Out of the Sails of the Defence

by introducing the evidence of what Lizzie had sworn to, but that was the conclusion which I drew as a result of my talk with him.

The counsel for defence after the adjournment of the court last evening gave

The Much Talked About Hatchet.

correspondents to understand that Lizzie will not be subjected to the ordeal of a public examination to-day. Counsel also said they were of opinion that they

Will Finish the Presentation of Their Evidence To-day.

There is speculation as to whether the completion of evidence will be followed by argument. It is an open secret that Mr. Knowlton would be only too glad to have an oppportunity to present in the able and concrete manner for which he is noted the points which he has grasped during the continuation of the examination. If the case was being at this stage presented to a jury Mr. Knowlton's argumentative powers would have great weight but when his words and facts are offered to a single individual it is a question if he will not waste "his sweetness on the desert air."

Mr. Adams has the reputation of being an able and eloquent pleader, and those who have sat under the spell which he weaves around his subjects affirm that even the district attorney, with all his ability, will not be able to overcome the impression left by the able counsel for defence.

The various avenues to the Central Station were thronged all this morning with the crowd, which has been always early and numerous, and the sights and sounds and scenes of other days before the opening of the court were duplicated to-day.

E. H. MARTIN.

THE SIXTH DAY.

Examination of Lizzie A. Borden Slowly Nearing Its Completion.

FALL RIVER, Aug. 31.—Court came in at 10 o'clock, but Lizzie and her counsel were not in their seats, and it was not until 10 minutes later that Lizzie appeared, leaning on the arm of Rev. Mr. Jubb, bearing upon her face the same look of stoical indifference which has characterized her appearance heretofore in general.

The first witness called was Rufus B. Hilliard, who said that his attention was called to the murder at 11 15 Aug. 4. He

Attorney Adams With the Hatchet.

sent Officer George W. Allen to the house and did not go to the house himself until 2 30 or 3 in the afternoon. The next officer sent was Doherty, then Mullaley, Medley, Gillen, Wilson and others he did not remember. When witness went at 3 o'clock he went with some men to search the barn and that vicinity, but knew nothing about the matter from what had been told by Medley, Fleet, and he thought, Riley. Medley is not in town now, but has been to look after everything. Rev. Mr. Buck placed in his hands, following out some supposed clew in connection with the murder, but witness declined to state what. When witness arrived at the Borden house he went to the back of the yard where the lumber was; a thorough examination was made of the hay in the barn, he was certain of that. Went in the back yard where the lumber was by the Chagnon fence, and looked over into the Chagnon property and also into the Crowe and Kelley yards and then he went to the wall or what was the wall, then to the vaults, then to the barn where they were overhauling the hay; then to the lower part of the barn, where they examined about the carriages; searched the stalls on the north of the barn and under the stairway; in fact, all downstairs; then sent officers to search other yards, and then witness went into the house. Saw no other officer in the house when he went in; this was 4 o'clock about; saw Drs. Dolan, Coughlin, Peckham, Dutra and Tourtellot, but was not positive whether Dr. Dolan was there or not. They were then in the dining-room where Mr. Borden's body lay and were talking; were in consultation; spoke to Dr. Dolan about the matter; looked at the sofa but couldn't say whether any part of it was cut.

Can't tell whether there were any blood spots on the head; (witness is speaking now of lounge in sitting-room.)

There Were Blood Spots on the Parlor Door,

but didn't notice the chair. Mr. Borden's body was then removed from the lounge; then passed into the front entry with Dr. Dolan and into the front room, where they said Mrs. Borden's body was found; saw some spots of blood on pillow shams. (Here witness was sent for pillow shams and the marble piece taken from the bureau.) Shams produced and identified. Witness said they were given to him on Wednesday the 10th. He saw them on the bed, however, on the 5th of August. The bed-spread of white was examined and also the shams. The sham with the blood lay near to the bureau.

Witness made no search of the house, but when he sent men to search the yard he also sent men to search the cellar, but has been informed that it had been searched; only know cellar was searched from what was reported to him; the officers were Fleet, Harrington, Riley, and Medley, and perhaps one or two others; they reported through the Assistant Marshal Fleet; nothing was delivered to witness as the result of the search that afternoon.

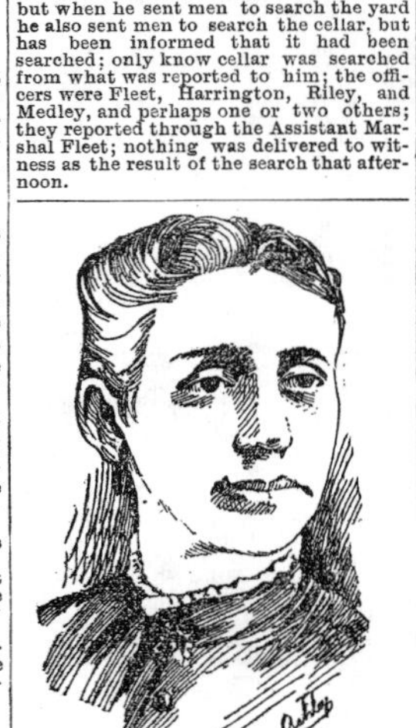

Mrs. Reagan, Police Matron.

Going back to the things found in the room where Mrs. Borden lay the marble was examined and one blood spot found on the top and two on the front edge. No orders were given by witness to search the upper part of the house, but know from reports of officers that such search was made. On Friday, the next day, witness didn't know that any search was made. That morning, however, he received two axes and two hatchets, and the hatchets were the same as shown in court yesterday. Did not make an immediate examination of the hatchets when he received them, but did later.

On Sunday morning a thorough inspection was made of the hatchet with a powerful glass. The hair was first discovered on the hatchet by Officer Edson, who brought it to him, witness thought; don't think Mayor Coughlin was the first one to call attention to that hair, but he did call the attention of witness to look to what looked like blood on one of the axes. The next search was made on Saturday about 12 30, caused by something which came to his knowledge; it was done after the funeral procession had started, and then three rooms, Lizzie's

[Continued on Fourth Page.]

GEORGE WILLIAM CURTIS DEAD.

Noted Author and Politican Expires at His Staten Island Home.

NEW YORK, Aug. 31.—George William Curtis died at 2 30 o'clock this morning at his residence, West Brighton, S. I.

George William Curtis was born Feb. 24, 1824, in Providence, and after obtaining an academic education only was taken to New York city by his father and placed in a mercantile establishment in 1839. As his mother died in his early boyhood, and he was by nature better fitted for almost any occupation than for a clerk or merchant, it is not necessary to add that he was peculiarly unhappy in the store. He has, in his novel called "Trumps", given us lively and entertaining sketches of his schoolboy life at Jamaica Plain, near Boston, but in his most genial moments he could not torture a joke out of his mercantile experience.

In 1842 he "cut the shop"—"bolted," as they said in those days—and with his brother joined the famous Brook Farm community of Roxbury, Mass. Of that ludicrous experiment almost every one who was in it has given a readable account, including Charles A. Dana of the New York *Sun*, but the best summary is by Nathaniel Hawthorne, who said: "I went for poetry, and I found muck. I went to drive the horses of the sun, and I sat in the manure milking a kicking cow." Not one of the experimenters regretted that he had been in it, but they all got out in good time, and Mr. Curtis and his brother tried farming on their own account for two years more.

It is scarcely necessary to say that they got tired of it and went into literature, where the fame of George William was soon secured. From 1846 to 1850 he lived abroad, travelling much in Egypt and Syria, as appears in his "Nile Notes" and "Howadi." In 1852-3 he joined with Parke Godwin and Charles E. Briggs in starting *Putnam's Monthly*, and when the magazine failed a few years later he voluntarily assumed his proportional share of the debts and paid every dollar of it, though it tied him down to hard work and rigid economy for ten years.

In 1853 he began the "Easy Chair" in Harper's Monthly. In 1857 he took the editorship of Harper's Weekly. In 1856 he became famous as a political speaker. From 1853 to 1865 he was a popular lecturer. Since 1870 he has been famous as a civil service reformer. In all these characters the reading world knows him well.

Mr. Curtis was a delegate to the National Republican Convention of 1860, 1864, and 1876, and in the latter year was an unsuccessful candidate for Congress from the 1st New York District. In 1862 he declined the consul-generalship to Egypt, offered by President Lincoln, and in 1867 was delegate-at-large and chairman of the committee on education in the Constitutional Convention in New York. In 1868 he was nominated a Presidential elector, and in 1869 declined the Republican nomination for Secretary of State of New York. In 1871, President Grant appointed him one of the commission to formulate rules for civil service regulation, and later, up to 1873, he was chairman of the commission and the advisory board. President Hayes asked him to choose a foreign mission, but he declined, and also declined the mission to Germany. He was chairman of a meeting of Independent Rebublicans in New York, that protested against the Chicago convention's action in nominating James G. Blaine and subsequently led the mugwumps in supporting Cleveland.

Since 1864, Mr. Curtis has been one of the regents of the University of the State of New York, and in 1886 was made its vice chancellor. He has been a prolific author, and his works are well known to the reading world.

WEATHER INDICATIONS.

COOLER—SHOWERS.

WASHINGTON, Aug. 31.—For the 24 hours from 8 a. m. to-day: For Massachusetts, Rhode Island and Connecticut, showers; cooler; brisk southwesterly winds.

LIGHT RAINS.

BOSTON, Aug. 31.—Local forecast for New England until Friday: Continued unsettled weather; probably light rains today and to-night; fair and cooler Thursday; southerly to westerly winds; Friday also cooler.

Duelists and Seconds Acquitted.

PARIS, Aug. 31.—Marquis de Mores and the four seconds in the duel in which the marquis killed Capt. Mayer have been acquitted.

HOME MATTERS.

HAVE BEEN INVITED.—Mayor Ashley and members of the City Council have received invitations to review the Labor Day parade.

LINCOLN GUARDS.—At the meeting of the Lincoln Guards, held last evening in Adelphi Rink, the following officers were appointed:

Colonel—Dr. J. W. Owen.
Lieutenant-Colonel—Charles Buckley.
Adjutant—J. G. Nicholson.
Sergeant Major—John Devlin.
Captain Company A—Edgar Potter.
Captain Company B—Ambrose Salt.
Captain Company C—John T. Champain.
Captain Company D—Frank T. Bentley.
And a staff of 13 members.

The enthusiasm in the regiment shows no signs of abating; a number of recruits were enlisted last evening. Dr. Owen is at work organizing a band for the regiment which he hopes to have complete in a few weeks. Companies are being formed in Boston, Fall River, Worcester and Taunton.

ODD FELLOWS.—The Fifth Regiment, Patriarchs Militant, I. O. O. F., will visit Warren, R. I., Monday, and the members of the order at that place are looking forward with considerable pleasure to the arrival of Canton New Bedford, which has voted to take part in the festivities of the day. Arriving at Warren the regiment will parade through the principal streets. The Warren Odd Fellows have engaged the National Band of Providence for the day. At the conclusion of the parade will be served an old-time clambake. A dress parade and review will be in order immediately after the parade. The Union Club of that place as well as the fire companies will keep open house. The New Bedford canton will be represented by about 40 members.

BIRTHDAY ANNIVERSARY.—At the residence of Patience Irish, No. 218 Purchase street, a company of about 20 of the relatives and friends of that estimable lady met last evening to congratulate her on the 89th anniversary of her birth. Although so far advanced in years she still enjoys a good degree of health and a remarkably retentive memory of all the important events that have occurred in the history of our country, as well as of those connected with her own life; of the joys and sorrows through which she has passed, and of the hopes that have cheered, comforted and sustained her during the long period of her existence. A pleasant hour was passed in rehearsing these reminiscences, after which she was presented a nice rocking chair and numerous other gifts by the friends present and some who were not fortunate enough to be there. The presentation speech was made by Deacon A. P. Manchester of the First Baptist church, of which she is an honored and consistent member of long standing. Though somewhat surprised, she responded in a graceful manner, and thanked the donors for their kind remembrance of her. A collation of cake and ice cream was partaken of, and the company retired to their homes after a very enjoyable evening, hoping to meet again when the 90th annive rsary comes round.

THE LAND OF SUNSHINE.—*A Unique Country where the Skies are almost Never Clouded, while the air is Cool and Bracing, like Perpetual Spring.*—As an anomalous Southern resort, by reason of the fact that there one may escape Summer heat no less than Winter cold, New Mexico is rapidly becoming famous. Averaging throughout the entire territory 5600 feet in altitude above sea-level, and characterized by dry air which, unlike a humid atmosphere, is incapable of communicating heat, the temperature in midsummer remains at a delightfully comfortable degree through the day, and at night becomes invariably brisk and bracing. The sunshine is almost constant, yet the most violent out-of-door exertion may be undertaken without fear of distressful consequences. Sunstroke or prostration are absolutely unknown there. It is an ideal land for a Summer outing. Its climate is prescribed by reputable physicians as a specific for pulmonary complaints, and the medicinal Hot Springs at Las Vegas are noted for their curative virtues. The most sumptuous hotel in the West, the Montezuma, is located at these springs. Write to Jno. J. Byrne, 723 Monadnock Block, Chicago, for "The Land of Sunshine," an entertaining and profusely illustrated book descriptive of this region, the most picturesque and romantic in the United States.

PERSONAL.—A letter received in this city states that Rev. W. J. Reynolds, the newly-elected pastor of the First Christian church, will be here and begin his labors on Sunday next.

William L. Peters left the city yesterday to attend the Baltimore College of Dentistry.

Alfred Chausse has gone to West Farnum, P. Q., to pursue a year's course in the Commercial College at that place.

Mr. Henry W. Smith and family and Mr. and Mrs. Lloyd Swain leave the city to-day for a short sojourn at Cuttyhunk.

Mme. Bruce, clairvoyant doctor, has returned from Cottage City.

Charles Howland of Nebraska, formerly of this city, is visiting Capt. J. E. Stanton.

Col. Tripp of the State Board of Charities is in town to-day.

COLORED ODD FELLOWS.—The District Grand Lodge of Massachusetts, G. U. O. O. F., will meet in the Grand Army Hall, Attleboro, Thursday, at 1 o'clock. An extract from the secretary's report shows that there are 17 lodges in the district, with a membership of over 1000. There has been paid to the sick, $2000; for funerals, $1800; to widows, $800; invested, $3000; for charity, $300; for various objects, $8360.10; remain in fund, $6000; value of property, $38,000; making a total value of property invested and in funds of $47,000, an increase over last year of about $4000. On Friday there will be a parade in honor of the District Grand Lodge. There will be speaking in the evening and also an entertainment.

LIBERTY THEATRE.—Manager G. F. Weeden has secured the Star Specialty Co. for the opening of the season at Liberty Theatre next Monday (Labor Day.) Two grand performances will be given, afternoon and evening. A neat and refined bill is offered, and according to Manager Weeden's programme there should be no hesitancy in giving him a rousing house in his endeavor to place attractive entertainers in this formerly popular house. One feature of his programme is the dog and bird circus of Mlle. Carretta, whom Tony Pastor stated to be the best in that line, Mlle. Carretta having played an engagement at his New York theatre.

BROKE HIS LEG.—John Cassidy, a laborer employed on the Propeller wharf, while assisting in moving a big gang plank on a gear this morning, stumbled, and the plank falling on his right leg, fractured the bone. He was removed to his home at Winterville in the police ambulance.

SCHOOL SHOES.—We can give you a bargain in misses' and children's school shoes. We are fixed so that we can sell you our regular $2 shoe for misses and children for $1.50. This is not a job lot, but straight goods. Union Shoe Store.

NOW IS THE TIME to buy your Winter overcoat. We will place them on special counters to-morrow—Thursday—and never will the people of New Bedford have the opportunity of buying an overcoat at the prices we will sell them. Wamsutta Clothing Co.

SO VERY CHEAP.—This week we will sell any laundered cheviot or madras shirt in our stock for one dollar each. This includes the $1.50, $2.00, and $2.50 grades, at Gifford & Cos., No. 139 Union street.

AT LAST the great and final mark down on children's clothing. School commences Tuesday, Sept. 6, and every suit will be closed out at greatly reduced prices. Wamsutta Clothing Co.

COME QUICK FOR BARGAINS.—Ladies' silver chatelaine watches $4.50, boys' watches $3.75, men's 15-year filled watches $13.50, clocks 93 cents. J. S. Kelley & Son, 15 Purchase street.

SCARLET FEVER.—Two new cases of scarlet fever have been reported at the office of the Board of Health this week. Both cases are in the same family.

MEN'S AND YOUTHS' black worsted pants that have retailed from $5 to $6. Your choice of this lot for $3. Wamsutta Clothing Co.

HATHAWAY, SOULE & HARRINGTON have written a letter that it will pay you to read on page 5. Union Shoe store.

REPORTED. — It is reported by those who know that Buchell's marked down bargains are just as advertised. Read adv. 5th page.

NORTH CONGREGATIONAL CHURCH.—Preparatory service will be held in the chapel this evening, instead of Friday evening.

B. F. COTTELLE, piano tuner and repairer. Orders left at Hutchinson's book store.

MEN'S $3 HATS in all the latest styles to be closed out at $2. Wamsutta Clothing Co.

BASS have struck on at Pasque.

HAND-SEWED HOUSE GAITERS $1. Devoll's

SCROFULA cured by Hood's Sarsaparilla.

THE UPS AND DOWNS OF YOUR WINDOW SHADES.

Do they Please You?

Why Not See Us About Them?

Making and Hanging Shades a Specialty with Us.

OIL OPAQUE SHADES,

Decorated or Plain.

The plain shades are handsomely furnished, mounted on a warranted roller, with a fine nickel pull; are 36 inches wide and 2 yards long.

READY-MADE SHADES,

By their convenience and low prices seem to have filled a real want. We have made up a pleasing variety of curtains in both Holland and Opaque, in the most approved colorings, using a high grade roller, which we believe at the very reasonable prices will meet the requirements of the majority of curtain buyers.

SPECIAL ORDER SHADES,

FOR CUSTOM CURTAINS.

We take great pleasure in referring to our *SUNFAST ROCKSONIA HOLLAND*, which we GUARANTEE to be STRICTLY FADELESS. Can we do more? In addition to this quality, it is the best fabric we have ever seen for nice curtains. If you will drop us a postal card we will send samples and give an estimate of cost free of charge.

C. F. WING,

34 to 40 Purchase st.

WHITING & CO.

Look Out for Our

GRAND

Fall Opening!

$30,000 worth of New Goods will be opened in a few days.

Due notice will be given in this column of the opening.

The remaining days of this week will be devoted in closing out odds and ends of all kinds of goods. Some goods will be sold awful cheap, to close them out.

100 Fine Black and White Wash Jersey Waists, sold by us at $2.50, $4.00 and $5.00, will be closed out at

LOT 1—$2.50 and $3.75 ones to be sold at 95c. a piece.

LOT 2 — $4.00 and $5.00 ones go on sale at $1.29 a piece.

At these prices it is almost giving them away.

WHITING & CO.

Fall Hats.

Buy

Your

New

Hat

Of

J. & W. R.

WING & CO.

Correct

Qualitie.

Correct

Shapes.

Correct

Prices.

Now Ready.

THE CRESCENT

22 Purchase St.

CORSETS.

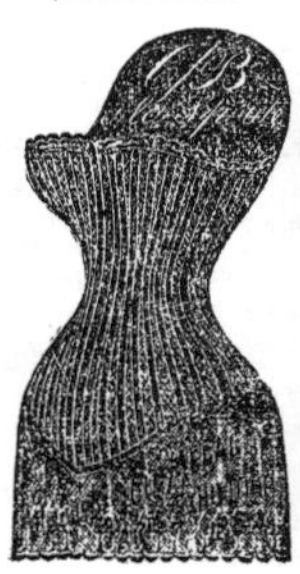

CORSETS.

We haven't begun to tell you all about our Corsets. It is

CORSETS,

and CORSETS,

and CORSETS.

A fresh stock coming in constantly. Don't forget we have a large line of Thomson's Glove-fitting Corsets. Prices at $1, $1.25, $1.50, $1.75, $2.25; satin $5. And we give you a new pair if the steels break.

Kalamazoo Corset Waists, very similar in style to the Jackson Waist, marked down from $1 to 75c. A very few Kabo Corsets left, drab only for 75c.; regular price $1.

Hoisery and *Hose Supporters.* Good Dress Shields only 10c.

Gingham Aprons of best quality and with two full widths only 25c. If you examine the make of them you will be satisfied. They sell *every time.*

UNABATED INTEREST.

Women Stood for Hours Listening to Evidence.

Miss Lizzie Borden's Testimony at Inquest Read.

Statements Contradictory in Several Particulars.

Discussion Over the Prussic Acid Evidence Standing.

Dr. Bowen the First Witness Presented by Defence.

It has only taken a few weeks time to make the square about the Fall River Police Station a magnet of public attention. On the merits of its own attractiveness it could never have attained any prominence, but as Miss Lizzie A. Borden's enforced home and the place of her preliminary trial it has become famous.

The usual caravan, which included a throng of women whose thoughts were in touch with things bizarre and bloody, hung around the alleyway yesterday morning at the side entrance to the station, the male portion discussing recent developments, and the women for the most part unusually quiet, and whenever opportunity afforded casting imploring glances at the blue coats. The police officials at the door disposed of favors in a manner complimentary to their tastes and good judgment, and few beside those were admitted who may now be termed the habitues of the court-room.

Lizzie's window was sought by every eye but with little satisfaction. Only a most disappointing view could be had of a bouquet of white and pink asters, which was another of the many tokens of friendship to the prisoner by the gallant and venerable Mr. Buck.

Lizzie Borden does not display the tendencies of a lady of leisure. She rose that forenoon as usual at about 7 30, and after breakfast fortified herself for the ordeal of the day with a few chapters from a book which resembled a tract or Christian Endeavor pamphlet. She did not move near the window, and only half of the blind was left swinging, that the public might not intrude with its gazes.

Miss Emma arrived nearly an hour before it was time for court. She came as usual in a hack, only the curtains were drawn closer than ever, to the supreme disgust of the loafers in the alley, who spread out in a serpentine coil around the vehicle, and threatened to overturn it in their scrabble to see who was inside.

Miss Lizzie Borden and Mr. Buck as usual led off in the march into the court-room. The reverend gentleman's very apparent courtliness has done much to screen the lack of grace of the prisoner.

Everybody gave their earnest attention to Prof. Wood, and during the forenoon were treated to some testimony that was mostly a sensation. During the several times that the hatchet was brought out or referred to Lizzie displayed the keenest interest. The eye of the entire court-room was upon her when she picked up the weapon and carefully looked it over. It was a refreshing change from her stereotyped demeanor of every day.

The matter of the hair on the hatchet being an animal's created such a surprise that even breathing was suspended for a few moments. That little statement by the professor has affected a good many people's opinion and was one of the most concise and important scraps of testimony yet given.

When the time for the afternoon session of the court arrived the court-room was too hot for pleasure, and crowded to the very limit. It was the largest crowd of the trial. The women who stood upright on the back seats looked like rows of human caryatides in modern robes. There was a row about the railing, so that the people on the seats were obliged to stand to look over their heads. The approach to every door was jammed so that the officers had to clear a passage for whoever wished to come in or go out. It is doubtful if the old court-room ever saw so many people before, most of them women, and well dressed women. Some of them stood for three hours without any support, listening to the reading of the report of the inquest.

LIZZIE BORDEN'S TESTIMONY.

Statements She Made at the Inquest Contradictory.

District Attorney Knowlton read the testimony advanced by Lizzie Borden at the inquest yesterday afternoon. It was as follows:

"Give me your full name."

"Lizzie Andrew Borden."

"You were so christened?"

"I was."

"What is your age?"

"32."

"Your mother is not living?"

"She died when I was two years of age."

The remainder of the testimony was as follows: "My father and stepmother were married 27 years ago. I have no idea how much my father was worth and have never heard him form an opinion. I know something about what real estate my father owned."

The next question was: "How do you know?" and Mr. Adams promptly objected. He said he did so on the ground of the admissibility of a statement which was detrimental to her.

Judge Blaisdell said he didn't know that any statement the defendant might make would not be competent. Mr. Jennings argued in support of his associate. He said any statement that did not bear directly on the issue between the prosecution and the defence was not material. Judge Blaisdell allowed the introduction of the question and the answer was "two farms in Swanzey, the homestead, some property on North Main street, Borden block, some land further south and some he had recently purchased."

"Did you ever deed him any property?" "He gave us some land, but my father bought it back. Had no other transaction with him. He paid in $5000 cash for this property. Never knew my father made a will, but heard so from Uncle Morse."

"Did you know of anybody that your father had trouble with?"

"There was a man who came there some weeks before, but I do not know who he was. He came to the house one day, and I heard them talk about a store. My father told him he could not have a store. The man said: I thought with your liking for money you would let anybody in. I heard my father order him out of the house. Think he lived out of town, because he said he could go back and talk with father."

"Did your father and anybody else have bad feelings between them?"

"Yes, Hiram C. Harrington. He married my father's only sister."

"Nobody else?"

"I have no reason to suppose that that man had seen my father before that day."

"Did you ever have any trouble with your stepmother?"

"No."

"Within a year?"

"No."

"Within three years?"

"No. About five years ago."

"What was it about?"

"About my stepmother's stepsister, Mrs. George Whitehead."

"Was it a violent expression of feeling?"

"It was simply a difference of opinion."

"Were you always cordial with your stepmother?"

"That depends upon one's idea of cordiality."

"Was it cordial according to your ideas of cordiality?"

"Yes."

Continuing: "I did not regard her as my mother, though she came there when I was young. I decline to say whether my relations between her and myself were those of mother and daughter or not. I called her Mrs. Borden and sometimes mother. I stopped calling her mother after the affair regarding her sister-in-law."

"Why did you leave off calling her mother?"

"Because I wanted to."

"Have you any other answer to give me?"

"No, sir. I always went to my sister. She was older than I was. I don't know but what my father and stepmother were happily united. I never knew of any difficulty between them, and they seemed to be affectionate. The day they were killed I had on a blue dress. I changed it in the afternoon and put on a print dress. Mr. Morse came into our house whenever he wanted to. He has been here once since the river was frozen over. I don't know how often he came to spend the nights, because I had been away so much. I have not been away much during the year. He has been there very little during the past year. I have been away a great deal in the day time during the last year. I don't think I have been away much at night, except once when I was in New Bedford. I was abroad in 1890. I first saw Morse Thursday noon. Wednesday evening I was with Miss Russell at 9 o'clock, and I don't know whether the family were in or not. I went direct to my room. I locked the front door when I came in. Was in my room Wednesday, not feeling well all day. Did not go down to supper. Went out that evening and came in and locked the front door. Came down about 9 next morning. Did not inquire about Mr. Morse that morning. Did not go to Marion at that time, because they could go sooner than I. I had taken the secretaryship of the Christian Endeavor Society and had to remain over till the 10th. There had been nobody else around there that week but the man I have spoken of. I did not say that he came a week before, but that week. Mr. Morse slept in the spare room Wednesday night. It was my habit to close my room door when I was in it. That Wednesday afternoon they made so much noise that I closed the door. First saw my father Thursday morning downstairs, reading the Providence *Journal*. Saw my mother with a dust cloth in her hand. Maggie was putting a cloth into a mop. Don't know whether I ate cookies and tea that morning. Know the coffee pot was on the stove.

Continuing, the testimony ran as follows: "My father went down town after 9 o'clock. I did not finish the handkerchiefs because the irons were not right. I was in the kitchen reading when he returned. I am not sure that I was in the kitchen when my father returned. I stayed in my room long enough to sew a piece of lace on a garment. That was before he came back. I don't know where Maggie was. I think she let my father in and that he rang the bell. I understood Maggie to say he said he had forgotten his key. I think I was upstairs when my father came in and I think I was on the stairs when he entered. I don't know whether Maggie was washing windows or not when my father came in.

At this point the district attorney had called Miss Borden's attention to her conflicting statements regarding her position when her father came in and her answer was: "You have asked me so many questions I don't know what I have said." Later, she said she was reading in the kitchen and had gone into the other room for a copy of the Providence *Journal*. "I last saw my mother when I was downstairs. She was dusting the dining room. She said she had been upstairs and made the bed and was going upstairs to put on the pillow slips. She had some cotton cloth pillows up there, and she said she was going to work on them. If she had remained downstairs I should have seen her. She would have gone up the back way to go to her room. If she had gone to the kitchen I would have seen her. There is no reason to suppose I would not have seen her when she was downstairs or in her room, except when I went downstairs once for two or three minutes."

"I ask you again what you suppose she was doing from the time you saw her till 11 o'clock?"

"I don't know, unless she was making her bed."

"She would have had to pass your room, and you would have seen her, wouldn't you?"

"Yes, unless I was in my room or down cellar. I supposed she had gone away, because she told me she was going, and we talked about the dinner. Didn't hear her go or come back. When I first came down stairs saw Maggie coming in, and my mother asked me how I was feeling. My father was there, still reading. My mother used to go and do the marketing."

"Now I call your attention to the fact you said twice yesterday that you first saw your father after he came in when you were standing on the stairs."

"I did not. I was in the kitchen when he came in, or in one of the three rooms, the dining room, kitchen and sitting room. It would have been difficult for anybody to pass through these rooms unless they passed through while I was in the dining room."

"A portion of the time the girl was out of doors, wasn't she?"

"Yes."

Lizzie Borden's testimony continued as follows: "So far as I know, I was alone in the house the larger part of the time while my father was away. I was eating a pear when my father came in. I had put a stick of wood into the fire to see if I could start it. I did no more ironing after my father came in. I then went in to tell him. I did not put away the ironing board. I don't know what time my father came in. When I went out to the barn I left him on the sofa. The last thing I said was to ask him if he wanted the window left that way. Then I went to the barn to get some lead for a sinker. I went upstairs in the barn. There was a bench there which contained some lead. I unhooked the screen door when I went out. I don't know when Bridget got through washing the widows inside. I knew she washed the windows outside. I knew she didn't wash the kitchen windows, but I don't know whether she washed the sitting room windows or not. I thought the flats would be hot by the time I got back. I had not fishing apparatus, but there was some at the farm. It is five years since I used the fish line. I don't think there was any sinker on my line. I don't think there was any fish lines suitable for use at the farm.

"What! did you think you would find sinkers in the barn?"

"My father once told me that there was some lead and nails in the barn."

"How long do you think you occupied in looking for the sinkers?"

"About 15 or 20 minutes."

"Did you do nothing beside look for sinkers in the 20 minutes?"

"Yes, sir. I ate some pears."

"Would it take you all that time to eat a few pears?"

"I do not do things in a hurry."

"Was Bridget not washing the dining-room windows and the sitting-room windows?"

"I do not know. I did not see her."

"Did you tell Bridget to wash the windows?"

"No, sir."

"Who did?"

"My mother."

"Did you see Bridget after your mother told her to wash the windows?"

"Yes, sir."

"What was she doing?"

"She had got a long pole and was sticking it in a brush, and she had a pail of water."

"About what time did you go out into the barn?"

"About as near as I can recollect, 10 o'clock."

"What did you go into the barn for?"

"To find some sinkers."

"How many pears did you eat in that 20 minutes?"

"Three."

"Is that all you did?"

"No. I went over to the window and opened it."

"Why did you do that?"

"Because it was too hot."

"I suppose that it is the hottest place on the premises?"

"Yes, sir."

"Could you, while standing looking out of that window, see anybody enter the kitchen?"

"No, sir."

"I thought you said you could see people from the barn?"

"Not after you pass a jog in the barn. It obstructs the view of the back door."

"What kind of lead were you looking for, for sinkers? Hard lead?"

"No, sir; soft lead."

"Did you expect to find the sinkers already made?"

"Well, no. I thought I might find one with a hole in it."

"Was the lead referred to tea lead or lead that comes in tea chests?"

"I don't know."

"When were you going fishing?"

"Monday."

"The next Monday after the fatal day?"

"Yes, sir."

"Had you lines all ready?"

"No, sir."

"Did you have a line?"

"Yes, sir."

"Where was your line?"

"Down to the farm."

"Do you know whether there were any sinkers on the line you left at the farm?"

"I think there was none on the line."

"Did you have any hooks?"

"No, sir."

"Then you were making all this preparation without either hook or line. Why did you go into the barn after sinkers?"

"Because I was going down town to buy some hooks and line, and thought it would save me from buying them."

"Now, to the barn again. Do you not think I could go into the barn and do the same as you in a few minutes?"

"I do not do things in a hurry."

"Did you then think there were no sinkers at the barn?"

"I thought there were no sinkers anywhere there. I had no idea of using my lines. I thought you understood that I wasn't going to use these lines at the farm, because they hadn't sinkers. I went upstairs to the kind of bench there. I had heard my father say there was lead there. Looked for lead in a box up there. There were nails and perhaps an old door knob. Did not find any lead as thin as tea lead in the box. Did not look anywhere except on the bench. I ate some pears up there. I have now told you everything that took place up in the barn. It was the hottest place in the premises. I suppose I ate my pears when I first went up there. I stood looking out of the window. I was feeling well enough to eat pears, but don't know how to answer the question if I was feeling better than I was in the morning, because I was feeling better that morning. I picked the pears up from the ground. I was not in the rear of the barn. I was in the front of it. Don't see how anybody could leave the house then without my seeing them. I pulled over boards to look for the lead. That took me some time. I returned from the barn and put my hat in the dining-room. I found my father and called to Maggie. I found the fire gone out. I went to the barn because the irons were not hot enough and the fire had gone out. I made no efforts to find my mother at all. Sent Maggie for Dr. Bowen. Didn't see or find anything after the murders to tell me my mother had been sewing in the spare room that morning."

"What did your mother say when you saw her?"

"She told me she had had a note and was going out. She said she would get the dinner."

The district attorney continued to read: "My mother did tell when she was coming back. I did not know Mr. Morse was coming to dinner. I don't know whether I was at tea Wednesday night or not. I had no apron on Thursday; that is, I don't think I had. I don't remember surely. I had no occasion to use the axe or hatchet. I knew there was an old axe down stairs and last time I saw it it was on the old chopping block. I don't know whether my father owned a hatchet or not. Assuming a hatchet was found in the cellar I don't know how it got there, and if there was blood on it, I have no idea as to how it got there. My father killed some pigeons last May. When I found my father I did not think of Mrs. Borden, for I believed she was out. I remember asking Mrs. Churchill to look for my mother. I left the screen door closed when I left, and it was open when I came from the barn. I can give no idea of the time my father came home. I went right to the barn. I don't know whether he came to the sitting-room at once or not. I don't remember his being in the sitting-room or sitting down. I think I was in there when I asked him if there was any mail. I do not think he went up stairs. He had a letter in his hand. I did not help him to lie down and did not touch the sofa. He was taking medicine for some time. Mrs. Borden's father's house was for sale on Fourth street. My father bought Mrs. Borden's half-sister's share and gave it to her. We thought what he did for her people he ought to do for his own, and he then gave us grandfather's house. I always thought my stepmother induced him to purchase the interest. I don't know when the windows were last washed before that day. All day Tuesday I was at the table. I gave the officer the same skirt I wore that day, and if there was any blood on it I can give an explanation as to how it got there. If the blood came from the outside, I cannot say how it got there. I wore tie shoes that day and black stockings. I was under the pear trees four or five minutes. I came down the front stairs when I came down in the morning. The dress I wore that forenoon was a white and blue stripe of some sort. It is at home in the attic. I did not go to Smith's drug store to buy prussic acid. Did not go to the rooms where mother or father lay after the murder. Went through when I went up stairs that day. I wore the shoes I gave to the officer all day Shursday and Friday."

"I now ask you if you can furnish any other suspicion concerning any person who might have committed the crime?"

"Yes; one night as I was coming home not long ago I saw the shadow of a man on the house at the east end. I thought it was a man because I could not see any skirts. I hurried in the front door. It was about 8 45 o'clock, not later than 9. I saw somebody run around the house last Winter. The last time I saw anybody lately was since my sister went to Marion. I told Mr. Jennings, may have told Mr. Hanscomb."

"Who suggested the reward offered, you or your sister?"

"I don't know. I may have."

Mr. Knowlton now stopped reading, and announced: "This is the case of the Commonwealth."

The defence now opened their side of the case."

PROF. WOOD—"NO SIR; THERE IS NO BLOOD ON THE HATCHET."

THE DEFENCE.

Mr. Adams Objects to the Prussic Acid Evidence of the Commonwealth.

Mr. Adams for the defence called Dr. Dolan to the stand.

"Have you completed and filed the records of the Oak Grove autopsy?"

"Yes, sir."

"When?"

"The day after I was on the stand."

Dr. Dolan then identified the records of the autopsy held on the Thursday following the tragedy.

Mr. Adams called for Miss Collette and

[Continued on Seventh Page.]

MOYNAN & CO

IMPORTING RETAILERS.

UNION ST. PURCHASE ST.

EMBROIDERED

Silk Handkerchiefs!

IMPORTER'S SAMPLES.

We have now on our counters at Handkerchief Department a large lot of Elegant Japanese Silk Handkerchiefs in white, black and colored, hemstitched and embroidered edges, at about half usual prices. It will pay you to come and see this lot if you anticipate buying now or at any time in the near future.

Lot 1—29c., worth 50c.
Lot 2—59c., worth 69c.
Lot 3—59c., worth 85c.
Lot 4—75c., worth $1.25.

A DRESS GOODS BARGAIN.

We shall offer while they last that special lot of 36-inch All-Wool Serges, in Black, Navy, Olive, Garnet, Brown, Green, &c., &c., a regular 50c. quality, now only **39 cents.**

Still a few of those imported Robes and Dress lengths left. Don't miss such a chance—just think of buying a

$12.50 Dress for $4.59.
$15.00 Dress for $5.98.
$22.00 Dress for $7.98.

Call and see for yourself.

PARASOLS.

We have only a few left, and they must go within the next few days. Some of them are the nicest goods and latest styles. All go at

Less than 1-2 Marked Price,

and although the season is far advanced it will pay you to buy now and keep it over for another season.

SILK WAISTS, SATIN WAISTS, CAMBRIC WAISTS.

All marked down to *must go prices.* Come in and see them; if you can get suited in the goods, there will be no difficulty about prices.

In Housefurnishing Dept.

Every kitchen necessary can be found here. Such as
Dish Strainers.
Knife Boxes.
Flour Sieves.
Kettles in Tin or Agate Ware.
Roasting Pans.
Chopping Trays.
Dish Pans,

and all the other hundred and one useful things required in kitchen work. Also here you find all kinds Glassware.

Fancy Vases and Ornaments in Japanese Ware.
Fancy Baskets.
Parlor and Banquet Lamps.
Pictures of all descriptions, &c., &c.

REMEMBER OUR SPECIAL SALE OF BLANKETS AT LOW PRICES.

MOYNAN & CO.,

185 and 187 Union St.
9 and 11 Purchase St.

The Evening Standard.

NEW BEDFORD, MASS.
WEDNESDAY EVENING, AUGUST 31.

THREE EDITIONS DAILY.
No. 87 Union Street.
PUBLISHED BY
E. ANTHONY & SONS.
INCORPORATED.
—TERMS—
Six Dollars a Year; Three Dollars for Six Months, in advance; Single Copies Two Cents.

FOR PRESIDENT:
BENJAMIN HARRISON
OF INDIANA.

FOR VICE-PRESIDENT:
WHITELAW REID
OF NEW YORK.

TEN PAGES.

This Evening's Issue Consists of Ten Pages, and Every Patron is Entitled to that Number.

CONTENTS OF THIS EVENING'S STANDARD.

THE REPUBLICAN STANDARD,

Issued this evening, contains all the local and general news of the past week, including latest reports from the examination of Miss Lizzie Borden of Fall River for the murder of her father, Andrew J. Borden, embracing Medical Examiner Dolan's testimony, the evidence of Bridget Sullivan, who gives a straightforward story, the testimony of John V. Morse, Prof. Wood, and a number of others, showing the movements of Lizzie Borden before the tragedy, some of which look unfavorable for the prisoner, while other portions seem to favor her, the attempt to purchase prussic acid by Miss Borden is also testified to by drug clerks of Fall River, and all other points made by the prosecution and defence, and the fullest particulars and latest developments are lucidly set forth in the columns of the *Standard:* valuation and taxes of this city, substantial increase of taxable property, rate of taxation $1 in excess of last year, debt statement of the city; meeting of School Committee, resignations of teachers accepted and routine business transacted; the eighth annual gathering of the Hathaway family at Dighton; letter from Cottage City, annual Ball of the Martha's Vineyard Association, big Sunday at the Methodist Camp-meeting, August meeting of the taxpayers; closing of the Camp-meeting at Onset Bay Grove, extensive improvements and additions predicted for next year; contracts awarded for furniture, and gas fittings for the new post office; meeting of the Board Public Works, business of importance transacted; particulars of the Chambers assault case at Harwich, which the authorities have in hand; Farm, Garden and Home; Bible Lesson for next Sunday; District Court reports; correspondence; with editorials, ship news, markets, miscellaneous reading matter, etc.

For sale by all newsdealers in this city, and at our counters, in wrappers ready for mailing, at 4 cents per copy.

There are three octogenarian writers of English poetry, Whittier, who is 85, Holmes, who is 83, and Tennyson, who is 83. Of these the last is incomparably the greatest, and has written verse which will live the longest. They have all passed the period of their best production, although Tennyson continues to be a verse writer. Tennyson published his first volume of poems in 1830, Whittier in 1836, and Holmes in the same year; but of course they had been writing verse for some years previous to these dates. Their poetry is marked by exquisite fancy and imagination, combined with melodious rhythm in the case of Tennyson, by patriotism and high moral feeling in that of Whittier, and by wit and sentiment in that of Holmes. They have contributed largely to the enjoyment of their readers for over half a century, and there is no line, which, so far as the thought is concerned, they could wish to blot. They have written enough, perhaps even too much, for their fame, but may they long live to enjoy the esteem with which they are held by all lovers of good and pure poetry.

The death of George William Curtis, announced to-day, removes one of the ablest and most prominent authors and politicians of the country. Opinions will, of course, differ as to the wisdom of his political notions, but as an author he has a high and undisputed rank, and he will be regretted by all lovers of good literature. New Bedford people were familiar with him in the palmy days of the Lyceum, of whose lecture courses he was always a leading feature.

When the Democrats in 1864 declared the war a failure, Gen. McClellan, their candidate for President, tried to evade that point. But it was of no use. The people of the country held the Democratic party to its platform, and left McClellan at home. It will be just so in 1892. The people hold the Democratic party to its tariff platform, and much as Mr. Cleveland may desire to avoid any discussion of it, he is to be judged by it; and he, too, will have to stay at home.

Hon. Henry Cabot Lodge informs a Boston *Journal* reporter that he is a candidate for Senator to succeed Mr. Dawes. He says the eastern part of the State has not had a Senator since 1877, and Essex County not since 1857. He means to make the best and most open canvass he can.

HOME MATTERS.

AT DEATH'S DOOR.—Aunt Keziah Randall of Mattapoisett is not expected to live but a few days. She is kindly cared for by her daughter, Mrs. John B. Francis of Fall River, who is 78 years old.

THE BRAVA PACKETS.—Bark Rapoza do Mar unbent her sails yesterday and will wait about two months for passengers to Brava.

Schooner Forest Fairy will sail for Brava Saturday.

THE VERBENA LAID OFF.—U. S. L. H. steamer Verbena, Capt. Peake, arrived here this morning and will haul off at Merrill's wharf for repairs. It is expected she will not again go into commission for several months.

BRAKEMAN KILLED ON THE OLD COLONY.—Daniel Creedon, an Old Colony railroad brakeman, was killed in the freight yard at Mansfield yesterday morning, being thrown under the cars through the engine jumping a switch.

ARRESTED.—James A. Scott was arrested by a police inspector in Brockton yesterday on a warrant from Cottage City, where he is wanted for selling liquor without license. He was sent to Cottage City yesterday afternoon.

CAME HERE SHOPPING.—E. C. Benedict's steam yacht Oneida arrived in port yesterday afternoon from Gray Gables with Mrs. Cleveland on board, who after making some purchases here returned in the yacht to her Summer home.

PATENTS have been granted to Edwin L. King, of this city, sash fastener; William H. Blaney, assignor to himself and E. B. Bullock, Attleboro, lock attachment for bicycles; John T. Hawkins, Taunton, graduating steam radiator; Horace E. Cunningham, Brockton, attachment for stapling machines.

PASTOR ORDAINED. — An ecclesiastical council was held at Yarmouthport yesterday for the purpose of ordaining E. L. Marsh of Leicester as pastor of the First Congregational church. The ordination sermon was by Rev. I. L. Wilcox of Worcester and the charge to pastor by Rev. A. H. Coolidge of Leicester.

ACTION AGAINST HIS ACCUSER.—Louis Quimmette, who has been accused by Henry Ledeaux of having kept money which was collected for Mr. Dupois, whose family were the victims of the fire at the north end some weeks ago, has brought an action of tort against Henry Ledeaux, and an attachment has been placed upon the goods of Henry Ledeaux for $5.0. George T. St. Germain is counsel for the plaintiff.

POLITICAL.—The Plymouth county Republican convention will be held in Red Men's hall in Brockton Thursday morning, Sept. 15, for the purpose of nominating a district attorney, a county commissioner, two special commissioners, a sheriff and three commissioners of insolvency.

The Republicans of Harwich have decided upon Augustus M. Nickerson for candidate for Representative to the General Court.

FINED FOR OVERDRIVING A HORSE.—On Sunday John Satchett hired a horse and buggy in Fall River to take his best girl to this city. When he returned to E. S. Chace's stable the horse dropped dead. The owner claimed that the animal was over-beaten and over-driven, while the defendant claimed that he only touched the horse with the whip a couple of times, and that he was driven very slowly. The girl held the reins. After the evidence was put in the judge held that the man was guilty and fined him $50 and costs, from which an appeal was taken.

N. B. V. F. A.—There was an adjourned meeting of the New Bedford Veteran Firemen's Association, last evening, which was largely attended and which proved to be an old-fashioned meeting. After electing W. A. Caswell and B. B. Johnson members of the association the comrades got right down to a discussion of the proposed visit to Boston on the occasion of the annual muster of New England League. It was decided to attend and a committee was appointed to make necessary arrangements and report at a meeting to be held on Saturday evening next. Another subject discussed was that of rolling out the old tub on Labor Day and it was voted to engage in a trial on the afternoon of Labor Day at 5 o'clock when every member of the working company was urged to be on hand.

SPINNERS' CALL.—Secretary Howard of Fall River has issued the following call:

Fellow workmen: Labor holiday will fall upon September 5, the first Monday in September, and we desire that all the preliminary arrangements be made at this meeting for its proper observance. Fall River should not be second to any district in the Commonwealth in grandly celebrating Labor Holiday, because most credit is due and is given to the representatives from this district for securing the passage of the Labor Holiday bill, than those from any other district in the State. After the Labor Holiday bill was reported and defeated in the Senate chamber it was Fall River's senator who moved and secured its reconsideration, and now owns the pen with which Gov. Ames signed the bill, which was purchased and presented to him by the Central Labor Union of Boston.

Therefore we trust members will turn out in full force Labor Holiday morning and join the procession, which will start from the Spinners' Hall at 8 45 o'clock. The larger the number that turns out in the procession the stronger evidence it will be of their appreciation of the efforts of their legislative representatives in advocating such legislation and the law which makes the first Monday in September a legal holiday to be known as Labor Day.

The trade emblems are now finished and will be on sale at the association's office on and after September 1st. They are splendid specimens of lithographic art, and no member of our craft should be without one.

We desire to remind collectors that contributions of members will be received only on Friday nights, and that the association's office will be closed on Saturday nights in the future, thereby giving the officers an opportunity to enjoy the Saturday half-holiday, as well as the other members of the association.

On behalf of the committee,
ROBERT HOWARD, Sec'y.

MARION.

Sadie L. Nye, one of the twin daughters of B. B. Nye, received the largest number of votes for the prize given on the last night of the entertainment given by the glass blowers. F. D. Ryder received the prize for the handsomest man and Edward W. Gifford that for the homeliest.

The desk in the Congregational church was ably filled on Sunday by Rev. William H. Cobb of Boston. His text was Acts xxviii, 4.

An excellent sermon was delivered by Rev. Leslie Moore in the Universalist church on Sunday evening from the following text: "But as for me and my house we will serve the Lord."

The net receipts of the recent Marigold fair held in the Club building were $142.

Everyone should visit the reading room recently opened by the Marion Library Association. It is open to all. The people of the town may well be proud of her educational and social advantages.

Mr. and Mrs. Albert Lees, recent guests of Miss Susie Conro, have returned to New Bedford

A son of W. G. McCormick was bitten last week by a dog belonging to A. W. Nickerson. The wound was not serious, but the dog was immediately killed.

S. D. Hadley, of the firm of Hadley, Cowing & Drury of Northampton, and J. E. Hadley, of the firm of Lusk, Bunn & Hadley of St. Paul, have been visiting in town several days.

Col. J. J. Emerson of Boston is stopping at Hotel Sippican.

THIRD DISTRICT COURT.

BORDEN, J.

WEDNESDAY, Aug. 31.

Edward R. Baldwin of Fairhaven got drunk yesterday and had some trouble with his brother-in-law. Officer Delano was called upon and arrested him last evening. Baldwin pleaded guilty and went up for 30 days.

Edwin Harkins belongs at the West End. It has been said of Harkins for a long time that there was not rum enough in the city to get him full, but last night the stuff got the best of him. He pleaded guilty of drunkenness. He said he was 45 years of age, but he looked to be nearer 65. He was sent to work-house for eight months.

Domino Pouper pleaded guilty of drunkenness and went up for 5 days.

One case of drunkenness was put on probation until September 30th next.

John Quirk of Fairhaven pleaded guilty of keeping an unlicensed dog in that town. Quirk said the dog belonged to a New Bedford man and that he was boarding the dog. From the statements of Officer Delano it was evident some one was attempting to evade licensing the dog. He was fined $15.

John Vernon pleaded guilty of assaulting Robert Thompson at the saloon of George Moss on South Water street yesterday afternoon. Thompson said he was at Moss's saloon playing cards and he heard Vernon talking with Moss about his (Thompson's) wife and calling her vile names. He spoke to him about it and was offered 10 cents by Vernon to have a drink. Thompson refused the drink and Vernon struck him and knocked him down. Thompson said the cause of the trouble originated last June, when he stopped buying his drinks at Vernon's saloon. He had been in the habit of spending most of his money for liquor at Vernon's, and his wife went to see Vernon and complained to him about his selling him liquor, and he had not bought any of him since. He saw Vernon after the warrant was sworn out, and was offered by him $3 to settle the matter, which he refused. Vernon then attacked him again and blackened his eye. Thompson further told the Court that Vernon's shop was open every day just as though there was no law. He had bought nothing there since last June, but saw people going in and out all the time. Vernon had nothing to say, and was fined $15, which he paid.

Ira Chase of Dartmouth pleaded not guilty of assaulting Lafayette Dean of the same town on the 17th of July last near Smith Mills.

Mr. Dean said he was driving some cattle from this city to his place in Dartmouth on the above day and met Chase near Smith Mills. Chase spoke to him and pointing to a cow said that is a nice looking cow, she would be a good one to steal. I told him he would get before the court if he did steal her. He then picked up a stone and threw it at me. I put up my hand to ward off the stone. It struck me and broke my arm. He had another stone in his hand and as he attempted to throw it at me I struck him with a stick.

Dr. Peterson testified to treating Mr. Dean and to his arm being broken and the flesh of the arm being badly lacerated.

Thomas L. Baker testified to seeing Chase throw the stone.

Chase took the stand and told a rambling, incoherent story and gave evidence of not being just right. The case was continued to Sept. 3d next that he may be examined as to his sanity. F. A. Milliken, Esq., for the Commonwealth.

Frank Veara pleaded not guilty of unreasonably neglecting to support his minor child, aged 9 years, for the past two years.

Mrs. Veara said he had done nothing for the child since she was born. She had asked him by letters which she had registered, and he would not answer them. She wanted him to pay $2.50 per week.

This case was suspended pending negotiations between the parties and the juvenile case against Joaquim Lomba for larceny of a bicycle valued at $30, the property of Thos. H. Mills was taken up. T. A. Codd, Esq., for defence.

After hearing the testimony, Lomba was adjudged guilty. At the request of Mr. Codd, who said the boy would be sent to sea, the case was laid on file on payment of $5 damages to Mr. Mills and the expenses, $6.78.

Six continued cases for drunkenness were defaulted, and one for assault and battery, one for non-support of child and one for drunkenness were placed on file, and 19 cases for various offences were further continued.

Peter Dufresne, who pleaded guilty to the larceny of a goat, the property of Joseph Jacinthe on the 29th inst., this morning said he did not understand the complaint when read to him, and wished to plead not guilty. He was allowed to do so. Federin Desgangue, the boy charged with being with Dufresne when the goat was stolen, pleaded guilty.

George T. King said he saw these two boys with the goat on the 24th, the day it was stolen. They went into the woods with it, where they had a camp.

Desgangue said Dufresne and he went to Jacinthe's and stole the goat. He untied him and they both took the goat into the woods. It was getting dark when they took the goat. Desgangue said he had been away from home some seven weeks. He first went away with Dufresne and Dufresne's father found us at Westport and took him home. I went to Fall River and then came back. I was in camp in the woods for about a week.

Dufresne denied stealing the goat and said the first time he saw him was in the camp.

At 1 o'clock the goat case was unfinished and the court took a recess until half-past two.

WESTPORT HARBOR.

Mrs. Nettie Rowland and children, who have been visiting Mrs. Charles D. Macomber and Mrs. Elmer Z. Brayton, have returned to their home in Harlem, N. Y.

Frederic L. Borden, wife and daughter Marian, of Providence, are stopping at his father's, Charles R. Borden's for a week.

Mrs. Elmer Z. Brayton has gone to Newburg, N. Y., on a visit.

VINEYARD HAVEN.

The funeral of the late Capt. William Cook took place yesterday afternoon at Oak Grove Cemetery from Grace Episcopal Church, where a short service was held. Dr. Oliver officiated, assisted by Rev. J. Dinzey of Woods Holl. Miss Mansfield of Hartford, Conn., sang very beautifully two hymns, "Abide with us" and "Jesus Lover of my Soul". The pall-bearers were Gen. William H. Rochester of Washington, D. C., Capt. Richard Luce of New Brighton, Staten Island, Capt. Gilbert L. Smith, Capt. Philander West, Mr. Foster H. Jenkins, and Mr. Charles Peakes of Vineyard Haven.

Contractor Horace A. Tilton is at present breaking ground for the Grace Church rectory on Main street, near the church building, and a store with dwelling over it for Capt. Owen Tilton on Main street.

It is expected that Senator J. N. Dolph of Oregon will deliver a short address at the Republican caucus to be held at Association Hall Thursday evening.

Capt. Joseph White, of the firm of Perkins and White of Boston, was here to-day aboard the tug William Cleary. He reports that no work has been done on the sunken yacht Alva for nearly a week, owing to the rough weather. He states that the yacht is all right and is confident of being successful in the attempt to raise her.

NANTUCKET.

Dr. F. A. Gardner has filed a bill in equity against the town of Nantucket for maintaining a nuisance in the shape of the Lily pond sewer, which empties into the harbor within 800 feet of the Gardner cottage. The tone of the bill would indicate that the nuisance must be abated, and not that damages are claimed for past annoyance.

IN DEFENCE.

[Continued from First Page.]

room, the north and the spare or front bed-room upstairs were then searched.

Dr. Learned's Evidence.

This examination was suspended for the time here, to allow Dr. W. T. Learned to testify. He said he was a practicing physician here and was at the Borden house at 3 15 on the day of the tragedy, and saw Mrs. Borden where she was lying. Her arms were on the body and not over her head. There were at least a dozen there; among them several doctors; that was just before she was taken downstairs for the autopsy.

Marshal Hilliard Recalled.

Marshal Hilliard resumed. The search was not a thorough one, but examined the bed thoroughly; did not examine the bureau drawers wholly, didn't think, in the guest room; this was about 12 30; there was another search made that day, about 3 o'clock; Officers Fleet, Desmond, Seaver, Dr. Dolan, Mr. Jennings, and witness were present; commenced in the attic and searched the whole landing, searching everything in a most thorough manner; those were the instructions.

Here the district attorney said he was willing to admit that a most thorough search was made in the house.

Witness said he judged from the looks of Fleet when he came down that he had examined everything under the roof; it was Officer Seaver who looked over the large closet in company with Fleet and Desmond.

In conducting the search in the cellar witness said a brick was removed from lower part of the chimney, to see whether there was anything thrown down the chimney flue from above. Witness said Miss Emma came into the kitchen where he was and said she wanted them to make as thorough an examination as possible in all parts of the house and if there were apartments unopened she would furnish the keys, and keys were handed by her to Mr. Jennings. There was one trunk in the upper part of the house which was hard to open and Lizzie, witness thought, showed him where the key was. In any and all of the searches, witness said, there was no attempt to hinder him from making a full examination.

On Monday witness sent Desmond and others to complete the search in the cellar; so far as he

Knew from Report to Him the Search Was Thorough,

not only in the cellar but in the barn; this he gathered from the report of his officers, not from personal observation. On the Saturday after the tragedy there was delivered to him a dress skirt with a blue ground and white figure waist or blouse similar to the skirt, also a white underskirt and a lounge cover, the one Prof. Wood referred to; witness didn't take the shams and spread that afternoon; took the shoes and stockings on the 10th, when the inquest was going on; Lizzie gave them to me, having offered to do so; the shams and spread were given to me the same day by Mrs. Holmes and he got the slab the same day.

Demand for Missing Dress Pattern.

On cross-examination witness said that in examining the attic he didn't recollect seeing any unmade dress pattern; had sent to inquire for such since, but had been unable to get it.

Here Mr. Knowlton made a demand on Mr. Jennings for that dress pattern, giving him until this afternoon to produce it.

Detective Seaver on the Stand.

George F. Seaver, State detective, was sworn. He said he was informed of the matter at 3 o'clock on the day of the murder by telegraph and went directly to the house, arriving there about 5 o'clock with Marshal Hilliard; made inquiries of several, but had no general conversation with Lizzie.

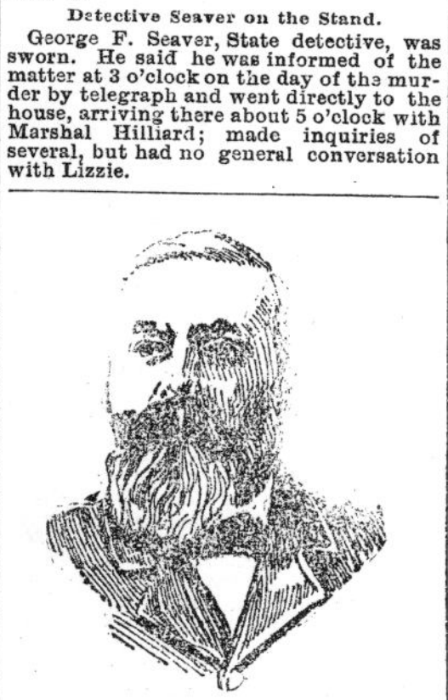

State Officer Seaver.

Went through the lower part of the house. Witness detailed his part in the various searches of the premises and said he saw the axes for the first time at the police station; talked with Bridget several times; had talked with her on Thursday, Friday and Saturday, and had a memorandum of the conversation. On Saturday at 12 30 he was engaged in searching the house, making a partial search, going through the beds in all the three rooms upstairs, just as Marshal Hilliard testified to.

Witness thought there was no running water in Lizzie's room, but that there were pitchers and bowls in that and other rooms upstairs; witness described the large store-room upstairs.

Referring to some dresses which were hanging there, Mr. Jennings asked him if he could say whether if there had been blood on any of the dresses he would have seen it, but the question was excluded. Witness did say he thought that he saw no blood on anything in that room. Witness saw no dress pattern during his search.

Hack Driver Donnelly Sworn.

John Donnelly, a hack driver, was the next witness. He said he went to the Borden house in the afternoon of the day of the murder; went into the barn about 15 minutes after he got there; the hay then was on the north side of the barn; it looked as though somebody had been lying on the northwest part of it, towards the window.

Cross-examined. It looked as though some one had been lying there. I cannot tell whether it looked most as if a man or a dog had lain there. The impression was rounding and about a foot long and six inches wide.

Because you saw a round hole in the hay about a foot long and six inches wide you thought that a man had lain there? asked the district attorney.

A ripple of laughter ran around the room when the witness said "Yes sir."

Witness said he never reported the fact to any officer.

Medical Examiner Draper.

Dr. Frank W. Draper, medical examiner for Suffolk county, was the next witness. At the request of the Attorney-General he came to Fall River and was present at the autopsy on the bodies; Drs. Dolan, Mr. Morrill and Mr. Holmes and two policemen were present at the autopsy. Witness said the injuries to Mr. Borden were in a group on the left side of the head between the left side of the nose and front of ear; in his opinion they were made by some edged instrument of considerable weight; should think a hatchet would be adequate to cause the injuries and thought a chisel sufficiently broad faced enough to have done so but said hatchets because of the length of the wounds; an ordinary axe would have caused the wounds, assuming the edge of the blade was at right angles and not rounded; by "rounded" witness meant a new axe that had not been ground off at the corners. The first cut he noticed was four inches, commencing above the nostril, going through the upper lip and partly through the lower one, and coming down near the angle of the jaw; that one would not be necessarily fatal. No. 2 was 4 1-2 inches long, parallel with the other, ending just above the edge of the jaw; not necessarily fatal. The third was two inches in length under the eye, and went through the cheek bone; that was not necessarily fatal. No. 4 began on the forehead, went towards the left half an inch, then down very nearly laterally, through the eye at the upper portion, then down in cheek bone; that was 4 3-4 inches long, not necessarily fatal; No. 5 was in forehead two inches long parallel with upper portion of No. 4, and not necessarily fatal. No. 6 was through the temporal bone and was four inches long; it penetrated the skull; not necessarily fatal. No. 5 was an extension upward in the same line with the one last described; was superficial. No. 8 was an extension upward of No. 5, one-quarter of an inch long, superficial; not necessarily fatal. No. 9 extended from the bottom of left ear up the left temple four inches; edges parting, extent two inches, bones crushed; probably fatal, but not necessarily. Next one was behind and fractured upper portion of skull; all were in front of opening of left ear, proceeding to opening of the left nostril; showed group wounds in left temple together as being sufficient to cause death.

The wounds which penetrated the eye lid were bevelled from the left toward the right as well as that near the eye. The skull was of an average thickness. One sixteenth of an inch at the left temple. I saw no crushing blow on the skull. In my opinion all the incise wounds would cause the appearance of the head. I have made experiments with blood from my finger, and proven that if blood was thrown from an instrument or wound on a perpendicular wall the stem end of the spot would be upward; a blood spot ending in a pear-shaped end would "skip" upward from the stem. Blood thrown on a horizontal surface would still retain its pear shape with the force outward.

I prefer not to give an opinion on the position of Mr. Borden's assailant at the time when he was struck. I have not formed a conclusive opinion yet on that subject. The injuries I have described on Mr. Borden's head disclose a distinct separation of one from another.

The instrument used on Mr. Borden was an edged one, but I cannot say if it was a sharp cutting one. The condition had been much modified at the time of the autopsy at Oak Grove. I cannot say if the hair on either head was cut. I have no opinion as to the force of the blows delivered on the bodies. I have no experience which will tell me if the blows were delivered with the right or left hand.

I do not know what causes coagulation of blood. I have an opinion about it, but authorities are not determined upon it. I can form an opinion from the coagulation of blood which has come from a body and been found near it as to the time of death, that is, within 15 minutes. Later than that is unsafe. I would not be willing to say within 60 minutes as to the time of death of a person judging from the condition of food found in the stomach. If an artery is cut there would be a spurting of blood in the direction in which the blood was flowing. I have seen blood from an artery spurt five feet. In case of an artery in the temple being cut the spurt would be upward. The spurting would leave a trail from the highest point reached back to the starting point.

I made notes on the body of Mrs. Borden at the autopsy at Oak Grove cemetery.

There were no injuries upon her apparent besides the cutting ones which would cause her death. I think the blow between the shoulders was a miss blow, one not intended to go there.

Cross-examination. I came down to attend the inquest in response to what I might call a double message, a telephone one from Dr. Dolan and a letter received from the Attorney-General.

At this point a recess was taken until 2 p. m.

VINEYARD HAPPENINGS.

Republican Flag Raising and a Wedding at Cottage City.

[Special Dispatch.]

COTTAGE CITY, Aug. 31.—Last evening the Republicans gathered in force about the post office and at precisely 7 45 unfurled a flag bearing the caricatures of their candidates. The Musical Exchange Band, stationed on a balcony across the way, played national airs, and the speakers from the Oakwood balcony predicted success and glory. Congressman Elijah A. Morse of Canton, Rev. J. B. Gould of Newton and Rev. S. F. Upham of Madison, N. J., were the principal orators. Rev. Mr. Gould made the hit of the evening in his concise remarks on topics of current interest.

Arthur Messenger and Miss Winnie A. White were last evening united in marriage at Trinity M. E. church before an audience that completely filled the audience room. The ceremony took place at a few minutes past 9 o'clock, or after the regular meeting of the church had been dismissed. The couple were driven to the church in a hack, accompanied by A. F. Caldwell, Jr., of New York city as best man and Miss Nelia Carr of New Bedford, who attended the bride. As the party walked down the aisle Miss Millie Worth, who presided at the piano, played Mendelssohn's wedding march. The ceremony was performed by Rev. W. Lenoir Hood, pastor of the church. The newly wedded couple departed from the church, reentered the hack, and were driven to their cottage at 63 Trinity Park. A reception followed and many beautiful presents were admired by friends of Mr. and Mrs. Messenger, who wished them all the joys that came from marital happiness.

Rev. W. L. Hood, who will superintend the children's festival on Friday afternoon, will have the assistance of twenty ladies of his society in the arduous work.

There were 40 guests at the Highland House last evening, against eight at a corresponding date last Summer. All the hotel men say that there is promise of a longer season than usual. The citizens' committee is perfecting a scheme whereby it is hoped that next season may be replete with attractions. It is proposed to inaugurate a series of entertainments early in June and to continue them as late as October 1. An effort will be made to induce managers of conventions to visit the Vineyard and as these gatherings of great bodies of people come as early as June and as late as October it is hoped that a great impetus may be given the resort.

During the week past there has been a boom in New York avenue, land and prospects are good for several fine residences west of that occupied by Christopher Look. The camp-meeting association has acquired considerable property in the vicinity of Trinity park, and on all sides there are indications of material prosperity.

Ex-Mayor B. B. Johnson of Waltham is a guest at the Pawnee.

State Officer Proctor of the Ocean Gem is cruising in the sound.

FALL RIVER.

It is understood that the Wyoming mill will start up under its new management in a few days.

SPECIAL NOTICES.

HONORARY MEMBERS NEW BEDFORD CITY GUARDS.

The annual meeting of this organization will be held FRIDAY, Sept. 2, 1892, at 8 o'clock P. M., at the Armory of Co. E, Pierian Hall. A full attendance is desired as business of importance will be transacted.

I. B. TOMPKINS, JR., Secretary.
au31-3t

Those Wonderful Christy Knives.

A GOOD ARTICLE IS WORTHY OF IMITATION.

We wish to caution the public against a knife that is being placed on the market made by the Clauss Shear Company. It is an infringement of the Christy patent, and parties selling or buying this knife are liable to prosecution. A word to the wise is sufficient. The Christy is being placed in this city and vicinity as rapidly as possible, and their great worth is attested by hundreds of our best families. *Right and left handed knives.*

WILLIAM S. HERSEY, Agent,
Telephone 110-7. 152 Mt. Pleasant St.
au31-s1-3

SPECIAL NOTICES.

NORTH CONGREGATIONAL CHURCH.

Preparatory Service of the North Congregational Church, in the chapel, THIS (Wednesday) EVENING, at 7 45, instead of Friday evening. P. A. MACOMBER.
au31-1t

MISS MATTHEWS' Private School,
OPENS SEPT. 6th.
au31-12t 24 Madison Street.

ALTON B. PAULL,
Teacher of Piano and Organ.

Would like pupils after Sept. 6. Address, Fairhaven. au31-WFM2w

NOTICE TO CONTRACTORS.

The Committee on City Property invite proposals or bids for building a fire engine house on the lot on the northwest corner of County and Hillman streets, in this city, in accordance with plans and specifications prepared by S. C. Hunt, architect, which will be ready for inspection at his office on and after TUESDAY, August 30th.

Bids should be addressed to the Committee on City Property, and left with the City Clerk, Library Building, on or before THURSDAY, Sept. 8th, at 12 o'clock noon.

S. A. BROWNELL,
au31-7t Chairman Committee.

FARMERS, ATTENTION!

Important Addition to the Autumn Fair of the South Bristol Farmers' Club.

EXHIBITION OF DRESSED POULTRY.

On FRIDAY, September 23d, the Club will provide space for, and give their attention to, an exhibition of dressed poultry.

All producers are cordially invited to contribute something towards this new and interesting feature of the Club's Autumn Fair.

All poultry to be dressed undrawn with heads on.

Premiums will be awarded by an impartial judge.

All exhibits may be sold at the pleasure of the owner, but must remain on exhibition until the closing of the fair Friday evening.

No exhibits, for competition, will be received after 1 o'clock P. M. Friday.

All exhibits should be plainly marked with the owner's name, breed of fowl, and class.

Thoroughbred and first-crossed stock alone accepted for exhibition.

CLASSES.

New York Broilers—To weigh not less than 2½ pounds nor more than 4 pounds per pair. To be exhibited only in pairs.
Chickens—To weigh under 4 lbs. apiece.
Chickens—To weigh over 4 lbs. apiece.
Fowl—To weigh over 5 lbs. apiece.
Green Ducks—Hatched in 1892, exhibited only in pairs.
Green Geese—Hatched in 1892.
Philadelphia Capons—Any weight.
For further information address,

HENRY M. PLUMMER,
Chairman Dressed Poultry Committee,
South Dartmouth, Mass.
au30-3t&w1t

NOTICE.

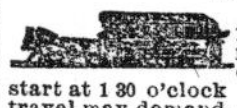

On and after September 1, 1892, on pleasant afternoons, the City Hall cars of the Fairhaven line will start at 1 30 o'clock and run as late as the travel may demand.

au30-tf UNION ST. RAILWAY CO.

WANTED TO HIRE

Furnished house by a small family without children, for the Winter season.

Address box 80 *Standard* office. a29-6t

ELMER E. TOLMAN, Violinist.

Leader at the Opera House, will be ready to receive pupils after Sept. 5th, 1892.

Apply at Box Office Opera House.
au27-tf

FRIENDS' ACADEMY.

The Fall Term Begins Sept. 22d.

Primary, Advanced and College Preparatory Courses. For particulars and catalogue, apply to

THOMAS H. ECKFELDT, Principal,
au24-WS4w Clinton Street, near Ash.

HEARING.

CITY OF NEW BEDFORD,
CLERK'S OFFICE, Aug. 25th, 1892.

Notice is hereby given that the Mayor and Aldermen will give a hearing in their chamber, City Hall Building, on THURSDAY, Sept. 8, 1892, at 7½ o'clock P. M., to all persons interested in the petition of T. A. Tripp, for a license to set up and maintain two (2) steam engines and boilers of fifty (50) horse power, at his place of business northeast corner of Prospect and Grinnell streets.

DANIEL B. LEONARD, City Clerk.
au25-tsep8

ARCHITECTS

Are invited to submit to the Committee on City Property, sketch plans for a new City Hall to be located on the present City Hall lot; with such suggestions as they may deem expedient. To be submitted on or before Sept. 1.

S. A. BROWNELL, Chairman.
au12-tsep1

NONQUITT HOTEL.

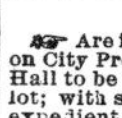

Now Open for the Season of 1892.

Special attention given to parties, clubs, &c., &c., for dinners and suppers. Escape the heat of town and pass a cool night at Nonquitt. Boats leave New Bedford 6 45, 8 50 A. M., 1 45, 5 00 P. M. Leave Nonquitt 7 45, 9 50 A. M., 3 00, 6 00 P. M. Fine macadamized road just finished to Nonquitt.

W. H. WINGATE, Proprietor,
au3-1m Nonquitt, Mass.

EXCURSION TO WHITE MOUNTAINS.

Messrs. Hatch & Abbott will run an excursion to Fabyans, starting Sept. 5th, returning Sept. 10th. From New Bedford, by rail to Boston, moonlight sail to Portland, and rail to Fabyans. Three days' board at first class hotel, with meals en route both ways, and all this for only $20. Persons desiring to join will send in names at once, as number is limited. Address or apply to HATCH & ABBOTT, at either 92½ or 796 Purchase St., New Bedford. au22-tf&wtf

Do you want the BEST, the CHOICEST, the Future Leader, In a Word do You Want

THAT PIANO?

which has more points of excellence, and a more brilliant record than can be found in any other. Call upon the

SOULE PIANO AND ORGAN INVT. CO.

who hold the finest line of Pianos to be found in New England. Satisfaction guaranteed. Prices reasonable.

147 Purchase Street.

Z. C. KEITH, Treas.
L. SOULE, Manager.

CHARLES F. SPOONER,

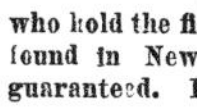

Piano Tuner and Repairer.
Residence 82 Thomas street.
Orders left with Briggs & Lawrence, 197 and 203 Union st. MWS

WILLIAM H. P. WALKER,
Counsellor at Law and Notary Public.
Room 23, over Citizens National Bank. jy6-WS

Mrs. WM. H. TAYLOR,
Teacher of the Pianoforte,
au6-SWtf 3 IRVING COURT.

Don't buy a blood-purifier because it is "cheap." The best—the Superior Medicine—Ayer's Sarsaparilla, is, in the end, the cheapest blood-purifier in the market. The ingredients of which it is composed are the most expensive and medicinally efficacious that can be obtained.

Dr. J. E. PEASE.

My office, No. 1 Bedford street, will be closed until SEPT. 1st. au12-17t

Dr. W. W. MANN.

My office, 174½ Purchase street, will be closed until SEPT. 1st. au12-17t

E. J. WEEKS, D. D. S.
Dental Rooms, 74 Purchase Street.
Office Hours—9 to 12. 2 to 4. au9-1m

TYPE-WRITING.
MRS. KENDALL, Copyist.
Room 21,............Robeson Building.
Copying of all kinds.
Supplies for all Type-Writers.

DR. H. E. MANN.

During months of July and August my office hours will be from 8 A. M. till 6 P. M.
jy27-tf

PENSIONS.

Soldiers, sailors, widows, orphans, desiring to apply for pensions, back pay or bounty, can consult J. F. VINAL, from Washington, D. C., at 107 Fourth street. au2-1m

Knowles & Co.

Cor. UNION & FOURTH STS.

Bargains in All-Wool Dress Goods, 40-inch all-wool goods, suitable for early Fall wear, 39c. Cheap at 50c.

Storm Serges in Black and Navy, all-wool, 40-inch, 50c.; 46-inch 75c.; 46-inch extra value, $1.00.

Black All-Wool Henriettas, 46-inch, 75c.; extra fine and heavy, $1.00 and $1.25; 46-inch, All-Wool, India Twill, 75c. and $1.00.

Beautiful styles in Ginghams at 10 and 12 1-2c. Large assortment to select from.

Ladies' full regular finished, Fast Black Hose, the best hose in the market for 25c. Also Ladies' Fast Black Hose, worth 50c. Three pairs in a box $1.00.

Ladies' Summer weight merino vests and pants 50c. each.

Gentlemen's Summer weight merino shirts and drawers 50c.

Gentlemen's unlaundered shirts, reinforced linen fronts and cuffs, double backs, good cotton, best shirt in the market, 50c.

Ladies' corset covers at 12 1-2, 25, 37 1-2 and 50c., in high, low, square and V shaped necks, handsomely trimmed, and decided bargains.

Ladies' and misses' night gowns, made of good materials and elegantly trimmed, at 50, 65, and 88c., $1, $1.25 and up.

Ladies' corsets, in all the popular makes, at from 49c. up to the very finest goods.

Best Germantown yarns, large full skeins, in 150 shades and colors, at only 12 1-2c. a skein.

Stamped Linens, Trays, Tidies, Splashers, Pillow Shams, Scarfs, all at popular low prices.

All kinds of embroidery and fancy working silk cheap. Knitting silk of best quality, large assortment of colors and shades at 30c. a ball. Best sewing silk in black and colors, 8c.

Table Linens, Brown and Bleached at 45c. worth 59c. Napkins at 50 and 75c, $1.00, $1.25, $1.50 and $2.00 per dozen. Towels at 12 1-2c., 19c., 25c., 37c., and 50c. up.

Lot of standard white ground prints, 5c. a yard. When out shopping don't fail to visit our store for we have just what you are looking for, and at lowest possible prices.

Knowles & Co.

HAS STOOD THE TEST 17 YEARS.

SEAL OF HAVANA

5¢ Londres Cigar.

No Other Cigar Equals it in Quality.

SWETT, SANBORN & CO.,
SOLE AGENTS,
55 Union Street, Boston.
FOR SALE BY ALL
Druggists and First Class Dealrs.
au6-SW8p

FINE CIGARS

—AND—

Tobacco.

Cigars by the Box a Specialty

—AT—

E. B. SHERMAN'S,

62 Purchase St.
jy19-8pMWS

Held Many Public Offices.

SAN FRANCISCO, Aug. 31.—Judge McMillin Shafter died here, aged 76 years. The deceased held the position of secretary of state of Vermont, his native state, for seven years, and subsequently became speaker of the house of representatives of Wisconsin. He served two terms in the California legislature and was appointed supreme judge. At the time of his death he was a regent of the Stanford university. He left an estate valued at $1,000,000.

Busy Day for Dr. Talmage.

LONDON, Aug. 31.—Dr. Talmage preached four times in Plymouth, to large audiences. A breakfast was tendered him in the guild hall. The mayor delivered a eulogy of Dr. Talmage, and thanked him for his sermons. Dr. Talmage gave an extensive account of his mission in Russia, and described his interview with the czar.

IT makes a luxury of oatmeal eating. . .

H-O Hornby's Oatmeal

And does it easily.

CHOLERA'S PROGRESS.

American Federal and Municipal Authorities Are on the Alert.

LONDON, Aug. 31.—A Hamburg special says: There has been an enormous increase in the number of persons who have been attacked and who have died of cholera, 810 new cases and 319 deaths having occurred yesterday. A feeling of deep gloom has settled over the city. The loss to the commercial community is reckoned at several million marks daily. The exodus from the city is unabated. The weather favors the progress of the epidemic.

A St. Petersburg special estimates that up to Aug. 22, 150,000 persons had died of cholera throughout Russia. The dispatch says the disease is steadily increasing in St. Petersburg.

A Brussels dispatch says two genuine cases of cholera appeared in a hospital there yesterday. One of the patients soon died. The news caused much exeitement throughout the city.

Ida Samyou, a Russian child, died last night. A post mortem examination showed that her death was not due to cholera, for which she has been under treatment at the hospital since Sunday.

Two cases of cholera have occurred in the city of London. The victims arrived Monday on the steamship Peregrin from Hamburg.

Another seaman belonging to the steamer Gerona, which arrived a few days ago at Middlesborough, has been attacked with cholera at Shields, to which place he went after leaving his ship.

In Prussian Districts.

BERLIN, Aug. 31.—It is officially announced that cholera is prevalent in six teen places in Schleswig and in three places in the district of Lunenburg. At Leipsic one case of disease has occurred and one case is reported at Neustadt, Mecklenburg. The patients at Leipsic and Neustadt both came from Hamburg.

The National Zeitung states that there are three distinct cases of Asiatic cholera at the Moabit hospital in Berlin. Two of the patients, it says, came from Hamburg, while the third is a Berlin wharf laborer.

During the past twenty-four hours seventeen new suspects have been taken to the hospital.

Is Spreading at Antwerp.

ANTWERP, Aug. 31.—The cholera returns show that there were twenty-two new cases here yesterday, and four deaths. Hitherto, the epidemic has been most prevalent in the quarters adjoining the Scheldt, but now it appears to be spreading into the city from the river.

More Cases, but Fewer Deaths.

HAVRE, Aug. 31.—There were reported yesterday in this city seventy-one new cases of cholera, an increase of eleven cases as compared with Sunday's returns. The number of deaths was seventeen, which is a decrease of seven compared with the returns of Sunday.

A Case in Holland.

THE HAGUE, Aug. 31.—A man who arrived here a few days ago from Hamburg was attacked with cholera last night. He was promptly removed to a hospital and the house where he was staying has been disinfected.

New York is Watchful.

NEW YORK, Aug. 31.—The saloon and second cabin passengers of the steamers Circassia, Friesland and Veendam were allowed to land yesterday afternoon. The steerage passengers remain on board, however, and the work of disinfecting their baggage progresses. The steamer Italia arrived from Naples with one cabin and 287 steerage passengers. All were found in a very healthy condition. As a precautionary measure, the passengers' baggage will be thoroughly disinfected.

Although every precaution is being taken by the health officials, prominent physicians say that the only safety lies in the stoppage of all immigration from infected districts.

Precautionary Measures.

PORT HURON, Mich., Aug. 31.—The collector of customs and United States Marine Surgeon Duff have received instructions from Washington to stop and thoroughly inspect and fumigate all effects of passengers coming from European and Asiatic points. Collector George appointed two physicians as inspectors, and they went on duty at once.

As Viewed at Washington.

WASHINGTON, Aug. 31.—Acting Secretary Spaulding says it has been suggested to him to establish a quarantine of twenty days against all vessels bringing immigrants into the United States. It could not be said that the treasury department was considering such an extreme step. The exigencies of the case would have to be very desperate to justify resorting to such an extreme measure, and it would not be done unless absolutely necessary for the public welfare.

CARLISLE AS EXAMINER.

Two Witnesses Before Him to Tell About Maverick Bank Complications.

BOSTON, Aug. 31.—On several distinct occasions the announcement has been made that the Maverick bank hearings were concluded, but in a few days the senators and their corps of stenographers would be found busily engaged in examining witnesses again. At the last hearing it was supposed that no more witnesses would be examined. Yesterday, however, Senator Carlisle was again at it, having summoned E. F. Smith, a discount clerk of the Maverick bank, and Wilmot R. Evans, brother of the late Irving A. Evans. Senator Carlisle was the only one of the committee present. The hearing was private.

It is hinted that, while the evidence obtained from the witnesses examined in public has not given the public much that was new, the evidence which has been given in private is decidedly interesting, and that before long it will be made public.

THE NEW ENGLAND FAIR

Opened at Worcester with an Address by Colonel Daniel Needham.

WORCESTER, Mass., Aug. 31.—The New England fair opened with every prospect of the usual great success. This is the twenty-ninth annual exhibition.

The address of Colonel Daniel Needham, the president, was devoted to a comparison of New England and western farming. He said: "There is no fiction in the declaration that today thousands of acres of farming land in the New England states offer far stronger inducements to the young or inexperienced farmer—means and market being duly considered—than any land in the newer states of the Union."

His chief reason was that the western lands are wearing out for want of fertilizers, while New England enjoys schools, churches and roads, and are near markets for every product.

Aldermen Vote Against Pure Water.

LAWRENCE, Mass., Aug. 31.—The aldermen have refused to pass the recommendations adopted by the water supply committee, looking toward purer water for Lawrence, as advocated by the state board of health. The aldermen say they want more time to look into the things before spending $20,000. There is much adverse comment among the citizens upon this dilatory action of the aldermen.

Tourists Will Appreciate It.

LONDON, Aug 31.—A railway train has arrived in Jerusalem from Jaffa, the railway between the two places having been completed.

Highest of all in Leavening Power.—Latest U. S. Gov't Report.

Royal Baking Powder

ABSOLUTELY PURE

LABOUCHERE IS FIRM

In His Statements Regarding the Gladstone Cabinet.

LONDON, Aug. 31.—The correspondence between Mr. Gladstone and Mr. Labouchere on the subject of the alleged objection of the queen to Mr. Labouchere's presence in the cabinet fills six pages of today's issue of Truth. In the first letter Mr. Gladstone writes from Hawarden on Aug. 22, saying that his attention had been called to Mr. Labouchere's letter to the Northampton electors. He assures Mr. Labouchere that the understanding conveyed therein is incorrect, and that he, Mr. Gladstone, was responsible for not having recommended Mr. Labouchere's name to the queen. He had considered the subject closely, and had arrived at the conclusion that there were incidents in Mr. Labouchere's career, in no way disparaging, which appeared to rend it not fitting for him, Mr. Gladstone, to ask Labouchere to become a minister.

Mr. Labouchere replied Aug. 23, saying that he recognized the difficulty of Mr. Gladstone's position, and, while he did not admit the sovereign's right to impose a veto on the premier's selections, he admired Mr. Gladstone for

Covering the Action of the Queen

in the matter and assuming the constitutional responsibility. He asked to be allowed to retain his conviction that Mr. Gladstone was not a free agent in the matter. Mr. Labouchere added that he was too stalwart a Radical not to support a government pledged to reforms. He only regretted that those reforms did not include the abolition of the house of lords and the endowment of the established church.

Mr. Gladstone replied on the 25th, confirming his previous note, which, he declared, was a true and succinct statement of the case.

Mr. Labouchere's final letter was sent on the 26th. In this he praised Mr. Gladstone's long and noble service, for which both Liberals and Radicals owed Mr. Gladstone an eternal debt of gratitude. Far from complaining, he hoped that many occasions during the coming session would show that the Radicals did not regret that Lord Salisbury had resigned, and that Mr. Gladstone was premier. Mr. Labouchere expresses regret that he had troubled Mr. Gladstone for a moment with a personal matter.

In his comments on the correspondence, Mr. Labouchere says that

He Proved Last Week

the queen's interference, and he now unqualifiedly asserts that the queen did interfere, although Mr. Gladstone was strictly within the bounds of truth in saying that he had not submitted Mr. Labouchere's name.

Mr. Labouchere reviews the criticisms of the press on the episode, and especially the severe remarks of the London Times, and he asks where he had ever maligned the queen or royalty. He scouts the notion that the Christmas issue of Truth contained anything that could be construed as maligning the queen or the royal family.

A PATRIOTIC EXECUTIVE.

Full Salary of His Office Refused by Acting President Caro.

PANAMA, Aug. 31.—Acting President Caro has refused to accept the presidential salary of $36,000 a year, although discharging the duties of president and will accept only the pay of vice president, $12,000 a year. Acting President Caro has chosen to live in a private residence, in preference to the presidential mansion, with its pompous surroundings. He is much commended for his disinterestedness and self-abnegation.

Coming to the United States.

HAVANA, Aug. 31.—An exodus from this city of 16,000 cigarmakers is threatened. The manufacturers are in despair because of the increased taxation, which leaves them little or no margin for profits. A Florida land company has been offering such inducements for the removal of factories from Cuba to Tampa and Ybor city that there is little doubt of many accepting. The employes are all eager for the change.

Would-Be Murderer Bound Over.

NORWICH, Conn., Aug. 31.—Manuel Rose, Portuguese, who shot and wounded Manuel Texerira in a quarrel over cards, two weeks ago, was bound over to the superior court for trial in $500 bonds. Texerira, whose wounds were at first supposed to be fatal, has recovered sufficiently to appear in court as a witness.

His Companion Was Rescued.

PROVIDENCE, Aug. 31.—Patrick F. McGinley, aged 26 years, was drowned in the Pawtuxet river, near Providence, by the capsizing of a small rowboat containing himself and a lady friend. The young lady clung to the gunwale of the boat and was easily rescued.

PLENTY OF MONEY ON HAND.

So Say the Officers of the Order of the Helping Hand.

SALEM, Mass., Aug. 31.—William H. Gove of this city, president of the Order of the Helping Hand of Lynn, was asked in regard to the published reports to the effect that the order was apt to pass into the hands of a receiver.

"Why," said Mr. Gove, "I never heard of that before. I suppose this trouble with the Iron Hall has made all members of endowment orders uneasy. I am sure that the Helping Hand has, or, at least did have in June, sufficient funds to pay all obligations. This trouble is probably being made by some persons who want what they have paid in refunded. We are not obliged to do this at the present time, although we could do it."

The officers of the Order of the Helping Hand in Lynn deny the stories published which state that a receiver would be asked for by the policy holders. They say the order is solvent, and exhibit a large amount of money to support that statement.

EASTERN MAINE STATE FAIR.

The Largest Exhibition in Its History Opens at Bangor.

BANGOR, Me., Aug. 31.—The tenth annual exhibition of the Eastern Maine state fair opened here under cloudless skies, and finer weather could not possibly be conceived. The fair managers have been working for weeks harder than ever before, and the result is an all-round exhibit never equalled or approached in Maine. There are probably 600 horses here, representing all the best bred stock in the state. The British provinces are represented by about 100 of the cream of their draft and race horses. The sheep, swine, poultry, farming implements, dairy and all other departments are filled to overflowing, while there are over 600 of the finest cattle in the country on exhibition. Although yesterday was devoted to organization, probably 5000 people were on the grounds, and the judges in all departments commenced work.

Protection Has Favored Farmers.

SYDNEY, N. S. W., Aug. 31.—The colonial parliament was opened yesterday. The Earl of Jersey, governor of the colony, in his speech, stated that since the passage of the protection tariff in March last the area of land under cultivation in the colony had increased 25 per cent.

Almost Ready for Sailing.

MADRID, Aug. 31.—The Caravels Nina and Pinta, which have been building some time at Barcelona for the Columbus celebration, have been launched, and will be completed shortly, as only the masts and a few of the fittings are now lacking.

SCROFULA 12 YEARS.

Always Sore. Burned Like Fire. Ashamed to be Seen. Got Worse Under Four Doctors. Cured by Cuticura.

For about ten or twelve years I have been troubled with scrofula. My head was always sore, my face was dry and scaly, and burned like fire most of the time. My body had big red spots on it, and I did not know what to do. I went to four different doctors and they helped me at first. In the Fall I got worse again; then I tried other remedies, but they did me no good. I was ashamed to go into public. I was a sight to look at. Every one would say, "What is the matter, why don't you take something?" Even at my daily labor I had to wear a sort of cap to keep the dirt from getting into the sores. After I would wash, I would be covered with big red pimples all over my face and neck. Some two or three people advised me to try the Cuticura Remedies. I did try them, and am glad I have done so. Glad to say I am a well man, and in the best of health since. I cannot praise the Cuticura Remedies too highly. I enclose my portrait.

LEWIS W. KATON, Larksville, Pa.

CUTICURA REMEDIES

Cuticura Resolvent, the new Blood and Skin Purifier, internally (to cleanse the blood of all impurities and poisonous elements,) and Cuticura, the great Skin Cure, and Cuticura Soap, an exquisite Skin Purifier and Beautifier, externally, (to clear the skin and scalp and restore the hair,) cure every disease and humors of the skin scalp, and blood, with loss of hair, from infancy to age, from pimples to scrofula, when the best physicians, hospitals, and all other remedies fail.

Sold everywhere. Price, Cuticura, 50c.; Soap, 25c.; Resolvent, $1. Prepared by the POTTER DRUG AND CHEMICAL CORPORATION, Boston.

"How to Cure Skin Diseases," 64 pages, 50 illustrations and 100 testimonials; mailed free.

PIMPLES, black-heads, red, rough, chapped and oily skin cured by Cuticura Soap.

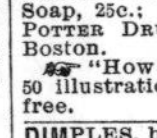

NO RHEUMATIZ ABOUT ME!

In one minute the Cuticura Anti-Pain Plaster relieves rheumatic, sciatic, hip, kidney, muscular and chest pains. The first and only instantaneous pain-killing strengthening plaster.

We Have Quite a Number of

REMNANTS

In all Grades of

CARPETING AND MATTINGS!

On which we have made

Special Low Prices

DURING AUGUST.

BRIGGS & LAWRENCE,

197 and 203 Union Street.

From Yesterday's Third Edition.

LIZZIE'S WORDS.

Notes Taken at the Inquest Read in Court.

Some of Prisoner's Statements Do Not Tally.

Testified She Was Upstairs When Her Father Came.

A Moment Later Said She Was In the Kitchen.

Story of the Trouble Between Step-Mother and Daughter.

Gift of Property to the Girls Satisfied Them.

But Lizzie Never After Called Mrs. Borden "Mother."

Government Rests and Defence is Putting in Evidence.

[Special Dispatch.]

FALL RIVER, Aug. 30.—When the court came in this afternoon every seat was crowded, a great many ladies were standing and hundreds outside were unable to obtain admittance.

The Stenographer on the Stand.

Annie M. White was the first witness. She said: I am the official stenographer of the courts of this county. I was present at the inquest and heard the testimony of Miss Lizzie A. Borden. I took notes of her testimony and have since transcribed them.

ATTY. ADAMS CONSULTING WITH MISS LIZZIE DURING INTERMISSION.

The witness was cross-examined. She said: I cannot tell who were present when Lizzie Borden testified. I know Mr. Seaver. Mr. Hilliard and Dr. Dolan were present. The statements that these people made, incuding that of a stranger present, were taken down by me. I made two copies of the testimony taken. I gave them both to Mr. Knowlton. That was the last I saw of them. The examination of Miss Borden was suspended once. At that time other witnesses were examined between the first and second time she was on the stand. I remember being here in the room with Mrs. Brigham, Miss Borden and Officer Harrington. The others were then out of the room. Some of them were in the judge's room. Mr. Knowlton was in that room. I know Miss Borden was at the inquest two days. Her examination was all the forenoon one day and not over an hour next day. The date of her last examination was Aug. 11. On refreshing myself from my notes I find that Miss Borden was at the inquest on the 9th, 10th and 11th. The examination on Wednesday was in the afternoon. On Tuesday she was perhaps an hour and a half engaged in testifying.

Mr. Adams said defence was willing to admit Miss White's report of testimony at the inquest provided defence can make its objection to what it deems irrelevant.

Lizzie's Testimony at the Inquest.

Miss White's report of the evidence taken at the inquest was then read by Mr. Knowlton. It was to the effect that Lizzie gave her name and said: My age is 32. My mother is not living. She died when I was two years old. My father and stepmother lived in the Second street house for 27 years. I have no idea what my father was worth. I know part of the real estate he owns. Do not know about all of it.

Mr. Adams objected at this point on general grounds to admitting this evidence but he was overruled.

The report was further read by Mr. Knowlton. The question was about what real estate Lizzie's father owned, and her answer as to real estate in Fall River and of farms was given. Then came the question "Did you ever deed any property to him?" (her father.) Lizzie answered that her father formerly deeded to her (Lizzie) and Emma her grandfather's real estate on Ferry street and then bought it back. A few months previously Lizzie said she had heard her Uncle John V. Morse say her father had made a will.

The report previously printed of Lizzie telling about a man calling at her house and having words about a store was stated and then Lizzie said the only man who has hard feelings against her father was Hiram C. Harrington, his brother-in-law. Lizzie's stepmother had some property. Her relations with her stepmother were "cordial," as some might call them.

Lizzie Did Not Call Mrs. Borden "Mother."

She had ceased to call her so five or six years before on account of an affair with a stepsister. Lizzie declined to state what the affair was, as she did not know how to answer it. She said she did not know how long John V. Morse had been east. Wednesday evening, August 3d, Lizzie spent the evening with Miss Russell. That day (Wednesday) Lizzie heard Morse's voice downstairs. She did not go down to supper. She did not feel well enough to do so. When she came home Wednesday evening she locked the front door. When Lizzie came downstairs on Thursday morning (the day of the tragedy she saw her father, mother and Maggie (Bridget.) When Lizzie came downstairs she said her father was reading a Providence paper, her mother was dusting and Bridget was getting ready to wash windows. She came downstairs about 9 o'clock. She got ready to iron some handkerchiefs. She did not know what time her father went down town. She had not finished ironing when her father went out. She went upstairs while her father was gone and sat in her room long enough to sew a little piece of tape on a garment.

When Lizzie's Father Came Home She Was Upstairs,

but was on the way down. A moment later witness said her recollection was that she was in the kitchen when her father returned home. She did not see her mother after she came down to breakfast. When her mother was dusting her mother said she had made the bed in the spare room and got everything ready for the next week. Mrs. Borden said she

Had a Note to Go and See a Sick Woman

and she would get the dinner while on the way. She did not tell Lizzie who the note was from or where she was going. It was usual for Mrs. Borden to go out in the morning.

In the questioning of the second day of the inquest

Lizzie Said She was in the Kitchen

when her father came home on the day of the tragedy. She did not go up stairs while her father was away. He did not go away from the house until about 10 o'clock. Lizzie did not see Bridget while she was washing the windows out of doors. Most of the time in her father's absence Lizzie was alone downstairs. The front door was locked.

When Lizzie Last Saw Her Father

she said he was lying down on the sofa in the sitting-room. He was not reading. She spoke to him about leaving the window open. She went to the barn and upstairs. She was after lead for a sinker. She knew there was lead downstairs in the barn, but there was a box of old things upstairs. Lizzie had no fish line at home but had lines at the farm. When Lizzie was in the barn chamber about 20 minutes as she said she ate three pears. When she got into the house she saw her father lying on the sofa and saw that he was cut. She did not see his face. It was all covered with blood. She called Maggie (Bridget) at once. Lizzie said she did not at that or any other time tell any one that she thought her mother was killed. She knew of no reason unless she was doing some sewing why her mother should be in the spare room for an hour or two.

The statement continued that Lizzie's mother told her she had received a note and was going out. After discovering that her father was dead Lizzie said she told Mrs. Churchill that she wished she would look and see where her mother was. After Lizzie's father came home she did not see him go upstairs before he said he would lie down.

Lizzie Did Not Fix the Pillow

on the sofa for him. The trouble had with her stepmother five or six years before was related in the statement. It was in effect that Mr. Borden had purchased a house for her step-

Pastor Buck and Lizzie Borden Entering Court.

mother's sister and Lizzie said if he would do this for people not his own that he should do something for his own flesh and blood. Mr. Borden then gave Emma and Lizzie their grandfather's house, and this satisfied them. It was

At the Time of This Trouble that Lizzie Stopped Calling Mrs. Borden "Mother".

At this point a recess of ten minutes was taken, and the hum of conversation and the sounds of laughter were heard all over the room. Lizzie had an earnest conversation with Mr. Jennings. Afterwards she leaned across Emma and talked with Mrs. Brigham. The heat in the court-room was something terrific and the biggest crowd of any day since the opening was in attendance. Not only were seats crowded, but the people were wedged in three or four deep inside the space reserved for reporters and counsel.

Court Reconvenes.

When the court was again called to order Mr. Knowlton resumed the reading of the record of the inquest. He showed that Lizzie had bought a dress pattern on Union street in New Bedford. Quoting from Lizzie's testimony he said: I did not go into the room where father was killed. The dress I gave the officer was the one that I wore that morning. The shoes and stockings I gave the officer were the ones that I had worn right along. I recollect about a man running around the house one night before the murder. I mentioned this fact before this time to Mr. Jennings. I have told my father about these incidents. Do not use prussic acid on anything that I have.

Here the Commonwealth closed.

GOVERNMENT CLOSES.

Evidence for the Defence Now Being Put in at the Borden Hearing.

For the defence Dr. Dolan was the first witness called. He made the autopsy and quoted from the records. He said that he made the autopsy on Mr. and Mrs. Borden Tuesday following the tragedy.

Miss Collett was called for and it was found that she was not present. Mr. Adams asked why she was not present and the district attorney said that she had come to the hearing at his request when she wanted to go to Canada. Perhaps she was in Canada now, he didn't know, and didn't know whether she could be summoned.

Miss Bridget Sullivan was called for, but was not present. The district attorney said that she was within call and could be present any time she was wanted, as she was in town.

Mrs. Churchill was the next witness. She said: I was not told who wrote the note to Mrs. Borden on that morning, but was told that Mrs. Borden had a note to go and see some one who was sick.

Mr. Adams addressed the court at this point, and asked that the evidence in relation to Lizzie's purchase or attempted purchase of prussic acid be stricken out as not pertinent, the government having charged that Miss Borden killed her father with an axe.

The district attorney argued that the evidence was pertinent and competent.

The court declined to rule out the eyidence.

Dr. Bowen then took the stand and told the familiar story of his visit to the house after the tragedy. He was on the stand when the last edition of the *Standard* went to press.

THAT WRECKED BRIG.—Tug Right Arm, which left this port this morning to go to the assistance of brig Woodbury, before reported as having lost sails and anchored off Menemsha Bight, took her in tow at 1 30 o'clock this afternoon, bound for an eastern port.

JUST OUT

Of their mattings and just placed on exhibit in our show rooms for your approval are

75

New patterns of Chamber Sets and

50

New styles of Parlor Suits; the finest and lowest priced collection of choice designs it has ever been our good fortune to offer you. These goods were personally selected from the great Furniture centres of the West and represent the latest conceptions in case and upholstery work. If you want to be sure of getting the latest and best productions

SLOCUM'S

IS THE PLACE,

354 & 362 Acushnet Av.

CASH OR LIBERAL TERMS.

Mr. Robert W. Denvir

An Exempt Fireman of Jackson Engine Co., Long Island City, N. Y., says that at Christmas, 1890, he could only take a smell of dinner, as he was in a fearful condition from **Dyspepsia.** The next summer he went to Europe for his health, but came home uncured. In the fall he decided upon a thorough trial of

Hood's Sarsaparilla

And by Christmas had a hearty appetite, healthy digestion, and was perfectly well. His cure was due wholly to Hood's Sarsaparilla.

HOOD'S PILLS cure liver ills, constipation, biliousness, jaundice, and [illegible]. Try them.

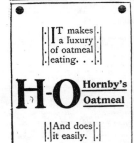

The Evening Standard.

ESTABLISHED FEBRUARY, 1850.

NEW BEDFORD, THURSDAY, SEPTEMBER 1, 1892.

TWO CENTS.

MOVED TO TEARS.

Miss Borden Breaks Down Under Counsel's Plea.

Lawyer Jennings Himself Gives Way Under Strain.

His Earnest Appeal for His Old Friend's Daughter.

Believes the Black Deed Work of an Insane Man.

Alleges That Lizzie Had No Opportunity.

Course of Government at Inquest Severely Condemned.

Counsel Demands the Release of the Prisoner.

Effort of Defendant's Attorney Greeted With Great Applause.

[Special Dispatch.]

FALL RIVER, Sept. 1.—According to the almanac we have reached the first month of the fall of the leaf, and at this period if ever in the year calm counsel should prevail and passion subside. This town—now the first in point of population in the country—furnishes a complete refutation of the philosophic suggestion made, for as I stated yesterday, the division into hostile camps here still prevails. Families as well as wards are divided, and in some localities it is hard to obtain an unbiased opinion regarding the guilt or innocence of Lizzie A. Borden.

All through the seething and turmoil she alone maintains the coolness which has marked her demeanor from the first. She does not seem to care for outside influences, and safe within her retreat she is to say the least totally indifferent as to what the general public may say. Attorney Jennings made a call upon her last night, and so far as can be gathered she was indifferent to what may be going on outside the walls of the granite edifice in which she has been confined for nearly two weeks. She lent an ear to what Mr. Jennings had to say but did not seem to care any more than would a casual visitor to the city what the course of proceedings will be to-day. All this may be the consciousness of innocence, but those who have followed the examination closely do not think so, and they think they have a right to say that either she does not realize the gravity of the situation or else that she is defiant. Mr. Jennings evidently feels in his innermost conscience the weight which is pressing on his client, that she is encompassed about and has to meet not only here, but in a court of competent jurisdiction, a charge the most serious that can be presented against any one.

Mr. Jennings has grown old and he looks haggard, and he seems to realize to its fullest extent all that he has got to meet. He knows full well that in argument in the court to-day he is to meet the brightest mind in the legal fraternity in Bristol county, and that District Attorney Knowlton is bound not only by his self-love but by his sense of duty to the government to make the strongest presentation of the case in his power. This summing up will be a masterly one, and as he has the ear of the judge after defence has presented its side, it is felt that he will rise to the occasion and will make one of the strongest pleas known in the history of the Bristol bar.

The same condition of affairs which has marked the last eight days around the Central police station was visible this morning, and crowds gathered before the hour for the opening of the Second District Court. The police were on hand in goodly numbers—the members of the night reliefs being as prompt and as wide awake as they have been all along. One thing which will go down into history by the pens of out of town reporters at least is the uniform courtesy they have met with from these same police officers, who in spite of the impatience of the crowd and the pushing and crowding done have at all times kept their tempers and done what they could to meet the exigencies of every occasion and forward the interests of the press representatives.

It is freely stated here this morning—and bets are offered upon it—that Lizzie will be held to await the action of the grand jury.

E. H. MARTIN.

PLEA FOR THE PRISONER.

Andrew J. Jennings Makes His Argument in Defence.

FALL RIVER, Sept. 1.—The court-room was filled with spectators at the opening of the last day of the examination of Lizzie A. Borden, charged with the murder of her father. In appearance the audience was about equally divided as to sexes, and all were alert and wide awake to catch even the faintest remarks when counsel come to sum up and make their arguments. The spectators included doctors, experts and other witnesses who had been present during the examination, and they overflowed on to all the space, and some of them seemed to feel very much hurt to think they were not admitted to places they had previously occupied.

Lizzie Borden came in accompanied by Pastor Buck, and it was noticeable that her sister was not with her.

Andrew J. Jennings opened for the defence. He said, among other things, that the complaint alleges that on the 4th day of August Andrew J. Borden was killed by his daughter. He appreciated the subject with feelings widely different from any other case he had ever handled. Mr. Borden was not only his client, but his friend, and had anybody told him four weeks ago that he should now be pleading for the daughter of his old friend he should have said it was beyond the bounds of credibility.

That Andrew J. Borden Was Murdered There Is No Doubt,

and that the time of the murder has been established there is also no doubt. Clegg, Shortsleeves and Bridget Sullivan have fixed the time by the City Hall clock, and some reliance can be placed on the fact that such time when Mr. Borden last entered his house has been fixed. Mrs. Kelley's time is wrong, and the others are to be relied upon. The alarm was given at 11 13 to 11 15, and we know so far as we can know from the evidence that the time between Mr. Borden's last entrance to the house and the alarm from 25 minutes to half an hour covers the time fully. What took place after he got there? Bridget Sullivan told her story and she left him in the sitting room reading a paper. Within half an hour Andrew J. Borden had to go into the house, have his talk with Lizzie, if he had one, go upstairs and downstairs and lie down on the sofa, unless he was killed and placed on the sofa afterwards. The time must be reduced to from 10 to 15 minutes of the commission of the deed.

It is found after the alarm has been given that the bodies were where they have been so often described, and any man of common sense would have said at once on seeing them that

This Was the Work of an Insane Man

or of one whose heart was as black as black could be. Blow after blow, cutting through the hair into the brain were rained on these persons, showing that the person who did that wanted to make sure; there was an unnecessary brutality about that that suggests infernal hatred and revenge or insanity. Every blow delivered shows its deep line of demarkation from the other, showing that the hand that struck these blows was powerful and that the hand had experience in handling a hatchet.

This case is one of circumstances and if there are those which have weight against Lizzie Borden you are bound to observe those which are for her equally as well. These wounds speak for themselves, and don't rest upon the statement of those who may have seen them. It becomes the duty of the Commonwealth to investigate a crime of this nature with the utmost care, that the guilty should be found.

The Theory of the Government

seems to have been that the crime was commited by inmates in that house; all their work seems to have been directed by that one idea. Now who are the inmates and what have they got to do with fastening it upon them. The isolation of that house has been shown. It is claimed that nobody could get out for there were people all around to see who passed and repassed if any there were—and they attempt to show that no persons were seen; what is the fact, however? They know the house has been burglarized within two years and the barn broken into within two months, and the facts are not disputed; we show something the police ought to have discovered, the stranger within the gate, as told by Mrs. Manley; they have spent night and day

Following Up Clews to Convict Lizzie Borden,

but know nothing about Mrs. Manley and the man she saw. Why? because they are not looking for anybody outside.

The extraordinary thing is that the police cannot find the man Dr. Handy saw but they can find the axe or axes Lizzie Borden killed her father with. There is the fact that

Strange Men Were There That Haven't Been Found.

Three men got there and the neighbors didn't see them and doesn't it follow that others might have gone in and yet not have been seen by the neighbors? Miss Collette didn't see Frank Wixon but he went over the fence while she was right there; neither Crowe's man nor the Frenchman saw him until he got down into the yard. Lizzie has told about seeing a man dodging about the house, and it hasn't been contradicted; isn't it entitled to some weight? Mrs. Chagnon hears somebody making a noise at the fence on the division line the night before.

We say that this goes to

Break Down the Government's Claim

that this deed was committed by somebody in the house. So far as we know Morse, Lizzie and Bridget Sullivan were the only persons in the house at the time with the murdered persons. Mr. Morse, having accounted for his time, leaves the others alone. The youngest daughter and the servant. And right here counsel called attention to the words "youngest daughter." She is the pet of the family; the one whose fingers were last clasped by the dead father, and the one whose head last rested against his breast.

Lizzie Here Burst Into Tears,

and Mr. Jennings was himself almost in tears.

Continuing, he said he didn't believe that either Bridget Sullivan or Lizzie committed the deed. Now, Andrew J. Borden couldn't have got into the house before 10 45, and there are 20 minutes of Bridget's time unaccounted for, and nobody has asked her on the side of the prosecution what she was doing all that time. If she could do three windows in 15 minutes did it take her three-fourths of an hour to wash the other four? The point is this, that if Lizzie doesn't explain everything as she goes along, if she trips in her testimony, then she must be the guilty party, think the government.

If Lizzie had an opportunity to commit this murder, Bridget Sullivan had an opportunity. Bridget says she was outdoors, but who else saw her out there but Mrs. Churchill? Counsel didn't desire to show that Bridget was guilty, but was only trying to show the extraordinary course of the government towards Lizzie. Now,

If Lizzie Did This, When Did She Do It?

The government has put in evidence to show that from the appearance of the digestion that these persons had been dead so long, but that is a very uncertain thing to build on; it is only approximate, for digestion varies.

Following Mr. Borden from his house at 9 30 counsel brought him back at the time testified to, and said that if Lizzie killed her mother she must have done it while her father was out of the house, but she has told her story about her movements at that time, and the telling of that story, counsel said, was in the line of an outrage, as he had told the District Attorney at the time; the inquest was taken for

No Other Purpose But to Put Lizzie on the Rack

and nobody who heard that testimony read the other day but what said so.

Over and over again she is asked the same questions to see if she cannot be made to change her story. Take the testimony of Mrs. Churchill, an intelligent woman, who couldn't tell where Bridget Sullivan went when they went to the upper room. And yet Bridget isn't so thin she couldn't be seen, nor could she vanish into thin air. Mrs. Churchill couldn't recollect what became of her, but here is Lizzie Borden, who had been subjected to a most severe strain condemned simply because she didn't remember some of the slightest details in in connection with her movements that morning.

It was stated that

Lizzie Laughed at Bridget

when she made that exclamation at the door, but it is beyond the bounds of human belief that any person could stand there and laugh over simple things like that when she had just come from the killing of her mother. Only an insane person could do that, and

Lizzie Borden Isn't Insane.

There wasn't anything inconsistent in the fact that Lizzie, although she had been sick, was eating pears that morning; her father and mother had been doing the same thing, and the government's own witness said so, for they were found in their stomachs.

When Mrs. Churchill saw Lizzie she was agitated because she had just found her father; if she had seen her mother before that wouldn't she have been likely to have shown some excitement and agitation then? Bridget says she was calm, and it has gone all over this land that she

[Continued on Fourth Page.]

THE PESTILENCE.

Quarantine Conditions at New York Unchanged.

Serious Talk of Postponement of the World's Fair.

Revolting Brutality of the Lower Classes in Berlin.

NEW YORK, Sept. 1.—The conditions at quarantine are unchanged, and the steamers Moravia, Veendam, Lahn, Teutonic, Gallia and Circassia are all below yet. No cases of sickness are reported on any of the vessels this morning. The Teutonic and Circassia will be released this morning.

Talk of Postponing the World's Fair.

CHICAGO, Sept. 1.—Dispatches from New York and Washington indicate that some apprehension is felt at those cities that the cholera abroad will have a harmful effect upon the prospects of the fair, so far as foreign exhibits are concerned. Many of these were to come from districts which are infected with the scourge and it might be dangerous to accept goods sent here under such circumstances. It is suggested that it might be well to postpone the exposition for another year.

Director General Davis does not think that the present condition of affairs warrants any action in the postponement of the fair.

"Do you think the reported condition of the cholera is such as would affect the prospects of the fair?" he was asked.

"I do not."

"Do you approve of a postponement?"

"Not at present."

"If the cholera should spread would you advise a postponement?"

"It would depend on circumstances. But I do not think such circumstances will develop. I have paid no attention to the scare."

President Hilanbotham is disposed to treat the scare lightly. "I have not heard of any desire to postpone the fair because of the cholera, and as far as I know it has not been discussed."

Several of the other directors are of the same opinion.

"I think it would be wise to wait until we know that the cholera is going to make trouble," said Director Gage, and that seems to be the general opinion.

Revolting Scene in Berlin.

LONDON, Sept. 1.—The Berlin correspondent of the *News* says: "Certainly the epidemic cholera is making rapid progress here. Dr. Guttman, the director of the hospital, says that, owing to the cooler weather prevailing at present and the sanitary precautions which have been taken, the disease will probably remain sporadic. The panic among the lower class, always coarse and brutal, gives rise to many revolting scenes. For instance, on Monday a poor old lady was taken ill in the street and began to reel. A workman supported her until she began to vomit, when he quickly bolted.

A crowd gathered about the woman at a safe distance, when suddenly a bricklayer, after carefully wrapping a handkerchief around his hand, seized hold of her, and dragged her in a brutal manner to the middle of the street, where he left her, after kicking her prostrate form and telling her in the vilest terms that he would stop her from infecting their house. In the meantime the woman's granddaughter, who was present during the revolting scene and who was crying bitterly, clasped the knees of a man in the crowd and implored him to have pity, when the wretch flung her with an oath on top of her unconscious grandmother, the child being stunned by the fall. Both were thus left lying in the street until other persons passing took compassion on them and helped them to reach their homes. Aid was summoned, and it was found they were suffering from choleraic diarrhœa.

Will Not Proceed to Hamburg.

The steamer Fuerst Bismarck from New York arrived at Southampton this morning. Under the new regulations of the American Packet Company, the vessel will not proceed to Hamburg. Her passengers will be landed and her cargo discharged at Southampton.

Discouraging Report from Paris.

PARIS, Sept. 1.—Twenty-one fresh cases of cholera were reported in Paris yesterday. There were ten deaths.

Ravages of the Pestilence in Russia.

ST. PETERSBURG, Sept. 1.—The official cholera returns for all Russia show a decrease in the ravages of the pestilence. The latest returns show a total of 4859 new cases and 2529 deaths, a decrease of 1285 and 212 respectively. The death rate, however, is excessively high, being slightly over 52 per cent. In St. Petersburg, there were 123 new cases and 40 deaths yesterday, as compared with 155 new cases and 51 deaths Monday.

FAST MAIL TRAIN WRECKED.

Fatal Disaster on the Hudson River Road at New Hamburgh, N. Y.

NEWBURGH, N. Y., Sept. 1.—The fast mail on the Hudson river road met disaster at the New Hamburgh drawbridge at ten minutes past 6 o'clock this morning. The draw had been opened to let a vessel pass through and was being closed when the train came along. A gap of several feet remained when the engine reached the draw going at the rate of nearly a mile a minute. The engine jumped the gap, but the rear end of the tender dropped enough to stop the passage of the train.

Then the mail car crashed into the tender, pushed it against the locomotive, the rear end of which and the forward end of the mail car were splintered. The engineer, Joseph Owens of Albany, and the fireman, Edward Best of East Albany, were crushed under the forward end of the cab and killed instantly. There were two clerks in the mail car. H. Kane of Cohoes was forced upward and landed on top of the debris of the mail car and instantly killed. The other clerk was not injured.

After the mail car came two baggage or storage cars. Conductor William L. Todd and Trainman John Hitchcock were in the forward end of the baggage car. J. H. O'Neil, a trainman, was in the rear part of the same car. Todd and Hitchcock were thrown against the end of the car. The former was hurt about the head and bruised about the body. Hitchcock had one finger cut. Otherwise he escaped injury. The engine, tender and mail car were utterly wrecked and much of the mail was torn into fragments. The debris obstructed the down track. This was soon cleared away and trains were run around the wreck on the up track.

FIRED UPON BY THE CORWIN.

San Francisco Codfishing Schooners' Experience in Bering Sea.

SAN FRANCISCO, Sept. 1.—The codfishing schooners John Hancock and Arcata have arrived from Bering Sea and the captain of the latter reports that he was overhauled several times by United States cruisers and cutters in the north and on one occasion the cutter Corwin signalled him to heave to. The captain said there was a dead calm at the time and it was impossible to obey. Accordingly the Corwin fired twice across the schooner's bows and afterward sent a boat's crew aboard who made a search of the vessel without finding evidence that she was engaged in sealing.

Ocean Steamers.

Arrived—At Boston, Ebro, Hull, Eng.

WEATHER INDICATIONS.

FAIR AND COOLER.

WASHINGTON, Sept. 1.—For the 24 hours from 8 a. m. to-day: For Massachusetts, Rhode Island and Connecticut, generally fair; cooler Friday morning; northerly winds.

FAIR.

BOSTON, Sept. 1.—Local forecast for New England until Saturday: Fair weather, cooler to-night and Friday morning; winds becoming northerly and variable. Saturday and Sunday probably fair and gradually warmer.

ACCIDENT TO THE PRESIDENT.

Thrown from a Carriage on a Rough Road but Only Slightly Bruised.

NEW YORK, Sept. 1.—President Harrison met with a slight accident last night on his way from Ophir Farm to White Plains station. The driver selected the "Madames road," the nearest to the station. This road is difficult to travel. It leads through the woods on Mr. Reid's farm for nearly a mile, and this part of the road is up hill and down. At night the way is pitch dark. Trees overhang it and cut off the light of the moon, and as it winds around with ditches on either side it is not easy for an expert driver to pilot a carriage over it safely.

Two carriages started ahead of the President last night. The first carriage got through safely because the occupants lighted the way and the horses walked. The second carriage came to grief against a rock. The victoria containing the President's party hustled along at a lively rate in the light shed by its side lamps. Just at the foot of the first steep hill, however, one of the front wheels ran into the ditch. The carriage came to a sudden stop, throwing the President out. The victoria was not overturned and the President was uninjured beyond a slight bruise on the leg. He had been sitting in the back in such a way that only a slight tilt of the carriage and a shock were needed to throw him out. The President picked himself up and jumped into the vehicle without aid, and the driver whipped up his horses and started for the station at a rapid rate.

FORT PAYNE STOCKHOLDERS

Discuss the Question of a Receiver at an Adjourned Meeting.

BOSTON, Sept. 1.—An adjourned meeting of the stockholders of the Fort Payne Coal & Iron Company was held Wednesday afternoon at Chickering Hall to discuss the affairs of the company relative to putting or not putting it in the hands of a receiver. W. P. Rice presided. There were about 100 gentlemen present. M. W. Howard, one of the directors of the company at Fort Payne, Ala., spoke of the prospects of the future. He believes in Fort Payne, and feels confident that an outlay of $50,000 now would save the property and pay the interest on the bonds and floating indebtedness. Judge Cochrane of Fort Payne has faith in the property. He is not a stockholder, but came because he is interested in the future of Fort Payne and wants to see the city grow into a flourishing manufacturing centre. He was followed by Col. W. H. Denson of Gadson, who also spoke in favor of the stockholders joining and saving their property. He is satisfied that there is iron in the Fort Payne mines, and that it only needs push and good management to develop the property and get good dividends. Lawyer Northfleet of Fort Payne gave a detailed statement of the condition of affairs as he had gleaned them from the books of the temporary receiver.

LIGHTNING'S WORK.

One Man Killed and Residences and Crops Destroyed in Alabama.

ANNISTAN, Ala., Sept. 1.—Lightning did fearful work in Henderson county yesterday. At Columbia, Charles Sumner Ford was struck and instantly killed. The same bolt struck and set fire to his stables and they were burned with contents. A house in the neighborhood was struck and demolished, but no one was injured.

At Dolhan, water and lightning did great damage. The open cotton was ruined. Corn was blown down and crops of all kinds greatly injured. Three residences were struck and wrecked. In one of them Lawrence Inniss, an old man, was sitting near an open fireplace and was rendered unconscious for several hours.

Leaf Tobacco Combine.

LOUISVILLE, Ky., Sept. 1.—A powerful combine, to be known as the Leaf Tobacco Company, was formed here yesterday to compete with the newly organized company at Cincinnati. The capital stock is placed at $2,500,000.

Small Pox in Illinois.

SPRINGFIELD, Ills., Sept. 1.—Small pox is reported in Iroquois and McHenry counties; the case in Iroquois county is among German immigrants.

The President at the White House.

WASHINGTON, Sept. 1.—The President arrived at the White House about 8 50 this morning.

HOME MATTERS.

PERSONAL.—Mr. William O. Hamblin left the city last evening to resume his position as Supervisor of Drawing in the public schools of Akron, Ohio.

Capt. Andrews is to take command of schooner Elisha Gibbs and Capt. Slocum will take the Warren B. Potter. The latter vessel will make three trips from Georgetown to New York with lumber.

J. C. Nowell, of this city, and Miss M. Stewart, of Fall River, are among the recent visitors at Mammoth Hot Springs Hotel, Wyo.

James Platt left this city to-day for Galveston, Tex., where he is to visit friends.

Mrs. Margaret Van Hovenberg-Morrill, soprano at the North Congregational church, will resume teaching a limited number of pupils on Monday mornings in the Y. M. C. A. parlors, commencing next week.

A party comprising Miss Mary L. Thompson, Miss Florence Parsons, Miss Lizzie Parsons and Mr. Howard Eldridge, leave this city to-morrow for a week at Cuttyhunk.

Miss Sarah J. Bailey arrived home yesterday from a four weeks' vacation in North Dartmouth.

TRAVEL IMPEDED.—A trench has been dug across Purchase street near the foot of Hazzard, necessitating the transfer of horse car passengers and greatly interfering with travel.

CURBING is being laid along the sidewalk on the east side of State street from Weld to Cedar Grove.

LAST DAY OF TESTIMONY.

Scenes When Witnesses for Defence Were on the Stand.

Marshal Hilliard Creates Excitement with the Spread and Shams.

The Prisoner Affected by the Proceedings of the Court.

The general opinion in the District Court-room in Fall River yesterday morning held by the regular attendants and those who were familiar with the proceedings from the newspapers was that the day would be the beginning of the end of the suspense. Whether the prisoner had thought anything about it is a question. If she had, from all appearances, the thoughts had not greatly disturbed her. She came in and was seated with her remarkable nonchalance and Mr. Buck made a courtesy before her.

Lizzie's friends are staunch. Mrs. Brigham was on board early, and Dr. and Mrs. Bowen sat on the end of her settee when she arrived. The accused woman ruled alone at her end of the seat, and every little attention which was conducive to her comfort was administered by her sister.

Upon being seated an old fashioned cashmere shawl was thrown over her shoulders, and strangely enough she wore it all the morning session though her dress is a thick one for the season. The court room was warm and most of the women there were comfortable in cotton waists, but the prisoner dressed in woollen required a shawl. Lizzie Borden seems to make it a specialty to keep cool when other people are warm or excited.

There were no seats to spare in the court room yesterday, but the number of distinguished people present seemed less than on some other occasion, and there were apparently in the room few people outside of Fall River.

Mr. Knowlton and Attorney Adams pulled their chairs together and leaned over on each other's shoulders, engaged in a very confidential whisper while Marshal Hilliard was being examined. Both were shaking with laughter and they belied the deadly hostility which has been frequently displayed during the hearing. Their disputes, in fact, have been the most entertaining exhibitions in court. On such occasions they address each other as brothers. Mr. Adams is blandly sarcastic, and Mr. Knowlton cutting and aggressive.

No one enjoys these professional bouts more than Judge Blaisdell, unless indeed it be the prisoner. She rarely fails to notice a witty retort, especially if it comes from Mr. Adams. Her confidence in that gentleman is evidently increasing. She consults with him much more frequently than at first. Mrs. Brigham is often questioned by the counsel for the defence, but Emma is never seen speaking with them.

As the name of Marshal Hilliard was announced, and that beau ideal of official manliness stepped before the clerk to be sworn, the spectators gathered themselves into shape expecting to hear an interesting story. The marshal's testimony was given in good style, but it revealed nothing new.

While he was on the stand the pillow shams and spread, stained with the life blood of Mrs. Borden, were brought to the court room. They were loosely wrapped in a copy of the *Standard*, and when the marshal untied the bundle every eye was fixed on its contents. "Oh, if only that sheet could talk," murmured a zealous reporter, as the marshal shook out the spread for inspection. The women on the back seats gaped and goggled. They thought the grand bloody scene had come at last, and they wanted to make the most of it. They looked and turned their heads away with disgust, but it was not at the sight of blood, however, rather the absence of the sight of it. The blood spots were too few and too scattering to be seen except on near examination.

These were a part of the bed coverings of the guest chamber in the Borden house, and they were of the most ordinary kind, such in fact as any man with $700 instead of $700,000 might use in his household. All the lawyers examined the articles very closely and Judge Blaisdell leaned forward, most interested, to get a good view of them. When not in use they were loosely spread over a table around which were seated Mayor Coughlin, Dr. Dolan, Mrs. Bowen and Dr. Bowen. These gentlemen gave the napery a general overhauling and made many remarks to each other in connection with it. Mrs. Bowen, who was a friend of Mrs. Borden, simply gave the spread sanctimonious little pats.

Marshal Hilliard, like most of the other witnesses, had to wrestle with the question of Lizzie's attire on the day of the tragedy. He did not distinguish himself as much as Mr. Doherty in his description of details.

While the marshal was being sharply questioned, a short gentleman with a heavy beard and pleasant face came into the room. As soon as he was seen by Attorney Adams he was securely buttonholed and escorted to the safety of the judge's room. The stranger was Dr. Draper, medical examiner of Suffolk county. People wondered what this conference of medical examiner and attorney could be over, but could tell nothing from the face of Mr Adams, which as always was composed and attentive on his return to court.

Mr. Knowlton's methods in a court room are so well known they scarcely will warrant description. His "delicious drawl" and disinterested expression have frequently been referred to in this case. There was one time yesterday when he not only seemed but was very much alive, and that was when cross-examining the hack-driver John Donnelly. This witness was so thoroughly "queered" by the district attorney that he left the stand with as much confusion as though he had been rolled down hill in a barrel.

The wife of Dr. Chagnon, a very Frenchy little French woman, created considerable amusement while on the stand. Madame is a rather pretty little woman. She was dressed in a very fetching walking hat with a Tyrolean crown and some nodding wheat in front, with a wonderful silk and lace arrangement in front. She spoke English with comparative ease, but with an accent which rivalled Rhea's for sweetness and grace. Her testimony contained much that was not necessary, but highly interesting. She seemed anxious that the district attorney should understand that they were having some piano music at her house when the alleged bold, bad man jumped over her back yard fence, and the family fete had to be postponed, everybody was so frightened. Several times she laughed outright, much to the disgust of the court officer and the amusement of Judge Blaisdell. As she had only partially mastered the English tongue she said a description of the Chagnon dog would be impossible without an interpreter. But Mr. Knowlton is prejudiced against these middle men, and with considerable tact coaxed his fair witness into saying that the animal was midway between St. Bernard and a greyhound, and that he was old and very lazy and not easily disturbed by men getting over the back fence, all of which things were very funny to Madame Chagnon and brought a smile on the face of "the court."

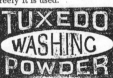

PRODUCTION OF THE BIOOD-STAINED SHAMS AND SHEETS IN COURT.

Martha Chagnon, madame's daughter and the girl who played the piano the night before the murder, testified after her mother. She was pretty enough to create a sensation when she mounted the stand. She wore a cherry-red hat trimmed with a profusion of red bows and rosettes, the color harmonizing with the rouge on her cheeks. A red veil concealed and yet revealed her features. She had a very, very sweet smile, with which she occasionally favored the district attorney. Her gown was a soft gray cashmere, with white silk drapery, as artful as a Delsartean robe.

With all Mr. Knowlton's chivalry he could not understand how a would-be murderer could be five minutes in jumping over a fence, as stated by Miss Chagnon, and on this point he asked so many questions that the witness became confused and a most enhancing blush that was real sported across her neck.

The hearing has very perceptibly told upon the prisoner. She has not so much color as on last Thursday morning, and there are deep lines across her cheeks which were not visible then. Whether she eats well or sleeps well, or how she employs herself when not in court, are questions which her guardians will not answer, but that she is far from happy is very evident. Though she is so undemonstrative as the days go by, public sympathy seems to broaden for the woman, even though evidences apparently against her accumulate. And, indeed, she presents a pitiful spectacle whether one believes her guilty or not, to many a spectacle quite as sad as though she were in tears. Yesterday must have been a trying day for her. She kept her eyes from the stand when Marshal Hilliard and especially her friend, Mrs. Bowen, were testifying. When the spread and shams were displayed she bowed her head on her hand and remained in that position some time. When she raised her eyes they were tearful, but her face wore a stolid expression. In one other thing she is changed. No longer the staring crowd appear to annoy her. She is apparently indifferent, almost unconscious of any one.

THE PICNIC AT PINE ISLAND.

To the Editor of the Standard:

Despite the unfavorable outlook and the unaccommodating attitude of the weather bureau, yesterday, the Universalists started upon their picnic to Pine Island. Both churches at Marion and Mattapoisett sent goodly barge loads to swell the number that came in private conveyances until the grove contained 140 bundles of picnicking humanity, each bundle intent upon obtaining in the least portion of time the greatest amount of enjoyment.

The pastor and a few from each society had their hands full with the duty, self-appointed though it was, of making all acquainted and of causing even those who at first had a tendency to sit like "little Miss Muffit, alone on a tuffet," to share the seat with a friend from the sister society.

As in all picnics there was an inclination among the "old" ladies, (pardon the remark, for no one is "old" at a picnic,) to sit upon a long seat by themselves, but upon being informed that the especial one upon which they were seated was to be called the "Old Women's Retreat," it was noticed that it was almost like drawing teeth to find any one to occupy it a few minutes later.

Tables were erected, swings fixed safely in the trees and hammocks swung, while those with more mathematical eyes gazed from stake to stake of the croquet set and superintended the placing of the middle wicket, through which hoop the balls, white and red, and green and yellow and black, soon began to wend their way. Rules were thrown to the winds, and if the black mallet was wielded by a bigger boy he went first, and if he was very much bigger took two turns to his opponents' one.

But when dinner was announced what a commotion there was! Hammocks stopped, mallets were dropped, and those who were in the swings, not even waiting to "let the old cat die," sprang out and made an assault upon the heavily laden table, that was braver, more headlong and fearless than that at Balaklava. Certainly there were bottles to right of them and bottles to left of them, although by their sallow complexion, it could readily be seen they were innocent of anything stronger than coffee and milk. A large jug standing beneath a lofty pine, was, however, of a more suspicious appearance, and many bent their eyes upon it with a questioning gaze, until a committee boldly approached it, and from its mouth, sparkling as it fell upon the brown pine needles below, issued forth a refreshing flow of cool Pine Island spring water, and having thus removed all seeming stains from its escutcheon, the old jug, with a last satisfying gurgle, settled back in its place, and awaited the coming of the next thirsty picnicker.

Soon all were too busily engaged to think of talking, and even the wanderer on his bicycle was welcomed to this feast "fit for the gods." The men straggled in and once more exemplified the truth of the lines in Lord Lytton's "Lucile":

"We may live without poetry, music, and art;
We may live without conscience and live without heart;
We may live without friends, we may live without books,
But civilized man cannot live without cooks."

"He may live without books,—what is knowledge but grieving?
He may live without hope,—what is hope but deceiving?
He may live without love,—what is passion but pining?
But civilized man cannot live without dining."

With a sigh of relief, (and in many cases a doughnut in either hand,) all now arose from the feast, but not to rest. Indeed there seemed to be "no rest for the weary," for soon games were started, and the grove rung again and again with the laughs of both players and audience, the latter now sitting upon the boards that had just served as a table, thinking perhaps of the days when the back could be more quickly bent and the feet touched more lightly on the sward. And some dear old, no, young souls spoke of the faces that had once beamed with joy near their own, but were now smiling only from above.

And now a stick has been cut over which the boys jump in quick succession, raised higher and higher at each trial until soon only one is left, and finally even the "lad in the brown suit" is obliged to cease his efforts. The large boys now try their hand at the sport, or to speak more correctly their feet, and at last even the "shepherd of the flock" is seen to start, leave dignity behind and land safely on the other side.

The boys depart to a neighboring field for a game of ball, but not alone, for peering through the trees you see each base guarded by a girl, who stands upon it as though it was the most important thing in the world that she depart not a foot from it, not even being enticed from her position by a "grounder" or a "fly," which technical terms she learns with the same ease displayed in telling whether a vessel is a ship, a schooner or a sloop.

The girls throng the woods, digging here and there in search of "Indian pipes," sassafras and checkerberry.

Singing? Yes, of course there was singing. And how natural it did all seem to sit there in God's own temple and join in those grand old songs, known everywhere where the church of God is known, and always beautiful and sweet.

And now the barges arrive and all depart to their various homes,—Pine Island and Marion and Mattapoisett all uniting in voting the day a great success.

And thus they are lost to sight down the different roads, tired and happy and better for having been "touched by the heart of Nature" for this one day.

"Good bye, folks," calls the parson, and the picnic is a thing of the past.

UNPRECEDENTED SCARCITY OF MENHADEN.—The supply of menhaden this season all along the coast north of the Capes of Delaware has been so scarce as to amount practically to a fish famine. William J. Brightman & Co., who have fish oil works at Tiverton, R. I., and a drying establishment at Cole's river, and who own three steamers and employ from 70 to 80 men during the season, have taken but 2000 barrels thus far this year. These were taken by steamer Seaconnet in one day early in April in four sets. The steamer quickly unloaded and hastened to the scene of capture south of Point Judith, but the school had disappeared, and since then the company has secured but 50 barrels of fish, which were taken last week. All the steamers are tied up and but two or three men are employed, and these as watchmen. Daniel Church, who runs four steamers and employs from 125 to 150 men, has all his vessels at the wharves. The fish make what are known as two runs, the first beginning early in April and the last about the first of August. It is now time that they should appear in the fall run, if at all, but the season has so far advanced that about all hope of getting a catch has been abandoned. The fall run usually lasts until the first frost, which drives the fish steadily southward, whither they are followed by the fishermen as far as the Chesapeake, beyond which it is not profitable to pursue them. The Maine fishing has been much the same as that in these waters, but more were found in Delaware Bay. As their transportation in a vessel's hold in Summer such a long distance renders them valueless for oil, the Rhode Island fishermen have not sought them in Southern waters. The scarcity is believed to be unprecedented. During many preceding seasons there have been months when no fish were taken, but there has been no previous year in the memory of the oldest fisherman when menhaden fishing could not be profitably carried on in some portion of the waters between Eastport and Long Island Sound. A fisherman of 25 years' experience attributes the present scarcity to the early arrival of bluefish, which voraciously attack the menhaden, and which, he alleges, drove the fish back into Southern waters.

PRESENTATION.—James Smith of East Bridgewater has made and presented to Judge B. W. Harris a cane made from the wood of the English frigate Somerset, which was stranded at Provincetown during the revolutionary war while trying to escape capture by a french man of war. The Somerset was buried from sight by the ever shifting sands for more than 50 years, having lain there for more than a hundred years. During the Winter of '85 and '86 the high course of tides so cut the beach away as to expose portions of her timber which were secured. This vessel took part in the bombardment of Charlestown during the revolutionary war.

STEAMBOAT FOR SEALING.—Capt. Buddington of sealing schooner Sarah W. Hunt of Stonington, now at West Mystic, has purchased a small steamboat, which he will take with him on his next voyage. She will be stowed away on the deck and used in the sealing country to run into shallow rivers and bays where seals are to be found and where the larger boats cannot go in. The Sarah Hunt has made several large fortunes in her different voyages, and Capt. Buddington with his new equipment expects to make this voyage as profitable as the last if not more so.

POLITICAL.—Bourne last evening elected a Randall delegate to the Congressional convention, giving Mr. Randall 35 delegates to Mr. Greene's 28.

At the meeting of the Republican committees of the towns of Marion and Rochester on Wednesday it was decided that the district should be represented in the Legislature this year by a Rochester man. Doubtless the caucus next Saturday evening will be fully attended. Capt. John G. Dexter is a candidate for the nomination.

Knowles &Co.

Cor. UNION & FOURTH STS.

Bargains in All-Wool Dress Goods, 40-inch all-wool goods, suitable for early Fall wear, 39c. Cheap at 50c.

Storm Serges in Black and Navy, all-wool, 40-inch, 50c.; 46-inch 75c.; 46-inch extra value, $1.00.

Black All-Wool Henriettas, 46-inch, 75c.; extra fine and heavy, $1.00 and $1.25; 46-inch, All-Wool, India Twill, 75c. and $1.00.

Beautiful styles in Ginghams at 10 and 12 1-2c. Large assortment to select from.

Ladies' full regular finished, Fast Black Hose, the best hose in the market for 25c. Also Ladies' Fast Black Hose, worth 50c. Three pairs in a box $1.00.

Ladies' Summer weight merino vests and pants 50c. each.

Gentlemen's Summer weight merino shirts and drawers 50c.

Gentlemen's unlaundered shirts, reinforced linen fronts and cuffs, double backs, good cotton, best shirt in the market, 50c.

Ladies' corset covers at 12 1-2, 25, 37 1-2 and 50c., in high, low, square and V shaped necks, handsomely trimmed, and decided bargains.

Ladies' and misses' night gowns, made of good materials and elegantly trimmed, at 50, 65, and 88c., $1, $1.25 and up.

Ladies' corsets, in all the popular makes, at from 49c. up to the very finest goods.

Best Germantown yarns, large full skeins, in 150 shades and colors, at only 12 1-2c. a skein.

Stamped Linens, Trays, Tidies, Splashers, Pillow Shams, Scarfs, all at popular low prices.

All kinds of embroidery and fancy working silk cheap. Knitting silk of best quality, large assortment of colors and shades at 30c. a ball. Best sewing silk in black and colors, 8c.

Table Linens, Brown and Bleached at 45c. worth 59c. Napkins at 50 and 75c, $1.00, $1.25, $1.50 and $2.00 per dozen. Towels at 12 1-2c., 19c., 25c., 37c., and 50c. up.

Lot of standard white ground prints, 5c. a yard. When out shopping don't fail to visit our store for we have just what you are looking for, and at lowest possible prices.

Knowles &Co.

PINKERTONS AS UNION MEN.

How They Discovered Inside Doings of the Amalgamated Association.

PITTSBURG, Sept. 1.—John Wippel and John Nebon were arrested in Homestead yesterday and brought to Pittsburg, charged by the Carnegie company with riot. Together with T. F. Gibson, previously held on the same charge, they were given a hearing before Alderman McMasters. R. H. Tyler and Joseph Knippe, Pinkerton detectives, were placed on the witness stand and caused consternation to the defense by producing their working cards, issued to them by the Duquesne lodge of the Amalgamated association, into which they had been initiated a short time before the strike. The cards gave them entrance to all gatherings of the workingmen. The Pinkertons testified that a short time before the riots at Duquesne, they had attended a meeting, at which a resolution, warmly supported by the defendants, was presented. It provided that the men organize themselves in squads, guard the mill, so that no one should be allowed to enter, and to keep out non-union men. Wippel and Nebon were sent back to jail, but Gibson furnished the necessary bail for court.

PECK AGAIN CHOSEN

As the Gubernatorial Standard Bearer for Democrats of Wisconsin.

MILWAUKEE, Sept. 1.—Governor Peck and the entire state ticket has been renominated by acclamation.

Governor Peck and all the others on the ticket made speeches. The platform is devoted chiefly to state issues, setting forth the fulfilment of the party pledges in repealing the Bennett school law, and in bringing suits against former state treasurers for repayment of interest on state funds. The platform opposes the doctrine of centralization and paternalism and all mischevious meddling with the rights of conscience and religion, and especially in the care and education of children; opposes sumptuary laws, and endorses the national ticket and platform.

Victim of a Brutal Husband.

BRIDGEPORT, Conn., Sept. 1.—Mrs. William Connor, residing on Humboldt street, this city, is thought to be in a dying condition as a result of a frightful beating inflicted by her husband yesterday. Connor was not satisfied with the breakfast his wife had prepared for him, and began abusing her. He finally threw her on the floor and repeatedly jumped on her abdomen. He is under arrest.

A New Scourge.

VIENNA, Sept. 1.—A frightful disease, called the black pestilence, has appeared at Funfkirchen and Batazek, Hungary. Sixteen cases are thus far reported. The victims are covered with black boils, from which infectious matter is discharged. The disease is thought to be akin to the mysterious malady which accompanied the cholera in Persia.

Killed on a Railroad Crossing.

NEW HAVEN, Sept. 1.—Joseph F. Kilbride of Newtown was killed at the Housatonic crossing, east of Hawleyville, by an express train. He was 26 years of age and unmarried. His wagon was thrown 100 feet.

Alleged Dynamiters May Be Freed.

LONDON, Sept. 1.—Mr. Asquith, the home secretary, has consented to consider the question of the release of the Irish prisoners who were sentenced for connection with dynamite plots.

At Work Again.

HAVANA, Sept. 1.—Many of the cigar factories that were closed as a protest against the minister of the colonies' refusal to remove the excessive tax on them, have been reopened.

New England Postmasters.

WASHINGTON, Sept. 1.—Fourth class postmasters appointed: W. Wilson, at Ballouville, Conn., and Effie P. Lane, Lanesboro, Vt.

IN DEATH'S EMBRACE.

Awful Details of Cholera's Ravages at Hamburg.

Moravia's Passengers Had the True Eastern Scourge.

American Authorities Realize Gravity of the Situation.

HAMBURG, Sept. 1.—During the twenty-four hours ended at midnight, the ambulances conveyed to the hospital 508 cholera patients. Of this number 268 have since died. A fearful feeling of apprehension hangs over the whole city, and the belief that the doctors are helpless to fight the scourge grows in strength.

The representative of the Associated Press here has seen in the military drill shed the bodies of 400 victims awaiting burial. Owing to red tape it is impossible to bury all the dead under the usual regulations, for the law requires the production of papers of identification before the body is consigned to the grave. Under ordinary circumstances these papers are easily procureable, but now, when whole families have been carried off by the the scourge, the greatest difficulty is experienced in getting the papers.

Already it is believed that the infection has been spread by the dead. Bitter imprecations are heaped upon the authorities for their pig-headedness in letting the victims lie unburied to scatter the contagion among the living, while they hunted for papers to show the age, occupation, etc., of the dead persons. A reign of terror prevails, and every person who can possibly do so is fleeing the city.

The ordinary form of burial will soon have to be abandoned, and trenches filled with quicklime will have to be resorted to. In many parts of the city the shops of grocers, bakers and butchers have been closed by the police, the owners and their salesmen having been stricken down while attending to business.

UNCLE SAM WIDE AWAKE.

World's Fair May Be Postponed Unless the Disease Soon Dies Out.

WASHINGTON, Sept. 1.—The reported arrival of Asiatic cholera at the port of New York has brought to the front the question of suspending immigration to this country altogether during the prevalence of cholera in the eastern hemisphere. It is admitted that such a measure would be justified only by the most pressing danger, but this danger, in the opinion of some high officials, is at hand. Government officials are ransacking records and reading up on former scourges. Assistant Secretary Spaulding, who has immediate control of the matter, was deeply immersed in a history of the smallpox epidemic of 1885. He said: "All the machinery of the government is at work on this cholera business, and all the precautions taken in 1885 have already been taken by us."

Continuing, Mr. Spaulding said that under the existing quarantine laws such restrictions could be imposed that would practically suspend immigration, but he would not say that such action was immediately contemplated. An eminent law officer of the government, who has given the subject much thought, said that in his opinion the president had the power to suspend all immigration, if, in his judgment, he deemed it necessary for the public welfare, while the scourge lasted. This opinion is entertained by others.

Every day's news seems to add to the gravity of the situation and to suggest new and far-reaching consequences. The question of postponing the World's fair is now being discussed. It is pointed out by treasury officials that most of the exhibits will necessarily come from cholera-infected countries, and that the fair would consequently serve as a great propogation garden for the general dissemination of the disease. Then, too, it is urged that the practical removal of all the customary restrictions from importations of goods intended for the World's fair would make such importations doubly dangerous as disease-breeders. A postponement of the monetary conference on account of the cholera is also more than a possibility.

HAS CROSSED THE OCEAN.

Vessel Infected with Cholera Detained at New York Quarantine.

QUARANTINE, S. I., Sept 1.—The steamer Moravia of the Hamburg-American line, had twenty-two deaths during her passage, which the ship's surgeon called cholerine. The first death took place Aug. 19, and the last Aug. 29. Twenty were children and two adults. Thirteen were natives of Poland, three natives of Hesse, one Austrian, five Prussians. All were buried at sea. The steamer was immediately ordered into the lower bay. The steerage passengers were carefully inspected and all of them found quite well. There are three cases of measles on board. The Moravia left Hamburg on Aug. 18.

The health officers who made the inspection of the Moravir's passengers pronounce the cause of death in the stricken cases as true Asiatic cholera. All the emigrants in the ship were transferred to Hoffman's island. The vessel and baggage of the passengers have been undergoing disinfection by steam.

The Situation in London.

LONDON, Sept. 1.—Tories and Liberals unite in urging the government to prohibit immigration during the prevalence on the continent of cholera. Experts are now pretty unanimous in declaring that the present system of inspection and quarantine is sufficient to protect the country from any serious invasion of the disease. The cases already reported as having broken out in London and elsewhere in England crept in before the government had had time to perfect its plans.

Spreading in Brussels.

BRUSSELS, Sept. 1.—While the conditions as to cholera are said to be improving in Antwerp, the disease is evidently extending in Brussels. There have been two fatal cases in the suburbs of this city.

Rouen Has It.

ROUEN, Sept. 1.—Three cholera patients have been admitted to the city hospital since yesterday afternoon. One of them died.

Nobility Not Exempt.

BERLIN, Sept. 1.—The deaths from cholera is reported of the Baroness Sidfok and her daughter, at Platten See, Hungary.

Liverpool's Cases.

LIVERPOOL, Sept. 1.—One of the cholera patients here is dead and two others are in a critical condition.

A Bad Wreck.

BROOKLYN, Sept. 1.—Two heavily laden freight trains on the Long Island railroad crashed together at Fresh Pond. Two men were seriously injured and three others badly hurt. Thirteen cars were demolished and traffic was delayed over six hours.

Long Island City's Affliction.

LONG ISLAND CITY, N. Y., Sept. 1.—Smallpox is spreading in this city. Several new cases were reported to the board of health yesterday. There is no pest house here and the patients cannot be removed.

Highest of all in Leavening Power.—Latest U. S. Gov't Report.

Royal Baking Powder

ABSOLUTELY PURE

PLATFORM AND CANDIDATES

Which Will Be Supported by Connecticut Prohibitionists This Fall.

HARTFORD, Sept. 1.—The platform, as adopted by the state Prohibition convention, deplores the liquor traffic as the chief menace of the state and nation. High license can afford no relief. It gives incentive intrenchment and monopoly to the traffic. The public welfare requires the entire suppression of the beverage—traffic in manufacture, sale, transportation and importation. The American school system is unequivocally indorsed and appropriations for sectarian purposes denounced. The ballot to all, regardless of sex, and equal pay to the sexes for equal work, is advocated.

On the tariff question the platform favors protecting American interests by a return to "a tariff for revenue to defray the necessary expenses of the government, and discriminating with special reference to the protecting of the domestic labor of the country. To these ends we propose that the tariffs levied to protect manufacturers shall in no case exceed the difference in labor cost between this and competing countries; and we believe that the present industrial conditions are such that free raw material will promote the economic welfare of the whole people. The residue of means necessary to an economical administration of the government should be raised by levying a burden on what the people possess, instead of what we consume."

Arbitration is favored to settle labor strikes. Stringent laws for the protection of the dairy interests of the state are favored. The election of the president and senators by direct vote of the people is favored.

After the adoption of the platform, the following ticket was nominated: Governor, Edwin P. Auger of Middletown; lieutenant governor, A. M. Bancroft of Ellington; secretary of state, Henry R. Palmer of Stonington; treasurer, Watson N. Hurlburt, Waterbury; comptroller, Eliakim E. Wildman, Danbury. All the nominations were by acclamation, except that of Mr. Hurlburt. William F. Dann of New Haven was placed in nomination against him, and a ballot was taken. Hurlburt received 110 votes to 41 for Dann. The electors were then chosen, and, after a few speeches, the convention adjourned sine die.

ATTACKED BY A MAD COW.

Premier Gladstone Has a Narrow Escape from Death at His Hawarden Home.

LONDON, Sept. 1.—A dispatch from Hawarden states that Mr. Gladstone had a narrow escape from being killed yesterday by an infuriated cow. The animal had been deprived of its calf. Mr. Gladstone was taking a walk about his estate when the cow made an impetuous rush at him. Mr. Gladstone stood his ground, hoping that it would go to one side. The cow dashed madly forward and knocked Mr. Gladstone down, trampling upon him, and endeavoring to gore him with its horns, which, fortunately, were not fitted to do as much injury as its feet. Others rushed to Mr. Gladstone's assistance and drove off the cow, which otherwise might have made a fatal ending to the attack. Mr. Gladstone was found to be not badly hurt, although much shaken and somewhat bruised by his encounter with the vicious brute. It appeared that the cow had gone entirely mad shortly before the attack. She was afterwards killed.

A WESTERN SENSATION.

Double Murder Said to Have Been Plotted by the Farmers' Alliance.

KANSAS CITY, Sept. 1.—Two years ago the whole southwestern country was startled by the brutal double murder of Frazier and Gibson, two of the most prominent cattle owners of Chautauqua county, Kan. The mystery of their deaths is now in a fair way of being solved, and the arrest at Sedan, Kan., of Jerry Hutton and Frank Kimsey, two prominent farmers of the county, is but the beginning of what is said to be one of the most sensational pieces of news that Kansas has ever known. These men are prominent in the alliance, and it is charged that the murders of Gibson and Frazier were plotted at a secret meeting held by members of that organization at the close of one of their regular meetings. Twelve more arrests will be made within a few days, and the whole country is excited over the developments in the case.

Was After a Reward.

ROCHESTER, Pa., Sept. 1.—George W. Adams, the man who claims to have saved the westbound New York and Chicago limited from being wrecked, near Enon, on the night of Aug. 26 last, by removing a pile of ties from the track, has confessed to having himself placed the ties upon the track as part of a scheme for obtaining a reward from the company. Adams, a few moments before the train was due, removed the obstruction, fired a bullet through his hat and another through his leg.

Day Was Unpleasant.

WORCESTER, Mass., Sept. 1.—Grange day of the New England fair was not a pleasant one. Rain began to fall at noon and kept down the crowds. There were 5000 people present.

CASES OF INSANITY

From the Effects of

"LA GRIPPE"

Are Alarmingly Prevalent.

Suicides

From the

SAME CAUSE

Are announced in every paper.

Would you be rid of the awful effects of La Grippe?

There is BUT ONE SURE REMEDY that NEVER FAILS, viz:

DANA'S SARSAPARILLA.

We Guarantee to CURE you or REFUND your money.

COULD WE DO MORE?

ISN'T IT WORTH A TRIAL?

je25-tf

WAITING FOR HILL.

The Senator May Explain Something About Commissioner Peck's Report.

NEW YORK, Sept. 1.—The Democratic state headquarters were formally opened yesterday. Chairman Sheehan of the campaign committee was seen there. To a reporter of the United Press he said: "I have nothing special to give out just at present, except that I shall at once take up the work of the campaign, and will remain here from the present time until the election in this city."

State Treasurer Danforth, in an interview with the reporter in regard to the famous report of Commissioner Peck, on the effects of the McKinley bill on the rate of wages, etc., said: "I do not think that Senator Hill knew anything about the intention to give out the report. I had a private conference with the senator the night before last on the subject, and he seemed very indignant that it happened as it did. I believe Senator Hill will make a very definite statement on the subject as soon as he arrives in the city.

"The people all over the state are very anxious to get the full particulars about the report, and it is certainly a matter of great interest to know if the McKinley bill has really increased wages. I now understand that Mr. Peck proposes to publish the full reports, but I do not know when this will be done." In conclusion, Mr. Danforth said: "I regret very much that the incident should have occurred."

Mr. Hill is expected to arrive in town at any moment.

MRS. LOGAN'S $1,000,000 FUND.

How She Proposes to Raise It for Women at the Washington University.

WASHINGTON, Sept. 1.—Mrs. John A. Logan defines her plans with regard to raising a fund of $1,000,000 for the American university as follows: "We propose to organize a national society, which will be under the control of a national president and vice presidents, who will represent every state and territory in the Union. These vice presidents will be vested with power to organize state leagues and to use the limits of each congressional district as their boundaries.

"All these sub-leagues are to hold meetings of a literary and social nature twice a month, at which the features of the plan will be thoroughly discussed and subscriptions received. Each sub-league will have a president, vice president, secretary and treasurer. They will report to their state leagues, who in turn will turn over all their funds to the national society, who has the power to receipt for the same. All the members of the league will be urged to solicit large subscriptions and endowments.

"The special provision made by the league is that all the money it collects shall be used exclusively for the women's branch of the university, and with the distinct understanding that men and women shall be recognized in it on precisely the same footing, either as professors or students, where women shall be found competent to fill the same positions."

"WILL DIE AS A MARTYR."

A Dangerous Crank Announces That He Will Kill Homestead Mill Managers.

DENVER, Sept. 1.—"I will get Carnegie, Frick and Lovejoy together and send them to the devil." The above is an extract from an anonymous letter which was received by the editor of The Times. It is decorated with the conventional head and crossbones, and reads like the raving of a demented brain, as follows:

I have read about that Secretary Lovejoy, belonging to Carnegie and Frick, hounding and persecuting continually those poor Homestead men, and I cannot bear it longer. My blood is all on fire and boiling worse than hell and damnation. I have fully made up my mind to kill old Frick, Lovejoy and Carnegie. Old Carnegie is sneaking away in Scotland until the excitement is over, and then will come back to Homestead. But I will get the three of them all together and send the trio to the devil. I am a cool-headed man and will carry out my plans to perfection. They won't have a chance to punish me, because I will quickly dispatch myself and die as a martyr. Sic semper tyrannis!

NINE PERSONS PERISHED.

Lumber Schooner Driven Ashore in a Gale on Lake Michigan.

MANISTEE, Mich., Sept 1.—The schooner City of Toledo, belonging to the Manistee Lumber company, cleared from this port Tuesday noon with a cargo of lumber. She was caught in the northwesterly gale and driven on the beach at Pierport, eighteen miles north of here. She turned completely over in a few minutes and all hands on board were lost. She was commanded by Captain John McMillan of this city. His two eldest daughters were on board with him. The crew consisted of six men. There was a heavy sea when the boat went out, so much that the crew had to take to the rigging. Three hours afterward she was sighted with her flag at half mast, making for the beach. The vessel now lies bottom up about fifty rods north of Pierport.

A Victory for Afghans.

LONDON, Sept. 1.—The forces of the Ameer of Afghanistan have won an important success over the Hazaras. The latter, after a severe conflict, in which 460 of the Afghan troops were killed, were compelled to evacuate Kamsan, which place was at once occupied by the Afghans. Much discontent prevails among the ameer's troops, owing to lack of supplies, and many are deserting.

Bad Men in Custody.

SOMERSET, Ky., Sept. 1.—A sheriff's posse came across members of the Foster gang near Steubenville. They were ordered to surrender, but refused. The sheriff's posse opened fire, killing one of the Foster boys and wounding Charles Denny. Two of the gang were captured.

Tough Characters Held for Trial.

WORCESTER, Mass., Sept. 1.—Edward D. Leslie and John Jones were held in $5000 each, for an assault with intent to kill Patrolman Romanzo Thayer, on midnight of Aug. 1.

Canada Choked Off.

WASHINGTON, Sept. 1.—The treasury department is fully prepared to carry out the Canadian retaliation proclamation of the president, which went into effect today. Collectors of customs promptly at 12 o'clock last night begun the enforcement of the law.

Hanlan Defeats the Australian.

TORONTO, Sept. 1.—The two-mile sculling match between Edward Hanlan and Charles Stephenson, champion of New Zealand, was won by Hanlan by two lengths.

From Yesterday's Third Edition.

THIRD DISTRICT COURT.

BORDEN, J.

WEDNESDAY AFTERNOON, Aug. 31.

Court came in at quarter of 3 o'clock and resumed the trial of the "goat case."

Adolph Dufresne, the father of Peter, said his son was with him all the evening of the 24th, the day the goat was stolen. He worked for him all day, and went home with him that night about half-past nine. He said the Desgangue boy was a bad boy and had the reputation of telling lies.

Dufresne was adjudged guilty. At the request of their parents each boy was fined $10, and they are to have a further trial, on their promise to behave in future.

The case against Frank Veara was disposed of by his giving his wife an order on their son for $100, which she was willing to accept, and the complaint was nol-prossed.

A case against James A. Wiley for stubbornness was further continued to Sept. 7th next, when he will be sentenced.

An old case against a Westport boy for breaking and entering and larceny was laid on file. One against Charles Cole for stubbornness was also laid on file, and a case of larceny against Frederick L. Avery was nol-prossed. Avery has been sentenced on another case.

NATURALIZATION.—Francis Morrison filed a primary declaration in the District Court today. William H. Johnson, Esq., for petitioner.

SEIZED BY RUSSIAN WARSHIP.

American and British Sealers' Crews Suffer Indignities.

VICTORIA, B. C., Aug. 31.—The American Bark Majestic from Petropaulovski reached here last evening, having aboard the captains and crews of the four sealing schooners Rosie, Olsen, Ariel and Willie McGowan flying the British flag and the American schooner C. H. White of San Francisco. They were sealing 40 miles off Copper Islands during the latter part of July, when the Russian warship Zeabraki, mounting 16 guns, and the Fur Company's steamer Kodiac bearing the governor of Bering's Island, rounded them up one by one, sent the schooners to be sold at Petropaulovski, and made the captain and crew prisoners. The former objected to the seizure, claiming they were free men on free waters, whereupon the marines pricked them with the points of their bayonets and informed them there was such a place as Siberia for those who spoke too loudly of freedom.

Both the British and American skippers recognized that it was no time for talking. Still they ventured to protest that they were outside the three-mile limit and were met with the information by the officers of the Zeabraki that "Russia is sovereign over the water a thousand miles from her shores."

The captain of the Russian cruiser braced his action on the ground that Russia exercised jurisdiction over all land and water westward of the line of demarkation. After being taken aboard the Zeabraki, the master of each vessel was ordered to sign a paper written in Russian and explained by the interpreter on an acknowledgment that he had been sealing in Russian waters. The skippers protested, and were told that those who did not sign would be sent to the mines. Under compulsion the papers were signed. They were then placed in a hut 11 by 11 feet, with a leaky roof and a broken floor. The men were finally placed out on the beach. The Majestic going away, a contract was entered into for transportation to American or British soil, and in the evening the prisoners were shipped away on board, no effort being made by the guards to detain them. The Majestic sailed at night, and next morning the Zeabraki started out on another hunting cruise.

POLICE STOPPED THE FIGHT.

How the Costello-Greggains Battle in San Francisco Was Drawn.

SAN FRANCISCO, Aug. 31.—In the Costello-Greggains fight last night there was little accomplished between the 32d and the 38th round. In the 39th the spectators urged the men to go in and fight. They made a show of doing so, but not until the 41st round, when Greggains pinned Costello in a corner with a left-hander, was anything done. In the 42d round a left-hander in Costello's face, a clinch and a right-hander from Costello on Greggains' neck as the latter broke away, marked this round.

In the 44th round the referee cautioned the men before the round opened and they made another effort, Greggains sending Costello half way across the ring with a left-hander. The latter fell near the rope. Costello dodged about the ring, followed by Greggains who jabbed him with his left and made a vicious pass with his right but failed to land. Costello scored some left-handers on the chest. About a dozen blows, none of them effective, were struck from the 47th to the 50th round. In the 50th Greggains landed a straight lefthander on the chin, getting Costello's right on the ear. Greggains rushed and Costello dropped. Greggains landed two stiff left drives and countered with force with his right. The police interfered at the end of the round and the referee decided the contest a draw.

PRESIDENT AT OPHIR FARM.

Ex-Senator Platt Cordially Greeted Upon His Arrival.

WHITE PLAINS, N. Y., Aug. 31.—President Harrison, accompanied by Chairman Carter and Russell Harrison, arrived at 10 40 a. m. and were met by Whitelaw Reid. There was a large crowd to witness the President's arrival, and he bowed in response to the cheers as he walked from the train to the carriage in waiting which was to convey him to Ophir Farm, Mr. Reid's country seat.

At 11 30 ex-Senator Platt arrived here with Mr. J. E. Milholland. They were taken to Ophir Farms, where they were received by Whitelaw Reid and D. O. Mills. Mr. Platt was ushered to the presence of President Harrison, who gave him a very cordial greeting.

FROM SEATTLE TO CHICAGO.

John Howard and His Wife Tramp the Journey and Get Their Wager.

CHICAGO, Aug. 31.—John Howard and his wife Lou of San Francisco, who started from Seattle on March 10th last on a tramp for Chicago for a $5000 purse, have arrived here, having 16 days to spare, their time limit ending Sept. 15th. Both looked emaciated when they reached the city, he having lost 40 pounds and his wife 22 1-2. Howard wore out seven pairs of shoes on the trip. They have walked 3700 miles and have wheeled a barrow with 100 pounds of camping outfit the entire distance. A check for the $5000 was handed Howard on his arrival.

WET DOWN AND WELL SMOKED.

Fire in Jones' Block in Taunton Causes Small Loss.

TAUNTON, Aug. 31.—Fire in Jones' block this morning gutted J. W. Sharkey's job printing office. Badeau, jewelry, Lawlor Bros., cigar makers, Jones, tobacco and pool room and W. M. & M. G. Smith, furniture store were wet down and well smoked. Losses all small; covered by insurance.

Mr. Goelet Will Not Serve.

NEW YORK, Aug. 31.—Robert Goelet, who was elected director of the New England railroad, states that his name was used without his authority and that he does not intend to serve. The belief prevails on the stock exchange that the traders arranged the entire matter in order to help them in a move to squeeze the shorts on the stock.

Campbell is the Tennis Champion.

NEWPORT, R. I., Aug. 31.—This was the last day of the tennis tournament, whose issue should determine the championship for another year. Promptly at 11 o'clock Joe Clark took the umpire's seat, and Campbell opened play with the service. The match went to Campbell, making him champion another year, making three consecutive years which he has held it.

EVIDENCE ALL IN.

Witnesses Finish Their Stories in Lizzie's Defence.

Strange Man Seen in the Borden Gateway.

Noise Frightened Neighbors the Night Before the Murder.

Sounded as if Some One Jumped Over the Fence.

Morse Modifies His Statement About Cellar Door.

Spring Lock Did Not Make Front Entrance Secure.

Hay in Barn Looked as Though it Had Been Lain In.

Arguments in the Great Case to be Made To-Morrow.

[Special Dispatch.]

FALL RIVER, Aug. 31.—In cross-examination Dr. Handy said: It was to my cottage in Marion that Miss Lizzie intended to go. I went to Marion on Friday. I cannot tell what there was in the appearance of the man to attract my attention. I saw him between 10 20 and 10 40 in the morning in front of Dr. Kelley's house. I was driving at the time. I saw no difference in his appearance in the two times I saw him. I did not observe the man very closely the first time I saw him. I am aware that efforts have been made by the police to find the man. At the time I saw him he was standing on the sidewalk acting very peculiar, and turned around several times.

Dress Pattern Seen.

District Attorney Knowlton said that he had seen the dress pattern about which he had questioned several witnesses. He told the court that he had examined it carefully and if it had been considered as in the case before could now be considered as out of it.

Saw a Man at Borden's Gate.

Mrs. Delia S. Manley testified. I was at the Borden house on the day of the murder; I saw a man on the premises that day; he was at the north gate; I was on the same side of the street as the Borden house; I was talking with a man in a carriage; the man I saw standing in the gateway was not Mr. Morse; he was a man about 35. He was leaning against the south gate post. I left him standing there when I came away down Second street. I cannot describe him. I cannot tell what clothes he had on. I do not think he had on black clothes. I never saw him before. This was about quarter or ten minutes of 10.

Cross-examined. There were four people in sight of the man I saw in the gateway. I do not know if they saw the man.

Heard a Strange Noise.

Mrs. Mary Ann Chagnon testified: I am the wife of Dr. Chagnon. I live on Third street. On the morning of the murder I went away at nine minutes of 7 o'clock. The night before the murder, between 11 and 12 o'clock, my daughter and I were alone, and my daughter said, "Do you hear some noise?" I listened and heard the noise as if some one was jumping the fence at the back of my house. In consequence of the noise we were very much frightened. We did not want to go into the cellar afterwards. Our windows were opened, and those leading to the piazza are very low. There is no piazza in front of my house. There is concrete on the front. Lucy Collett, (who testified yesterday,) was sitting on a bench on the concrete. She could not see the Borden house from the position where she sat.

Cross-examined. There was a dog at my house on the night when we heard the noise outside. He is a big dog—a cross between a St. Bernard and a greyhound.

The Doctor's Pretty Daughter.

Martha Chagnon, a pretty girl with black hair and eyes and a cardinal hat and veil, testified it was about 11 o'clock on the night before the murder that she heard the sound as of some one jumping over the Borden fence. The noise continued about five minutes.

In cross-examination Martha said she should think the noise continued fully five minutes. It was a sort of a scraping noise and came from the rear of her house.

Places Sunken in the Hay.

Arthur Clarkson testified. I am a steam fitter. I was at Mr. Borden's house on the morning of the murder at 11 o'clock. I went into the upper story of the barn. I noticed hay in the loft, mostly on the north side. The hay in two or three places appeared to have sunken. In one place, north of the west window, it appeared as if some one had lain in the hay. There were three other people in the loft. They were there in the barn very soon after I got there. Officer Medley was one of these men.

Cross-examined. I saw Officer Allen at the house when I got to Borden's. Other officers came soon after. I saw no one else go up into the barn but those I have spoken of.

Morse Modifies His Statement.

John V. Morse was next called. He said that when he was on the stand before he testified in regard to finding the cellar door open. He now desired to modify that statement somewhat and to state that he told Mr. Holmes about the door. He told him about it shortly after the murder, a day or two later, he thought. When he told Mr. Holmes about it he pointed the door out to him.

Lizzie's Intimate Friend.

Mrs. Mary E. Brigham, was the next witness. I am an intimate friend of Lizzie and have been to the house very frequently. The front door was fastened by a spring lock and bolt. There is nothing about the spring lock to prevent it from locking the door when the door is shut. I made an experiment this noon to see if I could see a form in Mrs. Borden's room between the bed and the dressing case while I was on the way upstairs and I found that I could not.

In answer to a question by the district attorney she said that Mr. Morse assisted her in making the experiment.

No Blood on Lizzie.

Charles H. Sawyer was the next witness. He testified that he went upstairs with Officer Allen. When he first saw Miss Lizzie on the day of the murder she was sitting in a chair in the kitchen. I went within three feet of her, and where I could see her very plainly. I could see no signs of any blood upon her. Her hair was not disarranged and there was no blood upon her hands or face.

Rubbed the Hatchet Blade.

He testified in regard to the axes and hatchet. He had rubbed the blade of the hatchet and could see no signs of blood upon it. The only thing he noticed after he rubbed it was that the dried yellowish rust came from it in a powder form.

Lock Did Not Fasten the Door.

Jerome C. Borden testified: I am a lumber dealer. I went to A. J. Borden's house the day after the murder. The door was closed. I took hold of the knob and pushed it open. There was a spring lock, which did not prevent my getting in. The people in the house I think seemed surprised at my coming in as I did.

Thought Lizzie Was Dead.

Mrs. Bowen, wife of Dr. Bowen, testified: I have always known Emma Borden. Have known Lizzie only since she came to live on the street. I knew about Mrs. Borden being sick the day before the murder. I saw Lizzie go down the street just before 6 o'clock on Wednesday, before I went into Mr. Borden's on that evening. On Thursday I did not go over to Bordens' before Dr. Bowen went. He came back afterwards and told me Mr. Borden was dead. Soon after Bridget came and told me Lizzie wanted me. I went over to the house. Lizzie was leaning her head on Miss Russell's shoulder. I thought Lizzie was dead. Miss Russell was bathing her face. There was no blood on Lizzie's hands, face or dress. She had on a blouse waist of dark blue with spots. Her skirt was one of a morning dress I have often seen her wear. I did not go into the sitting-room. I soon went home and did not go back that day.

Cross-examination. It was about 5 minutes past 11 when I went over to Mr. Borden's. I was watching for my daughter and so noticed the time. I could see the Borden yard and saw no one go out or in.

Messrs. Knowlton and Jennings then had a short consultation with the judge, and the court announced an adjournment until 10 30 to-morrow, when arguments will be made and the case completed.

STARTLING.

This Has no Uncertain Sound.

What Does This Mean To Our People?

It Rings With a Great and Grand Hope.

Something Thousands are Seeking For.

A Fact of Marvellous Import to All.

NEWBURG, N. Y.—A telegraphic dispatch from Newburg, N. Y., reveals the fact that a most marvellous change has taken place in the person of one of its oldest and best known citizens. H. S. Shorter, Esq., is an old man of 75 years, and lives at 391 Broadway, Newburg, N. Y. It appears that Mr. Shorter, who was an extensive lumber dealer, began to grow languid, got tired easily, was nervous and debilitated, until at last he became so weak and exhausted that he was just able to drag himself around. He lost flesh and strength so rapidly and became so alarmingly prostrated that his friends and relatives despaired of his life.

Now came the marvellous change.

Suddenly Mr. Shorter was transformed from his condition of extreme weakness to one of strength; his nerves grew quickly strong and steady, his muscles became vigorous, his blood was revivified and and enriched, he gained 15 pounds in weight, and today is in sound and perfect health.

Such a remarkable transformation in a man of his age was a nine days' wonder.

Of course the cause was eagerly looked for.

Your correspondent, determined to know the truth for the paper's readers, listened to the following astonishing facts from Mr. Shorter's own lips:

"I feel now like a new man!

"What do you think of taking an old man of 75 years, physically weak and broken down, *and making him feel like a boy again!* Giving him new life, health and strength, and adding 15 pounds of solid flesh to his weak and debilitated frame!

"And all in two months, with three bottles of Dr. Greene's Nervura blood and nerve remedy! Well, that is just what has taken place in me. Instead of being weak, debilitated and exhausted, just able to drag myself around, I feel now like a new man!

"I advise all to use Dr. Greene's Nervura blood and nerve remedy!"

Surely this wonderful remedy is a most marvellous health restorer, and, without doubt, the greatest medical discovery of the age.

If it can thus give back health and strength to an old man, weakened and exhausted by disease, how much more surely and certainly will it cure the thousands who are run down, weak, nervous and prostrated, who suffer from poor blood, weak nerves, dyspepsia, indigestion, constipation, malaria, kidney and liver complaints, etc. For debility it is a speedy restorer of strength and vigor. If you are run down in health and need a medicine to strengthen the nerves, invigorate the blood, tone up the stomach and regulate the bowels, kidneys and liver, Dr. Greene's Nervura blood and nerve remedy, which is purely vegetable and harmless, and is the best remedy known in the world.

Use it, for it will restore your health and strength. You can get it at any druggists for $1.

It is the discovery and prescription of the well-known and successful physician, Dr. Greene of 34 Temple Pl., Boston, Mass., the eminent specialist in the cure of nervous and chronic diseases, who can be consulted free, personally or by letter.

LAGUAYRA CAPTURED.

Revolutionary Forces in Venezuela Secure an Important Post.

NEW YORK, Aug. 31.—A Trinidad, W. I., special to the *Herald* says: News has reached here that the revolutionary forces have captured Laguayra. Business is suspended in Caracas, owing to the great excitement due to recent stirring events. The foreign residences in the capital of Venezuela are in danger. The diplomatic corps in Caracas, with the exception of United States Minister Scruggs, have protested in a body against the destruction of foreign property in Puerto Cabilo.

EXECUTIVE COUNCIL.

John I. Baker Reappointed Harbor and Land Commissioner.

BOSTON, Aug. 31.—At the meeting of the executive council to-day Gov. Russell withdrew the name of David Scates, whom he had nominated for bank commissioner. The withdrawal was made at Mr. Scates' request.

John I. Baker of Beverly was reappointed harbor and land commissioner and was confirmed.

Business Troubles.

GLOUCESTER, Aug. 31.—A voluntary petition of insolvency has been filed by Fitz J. Babson, Jr., lumber merchant, Gloucester. His liabilities are $40,000. His assets consist of office furniture, book accounts and land in equity mortgaged for $5000. He makes a proposition of 15 cents on the dollar.

Small Pox in New York.

NEW YORK, Aug. 31.—Two cases of small pox were discovered here to-day.

The Evening Standard.

ESTABLISHED FEBRUARY, 1850.

NEW BEDFORD, FRIDAY, SEPTEMBER 2, 1892.

TWO CENTS.

HASKELL & TRIPP.

About shoes.

Shoes for girls and boys.

Shoes that have been selected for good wearing qualities.

Shoes that are shapely.

Shoes that are lower in price than equal grades will cost you elsewhere.

Here, for example, we name a few sorts:

Children's spring heel kid button boots, self tip, 50c. a pair.

Children's fine kid spring heel button boots, plain or patent tip, 75c. a pair.

"Little Trojan" grain, heel shoes, usually sold for $1.00. Our price 84c. a pair.

"Little Trojan" kid button boots, usually sold for $1.25. Our price 96c. a pair.

Misses' spring heel kid button boots, plain or cap toe. $1.00 a pair.

Youths' and Boys' veal calf button and lace shoes, solid counter and inner soles, oak tanned outer soles. Sizes 11 to 2 and 3 to 5½. Price $1.00. These are made specially for us and are the best wearing goods possible to obtain for the price. *By no means the ordinary dollar sort, sold everywhere.*

Misses' straight goat button boots, plain toe, solid throughout.

Sizes 8½ to 10½. Sizes 11 to 2.

Price $1.25. Price $1.40.

The best wearing school shoes that are made bear the following stamp on sole:

{ Haskell & Tripp's Solid Leather School Shoes. Warranted. }

Made of grain leather, calf tip, solid counter and inner soles, oak tanned outer soles. Every attention paid to details that will produce a shoe to stand any amount of hard service. They cannot be improved upon. They are sold this way:

Sizes 5½ to 8. Sizes 8½ to 10½.

Price 80c. Price 95c.

Sizes 11 to 2.

Price $1.17.

Children's and Misses' heavy Dongola button boots, slipper foxed, spring heels. Sizes 8 to 10½ for $1.00 a pair. Sizes 11 to 2 for $1.25 a pair.

Misses' straight goat, tipped, button boots, spring heels. Sizes 11 to 2 for $1.50 a pair.

Mundell's celebrated "Solar Tip," kid button boots for misses. Sizes 11 to 13½, $1.50 a pair. A very handsome, serviceable boot.

We sell only *honest* shoe leather.

No shoddy shoe leaves this store.

Even the low price goods possess merit.

No paper counters.

No pasteboard soles.

No flimsy uppers.

Shall we not sell *you* some shoes?

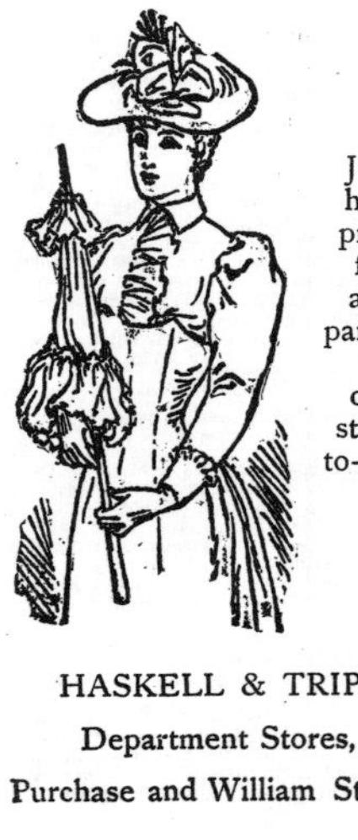

Just half price for any parasol in our stock to-day.

HASKELL & TRIPP.

Department Stores,

Purchase and William Streets.

PRESIDENT TAKES ACTION.

A Twenty-Days' Quarantine for Vessels Ordered.

Fresh Cholera Scare Breaks Out in New York.

Supposed Case of the Disease in a Crowded Tenement House.

QUARANTINE, N. Y., Sept. 2.—The situation remains unchanged. The steamship Island, of the Thingvalla line, has been passed by the doctor and will be allowed to go up this afternoon. She has no sickness on board and the emigrants—557 in number—are all Scandinavians and very clean.

Steamer City of Berlin brings 435 cabin and 658 steerage passengers. All well on board. The cabin passengers will be landed this afternoon.

The President Acts.

WASHINGTON, Sept. 2.—Following is the full text of a circular issued by the treasury department:

WASHINGTON, Sept. 1, 1892.

To collectors of customs, medical officers ot the marine hospital service, foreign steamship companies, state and local boards of health:

It having been officially declared that cholera is prevailing in various portions of Russia, Germany and France, and at certain ports in Great Britain, as well as in Asia; and it having been made to appear that immigrants in large numbers are coming into the United States from the infected districts aforesaid, and that they and their personal effects are liable to introduce cholera into the United States, and that vessels conveying them are thereby a direct menace to the public health; and it having been further shown that under the laws of the several states quarantine detention may be imposed upon these vessels a sufficient length of time to insure against the introduction of contagious diseases, it is hereby ordered that no vessel from any foreign port carrying immigrants shall be admitted to enter at any port of the United States until said vessels shall have undergone a quarantine detention of twenty days—unless such detention is forbidden by the laws of the state or the regulations made thereunder—and of such greater number of days as may be fixed in each special case by the state authorities.

This circular to take immediate effect, except in cases of vessels afloat at this date, which will be made the subject of special consideration upon due application to the department.

WALTER WYMAN,
Supervising Surgeon General, United States Marine Hospital Service.

CHARLES FOSTER, Secretary of the Treasury.
Approved, BENJAMIN HARRISON.

Speaking of the conference which preceded the issuance of this circular, and in which the postmaster general participated, Secretary Foster said:

"It is well for the public to know that state authorities and steamship companies are both acting in perfect accord and in hearty co-operation with the government, all being determined to exhaust their legal power to accomplish the prevention of the introduction of the dreaded disease. With everything we may do, except an absolute embargo of commerce, there is more or less danger, though remote, that it may creep in through seamen and otherwise. The postoffice department is cordially co-operating. From the moment that this department had knowledge of cholera in European ports, vigorous measures were taken to place a cordon of quarantine around the entire country. This department is gratified with the thoroughness with which the work has been done."

IS IT CHOLERA?

A New York Doctor Thinks He Has a Genuine Case in Hand.

NEW YORK, Sept. 2.—A suspected case of cholera has been discovered in the heart of the tenement house district on the east side. Shortly after 7 o'clock last night, Dr. Beck was summoned to the tenement 95 Orchard street. In a room on the fourth floor of the building he found a man lying on a sofa, suffering great agony. The man said that he felt pains in his bones, that his stomach ached him and that he vomited freely. Dr. Beck immediately became suspicious when he saw the case, and asked the man, who was a foreigner, his name and how long he had been in the country. The man replied that his name was Joseph Etuainiz, that he was 35 years old, and had arrived in this country on Sunday last by the steamship Russia by way of Hamburg. He said he was born in Russian Poland.

The doctor, after affording the patient some temporary relief, reported the case to the police, saying that the symptoms and the fact that the man only came to this country recently by way of Hamburg, led him to believe that the man was suffering from cholera. The police promptly notified the board of health, and an inspector was sent to the house.

The house is a five-story tenement, occupied by about twenty families. There are over 100 people living in the place. They became greatly alarmed when they heard that Etuainiz, who was living with his sister, was believed to be suffering from cholera, and many of them preferred to walk the streets rather than go to bed.

At the bureau of contagious diseases, those in charge declined to express any opinion in regard to the matter, saying that they were not at liberty to give out anything at present.

Deputy Health Officer Sanborn, who has been in charge of the Moravia since Wednesday, returned to quarantine last night and reported that there were no new developments.

Don't Get Frightened!

NEW YORK, Sept. 2.—The American Druggist gives some sound advice regarding the cholera scare. It says: A great many people are giving themselves unnecessary trouble about cholera. The disease is only formidable where inadequate means exist for grappling with it. Deficient and impure water supply is the primary cause of its origin in Asia. Dirt, ignorance and warm weather are the principal transmitters of the disease. While it may be well enough to quarantine the low class of immigrants that have been reaching us from the infected districts in Russia and Germany, or shut them out altogether for a time, there is no sense in people being panic stricken here. No person need fear the cholera if he exercises ordinary care in diet, cleanliness and sanitary surroundings.

No Place for Immigrants.

NEW YORK, Sept. 2.—The Inman line management has decided to carry only first cabin and second cabin passengers from Liverpool during the month of September.

Held at Detroit.

DETROIT, Sept. 2.—Detroit has one man in quarantine. He is Sylvester Kaminsky, who arrived from Hamburg yesterday. Inspector Corcoran found that Kaminsky had no certificate of inspection from New York, and as he came from an infected port, he was held to await developments.

Canadians Waked Up.

MONTREAL, Sept. 2.—The report that the United States government will put into effect a quarantine against the entire Dominion if cholera is allowed to pass Grosse Isle has had the effect of considerably awakening the authorities, who now express a determination to spare no expense to prevent the entry of the disease. The harbor authorities have decided to permit no vessel to enter the harbor without a clean bill of health be first submitted to the board of health for its supervision.

A Proper Proceeding.

PHILADELPHIA, Sept. 2.—The steamship Minnesota has been stopped from unloadby the deputy surveyor of the port, on account of having 119 bales of rags aboard from the cholera infected districts of Europe. The board of health has been notified.

THE SITUATION ABROAD.

No Danger in Liverpool.

LONDON, Sept. 2.—At a meeting of the health committee of the Liverpool municipality the medical officers reported that the emigrants who embarked yesterday were in excellent health, that the city of Liverpool was in the healthiest condition it had been for a long time past and that there was no reason to fear an epidemic. The passengers of the steamer Gemma, from Hamburg, have been released from quarantine at Gravesend.

Sanitary Regulations Ignored.

LONDON, Sept. 2.—There is both indignation and fright in Edinburgh over the fact that several Hamburg steamers have been allowed to discharge fruit and other cargo at Leith, the port of Edinburgh, although the sale of fruit is prohibited there, and that passengers arriving from Hamburg have been allowed to land at Leith almost without inspection as to their health.

A New Cure.

HAMBURG, Sept. 2.—Professor Northnagel and Professor Kahler have been giving cholera patients enemas of warm salt water. It is claimed by those who have followed this course of treatment that fully 50 per cent. of those treated in this way have recovered. Four hundred cholera victims were buried yesterday.

The Pestilence Decreasing.

ST. PETERSBURG, Sept. 2.—The official cholera returns for all Russia show a gratifying decrease in the ravages of the pestilence. The official statistics for St. Petersburg also show a decrease in both new cases and deaths.

How It Stands in Havre.

HAVRE, Sept. 2.—There were fifty-nine new cases of cholera in this city and nineteen deaths. The cholera has not spread to the quarters of the city in which the better classes live.

Emigrants' Luggage Fumigated.

QUEENSTOWN, Sept. 2.—The luggage of all emigrants, even of those from the healthiest parts of Ireland, is subjected to fumes of sulphuric acid in a sealed chamber, and is finally drenched with a solution of carbolic acid and certified to by the American consul here before being allowed to be taken aboard the Atlantic liners. On the other hand, the baggage of saloon passengers, even though they come from infected ports, is untouched by any disinfectant whatever.

Death Rate Doubled.

LONDON, Sept. 2.—The Moscow correspondent of the *Standard* says: "The heat has increased the fatalities of the cholera epidemic, and the death rate is now double what it was a week ago."

An Appeal to Nurses.

LONDON, Sept. 2.—Princess Christian, who is president of the Royal British Nurses' Association, writes to the papers a letter, in which she appeals to English nurses to enroll themselves for special cholera service.

Official Report from Hamburg.

HAMBURG, Sept. 2.—The official report of the total number of cases of cholera and deaths in this city since the first outbreak here shows that 3888 persons have been attacked by the disease and that death has resulted in 1728 cases.

Scheme to Escape Quarantine.

PARIS, Sept. 2.—Yesterday there were 15 cases of cholera and three deaths, a decrease of six new cases and seven deaths from Wednesday.

Considerable interest is manifested as to what would become of the Russian Jews who have been waiting for two weeks for the arrival of funds to permit of their proceeding to America. They were expelled from Odessa and travelled to Paris by way of Constantinople, under the direction of the Israelite Alliance. It was the intention to pack them off to the United States, but as the fact was that money was scarce among them and that quarantine was feared by the French steamers sailing for New York they found it impossible to proceed.

The difficulties in their way have now been removed and they started for Dieppe where they will go on board a vessel that will convey them to Canada. Their ultimate destination is the United States and their object in sailing for Canada is simply to escape the quarantine regulations at the various United States seaports. They expect to make a very short stay in Canada and then to proceed across the St. Lawrence into the United States.

Comment of a Medical Journal.

LONDON, Sept. 2.—The *Lancet*, the leading medical journal of England, says it believes the present state of affairs at some ports in the south of England is highly discreditable. Regarding the precautions taken to keep the cholera from obtaining a foothold in the country, the *Lancet* says: "No means of isolating the first attack by disease had been provided. If the present emergency passes, as we believe it will, we hope the few months interval will be utilized in preparing to combat the malady next year, which is likely to bring dangers in excess of any into which we are now running."

Ravages in Russia.

ST. PETERSBURG, Sept. 2.—The official returns for the empire Aug. 30th are as follows: New cases, 5273; deaths, 2722; being an increase over Aug. 29th of 414 new cases and 193 deaths. These figures, although official, are incomplete, as many of the smaller villages in which the disease exists are not heard from until too late to incorporate their returns in the official total.

It is not believed the scourge has spent its strength though false hopes are sometimes kindled by a marked falling off in the ravages of the epidemic. It is thought that before the disease dies out the total number of deaths throughout Russia will reach unparalleled figures. Estimates of the total reported places the number of cholera deaths at 150,000.

Canada Discussing Quarantine.

MONTREAL, Sept. 2.—The International Quarantine Inspection Commission held a conference with the health authorities and steamship representative yesterday regarding the precautions being taken to prevent the introduction of cholera into this country. The commissioners left for Quebec last night. They will visit Grosse Isle quarantine station, returning here on Saturday.

Ocean Steamers.

Arrived—At New York, City of Berlin, Liverpool; Island, Stettin. Passed Brow Head, City of Chester, New York.

ANDREW J. BORDEN'S ESTATE.

Miss Emma Appointed Administratrix by the Probate Court.

[Special Dispatch.]

TAUNTON, Sept. 2.—A matter of interest in relation to the celebrated Borden case appeared at a session of the Probate Court in this city to-day. On the 5th of August, the day following the murder of Mr. and Mrs. Borden, Emma L. Borden and Lizzie A. Borden appeared before Andrew J. Jennings as justice of the peace and swore that they were the surviving children of Andrew J. Borden, who died on the day previous intestate, and left no widow. They prayed that Emma L. Borden be appointed administratrix of the estate of Andrew J. Borden. On August 30 the bond of Emma L. Borden was approved by the Probate Court. The sureties are Joseph A. Borden, Franklin L. Almy, Jerome C. Borden, Frank S. Stevens and Andrew Borden of Fall River, and the amount is $50,000.

There was no application for administration upon any estate of Mrs. Abby Borden, and it is stated that she left no personal or real estate.

WEATHER INDICATIONS.

FAIR AND WARMER.

WASHINGTON, Sept. 2.—For the 24 hours from 8 a. m. to-day: For Massachusetts, Rhode Island and Connecticut, fair and warmer; northerly winds, becoming variable; light frosts are probable in exposed places in the interior Saturday morning.

TRAIN ROBBERS' MISTAKE.

Held Up a Freight Instead of a Passenger and Fled to the Woods.

KANSAS CITY, Sept. 2.—An unsuccessful attempt was made last night to hold up the Missouri Pacific eastbound passenger train. The train was late in leaving and a freight was sent out ahead of it on the passenger's track. When the freight reached Dead Man's Curve, near Lee's Summit, it was flagged and several masked men approached the engine, but finding that the train was a freight turned and took to the woods.

THREE BUILDINGS STANDING.

Town of Coneully, Wash., Entirely Destroyed by Fire.

SPOKANE, Wash., Sept. 2.—Word has been received that Conully, the county seat of Okanagan county, was burned to the ground Tuesday morning. Nothing remains of the town proper, except a school, the court-house and a drug store. The entire main street was swept away in less than an hour. Total loss $100,000; insurance not over 15 per cent.

VESSEL CAPSIZED.

Mate and Seaman of Schooner Lott Woodward Drowned.

SOUTHAMPTON, Ont., Sept. 2.—During a heavy gale from the north Wednesday the schooner Lott Woodward in trying to make Southampton harbor, and when about two miles out, was struck by a sea and turned over on her beam ends. Joseph Greathouse, mate of the vessel, and N. Mahen, seaman, were drowned. The captain and two sailors were rescued in the morning by the light-house keeper.

PRESIDENT BARROS ATTACKED.

Charged With Furnishing His Residence With Government Funds.

CITY OF MEXICO, Sept. 2.—The Guatemalan press is attacking President Barros furiously, accusing him of using the government funds for furnishing his residence. It has been learned that Barros made use of the police funds in payment of the house expenses of his servants whose names were carried on the police pay rolls.

Heavy Frost.

KINGSTON, N. Y., Sept. 2.—There was quite a heavy frost last night in various parts of Ulster county. In the Summer resorts in the Catskills grate fires are burning and tourists slept last night under heavy blankets.

Iron Hall Receiver Appointed.

CINCINNATI, Sept. 2.—Judge Wilson yesterday appointed J. R. Kinney receiver to take charge of the funds of the five branches of the order of the Iron Hall of this city.

The Anderson & Co. Failure.

PORT HURON, Mich., Sept. 2.—The total amount of Anderson & Co's liabilities is $423,000. Assets are said to exceed this amount.

Typhus Fever Raging.

CONSTANTINOPLE, Sept. 2.—The typhus fever is raging in the quarantine hospital at Synope, a seaport town of Asia Minor, on the Black Sea.

TELEGRAPHIC BREVITIES.

Five boatmen are missing from Bayfield, Wis.

The Perth Amboy, N. J., postoffice was robbed.

Smallpox is in Iroquois and McHenry counties, Ills.

A child was killed by its stepmother at Milladore, Wis.

Horace Russell of Watertown, Mass., committed suicide.

Philadelphia officials are inspecting Boston institutions.

There are more than 3000 cases of scarlet fever in London.

A new street railway company is to be established in Chelsea, Mass.

The crew of a wrecked German bark was brought to Boston in safety.

Rev. Mr. Worthington, said to be the oldest Harvard graduate, died at Jackson, Mich.

The New Haven schooner Harold C. Beecher rescued the crew of the bark Nevada.

Riotous mill hands at Rhinelander, Wis., prevented the factories from being operated.

Jack Clifford is said to have betrayed secrets of the advisory board of Homestead, Pa.

Two persons were killed and four fatally injured near Deadwood, S. D., by an explosion of powder.

George W. Creasy of Newburyport, Mass., was elected superintendent of the soldiers' home in Chelsea.

A powerful tobacco combine was formed in Louisville, to compete with the combine formed at Cincinnati.

Workingmen and manufacturers of Haverhill, Mass., are considering the establishment of a local board of arbitration.

Rt. Hon. John Morley, chief secretary for Ireland, has gone on a visit to Andrew Carnegie at the lodge at Loch Rannoch, Perthshire, Scotland.

Richard F. Connors, a prominent druggist of Haverhill, Mass., died suddenly at the age of 27 years. He was well known in business and political circles.

Lieutenant Blanchard, U. S. A., of Pembroke, N. H., who was graduated from West Point in June last, has been assigned to duty in Battery C, First artillery, Fort Wadsworth, New York harbor.

HOME MATTERS.

PERSONAL.—Hon. John H. Mitchell, United States Senator from Oregon, has been in this city a few days, the guest of Jonathan Bourne, Jr.

Mrs. Thomas G. Wing and son of Sioux City are in the city visiting relatives and friends.

George Wourm, superintendent of the harness shop at the House of Correction in this city, has accepted a position as superintendent of a large harness manufactory in Hudson.

Miss Nellie B. Crapo is spending her vacation in New York with her friend, Miss Davis.

Miss Rita Keith of Campello is visiting friends in this city.

C. J. R. Carson, who sold his marine collection to H. E. Weaver of Chicago for the Progress whaling museum, has accepted a position in connection with the management of that exhibit.

Roland G. Pray of this city has left the city to join Monroe's Celebrities in their musical farce comedy entitled Aunt Bridget's Baby. This makes the seventh year that Mr. Pray has been the business manager of one of the most successful companies on the road. The company opens in Cincinnati, Ohio, for one week, commencing Sept. 10th.

George St. Germain, Esq., Dr. J. H. Landry, Dr. L. Z. Normandin and Dr. Belanger have accepted invitations to deliver addresses to the Francs Tireur of this city at Cottage City next Monday.

SEPTEMBER.—Now that the Fall months have opened we are able to make some astonishing low prices, as we shall make the largest inducements to our customers than at any time before. We shall sell our best Christian's triple extra flour 68c. a bag; our best St. Louis 63c. bag; our best Mocha and Java coffee 28c. lb., or 4 lbs. for $1; fine early rose potatoes 75c. bushel, 20c. peck; extra fine sweet potatoes 10 lbs. for 25c.; 5 lbs. best starch 25c.; 4 lbs. best rice 25c.; fine Formosa teas 35c. lb.; eggs 28c. dozen; Sayena washing powder 10c. pkg.; Davis Bros.' pure lard 9c. lb.; and the best of all are those 10c. bottles pickles, now only 6c., at the White Cash Store, 134 Purchase street.

FACTS WORTH KNOWING.—People give too little attention to the repairing of shoes. They think the only thing to be considered is to have it done cheap. They make a mistake, spoil good shoes, or else have them look badly. Our prices are higher than most anyone's, but we do fine work. Pay our men the highest wages. Can make your shoes look like new, and wear better. See ad. page 5. Union Shoe Store.

H. C. HATHAWAY'S AUCTION BULLETIN for to-morrow, Saturday, Sept. 3d: At 10 o'clock a. m. at mart about 40 horses of all grades, including speed, gents' driving and some extra driving and work horses; also new and second-hand carriages, harnesses, &c., &c.

At 12¾ o'clock p. m. house and lot on Foster street.

At 3 o'clock p. m. mortgagee's sale of house and lot No. 24 Walnut street.

A SPECIAL SALE at Boston Beef Co's for Saturday only:

Best St. Louis Flour,	60 cents.
Best Haxhall Flour,	67 cents.
A Fine Formosa Tea,	28 cents.
Extra Fine Formosa Tea,	35 cents.
Fine Coffee,	28 cents.
Fine Mocha and Java,	28 cents.

BOSTON BEEF CO.

THERE IS NOTHING so useful as a light weight overcoat. We shall offer for Saturday 250 men's and youths' Fall overcoats that are retailed everywhere at $12, $15 and $18; our price for these coats Saturday $9.97. See them in our east window. Ashley & Peirce, 72 and 74 William street.

EVERGREEN PARK.—The management of this popular course has arranged an interesting series of turf events for Labor Day. Several good trotters are entered and an enjoyable day is promised. Read avertisement.

TO-MORROW, (Saturday) we will sell 250 Fall overcoats that are actually worth from $12 to $18, our price on this lot for Saturday $9.97; first come, first served. Ashley & Peirce, 72 and 74 William street.

TWO FISH ON ONE HOOK.—Joseph Dias, while fishing in Long Pond yesterday, had the remarkable good luck to catch two black bass at once with rod and reel. The two weighed five pounds.

$9.97.—Your choice from 250 Fall overcoats that are sold everywhere at $12, $15 and $18. This is for Saturday's sale. You can't afford to miss it. Remember they can't last long at this low price. Ashley & Peirce.

RAN AGROUND.—Tug Delavin Peck, Fall River, while towing a mud scow through the draw of the Coggeshall street bridge yesterday ran aground and rolled over on her side.

WE HAVE 300 children's suits in neat patterns that we must close out at once. The prices are so low that every boy can afford himself a new suit. Wamsutta Clothing Co.

BARGAINS BEFORE MOVING at No. 19 Purchase street. Imported corsets, worth from $1.75 to $3.50, going at $1 per pair. Children's $5 cloaks now $3.50.

GREAT FINAL MARK-DOWN on men's and youths' suits. Every suit must be sold before vacating our store. Wamsutta Clothing Company.

THE VETERAN CADET ASSOCIATION meets this evening in the Board of Trade rooms. See special notice.

CHILDREN'S KNEE PANTS 40 cents, ages 4 to 16 years; regular price 50 and 75 cents. Wamsutta Clothing Co.

CUT! CUT! CUT! $4.95 for best workingman's watch, Waltham make. Clocks 93c. J. S. Kelley & Son, 15 Purchase street.

NOW IS THE TIME to buy your Winter overcoat. *Every coat* will go at a great reduction. Wamsutta Clothing Co.

STREET LIGHT COMMITTEE.—The City Council committee on street lights will hold a meeting this evening.

REMEMBER Saturday, Sept. 24, is our last day for business with you. Wamsutta Clothing Co.

JUST RECEIVED at Hutchinson's Book Store some entirely new paper dolls at 1c., 10c., 15c.

CABBAGE FREE with corned beef at Boston Beef Co's.

LARGE VARIETY OF OVERALLS and jumpers at 55 William street.

PENSIONERS, read Capt. Howland's special notice.

MISS PARLOA'S APPLEDORE Cook Books 10 cents, at Hutchinson's Book Store.

NEW FALL HATS at 55 William street.

FALL HATS in all the leading styles at Ashley & Peirce's.

PANTS! PANTS! New lines at 55 William st.

CORNED BEEF from 3 to 6 cents. Cabbage free at Boston Beef Co's.

FANCY OUTING SHIRTS cheap at 55 William st.

BLACK CLOTH OVERGAITERS 50c. Devoll's.

BUY CLOTHING AND SAVE MONEY at 55 Wm. st.

Take Hood's Sarsaparilla for the blood.

REPEATED REQUESTS

Have induced us to have another

TABLE SALE.

Therefore

SATURDAY MORNING, Sept. 3

We shall offer a small lot, (not over 200 in number) of those

Handsome Oak Tables

—AT—

89 CENTS!

These Tables are made of Oak, with four handsome turned standards, supporting top 16 inches square, with middle shelf 10 inches square, well built and smoothly finished.

We cannot promise delivery on day of sale, but will use all possible dispatch in filling orders.

REMEMBER, THIS SALE IS FOR SATURDAY ONLY!

C. F. WING,

34 to 40 Purchase st.

WHITING & CO.

SPECIAL

SATURDAY SALE!

200 Roman Stripe, Silk Slumber Robes, go on sale at $1.25 apiece, such as we have sold at $3.00 apiece.

6 Dozen Suede Mousquetaire Kids, 5 3-4 to 6 1-2 only. Will be sold at 49c., regular $1.00 Gloves.

4 Dozen 5-hook Foster Suede Glove, our $1.00 Glove, to be sold at 69c.

25c. Black Taffeta Glove, now 17c. per pair.

500 Dozen of Ladies' fast black Hose, such as we have sold cases of, go on sale at same low price, of 25c. a pair.

WHITING & CO.

Fall Hats.

Buy

Your

New

Hat

Of

J. & W. R.

WING & CO.

Correct

Qualities.

Correct

Shapes.

Correct

Prices.

Now Ready.

THE CRESCENT!

22 Purchase St.

CORSETS.

CORSETS.

We haven't begun to tell you all about our Corsets. It is

CORSETS,

and CORSETS,

and CORSETS.

A fresh stock coming in constantly. Don't forget we have a large line of Thomson's Glove-fitting Corsets. Prices at $1, $1.25, $1.50, $1.75, $2.25; satin $5. And we give you a new pair if the steels break.

Kalamazoo Corset Waists, very similar in style to the Jackson Waist, marked down from $1 to 75c. A very few Kabo Corsets left, drab only, for 75c.; regular price $1.

Hoisery and *Hose Supporters.*

Good Dress Shields only 10c.

Gingham Aprons of best quality and with two full widths only 25c. If you examine the make of them you will be satisfied. They sell *every time.*

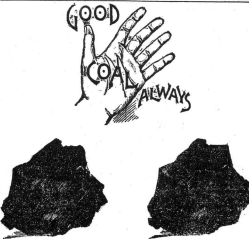
JUDGE BLAISDELL'S DECISION.

Touching Scenes in the Fall River Court-Room.

How the Verdict was Received by the Newspapers.

Dedham Story about Samuel Robinsky a Fabrication.

There was a murmur of surprise throughout the court-room at Fall River yesterday morning when Andrew J. Jennings rose to make the argument for the defence. It was supposed that his duty would devolve on Mr. Adams, and the early announcement that Mr. Jennings would present the case to the judge had created a furore of discussion about the hotels. But the surprise melted into admiration after Mr. Jennings had spoken for a few moments.

In her usual place at the centre front of the room was the prisoner. To her right and very near her sat Mr. Adams, and in his accustomed place at the left Mr. Buck. Mrs. Brigham and Marshal Hilliard were the other occupants of the seat.

Nothing was noticeably new in the character of the audience, unless it was the presence of many lawyers, and of those there were most of the members of the bar residing in Fall River and a number from other places. There was of course the same crowd of women chattering and laughing on the rear seats, in no wise apparently concerned over the happiness or misery of the prisoner in whose life's destiny so significant and fateful a link was to be woven.

When Lizzie Borden took her seat she wore the same expression and conducted herself in the same manner as on previous mornings of the trial, but she looked wearier than ever before. Her eyes were sad and heavy and suggested that she might have been weeping, though there were no traces of fresh tears. She watched with great interest her senior counsel when he rose for the argument. Perhaps no lawyer ever created a greater surprise than he as he proceeded. It undoubtedly would have saved his client from her fate if any plea could have done so.

Mr. Jennings stood immediately in front of the clerk's desk, at times with his hand resting on it, and kept his eyes fixed intently on Judge Blaisdell's face. His language was simple, his voice stir-

EVEN CHILDREN KNOW THAT **DR. HOUGH'S** COUGH AND LUNG BALSAM, IS THE BEST FOR Coughs, Colds, Croup or Whooping Cough. PRICE, 35 CENTS. Sold by all druggists and medicine dealers.

J. G. DOUGLASS' Sale and Exchange Stables, Mechanics' Lane, New Bedford, Mass. I keep constantly on hand and for sale or exchange a good stock of driving, family, business, and team horses. Horses bought and sold on commission. Fresh arrivals every Monday and Thursday. All horses warranted as represented.

THE **Lamson & Hubbard**

HAT.
For durability, style and comfort the best hat made.
For sale by leading hatters.   FM

THESE ARE BUT FEW
—OF THE—
MANY BARGAINS
WE ARE GIVING OUR CUSTOMERS.

If you see anything in the list that you can save money on give us a chance to save it for you. Remember anything you see advertised from our store is all right in quality. We don't keep poor goods that are not cheap at any price.

BEST St. Louis Flour, 66 cents per bag.
10 lbs. Large Sweet Potatoes for 25 cts.
3 lbs. Fresh Ginger Snaps for 25 cts.
4 lbs. Common Crackers for 25 cts.
A Can of Good Condensed Milk for 10 cts.
Much better Peaches at 18c. per can than you can buy fresh at 15 cts. a qt.
Quaker Oats at 1 1-2c. lb., or in packages at 10 cts.

Everything as low as any one, plenty of things lower than the lowest.

A. G. ALLEY, Jr.,
Sixth and Union Sts.

---

ring and his whole manner indicated that he had a personal feeling in his appeal.

The district attorney sat a desk near by occupied with the morning papers. He did not appear to be listening to Mr. Jennings, though the argument for the government shows that he must have been.

The prisoner was quite overcome for the first time with Mr. Jennings' remarks, at least she demonstrated that she was capable of tears. She was affected most when her counsel referred to her with some feeling as being the youngest daughter and the significance of those words. The tears were streaming down Lawyer Adams' face at this point as well. Before the speaker was a sheet of commercial note containing a skeleton of the argument. He finished a stick of licorice candy which he brought while talking, and was frequently handed some ice water by the court clerk, who also helped himself.

When Lizzie Borden took her seat she wore the same expression and conducted herself in the same manner as on previous mornings of the trial, but she looked wearier than ever before...

There were many congratulations for Mr. Jennings at the conclusion of his argument. He was pale and exhausted. Lizzie Borden was at his elbow, her eyes tearful and dropped to the floor. She was the object of many curious looks as the crowd pushed past her.

It was a very lively audience which gathered in the afternoon. The women brought boxes of candy and talked as gaily as though at a matinee. The pink peppermints and pears were devoured with as much relish as though one of their sex had not been sitting near by to receive a court's verdict on a charge of murder. There were children in white aprons and crimped hair who came with their mothers.

The district attorney began his argument immediately upon entering the room. For the first time in the course of the trial there was no other woman with Lizzie. Her sister had not been in court all day and Mrs. Brigham sat with the witnesses. Mr. Buck and Marshal Hilliard were alone with their charge.

Mr. Knowlton spoke in a most impassive manner, and much of the time his hands were encased in his pockets. He used no notes, save the report of the inquest. The prisoner hid her face, but she did not shed tears. People were not looking for any demonstration on her part after the exhibition of such an endurance. She was by all means the calmest person in the room when the district attorney with a few sweeping sentences closed his argument.

Mr. Knowlton's Closing Words.

There was no applause when the District Attorney took his seat. It was not because he had failed to make a masterly effort, but the court-room was quite a spell, and applause would have seemed out of place entirely.

Attention was almost immediately transferred to Judge Blaisdell, who needed no lapse of time to prepare for his ordeal. In almost the first sentence he revealed what his decision would be.

Perhaps there was never a more effective scene in any court-room than the closing one yesterday. Those who were present will never forget it. Judge Blaisdell's voice was low and tremulous. The profound sincerity of his grief was not to be questioned. Before those awful words "probably guilty," he paused and turned away, unable to utter them for a time. Even the clerk of the court, whose calmness is proverbial and who never was known to have been visibly touched before, nearly broke down. Men and women alike could not control their tears at the sorrowful spectacle almost too tragic to seem real.

When the crowd had left the room, Lizzie Borden on the arm of her most faithful friend, Minister Buck, left, perhaps forever, the court-room which must have been a scene of great trial to her. The mob in the alley were loudly discussing the only topic of the day, and the sounds could be distinctly heard through the matron's window. The lawyers for the defence did what they could for their charge, and the district attorney went away to sleep the sleep of the just.

The Superior Court Trial.

The Superior Court trial will possibly be held in this city. If the case is not tried in New Bedford, it will be in Taunton. It is thought the intense feeling in Fall River will be prejudicial to a fair trial.

ROBINSKY NOT IN DEDHAM.

Postmaster Riley and His Wife Deny Sending Letters to Fall River.

"A prominent citizen of Fall River" may have received a letter from some one in Dedham giving information that "letters have frequently been received" at the Dedham post office addressed to Samuel Robinsky, as was stated yesterday, but it was not written by the wife of the postmaster at Dedham, as was claimed.

"This is all a lie," said Postmaster Charles H. Riley of Dedham yesterday to a reporter when shown a newspaper clipping. "My wife will laugh when she hears about this. Why, she has nothing to do with my office. It takes all her time to look out for the children. We never saw any of the letters that come in here except her own. I don't know any such man as Samuel Robinsky in Dedham. No letters were ever received here for a person of that name. You can call on my wife if you wish. We live on Highland street."

The reporter found Mrs. Riley at home. She is a pleasant-faced, matronly looking woman, and laughed heartily when shown the newspaper clipping. "This is all news to me," she said. "I don't know anyone in Fall River, and don't even know where the city is. I wonder how such a mistake could get into the papers. Although my husband is postmaster here, I am very seldom in the post office."

Learning that there were a number of German and Russian Jews employed in the mills at East Dedham, the reporter walked up the railroad tracks to the East Dedham station, in which the branch post office is located. The postmaster is H. A. Hutchinson. Neither he nor his wife had ever heard of Samuel Robinsky being in Dedham and had certainly never written any letters to Fall River about him. At the Glendon Woollen Mills, where about 550 men and women are employed, the agent for the mills very kindly made inquiries among his employes. No one named Robinsky worked in the mills, nor did any one know such a man in East Dedham.

There are small branch post offices in the West Dedham station and at the Ash-

LAWYER ADAMS SITS WITH LIZZIE DURING MR. JENNINGS' PLEADING.

Opinions of the Press on the End of the Borden Hearing.

The Providence *Journal* says:

The decision of Judge Blaisdell in the Borden hearing, which came to an end at Fall River yesterday with the arguments of the counsel on either side, was exactly what everyone who has followed the testimony carefully and without prejudice must have anticipated. The champions of Miss Lizzie Borden, who have been much in evidence throughout, will doubtless continue to pursue a course the wisdom of which may be questioned, and will denounce it as an "outrage" that she is held for indictment before the grand jury. These friends are not content with saying that her guilt has not been proved, which is perfectly true, or that the evidence on which she is held is very flimsy, which is not true, although to say it would be pardonable under the circumstances. They go far beyond this. They proclaim her innocence without explaining away with any degree of success the facts, to say nothing of the inferences, which weigh against their theory. And they do not seem to see what ought to be tolerably obvious, that if she is an innocent woman suffering under an awful suspicion she ought to welcome a trial rather than avoid one. Whether the stigma placed upon her is deserved is not now the question. It is there, and letting her go free after this hearing would not have removed it. Furthermore, it was there the very first, before even the inquest was held or her arrest was ordered. In other words Miss Borden was the victim of circumstances, if nothing more, from the moment that her father's murder was discovered.

The counsel for the defence made a brilliant plea in her behalf. It unquestionably moved those who heard it, as it will move those who read it, more than any argument on the other side could do. In spite of the peculiar atrocity of the crime with which the prisoner is charged, the hope that she may be found innocent is so intense and so universal that it is almost as effective an instrument in her favor as an absolute presumption of innocence would be. Those who place the most reliance upon the evidence developed so far by the Commonwealth, and who deduct from it the conclusions least favorable to Andrew Borden's daughter, to whom alone any reasonable motive for the deed, so far as we can see, can be imputed, desire most ardently that they may find they have made a mistake. At all events they realize the gravity of the situation sufficiently to suspend pronouncing judgment. But eloquent as was the plea of Mr. Jennings, it did not in any way weaken the government case. It showed that if the prosecution rested upon a hypothetical basis, so did the defence at least to an equal degree. The chief point made in behalf of the accused was the assertion that she never tried to buy poison at all and that those who say she did are deceived by a case of mistaken identity. Yet the testimony that she did try to buy poison seems to be overwhelming.

We need not stop now however to analyze the evidence which has been presented before Judge Blaisdell during the past week, or even to argue that he was fully justified in deciding to hold Miss Borden upon this evidence. The two points which it is worth while to bear in mind involve opportunity and motive, and both necessarily tell heavily against this young woman. The revelations of the manner of life of the Borden household would be almost beyond belief were it not only too apparent that it is not the only case in New England where similar conditions obtain. As we have hitherto pointed out, it was to the last degree sordid, even squalid, especially when the wealth of Andrew Borden and the tastes of his daughters are borne in mind. They were not extravagant girls, but they demanded, and they had a moral right to expect, the means to meet the conditions of existence natural to those of their station. They moved among people who respected themselves too much to live as meanly as Andrew Borden lived. What wonder if they—and particularly the younger daughter, whose turn of mind seems to have been morbid—grew exasperated to the point of bitterness with the man who, even if he were their father, was keeping them from all the natural pleasures which belong to young womanhood? There is nothing improbable in assuming that Lizzie Borden's feelings toward her father were rancorous enough to lead to murder, however incredible the deed itself or the means taken to carry it out may be. And that this is assumption is hardly reason enough for saying that she should not be held for trial.

Boston *Post*:

Now that Lizzie Borden has been held for trial on the charge of murdering her father, it would be a good thing for the Fall River police to go to work and see if they cannot find the real murderer.

The committal of Lizzie Borden was a foregone conclusion when Judge Blaisdell, who conducted the star-chamber inquest, decided to preside at the examination. His opinion seems to have been formed by what he saw and heard at the inquest; and on this, rather than on what was presented at the examination, his decision appears to be based. Yet now that the evidence presented at the inquest has been made public, its force is seen to be destroyed by the light which has been let in upon it. The suspicion which this evidence aroused in the minds of those who were permitted

MANY VICTIMS.

Cholera Infantum's Dread Record.

A Serious Time for Little Babies.

Physicians Advise the Use of Pure Food.

Lack of Proper Knowledge Causes Suffering.

How the Health of Children May Be Preserved.

Mothers of New Bedford read what's here.

There is an epidemic of indigestion and cholera infantum in this and other states. Health boards everywhere are reporting a startling fatality from cholera infantum. Physicians say that in nearly every case the child is poorly fed and nourished, and hence the disease.

"It is absolutely certain," says a physician in one of the medical journals, speaking of the alarming Summer mortality among his patients, "that the cause of this high death rate among infants is indigestion."

At the beginning of Summer the best physicians gave warning that pure food must be used for babies. That this warning did not reach every city and town in this state is evident from the high infantile death rate. But in those places where the newspapers published the discussions that were going on large quantities of lactated food were sold and this best of diets for children was used. The result is statistics show that fewer deaths have occurred in those towns and cities where the larger amount of lactated food was used.

Comparisons of this sort are absolutely convincing.

September is a fatal month for the little ones, and unless lactated food is used the dreadful mortality and increasing amount of sickness among children will continue.

The one safe plan is to feed infants on lactated food.

"Your Honor, I demand the girl's release." —Lawyer Jennings.

to hear it in secret is not shared by any one who now sees it in its proper relation to all the facts as shown at the public examination.

Everything which was so carefully sought to give color to this suspicion has vanished. The stained weapons are found to be innocent of blood. The spotted garments are shown to be clean. The suspected motive of the crime disappears as soon as it is examined. There remains only the fact that the accused woman was present in or about the house at the time when the crime was committed. In fact, there is nothing to connect

the daughter with the murder that does not equally point to the servant. Mr. Knowlton might have demanded the committal of Bridget with as much reason as he demanded that Lizzie be held.

The real ground on which this decision is made is undoubtedly the testimony given by Lizzie Borden herself at the in-

TAKE WARNING!

Neglect Not the Signals of Danger.

An Object Lesson Taught by the Indians.

Let the Way Be Simple and the Remedy Safe.

If you are ailing, not exactly sick, but not feeling "just right," have a drowsy, dull feeling, bad taste in the mouth, variable appetite, occasional pains in the joints and muscles, and other signs of impending sickness, why not do as the Indian does—drive such symptoms out of the system by the judicious use of their vegetable remedy?

Don't neglect such warnings.

That pain in your shoulder may develop into rheumatism, and a month's sickness deprive you of the income of your toil.

That tarry tongue denotes you: liver is out of order, and a typhoid fever would easily take root in your system.

What could you do then?

Think of your business, your income, and your family.

Seek safety as you would fly from cholera or smallpox.

You are in danger if you neglect these warnings. They may pass off, but the chances are against you, and even then the poison is only latent in your system.

Do not, however, put your trust in the so-called "sarsaparillas" with which the market is flooded. Sarsaparilla bark is not a medicine, it is a flavoring, nothing more. The action of many of these decoctions comes from mineral poisons they contain, such as mercury, arsenic, strychnine, bismuth, iodide of potassium, and the like, and any druggist will tell you, if he tells you truly, that this is so.

Kickapoo Indian Sagwa and other Kickapoo Indian medicines contain only the product of the field and forest, nature's own vegetable growth of roots, barks and herbs, and of necessity are free from all mineral poisons whatever, because the Indian have no knowledge of them, depending wholly upon nature's laboratory for their cures, and upon their skill born of centuries of experience, in preparing them.

Kickapoo Indian Sagwa, made by the Indians from roots, barks and herbs of their own gathering and curing, is obtainable of any druggist at one dollar per bottle; six bottles for five dollars.

Send three two-cent stamps to cover postage, and we will mail you free a thrilling and interesting book of 178 pages, entitled "Life and Scenes Among the Kickapoo Indians." Tells all about the Indians. Address HEALY & BIGELOW, Distributing Agents, Grand Ave., New Haven, ct.

4

The Evening Standard.

NEW BEDFORD, MASS.

FRIDAY EVENING, SEPT. 2.

THREE EDITIONS DAILY.

No. 87 Union Street.

PUBLISHED BY

E. ANTHONY & SONS.

(INCORPORATED)

—TERMS—

Six Dollars a Year; Three Dollars for Six Months, in advance; Single Copies Two Cents.

FOR PRESIDENT:
BENJAMIN HARRISON
OF INDIANA.

FOR VICE-PRESIDENT:
WHITELAW REID
OF NEW YORK.

CONTENTS OF THIS EVENING'S STANDARD.

READ! READ!

It is not surprising that the prospect of the arrival of the cholera into this country should create some alarm. The dread of this disease arises from the suddenness of the attacks and the rapidity with which they prove fatal. But the visitations of the cholera are rare, while we have permanent epidemics among us, which, though more slow in their effects are more destructive of life. The grippe, which seems to have established itself here, is worse than cholera. So are typhoid fever, diphteria, and perhaps some other diseases. When the cholera visited this State in 1849 there were only 641 deaths from it in Boston, and only 1188 in the whole State. It lasted from June to the first of October, and the season is so far advanced here that it is not likely to be very serious. In 1854 there was another visitation of cholera and 765 deaths, of which 173 were in Bristol county. There is no occasion for a panic, but all proper precautions should be taken, especially in our cities, and individuals should be careful as to diet. If there are any dirty or unsanitary localities in our city they should be put into good condition at once, and the tenement houses of the mill operatives should be carefully looked after. Prevention is better than cure.

Union County, New Jersey, can boast of being the first in the country to have a complete system of improved county roads, opening up the entire county. There, says the Christian Union, one can drive a carriage, ride a bicycle, or go on foot from the county seat to any other city or township of the county on these Telford roads without soiling the tire of a wheel or the sore of his shoe. Burdens three times as heavy as heretofore can be hauled upon them with the same horse-power, with far less wear and tear to vehicles, and with much greater ease and comfort to draught animals and drivers.

The effect of this improvement has been an advance in the value of agricultural lands twice the cost of the roads already, and lands for building purposes have advanced in a still greater proportion. The whole of this section is developing at a rate before unknown for half a century. The work was largely accomplished through the energy of one man, Chauncey P. Ripley, a lawyer of Westfield, who spent much time and money for several years in advocating road reform.

Those who have followed the testimony in the hearing in the Borden case must feel that the Commonwealth holds Lizzie Borden on very insufficient evidence. The attitude of the officers of the law, in the inquest and at the hearing, has been singularly partial and cruel; if they have presented their case with any approach to fullness, they have small chance before a jury. The poison theory, the hatchet theory have both utterly failed, and it appears that all the case against Miss Borden rests on is the probability that she was in the house at least when Mrs. Borden was killed.—Springfield Republican.

If Mr. Gladstone can stand a thump in the eye from a chunk of stale gingerbread and being knocked down by an infuriated cow without serious injury, there would seem to be little doubt as to his ability to withstand the attacks of his political opponents when Parliament meets again. Salisbury can't get a quarter as mad as a cow driven to insanity by the loss of her calf.

The firm of Marden & Rowell, which commenced the publication of the Lowell Daily Courier twenty-five years ago to-day, has dissolved, and a corporation, called the Lowell Courier Publishing Co. has been formed to continue the business, of which Mr. Marden is president, and Mr. Rowell clerk and treasurer. The Courier has had several prominent Massachusetts men among its editors, such as William Schouler, William S. Robinson and John A. Goodwin, and since 1867 the present editor, George A. Marden.

MOYNAN & CO. are selling an extra size...

HOME MATTERS.

WILL BE CLOSED LABOR DAY.—Monday next being Labor day the banks in this city will be closed for business on that day.

NEW CITY HALL.—A picture of the proposed new City Hall, from drawings of J. L. Faxon, will be printed in the second edition of to-day's Standard on the sixth page.

CONTRACT AWARDED.—William Watkog has taken the contract to erect the building on County street for the new Primitive Methodist church.

THE BELT BROKE.—The big driving belt on the engine of the Hathaway, Soule, & Harrington's factory broke yesterday, necessitating the shutting down of the works till this forenoon.

BASKET PICNIC.—The pupils of Israel Smith's dancing class of last year, held a basket picnic at Fort Phenix yesterday afternoon. The children were accompanied by their parents and all thoroughly enjoyed the outing. The class are making plans for an excursion to Horse Neck soon.

YACHTING.—Sloop yacht Mull, Commodore B. F. Sutton of the Brooklyn Yacht Club, owner, arrived in port yesterday from the Vineyard, cruising. The yacht has one of the most expensively fitted cabins of any small yacht in American waters. She is commanded by Capt. C. G. Borden of this city. Steam Yacht Talisman arrived in port yesterday.

CONSUMPTION OF WATER.—The consumption of water from the distributing reservoir, as recorded at office of the Superintendent of Water Works for the month of August is 148,346,545 gallons. During the same month in 1891 the consumption was 139,065,188 gallons. As compared with July the consumption last month shows a falling off of 4,317,606 gallons.

PENSIONS have been granted as follows:—Original—J. H. Howard, F. T. Clayton (deceased), J. C. Weller, J. H. Bishop.
Additional—Thomas Higgins, Henry Young, G. P. Foos, William Dickinson, Daniel Neal, Hiram Loflin, E. F. Russell, Archibald McPhee, Lorenzo Hall, Thomas Dunn, Patrick Sullivan (deceased), C. C. Morrill.
Re-issue—Thomas Moore.
Original widows—Mary Hitch, Elizabeth V. Place, Ellen Sullivan, Mary E. Martin, minors of Thomas Moore, Pardena Taylor.

ACCIDENT.— William Ferguson, assistant engineer at No. 4 Wamsutta mill, met with a serious accident while at work this morning. While he was wiping the engine his right hand was caught in the machinery and badly mangled. The two middle fingers were severed and the rest of the hand terribly lacerated. He was taken to Dr. Normandin's office, where his wounds were dressed by Doctors Normandin and Landry.

WEDDING.—Pope's Island was the scene of a happy gathering last evening, when at the residence of Charles E. Holmes, Daniel L. Neff of Taunton and Miss Lillian M. Holmes were married in the presence of about a score of friends, some of them from Taunton. Rev. J. K. Wilson of Taunton performed the ceremony, and afterward a collation was served, and the newly wedded couple hold a reception. Mr. and Mrs. Neff left the city on the evening train and after a tour through central Vermont, will reside in Taunton.

GOLDEN WEDDING.—A reception in honor of the fiftieth anniversary of their marriage was given Mr. and Mrs. Harvey Rider of Rochester by their son, Mr. James Rider, at his residence on Bank street, Abington, Wednesday evening. A large number of relatives and friends were present. Mr. and Mrs. Rider were assisted in receiving by Mrs. Henry Hall, Mrs. Herbert Bliss, Sanford Rider and James Rider, all children, who with James Rider himself were the only surviving children. Mr. and Mrs. James Rider are in receipt of the reception.

GOOD TEMPLARS.—The annual meeting of the Plymouth district lodge, I. O. G. T. was held at Bridgewater yesterday. Charles F. Porter of Avon, district chief templar, presided. These officers were elected:
Chief Templar—Charles F. Porter of Avon.
Vice-Templar—Emily Crapo of Middleboro.
Councillor—John Sherman of Plympton.
Secretary—Mary E. Porter of Avon.
Treasurer—Miss Bessie Sherman of Plympton.
Superintendent of Juvenile Templars—George Beacon of Plymouth.

TEACHERS' ASSIGNMENTS.

Important Meeting of the Primary School Committee.

At a meeting of the primary school committee, last evening, the following teachers were assigned to the different primary schools in this city:

Acushnet Avenue School.
Principal—Jane C. Thompson.
Assistants—Sarah E. Kirwin, Hattie L. Finlan, Margaret H. Holmes, Caroline S. Silva, Susan M. Lucas, Harriet N. Hyatt, Hattie S. Gardner.

I. W. Benjamin School.
Principal—Jane E. Gilmore.
Assistants—Susan M. Tompkins, Nellie W. Davis, Helen J. Kirk, Rachael L. Denham, Sarah A. Winslow, Annie C. O'Connor, Mary C. Barstow, Annie L. Brownell, Mabel Bennett, Alice A. Taylor. On 3 not yet assigned.

Cedar Street School.
Principal—Annie S. Homer.
Assistants—Bessie F. Pierce, Abbie D. Whitney, Wilietta B. Nickerson, Annie L. Edwards, Mabel L. Hathaway.

Cedar Grove Street School.
Principal—Lucy F. Clark.
Assistants—Mary J. Eldridge, Eleanor V. Tripp, Edith E. Weeden, Annie G. Braley, Carrie A. Shaw, Flora E. Estes, Sara M. Hatch.
Special Assistant—Isabel Horr.

Cannonville School.
Principal—Adelaide J. McFarlin.
Assistant—Ethel W. Denham.

Dartmouth Street School.
Principal—Isadora F. Eldridge.
Assistants—H. Eva Schwall, Edith M. B. Taber, Annie F. Smith, Grace H. Potter, Sara H. Kelley, Nellie H. Cook.

Fourth Street School.
Principal—Sarah H. Cransten.
Assistants—Eliza H. Sanford, Sarah E. Sears, Annie L. Macreading, Lillie C. Tillinghast, Grace Covell.

Linden Street School.
Principal—Elizabeth P. Spooner.
Assistants—Isabella Luscomb, Isadora Foster, Lucy S. Leach.

Merrimac Street School.
Principal—Sarah H. Hewins.
Assistants—Addie West, Harriet S. Damon.

Maxfield Street School.
Principal—Mary B. White.
Assistants—Annie E. Pearce, Clara C. M. Gage, Mary B. Pamo.

William Street School.
Principal—Eleanor Commerford.
Assistants—Mary J. Graham, Kate E. Cleary, Amelia Lincoln.

Thompson Street School—Primary Department.
Leonora B. Hamblin.

Wood Street School.
Anna I. Dexter.

POLITICAL—The delegates thus far elected to the Republican Congressional Convention are as follows:

	Randall.	Greene.
New Bedford,	22	
Fall River,		27
Eastham,	1	
Gosnold,	1	
Wareham,	1	
Provincetown,	2	
Somerset,	2	1
Chatham,	2	
Harwich,	2	
Brewster,	1	
Bourne,	2	
Nantucket,	3	
Marion,	1	
Tisbury,	1	
West Tisbury,	1	
Barnstable,	3	
Total,	**44**	**28**

Nantucket has elected three Randall delegates—Henry Riddell, William H. H. Smith and Stillman Cash. There were 90 voters in attendance. Richard E. Congdon, Henry Riddell and Walter H. Burgess were chosen delegates to the senatorial district, D. E. Bacon, A. T. Morey and Mendell Rathenburg, to the State and Arthur B. Enos, J. S. Appleton, Jr. and Josiah F. Murphey to the councillor conventions. Great enthusiasm prevailed and redfire and cheers filled the air.

Tisbury has elected one Randall delegate—R. W. Crocker.

Barnstable endorsed Mr. Randall by acclamation, and chose three Randall delegates.

At the Republican caucus in Marion last evening Franklin B. Allen was moderator, and John F. Luce clerk. Delegates to the various conventions were elected as follows:
State—John Frank Luce.
Congressional—James H. Allen.
Councillor—Franklin B. Allen.
County—Charles D. Hall.
Senatorial—W. H. Mendell.
District—John Frank Luce, James H. Allen, Charles D. Hall, Franklin B. Allen, Lucius C. Kelley.
Charles D. Hall, John F. Luce and F. B. Allen were elected district committee.

The delegate to the congressional convention favors the nomination of Mr. Randall.

The Republicans of Fall River fired their opening gun of the campaign last night by an enthusiastic rally in Music Hall. The City Committee, with a band of music, marched to the Mellen House and received there the speakers of the evening, Hon. William E. Barrett, M. P. Murray, Hon. Milton Reed, ex-mayor William S. Greene, and other prominent Republicans.

A handsome Harrison and Reid flag was flung to the breeze in front of Granite Block, opposite City Hall.

There will be a Democratic caucus in City Hall, Sept. 8th, to elect delegates to the State, councillor and congressional conventions.

POLICE STATISTICS.—We are indebted to Harry N. West, clerk of the police department, for the following statistics contained in the monthly report of Chief Gardiner.

The whole number of arrests during August was 117, 27 of which were on warrants. Of these 20 were males.

The offences for which parties have been arrested are as follows: Drunkenness 63, assault and battery 13, larceny 9, 3 each for disturbing the peace, non-support and insanity, violation of the pharmacy law 4, idle and disorderly 2, illegal sale of liquor 2, tramps 2, and one each for indecent assault, exposure of person, keeping common nuisance, selling poison without label, trespass and violation of the Lord's day, and embezzlement. One person was arrested under the bastardy act.

The nativity of prisoners is as follows: United States, 63; Canada, 18; Ireland, 26; England, 12; Portugal, 3, and Russia 1.

During the month there has been 36 lodgers in the lockup.

The amount of property reported stolen during the month is $448, $115 of which was recovered.

Three buildings were found open and secured, and 148 cases were investigated, 3 defective streets and sidewalks reported, 1 dangerous dog reported, 1 dog notice served, 5 dogs killed, 1 intoxicated person helped home, 1 lost children found and restored, 3 cases of water running to waste and 11 disturbances suppressed.

THAT BUSY COMMITTEE.—Last evening the city property committee held another meeting, when George D. Richards was elected secretary in the absence of Councilman King.

Edgar B. Hammond was prepared to state to the committee the progress that has been made on the work of building the addition to the Cedar Grove Street school-house. The contractors asked the committee for two-thirds of the contract price and, on Mr. Hammond's statement of the progress of the work, it was voted to pay the contractors. The committee voted to pay one-half contract price for heating and ventilating. The building will not be ready for occupancy for several weeks.

Copies of the first directory of Fairhaven are being distributed.

PROBATE COURT.

FULLER, J.

Taunton, Friday, Sept. 2.

Wills proved and admitted to probate—Of John A. Wood of New Bedford, William H. Wood executor; of Anna Hutin of Fall River, Henry B. Hutin executor; of Mary Pratt of Mansfield, Hiram Rineley executor; of Hannah B. Watkins of New Bedford, James B. Watkins executor; of Edward R. Dean of Taunton, Mary A. Dean executrix; of John B. Hennessy of Providence, Mary G. Feeley executrix; of Allen Simmons of Somerset, Franklin Simmons and Franklin S. Simmons executors; of Rosanna M., alias Rose M., Keeley of Fall River, Catherine L. Keeley executrix.

Administration granted —To Mary F. Bowen, on estate of George L. Bowen of Raboboth; to Sarah Q. Smith, on estate of Rebecca S. Smith of Easton; to Alberta M. Brightwell, on estate of Charles E. Brightwell of Fall River; to Sarah M. Bates, on estate of Otis H. Bates of Swansey; to Sarah T. Cornell of Providence, on estate of Mary M. Ray, widow, North Attleboro; to George H. Gerrish of Rochester, Mass., on estate of Alice M. Miles of Fairhaven; to Arthur W. Reed, on estate of Jarvis B. Reed of North Attleboro; to James Casey, on estate of Bridget Casey of North Attleboro; to Phebe, on estate of Julia Pottras of New Bedford; to James Bonar, on estate of William Bonar of Mansfield; to Chloe M. Lee, on estate of Nathan B. Lee of Taunton; to John Drohan, on estate of Bridget Drohan of Fall River; to Susan Garnahy, on estate of Morgan Finnecane of Fall River; to Ernest U. Paull, on estate of Eben Paull of Fall River; to Ann Gallagher, on estate of James G. Gallagher of New Bedford; to Roby T. Snow, of New Bedford, on estate of James H. Snow of Acushnet; to Jesse Richardson, on estate of Susan E. Richardson of New Bedford; to George F. Tucker, on estate of Deborah Howland of New Bedford.

Accounts allowed—First and final of administrator estate of George L. Davis of Swansey; first of administrator estate of Michael Mahoney of Fall River; first of executor of the will of Elizabeth King of Taunton; first of executor of the will of Abby J. Pettce of New Bedford; final of administrator estate of Acheah Townsend of Berkley; first and final of administrator estate of Mary J. Harlow of Taunton; first of guardian of George C. Brown of Rehoboth.

Accounts rendered—First account of executor of the will of Ebenezer Leonard of Acushnet; first of guardian of Mary, Tessie and Maggie Clarkson of Fall River, minors; fourth account of guardian of Robert L. Yancy of New Bedford, minor.

Guardians appointed — Dennis Reiley of William, John H. and Margaret J. Reiley of Fall River, minors; Augustus White of Maria C., Walter A., Henry C. and Emma L. White of Acushnet, minors; Susan Garnahy of Ann, James and Susan Finnecane of Fall River, minors; George H. Evans of Martha F. and Eugene S. Hood of Taunton, minors.

Edward F. Potter of Dartmouth was appointed a trustee for the benefit of Charles W. Potter under the will of William Potter, 2d, of Dartmouth; also a trustee for the benefit of William G. Potter of Dartmouth and Annie F. Sweet of the same town; also a trustee for the benefit of Maria A. Potter and her minor children, Myron D., Mary H. and Carrie H. Potter of the same town. Henry B. Hitton was appointed a trustee under the will of Anna Hitton of Fall River for the benefit of Abraham Hitton.

The will of Joseph De Garis of Dartmouth was presented, and the matter of proof was continued to New Bedford, Sept. 23d, on account of the absence of a witness.

Leavitt Storer, of Waldoboro, Me., was appointed trustee under the will of Henry H. Winnell of Mansfield, Mass.

THIRD DISTRICT COURT.

BORDEN, J.

Friday, Sept. 2.

There was no business for the court this morning. Only one arrest was made by the police in the past 24 hours, and that being for drunkenness was released by the arresting officer.

CIVIL DOCKET.—Following is the trial list of the civil terms of the Third District Court to be held Monday morning at 9 o'clock:

153.	Schlesinger et al.	vs.	Gifford
550.	Clark	vs.	Lee
826.	Knowlton & Perry.	vs.	W. Clifford.
826.	Parker.	vs.	Genesky.
826.	Bernstein	vs.	Milliken
826.	Knowlton & Perry.	vs.	Benson
826.	Manchester	vs.	Nacreaster
882.	E. L. Barney.	vs.	Whie.
883.	Meaney et al.	vs.	Stanton et al.
977.	Desmond.		Knowlton.
977.	Kering	vs.	Rodgers et al.
995.	Willcox.	vs.	Da Terra.
994.	Cornell et al.	vs.	Deane et al.
998.	Knowlton & Perry.	vs.	Milliken.
995.	Bliss et al.	vs.	Finlan et al.
998.	W. Nickerson et al.		
	Dade.	vs.	Lynch
998.	Pokasoni et al.		Milliken.
1005.	Hastie	vs.	Bolvin
	Parker.		
1065.	Borden	vs.	Tripp
	Gillingham.		

POLICE STATISTICS...

REV. W. LENOIR HOOD.

From Yesterday's Third Edition.

PROBABLY GUILTY.

Lizzie Borden is Held for the Grand Jury.

Prisoner Weeps as She Leaves Court-room.

Audience Groaned When Decision Was Announced.

Judge Blaisdell Said He Only Did His Duty.

Bridget Sullivan and Morse Held as Witnesses.

Plea of the District Attorney was a Masterly One.

Lizzie To Be Taken to Taunton Jail To-Morrow.

Close of Preliminary Trial of the Great Murder Mystery.

[Special Dispatch.]

FALL RIVER, Sept. 1.—As usual long before the afternoon session of the Second District Court sitting, for the trial of Lizzie Borden for the murder of her father, bringing Harry Stewart, a wheelman, the opened the entrances were more bustling in appearance than the proverbial chickens around the dough dish. Humanity of all castes and classes pushed and jostled one another in a most plebeian fashion. There was the corpulent money-sordid aristocrat pushing side by side with the street laborer, and each and all clamoring and expostulating with the burly guardians of the public peace for admission to the court-room. Without exception a court-room of thrice its capacity would have been needed to hold them. They entered in groups, in twos and alone, filling the seats long before 2 o'clock and wearing away the long wait by chattering like so many magpies. The omnipresent "George" was in his element, bustling around the room, caring for the order and convenience of his large company of guests and otherwise displaying the importance of the Border City constabulary.

The friends of Lizzie, as they came in, were noticeably more smiling and buoyant than at any time previous in the trial. Attorney Jennings's forcible argument of the morning had aroused their hopes to a great degree, and they looked forward to the afternoon session with great expectancy.

THE DISTRICT ATTORNEY.

Mr. Knowlton's Presentation of the Case for the Prosecution.

The court came in promptly at 2 o'clock and the judge was received by the usual salute of the audience rising. Lizzie Borden came in a moment later, leaning on the arm of Mr. Buck, and took her seat. District Attorney Knowlton was supported upon the right by Attorney-General Pillsbury, who has made his second appearance here since the opening of the examination.

Mr. Knowlton said in his argument for the prosecution: I can easily appreciate Your Honor's feelings when near the close of one of the most important cases ever known in the county. The crime of murder is justly esteemed the most awful one in the calendar. Every woman who has heard of this crime which has been committed cannot but feel a thrill of horror, and even strong men are out-crept from such feeling. After the first shock, however, is over, everyone becomes a detective and willing to give his or her services to

Attempt to Discover the Author of the Crime.

I should have been deaf to the instincts of humanity if I had not listened to the call which came to me during the first vacation which I have enjoyed for twelve months if I had not come over here and endeavored to do what I could to unearth this most causeless of crimes. I have no wonder that the friends of this, the youngest daughter of the victim, have rallied to her defence. Does not Your Honor suppose that my own soul quickens with anguish at being called upon to accuse such a woman as this and to prosecute her for such a crime? The path of duty while not an easy one is a plain one, and I fully realize the responsibility which rests upon me at the present time.

There are

Three Stages to This Crime,

the first of which is outlined by the statutes. When a murder has been committed it is provided that there shall be held an inquest and witnesses summoned to give what testimony they can in regard to this case. Then there is another step in the course of inquiry. That step is to accumulate evidence which shall lead to the presentation of the crime to the grand jury. Then comes the duty of the grand jury and it is provided that they shall present their evidence to the court of competent jurisdiction.

Mr. Knowlton then entered upon the history of this crime, and said that a retired business man

and his aged wife, of a quiet and domestic disposition, have been murdered. The most pregnant fact in the case after the finding of the bodies was the knowledge of the murder of Mrs. Borden. The murder of the husband was but an incident to the first transaction. There is no motive shown for the murder that is adequate to the horribleness of the crime. I have never dealt with a man so utterly lost to sentiments of humanity as to believe him capable of such a deed without there is a suitable motive for it. When Dr. Draper in his evidence yesterday told of ten tapping blows we are struck by the fact that they are not such blows as a strong man would strike, but those of a weak, irresolute, imperfect

Feminine Hand, Not striking to Kill the First Time,

but striking and striking and striking until death was apparent. It was not even evidence of malice, because all were repeated successive blows, only one of which struck a fatal point. We stand upon the supposition that no one could have done the deed, but we are met with the fact that some one did.

Our first inquiry is, "Who would be benefited by the murder?" God forbid that I take that as full evidence of guilt. Take this girl as a babe with natural love for her mother, or at least the only mother she ever knew. I have learned that she repudiated the relation of mother and daughter which existed between them. Whatever cause there may have been for this murder we have this stubborn fact of a repudiation. Has Your Honor learned of any more fruitful source of hatred than that which grows out of the presence of a stepfather or stepmother. We do not know what was inside these doors, but we do know that here was a family, practically two families. Here we have a frugal old man, so frugal in fact that in the midst of a flourishing city does not even have gas or hot water, or even a bath tub in his home, married to a woman congenial to him but not to the daughters. Even as Lizzie tells it

There Was a Quarrel About Property,

and for five years Mrs. Borden was forced to be treated by the daughter she had brought up as not her daughter. Do you suppose love existed between them under these conditions? When Morse came he never saw Lizzie. When Lizzie's intimate friends came they saw her in her own sitting-room up-stairs. We have found the only person we ever heard of she was not in accord with.

Now, no one can imagine how anyone could have got into that house. I have listened to my learned friend and sympathize with him, but have heard no explanation of how anyone could have got in there, killed these people and got out again without being seen.

It was

The Most Completely Locked Up House in Fall River.

I tried to imagine how it could be done in my own house, where the doors are unlocked and free as air, but can see no way. Yet here is a house in the centre of Fall River where the doors are kept constantly locked and the windows shut. Even the barn was locked by Mr. Borden himself at night and unlocked by him in the morning. Lizzie says she locked her own room and you could not get from one part of the house to the other without a key.

Of course this is not conclusive evidence, but for that matter all evidence is circumstantial. In a house as open to public gaze as the City Hall of Fall River, where everybody who entered or left the house must have been seen, yet with everyone passing by and having a chance of seeing anyone, no one was seen to enter or leave.

The Front Door was Locked by Lizzie herself, and I fail to find in all the testimony a time when the back door was not locked. There is not a place accessible from the front stairs but Lizzie's room and the spare chamber.

I have not dwelt on the possibility or impossibility of a man secreting himself, of a man who would know when Lizzie Borden would be up stairs, and when Bridget Sullivan would be washing windows, and when he would meet no one in the way of the commission of his terrible crimes; neither of a man who would think it possible to stay in that house an hour

and a half after killing Mrs. Borden waiting his opportunity to kill the old man. I cannot conceive of any such man.

And so all the people in the house have been subjected to suspicion from the moment it appeared that the deed must have been done by some one in the house. First it was Morse, but his time was all suitably accounted for.

I Appreciate This Sympathy for the Prisoner,

but consider what Your Honor would do if John V. Morse were at the bar to be tried, but he is out of it.

Next comes the servant girl. Now I am a lover of fair play and in my eyes one class of people is no different from another. I know of no difference between reputable and honest Lizzie Borden, as she stood before, and reputable and honest Bridget Sullivan. Now I find Bridget Sullivan brought to this "star chamber," as my learned friend sees fit to call it, and examined as to her whereabouts the same as every one else. Star chamber? I ask my friend if he ever heard of my taking unfair advantage of a witness, or of showing discourtesy?

And what do we find? Let us assume that Bridget Sullivan told us the truth. She came down in the kitchen. The back door was locked. She waited in the kitchen while the rest ate breakfast. Saw Morse go out, saw Lizzie Borden come into the kitchen, she went into the yard and came in again. Mrs. Borden was then alive and told her about the windows. When she saw Mrs. Borden again she was dead. When she came into the sitting-room no one was in the lower part of the house and why? because they had gone up stairs, not by the back stairs. She must either have been in Lizzie's room or the spare chamber. Bridget goes to the barn to get a pail and when she comes in Lizzie goes out, says she need not lock the back door as she shall be there all the morning.

My friend says we have furnished proof only of an opportunity for crime. We have shown more. We have excluded the opportunity of leaving the house, and have left Lizzie and the woman she calls stepmother alone. They were alone until Bridget Sullivan came in to admit Mr. Borden. I don't care to comment on Lizzie's being at the head of the stairs laughing at this time, but Lizzie was there, where everyone who came in later and saw the body of the murdered woman says she was. I am now going to assume Bridget's testimony to be of importance. She left Lizzie with her father and went upstairs. Not over 20 minutes elapsed when Lizzie called her and said her father was murdered.

Lizzie Never Uttered a Cry or a Scream when she discovered the body of her father, which witnesses have well described was a most horrible sight. And no one has ever come forward to testify that they ever heard her utter a cry or a scream.

The district attorney then took up Lizzie's statement at the time of the murder and alluded to her saying she was in the kitchen or on the stairs. Mr. Knowlton said at the inquest

No Attempts Were Made to Confuse Lizzie

No adequate explanation has been made by Lizzie up to this time as to the manner in which she employed herself while her father was away from the house. When Assistant Marshal Fleet was at the house an hour after the killing, the house, and asked her what she wished the plea could have had more effect upon him.

Mr. Adams told a Standard reporter that no proceedings for a habeas corpus would be taken and the case would go the usual course.

Miss Borden will not be taken to Taunton jail until to-morrow, owing to the great excitement in this city this afternoon.

As Lizzie was taken to the matron's room for the first time she broke down and wept bitterly.

WILL WRITE A LETTER.

Mr. Blaine Will Make No Speeches During the Campaign.

AUGUSTA, Me., Sept. 1.—Senator Hale is in town to-day and visited the headquarters of the State committee. He informed a reporter that Mr. Blaine will make no speeches during the campaign, but is now engaged in writing a letter that is likely to appear any day, which will be devoted to some of the issues which are being discussed, and it is he thinks of deep interest.

The Famous Andover Case.

LAWRENCE, Sept. 1.—At the opening of the famous Andover case this afternoon Prof. Smyth's counsel argued for dismissal, because the case had been once decided on with a supreme decision in favor of Smyth. Judge Bishop of the trustee argued also for dismissal.

Died of His Injuries.

SALEM, Sept. 1.—William Walker, who was injured by a machine falling on him, died at the hospital this morning. He was 50 years old and leaves a family.

Cut in Two by a Train.

SALEM, Sept. 1.—An unknown man about 35 years old stepped in front of a freight train and was killed this afternoon, being cut in two.

POST OFFICE STATISTICS.—We are indebted to Postmaster Gifford for the following statistics of the money order business and sale of stamps at the post office for the month of August:

632 Domestic money orders issued, amounting to	$7,477.68
235 International money orders issued, amounting to	3,355.92
235 Postal notes issued, amounting to	381.57
1102	$11,215.17
383 Domestic money orders paid, amounting to	$5,971.00
49 International money orders paid, amounting to	1,422.69
215 Postal notes paid, amounting to	409.82
647	$7,802.91
Sales of stamps and envelopes amounted to	$4,315.89

REAL ESTATE SALES.—Francisco J. Oliveria has sold to Joseph Oliver a lot of land on the north side of contemplated Dudley street, containing 13.15 rods.

Simon Bousquet has sold to Alphonse Lachapelle a lot of land on Rock street.

Roble A. Emerson has sold to Cornelia W. Davis one undivided one-fifth part of house and land on the northeast corner of Bedford and Seventh streets, containing 6.39 rods.

We find here was the opportunity—the exclusive opportunity. Prussic acid couldn't be purchased and other means must be tried. Not a pistol. That would make too much noise, nor a knife as she would be seen by her victim, but a blow with some effective weapon delivered from behind. So we find this woman with another weapon.

In all this trial there is

Only One Person Who Has Never Expressed Emotion

and this fact takes away our horror at contemplating the bare facts. We never heard but one expression from Lizzie Borden, and that was when Assistant Marshal Fleet comes to the Borden house, she is annoyed that he searched her room to find who

Brutally Killed Her Father and Mother.

I know there is a discrepancy in not finding the cape that covered her when she struck the blows and another in our not producing the weapon. Long before Prof. Wood testified I was mystified for the reason why she could conceal the bloody clothing and not the hatchet.

This crime was planned by a cool, clear-headed person and she concealed the clothing and hatchet with such adroitness that they have not yet been found.

It would be a pleasure to be able to say that we could let this woman go, but we are constrained to find the evidence will not warrant it, constrained to find her trying to deal with murderous weapons, constrained because hers was the exclusive opportunity. The reward of such a release is not commensurate with the reward that attends the faithful performance of duty.

This closed the government's argument.

PROBABLY GUILTY.

Judge Blaisdell's Summing Up of the Facts Presented.

Judge Blaisdell spoke low and indistinct. He said this is a case where sympathy must be laid aside—duty must be done. In view of the evidence presented, there seems to me only one thing for a magistrate to do. Suppose a moment, instead of the defendant being a woman it was a man and he was found close to the guest-chamber,

That Chamber of Death,

as it proved for Mrs. Borden, and that man was the last to see Mr. Borden alive and the first to see his dead body. And suppose the only explanation of his conduct in the interim was as unreasonable as saying that he was in the barn looking for some lead for sinkers. Is there any question what a magistrate would determine under such circumstances as environ this case? So it seems to me there is

Only One Thing for a Magistrate to Do, and that is this: To announce that in the judgment of this court

The Accused is Probably Guilty, and order that she be held awaiting the action of the grand jury.

A Hum of Suppressed Excitement, almost a groan, ran around the room when Clerk Leonard arose.

"Lizzie A. Borden stand up," he commanded in solemn tones. Miss Borden arose with an effort trembling and pale. Clerk Leonard slowly read:

The judgment of this court is that you are probably guilty of the offence charged against you and it is therefore the order of this court that you be committed to the Taunton Jail, there to await the action of the Grand Jury, which meets the first Monday of November next."

Bridget Sullivan and John V. Morse were also held in $500 as witnesses and Hon. R. T. Davis went surety for their appearance.

Attorney Adams asked that the piece of plaster that created so much excitement a few days ago, be held in the custody of the court until the decision is rendered on his motion.

After court adjourned the judge stepped down and congratulated counsel for defence and said he wished the plea could have had more effect upon him.

NO NEW CASES ON BOARD.

Steamer Moravia Sent to Lower New York Bay.

NEW YORK, Sept. 1.—The steamer Moravia was sent to the lower bay two miles south of Swinburne Island this forenoon. Dr. Sanborn reports that there were no new cases on board. The Veendam's steerage passengers were this forenoon sent to Hoffmann Island, where the passengers will be bathed and disinfected, as Capt. Vanderse refused to allow the disinfecting process to be accomplished on board the steamer. When Dr. Talmage boarded the Gella at quarantine he found nine children suffering from measles and two from chicken-pox.

Acknowledge Themselves Beaten.

PALMER, Sept. 1.—The quarrymen at the flint granite company's works at Monson who were locked out some time ago, and refused to accept the terms offered by the manufacturers' association acknowledge themselves beaten this afternoon and will at once make application for their old places. Men that are needed will be hired but those employed since the lockout will not be discharged.

Ordered to be in Readiness.

SIMLA, Sept. 1.—A mountain battery and several battalions of Punjab infantry and cavalry have been ordered to hold themselves in readiness to re-inforce the troops in the Wana Gomul valley in the event of the ameer of Afghanistan failing to recall his agents, who are disturbing the peace of the Indian frontier.

Suspicions of Foul Play.

WILLIMANTIC, Sept. 1.—The body of William Ore, who mysteriously disappeared last Saturday, was found in the Willimantic river this morning, near the spot where he was last seen. The appearance of the body leads to a suspicion of foul play.

No Sign of Abatement.

LONDON, Sept. 1.—The scarlet fever epidemic shows no sign of abatement. There are to-day in the Metropolitan and London fever hospitals 356 cases of this disease.

Fire in Lowell.

LOWELL, Sept. 1.—On Suffolk street this morning fire destroyed the bottling establishment of P. H. Barry; also the barn of S. B. Pike with two horses. Barry loses $2000. Pike's loss unknown.

COLORED ODD FELLOWS.

Meeting of the District Grand Lodge G. U. O. O. F. in Attleboro.

The District Grand Lodge of Massachusetts, G. U. O. O. F., held its annual convention in Emmet Hall, Attleboro, Thursday afternoon, D. G. M. W. H. Clark presided. The following temporary officers were appointed:
Guardian—George Stevens of Royal Enterprise Lodge, Salem.
Warden—A. H. Roberts, Attleboro, Eastern Lodge.
Chaplain—A. M. Brown, Gordon Lodge, Springfield.

The chaplain offered prayer and the session was opened in due form. The roll of delegates was called.

The following grand officers were present: D. G. M. William H. Clark; D. D. G. M. Richard Carter; D. G. S. Isaac S. Millen; D. G. T. Michael R. Brown; D. G. D. Waldron Banks

D. G. M. Clark rendered his annual message. D. G. S. I. S. Mullen's report for the year ending Aug. 31, 1892, showed the number of the lodges in the district to be 17, with a membership of 1190. There has been paid to sick $3000, widows $200, charity $300, various objects $3360.10. There are in funds $6000, value of property $32,000, making a total valuation of property invested and in funds $47,000, an increase of $4900 over that of last year.

The secretary also reported the lodges in the State as being in a flourishing condition.

After the usual business was transacted, the following officers were elected for the ensuing year:
D. G. M.—W. H. Clark of Boston.
D. D. G. M.—G. A. Busby of Worcester.
D. G. S.—Isaac S. Mullen of Boston.
D. G. T.—Michael R. Brown of Boston.
Executive committee for one year—A. G. Gaskins of Boston, W. B. Smith of New Bedford, Waldron Banks of Boston.
Grand Marshal—George Stevens of Salem.
Grand Chaplain—A. N. Brown of Springfield.
Grand Warden—E. D. Treadwell of Pittsfield.
Grand Guardian—J. H. Roberts of Attleboro.

At the conclusion of the election the newly-elected officers were installed by N. P. Wentworth and W. G. Gaskins. The meeting then adjourned.

A RELIC OF THE PAST.—George F. Bartlett has purchased of Capt. Henry Clay the famous whaling schooner Franklin. He has been dismantled and towed to the cove at the foot of Howard avenue, where she will be moored as a relic of the whaling industry. At this point was commenced the first ship building of this port 75 years ago, two vessels of 275 tons each having been built there at that time. The old Howard house was erected at that time for the ship carpenters and was fitted for and occupied by five families. Another house of about this same size was built at the same time for the same purpose. Parts of the old ways from which the vessels were launched can be seen there now at low tide. The Franklin has her houses on deck and her pumps and rudder intact, and it seems fitting that one of the oldest and most successful whaling vessels of this port will be allowed to go to decay where the first were built.

INSANITY INDICATED.

Strong Doubts If Miss Borden Is Ever Tried.

An Official Thinks An Asylum May Be Her Lot.

A Pawtucket Woman Saw a Man Leave the Borden Yard.

One of the prosecuting officials of the Borden case is quoted by the Boston Globe as saying authoritatively on condition that his name be withheld from publication:

"On the day of the murder and very frequently since that time, I have talked with Lizzie A. Borden and have watched her closely. During her entire examination I sat in a position to command a full view of her face. At the inquest I heard her testimony. I believe I have observed her more closely than any other person connected with the prosecution case.

"What do I think?

"In answering that question I will first explain my reasons for framing my opinion of her. During 14 years official work for the State I have seen and dealt with many cases of insanity. I have been brought in constant contact frequently with the inmates of the Taunton Insane asylum during the Worcester asylum. I consider myself as well qualified to judge a case of mental irregularity in any man who is not an expert on insanity or a physician accustomed to the treatment of brain diseases.

With such experience, basing my opinion on what I have seen of Lizzie's eyes and movements, her physical make-up and mannerisms, I am led to believe her a victim of mania.

Her eyes have been very unnatural, and the way she has used them is identical with that of a person mentally deranged. This has been noted when her countenance was in repose, when it was not possibly assumed. The expression I have seen her wear time after time has been surely indicative of mental disturbance.

She has looked wilder and more irresponsible half of the time the past fortnight than any person I have seen in the Taunton hospital for months. My opinion has been corroborated by an expert who was led out of curiosity to attend the hearing one day and observe her.

As firmly as I believe she committed the murder, just so firmly do I think it the work of one insane. People may say, why doesn't she show signs of disturbance now? It is a well known fact that a person may be comparatively sound on all matters but one. That is the way I think it is with Lizzie.

When she has been looked up a few weeks, and the excitement of the examination is off, I shall look for a mental collapse and more definite signs of her trouble. In the event of my prediction coming true, it would be only necessary to procure two doctors to examine her, and then, without more ado, an order could be given for her removal to the insane hospital, and that would be the end of the prosecution of the Borden murder case.

This I really believe will be the ultimate result.

If Lizzie's condition is what I really think it is such an end will be certain.

If she is mentally sound, and her counsel appreciates the true strength of the government's case, with comparatively little trouble the same methods could be adopted with the same results. In either case I would not be the least surprised if Lizzie Borden never came to trial."

If the name of the official above quoted could be given, says the Globe, it would lend much weight to his statements. The gentleman in question has had greater experience than Marshal Hilliard, and is of sound judgment. He knows the facts in the Borden case as thoroughly as the former, and in his interview with the writer an unprejudiced opinion was sought and given.

A New and Important Witness.

Mrs. John Marshall of Pawtucket, R. I., has come forward with a statement to the effect that she was in Fall River on the day of the Borden murders, and while driving by the Borden house saw an ill-favored man come out of the front door. She says she remarked his appearance at the time to her lady companion. She explains her silence since then by the plea of illness and repugnance against appearing in court, but says that the case having gone so far, she now considers it her duty to tell what she knows. Her son has notified Mr. Jennings, and Mrs. Marshall's story will be at his disposal. Officer Medley of Fall River was in Pawtucket yesterday, but Mr. Marshall refused to permit him to see Mrs. Marshall.

Poor Peckham.

Charles H. Peckham, who gave himself up as the murderer of the Bordens, was heard from again yesterday morning, says the Fall River News. He says that he was the murderer and that Miss Borden is entirely innocent, and furthermore, the marshal and the judge have been bribed. The old man wanted a citizen of Central village to see the marshal this morning and try to persuade him that he (Peckham) is the criminal. He is still full of vagaries, and although half sick, desires to go to Washington and sit by the side of the President and tell Congress and the people that bribery and robbery must stop.

When asked why he happened to commit the murders, he says the devil prompted him. His explanation of the imminence of the Prince of Darkness involves the remark that the devil is inside of him (Peckham), and he is as big as a woodchuck.

Peckham was examined by three neighborhood physicians last Tuesday, who found his condition to be such that they will not be surprised to hear of his attempt at suicide later. During his verbal ramblings in discussing the part he had in the Borden case he said he thought the marshal would have him and hang him, and then his folks would have the $5000 reward offered by the Borden sisters, which was more than he was worth to his family.

DREDGING.—Dredger Yankee Notion of Fall River, with tug Delevan Peck of Providence as tender, has been dredging at Bennett mill for the laying of a new conduit for salt water for condensing purposes. The spruce conduit put down when the mill was built has been eaten out by worms. The new conduit will be of cast iron.

The Yankee Notion will now do some dredging for the Pierce mill for the purpose of a salt water conduit.

DR. FLOWER TO VISIT NEW BEDFORD TUESDAY.—Dr. R. C. Flower, the famous Boston physician, whose remarkable and extraordinary cures in seemingly hopeless cases, and whose no less remarkable method of diagnosing a patient's case correctly without asking a question has been the wonder of scientists and others, will, in response to numerous requests from friends and patients, visit New Bedford professionally next Tuesday, Sept. 6th, and will be at the Parker House on that day. This will give many an opportunity to consult Dr. Flower who might otherwise be unable to do so.

GOV. RUSSELL CANNOT ATTEND.—President Rotch of the Bristol County Agricultural Society has received word from Gov. Russell that his engagements will prevent his being present at the coming fair.

APPLIED FOR SUPERVISORS.—Among the cities that have applied to the United States Circuit Court for supervisors at the next national election are New Bedford, Fall River and Taunton.

None Such
CONDENSED
Mince Meat

Makes an every-day convenience of an old-time luxury. Pure and wholesome. Prepared with scrupulous care. Highest award at all Pure Food Expositions. Each package makes two large pies. Avoid imitations—and insist on having the NONE SUCH brand.
MERRELL & SOULE, Syracuse, N. Y.

C. W. HASKINS,

Having replenished his stock by liberal purchases of new goods, offers a choice selection of Diamonds, Watches, Fine Jewelry, Optical Goods, &c. The display of Sterling Silver Table Ware and Novelties is very attractive.

Attention is invited to a large collection of Souvenir Spoons, especially some in fine Enamel and Gold from various European countries.

Fine Watch and Clock Repairing done by competent and careful workmen and fully warranted

—AT—

C. W. HASKINS',
No. 20 Purchase Street.

THESE ARE BUT FEW
—OF THE—
MANY BARGAINS
WE ARE GIVING OUR CUSTOMERS.

If you see anything in the list that you can save money on give us a chance to save it for you. Remember anything you see advertised from our store is all right in quality. We don't keep poor goods that are not cheap at any price.

BEST St. Louis Flour, 66 cents per bag.
10 lbs. Large Sweet Potatoes for 25 cts.
3 lbs. Fresh Ginger Snaps for 25 cts.
4 lbs. Common Crackers for 25 cts.
A Can of Best Condensed Milk for 15c.
Much better Peaches at 18c. per can than you can buy fresh at 15 cts. a qt.
Quaker Oats at 3 1-2c. lb., or in packages at 10 cts.

Everything as low as any one, plenty of things lower than the lowest.

A. G. ALLEY, Jr.,
Sixth and Union Sts.

THE NAVAL RESERVE.

Col. Mathews Speaks Against the Transfer of Co. E.

The annual meeting of the honorary members of the City Guards was held in the Armory of Co. E last evening and was largely attended. The following officers were elected for the ensuing year:
President—William Banks.
Secretary and Treasurer—I. B. Tompkins, Jr.
Executive Committee—John Eldridge, Jr., James Delano, George N. Alden.

The treasurer's report showed the receipts by dividend has been $11.80 and the payments $119.11. Balance $237.94. There are at present 217 members. Two members were admitted during the year and one member died.

The proposition to transfer the company to the naval reserve was discussed. Capt. Perry explained the position of members of the company who desire to join the naval battalion.

Col. T. R. Mathews of the First Regiment, M. V. M., was a guest of the honorary members and delivered an interesting address.

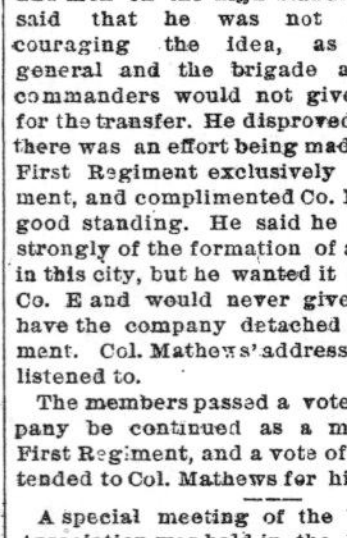

COL. MATHEWS.

Col. Mathews explained the meaning of the naval reserve and told of the duties of the organization. He said that it was not possible for Co. E to join the reserve, for as long as he was commander of the First Regiment he should never give his consent to it. A member of the company could not join the reserve until he had served his time of enlistment and is discouraged the idea of breaking up the company for any such purpose, speaking of the excellent record the company had made during its 45 years of existence, and complimenting the officers and men on the high standing to-day. He said that he was not alone in encouraging the idea, as the adjutant general and the brigade and regimental commanders would not give their consent to the transfer. He disproved the report that there was an effort being made to make the First Regiment exclusively a Boston regiment, and complimented Co. B on its present good standing. He said he approved very strongly of the formation of a naval reserve in this city, but he would have it independent of Co. E and would never give his consent to have the company detached from the regiment. Col. Mathews' address was attentively listened to.

The members passed a vote that the company be continued as a member of the First Regiment, and a vote of thanks was extended to Col. Mathews for his address.

A special meeting of the Veteran Cadets Association was held in the Board of Trade rooms last evening, President Mayhew B. Hitch in the chair. The meeting was for the purpose of listening to the report of a committee appointed at the annual meeting to look into the advisability of organizing a company of Naval Volunteers, among members of the association. In the absence of the chairman, President Hitch made the report, which was to the effect that the time had come when a company of Naval Volunteers is to be formed in this city and if the Veteran Cadets are to take a hand in the organization, now is their time to act. It was not for the association to organize the company, but merely to urge the members as individuals to enlist. Half the members of the company, at least, he thought, ought to be Veteran Cadets.

After an informal discussion of the matter a committee consisting of Mayhew B. Hitch, George N. Gardiner and John Holt, was appointed to act for the association in promulgating the formation of the company.

The Naval Reserve force in Fall River met in the armory Thursday night, and nominated Richard P. Borden and Edward Shove for ensigns. The membership list has 45 names on it, the regulation number being 58. The entrance fee is $2 and annual dues will be $4.

FALL RIVER.

A woman named Carter of Davis Street was cleaning a large looking-glass yesterday morning, when she slipped and struck it with her forehead, breaking it to pieces. Her head was cut in several places, also her right hand. It is feared that blood-poisoning will result from the wound.

The Fall River Yacht Club has decided to expel a Taunton member for conduct unbecoming a yachtsman in a race.

SOMERSET.

A wedding occurred Wednesday afternoon in Fall River, the interested parties being Mr. Frank H. Borden of Fall River, and Miss Josie E. Thrasher of Somerset. The ceremony took place at the home of the bride's mother, Mrs. A. C. Thrasher, corner of Clark and High streets. Rev. A. D. Spaulding officiated. The bride wore a princess gown of white silk, and carried a bouquet of white rosebuds. The room was decorated with golden rod, ferns, etc. The ushers were W. E. Dore and M. B. Deane of Fall River, E. A. Thrasher and W. B. Deane of Somerset. About 50 witnessed the ceremony. A reception and collation followed. Mr. and Mrs. Borden took the train for Boston, and after a short tour will return, and for the present reside at the bride's former home.

TAUNTON.

Fire in the picker room of Cohannet mill No. 2, yesterday afternoon damaged cotton to the extent of $3000; insured.

The writ in an action of tort for alleged libel by Dr. M. C. Golden against Thomas B. Eaton is returnable the first Monday in October at the Superior Court in Taunton. Dr. Golden and Mr. Eaton have furnished bonds.

The Taunton Cycle Club gave a reception to Hon. Edward Mott on Thursday evening to manifest its thanks for his efforts in behalf of good roads.

PLYMOUTH COUNTY.

Three public celebrations are to take place in Middleboro this month. On Sept. 14 occurs the reception and entertainment of the New England Water Works Association; Sept. 24 is Middleboro fire department "field day," and probably the last of September will be the joint celebration of the opening of the Plymouth & Middleboro railroad, Middleboro, Carver, Plymouth.

Police officers raided Dan Harrington's house on East Water street, Rockland, Thursday evening and secured 44 cases of lager beer.

The members of the First Free Baptist church of Brockton have voted to extend a call to Rev. D. G. Donnocker of Scarboro, Me., to the pastorate of the church.

NEWSPAPER CHANGES HANDS.—The Independent, published at Falmouth, has been sold, at sheriff's sale, to Charles F. Chamberlayne for $2500, the amount of his claim, less an $800 mortgage due to George E. Clarke of Falmouth. It is said it will continue to be published as a Democratic organ.

FREIGHT STEAMERS.—Steamer City of Fitchburg will go on the New York line tomorrow and will run with the City of Brockton.

When Your Liver
is torpid and sluggish, you cannot do business successfully. Everything goes wrong. You don't feel well. Get your liver in good working order by using Dr. Hale's Household Tea, the great blood purifier and nerve tonic. It has no equal as a health builder. For sale at Wright Drug Co., 18 Purchase street.

DROOP AND DIE.

Mothers Have Cause to Fear This Weather.

Interviews with Local Physicians of all Schools.

Infant Mortality Credited to Improper Food.

Lactated Food the Purest and Best Diet.

Happy New Bedford Mothers Whose Children Live on It.

The extraordinary mortality from various forms of infantile indigestion this Summer has led to careful inquiry, and the best authorities on the subject in this city have freely expressed their opinions. Several of the best known physicians in New Bedford were interviewed yesterday, and the following questions were asked:

"In view of the large death rate this Summer of infants in New Bedford, what do you recommend?"

The general sentiment of the profession was voiced in the following statement from one of the most successful practitioners among children. He said:

"There is nothing equal to lactated food, and its use is fast becoming general among the profession. We find that it is retained on the stomach where other things are not retained.

"For cholera infantum I find it most valuable, and I generally give small portions often repeated when called to attend such cases. In almost every case where mothers are unable to nurse their infants I find that lactated food answers well."

Many happy mothers in New Bedford have used lactated food successfully where everything else failed. They say that this food has kept their children strong and well during the dangerous Summer season and many of them have recommended it to friends, who have had the same happy experience.

The principal element of mother's milk is sugar of milk. This is the basis of lactated food. With it is combined the nutritious elements of the great cereals, wheat and barley, and when prepared it makes lactated food forming salts. This makes lactated food a perfect and natural substitute for mother's milk.

It must be borne in mind that lactated food is so inexpensive that it is within the reach of every family. 150 meals can be made from a dollar package of the food, and when prepared for the use of infants it costs less than five cents a quart.

Mothers should remember that cholera infantum can be more easily prevented than cured. Simply feed the baby with pure lactated food, and the child will keep well and strong.

WEST TISBURY.

The rate of taxation in West Tisbury is $11 per $1000. The following is a list of those who pay a tax of $20 and upward:

Freeman A. Athearn,	$32	Marshuns Luce,	24
Zadoc A. Athearn,	21	John A. Luce,	22
Benjamin Athearn,	25	Daniel Luce,	24
Heirs of Washing-		James Luce,	20
ton Athearn,	23	Hiram N. Luce,	21
Heirs of David B.		James F. Luce,	26
Athearn,	36	Mary C. Luce,	22
Heirs of Edmund		Sarah M. Luce,	27
Cottle,	22	Littlefield & Smith,	35
Timothy C. Cottle,	44	Jared Mayhew,	30
John Cottle,	32	David Mayhew,	25
William Cottle,	23	David W. Mayhew,	28
Walter G. Cottle,	35	Nathan Mayhew,	26
Edward Cottle,	48	Sereno M. May-	
William Chase,	23	hew,	30
Benjamin Chase,	25	Ulysses E. Mayhew,	20
James F. Cleveland,	26	S. M. Mayhew & Co.,	61
Heirs of Thomas G.		Adaline Manter,	29
Campbell,	67	Cyrus Manter,	34
Obed S. Daggett,	45	Heirs of Eliakim	
William N. Gray,	38	Norton,	21
George G. Gifford,	24	Heirs G. Norton,	45
John Huff,	29	Alfred Norton,	35
John E. Johnson,	37	Heirs of Thomas L.	
David N. Look,	22	Norton,	25
Mayhew Look,	21	Obed Nickerson,	25
John Look,	27	William L. Pease,	30
Frank L. Look,	39	William J. Rotch,	61
Allen Look,	23	Robert Raymond,	23
James Look,	26	John H. Smith, heirs of	27
Freeman A. Look,	31	Richard Thompson,	29
Constant D. Luce,	26	David B. West,	22
Heirs William H.		Hervey Weeks,	23
Luce,	35	Thomas Waldron,	97
Caroline M. Luce,	24	James F. Whiting,	48
William H. Luce,	21	Johnson Whiting,	68

Non-residents.

Anna S. Berry, Newport,			48
R. W. Crocker, Tisbury,			24
B. O. Cromwell Jr, Tisbury,			20
D. A. Cleveland, Middletown, Ct.,			20
Everett A. Davis, Boston,			42
Emmons & Morse,			24
Look, Washburn & Co.,			93
Frank H. Paine,			25
James L. Smith, Tisbury,			25
Herman Strater, Boston,			65
N. S. Shaler, Cambridge,			145
F. L. Smith, heirs, Tisbury,			30
Trustees Marthas Vineyard Associates,			51

The following statistics are furnished by the assessors: Number of polls assessed 159, dwelling-houses 189, horses 126, cows 200, other cattle 200, sheep 1895, assessed valuation—personal $52,598, real $229,018.

WAREHAM.

Rev. Daniel J. Griffin sailed from New York for Liverpool on first sill, thence to Africa. He is to engage in missionary work under Bishop William Taylor.

The Fall term of the High school will begin Monday, Sept. 12th.

Business is lively at the present time. The Franconia Works are kept running steadily to fill their orders; reports from the works at South Wareham are encouraging for the future, and at Tremont a large number of men are constantly employed. The works at Parker Mills, where but little has been done for many years, will soon be in full blast, employing a large force of men in the manufacture of nut nails.

The cranberry picking season has fairly opened, and hundreds of men, women and children are daily transported to and from the bogs.

There will be a larger number employed in the various industries of the town this Fall than there has been for a long series of years.

The annual meeting of the Wareham Free Library Association was held 28th ult. and the annual report was very encouraging. The library contains nearly 1200 volumes and their bank account shows $600. This year's bills of more than $275 have been paid by Miss Anna S. Amory of Boston, the founder of the library. The reading-room has been well patronized, and a large number of new and valuable books placed on the shelves.

GRAMMAR SCHOOL TEACHERS.—The grammar school committee has engaged Miss Helen Ring of Nantucket to fill the vacancy in the fifth grade at the Parker Street grammar school. Miss Lizzie Brightman has also been assigned to the same school.

Miss Julia P. Gifford is assigned to the vacancy at the Middle Street school.

It Strikes us as Remarkable
to hear of the wonderful record for curing enjoyed by Betton's Infallible Pile Salve. It cures every form of this troublesome ailment. If not to be had at your druggist's, send 50 cents to Winkelmann & Brown Drug Co., Baltimore, Md.

READ! READ!

SATURDAY

CLEARING PRICES

— AT —

MOYNAN & CO'S.

MOYNAN & CO. offer for Saturday Misses' School Coats, in medium weight, just the thing for early Fall wear, all sizes, 4 to 12 years, and worth from $7 to $12. Now marked down to $3.98, $4.98 and $5.98. Now is your chance to buy school garments cheap.

See our new stock of gloves.

MILLINERY DEPARTMENT. — For this day, new School Caps in all colors, 25 cents each. Boys' Straw School Hats were 48 cents, 75 cents and 98 cents, now only 25 cents each. Millinery Flowers, in Sprays, Wreaths, and Montures, formerly from 50 cents to 98 cents, your choice on Saturday 15 cents. A big variety of odds and ends in flowers will be offered for this sale at 5 cents each. Moynan & Co.

Don't Miss the Bargains in Millinery Flowers.

IN LINEN DEPARTMENT.—We offer for Saturday, 50 dozen Huck and Damask Towels, warranted all linen, some with knotted fringes, some with plain hem. These goods are worth 25 cents, for this sale only 19 cents each. Moynan & Co.

You should see those 36-inch all-wool serges we are selling at 39 cents, worth 50 cents.

MOYNAN & Co. are selling an extra size White Marseilles pattern Bed Spread, regular value is said to be $1.75, our price only $1.48; also at same counter you can buy a ¾-yard wide, cream white wool flannel, regular value 25 cents, our price being only 19 cents per yard.

Linen buyers should examine our remnants of Table Damasks, lengths of from 1 1-2 to 3 yards.

BIGGEST BARGAIN OF THE SEASON.—All our fine straw hats and bonnets, formerly sold at from $1 to $2.48, and recently sold at our bargain sales for 25 cents each, they are now offered for the last time on Saturday, when you can have your choice at *15 cents each.*

A few Blazer Jackets to be closed out at $2.98 each.

THOSE 50-CENT SERGES we are selling for 39 cents are making a wonderful stir in even these dull times. You should get one before they're gone. Remember no replacing at less than regular value. Moynan & Co.

Ribbons in all colors. Ribbons in all widths. Ribbons at half regular prices.

TRUTH ABOUT DRESS GOODS.—We have the best assortment in the city of Dress Goods, suitable for school wear, in good qualities. Especially have we made extra efforts to meet the demand this season, and those 50-cent, 59-cent and 69-cent all-wool Suitings we now offer at 37½ cents is the result. Come quickly, they cannot last long, as the quantity is becoming limited Moynan & Co.

Waists! Waists! All our 50-cent goods for Saturday only 39 cents.

MOYNAN & Co. are clearing up their wash goods department. All odds and ends are marked at ridiculously low prices; and to make things livelier still for Saturday, will throw in 20 pieces of Cocheco serges in dark colors only—regular 12½ cent goods—for 8¾ cents. *Come early.*

Visit our Housefurnishing Department for Bargains in Glassware and Kitchen Utensils of all kinds.

BARGAINS AT TRIMMING COUNTER.—Canfield dress shields (in seconds) only 12½ cents a pair; fine Nainsook dress shields 10 cents a pair; remnants of dress trimmings at your own price. Tuxedo veilings in colors, with chenille dot, 15 cents per yard. Embroidered flouncings and all kinds of laces at low prices. Moynan & Co.

Bargains on Saturday in Ladies' and Gents' underwear and hosiery.

FREE.—Call and get a copy of "Modes and Fabrics." September issue is now ready for distribution. Moynan & Co.

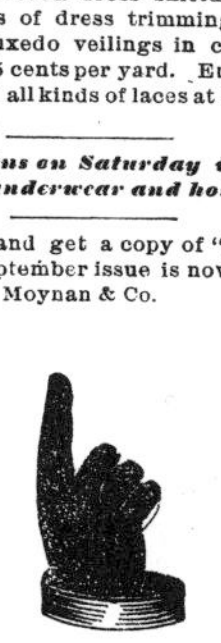

The Evening Standard.

NEW BEDFORD, MASS.

SATURDAY EVENING, SEPT. 3.

THREE EDITIONS DAILY.

No. 87 Union Street.

PUBLISHED BY

E. ANTHONY & SONS.

INCORPORATED.

—TERMS—

Six Dollars a Year, Three Dollars for Six Months, in advance: Single Copies Two Cents.

TWELVE PAGES.

This Evening's Issue Consists of Twelve Pages and Every Patron is Entitled to that Number.

TELEPHONE CALLS.

Counting Room, - - - - 308—2
Editorial Room, - - - - 308—3

BRANCH OFFICE AT NORTH END.

For the Convenience of the patrons of the EVENING STANDARD at the North End of the City, a branch office has been established at the stores of A. F. Wilde, Nos. 842 and 844 Purchase street, where advertisements will be received at office rates. Telephone number 32—4.

FOR PRESIDENT:
BENJAMIN HARRISON
OF INDIANA.

FOR VICE-PRESIDENT:
WHITELAW REID
OF NEW YORK.

CONTENTS OF THIS EVENING'S STANDARD.

Page 1.

Fall River Weavers' Association will again ask for an increase in wages.
Steamships with cholera on board arrive at New York to-day.
Home matters.
Late telegraphic news.

Page 2.

Indications of insanity in Miss Lizzie A. Borden.
Col. Mathews objects to the transfer of Co. E to the Naval Reserve.
Meeting of Veteran Cadets.
Convention of colored Odd Fellows.
West Tisbury's heavy tax payers.
Home matters.
Suburban news.

Page 3.

President's circular meets the approval of level-headed Britishers.
Progress of the cholera in the old world.
Suspicions of police in Cottage City infanticide case.
Portraits of Mrs. Grover Cleveland.
Early telegraphic dispatches.
Communications.

Page 4.

Opinions of New Bedford lawyers on Judge Blaisdell's conduct in the Borden murder case.
Third District Court.
Editorials.
Home Matters.
Suburban news.
Telegraphic dispatches.

Page 5.

Marine intelligence.
Marriages and deaths.

Page 6.

Financial news.
Second Edition — Telegraphic and local news.

Page 7.

Catcher Donahue badly injured in the New Bedford-Middleboro ball game.
Sports at New Orleans to see the big fights.
Sunday notices.
Yesterday's ball games.
Amusement and sporting news.

Page 8.

Outline of the President's plans during the Grand Army encampment.
A war movement in Hayti.
Peculiar case arising under the will of a Boston man.
More suits over the Order of the Rising Sun.
Business outlook is bright.
Third Edition—Telegraphic and local news.
Early telegraphic dispatches.

Page 9.

How stolen securities are disposed of in London with immunity.
Wives of the political leaders Carter and Harrity.
Friendly relations between the United States and nations to the South.
Joseph Rodman Drake.
People's party leader in Ohio.
Miscellaneous reading.

Page 10.

Wakeman writes from ancient Bath.
Kathleen Mavourneen sung by its author.

Page 11.

The G.A.R. re-union in Washington.
Olive Harper contrasts the costumes of today with those of long ago.

Page 12.

Bible Lesson.
Farm, Garden and Home.

☞ When the cholera visited this country in 1832, a town meeting was held here June 23, at which a report was made by Timothy G. Coffin, and a vigilance committee was appointed, of which James Arnold was president, to divide the city into districts for the abatement of nuisances. July 20 was appointed as a day of fasting and prayer on account of the epidemic. These causes combined proved so efficacious that no case of cholera was reported to have occurred in the town. The epidemic had practically disappeared by October 1. In 1854 four cases of cholera were reported here, two of which terminated fatally. There were rumors of others cases, but according to the papers of the day, they were without foundation.

The word cholera is said to be derived from a Greek word meaning a rain-gutter, as marking the fluidity, rapidity and copiousness of the discharges. The disease was known 400 years before Christ, and was said to have always originated in Hindostan, and it was said to have regular periods of twelve years, coinciding with the 12-yearly religious feasts there. In 1831 it made its first appearance in Europe, having been advancing eastward gradually since 1829, and in 1832 it first appeared in America at Quebec, and soon extended to this country, where it appeared again in 1848, 1854 and 1865. A great many remedies have been proposed and used, but no specific has been discovered, and the detection of the cholera bacillus has not been followed as yet by any means for its destruction. The best means to avoid it are not to use water which may contain the germs, unripe or indigestible fruits and vegetables, and intoxicating drinks, and to live on a healthy and substantial diet. The first thing to be done is for the patient to go to bed, remain absolutely quite and be kept warm, and the next to send for a competent physician instead of relying on nostrums.

☞ Methodists in this vicinity will no doubt be largely interested in this week's issue of *Zion's Herald*. It is known as the Wilbur Fisk number and includes a biographical sketch of this eminent divine so intimately connected with New England and American Methodism, by Abel Stevens, LL. D., a sketch of his life and character by Rev. William Rice, D. D., and a symposium of brief characterizations from the pens of the most noted professors, divines and others of the Methodist church. Nearly three pages of the paper are devoted to this feature, and every Methodist in the land should preserve a copy as a memorial of a great and good man.

☞ The Boston *Journal* suggests the names of Senator Dawes and Hon. John D. Long as the Republican candidates for electors-at-large.

☞ Gov. Tillman appears to have achieved a decided victory in the primary elections for Democratic candidates in South Carolina. This means that the old aristocratic democracy, composed of the great planters and slave holders, the fire-eaters and secessionists, has had its day, and that the Democratic Democracy, the hard-fisted farmers, who till their own fields and live by the sweat of their brows, has come to the top. As the Hartford *Courant* says, Tillman is not a handsome person, or a nice-spoken person, or a nice-mannered person, or an amiable person, or an intellectual person, or in any way the kind of person we have been in the habit of electing to governorships in this country; but the plain up-country Democrats of South Carolina seem to find him entirely satisfactory. But his success shows that there has been a revolution in the State, the full results of which are not yet apparent. The movement has not been a very intelligent one so far as matters of national policy are concerned, but the experience it will give will be an invaluable means of education in politics.

HOME MATTERS.

A HANDSOME SHOWING.

The circulation of the EVENING STANDARD for the last 10 days in August was as follows:

August 20,	9676	copies.
22,	8827	"
23,	8137	"
24,	8001	"
25,	9536	"
26,	9870	"
27,	9912	"
29,	9410	"
30,	9467	"
31,	9312	"

The daily average of copies was 9194 for the above period, and for the whole month was 8742.

AWARDS TO THE BELVEDERE.

Salvage for Bringing Down the William Lewis' Whalebone.

A telegram received in this city to-day from parties in San Francisco gives the award of the court on the question of salvage for the steam whaler Belvedere in bringing down from the Arctic ocean whalebone from steamer William Lewis, which was wrecked last season. The court has awarded $4006 to the owners of the Belvedere and $4092 to the officers and crew of the steamer.

POLITICAL.—The Republicans of Wellfleet have elected W. H. Tubman delegate to the Congressional Convention. He is a Randall man. Mr. Randall now has 45 delegates and Mr. Greene 28.

A Republican caucus will be held in Phœnix Hall, Fairhaven, on Tuesday evening to elect delegates to the State, District, First Councillor, Bristol County and Fourth Bristol Representative conventions. A town committee will also be elected.

There is some talk of holding the Councillor convention for this Republican district in Brockton.

The first Plymouth Prohibition Senatorial Convention was held at Banquet Hall, Whitman, yesterday, and John F. Kilbreth of Pembroke was nominated as candidate for Senator. George W. Severance was elected as a member of the State Central Committee. The Plymouth County Prohibition Association held a meeting afterwards. At 2 o'clock the executive committee held a conference with the town committees. It was decided to hold public meetings in every town in the county as often as possible until election day, and for the town committee to meet in conference on the afternoon of the day in which the meetings were held. J. R. Bartlett of Brockton was chosen to conduct the campaign. At 7 30 p. m. a public meeting was held, at which addresses were delivered.

The Democrats of Barnstable have formed a campaign club with the following officers: President, Frank M. Hinckley; vice-president, Zebina H. Jenkins; secretary and treasurer, George W. Kelley; executive committee, Elisha B. Fish, Frank B. Esterbrooks, William F. Makepeace, T. C. Day, Marcus M. Nye. A meeting of the Cleveland Club will be held at Barnstable on the 9th inst. when a flag will be unfurled.

SERIOUSLY INJURED.—Dennis Coughlin, a coal shoveller, employed at Garfield & Proctor's coal yard, was at work in the hold of schooner Wesley M. Oler this morning, when he wished to go on deck for a pail of water, and asked the engineer to hoist him with the falls. As Coughlin came up his head struck the combing of the hatch and he was thrown to the lower hold. He struck on his head and received a scalp would, and it is thought his skull is fractured. He was taken to St. Luke's Hospital for surgical treatment. He is 60 years of age, and therefore his chances for recovery are not so good as they otherwise would be.

MORTUARY.—The whole number of deaths the past week, as recorded at the office of the Board of Health, is 24, 11 of which were children under five years. There was one stillborn. Of the deaths there were five from infantile debility, three from cholera infantum, two each from paralysis, apoplexy and diphtheria, and one each from phthisis, tuberculosis pul., dysentery, pneumonia, heart disease, old age, cerebro spinal meningitis, convulsions and suicide, and also one from an unknown cause.

TIMELY DISCOVERY.—Officer James W Arnett discovered an incipient blaze in an ash barrel between buildings on the east side of Purchase street owned by Messrs. Saxon and Wilcox, and extinguished it before any damage was done. It was caused by hot ashes, and but for the timely discovery would have been serious, as it was communicating to the buildings.

THE COUNTY ROAD.—It is now ascertained that all abutters on the west side of County road, between Davis' corner and the city line, have consented to the setting back of their fences and walls to the orignal width of the road, with the exception of James Hathaway, who objects. It might be remarked that Mr. Hathaway has no buildings on his property.

RELIGIOUS.—The next all-day holiness meeting will be held in the Foster Street church, Thurday, Sept. 8th. Rev. M. D. Collins, D. D., of Scituate is expected to take charge.

The Friends' meeting-house, Spring street, opens to-morrow (Sunday,) having been closed during the Summer.

NEW CHURCH.—Mr. W. Walling, contractor, has broken ground to-day to build a Primitive Methodist church on East County street, north of Rivet, and south of Thompson street. We wish both contractor and Rev. Thomas Wilson every success in their enterprise.

CONTAGIOUS DISEASES.—Two new cases of scarlet fever, four new cases of typhoid fever, and one new case of diphtheria have been reported at the office of the Board of Health the past week.

NEW UNIFORMS.—The Monte Pio Association has contracted with Ashley & Peirce for 200 new uniforms. They are double-breasted, of blue cloth with gold trimmings

ACCIDENT.—Edward Lannie, employed by the Old Colony Railroad Co., while at work in a car this morning had his right arm broken by the door to the car falling on him.

HEAVY TAX PAYER.—Among the heavy tax payers in Providence is the Arnold Block estate, valued at $183,860.

FULL TIME.—The Morse Twist Drill & Machine Co's works will start up on full time next week.

LEGAL OPINIONS

Regarding the Action of Judge Blaisdell

Presiding at Inquest and at Miss Borden's Examination.

District Attorney Complimented by Lizzie's Staunchest Friends.

The action of Judge Blaisdell of the Second District Court in presiding both at the inquest into the cause of the death of Andrew J. Borden and his wife and at the examination which led to Lizzie A. Borden being held for the action of the grand jury, has created a good deal of discussion among the laity in this city, and among the members of the bar the feeling is even more pronounced. With the view of ascertaining how the action of Judge Blaisdell is taken among the lawyers a reporter of the *Standard* this forenoon called on a number of them. The selection of persons by the scribe was not made with design, but those who happened to be in (among a large number called upon) were interviewed.

The first man seen was Hon. Walter Clifford, of the well-known law firm of Crapo, Clifford & Clifford, and he was asked what he thinks of the decision of Judge Blaisdell in holding Lizzie A. Borden for the grand jury in the light of the testimony given.

"On that subject," said Mr. Clifford, "I have nothing to say, but I will give you my opinion on one subject. I am not surprised at the feeling which was engendered when it was learned that Judge Blaisdell had determined to act as a magistrate at the examination of Lizzie Borden when he had previously acted at the inquest. Although this determination was legal and in accordance with the recent statute, yet, the law being not generally understood by the people, and being so directly in contradiction with the common law in relation to criminal trials, it is only natural that feeling should be aroused that rights of accused were being somewhat violated. The theory which obtains in European countries under the civil laws—that accused persons should be at once subjected to a rigid cross-examination with the view of securing evidence which will place the accused in the position of being probably guilty unless innocence is clearly established—has never prevailed in this country, and the law which transferred from the coroner to the magistrate, before whom the question of the probable guilt is to be tried, the duty of first investigating the circumstances surrounding a tragedy partakes so strongly of the theory of the civil law as opposed to our own laws, that I think it would have never been passed by the Legislature had its effects been fully understood and appreciated by the people."

Wendell H. Cobb, Esq., on being asked as to his opinion of Judge Blaisdell presiding at the inquest and examination said: "I don't know as it is hardly proper for me to criticise without knowing all the facts. It seems to me that the action of Judge Blaisdell in presiding at the inquest and as judge at the preliminary trial were unprecedented, if not improper. In my judgment, having heard all the evidence at the inquest, it would be impossible in the nature of things that he could approach the trial with his mind entirely free and unbiased. Of course it was legal for him to preside, but in my opinion it was not in accordance with fine sense or judicial honor. In the minds of the public it was a foregone conclusion when the hearing commenced that Lizzie Borden would be held for the grand jury, but with the evidence so far made public I don't believe (and have yet to see the man who does believe) that the grand jury will indict her or that any jury could be found to convict her.

L. LeBaron Holmes, Esq., on being asked his opinion as to Judge Blaisdell's action, said the ordinary practice in murder cases has no parallel for judgment in this one. "I think," said Mr. Holmes, "Judge Blaisdell had a perfect right to sit. The rest must be left to his sense of judicial propriety. If the judge didn't preside, who could have done so? Who are the special justices of that court? That would have to be considered. Judge Blaisdell had heard the evidence at the inquest, and if he could conscientiously and honestly say that he had formed no opinion regarding the guilt or innocence of accused, and having a perfect legal right and no bias, and looking at the condition of things, I see no reason why Judge Blaisdell should not sit. I think no one can decide if Judge Blaisdell should not sit. It was a personal question for him."

E. D. Stetson, Esq., said: "It certainly could have been no pleasure for Judge Blaisdell to preside at the examination, and I feel that only a sense of duty could have caused him to do so. His age and experience qualify him to be the best judge of fitness."

William C. Parker, Esq., said among other things: "Unless Judge Blaisdell felt that in the hands of a special justice the interests of justice might suffer, I think as a matter of propriety it would have been better for him not to have presided after hearing the evidence at the inquest. For the same reason I think a magistrate who issues a warrant on a complaint in a common criminal case ought not to sit at its trial if he can avoid doing so. As to the legal right of Judge Blaisdell to preside, I have no doubt."

Judge Borden of the District Court was averse to talking for publication. He finally said as the law has made no other provision he thinks Judge Blaisdell was justified in presiding at both inquest and examination, and that he should not be subjected to severe criticism for doing so.

The District Attorney's Plea.

The Fall River *News* printed the following editorial last evening:

Whatever judgment one may form upon the merits of the question in view of the evidence submitted and analyzed by the contesting attorneys, no one will dispute that the case of the government has been in strong hands. District Attorney Knowlton has borne out his reputation as a sound and skilful prosecuting officer. He has not shown himself heartless, cold or apathetic. On the contrary his appearance as he entered upon and pursued his analysis of the evidence showed that he possessed no little feeling. His emotions were suppressed as they had to be. His argument was dispassionate, where that of his adversary was impassioned. His heart refused to follow the line of his argument.

The force of his desires and sympathies conspired with his deep convictions to give glow and fervor to the plea of Mr. Jennings. The exact reverse was the case with the plea of Mr. Knowlton. His convictions and sense of duty ran counter to the current of his desire. The one was impelled both by a sense of duty and the rush of his heart's impulse. The other was led by a sense of duty equally clear, against the tender sympathies of his nature, and therefore his appeal was not to the emotions, but to the rational judgment.

The manner of the district attorney comported with the solemnity of the task imposed upon him. Against every item of the cumulative evidence his heart reluctated. In manly fashion he took the responsibility of the arrest which his plea was to vindicate, and declared that for the decision to arrest, the judge on the bench had no responsibility.

The plea was an able, logical and cogent array of the items of evidence, and as formidable as the facts were susceptible of. It was a calm and cumulative recital of the incriminating facts of which the government is in possession, so far, at least, as the attorney judged is necessary to go to secure the holding of the accused. Mr. Knowlton was obliged to confess that the weapon with which the deed was committed has not been found. As Mr. Jennings most effectively urged, the closer Lizzie Borden is shut up in that house on the fatal day so much the closer are the bloody evidences of her crime shut in with her; and yet the repeated and careful searches have not disclosed them. That fact, of course, makes strongly against the guilt of the accused.

Mr. Knowlton's analysis of the movements of the two inmates of the house to whom suspicion might attach seemed to us more close than that made by Mr. Jennings.

The argument as to a motive will not seem conclusive to those who have best known the accused and her home relations, although it cannot be disputed that there is an unfortunate basis in fact for the allegation on which the district attorney rested his case as to a motive. Those who know the most as to the inside history of the family refuse to admit any family unpleasantness which would make even credible the government charge.

It is true, as the prosecuting officer alleges, that women have often shown savage impulses hardly to be eclipsed by those which men have displayed. It is true, as he said, that Shakespeare, the great analyst of human character and motive, makes women as well as men responsible for the crime of murder. He will admit that there is no more atrocious and virile instance of that kind in the pages of the great poet than Lady Macbeth, whose cold-blooded advocacy of the treacherous and bloody murder of the king, their guest, so astounded her less virile and resolute husband that he cried out to her in astonishment at her unwomanly proposition:

"Bring forth men-children only.
For thy undaunted mettle should compose
Nothing but males."

What she could do she tells him when she says:

"I have given suck and know
How tender 'tis to love the babe that milks me.
I would, while it was smiling in my face,
Have plucked my nipple from his boneless gums
And dashed the brains out had I so sworn as you have done to this."

And yet this woman, who thus protests her capability of dashing out the brains of her own child for the sake of fulfilling an oath, though she invoked the spirit of evil to unsex her and fill her from the crown to the toe top full of direst cruelty, and the night to pall her in the dunnest smoke of hell, so that her keen knife should not see the wound it makes, she failed to do the deed. And why did she fail? She thus states the reason:

"Hark! I laid their daggers ready;
He could not miss them. Had he not resembled
My father as he slept, I had done it."

Lady Macbeth, though such a woman, could not take the one life of the sleeping man because he resembled her father, though she knew he was not her father. Have we in Lizzie Borden a worse than Lady Macbeth, who slew her sleeping father after having slain her step-mother, while Lady Macbeth could not even slay a sleeping guest because he looked like her father?

This the government must make out in order to convict Lizzie Borden. The frightful import of the chain of evidence which the district attorney drew about her must be admitted. But we believe it to be weak in spots, and insist that the authorities keep an open eye toward every fact that may help to elucidate the awful mystery.

THIRD DISTRICT COURT.

BORDEN, J.

SATURDAY, Sept. 3.

The continued case against Arthur H. Jennings, charging him with being a tramp, was further continued to Dec. 31st next. Jennings has got work and is getting along well and the court was inclined to help him as much as possible.

The continued case against Ira Chase of Dartmouth, charging him with an assault on Lafayette Dean on July 17th last, was disposed of by a fine of $25, and he was also required to recognize in the sum of $300 with sureties to keep the peace towards all the people of this Commonwealth and more especially towards Mr. Dean for the space of six months from this date. Mr. Chase appealed to the Superior Court, and recognized in $300 with Edwin S. Spooner and Edward Tucker of Dartmouth as sureties.

One case of drunkenness was released by the officers.

OBITUARY.—Funeral services were held Thursday at 1 o'clock at the Stone Church, Tiverton, over the remains of Gideon Gray who died in this city, Tuesday evening. The Rev. Gilbert B. Cutler conducted the services. There was present quite a number of relatives and friends. The pall bearers were his four nephews, John G. Cory, Pardon Cory, Philip J. Gray and Stephen J. Crandall. The enterment took place in the family lot at Pleasant View cemetery. Mr. Gray was born in 1812, and followed the occupation of a farmer until about two years since, when he took up his residence in this city. Saturday he returned from a visit to Tiverton, and was taken with a fit the following day. He has been a widower about 10 years. He leaves two children, John A. Gray and Abbie, wife of Edward T. Almy of this city.

FAIRHAVEN.

The overseers of the poor of Wareham were in town yesterday looking for a girl who belongs in their limits and who had applied to Fairhaven for help. She had run away to New Bedford and was not to be found.

Wayfarers on Main street are remarking at the admirable methods in vogue by the street department authorities. In the early part of the week, to the especial joy of the car drivers who have been gorged to satiety with the soil of the earth, a trim-looking row of piles was swept up to the curbing and for the first time this Summer the cobbles were visible. But unfortunately the piles still remain, no longer trim, waiting for the superintendent to get back from his vacation or wake up.

Sunday evening Mrs. Eben Akin, Jr., fell from the steps of the house of Mary S. Delano, Green street, where she had been calling, and fractured her right wrist.

The Fairhaven Water Company has about completed negotiations for the mill pond property in East Fairhaven.

At a meeting of the Selectmen Saturday, Roswell W. Clark was drawn as a juror.

Rev. D. C. Stevens arrived home this week.

VINEYARD HAVEN.

Trial Justice Allen Look held a short session at Cappawock Hall yesterday, the only case on the docket being John Haft vs. Mrs. Joanna Haft, for assault. C. G. M. Dunham of Edgartown appeared for the defendant and L. T. Willcox of New Bedford for the plaintiff. Verdict rendered, "not guilty."

NANTUCKET.

Among the arrivals by yesterday's boats from New Bedford were Andrew G. Pierce and wife, B. Penniman and wife, Charles P. Rugg and wife, Mrs. L. A. Kollock, Miss May B. Pierce and Miss Bessie Handy. All registered at the Ocean House.

Hotel Nantucket closed for the season on Sept. 1st. The Veranda closed last night. The hotels generally are doing a good business for September. The Surf Side, Point Breeze, Sea Cliff and Ocean Houses will remain open the greater part of the month, while "The Springfield," the all-the-year-round hotel, will keep open as usual.

The attention of Nantucketers is now centred on the annual fair and cattle show to be held next Wednesday and Thursday. The exhibition of stock will take place at the Agricultural Grounds, commencing at 10 a. m. Wednesday. The ploughing match will take place at 2 p. m. Wednesday. Thursday, at 10 a. m., is the time set for the examination of horses. Horse racing both days. The display of vegetables, fruits, fancy and manufactured articles will be held at the rink. This exhibition continues day and evening both days of the fair. The usual Agricultural ball will come off at the Rink Friday evening. The Musical Exchange Band will furnish the music during the fair, the band going to Nantucket by Wednesday morning's boat.

TIVERTON.

About 400 guests were present at the garden party given by Mrs. Alice Thayer of Nanaquaket and Boston Thursday afternoon in aid of the mission of the Episcopal church under the charge of the Newport convocation. There were numerous attractive features connected with the entertainment, the principal one being the unique picture gallery. The proceeds (augmented by the sale of candy, fancy work and comestibles, all of which were donated) amounted to more than $200. Guests were present from Boston, New York, Tiverton, Fall River and Portsmouth, who helped to make the event one of the successes of the season. The Tiverton National Band was present.

A CONCRETE SIDEWALK is being laid on the west side of Fifth street between Wing and Grinnell streets.

LABOR DAY

To be Celebrated by a Procession, Picnic, Sports and Dancing.

There is every indication that the celebration next Monday will prove a grand success. Members of the various unions are enthusiastic and all the organizations will parade with full ranks.

The programme for the observance of the day is a long and varied one. The chief feature of the day is to be a grand street parade of all the labor organizations in the forenoon. Chief Marshal Holloway has appointed P. J. Lyons chief of staff. His aids are as follows:

First Division—Samuel Ross, James E. Savage, William A. Soule, H. F. Janell, A. Hough, J. Connolly and John I. Bryant.

Second Division — Chief, Matthew Hart; marshal, Thomas Gamble; aids, M. Roowan, James McAvoy, Herbert E. Hammond and Thomas Riley.

The line will be formed on French avenue, with the right resting on Water street, and will march through Water, Grinnell, Second, Union, Pleasant, Middle, Purchase street and Acushnet avenue to River View Park. The procession will be reviewed from the front of the Library Building by the Mayor, members of the city government and State representatives. At River View Park the line will countermarch, passing in review before the chief marshal and aids, and will then be dismissed. The first division will comprise the Musical Exchange Band, Bricklayers' and Masons' Union, Carpenters' Union, Loom Fixers and Stone Cutters. The second division will comprise Meyrelle's Band, Weavers' Union, Typographical Union, Card Room Help, Spinners' Union, including backboys and doffers, and female operatives among the weavers and card room help in carriages. At River View Park the Musical Exchange Band will give a concert, and members of the various unions and their families will enjoy a basket picnic.

At 1 30 p. m. a line will be formed at City Hall, and as many of the members of labor organizations as desire to participate will march to the Cove street grounds, escorted by the Musical Exchange Band, which is to render music during the progress of the various sports.

The following sports have been arranged: Base ball game, Weavers vs. Printers; pole vault, tug of war, Bricklayers vs. Stone Cutters; running high jump, three broad jumps, standing high jump, hundred yard dash, hundred yard race for boys under 16, potato race for boys under 16, hurdle race, fat men's race and hitch and kick.

Arrangements have been made to illuminate the Cove street grounds in the evening with arc electric lights, and an excellent dancing floor has been constructed, and dancing will be indulged in to the music of Sullivan & Gray's Orchestra.

It has been decided by the committee in charge to limit the entries in the fat men's race to men weighing not less than 195 pounds.

Bark Maria Lila has been towed to Marsh Island and stowed with tar, rags, petroleum oil and other inflammable material, for the purpose of burning to obtain her metal fastenings. She will be fired early Monday morning.

The post office will close at 11 a. m. and will open from 6 30 to 7 p. m. The money order and registry departments will be closed all day. Carriers will make one trip at 7 a. m. There will be one collection from street letter boxes at 4 a. m.

All the banks, manufactories, stores and places of business generally, will be closed throughout the day.

A FINE YACHT.—Yacht Water Witch on her recent quick trip from this port to New London, beat out of the harbor by Clarks Point light and around the Hen and Chickens. It was blowing great guns and some steam yachts that started put back. The yacht set three jibs and carried no topmasts. Her starboard sail was under water, but the deck about the foremast was dry.

WEDDING.—An attractive home wedding occurred in Mansfield on Wednesday last, at the residence of Mr. and Mrs. Matthew George, when their daughter, Miss Mary G. George was united in marriage to Mr. Frank S. Wilcox of this city, Rev. J. Ide officiating. The guests were limited to the family relatives on both sides. The house was profusely decorated. There were many handsome presents.

THEIR FIRST ANNUAL.—The High school class of '59, accompanied by their teacher, Mr. Ivory S. Cornish, and wife, yesterday chartered A. R. Caswell's "City of New Bedford" and proceeded to Perry's Grove, where they held their first annual clambake. Although many, on account of business, were unable to attend, those who were present felt amply repaid. Members from Foxboro and Providence were in attendance.

PUBLIC URINALS.—A gentleman from out of town who is interested in an advertising scheme has made a proposition to Mayor Ashley to erect several public urinals, which he proposes to maintain, if the city will allow him with the advertisements thereon. One space on the urinals, which by the way are made of iron, is devoted to fire alarm calls. The agent will be in the city on Labor Day.

PENSIONS have been granted as follows:

Original—G. L. Skerry, A. L. Hardy, John Sullivan, B. F. Wood, E. L. Hallett, Thomas D. Haney, Michael McGillicuddy, Samuel Lord, J. D. Whitney, J. H. Stevens, H. G. Gay, Joseph Brasseur, C. F. Barnard, W. H. Estes, John Hurley, Francis Smith, G. C. Lawrence, E. L. Woodbury, J. A. Schofield.

Increase—John Mahoney.

Original widows, etc.—Bridget Glinn, Mary Jane Matherson.

SPECIAL NOTICES.

NEW BEDFORD YACHT CLUB.

☞ There will be a hop at the Club House TUESDAY EVENING, Sept. 6th. All members are cordially invited to be present, with lady friends. Dancing 8 to 12 o'clock.
s2-2t Entertainment Committee.

A NEW EXHIBIT.

☞ At J. B. Wade's, corner of Purchase and Elm sts., ***tonight.*** Don't miss seeing it. s3-1t

THE SWAIN FREE SCHOOL,
391 County Street, Corner Hawthorn.
INSTRUCTION FREE.

☞ Fall term begins MONDAY, Sept. 26. French, German and Italian by Mr. A. Schumacher. Advance Italian by Mr. E. B. Celotta. Portuguese by some competent teacher to be announced later. Circulars sent free to any address. Apply early.
ANDREW INGRAHAM, Master.
s3-SThtf

FALL CLOAKINGS.

A large assortment of remnants in the latest styles of Fall Cloakings and Dress Goods now on sale at

ONEKO MILLS.
s3-6t-w1t

PENSION VOUCHERS.

☞ Sworn to from 7 A. M. to 6 P. M. daily at GRAND ARMY HALL.
Attendance at residence by notary arranged for sick pensioners. s2-2t

PENSIONERS, ATTENTION.

☞ Pension Vouchers executed on and after Sept. 5th, day and evening, at the Rubber Store, 58 Pleasant street, by
s2-2t JAMES W. LOOMIS, Pension Att'y.

PENSIONS.

☞ Pensioners will find me at 51 William st., Am. Supply Co., opp. post office, Sept. 5 and 6, from 7 to 8. Will call at private houses when desired. FRANKLYN HOWLAND, Pension Attorney. s1-3t

Mrs. VAN HOVENBERG-MORRILL,
Vocal Teacher,
OVERTONE METHOD.

☞ At Y. M. C. A. Parlors on MONDAYS, from 8 till 10 o'clock. s1-MWStf

ELMER E. TOLMAN, Violinist.

Leader at the Opera House, will be ready to receive pupils after Sept. 5th, 1892.
☞ Apply at Box Office Opera House. au27-tf

SPECIAL NOTICES.

NOTICE!

The Bennett Lot bounded by County, Ashland and Robeson Sts., is now on the market for sale. Can be bought either in lots or strips on very easy terms. For plans and further particulars apply to F. A. F. ADAMS,
38 North Second Street.
s3-6t

☞ Owing to the continued illness of Miss E. C. Case, the Sale advertised to Commence on TUESDAY, Sept. 6th, will be deferred for a few days. Due notice will be given the public. E. C. CASE.

DUNLAP HATS.

These Celebrated Hats are now ready in the
NEW FALL SHAPES.
The Genuine Dunlap can only be had at
CHARLES M. HASKELL'S,
178 Union Street, Cor. Fourth Street.
s2-3t

A FEW DAYS MORE

Before we can move.

Still Greater Inducements to Clear Up Stock.

LOT 1—Imported Corsets worth from $1.75 to $3.50. Your choice $1.00 per pair.

LOT 2—Children's Cloaks, old prices from $1.75 to $5.00. Prices to clear up from $1.00 to $3.50.

Fall styles in Domestic Paper Patterns, and our trade doubling up every day.

☞ Fashion Review for Fall, price 10c.

CHACE'S CORSET STORE,
H. B. DIMAN,
Proprietor.
19 PURCHASE ST.

NOTICE.

☞ Persons who usually put out ashes on Monday, will please put them out on TUESDAY, Sept. 6th.
s1-3t A. B. DRAKE, Supt. of Public Works.

MISS MATTHEWS' Private School,
OPENS SEPT. 6th.
au31-12t 24 Madison Street.

WANTED TO HIRE

Furnished house by a small family without children, for the Winter season.
☞ Address box 30 *Standard* office. au29-8

FRIENDS' ACADEMY.

The Fall Term Begins Sept. 22d.

☞ Primary, Advanced and College Preparatory Courses. For particulars and catalogue, apply to
THOMAS H. ECKFELDT, Principal,
au24-WS4w Clinton Street, near Ash.

INSTRUCTION IN GERMAN LANGUAGE.

☞ Perfect pronunciation. In short time to read, write and speak. Address
ROBT. LEUCHSENRING, 53 Cottage st.
au23-TTS1m

HEARING.

CITY OF NEW BEDFORD,
CLERK'S OFFICE, Aug. 25th, 1892.

☞ Notice is hereby given that the Mayor and Aldermen will give a hearing in their chamber, City Hall Building, on THURSDAY, Sept. 8, 1892, at 7½ o'clock P. M., to all persons interested in the petition of T. A. Tripp, for a license to set up and maintain two (2) steam engines and boilers of fifty (50) horse power, at his place of business northeast corner of Prospect and Grinnell streets.
DANIEL B. LEONARD, City Clerk.
au25-tsep8

NOTICE TO CONTRACTORS.

☞ The Committee on City Property invite proposals or bids for building a fire engine house on the lot on the northwest corner of County and Hillman streets, in this city, in accordance with plans and specifications prepared by S. C. Hunt, architect, which will be ready for inspection at his office on and after TUESDAY, August 30th.

Bids should be addressed to the Committee on City Property, and left with the City Clerk, Library Building, on or before THURSDAY, Sept. 8th, at 12 o'clock noon.
S. A. BROWNELL,
au31-6t Chairman Committee.

ON TO WASHINGTON.

☞ William Logan Rodman Post 1, G. A. R. and John A. Hawes Camp 35, S. O. V., have through their committee made the following arrangements for the excursion to Washington. Leave here SATURDAY, Sept. 17 at 5 55 P. M., via Fall River Line to New York and Annex boat to Jersey City, and by special train via Pennsylvania railroad to Washington, arriving there SUNDAY AFTERNOON. Fare for the round trip $10.05; tickets good to return until Oct. 10, on any train and stop over at any station. A portion of the state rooms on the boat will be reserved for our use and disposal. Tickets will be for sale about the 10th of September. We cordially invite all who intend to visit Washington about that time to join with us. For further information inquire of the following committee: S. C. Chamberlin, Thomas H. Soule, Holder R. Tripp, John Hall, George A. Taylor, Charles H. Forbes, James F. Tripp, Alexander O. Peirce of Post 1, G. A. R., William E. James, George H. Carpenter, Franklin H. Vinal, George T. Duckworth, Franklin E. James, Clarence E. Mathews of Camp 35, S. O. V., or at the Post room any evening from 7 till 9 o'clock. au18-S5t

EXCURSION TO WHITE MOUNTAINS.

☞ Messrs. Hatch & Abbott will run an excursion to Fabyans, starting Sept. 5th, returning Sept. 10th. From New Bedford, by rail to Boston, moonlight sail to Portland, and rail to Fabyans. Three days' board at first class hotel, with meals en route both ways, and all this for only $20. Persons desiring to join will send in names at once, as number is limited. Address or apply to HATCH & ABBOTT, at either 92½ or 796 Purchase St., New Bedford. au22-tf&wtf

Those Wonderful Christy Knives.
A GOOD ARTICLE IS WORTHY OF IMITATION.

☞ We wish to caution the public against a knife that is being placed on the market made by the Clauss Shear Company. It is an infringement of the Christy patent, and parties selling or buying this knife are liable to prosecution. A word to the wise is sufficient. The Christy is being placed in this city and vicinity as rapidly as possible, and their great worth is attested by hundreds of our best families. *Right and left handed knives.*
WILLIAM S. HERSEY, Agent,
Telephone 110-7. 152 Mt. Pleasant St.
au31-s1-3

WILLIAM H. P. WALKER,
Counsellor at Law and Notary Public.
Room 23, over Citizens National Bank. jy6-WS

Mrs. WM. H. TAYLOR,
Teacher of the Pianoforte,
au6-SWtf 3 IRVING COURT.

☞ You can never have a really good complexion until the impurity is cleansed from your blood. What you need is a thorough course of Ayer's Sarsaparilla, which is absolutely free from all harmful ingredients, and therefore, perfectly safe.

E. J. WEEKS, D. D. S.
Dental Rooms, 74 Purchase Street.
Office Hours—9 to 12. 2 to 4. au9-1m

FINANCIAL.

SECOND EDITION.

HOME MATTERS.

THE STONE CRUSHER which has been located on the County road will be started up on Tuesday preparatory to macadamizing that section.

BUILDING.—A. B. Kimball is building for Charles Sisson on the south side of Court street a cottage house 24 by 28 feet with 14 feet posts. It is to have bay windows and additions.

SAND CATCHERS.—A sand catcher is being put in on the northwest corner of Madison street and Acushnet avenue.

Another is being put in at the northwest corner of Bonney and Rockland streets.

ANOTHER BIG LAND DEAL.—It is reported that the Shaw property of nine acres, situated on Acushnet avenue and Belleville road, has been sold to a syndicate. The price is rumored to have been $21,000.

OIL AND WHALEBONE.—The stocks of oil and whalebone in first hands in this country today as compared with a year ago, are as follows:

	Sp. oil Bbls.	Wh. oil Bbls.	Wh. bone Lbs.
Sept. 3, 1892,	7,255	none.	107,720
Sept. 3, 1891,	15,310	2,055	94,000

THE STREETS.—A curbing is being set on the south side of Austin street from County to Ashland streets.

Curbing is also being set on the west side of Walden street north of Sycamore street, and continued on the south side of Smith street to County street.

A surface drain is being laid across Belleville avenue south of Howard avenue.

REAL ESTATE SALES.—George A. Briggs has sold to Joseph C. Warren 21.01 rods of land at the northwest corner of Kendrick avenue and contemplated Sycamore street.

The estate of Frederika W. Otto has sold to Nancy Moore, buildings and 14.26 rods land south side of Elm street.

Standish Bourne sold at auction to-day the 2½-story house and lot 162 North street to Susan M. Hathaway, for $4540 and two years' taxes.

Henry C. Hathaway sold at auction this noon, 2½-story house belonging to the city of New Bedford and situated on Foster street south of the Veteran Firemen's headquarters, with 6.74 rods of land, to William A. Kirby, for $3550.

CLAMBAKE.—The First Christian church will hold a clambake on the lawn of Loum Faunce, 63 Parker street, on Thursday. See special notice.

MARINE INTELLIGENCE.

ARRIVED THIS AFTERNOON.

Sch Sadie & Lilie, Norton, Boston.

Barges Buffalo, Brunswick and Buffet, Perth Amboy, in tow of tug R H Rathburn.

Sld from Bath 2d, sch Josie R Burt, Washington.

Ar at New Haven 2d, sch Golden Ray, Benjamin, Fall River.

Ar at New York 2d, steamer Richmond, Jenney, West Point.

Passed through Hell Gate 2d, schs Lillie A Warford, Handy, New York for Wareham; S L Thompson, Keefe, do for Taunton; Hattie M Howes, Handy, do for Providence.

Ar at Perth Amboy 2d, sch Chas H Trickey, Fiokett, New York. Sld, sch S L Thomeson, Keefe, Taunton.

Ar at Philadelphia 2d, sch John Paull, Whittier, Providence. Cld, sch Wm Neeley, Thompson, this port.

Sld from Norfolk 2d, schs Horatio, and Warwick, this port; C A White, Boston.

Sld from Newport News 2d, sch Jeanie Lippitt, Boston.

Sld from Savannah 2d, steamer Nacoochee, New York.

Ar at Fernandina 2d, sch Dora Matthews, Brown, Fall River.

FINANCIAL.

Markets Open Weak on Cholera Scare and Close Erratic—Sugar Booms up to 111½ and the List Responds Somewhat—No Boards on Monday—Money Markets Easy and a Trifle More Active—New York Bank Statement Shows Big Decreases—Late News Concerning Cotton—Lake Superior Iron Ore—Market Opinions—Gossip and News Notes.

SATURDAY, Sept. 3.

Yesterday's rally was a surprise inasmuch as few expected it to hold. It is true that some raiding of the coalers was attempted and succeeded, but the general market was strong throughout the day, although at times a slight sympathetic decline was noticeable. That this rally may continue is of course the hope of the bulls and there are many good reasons why their hopes should not be disappointed.

The local loan market closes the week steady. Rates are unchanged and little change is expected during the coming week.

Local bank clearances compare as below:

Week Ended To-day.

1892	1891.	Inc.
$440,302	$396,102	$44,200

A slightly increased activity in the Boston money market is apparent this morning. Although rates are unchanged it is very probable that next week will see an advance and before the first of next month a considerable advance in money rates is expected. What little business the banks are doing is mostly with the brokers. The large selling of securities has enabled some of the brokers to pay up loans, and their indebtedness to the Boston banks is probably not so large as heretofore. At clearing to-day loans were made at 3 per cent. New York funds sold at 12½ cents discount per $1000.

The advance in the rate for call money in New York yesterday was due to the calling of loans in Industrials. Time money is also in better demand in New York, the advance in the rate of new and renewed loans creating a feeling that the supply may be less during the month than it has been for some time past. Mercantile paper continues to be sold to out-of-town buyers.

Sterling exchange strong.

Bonds irregular.

Wall street gossip this morning said the *Chronicle* figures a loss to banks of a million and a half. Gold shipments seem as if they would never end, and this causes investors to hold off. The bears are more active and aggressive and it looks as if the bull movement this Autumn would start from a lower plane.

The New York market opened weak to-day on another cholera scare, and some further losses were made in the early dealing. Sugar then rallied over 2 per cent. and the whole list responded. The coalers recovered a large part of yesterday's decline. Notwithstanding a bad bank statement, the market boomed in the last half hour. Closing was erratic.

In Boston the market opened quiet and weak, with the only active stocks, Atchison 36 and B. & Q. 99½. Later Sugar developed much life and rose from 108¾ to 111. Atchison toward the close touched 37, Westinghouse 35, Bell 202. The close of the market was dull and stronger.

A 11 30 special says: "A movement in Sugar is said to have been started by insiders and considerable covering now in this and other stocks preparatory to the holidays."

To-day's New York bank statement follows:

Reserve decrease,	$2,257,375
Loans decrease,	3,566,000
Specie decrease,	2,212,200
Legals decrease,	2,064,200
Deposits decrease,	8,076,100
Circulation increase,	72,800

Banks are now $7,950,896 in excess. Same time last year $9,156,921 in excess. In 1890 $1,401,125 deficit.

Silver offered to the government yesterday amounted to 1,073,000 ounces. The amount purchased was 315,000 ounces at from 83.64 to 83.65.

The short interest in the market is estimated at 150,000 shares.

The London & General Bank suspended payment yesterday. The bank was founded in 1882.

The stock boards both in New York and Boston have closed this noon till Tuesday next, Monday being "Labor's Holiday."

Copper in London is quoted at £44 10s. for spot, £45 for futures.

Handy ships to-day 100,000 ounces silver; Zimmerman ships 50,000 and Colgate 60,000 silver and 15,000 Mexican dollars.

Cordley & Co. in their weekly market letter say:

The "bears" have had their innings, and the market this week, a good portion of the time, has been a genuine cholera market, and all sorts of rumors have been based on a few cholera facts. For instance, a rumor on Wednesday morning, "that the opening of the World's Fair would be postponed a year on account of the danger of cholera." The people who started that rumor evidently believed that the general public has very little acquaintance with, and knowledge of, the hard horse sense of the business men of Chicago who are in control of the world's fair business, for it must be patent to the most obtuse that postponement would be equivalent to failure, and "fail" is not in the vocabulary of the Chicago men referred to. Perhaps the best answer to the cholera scare, as applied to the stock market, was made by Mr. S. V. White, who is quoted as follows: "But I wish to make one point in this connection which I think is important; the effect of the scare will be to keep Americans at home next Spring, so that $75,000,000 of gold left by them in Europe every Summer will be saved to this country."

St. Paul earnings for the fourth week of August increased $90,252. Month of August increased $393,000.

Chicago & Eastern Illinois has declared a regular quarterly dividend of 1½ per cent. on preferred stock, payable Oct. 1. Books close Sept. 14, reopen Oct. 3.

Eighteen to twenty bushels wheat to the acre is the probable average of the State of Kansas.

Representatives of mining companies in Boston are very reticent regarding reports of a proposed copper combination. It is good opinion, however, that while no plans regarding such control of demand and supply have taken shape, that the subject has been discussed quietly and its feasibility is generally admitted.

The Boston cotton market is very dull, both at the South and here. Strict middling Texas is offered at 7¼ to 7¾ cents, landed, but only in a small way and the mills are uninterested. The estimate of the New Orleans Cotton Exchange puts the last crop at 9,035,000 bales. The spot market is steady. The contract market has declined slightly for the week.

The cotton statement for the full crop year to August 31, 1892, shows; Port receipts 7,137,900 bales, against 6,975,380 bales last year; overland movement, 1,253,560 bales, against 1,110,935 bales; Southern consumption net this year, 643,919 bales, against 565,282 bales. Total crop of 1891-92 9,035,379 bales, against 8,652,597 for the year preceding.

General Manager Chappell says Alton is the only road strictly maintaining rates in the Southwest.

Sales of Lake Superior iron ore have been very limited and at low prices the past six weeks. We hear of a non-Bessemer carrying from 56 to 58 per cent. being sold at Buffalo at $2.80 per ton, with freight added; this would mean about $4.30 to Lehigh Valley furnaces. The movement of tonnage from Lake Superior points continues very heavy. Arrivals last week aggregated 200,000 tons, while shipments to the furnaces were 35,000 tons, or about the volume which was shipped during the corresponding period last year. Ore freights from the mines have taken a tumble, the quotation from Escanaba being 70 cents, Ashland $1 and Marquette 90 cents. There is yet a considerable tonnage to be contracted for the Winter and Spring consumption, notwithstanding there are very few signs of activity.

The comparative production of anthracite coal last week and since Jan. 1 is given below:

Period.	1892. Tons.	1891. Tons.	Increase. Tons.
Week Aug. 27,	791,353	755,123	36,230
Since Jan. 1,	26,146,781	24,760,288	1,386,493

The net earnings of the Oregon Improvement Company for July are said to have increased $16,400 over last year.

LOCAL STOCK SALES AT AUCTION TO-DAY.

Sanford & Kelley sold the following shares of local stocks at auction to-day:

8 Potomska Mills	109
5 Grinnell Manufacturing Corpo'n	182
11 Wamsutta Mills	111

Fall River Print Cloth Market.

FALL RIVER, Sept. 3.

The cloth market has been active during the week, though brokers report that during the close of business the cholera scare affected trade somewhat. Thus far agents find that there is a call for more goods than they can produce, and buyers are willing to pay a half for very late deliveries. The regulars are scarce, and manufacturers have no stock of anything on hand. The majority of the mills are now running on a 3½ cent basis, and as fast as contracts expire they can be renewed at that figure. It enables the corporations to pay fair dividends and to lay by a reserve fund which will keep the plant in order and help the corporations to tide over a period of depression. The operatives are apparently contented. At all events they have been so deeply absorbed in the murder case that they have forgotten that an agitation was proposed, and as far as can be learned they are earning wages which satisfy them. They have certainly enjoyed a long stretch of steady work, have been subjected to no cut down for years, and with a single unimportant exception have marred their run of prosperity with but one strike. They ought to be fully as well off as stockholders who are just beginning to get the benefit of the boom.

The following is the print cloth statement for the week: Production 190,000 pieces, deliveries 194,000 pieces, stock on hand not any, sales 256,000 pieces, spots 190,000 pieces, futures 237,000 pieces. Market firm. Prices 3⅛ cents for 60x56s, 3¾ cents for 64x64s.

CALIFORNIA MINING STOCKS.

SAN FRANCISCO, Sept. 2.

The following are the official closing prices of mining stocks to-day:

Alta	—	Mexican	1 20
Best & Belcher	1 20	Mt. Diablo	—
Chollar	—	Ophir	2 25
Con. Cal. & Va.	3 20	Potosi	—
Crown Point	—	Savage	—
Eureka Con.	—	Sierra Nevada	1 60
Gould & Curry	—	Union Con.	1 20
Hale & Norcross	—	Utah	—

PROVISIONS AND GRAIN.

CHICAGO, Sept. 3.

	Lard.	Wheat.	Pork.	Corn.	Sh't Ribs
Opening.					
May	—	82½	—	50⅝	—
June	—	—	—	—	—
July	—	—	—	—	—
Aug.	—	—	—	—	—
Sept.	—	73¼	—	—	—
Oct.	—	—	—	—	—
Dec.	—	76⅜	—	—	—
Jan.	—	—	11.90	—	—
12 o'clock.					
May	—	82½	—	50½	—
June	—	—	—	—	—
July	—	—	—	—	—
Aug.	—	—	—	—	—
Sept.	—	73½	—	—	—
Oct.	—	—	—	—	—
Dec.	—	76¾	—	—	—
Jan.	—	—	12.07½	—	—

WEATHER INDICATIONS.

FAIR AND WARMER.

WASHINGTON, Sept. 3.—For the 24 hours from 8 a. m. to-day: For New England, fair and warmer; southerly winds.

WARMER AND FAIR.

NEW YORK, Sept. 3.—At 8 30 a. m. the weather was clear, wind southwest, temperature 62. The *Herald* says: In the Middle States and New England, fair and warmer weather may be expected.

FERRYBOAT BURNED.

The "Cornelia H." Consumed with a Wharf at Cape Elizabeth.

PORTLAND, Me., Sept. 3.—Early this morning the ferryboat "Cornelius H," was burned at her wharf at Cape Elizabeth. The fire caught from a steam pipe and the boat is a total loss. It cost $9000 and was insured for $4500. The wharf and waiting room were also burned. Loss $11,000 not insured.

Drowned.

FARMINGTON, Me., Sept. 3.—A Miss Thomas of Baltimore, aged 16, was drowned here yesterday by the capsizing of a boat. Miss Thomas was one of a party consisting of three ladies and a guide, who were boating on Greely Pond, Rangeley. The water was rough, and when a wave broke over the boat the ladies jumped to one side, overturning the craft. The guide rescued the other two. Miss Thomas's body was recovered.

Tried to Kill Her Lover, Too.

KANSAS CITY, Sept. 3.—Maggie Jonas, 18 years old, a domestic, attempted to shoot William Swartz, to whom she was engaged to be married, but the bullet went wide of its mark. She then turned the revolver on herself, firing a bullet through her heart. She died instantly.

Visitors to Gray Gables.

BUZZARDS BAY, Sept. 3.—Hon. W. C. Whitney and ex-Secretary Fairchild arrived here this noon from New York on a brief visit to Mr. Cleveland. Mrs. Cleveland met the party at the station. Messrs. Whitney and Fairchild return to New York this afternoon.

THE MURDER MYSTERY.

Dr. John H. Abbott's Opinion of the Case.

Question Raised Regarding the Dress Pattern Surrendered.

Mrs. Marshall Refuses to Tell Her Story to the Police.

[Special Dispatch.]

TAUNTON, Sept. 3.—Dr. John H. Abbott of Fall River, who has recently returned from the West, says that he examined the bodies of Mr. and Mrs. Borden within a short time after they were discovered and that both bodies were warm at that time. He is firmly of the opinion that Mr. Borden was killed first, that Mrs. Borden, coming downstairs, saw the murderer at work, turned and went back upstairs to get as far away from the murderer as possible and the assailant chased her and caught her as she was rushing to the window to give the alarm and struck her in the back. That blow in the back he thinks was the cause of death, striking as it did the spine. After she fell to the floor the other blows were given.

The fact that he was called West soon after the murders were discovered and that he has but recently arrived home and was not conversant with the evidence is the reason for his not saying anything about the matter before.

So far as the matter of digestion is concerned it is the opinion of leading physicians here that nothing can be told in regard to that matter, that it is a well-known fact that a glass of ice cold water will immediately retard digestion for an hour or more and it is thought that had Prof. Wood been interrogated upon this point that this fact would have come out.

Miss Emma Borden came up on the 8 45 train this morning but remained in the city only a short time.

THAT DRESS PATTERN.

Was it Possible for Defence to Have Duplicated the Goods?

[Special Dispatch.]

FALL RIVER, Sept. 3.—The day after the Borden murder City Marshal Hilliard put two New Bedford officers at work in that city with orders to trace Lizzie Borden's actions during the two weeks previous. They found that she had purchased a dress pattern of cheap material in a dry goods store in that city, and it was to this pattern that reference was made at the trial. Some importance was attached to the matter at the time of the discovery of the purchase. The police failed to find the dress pattern or any dress of it in their search at the Borden house. They made demand on the members of the family to produce the piece of goods or the made-up dress. If they could not do this the police wanted to know what had become of it. The family refused to move in the matter and the police at New Bedford searched the store to get a sample of the goods bought by Lizzie.

The last day of the trial the defence surrendered the piece of dress goods which Lizzie had purchased and it was still intact. The question has arisen in the minds of some people who believe as the prosecution does whether or not it was possible for the friends of the prisoner to have duplicated the dress pattern and surrendered the last purchased instead of the first, and that the first one might have been made up and used by Lizzie Borden at the time of the murder and afterwards destroyed or put out of the way.

FALL RIVER POLICE INDIGNANT.

Mrs. Marshall Says Not a Word by Advice of Lizzie's Counsel.

[Special Dispatch.]

FALL RIVER, Sept. 3.—Officer Medley of the police force arrived home last evening. He had been on a visit to Pawtucket by order of the City Marshal to see Mrs. Marshall, who, it is reported, has said that she saw a strange-looking man coming out of the door of the Borden house on Second street on the day that the murders were committed. Mrs. Marshall and her friends declined to talk to the officer about the matter. They state that the counsel for Lizzie Borden has been notified of what she saw and that counsel requested Mrs. Marshall not to have anything to say to anybody but himself in connection with the matter.

The police authorities here feel somewhat indignant in view of the fact that they are making every effort and have been doing so to chase down all clues, which might lead to the solving of the mystery that the counsel for the defence should thus endeavor to thwart their efforts.

Lizzie Talked in Her Sleep.

[By Associated Press.]

FALL RIVER, Sept. 3.—Lizzie Borden slept uneasily at times in the matron's room in this city, tossing her arms to and fro and talking in her sleep, but once she awoke and dressed she became as rigid and serene as she was when the police first interviewed her and placed her in their charge. It is this condition of things that makes it impossible for the officers to communicate with her friends or believe in her innocence.

LIGHT WIND AND SMOOTH SEA.

Harpoon Leading in the Eastern Club's Autumn Regatta.

MARBLEHEAD NECK, Sept. 3.—A light wind from the south-southeast and a smooth sea were given to the racers in the Eastern's Club Autumn regatta, which started at 10 45 this morning. No schooners had entered, but three 46-footers, Gloriana, Harpoon and Barbara, were again ready for a friendly fight over the usual open courses in Massachusetts Bay.

At 10 45 the preparatory whistle was blown from the judges' boat and the course to be sailed was indicated by a flag.

From Half-way-Rock the sloops were to go to a flag buoy off Nahant, thence to a stake-boat off Minot's ledge, thence back to the Nahant mark and to the line, a distance of 35 miles.

At 11 15 the starting signal was given. The Gloriana was close upon the line coming down from up to windward, the Harpoon smuggled in under her lee, not a length behind, and the Barbara was 30 seconds later in crossing. A club topsail and jibtopsail were carried on this first leg, a close reach to the Nahant mark. The Harpoon also crawled through the Gloriana's lee and opened out a couple of lengths of clear water between them. The wind freshened, and rails were well down as the boats skimmed along the shore. The Harpoon held her lead, carrying an intermediate jibtopsail.

Armour Interests to Unite.

CHICAGO, Sept. 3.—A local paper says that the entire interests of the Armour family, East and West, hitherto separate, representing a capital of perhaps $50,000,000, will be united on Oct. 1, and will be henceforth one and the same.

A CENTENARIAN'S FUNERAL.

It Is Largely Attended by Residents of Mattapoisett and Marion.

[Special Dispatch.]

MATTAPOISETT, Sept. 3.—The funeral of Aunt Keziah Randall, the centenarian of Mattapoisett, occurred this afternoon at 1 o'clock from the Friends' meeting-house at East Mattapoisett, which is at the entrance of the road leading to the forest home where this aged lady had passed so many days. The services were largely attended by Summer residents of this town and Marion, and there was also a large delegation of New Bedford people present. Rev. William Faunce of the Baptist church officiated, and John H. Dillingham of Philadelphia, a prominent Friend, also paid tribute to the deceased. The remains were interred in Pine Island cemetery. A. M. Jenney, Andrew Westgate, N. P. Hiller and J. Cummings were the pall bearers. The floral tributes were elegant and profuse, and among those who remembered the aged lady in this respect were Mrs. F. A. Bacon of Mattapoisett, a large wreath; Mrs. J. M. Clark of Mattapoisett, bouquet; Mrs. J. Thompson of New Bedford, sheaf of wheat; Mrs. S. A. Brownell of New Bedford, a cross. Besides the above relatives of deceased contributed many tributes of respect in this line.

BOATS' CREWS LOST.

Fears That They Have Been Captured by a Russian War Vessel.

VICTORIA, B. C., Sept. 3.—The schooner Annie C. Moor returned to port yesterday, having lost two boats' crews of three men each in a dense fog in the Copper Island neighborhood. The steam launch from the Russian cruiser Zabaka was looking for them at the time and Fred Hackett, master of the schooner, has reported his fears that they have been captured. The steamer Islander, which has returned from Alaska, brings word that small pox has broken out among the Indians. Precautions are being taken to prevent the spread of the disease.

TELEGRAPHIC BREVITIES.

Patrick Egan, minister to Chili, is homeward bound.

The belt line car stables, Washington, were destroyed by fire.

O. B. Culver has been appointed postmaster at Putnamsville, Vt.

Thomas Devine committed suicide by hanging in Bridgeport, Conn.

Lemuel S. Whitcomb, a prominent shoe manufacturer of Holbrook, Mass., is dead.

Eleven Massachusetts cities have applied for supervisors at the next national election.

Judge William E. Deck, for two terms chief justice of the supreme court of Colorado, was found dead in bed at Denver. He was 55 years old.

William Lively, at East Pepperell, Mass., has confessed that the motive that led him to murder his wife was the too frequent attentions paid her by another man.

STOCK AND BOND MARKETS.

Bids at close of the Stock Boards to-day.

NEW YORK, Sept. 3.

GOVERNMENT BONDS.

U.S. 2s, registered	100
" new 4s, registered	114¾
" new 4s, coupons	115⅝
" currency 6s, 1895, (Pacifics)	107

RAILROADS

Atchison	36⅞
Clev., Cin., Chicago & St. Louis	63⅛
Chicago & Eastern Illinois	—
Chicago & Eastern Illinois pref	—
Chicago, Burlington & Quincy	99⅞
Delaware & Hudson	131
Delaware & Lackawanna	152½
Erie	26⅛
Illinois Central	99
Lake Shore & Michigan Southern	131⅝
Louisville & Nashville	66½
Michigan Central	105
Missouri Pacific	59⅛
New Jersey Central	129½
New York & New England	34⅛
Northern Pacific	19⅞
Northern Pacific pref	54⅞
Chicago & Northwestern	114⅝
New York Central & Hudson River	110
North American	12½
Oregon Navigation	—
Oregon Improvement	—
Oregon Short Line	—
Philadelphia & Reading	54¾
Pullman Palace Car Co	194
Chicago, Rock Island & Pacific	80⅞
Chicago, Milwaukee & St. Paul	81
Chicago, Milwaukee & St. Paul pref	—
Richmond Terminal	9
St. Paul & Omaha	49⅛
St. Paul & Omaha pref	—
Union Pacific	37⅛
Wabash, St. Louis & Pacific	—
Wabash, St. Louis & Pacific pref	23⅞

MISCELLANEOUS

Ontario Silver	—
Pacific Mail Steamship Co	30½
Sugar, common	110⅞
Sugar, pref	103½
Western Union Telegraph	94⅝
Silver Certificates	83¼

BOSTON, Sept. 3.

BONDS

Atchison 4s	82
Atchison Incomes	56⅞
American Bell Telephone 7s	*114
Chicago, Burlington & Northern 5s	104
Chicago & West Michigan 5s	—
Mexican Central 4s	*67½
Illinois Steel Co. 5s	—

RAILROADS.

Atchison, Topeka & Santa Fe	36¾
Boston & Albany	205
Boston & Lowell	181
Boston & Maine	174½
Boston & Providence	251
Chicago, Burlington & Quincy	99⅝
Chicago & West Michigan	—
Cleveland & Canton	5
Cleveland & Canton pref	17
Flint & Pere Marquette	—
Flint & Pere Marquette pref	—
Mexican Central	14⅛
New York & New England	34⅜
New York & New England pref	85
Old Colony	*182
Oregon Short Line	20
Pullman Palace Car	—
Union Pacific	37⅛
Wisconsin Central	16½
West End	72⅞
West End pref	—

MINING.

Butte & Boston Mining Co	9
Calumet & Hecla Mining Co	290
Centennial	7
Franklin Mining Co	12¼
Kearsarge	10½
Montana	33⅛
Osceola Mining Co	29½
Tamarack	158

MISCELLANEOUS.

American Bell Telephone	202
Erie Telephone	45
Mexican Telephone	1
New England Telephone	57
Newport Land	*1½
Boston Land Co	5
West End Land Co	—
San Diego Land Co	—
Topeka Land & Development Co	—
Lamson Store Service	17¼
Illinois Steel Co	—
Am. Sugar Refineries, com	110⅝
Am. Sugar Refineries, pref	103⅝
Gen'l Electric	—
Gen'l Electric	—

*Asked.

Smallest Bone in the Human Body.

The smallest bones in the human body are to be found in the ear. The smallest of these is known by the anatomical name of stapes. It has a head, neck and two haunches and is shaped not unlike a stirrup iron. The full extent of its dimensions does not exceed that of a pea, and is frequently smaller. By some authorities it has been named the lenticular bone, from the idea that its shape and appearance resembled that of a lens. It is situated within the drum of the ear.—New York World.

King Humbert as a Fireman.

The king of Italy has a perfect fancy for attending fires. The other evening he was due at the German embassy, where Count Solms gave a ball. Her majesty Queen Marguerite, radiant in a toilet of pale yellow silk and dazzling with superb diamonds, came alone, and stated that his majesty the king had gone to a fire which had broken out at a manufactory of macaroni and Italian paste, and he remained at the scene until the flames were subdued.—St. Louis Globe-Democrat.

The distance between division points for changing engines has been increased in this country, and some roads are now running engines from 200 to 300 miles where they used to run 100 miles or less.

A BIG BARGAIN

—IN—

Ladies' Outside Jackets

—FOR—

EARLY FALL WEAR.

Knowles & Co.

1 lot of 20 Short Cloth Jackets for Ladies, have been sold at $2.50 and $4.00, now to close 75 cents.

1 Lot of Beaver Cloth Jackets for Ladies, have been sold for $6.50 to $8.00, now to close $1.98. You will miss it if you are not on hand early to secure one of these.

These cool mornings remind one of Flannels. We wish to state that we carry a full line of Red Flannels at 20, 25, 38, 42 and 50 cents. We guarantee these prices to be the lowest in the city. Blue Flannels at 20, 25, 38, 42, 50 and 62 1-2 cents.

A full line of Cotton and Wool and all Wool Flannel.

We are having special sales in our Cotton Underwear Department.

Corset Covers 12 1-2, 25, 37 1-2, 50, 62 1-2, 75, 87 1-2, cents and $1.00.

We have been looking over our Stamped Linen stock and have put prices on some little lots that will surprise you. Tidies, 27x17, at 10c.; Splashers, all linen, 12 1-2c., worth much more. Large Pillow Shams 19 and 25 cents.

KITCHEN FURNISHING DEPT.

We would draw your attention to our large assortment of German Steel Enamel Ware.

Preserving Kettles, in ten sizes, from 28c. for the pint to $1.25 for 12 quarts. Sauce Pans the same.

Coffee Pots, 73c. for 1 quart to $1.29 for 4 quart. Wash Basins, Fry Pans, Rinsing Pans, Cups, etc.; every piece fully warranted.

Flower Pots from 3c. up. Jardiniers 25 and 30 cents. We carry a line of Crockery, both white and yellow ware, prices the lowest.

Tin Ware. We carry the largest assortment of any dealer in the city. Prices always the lowest.

OFFICE ROOM

—AND—

Hall to Let.

APPLY AT

SHERMAN'S CIGAR STORE,

62 Purchase St.

jy19-spMWS

HE WANTED HIS HAT.

An Italian Jumps from an Express Train and is Instantly Killed.

SOUTH LAWRENCE, Mass., Sept. 12.—There was quite a chapter of railroad accidents here yesterday afternoon. At Haverhill, Frank P. Palmer, aged 35, an Italian, jumped from the Portland express train just beyond "White Peeps" bridge, and was instantly killed. He was on his way to Andover, where he was to join other Italians in extending the waterworks. His hat blew off and he leaped after it from the flying train.

At 5 o'clock, near the Boston and Maine overhead bridge, Andover, an electric car, bound for Lawrence, collided with a carryall containing James O'Donnell, his wife and two sons, from South Tewksbury. Mrs. O'Donnell was thrown before the car wheels and the promptness of the motorman alone saved her life. She fractured her ankle and received a severe cut on the head. A passenger on the car, Mrs. George Brown of this city, became excited at the collision and jumped from the car, badly spraining her ankle.

A Brutal Outrage.

NORTHAMPTON, Mass., Sept. 12.—The 8-year-old daughter of Louis Newkirk, who lives some distance out of the city, was ravished yesterday afternoon by an unknown young man. He was riding on a bicycle and enticed her into the woods near by. He afterward led her to Florence and put her on a street car going to her home. Late last night a young man, said to be from Springfield, was arrested on suspicion.

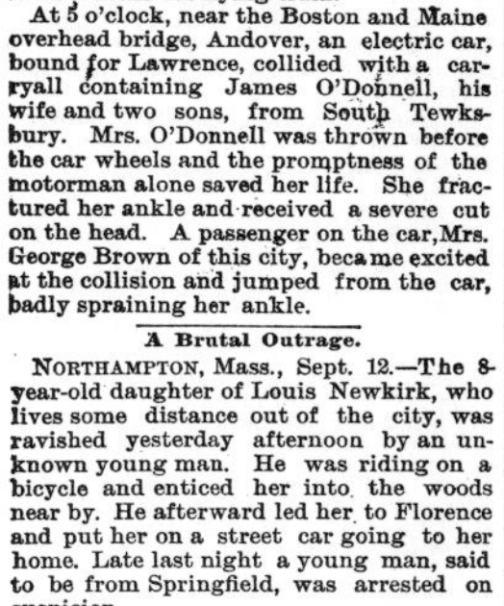

Mr. Chas. N. Hauer.

Of Frederick, Md., suffered terribly for over ten years with abscesses and running sores on his left leg. He wasted away, grew weak and thin, and was obliged to use a cane and crutch. Everything which could be thought of was done without good result, until he began taking

Hood's Sarsaparilla

which effected a perfect cure. Mr. Hauer is now in the best of health. Full particulars of his case will be sent all who address
C. I. Hood & Co., Lowell, Mass.

Hood's Pills are the best after-dinner Pills, assist digestion, cure headache and biliousness.

LIVES CRUSHED OUT.

An Awful Wreck on the Fitchburg Railroad.

Nine Deaths Have Resulted from a Collision in the Fog.

Many Others are Seriously Injured and Some May Die.

BOSTON, Sept. 12.—Nine dead, twenty-six injured, two dying. That is the story of a railway horror at the West Cambridge depot of the Fitchburg railroad Saturday night.

An accommodation passenger train left Boston at 10:15 p. m. An express train followed on the same rails at thirty miles an hour. The passenger train waited a few minutes at West Cambridge to cross an incoming accommodation.

The night was thick with fog. The standing train should have been protected by signal lanterns displayed 200 yards in its rear. It is stated that Brakeman Noon was sent back to flag the freight. There who only one man who could have seen his danger signal. That man, Driver Goodwin, in the engine of the freight—says he saw none. He thought the rails clear, and thundered on at thirty miles an hour.

His engine plunged into and almost through the rear passenger coach of the standing train. Death or injury fell upon the passengers

In a Rain of Flying Debris,

scalding steam and fire from the engine's furnace. One woman and four men were dead and terribly mangled when, after long and heroic efforts, the rescuers reached them. One woman and three men died from their injuries after removal to the Cambridge hospital.

Several are now at death's door. The piled one upon the other, and the engine with frightful momentum ploughed through two-thirds of the entire length of the passenger coach, crushing seats, flying timber and passengers in a confused mass before it.

Some passengers were crushed between the iron wedge and the walls of the car; others, driven before the storm of flying wood and fire, lay mangled in the ruin. Cries so awful that those who heard them wrung their hands in horror and despair, issued from the wreck.

Scalding steam entered the car, literally cooking the injured as they struggled helplessly in their agony. Men and women, frantic with pain and fear, beat upon the windows with their hands, prayed and shouted for air.

Fire Breaks Out.

Now fire added to the torture. The woodwork of the car had caught fire from the furnace embedded in it.

The firemen had come and were pouring water on the blazing wreck. Police were applying the axe to the sides of the car, in an attempt to liberate the imprisoned victims. Victim after victim was placed upon the floor of the station.

Rescuers swarmed. Ambulances were scarce. Express wagons were substituted. Splints ran out. The doctors used pieces of board as a substitute. Railway cushions

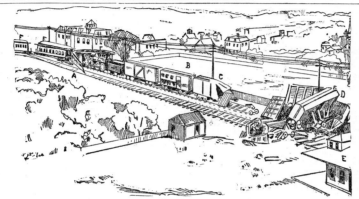

A BIRDSEYE VIEW OF THE WRECK.

A—Car in which victims were killed and injured.
B—Carload of horses which remained on track, uninjured.
C—Freight car which was partially burned.
D—Main wreck of freight train.
E—West Cambridge station.
FF—Cars on passenger train, taking the Watertown branch.

extent of the injuries in some other cases cannot yet be told by the surgeons.

The scene was one of almost unparalleled horror. Words fail when eye-witnesses would describe what they saw in and around the telescoped car.

The scene in the morgue-depot was marked by a display of heroism only to be appreciated by those who labored there and felt its sublimity.

The greater number of the victims lived in Waltham and Watertown. The dead have all been identified. Many who were reported missing have been found alive and well.

The Dead.

Retta Feyler, 22 years old, had been living at Waltham; home at North Waldoboro, Me.

Standish P. Sullivan, pawnbroker, Boston, residence at East Watertown.

John H. Barnes, Newton.

John Hudson, 60 years old, Watertown.

Leo Raymond, Winchendon, brakeman on the freight train.

Benjamin Tuck, Watertown, died at the Cambridge city hospital.

James Lane, East Watertown.

H. F. Merrifield, blacksmith, died at his home, Watertown, at 2:30 p. m., yesterday.

Margaret Adams, 35 years old, Waltham, died at the Cambridge hospital at 8:30 p. m.

Story of the Disaster.

Down the rails from Boston thundered the express freight. The night was thick, the train exceptionally heavy. It was making thirty miles an hour. The man at the throttle, Engineer Goodwin, was not billed to stop at West Cambridge. Unless he was unexpectedly signalled he intended to flash by at full speed. And on the rails at West Cambridge the passenger train was at a standstill—on Goodwin's rails.

It was 10:15 when the local accommodation train left the Fitchburg depot for Waltham. It was detained for a short time at Charlestown, but reached West Cambridge at 10:35, on time. The incoming train which was to be passed here had not arrived. It was necessary to wait for it. The fog was thick—so thick that it was

Impossible to See Fifty Feet.

The brakeman of the rear car was sent back to protect the train. His duty was to go far enough back to signal any train coming from Boston, and so render telescoping impossible.

The stop at West Cambridge was less than six minutes, probably four. It is, therefore, a question whether or not the brakeman had time to go back far enough to make his signal effective, retrace his steps and still catch his own train before it pulled out.

Meantime express freight No. 207, with thirty heavily laden cars, was thundering along from Boston at thirty miles an hour. The rear car of the standing train was near the station. It was only there that there was any light, and even there it was impossible to see except at close quarters, so thick was the fog.

Just as the passenger train began to pull out the fast freight

Crashed Into Its Rear Coach.

Signals or no signals there had been no diminution of speed. Engineer Goodwin, who lives to tell of it, says he saw no signals and believed he had clear rails before him. He saw nothing until within ten yards of the train ahead. Then he saw it. Goodwin knew what that meant at thirty miles an hour and thirty cars behind him.

Like lightning he reversed his engine and cried out to the fireman, but his voice was drowned by the terrific roar of solid wood and iron rent asunder in an instant.

Goodwin's engine, under a full head of steam and driven by the weight of the thirty loaded trucks behind it, had literally buried itself in the rear passenger coach of the passenger train. The solid platform of the car was cleft by a thirty ton wedge, its sides were torn from their setting, and the roof torn off and raised upward.

The Shock Was Terrific.

Behind the wild engine the freight cars

From Saturday's Third Edition.

THE ROGERS MURDER.

Officers Appear Satisfied That They Are on the Right Track.

WENDELL, Mass., Sept. 12.—A week ago yesterday Mr. Woodworth of Farley Village went to ride, and came home over the Mormon Hollow road, past the little cabin of Mrs. Rogers, found murdered four days ago. There was no light in it, and Mr. Woodworth said to his companion: "I guess the old woman's out."

This apparently trivial incident becomes important now, for the lonely dweller always kept a light burning all night on the table in front of the only window, overlooking Farley village and the Millers river valley. This light was always seen from below, and its absence was noted by others on Sunday night. The light hadn't been seen since Saturday, and on that night Eugene Baker saw her in her doorway.

All these things make Medical Examiner Wright confident that the woman was killed on Sunday. Certain other points that he does not care to make public are also confirmatory.

There is no desire to implicate the Bgors unjustly, but there is so much to directly connect them, and everything so far secured is so thoroughly consistent, that the officers feel sure they are on the right track.

Artie says he had been home about noon Sunday, and that Edward got home toward supper time, all of which is confirmed. Then, too, Ed was seen on the road coming from Mrs. Rogers' about 11.30 in the afternoon.

Officer Fowler spent most of the morning yesterday visiting the houses of the woodchoppers and others in the vicinity, and between Orange and Farley, where the Bgors were acquainted, and where the versatile story-tellers Artie and Ed also say they went. Nothing important was secured yesterday.

Mother and Daughter Died Together.

PHILADELPHIA, Sept. 12.—Mrs. Cora Targetta, a widow aged 30, and her daughter Ethel, aged 11, were found dead in their rooms yesterday. Four gas burners were turned on and the room was tightly closed to prevent the gas escaping. The mother had been a long sufferer from neuralgia and it is supposed became insane through despondency, imagining she had brain trouble.

Nebraska Bank Goes Up.

LINCOLN, Neb., Sept 12—Chief Justice Maxwell has appointed a receiver for the Nebraska state bank of Crete, at the request of the state banking board. George D. Stevens, the president and cashier, has been missing for three weeks. The affairs of the bank are supposed to be in bad shape.

For French-Canadians.

HAVERHILL, Mass ,Sept. 12.—The cornerstone of the brick building to be erected by the St. Jean Baptiste society was laid yesterday with an imposing parade and ceremony. The building will be the largest in the city devoted to social purposes, and will be the center of French-Canadian interests.

Thousands Looked On.

LOWELL, Mass., Sept. 12.—Under a great canvas that shaded the entire first floor, the services incident to the laying of the corner-stone of the new St. Peter's church on Gorham street, in this city, were conducted yesterday afternoon. Many thousand persons comprised the audience.

A PROSPEROUS UNION.—The britannia workers in the Fairpoint Manufacturing Co's works recently formed a union with 26 members, and since then has threatened to that extent that its ranks comprise about 75 names. The union will hold a meeting next Friday evening in Knights of Honor Hall, for the purpose of joining the American Federation of Labor.

STILL ALARM.—Permanent men from the Central Engine House were called to B. B. H. Waite's residence, corner Arnold and Cottage streets, this afternoon, where there was a fire between the partitions. Damage slight.

MRS. MAKEPEACE INDICTED.—Mrs. Anna Makepeace, who shot her husband at Acushnet and caused his death, was indicted to-day for manslaughter.

REAL ESTATE SALE.—Frederick C. Dawe has sold to Henry W. Bennett 82 rods land on the west side of Bullock street.

NO BAIL FOR LIZZIE.

Governor Has No Power in the Case of Miss Borden.

Prisoner will be Fairly and Considerately Dealt With.

Attorney-General Speaks Highly of Judge Blaisdell and Mr. Knowlton.

BOSTON, Sept. 10.—The rumored application to the Governor to have Lizzie Borden admitted to bail is not likely to produce any results. Competent lawyers say that the Governor has no power in the premises. The law puts criminal prosecution wholly in the control of the district attorney subject to the advice of the attorney-general and the action of the courts.

There is no known precedent for the admission to bail of a person charged with murder under these circumstances, but it can be safely assumed that Lizzie Borden will be fairly and considerately dealt with. It is stated on reliable authority that Attorney-General Pillsbury's attitude toward the case is still one of inquiry only, and that he has not allowed himself to form any opinion as to the probable guilt of Lizzie Borden, or determine anything as to the future course of the prosecution. He is reluctant to believe her guilty, and is disposed to examine every part of the evidence with the closest scrutiny before allowing it to influence his mind.

The attorney-general speaks in high terms of Judge Blaisdell, the district Attorney Knowlton and the other officers engaged in the case as conscientious men who have taken no step except from a sense of unavoidable duty, and have exercised great forbearance under unjust and unwarrantable criticism; but it may be regarded as certain that nothing will be assumed against Lizzie Borden by the attorney-general merely because she has been held, and this will not prevent a careful and impartial re-examination of the evidence before the course of the government is finally settled.

FAILURE TO FIND RETURNS.

Commissioner Peck May Be Obliged to Prove Figures in His Labor Report.

ALBANY, N. Y., Sept. 10.—Norton Chase of this city this morning presented Charles F. Peck, commissioner of State Board of Labor Statistics, with an order granted last night by Judge Edwards at Hudson, requiring him to show cause before Judge Furman at Kingston on Monday why a writ of mandamus should not issue directing him and his assistants to diligently search all the files, papers and records in his office, which include the returns made by manufacturing establishments in the city of New York, of which Mr. Peck's recent labor report was based, and make and furnish said petitioners a transcript therefrom, such transcript to include the names and addresses of the corporations which made such returns. The order to show cause was granted on the affidavits of E. Ellery Anderson and Norton Chase, who state their unsuccessful efforts to secure such returns.

Failures in Cotton Trade Expected.

LONDON, Sept. 10.—Several failures in the cotton trade are expected in the Preston district. The balance sheets for the past quarter show heavy losses. The privilege to workmen to continue at work at a reduction of 10 per cent. in wages until trade mends is growing in favor.

NATURALIZATION EXTRAORDINARY.

Largest Number of Simultaneous Applications Ever Granted.

Queen Victoria's subjects seem to have made a grand organized bolt from the honor of citizenship in her domain, and to have rushed bodily to attain the glory of American citizenship and the protection of Uncle Sam, if the appearance of the Third District Court this afternoon is to be counted as meaning anything.

When Judge Borden took his seat at 3 o'clock fully 150 men, mostly English, were crowded into the court-room, comprising petitioners and witnesses. Hon. William M. Butler represented the petitioners.

The following took out their primary declarations looking toward citizenship: Joseph H. Dearncale, William H. Gledhill, James McGovern, William H. Holland, William Skinner, Henry Allan, William Duckworth, Henry Clarke, John H. Chadwick, Edward Gelder, John Jones, John Brierly, Thomas Richardson, Samuel Jones, William Catenall, William Taylor, Greenwood Robinson, Thomas Woolley, John Walmsley, William Baxter Stephenson, William Stott, Thomas Prescott, Edmund Lees, Richard Woods, Thomas Slater, Robert E. Potter, John Thomas Francis, John Mercer, Joseph H. Garlick, John Norris, Thomas Hamlet, William Paul Catteral, Richard Hornby, Geo. Warning, Charles Key, James Key, Thos. Hoyle, John Jackson, Thomas W. Heap, William Ingham, William Clarke, Nathaniel Norvell, William H. Franklin, John W. Slater, James Brown, John Barker, John Ratcliffe, James C. Mather, William Blackburn, Jr., William Leary, John Henry Hoyle, Eli Higginbottom, Joseph Green, John Mc Manus, William Foster, Thomas Lownds, Edwin Lownds, William Pilling, Alexander Taylor, Lord Barker, Joseph Burgess and Jesse Simpkins, Hartley Pollard, John Cotter.

The following received their final papers and were admitted to citizenship: William H. Mulberry, Thomas Schofield, Samuel Whitlow, Edward H. Gregory, John Blackburn, William Blackburn, John Hollingsworth, James Wright, Thomas Aspen, John T. Champion, James Lees, Richard Lord, John Wilkinson, Joseph Lamb, James Crooks, Walter Allen Taylor, Richard Howorth, Robert Blackburn, William Pell, Sidney Lees, John Thomas Hesford, John Rycroft, John Howorth, William Reed, James Reed, Mark Stafford, John Durkin, Levi Pemberton, James P. Smith, Aaron Hesford, Percy Lees, Thomas Tattersall, James Swallow, James E. Gregory, William Money-peany, John Shore, Walter Jenkins, William Green, John W. Matthews, John Hall, Henry Gatie, Jr., Ibbetson Dawson.

FIRE ISLAND PURCHASED.

Cabin Passengers of Infected Ships Will be Taken There.

Twenty-five Cases of Cholera at Swinburne Island.

Surgeon of the Wyoming Stricken With the Disease.

SYRACUSE, N. Y., Sept. 10.—Gov. Flower, in an interview with a reporter, said he had wired instructions to Dr. Jenkins at New York to buy Fire Island for the use of the quarantined cabin passengers in lower New York bay. He said the cabin passengers would be provided for there and the steerage passengers at Sandy Hook. He said that he had also directed Dr. Jenkins to buy or hire a steamship for the accommodation of passengers.

Fire Island was this morning contracted to be sold by D. S. S. Sannis, the owner, to a party representing the State government. The price paid is understood to be $210,000.

Chamber of Commerce Takes Action.

NEW YORK, Sept. 10.—J. Pierpont Morgan, Seth Lowe and Samuel D. Babcock of the special committee of five appointed at the meeting of the Chamber of Commerce yesterday to cooperate with the health authorities about quarantine matters held a meeting to-day. After the meeting the following dispatch was ordered sent to Dr. Jenkins: "In conformity with your letter just received the following physicians have been invited to act as an advisory committee to this committee, and they will be asked to confer with you and to report to this committee.

Drs. A. S. Loomis, A. Jacobi, Stephen Smith, R. D. Derby, T. Mitchell Pruden and Dr. Hamilton. A similar dispatch was sent to Secretary of the Treasury Foster at the Fifth Avenue Hotel, stating that the invited physicians have been asked to confer with him or with Dr. Hamilton as his representative. The advisory committee has been asked to meet Seth Low at Columbia College this afternoon for a conference and to take suitable action to prevent the spread of cholera from the ships in the bay.

Crew Refused to Work.

QUARANTINE, N. Y., Sept. 10.—The crew of the tugboat Fletcher, which was ordered this morning to transfer the passengers of the Normannia and Rugia to the relief vessels Stonington and New Hampshire, have refused to do duty with the tug on this service and the health officer is now endeavoring to secure another crew.

Dr. Jenkins received the following from Dr. Byron at 11 o'clock: "Just back from the Scandia. Two dead and 11 cases." This is four additional cases and two more deaths over last night's figures.

The Stonington arrived at 11.15 o'clock, and the cabin passengers of the Normannia will be transferred to her as soon as possible.

The Scandia is the only one of the steamers in quarantine which is still flying the yellow flag.

The Columbia, from Southampton, was off Fire Island at 9.34 this morning.

Situation at Swinburne Island.

QUARANTINE, S. I., Sept. 10.—At 2.30 Dr. Jenkins stated that there are 25 cases of sickness on Swinburne Island and 62 persons who are not sick. The Stonington will take the cabin passengers to Fire Island to-morrow.

Surgeon of the Wyoming Sick.

News has just been received that the surgeon of the Wyoming has been taken to Swinburne Island, suffering from diarrhoea trouble and vomiting.

Yellow Flag Again Up.

SANDY HOOK, Sept. 10.—The yellow flag has again been hoisted on the Scandia.

No Immigrants to be Landed.

LONDON, Sept. 10.—A statement was telegraphed to London last night that President Harrison had directed that notice be given to all steamship companies that if they persisted in bringing immigrants from infected ports to the United States it might result in their vessels being denied entrance to American harbors. If such a course is definitely decided upon it will effectually stop the companies from hereafter dispatching special immigrant steamers.

The Hamburg-American Company has telegraphed to the agent of the Associated Press in this city, declaring that that company has entirely stopped the steerage passenger business. The steamer Bohemia, which sailed from Hamburg Sept. 1, and Polaris, which sailed from the same port Sept. 8, are the only vessels of the company now on the way to the United Stated with steerage passengers.

Fuerst Bismarck from Southampton.

LONDON, Sept. 10.—The steamer Fuerst Bismarck sailed from Southampton for New York this morning with 426 cabin passengers.

BIG SCANDAL AFLOAT.

Serious Charges Against Members of C Co. Sarsfield, 3d Conn. Regiment.

NEW HAVEN, Conn., Sept. 10.—A big scandal in one of the local companies of the second regiment has come to light. Three members of C Company, Sarsfield, are implicated in the affair, which when the facts become known will create a stigma on the regimental armory and prevent respectable ladies from entering the building.

On information furnished by the wife of Armorer Walker formal charges have been brought against three well known members of the company. The charges have been forwarded to Col. Doherty, who will order a court martial in a few days. The incident in question, whose details are unfit for publication, occurred in the company room Saturday Aug.20,the day of the regimental ball from the encampment at Niagara.

The affair is causing a lively sensation and nothing of the kind has ever before occurred in the history of the regiment. The men, if Mrs. Walker's story is substantiated, will be dishonorably discharged. The affair implicates a well known Waterbury woman. There has been an effort on the part of the officers to keep the matter quiet, but it has finally leaked out and is now the subject of much talk.

RESULT OF DULL TIMES.

Perry, Converse & Co., Leather Dealers of Boston, Make an Assignment.

BOSTON, Sept. 10.—Perry, Converse & Co., leather dealers at 13 and 15 South street, Boston, to-day, assigned to Mr. Everett G. Place, of Everett G. Place & Co. and Henry P. Stanwood, treasurer of the Reading Electric Co. The liabilities are from $75,000 to $100,000. The assets are unknown, but the firm is expected to make a fairly good showing. It has been rated as having a capital of from $50,000 to $75,000, with good collateral.

A gentleman in a position to know some of the facts of the failure said to a reporter that liabilities are borne principally by the banks and merchants of Boston. The Everett and Continental banks are the heaviest creditors. As to the cause of the failure he said it was owing to the general dull times in the business.

BGOR PLEADS NOT GUILTY

To a Charge of Murdering Mrs. Abigail Rogers at her Mountain Hut.

GREENFIELD, Sept. 10.—Edward Beauregard of Orange, known as Edward Bgor in the local anglo-French patois, was arraigned to-day, charged with the murder of Mrs. Abigail Rogers at her lonely mountainside hut on Sunday. He pleaded not guilty and the case went over to Sept. 15.

Held for Murder in the Second Degree.

MANCHESTER, N. H., Sept. 10.—Dr. Cynthia B. Stearns was to-day held without bail for the Supreme Court on a charge of murder in the second degree, in causing the death of Phoebe LeBarron.

Senator Hill will Speak.

NEW YORK, Sept. 10.—It is announced that Senator Hill will speak once during the campaign, and perhaps more than once.

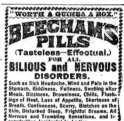

WENT DOWN IN THE GALE.

Loss of Schooner Cashier While Fishing on the Grand Banks.

HALIFAX, N. S., Sept. 10.—A schooner just returned to La Have from the Grand Banks brings the report of the loss of schooner Cashier of the same place. The vessels were fishing close together on the evening before the gale of Aug. 22. Next morning after the storm had abated nothing was to be seen of the schooner, but numerous pieces of wreckage were floating about. Without doubt the Cashier went down in the gale and her entire crew of 19 persons perished. The Cashier was one of the finest vessels in the business and was commanded by Capt. Reinhardt.

No Bill Against McCready.

BOSTON, Sept. 10.—The grand jury reported no bill against Hugh J. McCready of Montreal, who was arrested here some days ago on a charge of adultery preferred by his wife. He was alleged to have eloped with his sister-in-law.

Discovery Day.

HARTFORD, Ct., Sept. 10.—Gov. Bulkeley to-day issued a proclamation recommending that Friday, Oct. 21, Discovery Day, be observed as a holiday and advising that the public schools observe the day with appropriate ceremonies.

Whittier Memorial Exercises.

DANVERS, Sept. 10.—Whittier memorial exercises were held in the town hall this afternoon. There was a large attendance. Whittier poems were read and the school children took part songs.

Want Pauper Aliens Excluded.

GLASGOW, Sept. 10.—The Trades Union congress has adopted a resolution favoring the passage of a bill by parliament to exclude pauper aliens from Great Britain.

Indicted for Manslaughter.

BOSTON, Sept. 10.—A manslaughter was returned to-day against Frank Guilizinx for manslaughter in causing the death of Thomas Holland at Franklin Park.

Reuben Boynton Dead.

WESTBORO, Sept. 10.—Reuben Boynton, a prominent citizen, died this morning of heart trouble.

Continued text (West Cambridge wreck, left center column lower):

DISASTER ON THE BANKS.

Fishing Schooners Collide and Nineteen Fishermen Are Drowned.

HALIFAX, Sept. 12.—Great grief prevails at La Hava over the news of the loss of the schooner Cashier's crew, while fishing on the banks, collided with another fisherman, and both vessels were lost, with all on board. The Cashier was a fine vessel of 108 tons, owned by Reinhart Bros. and T. A. Wilson, and commanded by Captain Alfred Reinhart.

Among the crew are John Pernette, brother-in-law of the captain; William Wentzell, leaving a family of nine children of La Have; Eli Corkum, Spencer Ranby, Andrew Mosher, George Rickards and two brothers named Legge of West Dublin. The others were from Volgers Cove and vicinity. Young Ranby is the third son of the same family lost at sea.

Belgium Says No.

BRUSSELS, Sept. 12.—It is officially announced that the government of Belgium declines to allow the international monetary conference to be held here.

OUR STORE IS HEADQUARTERS

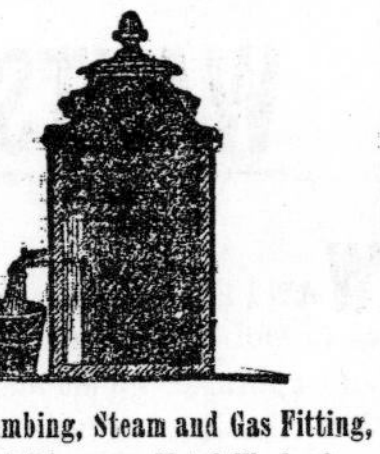

Pumps, Plumbing, Steam and Gas Fitting, Stoves and Furnaces, Metal Work, &c.

Diaphragm Pumps to Let for pumping out wells, cisterns, &c.

We sell the Best Rubber Bucket Pump made, and are agents for the celebrated "Buckeye" Lift and Force Pump.

Best of Workmen, Good Work, Prompt Attention, and Low Prices.

Wood, Brightman & Co.,
CORNER
North Water and William Streets.

To our Patrons:

The proprietors of the paper have kindly allowed us this space, in order to inform the people of New Bedford and all this part of Bristol County that there is no better place on earth to buy goods in the Kitchen Furnishing Line. Our line of Barstow's Bay State Ranges have a world-wide reputation. We have a full line of Kitchen Furnishings in stock and are ready to attend to all orders for Plumbing, Tinsmithing, Tinroofing and General Jobbing in our line of business. We propose to supply the wants of our customers to the best of our ability. We intend to call special attention to the various lines of our business as often as our time will permit. You are cordially invited to visit

HAYDEN'S
KITCHEN FURNISHING HOUSE;
Cor. Acushnet Ave. and Bedford St.

COLUMBIAS

Highest grade Bicycle in the world. Perfect in material, construction and finish, fitted with the Columbia Pneumatic Tire, guaranteed against puncture, bursting or leakage.

HOYLAND SMITH,
146 Pleasant Street.
Inspection solicited. Catalogue free.

COAL
—OF—
All Kinds and the Best Quality
—FOR—
DOMESTIC AND FACTORY USE
CONSTANTLY IN STOCK.

HAVING purchased the business and good will of Bates & Howard am prepared to fill orders at either my old office at yard or new office, No. 224 Purchase street.

YARD, ATLANTIC WHARF, FOOT OF CANNON STREET.

ALBERT W. HOLMES.
TELEPHONES:
YARD OFFICE, 92—3.
PURCHASE STREET OFFICE, 92—2.

GEORGE C. BLISS,
FLORIST.
34 Arnold Street,
CORNER COTTAGE.
TELEPHONE, DAY OR NIGHT.

BUSINESS CARDS.

WESTON C. VAUGHAN, JR.,
Funeral & Furnishings Undertaker

CASKETS, Coffins, Robes, and Flowers furnished at short notice; funerals attended in or out of the city; carriages furnished when desired. All orders from neighboring towns, by express or otherwise, will be promptly attended to. Telephone connection. 138 Purchase Street. Residence 142½ Purchase st. Night bell promptly answered.

E. T. WILSON,
Undertaker & Embalmer,
80 PLEASANT STREET.
(Odd Fellows' Building.)

CASKETS, Coffins, Robes, and Flowers furnished at short notice. All orders in or out of the city will receive prompt personal attention day or night.

Arterial Embalming a Specialty.
Persons wishing my services nights or Sun days will please call at my
Residence............... 15½ William Street
Telephone number 179—3. d&w

BOWKER & TRIPP,
Cor. North Water and North Sts.
MACHINISTS,
Steam Heating Engineers and Contractors.

Complete Outfits of Motive Power, Steam Heating, Hot Water Heating, and General Steam Fitting. A full line of Steam Fitting and Engineers' Supplies.

☞ Mill and heavy work a specialty. With our large machine shop, blacksmith shop and foundry attached, we have every facility for doing first-class work at moderate prices.

D. W. WILSON,
Steam Piping & General Machine Work
PIPE AND FITTINGS
Constantly on Hand.
21 Commercial Street, New Bedford, Mass.
☞ All orders promptly attended to. Satisfaction guaranteed.
Telephone No. 344—3. ap24-tf

GREAT SALE OF CARRIAGES.
—AT—
A. DAVIS ASHLEY'S,
947 Acushnet Avenue. cor. Coggeshall Street.

100 new and second-hand Carriages in endless variety: top phaeton, Stanhope, Corning and piano box buggies, Goddards, extension top surreys, canopy top surreys, buckboard changeable seats in the oak, new buckboard finished natural wood, $75.00; new open buggies $65.00 up; one $450.00 doctor's coupe nearly new, $165.00; two seated open and canopy top Ashley wagons, new and second-hand; also new and second-hand open and covered express wagons, best variety in the city; two and four seat dog carts; one new canopy top dog cart $50.00. If you want to buy or trade for any kind of a carriage that runs on wheels just look my stock over. I will guarantee the price and represent the goods just as they are; also have a fine assortment of harnesses; call early and you will get your money's worth. I also have some very desirable house lots and first-class business located lots which I will sell low for the location.

A. DAVIS ASHLEY,
947 Acushnet Ave., Cor. Coggeshall St.

ESTABLISHED 1884.
NEW BEDFORD
STEAM CARPET BEATING WORKS.
Cor. North Water and North Sts.

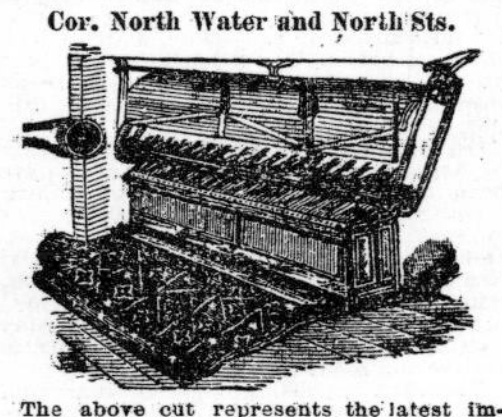

The above cut represents the latest improved Carpet Beating Machine now in use, and the only one of the kind in the city. When desired, Carpets can be steamed after having been beaten, by our

Patent Superheated Steam Vapor Process,
which destroys all moths and relieves the Carpets of all impurities. In doing this the colors are brought out wonderfully bright. Thanking my patrons for past favors and soliciting a share of their patronage in the future, I remain yours truly,

H. M. MAIN.
Telephone call 154—12. TTS

SOLICITORS OF PATENTS.
CROSBY & GREGORY,
GEO. W. GREGORY,
34 School Street,
BOSTON, MASS.,
and 318 F Street, Washington, D. C.

We have enlarged our office, increased our corps of draftsmen, and can intelligently prepare, successfully and properly prosecute, with broadest possible claims, and at reasonable cost, applications for U. S. and Foreign Patents on all subjects of invention.

DR. S. F. STOWE'S
Improved
Dyspepsia Lozenges

HAVE been before the public for the past seven years, and their success has established the high reputation they sustain in the cure of all Stomach Troubles. If you are subject to Heartburn, Sour Stomach, Distress after eating, Water Brash, Wind on Stomach, or Faintness and Sickness at Stomach, they are a certain remedy. For Hoarseness and Tickling Sensation of the Throat they stand unrivalled. Sold by all druggists and dealers in medicines at 10 cents per package or 3 packages for 25 cents. Observe my initials on each Lozenge, as none others are genuine, thus S. F. S.

MANUFACTORY, 555 HIGH STREET,
TTS PROVIDENCE R. I.

ORDERS FOR
LIVERY SUITS
—AND—
OVERCOATS!
Made and Trimmed in the Best Manner,
FIT GUARANTEED,
RECEIVED AT
SANDERS & BARROWS',
67 and 69 William St.

CLOSING OUT SALE
Of Summer Carriage Lap Robes, Horse Blankets, etc. Lowest Prices in the city for Harnesses, Ladies' and Gents' Riding Saddles, Bridles and Whips.

TRUNKS —AND— BAGS!

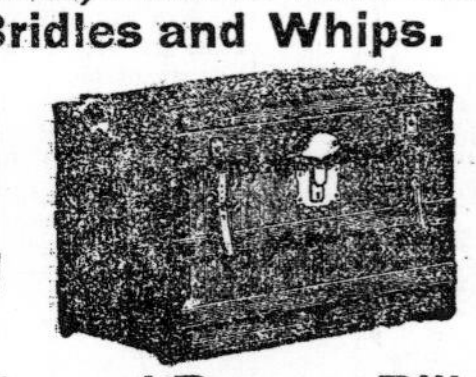

TRUNKS —AND— BAGS!

Pocketbooks and Purses, Bill Books, Umbrellas and all kinds of Travelling Goods, at
C. F. CUSHING'S,
HARNESS, TRUNK AND BAG EMPORIUM,
Opp. City Hall, and Branch Store 571 to 575 Purchase Street.

Every Day we are proving to Clothing Buyers who visit our store that we are selling Reliable, Well-made, Perfect-fitting Clothing for Men's and Boys' wear at Lower Prices than can be found elsewhere. Plain Figures and One-Price.

Larger, Better, and more attractive than ever our Fall and Winter stock of MEN'S AND BOYS' CLOTHING cannot fail to prove of interest to all who desire their money to do its best purchasing power.

H. V. SANDERS & Co.
Sell all Best Hats at Cut Prices. } OPP. CITY CLOCK, 92 Purchase St.

NEW BEDFORD BRASS FOUNDRY.

Machinists, Brass Finishers and Founders, Brass, Bronze and Composition Castings, Zinc and White Metal Pattern Castings, Phospor Bronze Castings a specialty, Lead Window Weights and High Speed Babbitt Metals, Chandelier Repairing and Brazing, Brass Finishing in all its branches. Machine Repairing promptly attended to. Lawn Mowers Sharpened and Repaired.

Foundry and Machine Shop, 108 North Water Street, foot of Elm.
WM. T. NICHOLSON, Manager, Formerly Foreman of the Armington & Sims Engine Company's Brass Foundry, Providence, R. I. je25-3m

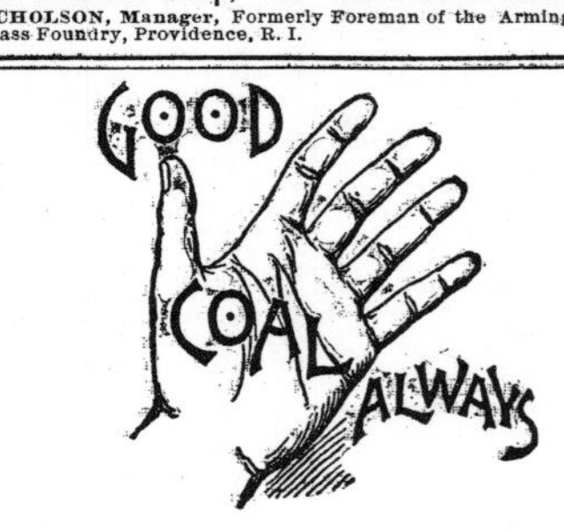

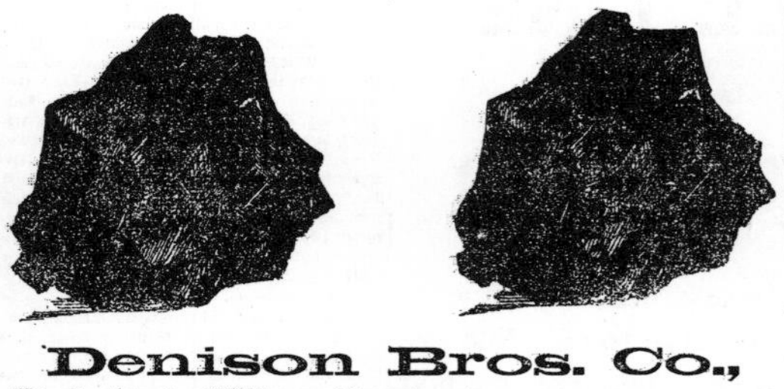

Denison Bros. Co.,
Yard—Foot of Hillman Street.
Offices—Cor. School and South Water Sts., and Cor. Hillman and North Water Sts.

A PILL
Errors of Youth.
NERVOUS DEBILITY PILLS.—All those suffering from Nervous Debility and Weakness and having been unsuccessfully treated, will find this famous remedy a certain and speedy cure for premature decay, inability, lack of confidence, mental depression, palpitation of the heart, weak memory, exhausted vitality, &c. Price $1 per box, or 6 boxes, which will cure most cases, for $5 postpaid. All correspondence confidential. Address or call on N. E. MEDICAL INSTITUTE, 24 Tremont Row, Boston, Mass. 118-TTS

A. B. HATHAWAY,
FLORIST.
Store 220 Union Street.
Greenhouses, Court Street.

POSTERS AND HAND BILLS
Printed at short notice at the
STANDARD PRINTING ROOMS.

HOME MATTERS.

PATENTS have been granted to William H. Johnson, Industry, assignor to Oliver Ames & Sons Corporation, North Easton, form for holding shovel handles; Frank Mossberg, assignor to Mossberg Manufacturing Company, Attleboro, wrench.

STRUCK BY A LOCOMOTIVE.—A. Horace Poole, superintendent of Sears' lumber yard at Middleboro, is at the Massachusetts General Hospital, in Boston, suffering from a fractured leg, received by being struck by the engine of the noon train from Boston yesterday, while crossing the freight yard.

PITCHED OUT.—Last evening two drunken individuals in a buggy driving rapidly down Russell street at the corner of Fourth street came to grief, the horse falling and throwing out the occupants. One of them, who refused to give his name, was badly used up, his face cut and scratched and his clothing was torn and mutilated.

NEWPORT CONVOCATION.—At the regular stated meeting of the Newport Convocation of the Episcopal churches of Newport county held at Emmanuel church, Newport, R. I., yesterday, the matter of appointing a missionary to Tiverton was referred to the Dean and Advisory Board, with power to nominate, to the Bishop. A communication from the Bishop, appointing Mr. Sturgess as missionary for one year to Portsmouth, was read.

LOSES $5000 WORTH OF STOCK.—The general rule of the common law that a thief can give no better title to stolen property than he himself possesses, is applied by Judge Putnam of the United State Circuit Court in Boston in a case decided yesterday, and as a result of the decision Mrs. Elizabeth R. Lee of Tisbury loses $5000 worth of the stock in the Bangor Electric Light & Power Company, which she took as security for a loan in good faith of broker Frank H. Williams, who some years ago left Boston and is now in parts unknown. The facts in the case showed that Augustus G. Robinson and Williams had a box at the Boston Safe Deposit & Trust Company, to which both had access. In the box was a certificate of the stock in question, belonging to Robinson, who was an army officer. During a temporary absence of Robinson, Williams pledged the stock to Mrs. Lee for a loan, but Robinson on his return claimed it, and the present suit was a bill of interpleader, to determine the rights of the parties, Mrs. Lee claiming that, inasmuch as Robinson had introduced Williams to her and given him an opportunity to impose upon her, although Robinson had no such intention, the pledge must stand and Robinson suffer the loss, but Judge Putnam says this is not the law. The judge says: "The certificate was not entrusted to the possession of Williams, either directly or implied, nor was he authorized to remove it from the box. His misdoing was not embezzlement or fraud, but criminal larceny at common law. Upon the whole case the court is unable to find any principle of common law that will protect Mrs. Lee.

Fashions for Children.

The endless number of dresses it takes to go through a season is often a heavy pull on the purse.

A sensible way is to use Diamond Dyes, which come in all colors, and make faded clothes look like new. The brown, bottle green and cardinal are fashionable and useful dyes, while fast stocking black will make cotton stockings a black that will not fade or crock.

Tutt's Tiny Pills
The dyspeptic, the debilitated, whether from excess of work of mind or body or exposure in malarial regions, will find Tutt's Pills the most genial restorative ever offered the invalid.

True merit sells and the presents advertise
TUXEDO WASHING POWDER.
Nothing made so perfect for the purpose of harmless cleaning as Tuxedo.
Read the ticket in every package.

SHAPE YOUR MUSTACHE.

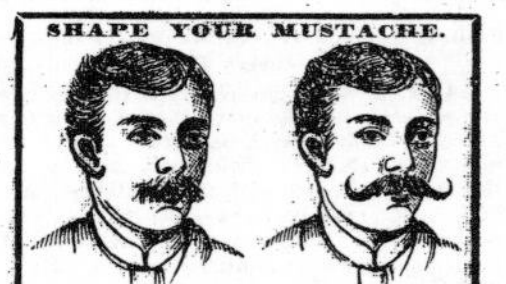

What is more disgusting than to see a man always twisting, twirling, and biting his mustache. Avoid the bad habit by using the instrument that will keep it always just right. Will be sent post-paid with complete outfit for 25 cents, two for one dollar. Postal note or stamps. Address the Mason Bartlett Co., Box 2480, Boston, Mass.

Oregon Red Cedar Shingles,
(NOT REDWOOD)
BEST SHINGLES MADE.
NEW LOT JUST IN.
THOS. W. CROACHER,
LEONARD STREET.

BEWARE OF
CHOLERA!

Nothing so promotes the spread of Asiatic Cholera as uncleanliness. The more filthy the condition the greater the danger, but no one is absolutely safe. Make sure your pores are all open and every particle of useless dead flesh or chance dirt is removed from your skin. Take a

Turkish Bath
No. 5 SOUTH SIXTH ST.

MISS BORDEN DIDN'T.

Denial that She Consulted a Providence Lawyer.

Last Startling Bit of Evidence Pronounced Bogus.

A Board of Trade Address on the Case Delivered in Watertown.

The announcement that the government is in possession of information which goes to show that Miss Lizzie Borden consulted an attorney in Providence in regard to the disposition of her father's estate, has greatly interested the lawyers of Fall River. Two members of the bar who were interviewed yesterday stated that they did not see how the prosecution could compel the prisoner's counsel to testify as to anything which she had said to him, but admitted that if the State kept on accumulating evidence it might force Miss Borden to talk. If it were true that she had applied for advice, as reported, the lawyers asserted that it would be damaging evidence in case it could be introduced. The fact that she was in Providence appeared to be well established, unless the authorities are very much at sea, but it was intimated that it was singular that a lawyer had dropped any hint which would betray his client. The police in Fall River are reticent and refuse to say anything beyond making the admission that the story, as it has been printed, is substantially correct. As nearly as can be learned, the Providence lawyer's mistake is explained in this way: On the night of the murder, while in a barber shop, and long before Miss Borden was suspected, he dropped a remark which found its way to the detectives, and which led to further important and interesting developments. It was too late to undo the mischief, and the State naturally took full advantage of it. Another version is that Miss Borden was seen in the waiting room of a prominent lawyer's office, on the Thursday before the tragedy, and that her presence there led to the investigation which brought to light the purchases she made at the Westminster street store.

Miss Borden Didn't.

It has been learned that Mr. Jennings was in Boston yesterday in consultation with Mr. Adams on the Borden case, and they were asked if they had anything to say with reference to the article recently published in the Fall River *Globe* and sent out by the Associated Press concerning the alleged discovery of evidence of Miss Borden being in Providence and having an interview with an attorney there about the disposition of the estate in the event of her father and mother, or either of them, dying. They both said they were prepared to state that the report was absolutely untrue; that Miss Borden did not then, or ever in her life, consult any attorney in Providence, R. I., or anywhere else, concerning the disposition of the property of her father.

Sheriff Wright's Orders.

Orders have been given by Sheriff Wright of Taunton to allow only Emma Borden to visit Lizzie during five days of the week. On Saturdays, when he is free from court duty, and is there himself, he can sift the wheat easily, and even then only friends of the family of long standing can see her for an extremely limited time.

A Lawyer's Address.

The Watertown Board of Trade met last evening and its members were addressed on the subject of Criminal Law, by Judge E. T. Luce of Waltham, of the Second Middlesex District Court, and Mr. John B. Goodrich of Newton. It had been announced that Mr. Melvin O. Adams, one of Lizzie Borden's counsel, would address the meeting, but as he was unable to attend Mr. Goodrich spoke in his stead. The first speaker was Judge Luce, who said he had been invited to speak on the Execution of Criminal Law.

John B. Goodrich was then introduced as a leading criminal lawyer and spoke at some length. He said the world was growing better. The better classification of prisoners, he thought, was an important subject. "Take the case at Fall River," said he. "It staggers every one. But the people must have some one arrested. A great many people think Miss Borden could have done it, but a great many people believe that a girl like her could not possibly have committed such a crime. In the meantime she is confined in a little hole in the wall, with only an iron grating window and door. This is simply because she has been charged with a crime. She has got to stay there three months, when she will certainly go free. Then the members of the grand jury will also be kept in confinement for several months.

"Why is this done? There ought to be some better system than this. It seems hard to thrust a woman of refined taste and manners into a cell formerly occupied by a low-class criminal."

In speaking of the grand jury he said that that body was not a very important nor useful body anyway. The district attorney, he thought, ought to serve all the purposes of a grand jury. It was perpetuated simply because it was an ancient institution.

As Mr. Goodrich concluded his speech a member asked what his opinion was about a judge presiding at an inquest and also at a hearing on the same case as was done by Judge Blaisdell at Fall River in the Borden case.

"Judge Blaisdell ought not to have done as he did," replied Mr. Goodrich. "It was a farce for him to preside at the hearing, and it was in shocking bad taste. He had associate justices who would have done just as well. He went a little further than he expected to, I think. As a Judge he might have given his decree and not his reasons, but he persisted in giving his reasons. He took the ground that no innocent person could have testified at the first hearing that she was only five or six minutes in the barn and at the next hearing testify that it might have been 15 or 20 minutes, as Lizzie Borden is said to have done. There is a well considered objection to the practice of doing as Judge Blaisdell did, and he showed very bad taste."

COLORED KNIGHTS TEMPLARS.—The colored Knights Templars of Massachusetts and Rhode Island held their annual convocation with Benjamin Gardner Commandery, No. 6, Newport, yesterday, and, besides the delegates, the following commanderies were present: Mt. Zion, No. 5, of Worcester; Van Horne, No. 8, of Springfield; Thomas Dalton, N. 7, of New Bedford; Lewis Hayden, No. 4, of Boston; George L. Gather, No. 2, St. Paul, No. 3, and Zion, No. 1, of Providence. In the afternoon they made a very creditable parade and in the evening held a reception and social. Grand officers were elected as follows: Right eminent grand commander, Rev. Malcolm Van Horne of Newport; deputy grand commander, Rev. W. B. Bowen of Worcester; grand generalissimo, Eli Welling of New Bedford; grand captain general, Mark N. G. Walker of Providence; eminent grand prelate, Charles C. Ringgold of Providence. The next convocation will be held at Providence.

TIVERTON.

The Rev. Donald Browne will preach his farewell sermon at the Congregational church next Sunday morning.

There are quite a number of cases of typhoid fever in town, confined principally to children.

Sickness Among Children,

Especially infants, is prevalent at all times, but is largely avoided by giving proper nourishment and wholesome food. The most successful and reliable is the Gail Borden "Eagle" Brand Condensed Milk. Your grocer and druggist keep it.

Good Sense if Not Poetry.

An official of the Gas Company received the following letter, through the Farmers' Fair P. O. last night, which shows the people are thinking:

I'ts meself has been using the gas-stove,
  I'd scorn to use any other,
When it kapes me kitchen so clane and nate
  Widout any fuss or bother.

And sure and faith I tell ye,
  The mon is a giutlemon true
Who has offered a way to get a watch,
  Which an Irish girl may do.

And I thought to send as foine a loaf
  As any farmer's leddy,
But alack-a-day, I fell out by the way
  A-riding with Patrick O'Greddy.

The horse was lively, and felt pretty good,
  And Pat was a bit onsteady,
And he fetched her a whack right on to her back
  For which the poor baste wasn't ready.

Ah! I didn't know any more at all
  Till I opened me eyes this morning,
And foind I was placed in the hospital ward
  For laving me place widout warning.

And I wanted just, by your lave, to say,
  Young man at the Farmers' Fair,
If it hadn't been for whiskey and gin
  It's I that am here would be there.

If you've got any coppers to spend for rum,
  Or whiskey, or lager beer,
Or even the wine that comes from the vine,
  Or tobacco's doubtful cheer,

For the sake of Mary, or rather St. Luke's,
  Hand em out for this good place of healing,
And faith in your heart, havin' acted this part
  It's no end o' good you'll be feeling.

THE HEBREW RELIGIOUS OBSERVANCES at this season of the year are undoubtedly of interest to participants, but they amount to nothing less than a disturbance of the peace to people living in the neighborhood of the building or hall where the meetings are held. This is particularly the case with people living in the vicinity of Pleasant and Market streets, where the Jews are now holding daily services. We say daily services, but most of them are in the evening or the early morning, and the loud voice of the leader and the full chorus of the people make a noise which disturbs everybody for the distance of a square at a time when they would like to sleep. The voices rise and fall and just as one gets into a drowse he is awakened by a fresh outburst which causes anything but kindly feelings toward those who are the cause of it. It is hard to tell exactly how much latitude a religious body is to be allowed in the way of making a noise, but if ever a case called for the interference of the authorities it would seem that this was one.

OBITUARY.—Deacon Stephen Buffington, the oldest person in Swanzey, died in that town Saturday night. He had been sick about four weeks before his death. He received a pension for many years for services rendered in the last war with England. In 1842 he represented the town in the Legislature. He was born in Swanzey, Dec. 19, 1794, and lacked three months of being 98 at the time he died.

Paul Sears, one of the oldest members of the Boston Marine Society, died Wednesday the 21st in Dorchester. He was born in Dennis, December 3, 1812. He went to Boston in 1840 and carried on the salt business under the name of Thacher & Sears. Afterward he devoted himself to the shipping business. Five sons survive him.

MARION.

The pulpit of the Universalist church will be occupied by the pastor of the church at New Bedford, Rev. William F. Potter, next Sunday, Sept. 25th.

FALL RIVER.

The new La France engine was given a trial yesterday afternoon. She threw a stream about 300 feet. The test was satisfactory and the engine will be accepted.

The Bedford street Democratic Club will fight against using the Australian ballot system at the approaching caucuses.

The Fall River Board of Trade is discussing the advisability of establishing a Board of Public Works in the city.

Applicants for a place in the Home for the Aged must be 65 years of age or over, and have resided in Fall River for at least ten years. They pay $100 and assign all of their property to the institution.

Tuesday afternoon, unknown persons broke into an unoccupied house at 325 Bay street, owned by Oscar Dubois. Tools and other articles to the value of over $100 were stolen.

TAUNTON.

The contract for building the new theatre has been awarded to Bryant & Slade of Fall River.

The Odd Fellows of the city are talking up a grand fair which will probably take place the last week in November. The order netted over $200 by the clambake Labor Day.

Yesterday morning fire was discovered in Strange's machine shop on Washington street. The whole interior of the lower part of the building was gutted and lathes and other machines seriously injured. The upper story was not so badly damaged. The cause of the fire is not known. The insurance was $800 on the building and $700 on the machinery.

BARNSTABLE COUNTY.

D. G. Whitlock of the Pavonia Yacht Club, Communipaw, N. J., has bought yacht Mayolin, formerly owned by E. O. Snow of Provincetown.

Capt. Thomas Sparks, aged 87 years, the oldest native born citizen of Provincetown, but one, was accidentally run over, knocked down and bruised by a horse and wagon yesterday.

Engineer Stearns of the State Board of Health has expressed his opinion that the Provincetown water is good for use and health.

A raid was made yesterday on the Union Fish Company's store at Provincetown, and a lot of salt mackerel stolen.

FOUND DRIFTING.

LOUELLA A. WARREN.

Found drifting, a boat out to ocean,
  Empty, all quiet and still,
With but an open journal
  Of the owner to tell good or ill.

It ran, "I, Therese, am an orphan
  Of some three years or more;
I know not what Dame Fortune
  Has for me in store.

I want to live on to the future
  And make my life noble, grand"—
'Twas ended; her journal was finished
  By God's much holier hand.

'Tis well we know not the future,
  Or see through the veil, the years
That stretch afar in the distance,
  Or know what in them appears.

Papers said, "Sad accident; drowning;
  Young lady went far from shore;"
Only a desperate struggle,
  And then—it all was o'er.

The waves danced on just as merry,
  A sea-bird screeched in its flight;
The sun shed one ray of crimson,
  And day faded into night.

The Father of Many Ills.

Constipation leads to a multitude of physical troubles. It is generally the result of carelessness or indifference to the simplest rule of health. Eugene McKay of Brantford, Ont., writes:

"I had for several years been a sufferer from constipation, had taken a great many different remedies, some of which did me good for a time, but only for a time, then my trouble came back worse than ever. I was induced by a friend, whom BRANDRETH'S PILLS had benefited, to try them. Took two each night for a week, then one every night for about six weeks. Since that time I have not experienced the slightest difficulty whatever, and my bowels move regularly every day. I believe firmly that for sluggishness of the bowels and biliousness BRANDRETH'S PILLS are far superior to any other."

ORDERS FOR

LIVERY SUITS

—AND—

OVERCOATS!

Made and Trimmed in the Best Manner,

FIT GUARANTEED,

RECEIVED AT

SANDERS & BARROWS',

67 and 69 William St.

CLOSING OUT SALE

Of Summer Carriage Lap Robes, Horse Blankets, etc. Lowest Prices in the city for Harnesses, Ladies' and Gents' Riding Saddles, Bridles and Whips.

TRUNKS —AND— BAGS!

TRUNKS —AND— BAGS!

Pocketbooks and Purses, Bill Books, Umbrellas and all kinds of Travelling Goods, at

C. F. CUSHING'S,

HARNESS, TRUNK AND BAG EMPORIUM,

Opp. City Hall, and Branch Store 571 to 575 Purchase Street.

Every Day we are proving to Clothing Buyers who visit our store that we are selling Reliable, Well-made, Perfect-fitting Clothing for Men's and Boys' wear at Lower Prices than can be found elsewhere. Plain Figures and One-Price.

Larger, Better, and more attractive than ever our Fall and Winter stock of

MEN'S AND BOYS' CLOTHING

cannot fail to prove of interest to all who desire their money to do its best purchasing power.

H. V. SANDERS & CO.

Sell all Best Hats at Cut Prices. OPP. CITY CLOCK, 92 Purchase St.

Denison Bros. Co.,

Yard—Foot of Hillman Street.

Offices—Cor. School and South Water Sts., and Cor. Hillman and North Water Sts.

NOTICE.

Having bought the bankrupt stock of the large harness factory of

GRANT & AMES,

Of SOUTH FRAMINGHAM, we can sell you a Full, Genuine Rubber-trimmed Harness at one-half the cost to make.

TRUNKS AND BAGS

At the LOWEST PRICES in the city.

WILLIAM CRONIN & CO.,

Corner Elm and Pleasant Sts.

A. B. HATHAWAY,

FLORIST.

Store 220 Union Street.

Greenhouses, Court Street.

Oregon Red Cedar Shingles,

(NOT REDWOOD)

BEST SHINGLES MADE.

NEW LOT JUST IN.

THOS. W. CROACHER,

LEONARD STREET.

POSTERS AND HAND BILLS

Printed at short notice at the

STANDARD PRINTING ROOMS.

J. O. DOUGLASS' Sale and Exchange Stables, Mechanics' Lane, New Bedford, Mass. I keep constantly on hand and for sale or exchange a good stock of driving, family, business, and team horses. Horses bought and sold on commission. Fresh arrivals every Monday and Thursday. All horses warranted as represented.

JAHN BROS., Florists,

CLARKS POINT.

ROSES AND CARNATIONS,

A SPECIALTY.

jy1-tf

LATEST STYLES OF TYPE

—AT THE—

STANDARD JOB OFFICE.

COLUMBUS DAY.

Recommendations for Its Observance in the Public Schools.

Following are the recommendations of the committee of five appointed by the public school principals to draw up a programme for Columbus Day. They have been approved by the special committee and will be brought before the School Board. Superintendent Hatch will issue a letter with their publication, requesting that teachers be governed by them in preparing for the celebration. The recommendations:

1. That all the public schools of the city have a celebration of Columbus Day at their respective buildings, in which celebration shall be included the first five numbers of the official programme.

It is further recommended, however, that in the primary grades the teachers explain the president's proclamation in their own language instead of simply reading it, and that instead of the Song of Columbus Day composed by Rev. Theron Brown, a portion of Hail Columbia be substituted.

2. That each principal be allowed to have such additional exercises as he may deem best.

3. That each principal be allowed to decide whether the exercises shall take place within or without the school building.

4. That the School Committee be requested to supply to each school building not already thus supplied a flag of suitable size for use in the salute to the flag, (No. 3.)

5. That the School Committee be requested to supply to the larger schools which hold out of door exercises a musician with some brass instrument to lead the children's singing.

6. That the teachers of all the public schools which are to have out of door exercises provide alternative exercises which can take place in the several school rooms in case the weather is unsuitable for open air exercises.

7. That the School Committee request the cooperation of the Grand Army of the Republic and any other organization of veterans of the civil war in the exercises at each school building.

8. That the length of the exercises be left to the decision of each principal, and that the several principals have authority to dismiss the pupils for the day on completion of the exercises.

9. That the School Committee be requested to take into consideration the question of providing badges appropriate for the occasion, to be worn by the pupils on that day, and to be retained as a memento of the occasion.

10. That the pupils be instructed to invite their parents and friends to be present and participate in the exercises of the day.

FALL RIVER.

The Board of Health has been notified that there is an unhealthy school at Nos. 5 and 7 Pitman street.

Andrew Porter, a master carpenter, died at his house on Pearl street yesterday, aged 59 years.

L. B. Sanford has been elected superintendent of the Wampanoag mills, and will enter upon his duty on October 3d.

A dressmaker named Lareau of Rodman street was badly burned Thursday afternoon by her son, who set her dress on fire by lighting matches while sitting at her side.

Ulderic Lambert of Bedford street was badly hurt on the legs and body yesterday by a barrel of coal falling on him.

While sliding on a balustrade yesterday a boy named Lefrance of Pleasant street fell and broke his nose. His forehead was badly cut.

TAUNTON.

Charles E. Holmes, a policeman of the city, died at the Insane Hospital yesterday.

The elevator in the rear of Union block came down several feet when the rope broke yesterday. The patent clamps did not work, and a man who was going up with a pail of thin tar to repair the roof came down with it. Luckily he was not hurt, but he had a tar bath.

At an inquest held yesterday relative to the death of William H. Baker, the finding of Judge Fox was as follows: "I find and report that William H. Baker, 23 years of age, was employed in carting water pipes for the water works extension. He had a pipe weighing about 3600 pounds on his wagon. As he was driving over sloping ground the pipes rolled off and crushed him to death. No other person was near. It was an accident.'

COTTAGE CITY.

Postmaster Scranton reports the Summer business of the post office exceeds any previous season. There were 563 registered letters dispatched; 547 registered letters received; 291 special delivery letters received and delivered; 693 money orders issued amounting to \$9373.69; 256 money orders cashed amounting to \$7481.13; postal notes issued amounting to \$1193.77; stamps and envelopes sold equal to \$2979.51; 23,473 postal cards sold equal to \$234.75; a total business amounting to \$21,262.82.

TIVERTON.

In the death of Mrs. Nancy S. Reid Tiverton loses the last of one of the oldest families, the homestead of her grandfather, Philip Seabury, and father, Cornelius Seabury, being at Packet Brook, south of the Four Corners.

Indigestion.

HORSFORD'S Acid Phosphate.

Promotes digestion without injury and thereby relieves diseases caused by indigestion of the food. The best remedy for headache proceeding from a disordered stomach.

Trial bottle mailed on receipt of 25 cents in stamps. Rumford Chemical Works, Providence, R. I.

BEWARE OF

CHOLERA!

Nothing so promotes the spread of Asiatic Cholera as uncleanliness. The more filthy the condition the greater the danger, but no one is absolutely safe. Make sure your pores are all open and every particle of useless dead flesh or chance dirt is removed from your skin. Take a

Turkish Bath

No. 5 SOUTH SIXTH ST.

SHERIFF WRIGHT DISGUSTED.

Strong Feeling Against Him as Miss Borden's Custodian.

His Sympathetic Generosity Shown in the Case of Dr. Vose.

Interest in the Fall River Case Unabated About Taunton Jail.

From the Standard's Staff Correspondent.

TAUNTON, Sept. 23.—As the days go by the interest in the Borden case abates not one jot, although in the absence of any particularly new matter it is necessarily hard for the general public to get at any new facts in connection with the case. There have been so many family circle trials of the case beforehand and theories are so well set that even when new matter is presented it will be difficult to turn those who have prejudged the case away from their chosen ideas.

Sheriff Wright said yesterday that he was never so sick of a case in all his experience; he was absolutely disgusted with the manner in which it had been conducted and would be heartily glad when it was ended. And the sheriff may well be glad, for there is a very bitter feeling towards him in the county, growout of his alleged discourteous treatment of persons who have visited the jail on business connected with the affair.

A prominent and usually well informed citizen told the *Standard's* representative the following story: "It will be remembered that the other night down in New Bedford every ward in the city was carried for Mr. Tompkins, and people were surprised that such should be the case. They appeared to know nothing of the caucuses until all was ended. The why and wherefore has just come to the surface, although it was well understood that there was opposition to Mr. Wright in that city, because he had insisted in putting a Fall River man in as keeper of the house of correction instead of a New Bedford man. It appears that some time ago the district attorney sent a certain man to the jail here in company with Inspector Hathaway of the New Bedford police, and the man was to see Miss Borden. Mr. Hathaway, so the story goes, wanted to go in where the cell was but had the door slammed in his face, and the man who did get a chance to go in was obliged to pick out the party he desired to see as best he could. He didn't make any mistake however, in the person, and identified Lizzie all right. But Inspector Hathaway didn't like his treatment; he considered it shabby, and the result was that every friend in the city of New Bedford turned out and defeated Mr. Wright in the caucuses. And to-day the feeling is so strong in Fall River over that interview which was allowed between Lizzie and the ex-Fall River woman that if the election of sheriff came off this week Mr. Wright wouldn't know what struck him. And yet, in the latter case, there seemed to be no other course open to him. He had no right to deny the request of Miss Borden's counsel, although he had turned away the woman twice when she came on her own account. Of course the whole thing was plainly arranged by the young woman who had worked very cleverly upon the feelings of the friends of Lizzie, and she did her work well. Her strenuous efforts on the Fall River police which she had been making for days before she enlisted Mr. Jennings in the matter all failed, although perhaps it was only natural that they should object to Lizzie's story going out in that way. And yet people about here are laughing at Lawyer Jennings in his allowing a young woman to interview Lizzie for the sake of presenting her side of the story, when he himself was engaged for that very business and had been and was working day and night in the matter. It showed, it is claimed, that the case is too big for him and that he was getting rattled;

Here is one thing that the newspaper men who were on the spot have never taken up, and why they haven't is a mystery. When Bridget Sullivan was on the stand she was subjected to a severe examination by Mr. Adams in regard to that last night at "Harrington's." The examination ran along something like this, after having fixed the time of her going home:

Question—Did anybody go home with you that night?

Answer—No, I went alone.

Q. Usually go home alone?

A. Not always.

Q. But you did go home alone that night?

A. I did.

Q. How did you go home, work or ride?

A. I walked.

Q. Walked all the way?

A. Yes.

Q. Didn't ride in the cars?

A. No.

Q. When you got home who was there?

A. The family.

Q. All of the family?

A. Yes.

Q. There had been a robbery at the house about a year before?

A. Yes.

Q. Where was the family then?

A. At home.

Q. All of them?

A. Yes.

Q. And something was taken out of the barn, too?

A. Yes.

Q. See anybody around at the time the robbery was committed?

A. No.

About this time Lawyer Jennings pulled the coat-tail of Mr. Adams and there was a whispered conference. The district attorney winked at Marshal Hilliard and the marshal smiled. The robbery business was dropped by Mr. Adams, after that conference with Mr. Jennings, like a shot. Why? Well, that's for some bright newspaper man to find out. And it wasn't once alluded to by Mr. Jennings in his argument except in a general way, when he referred to the police knowing that the house had been burglarized when nobody in the house knew of the circumstances. Yes, the police did know that the house was burglarized, and they knew that some money and a watch had been missing after the burglary. And the police know something more, without a doubt. They know why the case wasn't followed, but it is questioned by those who ought to know if the police have found out yet just what the whole resultof that robbery was, and how many articles disappeared besides the money and watch. It would not be surprising if it came out before this thing ended that the Bordens themselves stopped the police inquiry into that robbery, and it may be that Marshal Hilliard is backed up in his opinion of what course to take because in possession of certain facts which lead him to believe the worst of Lizzie Borden. It is hinted strongly that there were things taken from that house that an ordinary thief would have no use for, and that the money and watch were simply taken as a blind to throw Mr. Borden off the track. And when the real object of the thief was discovered proceedings were stopped and a family scandal checked right there. This is the theory of one or two who have been following the case pretty closely and who are well acquainted with all the parties interested.

But if Sheriff Wright is accused of being too much of a jailer in the case of Miss Borden, his treatment of unfortunate Dr. Vose shows an entirely different phase of character, providing the accusation is true. The doctor has been in jail for a long time now, awaiting a hearing on exceptions made by his counsel, after his conviction for abortion of a criminal nature at Somerset last year. He has almost entirely lost the use of his lower limbs, and every fine day the sheriff has him carried out into the pretty yard and allows him to take sun baths to his satisfaction. In his case, as well as in the case of Lizzie Borden, his friends have run wild in their ideas of how to handle the matter. They are actually talking of asking the Governor to pardon the doctor before he has been sentenced and before his case goes from the courts into the hands of the Governor and Council. Of course such a request cannot be granted if it is made.

A HANDSOME TROPHY.

Silver Cup to be Contested for by the Sheridan and I. A. Guards.

The accompanying cut gives an idea of the handsome silver cup to be awarded

the winner of the competitive drill between the Sheridan Guards of this city and the Irish-American Guards of Fall River at the Bristol county fair in Taunton.

MCKINLEY TALKS TARIFF.

Ohio's Governor has a Great Reception in Philadelphia.

PHILADELPHIA, Sept. 24.—One of the greatest gatherings that has ever greeted a public man in this city thronged the Academy of Music last night to hear Governor William McKinley speak upon "the pending issues of the campaign." Fully 5000 people were present, and hundreds were unable to gain admission. Governor McKinley was the guest of the Manufacturers' club, and was escorted to the stage by Thomas Dolan, president of the club, and a score or more of members of the club. As Governor McKinley entered, the audience arose and cheered veciferously. Mr. Dolan introduced Governor McKinley, and the latter was again given an ovation as he came to the front of the stage.

Governor McKinley's speech was mainly upon the tariff, which he designated as the great issue of the campaign. Again and again he was compelled to stop while the storm of applause rolled through the building. Every mention of President Harrison's name created the greatest enthusiasm. In the midst of the speech a local club came upon the stage bearing a banner of tin plate, with the arms of Pennsylvania painted upon it and this inscription: "American tin plate, made at Morristown, Pa., 1892." Governor McKinley said: "There is another trophy of protection," and the audience cheered itself hoarse. Governor McKinley said he favored a sound currency, and that free trade and debased money went hand in hand. The governor argued that a protective tariff was constitutional, and quoted figures to prove the beneficial effects of tariff on the industries of the country. He praised Harrison's administration.

Postmaster General Wanamaker also spoke.

STEVENSON AT RICHMOND.

A Vast Multitude Listens to His Remarks Upon Campaign Issues.

RICHMOND, Va., Sept. 24.—The ovation given last night to General Stevenson was almost unparalled in the history of politics in this state. He was escorted from the hotel to Mozart academy by a large torchlight procession which composed the various Democratic clubs of the city. The large building was packed with people, while thousands were unable to get within hearing distance. Colonel John B. Carey introduced General Stevenson, who was greeted with loud applause. General Stevenson contrasted the administration of Cleveland with that of Harrison, and said that during the former prosperity reigned, unknown since the war. He then discussed the tariff at some length but declared that the force bill was one of far greater importance to the people than a hundred tariff bills. He then discussed the force bill and denied that it was a dead issue.

He said the force bill meant to Viginia, North Carolina, South Carolina, Georgia, Alabama, Louisiana, Mississippi, the return of the "glorious days of reconstruction;" that its intent was to plunder the people, and that it was designed to take the government out of the hands of the people and place it in possession of federal agents.

Congressman Rainer of Maryland and James L. Gordon also spoke. The name of Cleveland, whenever mentioned, called forth vociferous applause. Among those on the stage were Governor McKinney, Congressman Wise and General Fitzhugh Lee.

Lodge Was There.

PROVIDENCE, Sept. 24.—The Garfield club of Pawtucket had as a guest at a banquet last evening Hon. Henry Cabot Lodge of Massachusetts and other gentlemen prominent in Republican counsels of the state. Congressmen Boutelle and Simonds sent regrets, as did Whitelaw Reid and General Clarkson. A resolution was adopted expressing sympathy with President Harrison in his present affliction in the sickness of his wife, and wishing her speedy return to health. Mr. Lodge spoke of the free trade issue, and referred to the Commissioner Peck of New York incident in a sarcastic vein. Other speakers followed and the meeting came to a close.

No Free Speech in Mexico.

MONTEREY, Mex., Sept. 24.—C. G. Hoag, an American merchant of this city, has been expelled from the republic for criticising the administration of President Diaz.

It Strikes us as Remarkable

to hear of the wonderful record for curing enjoyed by Betton's Infallible Pile Salve; it cures every form of this troublesome ailment. If not to be had at your druggist, send 50 cents to Winkelmann & Brown Drug Co., Baltimore, Md.

GEN. WEISSERT'S FIRST ORDERS.

Mrs. Wickens of Kansas Chosen President of the Women's Relief Corps.

WASHINGTON, Sept. 24.—The following was issued last evening:

HEADQUARTERS GRAND ARMY OF REPUBLIC, WASHINGTON, D. C., Sept. 23, 1892.

Having been elected commander-in-chief of the Grand Army of the Republic by the unanimous suffrages of my comrades, I undertake the duties of the position fully realizing the grave responsibilities assumed.

Whatever degree of success may attend the incoming adminis tration depends largely upon the cordial co-operation of the comrades throughout the nation, which is cordially invoked.

Headquarters will be established for the present at Milwaukee, Wis. All official business should be addressed to E. B. Gray, adjutant general, G. A. R., Milwaukee, Wis. By command of A. G. WEISSERT, Commander-in-Chief.

Notwithstanding the bad weather, the

Reunion of the Sons of Veterans

in Grant tent was a great success. Surgeon General Wilson presided and made the opening address. He was followed by Secretary Noble, E. Potter Dustin, Colonel P. H. Murphy of New York, Colonel Lang of Baltimore and several other comrades. Miss Daisy Tittle of Cincinnati, known as the daughter of the regiment, department of Ohio, added greatly to the success of the meeting by her several recitations.

The Union Veterans' union made an excursion trip to Riverview, a pleasure resort about fifteen miles down the Potomac river, and held a rousing camp fire. Patriotic speeches were made, incidents of the war were recounted and a tempting collation was enjoyed, although heavy showers spoiled out door recreation.

The Woman's Relief Corps.

The convention of the Woman's Relief Corps, auxilary of the Grand Army, was opened by singing and prayer. The commander of the departments of Colorado and Wyoming and staff, were introduced and welcomed. The commander made a stirring address. General Browning, past commander of the same department, also made an address, full of sympathy and appreciation of the work of the Woman's Relief Corps.

Mrs. Lynch, past national secretary, presented a report commending the able and just manner in which the national president performed her work. The report was adopted.

Sarah E. Fuller wanted it settled whether or not any officer should wear a souveneir badge or a regulation badge in order to be entitled to a vote. Mrs. Craig moved that all members entitled to a vote should do so without regard to badge. Agreed to.

Rev. Dr. Stakeley of the First Baptist church, in whose church the Woman's Relief Corps first assembled, was introduced. He said his church was loyal to the church and the flag and would welcome the Woman's Relief Corps in every way.

Gifts of elegant pieces of silver were made to the national president, Mrs. Sue Pike Sanders, in honor of the twenty-fifth anniversary of her wedding.

At the afternoon session General Weissert, the new commander-in-chief of the Grand Army, spoke briefly.

It was decided that the national pension committee be dissolved; that its unfinished business be transferred to the national Woman's Relief Corps home board and that this board be empowered to incur such expenditures as shall make the bill passed by congress operative at the earliest possible period. Mrs. Annie Wittenmyer was appointed special agent to prosecute the claims of army nurses at Washington. It was decided that the national Woman's Relief Corps be properly represented at the World's fair.

Mrs. Margaret R. Wickens of Kansas was chosen president. The retiring president, Mrs. Sue Pike Sanders, was extended a vote of thanks for her able and just administration of her arduous duties during the past year.

Quarter of a Million Visitors.

Now that the railroad officials have had an opportunity to consider the subject some approximately accurate figures are given of the number of visitors brought here to the encampment and reunion. The total is fixed at 225,000; 125,000 by the B. and O., 115,000 by the Pennsylvania and 15,000 by the Chesapeake and Ohio. This was fully 25 per cent more than the railroads ever handled; the largest crowd Washington ever entertained and the largest it will see again for a long time.

General A. G. Weissert, the newly-elected commander-in-chief of the Grand Army of the Republic, called at the White House to pay his respects to the president, but he was busy and could not be seen. He was accompanied by General Irvin Robbins and others of the Grand Army. General Weissert left a message of regard and sympathy for the president with Private Secretary Halford.

The Closing Event

in the official program of entertainment for the Grand Army encampment took place yesterday afternoon. The steamer Louise went on a trip down the river, having on board members of the encampment as guests of the citizens' committee.

BITTER CONTEST ENDED.

Granite Workers and Manufacturers Have Reached an Agreement.

BARRE, Vt., Sept. 24.—The last act of the trouble in the granite industry occurred yesterday afternoon when representatives of the union and the association signed the bill of prices and agreement, thus ending a long, bitter contest of five months duration. The dealers held a long session yesterday to discuss the wisdom of beginning work before a settlement was made elsewhere, but finally decided to do so and the bill was signed. It is understood that the association agrees to have Barclay Bros.' injunction removed, and all sheds will resume work as union yards Monday.

Union cutters are happy over the outcome of the struggle, and look upon the settlement as a partial victory. Men will be set to work rapidly, leading dealers notifying the trade to send orders soon, so that stock can be quarried before winter. Barclay Bros. and McDonald & Son of Quincy, Mass., have purchased the Dirigo Granite company's valuable dark quarry.

Nelson Trots at Springfield.

SPRINGFIELD, Mass., Sept. 24.—The stallion Nelson started in Hampden park to beat his record of 2:10 yesterday afternoon, but failed in two trials, the fastest of which was 2:11 1-2. The management of Hampden park, who have been opposed to the outlawed horse trotting on their track, tried to lock the park gates so as to prevent an attendance at the exhibition, but the management of the Hampden Agricultural society repulsed them, and a crowd of about 2500 saw the trials.

The Case of Edward Bgor.

GREENFIELD, Mass., Sept. 24. — This morning the preliminary examination of Edward Bgor, arrested on suspicion of being the murderer of Mrs. Abigail Rogers at Wendell on Sept. 4, was opened here. Judge Malone presides, and District Attorney John A. Aiken represents the commonwealth. Judge Edward Bicknell of Orange will defend the accused. Bgor still maintains a strict silence.

A Widow's Suicide.

BRATTLEBORO, Vt., Sept. 24.—Mary J., widow of John Harris, who was a well-known and wealthy Chesterfield (N. H.) farmer, committed suicide by hanging in the barn. She had lived with her son on the home farm since the death of her husband. Ill health and consequent despondency is supposed to be the cause for the deed. She was about 60 years old.

WARNING TO BUSY PEOPLE.

A New York Physician Gives Valuable Advice.

The Danger from Hard Work and Anxiety.

Experiences in Commercial Life in Manhattanville.

"You need rest," said the physcian to the business man. "The trouble is that you are just tired out. Unless you drop all thoughts of business and give your brain a complete rest you won't last much longer. You must take a rest, with change of scene, for at least three months."

"I can't do it," said the worker. "I am unable to leave my business for even three days. A vacation is out of the question."

He went back to business, toiled on, and the result was shown by an obituary announcement not long after. It stated that the toiler had died suddenly from heart failure. This is what the doctors called it. One who knew more about the cause said: "It was nervous exhaustion."

Now, there are hundreds of business men in just this condition. What are they to do? Those who are tired out, run down and debilitated at this trying season will do well to read the following remarkable statements of some well-known people:

Mr. John Blakely, the well-known tobacconist of No. 233 Broadway, says: "For a number of years past I have been troubled with insomnia, nervousness and overwork. It is impossible for me to sleep throughout the night without getting up several times to eat something. A short time ago my attention was brought to a remedy which has proven of great value to me. It is known as Paine's celery compound. I have used several bottles of it and am now able to sleep soundly. It cured me completely, consequently I am a great advocate of its use. I have advised dozens of my friends to use it and believe that it has helped them."

Oliver F. Berry, cashier Tradesmen's National Bank, No. 291 Broadway says: "While I am very seldom ill, I occasionally have been troubled with a pain in my liver. I procured some of Paine's celery compound, and was greatly benefited by it. In fact, it cured me, for I never had any further trouble. I have spread its fame broadcast among my friends."

There are thousands of men and women who have been enabled to follow their pursuits by the timely use of this preparation. It builds up the nervous system and sustains it. Brain and muscle alike are restored to their proper condition. It is not to be confounded with the common preparations so extensively advertised. Being the scientific discovery of a man of science—Prof. Phelps of Dartmouth College—it has the support of the leading physicians, and the many cases cured by its use prove that its support is merited.—*New York World.*

A PINKERTON AT WORK.

Traitor in the Ranks of Haverhill's Shoe Council.

HAVERHILL, Mass., Sept. 24.—Another Pinkerton detective is at work in this city Not since the day that it was discovered that Edward Laughran, the trusted member of the local shoe council, was a Pinkerton detective, have the shoeworkers felt so bitter against their employers as yesterday, when for the second time they learned that they had in their employ another Pinkerton man, who since Laughran's disappearance has pursued the self-same tactics, and has kept them posted of every move made by the international union.

Unlike Laughran this man concealed his idenity and may be still in the city and the lodge room for all the members of the union know. No one is suspected, but it is known that every act of the shoe council has been reported to the manufacturers, who

Being Forewarned Were Forearmed.

Of late the officials have been busy in preparing new price lists and it was very evident to them that some one was giving the manufacturers tips. But there is not even a suspicious character in the ranks of the union.

Coming at this time when business is rushing in every shop, and when a general strike would prove a serious blow to Haverhill, it is hoped alike by the officials of the international union and the public large that no trouble will follow the discovery of the manufacturers' underhand methods.

The shoe council has passed a resolution which tends toward peace. It is addressed to the shoe manufacturers, and, after attributing the troubles in the trade in the past two years

To the Work of Detectives,

makes the following proposition:

That you bring to us the reports of your agent and compare them with the official records of our meetings, and we feel sure that we will be able to prove to your entire satisfaction that your "Pinkerton" makes false statements and that his falsehoods have given you more trouble and worry than our organization ever did or can.

To the honorable manufacturers who have not stooped to the employment of such tools we say, select your committee, one, two or three, and to that committee we 'l open the doors of any and all our meeting will open our books to show the records of every meeting held by us during the last three years.

This proposition is an unheard of one in the history of the local unions and shows that the shoe council desires to set themselves right with the men who would be their enemies.

LABOR AND CAPITAL

Form the Basis of a Speech by Ex-Secretary of State Bayard.

BROOKLYN, Sept. 24.—There was a Cleveland demonstration at the Academy of Music last night. Edward M. Shepard presided and made a speech. He then introduced ex-Secretary of State Bayard, who was received with tumultuous applause. Mr. Bayard in the course of his speech said:

I ask you now if the signs are not plainly apparent that this government, which was framed by the people, is not palpably and rapidly becoming a government of the few, by the few and for the few. It is evident that all over this broad land, in the centers of population, wealth and industry, that domestic tranquility is daily disturbed by disagreements between organized labor and combined capital, in the settlements of which the public law seems never to be appealed to. The constitution was ordained expressely to provide remedies for these very troubles.

Mr. Bayard criticized President Harrison's letter of acceptance and the McKinley doctrine of protection. "If our flag," he asked, "is not to be seen on the high seas, is it not because Republican trade policies have driven it off?" He said that one effect that must survive the dreadful collision at Homestead is that no longer can it be pretended that high tariffs procure higher wages to American workmen. Mr. Bayard paid a high tribute to Mr. Cleveland.

A Peculiar Fatality.

LEWISTON, Me., Sept. 24.—Frank Weston, aged 23, of Minot, was killed instantly by the rebound of a broken chain. His neck was broken by the blow.

The Evening Standard.

ESTABLISHED FEBRUARY, 1850.]   NEW BEDFORD, TUESDAY, SEPTEMBER 27, 1892.   TWO CENTS.

HASKELL & TRIPP.

They say it's the biggest values in umbrellas *we* ever offered. You know what that means—prices unmatched by anything of the kind ever done in New Bedford.

Excellent umbrellas, made by one of the best manufacturers in this country. Fine "Gloria" cloth with neatly trimmed handles of oxidized metal that looks like silver. *Price $1 each.*

Have you a Mackintosh?

If not, price won't hinder. We are selling one at $6.78 and crowding big value into little money. Cloth outside, pretty styles, rubber inside, rain proof.

A better Mackintosh for $10.

Boys' Clothing Department. Here's great money's worth. A suit we call the *"Wear Resister."* Made from pure long fibre wool, double and twisted. Color is a serviceable gray and the pattern a stylish check. This suit we can furnish in any size from 6 to 14 years for only $4.50; and let us say right here that we have yet to see the suit at $6 that is its equal for durability. Send postal card and we'll mail you sample of the cloth.

Medium priced dress goods never offered more attraction. Their name is legion, their excellence surprising, even here.

At 25c., all plain colors, double-width chevrons.

At 25c., rough-faced homespuns.

At 42c., Knickerbocker suitings, ten colors, 1¼ yards wide.

At 50c., *hundreds!* Plaids, stripes, plains, mixtures, cheviots in natural colors, and camels' hair suitings, 44 inches wide, that never have been sold below 75c. until now. Plain cloths, 1¼ yards wide, pure wool, and in every wanted coloring.

At 75c., 85c. and $1, rich French dress goods in a hundred good styles, all new, and the *best for your money*, go where you may.

You are not likely to see any blankets this season that will give you equal service, look as well, or be as ample in size, for $2.50 a pair, as the special lot we are now offering.

A little finer, a little heavier, $3.50 a pair.

Superior family blankets, handsome borders, $5 a pair. A grand blanket.

Yes, there are still some of those infants' cloaks at about half cost. No two alike. Manufacturers' samples. $1.50 instead of $2.50, $3 instead of $5 and so on. Sharp buyers are getting them.

HASKELL & TRIPP,
Department Stores,
Purchase and William Streets.

THE DEMOCRATS' DAY.

State Convention of the Party in Boston.

Platform Upon Which the Democracy Will Stand.

Mayor Ashley Has a Place on an Important Committee.

BOSTON, Sept. 27.—The Democratic State Convention was held in Tremont Temple to-day. In the northern balcony a space was reserved abreast of the platform for the Governor's family and immediate friends and in their space was a large number of ladies, a feature somewhat novel in a Democratic convention here.

Upon the platform were a number of distinguished Democrats, including Congressmen Williams, Crosby, O'Neill and Stevens, Mayor Matthews, Hon. James S. Grinnell of Greenfield and many Senators present and past.

Mr. Josiah Quincy, Chairman of the State Committee, called to order at 11.35 a. m. and the call was read by Secretary Buckley.

Messrs. Quincy and Buckley were constituted temporary officers of the convention. Upon assuming his office Mr. Quincy made a speech which was heartily applauded. His hopeful prognostications, enforced by an emphatic utterance, aroused his hearers to enthusiasm, and his criticism of the Republican party of Massachusetts and laudation of the administration of Gov. Russell were also received with enthusiastic applause. The customary committees were then appointed.

WILLIAM E. RUSSELL.

The committee on permanent organization includes Sumner B. Sargent of Taunton and Charles S. Ashley of New Bedford; committee on resolutions, Robert Howard of Fall River; committee on balance of State ticket, Dexter E. Wilbur of Brockton, James A. Reed of Provincetown; committee on credentials, James S. Ozorer of Middleboro, Isaac Hill of Nantucket; committee on reporting 15 members of State committee, George T. McLaughlin of Sandwich, William F. Kennedy of Fall River.

The report of the committee on credentials showed the presence of 1951 delegates representing 28 cities and 324 towns.

Amidst mingled laughter and applause Representative Carr of Wakefield moved that "our most recent convert," Hon. F. A. Hobart of Braintree, be invited to a seat on the platform.

The motion was carried unanimously and Mr. Hobart was invited to come forward and upward, but Mr. Hobart did not make his appearance.

The committee on permanent organization made a partial report, recommending Hon. Charles Theodore Russell of Cambridge as permanent chairman and Daniel F. Buckley of North Easton as permanent secretary. The recommendation was adopted, and William M. Douglass of Brockton and James S. Grinnell of Greenfield escorted Mr. Russell to the platform, where he received a grand ovation. [His speech is given in full on the third and seventh pages.]

[Continued on Sixth Page, Second Edition.]

PORTSMOUTH COAL MINES.

Operations to Be Commenced with the Latest Electrical Appliances.

FALL RIVER, Sept. 27.—Preparations are now being made to open the mines at Portsmouth, R. I. It is proposed to purchase new machinery and equip the works with the latest electrical appliances for mining.

One of the great problems of the parties interested has been to find a method by which the coal dust could be burned under steam boilers. After trying all manner of experiments, with indifferent success, they have found a new one, which has recently been patented, that will burn the coal dust to perfection. This arrangement has been under test at the Boston weekly paper, and they are using this dust for fuel, and making a great saving in the coal bill.

Taunton and Natick parties have placed orders for the grate bars, and have ordered a supply of the coal. A Worcester steel manufacturer has just added six new boilers to his plant, and they will burn the new arrangement attached.

Two Children Burned to Death.

SHELBYVILLE, ILLS., Sept. 27.—A fire at the home of Washington Stucker burned his house and two small children Sunday. The father rushed through the flames and secured the children but not before they were fatally burned.

Verdict Against a Railroad Company.

DOVER, N. H., Sept. 27.—In the Supreme Court the jury in the case of James J. Hearn vs. Boston & Maine Railroad for injuries received at Rochester, two years ago, gave him $9000.

LIZZIE'S JAIL LIFE.

Flat Contradiction of Mrs. Livermore's Statements.

Miss Borden Apparently Suffering Neither in Body Nor Mind.

Sheriff Wright Indignant at the "Mess of Untruths" Recently Published.

[Special Dispatch.]

TAUNTON, Sept. 27.—There has been a great deal written anent the Borden case which was correct and quite as much far from being anywhere near correct. The latest addition to the incorrect material furnished is that which has emanated from the pen of Mrs. Livermore, relative to the jail life of Lizzie Borden and the "terrible" treatment which she is receiving every day from the hands of Sheriff Wright. If Mrs. Livermore would take the trouble to come to Taunton and look over the Taunton jail, she would be very sorry she ever wrote such a mess of untruths, for that is what they are; she does not mean to do any person an injustice, but she has undoubtedly been carried away by the excitement of the times and seems determined because that is so to make things out just as black as possible. But the people of this city who know Mr. Wright do not propose to have her story go uncontradicted.

In the first place Lizzie Borden is not being punished like a criminal, and she is not, judging from outward appearances, suffering in body or mind. She eats well, sleeps well, and in no way does she appear to be any different than she appeared when she last crossed the threshold of the jail. Sheriff Wright was naturally quite indignant when he read Mrs. Livermore's article. It was so unjust in its nature and so misleading in its character, that he asked where this thing was to stop. But when he was asked to express himself in regard to the matter he utterly refused. If his 24 years' of official life carried no weight against the attacks of people who so harshly misjudged him then he would allow all such statements to go uncontradicted. He was there to do his duty as he understood it and which had never been questioned, and he proposed to carry his ideas of what were right and proper under the circumstances out if it cost him his position. He was asked the source of the regulations under which Taunton jail was conducted, and replied that the regulations came from the prison commissioners or were approved by them; that in some instances the keepers were allowed to use their discretion on some points, but there was never any material change, and in any event any change must meet the requirements of the commissioners.

The charge that Miss Borden "sits shivering in the chillness of her temporary cell, wrapped in shawls for comfort," won't stand the light of investigation. As a matter of fact Taunton jail is heated by steam throughout, and every portion of it is kept at an even temperature the year around. If the thermometer shows a drop and artificial heat must be resorted to, the fires are lighted and the heat turned on. If Miss Borden sits shivering in chillness, etc., it is from some other cause than that of cold, and all the shawls in the county wouldn't keep her warm. "Lizzie Borden is not allowed the privilege of exercise in the open air," said Mrs. Livermore. The strongest yoke of oxen in Bristol county would be necessary to drag Lizzie Borden into the open air just now, when she shuns everybody but those whom she knows and who can sympathize with her in her unfortunate position. Her cell is whitewashed, but it isn't strictly speaking a confinement cell, any more than are hundreds of similar cells all over the Commonwealth. She is not treated as a prisoner but merely as one detained to profit or lose by the ends of justice. Lizzie Borden can sit in the sun all day, if she so chooses, for the women's wing of the jail has the sun pouring in at the windows from the time it rises until it sets, and when it first makes its appearance it looks directly into Lizzie Borden's cell.

"For exercise she may occasionally pace up and down the dreary corridor, breathing an atmosphere foul with the exhalations of prisoners of the lowest grade, etc.," said Mrs. Livermore. If anything were needed to prove that Mrs. Livermore was absolutely ignorant of her subject this statement does the matter. It would be impossible to find a cleaner apartment or one less entitled to such a sweeping condemnation than the apartment where the female inmates are placed. The lights are out every night at 7 30. That is one of the rules of the prison, made long before Miss Borden came to the jail, and one which the sheriff can find no adequate excuse for breaking at this time. If the sheriff could place Miss Borden in the guest chamber he would gladly do it, for he feels the position as keenly almost as does Miss Borden and her friends, and would be glad to do anything in his power, not to infringe the rules of the institution, which would make her more comfortable.

Miss Borden is not treated as a prisoner and she is not required to do anything at all as the other female prisoners are called upon to do, such as taking care of their cells, etc. She will not say herself that she is hardly treated since it would not be in accordance with the teachings of the Central church to say that which was untrue. There are more or less women confined in that jail all the time; women whose sensibilities may be somewhat more blunted than are Miss Borden's, and who may not be so susceptible to refining influences as she, but Mrs. Livermore has never uttered one word in regard to their terrible condition, and yet the writer has heard both men and women, time after time, plead in the district court when sentenced to the House of Correction to be sent to Taunton jail instead. They had been there before and wanted to go back if they must be confined in any such an institution. Why? Because they had been treated as near like human beings as it is possible under the restrictions of the law to be treated under such circumstances and they didn't propose to take chances with life in a stranger country."

RICH ON SECOND BALLOT.

Republican Contest for the Barnstable County Commissioner Nomination.

BUZZARDS BAY, Sept. 27.—The Republicans of Barnstable county held their convention this morning. Clarendon A. Freeman of Chatham was chosen chairman and F. O. Ellis of Sandwich secretary. Fifteen towns were represented by 80 delegates. The following nominations were made:

Sheriff—Joseph Whitcomb of Provincetown.

Special Commissioners—Freeman Howes of Yarmouth, Watson F. Baker of Dennis.

Commissioners of Insolvency—Eben B. Crocker of Barnstable, Frederick C. Swift of Yarmouth, George W. Jones of Falmouth.

There was considerable of a fight on the nomination for County Commissioner, there being four candidates. Richard A. Rich of Provincetown received the nomination on the second ballot.

COTTAGE CITY TOWN MEETING.

The Sea View House Matter Indefinitely Postponed.

[Special Dispatch.]

COTTAGE CITY, Sept. 27.—A special town meeting was held at town hall at 1 o'clock yesterday afternoon, of which Capt. Otis Foss was chosen moderator and E. R. Landers clerk. All the questions were brought up, but were laid on the table. In the Sea View House matter, Capt. F. U. Hart, proprietor, said that owing to the present condition of the hotel he could not give any intelligent information, and would prefer to have the matter indefinitely postponed.

SHOT HIMSELF IN THE HEAD.

Suicide of Col. W. P. Canady, Ex-Sergeant at Arms of the U. S. Senate.

WASHINGTON, Sept. 27.—Col. W. P. Canady, ex-sergeant, at arms of the United States Senate, committed suicide at his room to-day, by shooting through the head.

Mrs. Harrison's Condition.

WASHINGTON, Sept. 27.—Mrs. Harrison had a fairly good night and is reported resting quietly this morning.

HOME MATTERS.

STEAMER DISABLED.—The Marthas Vineyard has been disabled by a broken part of her starboard axle. The Island Home will take her place on the line.

RELEASED.—Augustus Meddy, committed to the House of Correction from this city July 9th for disturbing the peace, was released by the County Commissioners to-day on the recommendation of Probation Officer Coe.

NATURALIZATION.—Frank M. Bertram and Leon Benedict were admitted to citizenship in the Third District Court this morning. H. H. Crapo, Esq., appeared for Bertram and G. T. St. Germain for Benedict.

Primary departures looking toward naturalization were filed in the Third District Court this morning by Vitalice Benoit and Cyrille Beaudry, George C. St. Germain for petitioners.

COUNTY COMMISSIONERS MEET.

Capt. Sanders Explains His Position in Regard to Several Matters.

[Special Dispatch.]

TAUNTON, Sept. 27.—The County Commissioners met this morning to consider the matter of bridging Cole's river. This matter has been in abeyance for some time, but the plans submitted now are considered to be about right, and bids will soon be called for.

The feature of the meeting was the abook look upon the face of Commissioner Sanders as he read the stricture upon his conduct in this morning's *Mercury*. In regard to the matter of the draw at the Coggeshall street bridge Mr. Sanders said that he knew nothing whatever about it, that he had taken no part in the matter and only said what was told him by the man who fixed the draw.

Commissioner Gray said that it took two men to handle the draw on the bridge at Fall River.

Commissioner Babbitt said that he noticed the other day at a draw bridge in Boston three men were working, and that so far as they knew how the draw was all right and in good working order; that it was not supposed to work automatically.

Asked about the extension on the Registry of Deeds office, Commissioner Sanders said that that was a matter called for imperatively by the pressure of deeds, and that the law said he must be furnished with adequate quarters, and that before that extension was put on there was not room enough.

In regard to the new court-house matter, he said that was something lying entirely in the hands of the people of New Bedford. They have never asked for anything of the sort, and if they did ask for it and he was in office he should do his utmost to comply with their desires; the statement that Commissioner Babbitt has obtained a court-house for Taunton was simply rot; that the whole bar and the whole county in the end acted in unison, and he had no doubt that when the people of New Bedford made known their desires the whole county would act once more in unison.

The statement that Mr. Terry had built the jail in New Bedford, he said, was about on a par with the other statements. Mr. Terry single-handed could have done nothing. The building was called for by a county commissioner simply voiced the sentiments of the people and with the aid of the others the object was accomplished. Mr. Sanders said that he was of the opinion that the report was just a little biased and not strictly in accordance with the facts. He knew that the statement attributed to him as having been made to Mayor Ashley had been either curtailed or Mr. Ashley had reported him wrong. He not only said about what the mayor was reported to have said, but he said something more which would have explained the matter fully.

IN A COTTON MILL.

The Roofs of Manufacturing Co's Buildings Injured by Fire.

[Special Dispatch.]

FALL RIVER, Sept. 27.—Shortly before 12 o'clock to-day an alarm was rung in from the old Quequechan mill, which is now the property of the Fall River Manufacturing Company on Pocasset street. The cotton store-house fronting on the north end of the roof, and the flames communicated to the roofs of adjoining buildings. The old cotton store-house fronting on Central street sustained the greatest damage, and within 15 minutes after the alarm sounded the roof of this building was all in flames. The district fire apparatus worked well and with the assistance of the firemen of the Pocasset district from the department of the Pocasset mill got the flames under control after a stubborn fight. The high wind prevailing at one time led the firemen to fear a great conflagration. The fire was probably caused by sparks from the chimneys of adjoining mills and the loss will be about $1500, which is covered by insurance. The Quequechan mill is idle, undergoing repairs and refitting, and modern machinery is being put in.

JAMES B. CARROLL.

The Evening Standard.

ESTABLISHED FEBRUARY, 1850. NEW BEDFORD, FRIDAY, SEPTEMBER 30, 1892. TWO CENTS.

HASKELL & TRIPP.

Outside Garments

For ladies, misses and children. They've been rolling in for the last month till the cloak room will hardly hold tnem. Too many? Not if we can interest you to look at them, because they were never before so attractive in style, never before so reasonable in price, never before so excellently made, and never before such a desirable and almost bewildering assortment of beautiful cloths. From the little child of one year to the woman of 48-inch bust; all can be fitted and suited. It's a remarkable collection.

You can here see:

Dainty Bedford cord short coats, with white angora trimming.

Tasty cashmere short coats, with lace trimming.

Warm eider-down cape coats, with fur trimming.

Serviceable plaid woollen short coats with silk trimming.

(For little children from 1 to 4 years of age.)

Pretty Gretchens, with military capes.

Pretty Gretchens, with divided capes.

Russian blouse effects, with the new bishop sleeves.

Serviceable Gretchens, with fur-trimmed capes.

Watteau plaited back coats, with fur-trimmed hoods.

(For children from 4 to 12 years of age.)

The new box-plaited jackets, with belts.

The stylish Russian blouses.

The handsome box coats from plain cloths.

The nobby watteau plaited backs.

The serviceable plain reefers, with pearl buttons.

The 34-inch reefers, with the shirred back and flaring cuffs.

(For misses from 12 to 18 years of age.)

Black jackets in almost unlimited assortment of cloths.

Handsome embroidered capes.

Rich Sicilian cloth dolmans.

Satin-lined circulars.

Fur-trimmed reefers.

Fur capes in the new military shapes.

(For ladies from 32 to 48 inch bust.)

As usual, special shapes for stout, short-waisted ladies who never can get fitted anywhere else.

We'll be much pleased to show you this interesting collection. Come and look.

Special shoe item:

A woman's heavy dongola button boot, cut slipper foxed, welt edge sole and patent tip, comes on a medium opera last, with common-sense heel. Price $1.89. You've paid $2.50 for many a shoe not as good.

Special flannel item:

Remnants of heavy white domet flannel in lengths from 2 to 8 yards. 10c. per yard.

Special dress goods item:

Beautiful wool plaids, rich dark colors, relieved by narrow cross line plaid of gold and red. 40-inch. 50c.

HASKELL & TRIPP,

Department Stores,

Purchase and William Streets.

STITCHERS ON STRIKE.

Bleachery Girls at Assonet Quit Work Yesterday.

[Special Dispatch.]

FALL RIVER, Sept. 30.—It is reported that a number of the girls employed in the Crystal Spring Bleachery at Assonet left their work yesterday afternoon because of the refusal of the authorities to grant them an increase of $1 per week. The girls left the mill in a body at noon.

CLEVELAND AN ABSTAINER.

An Amusing Incident on Steamer Pilgrim Last Evening.

[Special Dispatch.]

FALL RIVER, Sept. 30.—The dining saloon of steamer Pilgrim, on her way to New York, was the scene of an interesting episode last evening. Among the passengers on board was ex-President Grover Cleveland, and at a table near the distinguished passenger was a Mrs. Goddard and her four daughters from Kentucky. The lady recognized the ex-President, and after opening a bottle of wine she filled a glass and dispatched the waiter with it to Mr. Cleveland. It was given him with the compliments of a Southern lady and the best wishes for his success this Fall. Mr. Cleveland received the glass with a smile, and gratefully bowing his acknowledgment, touched the glass to his lips and begged to be excused from drinking, as he had decided to be a total abstainer during the present campaign. Quite a smile went around among the passengers at this new role of the ex-President.

MR. CLEVELAND IN NEW YORK.

A Crowd of Two Hundred on the Pier to Receive the Ex-President.

NEW YORK, Sept. 30.—Ex-President Cleveland arrived in the city this morning from Buzzards Bay on the Fall River Line steamer Pilgrim. About 200 people were on the pier to receive him. He was accompanied by Richard Watson Gilder, editor of the *Century*, and Daniel J. Griffin of Watertown. Sergeant-at-Arms "Jimmy" Oliver was at hand to receive Mr. Cleveland and gave them a hearty greeting. The ex-President was hurried to a carriage by Mr. Oliver, in which were Messrs. Gilder and Griffin. He was driven to the Victoria Hotel, where he will put up while here. The duration of his stay here is not yet known. He will probably consult with the campaign managers during the day.

THE CHOLERA.

New York Health Board Bulletin—The Disease Abroad.

NEW YORK, Sept. 30.—The health board issued its usual daily bulletin this morning stating that no cases of cholera had appeared in this city since the 19th inst.

The Situation in Hamburg.

HAMBURG, Sept. 30.—The official cholera statistics for yesterday place the number of new cases at 33 and the deaths at 24. Compared with Wednesday's returns this is a decrease of 11 cases and an increase of 8 deaths. In Altona yesterday 9 new cases and 9 deaths were reported.

At Havre.

HAVRE, Sept. 30.—Three new cases of cholera and six deaths were reported yesterday. This is a decrease of one case and an increase of four deaths compared with returns for Wednesday.

Cholera Breaks Out in Servia.

BUDA-PESTH, Sept. 30.—It is reported here that cholera has broken out in a Servian village on the Danube. It is said the disease was imported by Russian vessels calling at the village.

Cholera Appears at Odessa.

ODESSA, Sept. 30.—It is announced that cholera is present in this city. From Friday, Sept. 23, to Wednesday, Sept. 28 there have been ten cases of the disease, four of which proved fatal.

SOMERBY, OF THE IRON HALL.

He Will Make it Interesting for Some Other Officers of the Order.

CHICAGO, Sept. 30.—A special from Indianapolis says: A friend of the late Supreme Justice Somerby of the Iron Hall says in a few days Mr. Somerby will be in Indianapolis and will make it interesting for some of the other officers of the order. "Somerby can send at least three men to the penitentiary," said this man, "and he is in a mood to do it now. He will come here and will tell the grand jury all he knows."

Proposed Duty on American Wheat.

NEW YORK, Sept. 30.—Colonel W. R. Nelson, editor and proprietor of the Kansas City Star, made the statement at Democratic headquarters that when parliament is again convened in England a bill will be introduced for putting a duty on American wheat. He says pamphlets have been circulated in England advising the measure.

Peck's Case Again Postponed.

ALBANY, Sept. 30.—The examination into the matter of the alleged burning of public records by Labor Commissioner Peck and his stenographer was to have proceeded yesterday. At the hour set for the case to go on, the court was informed that counsel for the defendants was out of town, and the case was adjourned till Oct. 7.

Columbus Day at Pittsfield.

PITTSFIELD, Mass., Sept. 30.—The Columbus day celebration here will consist of school children's exercises and a parade with the Grand Army in the morning, a general parade, including a trades parade, in the afternoon, and public exercises, with an address by prominent speakers in the evening.

Missing Woman's Body Found.

HARTFORD, Sept. 30.—While Thomas Scott was out hunting in a swamp near Farmington he came across the badly decomposed body of an old woman. The body has been identified as that of the widow of Robert Ray of Parkville, who disappeared early in August without leaving any trace. She was slightly demented.

Wants to Become a Citizen.

CHICAGO, Sept. 30.—Charlie Kee, a Chinese manufacturer of cigars, who employs none but white union cigarmakers, defies the recent edict of the Chinese Six Companies and has made application for a certificate of residence under the provision of the amended exclusion law.

Murderer Mancera Indicted.

LACONIA, N. H., Sept. 30.—The grand jury of the Belknap county supreme court returned an indictment against Giuseppe Mancera, alias Joseph St. Maria, who killed B. L. Perkins at Alton last Sunday. Manslaughter is the crime alleged in the indictment.

Disestablishment in Wales.

LONDON, Sept. 30.—Welsh newspapers declare that Mr. Gladstone has invited an eminent Welsh ecclesiastic to draft a bill disestablishing the church in Wales. They add that the bill will be prepared in a manner that will be acceptable to the Welsh clergy.

Took 372 Ballots to Settle It.

LOUISVILLE, Sept. 30.—Albert S. Berry of Newport was nominated on the 372d ballot at Warsaw as congressman from the Sixth district.

TREATMENT OF THE CHOLERA.

Prof. Rumpf of Hamburg and Prof. Klebs of Zurich Relate their Experience.

LONDON, Sept. 30.—A Berlin correspondent says: "Prof. Rumpf of the Ephendorfer hospital in Hamburg, has reported his experience in the treatment of 3000 cholera patients in his institution. He declares that all of the various vaunted remedies are useless. Among these he includes salol, cresol, creosote, lactic acid, and hydrochloric acid. The injection of sulphuric acid and morphia, as suggested by American doctors, he has found of no avail, but in mild cases the injection of tannin was successful.

Prof. Rumpf concludes that all methods aiming at the disinfection of the intestines failed and that remedies must be sought which remove the cholera bacilli from the intestines. He mentions hot coffee and tea, wine, champagne and camphor as useful in critical cases.

He adds that the injection of a solution of common salt cured 25 per cent. of cases so treated.

Prof. Klebs of Zurich, who has been treating patients in Hamburg with injections of a fluid obtained through the culture of the cholera bacillus, states that after the injection of the fluid the temperature becomes normal and that several apparently hopeless cases have recovered under this treatment.

THE DRINK QUESTION.

Lively Discussion of a Paper at the Pan-Presbyterian Council.

TORONTO, Ont., Sept. 30.—At the pan-Presbyterian council last evening a paper read by Dr. Hill of Montreal on "The Drink Question" caused an interesting discussion, in the course of which Rev. D. J. McDonnell of Toronto said he could not agree with some parties that a man could not use liquor at all and remain a Christian. Dr. McDonnell in his paper on the opium traffic had remarked that people who condoned or did not absolutely condemn the drink traffic could not consistently condemn the opium traffic. Later one or two speakers suggested that Dr. McDonnell was really apologizing for the conduct of the British government in carrying on the opium traffic. Dr. Mc Donnell admitted the evil, but said evil was mitigated by the traffic being in the hands of the government. The people of India were bound to have opium, and if not by way of the government a vast illicit trade would grow up.

The rest of the papers read dealt with the subject of Romanism in the different countries represented in the Congrees.

THE WAR IN VENEZUELA.

Gen. Colina, with His Forces, Joins Crespo's Army.

NEW YORK, Sept. 30.—Advices received in this city from Venezuela state that Gen. Leon Colina, with a heavy column of mounted spearmen and riflemen, has joined Crespo's army. Crespo and his troops had reached Maracai when Colina and his horsemen from Coro rode into Valencia. Maracai is a point almost midway between Valencia and Caracas. It is situated on the northeastern edge of Lake Valencia, just over the boundary line between the State of Carabobo and Miranda.

Gen. Crespo arrived at Maracai with his army on Sept. 22d, after a most fatiguing march over a rough country. Shortly after arriving there he learned of Gen. Colina's arrival at Valencia. He hastened with a mounted guard to Valencia, where he met Colina's men, who were ordered to join the main army at Maracai. After passing two days there Gens. Crespo and Colina started to join the troops at Maracai.

THE SMITH-SIDDONS FIGHT.

Battle Stopped at the Fifty-fifth Round and Referee's Decision Reserved.

SAN FRANCISCO, Sept. 30.—At the end of the 55th round in the Smith-Siddons fight last night, not a blow having been struck since the 50th, the referee announced that they could not finish the contest that night, and that he would reserve his decision until the meeting of the directors. Neither of the men had any advantage at the end of the fight.

TELEGRAPHIC BREVITIES.

A small labor riot occurred at Buffalo.

Argentina's new president, Senor Pena, is popular.

Two persons were killed in a wreck at Adrian, N. Y.

The town of Runnells, Ia., was destroyed by fire.

Increasing business is reported at the Boston postoffice.

The Kings county (N. Y.) reapportionment has been decided to be legal.

Cattle are being driven out of the Cherokee strip by means of prairie fires.

Further action against the coal combine has been taken by New Jersey.

Colorado coal may compete with that of the Reading combine at Chicago.

A Tennessee man is said to have fallen heir to Buckingham palace, England.

Home Secretary Asquith has decided to allow meetings in Trafalgar square, London.

Several blocks of buildings at Virden, Man., were destroyed by fire; loss over $50,000.

The steamer Coquitlam, seized by the United States authorities, has been released.

A British cruiser has been ordered to Russian waters to relieve seized British sealers.

Secretary of State Foster promises to attend the Woburn, Mass., anniversary celebration.

The corporate existence of the Natick (Mass.) National bank has been extended to Nov. 2, 1892.

Ex-Alderman Hiram C. Pearson of Haverhill, Mass., is dead. He was prominent in Odd Fellows circles.

The forty-third annual convention of the Vermont State Teachers' association opened a three days' session in Montpelier.

Michael Healy, 71 years old, was struck at Windsor Locks, Mass., by the White Mountain express train and fatally injured.

President Harrison may attend the Columbian celebration in New York and the dedication of the fair buildings in Chicago.

Kendall Flint, M. D., aged 85, a leading physician of Haverhill, Mass., is dead. He was born in Danvers, and graduated from Amherst college.

A teachers' convention will be held at Dillingham, Mass., Oct. 12, which Millis, Medway, Franklin, Mendon and Milford teachers will attend.

Rev. G. F. Kenngott, formerly of Newport, N. H., was installed pastor of the First Congregational church, the largest, numerically, in Lowell, Mass.

Milford (Mass.) Italians will have a Columbian celebration and ball Oct. 10, with a parade. An elaborate dinner and literary program are also being planned.

John Coffey, a brakeman on the New York and New England road, was thrown from the top of a car at East Hartford and run over by the freight train. He died at the hospital.

At Lancaster, N. H., ex-Congressman Jacob Benton was thrown by his runaway team, receiving injuries from which he died two hours later. His widow is a daughter of Neal Dow of Maine.

IMPORTANT DECISION.

Bankers are Interested in the Finding of Judge Smith.

CINCINNATI, Sept. 30.—Judge Smith in the superior court has rendered a decision of great interest to bankers. The action was on behalf of the Western National Bank of New York against the estate of E. L. Harper, the convict banker. Harper entered A. P. Gahr's note for $200,000 and pledging part of the new issue of Fidelity stock as collateral secured money representing the face value. The action of the bank was based on the prospectus of the Fidelity, which President Briggs Swift signed when the crash came.

The new bank sued Mr. Swift and a compromise for $50,000 was effected, with a loss of $150,000. The bank sued to recover the original amount from the Harper estate. The defence set up the compromise entered into by Mr. Swift. The court held that the bank is entitled to pay its claims for the full amount—$200,000, against Harper, and it is entitled to receive dividends on the face value. A compromise by another party could not affect the liabilities of the Harper estate for losses and damages.

CHARGES OF CORRUPTION.

Investigation by the Royal Commission Into Postmaster Cason's Case.

QUEBEC, Sept. 30.—The royal commission investigating the charges of corruption against Sir A. P. Cason, postmaster general, in connection with the subsidies to the Quebec & Lake St. John railway was continued yesterday. The principal witness was H. J. Beemer, the contractor of the building of the road. He denied ever saying to Sir A. P. Cason that if subsidies were granted the company would make sure of his election. He was entirely neutral on the political question, not being a British subject, and he left the men working under him to vote as they pleased.

The prosecuting counsel asked: "Have you in your possession books, papers or documents where an account was kept of moneys or subscriptions made to Sir A. P. Cason to help him in his election or that of his superiors in the House of Commons between 1889 and 1891?"

This was objected to by defence, and a long argument ensued.

POLICE CALLED IN.

Investigation of Boodle Charges Ends in a Riotous Manner.

OMAHA, Neb., Sept. 30.—The session last night of the special city council committee investigating the charges of boodle in connection with the construction of the city hall ended in a riotous fashion. Mayor Bemis on the witness stand refused to say who it was that told him the architect of the city hall had paid $2000 to defeat Lininger, Republican candidate for mayor two years ago, and also refused to give the names of parties who had said the committee was a whitewash affair.

The committee insisted that the mayor should give names and was told that he was plain Bemis on the witness stand and not mayor. City Attorney Connell coming to the mayor's aid was called a liar by a councilman. They were prevented from fighting by the chairman. Great disorder prevailed and bitter accusations were made. The chairman finally called the police who ordered those present to disperse but no arrests were made.

SOMETHING SUSPICIOUS.

Editorial Comment on the Manifesto of the National Federation.

LONDON, Sept. 30.—The *Standard* commenting editorially this morning on the manifesto of the national federation says: "The object of the manifesto being to persuade the Irish abroad that everything is going on swimmingly. The kindest things can be said about the government. But there is something suspicious about the earnestness with which it pleads that home rule is coming despite the opposition of the House of Lords. The whole moral of the manifesto is an old one. We have no money. Irishmen at home want home rule desperately, but do not want to pay for it. Contribute liberally, you Irish-Americans. This is positively the last application."

DON CARLOS INTERVIEWED.

No Doubt of the Overthrow of Queen Christina, He Says.

LONDON, Sept. 30.—A Vienna correspondent recounts an interview with Don Carlos, the Spanish pretender, in which the latter said: "No doubt of the overthrow of Queen Christina. Spain will become Republican, but she will finally return to Carlist allegiance. I am on good terms with ex-Queen Isabella, whom I recently visited, but I cannot give up my rights. Our principles admit of no reconciliation. I have ordered my adherents to abandon the passive attitude they have hitherto maintained towards Queen Christina."

STRIKING OPERATORS ARRESTED.

Charged with Tampering with the Wires, but Cases Were Dismissed.

CEDAR RAPIDS, Ia., Sept. 30.—The first sensational development in the operators' strike occurred yesterday when the company caused the arrest of three operators on a charge of tampering with the wires. The men appeared in court, but the proscution failed to appear and the cases were dismissed. There is no change in the strike situation.

FIRE IN A FREIGHT YARD.

Forty Carloads on the Nickel Plate Tracks in Chicago Burned.

CHICAGO, Sept. 30.—A disastrous fire broke out in the Nickel Plate freight yards at Eightieth street and Stony Island avenue, this morning. Forty carloads of merchandise were consumed and the loss is estimated at over $100,000.

A Gladstonian Victory.

LONDON, Sept. 30.—In the election yesterday to fill the vacancy in the House of Commons for South Bedforshire, caused by the elevation to the peerage of Mr. Cyril Flower, the Liberal Unionists were again defeated, Mr. Samuel Howard Whitbread (Gladstonian) receiving 4828 votes, against 4396 cast for Col. Duke, (Liberal Unionist.) The former Gladstonian majority was, however, reduced by 587 votes.

Harvey Plattenburg a Murderer.

LEXINGTON, Mo., Sept. 30.—Harvey Plattenburg, brother-in-law of the late Maj. John. N. Edwards, the well-known newspaper writer and author, shot James McDowell through the heart, killing him instantly. Police Officer David M. Gray attempted to arrest Plattenburg and was shot in the left breast and fatally wounded. The murderer was afterward locked up in jail.

Ranchmen Murdered by Cowboys.

SAN ANTONIA, Tex., Sept. 30.—James Coon and Charles Mosely, prominent ranchmen living near St. Hedierg, were murdered yesterday by two Mexican cowboys named Flores. The murderers rifled their victims' pockets and fled, but were captured and jailed.

Blown to Atoms.

DUBOIS, Pa., Sept. 30.—A pusher engine on the Buffalo, Rochester & Pittsburgh railroad was blown to atoms at midnight by the explosion of the boiler. The engine was standing on a side track near Grove Summit. Engineer Wise and Fireman Flynn were literally blown to pieces. Both resided in Dubois and leave families.

Ocean Steamers.

Arrived—At New York, Buffalo, London; Gothia, Stettin; Prince Wilhelm Amsterdam; Antonia, Rambrana, Gibara.

WEATHER INDICATIONS.

FAIR AND WARMER.

WASHINGTON, Sept. 30.—For the 24 hours from 8 a. m. to-day: For New England, fair, warmer, except in eastern Maine and on the Rhode Island and lower Massachusetts coast; south to west winds.

GRADUALLY WARMER.

BOSTON, Sept. 30.—Local forecast for New England until Saturday: Continued fair weather, gradually warmer, southerly winds.

HOME MATTERS.

PERSONAL.—Hon. William C. Lovering of Taunton is ill at his Boston residence with a severe attack of typhoid fever.

Mr. and Mrs. M. N. Gifford, Miss Fannie C. Gifford, Mr. and Mrs. James Gifford and Mr. and Mrs. J. H. Hopkins, of Provincetown, were guests at the wedding of Dr. Clement Caldwell Haskell of Boston to Miss Charlotte, daughter of Hon. and Mrs. Stephen S. Osgood at Georgetown yesterday.

Mrs. Clarence D'O. Russell, who lately went to Detroit, Mich., to live, is lying seriously ill with typhoid fever in that city.

Miss Inez Crabtree, vocalist, of Boston, is visiting her sister, Miss Crabtree, of the High school.

Harry Williams Waterman left the city to-day to attend Boston University School of Law.

Charles W. Milliken, son of L. E. Milliken, has entered upon a medical course at New York University.

A PLAIN STATEMENT OF FACT.—Granted that you want the finest butter for your table. The price to-day is 32 cents per lb. In a month or so you have to pay 36, and by the first of January 38. That means the *best Creamery Butter*. We can sell you this week the best selected, Fancy Vermont Dairy Butter, in 20, 30 or 50 lb. tubs, for 29 cts. per lb. We warrant every pound to keep till May, 1893, and at any time you are not satisfied between now and that time we will take what you have left, and pay you what you paid per lb. Our old customers know what this butter is, and we want the new ones to. Have you tried our cream yet? All we ask is a trial You will never buy any other. Alley, Union and Sixth streets.

FRESH PORK and sausage 12 cents lb.
Round steak 12 cents lb.
Rump steak 16 cents lb.
Legs of lamb 16 cents lb.
Legs of mutton 13 cents lb.
Rib roasts 10 and 12 cents lb.
Best corned beef 5, 6, 7 and 8 cents lb.
Fine mixed tea 38 cents lb.
Best and purest Java coffee 28 cents lb.
White beans 8 cents quart.
Yellow-eye beans 8 cents quart.
Whole hams 12 cents lb.
Good butter 28 cents lb.
Five gallons best oil 42 cents.
White Cash Store, 134 Purchase street.

SPECIAL SALE OF WINTER UNDERWEAR.—We have just bought $5000 worth of Winter underwear, and we propose to give our customers a great benefit. Double-breasted front and back, in white and gray shirts and drawers, all sizes, at 47 cents each; all wool camel's hair, 75c. each; Swits Conde, all wool, 97c. each; Portsmouth blue ribbed, all wool, 77c. each; fine white Australian wool, $2 each; Dr. Wright's health underwear, $2.50 each. You can't afford to buy any underwear until you have seen ours. Ashley & Peirce, 72 and 74 William street.

H. C. HATHAWAY'S AUCTION BULLETIN FOR TO-MORROW: At 9 o'clock a. m. at salesroom furniture, carpets, &c., &c.

At 10 o'clock a. m. at mart a fine lot of horses adapted for all purposes; also one small horse, harness and village cart, one black pony harness and back to back, carriages, harnesses, &c., &c.

At 3 o'clock p. m. two houses and lots on Nelson street.

KEEP YOUR SHOES IN CONDITION.—The wear of a shoe depends a great deal on the way it is cared for and polished. Knowing this, we have made arrangements to clean and polish your shoes free of charge, only asking that you come to our store and have it done. We make a specialty of russet shoes as well as black. Should be pleased to see you every day. Hours, 8 30 a. m. to 12 m., 2 to 6 30 p. m. Union Shoe Store.

FIRE ALARM BOXES.—New fire alarm boxes have been ordered and will be located as follows: Private boxes—On the Rotch spinning mill, No. 83; on Old Colony Steamboat wharf, No. 86; on Old Colony freight-house, No. 94; on Bristol mill, No. 95. The new street box, to be located at the corner of Linden and Purchase streets, will be numbered 127. In all there will be 69 boxes in the service.

HATS.—We are doing a big business in our hat department. Our $2 Freeman's reliable hat is better value than most of the $2.50 hats sold by other dealers. Soft hats are being worn this season, and we have what you want if you will only visit our store. Ashley & Peirce.

SPECIAL SATURDAY SALE.—All the *short lengths of every kind of carpet* are brought out to *sell to-day cheap.* Velvets, Brussels, Tapestries and all-wools; bring the measure and buy them *cheap*; all lengths that are short of an average room. B. H. Waite & Co., 71 William street.

STANDISH BOURNE sells at auction to-morrow at 10½ o'clock at salesroom, horses, carriages and misscellaneous articles.

At 2 o'clock, three houses and lot corner of Wall street and Acushnet avenue.

At 3 o'clock the Hurll house on Cottage street. See advertisement.

REMEMBER MR. SPARE allows us to remain till Saturday, Oct. 8. Buyers of clothing, now is your last chance to buy your clothing and furnishings at wholesale prices—every dollar's worth of clothing must be sold. Wamsutta Clothing Co.

COTTAGE CITY LIQUOR CASE.—Mrs. Hills was yesterday found guilty and fined $72 in the court at Edgartown, for the illegal sale of liquor at Cottage City last Summer.

HIBERNIANS.—The attendance of members of Division 7, A. O. H., is called to special notice requesting them to meet at Neptune Hall to-morrow evening.

CHILDREN'S SUITS and overcoats will be sold for the remaining few days for less than cost of manufacture. Wamsutta Clothing Co.

THE ANNUAL MEETING of the Union for Good Works will be held to-morrow afternoon at 4 o'clock.

TO-MORROW will be a big day at Whiting & Co's cloak room, ladies purchasing capes and jackets of all kinds.

MEN'S AND YOUTH'S overcoats that we have left will go for the remaining few days regardless of cost. Wamsutta Clothing Co.

IN WINTER QUARTERS.—Frederick Grinnell's schooner yacht Quickstep went into Winter quarters at Fairhaven yesterday.

GO TO WHITING & CO'S to-morrow for your hosiery, gloves and underwear of all kinds.

MASONIC.—Eureka Lodge, F. & A. M. will hold a special communication this evening.

BARGAINS in every department—Wamsutta Clothing Co.

HOOD'S Sarsaparilla is purely vegetable.

1892.

Fall Season

RENOVATION

Is the order of the day with the thrifty

HOUSEKEEPER.

Never before were we so well equipped to meet the demands of the most exacting and fastidious furnisher.

CARPETINGS

are the leading feature in our varied and extensive stock and the

NEW FALL STYLES

comprise many of the latest and choicest productions of the best designers in the country, which are confined to us for this city.

EVERY GRADE

—OF—

CARPETINGS

is represented in our stock, and can nowhere be purchased to better advantage than of us.

C. F. WING,

34 to 40 Purchase st.

WHITING & CO.

SPECIAL SATURDAY SALES

In all Departments.

No. 1—22 pieces of Silk Crepe, for Dresses and Scarfs, in Cream, White, Red, Blue, Yellow, Lavender, Pink, Light Green, Gray, Black and Old Rose. Regular $1.00 goods, to be sold at 62c. per yard.

No. 2—50 new Bernhardt Capes for Fall wear, at $9.00 and $12.00, in all sizes, 34 to 44 bust measure.

No. 3—1500 yards all wool French Bedford Cords, best $1.00 goods, for 50c. per yard.

No. 4—We have marked down some of our 50c. Dress Goods to 39c. Be on hand as they will go quick.

No. 5—1 case of White Blankets, 11-4, to be sold at $1.25 per pair.

No. 6—1 case fine White Domet Flannel, 5c. per yard, best ever sold at the price.

No. 7—1 case fine Towels to be sold at $1.50 a dozen, or 12 1-2c. apiece.

No. 8—1 case of fine Marseilles white Spreads, at $1.75 apiece.

No. 9—20 dozen more of those Ladies' Elegant Night Robes, at 50c. each.

No. 10—50 dozen of Ladies' Elegant Winter Jersey Vests and Pants to be sold at 50c. each. We had them made for us, so as to give you the best Vest sold at that price.

No. 11—200 dozen Fast Black Hose for Ladies and Children. The best ever sold in America for 25c. per pair.

No. 12—20 dozen Ladies' fine Embroidered White Handkerchiefs, to be sold at 17c. each, cheap at 25c.

No. 13—100 dozen Hemstitched Colored Border Handkerchiefs, all new styles, at 5c. each.

No. 14—100 pieces Fancy Gimps, for Dress Trimmings at 10, 12 1-2, 20, 25 and 37c. per yard, they are in Black and colors.

No. 15—20 dozen Gents' Colored Cotton Socks, 25c. ones for 12 1-2c per pair.

No. 16—50 dozen Gents' Silk Ties, in Teck and Four-in-Hand, at 25c. each, same as sold at 50c. in some stores.

WHITING & CO.

That Old Suit of Yours Looks Rather Seedy, Doesn't it?

Isn't it about time you were thinking of buying a new one? There's no excuse for wearing shabby clothes when you can get one of our nobby

Double Breasted Sack Suits

for $15. You'll be surprised at their handsome appearance and wonder how we can sell such excellent suits for so little money.

Our $16, $18 and $20 Suits are worthy of your attention from the fact that they represent the choicest products of the leading manufacturers of the country who have a reputation for making fine clothing only.

Better bring the boy along with you. We have some marvellous bargains in our

Boys' Department

that you can't afford to pass.

Boys' Short Pant Suits, 4 to 15 years, $2.50 to $10.

Lads' Long Pant Suits, 14 to 18 years, $5 to $16.

J. & W. R. WING & CO.

Clothiers for MEN and BOYS.

THE CRESCENT!

22 Purchase St.

JUST OPENED!

New Hats,
New Caps,
New Bonnets.

FALL STYLES.

A Turkish Fez in Tan, Brown and Navy Blue for only 50c. A nice little hat for the Autumn months.

The Latest Novelty for little boys—a Square Topped Hat of Eiderdown, 69c.

Good Cashmere Bonnets, all colors, 50c. We have many pleasing styles. Call and ex amine.

Infants' long and short Dresses, 25c. upward.

Infants' long and short Cloaks, $1.50 upward.

A new lot of infants' Sacks. A good variety at 25c. Better quality 50c., 75c. and $1 and upward to the dainty hand-embroidered ones at $2.50.

Infants' Socks, 15c., 25c., 37c. Silk Socks, Pink, Cream and Blue, $1.

We will close our gents' Tan Hose at 21c., *regular 25c. quality.*

Sateen Shirt Waists in dark colors, marked down to the lowest point to close.

More of those Gingham Aprons at 25c. Two widths, best quality, well made.

THE CRESCENT!

22 Purchase St.

Pages 1-8.

The Evening Standard.

Pages 1-8.

ESTABLISHED FEBRUARY, 1850.] NEW BEDFORD, WEDNESDAY, OCTOBER 5, 1892.---TEN PAGES. TWO CENTS.

HASKELL & TRIPP.

No dulness permitted.

Every part of the store is full of activity.

The regular stocks come rolling in. More by thousands of dollars in value than ever before.

Every day is "Opening Day" in this establishment.

You need to remember two things:

First—Our stock is double that of any similar store in this vicinity.

Second—*We are never undersold.*

Why enlarge upon things that everybody knows? Maybe there's no need to. But you *do* need to be told of the special things that come to the front daily among the great stocks, which literally crowd every available spot here.

Each department has a story to tell. This column is the express messenger to carry it to you. Only a little at a time.

To-day we're opening several hundred boxes of fancy feathers for millinery. Very latest from Paris, and from a third to a half of what you must pay at some milliner's.

To-day we display for the first time some rich white bone stick marabout feather fans, fresh importation, at 89c. each. Colors are: cream, pink, blue, gold, red. They are very cheap.

New gauze fans, exquisitely decorated, $1 to $2 apiece.

To-day we place on sale 50 new styles of beaded and plain passementeries, just out of the custom house. Narrow styles, now so fashionable, 12½c. and 17c. a yard. Wider from 25c. up. Beauty and cheapness go hand in hand.

New trimming braids.

New feather trimmings.

New Russian bands.

The special Blanket Sale is creating great interest among housekeepers. We have always been noted for startling values in blankets. We are *not* going backward.

Read on.

For $5 a pair— Fine family blankets, soft, heavy fine. Have handsome pink, blue or gold borders and are ample size.

For $3.50 a pair—Heavy and large fleecy white blankets, choice blue and pink borders.

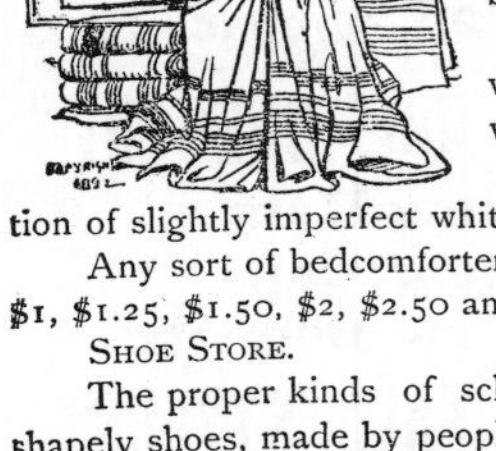

For $2.50 a pair—Ample size, very heavy white blankets that we are confident will excel any $3 blankets in the market.

For $1.75 a pair—Full size 11-4 white blankets that will wear and wear, and look well all the time.

For 59c. a pair—A mill collection of slightly imperfect white blankets; not injured for wear.

Any sort of bedcomforter you're likely to want. Prices $1, $1.25, $1.50, $2, $2.50 and up.

SHOE STORE.

The proper kinds of school shoes for girls and boys, shapely shoes, made by people who know how. Prices *absolutely the lowest* in town, quality considered.

Here's one of our great specialties for women:

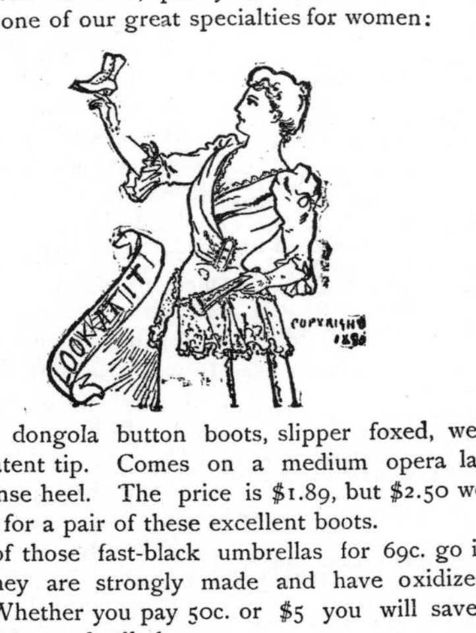

Heavy dongola button boots, slipper foxed, welt edge sole, and patent tip. Comes on a medium opera last, with common-sense heel. The price is $1.89, but $2.50 would be a fair value for a pair of these excellent boots.

More of those fast-black umbrellas for 69c. go in stock to-day. They are strongly made and have oxidized metal handles. Whether you pay 50c. or $5 you will save money by getting your umbrella here.

Merino and wool underclothing for the million.

New lines of men's flannel shirts, 50c., 75c., $1 and up.

HASKELL & TRIPP.

Department Stores: PURCHASE AND WILLIAM STS.

MISS LIZZIE'S DOUBLE.

An Important Disclosure Made in the Borden Case.

Young Married Woman the Living Image of the Prisoner.

Curious Case of Mistaken Identity in a Pawnbroker's Shop.

[Special Dispatch.]

BOSTON, Oct. 5.—The *Post* prints the following story:

FALL RIVER, Oct. 4.—Lizzie A. Borden has a double.

Her friends who know it are at work upon the story, feeling that it may go far to show that the identification of the prisoner as the woman who attempted to buy prussic acid at Smith's drug store on Aug. 3d was a grave error.

This is the story: In the building in which Andrew J. Jennings has his office there is a real estate office where loans are often negotiated on valuable personal property for persons who do not care to visit the ordinary pawnbroker. The proprietor of this office has been a resident of Fall River for years and knew the Bordens well. About 7 30 one evening in the Spring he was surprised to see a woman who, he felt sure, was Lizzie Borden, enter his office. Her social standing, the reputed wealth of her father and the unusual hour of the visit excited his surprise. With an eye to business he asked the lady what she wished.

She wanted $250 on some ornaments. He asked if they were diamonds. She replied in the negative. He then told her that he loaned money on diamonds only. She seemed bitterly disappointed and went away.

It was not until he escorted her to the door that he discovered his mistake.

It was not Lizzie Borden, but a young married woman whose face and figure were so like those of Andrew Borden's daughter that he had been deceived. His curiosity was so greatly excited at the peculiar visit and the urgency of the request that he scrutinized his visitor very closely. But for that she would have passed for Lizzie Borden, and his story, had it been made public before, would have served as another evidence of the premeditation which marked the crime laid at the prisoner's door.

Lizzie's double is a woman of good standing, whose relatives would be greatly shocked at the knowledge of her attempted loan, but it is thought the story will be told on the witness stand before the strange case is finished.

The importance of such an occurrence is evident. That a man who had been familiar with the prisoner from her youth could be so thoroughly deceived by the appearance of her double will illustrate the possibility of errors in identification. Two of the witnesses who identified Lizzie as the woman they saw in Smith's pharmacy within 24 hours of the murder were not familiar with her appearance. The third witness knew the prisoner by sight, but did not see her often.

So Lizzie's double is important.

[Special Dispatch.]

FALL RIVER, Oct. 5.—The *Standard's* correspondent made a careful investigation of the story of Lizzie Borden's double this forenoon. The authorities disclaim all knowledge of this "important disclosure," and an official told a *Standard* man that the whole thing emanated from the attorneys for defence.

TO DIVE FOR CHAMPAGNE.

There is About $10,000 Worth of It on Board the Sunken Alva.

CHATHAM, Oct. 5.—The yacht Alva is practically abandoned. The heavy wind storms of the past few days have completely undone all the work which has been done in the past two months. The vessel is now lying on her broadside, and for the first time her masts are nearly under water. Mr. White went to Boston yesterday to confer with Mr. Perkins, and upon his return it is expected that dynamite will be used to blow open the vessel's decks, and the work of saving the yacht's valuables will begin. The $10,000 worth of champagne and other liquors are in good order, and can be easily saved. All the machinery can be taken out without much trouble. The outcome of this undertaking is, of course, very disappointing to Messrs. Perkins and White, as, until the recent storm, the chances of saving the Alva they believed to be very good.

THE MULE SPINNERS.

Wages of Lowell Operatives the Subject Under Consideration.

DOVER, N. H., Oct. 5.—The greatest portion of the afternoon session of the National Mule Spinners' Association yesterday, was devoted to a discussion of the wages paid to the Lowell, Mass., spinners, who feel that they are the worst paid operatives in the country for the work performed. Able remarks were made by Senator Howard and Anthony Moore of Fall River, William Burke of Berkeley, R. I., Thomas Jackson of Lawrence and the delegates from Lowell.

These gentlemen claimed that they were being paid $10 a week where other parties doing the same work receive from $12 to $15 per week. The discussion was brought to a close by the appointing of a committee of three, to report at to-day's session as to what action should be taken regarding the matter.

Last evening the delegates held a reception from 7 to 8 at the hall of the Mule Spinners' Association, and afterward the local union tendered the delegates a complimentary ball at Lowell Opera House.

THE END VERY NEAR.

Lord Tennyson Slowly Passing Away at Haslemere.

LONDON, Oct 5.—A dispatch received from Haslemere, timed 2 p. m., states that Lord Tennyson is in the last stage of his illness and is slowly passing away.

NO IMPROVEMENT.

Mrs. Harrison Rested Better Last Night, But Remains the Same.

WASHINGTON, Oct. 5.—Dr. Gardner said this morning that Mrs. Harrison had rested better than usual last night and that there is no noticeable improvement in her condition.

Five Children Mysteriously Poisoned.

WICHITA, Kansas, Oct. 5.—Sunday night at Ferret Ind., the five children of F. Bailey were poisoned in some mysterious manner. Two died during the night and at last accounts the others were dying. The attending physician says the symptoms are those of poisoning by strychnine.

Democrats Will Contest the Election.

ROCKVILLE, Ct., Oct. 5.—The Democrats contemplate contesting the result of the town election Monday, which gave the town to the Republicans. They claim irregularities in the form of ticket similar to those at Thomaston, where the Democratic votes were thrown out.

Gladstone Honored.

LONDON, Oct. 5.—The corporation of Liverpool has decided to confer the freedom of the city upon Mr. Gladstone.

Death of Sculptor Dubray.

LONDON, Oct. 5.—Gabriel Vital Dubray, the French sculptor, is dead.

WEATHER INDICATIONS.

FAIR AND COLDER THURSDAY.

WASHINGTON, Oct. 5.—For the 24 hours from 8 a. m. to-day: For New England Thursday, fair, preceded by showers on the southeast New England coast to-day; brisk to high northerly winds; colder Thursday, with frosts; warmer Friday morning.

FAIR TO-MORROW.

BOSTON, Oct. 5.—Local forecast for New England until Friday: Threatening and rain, followed by clearing and fair weather Thursday; much cooler and frost to-morrow night; west to northwest winds.

THE PURITAN BEATEN.

Steamer Richard Peck Wins in a Race on Long Island Sound.

NEW YORK, Oct. 5.—A race on the Long Island Sound early this morning between the sidewheeler Puritan of the Fall River line and the Richard Peck of the New Haven line, resulted in a victory for the Peck, which is a twin-screw boat.

Ever since the Puritan was put into commission she has been regarded as the fastest boat on the sound, and Capt. Simmons has never had to lower his colors to any craft. Recently, however, the New Haven line has put the Peck in commission. She was completed two months ago and draws 10 feet of water. The Puritan draws 12 feet and has the most modern paddle-wheels. She is considerably larger than the Peck.

The agents of the Fall River line sent a challenge to the people of the New Haven line to test the speed of their fast boats. The challenge was accepted, and it was decided the race should take place between a point near Stratford Shoals to Fort Schuyler, 56 miles.

The Peck left New Haven at 10 30 last night. When she got out into the sound she slowed up and waited until the Puritan came up and the boats were stem and stem. Then they started and for the first 15 minutes neither seemed to gain an inch. The passengers on each boat share in the excitement, and though the weather was cold and stormy and rain was falling most of the time were on deck. Finally the Richard Peck began to forge slowly ahead. Gradually the distance between the two increased, and at last the Puritan was left far astern. When the Peck passed Fort Schuyler this morning the Puritan was a mile and a half astern and lost the race.

PLYMOUTH & MIDDLEBORO ROAD.

Its Opening. Oct. 13, to be Celebrated by Entertainment, Concert and Ball.

MIDDLEBORO, Oct. 5.—At a meeting of the directors of the Plymouth & Middleboro Railroad and committees from the Plymouth and Middleboro Commercial clubs last evening it was decided to open the road on Thursday, Oct. 13. There will be a day entertainment and dinner at Plymouth and a grand concert and ball in Middleboro in the evening.

CHOLERA REPORTS.

Epidemic Decreasing in Hamburg and Other Infected Ports.

HAMBURG, Oct. 5.—The official figures place the number of cases of cholera here yesterday at 30 and deaths at 11. This is a decrease from Monday of 13 cases and an increase of three deaths.

At Altona, yesterday, six new cases and four deaths were reported against three new cases and six deaths Monday.

HAVRE, Oct. 5.—There were reported yesterday one new case of cholera and one death. This is a decrease of two cases and four deaths compared with Monday.

ELECTION IN FLORIDA.

Majority of Mitchell, Democrat, Estimated at 25,000.

JACKSONVILLE, Fla., Oct. 5.—At midnight reports had been received from every county in the State, and from actual returns, coupled with careful conservative estimates, they show that Mitchell (Dem.) has a majority from 3000 in Hillsborough (his home) to 20 in Baker county, where the third party hoped for a victory by 100 majority. The footings of conservative estimates indicate that Mitchell's majority in the State will not be far from 25,000.

KEPT INDOORS.

Ancient and Honorables Have a Rainy Day in New York.

NEW YORK, Oct. 5.—The Ancient and Honorable Artillery Company of Boston, who are here, were kept indoors as a body this morning at the Grand Central Hotel by the rain. A few of them, however, visited points of interest individually. At 10 o'clock the Salem Cadet Band gave a concert in the rotunda of the hotel. This afternoon the visitors will come in front of the hotel, and escorted by a detachment of the Old Guard, will march down Broadway and Warren street to the Fall River boat and leave for home.

Sarah Linston Taken to Lowell.

[Special Dispatch.]

FALL RIVER, Oct. 5.—Detective Hayes of Lowell came to this city last night and took charge of Sarah Linston, who was arrested yesterday in company with Bagley, the Lowell character. She recognized the detective, and after shaking hands with him asked what she was wanted for. He replied: "I guess you know pretty well. Sarah you are wanted for receiving stolen property." He took the prisoner to Lowell this morning.

The First Snow Fall.

SCHENECTADY, N. Y., Oct. 5.—There was a slight fall of snow in this city about 2 o'clock this morning.

KINGSTON, N. Y., Oct. 5.—The peaks of the Catskills are covered with snow today. Early this morning snow fell to the depth of three inches and the ground was covered from Delhi to Big Indian.

Stranded on a Rock.

CITY OF MEXICO, Oct. 5.—The Spanish steamship Vera Cruz is high on a rock at Vera Cruz. It is believed that she will be a total loss.

Ocean Steamers.

Arrived—At New York, Manitoba, London; Johnnes Brun, Nassau; City of New York, Liverpool. At Boston (quarantine) Columbian, Liverpool.

HOME MATTERS.

PERSONAL.—D. D. Sullivan, of Fall River, is slated as the Democratic candidate for councillor in this district, and Z. W. Pease as the Senatorial candidate.

The Arctic Oil Works of San Francisco has appointed E. K. Austin of New York their eastern agent, in place of Sidney W. Knowles, deceased.

THE EVENING DRAWING SCHOOL opened last night in the High School building with 67 scholars. Principal George H. Nye reports that there are in the class for free hand and designing, 25 pupils; in machine drawing, 10; in geometry and architectural work, 25.

CEDAR GROVE STREET SCHOOL.—Work upon the addition to the Cedar Grove street school-house is progressing rapidly. The extension is all roofed in and is now ready for the slaters.

PIERCE MILL.—Four new boilers for the Pierce Mill arrived in this city yesterday, and were transported to the mill. They are to be placed in position to-day.

Three Peculiarities in Hood's Sarsaparilla.

FUNERAL.—The funeral of Capt. Elisha Gibbs took place at his late residence on South Sixth street this afternoon at 2 o'clock, a large gathering of friends being present. Rev. M. C. Julien officiated, and the choir of the Trinitarian church rendered musical selections. The exercises were simple and impressive. The floral tributes were numerous, among them being three links of white carnations from Acushnet Lodge, a basket of roses from the Trinitarian church, a wreath of ivy leaves from the New Bedford Cordage Co. and numerous others from relatives and friends. The burial took place at Rural cemetery, the bearers being Capt. Pardon G. Thomson, Capt. Matthew Fisher, Capt. Cornelius H. Springer and Sylvanus Bennett.

SOME ANXIETY is felt about the city in regard to the safety of whaling bark A. R. Tucker of this port, which spent last Winter in Hudson's Bay. The agents say there is not the slightest cause for anxiety. The vessel is not overdue, and indeed in view of the statements of the master of schooner Era, arrived at New London a day or two ago from Cumberland Inlet, the vessel could not yet have arrived home. The Era was 25 days coming down, having met with a succession of southwest winds, and the bark would have to get out of Hudson's Bay in addition to working her way down. Being a square-rigged vessel it would of course take her longer to make the passage as she cannot run so close to the wind.

THIS IS THE THIRD DAY of our great flour sale. By to-night we shall have put out over 200 barrels. By Saturday night we expect to reach the 500 mark; that means $500 worth of sugar given away free. Have you had your barrel yet? If you have not, don't delay, for this great offer closes Saturday night at 11 o'clock. Remember we give a dollar's worth of granulated sugar free with every barrel of "Cummings' Best Flour" at C. S. & B. Cummings.'

WILL THEY GO?—At a meeting of the committee of the Provision Clerks' Benefit Association last evening, reports from a subcommittee on closing up were made. This committee reported that the proprietors each and every one said that they would close a poriont of the day on the 21st if their neighbors would. The committee is in favor of visiting Waltham, and will so report on Tuesday night when action will be taken.

SENDING OUT BILLS.—The Board of Public Works is sending out bills due that department, some of which have been standing for three years. The superintendent has notified persons indebted to the department that if bills are not paid by Nov. 1st, they will be placed in the hands of the City Solicitor for collection.

OBITUARY.—Thomas Homes Dean of South Easton, a well known manufacturer of machinery, died Sunday, aged 73. He was a native of Taunton and a member of the Old Colony Historical Society. He leaves a widow.

PATENTS have been granted to Edward T. Covell of this city, fastening for horseshoes; Christian Washburn, Bridgewater, hammock swinging apparatus; Henry B. Baker, Dighton, lacing stud.

CITY HALL NOTES.—The City Council committee on street lights will hold a meeting this evening.

The Aldermanic committee on burial grounds will also meet this evening.

TAUNTON FAIR PREMIUMS.—By reference to special notice it will be seen that the premiums awarded at the Bristol County Agricultural Fair will be paid at the Taunton Court-House, Oct. 15th and 22d.

CONTRACT AWARDED.—Buchell being the lowest bidder, received the contract to furnish the firemen with rubber boots, another proof that prices are lowest at 75 William street.

NATURALIZATION.—Gilbert Brunette filed a primary declaration in the Third District Court this morning. J. C. Patnaude for petitioner.

WE ARE EXHIBITING a choice assortment of fine millinery which we shall be pleased to have the public examine. H. B. Coffin, 52 Purchase street.

GERMAN CLASS.—The Y. M. C. A. German class was organized last evening with 12 pupils. Several more will probably join. Miss Anne Lawton is teacher.

YOU WANT A MAN OF EXPERIENCE—Vote for Mr. I. B. Tompkins for Representative at the caucus this evening.

"GREAT EVENT OF THE SEASON"—Nooning's Millinery opening Wednesday, Thursday and Friday, Oct. 5, 6 and 7.

DON'T BUY carpets, furniture, draperies or upholsteries until you have been to Briggs & Lawrence's opening Oct. 11th and 12th.

YOU WANT A MAN OF EXPERIENCE—Vote for Mr. I. B. Tompkins for Representative at the caucus this evening.

MASONIC.—A regular convocation of Adoniram Royal Arch Chapter will be held this evening.

HAVE YOU GOT ONE of those dollars that are being given away at C. S. & B. Cummings'.

PATTERN HATS AND BONNETS on exhibition Oct. 7th, 8th and 9th at E. A. Boomer's, No. 18 Purchase street.

YOU WANT A MAN OF EXPERIENCE—Vote for Mr. I. B. Tompkins for Representative at the caucus this evening.

FALL OPENING of carpets, furniture, draperies and upholsteries at Briggs & Lawrence's Oct. 11th and 12th.

WEDNESDAY, THURSDAY AND FRIDAY, opening of fine millinery goods at E. A. Boomer's, No. 18 Purchase street.

VOTE for I. B. Tompkins, at the caucus to-night, for Representative.

OPENING at Mrs. F. H. Sargent's Thursday and Friday.

MILLINERY OPENING at E. A. Boomer's Wednesday, Thursday and Friday, Oct. 7, 8, 9.

GO TO CAUCUS TO-NIGHT; vote for Mr. Tompkins for Representative.

WAIT for Briggs & Lawrence's Fall opening Oct. 11th and 12th.

FALL MILLINERY OPENING at Nooning's this week Wednesday, Thursday and Friday.

VOTE for I. B. Tompkins, at the caucus to-night, for Representative.

LARGE ASSORTMENT of imported hats, Mrs. F. H. Sargent, 189 Purchase street.

DON'T FAIL to attend Nooning's Millinery opening this week.

GO TO CAUCUS TO-NIGHT; vote for Mr. Tompkins for Representative.

TEN CENTS for Miss Parloa's cook books at Hutchinson's book store.

VOTE for I. B. Tompkins, at the caucus to-night, for Representative.

SUBSCRIBE for the *Ladies' Home Journal* at Hutchinson's Book store.

GO TO CAUCUS TO-NIGHT; vote for Mr. Tompkins for Representative.

SAVE MONEY, burn oil, buy lamp. Bliss & Nye.

JUST AS ATTRACTIVE

As the hundreds of pleased visitors during the last three days have found our Draperies and Upholstery goods, will be found our

NEW FALL STYLES —OF— CARPETINGS.

All the knowledge gained by long experience and careful observation, has been used in the selection of the various grades of Carpets that make up our immense stock.

THE RESULT IS

We have brought together the most complete line of FLOOR COVERINGS that it has ever been our privilege to invite your inspection of. We were never so well equipped to supply the wants of Carpet buyers, whether it be the modest and serviceable *Ingrain*, the more pretentious *Tapestries*, the handsome and economical *Body Brussels*, the rich and durable *Moquette*, or the soft and luxurious *Axminster* that may be wanted, we are able to meet the demand.

SUPERIOR QUALITY!
EXCLUSIVE PATTERNS!
NEWEST COLORINGS!
LOWEST PRICES!

Is not this an attractive combination?

If you want to know what there is in the market and how much money you can save, do not buy until you have inspected our stock, and learned our prices.

C. F. WING,

34 to 40 Purchase st.

WHITING & CO.

FALL AND WINTER UNDERWEAR.

We have had made for us, a line of Ladies' extra quality Jersey Vests, Pants and Combination Suits, in all sizes.

Lot 1.—50 dozen Ladies' Jersey Vests and Pants, that we shall sell at 50c. each, extra quality.

Lot 2.—50 dozen Ladies' Jersey Vests and Pants that are very fine, at 75c. each as good as are sold at $1.00 each.

Lot 3—30 dozen Ladies' Jersey Vests and Pants, at 87c. each.

Lot 4—50 Dozen Ladies' Jersey Vests and Pants, elegant quality, at $1.00 each, regular $1.25 ones.

Lot 5—50 Ladies' Jersey Combination Suits, in all sizes, such as we sold so many of last season.

Lot 6—20 dozen Misses' and Children's Jersey Vests and Pants, from 50c. to 87c. each.

Also we have opened cases of Ladies', Misses', Boys' and Gents' Vests and Pants, of all makes, from 50c. to $1.75 apiece.

We invite all to call and examine the best stock of Fall and Winter Underwear, in the city, at lowest prices.

WHITING & CO.

Cool Weather This!

Don't put off buying your Winter Underwear too late. A month's sickness may be the result of your delay. There's no better time to buy Winter underwear than now while the assortment is unbroken. We are better prepared than ever to supply your wants.

Men's heavy Merino Undershirts and Drawers in White and Brown Mixed, 50c. each.

Men's Natural Wool Shirts and Drawers, $1.00, $1.50 and $2.00 per garment.

Men's White All-Wool extra weight undergarments, $1.00, $1.50, $2.00 and $2.50.

Our leaders in fine goods are our extra soft Australian Wool garments in three colors, White, Natural Wool and Buff, at $2.00 each. These are superior in quality and finish to the so-called health underwear that sells at much higher prices.

J. & W. R. WING & CO.

133 Union Street.

THE CRESCENT!

22 Purchase St.

TO BUY OR NOT TO BUY!

If that is the question, one only needs to SEE those Desirable Wrappers at $1.50 in order to be convinced. They are Warranted to fit, and sell readily.

SEEING IS BELIEVING and buying is the result.

We have a new supply of them in silver gray, mourning print, garnet, etc.

Good Wrappers at $1.00.

Outing Flannel $1.50.

Are you chilly? 29c. Jersey Vests and Pants will keep you warm during the Fall months.

Silk Hose Supporters in black, white, red, yellow and blue, only 25c.

More of those Kitchen Aprons at 25c., Best Gingham, two widths.

Perfectly Lovely!

Those Little Cloaks of Eiderdown for children. It makes one warm only to look at them. Prices from $2.00 to $5.00.

If Baby needs a Bib, 5c. will buy a good one.

If he needs a Sack we have them at all prices.

Socks, too, of different grades.

New lot of indigo blue and silver gray prints.

FLANNELS OF ALL KINDS.

We have Domets at 5c. per yard.

THE CRESCENT!

22 Purchase St.

The Evening Standard.

ESTABLISHED FEBRUARY, 1850.   NEW BEDFORD, MONDAY, OCTOBER 10, 1892.   TWO CENTS.

HASKELL & TRIPP.

So far as price for quality goes, these are two of the most remarkable offerings we have ever made in millinery feathers:

"Prince of Wales" ostrich tips, elegant line of colors, 57c. per bunch of three tips; worth 75c.

Much larger and finer "Prince of Wales" tips, all the stylish colors and black, $1.12 per bunch of three tips; worth $1.50.

One hundred new styles of fancy feathers, aigrettes, wings, jets, etc. Often a third to a half less than regular retail rates. This is worth looking into. Misses' trimmed hats, 45c. to $1.50, all new.

A great lot of women's colored walking skirts has invaded the department of such goods in our east gallery. Among these are prominent:

"Crow Brand" fast black skirts, made of sateen, lined, and finished in first-class style, warranted not to change color by washing, age or exposure. Prices $1.50 and $1.75.

Colored Mohair skirts, $1.75.

Gray melton skirts with silk-embroidered ruffle in contrasting colors, $1.58.

Rich, soft satin skirts, choice colors, deep ruffle at foot, $4.25.

Changeable taffeta silk ruffled skirts, "rustlers," $5 and $6 each.

Black "gloria" silk skirts, $5 each.

Merino underskirts, 50c.

Patent seamless stockinet underskirts, 75c. These are very warm and serviceable.

At the flannel counter are new arrivals. Gray twilled shirting or skirting flannels, 25c. a yard. Heavy, yard wide gray Shakers, 33c. a yard. Heavy, white Shakers, 25c. and 29c. a yard. Genuine unshrinking Shakers, 50c. a yard.

At the print counter. 2000 yards "Crepons."

Handsomer than calico, wider than calico, better than calico. } But at the same price: 8 cents a yard.

Think ahead. Blanket weather will be here some time. But don't hope then to get white blankets for 59c. a pair. They are not to be had any day we've a mind to send for them. Manufacturers blunder as little as possible. These are "blunders," hence the price. The imperfections are slight. We have a very big stock of good, large, heavy blankets for $1.75, $2, $2.50, $3, $3.50 a pair.

We have our famous fine and heavy Sierra Nevada blankets for $5 the pair. Best in the land for the money.

Elegant blankets, up to $10 a pair.

For your house plants—Jardinieres.

Handsome Jardinieres, attractive shapes, in these bright colors: wine or canary, 25c. each. Larger ones, 50c. and 75c. each.

Rich, new designs in granulated surface Jardinieres, with overlaid network in gold or silver finish, 50c. and 89c. each. For sunny Italy.

Brilliantly colored striped silk blankets, or slumber robes, at a lower price than ever. We offer to-day one hundred of these silk blankets at $1 each. Complete assortment of colors. Many people find these very effective for a portiere in a doorway or short window.

We have two very special bargains in lace curtains that should interest every housekeeper in need of draperies. The prices of these curtains are $2 and $2.50 a pair. They look like real Brussels, as the patterns are copied from those expensive curtains. Three yards long, 50 inches wide.

Full lines of fine lace curtains from $5 a pair up.

Printed sateen stand covers, beautiful designs and colors, every cover trimmed with knotted fringe on four sides, 36 inches square, 39c. each.

HASKELL & TRIPP.

Department Stores: PURCHASE AND WILLIAM STS.

A TISSUE OF LIES.

Lawyer Jennings Says the Boston Paper's Story is False.

Member of Fall River Police Force Asserts That It is True.

Names are Fictitious, but Statements Substantially True.

FALL RIVER, Oct. 10.—Andrew J. Jennings, counsel for the defendant in the Borden case, made the following statement to an Associated Press correspondent to-day: The matter published in a Boston paper this morning relating to the murders of Andrew J. Borden and his wife [see second page] is a tissue of lies. I have endeavored to find out about Mr. and Mrs. Fred Chace at the number indicated, 198 Fourth street. There is not only no such number, but not any within 50 of it. There is no such name George F. Sisson in the directory, nor can I find any person who knows anybody of that name. The kernel of the whole malicious story deals with a condition which is absolutely disproved by things found in the cellar by the prosecution and admitted to be what Miss Lizzie claimed they were. Subsequent events have confirmed her claim. Mr. Morse says that the whole story is absolutely false, not a word of truth in it. The Reagan story has already been denied by Miss Emma and Miss Lizzie, and was admitted by Mrs. Reagan to be false by at least six persons.

A member of the police force says to-day that the names used in the story are fictitious, but the matter is substantially true.

WEATHER INDICATIONS.

WASHINGTON, Oct. 10.—*Cooler and Warmer.*—For the 24 hours from 8 a.m. to-day: For New England, fair; winds shifting to southwesterly; slightly warmer on Tuesday; preceded by stationary temperature on the southern coast.

COOLER AND FAIR.

BOSTON, Oct. 10.—Local forecast for New England until Wednesday: Fair, cooler to-night and to-morrow; followed by warmer, westerly to southerly winds.

HELPLESS SEALER FIRED UPON.

Schooner May Belle has an Exciting Adventure with a Russian Cruiser.

VICTORIA, B. C., Oct. 10.—Schooner May Belle, which has arrived from Copper Island reports an exciting adventure on August 29. The schooner was anchored 70 miles north of Bering Sea in a dense fog, which lifted suddenly, revealing a Russian cruiser a short distance away. The latter made no signals and lowered no boats, simply sending a shot across the schooner's bow, which missed the rigging only by a few feet. The crew, in terror, hoisted all sails, the captain's orders being unheard or unheeded in the excitement.

Then came a second shot, better aimed, from the Russian which pierced the schooner above the water line, going completely through the forecastle. Still no boat left the cruiser, her commander apparently being satisfied with firing at the helpless sealer. Luckily for the latter, the fog thickened, and in it she escaped. The damages were patched up at the nearest beach and schooner saved.

EARL OF DUNRAVEN INTERVIEWED.

His Lordship will Build a New Boat to Compete for America's Cup.

PARIS, Oct. 10.—The *Herald's* European edition publishes the following from its correspondent at Vienna: I had an interview yesterday with the Earl of Dunraven on the subject of America's cup challenge. His lordship states that the match will take place in America. A new boat will be built, the builders being the Messrs. Watson & Co., of Glasgow, of Valkyrie and Thistle renown. The construction will be left entirely in Mr. Watson's hands.

Lord Dunraven's real intention is to do everything in his power to wrest the championship from Americans. He declines to explain the exact conditions of the challenge on the ground that it would not be judicious at the present juncture to do so.

FARMERS LOSE EVERYTHING.

Prairie Fire Doing Immense Damage in South Dakota.

HURON, S. D., Oct. 10.—A prairie fire started ten miles northwest of here yesterday, burning over a tract 10 miles wide and 20 miles long. The town of Hitchcock narrowly escaped destruction. A large force of men fought the fire till dark. The country burned over is thickly settled by prosperous farmers, many of whom have lost everything. Up to a late hour last night the fire was still raging. The wind blew at a velocity of forty miles an hour, driving the flames before it at a fearful speed.

FIREMEN BURIED IN THE RUINS.

Explosion and Fire in a Grocery Store in New Orleans.

NEW ORLEANS, Oct. 10.—A fire occurred yesterday in a grocery store, corner of Port Anthony and Canal streets, accompanied by a terrible explosion. The building was partially wrecked, burying firemen John Cavanaugh and B. F. Perreto beneath the burning debris. The former was brought out dead, while Perreto was fatally injured.

The Cholera in Hamburg.

HAMBURG, Oct. 10.—There were, according to figures, only two new cases of cholera and one death in this city yesterday.

Ocean Steamers.

Arrived at New York—Spain, London; Ben Lomond, Japan; Muriel, West Indies; Thingvalla, Stettin; Graffoe, Hamburg; Principia, Leith; Aller, Bremen; at Boston, Acandinavia, Glasgow.

HOME MATTERS.

A PETITION FOR A POST OFFICE at Lambert's Cove, Marthas Vineyard, is being circulated by residents of that village.

THE REGISTRARS OF VOTERS completed verifying the nomination papers of the Socialist party Saturday, and to-day are busy at work on those of the Prohibitionists.

SALE OF A BUILDING.—Standish Bourne sold at auction this afternoon the three-story partially burned building on Fish Island, to A. B. King for $61. The building is to be removed within ten days.

ACCIDENTS.—Daniel Godreau, an engine cleaner in the employ of the Old Colony Railroad, had two fingers of his right hand split at the second joint this morning while cutting a bad gash in the back of his head. He was taken to his home on Clark street in a jobbing wagon, where he received surgical aid.

Timothy Harrington while walking along Purchase street this forenoon tripped on the sidewalk, near Logan street, and fell, cutting a bad gash in the back of his head. He was taken to his home on Clark street in a jobbing wagon, where he received surgical aid.

PERSONAL.—Albion T. Brownell was elected vice-president of the Paint and Oil Club of New England at its annual meeting in Boston Saturday.

Rev. M. C. Julien left the city last evening for Minneapolis, where he will attend the National Congregational convention.

Jimmy Canavan isn't playing with the Chicago base ball club. He is detailed to take tickets at the gate. Jimmy has fallen off considerably in his batting, and Decker has taken his place at second base.

Rev. H. B. Cady intends writing a lecture from notes taken during his recent visit to the battle-fields of the South with the G. A. R. veterans.

F. G. Tripp of the New Bedford Steam Laundry left the city last evening to attend the ninth annual convention of the Laundrymen's National Association to be held in New York Oct. 10th, 11th and 12th. Headquarters, Broadway Central Hotel.

H. S. Francis, clerk with C. W. Haskins, has returned home after a month's vacation in Maine.

Jethro C. Brock, of this city, some years ago compiled a valuable list of the people who left Nantucket for California about the year 1849, some 700 in number, and this list is now being published in the Nantucket Journal.

Lieut. Kenneth Morton, of Plymouth, who recently graduated at West Point, has been assigned to the Third Artillery and stationed at Fort McHenry at Baltimore.

Charles E. Congdon, son of Richard E. Congdon of Nantucket, was among the successful candidates for admission to the Harvard Medical School last week, attaining a high average in the examination.

Engineer Rex, of steamer Nantucket, has resigned, and will remove from Nantucket with his family to New York.

COTTON WEAVERS CIRCULAR.—The following circular has been issued to the New Bedford Cotton Weavers' Protective Association:

Fellow Members:—The regular monthly meeting will be held in Spinners' Hall on Tuesday evening next, October 11th. You are earnestly requested to attend this meeting, as business of the utmost importance to the association will be brought before you for your consideration.

1. An itemized report of the income and expenditure for the past three months.

2. To elect three members for the executive committee.

3. Also to discuss the running of overtime in the different mills.

During the past quarter the progress of the association has steadily increased, both numerically and financially, and there is no reason why it should not do so, if the members in general will assist the collector in the proper discharge of his duties.

During the past month several complaints have been heard from the different mills in reference to fining, and it is about time that steps were taken to find out if the amendment to the original fines bill is of any benefit to the weavers.

Your attention will be called to other matters of minor importance. Hoping for a large attendance, on behalf of the executive committee. MATTHEW HART, Secretary.

PROF. SMITH'S DANCING CLASSES.—Saturday afternoon, on the forming of Prof. Smith's dancing class for children, there was a gathering of some 450 ladies and children in Odd Fellows' Hall, when a set of family party was held. Dancing was indulged in to the music of the following orchestra: Elmer E. Tolman, violin; D. J. Sullivan, cornet; Antone Mackish, clarinet; W. H. C. Smith, piano.

The reception of pupils for Prof. Smith's evening class and their friends will occur to-morrow evening.

On Monday afternoon last, Prof. Smith formed a large class in Fall River composed of the best people in the city.

The following dances adopted at the 15th annual convention of the American Society of Professors of Dancing in New York, will be taught by Prof. Smith during the season; The Aurora—waltz movement, Columbian polka quadrille, the Majestic polonaise, Academy waltz, Columbian lancers, Royal Gavotte, the Del Monte—waltz movement, the Manitou, the Wentworth—waltz movement.

OFFICE IMPROVEMENT.—The law office of Knowlton & Perry, North Water street, is undergoing improvement. In the northeast corner a room is being fitted for a private office, the folding doors between the main room and Mr. Knowlton's office have been removed, the partition extended and a door of ordinary dimensions put in, and the rooms are to be supplied with hot water heat.

PRESENTATION.—Mr. Carrie E. Dean started for Corning, N. Y., to-day, where she will join her husband, John L. Dean, and make it her home. A few of the employes at the Weeden Manufacturing Company presented her a very handsome gold chain and locket with a diamond setting. Mrs. Dean also received several other handsome presents from a number of her friends.

THERE ARE SOME THIRTY REMNANT pieces of tapestry carpets in B. H. Waite's stock, less than enough for large rooms and are marked down to remnant prices. Bring measurement of room and there's a bargain at 71 William street.

ONE HUNDRED AND NINETY-FIVE DOLLARS.—Beautiful mahogany upright second-hand piano, almost new, popular make, 71-3 octave, cost $350, warranted 3 years. E. B. Chase & Co., corner Union and Fifth streets.

MRS. E. O'NEILL, Dressmaker, having removed to 650 County street, corner of Smith, wishes to announce to her patrons in this city and Fairhaven that she will resume work Monday, Oct. 10.

LEASED BY SPORTSMEN.—Three thousand acres on Assonet Neck have been leased for three years by the sportsmen who conduct the field trials. There will be men and dogs present from all parts of the country.

ACKNOWLEDGMENT.—Capt. William Sanders, County Commissioner, sends us a fine lithographic engraving of the new Taunton Court House, with floor plans of the same, neatly framed, for which our thanks are extended.

TO BE MACADAMIZED.—The road roller is busy to-day picking up Harper street between Cedar street and Oak Grove cemetery, preparatory to laying new macadam.

SOME VERY CHOICE CARNATION FLOWERS might be seen at William Peirce's flower store. They are seedlings raised by a Jim Brothers, florists, Clarks Point.

TAXES.—The city treasurer had received up to the close of business Saturday afternoon $228,992.87 in taxes.

SUPPER.—Read the special notice of Sylvia H. Delano Circle, Ladies of the G. A. R., on the fourth page.

Y. M. C. A.—The annual meeting of the Y. M. C. A. will be held to-morrow evening. See special notice.

REPUBLICAN CONVENTION.

Hon. H. M. Knowlton Renominated for District Attorney.

The Republican convention to nominate a candidate for District Attorney for the southern district of Massachusetts was held in this city this noon.

The convention was called to order by Hon. Milton Reed of Fall River, who read the call, and was chosen temporary chairman. James L. Gillingham of Fairhaven was chosen temporary secretary.

L. LeB. Holmes, Esq., of New Bedford these days have found a committee on credentials. He reported Bristol, Barnstable, Dukes and Nantucket counties represented by six delegates. The report was accepted.

The temporary organization was made permanent.

Mr. Reed said although we meet in small numbers and in an informal manner, we must remember that no election of more importance has been held in this vicinity this year. While not in favor of this manner of holding the convention, considering the exigencies of the occasion and the law at the present time, this, perhaps, is the best method that could be pursued. An officer of such importance as district attorney should not be nominated by a district convention.

On motion of H. B. Worth, Esq., of New Bedford, L. LeB. Holmes was empowered to cast the vote of the convention for a candidate for district attorney for the southern district of Massachusetts.

The vote was for Hon. Hosea M. Knowlton, and he was declared the nominee of the convention.

Mr. Holmes thought it well to arrange for a permanent district committee, so that we might be again be called on to meet such an exigency as this year.

There was some talk as to the place of such a committee and then Mr. Holmes moved the committee consist of three members from Bristol county, two from Barnstable county, and one each from Dukes and Nantucket counties, with full power to call subsequent conventions for nomination of district attorney for the southern district, and with power to fill vacancies.

The chairman appointed the committee as follows: Lemuel Le B. Holmes of New Bedford, Lloyd E. White of Taunton, and L. Elmer Wood of Taunton for Bristol county, Charles F. Swift of Yarmouth and Hiram F. Harriman of Wellfleet for Barnstable county, Herbert L. Norton of Cottage City for Dukes county, Josiah F. Murphey for Nantucket county.

At this point Mr. Holmes, who had been appointed a committee to present Mr. Knowlton with the nomination (in the Third District Court room) returned, and introduced him.

Mr. Reed said it gave him great pleasure to welcome the candidate, and hoped he would accept the nomination.

Mr. Knowlton said he deeply appreciates the honor conferred on him. Although the convention is small in numbers the members represent a large constituency. The practical unanimity, said Mr. Knowlton, shown toward me, has induced me again to become a candidate for the position. There are younger men, perhaps, less hardened in criminal procedure, who might have been procured to accept the office, but as I have been unanimously nominated I will accept the position, and assure you that the office will know no party or set of men, but will be solely kept in the interests of the Commonwealth.

The convention dissolved, and by invitation the delegates dined with Mr. Knowlton at his residence.

POLITICAL.—The Republican county convention of Dukes county was held Saturday afternoon at Agricultural Hall, West Tisbury. E. D. Vanderhoop of Gay Head was chairman and Walter S. Osborn of Edgartown secretary. The following nominations were made:

For Sheriff—Jason L. Dexter of Edgartown.

Representative—Asa Smith of Chilmark—For Lodge for U. S. Senator.

Commissioner—Gilbert L. Smith of Tisbury.

District Attorney Convention—H. L. Norton of Cottage City.

Special Commissioners—William J. Rotch of West Tisbury and William A. Vanderhoof of Cottage City.

Commissioners of Insolvency—Stephen C. Luce of Tisbury, Thomas D. Crowell of Cottage City, and William E. Marchant of Edgartown.

Capt. Otis Foss of Cottage City was chosen chairman of the Republican county committee for the ensuing year. It was voted to hold the next convention at Cottage City.

The Democratic county convention of Dukes county will be held at 10.30 a.m. to-morrow at the room of the Democratic Club in Vineyard Haven.

Members of the Harrison and Reid battalion are referred to a special notice.

A meeting will be held in Phoenix hall, Fairhaven, to-morrow evening, to consider forming a Harrison and Reid battalion.

A Prohibitory rally will be held at Riverside Hall, Head of Westport, this evening, and the speakers will be Alderman C. H. Brownell of this city and Rev. Messrs. B. F. Simon and J. I. Bartholomew.

A meeting of labor leaders was held yesterday afternoon, when candidates for various offices were discussed. Among those present were Samuel Ross of the Spinners Union, Matthew Hart of the Weavers' Protective Union, Henry F. Janell of the Stone Cutlers' Union, Thomas Gamble of the Spinners and James Connelly of the card-room help. The candidacy of Samuel Ross, B. B. Barney and Frank W. Francis for representatives were indorsed by those present, also that of John I. Bryant for sheriff. A mass meeting of the workingmen of the city will be called and the action of the Independent Labor party will depend to a great extent upon the action of that meeting. The meeting will be addressed by prominent speakers. There is no doubt that candidates for the Common Council will be presented by the Labor party in wards one and six, and that the candidacy of Arod B. Holloway for aldermanic honors in ward one will be endorsed.

WHITING & Co. are having special sales on jackets, capes and children's garments. Why not? when they show you the largest stock and lowest prices in the city.

AUCTION SALE.—To-morrow at 2 o'clock, the stock of James Lowe & Co., grocers, corner Arnold and Ash streets, will be sold at auction by Standish Bourne.

DON'T BUY carpets, furniture, draperies or upholsteries until you have been to Briggs & Lawrence's opening Oct. 11th and 12th.

GUNTER'S NEW BOOK "Miss Dividends," is said to be his best. Sold at Hutchinson's Book Store.

LOOK at the white blankets Whiting & Co. are selling at $1.25 and $1.50 a pair, good size.

FALL OPENING of carpets, furniture, draperies and upholsteries at Briggs & Lawrence's Oct. 11th and 12th.

LEAVE YOUR SUBSCRIPTIONS for Harper's Monthly, Weekly and Bazaar at Hutchinson's.

WHITING & Co's price $5.00 blanket beats them all.

WARR for Briggs & Lawrence's Fall opening Oct. 11th and 12th.

HOOD'S Sarsaparilla tones the system.

YOU FURNISH THE BOY. WE DO THE REST.

BORDEN MURDER.

Motive for the Crime Given to the Public.

Lizzie's Secret was Discovered by her Father.

Startling Testimony of Twenty-Five New Witnesses.

Miss Borden Said to Have Been Seen at Window

Of the Room Where her Step-mother was Killed.

Her Head was Enveloped in a Rubber Cap.

Quarrel of the Sisters in Police Station Detailed.

Detective McHenry's Story of How the Case was Worked Up.

The Boston *Globe* to-day prints what purports to be a complete revelation of the government case against Miss Lizzie A. Borden. The *Globe* says besides those who testified for the government in the preliminary examination of Lizzie A. Borden before Judge Blaisdell fully 25 new witnesses will be called by the State at the trial of the defendant for murder in December.

Briefly stated, the result of the *Globe's* investigation is as follows: John H. Murphy, who resides on Bedford street, Fall River, will testify that he was standing on the sidewalk close to the Borden house when Mr. Borden entered his yard, about 10 40 o'clock on the morning of Aug. 4, and he saw him a minute or two later ushered into the house by Bridget Sullivan. Mr. Murphy will swear that while Mr. Borden was walking in the yard he saw a window blind of the room in which Mrs. Borden's body was afterwards found cautiously opened by a young woman, who had that same morning told him, when he called at the Borden house about 9 30 o'clock, that her "father" had gone down town and would not be back until noon or later. This woman he has identified as the defendant, Lizzie A. Borden.

The window Mr. Murphy designates as the one in which he saw Miss Lizzie is so situated that she must have been standing over the mutilated remains of her mother at the very time that her father was about to enter the house, between 10 30 and 10 45 o'clock.

The next witness of importance is Mrs. Gustave F. Ronald, whose husband is a well-known civil engineer, and whose home during the Winter is at Pawtuxet, R. I. She and her husband were guests at the Wilbur House at the time of the murder. About 9 30 o'clock on the morning of Aug. 4 she went out with her baby in its carriage for a walk. She wheeled the little one up Second street and stopped under the big trees near the Borden house about 20 minutes of 10 o'clock. A minute later she heard a terrible cry or groan and began looking around to see whence it came. She looked up at the Borden house and saw in a room through a partially open window a woman whose head was in part covered by a rubber cap or hood, and whose face she saw plainly, as the distance was short. This window she has designated to the authorities, and it is the one nearest to the murdered woman as she lay in the guest chamber of her home when found by the police.

Mrs. Ronald was almost that minute approached by Mr. Peter Mahany of 103 Pleasant street, Fall River, who is time-keeper in the Troy mill. He likewise had heard the groan, seen the woman at the window, who wore the peculiar head covering, and recognized her as the younger daughter of the Borden family, all members of which he knew quite well by sight. The window that he designates as the one in which he saw Miss Lizzie was the same as that pointed out by Mrs. Ronald.

Augustus Gunning, who now resides at 308 Plainfield street, Johnsonville, R. I., near Providence, was at that time a lodger in Mrs. Churchill's house, and he too, about 10 o'clock on the morning of Aug. 4, saw Lizzie Borden in the window of the guest chamber with a dark-colored garment on and a hood of similar color covering her head. As he looked across she seemed to be engaged in cleaning, but upon seeing him stepped aside from the window.

These witnesses fix Miss Borden at her mother's side almost at the minute when she probably was killed, and when Miss Lizzie, according to her own statement, was elsewhere.

The next witnesses of importance are Mr. and Mrs. Frederick Chace of 198 Fourth street, Fall River, and Mrs. Abigail Manchester, their daughter, who also resides in this city. They were friends of the elder Bordens, and visited them on the evening previous to the murder. They overheard a quarrel between Lizzie and her father. All heard Mr. Borden say: "You can make your own choice and do it to-night. Either let us know what his name is or take the door on Saturday, and when you go fishing fish for some other place to live, as I will never listen to you again. I will know the name of the man who got you into trouble." Then the Chaces and Mrs. Manchester heard Lizzie reply: "If I marry this man, will you be satisfied that everything will be kept from the outside world?" Then the visitors were announced, and conversed with Mr. and Mrs. Borden upon the subject of Lizzie's shame. Mr. Borden said, "I would rather see her dead than have it come out." When asked if he knew the cause of her trouble he said, "No; but I have my suspicions, and have had all along. If I am right I will never recognize this man in the world. She has made her own bed, so let her lie upon it."

Mr. G. Romaine Pittson, a wealthy New York dealer in machinery supplies, whose place of business is on Dey street, in that city, has made affidavit that a few days prior to the murder Mr. Borden consulted him, as a friend, about Lizzie, whose trouble he related in detail.

Mr. Pittson says he advised Mr. Borden to cut Lizzie off without a dollar if she refused to tell him the name of the man who got her into trouble.

Mrs. George J. Sisson of 189 Rock street, Fall River, who attended the funeral of Mr. and Mrs. Borden, heard Lizzie say to Bridget, "Are you a fool or a knave? Why don't you say how much money you want to keep quiet?" Bridget's answer was: "I don't know what you mean, but you are not the girl I took you to be."

Mr. George Sisson, among other important statements, will swear that less than a month before the murder Mr. Borden told him he had made a will, in which he had given Emma and Lizzie $25,000 each, which was more than he would have allowed them had it not been for his wife's intercessions.

Mrs. Sisson and Mrs. Mary J. Wilson, dressmaker at 110 Rodman street, Fall River, bear witness that Miss Lizzie Borden at one time offered the former for $10 her stepmother's gold watch, which had been stolen from the Borden house a short time before. They also, as well as do many of the other witnesses whose names are above mentioned, tell of the insolent treatment that Mrs. Borden received at the hands of Lizzie.

Bridget Sullivan again figures conspicuously in the case. She corroborates the quarrel overheard by the Chaces the night previous to the murder and the statement made to her by Lizzie, which was overheard by Mrs. Sisson at the funeral. Bridget also describes a conversation which she heard the night previous to the murder between Morse and Lizzie after the old folks had retired. Morse was talking to her about a will. Bridget says she heard him remark: "Quarrelling will not fix the thing. Something else has got to be done and I will do all I can."

Bridget swears that on the afternoon of the murder, about 6 o'clock, Lizzie said to her in a whisper, "Keep your tongue still and don't talk to these officers, and you can have all the money you want." Bridget also says that when she came down stairs when called by Lizzie, immediately after the murder of Mr. Borden, she asked Lizzie where she was when her father was killed. She says that Lizzie replied: "I heard a groan up-stairs and went to see if anything was the matter with Mrs. Borden, and when I came back I found that my father was dead, too"

Detective McHenry of Providence and his wife also give important evidence, which relates in part to the row between the sisters in the matron's room at the station-house after Lizzie's arrest. Not only does Mrs. Reagan affirm all that was at the time printed, but she adds much to it of a sensational nature that is corroborated by both Mr. and Mrs. McHenry, who overheard and saw the whole transaction through a hole in the wall that had been specially prepared by the authorities for the purpose of keeping a sleepless eye upon the accused inmate.

Mr. Gunning, above referred to, also furnishes interesting information of what he saw in the guest chamber of the Borden house on the night prior to the murder.

Mrs. Sarah Whitehead of 148 Fourth street and Miss Eliza J. Bell will swear that Mr. Borden told Mrs. Whitehead a week before the murder that he had made a will in which he had remembered Mrs. Whitehead sufficiently to keep her from want the remainder of her life.

Further corroborating the fact that Mr. Borden did make a will, the government has in its possession a slip of paper found in the wallet removed from the dead man's trousers pocket by Dr. Nolan, which reads substantially as follows: "These bequests appear in my will. To Mrs. Sarah Whitehead the farm in Somerset. To her daughter Abbie $5000 in trust. To Mrs. Fish of Hartford $3000 in trust. To her daughter Winifred ten shares of the new mill stock and $2500 cash. The rest to be attended to by my lawyer, as in the former will."

Bearing still stronger on the probable motive is the statement of Mr. Frank Burroughs, a well-known New York city lawyer, who formerly lived in Fall River. He will testify that about eight months previous to the murder Miss Lizzie Borden talked with him in Fall River about property rights. Again about five weeks before the murder he saw her. He was obliged to spend some time in New Haven, Conn., preparing a case at law for the New York, New Haven & Hartford railroad. While there he received a visit from Miss Lizzie, and she again inquired closely into the subject of wills and property inheritance, with especial reference to the legal disposition of property in the event of a step-mother's death before that of the husband. He told her that he would look the matter up at his convenience, as he was a little rusty on Massachusetts laws. Lizzie again called on him in New Haven just one week before the murder, and he then gave her the required information and she went off. The day after Mr. Burroughs' return to New York he read the facts of the murder, and his suspicions were aroused. When interviewed by Mr. McHenry he expressed willingness to come to court and testify. He made a statement for Mr. McHenry that was drawn by Mr. Geoffrey Williams of Providence, who was also in Connecticut on the same railroad case with Mr. Burroughs.

Mrs. Hannah Fish of Hartford, George F. Revere of Somerset, Minnie C. Wilson of Fall River and Detective Hathaway of New Bedford, and two others are the remaining witnesses on whom the government will depend.

Mrs. Reagan's testimony, which is a revelation, becomes particularly important, as it is fully corroborated by Mr. and Mrs. McHenry.

The Detective's Story.

The following is the story of Detective E. D. McHenry of Providence in detail:

I was called on to the Borden case Aug. 5, and after looking matters over in a general way, called my wife and domiciled her at the Wilbur House, to gather what information she could prior to having her interview with the Borden woman, if such action were necessary.

I concluded Bridget Sullivan was the first person to proceed against in the inquiry, after learning of her term of service, and my wife went and interviewed her in the garb of a sister of charity.

She elicited from her all that she knew about the family affairs, and then I called upon her, then Marshal Hilliard did, then two other officers on his force, and finally we all compared notes—that is, Marshal Hilliard and I compared them, and we found no discrepancies worthy of note in the servant girl's statement.

It was then proposed to investigate her record, as the statement about her being offered money is very material, and we held it back, personally feeling that she might have a spirit of revenge against Lizzie and my wife and I were not going to prejudice the case in any way.

I investigated her career from the time she landed in America to the time of the death of her intended husband a month before the murder.

Upon my return we made another examination, and she stood the test satisfactorily, and both Marshal Hilliard and myself were satisfied that she had told the truth.

I then turned her over to my wife again, and she worked her, thinking that we might have overlooked something in our inquiry, but the only thing new that we got were the names of the parties whose statements we procured and who have given their affidavits to the district attorney. I mean Mr. and Mrs. Chace and the others, whose testimony grew and was developed from that original source.

I was especially detailed to investigate

[Continued on Fourth Page.]

MONEY FOR POLITICS.

Cleveland Said to Have Given a Check for $10,000.

NEW YORK, Oct. 10.—In view of the call for funds by Chairman Harrity and Chairman Dickinson, there has been a natural interest to ascertain the size of the check contributed by ex-President Cleveland.

It will be recalled that four years ago he sent his check to Chairman Calvin S. Brice for $10,000. The announcement was made at headquarters that three weeks ago Mr. Cleveland contributed his check for $10,000. The check was turned over to Treasurer Roosevelt, and by him sent to the Holland Trust company. It is also reported that Mr. Cleveland's personal friends, E. C. Benedict, Mr. Whitney and Mr. Dickinson, have each contributed $10-000. The amount of Chairman Harrity's check was $25, but in view of the fact that Mr. Harrity contributes his services as chairman, nothing more was expected from him.

There were plenty of avenues opened for the expenditure of the contribution of Cleveland and his three personal friends. The Democratic national campaign of 1884, according to the best authorities, cost about $400,000, while that of 1888 cost about $1,000,000. The expenses of this campaign will run to higher figures, for the reason that the fight extends over more states.

Blaine May Speak.

Up at Chairman Carter's national Republican camp, the next important discussion was over the report of the committee which has just returned from Bar Harbor. The committee requested Mr. Blaine that, if his health permitted, he should make one or two speeches, either in Maine or in New York. The committee returned and reported that Mr. Blaine said that, while his health was greatly improved, his domestic afflictions had caused him great sorrow. He did not like the idea of appearing on a public platform, but if his health permitted he would waive his personal comfort, and do anything reasonable that the national committee desired. He is to answer definitely in a little while.

Republican Campaign Fund.

The subject of money also came up at Mr. Carter's bureau. At the beginning of the campaign it was thought necessary that a fund of $2,000,000 should be raised. While the committee have been very successful, the contributions have not yet reached that high water mark, but it is said that before the month is out everything will be all right.

Minister Phelps at Berlin cabled to James F. Burke, president of the Republican College league, $1000 to uniform Yale college Republicans. General Clarkson will uniform Harvard, and Columbia college has ordered 600 uniforms.

There is to be a big college Republican demonstration in New York on Oct. 29, Princeton, Yale, Harvard, Rutgers, the New York law school and other universities will send delegates.

Charges Against Democrats.

The Republican national campaign committee has issued a statement charging the Democratic national committee with conspiring to colonize in this city for election purposes large numbers of negroes from Philadelphia, Baltimore and Washington, and also to buy up thousands of colored floaters in this city and state.

These revelations of alleged crookedness, the statement says, have come to the committee through the exertions of Committeeman David Martin of Pennsylvania. Captain Elder of Washington is declared to be the chief instrument employed in this manipulation of colored voters, and it is asserted that he has three colored men as assistants.

CAMPAIGN FUND BOOKS.

Replies to the Cincinnati Post's Proposition to Have Them Examined.

CINCINNATI, Oct. 10.—The national committees of the four political parties have replied to the letters sent them by the Cincinnati Post, asking permission to examine their campaign fund books, for publication from time to time.

Chairman Harrity of the national Democratic executive committee says:

We are perfectly willing that any disinterested and fair parties examine our accounts and see for themselves the distribution of our funds, after the election. Before the election we would not, for, no matter how legitimately the fund may be used, we would be giving away our plan of campaign to the enemy. A good general never does that.

Chairman Carter of the Republican committee says:

The high character of Cornelius N. Bliss, treasurer of this committee, is a sufficient guarantee to the people of this country that all funds received by him will be correctly accounted for, and disbursed only for legitimate election expenses.

Chairman Taubeneck of the People's party replies to the letter as follows:

Send on your committee, but tell them to bring a microscope with them, or they will be unable to see the small amount of money that we have to run the campaign on, providing they should examine the expenses of some other party before coming here.

The response of the Prohibition committee was to the effect that the books were open to inspection to any and all persons who wished to see how the funds were disbursed.

Stevenson's Endorsement.

NEW YORK, Oct. 10.—The following letter has been received at the Democratic national headquarters:

BLOOMINGTON, Ills., Oct. 8, 1892.
Hon. W. F. Harrity, Chairman Democratic National Committee, New York:

MY DEAR SIR—I have returned here after a very satisfactory visit to the south. I have read with great pleasure Mr. Cleveland's letter of acceptance. I am in full accord with him upon all the questions discussed. Ably and tersely he reflects the views of the Democratic party upon the currency question. I need hardly say to you that I fully and earnestly endorse that part of his letter. He is the able exponent of the Democratic doctrines. Should I be elected I will, to the best of my ability, co-operate with him in giving practical effects to the views contained in his letter.

Yours very truly,
A. E. STEVENSON.

No Election Laws.

PROVIDENCE, Oct. 10.—Rhode Island Democratic leaders claim that the Republicans wiped all the election laws off the statutes at the recent special session of the legislature.

Confirmation and Dedication.

NASHUA, N. H., Oct. 10.—Rt. Rev. D. M. Bradley of Manchester issued the sacrament of confirmation to over 200 children at the Church of the Immaculate Conception yesterday afternoon. Following this he proceeded to the new convent building and performed its religious dedication.

OF PURITAN STOCK.

Death of Rev. Dr. Warren, Editor of The Christian Mirror.

PORTLAND, Me., Oct. 10.—Rev. Dr. Israel Perkins Warren died suddenly last night, aged 78 years. Deceased was born in Woodbridge, now Bethany, Conn., April 8, 1814, and was graduated from Yale college in the class of 1838. He was ordained pastor of the Congregational church in Granby, Conn., April 20, 1842, and was pastor there and at Mt. Carmel in Plymouth, Conn., for several years. He was corresponding secretary of the Seamans' Friend society, New York, from 1856 to '59, and secretary and editor of the American Tract society of Boston from 1859 to '69.

He engaged in book publishing and book selling in Boston and New York from 1870 to 1875. After leaving there he was engaged as editor of The Christian Mirror at Lewiston for a year and a half, and then bought the paper and removed it to Portland, where he has been a conspicuous figure in the councils of his denomination.

He was a descendant of Richard W. Warren, one of the exiles in the Mayflower, and possessed much of the Pilgrim spirit. He was a prolific writer, not only in the public journals, but also as editor of the publications of the two associations of which he was secretary and editor. He published numerous sermons, commentaries on the gospels and the Acts, and several volumes. He received his doctorate from Iowa college in 1868.

The best known and most discussed of his literary performances was his volume entitled, "The Paronsia of Christ," in which he took ground diametrically opposite that of the pre-millenarians.

BY A NARROW MARGIN

A Serious Accident is Averted by an Engineer's Prompt Action.

SALEM, Mass., Oct. 10.—There was a very narrow escape from a serious railroad accident in the Salem yard yesterday. As the Portland Pullman No. 11 (due in Salem at 9:50) came around the curve at Castle hill at a good rate of speed, the engineer saw the Rockport freight standing on the track ahead.

Engineer Waterman at once reversed his engine and set the air brakes, but the rail was wet and the train could not be stopped until it struck the freight. The headwork of engine 494, on the Pullman, was considerably damaged, the tank was sprung, and the baggage car was considerably smashed. The caboose on the freight was smashed.

Three Never Returned.

WINNIPEG, Man., Oct. 10.—Dr. Gray of this city, who was a member of the parliamentary expedition around Lake Winnipeg, has returned, bringing news of the drowning of three of those who accompanied him, during a severe storm.

PROFESSIONAL CARDS.

Moynan & Co.

UNION AND PURCHASE STS.

IN DRESS GOODS DEPT.

Every day brings us something to show. Illuminated Diagonals, Serges and Fancy Weaves are having an immense sale.

Those new ones at $1.48 (5 yards to the dress) are beauties and will wear like iron.

IN BLACK DRESS GOODS.

Monday we will place on sale 5 pieces Extra Heavy India Twills, in Jet and Blue Blacks, 46 inches wide and good value to-day for 85c. Monday and Tuesday only the price will be **69c. per yard.**

OUR SILK DEPARTMENT

Is an attractive corner just now. Besides being stocked with all the latest novelties of trimmings and combinations, we are showing some great values in Black Failles, Rhadames, Satin Duchess and Armures. Notwithstanding the advance of 10 to 15 per cent. in Black Silks, our prices are lower than ever.

ABOUT CLOAKS.

We have just received and added to our immense stock of garments a line of MEDIUM WEIGHT NEW-MARKETS for ladies and misses, made from the latest effects in Nobby Scotch Mixtures. A few imported samples among them which will not be duplicated.

Prices range from $10 to $38

IN MISSES' JACKETS.

We are now showing our complete line, which are so entirely different in style from last season. They are particularly interesting. Sizes from 12 to 18.

Prices from $3.98 to $25

Children's Gretchens,

with and without capes, from 4 to 14 years.

INFANTS' EIDER DOWN COATS,

In white and fancy colors, trimmed with Angora and Thibet furs. Sizes 1 to 4 years.

Remember we are headquarters for Mackintoshes.

(Cloak Room second floor.)

MILLINERY.

Our New Millinery Department is now complete and open for business, with a full line of Fur Felt Hats and Bonnets in all the new shapes at popular prices.

Our assortment of two toned effects surpasses anything ever shown in Southern Massachusetts. Trimmings and trimming effects in velvets, ribbons, birds and feathers in endless variety.

In Children's Hats, Caps and Bonnets we are showing the most complete lines ever offered in this city.

A BIG BOOK BARGAIN.

Don't wait for holiday time to buy your books. We are offering for the next six days 1000 Books, all the standard authors, in cloth and gilt binding, at 15c. each. See them and be convinced that they are worth from 25 to 35c. each.

Also a lot of paper bound at 5c., worth 10c.

IN LINENS.

We call special attention to our line of Fine White Table Damask, 70 inches wide, in new patterns, at **$1.00 per yard**

An odd lot of the celebrated John S. Brown's Table Cloths, in 2 1-2 and 3 yards, at greatly reduced prices to close.

Moynan & Co.

The Evening Standard.

NEW BEDFORD, MASS.

MONDAY EVENING, OCT. 10.

THREE EDITIONS DAILY.

No. 87 Union Street.

PUBLISHED BY

E. ANTHONY & SONS.

INCORPORATED.

—TERMS—

Six Dollars a Year, Three Dollars for Six Months, in advance; Single Copies Two Cents

The Best Family Newspaper in Southern Massachusetts is the REPUBLICAN STANDARD. Our Weekly Edition—a large twelve-page paper of 84 columns, containing more reading matter than any other weekly paper in Southern Massachusetts. It is published Thursday mornings. Subscription price only $1.50 a year, in advance.

REPUBLICAN TICKET, 1892.

For President,
BENJAMIN HARRISON,
OF INDIANA.

For Vice-President,
WHITELAW REID,
OF NEW YORK.

For Presidential Electors-at-Large:
GENERAL N. P. BANKS, of Waltham.
HON. JOHN D. LONG, of Hingham.
For Presidential Elector, 13th District:
JOHN SIMPKINS, of Yarmouth.

STATE TICKET.

For Governor:
W. H. HAILE,
OF SPRINGFIELD.

For Lieutenant Governor:
ROGER WOLCOTT,
OF BOSTON.

For Secretary of State:
W. M. OLIN, of Boston.
For Auditor:
J. W. KIMBALL, of Fitchburg.
For Attorney-General:
A. E. PILLSBURY, of Boston.
For Treasurer:
GEORGE A. MARDEN, of Lowell.

For County Commissioner:
FRANKLIN GRAY, of Fall River.
For Special Commissioner:
HENRY A. SLOCUM, of Dartmouth.
For Register of Deeds:
EURRILL PORTER, JR., of Attleboro.
For Sheriff:
ANDREW R. WRIGHT, of Fall River.

For Senator, Third Bristol District:
WILLIAM M. BUTLER, of New Bedford.

For Representatives to the General Court, Fifth District:
SAMUEL ROSS, ISAAC B. TOMPKINS.
For Representatives to the General Court, Sixth Bristol District:
GEORGE M. EDDY, CHARLES P. RUGG.

For Councillor, First District:
ZIBA C. KEITH, of Brockton.

For Representative to Congress, 13th District:
CHARLES S. RANDALL, of New Bedford.

CONTENTS OF THIS EVENING'S STANDARD.

☞ The Boston Herald declines the challenge of the Advertiser to a joint political discussion, the articles of each paper to be printed in the other.

☞ After being rotten-egged out of Georgia and Virginia Gen. Weaver is going to try it once more in Pulaski, Tenn., where he was post commander during the war. The General's courage is greater than his discretion.

☞ The Democrats are exulting over the letters of Carl Schurz and Wayne McVeagh against the Republicans. But as neither of them has acted with the Republican party for years we do not see what there is to boast of in the matter.

☞ The remains of the building damaged by fire on Fish Island were sold by auction to-day. The city should now step in promptly and purchase enough of the land on which the building stands to secure a broad road over the island, whenever the bridge is widened, which has got to be done sooner or later. The land can be bought more cheaply now than at any future time.

☞ A Munich paper urges German-Americans to vote for Cleveland on account of the injury it says our tariff has done to German industries. We doubt if they will view it in that light. They left their native land because they found better conditions of existence here; freedom from military service and crushing taxes, ample employment, high wages and perfect civil liberty. As American citizens they want to promote the interests of their adopted country than those of any other. Germany has always acted so as to promote her own interests. Americans should do all they can to promote American interests.

The German Emperor wants still more army, to cost $25,000,000 the first year and $10,000,000 a year afterwards. This means more taxation and a larger immigration from Germany to this country. It may be for her interests from the dynastic point of view, but it will not promote the welfare of her people, and German-Americans will sympathize with the people rather than with the dynasty.

MR. ROUSMANIERE. Fellows, of the Acushnet Congregational church. Secretary and Treasurer—Rev. James Mitchell, of the First Presbyterian church.

The reports of the treasurer and secretary were presented and accepted. Rev. W. J. Reynolds of the First Christian church and Rev. William F. Potter of the Universalist church were presented to the Union and admitted to membership. The various committees for the ensuing year were elected. Rev. B. F. Simon of the Fourth Street M. E. church addressed the Union on "Is Christian Science Scientific?" and the usual discussion of the paper's merits followed.

THE COLORED PYTHIANS.

Programme for the Sixth Annual Session of the District Grand Lodge.

The sixth annual session of the District Grand Lodge of Massachusetts, Rhode Island and Connecticut, Knights of Pythias of the Eastern and Western Hemispheres, will meet with Friendship Lodge, No. 11, of this city Oct. 20th and 21st. The first day's exercises will consist of a business meeting in the local lodge's castle hall, Union street, at which all business pertaining to the Grand Lodge will be transacted. The second day will occur the big parade. Forming at 1 o'clock and headed by the Musical Exchange Band the following societies will participate:

First Division—Uniform Ranks.
E. N. Hallowell Division, Boston.
Garnet Division, Cambridge.
David Walker Division, Boston.
Excelsior Division, Worcester.
Phoenix Division, Hartford, Conn.
Second Division—Subordinate Lodges.
U. S. Grant Lodge, No. 1, Worcester.
W. C. Nell Lodge, No. 3, Boston.
David Walker Lodge, No. 8, Boston.
William Murray Lodge, No. 7, Chelsea.
H. E. Garnet Lodge, No. 4, Cambridge.
Etta Lodge, No. 5, Hartford, Conn.
Lewis Hayden Lodge, No. 19, Boston.
Friendship Lodge, No. 11, New Bedford.

At 8 o'clock in the evening the exercises of the session will conclude with a grand public installation and ball in Odd Fellows Hall. Addresses will be made by Sir Knight Hon. E. G. Walker of Boston, Sir Knight Rev. J. T. Hayslett of Cambridge, and Sir Knight Rev. J. Horatio Carter of Chelsea. But to follow the Germania Orchestra will furnish music.

The committee of arrangements consists of R. C. Monroe, George F. Morton, C. J. Guinn, Charles H. Onley, A. G. Guinn, William H. Irons, Charles H. Easton, E. Hilton and J. T. C. Reed.

At the last meeting of Friendship Lodge the following officers were installed:
Chancellor Commander — Emanuel Sullathou.
Vice-Chancellor Commander—T. J. Guinn.
Master of Exchequer—William B. Smith.
Master of Finance—William J. Reynolds.
Prelate—Edgar L. M. Jackson.
Keeper of Records and Seal—Walter D. Poll.
Master at Arms—John Reed.

EXPENDITURES.—In a statement to Capt. William B. Topham, City Auditor, for the following expenditures in the various departments of the city for the month of September and week ending Oct. 1:

Board of Health	$1,079.14
Cemeteries	392.42
Com. of Mass., chap. 279	308.00
" 298 of 1889	142.00
" 301	647.75
Engineering Department	775.92
Fire Department	2,486.33
Free Public Library	501.17
" —Trustees of	417.30
" —Dog Fund	44.79
Highways and streets	6,877.37
Incidentals	1,144.87
Lighting streets	2,798.49
N. B. & F. Bridge	165.16
N. B. School Committee	129.63
N. B. Water Works	16,380.31
Parks and Squares	1,129.59
Police Department	2,221.52
Poor Department	2,791.68
Printing, Binding, etc.	397.61
Public Debt	150.85
Public Schools—Incidentals	1,899.55
Public Schools—Pay of Teachers	2,412.34
Public Schools—Repairs of buildings	1,705.85
Public Works—Permanent Improvements	
Repairs of City Property	392.42
Salaries	522.84
Sewers—General account	1,155.33
" Beadle and Howard streets	1,268.70
" Belleville avenue, No. 2	134.41
" Coggeshall street, No. 2	717.70
" Grape street etc.,	5.50
" North Front street No. 2	292.16
" Peckham street	13.33
Cedar Grove Street School-house and lot,	.20
City Stable Tool House and Workshop	4,000.00
Engine House alterations, No. 5,	259.33
	381.50
Total,	$58,091.01

PUBLIC BEQUESTS.—The will of the late A. G. Tompkins, the well-known fur merchant of Boston, and of a Little Compton family, has been offered for probate. After making bequests to the members of his family, he establishes two trusts, the first being the sum of $100,000, the income of which is payable to his mother during her life, and at her decease to his brother during his life, and at the death of both, this $100,000 is given to the Boston Museum of Fine Arts, to be known as the Tompkins fund, the income to be used in defraying the expense of making as many free days of admission as possible. He also establishes another trust, comprising all the rest of his property and estate, the income of which is payable to his mother and brother, and at the death of both is to be divided as follows: To the Massachusetts General Hospital $25,000; the Young Men's Christian Union, the Home for Aged Men, the Home for Aged Women, the Home for Aged Couples and the Home for Little Wanderers each the sum of $5000. The Boston Museum of Fine Arts is made the residuary legatee, and after paying the foregoing legacies, the entire balance and residue of the estate is to be paid to the Museum of Fine Arts, the income of such bequest to be used in purchasing the modern class of oil paintings, to be known as the Tompkins collection.

CHANNING CONFERENCE.—The session of the Channing Conference is to be held with the Unitarian society of Fairhaven, on Tuesday and Wednesday, promises to be an interesting one. Tuesday evening, at 7.30 o'clock, Rev. Stopford W. Brooke, pastor of the First Unitarian society of Boston, will preach. He is the son of Rev. Stopford Brooke, the noted preacher of London, England, and is one of the ablest young men of the denomination. Rev. N. L. Rexford of the Universalist church of Roxbury, who will preach on Wednesday at 11 o'clock, represents the progressive element in his church, and probably has done more than any other man to keep his denomination abreast of the times. He is one of the leading spirits among the Liberals, and will be listened to with interest. In the afternoon Rev. A. M. Knapp of Fall River will speak on Japan and the work that is being done there. The conference will close Wednesday afternoon.

INCREASE IN POPULATION IN GOSNOLD.—Mrs. Tilton, a resident of Cuttyhunk, last week gave birth to triplets. The father is a Chilmark man and a brother to Capt. Tilton of the steam whaler Mary D. Hume. This is certainly a successful season for the Tilton fraternity.

BORDEN MURDER.

[Continued from Third Page.]

her motive, and my wife was left to interview the parties mentioned, no matter where she found them.

She made several trips, one of which was into New York State, with success. I began my work by investigating Mrs. Borden's life.

Marshal Hilliard had his whole force at work upon two theories.

One was, has Mrs. Borden an enemy in the world outside of her home who could possibly have committed the murder? The other was an equally difficult line of action, and pertained to the movements of those in the Borden house on the fatal day.

I concluded my part of the work without discovering that Mrs. Borden had an enemy outside of her own family, and I had a long interview with the medical examiner, the mayor and the marshal, and learned from the doctors the estimated difference of time in the deaths of the two people.

I then began a different line of investigation taking the statements of Bridget and the ones that Lizzie had made to the marshal, the deputy marshal and others; then the time, then the condition of the weather, and other similar important facts.

I then spent 20 minutes in the hayloft of the barn, then had a weight dropped inside of the house to ascertain if I could hear it, and began writing a letter so as not to appear as if watching for the sound. From my position I heard a 20-pound weight dropped in the room where Mrs. Borden was killed, I being in the same position that Lizzie described at the inquest, that she was in at the time of the murder of Mr. Borden.

This experiment was tried at 10 o'clock in the morning on a day that corresponded in temperature to Aug. 4. I then ascertained how near the door there was any lead such as could be used for sinkers, and learned from those who went into the barn first without stating to anyone what my position was, the position of things in general.

I found by measurement that exactly three feet and six inches from the door was a box consisting of 21 1-2 pounds of sheet lead, of which I have a sample.

One glance of the eye to a stranger would locate the box beyond question as she entered the barn, while its position to one acquainted with the premises could not for a moment be detected. I then searched the outside premises in the rear, taking into consideration that the pile of boards had been shifted. I caused the adjacent yards and lumber piles and mortar boxes and cesspools to be examined for a weapon.

Moreover, the street door had no stain of any kind upon it such as it ordinarily would have if pushed open by a red-handed assassin. I examined all the interior of the house with especial reference to possible exits, but found no trace of any one's departure nor any stains.

The second day of my wife's sojourn in Fall River, she learned the complete story that Mrs. Ronald has told, and I got her statement in person.

Then Officer Harrington and myself began to hunt for Mahany. We found him, and he identified Mrs. Ronald as the person he had met.

My wife met me a despatch about the statement of the Chace people, whom she found in New York State, and as a result the order for breaking open the safe was given. I kept out of Mr. Jennings' way as much as possible, knowing that certain parties were shadowing me all the time in the interest of the defence.

I then had to pay own satisfaction secured a motive, being all the time cognizant of what the marshal's forces were procuring, I saw that our lines of action were coinciding at every stage.

When I detailed my sister to substitute my wife and sent the latter to Marion to interview people there.

She secured a copy of a letter that is in the hands of the district attorney, which I did not see, and therefore cannot speak as to its contents. I then returned home, procured my man, and put them on the train of Mr. Hanscom and Mr. Jennings.

Later they were taken off and back to Providence, there they found a lawyer's clerk who told them a few weeks before that Lizzie had been to Providence and purchased, among other goods, a lamp and some crockery.

I learned subsequently where she made these purchases, but they did not cut any figure in the murder beyond tracing her movements around the city, and from what was said to me it will be necessary to make further investigations before I can tell where else she went and whom she saw during that visit in the city. I am not at liberty to state the name of the lawyer from whom most of my information on this end of the case came.

During the inquest I was familiar with everything that occurred in Mrs. Reagan's room between Lizzie and her sister.

In the rear of the matron's room was a bath-room, with a thin partition dividing it from the sergeant's sleeping room that opens out of the patrolmen's dormitory. For several days I or my representatives were concealed under the bed in Lizzie's room, listening to the conversation that occurred, but finally, owing to the presence of Mr. Adams, counsel for the defence, whom I found would discover the deception practiced, the city marshal had two men sleep in the partition between the bath-room and sergeant's room taken out, and a cloth covering substituted, in which there were small holes, allowing me to see and hear comfortably.

I was within 17 feet of Lizzie Borden when the trouble between her and her sister occurred. Lizzie Borden deliberately kicked her sister three times, threw a biscuit at her and called her a "d——b——." I have full and complete notes of that interview.

Lizzie charged her sister with giving her away. She accused her of wanting to see her hanged, and said it was because with her out of the way Emma would come into the entire fortune. She said she never would give in; that she would die first. And she said that Emma, her sister, had been the one person whom she thought she could trust with her secret.

She said that she never would forgive her in the world. I found that her she only did what she did to benefit Lizzie's case, and Mr. Jennings had learned the fact only in her interest.

Lizzie added that she would under no circumstances have told him anything. It seemed to me that she was almost insane in her manner at the time.

Besides Mrs. Reagan, who has made affidavit to the above facts, there is another beside myself who has likewise deposed.

MAHANY'S STORY.

Peter Mahany, time-keeper in the Troy mill, residing at 102 Pleasant street, Fall River, will testify:

On the morning of Aug. 4, 1892, I left my house at 25 minutes of 10 o'clock, as I had to call at J. H. Kelly's home on Second street, next door above the late Andrew J. Borden's residence. As I reached there I was attracted by the window and then disappeared from it. I asked the young woman with the baby if she had heard that terrible cry or groan, and she said yes, and added it had scared her terribly and sent a chill through her. She told me

that she had also seen the woman looking down at her.

Mrs. Chace's Evidence.

Mrs. Frederick Chace, wife of Frederick Chace, owner of the Chace mills at Fall River, and residing at 198 Fourth street in that city, will testify:

I have known Lizzie A. Borden and his wife for over 15 years. On the 3d day of August, 1892, early in the afternoon, I met Mr. Borden on Main street in Fall River, and talked to him a few minutes. He asked me to come over that night with my husband, and I promised him we would and I asked him how he and how Mrs. Borden were.

He said she was very well, but he was troubled a great deal about what he had talked of previously, and he thought if I and my husband came over it would cheer him up a good deal. I told him we would certainly come and then left him. About 7.30 o'clock that evening my husband, my daughter, Mrs. Manchester and myself arrived at the Borden house.

My daughter had come to our house for ten, her husband being away for a couple of days. It thus happened that she accompanied us to the Bordens'. She is very jolly, and Mr. Borden thought a good deal of her, and we thought she would tend to cheer the old folks up, which was another incentive for us to take her along.

We were accustomed to enter the Borden house by the back door, as we were well aware, and had been for a long time, of the condition of affairs in the family. As we went to the door Maggie or Bridget, as she is properly called, was on the piazza way, and must have been coming down and stopped there, as we thought.

First we shook the screen door, and Bridget then came down toward us.

After we started up the stairs, intending to go to the sitting-room, we heard loud and angry voices in the dining-room, and above all heard Mr. Borden's voice. I was satisfied at once that the servant girl had been on the stairs listening to the quarrel.

The first words I heard were: "You can make your own choice and do it to-night. Either let us know what his name is or take the door on Saturday, and when you go fishing dish for some other place to live, as I will never listen to you again. I will know the name of the man who got you into trouble."

We felt awfully embarrassed, and turned around to each other, and I said to my daughter "Fay," as I always called her, "do go and get Bridget and send her ahead of us, as it would be awful to walk right in upon them."

This I said in a whisper. Just then I heard Lizzie answer: "If I marry this man, will you be satisfied that everything will be kept from the outside world?" Then Bridget came to us, and word was sent in to Mrs. Borden.

I said to my husband, referring to Lizzie: "That girl will be the means of great trouble if she is not wise to-night."

Mr. and Mrs. Borden received us in the dining-room, whither we repaired, and were received pleasantly.

Lizzie turned around and went off without recognizing us, to the front of the house. She was dressed in her street apparel, and we did not know whether she had just come in or not. The old folks later said that she was going out.

Pretty soon Mrs. Borden said to her husband: "You must not get so angry with Lizzie, as she has a terrible temper, and there is no telling what she might do to herself."

Mr. Borden said "I would rather see her dead than have this come out." I then spoke up and said "Now Mrs. Borden be right. You ought not to get so angry with her. Be gentle, and try to find out who this man is, and if he is made of anything at all he will marry her, and everything will be nicely settled." Mr. Borden said "No, I have my suspicions and have had all along, but if I am right I will never recognize this man in the world. She made her own bed, so let her lie upon it." Mr. Borden added, "To think at my time of life that such a terrible scandal is about to overtake me is terrible. You cannot advise or do anything with Lizzie; she will have her own way, come what may of it. By the way John Morse is visiting us. He may be here any minute. Now we know, Mr. Chace, that you never could bear him, as you say. But when he does come in don't let on a word to him about what has occurred to-night, as we don't want him to know that we have discovered anything as yet."

We then turned on to other matters, and did not refer to Lizzie's trouble again except saying we were sorry that things were so and hoped they would turn all right again. At 9.10 we left for home, bidding Mr. and Mrs. Borden good night.

Mr. Chace Corroborates.

Mr. Frederick Chace of 198 Fourth street, Fall River, will testify: I have known Andrew J. Borden and wife over 16 years and have visited him at his home, and he has visited me at mine. We were very close friends, and he has told me a great deal about his family troubles.

I knew his wife to be a most self-sacrificing woman. She has been insulted grossly in my presence by both of his daughters, and on one occasion Lizzie said to her, before me, that she wished her to make less noise in the room we were occupying, as she, Lizzie, was busy with a scholar and our conversation annoyed her. I asked Mrs. Borden if she were taken that way often, and the latter said, "Oh, she has spells when she is very nice."

One time later on she said that Lizzie had never addressed her by any title for over four years. I then said to my son-in-law, Mr. Manchester, just what I heard about her and the way I knew she treated her stepmother.

He said something derogatory of Lizzie afterwards, and she learned of it, and then we fell from grace so far as that end of the family was concerned.

Andrew has repeatedly told me about expecting trouble from her, and said he did not know how to avoid it. Then he said there had been a robbery at his house in 1891, and that nothing had been done since, as he did not wish to make any noise in the room over his stepmother, and that he had heard it said that way sister, Mrs. G. J. Sisson, had said that she had been robbed at Lizzie's possession after it had been stolen, and that she recognized it. "Now, Fred," said Mr. Borden, "find out the truth of this from your sister and let me know if it is true. I believe it is, but I want to be sure." I then told him that my sister had told me no some time before and that I believed her.

He said, "Well, I can account now for a great many things," and he called Lizzie to the door and said in my presence, "I want you to get Mrs. Borden's watch and other articles and have them returned at once; that is all I have to say." Lizzie gave me a look that I will always remember.

This was in February, 1892, about Washington's birthday week. I also corroborate, in detail, the statement of the quarrel at the Borden house the night prior to the murder as made by my wife in her statement for the authorities and confirmed by my daughter.

NEITHER AFFIRM NOR DENY.

District Attorney Thinks He Knows Where the Story Came From.

District Attorney Knowlton was seen this forenoon and asked concerning the developments in the Borden case published in another column. He said he had not read the story, but thought he knew from what source it came, but would not tell at the present time. He was asked in the light of the published story if he would not make a statement concerning certain phases of the case, and declined firmly but courteously to say anything for publication.

State Policeman George F. Seaver was asked concerning the published story. He said he knows nothing concerning its origin or truth.

ROCHESTER.

Mr. Rachel Lucas of Freetown was the clammonster cranberry picker at Mr. Chas. Freeman's bog, picking 11 and 4887 quarts, the largest of any one individual. The next in number was Mrs. Amie Reynolds of Freetown, with 3 and 2490 quarts. Miss Annie Antone is the family of whaler David Devoralmits, comprising four members, picking the combined figures of 10,076 quarts, and she said yes, and added it had scared her terribly and sent a chill through her. She told me

---

THIRD DISTRICT COURT.

BORDEN, J.
Monday, Oct. 10.

Daniel Sherman pleaded guilty of continuing his wagon in and upon Purchase street so as to obstruct the same, last Saturday afternoon, after having been ordered by one of the police force to move the same. Sherman was peddling grapes on William street and was ordered by Mayor Ashley to move along and not obstruct the street. He claimed he had a license and was allowed five minutes to stand in any one place. This the Mayor told him he had no right to do if he obstructed the street and farther that he had no license to peddle. After some further conversation Sherman said the man he worked for had a license and sent a man to get it. His Honor then instructed Officer Sisson to arrest Sherman if he continued to block up the street. Sherman by this time had moved along from William street into Purchase street and about 1 o'clock the man came along, whom Sherman said was the man to get his license and each pleaded guilty this morning. Ninety days each in the House of Correction was their sentence. Both appealed. Isabella secured bonds, and Susan went up to await trial in November next.

Susan A. Ward and Julia Foy got drunk last Saturday and were arrested by Messrs. Arnett and Moynan. They pleaded guilty, and one blamed the other for being before the court. A war of words passed between them in court, and it became necessary to take Susan below to keep her quiet. Susan was sentenced to four months and Julia to 60 days in the House of Correction. Susan appealed but failed to get bonds.

Henry J. Myers went to a clamsbake yesterday where they had no water, but had a barrel of beer. He was very thirsty after eating the clams and drank a large quantity of beer, so that when he got back from the bake to the Howland Village he was so drunk he was cared for by Special Officer Buckley. He pleaded guilty and was sent up for ten days.

In the civil suit of Josiah Benoit vs. George T. Squires, an action of contract tried two weeks ago, judgment was entered for the plaintiff for $24.10 and costs. Hon. E. L. Barney and G. T. St. Germain, Esq., for plaintiff; A. E. Perry, Esq., and H. A. Hervey, Esq., for defendant.

A STRANGE CASE.—Mrs. Minnie Quinn, nee Goyn, of Lowell, was put on an afternoon train Saturday in Lowell by her husband, and sent to Fall River to her mother, Mrs. Sarah Goyn, who lives at 124 Cedarwood street. By the help of two women, Mrs. Quinn got up town, and at 10 o'clock day found her moaning in the gutter on Sixth street, at the station house it was found that the woman's right side was paralyzed and she was unable to speak. Finally, by means of signs, she said she was assaulted by a man, who struck her in the face. The woman's mother was seen for. She said she had received no word of her daughter's coming, and could not understand the proceedings. Mayor Coughlin ordered Mrs. Quinn taken to the City Hospital, her mother being unable to care for her.

TWO BOARDS—THREE MEETINGS.

Mr. Tripp is Careful How He Goes Into History.

Ashland, Weaver, Field, John and Scott Streets Accepted.

More Plans Indorsed for Beautifying the Clarks Point Park.

The regular meeting of the Board of Public Works was held last evening with Mr. Kirschbaum the only absentee, and Mayor Ashley presiding.

Supt. A. B. Drake was chosen clerk pro tem, and read the records of several meetings.

When reading the records of the meeting at which Mr. F. A. Sowle criticised the Board's action and thereby so incensed Mr. Tripp that he left the room in a huff, the record was found to embrace that incident. Mr. Tripp objected to the act going on record, and at his request that portion of the record was stricken out. As thus amended, the records were approved.

John Mercer appeared in relation to the curbing of Bowditch street in front of his property corner of Cedar Grove street having petitioned for the same some time ago. His petition not having yet been acted on Mr. Mercer retired no wiser than when he came.

Pay roll No. 40 for the week ending Oct. 1st, was read and approved as follows:

Street department,	$2515.33
Grape street sewer extension,	682.99
Belleville avenue sewer,	262.29
General sewers,	105.50
Public Works—Permanent improvement,	83.21
Engineering Department,	50.23
New Bedford & Fairhaven bridge,	21.61
Parks and squares,	19.83
	$3740.99

Ellen O'Neil by Thomas F. O'Neil was granted permission to move a wooden shop, 22 by 12 feet in size, from 622 Purchase street, to 650 County street, the moving to be on wheels.

Cook & Smith's request for permission to erect a fence around their building corner of Acushnet avenue and Cedar Grove street, enclosing the whole side walk on Acushnet avenue and half of Cedar Grove street, until such time as the building shall be completed, was granted on condition that 12 feet only be used on Cedar Grove street, and that petitioners build a wooden walk four feet wide on the west side of Acushnet avenue.

Gladu & Tetault were granted permission to maintain a swinging sign over the sidewalk at 891 South Water street.

Hitching post permits were granted to Albert A. Chace for the north side of Butler street, west of East French avenue, and to Theodore F. Tillinghast at 37 Eighth street.

Borden & Crapo were granted leave to move a wooden dwelling, 24 by 26 feet, 13½ feet posts, from the north side of Allen street near Dartmouth street, to the south side of Allen street west of Borden street, subject to the usual conditions.

James H. Sherman's request for permission to cut down two trees on the northwest corner of Grinnell street and Acushnet avenue, was granted.

A petition of Calvin J. Slocum and 19 others that Francis street, contemplated from Court to Kempton streets, be laid out and accepted 40 feet wide, was placed on the visiting list.

A petition of Frederick Hazard and nine others, that North Front street be accepted and graded from Holly to Brown street, the petitioners stating that they contemplate the erection of $10,000 worth of property, was set down to be visited.

A petition of William Ingraham and four others, abutters on Holly street, asking that that street be accepted and that a sewer be laid in it from Acushnet avenue to Rock street, was also relegated to that little calling list.

A petition was received from Charles A. Sisson, asking that the side track of the Old Colony Railroad Co., now terminating at the north side of Bridge street, be extended across said street into his property.

Supt. Drake stated that Mr. Sisson has tried to get the railroad company to build the road and the corporation does not want to. It is willing to enter the premises from the south but Mr. Sisson doesn't like that plan. Agent Fisher had entered a remonstrance against granting the permission.

The Board decided that it would not be wise to grant the permit, and accordingly the petitioner was allowed to withdraw.

Corner curbing was ordered laid on the southeast and northwest corners of Cedar Grove and Bowditch streets agreeable to Mr. Mercer's petition.

It was voted to lay the Myrtle street sewer from a point in Myrtle street, half way between Linden and Weld streets to Weld street, and from another point in Myrtle street half way between Weld and Clark street to Clark street and up Clark street to Reynolds street.

Scott street was accepted 50 feet wide from County to Crapo streets.

The matter of laying out Bowditch and Church streets from the Nash road to Tarkiln Hill road came up, and hearings were ordered for Oct. 24th at 3 30 at Church street and Nash road, 3 45 at Nash road and Bowditch street, 4 15 at Tarkiln Hill and Bowditch street, and at 4 30 at Tarkiln Hill and Church street.

Ashland street, between Durfee and Clark streets, was accepted 40 feet wide.

The superintendent was authorized to purchase two more steam drills.

The Board of Public Works adjourned, and again convened as Park Commissioners.

Mayor Ashley read a communication from Acting Secretary Grant of the War Department urging the Board to outline its plans for remodelling the fort property on Clarks Point into a park. He read the following, which in answer he had signed and transmitted:

OFFICE OF THE BOARD OF PUBLIC WORKS,
NEW BEDFORD, Mass., Oct. 10, 1892.

Hon. L. A. Grant, Acting Secretary of War:

Sir,—I beg leave to acknowledge the receipt of your letter of Oct. 5th, relating to improvement upon government land at Clarks Point, and will now endeavor to give you as fully as possible the extent and plans of the work that we propose to do, with your approval, on said property.

Referring to the map submitted with this letter, we intend to lay out an avenue 100 feet wide on the extreme northern boundary of the property, running from the east to the west side of French avenue, to be used as a driveway. To remove all the old, tumble down walls upon the property, using the stone from the same in building up in a proper manner the walls on the east and west sides of the property; to clear out all the underbrush in the two groups of forest trees; to grade off all natural mounds and irregularities; to grade the rough ditch around the fort made at the time for excavating for its foundation, and to lay a pipe to carry off accumulating water; to tear down and destroy all the old barracks and buildings and storehouses, which were of a cheap character and erected during the war or prior to it and which have now gone to decay and are worthless; to continue French avenue, so called, around the fort on original foundation laid down for the road before work upon the fort was commenced, and when finished to close up the avenue west of the fort, as shown on the map; to collect the granite blocks scattered all over the property and place them in a continuous line along the sea line of the proposed extension of French avenue around the fort without in any way changing the form of or damaging the shape of said granite blocks, and placing them where the government can at any time remove them at less expense than can now be done.

This is all we propose to do on the property, excepting in the direction of beautifying it as a park by setting out trees and shrubbery under the direction of a landscape gardener, and everything done by the Board will be an improvement to the property.

Very respectfully yours.
CHARLES S. ASHLEY,
Chairman Board of Public Works.

The action of the Mayor in signing the plan was approved.

The Park Commissioners then adjourned and the Board of Public Works again came to order.

Weaver street from Dartmouth to Field streets and Field street from Stowell street to the cemetery wall were accepted, and damages were awarded to Mrs. Sophia Weaver of $30 a rod on a lot half way from Babbitt to Weaver street, and of $25 a rod north of Weaver street.

John street was accepted as Field street from Allen street to the cemetery wall.

The board then fell to considering filling in the cemetery pond and making it a grassy mound, with Field street passing around it in two driveways. No action was taken.

Adjourned.

TOWN MEETING.

MATTAPOISETT.

A special town meeting was held in Mattapoisett last evening to see what the town would do toward protecting its scallop fishermen from prosecution by the authorities of Marion. The two towns were originally a part of Rochester and the Mattapoisett fishermen claim the right to fish for scallops in any part of the original town. Town Clerk William B. Nelson read the call for the meeting, and Joseph L. Meiggs was chosen moderator. About 100 citizens were present. It was voted that the selectmen of Mattapoisett be authorized to grant licenses to any of its citizens to take scallops in any of the waters of the old town of Rochester and that the first one arrested and sued at law for taking scallops while having such permits be defended by the town of Mattapoisett.

LONG PLAIN.

Mrs. George James is to make alterations in her home and otherwise improve it by addition of new windows.

Mrs. Nancy Bennett, who has been in North Dartmouth the past three weeks amongst friends, has returned home improved in health.

The bog school-house district has received the balance required for its flag, through the kind efforts of Mr. George W. Bennett, who has been soliciting aid from his New Bedford friends. Mrs. Sarah Braley, the teacher, will purchase the flag this week.

THE BORDEN STORY.

Detective McHenry Sold it to a Reporter.

It is Proved to be a Lie in Several Particulars.

Branded as a Gigantic Fake by Reputable Persons.

How it is Looked Upon by the Citizens of Fall River.

Latest Developments Following the Publication of the Yarn.

BOSTON, Oct. 11.—The *Globe* to-day says that Detective E. G. McHenry furnished it with the Borden story published yesterday morning. He asserts that the the facts are true. He states that the names and residences of alleged witnesses were purposely given wrong for obvious reasons. The *Globe*, in the course of its investigation into the details of the story, interviewed Dr. and Mrs. Bowen and Rev. Mr. Buck on the question of Lizzie Borden's physical condition at the time of the murder, the result of which was the conviction that in this respect at least Mr. McHenry was wrong. The story may be wrong in some other minor particulars, but the weight of evidence favors the main facts as true.

TRICKEY'S STATEMENT.

The Boston Reporter Tells How He Purchased the Story.

The Boston *Globe* prints the following story of Henry G. Trickey this morning:

About 10 days ago the writer visited Providence for the purpose of learning if possible, through the assistance of Mr. Isaac Kirby, the Boston *Globe's* representative in this city, the correctness of the report in circulation that a providence lawyer had been approached by Miss Lizzie Borden some time previous to the murder of her father and stepmother, and consulted on property rights. The mission was not successful, as Mr. Kirby was not to be found. On leaving the office the writer was approached by Detective E. D. McHenry, who said: "Well, Trickey, I'm glad to see you. We haven't met since the Borden case was on and I then had no opportunity to offer my thanks for the good notice you gave me in the *Globe* at the time of the trouble between Lizzie and her sister. The *Globe* was the only paper that did use me decent at Fall River, despite the fact that I did a good deal of work there."

Mr. McHenry remarked that he was not prospering as well as he had wished since the preliminary examination closed, as he had only received one check from the city of Fall River for services and expenses, while another amounting to between $300 and $400 was unpaid. In consequence he was very short.

He made some reference to the great strength of the government's case and added that it would be great stuff for a newspaper if a journal like the *Globe* could only get it. The writer stated in reply that the *Globe* was anxious to get news and was ever ready to pay value received for information.

Mr. McHenry said it would be worth quite a lot of money if the *Globe* could exclusively print the government's case. The writer asked him if such a thing were possible? Mr. McHenry replied that it might be, under proper conditions. He then stated that he was in a position to secure the desired matter, and that as he had a family to support and had become financially involved, he thought he would be willing to do business if it were made an object for him to tell all he knew. The writer asked him how much money he thought the information he had in his possession was worth.

Mr. McHenry replied that it depended on who wanted it. The writer asked Mr. McHenry if his story could not be bought for less than $1000. Mr. McHenry said no, that he would not accept less money.

This conversation took place in the corridor, just outside the court-room.

Determining to get the information which Mr. McHenry had to sell into his possession, the writer upon his next search for Mr. McHenry met Mr. Kirby in Turk's Head square, took him into his confidence and related briefly his purpose in coming to Providence. In the afternoon Mr. Kirby accompanied the writer to Mr. McHenry's office, and there learned from the boy in charge that Mr. McHenry was in Fall River and that he would not be back until late that night.

The next day another visit was paid to Mr. McHenry and this also was in the forenoon. Mr. Kirby, whom the writer again met, accompanied him to Mr. McHenry's office and this time he was told that Mr. McHenry had been out all night on a case and had not arisen. The attendant said he would probably be up about 1 p. m. Owing to the breaking of the previous engagement, the writer sent up word that he wanted to see him then or not at all, and upon his return at the time stated he saw Mr. McHenry in bed.

The latter explained that he had been away on business at Attleboro, and when the matter in issue was referred to he became much interested. Mr. McHenry suggested if it were possible he ought to have some financial guarantee that he would not be "thrown down," as he expressed it. Mr. McHenry said he would be willing to do business if he were advanced a small sum as a guarantee. He was given $30 as a starter. He then called his man "Jim," and told him to go down stairs to his private office and get some papers that he would find on top of the contents of the drawer, which was to be unlocked with the bent key. The man presently returned with the papers. They were written in a close hand on foolscap pages, and there were five or seven sheets among them. Mr. McHenry read therefrom, withholding the name of the witnesses, but read what purported to be their testimony.

His reading continued until he had covered what appeared in the first seven affidavits designated in the *Globe's* publication of Monday. He said he would call that the initial instalment.

The writer then told him it was worth a $100 guarantee if the things were true and he agreed therewith to go to Boston and procure more funds and return that night so that McHenry could have his $100 before he continued. Then the *Globe* man went to Boston and procured funds, returned to Fall River and at the outset paid Mr. McHenry $50 more on account, making $80 in all advanced. This warmed him up and he related many other facts in the case during the evening. Before leaving him at the door of his house he was handed the remaining $20, and therewith all suspicion vanished from the writer's mind that he was being in any wise victimized, for Mr. McHenry's expressions of thanks were profuse.

An engagement was then made to meet again on the following Sunday night at Mr. McHenry's office. The writer was then to receive from the detective the written statements of all the "witnesses," whom Mr. McHenry said at first were 19 in number and afterwards 25. It was about 3 15 o'clock in the afternoon when the writer left Mr. McHenry's house to go to the depot to catch the train for Boston for the purpose of getting the money referred to above. On the way to the station he met Mr. Kirby, to whom he narrated in a general way the story of the McHenry interview. Mr. Kirby also went to the train, saw him on board, and promised to meet him upon his return on the Shore line express, but did not, owing to an unexpected engagement. The writer after completing the evening interview above stated, went to Boston and did not return to Providence until Sunday evening. Mrs. McHenry said her husband had waited until after 8 o'clock, and had then gone out and would not be in until late. The *Globe* man sat talking with her for fully half an hour. Mrs. McHenry seemed to suspect that the *Globe* man was acting a part, and she asked more questions than she volunteered information. The writer called at Mr. McHenry's office the next morning. He was told that Mr. McHenry was away and likewise that his wife was out. Through the day the *Globe* man waited patiently and towards night was told by the man in attendance that Mr. McHenry had telephoned that he would be home that evening. He did arrive that night and the writer saw him. Mr. McHenry came in with a bag in his hand between 8 and 9 o'clock, and said he had been to Pawtucket or Attleboro. He said it was a work of recovering some stolen property and had kept him longer than he had expected it would. He said he was all ready to complete the work that night, however, and if the writer called early in the morning he would be given the statements. The writer said he would call at 4 a. m., as he much desired to go to Boston on the Stonington line express that leaves Providence at 4 35 o'clock. This was agreed to, and then the *Globe* man left, went to the Narragansett Hotel, left a call for 3 15 a. m. and went to bed. Before retiring, however, the writer telephoned to the *Globe* that the matter was to be in his possession at 4 o'clock, and made arrangements for taking an immediate transcription of the manuscript on reaching Boston.

This was done for the reason that the writer was to see Mr. Adams again to ascertain if in the interim since last seeing him anything had happened to make negotiations again possible on a basis that would meet the expense necessary to be incurred in getting the story.

Mr. Adams was sick in bed and was unable to talk business. He said the defence was not prepared to proceed with the matter on any basis, and therefore nothing could be done.

The writer had previously dictated a transcription of the matter, and had the original and a copy with slight variations that had been suggested by Mr. McHenry with him at the time. Mr. McHenry's proposition was then discussed, and the writer then telephoned him to the Park Hotel, Attleboro, where he said he would be in the afternoon, that the *Globe* man would meet him and transact the remaining business there.

The writer left Boston at 3 o'clock, and on reaching Attleboro, met Mr. McHenry in front of the hotel.

He said he had been there doing business with the deputy sheriff. The writer then walked with him up a side street and told him that the *Globe* would pay him $500. He would not lose anything from his later proposition.

The deal was then consummated in this way: The writer gave McHenry $300 cash, making all that he had received up to that time the sum of $400. The remaining $100 the writer told him he thought he ought to withhold until after the publication of the story. To this Mr. McHenry was perfectly agreeable, but requested explicitly that he be given 24 hours' notice of the publication. This was promised and then Mr. McHenry said how he had captured the entire mass of testimony. He said he was an old-time friend of Mr. Hilliard, and that eight of the affidavits in question were taken and sworn in his office. He said Mr. Hilliard had given him all of the typewriting of the entire lot of affidavits to do, so that the thing would not leak out. He said that what appeared in the written statements he had furnished the *Globe* was contained in substance in the original papers, a copy of which he had kept. Mr. McHenry then left, saying he had got to see the deputy sheriff again and that he was afterwards going to Fall River. The writer agreed to see him on Sunday morning early, when Mr. McHenry promised to get two or three other affidavits, among which was one from a "new witness Mr. Harrington had discovered," and also Mrs. Reagan's second statement and what Officer Hathaway of New Bedford knew. Mr. McHenry cautioned the writer about bringing his name too conspicuously to the front, as it might make the marshal suspect him as the author. The matter printed in the *Globe*, Monday, was all forthcoming from Mr. McHenry. He bestowed liberal praise on all members of the department of Fall River, and told which witnesses were secured by himself and wife. The original matter secured from Mr. McHenry was inclosed in a large envelope bearing the official stamp of the sheriff's office, Providence. The contents were placed in the *Globe's* safe, where they are now. As the writer remembers, there were some other meetings and additional conversations.

THE STORY FALLS FLAT.

Since It Has Been Digested People Pronounce It a Fake.

FALL RIVER, Oct. 11.—The defence is perfectly calm in the face of the startling story, published in a Boston paper yesterday, in relation to the Borden murder mystery; calm with regard to its bearing upon the guilt of their client, but very indignant when discussing the motive for its publication, and searching for grains of truth through its fourteen columns of alleged affidavits.

Early yesterday the story with its terrible array of minute details carried conviction with it. Last night, after a full day's winnowing of those affidavits, it is looked upon as the most remarkable fabrication that was ever built for a newspaper.

There is only one theory under which it may yet appeal for credence, and that is that the very details which gave it weight, the names and residences of the witnesses, are all fictitious, all save Mr. and Mrs. McHenry.

It is well authenticated that the story was given out by Detective McHenry. There are those who say, and are also ready to make affidavits, that this story was offered to the Boston *Herald* some weeks ago for the sum of just $150 by McHenry, and the offer was not accepted. It was again offered to the Fall River *Globe*, but the price was too high. It remains to be seen whether the price finally paid for it was altogether too high, low as that price may have been.

The argument offered everywhere against it being a fake out of the whole cloth is that it is beyond credence that such a story could be coined, and especially that it could be given publicity by a newspaper of to-day unless it was at least based on truth. Certain it is, however, that no one of the really important witnesses can be found, and the others deny or refuse to confirm it. Many whose residences were given here can be found to have no existence in Fall River.

More than that, of the facts and circumstances cited nearly all can be clearly shown to be false. I have gone over the ground carefully, so far as possible within the time, and find it so.

In the first place, Emma Borden, with whom I had a long talk last night, says she does not know any such people as the Chaces who were such close friends of the family that they were admitted by the back door, and standing on the stairs overheard old man Borden charge his daughter with her shame and the daughter's reply. She does not know such a person as George Sisson, who was so close a friend that he attended the funeral and overheard Lizzie Borden ask Bridget why she did not name her price for silence.

Furthermore she says Lizzie is not sick, is not in a condition to have brought shame upon herself and her parents. The proofs of this she says were found in the cellar by the officers themselves during their search, and she has further proofs secured since Lizzie has been confined in the Taunton jail.

Dr. Bowen, the family physician, who was a witness for the defence, and Dr. Dolan, the medical examiner, who was a witness for the prosecution, both corroborated this statement, that Lizzie Borden is not in the delicate health that it is alleged offered the motive for the terrible crime. This would seem to answer the very core of the whole matter.

Fictitious names and residences, say

The Evening Standard.

NEW BEDFORD. MASS.

WEDNESDAY EVENING. OCT. 12.

THREE EDITIONS DAILY.

No. 87 Union Street.

PUBLISHED BY

E. ANTHONY & SONS,

INCORPORATED.

—TERMS—

Six Dollars a Year; Three Dollars for Six Months, in advance: Single Copies Two Cents

TEN PAGES.

This Evening's Issue Consists of Ten Pages, and Every Patron is Entitled to that Number.

REPUBLICAN TICKET, 1892.

For President,
BENJAMIN HARRISON,
OF INDIANA.

For Vice-President,
WHITELAW REID,
OF NEW YORK.

For Presidential Electors-at-Large:
GENERAL N. P. BANKS, of Waltham.
HON. JOHN D. LONG, of Hingham.
For Presidential Elector, 13th District:
JOHN SIMPKINS, of Yarmouth.

STATE TICKET.

For Governor:
W. H. HAILE,
Of Springfield.

For Lieutenant Governor:
ROGER WOLCOTT,
Of Boston.

For Secretary of State:
WM. M. OLIN, of Boston.
For Auditor:
J. W. KIMBALL, of Fitchburg.
For Attorney-General:
A. E. PILLSBURY, of Boston.
For Treasurer:
GEORGE A. MARDEN, of Lowell.
For County Commissioner:
FRANKLIN GRAY, of Fall River.
For Special Commissioners:
HENRY A. SLOCUM, of Dartmouth.
BURRILL PORTER, Jr., of Attleboro.
For Sheriff:
ANDREW R. WRIGHT, of Fall River.
For Senator, Third Bristol District:
WILLIAM M. BUTLER, of New Bedford.
For Representatives to the General Court,
Fifth Bristol District:
SAMUEL ROSS, ISAAC B. TOMPKINS.
For Representatives to the General Court,
Sixth Bristol District:
GEORGE M. EDDY. CHARLES P. RUGG.

For Councillor, First District:
ZIBA C. KEITH, of Brockton.

For District Attorney Southern District:
HOSEA M. KNOWLTON of New Bedford.

For Representative to Congress, 13th District:
CHARLES S. RANDALL, of New Bedford.

☞ The Fall River Herald finds relief occasionally from publishing matter about the Borden case in trying to be funny about citizens of New Bedford. We recently quoted an instance which the victim probably looked on as a silly attempt at wit, as indeed it was. And now Mr. Pease, the Democratic candidate for Senator, takes his turn. The Herald cannot tolerate bangs among women, and its opinion of men who ape the fashion is not very favorable. It thinks Mr. Pease's portrait represents a very handsome man, but is of the opinion that the minute adornment detracts from the air of masculinity which the contour reveals; it gives him credit for being ordinarily sensible, and it tries to persuade itself that the sanguine views about the prospects of Mr. Pease's party in his speech accepting the nomination have some foundation, in which it is wrong. We are glad to see that the Herald recognizes the fact that Senator Butler is an able man, and it gives the Fall River Democrats good counsel in advising them to copy our example of selecting candidates who possess capacity and not check alone. But it won't do for them to have their hair banged if they want its favor.

☞ The number of cotton manufacturing establishments in this country increased from 756 in 1880 to 904 in 1890; of spindles from 10,653,435 to 14,088,103; and of cotton used from 750,348,918 pounds to 1,117,445,776. Massachusetts and Rhode Island have 56 per cent. of all the spindles of the country. The great bulk of the cotton manufactures of the United States consists of sheeting and shirtings, and prints cloths. Of the total number of square yards of cotton goods made in 1890 over 60 per cent. consisted of these fabrics. The manufacture of sewing-cotton thread has made very important progress since 1880, till now substantially the whole supply is the product of American mills.

☞ The Attorney-General argued the case in favor of the appeal from the decision of the Supreme Court of Michigan, affirming the constitutionality of the law providing for the choice of presidential electors by districts, before the Supreme Court in Washington yesterday. He admitted that his own party had robbed the people by unjust apportionments, as well as the Democratic, but declared that it is high time that the courts should, once for all, say to these wordlists: "It is just as much larceny to steal a political right as it is to steal private property."

CONTENTS OF THIS EVENING'S STANDARD.

THE REPUBLICAN STANDARD,

☞ Issued this evening, contains all the local and general news of the past week, including particulars of the dedication of the Veteran Firemen's Headquarters, an entertainment complimentary to the lady friends of the members; Democratic senatorial and Councillor Conventions, Z. W. Pease of this city nominated for senator and D. D. Sullivan of Fall River for councillor; caucuses and convention of the Fifth Republican Representative District, which resulted in the nomination of Samuel Ross and Isaac B. Tompkins; Sixth Representative District Republican caucuses and convention, Charles P. Rugg and George M. Eddy the candidates; convention to nominate a candidate for District Attorney, Hon. Hosea M. Knowlton renominated; 4th Bristol Representative District nominates Moses S. Douglass of Acushnet; meetings of the Board of Public Works, and Park Commissioners, plans indorsed for beautifying the Clarks Point Park, several streets accepted and other business transacted; annual meeting of the New Bedford Pastoral Union; Detective McHenry of Providence gives in the Boston Globe the motive for the Borden murder to the public, startling testimony from 10 new witnesses, Lizzie Borden said to have been seen at the window of the room where her stepmother was killed, Lizzie's secret discovered by her father, the quarrel of the sisters' in police station detailed, the whole thing denounced as a tissue of lies by Counsel Jennings, and it is generally discredited in Fall River by the newspapers, and by the public, the Globe retracts and makes an apology for the statements against Lizzie Borden; welcome to Father Clark from his four months visit abroad; annual meetings of the Woman's Exchange, Ladies' Auxiliary of the Y. M. C. A. and of the Y. M. C. A., with interesting reports, election of trustees, etc.; meeting of the Water Board, routine business transacted; description of Savory C. Hathaway's new house on Hawthorn street; meeting of Board of Aldermen, list of precinct officers nominated and approved and polling places established; the return of steamer Mary D. Hume to San Francisco, story of her long stay in the Arctic Ocean as related by Capt. Tilton; 54th session of the Channing Conference of Unitarian Churches in Fairhaven; Brockton Cattle Show, great crowd and excellent exhibit of stock; unveiling of Union Neighborhood Convention at Marion; George H. St. Germain adjudged guilty of extortion and bound over to the Superior Court; Farm, Garden and Home; Bible Lesson for next Sunday; superior, Probate and District Court reports; correspondence; with editorials, ship news, markets, miscellaneous reading matter, etc.

For sale by all newsdealers in this city, and at our counters, in wrappers ready for mailing, at 4 cents per copy.

HOME MATTERS.

DID NOT INSPECT.—As there was no quorum of the city council committee on street lights last evening the proposed inspection was given up.

RELIGIOUS.—Elder John G. Hook, the noted Advent preacher of Concord, N. H., will preach in the Advent chapel at Fairhaven, Thursday evening, at 7 30. All are invited.

NATURALIZATION.—John Flood was admitted to citizenship in the Third District Court this morning. M. R. Hitch, Esq. for petitioner. Charles Zaloudek filed a primary declaration. B. B. Barney, Esq., for petitioner. Patrick McLaughlin filed a primary declaration. B. B. Barney, Esq., for petitioner.

PATENTS have been granted to Joseph H. Croquette, Fall River, pattern for drafting garments; Robert L. Ellery, assignor of one-half to F. E. Fuller, Taunton, running gear for vehicles; Frank Mossberg, assignor to Mossberg Manufacturing Company, Attleboro, jeweller's turk's head roll; Henry H. Arnold, Rockland, channel ling machine.

THE CITY PROPERTY COMMITTEE will meet this evening and again consider the plans for a city hall building, which were submitted by Architect Brigham. The committee will also take up the subject of a hospital for contagious diseases, which was referred to them to investigate several weeks ago. It is probable that the committee will decide to further investigate.

SUPPOSED TO HAVE BEEN KILLED.—William Bishop, whose family resides at 35 Davis street, Fall River, left home a year ago last July, and with two companions started to tramp to Providence. After that the family lost trace of him. He is now supposed to have been killed by the cars at indis point, Providence, and the police are trying to find his companions.

GRAND ARMY CONVENTION.—The quarterly convention of Bristol County Association, G. A. R., was held at Mansfield to-day. No delegates were present from William Logan Rodman Post 1, but Rufus A. Soule, N. B. Mayhew, Fred. W. Wood, Cornelius Sullivan, George P. Brock, A. E. Benton, and others represented the Manhattan House last evening. Twenty-two plates were occupied and the menu was of the nicest kind. Speeches were made and the evening was passed in a delightful manner. The supper was given under the superintendence of Mr Knight Eben C. Milliken, and the occasion was a complete success.

SUPPER.—The members of Sutton Commandery, Knights Templars, who occupied room 11 at the Loree House, Washington, D. C., on the occasion of the Masonic pilgrimage to that city three years ago, had a reunion and supper at the Manhattan House last evening. Twenty-two plates were occupied and the menu was of the nicest kind. Speeches were made and the evening was passed in a delightful manner. The supper was given under the superintendence of Mr Knight Eben C. Milliken, and the occasion was a complete success.

BROKEN, UNDERMINED, WASHED AWAY.

A High Tide Makes Sad Havoc,

Before the Eyes of Thousands of People.

NEW BEDFORD, Oct. 12.—It has been demonstrated within the past year, in fact ever since Buchell opened store at 75 William street, that high prices on boots, shoes and rubbers have been broken and washed away. The high tide of patronage which has constantly flowed into our store has made sad havoc with competition, and our low prices have been placed before the eyes of thousands of people who are looking for good shoes. We call your attention to our new "Vici Kid" Goodyear welt boot for ladies at $2.50. See our new line of $3.00 shoes "The Buchell" made to our own order and wearers. We make a point to buy only the best makes and goods that fit. Our prices on Shoe Dressing we know are below cost, but these are the prices every day in the year:

GILT EDGE,	
GLYCEROLE,	
RAVEN GLOSS,	
WHITE EGG FINISH,	
Alma Polish, 10c.	**15c.**

BUCHELL'S, 75 William Street.

WHAT IT COST.

Itemized Statement of Expense for Building the Coggeshall Street Bridge.

When, on March 12, 1889, the Legislature passed an act to authorize the County Commissioners of Bristol County to cause a bridge to be constructed across the Acushnet river, between the City of New Bedford and the town of Fairhaven, it specified that its expense should not exceed $50,000. But later on in the act, reference is made to authority for the County Commissioners to borrowing for the expense. It is not stated whether the interest for the same is to be exclusive of the $50,000 or not; but to the present time the cost of the bridge has been about $1331 in excess of that amount. The total expense of the structure as per itemized statement filed in the office of the Clerk of courts at Taunton, is as follows:

Detailed Statement of the cost of a Highway and Bridge over the Acushnet river, between New Bedford and Fairhaven, (Acts of 1889, chap. 321.)

1888.			
Aug. 5	E. Anthony & Sons, advertising,	$14.25	
	Mercury Publishing Co., advertising,	28.00	
	Engineering News advertising,	8.20	
Oct. 3	Mercury Publishing Co.,	2.50	$52.95
1890.			
Jan. 3	George J. Briggs, plans, &c.,	$495.00	
	Brownell & Murkland, on contract,	6,400.00	
March7	Brownell & Murkland, on contract,	4,800.00	
April 14	Brownell & Murkland, on contract,	7,378.00	
May 17	Brownell & Murkland, on contract,	8,987.90	
July 9	Brownell & Murkland, on contract,	8,900.00	
Sept. 4	Brownell & Murkland, on contract,	8,000.00	
Oct. 17	Brownell & Murkland, on contract,	6,000.00	$43,866.72
1891.			
March9	George A. Briggs, engineer,	$400.00	
	George R. Richmond, register, recording,	1.40	$401.40
1891.			
Jan. 8	William H. Sherman, transportation,	$2.53	
April 6	D. W. Holmes, visits,	22.07	
April 9	Brownell & Murkland, on contract and ex.,	2,823.83	
May 6	George A. Briggs, engineer,	200.	$3,051.32
			$47,372.39

Interest.

1890.			
Nov. 22	N. B. Five Cents Savings Bank, interest,	$375.00	
Dec. 20	Commonwealth of Massachusetts,	561.25	
1891.			
May 22	N. B. Five Cents Savings Bank,	375.00	
June 20	Commonwealth of Massachusetts,	561.25	
Nov. 20	N. B. Five Cents Savings Bank,	375.00	
Dec. 18	Commonwealth of Massachusetts,	561.25	
1892.			
May 21	N. B. Five Cents Savings Bank,	475.00	
June 20	Commonwealth of Massachusetts,	675.00	$4,518.75
			$51,391.14

The statement is endorsed as a correct one of the cost of the bridge and of interest on borrowed money, by Francis S. Babbitt, Franklin Gray and William Sanders, County Commissioners.

A hearing on a petition for the appointment of commissioners to apportion this cost on those cities and towns benefited, has been called for the first Monday of November.

POLITICAL.—About 30 men gathered in Phoenix Hall, Fairhaven, last evening and organized a Harrison and Reid company, with the following officers:
Captain—Fred B. Fish.
First Lieutenant—J. W. Marsten.
Second Lieutenant—C. H. Coombs.
After a long drill the meeting adjourned to Friday evening.

At the Democratic rally to be held Tuesday evening the speakers will be John E. Fitzgerald of Boston and Charles S. Hamlin of Brookline.

The Republican caucus was held in Plymouth last evening. Capt. Edward B. Atwood was renominated by acclamation for the Legislature. The meeting indorsed Hon. Henry Cabot Lodge for Senator. The following town committee was chosen for the ensuing year: Edward, B. Atwood, Stephen Holmes, Freeman Edward Holmes, William H Wall, Martin V. B. Douglass, David E. Avery, Charles C. Doten, Barnabas Hedge, Jr., Charles Holmes, James C. Bates, Winslow B. Standish, Alonzo Warren, William S. Kyle and Arthur Lewis.

A Republican convention was held in the eleventh Plymouth district in Brockton last night, and R. M. Lowe was renominated by acclamation. He is a Barrett man. In the twelfth district Representative Battles, a Barrett man, failed to secure a renomination. Fr d W. Hathaway, a Lodge supporter, was nominated; the vote being 102 to 106.

Democratic caucuses were held under the Australian ballot system last night in the eighth and ninth Representative districts in Fall River. Patrick Delaney and Michael B. Sullivan were renominated in the ninth district without opposition. Returns from the eighth are not yet in.

Stephen D. Pierce, Joseph Dawson and Thomas Donaghy, Jr., are in Boston to-day attending a meeting of the 18th Congressional District Democratic committee.

ORDINATION—Mr. A. L. Beaublossom was ordained as pastor of the Christian church in Assonet last evening, with the following programme:
Organ voluntary.
Anthem—I Will Set Watchmen.
Invocation,   Rev. E. C. Fry
Scripture reading,   Rev. G. A. Conibear
Hymn—Go preach my gospel, saith the Lord
Sermon,   Rev. Warren Hathaway, D. D.
Anthem—Nearer My God to Thee
Presentation of candidate.
   Rev. G. A. Conibear
Ordination prayer,   Rev. I. H. Coe
Hand of fellowship,   Rev. B. S. Batchelor
Charge to candidate,   Rev. J. McCallum
Address to church,   Rev. G. B. Merritt
Hymn—Lot Zion's watchmen all awake
Benediction by the candidate.

THE NEW RAILROAD DIRECTORS.—Rail road Commissioners Dole and Stevens, Presidents C. F. Choate, Division Superintendent E. G. Allen, Trainmaster Sanborn, Master Mechanic Willis, Division Master R. H. Bryant and Engineer Swain of the Old Colony Railroad, with President Shumway and Directors Edw. B. Atwood, Nathaniel Morton, William P. Stoddard, Jason W Mixter, Leavitt T. Robbins and Benjamin A. Hathaway of the Plymouth & Middleboro Railroad went over the road yesterday to inspect it.

ADMITTED TO MEMBERSHIP.—At a meeting of the executive committee of the Young Men's Republican club last evening the following were admitted to membership:
J. W. Cunningham, Charles M. Hussey, John Flood, Dennis Leary, Jr., Michael McDonald, Thomas Edmonson, James Garrington, Edward Garrington, Frederick W. Treen, Antone L. Sylvia, James L. Blackmer, Fenwick A. Winchester, Charles H. Hazzard, Jr., Edmund L. Wilcox, George N. Alden.

Crew List

Of schooner Sun, Capt. John Gonsalves, of Providence, which sails Oct. 13 from this port, on Atlantic ocean whaling voyage.
Frank Manuel, New Bedford, boatsteerer; Antonio Carlos Lisbon, Peter Lopes, New Bedford, boatsteerers; Manuel Texeria, do., steward; Henry Pepi, do., cook; Theodore Bravos, do., shipkeeper; Fidel Pena, do., mate's loft; Manuel Rodrigues, Jose Martins, Manuel Silva, Serafs Almeida, John Lomba, John Sima, Pera Lobo, Luis Turvera, all of do., seamen.

ROCHESTER.
Carpenter work is in brisk demand here, and all our carpenters have their hands full. James A. Hartley is having the old Davis school-house fitted over into a dwelling-house for the occupancy of one of the men in his employ.

YACHTING.—Schooner yacht Diona, of which Capt. Edward Colbert of this city is master, arrived in port yesterday and sailed for Gloucester to-day.

CHANNING CONFERENCE.

If I had one message to give all humanity I would say, "Take the mind of Christ."
After prayer by Rev. Mr. Horton, the choir rendered a trio by O. P. Brown, "I Will Lay Me Down," and the benediction was pronounced by Rev. Herbert Mott.

This morning the session opened at 9 o'clock and Rev. Herbert Mott for an hour conducted a conference meeting. Other speakers were Rev. Alfred Manchester of Providence and Rev. C. F. Nicholson of Rockland.

At 10 o'clock occurred the business meeting. In the absence of President L. S. White of Taunton and Vice-President Thomas Coggeshall of Newport, Job C. Tripp of Fairhaven was chosen chairman.

The records of the 53d session at Newport last April were read by the secretary, C. F. Nicholson of Rockland, and approved.

The treasurer's report, presented by Mr. Manchester of Providence, was approved. It shows a balance on hand of $210.19.

The committee on Christian work reported through Mr. Manchester. It referred with regret to the separation of Dr. Woodbury from the Westminster church but with congratulation at the happy choice of his successor, Rev. Herbert Mott. Regrets were expressed that Rev. C. F. Nicholson had decided to sever his connection with the Norton church, but is called to a broader field in Rockland Welcome was expressed toward Rev. Messrs. Law and Knapp on their return from foreign lands. In brief the whole state of the conference was reported in a flourishing and harmonious condition. The report was adopted and filed.

A resolution to raise $400 for annual expenses of the conference was adopted.

The resignation of Rev. C. F. Nicholson as secretary of the conference was presented and accepted, and resolutions of regret at the withdrawal of the gentleman were adopted.

The report of the Sunday school committee was presented for Mr. Hodges of Dighton by Rev. D. C. Stevens. It showed the Taunton school with 18 classes and 125 pupils; Fall River in a flourishing condition; Newport with 13 teachers and 125 pupils; Fairhaven with 11 teachers, 81 pupils and 4 officers, a library of 500 books, and Dighton with 20 pupils and 5 teachers. No reports were received from Providence and Norton. The report was placed on file.

The next business was to choose a secretary pro tem. to fill the vacancy caused by Mr. Nicholson's resignation. On nomination of Mr. Manchester, Rev. D. C. Stevens of Fairhaven was chosen secretary pro tem. to serve till April, 1893.

Mrs. Cleveland of Providence presented the reports of the Women's Alliances at Newport and Providence, and they were placed on file.

Rev. A. M. Lord of Providence brought before the conference the matter of establishing a church at Vineyard Haven, referred last April to a committee. He quoted from a letter from Rev. Grindall Reynolds, urging the conference to immediate action in the matter. The late Rev. D. W. Stevens was very anxious that a church be established there, and his son has agreed to give a lot of land if the conference will erect the church. Mrs. Emmerton of Salem, a Summer resident at Vineyard Haven, has agreed to give $500, on condition that the church is decided on this month. So hasty action is necessary, and the association at Vineyard Haven will do nothing unless the conference take the initiative. About $1900 to $1000 are needed, it being Mr. Stevens' wish that a church be erected costing about $3000. The younger Mr. Stevens has an offer for the land and desires a speedy decision. Mr. Lord thought the conference ought to raise $700.

Dr. G. W. Cutler of Newport said other denominations have the field in view and unless the Unitarians do something at once others will step in and reap the harvest. He moved that a committee of three be chosen to apportion the expense among the churches.

Mr. Manchester said that $200 of the $400 of current expenses already voted is for the sustenance of the mission at Vineyard Haven, and amended the motion that the amount raised be $900 and that the treasurer and committee on Christian work act in conjunction with the committee of three appointed last Spring.

Dr. Cutler accepted the amendment and the motion was passed unanimously.

The convention then listened to an address by Rev. R. L. Rexford of Roxbury on "Progressive Revelation."

At 1 o'clock a recess was taken during which a collation was served in the vestry.

Rev. Alfred Noon of Boston, secretary of the Massachusetts Total Abstinence Society, spoke at 2 15 p.m., on the general work of the society; and at 2 30 Rev. Arthur May Knapp of Fall River addressed the conference on "Unitarianism in Japan."

The conference will dissolve about 4 o'clock, to meet next April with the First Congregational Church, Providence.

CHARGED WITH POLYGAMY.

William Cartledge on Trial in the Third District Court.

One case of drunkenness was placed on probation in the District Court to-day until Nov. 20th next, and one case of drunkenness was released by the officers.

Ida F. Phillips pleaded not guilty of being idle and disorderly. She was adjudged guilty on the testimony of her father and Officer Arnell and was sent up for six months.

Hugh Finlan was adjudged probably guilty on a complaint sworn out by Bridget Mc Kanna under the bastardy act, and was ordered to give bond to the complainant in the sum of $300, with sureties, for his appearance at the November term of the Superior Court.

Judge Borden having advised William Cartledge and Bridget Cox as to their marriage declined to sit on the cases against them and Special Justice Milliken was called in to preside.

The case against William Cartledge for polygamy was first taken up. Hon. E. L. Barney appeared for the Commonwealth and Messrs. Desmond & Cobb appeared for the defence.

Jane Cartledge was the first witness. She said she was married in England in the English church, and lived with William Cartledge as his wife in one street eleven years, she came to this country one year before he did, and when he came they lived together at 52 School street as husband and wife until she went to California in 1889. She returned a short time since and found her husband married to Bridget Cox. Her husband told her he was a windower when he married her, and that his first wife died in child-birth.

Mrs Andrews said she lived in Fall River, and knew Jane and William Cartledge. She was present at their marriage in England. They lived together as husband and wife in England for eight years Jane then came to America and William one year after. William came to her house when Jane went to California. He told the clergyman he was a widower and we all signed the book at the church.

William Tomlinson said he knew Jane and William Cartledge. He wrote a letter for William Cartledge to Jane Kelly in California. He wrote that if she did not come home soon he should get married again. Home to point. Mr. Desmond asked for a continuance until afternoon to enable him to produce certain letters written by Jane to her husband while she was in California, in which he said his oldest morned his wife statements showing she knew his first wife to be alive who also married Cartledge.

The request was granted by the court and a recess was taken until afternoon at 2 30.

THE BORDEN "FAKE."

Boston Globe Makes a Humiliating Confession.

Retracts Its Story and Admits Its Falsity.

Who Was to Blame for the Latest Developments in the Case.

BOSTON, Oct. 12.—The Post's special correspondent at Fall River has this to say of the Borden "fake" this morning:

The more the Globe's backdown is discussed, the more people begin to ask: Is it possible that McHenry, who is admitted even by his enemies to be very keen and clever, could have been such a fool as to approach a man like Trickey, to ward whom he cherished no kindly feelings after the developments of the Saunders case? Dr. Graves tried at Denver, and unhesitatingly solicit a bribe to disclose that which, by every consideration of honor, he was bound to protect with absolute secrecy? Even if he did this, people ask, would a man of McHenry's cleverness and experience be such a colossal idiot as to palm off that which he knew must instantly be exposed as false, thus ruining his reputation

DETECTIVE EDWIN D. McHENRY.

and wisdom, and laying himself liable to prosecution, when, having the true facts in his possession, he could disclose them and have nine chances out of ten escaping the discovery and exposure of his perfidy?

On the contrary, it is generally asked, is it not probable that Trickey and his paper, eager for a sensation, approached the detective and offered to bribe him, and that he, perhaps, seeing the chance to get even with a man for whom he, at least, had no liking, and at the same time to get some free advertising, to which some say he is not averse, led him on into a trap, and then let him get out of it as best he might?

That seems to be the almost universal conclusion reached by many people here. Of course they have

No Proof

upon which to base it; but it is generally felt that the conclusion rests upon pretty sound common sense, and that it is quite as reasonable as the conclusion of Lizzie Borden's guilt that so many have adopted.

Another thing that has occasioned general comment and the greatest astonishment is that The Globe should accept and publish such a story without the slightest attempt at verification, as it confesses having done, especially since it was full of statements that must have been known to Trickey, in view of his familiarity with the case, to be absolutely false, contradictory and impossible.

The humble, abject apology published by The Globe occasioned another flurry. The general comment was that The Globe had done the only honorable thing possible, though it would have come with a better grace yesterday morning; but almost everybody attributed the apology to the promptness with which libel suits and criminal libel proceedings were said to have been ordered unless satisfactory reparation were made.

The Globe's Apology.

The following appeared in last evening's issue of The Globe.

The Lizzie Borden Case.

The Globe is, first of all, an honest newspaper. To err in human, and as newspapers have to be run by men and not by angels, mistakes are inevitable.

The Globe feels it a plain duty, as an honest newspaper, to state that it has been grievously misled in the Lizzie Borden case. It published on Monday a communication that it believed to be true evidence. Among all the imputations which newspapers have suffered, this press unparalleled in its astonishing completeness and irresistible plausibility. Judging from what we have heard, it impressed our readers as strongly as it did The Globe. Some of this remarkably ingenious and cunningly contrived story is undoubtedly based on facts, as later developments will show. The Globe believes, however, that much of it is false, and never should have been published.

The Globe, being thus misled, has innocently added to the terrible burdens of Miss Lizzie Borden. So far as lies in our power to repair the wrong, we are anxious to do so, and hereby tender her our heartfelt apology for this inhuman reflection upon her honor as a woman, and for any injustice the publication of Monday inflicted upon her. And the same sincere apology is hereby tendered to John V. Morse, and any other persons to whom the publication did an injustice.

The Globe comes out in this manner because it believes honesty is the best policy, and because it believes in doing what is right. We prefer to build up rather than to tear down, to help rather than to injure, to carry sunshine and not sorrow into the homes of New England.

When we make a mistake, whether through our own fault or not, we believe that justice to our readers demands that we should fairly and frankly proclaim the fact in the same conspicuous place in The Globe where the error was committed.

Something About Trickey.

Henry G. Trickey, who has become so prominent because of his connection with the late "Lizzie Borden story," which he claims was sold to him by Detective Mc Henry, and which was printed in Monday's Globe, is yet a young man, and had already achieved considerable fame in the journalistic fields from his connection with the Sawtelle and other noted criminal cases. He is a native of Dover, N. H., and was born in that city July 7, 1868. He lived in Belmont until 1884, when his parents removed to New Hampshire. Then he came to Boston to board. He was married not long ago.

His early education was received in the public schools of Belmont, and he graduated from the High School the same year that his parents moved into the Granite State. He was, at that time, the youngest graduate of the institution, being only 16 years of age.

In Boston he was employed about a year by Hon. P. C. Chandler in his law office. He added to his income by doing small special work on country papers. In 1884 he became a regular reporter for the Globe, having previously reported for the Cambridge Tribune.

The special work he has done for the Globe has always been noted, and degree by degree his name has become famous. For the past seven years he has been engaged on different letters written by Jane to her husband, first being concerned in that expose of Boston opium joints in 1885. Next he did promising work in the Mellen conspiracy case at Baltimore.

He became famous again as the writer

MARION.

Schooners W. D. Mangan and Oliver Chase are at Marion Upper Village.

The high fence now being cut down in front of Mrs. C. Callen's land on Main street is another village improvement.

The scallop war between Marion and Mattapoisett has begun. If the boats from Mattapoisett appear again to-day arrests will be made.

YOUNG AMERICA'S DAY.

Children Sing Praises to Their Beloved Country.

Guests Attend a Brilliant Ball in Chicago Auditorium.

All Nations Represented by Famous Men and Women.

CHICAGO, Oct. 20.—A crisp, invigorating atmosphere, its touch of frost gently tempered by the genial rays of the sun, as it looks down from a cloudless sky, might be interpreted as a special recognition from the elements of the opening day of the festivities incident to the dedication of the structures designed for the use of the World's Columbian exposition. The Stars and Stripes and tri-colored bunting are floating proudly. Apparently, the hotels are already as full as they need be. There are crowds at the larger ones and smaller ones alike, and at some of them, notably at the Auditorium, the Palmer and the Grand Pacific, it is difficult at times to force a way through the crowds that fill the rotundas.

Special trains packed with men and women of note and distinction are

Speeding Chicagoward

from every state and territory, while the ordinary trains are running in two, three and four sections. Governor Tuttle of New Hampshire with his staff and party reached the city several hours late. The carriages on hand were barely sufficient for the accommodation of the ladies, and so the governor headed the procession on foot to the Wellington. There was a large crowd at the Union station to extend a welcome to Governor McKinley and the nelegation from the Buckeye state. They came in force, over 250 of them, members of both branches of the legislature, representatives of the judicial bench, of the various state departments and the members of the state board of World's fair managers. The Buckeye train had barely been gotten out of the depot when that having the delegation from the Keystone state rolled in. Governor Pattison was one of the first to alight from the front end of the second car. The remainder of the party, to a total of nearly 100, was made up of the governor's staff, officials and members of the state World's fair commission.

An imposing procession, indicative of peace, prosperity and patriotism, participated in by fraternal and other civic organizations, started on a march through the business portion of the city at noon today. The parade is under the direction of General Joseph Stockton of Chicago, and 80,000 people are in line.

Children's Day.

The little ones who toddle to the infant school to learn their first letters, the big ones who have mounted step by step on the ladder of instruction to the high school, and are now about ready to go forth and battle with the world—these it is who were elected to inaugurate the celebration of the week.

Tens of thousands of youthful voices—voices robust and strong, voices weak and piping—joined all over this city and its suburbs in the grand strains of "America," and it was sung with an enthusiasm and patriotic fervor that in itself was an inspiration. It was a grand day for the children, and very few seats were empty in any of the schoolhouses.

The program of one school was that of all. As an overture the principal read the proclamation of President Harrison declaring Friday a general holiday. After this, the pupils, four abreast, marched out to the playground, where they stood in battalions, heads uncovered, while the Stars and Stripes were hoisted and unfurled. A word of command from the teacher, and every hand touched the forehead in military salute, while every tongue repeated a solemn pledge of allegiance to the flag and to the Republic, "one nation indivisible; with liberty and justice for all."

The Grand Ball.

Chicago's Auditorium, the greatest assembly hall of the continent, was ablaze with light and beauty last night. Lovely women were there, women whose presence would create a furore at a drawing-room in Buckingham palace; women in toilets that would put to shame the greatest creations of a Worth. And there were men—men who have made their imprint on the history of this and other nations, statesmen and diplomats; warriors that have faced the dusky foe in the jungles and tried conclusions with the enemy on the briny deep; men of letters and law, of science and art; merchant princes, whose early days tell stories of toil and poverty, and who stand today as gigantic monuments of the opportunities afforded to energy and independence under the flag of a free republic. Patriotism was the animative motive of the occasion and the event, love and exaltations for native land, the tribute of the four hundred to an event that has dignified the present metropolis of the west.

So far as the official program or dedication was concerned it had no recognition beyond the formal endorsement of the committee on ceremonies of the World's Columbian exposition, an endorsement that carries with it neither financial liability or responsibility. A thousand or more of the leading citizens of Chicago were the hosts, two thousand or more of distinguished women and men of the civilized nations of the earth the guests. As a social function there was an effervescence of patriotic fervor on the part of the ruling element of the Garden City. It was, perhaps, the most notable event, so far as society was concerned, in her entire history. It was a scene of

Almost Indescribable Brilliance

that presented itself to the vision of the Vice President of the United States, when, at 9 o'clock, leaning upon the arm of President H. N. Higginbotham of the World's fair directory, he appeared upon the floor of the ballroom. The brilliant hues of bunting seemed to struggle for recognition with the rays of the electric light.

The steel curtain of the stage had been raised, and in its place half fluttered the Spanish royal banner. To the right and left, above and below, were banners upon which were embroidered the initials of Queen Isabella and her consort, the rulers of Spain in the time of the great discoverer. In the space between the boxes and the proscenium arch loomed up a massive United States shield. It was surrounded by a stand of colors, and supported on the right and left by tht flags of all the American Republics. To the south, on the corresponding panel, was the shield of Spain, surrounded by the flags of all the nations of the Old World, a bouquet of national emblems, in which the colors of Spain and Italy were conspicuous. To the right and left, before and behind, above and below, fluttering in the air from the balconies, and hiding from view the primitive nakedness of the marble pillars, were the stripes in profusion, almost beyond arithmetician's art of calculation or guess work.

Queen Flora also played no insignificant part in the decoration. There were festoons of wild smilax running in front of all the boxes, and running thence along the balcony and the gallery proper. Here and there the green of nature was relieved with rosettes of red and yellow. Towering banks of palms and ferns supported the panels to the right and left of the proscenium, while a mass of green foliage formed a centerpiece for the stage, and a rising bank of ferns and tropical plants hid from view the military band, directed by Sousa of Marine band renown, that furnished the music for the grand march.

The Appearance of Mr. Morton

was recognized by a flutter of feminine apparel, but decorum militated against any demonstration of joy and gladness on the part of the sterner sex. The vice president was escorted to a position in the eastern corner of the hall, and the reception was at once inaugurated. The guests passed over the floor in procession, being first introduced to the managers, then to the committee of arrangements, next to the patronesses, and finally, after running the gauntlet, to the vice president and distinguished guests.

At the conclusion of the reception, which continued until nearly 11 o'clock, the vice president was escorted to the loge on the immediate right of the stage, and the remainder of the distinguished guests followed.

After the reception considerable time was occupied by the managers in arranging the floor for the opening quadrille, and it was after 11 o'clock when the strains of the cornet, violin and harp summoned the devotees of the terpischorean art to the center of the floor to inaugurate a tripping of the light fantastic toe.

The ball terminated at daylight, thus allowing the participants a brief medium of repose preparatory to the review of the grand civic parade. An elaborate supper, however, was by no means an insignificant feature of the night's program.

The Temperance Question

came up for consideration by the national World's fair commission, in the shape of bundles of petitions demanding the prohibition of the sale of liquor on the exposition grounds. Several prohibition speakers were present. Commissioner Hundley of Alabama declared that the commission had no right to prohibit the sale of liquor on the grounds, and offered a resolution that, as the commission only has the right to modify the rules made by the directory, the commission should take no action on the prohibition question until the directory has acted. A long debate followed, after which Mr. Sewell of New Jersey moved that the question be referred to the judiciary committee. The motion was lost by a vote of 43 nays to 37 yeas.

Commissioner King's motion was then amended to grant the prohibition speakers an hour in which to address the commission in favor of a dry fair on condition that the liquor interest be given a similar hearing in the future. An adjournment was then taken until 3 o'clock, when the arguments for a dry fair began.

The commission upheld General Miles in his desire to confine the military parade Friday to Washington park, but not without a parting shot, however, from Governor Waller of Connecticnt, who urged the right of the general public to witness the display in a down-town review.

Slashed His Wife.

BOSTON, Oct. 20.—The midnight quiet was rudely broken by screams in the house of John Flaherty, 93 Mercer street, South Boston, and officers of station 12 found John's wife, Honora, bleeding from a cut two inches long over her right eye, which, she alleged, was inflicted by her husband. Mrs. Flaherty's wounds were dressed by a physician, and Flaherty was arrested, charged with assault.

Startling Case of Crookedness.

TOLEDO, Oct. 20.—City Solicitor Reid laid before the county prosecutor the evidence and finding of the board of revision in the case of Street Commissioner Bower, who was accused of carrying the names of dead men on his pay-roll and appropriating the money to his own use, and recommended that the matter be presented to the grand jury.

Associates Think He Is Crazy.

OMAHA, Oct. 20.—The injunction sought by Judge C. R. Scott, to prevent an insanity commissioner from examining him as an insane person, was denied by three of his associate judges sitting upon the case. A bar committee will begin an investigation into charges upon which Scott, it is thought, can be impeached.

More Trouble at Crete.

LONDON, Oct. 20.—Advices from the island of Crete state that serious affrays have occurred there, between the Christians and the Turks. In the encounters reported, four Christians were killed, and 149 Turkish soldiers lost their lives, besides twenty being wounded.

Their Sentences Lengthened.

BOSTON, Oct. 20.—A further sentence of one year was imposed upon Felix Golding, Daniel Coffey and John Booth, three state prison convicts, who escaped from that institution on July 8 last, with seven others, by crawling through a sewer main.

Killed by a Robber.

WILKESBARRE, Pa., Oct. 20.—Joseph Dirk, a Polander, residing in this city, was murdered by an unknown man, who entered his house for the purpose of robbery.

A FAMOUS LAW CASE

Which Has Been Pending Several Years Bids Fair to Be Soon Settled.

RUTLAND, Vt., Oct. 20.—George L. Mussey brought suit against A. C. Bates and S. P. Curtis in the county court yesterday to recover $100,000 damages. The case has been pending for several years, and is now celebrated in this county. The property out of which Mussey claims to have been defrauded, is situated near Rutland, and was formerly the property of his father, who died leaving ten heirs, of whom Mussey was one.

He claims to have purchased the remainder of the estate nine years ago for $12,685, the figures being fixed by court, and Bates and Curtis, who were the last owners of the property, he claims, would not allow him to take possession, and have since then forbidden him to even visit the premises. The case has been tried half a dozen times in nearly as many courts, decisions, at times, having been rendered for both parties without a settlement.

The property has been increased in value since the lawsuit was begun by the building of manufacturing enterprises, and is now valued at ten times what it was once. Mussey claims that he should receive the benefit of the increased value. There is great interest in the case and the decision will be an important one.

Diven Acquitted.

NEW YORK, Oct. 20.—The trial of Edward Diven, who murdered Max Clerget, the betrayer of his sister, in open court, ended in a verdict of acquittal on the ground of insanity. Diven is a harrowing spectacle of idiocy.

Mysteriously Missing.

NYACK, N. Y., Oct. 20.—George Bilyen, a prominent business man of Suffern, has mysteriously disappeared. An active search is being made for him. He was doing a large business and had no financial trouble.

From Yesterday's Third Edition.

SUPERIOR COURT—CIVIL TERM.

MAYNARD, J.

FALL RIVER, Oct. 19.

In the case of Joseph Fremont vs. Joseph Tetrault decision was reserved.

In the case of David Paddleford vs. Harriet Paddleford, action for divorce, the evidence was heard and the case rested for a while.

In the case of Joseph Healy vs. Katherine Healy, for divorce, a divorce nisi was granted

SENTENCE REVISED.—The Third District Court held a session at 3 o'clock this afternoon when the sentence of Bertha F. Thomas, sentenced this morning to the State Industrial School for Girls at Lancaster was revised. She was ordered to be committed to the custody of the State Board of Lunacy and Charity. State Agent Whiting was present, and the change was at his request, he thinking it better for the girl.

STRICKEN WITH PARALYSIS.—John Lisle, of Cold Spring, N. Y., captain of barge Bluster, discharging coal at Hart & Akin's wharf, was on Taber's wharf this afternoon when he was stricken with paralysis. Word was sent to the Central Station, but by mistake the patrol wagon answered. Some delay was occasioned in getting the ambulance, but finally Capt. Lisle was taken to his barge and attended by Dr. Potter.

WEDDING.—At St. James (Catholic) church this morning James Francis Hutchinson and Miss Ellen Welch were married before a large gathering of friends. John Carney was best man and Alice Welch was bridesmaid, while Rev. James F. Clark performed the ceremony. A reception followed at the bride's residence, County street, near Thompson, and presents galore were exhibited.

DEDICATION WEEK.

School Children Inaugurate the Celebration at Chicago.

CHICAGO, Oct. 19.—The weather to-day is bright and cool. An army of decorators is at work throughout the city putting on the finishing touches to Chicago dedication week attire. Special trains are arriving with distinguished persons from all over the country, while the influx of visitors is already of stupendous proportions. A bright silken flag floats proudly to-day from the roof of every public school-house in the city and Cook county. This is Children's day. The school children, big and little, have been selected to inaugurate the celebration of welcome. Thousands of youthful voices joined this morning all over the city and suburbs in the grand old strains of "America." While the boys sported a button bearing the stars and stripes, the girls had tiny American flags fastened to the bosoms of their dresses. Programmes calculated to inspire youth with sentiments of patriotism were executed in all the schools.

Operator Carroll Gives Himself Up.

WILLIMANTIC, Conn., Oct. 19.—Telegraph Operator Charles F. Carroll of Norwich, whose criminal carelessness caused the railroad collision at New London last Friday and who disappeared, arrived here this forenoon and gave himself up to the police. He was taken to New London where he will be tried.

CHANGE OF VENUE IN BORDEN CASE.

Miss Lizzie May be Tried in Plymouth County.

Pinkerton Detectives Now Working in the Prisoner's Behalf.

Proof that the Man Arrested in Richmond is Not Guilty.

[Special Dispatch.]

TAUNTON, Oct. 19.—It is rumored that a change of venue may be asked for in the Borden case, should it ever come to trial, and, if granted, Plymouth county will probably be the locality selected. Two Pinkerton detectives are now at work on the case in and about Fall River for defence, it is said.

He Was in Europe.

FALL RIVER, Oct. 19.—It is learned that the real name of the man arrested in Richmond, charged with being implicated in the Borden murder case is Henry Mahr, but he was known as John Wood. He came to Fall River two years ago and boarded at the house of Mrs. Cross at 17 John street. He was employed for three months in Marshall's hat factory. Last April he left this city and went to New York, where he visited a brother, who is a well known theatrical agent. While in New York he wrote to friends in this city saying that he intended to go to England and that they would not hear from him again for some time.

About the time of the cholera scare a letter was received from him saying that he had just arrived in New York on an infected steamer and would be in Fall River the next night, at the same time requesting Mrs. Cross to meet him on the arrival of the boat. Mrs. Cross went to the boat to meet him, but Mahr did not show up and has not been heard from since. Mrs. Cross says she has in her possession letters and telegrams which prove conclusively that he was in London during the time of the Borden murders.

SENSATIONAL SHOOTING.

Wealthy Stock Raiser and Mine Owner Puts Three Bullets Into His Wife.

PEORIA, Ill., Oct. 19.—Great excitement prevails at Pekin, ten miles below this city, over a sensational shooting affair there late on Tuesday night. Mrs. Norman Hawley, the wife of a wealthy stock raiser and mine owner, appeared in Pekin about midnight, covered with blood, and swore out a warrant for the arrest of her husband, charging him with an attempt to kill her.

She had been in Pekin during the day, shopping, and did not start for home, a distance of three miles, until evening. As she neared her home, her husband approached the buggy and said he would ride home with her. As soon as she had stopped the horses, he fired at her with a revolver, the bullet striking her in the head and passing around the skull. He fired two more shots, both taking effect in her body.

Meanwhile she had turned the frightened horses around and drove back in the direction of Pekin. It is thought that Mrs. Hawley must have fainted. The horses stopped somewhere along the road, for she did not reach the city for several hours.

Her husband was arrested and is now in jail. He denies that he did the shooting and attributes it to tramps. It has been an open secret for years that the couple did not agree and something sensational has been expected. The wealth and position of the family have saved them much scandal. It is thought Mrs. Hawley will survive, but she is in a critical condition.

EPISCOPAL CONVENTION.

Proceedings of the House of Delegates on the Thirteenth Day.

BALTIMORE, Md., Oct. 19.—The proceedings of the house of delegates at the morning session of the thirteenth day of the general Protestant Episcopal Convention were very dry and uninteresting. Hon. J. C. Bancroft Davis of Maryland presented from the committee on legislation amendments to an adverse report on the memorial to set apart Western Tennessee as a new diocese because of irregularities in the vote on the question. The memorial had been rejected by the committee on new dioceses.

Judge Bennett of Massachusetts offered a minority report. A motion was made to substitute the minority report and its accompanying resolution for the report of the committee. Dr. Kedney of Minnesota favored the motion. He was followed by Rev. Mr. Lightner and Mr. Caustin Brown of Massachusetts, who also favored the views of the minority. These were opposed by Mr. Stinness of Rhode Island and others. After a long debate Dr. Seth Low of Brooklyn desired to offer an amendment to the motion to substitute, but here Dr. Dix declined to entertain it.

CAUGHT DIGGING HER GRAVE.

Arrest of a Man for the Brutal Murder of His Wife.

LONDON, Oct. 19.—A horrible affair has come to light at Oldham, near Manchester. A man named Mellor lives in a house on the Hollings road. His wife has been missing for some time, but apparently nothing had been seriously suspected. Some neighbors to-day paid an unexpected visit to the house, noticed that a hole had been dug in the kitchen having appearances of being intended as a grave. They informed the police, who proceeded to the house. A search was made and soon a body was found in the cellar which was thought to be that of Mellor's wife. Her throat was cut and the body covered with stab wounds. The remains were in such a condition as to indicate that the woman had been dead for weeks. A barrel of quick lime was found, no doubt intended for use in the grave. Mellor is under arrest.

CONNECTICUT BAPTISTS.

Reports and Addresses Made at the State Convention at Willimantic.

WILLIMANTIC, Conn., Oct. 19.—The Baptist State convention reassembled this morning, Rev. J. D. Herr, D. D., of Norwich presiding. The report on the state of the church was read.

At 9 30 a. m. the 73d annual meeting of the Connecticut Baptist Educational Society convened. Hon. James Howard of Hartford presided and gave an address on the origin and growth of the society. The treasurer's report showed receipts of $1474, disbursements $1350, balance $124.

An address was made by Rev. J. D. Herr, D. D., of Norwich, and Rev. J. W. McKinney of Deland, Fla., and Rev. F. D. Elmer of Brown University, beneficiaries of the societies, spoke interestingly, and officers were elected for the ensuing year.

ANNUAL CONCLAVE.

American Gas Light Association Holds a Session in Boston.

BOSTON, Oct. 19.—The American Gas Light Association held its annual conclave to-day. Papers were read as follows: "The relation of theory to practice," A. C. Humphreys of Philadelphia; "Water gas condensation," J. W. Rushby, Jersey City; "A gas association and its members," W. R. Addicks, Boston; "Saving and proper concentration of ammoniacal liquors," George Osins, Detroit; "Anthracites of the United States," C. R. Collins; "Some experiences as to the best burner for a mixture of coal and water gasses in about equal proportions," A. E. Forstall.

Daley Found Guilty of Murder.

PROVIDENCE, Oct. 19.—In the Court of Common Pleas this morning the jury in the trial of Timothy Daley for wife murder brought a verdict of guilty, after deliberating an hour and a quarter. Sentence reserved.

THE FENIAN MOVEMENT.

Reminiscences of Dr. Le Caron are Made Public.

Plots to Blow up Parliament and Assassinate the Queen.

President Johnson Declared Himself in Sympathy with the Cause.

LONDON, Oct. 19.—The Reminiscences of Dr. LeCaron, or Thomas Philip Beach, the spy for the British government who gained such unenviable notoriety in 1889 by his disclosure on the part of the *Times* before the Parnell commission, have been made public.

He declares when he and Gen. O'Neil were received at the White House in Washington by President Johnson, the President told Gen. O'Neil that he sympathized with the Fenians, and was willing to do all in his power to assist the Fenian movement. "You must remember," said President Johnson, "that I gave you full five days before issuing the proclamation stopping you. In God's name what more did you want? If you could not get there in five days you could never get there. And then, as President, I was compelled to enforce the neutrality laws or be denounced on every side."

Le Caron described to the utmost detail the whole Fenian movement against Canada, showing how he became acquainted with every man of any important connection with the move. He says only twice was he in danger of discovery. The first occasion was when he incautiously took down the names of Fenians in his notebook. He was denounced, tried and acquitted by comrades. He resigned his position in order to emphasize his innocence, and was begged to remain in the order. After much persuasion he relented and secured a stronger position.

The second occasion was when he was arrested in Canada as a Fenian, and only escaped the fury of the populace and death by making a clean breast to the mayor of the place, who conveyed him secretly from the city.

LeCaron relates that some of his less fortunate Fenians, suspecting one of his government accomplices Rose, as a spy on the Fenian movement, waylaid, robbed and thrashed Rose, while he (LeCaron) was obliged to applaud their action.

The Irish part of the memoirs is of less interest from the fact that all was revealed before. LeCaron says the Clan-na-Gael's wild plans included a treaty with Russia, the manufacture of a submarine torpedo boat to inflict damage on the British navy, plots to assassinate the Queen, and to kidnap the Prince of Wales.

He says: "Parnell confessed his belief that nothing but force of arms would accomplish the redemption of Ireland. He went into details on the league's resources for a movement of insurrection and said they had £100,000 in the treasury. He discussed the position of home and American revolutionary organizations and defended the American policy. I parted with him by assuring him that I would do all he wished."

LeCaron then gives the text of a secret circular prepared for a dynamite campaign in the event of Mr. Gladstone's home rule scheme being inadequate.

In regard to the modern Irish-American agitator he says: "Gold is his god. He attains his ends by jobbery, trickery and delusion of the meanest and most despicable type. He bravely and blusteringly advocates desperate enterprises from the safe distance of 3000 miles."

Le Caron says "Dr. Gallagher, who controlled the compaign, was often in Parliament and he heard, had been introduced to Mr. Gladstone."

One plot was to blow up Parliament by throwing bombs on the table in front of the speaker. Another was to steal the Stone of Scone, which serves as the seat of the coronation chair in Westminster Abbey, on which the Irish Kings were believed to have been crowned for centuries on the hill of Tara. Le Caron makes hardly a trace of an effort to justify the statements he made before the Parnell commission; still he gives his readers the impression of truthfulness that he conveyed at the time of the commission's inquiry.

PRISONERS' TERMS LENGTHENED.

Booth Makes a Dramatic Appeal for Justice.

BOSTON, Oct. 19.—Felix Golding and Daniel Coffey, two State prison convicts who escaped July 8 last with seven others by crawling through a sewer, pleaded guilty to-day and were sentenced each to one year imprisonment, to take effect when their present terms shall have expired. John Booth, another of the escaping party, pleaded not guilty, and will be tried later on the charge of having escaped.

When testimony in Booth's case had been submitted, Booth made a dramatic appeal for justice, declaring that he was the victim of a conspiracy and wholly innocent of the crime for which he is serving a 15 year sentence. The jury found him guilty and he received an additional sentence of one year. Booth was convicted of assault on a young girl in Lowell. He told the court to-day that a corporation, which had tried to force him to come to terms that he would not submit to, hired a girl and witnesses to testify against him. He had 11 witnesses, he said, but despite their evidence he was unjustly convicted.

GIGANTIC FRAUDS.

Dr. Hale of Philadelphia Arrested in Belfast for Swindling.

LONDON, Oct. 19.—Dr. Hale of Philadelphia has been arrested at Belfast on a charge of conspiracy with others not yet known to defraud merchants of Liverpool and other places by a system of swindling. The prisoner has been remanded. The police believe that they are on trail of immense frauds in which Hale is a principal.

Alleged Counterfeiters Held.

BOSTON, Oct. 19.—Charles B. Byron and Daniel Kelley, the men arrested Tuesday on a charge of having moulds for making counterfeit money in their possession, were before United States Commissioner Hallett to-day, and held in $1500 each for the United States Circuit Court grand jury.

Ocean Steamers.

At Boston—Colorado, Hull, Eng.

WHAT SHE SAYS.

Her Testimony and Evidence Clear and Strong.

Ringing Words of Hope and Cheer Which Will Comfort Many Hearts.

The Great Information and Good Advice A Talented Woman Can Give.

One of the most skilful nurses in this country is Mrs. Elizabeth D. Berry, of Hampton, N. H. She is a lady of the widest experience among diseases of all kinds, and has cheered many a sickroom by her hopeful and encouraging words.

She has sent a communication to this paper which will be read with great interest by all. Her advice is worthy of the greatest consideration on account of the high reputation she has as a nurse, and her words are especially valuable because of their great encouragement to all classes of sufferers.

"Through trouble and overwork," she writes, "I grew fearfully nervous, weak, dizzy, faint and exhausted from nervous prostration, until I became entirely helpless. Thanks to Dr. Greene's Nervura blood and nerve remedy, I am now so well and strong that everyone who sees me is very much surprised. I would like to tell the whole world of women what Dr. Greene's Nervura blood and nerve remedy has done for me, and to recommend all women to use this wonderful medicine.

"I am a nurse, and when nursing my sister I gave her this wonderful medicine. She says she has never felt better than since using

MRS. ELIZABETH D. BERRY.

it. I gave it also to a lady suffering from great nervous prostration, who could not get help from three physicians. She is now well, strong and fleshy, and says she should have been in her grave if it had not been for Dr. Greene's Nervura blood and nerve remedy.

"I have recommended it to many others with the same wonderful success, and I would especially say that if women between the ages of 40 and 60 years would take it there would not be so many die when they came to the change that takes place. I hear this wonderful medicine named and blessed everywhere, and I am glad to add my testimony to its great value, and truly call it a savior of us women."

We would say that Mrs. Berry's advice as a nurse is endorsed by physicians generally. Dr. Greene's Nervura blood and nerve remedy is indeed a wonderful discovery and of incalculable and inestimable value to the sick everywhere. It has been proved over and over again, in thousands upon thousands of cases, that it does cure, that it makes the sick well.

Physicians know of its great value, for they have seen it perform wonders in restoring health, and they recommend it freely to the sick because it is the discovery and prescription of the famous specialist in the treatment of nervous and chronic diseases, Dr. Greene of 34 Temple Place, Boston, Mass., the well-known physician, who gives consultation to sufferers from any disease free of charge, personally or by letter.

The great remedy costs but $1 of druggists, and we know it will make you well.

Railroad Meeting.

NEW HAVEN, Ct., Oct. 19.—The twenty-first annual meeting of the stockholders of the New York, New Haven & Hartford Railroad was held here to-day. Directors were elected and leases ratified.

TELEGRAPHIC BREVITIES.

The Gulf, Colorado & Santa Fe Railroad is employing operators to take the place of strikers. It is thought this action means a suspension of negotiations with the men. Railroad employes at Clebourne, Tex., decided at a meeting that the strike was ill advised.

Gen. Nelson A. Miles is having a hard time with Chicagoans in reference to the much wanted military parade. He now proposes to have a grand spectacular display of military tactics at night.

Silas W. Gordon, the Wakefield man who attempted to shoot his wife and take his own life last night, is much improved and will recover.

A dispatch has been received at the Ministry of Marine in Paris that removes whatever little anxiety was felt regarding the safety of the French forces in Dahomey.

J. G. Ernst Krause, keeper of the bath in the new Yale gymnasium in New Haven, committed suicide by hanging to-day.

Stamford, Conn., entered upon the last day of its 250th anniversary celebration this morning.

The British government has decided to permit meetings to be held in Trafalgar square, but precautions would be taken to insure order.

The wife of the murdered Hans Gerson, proprietor of a great dry goods house and Westheim flour mills, who was killed and robbed in Mosbach Baden last week, has been arrested together with Gerson's bookkeeper, Billigherim, on charge of having committed the murder.

A wild freight train backed into the rear of the local freight at Union Market, Watertown, at 10 45 this morning. Four cars were smashed. A brakeman named Paul Tiernan of Fitchburg had a leg broken and a drover named Casey was thrown from a car and badly shaken up.

Column 1

SECOND EDITION.

HOME MATTERS.

RELEASED.—James W. Eastwood of Fall
River, committed to the House of Correction
Aug. 5th for assault and battery, was released
by the County Commissioners to-day on the
recommendation of the probation officer,
concurred in by the justice of the Second
District Court.

THE STALLION GEMARE.—A magnificent portrait of the celebrated stallion Gem are may
be seen in the Wright Drug Co's window.
This fine trotter is owned by J. S. Sanborn of
Chase & Sanborn, and he has his pedigree for
211 years without a break. He was raised by
the French government and is bred 16 trotting lines. He is a bright bay, 16½ hands
high, and weighs 1250 pounds, and we have it
on good authority that he will trot 30 miles in
two hours, carrying two men with a road
wagon.

Voters of the Sixth Bristol Representative
District, mark the Republican candidates,
Eddy and Rugg.

LAND BEING FILLED IN.—The tract of low
land lying between the Old Colony railroad
and Purchase street south of Weld street, is
being filled in, a pipe having been put in to
drain the brook there and a story has arisen
that on the land the Union Street Railway
Co proposes to erect a building to be used
for a car shop, blacksmith shop and machine
shop. A reporter of the *Standard* this forenoon asked a prominent official of the road
in regard to the reported buildings. He said
the company already has car, blacksmith
and paint shops, and he has heard nothing
about any others being erected.

Do the Republican voters of New Bedford
wish to see a Democratic sheriff? If not,
vote for Andrew R. Wright.

REAL ESTATE SALES.—Betsey A. Webster
has sold to Henry W. Bennett a lot of land on
the east side of Vine street, containing 17.82
rods.

P. J. Driscoll has sold for Rodolphus Beetle
to Stanislas Vigneault a lot of land on the
west side of Rock street containing 25.58
rods; also a lot of land on the north side of
Sawyer street containing 18.64 rods to Bruno
Forcin.

F. A. F. Adams has sold for J. F. Kilburn
two and a half story house and 25 rods of land
on Crapo street to J. B. Watkins.

Standish Rourse sold at auction Saturday
afternoon house and lot of land on Washburn street to Joseph C. Janson for $2100.

The same gentleman also sold at auction
Saturday afternoon lot of land containing
21¾ rods, together with barns on North Front
street, near Washburn street, to D. J. Sullivan for $1970.

Mr. Bourne also sold at the same time a lot
of land on Washburn street, east of Front
street, to D. Sullivan for $35 a rod. The lot
contained 25½ rods.

H. A. Leonard has sold for John Paul to C.
F. James a lot of land situated on Palmer
street, between Court and Union streets, containing 68.35 rods.

Charles F. Jennings has sold all his interest
in his mother's estate in this city to Clark H.
Jennings.

Dinah Briggs has sold to Mary E. Borden a
lot of land in Westport.

Column 2

IT HAS COME TO THIS.

That every successful, meritorious article has its
imitations. This is a grave injustice, for the genuine
pure article will be often judged by the imitation.
No preparations require for their manufacture more
care and skill, more costly and purer materials, than
flavoring Extracts.

In this instance cheap materials means inferior
flavors. **Dr. Price's Delicious Flavoring Extracts**
have won their way to public confidence by the pure
and costly materials used, the new processes employed
for extracting from the fruits their natural flavoring
principles. In using

Dr. Price's Orange, Lemon, Vanilla

or other flavors the housewive will never fail to obtain
the grateful flavor desired.

THIRD DISTRICT COURT.

BORDEN, J.

MONDAY, Nov. 7.

Mary Sweeney pleaded guilty of drunkenness, and as she has a very sick child her
case was continued to Saturday nex'.

William V. O'Leary pleaded not guilty of
assaulting Margaret Donohue at the Howland Village Saturday afternoon. O'Leary
is collecting agent for an installment house,
and while under the influence of liquor committed the assault. He was fined $20 and
settled.

John Allen, Henry Boivin, Albert Boivin
and Walter Chausee, juveniles, pleaded
guilty of breaking and entering the shop of
Telesphore Vigneault on the 4th inst., in the
night time and stealing cigars and $2 in
pennies. Their cases were continued to
Wednesday next.

A vote for Congressman Randall is a
vote for a man who believes in sound currency; a vote for Henry F. Thacher is a
vote for a man in favor of a bogus banking
system.

NEW POLITICAL CLUB.—Another political
club has just been organized at the South
End, its object being principally to have an
interest in municipal affairs. The officers are
as follows:
President—John Walsh.
Vice-President—Edw O'Malley.
Secretary—James Kelley.
Treasurer—Michael Flannery.
Republicans, go to the polls early to-morrow and help swell the vote of the old Bay
State for the Republican party.

FOR BUTLER AND EDDY.—The South End Independent Political Club held a largely attended meeting on Grinnell street yesterday,
when addresses were made by several members. It was decided to support the candidates of William M. Butler for the Senate
and George M. Eddy for Representative from
the Sixth Bristol District.

Haile and Wolcott are in sympathy with
the American workingman, Russell and
Carroll with the foreign laborer.

ACUSHNET.

Revival services have been commenced,
and will be continued each evening this week
excepting Saturday. A cordial invitation is
extended to all.

Place an X against the word Republican
wherever it appears on the ticket.

POSTAL OR TELEPHONE 158-12 and John Mc
Cullough will send for rags, rubbers, bottles, &c.

MARINE INTELLIGENCE.

Sld from Stonington 6th, sch A W Parker,
Snow, Port Johnson for Nantucket.
Sld from New Haven 6th, sch John J Beckerman, Gammons, Baltimore.
Ar at New York 5th, steamers Nacoochee,
Smith, Savannah; City of Colombia, Jenney,
West Point; schs P G Thomson, Chase,hence;
Julia Francis, Anderson, Fall River.
Passed through Hell Gate 4th, sch Annie
Louise, Cole, New York for Dennis.
Ar at Philadelphia 5th, steamer Hercules,
Hand, Fall River; sch Van Name & King,
Curtis, hence. Cld,schs Gardner B Reynolds,
Raynor, Greenwich; 6th, Kate Markee, Perry,
Allyn's Point.
Ar at Newport News 5th, sch Josie R Burt,
Hammett, hence.
Ar at Charleston 5th, Gov steamer Azalia,
hence, with Martin's Industry light-ship in
tow.
Ar at Savannah 6th, steamer City of Macon,
Lewis, Boston.

FINANCIAL.

Day Before Election Dullness—Stocks do
Not Move Much EitherWay—Quincy Mining Co. the Feature in Boston—Money
Rates Unaltered for Most Part—In Chicago
Money is Active and Firm—Flint & Pere
Marquette Earnings—Latest Statement
Shows a Big Decrease—Favorable Report
on Union Pacific—In General.

MONDAY, Nov. 7.

The day before election is always marked
with dullness in stock circles. To-day has
been no exception. Prices have been well
supported, however, and in some cases small
advances have been scored. To-morrow
stock business will be suspended in both
Boston and New York, election day being a
legal holiday in New York State.
Local money rates are unaltered.
In Boston money is more freely offered and
rates are easier if anything. At clearing today loans were made at 4 per cent. New
York funds sold at 10, 8 and 5 cents discount.
In New York money is reported as dull and
steady to-day.
Sterling $4.84 and $4.87¼.
Bonds firm.
Wall street gossip this morning said:
"Movement made by the bulls last week
may be renewed to-day, but if so there will
be naturally some temptation to realize before the election. London up ¼ to ½ per
cent."
Trading was very light in the New York
market to-day. The brokers on the floor were
little inclined toward business, preferring to
await the result of the election. On the opening, the market showed some slight advances. Rock Island
up ¼ and Union Pacific up ⅛ to ⅜. At noon
these prices were still ruling, and the afternoon commenced with a dull and steady
range of values.
Quincy Mining was the feature of the Boston stock market. Opening was at 135 and at
noon the price was up 5 at 140. Atchison, B.
Q., and the general list of railroads was firm.
Poor earnings knocked Flint preferred to 68.
Bell sold at 207¼. In the early afternoon the
market was dull and featureless.
Prime's weekly crop report says that
drought in Winter wheat sections is broken.
Ground now in fine condition for ploughing
and for recently sown wheat.
A Chicago dispatch says: "Money is active
and firm here."
Aggregate earnings 21 railroads for October show a gross increase of $647,722.
Sales to noon in Boston to-day were: Bonds
$13,000 and 6100 shares of stock.
Painter & Holt say London up ¼ to ½ per
cent. We do not look for much of a market,
but a firm one.
Director F. L. Ames has returned from a
trip over the Union Pacific road and expresses himself as more than satisfied with
the condition and prospects of that property.
It is understood that the Union Pacific earnings for October are the largest in the company's history, while the rolling stock and
road bed, Mr. Ames believes, are in a condition never before surpassed.
The Osceola mine is looking remarkably

Column 3

well. The company has paid $2 per share in
dividends this year and will pay short'y $1
per share more, making $3 for the year. Besides it will carry over from $15,500 to $27,500
surplus.
The market for steel rails continues quiet,
no sales of any size being placed. The meeting of the rail manufacturers held in New
York on Satur lay last continued the present
agreement as to output and price. Standard
sections are still quoted firm at $30 at Eastern
Mills.
The earnings of Canadian Pacific for September were, gross increase, $33,372; net increase, $13,758; since Jan. 1, gross increase
$941,303; net increase, $409,627.
Flint & Pere Marquette earnings for the
last week of October compare as below:

	1892.	1891.	Dec.
Fourth week Oct.			
Freight,	$49,675	$62,892	$13,217
Passenger,	23,789	25,157	1,368
	——	——	——
Total	$73,464	$88,049	$14,585
Month of October,	$238,427	$255,839	$17,412
Since Jan. 1,	$2,367,678	$2,403,855	$36,177
Mileage,	625	625	

A comparative statement of salt and log
earnings of the Flint & Pere Marquette for
the fourth week of October shows as below:

	1892.	1891.	Dec.
Working days,	3	3	
Salt earnings,	$246	$3,908	$3,662
Log earnings	5,446	9,945	4,499
	——	——	——
Total,	$5,692	$13,853	$8,161

STOCK AND BOND MARKETS.

Bids at the close of First Board.
NEW YORK, Nov. 7.

GOVERNMENT BONDS.

U.S. 2s,	100
4s, registered	......114¼
4s, coupons	......114¾
" currency 6s, 1895,	......107½

RAILROADS.

Atchison	39¾
Clev., Cin., Col. & St. Louis	64½
Chicago & Eastern Illinois	......
Chicago & Eastern Illinois pref	......
Chicago, Burlington & Quincy	103
Delaware & Hudson	......
Delaware & Lackawanna	153¾
Erie	27⅛
Illinois Central	103½
Lake Shore & Michigan Southern	......
Louisville & Nashville	69⅞
Michigan Central	......
Missouri Pacific	62¼
New Jersey Central	......
New York & New England	44¼
Northern Pacific	18¾
Northern Pacific pref	51½
Chicago & Northwestern	116¼
New York Central & Hudson River	111¾
North American	12¼
Philadelphia & Reading	56½
Pullman Palace Car Co.	......
Chicago, Rock Island & Pacific	83½
Chicago, Milwaukee & St. Paul	80½
Chicago, Milwaukee & St. Paul pref	......
Richmond Terminal	......
St. Paul & Omaha	......
Union Pacific	40¼
Wabash St. Louis & Pacific pref.	26½

MISCELLANEOUS.

Ontario Silver	......
Pacific Mail Steamship Co.	31
Sugar, common	112¼
Sugar, pref.	......
Western Union Telegraph	93½
Silver Certificates	85½

BOSTON, Nov. 7.

BONDS.

Atchison 4s	82¼
Atchison Income	78
American Bell Telephone 7s	113
Chicago, Burlington & Northern 5s	......
Chicago & West Michigan 5s	......
Mexican Central 4s	67
West End 6s	......
Illinois Steel Co. 5s	100

RAILROADS.

Atchison, Topeka & Santa Fe	39¼
Boston & Albany	*204¾
Boston & Lowell	182
Boston & Maine	176
Boston & Providence	262
Chicago, Burlington & Quincy	104
Chicago & West Michigan	......
Eastern	147
Eastern 6s	......
Fitchburg pref.	......
Flint & Pere Marquette	......
Flint & Pere Marquette pref	68
Mexican Central	14½
New York & New England	45
New York & New England pref.	94
Old Colony	......
Oregon Short Line	28
Pullman Palace Car	*190½
Union Pacific	40¼
Wisconsin Central	......
West End	72½
West End pref	......

MINING.

Butte & Boston Mining Co	39½
Calumet & Hecla Mining Co	288
Centennial	32
Franklin Mining Co	*12½
Kearsarge	15½
Montana	32
Osceola Mining Co.	24¾
Tamarack	155
Quincy	137½

MISCELLANEOUS.

American Bell Telephone	208
Erie Telephone	......
Mexican Telephone	......
New England Telephone	60
Newport Land	......
Boston Land Co	5½
West End Land Co	17½
San Diego Land Co	13½
Topeka Land & Development Co.	.50
Lamson Store Service	......
Illinois Steel Co	72½
Am. Sugar Refineries, com.	110½
Am. Sugar Refineries, pref.	103
Gen'l Electric	115¼
*Asked.	

PROVISIONS AND GRAIN.

[CHICAGO, NOV. 7.

Opening.
	Lard.	Wheat.	Pork.	Corn.	Sh't Ribs.
Nov.		71½		41½	
Dec.		71½	12.45		
May		77¼		45½	

9 o'clock.
Nov.		71½		41½	
Jan.			13.56		
May		77¼		46¼	

Keep New Bedford Republican by an old-time majority.

Egyptian Cotton Crop.

LONDON, Nov. 7.—A Cairo dispatch to
the *Times* says the Egyptian cotton crop
is expected to exceed 5,000,000 cantars
(495,000,000 pounds,) a yield greatly exceeding the best previous record.

Workingmen, remember the Democratic
party's plank indorses the wildcat bank.

Ocean Steamers.

Arrived—At New York, Rosse, Santos;
Ocean, Amsterdam; Dunmore Head, Belfast; La Bretagne, Havre.

When Baby was sick, we gave her Castoria.
When she was a Child, she cried for Castoria.
When she became Miss, she clung to Castoria.
When she had Children, she gave them Castoria

Column 4

THE BORDEN CASE.

Mr. Adams Asks for Special Instructions to Grand Jury.

**Request Made on Petition of Lizzie
to the Court.**

**Judge Refuses to Repeat Instructions
of the District Attorney.**

[Special Dispatch.]

TAUNTON, Nov. 7.—The criminal term
of the Superior Court opened here this
morning with Justice Thompson of
Gloucester on the bench. After the
grand jury's roll call had ended some little excitement was caused by the appearance of Mr. Adams, associate counsel for
Miss Borden, at the bar. He addressed
the court as follows:

Mr. Jennings and I appear as counsel for
Miss Borden in the District Court at Fall
River when she was charged with the
crime of murder. She desires us to represent her in this court, but I am doubtful
whether or not we have full standing
here. But I hope your honor will hear
what I have to say. We have felt that in
her interest we were entitled to speak
in this court without being specially
assigned to the case since she has petitioned that we represent her here. This
case has been one extraordinary in its
character and one which has excited great
interest in the minds of the public and in
the newspapers. There is no doubt in
our minds that the grand jury ought to
be cautioned, especially in reference to
the formation of any opinion in
their minds because of reading
the accounts of the trial of the
case in the papers. We think they
ought to be cautioned in addition to their regular instructions, and
that the court may fairly warn them in
regard to their duties. I have here in my
hand the petition of Miss Borden in
which she asks us to represent her in this
court, and also asks the court that the
grand jury may be instructed, and that
to justify any finding the jury must be
satisfied upon the evidence before it that
the accused is guilty.

District Attorney Knowlton, asked by
the court if he had anything to say in
reference to the matter, appeared to be
somewhat indignant and replied that he
only had this to say, that in all his service as District Attorney the grand jury
has never considered an important case
but what he had fully instructed them in
regard to their duties and he was
at a loss to understand why it
was assumed that he would not
do his duty in the present case. If your
honor thinks, he said, there is any danger of my not warning them to do their
duty impartially and to instruct them in
regard to the weight of evidence, I have
no objection to your honor re-instructing
them.

The court said Mr. Foreman and gentlemen of the Grand Jury: You have
already been instructed in your duties
and have taken upon yourselves the oath.
I have been asked to repeat to you the instructions already given you and to refer
especially to the rules regarding the burden of proof. You are to consider only
the testimony presented by the witnesses
before you, and if any of the grand jury
have facts in their possession relating to
this or any other case, reduction in wages
their duty to act as witnesses themselves. They cannot act upon hearsay
evidence or newspaper reports, since they
are not competent testimony. You will
have the assistance of the district attorney in all questions of law and I do not
feel that I am called upon or am under
any necessity to give you any particular
instructions in regard to any part of this
or any other case.

The court then adjourned and the grand
jury took possession of their room.

Mr. Adams was seen after the court had
adjourned and expressed himself as being
well satisfied with what he had accomplished.

Old soldiers to-morrow will remember
their gallant comrade, Benjamin Harrison,
at the polls.

WEATHER INDICATIONS.

A CLOUDY ELECTION DAY.

NEW YORK, Nov. 7.—At 8 30 a. m. the
weather was cloudy; wind east, temperature 56. The *Herald* says: In the Middle
States and New England on Tuesday
generally partly cloudy weather will
probably prevail with nearly stationary
temperature, preceded by rain or snow—
at least in the northern and western districts—and followed by clearing, colder
weather and brisk or high northwesterly
winds, and on Wednesday fair weather,
with no very decided changes of temperature.

William E. Russell has nothing in common with the industrial classes of this
Commonwealth.

Diseased Cattle.

LONDON, Nov. 7.—The *Times*, referring
to the outbreak of pleuro-pneumonia and
the prohibition of the importation of
Canadian cattle, urges that the British
government issue a permanent order for
the slaughter of all cattle shipped to this
country from New York to this
city. He said that he was on his way to
Attleboro to purchase a stock of jewelry.
He was unable to procure a stateroom
and was obliged to occupy a berth in one
of the rooms off the dining hall. There
was a stranger in the room with him. Before retiring he took his money, which
consisted of a roll of bills, and placed it
under his pillow. During the night he
had occasion to leave the room, and when
he returned he found it empty. His
sleeping companion had disappeared and
with him the $600. He was unable to give
any accurate description of the man, as
the latter was in the upper berth apparently asleep when he went into the
room. The robber made his escape and
there is no clue to his identity. The police of this city in company with the
steamboat officers are investigating the
matter.

William E. Russell has nothing in common with the industrial classes of this
Commonwealth.

RAN OVER A COW.

Train Ditched, Engineer Killed and Three
Others Badly Hurt.

PARSONS, Kan., Nov. 7.—A northbound
train on the Missouri, Kansas & Texas
railroad yesterday was wrecked at Maxai,
Indian Territory, 60 miles south of here,
ditching 17 loaded cars, and overturning
the engine. Engineer was killed, Fireman
Ely, Brakeman Ayers and an unknown
man were badly hurt. The wreck was
caused by running over a cow.

New Bedford's great prosperity is due
due to the Republican party's protective
policy.

The Wage Question in Fall River.

[Special Dispatch.]

FALL RIVER, Nov. 7.—A general meeting of the Weavers' Association will be
held Thursday evening, at which time action will be taken on the proposed advance in wages. Secretary Whitehead
said to a *Standard* reporter to-day that he
could not definitely answer the question
whether the weavers would demand 10
per cent. or not. He said they were hunting talked with the agents and collectors
of the Weavers' Association who have
visited all the mills that it seemed to be
the will of the weavers to accept the situation. There are many members of the
association, however, who claim 10 per
cent. is wanted and will try to have the
demand made.

The attitude of the spinners is unchanged.

Senator William M. Butler has won an
honorable name at the State House and
deserves reelection.

Column 5

FORGET IT NOT.

We are making our own Boots and Shoes, and we
know they are better for the money than any other
makes. If you doubt it come in and we will show
why they are better.

We also make to order any kind or style of footwear at from $1.50 upwards.

FORGET IT NOT.

SCHULER BROS.

Factory Connected.   76 and 78 Purchase Street.

The above cut shows how the people will
rush to our store for clothing when the announcement is made who is the successful man.

M. C. SWIFT & SON,

153, 157 and 159 Union Street,

NEW BEDFORD, MASS.

LOCKOUT IN THE COTTON TRADE.

Victory for Operatives Believed to be a
Practical Certainty.

LONDON, Nov. 7.—As the lockout in the
cotton trade began at the usual midday
closing hour on Saturday, the exact
number of operatives affected will only
be known to-day.

Mr. Howdelwy, secretary of the amalgamated Association of Operative Cotton
Spinners, things that 53,900 persons will
be rendered idle by the lockout or strike,
the trouble partaking of both features.
His estimate may be modified should the
stampede among the employers spread.

The federation of master cotton spinners has never been successful in its
lockouts, and the present trouble promises to be no exception to the rule. Since
the masters issued their notices that the
spinners would have to submit to
a 5 per cent. reduction in wages
there has been an improvement
the trade and manufacturers are loth to
shut their mills and forego the profits
in sight. Should the manufacturer spinning American cotton offer their employes the old rate of wages it is probable that about 15,000,000 spindles would
continue to run and the number of idle
spinners would be reduced to 30,000. A
victory for the operatives is a practical
certainty. Only one mill in Haywood
stands out to-day. With so many mills running the position of the strikers is materially strengthened. The spinners at
work pay a part of their wages into the
strike fund, which is very large, and this
will allow the operatives to stay out for a
long time.

Do the Republican voters of New Bedford
wish to see a Democratic sheriff? If not,
vote for Andrew R. Wright.

ROBBED ON STEAMER PILGRIM.

Western Man Loses $600 and the Thief
Escapes.

[Special Dispatch.]

FALL RIVER, Nov. 7.—Yesterday morning a Western man arriving in this city on
the steamer Pilgrim reported to the officers on duty at the dock that he had
been robbed of $600 on board the steamer
coming from New York to this

A TONIC

HORSFORD'S Acid Phosphate.

A preparation of the
phosphates, that acts as
a tonic and food to the
exhausted system.

There is nothing like it;
gives great satisfaction.

Trial bottle mailed on receipt of 25 cents
in stamps. Rumford Chemical Works,
Providence, R. I.

HAT.

For durability, style and comfort the best
hat made.

Sold by leading hatters.   FM

IF you wish to advertise anything, anywhere at any time write to GEO. P.
ROWELL & CO., No. 10 Spruce St., New York.

EVERY one in need of information on the
subject of advertising will do well to obtain a copy of "Book for Advertisers," 368
pages, price one dollar. Mailed, postage
paid, on receipt of price. Contains a careful
compilation from the American Newspaper
Directory of all the best papers and clases
of publications; gives the circulation rating of every
one, and a good deal of information about
rates and other matters pertaining to the
business of advertising. Address ROWELL'S
ADVERTISING BUREAU, 10 Spruce St., New
York.

W. L. DOUGLAS
$3 SHOE FOR GENTLEMEN

THE BEST SHOE IN THE WORLD FOR THE MONEY.

OTHER SPECIALTIES in footwear are of
the same high grade, and represent a money value
for prices asked, as the following lines. Every
pair stamped on bottom of shoe with price and
name of maker. TAKE NO SUBSTITUTE.
W. L. Douglas, Brockton, Mass. Sold by
BUCHELL'S Shoe House and THOS. DONAGHY.

Column 6

Pages 9-10.

The Evening Standard.

Pages 9-10.

NEW BEDFORD, MONDAY, NOVEMBER 7, 1892.---TEN PAGES. TWO CENTS.

ADVERTISEMENTS.

HE IS AN ABLE YOUNG MAN.

Republicans Decide to Help Reelect Representative Barney.

A Remarkable Compliment Since He is a Democratic Candidate.

Ranks Among the Brightest Men New Bedford Ever Sent to State House.

One of the most prominent Republican voters, as well as one of the most conservative in the Fifth Bristol Representative District told a *Standard* reporter this forenoon that he should vote for the reelection of Benjamin B. Barney, Democratic candidate for Representative. In answer to a request to give his reasons for supporting a Democratic candidate, the gentleman said he was fully convinced that he was only one of a very large body of Republicans who would vote for Mr. Barney, and their action was based simply on a desire to do justice to a young man who has been conceded by representatives of every political faith at the State House to be one of the cleanest and brightest men ever sent there from this city.

Representative Benjamin B. Barney,
The Youngest Man Who Ever Presided Over Massachusetts House of Representatives.

"There is certainly not the slightest reason why any good Republican cannot vote for Mr. Barney," continued the speaker, "when the Boston *Journal*, the representative Republican paper of the State, pays a man as pretty a compliment as it did young Mr. Barney when he occupied with honor the chair of the speaker of the Massachusetts House of Representatives. Mr. Barney has voted uniformly with good judgment. It is an honor to the Democratic party to have so good a candidate and the only pity is he is not a Republican for Republican votes will swell his majority."

The reporter found the same feeling above expressed to exist very generally among the Republican voters of the district, and a careful survey of the situation shows that Mr. Barney, as he deserves to, will poll far more than his party strength. In this connection it will be interesting to the *Standard's* readers to know that Mr. Barney is the youngest man who ever occupied the chair of the Speaker of the Massachusetts House of Representatives. On no less than ten times has he been so honored, and for five full legislative days he presided over the deliberations of the House. The past Summer Mr. Barney was a valued member of the joint special committee on the revision of the judicial system of the Commonwealth.

Do You Smoke

THE
Pickwick
Social
Cigar?
PROCLAIMED
THE BEST 5c CIGAR
IN THE WORLD'
BOSTON CIGAR & TOBACCO CO

THE BEST Home-Made Drink.

MASON'S NON-ALCOHOLIC ROOT BEER,

Tonic—Stimulating—Refreshing—Delicious. . . Sold in Melbourne and Calcutta, as well as in New York and Boston. . . One bottle makes six gallons. . . No other Root Beer has such a variety of flavors.

U. S. Agency, 408 Chamber of Commerce, Boston.

SOLICITORS OF PATENTS.
CROSBY & GREGORY,
GEO. W. GREGORY,
34 School Street,
BOSTON, MASS.,
and 318 F Street, Washington, D. C.

We have enlarged our office, increased our corps of draftsmen, and can intelligently prepare, successfully and properly prosecute, with broadest possible claims, and at reasonable cost, applications for U. S. and Foreign Patents on all subjects of invention.

ENGRAVED CARDS & INVITATIONS
A Specialty at Reasonable Prices
—AT THE—
STANDARD OFFICE.

A GREAT INVENTION.

The Art of Hardening Copper Rediscovered by Ferdinand Allard.

Success comes early in life to some people and late to others. Some, like Byron, 'wake to find themselves famous, while others are crowned with laurels only after long years and many efforts.

This last is the case of Ferdinand Allard, the inventor of hardened copper. Allard can render copper so hard that it can be ground to an edge, and not only can it be used to replace steel, but its substitution is often an improvement.

The reality and genuineness of the invention has been attested by such a well known scientist as the Abbe Professor Laflamme, of Laval university, Quebec, and Sergeant Major Richard, of the Quebec Rifle corps, who fired three times with a Snider rifle at a sheet 1¾ inches thick. In every case the bullets were shattered. Experiments made in the British Royal dockyards on a piece of the same thickness have been eminently successful also.

Allard has already made axes, razors and other cutting tools of this prepared copper, which takes an excellent edge, and such pieces of cutlery have the advantage, as he carefully pointed out, of being tempered throughout, whereas tools of iron and steel have only the edge tempered.

The inventor himself, Ferdinand Allard, is a typical French-Canadian—honest, industrious and good tempered.

He was born at Cap Sante, Que., seventy-six years ago. Allard early showed a marked preference for blacksmithing, and when he was about twenty-six he went to New York to learn his trade more thoroughly.

"For sixteen years," Allard said, in speaking of his invention, "I lived in New York working at my trade. Well, one day while we were eating dinner a comrade

FERDINAND ALLARD.

began reading the newspaper to me—for I cannot read," he added diffidently, "and there was one item that interested me very much. It said that the Egyptians had known of a method of hardening copper, but that this was now one of the lost arts, and that a fortune awaited the man who should rediscover it.

"That made a great impression upon me. I thought and thought about it, and all my spare moments I experimented. When I came back to Quebec I still experimented. At last I resolved to try just once more and then give up forever, for I had tried all sorts of experiments for thirty-three years without success. This time I succeeded. When I was convinced that I had really made a genuine discovery I went to the Abbe Laflamme and told him, and he advised me what to do."

All this was of course in French, for Allard does not speak English, though he understands it fairly well. As for himself and his surroundings, he is a man seventy-six years of age, and has a family of twelve children—nine girls and three boys—all living and grown up, and as hale and hearty as himself and his wife, who is about his own age. His expression is honest, good tempered and pleasant, and his black eyes beam with intelligence. He is a broad shouldered, rather thickset man, 5 feet 8½ inches in height and weighing about 200 pounds. He is proud that he has never had a day's illness in his life.

For some years past Allard has lived at Point Levis, which lies on the opposite side of the St. Lawrence to Quebec. Here in his little blacksmith shop, only 16 by 24 feet in size, he made his great discovery. The shop and cottage were both built by himself and his sons, and for many years Allard, his wife, four unmarried daughters and one son have lived here content and happy in their humble sphere of life, the father earning a scanty living, but always hopeful of success in his lifelong ambition.

In addition to copper plates Allard makes hardened copper carriage springs that have all the elasticity of the best steel springs, and are not so liable to break. He uses a great deal of charcoal, and the length of time required depends upon the thickness of the sheet or the size of the article to be hardened; a piece of copper 8 feet long by 4 wide requires about twenty-four hours, and the process has the further advantage of being simple and inexpensive.

Besides its many other uses hardened copper will doubtless be of great service in the manufacture of the commutators and brushes of dynamos.

So soon as he realizes from his discovery Allard says it is his intention to place the money in the hands of the Roman Catholic clergy, who will pay him the interest on it.

A Novel World's Fair Display.

There will be sent to the exposition at Chicago a most beautiful model of the Island of St. Thomas, Danish West Indies It is now being constructed on that island by Dr. Charles E. Taylor and his son Clarence, is about 8 by 4 feet, built to a scale of six inches to the mile, and will be painted in natural colors, showing the roads, country houses, ships and steamers in the harbor and the pretty town of Charlotte Amalia, with its two old legendary towers of Blackbeard and Bluebeard. It will be set into a table enameled in black edged with gold, with terra cotta paintings by Mr. Clarence Taylor of various spots of interest on the island. The whole will be covered with plate glass.

THE BORDEN MYSTERY.

This Week Will See Additional Chapters Enacted.

Application of Howell's Description of a Fake Reporter.

Criticism on the Manner of Handling the Case by some Newspapers.

[Special Correspondence of the Standard.]

TAUNTON, Nov. 7.—With the opening of this week will come more chapters in the terrible Borden mystery. Only those inside the grand jury room will know anything tangible about those new chapters, presuming, of course, that the jury is to hear additional evidence, but there will be all sorts of rumors and hints, worked into readable stories for the newspapers, and once again the reporter of vivid imagination will get down to his work. I am glad to know that none of the papers in this section treated this matter in quite the same manner as did the papers of perhaps wider range, and certainly published further away from the scene. The *Standard*, it seems to me, treated the subject in the best manner possible, and while giving to the world the essential facts at all times, yet forbore adding to the heaps of nauseating material sent broadcast and apparently demanded by all classes of readers.

There is a vast difference in newspaper men and their style of handling such cases as the Borden mystery. When Howells wrote his "The Quality of Mercy" he drew, and undoubtedly intentionally, for the benefit of his readers, a contrast between two classes of newspapers and two classes of reporters, which leaves no doubt in the minds of those who are posted as to just where he intended to hit, exactly what papers at least were meant by the allusion. He styles the papers the *Events* and the *Abstract* respectively. The *Events* is hit off in this manner: A journal without principles and without convictions, but with interests only; a map of busy life indeed, but glaringly colored, with rude endeavors at picturesqueness and with no more truth to life than those railroad maps where the important centres converge upon the broad black levels of the line advertised and leave rival roads wriggling about in uninhabited solitudes. The *Abstract* is described as a paper whose managing editor had a fixed idea of a conscience in journalism. The story deals, as probably most of your readers are aware, with the defalcation of a bank president, but the way in which it was written up by the reporter of the *Events* is almost identical with the method of handling the Borden case by some of the newspaper men detailed for the work. Here is Howell's description of the way in which the matter was handled in general: "Day after day the papers were full of the facts and it was weeks before the editorial homilies ceased. From time to time fresh details and unexpected revelations, wise guesses and shameless fakes renewed the interest of the original fact. There were days when there was nothing about it in the papers and then days when it broke out again in vivid paragraphs and whole lurid columns again."

Mr. Howells was evidently familiar with the fake writer, and his respect for him was about on a par with that accorded him by many others. Do you recognize a familiar spirit in the following description of how the reporter of the *Events* wrote up the case? This reporter "made the report of the affair the work of art which he boasted should come off his hand. It was really a spaceman's masterpiece, and it appealed to every nerve in the reader's body, with its sensations repeated through many columns, and continued from page to page with a recurrent efflorescence of scare heads and catch lines. In the ardor of production all scruples and reluctances became fused in a devotion to the interests of the *Events* and its readers. With every hour the painful impressions of his interview with Miss Nothwick became fainter and the desire to use it stronger, and he ended by sparing no color of it. * * * * He worked in all the pathos which the facts were capable of holding and at certain points he enlarged the capacity of the facts. He described with a good deal of graphic force the Northwick interior. Under his touch the hall expanded, the staircase widened and curved, the carpets thickened, the servants multiplied, the library into which "the *Events* representative was politely ushered was furnished with all 'the appliances of a cultured taste.' The works of the standard authors graced its shelves; magnificent paintings and groups of statuary adorned its walls and alcoves. The dress of the lady who courteously received the *Events* reporter was suitably enriched; her years were discounted and her beauty approached to the patrician cast. * * *

While he was at it he lavished a manorial grandeur upon the Northwick case outside as well as inside. He imparted a romantic consequence to Hatboro itself—a thriving New England town, proud of its historic past and rejoicing in its modern prosperity, with a population of some 5000 or 6000 souls, among whose working men and women modern ideas of the most advanced character had been realized in the well-known Peck Social Union, with its cooperative kitchen and its clientele of intelligent members and patrons."

People of all occupations became leading residents in virtue of taking this reporter into their confidence, and "A Prominent Proletarian" achieved the distinction of a catch line by freely imparting the impressions of Mr. Northwick's character among the working classes. "Pinney's (the reporter) masterpiece was in fine such as he could write only at that moment of his evolution as a man, and such as the *Events* could publish only at that period of its development as a newspaper. The report was flashy and vulgar and unscrupulous" and it "was helplessly and thoroughly personal."

How much all this reminds us of the Borden case; how close to the line of conduct of some newspaper men this brings us. For all of Howell's peculiarities it must be said that he understood some kinds of newspaper men thoroughly, for he has in this given us an excellent description of men we are now familiar with. And yet that reporter, in all probability, did just what he knew his chief expected him to do. In direct contrast to this report was that of the reporter of the rival paper, and while it was looked upon as "a work of art" undoubtedly by the person who wrote it, there was no shadow of resemblance between the two reports. One dealt in unembellished facts; the other used the talents given him and the opportunity offered to, well, do just as has been said before, produce a report that was flashy, vulgar and unscrupulous.

There is one thing quite certain; if Lizzie Borden should be allowed to go free, there will not only be very many young men who will hang their heads in shame, but there will be the liveliest kind of dodging among those who have been the most unscrupulous and the most outspoken on matters which had better been left untouched for the time being. And it would not be in the least surprising if after all a jury by disagreement or by direct acquittal should say that it could not bring itself to call her a guilty woman or that it was all a horrible mistake. While those who know the men have the highest opinion of the ability of the district attorney and the attorney-general, yet it appears to be open an secret, as indeed about all of the Borden matter has been, that there is very little additional evidence to be presented. It is asserted that it will be an utter impossibility to find a jury of 12 men who will be willing to say that this girl committed the deeds laid at her door, but of course, if there is fresh evidence the complexion of things will be changed.

HELPED TO NOMINATE LINCOLN.

A Modest Massachusetts Man Claims That Distinction.

Mr. Edward R. Tinker, of North Adams, Mass., modestly claims to have nominated Abraham Lincoln. The world has been a little slow of recognizing him and according to him the honor, but the proof is ample that he did devise the plan which united the opposition to Seward and brought it to the support of Lincoln.

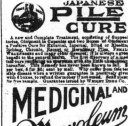

EDWARD R. TINKER.

All readers remember that Horace Greeley went to the Chicago convention of 1860 with the avowed object of defeating Seward, and that on Thursday evening, May 17, he telegraphed to The Tribune that it could not be done; that the opposition could not concentrate on any other candidate. After that dispatch was sent Mr. Tinker proposed that the delegations from Indiana, Pennsylvania and New Jersey express their first, second and third choice and submit it to a conference of three—one from each state.

It was done, and showed that while Pennsylvania would first cast her vote for Simon Cameron, her third choice was Lincoln, and outside of his own state Mr. Cameron's support was practically nothing. It also showed, and all the Pennsylvanians in the convention confirmed it, that the state would not give her electoral vote to Seward. The conclusion was obvious—as all could unite on Lincoln for third choice, and as he was already next to Seward in the count the only thing to do was to unite on him, and it was done accordingly.

Mr. Tinker was born July 20, 1822, and has been a zealous politician ever since he was old enough. He helped organize the Republican party, and was a member of the state committee all through the stirring times of Sumner, Wilson and Boutwell. Aug. 26, 1862, President Lincoln appointed him collector of internal revenue, and he held that position continuously till July 1, 1885. Being active in state politics, and a firm believer in the old theory, "to the victors belong the spoils," he naturally acquired the title of "Boss Tinker," but it did not lessen his activity.

There was some material for humor in the famous Chicago convention, one feature being that Horace Greeley was laughed out of court on his first proposition, but went home victorious. Another was that the convention rejected Seward because of his very radical utterances on the "higher law," "irrepressible conflict," etc., which the delegates said would certainly cause the loss of Pennsylvania, and then nominated a man who had made a far more radical utterance than any other Republican. Pennsylvania, too conservative to vote for Seward, practically elected the man who had made the "house-divided-against-itself" speech, and a few months later, when Seward was for compromise, Lincoln and Pennsylvania were against it, and Horace Greeley was for saying, "Erring sisters, depart in peace!" On all these things and all other issues of the olden time the septuagenarian, Mr. Tinker, is a most entertaining talker.

India has one missionary to 275,000 people, Persia one to 300,000 and Thibet one to 2,000,000.

It is a warm situation when you are troubled with indigestion, or, in fact, any of those ills that arise from derangements of the digestive apparatus. You go to the drug store and you will probably take some pepsin preparation, some mercurial doses which will injure you for life. Stop it. The medical fraternity throughout the world are now recognizing Johann Hoff's Malt Extract as a standard remedy. It is specially recommended for invalids where a delicate yet strengthening tonic is necessary to build up a debilitated constitution. There are lots of counterfeits on the market. The genuine have the signature of "Johann Hoff" on the neck of bottle. It is beneficial alike for man, or woman, or child. Eisner & Mendelson Co., N. Y., Agents.

External Use.

You can cure skin affections by pouring medicines into the stomach, but it is a long way around, and a slow process.

"A HEALING WONDER."

Comfort Powder

Is quicker, safer, and more certain.

It never drives the disease in.

CAPT. JAMES MAY, Quincy, Mass., used Comfort Powder for Erysipelas, and he says it relieved the burning and itching instantly.

MRS. LUCY E. RICE, Bridgeport, Vt., says: "I had a humorous sore on my nose for a long time. Comfort Powder completely cured it."

ALL DRUGGISTS SELL IT.
SEND POSTAL FOR FREE SAMPLE.
COMFORT POWDER CO., Hartford, Conn.
E. S. SYKES, SECRETARY.

JAPANESE PILE CURE

A new and Complete Treatment, consisting of Suppositories, Ointment in Capsules and two Boxes of Ointment a Positive Cure for External, Internal, Blind or Bleeding Itching, Chronic, Recent or Hereditary Piles, FEMALE WEAKNESSES and many other diseases; it is always a great benefit to the general health. The first discovery of a medical cure rendering an operation with the knife unnecessary hereafter. This Remedy has never been known to fail. $1 per box, 6 for $5; sent by mail. Why suffer from this terrible disease when a written guarantee is positively given with 6 boxes, to refund the money if not cured. Send stamp for free sample. Guarantee issued by WRIGHT DRUG CO.

MEDICINAL AND Myroleum TOILET SOAP

A COMBINATION of pure Petroleum and Olive Oil. Contains all of their healing properties. Unrivalled for Medicinal and Toilet use. Gives a smoothness and softness to the skin not obtained by any other preparation. *Guaranteed to cure* all skin diseases that can be reached by external application. *Used by Physicians.* All dealers have it.

The Barney Co., Boston, Mass.

A SOCIETY LEADER.

This Youthful McAllister Directs Entertainments and "Classifies Society."

Those who go to Saratoga in the summer, or to the Ponce de Leon at St. Augustine in the winter, have doubtless had the privilege of becoming acquainted with a young man who figures as the Ward McAllister of these two places.

DAVID H. NOON.

Technically described, he is the master of ceremonies at the hotels, but so valuable has he proved himself in this capacity that his social talents have been brought into requisition in the way of directing all the entertainments, both at Saratoga and St. Augustine, during their respective seasons.

Like his illustrious master, Mr. David H. Noon devotes much time and thought to dress, and spends many an anxious hour over a new menu card. In addition to devising new figures for the cotillon, arranging dances, inventing new dishes and criticizing gowns, Mr. Noon's mission is to classify the society of the two resorts, dividing it into cliques and making agreeable arrangements for all to enjoy themselves.

In appearance Mr. Noon is worthy of notice. A stalwart frame, handsome eyes and a noble bearing make up a fine personality. But it is not of his personal appearance that this youthful McAllister is most proud. He takes pride only in his social skill, or, as he expresses it, in his cleverness in separating "the sheep from the goats."

Last of a Famous Tower.

The famous leaning tower of Saragossa is being pulled down at last, after repeated threatenings. It was repaired in 1860, but had long been pronounced unsafe. The "New tower" was built in 1504 to hold the town clock, and was a brick construction of Arabic style.

THE NEW GLOBE

The Latest Grand Triumph of Mechanical Genius,

THE GREAT PARLOR OIL HEATER AND ILLUMINATOR,

Will Heat and Light a room 16 feet square at less than one cent per hour. It has the Genuine Central Draft, and is absolutely safe.

No. 8 GLOBE 8

Sold only at the Oil Stove Headquarters,

E. B. CHASE & CO.,
Corner Union and Fifth Streets.

DAVID DUFF & SON.

COAL!

All Best Grades at Lowest Market Prices. Well Screened and Properly Delivered.

Office 99 William Street, - - (Liberty Hall Building.)

TELEPHONE 22—2. MWS

MERIT WILL WIN.

CANFIELD DRESS SHIELD.

SALES 15,000 PAIRS A DAY.

CANFIELD RUBBER CO.

Offices: NEW YORK, LONDON, PARIS, HAMBURG AND VIENNA.

For Sale in New Bedford at the Following Stores:

Haskell & Tripp. Knowles & Co. Ed. B. Whiting & Co.

"That boy!

He is late again." Don't blame him. You may have no reason to. Has he a watch to go by? Why don't you buy him a new, **quick-winding** Waterbury? It costs only $4 for time; (up to ten dollars if you include style.) It winds in *five seconds* and looks as handsome as a fifty-dollar watch.

It *keeps time* and will keep him up to time; will teach him the value of saved minutes—and help you to keep sweet. Get him a watch.

All jewelers sell the new **quick-winding** Waterbury in every style: nickel, coin-silver and filled gold; for men, women and youngsters. $4 to $15. N2

RUBBER
ROOFING

Is unequalled for house, barn, factory or outbuildings, and costs half the price of shingles, tin or iron. It is ready for use and easily applied by anyone. For Shed or Henhouse. On steep or flat surface. Excellent roof, complete. $2.00 Per 100 square feet. $2.00. Send stamp for sample and state size of roof. Ind. Paint and Roofing Co., 42 W. Broadway, New York. Catalogue free if mention this paper. s14-MWS&w3m

For Heating Dwellings, Public Buildings, etc., by Hot Water Circulation, the

Gurney Hot Water Heaters AND RADIATORS

are the original and best. They have never failed to take the highest awards wherever shown.

Send for our new illustrated book "How Best to Heat our Homes," a work of art on the subject of house-warming.

GURNEY HOT WATER HEATER CO.,
163 Franklin St., Boston, Mass.

GEORGE E. GIFFORD,
UNDERTAKER AND EMBALMER,
Westport, - - Mass.,

FURNISHES everything pertaining to the business. Parties wishing his services can telephone to C. A. Gifford's store, Head-of-Westport, where all calls will be promptly attended to. s8-d&w3m

LINEN PAPER AND ENVELOPES
Large Variety and Low Prices
—AT THE—
STANDARD OFFICE.

WELCOME SOAP

Is not advertised to preserve clothes, but will do less injury and give better results than any soap in the world.

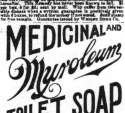

The Evening Standard.

ESTABLISHED FEBRUARY, 1850.]   NEW BEDFORD, THURSDAY, NOVEMBER 17, 1892.   TWO CENTS.

HASKELL & TRIPP.

"TAMS"

We have the *genuine* Scotch Tam O' Shanter caps now so stylish for youngsters, both girls and boys. Our prices are 50c. and 69c. each, and are less than similar goods can be bought elsewhere.

Girls' trimmed hats, 79c. and $1; exceedingly pretty styles.

Young women's walking hats, trimmed, ready to put right on, 75c. each.

Every style of headwear for babies and small children. Those handsome changeable silk bonnets, trimmed with fur, go out as fast as we can get them. Price only $1.

Skirts.

Beyond a doubt this is *the* place for skirts. Our fast black sateen skirt, lined throughout, and with deep gathered ruffle at foot, is a "hummer" for $1.

Good melton skirts, all the way from 79c. to $2.

Silk skirts, $5 and $6.

White merino underskirts, 50c. each.

Cut in halves.

The prices on Dress Goods are now but half what they were a month ago. If you are in no immediate need of a dress, never mind. You can afford to buy a pattern now and keep it until you do need a new gown even if it isn't until next year.

Dollar dress stuffs for 50c.,
Half-dollar material for 25c.,
Quarter-dollar suitings for 12½c.,

"don't go a-begging."

We have had a lively time since starting the sale of the above at slaughtered prices. We propose to keep up the fun several days longer, as we need the room for other things.

Two very good hosiery items:

No. 1—*For women.*
Better fast black, fleecy lined hose for 25c. a pair than generally sold so low. Every seam woven.

No. 2—*For men.*
The thickest, softest camels' hair and natural wool socks ever offered for 25c. a pair. *Seamless.*

Yes, this is the store for down pillows.

No doubt about it.

Cotton covered:

18-in.	20-in.	22-in.	24-in.
$1.00	$1.25	$1.50	$2.00

Silk covered:

16-in.	18-in.
$1.25	$2.00

Sateen covered:

16-in.	18-in.
$1.00	$1.25

Hair filled, silk covered pillows, $1 and $1.25.

Novelties in silk tidies, hand painted, now on display in our upholstery gallery.

You have forgotten that small bill. It was due Oct. 1st.

HASKELL & TRIPP,

Department Stores,

Purchase and William Streets.

NO BILL AGAINST SMITH.

Grand Jury Ends One of the Complications Arising from the "Rustler" War.

CHEYENNE, Wyo., Nov. 17.—The report of the grand jury in the U. S. Court of Wyoming yesterday ended one of the complications arising out of the late "Rustler" war in this State. After the invasion suits were commenced in the federal courts by the big stockmen against 40 small stockmen, or so-called rustlers, of Johnson county, to restrain them from holding so-called illegal round-ups. While on his way to serve processes in these suits George Wellman, a deputy U. S. marshal was assassinated. Frank Smith, one of the defendants on the injunction suit, while in Cheyenne a few weeks later, was arrested on a charge of conspiracy to deprive H. M. Blair of Chicago, one of the plaintiffs, of his rights under the United States law.

Smith was held a month in jail without a hearing. Then his bail was fixed at the excessive sum of $40,000. He furnished this, but was held in jail a week and was rearrested as soon as released on the charge of conspiring to kill a deputy marshal. Habeas corpus proceedings were commenced by Smith's attorney before Judge Riner, and Smith was discharged. He was again arrested, and on the hearing held without bail. Yesterday the case presented by District grand jury, which returned "not a true bill" on all the indictments against Smith.

Smith will at once commence civil suits against several prominent stockmen here for false imprisonment. An investigation of the proceedings by which he was held for a month without a hearing and excessive bail was demanded will be begun by the Department of Justice at Washington. The question of the constitutionality of the Wyoming round-up law will be tested at the present term of the Federal Court.

CLAIMS TO BE A PROPHET.

Frederick Engels Says He Predicted Downfall of Protection in America.

LONDON, Nov. 17.—The Berlin correspondent of the *Times* says: "Frederick Engels, in the socialist organ, *Forwarts*, claims that he predicted four years ago the downfall of protection in America, and that now the second portion of his prophecy is on the eve of fulfilment, namely, the destruction of English monopoly of the world's trade through the advent of free trade in America. Engels says there will be an industrial struggle such as the world has never before seen; that the dismal story of the last decade with respect to cotton and woollen factories so familiar to every Lancashire operative will repeat itself in every other field of industry; and that Great Britain will sink to the position of Holland, unless the working classes come to the rescue by adopting socialism."

An article in the *Hamburger Nachrichten*, inspired by Prince Bismarck, criticises unfavorably Dr. Miquel's proposals for financial reform.

THE PANAMA PROSECUTION.

Interview with M. Charles De Lesseps on the Situation.

PARIS, Nov. 17.—The directors of the Panama Canal Co. who are to be prosecuted by the government will be allowed three months to prepare their defence.

LONDON, Nov. 17.—The *Standard's* Paris correspondent sends to his paper an interview with M. Charles De Lesseps, quoted from *La France*, regarding the government's decision to prosecute the directors of the Canal Company. De Lesseps said his father, Count De Lesseps, has been so much affected by the decision that he has been unable to leave his room for three days. "As far as my father and myself are concerned," M. De Lesseps added, "we have nothing to fear from an inquiry. Those who accuse us of squandering millions will be astonished to learn that in many instances we have ourselves been a prey." An eminent colleague of M. Eiffel's said that M. Eiffel would prove the charges against him were calumnious.

CHANGE MUST SURELY COME.

The London Times Talks About the "Absurdities of McKinleyism."

LONDON, Nov. 17.—The *Times*, commenting on the speeches of Messrs. Depew and Reid at the New York Chamber of Commerce banquet on Tuesday night, says: The eagerness of the defeated party to abrogate the McKinley law is in itself sufficient to inspire the victors with caution. Mr. Cleveland has other and better reasons for delay. The McKinley tariff enlists the support of a powerful body of capitalists and numbers of workingmen, and although their forces were vanquished by the overpowering movement of public opinion, it is not desirable to make their defeat too painful and ruinous. A change from the most monstrous absurdities of McKinleyism to something like an endurable tariff will probably be slow; but it cannot be long postponed, nor can it be restricted within narrow bounds."

EXPLOSION OF POWDER.

Democratic Jollification Ends in a Terrible Disaster.

FAYETTEVILLE, Ark., Nov. 17.—The Democrats of Mountain View had a presidential election celebration in the district school-house last evening and a terrible disaster ended the proceedings prematurely. During the speeches and while the building was packed two kegs of powder exploded. The school-house was wrecked and a number of its occupants buried in the ruins. Shrieks and moans came from the mass of timbers, and it was evident that the calamity was terrible. The debris took fire in several places and it was hard work to prevent the cremation of the persons imprisoned. A son and a daughter of Silas Graham were taken out dead, and Berry Sheed was so badly injured that he has since died. Another, name unknown, has been killed. Fifteen were injured, some fatally, but their names have as yet not been learned.

Knights of Labor Assembly.

ST. LOUIS, Mo., Nov. 17.—At the afternoon session yesterday of the K. of L. the reports of the committee on law was submitted. A clause was adopted advocating the establishment of labor employment bureaus in each State. The committee was instructed to frame a plank demanding a graduated income tax and a tax on inheritance.

Stage on a Cliff Fell.

OURAY, Col., Nov. 17.—By the falling of a stage over a cliff near here four persons were seriously injured, one of whom will die. Harry Hoopitaller was fatally injured, the others injured are George Schrieber, Frank Niero and W. N. Allis on.

Evicted Tenants and Landlords.

DUBLIN, Nov. 17.—The executive committee of the Irish landlords' convention intend to issue with the appearance of the report of the evicted tenants' commission a counter report giving the landlords' side of the question.

Syndicate Wants to Buy.

HALIFAX, N. S., Nov. 17.—At a meeting of the directors of the Nova Scotia Midland Railway & Iron Company yesterday Mr. Richmond, president, said that he had an offer to sell the road and iron properties to a wealthy syndicate.

LONDON, Nov. 17.—The *Chronicle* says there is a rumor current that Lord Randolph Churchill has purchased the *Pall Mall Gazette*.

NEW WITNESSES

Before the Grand Jury in the Borden Case.

District Attorney Knowlton Putting in Important Evidence.

New Bedford Druggists Among those Examined To-day.

[Special Dispatch.]

TAUNTON, Nov. 17.—The grand jury sitting on the Lizzie Borden case came in at 9 30 this morning at the court-house in this city. Owing to the bad ventilation and poor heat in the grand jury room adjournment was made to the First District Court room, across the street, where the examination of witnesses proceeded.

The full grand jury was present and the facts of testimony were collected and presented by District Attorney Knowlton and Attorney-General Pillsbury. A little knot of interested and expectant newspaper men gathe red around the entrance, but were debarred the satisfaction of seeing the witnesses. City Marshal Hilliard of Fall River then steadfastly guarded in the clerk's room, with the doors closed tight as a drum and the only inklings of proceedings obtainable were gleaned from garrulous witnesses as they came out.

It is learned that nothing particularly new or startling in the line of evidence was produced, most of the witnesses having testified in the lower court at the preliminary trial, and facts developed were not of as interesting a nature as those of yesterday. Among the witnesses examined were Officers Connors, Mullaley, Chase, Hyde and Edson of Fall River; Police Matron Reagan, who told of Lizzie's conduct in the police station and the interview between the sisters; Frank H. Kilroy, a Harvard medical student, who happened to be in Smith's drug store when it is alleged Lizzie Borden tried to buy hydrocyanic acid; Eli Bence and Fred Hart, drug clerks there; Thomas Brown, who worked for the company on Third street opposite the Borden house; Thomas Boulds, Charles Sawyer and Harry Peirce, who were called in on the discovery of the murder; Dr. Bowen and his wife and Mrs. Churchill, the intimate neighbors of the Bordens; Mrs. Kirby, an old lady on Third street, back of the Borden house, who heard noises the night preceding the murder; Miss Johnson, a school teacher; Mark Chase, an express driver; James E. Cuneen, superintendent of the Seaconnet Mill; Charles Cook, William L. Hacking, George L. Douglass and Oliver Durling, who together were sitting talking on Mrs. Churchill's steps when the terrible deed was done and who saw no one enter or leave the Borden premises; Hiram Harrington, a relative of the Bordens, who, it is said, knows more of the internal affairs of the household than the prisoner wishes he did; Miss Carrie Rogers, a saleslady in the Troy dry goods store, a new witness who is said to have novel testimony; Orrick Smalley of New Bedford, whose friend at Craigville, George W. Hathaway, told him about a conversation with Andrew J. Borden in which Mr. Borden was said to have told of family infelicity, and Edward E. Wright and William R. Martin, New Bedford druggists, who think it was Lizzie Borden who tried to buy hydrocyanic acid of them.

More witnesses are to be examined and it is difficult to tell when the sitting will be completed. City Marshal Hilliard told a *Standard* man that in his opinion the jury would not report to Judge Thompson much before Friday and probably not until Saturday.

LOOKING FOR AGNES.

Mrs. Brewster Makes Inquiries in Fall River for Her Missing Daughter.

FALL RIVER, Nov. 17.—Agnes J. Brewster, 17 years of age, left her home in West Brewster, Mass., about four weeks ago in company with an employe of the Old Colony company and has not returned since. To-day her mother made a complaint at the Central Police Station and a search for the missing girl has been commenced in this city.

TRUNK LINE AGREEMENT.

Pool Which Will Remove Antagonism and Give All a Fair Recompense.

NEW YORK, Nov. 17.—The *Herald* says that the presidents of the trunk lines at a meeting yesterday entered into an agreement which, if carried out, will end most of the warfare between the companies and be a cause of thanksgiving to the stockholders. The agreement, it is said, is in the nature of a pool by which all the roads will get a fair recompense for hauling traffic and by which all antagonism will be removed.

Syndicate Buying Uruguayan Bonds.

LONDON, Nov. 17.—A syndicate of bankers and financiers yesterday bought all the Uruguayan bonds obtainable. The purchasers advanced the price to near 40. The syndicate offered 40 for all these bonds held by the Bank of England on account of the Baring estate. The bank declined to sell. The syndicate intends to force the price to 50.

Assaulted by a Negro.

PROVIDENCE, Nov. 17.—This morning Frank Horton was assaulted by a negro named William R. Fitzgerald, who had done some work for Horton and was not satisfied with the pay. The negro hit Horton on the head twice with a stone tied in a handkerchief, cutting severe gashes. Fitzgerald was arrested and bound over to a higher court.

M. Eiffel Not Included.

PARIS, Nov. 17.—The *Dix Neuvieme Siecle* says that M. Eiffel will not be included among the directors of the Panama Canal Co. whom the government intends to prosecute for attempting to swindle the stockholders.

Funeral of John Hoey.

NEW YORK, Nov. 17.—The funeral services over the remains of John Hoey was conducted this morning at St. Leo's church at Woodlawn cemetery. The interment was at Woodlawn Cemetery.

Drowning Accident.

RUMFORD FALLS, Me., Nov. 17.—Charles H. and John A. Heming of Calais were drowned this morning while crossing above the upper dam.

Big Haul of Mackerel.

HALIFAX, N.S., Nov. 17.—The American seiner Joseph Rowe got 80 barrels of magnificent mackerel 150 miles off Sambro Tuesday night.

WEATHER INDICATIONS.

FAIR AND WARMER.

WASHINGTON, Nov. 17.—For the 24 hours from 8 a. m. to-day: For Massachusetts, Rhode Island and Connecticut, fair, followed by rain in the interior; warmer Friday morning, southerly winds.

FAIR, FOLLOWED BY RAIN.

BOSTON, Nov. 17.—Local forecast for New England until Saturday: Fair to-day followed by increasing cloudiness and rain, slight changes in temperature; winds mostly westerly to southerly.

SENATOR VEST'S IDEA.

How the Democracy Should Handle the Tariff in the Coming Congress.

KANSAS CITY, Mo., Nov. 17.—Senator Vest in an interview yesterday expressed himself freely as to how the democracy should handle the tariff in the coming session of Congress. Said he: "There is no danger to the country in our victory. We do not propose to smash the business interests as the blacksmith should destroy a fine watch. We will proceed cautiously, deliberately, but firmly, to readjust the tariff taxes so that tariff shall not be a shield for trusts and monopolies. Free trade, pure and simple, is impossible, for we must raise a large amount of money necessary to carry on the government but by which to carry on the government the import duties, but in doing so we should act cautiously.

It is impossible to specify the details of proposed legislation, but I can venture to say for myself that I would remove the duty on refined sugar and on binding twine, and decrease the duties on tin plate. I would also make wool free, and reduce the duties on woollen goods and hardware and cutlery. There are many incongruities and outrages in the McKinley act which should be remedied. I might give many instances, but they have been already discussed. McKinley's law has defeated his party. It was made by the manufacturers, and failed to humbug the people with the pretence that the consumer did not pay the tax."

Senator Vest discussed the idea of an extra session. "Mr. Cleveland is too wise headed for any such nonsense," said he. "He does not believe in a cavalry charge upon the existing system of taxation and finance. He is firm, but also conservative, and knows that we must make haste slowly.

We intend to do the work thoroughly, but not like boys at play. Our first duty when we meet in December will be to provide for the deficit created by our Republican friends in the billion dollar congress. We must redeem our promises to the people and prove ourselves worthy of their confidence. If we do, the Democratic party will remain in power for the next quarter of a century."

FREE TRADE AND AN 8-HOUR DAY.

Subjects Touched Upon by Mr. Fogg of the Manchester Statistical Society.

LONDON, Nov. 17.—An interesting address was delivered before the Manchester Statistical Society last evening by its president, Mr. Fogg. The speaker said that while America, in four years, with protection had increased the number of her spindles only about 8 per cent., India had, with free trade, increased the number of her spindles 32 per cent. He could not see why the operatives should demand a working day of eight hours. England now takes only one-third of the cotton grown, instead of one-half, as she did 20 years ago; and the dividends paid in Oldham, a fair example of trade, have averaged under 3 1-2 per cent. in the last 16 years. That profit, with the certainty of a large loss on the principal, is hardly likely to induce investment in the industry when the eight-hour day is added to the differences pressing on the trade.

CLAIMS TO BE A RUSSIAN NOBLEMAN.

Vladimir Nicholas Rumin in Prison at San Francisco.

SAN FRANCISCO, Nov. 17. — Vladimir Nicholas Rumin, who claims to be a Russian nobleman and chief of the Russian prisons of Siberia, is in custody at the city prison, charged with intemperance and disorderly conduct. According to his story, as told by friends who visited him, Rumin, who arrived here about two weeks ago, had his attention attracted to the prisoners at the city hall yesterday, and he proceeded to examine the prison. The turnkey objected and ordered him away. Rumin, not understanding English, did not comply, and he was accordingly hustled into the jail after a desperate resistance, and was strapped to a cot in the prison hospital. Rumin declares he will report the affair to his government.

SEVERED HIS VICTIM'S HEAD.

A Kentucky Farmer Brutally Murders a Neighbor in a Cornfield.

DANVILLE, Ky., Nov. 17.—James Christman, a farmer, living near High Bridge, in Jessamine county, north of this city, brutally murdered his neighbor, George Woods, yesterday. Woods was at work gathering his corn crop, when a charge of buckshot fired by Christman struck him in the stomach. Woods fell mortally wounded and his assailant rushed from behind a shock of corn and attacked his victim with a knife and with the fury of a madman cut his head from his body. The murder is the result of a little trouble between the men two years ago. Christman made his escape and a posse is now searching for him.

Republican Counted In.

DANVERS, Nov. 17.—The recount in the fifth Essex Senatorial district elects Samuel Sawyer, rep., over L. M. Brock, dem., by 18 votes. The first count gave Brock 38 plurality.

HOME MATTERS.

POOR TERMINAL FACILITIES.—The insufficiency of the railroad terminal facilities in this city were never more apparent than at the present time. Contractors who are building the new mills and the other buildings in the process of construction are greatly hindered and delayed through their inability to secure supplies promptly. It is said that there are now on the sidings over 300 loaded cars and only room to work on the unloading of 66 at one time.

THE CHRYSANTHEMUM SHOW.—The proceeds from the Gardeners' and Florists' Club exhibition netted nearly $225. This will just about cover expenses and pay the premiums. Hill's Band played in front of the hall last evening, but the weather was such that the attendance was very small. During the evening the plants and cut flowers of George C. Hilss and Robert H. Woodhouse found a ready sale.

LARCENY.—Yesterday afternoon, in the temporary absence of Mrs. Ann J. De Wolf from her furniture and clothing store, No. 305 Purchase street, some one entered the rear door and stole and carried away two overcoats. Charles McKenna was this morning arrested by Inspector Parker and Officer Cannavan for the crime. He was arraigned in the District Court and the case continued till tomorrow. The overcoats were not recovered.

RECOVERED.—A Frenchman from Taunton, who yesterday let a horse and carriage to a man who had not returned them, was in the city to-day looking for the turnout. He recovered them in a stable here and took them back to Taunton.

RELEASED—James Cody of Taunton, committed to the House of Correction Aug. 19th for drunkenness, was released by the County Commissioners to-day.

WE HAVE a few of those nice Florida Oranges, 19c. dozen. White Cash.

PERSONAL.—

Andrew M. Bush, Jr., left this city yesterday for El Paso, Texas, for the benefit of his health.

Holder M. Brownell was attacked with illness at the matinee at the Opera House yesterday afternoon, but is comfortable to-day, although he is not yet out of bed.

At the annual meeting of the Home Market Club at Boston yesterday, William H. Bent of Taunton was elected president and Arnold B. Sanford of Fall River one of the executive committee.

Edward Atkinson was the guest of Andrew G. Pierce.

Rev. Dr. Mark Trafton, formerly of County Street M. E. church, this city, has consented to write for the *Zion's Herald* a series of articles upon "The Men Whom I Have Heard in Pulpit, in Congress, and on the Platform."

OBITUARY.—Mr. James S. Morrison, after a severe illness, passed peacefully away at his residence, 48 Forest street, last evening. Born in Hawick, Scotland, he came to this country at the age of seven. His people settled in Ballardvale, Andover, Mass., where he spent his boyhood, attending the village school and Phillips Academy. When his school days were completed he chose the trade of carriage trimming, and by strict faithfulness to his duties he became a most successful workman. For the past 13 years he has worked for Brownell & Ashley, and was greatly respected both by employers and shopmates. By nature a quiet, retiring man, he preferred the life and associations of home to mingling with the outside world. He tried to live an upright and honorable life, and the strength and sterling loyalty of his character won the esteem of all who knew him. He leaves a wife and three sons who deeply feel their loss.

Benjamin Covel, one of the oldest residents of Fall River, died suddenly at noon yesterday of heart failure. He was a wellknown master carpenter, and had constructed many mills, and large buildings for the Old Colony railroad. He leaves three sons.

THE UNION STREET RAILWAY COMPANY has purchased Thomson-Houston motors with which to equip the cars on the electric line of the road, and it is expected that they will be running with them some time next week. Several weeks ago Weightman motors were ordered, and soon after they arrived the company furnishing them failed and the railway company refused to accept them. The new motors are said to be superior in every way to those now in use. They are easier to operate, perfectly noiseless, water-proof, and there is no possibility of the motorman or passengers receiving a shock.

NEARLY COMPLETED.—United States Inspector Cluss was in the city Monday and Tuesday, made a thorough examination of the new post office building, and pronounced the work very satisfactory. Some of the furniture has arrived and the building will be ready for occupancy at an early date.

EDMOND O'KEEFE, the superintendent of construction, will remain in New Bedford for two or three weeks longer on the approaches and a few other matters relating to the building.

A NOVEL MOUSE TRAP.—A little girl in this city recently had made for her by an older sister a worsted rabbit, which, for want of cotton, was stuffed with meal. The little girl kept her rabbit in the attic, and a few days ago after going up to play with bunnie the child came down and said there was a mouse in her rabbit. Investigation showed that the mouse had gnawed through the covering and eaten his way so far into the interior that he was unable to extricate himself and was captured.

EDUCATIONAL ASSOCIATION.—The Dukes County Educational Association began its 44th annual meeting by an instructive address on "Canada" by Rev. John E. Locke in the Baptist church, Vineyard Haven, last evening. A business meeting was held this morning in Association Hall, after which a discourse on "History, and How to Teach It" by Mr. T. P. Weeks, principal of the Vineyard Haven schools, followed. An interesting programme will be carried out this evening and to-morrow.

HOUSE WARMING.—The fellow clerks of Howard Collins at I. C. Sherman & Son's last evening with lady friends called on him at his residence on Scooticut Neck, Fairhaven, and gave him a house warming. Dancing was indulged in, a nice supper was served, and the company did not separate till a late hour.

NEW TURNOUT.—Josiah Hunt has just put on a new oil tank wagon to meet the demands of his rapidly increasing business. The wagon is a beauty. It is a complete new turnout, including new horse and harness.

LOSS BY THE STORM.—During yesterday's storm William T. Dunn's fish trap at Ricketson's Point was broken by the wind and high tide. Fully 20 barrels of fish escaped, causing a considerable loss.

FISH PLENTY.—Trap fishermen report fish very plenty and good hauls are secured after every tide. William T. Dunn took 25 barrels of frost fish in his trap at Ricketson's Point this forenoon.

"THE CARE AND FEEDING OF INFANTS" will be interesting to every mother. A copy will be mailed free to any one who sends her address to the Doliber-Goodale Co., Boston, Mass.

MORE LONG, woolly white rugs you were waiting for have arrived at B. H. Waite & Co's, 71 Wm. st.; also very handsome bear and wolf skins in two colors, beauties.

THE SEA VIEW SHOAL.—John McCullough has purchased the ruins of the Sea View House in Cottage City with the engines, boilers, etc.

DIPHTHERIA.—Three new cases of diphtheria have been reported at the office of the Board of Health since Saturday.

EUREKA LODGE, F. & A. M. will hold a special communication to-morrow evening. See special notice.

UNION LODGE, K. OF P.—Members of this lodge and uniformed members are requested to meet at Castle Hall at 6 45 this evening.

SEWING will be given out at the Union for Good Works rooms Saturday afternoon at 2 o'clock.

M. S. AYER of Boston and of Ayer's Hygienic Coffee fame has written a book on "Diet Reform." Send for it. Price 15c.

ANOTHER LOT of four-crown Raisins, 9c. lb. White Cash.

PRECINCT OFFICERS will be paid off to-morrow.

BONBERRIES, 7c. qt. White Cash.

CUT FLOWERS and floral designs, bouquets and baskets of flowers at 5 Purchase street.

WE SHALL BE ABLE to make you the prices on Beef this week. White Cash.

MASONIC.—Sutton Commandery will hold a special conclave this evening.

JUST RECEIVED, another lot of Country Butter, very low. White Cash.

A SPRING MORNING after the rain.

FIVE POUND boxes Glendon. White Cash

DYSPEPSIA cured by Hood's Sarsaparilla.

HASKELL & TRIPP.

Thanksgiving hints.

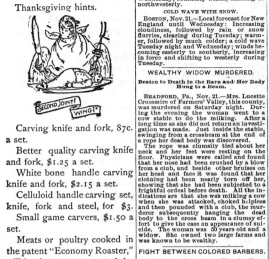

Carving knife and fork, 87c. a set.

Better quality carving knife and fork, $1.25 a set.

White bone handle carving knife and fork, $2.15 a set.

Celluloid handle carving set, knife, fork and steel, for $3.

Small game carvers, $1.50 a set.

Meats or poultry cooked in the patent "Economy Roaster," will be done to a turn and deliciously tender, all juices and flavor being retained in the meat. Five sizes: 69c., 98c., $1.17, $1.50, $1.75.

Tray cloths, new pattern, hemstitched and openwork, 50c. each.

Sideboard scarfs, hemstitched and openwork, 50c. each.

Special napkin values at $1.25, $1.50 and $2 per dozen. (Of course we have finer and cheaper as well.)

Bleached satin damask table linen, handsome design, 72 inches wide, costing $1 a yard, is worthy of note.

The Book Department is now ready for early buyers of holiday presents. Everything marked way down to smallest possible notch. Superb display of children's books.

Games.

We don't ask you to read a list of *all* the games, but the following will give you a good idea of this attractive line:

Authors, 8c.
City Life, 17c.
Checkers, 21c., 47c., 87c.
Derby Steeple Chase, 18c.
Errand Boy, 18c.
Foot Ball, 35c.
Fish Pond, 18c.
Golden Locks, 35c.
Halma, 69c.
Jack, the Giant Killer, 35c.
Klymo, 18c.
Lotto, 18c., 35c., 58c.
Messenger Boy, 87c.
McAllister, 35c.
Parcheesi, 81c.
Kings and Queens, 47c.
Round the World with Nellie Bly, 35c.
Steeple Chase, 35c.
Twiddles, 18c.
Telegraph Boy, 69c.
The Judges, 17c.
Tiddledy Winks, 18c.
What D'ye. Buy, 17c.
Yacht Race, 87c.

Blocks.

A B C Blocks, 18c. Christmas blocks, 35c. Cat and Dog Blocks, 18c. Columbian Exposition Blocks, 53c. And many others.

Grand opportunity to buy California Blankets. Special sale this week. Elegant goods at about the prices usually charged for much commoner Eastern Blankets.

HASKELL & TRIPP,

Department Stores,

Purchase and William Streets.

WEATHER INDICATIONS.
COLDER.

WASHINGTON, Nov. 21.—For the 24 hours from 8 a. m. to-day: For Massachusetts, Rhode Island and Connecticut, fair, slightly warmer Tuesday morning, followed by much colder weather on Wednesday; southerly winds, shifting to northwesterly.

COLD WAVE WITH SNOW.

BOSTON, Nov. 21.—Local forecast for New England until Wednesday: Increasing cloudiness, followed by rain or snow flurries, clearing during Tuesday; warmer, followed by much colder; a cold wave Tuesday night and Wednesday; winds becoming easterly to southerly, increasing in force and shifting to westerly during Tuesday.

WEALTHY WIDOW MURDERED.
Beaten to Death in the Barn and Her Body Hung to a Beam.

BRADFORD, Pa., Nov. 21.—Mrs. Lucette Crossmire of Farmers' Valley, this county, was murdered on Saturday night. During the evening the woman went to a cow stable to do the milking. After a long time as she did not return an investigation was made. Just inside the stable, swinging from a crossbeam at the end of a rope her dead body was discovered.

The rope was clumsily tied about her neck and her feet were resting on the floor. Physicians were called and found that her nose had been crushed by a blow from a club, and beside other bruises on her head and face it was found that her clothing had been nearly torn off her, showing that she had been subjected to a frightful ordeal before death. All the indications are that she was milking a cow when she was attacked, choked helpless and then pounded with a club, the murderer subsequently hanging the dead body to the cross beam in a clumsy effort to give the case an appearance of suicide. The woman was 50 years old and a widow. She owned two large farms and was known to be wealthy.

FIGHT BETWEEN COLORED BARBERS.
One Slashed with a Razor Dies in Three Minutes.

WASHINGTON, Ind., Nov. 21.—About 8 o'clock Sunday morning Henry Stewart, Ed Harmon and another colored man were in a saloon playing cards. A dispute arose and the lie passed. Stewart jumped to his feet and seized a razor. Harmon then knocked him down with a chair. But Stewart seemed bent on a fight, and he was knocked down four times in succession. Harmon tried to escape, but Stewart rose to his feet and rushing at Harmon struck him a blow that almost severed Harmon's right arm. The man bled to death in three minutes. Stewart is in hiding, and the police and several deputies are on his track. There is strong talk of lynching. Stewart and Harmon are both colored.

A FIGHT FOR LIFE.
Disastrous Prairie Fire in Clark County, Nebraska.

NEWPORT, Neb., Nov. 21.—One of the worst prairie fires Clark county ever witnessed started yesterday while the wind was blowing a hurricane. The fire is supposed to have started from a spark from a farm-house a mile east of Clarkville. But Stewart seemed bent on a fight, and he was knocked down four times in succession. Harmon tried to escape, but he was blowing a hurricane. The fire is supposed to have started from a spark from a farm-house a mile east of Clarkville. The farmers, with the help of about 200 persons from Newport and Bassett, by hard fighting saved thousands of dollars worth of property which otherwise would have been lost. It seemed to be a fight for life as well as property. Several families were compelled to seek lakes, wells and caves to save their lives. Four or five farm-houses with farms and granaries were burned. As near as can be learned no lives were lost.

BRIGANDAGE IN SPAIN.
A Contractor Beaten and Robbed and His Wife and Niece Bound.

LONDON, Nov. 21.—The Standard's correspondent at Madrid sends particulars of a daring outrage perpetrated yesterday by Spanish brigands near Bilbao. Nine robbers, armed with rifles, pistols and knives went to the house of Senor Sandiaga, a contractor, building a railway from Bilbao Lezama and demanded wine. This being refused them and the master of the house being absent they gagged and bound the wife and niece of Senor Sandiaga and awaited his return. When he reached home the brigands brutally beat him, severely injuring both his eyes and robbed him of £2000 which he had brought to pay his workmen.

THE ANTI-TRUST BILL.
Ex-Senator Edmunds Believes It Is Constitutional and Should Be Enforced.

CHICAGO, Nov. 21.—The Inter-Ocean publishes an interview with ex-Senator Edmunds, in which he declares his belief in the constitutionality of the Sherman anti-trust bill, and advocates its rigid enforcement. He declares that the framers of the bill intended to reach all railroad pool and traffic agreements where they related to putting up of rates. It is claimed that if the courts hold to Mr. Edmunds' views the pooling arrangement between the railroad presidents will be illegal, as well as the agreed rates for World's Fair business next year.

A Maniac's Deed.

READING, Pa., Nov. 21.—Three miles from this city last evening John S. Heller, age 42, shot Sebastian Muhringer through the head and then put a bullet through his own heart. The excitement caused by the tragedy is tremendous. Heller was undoubtedly seized with sudden insanity. Muhringer was brought to Reading in a critical condition.

TELEGRAPHIC BREVITIES.

Dynamiters are at work in Lisbon.

Secretary Foster is confident there will be no deficit this year.

Emperor William and the King of Saxony disagree about Prince Bismark.

The Democratic victory in the United States pleases Canadian mining men.

Well, Dreyfus & Co. of Boston have yielded to the demands of their women shirtmakers, who were on strike.

New York detectives raided a den of thieves, captured a dozen crooks and recovered $6000 worth of stolen property.

Cars were wrecked and several passengers injured by a collision of trains on the Boston and Albany at Newton Highlands.

Matthew T. Trumpour, one of the defaulting officers of the Ulster county (N. Y.) Savings Institution, was found guilty.

New York and Massachusetts are to make no display in the World's fair educational section unless adequate space is provided.

Mrs. Mary Cantwell of Pawtucket, R. I., aged 50 years, was found drowned in the Blackstone river at Valley Falls, R. I. Her death was accidental.

Miss Louisa Harrison, a member of the King's Daughters, while suffering from religious mania, attempted to jump from a third-story window in New York.

Francis A. Boothby, a former member of the city government, and for many years a member of the board of overseers at Saco, Me., died in that city, leaving a family.

A hurricane in Chesterfield, N. H., unroofed barns and blew down chimneys, timber and shade trees. A summer residence on Prospect Hill, Hancock, was also destroyed.

Ocean Steamers.

Arrived—At Boston, Catalonia, from Angloman, Liverpool; Alier, New York.

THE GRAND JURY DISMISSED.
Members Paid Off and Permitted to Go to Their Homes.

New and Important Evidence in the 'Borden Murder Case.

Will Be Ready and Presented by Thursday, Dec. 1.

[Special Dispatch.]

TAUNTON, Nov. 21.—The grand jury came in this morning and after hearing evidence in one or two minor cases the jurymen were paid off and dismissed until Thursday, Dec. 1. This means that new, and a *Standard* reporter learns from the best authority, very important evidence in the Borden murder case is yet to be presented.

BANKRUPT SPAIN.
Parisian Bank Advances the Government Another Twenty-five Million Francs.

PARIS, Nov. 21.—The Banque de Paris et de Pay Bas has advanced the Spanish government another 25,000,000 francs. This makes 75,000,000 francs advanced by the bank. In loaning the money the bank imposes a condition that the Cortes meet at the beginning of December and authorize the government to raise a large loan, part of which shall be used to repay the bank. Opposition is organizing to compel a full discussion of the financial embarrassment and to prevent the ministers from rushing a loan bill through. If the debate is protracted it may end in the suspension of the payment of the interest on the national debt.

The Rothschilds having declined to advance more money they are now clamoring for the payment of advances made by them. Spanish bankruptcy coming on top of the collapse of the Panama Canal Company would be a heavy blow to French industry.

RAILROAD TRAFFIC PARALYZED
Through the Heavy Damage by Wind and Rain in the Northwest.

SEATTLE, Wash., Nov. 21.—There has been a heavy rainfall throughout this country for the past two days, and the prevailing high wind has played havoc with nearly every railroad in the state. Between Seattle and Tacoma the tracks on all the railroads have been washed out in several places. No trains are running to the north either on account of bad washouts or slides on Seattle lake shore. The Eastern and Great Northwestern, Columbia and Puget Sound Narrow Gauge roads also suffered by two slides, one at Cedar Mountain and the other on the bluff between Black Diamond and Franklin. Through traffic is paralyzed. The Union Pacific has been the heaviest sufferer. A slide on this road occurred at Bonesville, Or., which will stop trains for several days. The road has also suffered in the eastern part of the state. The Northern Pacific has had several washouts west of the Cascades. Telegraph wires are down in all directions, and the thorough extent of the storm cannot now be learned. All the rivers are reported phenomenally high. Considerable damage is reported to small crafts at the coast towns.

A POLITICAL ROW
Results in a Probably Fatal Stabbing Affray at Norwich, Conn.

NORWICH, Conn., Nov. 21.—As a result of a political quarrel, Charles Caswell was probably fatally stabbed by Edgar Sparrow. The stabbing occurred at the Miantomah Hotel, two miles from this city.

James Mulholland, proprietor of the hotel, settled his election bet with Peter Lumsden Saturday night, by wheeling him from the hotel to this city and return, Lumsden the while playing the bagpipes. The affair attracted a great crowd, and more or less drunkenness was the result.

The party left this city to return at 11 o'clock, and, on reaching the hotel, more drinking was indulged in, and a row broke out, in which knives were used. Caswell received a deep cut in the bowels. Sparrow was arrested and Caswell is also at the station house under the care of the surgeon.

Was an Old Politician of Boston.

BOSTON, Nov. 21.—Vincent Laforme, an old resident of South Boston, died yesterday. His connection with local politics brought him into public life, which ended when certain charges, which were not proven, were made against him, alleging an attempt to bribe an alderman. Shortly after the charges were made Mr. Laforme had a stroke of paralysis, which was probably the primary cause of his death.

Killed His Friend.

BELLAIRE, O., Nov. 21.—In Proctor, a small town south of here, Franklin Huff and Michael Powell had engaged in a wrestling match. Powell threw Huff to the ground with great force and held him, which so enraged Huff that when he gained his feet he drew a dagger and stabbed Powell in the breast and he dropped dead. The men were among the most prominent residents in the valley and had always been friends. Huff is in jail.

Gloucester Sailors Lost.

PORTLAND, Me., Nov. 21.—Schooner Edith M. Prior arrived here and reports the loss of six men while taking in trawls off Matinicus. The lost men were: William Delano, Ames Simmons, Martin Butler, Joseph Hanlon, William Goodwin and David Merrow, all of Gloucester, Mass.

Crew Rescued by Life Savers.

PROVIDENCE, Nov. 21.—Schooner Vandalia, Captain Betts, of Ellsworth, Me., from New York for Rockland, laden with kerosene oil, ran ashore outside of the Far buoy off Watch Hill. The life-saving crew assisted in saving the schooner's crew and baggage. Loss is full of water.

New Job for Mr. Foster

WASHINGTON, Nov. 21.—When Mr. Foster retires from the state department he will go to Paris as agent of this government in charge of its case before the Behring sea arbitrators. Mrs. Foster will accompany him and they expect to be absent a year or more.

The Monongahela's Cruise.

NEWPORT, R. I., Nov. 21.—United States training ship Monongahela sails yesterday for her winter's cruise. She will cross the Azores, visit several ports there, then go to the Azores and return to the United States in time for the Columbian celebration at New York.

Three Bad Men Arrested.

HAMBURG, Nov. 21.—Three anarchists, suspected of complicity in the last explosion in Paris, have been arrested in this city.

N. Y. & N. E. STOCKHOLDERS.
Rather an Inharmonious Special Meeting in Boston This Forenoon.

BOSTON, Nov. 21.—The special meeting of the N. Y. & N. E. stockholders to-day was called to order at 10 a. m. Ex-Gov. Howard was elected chairman. The election was objected to by N. F. Goldsmith, who wanted President Parsons chairman. W. F. Brandies, counsel for Goldsmith, read the bylaws, which said the president should preside at all meetings of the stockholders of which he is present, and demanded that Mr. Parsons preside. He wished his protest entered on the records. Mr. Howard requested President Parsons to take the chair and he did so, explaining that he was indisposed.

The reading of the records was dispensed with.

The third article of the call to authorize and provide for the issue of consolidated mortgage bonds under the provision of the act of the State of Rhode Island was brought up.

Mr. Brandies moved that the resolution be laid on the table, but was voted down. He asked to have it put on record that he objected to this act.

It was voted to recommend so much of the vote of the stockholders passed March 8 as contemplated the possible exchange of shares of the preferred stock for consolidation bonds.

A motion was put to open the polls, but Mr. Brandies objected.

Mr. Brandies then asked why the stockholders were called now to ratify the lease of the Providence & Springfield, which was executed in October, 1890.

No one answered.

He then asked if a suit was not in progress to set aside this lease as it was made largely for the benefit of the directors and not for the company, and he wanted to know if there were not $500,000 of the Providence & Springfield bonds overdue and if the mayor of Providence had not taken possession of the road.

Mr. Lummis said the first two questions could be answered in the records of the court.

Mr. Parsons said it was the interest of the company to ratify this lease, but Mr. Brandies said that that did not answer his question.

President Parsons said Mr. Brandies was fooling away time. Mr. Brandies read a letter from Providence stating that default was made on the Providence & Springfield bonds and the default had continued 90 days, and that the Mayor of Providence demanded the sale of the road.

Mr. C. A. Prince said the counsel for Mr. Goldsmith was wasting time and his course led to delay as he was asking questions when he had the information. There had been a technical default on the Providence & Springfield bonds.

BOYCOTT ON A BROCKTON SHOE.
Manufacturers Charged with Refusing to Recognize Organized Labor.

NEW YORK, Nov. 21.—At the meeting here yesterday of the Central Labor Union, a delegate of the Lasters' Protective Union of America stated that there was a boycott on the shoes made by Bouve, Crawford & Co. of Brockton, Mass., for refusing to recognize organized labor. The boycott was unanimously indorsed.

ASHORE AND AFLOAT.

Sch. Sayanara Pulled Off Great Ledge by Tug Elsie.

VINEYARD-HAVEN, Nov. 21.—Schooner Sayanara, from St. John for New York with a cargo of piling, was ashore on Great Ledge, entrance to Woods Holl, this morning, but was floated by steam tug Elsie and proceeded apparently uninjured.

Sch. Eva May on Hawkerchief Shoal.

CHATHAM, Nov. 21.—Schooner Eva May, coal, Perth Amboy for Gardiner, Me., went ashore on the northwest part of Handkerchief Shoal at 3 o'clock this morning. Wreckers are throwing out the cargo and hope to float her to-night.

Murder and Suicide.

FRAZEE, Minn., Nov. 21.—T. L. Van Sickler, during a quarrel last night shot his wife twice through the body, one ball passing through her heart killing her. He then turned the weapon on himself and sent a bullet through his lungs. Then he shot F. C. Brown through the legs, following this with again shooting himself in the mouth, blowing the top of his head off.

MILWAUKEE, Wis., Nov. 21.—William Binder, book-keeper for the Leidersdorf Tobacco Company, this morning shot and killed his wife, his 7-year old daughter and himself. The affair occurred at the home of the family on Cambridge avenue.

Grand Army Encampment.

BOSTON, Nov. 21.—The annual encampment of the Grand Army of this State will be in this city Feb. 8 and 9. Junior Vice Department Commander W. A. Wetherbee, Chief Mustering Officer Charles S. Anthony, Department Inspector Joseph W. Thayer and Comrades John J. Warden and William R. Warner of the council have been appointed a committee to make arrangements for the banquet, and Department Commander James K. Churchill, Senior Vice Department Commander Eli W. Hall and Junior Vice Department Commander Wilfred A. Wetherbee, with the recipient of many valuable gifts, among them a gold watch, the present of her father. A bountiful collation was served and a fine time enjoyed.

Price Set Upon Desperadoes Heads.

PHOENIX, Ari., Nov. 21.—Gov. Martin has offered a reward of $6000 for the capture of "Kid," the notorious Apache cattle rustler, alive or dead, and $300 each for the capture of his companions. A number of old Indian hunters, allured by the price set upon the desperadoe's heads, have gone on his trail.

Salt Sheds Destroyed by Fire.

CHICAGO, Nov. 21.—Thirty sheds containing 230,000 barrels of salt belonging to the Michigan Salt Co., were almost totally destroyed by fire in Cummings last night. The loss is estimated at $250,000.

Hotel Burned.

WILMAR, Minn., Nov. 21.—The Merchants Hotel was burned early yesterday morning. All the guests escaped except West River, who perished in the flames. Loss $15,000; insured.

Cholera at St. Petersburg.

ST. PETERSBURG, Nov. 21.—Eleven new cases of cholera and three deaths were reported here yesterday.

HOME MATTERS.

ANOTHER RESCUED SAILOR.—It is reported in San Francisco that bark Jesse H. Freeman had rescued another of the crew of the Helen Mar floating on an ice-cake the day after the disaster. If the report proves true, another survivor will be added to the few previously named.

FUNERAL.—The funeral of the late Charles Browning took place at his late residence, 570 Purchase street, this noon. Rev. E. B. Rousmaniere officiated and the Orpheus Quartet sung. The burial took place in Oak Grove cemetery, the bearers being John G. Remington, Seth C. Caldwell, George W. Bennett and John Whitehead.

STILL UNDER CONSIDERATION.—It is understood that the mill authorities are considering the demand of the labor unions for an increase of 10 per cent.

NOTHING LIKE IT, Taber's mince meat.

The Evening Standard.

NEW BEDFORD, MASS.
TUESDAY EVENING, NOV. 22.

THREE EDITIONS DAILY.
No. 87 Union Street.
PUBLISHED BY
E. ANTHONY & SONS,
INCORPORATED.

—TERMS—
Six Dollars a Year, Three Dollars for Six Months, in advance; Single Copies Two Cents

A NEW THEORY.

Cause of the Delay in Finding an Indictment.

Belief That Lizzie Borden Had an Accomplice.

Worker on the Farm May Possibly Have Been Involved.

FALL RIVER, Nov. 22.—Attorney-General Pillsbury caused a surprise yesterday in the case of the government against Lizzie A. Borden. The grand jury, sitting at Taunton, would have, under ordinary circumstances, had the whole whether or not they found evidence enough to indict the young woman accused of the brutal murder of her father last August. Instead of that they were told that the consideration of the Borden case was adjourned until Dec. 1, when further evidence on the matter would probably be offered them.

Saturday the presentation of the government's case was practically finished. Ninety-four witnesses had given their testimony, and four minor ones were to be heard yesterday morning. With their evidence finished, the grand jury would have been ready to report, and it was given on high authority that an indictment would have been found.

A short presentation of the principal points was to have been made by District Attorney Knowlton, but, instead of that, Attorney-General Pillsbury made a little speech. He said he had certain reasons—a number of them—why he desired the case left open, and he told the jurors what those reasons were. They were sufficient to satisfy the gentlemen composing the jury, and it was at once unanimously decided to adjourn until Dec. 1 next, when the case will be again taken up.

But while that was going on the surprise was getting in its work at Fall River. Miss Emma Borden was told that her presence was desired in Taunton, and it was suggested that it would be a good idea for Rev. Mr. Buck to go along, too. Hon. Charles J. Holmes, who has been the firm friend and counsellor of the young women all through their time of trouble, was also invited to go, and Dr. Handy was requested to appear with them. So the morning train for Taunton had among its passengers all these distinguished personages.

Word was sent for Lawyer Jennings to see Mr. Knowlton in the shire town, but the senior counsel for Lizzie had been taking a little vacation in Connecticut, and was not at his office when an officer from the Fall River police headquarters called there, but Attorney Arthur S. Phillips, Mr. Jennings' assistant, told him that his chief would receive word in time to be in Taunton before the business of the day closed. It happened that Mr. Jennings telephoned to his office on his way home yesterday, and Mr. Phillips had a chance to deliver the message which was sent by District Attorney Knowlton.

About noon there was quite an interesting gathering in the Taunton court-house. Messrs. Pillsbury and Knowlton explained the government's decision, so far as they could without divulging state secrets, and the government's reasons why the adjournment was desired.

This was before Mr. Jennings arrived. Mr. Knowlton met Lizzie's attorney in the City Hotel, and they went at once to a room and had a long, confidential talk, the first one since the case opened. Contrary to the usual custom Mr. Knowlton has not conferred with the lawyer for the defence at all until yesterday. What the principal point in that conversation was neither gentlemen would tell, but Mr. Jennings admitted that it was not displeasing to him.

The decision to adjourn the grand jury was not reached by Atty.-Gen. Pillsbury until yesterday afternoon. Then, after mature consideration, he made up his mind that before the grand jury made its report a number of points should be cleared away before the government had gone too far in the prosecution.

These points at present seem to indicate that another person should be indicted, either as principal or accessory. Unexplained, they leave the government's case a little cloudy; that is, while the evidence against Lizzie has been sufficient to warrant an indictment against her, two or three little threads are sticking out which might change the entire aspect of the case.

These threads, properly gathered and worked together, may show another hand in the affair. It is possible that developments may show that person to be the only guilty one. With these threads hanging as they now are, it appears that Lizzie had an accomplice—a worker on the farm—and it is looking up that man and his record and investigating certain evidence in connection with him that largely causes the delay. Those are not the only reasons for the adjournment, but they are some of the principal ones.

The government officials are clinging tenaciously to the theory of Lizzie's guilt, but there is a doubt as to the young woman having been alone. Dr. Handy's wild-eyed man is thought of again in this consideration, and also the mysterious Portuguese who purchased a hatchet in New Bedford two or three days before the murder, and the suspicious man of the same nationality who was seen in the vicinity of the Borden house the day of the tragedy, and who has never been found. There are also two or three points in connection with this unknown individual which to-day can be considered peculiar, to say the least. Now these threads may, on investigation, fail to establish anything, but Attorney-General Pillsbury was determined that they should be examined before an indictment was returned.

It is thought the Portuguese may be connected with a farm hand who, from the first, has been somewhat under suspicion, and whose movements on the day of the murder have never been thoroughly explained. The coming 10 days will be directed toward determining whether or not that individual has a perfectly established alibi. The hardware dealer of New Bedford who sold a hatchet to a mysterious Portuguese will be given an opportunity to identify him, and Dr. Handy will also be called on to look at him.

If all this amounts to nothing, and the investigation fails to show further signs of an accessory's hand in the murder, then the wheels of justice will commence to revolve at the point where they stopped, and the indictment proceedings will go on.

In connection with this mysterious hatchet purchaser comes another young man whose movements have been carefully "piped" by the Fall River police. He has visited the Borden house several times since the murder, and on every occasion a police officer has quietly tracked his movements. Why this person is only the shadowing officer and the principal government officials know.

Those are some of the threads which District Attorney Knowlton will have gathered before the grand jury gives its final finding, for it is possible that on them very much depends—possibly another indictment. It is not because of lack of work that these points remain unexplained, but because they have grown more and more complicated as the detectives' labors went on. Now they will be followed to the end. They may show that Lizzie had an accomplice—they may be satisfactorily explained away. But, whatever the result, Attorney-General Pillsbury does not want any indictment reported until the government's case is made more clear.

The evidence which has thus far been given before the grand jury was much more thorough and complete than that offered at the preliminary hearing that opened Lizzie Blaisdell, even by the same witnesses. Bridget Sullivan, for example, went into extensive details in regard to matters in the Borden family before the murder, and told a great deal of Lizzie's attitude towards her mother, as exhibited before the servant girl.

She was, however, unable to give any evidence bearing directly on the tragedy itself, but, beside describing Lizzie's actions and appearance after the murder, she mentioned one very peculiar and significant circumstance. It was this: Just before Bridget went up stairs to her room to lie down there was a kettle full of hot water on the stove and a roaring hot fire. Directly after she was called down stairs by Lizzie she noticed that the water in the kettle had disappeared, and that the roaring hot fire was almost out, notwithstanding that less than 20 minutes had elapsed.

Chief Hilliard also told the members of the grand jury why it was that the mysterious burglary who stole Mrs. Borden's watch and property about a year before the murder was never publicly accused. This peculiar burglary has been frequently referred to as showing the possibility of an assassin entering the house and committing his bloody deed without discovery. The chief said he was satisfied that Lizzie committed the theft, and went on to say how he convinced Mr. Borden that such was the case. All the articles stolen at that time were the property of Mrs. Borden, and included beside the watch and money, a quantity of free horse railroad tickets. A number of persons were found presenting free tickets who were not entitled to them. The police asked them where they secured these little pasteboards. They said Lizzie Borden gave them to them. Lizzie never had any of these tickets until after the theft from Mrs. Borden, so Mr. Borden requested that there be no further investigation of the matter.

A number of such points were brought to the attention of the grand jury which never before have been made public, and they added much strength to the case. Now, when the police are ready to answer the question, Who is the strange man? the case will go on to the next step.

POLITICAL.

What is Heard on the Streets Concerning the Municipal Campaign.

As the time draws near for the municipal election the interest in that event increases, and there is considerable speculation as to the result. Bets have been numerously made as to the winner of the head of the tickets in the field, and thus far the betting head of has been even.

All nomination papers must be filed with the City Clerk by Friday at 5 p.m. Certificates or caucus nominations must be filed by Wednesday at the same hour.

The Brock party will endorse the nomination of S. H. Shepherd as school committeeman from ward three.

Hon. William M. Butler, Hon. Alanson Borden and Edmund Wood are the committee on ratification meeting of the Brock party. This meeting is to be held to-morrow evening, and the plans are being made for that event. At the time of going to press it had not been decided who would preside.

Frank Paull will receive the nomination of assistant assessor for ward six from the Brock party.

It is probable that John H. Barrows will be selected by the Brock party as a Councilman from ward three, and it is said the same party will indorse the nomination of Councilman Lemuel W. Hayes from the same ward. In ward four this party will probably place in nomination for the lower branch of the city government Charles H. Vinal and Clifton W. Bartlett. Dr. George H. Dunbar will be indorsed for School Committee and M. T. Mills for assistant assessor. Nothing has been determined as to ward five, except that Robert W. Taber will receive the nomination for School Committee should he desire to be a candidate.

The friends of William A. Twist, superintendent of the Hathaway mills, are urging him to allow the use of his name for aldermanic honors from ward six.

It is said that Charles S. Paisler is to be nominated for alderman from ward three on the Brownell ticket.

The following are the signatures to the nomination papers of Arod B. Holloway, independent Labor candidate for alderman from ward one:
William Sanders,
Frank C. Barrows,
Stephen R. Potter,
Samuel S. Boardman,
John F. Cleary,
George H. Salters,
Samuel S. Gibson,
Albert D. Milliken,
Albert White,
George W. Taylor,
William Ogden,
William Armitage,
William Sharples,
Frank E. Foley,
Frank Pickering,
Samuel Brierly,
Hoyland Smith,
Perry P. Jenney,
George W. Hillman,
James Livesley,
Beecher Burns,
Charles F. Faums,
Henry F. Janell,
William Whitehead,
Stephen Neary,
James F. Collins,
Michael Leady,
John H. Mahoney,
Patrick J. Jordan,
Michael Lee,
Thomas Bertwistle,
Timothy E. Manchester,
George H. McCulloch,
Walter A. Taylor,
Michael R. Daley,
Isaac W. Greenup,
John Nelm,
Samuel Dalton,
Bernard McCarthy,
John Kenney,
John E. Enns,
James H. Kennedy,
Jeremiah D. Sullivan,
James B. Cook,
Frank H. Harrell,
Thomas J. Clynes,
William J. McRay,
Harry W. Butler,
Frank McMahon,
Robert W. Castle,
Walter A. Jenney,
George E. Braman,
James K. Savage,
Samuel C. Trueman,
Eli Idell,
J. O. Sullivan,
Hartley Spencer,
Elon F. Fish,
Henry Thorns,
Francis N. Howes.

THREE DESPERATE THIEVES.

Attempt to Murder a Storekeeper and His Son at Phenix, R. I.

PROVIDENCE, Nov. 22.—A bold robbery and attempt at double murder was made at Phenix, on the New York and New England railroad. In that manufacturing village Jmes L. Pierce keeps a grocery store. About 7 o'clock last night, when the train arrived there from Providence, three young men who had come in on that train went to the store and made a raid upon it.

Their objective point was the cash drawer. Mr. Pierce resisted the marauders, and called upon his son to aid him. The thieves opened fire, and Mr. Pierce and his son were shot down. Then the visitors went through the drawer, securing $80, after which they cut to the railroad track and disappeared in the darkness, coming in this direction.

Dr. Hammerford was called to attend the injured men, and it is thought that neither will lose his life by reason of the shooting. The city police were promptly notified, and are now waiting for the culprits to walk into the trap set for them.

PLAYED WITH MATCHES.

A Little Child Burned to Death and Her Guardian Fatally Injured.

CAMBRIDGE, Mass., Nov. 22.—Mrs. Lizzie Poole of 2 Gray place left her little 3-year-old daughter in the care of Mrs. Ellen Chambers, a neighbor, while she went shopping in Boston yesterday afternoon. The child was playing around the room, and in some way got hold of matches and set her clothes on fire. Mrs. Chambers was horrified when, attracted by the child's screams, she found her enveloped in flames.

In her fright the woman grabbed the child in her arms and rushed out of doors into the court. The woman's screams attracted the attention of the neighbors, but they seemed not to be ready to render assistance. Rev. Thomas Scully happened to be passing by, and he pulled off his coat and wrapped it around the burning form. The flames were smothered, but not before fatal work had been accomplished. The child died in about two hours. Mrs. Chambers was horribly burned about the breast. Her recovery is extremely doubtful.

Cabinet Talk.

NEW YORK, Nov. 22.—Politicians say that W. H. Harrity is booked for the postmaster generalship, and that Hon. Don M. Dickinson will probably be made secretary of state, although it is said he is not anxious for the office.

THIRD DISTRICT COURT.

BORDEN, J.

TUESDAY, Nov. 22.

John C. Tierney was brought into court by Keeper Hunt and withdrew his appeal from a sentence of six months in the House of Correction for drunkenness. Sentence was reaffirmed.

Jacob Harwood pleaded guilty of unreasonably neglecting to provide for the support of his minor child, Sarah Harwood, aged 2 years, from the 1st day of July, 1889, to the 7th day of November, 1889. Mrs. Harwood said she had been married six years and during that time had started housekeeping with her husband three times. Twice she had paid for the furniture herself unaided by her husband. When her baby was two weeks old he wanted her to go to work in the mill and he would take care of the baby. He went away in July, 1889, and did not return to this city until yesterday. The baby died when she was 28 months old. Her father, Thomas Booker, had taken care of her when sick and when unable to work. Since her marriage her husband had left her several times and had done nothing for her or the child's support since July, 1889. Harwood told the Court he was sorry for what he had done, and that he desired to be friends with everybody. He got a letter in Providence a few days ago, informing him of this warrant, and he at once came to this city and called at the police station to see about it. Harwood seemed rather simple minded and talked to the Court more like a child than like a man 31 years of age. Accordingly he was given a hearing and referred to the Probation officer for a period of six months. E. Sullavou, Esq., for Commonwealth.

One case of drunkenness was released by the officers.

☞ What did Mr. Cleveland mean in his last speech, which though made at a private dinner table was circulated extensive over the whole country, by warning his audience against being "misled to our undoing by other lights of false democracy, which may be kindled in broken faith, and which, shining in hypocrisy, will, if followed, lure us to the rocks of failure and disgrace"? What is this danger to the Democratic party? Who are they who are holding out false lights to lure the Democratic vessel, with Cleveland at the helm, onto the rocks? Will some Democrat expound the enigma, and tell the faithful in plain English what it all means, and how to distinguish the true from the false lights?

☞ The Homestead strike is over. What was gained by it? The power of the owners of the mills to manage their own property in their own way. But it has been a costly gain on the one side and a costly loss on the other. A number of lives have been lost, a dastardly murder has been attempted, and millions of dollars lost in the sacrifice of property and wages, in the interruption of business, and in the expense to the State of Pennsylvania of maintaining order. Is there not some better way than this of adjusting differences between employers and employed?

☞ At the meeting of the Executive Council to-morrow the Pardon Committee will probably report their finding in the cases of life-term men in the Charlestown prison, two of whom the Governor will pardon on Thanksgiving Day. The Pardon Committee have made a visit to the prison and looked up the behavior records of some ten or more convicts with a view of selecting two deserving cases. It is the custom to pardon on this day only those who are serving life sentences and those who have served ten or more years of their sentences.

☞ The action of the Catholic Archbishops on educational matters at their recent meeting in New York is claimed as a triumph for the Liberal side, led by Cardinal Gibbons and Archbishop Ireland. There is no condemnation of the public school system, but special provision is to be made in Sunday schools, and by special instruction, for the care of those children who attend public schools.

☞ Now that pretty much all the millionaires of New York have dined Mr. Cleveland, would it not be a good idea for the poor farmers of the West and South to tender him a banquet and invite him to partake of their homely fare? We should think corn pone and fried pork would be a welcome relief to him after the high diet he has been partaking of.

☞ The change of the grade of the Old Colony road at West Fourth street, Boston, which is to be commenced immediately, involves the transfer of the freight yards of the Old Colony from Kneeland street to South Boston, and it is semi-officially said the enlargement of the passenger station.

THE EVENING STANDARD

is on sale every afternoon by the following newsdealers in this city:
Edwin Dews—No. 129 Union st., and 147 Purchase st.
C. H. Spooner—No. 600 Purchase st., foot of Hazzard st.
B. S. Booth—No. 174 Acushnet ave.
David Tomlinson—No. 729 So. Water st.
A. F. Wilde—842 and 844 Purchase st.
B. Frank McCabe—Washington Square.
William Ferguson—No. C. Water st.
N. S. Gibbs—No. 343 Purchase st.
Wm. Upjohn—No. 1039 So. Water st.
Jno. Cobb—No. 181 Kempton st.
Robert W. Taber—No. 198 Union st.
Mrs. B. S. Burdick—No. 34 Dartmouth st.
James Owen, Jr.—No. 256 Purchase st.
E. L. Peckham—No. 26 Pleasant st.
F. H. Wilde—No. 526 County st.
Ambrose E. Luce—No. 82 Smith st.
David S. R. Durfee—Cor. County and Smith sts.
Mrs. Mary Wilbur—No. 261 Middle st.
Thos. W. Jackson—No. 531 County st.
Mary A. Jackson—Smith street, near Cedar.
B. F. Card—No. 292 Cedar st.
James Lettice—113 No Water st.
Wm. S. Jenney—98 Mill st.
Wm. J. Macy—Cor. County and Wing sts.
Jos. Lemos—South Water st., below Howland st.
A. N. Bolles—Cor. Arnold and Ash streets.
John Blood—Tremont, cor. Court.
E. L. Blowell—Cor. Summit and Kempton sts.
Frank J. Gildea—Howard st.
Cor. Shawmut ave. and Durfee st.—B. H. Reed.
Cor. Acushnet ave. and Coggshall st.—Caleb Slade.
Bliss' Corner—Charles W. Gifford.
Jas. Wilbur—Lund's Corner.
In Fairhaven—H. L. Card—Phoenix Block; H. Tucker—Center st.; W. D. Eldridge, Bridge and Main sts.
In Mattapoisett—Central R. R. Station.
In Mansfield—Railroad Station.
In Boston—Park Square Station

The Best Family Newspaper in Southern Massachusetts is the REPUBLICAN STANDARD.

Our Weekly Edition—a large twelve-page paper of 84 columns, containing more reading matter than any other weekly paper in Southern Massachusetts. It is published Thursday mornings. Subscription price only $1.50 a year, in advance.

☞ This Paper has a very much Larger Circulation than any other paper in the State south of Boston. Its Circulation in this city is FOUR TIMES that of any other paper. Our Weekly has a circulation double that of any other in Southern Massachusetts, and more than THREE TIMES that of any other Weekly printed in this city. These papers are the best advertising mediums in this section.

CONTENTS OF THIS EVENING'S STANDARD.

Page 1.
Month or six weeks shut down at No. 6 Wamsutta mill, caused by an accident to the engine.
Emperor William's speech at the opening of the Reichstag.
Home matters.
Late telegraphic news.

Page 2.
Golden wedding anniversary of Mr. Warren Ladd and wife.
Board of Public Works meeting.
Y. M. C. A. directors meet.
Petition to quash the indictment against Walter Paine.
Suburban news.
Home matters.

Page 3.
Business transacted last evening by the political committees.
North Baptist Christian Endeavor Society.
Report of the true tree of the Taunton Lunatic hospital.
Edgar M. Ward's picture, "A Corner in the Old Homestead."
Suburban news.
Home Matters.
Early telegraphic dispatches.

Page 4.
Grand jury to consider new evidence about an accomplice in the Borden murder case.
Story that the Boston & Albany is coming to this city.
Municipal campaign news.
Superior Court.
Third District Court.
Editorials.
Home Matters.

Page 5.
Marine Intelligence.
Marriages and deaths.

Page 6.
Annual meeting of the Grinnell Manufacturing Corporation.
Second Edition—Telegraphic and local news.

Page 7.
Political cartoon.
Astronomers puzzled by the comet orbit news.
Amusement and sporting news.

Page 8.
A father's brutality lead to a suspicion that he has killed his son.
Disgraceful scene in French Chamber of Deputies over Panama canal frauds.
Fearful powder explosion in an Ohio coal mine.
Democrats must assume the responsibility for national legislation.
National congress of the Salvation Army in New York city.
Mr. Blaine's condition said to have assumed a very serious phase.
T. V. Powderly reelected chief of the Knights of Labor.
Early telegraphic dispatches.
Third Edition—Telegraphic and local news

HOME MATTERS.

NATURALIZATION.—Bernard Goldman filed a primary declaration with a view to future citizenship in the Third District Court this morning. James Smith for petitioner.

G. A. R. INSPECTION.—William Logan Rodman Post 1, G. A. R., will be inspected to-morrow evening by Chief Mustering Officer Charles S. Anthony of William H. Bartlett Post 3 of Taunton.

STABBED IN THE NECK.—Two Italian laborers on the railroad at Middleboro got into a quarrel last night. One drew a knife and slashed the other in the neck. Dr. George L. Ellis, who was called, says it is an even chance whether the injured man lives or dies. His assailant has been arrested and is held to await developments.

AUDITOR'S REPORT.—Wendell H. Cobb, Esq., auditor of the Superior Court, in the case of Antone Brown vs. Mary J. Menterio, an action of contract, upon an account has filed his report in the court, in which he finds for the plaintiff for $33.23. Edwin A. Douglass, Esq., was counsel for the plaintiff, and Hon. W. M. Butler for defendant.

REVENUE CUTTER PATROL.—The President has issued an order for revenue vessels to patrol the Atlantic coast from Dec. 1 to April 1, in order to assist vessels that may require their services. The Levi Woodbury will cruise from Eastport, Me., to Cape Elizabeth, Me.; the Alexander J. Dallas from Mount Desert, Me., to Gloucester, Mass.; the Samuel Dexter from Gloucester, Mass., to Newport, R. I.; the U. S. Grant from Newport to Delaware Breakwater, including Long Island Sound.

BIRTHDAY SURPRISE.—Eddie M. Wood, living at No. 297 Cottage street, was 19 years old yesterday, and the Sunday school class at the Middle Street Christian church, of which he is a member, gave him a surprise party in the evening. About 20 young ladies and gentlemen came to his home and presented him a ring, and his teacher, Miss Susie Townsend, gave him a year's subscription to The Golden Rule. The evening was passed in singing and games and in the enjoyment of ice cream and cake.

SUDDEN DEATH.—Ann Gibba, aged 55, of Edgartown, died suddenly at his residence in that town yesterday, of apoplexy. It was his usual custom each morning to visit certain of his relatives, and having failed to do so yesterday caused some anxiety among his friends, who went to his residence and found the door locked. They went away, but returned in a short time and forced the door open, when they found Mr. Gibbs lying underneath his bed in a gasping condition, and life became extinct in a few moments. He was born on Marthas Vineyard, and was a seafaring man for the greater portion of his life. He entered the navy during the civil war and held the rank of master's mate.

TIVERTON.

The Rev. Mr. Byron, from Los Angeles, Cal., occupied the pulpit of the Congregational church Sunday.

J. W. Maynard of Boston, the blind pianist and vocalist, has been visiting friends in town.

WEST TISBURY.

Mr. and Mrs. Ellen Raymond are spending Thanksgiving with friends in Pocasset.

Arthur Mayhew and family from Chilmark are occupying the residence of David Mayhew at the Oaks, while Mr. M. and family are spending the Winter at Somerville.

M. C. Mitchell, A. M., has sent $10 to the Library Association and expressed his delight that the ladies had put his former school building to such a good use.

Mrs. Rebecca West has gone to Jamestown, R. I., to visit her daughter, Mrs. Elizabeth Flanders.

Rev. W. R. Terry will preach his farewell sermon in the First Baptist church at 11 a.m. next Sabbath, and the second Baptist church at 2 p.m. same day

LITTLE COMPTON.

At a meeting of the Court of Probate the business transactions were as follows: Abraham Manchester appointed administrator on the estate of Frederick Brownell. Follen Beebe appointed administrator on the estate of Lydia R. Beebe. Inventory received on the estates of Sarah T. Head and George S. Pierce.

A musicale was held at the residence of Miss Mattie Almy Saturday afternoon.

Mrs. Lorenzo Smith and family have removed into their new home, their former house having been destroyed by fire in the early part of this year.

IN RECEIVER BEAL'S FAVOR.

Insolvency Decision Concerning the Maverick Bank and Evans & Co.

CAMBRIDGE, Mass., Nov. 22.—Receiver Beal of the Maverick National bank is a creditor of the firm of Irving A. Evans & Co. Judge Brooks in the Middlesex insolvency court has so decided. The decree of the court upsets the arrangement of settlement made by the directors with the firm of Evans & Co. ten days before the bank failed.

This settlement was, in substance, that the bank should release all the obligations of the firm of Evans & Co. to it, amounting, it is claimed, to $641,000, and the bank was to retain in consideration thereof $100,000 of pledged securities. The receiver claimed that this settlement was in fraud of the bank, as Asa P. Potter, a director, was released from paying a personal indebtedness due Evans & Co.

Receiver Beal presented a petition to the insolvency court, asking the court to instruct him to sell the collateral held by him as receiver of the bank and apply it to the payment of the claim of $641,000 and prove for the balance against the insolvent firm of Evans & Co. Several hearings were held on the petition with the result that the court holds that the receiver is a creditor of the firm and entitled to prove whatever and above the amount he will obtain by sale of the securities. The court decrees that the securities are to be sold under the directions of the United States district court, and the proceeds to be applied to the payment of the debt of the bank.

The firm of Evans & Co. have assets amounting to $150,000, with liabilities of about $750,000. It is not the bank's debt of the firm, should the bank's debt be finally allowed to be proved, would not be more than 20 per cent of their claims. An appeal to a higher tribunal will be taken.

COMPETITOR FOR THE OLD COLONY.

Rumor of the Boston & Albany Coming to This City.

The Fall River correspondent of the Providence Journal says:

Surveyors employed by the Boston & Albany Railroad Co. have been in evidence in these parts for the past few days and rumors are afloat to the effect that the Old Colony is to have a competitor. This story will probably interest the latter concern less than any corporation in town. When a couple of railroad companies quarrel long-established custom demands that one of them shall straightway invade the territory of the other, and in doing so to save of stakes and map out a first class road. Accordingly, just now people are building a brand new line for the Boston & Albany. It will come in by way of New Bedford, will be fitted with numerous spur tracks and will land the passenger at all the mills at their doors. Thus far, however, the construction has been confined to a survey of a farm in Somerset, which the owner says has been blocked out three times already. The Boston & Albany may intend to cover this section and it may be shutting off from shipping which it recently had with the Old Colony.

THE VINEYARD.

J. H. Rostock of the United States Engineer's Office at Newport, R. I., is at present engaged in making a survey of Vineyard Haven and also West and East Chops for the purpose of ascertaining the results of the jetties erected at the Chops several years ago under the supervision of Major Livermore.

The Evening Standard.

NEW BEDFORD, MASS.
WEDNESDAY EVENING, NOV. 23.

THREE EDITIONS DAILY.
No. 87 Union Street.
PUBLISHED BY
E. ANTHONY & SONS,
INCORPORATED.

Six Dollars a Year, Three Dollars for Six Months, in advance; Single Copies Two Cents

TELEPHONE CALLS.
Counting Room, - - - 308-2
Editorial Room, - - - 308-3

TEN PAGES.

This Evening's Issue Consists of Ten Pages, and Every Patron is Entitled to that Number.

THE REPUBLICAN STANDARD.

Issued this evening, contains all the local and general news of the past week, forming an interesting account of a new tie ry in the Borden murder case, cause of delay in finding an indictment, belief that Lizzie Borden had an accomplice; Golden wedding of Hon. Warren Ladd and his wife, Mrs. Lucy Washburn Ladd, congratulations and beautiful gifts from a host of friends, the crowning event of a useful and prosperous career; continuation of Capt. Borden's whaling experiences; first indoor meeting of the season of the South Bristol Farmers' Club, which reports gratifying success of Autumn fair, and interesting addresses by President Howland and others; annual report of the Taunton Lunatic Hospital, an appropriation of $15,500 asked for by the Board of Trustees; interesting statistics of the business of the Union Street Railway during the past year; a new four-story brick block to be erected immediately on the northeast corner of Union and Pleasant streets, all old buildings to be removed and operations begun by January; Winter programme for the meetings of the South Bristol Farmers' Club; Board of Trade Annual Dinner, brilliant flow of oratory, L. LeB. Holmes attacks the old bridge and national facilities, Edward Atkinson talks on Free Trade to Cotton Manufacturers; successful Convention of the Acushnet Sunday School Association at North Rochester; autobiography of Capt. Gilbert B. Borden, late superintendent of the House of Refuge, at Point Barrow, Arctic ocean; meeting of the Board of Public Works, Pleasant street abutters accept the Board's award for damages, hearing granted remonstrants against Fourth street turnout; a Fall River Alderman charged with protecting dives, and police man warned to be careful in his rants; another story of the wreck of the Helen Marr by one of the survivors; semi-annual statement of the New Bedford Cooperative Bank; annual meeting of the Bristol County Agricultural Society, officers elected, President Rotch congratulates the society on its success, auditor's report submitted and other business transacted; a six weeks' shut-down necessitated by the breaking of the steel shaft of No. 6 Wamsutta engine, six hundred operatives thrown out of employment by the accident; meetings of the executive committees of the Citizens' and Independent Citizens' parties and the completion of the tickets for the election in December; Single Lesson for next Sunday; correspondence; with editorials, ship news, markets, miscellaneous reading matter, etc.

For sale by all newsdealers in this city, and at our counters, in wrappers ready for mailing, at 4 cents per copy.

We publish elsewhere nearly full lists of the candidates of both parties at the coming municipal election, which we commend to the careful consideration of the voters. With regard to minor offices there will be abundant room for the exercise of private judgment. But with regard to the Mayor and City Council we hope that the issue is one of principles and not of men. We have no charges to bring against Mr. Brownell for anything he has done in the past. But we regard it as exceedingly important whether the policy which has actuated the present city government shall be continued for another year; whether the neglect to enforce the laws which has been its most conspicuous feature shall be allowed to continue. Mr. Brownell has given no assurances to the public with regard to this matter, but in his addresses has confined himself to personal matters which are not a matter of contention. We know where Mr. Brock stands, and we commend the ticket of which he is the head to the support of our citizens.

☞ The Boston Journal thinks that the dinner of the Young Men's Democratic Club in this city in February last, which was addressed by Representative George Fred. Williams who expressed the determination to carry on the battle till his party had secured both Houses in the State Legislature and the two United States Senatorships, was not productive of very satisfactory results from his point of view. Instead of gaining the Legislature and a United States Senator, his party lost five members of Congress, including his own inestimable self, it has smaller minorities in both branches of the Legislature than last year, and its prospects of securing another Senator are as remote as those of a second Noachian deluge. But Mr. Williams is going to carry on the war unceasingly, for which he will have abundant leisure after March 4, 1893. The Republican will be pleased to see this mighty warrior keep on his armor and wield his potent lance, but the leaders of his own party will be likely to sit down upon him. We doubt if they will find any further use for him.

☞ The last number of Printers' Ink contains some suggestions with regard to the construction of the law regulating second class postage, which under present rulings it claims works great injustice to publishers. It says that inquiries as to what the law is should receive definite and comprehensive answers, and not such vague ones as are now given by the department; that all decisions once made should be treated as precedents until overruled, and that they should be published in the Postal Guide; that if the right to second class postage is withdrawn from a publisher he should be notified and the reasons given, and saved the expense of a trip to Washington to obtain a renewal, and that under-clerks should not be allowed to issue unlawful decrees, which are a discredit to the department. These suggestions appear to be eminently reasonable.

The man in the moon has disappeared and has been replaced by a woman. At least one W. H. Burr claims to have discovered a woman's profile in our satellite. He does not inform us, however, whether he identified the sex by her high hat.

In eight counties, representing one-third of the total vote in the State, 10,500 votes were cast for Governor which were classed as blanks, of which 2450 were in Bristol, 1300 in Plymouth and 280 in Barnstable. In Fall River alone there were over 1100 blank and defective ballots for Governor. This certainly shows a remarkable indifference on the part of voters.

On the eighth page of this evening's Standard will be found a Boston dispatch telling of the mistakes of thousands of Republican voters. As we quoted from the Boston Traveller Monday, confusion of the names of Wolcott Hamlin and Roger Wolcott was evidently the stumbling block.

Mr. Cleveland has given a warning to office seekers to let him alone, in which there are the usual number of capital I's. The warning is doubtless a needed one, but hasn't Mr. Cleveland given the public about enough of his personal feelings? We doubt if his warning will have much effect, for office seekers are as pertinacious as autograph fiends. We have considerable sympathy for Mr. Cleveland in the annoyance he is subjected to, but it is one which all in his position have had to experience.

HOME MATTERS.

Another Aspirant.—The friends of Dr. Asa Messer are urging his name as a candidate for the postmastership.

Adjusted.—The losses occasioned by the wreck of steamer William Lewis last season have all been adjusted and the owners have received the money.

Registration.—Fifteen new names were added to the voting lists to-day, making a total of 36 since registration began. Three of those registered to-day were women.

Board of Aldermen.—There will be a special meeting of the Board of Aldermen Friday afternoon at 2.30 o'clock to draw traverse jurors to serve at the Superior Court.

Work on a Big Cellar.—Work on the cellar wall of Cook & Smith's big block, corner of Acushnet avenue and Cedar Grove street, was commenced this morning. This is the largest single cellar in the city.

St. Luke's Hospital.—To-day occurs the annual donation at St. Luke's Hospital, and bountiful supplies of groceries, dry goods, blankets, underwear, etc., and some money have been received, and there is a prospect for a large increase in gifts later in the day.

Thrown from a Car.—William Foley of 13 Hazzard court, while riding north on a street car last night, about 10.45 o'clock, was accidentally thrown off near Hazzard street. He struck heavily on the pavement and was dragged for a considerable distance. He was picked up insensible and removed to his home, where Dr. Belanger attended him. He was found out how badly cut and he did not regain consciousness for a long time.

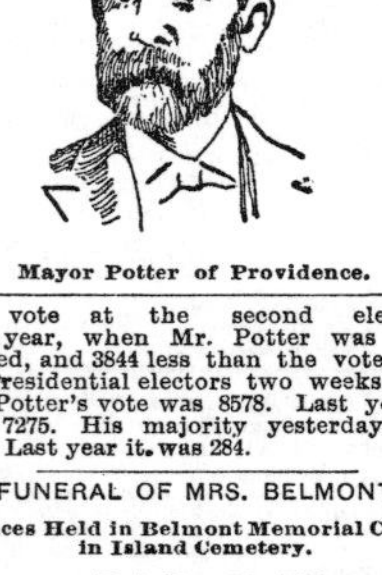

Religious Monomaniac.—James Miller, a man about 40 years of age, entered the tenement house at No. 2 Delano street this forenoon, and thoroughly frightened the inmates. He acted strangely, gesticulated wildly and talked incoherently about religion, and demanded to know if the ladies prayed. Officer Timothy Sullivan was called and turned the man over to the charge of Thomas Richardson, who offered to be responsible for him. He is evidently a religious monomaniac, and will be examined as to his sanity. It was later learned that he was at one time an inmate of a lunatic asylum in England.

Expenditures.—We are indebted to Frederic A. Brownell, City Auditor, for the following list of expenditures in the various departments of the city for the week ending Nov. 19:

Cemeteries,	$97.51
Engineering Department,	53.74
Fire Department,	473.95
Free Public Library—Dog fund,	15.44
Highways and Streets,	1,384.81
Incidentals,	181.65
N. B. & Fairhaven Bridge,	21.66
N. B. Water Works,	672.12
Parks and Squares,	172.20
Police Department,	1,176.90
Schools—Incidentals,	235.44
Public Schools—Pay of Teachers,	2,556.83
Sewers—General Account,	170.89
Belleville avenue, No. 3,	162.17
Court street, No. 3,	391.39
Grape street extension,	675.66
Harbor street,	3.50
Hemlock street,	221.09
	$9,346.98

A Good Record on the Track.—The following table of winnings gives the record and number of races in which N. J. Stone has handled horses during the past season:

	Reg. No.	1st.	2d.	3d.	4th.
Johnny Knott,	13	2	3	0	2.23¼
Sylvester K.,	11	2	8	0	2.25¼
Hy-Wilkes,	7	2	0	2	2.29
Woodland Boy,	4	1	1	1	2.27¼
Elcho,	4	0	1	0	
Capt. John,	3	2	0	0	2.21¼
Joe,	1	1	0	1	2.24¼
Charlie H.,	1	1	0	1	2.34¼
Harry A.,	1	0	0	0	2.34¾
	41	12	7	5	

Johnny Knott began the season with a record of 2.25¼, and has reduced it as above, while Sylvester K. lowered his record from 2.31¼ to 2.25¼.

The Evening Standard.

ESTABLISHED FEBRUARY, 1850.

NEW BEDFORD, FRIDAY, NOVEMBER 25, 1892.

TWO CENTS.

HASKELL & TRIPP.

After the turkey—what?

A sale of cold weather underclothing on Saturday.

The following are *great* values, and need only to be seen to prove that claim. Even inexperienced buyers of underwear may purchase, confident that they are getting the best in the market for their money.

Men's heavy, clouded merino shirts and drawers, 50c. apiece. White, if preferred, same price.

Men's double-breasted, dark blue, woollen ribbed shirts, 58c. Drawers to match, 58c.

Men's camel's hair shirts and drawers:

First quality, $1.50 each garment.

Second quality, 75c. each

garment.

Women's "Jersey ribbed" vests and pants, heavy weight, 50c. each. Your choice of two excellent sorts.

Women's Australian wool "Jersey ribbed" vests and pants, 75c. and $1 each garment.

Women's "flat" merino vests and pants, 50c.

Women's fine Australian wool "flat" underwear, $1.25.

Underclothing for girls, boys and babies at proper prices. We can suit you.

Hosiery items:

For men—Seamless camel's hair socks, 25c. English merino socks, 37½c. Scotch wool socks, 50c.

For women—"Gloria" fast black fleecy lined hose, 25c. Seamless black cashmere wool hose, 25c. English cashmere hose, 50c.

For children — Seamless black woollen hose, 25c. Stout bicycle hose, 25c. English wool hose from 25c. up, according to size.

Glove items:

Gauntlet gloves, very stylish, $1.50 a pair. Fleecy lined silk gloves, 50c. a pair. Lambskin lined gloves, fur wrists, for men or women, $1 to $2.50 a pair. Great assortment.

Children's lined and fur trimmed lambskin gloves and mittens, 50c. and 75c. a pair.

Kid Glove Bargains:

Best Biarritz, plain wrist or laced. $1.

Four-button gloves, good quality, choice colors, 59c.

Cut-price sale of Dress Goods continued. Imported fancy stripes cost 90c. last month. *Our retail price today 50c. a yard.*

French crepons and crinkly crepes cost to land this season more than 80c. a yard. *Our retail price to-day 50c. a yard.*

Magnificent quality black, all-wool Henriettas, 45 inches in width, real value 90c. *Our retail price to-day 75c. a yard.*

Scotchy, rough-faced cheviots and camel's hair suitings; 3 lots:

Lot 1, 50c. a yard. Reduced from 75c.

Lot 2, 39c. a yard. Reduced from 50c.

Lot 3, 25c. a yard. Reduced from 39c.

Book Department now open in our light cheerful basement salesroom.

Prices are light, too.

HASKELL & TRIPP,

Department Stores,

Purchase and William Streets.

NO INDICTMENT.

Lizzie Borden Likely to Go Free.

Evidence too Flimsy to Warrant a Finding.

Attorney-General Wants No Mistakes Made.

Must Have Something More Tangible Presented.

Mr. Knowlton Differs in His Opinion of the Case.

State Given Ten Days to Produce What It Can.

Grand Jury Not Satisfied With Government Testimony.

The Future Now Left to Clear Up the Awful Murder Mystery.

[Special Dispatch.]

TAUNTON, Nov. 25.—Lizzie Borden will not be indicted by the grand jury.

In another week, without any doubt from present indications, she will be a free woman and the whole miserable farce will be ended—the life of one woman blighted forever—albeit the verdict of a jury of her peers will be in substance that she is innocent of the crimes laid at her door so far as can be determined upon the evidence presented—crimes about which

MISS LIZZIE BORDEN.

all the world has been wondering and speculating for months.

The evidence offered at Fall River was essentially the evidence produced before the grand jury, neither more nor less, but it was not sufficient to warrant the finding of an indictment simply because there is no assurance that there is anything back of it.

The police of Fall River think Lizzie Borden had something to do with these crimes. They believe this in spite of the fact that there is not one scintilla of evidence to prove this theory, beyond the fact that she was in the house at or about the time; that the family relations were unpleasant, and that there were apparent discrepancies in the story of the young woman. And even up to the last, when it was established beyond a possible doubt that no additional evidence could be secured, despite the efforts of some of the brightest officers in the county, they still held a bold front and declared that an indictment was sure—that there was nothing but that course for the grand jury to take.

Now that body is not what can be considered a responsible body, i. e., its findings are not necessarily binding, since the evidence given before them is of a strictly ex parte nature, and they are supposed to know nothing whatever of the defence. If the government presents sufficient evidence to make it appear to the jury that so far as has been shown the government has a good case, without reference to what is to be set up by the defence, then it is customary to find an indictment and let the government try issues with the defence, trusting in the superiority of the former's cause to have its renderings sufficiently backed up. If there is a miscarriage it is no fault of the jury, and shows no lack of judgment on its part.

In this case the issue was a serious one. It had become a celebrated case and more than Bristol county had become interested onlookers. The question was not whether an indictment should be found, but whether upon the evidence brought forward an indictment ought to be found, it being reasonably certain that there was absolutely no chance from the present outlook of combatting the defence in the slightest degree.

It was all very well to say that these murders were committed by some one who had strength enough and skill enough to wield a hatchet or some sharp and sufficiently heavy instrument, but the most essential point was to learn who handled that instrument. It was not enough to hold that because there had been unpleasantness in the family, that the family disposition was a peculiar one, and that a property consideration might have some weight in the matter, that therefore Lizzie Borden, who was about the house at the time, committed these murders. This was simply a theory, and the juries and the courts desire evidence.

From the first appearance in this case of the District Attorney his motives have been impugned and erroneously set out by these prejudged matters. He has been pictured as a bloodthirsty individual, whose only object in life was to go about the county under license from the powers that be to hunt up evidence and spy out reasons why such and such persons should be put away from the usual haunts of men and branded as dangerous; that he was a fiend in human form; his only object was gore, and lots of it. The very reverse of this is correct. Mr. Knowlton is one of the most humane men who ever pleaded a cause before a jury or worked up a case for presentation to court. In spite of his brusqueness and his apparent indifference to the feelings of others he is one of the most tender-hearted of men, as well as one of the most sensitive to public opinion. He has felt keenly the shafts which have been levelled at him, and their pricks will be felt for long years after the excitement consequent upon this case has subsided. But yet there was a line of duty to be followed, and he followed it.

Atrocious murders have been committed, the police have made an arrest on suspicion, everything pointed to the murders having been done by some one on the premises, the answers to interrogatories by Miss Borden were not satisfactory in many respects—whether because of actual guilt or not remains to be proven—it was the sworn duty of the District Attorney to get at the truth, and if his methods smacked of the mysterious and unexplainable it made no difference to him, he was apparently impervious to public criticism, although feeling its force as few men in his position could feel it, and plodded on in his chosen and what undoubtedly seemed to him the only proper way.

The net results have been as nothing. The government is actually no nearer a correct solution of the horrible mystery than when the case was first opened.

Ever since the grand jury first began its work upon the matter Miss Borden's nerves have been at a tension which at times threatened to tear them apart and place her in a condition for the madhouse. Her face has grown a shade or two paler and her nervous force has spent itself in trying to foresee the end without a breakdown at last. Thus far she has succeeded admirably in controlling herself, but the temptation to scream and tear her hair in agony has been a terrible one and hard to withstand, and there was not a man in that grand jury room but what could see the face of that girl day after day as the case proceeded and the old evidence was unfolded. And when all was over on that day when the grand jury went to Fall River—for that was practically the end of it all—there was nothing but suspicion, and suspicion is not sufficient for the indictment of one for murder.

All of the matter introduced at the other hearing, and but very little more, was given out here, and still there was nothing. The statement of Mr. Jennings from the first that his client was not guilty seems to have been borne out by the facts, although he knew no more about the affair than there was told him by that client and by her friends.

The prussic acid affair was fully ventilated, but it was of no consequence. Even if she did go to that store she did not get what she wanted, and there was no poison in the system of the victims. Every theory was worked for all it was worth, and not a particle of comfort came out of it for the government, and the groping in the dark continued right along with painful regularity.

The attorney-general saw that there was no use in the government pursuing this line any further, and the day that the grand jury went to Fall River he told Mr. Knowlton to shut off, and the shut off was accomplished at once. But the two did not agree as to the work to follow. There was a slight difference of opinion between the two, and Mr. Knowlton became provoked for the time only. Mr. Pillsbury was determined that unless something more tangible was brought forth there would be no sense or reason in asking the jury to indict. It would be like erecting a barricade to stand off the enemy and then running away and leaving it defenceless. If within 10 days there was any further matter bearing upon the case produced, and if it was of sufficient weight, then the delay would not have been fruitless and some benefit would have been accomplished.

But the confident look of the members of the Fall River police force has vanished. There is no longer any feeling of confidence in the grand jury returning an indictment to let a traverse jury after it concur in or reject, as the case might be. The grand jury has taken the initiative in the matter, and if whispers have sent the news broadcast it is little wonder. The discussion of this case has been carried on in so many different forms ever since the first intimation that murder had been done that to every one it comes much as a matter of course to talk about it, and discuss and weigh every particle of evidence for and against this woman. No one has intentionally betrayed secrets of the grand jury room, and no one pretends to say just what was done in that room except by inference, and the inference has become so strengthened by actions and results that there is little doubt as to the actual condition of affairs.

And there is one very important feature of this result that must not be overlooked by those who may doubt the wisdom of the decision not to indict. Lizzie Borden set free by a jury after trial for murder means that she is free forever. Nothing brought up against her in the future can affect her standing in the community in the slightest degree. Lizzie Borden tacitly cleared by the grand jury because of the fact that no indictment is returned means only that hereafter she may be just as much under a cloud as ever and her every action scrutinized with a view to future possible results of an embarrassing nature. She can be brought before the grand jury again at any time, and when the weight of evidence says that it is feasible.

The Attorney General undoubtedly believes that it will be better for the interests of justice to make no mistakes now more than have been made, trusting to the future to clear up all the mystery which surrounds this case, and at the same time placing Miss Borden in a position where she can be easily brought to bar again.

THE SCALLOP WAR CASE.

Judge Alden Fines the Mattapoisett Fishermen $20 Each.

[Special Dispatch.]

WAREHAM, Nov. 25.—In the Fourth District Court at Wareham this forenoon, Judge Alden rendered his decision in the famous scallop warfare between Marion and Mattapoisett. The court came in at 10 45 o'clock. The defendants, Francis A. Bowman, Walter E. Bowman and Frederick L. Dexter were represented by Frank M. Sparrow, the senior counsel for Mattapoisett, Lemuel LeBaron Holmes and Hosea Kingman of Bridgewater counsel for Marion were not present, as it was naturally expected the case would be decided in favor of the government, to take it to a higher court as a test case. The court was not in session five minutes. Judge Alden gave his decision in the case of Commonwealth vs. F. A. Bowman et al. as follows: "I find that the government has made out its case and fine the defendants $20 each." An appeal was entered by each and defendants were bound over to the Superior Court to be held in Plymouth in February, each being held in their personal recognizance of $100.

"AN INFAMOUS STORY."

Denial of the Dispatch About Mrs. Cleveland's Runaway.

NEW YORK, Nov. 25.—The following dispatch has been received from Mrs. Cleveland for publication:

Lakewood, N. J., Nov. 25.—To the Associated Press: Please contradict in all evening papers the infamous stories in the morning papers of a runaway accident. There is not one word of truth in it.

(Signed) MRS. GROVER CLEVELAND,
FRANCIS P. FREEMAN.

[The dispatch referred to was sent out to the morning papers and is printed on the second page.—ED.]

COLLISION WITH THE COMET.

It Will Strike the Earth—if it Strikes—at 9 45 p. m. Sunday.

CHICAGO, Nov. 25.—If Biela's comet, which is now attracting so much attention, is to collide with this planet, the ceremonies will be over by 10 o'clock next Sunday evening. Prof. Elias Colbert, who is observing the comet closely, has this to say upon the subject: "If any one is afraid of the consequences of a collision with the comet he may reassure himself after 9 45 Sunday night.

As near as can be computed the earth will be at that point in its orbit which is crossed by the Biela comet at 9 30 on Sunday evening, providing there has been no shift in the position of the plane of the comet's orbit in the last 40 years. If there has been such a change it would be a slight retrogression, making the limit of possible contact earlier than above stated.

While he has no means of knowing the exact position of the comet, owing to cloudy weather, it seems probable that the comet is moving toward us in spite of assertions to the contrary and that it must cross the earth's orbit, but possibly not until some days after the earth has got beyond the collision point, if there be any.

The comet ought to have moved more than one degree in position between 8 o'clock Wednesday night and the same time last night, provided that it be due to cross the earth's orbit not later than Sunday evening, while an indistinct observation of it through the haze does not warrant the belief that it has changed its position by as much as one degree."

HIGHWAYMAN IN A BIG CITY.

Daring Young Man on Horseback Terrorizes a Suburb of Chicago.

CHICAGO, Nov. 25.—A masked highwayman, who is terrorizing Lake View was hunted by 50 extra policemen and an army of volunteers. He robbed one man yesterday, making a total of eight victims who have stood and delivered since Tuesday. The man, splendidly mounted, showed his contempt for the police by riding up to the Sheffield avenue police station and asking for a description of the much wanted man. The police went after him in patrol wagons, on horseback, on bicycles and on foot. They saw the fellow several times and a dozen shots were exchanged, but each time the thoroughbred on which the robber rode carried him off in safety. The strange feature of this lone highwayman's work is he holds up all his victims in daylight. He is a young man and from his splendid horsemanship is believed to be a cowboy.

THE TRAVE'S NARROW ESCAPE.

Ocean Steamship Almost Dashed Upon the Rocks.

NEW YORK, Nov. 25.—A London special to the *Herald* says: The passengers by the Trave, who were landed at Southampton Thursday, report that the ship had a narrow escape from being dashed on the rocks Wednesday night. They had passed the Lizard and were proceeding through a thick fog. Shortly after 5 o'clock the passengers were startled by the sudden stoppage of the engines and on reaching the deck they saw the great rock known as "Start Point" looming up scarcely a hundred yards away. Many passengers became hysterical and a panic would have ensued but for the admirable behavior of the officers and crew, who succeeded in restoring confidence. The prompt response of the engines to the call to reverse was the only thing that saved the ship going on the rock.

FIENDISH PUNISHMENT.

Russian Peasants Burn a Horse Thief and His Family to Death.

LONDON, Nov. 25.—The *Telegraph's* correspondent at St. Petersburg sends an account of a horrible crime committed by peasants at Zastrzki in Lithuania. The peasants assembled in the night at the hut of a horse thief whom they wished to punish. The thief was asleep at the time with his wife and five children. The peasants set fire to the hut and kept watch for the occupants. When the shrieking inmates tried to escape they were met with fiendish yells by the heartless wretches and driven back into the flames with knives and other weapons. One of the inmates was murdered. The others were burned to death. The culprits afterward surrendered in a body to the police.

STRIKING FIREMEN.

New York Steam Company's Employes Will Fight Reduction in Wages.

NEW YORK, Nov. 25.—All the firemen employed in the New York Steam Company's plant in Greenwich and Washington streets struck at 12 10 o'clock this morning against a reduction of wages. The company employs about 50 firemen on the 46 boilers located around the bases of the great chimneys which are among the most prominent landmarks of the city. Before 1 o'clock the steam had fallen from the regular pressure of 85 pounds to the square inch to less than 50 pounds and was still rapidly falling. The elevators in the Western Union telegraph building had to stop running and in this building and in the general post office the electric lights went out as there was not power enough to run the dynamos.

Ocean Steamers.

Arrived—At Boston, Norseman, Liverpool. At New York, Rhynland, Antwerp; Flamborough, Barbadoes.

WEATHER INDICATIONS.

FAIR AND WARMER.

WASHINGTON, Nov. 25.—For the 24 hours from 8 a. m. to-day: For New England, generally fair; warmer; northwesterly winds.

SNOW FLURRIES OR RAIN.

BOSTON, Nov. 25.—Local forecast for New England until Saturday night: For Massachusetts and Rhode Island, generally fair, probably followed by snow flurries or rain by Saturday evening or night; gradually warmer, westerly to northerly winds.

MINISTER PHELPS' SPEECH.

Tribute to President Harrison at a Thanksgiving Banquet.

BERLIN, Nov. 25.—At the Kaiserhof Thanksgiving banquet yesterday Minister Phelps said: "President Harrison has given the country the cleanest and most successful administration in American annals. When history makes up its record, on every page will be written the name of Benjamin Harrison."

Mr. Phelps gave a toast to "The Republican party," which, he said, was "temporarily withdrawing for repairs, because it has given some of us offence."

"America," Mr. Phelps added, "is the only land in which God has poured forth such a river of good things that it takes Thanksgiving day to dispose of them. America is the only nation that could have a national Thanksgiving. Other nations try it and the day, instead of being a day of thanks, becomes a day of prayer. When other nations pray they pray for just what the United States has got. The Jew and the Gentile are the same in America. A man's faith, or his lack of faith, does not hurt him there."

Mr. Edwards, the American consul-general, replied for the United States.

Dr. Martindale responded to the toast "American Students Abroad," and Dr. Queen to the "Ladies."

Mr. Blaine Improving.

WASHINGTON, Nov. 25.—It is stated at ex-Secretary Blaine's home that he passed a comfortable night and is improving this morning.

HOME MATTERS.

PERSONAL.—Mr. and Mrs. Harry M. Peirce of this city were registered at the Arlington, Washington, on Wednesday last and will remain there about a week.

Henry James, mate of bark Mermaid, Mr. Enos, second mate of brig F. A. Barstow, Thomas Gifford of Acushnet, boat-header of bark William Baylies, Silas Pope of Acushnet, boatheader of bark Mermaid, and Joseph Blain, mate of steamer Belvedere, arrived in this city yesterday from San Francisco.

Richard S. Taber has been appointed chief of construction of the New Bedford Exchange of the Southern Massachusetts Telephone Company.

BOY MISSING.—Robert Boardman, residing at No. 387 Pleasant street, wishes information concerning his son Peter Boardman, 16 years old, who ran away from his home in this city on Aug. 5th last. The father has personally visited Boston, Lowell, Lawrence and other cities without gaining information of the son and he has now had descriptive cards printed which will be sent to all cities and towns in this part of the State at least.

H. C. HATHAWAY will sell at auction tomorrow morning at 9 o'clock at sales-room furniture, 1 New England organ (nearly new,) oil cloths, &c., &c.

At 10 o'clock at mart 25 horses of all grades, including several very fast ones, in fact the most speed we have ever shown, also three extra good saddlers showing all the gaits; also 4 very good cows, lot fur and plush robes, blankets, harnesses, &c., &c.

SKATING is good, and hundreds of girls and boys are earning a pair of Barney & Barry's nickled club skates with only an hour's work, selling three to eight pounds of tea. See advertisement in miscellaneous wants. C. Y. Wilcox, 28 Pearl street.

IF YOU BUY A NEW ULSTER this Winter see the new hood ulster, the latest style. We have them for men, and also in boys' sizes ages 14 to 19. Prices always the lowest. Reliable goods always. H. V. Sanders & Co., opp. City Clock, 92 Purchase street.

THE COLD WAVE has come, you want to keep warm. We want to sell you an ulster or overcoat. We have got them and we want to sell them. We can save you money on overcoats and ulsters. Ashley & Peirce.

LADIES, we never deceive you by asking fancy prices for your millinery and trim your hat or bonnet free, but plain figures and estimates always given, La Mode, 10 Purchase street.

AN AGED TRIO.—At Barnstable yesterday Ansel D. Lothrop and his two sisters ate their Thanksgiving dinner together. Their ages aggregate 249 years.

NEVER IN THE HISTORY of the cloak trade have Whiting & Co. sold so many jackets and wraps for Winter as this season—the style, quality and low prices have done it.

BIG DRIVES IN UNDERWEAR, merino and all wool. We want you to come in and see our big stock. You can find underwear at your own price from 47c. to $2.50. Ashley & Peirce.

HUMAN HAIR GOODS.—We are showing a large stock of strictly first quality hair at much less than regular prices. Gray hair a specialty. Coffin, 52 Purchase street.

GREATEST THANKSGIVING BARGAINS in millinery on Saturday, La Mode. Visit the store and you will be more than surprised at the reduction in prices.

LARGEST STOCK of trimmed hats in the city, the products of our own artistic designers and trimmers, at remarkable low prices. Coffin's, 52 Purchase street.

READ MOYNAN & Co's advertisement on page 4, under the heading of "Unparalleled Values."

HOW IS IT WHITING & Co. are selling so many blankets? Because they are selling the best quality at the lowest prices.

GO TO MOYNAN & Co's on Saturday—big special sale of trimmed hats and bonnets ⅓ off former prices.

THE COLD WAVE has come—secure your nice, warm, Winter underwear at Whiting & Co's.

UNITY CLUB.—The regular meeting of the Unity Club will be omitted this evening. See special notice.

MOYNAN & Co. are offering some excellent values in Newmarkets, capes and jackets. Read advertisement on page 4.

SPECIAL PRICES on all our trimmed hats and bonnets regardless of cost, La Mode.

THOSE REMNANTS of mouldings at half price are ready at Hutchinson's.

CHILDREN'S OVERCOATS AND ULSTERS in great variety at Ashley & Peirce's.

EXAMINE regular $1.25 black velvet for 89 cents a yard. Coffin's, 52 Purchase street.

ANNAWAN ENCAMPMENT.—A special meeting will be held this evening at 7 30 o'clock.

MASONIC.—Eureka Lodge, F. & A. M., will have a special communication this evening.

ETCHINGS all marked down at Hutchinson's.

THIS season take Hood's Sarsaparilla.

SATURDAY'S SPECIAL!

20 Per Cent. Discount from Regular Prices.

SCREEN FRAMES, FILLED.

SCREEN FRAMES, UNFILLED.

A very handsome line in

OAK, CHERRY OR BAMBOO.

In a great variety of styles and sizes, varying in price from

$2.50 to $15.00.

EASELS!

OAK, CHERRY, BRASS OR BAMBOO.

Splendid assortment, comprising the newest designs and many novelties never seen in this city before, ranging in price from

62 1-2c. to $5.00.

20 Per Cent. Discount from Regular Prices.

That we have the largest and finest assortment of Screens and Easels in the city, goes without saying. These articles make an ornamental and useful present for the holidays. Why not improve the opportunity to make a handsome saving? Come in and see the styles.

We also offer a line of Art Photogravure Dado Shades, mounted complete, with silk tassel for

75 CENTS EACH!

The regular price is $1.25.

C. F. WING,

34 to 40 Purchase Street.

WHITING & CO.

THE COLD WAVE HAS COME!

TO-MORROW

Will be

A Great Cloak Day

AT OUR STORE.

100 new Cape Newmarkets in all the new Cloths and in all sizes and prices.

400 Ladies' Jackets in Black, Navy and Tans, in all styles of make and all prices.

25 new Seal Plush Sacks for to-morrow's sale and to be sold at $25 apiece; they are beauties.

10 new Circulars, all Fur trimmed and at low prices.

50 new Bernhardt Capes in Black and Tan color; they are in all sizes and prices.

62 Fur Capes in 3 lengths, that we are selling very cheap.

Our Children's Garment stock is large and we can suit all that give us a call.

A few more of those Children's Gretchens left at $5.00 apiece. 6, 8 and 10 years of age; these are $8 and $10 Garments.

We want every Lady that wishes a good Winter Garment cheap to call at our store TO-MORROW.

WHITING & CO.

Children's Overcoats.

How people look at the stylish little lads in Overcoat time, and how much time and brains we spend over these patterns, but we commence far enough ahead to get 'em just right.

It isn't the style only that we look out for. The wear has attention too—that means the foundation, the linings and the finish, the button-holes and buttons, and we don't neglect the prices. We make them as they should be.

Any price from $3.50 to $9.00.
Extra Long and Extra Long Capes.

Ulsters and Reefers also occupy a conspicuous place in our Children's Department, for we have provided an enormous variety of these useful garments for boys from 6 to 18 years of age.

Ulsters $6.00 to $15.00.
Reefers $3.50 up to $10.00.

J. & W. R. WING & CO.

133 Union Street.

THE CRESCENT!

22 Purchase St.

A New Stock of Outlining

RECEIVED.

Black Sateen Shopping Bags,	39c.
Black Mohair Shopping Bags (larger)	50c.
Cream Laundry Bags,	50c.
Velvet Covers for Sofa Pillows,	50c.
Stand Covers,	50c.
Stand Covers in Bedford Cord,	62c.
Stand Covers in Velvet,	87c.
Pillow Shams (per pair),	15c.
Pillow Shams (per pair),	25c.
Commode Scarfs,	19c.
Commode Scarfs,	39c.
Commode Scarfs,	83c.
Bureau Scarfs,	25c.
Bureau Scarfs,	50c.
Bureau Scarfs,	1.00
Bureau Scarfs,	1.25
Hmestitched Doylies,	12 1-2c.
Tidies,	5c.
Tidies,	29c.
Tray Cloths,	10c.
Tray Cloths,	12 1-1c.
Tray Cloths,	25c.
Tray Cloths,	50c.
Tray Cloths,	62c.
Infants' Bibs,	9c.
Infants' Bibs,	25c.
Wash Silk, Rope Silk, Zephyr Silk,	5c.
Filosene Silk, Rope Linen,	5c.
Linen Fringes,	17c.
Germantowns and Saxony, (good size and quality),	12 1-2c.

N. B.—These goods as cheerfully shown to lookers as to buyers.

At the same time please ask to see our new line of INFANTS' LONG DRESSES. The prices are varied and the styles are the daintiest we have seen yet. Also the beautiful Flannel and Cashmere Embroidered Sacks and Wrappers for Baby. You will all agree they are as pretty as any you have seen.

We have, too, more Bonnets for little girls of 5 or 6 years of age, style entirely new.

Infants' Bonnets in white and colors, good variety.

Ladies' Wrappers,	$1.00
Ladies' Wrappers,	1.25
Ladies' Wrappers, (Mourning Prints)	1.50
Ladies' Wrappers, (Eiderdown Flannel),	2.50

Hosiery, Underwear, Corsets.

Special Sale of Buttons at greatly reduced prices. We wish to close them out this week as we need the space which they occupy.

THE CRESCENT!

22 Purchase St.

Pages 1-8.

The Evening Standard.

Pages 1-8.

ESTABLISHED FEBRUARY, 1850.

NEW BEDFORD, WEDNESDAY, NOVEMBER 30, 1892.---TEN PAGES. TWO CENTS.

HASKELL & TRIPP.

The department of Toilet Articles is an important one in this store.

Do you keep track of the stock? Your favorite soaps and perfumes are sold here, very likely for less than you've paid somewhere. Imported hair brushes are a special feature.

Just now we are offering a bargain lot of really good hair brushes at 25c. each.

Three lines of French hair brushes at 50c., 67c. and 75c. are great values. Celluloid sets, brush, comb and hand mirror in neat box, cost $1. More showy sets in brocade plush cases, $1.

Silver-mounted sets of brush, comb, mirror and manicure, in handsome plush case, $2.50. Same in elegant hard wood case, satin lined, $3.89.

Smokers' sets in cases, $1.25 and $1.75.

Complete shaving set in case, good fittings, $2.39.

Here's a big bargain, worth 85c., our price 50c. { 8-oz. bottle of fine-quality Violet toilet water.

Extracts, Soaps, Powders, from Famous Makers. | LUBIN, COLGATE, LADY GREY PERFUMERY CO.

Colgate's Florida water, (new) 25c.

"Mountain Violets," finest handkerchief extract ever prepared. 50c. a bottle. Try it. *It is simply exquisite.*

Cold cream soap is the latest; prepared by Colgate & Co. 3 cakes in a box. Price 50c. a box.

Pierce's pure Bay Rum in sprinkler top bottle, 35c.

Farina cologne, "4711," 48c. a bottle.

Imitation cut glass toilet bottles, 8-oz. size, 25c. a pair. Same size, covered with filagree silver, 78c. a pair.

Correct prices on these ever popular soaps. | Lubin's. Pear's. Rose Glycerine. Cuticura. Old Brown Windsor. Carmel Castile.

Our own brand pure Witch Hazel, 10c. per bottle.

Ribbons.

The great demand for Christmas ribbons can be fully met here. Our unrivalled ribbon stock can supply every known shade. Specialties for fancy work now ready in great abundance. One lot of very rich satin and watered ribbons, worth 50c. a yard, closing out at 25c. a yard. The new "bull's eye" moire ribbon, for decorative uses, only 6c. a yd.

Stir at the hat counter. A mark-down of misses' beautiful quality felt hats, new shape, ready trimmed. Formerly 75c. Now 50c. each.

Rich plush Tam O'Shanter caps, formerly $1.25. Now 89c. each.

Bedford cord caps, sailor shapes. Formerly 45c. Now 25c. each.

HASKELL & TRIPP,

Department Stores,

Purchase and William Streets.

WEATHER INDICATIONS.

FAIR.

WASHINGTON, Nov. 30.—For the 24 hours from 8 a. m. to-day: For Maine, New Hampshire and Massachusetts, fair; clearing on the coast; northwest gales; fair Friday.

SNOW.

BOSTON, Nov. 30.—Local forecast for New England until Friday: Snow for coast sections, followed by fair, generally fair in interior; no decided changes in temperature; north to west winds, high along the coast.

M. BRISSON'S PROMISE.

He will Undertake to Form a New French Cabinet.

PARIS, Nov. 30.—President Carnot has requested M. Brisson to form a new cabinet, and M. Brisson has consented. It is rumored that neither M. de Freycinet nor M. Ribot will accept office under M. Brisson, who, it is said, intends to take the ministry of justice in addition to

M. Brisson.

assuming the duties of prime minister. A strong feeling in favor of M. Brisson prevailed last evening in the lobbies of the Chamber of Deputies.

THE FRENCH POLITICAL MUDDLE.

Press Condemns M. Loubet's Weakness, but Esteems His Honor and Courage.

LONDON, Nov. 30.—The Paris correspondent of the *Times* says the utter absurdity of the political situation is ridiculous. The hopelessness of the muddle is the aspect that chiefly strikes the spectator. The Panama Canal Co. has expanded into a kind of irresponsible committee on public safety, the president of which is forced into the position of the head of the legislative and executive power. The committee, therefore, possesses dictatorial powers and claims universal obedience, although the judicial power, jealous of its authority, is fighting the committee both tooth and nail. Nothing could better illustrate the French temper than the tremulous comment of certain journals in seeking with bated breath to draw a historical parallel between Brisson and the incipient Robespierre. While the press condemns M. Loubet's weakness it esteems his courage and honor."

GLADSTONE'S HOME RULE SCHEME.

Sneering Headlines Appear in Pall Mall Gazette Columns.

LONDON, Nov. 30.—"Yankee Details" and "Exclusive Information" are the sneering headlines under which the *Pall Mall Gazette* to-day publishes a summary of the details of Mr. Gladstone's new home rule scheme for the Irish provinces as cabled here. A few papers print the cable dispatches, but none comment on it.

The representative of the Associated Press to-day had an interview with Herbert Gladstone, and asked whether the scheme as published was based on an autograph letter of his. Mr. Gladstone said there was not a word of truth in the report that any such letter was in existence.

In regard to the alleged scheme, which purports to be a plan of government, Mr. Gladstone said it was unworthy of notice, adding that it contains its own most effective denial.

The Socialist leaders have requested Mr. Gladstone to receive a deputation; their intention, it is declared, is to get a plain answer to the question whether the government will supply work to the unemployed of London. It is not likely that Mr. Gladstone will give his consent to recognize the deputation.

TRAIN HELD UP.

Messenger Forced to Open a Safe but Only $25 Was Secured.

GREAT FALLS, Mont., Nov. 30.—The great northern west-bound passenger train was held up by three robbers near Malta yesterday morning. A few minutes after leaving Malta two men climbed over the tender, covered the engineer and fireman, made them stop and asked the messenger to open his car, while the third held the conductor and brakeman in the snow at the end of a gun when they jumped off to see what the matter was.

The messenger was forced to open the local safe, in which it is claimed only $25 was secured. He did not know the combination of the big safe. The robbers evidently did not have the tools to break open the safe.

CLAYTON UNSEATED.

Mr. Gladstone's Majority Now Increased to Forty.

LONDON, Nov. 30.—The unseating of Mr. Nathaniel George Clayton, Conservative, increases Mr. Gladstone's majority to 40.

Mr. Frank C. James, the Conservative who was elected in Wallsall, was deprived of his seat by the courts because he provided hat cards or favors for his adherents.

The petition which resulted in the unseating of Clayton charged him with bribery. His offence consists in giving a check to an ardent Conservative who used the money to organize a picnic. This was held by the court to come within the provisions of the act prohibiting treating.

TONS OF STONE FROM THE SKY.

People of a Colorado Town Think They Have a Piece of the Comet.

NEWCASTLE, Col., Nov. 30.—About 9 a. m. yesterday a stone weighing probably ten tons fell from the sky, striking the earth a mile northeast of the town. There were no witnesses, as far as known, but the fact that it sank deep into the earth and was in a heated condition when discovered leaves no doubt in the minds of the inhabitants as to where it came from, and great excitement prevails. The stone is of a color entirely foreign to the locality, being slate colored, and the people are convinced that it dropped from the much-talked-of comet.

Struck a Sunken Rock.

NEW YORK, Nov. 30.—The steamer Orinoco, which was due here from Bermuda last Sunday morning, has returned to Bermuda with a hole in her bottom, having struck a sunken rock while leaving the harbor. She had on board a number of passengers who were returning to New York.

SEVERE NORTHEAST STORM.

No Steamers from the Vineyard or Nantucket.

Schooner Ashore on Chappaquiddic Floated by Wreckers.

Government Telegraph and Telephone Lines on Islands Prostrated.

[Special Dispatch.]

VINEYARD HAVEN, Nov. 30.—A severe northeast storm has been blowing three days with violent gusts of wind and heavy rain. The wind last night attained a velocity of 48 miles per hour. Over one inch and a half of rain fell.

Schooner Idaho, Hall, of and for Rockland, Me., in ballast, having discharged at Edgartown, dragged her anchor yesterday morning and went ashore on Chappaquiddic Point. She was floated at high water by Edgartown wreckers apparently uninjured.

Nantucket had no boat yesterday and will have none to-day.

The Vineyard boat did not make her trip to New Bedford to-day.

Steam tug Elsie brought the Vineyard mail and passengers from Woods Holl.

Fortunately no serious wrecks are reported in this vicinity.

The government telegraph and telephone lines on the Vineyard and Nantucket are prostrate. Heavy north wind and light snow now prevail.

The General Banks Ashore.

Schooner Gen. Banks of Boston, New Bedford for Sullivan, Me., in ballast, parted one chain in this harbor last night during the northeast gale and dragged afoul of another vessel. To prevent sinking, she was compelled to slip the remaining chain and run ashore at the head of the harbor, where she now lies.

No Fall River Boat at Newport.

NEWPORT, Nov. 30. — Newport's first storm of the Winter is a real one. Rain and snow have alternated for nearly 48 hours and the end seems yet afar off. The wind blew a gale all night and the air was filled with snow, which failed to accumulate to any great quantity. The Fall River Line sound boat has not yet arrived. The early mail from New York over the Shore Line failed to connect and telegraphic communication with the outside world has been difficult. No serious disasters on sea or land are as yet reported.

Ocean Steamer Delayed by Weather.

BOSTON, Nov. 30.—Steamers Lancastrian, hence for Liverpool, and Peruvian, hence for Glasgow, which left their docks at 7 30 this morning, were obliged to anchor in the stream on account of the storm.

Worst Storm on Long Island Since the Blizzard of 1888.

LONG ISLAND CITY, L. I., Nov. 30.—The snow storm on Long Island was the heaviest since the blizzard of 1888, the fall being from 18 inches to two feet. At East Minola and other points the snow is a foot or over in depth. Heavy drifts have formed in many places, impeding travel on the roads. All trains are behind time. Snow-ploughs have been sent out to aid the stalled trains.

COMMITTEE AT WORK.

Exhaustive Report on Plans Submitted to be Presented to the Monetary Conference.

BRUSSELS, Nov. 30.—The committee of 12 appointed by the International Monetary Conference to examine into and report on the proposals submitted by Alfred De Rothschild, sat yesterday for eight hours, with only a short interval for luncheon. The members have arranged to give their exclusive attention to the work so as to be able to present an exhaustive report to the conference.

Several experts, who are not delegates, offered to give evidence on the production of precious metals and other points relating to the deliberations, but the committee declined to hear witnesses on any side of the question.

It is understood the committee take as nearest approaching accuracy the statistics prepared by Ottomar Haup, especially for the use of the conference, giving estimates compiled from the latest data of the monetary stocks of the world. Senator Jones, one of the American delegates, has prepared a special statement of the consumption and production of silver.

The committee has consented to request the Danish delegate, C. T. Teitgen, to submit his plan as an addendum to the DeRothschild plan. Mr. Teitgen is a mono-metallist. He proposes the coinage of silver five-franc, four-shilling or dollar pieces, rated to gold according to the price of silver in the year previous to the adoption of the agreement, with a seigniorage of ten per cent. He also proposes the appointment of a permanent international commission to fix the initial price. Should the price of silver fall to 5 per cent. below the coinage ratio the committee will have authority to fix a new ratio and order the recoinage of the pieces. These coins will be legal tender internationally; banks to keep them as a reserve against notes and to have the right to demand gold in exchange for them at any time from the government issuing the particular coin held.

The members of the committee declare that their proceedings must be kept completely private until definite decisions are attained.

Newspaper Comments.

LONDON, Nov. 30.—The *Telegraph* in an editorial article suggests that silver be made legal tender up to the amount of £4, in order to secure the inviolability of the £5 pieces. It continues: "Even if the monetary conference should adopt the Rothschild plan there might be months and perhaps years of negotiations between the different governments before anything could be done. But it is universally felt that M. DeRothschild has done a great service to commercial interest by averting an utter smash of silver, through the collapse of the conference."

The *Standard's* article says: "The silver market is not favorably impressed with M. DeRothschild's scheme. The more the scheme is examined the more potent becomes its impracticability. The collapse of the conference is expected in all thoughtful circles."

SOCIETY WEDDING.

Whipple-Weaver Nuptials Take Place at Newport This Forenoon.

NEWPORT, R. I., Nov. 30.—November weather is evidently not the best adapted to society weddings. Yesterday's event of that kind took place in a snow storm, while to-day's came close upon the end of a small blizzard. The bride was Miss Eleanor Whipple, daughter of Mr. and Mrs. John Whipple of this city, and granddaughter of ex-Gov. Thomas Swann of Maryland. The groom was Benjamin Weaver, associated with his father, John G. Weaver, in the management of the Ocean House and the Everett House, New York. The best man was J. Baucel Lafarge, and the bridesmaids Miss Sallie Smith and Miss Helen Gammel of Providence, the latter herself to become a bride within a fortnight. There were no ushers, the wedding being a home affair, taking place at the Whipple residence on the Cliffs, which was handsomely bedecked with flowers for the occasion. The ceremony was performed at noon by Rev. E. H. Porter, rector of Emmanuel church, a reception following.

TRICKEY'S STORY.

Officer Heard What Passed Between Reporter and McHenry.

The Third Person was Concealed in the Detective's Office.

Police of Fall River Suspect an Attempt to Tamper with Grand Jurymen.

[Special Dispatch.]

FALL RIVER, Nov. 30.—A feature of the Borden case which has aroused considerable interest is the report from time to time that evidence was introduced in the grand jury room to prove that Henry G. Trickey had attempted to bribe a witness. That story in regard to the evidence is not true, but nevertheless all has not been told in connection with the startling story which was signed by Mr. Trickey and which still stands as one of the sensations of a most sensational tragedy.

When Mr. Trickey applied to Detective McHenry for exclusive information, a third person, an officer in the employ of the government was concealed behind a curtain in McHenry's office in Providence. Mr. Trickey there represented that he wanted the McHenry story for the use of Lawyer Adams of counsel for defence, though behind that bald assertion there is not the slightest particle of evidence to show that Mr. Trickey had any right to use Mr. Adams' name or that he was not working entirely in the interests of his paper.

However, he was taken at his word, and McHenry led him on with the assistance of the government. Then came what Mr. Trickey himself confessed was a premature publication and the explosion followed. Just how far McHenry and the ally concealed in his office had been authorized to go in determining what game Mr. Trickey was playing is not known. If they thought they were at the beginning of a valuable clew, Mr. Trickey threw them down as hard as they threw him down, which was certainly hard enough.

On what appears to be reliable authority the affidavits made in that story did not originate with McHenry, but were prepared in this city with the evident intention of boring into the mine which was supposed to have been laid under the government's case.

As to the liberty the grand jurymen are enjoying the police here have good grounds for suspecting that attempts are being made to tamper with them, and they have been keeping close watch on a person who has figured very prominently in the case.

Is Miss Borden Insane?

The latest story in connection with the Borden case is that the grand jury took a recess to enable an examination as to Miss Borden's sanity and that when that body reassembles to-morrow it will be confronted with experts who will give their opinions whether Lizzie Borden is of sound mind or whether she is a maniac. The Attorney-General believes Lizzie was irresponsible, but that she committed the crime. The district attorney thinks she is sane. The rumors that Henry G. Trickey, the newspaper man, is wanted for attempting to interfere with a government witness, are believed to have foundation in fact.

THE PRESIDENT'S MESSAGE.

Personal Afflictions Will Delay its Tns-ra mission One Day.

WASHINGTON, Nov. 30.—The President has virtually decided that the exigencies of the public business require that he shall temporarily disregard his personal afflictions, and he therefore devoted himself to-day to the consideration of his message to Congress with a view to having ready it Tuesday next. It is said to be the President's purpose to elaborate several important topics, only briefly touched upon in the original draft, but he has now abandoned that idea and will confine himself to the strict necessities of the case. The report that there might be several days' delay in presenting the message was based on the President's original purpose of a total abstention from duty until after his return from the funeral of Dr. Scott on Friday next. In view of his modified plans it is now settled that there will be but one day's delay in the transmission of the message.

OBITUARY.

Death of Henry C. Perry, the Oldest Active Merchant in Taunton.

TAUNTON, Nov. 30.—Henry C. Perry, the oldest active merchant in this city, is dead in his 73d year. Mr. Perry has been engaged in the boot and shoe business in this city for more than half a century.

To Guard Against Cholera.

LONDON, Nov. 30.—The local government board are preparing a new and stringent series of regulations to guard against the recrudescence of cholera next Spring.

Ocean Steamers.

Arrived—At New York, Spain, London; Sorento, Hamburg; Newport, Colon; Arecuna, Grenada; Wyoming, Liverpool. Passed Kinsale, Virginian, Boston.

HOME MATTERS.

SNOW BEGAN FALLING last night, and before noon to-day between three and four inches had gathered. The weather moderated this forenoon and the snow melted about as fast as it fell. The schools held no afternoon session, on account of the bad walking.

TO CONSIDER THE SUBJECT.—The Board of Public Works will consider the subject of insuring the employes of the street department against accident, and it is thought that the Water Works department will also look into the matter.

ANOTHER POLITICAL CLUB.—The West End Independent Political Club was organized, last evening, with a large membership. There will be another meeting of the club to-morrow evening to take action on the coming election and decide as to which candidates shall be supported.

WIDENING THE BRIDGE.—The directors of the Board of Trade held a meeting this forenoon, when the matter of widening the New Bedford and Fairhaven bridge was fully discussed. It was voted to refer the subject to the committee on public affairs of the Board, of which Hon. W. W. Crapo is chairman, with full powers. The committee was instructed to procure plans, ascertain the cost, etc.

RESTRICTED IMMIGRATION.—The restrictions put upon immigration by the United States government have nearly ruined the business of local steamship agents. Prepaid tickets furnished the great bulk of their business, and owing to the strict enforcement of the laws, hundreds of citizens of Great Britain who have friends and relatives in this city and who had intended to take up their residence here have been temporarily prevented from doing so. Local agents of the Anchor Line have been notified that several steamers of that line have been withdrawn from the regular passenger service.

LIQUOR DEALERS DISAGREE.

Contention Among Them About Dispensing $8000 Campaign Fund Effectively.

It is said that a meeting of liquor dealers was held yesterday and that the municipal campaign was the topic under consideration. It is rumored that considerable ill-feeling was engendered among the dispensers of the "ardent," because only those who held licenses last year were notified of the meeting. It is said there is also considerable disagreement among them as to the manner of dispensing the campaign fund most effectively. Many of the dealers who have entered into the business during the present year claim that they have contributed to the fund and received no invitations to the meetings called for the purpose of discussing what use is to be made of it. It is said that $8000 have been contributed. Some are in favor of putting it at once into the hands of a committee to be used, while others claim that it should all be dispensed on election day.

SUPERIOR COURT—CRIMINAL TERM.

THOMPSON, J.

TAUNTON, Nov. 30.

The jury brought in a verdict of guilty in the case of Michael O'Brien of Fall River. Charged with disturbing the peace and assault and battery.

Mary, the wife of Sewell P. Ellis of Fall River, asked the jury to compel her husband to support her. The case is an appealed one from the lower court, and it lasted all yesterday afternoon and a part of this forenoon, because of unlooked-for legal complications. As a matter of fact the wife was out of the case as she stated that she is able to support herself. The question then came upon the liability of Ellis for the support of his minor child. The husband and wife have been quarrelling for some years and have not lived together. Two years ago he tried to get a divorce from her on the ground of gross and confirmed habits of intoxication, but did not succeed, and some time after he was charged in the lower court for non-support of a minor child, whose paternity he denied. He was found guilty and was then sentenced to three months in the House of Correction, from which sentence he appealed. It was upon the fact that he had once before been sentenced that the complications ensue, the judge holding it to be a fact that he has once been sentenced and ruling that he is bound to support the child. The court said: "I rule as a matter of law that the question having been tried and determined in the lower court in the previous action that the fact that this child is his, defendant is not at liberty in this court to say that this is not his child." The case goes to the Supreme Judicial Court on exceptions, as a test case.

James Atkinson of Fall River. Indicted for manslaughter in having caused the death of Maria E. Tobin at Fall River, Sept. 23d, in having run over her. On trial. R. C. Brown for defendant.

Joseph Noreau of Fall River. Complaint for disturbing the peace. Tried. Verdict guilty. Fined $15 and expenses. A. E. Bragg for defendant.

PERSONAL.—Capt. C. H. Foley, who was master of bark Bounding Billow last season, will command steamer Jesse H. Freeman next season. Capt. Foley is now at home in this city, enjoying a well-earned vacation.

Wallace S. Ashley, who was first officer of the Bounding Billow last season, it is stated, is to command her the coming one.

Capt. William Hegarty, late master of bark Alice Knowles, will command bark Triton next season. He is now in this city, but will soon return to San Francisco.

Capt. George L. Donaldson, who was master of bark Andrew Hicks last season, will be her commander again next season.

James Wing, who was first officer of steamer Karluk last season, will command her next season.

Henry C. Thacher of Yarmouthport was in town to-day. He made a pleasant call on Mayor Ashley.

Miss Ruth Tripp, of this city, who went to Tiverton Monday to attend the funeral of her mother, the late Mrs. A. G. Tripp, was taken quite seriously ill in Fall River while returning to this city.

Isaac B. Tompkins, Jr., James Delano and Henry C. Hutchinson of the New Bedford Board of Trade, were in Boston yesterday at the annual meeting of the Massachusetts Board of Trade.

E. Gerry Brown, formerly proprietor of the *Bunker Hill Times*, has removed to Brockton and will soon commence the publication of a Sunday paper.

A WONDERFUL DISCOVERY. — "Carbonite." What is Carbonite?" The perfect coal, a simple non-explosive fuel composed of almost pure carbon. Burns *anywhere without chimney or flue* in *portable* heaters. No smoke, no smell, no gas. Manufactured by the American Safety Fuel Co. of New York. Now on exhibition by E. B. Chase & Co., cor. Union and Fifth streets.

BREAK DOWN. — Napoleon Normandin's grocery wagon broke down on Purchase street near Franklin street last evening, the rear axle breaking in two in the middle. The snow came providentially, for it enabled the owner to drag his wrecked vehicle home this morning on sled runners.

THE BOARD OF TRADE will hold its monthly meeting at the rooms to-morrow evening. A full attendance is requested, as the committee on transportation will give a hearing to patrons of the Old Colony railroad in regard to better freight facilities.

DANCE POSTPONED.—The dance advertised on the seventh page to occur this evening, at Purrington Hall, Mattapoisett, has been postponed one week, and will occur next Wednesday evening.

PARLOR SALE of useful and fancy articles will open on Dec. 1st and continue afternoons and evenings, at 116 Fifth street. Mrs. Wm. W. Sayer.

"A YARD OF POPPIES" given away at *Hutchinson's* with the Home Magazine for December. Price 25c.

GATES AJAR.—The gates at the Weld street railroad crossing are out of commission to-day, being so heavily loaded with snow that they are difficult to operate.

FINEST LINE of Christmas Booklets, etc., in the city at Hutchinson's Connecting Stores, 194 and 202 Union street.

SIPPICAN TRIBE of Red Men held a meeting last evening, when four palefaces were adopted.

VIOLETS and velvet roses in all the new shades at Nooning's.

SPECIAL.—Celluloid Frames, all colors, for cabinet pictures, only 10c. this week at Hutchinson's Connecting Stores.

TOURISTS' and Tam O'Shanter hats at Nooning's very cheap.

IT WILL INTEREST you and pay you to visit Hutchinson's new Connecting Stores.

REMEMBER that Nooning's is the place to buy nobby felt hats in all colors at 79c. each.

CHIROPODIST.—Mrs. L. W. Williams, No. 190 Purchase st., Webster Block, every Friday.

GO TO H. H. NOONING'S for Christmas ribbons.

BE made strong by Hood's Sarsaparilla.

CARPETS,

FURNITURE,

DRAPERIES,

UPHOLSTERY GOODS,

WALL PAPERS,

OIL CLOTHS,

LINOLEUMS.

We are Sole Agents for the famous

Glenwood Stoves!

THE GLENWOOD RANGE

Is superior to all others.

THE GLENWOOD PARLOR

Has no equal.

THE ELECTRIC OIL HEATER

Is the best Oil Stove in the market. Hundreds of these stoves are in use in this city and vicinity and give perfect satisfaction.

C. F. WING,

34 to 40 Purchase Street.

WHITING & CO.

THIS WEEK

We shall make

SOME EXTRA LOW PRICES

on our

DRESS GOODS!

To reduce stock and make room for our

Holiday Goods!

All of our French novelty pattern dresses, to be closed out very cheap, get the prices.

22 French pattern dresses, to be sold at $5.95, $6.95 and $7.95, just half price.

800 yards left of those $1.00, plain, French dress goods, in Black and Colors, at 50c. per yard, that we have sold so many thousands yards of the past few weeks.

You want to see the Dress Goods we are selling at 39c. per yard, and try to match them for less than 50c.

300 yards remnants of Printed China Silk same as we had such a rush for in September, $1.00 goods at 39 cts. per yard, just right for dress trimmings and fancy work.

Look at New Jackets Opening in our Cloak Room to-day.

We can show you a large stock of Fur Capes, and Muffs, at lowest prices.

Our Glove, Hosiery and Underwear departments are busy places.

Do not forget to look at our Blankets, Puffs, Spreads, Flannels, Cotton and Linen Goods, as we have the largest stock, and at the lowest prices.

WHITING & CO.

Don't You

WANT

—AN—

ULSTER?

One so full of generous warmth and solid comfort that no matter how sharp the weather you'll feel just as comfortable as though "toasting your shins" around a warm fire.

Your size and style is here at your price—$8, $10, $12, $15, $16, $18, $20, $25, $30, $35. Don't you think your kind is among them.

Ulsters for Big Boys are here too.

J. & W. R. WING & CO.

133 Union Street.

THE CRESCENT!

22 Purchase St.

Special Bargains

THURSDAY, FRIDAY & SATURDAY

Dec. 1, 2 and 3.

Ginghams in apron checks, only 5c. per yard. Regular price 8c.

75c. for 2 1-2 yards of Table Linen, good quality.

42c. per yard for regular 50c. Table Linen.

6 1-2c. per yard for Crocodile Cloth, much wider than common print. Regular price 8c.

29c. per yard for Striped Flannels suitable for Wrappers or Dressing Sacks, regular price 37c.

$1.00 each for Plush Hats and Bonnets in Red, Blue, Brown and Old Rose, regular prices $1.25 and $1.50.

89c. for Plush Hats, regular price $1.25.

39c. for a 50c. Turkish Fez in Brown, Red and Blue.

59c. for 75c. Cashmere Bonnets.

Pretty Plush Hats for Boys $1.00 each, former price $1.33.

Only 21c., Infants' Cream Brocade Bonnets with full ruche and lined with Flannel.

19c. for a nice little Hood for Baby.

Only 79c. for Kid Gloves in Tans, Black and Slates, regular price $1.00.

☞ Please Remember these goods are offered for THURSDAY, FRIDAY and SATURDAY ONLY.

THE CRESCENT!

22 Purchase St.

HASKELL & TRIPP.

A marked day.

Saturday will be a marked day in the Cloak Department. If any of our readers have been waiting for the usual cut-price sale of high-class garments, customary at this time of the year, they have not delayed in vain. Here's the story:

A jacket-maker overdid it. Result 1 — Jackets plenty, money scarce. Result 2 — Goods here, jacket-maker happy, and something of special interest for 75 jacket wearers.

Fine navy blue jackets, satin faced, with full shawl collar of mufflon fur, actually worth $20. Our price $6.95.

Fine black cheviot jacket, with full shawl collar of raccoon fur, actually worth $15. Our price $6.95.

Fine navy jacket, with deep, full collar of blue gray Angora fur, worth fully $15. Our price $6.95.

Black cheviot, satin-faced jacket, with collar of handsome black Angora fur, worth fully $12. Our price $6.95.

Black cheviot jacket, satin facing, shawl collar of natural opossum fur. Actual value $12. Our price $6.95.

Black cheviot jacket, satin faced, with shawl collar of black Persian lamb, really worth $12. Our price $6.95.

Besides the styles quoted above there are a good many sample jackets, not more than two of a kind, trimmed with all the popular sorts of furs, regular prices $10, $12 and $15, comprising:

Misses' sizes from 12 to 18 years. Women's sizes, 32 to 40-inch. — All to go $6.95 each.

Remember, the above lots are all to be sold at one price, and will be ready Saturday morning at 9 o'clock.

Remember, many of these were sample garments and are extra well made, as the manufacturers have a way of turning out their samples in the best possible manner.

Remember, none of these garments have been made up from poor but showy materials on purpose for a so-called "bargain sale," but are straight, right, first-class, and you will get a great return for your money—$6.95.

Now boys.

A first-class rubber foot ball, measuring 24 inches in circumference, *goes free of any charge whatever* with one of our "wear-resister" suits. Price $4.50.

We have just had made up to our order a large lot of suits, strictly all wool, "double and twisted" cloth, and have named them the *"wear-resister."*

The name fits.

The price is $4.50, but the suit is worth more money, and besides that the foot ball is complimentary.

A large assortment of these handsome suits ready Saturday.

HASKELL & TRIPP,

Department Steamers,

Purchase and William Streets.

INDICTED!

Miss Borden Will be Tried for Double Murder.

Grand Jury Charges Her With Both Crimes.

True Bill Found Against Another Party.

Not Given Out as the Person Is Not in Custody.

Henry G. Trickey Supposed to be the Man.

Hearing in the Great Case Over at Last.

Lizzie Preserves Stolid Demeanor on Hearing News.

She Learns of Indictment First Through Medium of Friends.

[Special Dispatch.]

TAUNTON, Dec. 2.—The grand jury assembled promptly at 9.30 o'clock this morning and occupied their usual room in the lower story of the court-house.

The usual large number of reporters was on hand, and a number of officers, both State and county.

After the Superior Court took a recess, Mr. Knowlton joined the grand jury in their room.

There were before the grand jury as witnesses Bridget Sullivan, Detective McHenry of Providence and his wife and Assistant Marshal Fleet of Fall River.

At 12.35 the grand jury came into the court-room and took their seats back of the prisoner's dock. District Attorney Knowlton came in and a moment later Judge Thompson followed and took his seat.

Ready to Report.

Mr. Knowlton addressing the court said: "Your honor the grand jury is ready to make a further report.

The grand jury polled and 21 men who are now on the panel answered to their names.

Assistant Clerk of the Court Borden addressed the jury, saying: Mr. Foreman, have the grand jury any further presentments to make?

The foreman answered: We have.

Mr. Knowlton said this is the last session of the grand jury for the year, although they may be called on for a special session at any time before February.

Judge Thompson thanked the jury for its attention and informed them that their services would not be required unless called in special session.

The Indictment.

Copies of the indictment against Lizzie Borden were given to the reporters. There are two indictments of one count each and one of two counts, all of which are embraced in the following documents: Commonwealth of Massachusetts, Bristol, ss. At the Superior Court begun and holden at Taunton in and for said county of Bristol on the first Monday of November in the year of our Lord 1892:

The jurors for the said Commonwealth on their oaths present, Lizzie Andrew Borden of Fall River in the county of Bristol at Fall River in the county of Bristol, on the fourth day of August in the year 1892, in and upon one Abby Durfee Borden feloniously and wilfully and of her malice aforethought an assault did make, and with a certain weapon, to wit, a sharp cutting instrument, the name and a more particular description of which is to the jurors unknown, her, the said Abby Durfee Borden, feloniously and wilfully did strike, cut, beat and bruise in and upon the head of her, the said Abby Durfee Borden, by the said strik-

THE INSANE STORY.

Exact Words of the District Attorney in Denying Its Accuracy.

[Special Dispatch.]

TAUNTON, Dec. 2.—The New Bedford morning paper to-day states that District Attorney Knowlton denied that he said to a *Standard* reporter that the *Mercury's* story concerning Attorney-General Pillsbury's theory that Miss Borden is insane "was far off from the truth as any other reports which have been published," and also that he said the story was "all bosh" as the Associated Press dispatches stated.

In regard to the denial that the district attorney said that the insanity story in the *Mercury* was untrue, it is only necessary to say that the district attorney and the *Standard* reporter were speaking about the case, and the district attorney volunteered the remark when speaking directly of the insanity issue, "Zeph (Mr. Pease, a *Mercury* reporter who wrote the story) is as bad off as any of you."

Despite this denial there is undoubtedly some foundation for the story. *Standard* readers will remember that in the columns the insanity story was first hinted at in a special from Fall River, in which those interested in the tragedy were significantly told to watch the visitors at Taunton jail. Several persons have been seen who say that they have been interviewed within a few days as to the probability of insanity, and that their interviewer said he was sent to them by the district attorney to collect information on this point, and gave the name of some eight or 10 persons whom he was instructed to call upon for this purpose.

WEATHER INDICATIONS.

FAIR.

WASHINGTON, Dec. 2.—For the 24 hours from 8 a.m. to-day: For New England fair weather; northwesterly winds, becoming variable.

FAIR.

BOSTON, Dec. 2.—Local forecast for New England until Saturday night: Generally fair weather, little change in temperature, westerly winds, becoming variable.

Illinois' Vote.

SPRINGFIELD, Ill., Dec. 2.—The State board of canvassers have completed the canvass of the vote of Illinois as follows: Cleveland 426,281, Harrison 399,288, Weaver 22,207, Bidwell 25,907.

HOME MATTERS.

PERSONAL.—Hon, Charles S. Randall left the city this forenoon for Washington, and will probably not return until April. His home this Winter will be at the Shoreham.

L. D. Eldred, the well-known artist, who has been the past season in Fairhaven, has returned to his studio in New York city.

Herbert R. Wilbor and wife and little son, Robert Rushmore, left for Titusville, Brevard county, Fla., last week to spend the Winter.

Mr. E. E. Baker of West Falmouth, late first officer, and Capt. George F. Allen, late boatheader of steamer Jesse H. Freeman, came through this week from San Francisco to remain for the Winter.

H. C. Hathaway will sell at auction tomorrow morning at 9 o'clock at salesroom, furniture, oil cloths, &c., &c., and at 10 o'clock at mart about 30 horses of all grades, including some very fine ones. He is the lot is the blood bay stallion Dick Tate, foaled June 18, 1886, by Dictator, Jr., standard 2193, full brother to Dexter (2.17,) sire of Jay Eye See 2.10, Phillus 2.13½, Dictator 2.17, and other noted horses. Full description at sale. Dick Tate is very fast, without any tricks and perfectly safe for any one to drive. Also a lot of harnesses, robes, blankets, carriages, &c., &c.

ODD FELLOWS' VISIT.—Members of Vesta, Pacific and Acushnet Lodges, I. O. O. F., to the number of 125, made a visit to Taunton last evening, to attend the fair of Good Samaritan and King Philip Lodges of that city. They were met at the Taunton depot by a brass band and escorted to the hall where the fair was held. As a part of the entertainment during the evening a mock third degree was given. The New Bedford men were finely entertained and had a most enjoyable visit.

HAVE YOU SUPPLIED your wants in Winter underwear? If not you cannot afford to miss our special sale. We have about $6000 worth of underwear that we want to sell, and we can surely save you 25 per cent. from other dealers' prices. Our 47c. underwear is great value; our Blue Ribbed, all wool, &c., less than cost to manufacture. Come in and buy your underwear at headquarters, Ashley & Peirce, 72 and 74 William street.

THE NEW PACKET LINE.—The new packet which is to be put on between this port and St. Helena is now loading at Boston with general supplies. She will be commanded by Capt. Willis Clark of Everett, Mass. A mail bag for the accommodation of New Bedford people will be at the office of Thomas Luce until Dec. 15.

TRIAL LISTS.—We have received from Simeon Borden, clerk of the courts, a copy of the Trial Lists for the December sitting of the Superior Court in this city. There are 132 cases for jury trial, 22 by the court, and 38 divorce cases.

MR. SHERMAN SURRENDERS.—James H. Sherman has withdrawn his objection to the location of the turnout on the west side of Fourth street, between Bedford and Grinnell streets, and says that he is tired of the controversy.

LOADED WITH BEER.—A heavy dray covered with canvas broke down on Union street, at the corner of Water, this noon, and when the canvas was removed to unload the vehicle a pile of beer barrels was exposed and excited the derision of passing Breck men.

MILLINERY.—Don't miss seeing what we are doing in this department for Saturday. Bargains all along the line, many goods at less than half price. Read advertisement on page 4. Moynan & Co.

THE NEW PACKET LINE.

CONCERT POSTPONED.—Miss Orr's concert, which was to have been given in the Y. M. C. A. Monday evening, has been postponed. See special notice.

MOYNAN & CO.'S SPECIAL Saturday advertisement on page 4. Bargains all along the line. Get a copy of "Modes and Fabrics," Christmas number, free. Ready Saturday.

SONS OF VETERANS.—Members of John A. Hawes Camp are referred to special notice in regard to assembling to-night.

DON'T MISS SECURING one of those cashmere waists at Moynan & Co's on Saturday. For other specials read advertisement on page 4.

ONE HUNDRED SEVENTY-NINE TRIMMED HATS marked down to close. Please examine. Coffin's, 52 Purchase street.

CHILDREN'S OVERCOATS and ulsters at low prices, Ashley & Peirce, 72 and 74 William st.

AT O'NEILL'S you will find trimmed hats and bonnets for $3.00.

ONE LOT SWEET Florida oranges 12c. dozen. White Cash.

FINE upright pianos just arrived from the factory, 222 Acushnet avenue, near School st.

SPECIAL BARGAINS at Whiting & Co's tomorrow on all kinds of Winter garments.

FOR BOOKS and BOOKLETS, go to Moynan & Co's on Saturday.

DON'T FORGET to examine our stock of poultry. White Cash.

FOR A HUMAN HAIR SWITCH go to Coffin's. Largest stock, lowest prices. 52 Purchase st.

OLD PIANOS and organs taken in exchange for new upright pianos at Coffin's.

FUR CAPES, fur muffs, selling cheap at Whiting & Co's.

ONE LOT killed chickens, fowl and turkeys just arrived, 12c. lb. White Cash.

IT WILL PAY YOU to call at Whiting & Co's cloak room to-morrow.

ONE LOT SWEET Florida oranges 25c. dozen. White Cash.

BIG BARGAINS in ulsters and overcoats at Ashley & Peirce's, 72 and 74 William street.

FANCY FEATHERS 5, 10, 15 and 25c. at O'Neill's.

PRINCESS TIPS in all shades only 59c.; O'Neill's millinery parlors, over Kempton street.

TAM O'SHANTERS CHEAP at O'Neill's.

Hood's Sarsaparilla sharpens the appetite.

PROBATE COURT.

FULLER, J.

TAUNTON, Friday, Dec. 2.

Wills proved and admitted to probate—Of Franklin Hathaway of New Bedford, Annie K. Hathaway executrix; of Margaret White, formerly of New Bedford, Benjamin B. Barney executor; of Carrie C. Davoll of New Bedford, Pardon G. Thomson executor; of Hugh Gallagher of Taunton, Richard Powers executor; of Jones Godfrey, Jones W. Godfrey executor; of Eliza B. Mitchell of New Bedford, Walter Mitchell executor; of James D. Thompson of New Bedford, George A. Bourne administrator; of Orcelia Willis of Easton, Martin H. Willis executor; of Christopher S. Andrews of New Bedford, Ruth Andrews administratrix; of Samuel Doran of New Bedford, Thomas Doran and William Clark executors; of James H. Doran of Fall River, Paul H. Doran, Jr., executor; of Edwin P. Hall of Raynham, Matthew Hall executor.

Administration granted—To John P. McKenna on estate of Ellen McKenna of New Bedford; to Mary E. Hathaway on estate of Arvin smith of New Bedford; to Emma Taylor on estate of Thomas Taylor of Fall River; to Henry H. Earle on estate of Angeline Covel of Fall River; to Henry H. Earle on estate of Benjamin Covel of Fall River; to Mary Galvin of Fall River on estate of Michael Gallivan, alias Galavan, alias Galvin; to John S. Bassett on estate of Henry C. Perry of Taunton; to Mary Ann Raymond on estate of Arthur W. Raymond of Fairhaven; to Arthur C. Browning on estate of Clark Browning of New Bedford; to Rose Annie Kelley on estate of Henry E. S. Kelley of Fall River.

Accounts allowed—First and final of administrator with will annexed on estate of John S. Stowell of New Bedford; first and final of administrator on estate of Johanna, alias Joanna, Gallagher of Fall River; first and final of administrator on estate of Mary Ann Mason of Swansey; first of administratrix on estate of Nathaniel G. Thurston of Fall River; final of administrator de bonis non on estate of David G. Saunders of Attleboro; first and final of administrator on estate of Fannie E. Smith of Attleboro; ninth, of executor of the will of Gilbert Howland of Dartmouth; first, of executrix estate of Cecile C. Ricketson of New Bedford; final, of executor estate of Charlotte Nelson of New Bedford; first and final, of administrator, with will annexed, estate of Lydia M. Webster of Westport; first and final, of executor estate of Horatio L. Brownell of Westport.

Accounts rendered—Fourth of trustee under the will of Susan Chace of Fall River; first of executor will of Hannah T. Wordell of North Westport.

License to sell real estate—George A. York, trustee under the will of John W. Sullings of New Bedford, was licensed to sell real estate at Nonquitt for investment; Earl B. Smith, guardian of Irene B. and Mary W. Smith, to sell their interest in land in Attleboro; Thomas H. Knowles and C. D. Prescott, guardians of Louisa and Thomas C. Knowles of New Bedford, to sell real estate in New Bedford for investment.

A petition of Ellen F. Chace for the partition among tenants in common of land in Rehoboth was granted, and Elijah P. Chase and Henry A. Baker of Swansey appointed commissioners.

A division of the balance of the estate of Katie A. Batty of New Bedford was decreed, agreeable to petition of William C. Parker administrator.

Emma Fenner of Fall River was granted authority to adopt Emma P. Fenner, a child of George A. and Almie R. Fenner of Fall River.

William J. and Selina Mills of New Bedford were decreed permission to adopt Horace Lincoln Cushing, an orphan child of George Francis and Bazilla C. Cushing, and his name was changed to Horace Cushing Mills.

Augustus W. and Alice A. Goff were authorized to adopt Malvina F. Holman of Fall River, an orphan.

Franklin Copeland and Carrie Ella Wade of Easton were granted leave to adopt Mary H. Connelly of Fall River, by consent of the State Board of Lunacy and Charity, and her name was changed to Hester Crawford Wade.

Elizabeth C. Dean's request to be relieved from further duty as executrix of the will of Thomas H. Dean was granted and John Everett, joint executor, was made sole executor.

The resignation of Francis C. Terry, formerly of New Bedford, now of Fort Payne, Ala., as trustee under a clause of the will of Susan P. Mayhew, was accepted and Adelaide V. Wilbur was appointed trustee under the will of Henry Taber of New Bedford.

The distribution of the estate of Jane R. Hatch of Dartmouth was decreed in favor of heirs residing in Alleghaney, Pa.

FOR SATURDAY at B. H. Waite & Co's., 71 Wm. street, a discount of 20 per cent. on all oil cloths in any quantity desired. 75 cents for a tapestry carpet that you can't begin to match for the price. White fur rugs $2.25. Heavy door mats 50c., worth 87c. Jointless straw matting 19c., worth 32c.

THE STREET RAILWAY.—It is stated authoritatively that when the Union Street Railway builds its belt track from Mt. Pleasant to Purchase street, through Clark street, as stated in the *Standard* yesterday, the Mt. Pleasant barn will be discontinued.

READ MOYNAN & CO'S SPECIAL Saturday advertisement on page 4. Bargains all along the line. Get a copy of "Modes and Fabrics," Christmas number, free. Ready Saturday.

SONS OF VETERANS.—Members of John A. Hawes Camp are referred to special notice in regard to assembling to-night.

Center column continued (Indictment)

ing, cutting, beating and bruising in and upon the head of her, the said Abby Durfee Borden, divers to wit: twenty mortal wounds, of which said mortal wounds the said Abby Durfee Borden then and there instantly died.

And so the jurors aforesaid upon their oath aforesaid do say that the said Lizzie Andrew Borden, the said Abby Durfee Borden in manner and form aforesaid then and there feloniously, wilfully and of her malace aforethought did kill and murder; against the peace of the said Commonwealth and contrary to the form of the statutes in such case made and provided.

And the jurors for the said Commonwealth on their oath do further present, That Lizzie Andrew Borden, of Fall River, in the county of Bristol, at Fall River, in the county of Bristol, on the 4th day of August in the year 1892, in and upon one Andrew Jackson Borden feloniously, wilfully and of her malice aforethought an assault did make, and with a certain weapon, to wit, a sharp cutting instrument, the name and a more particular description of which is to the jurors unknown, him, the said Andrew Jackson Borden, feloniously, wilfully and of her malice aforethought did strike, cut, beat and bruise in and upon the head of him, the said Andrew Jackson Borden, giving to him, the said Andrew Jackson Borden, by the striking, cutting, beating and bruising in and upon the head of him, the said Andrew Jackson Borden, divers, to wit, ten mortal wounds of which said mortal wounds the said Andrew Jackson Borden then and there instantly died.

And so the jurors aforesaid upon their oath aforesaid do say that the said Lizzie Andrew Borden, the said Andrew Jackson Borden in manner and form aforesaid then and there feloniously, wilfully and of her malice aforethought did kill and murder against the peace of the said Commonwealth contrary to the form of the statutes in such case made and provided.

After the indictment was read the district attorney said in accordance with the law a copy of the indictment will be taken to the prisoner and one sent to the Superior Court.

Miss Borden did not appear in court and Sheriff Wright says that she will not be brought into court until the time fixed for her arraignment. She remains in apparent good health, has not lost any flesh and still possesses the wonderful nerve which has upheld her so long.

Rumors of Another Indictment.

Inquiry as to whether an indictment was found against Henry G. Trickey failed to discover that it was, although it is very generally understood that such an indictment was drawn against him in view of the fact that a Fall River police officer sat behind a curtain and heard Trickey say to McHenry, "I will give you $1000 for the government's evidence; I do not want it for myself, but for Mr. Adams," (defendant's counsel,) is strong presumptive evidence that an indictment was found against him.

Immediately on an indictment being found the court took up other matters.

The great sensation of the Borden case is over for the present.

THE THIRD INDICTMENT

Supposed to be Against Trickey of Sensational Story Fame.

[By Associated Press.]

TAUNTON, Dec. 2.—The third indictment found by the grand jury was kept a secret, as the party indicted is not in custody. The jury made no public report in court. It filed it, handed its paper to the court and then was dismissed and disappeared in the region of the treasurer's office for payment. All looked tired and much as if each had passed through the trying scenes of a town meeting. None was disposed to be communicative.

District Attorney Knowlton will neither admit or say that the third indictment relates to Mr. Trickey of the late sensational story matter, but such is the impression at the court house.

It is understood that Miss Borden will not be immediately arraigned to plead, but that the indictments will be served on her at her quarters in Taunton jail. She will be unmoved by friends of the return of the indictments by the grand jury, and is said to have preserved the same stolid demeanor which has marked her course during the trial.

Ocean Steamers

Arrived—At New York, St. Ronans, Liverpool; Neptune, Montego Bay. At Boston, Colorado, Hull.

LIZZIE ANDREW BORDEN,
Indicted for the Murder of Her Father and Step-Mother.

Pages 1-8.

The Evening Standard.

Pages 1-8.

ESTABLISHED FEBRUARY, 1850.]

NEW BEDFORD, MONDAY, DECEMBER 5, 1892.---TEN PAGES.

TWO CENTS.

HASKELL & TRIPP.

Suppose you could buy choicest tints in Chiffon Handkerchiefs, silk embroidered, for 12 1-2 cents a piece, such as are usually sold for a quarter of a dollar.

Would you?

We think you will be only too happy to buy the splendid lot we place on sale to-day, in cream, light blue, pink, ecru, silk embroidered edges and a graceful design in the corner. These styles are not to be had elsewhere in this city. 12 1-2 cents is absurdly little to ask for such quality.

Other Chiffon Handkerchiefs, more elaborately embroidered, 19c., 25c., 50c. each.

White Mull Handkerchiefs, choice embroidered edges and with a large handsome initial in one corner, 25c. apiece.

Very fine linen hemstitched Handkerchiefs, with hand embroidered initial, 29c., worth half a dollar. Only a small quantity to go at this sacrifice.

Mufflers.

Just a few hints at an overflowing stock.

Rich silk brocades 75c. to $1.75.

Cream cashmere, with colored spots, 25c.

Cream cashmere, with fancy silk stripes, 50c.

Suspenders.

Bargain lot of good webs, nicely made and trimmed, only 12 1-2c. a pair.

Handsome satin suspenders, each pair in glass top box, 50c., worth more.

Neckwear.

Immense variety Windsor ties 25c. each.

China silk hemstitched scarfs 50c. each.

Men's tecks, puffs and four-in-hands, rich quality and latest styles, 29c. each.

Men's holiday scarfs, light fancy colors, novel and neat designs, 50c. each.

Gloves.

Fur top lined calfskin gloves, both women's and men's sizes, best possible qualities, at $1, $1.50, $1.75 a pair.

Men's Scotch wool gloves 29c. and 50c.

Boys' Scotch wool gloves 25c. a pair.

Note this: We guarantee these gloves to give superior to any knit glove of equal price in the market. They no means between the fingers, have all other makes, consequently no sewing to give out.

Miscellaneous.

Sterling silver thimbles 25c.

Novelties in Vienna purses 25c.

Pin "sweepings," about 1000 assorted best quality in a box, 10c. box.

Cold cream soap, 3 cakes in a box, for 50c.

Rose glycerine soap, 3 cakes in a box, for 48c.

Eight ounce bottle fine quality violet water 50c.

Remarkably good hair brush 25c.

Celluloid soap box 25c.

HASKELL & TRIPP,

Department Stores,

Purchase and William Streets.

THE ARRAIGNMENT.

Clerk Borden Says It Will Come in a Week or Two.

Miss Borden Not Yet Served with Copy of Indictment.

Belief that Trial Will be in Taunten if Left to the Judges.

[Special Dispatch.]

TAUNTON, Dec. 5.—In a Boston paper it has been stated that Miss Borden would be arraigned here to-morrow. As a matter of fact neither Miss Borden nor Chief Justice Mason have as yet received copies of the indictment because they have not yet been returned from the printer, but it is expected they will be sent out this afternoon or to-morrow morning.

In conversation with Clerk of Courts Borden this morning, he stated that it would probably be a week or two before Miss Borden would be arraigned, and that the arraignment would of course take place in Taunton. He was doubtful in regard to the place of trial and the time, but was inclined to believe that the trial would take place in Taunton, if left with the judges, although it was well understood that District Attorney Knowlton desired the trial to take place in New Bedford.

In regard to the matter of expense it would be much less if the trial should take place here rather than in New Bedford, but on the other hand so far as hotel accommodations were concerned he considered New Bedford the better place. The Taunton court-house is better adapted to a trial of that nature than the New Bedford court-house, because of the fact that the law library is here and that also there would be better accommodations below stairs for the small army of stenographers and typewriters necessary in the hearing of such a case. He also believed the Taunton jail would be a much better place than the New Bedford institution.

It would not be surprising, he said, if the trial should take place immediately at the close of the regular criminal session here in February, although it would depend very much upon the work of the other judges.

LOUIS KOSSUTH DYING.

The Well Known Hungarian Patriot at Death's Door in Turin.

VIENNA, Dec. 5.—It is reported that Louis Kossuth, the Hungarian patriot, is

LOUIS KOSSUTH.

dying at his residence in Turin. He recently celebrated the 90th anniversary of his birth.

FATAL BURNING ACCIDENT.

A Two-Year-Old Child Played With Live Coals.

NEW HAVEN, Dec. 5.—A horrible burning accident occurred shortly after 10 o'clock this morning. While Mrs. Levi Berkofski, who lives at 32 Madison street, was out in the yard sifting ashes her two-year-old child Fanny, having seen her mother clean the stove just before, took an ash shovel full of hot coals and bearing her mother open the door she dumped them into the baby carriage in which Mrs. Berkofski's six months old child was sleeping. The clothing in the carriage took fire at once, as did the little girl's garments. In a moment all was ablaze. The screams brought the mother to their aid, but the little girl died about half an hour after the accident. The baby was taken to the hospital where she is expected to die.

Steerage Passengers Landed.

PORTLAND, Me., Dec. 5.—Steamer Vancouvre of the Dominion Line arrived today from Liverpool with 60 steerage passengers. She proceeded to the new disinfecting station at House Island, where these passengers were put ashore. During the day she will be disinfected. The station is fitted with the most modern appurtenances for this business.

Suicide of a Youth of Eighteen.

ROCKFORD, Ill., Dec. 5.—Albert Furlong, aged 18 years, shot himself yesterday afternoon and will die. He left a letter addressed to an aunt, a Mrs. Faulkner, saying he had but $2 left after a year's work and death would be a relief. He also asked to be buried beside his mother and urged his aunt to embrace a religious life.

Death of a Prominent Politician.

READING, Pa., Dec. 5.—Charles F. Evans, mayor of Reading for three terms, from 1873 to 1879, and formerly prominent in Republican county and State politics, was found dead in his bedroom this morning from heart disease. He was 50 years old.

Lost on the Mexican Coast.

NEW YORK, Dec. 5.—Steamer Orizaba, from Mexico, which arrived this morning, brought Capt. Hall, of schooner Hayes, which went ashore in a storm at Casmonos, Mex., Sept. 29. One of the crew was drowned.

TELEGRAPHIC BREVITIES.

There is a severe famine at Khiangmai, and the American missionaries are feeding the starving people.

Prof. Hubert Herkomer, who painted Jay Gould's picture, says the true index of his power was the fine fibre of his sensitive nerve structure.

The London *Times* says that political questions in France are all subordinate to the Panama inquiry.

There was a riot at Ichang, China, 2d, and sailors were landed from naval vessels to quell it. No Europeans were injured.

A Caracas special says that the blockade has been raised. Yellow fever still exists at Laguayra.

The expedition of the British commissioner to Uganda discloses the thoroughness of the plans of the government for the occupation of the territory.

IN THAT GRAND JURY ROOM.

What Took Place as Told by One of the Jurors.

Penitent Witnesses for Defence Told All They Knew.

Jury Threatened by White Caps if They Found a Bill.

[Special Dispatch.]

FALL RIVER, Dec. 5.—One of the Fall River members of the grand jury which recently had before it the case of Lizzie A. Borden called at the office of the *Globe* this morning and entered into conversation and said in the presence of a *Standard* reporter:

"I want to have one thing corrected. It has been stated that Mr. Buckman, the foreman of the jury, stood out against an indictment. This is not true. There was a little which leaked out [at a recess before the jury had been cautioned] which the government did not mean should, but nothing about the position of the foreman."

"I suppose you know Trickey is dead?" was asked?

"I heard so," was the juror's reply.

"I suppose that ends the case so far as Trickey is concerned," was said.

"No, it doesn't," was the reply.

"I don't see how anything more can be done in that matter if the man is dead," it was asserted.

"There are other parties concerned. Trickey is not the most conspicuous one by any means. I tell you there is some dirty work, and when the case comes before the other jury the real surprise is to come," said the juror. "It has been said that we have got to hear from defence," said the juror, "but as a matter of fact we have heard the story of defence. The attorney general, and the district attorney in particular, were so much worked up over the abuse and vilification to which they were subjected that they sent for Andrew J. Jennings to put in the evidence for defence, and he did so. Mr. Knowlton sat back and took no part in the big matter, and left it to the jurors to ask questions. No one, as a matter of fact knew how he stood as to the guilt or innocence of the accused. My gracious! I wish you could have been there. The government witnesses were reluctant and acted as if they wanted to believe Lizzie A. Borden innocent. Then the engines were gradually called off with the exception of two of the local volunteer firemen, who remained at the scene. All danger was passed at 8 o'clock. The fire had done $100,000 damage. On this there is considerable insurance.

voted. The one word freely and handed the truth carelessly, to say the least. At the eleventh hour the friends of Lizzie A. Borden came up penitent and conscience-stricken and told that which clinched the case in the minds of the jurors. I think the District Attorney was satisfied he could get an indictment without the admissions made by defence. The government through and through and as fair and impartial as a man could be in spite of the threats which were made."

"Threats did you say?" was asked.

"I should think so," said the juror. "Why during the recess of the jury when I was at the Hargraves mill I heard a man who did not know I was a member of the jury say he would be one man who would kill the juryman. Then I made myself known and told him if anything happened to any of the jury he would be the first man to be looked for. He then weakened and apologized, saying he didn't 'mean anything.'"

"We found a bill against Lizzie A. Borden the day before we came in," said the juryman, "and the next morning, when we were considering another case, the district attorney read us a letter which he had received from Brattleboro, Vt., which was to the effect that the best thing he (the district attorney) could do was to let Lizzie A. Borden out and give her her freedom and then lock Bridget Sullivan up in one cell and John V. Morse in another." And the letter ended: "Now if the jurors find a bill against Lizzie A. Borden look out for White Caps."

"The district attorney got lots of letters about the case, and it was after the recess that the friends of Lizzie said they might as well tell all they knew about the case."

The juror was asked if he was willing to give the exact vote of the grand jury, and said he could not consistently do so. He said, however, that there were two polls of the jury, the first informal, but after the story of defence had been put in a second ballot was had by permission of the district attorney, the vote was reconsidered and the result was practical unanimity for the indictment.

DECISION OF THE FULL BENCH.

Fall River Mill Men Will Not Be Ordered to Respond to a Suit.

BOSTON, Dec. 5.—Treasurer James Waring of the Narragansett mills of Fall River and John Harrison, superintendent of the same mills, will not be ordered to respond to a suit brought against them by certain employes, wherein, it is alleged, they had blacklisted for refusing to work at a scale of wages fixed by the mill. This is the decision of the full bench of the Supreme Judicial Court sent down in the case of Dinah Worthington and others against Treasurer Waring and Superintendent Harrison.

YALE STUDENTS' CRAZY ESCAPADE.

Faculty May be Induced to Make an Example of the Rowdies.

NEW HAVEN, Conn., Dec. 5.—The crazy escapade of the Yale students late Saturday night is the talk of the town. The exhibition of rowdyism in Proctor's Family Theatre is being condemned. In the past this morning the cases against Frederick Wienhauser, Frederick W. Hendrick, John Long and Joseph Lentillon were continued till Wednesday. They are charged with breach of the peace, assault, etc. John Adler, the member of the theatre orchestra who was hit in the eye with a torpedo thrown by one of the students, will, it is thought, lose the use of that member. An effort will be made by the better class of citizens to induce the faculty of the college to make an example of the leaders in this affair.

HE OF "CIRCUS" FAME.

Gardner, Mr. Parkhurst's Agent, Charged With Blackmail and Extortion.

NEW YORK, Dec. 5.—Charles A. Gardner, the agent of Dr. Parkhurst's society, was a prisoner in the Tombs Police Court this morning in charge of two detectives. At the request of Supt. Byrnes the case was put over until to-morrow. It is said that Gardner is accused of blackmail and extortion.

Mr. Cleveland at Home.

NEW YORK, Dec. 5.—President-elect Cleveland arrived this morning at 7.30 from Exmore, Va. Mr. Cleveland seemed in the best of health and spirits. With the exception of two of the reporters, there were few people to greet him on his arrival. Mr. Cleveland entered a carriage, accompanied by his valet, and was driven up town to his house.

Mill and Offices Burned.

TOLEDO, O., Dec. 5.—The annealing mill of the Malleable Casting Company of this city, with offices of the company, was burned yesterday. Loss to building, $25,000; partially insured.

WEATHER INDICATIONS.

FAIR.

WASHINGTON, Dec. 5.—For the 24 hours from 8 a. m. to-day: For New England, generally fair weather, northwesterly winds, becoming variable.

FAIR AND COLDER.

BOSTON, Dec. 5.—Local forecast for New England until Wednesday: Fair weather, slightly colder to-night and to-morrow morning; westerly to northerly winds, becoming variable.

FR. DALEY'S FUNERAL

Sad and Impressive Ceremonies at St. Lawrence Church.

Bishop Harkins and Vicar General McCabe in Attendance.

Large Number of Clergymen and Vast Concourse Present.

Yesterday the interior of St. Lawrence church was draped in mourning for the late Father Daley by the Sisters of Mercy. Heavy festoons of black caught up at intervals with bows of white ribbon extend the length of the church, while across the rear in front of the gallery are draped streamers of white and black. The altar is nearly buried in a profusion of black crepe.

At about 3 o'clock yesterday afternoon the remains were borne into the church, where a congregation that completely filled the edifice and the beloved pastor whose life work is ended.

HOME MATTERS.

WHAT IT COST.

Interesting Facts in the Statement of Republican Campaign Expenses.

The statement of expenditures by the Republican City Committee in the recent campaign has just been filed with the city clerk by the treasurer, Fred S. Potter. The official figures afford considerable interesting information. The total amount of receipts was $2206.39, expenditures $2176.30, leaving a balance on hand of $30.09. Among the expenditures the following items are found:

Support of Harrison & Reid Battalion,	$250.00
Maintenance of headquarters,	188.54
Damages to Rideteau Block,	10.17
Expended in aid of naturalization,	104.00
Flags and fittings,	111.95
Printing, distributing and advertising,	403.94
Rallies, music, &c.,	658.11
Carriage hire,	149.75
Checkers and advisers at polls,	123.52
Incidentals,	176.42
	$2176.30

SUPERIOR COURT.—The Superior Court, civil session, commenced its December sitting in this city to-day, Hon. Francis H. Dewey presiding.

MISS BURKE, a teacher with eight years' experience, will be at the Parker House on Thursday, Dec. 8th, from 2 to 5 p. m., to meet parents and their friends interested in forming a school children's drawing class. Ladies' parlor private entrance on Middle street.

COLD BATH.—Henry Nelson took a rather cold involuntary bath this morning near Merrill's wharf. He slipped on the deck of catboat Tramp and went overboard, but was immediately rescued.

SPECIAL SALE of real Daghestan rugs at Walte's, 71 Wm. st., for lower prices than any comparable bought in any market. A most valuable Christmas gift.

ROBERT HALL, shoe dealer, County street, has sold his entire stock of boots and shoes to Buchell, to be closed out at once regardless of cost. Read adv. on 8th page.

READ THIS.—I will compel respect and obedience to all laws, says S. A. Brownell. What more could any honest man say?

A FREE ENTERTAINMENT will be given by Bristol Colony, U. O. P. F., to-morrow evening in China Hall. See advertisement on sixth page.

A VOTE for Brownell and the Independent Citizens' Ticket is an assurance that the platform of just taxation will be continued.

HARPER'S MONTHLY, Weekly, Bazar and Young People. Subscriptions received at Hutchinson's.

TO-MORROW.—Citizens of Ward One be sure and vote for Cyrus T. Lawrence for one of your common councilmen.

YOU WANT TO CALL at Whiting & Co's store daily, as you will see new goods for the holidays.

A VOTE for Brownell and the Independent Citizens' Ticket is an assurance that the just taxation system for just taxation will be continued

FINEST LINE of Christmas Booklets, etc., in the city at Hutchinson's Connecting Stores, 194 and 202 Union street.

READ THIS.—I will compel respect and obedience to all laws, says S. A. Brownell. What more could any honest man say?

VOTE for William H. Sherman for Alderman from Ward Five.

SOMETHING OF INTEREST to marketmen in special notices.

VOTE for Frank B. Carr for Alderman from Ward One.

VOTE for Charles S. Paisler for Alderman from Ward Three.

VOTE for Henry C. Hathaway for Alderman from Ward Two.

VOTE for Charles S. Paisler for Alderman from Ward Three.

VOTE for William G. Kirschbaum for Alderman from Ward Four.

NEW ROOM opening at Whiting & Co's for Holiday Gifts.

VOTE for S. A. Brownell for Mayor. He is an honest man and will enforce all laws.

VOTE for William H. Sherman for Alderman from Ward Five.

SOMETHING OF INTEREST to marketmen in special notices.

VOTE for Henry C. Hathaway for Alderman from Ward Two.

NEW JAPANESE WARE will be open in a day or two at Whiting & Co's.

VOTE for William H. Rankin for Alderman from Ward Six.

VOTE for S. A. Brownell for Mayor. He is an honest man and will enforce all laws.

CITIZENS of Ward One see to it that you elect Cyrus T. Lawrence for common council.

WHITING & Co's Handkerchief Sale will attract the attention of the ladies.

VOTE for Frank B. Carr for Alderman from Ward One.

VOTE for William H. Rankin for Alderman from Ward Six.

GOOD CLEAN COAL. Denison Brothers Co.
GOOD CLEAN COAL. Denison Brothers Co.
GOOD CLEAN COAL. Denison Brothers Co.
GOOD CLEAN COAL. Denison Brothers Co.
GOOD CLEAN COAL. Denison Brothers Co.
GOOD CLEAN COAL. Denison Brothers Co.

Ocean Steamers.

Arrived—At New York, America, (Br., London); America, (Ger.) Bremen; Werra, Genoa; Orizaba, Havana; Schiedam, Rotterdam.

HOOD'S Sarsaparilla cures biliousness.

AMANDA'S CASE CONTINUED.

Gen. E. W. Peirce Too Ill to Appear in Court To-Day.

[Special Dispatch.]

FALL RIVER, Dec. 5.—In the Second District Court, before Judge Blaisdell today, the continued case of Amanda Watts for assault on Mary A. Gardner, mother-in-law of Gen. E. W. Peirce at Assonet Village, Freetown, came up. George Grime, of the firm of Swift & Grime, counsel for defendant, stated that Mrs. Gardner acknowledges satisfaction, and so far as she is concerned the charge is withdrawn. As Gen. Peirce is too ill to be present in court the case was further continued until 10.30 o'clock on 12th inst.

Heavy Snow in Great Britain.

LONDON, Dec. 5.—Half a foot of snow covers the ground in South Wales and the storm continues. Nearly all out-door work has been suspended. Railroad traffic is delayed. In the north of Scotland the snow is 15 inches deep. In the railway cuttings the drifts are many feet deep. A mail train was stopped by the drifts and the passengers were rescued with difficulty.

The Fire at Cranford.

CRANFORD, N. J., Dec. 5.—It was 4 o'clock this morning when the fire which broke out about 11 o'clock last night and threatened to annihilate the town, was entirely under control.

Pages 1-8.

The Evening Standard.

Pages 1-8.

ESTABLISHED FEBRUARY, 1850.

NEW BEDFORD, SATURDAY, DECEMBER 17, 1892.---SIXTEEN PAGES.

TWO CENTS.

HASKELL & TRIPP.

Will you not read carefully the NINTH PAGE of this evening's *Standard*

IN

THE

INTERESTS

OF

YOUR

POCKET?

We think you will.

Every one in this city and vicinity has a personal interest in our goods and prices.

Thousands of dollars will change hands during the week before Christmas, and we have made ample preparations to direct several of those thousands through the bargain channels of this store.

AN

ORDINARY

OBSERVER

Would hardly credit the quantity of merchandise that is daily turned in and out of this busy store.

ON

ALL

HANDS

We are told that we keep the kind of goods the people want, and the quick way in which sales are made is the best possible proof that our prices are as popular as our goods.

THE

CHRISTMAS

BUSINESS

So far is greatly in excess of previous years and increasing every day. It is proceeding with accuracy and dispatch never attained before, but the vast amount of work compels us to ask patience and cooperation from buyers.

Where possible, please carry your small parcels; and for goods to be sent by our delivery, please be patient. Nearly all purchases are sent out the same day made and the balance by early deliveries the following morning.

We begin Monday, Dec. 19th, keeping open evenings until Christmas.

Mornings and stormy days are the very best times to do your Christmas shopping, as you have

MORE

ELBOW

ROOM

And get better attention. Everybody in the store is anxious to please and serve you, but everybody is taxed to the highest point during these few days; and we therefore ask that you will, as far as possible, help our people to do their best for you.

HASKELL & TRIPP,

Department Stores,

Purchase and William Streets.

WITH PURIFYING FORCE

The Wave of Reform Strikes the City of Fall River.

Keepers of Gambling Dens Warned to Shut Up Shop.

Elegant Apartments Vacated in a Hurry by Chief Hilliard's Orders.

[Special Dispatch.]

FALL RIVER, Dec. 17.—There was intense excitement in sporting circles yesterday afternoon over the action taken by the city marshal. Officer Harrington left the Central Police Station and at once paid a visit to six or seven well known keepers of gambling places in this city. They are all situated almost within a stone's throw of the Central Station, and it is said of late have been doing an unusually large amount of business.

The officer notified the men that every scrap of furniture and everything else pertaining to the gambling system should be removed from their places within three hours from the time of notice or they would all be raided during the night and all their possessions captured and taken to the station-house.

In almost every case the keepers of the rooms paid immediate attention to the orders and there was a great hurrying of express wagons engaged in carting off the paraphernalia and fixings in the different places.

The *Standard* reporter had a talk with Chief Hilliard in regard to this move and asked him as to some of its causes. He had not much to say for publication but intimated that he was really in earnest and that if it were necessary he would serve a warrant of seizure and search every day for the next twelve months to clean out the gambling houses.

The general opinion is that many complaints have been made of late from parents in regard to the action of their sons and from employers in regard to those who work for them and have been constant visitors at these places for the last couple months. Another source of complaint, it is said, is that one of the most patronized places has recently fitted out a magnificent suite of rooms and that this fact has caused jealousy among some of the keepers in the smaller places and who have thus reported the fact to the police.

Be that as it may, it is well known that the vice has flourished more during the last six months than ever before in the history of the city, and that this fact also has been well known to almost everybody about the centre of the city.

The marshal says that this order also includes policy shops and other small systems of gambling which are known to have existed here, and that they, also, will be prosecuted to the bitter end if they do not at once cease business. He is in possession of a list of names of men, young and old, who have been in the habit of constantly patronizing these establishments, and while he says it is not for publication he intimates that a social sensation would be created in town were he to announce one-half or even one-quarter of the prominent names he has on the list.

THE COBDEN CLUB MEDAL.

Problems to be Solved in Order to Win the Prize.

NEW HAVEN, Dec. 17.—The Cobden Club medal for 1893 will be awarded to that undergraduate who shall present before June 1, 1893, the best solution of the following problems:

1. Discuss the effects on the treasury and the people of a reduction of letter postage to one cent.
2. In what ways, if any, does a country get a return for the money spent in subsidizing shipping?
3. It is said that by the payment of the national debt we are losing the advantages of the national banking system. How far is this true?
4. Criticise the maxim: "The longer the hours, the shorter the pay; whether you work by the piece or the day."
5. Under what conditions can the profits of the speculators be regarded as a tax on the investor, the consumer, or neither?
6. Discuss the economic effects of a great international exhibition on the different classes of people in the city in which it is held.

TWO TOWNS IN DANGER.

Great Volcano of Hawaii is Again in Eruption.

SAN FRANCISCO, Dec. 17.—Honolulu advices state that Maunaloa, the great volcano of Hawaii, is in eruption again and threatens the destruction of the villages of Hilo and Waiakea at its eastern base and extensive plantations of cocoanuts and cane. For five days previous to Dec. 5 the illuminations were on a grand scale and the whole country was shaken by a prodigious earthquake. Maunaloa for a distance each way of 60 miles threw weird light over the ocean and all the country around about.

No Cheap Tickets to the Fair.

LONDON, Dec. 17.—The Berlin correspondent of the *Times* says that the decision of the steamship association as to the trans-Atlantic passenger trade applies also to the Belgian and Dutch companies. All arrangements for creap tickets to the World's Fair have been cancelled. The companies declare that interest in the fair has declined to the minimum, probably in consequence of the immigration regulations.

Governor is Fleeing for His Life.

NEW YORK, Dec. 17.—A special to the *Herald* from Valparaiso says: News reaches here from Rio Janeiro that the federalists are entering the city of Rio Grande do Sul and Gov. Castilho of Rio Grande do Sul is flying south. He will resign. Costilhistas have signed a petition asking the federalist government to declare war against Uruguay.

In the Path of Ocean Steamers.

NEW YORK, Dec. 17.—The Steamship Elbe from Bremen, which arrived last night reports: December 10 at 11 a. m., lat. 50 14, long. 23 17, passed ship Cubana (of London) abandoned, fore and mainmasts and jibboom gone and main hatch open; lies in a very dangerous position for westward steamers.

Troops will Scout for Mexican Bandits.

GALVESTON, Tex., Dec. 17.—A special from San Antonio says troops D and K of the Third U. S. cavalry at Fort Sam Houston, that city, have been ordered to proceed to the lower Rio Grande border and scout for the Mexican bandits. They will leave to-day.

A $60,000 Fire in New York City.

NEW YORK, Dec. 17.—Early this morning the Empire Storage Co's warehouse, at 386 to 392 Hudson street, was destroyed by fire. The loss, $60,000, is covered. Cause of the fire unknown.

Fire in Cincinnati.

CINCINNATI, O., Dec. 17.—Fire this morning destroyed the Cincinnati Lead Pipe & Sheet Lead Works, located at 21 and 23 Ninth street. Loss $70,000.

Ocean Steamers.

Arrived—At Boston, Martello, Hull, England; Pontiac, Mediterranean ports. Passed Lizard, 16th, Westernland, New York.

BORDEN MURDER TRIAL.

Attorney Jennings Lies Awake Nights Forming Plans.

He Expects the Case to Come up at Any Time.

Chief Justice Mason Thinks it May Not be Reached Until April.

[Special Dispatch.]

TAUNTON, Dec. 17.—On the 5th day of December Chief Justice Mason was sent notice from the clerk's office in this city of the action of the grand jury in relation to the case of the Commonwealth against Lizzie A. Borden.

On Monday last the chief justice stated to a member of the Bristol county bar that he had as yet received no official notice in regard to the matter.

During the present term of the court in New Bedford Mr. Jennings was present one day and was requested by a brother member of the bar who had some cases to try with him, to have the causes heard at this term of court. Mr. Jennings replied that he could not think of it, but wanted them postponed until the February term. The other member laughed at him and told him that it was much better for him to take the cases up now than to wait. Mr. Jennings was of the opinion, however, that the Borden case was liable to come in on him at any time and he wanted to be prepared for it, and not be bothered with any other outside cases. He stated that he could not get the case out of his mind, and that in a great many instances he lay awake half of the night thinking about it and arranging matters in his head. His brother lawyer intimated that it would be much better for him to take up some other cases and drive the Borden affair out of his mind, and at the same time offered to bet Mr. Jennings a new hat that the case would not be reached before the middle or last of February. The bet was taken.

In conversation with Chief Justice Mason on Monday, when the Chief Justice stated that he had received no official notice of the matter, this fact was laughingly brought up, and the Chief Justice said that there wasn't any question at all but what the man who made the bet was safe, as it seemed to him quite impossible that the case could be reached before that time, if then. He said that there were a great many matters pending before the courts of a similar nature to that of the Borden case which take precedence of that and he intimated that it might be impossible to get at the case much before the latter part of April or even May; that during the early months of the year the courts were very busy naturally and to take three justices away and put them on a case which might occupy two or three weeks and in fact use up all the time of an ordinary term of court be rather hard upon the justices coming so early in the year.

Therefore it seems quite possible that the case may not be reached until the third or fourth month of the year. Chief Justice Mason said that when the counsel were ready they would assemble before him and a place and time satisfactory to all parties would be then and there arranged. It is still thought, however, in certain official circles here that the arraignment may come the latter part of next week.

WEATHER INDICATIONS.

CLOUDY WITH SNOW.

WASHINGTON, Dec. 17.—For the 24 hours from 8 a. m. to-day: For Massachusetts, Rhode Island and Connecticut, cloudy, threatening weather and occasional snow; northerly winds.

RAIN OR SNOW TO-NIGHT, FAIR TO-MORROW.

BOSTON, Dec. 17.—Local forecast for New England until Monday night: Fair, followed to-night by rain or snow for coast sections; fair Sunday, except clearing along the northern coast; stationary followed by lower temperature; decidedly colder to-morrow night; northerly to westerly winds.

SUNK A SPANISH STEAMER.

Ship Mary L. Stone in Collision While Entering Manila Bay.

LONDON, Dec. 17.—The American ship Mary L. Stone from Shanghai via Manila for New York or Boston while entering Manila Bay on the night of Dec. 7 collided with a Spanish steamer. The latter vessel was so badly damaged that she filled and sank. It is supposed that several passengers aboard of her were lost. The Mary L. Stone sustained only trifling damage.

TWELVE FIREMEN BURIED.

Crushed by the Falling Wall of a Burning Cotton Warehouse.

BROOKLYN, N. Y., Dec. 17.—Shortly after 9 o'clock this morning fire was discovered in the large cotton storage warehouse of Davis S. Arnot, on the river front between 27th and 28th streets, South Brooklyn. At 10 o'clock, while the fire was still burning fiercely, one of the walls fell, burying, it is said, 12 of the firemen, many of whom, it is thought, were killed. The loss will be very heavy.

Safe Blowers Make a Haul.

CHARLOTTE, N. C., Dec. 17.—Safe blowers got in some successful work at King's Mountain, N. C., Thursday night. They blew Carpenter Bros.' safe open with dynamite and got away with $2000 in cash. The burglars effected an entrance to the store by boring a hole in the door and removing the lock. The town was alarmed and on the move within 10 minutes after the explosion, but no trace of the burglars could be found.

"CAVALIERIA RUSTICANA."—The Rheinberger Club held its second rehearsal last evening on Mascagni's famous opera, "Cavalieria Rusticana," and made much progress in the difficult choruses. The Opera House has been secured for Jan. 2 for the concert, and the talent has been nearly all engaged. As far as cast the soloists are:

Santuzza,	Mme. Lillian Nordica
Alfio,	Signor Guiseppe Del Puente
Lucia,	Miss Helen Dudley Campbell

Signor Campanini, who was to have sung the role of Turidu, a most difficult tenor part, will not be engaged, but another substituted, probably Paine Clark of New York. Luckstone, the famous New York pianist, who accompanied Roumania, the violinist, on his recent tour, has been engaged as accompanist.

MANCHESTER UNITY.—Alpha Lodge, No. 6463, I. O. O. F. M. U., held its annual election last evening when the following officers were chosen for the ensuing year:

Grand Master—Herbert H. Roscoe.
Noble Grand—John Slater.
Vice-Grand—William Burt.
Recording Secretary—Samuel Bancroft.
Permanent Secretary—Nelson L. Parke.
Treasurer—Charles N. Buchell.
Surgeon—William E. Browaell, M. D.
Inner Guardian—William Ratcliffe.
Outer Guardian—Benjamin Chace.

The officers will be installed Friday evening Jan. 6th, at which time Puritan and Unity Lodges of Fall River will make a fraternal visitation. The occasion will be celebrated in a fitting manner with concert and collation.

AMERICANS WILL RULE.

Syndicate Buys Control of San Domingo's Custom Revenues.

Mr. Wanamaker and Senator Quay Interested in the Scheme.

Concessions Give the United States a Harbor for Coaling.

NEW YORK, Dec. 17.—The *Herald* says: A syndicate of American capitalists has acquired virtual control of the island of San Domingo by purchase of the right to control the customs revenues of the country, which are principally derived from the tobacco monopoly. The precise terms are withheld, but it is understood that $3,500,000 is agreed upon. The members of the purchasing syndicate are, as far as known, Charles W. Wells and Willard Brown of New York and John W. Taylor of Newark.

A hitch which has occurred will call several members of the syndicate to the island, but the time of their departure is kept secret.

The scheme in which Postmaster General Wanamaker and Senator Quay are mentioned as members makes the holders of the concessions the practical rulers of the republic, because they pay the officials. The concessions will also give the United States a harbor for coaling.

HOME MATTERS.

PERSONAL.—Henry H. Lyman, Esq., collector of the port of Oswego, N. Y., is visiting friends in this city.

George A. King of Taunton was yesterday elected secretary of the Association of Assessors of Massachusetts.

Mrs. Herbert A. Blackmer and child are passing the Winter at Jamaica for the benfit of Mrs. Blackmer's health.

Col. S. C. Hart has returned from a week's trip in the South.

George W. Parsons, formerly in the laundry business in this city, is visiting old New Bedford friends.

Patrick Hyland, well known at the North End, who has been ill for several weeks is reported better and able to sit up.

Mrs. Lyman Montague arrived in this city to-day from Savannah, Ga., and will take up her residence here.

CHRISTMAS WINDOW.—Briggs & Lawrence's west curtain came up to-day displaying a very pretty holiday window. It is a representation of a finely furnished bed chamber, with all the appointments that perfect taste could suggest. The bed itself is a work of art. It is very prettily draped, and the dressing case is treated in the same fetching way. In the rear are represented two windows with dainty curtains. Palms and ferns assist to further enliven the scene. The east window is filled with beautiful Christmas fur rugs.

MORTUARY.—The whole number of deaths reported at the office of the Board of Health the past week is 23, 12 of children under five years. There was one stillborn. Of the deaths there were three from infantile debility, two each from heart disease, bronchitis and pneumonia, and one each from pul. tuberculosis, alcoholism, cancer of the bowels, peritonitis, asphyxia, phthisis, cap. bronchitis, congestion of the lungs, cancer of liver, brain fever, uræmic convulsions, diphtheria, convulsions and meningitis.

ACCIDENTS.—A horse belonging to C. A. Sisson stumbled, fell and broke a shaft of the wagon to which he was hitched, on Hawthorn street, west of Ash street, this morning.

An engine fitter who has recently been putting in an engine at Benjamin Dawson's bottling establishment on Hazzard street, had one of his fingers nipped in the slide of the engine yesterday afternoon, and severed it below the first joint.

IMPROVED FREIGHT RATES.—There is a general awakening among the people as to the importance of securing a more equitable adjustment of freight tariff to this city via the Old Colony railroad, and the work of the Board of Trade committee on transportation in this direction is warmly approved. Petitions favoring the movement are being circulated, and one of them has already received about 1500 signatures.

WAGON DAMAGED.—On Cedar street, near Maxfield, last evening, an electric car came in collision with a horse and wagon belonging to F. A. Bates of Fairhaven, which was crossing the track. The wagon was struck and one shaft broken and some other damage done, but neither horse nor driver were injured.

THE SALE OF THE GRINNELL IRON FOUNDRY. The administrators of the estate of Edmund Grinnell have sold for $43,000 to the Smith Carleton Iron Co, the Grinnell Iron Foundry, consisting of buildings and 440 rods land on South Water street.

CHAMBER CONCERT.—The last of the series of chamber concerts will be given in Odd Fellows' Hall by the Kneisel Quartet on Wednesday evening next. Tickets may now be procured. See advertisement on sixth page.

TO BE FINISHED IN THE SPRING.—The City Property Committee has ordered the work of constructing the new engine-house on Hillman street stopped in consequence of the approaching cold weather. Work will be resumed early in the Spring.

WE SHALL GIVE AWAY on Monday to purchasers of from $1 to $50 worth of Holiday goods one ounce of Belding Bros.' Black Sewing Silk, containing about 1500 yards. E. B. Chase & Co., cor. Union and Fifth streets.

CONTAGIOUS DISEASES.—Four new cases of diphtheria, four new cases of scarlet fever and two new cases of typhoid fever have been reported at the office of the Board of Health the past week.

TEN THOUSAND DOLLARS.—Fine etchings and steel engravings in the sheet and framed at 50c. on the dollar. E. B. Chase & Co., cor. Union and Fifth streets.

THE COMMON COUNCIL.—Col. Samuel C. Hart, Common Councilman-elect from Ward Five, is a candidate for the presidency of that body next year.

THE OVERSEERS OF THE POOR report many cases of sickness among the poor. There have also been a great number of demands for aid.

CONTRACT AWARDED.—The contract for building the apparatus house on the west end of Cuttyhunk has been awarded to Ansel F. Blossom of this city.

CLASS REUNION.—The High school class of 1892 has voted to hold a reunion in the High School Hall on Jan. 5th.

SEE OUR 6c. roasts. Gray Bros.

FOR SMOKING SETS, go to Cheap John's.

ORANGES lower at Gray Bros.

MUSIC BOXES, at Boden's music store.

DATES 5 lbs. for 25c. Gray Bros.

WIDENING THE BRIDGE.

The Standard's Plan for Abolishing the Grade Crossing Approved.

The proposal recently formulated by the *Standard* for abolishing the dangerous grade crossing of the Old Colony railroad at the bridge causeway in this city meets with general approval.

The Board of Trade committee on public affairs, of which Hon. William W. Crapo is chairman, has had several meetings at which the subject of widening the New Bedford & Fairhaven bridge has been discussed, and the urgency of the matter fully recognized. The committee is alive to the importance of widening the bridge, and as a preliminary to that work of doing away with the grade crossing at the west end. Mr. Crapo has been appointed a subcommittee to confer with the Old Colony railroad officials, and he will correspond with President Choate or General Manager Kendrick and bring about a conference with either or both of them with the committee, a meeting which cannot fail to be of interest and result advantageously.

It is thought the Legislature, early at its coming session, will be asked for and grant permission to issue bonds to widen the bridge, and that the work will be begun the coming Spring.

WOULDN'T ONE of those handsome parlor or library tables at C. F. Wing's be just the thing for a Christmas present? Owing to the extensive alterations to be made prices are very favorable for the buyer.

YOU BRING THE MONEY, we do the rest. Come and get your share of the bargains in watches, clocks, jewelry, etc. We are closing out. J. S. Kelley & Son, opposite Cummings', 101 William street.

GREAT BRRGAINS.—Odd sizes on fur capes to be closed out cheap: $15 capes $7; $18 capes $10; $85 capes $50; 12 plush capes $6. Now is your chance. Come early. H. H. Tilson, 43 Purchase street.

WE DO NOT WONDER that ladies find C. F. Wing's drapery department such an attractive place. The stock comprises many novelties not to be seen elsewhere in the city and holiday buyers are present in force.

SPECIALTIES.—Misses', boys' and youths' fancy slippers, dolls' slippers, ladies' spring heel storm rubbers, Turkish slippers 50 cents. Buchell, 75 William street.

A REGULAR EXHIBIT.—A place on the exhibition grounds of the World's Fair in Chicago is being dug for bark Progress, and she will soon be taken in as a regular exhibit.

N. E. O. P.—Attention is called to special notice in another column advertising a regular meeting of Bay State Lodge for Monday evening, when officers are to be elected.

FOUR OURS.—*Our* good shoes, *our* low prices and *our warrant* is the reason you always find a crowd in *our* store. Buchell, 75 William street.

RUGS! RUGS! fur rugs, in all colors, at lower prices than you ever saw them on sale, at Whiting & Co's for the holidays.

IF YOU ARE LOOKING FOR HOLIDAY GIFTS you will be interested in the advertisement of Bliss & Nye, page 5.

TWELVE HUNDRED pairs of kid gloves and silk mittens on sale, for the holidays, at Whiting & Co's.

ORIENTAL RUGS and carpets make useful presents. See the assortment and get the prices at C. F. Wing's.

A FEW MORE of those Tam O'Shanters at 39c. at O'Neill's, one door north of Peirce Furnishing Co.

YOU MUST GO TO Whiting & Co's and see the handkerchiefs they are selling, best styles and lowest prices in the city.

POCKETBOOKS, purses, card cases, bill books toilet sets, &c., cheap at Cushing's, opp. City Hall.

GENTS' MACKINTOSH COATS, silk umbrellas, silk hosiery, silk gloves, ties, silk braces. Popular prices. H. H. Tillson.

THE PROFESSOR and his banjo will be at Cheap John's every evening this week from 8 to 10.

ONE THOUSAND ladies' white aprons on sale at Whiting & Co's for the holidays, from 25 cents to $2 a piece.

WHY NOT LOOK at those writing desks and bookcases at C. F. Wing's. Nothing better for a present. Prices are way down.

SHOPPING AND TRAVELLING bags, just the thing for holiday presents, lowest prices at C. F. Cushing's.

AT LAST we have got them—those fine cloth side bags. Cushing's, opp. City Hall.

FIFTY CENT music books 25c. at Boden's, opposite Haskell & Tripp's.

CONCERT at Cheap John's this evening from 8 to 10.

PRETTY TRIMMED walking hats for children $1.25 at O'Neill's.

FAIRHAVEN BOWLING ALLEY has reopened for engagements.

TEN CENT MUSIC 3c. a copy, two for 5c., Boden's music store.

CHRISTMAS PRESENTS for ladies and gents at Cushing's, opp. City Hall.

MRS. H. BOWLED 197 at Fairhaven Bowling Alley one day this week.

VERY LARGE ASSORTMENT of boxing gloves at 125 Purchase street. J. T. Tobey.

GOOD BY CORN REMOVER guaranteed cure by Wright Drug Co. 25c. a bottle.

FUR ROBES, horse blankets, harnesses, whips, etc., closing out prices at Cushing's.

MRS. T. BOWLED 287 at Fairhaven Bowling Alley the other evening.

NICE NEW LINE of harmonicas, 125 Purchase street. J. T. Tobey.

BANJO, guitar, violin and mandolin cases, in wood, canvas and leather, Boden's music store.

BLISS & NYE'S bargain counter is worthy of your attention.

ENJOY AN EVENING at Fairhaven Bowling Alley.

THE TILLER CLUB will meet at 1 30 p. m. to-morrow.

TOY TRUNKS for the children 45c. to $3 at C. F. Cushing's.

FOR SNUFF BOXES, go to Cheap John's.

DOLLS' HAT FRAMES at Nooning's for 15c. each.

BAY STATE GUITARS, Boden's music store.

4½ pounds of raisins 25 cents. Gray Bros.

FOR Christmas presents, go to Cheap John's.

SWEETEST ORANGES. Gray Bros.

REMOVAL—Boston Shoe Store to 124 Purchase.

BIG CUT on roasts. Gray Bros.

GATCOMB BANJOS at Boden's music store.

CHEAPEST ORANGES. Gray Bros.

STYLISH trimmed hats at Nooning's for $3.

SAVE 4c. a lb. on roasts. Gray Bros.

FOR CIGAR CASES, go to Cheap John's.

FOWL 12 and 14c. at Gray Bros.

MUSIC ROLLS at Boden's music store.

HOOD'S Sarsaparilla is sold by all Druggists

Alteration Sale!

Early in January we shall make extensive alterations in our stores which will necessitate moving a large part of our heavy stock. In order to do as little of this work as possible, we have decided to have an ALTERATION or CLEARING SALE, and shall make prices that will enable us to move a goodly part of our stock from our own floors to the homes of our customers. In order to do this in so short a time, we realize that we must sacrifice our profit (and more in some cases) and make prices that will be irresistible.

PARLOR SUITES
CHAMBER SUITES
DINING ROOM SUITES
WARDROBES
SIDEBOARDS
CHIFFONIERS
DESKS
BOOK CASES
SECRETARIES
CHINA CLOSETS
LOUNGES
BEDSTEADS
CHAIRS
MIRRORS
RATTAN CHAIRS
EASELS
MATTRESSES
PILLOWS
FOLDING BEDS
ODD PIECES
HAT RACKS
SPRING BEDS
CHILD'S CRIBS
PARLOR CABINETS
TABLES
&c., &c., &.

The Time is Opportune, and This Sale will Give Christmas Buyers a Benefit which we are confident will be appreciated, and as a result many a handsome piece of Furniture will be ordered for a holiday gift, which probably would be passed by at the regular price. We mention a few of the many articles in our stock suitable for presents, and if you want to know how wonderfully far a little money will go in making a home attractive and inviting, come and examine our stock; the inspection will surprise you into making a purchase.

Sale Commences To-day and will continue through the month.

C. F. WING,

34 to 40 Purchase Street.

WHITING & CO.

WE ARE OPENING

New Holiday Goods

TO-DAY,

You Want to Call Often.

We have a large stock of new India Rugs, also Fur Rugs for Holiday Gifts.

You should see our new Table Linens, in sets, and by the yard, they are elegant.

In our Blanket Department we are having great sales. The quality and low prices are doing the business.

Our Gents' Furnishing Department will be, as usual, one of the busy places. See the New Umbrellas, Handkerchiefs, Neckwear, Hosiery, Gloves and Underwear, and get our prices.

200 New and Choice Patterns of Real Shell Pins, from 25c. to $3.50 apiece.

On our first circular counter will be found Handkerchiefs, Gloves, Hosiery, Laces, Ribbons, Shopping Bags, Pocket Books and Purses.

If you want to purchase a Dress Pattern for a holiday gift we can sell you $1 all-wool goods at 50c. per yard, and for 39c. per yard the best bargains ever shown.

200 New Mackintosh garments open to-day for ladies for holiday gifts.

See our Wares and Fancy Goods on the last circular counter.

WHITING & CO.

J. V. SPARE,

41 Purchase St.

HOLIDAY GOODS,

HOLIDAY GOODS,

HOLIDAY GOODS,

FOR GENTLEMEN.

Large Cashmere Mufflers, assorted colors, 25 to 75c. each.

Large Silk Mufflers, white, black and navy brocaded patterns, at $1.00, $1.25 $1.50.

Japanese Silk Handkerchiefs, with and without initial, at 50c., 62c., 75c., $1.00.

Excellent Linen Handkerchiefs at 25c. and 33c.

Silk neckwear in Tecks and Four-in-Hands at 25c. and 50c.

Suspenders assorted styles at 12 1-2c. to 50c. pair.

Cardigan Jackets at $1.25c. upward.

Lined Kid Gloves with fur wrists at $1.

Laundered Shirts, Night Shirts, Linen Collars and Cuffs.

For Ladies' and Children, we have Handkerchiefs from 5c. upwards.

Silk Handkerchiefs, an endless variety.

Initial Handkerchiefs.

Cashmere Gloves, Kid Gloves, Neckwear, Ruches, Windsor Ties, &c., &c.

Hoods, Shawls, Leggins, Mittens.

Letter Paper by the box at 10c., 15c., 20c., 25c. and 50c.

Booklets and Cards, Jewelry, &c., &c.

A nice assortment of Shawls at $2.00 and upwards.

Stamped Linen Goods, all the popular kinds and prices.

HANDKERCHIEFS,

HANDKERCHIEFS,

HANDKERCHIEFS.

Indian Baskets from 5c. upwards.

Scrap Baskets, 25c.

Albums, Vases, Trays, Calenders, Hairpin Cases, &c., &c.

Aprons, Aprons, Aprons, Aprons.

Chenille Table Covers.

Linen Table Sets.

Towels.

Beautiful Towels at 25c., 50c. and 75c.

Linen Table Covers, fancy borders, at $1.00, $1.25, $1.50 and $2.00.

J. V. Spare,

41 Purchase St.

Christmas Shoppers

In Search of Gifts for

Gentlemen are invited

To inspect our attractive

Furnishing Department.

Here are some of the things

You will find to interest you.

Elegant Neckwear bought

Especially for the Holidays.

Gloves of all descriptions,

Mufflers and Silk Handkerchiefs

In large variety.

Fancy Suspenders and

Silk Umbrellas,

Underwear & Hosiery, all grades

Collars, Cuffs and Shirts of

The best makes only.

Our assortment is the largest,

Our goods are the best

We can find.

Our prices are as low as we can

Possibly make them.

J. & W. R. WING & CO.

Clothiers and Furnishers.

Knapp's ROOTBEER EXTRACT

SCENES OF GRANDEUR.

Greeted Those Who Saw the World's Fair Opened.

Dedication of the Magnificent Woman's Building.

Multitude Was Countless and Greatest Enthusiasm Prevailed.

CHICAGO, May 2.—It is impossible to convey by words from the adequate conception of the framework in which Chicago's panorama of action was set. "It is the most beautiful scene in all the world," was the exclamation uttered by a man who has traveled in every clime and has seen nature adorned and unadorned by art in all its phase. No name has yet been formally, or even by common consent, conferred upon the theater of yesterday's action. That it will have a name in time is beyond question, for it is a place by itself, and, though composed of many parts, makes a distinct and magnificent whole.

"The central court" as it is often termed, is in reality a vast unroofed court, but of dimensions so enormous as to make it seem as though a section of all outdoors had been set apart and enclosed within a series of lofty and noble facades, composed of porticos, columns, cornices, friezes, and heroic statuary, and as if the space thus enclosed had received with lavish hand all the beauty that arts most lavish and thapsady guided hand could confer.

Imagine, if you can, this vast space flanked by the white facades of the tremendous palaces of manufactures on one side and agriculture on the other. The head of this enclosure, crowned by the aspiring front and soaring dome of the administration building, while its foot outstretched toward the dancing waters of Lake Michigan, is

Girdled as by Jewels

and lit with the peristyle, a gleaming portice of columns supporting a graceful frieze upon which stands heroic statues.

The place thus inclosed is laid out in gravelled walks, winding amid velvety lawns, whose emerald hue is made still brighter by contrast with the dazzling marble surrounding it on every side. In the centre of all, stretching from the front of the administration building to the peristyle and passing beneath that structure by flying arches into the lake itself, is the central basin, a long lagoon of sparkling water. In this lagoon, at either end, are two of the most beautiful and imposing objects of art within the white city.

The first of these is the triumphal barge of state, magnificent, yet light and full of action. Planking this, directly in front of the administration building are two electric fountains which all summer long will throw jets of 50 feet into the air. At the other end of the lagoon, facing the flying barge, rises the colossal statue of the Republic, 115 feet high, entirely covered with gold. The effect of this rich decoration, from the midst of its surroundings of almost universally pure white, is peculiarly striking.

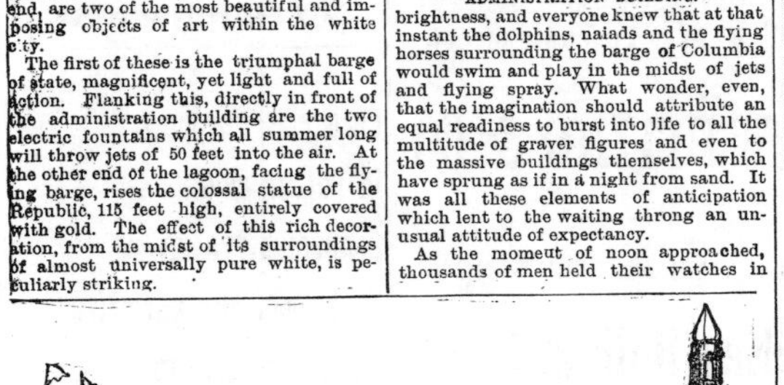

ON THE LAGOON.

This impression of life ever ready to burst into activity was heightened by the knowledge which everybody possessed of just what was to happen at 12 o'clock when President Cleveland was to touch the magic button. Everybody knew that at that instant away over in the palace of mechanic arts a huge mass of metal, now lying seemingly inert and dead, would have breathed into its lungs a force which would cause it to live itself and to send the forces of life pulsing to every part of the exposition. Everybody knew that at the same moment a thousand flags of

Every Nation on the Earth

would be broken from the compact balls of bunting into which they were now rolled upon the top of as many flagstaffs and swung to the breeze a blaze of variegated and fluttering color.

Everyone knew that at that instant the great white veil would drop from the lofty figure of the Republic. Everyone knew that at that instant the electric fountains would add two new columns to the scene of translucent and quivering brightness, and everyone knew that at that instant the dolphins, naiads and the flying horses surrounding the barge of Columbia would swim and play in the midst of jets and flying spray. What wonder, even, that the imagination should astretche and pressed the button which was to thrill the city with the spark of life. The strain of waiting were intense with every moment of delay, men almost held their breath and women were still with the silence of tense eagerness. At last,

When the Climax Came

when all the flags fluttered, when the noble upturned face of the republic was revealed, when the fountains shot into the air and the first gun of the salute by the revenue cutter anchored outside in the lake rent the gray atmosphere, this intense and silent expectancy cracked like an overstrained violin string.

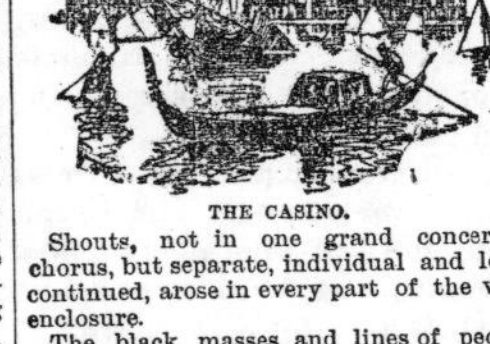

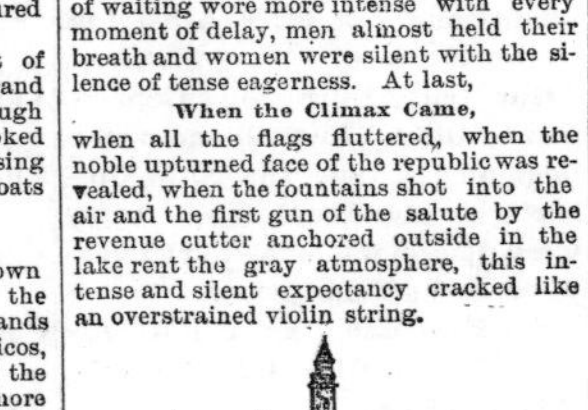

ADMINISTRATION BUILDING.

The most methods consist of elementary, high school and academic courses. The list of instructors includes some of the most prominent professors in the country. They are:

Dr. C. Wesley Emerson, president of the Emerson School of Oratory, Boston; Professor A. Guilliner, New York city; Professor George Sternberg, L. D., Ph. D., New York city; Miss Amelia M. Watson, East Windsor Hill, Conn.; Mr. Louis Collin, Boston Normal School of Gymnastics; Mr. Everett Schwartz of Waltham, George I. Aldrich, A. M., superintendent of schools, Newton; W. A. Mowry, Ph. D., superintendent of schools, Salem; Miss Augusta L. Balch, supervisor of drawing, Somerville, Mass.; F. F. Murdock, Bridgewater Normal school; J. C. Greenough, A. M., principal Westfield Normal school; C. E. Meleney, A. M., superintendent of schools, Somerville; Miss Lucy Wheelock, principal Chauncy Hall kindergarten, Boston; Miss Kate K. Fowler, superintendent of music, Brooklyn; A. C. Boyden, A. M., Bridgewater Normal school; T. M. Balliet, Ph. D., superintendent of schools, Springfield; Miss Anna E. Hill, supervisor of penmanship, Springfield; J. W. Dickinson, LLD, secretary Massachusetts board of education, Boston; A. W. Edson, A. M., agent Massachusetts board of education, Worcester; E. S. Burgess, high school, Washington, D. C.; Daniel Dorchester, Jr., Ph. D., Boston university; Professor Rene Dreyfuss, A. B., New York; Professor Adolph Meyer, New York; Carlton B. Stetson, A. M. Cambridge; J. W. MacDonald, A. M., agent Massachusetts board of education, Stoneham; Rev. J. D. King, Ph. D., Cottage City, and Charles E. Adams, Salem Normal school.

THE TRIAL OF LIZZIE BORDEN.

COURT ROOM IN THIS CITY WHERE THE CASE WILL PROBABLY BE HEARD.

It is generally believed that the trial of Lizzie Borden will be held in the court house in this city.

Attorney General Pillsbury has thus early determined his course. He was very short and sharp to a reporter, who simply asked him how the trial would continue. His reply was:

"I have nothing to say in regard to the Borden case, and it is as well to have it understood now as later. When there is any information to be given to the public in regard to it, I shall not wait to be asked in order to give it. At present there is nothing to be said in regard to it."

The latest newspaper comments on the case are these:

It is to be hoped that nothing will prevent the trial of Lizzie Borden next month. Whether the woman is innocent or guilty, she is to be considered innocent, and it is an act of injustice to delay the trial.—Springfield Union.

The demand by the newspapers that Lizzie Borden be given speedy trial has reached such proportions that those who are responsible for the delay are unable to withstand it longer. The idea which the public entertains is that Lizzie Borden was held because there is no one else who could be. Unless the government is in possession of new evidence that opinion is not liable to change by the trial.—Worcester Telegram.

"IT WAS INHERITED."

The Fearful Effect of Heredity Upon the Lives of Men and Women—A Striking Case.

"The man or woman does not live who is free from hereditary influences." This remark was made by the celebrated Dr. Vanderville, to the Rev. Dr. McArthur, at a convention of scientists.

"I agree with you, doctor," said the divine.

"Pure blood," continued the doctor, "is the great cause of health; impaired blood the source of most diseases. It may even go back to the grand or great grand-parents."

"I have in mind a prominent man," said the reverend gentleman, "General Alfred C. Monroe, of No. 1 Pemberton square, Boston. He inherited kidney troubles from both parents, one of whom died with it. He suffered terribly from pains in the back and head, and at times when walking, the dizziness became so bad that he was compelled to lay hold of some convenient post for support. He was in a most desperate condition."

"And is he so still?" asked the doctor.

"No, he is in perfect health. Dr. McGregor, I believe of Maine, who had amputated an arm for the general, cured him."

"Do you know what medicine he used?"

"I understand it was Hunt's Remedy."

"Oh, Hunt's Remedy. I know it very well," said Dr. Vanderville. "I consider it the best remedy for kidney, liver, heart troubles, and female difficulties in the world. It is in no sense a patent medicine, but a standard remedy, which deserves to be used by all intelligent people. The fact is, no blood taint can exist when the kidneys are in perfect order, and there is where Hunt's Remedy shows its marvelous superiority."

"I only wish," said Rev. Dr. McArthur, "that all people who inherit a tendency to disease, could know of this remedy of which you speak so highly, and use it. I am positive it would greatly lessen suffering and death."

TRANSFERS TO FAIRHAVEN.

May be Abolished by Street Railway Owing to Abuse of System.

The directors of the Union Street Railway company are to consider the advisability of discontinuing the sale and acceptance of transfers on the Fairhaven line. General Manager Smith states that the reason for this is that the system has been abused. Transfers are good only on the line for which they are punched. It has become the custom of some of the passengers to purchase transfers to some other line and then tender them in payment of a return trip on the Fairhaven line and give the conductor the option of taking the transfer or nothing. Mr. Smith says that his present feeling is not to prosecute the men for evading fare, but to discontinue the transfers. If this action is taken a passenger on the Purchase street or Mt. Pleasant lines who connects with the Fairhaven line will be compelled to pay 10 cents fare.

FALL RIVER.

The mayor explained his position on the recent grant to the Globe Street Railway company at the board of aldermen meeting night of 1st, and Frank S. Stevens, who represented the road, offered to repair the causeway at the Narrows and give the city $4,000 to build an iron bridge there, so that the matter has been amicably settled. The claim of Rev. W. Walker Jubb for damages for injuries to his wife was allowed. The water commissioners have organized with Joseph Walters chairman.

A young man named Shea was thrown around a shaft in the bleach house of the American Printing company, 1st, and badly hurt.

CUTTYHUNK.

Frederick S. Allen, keeper of the Massachusetts Humane society's life boat at the east end of the island, is building a light weight life car to be used by means of whip and hawser, or by whip alone. The life car is built of white oak timbers, cedar planking and ceiling and covered with thick canvas, around which cork is lashed. The dimensions are 7 feet 6 inches in diameter, 8 feet long, capacity 32 cubic feet, weighing about 100 pounds when completed. Mr. Allen thinks that had one of these cars been in readiness at the wreck of the ill-fated Aquatic the crew would have been saved long before they were. The car will be on exhibition in New Bedford on the fourth day of July.

Mrs. Martha Tilton of the Vineyard is visiting her daughter-in-law, Mrs. Lottie Tilton.

Frederick S. Allen visited New York last week to witness the grand naval review.

The trap fishermen have finished driving stakes and are now ready for the spring fishing.

Edgar Veeder has been offered a position as captain of a steam yacht during the summer by parties at Woods Holl.

VINEYARD SUMMER INSTITUTE.

Sixteenth Annual Session Will Commence on July 10.

The 16th annual session of the Marthas Vineyard summer institute will commence on July 10. This institution has grown in popular favor since its incorporation, and last summer the attendance was the largest in its history. There were 600 students from 44 states in the Union.

The directors of the school are William A. Mowry, Ph. D., president; Rev. John D. King, Ph. D., vice president; Arthur C. Boyden, A. M., clerk; C. E. Meleney, A. M., treasurer; William B. Dwight, Ph. B., auditor; A. W. Edson, A. M., manager school of methods; C. W. Emerson, president Emerson college of oratory; Edward S. Burgess, A. M.; J. C. Greenough, A. M.; G. I. Aldrich, A. M.; Daniel Dorchester, Jr., Ph. D.

The institute was established for the purpose of affording teachers and others an opportunity of combining the study of some specialty with the rest and recreation of a delightful and inexpensive seaside resort. The class instruction for the most part is given in the morning between 9 and 11. In the afternoon between 3 and 5. The middle of the day is set apart for sea bathing and rest. On Monday and Wednesday evenings a series of public lectures are given in Agassiz Hall.

A popular course of first-class entertainments will be given in Union chapel on Tuesday and Thursday evenings. Friday evenings will be devoted to receptions of professors, students and invited guests. Saturdays will be devoted to excursions to nearby summer resorts and historical places.

LANE'S MEDICINE

C. W. HASKINS

No 20 PURCHASE STREET,

Has replenished his stock since the holidays, and now offers at very low prices a good variety of Diamond Rings, Fine Jewelry, Gold and Silver Watches, Chains, &c.

His stock of Sterling Silver Spoons, Forks, Fancy Table Ware and Novelties is very extensive; these goods are lower in price than ever before.

18 KARAT WEDDING RINGS

A SPECIALTY.

You can save money buying of him your Spectacles and Eye Glasses, fit and quality guaranteed.

Watch, Clock and Jewelry repairing by experienced workmen.

Ice! Ice! Ice!

Having assumed the agency of the South Dartmouth Ice Co. we are prepared to receive orders for Ice in any quantity.

A stock constantly stored ready for immediate delivery at our store house foot of Walnut street.

Call at or telephone to

HART & AKIN,

Corner Water and Walnut Streets.

HARDY HITCH, JR.,

Awning, Carpet and Shade Upholsterer,

195 UNION STREET.

(Masonic Building.)

Telephone - - - 153-12

Knowles & Co.

We are offering special bargains in seasonable dress fabrics.

Broadcloths in all the new and elegant shades of Tan, Golden Browns, Navy, Greens and Black, 54-inch wide, and at the very low price of 89c. and $1.25. The shades and quality are just what you want.

The largest assortment of Fancy Weaves in all wool dress novelties at 50c. a yard to be found in the city.

In India Twills we have every conceivable shade, Navys, Light Greens, Heliotrope, Golden Browns, Tans and Grays, 40-inch at 50c., and 46-inch at 75c. and $1.00.

Storm Serges in Navy and Blacks, good values at 50c., 75c., $1.00, $1.25.

Black Dress Goods. We are headquarters in plain and fancy weaves. We deal in nothing but the most reliable and desirable fabrics. Prices range from 50c. up.

We wish to call your attention to the special values we are offering in Black Silks and Wool Henriettas at $1.00, $1.25, $1.50, $1.75 each, and every one of better value than can be bought in any store in this section of the state. If you are thinking of buying a black dress, you will save money by buying here. Give them a look and see for yourself.

Our assortment of Velvets and Fancy Trimming Silks was never so large as now, and prices so reasonable. We can suit you in Trimming Silks and Velvets.

Ladies' outside Wraps, Suits and Capes. One line Capes at $5.00 in Black, Brown and Tan, a leader. One lot Ladies' Jackets, Blacks, Blues, Tans and mixtures at $5.00, and many other prices from $5.00 to $12.00. Our line Ladies' Wrappers, the best in the city, from 79c. to $2.50; these are the best prints and percales. A line of Silk Waists, Black, Blues, Scarlet and striped at $6.00. A line of very attractive Cambric and Sateen Waists from $1.38 to $3.00. Suits; in this line of goods we carry a suit at $6.00 that beats the world, and also suits at $10.00 and $12.00.

Knowles & Co.

UNION and FOURTH STS.

BROOKLYN OFFICIALS ARRAIGNED.

Columbus Day Celebration Frauds Being Probed to the Bottom.

Brooklyn, N. Y., May 8.—The first cases of the Brooklyn city officials and tradesmen indicted for auditing and presenting alleged fraudulent and exorbitant bills in connection with the city's celebration of Columbus Day, were called this morning. The cases of five men were called, namely: Aldermen Arthur J. Heney, Moses J. Wafer and McKee; City Plan Clerk James H. Pigott of the building department, and Patrick Ross, a plumber. The case of Pigott was first heard. His counsel endeavored to show that Mr. Pigott was not guilty of the charges as set forth in the indictment. Thirty-three men in all are under indictment for being concerned in the frauds.

WIRES UNDERGROUND.

Bill Reported by the Committee on Mercantile Affairs.

Boston, May 8.—The committee on mercantile affairs reported this afternoon a bill to compel the placing of electric wires underground with the exception of trolley wires. The bill applies to that portion of Boston bounded by Dover, Berkeley and Charles streets, the harbor and Fox point channel. The bill constitutes the city engineer, the superintendent of streets, and inspector of works, commissioners on electrical wires. The wires are to be all underground by 1900. The act is to go into effect Jan. 1, 1894.

The committee on cities this afternoon reported a bill providing that cities and towns may require reasonable payment for permission to open streets.

BAD ECZEMA ON BABY

Head one Solid Sore. Itching Awful. Had to Tie His Hands to Cradle. Cured by Cuticura.

Our little boy broke out on his head with a bad form of eczema, when he was four months old. We tried three doctors, but they did not help him. We then used your three CUTICURA REMEDIES, and after using them eleven weeks exactly according to directions, he began to steadily improve, and after the use of them for seven months his head was entirely well. When we began using it his head was a solid sore from the crown to his eyebrows. It was also all over his ears, most of his face, and small places on different parts of his body. There were sixteen weeks that we had to keep his hands tied to the cradle and hold them when he was taken up; and had to keep mittens tied on his hands to keep his finger-nails out of the sores, as he would scratch if he could in any way get his hands loose. We know your CUTICURA REMEDIES cured him. We feel safe in recommending them to others.

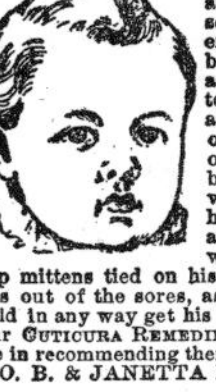

GEO. B. & JANETTA HARRIS, Webster, Ind.

Cuticura Resolvent

The new blood and Skin Purifier, and greatest of Humor Remedies, cleanses the blood of all impurities and poisonous elements, and thus removes the cause, while CUTICURA, the great skin cure, and CUTICURA SOAP, an exquisite skin beautifier, clear the skin and scalp, and restore the hair. Thus the CUTICURA REMEDIES cure every species of itching, burning, scaly, pimply, and blotchy skin, scalp, and blood diseases, from pimples to scrofula, from infancy to age, when the best physicians fail.

Sold everywhere. Price, CUTICURA, 50c.; SOAP, 25c.; RESOLVENT, $1.00. Prepared by the POTTER DRUG AND CHEMICAL CORPORATION, Boston.

☞Send for "How to Cure Skin Diseases," 64 pages, 50 illustrations, and 100 testimonials.

BABY'S Skin and Scalp purified and beautified by CUTICURA SOAP. Absolutely pure.

PAINS AND WEAKNESSES Of females instantly relieved by that new, elegant, and infallible Antidote to Pain, Inflammation, and Weakness, the Cuticura Anti-Pain Plaster.

[From Yesterday's Extra Edition.]

ARRAIGNED.

Lizzie Borden Brought to This City.

Taken Before Judge Hammond in Superior Court.

Pleads Not Guilty to the Terrible Charge.

A Momentary Faltering at the Door but Quick Recovery.

Preserves a Calm Demeanor and Answers Clearly.

She is Returned to the Jail at Taunton by the 5 50 Train.

Lizzie Borden was taken from Taunton jail this afternoon at 3 25, hurried to the railway station in a close carriage, and in charge of Sheriff Wright started for this city at 3 33, to be arraigned in the superior court.

The utmost secrecy was observed, the sheriff coming to this city alone as a blind, and then going back at noon to get the prisoner. Miss Borden was looking well, but pale. Her sister was with her all the afternoon.

THE ARRIVAL IN THIS CITY.

Crowd About the Station Didn't Recognize the Prisoner.

Lizzie Borden in company with Sheriff Wright and his wife arrived in this city this afternoon on the 4 20 train. Miss Borden came for her arraignment.

On the Fall River train 15 minutes before came Andrew J. Jennings. He stepped from the platform and wandered anxiously about the platform for five minutes before he drove off in a coupe.

John V. Morse was also at the station in an open carriage.

Miss Borden looked pale when she alighted, and was immediately hurried into a cab.

She was not in sight more than two seconds.

Many people on the cars were aware of her identity, but few of the crowd on the platform recognized her.

On the way from Taunton Miss Borden attracted the attention of passengers, but to their credit there was a marked degree of decency shown, and the prisoner was not the object of annoying curiosity.

AT THE COURT HOUSE.

Miss Borden Shielded From the Public in the District Attorney's Office.

Upon arrival at the court house there were not more than half a dozen spectators visible. The hackman sprang from his seat and in a twinkling the door was opened. Miss Borden, heavily veiled, alighted, and between the sheriff and his wife hurried up the concrete walk and broad stone steps and disappeared into the dark corridor of the court house. Officers McBay and Telford blocked the way for venturesome onlookers and the trio were unmolested as they passed the length of the building.

They entered the district attorney's private office and Sheriff Wright locked the door.

That was all the evidence noticeable that Miss Borden had arrived, except that a steady stream of citizens began to pour in, momentarily growing denser, the legal profession being largely in the predominance.

Miss Borden and her attendants remained in the district attorney's room till the counsel on the Reilly-Smith case were through their arguments. Then she was escorted to the court room.

AN OPEN SECRET.

News of the Arraignment Leaked Early in the Afternoon.

Outwardly the superior court room in this city this afternoon wore an air of quiet, but soon after 4 o'clock there was noticeably a small increase of numbers in the spectators, and those who came in wore an air of expectancy, and they took care to get seats as near the front as they could. It had been quietly whispered from one to another that Lizzie A. Borden, who for more than eight months has been held in the jail at Taunton under indictment from the grand jury charging her with murdering her father and stepmother in Fall River in July last, was to be arraigned, and that even then she was speeding on her way to this city as fast as the iron horse could bring her.

At 4 15 o'clock Andrew J. Jennings of Miss Borden's counsel entered the court room carrying with him the customary little green bag which counsel have when they have court matters to attend to. He took off his overcoat, threw it across the seat and leaned back and listened to the evidence in a civil cause which was on trial. He was asked by a Standard reporter what the method of procedure would be and he said he had no idea what course District Attorney Knowlton would pursue, all he knew was that Miss Borden was to be arraigned.

From 4 15 to 4 30 reporters in considerable numbers from Fall River and Taunton arrived, and by this time the fact that Miss Borden was expected was an open secret.

Significant of the expected arrival of Miss Borden was the course pursued just after 4 30 o'clock by Deputy Sheriff John W. Nickerson, who walked along back of the prisoners' dock and requested a number of spectators sitting there to vacate, which they did. By this time members of the bar in considerable numbers, who had somehow got the "tip," arrived and took seats inside the rail reserved for them, but so quietly had matters been kept that not 50 spectators were on hand.

MISS BORDEN ENTERING THE COURT HOUSE.
[From a Sketch by a Standard Artist.]

LIZZIE BORDEN,
Arraigned in This City This Afternoon.

MISS BORDEN IN THE DOCK.

Pleads Not Guilty of the Crime with Which She is Charged.

At 5 10 o'clock Thomas F. Desmond completed an argument in the civil case which had been on trial, and then there was a stir in the court room, the jury retired, and into the south door came Sheriff Andrew R. Wright, followed by his wife and then Lizzie A. Borden appeared, framed in the doorway. As she crossed the doorway it was noticeable that for the smallest instant of time she faltered.

It was but an instant, however, for she seemed to brace herself and then walked steadily to the dock and took her seat. Her face was flushed, and she looked from one side to the other, but her eyes did not rest on any one.

After Miss Borden had taken her place in the dock District Attorney Knowlton arose and said "Your honor, it is provided by law that in a capital case the prisoner may be arraigned at any regular session of the court. If your honor please there is a prisoner to be arraigned."

"Lizzie Andrew Borden," called Clerk Simeon Borden, and she arose in her place.

The clerk then read the indictment, which has been printed in full in the Standard, and at times his voice was noticeably tremulous. "What say you to this indictment," he asked, "are you guilty or not guilty?"

Without the least hesitation and in a voice firm, clear and resonant, she replied: "I am not guilty," and this she repeated three times as as many indictments were read.

After Miss Borden had pleaded to the charges and taken her seat, Andrew J. Jennings walked to the clerk's desk and said:

"Will your Honor assign counsel in this case?"

Judge Hammond asked if counsel has not acted in the case.

Mr. Jennings said he has and associated with him George D. Robinson and M. O. Adams.

Judge Hammond asked if it is the desire of prisoner that they shall act.

Mr. Jennings replied affirmatively.

Judge Hammond said: "You may enter your appearance. There is no occasion to assign counsel."

This finished the proceedings, and Deputy Sheriff Butman adjourned the court till 10 o'clock tomorrow morning.

AFTER ADJOURNMENT.

Pointers Gleaned by Prying Eyes Around the District Attorney's Room.

After the adjournment Miss Borden and her two attendants did not start at once, but kept their seats some minutes. Then Sheriff Wright arose and came out of the dock. Miss Borden came next, but stepped aside to allow Mrs. Wright to pass first.

The prisoner came last and Deputy Sheriff Kirby brought up as a rear guard. The procession moved down the stairs and in less time than it takes to tell it was locked in the district attorney's office again.

As a Standard man caught a glance through the door Mrs. Wright was more agitated than Miss Borden. The latter sat calmly in the district attorney's chair and gazed quietly out across the Morgan estate, while Mrs. Wright was apparently nervous and agitated. Sheriff Wright walked back and forth, gazing now and then at his watch to see the approach to train time.

Soon he emerged, and, walking to the rear entrance, saw that the hack was still waiting. Then he paid the hackman to save delay at the station, and immediately went back to his prisoner.

A few minutes later Attorney A. J. Jennings came hurrying down stairs and, sticking his head inside the door, asked the sheriff to wait for him and to allow him to accompany the party to the station. The request was granted, and Mr. Jennings returned to the court room.

SOON GATHERED.

Crowds Around the Court House After Arrival Became Known.

Before Lizzie Borden was removed from the court house the fact that she was there had become pretty thoroughly noised abroad, and crowds began to gather around the building.

Carriages were in waiting at both ends of the building, and the spectators paced anxiously up and down the sidewalks, determined to catch a glimpse of her as she emerged, and completely in doubt as to which way she would appear.

Sheriff Wright made his appearance at the rear entrance of the building to pay the hackman who brought her and his charge to the court house from the depot, and the crowd, taking this as evidence that Miss Borden was soon to enter the hack, surged up to the door, but were disappointed.

OFF FOR TAUNTON.

The Suspected Woman as Self-Possessed as Ever.

It was just 25 minutes of 6 o'clock when four persons who have been prominently identified with this celebrated case filed out from the district attorney's room. Sheriff Wright headed the little procession, next came his wife, Mrs. Wright, then followed the prisoner, Lizzie A. Borden, with Andrew J. Jennings, her counsel, bringing up the rear.

The party entered one of Kirby & Hick's carriages, driven by Hiram Tilghman, and were immediately driven to the depot, where they took the 5 50 train for Taunton.

Miss Borden was as self possessed as ever, not even noticing the crowd of curious lookers-on who had assembled in the court yard to witness her exit.

The New York Tribune today says:

A Boston dispatch says that the trial of Lizzie Borden has been set down for Monday, June 5, "unless some reason hereafter appears to the contrary." At this distance it looks as if the burden of proof was upon the prosecuting authorities to show why there has been so much delay in bringing this case to trial. The Borden murders occurred in August last, and the arrest of Lizzie Borden, and the action of the coroner's jury in holding her for trial, followed soon afterward. The inalienable right of every person accused of crime is a speedy trial. Such a trial would especially seem to be in order where a young woman is charged with the horrible crime of murdering her father and mother. There may be a good explanation for the delay which has already occurred, but surely nine or 10 months ought to be ample time to obtain all the evidence procurable. In fact, half that time would seem to be quiet sufficient for the purpose. Strict regard for justice requires that Lizzie Borden should be put on trial at the earliest day possible, and no further excuse for delay should be tolerated.

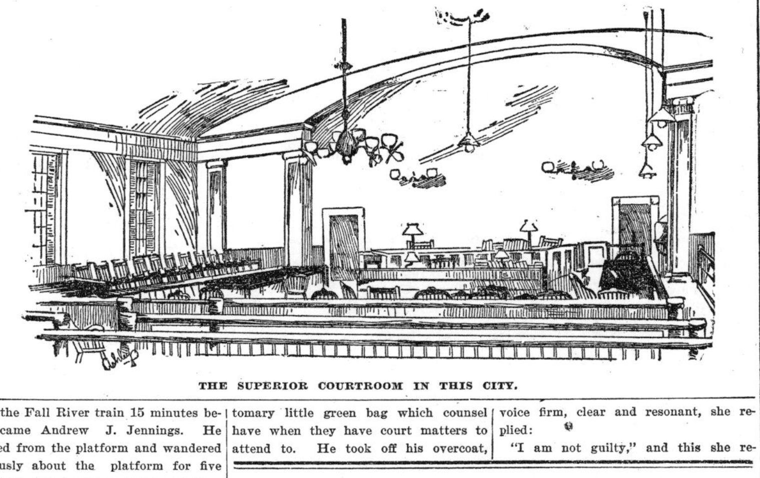

THE SUPERIOR COURTROOM IN THIS CITY.

Highest of all in Leavening Power.—Latest U. S. Gov't Report.

Royal Baking Powder

ABSOLUTELY PURE

JAMES PYLE'S PEARLINE WASHING COMPOUND THE GREAT INVENTION FOR SAVING TOIL & EXPENSE WITHOUT INJURY TO THE TEXTURE COLOR OR HANDS. NEW YORK.

Is It Like This

—your package of washing compound that you call "Pearline?" Look at the front of the package, and see. It will be for your own good and your own protection, quite as much as ours. The popularity of Pearline has led to the calling of anything in the shape of powder, which is used for washing or cleaning, by that name.

If you find you are using the genuine, we will guarantee that you are well pleased. If you have any complaints to make, we will guarantee that what you have is not Pearline, but some worthless or dangerous imitation of it. Many grocers send these imitations when Pearline is ordered—more profit to them—sure loss to you. Send them back, please. 287 JAMES PYLE, New York.

SUPERIOR COURT.

Defense in the Suit of Mrs. Reilly Against James F. Smith.

At the afternoon session of the superior court the case of Juliet F. Reilly vs. James F. Smith et al. was resumed.

John Quinlan was the first witness for the defense, but gave no evidence of importance.

Dr. Manuel B. Sylvia saw Mrs. Reilly directly after the accident, while she was lying on the snow, and examined her injuries. He came to the conclusion at the time that she was not seriously injured.

Cornelius Collins, a second hand in Acushnet mill, was on County street the day of the accident and saw the collision. He thought Mr. Smith's horse was running away and uncontrollable. He heard Mr. Smith tell Mr. O'Neil to pull on the rein and saw him pull the left rein. There was no team in the way of his passing Reilly on the left without colliding.

Daniel F. Driscoll, a Linden street grocer, saw the collision. Mr. Smith's horse was going rapidly, and he saw him try to pull him down. There was a space reserved in the center of the street for the horses which were being driven fast, and if Reilly hadn't turned into this space Smith would have gone by without injury.

Charles Cotter, a teamster for Smith Brothers, saw the accident. Smith's horse broke, and before he had struck Reilly's sleigh the animal was under control. Smith was sitting on the right hand side of the sleigh.

William H. Daley, an employe of the Copper works, was in Washington square watching the sport the day of the accident. He saw O'Neil take hold of the rein when they were about to run into Reilly's sleigh and turn the horse to the left.

Andrew E. Hathaway saw considerable trotting on County street the day of the accident, and 20 or 30 were speeding their horses at the time. He was out driving himself, and imagined he had a trotter.

John E. Harrington, Jr., saw the sleighs when they struck, and saw Reilly haul out to pass a sleigh ahead of him just before the collision.

Thomas F. O'Neil, one of the defendants in the case, testified that the horse broke just as they were passing Sherman street, but was under control when they struck Reilly's sleigh.

BOARD OF ALDERMEN.

Another Special Club Liquor License Granted This Afternoon.

The board of aldermen held a special meeting this afternoon to give a hearing on the petition of Hedge, Lewis & Co., for leave to maintain a steam engine and boiler of 50 horse power in the stone building corner of Rivet and First streets. The mayor presided and Alderman Barrows and Cobb were absent. As no one appeared to oppose the petition it was granted.

The petition of Frederick Winship for an innholder's license at the Whitcomb House was granted.

The petitions of Frank T. Perry and Fannie M. Washington for common victualers' licenses with Sunday privileges were granted.

The petition of Israil Gerstein for leave to deal in junk and secondhand articles was referred to the committee on licenses.

The petition of the New Bedford Turkish Bath and Athletic club corporation for a special club license at 5 South Sixth street was granted.

Anthony V. De Costa was nominated and confirmed as a special policeman, to serve without pay from the city, at the Spiritualistic meetings 168 Chestnut street.

Adjourned.

MUST WAIT.

New Bedford and Fall River's Petitions Referred to Next Legislature.

Boston, May 8.—The committee on cities reported reference to the next legislature on a petition for a board of public works in Fall River; also on the petition of the city of New Bedford for control of the board of public works.

Plea for a Union Station.

Boston, May 8.—Hon. J. E. Sanford, chairman of the state railroad commissioners, made an earnest plea before the treasury committee of the legislature today in behalf of the Boston & Maine and Fitchburg union station, as recommended by the rapid transit commission. Senator Kittredge explained the rapid transit bill for the city of Boston to the finance committee. He estimated the cost at $5,050,000. Other members of the rapid transit committee appeared, and urged the necessity of a state loan.

Ocean Steamers.

Arrive—At New York, Berlin, Southampton.

THE NEW YORK FAILURES.

Experts Hard at Work on the Books of the National Cordage Company.

New York, May 8.—Henry Allen, of Henry Allen & Co., whose suspension was announced on the exchange on Thursday, stated today that the extent of their liabilities was $670,000.

The experts appointed to examine the books of the National Cordage are still hard at work, but say they have not yet got to a point where they can make any statement. The rumor current to the effect that the firms comprising the trust are in the difficulty more deeply than the company itself is still refused affirmation or denial by the officer who speaks for the company, and the heads of the firms said to be implicated decline to be seen.

Persons closely connected with the affairs of the company declare that the notes unpaid are those of the individuals of the pool, which are guaranteed by the separate companies comprising the National Cordage company. If this be so then the receivers of the trust are engaged chiefly in disentangling the complications arising from the confusion between the cordage company, the firms in that company and the individuals comprising the firms.

SUIT FOR HEAVY DAMAGES.

National Paper Box Corporation of New Haven Sued by an Employe.

New Haven, May 8.—Suit is to be instituted against the National Paper Box corporation of this city in an action for serious, and perhaps fatal illness, resulting from the use of certain chemicals in the paper necessary for box making. The injured person is J. J. Keefe. It was part of his duty to steam the paper, and he alleges that his system absorbed arsenic and other chemicals, to the detriment of his physical well being. His eyes are sightless, possibly permanently so; his body a mass of ulcers, and it is a question whether he can long survive the horrible agony in which he now is. Keefe's attorney, J. P. Goodhart, of this city, claims $25,000 damages for his client.

AT THE CONEY ISLAND CLUB.

Billy Smith Signs an Agreement to Meet Dempsey on June 30.

Boston, May 8.—Judge Newton of the Coney Island Athletic club met Billy Smith at the office of Captain A. W. Cooke today, and as a result Smith signed an agreement to box Dempsey 20 rounds, or until a decision is rendered by the referee at the Coney Island Athletic club, under its rules, on the evening of June 30, the contest to be under Marquis of Queensberry rules, with five ounce gloves, and such referee and timekeeper as the club selects, for $6,000 given by the club, $5,500 to the winner and $500 to the loser. The principals are not to exceed 142 pounds each and the forfeit is $500.

CASHIER SHAW ARRAIGNED.

Sentence Suspended to Give Him Time to Settle Up His Affairs.

Portland, Me., May 8.—In the United States circuit court this morning Cashier William Shaw of the Lincoln Bank of Bath was arraigned on four indictments charging him with embezzlement and misapplication of the funds of the bank and false entries on the books. He pleaded nolo contendere to each. The judge suspended sentence until July 1, presumably to give the prisoner time to settle up his affairs, procure guardians for his children, etc.

THE GOLD RESERVE.

Treasury Department Gradually Building It Up.

Washington, May 8.—The treasury department is gradually building up its gold reserve, which was depleted to a considerable amount on April 24. Today the gold in the treasury foots up $97,864,505. The "low water" figure was reached April 25, when it was $93,753,910. Since then the export of gold has been comparatively light, and the gold has crawled up to the figures stated. It is probable, however, that during this week gold to the amount of a million dollars will be taken for shipment to Europe.

Moulders Still Out.

Wakefield, Mass, May 8.—The 75 moulders at Smith, Anthony & Co's foundry did not go to work this morning because of the refusal of the firm to grant a 10 per cent. increase over the present wages. The men claim that eight years ago they were promised the increase they now demand.

Strike of Linemen and Inspectors.

New York, May 8.—The Brotherhood linemen and inspectors employed by the New York & New Jersey Telephone company in New Jersey, 150 in number, struck this morning. They demand an increase of wages and other concessions.

Asa Potter's Bail.

Boston, May 8.—Asa P. Potter's bail of $10,000 on the indictment charging him with false entries on the books of the Maverick bank was renewed today in the United States circuit court. The surety was G. T. W. Braman, the bondsman in the former instance.

Assistant Justice Smith.

Washington, May 8.—The president today announced the appointment of H. W. Smith of Utah to be assistant justice of the supreme court of the territory of Utah.

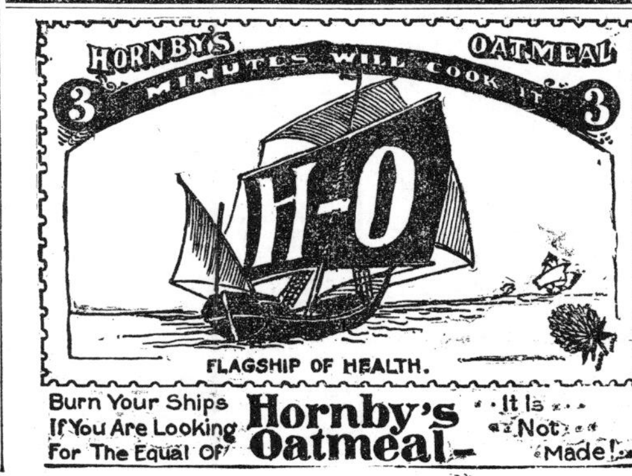

Burn Your Ships If You Are Looking For The Equal Of Hornby's Oatmeal—It Is Not Made!

Pages 1-8.

The Evening Standard.

Pages 1-8.

ESTABLISHED FEBRUARY, 1850.

NEW BEDFORD, WEDNESDAY, MAY 10, 1893.---TWELVE PAGES.

TWO CENTS.

HASKELL & TRIPP.

Basement.

A sale of great interest to housekeepers.

Steel enameled ware, every piece warranted.

You know what a treasure steel enameled ware is. Below find a partial list of the many shapes and sorts now ready for your orders:

Teapots—
1qt. 1½ qts.
65c. 69c.
2 qts. 3 qts
75c. 89c.

Coffee pots, same sizes and prices.

Lipped sauce pans—
1 qt. 1½ qts. 2qts.
25c. 29c. 33c.
3 qts. 4 qts.
48c. 57c.

Pudding pans—
1 qt. 2qts. 3 qts.
25c. 33c. 37c.
4 qts.
42c.

Wash basins—
26 in. 28 in.
35c. 39c.

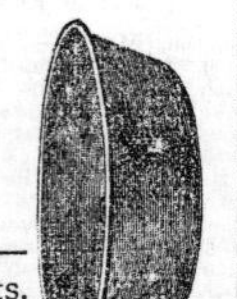

Pie plates—
10 in. 11 in.
21c. 25c.

Preserve kettles—
2¼ qts. 3 qts. 4qts.
42c. 45c. 57c.
6 qts. 8qts. 10 qts.
72c. 87c. $1

Rice boilers, $1.39.

Buckets—
2 qts. 2½ qts. 3 qts.
48c. 54c. 60c.

Soap dishes, 23c. Cuspidors, 69c. Round trays, 25c. and 35c.

For flytime—

Adjustable wire covered window screens and screen doors at *right prices*.

Dress Goods.

Overloaded importers must sell. We are on the lookout for chances to get fresh, desirable suitings below cost and have secured a few this week.

On sale today.

French serges, 45 inches wide, choice line of colorings. Would be extra cheap even at 75c. a yard. Our price 59c.

Fashionable shades in self-colored figured wool suitings. Never sold below one dollar a yard until today. Our price 59c. a yard.

World's fair traveling dresses cost but little if made from the handsome iridescent serges that are on our counter today marked 39c. a yard. Ten colorings—all good.

Russet and tan shoes for women, misses and children.

Russet and tan hosiery to match in many qualities.

Parasols by the hundreds now ready.

HASKELL & TRIPP,

Department Stores,

Purchase and William Streets.

DID NOT ESCAPE DEATH.

Body of Murderer Rohle Found in Hudson River.

Cheated the Electrical Chair Only to be Shot.

Belief That the Remains of Pallister Will Also be Recovered.

Sing Sing, N. Y., May 10.—The body of Frank W. Rohle, who with Thomas Pallister escaped from the death house in Sing Sing prison on April 20, was found at 8 45 this morning in the Hudson river, directly across the river from Sing Sing. The body was found by three fishermen, who towed the remains to the upper dock and notified the prison officers. State Detective Jackson and Prison Keeper Connaughton at once re-

Frank W. Rohle.

paired to the spot and identified the body by means of a picture and the prison shoes which the dead man wore. The body was very much decomposed.

One of the fishermen says he thinks he saw another body further down the river, but did not go after it, as he had the body of Rohle in tow. Searching parties are now trying to find the body of Pallister in the river.

When the body had been washed it was found that Rohle had been shot in the right side of the head, and the supposition is that Pallister shot him.

THE REPUBLICAN LEAGUE.

A Cordial Welcome from Democratic Mayor of a Democratic City.

Louisville, Ky., May 10.—Undismayed by the rout of a few months ago, when their principal adversaries for the first time in nearly three decades secured control of every branch of the government, but full of enthusiasm and their future, the representatives of the Republicans of the United States assembled in national convention in McCauley's theatre this morning. It was a pretty sight that greeted the advance guard of delegates to the league of clubs when the doors were opened. The platform had been decorated with the choicest flowers, palms and exotics which shed their fragrance through the auditorium.

Before the chairman's table rested a mammoth shield, supported on either side with silken flags. Stretched across the parquet from the proscenium rail was a silver filigree transparency bearing the names of all the states and territories of the Union. From gallery to floor the pillars were twined with tri-colored bunting and thousands of flags encircled the balconies, suspended from chandeliers and formed an archway through the long corridor and over this there was an immense "Old Glory."

Spurred to promptitude by an invitation to witness the Kentucky Derby in the afternoon, the delegates were lively in getting together, and by 10 o'clock, the hour designated in the call, every seat on the main floor, as well as in the balcony and gallery, had its occupant. Several hundred people were content with standing room, while fully 1,000 more were denied admission, as a result of the crowded condition of the interior.

The convention was opened with prayer by Dr. Heywood, of the Unitarian church. Mayor Tyler, who was heartily cheered, delivered the address of welcome. He said that he was glad, as the Democratic mayor of a Democratic city, to greet so large and influential a gathering of their Republican brethren, and the city of Louisville would do its utmost to give them a genuine Kentucky welcome.

General J. L. Crawford welcomed the convention for the state league.

Upon being presented as presiding officer of the day, Colonel Andrew Cowan, a local merchant, and one of the oldest Republicans in the state, was greeted with repeated cheers. He briefly spoke his appreciation of the compliment, and then the official call for the convention was read by Secretary Humphrey.

BIG SHORTAGE DISCOVERED.

Treasurer of an Ohio County for the Past Ten Years Charged with Embezzling.

Columbus, O., May 10.—The recent investigation of the accounts of the treasurer of Putnam county, ordered by the state auditor a month ago, was made to him yesterday and reveals a shortage of nearly $25,000. The investigation covered the last ten years and the administration of Treasurers H. L. Mc Dowell, L. L. Parker, O. F. Crawfis, and W. E. Lenart, the last the present incumbent. All of them charged excessive fees, but, except in the case of Crawfis, the money illegally taken is inconsiderable. In the four years of Crawfis' administration of the office the expert also finds $24,366 unaccounted for.

BISHOP BROOKS' SUCCESSOR.

Bishop Scarborough Rebukes the Political Methods Employed.

New Brunswick, N. J., May 10.—The diocesan convention opened here yesterday. Bishop Scarborough's address was a resume of the progress and policy of the church, and a rebuke of the methods used at the election of a successor to Bishop Brooks. "We cannot but regret," he said, "that methods of political caucus have been introduced into the election of a bishop. When delegates meet, agree upon a candidate, proclaim their choice through the daily press, demand that candidate's acceptance or refusal, and then, going into the convention kneel down and ask the guidance of the holy ghost upon their choice, it seems to me like trifling with holy things."

Will Retire from Parliament.

London, May 10.—William Saunders, Liberal M. P. for Newington Walworth, who showed a disposition to vote against the second reading of the Irish home rule bill, but finally voted with his party, is about to retire from parliament in deference to the wishes of his constituents, who are displeased with his course.

WEATHER INDICATIONS.

Fair and Warmer.

Washington, May 10.—For the 24 hours from 8 a. m. today: For New England, fair weather; slight changes in temperature in the night, but warmer during day; south winds.

Slightly Cooler Tomorrow.

Boston, May 10.—Local forecast for New England until Thursday night: Continued fair; warmer today, slightly cooler Thursday; northwesterly winds, changing to easterly on the coast during the day Thursday.

STUPENDOUS PENSION FRAUDS.

Attorney of Norfolk Va. Arrested—Used Colored Persons as Instruments.

Washington, May 10.—The pension department believes that it has unearthed stupendous pension frauds. An attorney of Norfolk, Va., named W. R. Drewrey, now under arrest, is charged with securing fraudulent pension claims by the wholesale, using as his instruments in many cases colored women and men who could not read or write.

About 16 months ago Secretary Noble ordered three cases dropped from the pension rolls that Drewrey had secured, and later on he was debarred from practice. When the present administration came in a thorough examination was made into the cases that Drewrey had secured, and when it was concluded a few days ago it was discovered that 98 of the cases he had handled under the act of 1890 were secured through the filing of false declarations.

The extent of the frauds can be understood when it is stated that 166 cases were granted and that every one of them carried arrears. The importance of the discoveries necessitated prompt action, and A. D. Albert, supervising examiner of the southern district, and several assistants, were sent to Norfolk, where they are now pursuing their investigations.

They have learned that Drewrey did a thriving business. In his office, occupying desk room, was a notary public named B. A. Richardson, Jr. When Richardson went out of the office Drewrey used Richardson's seal, attesting the false evidence which he had prepared, and forwarded the papers to the secretary.

Richardson is said to have been ignorant of the use to which his seals had been put. The result of the examiner's work will be shown next Monday. The United States court meets on that day and several pension cases will be brought before it. It is said that a large number of fraudulent pensioners will soon be dropped from the rolls and prosecutions begun. The amount of the steals will probably amount to $100,000.

"I THINK I'M DONE UP."

Last Words of George Slater as He Fell Dead on the Floor.

(Special Dispatch.)

Fall River, May 10.—"I think I'm done up," were the words heard by a kitchen girl in the Perry House on Pleasant street about 6 o'clock this morning. At the same time she heard a heavy fall, and turning quickly she saw a man, named George Slater, about 60 years of age, lying on the floor near the range. The girl was alarmed at his appearance and quickly summoned help. Physicians were at once called, but before they arrived the man was dead. Medical Examiner Dolan pronounced death the result of heart disease. Slater had been employed about the house for some time and had just completed his rounds of the upper stories awakening the boarders.

CHINAMEN HELD FOR TRIAL.

Actors Intending to Go to Chicago Prevented from Landing.

Tacoma, Wash., May 10.—Three Chinese merchants, who were deported on the steamer Victoria, were taken from the ship yesterday on writs of habeas corpus, issued on complaint of Moy Yuck, a merchant of this city. The Chinese were taken before the United States commissioner and held for trial next Wednesday.

Habeas corpus writs were served on Collector Wasson and the captain of the steamship for the bodies of 14 more Chinamen, who have been merchants in Portland for years past. They will land today and be held in custody until trial next Monday.

A telegram was received last evening from the Wash Young company in Chicago, which is importing the 215 actors on board the ship, stating that the company has no further concession from the government. This precludes the actors from being landed, and they will return today on the ship.

TO AVOID DISGRACE.

Suicide of a Young Capitalist and Real Estate Man.

New York, May 10.—The Sun's San Francisco special says: William T. Morgan, a young capitalist and real estate man, committed suicide yesterday in the rear of his office. Financial troubles, probably including embezzlement and breach of trust, furnished the principal motive. He was only 35 years old and well known and popular. At the time of his death he was president of the Belvedere Land company, and in popular estimation he was a millionaire.

Yesterday Morgan was jovial as usual at luncheon, but on returning to his office he went into a back room and ended his life with a bullet. It is said he discovered shortly after noon that the directors of the land company had begun to overhaul the books and that he killed himself to avoid inevitable disgrace.

REVOLUTIONISTS GAINING.

War in Nicaragua Will be a Long and Bloody One.

New York, May 10.—The Herald's San Juan Del Sur, Nicaragua, special says: The revolutionists against the power of President Sacaza are gaining. They have taken possession of this port and control most of the country between here and Granada. It is reported that Managua is under siege and that several engagements between the government troops and the insurgents have taken place.

Many of the leading merchants have openly declared their sympathy for the revolutionary cause. Among the laboring classes great enthusiasm is shown. It is quite evident that the outbreak is the most serious which has taken place in Nicaragua for many years. The war may last for some time, and it promises to be a bloody one.

A VILLAGE BURNED.

North Galveston, Ind. Almost Totally Destroyed.

Warsaw, Ind., May 10.—The village of North Galveston, 10 miles northwest of here was almost totally destroyed by fire yesterday. The residence of J. J. Jackson, among others, was consumed and the entire family, consisting of himself, wife, two sons and a daughter perished in the flames. Several other persons were badly burned. Many families lost their entire possessions and they escaped clad only in their night clothes. The loss is estimated at $75,000. The origin of the fire is unknown.

Farm Buildings Burned.

Laconia, N. H., May 10. — The farm buildings of Thomas Britton on Prospect hill, Belmont, were burned with their contents this morning. Loss $6,500; insurance $1,900. Cause unknown.

THE BORDEN CASE.

Another Hatchet Said to Have Been Found.

Officials Will Neither Affirm Nor Deny.

Defence Concedes Government Case is Strong.

Prisoner to be Brought Here a Week Before Trial.

Some Interesting Facts About Impaneling the Jury.

It was reported in connection with the Borden case this forenoon that another hatchet had recently been found in Fall River and that it is without a handle. Those who are in a position to know as to the truth of this matter will neither contradict or affirm the statement.

Notice was sent from this city today to Simeon Borden, Jr., assistant clerk of courts, that lists would be sent him today or tomorrow from which he could make up venires for jurors to be used in the Borden case. At the Tighe trial 80 jurors were drawn from all parts of the county, and every one of them was called, but there being so many challenges and excuses the necessary 12 was obtained out of that 80 only because one man who had given an excuse changed his mind and was put on the jury. But for this fact an additional call would have been necessary.

Because of the peculiar circumstances attending the Borden case it is estimated that over 100 jurors will be summoned into court. As is probably well known each side in a capital case has the right to challenge 22 men. This disposes of 44 out of the number which may be summoned. They have then a right to challenge for cause any number they may see fit to, and this fact taken in connection with the fact that a large number of those summoned may have decided opinions as to capital punishment and may have formed ideas of their own in regard to the innocence or guilt of the prisoner, it can be readily seen that quite a number of jurors will be needed to fill the bill. A man who has an opinion that the prisoner is innocent is liable to find a place on the jury for the simple reason that this opinion is just exactly the same as that held by the court, in that all persons are considered innocent until their guilt is proven. If a person gives as his opinion that the prisoner is guilty then, of course, there is no show for him.

It is estimated that because of the large number of jurors to assemble on the first day of the trial, there will be little room for ordinary spectators until the jury is impaneled. County Treasurer Pratt says that he will need at least two rooms on the first floor of the building until the jury is impaneled. After that these rooms, he believes, ought to be given over to the type writers who may be in attendance at the trial.

The statement alleged to have emanated from Sheriff Wright, that he would allow no tables within the bar proper during the trial, for the use of reporters, if correct, will place the newspaper men in a bad position. The clerk of courts, however, is of the opinion, as is also Chairman Babbitt of the county commissioners, that Captain Sanders, who has charge of the court house in this city, will see to it that the newspaper men have ample accommodations. It is thought that many of the seats now reserved for spectators will be removed and long tables put in. The space inside the bar will admit of several tables if the objection supposed to come from Sheriff Wright can be overcome.

It is suggested by court officials that room might be made in the court house, either on the first floor or in the basement for the telegraph companies to locate at least a dozen men, if it can be arranged there, that the wires can be run into the building. The distance between the court house and the offices existing at present and the need of promptness in filing reports, will make it very bad for newspaper people if the present arrangement continues. It is understood that the county commissioners so far as they are concerned will do everything possible to make it easy for newspaper men in this respect, and will give every encouragement to the telegraph companies to offer all the facilities possible.

It is well understood now that Miss Borden will be brought to this city the week before the trial, and if there is any secrecy to be observed it is also well understood that the newspaper men will be around about the time she gets here.

It is stated on the best authority that the prosecution feels confident that the government will make out a strong case.

Court officials of long experience predict that the trial will run through three weeks, and possibly last four.

City Marshal Hilliard of Fall River was in the city yesterday, and for a time was closeted with District Attorney Knowlton, probably mapping out work for the future.

THE 54-HOUR BILL.

Lowell and Lawrence Operatives Fail to Have It Postponed.

Boston, May 10.—The house—82 to 34—agreed to the conference report on the World's fair resolution, a roll call being refused. As agreed to, the delegation will include eight senators and 20 representatives, also all living ex-governors, the governor and 10 of his staff and the executive council.

The bill to compel the burying of electrical wires in Boston was advanced one stage without debate.

The gas investigation committee was given until May 17 to make report.

Mr. Farley of Lowell tried to have the 54-hour bill postponed to next week in order to give time for the Lowell and Lawrence operatives to find where they stood on it, but he could not get the necessary two thirds vote.

Moorefield Story, counsel for the New York & New England railroad, made his closing argument this morning before the railroad committee on the charges of discrimination by the New York, New Haven & Hartford against the New York & New England.

The treasury committee gave a hearing on the bill to give titles to land to the squatters now occupying the state's land at Provincetown.

The Essex county street railway bill was engrossed, with an amendment that the capital shall not exceed $30,000 a mile instead of $35,000, and that no bonds shall be issued without the approval of the railroad commissioners.

HOME MATTERS.

PERSONAL.

Miss Caroline L. Thomas of North Dartmouth was one of the graduates last week from the College of Physicians and Surgeons in Boston. Miss Bernice L. Howland spent a few days in Boston and attended the exercises. Miss Thomas is stopping for the present with her sister, Mrs. Lottie Howland, of Apponegansett.

The approaching marriage is announced of Timothy W. Coakley, the well known lawyer and politician, who defended Charles Tighe when on trial for his life, to Miss Lizzie Smith, a popular young lady of Mt. Pleasant, Boston.

Bishop Cyrus D. Foss, while in attendance at the meeting of the bishops at Evanston, fell down a stairway in the house where he was stopping, and dislocated his left shoulder.

Rev. Dr. William McDonald and wife returned from Los Angeles, Cal., last week, and have gone to their summer home in Waltham. Mrs. McDonald is in feeble health.

Sarah Morris of this city is booked as a cabin passenger on steamship Pavonia, which sails from Boston May 13 for Liverpool.

I. W. Thomas, of the firm of Roberts & Thomas, has returned from a four months business trip to Florida.

James L. Humphrey, Jr., and wife left home yesterday for Chicago and the West.

Stephen D. Peirce is confined to his home by an attack of la grippe.

THE NEW CORDAGE FACTORY.

Work to Begin Upon Mr. Brigham's Return from England.

The new cordage factory to be started in this city, as previously stated in the Standard, will be managed by a corporation having a capital stock of $125,000. Already $85,000 have been subscribed, and as soon as all subscriptions are in the new corporation will meet for organization. Mr. Brigham, who is in England in the interest of the new concern, has secured the right to use the machinery necessary, and the projectors feel confident that they are in possession of a good thing. The factory will be located on the Hawes' farm in Acushnet, the land for which having been donated by the syndicate owning the property. The new concern will manufacture cotton rope, hawsers, etc., and the material used is either cotton, manilla, hemp, silk, vegetables, metal, etc. The buildings will be constructed of brick and wood and similar in design to those in use on Court street. Work will be commenced towards erecting the structures immediately upon Mr. Brigham's arrival home.

LATEST FROM THE BLACK WONDER MINE.

Mr. Frank C. Smith, 47 William street, New Bedford, who is agent for the Black Wonder Gold & Silver Mining company, received word from Mr. Davis, general manager of the company, that a letter had just been received from the superintendent of the mine stating that they were having great success at the mine, and that the ore was of exceeding richness, and further that he had that day made nine assays for both gold and silver with the following results per ton. "No. 1, 15 oz. silver; No. 2, 175 oz. silver, 23 oz. gold; No. 3, 286 oz. silver, 19 oz. gold; No. 4, 180 oz. silver, 20 oz. gold; No. 5, 198 oz. mostly gold; No. 6, 25 oz. mostly gold; No. 7, 4 oz. silver, 22 oz. gold; No. 8, 22½ oz. silver, 2½ oz. gold; No. 9, 23 oz. silver, 99 oz. gold."

The Black Wonder is certainly proving a bonanza mine. With gold worth $20 an ounce and silver 84 cents an ounce and a vein from two to four feet wide of such rich mineral as the above assays show, there is no question but what those who invest in its stock will reap a golden harvest in a few months.

CONDENSED LOCALS.

Joseph Deacon, who is employed at the establishment of J. H. Sherman, corner of Union and Water streets, met with a severe accident yesterday while assisting a teamster to load a stove into his wagon. The stove slipped and caught Mr. Deacon's left hand, tearing the flesh across the back and bruising the tendons badly. F. B. Sistare, who was present with his carriage, took the man to Dr. Bullard's office, where the wound was dressed. The doctor thought no bones were broken, but it was a very bad flesh wound and he was obliged to take many stitches in dressing it.

Ladd's squash is well known, always sells for 15c. We offer it at 13c., 2 cans for 25c. A splendid can pineapple at 15c. can; 3 bottles piccalilly for 25c.; don't pay 25c. for ½ lb. box of cocoa when you can buy a pound of Hasty Lunch cocoa for 30c. Our confectionery department is worthy of your attention. We have something new every day at just about half the regular price. Always step in to the Boston Branch.

At the meeting of the city council finance committee this evening the subjects of providing increased accommodations in the Benjamin, Acushnet avenue and Dartmouth street schoolhouses will probably be presented. Something will probably also be said of the need of another new primary schoolhouse in the south part of the city.

Special bargains in stamped stand covers until we move. Cream atlas, 20c.; old gold, ecru and tan, 38c.; Bedford cord, 33., regular price, 50c.; diagonal, 55c., usual price, 75c.; red denim, 70c.; bureau scarfs, 38c.; doilies, 6, 7, 8 and 10c. These must be sold within 10 days. Miss Nye, Cheapside.

Ceresota flour, the finest, whitest and most economical flour ever produced, our price $5 per barrel; sold in Boston and everywhere else at $5.50. Our only object in making this low price is to introduce it. A. G. Alley, Jr., Boston Branch.

The meeting of the St. Lawrence Catholic union which was held in Ashley's hall last evening was largely attended. A varied musical and literary programme presented by members was thoroughly enjoyed.

The police this morning received a telegram announcing that a Victor bicycle was stolen yesterday from Dr. George W. Bosworth at North Plymouth.

A boat belonging to Cajatan Cassey which was stolen from its moorings just east of the depot last Monday has been returned.

E. C. Brownell invites you to try a dish of the National Pure Food Soup, which is the best.

Royal Arch chapter, F. & A. M., will have a special convocation at Masonic hall this evening.

Be sure and stop in on your way down town and try a dish of the National Pure Food Soups at E. C. Brownell's.

Everybody uses "London Cream Biscuit." They are simply elegant. Your grocer sells them.

Judge for yourself the merits of a dish of the National Pure Food Soup on exhibition at the Fourth Ward Market.

Dr. C. H. Strong of Providence will be at his office in the new bank building tomorrow and Friday till 4 p. m.

A special meeting of the North American Endowment associates will be held tomorrow evening. See special notice.

A dish of the National Pure Food Soup is well worth sampling. E. C. Brownell.

Chiropodist.—Mrs. Williams, 190 Purchase st., Webster block, every Friday.

Do you like soup? Call and try some at E. C. Brownell's.

Take Hood's Sarsaparilla for the blood.

$ $ $ $ DOLLARS CAN'T BUY GOOD TASTE!

VISIT OUR CLOSING SALE —OF— FURNITURE! —AND— Save Money.

Costly Furniture, Expensive Draperies, Elaborate Decorations, do not always produce

A PRETTY ROOM.

A lot of elegant things brought together at random will not do it. The first essential is

HARMONY OF COLOR

in floors, walls and ceilings. Then come the Furniture, Pictures and Ornaments. There are in New Bedford and vicinity

MANY LADIES WHO KNOW

how to bring all these things into harmonious relations, without spending a great deal of money. When in want of CARPETS, FURNITURE, WALL PAPERS AND DRAPERIES, they have learned to go directly to

C. F. WING'S,

where they have no difficulty in selecting from his extensive stock just the design, coloring, style, and quality wanted, at a price in keeping with the correct ideas of

TRUE ECONOMY.

The steady and constantly increasing inflow of orders for Repairing, Renovating, and Re-upholstering old Furniture, is evidence, not only of the skill and good taste of our cabinet makers and upholsterers, but that the important item of cost is most reasonable and satisfactory.

C. F. WING,

34, 36, 38, 40 Purchase St.

WHITING & CO.

SPECIAL BARGAINS

All This Week on

LACE CURTAINS, RUGS and PORTIERES.

500 pairs of Lace Curtains to be sold at lower prices than they were ever sold. See our $1, $1.50 and $2 curtains.

We are closing out all of our Rugs under price. See our Hall, Parlor and Dining room Rugs and get our prices.

10 pairs of Portieres left, to be closed out at same low prices, $3.95 a pair. Do not fail to see them.

We want you to see our stock of Sheets and Pillow Slips, made of fine Cotton, and all made well.

WHITING & CO.

Men Who Won't

Wear Ready-made Clothing

Will

Wear our Blue Serge Suits.

Why?

Because they are ready made in name and price, not in fact.

They are built by tailors who know how to build good clothes; consequently they are well made and fit better than a cheap custom-made suit.

We have two qualities of Blue Serges—one at $15 and one at $18, cut into both single and double-breasted sack suits, which we guarantee to be absolutely fast in color, perfect in fit and style and thoroughly well made.

J. & W. R. WING & CO.,

133 Union Street.

THE CRESCENT!

22 Purchase St.

SHIRT WAISTS!

Print Shirt Waists, 50c.
Percale Waists, 75c.
White Lawn Waists, $1.00.
Sateen Dark Waists, $1.25.
Fancy Waists, $1.50.
Embroidered Chambray, pink and blue, $3.00.

Try "Crescent" Hosiery and you'll buy "Crescent" Hosiery for the Dye of "Crescent" Hosiery is warranted.

The Popular Tan Shades for Ladies and Children; also a good assortment of Black, at fair prices.

SUMMER CORSETS.

A Bargain for 50c.
Thompson's $1.00.
C. B. a la Spirite, 75c., $1.25.
P. D. Summer Corsets, $2.00,
Ferris Ventilated Waists for Ladies and Misses.

SUMMER VESTS.

A Good Variety

Prices 10c., 12 1-2c., 15c., 20c., 25c. and 39c.

Lisle Thread, White and Ecru, 50c.

Infants' and Children's Cloaks.

Fine assortment of dresses, both white and gingham.

THE CRESCENT!

22 Purchase St.

THE REPUBLICAN STANDARD,

Issued this morning contains all the local and general news of the past week, including arraignment of Lizzie Borden at the superior court in this city, charged with killing her father and step-mother, pleaded not guilty to the several indictments, little trace of suffering in her appearance, and showed the same stolid spirit in court, the announcement of date of trial, Chief Justice Mason to preside and Justices Blodgett and Dewey will sit with him; annual meeting of the New Bedford Day Nursery, reports of the secretary and treasurer and election of officers for the ensuing year; annual meeting of the Orphans Home, reports of secretary and treasurer and election of officers for the ensuing year; meetings of the board of public works, Superintendent Drake re-elected for another year, unexpected developments, interesting discussion on street railway hearings, Hillman street to be graded at once, sewer construction discussed, work to be given out by contract, with other important business; special meeting of the board of aldermen at which Paul J. Oesting and Daniel H. Harrington secure licenses, also Wamsutta, Washington Social and Bohemian clubs get licenses; neighborhood convention with the Congregational church, at Rochester; complete and illustrated description of the Standard's new type machine plant, a complete revolution in the art of composition, a new dress of type every day, marvelous evidence of the progress of the age, three times as quick work as that of hand compositors; the finding of Eugene Brightman's body, one of the Cuttyhunk heroes; the close of the carriage makers' strike, the manufacturers come to the terms made by the men; personnel of the church choirs, singers who will furnish music for the coming year, changes and reorganizations that transpire; another disaster at Cuttyhunk, schooner Wm. Flint hauled off by tug Volunteer and towed to this port, story of the rescue and heroic conduct of the Cuttyhunkers; Isaac F. B. Perry of Rochester thrown from his carriage and killed in Wareham by a runaway horse; superior, probate and district court reports; Farm, Garden and Home; Bible lesson for next Sunday; the electrocution of Carlyle W. Harris for the murder of his wife, Helen Potts Harris; correspondence; with editorials, ship news, markets, miscellaneous reading matter, etc.

For sale by all newsdealers in this city, and at our counters, in wrappers ready for mailing, at 4 cents per copy.

PLYMOUTH AND BAY CONFERENCE.

Twenty Sixth Annual Meeting of the Unitarians.

The 26th annual meeting of the Plymouth and Bay conferences of Unitarian churches was held at the Second Unitarian church, Rev. C. T. Billings pastor, at South Hingham, yesterday. The exercises included devotional service, led by Rev. Watson Weed of Scituate; reading of the secretary's report; reports from the various churches in the district; election of officers; essay by Rev. F. B. Hornbrooke of Newton, subject, "Is the Church a Luxury or a Necessity?"

At the afternoon session there were addresses by Mrs. Kate Gannett Wells, Rev. D. M. Wilson, and Grindall Reynolds of Boston.

The officers chosen for the ensuing year are:

President — Mr. Swaine of North Easton.

Vice Presidents—Rev. Joseph Osgood of Cohasset, C. D. Nash of Whitman.

Treasurer—William S. Danforth of Plymouth.

Secretary — Rev. John W. Day of Hingham.

Executive Committee—Rev. C. T. Billings, Rev. C. Y. De Normandie, Rev. J. W. Quimby, Eben L. Ripley and C. A. Turner.

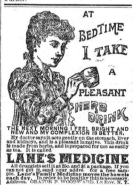

ITEMIZED ACCOUNTS.

Lively Discussion by City Council Committee on Finance.

The finance committee of the city council held a meeting last evening and continued its deliberations until nearly 1 o'clock this morning. Mayor Brock presided, and there were present Alderman Crapo and President Hart and Messrs. Holmes and Sherman of the common council.

The last hour of the session was an interesting one, and Mr. Holmes remonstrated against the transfer of $128 to the account of the city toolhouse and workshop which the auditor said was necessary.

Mr. Holmes said he had remonstrated again and again against the bills to this account, which had already overrun the appropriation made for the entire year. The purpose of the itemized appropriation scheme was to regulate the expenditures. He didn't believe the board of public works was conforming to the order of the city council. It was charging to the city toolhouse and workshop account items which should be charged to macadam and other accounts.

Mr. Holmes asked some questions for information on this point. He failed to receive a reply that satisfied him, and remarked that "the advantage of adding the mayor and president of the common council to the board of public works for the enlightenment of the city council was quite apparent."

Mr. Hart replied: "I have not investigated Mr. Drake's system of bookkeeping."

"Why don't you investigate it, then?" demanded Mr. Holmes, with warmth.

Mr. Hart said he doubted if he would understand a great deal more about the matter if he made an investigation than he did at present.

Mr. Crapo declared that itemized accounts have been demonstrated to be a failure.

Mr. Holmes thought it had been demonstrated that they were a pretty weak lot to allow things to go on in this way.

Mr. Hart understood a stump puller was being made in the workshop.

Mr. Holmes thought there was a gang of men in the shop who must be kept busy even if they had to "scour the anchor." Money is being spent for tulips which might be used for sewers at Nash's point.

Mr. Sherman thought the re-election of Mr. Drake as superintendent of the board of public works was an indorsement of the system.

Mr. Crapo considered this remark "rather a hard clip at the board of public works," and this pleased Mr. Holmes.

Mr. Holmes would like to refuse to make the transfer to watch the effect and at this suggestion Mr. Hart promptly moved that it be refused. Mr. Holmes seconded the motion, and it was unanimously carried.

As this vote would deprive the laborers of their wages, Mr. Holmes was willing to recede if the mayor and Mr. Hart would agree that the labor bill in the account would be itemized to correspond with blanks furnished the superintendent.

A motion made by Mr. Holmes that the sum be transferred from the macadam account, instead of from the private works account, was carried.

It soon appeared that this week's pay roll had been approved by the mayor and Superintendent Drake, and that it would be paid this week, although it would not be approved by the board until next Monday evening.

Mr. Holmes was amazed at this statement.

The mayor said this course seemed necessary because the meeting nights did not come right this week to approve the bills before they were paid.

Mr. Holmes thought if this were true the meeting nights should be changed.

Mr. Holmes asked Mayor Brock to consider whether he could justify this course in signing the pay roll before it was approved by the board with his oath.

Then Mr. Hart and the mayor explained the manner in which the board of public works approved bills. Mr. Hart said the board waited until nearly 12 o'clock, when every one was busy, then one man called off the vouchers which another checked on the pay roll. He doubted if any one knew anything about the bills excepting Mr. Drake.

Mr. Holmes declared such a system to be rotten.

By and by last week's pay roll was brought in, and Colonel Hart detected an item of $27 for an engineering account.

Inasmuch as the engineering department of the board has been abolished, every one wanted an explanation and nobody could give it.

Mayor Brock said he approved the bill without noticing the item. He promised to inquire into it.

In the course of the discussion Mr. Holmes complained of the elaborate plant of the public works department.

"Mr. Drake's annual report details the need of another shed at the city yard," said Mr. Holmes. "I had an idea that I knew what a 'shed' was, but I find that the estimated cost of this 'shed' is nearly $10,000. I guess my idea and Mr. Drake's don't quite agree."

Mayor Brock brought up the fee of $2 which is paid to the city messenger at each meeting of the city council, and asked if the committee considered that he could approve it in view of the ordinance which requires that the messenger shall give his entire time to the city at a fixed salary.

It was finally agreed that this was a matter for the board of aldermen to decide.

Superintendent Hatch and Mr. Howland of the expenditure committee of the school committee were before the board, explaining the necessity for additional appropriations for the use of the department.

The statistics showing the crowded conditions of the schools were presented. It was stated that a new building would be needed in the Linden street district and that Fourth Street school is inadequate. At the Acushnet Avenue school an addition was recommended which would give a three-story building with 13 rooms. Mr. Slack estimates the expense of the changes at $20,000, not including the heating. The Benjamin school is over-crowded, and the fitting of another room at Dartmouth Street school, at an estimated expense of about $1,375, was recommended. The wishes of the committee concerning the establishment of a manual training department, which will require an additional appropriation, was also set forth. A report on the above will be presented at the meeting of the city council tonight.

BAY STATE AT THE WORLD'S FAIR.

Curiosities Contained in the Old John Hancock House.

The exhibit of revolutionary antiquities prepared by the state of Massachusetts for the World's fair is a remarkably interesting one. The state headquarters building, John Hancock House, is a fine piece of architecture.

The front hall on the second floor contains many Nantucket relics belonging to Mrs. C. P. Hills, a descendant of the celebrated Coffin family, and to S. B. Phinney of Barnstable. There is a card table used on Nantucket island in 1790, an old chair which belonged to the Coffin family and is dated 1775, and an altar chair from the Barnstable Congregational church which bears 1780 as its date.

Mrs. Otis Washburn of Taunton has contributed many interesting old autographs and relics of this collection. The cases contain some old-fashioned dolls, great hoopskirts and the clinging draperies which were in vogue in the empire era. Poke bonnets are there also, and each case is surmounted by a bandbox covered with bright wall paper of Dolly Varden design.

BORDEN HATCHETS AGAIN.

This Time It is Probably a New Discovery of an Old Weapon.

The news to the effect that a hatchet had been discovered in Fall River and that it might be the weapon with which the Borden murders were commited, created more or less curiosity in Fall River as to which hatchet had now come to the surface, says the Providence Journal. Ever since the tragedy there has been no end of hatchets, but as nearly as can be ascertained, none of them has satisfied all the claims made for it. There was a "very sharp" hatchet with which wood for a camping party at Marion was to be chopped, and there was a hatchet in the cellar of the Borden house which looked as if it had been scraped with ashes. Then the authorities unearthed an instrument, the handle of which was said to be covered with blood stains. This axe was subjected to an examination which seemed to confirm suspicions, until Professor Wood testified that it was free from anything that indicated that it had been used for an illegitimate purpose. After that there followed the story of a flat-headed, mysterious kind of a hatchet, with no handle, which had been found by Officer Midley. This blade, it is understood, was on exhibition when the grand jury met and it has thus far figured as a possible instrument of destruction, though the prosecution did not claim that no further search was necessary. Yesterday the New Bedford dispatch was shown to City Marshal Hilliard, who did not appear to be surprised by the information it contained, and who said that perhaps Dr. Dolan could offer some explanation. Dr. Dolan has concluded to do all his talking on the witness stand, and the impression prevails that the discovery is not deserving of very serious consideration. At all events there have been no hatchets found in Fall River of late, and, if the police are to be believed, they completed their work on the case weeks ago, and have long been ready for trial. If they haven't the axe which is wanted, they do not expect to come across it at this late day, and considerable allowance will be made on developments that crop up outside of the court room.

The Defense in the Coming Trial.

A gentleman who has closely followed the testimony in the Borden case and whose profession has made him familiar with value of evidence, says the Fall River Globe, said last evening that he expected that the defense would rely entirely on the inability of the prosecution to prove to the satisfaction of a jury that the prisoner committed the deed of which she is accused.

In other words, there is nothing except denial, which in the main, is unsupported, to offset the points which the government will make, and by which it means to demonstrate that its position is correct. In the opinion of the gentleman in question, the weakest spot in the prosecution lies in the failure to show an adequate motive.

Thus far, nothing has been gleaned from Bridget Sullivan, who lived in the family for a considerable period, which would indicate that the relations among the members of the household were strained to such a degree as to warrant the supposition that the unpleasantness would result in murder. All may not have been harmonious, but so far as evidence goes, there was no strife bitter enough for the brutal butchery.

There have been reports without number floating around on the outside, relating to Miss Borden's hatred of her stepmother, but unless the grand jury heard more than has yet been made public in court, there is nothing very damaging against the defendant under this head. In fact, Miss Borden has herself furnished the prosecution with most of its evidence on the subject, inasmuch as she admitted frankly that she was not on good enough terms with her stepmother to call her mother.

The only alternate in the matter of motive, is to plead avarice, and that is generally regarded as dangerous ground on which to proceed. Mr. Borden may not have been generous, but his daughter did not want for the necessaries of life, and in families innumerable it might be contended that the purse was as tightly closed. Miss Borden might have desired a more liberal allowance, but it may be difficult to convince twelve men that she would use an axe to obtain it; she may have objected to her stepmother receiving any portion of the estate, but it has not appeared that her objections were so strong as to prompt her to murder.

It is possible, of course, that the government has witnesses who will testify that the prisoner was greatly incensed against Mrs. Borden, and it is no secret that there is such testimony, but it has not yet been produced either at the inquest or the preliminary hearing.

There is another point which has not been argued in full, though it will undoubtedly receive attention later on, and that is the statement of John V. Morse to the effect that Mr. Borden told him he intended to make a will, and that he meant to leave property to certain charities. Mr. Morse may, or may not have reported this interview, but if he did, it could be urged that the decision on Mr. Borden's part, contributed to the fatal termination of the family feud which existed.

A. M. E. ZION CONFERENCE.

Election of Officers and Other Business of the Session in Boston.

At the session of the New England conference of the A. M. E. Zion church in Boston yesterday, the election of officers for the conference resulted as follows: Secretary, Rev. J. B. Colbert; assistant secretary, Rev. J. F. Waters; compiler, Rev. G. L. Blackwell; reporter of the Star of Zion, Rev. W. B. Bowen; marshals, Rev. J. H. Young, J. S. Johnson; postmaster, Rev. N. J. Young.

Bishop Hood, who presided, read the list of standing committees.

The Daughters of the Conference served a collation in the vestry of the church after the morning session.

At the opening of the afternoon session Bishop Hood made a stirring address, after which collections from the various societies of the church, for church work, were received.

Bishop Hood explained the educational work at Tuscaloosa, Ala., which is making itself felt in that locality.

Rev. E. George Biddle moved that all sums raised for educational purposes be used for such purposes only.

Miss Eliza Gardiner spoke on "New England's Position in Missionary Work."

Letters were read from Editor Dancy of the A. M. E. Zion Quarterly, J. W. Allsop, general steward A. M. E. Zion church, St. Luke's A. M. E. Zion church, Franklin, Va.

A recess was taken at 4 30 until 8 o'clock, to enable the visiting clergymen and delegates to see the city.

The evening session included music by the choir, Rev. Mr. Manley and Blind Tom No. 2, the annual sermon by Rev. Mr. Fenderson of Cambridge, address of welcome by Mr. Jacob W. Powell, address on the part of the Sunday school by Mr. Philip J. Allston, and responses by Rev. George W. Clinton, Rev. J. B. Colbert, Rev. Mr. Blois and Rev. J. F. Waters.

BARNSTABLE COUNTY.

Two cows owned by Joel B. Cahoon of Harwich were badly injured by being bitten by dogs 30th ult. Mr. Cahoon was awarded $25 by the selectmen. The dogs were owned by R. F. Hopkins of South Brewster and Antone P. Lucas of Harwich.

TIVERTON.

At a meeting of the town council a large number of bills were ordered paid, and Edwin R. Short, Daniel C. Durfee and Philip Sanford were appointed special constables. Henry Durfee, Jonathan Hart, George F. Nickerson were appointed justices of the peace.

SHOULD BE REMOVED.

Senator Butler After the Medfield Asylum Trustees.

In the senate Wednesday Mr. Butler of Bristol declared that the trustees of the Medfield asylum ought to be removed because they had subverted the will of the last legislature.

When the measure came up appropriating $200,000 additional funds to finish the asylum, whose estimated cost originally was but $500,000, Mr. Butler criticised the commissioners for going on as they had, and was inclined to move to substitute a bill to remove them from office.

Mr. Lawrence admitted that the commissioners had been derelict in not sooner calling attention to the facts in the case, but the state is held legally to their acts and contracts.

Mr. Stevens of Worcester held that the report of the treasury committee was practically an indorsement of the commissioners, and that the state is to get its money's worth in the buildings they now have under process of construction.

Senator Butler said it was a mistake to keep in office men not fitted to do the work. If the governor would not remove them it was about time the legislature dealt with them. When the bill was up originally the governor blocked it for two or three years on account of a fad for trustees instead of a commissioner, though nobody could see the difference. If it had not been for this pet theory on the part of the executive the asylum would have been built before now. The governor delayed it for two or three years, when the asylum was greatly needed for the chronic insane, who were suffering from insufficient accommodations.

Mr. Butler said this was purely a question of business, and as the commissioners have admitted that they have subverted the will of the legislature, and that they should have done differently, they ought to be removed without any regard to politics. Mr. Stevens denied that the trustees had exceeded their appropriation. Mr. Butler replied that the contracts call for an expense of $700,000 when only $500,000 was authorized. Mr. Stevens said the appropriation was made on insufficient estimates, and the trustees had been obliged to make the changes causing this excess over the appropriation. The trustees are honest, conscientious men, who have given their best service to the state. Mr. Reed of Middlesex also criticised the course of the trustees. Mr. Butler said he might want to move a reconsideration tomorrow, and put in an amendment embodying his views. The bill was then engrossed.

GONE WEST.

William Fisher Takes a Sudden Departure from His Home in North Abington.

North Abington, May 11.—William Fisher, a well-known young man, disappeared suddenly from this village last Saturday night. He was engaged in the kerosene oil business, acting as agent for Boston firms, and it is alleged that a shortage in his accounts was the cause of his hasty departure. He was a young man of no very bad habits, and to all appearances was doing a successful business.

Saturday morning he collected some of his clothing and wrapped it up, representing to his wife that he was going to take the bundle to the laundry. He then harnessed his horse and drove to Rockland, where he collected money from customers and sold the team. Returning at dusk, he kissed his wife and two children and left the house, stating that he would return shortly. He took the 7 45 p. m. train, and it is supposed that he has gone west to seek his fortune.

Mrs. Fisher says a month or more ago he talked of going to Michigan, where a friend offered him a position, but she persuaded him not to accept. He apparently had given up the notion, but for the past week had been uneasy and restless. He was doing fairly well in the oil business and to her knowledge was not indebted to any great extent to Boston firms. She received a letter from him, which he wrote in Boston Sunday night, saying that he was going to New York, and then west, where he intended to travel as salesman for an oil firm.

Fisher came here from Brockton some three years ago, and previous to starting in the oil business was employed as clerk in a grocery store here.

A HOME WEDDING.

Chester T. Cornish Weds a Daughter of Hon. W. O. Clough of Nashua.

Nashua, N. H., May 11.—The residence of Hon. W. O. Clough, 17 Terrouse street, was the scene of an event of a happy nature yesterday afternoon, the occasion being the marriage of Chester T. Cornish, night editor of the Lowell Morning Mail, a son of Ivory S. Cornish of New Bedford, to Miss Charlotte M. Clough, eldest daughter of Hon. W. W. Clough, associate police judge of this city.

The wedding was a strictly private one, only the parents and immediate friends of the contracting parties being present. Rev. William Hall Marland performed the marriage ceremony.

The happy couple were the recipients of a very handsome and costly array of presents from their many friends. Both are well and favorably known in this city. Mr. Cornish resided in Nashua about three years, in which time he was city editor of the Nashua Gazette for over two years, and later was city editor of the New Hampshire Republican until that paper went out of existence. The bride is a very popular and accomplished young lady. She was a teacher in the Main street school of this city for several terms. The bride and groom will take a short wedding tour, after which they will reside at 46 Elm street, Lowell.

NEW QUARTERS LEASED.

Business Transacted by Republican State Committee.

The meeting of the Republican state committee was held in Boston yesterday, and it was voted to accept the resignation of Walter Clifford of New Bedford as a member of the committee. The reason given for his resignation was that has so much private business that he cannot give any further time to the committee. Another vacancy was declared in the committee by the death of Dr. Hodges of Nahant. The committee was also notified that there had been leased a suite of six rooms in the Albion building, No. 1 Beacon street, Boston, for future headquarters. It is expected that the rooms will be ready for occupancy about the first of August. Chairman Winslow, who has been sick for quite a while, presided at the meeting.

LITTLE COMPTON.

Nathaniel Church has been awarded the contract for carrying the mails to and from Little Compton to Tiverton station, to take effect the 1st of July.

One of the largest barns in the town has been erected for Miss Edith Church. Its main length is 100 feet, with a frontage of 56 feet, the L 62 by 35. The east main barn is 38 by 56. The carriage room is 26 by 8 by 38 by 4 in depth. The driveway is 16 feet 6 inches. The room for washing carriages 6 by 8 by 19 by 7. The harness room is 9 by 11 by 20 by 3. The horse stables are 36 by 35, to accommodate eight horses. The cow barn is 29 by 35, capable of holding six cattle stanchions. The haymow 40 by 60. There are 57 windows in the upper part, and 20 windows in the cellar. The cupola is covered with copper and ornamented with the old King Philip weather vane. The architect is S. D. Kelley of Boston. Two hundred and nine thousand feet of hard pine has been used in its construction.

TAUNTON.

The barn of Miss Myra Eldredge, together with four tons of hay, one horse and some farming tools, was burned Wednesday afternoon. Loss estimated at $2,500; insured.

A REPLY TO MR. ROSS.

Rev. John Brown Writes Still Another Communication.

To the Editor of the Standard:

I beg to say a word or two in reply to Mr. Ross' recent communication. I would have taken no notice of it were it not for the misstatements which he makes in it with so much coolness. There are none so blind as those who will not see. I am, therefore, perfectly willing to leave outside competition with the logic of future events.

As for his questions I will say that I advocated 58 hours for women and children last year, and I do so still, as the right period of time for them to be confined in our mills. This is the ideal standard, but as I said last year I say now, it is to be procured as circumstances will allow. If the product of our mills were all consumed in this state, I would advocate strong measures at once in behalf of our women and children, but as our mill products have to go out to other states, where the labor of women and children working from 60 to 72 hours weekly comes into competition with it, I hold that the ideal is possible for this industry as it is affected by the same industry elsewhere. I hold, also, that any attempt to procure the ideal, or any part of it, is often very seriously hindered by rash and foolish attempts at the impossible. This is what is now being done and it is going to put further benefits back a long ways. I last year felt that a reduction to or towards the ideal ought to be made. There was still a probability that the tariff protection would be continued for at least a number of years, the cloth market was good and the outlook was hopeful. This year my judgment tells me that as a step forward has but recently been made, matters should be allowed to regulate themselves; the operatives should consider the changed circumstances, and instead of insisting on taking another step at once, help prepare favorable conditions for another step. I have stated this so often and tried, in the simplest language possible, to make Ross understand it, that I am surprised to see him, and others of his class, rushing into print with indecent haste to proclaim my condemnation, as if it amounted to a row of beans to the public what they might think of me. As for Mr. Ross he is either defective in his moral or his intellectual perceptions, for he so misrepresents what I plainly stated to him on the matter in dispute, that I believe it is only a waste of time to take further notice of him. His reference to what I said on the low condition of some of the poor whites among the mountains of Tennessee before and after the war and applying this to the whole of the southern whites is positively dishonest. He must know that a half truth is often a whole lie.

One thing more, Mr. Ross is a member of the labor committee of the legislature. Now I always understood that it was the duty of such to weigh carefully what might be said by both petitioners and remonstrants. Ross is evidently such a one-sided man that he can only see one side, hence he claims that I have my arguments from the remonstrants. I say in reply that this is a falsehood, and he knows it, as I showed him more than once that my present ideas regarding the south have been well known in Fall River since I came there. Why listen to remonstrants at all? The thing for Mr. Ross and all others interested in the discussion is to lay aside worthless reports about what this or that man said about southern competition and go and see for themselves how it is. One half the expenses for Mr. Ross is provided for if he goes. If he will not go, he should shut up at once.

To your labor unions of every sort in New Bedford I would say that they are simply making themselves ridiculous by their condemnatory resolutions. They had better wait till they see how I do vote on this bill before they go into the denouncing business. It is indecent just yet while the bill is under consideration. Politics! politics!! politics!!!

J. BROWN.

LEWISTON SPINNERS AT WORK.

Trouble with the Hill Manufacturing Company Settled.

Lewiston, Me., May 11.—The trouble between the mule spinners and the agent of the Hill Manufacturing company of this city has been finally and amicably settled. A meeting of the Mule Spinners union was held recently at which a special committee was appointed to confer with Agent Pennell in regard to their alleged grievances. Mr. Pennell met the committee and the whole matter was discussed very carefully. The committee reported that Mr. Pennell had lived up to his agreement made with the mule spinners in every particular and that the spinners were not justified in the action taken by them. The spinners resumed work this morning. The result is very satisfactory. It is pleasant for Mr. Pennell to be fully sustained in the position taken by him and a credit to the spinners that having seen their error they so manfully acknowledge it.

The Evening Standard.

ESTABLISHED FEBRUARY, 1880.]

NEW BEDFORD, FRIDAY, MAY 12, 1893.

TWO CENTS.

HASKELL & TRIPP.

Those heavy, handsome "Point de Gene" laces.

To get such beauties *below wholesale cost* is a rare happening indeed. But that's exactly what hundreds of wide-awake buyers have been doing here for two days past.

Fashionable laces for dress trimmings.

Now 29c. a yd., worth 39 to 60c
Now 39c. a yd., worth 62c.to $1

A list of attractions for Saturday, arranged for quick readers.

HOSIERY.

Richelieu ribbed silk hose, all sizes for women, 75c. a pair, in russet tan and brown, also fancy colors. This eclipses any offering we ever made.

Drop stitch fine cotton hose in every nice shade of tan and leather, 25c. a pair.

Tan and leather shades for children, 25c. a pair, narrow ribbed, very durable.

Men's black socks, front embroidered with silk in small figures, 25c. a pair.

GLOVES.

Gauntlet lisles, 25c. a pair.

Extra quality fast black taffetas, 25c. a pair.

Four-button tan shades kid gloves, 59c. a pair.

Fancy greens and heliotrope kid gloves with four large pearl buttons, $2 a pair.

UNDERWEAR.

100 dozen women's ribbed cotton undervests, 7c. each.

Pink, blue and ecru Jersey undervests, 25c. each.

Men's Shetland mixed summer merino shirts and drawers, 37½c. Camel's hair, 50c. and $1.

PARASOLS.

Complete stock of the novelties of the season. See our window display.

Special line of changeables, surahs and printed India silk parasols, with and without ruffles, worth from $2.50 to $4. Your choice $1.89.

BELTS AND BAGS.

Novelties in leather and metal belts, 25c. to $1.50.

Cloth and leather shopping bags, 50c. to $1.50.

World's Fair shawl straps, 17c., 25c., 50c.

SHOES.

Brown shoes are correct for the season now opening. We can supply handsomely finished russet leather footwear for women, misses and children at prices that will surprise you unless you've been a customer of this department.

BOOKS.

Ten cents for a well-printed, paper-bound novel. Over 3000 in stock today. *Your favorite author* among them, most likely.

CANDY.

We sell exquisite Chocolates, Bonbons, Marshmallows and a great variety of "sweets" at lower prices than *strictly first-class, pure confectionery* is usually obtained. *Try ours.*

HASKELL & TRIPP,
Department Stores,
Purchase and William Streets.

THE BORDEN MURDERS.

Politics Connected with World Famous Case.

Pillsbury for Governor and Knowlton for Attorney-General.

One Believes the Prisoner is Innocent the Other That She is Guilty.

(Special Dispatch.)

Boston, May 12.—The Record had a half column story today about the Lizzie Borden case. Beyond intimating that Attorney General Pillsbury does not believe her guilty and saying that District Attorney Knowlton does, the only news is in regard to the politics connected with the case.

It announces Mr. Knowlton's candidacy for the attorney generalship in the following manner: "Mr. Pillsbury will not be a candidate for re-election as attorney general. He has communicated that decision to many friends at the bar and it is final. Of course, this is interpreted to mean that he will be in the field for governor, and of that no one in this vicinity (meaning New Bedford) has any doubt, or that he will receive the practically unanimous support of the delegates in the convention from this part of the state. He has always been popular in this section, and as against any one else suggested he will be the choice.

Anyway, Mr. Knowlton will be in the field for attorney general, and his long and successful career as district attorney will help him greatly. His opponent will probably be Mr. Moody of Haverhill and United States District Attorney Allen of Lynn. They are both from Essex county and it will probably unite in support of Mr. Allen. Between him and Mr. Knowlton the position will probably rest. As neither Essex nor Bristol has had a nomination on the state ticket for years the fight will be a pretty one. The people down here have so often seen Mr. Crapo set aside by the state convention that in case Knowlton is turned down they are likely to be very tired on election day."

THE CAMPANIA WINS.

Fastest Time on Record in the Great Ocean Race.

Queenstown, May 12.—The new Cunard line steamer Campania, which sailed from New York for Liverpool May 6, arrived at Queenstown at half-past 9 this morning, having made the passage from Sandy Hook to Queenstown in 5 days, 17 hours and 42 minutes, the quickest passage eastward yet made by any steamer. The passengers cheered enthusiastically upon coming into the harbor, and the crew of the Campania showed much jubilation over their victory.

The Campania passed the Paris, of the American line, when 109 miles east of Sandy Hook. The Campania had passed the Sandy Hook lightship at 11 13 a. m. Saturday, May 6, and the Paris had passed the lightship at 10 58 a. m. The Paris made the best time to Fire Island, but the Campania improved as her machinery got thoroughly at work. Passing the Paris, the Campania did not sight her again during the voyage to Queenstown, although the ocean track for Southampton does not diverge from that to Queenstown for about 1,800 miles.

From passing Sandy Hook until noon of Saturday the Campania made 429 miles; during the next 24 hours, ending Sunday noon, 481 miles; during the next 24 hours, ending Monday noon, 490 miles; during the 24 hours ending Tuesday noon 474 miles; during the 24 hours ending Wednesday noon 517 miles; during the 24 hours ending Thursday noon 495 miles.

The best previous eastward record was that of the American liner New York, 5 days, 19 hours, 57 minutes, as against the Campania's 5 days, 17 hours and 42 minutes.

The Cunard company has made arrangements to land the passengers of the Campania on the arrival of the steamer. This is unprecedented in the history of the trans-Atlantic travel. The office of the company is thronged with excited people betting whether the passengers by the Campania will be landed in Liverpool before or after the passengers on the Paris will be landed in Southampton.

ASSETS AND LIABILITIES.

Condition and Liabilities of Several Suspended Concerns.

Sioux City, Ia., May 12.—E. H. Hubbard, assignee of the Union Loan & Trust company, the Hedges Trust company and D. T. Hedges, yesterday filed his estimates of the value of the assets schedules in the three assignments. The Union Loan & Trust company's assets are placed at $1,351,574, as against an original estimate of $1,468,038. The company's liabilities are placed at $7,000,000. The assets of D. T. Hedges, originally placed at $2,247,000, are cut down to $307,577. His liabilities are placed at $1,022,000. The Hedges Trust company estimates its assets at $4,475,000. The assignee cuts the sum down to $183,018. The company's liabilities are $250,000. The discrepancies in both cases lie between the face value of the securities and the assignee's estimate of their values.

Yesterday W. M. Thompson was appointed receiver for the Sioux City Engine works. The failure is charged to the Sioux National bank, which failed to give credit for $35,000. The assets of the company are placed at $231,000 and its liabilities at $200,000.

San Jose, Cal., May 12.—The liabilities of the Santa Clara bank, which failed yesterday, are stated to be $3,000,000. Assurances had been given by the officers of the bank that depositors would be paid in full, but it is now believed that settlements must be effected at very much less.

Wilmington, Del., May 12.—The liabilities of E. R. Robinson & Co. of the suspended banking firm are placed at $320,000 and the assets at $204,000. S. J. Willey, supreme master of the exchequer of the Sir Knights of Pythias, says that he had a large amount of the order's own money in the bank, but that it is fully covered by collateral. He does not say what the amount is, but it is placed as high as $70,000. Willey is mayor of the city.

THE BECKWITH WILL.

His Niece in Fairhaven Bequeathed the House she Occupies.

Taunton, May 12.—By the will of the late Henry T. Beckwith of Providence $2,000,000 is disbursed. The will is probated in Taunton because there was property located in Swansey and some in Fairhaven. Among the bequests the sum of $5,000 each are given to the American Church Missionary society of the United States, located in New York; and to the Evangelical Education society of the Protestant Episcopal church. The Rhode Island Episcopal State Convention, for missionary and other purposes, gets $3,000. His niece, Alice B. Train of Fairhaven, gets the house now occupied by her there.

WEATHER INDICATIONS.

Thunder Showers.

Boston, May 12.—Local forecast for New England until Saturday night: Fair today; showers Saturday, probably thunder showers; continued warm today; cooler Saturday and southwest winds.

Washington, May 12.—For the 24 hours from 8 a. m. today: For New England generally fair, followed by light showers tonight or Saturday morning in northern portion of Vermont; south winds and slightly cooler on the southern New England coast.

AN OLD WHALING MASTER DEAD.

Capt. Isaac Chase Daggett Expires at His Home on the Vineyard.

(Special Dispatch.)

Vineyard Haven, May 12.—Captain Isaac Chase Daggett, who has been sick for some time with a cancer, died at his residence on William street, yesterday. He was born in Tisbury, near what is now the village of West Tisbury, a little more than 77 years ago. He married in March, 1844, Eliza Robinson, who with an only son survives him. The son, Francis L. Daggett, resides in St. George, Utah, where he has for many years. Captain Daggett was much respected. As a young man he followed the sea, which he continued until about 20 years ago, since which time he has lived a retired life. His first voyage was aboard whaling ship Emerald, Captain Joseph Dexter, of the Vineyard, sailing from Salem, in which he made two voyages. He commanded ship Java for ten years; his last vessel being the Oil of Montreal, running between New York and Liverpool. Since having lived retired, he has served the town of Tisbury as a selectman, assessor and overseer of the poor for four years. The interment takes place at 2 p. m. today at Oak Grove cemetery here.

BARNSTABLE COUNTY TEACHERS.

Annual Convention Being Held at Buzzards Bay.

Buzzards Bay, May 12.—The annual convention of the Barnstable County Teachers' association was held here today. The morning session opened at 9 in Franklin Hall, 125 teachers being present. M. C. Waterhouse delivered an address of welcome, after which H. E. Harriman discussed the benefits of "Topic Teaching." Elmer L. Curtis spoke in an instructive manner on "Nature study in the primary grades," and I. A. DeWolf of Wellfleet on "Lower school work in preparing for the high school." J. W. McDonald, agent of the state board of education, occupied the rest of the morning session in an able and instructive paper on "The meaning and use of graduation."

OBITUARY.

Death of General S. C. Armstrong, Founder of Hampton, Va., Normal Institute.

Richmond, Va., May 12.—General S. C. Armstrong, founder and superintendent of the normal institute at Hampden, died last evening, aged 56.

Burglary at Bourne.

Buzzards Bay, May 12.—The Old Colony passenger depot at Bourne was broken into early this morning and a small quantity of tickets stolen.

HOME MATTERS.

EX-GOV. ROBINSON AT THE JAIL.

Has a Two Hours' Conference with Lizzie Borden at Taunton.

Ex-Governor Robinson was in Taunton yesterday and visited Taunton jail, where he had a two hours' conference with Lizzie Borden in relation to her case.

Those who are acquainted with the accommodations at the woman's building at the county jail in this city are much interested in where Keeper Hunt will place Miss Borden. While awaiting trial female prisoners must occupy cells in the women's prison, and as it is seldom that women of refinement are lodged in jail everything has run along smoothly. The last instance of lodging a woman in jail where there was fault found with the accommodations was during the three days' confinement of Dr. Ann Chase, who was compelled to occupy one of the cramped up cells for female prisoners serving time. She objected to her quarters, but she remained there just the same until released on bail. Will Lizzie A. Borden be assigned one of these cells? It is thought by some that the room formerly occupied by the matron will be fitted for her use. This room is located at the north end of the women's prison, and is apart from the prisoners. The room is of small size. If she is not assigned to this room it may be decided to place her in one of the old hospital cells on the third tier at the south end of the women's prison. These cells, and there are two of them, are roomy, being about eight feet square, and are well ventilated. The floors are carpeted.

THE STRIKING BACKBOYS

Still Out and as Obdurate and Confident as Ever.

There is no change in the labor situation at the north mill. All the strikers are still out and appear as determined as ever. They gathered at the mill gate this morning and waited for a time to see if they were to receive notice that their demands were granted, and failing to receive such notice, held a short meeting and then dispersed.

The youngsters are jubilant and claim that the backboys in Wamsutta mills No. 1 and 6 have promised to join them Monday, providing the concessions they are demanding are not made in the meantime.

The boys grow more bitter toward the spinners and threaten to take their places the first time they get an opportunity. Work is progressing rather slowly in the spinning departments where the boys are out, and the lads express themselves as confident that they will be called in Monday.

The nine doffers who quit work at the New Bedford Manufacturing company's mills yesterday afternoon are still out. All the rest of the doffers are at their work. The strikers demanded an increase of 40 cents per week in their pay, but contrary to the usual mode of procedure struck and made the demand afterward.

Deputy United States Marshal Albert Tuttle has written Thomas A. Codd that he will be in this city Tuesday, May 16th, to pay off the people who served on election day. For some unknown reason the supervisors are "not in it," and will have to wait a while longer for their money.

WEATHER INDICATIONS.

CONSULTS A LAWYER.

Supt. E. S. Haskell Denies the Charges Made by Alderman Duff.

There is more or less talk this morning concerning the charges made last evening by Alderman John Duff at a regular session of the aldermen, the particulars of which are printed on the second page. This forenoon a Standard representative called on Mr. Haskell, who, replying to questions, said he did not care for an extended interview. He informed the newspaper man that he had taken legal advice. The charges he further stated were false and he denies in every particular statements made by the aldermen. There is liable to be some interesting developments before long, and it is rumored that one of the next moves will be an attempt to remove Mr. Haskell from office.

A NEW BRICK STRUCTURE.

Charles A. Sisson Having Plans Perfected for a Proposed Building.

Charles A. Sisson contemplates the erection of a large brick building at the foot of Middle street, which is to be used as a wholesale meat establishment and for the ice business, in which he is interested. The meat business will be conducted in the north half of the building on the first floor, while the ice establishment will be in the south half. The second and third stories will be utilized for manufacturing industries. This structure will have a frontage of 69 feet on Front street and an average depth of 80 feet. It will be four stories high. S. C. Hunt is drawing plans for the proposed building.

CONDENSED LOCALS.

For Saturday because you're needing oil cloths we'll sell this day very best quality made, 2 yards wide, for 94 cents, worth $1.20; and 65-cent quality for 50 cents; also best Brussels remnants, 1½ yards long, for 58 cents apiece; a heavy door mat for 50 and 75 cents, worth 75 and $1; a pair of lace curtains, with brass trimmed pole and "tie back," complete for window, for just $2, worth $3.50; and our regular Saturday straw matting sale at a discount of about 25 per cent. on all qualities. Will give you cheaper price for the day than you've ever seen. B. H. Waite & Co., 71 Wm. st.

The work of relaying the track of the Mt. Pleasant division of the street railway from Durfee to Kempton street has been completed. A force of 65 men has commenced to lay the new track in Ash street from Kempton to Court. This is really the beginning of the Fall River road. Seventy-five tons of rails were shipped from Pennsylvania for this road yesterday, and 200 tons are now on the way here.

The buyers and jobbers of strawberries held a meeting on Tuesday to set on foot a movement for free strawberry crates. The crates now in use by shippers must be returned or paid for, thus reducing the profit to the dealer. A resolution was adopted demanding of shippers that when strawberries and blackberries are sold on the market no charge shall be made for crates.

The Y. M. C. A. has voted to have a public meeting next Tuesday evening, when members will be admitted with lady friends on showing their tickets. Miss Stanley, the well known reader, and Miss Hodgdon, the whistling soloist, both of Boston, have been engaged for the occasion. There will be short addresses by business men.

H. C. Hathaway will be stationed morning at 9 o'clock, at stateroom, 1,000 yards No. 1 oilcloth, lot rugs, clocks, furniture, etc. At 10 o'clock, at mart, a carload of horses of all grades, including several good seconds that have been worked in the woods all winter. Also two express wagons, carryall, buggies, business wagons, harnesses, etc.

Ribbons, flowers, laces, together with a full line of millinery, at retail, at wholesale prices. The great bulk of our goods is purchased of the largest importers and manufacturers in the country. We save you one profit. All bonnet frames, wire and others, 10 cents. B. B. Coffin, 52 Purchase street.

The generous sum of $138.75 has been received by the Woman's board of St. Luke's hospital, as the result of Mrs. Sherwood's reading in this city May 5. The amount will form the nucleus of a fund for furnishing the new building.

Mary Forsythe, committed to the house of correction from this city April 22d for drunkenness, was released by the county commissioners upon the recommendation of the probation officer.

Horses, mares, colts, family, trotting, work and draft, at the Mart of Mrs. Sate, Wareham, administratrix's sale. Descriptive catalogue mailed free. Seed—Loring & Carroll, 272 Franklin street, Boston.

Special sale of tomato plants this day. Look at our styles and prices, then compare with our competitors. We leave our patrons to judge of quality and price. B. B. Coffin, 52 Purchase street.

Bargains! Bargains! We have 50 men's suits that cost $15, $16 and $18 that we shall put on sale Saturday at $12 a suit. Gifford & Co.

A first class pineapple at 15c. can; fresh lot sugar-cured hams and shoulders at 14c. and 16c. Boston Branch.

Rev. M. B. Rousmaniere was present at the laying of the corner stone of St. Paul's Episcopal church, Brockton, yesterday.

Henry L. Draycott was arrested on a warrant today charging him with nonsupport of a minor child.

Eureka lodge, F. & A. M., will hold a special communication in Masonic hall this evening.

Work on a sewer in Phillips avenue was commenced this afternoon by George E. Briggs.

The annual meeting of the Acushnet Co-operative association occurs tomorrow evening.

Boys! Boys! Don't forget that a mystery package goes with every suit at Gifford & Co's.

The annual meeting of the New Bedford Co-operative bank takes place on the evening of the 19th inst.

All styles of flange brim and stiff hats and the new shape Kodak cap at lowest prices. Gifford & Co.

Beef has advanced 50 cents a hundred at wholesale.

Go to Whiting & Co's tomorrow for your Hosiery, Gloves and Underwear.

Pure and healthy—Colby's Baking Powder. Try it and be convinced.

Go to Whiting & Co's tomorrow for your Cents' Furnishing Goods of all kinds.

We shall have a fine display of corned beef, this morning. F. E. Hickham, 9 North Sixth street.

Car after performance, Fairhaven, tonight.

Go to Whiting & Co's tomorrow for your Capes and Jackets.

"FaithTriumphant," Phoenix hall, tonight.

No heavy food, if you use Colby's Favorite Baking Powder.

New spring spinach, rhubarb, strawberries and new potatoes. White Cash.

Fairhaven Improv't Ass'n chorus tonight.

Another lot of French prunes, 3 lbs. for 25c. White Cash.

Phoenix hall, this evening, admission 35c.

New potatoes 80c. peck. White Cash.

"FaithTriumphant," Phoenix hall, tonight.

Five good soloists in "Faith Triumphant." Hood's Sarsaparilla vitalizes the blood.

PERSONAL.

The injuries of Joseph Rock who fell from the roof of a house at the north end, Wednesday afternoon, a distance of nearly 20 feet to the ground, are much more serious than they were thought to be. He struck upon his back and was injured internally. He lies at his home on Purchase street, near the foot of Franklin, in a precarious condition.

Captain Edward Akin of this city, who has been recently appointed keeper of the Point Barrow relief station, will leave this city next Tuesday for San Francisco and will sail from there on steamer Jennie, June 1st, for Alaska.

Major General James O. Woodward, commandant of the Burgess corps of Albany, N. Y., an organization composed of past officers of the National guard of that state, is in the city today as the guest of William B. Wood.

George H. Kidd, who is to have charge of the cloth room of the Bristol mill, has been presented by the employes under his charge at the Cornell mill, Fall River, an elegant easy chair.

George A. Smith was elected a director of the Vineyard Grove company, in place of E. G. Eldridge, resigned, at a recent meeting. H. J. Greene was appointed the agent of the company.

H. S. Barnes and John Maynard of Plymouth and Clara Howes Bodfish of Vineyard Haven were among the New England arrivals on the World's fair grounds, Chicago, yesterday.

The North Congregational church has elected Rev. John A. MacColl delegate to the general association of Congregational churches to be held in Boston May 16 to 18.

Hon. Charles S. Randall is spending several days on the Vineyard, enjoying the trout fishing on R. W. Crocker's trout preserve at North Tisbury.

Robert L. Williams of Fall River has been appointed district deputy over the Royal Arcanum lodges in this city, Fall River and Plymouth.

Miss Sarah B. Bullard was one of the Raymond & Whitcomb World's fair excursionists who left Boston yesterday for Chicago.

Captain Bessie Kingsland of the Pennsylvania district of the Salvation Army, formerly stationed in this city, is here on furlough.

Captain Shepherd of steam yacht Aida has resigned his position, and Captain Charles Stubbs will succeed him.

George W. Penniman, who is well known in this city, has become city editor of the Boston Evening Traveller.

Charles W. Clifford, Esq., who has lately made the month of June in Chicago at the World's Fair.

Stephen A. Brownell and wife and Pardon Cornell leave the city to-morrow for Chicago.

Hon. Charles S. Ashley arrived home from Washington this morning.

ANOTHER LAND DEAL.

The New Cordage Company Interested in Purchase.

It is stated that gentlemen who are largely interested in the new cordage company, which is to locate on the Hawes farm in Acushnet, have purchased 100 acres of land adjoining the site of the proposed factory and will at once begin the erection of a number of dwelling houses, some of which will be reserved for men in the employ of the new company.

BETTER THAN BANKS OR MILL STOCKS.

Why deposit your money in banks or invest it in bonds or mill stocks? when you can invest it in the stock of the Black Wonder Gold & Silver Mining company and have it at least double in one year, besides earn you handsome dividends, beginning July 1st. Stock can be had on or before May 15th at 55 cents per share, par value $1, of Frank C. Smith, agent, 47 William street, New Bedford, Mass. Mr. E. C. Davis, vice president and general manager of the company, will be at Mr. Smith's office all day Saturday, May 13th, and it will pay every body having money to invest to call upon him.

WARM WEATHER REMINDERS.

Three bottles Hires' or Williams' Root Beer extract for 50 cents; 18c. single bottle. Large bottle lime juice for 23c. Moxie nerve food 25c. bottle, $2.40 doz. Dried beef, shaved thin, fresh crackers, wafers and biscuits of very description at a lower price than you can buy. We can show more kinds than you ever saw. The confectionery manufacturers are making the lowest prices ever known for good goods—we are giving our customers the benefit. Boston Branch.

THE VINEYARD.

Fred A. Mayhew will carry the mail for four years, beginning July 1, to the western points on the island.

The repairs to the Cottage City Street railway tracks have all been completed, and the ground wires placed throughout the entire line, but it is hardly probable that the electric car will be established this summer.

Robart & Butler have contracted for the building of an observatory at Chappaquiddic on Israel's hill. The property has been recently purchased by Mr. Gantz of New York. The tower will be 50 feet high, 24 feet square at the base and 10 feet at the top. There will be six platforms. Work has been commenced and will progress rapidly.

Charles Snow, real estate agent, reports the following transactions:

Has let Seavel's hotel, Circuit avenue, for Captain Gilbert L. Smith of Vineyard Haven, to C. J. Read of Providence.

Cottage No. 51 Narragansett avenue, for M. F. Cummings of Vineyard Haven, to F. G. Sanborn of Boston.

Cottage No. 11 Kennebec avenue, for Mrs. C. M. Luce of West Tisbury to Mrs. M. L. Lander of Brockton.

Cottage No. 12 Clinton avenue, for J. S. Spinney of New York, to Mrs. E. H. Viall of Providence.

Cottage No. 8 Clinton avenue, for J. S. Spinney of New York, to Miss Jennie L. Irwin of Brookfield, Mass.

Store on Circuit avenue, for Mrs. E. E. Moore of Cottage City, to S. T. Bacon of St. Augustine, Fla.

Pierce villa, for L. Sprague of Fitchburg, to E. D. Johnson of Auburndale.

Cottage on Pequot avenue, for Miss E. H. Twitchell, to G. N. Proctor of Fitchburg.

Forest Grove House, for estate of J. S. Spinney, to James B. Young of West Medway.

Cottage on Fiske avenue, for A. N. Niles of Hartford, to John Sandiford of Cottage City.

Cottage on Penacook avenue, for Mr. Monroe of Edgartown, to Wellington J Rodgers of New York.

Cottage on Massasoit avenue, for E. R. Chapman of New York, to E. O. Hopp of New York.

Sold cottage and four lots on Ocean and Kennebec avenues, for S. G. Tripp of Providence, to B. A. Morse of Rutland, Vt.

Sold four lots on Morse Court avenue, for B. A. Morse of Rutland, Vt.

B. A. Morse of Rutland, Vt.

T. J. Murphy says his horse did not shy yesterday and cause the collision with D. H. Demoranville's wagon. Mr. Murphy was coming south on Purchase street and Mr. Demoranville's horse which was backed up in front of Levi Hawes's candy store, Mr. Murphy says, turned to one side and came in collision with Mr. Murphy's buggy, breaking one wheel and causing his horse to run.

Native asparagus now on hand. White Cash.

Five good soloists in "Faith Triumphant."

Hood's Sarsaparilla vitalizes the blood.

Pages 1-8.

The Evening Standard.

Pages 1-8.

ESTABLISHED FEBRUARY, 1850.]   NEW BEDFORD, SATURDAY, MAY 13, 1893.---TWELVE PAGES.   TWO CENTS.

HASKELL & TRIPP.

Items worth study, first in the paper, then on our counters.

More "Hop Sackings" have arrived. The popular fabric of the season for traveling, boating, mountain wear, etc.

"Hop Sacking," all wool.
Navy, 36 inch, 50c.
Black, " " 50c.
Navy, 54 " $1.00
Black, " " $1.00

Iridescent serges, 12 good mixtures, very durable, 36 inches wide, 39c. a yard. Hold them up to the light; they shade and shimmer in changeable effects much like the more costly materials.

Boadcloths for capes are here in the wanted colors.

"Cravenette," shower-proof cloth, 60 inches wide, $1.75 a yard.

Hats for misses and small girls have been moved up in the east gallery. Novelties in caps, 25c. Novelties in trimmed sailors, 33c. and 62c.

Hats and caps for boys, big and little, you will find in the Boys' Clothing Department-annex. Prices are lower than in any other place we've heard of—and we would be likely to hear.

Brown and russet and tan. These are the colors for shoes. We have them, and what's more we have hosiery in the right shades to match.

These specials in hose may interest you:

Russet Tan and Brown Hose.
Women's "dropstitch" 25c.
Women's brilliant lisle, 37c.
Women's ribbed lisle, 50c.
Women's ribbed silk, 75c.
Children's embroidered, 37 to 50c.
Children's ribbed cotton, 25c.

White Skirts.

We can show you a big collection from 50c. to $2 with very great bargains, well made and trimmed with flouncings for a dollar.

Skirts for little girls come in seven sizes and the prices run from 60c. to 80c. These skirts have tucks, above a pretty Hamburg trimming.

Prices on fine laces are badly "rattled." We are offering high class "Point de Gene" laces in white and ecru, from one-half to one-third the cost of importation. There is still good picking among these laces at 29c. and 39c. a yard.

See the new fancy collars and cuffs, 25c. and 50c. the set. Chemisettes with cuffs to match, 50c.

Have you a "sweet tooth?" Our Candy Department offers *exquisite*
Chocolates,
Nougatines,
Bonbons,
Marshmallows,
At prices that cannot be matched for pure confectionery of *equally high grade.*

HASKELL & TRIPP,
Department Stores,
Purchase and William Streets.

WEATHER INDICATIONS.
Rain and Northeast Gales.

Washington, May 13.—For the 24 hours from 8 a. m. today: For New England and northeast gales. Cool, Cloudy, and Rainy.

Boston, May 13.—Local forecast for New England until Sunday night: Continued cool, cloudy and rainy weather; high, northeasterly winds, decreasing in velocity by Sunday.

FINANCIAL PANIC.
Scores of Small Banks Fail in Western States.

New York, May 13.—A financial panic prevails throughout the western states, a score of small banks have failed. Most of the failures are of small country banks and banking institutions, and are due to the failure of other and larger banks in the cities. Failures are recorded of banks at Moreystown, Russiaville, Brookston and Geneva, Ind., Casey, Ill., and Convoy, O. The capital of each of the banks is small, and the liabilities in each case are from $10,000 to $80,000.

Depositors Will be Paid in Full.

Hillsdale, Mich., May 13.—The First State bank of this city has gone into liquidation. The business has been transferred to the Hillsdale Savings bank, which will assume all the liabilities and pay depositors in full.

Lumber Company Fails.

Seattle, Wash., May 13.—A special from Wardner says: "The Small & Colby Lumber Co. failed yesterday. Attachment suits and mortgage liens which have been placed against the concern will probably aggregate $40,000. The assets are supposed to be of nominal value of $100,000. The liabilities will probably not exceed $50,000.

A Michigan Bank Closes Down.

PAWPAW, Mich., May 13.—Great excitement prevails at Lawton. The managers of a local bank there did not open up the institution yesterday. Citizens have some $18,000 deposited in the bank and are taking legal steps in the hope of realizing something.

ONLY TWO SMALL FAILURES.
Members of New York Stock Exchange Agreeably Surprised.

London, May 13.—The members of the Stock exchange gathered on the floor this morning expecting to hear the failure of several firms officially announced. They were agreeably surprised, however, when they found that only two small failures had occurred and that some of the firms that were supposed to be in difficulty had effected their settlements. This knowledge produced much relief and added steadiness to the market. A number of firms, including that of the Greek speculator mentioned in yesterday's dispatches, who was said to have been deeply involved, received sufficient assistance to carry them over the settlement.

AN ABSCONDING OFFICIAL.
President of a Wisconsin Land Company Flees to Canada.

New York, May 13.—The Tribune's special from St. Paul, Minn., says: The announcement that Francis H. Weeks, the president of the Land & Improvement company, and some of the several hundred thousand dollars caused little surprise at West Superior, Wis. It is now known that Mr. Weeks, as president of the Land company, loaned to the steel works of which he was treasurer $375,000 without the knowledge of the other directors, taking the steel company's notes unsecured. This transaction led to a call for his resignation and the investigation of the books. The Land company attachments against the steel works fully cover this loan. The J. Wemyss, vice president of the Land company, says: "I knew there was something wrong. I think, however, that Weeks is in Canada and will appear when he is wanted." Another Land company official admitted that a $20,000 shortage was shown by the Land company's books. This $20,000, it is claimed, will be made good and there was no need for Mr. Weeks to leave the country because of it.

DONNELLY'S BOLD CHARGE.

He Invited a Suit for Libel and Now He Has It.

St. Paul, Minn., May 13.—The war between the two factions of the Minnesota Farmers Alliance reached a climax last evening, when Dr. Everett W. Fish, editor of the Great West, brought suit against Ignatius Donnelly for $25,000 for defamation of character, and against George L. Stoughton, editor of the Representative, for criminal libel. In the issue of the Representative yesterday afternoon Senator Donnelly said over his own signature: "I plainly, distinctly and unequivocally charge Everett W. Fish, while editing a newspaper called the Great West, with having at different times, and especially during the political campaigns of 1890 and 1892, while pretending to support the reform ticket, of having taken large sums of money amounting to thousands of dollars from officers of the Republican State Central committee. I make this charge deliberately, and invite Everett W. Fish to begin proceedings against me for libel."

TWO DAYS IN AN OPEN BOAT.

Rescue of Shipwrecked Crew of Bark Cushing of Portland, Me.

Halifax, N. S., May 13.—On her last voyage to the West Indies from this port the schooner Helena picked up the shipwrecked crew of the foundered American bark Edward Cushing and landed them at Porto Rico. The men had been in an open boat about 48 hours. The United States consul will protect Captain Martell of the Helena with a gold watch and his crew with a liberal money reward for their exertions in rescuing the castaway. The Cushing belonged at Portland, Me. She left Canning, N. S., Jan. 15, encountered a hurricane in the tropics and foundered and the crew had taken to the boats.

GRAND TREASURER MISSING.

Members of the Order of Germania Look to His Bondsmen.

New York, May 13.—The Herald says: John Weiss, grand treasurer of the Order of Germania, a relief fund, death, sick and benefit association, has disappeared from his home and place of business in this city. He is last seen by his family about ten days ago. The officers of the association, which has branches in the various states and a membership of 20,000, charge Weiss with having taken with him between $5,000 and $6,000 of their funds. The loss is fully covered by his bondsman. It is thought possible he may have been the victim of foul play.

CAMPANIA THE FASTER FLYER.

Steamer Paris Arrives at Southampton This Morning.

London, May 13.—The steamer Paris, which sailed from New York May 6 for Southampton, passed the Lizard at 3 55 o'clock this morning. The Paris left New York on the same day as the Campania, which arrived at Liverpool about 10 o'clock last night. It was expected that a close race would follow the sailing together of the two crack ocean steamers, but the result has proved that the Campania is much the faster of the two vessels.

MILLS BURNED TO THE GROUND.
Plant of the Wilbraham Woolen Company Destroyed This Morning.

North Wilbraham, Mass., May 13.—The mill of the Wilbraham Woolen Co., situated about one mile east of this village, caught fire at 6 30 o'clock this morning, and was burned to the ground. Loss $75,000; partly insured. The fire started in the card room, and almost immediately got beyond control, owing to the grease and oil with which the room was saturated. Practically nothing was saved, only a small quantity of cloth from the finishing room being taken out. The burned buildings comprised the main mill 40 feet by 80, and three stories high; an ell 30 by 50 feet, and the office and sheds. Some of the books and papers in the office were also destroyed. The mill was a three-set, making cloakings and fancy cassimeres, but spinning and carding were run extra, thus making the product equal to that of a four-set mill. The mill will undoubtedly be rebuilt. The owners are D. W. Ellis & Bro. The firm is composed of L. B. Baker of Springfield; F. B. Baker of Stafford Springs, Conn., and Thomas H. Mack of this place.

OBITUARY.
Death of Major A. R. Hale the Widely Known Hotel Man.

New London, Conn., May 13.—Major A. R. Hale, one of the most widely known hotel men in New England, died this morning, aged 70. He was born in Glastonbury, Conn., and went into the hotel business in Bridgeport as manager of the Atlantic hotel, which house he conducted until 1872, when he purchased the Watch Hill House at Watch Hill, R. I., which he has operated as a summer resort ever since.

He had been south this winter, and since 1872 had managed winter resorts in Florida at Green Cove Springs, St. Augustine, and Sanford. He came to the Crocker House in New London in 1881, and conducted it in partnership with his sons until 1889, when he retired from the partnership to give his exclusive attention to his summer and winter resorts.

He was the oldest commissioned officer in the Connecticut National guard, his commission dating back to 1850. He had served in the New London city government as alderman and had held other offices of trust.

GOV. M'KINLEY'S OPINION.
Thinks Republican League Should Have Affirmed the Minneapolis Platform.

Columbus, O., May 13.—Governor McKinley was asked last evening what he thought of the platform adopted by the National league of Republican clubs at Louisville, and said he thought the league ought to have affirmed the platform adopted by the national convention at Minneapolis last year. Asked whether he approved the woman suffrage plank, he said he was hardly decided on that point, but would admit that he did not see any immediate or urgent need of woman suffrage.

WOMAN FATALLY SHOT.
Waiter at Bowery Music Hall Under Arrest for the Crime.

New York, May 13.—Mary Sexton, an unmarried woman, 19 years old, was fatally shot early this morning in her apartments at No. 232 Crosby street, and it is supposed that William Planert, aged 23 years old, a waiter in a Bowery music hall, did the shooting. He is now under arrest.

Burned at Sea.

San Francisco, May 13.—Honolulu advices say the ship Greta, from Newcastle, which reached Honolulu May 3, reports having sighted about 1,200 miles from that port the hull of an iron four-masted ship, totally dismantled and evidently having been completely burned, as steam was still issuing from the hold. The name of the derelict could not be learned.

Scotch-Irish Congress.

Springfield, O., May 13.—At the Scotch-Irish congress yesterday the old officers were re-elected, with Robert Bonner as president. The only other business transacted was the report of the executive committee. A meeting was held last evening with President Bonner in the chair. Dr. John Hall made a few remarks. General Gibson and others also spoke.

HOME MATTERS.

The board of health will move into new quarters in the Bates & Kirby building this afternoon. The rooms are handsomely furnished. The woodwork is hard pine finish and the counter and gate is of ash. There are three rooms, a sliding door separating the public room from that occupied by the board. A smaller room leads from the board's room, and is used as a private office. The floors are neatly carpeted.

There have been fifteen deaths reported at the office of the board of health during the past week and one still born. Of the deaths three were children under five years. There were four from pneumonia, two each from infantile debility and phthisis, and one each from internal strangulation of bowels, measles, atrophy of liver, convulsions, embolism, cancer and erysipelas. The resolution introduced by Alderman Crapo at the meeting of the city council on Thursday evening, calling the attention of the board of assessors to certain slight inequalities of taxation, was unanimously adopted by both branches in concurrence, and not placed on file as reported yesterday. The city clerk has transmitted a copy to the chairman.

John Walsh was arrested this noon by Officer Wing for disturbing the peace. Walsh, with several other companions, was standing near the stone quarry on Independence for fooling with the laborers, and hazing them, when one of them, a Portuguese, objected, and led Walsh arrested.

A final decree has been entered in the divorce case of Elizabeth Bromley vs. James Bromley in favor of the wife, and she has also been allowed to resume her maiden name of Elizabeth Chadwick. Edwin A. Douglass, Esq., was counsel for the wife.

A runaway horse struck the gate at the Wamsutta crossing last evening and broke it. The buggy to which the animal was attached was badly smashed. The occupants of the vehicle escaped injury.

A handsome bay horse, weighing over 1,400 pounds, has been purchased by the city council committee on fire department to run on the hose wagon at Onward engine house.

There will be a special meeting of the city council on Tuesday evening of next week to act on the numerous orders which were left over at the last session of the government.

The Silver Star Monogram Minstrel company, an organization of boys connected with the Union for Good Works, is to give an entertainment at Mattapoisett this evening.

The Interscholastic League ball game between the High School and Rogers School (Newport) team did not come off today on account of the storm.

Seven new cases of scarlet fever and two new cases of typhoid fever have been reported at the office of the board of health the past week.

THE BORDEN TRIAL.

No Jurors to be Drawn from Fall River.

Secrets Connected with the Mystery Now Coming Out.

Insanity Theory the Real Cause of Grand Jury Recess.

No Hatchet in the Case Say Those in Authority.

Stanchest Friends of Lizzie Borden Changing Their Opinions.

The venires for the jurors in the Borden trial will be handed to the sheriff next week, and the jurors will be drawn during the week, as it is necessary that seven days at least should elapse between the time of drawing and the trial. Thirty will be drawn from Taunton, 45 from this city, none from Fall River, and 75 from the towns in the county, making a total of 150 in all from which to select a jury of twelve men. This is nearly double the number drawn altogether in the Tighe case.

Now that the Borden case is practically on a great deal that was kept within the bosoms of those acquainted with the circumstances is coming to the surface. They felt in the uncertainty of the disposition of the case that they were harboring secrets, and had no right to disclose them, but now that the trial is assured and the date set, all of these things are coming out. It is an open secret now that the real cause for the recess of the grand jury was just what was hinted at at the time, to wit, that the attorney general desired a consultation of medical experts on the mental condition of Miss Borden. It has been stated that Mr. Pillsbury believes Miss Borden is innocent. This assumption is hardly correct, and if it was so, Mr. Pillsbury would be the last man to allow it to go out as a fact. While he understands there are many strange circumstances connected with the case he has no right, nor would he state that the woman was innocent or that the crimes charged to her, but he does believe, and has all along believed since hearing the evidence before the grand jury, that she is mentally unsound.

Mr. Jennings, it will be remembered, at the preliminary trial in Fall River asserted that his client was not insane. When, therefore, it was proposed by Mr. Pillsbury to hold a consultation in regard to her sanity he strenuously objected, and as can be readily understood there was for weeks seeing wild-eyed men and all sorts of visions will not be bothered with to any great extent. Neither the government nor the defense will waste any time in working insanity theories. Facts are what is wanted by both parties. Ex-Governor Robinson is devoting a great deal of time to the case, and it may be asserted with truth that upon him and Mr. Adams lies the burden of the defense. Ex-Governor Robinson, aside from the fact that he is retained in one of the greatest cases of the age, realizes plainly with mystery and uncertainties, realizes also the fact that he is to be pitted against two of the strongest criminal lawyers in the commonwealth of Massachusetts, if not in this section of the country. The strongest witnesses for the government are Bridget Sullivan and Mrs. Churchill. It is estimated that the cross-examination of the witnesses for the government may be the longest siege of any during the trial. The hatchet story recently resurrected has no foundation in fact, if statements from those in authority are good for anything. As a matter of fact, there is no hatchet in the case; there never was any that fitted where the government wanted it to fit. Some time ago the district attorney gave very much to have the Borden house and barn torn down, the ground plowed up and every article of the Borden property thoroughly examined. He had this theory in regard to the disposition of whatever weapon may have been used, and to those who know how old fashioned houses were constructed his theory was not very far out of the way. But unfortunately for him there is no law which would allow to touch the house, barn or grounds, and the Borden family is not in sufficient need of money or so thoroughly in love with the government that it will give over any part of the property for that purpose. The fact that Miss Emma Borden and a servant holds possession of the property today, as Miss Borden has ever since the tragedy, is additional weight in the minds of the government that there is something on those premises which the government ought to have.

It is asserted that in Fall River, at least, there has been a great change of opinion within the last few months, and even the stanchest friends of Miss Borden are saying now that they fear they have been led astray in their opinions formerly expressed. The fact that no jurors are to be drawn from Fall River seems to indicate that the government has little faith in any such weight as the sheriff will have a tendency to show that the government is just a little bit afraid of people from that section. The jury will be very carefully selected.

THE RECORD'S STORY.
Fall River Globe Thinks the Boston Paper May Find it is Mistaken.

The Fall River Globe this afternoon says:

"For some reason or other the Boston Record has shifted ground in its views on the Borden case. It has maintained all along that there was little or nothing in the testimony in this city at the preliminary hearing which pointed

(Continued on Fourth Page.)

THE BORDEN MURDER TRIAL.

The Evening Standard is perfecting arrangements to give the public as complete and accurate reports of the great murder trial as can be printed. Orders should be early placed with your nearest newsdealer, or word sent to this office, and the Standard will be sent regularly during the trial.

PERSONAL.

Mrs. O. Walton Longley, who is to have charge of Hotel Westport the coming season, conducted the West Chop Inn last season and not the Cedars, which has always been conducted by Miss Clifford of Boston.

Mrs. Captain W. A. Clark and daughter, Miss Susie G. Clark of Brockton, arrived at San Francisco 6th inst., having been passengers on the steamer Acapulco, of which vessel Mrs. Clark's husband is captain.

William T. Nicholson of the New Bedford brass foundry has just returned from a business trip to New York and New Jersey. Mr. Nicholson has an electrical invention, on which he held a consultation with Thomas A. Edison.

Governor Russell, Colonel Wheelwright and A. H. Wood arrived in Sagamore last evening, and are guests of John P. Knowlton. They are trying their luck at trout fishing today and will return to Boston this evening.

Elizabeth H. Brayton, Edith E. Raymond and Dana D. Brayton of Fall River, and A. A. Shepard of Plymouth were among the New Englanders who visited the World's fair yesterday.

Rev. William Carruthers has been chosen by the Trinitarian church as delegate to the Massachusetts state association which meets in Boston next week.

M. V. P. D. B. Allen and Charles E. Sulis left for Cambridge yesterday afternoon to attend the annual election of the Cambridge patriarch, U. O. O. of O. F.

Mrs. Herbert W. Blanchard, of Boston, late of Dr. Quint's church, Roxbury, has accepted the position as soprano at the North Congregational church.

Robert F. Bayliss has been appointed inspector of immigration at this port and installed today before James Taylor, Esq.

Miss Manley, sister of John Joseph H. Manley of Maine, is visiting at Mr. William J. Kilburn's, County street.

Lieutenant George F. F. Wilde, inspector of lighthouses in this district, was in the city yesterday.

Hoyland Smith is a scratch man in the big bicycle road race from Chelsea this afternoon.

Miss Sadie Taylor, bookkeeper for S. C. Lowe, is spending a short vacation in Plymouth.

Captain Charles Weeks of steam whaler Thrasher has arrived in the city.

LAST CALL, MAY 15TH.

Monday, May 15th, is the last day you can buy the stock of the Black Wonder Gold & Silver Mining company at 55 cents per share, par value $1.00. This is another Mollie Gibson opportunity to make money. Don't let it pass by. Dividends will begin July 1st. For stock and full particulars call upon Frank C. Smith, Agent, 47 William street, New Bedford, Mass.

CONDENSED LOCALS.

Laundry men have long felt the need of a machine that would iron a turn down collar acceptably and fold it without breaking the edge. There is nothing that is any more provoking to a customer than to send round new collars to the laundryman and have them returned to him with edges broken almost the entire length. A machine that will do the work to perfection and in a much better manner than it can be accomplished by hand has at last been invented and the New Bedford Steam laundry, with characteristic enterprise, is the first and only one in this part of the state to adopt them. By the use of this machine a turn down collar will wear as long as one that stands up and it works equally well with collars on both bosom and cutting shirts. By its use collars will sit better, look neater and wear longer.

Fajardo Testimonials.—Myron W. Whitney, Madame Nordica, Madame Eugenie Pappenheim, Henrietta Markeen, and John S. Hiller, all special artists in their line, indorse the New England piano. If you are interested read their testimonials on 5th page. E. B. Chase & Co., agents for New Bedford and vicinity.

Ribbons, flowers, laces, together with a full line of millinery, at retail, at wholesale prices. The great bulk of our goods is purchased of the largest importers and manufacturers in the country. We save you one profit. All-bonnet frames, wire and others, 19 cents. H. B. Coffin, 52 Purchase street.

Horses, mares, colts, family, trotting, Ware estate, Wareham, administratrix's sale. Descriptive catalogue mailed free. Send—Loring & Carroll, 272 Franklin street, Boston.

Special sale of trimmed hats this day. Look at our styles and prices, then compare with our competitors. We have our patrons to judge of quality and price. H. B. Coffin, 52 Purchase street.

Bargains! Bargains! We have 50 men's suits that cost $15, $16 and $18 that we shall put on sale Saturday at $12 a suit. Gifford & Co's.

There will be a special meeting of carriage workers at the Musical Exchange band room this evening. See special notice.

Ask your grocer for "London Cream Biscuit." They are the finest crackers in the world. The words London Cream stamped upon every cracker.

The annual meeting of the stockholders of the Acushnet Cooperative association will be held at the store this evening.

David Tomlinson, the south end newsdealer, has opened a branch store on Hemlock street.

Rex Gelatine is the simplest, purest and cheapest. Free at the Boston Branch grocery.

Boys! Boys! Don't forget that a mystery package goes with every suit at Gifford & Co's.

Dinner is not complete without a dessert. See Rex Gelatine at Boston Branch grocery.

Only Reliable Cough Remedy—Compound Syrup of Wild Cherry. Wright Drug company.

Call at Boston Branch grocery and taste the new dessert, Rex Gelatine. Free today.

All styles of flange brim and stiff hats and the new shape Kodak caps at lowest prices. Gifford & Co's.

Are you fond of jellies? Something new at Boston Branch grocery. Free today.

Horse Neck.—Fish dinners now served at Ocean Cottage with broiled lobsters.

A. O. H., Div. 91, meet at Hibernian hall this evening. See special notice.

Bluefish 12c. per pound. F. E. Tinkham, 9 North Sixth street.

Have you tasted the new dessert, Rex Gelatine? Free at Boston Branch. Visit Waite's carpet rooms Saturday evening. Catarrh cured by Hood's Sarsaparilla.

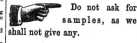

SOMETHING WHICH IT WILL PAY YOU TO READ!

Saturday,

(AS USUAL,)

BARGAIN DAY!

BOYS' SUITS—Boys' Reefers, sizes 2 to 6 years, $1.50 and $1.75. Boys' School Suits, best values in the city, at 98c., $1.48, $1.59, $1.75 and $1.98. Boys' Pants, in sizes 5 to 14 years, only 29c. a pair. Boys' all wool Caps, only 25c. each. Boys' Shirt Waists, 25c., 39c. and 48c. The celebrated "Star" Shirt Waist, laundered, at 98c. MOYNAN & CO.

☞ Millinery—Flowers in endless assortments. Prices from 15c. to $1.25, and they are beauties.

CLOAK DEPT. SPECIALS—For Saturday we offer the following specials: Light mixed Jackets with Butterfly Capes, $4.98. Plain Tan Jackets with Butterfly Cape, $6.50. Tan, Navy and Havana Brown Jackets, Butterfly Cape, $7.98. Fine mixtures, also all the plain colors, including Black, with silk lined capes, $9.98. Special lot of Short Capes in Tan, Navy and Black, while they last, $3.50. MOYNAN & CO.

☞ Boys, remember the "baseball and bat" given away with every suit on Saturday.

MILLINERY SPECIALS—New Ribbons in all colors and widths, at 5c., 10c., 15c., 19c. and 25c. a yard, for hair, millinery and dress trimming purposes; also Windsor Ties and Scarfs for ladies and children in all the "Chic" colors and shadings. Don't forget our new Silk and Muslin Caps and Bonnets, special display, some at 19c., others at $5, and every price between. MOYNAN & CO.

☞ Specials in Boys' Jersey Suits, sizes 3 to 10 years. Regular price $4.50, for $2.50.

BASEMENT SPECIALS—Shelf Paper in lace designs, 10 yards in each roll, for 10c. Sewing Lamp with decorated stand, glass fount, trimmed complete with burner, wick and chimney, 47c. Mrs. Pott's nickel plated Sad Irons, viz.: 3 irons, 1 handle and 1 stand, regular price $1.25, Saturday's price 97c. One burner Oil Stove for 47c. Carpet Sweepers, $1.97 and $3.00. See our "Gem" Coffee Pot at reduced prices. MOYNAN & CO

☞ New Veilings, New Ruchings, New Embroideries, New Laces. Come in and see for yourself.

LINEN AND COTTON SPECIALS—For Saturday, 50 Fringed Damask Table Cloths, 2 1-2 and 2 3-4 yards long, in plain, white and fancy borders, regular $1.98 quality, our price $1.19 each, (one to a customer.) 200 pairs ready-made Pillow Cases, 42-inch cotton and worth 16c. each, on Saturday you can buy (six pairs the limit to one customer) at 12 1-2c. each.

☞ For Saturday—25 Chenille Table Covers, 1 1-2 yards square, with heavy ball fringe, regular $2.00 quality for $1.50.

WAISTS—We have the largest and best assorted line of Waists to be found in this city. See our Leader at 39c.—at the money asked it cannot be beaten—and it's a dandy, our 50c. Waist. Also a regular 75c. Waist at 59c. Lined China Silk Waists, Navy, Black and Red, a few to sell for $2.98. MOYNAN & CO.

☞ Millinery goods of all kinds, latest styles, popular prices. Specials for Saturday,

DRESS GOODS BARGAINS—At 50c. per yard, balance of 100 pieces 75c. and $1.00 suitings, on sale Saturday with new fabrics and styles added; your last chance this season for a choice Dress at 50c. per yard. Have you seen them yet? Your choice of 15 pieces plain and mixed Suitings, imported this season to sell at $1.00 and $1.50 per yard, all the new and exquisite shades are represented in this lot, and the price is only 75c. per yard. MOYNAN & CO.

☞ Wash Goods — 12 1-2c. Ginghams, 50 pieces and as many styles to choose from for 7 1-2c. per yard. 25c. Fast Black Satine, 1,000 yards in jet and blue blacks for 17c. per yard.

GLOVE SPECIALS — 8-button White Chamois Gloves, regular $1.00 quality, for Saturday 85c. a pair. Ladies' 6-button Suede in Tans, worth $1.00, for 79c. a pair. Ladies' Glace Biarritz were $1.00, now at 79c. a pair. 5-hook Gloves in New Tuscan shade, regular $1.00, for 59c. a pair. Odd size in Black Taffeta Gloves, for Saturday 10c. a pair. MOYNAN & CO.

☞ See our special in Children's Gingham Dresses, a fine Gingham, trimmed with Insertion and Hamburg Edging, (only a few in stock,) regular price $1.19, to close out at 69c. each.

MOYNAN & CO

UNION ST. PURCHASE ST.

The Evening Standard.

NEW BEDFORD, MASS.

SATURDAY EVENING, MAY 13.

THREE EDITIONS DAILY.

No. 87 Union Street.

PUBLISHED BY

E. ANTHONY & SONS.

INCORPORATED.

—TERMS—

Six Dollars a Year; Three Dollars for Six Months, in advance; Single Copies Two Cents.

TWELVE PAGES.

This Evening's Issue Consists of Twelve Pages and Every Patron is Entitled to that Number.

George Fred Williams has occasionally deviated into sense. But not for long. In a very recent speech at Manchester, N. H., he expressed the hope that when the silver issue comes before congress the president "will put the thumb screws on every recalcitrant senator until he howls aye on every administrative question." This displays a remarkable appreciation of the relations between the executive and the legislative body of the Union. Williams seems to regard the president of this country as having as absolute authority as the Kaiser William arrogates to himself. But there is one thing the president cannot do. He cannot dissolve congress as the kaiser dissolved the reichstag the other day because it refused to comply with his wishes. Senators are selected for six years and there they stay in spite of presidential thumb screws.

New Hampshire seems to be a favorite resort for Massachusetts politicians to display their vocabularies. Governor Russell went up there the other day and denounced our entire pension system as highway robbery. Does he think this wild talk will make him more popular at home?

The Springfield Republican is kept very busy in comparing the civil service reform practice of the administration with its professions. It was just the same in Mr. Cleveland's first term. But that didn't hinder the Republican from continuing to worship its idol. It still expects the president, or rather says the people expect him, to do something in the present juncture. But has it noticed Secretary Carlisle's question, What was the election for?

The New York Nation gives an interesting account of a town meeting in Hyannis, where that New England institution exists in all its vigor. Perhaps the most interesting incident of the gathering was the voting down of a motion that no man should be permitted to call another "a darned fool" in town meeting. There is great freedom of speech in our little municipalities.

For two days it has been possible to go without an overcoat, the open street cars have been running well patronzed, and even an occasional straw hat has made its appearance. But the change of wind to the northeast has been a slight set back to dreams of summer.

Invitation cards to the 25th anniversary of the Hampton Normal and Agricultural institute have been received for which our thanks are extended. The exercises, which promise to be interesting, will take place Thursday, May 25.

The way to see the exposition cheaply is to become a resident of Chicago. Then you can get a free pass without much difficulty. The dead heads are said to be more numerous than the paying visitors.

We Give $10.00 WORTH —FOR— $2.00.

A SPECIAL OFFER FOR TEN DAYS ONLY.

The Perfection Portrait Co., of New York desiring to introduce their celebrated

CRAYON PORTRAITS

in this section of the country have decided to offer for the next 10 days only an Elegant Life Size Crayon Portrait completely framed in an attractive White and Gilt frame at the remarkable low price of

TWO DOLLARS.

Our regular price for this work is

TEN DOLLARS

and this offer is made by us to introduce our work only.

The Artists employed by us received the HIGHEST AWARD FOR PORTRAIT WORK at the convention of the PHOTOGRAPHERS ASSOCIATION OF AMERICA held at WASHINGTON, D. C.

This offer includes Frame and Glass.

There is no extra charge for boxing or any other EXTRAS.

DIRECTIONS.

Clip out the coupon printed below and send it by mail with the photograph or picture you desire copied.

The Two Dollars should also be enclosed, either in Postal Note or P. O. Money Order.

Be sure and write your name and address plainly on back of the picture.

Be sure to address your package plainly,

THE PERFECTION PORTRAIT CO.,

466 and 468 Broadway, New York.

As to our responsibility we refer to The Citizens National Bank, New Bedford, Mass.

CUT OUT THIS COUPON AT ONCE

As this advertisement will not appear again.

This Special Coupon to the readers of The Evening Standard, New Bedford, Mass. May 13th, 1893, entitles the holder to an elegant Life-size, 16x20 inches Head and Bust Crayon Portrait, copied from any Photograph, Tintype or Daguerreotype, completely framed in an attractive White and Gilt Frame, with glass, at the special price of $2.00, provided this coupon is returned within ten days from date.

THE PERFECTION PORTRAIT CO.,
466 & 468 Broadway, New York.

CONTENTS OF THIS EVENING'S STANDARD.

Page 1.
No jurors from Fall River will be drawn in the Borden Case.
Fall River Globe's comments on "The Record sensation."
Failures of small banking institutions in the west.
Rescue of shipwrecked crew of bark Cushing of Portland.
Absconding president of a Wisconsin land company.
Arrival of the Paris at Southampton.
Ignatius Donnelly's bold charge.
Woolen mills burned today.
Home matters.
Telegraphic dispatches.

Page 2.
Third District Court.
Meeting of the board of public works.
Yacht Mildred stolen.
Barnstable county teachers' election.
Local and suburban news.

Page 3.
Bridgewater sensation.
Arrival of the Iron Spoon sloop Nautilus.
A. M. E. Zion conference.
Sunday notices.

Page 4.
Gay couple from Fall River wreck a buggy by reckless driving.
Situation among the striking back boys.
Sudden Death of a South end man.
Fairhaven water works and talk of a new mill.
Baseball News.
Editorials.

Page 5.
Marine intelligence.
Marriages and deaths.

Page 6.
Local stocks at auction.
Financial news.
Second Edition — Telegraphic and local news.

Page 7.
Cantata by the Fairhaven singing class last evening.
Two little misses entertain friends in Odd Fellows hall.
Opening of the racing season at Manchester.
Amusement and sporting news.

Page 8.
Statement of President Warner Miller of the Nicaragua Canal company.
Faithless lawyer said to have embezzled $70,000 from one of his clients.
A wronged woman's attempt to murder her betrayer in Somerville.
Legislative proceedings.
Third edition—Telegraphic and locals.
Early telegraphic dispatches.

Page 10.
World's fair building designed by Architect Jenney for the Fairhaven Hustler.
The new flagship of the New York yacht club.
Miscellaneous reading.
Old publications.

Page 11.
"Beyond the City," by A. Conan Doyle.

Page 12.
Blarney and other Irish castles described by Wakeman.
Drunkenness in France.

HOME MATTERS.

ARRIVED BELOW THIS AFTERNOON.

Schooner Lottie Beard, Marquand, from St. Helena, with oil and bone on freight, is below as the first edition goes to press.

SUDDEN DEATH.

A South End Man Expires Before a Physician Arrives.

Timothy McGlynn, living on the south side of Delano street, between Acushnet avenue and Second street, died suddenly last night. He formerly worked at the coal pockets, but was not employed yesterday. He was about home during the day apparently as well as usual, except that he complained of a headache. He retired to bed between 9 and 10 o'clock, and his wife soon followed. Just after this Mr. McGlynn threw himself quickly from one side to another, and when his wife asked him what was the trouble, he complained of a violent pain in the region of his heart, and said he was trying to secure an easier position. She became alarmed and wished to go for a doctor, and in a short time she went out after her brother, returning almost instantly, when Mr. McGlynn was at his last gasp. Dr. St. Germain was sent for, but the man was dead before his arrival. Mr. McGlynn was 27 years of age, a man of temperate habits, a member of St. Lawrence Catholic Temperance society, and leaves a wife and two children, the youngest 10 days old. Dr. G. DeN. Hough, medical examiner, was notified.

THE BACKBOYS' STRIKE.

Little Change in the Situation and Strikers Still Out.

The striking backboys gathered at the Wamsutta mill gate this morning, and after waiting a little while to see if they were to be called in, dispersed. They are inclined to view the situation with complacency, and say that they will remain out another week if necessary to secure the advance, but hope they will have good weather.

The doffers who came out with them show signs of weakening, and it would not be surprising if they returned to work Monday.

The backboys say that the spinners have been able to make comparatively little headway without them, and if the mill people had rather pay the spinners standard wages than to grant them the advance they demand they will give them an opportunity to do so a while longer.

Some of the spinners say that they have been told by their overseers if they would give the advance the boys demand out of their pay the strike could be settled at once, and fear that this course may yet be adopted. This they would not submit to, and would strike at once.

The boys declare that they would be only too glad to have the spinners go out, as this would give them a chance to square accounts with them.

Many of the spinners are of the opinion that now the boys have had the vacation they were looking for, they will return to work Monday. On the other hand, the boys agreed this morning that regardless of what course the spinners, doffers and piecers pursue, they would remain out until they were conceded an advance of 50 cents per week in their wages.

NEW BASEBALL PARK.

Admirable Arrangement of Grounds—Work to be Pushed Rapidly.

The work of putting the new baseball park on Kempton street into condition is progressing rapidly. The fence is well under way, and will be completed in a day or two. The space enclosed is considerably larger than the old park, being 400 feet in length and 350 feet wide. Work on the grand stand is to commence Monday. It is to be 100 feet in length and 20 feet deep, with a seating capacity of 500. Comfortable bleachers are to be erected near the first and third bases, each seating 500 persons. It is 333 feet from the home plate to the fence in the rear, and it is 75 feet from the home plate to the catcher's fence. Under the grand stand will be commodious dressing rooms, one for each team.

T. A. Duffy has been awarded the contract for grading the grounds, and will commence the work Monday and push it as fast as possible. Under the grand stand will also be a large room for the storage of sawdust and the tools of the janitor in charge of the grounds. The sanitary arrangements have not been overlooked, and the city water is to be conveyed to the grounds. Bicycle racks will be provided for the convenience of wheelmen, and there is an abundance of room for carriages. A well graded driveway 30 feet in width will lead from Kempton street to the grounds, and the layout is such that no one will be obliged to cross the diamond or encroach in any way on the players' room. Ticket offices will be so situated that parties in carriages can secure their tickets without alighting. A large flag pole is to be stationed right in the rear of the grand stand. In fact, everything that suggests itself as in any way enhancing the convenience and enjoyment of the patrons of the sport will be provided.

THE BORDEN TRIAL.

(Continued from First Page.)

to the guilt of the accused, but it now assumes that the community is convinced that she committed the murders and analyzes her disposition and temperament in a cold-blooded fashion.

The same paper also assumes that District Attorney Knowlton will have to bear the brunt of the trial and that Attorney General Pillsbury will not figure as prominently as he has on certain occasions which might be mentioned. At least it is fair to state that this is assumption, for it is not probable that either the attorney-general or the district attorney has confided his plans to anybody. It is barely possible, therefore, that before many weeks have passed the Record will find that it has made a mistake. It may be that Attorney-General Pillsbury will conduct the prosecution with all the ability and enthusiasm for which he is noted, and that District Attorney Knowlton will fill the usual role of assistant counsel. It is probably true that Mr. Pillsbury does not regard the duty as a pleasant one. No lawyer who could have his choice would care about trying a woman for her life, but he has no alternative, and he cannot afford to betray any indifference when he has entered upon his task.

Neither is there anything to prove that he has his doubts concerning Miss Borden's guilt. He was present in this city when the district attorney ordered her arrest, and conferred with Mr. Knowlton on the subject. While he did not, as the Record asserts, attend the hearing, he is, of course, familiar with the evidence, and heard the counsel sum up the last day. If he does not agree with Mr. Knowlton, nobody knows it, though there were rumors to that effect afloat while the grand jury was in session. Nevertheless they have not been confirmed by developments up to date, and it would be a singular spectacle to see the attorney general dragged unwillingly into a trial which he did not believe ought to take place.

So far as the element of politics is concerned there is nothing new in it. Mr. Pillsbury has never denied that he had gubernatorial aspirations, and probably Mr. Knowlton would accept the attorney generalship if the position were offered to him. But just at present they are, before everything else, counsel for the state in a capital crime, with professional reputations to guard. So far as a forecast of the result goes the public is free to guess for itself. The venture was boldly made that Miss Borden would not be held when the inquest was concluded. It was then said that she would never be bound over, and later the country was informed that the grand jury would fail to indict her. It is now given out that the prisoner will be acquitted in June. But there is nothing in the previous predictions which makes these statements at all reliable."

A GAY BORDER CITY COUPLE.

Wreck a Buggy in Their Reckless Driving About Town.

A Frenchman and a female companion came over here from Fall River yesterday afternoon in a livery stable turnout. They couldn't talk English, but they could imbibe liquor, and proceeded to do so with such success that before the night shades had fallen they were gloriously "corned." They still continued their ride, however, and were driving at a furious gait down Fourth street when they encountered a farmer's wagon coming east on Wing street. The two turnouts collided with disastrous results to both. The farmer's horse cleared himself and ran a short distance, while his driver was thrown out, but not hurt half as much as the wagon was. The erratic couple mended their shafts and continued south again. On County street, near Rivet, they again came in collision with a wagon and still further reduced the buggy to a wreck. Then a friendly bystander took a hand to help matters out, and tried to drive the turnout to a place of safety. But the Frenchman objected, and a lively scrap ensued, in which the female companion took a hand, while a crowd numbering hundreds gathered around. In the midst of the fracas a policeman appeared, whereupon the Fall River couple deserted the buggy and in the crowd escaped and disappeared up the street. The turnout was taken to Sylvia & Mitchell's stable, where the owner claimed it this morning by telephone message from Fall River.

WILL IT BE CONDEMNED?

Holy Acre Talked of as a Park for Mill Operatives.

Yesterday afternooon the board of public works made an official visit to Holy Acre, which locality has been the subject of more or less comment for several years. By invitation the members of the board of health accompanied the public works officials, and after looking over the ground and discussing the advisability of accepting Turners lane, and putting it in first class condition, which would necessitate the filling in of the land on either side of the thoroughfare, the suggestion was made by one of the members of the board of public works that the whole section including the lagoon south of the Wamsutta mills ought to be condemned and the whole territory fitted for park purposes for the large number of mill operatives who frequent that section. This, it is said, is looked upon as the best possible way of remedying an evil which has long existed.

AN EXCITING RUNAWAY.

Four horses attached to one of Simeon Hawes' heavy ice carts started to run from in front of the New Bedford Ice company's house on Fourth street this forenoon, turning north into Purchase street. North of William street an open horse car is kept standing on the track while relaying water pipes is in progress. Toward this car the horses dashed, but just before they reached it Rufus Norris, at considerable personal risk, grabbed one of the leaders, and at almost the same instant Officer Telford caught the off pole horse, and they succeeded in bringing the team to a standstill, but so near to the car that Mr. Norris had to swing the leaders one side to prevent collision with the car. The horse Mr. Telford caught got one hind leg over the traces, and had one of his fore legs cut by contact with the leaders' whiffletree. Nathan B. Brooks caught the bridle of the nigh pole horse.

BARNSTABLE COUNTY.

The will of Theophilus Chase, of South Yarmouth, was disallowed in the probate court by Judge Harriman, 9th. The question was on the execution of the same, the respondents claiming that the will was not signed by the witnesses in the presence of the testator, as required by law. The evidence went to show that it was signed by two of the witnesses in a room adjoining the testator's bedroom, where he could not see them sign. The question of undue influence was not gone into at this hearing. Charles Bassett for executors; T. C. Day for respondents.

In the case of petition of Z. J. Avery, of Bourne, for guardianship of his minor children, and his wife's petition for separate maintenance, the evidence was all put in, and the arguments of counsel will be heard later. F. C. Swift for respondent; T. C. Day for petitioner.

Train Robbers Located.

St. Louis, Mo., May 13.—Word was received from Cairo late last evening that the four men who robbed the Mobile & Ohio train near that place had been located and their arrest would follow.

Fatal Railroad Wreck.

Cairo, Ill., May 13.—The south bound passenger train on the St. Louis and Southwestern road was wrecked at 5 o'clock last evening, seven miles below Bird's Point, Mo. Engineer and fireman were instantly killed.

FAIRHAVEN WATER WORKS.

Material Soon to Arrive—Prospect of a New Mill.

The special town meeting, to consider what contract will be made with the water works, has been called for next Saturday. It is probable that the Fairhaven people wish for a contract much like the specifications in the warrant, and the meeting will go off smoothly. But whatever the town may adopt there is no doubt that the works will be commenced at once, as permission for laying pipes has been granted by the legislature. The material for construction has already been purchased. A vessel load of 6 and 8-inch pipes will arrive about the first of June, and a contract for 80 nonfreezing hydrants is now being filled. For a long time it has been an open secret that the capital of H. H. Rogers, Esq., is behind the whole scheme, and it is he who has so far conducted the tests, and will build the works. The pipes are to be laid in the center of the town first, where the water will benefit the largest number of people. The introduction of water will undoubtedly create a revolution in the commercial affairs of the town. A prominent New Bedford mill man said yesterday that a big mill would be put up on the site of Union wharf property as soon as the pipes were laid. This is owned by Mr. Rogers, and though it is in the market for occupancy by a manufacturing corporation, it is well known that Mr. Rogers does not favor a mill, and would not be likely to give up the land for such usage. The prospects look bright for a mill, however, and it may be on another location. The contract to be made between the town and the water works is for not more than 20 years, and it is probable that Fairhaven will own the plant in a much shorter time than that.

A scroe or more of new wells are to be driven at Naskatucket as soon as workmen can be procured.

In the town meeting warrant is an article calling for a provision to be made for the transportation of children in the rural districts to the Rogers school. There is at present enough room in the building to accommodate more pupils and it is thought the expense of transportation will be less than the support of the country schools, and the children will have much better advantages.

At last, after three weeks, the cemetery committee has got together and voted to macadamize the avenues in Riverside annex. They have called upon Superintendent Bryant to do it at once, but as he has been waiting their movements so long they will have to wait a week at least for him. At present the street department is busy cleaning up, and it is Mr. Bryant's intention to have the streets in first class condition by Memorial Day.

About 70 trees have been set out in all parts of the town this week, and the work still goes on.

Oesting and Bertram, who recently purchased that part of the town farm lying west of Main street, have contracted with James H. Murkland to do grading of the land. He will commence work immediately. A track will be laid from Main street to the low land near the river, on which dump cars will be run up and down the hill by a stationary engine and fall. This is one of the largest contracts for grading ever given in this vicinity. When the work is finished Mr. Oesting will put several houses on the site. He will begin two cellars for houses on Winsor street on Monday.

The faced wall on the property foot of Fort street is being continued south. A stone gateway has been put in on Fort street, and several cottages are to be erected.

Frank Nolan caught five sea perch in the Mill pond, which altogether weighed seven pounds.

Rev. Donald Lee will preach in the Congregational church tomorrow, and a Japanese student from the Harvard Divinity school in the Unitarian church.

Work on the sewer to lead from the rear of the horse car barn to the water was begun Thursday. Nearly 300 feet of 5-inch pipe has already been laid. Some trouble is already experienced from the caving in of the sides of the trench, and one accident happened which came very near resulting fatally. About four or five tons of dirt caved in from the side and buried one man up to his neck. If instead of standing up he had been stooping over at the time, he have been completely buried, and probably would have smothered before any one could dig him out. The work is under the supervision of Anthony Pierce, Jr., of New Bedford.

MARION.

Emma Butterworth, the brave young girl in Warren who tried to save her father's life, and in so doing sacrificed her own life, was in Marion last summer, a guest of Miss Nellie Hathaway, at Captain Hathaway's cottage in East Marion. Miss Butterworth was beloved by every one.

Silas B Allen, Sr., is making a short visit at his former home in Marion.

Captain Zenas H. Crocker, successor of Captain George L. Luce in the coal and lumber business, has been appointed a justice of the peace.

A valuable gold watch, lost last summer by Mrs. M. G. Van Rensselaer while driving, was found by the roadside in Rochester recently near the residence of Stephen Mendell. It was apparently uninjured.

ROCHESTER.

A special town meeting will be held Saturday, May 20th, at 2 p. m. to choose a selectman to fill the unexpired term of the late Isaac F. B. Perry; to see if the town will vote to reconsider the vote in relation to buying a stone crusher, and to accept any propositions that may be made by Mr. Z. H. Thompson and act on anything thereon.

SPECIAL NOTICES.

MEMBERS OF DIV. 9, A. O. H.

Are requested to meet at Hibernian hall THIS EVENING (May 13) at 7 30 to take action on the death of Brother Timothy Mc Glennon. Per order,
*my13-1t T. J. CLYNES, Pres.

CARRIAGE WORKERS, ATTENTION.

There will be a special meeting of carriage workers at Musical Exchange Band rooms THIS EVENING (Saturday) at 7 30 sharp. Business of importance. Per order.
my13-1t* PRESIDENT.

APPLICATION FOR TRANSFER OF LIQUOR LICENSES.

Michael Hines makes application to transfer his first and fourth class liquor licenses from the southwest corner Coggeshall and Belville avenue to Nos. 870 and 876 Acushnet avenue. my13-1t*

PLANTS! PLANTS! PLANTS!

All my stock of Plants to be sold out at a great reduction, among them a fine lot of Hydrangea, sale commencing **MONDAY, May 15th,** to continue until all are sold.

JOHN F. TYNAN,
341 Cedar Street.
my13-6t*

VETERAN FIREMEN, ATTENTION!

Every member of the New Bedford Veteran Firemen's Association is requested to turn out MONDAY NIGHT to work the engine. Come one, come all! Meet at 7 sharp.
B. F. LEWIS, Foreman.
W. A. Gibbs, Secretary. my13-2t

SPECIAL NOTICE.

The annual meeting of the stockholders of the Acushnet Co-operative Association will be held at the store SATURDAY, May 13th, at 8 p. m. WM. COLE, JR., Secretary.
my12-2t*

BUSINESS.

JENNEY & BUFFINGTON have established a permanent office at No. 1 Crapo street, corner Grinnell, which will be open daily for business from 8 a. m. to 5 p. m., during which time they can be reached by telephone at any hour. my11-3t*

RHODE ISLAND, East Greenwich.
East Greenwich Academy,
FOUNDED 1802.
Both sexes. On Narragansett bay. Steam heat and electric light. Endowed. Twelve courses. $200 a year. Sept. 12. Write for illustrated catalogue. F. D. BLAKESLEE, D. D. Principal. my6-8t*

Attention, New Bedford Grocers.

Driscol, Church & Hall are wholesale distributing agents for "London Cream Biscuit" and other specialties from Young & Larrabee. my1-1m*

ADELPHI RINK.

The Riding School having closed the rink will at once be put in first class condition to rent for Balls, Fairs, etc. For particulars inquire of A. E. HATHAWAY,
my2-1m* 100 Pleasant Street.

REMOVAL.
JOHN N. PIERCE.
Attorney and Counsellor at Law,
Room 14, Five Cents Savings Bank Building

GEORGE PEIRCE,
ORGANS AND PIANOS
TUNED, REPAIRED AND POLISHED.
5 Dover Street.
Telephone.............259-12

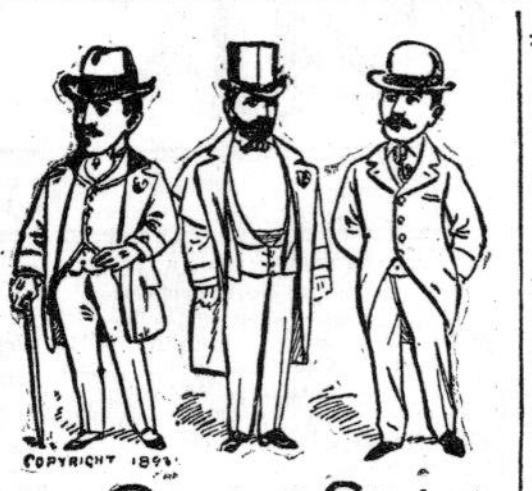

The Correct Styles

are the correct thing to have, and our store is the correct place to find them. Correctness is the essential point in one's attire—correctness of fit and style, supplemented with the employment of appropriate materials. Only suits made to order by artistic tailors have perfect fit and can give perfect satisfaction. Make your

Spring Outfit Perfect

in every particular by having it made up by us of cheviot, etc., in the frock, sack, or cutaway style. All our suits have cut a way into unbounded popularity because those who wear them, cut an elegant figure in perfectly correct attire. What can be more elegant than correctness. We have them at $10.00, $12.00 and $15.00.

M. C. SWIFT & SON,
153, 157 and 159 Union St.
NEW BEDFORD, MASS.

SPECIAL NOTICES.

MISS E. C. CASE'S GREAT CLOSING SALE!

Ladies should take advantage of this sale to secure fine goods at

EXTREMELY LOW PRICES.

E. C. CASE, - - 13 Pleasant St.
BRICK BLOCK.
TTS*

SEALERS OF WEIGHTS AND MEASURES' NOTICE.

The law of this Commonwealth compels all persons using scales, weights and measures for buying or selling, to have them sealed annually. I would give notice to all persons using scales, weights and measures, that if the same are brought to my office, Rooms of Registrars of Voters, basement of City Hall, by May 24, no charge will be made for sealing the same, except for alteration or repairs. After the above date I shall proceed to call on such as do not bring in the above and shall charge the regular fees.
Office Hours 10 30 to 12, 3 to 5.
JAMES H. PEASE,
Sealer of Weights and Measures.
my1tmy25*

AT THE PARKER HOUSE
You can get a
TEN MEAL TICKET FOR $5.00.
Good for breakfast, dinner and supper. Not transferable. *my8-6m

CARD.

Mrs. M. B. Rounsvell, for many years with Purrington & Brown and lately with C. F. Wing, will be pleased to meet her old customers at the new store, No. 73 William street, Waite Building, under the firm name of A. S. Rounsvell & Co., dealers in crockery, art novelties and wall paper. my5-8t

FOR SALE
Chickering Baby Grand Piano.

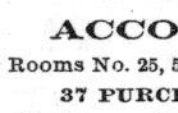

In good order. Real Cheap. Call at 5 Dover st., in rear of Bourne's salesroom.
GEORGE PEIRCE.
ap17-tf*

G. D. POPPLE
ACCOUNTANT.
☞ Rooms No. 25, 5c. Savings Bank Building.
37 PURCHASE STREET.
Your business solicited. Take the elevator.
mh7-2m

PARTNER WANTED.
Prefer a Practical Printer or Good Salesman.

☞ This is no bonanza, but an excellent chance for an intelligent young man, who will attend strictly to business, to draw a good salary for his labor and realize a handsome interest on his capital invested.
Apply to PAUL HOWLAND, JR.,
d20-tf 45 William Street.

WHY NOT BUILD A HOME?
THROUGH THE CO-OPERATIVE BANKS
You can buy or build a Home.
Call for Circulars.
WINSLOW BUILDING.
W&S CHARLES R. PRICE, Sec'y.

O'Neil
ARTIST PHOTOGRAPHER
High Class Work at Low Prices.
(Hastings Building.) TTS

E. E. TOLMAN,
Leader of the Grand Opera House orchestra, teacher of violin; Will also furnish the best music for all occasions. Apply at residence, 238 Acushnet avenue, or box office of theater.
mh28-tf

REMOVAL.
ALEXANDER McL. GOODSPEED,
ATTORNEY AND COUNSELLOR AT LAW.
New Five Cents Savings Bank Building,
37 Purchase St., Room 13. s30-tf

T. F. DESMOND. WENDELL H. COBB
DESMOND & COBB,
Attorneys and Counsellors at Law.
Rooms 6, 7, 8 Five Cents Savings Bank Building, 37 Purchase st., up one flight.
o14-tf

MAYOR'S OFFICE HOURS.

☞ On and after MONDAY, January 2d, the office hours of the Mayor will be from 11 A. M. until 12 30 P. M. ja6-tf

M. C. ROGERS, . . 30 Purchase St.
OPEN
For the Spring and Summer Season.
ap1-tf

TYPE-WRITING.
MRS. KENDALL, Copyist.
Room 21,............Robeson Building.
Copying of all kinds.
Supplies for all Type-Writers.

MADAME DEVOLL.
CLAIRVOYANT, DOCTRESS & BUSINESS MEDIUM.
Has moved from No. 70 Mill st., to No. 10 Bedford St. Office hours from 9 to 12 A. M. 2 to 9 P. M. jy25-tmy22

Clairvoyant, Business and Test Medium.
☞ MRS. EDDY can be consulted at 128 Union street. Hours strictly from 10 to 12 A. M., and 2 to 9 P. M. Ladies 50 cts.; Gents $1.00

SPECIAL NOTICES.

DON'T DELAY

Until about to go away, but leave your order with us now for an

ENGRAVED PLATE

and Cards.

GOOD WORK,
LATEST NEW YORK STYLES.

ROBERT W. TABER,
Bookseller and Stationer,
PURCHASE cor. HIGH STREET

WHEELS.

LOVELL DIAMOND.

We have them in Ladies', Gentlemen's and Convertible styles.

PNEUMATIC TIRES:
$85, $100, $115.

CUSHION TIRES:
$75, $90, $105.

A Year's Warrant with each wheel.

PURRINGTON, BROWN & RICHARDS,
ODD FELLOWS BLDG.

Formerly Geo. D. Richards.

PAPER HANGINGS!

Spring has now really come, and house cleaning has come with it. In the general renovation the walls must be papered, for there is nothing for so little money which brightens up and makes the rooms look so clean and pleasant as new paper. Wall paper is so cheap now, especially in our store, that it is better economy to have it than to go without it. Come and see us before you buy and be convinced. If you need

NEW CURTAINS

at the same time, our prices are the lowest.

HENRY J. TAYLOR & SON,
Cor. William and Sixth Sts.

REMEMBER!

That we re-upholster and re-finish Old Furniture, and in many cases make it more desirable than when new.

OUR STOCK OF FURNITURE COVERINGS

Comprises a most complete assortment of both foreign and domestic fabrics. A postal will bring our chief upholsterer to your house, who will give you a careful estimate of cost.

☞ We guarantee very best work at moderate prices.

CHARLES F. WING.
34 to 40 PURCHASE ST.

☞ If you have Neuralgia, Headache or Rheumatism, try the New Remedy and get relief. For those excruciating pains in the Eyes, Jaws, Temples, Cheek Bones or Facial Neuralgia, and for Rheumatism in all its various forms, such as Lumbago, Sciatica and Rheumatism of the Heart it acts like magic relieving you almost instantly. It is an Alkaline Compound free from Opium, Morphine, Strychnine, Arsenic, Belladonna, Hydrate of Chloral and all other poisonous ingredients and operates by neutralizing the poisonous Uric Acid in the blood, which the Kidneys fail to eliminate. Every bottle warranted to give perfect satisfaction or your money refunded. It is not a cure all, but it is remarkable how many aches and pains it will alleviate.

Manufactured and for sale by

C. H. CHURCH,
Cor. Purchase and Middle, and Cor. Union and Pleasant Sts.,
NEW BEDFORD, MASS.

AGENT FOR THE FOX EYE GLASS.

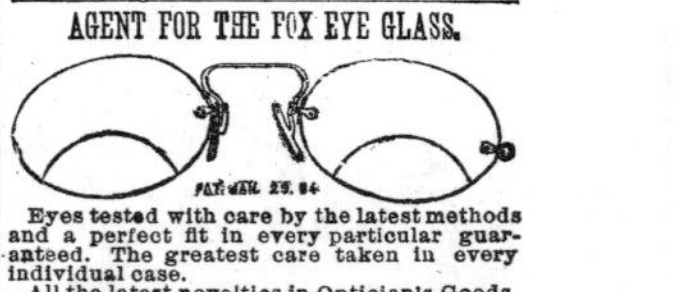

Eyes tested with care by the latest methods and a perfect fit in every particular guaranteed. The greatest care taken in every individual case.

All the latest novelties in Optician's Goods added to my stock as soon as out. Oculist orders a specialty. Repairing neatly done.

JAS. T. ALMY, - - - Practical Optician.
188 UNION STREET.
Opposite Moynan & Co. TTS

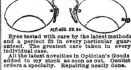

Pages 1-8.

The Evening Standard.

Pages 1-8.

ESTABLISHED FEBRUARY, 1850.

NEW BEDFORD, MONDAY, MAY 15, 1893.---TEN PAGES.

TWO CENTS.

HASKELL & TRIPP.

Anything you'll be likely to want in

Parasols:

A bewildering assortment now ready. The entire stock is "fresh as a daisy." As a leading bargain we are giving early buyers a choice from several extra good styles in both plain and ruffled parasols, including China silks, plain and changeable surahs and printed Indias, worth all the way from $2.50 to $4. *Our price for this line only $1.89 each.*

Stamped table covers ready to embroider.

Just opened a new line of patterns on much better quality twilled cloth than ever before shown for the price.

And that price?

Only 25c. The covers are a yard square and the colors are nice browns, tans and modes.

Still running that marvelous bargain in all-linen stamped tray cloths, 12½c. apiece.

The cut-price dress goods.

From $1 down to 59c. a yard is a big break, especially when you take into consideration the fact of the goods being entirely new, imported from France for this season's trade.

Wide (45-inch) French serges, considered cheap at 75c. in any store in the land, our present price 59c. a yard.

"Iridescent" serges, first-class colorings, 39c.

At the trimming counter are these desirable things:

Eton jackets (imported passementerie).

Pearl and metal buckles.

Satin and linen back velvet ribbons.

No. 1 width, velvet ribbons, millinery shades.

Immense variety of stylish braids.

The wanted widths, plain and beaded headings.

Big pearl buttons for jackets.

Velveteen dress facings, 6 yard pieces.

Ginghams that truly the real Scotch goods are being offered on our counter at retail for less than the actual cost to manufacture. Just glance down the long line marked 12½c. a yard. No, neither you nor we have *ever before* seen the time when 12½c. a yard would take *such quality* as this.

Every department of the great store is filled with seasonable merchandise--the kinds that people want--marked at prices you can afford to pay. *The producer and consumer meet with only one agent between them.* This reduces the three or four profits of the past to a single one, and that is smaller than it used to be.

We can help you to save money.

HASKELL & TRIPP,
Department Stores,
Purchase and William Streets.

THE POST OFFICE FIGHT.

No Change in the Situation as Viewed in Washington.

Comments on Candidate Ashley's Stay at the Capital.

Applicants' Chances Injured by Calling on Cabinet Officers.

(Special Dispatch.)

Washington, May 15.—No charges against Postmaster Gifford of New Bedford have yet been filed at the post office department. It does not necessarily follow that Assistant Secretary Quincy has not seen any, and does not know of any, though the officials here who are familiar with Mr. Gifford's record will not admit for a moment that any charges could be brought with the slightest trace of decency. Postmaster General Bissell is as firm as ever in his determination not to make removals except for offensive partisanship or for inefficiency or other cause, and it is as true as ever that appointments in the postal service are not made until the expirations of terms, and terms are considered as beginning with the dates of commissions.

It is entirely possible that Candidate Ashley may have come to town and found it likely to be useless, or even hurtful, to appear at the post office department and urge his candidacy, for he did not appear there nor at any of the usual lounging places of visiting politicians. The recent order of President Cleveland excluding office seekers from the White House has had a most depressing effect upon all visiting candidates. They have not only seen the wisdom of keeping away from the president, but they are also beginning to reflect whether their chances are not injured by applying to the cabinet officers, especially since it has been rumored here that each one of these intends shortly to issue an order similar to the president's. If this is the true supposition with regard to Mr. Ashley, he may very likely have called upon Josiah Quincy, either at the state department or at the assistant secretary's lodgings at the Albany after dark; and it would be almost certain that he would be advised by Mr. Quincy, even if it were admitted that this particular candidate's chances for appointment were the best, or even if he had been slated for the position of postmaster at New Bedford by the state boss, with the assistance of his local Democratic advisers, that he should be advised that it would be better to go quietly home and say nothing. It is doubtful, however, if Mr. Ashley has any assurances so definite as the ones mentioned, for the real fight over the position is yet months away, according to all indications, and evidently it would not be good politics to take some action which might have to be undone later, or which, in view of any contingency likely to arise might not prove to be "the best politics" in November or December.

The fact is that the Democratic bosses of Massachusetts, as in other states, are proceeding with great caution in the apportionment of the offices, especially where contests are involved, and they have almost invariably settled their disputes at home, so the annoyance and scandal of them shall not be dragged hither. It would be likely, therefore, to do any one of the New Bedford candidates very little good to come to Washington, except, of course, as he might profit by a conference with Mr. Quincy; for he might find out in that way that certain local indorsements were necessary, and then he might proceed more intelligently to get them. The Republican administration reappointed a number of New England postmasters, though that custom was very rare in other states. The Democrats are not expected to be so generous, however much the civil service reformers, who are stronger in Massachusetts than elsewhere, may insist on reappointments. At any rate, the present administration is taking its time, and though practically all of the offices are to be changed, it is more convenient to have the office-hunting and office-giving indulged over a long period; and hence the custom of waiting for the expiration of terms.

It is entirely possible, of course, that New Bedford Democrats, to whom Mr. Quincy must look for counsel, may settle among themselves very soon whom they will recommend, and that man will be recommended in due course to the postmaster general. A selection like this, however, would give notice to all unsuccessful candidates that they had been passed over, though, as previously hinted, a course like this would also avoid the risk of conflicts between the present time and the time when the appointment should be made. It is a common and a very natural error to suppose that the whole of the ten thousand post office fights, now going on, attract the same amount of attention in Washington that they attract locally. The division of the department do not take cases up, and have no knowledge of them, except as the petitions or letters come straggling in (all of which are filed mechanically away without any particular notice) until the referee, as he is called—in this case Mr. Quincy—finally recommends to the postmaster general the appointment of some particular man.

BIT OF A POLICEMAN'S EAR.

Fall River Policeman Badly Used Up in a Sunday Night Fight.

(Special Dispatch.)

Fall River, May 15.—Last night about 9 o'clock Patrolman John Wadsworth of the northern police station, who was covering his beat near the Narragansett mill house heard a disturbance in the tenement of Antone Corie. On entering the house the policeman found himself confronted by six Portuguese men who were anxious to fight. The men attacked Wadsworth, knocked him down and kicked him. A desperate melee followed. The officer drew his club, but it was taken from him and used with terrible effect on his own head. After knocking Wadsworth down one of the men grabbed him by the neck, and hugging him closely to his body, bit off one of his ears. The officer was so badly used up that he had to be carried to his home. Three of his assailants were arrested, arraigned in court today and held in $1,100, as the officer was unable to appear.

WEATHER INDICATIONS.

Fair and Warmer.

Washington, May 15.—For the 24 hours from 8 a. m. today: For New England, generally fair, southwest or west winds.

Boston, May 15.—Local forecast for New England until Tuesday night: Generally fair, except local rains this afternoon or tonight in Vermont and western Massachusetts; slight changes in temperature, except warmer Tuesday in southern portions.

Ocean Steamers.

Arrived—At New York, Aurania, Liverpool; Cicinda Condal, Vera Cruz; Wakefield, Girgenti; Aurilla, Belfast; Europe, London; Arizona, Liverpool.

LIZZIE BORDEN ILL.

No Serious Results Anticipated from Her Sickness.

Only Limited Space for Press Representatives at the Trial.

Testimony of Medical Experts to be Introduced in the Case.

For the first time since the incarceration of Lizzie Borden at Taunton jail she is under the care of a physician. She has a slight attack of tonsilitis, and it is thought that no more alarming symptoms will appear. She caught cold on the day of her arraignment.

A special to the Standard says the report from Taunton jail this morning is to the effect that Miss Borden is somewhat improved in health and no serious consequences are anticipated.

Dr. Paige, jail physician, said to an Associated Press reporter that Miss Borden's illness is of bronchial nature and came on after her return from the arraignment. The following day she experienced a sudden chill and has since been under his care. Owing to noise in the women's quarter, she has been taken into the keeper's house, where it is quiet. She will undoubtedly be in fair condition at the time of her trial.

The generally accepted idea that anywhere from 40 to 50 newspaper men are to be accommodated at the court house is far fetched. As a matter of fact, the accommodations will be exceedingly limited, the chief justice having decided opinions in regard to this matter. He believes that the body politic has quite as much right in the court room during the hearing of a case like this as newspaper people. The trial will take place before what might be called the second jury as the jury will occupy the seats usually occupied by the second jury. The witness box on the right hand side of the court room, facing the bench, will be given up to newspaper men and this space will admit of about, 12 or 15 persons. If there are other newspaper men to be accommodated they must take their chances elsewhere in the court room, and do their writing at a decided disadvantage, for no other tables or conveniences will be allowed. The aisles will all be kept clear throughout the trial, nobody will be allowed to stand and at the slightest sound of applause or disturbance the sheriff will be ordered to clear the room. It is stated that the case will be conducted to a large extent upon scientific grounds, that is to say, medical expert testimony will be introduced to a considerable extent.

The venire for the jurors in the Borden case was received by the Bristol county clerk this morning. It calls for 45 men from this city.

In the Providence Sunday Journal there was an intimation that Bridget Sullivan may be expected to testify in reference to the strained relations existing between Lizzie Borden and her stepmother, but Miss Sullivan has little definite information on this point and she will not be called upon to testify concerning the family relations. The government, it is said, lost one of its strongest links through the death of Henry G. Trickey. The argument has been employed in Miss Borden's defense that she could not have committed the murders and have avoided being covered with blood, and the absence of blood on her clothing when she summoned assistance so soon after the murders were committed has been unreconcilable with her guilt in the minds of many people. The theory upon which the government will proceed at the coming trial is said to be partly based upon the blood stains found on the inside panel of the dining room doorway. Professor Wood said to the district attorney at the preliminary trial that there was nothing to conflict with the theory that the assailant stood behind the dining room partition and struck Mr. Borden through the doorway. The position of the sofa upon which Mr. Borden lay in the sitting room would make this entirely feasible. This, the government thinks, would account for the fact that there was no blood on Lizzie's dress. It is agreed that it would have been difficult for Miss Borden's assailant to have avoided blood spurts, for in this case the murderer stood over her and swung the weapon. But the government theory, it is said, is that the assailant of Mr. Borden stood behind the doorway when the killing blows were struck, and that sufficient time elapsed between the two murders for the murderer to have made a change of clothing.

HOME MATTERS.

THE FIRE DEPARTMENT.

Appointments at a Meeting of the Board of Engineers.

A very important meeting of the board of fire engineers was held Saturday evening at which every member of the board was present. The board approved the list of officers recently elected by the different engine companies, and besides appointed Charles Haskins, the spare driver, tillerman for ladder truck No. 1, in place of Charles Vining, who leaves the department on Friday next to accept a position in Providence, where it is said Mr. Vining will be attached to the water tower in the fire department of that city. Edward Cowperwaite, for a number of years brakeman on the Old Colony railroad, was appointed spare driver in the department to fill the vacancy caused by the promotion of Charles Haskins as stated above.

FOR ST. LUKE'S.

Collections Made at Different Churches in This City.

Yesterday was hospital day at many of the churches in this city, when collections were taken as follows:

Unitarian church, $250, and more expected this week.
Grace church, $143.54.
North Christian church, $50.
William Street Baptist, about $40.
North Congregational church, about $25.
Universalist church, about $20.
Pleasant Street M. E., about $20, a very small collection.
County Street M. E. church, it is thought about $40.

A black T. D. pipe in the mouth of the eagle that adorns the gable on the Pleasant and school house has arrested the attention and excited the merriment of passers by for the past two or three weeks. All who have seen it have been in a quandary as to how it came there. The mystery is easily explained. A painter who had been smoking while at work, laid his pipe, bowl up, on the eagle's bill and got it. Shortly afterwards the staging was taken away, and when the man's attention was drawn to his pipe by a desire to smoke there was no way to reach it.

The work of putting in sewers at the Wamsutta mills village was commenced this morning.

Scup 10 cents per pound, F. E. Tinkham, 9 North Sixth street, telephone 252-1.

BODY FOUND.

Floating in Buzzards Bay North of Black Rock.

Towed to This Port and Placed in Wilson's Morgue.

Thought to be the Body of a Man Lost from a Steamer.

This forenoon the schooner smack J. L. Berry, Joseph L. Sylvia owner, was sailing from West Island to this port for a load of lumber. When about half a mile north of Black rock, and about an equal distance from the west shore of Sconticut Neck, Captain Sylvia saw something white floating in the water, and took it to be the buoy of a lobster pot. He bore up for it, and as the schooner drew near he discovered it to be the body of a man. The dory was launched, and Captain Sylvia pulled to the body, which was floating with the head down. A rope was passed around the body and attached to the stern of the schooner, which, with colors at half-mast, put away for this port. Steamer Volunteer came within hail, and Captain Sylvia requested Captain Doane to notify the authorities of the finding of the body, and that he would put in at Greene & Wood's wharf. Captain Doane did as requested, and the police notified Undertaker Wilson, who sent a carriage to the wharf. On the arrival of the schooner at the wharf the body was taken from the water, and took it for grown, it was apparently of middle age, about five feet nine inches in height, of stout build, with iron gray hair, and dressed in grayish mixed pantaloons, brown cardigan jacket buttoned up, checked shirt, and heavy, laced brogan shoes, with both nails in the taps. The face and hands are badly disfigured, and the features are unrecognizable. All the hair on the head was one tuft of brown on top. It is thought the body may be that of a man from Fall River, it is reported who was lost overboard from a tugboat in Vineyard sound about the 20th of March last. The remains were taken to Mr. Wilson's morgue, and Dr. Hough, medical examiner, notified.

PERSONAL.

Louie A. Pratt, who has been principal of the schools at Cottage City, left this morning for Chester, where he will assume charge of the superintendency of the Hampden county schools, to which position he was recently elected at a salary of $1,500 per year. Mr. Pratt's brother, Linwood S. Pratt of Ogdensburg, N. Y. will assume charge of the Cottage City schools for the unexpired term.

At a recent meeting of the Massachusetts Association of Minute Men of '61 the following comrades were among those chosen delegates to the national convention to be held at Indianapolis in September: At large, General David W. Cowdroy; Third Infantry, Major Austin S. Cushman; Fourth Infantry, Hon. Elijah A. Morse.

The Advent Christian church of this city has extended a call to Elder J. F. Clothy of Bangor, Me., to become its pastor. Elder Clothy has accepted the call, and will finish an eight years' pastorate with the church in Bangor the first Sunday in June, and will immediately remove to this city and begin his labors.

President Minnie E. Vincent of Corps 134 of Cottage City has contributed much to the decoration of the W. R. C. headquarters in sending to the department officers some rare and beautiful sea weeds mounted upon cards. They have been very much admired, and were arranged by her son, a student at Yale college.

James H. Manning, formerly engineer of the Cornell mill, Fall River, who has been secured by the Bristol mill of this city to take charge of its engines, assumed his duties today. Thomas Daily, formerly of the Crescent mill, Fall River, is to become master mechanic at the Bristol.

The condition of Bishop C. D. Foss of the Methodist Episcopal church, who fell down stairs recently at Evanston, Ill., has taken a serious turn, as erysipelas has set in. The doctors have forbidden his going to Japan for a year, and Bishop Foster of Roxbury will take his place.

Hennessey says in the Boston Globe's state house column: "Mr. Smalley of Nantucket has been reported as the victim of the sugar market during the recent panic. Barring the loss of a little pin money the one member is all right, he says."

Mrs. Julia F. Weeks has been elected president of the W. C. T. U. Mrs. Mary N. Nind, Mrs. Alice S. Feltz, Mrs. Dr. Lilley and Mrs. Deborah Lucas were chosen delegates to the county convention to be held in Dighton, 17th inst.

It is highly probable that Manager William B. Cross of the Opera House will soon become a member of the Jefferson colony on Buttermilk bay, as negotiations are pending looking to his becoming a land and cottage holder there.

T. J. Murphy is confined to his house as a result of the injuries he received in the runaway, 11th inst. He was more badly injured than was at first supposed, having had three ribs fractured.

Rev. J. S. Swaim and son Roger are to leave this week for Chicago to visit the World's fair. Before his return Mr. Swaim will attend the national convention of the Baptist denomination at Denver.

Mary Mercier of this city sailed Saturday on steamer Bergenland of the Red Star line from New York for Antwerp.

William B. Fisher, John and Joseph Kennedy have gone to Chicago and the World's fair.

A special meeting of Potomska lodge 1518, G. U. O. of O. F., will be held tomorrow evening. See special notice.

The rite of baptism was administered to two persons at the First Baptist church Sunday.

Anything and everything bought by John McCullough. Postal or telephone 158—12. Rags, bottles, iron.

Every member of the Veteran Firemen's association is requested to meet this evening at 7 o'clock to help work the engine. Pleasant street, between Mill and Maxfield streets, is being put in thorough repair.

Scup 10 cents per pound, F. E. Tinkham, 9 North Sixth street, telephone 252-1.

Horse Neck—Fish dinners now served at Ocean County with broiled lobsters, by A. Macomber. Hood's Sarsaparilla makes the weak strong.

THE BORDEN MURDER TRIAL.

The Evening Standard is perfecting arrangements to give the public as complete and accurate reports of the great murder trial as can be printed. Orders should be early placed with your nearest newsdealer, or word sent to this office, and the Standard will be sent regularly during the trial.

COURT INSTITUTED.

On Saturday evening Dionysesus court of Collanthe, No. 10, was instituted by the supreme chancellor, W. S. Mower, of Philadelphia. The following officers were installed:

Past Worthy Counselor—Mrs. Jennie Hopewell.
Associate Counselor—Mrs. Susie M. Sullavou.
Worthy Counselor—Mr. William D. Reynolds.
Associate Counselor—Mrs. Laura G. Swan.
Worthy Orator—Mrs. Sarah King.
Worthy Register of Deeds—Mrs. Clara L. York.
Worthy Register of Accounts—Mrs. Flora Reynolds.
Worthy Receiver of Deposits—Mrs. Carrie Post.
Worthy Escort—Mrs. Bessie Bryant.
Worthy Conductress—Mrs. Bianca Howland.
Worthy Guide—Mrs. Martha Reed.
Worthy Herald—Mrs. Helen Guinn.
Worthy Protector—Mr. John Barbour.

The court started with a membership of 23, and is the auxiliary branch to Friendship lodge, No. 11 K. of P.

SONS OF VETERANS.

The 11th annual convention of the Massachusetts Division Sons of Veterans will be held in this city Wednesday and Thursday, June 14 and 15, 1893. Convention to open at 8 a. m. June 14. Division headquarters will be established at the Parker House. A division council meeting will be held June 14 at 3 p. m. at the Parker House for the purpose of auditing the books and other business. Credentials should be presented to Adjutant H. Frank Williamson upon arrival at the convention. Camps or private parties desiring hotel accommodations should apply to Arthur W. Forbes, 67 Purchase street, New Bedford, at once.

CONDENSED LOCALS.

There is little change in the strike of the backboys at Wamsutta mills this morning. The differs in No. 6 mill have returned to work. The mill management have made a proposition to give the boys 25 cents per week increase if the spinners will do the same. This amounts to the same as cutting the spinners down 25 cents per week, a suggestion to which they will not give the slightest consideration. The boys at a meeting held this forenoon agreed to remain out until their demands were granted.

An inquisitive employe at the Bristol mill this morning had curiosity enough to see how the fire alarm box at that mill operated, and upon opening the door learned for the first time that he could not withdraw the key. Master Mechanic Briggs was obliged to repair to the scene and remove the key for him. That man will probably be instructed to let the box alone except in cases of fire.

Unsuccessful searches for liquor were made Saturday evening at the tenements of Charles Nye and James Bradley on North Friar street, the Plainville House, kept by John Doyle, and at the house in Evergreen park kept by Albert Aldritch Sunday evening the police made an unsuccessful search for liquor at the house of Amalic Peckham on Topham street.

All the police officers of the day force have been ordered to send their light helmets to police station 1 in order that the new numbers may be changed to correspond with the new numbers given the day force. The day officers have also been ordered to report at $45 tonight to draw lots for furloughs.

A horse attached to a buggy which was unoccupied ran furiously down Blackmer street this morning and struck a telephone pole. The top of the buggy and one wheel was taken off. The horse continued down South Water street.

The work of laying the new sewer in Wamsutta village commenced today. The cars on the Purchase street line are considerably delayed in consequence and the passengers are obliged to transfer at the head of Wamsutta street.

The lathers of this city have formed a branch of the National Lathers' union, with 25 charter members. The prices paid here for laying laths is from $1.50 to $1.75 per 1,000. June 15th the union men will demand $2 per 1,000.

The members of Hill's band are to be supplied with new pantaloons of dark blue Middlesex flannel, with a half-inch mohair stripe, by Joseph Tessier. They are also to have new ponchos and hats.

Quick Dessert—Nothing better than Puddine or Rex Gelatine. Call and see a practical illustration and try the goods. We make a very low price, three packages for 25c. Boston Branch.

The A. M. E. Zion conference held in Boston have decided that the annual convention of Sunday schools shall be held in this city instead of Great Barrington, as at first intended.

Twelve members of the class of '90, Sanborn B. Bridgewater Normal school, dined at the Parker House, Boston, Saturday afternoon, Mr. Frank E. Gurney of Brockton presiding.

The permanent men at the Bedford street fire station were called to the house of John Southwick on Spring street, Saturday, where they looked after a chimney fire.

Horses, mares, colts, family, trotting, Warr estate, Wareham, administratrix's sale. Descriptive catalogue mailed free. Send—Loring & Carroll, 272 Franklin street, Boston.

Dr. Parker will examine afflicted free at Mansion House, New Bedford, Wednesday, May 17. Ruptures, varicoceles and hydroceles cured without operations, pain or detention from business.

Ask your grocer for "London Cream Biscuit." They are the finest crackers in the world. The words London Cream stamped upon every cracker.

Colonel Thomas E. Barker, treasurer of the Soldiers' home, reports a donation of $5 from Woman's Relief corps 95 of this city.

A valuable setter dog was killed by the cars at the Weld street crossing this morning.

Some valuable Pekin bantam fowls belonging to Mrs. Smith, 83 Parker street. were killed by dogs last night.

Seup 10 cents per pound, F. E. Tinkham, 9 North Sixth street, telephone 252-1.

Pages 1-8.

The Evening Standard.

Pages 1-8.

ESTABLISHED FEBRUARY, 1850.

NEW BEDFORD, WEDNESDAY, MAY 17, 1893.---TWELVE PAGES.

TWO CENTS.

HASKELL & TRIPP.

Furnishings for the summer cottage.

The springing grass,
The balmy air,
The budding trees,
The lengthening days,
} Harbingers of Summer.

Already the vacation thought begins to assert itself, and anticipations of the summer outing lighten the burden of the toiler.

About time to think of getting the summer home in readiness.

Our great stock furnishes a satisfying assortment of all the needfuls. Wonderfully convenient, too, to be able to supply nearly all your wants in this direction under one roof, without the bother and annoyance of running hither and thither about town.

Here are some of the things you'll likely want:

Summer Blankets, { White, $1.25, $1.75, $2.50, $3.50. Colored, $1, $1.25, $2, $3.

Summer Bed-spreads. { White, 75c., $1, $1.25, $1.50. Colored, $1.25, $2, $2.50.

Feather pillows, 69c., 89c., $1.25, $1.50. All made from feather-proof ticking.

Pillowcases from good cotton, 12½c.

Bleached sheets, 2¼ x 2¾ yds., 70c.

Portieres for the doorways. Select from nine different colors in either plain or bordered, $3.50, $4.50, $5 the pair.

Lace curtains for the windows, $1. $1.50, $2 pair.

Window shades mounted on spring rollers ready to hang, 25c. Eight tints.

Venetian window blinds, 69c.

Adjustable fly screens, fit any window, 25c.

India jute rugs, 26 x 54 in., $1.50.

White dotted muslins make cool-looking window draperies, 19c., 25c., 37c. a yard.

Double-faced canton plushes for door draperies, cost 25c. yd.

Turkey red tablecloth by the yard, 25c. and 50c. Fast colors.

Excellent values in half-bleached table linens by the yard at 39c. and 50c.

Turkey red covers: 8-4, $1.75; 10-4, $2.

Wonderfully pretty half-bleached linen covers, bordered, 9-4, $1.

Half-bleached doilies, 69c. a dozen.

Turkey red doilies, $1 a doz.

Best towels you ever saw at the price, 12½c.

Look over the following list and see if the kitchen or pantry service couldn't be improved by a generous selection:

Tea spoons, 45c. doz. Table spoons, 90c. doz. } Excellent plate.

Set of one-half dozen each knives and forks, 57c., 75c., $1.13 the set.

Glass salts and peppers, 5c. each.

Wonderfully pretty glass pitchers, 17, 21, 37, 42c.

Glass set, 4 pieces, sugar, butter, creamer, spoon holder. } 50c set.

Etched glass tumblers, 59c. a dozen. Bowls, 7c. each. Tin coffee pots, 25c. and 37c. each. Granite Iron coffee pots, $1 and $1.25. Tea kettles, nickel plated on copper, 89c. Tin tea kettles for gas stoves, 25c. Wooden pails, 23c. Fibre pails, 42c. Good brooms, 19c., 25c., 39c. Feather dusters, 20c., 25c., 67c., according to size.

And a hundred other things you are likely to need. All of excellent quality and at proper prices.

HASKELL & TRIPP,
Department Stores,
Purchase and William Streets.

WEATHER INDICATIONS.

Fair and Cooler.

Washington, May 17.—For the 24 hours from 8 a. m. today: For New Hampshire, Vermont, Massachusetts, Rhode Island and Connecticut, showers, followed by fair Thursday, slightly cooler in the interior, southwest gales, becoming northwest.

Fair and Warmer.

Boston, May 17.—Local forecast for New England until Thursday night: Generally fair weather, preceded by rain today in Maine, New Hampshire and Vermont; warmer this afternoon, slight change Thursday, winds becoming westerly.

CREEKS SWOLLEN.

Culverts and Bridges Destroyed and a Part of Erie, Pa., Under Water.

Erie, Pa., May 17.—Heavy rain has been falling for the past 48 hours and all the creeks in and about Erie are raging torrents. Culverts and bridges have been destroyed in all parts of the city. A large section of the First Ward is under water. The Nickel Plate railroad bridge is threatened with destruction and is already in a shaky condition. One boy was drowned in Mill creek yesterday. The water is still rising.

Arkansas City, Ark., May 17.—The river gauge reads 49.6, a rise of .1 in the past 24 hours. At the mouth of White river, 70 miles above, the river is stationary, which is evident that the rivers have spent their force, which will be needed to offset the increased rise at Helena. The levees are holding in this neighborhood, and are being watched closely by 400 or 500 men. The back water in the city is rising rapidly, and families are constantly moving. Nearly all of the territory in five miles of here to the Arkansas river is submerged.

Cleveland, O., May 17.—A furious storm, which commenced last Sunday night, still prevails today. Up to 9 o'clock this morning nearly 3½ inches of rain had fallen. The wind reached a velocity of 40 miles an hour last night. Many half completed houses were blown down, and cattle sheds were demolished in large numbers. The Cuyahoga river is over its banks in the lumber district on the flats, and great quantities of lumber are being carried out into the lake. The loss to lumber firms will be very heavy. A bad washout is reported just east of the city on the Cleveland, Canton & Southern railroad. Railroad traffic on that line is cut off.

FITTED FOR THE MINISTRY.

Commencement Exercises of Yale Theological School.

New Haven, Ct., May 17.—The first of the departments of Yale to hold its commencement exercises is this year, as usual, that of the Theological school. They were begun in Battel chapel at 10 30 o'clock this morning and attended by about 500 people. President Timothy Dwight presided, and after opening the services with a prayer and hymn the following essays were delivered by members selected from the graduating class:

"The Ministry as a Stewardship," George Henry Flint, M. A. Williams college, Lincoln, Mass.

"The Christian Ideal of Education," Frank Curtiss, Putnam, B. A., Amherst college, Buffalo, N. Y.

"Vested Rights in the House of God," Charles Edward Harris, B. A., Yale university.

"The Modern Prophet," Lincoln Baker Goodrich, B. A., Amherst college, Plainfield, N. J.

Anthem by the divinity school octet.

"Savonarola, the Reformer," Evan Evans, B. A., Marietta college, Cincinnati.

"What China Needs," Charles Edward Ewing, B. A., Amherst college, Danvers, Mass.

"The Unrealized Idea in Journalism," Warren Joseph Moulton, B. A., Amherst college, Centre Sandwich, N. H.

"The New Education and the Christian Spirit," Albert Putnam Davis, B. A., Amherst college, Hyde Park, Mass.

Professor Fisher of the theological department delivered the annual parting address to the class. He remarked upon the high standard set by the class in meritorious scholarship and character, and bidding them God speed in their future life work.

The parting ode, written by B. Francis Case, of Granby, Ct., was then sung, after which the affair closed with the benediction.

After the exercises a collation was served to the alumni members of the divinity school and guests. At 2 o'clock the meeting of the alumni of the school was held in Marquand chapel. The reception to members and friends this evening will close the exercises of the school.

TRAMP BURGLARS.

Officers Capture Three of the Gang After a Hard Fight.

Grand Rapids, Mich., May 17.—A gang of ten tramps, armed with revolvers, and with jewelry about them, took possession of the Detroit, Grand Haven & Milwaukee railroad junction late Monday evening, and terrorized the neighbors. A saloon keeper was held up at the point of a revolver, and relieved of a gold watch and some money. The police were notified and three officers had a pitched battle with them, the tramps hiding in the woods and opening fire. The officers responded, and over 40 shots were exchanged, but owing to the intense darkness their aim was necessarily bad.

The officers succeeded in capturing three of the tramps after a hard fight, and one of them, giving the name of George J. Wilson, was badly cut and pounded, and covered with blood. On his person were found a revolver, the saloon keepers' watch, and a kit of burglars' tools. After the battle the tramps escaped in the darkness, and meeting Patrolman Starr, who was attracted by the firing, and was hastening to the scene, they surprised him, and at the point of a revolver, compelled him to throw up his hands while they relieved him of his handcuffs and revolver. A large squad of policemen searched all night for the other tramps, but were unsuccessful.

Cruiser Baltimore Sent to China.

Washington, May 17.—The navy department has decided to send the cruiser Baltimore to China as the flagship of the Asiatic station. While this determination has no direct bearing on the present agitation over the Chinese exclusion act, the decision of this subject has probably operated to precipitate the decision of the department to carry out its long contemplated purpose of sending a new flagship to China.

London Stock Exchange.

London, May 17.—The stock exchange opened today with a better tendency, but afterwards weakened. Buyers were scarce, and there were many liquidations.

At 2 p. m. the stock exchange was very flat. American railroad securities dropped from 2 to 2½, notably Louisville & Nashville, and also Canadian railway shares generally.

Fatal Accident in a Mill.

Lewiston, Me., May 17.—David Shelby, aged 35, employed in the Cumberland mill, was drawn into a picker today and so badly injured that he died in a few minutes. He belonged in Canada.

RECEIVER ASKED FOR.

Northwestern Guaranty Company Failure.

President Menage Says Depositors Will Not Lose.

Confident That Assets Are Sufficient to Pay Liabilities.

Minneapolis, Minn., May 17.—The Citizens bank has suspended, and a receiver has been asked for the Northwestern Guaranty Co. A good deal of surprise was manifested when the Citizens bank suspended payment. The notice on the door says that depositors will be paid in full. The officials declare that the bank is solvent, and that the suspension is due simply to its inability to realize promptly on its securities. The Citizens is one of the smaller state banks of this city. Its statement at the close of business May 4 shows loans and discounts $478,844; cash on hand and due from banks, $60,000; deposits, 283,913; surplus and profits, $16,800; rediscounts, $76,500. The capital is $250,000. The suspension is only temporary.

What the Northwestern Guaranty Loan Co's Officers Say.

Minneapolis, May 17.—The officials of the Northwestern Guaranty Loan company are not ready to make a statement of its condition in advance of suspension, which, however, they say will probably become necessary. The Journal says that the investors in the company will probably not lose a dollar; that the security taken is ample to pay every dollar; that the only possibility of loss is to the stockholders, and that President Menage is sure that they will be protected from loss also, providing the company is left to carry on business without forced liquidation. The statement was made in a dispatch from Troy, N. Y., that the company had $16,000,000 in debentures. The Journal says the debentures are only a little over $2,500,000. It is also stated that the commercial paper held by the company amounts to about the same amount as the debentures, and that this is well secured. President Menage is said to be confident that the assets are sufficient to pay the liabilities without calling on the stockholders.

More Cash on Hand Than Before the Run.

After a heavy run of two days the Farmers & Mechanics bank will commence business today with more cash in its vaults than it had when the run started. It is expected that there will be no further trouble. The other banks did not feel the effects of the run in any way.

Will Pay Dollar for Dollar.

Munroeville, Ind., May 17.—The Citizens bank of Munroeville, which closed its doors last Friday after a run of one hour had depleted its cash on hand, has opened its doors for business, with the statement that it would pay dollar for dollar on all indebtedness.

SUNDAY OPENING.

Opinion of Two of the Fair Commissioners in Regard to the Subject.

Chicago, May 17.—The rule adopted by the directors of the World's fair yesterday is the result of the conference with a number of lawyers from the national commission now in session. At this conference the plan proposed by Edward Walker and adopted by the board of directors was discussed at length. This proposition was to open Jackson park and keep the big buildings closed on Sunday. What the national commission will do with the new rule can only be conjectured. There is little doubt that with a full attendance the course mapped out by the directors yesterday will be indorsed.

Commissioner Smith of New Jersey said last night: "When it is made plain to me that the refusal of the local directory to accept the congressional appropriation makes the Sunday closing clause ineffective, I will vote to open the fair each and every Sunday. The directory has a right to make the new rule, subject to the sanction of the national commission. There is nothing equivocal in the reading of the law; we are here to support it, and as long as the law remains law it shall be supported. The proposal to pay congress the money advanced seems to make it possible to legally open the exposition."

Commissioner Breslin of New York says: "I regard an open fair on Sunday as a distinctly educational proposition, and I can speak for a majority of the national commissioners. We are not Sabbath desecrators; on the contrary to open the fair on Sundays is a recognition of the true purpose of the Sabbath, which cannot be overlooked. Of course I am in favor of Sunday opening. The national commissioners meet again tomorrow and it will be seen that a majority favor Sunday opening. As to repaying to the government the remainder of the $2,500,000 appropriated for souvenir coins, I do not think the fair management ought to promise anything of the kind."

LANSING LUMBER CO.

Report of the Committee on Condition of Its Affairs.

Lansing, Mich., May 17.—The committee appointed by the creditors of the Lansing Lumber company to inquire into and report upon the condition of its affairs, made a report at the second meeting of the creditors which shows the total assets to be $573,832, with liabilities of $461,163. A proposition was adopted for the transfer by O. M. Barnes to a trustee of security for the entire indebtedness upon all the company's property now held by him, and to issue bonds payable in five years from May 1, with interest at 6 per cent., payable semi-annually. The paper with Mr. Barnes' personal indorsement, aggregating $278,000, will be made preferred indebtedness.

AUSTRALIAN BANKS.

Court of the Queen's Bench Orders the Winding Up of Three Corporations.

London, May 17.—The court of queens bench has made an order for the winding up of the London Chartered bank of Australia, whose head office was at Melbourne, and has adjoined similar petitions for the winding up of the Australian Joint Stock bank of Sydney and of the National bank of Australia.

London, May 17.—Advices from Australia show that the financial crisis is still acute. It is announced that the Royal Bank of Queensland had suspended.

TO MEET IN FALL RIVER.

Next Session of the Primitive Methodist Conference in May, 1894.

Lawrence, May 17.—The annual session of the Primitive Methodist conference, which has been holding here the past week, was brought to a close today. The following district secretaries were elected: Brooklyn district, Rev. J. J. Arnand; Lowell district, Rev. W. H. Yarrow; Fall River district, Rev. L. G. Spencer. Rev. Mr. Blandy and wife and Miss Sarah Etchells were appointed evangelists. The conference meets at Fall River the second Tuesday of May, 1894.

THE WESTPORT BRIDGE.

County Commissioners Holding Another Hearing Today.

(Special Dispatch.)

Fall River, May 17.—The county commissioners are having a hearing in Westport today for the benefit of all parties interested in the proposed construction of a bridge from Westport Point to Horse Neck beach. The proposed structure would cut off four or five miles, it is believed, and there is little doubt it will be constructed at an early date. Civil Engineer Tiernan of this city is present at the hearing to answer questions as to the cost and other matters relative to the construction.

A MAN IN HER ROOM.

A Fall River Girl Frightened by a Prowling Negro.

(Special Dispatch.)

Fall River, May 17.—A young girl, 16 years of age, named Rose Murry, had a startling adventure at her home on Pearl street about 2 o'clock this morning. She awoke at that time, hearing footsteps about the house, and was thunder struck to see a big negro prowling about the room. She screamed for help at once and the intruder made a dive through the window, which was on the ground floor, carrying the sash along with him in his jump. The police were notified and are making an active search for the man.

THE BUNCO MEN.

Anthony Comstock Is Endeavoring to Protect Connecticut Farmers.

HARTFORD, May 17. — Anthony Comstock appeared before the judiciary committee yesterday afternoon in favor of a bill to prevent buncoing in Connecticut by green goods men. With him was United States Marshal Strong of Bridgeport, who assisted in the great raid upon the Bridgeport gang of green goods men last week.

They advocated the passage of a law similar to those of New York and New Jersey and said that Connecticut had not a law of any use to protect her citizens from the green goods men. He showed a list of persons who had been robbed by the gang from April 1, 1893, to date, taken from their books. The amounts aggregated $40,185, and the victims are scattered all over the country, principally in the far west.

Blame Laid on Strikers.

BUENA VISTA, O., May 17.—While a heavily loaded stone car was decending a tramway here the cable broke, sending the car down the steep grade. It struck a saw at which five men were working, instantly killing them. Strikers are accused of cutting the cable.

Big Strike at Indianapolis.

INDIANAPOLIS, May 17.—Over 2000 men who are laying asphalt on the street went on strike for an eight-hour day and increased wages. Men who remained at work were driven away by the strikers and details of police were called out to preserve order.

An Interesting Admission

ST. PETERSBURG, May 17.—The Russian government has warned members of the Panelavist committee to abstain from making any speech of a warlike character, which might furnish Chancellor Caprivi with arguments in favor of the German army bill.

She Wore Pants.

NEW YORK, May 17.—Ida M. Stewart was arrested in the Hunters Point ferryhouse for masquerading in male attire. She was accompanied by her husband. She was arraigned before Justice Noble and remanded.

A Dangerous Lad.

NEWARK, N. J., May 17.—Robert Alden Fales, the boy murderer of Thomas Hayden, who tried to escape from jail, is kept in his cell and closely watched. Warden McMonagle will not permit any person to see him.

Has Been a Hard Winter.

NEW YORK, May 17.—Incoming ships from the south Atlantic report universal quantities of pack ice and immense isolated bergs adrift in the track of ships bound either way around Cape Horn.

France and Russia.

BERLIN, May 17.—The mayor of Dantzic declares that M. Herbette, the French minister here, assured him that no treaty or agreement existed between France and Russia.

TELEGRAPHIC BREVITIES.

Commander Ballington Booth addressed a large audience of Salvation Army members in Springfield, Mass. Delegations were present from various corps in Massachusetts and Connecticut.

Schooner Kate Walker, of and from Bangor, Me., for New York, with a cargo of lumber, experienced a heavy easterly gale and sprung aleak. She arrived at Vineyard Haven, Mass., leaking badly.

The Rockville Water and Aqueduct company has been organized with a capital of $195,000, for the purpose of furnishing the city of Rockville, Conn., with an improved water service with high pressure.

The committee in charge of the temperance meetings recently held in New Britain, Conn., by T. E. Murphy have presented him with $750, and a committee has been appointed to take steps for continuing the work.

HOME MATTERS.

PERSONAL.

Captain William Whittier, who was wrecked with his crew on the schooner John Paull at Green Hill, R. I., on Feb. 10, has just taken charge of the four-masted coal schooner Job H. Jackson, Jr., of Perth Amboy, N. J., and sailed from Salem, Tuesday, in her.

Rev. J. S. Swaim is in attendance at the alumni meeting dinner and session of the board of trustees, of which he is a member, at Newton Theological seminary today.

Jesse H. Jones, North Abington, and William White of Mansfield were among those who registered at the Massachusetts building at the World's fair yesterday.

Mary J. Frates, forewoman at the Mt. Washington Glass works, is to leave Saturday on a vacation that will probably continue through the summer months.

Dr. Ann H. Chace, of this city, has accepted a position in the emergency hospital at the World's fair grounds in Chicago during the exposition.

R. Swain Gifford has been elected a member of the jury of selection of the National Academy of Design.

Miss C. A. Hersom, of this city, is spending three weeks at the World's fair.

Lizzie Borden's condition is very much improved today, and she will be fully recovered in a few days.

THE BORDEN MURDER TRIAL.

The Evening Standard is perfecting arrangements to give the public as complete and accurate reports of the great murder trial as can be printed. Orders should be early placed with your nearest newsdealer, or word sent to this office, and the Standard will be sent regularly during the trial.

EDISON COMING HERE.

Interested in a New Bedford Man's Invention for Electrical Apparatus.

Thomas A. Edison, the famous electrician, is expected in this city next Friday to investigate an invention of a New Bedford man that may revolutionize the manufacture of electrical apparatus.

The inventor in question is William T. Nicholson of the New Bedford Brass Foundry, and his invention is a new metal, the principal feature of which is a marvelous degree of conductivity. Some time ago Mr. Nicholson was attempting to harden copper and make a substitute for German silver when he suddenly produced a compound that exhibited surprising results as a conductor. In fact, tests made showed it to transmit electricity to as high a percentage as 90 to 98, and in one instance very close to 100. Now the average conductive percentage of the metals commonly used in the construction of electrical apparatus is 45 to 50, and rarely above 60. Hence the important economy of the electric fluid by the use of Mr. Nicholson's metal is evident at a glance.

Samples of the metal were sent to the Massachusetts Electrical Engineer-

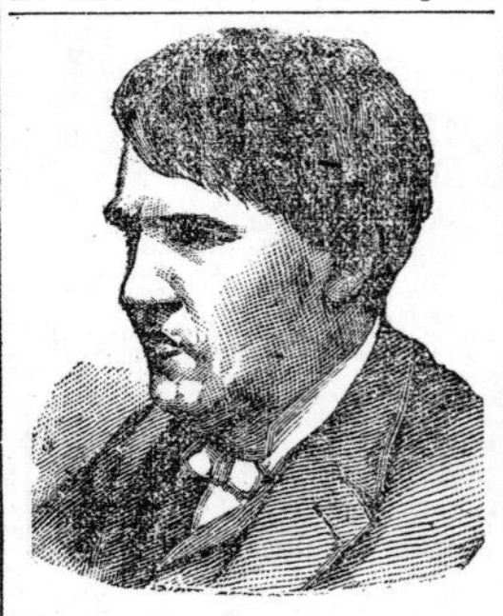

Thomas A. Edison.

ing company at Boston, and the results of their tests created an immediate sensation. Mr. Nicholson was soon made to realize the value of his invention, and placed his affairs in the hands of an attorney. Mr. Nicholson has just returned from a business trip in the course of which he visited Thomas A. Edison. That famous electrician was at once impressed with the appearance of the invention and promised to come to this city next Friday and look more closely into it.

Mr. Nicholson's backers mean to sell rights to the Edison company if agreeable terms can be made, but if not a plant will be established in this city to manufacture the goods. Already such a possible concern has received the promise of plenty of orders to start up a big factory.

The metal, if generally adopted, will largely supersede copper, brass and German silver castings and can be made for about one half the cost of drawn copper.

SONS OF VETERANS.

Preparations for a Banquet in City Hall During the Convention.

At a meeting of the joint convention committee of the Sons of Veterans last evening it was voted to circulate subscription papers for the purpose of raising money to help defray the expenses of entertaining the delegates to the convention here, June 14 and 15. It is the plan of the committee to provide a banquet on the evening of June 14 in City hall, and invite the mayor, president of the common council and other prominent officials. Subcommittees have been appointed and are now busily at work, and all interested in the work of the order and wishing to make the convention the largest and most successful one yet held will be given an opportunity to contribute.

DISLIKE THE CHINESE.

President Shaw of the Laundrymen Congratulates Mr. Geary.

William C. Shaw, president of the Laundrymens National association, who arrived here last evening, today telegraphed Congressman Geary congratulating him on the decision of the supreme court, sustaining his famous Chinese bill. Mr. Shaw in speaking of the inforcement of the Geary law, says it will make a great difference to laundrymen in this country if it is strictly inforced, but he looks for no such revolution.

H. C. HATHAWAY

will sell at auction tomorrow morning at 10 o'clock, at mart, about 35 horses from Vermont, New Hampshire and Maine. This lot consists of gents' driving, business and work horses. Also two trotters from the state of Maine, very fast. Full description given at sale. Be sure and attend this sale, for they are as nice a lot as have been brought to this city this season. Harnesses, carriages, etc.

CONDENSED LOCALS.

A large gang of laborers in the employ of the Union Street Railway company struck on this morning taking up the old rails on Ash street, between Union and Morgan streets.

Petomska lodge, No. 1,518, G. U. O. O. F., meet tomorrow at 11 a. m. to attend the funeral of the late Isaac Guinn. See special notice.

Ask your grocer for "London Cream Biscuit." They are the finest crackers in the world. The words London Cream stamped upon every cracker.

Dr. C. H. Strong of Providence will be at his office in the new bank building tomorrow and Friday till 4 p. m.

Members of the St. Lawrence C. T. A. & B. society are referred to special notice of a meeting Thursday evening.

The work of filling in the creek at Nash point was commenced this morning.

A special meeting of the South P. M. society will be held tomorrow evening. See special notice.

Cumberland Association of Naval Veterans are referred to special notice.

Introducing the famous platinotypes at Headley & Reed's.

Chiropodist.—Mrs. Williams, 190 Purchase st., Webster block, every Friday.

Adoniram Chapter Masons should read the special notice on the fourth page.

See new style mounts and artistic platinum photos at Headley & Reed's.

Blood diseases cured by Hood's Sarsaparilla.

$ $ $ $
DOLLARS
CAN'T BUY
GOOD TASTE!

VISIT OUR
CLOSING SALE
—OF—
FURNITURE!
—AND—
Save Money.

Costly Furniture, Expensive Draperies, Elaborate Decorations, do not always produce

A PRETTY ROOM.

A lot of elegant things brought together at random will not do it. The first essential is

HARMONY OF COLOR

in floors, walls and ceilings. Then come the Furniture, Pictures and Ornaments. There are in New Bedford and vicinity

MANY LADIES WHO KNOW

how to bring all these things into harmonious relations, without spending a great deal of money. When in want of CARPETS, FURNITURE, WALL PAPERS AND DRAPERIES, they have learned to go directly to

C. F. WING'S,

where they have no difficulty in selecting from his extensive stock just the design, coloring, style, and quality wanted, at a price in keeping with the correct ideas of

TRUE ECONOMY.

The steady and constantly increasing inflow of orders for Repairing, Renovating, and Re-upholstering old Furniture, is evidence, not only of the skill and good taste of our cabinet makers and upholsterers, but that the important item of cost is most reasonable and satisfactory.

C. F. WING,
34, 36, 38, 40 Purchase St.

WHITING & CO.

Commence Monday Morning
A GREAT SALE
—OF—
ALL WOOL
French Dress Goods!
At a Fearful Loss to the Importer.

2,500 yards of French Poplins, Whip Cords, Serges, Bengalines and Crepes in Black, Grays, Tans, Greens, Browns and Navy, all to go on sale at 59c. per yard.

No samples given. Do not miss this sale, if you ever want to purchase first quality Dress Goods cheap.

2,000 yards of the best imported Scotch Ginghams, regular 33 and 37 1-2c. quality, all to go on sale at 17c. per yard. Now is your time, as the hot season has commenced

Do not ask for samples, as we shall not give any.

WHITING & CO.

Double Breasted
SACK SUITS!

Are the leading style in men's wear for this season. You'll want one, of course. A look at our immense variety will convince you that you can do no better than by buying of us. We show about 100 different patterns in double-breasted Sack Suits made from Cheviots, Serges, Tweeds, Cassimeres and Worsteds at prices ranging from

$10 to $18.

Light Suits, Dark Suits, Medium Shades, Blues, Blacks and Grays—every conceivable pattern and color that experience and good taste could suggest you will find in this magnificent showing of Summer Suits.

It's for your advantage to buy early before the assortment is broken. Your size and kind are here now. Others are selecting theirs. Why don't you?

J.&W.R.WING&CO.,
Reliable Clothiers.

THE CRESCENT!
22 Purchase St.

SHIRT WAISTS!

Print Shirt Waists, 50c.
Percale Waists, 75c.
White Lawn Waists, $1.00.
Sateen Dark Waists, $1.25.
Fancy Waists, $1.50.
Embroidered Chambray, pink and blue, $3.00.

Try "Crescent" Hosiery and you'll buy "Crescent" Hosiery for the Dye of "Crescent" Hosiery is warranted.

The Popular Tan Shades for Ladies and Children; also a good assortment of Black, at fair prices.

SUMMER CORSETS.

A Bargain for 50c.
Thompson's $1.00.
C. B. a la Spirite, 75c., $1.25.
P. D. Summer Corsets, $2.00,
Ferris Ventilated Waists for Ladies and Misses.

SUMMER VESTS.

A Good Variety

Prices 10c., 12 1-2c., 15c., 20c., 25c. and 39c.
Lisle Thread, White and Ecru, 50c.

Infants' and Children's Cloaks.

Fine assortment of dresses, both white and gingham.

THE CRESCENT!
22 Purchase St.

Pages 1-8.

The Evening Standard.

Pages 1-8.

ESTABLISHED FEBRUARY, 1850.

NEW BEDFORD, MONDAY, MAY 22, 1893.---TEN PAGES. TWO CENTS.

HASKELL & TRIPP.

Fine Ginghams.

Possibly you've looked in our show window, seen the beautiful styles, observed the silky appearance of the cloth, noticed the "imported" look of the goods, and said to yourself "Scotch ginghams." But the eye has caught sight of the price mark—12½c.—and you have become sufficiently interested to come inside, and now notice that the goods bear the mark of a well-known domestic manufacturer; but the favorable impression remains, because the goods so closely resemble their imported sisters at double the price that you'll not pay the difference. 40 styles. 32 inches wide.

Women's Capes.

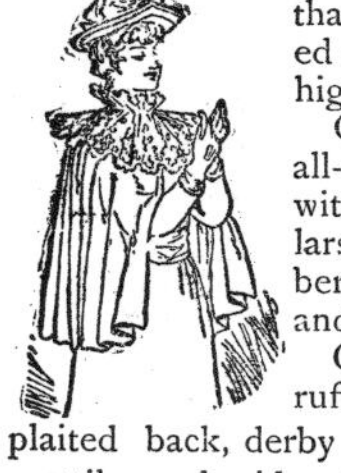

The kinds that are wanted at not too high prices.

Capes from all-wool cloths with ruffle collars and deep bertha, in tan and black, $5.

Capes with ruffle collar, plaited back, derby top cape prettily embroidered, come in black and are very saleable at $6.50.

Capes cut 40 inches long, tight-fitting backs, made from an imported, silk-finished diagonal cloth richly embroidered, are very handsome and appropriate for elderly ladies. Price $10.

Beautiful examples of the cape maker's skill cost $12, $15, $17.

At the Silk Department.

More of those changeable merveilleux, of which we have had such a wonderful sale, are direct from the looms to our counter.

These colorings:

Navy and cardinal,
Myrtle and black,
Cardinal and black,
Brown and gold,
Black and gold,
Brown and gobelin,
Cardinal and gray,
Blue and gold.

22 INCH. $1.00.

Ask to see those very excellent printed pongee silks in proper styles for waists and blouses. 19 inch, 39c. 12 designs.

Every color you'll likely ask for in the very fine Japanese pongees. 19 inch at 50c.

White and cream washable canton pongees for the coming graduation dresses cost 50c., 75c. and $1.

A bewildering assortment of fancy plaid surahs for waists, sleeves and combinations. 21 inch, $1.

Any scarce shade in plain velvet that can be found elsewhere can be had here. $1, $1.25, $1.50. 18 and 19 inch.

HASKELL & TRIPP,

Department Stores,

Purchase and William Streets.

MAY NOT BE TRIED.

Lizzie Borden Breaking Down Under Strain.

Her Strength Rapidly Failing as Trial Approaches.

Recovered from Tonsilitis but is Not Herself.

Condition at Present is Considered to be Serious.

Fears That Her Mental Capacity May be Impaired.

Burden Resting on the Prisoner Weighs Heavily Upon Her.

Acknowledges Herself That She May Not Hold Out.

The Woman of Eight Months Ago and Today Two Different Persons.

(Special Dispatch.)

Taunton, May 22.—Two weeks from today Lizzie A. Borden may be called upon to face her accusers once again in court, and the greatest trial of the age may be commenced. The word "may" is used advisedly. While it is true she has been notified that on the 5th of June the government will take up her case, that the justices have made up their minds to be prepared to listen to the evidence and the 150 men from whom a jury of 12 is to be selected have been warned to be on hand at that time, still there is a possibility of the case not coming up then or even later on, for Lizzie Borden is a sick woman.

It was given out a short time ago that she had a severe cold, that she caught cold on the day she was taken to New Bedford for arraignment and that a slight attack of tonsilitis was the result, there was even a possibility of her being afflicted with pneumonia. It has been stated since that she had quite recovered from that attack and was herself again. This, so far as relates to the cold contracted on the 8th day of May, is correct, but there is something deeper than this, something far more serious. Miss Borden with all her firmness, her apparent insensibility to what has been said and done has felt and still feels keenly the peculiarity of her position, and she would be much less than human if the result of all this trouble did not affect a vital spot.

If she is guilty one can readily bring within reasonable distance the feeling that, given a fairly good mental condition and a not too elastic conscience, she must suffer from a burden which not many of us would care to assume. If she is innocent there must naturally come upon her another burden in a totally different form undoubtedly, but none the less a burden, and she must suffer in bearing that.

She has been kept a close prisoner all these months. Her mind, whether she is guilty or innocent, must have been in constant motion all the time through her waiting hours; whether weighing the chances either way, whether troubled by remorse or bowed down in sorrow under the terrible load fastened upon her seemingly by circumstantial evidence, the woman has been in a position most unenviable. It is against nature to suppose that one being possessed of even the strongest of mental capacities should be able to endure all this without some symptoms of breaking down. Lizzie Borden, with all her apparent strength, has not been able to stand up fully under this load, and it is said that she is rapidly breaking down under the pressure.

When she went down to New Bedford the other day there was not the slightest sign of anything tending to show that she had been affected in the slightest by her long imprisonment beyond a pale face and slight tremor in her movement. Certainly when she said "I am not guilty," in answer to the indictment the words were spoken as calmly and as strong as one could possibly expect to hear such words from any person, and coming from Miss Borden, all things considered, in such a manner they deeply impressed those who heard them. But in whatever spirit that pleading was made, however she may have turned the matter over in her mind, whatever her thoughts, it is not for outsiders to interpret. Suffice it to say that the end is rapidly approaching, and unless some sudden change is made, and for the better, there must soon come an end to Miss Borden's strength.

But for the fact that she has had the kindly ministrations of Mrs. Wright it is extremely doubtful if Miss Borden would be even in as good condition mentally as she is today, and even Mrs. Wright, kind, good, faithful, womanly woman that she is, would not and cannot prevent Miss Borden from thinking all the live long time.

We have been told that she has occupied her time in reading, in sewing, in tending flowers and in seeing such of her friends as she cared to see, but we have been left to guess at the other side of the terrible life which she must have been leading through all these terrible months. Not all the books, flowers and friends of the universe could shut from her eyes the unalterable fact that she was a prisoner and suspected murderer Only the other day she is reported to have said to a friend, "I do not know how I can stand much more of this. I am glad the end is approaching, but I am fearful of my strength. I have been sorely tried."

During the next two weeks preceding the opening of the case she is going to do more thinking than ever. She is going to condense into 12 or 14 days the sorrows of the past and the uncertainties of the future, and if she can keep her brain free from inroads of a nature which might tend to overthrow her reason she will furnish an additional incentive for praise and proof of an unusual mental capacity.

There is no question but that her cough is better, that she is quite recovered from the effect of the cold contracted on the trip to New Bedford, but when the idea is sought to be conveyed that she is in as good condition mentally and physically as she was when she first entered upon her long imprisonment, the idea is erroneous. It is not reasonable to expect that she could be, unless she was utterly devoid of the powers of thought and feeling. The Lizzie A. Borden of today and of eight months ago are two different persons. It must not be forgotten that a weak mind never accumulates force enough to hurt itself and that stupidity often saves a man from going mad. Miss Borden's mind is not naturally a weak one and no one can say that she is stupid.

Lizzie Borden's Trial.

BOSTON, May 22.—It has been definitely decided that Chief Justice Mason and Judges Blodgett and Dewey are to preside at the trial of Lizzie Borden at New Bedford, next month.

GOLDEN WEDDING

Of the President's Pastor, the Rev. Byron Sunderland.

Washington, D. C., May 22.—Today the president's pastor, Dr. Byron Sunderland, and Mrs. Sunderland are celebrating their golden wedding by a reception, which will be attended by both the president and Mrs. Cleveland and a host of the famous clergymen now gathered here in attendance on the Presbyterian general assembly. Over 40 years ago Dr. Sunderland preached a sermon in Fayetteville, near Syracuse, N. Y., where he replaced Rev. Stephen Cleveland. Grover, the son, was present, and was deeply impressed. Years afterward, when the boy became president, he remembered the man and chose the church where Dr. Sunderland officiated as his own. There is nothing fashionable or showy about the church or its pastor. Dr. Sunderland preaches a long sermon, but he possesses a vein of dry Scotch humor which Mr. Cleveland appreciates.

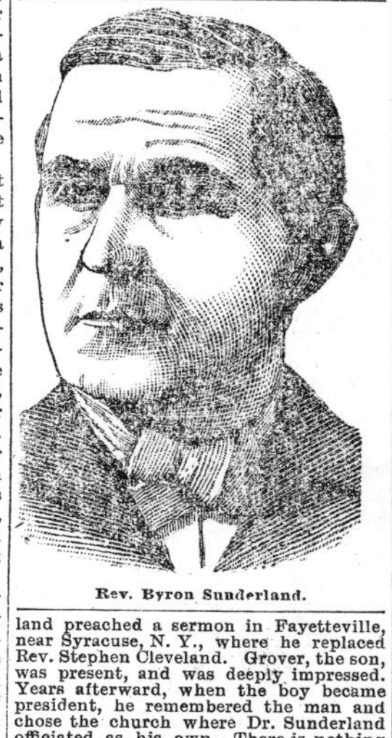

Rev. Byron Sunderland.

A $200,000 FIRE IN ST. LOUIS.

Great Property Loss and a Life Sacrificed in a Burning Stable.

St. Louis, May 22.—A fire which broke out at midnight destroyed $200,000 worth of property and caused the loss of a human life. A few minutes before 12 an alarm was sent in from the corner of Channing avenue and Locust street. The fire, which was of incendiary origin, completely destroyed the three-story brick block on the corner mentioned, occupied by the C. M. Crumm Livery company. One hundred and fifty horses are burned to a crisp, and the entire lot of buggies, phaetons and other vehicles, harness, etc., were destroyed. On the second floor James Quinn, foreman, his wife and eight children, were asleep. All had narrow escapes except Eddie, a seven years old boy, who was fatally burned before he could escape. Crumm's insurance is $17,000.

A SALOON TRAGEDY.

Three Italians Shot in Chicago During a Drunken Row.

Chicago, May 22.—Gathered about a table in a beer saloon at 203 West Taylor street last evening, was a crowd of Italian laborers. Suddenly there was a quarrel and a fight. In his drunken rage John Gorlong, one of the company, drew his revolver and turned it upon the crowd. Tony Costlucci, proprietor of the saloon, fell to the floor shot through the left lung. John Luccova fell on the sidewalk just outside the door, shot in the lower part of the back. Joseph Spangola was shot through the back of the neck. Before leaving the place Gorlong turned the weapon on another man, and would have had another victim had not the cartridge failed to explode. He was pursued and arrested at the point of a revolver. At the station Gorlong admitted the shooting and justified himself by a claim of self-defense, saying the others had cheated him at gambling.

FIGHTING IN NICARAGUA.

Battle Now Ensuing Believed to be the Final One.

New York, May 22.—The Herald's Granada, Nicaragua, special says: What is believed will be the decisive battle of the revolution against the authority of President Sacaza has been opened. After days spent in preparation the government troops began their advance Sunday morning at 9 o'clock. Their purpose was to attack the revolutionists at Barranca, near Masaya. As the government forces advanced the battle was begun by the revolutionists, whose artillery opened a vigorous fire upon the attacking columns. The revolutionists are enthusiastic. They believe the engagement will result favorably to their cause.

The Advertiser's special from Managua, Nicaragua, says: President Sacaza declared himself dictator last Saturday night and proclaimed martial law throughout the entire republic.

Ice Houses Burned.

Boothbay Harbor, Me., May 22.—The buildings of the Echo Lake Ice company were burned last night. Cause unknown. Insured.

WEATHER INDICATIONS.

Rainy and Cooler Tomorrow.

Boston, May 22.—Local forecast for New England until Tuesday night: Fair weather, followed by rain beginning Tuesday afternoon or night; cooler Tuesday; variable winds, changing to south and east and increasing in velocity by Tuesday night.

Fair Today, Thunder Showers Tuesday.

Washington, May 22.—For the 24 hours from 8 a. m. today: For New England, generally fair today and tonight, followed by thunder storms Tuesday; west winds.

THE NEW YORK'S TRIAL TRIP.

Fine Weather for the Run of the Big Cruiser.

Boston, May 22.—United States cruiser New York, sailed from her anchorage off Boston light at 8 15 this morning, for her official trial trip.

Rockport, May 22.—The weather off shore is grand for the trial of the cruiser New York. The sea is as smooth as glass. The headlands are covered with people watching the trial. When the New York passed the Vesuvius she presented a grand spectacle, and plowed the sea up her bow to the rail. Although the day is clear, she was out of sight in a few minutes.

Kennebunkport, Me., May 22. — The cruiser New York passed the flagship off Cape Porpoise at 11 29 a. m.

Portland, Me., May 22.—The cruiser New York made the turn on her way homeward at 11 45.

WOMEN'S BICYCLE RACE.

The Young San Francisco Rider Wins in the Chicago Tournament.

Chicago, May 22.—At 1 o'clock this morning the women's bicycle tournament at the Second regiment armory terminated, Baldwin, the young rider from San Francisco, being victorious, with Williams second and Armaindo third. The following was the score: Baldwin 467 miles 3 laps, Williams 462 miles 9 laps, Armaindo 452 miles 2 laps, Standley 263 miles, Harvey 233 miles.

OBITUARY.

Death of Chauncey H. Snow, Journalist and Civil Engineer.

Washington, May 22.—Chauncey H. Snow, journalist and civil engineer, died here yesterday, aged 60. Mr. Snow was one of the corps of engineers who constructed the Hoosac tunnel and rendered valuable services to the government by his feats of engineering during the late war. He was a government director of the Union Pacific railroad and his report led to the Credit Mobilier investigation.

A Minnesota Town in Flames.

St. Paul, Minn., May 22.—A dispatch from Rock Creek at a late hour last night said that the town was in flames and among the buildings destroyed were two general stores, a depot and several residences. The losses will probably reach $30,000.

HOME MATTERS.

PERSONAL.

Thomas Pennington, late second hand in Potomska mills, has left the city to take a similar position in the King Philip mills, Fall River. Mr. Pennington leaves a host of friends here, for he had won the esteem of all his employes. His thorough knowledge of the designing of fancy textiles, together with his ability to manage help, of which he always had a plentiful supply, owing to his popularity, has demonstrated the fact that he is a practical weaver and a man who will make his mark as such. The best wishes of his numerous friends go with him.

H. T. Soule, formerly of the old Liberty theatre, made a short visit here Sunday, combining business and pleasure. Mr. Soule is and intends to remain general advertising agent for the Abe Spitz Amusement company with three theatres and four road companies. He requests The Standard to state that he is not to join any other company, as has been reported.

Rev. Dr. Charles S. Murkland of Manchester, N. H., a brother of James H. Murkland of this city, has been unanimously elected president of the New Hampshire College of Agriculture and Mechanic Art at a meeting of the trustees at Concord, N. H.

Miss Etta Sharples gave a party to her friends at her residence, Middle Point road, Saturday evening, and a most enjoyable time was passed. Dancing was enjoyed to the music of Frawley's orchestra.

Mayor Brock is to be invited to preside at the labor meeting to be held in Y. M. C. A. hall Thursday evening, and invitations will be extended to all the representatives in the legislature to be present.

Among the subscriptions just acknowledged for the erection of the Phillips Brooks house at Harvard are Charles W. Clifford, $25; Rev. Edmund S. Rousmaniere, $15, and Milton Reed, $50.

Mrs. George M. Eddy and Elizabeth H. Eddy of this city registered at the Massachusetts building at Chicago Friday.

Louis P. Slade of Fall River has been appointed one of the commencement speakers by the Williams college faculty.

Walter Cunliffe, Edward M. Slocum and Horace Carpenter made a bicycle run to Providence and return yesterday.

Mrs. Albert Lord and Mrs. Edwin Whittaker are in Washington, where they will spend their summer vacations.

THE BORDEN TRIAL.

Press Representatives to Meet in This City May 30.

The representatives of the newspapers of Bristol county will meet in this city on Tuesday, May 30, at 11 30 a. m. and draw for seats in the press box for the Borden murder trial. Sheriff Wright and County Commissioner Sanders have deputized Z. W. Pease of this city to have charge of the matter and the selection is one that commends itself to newspaper men throughout the county. After the Bristol county papers the Boston dailies will have the preference.

A report current in Boston that Lawyer O'Sullivan, who made himself famous in tangling up witnesses in the Buchanan poisoning case in New York, had been engaged by the defense in the Lizzie Borden case is denied by M. O. Adams. Mr. Adams said: "We have heard of the gentleman, but he has not up to this time, been engaged to assist in the defense."

Attleboro selectmen have drawn the following 10 men: Henry M. Goss, overseer of a cotton mill; Willard F. Ashley, laundryman; Isaac Alger, a farmer; George W. Currien, jeweler; Harold V. Hopkins, leather tanner; Frank G. Cole, jeweler; Leon H. Tingley, farmer; Charles E. Briggs, jeweler; George A. Austin, jeweler; Charles F. Forrester, jeweler.

Miss Lizzie Borden has secured one of the prizes offered by the Boston Journal to the leaders on the vacation list, and she will soon have a complete set of Thackeray's works Miss Borden has received 5,936 votes.

Car No. 53 of the Fairhaven line, heavily loaded with passengers bound for city churches, broke down on Second street about 10 o'clock yesterday morning, one of the axles breaking, and many passengers in consequence were late at church.

THE BORDEN MURDER TRIAL.

The Evening Standard is perfecting arrangements to give the public as complete and accurate reports of the great murder trial as can be printed. Orders should be early placed with your nearest newsdealer, or word sent to this office, and the Standard will be sent regularly during the trial.

WILL OBJECT.

A Strong Remonstrance Against Opening North and Mill Streets.

When those who are interested in the establishment of a home for the aged poor and orphans of the Catholic church in this city purchased 400 rods of land at the west end of the city between Hillman and Kempton streets they little thought that land so far remote from the business center would be opened up and laid out in streets, and now that a petition is before the authorities asking that Mill and North streets be extended west through their land naturally enough they object, and this afternoon, when the public works officials visit the proposed layout of North street they will meet Rev. James F. Clark of the St. James Catholic church, who as a representative of St. Lawrence, St. James and St. John the Baptist parishes, will present a remonstrance signed by as many of the parishioners as he has been able to secure in a very short space of time. The three parishes named above are the ones interested in the proposed home, and should the two streets named be opened up the idea of constructing the home at present will have to be abandoned.

"The extension of these streets," said Father Clark to a Standard man this morning, "will be a great drawback to our plans. Our land will in reality be cut up into three lots, and if we build as proposed we shall be obliged to look for another location, and that is quite a difficult task, you know, with real estate at the prices now held."

Continuing his remarks the reverend gentleman said, "I do not want to stand in the way of any public inprovement, but I fail to see the necessity of extending these streets for public convenience."

"How would your lot be affected if but one of these streets should be extended?" asked the newspaper man.

"If Mill street is not extended," said he, "we can carry out plans by building south of North street, but even then we will be cramped for yard room, which is a valuable acquisition in such an institution as we propose to build."

"You can also say," he further remarked, "that if we succeed in establishing this home it will be of great benefit to the city, as the authorities and taxpayers will be relieved in a great measure from looking after the destitute residents whom we propose to care for, who otherwise would of necessity be dependent upon the city."

Bishop Harkins was in the city Friday evening, and completed the arrangements for constructing the building. All that now remains to prevent awarding the contract and proceeding to break ground at once is the uncertainty about the action of the board of public works as to the layout of the new streets. The new ball park is doomed if the streets are extended, but the management of the baseball association would have a year in the present location, whereas the projectors of the new institution are desirous to know that their location is permanent before proceeding to erect buildings at a great expense.

The remonstrance presented at the St. James church yesterday was signed by every voter present at the service, and at the St. Lawrence church every property holder was eager to sign a protest against the proposed extension.

BUTLER'S FLAT GAS BUOY.

Congressman Randall was notified last night that the gas buoy on Butler's flat was not lighted. He immediately wired Commander Wilde of the lighthouse board, who telegraphed instructions for Babbitt & Wood to examine the buoy, and if they find it impossible to make immediate repairs a temporary lantern will be placed on the buoy until the light can be restored, which will be in a few days.

CONDENSED LOCALS.

What, again! Well, here we go again. Here is what we are going to do now. Yes, right off. A lot of raisins for 6c. lb., a new lot of Golden Creamery butter, right from the green fields, for 28c. lb.; fresh strawberries arriving every day. We have a season's contract with several enterprising farmers for fresh asparagus and lettuce, which enables us to have a fresh stock always on hand.

P. S.—We will make special prices on butter for 5 lbs. and upwards. White Cash Store. 134 Purchase street.

Howard P. Eldridge, shipping clerk at the Howland mills, and Miss A. A. Florence Parsons were married at St. James Episcopal church this morning. Only the immediate friends of the contracting parties were present. An elaborate repast was served at the home of the bride's mother, 176 Mill street. The couple were the recipients of many beautiful and valuable presents. They left this afternoon for a short bridal tour to the White mountains.

Funeral services over the body of James McPhee took place at the Sacred Heart church Saturday afternoon, Rev. Fr. Payan officiating. A dispatch from deceased' brother, dated at Georgetown, P. E. I., was received, stating that it was impossible for him to be present, and he would write full particulars and instructions.

Thomas A. Edison met William T. Nicholson of this city in Boston, Friday, and examined the new conducting metal invented by the latter. He expressed himself as much interested in the matter and took samples to his laboratory for experiment and test. It is said surprising developments will be heard in a few days.

Local Knights of Pythias have recently received circulars from Edward Waldo & Son of Chicago, announcing the opening at 389 Bowen avenue of a special hotel, and it is said many from this city will make their quarters there during their visit to the World's fair.

Daniel Donovan of Fall River, committed to the house of correction in this city March 22 for drunkenness, was released today by the county commissioners.

William Bloomer, who resides on Brooks street near Sawyer, is anxious to arrange a match of homing pigeons of from 100 to 200 miles for $25 a side.

Rheinberger club popular concert Tickets on sale at Hutchinson's and E. Boden, Jr.'s. Twenty-five cents to all parts of the Opera house.

Gutters are being paved on either side of Wing street, between Fourth and Fifth streets, and new curbing is also being laid.

Ask your grocer for "London Cream Biscuit." They are the finest crackers in the world. The words London Cream stamped upon every cracker.

Whiting & Co. are having a rush for French challies and Scotch ginghams at the great mark-down in prices.

Eight deaths have been reported at the office of the board of health since last Saturday.

Go to Whiting & Co's and secure your summer dress goods at the fearful low prices they are selling them.

Blood poison cured by Hood's Sarsaparilla.

(Continued from Saturday's Standard.)

The Gurney Patent Refrigerator.

To substantiate the claim of superiority, as set forth in Saturday's paper, we beg to call your attention to the following discussion of the separate claims.

1. Cleanliness.

By the use of the removable galvanized ice compartment, we are able to challenge comparison as to Cleanliness with any refrigerator made. By the use of which we do not permit any of the vapors arising from the provision chamber to enter the inner walls or pass through end flues, depositing unwholesome gasses where they cannot be got at and cleaned as in the Old Style Refrigerator. In the Gurney, the air from the provision chamber rises, passes directly against, and through holes in the four side walls of the ice compartment, which can be lifted out when necessary, and the refrigerator made as sweet and clean as a milk pan. By the use of the Removable Ice Compartment, we get the most perfect interior construction, we do not cut our zinc side walls, all wood is zinc lined with no exposed wood to become sour and unwholesome.

2. Free Circulation.

An examination of our front sectional cuts will show that in the Gurney system the air from the provision chamber is not restricted as in the old style refrigerator, to small end flues, to gain access to the ice compartment, but is admitted through both Ends, Back and Front. In fact, the ice compartment, constructed as it is of galvanized iron, partakes of the same temperature as the ice, and is practically the same as a suspended cake of ice in the top of the refrigerator. By the natural laws of gravitation, the cold air descends to the provision chamber, displacing the warmer and lighter air, which rises to the ice, and in turn falls to the provision chamber, which operation being repeated, produces perfect and free circulation of pure, dry air between the ice and provision chambers.

3. Greater Condensation and hence Dryer Air.

Both side and end walls of our Removable Galvanized Ice Compartment form the largest condensing surface of any refrigerator in the market, and hence dryer air.

4. Lower Average Temperature.

The Gurney reaches a lower average temperature than any other refrigerator by reason of its freer circulation. A test will prove that the Gurney will reach the lowest temperature possible to be attained in from one quarter to one sixth of the time required under the old system. When the doors are often opened the importance of our free circulation is apparent.

5. Freedom from Condensation on the Inner Walls.

In the Gurney the ice is not permitted to touch the zinc side walls, and hence no condensation on the back of the zinc walls. The Gurney gets its condensation on the back walls of the galvanized ice compartment, which runs into the drip pan and passes off through the waste pipe.

6. Freedom from Damage by Use of Ice Pick.

If in using the Ice Pick a hole is made in the Galvanized Ice Compartment of the Gurney, no damage is done, as the walls are purposely perforated with holes for admission of air to the ice, and any water that runs through passes to the drip pan and escapes.

[Continued in Tuesday's Standard.]

C. F. WING,

Carpets, Furniture, Draperies and Wall Paper,

34 to 40 Purchase St.

WHITING & CO.

MONDAY MORNING

WE COMMENCE A

Special Sale

—ON—

DRESS GOODS!

1000 yards of the best 60c. French all wool Challies at 41c. per yard. This is lower than you can purchase them in New York or Boston,

2000 yards of Figured Organdie Muslin for summer dresses at the low price of 12 1-2c. per yard.

Our great sale of Scotch Ginghams is going on with a rush, regular 33 and 37 1-2c. ones, all at 17c. per yard. Elegant goods.

We are having a rush on our French all wool Dress Goods at 59c. per yard. No wonder, when we sell you goods that are sold from 75c. to $1.00 per yard. Come and see.

If you want a Cape or Jacket, do not fail to see our stock. All of the latest styles and at the lowest prices.

WHITING & CO.

Double Breasted

SACK SUITS!

Are the leading style in men's wear for this season. You'll want one, of course. A look at our immense variety will convince you that you can do no better than by buying of us. We show about 100 different patterns in double-breasted Sack Suits made from Cheviots, Serges, Tweeds, Cassimeres and Worsteds at prices ranging from

$10 to $18.

Light Suits, Dark Suits, Medium Shades, Blues, Blacks and Grays—every conceivable pattern and color that experience and good taste could suggest you will find in this magnificent showing of Summer Suits.

☞ It's for your advantage to buy early before the assortment is broken. Your size and kind are here now. Others are selecting theirs. Why don't you?

J. & W. R. WING & CO.,

Reliable Clothiers.

THE CRESCENT!

22 Purchase St.

MUSLIN HATS!

Only 19 Cents.

Pink and White, Blue and White, Red and White, and White.

MUSLIN BONNETS!

25 Cents Upward.

Infants' Long Cloaks!

From $2.00 to $9.50.

Children's Short Cloaks!

From $2.00 to $10.00.

Children's Dresses!

Good assortment.

Long and Short Skirts!

Flannel and Cotton.

Guimpes!

Guimpe Dresses!

SUMMER CORSETS!

50 Cents Upward.

Ferris' Ventilated Waists.

Equipoise Waists.

Double Ve Waists.

Wrappers.

Shirt Waists.

Hosiery!

Ladies' Tan Hose, 25, 33 and 50 cents. Ladies' Black Hose, 25, 33 and 50 cents. Children's Tan Hose, 25 and 37 cents. Warranted fast colors.

THE CRESCENT!

22 Purchase St.

Pages 1-8.

The Evening Standard.

Pages 1-8.

ESTABLISHED FEBRUARY, 1850.

NEW BEDFORD, WEDNESDAY, MAY 31, 1893.---TWELVE PAGES. TWO CENTS.

HASKELL & TRIPP.

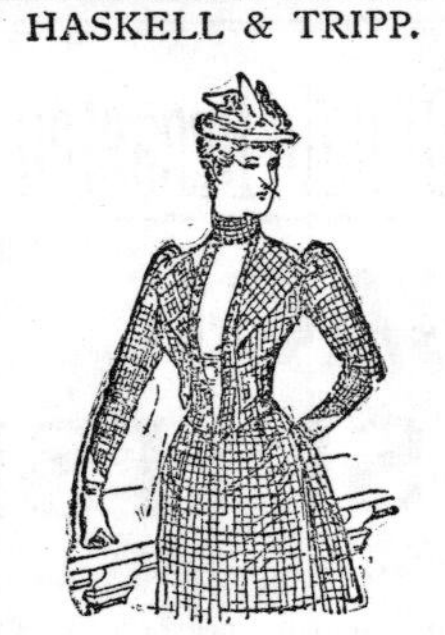

There are plenty of ginghams in every dry goods store in the land. Plenty at just such prices as we ask for ours. But how about quality? We claim for those beautiful ginghams now on our counters at 12½c. per yard—

1st: *The quality is finer than any ever offered for such a price.*

2d: *The styles are such as you seldom see in other than real Scotch ginghams.*

Such choice goods at this small price is simply the result of overstocked market in a backward season. They cost to manufacture more than our retail price.

Tomorrow we expect on the New York boat another case of all-wool Henriettas, 36 inches wide, to retail at 39c. per yard. Fifteen choice plain colors in the new spring shadings, including the favorite greens, heliotropes and tans. There is a quick demand for double-width changeable serges; also 39c. a yard. They are very close copies of French goods at a dollar per yard. Ten colorings.

We continue the bargain sale of French all-wool suitings at 59c. a yard. Attractive fabrics, recently sold as high as $1.

"Hop Sackings," stylish for traveling gowns, 50c., 75c. and $1 a yard.

Broadcloths, 89c. and $1.25 a yard in the colors you want.

Special.

Black dress goods below the cost to import. Your choice of five different weaves, genuine French fabrics, for 59c. a yard. A black dress is never out of the fashion, and this chance to get a new and handsome one doesn't come every day. You'll wonder when you look at them how such a little price ever came to such goods.

Laces.

Still selling choicest "Point de Gene" laces for 29c. and 39c. a yard, *actually worth double.* Plenty of people get their wits about them after the chance has passed. Don't let that be your case with these beautiful laces.

Japanese Fans.

Twenty new sorts ranging in price from 5 to 50c. apiece, will make their first appearance in our stock today. Among them are some unique decorations.

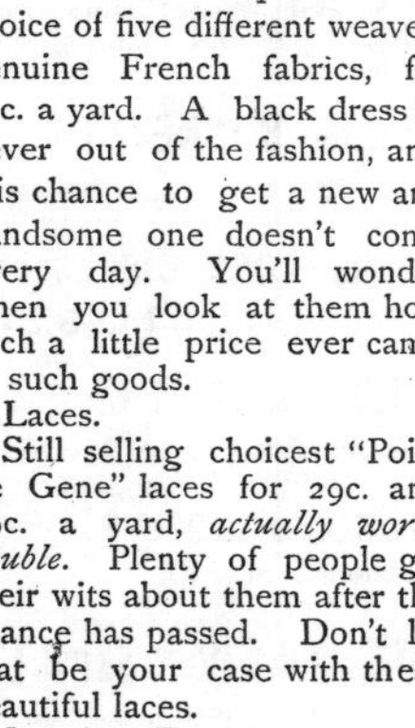

HASKELL & TRIPP,
Department Stores,
Purchase and William Streets.

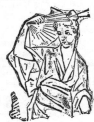

☞ *A well-recommended boy wanted at once.*

HORRIBLE CRIME.

Bloody Work of a Fiend in Fall River.

Further Particulars of the Memorial Day Murder.

Victim of the Butchery Was a Most Lovable Girl.

Did a Man's Work on Her Father's Farm.

Perpetrator of the Crime Still at Large.

Family Strongly Object to the Removal of Mutilated Body.

Scene at the House in Which the Medical Examiner Figured.

A Suspect Run Down by the Police in This City.

The New Bedford police have been on the alert for the assassin who butchered Bertha Manchester in Fall River Tuesday. This forenoon one suspect was run down in this city. A man was reported as making inquiries about the gatehouse to the Old Colony railroad on Weld street of the nearest way to Providence without going through Fall River. The man had gone north after making inquiries. Captain Allen ordered Officer McBay to look into the affair, and he mounted a bicycle, started up Acushnet avenue and overhauled the man, who did not answer the description of the man wanted, and as he gave a satisfactory explanation Mr. McBay allowed him to proceed.

THE MANCHESTER MURDER.

Details of the Horrible Memorial Day Crime in Fall River.

(By Associated Press.)

Fall River, May 31.—At 8 o'clock this morning the murderer of Bertha Manchester had not been discovered. Further details of the affair are now in the hands of the police. The Manchester house is a cottage sitting about 30 feet in from the road. It is one and a half story, with an L of the same height at the south and west. There is a piazza on the south of the main house and at the front; running west of the L is still another porch, one story in height. This is the kitchen, the scene of the awful butchery, a room about 10 by 20 feet. The main house rests upon a stone foundation, accessible from the inside by stairs and on the outside from the west. The porches also rest upon a stone foundation, accessible only from the outside and on the north. The door leading to this was closed and the padlock was found clasped, but not locked. On the piazza were two large dogs, one a mastiff, chained to a kennel near the cellar entrance to the main house, and the other an old and large black dog, with a ferocious bark, the terror of all well-meaning people who had occasion to visit the place. This dog was at large. The neighbors report they heard loud barking by the dogs about 10 o'clock, but "as the dogs are always barking," thought little of the circumstances.

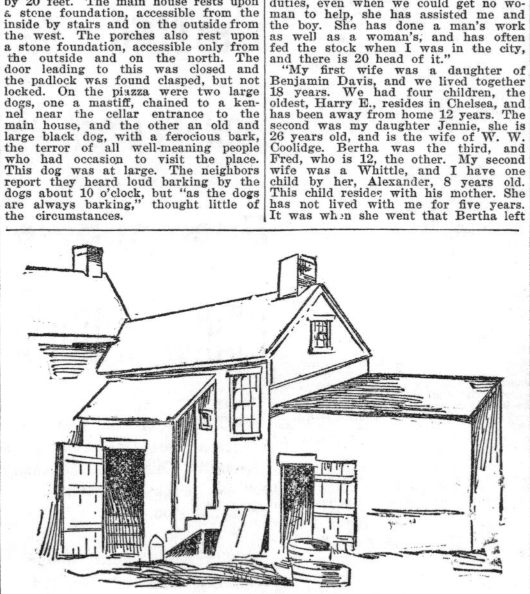

SCENE OF THE MANCHESTER MURDER.
Entryway and Kitchen Where Bertha was Found Dead.
[From a Sketch by a Standard Artist Today.]

Stephen C. Manchester, father of the murdered girl, is a farmer and milkman. His farm consists of about 40 acres of land, and on it are 20 head of cattle and three horses. He is 63 years of age, and his disposition is such that he has great difficulty in keeping help. The girl lay close beside the stove in the kitchen of the house, her head about on a line with the front of the hearth. Her face was not really straight downward, but a little turned to the right, so that the features could be discerned. Her long brown hair was extended and matted with blood. The head rested upon her right arm, and her right hand tightly and convulsively clutched the hair near its roots. The left arm was doubled under the body. The right leg was also doubled beneath her, bended back against her hip from the knee joint. The left leg was extended and exposed from the knee, the foot resting top down upon an old red and black check shawl. The bleeding had been profuse. It extended from her head in a strip about a foot wide without diminishing until it was lost under her body. It was still bright at six o'clock, but coagulation had taken place to a considerable extent. The top was of thick blood, but by putting one's finger into it the lower part was watery, and left no stain on the finger. The stream had appreciable depth, and was apparently an eighth of an inch or more through. Behind the body ran a stream about an inch in width, prevented from spreading by the coal hod that stood behind and in line with the north side of the stove. In a semicircle behind the foot of the girl were smooches of blood three feet in diameter that looked as if they might have been made by the girl's dragging herself on the floor.

As yet the police have no decidedly strong opinions as to who could have committed the murder. In the Borden case it was argued that none but a woman would have so hacked her victim, yet the appearance of Miss Manchester, due largely to the great flow of blood, was fully as revolting as the appearance of either victim in the Borden tragedy, while the hacking was repeated with the back of the axe a number of times, and at least five blows were struck with the edge.

On the other hand it has been claimed by friends of Miss Borden that a murderer always has a horror of being connected with the crime by means of finding the instrument and will take it with him to avoid all risk. This they think is why no hatchet has been found by the police. Yet in this fresh tragedy the bloody axe is left exposed upon the wood pile near the house.

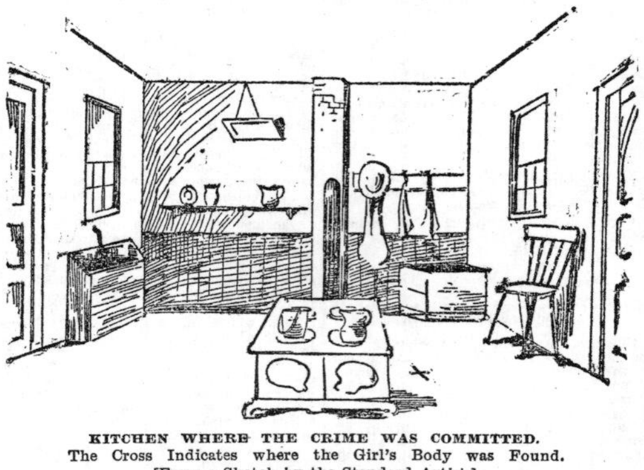

KITCHEN WHERE THE CRIME WAS COMMITTED.
The Cross Indicates where the Girl's Body was Found.
[From a Sketch by the Standard Artist.]

Naturally, knowing the disposition of Mr. Manchester, his difficulty in getting and keeping help, the police have sought for information of recent employes. One of them, a Portuguese, is wanted for a robbery committed at Charles Frank's clothing store in April, for whom a warrant has been out for some time, and whose associate is now serving sentence. He was at Manchester's for two days about two weeks ago and has been there for one night since. Mr. Manchester says he saw this man in the city Tuesday on the Crab pond bridge about 11 o'clock. Another man who will probably be locked up and made to account for his time is well known to the police and worked for Manchester a few days ago; he can't remember just when. Two others are French, the last he had. They hailed from Lowell, and one claimed to be a mason, but said he could not get work because he did not belong to a union. They were pleasant and well intentioned fellows, Mr. Manchester thinks, but knew nothing of farm work and could not talk much English. He paid them so as to satisfy them and there was no trouble when they were there or when they left.

"I can't think of a person who would have done such a deed," said Manchester to a reporter. "I wish to God it had been me instead of her. This girl was everything to me, and since my wife left me has done what few men or women would. In addition to doing all the work of the house, looking after the milk, making butter and its regular duties, even when we could get no woman to help, she has assisted me and the boy. She has done a man's work as well as a woman's, and has often fed the stock when I was in the city, and there is 20 head of it."

"My first wife was a daughter of Benjamin Davis, and we lived together 18 years. We had four children, the oldest, Harry E., resides in Chelsea, and has been away from home 12 years. The second was my daughter Jennie, she is 26 years old, and is the wife of W. W. Coolidge. Bertha was the third, and Fred, who is 12, the other. My second wife was a Whittle, and I have one child by her, Alexander, 8 years old. This child resides with his mother. She has not lived with me for five years. It was when she went that Bertha left the High school, and has had charge of the house since."

The second Mrs. Manchester is a sister of the late Samuel Whittle, who was drowned with six others while crossing North Watuppa pond three years ago. The marriage was an unhappy one, and both have recently had counter-trials for divorce, which libels are now pending, Mrs. Manchester being decreed a monthly allowance, which Manchester is paying. He is a man of considerable property, both acquired and inherited. The latter may be said to be in a sense prospective, as there has been constant wranglings over the estates by the different heirs. In court he testified that he had braved the deep, had been on angry seas, heard the thunders of war and seen vivid lightning, but never anything like that woman. His daughter Bertha accompanied him at the court hearing. (Between her and her father there is said to have existed the pleasantest of relations.)

The girl herself is spoken of by her neighbors and all along the road as a fine woman. The Reeds did not like the old man, but the daughter was a noble girl. She is not known to have had any lover or regular callers. All speak of her as modest, retiring, self-sacrificing. She would seldom take any outing or attend church services, even except at repeated urging, and then rather to please others than to gratify her own wishes. She possessed a good figure and face and was attractive and loveable.

If the motive was robbery the thief probably gained access to the house by some way as yet unknown. His rifling of her room called her from the closet, where she was mixing ginger bread, and pursuing her to the kitchen he struck her and secured the axe with which the murder was committed.

It is reported that some bruises were found upon her.

One story is that certain neighbors heard shrieks from the Manchester house about 11 o'clock, but that they were not accustomed to pay much attention to noises at the Manchesters.

Medical Examiner Dolan states that in his opinion the girl had been dead six or seven hours when he first saw the body not far from half-past 3 o'clock. If the shorter time, this would make the hour of the murder at 9 30 a. m., not far from "the about 10 o'clock" that the neighbors heard the dogs barking.

A woman is reported to have seen Mr. Manchester near Orange street about 8 o'clock yesterday.

About 6 o'clock last night, the medical examiner having completed his work preliminary to the removal of the body, word was communicated to the father and aunt of Miss Manchester, who were in the room next the kitchen, that the body was to be removed. An undertaker had been summoned an hour or more before, but was very late in appearing. When this word was given, both relatives protested to the medical examiner against removing the remains, showing both a sense of shock and indignation at the proposal.

Dr. Dolan calmly assured them he was acting in the interest of the state, and that it was his duty to remove the body, and added that he should do it; the father insisted, with an oath, that enough violence had already been done to his child, and he would not allow any more to be done—evidently decapitation after the removal—and he maintained that she could be examined as well in that house as anywhere. He was reinforced by his sister, who piteously pleaded for the retention of the body, and be allowed to call Dr. Dwelley to examine the body, and who at the same time said that the medical examiner had no right to prevent her from doing her pleasure in this matter.

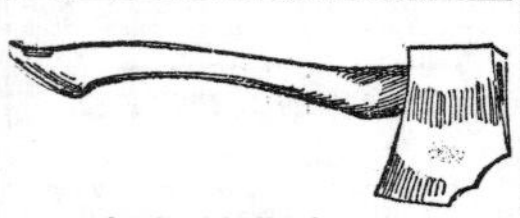

Axe Used by the Assassin.

After Dr. Dolan had reiterated his authority and his duty, and his determination to do as he was told by superior officers, and after the assistant marshal and several members of the police force had emphasized Dr. Dolan's claims, Mr. Manchester and Mrs. Terry were sent back into the other room and the door was forcibly shut upon them. They were still firm in their protest, however, and referred to the decapitation of several persons by Dr. Dolan in an accusatory manner. Mrs. Terry came at least once afterwards to the kitchen door and looked sorrowfully upon the dead girl. After a few minutes Captain Harrington came into the kitchen and announced that the medical examiner had ordered the family to leave the house and would close it up, taking full possession.

The reporters who were in the kitchen at this time continued their work and it was about 7 30 when the room was cleared of all but the family. The medical examiner kept his eyes strained for the undertaker, and finally, as the clock neared the strike of 8, D. D. Sullivan & Sons' wagon arrived. The father and aunt renewed their protestations against the removal of the body and against closing the house against them, but the authorities prevailed and the body was carried away.

Officers Ferguson and Wilson were detailed for guard duty at the house during the night, and the family were ordered to provide themselves quarters elsewhere.

Joseph Corri, the Portuguese for whom the police are looking, is 19 or 20 years of age, but looks to be 22, and has a smooth face.

At 1 30 this afternoon the police authorities gave out the fact that nothing new had transpired in the Manchester case toward developing a positive clew to the murderer. An autopsy is being held at an undertaker's warerooms under the direction of the medical examiner, Dr. Dolan, but little has yet been determined, except that the girl was not outraged. Even this has not yet been given out officially. Every inspector and police captain is at work on the case. The house is still in the hands of the authorities.

Stephen Manchester, the father of the murdered girl, would not leave the premises last night, but insisted in sleeping in the barn, where he was watched continuously by a policeman. The men employed at different times by Manchester bore bad characters in many instances, and these are now being sifted by the police and the whereabouts of the men are being traced.

WEATHER INDICATIONS.

Fair.

Washington, May 31.—For the 24 hours from 8 a. m. today: For New England fair, south and southwest winds.

Colder with Rain.

Boston, May 31.—Local forecast for New England until Thursday night: Cloudy or partly cloudy weather today, rain Thursday, continued cold, southerly to easterly winds.

BURGLARS IN MANSFIELD.

Residences Entered and $150 in Money and Valuables Stolen.

(Special Dispatch.)

Providence, R. I., May 31.—Burglars raided residences in Mansfield, Mass., again last night and succeeded in escaping with considerable property. At the residence of Henry Hodges on Central street they stole $150 in money and valuables. Sheriff Cobb has this and one other case under investigation.

HOME MATTERS.

WATER WORKS MEETING.

Proposal for Plans for Increased Supply Accepted.

At a meeting of the water board this morning a proposition was accepted for furnishing plans for an enlargement of the city water supply. The proposition is contained in the following communication:

New Bedford, May 31.

To the New Bedford Water Works:

Gentlemen—We will make the preliminary studies and surveys and furnish necessary plans, labor and estimates, and make a request for an additional water supply for the city of New Bedford for the sum of $3,400, the work to be done at the earliest practicable time and not later than Nov. 1, 1893. Partial payments to be made in August and September as may be agreed upon.

GEORGE S. RICE,
GEORGE E. EVANS.

Messrs. Rice and Evans are expert engineers, the former being particularly well known as having unearthed the frauds in the construction of the New Croton aqueduct. He was formerly assistant engineer of the Boston water works and chief engineer of the Boston rapid transit commission. Among other positions which Mr. Evans has filled have been those of assistant engineer of the Portland & Ogdensburg railroad, assistant and chief engineer of the Lowell water works and chief engineer of the Helena, Mont., water works.

Both gentlemen were in town today and were driven over the ground by Superintendent Coggeshall.

AFTER THE ANTIQUE.

Some of those wooden rocking chairs, which F. R. Slocum is now selling at a discount, are modeled after the graceful rockers which adorn the chimney corners of old-fashioned farm houses. He has a variety of rocking chairs, some with embossed leather and cane seats, and a few of the oak seated style which are so difficult to procure. A large floor space is devoted exclusively to rocking chairs, and it is worth your time to see them.

TRAIN SERVICE TO FALL RIVER.

It is reported that commencing June 12th, when the time table changes, additional train service will be provided between this city and Fall River by way of the branch road. An additional train will make a round trip from this city near the middle of the day, and another train will be put on each evening during week days.

CONDENSED LOCALS.

A man sitting on the end of a seat on a Fairhaven car yesterday afternoon tried to shake hands with a similarly seated man on another car going in an opposite direction on a turnout. The result was that he miscalculated the speed of the cars and was pulled from his seat and thrown under the running boards. By almost a miracle he escaped with but few bruises, though every passenger paled at what seemed fated to be a serious accident.

A sailboat on Assawampsett pond, in which were three men, a lady and little girl, was capsized by a flaw of wind yesterday when about three quarters of a mile from the shore. Boats put off, and all the occupants of the capsized boat, who had held on to the craft, were rescued and taken to Sampson's where they were furnished dry clothing at a cottage.

Mrs. Van Hovenberg-Morrill, who has been singing and teaching in the city for the past year, will continue her class in vocal work until the last of June. September 1st she will renew for the coming year. Mrs. Morrill will be pleased at any time to try all voices free of charge on Mondays at the parlor of the Y. M. C. A.

A turnout of the board of public works was standing at the corner of Howland and Front streets last evening, while an employe was placing lights on a pile of curbing, when the horse became frightened and ran away up Howland and Wing streets. He encountered no obstacles and was stopped near the Portuguese church.

The union of mill firemen met at the corner of County and Penniman streets Monday evening and completed the organization. Another meeting will soon be held and the schedule of prices to be presented to the employers will be adopted.

Remember Babo's German Medicated Tea does not debilitate but invigorates and strengthens the system; positive cure for sick headaches, indigestion, etc. For sale at all druggists, 25 and 50 cents per package, or sent by mail postpaid. Send postal for sample.

The Francs Tireurs dedicated their new building on Hicks street Monday evening. Congratulatory addresses were made by Dr. L. Z. Normandin, Dr. Thuot, and Delphis Duval, president of the French zouaves.

Hugh Beck, a boy 10 or 11 years old, was run over by a double team on Park street yesterday afternoon, and had one of his ears nearly torn off. He was attended by Dr. St. Germain, who rendered the necessary surgical aid.

H. C. Hathaway will sell at auction tomorrow morning at 10 o'clock at mart about 30 horses adapted for general purposes; also several secondhand horses; been used about the city. Also carriages, harnesses, whips, etc.

The Guard of Honor of this city has received an invitation to parade with the other French societies in the St. John's day festivities at Montreal, June 24th. A meeting will be held Sunday to consider the matter.

Mayor Brock and a party of friends visited training ship Enterprise this forenoon. Miss Mary B. Hathaway, who so kindly entertained those in the Memorial day parade yesterday, was in the party.

Dr. Parker will examine the afflicted free at the Mansion House, New Bedford, Friday, June 2. Ruptures, varicoceles and hydroceles cured without operations, pain or detention from business.

Elegant Wine for family use, $1.50 per gallon, delivered in city—Port, Sherry, Madeira, Angelica, Muscatel, or Tokay, at Hiram Wheaton & Sons, 45 to 51 School street.

Manuel Pedro, well known as a Standard carrier for David Tomlinson, has opened a poolroom in the shop recently vacated by Edward Murphy on South Water street.

Two large trees on the west sidewalk of South Water street south of Grinnell are being cut down today by city employes.

Ask your grocer for "London Cream Biscuit." They are the finest crackers in the world. The words London Cream stamped upon every cracker.

A valuable dog belonging to Thomas Booker on Locust street, was strangled yesterday by jumping over a fence while attached to a chain.

The Iron Spoon yacht Nautilus went to Cuttyhunk yesterday.

Nice large, fresh mackerel at Tinkham's, 9 No. Sixth st. Telephone 252—1.

Chiropodist.—Mrs. Williams, 190 Purchase st., Webster block, every Friday.

McCullough sends to all parts for iron, metal, rags, bottles. Postal or Tel. 158-12.

You get old, pure whiskey when you purchase genuine Cutter.

Nice large, fresh mackerel at Tinkham's, 9 No. Sixth st. Telephone 252—1.

Bamboo Fishing Poles at McCullough's, 10 cents apiece.

Now is the time to take Hood's Sarsaparilla.

THE UPS AND DOWNS
—OF—
Your Window Shades

Do they Please you?
Why not see us about them?
Making and Hanging Shades
A Specialty with us.

SPECIAL ORDER SHADES
FOR CUSTOM CURTAINS.

We take great pleasure in making reference to
OUR ROCKSONIA SUN FAST HOLLAND,
Which we are prepared to
GUARANTEE TO BE STRICTLY FADELESS.

Can we do more? In addition to this quality, it is the best fabric we have ever seen for Fine Curtains. It will give us pleasure to submit sample colors by mail, or we will send a competent man with samples, who will measure your windows and furnish estimate of cost, free of charge.

OIL OPAQUE SHADES.
DECORATED OR PLAIN.

We solicit your attention to the superior quality and finish of these Window Shadings, with the assurance that they are not surpassed in excellence by any Opaque goods in the market. The shades are 36x72 inches, handsomely finished, mounted on a reliable spring roller, with a fine nickel pull, all ready to hang at the window. Numbers 258, 264 and 266 are 35 cents each. Numbers 52, 58, 62 and 68 are 50 cents each.

READY-MADE SHADES

By their convenience and low prices seem to have filled a real want. We have made up a pleasing variety of Curtains, both plain and ornamental, using a high class roller which we believe will give you good satisfaction.

The prices have been made VERY LOW.

C. F. WING,
34 to 40 Purchase Street.

WHITING & CO.

Have made a big purchase of Chenille Portieres and Lace Curtains at less than 50 cents on the dollar, and they propose to give the trade the advantage of the low prices.

100 pairs of heavy fringed Chenille Portieres that you never have bought for less than $7 to $8. Our price for this lot only $3.95 a pair or $2 singly.

20 pairs Chenille Portieres, edged with narrow fringe, to be sold at the low price $2.95 per pair, $1.50 singly. No more when these two lots are sold, as we closed them all out.

400 pairs of Lace Curtains that we are going to sell at $1, $1.25, $1.50, $1.75, $2, $2.50, $3, $3.25, $3.50, $3.75, $4, $4.50, $5, $7, $7.50. Every pair is a real bargain.

This sale commences WEDNESDAY MORNING, May 31, and lasts until all are sold.

WHITING & CO.

Boys' Clothing!

Have you examined our stock of Boys' Clothing this spring? If you haven't you are probably not aware that we have an unusually attractive assortment of small and big boys' wearing apparel. Our Boys'

DOUBLE BREASTED
TWO-PIECE
KNEE PANT SUITS

from 6 to 15 years are right in every way—style, quality and price. The newest styles and handsomest patterns cost from

$5 to $7,

but we have some carried over suits which are just as good in quality but not as late style, which we are selling out at half price. These are bargains it will pay you to examine.

In lads' long-pant suits, 15 to 19, we show a choice variety of light shades, together with blue and black Serges, Cheviots and Dress Worsteds from

$5 to $16.

J.&W.R.WING&CO.,

HEADQUARTERS FOR THE

Celebrated Star Shirt Waists—the best in the world. New spring patterns now on view.

THE CRESCENT!
22 Purchase St.

MUSLIN HATS!
Only 19 Cents.
Pink and White, Blue and White, Red and White, and White.

MUSLIN BONNETS!
25 Cents Upward.

Infants' Long Cloaks!
From $2.00 to $9.50.

Children's Short Cloaks!
From $2.00 to $10.00.

Children's Dresses!
Good assortment.

Long and Short Skirts!
Flannel and Cotton.

Guimpes!
Guimpe Dresses!

SUMMER CORSETS!
50 Cents Upward.

Ferris' Ventilated Waists.
Equipoise Waists.
Double Ve Waists.
Wrappers.
Shirt Waists.

Hosiery!
Ladies' Tan Hose, 25, 33 and 50 cents. Ladies' Black Hose, 25, 33 and 50 cents. Children's Tan Hose, 25 and 37 cents, Warranted fast colors.

THE CRESCENT!
22 Purchase St.

FOR BILIOUS AND NERVOUS DISORDERS.

No mineral water will produce the beneficial results that follow the taking of ONE or more of "Beecham's Pills" with a glass of water immediately on rising in the morning.

BEECHAM'S PILLS

PAINLESS EFFECTUAL

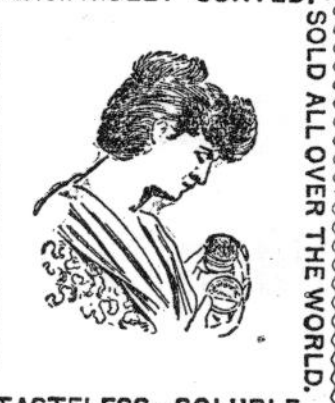
BEAUTIFULLY COATED.
"WORTH A GUINEA A BOX."
SOLD ALL OVER THE WORLD.
TASTELESS---SOLUBLE.

In many towns where this wonderful medicine has been introduced, and given a fair trial, it has abolished the family medicine chest, and been found sufficient to cure nine-tenths of the ordinary complaints incident to humanity; and when diseases of months and years are thus removed or palliated in a few days, it is not surprising that Beecham's Pills should maintain their acknowledged popularity in both hemispheres. **They cost only 25 cents,** although the proverbial expression is that they are "worth a guinea a box," for one box will oftentimes be the means of saving more than one guinea in doctor's bills. They

CURE

SICK HEADACHE

What a world of Misery is embodied in Sick Headache! Physical and mental anguish combined! Why WILL people suffer from this evil when they can free themselves from it permanently by the use of Beecham's Pills, which also cure

Constipation
Weak Stomach
Loss of Appetite
Impaired Digestion

DISORDERED LIVER AND ALL KINDRED DISEASES.

Prepared only by THOS. BEECHAM, St. Helens, Lancashire, England. B. F. ALLEN CO., Sole Agents for United States, 365 Canal St., New York, who (if your druggist does not keep them) will mail Beecham's Pills on receipt of price, 25c.—but inquire first.

"Nearer, My God, to Thee," and then at General Howard's request played "Yankee Doodle." The orator was introduced by Commander Chamberlin of Post 1 in fitting terms, and he was warmly received. In opening, General Howard spoke of meeting a few days previously Drs. Prentiss and McKenzie, and then alluded to New Bedford as the present or former home of several eminent men, among whom are Dr. Quint, the foremost clergyman in the country, and Israel Smith, the leader of the famous Thirty-third Massachusetts Regiment band, which did so much to cheer the hearts of the men in Sherman's march to the sea. Continuing, the speaker said he has dodged prohibition all his life, but today he has run into a prohibition mayor, whose cheerful presence has contributed toward making him happy, even under the influence of two memorial services and those at the common. The editors are responsible, said General Howard, for my having written my speech, a thing I never did before, but they sent to me asking for my notes, and I dictated to my stenographer what I am to deliver this evening. He then proceeded to deliver his oration, which is printed in full on the ninth page. It was of much interest, and telling points made and allusions to prominent statesmen and generals were greeted with hearty applause.

Notes of the Day.

Present with General Howard in the city was First Lieutenant Charles G. Treat of the artillery branch of the regular army, who is one of his aids-de-camp.

The City guards appeared in their new service leggings for the first time.

The police arrangements under charge of Captain Wilber were of the best, and were universally commended.

PURE BLOOD.

"Long Life and Good Health" In Kickapoo Sagwa.

Take Nature's Remedy Now.

All Persons Suffering from the Impurities of the Blood are Ready Prey of Epidemical Malarial Fevers and all Forms of Prostration.—Kickapoo Indian Sagwa is the Safest, Best and Most Reliable Blood Remedy Made.

Kickapoo Indian Sagwa will cure all troubles originating in impure blood, safely, speedily, permanently, and with economy. Impure blood is manifest in Pimples, Blotches, Boils, Carbuncles, Eruptions or Sores, Sallow Skin, Salt Rheum, Etc.

The only way in which to alter this state of things is to Cleanse the Blood from all Impurities and allow a Free, Unobstructed Circulation Through Every Vein and Artery of the Body.

Kickapoo Indian Sagwa as a *Blood-making, Blood-cleansing and Life-sustaining* medicine has eclipsed any blood purifier yet produced.

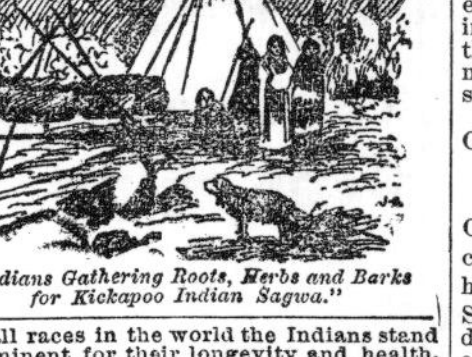

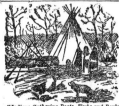

"Indians Gathering Roots, Herbs and Barks for Kickapoo Indian Sagwa."

Of all races in the world the Indians stand pre-eminent for their longevity and health. Why is it? Listen! If perchance sickness attacks them, no Poisonous Drugs are resorted to, nothing but nature is consulted and nature's gifts appropriated to their cure. The best and most reliable of roots, herbs, barks and gums constitute their medicines—hence the Indian's noble physique, pure blood, high muscular development, strong frame, and sound lungs.

Scrofula Cured By Sagwa.

WINCHESTER, N. H., March 17, 1892.

For the past 25 years I have been terribly afflicted with Scrofula, and have tried everything there was in the market, but could get no relief. A year ago I purchased six bottles of the Kickapoo Indian Sagwa, and by its use was completely cured, and the entire poison was eliminated from my system. I always keep it in the house, and my wife and myself both take it whenever we feel the least bit "run down." I would rather pay $5 a bottle for Kickapoo Indian Sagwa than to be without it.

CHARLES D. SEAVER.

SUFFERED FOUR YEARS.

Doctors Powerless—Kickapoo Indian Sagwa Cures.

MERIDEN, N. H., Dec. 3, 1892.

I have been a constant sufferer from blood and skin diseases for four years, and employed the best medical skill obtainable in this state, besides trying the Boston doctors. Kickapoo Indian Sagwa afforded me more relief in two weeks than all the different physicians in four years, and today I am a well man, thanks to this splendid medicine.

JOHN H. MOORE.

Kickapoo Indian Sagwa,

made by the Indians from roots, barks and herbs of their own gathering and curing, is obtainable of any druggist, at

$1 per Bottle, Six Bottles for $5.

MEMORIAL DAY AT ASSONET.

The morning of the 30th, the sky overcast till nature seems ready to weep. The aged veterans, solemnly wending their way among the graves of their companions in arms; these graves now decked with floral tributes and a miniature flag, speaking a language more eloquent than audible eulogies, chanting an imaginary requiem more fervent and touching than human melodies, till generations unfamiliar with the stirring scenes that caused these results and prompted these measures; catch in a degree the inspiration that fills the veteran's breast as each successive Decoration Day comes and the years creep on apace. Later the day becomes exceptionally beautiful, and a large audience assemble in the hall to listen to the exercises as prepared by the Memorial Day committee. First singing by the choir, followed by devotional exercises by the chaplain, the Rev. A. L. Beanblossom, pastor of the First Christian church. The oration, dealing primarily in generalities and reminiscences; secondarily, eulogistic of General Philip H. Sheridan by Captain A. M. Dudley of Salem, who was an officer in the Fifty-eight regiment, Massachusetts volunteers, for three years, and post commander of General Phil Sheridan post of Salem. Captain Dudley's address was extremely interesting and impressive. His allusion to Comrades Winslow and Haskins was exceedingly touching and opportune. Winslow died in Danville prison, and Haskins was reported missing after the battle of Poplar Grove, Sept. 30, 1864—never heard from. The choir rendered two fine selections. A quartet of male voices sang "Silently, Tenderly, etc." Reading by Mrs. L. G. Gove. Remarks by Colonel S. P. Richmond and the Rev. A. L. Beanblossom, the first named recalling Captain Dudley's first appearance at Taunton, then but a boy, and his prompt action and enlistment in the service of his country, and the latter enjoining upon the veterans present the thought that although they had fought a good fight that their battles were not o'er, but that a continual warfare should be kept up against the world, the flesh and the devil. Chairman Tinkham got his foot in it when he searched the audience for Mrs. Gertie Anthony, but otherwise officiated admirably. The veterans were ranged in front, each wearing a tasty bouquet upon the lapel of their coats. The sitting, which occupied nearly two hours, was concluded by singing "America" by the audience.

CHRISTIAN ENDEAVOR CONVENTION.

The semi-annual convention of the Cape Cod Union of Young People's Society of Christian Endeavor, is to be held in the First Congregational church, Sandwich, morning and afternoon, Saturday, June 3. The following is the order of exercises:

9 a. m. Convention called to order. Scripture lesson and prayer.
9 15. Address of welcome, Dr. J. E. Pratt, Sandwich.
9 30. Roll call of delegates; business meeting; report of secretary; report of treasurer.
10. Paper, "The Importance and Duty of the Lookout Committee," Miss S. Evie Hall, Dennis.
10 20. Report from societies.
11. Address, "Power for Service; What it is and How Obtained," Rev. E. L. Marsh, Yarmouth.
11 20. Question Box, conducted by Rev. E. W. Florence, Orleans.
12. Collation.
1 30 p. m. Praise service, led by Rev. D. W. Clark, Wellfleet. Scripture lesson and prayer.
1 50. Report of floating Christian Endeavor societies, Miss A. P. Jones, superintendent, Falmouth.
2 05. Address, "Winning Souls for Christ," Rev. H. S. Kimball, Hyannis.
1 25. Consecration meeting, led by Miss Amelia Snow, Orleans.
3 10. Papers, "Why are not More Young Men and Women Actively Interested In Christian Endeavor Work," Rev. H. L. Strickland, Hatchville. "What Can we Do to Secure This Result," Miss Mary E. Jenkins, West Barnstable.
3 35. Address, "Successful Personal Work," Rev. R. L. Rae, West Wareham. Singing, "God Be With You till We Meet Again." C. E. Benediction.

The Portuguese societies of Fall River and this city celebrated the dedication of a church in Fall River by a street parade yesterday. At the church interesting exercises were held.

TO REPORT THE BORDEN TRIAL.

Sheriff Wright Assigns Seats to Newspaper Representatives.

Representatives of the newspapers of Bristol county met Sheriff Wright and County Commissioner Sanders at the court house in this city Tuesday forenoon when seats were assigned for the Borden trial. Two seats were assigned to each of the daily newspapers in this city and Fall River, which took 12. Four seats were assigned to the Associated Press, one more went to Taunton and another to Attleboro, making 18. Seven seats remained and it was decided that these should go to the Boston papers. Two were assigned to the Boston Herald and Globe and one each to the Journal, Post and Advertiser.

The sheriff issued tickets bearing numbers corresponding with numbers on the tables in the press box, which is on the north side of the court room, east of the jury seats.

Deputy Sheriff Nickerson was present and made a record of the numbers assigned, that there may be no dispute on Monday.

The entire 25 seats at the disposal of the press have been assigned and Sheriff Wright says, absolutely that no other newspaper men may expect any accommodations excepting such as are open to the general public. The New York newspaper men and others, under present arrangements, must take chances at getting into the court house along with other spectators and will not even be vouchsafed a card of admission to the building.

Representatives of papers in all sections of the country are still applying in vain for places. The New York Sun enlisted the sympathies of a Massachusetts senator. Artists representing the leading illustrated weeklies will be here. Mr. Wright yesterday received an application for a seat from Yarmouth, Nova Scotia.

Mr. Pillsbury's Duty.

It is customary for the attorney general to take charge of capital cases and there are some laws about it, but we suppose he can delegate his authority to a district attorney alone, if he sees fit, but it would be regarded as avoiding his duty.—Worcester Gazette.

This is hardly fair to Mr. Pillsbury, who has been advised by his physician that he is not physically able to undertake the strain of the Borden trial. If he cannot go through with it, certainly he had better not begin with it. In addition to that, Mr. Pillsbury has never had, since the preliminary trial, any great confidence in the guilt of Lizzie Borden. Mr. Knowlton is thoroughly convinced of it. The latter will try the case with the firm belief in her being the slayer of her father and mother, and no one need fear but that the state's case will be ably conducted.—Boston Advertiser.

FAMILY REUNION.

A reunion of the relatives of Weston C. Vaughan, Sr., was held at his home in Mattapoisett on Monday. Rev. William F. Faunce and wife, father and mother of Mrs. Vaughan, were present also, and in all four generations were represented. Mr. Vaughan has four sons, two daughters, and eighteen grandchildren, all of whom were present and enjoyed the day with the old folks. At 5 p. m. supper was ready, and 34 persons sat down to the tables. During the evening the members gathered in the parlors, and a programme of singing, recitations, etc., was carried out. While this was going on a monstrous May basket, carried from this city, was hung to the old gentleman. He was greatly surprised at such proceedings, and was compelled to call for help to bring in the load, which consisted of groceries, fruits, candies, etc. After singing "Blest be the tie" and "Auld Lang Syne" the gathering broke up, and the party from this city returned by moonlight. The oldest person present was Rev. Mr. Faunce, who will be 80 years old in June, while the youngest was a babe but two weeks old. The reunion was the first one of its kind, and was a memorable occasion to all who were there.

OBITUARY.

Caroline B., widow of the late Principal Robert F. Leighton of the B. M. C. Durfee High school, Fall River, died Sunday at her residence on Pine street. It is only thirteen months since her husband passed away, shortly prior to which they had been called to bury their youngest child. The death of the mother leaves three orphan children, two daughters being members of the High school, and a son younger. They are left with no living relative nearer of kin than cousins of the parents. Mrs. Leighton was not well known outside the Church of the Ascension, which the family attended. Like her husband, Mrs. Leighton was a person of scholarly attainment, being as much at home in the German as in the English language.

TRUANT SCHOOL.

The quarterly report of the Norfolk, Bristol and Plymouth Union Truant school at Walpole has been filed in the office of County Treasurer Smith at Dedham. The cost of keeping truants for the past quarter has been $1,050. There are 13 truants in the school from New Bedford, 17 from Fall River, two from Taunton and one each from Easton and North Attleboro credited to Bristol county; four from Brookline and one each from Holbrook, Wrentham, Norwood, Hyde Park and Weymouth credited to Norfolk county; and two from Norwell and one each from Brockton and East Bridgewater credited to Plymouth county.

LONG PLAIN.

The Ladies' Aid society of the Baptist church have a strawberry festival and entertainment at the home of L. T. Jennings on Thursday evening. A feature of the entertainment will be a whistling soloist.

Walton S. Braley, at present in New York, is spending a few days with his parents here.

Joseph R. Davis is having a barn built at his new place. Augustus Wright is the carpenter.

Mrs. E. W. Ashley and Miss Florence Manter, who have been in Boston several weeks, have returned.

The Library association will meet with Miss Anna Davis this evening.

Mr. Erford Newcomb, of Taunton, is visiting his sister, Mrs. W. W. Jordan.

The public schools had a holiday yesterday. They will close for the term June 16.

Strawberry beds are looking very well, and the crop promises to be up to the average, although perhaps a little later.

It has always been customary with the Chilton Paint Co. to use in their roof paints the same quantity of oil and dryer as used in the Chilton Paints. We could never see the reason for putting a good paint on a house, and a poor paint on a roof or barn. Any paint bearing the name of Chilton is made with pure linseed oil and a turpentine dryer. We wish we knew what "the old red school house" was painted with where we went to school when a boy. Not Chilton by any means, for it was painted beyond the memory of man. If you want about the same effect, get shade number ten of the Chilton Roof Paint. DeWOLF & VINCENT, Agents.

THE REPUBLICAN STANDARD,

Issued this evening contains all the local and general news of the past week, including the local observance of Memorial Day, list of graves decorated by the G. A. R., and the names of those who sleep in southern graves, General Howard's address, and full particulars of the observance of the day; meeting of city council, large amount of important business transacted, report of investigating committee on city stables, recommendations by the mayor for better school accommodations; destruction of Washburn's planing mill and the Ullman Manufactory building by fire, loss on buildings and stock $60,000, full particulars of the conflagration; picture of Dartmouth's new town hall; two Dartmouth town meetings, new town hall to be located on Hawes' lot at Smith Mills, Bliss corner school to be removed and new building erected, town refuses to appropriate money for school superintendent's salary; William Bradford's memorial, a boulder from the Fort Phenix shore; drowned in the harbor on Sunday, two men went rowing and but one returned, the survivor gave no information until next morning, and was held while investigation was made; reports from the Antarctic whaling fleet, vessels returning home having taken a great number of seals and whales; photograph studio of Starr Brothers destroyed by fire; Attorney General Pillsbury withdraws from the Borden murder case and District Attorneys Knowlton and Moody will prosecute the case; enthusiastic labor meeting in Y. M. C. A. hall, address by Rev. Paul R. Frothingham on labor movements in general, and speeches by Senator Howard, Mr. Ross and Rev. N. W. Matthews; Rev. W. F. Crafts' lecture on the opening of the World's fair on Sundays; summer outings of the pastors of this city, where they will spend their vacations; Westport town meeting, layout of a road precipitates a discussion; the canal across Cape Cod, the senate discusses the Old Colony and Interior company bill; another murder in Fall River, a young woman hacked to pieces with a hatchet, no clew as yet to the murderer; Farm, Garden and Home; Bible lesson for next Sunday; superior and district court reports; correspondence; with editorials, ship news, markets, miscellaneous reading matter, etc.

For sale by all newsdealers in this city, and at our counters, in wrappers ready for mailing, at 4 cents per copy.

DARTMOUTH.

Archibald Crosbie, an approved minister of the society of Friends from Iowa, is expected to attend Friends' meeting at North Dartmouth (Smith Mills) on fifth day next (6th month, 1st.) The meeting commences at 11 o'clock a. m.

FALL RIVER.

Inspector Feeny arrested a woman who gave the name of Smith 30th. She immediately surrendered a watch, with the explanation that the timepiece looked just like hers. The mistake occurred a few weeks ago, when Mrs. Smith entered Boyd's jewelry store and picked out a watch which she said had been stolen from her home. It needed a new mainspring, she added. It was true that it did need a new mainspring and the jeweler gave it up. On Saturday night the owner of the watch, who had left it in the store three months before, called for it and found that he was too late and he entered a complaint.

The searching party that was scouring the woods for Frank McDonald has secured no clew to the whereabouts of the missing man, and his friends fear that he has committed suicide.

A peddler called at the house No. 6 Conanicut street 29th, and finding 13-year-old Maggie Duddy alone attempted to indecently assault her. Her screams drove the man away from the house. The police are now looking for the scoundrel.

Some of the mills in the central part of the city are going back to the practice of running overtime and State Inspector Tierney is keeping his eyes on them.

The deckhands of steamer Richard Borden struck for an increase of wages 29th and their demands were granted.

Seymour Cummings, a barge man employed by the Globe Coal company, was drowned yesterday afternoon near the company's dock in Fall River.

Fire caused $2,000 damage in an eight-tenement block owned by a man named Walsh afternoon of 30th.

TAUNTON.

Levi Goldstein's barn at Whittenton was broken into Saturday night and his cart, containing fancy articles of all kinds, was pilfered to the extent of about $100.

DIGHTON.

A call has been posted for a town meeting to take action on the proposed widening of the road near the cove, and over which electric railway tracks are to be laid. There is some hope on the part of the townspeople that the county commissioners may take the matter into their hands.

PLYMOUTH COUNTY.

Miss Mary A., daughter of Mrs. Jane Corcoran of Spring street, Bridgewater, disappeared from her home last week and has not been seen since. She was engaged in the stitching department in the Commonwealth factory at Whitman and was accustomed to take the train at Bridgewater early in the morning, and in order to reach Whitman in time for work was obliged to change cars at Westdale. On the 19th she left home as usual, and instead of changing cars at Westdale she went to Brockton or Boston. Her brother, who is employed in Whitman, received a letter from her dated at South Hanson. The letter stated that her friends might never see her again, and she also stated her intention of making a long visit, but where was not stated.

The assessors of Middleboro will tax bicycles this year wherever their ownership can be located.

Post 8, G. A. R., of Middleboro has been presented by General E. W. Pierce the sword carried by him during his connection with the Assonet artillery company nearly half a century ago. The sword was in use by Sylvanus S. Payne, of the Assonet light infantry, some 20 years before coming into the general's hands, and is a handsome weapon, with its handle finished in gold and ivory, and engraved upon a gold shield just below the handle is the following inscription: "Sylvanus S. Payne, Ensign of Assonet Light Infantry, May 4, 1824, Captain, 1825; E. W. Peirce, Lieutenant of Artillery, Aug. 7, 1844, Major of Artillery, Aug. 31, 1844, Lieutenant Colonel of Artillery, Sept. 5, 1846." The post took appropriate action upon the acceptance of the sword, and it will be placed with the trophies in the war museum.

A large stable on Brighton street, North Abington, owned and formerly occupied by H. B. Russell as a livery stable, was destroyed by fire 30th. A concreting outfit, stone drag, and a quantity of farming tools were also destroyed. The cause of the fire is not known. Loss, $1,000; insured for $400.

John E. Hunt's house, 26 Hunt street, Brockton, occupied by Frank Kammaiski, was damaged $1,000 by fire 30th. Kammaiski's furniture was damaged $500. The losses are covered by insurance.

The police discovered two burglars in Norman McKenzie's store in Brockton, 30th. They gave their names as William Robertson and Hammond Cannon.

BARNSTABLE COUNTY.

At a joint meeting of the selectmen of Bourne and trustees of the public library to fill two vacancies on the board of trustees, made vacant by the removal of Rev. C. S. Davis from the town and the failure of the town to elect one at the last annual meeting in place of L. R. Leavitt, whose term expired, David D. Nye and Levi R. Leavitt were elected, and at a meeting of the trustees held after the election Levi R. Leavitt was chosen chairman and D. D. Nye secretary.

TIVERTON.

The proceeds of the cantata "Esther," given at the Congregational church last week, netted $42, which will be appropriated to the repairs and refurnishing of the church.

NICARAGUAN REVOLUTION.

Rebels are Within Four Hours' March of the Capital.

New York, May 31.—The World's special from San Salvador says: The revolutionists are within four hours' march of Managua, the capital of Nicaragua, and are getting ready to attack President Sacasa. Sacasa is still in Managua, and is expected to leave at any moment, unless his terms are accepted by the revolutionists. He has made a strong appeal to Monteil, a member of the revolutionary junta, whom he considers his personal friend, for guarantees of personal safety. A number of the leaders of the revolution are clamoring for Sacasa's life. Sacasa knows this, and is in mortal dread. He has applied to the government of San Salvador for an asylum. This will be granted him upon condition that he comes here alone. His family is now on one of the Pacific mail steamers.

The Herald's Granada, Nicaragua, special says: Three peace commissioners appointed by President Sacasa met the three representatives of the insurgents in Sabana Grande at noon Tuesday. Those representing the insurgents returned to Granada at 10 o'clock at night. They declined to make public the various propositions advanced by each side, but report that no agreement was reached. It is probable that hostilities will be resumed at the end of the 48 hours during which it was agreed that the truce should prevail.

FIFTY CENTS ON THE DOLLAR.

Creditors of Ex-Secretary Foster Accept His Offer of Settlement.

Cleveland, O., May 31.—A largely attended meeting of the creditors of ex-Governor Foster was held at Fostoria last night. Resolutions of sympathy were adopted, after which it was agreed to accept 50 cents on the dollar in payment of claims, leaving it entirely with Mr. Foster whether he should pay more if he became financially able to do so. A statement from the governor was read, saying that he could pay 50 per cent. of his liabilities soon and that he wanted to pay in full.

Gilbert Moves Feebly.

London, May 31.—Father Matthews, chaplain of the Portland prison and nephew of the home secretary in the last Salisbury cabinet, accompanied Gilbert, the released convict, to London. Gilbert's appearance corroborated the recent reports as to his ill health. He moves feebly and stoops. His face and figure have aged 20 years since he was taken to prison.

The Pope and the School Question.

Rome, May 31.—It is reported that the pope is about to publish a rescript on the school question, with special application to the church in the United States. The rescript is expected to show a considerable modification of the pope's former views on the subject, and is said to differ radically in many points from the opinions held by archbishop Ireland.

Quarantine Against Cholera.

Madrid, May 31.—The Spanish government has declared a five days quarantine against all vessels arriving from Hamburg. Spanish consuls in France report that cholera prevails in Cette, a Mediterranean port. Several cases have ended fatally.

The Foot Relay Race.

NEW YORK, May 31.—At 2:33 o'clock yesterday Thomas Mallon of the Harlem Young Men's Christian association reached the clubhouse with the letter in the foot relay race. The banner offered to the association making the best time was won by the New Haven association. The prize for the best time by any man for five miles was won by William Hunt of the New Haven association. His time was 27:01. The distance is 76 miles.

By One Vote.

LONDON, May 31—In the house Viscount Wolmer moved an amendment forbidding the Dublin legislature to discuss subjects on which they were not allowed to make laws. Mr. Gladstone objected to the amendment. Eventually the amendment was lost by a vote of 239 to 238. The smallness of the government majority provoked prolonged Unionist cheers.

The Marblehead at New York.

NEW YORK, May 31.—The United States twin screw cruiser Marblehead arrived here in tow yesterday morning. She went to the Brooklyn navy yard. The Marblehead comes from the ship yard of Harrison Loring of Boston, and started for this port Sunday. She will probably make her trial trip in July and is expected to make over 18 knots an hour.

Dynamiter Gilbert Released.

LONDON, May 31.—It is learned that the released dynamiter is not John Daly but James Gilbert, who was sentenced in 1885 to penal servitude for life, for having caused dynamite explosions at the tower and houses of parliament. The sole reason for Gilbert's release is said to be the breaking down of his health.

Attacked by a Snake.

NORTH SCITUATE, Mass., May 31.—While Mrs. Davis Jenkins and daughter of Mott Farm were walking they were attacked by a huge snake, which they killed after a hard tussle. The serpent was 5 feet 8 inches in length and as large as a man's arm. Parties are searching for its mate.

Was Bitten by a Hog.

NEW YORK, May 31.—Dr. Gibier of the Pasteur institute is treating a man for hydrophobia who was bitten by a hog. The man is John P. Smithson, a farmer from Washington, Md. He owned a dog which went mad and bit the hogs, which afterward showed all signs of hydrophobia.

Took a Dose of Laudanum.

BRIDGEPORT, Conn., May 31.—Mrs. William Brill, aged 50 years, drank laudanum and died. The woman had endeavored to run an unlicensed resort here, but had been frequently raided. The Brills were once wealthy, but are now poor and have been harassed by the police. This discouraged the mother and probably led to suicide.

JOHNSON'S ANODYNE LINIMENT

UNLIKE ANY OTHER FOR HOUSEHOLD USE.

Was originated and first prescribed by AN OLD FAMILY PHYSICIAN in 1810. Could a remedy without real merit have survived over eighty years?

Generation after Generation *Have Used It,*

For INTERNAL as much as EXTERNAL use.

It is Soothing, Healing, Penetrating. Once used always wanted; and dealers say "Can't sell any other kind."

Every Mother Should have Johnson's Anodyne Liniment in the house for Croup, Colds, Sore Throat, Tonsillitis, Colic, Cuts, Bruises and Burns. Stops Pain, Cramps, Inflammation in Body or Limb. Cures Coughs, Asthma, Catarrh, Bronchitis, Cholera Morbus. For Muscular Rheumatism, Lame Back, Stiff Joints, Strains, best remedy made. Inhale for Nervous Headache. Full particulars sent free. Sold everywhere. Price, 35 cents, Six, $2.00. If you can't get it send to us. I. S. JOHNSON & CO., 22 Custom House St., Boston, Mass.

AGAIN A WIFE.

Mrs. Mary Nevins Blaine Weds a New York Physician.

NEW YORK, May 31.—Mrs. Marie Blaine, nee Nevins, the divorced wife of James Gillespie Blaine, Jr., was married at high noon yesterday to Dr. William Tillinghast Bull, one of New York's leading physicians. The ceremony was performed in the South Reformed church, Madison avenue and Thirty-eighth street, by Rev. Dr. Roderick Terry, pastor of the church.

The bride, accompanied by her parents, Colonel and Mrs. Richard Nevins, her sister, Miss Anna Nevins, her brother, Frank Nevins, and her little son James, arrived at the church in a private carriage from the Belmont hotel, where they have been staying.

Mrs. Blaine was dressed in a light gray travelling dress trimmed with pearl gray silk. She wore a small toque bonnet, corresponding to her costume. Her father carried her wedding bouquet of choice mixed spring blossoms.

Dr. Bull reached the church after the bride and took a seat in one of the front pews. He was soon joined by his best man, Dr. Bradford of Boston. The wedding ritual was very simple, and lasted but a little while. Colonel Nevins gave away the bride. During the ceremony selections from Lohengrin, Cavalleria Rusticana and Mendelssohn were played by the church organist, Gerrit Smith. There was no music by the choir. The couple left at once for Newport, R. I., and will sail tomorrow for Europe.

Will Be Launched June 10.

PHILADELPHIA, May 31.—The United States battleship Massachusetts will be launched from Cramps' shipyard on Saturday, June 10. The vessel is an exact counterpart of the Indiana, which left the ways last February. It is probable that a delegation from Massachusetts will attend the ceremonies, and that the daughter of a Massachusetts statesman will christen the ship.

A Young Firebug.

ROCKLAND, Me., May 31.—Appleton has been excited over a firebug. A few days ago an 11-year-old boy named Llewellyn Newbert came to town from the Little Wanderers' home in Boston. Shortly after three fires were discovered in one day in populous parts of the town. The boy was at last apprehended, brought to Rockland and sent to the state reform school.

Both Must Die.

NEW YORK, May 31.—Governor Flower who has had the cases of Martello and Osmond, two murderers, under consideration for some time, decided yesterday to let the law take its course, and they will both be killed by electrictricity. Martello will be killed some time during the first week in June, and Osmond will be executed the second week in June.

President Cleveland in Virginia.

WASHINGTON, May 3.—President Cleveland, accompanied by L. Clark Davis of Philadelphia, left Washington for Hog Island, Va., yesterday afternoon, where he arrived at 5 o'clock this morning. His determination is to return to Washington Saturday evening.

Suffocated by Gas.

HAVERHILL, Mass., May 31.—Mrs. Jane Craston, aged 49, was found dead in her sleeping room at 59 Pecker street, having been suffocated by escaping gas from an open gas jet. Mrs. Craston belonged in Lynn.

Won by Zimmerman.

PARIS, May 31.—A. A. Zimmerman, the noted bicyclist of the New York Athletic club, easily won the mile amateur bicycle race here yesterday, but failed to lower the record. He started back for London today.

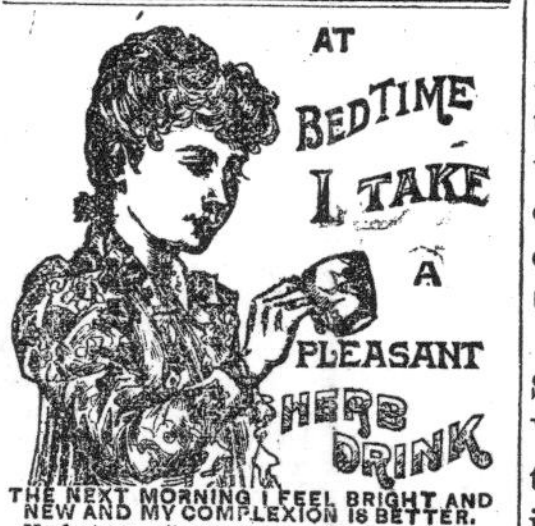
AT
BEDTIME
I TAKE
A
PLEASANT
HERB
DRINK

THE NEXT MORNING I FEEL BRIGHT AND NEW AND MY COMPLEXION IS BETTER.

My doctor says it acts gently on the stomach, liver and kidneys, and is a pleasant laxative. This drink is made from herbs, and is prepared for use as easily as tea. It is called

LANE'S MEDICINE

All druggists sell it at 50c and $1 a package. If you can not get it, send your address for a free sample. Lane's Family Medicine moves the bowels each day. In order to be healthy this is necessary. Address, ORATOR F. WOODWARD, LeRoy, N. Y.

GEORGE C. BLISS, FLORIST.

34 Arnold Street,

CORNER COTTAGE.

TELEPHONE, DAY OR NIGHT.

BRICKS. Large variety Common and Pressed Bricks.

LIME. Both Lincolnville and Rockland.

CEMENT. Both American and English.

PLASTERING HAIR, DRAIN PIPE, etc.

S. S. PAINE & BRO.,

Front Street, Just South of Bridge.

CITY NOTICES.

POLICE NOTICE.

CITY OF NEW BEDFORD, IN BOARD OF ALDERMEN, May 11, 1893.

Ordered—That the Chief of Police is hereby authorized to assign stands at such places as to him seems proper for hackney carriages, under the provisions of section 4 of chapter 29 of the ordinances.

Ordered—That the Chief of Police is hereby authorized on behalf of the Board of Mayor and Aldermen to designate the public stand or stands within the city which jobbing wagons and other vehicles mentioned in section 9 of chapter 29 may occupy. Adopted.

D. B. LEONARD, City Clerk.

City of New Bedford, Mass., Office of Chief of Police, May 22, 1893.

In pursuance of the foregoing orders to me directed, I hereby designate Spring street, on the north and south sides of said street, between Water street and South Second street, as a public stand which jobbing wagons may occupy.

I would also designate Elm street, between Purchase street and Acushnet avenue, on the north side of said Elm street; also Middle street between Purchase street and Acushnet avenue on the south side of said Middle street, as a public stand which hackney-carriages may occupy.

All other places designated or occupied as stands for hackney-carriages, baggage wagons, and jobbing wagons, in any public street, square or way of the city is hereby abolished. Per order,

GEORGE DOUGLASS, Chief of Police.

my24-6t*

DOGS MUST BE LICENSED

On or Before May 1st, or the Owners or Keepers Thereof Are Liable to Fine.

CITY CLERK'S OFFICE, NEW BEDFORD, April 1, 1893.

All Dog Licenses expire May 1st next. The undersigned is now prepared to issue licenses for the year ending May 1st, 1894. DANIEL B. LEONARD, City Clerk.

(LICENSE NOW. DON'T DELAY.)

Extract from Chapter 102 of the Public Statutes.

SECT. 80. Every owner or keeper of a dog of THREE MONTHS OLD or over shall annually on or before the 30th day of April, cause it to be registered, numbered, described and licensed for one year from the first day of the ensuing May, in the office of the clerk of the city or town wherein said dog is kept, and shall cause it to wear around its neck a collar distinctly marked with its owner's name and its registered number.

SECT. 81. An owner of a dog may at any time have it licensed until the first day of the ensuing May; and a person becoming the owner or keeper of a dog after the first day of May, not duly licensed shall cause it to be registered, numbered, described, and licensed, as provided in the preceding section.

SECT. 87. Whoever keeps a dog contrary to the provisions of this chapter shall forfeit fifteen dollars, five dollars of which shall be paid to the complainant and ten dollars to the treasurer of the county in which the dog is kept.

ap3tje1

To Keepers of Billiard, Pool, Sippio and Bagatelle Tables for Hire.

CITY OF NEW BEDFORD, City Clerk's Office, April 1, 1893.

Notice is hereby given that licenses to keep billiard, pool, sippio and bagatelle tables for hire expire on the the thirtieth (30th) day of April, instant. Applications for such licenses for the ensuing year should be made at once to the Mayor and Aldermen. Blanks for the purpose may be had at this office.

DANIEL B. LEONARD, City Clerk.

ap3toje1

C. W. HASKINS

No. 20 PURCHASE STREET,

Has replenished his stock since the holidays, and now offers at very low prices a good variety of Diamond Rings, Fine Jewelry, Gold and Silver Watches, Chains, &c.

His stock of Sterling Silver Spoons, Forks, Fancy Table Ware and Novelties is very extensive; these goods are lower in price than ever before.

18 KARAT WEDDING RINGS A SPECIALTY.

You can save money buying of him your Spectacles and Eye Glasses, fit and quality guaranteed.

Watch, Clock and Jewelry repairing by experienced workmen.

GOLDSMITH, SILVER & CO'S

M.C.A.

10c. CIGARS LEAD ALL OTHERS.

EVERYBODY SHOULD TRY THE

"108"

Havana Filled 5c. Cigar.

C. R. DEAN, Agent, - Taunton.

Baggage Tags

ALWAYS IN STOCK AT STANDARD OFFICE.

Lawn Mowers!

We carry the Philadelphia, Magic, New Departure, Union, Diamond and New England High Wheel.

You must be suited with some one of these makes. We are selling a warranted mower, parts for which can be supplied at any time, for **$3.50.**

F. L. SOWLE & CO.,

OPPOSITE CITY CLOCK.

The Evening Standard.

ESTABLISHED FEBRUARY, 1850. | NEW BEDFORD, THURSDAY, JUNE 1, 1893. | TWO CENTS.

HASKELL & TRIPP.

As The Old Farmer's Almanac used to tell us, "About this time look out for a warm spell."

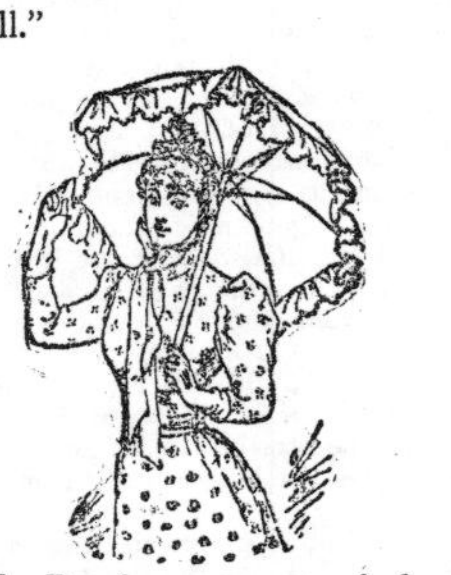

A Purchase street window of parasols, ruffled, changeable, surahs, printed Chinas, etc., well-made, all stylish silks for the *sunshiny season*—it's coming, sure, even if a long time on the way. Take your pick from this beautiful collection of parasols for $1.89; and mind you, they are worth a great deal more money. How they happen to be sold so low wouldn't interest you, *but the fact will.*

We have ready some extra good things in thin gloves, notably taffetas, for 25c., and pure Milanese silks for 29c. a pair.

Kayser's perfection finger-tipped silk gloves, 75c. a pair. Finger ends last as long as any part. If you don't find it so bring 'em back and get a new pair.

Some new belts from France are of metal, will not tarnish, exceedingly handsome and cost 89c. each.

Japanese screens. *A bargain lot* way below importation price.

We will open today 500 handsomely decorated Japanese screens, in a large assortment of colorings and designs, and offer you a choice from the entire collection for 25c. each. For the summer sitting room or the seashore cottage these help to brighten up the furnishings, and the price is ridiculously little. For sale in Upholstery gallery.

Thin dress stuffs for hot weather.

Swiss muslins, plain and dotted, 25c. a yard.

Colored Swiss muslins, delicately tinted grounds with neat figures and stripes, 25c. a yard.

Sheer, cool-looking dimities, 25c. a yard.

Cotton pongees that closely resemble India silks come in the same colors and styles, 12½c. a yard.

Canton cloths, beautiful fabric, charming assortment of colors, 12½c. a yard.

Forty nice styles challies, 5c. a yard.

Openwork plaids and lace striped white lawns and nainsooks, 12½c. a yard.

Irish lawns, white grounds, neatly printed, 12½c. a yard, 38 inches wide.

Twenty-nine cents for a well-printed, well-bound book. As handsome in get-up as the $1 books used to be—handsomer than most of them.

At 29c. we include a large assortment of novels in library edition of 12 mos.

At 29c. each we offer the following in white, green, red and gold, cloth bindings:

Twice Told Tales, HAWTHORNE.
Mosses from an Old Manse, "
Hyperion, LONGFELLOW.
Outre Mer, "

3000 paper novels, 10c. per copy.

HASKELL & TRIPP,
Department Stores,
Purchase and William Streets.

A CLEW.

Police on the Track of a Farm Hand.

He Quarreled with Old Man Manchester.

Farmer Slapped His Employe's Face.

Laborer Mysteriously Disappeared on Tuesday.

Said He Was Going to Newport for Work.

The Suspicious Character is Manuel Carreiro.

Officers Will Not Tell What They Know of Him,

But Think They Have Their Work Well in Hand.

(Special Dispatch.)

Fall River, June 1.—The Globe says the police have a clew which may lead to the capture of the villian who murdered Bertha Manchester. They are working it with commendable activity and with a well grounded hope that he will be captured in the near future. All day yesterday officers scoured the woods in the vicinity of the house, and interviewed every person living within a radius of three miles of the premises, and when their work had been finished a consultation was held at headquarters. It was then determined that there were several possible clews to be worked. But there was one which gave promise of splendid results. It is the important feature of the case today and is so plausible that the marshal and his men are feeling that the work is well in hand and can be successfully accomplished.

It is the accepted theory of the police that Bertha was killed by a former employe of her father. They think that the murderer went to the house about 9 o'clock Tuesday morning, and with the intention of robbery primarily, and finding much opposition in the person of the girl added murder to the original motive which prompted the visit. They are fully convinced that a former employe of Mr. Manchester killed the girl. With this idea in view they found traces of a suspicious character, a Portuguese named Manuel Carreiro, and the last man who was employed by Mr. Manchester on the farm. He is described as a man about 22 years old, small in stature, with black hair, clean face except a small black mustache, and a comparative stranger in this city. He worked three days on the farm last week and left because of the manner in which he was treated by the old gentleman.

Carreiro came to America from the Western Islands about two months ago and went to board with a distant relative, Jacinto Muniz, who lives in the mill tenement on the eastern row of the Narragansett mill blocks. Muniz is a mill operative, and also directs a band of Portuguese musicians. Last Monday Carreiro called on a very prominent Portuguese resident and asked to be directed to a farmer who might need a laborer. He was sent to Manchester's place and was employed. He worked three days and then left. In speaking of his experience to his relatives he said that Manchester fed him on codfish three times a day, and that he didn't like that article as a steady diet. For that reason he says he left.

But the police have another story of how he happened to leave the farm. They learn that Mr. Manchester pays his help according to the amount of work done, and that when Carreiro asked for a settlement there was a quarrel, and that the old farmer slapped the Portuguese's face. This took place about the middle of last week, and Carreiro returned to the city and located at the residence of Manuel Peters on Eagle street. The police also learn that he left Peters' place early Tuesday morning, saying that he was going up to the Narragansett block to get his trunk, and that he intended to go to Newport. He expected to get employment at some farmhouse in the vicinity of that city.

Since that time Carreiro has not been seen. He did not visit his relatives in Border City, and they have not heard from him. Inspectors Feeney, Medley and Wordell and Captain Desmond are following his clew today to the exclusion of all others, if indeed there be any others.

The gentleman who referred Carreiro to Manchester told a reporter this morning that within the past year he had sent at least 20 workmen to the Manchester farm, and that most of them came away, after failing to agree with the old man. Manchester came to this gentleman within two weeks and said that he was short of help, and wanted more men. He was told that he would be accommodated, and the very next man who applied for work was Carreiro, and he was employed, as before stated.

While the police do not accuse this man of the murder, they believe that his mysterious disappearance is significant, and they intend to find him and get an explanation of his conduct.

When a reporter called at the home of Jacinto Muniz this morning, a daughter who speaks good English denied that there was any such person as Carreiro, but it was learned that the police had been to the house and secured information to the contrary.

The officers refuse to tell what they know of Carreiro's whereabouts, but they admit that he is the man wanted at this time. A squad of policemen crossed Slade's Ferry bridge this morning, going in the direction of Swanzey, but it is probable that they were on a less important clew.

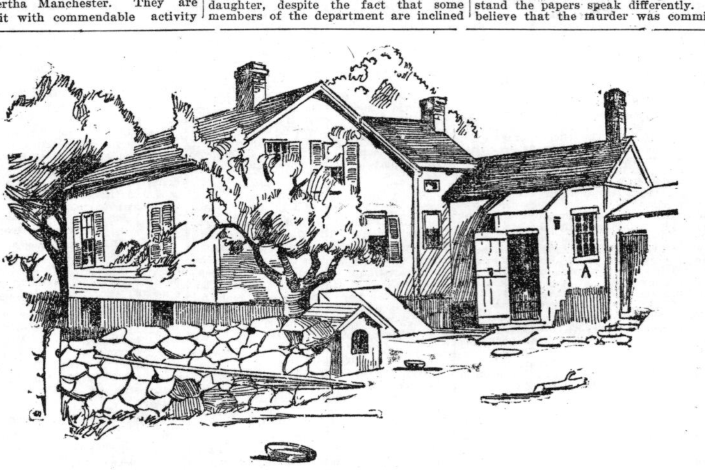

THE MANCHESTER HOUSE.
The body lay directly under window—A.

MARSHAL HILLIARD TALKS.

He Has No Doubt of the Motive of Miss Manchester's Murderer.

(By Associated Press.)

Fall River, June 1.—The Manchester murder is no longer a mystery as far as the police are concerned. Many newspapers are putting forth prettily written, but deliciously untrue stories, of the affair, and are contradicting themselves in almost the same columns. But the officers looking on the case are well satisfied as to what went on in the Manchester kitchen last Tuesday morning.

The murder was committed either as a result of anger because of an unsatisfied passion or, what seems more probable, because of a combination of uncontrolled desire and robbery. The authorities of the force are not casting the slightest suspicion on "Old Steve" Manchester as the murderer of his daughter, despite the fact that some members of the department are inclined to suspect him. He not only did not commit the awful deed, but by the testimony of two boys and by the evidence given by the old man himself he had no opportunity to do so had he so wished. The person who committed the murder was a former employe, probably one of the men hired within six weeks, and perhaps not as remote as that.

The police worked all last night and Wednesday afternoon hunting up a man called "Joe," a reckless, shiftless Portuguese, who worked on the Manchester farm less than three days and quarreled with both daughter and father before leaving the premises. This man had knocked about a great deal in the vicinity of Eagle street and in the Bowenville colony of Portuguese, but the combined efforts of Inspectors Feeney, Perron, Medley and Wordell under the direction of Assistant Marshal Fleet and other officers failed to disclose his whereabouts during the past three days.

The story got abroad Wednesday that Medical Examiner Dolan had found it advisable to remove the skull from the body of Bertha Manchester for evidence in a trial when the murderer is apprehended.

In conversation with a reporter, Dr. Dolan said that the head had not been removed from the body. Only just so much work had been done at the autopsy as was necessary in the circumstances.

Much is being said in the newspapers about the similarity of the Manchester and the Borden murders and the respects in which the murders present like conditions. They were all committed in the light of day and the instrument used in both cases was an axe. The victims were hit about the head in all cases. Beyond these points it is not possible to go. The Bordens were old people, living on one of the principal streets of the city. Bertha Manchester was young, living in a lonely farming district. The Bordens were stricken down in their own homes, but at times two hours apart. Their house was occupied by one or more persons at the time of the murders, and the discovery of the deaths was within 20 minutes of the time when one of them took place. Bertha Manchester was stricken down in her own home, where she, with the murderer was the sole occupants and it was at least five hours after the murder when a police authority looked on the stricken form. The cuts in all cases were on the head, as has been stated, but the cuts on the Bordens and those on the Manchester girl were of an entirely different character. Mrs. Borden was struck in about the same place on the back side of the head, and when the exhausted arms that gave the blows were about to end their work the deadly axe fell on the poor woman's back. The blows on Mr. Borden's face were 13 or 14 in number, but none of them extended beyond the limits of the ear on one side or the edge of the mouth on the other. The blows that killed Bertha Manchester were given on the back of the neck, the back of the skull and directly in the face, just as a frenzied man would strike his struggling, dodging victim.

Then, too, no adequate motive for the Borden murder has been discovered beyond such as has been inferred from family relationship. In the Manchester murder the house is located on an unfrequented country road; escape into the woods was possible from the rear of the house without even an opportunity for detection. Everything about the Borden mystery points to a well-concocted plan to kill, while the evidence in the Manchester case points to a struggle and sudden impulse to murder.

Marshal Hilliard has said in an interview he could not understand why there should be talk of a mystery in connection with the horrible murder of the innocent Manchester girl. No one could doubt the motive for the murder. The girl's old father himself showed what the cause of the murder was. Her money and watch were missing and her position when found indicated that she struggled for her honor and her life. It is idle to think of the old man as the murderer of his daughter. The officers satisfied themselves of this fact after examining the house and the old man collectively and separately.

"The old fellow isn't very expressive in his affections, I guess," quizzed the reporter.

"Now don't run away with that idea," said the marshal. "He may not strike you very favorably, but that old man loved that daughter better than his own life. He may not have a great deal of love for humanity in general, but we can't talk with him about this girl unless he shows feeling. He considers it his duty to go over his milk route every day, just as many people consider prayer the first thing to do in the morning and the last at night. He didn't consider it unusual or cruel that the girl should work like a slave. He prided in her because she could do it. Why, my officers have heard lots of stories about the old man's travels among his customers today, and in every case where he was spoken to at length he showed his sorrow. I don't live as he does, you don't live as I do, but that isn't any reason that we would commit murder."

The marshal was asked how it could be possible for a sane man to hack a victim so because of robbery or unsatisfied desire.

In answer he recalled to the reporter's memory the case of the murdered egg man, Lawton, who was killed in Wareham by Besse, afterwards hung. After killing and robbing his victim, he cooly drove along the highway with the murdered man's body in the bottom of the wagon. There is nothing impossible in crime, and life is often brutally taken for very slight cause."

"Have you any clew at all, Mr. Marshall?" asked the reporter.

"Yes, sir, we have, although I understand the papers speak differently. We believe that the murder was committed by some of the curious hired help that worked on the farm, and we are after two men who have suddenly disappeared. We are not saying much about the work for reasons the public will appreciate and understand, and it is easy to see that the officers are working harder than policemen ever worked in a crime in this city before."

"What do you think about the similarity of this murder and that of the Bordens?" he was asked.

"They are not similar," he replied; "there is a motive, possibly two, for murder. In the other case there was no robbery, no rape, not the slightest shadow of a motive for hours, and we were all at sea. At Manchester's we were on the scene first, but the poor victim had been dead for hours. At Bordens' we were on the scene early, but we were not the first who were there, and one at least of the victims had been dead only a short time."

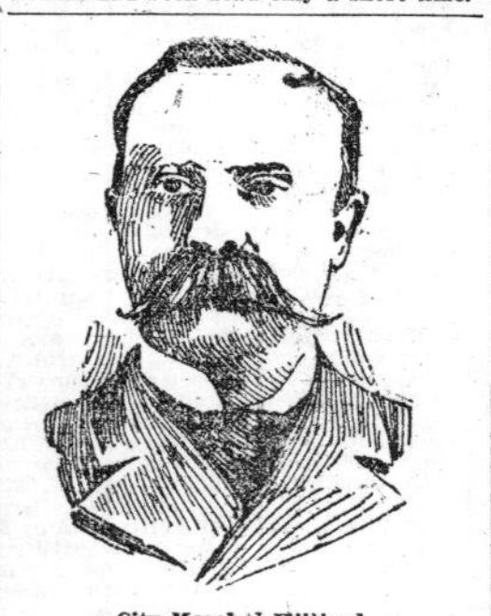

City Marshal Hilliard.

"It's curious about these two crimes in this respect." He said in conclusion: "When the Bordens were killed the police force was away at Rocky Point; when this girl was killed most of the people in her neighborhood had started for the city to see the parade and look on at the Memorial Day exercises."

The board of aldermen will hold a special meeting tonight, and a reward will be offered for the detection of the criminal.

THE HOUR OF THE MURDER

May be Ascertained from an Examination of the Stomach.

(Special Dispatch.)

Fall River, June 1.—The stomach of the murdered Manchester girl was removed by the physician making the autopsy and will be sent to an expert for analysis, to establish, if possible, the hour of the murder as indicated by the point reached in the process of digestion. The body is still lying in the undertaker's rooms and a host of people, including a large number of morbidly curious women, are availing themselves of an opportunity to view the remains.

TRIED TO AVOID RECOGNITION.

Strange Action of a Man on the Road to Fall River.

Superintendent of Construction Slade, of the Rotch mill in this city, reported today to Captain Allen of the police that about 6 15 o'clock yesterday morning he was coming to this city and when on the new road west of Smith Mills village and near the ledge he passed a man going the other way. This man, Mr. Slade says, is named Will Davis, and he was brought up on the Somerset poor farm. He knows him well, and what surprised him was that when Davis approached he hung his head, did not once look up, and seemed desirous to avoid recognition. Mr. Slade has not previously seen the man for two years. He describes Davis as 30 years old, five feet eight inches tall, dark mustache and quite good build. The police here have telephoned the account received from Mr. Slade to the Fall River authorities.

WEATHER INDICATIONS.

Cloudy and Showery.

Washington, June 1.—For Massachusetts, Rhode Island and Connecticut, for the 24 hours from 8 a. m. today: Increasing cloudiness and showers; slightly warmer tonight; southerly winds.

Fair and Warmer.

Boston, June 1.—Local forecast for New England until Friday night: Fair, warmer, southwest winds.

HOME MATTERS.

PERSONAL.

Stephen Manchester, father of the latest victim of the murderer in Fall River, when a young man was engaged in the whaling business, having made one or more voyages on ship Caravan of Fall River, and also on ship Polar Star from this port, rising to the position of mate.

Rev. William J. Potter's stay in California is drawing to an end, at least for this season. He will preach in Sacramento June 4th, and then move eastward toward Colorado, stopping a few days at Salt Lake City, where he is to speak June 11th.

Among the Raymond & Whitcomb excursionists leaving Boston yesterday for Chicago via Niagara Falls was Mrs. Colonel S. P. Lee.

Mr. and Mrs. Thomas N. Doutney of Burlington, Vt., are receiving congratulations: "Sylvia Doutney, 10 a. m. Monday, May 8, 10½ pounds."

John Connelly, chairman of the Democratic city committee of Fall River, is understood to be a candidate for the position of collector of that port.

GUNN FOLDING BED.

This is one of the renowned modern inventions that every one knows about. F. R. Slocum sells the Gunn mantel bed. If you want one examine into the merits of that $25 bed, with woven wire springs and a wool mattress, that he has had such a trade on. There are other styles, some with mirrors and chiffonier backs, some with mirrors and for ornaments as they are for convenience.

CONDENSED LOCALS.

The report of Probation Officer Coe for the month of May gives the number of cases investigated, 125; statements of defendants found true, 116; statements of defendants found untrue, 6; no statements made by defendants, 3. Placed on probation during the month, 44. This is the largest number placed on probation by nearly one-half of any month since the law was passed.

F. E. Tinkham's bulletin for tomorrow: Cod, haddock, halibut, Penobscot river salmon, striped bass, rock bass, scup, tautog, flounders, bluefish, shad, both with and without roe, kingfish, perch, lobsters, clams, quahogs, oysters, butterfish, smoked salmon, smoked halibut, new smoked alewives, etc. The place is 9 No. Sixth st. Telephone 252-1.

Frank Bonneaux has reported to the police that his store at the corner of Front and Hicks streets was burglariously entered Monday night, and that a quantity of cigars and a nickel clock were stolen. The thieves gained entrance by breaking a light of glass and raising a window.

The search for the body of Duncan McNeil still continues, but so far without success. An account of proceedings against George E. Bradley, who was in the boat when McNeil was drowned, will be found in district court proceedings.

Foster M. Blake, a somewhat notorious character, was arrested today by Inspector Parker for the larceny a few days ago of a coat and vest belonging to William Simpson, which was hanging on a line at No. 321 Pleasant street.

The Washington Social club gave an oyster supper complimentary to its friends at its rooms on Harmony street last evening. About 40 or 50 were present, and after the repast a pleasing musical entertainment was given.

New potatoes, radishes, string beans, asparagus, strawberries, new cabbage, thick rib corned beef, choice legs of mutton and a lot of handsome fat fowl now ready for Friday and Saturday's trade. White Cash.

Standish Bourne sold at auction this morning Police Station No. 2 on South Water street, to be removed, to Manuel J. Moura for $215; also the woodhouse on premises to William Wilkinson for $8.

It will pay all who intend papering this season to see the fine line of paper hanging shown by Bliss & Nye. They carry the largest stock of the best selected patterns at the lowest prices in the city.

Our great tea sale is meeting with great success. We have only a few more chests. Our sale closes Saturday night. The price will then be 50c. per pound. Come now while the price is only 30c. per pound. White Cash.

Dr. Parker will examine the afflicted free at the Mansion House, New Bedford, Friday, June 2. Ruptures, varicoceles and hydroceles cured without operations, pain or detention from business.

Elegant Wine for family use, $1.50 per gallon, delivered in city—Port, Sherry, Madeira, Angelica, Muscatel, or Tokay, at Hiram Wheaton & Sons, 45 to 51 School street.

"All sorts and conditions of men," and of babies too, make up this world of ours, but the Mellin's Food babies are all of one and the same sort—healthy, happy and good.

Teamers are requested to meet at the corner of Pleasant and Kempton streets this evening and discuss the question of nine hours' work.

The New Bedford Blues are trying to arrange a game with the High Schools or Bay Views for next Tuesday afternoon.

A wail is heard at the south end for the return of the seats on the South Water street park.

Gentlemen, the finest line of Russia leather shoes found at Buchell's. See our $4 shoe.

A belt given away with every boy's suit at Gifford & Co's.

See F. E. Tinkham's bulletin for tomorrow on this page.

Cutter Whiskey comes high because of its age and the care taken in making it.

A nice black bicycle stocking for 50 cents at Gifford & Co's.

In using Ayer's Hygienic Coffee don't make it too strong. Grocers sell it.

The 25 cent straw hats have arrived at Gifford & Co's.

Another lot of fresh eggs 20c. per dozen. White Cash.

See F. E. Tinkham's bulletin for tomorrow on this page.

Good Sweaters at Gifford & Co's, $2.50.

Hood's Sarsaparilla tones the system.

Saturday, JUNE 3d,

The Special Drives will be:

FIRST.

Art Squares.

These well nigh indispensable floor coverings are in extra super all-wool Ingrain quality of good styles and colorings.

Size.	Regular Price.	Saturday's Price.
2 x 3 yards	$5.50	$4.45
2½ x 3 yards	7.50	5.95
3 x 3½ yards	10.50	8.25
3½ x 4 yards	14.00	10.70

We don't expect to be able to repeat this offer.

SECOND.

We sell the balance of the odd lots of

Wall Paper.

8 rolls Paper, 16 yds. Border, } 65 cents.
10 rolls Paper, 20 yds. Border, } 83 cents.
10 rolls Paper, 20 yds. Border, } $1.17.

None of these papers sold regularly for less than 15c. a roll; many of them were 45c. goods.

THIRD.

A beautiful line of extra fine WASHABLE

Art Muslins.

These goods are as beautiful as China Silks and far more serviceable. We are told "they wash like white cotton cloth." The designs and colorings are truly artistic. All the season we've been selling them for 50c. a yard. Saturday you can buy them for

32c. Per Yard.

FOURTH.

A lot of fine

Holland Shades.

Made in our own workrooms from colors which were "a little slow." Aside from the labor of making the stock in these curtains is worth 70c. each. You can buy them complete ready to hang for

35c. Each.

FIFTH.

Two lots of

Carpet Samples.

The best of Tapestry, 1 yard to 1¼ yards long, for 50c. a yard; and the best of all wool Ingrains, 1 to 1¼ yards long, for 29c. each.

COME EARLY.

C. F. WING,
34 to 40 Purchase Street.

WHITING & CO.

We have closed out all the Remnants of White Check Crinolines, some 1,500 yards of the manufacturer, in lengths from 1 to 5 yards in a piece, and shall sell them at the low price of

5 Cents Per Yd.

Now is the time to get Crinoline cheap.

You will always find we are headquarters for all kinds of Dress Linings, and of the best makes, and all of our black linings are sterling fast dye.

WHITING & CO.

J. V. SPARE,
41 Purchase St.

SPECIALS
—IN—
HOSIERY
—AND—
UNDERWEAR.

Ladies' 40 gauge tan hose in either plain or drop stitch, with double heels and toes in all sizes at 25c. pair.

Ladies' extra fine tan hose in fancy drop stitch with high spliced heels at 39c. pair, well worth 50c.

Tan hose for children in both plain and ribbed sizes, 6 to 8 1-2 at 25c. pair.

Ladies' jersey vests with low neck and no sleeves trimmed with silk stitch and silk ribbon at 19c. each, regular value 25c.

Ladies' jersey vests with high neck and short sleeves, and finished with pearl buttons and made of pure Egyptian cotton at 25c. each.

Ladies' plain white medium weight vests, silk cat stitch and finished with pearl buttons in either long or short sleeves at 50c. each.

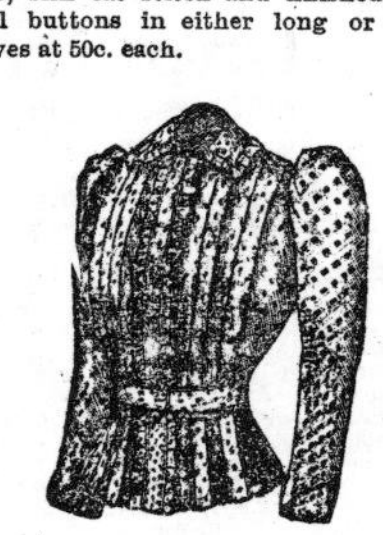

We have just received a beautiful assortment of ladie's white muslin waists with neat tucks in front and back and trimmed with pretty ruffle of white or colored embroideries at neck, down the front and on the sleeves at $1.00 and $1.25 each.

Ladies' fine cambric waists plaited front and back with neat stripes, figures and spots at 50c. each, sizes 32 to 40 inch.

J. V. Spare,
41 Purchase St.

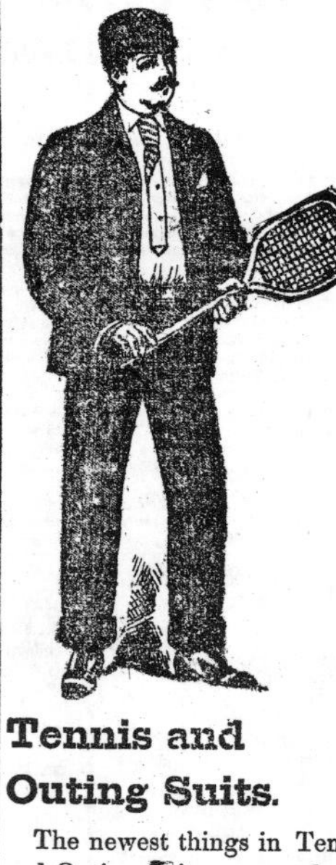

Tennis and Outing Suits.

The newest things in Tennis and Outing Suits are ready for your inspection. Blue Serge Skeleton coats and White Duck Trousers will be the "go" this Summer, and we have provided an unusually large stock of these comfortable goods for the hot weather.

The new styles in Tennis Flannels are very handsome and especially moderate in price.

Our assortment of Negligee Shirts, Leather Belts, Straw Hats, Tennis and Bicycle Caps, Stockings, etc., is most complete and comprises everything that is newest and best.

J. & W. R. WING & CO.,
Men's Furnishers.

FINANCIAL.

SANFORD & KELLEY.

GARDNER T. SANFORD, CHARLES S. KELLEY, } **Bankers,**

Members Boston Stock Exchange,

47 North Water St., New Bedford.

STOCKS AND BONDS BOUGHT AND SOLD ON COMMISSION

At the New York and Boston Stock Boards.

Local manufacturing stocks a specialty.

Outside investments of a conservative character, paying good rates of interest, on hand and for sale.

Also strictly high class investments for trust funds.

Auction Sale of Stocks and Bonds

WEDNESDAYS AND SATURDAYS, at 10 45 A. M.

ORDERS SOLICITED.

Will be sold at auction SATURDAY, June 3, 1893, at 10 45 a. m., at office—

11 shares Wamsutta Mills.
20 shares City Manufacturing Corp.
10 shares Morse Twist Drill & Machine Co.
8 shares N. B. Manufacturing Corp.
10 shares Potomska Mills.
15 shares N. B. Gas & Edison Light Co.
20 shares Columbia Spinning Co.
5 shares National Bank of Commerce.
10 shares Bristol Mfg. Corp.

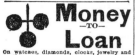

Money —TO— Loan

On watches, diamonds, clocks, jewelry and anything of value; also on pianos, organs, furniture, horses, carriages, merchandise, &c. All business confidential. I have on hand a large assortment of unredeemed pledges for sale; also one Hallett & Davis piano and one Wheeler & Wilson sewing machine; one N. E. Organ. A. L. BRALEY, successor to L. Braley, licensed pawnbroker, 99 Union st. ap20-TTStf

T. E. BOWMAN & CO.,

Topeka, Kansas,

NEGOTIATORS OF

Conservative Mortgage Loans in the Eastern Counties of the State.

WE know every security and give personal attention to every detail. Parties desiring absolute safety and satisfied with six per cent. interest paid promptly by check in their office or home, are invited to investigate our loans.

MONEY TO LOAN!

IN large or small amounts at low rates and easy terms on Real Estate, Pianos, Organs, Horses, Carriages, &c., which can remain in possession of the owners. Loans taken from 30 days to 5 years. All business strictly confidential. Office Hours 8 to 12 A. M., and 1 to 6 P. M. H. F. DAMON, 34 North Second St., (up one flight) opposite old Post Office. sep17-TTS6ptf

ANNUAL MEETING.

The Morse Twist Drill and Machine Company.

THE ANNUAL MEETING of the Stockholders of the Morse Twist Drill and Machine Company, will be held MONDAY, June 5th, 1893, at 3 o'clock p. m., at the Banking Rooms of Sanford & Kelley, No. 47 North Water street.

First—To hear the report of the Treasurer

Second—To elect Directors, Treasurer and Clerk.

Third—To transact any other business that may legally come before the meeting.

my26-7t GILBERT ALLEN, Clerk.

SECOND EDITION.

HOME MATTERS.

REAL ESTATE AND BUILDING.

F. A. F. Adams has sold to Mrs. William H. Taylor a lot of land on the south side of Grove street adjoining the premises of Thomas M. Stetson.

Bates & Kirby have sold to Charles F. Cushing about eight rods of land on the north side of Sears lane for $20,000. So far as known, this is the highest price ever paid for land in this city. The land has a frontage on Pleasant street of about 22½ feet and a depth in the lane of 98½ feet. The building on the property is now occupied by the Wheeler & Wilson Sewing Machine company. Mr. Cushing will erect a building there which will be occupied for his business.

Narcisse Roy requests leave to erect a dwelling house at the southeast corner of Washburn street and Belleville avenue. It is to be 28 by 35 feet, 35 feet posts.

Fred Denault asks leave to erect a dwelling house on the south side of Mitchell street between Sawyer and Coggeshall streets. It is to be 40 by 26 feet, 28 feet posts.

Work on the St. Hyacinthe church will be completed this summer, a petition having been presented to carry forward the work. The building is 112 by 55 feet, 31 feet posts. The first story, which was finished some time ago, is of brick, and the rest of the structure will be of wood.

Manuel F. Sylvia has petitioned for leave to raise a dwelling house at 223 South Front street. It will be raised 6½ feet and moved back 3½ feet.

William Shumway, who has had charge of the business of Norcross Brothers in this city for the past few months was superseded yesterday by George Conner, who had charge of the erection of the Millicent library. Mr. Shumway will go to Norwich, Conn., to erect a bank building, for which the firm has the contract.

Work on the foundation of the Merchants bank building is going forward rapidly. Blasting with dynamite has been conducted so quietly that very few people knew that explosives were being used.

OBITUARY.

Samuel Blythe Rogers, a young lawyer connected with the New York firm of Davies, Short & Townsend, died on Tuesday morning at his home, No. 550 Park avenue, New York. His death was due primarily to an attack of grip contracted in February; it resulted in an affection of the brain which caused his death. Mr. Rogers was born in Philadelphia in 1864. He was the son of Samuel B. Rogers, a merchant of that city, and at one time the president of the Planters Sugar Refining company of New Orleans. His mother was Clara A. Dupuy Rogers. Mr. Rogers was educated at Phillips academy, Andover, and later entered Harvard. He was graduated from the Harvard law school in 1888, and shortly afterward came to this city and entered the office of Davies & Rapallo, and afterward became associated with Roger Foster. Later he was retained by Davies, Short & Townsend as one of their trial counsel, and he achieved some prominence in elevated road litigation, his arguments in the court of appeals winning commendation for him. He was unmarried, and was a member of the Reform and Harvard clubs and the Bar association.

The funeral was at his home today at 2 p. m., and the burial will be in Riverside cemetery, Fairhaven.

The exports from New York the past week include 1,027 gallons sperm and 17,535 do. whale oil.

J. O. Douglass has shipped 11 horses to Nantucket.

Dr. A. L. Shockley and wife leave for the World's fair tomorrow.

OVERSEERS OF THE POOR.

A regular meeting of the board of overseers of the poor was held this afternoon, with every member in attendance. Chairman Smalley presided, and the session was held in the private room of the board for the first time.

Bills for the month of May were examined and approved as follows:

Groceries,	$627.85
Salaries,	329.83
State hospitals,	73.11
Cities and towns,	63.00
Clothing and supplies,	8.25
Burials,	162.00
Fuel,	118.47
Incidentals,	165.95
Grain and provisions,	314.84
Furnishings and supplies,	144.52
Incidentals and pay-rolls,	316.19
	$2,324.01

P. S. Macy, superintendent of the almshouse, submitted his monthly report as follows:

Whole number of inmates April 30,	65
Admitted in May,	8
	73
Discharged in May,	12
Remaining May 31,	61

William G. Potter, physician to the overseers of the poor, submitted the following report: Made 135 house visits during the past month; had 77 office calls, and made 6 visits to the almshouse. He reports five deaths and three births. One death occurred at the almshouse.

Samuel Dammon, superintendent of the wood and coal yard, reports that during May he received no wood and but 15 tons and 1,230 pounds of coal. In the same period he has delivered on 71 orders 8 cords, 3 feet and nine inches of wood, and three quarters of a ton of coal.

Adjourned.

OIL AND WHALEBONE.

The stocks of oil and whalebone in first hands in this country today, as compared with a year ago, are as follow:

	Sp. oil. Bbls.	Wh. oil. Bbls.	Whalebone. Lbs.
June 1, 1893,	2,770	405	126,400
June 1, 1892,	6,520	410	93,800

In New York a sale has been made of 2,500 pounds South Sea whalebone, reported at $3 per pound.

DIVIDENDS.

The Acushnet mills is paying a dividend today of $4 per share.

The Wamsutta mills is paying its usual semiannual dividend of $3 per share today.

The Grinnell mill is also paying the dividend recently announced.

MARRIED.

In Attleboro, May 30th, Elmer Ellsworth Langill to Miss Edith Bertha Smith.

MARINE INTELLIGENCE.

Steamer Monowai, which sailed from San Francisco May 25th, had on freight 2,518 gallons whale oil for Sydney.

Sld from Fall River 31st, schs Bertha Louise, New York; Lizzie H Brayton, Norfolk.

Ar at Providence 31st, sch Jonathan Bourne, Ellis, Georgetown.

Ar at New Haven 31st, sch Marion F Sprague, Fisher, Norfolk.

Ar at Stonington 31st, sch Fred Snow, Tate, New York.

Ar at New York 1st, steamer City of Columbia, Jenney, Norfolk; schs Thos H Lawrence, Kelley, Boston; Ira Laffrinier, Crowell, do; Hattie M Howes, Handy, hence; Henry P Hallock, Tisdale, Taunton.

Passed through Hell Gate 1st, sch Hastings, Corey, New York for this port.

Passed Highland Light 30th, schs Rose Esterbrook and King Philip, Philadelphia for Salem.

Ar at Philadelphia 31st, schs R R Nickerson, Nickerson, Lanesville; Massasoit, Babbitt, do; Van Name & King, Curtis, Providence; Jesse Murdock, Perry, Saco. Cld, sch R & T Hargraves, Allen, Boston; Josie R Burt, Burt, Salem; A H Perry Perry, Wareham; John J Hanscom, do; Three Marys, Birdsall, this port.

Ar at Norfolk 31st, sch R H Rathburn, Crowell, Bridgeport. Sld, sch Katherine D Perry, Garfield, this port.

Ar at Bahia April 25th, bark Moses B Tower, Freitas, Rio Janeiro.

FINANCIAL.

Another Rise in General Electric and a Further Decline in New England—Price on Former Crosses 75 and Latter Touches 22—Bell Strong—Money Easy, Though Some Clearing Loans are Made at 6 Per Cent. Today—Bank of England Rate Unaltered—C. B. & Northern April Earnings—Bull Pool Formed in General Electric—General Matters.

Thursday, June 1.

The rally in General Electric in yesterday's trading started a better feeling among operators and commission houses as to the balance of the list. The declines in Reading and New York & New England did not counterbalance the feeling in the least. Evidently the buying of the stock by Drexel, Morgan & Co. at 64 to 65 meant something, though naturally the greater part of the swift rise was due to covering by the large short interest in the stock. Whether the movement will reach its height today or not is an open question, and the opinions of those in a position to judge the market are widely at variance. There is much of the Electric company's stock which is believed to rest in weak hands and has yet to be marketed. If this comes out on the rally the price will naturally fall again, otherwise the rally may carry the price considerably above the close of yesterday—74.

The local money market is quiet and firm over the first of the month. New money where put out finds a ready market at 6 to 6¼ per cent.

In Boston today call money is nominally 5 per cent. There is really little feature to the market. Money will not tighten over the first of the month, and this is a satisfactory condition. Time money is in good supply where the name and collateral are acceptable. At clearing today loans were made at 5 and 6 per cent. New York funds sold at 15 and 20 cents discount per $1,000.

In New York call loans average 3 per cent. Time money is in stronger demand. Banks are holding off from making these loans in large quantity today. Private lenders are putting out considerable amounts.

Sterling retains its strength and bills are in demand.

The bond market is dull without feature.

The New York market opened steadier this morning with most of the business in Industrials, General Electric leading, selling at 74 and 73¾. Sugar firm near 88. Chicago Gas 73¼. Grangers steady. C. B. & Q. 86.

At 11 o'clock the market was quiet and fairly steady, save for New England feverish at 23. Sugar touched 89, Reading 17.

At noon the market was off. General Electric, which had touched 75⅛, declined quickly to 73⅛ and 72¾, New England weak at 22⅜, Union Pacific 29. Feeling a trifle bearish.

The following table shows the fluctuations of the leading active stocks during the forenoon:

Stocks.	Opening.	11 a. m.	12 m.
Atchison,	26	25¾	25½
New England,	24⅛	22⅞	22⅛
No. Pacific pfd.,	35⅜	34⅞	34⅛
Reading,	16⅞	17	16⅞
St. Paul,	68⅞	69	68¾
Sugar,	88⅜	89	88¾
General Electric,	74	75	72½

At 1 o'clock the market was lively, but soft. A fresh break carried New England down to 20⅞.

At 2 o'clock the market was weak. C. B. & Q. off to 85½, New England 20⅞, General Electric 72½.

The Boston market opened quiet and firm, except for New England off on a large business to 22½. Bell strong up to 194. Some sales at 193. Atchison lively at 26.

At 11 o'clock the market was firm and New England rallied from 22½ to 23¼, but looked like going off again. Bell out once more at 194. Boston & Maine 165.

At noon the market was unsettled, owing to a break in General Electric to 72½; Bell 196 asked.

The following table shows the fluctuations of the leading active stocks during the forenoon:

Stocks.	Opening.	11 a. m.	12 m.
Atchison,	26	25⅜	25⅛
C. B. & Q.,	86	85⅞	85⅞
New England,	24⅛	23	22⅛
General Electric,	74	75	72½
Sugar,	88⅜	88¾	88⅛
Bell,	193	194	196

At 1 o'clock the market was active and weak. New England off to 21, Atchison 25⅛.

At 2 o'clock the market was weak. Montana copper off to 20, New England 20⅝, Atchison 24⅝.

C. B. & Northern earnings for the month of April show a gross increase of $101,395. Net earnings for the same time increased $64,608. For the four months of 1893 net earnings increased $52,912.

Gross earnings of the West End Street railway for the first 29 days of May show an increase over last year of $64,000. The total gross for the month will show over $66,000 increase.

Delaware & Hudson has declared 1¾ per cent., payable June 5th.

C. B. & Q. is loaning flat. General Electric ⅛ premium.

Gossip on General Electric is to the effect that the formation of a 30,000 share pool to put the stock back to 90 has been consummated. It is further stated that the company will issue a statement to stockholders at an early date.

A Chicago dispatch at 1 o'clock says: "Reported that the Plankinton bank of Milwaukee has failed." This is the bank that Armour recently sent a cool million dollars in cash on a special train from Chicago to help out.

A later dispatch from Milwaukee confirms the previous rumor that the Plankinton bank of Milwaukee has closed its doors.

The annual report of the Pacific Mail company makes a poor showing. Net earnings decreased $777,947 during the year, and the cash assets have fallen off from $775,871 to $558,700.

Gold shipments today amount to $750,000.

G. M. Pullman says that so far as he has heard there is no hitch in the reorganization of Reading. It is a fact, nevertheless, that certain Philadelphia newspapers are opposed to the plan as proposed.

Taintor & Holt say: "London up ¼ to ⅜ per cent. Bank of England rate of discount is unchanged. We look for a further rally this morning in shorts covering."

Edward Sweet & Co say: "In face of the enormous gold shipments the market is showing strength and the shorts take fright easily. This is accounted for by the belief in many quarters that an extra session of congress will be called in September, and that bonds will be issued when necessary under the decision of the attorney general.

Commercial paper is still slow of sale. Banks are generally taking care of their best customers at from 6 to 6½ per cent. Note brokers are doing very little business. Western paper is practically without a market. A bank in one of the large cities of western Massachusetts has recently bought New York paper, of which it always carries a line, at 12 per cent.

It is stated that Northwest annual report, to be given out today, will be very good. It will show great growth on the part of Nebraska and western lines. Regular dividends of 3 and 1¾ will be declared.

Cash receipts of Westinghouse during April were the largest in the history of the company.

Mr. Theodore Havemeyer says: "We have not the slightest intention of retiring from control of the Sugar property. I do not believe any administration or any party will do anything to injure a staple industry, and with that belief I do not expect any change in the tariff that will hurt the business of sugar refining."

General Freight Agent Hamblin, of Chicago, Burlington & Quincy, says that a big acreage has been planted and the present outlook for the crop is extremely good. He says that freight rates are well maintained.

STOCK AND BOND MARKETS.

Bid Prices at 12 o'clock Today.

NEW YORK, June 1.

GOVERNMENT BONDS

U. S. 2s,	99
" 4s, registered	111⅛
" 4s, coupons	112⅜
" currency 6s, 1895	102½

RAILROADS

Atchison	25⅛
Clev., Cin., Col. & St. Louis	42⅛
Chicago & Eastern Illinois pref	94
Chicago, Burlington & Quincy	85⅞
Delaware & Hudson	122
Delaware & Lackawana	140⅛
Erie	17⅞
Illinois Central	92¾
Lake Shore	122¼
Louisville & Nashville	66⅛
Manhattan	129⅛
Michigan Central	95
Missouri Pacific	37⅝
New Jersey Central	108⅛
New York Central	101⅜
New York & New England	22⅛
Northern Pacific pref	34⅛
Northwest	103⅛
Philadelphia & Reading	16⅜
Rock Island	72⅝
St. Paul	68⅝
St. Paul pref	117⅛
Richmond Terminal	3
St. Paul & Omaha	41⅛
Union Pacific	29⅞
Wabash pref	16⅛

MISCELLANEOUS

Chicago Gas	72⅞
National Cordage	17⅛
Ontario Silver	15
Pacific Mail	20⅛
Pullman	173⅜
Sugar	88⅛
Sugar, pref	87⅞
Silver Certificates	82⅛
Western Union Telegraph	82½

BOSTON, June 1.

BONDS

Atchison 4s	79¾
Atchison 2ds	46⅛
Bell Telephone 7s	109
Chicago, Burlington & Northern 5s	100
C. B. & Q. Cons. Mort. 7s	116½
C. B. & Q. Conv. 5s	101
Chicago & West Michigan 5s	94
Mexican Central 4s	57
Illinois Steel Co. 5s	*90

RAILROADS

Atchison	26
Boston & Albany	211
Boston & Lowell	188
Boston & Maine	164
Boston & Providence	250
Central Mass. pref	49
Chicago, Burlington & Quincy	86
Chicago Jun. & Un. Stk. Yds	85
Chicago Jun. & Un. Stk. Yds. pref	88
Chicago & West Michigan	29
Cleveland & Canton & Southern	4
Cleveland, Canton & Southern pref	14
Fitchburg	84
Flint & Pere Marquette pref	61⅛
Mexican Central	8⅛
New York & New England	23
New York & New England pref	63
Old Colony	184
Oregon Short Line	13
Pullman Palace Car	174
Union Pacific	29
Wisconsin Central	9
West End	56
West End pref	79½

MINING

Butte & Boston	6½
Calumet & Hecla	*285
Centennial	6⅛
Franklin	12
Kearsarge	*7
Montana	21½
Osceola	27
Quincy	112
Tamarack	141

MISCELLANEOUS

American Bell Telephone	*196
Erie Telephone	*45
New England Telephone	56
Boston Land	4
West End Land	13⅛
Topeka Land	.25
Lamson Store Service	17
Illinois Steel Co	*60
Sugar common	88⅛
Sugar pref	86⅛
Gen'l Electric	74
Westinghouse	26
Bay State Gas	9
National Lead	30⅛

*Asked.

PROVISIONS AND GRAIN.

Chicago, June 1.

	Wheat.	Pork.	Corn.
Opening.			
July,	71⅛	—	41⅛
September,	74⅞	21.25	42⅛
Twelve o'clock.			
July,	69⅜	—	40⅛
September,	73⅛	21.30	41⅝

CALIFORNIA MINING STOCKS.

San Francisco, May 31.

The following are the official closing prices of mining stocks to-day:

Best & Belcher	1 15	Mexican	1 25
Bulwer	—	Mount Diablo	1 80
Chollar	1 10	Ophir	—
Con. Cal. & Va.	1 85	Potosi	3 55
Crown Point	—	Savage	—
Eureka Con.	—	Sierra Nevada	—
Gould & Curry	—	Union Con.	—
Hale & Norcross	—	Belcher	1 40

WEATHER INDICATIONS.

Partly Cloudy.

New York, June 1.—At 8 30 a. m. the weather was partly cloudy, wind east, temperature 60. The Herald says: In the Middle States and in New England: On Friday, partly cloudy weather will prevail, with fresh southerly and easterly winds, slight temperature changes and rain, and on Saturday cloudy and partly cloudy, slightly cooler weather and rain, followed by clearing.

Arrested for Assault.

Boston, June 1.—Arrion Walton, a mulatto, 23 years old, was arrested today charged with assault upon Charles F. List, colored, who was found lying on the sidewalk in Eliot street this morning with his skull crushed.

THE MURDERER SEEN.

Stranger Accosted a Fall River Alderman.

Inquired the Way to St. Mary's Cemetery.

Man Was Nervous and Concealed His Right Hand.

Same Suspicious Character Seen by Two Others.

Answers Description of Portuguese Farm Hand.

Fall River, June 1.—About 7 o'clock Tuesday evening, as Albert F. Dow and his wife were leaving the Oak Grove cemetery, they were accosted by a man who inquired the way to St. Mary's church. The fellow was rather stout and thick set, of a dark and sallow complexion, and wore a suit of dark clothes. He appeared to be greatly agitated, and acted in a nervous and excited manner. He had approached from Orange street, and was covered in dust from head to foot, as if he had been traveling for some time along a dusty country road. While talking the fellow glanced about him nervously as if pursued or fearing pursuit.

Mr. Dow told him that the easiest way to find the St. Mary's would be to follow Prospect street, down until he struck the horse car tracks, which would lead him into the center of the city, and almost any one would then direct him to the church.

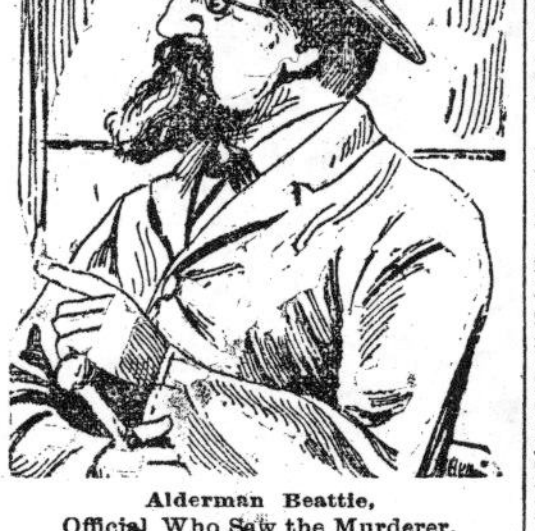

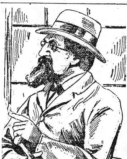

Alderman Beattie,
Official Who Saw the Murderer.

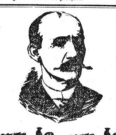

The man walked along with Mr. Dow and his wife for a short distance, and showed no disposition to move ahead or fall behind, and evidently intended to accompany them. Realizing this, Mr. and Mrs. Dow stopped and went into Shaw's greenery, a short distance from the cemetery, and the man passed on. Just as they left the hot house they saw the man turn south into Hanover street, and when they reached the corner he was in conversation with Alderman Beattie.

The alderman's story is in substance as follows: He had just left his house, and was passing through the gate, when the man addressed him, asking to be directed to St. Mary's church. Mr. Beattie gave him the necessary instructions, but while talking was attracted by the man's appearance and nervous actions. He noticed that all the while the fellow kept his right hand under his coat, as if in his hip pocket. Mr. Beattie said: "I never see a man put his hand there without I get just as close to him as I can, and look him square in the eye." The stranger turned to go, but Mr. Beattie was so impressed that he called him back to get a further look at him, and gave him more detailed directions.

After the man had gone, Alderman Beattie met Mr. Dow, and after comparing notes and seeing a police officer on the beat pass by, Mr. Beattie ordered him to shadow the stranger. The alderman says he is not certain, but it looked to him as if the hand which the man kept under his coat was either cut or blood-stained. The police are looking for Jose Correio, who answers the description given by these men. He boarded on Eagle street with Frank Peters, but since Tuesday he has been missing. At that time he left to go the farm, he said, and his landlord thought he meant to go to the Manchester farm, where he had previously worked.

The Herald will say tonight: "The time seems to have come when the neck of some villain should be stretched in Bristol county. The reputation of this peaceful, industrious locality is in danger, and every good citizen is ready to co-operate with Mayor Coughlin, Mr. Hilliard and the county authorities, if necessary, to wipe the stain off the fair name of this community. Two murders in a year where only one had been perpetrated in a generation are two too many, and nobody understands that better than the authorities. That is the inspiration that is urging them on, and the method of their work is grimly serious, even if they are making little display about it."

Uganda Evacuated.

Berlin, June 1.—Eugene Wolff, the African correspondent of the Tageblatt, cables to that paper that the British East Africa company evacuated Uganda on April 1, and that Sir Gerald Portal, the special commissioner to Uganda, hoisted the British flag and proclaimed a protectorate over the region.

Outbreak of Cholera.

London, June 1.—Lloyds' sanitary inspector at Bagdad, Asiatic Turkey, announces the outbreak of cholera at some of the stations on the Tigris and at Bussorah, a port on the Shat-El-Arab.

Trial Trip of the Machias.

Bath, Me., June 1.—The gunboat Machias on Saturday afternoon will leave for her trial trip in Long Island sound.

In the Hands of a Receiver.

Beebe, Ark., June 1.—The White County bank of Beebe, a private concern instituted by George D. Foster, is in the hands of a receiver.

Remarkable Record of the Moxie Nerve Food Co.

This company is now six years old, and already it has 18 factories in the United States, and last year the company made and sold 438,231 cases of its goods. Boston alone consumed 58,000 cases, necessitating a factory there. The goods are generally used by women for the vitality they give to the nervous, weakly and overworked. It is not a medicine or tonic, and contains no alcohol. In Boston many of the richest families use it in place of tea and coffee. It has been thoroughly examined by chemists, by order of the United States courts, and found to be a pre-digested nerve food, flavored into a luscious beverage; therefore it is used by all classes, sick or well. When they drink, the public prefer the most useful and harmless drink, and that fact has caused the moxie business to overshadow every other in the country in its line.

Drisco', Church & Hall are the agents for New Bedford and vicinity.

COAL

FREE FROM SLATE AND DIRT, Promptly Delivered, AT LOWEST MARKET RATES.

DAVID DUFF & SON,

NEW FIVE CENTS SAVINGS BANK BUILDING. Telephone 22-2.

CYCLONIC STORM.

Loss of Life and Great Destruction of Property Result.

Milan, Tenn., June 1.—One of the most disastrous and destructive wind and rain storms known for years struck this section yesterday morning and continued throughout the day. Destruction to crops, buildings, etc., will be enormous. The sewers on Main street became obstructed, flooding business houses and converting that thoroughfare into a roaring torrent and sweeping away several bridges. John Morgan attempted to ford a stream, and was swept away and drowned.

Washouts on the Louisville & Nashville road are reported at Gadsden and Gwens Switch. The Illinois Central track is covered with trees.

No definite news has been received from surrounding country districts, although several fatalities have been reported.

Memphis, Tenn., June 1.—An Appeal-Avalanche special from Rosedale, Miss., says: A cyclone struck this town yesterday afternoon, leveling many houses and the roar of the wind drowned the cries of the wounded. W. L. Boudre, colored preacher, and wife were killed. The list of the wounded embraces the following: Mrs. Captain Miller, John Water, A. V. Foote, Lucas Vead, Linn Robinson, the last two colored. Twenty houses were either wrecked or badly damaged. Among them were the Baptist and Methodist churches and the City bank. Many cabins occupied by colored people were blown down and trees and fences were carried away by the wind like straws.

Nashville, Ark., June 1.—The wind was very destructive all over this county yesterday, fences, barns, trees and crops of all kinds being destroyed. A negro's cabin was blown down on the edge of the town with a family of four in it, but they escaped without fatal injury. Lightning struck the house of Joseph Stuart, fatally injuring one of his daughters. At Center Point a number of business houses and the Baptist church were blown down. A negro was killed in the church. The Arkansas & Louisiana railroad sustained serious injuries from water. The bridge at Mine Creek was destroyed. The fronts were torn from the store buildings of Ainslee Brothers, Cannon & Owens and James A. Hughes, and the mill and factory of Mr. Hughes were wrecked. News from the country north of here, where the storm is supposed to have done most serious damage, has not yet been received.

Paducah, Ky., June 1.—A severe wind storm struck Paducah yesterday morning at 11 o'clock, and for one hour buildings rocked and cracked as if about to fall and engulf their terrorized occupants. Trees were blown down on every street, and many people fled from their houses and sought refuge in the government building. The buildings unroofed were the Opera House, W. H. Ricke's Sons' dry goods store, Sam William's saloon, George O. Hart & Son's hardware store, several warehouses and two planing mills. About 50 business houses and dwellings were partly unroofed. The two wharf boats were torn from their moorings and carried into the river. The steamers B. S. Resea and John K. Speed tried to bring them to shore, but the wind proved the stronger, and all were carried down the river. The two wharf boats went ashore on the Illinois side.

At Brooklyn, Ill., three miles down the river, the damage to boats was disastrous. The Dick Clyde was torn to pieces, part of it sinking and part floating down stream. The towboat Camasco was driven ashore and sunk. It will be a total loss. The towboat Fannie met with the same fate, but probably she can be raised. About 20 barges, mostly loaded with lumber and ties, were torn to pieces and sunk. The total loss of floating craft at Brooklyn will be about $25,000.

At Smithland, 12 miles up the river, the court house and seven churches were unroofed, and the house of Rube Clifton was demolished.

Little Rock, Ark., June 1.—The whole amount of damage done by the cyclone which struck the southern portion of the state Tuesday afternoon is not yet known, but it is feared that incalculable damage has been done. At Hope several buildings in the course of erection were completely demolished. Roofs were blown from buildings, trees were uprooted, fences are all gone and the entire country is wrecked from two to seven miles southwest. Hail fell to the depth of eight inches. No one is known to be killed.

At Guernsey houses were blown down and the inmates of a good many of them hurt, two fatally.

At New Lewisville a destuctive hail storm did great damage to crops and residences. The hail killed a large amount of stock and the damage in that line will be great. Oat and corn fields were laid waste. Many persons were seriously injured by the hail stones.

BITTER COMPLAINTS.

French Exhibitors Dissatisfied with Treatment in Chicago.

London, June 1. —The Paris correspondent of the Morning Post says that French exhibitors complain bitterly of the treatment received by them at the hands of the managers of the World's fair in Chicago, and of the customs and railway officials in the United States. They also complain of the intolerable dirt and general disorder around the exhibition grounds.

The Pope and the School Question.

London, June 1.—In regard to the report that the pope was about to publish a rescript on the school question, which was published Tuesday, a special dispatch from Rome to The Chronicle says: "The enemies of the pope, and of Monsignor Satolli and of Archbishop Ireland declare that the rescript is prepared. It is evident that the conspiracy in Rome and the United States is reviving. If the document exists the pope is keeping it dark, lest it should injure Mgr. Satolli, whom his holiness continues to approve and encourage. The pontiff has recently declared again his wish to continue and confirm the school proposal of Mgr. Satolli."

The Seal Fisheries Question.

London, June 1.—The Daily News, in an article on the seal fisheries question, says: "Even if England and the United States agree to protect the seals, in the event of judgment being rendered by the court of arbitration against the American claim, we fail to see how the two powers can do more than prevent the seizure by their own subjects of vessels caught poaching. A Norwegian dealer, for instance, might still claim the liberty of seizure on the common highway of nations. If a convention is made it must include all maritime nations."

AT THE BLACK HORSE CLAIM.

Battle Between Miners in Which a Claim Jumper was Injured.

Carson, Nev., June 1.—Henry Morrison arrived yesterday after a 30-mile journey on foot with news of a battle between miners at the Black Horse claim in the Buckeye mining district. Three claim jumpers appeared at the mine with Winchesters and drove out Morrison and George Jaqua, who were at work. Thirty shots were fired in the trouble that followed, the cabin of Arthur Raycroft, one of the owners of the mine, being riddled. Pete Millich, one of the jumpers, was slightly wounded. Twenty armed men now hold the mine.

FACTORIES CLOSED.

Diamond Company Has $600,000 Worth of Plate Glass on Hand.

Kokomo, Ind., June 1.—The Diamond Plate Glass company of this city, employing 800 men, has been closed indefinitely. The same company's branch plant at Elwood has also been closed, throwing 600 men out of work. An official of the company said: "We have more than $600,000 worth of glass on hand, and the market is utterly demoralized. The threatening financial situation has paralyzed new construction."

Lumber Firm Assigns.

St. Joseph, Mo., June 1.—The wholesale lumber firm of Muthleisen & Co. filed a deed of assignment at midnight last night. The firm has several yards in this section and also in Kansas. The liabilities are not fully known, but an estimate places them at $150,000.

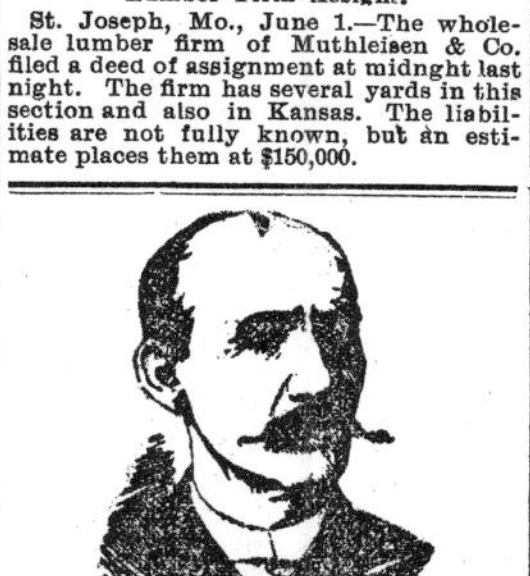

J. O. DOUGLASS' Sale and Exchange Stables, Mechanics' Lane, New Bedford, Mass. I keep constantly on hand and for sale or exchange a good stock of driving, family, business, and team horses. Horses bought and sold on commission. Fresh arrivals every Monday and Thursday. All horses warranted as represented.

COAL

—OF—

All Kinds and the Best Quality

—FOR—

DOMESTIC AND FACTORY USE

CONSTANTLY IN STOCK.

HAVING purchased the business and good will of Bates & Howard, am prepared to fill orders at either my old office at yard or new office, No. 224 Purchase street.

YARD, ATLANTIC WHARF, FOOT OF CANNON STREET.

ALBERT W. HOLMES.

TELEPHONES;
YARD OFFICE, 92—3.
PURCHASE STREET OFFICE, 92—2.

We Must Have Room

SECOND HAND

CARRIAGES

Must Go.

Brownell, Ashley & Co.,

24 to 38 FOURTH ST.

FINE CARRIAGES.

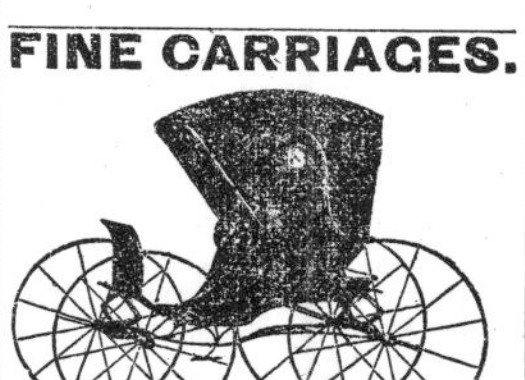

GEO. L. BROWNELL

OFFERS FOR SALE AT HIS

Carriage Manufactory and Repository,

Cor. Acushnet Ave. and Cannon St.,

NEW BEDFORD,............MASS.,

A FINE assortment of Carriages, namely: Landaus, Coaches, Coupe Victorias, Coupe Rockaways, Extension and Standing Top Family Carryalls, Phaetons, Goddard Box Top Buggies, Open Road and Business Wagons. Also a very large assortment of *SECOND-HAND CARRIAGES* of all descriptions, which will be sold low.

GILES G. BARKER, Supt.

MILK RECEIPTS.

Get Them Printed at the

STANDARD JOB ROOMS.

AUCTION SALES.

By STANDISH BOURNE,

(Successor to Geo. A. Bourne & Son,)

Auctioneer, Commission Merchant, Real Estate Dealer and Appraiser.

Cash advanced on goods consigned for auction. Ready buyer for personal property of every description.

Office and Salesrooms 47, 49 and 51 North Second Street, near the Post Office.

Horses, Carriages and Harnesses.

On SATURDAY, June 3d, at 10½ o'clock, at salesrooms, will be sold horses, new and second hand carriages, harnesses, etc. Executor's sale, one second hand extension top carryall in good order.

Mortgagee's Sale.

By virtue of a power of sale contained in a certain mortgage deed given by William A. Macomber to Sarah B. Refuse dated October 14th, 1892, and recorded in records of mortgages of personal property in the clerk's office of the city of New Bedford libro 23, folio 444, and for breach thereof will be sold at public auction at the auction rooms of Standish Bourne, on North Second street in New Bedford on SATURDAY, June 3d, 1893, at 10½ o'clock, a. m., one dark bay mare about eight years old, 1,050 pounds weight, called Nellie, one express wagon, one phaeton buggy, the property described in said mortgage. Terms cash.

ROBERT T. REFUSE,
Assignee of said mortgage.

Mortgagee's Sale.

On SATURDAY, June 3, at 2 30 o'clock on the premises, will be sold the two-story house and lot of about 15 rods situated on the north side of Middle street, west of Summer street. For legal advertisement see N. B. Evening Standard of May 9th, 16th, 23d, June 1st.

Mortgagee's Sale of Real Estate in New Bedford.

By reason of breach of the conditions of a certain mortgage given by Ellen S. Harding and John N. Harding, her husband, in her right, to Elizabeth P. Briggs, dated February 4, 1891, and recorded in Bristol county, S. D., Registry of Deeds in book 142, pages 353, 354 and 355, and by virtue of a power of sale in said mortgage contained, will be sold at public auction, on the premises, on SATURDAY, June 3, 1893, at two and one half o'clock in the afternoon, all and singular the property described in and conveyed by said mortgage, to wit:

A certain lot of land, with the buildings thereon, in said New Bedford, bounded and described as follows, viz: Bounded south by Middle street, there measuring forty-two (42) feet. The west line measures one hundred five (105) feet eight (8) inches, the north line measures forty-one (41) feet two (2) inches; the east line measures one hundred five feet (105) feet two (2) inches Said lot contains fifteen (15) square rods more or less. WILLIAM T. SCHULTZ,

Assignee and owner of said mortgage.

New Bedford, May 9, 1893. my9-16-23-je1-2

Arnold Street School House and Lot.

On SATURDAY, June 3d, at 3 o'clock on the premises, will be sold the Arnold street school house and lot of 22 47-100 rods. This lot has a frontage on both Arnold and Clinton streets of 45 feet or a depth of 135 1-2 feet, thereby making two desirable house lots of about 11 1-2 rods each.

For Rent.

A furnished house from June 1st to Oct. 1st. Location first class.

Also north half of the double house corner of Orchard and Clinton streets.

A very desirable residence, centrally located, containing all the modern conveniences. Apply to STANDISH BOURNE'S office.

To Let in Our Storage Warerooms.

We constantly have on hand first-class rooms for the storage of household goods, to be rented by the month or year.

Good dry storage room for stoves.

By JOHN B. BAYLIES,

121 and 123 Union Street,

Commission Merchant, Appraiser, and Auctioneer for the sale of Real Estate and every description of Personal Property. Furniture Bought.

Saturday's Sale.

On the 3d inst., at office, at 9½ a. m., will be sold furniture, carpets, bedding, springs, oil cloth, and many other articles.

H. C. HATHAWAY,

Auctioneer, Real Estate Agent and Appraiser,

Corner Acushnet Ave. and Elm St.

One of the best auction marts in the State for the sale of horses and carriages. Keeps constantly on hand carriages of every description, carriages made to order and repairing in all its branches attended to under the superintendency of J. R. Forbes. Consignments of every description solicited. Cash advanced on goods for auction. Personal property of every description bought at short notice for cash. Negotiable notes bought and sold.

ALFRED WILSON,

Auctioneer and Real Estate Agent,

Room 22, - - - Robeson Building.

Houses and land in all parts of the city for sale: tenements for rent: rents collected

House Lots.

The best location in the city for homes. The land bounded by Union, Court, Tremont and Ocean streets, has been laid out in lots, and offers a rare chance to get a home in a good neighborhood. Sewers, water, and prospective electric cars to the new park makes it the most desirable to be had. Call at room 21 Robeson building and see plan.

ALFRED WILSON.

HEALEY & JENNEY,

Real Estate Brokers,

Successors to T. F. Healey.

Real estate bought and sold on commission at lowest rates.

Farms, houses, house lots and strips of every description always on hand and offered for sale on easy terms at lowest prices.

Any and all parties desiring of buying or selling will do well to call at our office, which will be open day and evening.

Office, 555 Purchase St., Cor. Franklin.

T. F. HEALEY. Telephone 28-5. N. H. JENNEY

REAL ESTATE.

FRANCIS W. TAPPAN,

Agent for Purchase, Sale, and Lease of REAL ESTATE.

Office, 15 North Water St., New Bedford. d&w

FRANK C. SMITH,

BROKER & AUCTIONEER, Office, 47 William St.

Public Auction.

SATURDAY, June 3d, at 3 o'clock in the afternoon at or near the corner of Chancery and Willis sts., three house lots containing about 60 rods. je1-2t

M. E. SMITH,

REAL ESTATE BROKER,

Real Estate bought, sold, mortgaged or auctioned. Employ 10 assisting agents. Facilities unsurpassed. Call at

M. E. SMITH'S,
REAL ESTATE EXCHANGE,
619 Purchase Street. Telephone 16-11.

H. A. LEONARD,

REAL ESTATE AGENT,

126 UNION STREET.

Houses and house lots in all parts of the city for sale. Three fine residences. Good bargains. Call and examine tenements to let.

LAND—50 rods corner Hillman and Florence sts. Apply to CYRUS T. LAWRENCE, 329 Cedar st. my18-ThSTu-6t

FOR SALE.

House and Lot, 86 Walden St.,

Inquire

J. M. WILLIS, 43 Purchase St. my11-tf

FOR SALE—Residence of the late Charles Briggs, 175 Acushnet ave.; cottage house, 10 rooms, steam heat, set bowls, marble mantles, four fireplaces; large barn; laundry, containing set tubs, etc. All buildings in A1 order; 20 rods land. Apply on premises. my27-12t

VERY DESIRABLE COTTAGE HOUSE—Stable and about 4 acres land on the Old County road, north of Acushnet Village. Practically new buildings, orchard, henery, carriage house, etc. Will be sold cheap if applied for at once. May be seen at any time. Keys at Mrs. Ashley's opposite. Address, J. W. LEONARD, 59 Commercial st., Boston. ap27-tf

FINE BOOK AND JOB PRINTING

AT REASONABLE PRICES,

—AT THE—

STANDARD OFFICE.

Pages 1-8.

The Evening Standard.

Pages 1-8.

ESTABLISHED FEBRUARY, 1850.

NEW BEDFORD, SATURDAY, JUNE 3, 1893.---TWELVE PAGES.

TWO CENTS.

HASKELL & TRIPP.

Sensations of the day.

These things are creating lively business for us. By no means fail to get your share of the bargains.

Sensational sale of fancy ribbons, 29c., worth 50c.

Sensational sale of women's "Eton" suits, $5.89, worth $12.

Sensational sale of Japanese screens, 25c., worth 50c.

- - - - - - - - -

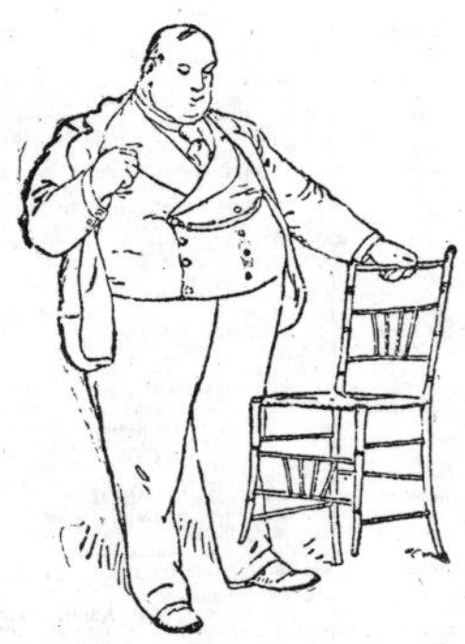

Men's furnishings.

Here are some items worthy the attention of all who want the best possible values for every bit of their money.

Balbriggan shirts, good quality, have French necks, 25c. each.

Fine balbriggan shirts, have pearl buttons, long or short sleeves, 50c. each. Drawers to match, 50c.

Clouded or natural gray summer merino shirts and drawers, 37½c.

White summer merino shirts and drawers, 50c. each.

Camel's hair, light weight shirts and drawers, 50c. each.

Bleached jean drawers, nice-fitting, 50c.

Very fine all-wool, tan-colored shirts and drawers, $1 each.

Excellent styles in negligee shirts are made from Madras cloth and cost (unlaundered) 50c. each.

Finer negligee shirts, including laundered collar and cuffs, cost $1.

Night shirts, cut ample, well made and trimmed with fancy embroidery, 50c. each.

Seamless half hose, various mixtures, 10c. and 12½c. a pair.

Imported fast black socks, 12½c. and 25c. a pair.

Finest unbleached Balbriggan half hose, 25c.

Ingrain lisle socks, 50c.

Summer merino socks, 50c.

Suspenders.

One lot at 12½c. a pair that you would guess 25c. on, if we didn't quote the price. Another lot of the so-called "American Guyot," because they copy the French exactly and cost only half as much, viz: 25c.

Washable four-in-hand scarfs. Japanese cotton crepe four-in-hands. } Either for 25c.

Satin bows to wear with negligee shirts, 25c.

Teck scarfs, made from high-grade silks and satins, 29c.

- - - - - - - - -

Our Corset Department

Has the best summer corset for half a dollar that has ever been offered to the women of New Bedford;

Has the favorite Jackson corset waist;

Has the corded waist for children, of which *thousands have been sold* for 29c. each;

Has a splendid-fitting Jersey ribbed corset cover for 25c.

"*Home-made*" underwear for warm weather may be had in fine cambric, beautifully trimmed.

HASKELL & TRIPP,
Department Stores,
Purchase and William Streets.

THE MANCHESTER MURDER.

An Important Arrest Made in a Vermont Town.

Marshal Hilliard Dispatches an Officer There.

Old Man Manchester and His Son Not Reconciled.

(By Associated Press.)

Fall River, June 3.—It has been definitely determined by the police that Jose Correiro is not the man wanted for the Manchester murder. The police practically arrived at this conclusion last night, but were unable to give it out officially until this forenoon. There seems but little doubt that the murderer is many miles away.

The city marshal has just received a second dispatch from Barre, Vt., giving details of the capture of a suspicious Frenchman, and they are inclined to attach considerable weight to it. They now admit that for two days they have hunted Correiro, but not with the hope of tracing the crime to him.

MAY BE THE MURDERER.

Importance Attached to an Arrest in Vermont.

Barre, Vt., June 3.—Police Officer Nason last night arrested a Portuguese answering the description of the suspected murderer of Bertha Manchester in Fall River. He told many conflicting stories. He finally gave his name as George Corbus, but later said it was Alexander Bisonette, that he was born in Hinesburg and was a resident of Montpelier. While under examination he had or feigned to have a fit. He is 22 years old and five feet in height. He admitted that he shaved off his mustache yesterday. The authorities have wired the Fall River police for an accurate description of the suspected murderer.

POLICE STILL AT SEA.

Nothing New Regarding Whereabouts of Suspected Man.

Fall River, June 3.—Two, and possibly three, of the local detectives are out of town today, and it is surmised that the police have given up all hopes of finding the Manchester murderer in this vicinity. The news from Barre, Vt., has caused a sensation here, and while the city marshal will not say directly that a detective has been sent there, it is assumed in police circles that Officer Perron, a French Canadian inspector, left for the place this morning. The old man Manchester has not yet become reconciled to his son Harry, who still remains here, and there is no likelihood that he will make the first advances.

There is no disposition on the part of the marshal to give out any facts for widespread circulation, but the assistant marshal assured the Associated Press representative at 1 o'clock that there was nothing new regarding the whereabouts of the man toward whom the department directs strong suspicion.

This Man is All Right.

The man who stopped at Mrs. Jenney's in this city a night or two ago and left a suit of clothes there, as stated in the Standard yesterday, called for the garments in the afternoon and took the clothes away with him to Rochester, where he has been at work, and where he returned by stage, the driver of which vouches for the man being all right.

WELSH IS DYING.

Makes a Sworn Statement of the Assault by Luke Burke.

(Special Dispatch.)

Fall River, June 3.—Henry Welsh, who was thrown from the third story of the Merchants mill by Luke Burke, was reported to be in a dying condition this forenoon at 10 o'clock. He had spent a very restless night, and the physicians concluded that there was no hope for his recovery. The police were notified, and Lieutenant Edson went to the hospital accompanied by Justice of the Peace A. M. Lincoln, to take Welsh's ante-mortem statement of the manner in which he was assaulted by Burke.

Welsh was told by the nurses that he could not live but a few hours, and that the officers had come to hear his last declaration. He was perfectly resigned to his fate, and replied to the nurses: "It is too bad, but God is good." He then gave his name, address and age, and said that he knew no reason why Burke should shove him out of the door. All he remembered of the affair was that he felt somebody place their hands upon his back, and then felt a violent push, which hurled him through the door face foremost, and to the ground below. That was all he knew about the assault. He signed the statement, and swore to its truthfulness before Justice of the Peace Lincoln.

Yesterday Welsh's two brothers and sister came over from New Bedford, and made a visit to the hospital. They were notified this morning that Welsh cannot live longer than today.

STILL ANOTHER CRIME.

Murder of a German Near the Natick Line in Wellesley.

Natick, June 3.—A German, named Jacob Lettig, was murdered last night just across the line in Wellesley. Particulars later.

WEATHER INDICATIONS.

Local Rains.

Washington, June 3.—For the 24 hours from 8 a. m. today: For New England fair, preceded by showers today near the coast; warmer in Maine, and eastern Massachusetts; tonight southerly winds.

Boston, June 3.—Local forecast for New England until Sunday night: Local rains on the south coast today; fair tonight; and Sunday warmer on the coasts, winds becoming southerly.

Negro Fiend Lynched.

Decatur, Ills., June 3.—Early this morning a mob attacked the county jail and lynched Samuel J. Bush, the negro who made a criminal assault on Mrs. William H. Vest in Mt. Zion township last Tuesday

LIZZIE BORDEN HERE.

Very Quietly Removed to New Bedford Jail.

Sheriff Wright Brought Her from Taunton Today.

Bridget Sullivan Watches Arrival of Her Mistress.

Some Secrecy Observed as on Day of Arraignment.

Standard the Only Newspaper to Have Men on Scene.

Lizzie A. Borden left the Central station, Taunton, on the 10 31 train for this city this morning in company with Sheriff Andrew R. Wright. The hack in which Miss Borden was brought to

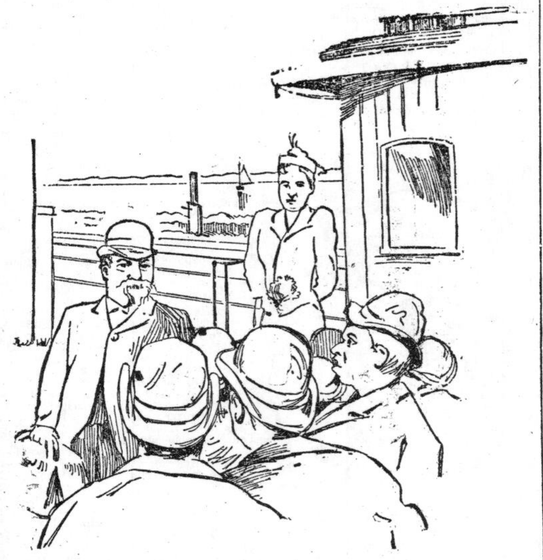

MISS BORDEN AT PEARL STREET STATSON.
[From a Sketch by an Evening Standard Artist.]

the station was driven to the extreme end of the platform, and so quietly had the arrangements been perfected that only the policemen on duty and a Standard man was there to see her step from the hack, walk across the platform unassisted into the rear end of the rear car and take her seat alone. Sheriff Wright took a seat behind her on the left side of the car. Had Miss Borden been going on an outing she could not have looked more unconcerned as to what she was leaving behind her than she did this morning. She was dressed as she usually has been on her little jaunts about the county during the last eight months, and her face wore no

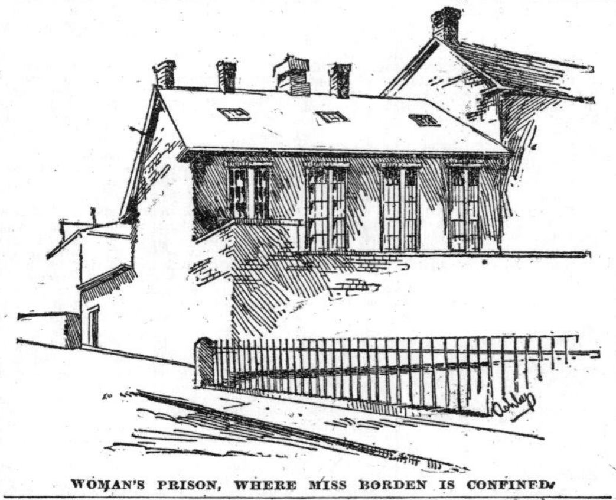

WOMAN'S PRISON, WHERE MISS BORDEN IS CONFINED.

traces of recent suffering other than a natural paleness and considerable fullness about the eyes. She had in her hand a large bunch of pansies which some kind friend had given her and a book. As she took her seat she opened the book and began to read, occasionally smelling of the pansies, glancing out of the window once in a while, and appearing to be perfectly contented with her lot.

In the waiting room, as the train rolled in from Boston, sat Emma Borden and a lady friend. The good byes for the present had been said at the jail, and

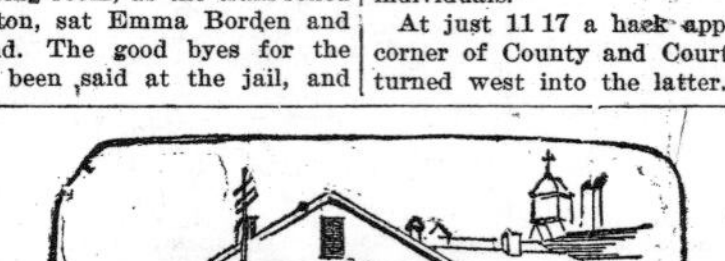

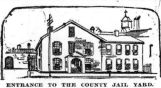

ENTRANCE TO THE COUNTY JAIL YARD.
Miss Borden Entered the Big Gate on the Left.

she only came out to take the Fall River train and go to her home.

When the locomotive and its three coaches rolled up to the Old Colony station in this city the train was just five minutes late schedule time.

On her way down the woman whose name is upon every tongue seemed unconcerned as to those around her, and although engaged in reading a magazine, it was evident to some in the car who had seen her before that her mind was not riveted on the book which she was reading. Twice she spoke to the sheriff, who sat behind her, and once smiled at a reply which he made. To those on the car she appeared to have indulged in tears previous to her start, for her eyes were somewhat swollen.

Arriving at the Pearl street station Sheriff Wright, with his companion, left the car by the rear platform. He assisted her to alight, and signaling Hiram Tilghman, driver for Kirby & Hicks, who had a carriage stationed at the edge of the north walk of the depot, he proceeded to the carriage with Miss Borden following. In her right hand she carried the bunch of pansies mentioned, and walked with a firm step to the carriage door. Entering she took the back seat, and then Sheriff Wright entered and sat beside her, first pulling down the curtains to shut out the view from some 30 people, mostly passengers on the train, who had got word that Miss Borden was on the train.

The only newspaper man on the spot was a Standard reporter. As the carriage went on its way to the house of correction a few of the sight-seers gathered in groups and discussed some points in the great tragedy in which so much interest is felt.

The arrival of Miss Borden at the county jail attracted little attention. At 11 o'clock two prisoners were sweeping the sidewalk on Court street in front of Keeper Hunt's house, Keeper Hunt was standing in the side entrance to his residence, a Standard reporter was talking with a bystander on the corner of Cedar street, and Bridget Sullivan and one other domestic were ostensibly working in a second floor room of Mr. Hunt's house, though their frequent glances down Court street showed that they were anxiously awaiting an arrival.

Miss Sullivan was apparently very nervous and as the minutes sped past her curiosity got the full possession of her and most of her time was spent at the window. Keeper Hunt was also somewhat agitated lest he should not be quick enough in opening the big gates and cause some delay in which his coming guest might be scrutinized by curious individuals.

At just 11 17 a hack appeared at the corner of County and Court streets and turned west into the latter. Mr. Hunt held his key in readiness for use and the seven onlookers pressed forward to catch a glimpse of the hack and its occupants.

Three minutes later the carriage turned into the entrance at the foot of Cedar street, east of Mr. Hunt's

(Continued on Fourth Page.)

HOME MATTERS.

AN INTERESTING EXHIBIT.

Automatic Train and Switch Signaling Device.

There is a very interesting exhibit in room 10 in the Parker House, which interested citizens are invited to inspect. Moreover it offers an opportunity for an investment which many conservative business men believe will be a repetition of the Bell telephone success. New Bedford investors will be given the privilege of getting in on the "ground floor," inasmuch as not a share of stock has yet been offered, and the books will be opened here on Monday.

The invention is an automatic train and switch signaling device for steam railroads, whereby the dangers of railroading and the loss of life and property thereby, will be minimized to a degree which will make it practically safe.

The exhibit is made by the American Electric Train & Switch company, of Portland, Me. This company has just been organized under the laws of the state of Maine, capitalized at $250,000. The stock will be issued in 25,000 shares at $10 per share, and the first issue ordered is of 10,000 shares of treasury stock.

The company is now negotiating with three of the largest railroads in the New England states to equip experimental sections of their roads, and these roads will be under contract with to adopt the systems throughout the entire line if its operation is successful.

The president and inventor of the system is George E. Miller, and the company is fully protected by patents. E. P. Francis, of Fall River, whose financial standing is vouched for by the Pocasset National bank, and the city treasurer of that city, is treasurer of the company. Dr. E. S. Williams, the secretary and general manager, is in the city, and extends a cordial invitation to every one to inspect the model, which is well worth seeing.

The proceeds of the first issue of stock is to be applied for the purpose of putting the system into practical operation. Subscriptions are taken in amounts from $10 to $1,000, and the right to reject any subscriptions is reserved by the officers. See advertisement on sixth page.

LIZZIE BORDEN'S TRIAL.

Graphic Pen-Pictures of It by Joe Howard, Jr.

Boston, June 3.—The trial of Lizzie Borden of Fall River will be one of the most famous in the annals of New England. It will be begun on Monday, June 5, at New Bedford. THE BOSTON DAILY GLOBE will not only have a complete phonographic report of the evidence, but the most brilliant pen-pictures of the scenes and people in court will be given in THE DAILY GLOBE each day by Joseph Howard, Jr. Order THE GLOBE of your dealer today if you do not take it regularly.

RUNAWAYS RETURNED.

One of Them Stole $10 from his Father and Both Went to Fall River.

A few days ago Manuel and John Enos, sons of Antone Enos of this city, left their home in this city and wandered away to Fall River. They returned to this city were arrested and are now locked up in station 1. Their father went to see them this morning, and after he came out he told a reporter that one of the boys before leaving stole $10 from him.

AN IMPORTANT DISCOVERY.

For some people to know that F. R. Slocum sells carpets would be an important discovery, because it would save them money. One large store is entirely devoted to carpets, all grades and styles. All novelties in carpets such as imported straw mattings and art squares may be found at discounted prices. These are the proper things to furnish your summer cottages with. The best ingrains and tapestries always in stock.

MORTUARY.

The whole number of deaths for the week ending today at noon, as recorded at the office of the board of health, is 20, of which five were children under five years of age. There was one stillborn. Of the deaths five were from pneumonia, three from phthisis, two each from old age and infantile debility, and one each from peritonitis, meningitis, broncho pneumonia, drowning, apoplexy, bronchitis, Bright's disease and convulsions.

CONDENSED LOCALS.

It will pay all who intend papering this season to see the fine line of paper hanging shown by Bliss & Nye. They carry the largest stock of the best selected patterns at the lowest prices in the city.

Elegant Wine for family use, $1.50 per gallon, delivered in city—Port, Sherry, Madeira, Angelica, Muscatel, or Tokay, at Hiram Wheaton & Sons, 45 to 51 School street.

Don't buy your berries for Sunday till you have seen our display. Best this season, three boxes for 25 cents at Boston Branch.

Dr. Thayer of Boston says Ayer's Hygienic Coffee is an admirable beverage, possessing none of the pernicious effects of coffee. Grocers generally sell it.

Eureka lodge, F. & A. M., will hold a special communication at noon Sunday, to attend the funeral of John D. Silva. See special notice.

The Portuguese Political and Naturalization club meets next Wednesday evening. See special notice.

Stuzz Bros.' fine upright pianos. Other makes in new and second-hand pianos and organs. 292 Acushnet ave., near School.

Gentlemen, the finest line of Russia leather shoes found at Buchell's. See our $4 shoe.

The Demorest medal contest announced in this paper for 6th will be postponed to the 13th inst.

Large strawberries tonight for your Sunday dinner. White Cash.

McCullough sends to all parts for iron, metal, rags, bottles. Postal or Tel. 158-12.

We make it interesting for Saturday night buyers. Boston Branch.

A belt given away with every boy's suit at Gifford & Co's.

Boys, this beats them all
With Bucheli shoes a bat and ball.

A nice black bicycle stocking for 50 cents at Gifford & Co's.

Special sale of trimmed hats and sailors Saturday. O'Neill's, 176 Puchase st.

100 bats and balls given away this week. Boys, read Buchell's ad. 5th page.

One thousand boxes of strawberries to be sold cheap at Boston Branch.

For a fancy roast tonight call at the White Cash.

A rare chance for investment, beautiful house on Morgan street, see advertisement.

B. F. Cottelle, piano tuner and repairer. Address to New Bedford post office.

The 25 cent straw hats have arrived at Gifford & Co's.

Special sale on strawberries, three boxes for 25 cents, at Boston Branch.

Bamboo Fishing Poles at McCullough's, 10 cents apiece.

Large, handsome strawberries, three boxes for 25 cents at Boston Branch.

Cutter Whiskey will help lung troubles.

Fine, fat fowl tonight. White Cash.

Good Sweaters at Gifford & Co's, $2.50.

Visit Waite's carpet rooms Saturday evening

Strawberry day at Boston Branch.

Languor thrown off by Hood's Sarsaparilla.

LADIES

SOMETIMES

You feel uncertain where to buy

CARPETS.

NOW WE WISH TO TELL YOU THAT WE ARE FULLY PREPARED TO SUPPLY YOUR WANTS.

OUR STOCK IS MORE ATTRACTIVE AND COMPLETE THAN AT ANY TIME DURING THE HISTORY OF OUR BUSINESS.

New Carpets.
New Mattings,
New Furniture,
New Curtains.

YES

WE ATTEND STRICTLY TO THE
Furniture,
Carpet and
Curtain
Business.

FURNISHING HOUSES IS OUR SPECIAL WORK, AND THIS WE DO TO THE ENTIRE SATISFACTION OF EVERYONE WHO FAVORS US WITH THEIR BUSINESS.

We handle the best makes.
We guarantee our prices to be as low as the lowest.

CASH or CREDIT.

C. F. WING,
34 to 40 Purchase Street.

WHITING & CO.

GREAT BARGAINS

—IN OUR—

Cloak Room

—FOR—

SATURDAY.

11 Navy Blue and Black Serge Suits, that we sold at $15, $16.50, $19, $23 and $25, all marked down to just $10 apiece. This is a great bargain if you can get your size.

Also 8 Ladies' Jackets that we sold at $6.50, now $3.95.

Also 16 $9, $12 and $15 Jackets, all marked down to $5, some are lined with silk.

Also 10, 12 and 16 years of age Misses' Jackets that sold at $10, now $5 apiece.

Also 8, 8 to 10 years of age Children's Jackets, that sold at $5, now are $2.95 apiece.

If you want a nice made and finished suit, do not miss this chance to get one at less than half price.

None sent out on memorandum or exchanged after leaving the store, as we expect to close them out before the day is over.

WHITING & CO.

J. V. SPARE,
41 Purchase St.

SPECIALS

—IN—

HOSIERY

—AND—

UNDERWEAR.

Ladies' 40 gauge tan hose in either plain or drop stitch, with double heels and toes in all sizes at 25c. pair.

Ladies' extra fine tan hose in fancy drop stitch with high spliced heels at 39c. pair, well worth 50c.

Tan hose for children in both plain and ribbed sizes, 6 to 8 1-2 at 25c. pair.

Ladies' jersey vests with low neck and no sleeves trimmed with silk stitch and silk ribbon at 19c. each, regular value 25c.

Ladies' jersey vests with high neck and short sleeves, and finished with pearl buttons and made of pure Egyptian cotton at 25c. each.

Ladies' plain white medium weight vests, silk cat stitch and finished with pearl buttons in either long or short sleeves at 50c. each.

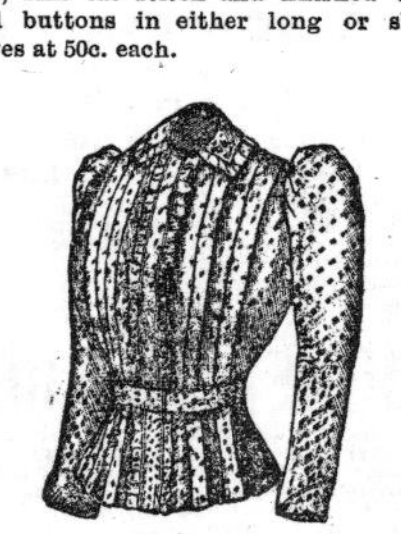

We have just received a beautiful assortment of ladie's white muslin waists with neat tucks in front and back and trimmed with pretty ruffle of white or colored embroideries at neck, down the front and on the sleeves at $1.00 and $1.25 each.

Ladies' fine cambric waists plaited front and back with neat stripes, figures and spots at 50c. each, sizes 32 to 40 inch.

J. V. Spare,
41 Purchase St.

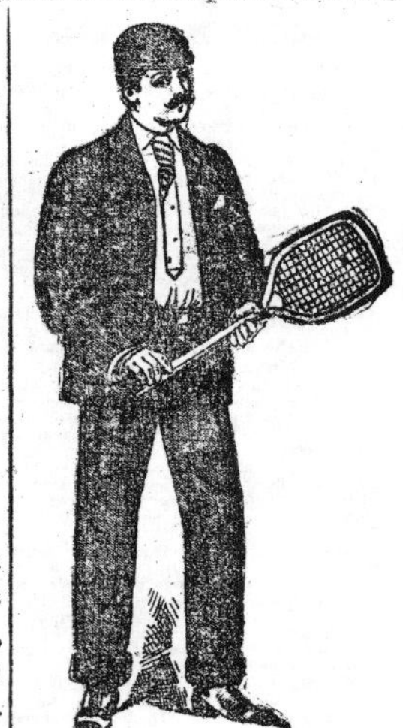

Tennis and Outing Suits.

The newest things in Tennis and Outing Suits are ready for your inspection. Blue Serge Skeleton coats and White Duck Trousers will be the "go" this Summer, and we have provided an unusually large stock of these comfortable goods for the hot weather.

The new styles in Tennis Flannels are very handsome and especially moderate in price.

Our assortment of Negligee Shirts, Leather Belts, Straw Hats, Tennis and Bicycle Caps, Stockings, etc., is most complete and comprises everything that is newest and best.

J. & W. R. WING & CO.
Men's Furnishers.

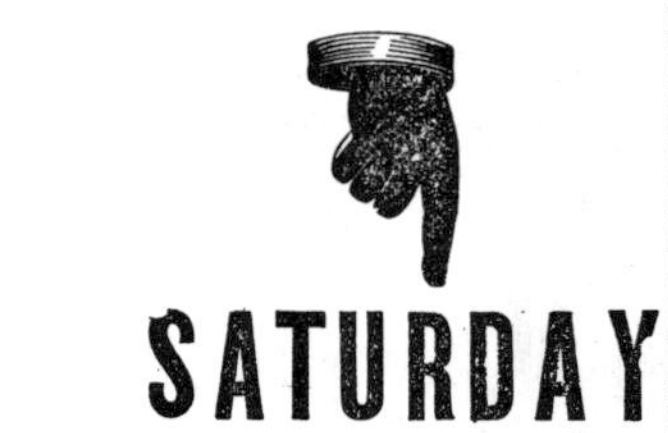

SATURDAY

The People's Bargain Day!

It will be the record breaking day of the season, and no wonder, when such bargains as these are on the list. To fully appreciate our wonderful values, we want you all to come to our stores on SATURDAY, June 3d, 1893.

LADIES' AND MEN'S FURNISHINGS. Ladies' fancy two-toned fine hose, with black boot, in all sizes at 25c. a pair. Ladies' fine Lisle Thread and Maco Yarn Ribbed Vests at 15c. and 25c. each. Men's Negligee Shirts, all sizes and in a great variety of styles, at 49c. and 75c. Gents' Wash Neckwear, new designs, at 19c. and 25c. each. MOYNAN & CO.

What an enormous variety of Millinery Flowers, prices from 15c. upwards.

MUSLIN UNDERWEAR AND CORSETS —For Saturday's sale we offer Ladies' White Skirts with tucks and lace ruffle at 49c. each. Ladies' fine White Skirts with tucks and beautifully hemstitched at 65c. each. Ladies' Robes with insertion and Hamburg trimming, our price only 47c., each. Summer Corsets at 49c., 75c., and $1.00 a pair. See our glove fitting Corsets at $1.00. MOYNAN & CO.

A big purchase of choice styles in White Embroidered Flouncings—you can buy at one-half usual prices.

CLOAK DEPT.—For Saturday we offer 25 Tan, Navy and Havana Brown Capes, handsomely braided, regular $10.00 for $6.98. 50 Jackets with Butterfly Capes, in Navy, Tan and Havana Brown, prices were from $10.00 to $15.00; now we give you a choice at $6.98 (sizes 32 to 38.)

Remember our Closing Out Sale of Jackets and Capes on Saturday.

MOYNAN & CO.—Continue on Saturday the great 50c. Dress Goods Sale, the lot includes 45-inch vigoreaux that sold for 75c. 40-inch Crepons, were $1.00, and 38-inch Corded Beiges that were $1.00. You are now offered your choice from the pile at 50c. per yard.

See our Boys' "Hardwear Suit," with a pair of Pants extra, all at $1.39. Without doubt it is great value.

MILLINERY SPECIALS — Still they come, new Ribbons in all widths at 5c., 10c., 15c. and upwards. Children's Silk and Muslin Hats and Bonnets. New goods, new styles. Prices begin at 15c. each. Ladies', Misses' and Children's Untrimmed Hats, in every new braid and mixture, beginning at 25c. each. MOYNAN & CO.

See our splendid assortment of Windsor Ties and Scarfs for Ladies and Children from 25c. upwards.

SPECIALS IN WASH GOODS—Dark and white ground full standard Prints and Shirtings, regular 7c. and 8c. quality for 5c. per yard. Best quality Outing Flannels in desirable styles, sold everywhere at 10c. and 12 1-2c. per yard, our Saturday price is 8 1-2c. per yard. MOYNAN & CO.

Summer Gloves in White Chamois, the $1.00 kind for 85c. a pair.

IN HOUSEKEEPERS' DEPT. — Three big bargains in full size Toilet Spreads as follows:
Worth 89c. each, price now 69c.
" 98c. " " " 79c.
" $1.25 " " " 89c.
Heavy German Linen Table Cloths, satin finish and heavy fringe, all pure white, regular value $1.98; for Saturday $1.19. A heavy Chenille Table Cover with deep ball fringe in elegant designs, regular $2.25 quality, for $1.75. MOYNAN & CO.

Saturday we present "base-ball and bat" free with every Boy's Suit.

WAISTS AND SUITS—On Saturday we will sell our 39c. Waists at 29c. each. More new Waists arrived at 50c. and 75c. each. White Waists at 59c. each. Full line of Ladies' Navy Eton Suits at $5.00. All Wool Serge Suits from $8.50 to $25.00. MOYNAN & CO.

Hammocks and Hammock Chairs now ready for the Piazzas.

BASEMENT—Window Screens to fit any size window, 23c. and upward. A bargain in Whisk Brooms at 7c. each. Bread and Butter Plates, 23c. and 25c. each. Cake and Fruit Plates, 25c., 33c., and 48c. each. Special, 3c., 5c. and 10c. Bargain Table. CALL ON SATURDAY. MOYNAN & CO.

Come early and avoid the crush which usually characterizes our Bargain Sales.

Moynan & Co.
Importing Retailers,
UNION ST. PURCHASE ST.

The Evening Standard.
NEW BEDFORD, MASS.
SATURDAY EVENING, JUNE 3.
THREE EDITIONS DAILY.
No. 87 Union Street.
PUBLISHED BY
E. ANTHONY & SONS.
INCORPORATED.
—TERMS—
Six Dollars a Year; Three Dollars for Six Months, in advance; Single Copies Two Cents.

ORDER THE EVENING STANDARD TO YOUR VACATION ADDRESS.

Mailed direct from this office for any length of time desired; 50 cents a month, including postage.

TWELVE PAGES.

This Evening's Issue Consists of Twelve Pages and Every Patron is Entitled to that Number.

The scenes which have been enacted in the Rhode Island legislature at its recent session, arise partly from the maintenance of the old practice of requiring a majority to elect, partly from the peculiar laws in relation to members holding over, and partly from the endeavor of the Democrats to make political capital out of the anomalous state of things which has arisen. We suppose it was within the power of the governor to prorogue the legislature as he did yesterday, or he would not have done so, so that the house by continuing in session by itself cannot effect any valid legislation, although it has prepared questions to be submitted to the supreme court to test the legality of the recent proceedings.

The whole game does not seem to be worth the trouble, inconvenience and expense it will occasion. Rhode Island should revise its election laws, so as to prevent such things in the future; and the Democrats should not undertake the illegal unseating of members and other revolutionary proceedings, as they have shown a disposition to do in several states.

The Boston Advertiser makes a strange mistake in saying that in 1837 the general assembly of the Presbyterian church of the United States, tried and convicted of "heresy" Rev. Albert Barnes, D. D., pastor of the First Presbyterian church in Philadelphia, and that the penalty inflicted upon him was a sentence to silence. Appleton's Cyclopedia of American Biography says that Dr. Barnes was tried for heresy on account of certain passages in his commentary on the epistle to the Romans, and was acquitted, but was advised to alter the phraseology of his notes, which was accordingly done. Dr. Briggs's heresy is much more far-reaching than that of Dr. Barnes, which was chiefly of what might be called a metaphysical cast, and he has been found guilty and suspended from the ministry till he gives satisfactory evidence of repentance. The chief analogy between the two cases is that Dr. Barnes was one of the leaders of the "new school" Presbyterians, who seceded soon after his trial. Whether the present heresy trial will be followed by another rupture remains to be seen.

The Springfield Republican points out that Fall River has an unenviable record with regard to murders. Out of twelve indictments for murder found in Bristol county from 1871 to 1892, inclusive, eight were for homicides committed in Fall River. The Manchester murder adds another, and the Burke-Walsh affair perhaps another. The proportion of murders to population is greater than in any other city of the state, even including Boston. This is not a pleasant reputation for our sister city to have.

At the yearly meeting of Friends in New York this week it was stated that their number is fast decreasing. The records show that the deaths far exceed the births among them, and that accessions from conversions are extremely few.

NOTE AND COMMENT.

PEOPLE IN NEW ENGLAND wondered when it was announced that Judge Stein of Chicago had granted an injunction against closing the World's fair on Sunday and many asked how it could be done. A perusal of the Judge's decision makes that point very plain. The decision is based on the ground that the exposition buildings being located in a public park have become part of the same. As such, the right of the people to the use of all parts of the parks on Sunday would be violated by closing the exposition on that day.

CHARLES H. CRAMP, THE SHIPBUILDER, unlike some men who have an axe to grind, is not given to bluff and bluster about the steamships his firm has built or is building. They are never "marvels of speed" or record breakers. Mr. Cramp simply refers to them as having been "built in compliance with the conditions of the contract," but, he adds with the faintest suggestion of a knowing look, "if the vessel turns out to be a wonder it will simply be because we have done our best." That kind of man deserves prosperity and every citizen of the United States can wish him good luck in his efforts to serve the government and give us a navy to be proud of.

Mr. E. S. Drone has been made editor-in-chief of the New York Herald. He has been connected editorially with that paper for about fifteen years. He is considered an authority on the laws of copyright and libel, and has written all the editorials on legal topics for years. Although unacknowledged until Thursday last, he succeeded to the chair of editor-in-chief early in the month, when Mr. Bennett paid his flying trip from Paris, Rev. George W. Hepworth, Mr. Drone's predecessor, being placed at the head of The Evening Telegram forces. Mr. Drone is about 57 years old, and is said to hail from Vermont.

You need not go to Boston or New York to consult a Specialist.
Services First Three Months Free.
DOCTORS
MILLER & VON HEILMAN,
The noted German specialists, permanently located at 202 Union Street, (over Hutchinson's Book Store,) give services *free* for three months to all who visit them BEFORE JUNE 16TH. But medicines of course, charged for. These eminent doctors treat all forms of chronic disease, especially *male and female weakness, catarrh and catarrhal deafness, etc.*, but accept no incurable cases. The doctors examine each case thoroughly *free of charge* and if incurable will frankly tell you so. Catarrh and catarrhal deafness is positively cured by their German treatment.
N. B.—The New Bedford office is permanent, but free service ends June 15th.
Hours 9 a. m. to 8 p. m. Sundays 10 to 4. my27-6t

CONTENTS OF THIS EVENING'S STANDARD.

Page 1.
Lizzie Borden brought to this city to await her trial Monday.
Henry Welsh of this city dying in Fall River makes his ante mortem statement accusing Luke Burke of pushing him from the Merchants Mill in Fall River.
A man arrested in Vermont who it is thought may be the Manchester murderer; police no longer looking for Correiro.
Still another murder in Massachusetts.
Runaway boys who went to Fall River returned.
Home matters.
Telegraphic dispatches.

Page 2.
Details of the hunt for the murderer of Bertha May Manchester with all the suspicious incidents brought to the attention of the New Bedford police.

Page 3.
The 56 hour and weavers particulars bills referred to the next general court.
Death of A. E. Covil the well known stable keeper.
Press seats at the Borden murder trial.
The uncertainty of circumstantial evidence by D. R.
Third district court.
World's fair news.
Suburban news.

Page 4.
Text of the Anglo-Russian Bering sea argument.
Suburban news.
Editorials.

Page 5.
Marine intelligence.
Marriages and deaths.

Page 6.
Reign of terror caused by striking quarrymen in Illinois.
Financial success of the World's fair assured.
Today's telegraphic news.
Financial news.
Second Edition — Telegraphic and local news.

Page 7.
Georgetown again defeats Brown; other ball games.
Amusement and sporting news.
Sunday notices.

Page 8.
Gov. Brown adjourns the Rhode Island general assembly until January 1894.
The trade review.
Uneasiness as to the result of iron and steel workers conference.
Legislative proceedings.
Third Edition—Telegraphic and locals.
Early telegraphic dispatches.

Page 9.
Sons of Veterans camps in New Bedford and the stories of their existence.
Simple ending of a perilous adventure.

Page 10.
Historic Veneration in the Pennsylvanians of 1816.
Wakeman's foreign letter.
In Amsterdam—poem by Eugene Field.
Chicago and the fair.
James Berry the hangman relates his experience to a Glasgow audience.

Page 11.
A Nymph of the West—Howard Seeley's serial story.

Page 12.
The sights of Chicago.
Christian Endeavor column.
The anarchist memorial to be unveiled in Chicago.
Italy's young premier.
An airship resembling a fish and a windmill.
Interesting personality of Logan Carlisle.

HOME MATTERS.

PERSONAL.

H. Winfred Goff, Ellis L. Howland and Edgar R. Lewis of this city and Fred. S. Sprague and Fred. S. Barden of Taunton were among the members of the Bach and Brahms club that participated in the club's third annual recital at Sleeper hall, New England Conservatory of Music, Boston, last evening. Bach's cantata "My Spirit was in Heaviness" was presented, and Messrs. Howland and Sprague sustained solo parts.

Edward J. Egan, one of the most popular and efficient conductors on the Old Colony railroad, has been appointed night station master at Park square station, Boston. Mr. Egan has been with the company for many years, and for a long time has had charge of the Shore Line express, leaving Boston at 10 a. m.

Edgar R. Lewis and H. Winfred Goff of this city will be members of a party of pupils of William L. Whitney at the New England Conservatory of Music, who will sail from New York June 24th on the Etruria for a two months' trip through Europe under Mr. Whitney's guidance.

Lieutenant William E. Reynolds, LL. B., formerly of revenue bark S. P. Chase of this port, is to receive the degree of master of laws at the commencement exercises of Georgetown university, Washington, Monday evening.

Henry T. Corson of this city and Dominick F. Corrigan of Fall River were granted certificates Friday by the board of registration in pharmacy.

Rev. E. S. Rousmaniere has been invited by the graduating class of the High school to offer prayer at the graduation exercises June 30.

Edward C. and Benjamin F. Mosher of this city will leave Monday evening for Hot Springs, Ark., where they will spend a vacation for the benefit of their health.

Mrs. Franklyn Howland joins a party of her friends in Providence on Monday for a visit to the Columbian exposition.

Dr. Frederick W. Abbott of Taunton was Friday chosen vice-president of the Massachusetts Eclectic Medical society.

Mr. and Mrs. George F. Kingman are at Saratoga Springs.

CONDENSED LOCALS.

John W. Dean, the Quaker evangelist, gives another Bible reading at Y. M. C. A. hall this evening. His subject will be "The Second Coming of Christ." Tomorrow afternoon Mr. Dean will conduct a union service in Association hall, which will close his work in the association; and he will speak in a union service in North Congregational church in the evening. Last evening some 300 persons were present at the "chalk talk" of Rev. N. S. Greet to hear his exposition of the Sunday school lesson for tomorrow.

The first supper of the Brooks club was held in the banquet hall of Grace House last evening. Fifty-eight gentlemen were present, and an excellent spread was enjoyed. At the post prandial exercises addresses were made by Rev. B. M. Addison of Fitchburg, Rev. Henry Bassett of Providence, City Treasurer D. L. D. Granger of Providence and George Fox Tucker of this city.

A meeting was held last evening of the real estate men interested in the electric line to run down the Middle Point road. The road will be made 60 feet wide and the line will probably be built this summer.

The meeting of the Labor party which was to be held at Spinners' hall tomorrow has been postponed one week. The committee having charge of the recent mass meeting will meet at the hall in the afternoon.

The first electric car over the new Kempton street route was run this noon to Cannonville under charge of Superintendent Arthur F. Taber. Twenty minute trips will be established at once.

A horse attached to one of Richmond's bread carts slipped on the car track at the corner of Weld and Purchase streets last evening and broke the shafts of the vehicle.

The Elks meet tomorrow evening to arrange for the reception of the remains of the late Walter Emerson. See special notices.

Eleven new cases of scarlet fever and two new cases of typhoid fever have been reported at the office of the board of health, the record for the past week.

The next monthly mass temperance meeting will be held at the Spruce Street Christian church Monday evening, June 5th.

Pensions have been granted as follows:
Original—Thomas Shin.
Renewal and Increase—George Dole.
Original, Widows, etc.—Minors of H. W. Hathaway, Mary Fee, Aaron Mitchell, minors of William M. Towle, minor of John Emery, Mary Blanchard, Catherine O'Connors, Sarah Sipperly, Mary Severance, minor of Thomas Doyle.

LIZZIE BORDEN HERE.

(Continued from First Page.)

residence. The windows were down and seated on the back seat were Sheriff Wright and Lizzie A. Borden. She appeared unconcerned and gazed out of the window in a disinterested way, drawing back somewhat as the newspaper man and the other spectators approached. The prisoners stopped sweeping, but did not dare to approach.

Mr. Hunt hurried to the gate and in a twinkling had the big iron bolt disengaged. The solid iron bound gates

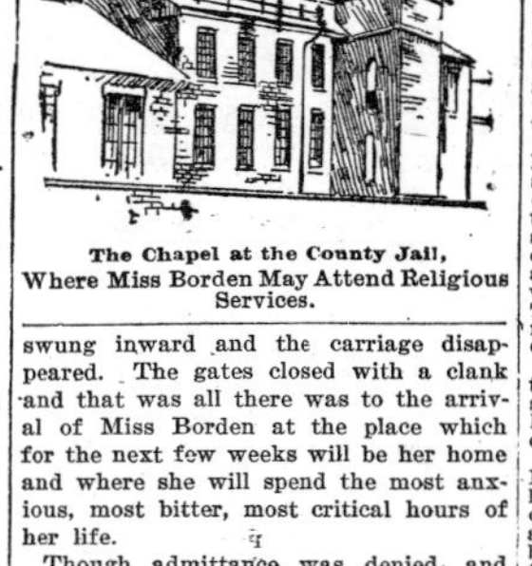

The Chapel at the County Jail, Where Miss Borden May Attend Religious Services.

swung inward and the carriage disappeared. The gates closed with a clank and that was all there was to the arrival of Miss Borden at the place which for the next few weeks will be her home and where she will spend the most anxious, most bitter, most critical hours of her life.

Though admittance was denied, and though Mr. Hunt was silent, it was stated that Miss Borden was taken at once to the women's apartments of the jail. She was not even obliged to answer the formal questions before the clerk, but the necessary passage of transfer papers was accomplished by Mr. Hunt.

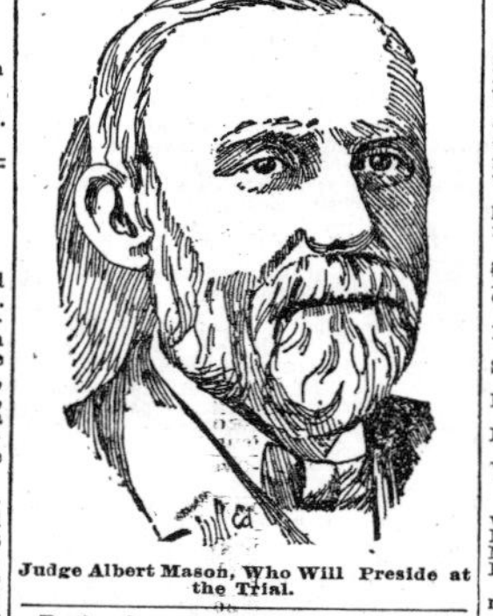

Judge Albert Mason, Who Will Preside at the Trial.

During her confinement here Miss Borden will occupy one of the ordinary cells of the women's apartments. These are situated in the old jail south of the chapel. The cells are 42 in number and very simple in their appointments. Each is seven and three-quarters feet long, seven feet high and four feet wide. The sides and back are of masonry and the front is closed by an iron door. The furnishings are a simple iron cot and a few necessary articles of cheap furniture. Mr. Hunt declines to state whether Miss Borden will have any better accommodations than other prisoners, but it is said, she may be transferred to one of the hospital cells; equal in size to two ordinary ones adjoining them.

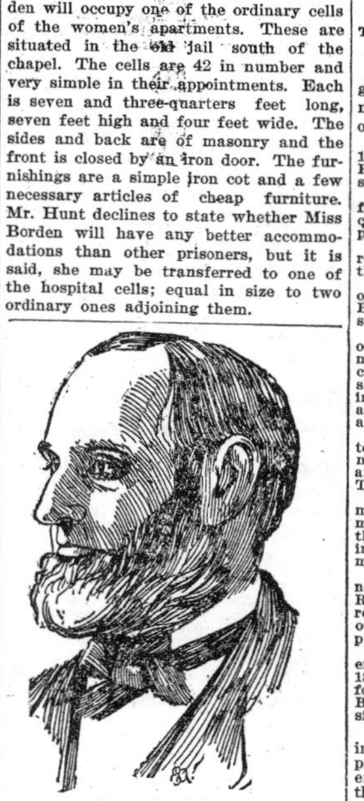

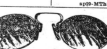

Judge Caleb Blodgett.

John V. Morse was in the city early this morning, having come from South Dartmouth with William A. Davis in a butcher's cart. He called on several friends during the morning and left on the 10 o'clock train for Fall River for the purpose of consultation with Lawyer Jennings.

A force of men are engaged today in inclosing the court house grounds with a fence.

THE LOOM FIXERS.

The New Bedford Loom Fixers union is entertaining the Whittenton Loom Fixers union this afternoon. The local union met at Spinners hall soon after 1 o'clock this afternoon, and headed by the Lincoln Guards band, Thomas Walley leader, proceeded to the Pearl street station, where the Whittentons were met. The chief marshal was Thomas Fowler, and Peter Slater acted as his assistant. After the line had been formed the route was taken up through Pearl, Pleasant, Weld, Purchase, Fourth and Grinnell streets, Acushnet avenue and Union street. At Spinners hall the parade was dismissed and the afternoon was spent in a reception to the visitors. A collation of cold meats and sandwiches was served, and in the evening an entertainment will be furnished with speeches by local officers and visitors.

VINEYARD HAVEN.

Mrs. E. A. Bush, wife of Lieutenant J. C. Bush, of Governor's Island, has arrived, and will occupy Grace Episcopal church's new rectory this summer. Mrs. Bush is a daughter of the late Secretary Stanton.

James A. Harding and family will occupy the Douglass residence "Glenwood," on Franklin street, this summer.

Miss L. B. Bradford, of Medford, is spending a ten-days' vacation with Captain and Mrs. Wilcox at Pasque island.

FELL IN A FIT.

An Unknown Woman Found in the Street and Taken to St. Luke's Hospital.

A woman, apparently about 35 years of age, created some excitement by falling in a fit on the sidewalk of Fourth street, near St. Luke's hospital, about 9 o'clock last evening. She was taken into the house of Thomas C. Case, where Dr. Leonard attended her. As she did not recover consciousness she was afterwards taken to the hospital. She was neatly dressed in black and her underclothing was marked L. P. or E. R. Green. As no one called to inquire about the woman the case was considered mysterious. The woman recovered consciousness this morning and gave the name of Mary Green and said she came from Westboro and was going to Westport. It has been ascertained that her name is Mary Green, that she lives in Dartmouth, has been afflicted with mental trouble and has been in an asylum.

FAIRHAVEN.

There was a meeting of the school committee last evening to hear from A. B. Collins, Esq., the attorney for the town, on the present status of the town's claim to the Pease school fund, and also to get a list of all schools in the so-called Pease district. This was originally a legacy of $5,000, left by the late Abner Pease to his widow, and after her death to be held in trust by the town for the improvement of the schools in the district between the Mill pond and Oxford. Since the Rogers school has been built the school in this district has been abandoned, and the matter for adjustment is whether the money still belongs to the town. There are two other claimants—the heirs of Abner Pease and the Long Plain Friends' meeting, to which the residue of the estate was willed. The fund now amounts to $7,500. The difficulty will probably be settled at the October term of the supreme court.

Some of the small boys in town are getting themselves into trouble by throwing stones at the town hall after the workmen have gone home. They may do serious damage.

The Oxford car makes its first trip from Riverside cemetery at 9 15 a. m. and the last trip at 7 15 p. m., connecting with cars going west. Before the hour of 9 15 and after 7 15 the terminus of the line will be at North street, the car connecting as formerly. Two horses and an open car are now used on the Oxford line in pleasant weather.

Dr. and Mrs. C. C. Cundall leave next Monday for Chicago and Tacoma. Dr. A. P. Webber of New Bedford will have charge of the practice. The house will be occupied by Rev. Joseph Danielson and family of Southington, Conn., during the summer.

A debate will be held at the High school next Friday morning, the subject being, "Should the World's Fair be Opened on Sunday?" Ralph Bryden and Jane Alden will support the negative, while they will be opposed by Nellie Maxfield and Herbert Terry on the affirmative.

Samuel Hunt of New Bedford says that as soon as he is assured of the water works running its mains to Coggeshall street or Howland road, he will build six houses on that street.

Miss M. A. Noland has returned from a trip through the west and south, spending three months at New Orleans, accompanied by Sydney H. Noland of Denver, who will spend the summer in Fairhaven.

Mrs. H. H. Wotherspoon of New York has arrived at her summer residence at Oxford.

The following is the complete programme of the graduating exercises of the High school class:
Class History.
Cordie Hillman.
Essay—The Rocks of Fairhaven
Florence Howard.
Scene from Merchant of Venice.
Grace Nickerson and Gertrude Sisson.
Essay—Historic Landmarks.
Edward Wrightington.
Piano Solo.
Grace Nickerson.
Valedictory.
William Benson.

During the exercises the following pieces will be sung:
Now is the Month of Maying. Morley
Mice in Council. Arr. from Filby
Farewell to the Forest. Mendelssohn

The class color is yellow and white; the motto, "Not for ourselves, but for others."

BERING SEA.

Text of the Anglo-Russian Argument Submitted May 12.

London, June 3.—The text of the Anglo-Russian Bering sea argument submitted to Privy Councillor Schischkine on May 12, 1893, is as follows:

First—During the year ending Dec. 31, 1893, the British government shall prohibit British subjects from killing and hunting seals within the following limits:

(A) Within a zone of ten marine miles following the sinuosities of the Russian coasts which border Bering sea and other parts of the North Pacific ocean.

(B) Within a zone of 30 marine miles round the Komandorsky islands and round the Robbin islands and Tulinew.

Second—The British government shall co-operate with British cruisers in preventing British subjects from killing or hunting seals within the aforesaid limits.

Third—British vessels engaged in killing or hunting seals within the aforesaid limits may be seized by either British or Russian cruisers; but if seized by the latter they shall forthwith be handed over at any port in British possessions or the commander of any British warship for trial by the British authorities.

Fourth—The Russian government engage to limit to 30,000 the number of seals that may be killed in whole year of 1893 upon and around the islands of Komandorsky and Tulinew.

Fifth—It is agreed that a British agent may, when desired by the British government, visit the islands, confer there with the authorities and inquire into the working and the results of the present agreement.

Sixth—The present agreement shall in nowise affect facilities hitherto accorded at Russian ports to British vessels regarding refuge, repairs, obtaining supplies and other necessaries wherefore they may properly require access.

Seventh—It is understood that the present agreement relates solely to the year 1893. It has consequently no retroactive force or effect, more especially as regards British vessels captured previously by Russian cruisers.

Schischkine replied on the 22d accepting the terms of the agreement, but expressing a preference that it may be embodied in an extension of notes, as the draft as it stood was too concisely worded and therefore left room for a misunderstanding and perhaps for complications. The Russian government, he says, moreover, could not agree to the draft without a few reservations designed to safeguard their freedom of judgment in the future.

"It is understood," he continued, "the agreement leaves intact all rights of Russia in her territorial waters. Our reservations refer them to the following points:

First, in consenting to hand over to the British authorities enough ships sealing in prohibited zones we do not wish to prejudice generally the question of rights of a power to extend its territorial jurisdiction in special cases beyond the waters properly called territorial.

Second, the Russian government desires to preserve complete liberty of action either by the method of a prohibition zone, entirely to prohibit in the future pelagic sealing or to regulate it in the open sea.

Third, the present arrangement cannot be considered in anywise as a precedent, and is looked on by us essentially as a provisional arrangement intended to meet present circumstances.

Schischkine closes his note with an expression of hope that the "British government will consider the understanding as established henceforward for the present year."

Lord Rosebury, in his reply, dated the 29th, accepts the arrangement for the current year, and states that he will take steps to carry it into operation. Regarding the reservations made by the government he says that they need not be stated or discussed at present, but it may be mutually understood that the rights of either power remain unaffected by this provisional agreement.

Terrific Rain Storm.

Elgin, Tex., June 3.—A terrific rain and electric storm raged in the country near here Thursday night and yesterday morning. The dwelling house of Carl Bien was blown down and Bien fatally injured.

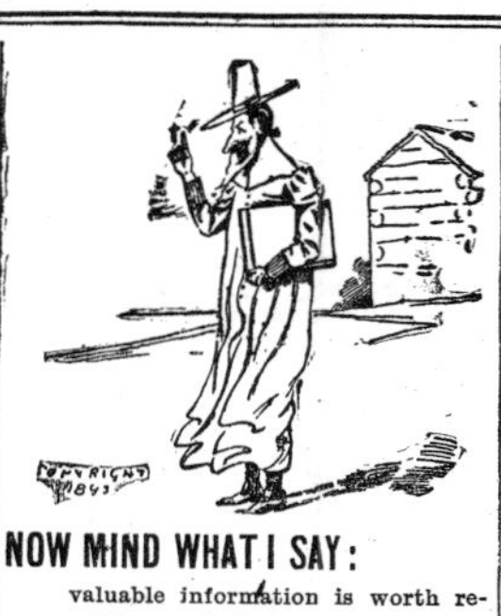

NOW MIND WHAT I SAY:

valuable information is worth receiving and better worth acting upon. The best information you can possibly receive this week is about the new stock of clothing at Swift's, No. 157 and 159 Union street. It's a

New Stock of New Goods

for the Summer trade, and beats anything of the kind ever before seen in town. Swift & Son's establishment is a perfect storehouse of taking novelties, and is as crowded with bargains as it is with buyers. Bargains draw buyers, especially at Swift & Son's, where buyers are always carrying off bargains. They have choice suits at $8.00, $10.00, $12.00 and $15.00.

M. C. SWIFT & SON,
153, 157 and 159 Union St.
NEW BEDFORD, MASS.

FINANCIALLY EMBARRASSED.

Grant Locomotive Works Calls a Meeting of Stockholders.

Chicago, June 3.—A call has been issued for a meeting of the stockholders of the Grant Locomotive works to devise means to tide over a temporary financial embarrassment which confronts the concern. The financial difficulty which the gigantic establishment is called upon to meet and overcome was brought about mainly through the recent strike of the machinists employed at the works, but the financial stringency prevailing all over the country has also had something to do with the trouble.

SPECIAL NOTICES.

CARD OF THANKS.

The Memorial Day Committee of the New Bedford Grand Army Posts, hereby return their sincere thanks to all organizations and all individuals who assisted them in making a complete observance of Memorial Day. Especially would they thank our friends who by their generous contributions of flowers enabled them to fittingly decorate the graves of the nation's dead.
S. C. CHAMBERLIN, Chairman.
RUFUS A. SOULE, Secretary.
New Bedford, June 3, 1893. je3-1t*

ELKS, ATTENTION.

You are earnestly requested to meet in Elks' Hall on SUNDAY (tomorrow) EVENING, June 4th, at 8 o'clock sharp, to arrange for the reception of the remains of our late Bro. WALTER EMERSON, accompanied by a delegation from Boston lodge.
F. B. CARR, Exalted Ruler.
H. A. FITCH, Secretary. je3-1t*

TO PORTUGUESE.

The Portuguese Political and Naturalization Club will meet in Monte Pio hall at 8 o'clock p. m., on WEDNESDAY, June 7th.
Per order,
je3-1t* MANUEL ANDREWS, Sec'y.

HOTEL BANCROFT, CHICAGO.

Fireproof, Calumet avenue and 29th st. 244 fine rooms, steam heat, baths on every floor; first class family hotel, best location in Chicago, near World's fair; European and American Plan, $1.00 to $3.00 per day. Write for Circulars if you wish to reserve rooms. je3-S4w*

Eureka Lodge, F. & A. M.

A Special Communication will be held in Masonic Hall, SUNDAY, June 4th, at 12 m., to attend the funeral of Brother JOHN D. SILVA. Members of Star in the East and Concordia Lodges and all sojourning brethren are cordially invited.
je2-2t* Per order W. M.

NOTICE TO PENSIONERS.

Pension vouchers executed on and after June 5th, day and evening, at Room 1, Waite's building, William street, by JAMES W. LOOMIS, Pension Attorney. je2-2t*

PENSIONERS

Will find the undersigned at 51 William st. office American Supply Co., opp. P. O., June 5 and 6, from 7 to 3. Will call at residence if desired. FRANKLYN HOWLAND,
je1-3t* Pension Attorney.

BEDDING PLANTS AND CUT FLOWERS,
for sale by E. W. DREW, 185 Summer st. *

B. OTHEMAN,
Goldsmith.
Room 1, Bates & Kirby's New Block, opposite City Hall,
52 Pleasant Street.
Fine Violins, Bows and Cases, Violin, Viola, Cello, Guitar and Banjo Strings of the best quality. Violin varnish and all Trimmings. A few small sized Violins suitable for beginners. my26-2w*

NOTICE.

Dr. A. M. Pierce will be absent from the city until June 10. my27-TTS-tje10*

HOTEL WESTPORT,
Westport Point, - - - Massachusetts.
Location and Sanitary conditions perfect, safe ocean bathing, pleasant drives and groves, spring water, modern toilets, electric bells, superior cuisine, terms right. Address H. A. BROWN, Saxonville, Mass., until June 20, then Westport Point, Mass. Opens July 1, 1893. *my31-MWFtf

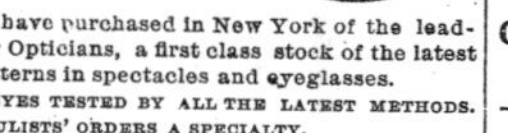

I have purchased in New York of the leading Opticians, a first class stock of the latest patterns in spectacles and eyeglasses.
EYES TESTED BY ALL THE LATEST METHODS.
OCULISTS' ORDERS A SPECIALTY.
R. H. CUBBERLY,
OPTICIAN,
12 PURCHASE STREET.
Up one short flight. MWS*

TO CURE
MOTE AND FRECKLES!
Use Mme. Bush's Obliteration
The great skin remedy.
For sale by Druggists. Wholesale and retail by
Mme. B. M. BUSH, Sole Proprietor.
No. 383 Purchase St., cor. Campbell. MWS

AT THE PARKER HOUSE
You can get a
TEN MEAL TICKET FOR $5.00.
Good for breakfast, dinner and supper. Not transferable. *my8-6m

MAYOR'S OFFICE HOURS.

On and after MONDAY, January 2d, (excepting Saturday) the office hours of the Mayor will be from 11 A. M., until 12 30 P. M.

SPECIAL NOTICES.

SPECIAL!

We have received direct from the factory a small lot of
COMBINATION POCKETBOOK AND CARD CASES,
In real Seal and Morocco Leather.
PRICE, $1.00.
They are the best value that we have seen.

HUTCHINSON'S
BOOK STORE,
198 AND 200 UNION ST.

NEW MAGAZINES!
NOW READY AT
HUTCHINSON'S BOOK STORE.
Century, Cosmopolitan, Outing,
FOR JUNE.
Album of Fashions, Le Bon Ton, L' Art De La Mode, Toilettes,
A very popular magazine, price 15c.
FOR JULY.
HUTCHINSON'S BOOK STORE,
198 and 200 Union St. je2-2t

SEASONABLE GOODS!

WALL PAPERS!
The patterns are handsome and prices so low you cannot fail to purchase if you will look them over.

BABY CARRIAGES!
With the advent of warm weather the baby needs fresh air. We would call attention to the carriage we are offering at $12. It's a decided bargain.

REFRIGERATORS!
You never heard of an "Alaska" that did not give perfect satisfaction. They are well made and yet very low in price.

PURRINGTON, BROWN & RICHARDS,
Odd Fellows Building.

WATCHES
Carefully Repaired.

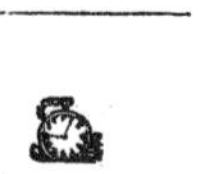

Headquarters for **DIAMONDS** —AND— **WATCHES!**

H. B. HOWLAND,
28 Purchase St.,
NEW BEDFORD.
Sign of street clock.
ap29-MThS

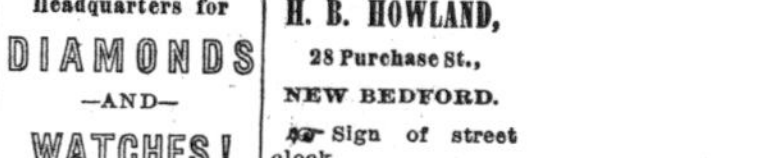

Having all the tools and material, including imported finishing stones, and having experienced Boston help, I am prepared to do all kinds of repairing and new work neatly and quickly. I use the first quality of crown glass, the clearest and finest of lenses. The celebrated frameless glasses which are made in my own establishment, are finding many admirers.
C. W. HURLL, Jr., Optician,
34 Purchase Street,
Over C. F. Wing's Carpet Store. TuThS

CLOSING SALE
—OF—
RIBBONS
At Half Price.
FINE SHELL COMBS and HAIRPINS,
At a great reduction.
DRAPERY MUSLIN, DRAPERY SILKS,
In a variety of lovely designs.
SOFA PILLOWS TO COVER,
In all sizes.
E. C. CASE, - - 18 Pleasant St.
BRICK BLOCK.
TTS*

GUIMPES.
Also Dresses to Wear with Guimpes.
From Two Years to Six.
C. T. JOHNSON - - - - - - 7 PLEASANT ST.
FS

A. B. DRAKE,
CIVIL ENGINEER AND SURVEYOR,
OFFICE 164 WILLIAM STREET.
Telephone, 236-5.

CHARLES F. SPOONER,

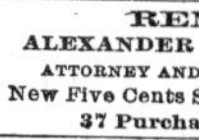

Piano Tuner and Repairer.
Residence 82 Thomas street.
Orders left with Briggs & Lawrence, 197 and 203 Union st. MWS

REMOVAL.
ALEXANDER McL. GOODSPEED,
ATTORNEY AND COUNSELLOR AT LAW.
New Five Cents Savings Bank Building,
37 Purchase St., Room 13. s30-tf

Mrs. VAN HOVENBERG-MORRILL,
Vocal Teacher,
OVERTONE METHOD.
At Y. M. C. A. Parlors on MONDAYS, MWS

TYPE-WRITING.
MRS. KENDALL, Copyist.
Room 21,............Robeson Building.
Copying of all kinds.
Supplies for all Type-Writers.

T. F. DESMOND. WENDELL H. COBB
DESMOND & COBB,
Attorneys and Counsellors at Law.
Rooms 6, 7, 8 Five Cents Savings Bank Building, 37 Purchase st., up one flight.
o14-tf

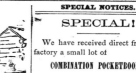

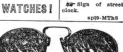

Pages 1-8.

The Evening Standard.

Pages 1-8.

ESTABLISHED FEBRUARY, 1850.] NEW BEDFORD, MONDAY, JUNE 5, 1893.---TEN PAGES. TWO CENTS.

HASKELL & TRIPP.

The days are not long past when the phrase "only an advertisement" was sufficient to condemn, unread, all advertising.

But there are proper appeals to your intelligence and self interest—advertisements worth your time and care in reading. We believe it will pay you to read ours.

The sales are big, and growing always. We want June sales to show more than their average of gain. We shall strive for it with an unapproachable stock of seasonable merchandise that we own at right prices.

There is a big ribbon sale in progress now.
Ribbons in every fashionable shade.
Ribbons in more than a score of fancy designs.
Ribbons from 3 to 6 inches in width.

Ribbons figured. Ribbons striped.	19c. a yard, worth on an average 33c. yd.
Ribbons plaided. Ribbons for all purposes.	29c. a yard, worth on an average 50c. yd.

Lace slaughter.

You know those handsome, heavy "Point de Gene" laces, of course?

Nothing so stylish, nothing as effective for dress trimmings has been brought out for many seasons. Nevertheless, importers will overstock with the usual result: goods forced off at a loss.

We are offering these beautiful laces for 29c. and 39c. a yard. *Actually worth double those figures.*

Dress Goods bargains are plentiful.

A lot of French suitings, five styles of fancy weaves in blacks and several lines of choice colors, including suitings sold early this season for 75c., 87c. and $1 a yard. *Now going at 59c. a yard.*

All-wool, double-width Henriettas, every color strictly first class. Now 39c. a yard.

Three tan shades, two brown shades, two shades of navy, old rose, the new green, heliotrope, cardinals, slates and black.

Hop Sacking, navy and black, 50c. a yard.

Storm serges, navy, brown, slate, wine, black, 50c. a yard.

Cream Danish cloth, $12\frac{1}{2}$c. yd.

Cream twilled tennis suiting, 25c. and $37\frac{1}{2}$c. a yard.

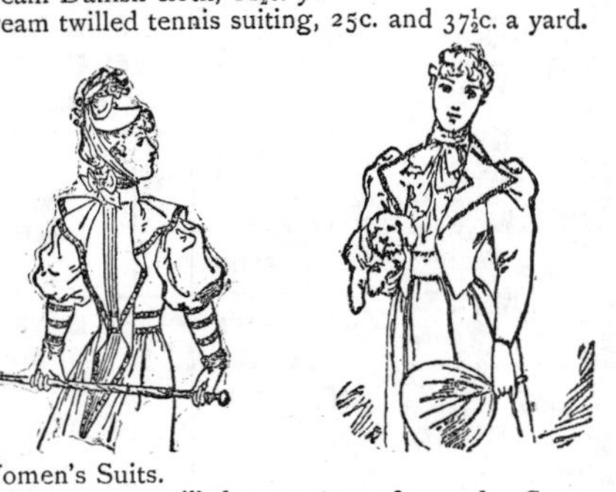

Women's Suits.

This summer will be an era of travel. Suppose you could get a stylish suit, just the thing for traveling or any outing wear, either at home, in the mountains or by the shore, and pay only half the actual value?

Wouldn't it strike you as being worth investigation?

That's the offer we make today.

For $5.89 you can take your choice of suits worth actually $12 apiece.

"Eton suits."
"Blazer suits."
"Reefer suits."

Some of these suits are made of navy storm serges, others of the famed "Clay" diagonals. There are blacks, navy, browns and mixtures in other nice fabrics. Part of them have half silk linings, others have fancy silk fronts. Many of the jackets are adorned with large pearl buttons.

And all this style and value are yours for half the ordinary price, simply because, armed with "nerve" and cash, we closed out the sample lines of two manufacturers at the close of their season.

Will you buy $12 worth of fashionable garments for $5.89?

We think so.

HINTS FROM VARIOUS STOCKS.

Sailor hats, ready trimmed, are here in the wanted styles. 50c. to $1.25 each.

Women's summer weight Jersey ribbed undervests in white, ecru, blue or pink. Fine quality for 25c. each.

Tan hosiery to match the colored shoes. A full assortment for women and children.

Women's open ribbed silk plaited hose at 75c. a pair may be had in leather shades, light blue, pink, green and red. This is an extra low figure for silk stockings.

Shopping bags with leather sides, change pocket, cloth top, with drawing strings and two leather handles, begin as low as 50c.

This is the fitting time to repeat some old advice. It is: "Explore the store." Know it as you never knew it before. Do not confine your walks to the main floor and the centre aisle. The basement, the annex and the galleries are just as interesting as the main floor.

HASKELL & TRIPP.

Department Stores: PURCHASE AND WILLIAM STS.

ON TRIAL.

Lizzie Borden at Bar of Justice.

Presents Same Calm Appearance.

Undisturbed by the Many Eyes Upon Her.

Entered Court With Apparent Indifference.

Challenges Jurors in Clear, Sharp Tones.

Five Men Drawn at Hour of Noon Recess.

No Curiosity Seekers Allowed in Court.

Everyone Present Was There on Business.

Disappointed Crowds Hung About Building

Vainly Striving to Gain Admittance.

Miss Borden Given Matron's Room at the Jail.

Prayers Offered for the Prisoner and Her Sister.

Ever since the electric spark flashed the news throughout the length and breadth of the land 10 months ago that one of Fall River's representative business men, Andrew J. Borden, and his wife, Abbie D. Borden, had been fiendishly murdered at their home on one of the principal streets of the Border City and almost within a stone's throw of the center of business activity the public has evinced the greatest interest in all that has pertained to the great tragedy, and has perused anything and everything that has been written upon the terrible crime with extreme avidity. Ardent as was the interest, contrary to the general rule, it has increased in intensity as time has passed, until at its culmination in the placing of the youngest and favorite daughter of the murdered man, Lizzie A. Borden, at the bar to be tried for her life, confronted with the charge of having committed the most inhuman and barborous as well as the most mysterious deed in the annals of New England crime, it has become of absorbing concern. The murder was without a parallel in the history of vice, in many particulars, and in no capital case of recent years has the accused had the sympathy of so many distinguished friends of various callings as Lizzie Borden, and they have sustained and comforted her during the nine months of her incarceration under the shadow of the awful charge by constant reiteration of their belief in her ability to establish her innocence of any complicity in the horrible deed, and their utter disbelief that she is the embodiment of depravity that the accusation presupposes.

To those who have watched the disclosures in the case from the very first in a disinterested manner, however, Marshal Hilliard's course seems to have been the only one that would suggest itself to any man in his position whose only aim was to subserve the cause of justice, and the accusation of Lizzie seems to be the logical result of the developments. In nothing perhaps have the police been so censured by many, as for the great leniency and consideration shown the members of the ill-fated household during the week following that fearful fourth of August, and the idea is entertained that their forbearance is responsible for the absence or destruction of many things of vital importance in determining the result of the trial now commenced.

Certain it is that very early in the investigation, when some solution of the mystery of the diabolical and sickening crime was most eagerly sought, when even the thought that a member of the household and a relative could unravel the dark secret was absolutely repulsive to the police, many things kept forcing themselves to their attention which they could not escape, and finally, much against their will they were compelled to take Lizzie into custody.

From the day of the murder she has preserved the air of stoical indifference which seems to fit her like a glove, and whatever her nervy exterior may conceal, there is nothing in her appearance to denote that she is anything but the least interested person of any concerned in the solemn business now occupying the attention of the court.

On the afternoon of the day of the murder Captain Harrington attempted to interview her on many salient matters in connection with the case and was dumbfounded at her careless demeanor and display of nerve, and from that time until the present she has maintained that manner which has made her an enigma to even the closest students of human nature. The predictions freely made that the severe strain would prove too much for even her wonderful vitality have proved to be in error, and the springy, elastic step and self-contained bearing displayed by her when she alighted from the train Saturday and walked across the platform to enter the carriage which conveyed her to the jail, where will be her home until

(Continued on Third Page.)

NOW HE IS A FREE MAN.

Indictment Against Walter Paine Quashed.

District Attorney Knowlton Sets Forth the Reasons.

His Exile, Old Age and Petition for Clemency Had Weight.

It was agreed that the indictment against Walter Paine, the Fall River embezzler, be nol prossed in the superior court this forenoon. The following was offered by Mr. Knowlton:

Walter Paine, 3d.

The entry in this case may be:

Indictment nol prossed.

The reasons for the foregoing entry are—

First—Upon the examination of the facts of the case I am satisfied that the embezzlements committed by the defendant were not to obtain money to be extravagantly expended, or to increase his income, but were incurred by reason of losses in cotton speculations, in which he was engaged, both for himself and for the mill of which he was agent, with the full knowledge of some of the directors of the corporation, and being the only indorser on many of the notes of the corporation, which at the time was largely indebted, he feared that if his own credit should become impaired it would be disastrous not only to the corporation, but to many of the men interested in it.

Second—The defendant is now seventy years of age, and since the finding of the indictment in September, 1879, has been a fugitive from his native country, living in exile in Canada, a punishment in many respects more severe, in view of his previous social position and family connections, than if he had been convicted and sentenced to a term of imprisonment.

Third—A petition asking for this action has been addressed to me which bears the signatures of very many citizens of respectability and high standing in Fall River, including all now living who were affected by his embezzlements. I have not learned of any opposition to such a course from any source whatever.

HOSEA M. KNOWLTON,
District Attorney.

WEATHER INDICATIONS.

Showers.

Washington, June 5.—For the 24 hours from 8 a. m. today: For New England, showers; cooler Tuesday; southwesterly winds.

Fair Today, Thunder Showers Tomorrow.

Boston, June 5.—Local forecast from 8 a. m. today for New England until Tuesday night: Fair today; thunder showers Tuesday; cooler Tuesday evening; winds mostly southwest.

THREATENED REVOLUTION.

Departments in Washington Have War News from Peru.

Washington, June 5.—Semi-official reports continue to reach here from Peru indicating a threatened revolution in that country. The unpopularity of the candidate for presidency and the old controversy about the nitrate beds, which Chile assumed control of at the close of the war with Peru, is given as the cause of the unrest. At the coming election it is decided by ballot whether Chile is to be paid a certain portion of the reveune from the beds. The argument of the question has aroused much of the old war spirit, and further complications between the countries are feared. Both the state and navy departments here are manifesting intense interest in the departure for the Pacific coast of the United States steamers Charleston and Philadelphia. It is probable that the Philadelphia will sail from New York on the 17th inst. for Callao.

MISPLACED SWITCH.

Cannonball Train Wrecked and Seven Passengers Injured.

St. Louis, Mo., June 5.—The southbound cannon-ball train on the Iron Mountain, which left here at 9 p. m. Saturday for Texas, was wrecked by a misplaced switch at Leeper station, 135 miles south of here. Seven passengers were injured. The wires are prostrated by storms and no other particulars can be learned.

At 6 o'clock last evening another wreck occurred a few miles from Poplar Bluff. A stock train was in collision with a freight, causing a loss of $75,000. Upwards of 100 head of valuable live stock were killed.

FRESH CASES OF CHOLERA.

Epidemic Spreading Despite Denials of Authorities.

Madrid, June 5.—Despite the denials of the French local authorities Spanish consuls in France continue to report the spread of the cholera epidemic at several ports. Four fresh cases they say developed Saturday in Marseilles, two in Cette and one case in Toulouse. Between May 22 and June 1 there were 14 cases and 11 deaths in Marseilles. The Spanish government has ordered that all vessels arriving from Marseilles be detained seven days in quarantine, and that vessels from other Mediterranean ports of France be kept under observation for three days.

THE BRIGGS CASES.

Rev. Lyman Abbott Preaches in Defense of the Clergyman.

New York, June 5.—Rev. Dr. Lyman Abbott, in his sermon on the Briggs cases today at Plymouth church, Brooklyn, endeavored to prove that Dr. Briggs and not the general assembly during the last two years had defended the true faith; that it was not Dr. Briggs who was heretical; that the stand taken by the general assembly was one whose logical result was infidelity.

BIG STRIKE THREATENED.

Dissatisfaction Among Standard Oil Help in Illinois.

Chicago, June 5.—The 2,500 hands of the Standard Oil company's plant at Whiting, Ill., have decided to strike unless the company accedes to their demand for a nine-hour working day with 10 hours pay. There seems to be small likelihood of the company making the concession.

Niver Will Not Resign.

Boston, June 5.—Vice President Niver of the Boston & Maine road says: "I have never contemplated for a moment the idea of resigning as vice president of the Boston & Maine Railroad company. I shall not under any circumstances resign."

TELEGRAPHIC BREVITIES.

William H. Whitin, a prominent citizen of Northbridge and a well known cotton manufacturer, died at his home in Whitinsville last evening of Bright's disease. He had but recently returned from a southern trip for his health.

An engine and 18 box cars were derailed and thrown down a steep embankment at Pomfret, Ct., last night. A brakeman was injured.

In obedience to the orders of the French residents the Siamese have withdrawn from Cammon, the principal military post of northern Annam.

William Shannon, aged 48 years, serving time for forgery, made his escape from the Monroe county (N. Y.) penitentiary yesterday.

John R. Sanborn hanged himself at Norway, Me., last night.

Steamer Cephalonia, from Boston, passed Brow Head this morning.

STANDARD EXTRAS.

Newspaper readers of southeastern Massachusetts look to the Standard for the very best reports of the Borden murder trial printed in this section. They will not be disappointed. In addition to elaborate reports of the proceedings of the Borden trial in all the regular editions of the Standard, an extra edition will be printed every evening upon adjournment of court, with a complete record of the day's events.

CONTENTS OF THIS EVENING'S STANDARD.

Page 1.

The Borden murder trial.
Walter Paine a free man.
More news from Peru.
A train wrecked and passengers injured.
Cholera in Spain.
A big strike threatened.
Home matters.
Telegraphic dispatches.

Page 2.

Jose Correiro surrenders himself to the Fall River police; damaging evidence against him convinces the officers he is the murderer of Bertha Manchester.
Sunday's fire.
Amelia Wignall supposed to have committed suicide at Fall River.
Home matters.
Suburban news.

Page 3.

The Borden murder trial continued.
Third district court.
Memorial service.
List of unclaimed letters.
Telegraphic dispatches.
Suburban news.

Page 4.

The Borden murder trial continued.
Editorials.

Page 5.

Marine intelligence.
Marriages and deaths.

Page 6.

Financial news.
Second Edition — Telegraphic and local news.

Page 7.

First infantry orders on the camp at Framingham.
Dr. Lyman Abbott's remarks concerning the Briggs case create a sensation.
Edwin Booth's condition critical.
Base ball.
Communications.

Page 8.

The Natick murder shrouded in mystery.
Stabbing assault in Boston.
Open Sunday at the World's Fair.
An Arkansas preacher in trouble.
Mexican murderers to be shot to death.
Third Edition—Telegraphic and locals.
Early telegraphic dispatches.

Page 9.

His Revenge—story.
Miscellaneous reading.

Page 10.

New York fashion letter.
Miscellaneous reading.

HOME MATTERS.

PERSONAL.

George L. Smith of Houston, Texas, who has been visiting his old home in this city for some time, will return home in a few days. During his stop here he has been impressed with the marvelous development of New Bedford, and has collected much statistical matter relative to the textile industry, which he will present to the Houston board of trade.

John Q. Ryder, local manager for the Western Union Telegraph company, is in charge of the operators detailed by that company at the court house on County street. Chester G. Rogers and Frank E. Murphy have charge of the Postal's service at the court house.

Captain William Lewis, David A. Snell and William B. Wood of this city, members of the Ancient and Honorable Artillery company of Boston, are in that city today in attendance at the annual meeting of that corps.

Sheriff Wright has appointed George F. Weeden a deputy sheriff, and Mr. Weeden has qualified before Mayhew R. Hitch and James L. Gillingham as commissioners.

At the meeting of the New England conference of educational workers in the English high school, Boston, Saturday, Elmer L. Curtis of Sandwich was admitted to membership.

Fred W. Bancroft has very successfully passed the examinations for the school ship Enterprise.

David G. Pratt of North Middleboro has been elected a member of the Boston Art club.

THE BEST IN TOWN.

F. R. Slocum has about 175 patterns of lounges and couches to dispose of during the next few weeks. This is the largest stock carried by any furniture dealer in town. They are all modern in style and handsome in material and will be sold at prices within the reach of every one.

CONDENSED LOCALS.

The body picked up off Black rock recently is believed by parties at Cuttyhunk to have been that of Second Engineer Rogert McManus of Philadelphia, who was washed overboard from steam tug Sea King, which arrived at Vineyard Haven Feb. 20th from Philadelphia, and which reported the loss of their engineer off Cuttyhunk, and whose body was not recovered.

At a meeting of the aldermanic committee on soldiers' aid four persons were granted $4 per month under chapter 301, who formerly had $8 per month under chapter 279. The change was made because the persons have been granted pensions. Under chapter 279 one applicant was granted $6 a month.

Remember Babo's German Medicated Tea does not debilitate but invigorates and strengthens the system; positive cure for sick headaches, indigestion, etc. For sale at all druggists, 25 and 50 cents per package, or sent by mail postpaid. Send postal for sample.

Permanent men from the Weld street fire station were called on Saturday night to extinguish a blaze in the boiler room of the North End planing mill on Bowditch street. The loss was trivial.

Elegant Wine for family use, $1.50 per gallon, delivered in city—Port, Sherry, Madeira, Angelica, Muscatel, or Tokay, at Hiram Wheaton & Sons, 45 to 51 School street.

The police seized ten quarts of whiskey at the house of James Driscoll on Merrimac street Saturday night. Driscoll cannot be found, and is understood to have left town.

Nearly all the cars returning last evening from the band concert at the north end were delayed fully 15 minutes by a balky horse on one of the first cars.

Joao F. da Silva, Jr., was admitted to citizenship in the district court this morning. J. I. da Terra for petitioner.

Go to Whiting & Co's tomorrow and get a gingham or pongee dress at the great mark down prices.

Gentlemen, the finest line of Russia leather shoes found at Buchell's. See our $4 shoe.

Have you seen the 4-button $1 kids Whiting & Co. are selling at 75 cents per pair.

Wednesday will be visiting day at the Middle street grammar school.

All first class druggists keep Cutter Whiskey.

For your hosiery and underwear go to Whiting & Co's.

Weariness overcome by Hood's Sarsaparilla.

LADIES

SOMETIMES

You feel uncertain where to buy

CARPETS.

NOW WE WISH TO TELL YOU THAT WE ARE FULLY PREPARED TO SUPPLY YOUR WANTS.

OUR STOCK IS MORE ATTRACTIVE AND COMPLETE THAN AT ANY TIME DURING THE HISTORY OF OUR BUSINESS.

New Carpets.
New Mattings,
New Furniture,
New Curtains.

YES

WE ATTEND STRICTLY TO THE

Furniture,
Carpet and
Curtain
Business.

FURNISHING HOUSES IS OUR SPECIAL WORK, AND THIS WE DO TO THE ENTIRE SATISFACTION OF EVERYONE WHO FAVORS US WITH THEIR BUSINESS.

We handle the best makes.
We guarantee our prices to be as low as the lowest.

CASH or CREDIT.

C. F. WING,

34 to 40 Purchase Street.

WHITING & CO.

Great Summer Cotton Wash Goods Sale.

One case 1,632 yards of the best 12 1-2c. American Ginghams will be sold by us at 7 1-2c. per yard. Only 75c. for 10 yards of nice Gingham.

500 yards of Bedford Cord Ginghams, made to sell at 25c., our price 12 1-2c.

250 yards of Cheviots that sold at 33c. per yard, our price 12 1-2c. today.

2,500 yards of the finest American Ginghams, made and sold this season at 17c., will be sold by us at 12 1-2c. per yard.

2,800 yards of the best Scotch Ginghams, made by R. A. Whythan & Son of Glasgow, Scotland, that have been sold at 33c. the first of the season, now sold by us at 17c. per yard.

1,000 yards of our best Printed Pongees, mostly white grounds, carried over from last season and sold at 15c. per yard, we shall put on sale at 9c. per yard. Do not wait, but come as soon as you read this, as the case price today for same goods is 12 1-4c. cash.

☞ Do not ask for samples of any of these goods, as we shall not give any.

WHITING & CO.

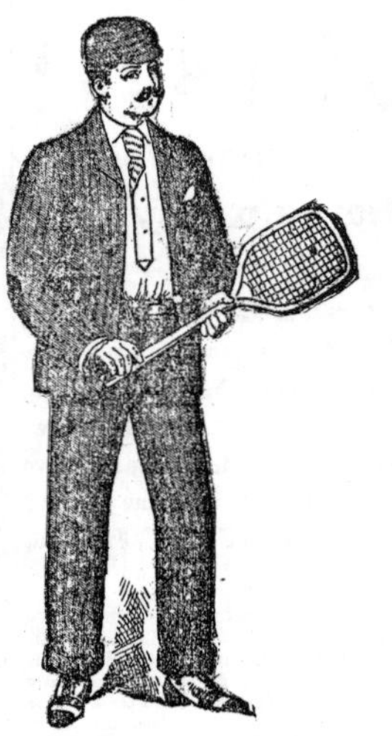

Tennis and Outing Suits.

The newest things in Tennis and Outing Suits are ready for your inspection. Blue Serge Skeleton coats and White Duck Trousers will be the "go" this Summer, and we have provided an unusually large stock of these comfortable goods for the hot weather.

The new styles in Tennis Flannels are very handsome and especially moderate in price.

Our assortment of Negligee Shirts, Leather Belts, Straw Hats, Tennis and Bicycle Caps, Stockings, etc., is most complete and comprises everything that is newest and best.

J. & W. R. WING & CO.,

Men's Furnishers.

THE CRESCENT!

22 Purchase St.

ONLY 19c. PER YARD.

VERY WIDE HAMBURGS.

Just right for Skirts.

Excellent Hamburgs at 12 1-2c.

A good assortment at 5c.

To close at 19c. per yard.

A Lot of Silk Gloves,

Black and Colors, regular 25 and 29c. quality.

Mitts, good quality, 25c., a better grade at 50c.

Shirt Waists, at 29, 50, 75c.

Better quality at $1.00 $1.25, and $1.50, etc.

An entire new lot of belts, all styles.

Try THE LATEST, Empire styles, in tan and black, at 50c.

GUIMPES.

Guimpes at 39, 50, 58c.

Guimpes at 62, 75, 83c., $1.

Children's Dresses!

Gingham dresses from 50c. to $1.75.

White dresses, all styles and prices.

MARKED DOWN—Children's Short Cloaks.

TAN COLORED HOSIERY.

Children's Tan Hose, 25 and 37c. Ladies' Tan Hose, 25, 33 and 50c. Black Hosiery in all grades.

SUMMER CORSETS.

Good ones at 50c. Better grades at 75c., $1, $1.25 and $2. Corsets of all kinds. Equipoise Waists, Double Ve Waists, Ferris Ventilating Waists. Misses' and Ladies' Summer Vests of all kinds. Gingham aprons, two widths, 25c.

THE CRESCENT!

22 Purchase St.

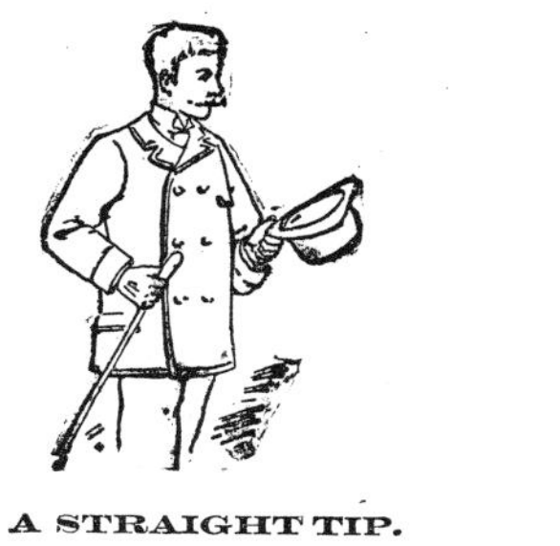

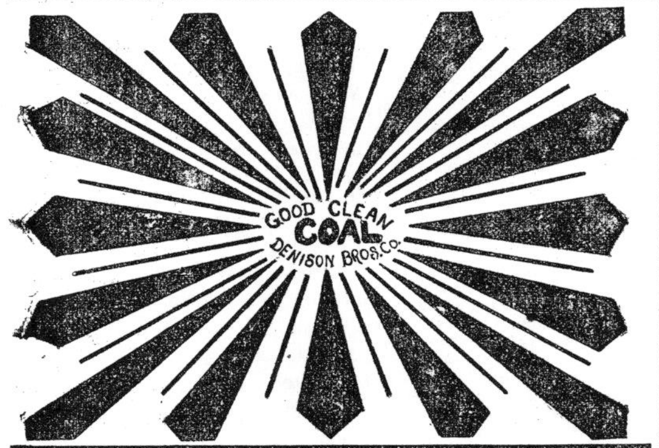

IN CUSTODY.

Evidence Strong Against Jose Correiro.

Police Believe He is Miss Manchester's Slayer.

Passed Coins Known to Belong to Murdered Girl,

When Purchasing Shoes on Memorial Day.

Damaging Details Withheld by the Police.

Man Arraigned and His Case Continued.

The Dead Girl's Funeral Held on Sunday.

It Leads to the Disclosure of a Peculiar Incident.

There is circumstantial evidence which points strongly to Joseph Correiro as the murderer of Miss Bertha M. Manchester at Fall River. It has its weak points, but perhaps the police are holding back the full story. At 3 30 yesterday afternoon City Marshal Hilliard granted an audience to the newspaper men and gave them the following account.

On the forenoon of Memorial Day Correiro called at the shoe store of Joseph La Croix, 364 North Main street. The shop is near the Sagamore mills and is patronized exclusively by Portuguese. One of that nationality named Sousa, who resides in South Somerset, and who has been detained as a witness, happened to be present when Correiro entered the shop, and acted as interpreter. The prisoner asked for a pair of shoes, made a selection and inquired the price. He took from his pocket a woman's purse containing a silver trade dollar, a half dollar with a hole in it and two silver quarters. He was to pay $1.50 for the shoes.

The discussion which followed fixed Correiro permanently in the minds of La Croix and Sousa. The former valued the dollar at 90 to 95 cents, and would have nothing to do with the imperfect half dollar. Correiro, through the interpreter, argued in vain. He had, according to La Croix's calculation, $1.40 or $1.45, and the shoes were worth $1.50.

After more or less haggling, Correiro said that if he must pay five cents extra, La Croix would have to break a bill. The shopkeeper demurred. There was trotting at Riverside park, he said, and his safe was locked. Rather than be late for the races, he would let the five cents go.

Correiro took off his old shoes, which were done up in a paper. They were covered with dust, as was the man's clothes. The prisoner slipped on the new shoes, put the cast-off pair under his arm and disappeared. La Croix went to the horse trot, and later in the day came the announcement of the brutal crime which had been committed on the New Boston road.

The police began to hunt for clews in the Sagamore mill neighborhood, where the

Missing Portuguese Had Made His Home,

and the trail led them to the shop of La Croix. They learned of the purchase on the morning of Memorial Day and secured the coins. Mr. Manchester examined them. He said that they belonged to Bertha M. Manchester, his daughter. Thirteen or fourteen years ago Mr. Manchester gave Bertha and Jennie, her sister, a couple of bright, new, silver trade dollars. They bore the date of 1878, and the girls put them away as keepsakes. The dollar which Correiro handed to La Croix is bright as it was the day it was stamped, and it bears the date mark 1878.

It isn't strange that the authorities hunted for Correiro. Two farmers were also found who could tell something about the Portuguese. They were working on their land on Wilson road, which runs from Steep Brook to New Boston road on the morning of the tragedy. They think it was between 9 and 10 o'clock when

They Saw a Man Running Down the Highway.

They observed him closely because a number of bicycle riders had passed, presumably on their way to Riverside park, and it occurred to the tillers of the soil that this fellow was more in a hurry than any of them. The report of Correiro's surrender has been published. The city marshal, the assistant marshal and all of the captains and the inspectors worked on him until 4 o'clock yesterday morning. He admitted that he had purchased a pair of shoes, but denied stoutly that he had any purse or that the money which he offered in payment resembled the coins which have been described. At 11 30 p. m. inspectors entered the station with La Croix and Sousa. They identified the Portuguese prisoner as the man who had given them the coins. There could be no mistake about it, they said. Yesterday the Wilson road farmers, whose names the police withhold, drove in, and after examining the suspect, stated that he resembled closely the man who ran past them on Memorial Day.

Correiro still sticks to the original account of his movements on that day. He did not go near the Wilson road or the New Boston road, he says. He followed the procession for a while, went to Crab pond bridge and at noon took the train for Taunton. He

Does Not Explain Where He Got the Money

with which he paid for the shoes, and the police intimate that they can prove that he did not take the noon train for Taunton. It is whispered about at headquarters that there is more evidence, equally damaging, which will be made public later.

There are these points in the prisoner's favor, provided the details given above are correct: If he ran down Wilson road between 9 and 10 o'clock in the morning, stopped on North Main street to purchase shoes, haggled over the price and reached Crab pond bridge at 11 o'clock he traveled on the wings of the wind. He says that he met Mr. Manchester on the bridge, and Mr. Manchester says the same thing. Again, if he is guilty it is strange that he surrendered. The police argue that he didn't surrender. They state that they gave the prisoner's uncle a certain number of hours in which to produce him and threatened to arrest Correiro unless the uncle brought him in of his own accord. The bluff worked beautifully, for it must have been a bluff pure and simple.

If the Police Could Have Located Correiro

they would have wasted precious few words on his uncle. Furthermore, the finding of the coins in Correiro's possession does not necessarily connect him with the farmhouse on the day that Miss Manchester was killed. He had worked there a couple of days a month ago, and it has been given out that Mr. Manchester's help labored at cut rates. Correiro may double on his tracks if hard pressed and admit that he stole the purse and coins before he gave up the job. In that event it will be urged that a man in his circumstances, crippled as he was for board money, and a drag on his relatives, couldn't have held on to $1.75 for 30 days. There are occasions when it is necessary to part with money, no matter how strong the disposition to save may be. There is

One More Black Mark Against Him.

He flatly contradicts Sousa and La Croix regarding his movements in their store. He says that he wore his old shoes out of the shop and changed them afterwards. He

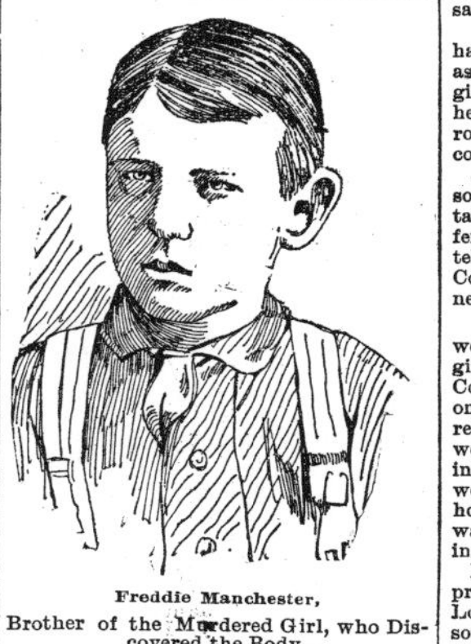

Freddie Manchester,

Brother of the Murdered Girl, who Discovered the Body.

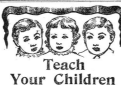

threw them behind a door in the tenement where he was stopping. Officers have searched this tenement from cellar to garret, and they found no shoes. Neither can Correiro's friends produce a pair which will answer the purpose. The conclusion reached is that the prisoner threw away his old shoes soon after he left La Croix, and it would help his case if he could locate them. Captain Medley and other officials were in Taunton yesterday, making inquiries regarding Correiro's conduct at the brick works, and the exact time of his arrival. City Marshall Hilliard declined to answer many of the questions put to him by his audience, and refused to say anything concerning the condition of the prisoner's clothing. If he wears the suit which covered him on Memorial Day and is guilty, there are blood stains on it. If he has changed his garments it will be in order for him to tell what he did with them.

Considerable Excitement Prevail in the City

when it was known that the circumstantial evidence was so strong against Correiro, and there was a feeling of relief over the prospect of clearing up at least one mystery. The prisoner's uncle, Jacinto Muniz, will say nothing about the case. He insists that his nephew is innocent, and La Croix is also inclined to believe that his customer is all right. The latter is not at all pleased to find that he has been drawn into the prosecution, if his actions count for anything, and the authorities have probably cautioned him not to talk.

Funeral of Miss Manchester.

The funeral of Miss Bertha M. Manchester took place from the residence of her brother in law, W. W. Coolidge, corner of Stafford square and Quarry street, Fall River, at 1 15 o'clock yesterday afternoon. Some 30 mourners were present, including the members of the Reed family, who live opposite the Manchester farm, anl 15 carriages followed the hearse to the grave. The body of the murdered girl rested in a white plush casket, and was covered with a profusion of flowers. Rev. D. B. Jutton of the Baptist Temple officiated. He prayed that the assassin might be speedily brought to justice, and after reading appropriate selections from the Scriptures spoke briefly on the admirable character of the deceased and her sad and untimely end. Mr. Manchester and other relatives were overcome by grief as they viewed the face of the daughter and sister for the last time, and the scene was a touching one. The bearers were Arthur Brown, Henry Reed, Mitchell Nicholson and Arthur Loun. The coffin was deposited in the tomb near the entrance of Oak Grove cemetery.

One More Capture.

William Smith, one of the trio of lunatics who have been at large, spent Sunday in the Central police station, Fall River. He did not murder Miss Bertha Manchester, however, and will be returned to the Wesport poor farm, from which he escaped. Officers McNulty and Pierce saw Smith on the streets of the city last Saturday, and his peculiar conduct aroused their suspicions. They followed him into a barber shop on Montaup street, and heard him tell the proprietor that he had just spent $1,000,000, and was about to indulge in further extravagances. That settled his case and he was locked up. He belongs in the Bear's Den country. There remain wandering around one Davis, who escaped from Taunton a few days ago, and an insane man named Holland, who is wanted at the Bridgewater asylum.

LOOKS BAD FOR HIM.

Police Think Correiro is Bertha Manchester's Murderer.

(Special Dispatch.)

FALL RIVER, Mass., June 5.—Saturday night Joseph Correiro walked into the Central police station with his uncle. He was merely a suspect then; a man whom the police wanted just because he had worked on the farm and was missing. Now he is regarded by the police and reporters as guilty of the terrible slaughter of Bertha May Manchester on the morning of May 30. He may not have been alone in the terrible deed, but that he was the author of the crime and the robber of the girl's money is practically established beyond a peradventure of a doubt.

The facts elicited from the eight-hour investigation are the basis of the assumption. It is from

No Idle Theories

that the terrible charge is made, for, as the mayor said: "This is no fake, but tangible clues pointing to the guilty person."

Too much cannot be said in praise of the work of the police. Since the day of the shocking tragedy there has been no such thing as rest for anyone connected with the department.

The people have been fooled by the alleged clues from Bridgewater, Providence, Natick et al.—not so the police. Their work was systematic; they wanted everyone who had worked for old Manchester—those who were familiar with the place.

They wanted Correiro most of all; they got him. They had located Correiro in Taunton before Saturday, but had not at that time put their hands on him. To save trouble, and for other purposes, they sent his uncle, Jacinto Muniz, after him. They told Muniz that if his nephew was not there by 7 o'clock that night the police would bring him in. It was a fact, for the marshal and his men were hot on the trail.

It is well known that the police have yet much important information in their possession. Among other things they will prove that the murderer

Slept In the Farmhouse

one night after he was suspected to have ended his work for Mr. Manchester, and it is very probable that he planned the robbery at that time. He, perhaps, never intended to commit murder, but the fact that Bertha was not to be trifled with led to his shocking brutality.

Although it has all along been denied there had been any violation of the girl's honor, there is a well established opinion among the police that such an attempt was made with some success. A microscopical examination may be required to determine some things in connection with this matter.

This is about all that Dr. Dolan cares to say about this part of the affair. It is said that

New Blood Stains

have been discovered in the dining room, as though, before the death blow was given, the girl had tried to escape from her assailant by running through another room. Many new things are being discovered hour by hour.

Joseph Lacroix was the shoe dealer who sold the shoes to Correiro. He would not talk about the case, saying that he preferred to wait until the proper time before telling what he knows. Jacinto Muniz, Correiro's uncle, is still confident of his nephew's innocence.

Funeral Services

were held over the remains of the dead girl yesterday at the house of W. W. Coolidge, brother-in-law of the dead girl, on Quarry street. Only a few invited relatives and two local newspaper men weie present. The remains were enclosed in an embossed white cloth casket and were exposed to the view of those in the house who cared to see them. The casket was surrounded with many floral offerings.

Rev. Mr. Jutten made an impressive prayer, and there was no singing. Arthur Lowne, Arthur Brown, Mitchell Nicholson and Henry Read removed the body to a plain black hearse. When the services began there was a small crowd around the house, but by the time the funeral cortege of 14 carriages moved off a large crowd had gathered.

At the cemetery the carriages were surrounded by 1500 people, principally women and children. The remains were taken from the hearse and placed in the tomb, because the widow of the deceased brother of Mr. Manchester objected to the intermen of the body where her husband lies.

This incident is one of the many indications of the

Strange Family Relations

that have existed among the Manchesters for many years. The mourners did not leave their carriages at the cemetery, but as they passed the tombs they lifted the curtains and took a farewell glance at the casket. The most noticeable of all the many mourners was Mr. Manchester's wayward boy, Harry, who has returned home, probably to stay. He sat in the carriage with his father. He went over the old homestead after the funeral in company with his brother-in-law.

CORREIRO ARRAIGNED.

His Case Continued This Morning Until Thursday, June 15.

(By Associated Press.)

Fall River, June 5.—Joseph Correiro was arraigned before Judge John J. Mc Donough in the second district court this morning charged with homicide, causing the death of Bertha M. Manchester. Through the interpreter he entered a plea of not guilty, and announced himself ready for trial. Assistant Marshall Fleet asked for a continuance on the part of the government, as many of the officers and important witnesses were in New Bedford attending the Borden trial. The case was continued until Thursday, June 15.

The news of his arrest caused the greatest excitement in the city, and the court room was crowded with spectators this morning, all anxiously awaiting to obtain a glance at the prisoner. He entered the court room a few minutes after 9 o'clock in charge of Steward Leonard, and was assigned a seat next to the officer on the last row of the dock. He was dressed as he was on the night of his arrest, wearing a light-colored coat, a dark vest and pants. He was pale and haggard looking, and evidently fully realizing his position. His eyes roved nervously around the court room, and as Judge McDonough entered the room and the court officer announced "Court," there was a perceptible twitching of his face, and his eyes became riveted on the judge. His case was the first called, and Dr. Dutro, a local physician, acted as interpreter and translated to the prisoner the rather lengthy charge. He listened attentively throughout its reading, and at its close smiled faintly and pleaded not guilty. Upon the government's request for a continuance the prisoner was committed without bail to await his trial. Manuel Souci, the principal witness for the government in the case, was held in $2,000 bonds.

SUNDAY'S FIRE.

The alarm from box 58 at 2 45 p. m. Sunday was rung in for a lively blaze amongst a pile of empty machinery cases on a vacant lot just east of the Hathaway mill on Cove street. Mill employes had a stream of water, from a mill hydrant, on the fire when the department arrived. As there was an abundance of dry excelsior in and about the boxes the firemen had an hour's smoky work before the fire was declared all out. The damage will be slight. It is supposed that the fire was started by boys. While responding to the alarm the spring on truck 3 which holds the brakes back from the wheels broke, and in consequence the apparatus was detained in arriving at the fire.

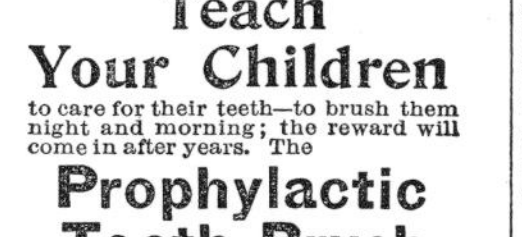

PUBLIC SCHOOLS.

Some Interesting Statements Anticipated at the Meeting.

The regular monthly meeting of the school committee will be held this evening, when the annual election of teachers in the public schools will occur. It is anticipated that the meeting will be a very interesting one. The sub-committees this year have been very thorough in their work, and the needs of the schools, the qualifications of the teachers and their success or non-success have received careful attention.

In the High school the relations of principal and teachers, matters of discipline, etc., have received attention, and the sub-committee will hold a final meeting this afternoon. It is not anticipated that a change in the corps of instructors will be made, but some interesting suggestions will likely be made.

In the grammar schools one vacancy at least will occur, Miss Mary R. Hinckley of the Middle Street, who has for many years been a valued instructor, has found that her health will not permit her to continue the work, and she has announced that she will not be a candidate for re-election.

In the primary grades there are likely to be one or more vacancies.

There is quite a large class to graduate from the training school, but still the supply is likely to be less than the demand. Every year the tax on the time and ability of instructors becomes more onerous and constant study and attention is required on the part of teachers to keep them abreast of the requirements of the times.

A PROBABLE SUICIDE.

Amelia Wignall Believed to Have Drowned Herself at Fall River.

The woman known to the Fall River police as Amelia Wignall, supposed to belong in this city, who attempted to drown herself in the river the other afternoon, is missing, and it is believed that she has taken her life. As nearly as can be ascertained, she went from her house to the new Hargraves mill last Saturday, taking with her one of her children, a little boy. She left the lad near the factory, telling him that she would return in a few minutes. He waited for her until his patience was exhausted and then made his way to his father's place of employment at Davis Brothers' establishment. The police say that the boy asked his father to take care of him, and that he refused. Young Wignall then proceeded to the police station and told his story. A searching party was sent out, and the streams in the neighborhood of the Hargraves mills were dragged all day yesterday, but without success.

PRISON REPORTS.

Josiah A. Hunt, Esq., keeper of the jail and house of correction, reports 31 prisoners in the jail a week ago; since committed, 5; transferred from Taunton jail, 1; sent to court and not returned, 2; sent to court and returned to house of correction, 3; remaining 32, now in confinement.

In the house of correction a week ago there were 252 prisoners; since committed, 13 for being drunk, 2 for assault and battery, 1 for larceny, 1 for vagrancy, 2 for disturbing the peace, 2 for common nuisance and keeping disorderly house, 1 for keeping liquor unlawfully, and 1 for keeping open shop on Sunday; discharged as poor convicts, 4; on payment of fine, 0; at expiration of term of sentence, 14; conditionally released by county commissioners, 0; remaining 257.

The commitments to the house of correction include 15 sentences from New Bedford, aggregate 25 1-3 months; 10 from Fall River, aggregate 34 2-3 months. The number of commitments of prisoners of temperate habits is 1; intemperate, 22.

SUPERIOR COURT CASES.

The following cases were sent to the superior court today by the clerk of the district court to be acted upon during the present June term, viz: Appeals from sentences imposed in the lower court 60. Of these 37 are for drunkenness, 13 for liquor selling, 4 for assaults, 2 for disorderly house keeping and 1 each for keeping a policy shop, violation of the school law, disturbing the peace and receiving stolen goods.

For investigation by the grand jury there are 10 cases, viz: Larceny from person, 1; assault, 2; perjury, 1; seduction, 1; obtaining goods by false pretense 1; robbery, 1, and for breaking and entering in the night time and larceny, 3.

INCREASED INSURANCE RATES.

At a recent meeting of the New England Insurance exchange, Chairman Emerson of the Nantucket committee reported that the contract between the town of Nantucket and the water company formerly supplying the town for fire purposes expired May 14 last and had not been renewed. An increase in the insurance rates of 25 per cent. was made on all risks formerly under the protection of the water works. Dwellings were excepted, the rates on these being made $1.50 for five years.

CONDENSED LOCALS.

At the Hammond-Fiske nuptials at Falmouth on Thursday the four bridesmaids will be Miss Olga Gardner, Miss Cabot, Miss Tudor and Miss Lyman of Boston. Mr. Herbert Otis, who has lately become engaged to Miss Whiting, is to be best man, and Mr. Gordon Dexter, Dr. W. A. Dunn, Sam Hammond, Jr., Mr. Frank Beebe, one of Miss Fiske's bachelor uncles, Mr. Lewis Strong of the Calumet club, New York, and Mr. Robert Dudley Winthrop of the Knickerbocker club, New York, and a Harvard, '93, classmate, will be the ushers.

Edward Shaw of Boston, a well known engineer, will be secured by the county commissioners to make the preliminary surveys and drawings for the new bridge across the Acushnet. Mr. Shaw had charge of the construction of the railroad bridges at Springfield, and has drawn the plans for two bridges across the Connecticut river. Mr. Shaw will come to this city at once, and will complete his work before the summer is over. Captain Sanders is of the opinion that the bridge cannot be finished in less than three years.

The president of the board of trade of New London through the collector of the port requested the treasury department to furnish a government vessel to keep the course clear during the Harvard-Yale boat races on the Thames. In response to this request the collector was notified on Saturday that the commander of the revenue cutter Dexter had been directed to have that vessel at New London on the 30th inst. to assist in enforcing the navigation laws.

The Guard of Honor met at headquarters Sunday afternoon for the purpose of talking over the matter of the proposed trip to Montreal June 24th. Nothing definite was decided, but another meeting will be held Tuesday evening, when the Guard of Honor will meet with the L'Union Ouvriere society to vote on the matter. It is expected that of the 500 French societies invited at least half of the number will attend.

D. J. Lanagan, chief ranger of Court New Bedford, A. O. F., has presented Deputy John F. Quinn of Fall River a bugle which has a history. The instrument is of English manufacture and was used in the war of the revolution and in the war of 1812, where it did royal service. It was presented to Mr. Quinn as a tribute for services rendered by him to Court New Bedford.

Last Saturday afternoon the superintendent of the Lily of the Valley Temple, at the close of the meeting, invited all to Bates & Kirby's and they each one had a fine treat of ice cream.

One person was admitted to full membership in the Pleasant Street M. E. church yesterday from probation and three by letter.

CUTTYHUNK.

Great Excitement Over Supposed Appearance of the Sea Serpent.

Quite an excitement prevailed at the west end for a time Friday evening. A floating object was seen in the water near the Sow & Pigs ledge that to the naked eye resembled the much talked of sea serpent very much. It was a long, black, slender body with a flat head rising high above the waves. It appeared to be moving rapidly toward the entrance of the sound. Upon looking through the glass, however, it was found that instead of a sea serpent it was an old tree with part of the branches projecting above the water and drifting with the tide.

A large piece of wreckage from the Aquatic has drifted ashore directly across the rocks where a fishing stand is to be put. Mr. Clifford has received orders from the club to have the wreckage blown to pieces so that the stand may be put in its usual place.

Mrs. Sadie Veeder and Master Chester have been visiting Mrs. Mary Keeny in New Bedford.

Quite a number of excursions have been made to Penikese after gulls' eggs. They are quite plentiful.

The trap fishermen say that the fishing is about over for this season.

Captain Akin brought a party on the island in the Nautilus Decoration Day.

Fred Veeder is building a piazza on his house.

Mr. Hammond of Fairhaven has been helping Oscar Stetson build his cellar.

Thomas Jones is employed painting in New Bedford.

Tug and lighter are engaged in moving rocks off Cannapitsett in order to make the channel wider. The work began Thursday.

Mr. James Connor of New York, late from Paris, is boarding at Mrs. George Bosworth's.

A pleasant little entertainment consisting of recitations, music, tableaux and dialogues took place at the schoolhouse Saturday evening.

Mr. and Mrs. Russell Rotch have moved in the house formerly occupied by Mrs. Isaiah Tilton.

Quite a number of the island people spent Memorial Day in the city.

Lobsters are rather more plenty than they have been.

Elliott Cornell of Westport is visiting on the island.

Mrs. William Haskins has been on a short visit to friends in New Bedford.

BEULAH GROVE.

Beulah Grove will be open as usual this summer for out-door gatherings of various kinds. Sunday schools are the first to use it for their annual picnics. Some are already discussing the matter of going there. It is easily reached, a quiet, pleasant grove, and the railroad fare is low. Gatherings in the interest of the farming community, of the Sunday school and temperance cause are being planned for about the middle of July. The annual camp-meeting of this division of the Salvation Army will commence July 29th and continue till Aug. 7th. Great preparations are being made for this jubilee of the Salvationists, and a grand time is anticipated by them. No charge is made for space to erect tents and cottages, and application has already been made for such of the agent, G. R. Wordell of Westport.

WALTER EMERSON'S FUNERAL.

The funeral of Walter Emerson took place at 10 a. m. today from St. Paul's church, Tremont street, Boston. After the services a special train left the Providence depot at 12 m. for New Bedford, where interment will take place this afternoon. Delegations from the Elks, St. Andrew's Royal Arch chapter, DeMolay commandery, K. T., and Wapiti tribe, I. O. R. M., accompanied the remains. On the arrival of the train at Pearl street station at 1 40 p. m. Exalted Ruler F. B. Carr, Secretary H. A. Fitch and Chaplain G. W. Parsons of New Bedford lodge of Elks, with a delegation of other members of the lodge, will escort the remains to Rural cemetery.

FALL RIVER.

Henry Tetrault, alias Nichols, was arrested night of 3d at his home on Snell street, charged with adultery. Ten years ago in Augusta, Me., Tetrault was married to an estimable woman by Rev. Fr. Murphy. He deserted his wife and went to Norwich, Ct., where, under the name of Nichols, he met and marrier a divorced woman named Cross. His first wife, who had heard of the affair, went to Fall River a short time ago, and obtained work in the mill where he was employed. She tracked him to his home and the police took him into custody. It is very probable that a charge of bigamy will be preferred against him.

Richard Wamsley was struck by an engine at the Eagle street crossing of the Old Colony road Saturday night and seriously injured. He is at the hospital of the Good Samaritan.

MANSFIELD.

Mansfield was visited Saturday night by the worst fire it has had for a number of years. The large machine bakery of G. E. Bailey & Sons, together with a large barn close by, was totally destroyed, and a cottage house owned by George Bailey was so badly burned that it will have to be rebuilt. The loss is estimated at $20,000, and there is no insurance. The fire is said to have been started by a spark from a locomotive.

EXPELLED FROM HIS NATIVE LAND.

Interesting Case of An American Citizen in Austria.

Washington, June 5.—The volume of "Foreign Relations" for 1892, just published by the state department, contains an account of the case of Leon Spitzer, a naturalized American citizen who returned to his native land, Austria, and was expelled from that country. The Austrian minister of foreign affairs claimed that Spitzer had emigrated from Austria to escape military duty; that his expulsion was in the interest of public order; that every state has a right to expel foreigners for reasons, and that the question whether and when reasons for such expulsion exists can be judged only by an international point of view. This accords with the views expressed by Justice Gray in delivering the recent decision of the United States supreme court on the Chinese exclusion act. United States Minister Grant protested in vain that Spitzer's expulsion was in violation of the treaty of 1870 between the United States and Austria.

Home Again.

NEW YORK, June 5.—Jefferson Coolidge, ex-minister to Paris, and family, arrived here yesterday on the steamer La Bourgogne.

ON TRIAL.

(Continued from First Page.)

12 men have passed upon the question of her guilt or innocence, clearly betokened that her health and strength are, unimpaired, and if appearances are indicative, she is in even a better condition, both mentally and physically, than at the time of her arraignment before Judge Blaisdell. The impression has been freely entertained that the case would never come to trial, and that something in the nature of a confession would forestall court proceedings, though it is difficult at this time to determine upon what such theories were based.

It is evident that the case is to be

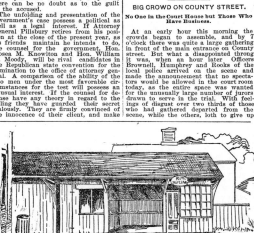

THE EVENING STANDARD'S HEADQUARTERS,
Where Stenographers and Typewriters are Busy.

stubbornly contested every inch of the way as it drags out its weary length. In no criminal trial of recent years has there been arrayed a brighter aggregation of legal lights and their efforts will be by no means the least interesting or important feature of the trial. The government's case will be based upon circumstantial evidence and the effort will be to prove Lizzie's exclusive opportunity to commit the crime to the satisfaction of a jury which will be instructed to give the prisoner the benefit of every doubt. Exclusive opportunity as contemplated in the government's case means that Lizzie is the only person to whom the opportunity to butcher Andrew J. Borden and his wife at the time and place they were so foully murdered presented itself and, if proven, there can be no doubt as to the guilt of the accused.

The unfolding and presentation of the government's case possess a political as well as a legal interest. If Attorney General Pillsbury retires from his position at the close of the present year, as his friends maintain he intends to do, the counsel for the government, Hon. Hosea M. Knowlton and Hon. William H. Moody, will be rival candidates in the Republican state convention for the nomination to the office of attorney general. A comparison of the ability of the two men under the peculiar circumstances for the test will possess an unusual interest. If the counsel for defense have any theory in regard to the killing they have guarded their secret jealously. They are firmly convinced of the innocence of their client, and make the claim that the government cannot show "exclusive opportunity," and believe that there was nothing to prevent an unknown and mysterious villain from stealthily entering the house, accomplishing his purpose, while Lizzie was at the barn and Bridget in her room, and as stealthily departing. The government will bring forward as a motive not only money, but revenge as well. The government will introduce evidence tending to show that the relations between Lizzie and her stepmother were far from pleasant, and that she had come to believe that her father would leave the major portion of his estate to the woman she had cause to despise.

The prosecution will claim that the killing of the father was incidental to the putting of the mother out of the way in a horrible manner. That the father's concern at the non-appearance of his wife after his return from his trip about the city, on that fateful day, was what led to his butchery, and was believed by Lizzie to be necessary to escape detection in the first deed.

The defense will insist that Lizzie Borden is as innocent as the unborn babe of any complicity in any way, and will combat every theory of the prosecution, fully realizing the tremendous responsibility resting upon them to conserve in

HEALTH RESTORED.

Kickapoo Indian Sagwa Cures a Severe Stomach Trouble.

Gains Thirty Pounds in Weight.

Kickapoo Indian Sagwa has been a good friend to me. In the Spring of 1892 I **Cured Me of Gastritis,** from which I had been a sufferer for over a dozen years and had vainly sought relief both from the medical profession and various remedies.

When I began taking Kickapoo Indian Sagwa I was all run down. After taking the medicine a short time I **grew Stronger, Regained my Appetite,** and **Increased my Weight,** gaining over Thirty Pounds in a few months, and I have never had any recurrence of my troubles. It is only cured the Gastritis, but improved my General Health.

It gives me great pleasure to say a good word for Kickapoo Indian Sagwa and Endorse its Curative Powers. THOS. P. FLANAGAN, Charlestown, Mass.

Kickapoo Indian Sagwa,
$1 Per Bottle, 6 Bottles for $5.
Sold by All Druggists and Dealers.

---

every way the interests of the client in whose innocence they have the most implicit belief, and whose life it may be in their hands.

Early Astir.

Those in charge of the arrangements for the trial of Lizzie Borden were astir early this morning, looking into every detail and satisfying themselves that nothing necessary had been lost sight of in the bustle and activity incidental to the last week of preparation for this greatest event in the criminal history of Bristol county. From an early hour the incessant click of the telegraph instruments in the shed in the rear of the court house told plainly that the newspaper representatives were already busily plying their pencils and that the latest details were being spread broadcast to the millions of readers throughout the country who are eagerly waiting to receive them. Despite the limited means at the disposal of the

Hon. George D. Robinson,
Counsel for Defense.

arrived, accompanied by Sheriff Wright. Philip King drove the party to the court house.

Two minutes later the prisoner arrived in Kirby & Hicks' new coupe in charge of Abraham Lee. Beside Miss Borden sat Deputy Sheriff Kirby. He has been assigned to this duty during the trial. As she passed up the concrete walk the crowd separated, and when she alighted the many hundreds at the Court street entrance watched every movement.

At 11.05 o'clock the bell in the tower on the court house rang out the tidings that the court had come in, and the beginning of this famous trial was inaugurated.

The Busy Deputy Sheriffs.

Deputy Sheriffs Kirby of this city and Lincoln of Raynham are guarding the front door and Deputy Sheriff Cobb of Mansfield is in charge of the west door. Deputy Sheriff Spooner has his stand at the foot of the stairs at the rear of the corridor leading to the court room above, and promptly challenges all comers, lest perchance some one who has eluded the vigilance of the other officers make to gain entrance through this avenue, and there are more imposters than one would imagine. Several young men informed him with considerable assurance that they were representatives of the press, but retired in confusion when their tickets were demanded. After the jury is impaneled it will be in charge of Deputy Sheriff John W. Nickerson of New Bedford and Deputy Sheriff Russell Lincoln of Raynham. Frank H. Burke, the official reporter

---

THIRD DISTRICT COURT.

Borden, J.

Monday, June 5.

The attractions at this court this morning were so light as compared with those at the superior court, that the attendance fell off to a marked degree and not even the case against Rosa Francis Bourbo for keeping a disorderly house at 37 Hillman street could raise a ripple of excitement or interest among the small audience. Rosa pleaded not guilty and asked for a continuance until Wednesday next, which was granted.

Max Abrahamson and Marien Solen pleaded guilty of peddling without a license and were each fined $15, which they paid.

Paul Champgay pleaded guilty of allowing minors to frequent his pool room, 422 Purchase street, without the written consent of their parents, and paid a fine of $10.

Michael J. Shea and John Moore were each sent up for three months for drunkenness and appealed.

Daniel J. McGurk for drunkenness was given 60 days and appealed.

Thomas Seddon for a similar offense got six months, and took his medicine without a murmur.

MEMORIAL SERVICE.

There was a very large attendance at the memorial service held last evening in the South Mission chapel. The chapel was tastefully decorated with flags and bunting. Two small flags draped the portrait of the sainted Dennison. The Grand Army was well represented. Sergeant Carney executed a hearty welcome and his fine rendering of "Soldier, Rest," was one of the leading features of the evening. The closing number of the programme, "The Army Canteen," was most effectively recited by Mr. Freeman Luce. Among those who took part in the service were Lizzie and Jennie Allen, the latter giving "The Old Blue Coat the Soldier Wore;" Miss Maggie Watson, who sang "The Star-Spangled Banner," and recited "Barbara Frietchie;" Miss Jennie Frates, who sang "Only a Picture," and recited "The Roll Call;" Miss Beatrice Carter, who gave "Left on the Battlefield;" Miss Nannie Farnham, singing "The Blue and the Gray;" Mrs. L. Chadwick, "The Boys Who Wore the Blue Are Turning Gray;" Mr. T. C. Robbins, "Relic of the War;" Mrs. S. Carter, who sang "The Vacant Chair;" Mrs. Taylor, reading, "The Silent Grand Army;" Mrs. E. Kimball, "Decoration Day;" Mrs. T. C. Robbins, who sang "The Faded Coat of Blue;" Miss Lizzie Durant, who gave "Reminiscences of the War;" Mrs. Howland, who recited a selection from the history of the war.

Mrs. T. C. Robbins, on whom devolved mainly the preparation for the service, must have been greatly pleased with the evening's success.

UNCALLED FOR LETTERS.

The following is the list of uncalled for letters remaining in the post office June 5th:

Gents' List—Alfred E. Bird, Milford Bruette, Elwin L. Braley, Pierre Boutin, Emile Cabana, Manoel Cabrae Caulisto, H. A. Cook, John F. Clapp, Michael Cowan, Joseph Eams, Captain Albert Ellis, Seabow Frunisee, Placeds Gautreau, Eugene Genereau, Horace George, Thilesphore Goselin, John Gordan, Charles A. Godfrey, W. H. Holliston, Joseph Nenoad, Owen Larkin, Herbert Manchester, John Mc Donnold, John McManus, E. W. Parson, A. J. Stanley, Philander Shaw, D. Springer, Emanerelle Satimeli, M. Silva, Paul Therrien.

Ladies' List—Mrs. Nellie Ashley, Mrs. T. Clarke, Miss Elly Crowley, Miss Marlquinhas Coelho, Mrs. Arthur Coutoin, Kate Green, Elizabeth C. M. Gifford, Mrs. H. O. Larch, Miss Mary Hurbert, Mrs. Annie McGurk, Mrs. Eugenie Penbero, Miss Alice Richardson, Mrs. Matilda Layeux, Miss Etta L. Smith, Mrs. Wild, Emily Zola.

FAIRHAVEN.

A vessel load of pipe for the water works left Burlington, N. J., May 31st, and is expected to arrive here today. This is one third of all pipe to be sent, and after the second vessel comes the work will commence. A pumping station will be built the first thing, and an engine has already been contracted for.

William E. Ellis, who was bound over in the third district court Saturday under the bastardly act for the superior court, applied to Town Clerk Tappan for a marriage license this morning, and proceedings will therefore be quashed.

Some of the Fairhaven people, it seems, are not disposed to assist the Improvement association and the benefactors of the town in beautifying the streets by planting elm trees. There is one case on the corner of Main and Union streets where trees have been planted for the past three years, and have been taken up dead every spring. The town officials have "caught on" that somebody in that quarter has been dosing the elms, and this year they planted a sickly looking tree, which it will be a mercy to kill. This is one of the only instance where the trees have been killed, though in most instances they are carefully protected by abutters.

Rev. Dorrell Lee has accepted his call to the Congregational church, and will preach his first pastoral sermon July 2.

Rev. Mr. Whitney, of Cambridge, preached at the Unitarian church yesterday, and made a most favorable impression with the members of the congregation. He may be given a call.

Mrs. N. C. Alger is to deliver a course of ten lectures in Vermont towns. Her subject will be "Missions."

A petition is in circulation for a private way from the Sconticut Neck road to West island to accommodate the summer cottagers, which it is expected will soon locate there. Horace Crowell spent Sunday on the island.

VINEYARD HAVEN.

Mrs. W. S. Woods of Nashville, Tenn., widow of the late Chief Justice Woods, accompanied by her son, has arrived and taken rooms at the Tashmoo, to remain during the entire season.

The many friends of Rev. John N. Jenkins will regret to learn of the death of his wife, which occurred on Thursday last at Madison, S. D., where they reside. Rev. Mr. Jenkins is a son of Foster H. Jenkins of Vineyard Haven.

Mrs. E. L. Richardson of Framingham has arrived and taken possession of her cottage for the summer.

SOUTH DENNIS.

The North High School team of this town crossed bats again with the South High Schools Saturday, June 3, the result being a second victory for the latter, with a score of 13 to 12. The weather was fine and attendance large. The game was fought sharply, and the crowd followed it enthusiastically to the close.

The Accident to the Kaiser Wilhelm.

Genoa, June 5.—The accident to the steamer Kaiser Wilhelm II turns out to have been very serious, and will entail heavy loss to the owners or underwriters. She sank alongside her wharf just as she was ready to sail for New York. Part of the cargo will be saved in a much damaged condition.

Electric Bitters.

This remedy is becoming so well known and so popular as to need no special mention. All who have used Electric Bitters sing the same song of praise. A purer medicine does not exist and it is guaranteed to do all that is claimed. Electric Bitters will cure all diseases of the liver and kidneys, will remove pimples, boils, salt rheum and other affections caused by impure blood. Will drive malaria from the system and prevent as well as cure all malarial fevers. For cure of headache, constipation and indigestion try Electric Bitters. Entire satisfaction guaranteed, or money refunded. Price 50 cents and $1.00 per bottle at H. A. Blackmer's drug store, 215 Purchase street, or North.

NOW TAKES MARITAL VOWS.

Former Sister of Mercy Weds a Brockton Physician.

Waterbury, Conn., June 5.—An event which excites much interest in Catholic circles in this state is the marriage of Dr. Thomas P. Conlon of Brockton, Mass., and Miss Lulu Wilcox, which is to take place in New York today.

About a year ago Miss Wilcox surprised those of her friends who were not aware of her intention by renouncing her vows as a sister of the order of mercy and retiring from Mt. St. Joseph's convent at Hartford. She had spent 10 years in that well known religious and educational institution. Miss Wilcox was a convert to the Catholic church, and it was assumed by many that in laying aside her religious robes she would return to her first religious belief. Miss Wilcox's course did not justify the assumption.

The vows taken by the sisters of mercy are not perpetual, and when Sister Calixtus after mature deliberation decided that life in the world was more to her tastes and desires than that of a recluse, it needed only the recommendation of Bishop McMahon to secure from the pope a release from these vows. Miss Wilcox's well known talent as a musician in all probability suggested the rumor, after her retirement from the convent that she was to adopt an operatic career. Nothing was further from the young lady's intention. Her life on re-entering the world has been almost as quiet as the days she passed at Mt. St. Joseph's. For several months she resided with her mother at Hartford, and her evident desire to avoid notoriety or even attention was universally respected. That she is esteemed as a woman is attested by her popularity with the sisters and pupils of the convent.

Miss Wilcox is wealthy in her own right.

The romance in Miss Wilcox's life recalls a no less interesting romance in the life of her mother. That lady first married a man named Tiffany, but a few years later she secured a divorce from him and married a Mr. Wilcox. At the end of a few years she secured a divorce and re-married Mr. Tiffany.

Later still she secured a divorce from Mr. Tiffany and married Mr. Wilcox for the second time.

A BRUTAL NOBLEMAN.

Outrageous Assault by an Austrian Count on the Race Track.

Vienna, June 5.—Considerable dissatisfaction has been aroused in aristocratic circles here by the action of Count Zdenko Kinsky at the race course yesterday morning. It appears that the count, who is the owner of a number of race horses, became involved in a dispute with his trainer. The count was on horseback, and, infuriated with the trainer, he drove the animal at him, the horse knocking the man down and trampling upon him. After the horse had passed over the prostrate trainer, the count wheeled about and again rode over him. The trainer was very seriously injured. As yet the count has not been arrested. The details of the quarrel are not known.

Oldest Son of Veteran.

The "oldest son of a veteran" in the United States is said to be John E. Mills of Bradford, Mass., who is seventy-nine years old. His father, who was principal musician in the First United States Infantry, though nearly eighty years old when the war broke out, was assigned to active duty, and was commissioned second lieutenant by President Lincoln. John E. Mills, his son, enlisted at the outbreak of the war, and had three sons who enlisted with him, so that three generations of the family saw service at the same time in the rebellion.

PERSONAL.

Ex-Adjutant General Kelton, governor of the Soldiers' Home at Washington, is dying from cerebral hemorrhages. He cannot live more than a day or two.

Amos Barnes of the Brunswick, Boston, has given $250 to aid in the erection of a statue at East Lebanon, N. H., and will furnish a carpet for it when completed.

Rev. Daniel E. Land of Lisbon, N. H., attended the Memorial day oration at Gilmanton Iron works. Mr. Land was born and lived a slave at Norfolk, Va., until he was 14 years of age, when he escaped into the Union lines.

Mgr. Satolli is to be invited to be present at the celebration this summer of the 50th anniversary of the Pittsburg Roman Catholic diocese. Cardinal Gibbons, Archbishop Ryan and many other church dignitaries are expected to be present.

Robert T. Lincoln, ex-minister to England, returned to his home in Chicago Wednesday, and will resume his law practice. Mr. Lincoln said that night that he was entirely out of politics, and had no longing except to pass the remainder of his life as a private citizen.

It is reported that the library of manuscripts and other historical antiquities collected by Hubert H. Bancroft in preparing his Pacific coast histories has been sold to the University of Chicago for $80,000. The collection was offered to congress for $50,000, but it was refused.

THE SENATE COMMITTEE on immigration seems to be digging to some purpose in some directions and perhaps may explain how some of our gold gets out of the country. The other day a question pro pounded by Senator Hill brought out the interesting information that Italian laborers in America send home to their relatives in Italy not less than $20,000,000 a year. One Italian banker of New York testified that he alone had been sending away for his clients about $4,000,000 a year, but owing to the money stringency he would forward not much over $1,000,000 this year. The $20,000,000 referred to seems to be sent through bankers in New York only, and while it probably represents the bulk of the amount sent away, does not represent it all. The evidence also developed the fact that contract laborers arrive at this port every year, notwithstanding the law which is supposed to govern that matter.

Oculists profess to have discovered a connection between wood pavements and ophthalmia. It is said that the gaseous emanations from the pavement are very injurious to the organs of vision.

A club of amateur shoplifters in Vienna was found to have secreted queer things of no earthly use to them, like hardware, mathematical instruments, prayer books and the like. None of them were needy.

Interesting experiments on the sense of taste in ants have been made by H. Devaux. Among other results, says Nature, he has found that Lasius flavus, while fond of sugar dislikes saccharine. The ants swarmed around sugar laid out for them, but turned away from saccharine as soon as they had tasted it. Even sugar became unpleasant to them when it was mixed with saccharine. It seems, therefore, that sweetness is not the only quality which attracts them to sugar.

Professor Huxley says that the bottom of the Atlantic ocean is one of the widest and most even plains in the world. If the sea was drained off, a wagon might be driven from Valentina, on the west coast of Ireland, to Trinity Bay, in Newfoundland. From Valentina the road would lie down hill for about 200 miles, to a point at which the bottom is now covered by 1,700 fathoms of sea water. Then would come the central plain, more than 1,000 miles wide, the inequalities of the surface of which would be hardly perceptible though the depth of water upon it now varies from 10,000 to 15,000 feet.

General Directions in Painting

are to see that no paint is put over a moist or even damp surface. To have thin coats of paint applied instead of thick. Chilton Paint should be thinned with the best raw linseed oil. Many people think there is little or no difference in linseed oil. The Chilton Paint company, in buying oil, obtain only the best brands from people who have a reputation of buying the best and cleanest flaxseed, and allowing their oil to settle. By this means the oil is clean and can be classed as Strictly Pure. Chilton Paint is now covered by 1,700 fathoms of sea water. Then would come the central plain, more than 1,000 miles wide, the inequalities of the surface of which would be hardly perceptible though the depth of water upon it now varies from 10,000 to 15,000 feet.

---

county commissioners the arrangements for the telegraphic dissemination of the happenings at the court house are really admirable. The horse shed in the rear of the court house has been floored and divided into three compartments. In the west end are the quarters of the Postal Telegraph company, which are also the headquarters of the Boston Herald. The middle compartment is devoted to the Western Union and has eight instruments installed, while the office to the east is that of the Standard and Associated Press. Next signs designate the various offices and the interior arrangements in each office are similar, there being shelves extending around three sides of the room, with plenty of comfortable chairs.

After the jury is impaneled it will be in charge of Deputy Sheriff John W. Nickerson of New Bedford and Deputy Sheriff Russell Lincoln of Raynham. Frank H. Burke, the official reporter

Hosea M. Knowlton,
District Attorney, Senior Counsel for State.

It is understood that the court will adjourn at an early hour to allow the justices to return home for the Sunday following, and that the jury will visit Fall River and make an inspection of the Borden house, where the tragedy occurred. A special car will be secured for the use of the jury.

Miss Emma Borden arrived from Fall River this morning, and will remain with friends in the city.

Police Regulations.

Officer Humphrey guards the passageway to the rear entrance. The police regulations are excellent, and today only those having business in the court house or on the premises are permitted to enter the inclosure. What interest the crowd could find in looking on at those permitted on the grounds is difficult to imagine, but there they stood for hours, watching every move made by sheriff or newspaper representative.

That there will be plenty of work for the newspaper men assigned to the trial goes without saying. Many of them are armed to have their dinners sent up to them at the noon hour.

Yesterday morning Bridget Sullivan, the domestic in the Borden family, who will figure conspicuously in the trial as a witness, attended mass at St. Lawrence church.

Joseph Howard, Jr.

of the Norfolk county courts, is in charge of the stenographers, and he is assisted by Messrs. William B. Wright, W. H. Haskell, C. E. Barnes of Boston. Messrs. A. M. Dollard, Cushing and Ross and Mrs. W. H. Haskell, all of Boston, are the official typewriters to whom the stenographic notes are being dictated.

THE COURT ROOM SCENE.

Prisoner Entered with a Steady Step and Without Hesitation.

The jurors were early in their seats and they filled the entire space usually allotted to spectators as well as the jury seats on both sides of the court room. There was a large attendance of the members of the Bristol county bar and seated within the rail were some of its most distinguished members. Judge B. H. Bennett was one of the first to arrive and busied himself while waiting for the appearance of the prisoner in perusing a newspaper. Minister Buck was in his seat in front of the prisoner's dock a good half hour before the time announced for the court proceedings. As early as 10 o'clock the newspaper seats were occupied by the representatives of the papers who had been fortunate enough to secure seats, and it is doubtful if a more notable array of newspapers writers were ever assembled in any one place. Joe Howard, the veteran journalist, who has probably attended more notable murder trials during the past 30 years, including those of Mrs. Surratt and the Malleys for the killing of Jennie Cramer, than any other newspaper man alive, was the observer of all observers and the cynosure of all eyes. His individuality crops out in spite of himself, and he was especially noticeable as being the only man in the court room who had utterly disregarded conventionality and appeared in genuine summer apparel. He represents the Boston Globe and the New York Recorder.

Among other bright lights of the newspaper world present was noticed Julian Ralph, the famous New York Sun correspondent, with a reputation for brilliant achievement as wide as the world. Mr. Caldwell, whose articles descriptive of the arraignment of Lizzie Borden at Fall River, which attracted wide spread attention at the time of their publication, is representing the New York Herald.

John W. Carberry is representing the Boston Globe, and he is accompanied by L. F. Grant and Bert Poole, staff artists.

Judges and Prisoner Arrive.

At 10.55 o'clock the presiding justices

TELEGRAPH OFFICES AT THE COURT HOUSE.

the idea of getting a seat remained about. Among these were three women who had got an early start and had the best places in line when Officers Brownell and Rooks furnished the information which was so disappointing. Then some of the more venturesome resorted to the press dodge, but again they were left, for they hadn't the necessary piece of pasteboard which was a guarantee of admission.

Julian Ralph.

(Continued on Fourth Page.)

BIG CROWD ON COUNTY STREET.

No One in the Court House but Those Who Have Business.

At an early hour this morning the crowds began to assemble, and by 7 o'clock there was quite a large gathering in front of the main entrance on County street. But what a disappointed throng it was, when an hour later Officers Brownell, Humphrey and Rooks of the local police arrived on the scene and made the announcement that no outsiders would be allowed in the court room today, as the entire space was wanted for the unusually large number of jurors drawn to serve in the trial. With feelings of disgust over two thirds of those who had gathered departed from the scene, while the others, loth to give up

---

NICHOLS & DAMON,

F. L. SOWLE & CO.,

Moynan & Co.

Importing Retailers,

UNION ST. PURCHASE ST.

Going on Sale Today.

For Tennis and Outing Suits—One case of Bedford Cords, white grounds, with colored stripes, just as handsome as the all-wool goods at 50c. per yard, our price on this lot is **15c. per yard**

French Cotton Crepes.

Just what's so much wanted, all the desirable colors are here, Heliotrope, Red, Blue, Yellow, Cream, Pink, Green, etc. These are regular 20c. quality, we now offer at **15c. per yard**

In Linen Department.

Commencing today we will sell all our 72-inch heavy full bleached Damasks, regular $1.25 and $1.35 qualities, at **$1.00 per yard**

10 pieces extra heavy Cream Table Damask, never sold below 75c. per yard, now at **50c. per yard**

50 dozen full bleach Damask Towels with deep knotted fringe and fancy borders, regular value 25c., now for **19c. each**

Corsets and Muslin Underwear.

These departments are now replete in all the different lines of goods, and in all qualities from the cheapest to the high priced. Some favorites in corsets are:

Thomson's Glove Fitting in White, Drab and Black, at any of these prices according to quality, **$1.00, $1.25, $1.50 and $1.75**

The ever popular S. C. Corsets in White, Drab or Black at prices from **$1.00 to $2.50**

Summer Corsets in different styles at **49c., 75c. and $1.00**

Ladies' Gowns, trimmed with insertion and Hamburg edging, **50c.**

Ladies' Gowns, in finer qualities and more elaborately trimmed, **75c., $1.00, $1.25, etc.**

Corset Covers, V neck, made from fine Lonsdale and trimmed with very fine Hamburg edging, **50c. and 75c.**

Boys' Clothing Department.

This is the place where you find all the latest styles for the boys at prices the lowest.

Boys' "HARD WEAR" Suits with a pair of pants extra for **$1.39**

Extra good value in Boys' School Suits, all sizes, at **$1.98**

Jersey Suits, trimmed with braid and sailor collar, all wool, and our price only **$2.50**

Boys' Suits in a dozen other styles at prices from **$1.00 to $10.00**

Boys' Hats and Caps of all kinds, suitable for Summer wear, at very reasonable prices.

Shirt Waists for boys, all sizes, at **25c., 39c., 48c. and 98c.**

SPECIAL REDUCED PRICES

In Garments, Dress Goods, Millinery, Kitchen Furnishings, Etc., Etc.

We want you to see for yourself, so PLEASE COME IN.

Moynan & Co.

UNION ST. PURCHASE ST.

The Evening Standard.

NEW BEDFORD, MASS.

MONDAY EVENING, JUNE 5.

THREE EDITIONS DAILY.

No. 87 Union Street.

PUBLISHED BY

E. ANTHONY & SONS.

INCORPORATED.

—TERMS—

Six Dollars a Year; Three Dollars for Six Months, in advance; Single Copies Two Cents.

ORDER THE EVENING STANDARD TO YOUR VACATION ADDRESS.

Mailed direct from this office for any length of time desired; 50 cents a month, including postage.

TEN PAGES.

This Evening's Issue Consists of Ten Pages, and Every Patron is Entitled to that Number.

The most important criminal trial ever held in Bristol county commenced in this city today. It is a trial for one of the most shocking crimes known to the law, a double parricide, and to add to its intensity the accused person is a woman. These circumstances have given it an extraordinary interest, and the proceedings as they appear in the daily papers will be read with the closest attention far and near. It will not be within the province of the press to comment on these proceedings during the progress of the trial. Its duty is confined to giving a full and accurate report of what is said and done every day; and in this the Standard does not propose to be outdone by any of its contemporaries. It has made arrangements which will enable it to give every day an exact report of all that occurs up to the hour of the issue of the regular editions, and a later issue will carry them up to the time of the daily adjournment of the court. The public may be assured that there will be no better or fuller account of the trial than that contained in the daily Standard, and the Republican (weekly) Standard will reprint them up to date.

There is a difference of opinion between the Springfield Union and one of its correspondents with regard to the method of conducting the Republican gubernatorial canvass. The Union thinks the names of candidates should be presented now and discussed until the convention meets. The correspondent would have the state committee consult with the leaders of the party, the very men talked of as candidates, and decide on some one who they believe is the strongest man, and then present his name to the people, and when the convention meets to nominate let the committee present the same name to the convention, and the delegates would vote unanimously for the name presented, which he thinks would be a better way than to have two or three names presented to the convention, and then have a fight over which one should be nominated.

But does not this smack a little too much of Tammany methods, by which a few bosses dictate the action of the party conventions? Republican opinion in this state would hardly be willing that a state committee should dictate a nomination for governor, though it is conceivable that it might be best in some emergencies. Nor is the Union's plan much better. Discussing candidates means setting up Mr. A in one section of the state, Mr. B in another, Mr. C in third, and so on. And although Messrs. A, B and C may be all of them very good men, neither one of them is likely to show any remarkable superiority over the other. The friends of each would go into the convention and do their best to prevent the success of the others; and that is what seems to be the trouble with the Republican party of Massachusetts. We haven't any panacea of our own, but we feel convinced that, as we have said before, if the party wants to elect a governor it must take up some man who can go before the people in a campaign and produce a stronger impression on them than either of its last two candidates did. In this we do not intend any disparagement of the personal merits of those estimable gentlemen. But they failed to impress the people.

In this country fortunate editors get consulships or ambassadorships, which are supposed to carry something substantial with them. In England they have to be satisfied with knighthood, an honor which is doubtless flattering to their vanity, but has no emoluments, and entails no expense on the public treasury. An American is generally satisfied with a military title like colonel or general, very often self-bestowed.

The charter of Farnham Post, G. A. R., in New York, was revoked not for passing resolutions in regard to pensions, but for violating the rules in not submitting them for approval before promulgation. As soldiers the members should have known that discipline must be maintained. The Lafayette post obeyed the rules in forwarding similar resolutions to General Weissart for approval, which was promptly given.

To the presence of unusual quantities of ice in the Atlantic may perhaps be attributed the unpleasantness of the present season. Unlike that recorded by Emerson when every wind brought a clear sky or the smell of a clover field, whichever way it blows now it brings dampness, coolness and grippy sensations.

Seventy-five children in Hingham have collected 68,000 caterpillar beds, representing at least 15,000,000 caterpillars. This is a good deal better than if they had been destroying birds' eggs.

The line of plain Sheila Portieres at Sisson & Ring's, New Bank Building, 37 Purchase street, are marked at prices lower than this class of goods were ever sold before. Have Sisson & Ring cleanse your lace curtains.

ON TRIAL.

(Continued from Third Page.)

The Boston Herald is represented by Messrs. Billings and Brennan, and with them is Mr. Blair, the artist, whose cartoons in the Sunday Herald are famous.

"Amy Robsart," Mrs. Worwich, represents the Boston Post, with "Norman" Ritchie, the Post's artist.

There are upwards of 30 other newspaper men in the court room, besides quite a number on the outside who were unable to gain entrance.

Mr. Rosenfield is here for the Providence Journal, with W. H. Loomis, its artist, and W. F. Greenough, a well known correspondent of the Standard, and Mr. Foley are representing the Associated Press.

District Attorney Knowlton was in the court room before 10 o'clock, and by his manner one would never mistrust that he was about to enter upon the trial of anything other than an ordinary or every day criminal court case.

Colonel Adams was the first of the counsel for the defense to enter the court room, and after casting a careless glance around commenced to chat pleasantly with acquaintances.

It was just precisely 11 o'clock when the ripple of excitement that passed around the room announced Lizzie's arrival, and an instant later she entered the door, preceded by Deputy Sheriff Kirby, and took her seat in the dock. She walked steadily and without hesitation and her bearing was in no way different than at her previous appearances before the public since her accusation of having put her father and mother to death. There was nothing to indicate that she was enduring the mental and physical suffering her friends have spoken of. She was attired in a new dress of black mohair cut in the latest style, with leg of mutton sleeves, and which fitted her by no means inferior form to perfection. Upon her head was a jaunty black lace hat trimmed with rosettes of blue velvet and a blue feather. She appeared wholly unmindful of the fact that every one's gaze was directed toward her, and was apparently altogether unembarrassed. Shortly after her entrance, Lawyer Jennings glided into the room and nodded pleasantly to Lizzie. District Attorney Moody had arrived a few minutes before and busied himself looking over some papers which appeared to possess a deep interest for him.

Ex-Governor Robinson was the last of the counsel to put in an appearance. After shaking hands with several of those within the rail with whom he was acquainted he stepped forward to grasp Lizzie by the hand, and a smile of recognition overspread her features for an instant and then disappeared. They conducted a conversation for a few minutes, but it was soon interrupted by the announcement of "the court."

Two handsome bouquets of pinks, one pink in color and the other red, adorned the judges' bench, and upon these Lizzie's eyes seemed to rest unconsciously.

THE FORMAL PROCEEDINGS.

Rev. M. C. Julien Prays That Soul Innocence be Revealed and Guilt Exposed.

At precisely 11 28 o'clock Chief Justice Albert Mason, who will preside, and Judges Blodgett and Dewey entered the court room and took their places.

After the opening of the court by the crier the names of the jurors drawn from which a panel of 12 will be selected to try Miss Borden were called and the jurors responded to their names.

Prayer was offered by Rev. M. C. Julien of this city, who prayed as follows:

"Almighty and all wise God, our Father, we look to thee as the only source of wisdom, as the only source of courage. We pray thee that thou wouldst grant that in entering upon the solemn duties of this court we shall have not only such help as comes from the experiences which pass through the history of the world, but such help as

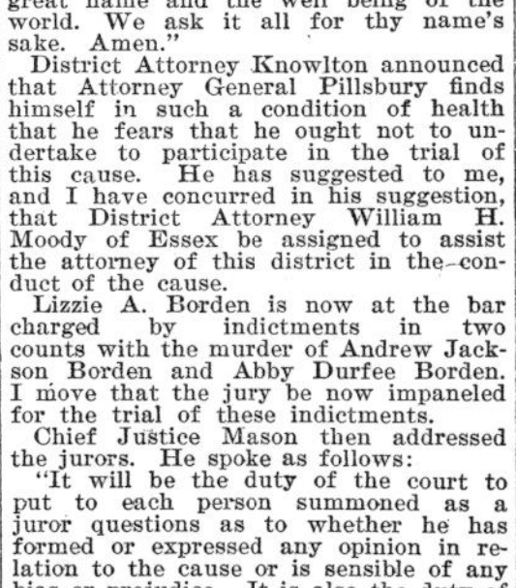

Rev. M. C. Julien.

thou by thy providence will give to thine earthly children. We pray thee that soul innocence may be revealed and guilt exposed to the glory of thine own great name and the well being of the world. We ask it all for thy name's sake. Amen."

District Attorney Knowlton announced that Attorney General Pillsbury finds himself in such a condition of health that he fears that he ought not to undertake to participate in the trial of this cause. He has suggested to me, and I have concurred in his suggestion, that District Attorney William H. Moody of Essex be assigned to assist the attorney of this district in the conduct of the cause.

Lizzie A. Borden is now at the bar charged by indictments in two counts with the murder of Andrew Jackson Borden and Abby Durfee Borden. I move that the jury be now impaneled for the trial of these indictments.

Chief Justice Mason then addressed the jurors. He spoke as follows:

"It will be the duty of the court to put to each person summoned as a juror questions as to whether he has formed or expressed any opinion in relation to the cause or is sensible of any bias or prejudice. It is also the duty of the court to ask each juror if he has any opinions which will prevent him from finding a verdict of guilty in a cause where the crime is punishable by death. It has been said by Chief Justice Shaw and it has never been questioned as law that the statute intends to exclude any person who has made up his mind or formed a judgment in advance, no matter in favor of which side. Still the opinion or judgment must be something more than a vague impression formed from casual conversation with others or from reading abbreviated newspaper reports. It must be such an opinion upon the merits of the question as would be likely to bias or prevent a candid judgment upon a full hearing of the testimony. I desire to call the attention of all those persons who are summoned as jurors to this statement in reference to the opinions to which the statute refers. And I also wish to remind every juror that he will be called to answer these questions under oath, that he must answer them truly, not availing himself of the question to escape unpleasant duty, but must answer them truly and accept what may follow; also with reference to the question as to whether opinions which would preclude one from finding defendant guilty of an offense punishable by death. It is not at all what opinions are entertained with reference to capital punishment, but there are some persons so constituted mentally that they could not sustain a law of the land which they deemed wrong. There are some persons so mentally constituted that they could not declare the simplest axiom of mathematics if it were to follow that death was to be inflicted in consequence of the declaration. If any person thinks and is satisfied that he is so mentally constituted that he cannot find upon evidence that the defendant is guilty of an offense punishable with death then in response to that question he will so answer. But in answering that question as the others each juror will keep in mind that he is answering upon oath."

The complete list of those drawn for juror service follows:

Herbert L. Atherton, Taunton; Willard F. Ashley, Isaac Alger, George A. Austin, Attleboro; Henry B. Almy, Charles N. Allen, New Bedford; Hobart Ames, Oliver Ames, 2d, Easton; William A. Bennett, North Attleboro; Ziba F. Bliss, Ansel O. Burt, Taunton; George P. Bailey, Mansfield; Charles E. Briggs, Attleboro; William F. Butler, Francis A. Booth, Eugene M. Barrows, Bourne S. Bartlett, Gilbert K. Brownell, Ansel G. Baker, New Bedford; Frank M. Bates, Fairhaven; Jeremiah N. Brown, Swanzey; Nathan Clark, Oliver B. Crossman, Taunton; James H. Cobb, Acushnet; Geeorge W. Currien, Frank G. Cole, Attleboro; Jireh W. Clifton, Robert H. Carter, Orville W. Cranston, George A. Cobb, Joseph Chausse, New Bedford; Harry C. Dean, Elihu M. Davis, Ezra Davol, William F. Dean, John W. Dickson, Taunton; George W. Davis, Dartmouth; Thomas Donaghy, Jr., Daniel F. Driscoll, Charles H. Dias, Silas D. Dammon, New Bedford; Albert E. Dean, Berkley; Oscar R. Douglass, Swanzey; T. W. Driscol, Easton; Thomas B. Earle, Westport; Ezekiel P. Francis, John C. Finn, Taunton; David Fisher, Mansfield; Charles F. Forrester, Attleboro; Frank W. Francis, Charles F. Folger, New Bedford; Jason T. Guild, North Attleboro; Dexter F. Goff, Gordon H. Godfrey, Taunton; William Graves, Mansfield; Henry M. Goss, Attleboro; James Grundy, Oliver E. Gifford, New Bedford; Eben S. Grinnell, East Freetown; Edwin Gusher, Raynham; Olney Greene, Seekonk; Augustus O. Hall, North Attleboro; Joseph W. Hathaway, Edmund E. Hill, Louis D. Hodges, George L. Hathaway, Henry A. Hodges, Taunton; John F. Hammett, Acushnet; Josiah G. Horton, Dighton; Gideon Howland, Dartmouth; Harold V. Hopkins, Attleboro; George A. Howe, Joseph W. Hatch, New Bedford; Henry M. Hoxie, Fairhaven; Stephen A. Hathaway, Assonet; Charles F. Hathaway, Swanzey; Gilbert M. Horton, Dexter E. Horton, Jr., Rehoboth; Henry P. Jenney, New Bedford; Henry W. Kenyon, Charles W. Knight,

CONSULTATION OF COUNSEL FOR DEFENSE.

New Bedford; George F. King, Easton; Charles Lamphier, J. O. Leary, Jr., North Attleboro; Augustus Leonard, Mansfield; Dwight F. Lane, Dighton; Harry J. Leach, New Bedford; James A. Lewis, Frederick E. Lawton, Fairhaven; Harrison T. Lincoln, Lloyd S. Lincoln, Norton; Augustus M. Mosher, Westport; Thomas McKeon, Henry B. Macomber, John F. McCarthy, Taunton; George H. Milliken, William J. Mills, Edward M. Murphy, New Bedford; Willard B. Monroe, Rehoboth; George E. Nye, New Bedford; F. William Oesting, New Bedford; George Potter, Westport; Joseph Peltier, Henry N. Pratt, Lyman Palmer, Taunton; Francis H. Pasell, James H. Pease, Frederick Parker, New Bedford; Walter Pease, East Freetown; Charles I. Richards, North Attleboro; Eugene F. Rose, Dighton; Augustus S. Russell, Dartmouth; John Ratcliffe, New Bedford; Otis S. Springer, Herbert K. Sturdy, North Attleboro; Charles L. Seaver, Mansfield; Walter C. Slocum, Dartmouth; Isaac C. Sherman, Ezra J. Swift, Mortimer Searles, Augustus Swift, New Bedford; George E. Smith, Norton; John F. Sharples, Berkley; Elijah Smith, Easton; Philip Thomas, North Attleboro; Leon H. Tingley, Attleboro; Edward S. Taber, Otis Tinkham, John H. Taber, New Bedford; D. B. Tinkham, Easton; Daniel Whalon, Westport; George H. Wheeler, John B. Wade, Simeon A. Wheeler, John T. Williams, George A. Wood, Taunton; George Winslow, Mansfield; Nathan O. Walker, Dighton; Allen H. Wordell, Dartmouth; William H. Willis, Thomas H. Weaver, New Bedford; Albert M. Wilcox, Fairhaven; Cyrus Washburn, Frederick C. Wilbur, Raynham; William Westcott, Seeconk; L. K. Wilber, Easton; Benjamin T. Cundall, George Lynch, John Wilbur, Matthew Costello, Somerset.

The prisoner, in response to her name, stood up and received the instructions of the clerk as to her right of challenge.

Ansel G. Baker, a foreman at the Morse Twist Drill & Machine company, was the first to have his name drawn from the box.

Are you related to the prisoner at the bar? asked Chief Justice Mason.

No sir, replied Mr. Baker.

Have you any interest in the cause about to be tried? was the next question asked. Mr. Baker replied in the negative.

Have you formed any opinion in the case which in your judgment would preclude you from serving as a juror?

To this question Mr. Baker replied: I have, and I do not think any evidence could be introduced which would cause me to change my mind.

Step one side, was the command of Chief Justice Mason.

George Winslow, a rather good-looking man of 45, who hails from Mansfield, was then asked the usual questions. In reply to the question: Have you formed any opinion which would preclude you from serving as a juror? he said: I have not, and then he was turned over to the commonwealth, with whom he also passed muster. He, however, was not so fortunate, or unfortunate, as the case might be, with the defense, for at the request of Mr. Jennings, one of the counsel for the prisoner, he was challenged by Miss Borden, who in a clear and distinct voice, which resounded throughout the court room, said: Challenge.

George Potter of Westport walked calmly to the front, was sworn, and answered the usual interrogatives. He had formed no opinion, was not biased, and held no opinion which would preclude him from serving as a juror. Passing the commonwealth, he was also accepted by the defense, and was then sworn in by Clerk Borden as the first juror in the Borden trial. Mr. Potter took his seat in the jury box on the north side of the court room.

Mortimer Searles of New Bedford, a dealer in rubber stamps, walked to the front in a business-like manner. He had no interest in the case, had formed an opinion, and thought it would be a hard matter to cause him to change his mind.

"Step one side," was again the command of Chief Justice Mason.

William H. Willis of New Bedford, a retired harness maker, was next called to the front, and was likewise sworn. He was put through the same ordeal as the others. Mr. Willis had formed no opinion, and receiving instructions from the chief justice the district attorney said, "We do not challenge."

At this point Mr. Jennings handed Chief Justice Mason a lengthy document, which was read by that gentleman and then submitted to his associates at the bar on the bench.

Then was held a whispered conference between Chief Justice Mason and Mr. Jennings, while the newspaper men perched on the platform, as well as Mr. Knowlton, were kept in blissful ignorance as to what it was all about.

Suffice it to say that that document touched on something concerning Mr. Willis and his ability to serve as a juror, for he was again questioned quite sharply by the chief justice, and some of these questions were decidedly pointed. He denied ever saying that Lizzie Borden was guilty and that he desired to serve on the jury for the purpose of convicting her

Are you a client of the prosecuting officer, Mr. Knowlton? was the question then asked by the chief justice.

"No, sir, I am not," was Mr. Willis' reply.

Mr. Knowlton then arose, and referring to the document submitted to the chief justice, suggested that he should have the right to exercise his privilege in the matter before the court.

Mr. Willis, passing muster, was then turned over to the defense, and again came from the lips of Miss Borden the word "challenge."

The name of Jonah G. Horton, of Dighton, a sunburnt farmer, was then taken from the box.

He passed muster at the hands of the chief justice, and was turned over to the district attorney, who challenged for the commonwealth.

Otis A. Springer, of North Attleboro, was the next person to have his name drawn from the box, and after stepping to the front was ordered to step aside, as his name had not been properly handed to the court.

William F. Dean, of Taunton, had formed no opinion.

The juror stands indifferent," said the chief justice, and after District Attorney Knowlton had consulted with Mr. Moody he said "the commonwealth will not challenge." Then Mr. Jennings, for the prisoner, said "neither does the defense," and Mr. Dean, after being sworn in to serve as a juror, took his seat beside Mr. Potter.

James Grundy of New Bedford had formed no opinion. He was challenged by Lizzie Borden.

Gilbert K. Brownell of New Bedford was called. It was established that he had done jury duty within the limit, having served at the last term, and he was excused.

William Graves of Mansfield said he was 68 years old, was not related to the prisoner or the deceased Andrew J. and Abby Borden, had formed no opinion, was not prejudiced in any way, and knew of nothing to preclude him from rendering a verdict finding the defendant guilty of an offense punishable by death. Mr. Graves was challenged by the government.

John Wilbur of Somerset was not related to the prisoner or the murdered couple, had formed no opinion, was sensible of no prejudice and had no opinion that would prevent him from rendering a candid judgment upon hearing the full evidence. He was accepted and sworn in as a juror by Clerk Borden.

Frederick C. Wilbur of Raynham gave satisfactory answers to the questions put to him by the court, was not challenged by either government or defense and took his place beside the other jurors already impaneled.

Elijah Smith of Easton said that he held opinions that would preclude him from rendering a finding of guilty in an offense punishable by death, notwithstanding the explanation of the court in regard to opinions on the matter of capital punishment. He was excused.

Joseph W. Hatch of New Bedford presented a certificate which was sufficient to excuse him from jury duty, but the certificate was not sworn to. After a consultation by the judges he was allowed to retire.

John F. Staples of Berkley said that he had opinions which would prevent him from giving a candid judgment, and he was ordered to step aside.

Benjamin T. Cundall of Somerset said he was 69 years of age; he had formed no opinion, and was not biased or prejudiced; would be willing to render a verdict of guilty in an offense punishable by death. In answer to a question by the court he said that his eyesight was very poor. He was challenged by the commonwealth.

George H. Wheeler of Taunton had opinions that would preclude him from finding defendant guilty of a crime punishable by death, and was therefore excused.

Lemuel K. Wilbur of Easton was accepted as a suitable person to serve as juror in the case about to be tried, and was sworn in.

Hobart Ames of Easton had formed no opinion, was not sensible of any bias, and had no objection to giving a candid judgment according to the evidence. He was challenged by the government.

Orville W. Cranston of this city had formed and expressed opinions in regard to the guilt or innocence of the accused. He was sensible of bias and prejudiced in the matter. Excused.

Henry P. Jenney had also formed opinions in regard to the case. He was, like Mr. Cranston, sensible of both bias and prejudice, and was likewise excused.

Frank W. Francis of New Bedford was called and stated to the court that he was positive he served as juror in September, 1890, in Fall River. He had no certificate to that effect. The court determined that Mr. Francis should stand aside until after recess.

At this point the court took a recess for dinner until 2 15.

The jurors thus far drawn are as follows: George Potter, Westport; William F. Dean, Taunton; John Wilber, Somerset; Frederick C. Wilber, Raynham; Lemuel K. Wilbur, Easton.

Prayers for the Borden Sisters.

At the morning service in the Central Congregational church in Fall River Sunday the pastor, Rev. W. Walker Jubb, prayed fervently for Miss Lizzie Borden and her sister, Miss Emma Borden, referring to the former as an innocent victim of circumstances, and asking for divine assistance to support them in the ordeal which they were about to face.

THE FIVE JURORS DRAWN.

Appearance of the Men Upon Whom Miss Borden's Life Depends.

George Potter, of Westport, the first juror who passed muster, is a pleasant featured man, apparently about 40 years of age, and if we can judge by appear-

George Potter,
The First Juror Drawn.

ances, is a man who will render a verdict strictly in accordance with the evidence.

William F. Dean, of Taunton, is a man whose hair is plentifully sprinkled with gray, and is evidently about the middle age. He has a searching eye, takes close note of all that takes place about him, and is an interested spectator of all that is transpiring.

John Wilber, of Somerset, is a man whose well tanned features clearly show that he is employed in the open air, and his well whitened locks show that he has well passed his youth. He is of a nervous temperament, and twists his moustache incessantly while listening to the proceedings.

Frederick C. Wilber, of Raynham, is apparently not over 40 years of age. He has a look of determination, and does not bear the appearance of one who could easily be shaken in his opinions after they were first formed.

Lemuel K. Wilbur, of Easton, is a fine looking man of ruddy complexion, and has a face betokening intelligence. He looks like one who would be slow to form an opinion, and having once formed it would maintain it against all comers.

THE PRESIDING JUDGES.

How They Looked to One of the Standard Representatives.

Chief Justice Mason is a man of striking personality, and presides with rare grace. His interrogatories are sharply put and are clearly cut and incisive, yet there is something so suave and reassuring in his manner that the juror or person under examination is immediately put completely at his ease. He possesses wonderful executive ability, and has a way of expediting business without giving it any appearance of unseemly haste.

Justice Blodgett is a mild-featured man, whose face fairly beams with good nature, yet he is completely absorbed in the proceedings, and gives the most earnest attention to all that is transpiring.

Justice Dewey possesses a very distinguished air and a quiet dignity that completely harmonizes with the solemn matter now engrossing his attention. Nothing of importance in the case, no matter how slight, evades his watchfulness, and he takes copious notes of the proceedings.

THEIR OPINIONS KNOWN.

Both Sides Alleged to Have Been Sounding the Views of the Jury Panel.

District Attorney Knowlton and others representing the defense have been busy the past week or ten days gathering the opinions of the men who have been drawn for jury service. It is said that so thorough has the work been that each side knows the opinion of almost every man summoned. The government has been specially thorough in its work, and a man whom its officers do not know the opinion of must either not have one, or he has been more close mouthed than the majority. In getting this information the officers have worked in various ways. Some of the men have been approached by officers in person and have freely said that they did or did not think Lizzie guilty. But most of the information has been obtained second hand.

THE PRISONER'S QUARTERS.

Miss Borden Occupying Matron's Room in Woman's Prison.

A Standard reporter has learned that Lizzie Borden will occupy the matron's room in the jail during the time the trial is in progress. No special arrangements were made in the way of fitting the apartment for Lizzie's use, and even the matron herself was not aware that such arrangements had been made until she had occasion to enter the room and found Lizzie installed there.

Insufferably Hot in Court Room.

During the forenoon the court room was almost insufferably hot and fans were in great demand. Lizzie waved one that had been furnished her by Deputy Sheriff Kirby almost incessantly and seemed to feel the effects of the heat to quite a degree.

TRAINING SHIP ENTERPRISE.

U. S. steamer Enterprise, with the Massachusetts Nautical Training school on board, sailed from this port today for a two weeks' cruise. Of the 14 young men who took the examinations in this city for positions in the school five passed. Commander Merry of the Enterprise has considerable discretion in the matter of the cruise, but it is expected that he will take the ship into Gloucester on or about June 18. She will then go to Boston and have a slight overhauling preparatory to the four months' cruise in foreign waters. It is likely the cadets will make their first public appearance in a body at the dedication of the Farragut statue June 28, when they will parade as infantry with their own band.

CONDENSED LOCALS.

The funeral of the late Captain John D. Sylvia occurred in the Bonney street church yesterday afternoon, and was largely attended. Hev. I. H. Coe conducted the services. After the church service the remains were taken in charge by Eureka lodge, F. & A. M., of which deceased was a member, and headed by Hill's band, the procession took up the march for Rural cemetery. Members of several other Masonic lodges participated. At the grave the exercises were in accordance with the Masonic ritual, and the bearers were Captain Cornelius H. Springer, Captain Charles H. Robbins, Captain Joseph W. Lavers and Captain Prince S. Borden.

Ground was broken this morning for the foundation of Hathaway, Soule & Harrington's new chimney. It will be 75 feet high, 10 feet square at the bottom and 5 feet square at the top. A contract has been placed with the Cunningham Iron Works company of South Boston for a new 150 horse power boiler. It will be put in during the annual shut down which commences July 1.

City officials are being summoned as witnesses to attend the hearing on the Coggeshall street bridge at the City hall on Thursday at 10 o'clock a. m. The public generally will be interested in the special notice.

Jacob Steinman was arrested this morning by Edwin R. Smyth of Boston, agent of the Society for the Prevention of Cruelty to Children, for non-support of his wife. He was later released on bail.

A GOOD PLACE TO STOP

is at our store, if you want to purchase anything in the line of clothing. We have the goods, have more of them, and of better quality, and at

Lower Prices

than at any other store in this county. The bigger the stock, the more room for choice for the buyer. You can take what you want at our store, because we're sure to have it in stock, and won't be obliged to take something else as a substitute. Look at our stock and you'll recognize its superiority; a glance at our price list will demonstrate that we can't be approached, much less undersold. We have suits at $10.00, $12.00 and $15.00.

M. C. SWIFT & SON,

153, 157 and 159 Union St.

NEW BEDFORD, MASS.

Fire at Williamstown.

Williamstown, June 5.—Fires here at 3 30 this morning consumed two barns on Main street, owned by Mrs. John M. Cole. It required a hard fight by the firemen and a large number of spectators to keep the house from burning and rescue the stock and carriages from the barn. The loss is heavy, as the barns and contents were valuable.

Bankers Fail.

Chicago, June 5.—Meadowcroft Bros. & Co., private bankers doing a commercial paper business, closed their doors this morning. The concern was one of the oldest here. Their assets and liabilities are unknown.

Lyman E. Crandall has been appointed receiver.

Fishing Schooner Ashore.

Gloucester, June 5.—Fishing schooner A. T. Gifford, from Grand Bank, ran ashore at Magnolia this morning, and lies in a dangerous position.

Postmaster for New York.

Washington, June 5.—The president has appointed Charles W. Dayton, of New York, to be postmaster of that city.

TO AID THE INDIANS.

Emma C. Sickels Heads the National Indian Land Adjustment League.

There was organized in New York city recently a society which proposes to take a radical departure in the field of Indian philanthrophy. Its chief promoters have had considerable experience on the plains of the west and have not only a practical knowl-

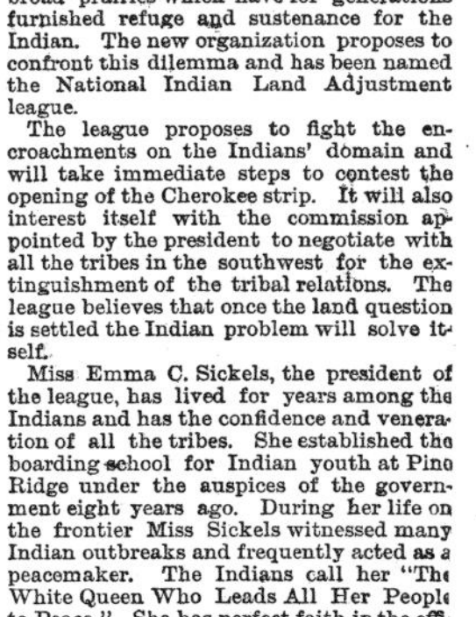

EMMA C. SICKELS.

edge of the situation, but definite plans for the solution of the difficulties which environ the red man. One of the dangers that threaten the existence of poor Lo is the rapid appropriation by white settlers of the broad prairies which have for generations furnished refuge and sustenance for the Indian. The new organization proposes to confront this dilemma and has been named the National Indian Land Adjustment league.

The league proposes to fight the encroachments on the Indians' domain and will take immediate steps to contest the opening of the Cherokee strip. It will also interest itself with the commission appointed by the president to negotiate with all the tribes in the southwest for the extinguishment of the tribal relations. The league believes that once the land question is settled the Indian problem will solve itself.

Miss Emma C. Sickels, the president of the league, has lived for years among the Indians and has the confidence and veneration of all the tribes. She established the boarding school for Indian youth at Pine Ridge under the auspices of the government eight years ago. During her life on the frontier Miss Sickels witnessed many Indian outbreaks and frequently acted as a peacemaker. The Indians call her "The White Queen Who Leads All Her People to Peace." She has perfect faith in the efficacy of education for the civilization of the Indians, but believes that an immediate adjustment of the land difficulty is an urgent necessity.

Concerning one effect of placing Indian children for a temporary term in eastern schools Miss Sickels says: "The eastern schools are valuable for showing white people the capability of Indian youth, but the contrast is very painful when students return to their homes after an absence of three years. The look of desperation which came over the faces of some girls who amid the joy of home coming had forgotten that they must go back to their life in the tepee, with all that meant for them, accounted to a large degree for the fact that those who do go back to barbarism sink to lower depths. They are driven by a desperation born of a knowledge of better things."

Miss Sickels is tall and willowy, with dark complexion and dark hair streaked with gray. She was one of the best horsewomen in the west.

A New Rainmaker.

A European living in the tropical regions of India has invented a novel rain producer. His apparatus consists of a rocket, capable of rising to the height of a mile, containing a reservoir of ether. In its descent a parachutelike attachment opens out, causing the apparatus to descend slowly. At the same time the ether is thrown out in a fine spray. The absorption of heat by the ether is said to lower the temperature of the surrounding air sufficiently to condense the vapor, and hence cause rain.

The Evening Standard.

ESTABLISHED FEBRUARY, 1850.] NEW BEDFORD, TUESDAY, JUNE 6, 1893. TWO CENTS.

HASKELL & TRIPP.

A Big Store
With light in every corner.
A Stock
That will bear looking at, and
Prices
That will bear comparing.

Weather for waists.

Women's percale waists, with the new large sleeves, ruffled front, cuffs. A stylish garment and as good as you expect to pay 75c. for. We ask you only 59c.

The new and very stylish Madras waists have laundered collar and cuffs, and come in pinks, blues and heliotrope shades. Some have a cording of white on collar, cuffs and front. Our prices are $1, $1.25 and $1.50 for these very choice waists.

Excellent silk waists $5 each.

Isn't 52c. worth saving on a gingham dress for the girl?

That's precisely the amount we can help you to save on a special line of gingham dresses to fit girls from six to fourteen years. Not common styles but finest of this season's 12½c. ginghams. Our price 98c. Real value $1.50.

Parasols.

We have a big stock of parasols and we are not making the mistake of trying to see how high a price we can get for them. The season is to be short this year and we have determined to make the prices so attractively low that you can't resist them.

Specials in navy blue sun umbrellas today. "Gloria" cloth, with blue ball handles and cases only $2 each.

"Union" silk with cases to match and plain wood or ball mounted sticks, your choice for $2.50.

Elegant white, cream and black, plain or lace trimmed parasols and many striking novelties await your pleasure. *Glad to show you.*

Sailor Hats.

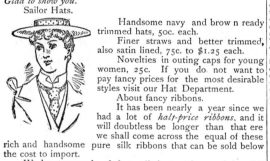

Handsome navy and brown ready trimmed hats, 50c. each.

Finer straws and better trimmed, also satin lined, 75c. to $1.25 each.

Novelties in outing caps for young women, 25c. If you do not want to pay fancy prices for the most desirable styles visit our Hat Department.

About fancy ribbons.

It has been nearly a year since we had a lot of *half-price ribbons*, and it will doubtless be longer than that ere we shall come across the equal of these rich and handsome pure silk ribbons that can be sold below the cost to import.

We have upwards of forty distinct styles, each in a full assortment of fashionable colorings, and it makes a brilliant collection.

One lot all at 19c., worth 33c. a yard.
One lot all at 29c., worth 50c. a yard.

Suppose you don't need these ribbons just at this moment. If you ever trim a house gown, a summer dress or hat, or if you do any sort of fancy work that calls for ribbon decorations they will come in play and you'll be thankful that your attention was called to them when they were selling for about half cost. Extra counter space for this sale.

Belts.

Stylish leather belts as low as 25c.
New leather and metal belts from 25c. to 89c. each.

At the Silk Department.

More of those changeable merveilleux, of which we have had such a wonderful sale, are direct from the looms to our counter.

These colorings:

Navy and cardinal, myrtle and black, cardinal and black, brown and gold, black and gold, brown and gobelin, cardinal and gray, blue and gold. } 22-inch $1.00

Ask to see those very excellent printed pongee silks in proper styles for waists and blouses. 19-inch, 39c. 12 designs.

Every color you'll likely ask for in the very fine Japanese pongees. 19-inch at 50c.

White and cream washable Canton pongees for the coming graduation dresses cost 50c., 75c. and $1.

A bewildering assortment of fancy plaid surahs for waists, sleeves and combinations. 21-inch, $1.

Any scarce shade in plain velvet that can't be found elsewhere can be had here. $1, $1.25, $1.50. 18 and 19-inch.

Five hundred Japanese screens in more than a score of bright decorations, are offered today for 25c. each. An absurdly small price.

HASKELL & TRIPP.

Department Stores: PURCHASE AND WILLIAM STS.

SWOONED.

Miss Borden Gives Way Under Strain.

Fainted After Hearing Words of Accuser.

Lay Unconscious in the Court Room.

Kindly Hands Ministered to the Prisoner.

District Attorney Moody's Opening Address.

Case of the Government Outlined by Him.

Alice Russell to be an Important Witness.

Jury Goes to Fall River to Visit Scene of Crime.

Court Adjourns at Noon Until 9 a. m. Tomorrow.

There was almost an entire absence of the hustle and bustle about the court house this morning that characterized the opening of the famous case now occupying the attention of the court.

The failure of any of the large crowd that hung around the court house yesterday from early in the morning until the close of the day's proceedings, to evade the vigilance of the officers, had the effect of keeping many away today, and a much smaller crowd put in appearance this morning than was expected. There were some, however, whose curiosity to see the prisoner and the interior of the court room was almost overpowering, and lest they might lose the coveted opportunity, they were on hand as early as 6 o'clock. Several women were seen to take their station on the curbing opposite the court house at a little after 6 o'clock, and there they remained until the bell

District Attorney Moody.

announced that the proceedings were about to begin. Officer Humphrey was at his station at the rear door at a little after 7, but found little to do, except to hustle a small crowd who had come to the conclusion that the best place to make the attack was from this direction. Officers Gendron and Eldridge were on duty at the front entrance.

The jury marched up to the court house, arriving at half past eight. It is unnecessary to say that they were carefully looked over by every one, who caught a glimpse of them as they passed through Purchase, William, Water and Union to the court house in twos, led by Deputy Sheriff Nickerson, and followed by Deputy Sheriff Arnold.

At three minutes of 9 o'clock Deputy Sheriff Kirby arrived with his charge. She looked none the worse for her night's rest. Sheriff Wright made a wise selection when he appointed Mr. Kirby to look after Miss Borden. He has attended to his duties faithfully. His charge has proved most retired, and although the two have sat side by side in court, but once in that time has she spoken to the official, and then only to ask for a drink of water. On the way to and from the court house she has kept the same reserved demeanor, commenting once on the excessive heat of the day while on her way to prison yesterday afternoon. The carriage in which she rides to court enters the jail yard, when Miss Borden is turned over to the deputy sheriff by Keeper Hunt.

Spectators Admitted.

At the time announced for the court the officers in charge of the doors allowed all those hanging about the doors to enter, an opportunity that they eagerly embraced, and in a minute the seats allotted to the spectators were about half filled.

The counsel were in their seats some considerable time before the opening,

(Continued on Third Page.)

THE BLACK WONDER MINE.

A Property That Has Developed Into a Steady Producer.

Favorably Located in Hinsdale County.

Sunshine Mountain, Near the Backbone of the Continent, the Home of the Black Dyke, the Base of Operations—The Mine's Present and Future.

(From The Daily State Mining Journal, Denver, June 1, 1893.)

The Black Wonder mine, owned by the Black Wonder Gold & Silver Mining company is located directly above the mining camp of Sherman, on Sunshine mountain, sixteen miles from Lake City, in Hinsdale county, Colorado. Sherman is connected by a good wagon road with Lake City, the present terminus of a branch of the Denver & Rio Grande railroad; a good trail leads from Sherman to the mine, which has an elevation above the town of about 600 feet. Over this trail and wagon road ores can be easily transported to the railroad at a cost not exceeding $5 per ton. Several freighting outfits now in camp have contracted with the Black Wonder and other companies for the delivery of their ores at Lake City at this figure.

In the town of Sherman is located the Black Wonder boarding house, the superintendent's office, miners' cabins, stables, etc., belonging to the company, besides a number of cabins occupied by miners operating upon other mines in the vicinity.

Sunshine Mountain.

Sunshine Mountain lies to the north of the camp, and derives its name from the fact that it receives the direct rays of the sun more hours every day in the year than any other mountain in this section of Colorado. Mines located on the south side of this mountain, as is the Black Wonder, can be worked every day in the year,—a very desirable point in favor of such properties. Sunshine Mountain is the home of the greatest trachyte dykes ever discovered in this country, and which are said to equal those of the most famous portions of Hungary. These dykes cut through the granite formation, and vary from 40 to 80 feet in width, carrying mineral veins of more or less strength throughout their entire length and breadth. The mineral veins of this mountain are found in the dykes, the largest and most distinct of which is the one upon which the Black Wonder mine is located. This dyke can be traced for a distance of from four to five miles, the granite on either side being of a redish brown hue

The Lake Fork of the Gunnison river, which skirts this mountain, furnishes ample water for all purposes, including mining, milling, and for the domestic uses of the people of Sherman; there is also an abundance of timber upon this and surrounding mountains.

Character and Value of the Ore.

The accompanying map (cut omitted) shows the southern slope of Sunshine mountain, a number of the mining claims, and the trend of the two principal veins so far as the same have been determined. The upper or western portion of the vein is in the direction of Burrows Park, one of the best mineral sections of Hinsdale county, where a large number of promising properties are being developed at the present time. The character of the vein matter in the dyke is conglomerate, being composed in the upper part, as shown by the workings, of silicates, oxides, sulphurets, fluor-spar (valuable at smelters' for fluxing purposes) which carry their principal values in silver. A fair sample, taken by the writer, from the vein in the upper stope of the first level in the shaft to the west of the same at a depth of about 35 feet from the surface, and assayed by Henry E. Wood, assayer of this city, gave returns of .4 ounces of gold and 173 ounces of silver to the ton. The breast of the stope from which the sample was taken is from 18 inches to 3 feet in width, the ore lying upon the foot wall. In this stope miners were busily at work taking out the ore and hoisting it to the surface. There can be hundreds and perhaps thousands of tons of mineral taken from this drift and stope.

In the lower workings, about 200 feet down the mountain side, entrance to which is gained through the cross-cut tunnel shown herewith, (cut omitted,) which tunnel is in 250 feet, cutting the vein at that point, the character of the ore is somewhat changed from that found in the shaft. The vein matter is of a light-colored quartz, streaked with brown and yellow, carrying some purple, yellow and rose quartz, spar, talc, iron and copper pyrites, black oxide of manganese and considerable tellurium ore, with a small streak of nagyagite, all being mineralized, and everything taken from between walls showing some value.

Drifts have been run on the vein both east and west from the tunnel. The west drift is in about 100 feet and the east drift about 175 feet. The large quantities of ore now on the dump were extracted in driving these levels. The ore runs in compact strata through the vein matter separated only by a talcous substance and these strata are generally a very high grade of mineral, varying in places from six inches to one foot in width. Several of these strata occur in the vein which is of an average width of about four feet between walls in these workings. I took a fair sample from all of the strata except a small one about four to six inches wide which ran parallel with the larger ones but of a different character of mineral. This sample was also assayed by Henry E. Wood and returned 25.8 ounces gold and 52.2 ounces silver per ton. A sample taken from the small streak above mentioned ran as per assay certificate 43.88 ounces gold and 94 ounces silver per ton. This sample also carried some lead value which was not taken into account. The nature of the ore of this small stratum is a form of nagyagite, (a telluride of gold and lead,) and is the most valuable ore found in the mine. The ore from these workings is carefully sorted into three grades, the first two being shipped to the smelter and the low grade stacked up on the dump awaiting the construction of a mill to treat the same. The company is now at work raising funds for the erection of a mill, which will be located at Sherman and a tramway built to connect the mine and mill. These improvements should be made at an early date in order to facilitate the economical handling of the ore, and to get the value of the product mined. Milling ore predominates in the mine in the ratio of about five tons of mill ore to one ton of the smelting product, hence the necessity of the mill is apparent. Indications lead to the conclusion that as depth is gained on the vein the ore strata will come together, forming one solid body of ore, in which event the smelting product will no doubt increase, yet there will always be a sufficient milling product to keep a mill going profitably. The necessity of a mill cannot be too strongly recommended. The Monster vein, shown in the map, joins the Black Wonder vein in the Come Up claim, owned by the Come Up Gold & Silver Mining Co., which company also own the Mineral Flower. These operations together with the steady output of the Black Wonder will make Sunshine Mountain a veritable bee-hive of industry from this time on.

During my visit to these properties Superintendent A. A. Allen of the Black Wonder company showed me every attention, thereby making it possible to gain every detail of interest to our readers. It is justly due Mr. Allen to state that he is a careful, conservative superintendent, always on the alert when the interests of his company are concerned. There is no waste of time or money, and every movement evinces careful forethought and judgment. During the winter, while the snow was deep and the roads almost impassable, making ore shipments impossible, while other mines closed down, Mr. Allen kept a small force at work, steadily opening up the property and increasing the ore reserves on the dump. Now that the roads are open and in good condition, ore shipments have begun and five-yoke bull teams are making tri-weekly trips from the mine to the sampler located at Lake City. The first lot delivered to the sampler ran 5.7 ounces gold and 47 ounces in silver per ton. While this is a very flattering return, yet the fact must not be lost sight of that it was only second grade ore taken promiscuously from the large dump, and that the mine produces a much better grade of ore, although in smaller quantities. Superintendent Allen is increasing the working force as rapidly as room can be found for men in the mine, and he expects to treble the output in less than 30 days.

All things considered, the Black Wonder is truly a wonderful mine, the possibilities of which are beyond the ken of man. Conditions are favorable for economic mining, and with the further equipment of a tramway and mill, the mine could be placed on a handsome, dividend-paying basis in a very short period of time.

(Signed) W. F. REINERT.

THE STANDARD'S LEAD.

The Evening Standard printed an edition yesterday unprecedented in Southern Massachusetts, and the demand, which was an extraordinary one, showed the public's appreciation. The Standard's corps of reporters and artists are determined to continue to give the very best and most complete report that can be printed. Residents of suburban towns and of Cape Cod, by ordering the Standard, have all the news twelve hours before it can reach them in the Boston dailies. Standard extras will be issued every night during the Borden trial with the complete record of the day's proceedings.

As the court has adjourned till tomorrow there will be no extra this evening.

WEATHER INDICATIONS.

Showers and Cooler.

Washington, June 6.—For the 24 hours from 8 a. m. today: For New England increasing cloudiness and showers; cooler Wednesday, south to west winds.

Boston, June 6.—8 a. m.—Local forecast for New England until Wednesday night: Thunder showers in afternoon or evening; much cooler tonight and Wednesday morning; fair and cool Wednesday; southwest, changing to west and northwest winds.

HOME MATTERS.

ONE ADVANTAGE

To people who are beginning housekeeping is to be able to purchase a complete outfit of furniture on the start. There is only one safe way to do it, and that is to buy on installments. Everything in F. R. Slocum's store is available to installment purchasers. That is a fact which young housekeepers should keep in mind. The terms are the lowest in town.

CONDENSED LOCALS.

As a heavy truck was coming down North second street, near Middle, last evening, a little son of Michael Collins, who resides at the corner, ran into the street and tried to get on the truck. Instead, he fell between the wheels and the heavy wheels passed over his left wrist. By almost a miracle no bones were broken.

The verdict of the people—that B. H. Waite & Co., 71 William street, offer best inducements to carpet buyers. The stock of Brussels, tapestries and ingrain carpets is complete in choice styles. The variety and styles of straw matting excel any previous year. The prices are the lowest.

It will pay all who intend papering this season to see the fine line of paper hanging shown by Bliss & Nye. They carry the largest stock of the best selected patterns at the lowest prices in the city.

Elegant Wine for family use, $1.50 per gallon, delivered in city—Port, Sherry, Madeira, Angelica, Muscatel, or Tokay, at Hiram Wheaton & Sons, 45 to 51 School street.

Everybody says the cake and hot biscuit made with the Winner Baking Powder are fine. Come and try them tomorrow at my store. Remember they are free to all. F. C. Bliss & Son, Washington square.

A lost child was found sitting on Dr. Seip's steps, corner of Union and County streets, this morning, and was taken to the Central station awaiting her parents.

There will be a meeting of the W. C. T. U. in the Woman's Parlors, 190 Purchase street, on Wednesday, June 7th, at 3 o'clock p. m.

Early Closing.—Commencing June 1st, the White Cash store will close every evening at 6 30 until Oct. 1st, except Fridays and Saturdays.

Denison Bros. have made the Standard editorial rooms an acceptable gift of a quantity of fans with World's Fair scenes pictured on them.

Call at Nooning's and we will show you the largest and best selected stock of sailors that are in the market today at extremely low prices.

The city council committees on city property and fire department will meet this evening to approve bills.

Gentlemen, the finest line of Russia leather shoes found at Buchell's. See our $4 shoe.

The first bluefish of the season were received today by J. G. Childs & Son from Andrew R. Reid.

J. P. Hanson captured two young owls in the woods north of Nash road Sunday.

Wrappers and Waists are in great demand, you will find them at Whiting & Co's.

Special sale of trimmed children's hats at Nooning's at greatly reduced prices.

"The duty of every mother" of a hand-fed infant is to give him Mellin's Food.

The Majestic Light Roadster Bicycle has been reduced to $85. See fifth page.

Go to Whiting & Co's and purchase a nice cool waist, for this hot season.

Physicians universally recommend Ayer's Hygienic Coffee. Grocers sell it.

Do not miss the great Gingham and Pongee sale going on at Whiting & Co's.

Cutter Whiskey costs $1.25 per bottle.

Hood's Sarsaparilla enriches the blood.

LADIES SOMETIMES

You feel uncertain where to buy

CARPETS.

NOW WE WISH TO TELL YOU THAT WE ARE FULLY PREPARED TO SUPPLY YOUR WANTS.

OUR STOCK IS MORE ATTRACTIVE AND COMPLETE THAN AT ANY TIME DURING THE HISTORY OF OUR BUSINESS.

New Carpets.
New Mattings,
New Furniture,
New Curtains.

YES

WE ATTEND STRICTLY TO THE

Furniture, Carpet and Curtain Business.

FURNISHING HOUSES IS OUR SPECIAL WORK, AND THIS WE DO TO THE ENTIRE SATISFACTION OF EVERYONE WHO FAVORS US WITH THEIR BUSINESS.

We handle the best makes. We guarantee our prices to be as low as the lowest.

CASH or CREDIT.

C. F. WING,
34 to 40 Purchase Street.

WHITING & CO.

Great Summer Cotton Wash Goods Sale.

One case 1,632 yards of the best 12 1-2c. American Ginghams will be sold by us at 7 1-2c. per yard. Only 75c. for 10 yards of nice Gingham.

500 yards of Bedford Cord Ginghams, made to sell at 25c., our price 12 1-2c.

250 yards of Cheviots that sold at 33c. per yard, our price 12 1-2c. today.

2,500 yards of the finest American Ginghams, made and sold this season at 17c., will be sold by us at 12 1-2c. per yard.

2,800 yards of the best Scotch Ginghams, made by R. A. Whytlaw Sons & Co. of Glasgow, Scotland, that have been sold at 33c. the first of the season, now sold by us at 17c. per yard.

1,000 yards of our best Printed Pongees, mostly white grounds, carried over from last season and sold at 15c. per yard, we shall put on sale at 9c. per yard. Do not wait, but come as soon as you read this, as the case price today for same goods is 12 1-4c. cash.

☞ Do not ask for samples of any of these goods, as we shall not give any.

WHITING & CO.

J. V. SPARE,

41 Purchase St.

SPECIALS

—IN—

HOSIERY

—AND—

UNDERWEAR.

Ladies' 40 gauge tan hose in either plain or drop stitch, with double heels and toes in all sizes at 25c. pair.

Ladies' extra fine tan hose in fancy drop stitch with high spliced heels at 39c. pair, well worth 50c.

Tan hose for children in both plain and ribbed sizes, 6 to 8 1-2 at 25c. pair.

Ladies' jersey vests with low neck and no sleeves trimmed with silk stitch and silk ribbon at 19c. each, regular value 25c.

Ladies' jersey vests with high neck and short sleeves, and finished with pearl buttons and made of pure Egyptian cotton at 25c. each.

Ladies' plain white medium weight vests, silk cat stitch and finished with pearl buttons in either long or short sleeves at 50c. each.

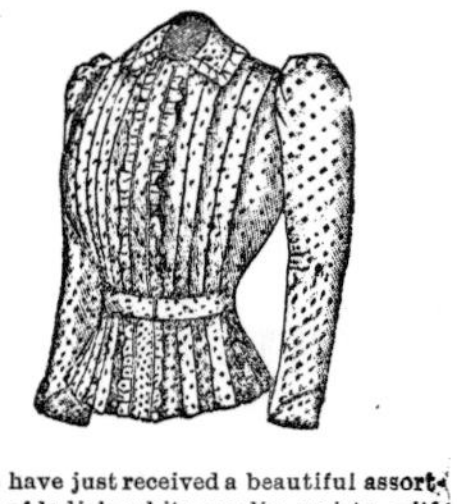

We have just received a beautiful assortment of ladie's white muslin waists with neat tucks in front and back and trimmed with pretty ruffle of white or colored embroideries at neck, down the front and on the sleeves at $1.00 and $1.25 each.

Ladies' fine cambric waists plaited front and back with neat stripes, figures and spots at 50c. each, sizes 32 to 40 inch.

J. V. Spare,

41 Purchase St.

Tennis and Outing Suits.

The newest things in Tennis and Outing Suits are ready for your inspection. Blue Serge Skeleton coats and White Duck Trousers will be the "go" this Summer, and we have provided an unusually large stock of these comfortable goods for the hot weather.

The new styles in Tennis Flannels are very handsome and especially moderate in price.

Our assortment of Negligee Shirts, Leather Belts, Straw Hats, Tennis and Bicycle Caps, Stockings, etc., is most complete and comprises everything that is newest and best.

J. & W. R. WING & CO.,

Men's Furnishers.

SCHOOL COMMITTEE.

The Most Exciting Meeting Held for a Number of Years.

Teachers Elected in Some Grades and Salaries Fixed.

Interesting Discussion About Mabel Cleveland of High School Corps.

The regular monthly meeting of the school committee was held Monday evening. In the absence of the mayor at the opening, Vice Chairman Pitman presided. There were no other absentees. The mayor afterward came in and took his seat.

The records of the last meeting were read and approved.

The superintendent's report for April was as follows:

Total enrollment	5,629
Boys, 2794; girls, 2835.	
Average number belonging	5,316.6
Average daily attendance	4,834.5
Per cent of attendance	90.
Total half days' absence	19,791
Cases of tardiness	1,550
Cases of dismissal	2,616
Cases of truancy	6
Cases of corporal punishment	90
Half days teachers' absences	122
Times teachers were tardy	7
Visits by superintendent	49
Visits by committee	21

The superintendent's monthly report for May was read as follows:

Total enrollment	5,515
Boys	2,730
Girls	2,785
Average number belonging	5,404.8
Average daily attendance	4,850.7
Per cent attendance	89.7
Total half days' attendance	21,997
Cases of tardiness	1,823
Cases of dismissal	3,172
Cases of truancy	27
Cases of corporal punishment	102
Half days teachers' absence	102
Times teachers were tardy	4
Visits by superintendent	54
Visits by committee	52

Mr. Howland, from the Sylvia Ann Howland fund, recommended the following appropriations, which were authorized:

High School.

250 Abide with Me, 1 Outlines of Lessons in Botany, Part II, Newell, 1 How to Know the Wild Flowers by Mrs. Dana, Apparatus, $18.10.

Fifth Street Grammar.

4 Dale's American Citizen, 5 Brown's Manual of Commerce, 1 International Dictionary, 4 Youman's First Book of Botany, 61 camera views with lecture on America, $49.46.

Parker Street Grammar.

1 Flora of New Bedford and the Shores of Buzzards of Bay, by E. W. Hervey, 1 Trees of the Northern U. S., by Apgar, 1 Edward's Historical Caads, 1 set Edwards Geographical Cards, 2 Lessons on Common Minerals, 1 On Common Birds and How to Know them, 20 Higginson's U. S. History, 30 Normal Music 2d Readers, 2 maps of New Bedford, $40.70.

Middle Street School.

2 piano covers, 2 Brinbi, $7.00.

Thompson Street Grammar.

3 Potter's Primary Geography (teacher's edition), 3 Potter's Advanced Geography (teacher's edition), 3 Montgomery's U. S. History, 3 At the Back of the North Wind, 1 Peaslees' Graded Selections, 1 Youth's Companion, $17.10.

Cedar Grove Primary.

1 set wall maps, 50 Sea Side and Way Side, No. 3, 50 Scribner's Geographical Readers, 50 Grandfather's Chair, by Hawthorne, 1 Johnston's U. S. History, 1 Montgomery's U. S. History, 1 American History Stories by M. L. Pratt, volumes 1, 2, 3 and 4; 1 Swinton's Grammar School Geography, 1 Mawry's Geography, 1 Barnes' Geography, 1 Butler's Complete Geography, 1 King's Geog- King's Geographical Readers, Vols. 1, 2, 3 and 4; 2 Popular Educator Arithmetics, 1 Rickoff's Number Applied, 1 Our Bodies and How We Live, 1 Huxley's Physiography, 1 Blaisdell's Physiology for Little Folks, 3 Fables and Folk Stories, $112.23.

Dartmouth Street Primary.

2 Lessons on Manners, 1 Prang's Primary Course in Art Education, 50 Parker & Marvel's Reader, Part I, $13.60.

Acushnet School.

2 Story of Our Continent, 3 The Peasant and the Prince, 3 The Prince and the Pauper, 3 The Arabian Nights, 2 Primer of American Literature, 2 The World by the Fireside, $13.55.

North School.

14 Eggleston's Smaller U. S. History, 13 Hawthorne's Grandfather's Chair, 1 Monroe's Reading Chart and Easel, 1 Monroe's Chart Primer, 12 Parker & Marvel's Reader, first book, part 1; 12 Wood's Natural History 1st reader, 12 Wood's Natural History 2d reader, 12 Wood's Natural History 3d reader, 1 set maps, 1 Joslm 12-inch Globe, 1 Webster's International dictionary, 25 pairs scissors, St. Nicholas for one year, $92.96.

Clark's Point School.

10 Holme's 2d Reader, 10 Normal 2d Readers, 1 Youth's Companion, $7.44.

Recapitulation.

High school	$18.10
Fifth street grammar	49.46
Parker street grammar	40.70
Middle street grammar	7.00
Thompson street grammar	17.10
Cedar Grove primary	112.23
Dartmouth street primary	13.60
Acushnet school	13.55
North school	92.86
Clarks Point school	7.44
Total	$372.04

Mr. Howland stated that the city council had been asked for money for a cooking school and for a manual training school. Notice has been received that the appropriation of $600 has been made for the cooking school; as also appropriations for furnishing increased accommodations at the Dartmouth Street and I. W. Benjamin schools. For the manual training school the city council adopted an order that the committee on city property furnish the tools necessary at an expense not to exceed $1,000, the same to be charged to incidental expense account.

The order, Mr. Howland said, is in violation of statute law, which provides that the school committee alone shall be authorized to purchase supplies for the schools.

It was voted that the secretary be instructed to inform the city council that the order adopted relating to tools for the manual training school is illegal, and in view of that ask that the appropriation be transferred to the school committee.

Mr. Howland said that the committee on expenditures has come to the conclusion that the time has arrived for a new school house on the site of the present one on Fourth street, which is of great age, illy-ventilated, and dangerous to life in case of fire. The committee has decided to ask that an eight room building be placed on this lot and that the Acushnet avenue schoolhouse be increased in size to a ten-room building.

It was ordered that a new schoolhouse be asked for on the Fourth street lot, and that the secretary be instructed to notify the city council of the vote.

On motion of Mr. Sayer it was voted that the committee on expenditures be instructed to take charge of fitting up the cooking school, and that the committee on manual training be instructed to report a candidate for teacher to the full board.

Mr. Tompkins moved to proceed with balloting for teachers, commencing with the primary school list, and that reporters be requested not to publish the number of votes cast for each teacher.

Mr. Taber amended that balloting begin with the grammar school list.

Mr. Tompkins said the grammar school committee has a report to make, and will ask further time.

Mr. Taber asked if the report affects all the grammar school teachers.

Mr. Tompkins said perhaps not all, but one school is affected. The committee would rather report on all at one time, and hope to report at an adjourned meeting to be held not later than two weeks hence.

Mr. Taber's motion was not seconded, and Mr. Tompkins' was declared carried.

The resignation of Miss Eleanor Commerford, principal of the William Street Primary school, was accepted, and the vacancy was referred to the primary school committee with instructions to report back.

Primary school principals were elected as follows, the figures appended showing the number of votes each received:

Linden street school—Elizabeth P. Spooner, 19.
Merrimac street school—Sarah H. Hewins, 19.
Maxfield street school—Mary B. White, 18.
Cedar street school—Annie S. Homer, 19.
Acushnet avenue school—Jane C. Thompson, 19.
I. W. Benjamin school—Jane E. Gilmore, 19.
Fourth street school—Sarah H. Cranston, 19.
Dartmouth street school—Isadore F. Eldridge, 19.
Cedar Grove street school—Lucy F. Clark, 19.
Cannonville school—Addie J. McFarlin, 19.

Mr. Tompkins called up again that section of his motion that the number of votes each teacher received should not be printed, and asked if it was passed.

Vice Chairman Pitman decided that it had.

Mr. Sayer questioned whether such a vote had been passed, and said the chairman put the vote as simply that the board proceed to a ballot. He was connected with a newspaper, and so far as he is concerned the figures will appear in that paper, while he should be sorry to go against the wishes of the school committee.

The chairman asked if the member wished to intimidate the board, and the answer was a negative one.

Mr. Tompkins said such a course as not printing the votes has been pursued in former years. He renewed his motion, and said if it is carried he will move that each teacher be officially notified of the vote he or she received.

Mr. Taber asked why the figures should not be printed.

Mr. Tompkins said sometimes there is a personal feeling against some teacher among members of the board which lessens the vote, and if the vote is published the teacher's influence is lessened, and it is more difficult for her to maintain discipline.

Colonel Hart inquired what the vote really was which had passed.

The secretary read the vote as he understood it, to the effect that balloting begin for teachers, and that reporters be requested not to publish the number of votes cast.

Mr. Milliken moved to reconsider the vote.

Mr. Taber raised the point of order that the vote has not been adopted, and therefore there is nothing to reconsider.

The chairman decided that the vote as read by the secretary was the one passed.

Mr. Milliken appealed from the decision, but the chair was sustained.

Colonel Hart moved that no member of the board be allowed to divulge the vote cast for any teacher.

Mr. Taber said. "You can't muzzle free speech."

Colonel Hart said he had voted against Mr. Tompkins' motion. He thought any action taken by this board is a proper subject to be reported, if correctly reported.

Dr. Kennedy said the board could request and the reporters would do as they had a mind to. The board would thus gain some experience which might be of value.

Colonel Hart withdrew his motion.

Primary school assistants were elected as follows, the figures showing the number of votes each received:

Amelia Lincoln, 20.
Mary J. Graham, 20.
Helen J. Kirk, 20.
Lucy S. Leach, 20.
Isabella Luscomb, 20.
Isadora Foster, 20.
Addie West, 20.
Harriet S. Damon, 20.
Anna I. Dexter, 20.
Annie E. Pearce, 20.
Clara C. M. Gage, 20.
Mary E. Pasho, 20.
Abby D. Whitney, 20.
Bessie P. Peirce, 20.
Willetta B. Nickerson, 20.
Annie L. Edwards, 20.
Mabel L. Hathaway, 20.
Sarah E. Kirwin, 20.
Hattie L. Finian, 20.
Carrie S. Silva, 20.
Margaret H. Holmes, 20.
Harriet N. Hyatt, 20.
Julia M. Pilling, 20.
Harriet L. Cornell, 20.
Susan M. Tompkins, 20.
Annie C. O'Connor, 20.
Nellie W. Davis, 20.
Mary Barstow, 20.
Sarah A. Winslow, 20.
Annie L. Brownell, 20.
Alice A. Taylor, 20.
Mabel Bennett, 20.
Eleanor V. Tripp, 20.
Dora A. DeWolf, 20.
Lizzie M. Briggs, 19.
Eliza H. Sanford, 19.
Sarah E. Sears, 20.
Lillie C. Tillinghast, 20.
Annie L. Macreading, 20.
Grace Covell, 20.
M. Eva Schwall, 20.
Sara H. Kelley, 20.
Grace H. Potter, 19.
Annie F. Smith, 20.
Edith M. B. Taber, 19.
Nellie H. Cook, 20.
Mary J. Eldridge, 20.
Carrie A. Shaw, 17.
Flora E. Estes, 20.
Annie G. Brawley, 20.
Edith K. Weeden, 20.
Sara M. Hatch, 20.
Caroline E. Bonney, 20.
Ruth E. Pease, 20.
Ethel W. Denham, 20.
Leonora B. Hamblin, 20.
Charlotte M. Allen, 20.

Special teachers were elected as follows:
Drawing—Mary W. Gilbert, 20.
Singing—F. H. Butterfield, 20.
Sewing—Carrie H. Richmond, 20; Eliza A. Smalley, 20; Gertrude H. Leonard, 20.

Teachers in the Harrington training school were elected as follows:

Josephine B. Stuart, principal, 20.
Anna W. Braley, principal's assistant, 20.
Belle Almy, assistant, 20.
Fannie M. Spooner, assistant, 20.

Mill school teachers were elected as follows:

North Mill school—Emma R. Wentworth, 19; Kate Sweet, 19.
South Mill school—Lucy J. Remington, 19.

A communication from Miss Mary E. Haney of the Plainville school, tendering her resignation, was laid on the table till the next meeting.

On motion of Mr. Lowe it was voted that the election of teachers for the country schools be postponed till the next meeting.

The election of teachers for the grammar schools was laid on the table till the next meeting.

Mr. Pitman, from the subcommittee on High school, recommended the re-election of the entire corps of teachers for that school, except Miss Mabel W. Cleveland, one of the assistants.

Mr. Taber asked for the reasons for not recommending Miss Cleveland.

Mr. Pitman said he would prefer not to go into the reasons. In the committee the vote on recommending Miss Cleveland stood four to four, and she was not, therefore, indorsed. There were reasons why she should not be recommended. She has never had a hearing before the committee, although she has talked with individual members.

Mr. Taber said this is the time and place to know the reasons for not recommending Miss Cleveland, if there are any. She was transferred from the grammar grade to the High school and was highly recommended. If she is inefficient or not giving satisfaction the board has a right to know it, and if the feeling against her is a personal one it should be so stated.

Mr. Pitman said he regretted being forced into a discussion on this matter, which will be made public, when the whole matter might have been settled inside of the High school committee. Miss Cleveland was not appointed to the High school for any special qualification. There have been repeated complaints against her from parents as to the manner in which she used their children. Mr. Hatch has been to her, although not in an official manner. She was on the defensive with him and did not yield at all, and she made a remark to him, which Mr. Pitman said he did not care to repeat unless he was oblige to. Only since she has known she was not to be recommended for re-election has she shown any desire to accede to the wishes of the committee.

Mr. Taber said the members of the board ought to have a chance to vote for Miss Cleveland if they wish to do so, and he moved that the ballot be for nine assistant teachers in the High school instead of eight, as recommended by the committee.

Mrs. Borden said Miss Cleveland is a vigorous teacher, and in full sympathy with her work. In her ambition to have her pupils stand well she may have taxed them a little too much, but she is willing to carry out the wishes of the committee.

Dr. Kennedy called attention to the fact that in the case of Miss Cleveland the rule requiring three months' notice to a teacher who is not to be retained has not been complied with.

The chairman ruled that such notice should have been given.

Mr. Pitman said there is something else besides a rule to be considered. Failure to recommend was all that could be done by the minority. Miss Cleveland has not regarded the committee, and she would not come before it. She has been to members of the school board, however, and has asked them to vote for her. Those whom she has seen have heard but one side of the story. It seems to be almost considered a crime not to vote to recommend a teacher for re-election year after year in this city. In other cities this is not so, but if the teachers are not satisfactory they are at once discharged. The speaker said he would not care to serve on a subcommittee whose adverse report was overridden by the board. He moved that the matter of electing a ninth assistant be referred back to the High school committee.

Mr. Taber said if we have rules we ought to go by them. There appears in this matter to be two reports, and that the committee is divided against itself.

Dr. Tucker thought the committee ought to be willing to give Miss Cleveland another chance if she is willing to be amenable in matters of discipline.

Mr. Sayer said he was opposed to recommending Miss Cleveland. An attempt had been made to induce her friends to consent that the matter be referred back to the High school committee with the understanding that she would be recommended for one term, and if her work was satisfactory for that time, then for the year. This proposition was refused. In justice to the High school committee, Mr. Sayer said he did not believe Miss Cleveland should be elected for a year.

Mr. Pitman moved that the matter of the ninth assistant be referred back to the High school committee.

The motion was lost—9 to 9—the mayor casting the deciding vote in the negative.

High school teachers were then elected by the following votes:

Ray Greene Huling, principal, 14.
Charles T. Bonney, Jr., sub-master, 19.
Charles R. Allen, teacher of sciences, 20.
Sarah D. Ottiwell, assistant, 20.
Elizabeth P. Briggs, assistant, 18.
Lydia J. Cranston, assistant, 20.
Mary E. Austin, assistant, 20.
Lucretia N. Smith, assistant, 20.
Emma K. Shaw, assistant, 20.
Helen L. Hadley, assistant, 20.
Mabel W. Cleveland, assistant, 14.
Catharine M. Crabtree, assistant, 20.
John K. McAfee, military instructor, 20.

Mr. Pitman moved the election of country school teachers be taken from the table. Carried.

Colonel Hart made the point of order that the election of these teachers having been postponed to a certain time, the matter could not be taken up again tonight.

The chairman decided the point well taken, and the election was not proceeded with.

Mr. Tompkins moved that when the board adjourn it be to meet again on Monday evening, June 12th, at 7 30 o'clock. Carried.

The salary list of teachers was then taken up, and Mr. Sayer said that under the rule Miss Cleveland's salary should be increased to $800, and he moved that it be fixed at that sum. Lost—only 9 votes being cast in the affirmative.

(Eleven votes are necessary to establish salaries, and at this time Drs. Dunbar, Brownell and Channing and Mr. Bentley had gone home.)

Salaries were then established as follows:

High School.

Ray Greene Huling	$2750
Charles T. Bonney, Jr	1600
Charles R. Allen	1600
Sarah D. Ottiwell	900
Elizabeth P. Briggs	900
Lydia J. Cranston	900
Mary E. Austin	900
Lucretia N. Smith	900
Emma K. Shaw	900
Helen L. Hadley	800
Catharine M. Crabtree	700
John K. McAfee	300

The salary of Miss Cleveland was not fixed. Mr. Sayer moved to make it $800, which it would be under the rules, but the motion was not carried.

Harrington Training School.

Josephine B. Stuart	$1300
Anna W. Braley	900
Belle Almy	450
Fannie M. Spooner	425

Special Teachers.

Mary W. Gilbert	$1200
F. H. Butterfield	1700
Carrie H. Richmond	600
Eliza A. Smalley, at rate of	525
Gertrude H. Leonard, at rate of	525

Primary School Principals.

Elizabeth P. Spooner	600
Sarah H. Hewins	600
Mary B. White	600
Annie S. Homer	650
Jane C. Thompson	700
Jane E. Gilmore	775
Sarah H. Cranston	650
Isadore F. Eldridge	675
Lucy F. Clark	750
Addie J. McFarlin	550

Primary School Assistants.

Amelia Lincoln	550
Mary J. Graham	550
Helen J. Kirk	550
Lucy S. Leach	550
Isabella Luscomb	550
Isadora Foster	550
Addie West	550
Harriet S. Damon	550
Annie I. Dexter	550
Annie E. Pearce	550
Clara C. M. Gage	475
Mary E. Pasho	475
Abby D. Whitney	550
Bessie B Peirce	550
Willetta B. Nickerson	550
Annie L. Edwards	550
Mabel L. Hathaway	450
Sarah E. Kirwin	550
Hattie L. Finlan	550
Carrie S. Silva	550
Margaret H. Holmes	450
Harriet N. Hyatt	425
Julia M. Pilling	425
Harriet L. Cornell	425
Susan M. Tompkins	550
Annie C. O'Connor	550
Nellie W. Davis	550
Mary Barstow	550
Sarah A. Winslow	550
Annie L. Brownell	550
Alice A. Taylor	550
Mabel Bennett	450
Eleanor V. Tripp	450
Dora A. DeWolf	425
Lizzie M. Briggs	425
Eliza H. Sanford	550
Sarah E. Sears	550
Lillie C. Tillinghast	550
Annie L. Macreading	550
Grace Covell	450
M. Eva Schwall	550
Sara H. Kelley	550
Grace H. Potter	550
Annie F. Smith	550
Edith M. B. Taber	450
Nellie H. Cook	450
Mary J. Eldridge	550
Carrie A. Shaw	550
Flora E. Estes	550
Annie G. Brawley	550
Edith K. Weeden	550
Sara M. Hatch	450
Caroline E. Bonney	425
Ruth E. Pease	425
Ethel W. Denham	425
Leonora B. Hamblin	550
Charlotte M. Allen	425

North Mill School.

Emma R. Wentworth	$15.50 per week
Kate Sweet	

South Mill School.

Lucy J. Remington	$15.50 per week

Miss Sweet was given an advance of $25 a year under the practice with regard to primary teachers who do similar work. She has been paid at the rate of $11.25 per week.

Mrs. Borden, the chairman of the committee on mill schools, recommended an increase in pay of 50 cents per week for the principals of mill schools, and argued that their labor is arduous, that they have to keep up the work of several grades in other schools, that many of the pupils do not understand English, etc.

Mr. Pitman strongly opposed the increase, arguing that the attendance at these schools are constantly growing smaller in point of numbers, that it costs more to maintain them per capita than any other schools in the city except the High school, that instead of increasing their expense it would be better to abolish them, and asserting that the mill school teachers do not have the difficulties to encounter in the way of pupils not understanding English which are met by primary teachers in the Cedar Grove street and I. W. Benjamin schools.

Mr. Tompkins spoke in a similar strain, and the increase recommended was not granted.

Mr. Shepherd offered the following resolution, which was unanimously adopted:

Resolved, That the thanks of this board are due are and hereby tendered to Miss Eleanor Commerford, for the uniform courtesy and faithfulness with which she has discharged the duties devolving upon her as prinicpal of the William street primary school and as a teacher in the public schools of New Bedford; and for the unswerving devotion and fidelity to the trust committed to her care during a long and successful term of years, and it is further

Resolved, That this board manifests its appreciation of said service by spreading these resolutions upon its records.

Adjourned.

WATER BOARD.

Petitions for Main Pipe Granted and Ordered Laid.

At a regular meeting of the water board last evening the president and Messrs. Church, Howard and Kempton were present.

Bills were presented, examined and allowed amouuting to $16,734.11. Labor pay roll for week ending June 3d was presented, examined and allowed amounting to $913.75. Weekly pay rolls for the following stated amounts have been paid since the last meeting. These rolls have been certified to by the clerk and approved by the president previous to payment being made. Date of approval: May 8th, $905.20; May 15th, $915.38; May 22d, $955.82; May 29th, $848.76; $3625.16. Total expenditures for the month, $21,273.02.

The following list of petitions for main pipe were received. Each was accompanied by a guarantee whereby petitioner agrees to provide for the payment of a rate equal in amount to 6 per cent of placing the work indicated. Each petition received separate action as stated.

Hillman street from present terminus 85 feet west of County street west 36 feet; petition and guarantee signed by Benjamin Irish, trustee. Petition granted and pipe ordered laid westerly and connected with the Summer street main, a distance of 219 feet.

Maxfield street, from present terminus 92 feet west of Ash street west 248 feet; petition and guarantee signed by Nathan Wheaton. Petition granted and pipe ordered laid.

Union street, from Chancery street west 118 feet; petition and guarantee signed by Seth W. Godfrey. Petition granted and pipe ordered laid.

Armour street, from present terminus 130 feet south of Court street south 280 feet; petition and guarantee signed by James H. Winslow. Petition granted and pipe ordered laid.

Weaver street, from present terminus 197 feet west of Dartmouth street west 132 feet; petition and guarantee signed by Lester F. Reynolds Petition granted and pipe ordered laid as soon as street is lowered to its proper grade.

Scott street, from present terminus 171 feet west of County street west 196 feet; petition and guarantee signed by Alvina Noel. Petition granted and pipe ordered laid as soon as the street is placed in proper condition to receive the pipe.

Franklin street, from Purchase street west 118 feet; petition and guarantee signed by Edwin G. Tilton. Petition granted and pipe ordered laid through to and connected with the Pleasant street main, a distance of 240 feet.

Sawyer street, north side of sewer and from Belleville avenue east 520 feet; petition and guarantee signed by Alfred G. Brownell. Petition granted and pipe ordered laid.

Shawmut avenue, from present terminus at south line of Grand street north 250 feet; petition and guarantee signed by Edward D. Kenney. Petition granted and pipe ordered laid.

Coffin avenue, from Belleville avenue east 197 feet; petition and guarantee signed by Joseph P. Silvia. Petition granted and pipe ordered laid.

The committee consisting of Messrs. Church and Kempton, appointed at the meeting held May 1st to ascertain the cost of placing a suitable plant for electric lighting at the pumping station reported that the cost of such a plant would not exceed $1000 and that it would be sufficient to supply 75 lights.

At present the cost of lighting the building is about $272 per annum and this amount will be reduced over 50 per cent and a better light secured by introducing an electric lighting plant. The report of the committee was accepted and the superintendent was instructed to procure and place a plant for electric lighting at the pumping station.

A communication was received from the city clerk stating that at a meeting of the city council held on the 11th day of May, a report from the committee on water works and water supply was received recommending that the water board be empowered to establish a meteorological department at the pumping station and to procure meteorlogical instruments to equip the same at an expense of about $1100. This report was received, placed on file, and recommendation adopted in concurrence. This communication was received, placed on file and Messrs. Kempton and Church were appointed a committee to procure the instruments.

The board then adjourned.

OFF FOR MUSTER.

Company E, first regiment of infantry, left this city by the 7 25 train this morning, with full ranks, under command of First Lieutenant Abner P. Pope, for South Framingham, where they will remain for the next five days performing the annual tour of duty required by the state.

Captain Perry will join the company this afternoon, leaving by the 3 40 train.

The camp detail of the company, consisting of seven men, went to camp yesterday morning.

DARTMOUTH.

Archibald Crosbie of Iowa, an approved minister of the Society of Friends, has appointed a meeting for worship at Apponegansett meeting house on 4th day, 6th mo., 7th, at 2 30 o'clock, p. m., and expects to attend Friends' meeting at Smith Mills on the 5th day, the 8th inst., at 11 o'clock a. m. He is desirous of the company of all who are disposed to attend.

LOOKS BLACKER.

Chain of Evidence Against Correiro.

Blood Spatter Found Upon His Shirt.

Shoes Sent to Prof. Wood for Analysis.

Prisoner Nearly Fainted When He Saw Them.

Police Suppressing Much of Their Evidence.

Contradictory Statements of Correiro's Countrymen.

Officers Overworked with Cares of Borden Case.

Marshal Hilliard Busy on His Return from New Bedford.

The police force of Fall River was hard put to it Monday. Superior officers and patrolmen were compelled to divide their thoughts between New Bedford and Bowenville, and they were working in a heat that was bred in the torrid zone. Many of them worked night and day in perfecting the link in the chain which surrounds Miss Lizzie A. Borden, and they are anxious to follow every detail of that case. At the same time their attention is pretty fully occupied with the Manchester murder. Already the public is beginning to weigh the evidence against the prisoner. Monday a pair of shoes was produced and examined at the Central station, but whether they are the shoes, or simply shoes, remains to be seen. Nobody knows what the authorities are keeping back, but the impression prevails that even if they are keeping back nothing Correiro is in a close corner. When the time comes he must make it clear that the coins which he gave in payment for the shoes came to him honestly. The bare fact that he had a new trade dollar of the date of 1878 will not convict him unless the prosecution can prove that that is the only dollar of the kind in the city. But he did buy shoes, and he admits himself that he settled for them. He ought to be able to explain

Jose Correiro,
Held for Murder of Bertha Manchester.

how the money which he handed to the storekeeper La Croix happened to be in his possession. Funds were not so plenty with him as to make it impossible for him to trace the source of it. His relatives have testified that he wasn't a paying investment as a boarder, and he probably knows where he last worked before he went to the brick yard in Taunton. It is probable, too, that the police will be able to fix accurately the time at which

The Suspect Made His Purchase at La Croix's Store.

If he were there near the hour when Mr. Manchester saw him on the Crab Pond bridge, then either Mr. Manchester is mistaken, or La Croix and Sousa, the Somerset Portuguese, are off in their reckoning. The authorities will not talk regarding time, but it is known that La Croix was so anxious to get to the race track that he didn't care to stop to unlock his safe. The trotting didn't begin until 1 30, however, and this seems to bring Correiro perilously near the hour when Mr. Manchester saw him. There is another point in dispute. In one quarter of the department it is stated positively that Correiro did not give himself up; that his arrest would have followed in short order, and that he was trapped when his uncle induced him to come in to headquarters. It is stated as positively in other quarters that the inspectors could not locate him. If that is the case, and he is guilty, it is strange that he surrendered, uncle or no uncle. The latter certainly had no authority over his nephew, and could not

Continued on Seventh Page.)

SWOONED.

(Continued from First Page.)

and busied themselves poring over papers.

All eyes were turned toward Lizzie as she came into the court room preceded by Deputy Sheriff Kirby some minutes before the arrival of the justices, but the same self-contained, apparently careless and wholly unconcerned manner that has marked her throughout was as noticeable as ever, and she walked with a firm step to her place in the dock. From her manner one would little think that the business of the court was so freighted with import to her.

Scarcely had the bell ceased ringing, when the announcement of "the court" was made. After the formal proclamation had been made by Deputy Sheriff Butman, the roll of the jury was called. Immediately after Clerk Borden in a voice in which there was much feeling read the indictment as follows:

The Indictment.

Commonwealth of Massachusetts, Bristol s.s. At the superior court begun and holden at Taunton, in and for said county of Bristol, on the first Monday in November, in the year of our Lord, 1892.

The jurors of the said commonwealth on their oaths present Lizzie Andrew Borden of Fall River, in the county of Bristol, on the fourth day of August, in the year 1892, in and upon one Abby Durfee Borden, feloniously and willfully, and of her malice aforethought, an assault did make, and with a certain weapon, to wit, a sharp cutting instrument, the name and more particular description of which is to the jurors unknown, her, the same Abby Durfee Borden, feloniously, willfully, and of her malice aforethought did strike, cut, beat and bruise in and upon the head of her, the said Abby Durfee Borden, giving to her, the said Abby Durfee Borden, by the said striking, cutting and bruising in and upon the head of her, the said Abby Durfee Borden, divers, to wit, 20 mortal wounds, of which said mortal wounds the said Abby Durfee Borden then and there instantly died.

And so the jurors aforesaid, upon their oath aforesaid, do say that the said Lizzie Andrew Borden, the said Abby Durfee Borden in manner and form aforesaid, then and there feloiously, willfully and of malice aforethought, did kill and murder; against the peace of the said commonwealth and contrary to the form of the statutes in such case made and provided.

And the jurors for the said commonwealth on their oaths do further present; that Lizzie Andrew Borden of Fall River, in the county of Bristol, at Fall River,

Simeon Borden,
Clerk of Courts.

in the county of Bristol, on the fourth day of August, in the year 1892, in and upon one Andrew Jackson Borden, feloniously, willfully and of her malice aforethought, an assault did make, and with a certain weapon, to wit, a sharp cutting instrument, the name and a more particular description of which is to the jurors unknown, him, the said Andrew Jackson Borden, feloniously, willfully and of her malice aforethought did strike, cut, beat and bruise in and upon the head of him, the said Andrew Jackson Borden, giving to him, the said Andrew Jackson Borden, by the striking, cutting, beating and bruising, in and upon the head of him, the said Andrew Jackson Borden, divers, to wit, 10 mortal wounds, of which said mortal wounds, the said Andrew Jackson Borden then and there instantly died.

And so the jurors aforesaid, upon their oaths, aforesaid, do say that the said Lizzie Andrew Borden, the said Andrew Jackson Borden in manner and form aforesaid then and there feloniously, willfully and of her malice aforethought did kill and murder against the peace of said commonwealth, contrary to the form of the statutes in such case made and provided.

During the reading of the formal charge Lizzie's eyes were turned to the floor, and she kept them riveted on one spot until after the last word of that terrible accusation had fallen from the lips of the clerk. Then her eyes were

Judge Dewey.

raised and her ears strained to catch the first words of the opening by District Attorney Moody of Essex county, who at once commenced to outline the case the government proposes to present in proof of her guilt. Her whole feeling during the reading of the indictment, if outward appearances may be relied upon, was one of careless indifference, and that of a person who was listening to an oft-told tale. From the instant Mr. Moody commenced, however, she was an attentive listener, and it is safe to say not a word fell from his lips which escaped her. Mr. Moody's manner was that of one who is fully convinced of the truth of his cause, and throws himself into the presentation of it with much earnestness. He spoke as follows:

District Attorney Moody's Opening.

Mr. Foreman and Gentlemen of the Jury—On the fourth day of August last year an old man and woman, husband and wife, in their own home upon a frequented street in the most populous city in this county, in the light of day

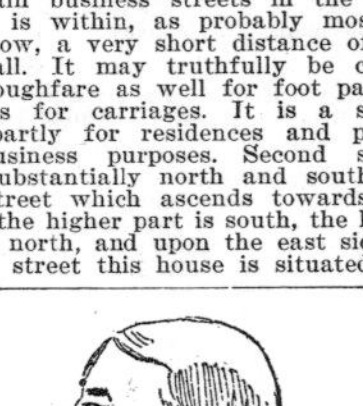

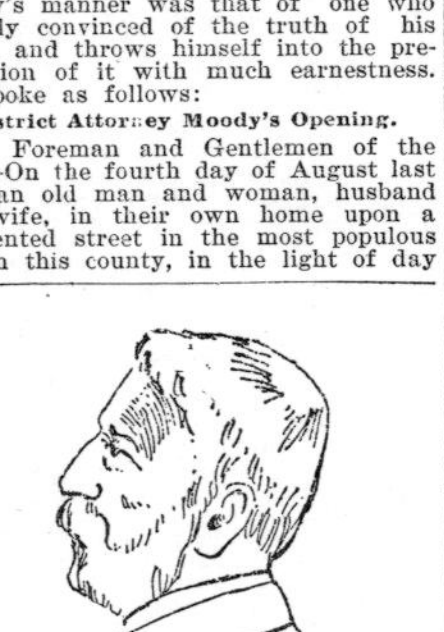

Foreman of the Jury Chas. I. Richards.

and in the midst of its activity were first one, then, after an interval, another, severally killed by or under the auspices of human agencies. Today a woman of good social position, of hitherto unquestioned character, a member of the Christian church and active in its good work, is at the bar of this court accused of these murders.

There is no language, gentlemen, at my command which can better measure the solemnity of the inquiry which we are about to begin than this simple statement of facts.

For the sake of these crimes and for the sake of these accusations every man may well pause at the threshhold of this trial and carefully search for any vestige of the truth. It is my purpose, gentlemen, and it is my duty, to state to you at this time so much of the history of the cause and so much of the evidence which is to be introduced upon this trial as shall best enable you to understand the claim of the government and to appreciate the force and the application of the testimony as it comes from the witnesses upon the stand. It is my purpose to do that in the plainest, simplest and most direct manner, and it is not my purpose to weary you with a

MISS BORDEN AS SHE ENTERED THE COURT ROOM

recital of all the details of the evidence which is to come before you.

Andrew Jackson Borden, the person named in the second count of the indictment, was at the time of his death a man, I believe, 70 years of age. He was a man of considerable property, somewhere, I believe, between $250,000 and $300,000. He had been retired from business for a number of years. He was a man who had obtained his property by earning and saving, and he retained the habit of saving up to the time of his death. It will appear in the course of this trial that the family establishment was upon what might well be called, for a person in his circumstances, a narrow scale. He had been twice married. The first wife died some 27 or 28 years before he died, leaving two children now alive—the prisoner at the bar, Lizzie Andrew Borden, the youngest, and then somewhere between two and three years of age; a sister, Miss Emma Borden, being a woman at the present time in the

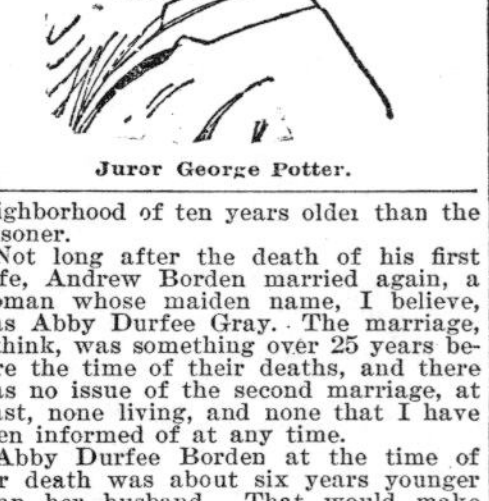

Juror George Potter.

neighborhood of ten years older than the prisoner.

Not long after the death of his first wife, Andrew Borden married again, a woman whose maiden name, I believe, was Abby Durfee Gray. The marriage, I think, was something over 25 years before the time of their deaths, and there was no issue of the second marriage, at least, none living, and none that I have been informed of at any time.

Abby Durfee Borden at the time of her death was about six years younger than her husband. That would make her, of course, 64 years of age. Mr. Borden was, I may say here, a man spare and thin, and somewhat tall. Mrs. Borden was a short, fat woman, weighing, I believe, in the neighborhood of 200 pounds.

The house in which these homicides were committed had been occupied by the Borden family for some 20 years. I shall have occasion to consider its construction and its relation to other buildings and streets later on in the course of this opening.

There was or came to be between the prisoner and her stepmother an unkindly feeling. From the nature of the case, from the fact that those who know the most about that feeling, except the prisoner at the bar, are dead, it will be impossible for us at this hearing to get anything more than suggestive glimpses

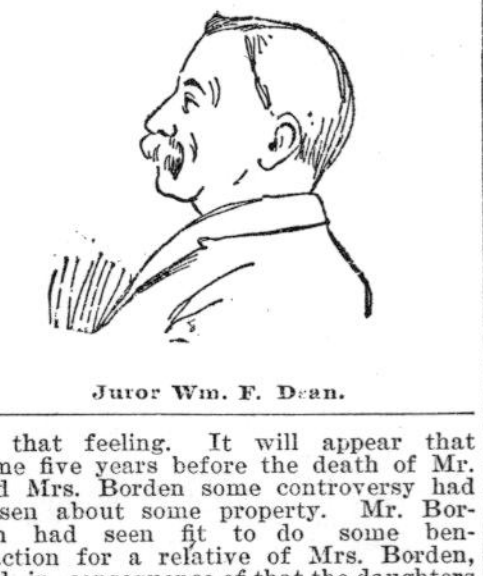

Juror Wm. F. Dean.

of that feeling. It will appear that some five years before the death of Mr. and Mrs. Borden some controversy had arisen about some property. Mr. Borden had seen fit to do some benefaction for a relative of Mrs. Borden, and in consequence of that the daughters thought that something should be done for them by way of pecuniary provision as an offset.

The details of what happened at that time are, as I have said, by no means important. It is significant, however, that enough of feeling had been created by the discussion which arose to cause a change in the relations between the prisoner and Mrs. Borden. Up to that time she had addressed her stepmother as "Mother;" from that time she substantially ceased to do so. We shall show to you that the spring before these homicides upon some occasion a talk arose between the prisoner and a person who did cloak making for the family, in which the latter spoke of Mrs. Borden as mother. The prisoner at once repudiated that relation and said, "Do not call her mother, she is a mean thing, and we hate her. We have as little to do with her as possible."

"But don't you go to meals with her?"

"Yes, we do sometimes, but we try not to, and a great many times we wait until they are through their meals, and we stay in our own room as much as possible."

I know of nothing that will appear in this case more significant of the feeling that existed between Mrs. Borden and the prisoner than a little incident which occurred not long after the discovery of these homicides. When one of the officers of the law was seeking, while the father and the stepmother lay in the very place where they had fallen under the blows of the assassin, were seeking information from the prisoner, he said: "When did you last see your mother?" "She is not my mother, she is my stepmother; my mother is dead."

You cannot fail, I think, to be impressed in this respect after what will appear as to the method of living of this family. It will appear later on in the evidence that although they occupied the same household there was built up between them by locks and bolts and bars almost an impassable wall.

In the early part of August of last year the elder daughter, Miss Emma, was away, I believe in this city at the time, or in Fairhaven. When Miss Emma was away the household that was left consisted of Mr. and Mrs. Borden and a servant who had been in the service of the family nearly three years, Bridget Sullivan, and the prisoner. Upon

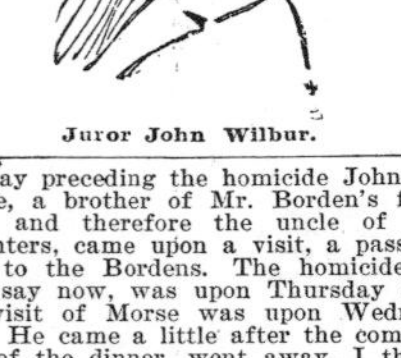

Juror John Wilbur.

the day preceding the homicide John G. Morse, a brother of Mr. Borden's first wife, and therefore the uncle of his daughters, came upon a visit, a passing visit to the Bordens. The homicide, I may say now, was upon Thursday and the visit of Morse was upon Wednesday. He came a little after the completion of the dinner, went away, I think during the afternoon, returned in, the evening and slept at the house upon the Wednesday night.

Upon Tuesday night, Aug. 2d, an illness occurred in the household. Mr. and Mrs. Borden were taken suddenly ill with a violent retching and vomiting sickness and it is said that to a less degree the prisoner herself was affected by this illness. Bridget, the servant, was not. Upon the Wednesday morning Mr. and Mrs. Borden arose feeling, of course, in a condition that people would be in after a night of that character, and Mrs. Borden consulted a physician with reference to her condition.

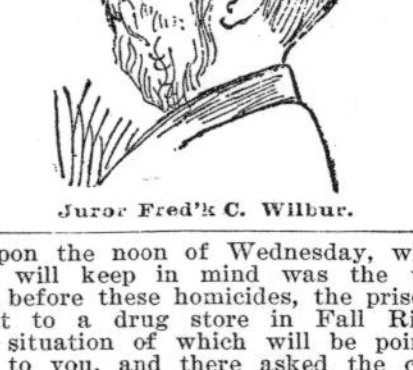

Juror Fred'k C. Wilbur.

Upon the noon of Wednesday, which you will keep in mind was the very day before these homicides, the prisoner went to a drug store in Fall River, the situation of which will be pointed out to you, and there asked the clerk for ten cents' worth of prussic acid for the purpose of cleaning a seal skin cape. She was told that that was poison which was not sold except upon the prescription of a physician, and after some little talk went away.

I think, gentlemen, that you will be satisfied that there could be no question that the person who made this application for this deadly poison was the prisoner. There were three people in the drug store, two of whom knew her by name and sight. One of these two knew her as the daughter of Andrew J. Borden and the third recognized her at once as he saw her.

Upon the evening of Wednesday the prisoner made a call, not in itself unusual or peculiar, upon a friend of hers, Miss Alice Russell, and we shall commend to your careful attention what occurred during that interval. It will appear that the prisoner had been intending to spend a vacation with a number of her friends at Marion, and had made

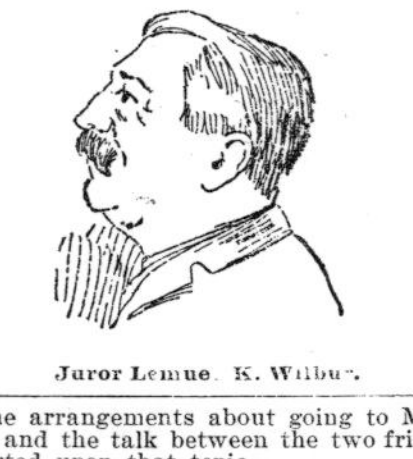

Juror Lemue K. Wilbur.

some arrangements about going to Marion, and the talk between the two friends started upon that topic.

The prisoner said: "I have made up my mind, Alice, to take your advice and go to Marion, and I have written there today that I shall go, but I can't help feeling depressed. I can't help feeling that something is going to happen; I can't shake it off." "Last night," she said, "we were all sick. Mr. and Mrs. Borden were quite sick, and vomited. I did not vomit. And we are afraid that we have been poisoned. The girl did not eat the baker's bread, and we did, and we think it may have been the baker's bread."

"No," said Miss Russell, "if it had been that some other people would have been sick in the same way."

"Well, it might have been the milk. Our milk is left outside upon the steps."

"What time is your milk left?"

"At 4 o'clock in the morning."

"It is light then, and no one would dare to go in and do it at that time."

Juror Wm. Westcott.

"Well," said the prisoner, "probably that is so, but father has been having so much trouble with those with whom he has had dealings that I am afraid that some of them will do something to him. I expect nothing but that the building will be burned down over our heads. The barn has been broken into twice."

"That," said Miss Russell, "was merely boys after pigeons."

"Well, the house has been broken into in broad daylight when Maggie and Emma and I were the only ones in the house. I saw a man the other night

Juror Lewis B. Hodges.

as I went home lurking about the buildings, and as I came he jumped and ran away. Father had trouble with a man the other day about a store. There were angry words, and he turned him out of the house," and so the talk went.

That I beg you to keep in your minds. It was with Miss Alice Russell.

It becomes now the most difficult duty which I have in this opening. I am consoled, Mr. Foreman and gentlemen, by the fact that you will be aided beyond any explanation that I can give you by a view of these premises that I am

Juror Augustus Swift.

about to explain. I hope I shall be able to make myself entirely intelligent to you, because no one can understand the testimony that is to come and rightly reason upon it without an exact knowledge of the interior and exterior of that house.

Juror Frank G. Cole.

In the first place I may say that the house occupied by this family was the type of houses in this community and in this state, a house with the end to the street and the front door upon the end. It had, I believe, no ell; it was a rectangular house. It was situated upon Second street in Fall River, which is one of the most frequented outside of the main business streets in the city, and it is within, as probably most of you know, a very short distance of the city hall. It may truthfully be called a thoroughfare as well for foot passengers as for carriages. It is a street used partly for residences and partly for business purposes. Second street runs substantially north and south. It is a street which ascends towards the south, the higher part is south, the lower part is north, and upon the east side of Second street this house is situated.

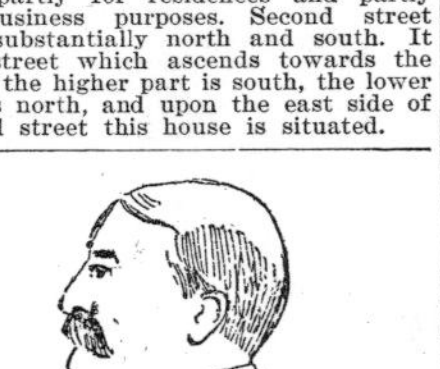

Juror John C. Finn.

At the south of the house is the residence of Dr. Kelly, and very near; to the north of the house, and also near it, is the residence occupied by Mrs. Churchill, and diagonally in the rear of the house is the residence occupied by Dr. Chagnon. The house is separated from the sidewalk by a wooden fence, two gates, and in the rear of the yard, in which is situated a barn, there is a high

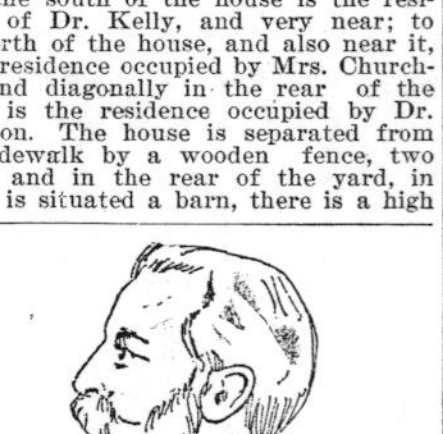

Juror Allen H. Wordell.

board fence, on the top and bottom of which there was at the time, and is, I believe now, a line of barbed wire.

There are three exterior doors, three entrances to these premises, and only three, the front door leading directly from the sidewalk up a pair of steps into the hall. There is a side door upon the north side, facing Mrs. Churchill's house,

(Continued on Fourth Page.)

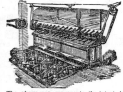

Moynan & Co.

Importing Retailers,

UNION ST. PURCHASE ST.

Going on Sale Today.

For Tennis and Outing Suits—One case of Bedford Cords, white grounds, with colored stripes, just as handsome as the all-wool goods at 50c. per yard, our price on this lot is **15c. per yard**

French Cotton Crepes.

Just what's so much wanted, all the desirable colors are here, Heliotrope, Red, Blue, Yellow, Cream, Pink, Green, etc. These are regular 20c. quality, we now offer at **15c. per yard**

in Linen Department.

Commencing today we will sell all our 72-inch heavy full bleached Damasks, regular $1.25 and $1.35 qualities, at **$1.00 per yard**

10 pieces extra heavy Cream Table Damask, never sold below 75c. per yard, now at **50c. per yard**

50 dozen full bleach Damask Towels with deep knotted fringe and fancy borders, regular value 25c., now for **19c. each**

Corsets and Muslin Underwear.

These departments are now replete in all the different lines of goods, and in all qualities from the cheapest to the high priced. Some favorites in corsets are:

Thomson's Glove Fitting in White, Drab and Black, at any of these prices according to quality, **$1.00, $1.25, $1.50 and $1.75**

The ever popular S. C. Corsets in White, Drab or Black at prices from **$1.00 to $2.50**

Summer Corsets in different styles at **49c., 75c. and $1.00**

Ladies' Gowns, trimmed with insertion and Hamburg edging, **50c.**

Ladies' Gowns, in finer qualities and more elaborately trimmed, **75c., $1.00, $1.25, etc.**

Corset Covers, V neck, made from fine Lonsdale and trimmed with very fine Hamburg edging, **50c. and 75c.**

Boys' Clothing Department.

This is the place where you find all the latest styles for the boys at the prices the lowest.

Boys' "HARD WEAR" Suits with a pair of pants extra for **$1.39**

Extra good value in Boys' School Suits, all sizes, at **$1.98**

Jersey Suits, trimmed with braid and sailor collar, all wool, and our price only **$2.50**

Boys' Suits in a dozen other styles at prices from **$1.00 to $10.00**

Boys' Hats and Caps of all kinds, suitable for Summer wear, at very reasonable prices.

Shirt Waists for boys, all sizes, at **25c., 39c., 48c. and 98c.**

SPECIAL REDUCED PRICES

In Garments, Dress Goods, Millinery, Kitchen Furnishings, Etc., Etc.

We want you to see for yourself, so PLEASE COME IN.

Moynan & Co.

UNION ST. PURCHASE ST.

The Evening Standard.

NEW BEDFORD, MASS.

TUESDAY EVENING, JUNE 6.

THREE EDITIONS DAILY.
No. 87 Union Street.
PUBLISHED BY
E. ANTHONY & SONS.
INCORPORATED.
—TERMS—
Six Dollars a Year; Three Dollars for Six Months, in advance; Single Copies Two Cents.

ORDER THE EVENING STANDARD TO YOUR VACATION ADDRESS.

Mailed direct from this office for any length of time desired; 50 cents a month, including postage.

CONTENTS OF THIS EVENING'S STANDARD.

The testimony of those who have been to Chicago is the best evidence in its favor. All those from this city whom we have conversed with agree that it is well worth seeing, and that they find no difficulty in getting good accommodations at reasonable prices. This outweighs all the anonymous newspaper talk. No one need be imposed upon if he has a fair degree of Yankee shrewdness. As to Sunday opening the testimony is that there never was a more quiet and orderly crowd than that which has visited the grounds on the two Sundays it has been opened. Two thousand four hundred Massachusetts visitors have registered at Chicago.

There are 22,248,000 soldiers in Europe, and it costs over $800,000,000 a year to support them. Yet the German emperor has not soldiers enough, and wants more, with, of course, more taxes to maintain them. This does not look much like universal peace. The population of Europe is about 300,000,000, so that about one person in every 14 is a soldier, withdrawn from production, and kept armed for purposes of slaughter.

In an address at Vienna yesterday Count Kalnoky ridiculed the idea of a general disarmament of European powers, but he admitted it would be a relief could the present process of increasing military and naval forces be brought to a standstill.

Dr. Paul Geraud has constructed a stove which will heat a room 23 feet square, and, while heating it generates a current of electricity sufficient to run an electric lamp of eight-candle power continuously, or several such lamps for part of the time. This work is accomplished by the consumption of forty pounds a day of a mixture of anthracite coal and coke, or either alone, although the combination is found to give the best results. The electric current is stored during the day in accumulators.

It is a matter of congratulation that the jury in the Borden case was fully impaneled the first day of the trial, which is almost an unprecedented thing. It is to be hoped that similar promptness may characterize the whole trial, and that it may not be spun out through the whole heated term.

The hot term is upon us, and as usual it comes unexpectedly and with all its force. Yesterday was a scorcher, and today is about the same. But, after all, it is a welcome relief after the damp and uncomfortable weather we have had so long.

ROSE WESTON FOUND DEAD.

Her Husband Arrested on Suspicion for Assault.

Rosanna Weston was found dead in bed at 116 North Water street this morning, and the police on the report of the condition of the body, arrested her husband, Frederick W. Weston.

The woman has been sick for five days, and attended by Doctors Hough and Potter. The last time the physicians saw her alive was Sunday night. She had then a fever, which the medical examiner thinks may have developed into typhoid.

This morning when her death was reported Dr. Potter was sent to view the body, as the medical examiner could not be secured.

On Dr. Potter's report a warrant was sworn out, and Officers Wing and Moynan were sent to arrest the husband, Frederick W. Weston. It was then the opinion of Chief Douglass that there were bruises on the woman's body, and the charge brought against Weston was for assault. In the district court this morning the man was held in $1,000 for his appearance next Saturday.

Later on in the morning Medical Examiner Hough went to the Weston house and viewed the woman's body. He then reported to Chief Douglass that the woman had been suffering from varicose veins, which gave her body an unsightly appearance, but there were no indications of an assault. After further investigations the chief told Judge Borden there was nothing to justify the court in holding Weston under bonds, and the decision was revised and the man ordered to appear on his personal recognizance.

The Weston woman was recommended by Dr. Hough for admission to the hospital some days ago, but there were no vacant beds.

Coca-Cola
A DELICIOUS SODA FOUNTAIN DRINK.
For TIRED NERVES and BRAIN
Cures Headache. 5c. a Glass.
SETH W. FOWLE & SONS, Boston.

SWOONED.

(Continued from Third Page.)

leading into a small entry way which leads into the kitchen. There is a third door exactly in the rear of the house which leads down to the cellar. There is what might be called a porch and a door leading into it, as you will see.

As you enter the front door you enter a hall, from which leads two doors, a door into the parlor, which is the front room in the house, making the northwest corner of the first story; a door leading into the sitting room and a stairway leading upstairs.

Let us in the first place go up stairs and see the arrangements there. It will aid you in considering these arrangements to remember that this house was originally a double tenement house. The arrangement upstairs is as it is upon the first story.

As you are about to see the premises, gentlemen, I do not think it wise to detain you at the present time by explaining these plans in detail. I will try to make it as clear as I can.

Then turn and go upstairs from the front entry. You go into the hallway. From that hallway leads three doors, the first a door which leads into a large closet used at this time for keeping dresses, and which is almost large enough to be a small bedroom. Another door leads into the guest chamber, which is directly over the parlor below, and corresponds to it in every respect. The guest chamber is the chamber in which subsequently you will hear that Mrs. Borden was found dead.

It is a matter which is to be carefully considered that as you turn upon the journey upstairs, as the stairs wind about and begin to face into the hall toward the north, you can look directly into the door of the guest chamber. The other door which leads from this hall is a door which leads into a bed room and leads towards the rear of the house.

Following then my direction, as you go up the stairs, turn to the left and approach the entry. In front of you is a door leading into the guest chamber, and to your right is a door leading into a chamber which at that time was occupied by the prisoner.

There was another door, and I may as well dispose of it now for good. It was a door which always, including the day of this homicide, was kept locked upon both sides, and upon the side towards the prisoner's room there was against the door a desk, in other words it was not a practical opening.

When you have got into this part of the house, gentlemen, you cannot go anywhere except into this clothes closet, into this guest chamber, and into the room occupied by the prisoner.

It is important to remember that all access to the other part of the house is cut off, not by the natural construction of the house, but by the way in which the house was kept.

Follow me, if you please, then into the prisoner's bedroom. As you enter her bedroom a door leads to the left into a room which has no other entrance than that door. That is the room that was occupied by Miss Emma when she was at home.

The only access to it was through the prisoner's room. There is another door at the rear of the prisoner's room and directly opposite the door of entrance which leads into the room occupied by Mr. and Mrs. Borden. It is over the kitchen. The prisoner's room was exactly over the sitting room. The room in the rear of the prisoner's room was exactly over the kitchen, and was occupied as a bedroom by Mr. and Mrs. Borden. The door leading into that room was kept always locked on both sides. It was locked on the Friday toward the prisoner's room by a hook; it was locked in the rear towards Mr. and Mrs. Borden's room by a bolt and I may as well say here as at any time that the proof that that door was locked upon both sides upon this morning, Friday morning, down to the time of the arrival of those who came alarmed by this homicide will be ample and complete.

Passing to the rear into Mr. and Mrs. Borden's room we find a door, and only a single door, leading out into the entryway, the entryway leading into the kitchen. That door it will be clearly and

ENTRANCE OF MISS BORDEN, PRECEDED BY DEPUTY SHERIFF KIRBY.

amply and satisfactorily proved was locked all through this day up to and beyond the time of this homicide.

Now then, gentlemen, if I have made myself clear upon this description, it is wearisome, I know, but it is one of the wearisome duties which we must undertake in this cause, I have made it clear to you that as you go up the hallway you get access to but four rooms; the hallway itself, if you call that a room, the closet, the guest chamber, in which Mrs. Borden was found, and the room of the prisoner and the room leading out of that was occupied by Miss Emma when she was at home. And there was no access whatever to the rear of the house.

Now, gentlemen, let me go below. As you know, the hallway below is, I believe, exactly as above, except of course there is no closet there as there is above. There are two small closets, very small. To your left as you enter is the door which leads to the parlor, a room under the room where Mrs. Borden was found dead. Going straight ahead you enter into the sitting room, it is a room in the rear of the hall at the south of the house and directly under and corresponding to the prisoner's room.

You turn to the left from the sitting room and you enter the dining room, on the north side. This is directly under Miss Emma's room, and a large room used as a closet by Mrs. Borden. These rooms are separated by a partition, so that the effect of that partition it will be readily seen is to reduce these rooms to one, while at the same time they can be used separately. These rooms are

BIRD'S EYE VIEW OF VICINITY OF THE BORDEN MURDERS.

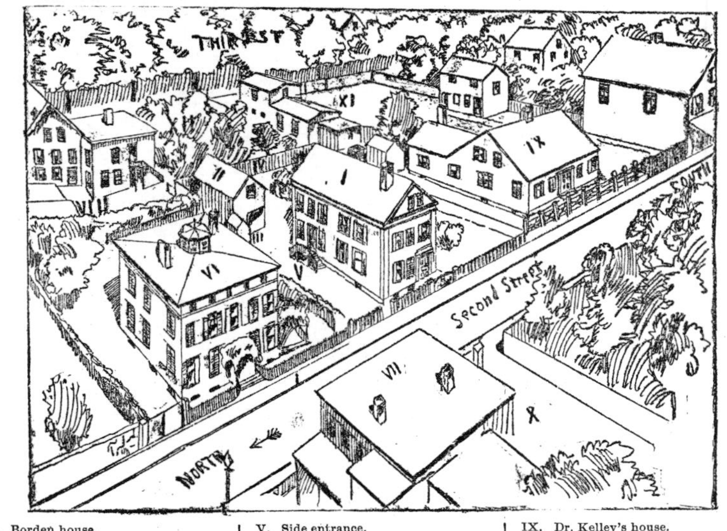

I. Borden house.
II. Borden barn.
III. The well.
IV. Fence with barbed wire on top.
V. Side entrance.
VI. Churchill residence.
VII. Dr. Bowen's house.
VIII. Dr. Chagnon's house.
IX. Dr. Kelley's house.
X. Yard from which officers watched Borden house.
XI. Kelley's barn.
XII. Pear orchard.

barred by two doors. Again, gentlemen, I see the difficulty of explaining this plan, but you will be aided by a view of the premises. Mr. Morse returned upon Wednesday night. Who occupied the house that night? Let us first go to the front part. The person who came in last was the one who locked the front door. There are three fastenings on that door. These three fastenings were drawn by the last person in the night before. The door leading to the cellar had been closed by Mrs. Borden, and by the evidence it will be shown that that door was locked during the day of the murder. Bridget came in the night before by the back door and locked it, so when the prisoner and Bridget came in every exit was closed. Now in the front part of the house that night the prisoner slept in her own room. Mr. Morse slept in the guest's chamber. Mr. and Mrs. Borden slept in their own room. Bridget slept in her room in the third story. Now then it becomes my duty to relate all that occurred down to the time of the discovery of the awful crime committed in that house. In the morning Bridget was up first. She went down stairs and into the cellar to get her fuel for building a fire. Then she went to the door and took in the milk. The rear door I may explain was a double door, the inside or screen door being kept fastened, while the outside door was open. When opened by Bridget the outside door was opened for the day.

Then Mr. Borden came down stairs. He went out into the yard and to the barn. Bridget saw him do that. Bridget did not see Morse until after Mr. and Mrs. Borden had taken breakfast. After breakfast Mr. Morse was first to depart. He went out at 7 45 o'clock, and Mr. Borden let him out and bolted the door behind him. Soon after Morse went away the prisoner came down stairs, and began cooking her breakfast in the kitchen. While she was there Mrs. Borden went up stairs, and while up stairs Bridget went out into the yard because she was sick. When she came back Mr. Borden had apparently gone down town. Mrs. Borden was dusting the dining room, while the prisoner was in the kitchen. There was some conversation, we believe, between Mrs. Borden and Bridget about washing windows, and Bridget received her directions. Mrs. Borden disappeared at about that time, or at the time she went up stairs

to put two pillow cases upon two pillows there. You will be satisfied that this was not far from half past 9 o'clock, and upon the evidence you will be satisfied that she never left that room alive.

But one living person saw Mrs. Borden from that time until found dead. In the course of beginning the duty of washing windows Bridget had to go to the cellar and as she was about to go out the prisoner appeared at the screen door. "You need not shut that door because I am coming in," was the remark of Bridget. The prisoner said nothing, and I believe it to be fact that the door was not locked at that time. Then Bridget went into the dining room and sitting room to close the windows, and there was nobody there. Two of the sitting room windows were out of sight, because they are on the other side of the house. Then Bridget came to the front of the house, then to the north and washed the parlor and dining room windows. During all this time she saw neither Mrs. Borden or the prisoner. When she finished on the outside she came in at the screen door to wash the windows on the inside. She had partly washed one or two when some one was heard at the front door.

Mr. Borden left the house at between 9 o'clock and 9 30, and during that forenoon was at two banks, as we shall show to your entire satisfaction. At 25 minutes of 11 he was at the store of Mr. Clegg, who fixes the time satisfactorily. The next place we find him is at another store belonging to him on South Spring street, and we shall show that he left this place at 20 minutes to 11. The next that is heard of him he is seen by Mrs. Kelly, who is going down town, and he is coming out of the screen door and going around to the front door of his own house. Mrs. Kelly will fix the time, and it will not be the same as some others will say, but the discrepancy will be accounted for, in that we shall show to your entire satisfaction that the clock upon which Mrs. Kelly depends is not wholly reliable. When Mr. Borden attempted to enter the house by unlocking the front door with a key he found that the door was not secured as usual, but was bolted. When he came into the house we shall show it was by being admitted by Bridget. The prisoner at his entrance made some laugh or exclamation from the hall above, and at that moment Mrs. Borden laid dead within plain view of any one who stood in just the position the prisoner stood at that time, and had been dead for more than an hour. Mr. Borden was asked by the prisoner if there was any mail. "Mrs. Borden has gone out," said she. Had she a note calling her away? This, gentlemen, we shall put to you as a lie, and asked for no purpose except to stifle any inquiries of Mr. Borden in regard to the whereabouts of his wife.

Lizzie Borden went to the kitchen and commenced to iron handkerchiefs. Lizzie asked Bridget if she intended to go out, and cautioned her if she did so to lock the doors. To Bridget was told exactly the same story. Bridget finished her work of washing the windows and put her pails away. Then Lizzie tells Bridget there is a sale of cheap goods down town, and that something very desirable can be bought for 8 cents a yard, and Bridget, after saying that she guessed she would have some, went up stairs. The next thing of interest is the alarm. Bridget is sent across the street to Dr. Bowen's, and after she has returned, unable to find him, is sent to Miss Russell's. In the meantime Mrs. Churchill has arrived, altogether accidentally, and she gives the alarm. She saw Mr. Cunningham, and the telephone message reaches the station. An officer is sent at once to the scene of the homicide, and having duty which called his attention to the matter fixes the time at 11 15. It could not have been far from quarter of 11 when Mr. Borden arrived at the house, nor far from 11 15 when the alarm was given. You can measure time best perhaps by what was done by Bridget and others during the interim. Bridget had time to wash a window and a half in the sitting room, two windows in the dining room and the putting away of various articles and the dishes. After the alarm was given there instinctively leaped to the lips of every one this question, which was put to the prisoner, "Where were you, you were the last person who was left with your father alive?" Bridget asked "Where were you, Miss Lizzie?" She said she was out in the back yard, heard a groan and came in and found her father murdered. Bridget was sent to Dr. Bowen's, and not finding him returned. There had been no scream and no alarm up to the time Bridget returned unsuccessful in her search. Mrs. Churchill appears and saw Lizzie inside the screen door. Bridget was told by the prisoner to go down to Miss Russell's, whom you will remember as being the very person to whom Lizzie had predicted that disaster was about to occur. Mrs. Churchill asks the question, "Where were you?" and receives the reply, "I was out in the barn to get a piece of iron." Lizzie said, "I wish you would find Mrs. Borden," whereupon Mrs. Churchill and Bridget went up stairs and at once discovered Mrs. Borden's dead body.

It is to be regretted that Dr. Bowen was not found by Bridget when she went for him. Here would have been a witness who was trained to observation; he thought Mrs. Borden had died of fright and so expressed himself. After the alarm had been given the prisoner did not stop to make any inquiries regarding Mr. or Mrs. Borden, but went up stairs and put on a pink wrapper. We will show to you that Lizzie told Dr. Bowen that she went after a piece of iron when she left the house, to another she told she went for a piece of tin to fix a screen, to Mrs. Churchill that she heard a groan, to an officer that she heard a peculiar noise. Again she tells that she went into the barn to get lead to make sinkers, and to another in detail she says she came back and looked at the stove to see if the fire was hot enough for her to iron, put down her hat and accidentally discovered the homicide. Gentlemen, it isn't a difference of words. In one case she tells that she discovers the murders while about her regular duties, and in another case that she heard groans. We will ask you to remember that the 4th of August was one of the hottest days of the last summer in this locality and that the loft of the barn was stifling. Officer Medley was among the first to enter the barn after the tragedy. He had heard the story and went upstairs to the loft. He found when he had touched the floor above with his hands that it was thickly coated with dust. Later he found that every foot print was plainly to be seen. It is our duty to offer proof to you that Mrs. Borden died before her husband. We have evidence that when discovered Mr. Borden's body showed freshly running blood and was warm. The blood of Mrs. Borden was coagulated and the body was stiffened in death. The judgment of professional men who examined the bodies will be presented to you. The stomachs were sent to Professor Wood and examined and prepared with exactness. Mrs. Borden's stomach contained 11 ounces of food in the process of digestion, one fifth of which was water and four fifths solid matter partly digested. Mr. Borden's stomach contained six ounces, nine tenths water and one tenth food or solids. In the autopsy it was found that the upper intestines of Mrs. Borden contained partially digested food, while Mr. Borden's were empty. Mrs. Borden's lower intestines were empty, while those of Mr. Borden contained the matter which had been digested during the forenoon. Upon these facts the experts have determined that Mrs. Borden died at least an hour before her husband.

It will be shown that about two rooms of the house blood was spattered in various directions, which would make it appear there would be blood upon the clothing of the assailant. There was produced for the inspection of the prosecution some days after the crime, clothing which was said to have been worn by the prisoner on the day of the murder. The most rigid examination fails to produce any blood upon this clothing. Upon the skirt there is one minute trace of blood which is hardly worth while to call to your attention.

Let us go back on the story and consider the interval which elapsed between the deaths. The prisoner says she left off ironing because the fire became low. She says she put a stick of wood in the stove and left it smouldering and thought it would catch, but when she came back the fire was all out.

An officer discovered, it would appear by pure accident, that the prisoner had a light blue cotton dress with a fixed geometrical figure which she wore in the morning of that day. Dr. Bowen will say that she wore a cheap calico dress.

Mrs. Churchill says that she had on this morning a dress of light blue ground with a fixed diamond figure of darker blue, without a white spot. Upon being shown the dress referred to by Dr. Bowen she will say it is not the dress the prisoner had on. You will recall that the prisoner expressed a preference for a particular undertaker, and Miss Russell went for him, and when she came back Lizzie had on a pink wrapper.

It was on Saturday following the crime that the chief executive officer of Fall River, Mayor Coughlin, informed Lizzie that she was suspected.

Another dress will be described, one which was bought early in the spring. It will be shown that this dress was burned, and as Emma saw Lizzie at the stove she asked her what she was going to do. She replied, "I am going to burn this dress, it is all covered with paint." It will be shown that Miss Russell said "I wouldn't do that where folks can see you." Lizzie's only answer was to move away where she couldn't be seen from without.

Officer Hanscom, a Pinkerton detective not employed by the government, when this incident was called to his attention made the remark, "This is the worst thing you could have done."

We shall show to you that the search of the officers at that house was such that no dress covered with paint could escape their detection.

Upon the premises were found two hatchets and two axes, (which the counsel exhibited to the jury,) and upon one of these hatchets are spots which were once thought to be blood. Professor Wood says that it is utterly impossible to determine that the spots are blood and the axes are out of the question and could not be the weapons used by the assailant.

Both these hatchets have ragged edges and Professor Wood will say that they could not have been used for the murder and washed so as not to show the traces of blood.

Upon the day of the homicide another weapon was found that attracted little attention of the officers at the time from the fact that the weapon by which the deed was committed was supposed to have been already discovered. (Here the counsel produced a handleless hatchet and exhibited to the jury, and resumed.) At that time the handle was in its place, while the hatchet itself was covered with ashes, not ashes meaning dust, but with a firm adhesion. Monday it was taken away, and its custody up to this time will be traced for you. Both hatchets I hold in my hand are rusty, and one of them is known to be innocent. But you will observe that the rust on the handleless one is such as might result from an exposure to the night's dews or an exposure that was uniform on all parts of its surface. Professor Wood will say that if the hatchet was as smooth as the others the application of water soon after its use would cause it to part with all traces of blood. A test that was made will show that a break which appears in the weapon was a fresh one.

According to the practice in this commonwealth, either to protect the innocent or to establish guilt, such portions of the victims' bodies must be produced as are necessary, and the skulls of Mr. and Mrs. Borden will be shown to you, and you will carefully examine them.

(Here the skulls were produced by Dr. Dolan.)

There is another thing told—the weapon which brought Mr. Borden to his death was just 3½ inches in width. Let there be no mistake, gentlemen. The one significant fact is that the bloody weapon was not found on the premises beside the victims of that homicide. Whether this was the work of a maniac or of some one familiar with the house, is for you to determine. When the bodies were found, it was found that not a thing in the house had been disturbed. Mr. Borden had a considerable sum of money about him as well as his watch and chain. In or about the room there was not the slightest evidence of a struggle. The person, whoever he or she might be, was able to fell them down without a struggle. Mrs. Borden was found on the floor between the bureau and the bed, with her head hacked. Mr. Borden, found on the sofa, bore the same marks as those on the head of his wife. It will appear by confirmatory evidence, that no one was seen to escape from the house on that morning. The commonwealth will prove that there was an unkindly feeling between the prisoner and her mother; that on Aug. 3 she was preparing a murderous weapon; that from the time Mrs. Borden left the dining room until the prisoner came down no human being was in the house; that these were the acts of a person who from the time and place was familiar with the premises; we shall prove that the prisoner has made contradictory statements; that Mrs. Borden's was a prior death, and now, gentlemen, my duty with you is drawing to a close. We are to be governed from this time forth by the evidence. He closed with an appeal to the jury to exercise the best judgment as men.

Seasonable hats are now in season, and they're in our stock in all the latest styles. That's the magnet that's drawing crowds of buyers to our store. Everyone is eager to see a display of

All the New Styles,

and they come where the display is to be found. We have hats for all purposes, in all styles and in all sizes. Our stock is a hat exposition worth a place in the World's Fair. It's a fair sight to see, and you can't do the fair thing by yourself unless you see it. We have all the new colors in Soft and Stiff Hats.

M. C. SWIFT & SON,
153, 157 and 159 Union St.
NEW BEDFORD, MASS.

LIZZIE FAINTS AWAY.

Swooned Under the Terrible Strain of the Morning.

Immediately after Mr. Moody had finished the opening of the case, the prisoner swooned, and for several minutes was in an unconscious state. Deputy Sheriff Kirby, Mr. Jennings and Rev. Mr. Jubb were at once at her side, and through their efforts the woman, who up to this time had withstood the terrible strain which had been sufficient to break down the strongest, was restored to sensibility.

At this point the jury was excused for a few minutes.

The First Witness.

Thomas Kerian, the first witness, testified that he had drawn plans of the house and had made a survey of distances. From the Borden house to city hall he testified the distance was 900 feet, and from the Central police station to the Northern police station 1 14-100 miles. He went into detail as to distances of certain locations in the Border city. From Mr. Clegg's store to the Borden house it was about 540 feet. Had drawn plans showing the Borden premises and premises adjoining on three sides. Had also drawn plans of the Borden premises separate, also plans of the floors, showing the rooms where the bodies of Mr. and Mrs. Borden were found, as well as other rooms on the premises.

To Mr. Jennings witness said he had also prepared blue prints exhibited by that lawyer. They were correct and showed Mr. Borden's house and the house adjoining. A man standing on Second street south of the Borden house with his eye directly in line between the corner of Dr. Kelly's house and the southeast corner of the Andrew Borden house, he could see 12 inches of the door of the Andrew Borden barn.

At this point Mr. Knowlton arose and said with our desire and at the consent of defense I now move that the jury take a view of the house in Fall River.

Governor Robinson acquiesced, and claimed the privilege of his client accompanying the jury if she desired. He consulted with his client, and then said: "Your honor, she does not feel equal to the task."

Whom do you appoint, Mr. Sheriff, to look after the jury?

Deputy Sheriffs Nickerson, Arnold, Hodges and Brown, and these officials were duly sworn.

Mr. Moody will be represented by the commonwealth.

Judge Mason then stated to the jury that the view was not for the purpose of testimony, but only that they might be able to fix locations. You must keep together and not separate, and you will report at this court room at 9 o'clock.

At this point the court adjourned until tomorrow at 9 a. m.

At the request of District Attorney Knowlton the Old Colony company furnishes a special car for the jury, and, if necessary, the train will be held over ten minutes for its accommodation.

THE JURY IN FALL RIVER.

They Will Make a Thorough Examination of the Borden Premises.

(Special Dispatch.)

Fall River, June 6.—The train with the Borden jury left the Old Colony station in New Bedford at 12 45 and arrived here at 1 15.

The forward car was reserved for the jury in charge of Deputy Sheriffs Nickerson, Arnold, Hodges and Brown. Governor Robinson, A. J. Jennings, District Attorney Knowlton and Mr. Moody were allowed seats in the car with the jury.

Arriving at Fall River the jury proceeded at once to walk to the Borden house to examine the premises, and as they had their lunch in New Bedford they will be enabled to devote the whole afternoon to a most thorough examination of the premises.

THE NEW TESTIMONY.

Effort to Show that Miss Borden Spoke of "a Presentment of Murder."

Haverhill, June 6.—Ex-Senator Benjamin F. Brickett, an intimate friend of Mr. Moody, is authority for the statement that very little new evidence will be introduced into the Borden trial. The only important bit of testimony yet unpublished which will be offered will be to prove that a few days before the tragedy Miss Borden, in conversation with some neighbors, said that she had a presentment that within a few days there would be a murder in her family. The trial of Miss Borden attracts more than usual attention here on account of the connection with the prosecution of District Attorney Moody. Many of the friends of Mr. Moody are inclined to the opinion that he will lose in popularity and prestige by being upon the unpopular side of the case. Friends of Mr. Moody, however, say that it was a case of being drafted. Law requires that important criminal cases must be tried by officers of the state and not by attorneys hired for the occasion. The attorney general was therefore obliged to seek an assistant for Mr. Knowlton from among one of the district attorneys, and his choice fell upon Mr. Moody. It was then either accept or resign.

Burke Has Delirium Tremens.

(Special Dispatch.)

Fall River, June 6.—Luke Burke, who it is alleged pushed Henry Welsh from the tower of the Merchants mill in Fall River a week ago, was not arraigned this morning, as he is suffering with delirium tremens.

ULCERS, CANCERS, SCROFULA, SALT RHEUM, RHEUMATISM, BLOOD POISON.

these and every kindred disease arising from impure blood successfully treated by that never-failing and best of all tonics and medicines,

SWIFT'S SPECIFIC SSS

Books on Blood and Skin Diseases free.
Printed testimonials sent on application. Address
The Swift Specific Co.,
ATLANTA, GA.

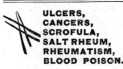

AMUSEMENTS.

Base Ball.

NEW KEMPTON STREET GROUNDS,
Wednesday, June 7th,
High Schools vs. Acushnets.
Game at 3 o'clock
ADMISSION........................15 CENTS.
je6-1t

GRAND OPERA HOUSE.

WEDNESDAY, JUNE 7th, 1893.
Complete production, same as at Park Theatre, Boston.
The Star Event!
The Interstate Satire by a New Hampshire Playright,
HOYT'S
A TEMPERANCE TOWN.
It points a moral and adorns a tale. The action of the play is laid in New Hampshire and Vermont, and it will interest every person in the state. It has held Boston six months after taking it by storm. It is true to life and full of points illustrated by brilliant actors.
Prices.......$1.00, 75, 50, 35 and 25 Cents.
Seats on sale Monday.

The Sewing Society
—OF—
ST. MARTIN'S CHURCH,
Will hold a Strawberry Festival and Sale in the Parish Rooms, Rivet street, foot of Fourth,
WEDNESDAY AND THURSDAY AFTERNOON AND EVENING, JUNE 7th and 8th,
On Wednesday evening there will be an exhibition of Wax Works, and on Thursday evening the drama entitled "Bread upon the Waters," will be given.
Admission............................15 Cents.
Refreshments will be served at reasonable prices. je5-3t

FRIENDS UNION.
The Friends Union will give an unique supper and attractive entertainment in
CHINA HALL,
THURSDAY EVENING, June 8th,
To which the public is cordially invited.
Supper from 6 to 7 30; tickets, 25 cents. Entertainment, 10 cents. Music by Maxfield and Andrews. je6-2t

THE LADIES' SOCIAL UNION
—OF THE—
Fourth Street M. E. Church,
Will hold their Annual Strawberry Festival and Entertainment, on
Thursday Evening, June 8th.
Entertainment at 8 o'clock.
ADMISSION.........................10 CENTS.
Cake, Cream and Berries will be on sale. je6-2t

NEW BEDFORD HIGH SCHOOL CADETS.
SEMI-ANNUAL
PRIZE DRILL AND DANCE
—AT—
GUARDS ARMORY,
Friday Evening, June 9, 1893.
Admission..............................35 Cents.
Reserved Seats.........................50 Cents.
Seats on sale at box office at Armory, Wednesday, June 7, at 2 30 p. m. je6-7-9

ENTERTAINMENT DIRECTORY.

WEDNESDAY.

St. Martin's Parish Rooms—Afternoon and evening, festival and sale.
Opera House—8 p. m., A Temperance Town.

FUTURE EVENTS.

Fourth Street Church—8th, Strawberry Festival and Entertainment.
China Hall—8th, Friends' union supper.

AMUSEMENTS.

The Friends union will give a unique supper and attractive entertainment on Thursday evening in China hall, to which the public is invited. See advertisement.

A strawberry festival and entertainment will be given by the Ladies Social union of the Fourth Street M. E. church Thursday evening. The delicacies of the season will be on sale.

The High School cadets' semi-annual prize drill and dance will take place at the Guards' armory next Friday evening. The prices are 35 and 50 cents, and seats go on sale Wednesday afternoon. Read advertisement.

A strawberry festival and sale will be held by the Sewing society of St. Martin's church in the parish rooms, Rivet street, tomorrow and Thursday afternoons and evenings. Wednesday evening there will be an exhibition of wax works, and on Thursday evening a drama, "Bread upon the Waters," will be given.

At the Opera House tomorrow evening Charlie Hoyt's latest and most popular play, "A Temperance Town," will be presented by an excellent company. Mr. Hoyt has mingled humor and pathos with flashes of his brightest wit and bits of excruciatingly funny stage business, in his most crafty manner, so that the Prohibitionist and anti-Prohibitionist forget that they are severely scored, and one side can join with the other in a hearty laugh, which is sure to be repeated by the score.

THE SPINNERS.

At a meeting of the executive committee held last evening several spinners employed at the Hathaway mills appeared with a grievance. They complain that they are paid by the day when they should work by the piece. The new mill has now been running four months and they think it is time they were put on piece work, as the mules are working nicely and the weekly wages they receive, $12, represents $18 worth of labor. The executive committee took the matter under consideration and decided to place the matter before a special general meeting to be called either tonight or tomorrow night.

Among the visiting clergymen who will participate in the work of the annual conference of New England Christian churches in session at Portsmouth, N. H., are Rev. Messrs. W. J. Reynolds and J. McCalman of this city.

A Pitiable Sight

It is to see an infant suffering from the lack of proper food. It is entirely unnecessary, as a reliable food can always be obtained; we refer to the Gail Borden Eagle Brand Condensed Milk. Sold by grocers and druggists everywhere.

METHODIST SOCIAL UNION.

Final Meeting for the Year in County Street Church.

Officers Elected and a Banquet Served to Many Guests.

Speeches by Various Pastors and Lay Members of the Organization.

The annual and final meeting of the present season of the Methodist Social union was held in the vestry of the County Street M. E. church last evening.

The exercises opened at 7 30 o'clock with a supper. The big vestry had been prettily set with a dining room in one half and reception room in the other, the division being marked with potted palms and shrubbery.

Grace was asked by Rev. A. Cameron, after which the 150 guests enjoyed an excellent spread of cold meats, sandwiches, cake and ice cream. An orchestra, embracing William Baylies, Jr., cellist, George W. Burgess violinist, and Miss Alice G. Anthony pianist, rendered incidentally several orchestral selections.

After the supper, Vice President George M. Eddy, acting in the absence of the president, Robert F. Raymond, called the meeting to order and after a brief address called on Rev. G. A. Sisson to offer prayer.

The meeting then proceeded to the annual business session.

On motion of Rev. B. F. Simon, a nominating committee of six was chosen and retired to choose officers for next year.

Rev. B. F. Simon acted as toastmaster at the post prandial exercises. He expressed regret at the inability of Mayor Brock to remain, as had been expected, and respond to the toast "Municipal Morality." Mr. Simon declared him a stalwart son of Methodism, placed in the vanguard—a shining figure of the church in the political life of the community. The church rejoices in the achievements of her fathers, she rejoices in what she herself has achieved, and most of all in what her young people are to achieve in the future for God and their country. Even though the mayor could not be present, other stalwart sons were, and Mr. Simon called on Rev. R. C. Miller of Acushnet as the first speaker, responding to the toast, "Our Young People."

George M. Eddy,
President Methodist Social Union.

Rev. Mr. Miller said he was proud of the young people. And as for that there is very little distinction between young and old people—they are all young people. The tendency of the age is to draw in the young. Of course they are the hope of the future; the life of the Methodist church today. The young people of the Methodist church are ahead of those of other denominations in their activity, and it is an inspiration to get into one of their meetings. They are coming into the church as workers to lead the world to Christ. He was proud of them in social life—in their firmness of purpose and disregard for popular scoffing. In his opinion they should have all the liberality accorded them that the spirit of Methodism will allow. Those churches are most successful which are most liberal to the young people. He felt that the young people of his church are earnest workers, and he felt sure that if desired, he has plenty of them to spare a few to help the city workers in the great work.

Mrs. Arthur G. Luce sung a soprano solo most acceptably.

Lewis C. Small responded to the toast "The Mission of the Methodist Social Union." Primarily, he said, the mission is to bring together the Methodists of all the different churches for the purpose of promoting their mutual acquaintance. It is not wise to isolate each church in its work. In union there is strength, and the time spent in the union meetings is by no means wasted. All the good people are not in any one church, and the best way to find it out is by seeking the intimacy of friendly fellowship with one another. Missionary work is better promoted by the union than by any individual church. The union seeks to make it possible for every dollar spent to yield 100 cents in equivalent. It has its literary as well as social advantages, and many a good speaker may there develop his talents. Its work might be even better promoted by the establishment of a permanent time and place for meetings, and a more regular system of affiliation. In closing, Mr. Small quoted and adapted the familiar hymn: "We are not divided, All one body are we; One in faith and doctrine," let us be one in charity.

Rev. C. S. Davis spoke on "Aggressive Methodism." In opening he expressed a firm belief in the efficacy of social gatherings and declared companionship the greatest gift of fortune and the ground on which the future of the church depends. He declared himself glad he was born a Methodist, and attributed to the fact all he is and all he has. The meetings are not a merely pleasurable, social affair, but to gain strength for labor in the world by communion of ideas. From its beginning to the present the history of Christianity has been one of effort and endeavor. Its eras of progress have been exactly contemporary with its most earnest emphasis of primitive truth and primitive sacrifice. The Methodist church was born in a revival and its whole career has been one of effort and endeavor. A church to be aggressive must have its members emphasize the power of personal Christianity and personal consecration to the work. They must be aggressive or nothing. They must be consecrated and believe the church not only worthy and an essential, but supremely so. The church must have the best young people of the church now—with all the best endowments nature and the church can give them. The enthusiasm that should be expended for the church is now too much diverted to other societies. With a hundred more of them there will be no churches. Methodism, to live, must grapple with issues of the hour and can be successful only when pushed by one vast body of consecrated workers.

William Baylies, Jr., rendered a cello solo very pleasingly.

The nominating committee reported the following candidates for office for the ensuing year:

President—George M. Eddy.
Vice Presidents—Lewis C. Small and Robert H. Taber.
Secretary—Miss Emma C. Haskell.
Treasurer—Louis Tilden.
Corresponding Secretary—R. F. Raymond.
Executive Committee—Alfred G. Studley of Pleasant Street church, Stephen H. Briggs of Allen street, Mrs. H. K. Nye of Fairhaven, Savory C. Hathaway of County street, Gilbert B. Borden of Acushnet and Mrs. C. H. Gifford of Fourth street.

George M. Eddy sought to decline an election, but after considerable urging consented to stand. It was unanimously voted that the list be elected as a whole.

On motion of Rev. C. W. Holden it was voted that each pastor select a committee of three from his church to solicit members to the union.

After the singing of the doxology and the pronouncing of the benediction the meeting adjourned.

The success of the meeting was due to the efforts of a large committee of ladies. They were: Chairman, Miss E. M. Haskell; secretary, Mrs. H. K. Nye; treasurer, Mrs. S. H. Briggs; County Street members, Mrs. Job Wade, Mrs. A. J. Rice and Mrs. H. M. Parker; Pleasant Street, Mrs. Dr. Lilley, Mrs. C. H. Spooner and Miss Anna Jennison; Fourth Street, Mrs. Horace Tilden, Mrs. Charles Gifford and Mrs. James Russell; Allen Street, Mrs. S. H. Briggs and Mrs. A. E. Clarke; Acushnet, Mrs. Franklyn Howland, Rev. R. C. Miller, Mrs. Thomas Denham and Mrs. Addie Poulson; Fairhaven, Mrs. Alfred Nye, Mrs. Robert Swain and Mrs. Robert H. Taber.

NEIGHBORHOOD CONVENTION.

Resolutions of Regret at Rev. R. L. Rae's Departure Adopted.

The neighborhood convention met Monday in the Congregational church at East Rochester. The devotional services were conducted by Rev. R. P. Gardner. In the absence of the moderator, Rev. J. W. Goodwin, Rev. B. E. Smith opened the discussion of the morning on the topic, "What place shall we give music in our church service?" Mrs. Edington, of Wareham, Rev. J. S. Thomas, Rev. R. L. Rae, and Rev. R. P. Gardner spoke briefly, and the exercises were valuable and instructive.

During the noon intermission an abundant collation was served in the vestry.

A business session followed, in the course of which the following resolutions were unanimously adopted:

Resolved, That we, the Union Neighborhood convention, in session at East Rochester, do hereby say that we regret the departure of our Brother Rae and his estimable wife from the limits of our convention.

Resolved, That we bear testimony of his faithfulness in helping to make these meetings a success.

Resolved, That our prayers shall be offered up that in his new field even greater success shall be his than in this place, where so many have found the light under his faithful ministrations.

The topic for the afternoon was, "Wasted Spiritual Resources." Revs. R. L. Rae, J. S. Thomas, R. P. Gardner and B. E. Smith and Messrs. Gifford, Morse and Sherman carried on a spirited discussion.

At 3 40 the convention adjourned to meet in July with the Christian church at Perry Hill, Acushnet.

BROWN'S 11-INNING VICTORY.

The Providence Nine a Winner Over Holy Cross Ball Players.

Worcester, June 6.—The rubber game between the Holy Cross and Brown university ball teams was the most exciting of the season in this city yesterday. It took 11 hotly contested innings to reach a decision.

Neither side had its star pitcher in the box, but both the substitutes did good work. Bannon is the regular second baseman of Holy Cross, and the change brought in an outfielder to play short, which weakened the infield.

The Browns scored in the first inning, after two men were out. Jones hit safely, and went to third on McGill's single. McGill started to steal second, and Jones came home, Hickey making a slow return of the ball to the plate. In the sixth Brown had three men on bases and nobody out, but was prevented from scoring by sharp work.

Holy Cross tied the score in the ninth on a three-bagger by McCarthy and Stafford's long fly to McGill.

In the last half of the 11th, after Lang had struck out, White made a single, Sexton hit a hot ball, which Lowney fumbled, Steere lined out a single and White scored the winning run. The score:

BROWNS.

	ab	r	bh	tb	po	a	e
Sexton, 3b.,	5	0	0	0	2	0	1
F. Steere, s.s.,	5	0	1	1	0	4	1
Jones, 2b.,	4	1	1	1	4	3	0
Magill, r.f.,	4	0	1	1	2	0	0
George, c.f.,	4	0	0	0	2	0	0
McLane, l.f.,	4	0	0	0	3	1	0
Greene, 1b.,	4	0	0	0	11	0	2
Lang, c.,	4	0	0	0	9	3	1
White, p.,	4	1	2	2	0	4	0
Totals,	38	2	5	5	33	15	5

HOLY CROSS.

	ab	r	bh	tb	po	a	e
Leahy, c.,	5	0	2	2	7	2	0
Bannon, p.,	5	0	2	2	0	3	0
Cotter, 1b.,	5	0	1	1	12	0	0
Hickey, 2b.,	5	0	0	0	3	2	0
McCarthy, l.f.,	5	1	2	4	3	2	0
Stafford, r.f.,	4	0	0	0	0	0	0
Lowney, 3b.,	3	0	0	0	1	3	1
Kelley, s.s.,	4	0	0	0	1	2	3
Johnson, c.f.,	3	0	0	0	4	0	0
Totals,	39	1	7	9	*31	12	4

Innings,	1	2	3	4	5	6	7	8	9	10	11	
Browns,	1	0	0	0	0	0	0	0	0	0	1	—2
Holy Cross,	0	0	0	0	0	0	0	0	1	0	0	—1

Earned runs—Browns 1, Holy Cross 1. Three-base hit—McCarthy. Sacrifice hit—Stafford. Stolen bases—Bannon, Jones Magill. First base on balls—Lowney. First base on errors—Browns 4, Holy Cross 4. Struck out—Johnson 2, Bannon, Hickey, Cotter, Lowney, Sexton, Greene 2, George, Lang. Double plays—Bannon, Leahy and Cotter; McLane and Lang. Wild pitches—White 1. Hit by pitched ball—Johnson. Time—2 hours 20 minutes. Umpires—Murphy and McMurray.

*Winning run made with one man out.

The High Schools and Acushnets will play on the new Kempton street grounds tomorrow at 3 p. m.

TIVERTON.

Mr. and Mrs. Charles Morse of Acushnet were the guests of Mrs. Hammond Skewis over Sunday.

Mrs. Delano of Fairhaven arrived Saturday on a visit to her daughter, Mrs. Samuel E. Almy.

Mrs. John Delano and two children of New Bedford were in town over Sunday, the guests of John G. Cory and family.

Mr. and Mrs. Levi Wing of Acushnet were the guests of Samuel W. Hathaway and family over Sunday.

Mr. and Mrs. Marshall of Fall River are occupying for the season the Queen Anne cottage owned by Alphonso Covell of Boston.

PLYMOUTH COUNTY.

Saturday night Officers Ashport and Boyden arrested Joseph Korvikiby, aged 29, and Mrs. Rosa Martin, aged 42, both Poles, for adultery. They were found together. The man drew a revolver at the entrance of the officers, but got no chance to use it. In the district court they were held in $800 each for the grand jury.

HAS WORKED ITS WAY

Into nearly every house.
DR. HOUGH'S
COUGH AND LUNG BALSAM.
The best remedy for Coughs and Colds. Price 35 cents. Sold by all druggists and medicine dealers.

LOOKS BLACKER.

(Continued from Third Page.)

compel him to act against his own wishes. He might have threatened to reveal the whereabouts of the man that was wanted, but there was nothing to anchor the Portuguese to that spot once he had learned that the police were after him. However, he has no easy task before him if he is to free himself from the net and those who trapped him.

Made a Clever Job of It.

For several days they have known of the shoe purchase, have been familiar with the history of the coins and have persisted that the capture was of the utmost importance. They were certainly right in their assumptions, and if the examination of the stomach of the murdered woman indicates that she was killed early in the morning, it will be difficult for Correiro to get away from La Croix's shoe store, whatever may be said concerning his presence on the bridge. Guilty or innocent, it is a little singular that he spent all the money he had on shoes. He had shoes, such as they were, and he was short on food and car fare. He had a plugged half dollar left when he concluded his bargain with La Croix, and a bill, which it is thought, only existed in his imagination, so far as has appeared. There was no blood on the shoes he discarded which attracted attention, and he ran into danger when he renewed his footwear. It is hoped, of course, that the police will not have to look further for an assassin and from their movements yesterday it was evident that they were pretty well satisfied with their case.

Looks Blacker for the Prisoner.

Things are now looking even blacker for the prisoner. Manuel Sousa, the chief witness for the government, was admited to $2,000 bail yesterday afternoon.

Captains Doherty and Connors, who have been at work on the case from the beginning, and to whose efforts the arrest of Correiro is due, started out for new evidence immediately after the court proceedings. Following up the theory that Correiro had started for Crab Pond bridge immediately on leaving La Croix's store, the officers took a walk up the railroad track at a point on the track opposite St. John's cemetery.

The old shoes were found in a pasteboard box and the paper wrapping of the box was found a short distance from the shoes. They were taken to the shoe store, where the proprietor identified them as those Correiro had removed in his store, and which he had sold to him some time ago. The shoes bore traces of having been lately washed with salt water, so that if there are any traces of blood on them it will be difficult to find them. They will, however, be sent to Professor Wood of Harvard for examination.

Spatter of Blood on His Shirt.

Despite all efforts the police have been unable to find any bloody clothing, although on Correiro's shirt was a splatter of blood that he says came from a cut on his finger. In the afternoon Captains Doherty and Connors went to Taunton and made a search for the watch.

They were unable to get any clew to it and will continue the search today in Fall River. The finding of this and the pocketbook would fix the crime beyond all shadow of doubt, although all the city officials and the people at large are confident that the police have the right man under arrest. Mr. Manchester's son-in-law has been assisting Mr. Manchester for the last two days on the farm, and is sure that the right man has been caught. On examining the kitchen today he discovered a cent, covered with blood, that had escaped the scrutiny of the police and the medical examiner. It was lying slightly under the kitchen stove near one of the large pools of blood. In connection with this find Mr. Coolidge says that to his mind it indicates that the robbery was committed previous to the murder, and that in the attempt to prevent the robber from getting out of the house the murder was committed, and that this coin was dropped in the fierce fight that ensued.

In accordance with the theory of the police to suppress from the press a portion of the evidence, as was evidenced when the medical examiner refused to give to the press the complete result of the autopsy, the police have made no mention of the bloody spots leading from the kitchen to the dining room. These spots are plainly to be seen and were seen this afternoon by a Standard reporter. There is a spot of blood in front of the pantry door and two large ones on the seat of a chair near one of the dining room windows. This indicates either one of two things to the investigators. First, that Bertha, who was at work in the pantry, surprised the murderer as he was coming out of her bedroom, and attacked him in the dining room, and in the struggle was dragged to the kitchen, where the robber took the axe from the woodbox and killed her. Second, that he killed her in the kitchen first, and then walked into the dining room and from there to the bedroom. In the latter case the blood was carried in on his feet, and possibly some blood dripped from his hands, which, the police are inclined to think, were covered with blood.

If the first theory is correct, then in the struggle in the dining room Bertha must have received a blow that caused her to bleed freely, and that she was finished after following the assailant to the kitchen. Her brother-in-law inclines to the second theory, as he thinks it was the knowledge that the robber had her watch that caused her to fight so fiercely. The coin still remains on the floor where discovered, and will be left there until removed by the police, as Mr. Manchester is trying to assist the police all that he can. The trade dollar, the companion piece to the one owned by Bertha, which Mr. Coolidge took to the bank to ascertain its value, has not yet been found.

The latter is confident that the trade dollar passed by Correiro, and which is now in the possession of the police, is the one that was stolen from the Manchester house.

It had been his wife's custom to allow the baby to play with the one she had, and when he visited the Manchester house a few Sundays ago the baby was restless and Bertha went and got the trade dollar for the baby to play with. Mr. Coolidge noted at the time that it had the appearance of having just been issued from the mint, and so remarked to Bertha.

The half dollar with the hole in it was also a keepsake, one she had when a child, and both pieces of money were kept together. The crisp new bills Correiro is said to have possessed is accounted for by the statement that her father always made it a point to give her new crisp bills when he gave her money, always saving them for her.

Marshal Hilliard returned from New Bedford last night and was immediately closeted with Captains Doherty and Connors, as well as the inspectors who have been working on the case. He said nothing new had been developed during the day, save the finding of the shoes.

The alibi set up by the countrymen of Correiro evidently causes the police no uneasiness, for previous to the charge the Portuguese had accounted for his movements in such a manner as to allow of his being in the places indicated by the witnesses for the prosecution. Since then they have changed their story materially as to the time Correiro was seen in the place previously mentioned.

The police have witnesses who heard the first statements of these men. Muniz, the uncle of the prisoner, changed his story Sunday afternoon when he had a conversation with a Standard representative, but at that time Muniz did not know of the evidence the police had in their possession as to the shoes and the money.

When Correiro was shown the shoes found by the police and identified by the shoe dealer he is said to have nearly fainted.

Today the police will search the city for the watch.

The Reward.

If it turns out that Correiro is the murderer some question may arise regarding the reward which has been offered for the capture of the murderer. In case the police who worked up the clew are barred, the prisoner's uncle may put in a claim which could be disputed, should it appear that he brought in his nephew under orders. There is a law which makes it necessary for any citizen who is called on to assist in an arrest, and perhaps the money belongs to nobody. However, the city will take no pains to economize in this direction, provided the real villain is safe behind the bars.

Is Correiro a Fugitive.

About 16 days ago a murder was committed at Arlington, Md., back of the Pimlico Race track, about seven miles from Baltimore. The murder in every respect was similar to the slaughter of Bertha Manchester at Fall River. Istabelli, a hard-working, honest man, who had saved up some $600, was found chopped to pieces. The money was missing. Among the money stolen at the time of the murder was $4 in counterfeit coin, which was all he had left of about $30 passed on him by a gang of counterfeiters in Philadelphia. An Italian named Dennari, answering in every respect the description of Correiro, is wanted for the murder. The police learned that he had left for the north. He was traced as far as Fall River and there the search ended, as they were unable to connect with any clew. Louise Ferravia, a bright young Italian, is of the opinion that these men are one and the same person. He says that it is in his belief a case of thirst for human blood on the part of the assassin. Dennari, he says, is an escaped criminal from Lombardi, and the majority of his class in this country are of a similar stamp. In Italian the word carreiro means police guard or picket.

CITY NOTICES.

CITY OF NEW BEDFORD.

Assessors' Notice.

To the Inhabitants and Other Persons Liable to Pay Taxes in the City of New Bedford.

ASSESSORS' OFFICE,
LIBRARY BUILDING May 1, 1893.

The Assessors of the City of New Bedford hereby give notice to the inhabitants of said city, and all other persons liable to pay taxes therein, that their office will be open on and after the First Day of May until and including the Fifteenth Day of June, and all persons liable to be taxed in said city are hereby required to bring in at the said office true and perfect lists of all the polls (males twenty years old and upwards) and schedules of the real and personal estates for which they are liable to pay taxes.

Financial officers of LITERARY, BENEVOLENT, CHARITABLE OR SCIENTIFIC CORPORATIONS, incorporated under general laws, are hereby notified to bring in to the Assessors on or before July 1st, true lists of all *real and personal estates* held by such persons or corporations for such purposes, in accordance with Chapter 217 of the Acts of 1882, a copy of which is hereunto appended.

[CHAP. 217.]

AN ACT providing for returns of property held for literary, benevolent, charitable or scientific purposes.

Be it enacted. &c., as follows:

SECT. 1. The notice to be given by assessors under the provisions of section thirty-eight of chapter eleven of the Public Statutes shall require all persons and corporations to bring in to the assessors, within a time therein specified, not later than the first day of July in the then current year, true lists of all real and personal estate held by such persons and corporations respectively for literary, benevolent, charitable or scientific purposes on the first day of May in said year, together with the statements of the amounts of all receipts and expenditures by such persons or corporations for said purposes during the year next preceding said first day of May; such lists and statements to be in such detail as may be required by the tax commissioners; *provided*, that the assessors may accept any such list and statement after the time so specified if they shall be satisfied that there was good cause for the delay; but no list or statement shall be received after the first day of August in the then current year.

SECT. 2. If any person or corporation wilfully omits to bring in the list and statement of real and personal estate as herein required, the estate so held shall not be exempt from taxation in the then current year under the provisions of the third clause of section five of said chapter.

Mortgaged Real Estate.

"Any mortgagor or mortgagee of real estate may bring in to the assessors of the town or city where such real estate lies," within the time specified in this notice, "a statement, under oath, of the amount due on each separate lot or parcel of such real estate, and the name and residence of every holder of an interest therein as a mortgagee or mortgagor. When such property is situated in two or more places, or when a recorded mortgage includes for one sum two or more estates or parts of an estate, an estimate of the amount of the mortgagee's interest in each estate or part of an estate shall be given in such statement." (Chap. 175 of the Acts of 1882.) When a statement in conformity with the law above quoted is brought in, the real estate therein returned will be assessed under sections 14, 15 and 16 of chapter 11 of the Public Statutes. But in case where the mortgagor of the real estate has agreed in writing to pay all taxes assessed thereon, NO STATEMENT OR RETURN IS REQUIRED from either mortgagee or mortgagor, unless requested by the Assessors in writing.

Estates in Trust.

Persons holding estates in trust, whether for minors or otherwise, are particularly requested to furnish the Assessors with statements in relation to such estates. *When trust estates, or estates of persons deceased have been divided during the past year, or have changed hands from other causes, the trustee, executor or administrator, or other person interested, is required and warned to give notice of such change; and in default of such notice, will be held to pay the tax assessed, although such estate has been wholly distributed and paid over.*

Any person bringing in a list of all his taxable personal property will be assessed upon the valuation thereof, and any one neglecting to furnish the Assessors with such list, within the time above specified, will be doomed at a legal meeting of the Board of Assessors, agreeably to the law of the Commonwealth. *All persons will take notice that statements of personal property must be in writing, subscribed and sworn to, and handed in to the assessors' office, on or before the Fifteenth day of June. Also that the personal property of all taxable persons must be estimated by the Board, notwithstanding a Verbal Statement or Informal Written Communication to any one or more of the Assessors.* (Pub. Stat., chap. 11, sec. 39 and 41.) When a person has failed to bring in a list or schedule of all his taxable property, in conformity to this notice, no abatement of a tax so assessed upon such person for personal property can be granted, "unless such tax exceeds by more than fifty per cent. the amount which would have been assessed to that person on personal estate, if he had seasonably brought in said list; and if said tax exceeds by more than fifty per cent. the said amount, the abatement shall be only of the excess above the said fifty per cent." (Pub. Stat., chap. 11, sec. 73.)

Special Notice to Owners of Merchandise.

The amount of goods, wares, merchandise and stock in trade, must be given as the same was held on the first day of May of the current year.

Special Notice to Women.

In accordance with the provisions of chap. 351, sec. 7, of the Acts of the year 1892, the Assessors will "receive the request of every woman, twenty-one years of age and upward * * * * * who shall in a writing signed by her, request that her name be transmitted to the Registrars for purposes of registration." These requests should be ready at the time the Assessors call at the residences.

CHAS D. TUELL,
WM. A. RUSSELL,
JOHN A. RUGGLES,
Assessors.

Office Hours—Until further notice, from 8 a. m. to 12 m. and 2 to 6 p. m.
ap29-TTStje15

Baggage Tags
ALWAYS IN STOCK AT
STANDARD OFFICE.

UNDERTAKERS.

E. T. WILSON,
Undertaker & Embalmer,
80 PLEASANT STREET.
(Odd Fellows' Building.)

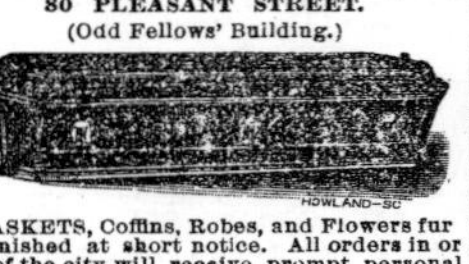

CASKETS, Coffins, Robes, and Flowers furnished at short notice. All orders in or out of the city will receive prompt personal attention day or night.

Arterial Embalming a Specialty.
Persons wishing my services nights or Sundays will please call at my
Residence................ 152 William Street
Telephone number 179—3. d&w

R. G. BENNETT,
UNDERTAKER and EMBALMER,
356 Acushnet Avenue,
(Third door South of New Post Office.)
A choice stock of Caskets, Robes and Funeral Supplies. All orders in or out of the city receive prompt attention. Office Telephone, 151—5. Residence Telephone, 346—4. Residence, 47 Chestnut Street, corner Hillman. Orders nights and Sundays received at residence or at Kirby & Hicks' Stable, 60 Elm street, corner Pleasant. d19-d&wtf

WESTON C. VAUGHAN, JR.,
Undertaker and Embalmer,
321 AND 323 PURCHASE STREET.

CASKETS, Coffins, Robes and Flowers, furnished at short notice. Funerals attended in or out of the city. All orders from neighboring towns by express or otherwise promptly attended to. Telephone connection day or night. Residence, 323 Purchase street. Night bell promptly answered. Telephone number 201—7.

STEAMSHIP LINES.

ANCHOR LINE.
United States Mail Steamships
Sail from New York every Saturday for
GLASGOW VIA LONDONDERRY
Rates for Saloon Passage
By S. S. CITY OF ROME, $50 and upward.
OTHER STEAMERS, Cabin, $45 and upward, according to accommodation and location of Room. Excursion Tickets at reduced rates. Second Cabin, $30. Steerage, $24. Second Cabin from Glasgow or Derry, $35.
Drafts at lowest Current Rates.
For Book of tours and other information apply to HENDERSON BROTHERS, 7 Bowling Green, N. Y., Thomas Donaghy, Corner Union and Water sts. or Edwin Whittaker 884 Purchase st., or David Waugh, 773 South Water street, New Bedford.

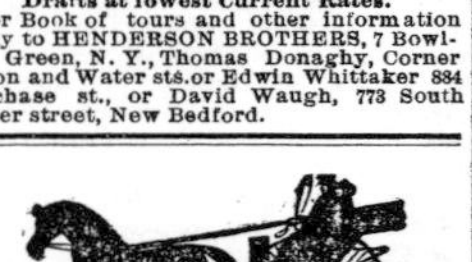

CARRIAGES!
—AT—
A. DAVIS ASHLEY'S,
947 Acushnet Avenue,
IN ENDLESS VARIETY.
New and Secondhand for sale and exchanged. We trade quick and often and give you an equivalent for your money.

—ALSO—
Several Horses!
For sale LOW to clean out the lot. Call early and get your money's worth at
A. DAVIS ASHLEY'S,
947 Acushnet Avenue,
Cor. Coggeshall Street.

We Must Have Room
SECOND HAND
CARRIAGES
Must Go.
Brownell, Ashley & Co.,
24 to 38 FOURTH ST.

HATCH & COMPANY'S
EXPRESS,
No. 5 Ricketson Block, New Bedford,
DAILY,
By Passenger Trains, to all Points on the Old Colony Railroad and its Connections.

GEORGE C. BLISS,
FLORIST.
34 Arnold Street,
CORNER COTTAGE.
TELEPHONE, DAY OR NIGHT.

POSTERS AND HAND BILLS
Printed at short notice at the
STANDARD PRINTING ROOMS.

TRAVELLERS' GUIDE.

THE NEW YORK, NEW HAVEN AND HARTFORD RAILROAD COMPANY, LESSEE.

OLD COLONY RAILROAD.

TIME tables showing local and through train service between all stations may be obtained at all ticket offices of this company.

Week day passenger trains Leave New Bedford for Boston (Park Square Station) at 5 25, 7 25, 8 45, 10 55 A. M., 1 30, 3 40, 5 50, 9 40 P. M., Return, 8 00, 9 30 A. M., 12 M., 2 30, 5 10, 6 30, 11 00 P. M. Boston (Kneeland Street Station) at 5 50 P. M. Return, 5 45 A. M. Providence at 5 25, 7 25, 8 45, †10 55 A. M., †1 30, 3 40, †5 50, †9 40 P. M. Return, †6 00, 8 15, †9 00 A. M., 12 10, †2 00, 5 05, †6 22, †10 05 P. M. Lowell at 5 25, 8 45 A. M., 3 40 P. M. Fitchburg at 5 25, 8 45, 10 55, A. M., 3 40, P. M. Mansfield at 5 25, 7 25, 8 45, 10 55 A. M., 1 30, 3 40, 5 50, 9 40 P. M. Taunton at 5 25, 7 25, 8 45, 10 55 A. M., 1 30, 3 40, 5 50, 9 40 P. M. Return 12 08, 7 18, 9 12, 10 31 A. M., 1 05, 3 33, 6 06, 7 58 P. M. Newport at 8 45, A. M., 3 40 P. M. Fall River at 8 45 A. M., 3 40, 9 40 P. M. New York, via Fall River Line, at 5 50 P. M. New York, via Shore Line, at 7 25, 8 45, 10 55 A. M., 8 40, 9 40 P. M. Myricks at 5 25, 8 45, 10 55 A. M., 1 30, 3 40, 5 50, 9 40 P. M. East Freetown and Braley's, 5 25, 8 45 A. M., 1 30, 5 50, 9 40 P. M.

Fall River and Way Stations, via Fall River Branch, at 7 05, 10 00 A. M., 12 35, 5 45 P. M., S10 00 P. M. Return, 8 50, 11 50 A. M., 3 30, 6 35, P. M. S 10 45 P. M.

†Via Mansfield. S Saturdays only.

SUNDAY TRAINS.

Leave New Bedford for Fall River, at 6 30 P. M. Providence, Taunton and Boston at 7 25 A. M., 12 50, 6 30 P. M. Return—Boston, Park Square Station, 4 15 A. M., 6 00 P. M. Providence 6 45 A. M., 6 30 P. M. Fall River, 7 10 A. M., 6 40 P. M.

FAIRHAVEN BRANCH.

Leave Fairhaven (week days) for Boston, Brockton, Bridgewater and Middleboro, at 8 00 A. M., 4 40 P. M. Tremont, Marion, Mattapoisett, Sandwich, Hyannis, and all points on Cape Cod, at 8 00, 9 45 A. M., 4 40 P. M.

Horse cars will leave William street at 7 30 and 9 10 A. M., 4 00 P. M., to connect with trains at Fairhaven.

J. R. KENDRICK, General Manager, Boston.
GEO. L. CONNOR, Gen'l Pass. Agent, Boston.
WILLIAM B. FISHER, Agent, New Bedford
April 5th, 1893.

NEW BEDFORD, MARTHAS VINEYARD & NANTUCKET STEAMBOAT CO.
SPRING ARRANGEMENT,
Commencing MONDAY, April 17th, 1893.
Nantucket, Marthas Vineyard, Cottage City, Oak Bluffs, Edgartown, Vineyard Haven and Woods Holl.
(Weather Permitting,)
Steamers will run daily (Sundays excepted.)
Leave New Bedford for Nantucket, Woods Holl, Vineyard Haven, Cottage City and Edgartown, 1 50 p. m., (arrival of train leaving Boston Park Square Station 12 00 m., Providence 12 10 p. m., Taunton 1 05 p. m., and Fall River (via Branch) 11 50 a. m.
Return leave Nantucket 7 00 a. m., Edgartown 7 00 a. m., Cottage City 7 35 and 9 15 a. m., Vineyard Haven 8 10 a. m.. Woods Holl 8 50 and 10 00 a. m., connecting with train at New Bedford due in Boston (Park Square Station) 12 40 and 3 20 p. m., Providence 1.15 and 3 30 p. m.
Leave Woods Holl for Martha's Vineyard and Nantucket 3 05 p. m.
Leave Cottage City for Nantucket 3 45 p. m.
EDWARD T. PIERCE, Agent.
New Bedford, April 13, 1893.

Mattapoisett Stage.
On and after MONDAY, May 8th, and until further notice, the Mattapoisett and New Bedford stage will run twice daily leaving Mattapoisett, from H. A. Shurtleff's store, at 8 00 a. m., and 1 15 p. m. Returning, leave New Bedford at 11 a. m., and 5 00 p. m., from Nichols & Damon's shoe store, 71 Purchase street. All express business promptly attended to.
C. E. FULLER, Proprietor.

South Dartmouth Stage.
Will leave South Dartmouth on and after MONDAY, Oct. 10, at 7 45 A. M. and 1 30 P. M. Returning, leave New Bedford at 11 00 A. M. and 5 P. M. Office at Hatch & Co's express office, No. 5 Ricketson Block, New Bedford, and at Post Office in South Dartmouth. Passengers to be called for must book their names 30 minutes before starting.
FREDERICK C. SWAIN, Prop'r.

Little Compton Stage.
On and after this date the stage will leave Little Compton at 6 30 A. M., passing through Adamsville, Central Village, South Westport, Russell's Mills, Apponegansett. Returning, leaves office 104 North Second street, New Bedford, at 3 P. M. Order slate at Nichols & Damon's shoe store, 63 Purchase street.
A. RICHARDS, Proprietor.

Westport Point and New Bedford Stage.
Leaves Westport Point at 7 A. M., passing through Central Village, Head of Westport, Westport Factory and Smith Mills. Returning, leaves No. 104 North Second street, New Bedford, at 3 P. M. Order slate at Nichols & Damon's shoe store, 63 Purchase st.
A. RICHARDS, Proprietor.

Long Plain Stage.
Leaves Long Plain at 7 A. M. Return, leaves Hatch & Co's Express Office, Union street, at 3 45 P. M., Post Office at 4 P. M. Express and errands attended to carefully and promptly. A. C. SHATTUCK.

Rochester and New Bedford Stage.
On and after MONDAY, April 24th, the stage will run daily, leaving Rochester at 7 30 a. m., returning leave Douglass' stable, Mechanics lane at 4 30 p. m. Express business and errands promptly attended to.
ap22-tf A. D. WATSON, Driver.

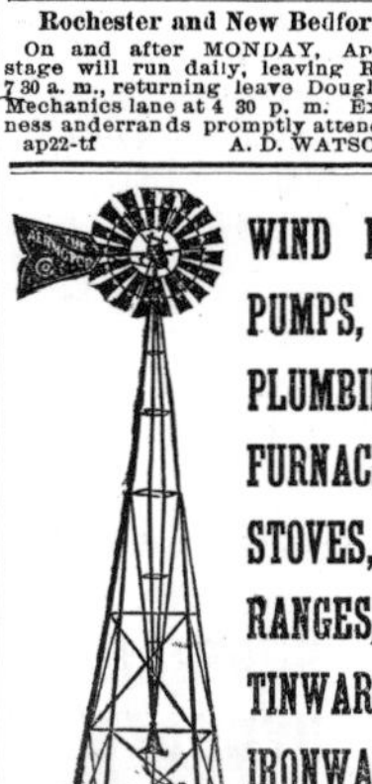

WIND ENGINES,
PUMPS,
PLUMBING,
FURNACES,
STOVES,
RANGES,
TINWARE,
IRONWARE,
ETC., ETC.

Diaphragm Pumps to let for pumping out wells, cellars, etc.

Wood, Brightman & Co.,
CORNER
North Water and William Sts.
TTS&wky

BRICKS.
Large variety Common and Pressed Bricks.
LIME.
Both Lincolnville and Rockland.
CEMENT.
Both American and English.
PLASTERING HAIR, DRAIN PIPE, etc.

S. S. PAINE & BRO.,
Front Street, Just South of Bridge.

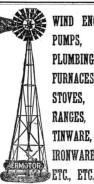

Knowles & Co.

Our Dress Goods Department is a very busy place this season and we are constantly putting out bargains which are bound to attract.

We have a line of all-wool, imported, full 40-inch Dress Goods that cost to land in this country 75c., our price 59c. until sold; regular price $1.

A nice line of Lace Drapery Net for dresses 49c. to $2.50.

A full line of Lisle Gauntlet Gloves at 50c. Also a pretty line of Gauntlet Gloves at 25c. in black and colors.

We are showing an elegant line of Laces in black, cream and white from 10c. to $1 a yard.

The largest line of Ladies' Belts to be found in the city, all styles, black, white, reds, tans, modes, blues, and any color you could wish for from 19c. to 62c. Also a full line of colors in Silk Belts, 25c., 33c., 37 1-2c. and 50c.

SHOE DEPARTMENT.—In this department we are now prepared to show a full and complete line of Spring and Summer Shoes. The light-colored shoes will be worn a great deal and we have made extra preparations for the great demand which will surely be made for them. In Tan Oxfords we have them from $1.25 to $3.50, and in Tan Boots we have a fine one, "Blucher" cut, at $3. Misses' and Children's high and low cuts, tans and blacks, in many styles and prices. Don't forget our Ladies' Kid Boots and Low Shoes. We can show you the nicest and most varied assortment to be found in any store in this city, at all prices from $1.25 to $6. West door on Union street.

Now is the time to buy Oil Stoves. We have them; all prices.

No. 1—Oil Stove fount, all one casting and warranted not to leak, tin chimney with mica front, 1 burner, 59c.; 2 burner, $1.25; 3 burner, $1.89.

No. 2—Solid fount, brass tubes, nickel frames, as good a stove as you can buy at any price. One burner, 75c.; 2 burner, $1.50; 3 burner, $2.25. Every stove warranted. Extension tops 50c. and 75c. each. Ovens 59c., $1.50, $2 each. Three-quart Oil Stove Tea Kettle 25c.

We are having a large sale of the Stove Polishing Mittens at 25c. for Mitten and dauber. Have you got one? Columbia Tacks, four papers of tacks with metal cup, all in a neat box, 10c. each. Carpet Tacks, 1-4 lb. papers, 8c. 1 lb. boxes, assorted tacks, 6c. Shelf Paper, 1c. per dozen.

Knowles & Co.

UNION and FOURTH STS.

SPECIAL NOTICE.

The demand for the famous "J. H. CUTTER" WHISKIES, (for which we are the sole agents in this city) having become so great, many houses out of the State are sending their travelers in here, with the hope of inducing our trade to buy the "Cutter" whiskies from them, by underselling us, or rather trying to. We therefore beg to say to our friends and the public generally, we will NOT allow ourselves to be undersold, by any house dealing in the genuine "J. H. CUTTER" WHISKIES, and we are prepared to protect our trade, not only in QUALITY but in PRICES as well.

Very Respectfully,

BENJAMIN DAWSON,
597 Purchase Street.

Sole agent for New Bedford, Mass., for the famous J. H. Cutter Whiskies. 8p

DRINK
ROXBURY RYE WHISKEY.

Equaled by few, Excelled by None.

je6-6t8p

MASSACHUSETTS LEGISLATURE.

Story of the Doings of the Senate and House Briefly Told.

BOSTON, June 6.—Mr. Parkman explained to the senate that the governor and council had already remedied the cause of complaint against Commissioner Hovey, covered by the Roe resolutions in the house, and the latter were therefore refused admission.

The order relative to the investigation by the insurance commissioner into industrial and other life insurance business was rejected because the present law is all that is necessary.

Mr. Ray had a substitute bill adopted establishing the southern district court of Norfolk, to include Bellingham, Foxboro, Franklin, Medway, Medfield, Millis, Norfolk, Walpole and Wrentham, with a judge at $1100, a clerk at $700, and two associate justices, with sittings at Franklin and Walpole.

Mr. Kennedy explained and advocated the house bill to provide an open space on the east side of the state house, urging that there would never be so good a chance as now. After some discussion the bill was then referred to the next general court—19 to 13.

Without any debate the house concurred with all the senate amendments to the Cape Cod canal bill.

The house insisted upon its amendments to the McTammany voting machine bill, and Messrs. Moriarty, Hoyt and Bacon were appointed a committee of conference.

EGYPT AND BIBLE LANDS.

Prof. John Moore's Interesting Lecture Closing His Course.

Professor John Moore gave the last lecture in his course last evening in the Y. M. C. A. hall. The lecture abounded with interesting facts and thoughts relating especially to Egypt.

One of the striking features of our age is the wonderful discoveries made in Egypt and other Bible lands. Egypt is the monumental land of the earth; no written history having come down to us, we rely mainly on the monuments. The ancient Egyptians aimed to perpetuate in such permanent forms the record of their customs, institutions and achievements through future ages. How far back it existed as a nation is uncertain. The great antiquity sometimes claimed for it is not sustained by monumental evidence. In the time of the first Napoleon temples were discovered in Esneh and Denderah that French skeptics asserted had been erected 17,000 years before the Christian era. That rash conclusion was soon overthrown by the key to the inscriptions derived from the Rosetta stone. According to the best authorities the oldest of the monuments is the Great Pyramid, the age of which has been ascertained astronomically. This remarkable structure was erected 2,170 years B. C., and is therefore the first link in the chain of monumental history. This contains a body of masonry amounting to 7,000,000 tons, sufficient material to build quite a city. It is so high that the Washington monument is only a few feet higher. The age of the oldest structure being ascertained we cannot go back of it with confidence.

The tombs furnish striking records of ancient Egypt. The limestone rock, in the vicinity of Thebes, abounds with these, some of which are as large as a city church. In one of them has been found a manuscript in a state of perfect preservation written in the time of Moses. The walls and ceilings are covered with representations of how the occupants lived thousands of years since. This manuscript is a roll of papyrus 100 feet in length, a facsimile of which the lecturer had seen. It is a medical treatise, and all the characters are legible. In one of these tombs, the date of which goes back 3,000 years, a harp of many strings was found. One of an exploring party applied his hand to the instrument, and the chords vibrated to the touch, which had been motionless and silent for thousands of years, and awoke the echoes of the tomb with musical sounds. The ruins of Thebes show that it surpassed in some respects any city today on the globe. This reached its zenith when the patriarchs were herding their flocks and dwelling in tents. This temple covered several acres. There are pillars in it 70 feet long and 36 feet in circumference covered with sculpture, the colors of which remained bright and vivid for ages. On the outer wall is the record of a great event in Old Testament history, about 1,000 B. C. Near it lies a statue which was thrown down 525 years before Christ, which on its pedestal stood 75 feet and weighs 887 tons. It was carved out of a single block of stone quarried 100 miles distant.

The most remarkable modern discovery, which occurred a few years since, was that of over 30 royal mummies. Among them is that of Pharaoh, the chief oppressor of the Israelites, the identity of which cannot be called in question. Among them is said to be that of Pharaoh's daughter, who rescued Moses from the waters of the Nile.

In the city of On or Heliopolis was the great university of learning, and where Joseph married his wife. Moses was educated there, and Plato, one ancient writer tells us, studied there 13 years. All that remains of that city is a single obelisk, standing in its solitary grandeur in a grove of orange and lemon trees. In that city was the famous Temple of the Sun, leading up to which was an avenue, on each side of which was a row of obelisks. These began to be removed at an early period after the Roman dominion. The largest of which is that of St. John Lateran at Rome, which was brought to Alexandria by Constantine, and was conveyed to Rome by Constantius. Its height is 105 feet and 7 inches. Two more brought to Alexandria 2,000 years ago and there set up, are commonly called Cleopatra's Needles. One fell down and was covered for ages in the sand. This was presented to George IV. of England, but was not removed till a few years since, and now stands on the Thames in London. The other, which remained standing, was presented to the United States, and now stands in the Central park in New York. The lecturer critically examined it in the hold of the steamer before it was landed. This may be regarded as a link connecting the oldest of the great nations of antiquity with the youngest of the great modern nations. It ought to be highly prized. On it Moses and Joseph often gazed and read the inscriptions, which are now legible in the light of modern research. All the discoveries made in Egypt go to illustrate and confirm directly and indirectly the truth of the Book. Monuments and ruins that have laid covered or buried in dust for thousands of years are now rising and bearin their testimony.

LONG PLAIN.

Rev. C. E. Cockril of Boston preached on the Sabbath in the M. E. church, in exchange with the pastor.

The earnest sympathy of this community goes out to Mr. James H. Sears in his affliction, caused by the death of his wife on Saturday night last. Mrs. Sears recently while out in the yard adjoining her home was so unfortunate as to puncture her foot with a common wire nail. The wound almost immediately caused her trouble, and its result was her death, as before stated, the case having developed a very marked one of lockjaw. Her suffering during her hours of illness was most intense, and during it all she bore up with great patience and fortitude. Mrs. Sears was an English lady, with none of her immediate family in this country, and although a stranger to our people until her advent here a short time since as the bride of Mr. Sears, had easily won the respect and friendship of a large circle of acquaintances.

Joseph T. Brownell has let his house to parties from New Bedford for the summer.

The Ladies Social society of the M. E. church will in a few days have their annual strawberry festival.

George Devoll of New Bedford is papering and painting at the Bloomfield house.

Joseph R. Davis has his new barn all raised and boarded.

In the notice of the strawberry festival given a few days ago, it read "Piano duet, the Misses Bassett." This was a mistake, and should have read, Piano duet, Maud Bassett and Bessie Russell.

Joseph Jefferson, the veteran actor, with his wife and family, are expected in Buzzards Bay Wednesday. They will occupy the Whittier cottage. Mr. Jefferson will at once arrange for the building of a residence on the site of Crow's Nest, which it is expected will be far superior to the beautiful villa so recently destroyed by fire.

Dr. Perevia

Speaking of H-O says,

I have carefully looked into the matter of

H-O Hornby's Oatmeal

being overheating, and I find such a complaint to be without just grounds.

Highest of all in Leavening Power.—Latest U. S. Gov't Report.

Royal Baking Powder

ABSOLUTELY PURE

THE LOSS OF THE ALVA.

Mr. Vanderbilt Suing Owners of the Dimock for $350,000.

Mr. Vanderbilt's suit against the Metropolitan Steamship company to recover $305,000 for the loss of the yacht Alva and her contents was begun in the United States circuit court in Boston Monday.

The bell of the Alva was in court, and will probably play an important part in the case.

Frederic and E. S. Dodge of Boston, Harrington Putnam and G. E. B. Howard of New York appeared for Mr. Vanderbilt, and Judge Lowell, W. D. Sohier and E. P. Carver for the steamship company.

The case was opened by Mr. Sohier, who read the deposition of the captain of the Pollock Rip lightship. This was to the effect that he heard the bell of the Alva on the night of the collision, and that it was customary for sailing vessels to anchor where the Alva had anchored.

Captain Morrison of the Alva was the first witness. He testified that the bell of the Alva had been sounded regularly. He had no doubt that the bell could be heard on the Dimock. He said that the whistle of the Dimock showed that the bell had been heard. The steamer, he said, must have been going at the rate of ten knots an hour. Though the Alva had six water-tight compartments its bow touched bottom ten minutes after it was struck.

On cross-examination Captain Morrison testified that he had never before passed through the "slew" in a fog.

At this point the court adjourned.

FALL RIVER.

The new excursion steamer, King Philip, which arrived from Bath, Me., Friday, was taken for a trial trip down the bay Sunday, and she proved to be as smart a craft of her rating as floats in the waters in this vicinity. The steamer is a screw propeller, capable of carrying 800 passengers.

Officer Ferguson discovered a slight incendiary fire in the Harris building on South Main street Sunday morning, and permanent firemen put it out. Paper had been placed under a door and ignited.

The police have been so occupied since the Manchester murder that the accumulation of suspects, lunatics and cranks is very large. By the end of the week it is thought that the cell rooms will once more be ready for the reception of the plain drunks, and that the unwelcome furor will be over.

The horribly mutilated remains of James McCarty of Fall River were found on the Pennsylvania railroad near Columbia, Pa., Sunday. It is supposed he tried to board a freight train and fell under the cars.

The Globe Street Railway company has served a notice on the city council to the effect that it would pay the city $4,000, in full discharge of all obligations entered into when the grant for a location was given in Pleasant street to the town line of Westport, the sum to be expended in reconstructing the streets in the vicinity and the bridge over the Narrows, provided certain conditions are carried out.

The aldermen last night passed an order appropriating $2,500 for a Fourth of July celebration and sent it to the council. The lower branch cut down the amount to $1,000, and otherwise mangled the measure. The aldermen considered that they had been trifled with and refused to concur.

The residence of Samuel Benoit was entered on Sunday afternoon, but an alarm was given while the thieves were in the house and nothing of value was taken.

BABY ONE SOLID SORE

Tried Everything without Relief. No Rest Night or Day. Cured by Cuticura Remedies.

My baby, when two months old, had a breaking out with what the doctor called eczema. Her head, arms, feet, and hands were each one solid sore. I tried everything, but neither the doctors nor anything else did her any good. We could get no rest day or night with her. In my extremity I tried the CUTICURA REMEDIES, but I confess I had no faith in them, for I had never seen them tried. To my great surprise, in one week's time after beginning to use the CUTICURA REMEDIES, the sores were well, but I continued to use the RESOLVENT for a little while, and now she is as fat a baby as you would like to see, and as sound as a dollar. I believe my baby would have died if I had not tried CUTICURA REMEDIES. I write this that every mother with a baby like mine can feel confident that there is a medicine that will cure the worst eczema, and that medicine is the CUTICURA REMEDIES.

MRS. BETTIE BIRKNER, Lockhart, Texas.

Cuticura Remedies

Cure every humor of the skin and scalp of infancy and childhood, whether torturing, disfiguring, itching, burning, scaly, crusted, pimply, or blotchy, with loss of hair, and every impurity of the blood, whether simple, scrofulous, or hereditary, when the best physicians and all other remedies fail. Parents, save your children years of mental and physical suffering. Begin now. Cures made in childhood are permanent.

CUTICURA REMEDIES are the greatest skin cures, blood purifiers, and humor remedies of modern times, are absolutely pure, and may be used on the youngest infant with the most gratifying success.

Sold everywhere. Price, CUTICURA, 50c.; SOAP, 25c.; RESOLVENT, $1. Prepared by the POTTER DRUG AND CHEMICAL CORPORATION, Boston.

Send for "How to Cure Skin Diseases," 64 pages, 50 illustrations, and 100 testimonials.

PIMPLES, black-heads, chapped and oily skin cured by CUTICURA MEDICATED SOAP.

FREE FROM RHEUMATISM

In one minute the Cuticura Anti-Pain Plaster relieves rheumatic, sciatic, hip, kidney, chest, and muscular pains and weaknesses. The first and only instantaneous pain-killing plaster.

[From Yesterday's Extra Edition.]

BORDEN JURY.

Work of Selecting It Now Completed.

Charles I. Richards, of Attleboro, Foreman.

Only One New Bedford Man Among the Twelve.

Court Adjourns Until 9 a. m. Tuesday.

Everyone Glad of Release from Oppressive Heat.

The twelve jurors who will bring in the verdict in the Borden murder case are all selected. They are:

Allen H. Wordell, of Dartmouth.
Augustus Swift, of New Bedford.
John C. Finn, of Taunton.
Louis D. Hodges, of Taunton.
William F. Dean, of Taunton.
George Potter, of Westport.
Frederick C. Wilber, of Raynham.
John Wilber, of Somerset.
Frank G. Cole, of Attleboro.
Charles I. Richards of North Attleboro.
Lemuel K. Wilbur, of Easton.
William Wescott of Seekonk.

There was but a very small number of spectators in front of the court house at the opening this afternoon, people evidently having received the tip that spectators were "not in it" during the impaneling of the jury. Officers Gifford and Mather, of the local police, relieved the two officers who were on duty this forenoon.

It might be stated that Officer Humphrey, who is guarding the Court street entrance, is on his annual vacation, and he has been secured by County Commissioner Sanders to look after the entrance to the court house at the west end of the building during the first two weeks of the trial.

Chief Douglass was at the afternoon session, and occupied a seat within the rail. He was a close observer of what was going on, and nothing of interest escaped him.

At 10 minutes past 2 o'clock Miss Borden was again brought from the house of correction by Deputy Sheriff Kirby and entered the court house. It was a fact worth noting that but few persons knew of her coming and Abraham Lee, the driver, had little difficulty in reaching the granite steps upon which she alighted from the carriage.

It is excessively hot, and the newspaper men, telegraphers, typewriters and others engaged in the herculean task before them for the next few weeks are looking for that long-desired and refreshing cool southwest breeze.

The Afternoon Session.

Promptly at 2 15 o'clock the justices were in their seats, and an instant later the five jurors already drawn, which had been in charge of Deputy Sheriffs John W. Nickerson of this city and Arnold of Norton, filed in and took their seats. Lizzie was brought into the court room just before the time the court resumed its session, and eagerly embraced the opportunity to exchange a few words with Rev. W. W. Jubb, who has been present during the day, and whose friendship for the prisoner at the bar makes him one of the deepest interested spectators.

Chief Justice Mason stated that during the recess the clerk of the court had made inquiries, and ascertained that the memory of Juror Frank W. Francis was correct, that he had served as juror in September, 1890, and was therefore exempt.

William Wescott of Seekonk was not related to the prisoner and answered all questions satisfactorily. He was accepted and sworn in as a juror.

Lyman Palmer of Taunton said that he was sensible of bias and prejudiced and held opinions that would prevent rendering a candid judgment. He was excused.

Charles N. Allen of New Bedford said that he held opinions and had expressed them, but thought that he was not biased or prejudiced. He said, however, that he thought he did hold opinions that would preclude him from finding the defendant guilty of an offense where death was the penalty. Excused.

Edmund E. Hill of Taunton gave satisfactory answers to the questions put to him by the court, but was challenged by the prisoner.

Gordon H. Godfrey of Taunton said he was prejudiced in the case and was therefore excused.

Edward S. Taber of this city said that he was not related to Lizzie Borden or her father or stepmother. He had formed opinions, but was not prejudiced. He said that he could render candid judgment according to the evidence, but asked to be excused on account of his age, which he gave as 67 years. The court granted his request.

Gilbert M. Horton of Rehoboth, who is 66 years of age, was next called. He did not care to be excused because of his age, and said: "He was neither related to Lizzie A. Borden or her father or stepmother." He had formed no opinion, and passing the examination of Chief Justice Mason, was turned over to the lawyers.

At a hint from District Attorney Knowlton the chief justice put this query: "Are you a client of either counsel in this cause?"

To this Mr. Horton replied: "No sir." Whereupon the chief justice remarked, "The juror stands indifferent."

After consultation with Mr. Moody Mr. Knowlton said: "We do not challenge."

Then Mr. Jennings stepped up to Miss Borden and she challenged in her usual firm and clear tone.

George W. Currien of Attleboro had formed no opinion and was unbiased. "The government does not challenge," said Mr. Knowlton, but Miss Borden arose in the dock and sent Mr. Currien to his seat with another peremptory challenge.

Joseph W. Driscoll of Easton, a young man of 30 years, had no interest whatever in the case. He had, however, formed an opinion, but did not think it would prevent his rendering a verdict from the testimony which might be put in.

After consultation with Mr. Moody, the district attorney announced that the government would not challenge. Mr. Driscoll, however, like his predecessor, took his seat on another challenge from Miss Borden.

Louis D. Hodges, an elderly looking Tauntonian, was next called. He was not related to the prisoner nor her father nor her stepmother. Neither had he any interest in the cause. He didn't think his opinion formed would interfere with his duties as a juryman.

"The juror stands indifferent," was again the remark of the chief justice. "The commonwealth does not challenge," was the ready response of Mr. Knowlton, and Mr. Jennings was equally as prompt by saying, "We accept."

And Mr. Hodges was sworn in as the seventh juror and took his seat with the others in the jury box.

Harry J. Leach, a carpenter doing business in this city, was not related to the prisoner at the bar, neither had he formed an opinion, was not biased in the matter, but he had decided opinions as to capital punishment, and Chief Justice Mason very politely informed him that he might take his seat.

Augustus Swift, proprietor of the Acushnet Iron foundry located in this city, next came to the front with a smile upon his face. He was not biased and believed that he could serve as a juror without prejudice. In answer to the query he said he was not a client of either of the counsels in the cause, and after consultation on the part of Messrs. Knowlton and Moody he was accepted by the commonwealth. It was somewhat of a surprise when Mr. Jennings informed the court that his client would accept. Immediately after Mr. Swift was sworn in and took his seat with the others.

David B. Tinkham of Easton said that opinions he held would preclude him from rendering a verdict of guilty for an offense punishable with death. He was told by the court to step aside.

Daniel Whallon of Westport said he had expressed opinions in regard to the case, but was not prejudiced. His opinion would, however, prevent him from finding defendant guilty of a crime punishable with death. Excused.

Augustus M. Mosher of Westport had formed an opinion. He would not be willing to render a finding of guilty. Excused.

Oliver Ames, 2d, of Easton had formed and expressed opinions in regard to the case. He said also he was prejudiced. He was excused.

George A. Cobb of this city said that he was prejudiced, and the court said he was exempt.

Frank G. Cole of Attleboro said that he had formed opinions in regard to the case, but was not prejudiced. Mr. Cole was accepted and sworn in to serve on the jury.

Oscar R. Douglass of Swanzey was challenged by the government.

John C. Finn of Taunton was satisfactory to both government and defense and his name was added to the list of jurors already drawn.

John H. Taber of this city said that he was 70 years of age. He was asked by Chief Justice Mason if he wished to be excused on that account, and he said that he did.

Isaac Alger of Attleboro was satisfactory to the government, but Lizzie Borden challenged him.

Nathan O. Walker of Dighton said that he was prejudiced and he was excused.

William J. Mills of New Bedford was indifferent, but was challenged by the commonwealth.

Charles F. Folger of New Bedford proved objectionable to Lizzie Borden, although he said he was not prejudiced and had no opinions that would prevent giving a candid judgment in the cause. Mr. Folger said in answer to a question that he was not a client of the counsel on either side of this cause.

Gideon Howland of Dartmouth had formed an opinion and said that he was prejudiced. Excused.

George F. Keen of Easton said that the opinion he had formed would preclude him from rendering a verdict of guilty in this case and he was therefore excused.

Henry A. Hodges of Taunton was next called, but he did not materialize.

Willard D. Monroe of Rehoboth was one of the youngest drawn as a juror. He went through the usual examination by Chief Justice Mason, but the commonwealth saw fit to challenge, and Mr. Monroe stepped one side.

Nathan Clarke, another Tauntonian, was not long in getting before the justices. He said his hearing was very much impaired, and thought he would have much difficulty in hearing the testimony. He said he was 68 years of age, whereupon Chief Justice Mason replied, "You are exempt because of age."

George A. Howe of New Bedford, a bright looking young fellow, had no interest whatever in the cause, but had formed an opinion, and was so biased that he did not think such opinion could be changed. He was also invited to take a seat with the spectators.

George E. Hathaway of Taunton, who perhaps was not over 35 years of age, was next called. He was not related to the prisoner at the bar nor her parents. He had formed an opinion, but was not prejudiced, and had no scruples as to capital punishment.

"The juror stands indifferent," again announced Chief Mason.

"The commonwealth challenges," said Mr. Knowlton.

Albert M. Wilcox of Fairhaven had scruples against capital punishment and was ordered to step aside.

George W. Davis of Dartmouth, a manly looking type of the New England farmer, was next called. He said he had formed an opinion, but could give a candid verdict, and when asked if he had prejudices against capital punishment, replied that he had, and he, too, was sent to his seat.

Walter Pease of East Freetown was another young man, and like the other young fellows drawn, he didn't believe in capital punishment, and went to his seat thankful that he had been excused from a most unpleasant task.

Olney Green of Seekonk, another young man, went through the usual questions. He passed muster, and after nearly a minute's consultation with Mr. Moody the district attorney broke the silence by announcing that the commonwealth would challenge.

Joseph Pelton, a Tauntonian, said he did not understand English clearly enough to serve as a juror, and he, too, was excused.

Edward Gushee of Raynham passed the ordeal all right and the commonwealth was satisfied with his choice, but Miss Borden, receiving the tip from Mr. Jennings, stood up in the dock and sent him to his seat with a challenge.

Dexter D. Horton, Jr., of Rehoboth, who is scarcely 25 years of age, like his younger brethren, did not believe in capital punishment, and he, too, took a back seat with a smile on his face.

Frederick E Lawton of Fairhaven hesitated about the opinions he had formed about the case and was excused from jury duty.

George H. Milliken of New Bedford presented a medical certificate and was therefore excused.

Ezra J. Swift of New Bedford said his opinions would preclude his finding the defendant guilty of a crime punishable by death. Excused.

Henry W. Kenyon of New Bedford said that he was a client of one of the counsel in this cause and the court excused him.

F. William Oesting of this city said that he had formed opinions and was biased. Excused.

Henry C. Dean, of Taunton, was indifferent, but the government challenged him.

William A. Bennett, of North Attleboro, said that the opinions he held would preclude him from rendering a verdict of guilty, even if the evidence should warrant it. He was allowed to retire.

John H. Tingley, of Attleboro, satisfactorily answered the questions. Lizzie Borden challenged him and he retired.

Elihu M. Davis, of Taunton, had expressed an opinion, but was not biased. He was, however, hard of hearing, and was excused on this account.

George A. Wood of Taunton held opinions that would prevent him rendering a verdict of guilty in a case where the crime was punishable by death. Excused.

George P. Bailey of Mansfield had formed an opinion and was biased.

Charles I. Richards of North Attleboro was acceptable to the government and defendant, received the oath and took his seat with the jury.

Eugene M. Barrows of New Bedford was neither biased nor had any opinions that would prevent him from rendering a finding strictly in accordance with the evidence. He answered all questions promptly, and Lizzie Borden as promptly challenged him.

Walter C. Slocum of Dartmouth, a young man, had formed no opinion. He had no scruples against capital punishment and stood before the court ready for acceptance or rejection. "The commonwealth does not challenge," said Mr. Knowlton, but as Miss Borden did not like his appearance, Slocum took his seat with the rejected.

Harold B. Hopkins of Attleboro was another young man. He was not related to the prisoner at the bar, neither had he formed an opinion in the case in hearing, and furthermore he had no scruples against capital punishment. He, however, was challenged by the commonwealth.

John B. Wade, of Taunton, answered the usual questions. He was not biased, and thought he could serve faithfully as a juror. The commonwealth does not challenge, said Mr. Knowlton.

Again Miss Borden arose in the dock and uttered that magic word so pleasing to the ears of those in the court room: "Challenge;" and Wade took his seat with the others.

John W. Dickson, of Taunton, was not related to the prisoner, but he was biased in the matter, and he stood aside.

Charles F. Hathaway of Swanzey then made true answers to the court, when it was learned that he was qualified to serve as a juror.

At the request of District Attorney Knowlton, Chief Justice Mason asked this question: "Are you a client of either of the counsel in this cause?"

To this Mr. Hathaway replied: "I am not," but Mr. Knowlton saw fit to challenge in behalf of the commonwealth, and Mr. Hathaway took his seat.

Augustus O. Hall of North Attleboro had no interest in the cause. He passed muster to the court, but the commonwealth challenged.

Henry B. Almy, of the firm of Almy & Hitch, was next called. He was sworn and made true answers, when it was revealed that he was not related to the prisoner at the bar, but he had formed and expressed an opinion. He did not believe in capital punishment and was asked to step aside.

Thomas Donaghy, Jr., a shoe clerk, who resides in New Bedford, and is in the employ of his father, doing business on Union street, was next called. It was not long before the chief justice was satisfied that Mr. Donaghy had better be seated with the excused, and with a smile Mr. Donaghy took his seat.

Daniel F. Driscoll of New Bedford was biased in his opinion and was therefore allowed to retire.

Ezra Davol of Taunton presented a document to the court and was exempted by the statement contained therein.

Charles W. Knight of New Bedford was called. The objection to him was that he had opinions that would prevent him from finding the defendant guilty of an offense punishable by death. He was excused.

Oliver E. Gifford was asked if he was related to the prisoner at the bar and he said he was. Excused. Mr. Gifford is an uncle, by marriage, of the defendant.

Simeon A. Wheeler of Taunton said that he was prejudiced, and the court ordered him to retire.

Francis H. Pasell of New Bedford was biased in his opinions, and was excused on that account.

Eben S. Grinnell of East Freetown had opinions that would prevent him rendering a verdict of guilty in a capital case. Excused.

George E. Smith of Norton, when asked if he had any opinions that would preclude him from rendering a verdict of guilty in an offense punishable by death, said that he thought he had one. He was told that he might step aside.

Charles L. Seaver of Mansfield was satisfactory to the government, but was challenged by Lizzie Borden.

Dwight F. Lane, of Dighton, stood indifferent according to the statement of the court. Mr. Knowlton, for the government, challenged him.

John F. Hammett, of Acushnet, said that in his opinion he could not render a verdict of guilty in a case of this kind. Excused.

James O'Leary, of North Attleboro, objected to capital punishment, and said that his opinion would preclude him from finding the defendant guilty in a capital case. Excused.

Robert H. Carter, of New Bedford, was biased, and was excused.

Joseph Chausse, of this city, was also prejudiced, and the court asked him to retire.

David Fisher, of Mansfield, was not biased, but had opinions that would preclude him from finding the defendant guilty.

Silas D. Dammon of New Bedford was biased and was allowed to retire.

Frederick Parker, a retired merchant of New Bedford, had no interest in the cause, but he did not believe in capital punishment and was sent to his seat.

Francis A. Booth, a New Bedford accountant, next passed muster in every respect, even with the commonwealth, but Miss Borden challenged.

Matthew Costello of Somerset was not related to the prisoner, had no interest in the cause, but had formed an opinion and was so strongly prejudiced against capital punishment that he was asked to step aside.

Cyrus Washburn of Raynham was exempted because of age, he being in his 69th year.

John T. Williams of Taunton had scruples against capital punishment, and took a seat with those who had previously been rejected.

Lloyd S. Lincoln, of Norton, had formed and expressed an opinion, and not believing in capital punishment, was also asked to step aside.

Henry M. Hoxie, of Fairhaven, had no interest in the cause, neither was he related to the prisoner at the bar. He was not biased in his opinion, and thought he could render a candid verdict from the testimony submitted, but he had decided scruples against capital punishment, and he too was asked to step aside.

Jason T. Guild, of North Attleboro, was exempted because of age. He was also 69 years of age.

Ezekiel B. Francis, of Taunton, passed muster with the court and the commonwealth, but the defendant challenged, and he too retired.

Henry M. Gross, of Attleboro, stepped aside because of decided opinions.

George Lynch of Somerset was prejudiced in the case and therefore could not serve.

Oliver H. Crossman of Taunton was in a similar predicament and he likewise stepped aside.

Allen H. Wordell of Dartmouth was wholly unbiased, and as he was unchallenged by either prosecution or defense he took his seat in the panel and completed the jury.

Half an Hour Recess.

After the names of the jurors on the panel were called a recess of half an hour was given them, as is customary, to allow them to make such arrangements as are necessary on account of their enforced absence from their homes and vocations. To all intents and purposes they are dead to the world during the progress of the trial, and this is the only opportunity they will have to communicate with their friends in any way until after they shall have rendered a verdict upon the evidence that is about to be presented to them.

Court Room Incidents.

Dr. Dolan of Fall River, medical examiner, came into the court room during the afternoon, and in taking his seat within the rail unwittingly sat in such a way as to obstruct Lizzie's view of the judges' bench and the witness stand. He was at once asked to move his seat by Sheriff Wright.

A ripple of laughter passed around the court room as a colored juror was solemnly asked if he was related to the defendant.

Prisoner Chats with a Friend.

During the recess Lizzie conversed earnestly with her trusted friend, Deacon Charles J. Holmes, who is a prominent member of the church in Fall River that has been the place of worship of the Borden family for years. Lizzie apparently threw off all restraint and conducted the conversation in much the same manner as if it had occurred in her own home long before the occurrence of the fearful tragedy for which she is now on trial.

110 Names Brought Forward.

Before the jury of 12 men, in whose hands the fate of Lizzie Borden now rests, were secured, 110 of the 150 jurors who were brought forward by the venire were examined. Out of the 150 men whose names appear on the list 145 answered to Clerk Borden's roll call.

Hon. Charles S. Randall strolled in to the court room shortly after the jurors in the case had retired, and after a pleasant recognition of his various friends, entered into an earnest conversation with Colonel M. O. Adams, counsel for defense.

Clerk Borden arose and called the roll of the jurors on the venire who will serve at the coming session of the court, and notified them to appear July 10th at 10 o'clock a. m. All others were notified that they were excused. The heat of the room had proved too much for their curiosity, and the minute they were allowed to depart they availed themselves of the opportunity, and in a trice the room was cleared of all save the officers in attendance and the busy scribes, while those drawn as jurors called upon County Treasurer Platt and received their pay.

When the jury returned to the court room Charles I. Richards was appointed foreman of the 12 and was sworn by Clerk Borden. The court then adjourned until tomorrow morning at 9 o'clock.

As soon as the court adjourned Lizzie's counsel, Messrs. Robinson, Jennings and Adams held a consultation with her. They talked too low to be heard, but it was plainly to be seen that they were holding out encouragement to her as the faintest sort of a smile played across her features. After cordially shaking her by the hand, they turned away and Deputy Sheriff Kirby showed her to the carriage in which she was conveyed to the jail.

"UNCLE JOHN" HAS LISTENERS.

Making the Best of His Enforced Attendance at Court.

John V. Morse spent the afternoon in the corridor of the court house, and entertained a large number of listeners with tales of his experiences and life in the west. A coterie of farmers were much interested in his description of the methods of planting, caring for and harvesting crops in the section of Iowa in which he lived, where 640 acres of land is regarded as an average sized farm. His tale was told in a remarkably straightforward way, that held the close attention of the listeners. He seemed to be making the best of his enforced attendance at the court house in a philosophical way.

THE ACCEPTED JURORS.

Pen Pictures of the Men Now Seated in the Box.

Louis D. Hodges, of Taunton, is a man whose snow white locks and beard give evidence that he has seen many summers' suns and winters' snows. His overhanging eyebrows and strongly set features denote a large degree of intelligence and firmness of character.

Augustus Swift is a well-known New Bedford business man, and those who are familiar with him are assured that any verdict that might have his assent will be strictly in accordance with the evidence.

Frank G. Cole, of Attleboro, has reached middle age. He is a good looking man with a sharp, searching black eye. His features are sharp in outline, and firmness is a characteristic of his physiognomy.

John C. Finn, of Taunton, is the youngest man in appearance of any who have taken their seat in the jury box. Judging from his countenance he will render a verdict strictly in accordance with the evidence that is presented to him, and having once formed his opinion, it will be useless for his associates to attempt to win him over in case of a disagreement.

Mr. Wescott is a man who appears to have reached the middle age and has a countenance that denotes more than an average degree of intelligence.

Charles I. Richards of North Attleboro is a kindly featured man with a full head of hair of silvery white. In appearance he is one given to weighing matters well before passing judgment, and one to whose opinions weight is to be attached.

Allen H. Wordell of Dartmouth, the last juror accepted, is a man about 45 years of age, and is evidently employed in the open air, being well browned from exposure to the weather. He has a frank, open countenance, and looks as if any verdicts or conclusions he might reach would be the result of careful consideration of all the facts presented to him.

Ex-Gov. Robinson's Methods.

It was interesting to watch ex-Governor Robinson's method of work. He applied himself diligently, and would pause just long enough as each juror's name was called to give him a searching glance, which evidently satisfied him as to whether he had any objections to his sitting upon the jury. He had in his hand a paper upon which was evidently written the names of each of the jurors and notations in regard to their antecedents.

MEETING POSTPONED.

The annual meeting of the Morse Twist Drill & Machine company, which was to have been held at the office of Sanford & Kelley this afternoon, was postponed till Friday, June 9th, at 11 a. m., at the same office, no quorum being present.

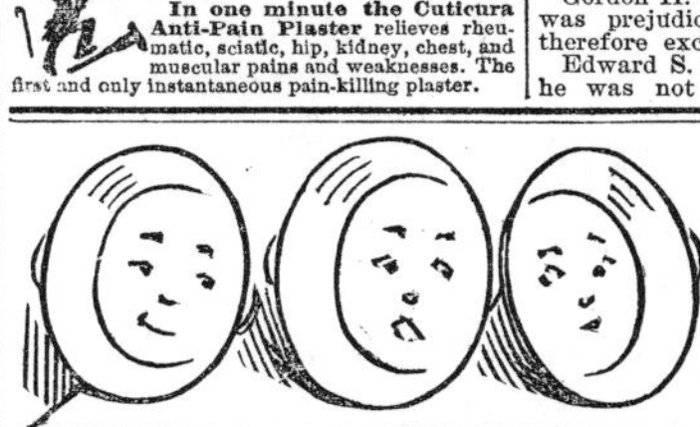

Milk Pans,

and pails, and cans, and bottles (even baby's)—or anything that you want particularly clean, ought to be washed with Pearline. You'll save work in doing it, and it's a great deal more thoroughly done. Dairies and dealers use Pearline extensively. Just try it once, on your milk-ware or butter-ware—and then say if it isn't the most satisfactory way of cleaning. Pearline is the most economical thing you can use, too. You get so much more out of it.

Send it Back

Peddlers and some unscrupulous grocers will tell you "this is as good as" or "the same as Pearline." IT'S FALSE—Pearline is never peddled, and if your grocer sends you something in place of Pearline, be honest—*send it back*. 393 JAMES PYLE, New York.

Pages 1-8.

The Evening Standard.

Pages 1-8.

ESTABLISHED FEBRUARY, 1850.

NEW BEDFORD, WEDNESDAY, JUNE 7, 1893.---TWELVE PAGES. TWO CENTS.

HASKELL & TRIPP.

In double harness.

The merchandise side of this business runs on two well-matched ideas—regular goods and bargains.

Regular goods at regular times and seasons.

Bargain lots at any time and all seasons.

The pace will be a lively one the whole of June.

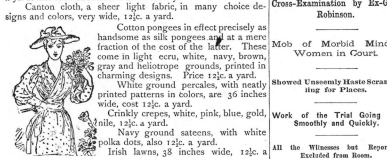

Hot weather dress goods.

Airy weaves that this weather sets you thinking of.

Thousands of yards of summer cotton dress stuffs are now on our counters. All new styles; nothing carried from last season.

Glance at a few of them.

Cream ground challies, prettily printed, 5c. a yard.

Corded ginghams in all the wanted colors, our price 10c. a yard, intended to retail for more money.

Canton cloth, a sheer light fabric, in many choice designs and colors, very wide, 12½c. a yard.

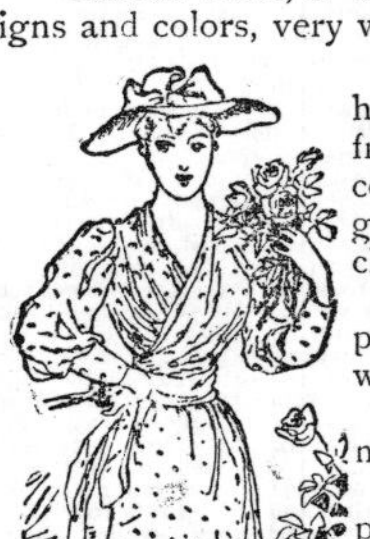

Cotton pongees in effect precisely as handsome as silk pongees and at a mere fraction of the cost of the latter. These come in light ecru, white, navy, brown, gray and heliotrope grounds, printed in charming designs. Price 12½c. a yard.

White ground percales, with neatly printed patterns in colors, are 36 inches wide, cost 12½c. a yard.

Crinkly crepes, white, pink, blue, gold, nile, 12½c. a yard.

Navy ground sateens, with white polka dots, also 12½c. a yard.

Irish lawns, 38 inches wide, 12½c. a yard.

The two last named are specially good for shirt waists.

Ginghams at 12½c. a yard that cannot be distinguished from Scotch goods at twice their cost are selling freely. This great bargain eclipses anything of the kind in our own past. The retail price today is less than the wholesale cost of last month.

Cool, crisp Swiss muslins, plain white, dotted white, figured white, figured tinted, all at 25c. a yard—a collection *difficult* to match, *impossible* to surpass.

Fine India linens, 20 and 25c. a yard.

Tuckings, plain and fancy, 50c. a yard.

English cambrics, nainsooks, mulls at the lowest prices possible for high-class qualities such as we sell.

Summer flannels for tennis or outing dresses or waists. They look like the French goods at 50c. a yard. No, they are their "Yankee" cousins, and the price is 12½c. a yard.

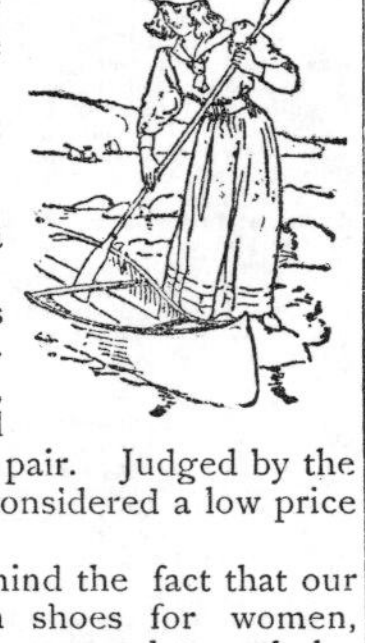

Cream twilled cotton and wool tennis suitings, 25c. and 37c. a yard.

Cream Danish cloth, 12½c. a yard.

Cream cashmeres, 25c., 37c., 50c. a yard.

A new arrival in our shoe store is *a Russian calf Oxford* on either "common sense" or "opera" last, hand turned, flexible sole, a nicely made shoe, all widths, and our price is only $1.50 a pair. Judged by the usual shoe store standard, $2 would be considered a low price for such excellent shoes.

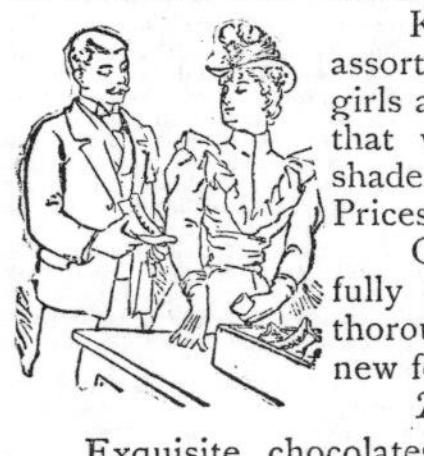

Keep bright in mind the fact that our assortment of brown shoes for women, girls and boys is very complete and also that we have the new russet and tan shades in hosiery to match the leathers. Prices invariably at the bottom.

Our basement salesroom is delightfully cool these June days, and you can thoroughly enjoy a glass of soda from our new fountain there.

Try it.

Exquisite chocolates, marshmallows, bonbons and al high-grade candies at popular prices.

Think of 29c. a yard for Magnificent Ribbons that the wholesaler meant to get 40c. for, and that the retailer hoped to sell for half a dollar per yard; then think of our price today, and you'll become a buyer at once if you care anything about possessing beautiful fancy ribbons, for millinery, dress trimming or fancy work.

Plaids,
Stripes,
Figures,
Cords,
Tinsel edge.
} Rich Silk Ribbons. 29c. a yard.

HASKELL & TRIPP.

Department Stores: PURCHASE AND WILLIAM STS.

THIRD DAY.

Prisoner Pale but Self-Possessed.

Her Uncle, John V. Morse, Testifies.

Bridget Sullivan Also on the Stand.

Her Story One of Greatest Importance.

Lizzie Closely Follows Servant's Words.

Cross-Examination by Ex-Gov. Robinson.

Mob of Morbid Minded Women in Court.

Showed Unseemly Haste Scrambling for Places.

Work of the Trial Going on Smoothly and Quickly.

All the Witnesses but Reporters Excluded from Room.

As early as 6 o'clock this morning the vanguard of the curiosity seekers put in an appearance at the court house and immediately composed themselves on the curbing to await the opening of the court. The knowledge that yesterday there was an opportunity for nearly twice the number of spectators to gain admission to the proceedings and listen to the unfolding of this fascinating though terrible mystery as put in an appearance, was sufficient to make those who are determined to gratify their curiosity resolve that they would never allow another such chance to escape them.

Among the early comers was a woman, who vouchsafed the information to a bystander as she contentedly munched a lunch that she had hastily wrapped up in a newspaper before her departure from home that she had left one of the children with her mother, another with her sister, who lived nearly a mile away, and the baby with the woman who lived up stairs, and had started for the court house before 6 o'clock, leaving her "old man" to prepare his own breakfast.

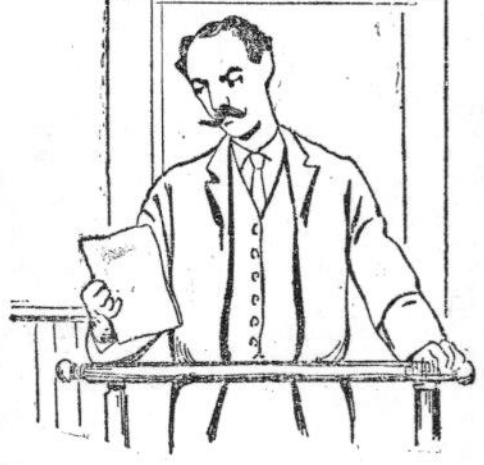

Thomas Kieran,
When Recalled This Forenoon.

Officers Taber and Callanan were on duty at the front entrance shortly after 7, but found little difficulty in keeping the crowd within bounds, as the lesson that no encroaching on the inclosure will be allowed has been pretty well learned. Officer Humphrey had little to do at the rear entrance, as several attempts to elude his vigilance have convinced those who have tried it that it is of no avail.

The witnesses began to arrive before 8 o'clock and as soon as they put in appearance were met by the deputy sheriffs and conducted to the witness room.

The Prisoner's Appearance.

Miss Borden arrived at the court room at 8 minutes of 9 and stepped from the cab unassisted by Deputy Sheriff Kirby, who accompanied her. She paid not the slightest attention to the crowd who gathered to scan her features, to see if any sign of a night of intense mental suffering was denoted by her features. Although she appeared to be somewhat more pale than yesterday, she tripped lightly up the steps and followed Deputy Sheriff Kirby into the corridor and was lost to view. Many who expected her condition today to be such as to require attendance or assistance were greatly disappointed. Her step was as firm and her bearing as self-contained as it has been at any time since her arrest, and she appeared utterly oblivious to the crowd which gathered around and looked directly into her face at close range.

After as many spectators had been admitted at the opening of the court as could be accommodated fully as many more hung around on the outside in the hope that some one whose curiosity had been satisfied would leave the room, in which case there would be half a hundred ready and eager to replace him.

John V. Morse was on hand and comfortably seated in the corridor. He conversed pleasantly with all comers

(Continued on Second Page.)

WEATHER INDICATIONS.

Fair.

Washington, June 7.—For the 24 hours from 8 a. m. today: For New England: Fair tonight and Thursday; warmer in the interior; west to north winds.

Fair and Cooler Tomorrow.

Boston, June 7.—8 a. m.—Local forecast for New England until Thursday night: Fair weather, cooler Thursday morning; warmer Friday; westerly winds.

GREAT BRITAIN'S DEMANDS.

Reparation Pecuniary and by Apology for an Arrest at New Orleans.

New York, June 7.—A dispatch from New Orleans says: Reparation, pecuniary and by apology, has been asked from the state department by the British ambassador at Washington for the arrest by a customs officer in New Orleans May 2 of First Mate Maile of steamer Nigretia.

BIG FIRE IN SAN FRANCISCO.

Flames Beyond Control—Firemen Killed by Falling Walls.

San Francisco, June 7.—Fire broke out this morning on Page street, between Baker and Lyons streets, in the western part of the city. In less than an hour a whole block had been consumed and the fire was beyond control. Two firemen were killed by falling walls.

LARGE DRAFT OF MEN

Ordered from the Mare Island Navy Yard for Honolulu.

San Francisco, June 7.—Orders have been received at Mare Island Navy yard to send a large draft of men by the next steamer to Honolulu to reinforce the crews of the United States steamer Adams and the cruiser Boston.

Carboy of Vitriol Exploded.

Buzzards Bay, June 7.—A carboy of vitriol exploded yesterday at the bottling establishment of L. E. and C. E. Ames, severely burning D. C. Besse about the legs. C. E. Ames wore rubber boots, and escaped with a few slight burns.

Chicago Lumber Dealers Assign.

Chicago, June 7.—Joseph Rathborne & Co., lumber, voluntarily assigned this morning. Assets scheduled at $500,000, liabilities $250,000. Inability to realize on commercial paper is given as the cause.

Grant Locomotive Works Assign.

Chicago, June 7.—The Grant locomotive works assigned yesterd. Liabilities May 1 were $410,950, assets $1,161,020.

Washington Banks Fail.

Spokane, Wash., June 7.—The Citizens National bank closed yesterday. The Palouse City bank of Palouse City also closed yesterday.

HOME MATTERS.

BAPTIST SUNDAY SCHOOLS.

Proceedings of the Convention at the William Street Church.

An all day's convention of the Sabbath schools in the Taunton Baptist association opened in the First Baptist church in this city at 10 o'clock this forenoon. The convention covers the churches in the county, comprising four in New Bedford, eight in Fall River and eleven others in Taunton and suburban towns.

The convention was called to order by President A. G. Hart, of Fall River, and Frank L. Tinkham, of Taunton, acted as secretary.

Rev. J. S. Swaim, of this city, made the opening prayer, which was followed by a brief praise service. Addresses of welcome were made by George C. Hatch and Mr. Swaim.

Frank L. Tinkham, of Taunton, secretary and treasurer of the association, made his report for the year, and only four schools responded, as many of the delegates had not arrived.

Following Rev. Brown E. Smith, of Long Plain, read a paper on the "Home and the Sunday School." The address which was to have been given by Rev. T. J. Villers was substituted by one on "The Child as a Church Member," by Rev. D. B. Jutten of Fall River.

The following committees were appointed to report at the afternoon session:

On Nominations—J. L. Buffington, Fall River; Rev. H. C. Graves, New Bedford; E. W. Fuller, Mansfield; J. F. Hatch, New Bedford; C. W. Turner, Dighton.

Resolutions—J. A. Borden, North Attleboro; George A. Phillips, New Bedford; Dennis S. Smith, Long Plain; Edwin Southworth, Fall River; T. H. Greene, Fall River.

Place of Next Meeting—Rev. W. D. Athern, Dighton; Nathan Clark, Taunton; J. M. Manning, Raynham; Rev. Walter Gay, New Bedford; A. C. Cook, Fall River.

New School—Rev. T. S. Barbour, Fall River; C. A. Lawrence, Taunton; G. A. Petty, Fall River; C. C. Wood, Raynham.

This new school is the Oak street chapel, which is a branch of the First Baptist church and is supported by voluntary contributions.

After the morning session the visiting clergymen and delegates were dined by the ladies of the church in the vestry.

AN AGE OF IMPROVEMENT.

There are many different refrigerators on the market, some of which are not worthy of the name; others that are first class in style, finish and workmanship. But this is an age of improvement and invention that recognizes that the usefulness of a refrigerator does not depends on style and finish alone; that a perfect refrigerator must be so constructed that it can be kept pure and clean, exclude as far as possible the heat from without, and produce and retain at the least expense of ice, pure, dry, cold air. As the only refrigerator that possesses all these requirements, we desire to call your attention to the Gurney Patent Refrigerator. Sold only by C. F. Wing.

ONLY $13.50.

Compact.

Ornamental.

Made of iron.

Painted in white and gold.

Displayed in the window.

This is the new folding-bed for summer cottages, of which F. R. Slocum is the exclusive agent. It occupies no room, and the bedding can be folded inside. A set of the finest woven wire springs goes with every bed. Don't go off for the summer without seeing this novel invention.

Mrs. Lizzie S. Green is the woman previously reported as Mary Green who created an excitement on Fourth street Saturday night. The woman says she did not fall in a fit, but was suffering from the effects of chloroform given her for a sprained foot.

Witnesses are being summoned by the police today to attend the hearing before the special commissioners on the cost of construction, maintenance and repairs on the Coggeshall street bridge in the city hall at 10 o'clock tomorrow forenoon.

Pensions have been granted as follows: Original—George Jillson.

Original widows, etc.—Lucy J. Jones, E. Armstrong, Catherine Cannon, Maria L. Caldwell, Ellen E. Thayer.

Great glove and hosiery sale going on at Whiting & Co's.

Hood's Sarsaparilla cures sick headache.

EVENING STANDARD EXTRAS.

The Evening Standard yesterday printed an enormous edition, yet in many cases newsdealers found their supply was insufficient to meet the demand. Never in the history of the Standard have subscriptions poured into the office as at present and that signifies a permanent growth in circulation, for past experience has proven that every new reader of the Standard soon becomes a steadfast friend of the paper. The transient sale of Standards has never been equaled. Standard extras will be issued tonight and every night after the close of the court, with a complete report of the day's proceedings in the Borden trial. Order of a newsdealer or write to the Standard.

CONTENTS OF THIS EVENING'S STANDARD.

Page 1.

John V. Morse and Bridget Sullivan the two important witnesses at the forenoon session of the third day of the Borden murder trial.

Great Britain's demands from the United States.

Baptist Sunday school convention in this city.

Big fire in San Francisco.

Telegraphic dispatches.

Home matters.

Page 2.

The Borden Murder trial (continued.)

Correiro, the alleged murderer of Bertha Manchester, son of a well-to-do resident of St. Michael.

Letter from William J. Potter.

Page 3.

Borden murder trial (continued.)

Union of local textile workers elect officers for the ensuing year.

Page 4.

Borden murder trial (continued.)

Editorials.

Page 5.

Marine intelligence.

Marriages and deaths.

Page 6.

The district court record.

The de Lesseps relected directors of the Suez canal.

Repeal of Sherman act predicted in financial article in the London Times.

Suburban news.

Financial news.

Second Edition — Telegraphic and local news.

Page 7.

The World's fair news.

Marriage of Thomas Nelson Page, the novelist.

Programme of Children's day observance at County Street M. E. church.

Edwin Booth's death at the Players' Club, New York, early this morning.

New England field trials at Assonet.

New Bedford retail market.

Cattle markets.

Legislative proceedings.

League and other ball games.

Amusement and sporting news.

Page 8.

The visit of the jury in the Borden case to the scene of the murders.

Third Edition—Telegraphic and locals.

Page 9.

Board of public works and park commissioners meet, Catholics say an extension of North street will ruin their home.

Editorial.

Suburban news.

Page 10.

Farm, Garden and Home.

Bible lesson.

The Indian exhibit at the World's fair.

Page 11.

A Nymph of the West—Howard Seely's serial story.

Page 12.

New office building in New York higher than Trinity steeple.

James Gordon Bennett, the man of mystery.

New York fashions.

Miscellaneous reading.

CONDENSED LOCALS.

The fuel of the future,—a fire that is many times hotter than heat produced from either coal, wood, or oil. For cooking it has no equal. The new system is sold by the following first class dealers: New Bedford—Wood, Brightman & Co., Thomas J. Gifford & Co., Otheman & Dunham, A. Knowles, Joseph Greenwood, William G. Hayden, E. F. Penney, C. A. Galligan and J. B. Dion. Fairhaven—Robert H. Taber and Forrest & Long.

The summer arrangement of the New Bedford, Marthas Vineyard & Nantucket Steamboat company will commence Monday, June 12th, four boats daily to Cottage City, two boats to Nantucket. First Sunday boat June 18th. Time of leaving will be about the same as last year. Look for advertisement in tomorrow's issue.

H. C. Hathaway will sell at auction tomorrow morning, 10 o'clock, at mart, about 30 horses adapted for general purposes, one load to arrive tomorrow morning; also three horses and one heavy express wagon, been used about the city; 3 p. m., at salesroom, lot of plants. See advertisement on page 6.

The Guard of Honor met recently to consider an invitation to join with other French Canadian societies in the celebration of St. John's Day, June 24th, at Montreal. On account of the expense it was voted not to accept the invitation.

Division 7, A. O. H., will hold its annual election of officers Friday evening. It is understood that Matthew Hart, the president, declines a re-election. The organization is planning an excursion to Nantasket Beach on June 18th.

The barber shop of Anthony Gomes, Union street, has been thoroughly renovated, with new paper, mirrors, cupracks, portiere, etc., and these adjuncts, aided by a fresh coat of paint, make it a very attractive place.

Removal—Mrs. J. F. Corcoran, dressmaker, has removed to 138 Washington street, where she will resume work as usual. Perfect fit guaranteed. S. T. Taylor system used.

The tulips in the flower beds in front of the court house have been replaced with begonias of a rare variety, geraniums and lichens by William Peirce.

Stockholders in the Morse Twist Drill & Machine Co. will be interested in the call for the adjourned annual meeting Friday morning. See sixth page.

The telephone service was interrupted last evening because the lights at the Central office went out and the operators could not see to work.

Division 9, A. O. H., meets this evening to make preparations for the funeral of Peter E. Harrington. See special notice.

Now is the time to purchase your gingham and pongee dress goods at the great mark-down sale at Whiting & Co's.

Gentlemen, the finest line of Russia leather shoes found at Buchell's. See our $4 shoe.

Don't forget to attend Nooning's great Flower Sale commencing Friday morning at 9 o'clock.

L. A. Davenport has recently bought a fine three-year old Hambletonian.

Chiropodist.—Mrs. Williams, 190 Purchase st., Webster block, every Friday.

Call and see Nooning's Trimmed Sailors for 69c.

The place to purchase waists and wrappers is at Whiting & Co's.

A rare chance for investment, beautiful house on Morgan street, see advertisement.

Greatest event of the season—Nooning's great Flower Sale on Friday morning.

The proprietors carry in stock 12,000 barrels of Cutter Whiskey.

LADIES

SOMETIMES

You feel uncertain where to buy

CARPETS.

NOW WE WISH TO TELL YOU THAT WE ARE FULLY PREPARED TO SUPPLY YOUR WANTS.

OUR STOCK IS MORE ATTRACTIVE AND COMPLETE THAN AT ANY TIME DURING THE HISTORY OF OUR BUSINESS.

New Carpets.
New Mattings,
New Furniture,
New Curtains.

YES

WE ATTEND STRICTLY TO THE

Furniture, Carpet and Curtain Business.

FURNISHING HOUSES IS OUR SPECIAL WORK, AND THIS WE DO TO THE ENTIRE SATISFACTION OF EVERYONE WHO FAVORS US WITH THEIR BUSINESS.

We handle the best makes.
We guarantee our prices to be as low as the lowest.

CASH or CREDIT.

C. F. WING,

34 to 40 Purchase Street.

WHITING & CO.

Great Summer Cotton Wash Goods Sale.

One case 1,632 yards of the best 12 1-2c. American Ginghams will be sold by us at 7 1-2c. per yard. Only 75c. for 10 yards of nice Gingham.

500 yards of Bedford Cord Ginghams, made to sell at 25c., our price 12 1-2c.

250 yards of Cheviots that sold at 33c. per yard, our price 12 1-2c. today.

2,500 yards of the finest American Ginghams, made and sold this season at 17c., will be sold by us at 12 1-2c. per yard.

2,800 yards of the best Scotch Ginghams, made by R. A. Whytlaw Sons & Co. of Glasgow, Scotland, that have been sold at 33c. the first of the season, now sold by us at 17c. per yard.

1,000 yards of our best Printed Pongees, mostly white grounds, carried over from last season and sold at 15c. per yard, we shall put on sale at 9c. per yard. Do not wait, but come as soon as you read this, as the case price today for same goods is 12 1-4c. cash.

☞ Do not ask for samples of any of these goods, as we shall not give any.

WHITING & C

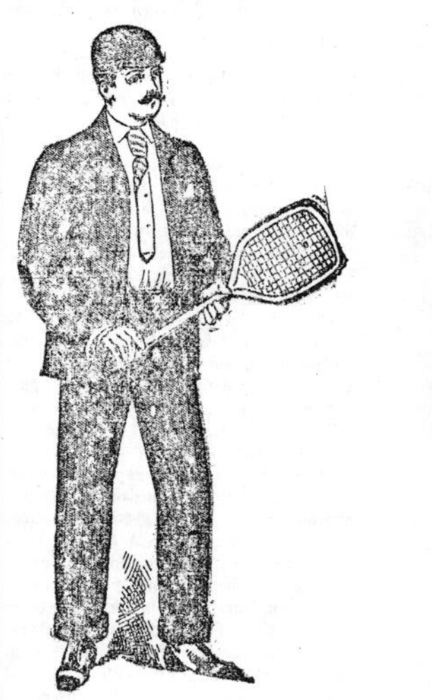

Tennis and Outing Suits.

The newest things in Tennis and Outing Suits are ready for your inspection. Blue Serge Skeleton coats and White Duck Trousers will be the "go" this Summer, and we have provided an unusually large stock of these comfortable goods for the hot weather.

The new styles in Tennis Flannels are very handsome and especially moderate in price.

Our assortment of Negligee Shirts, Leather Belts, Straw Hats, Tennis and Bicycle Caps, Stockings, etc., is most complete and comprises everything that is newest and best.

J. & W. R. WING & CO.,

Men's Furnishers.

THE CRESCENT!

22 Purchase St.

ONLY 19c. PER YARD.

VERY WIDE HAMBURGS.

Just right for Skirts.

Excellent Hamburgs at 12 1-2c.

A good assortment at 5c.

To close at 19c. per yard.

A Lot of Silk Gloves,

Black and Colors, regular 25 and 29c. quality.

Mitts, good quality, 25c., a better grade at 50c.

Shirt Waists, at 29, 50, 75c.

Better quality at $1.00 $1.25, and $1.50, etc.

An entire new lot of belts, all styles.

Try THE LATEST, Empire styles, in tan and black, at 50c.

GUIMPES.

Guimpes at 39, 50, 58c.

Guimpes at 62, 75, 83c., $1.

Children's Dresses!

Gingham dresses from 50c. to $1.75.

White dresses, all styles and prices.

MARKED DOWN—Children's Short Cloaks.

TAN COLORED HOSIERY.

Children's Tan Hose, 25 and 37c. Ladies' Tan Hose, 25, 33 and 50c. Black Hosiery in all grades.

SUMMER CORSETS.

Good ones at 50c. Better grades at 75c., $1, $1.25 and $2. Corsets of all kinds. Equipoise Waists, Double Ve Waists, Ferris Ventilating Waists. Misses' and Ladies' Summer Vests of all kinds. Gingham aprons, two widths, 25c.

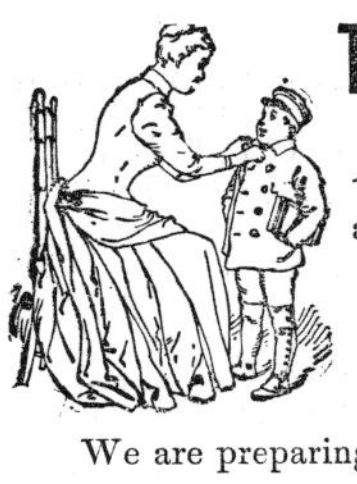

The Boy Wanted a Reefer,

And his parents came to our sale that we are having on all kinds of

CHILDREN'S SUITS.

We are preparing to move next Spring, and shall carry no stock over.

Shall sell everything at some price.

Children's Suits at astonishing low prices.

Now is your time to get a suit for the boy at little cost.

REMEMBER THIS WEEK.

SANDERS & BARROWS,

67 and 69 William St.

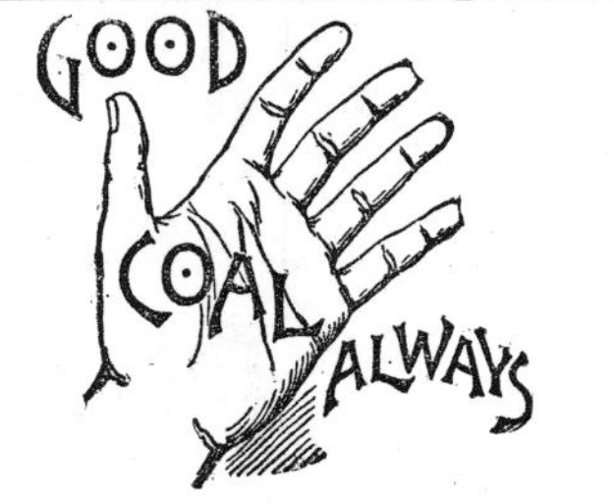

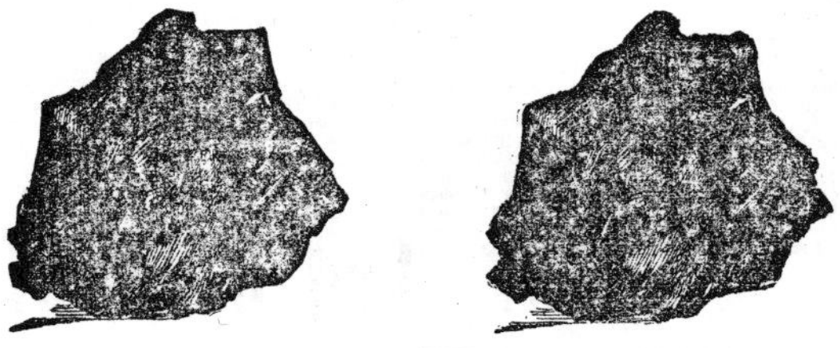

Denison Bros. Co.,

Yard---Foot of Hillman Street.

Offices---Cor. School and South Water Sts., and Cor. Hillman and North Water Sts. TTS

HIRAM WHEATON & SONS,

Wine and Spirit **Merchants.**

Dealers in the finest brands of Kentucky and Maryland Whiskies, Rums, Gins, Brandies, Champagnes, Wines, etc., Foreign and Domestic, Bass Ale, Guinness Stout, Mineral Waters,

Milwaukee . . and Ballantine Export . . . . . Lager Beer Bottled . . Fresh . . . Every Day.

48 to 51 School Street, New Bedford, Mass. Orders by Mail, Telephone or Express Will Receive Prompt Attention.

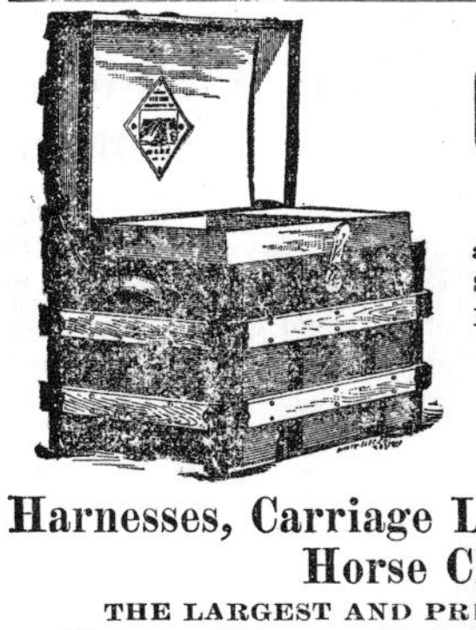

This Cut Represents the

Clinton Wall Trunk!

Five kinds of Wall Trunks, and all other kinds of Trunks, Shopping and Traveling Bags, Pocketbooks, Purses, etc., at

CUSHING'S.

Our Stock of

Harnesses, Carriage Lap Robes, Horse Clothing, Whips, etc.,

THE LARGEST AND PRICES THE LOWEST AT

C. F. CUSHING'S,

OPPOSITE CITY HALL.

Men's Summer Clothing.

SUMMER COATS,
SUMMER SUITS,
SUMMER HATS,
SUMMER HOSIERY,
SUMMER UNDERWEAR.

STRAW HATS, 5c. to $2.00.

H. V. SANDERS & CO.

OPPOSITE CITY CLOCK. | One Price Clothiers, | 92 PURCHASE ST.

NOTICE.

THE LARGEST STOCK OF HARNESSES. and Bags

GOLDSMITH, SILVER & CO'S

M.C.A. 10c. CIGARS LEAD ALL OTHERS.

EVERYBODY SHOULD TRY THE "108" Havana Filled 5c. Cigar.

DEAN, Agent, - Taunton.

THE REPUBLICAN STANDARD,

Issued this evening contains all the local and general news of the past week, and it will be a valuable number to send to New Bedford people abroad. The main feature of the number is a full and illustrated account of the famous trial of Lizzie Borden on the charge of murdering her father and stepmother—she presents a calm appearance at the opening of the court, and challenges jurors in clear, sharp tones, full particulars of the process of securing a jury, which was accomplished upon the first day of the trial, portraits of the jury, the reading of the indictment, and opening address of District Attorney Moody, Miss Borden gives way under the strain and faints away after hearing the words of her accuser, the jury goes to Fall River to visit the scene of the crime, and makes a thorough examination of the premises, progress of the trial, testimony for the government being put in; arrest of a Portuguese named Manuel Correiro for the murder of Bertha Manchester, who surrendered himself to the Fall River police, he is arraigned for the crime and the case postponed till June 15th, circumstances are unfavorable for him, and the police are suppressing much evidence; Henry Welsh of this city pushed from a third story window in Fall River and he receives fatal injuries, his assailant, Luke Burke, surrenders himself, and is believed to be demented, Welsh makes a sworn statement of the assault by Burke; the body of Duncan McNeil found in the river, and Medical Examiner Hough says there was no foul play, but that he died from drowning; meeting of the school committee, most exciting meeting held for years, teachers elected in some grades and salaries fixed, interesting discussion on the High school corps; a canal to be cut through the sandy soil of Cape Cod via Bass river by the Old Colony and Interior campany and the Cape Cod Canal company, which unite for the purpose; indictment against Walter Paine quashed, District Attorney Knowlton sets forth the reasons, as his exile, old age and petition for clemency; Farm, Garden and Home; Bible lesson for next Sunday; probate and district court reports; correspondence; with ship news, editorials, markets, miscellaneous reading matter, etc.

For sale by all newsdealers in this city, and at our counters, in wrappers ready for mailing, at 4 cents per copy.

INSOLVENCY COURT—PLYMOUTH CO.

Harris J.

Brockton, June 5.

The following business was transacted:

Henry M. Dunham, Mansfield, adjourned third meeting in September; Fayette C. Morris, Middleboro, first meeting in composition in July; Hugh P. James, Brockton, adjourned second meeting in July, James P. Barlow, assignee; Winsor & Stone, Brockton, second meeting in July, David A. Andrews, Jr., assignee; Charles Wakeling, second meeting in July, Joseph O. Harrington, assignee; Bert H. Shurtleff, Scituate, third meeting in September; Hiram Whittemore, Middleboro, third meeting in July; Fowler & Cousins, Brockton, third meeting in July.

Algernon S. Lyon, Bridgewater, adjourned to September; Edward C. Howland, Abington, final meeting in composition, closed; Daniel C. Murray, Brockton, adjourned second and third meeting, dividend of 50 per cent. preferred, case closed; William C. Sturtevant, Pembroke, adjourned third meeting, adjourned to October; Fred Stetson, Brockton, adjourned third meeting, adjourned to October; Charles E. Tucker, Abington, adjourned third meeting, adjourned to October; Mabel S. Howard, Brockton, adjourned third meeting, adjourned to October; Nathaniel T. Ryder, Brockton, adjourned third meeting, adjourned to January, 1894.

TRINITARIAN CHURCH CLUB.

The annual meeting of the Trinitarian Church club was held Tuesday evening. The following officers were elected:

President—Rev. M. C. Julien.
Vice President—David L. Parker.
Secretary—Miss Helen L. Hadley.
Treasurer—Mrs. Thomas B. Tripp.

Officers of sections were elected as follows:

Literary Section—Chairman, Charles T. Bonney, Jr.; vice chairman, Miss Marian Swasey; secretary, Mrs. Robert W. Taber.

Charity Section—Chairman, Mrs. Lydia Adams; secretary and treasurer, Mrs. William N. Weeden.

Social Section—Vice chairman, Miss Elmira Watson; secretary, Miss Fannie Spooner.

Following the election refreshments were served and then came an enjoyable original play with the following cast: Miss Josie Cobb, Miss Bessie Cobb, Miss Gertrude Sayer, Miss Caddie Bly, Miss Sophie Anthony, Miss Jennie Paine, Miss Stella Paine, Miss Susie Reed.

The Dentist

when he cleans your teeth, runs a strip of floss between them. Did you ever wonder why an ordinary tooth brush wouldn't do as well? Simple enough. The ordinary tooth brush cleans the surface only. The danger of decay lies between the teeth. The

Prophylactic

Tooth Brush is an improvement upon the old fashioned brush as well as the dentist's floss. It removes every particle from between the teeth, and cleans the surface too. It is the only brush constructed on strictly hygienic principles. The best dentifrice to use with the Prophylactic brush is

Operle Cream

Sold in large embossed tubes only. It makes the teeth like pearls, arrests decay, hardens the gums, leaves a delicious flavor of roses.

Both sold by Druggists.

A sample tube of cream, and dainty book about the teeth, free. Florence Mfg. Co., Florence, Mass.

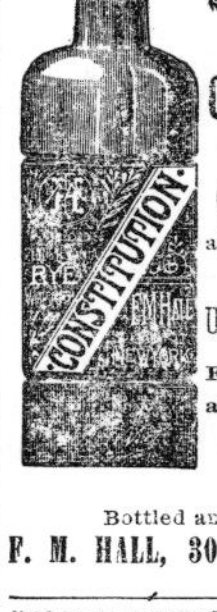

Why Buy Whiskey by measure and not know what you get? BUY THE

CONSTITUTION

—IN—

Quart and Pint Bottles, and get uniform High Grade goods always.

Unsurpassed for Medicinal Use

For Sale by all Druggists and Licensed Dealers.

QUARTS. $1.25.
PINTS. .75.

Bottled and at Wholesale by

F. M. HALL, 30 Front St., New York. ws

Town Talk,

The new High Grade Flour. Makes MOST, BEST, WHITEST, SWEETEST BREAD.

DENISON BROS. CO., Wholesale Agents.

CORREIRO'S COUSINS

Ask to Provide Clothing for the Prisoner.

His Family Well-to-do Residents of St. Michael.

Old Man Coming to Fall River with Funds to Pay Counsel.

(Special Dispatch.)

Fall River, June 7.—Manuel Vera, Joseph Siero and Michael Correiro, three cousins of Jose Correiro, the accused Manchester murderer, called at the Central police station yesterday afternoon to inquire of Captain Harrington if they could supply their friend with clothing and victuals. They had been informed that such things had been done before, and they came for information. They did not want the "poor boy," as they designated Correiro, to be left without his necessary changes of clothing.

The captain informed them that the accused had all his wants supplied, and if he needed anything all he had to do was to speak. The trio were surprised and departed well satisfied.

Before leaving the station they informed a Standard reporter that a telegram had been sent to St. Michael, where Michael Correiro, the father of the accused, lived, and it was expected that he would take the first boat for Fall River.

Correiro, it seems, is the oldest boy, and has two sisters and a younger brother at the home in the Western islands. The mother of the accused, they said, was a very good woman and thought the world of Jose, in spite of the fact that he was a little wild and careless. Correiro's parents are said to be in pretty comfortable circumstances. They own two grocery stores and a large farm, on which the family is employed.

When Correiro's father comes he is expected to bring funds with him to provide counsel, so that his boy will have a fair trial. The cousins are confident that the old man will spare no efforts or expense in proving the innocence of his son on the terrible crime charged against him.

A CLEW RUN DOWN.

Fall River Man Suspected on Account of an Injured Eye.

Boston, June 7.—About the time of the Manchester murder there was admitted to the Eye and Ear Infirmary on Charles street, this city, a man from Fall River by the name of Jansen, who had one of his eyes partially knocked out. He was accompanied by a younger man. Nothing was thought of the matter, and he was treated for his bad eye.

In some way the fact of Mr. Jansen being there got to the Fall River police, and it was noised about that he would be seen and questioned in regard to how he came to have his eye blinded in such a manner. The facts, if ever told, were greatly exaggerated, and the police thought that the man might prove to have had some connection with the Manchester murder.

It was intimated that the Fall River police had communicated with the physician in charge at the infirmary, and that they were satisfied that the case was worth looking up, and would be in Boston yesterday.

A reporter called at the infirmary yesterday afternoon, and the story was at once exploded. It is true that the man is there; he also came from the Border City, and one of his eyes is under treatment. But this is all there is to it. Mr. Jansen was brought to this city by his son. He is an old resident of Fall River, and has been known by one of the attendants at the infirmary for thirty years.

The police of Fall River had not communicated with the officials at the Charles street institution, and the story as told in detail was far from true. Thus goes to the wall another clew.

THE ALVA SUIT.

The $305,000 damage suit of Vanderbilt vs. the Metropolitan Steamship company, for the sinking of the yacht Alva, was resumed in the United States district court Tuesday morning. The Vanderbilt side first submitted the deposition of Stephen D. Horton, pilot of the Alva, and then put George Eldridge, the hydrographer, on the stand. At this point the steamship people introduced, out of course, the testimony of F. W. Howes, who was on the steamer Dorchester. He did not see the collision and only testified to conditions. Lieutenant Burdick, U. S. N., was on the stand at the hour of adjournment.

OBITUARY.

William Carr, an ex-alderman of Fall River, died Monday evening. He was formerly agent of the Fall River and Providence Steamboat company and a director of the Metacomet bank from its organization. He was prominent in promoting measures for the relief of suffering operatives in the winter of '57.

PROVISION CLERKS.

At the annual meeting of the Provision Clerks Benefit association Tuesday evening the following officers were elected:

President—Frank P. P. Tuell.
Vice President—Horace D. Bradley.
Recording Secretary—William D. Linton.
Financial Secretary—Samuel W. Mitchell.
Treasurer—Frank C. Dunham.
Directors—One year, Joseph A. Wright, James Lowe, Jr.; two years, Edward N. Bennett, Walter F. Jenney; three years, Charles M. Miller. Edgar C. Tripp.

NANTUCKET.

What was supposed to be a large steamer ashore on the shoals near Muskeget channel, was discovered Monday noon, and the same wrecking boat, under command of James A. Holmes, with substantially the same crew that boaded the derelict bark Mentor, started for the scene of the disaster. The mists hung low over Muskeget channel, but the valient crew pushed on, and returned about 9 o'clock p. m., reporting a porgy steamer there with her seines set for porgies and needing no assistance.

By auction, Monday, George E. Mooers sold for taxes a large number of pieces of dividend lands for small prices. Sheep commons sold for $7 per common.

Walter May, son of George W. Burdick, while bathing near Old Commercial wharf, jumped upon a broken glass bottle and cut one of his feet severely, severing an artery. Dr. E. B. Coleman rendered the surgical aid.

The announcement that the Old Colony Railroad company will run trains in connection with the steamers for Nantucket, so that Boston morning papers, mails, and passengers can arrive at the island by the noon boat instead of being detained till the night boat, gives general satisfaction to both residents and visitors.

The Wannacomet Water company has sent to the fire department a bill of $500 for use of water and hydrants at the late fire in the store of John Harps & Co., the contract between the town and the company having expired. It was the first fire in over two years and occurred within a month after the contract expired.

The bills of the late committee of the town on a water supply for fire purposes thus far foot up $473, and they are not all in.

The school committee has taken prompt action to renovate the outbuildings connected with the Academy Hill school, in accordance with the suggestions of the board of health.

The mosquito fleet of sailboats is fast being placed in commission for the summer campaign. No accidents resulting in loss of life have ever occurred in the employment of these regular boats commanded by competent skippers.

The Nantucket railroad to Siasconset will be in running order the last of this month.

REV. WM. J. POTTER'S LETTER.

To the Editor of the Standard:

Since my last letter to the Standard I have seen considerable of that part of Californian life not usually sought after by tourists for pleasure, nor by those who come here for the charms of climate. In a figurative sense, at least, this land is not all sunshine, nor the atmosphere entirely balmy. Just now particularly there is a cry of hard times. And this complaint appeared previous to and independent of the present condition of semi-panic throughout the country. The truth is the state is still suffering from the collapse of its speculative boom of a few years ago. Many people who then invested in ranch lands or in corner lots in prospective cities are now "land poor." Heavy taxes are called for, but the promised income is not yet in sight. At Fresno, also, the center of of one of the richest agricultural districts of the world—the great San Joaquim valley—there seemed to be a horde of laboring people vainly seeking work. At least, it was so said of them. But to me many of them bore the insignia of the professional tramp.

And Fresno's saloons are the bane of those who do find work, as well as of those seeking work. The vineyards and fruit orchards in the surrounding country give work and good wages at certain times of the year, and after that the workmen are idle or must go elsewhere. But the saloons are ever open to catch either the idler or the worker. They appeared to me to occupy about every third or fourth place in the best locations on the best streets, and many of them are open through the night as well as the day, and without even the Sunday for a day of rest. It was evident where the wages of the working people and of the poor were largely vanishing. The liquor traffic, now a flourishing business, but ruinous in its effects, is one of the problems which the state has yet to solve. A few of the smaller cities are trying restrictive laws and even prohibition.

In San Francisco, a great bustling, smoky metropolis, there is yet now a special feeling of business depression. This appears to come, to a large extent, because its commercial interests, so far as its Oriental trade is concerned, are seriously imperiled by the opening of the Canadian Pacific railway and the establishment of the British steamship line from Vancouver across the Pacific. And now to this fact is added "the Chinese question" as involved in the enforcement of the Geary law. If this law is enforced there seems little doubt that San Francisco will lose still further its trade with China. Yet this probability seems to be ignored by the newspapers here. Indeed, it is difficult to get at the exact status of public sentiment in the state on this Chinese question. I have discovered that it will not do to take for test the newspaper utterances. The daily newspapers, for the most part, reflect the political party platforms, and the party platforms were adopted, from motives of policy, to catch the labor vote; and the Geary law, with all its inhumanities, was passed by congress for the same reason. The laboring people and labor organizations are as a whole opposed to the Chinese. But aside from these, I do not discover much opposition to them. Here they are employed by those who need labor almost universally. And if it were possible for the law to be enforced at once, and this large number of laborers expatriated, the industries of the state, in the agricultural districts particularly, would for the time be completely upset. Not all Californians, by any means, approve of the Geary law. Rev. Mr. Wendte has recently preached in the Oakland Unitarian church a sermon in condemnation of the law befitting the latitude of Boston, and I have seen and heard other similar expressions of opinion from old residents here.

It should be added that the question of further restricting immigration from China is entirely separate from the questions involved in the Geary law. The latter deals with people already domiciled here, and deals with them in ways which, though they may be constitutional, are not such as have hitherto been recognized in this country as American, or are now recognized in civilized countries as humane.

William J. Potter.

San Francisco, May 31.

AN INDIAN LETTER.

Methods of Communication Among the Indians.

The Picturesque of Eloquence.—Thoughts Expressed in Silence.—How Indian History is Preserved.—Letter from an Indian about Kickapoo Indian Sagwa.

The sign language of the Indians is a wonderful thing. Two Indians different in their speech as a German and a Spaniard will readily communicate with each other.

It is the picturesque of eloquence to watch an Indian addressing a council and without speaking a word, making his meaning clear to all present by signs.

Histories and all written communications are made by pictures. The family history of a chief will be painted on a tepee. The following is a specimen of this method of communication.

The "letter" was written by KEE-EL-NAH-WE, "The one who knows secrets," a Kickapoo Indian Medicine Man.

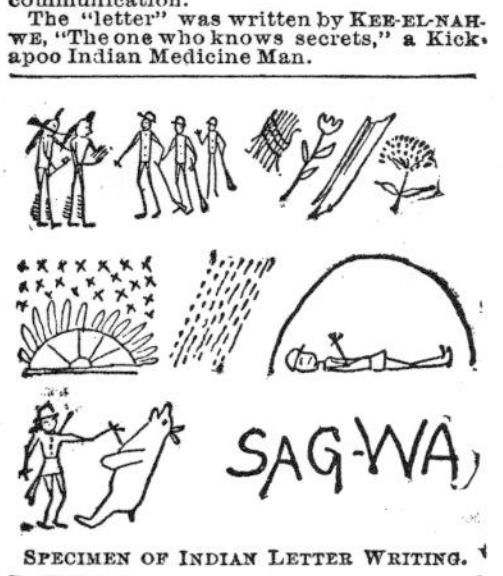

SPECIMEN OF INDIAN LETTER WRITING.

The above letter translates as follows:

"The Indians offer to their white brothers flowers, leaves, roots and barks, made by the sun, the stars, and the rain (nature.) If the white brother is sick, this will make him stronger than the bear who will fall before him."

"SAGWA" is a medicine word meaning good or best, and signifies "best medicine."

Here are the sincere statements of a noble son of a grand race.

Every word is true.

Catlin, the highest authority on the Indians and who lived among them for years, says "the word of an Indian can always be relied upon," and he is right.

Here is proof of the genuine value of Kickapoo Indian Sagwa.

Here is a letter from a far different source. The following is from the Professor of Physiological Chemistry at Yale College, and this scientist says:—

"After a chemical analysis of Indian Sagwa, I find it to be an Extract of Roots, Barks and Herbs of Valuable Remedial Action with no Mineral or other Deleterious Admixtures."

Heed the teachings of these letters.

Take Nature's Remedy in season. If your blood is impure and your skin is marked by pimples, blotches and boils; if you have dull pains in your back and side; if your appetite is poor; if you do not get sound, refreshing sleep, so necessary to your health and strength, *you are in Danger*. These, and other symptoms are the warnings of nature.

Arouse yourself, and drive off the enemy—Arm yourself with Kickapoo Indian Sagwa—build up your system by its use and all danger is averted.

Kickapoo Indian Sagwa and other Kickapoo Indian medicines contain only the products of the field and forest, nature's own vegetable growth of roots, barks and herbs, and of necessity are free from all mineral poisons whatever, because the Indians have no knowledge of them, depending wholly upon nature's laboratory for their resources, and upon their skill, born of centuries of experience.

KICKAPOO INDIAN SAGWA

Is sold by Druggists and Medicine Dealers Only. $1 per Bottle, 6 for $5.

THIRD DAY.

(Continued from First Page.)

upon a wide variety of topics, but studiously avoided any allusion, however remote, to the murder and positively refused to answer any and all inquiries in regard to it.

A RUSH FOR THE DOORS.

Crowd of Curious Women Anxious to See Miss Borden.

When the doors leading to the court room were opened at ten minutes before 9 o'clock there was a much greater rush than at previous sessions. There was a goodly number of women in the rush, and as the jury filed in from their room the best seats in the room were at once taken by these followers of Mary Livermore. Sheriff Wright found it necessary to put a stop to some crowding on the part of women, and while he was ordering them to find seats in another part of the room the prisoner, accompanied by Deputy Sheriff Kirby, put in an appearance. This was at 8 55 o'clock. At 9 o'clock Governor Robinson entered, and from the women's row on the south side there was a buzzing among the gayly dressed females, who had rather neglect most any work than miss an opportunity to be present at this famous trial. Just before the justices entered the prisoner held a whispered consultation with Mr. Jennings.

The jury was tolled off and found present.

It is noticeable that in "women's row," which is filled to its utmost, most of the occupants of the seats are women advanced in years. In one instance a young mother of perhaps 22 years could not content herself at home, and brought with her a child of less than three years, who was compelled to sit through the agony the whole forenoon.

The air in the court room is a great improvement on the last two days, a cool northeast wind making it very much more comfortable.

There is a suspicious box in the back entry, and when Ike Wordell of Fall River informed the attendant that it was for Dr. Dolan there was an immediate inquiry, which revealed the fact that it contained the skulls of Mr. and Mrs. Borden.

Mr. Kieran Recalled.

Thomas Kieran, recalled, in cross-examination said upon being shown the plans exhibited yesterday, made further statements in relation to the door of the Andrew J. Borden house. The 12 inches referred to was the east part of the door.

Then followed a dispute between counsel as to the putting of a question in relation to the best point of observation from the street.

Resuming testimony, witness said he thought he could see more of the door from the line designated by white lines on the blue prints. He had made observations from other points, from the vicinity of the line for a distance of a foot or so. The barn door is lost sight of the instant you leave the line for the south. A very few inches north of the line the door is lost sight of. At that point of contact there is at the southeast corner of the Borden house a climbing plant, which partially obstructs the view. The fence near the sidewalk did not obstruct the view. The dividing fence between Dr. Kelley's and Andrew Borden's house is a picket fence, 4 feet 10 inches high. At the east end of Dr. Kelley's house is a shed and east of the shed a high board fence. Between Mr. Borden's and Mrs. Buffington's premises is a low board fence. Witness was then questioned as to the size of the front door of the Borden barn which is on the south side of the west end of the barn. He said he could not tell the size accurately, as he had never taken any measurements.

Mr. Moody—We do not want any guess work.

Being shown another plan witness said that it was a representation of the barn door on the south.

Mr. Jennings here stated that this plan has been put in since Tuesday night.

Resuming witness stated that the plans submitted yesterday showed the closets down stairs. His attention had been called to the front closet in the front hall.

Could a person shut himself in that closet? asked Mr. Jennings.

Then came an objection from the prosecution, but the objection was overruled.

And witness said that a person could shut himself up in the closet in question.

Could he be seen from the hall if the door was ajar?

Witness answered in the negative.

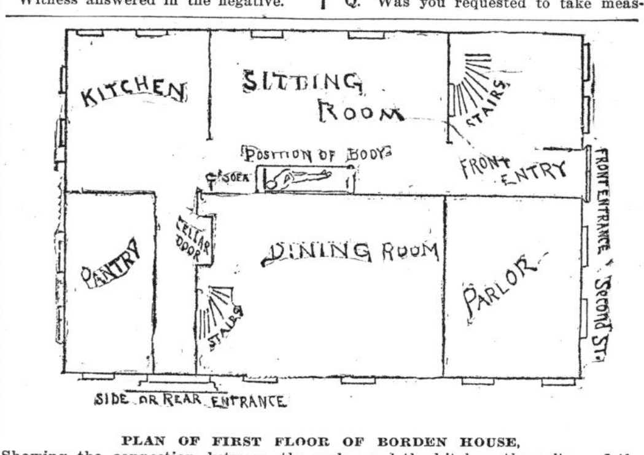

PLAN OF FIRST FLOOR OF BORDEN HOUSE,
Showing the connection between the parlor and the kitchen, the exits, and the stairs leading to the upper floor.

Could this man used in the experiment you speak of be seen from the parlor?

To this the witness said when he moved the door a trifle more he could see the man in the closet.

Q. Did you take any observation of whether a body could be seen between the bureau and the bed?

A. I did. A man laid down on the floor.

Q. How tall was he?

A. Just about my size.

Q. How tall are you?

A. I do not know, sir. Then I went down stairs and came up stairs. I was about in the middle of the stairs.

Judge Mason—The witness must be very careful to observe the question as it is put.

Q. Did you go up stairs in the ordinary way that you would go up stairs?

A. I did.

Q. Could you see the body?

A. I looked under the bed as I went up stairs and saw the man stretched on the floor.

Q. What were you doing when you saw him under the bed, and where were you on the stairs?

A. I was looking for him when I went up stairs.

Q. Do you mean to say that there was any point at which you could see him? If so what was that point?

A. From the stairs I could see under the bed and see the man.

Q. Could you at any other point passing up the stairs except the point where your eyes were on a level with the floor?

A. Well, from a short distance above there.

Q. And that you say was when you were particularly looking to see him?

A. Yes sir, when I tried to see him.

Q. How was it when you went up as you ordinarily went up?

Judge Mason—That question is not proper.

Q. You saw it when you stood upon the floor of the hall upstairs in front of the door which we would call Miss Lizzie's room?

A. I could not see him.

Q. Do you know whether the position of the bed and the bureau, as you had them that day you were taking the observations, corresponded at all with what it was when Mrs. Borden's body was found?

A. I do not.

Q. Was you requested to take measurement by Dr. Dolan or Marshal Hilliard of the distance between the bureau and the bed at any time?

A. I was.

Q. How soon after the tragedy?

A. I went there at Dr. Dolan's request on the 16th of August.

Q. Do you know whether the bed and the bureau were adjusted in the positions at that time for you to take the measurements by Dr. Dolan?

A. I do not.

Q. What was the distance at the time you took these measurements of the bureau from the bed?

A. (The witness here referred to notes.) Thirty-four inches.

Q. What was the distance of the bureau from the bed at the time you were making the experiment you have just described?

A. The same.

Q. In what position did you place

THE BLIND BARD.

Will Carleton Admires Her Writings.

Shut Out for Twenty Years from Nature's Beauties.

For Years a Helpless Wreck---Now She is Well.

Had to be Carried About in Stronger Arms.

She Writes of Her Miraculous Restoration.

For nearly 20 years Ida Glenwood, "the blind bard of Michigan," to use her own language, has been shut out from "all the bright beauties with which nature gladdens the soul and invigorates the mind."

Of her last fascinating story, which was instantly popular with young and old, Will Carleton says: "I have admired it much, and can only wonder that one deprived of sight could paint such vivid pictures."

The Independent calls it "intensely interesting from first to last."

Ida Glenwood's real name is, as every one knows, Mrs. C. M. R. Gordon. The story of the last few years of her life is almost miraculous.

"For several years," she writes, "I have been for the greater part of the time a helpless wreck, caused by nervous prostration and dyspepsia of the stomach and bowels."

She owes her health today, as do thousands of others, to the glorious remedy first prescribed by Dartmouth's great professor, Dr. Phelps.

"I was so low at the time of commencing its use," she continues, "that I was able to walk but a few steps, having to be carried about in stronger arms, like a child. My friends had no hope of my recovering so as to be about again. But two bottles of Paine's celery compound did the work of placing me on my feet again. I have been better for the last year than for many previous years.

"I have a wish that every one in a like condition should try Paine's celery compound. I cannot fail to preach its merits, as it has not failed one of the hundreds who have tried it with whom I am personally acquainted. If you wish to use my name in recommendation of the priceless compound, you are at liberty to do so. I have been glad to speak of its merits through the Open Window, the organ of the "Shut In" band, believing that a large number could be reached with its benefits.

"I have divided part of my celery compound with my aged husband, who was run down and feeble, three bottles relieving him to such a degree that he has been active and busy ever since. This spring I have taken one bottle of the compound and it has apparently driven back another attack of my old trouble.

"My wishes to the afflicted are that they may be persuaded to use Paine's celery compound, which will not fail in giving strength and vitality when these necessities fail them."

Worth a Guinea a Box.

Stubborn tendencies to digestive troubles in *children* will always yield to a *mild* dose of

Beecham's Pills

(Tasteless)

25 cents a box.

31

the man who was lying between the bureau and the bed on the day you made the experiment relative to the mopboard at the head of the bed? What I want to get at is, if you know what the distance of the man's head was who was lying down from the mopboard behind the head of the bed.

A. His head was about three feet from the mopboard.

Q. Do you know how tall he was?

A. I do not.

Q. Did his feet project beyond the head of the bed?

A. They did.

Q. As you stood in the hall did you stand in front of Miss Lizzie's door and look for him?

A. I did.

Q. Could you see any portion of his body from that position?

A. No, sir.

Q. Do you know how far his feet projected beyond the foot of the bed?

A. I do not.

Q. Do you know the length of the bed?

A. It was 6 feet and 7 inches.

Q. Could you see the feet from any portion of the stairs?

A. I could not.

At this point there was a break in the proceedings, as Mr Jennings stopped to examine some plans, and Joe Howard attracted considerable attention by walking across the court room and making an ineffectual attempt to engage Sheriff Wright in conversation. He settled contentedly into Deputy Sheriff Butman's seat, and as that official good-naturedly made no objection upon his return, he retained it.

Mr. Jennings resumed the cross-examination of the witness.

Q. I observe on the plans that between the southwest corner of Dr. Chagnon's house and the northeast corner of the fence around the Borden estate there is an open space. Does this represent the condition of things?

A. No sir, there is a fence at that point.

Q. Can you tell what the height of that fence is?

A. I cannot.

Redirect examination was resumed by Mr. Moody, and the witness gave various measurements of the sofa in the sitting room upon which Mr. Borden's body was found.

Q. Will you state the distance from the sofa to various parts of the room?

A. It was on the east side of the door leading from sitting room, and projected by the door just half its distance.

Q. How far is the east sofa pillow from the kitchen?

A. I did not make the measurements.

Q. With whom was it you made the experiments alluded to?

A. Mr. Jennings.

Q. Is there any ventilation in the closet referred to?

A. I didn't see any.

Q. How long did he stay in the closet with door closed?

A. Mr. Jennings did not go into the closet. He called my attention to the experiment. Mr. Phillips went into the closet.

Q. Well, then how long did Mr. Phillips remain in the closet?

A. Not more than a few minutes.

Q. Where were the measurements up stairs made by you?

A. The measurements in relation to the sofa were made August 16, 1892.

At this point Mr. Moody requested witness to furnish prosecution with duplicate plans of the cellar, and resuming redirect examination asked:

Q. Did you notice whether the front door of the Borden barn moved on rollers or wheels?

A. I did not.

Q. Will you state what was observed as to barbed wires on any of the fences adjoining the Borden property?

A. All of the fences had barbed wires on top. The fence between the Borden yard and Mr. Crow's yard has a barbed wire on the side of the top stringers.

Q. Did you notice barbed wire at the bottom of this fence?

A. I did not see any.

Q. Did you notice any at the corner of this fence?

A. I did not see any.

Again cross-examined by Mr. Jennings:

Q. Did you notice blood spots about the rooms?

A. I did.

Q. Who pointed them out to you?

A. Dr. Dolan.

Q. What was noticed on the door opening from the sitting room to the kitchen, and how far was it?

A. Noticed a blood spot. It was 8 feet 6 inches from the sofa.

Q. Where was it in respect to the door?

A. It was on the architrave on the side of the door farthest from the dining room wall.

Q. How far from the floor?

A. I don't know.

Q. Was your attention called to a spot in the dining room?

A. On the casing of the door opening from the sitting room from the dining room.

Q. How far from the floor?

A. There were two spots—one 12 and one half inches from the floor, the other 14 inches.

Q. Who pointed them out?

A. Dr. Dolan.

Q. Were any pointed out on the wall?

A. No sir.

Photographer Walsh.

James A. Walsh of Fall River was then called and sworn. He had taken photographs of various parts of the Borden house, and identified several photographs shown him as his handiwork. In cross-examination by Governor Robinson he said that the views were all taken on the afternoon of the same day.

THE PRISONER'S UNCLE.

John Vinnicum Morse on the Stand as a Witness.

John V. Morse, an uncle of the prisoner, was next called to the stand, and was examined by District Attorney Moody.

Q. Your full name.

A. John Vinnicum Morse.

Q. Where is your present residence?

A. South Dartmouth.

Q. Be kind enough to give us your age, sir.

A. Sixty years.

Q. How long has your residence been that that you have just stated?

A. Something over a year.

Q. Prior to that time your residence had been in the west?

A. Yes sir; three years ago I came here.

John V. Morse, Uncle of the Prisoner.

Q. Prior to the time of your coming here had you been a resident of the west for a number of years?

A. I did.

Q. Did you bear any relation to the first wife of Mr. Borden?

A. Yes sir, she was my sister.

LIZZIE BORDEN'S FAINTING SPELL.
Deputy Sheriff Kirby Holding the Fan and Rev. W. W. Jubb and Andrew J. Jennings in Front of the Prisoner.

Q. You are therefore the uncle of the present Miss Emma Borden?

A. Yes, sir.

Q. Mr. Borden's first wife then was a Morse?

A. Yes, sir.

Q. Do you now recall when Mr. Borden was married?

A. I think I could if I studied over it a little.

Q. If you could give us a date approximately without delay I wish you would be kind enough to do so.

A. I think about 47 years ago.

Q. By that marriage how many children were there?

A. Three.

Q. One died a good many years ago?

A. Yes, sir.

Q. The two others were the prisoner and Miss Emma Borden?

A. Yes, sir.

Q. Do you remember when your sister died?

A. She died in '61, I think.

Q. The child of the first marriage who died, was he or she older or younger than the surviving children?

A. Younger than Lizzie.

Q. Your answers seem inconsistent?

A. Emma is the oldest, then Alice, her name was, and then Lizzie.

A. J. Jennings.

Q. Do you remember when Mr. Borden's second marriage occurred?

A. It was in '64, I think.

Q. What was the name of the lady whom he married the second time? Was it Abby Durfee Gray?

A. Yes, sir.

Q. And the wife of the second marriage is the subject of this inquiry?

A. Yes, sir.

Q. How old was Andrew Borden at the time of his death?

A. Seventy.

Q. How old was his wife at the time of her death?

A. I think 63 or 4.

Q. Were there any children of the second marriage?

A. No.

Q. Never had been a child?

A. No.

Q. Are you able to give the age of the prisoner?

A. I think about 33.

Q. Do you know how old Miss Emma Borden is?

A. Forty-one, I think.

Q. Upon Wednesday, Aug. 3d, last

A. I do not know.

Q. Where did you go when you left the house in the afternoon?

A. To Swansey.

Q. Did you return again on Wednesday?

A. I did.

Q. What time did you return?

A. About half past 8.

Q. In the evening?

A. Yes, sir.

Q. When you returned to the house in the evening what door did you enter?

A. The front door.

Q. How did you get in?

A. Mrs. Borden let me in.

Q. How did you announce your presence at the door?

A. I rang the bell.

Q. And Mrs. Borden came to the door?

A. Yes, sir.

Q. Did you notice after you entered whether the door was shut or not?

A. It was shut after I went in.

Q. Was any one except Mr. and Mrs. Borden in the house that you saw on Wednesday night when you returned?

A. No sir.

Q. Did you see Bridget Sullivan at all that night?

A. No sir.

Q. Did you see Miss Lizzie Borden at all that night?

A. No sir.

Q. When you went into the house into which room did you go?

A. The sitting room.

Q. How long did you remain in the sitting room?

A. Until a few minutes past 10.

Q. Who went to bed first?

A. Mrs. Borden.

Q. Which way did she go to go to bed?

A. Out the rear door to the back stairs.

Q. Who next went to bed?

A. Mr. Borden and I both left at the same time.

Q. Did you see any one before you went to bed?

A. No, sir.

Q. Describe what you heard when you went to bed.

A. Somebody opened the front door and came in and went up stairs to Lizzie's room.

Q. Did you see the person who went up stairs to Lizzie's room?

A. I did not.

Q. In which room did you go when you went to bed?

A. The guest chamber; up stairs in the northwest corner of the house.

Q. Directly over the parlor?

A. Yes, sir.

Q. The room in which Mrs. Borden was found dead the next day?

A. Yes, sir.

Q. When you got up stairs did you notice anything in respect to the door leading into the prisoner's room?

A. No, sir.

Q. Do you know whether it was locked or not?

A. I do not.

Q. You slept all night, I suppose, in the guest chamber?

A. That's trouble. The

Q. Do you recall whether your door was opened or not during the night's sleep?

A. No, sir.

Q. Did anything occur until you arose in the morning?

A. No, sir.

Q. Did you see any person or hear any person?

A. No, sir.

Q. Did you bring with you, Mr.

Holmes and the experts who are to testify to retire and hold themselves in readiness to be called.

Mr. Moody then resumed his examination.

Q. What sort of a day was this Thursday in regard to temperature?

A. Hot.

Q. Was there any one else in the sitting room when you came down stairs?

A. No sir.

Q. Did you remain in the room until some one else came down?

A. Yes.

Q. Was the door leading out of the room open or closed?

A. Closed.

Q. Who did you first see in the morning?

A. I did.

Q. Work about the kitchen.

Q. What occurred as you went out?

A. Mr. Borden hooked the door.

Q. How was the door hooked?

A. The hook went into an eye fitted to a screw.

Q. Was the door hooked when you came to it?

A. It was.

Q. Did you see what was done after you crossed the threshold?

A. Mr. Borden hooked the door.

Q. Where were you until you returned to the house?

A. In Fall River.

Witness then stated where he was. He said he called on a nephew and niece on Weybosset street about 1¼ miles from the Borden house. In answer to the query he said he walked there. Continuing, he stated that the nephew was not at home, but that he saw his niece named Morse; left that house about 20 minutes past 11 and returned to the Borden house.

Q. Did you walk?

A. No sir, I took the car.

Q. Where did you take the car?

A. Just off of Weybosset street.

Q. Where did you leave the car?

A. At the corner of Second and Pleasant streets.

Q. And then where did you go?

A. Went immediately to the Borden house.

Q. Was there a light in the room?

A. I do not think that there was.

Q. Was the sitting room door to the hall open?

A. It was.

Q. Was there any hall light?

A. I think there was.

Q. Where did you sit while with Mr. and Mrs. Borden?

A. I sat in the south part of the sitting room.

Q. Did you receive any instructions in regard to the fastening of the front door?

A. I did not.

Q. After you went upstairs to your room did you hear anybody come into the house?

A. No sir.

Q. Yes sir; somebody came in and passed up to the room of Miss Lizzie.

Q. Do you know who this person was?

A. I do not; the person came in before I retired.

Q. When you went into your room did you find the door open?

A. I did.

BRIDGET SULLIVAN,
The Bordens' Servant at the Time of the Tragedy.

Q. Mr. Borden.

Q. Who did you next see?

A. Mrs. Borden.

Q. Into what room did they come when they came down stairs?

A. Sitting room.

Q. You took breakfast in the dining room, of course?

A. Yes, sir.

Q. Who breakfasted with you?

A. Mr. and Mrs. Borden.

Q. At about what time did you eat breakfast?

A. About 7.

Q. Can you tell what you had for breakfast?

A. Mutton, bread, coffee and cake.

Q. What kind of cake?

A. Sugar cake.

Q. Do you recall anything that was on the table?

A. Fruit.

Q. What kind of fruit?

A. Pears.

Q. Do you recall having johnny cake on the table?

A. I don't remember anything about seeing it on the table.

Q. Do you remember how long you were at the breakfast table?

A. About half an hour.

Q. Did you all arise from the table at the same time?

A. Yes, sir.

Q. Did all who sat at the table partake of the food?

A. Yes, sir.

Q. After completing breakfast, what room did you go into?

A. Sitting room.

Q. Did any one go with you?

A. Mr. Borden.

Q. Did Mr. and Mrs. Borden remain in the sitting room until you started to go away?

A. Not after breakfast. Mr. and Mrs. Borden were in and out several times.

Q. Did you notice where Mr. Borden went when he left the room?

A. Out doors.

Q. Did you notice where Mrs. Borden went?

A. She went into the front hall.

Q. How long before you went away did Mrs. Borden go into the front hall?

A. Some little time.

Q. Did Mrs. Borden do anything in the way of housework that you observed?

A. Mrs. Borden was dusting with a feather duster.

Q. Did Mrs. Borden go into the dining room after breakfast?

A. Not after breakfast.

Q. Did she have anything on her head while she was dusting?

A. I don't think she did.

Q. Was Miss Lizzie sick?
This question was objected to.

Q. After you returned at night was you in the sitting room with Mr. and Mrs. Borden?

A. Yes sir.

Q. Did you hear any conversation between Bridget and Mrs. Borden about washing windows?

A. I did.

Q. What did Mrs. Borden say?

A. I want these windows washed today.

Q. Had you noticed anything about the screen door on the front door?

A. Yes sir. If you shut the door hard it will catch, and if you do not it will not catch.

Q. When did you notice this?

A. After the tragedy.

Q. Was the room closed?

A. Yes.

Q. Of course you did not ascertain whether it was locked?

A. I did not.

Q. When you went up to your room by the front way did not Mrs. Borden go up to her room by the back way?

A. She did.

Q. Was Bridget up before you got up the next morning?

A. I do not know.

Q. Did you hear her about in the kitchen?

A. I did not.

Q. How was the table set for breakfast?

A. With ordinary appliances.

Q. Didn't you have a good fair breakfast and plenty of it?

A. I did.

Q. There was nothing mean or stingy about it?

A. I did.

Q. Is the distance far?

A. It is not.

Q. How did you approach the house?

A. Went around to the rear. Picked up a couple of pears and ate a part of one of them.

Witness said he first saw Mrs. Borden's body upon entering the house, he describing his passage upstairs into the room occupied by him the night before he saw the body lying on the floor between the bureau and the bed.

Q. Where was your head when you saw it?

A. It might have been six inches above the floor.

Q. Did Mr. Borden have a farm in the neighborhood of Fall River?

A. In Somerset.

Q. Before you went away on the day of the murder did you see Miss Lizzie Borden?

A. No sir.

Q. You saw her then on your return?

A. I did.

Q. Who was in the house when you got there?

A. Dr. Dolan and two or three officers.

Q. Was there a lady there?

A. Mrs. Churchill, I think.

Q. Was Miss Russell there?

A. I don't remember.

Governor Robinson began cross-examination:

Q. Did you see Bridget Sullivan on the day before the murder?

A. I did not.

Q. Were Mr. and Mrs. Borden sick the night before the tragedy?

A. They were.

Q. Was Miss Lizzie sick?

This question was objected to.

Q. After you returned at night was you in the sitting room with Mr. and Mrs. Borden?

A. Yes sir.

Q. Did you hear any conversation between Bridget and Mrs. Borden about washing windows?

A. I did.

Q. What did Mrs. Borden say?

A. I want these windows washed today.

Q. Had you noticed anything about the screen door on the front door?

A. Yes sir. If you shut the door hard it will catch, and if you do not it will not catch.

Q. When did you notice this?

A. After the tragedy.

(Continued on Fourth Page.)

EX-GOVERNOR ROBINSON
As He Appears Listening to the Evidence.

year, did you go to the Borden house at any time?

A. I did.

Q. Prior to that Wednesday had you been a visitor recently?

A. Well, several weeks before that I was there about three or four weeks.

Q. How long before Aug. 4th was the last time you saw Miss Lizzie Borden?

A. I do not recollect seeing her for three or four months previous.

Q. What time in the day on August 3d did you arrive at the Borden house?

A. About half past one.

Q. Had they had their noonday meal?

A. I ate separate; they had been to dinner.

Q. When did you see the prisoner at any time during your stay at noon?

A. The sitting room.

At this point ex-Governor Robinson and District Attorney Knowlton entered into a discussion as to the exclusion of witnesses from the room, and Chief Justice Mason ordered all witnesses in the case except Reporters Manning, Stevens and Caldwell, Messrs. Buck, Jubb and

Morse, any luggage, any baggage, a grip, or anything?

A. No, sir.

Q. What time did you get up in the morning?

A. About 6 o'clock.

Q. You dressed, of course, and went down stairs?

A. Yes.

Q. Did you leave the door of your room open or shut?

A. Open.

Q. Was Lizzie's door open or closed when you got up?

A. Closed.

Q. Into which room did you go when you went down stairs Thursday morning?

A. The sitting room.

THIRD DAY.

(Continued from Third Page.)

Q. Did you have your attention called to it?

A. No sir; I learned this by finding that the door failed to lock at times. It was discovered by accident and I then had the lock changed.

Q. How long after the tragedy did you make this discovery?

A. A day or two.

Q. Was there any one else around at the time?

A. I don't think that there was.

Q. What time did you say that you returned to the house that morning?

A. About 20 minutes of 12.

Q. By what street did you approach the house?

A. By Second street.

Q. By which door?

A. The rear door.

Q. This is a well-traveled thoroughfare?

A. Yes sir.

Q. It is a noisy street, isn't it?

A. Yes sir.

Q. When the windows are open you can hear the clatter and noise of the street, upon which there is a good many teams passing and repassing?

A. Yes sir.

Q. When you came in the side entrance you saw some one?

A. Mr. Sawyer.

Q. You had some conversation with him?

A. Yes sir.

Q. Where was he?

A. He was on the outside?

Q. On the broad stair outside?

A. Yes sir.

Q. Was there any conversation between Mr. Sawyer on the outside and Miss Sullivan on the inside?

A. I didn't hear any.

Q. Outside there was nobody with Sawyer?

A. No sir.

Q. Inside nobody with Bridget?

A. No sir.

Q. Was there any one around on the outside of the premises?

A. I didn't see anybody.

Q. As you passed into the yard you saw no policemen about the house in any direction?

A. No sir.

Q. Was the barn door open or closed?

A. Closed.

Q. Your only errand as you passed around the house was to get a pear?

A. Yes sir.

Q. Did Mr. Sawyer follow you in?

A. I think not.

Q. What did Miss Sullivan do?

A. Nothing that I know of.

Q. Continued to stay there?

A. Yes sir.

Q. Where did you go?

A. I went into the sitting room.

Q. After going into the sitting room did you go into the dining room?

A. Not at that time.

Q. Did you go up stairs before you went into the dining room?

A. I went part way up.

Q. And did you go up stairs before you saw Miss Lizzie?

A. Yes sir.

Q. When did you first see her and where?

A. When I came down after I had got partly up the stairs; she was sitting in the dining room on the lounge.

Q. Do you know who were there with her?

A. I do not think of any one; there was no one on the lounge.

Q. Don't you remember there were some ladies there?

A. Yes, I saw Mrs. Churchill, but she was in the other room.

Q. In the sitting room?

A. Yes sir.

Q. Where Mr. Borden was lying on the sofa?

A. Yes.

Q. Did you remain from that time on at the house?

A. I was about the house all the afternoon.

Q. I think you said that there were two or three policemen there as you went in the house, and you did not know who they were.

A. I did not know them.

Q. In what part of the house were they?

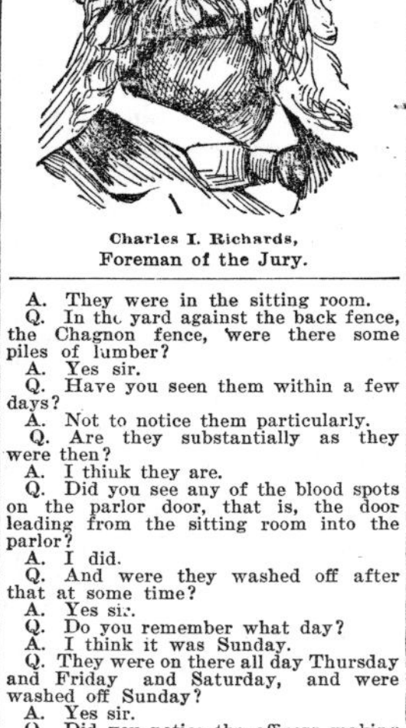

Charles I. Richards,
Foreman of the Jury.

A. They were in the sitting room.

Q. In the yard against the back fence, the Chagnon fence, were there some piles of lumber?

A. Yes sir.

Q. Have you seen them within a few days?

A. Not to notice them particularly.

Q. Are they substantially as they were then?

A. I think they are.

Q. Did you see any of the blood spots on the parlor door, that is, the door leading from the sitting room into the parlor?

A. I did.

Q. And were they washed off after that at some time?

A. Yes sir.

Q. Do you remember what day?

A. I think it was Sunday.

Q. They were on there all day Thursday and Friday and Saturday, and were washed off Sunday?

A. Yes sir.

Q. Did you notice the officers making any examination of any part of the premises at the time you were there?

A. Yes sir. I was with them a part of the time.

Q. Where did you go?

A. To the second and third stories.

Q. What did they look at?

A. Everything, I guess.

Q. Were they thorough about it?

A. I think so.

Q. What did you see them do?

A. I did not take particular notice.

Q. Did they have full opportunity to look about, was anybody there to stop them?

A. No, sir.

Q. Did you impose any objection?

A. No, sir.

Q. Your observation was that they had free access to everything?

A. They had free access to everything.

Q. This was right after you got there?

A. Well, I think it was Friday that I was with them up stairs. On Thursday afternoon when they searched I was not with them.

Q. At any time did they search in the cellar when you were present?

A. Yes, sir.

Q. Well, where did they go then?

A. They went all over it.

Q. What do you mean by going all over it?

A. Well, in the different rooms, the wash room, the coal room and the wood room.

Q. I understand you were there?

A. I was there a part of the time; not all the time.

Q. When you were there what did they do?

A. They looked over the different rooms.

Q. Did they find anything down there?

A. Some axes and hatchets.

Q. Did you see them find these?

A. I saw them after they were found.

Q. How many officers were there?

A. I do not know; three or four.

Q. Would you know the axes or hatchets that were found?

A. I would not.

Q. Could you tell us anything as to whether they were axes or hatchets?

A. I think one was a hatchet.

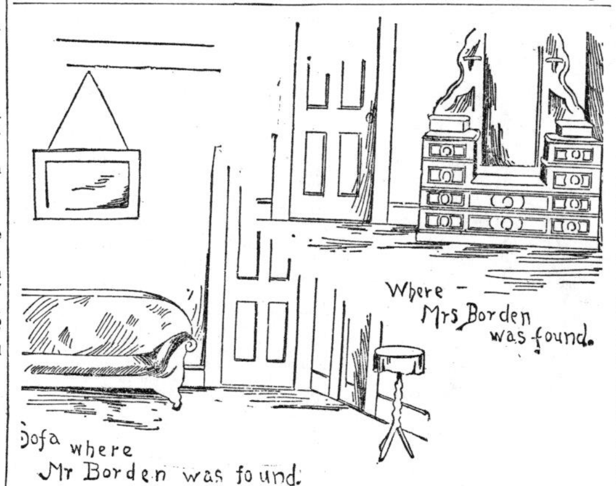

WHERE THE BODIES OF THE BORDENS WERE FOUND.

Q. Did you examine them?

A. No sir.

Q. Did you see these implements again at any time?

A. Several days afterward I saw a man put them into a sack in the yard.

Q. Did you know the man?

A. I did not.

Q. Did he have a uniform on?

A. I think not.

Q. Do you know whether Dr. Dolan was there at that time or not?

A. He was not outside.

Q. Did you attend the preliminary hearing in Fall River?

A. I did.

Q. Were there axes produced there?

A. Yes

Q. Could you say whether these were the same ones or not?

A. I could not say.

Q. Were you at the Borden house on Saturday?

A. I was there every day afterwards for three or four months.

Q. After you came back to the house from the cemetery was a search of the house being carried on?

A. I think there was.

Q. How many officers were participating in that?

A. Four or five, I should think.

Q. Did you know any of them?

A. No, sir.

Q. Did you know the marshal?

A. No, sir.

Q. So far as you saw them that day where did they go?

A. All about the house.

Q. What part of the house?

A. I do not know, I judge from the sound all over it.

Q. Up in the third story as well?

A. I should think so.

Q. And Miss Lizzie, the defendant, was there?

A. Yes sir.

Q. And Miss Emma, her sister.

A. Yes sir.

Q. Was there any objection, the slightest, made to their looking where they wanted to?

A. No sir.

A Recess.

A recess of five minutes was then given the jury.

During the testimony of Mr. Morse Miss Borden listened attentively, leaning forward in her desire to catch every word, and afterwards leaning back and taking in his statements.

At 11 45 o'clock Deputy Sheriff Kirby took the coupe kept on the premises and went to Keeper Hunt's house for Bridget Sullivan.

During the recess ex-Governor Robinson and Mr. Adams held a consultation with Lizzie, and though brief, from her manner, she gained much encouragement.

Mr. Morse Recalled.

After recess Mr. Morse was recalled, and Mr. Robinson resumed.

Q. I would like to ask you about the death of your sister. There is apparently some error; is your recollection positive?

A. It is the best of my recollection. I am not quite sure; I know it was in war time.

Q. Did you not put your sister's death a year or two early?

A. I thought Lizzie was about three years of age when her father married a second time.

Q. You might be in error in regard to the time?

A. Yes sir.

In reply to Mr. Moody witness said that his sister's full name was Sarah Anthony Morse, and that she died in Fall River. Mr. Borden was married the second time at Fall River. All the hatchets and axes that were taken away from the house had handles, and he had no recollection of hearing a man testify at Fall River about taking them away. The street in front of the Borden house was macadamized. He used a lamp while at the house, as it is not provided with gas. To the best of his recollection he went to bed at 9 15 on the night preceding the murder.

ABRAM G. HART.

Testimony of the Treasurer of the Union Savings Bank.

Abram G. Hart, treasurer of the Union Savings bank, was the next witness. He testified that the bank is in what is known as Market square, on North Main street, Fall River, and it is on the east side of the street just north of City hall. Of this bank Mr. Borden was the president. Mr. Borden came into the bank at 9 30 on the day of the murder and remained about five minutes. He did not notice where Mr. Borden went when he left the bank, but he turned to the right. There is another bank in the same building.

Under cross-examination by Mr. Robinson, witness stated that he hesitated to say under oath that Mr. Borden turned to the right, but that was his impression. Mr. Borden did not seem to be in his usual good health and to use a common expression, seemed to be "a little under the weather."

John T. Burrill,

cashier of the Union National bank of Fall River, saw Mr. Borden on the morning of August 4th, 1892, standing in conversation with A. G. Hart in regard to a loan. This must have been between quarter past nine and quarter of ten. Mr. Borden remained about 15 minutes. He was sure that Mr. Borden was out of the bank before quarter of 10.

Everett M. Cook,

cashier of the First National bank, which is on North street in Fall River, and farther removed from the Borden house than the Union bank, saw Mr. Borden transacting business at his bank, of which Mr. Borden was a director, at about 9 45 on the morning of the murder. It could not have been far from quarter to 10 when he left the bank.

Jonathan Clegg of Fall River.

Witness said he was a hatter. First saw Mr. Borden on the morning of the tragedy at his store, 6 North Main street. Had some talk with him in the store. He remained eight or nine minutes. Leaving the store he went south toward the City hall. Witness said Mr. Borden left the store at 29 minutes past 10 o'clock. Witness also stated that he had a reason for fixing the time, and in answer to the query said he never saw Mr. Borden again alive. Had dealings with Mr. Borden in relation to hiring another store, and had called on him at his house in relation to the new arrangement. Went there on August 2d, and again on the 3d, the two days previous to the homicide. Remained in the house perhaps ten minutes, the conversation between witness and Mr. Borden being in relation to the new store which Clegg now occupies.

In cross-examination, witness said he did not see Mr. Borden at the new store. It was at 6 North Main street that he saw deceased. This store, he said, was about 80 yards from City hall, and from the old store to the one now occupied by him the distance was about 150 yards.

Q. Are you positive that Mr. Borden left your store at exactly 29 minutes past 10 o'clock? asked Governor Robinson.

A. I am, sir.

Governor Robinson—That will do.

Joseph Shortsleeve.

of Fall River, had lived in that city 16 years. He was a carpenter by trade, who had known Mr. Borden about 10 years, during which time he had done more or less work for him. Witness was at work on the store now occupied by Mr. Clegg Aug. 4, 1892. Saw Mr. Borden that morning coming up Main street from the direction of the store then occupied by Mr. Clegg. Reaching the store he came in, and after picking up a lock he went out with it. He was there somewhere between half past 10 and quarter of 11. Did not notice any timepiece, but arrived at this conclusion from an estimate of the day's progress. Mr. Borden left the store, crossed the street, looked up at the building and returned to the front of the store, and while standing on the sidewalk held a conversation with witness. When asked what was said witness replied, "We merely said good morning." In reply to Mr. Moody's question witness said that the town clock is in sight of the sidewalk in front of the store.

Cross-examination: Witness said that James Mathews was working with him when Mr. Borden returned to the front of the store. Witness also stated that he first saw Mr. Borden coming up Main street about 75 feet from the store where he was at work.

Q. How long was Mr. Borden in the building?

A. About three minutes.

Q. Then he did not say good morning when he first entered the building?

A. No sir, he did not. He said "Good morning" after he returned from across the street to the front of his store.

Q. Then from the time he crossed the street until he left you on the sidewalk what was the time consumed?

A. Perhaps another three minutes.

In redirect Mr. Shortsleeve was asked if his companion looked at the clock before or after he said "Good morning, Mr. Borden?" He answered "He looked down the street." I do not know whether he looked at the clock then or not; I can't exactly say that he did."

James Mather.

of Fall River, was sworn and said that he was at work with Mr. Shortsleeve on the 4th of August. He said that he did not know Mr. Borden in his life time. He never saw him before the 4th of August. On that day he was working at John Clegg's new store, with Mr. Shortsleeve, lowering the windows; he was working at the outside at the time. He was on the outside all the time between 10 and 11. The window he was at work upon was the one nearest the City hall clock. The City hall clock was within his view. He recalled a person coming to the store that morning who he was told was Mr. Borden. He said he heard a conversation between Mr. Borden and Mr. Shortsleeve. He did not see him on his way to the store. He did not see him till he got there. After Mr. Borden arrived he went into the store, went up stairs a few moments and then came down again, went part way across the street and came back and spoke to Mr. Shortsleeve. When he went out to go home he walked up towards Spring street. The witness said when he went away from the store it was about 20 minutes to 11. He looked at the City hall clock about that time. He did not notice whether Mr. Borden turned up Spring street, because he did not see him get that far. He did not come back to the store again that day.

In cross-examination, Mr. Mather said that he could not say whether it was when Mr. Borden came to the store or just before he went away that he looked up at the clock. When he looked up at the clock it might have been 19 or 21 minutes of 11, but it could not have been more or less. Mr. Borden was there some three or four minutes, upstairs. He talked with Mr. Shortsleeve a minute or two. Witness did not notice how fast Mr. Borden walked when he went away.

BRIDGET SULLIVAN.

Prisoner Closely Followed Words of the Family Servant.

Bridget Sullivan was the next witness. She was dressed in maroon-colored fashionably made dress, wore black hat with large feather, and black kid gloves. She leaned left side against rail, looked straight at Mr. Moody, and spoke so low he had to tell her to speak louder. The prisoner remained leaning back in her seat, but changed posture so as to see witness plainly, and watched Bridget steadily with large eyes wide open.

Bridget was asked to remove her veil, and lifted it from her face.

Q. What is your full name? asked Mr. Moody.

A. Bridget Sullivan.

Q. And were you in the Borden house sometimes called Maggie?

A. Yes, sir.

Q. By whom were you called Maggie, every one?

A. No sir, by Miss Emma and Miss Lizzie.

Q. Will you be kind enough to tell us how old you are?

A. Twenty-six years.

Q. I believe you have never been married?

A. No, sir.

Q. How long have you been in this country?

A. Seven years last May.

Q. Were you born in Ireland?

A. Yes, sir.

Q. Where did you go upon coming to this country?

A. To Newport, R. I.

Q. Had you any folks when you came here?

A. No, sir.

Q. Have you any here now?

A. No, sir.

Q. When you went to Newport did you stay there quite a while?

A. I stayed there about a month.

Q. When you left Newport where did you go?

A. I went to a place in Pennsylvania.

Q. When did you go to Fall River?

A. About two years ago.

Q. When did you go to work for the Bordens?

A. I had been there two years.

Q. Were there any other domestic servants except yourself?

A. No sir, not while I was there.

Q. Was there any man employed there while you were there?

A. No sir: there was a man who came to do the chores and then went away again.

Q. Did he come from the farm?

A. Yes sir.

Q. What was his name?

A. I do not know.

Q. What was the barn used for, there was no horse there, was there?

A. No sir.

Q. When did they cease to have a horse there?

A. About a year before, as near as I can remember.

Q. After the horse had been discontinued did they use the barn for anything?

A. No sir, I don't think they did.

Q. There was some hay in the barn. Was that hay that had been left there from the time that the horse had been kept there?

A. I suppose so. I do not know.

Q. Tell us how the barn door ran. Did it go on wheels or did it open?

A. It opens.

Q. Have you seen that door open?

A. Yes, sir.

Q. Do you know whether it was kept locked or not?

A. No sir.

Q. Have you seen it open recently before the death of Mrs. Borden?

A. Yes, sir.

Q. How long was it before this?

A. I do not know.

Q. Have you seen it open since that time?

A. No sir.

Q. What were your general duties in the household?

A. Washing, ironing and cooking.

Q. Did you have care of any of the chambers except your own?

A. No sir.

Q. You slept in the third story of the house?

A. Yes, sir.

Q. Can you tell the location of the room you slept in?

(Here Bridget was handed a photograph and asked to point out the window of her room, which she did.)

Q. What way does your window look?

A. Into the rear of the house.

Q. Do you know whether your room is the room next to Mrs. Churchill's or Mrs. Kelly's house?

A. Next to Mrs. Kelly's house.

Q. Who occupied the other room in the third story?

A. No one.

Q. Do you know who took charge of the rooms in the front part of the house?

A. I think Mrs. Borden took charge of the front chamber.

Q. Do you know who took care of the rooms belonging to the daughters?

A. They took care of their own rooms.

Q. And did this include sweeping and dusting, as well as making beds?

A. Yes sir.

Q. You had nothing of any kind to do in any of the bedrooms then?

A. No sir.

Q. Did you know Mr. Morse before the time of Mr. Borden's death?

A. Yes sir.

Q. How long had you known him?

A. Quite a while. I don't know how long.

Q. He had occasionally come to the house had he?

A. Yes sir.

Q. And stayed over night?

A. Yes sir.

Q. Can you tell me who took charge of the parlor, the sweeping, dusting and cleaning?

A. I cannot say.

Q. Did you have anything to do with it?

A. No sir.

Q. Do you remember Mr. Morse coming to the house on Wednesday?

A. Yes, sir.

Q. Did you see him?

A. Yes, sir.

Q. When did you first see him on Wednesday?

A. I can't tell whether it was before 2 o'clock or after. It was about that time.

Q. Where did he come from, what door?

A. The back door.

Q. Who let him in?

A. I do not know, I can't tell.

Q. Did you get any dinner for him?

A. No sir.

Q. Do you know whether any dinner was got for him?

A. Mrs. Borden got him some dinner.

Q. Did you go out that afternoon?

A. No sir.

Q. Where did you remain on the afternoon of Wednesday?

A. I was in the kitchen till about four or half past.

Q. When did you do your washing?

A. Monday.

Q. When did you do the drying of your clothes?

A. I dried them Tuesday.

Q. Where did you do your washing?

A. Down cellar.

Q. When you did your washing what was the condition of the door leading out of the back yard into the cellar, was it opened or closed?

A. It was open when I was down there.

Q. When you did your drying on Tuesday was it opened or closed?

A. It was open.

Q. When you got through using the door did you lock it?

A. I locked the door as I hung out the last of my clothes.

Q. How did you lock that door?

A. With the bolt.

Q. The bolt on which side of the door?

A. The inside.

Q. Did you notice any change in that door down to the time of the death of Mr. and Mrs. Borden?

A. I do not know of any

Q. So far as you know it remained bolted?

A. Yes sir.

Q. Describe the character of the travel on Second street. Were there few or many people passing?

A. There were many people going past the house all the time.

Q. When you came in how did you leave the screen door?

A. Hooked.

Q. Did you get the supper Wednesday night?

A. Yes, sir.

Q. Did you notice anything about Mr. and Mrs. Borden's condition Wednesday night?

A. Yes, sir.

Q. What did you observe in their appearance?

A. They were sick.

Q. Were they sick before Thursday?

A. Yes, sir.

Q. Did you have occasion on Wednesday after the dinner hour to go into the front part of the house?

A. No sir.

Q. What time did you go and return on Wednesday evening?

A. I left at 7 o'clock, and after seeing several friends I returned at about five minutes past 10, I think.

Q. Was there a light in the house when you returned?

A. Yes sir.

Q. You did not light the lamp?

A. No sir. There was always one left in the house for me when I was out.

Q. Were there any lights to be seen in the chambers or in any part of the house when you returned?

A. There were no lights in the house.

Q. How did you leave the back doors when you entered the house?

A. I left them locked.

Q. When you came back how did you find the doors?

A. I found them all locked.

Q. Had any one beside you a key to the back door?

A. Yes, Mr. Borden.

Q. When you passed in how did you leave the door?

A. I hooked the spring door; the inside door locked with a spring lock. I bolted the inside door besides.

Q. Did you go directly to bed?

A. Yes sir; only I stopped and got a glass of milk out of the ice-chest.

Q. What milk was it; was it some that came that day?

A. Yes, sir.

Q. It was Wednesday's milk?

A. Yes, sir.

Q. What time in the morning did the milkman come?

A. It was before I got up.

Q. How was it left?

A. It was left in a can.

Q. It was your habit to exchange cans with the milkman, and you had two cans, so that one was always in your possession, and the other with the milkman?

A. Yes sir.

Q. Were you sick during Wednesday night?

A. No sir.

Q. In the morning?

A. In the morning I had a headache and felt bad.

Q. Did you hear any noises during the night, or anything to attract your attention?

A. No sir.

Q. No unusual noise of any kind?

A. No sir.

Q. At what time did you get up Thursday morning?

A. At quarter past 6.

Q. All the house is carpeted, except the stairs leading to your room from the second story?

A. Yes sir.

Q. Did you have a time piece in your room?

A. Yes sir.

Q. Was it a small round metal clock?

A. Yes sir.

Q. You observed the time on Thursday morning when you came down stairs by the clock in the kitchen?

A. Yes sir.

Q. Where did you go when you came down stairs?

A. I went to the cellar to get some wood and coal to kindle a fire.

Q. What way did you go to the cellar?

A. I went down the back way.

Q. Did you have any occasion to go by the back part of the cellar or through it?

A. The door leading to the wash room was wide open, and I could see through it.

Q. After you got the coal what did you do next?

A. I unlocked the doors and went out and got the milk.

Q. When you came to the door to get your milk how did you find the door?

A. The same as I left it.

Q. After you had taken in the milk how did you leave the door?

A. I locked it.

Q. The panel door was left open then?

A. Yes sir.

Q. When you left the inside door what did you do?

A. I hooked it.

Q. Did you go into any of the rooms before breakfast?

A. Yes sir, I went into the dining room.

Q. Any other room?

A. No sir.

Q. What was the condition of the door between the dining room and the sitting room?

A. It was locked.

Q. How about the kitchen door?

A. It is always locked.

Q. Who first appeared that morning?

A. Mrs. Borden.

Q. Did she go out?

A. No sir.

Q. What did she do when she came down?

A. She went into the sitting room.

Q. Did you receive any directions about breakfast?

A. Yes sir.

Q. Did you make any preparation before she came down?

A. No sir.

Q. Who next came down?

A. Mr. Borden.

Q. By what way did he come down?

A. He came down the back stairs.

Q. Have you ever known of any communication on the second floor between the front part of the house and the back part?

A. Yes, sir. There is a door.

Q. What time was it that Mrs. Borden came down stairs?

A. About half past six.

Q. How long after that did Mr. Borden appear?

A. About five minutes.

Q. What did he do?

A. He put a key on the shelf in the sitting room.

Q. What did he do afterwards?

A. He then went out doors.

Q. Did he bring anything else down besides the key?

A. Yes, sir, a slop pail.

Q. When he went out was the screen door locked?

A. Yes sir, but not locked while he was out.

Q. While he was out what did he do?

A. He unlocked the door to the barn.

Q. Not the carriage door, you mean the door this side of the privy, pointing to a photograph?

A. Yes sir.

At this point the court took a recess until 2 15.

When the prisoner and Bridget Sullivan, the two most prominent persons in this trial, left the court house there was a very large gathering of spectators on Court street.

THE PRISONER'S COLLAPSE.

Denouement of Tuesday's Court Proceedings Not Unexpected.

The denouement of yesterday's proceedings at the court house when Lizzie Borden at the close of District Attorney Moody's cogent and minute description of the events that transpired at the Borden house on the terrible 4th of August, succumbed for the first time since the tragedy, was not wholly unexpected and unanticipated by those who have been careful observers. Even as long ago as the 22d of last month it was predicted in the Standard, which regarded her remark to a friend, "I do not know how I can stand much more of this. I am glad the end is approaching, but I am fearful of my strength. I have been sorely tried;" as suggestive that she might give way at any time under the terrible burden she was bearing.

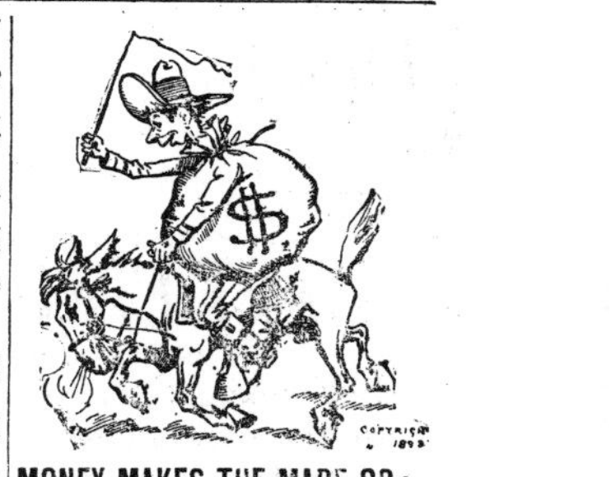

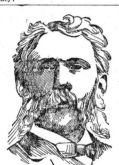

Pages 1-8.

The Evening Standard.

Pages 1-8.

ESTABLISHED FEBRUARY, 1850.

NEW BEDFORD, THURSDAY, JUNE 8, 1893.—TEN PAGES.

TWO CENTS.

NEW FACTS

Pointing to Guilt of Lizzie Borden.

Intimate Friend Her Accuser.

Alice Russell's Story on the Stand.

Why Lizzie Did Not Go to Marion.

Predicted Harm Would Come to Family.

Burning of Dress Covered with Paint.

Strange Action After Discovery of Crime.

Visit to Wash Room in Cellar at Night.

Evidence of Absorbing Interest in Great Trial.

This morning there was by far a larger number of people hanging around the court house than any time since the opening of the trial. They were on hand not as heretofore by 6 o'clock, but some fully as early as 5 o'clock. To many who know that their chances of getting an opportunity to gain entrance to the court room are infinitesimal, a glimpse of the prisoner as she alights from the cab, is a wonderful satisfaction, and they cluster around the rear entrance to the court house inclosure by the hundreds. This morning a large number of young men, and some not so young, took up their station on the top of the high board fence surrounding the estate opposite, where they remained with no thought of their discomfort, feeling amply repaid by just catching sight of Lizzie for an instant as she passed into the corridor. Among the crowd were many young children on their way to school, and they remained until Lizzie appeared, with never a thought as to whether they would be tardy or not. This morning the crowd forced its way up the concrete walk in front of the court house, and stationed itself well within the ropes before the officers came on duty at about half past 7. The wisdom of roping in the inclosure was pretty thoroughly demonstrated, and without the assistance of the fence, much difficulty in keeping the throng in check would have been experienced.

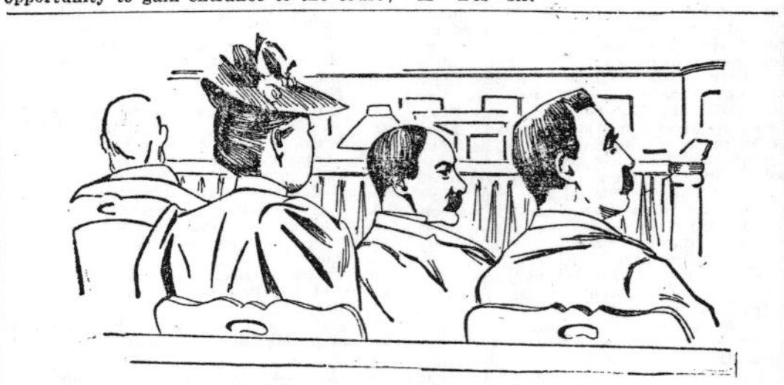

MISS BORDEN SEATED WITH HER COUNSEL.

NOT AS COOL AS A SHADY DELL.

Only a Comparative Degree of Comfort in Crowded Court Room.

The air of the court room was not as cool as that of a shady dell when the court was announced on the morning of the fourth day, but there was a comparative degree of comfort when contrasted with that of the opening.

One question which might suggest itself to a stranger suddenly introduced to this room, without any foreknowledge of the grave issue being tried, would be, "Am I in an asylum for the deaf?" This would be suggested by the intense look, the slightly forward leaning, and the apparent straining to catch the words which are being uttered. There is no need for this close attention, for nine out of ten words uttered by counsel or witnesses are plainly to be heard at the remotest corner of the room. I have come to the conclusion that the raptness is simply the result of habit, and this shows how quickly habits of Fall River are acquired. It is, by the way, a very democratic audience, and side by side may be seen the fair-haired, white-skinned blonde of Anglo-Saxon origin and the dusky woman whose ancestors were born and reared under African skies. It is all one to them. They are bound by a common sentiment of curiosity, (or perhaps interest would be a fairer term,) which raises them above all narrow and vulgar prejudices.

The Sedate Jury.

The jury does not seem to be weary and are apparently bearing their incarceration with much equanimity. It was noticeable that among them as they filed in and took their seats nearly every other man was chewing a toothpick, or was it a straw? Probably not the latter, which would be too suggestive of sherry cobblers. They were very sedate, serious and attentive, however, and were models in their way.

The Prisoner's Appearance.

The prisoner came into the court room at 8.50 o'clock bearing in one hand an envelope, which was handed to Mr. Jennings, and he and ex-Governor Robinson inspected the contents. Miss Borden took her seat inside the rail close by her counsel and at once gave undivided attention to the proceedings.

When "court" was called Dr. Bowen was called. He looks more like a clergyman than a physician, with his clear cut face, short side-whiskers and Prince Albert frock buttoned closely in front. He stood easily with one hand resting on the rail of the witness stand, and answered questions clearly and readily.

DR. BOWEN ON THE STAND.

Defense Shows that He Prescribed Morphine for Lizzie.

The first witness called to the stand this morning was Dr. Bowen of Fall River, who was examined by Mr. Moody.

Q. Your full name?

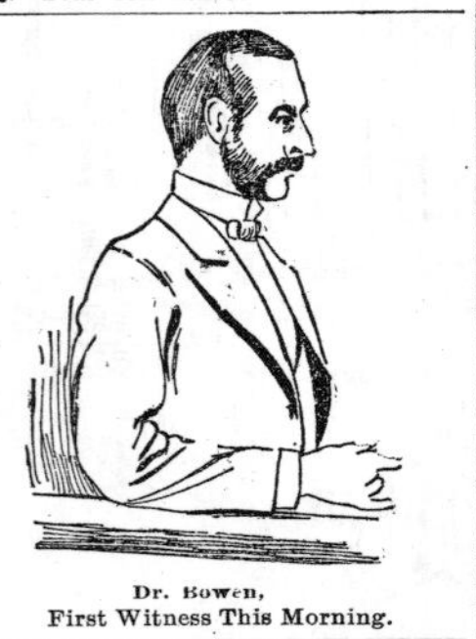

Dr. Bowen,
First Witness This Morning.

A. Seabury W. Bowen.

Q. You are in practice in Fall River?

A. Yes sir.

Q. How long have you practiced there?

A. Twenty-six years.

Q. How long have you lived at your present residence?

A. Twenty-one years.

Q. That is, I believe, diagonally opposite to the northwest from the Bordan house?

A. Yes sir.

Q. It is a double house?

A. Yes sir.

Q. And you live on the northerly or lower side of the house?

A. Northerly side, yes sir.

Q. During the time that you have lived at that house Mr. Borden and his family have lived at the house opposite you?

A. Yes sir.

Q. Have you been the family physician for some time?

A. Yes sir.

Q. During that time had you had social as well as business and professional relations?

A Yes sir.

Q. What have been your dealings with them, largely, business or social?

A. About equal.

Q. Do you recall the morning of August 4, 1892?

A. Yes sir.

Q. On the day preceding Aug. 4 did you see Miss Lizzie Borden at any time on the street?

A. I saw her between 6 and 7.

Q. Going in what direction?

A. Going down the street.

Q. Did you at any time see her going up the street?

A. No sir.

Q. By the street you mean Second street?

A. Yes sir.

Q. You testified at the inquest did you not?

A. Yes sir.

Q. That time was very soon after these occurrences that we are inquiring into?

A. Yes sir.

Q. Do you recall whether you said anything at that inquest as to seeing Miss Lizzie Borden going up the street on Wednesday?

A. No sir.

Q. Perhaps I may aid you. Do you remember being asked this question and replying in the manner that I state: "Where did you afterwards see Mr. Borden? Did you see him Thursday?" "I might possibly. I saw him Wednesday walking along between the side door and gate. Lizzie I saw walking up the street and I concluded that they were all right, all of them."

A. That was a mistake.

Q. You start out, I suppose, upon your professional calls?

A. Yes sir.

Q. You did on the morning of Aug. 4th?

A. Yes sir.

Q. Do you recall what time you returned to your house on Aug. 4th?

A. No sir.

Q. Can you give us the time approximately?

A. Well, I returned in about half an hour. Somewhere between 11 and half past.

Q. We may safely assume it was after 11 and before 12?

A. It was before half-past 11.

Q. Had you any occasion to notice the time?

A. No sir.

Q. When you came to your house you had some talk with Mrs. Bowen?

A. I did not go into my house.

Q. But she said something to you as you came up to the house?

A. She came to the door.

Q. In consequence of that where did you go?

A. I went across the street to Mr. Borden's house.

Q. To which door did you go?

A. To the side door.

Q. Did you see any one there when you arrived?

A. Yes sir.

Q. Whom did you see?

A. Miss Lizzie Borden and Mrs. Churchill.

Q. Where were they?

A. They were in the back entry close to the kitchen door.

(Continued on Third Page.)

BORDEN TRIAL REPORTS.

The Evening Standard's reports of the Borden trial are as full and accurate as those of the metropolitan dailies. Outside of the big cities no paper even approaches the Standard's work in the great case. The Standard reaches the newspaper readers of Southern Massachusetts hours ahead of all competitors. The Standard extra is the only paper printing the evidence complete on the day it is given in court.

WEATHER INDICATIONS.

Fair and Warmer.

Washington, June 8.—For the 24 hours from 8 a. m. today: For New England, fair, slightly warmer weather, winds shifting to south.

Boston, June 8.—Local forecast for New England; until Friday night: fair and warmer, much warmer during the day in eastern sections Friday; winds, southwest; continued warmer and probably showers Saturday.

HOME MATTERS.

VISITED THE BLACK WONDER.

[From Lake City Times, June 1.]

Hy May of this place, who has had thirty-two years' experience at mining in Colorado, and who is perhaps as good a judge of mines and minerals as any man in the state, visited the Black Wonder mine Monday of this week. To the writer Mr. May expressed himself as more than pleased with the mine, in fact was surprised to see so much rich ore in sight. The vein in the stopes where the men are now at work is three feet wide, and on each side of this rich vein or pay streak and between the walls is a wide mass of mineralized quartz. He brought down with him a chunk of the ore that will perhaps weigh half a pound, that the foreman of the mine, Jake Long, says will run 500 ounces gold to the ton. Mr. Long says he placed a chunk of the ore just like that Mr. May has on the blacksmith's forge and "sweated" it, and the gold stood out on it in drops like sweat on a man in a harvest field. This may be putting it a little strong, but the ore will stand the test if any one wants to try it.

SIDEBOARDS.

To state it briefly, F. R. Slocum has the largest, best, and cheapest line of sideboards of any dealer in the city. One pattern which defies superiority is of polished quartered oak, large mirror, velvet lined plate drawers, bottle drawers, and linen drawers, and exceedingly graceful in design. There are 27 other patterns, and all of them are bargains. You can get a good board for $13.50.

CONDENSED LOCALS.

Everybody certainly is aware that summer has arrived, and that the proper thing to eat in this season is fish; also that F. E. Tinkham, 9 North Sixth street, has the largest stock of the finest fish. Read the following assortment, and be convinced as to the quantity. Call and buy and be convinced as to the quality. Penobscot river salmon, 25c. per pound; fine white halibut, 15c. per pound; stripped bass, rock bass, roe shad, bluefish, fresh mackerel, scup, tautog, perch, cod, haddock, flukes, kingfish, lobsters, fresh boiled every day, new smoked Penobscot river herrings, "the finest," also all other kinds of smoked and salt fish, oysters, clams, quahogs, etc. The place is 9 North Sixth st. Telephone 252-1.

It is stated by all first class dealers in this vicinity that the new system of cooking without coal, wood or oil is meeting with marked success. Over three millions in use. For sale in New Bedford by Wood, Brightman & Co., Thomas J. Gifford & Co., Otheman & Dunham, A. Knowles, Joseph Greenwood, William G. Hayden, E. F. Penney, C. A. Galligan, and J. B. Dion. Fairhaven, Robert H. Taber and Forest & Long.

How is this! New spring spinach, fresh asparagus, new tomatoes, fresh legs of mutton, fine thick rib corned beef, cucumbers, lettuce, string beans, and strawberries, now all ready for our great Friday and Saturday trade. White Cash.

It will pay all who intend papering this season to see the fine line of paper hanging shown by Bliss & Nye. They carry the largest stock of the best selected patterns at the lowest prices in the city.

Patents have been issued to John H. Wells, Fall River, for a comb making machine; to John W. Maillot, North Attleboro, for combined match box and cigar tip cutter; to George B. Goddard, Brockton, bicycle handle.

The insurance on the property of the Ullman Manufacturing Co., recently destroyed by fire, has been satisfactorily adjusted through the agency of George N. Alden.

The great merit of Ayer's Hygienic Coffee is not due to advertising, but from its superiority over coffee. Principal grocers sell it. Try a package.

Don't fail to see the ballon ascension and fire works at the steam Merry-go-Round on Acushnet avenue near corner Sawyer st. tonight. Come one, come all.

Over 100 men are now at work on the Dartmouth & Westport street railway. The track will be laid by tonight to the Dartmouth town line.

Be on hand for Nooning's Flower Sale, commencing Friday morning at 9 o'clock. Elegant French Sprays for 49 and 69c. per bunch, worth $1.00 and $1.75.

Adam J. Shaw filed a primary declaration for naturalization in the district court this morning. James Smith for petitioner.

At a meeting of the Portuguese Naturalization Society, last evening, seven new members were admitted. The total membership is now 150.

A car of Christian's triple extra flour just arrived, and the price for bags or barrels is almost for you to say. White Cash.

The foot way in Sears' Court, between Pleasant and Purchase street, is used by pedestrians to considerable extent.

Gentlemen, the finest line of Russia leather shoes found at Buchell's. See our $4 shoe.

A good night's rest and a happy day when the baby has been fed on Mellin's Food.

Eureka lodge, F. & A. M., holds a special communication tomorrow evening. See special notice.

Divisions 9 and 7, A. O. H., meet to-morrow at 8 a. m., to attend the funeral of Peter E. Harrington. See special notice.

Foresters, A. O. F. of A, Court of New Bedford, 8141, meet tomorrow evening. See special notice.

Another great trade on creamery butter. White Cash.

Just received a large assortment of stylish Veiling in all colors at Nooning's.

See F. E. Tinkham's bulletin on this page for tomorrow.

The Majestic Light Roadster Bicycle has been reduced to $85. See fifth page.

Elegant Flowers at Nooning's for 49 and 69c. per bunch on sale Friday morning.

Cutter Whiskey owes its popularity to its great purity.

New potatoes are taking quite a lead at the White Cash.

See F. E. Tinkham's bulletin on this page for tomorrow.

Salt Rheum cured by Hood's Sarsaparilla.

NEW FACTS.

(Continued from First Page.)

Q. Was there any one else there at that time?
A. No sir.
Q. Will you state what talk there was between you and the prisoner at that time?
A. I said as soon as I got to the house: "Lizzie, what is the matter?" Her reply was: "Father has been killed or stabbed."
Q. Does anything else in that conversation occur to you?
A. I asked Lizzie, "Where is yout father?" She said, "In the sitting room."
Q. Do you recall anything else said in that connection?
A. No sir, not then.
Q. Let me ask you if anything was said with reference to her father's tenants at that time?
A. Not then, it was afterwards.
Q. What did you do then?
A. I went into the dining room and from there into the sitting room.
Q. Will you describe what you saw as you came into the sitting room?
A. I saw the form of Mr. Borden lying on the sofa at the left of the sitting room door.
Q. Will you give further description

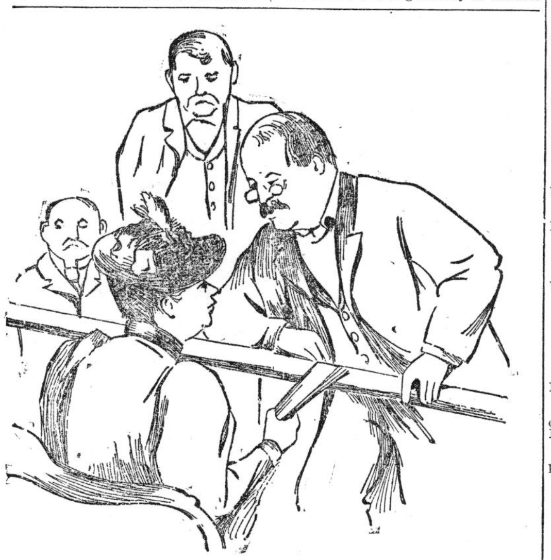

MISS BORDEN AND EX-GOV. ROBINSON IN CONSULTATION.

as far as you can as to the injuries that appeared upon inspection?
A. Upon inspection I found his face was very badly cut with apparently a sharp instrument. His face was covered with blood too. I felt his pulse to satisfy myself that Mr. Borden was dead. I took a glance about the room; there was nothing disturbed.
Q. None of the furniture or anything else disturbed about the room?
A. No sir, not that I know of.
Q. Will you describe the position of the body on the sofa?
A. He was lying with his face towards the south, on his right side, in the position he would lie in if asleep.
Q. Was the face to be recognized?
A. Hardly, I should think.
Dr. Bowen was handed a photograph and asked if he had seen it. He said "yes."
Q. Will you be kind enough to tell us in what respect Mr. Borden's position differed from that photograph, if it differed at all?
A. I do not think the photograph shows a position that is natural to a person who is asleep or lying down. I think in this case the form had sunk down a little from what it was when I saw it.
Q. Otherwise than the sinking down is there any change in the position of the body upon the sofa?
A. No sir, I do not think there is.
Q. And the sinking down would be due to general collapse?
A. Yes sir.
Mr. Moody asked the judge if he might show the photograph to the jury and he was allowed to do so.
Dr. Bowen was asked if there was any change in the position of the sofa from its position as he saw it?
Dr. Bowen said when he saw it he thought it was even with the door. It looked to him in the picture as if it was moved a little away from the door.
Q. With reference to the back of the door, is the head the same that it was when you saw it, or substantially the same?
A. Yes sir, it is about the same.
Q. How did you ascertain that Mr. Borden was dead?
A. I felt of his pulse.
Q. Did you make any examination at this time other than to feel of his pulse?
A. No sir, not at this time.
Q. What else did you do?

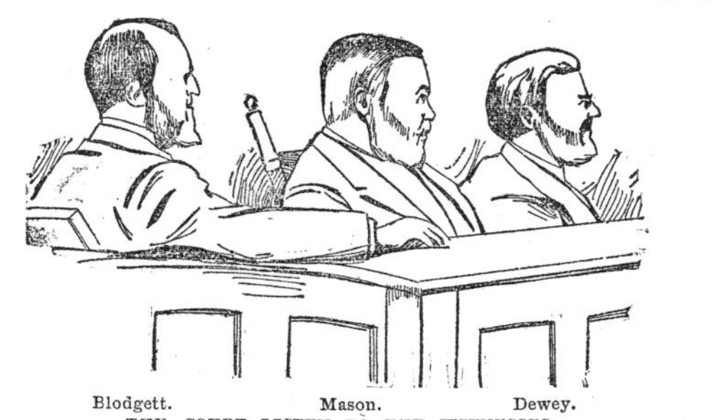

Blodgett. Mason. Dewey.
THE COURT LISTEN TO THE WITNESSES.

A. When I found he was dead I asked Lizzie several questions. The first one was "Have you seen anybody?" and her reply was "I have not." The second question was "Where have you been?" and her reply was "I have been to the barn looking for iron." She then said she was afraid that her father had had trouble with his tenants, as she had overheard his conversation with them several times. Lizzie made a request that some one look for Mrs. Borden.
Q. What was done in consequence of this request?
A. Bridget Sullivan went up stairs.
Q. Do you know who, if anybody, went up stairs with Bridget?
A. I do not.
Q. Do you remember anything about a key?
A. Not at that time.
Q. How did Bridget get into Mrs. Borden's room?
A. I do not know; the key was usually placed on one end of the mantelpiece in the room below.
Q. Did you get the key or did any one get it for you?
A. I would not say.
Q. You asked for a sheet to cover Mr. Borden's body?
A. Yes sir.
Q. When the sheet was brought back do you know by whom?
A. I cannot say by whom it was brought.
Q. What occurred next?
A. Lizzie wanted me to telegraph for Emma.
Q. You went to the telegraph office?
A. Yes sir.
Q. State what was said before you went to the telegraph office.
A. Lizzie said that Mrs. Borden received a note in the morning asking her to come and see a sick person.
Q. What was next done?
A. The officers were notified of the affair and I satisfied myself that they had arrived before I went away.
Q. Do you remember any officer you met?
A. Yes sir, Mr. Allen.
Q. Did you make any observation about the manner of the killing?
A. Nothing better than guess work.
Q. Nothing more valuable than guess work?
A. No sir.
Q. What occurred after you returned from the telegraph office?
A. The body of Mrs. Borden was found.
Q. Where?
A. Upstairs in the front room.
Q. State what else you observed or that occurred?
A. I went directly through the dining room and up stairs. I stopped a moment and saw the prostrate form of Mrs. Borden lying under the bed.
Q. Where were you standing when you observed the body?
A. I was standing directly in the door of the room.
Q. What did you then do?
A. I went around back of the bed and placed my hands on her head. I found the wounds and then felt of her pulse. I found that she was dead.
Q. Did you form any opinion as to the cause of the death the first time you saw the body?
A. Yes sir, I did.
Q. Did you make any statement at that time, or have you made any statement since that she died of fright?
A. No sir, I never have made any such statement.
Q. What did you next do?
A. I went down stairs and told them that she had been killed, probably by the same instrument that had been used on Mr. Borden, and I told Lizzie that it was fortunate that she was out of the way at the time.
Here witness was shown several photographs, and pointed out some slight differences between the positions as shown by the pictures and observed by him.
Q. Did you notice anything about the dress Miss Lizzie wore on that morning?
A. She changed her dress after she went into the room.
Q. What was the last dress she had on?
A. It was a pink wrapper.
Q. He read from the inquest and then said, "What do you now say was the color of the dress?"
A. It was indefinite.
Q. Do you mean to say that the color was drab or not?
A. I don't attempt to describe the woman's dress.
Q. Did you describe it at the inquest?
A. I did not.
Q. Didn't you say it was drab?
A. I don't think I did.
Q. Do you now desire to modify your statement made at the inquest?
A. I don't know that I do.
(Mr. Moody holding up a dark-blue figured dress.)
Q. Does that appear to be a sort of a drab calico dress?
A. No, it does not.
Q. Is that the dress she had on that morning?
A. I don't know.
Q. Give us your best judgment if it was.
Mr. Robinson objected and the question was withdrawn.
Q. What color do you call this dress?
A. Dark blue.
Cross-examination was then begun by Mr. Adams.
Q. Doctor, when you first went to the Borden house what way did you go?
A. I came from the south and drove.
Q. Had you a boy with you?
A. Yes.
Q. Did he stay out?
A. Yes.
Q. You have stated that after seeing Miss Churchill you had a telegraphic message to send. Is that so?
A. Yes.
Q. Did you drive back from the house to the office?
A. Yes, after making one stop.
Q. Was there any other officer at the house but Allen at that time?
A. No.
Q. When you came from the telegraph office was Mr. Borden's body covered by a sheet?
A. It was.
Q. When you went up the stairs was any one there?
A. No.
Q. When you went up the stairs did you see the prostrate form?
A. No.
Q. Not until you looked over the bed?
A. No.
Q. How was the body lying then?
A. With the feet to the west.
Q. In what position was the body?
A. She was lying directly on her face with the hands underneath.
Q. Will you illustrate her position?
Witness clasped his hands across his chest in a horizontal line.
Q. Do you recall how much space there between the bureau and the bed she took up?
A. I did not ascertain.
Q. When you went to look at the body on what side did you go?
A. I went to the right side.
Q. Was life extinct?
A. Yes.
Q. Which wrist did you take hold of when you went to feel the pulse?
A. The right.
Q. When you took the wrist did you draw it out?
A. Yes, slightly.
Q. No doubt about that?
A. No.
Q. Didn't you leave the right arm drawn out more than the left?
A. Yes.
Q. Was the room dark?
A. Not very light.
Q. How about the shutters?
A. The inside shutters were partly closed.
Q. The inside shutters were of board, not slats, like these in the court room, weren't they?
A. Yes.
Q. You have ascertained since that time at what hour you sent the telegram haven't you?
A. Yes; it was 11 25.
Q. Then you arrived back at the house at 11 35?
A. It would take four or five minutes to go there.
Q. Then it was 11 40 when you got back?
A. Yes; about.
Q. When you went down stairs how soon after did Dr. Dolan arrive?
A. I think it was 10 or 15 minutes.
Q. Did you then go up stairs with Dr. Dolan again?
A. Yes sir.
Q. Any one else go?
A. No.
Q. Had any one interfered with the body?
A. I don't think they had.
Q. Was the body raised when Dr. Dolan went with you to see it?
A. Yes.
Q. By whom?
A. The doctor and myself.
Q. Did you put it back in the same way in which it laid?
A. Yes.
Q. Were you present at the autopsy?
A. Yes.
Q. Did you take notes at that time?
A. Yes.
Q. Did the notes concern Mrs. Borden?
A. Yes.
Q. Was the autopsy on the body of Mr. Borden in the afternoon?
A. Yes.
Q. After seeing the body of Mrs. Borden the first time where did you find Lizzie?
A. In the kitchen.
Q. What were those who were with her doing?
A. Leaning over and fanning her.
Q. Did they go into the dining room?
A. Yes.
Q. Did you give her any direction?
A. Yes.
Q. What?
A. I told her to go to her room.
Q. What way did she go?
A. Through the sitting room and up the front stairway.
Q. Was Mr. Borden's body covered then?
A. Yes.
Q. Did you see Lizzie in her room?
A. Yes; it was later in the day.
Q. Did a message come from Alice Russell?
A. Yes.
Q. Did you prescribe for Lizzie?
A. Yes.
Q. What did you prescribe?
A. It was something quieting.
Q. Did you give other medicine of the same kind that day?
A. Yes sir.
Q. In what way?
A. The same dose.
Q. Did you carry some bromo-caffeine over there?
A. I carried a bottle.
Q. Did you have occasion to prescribe for her on account of this mental distress and nervous excitement after that?
A. Yes sir.
Q. When was it?
A. Friday.
Q. Was the prescription the same?
A. No, it was different.
Q. What was it?
A. It was morphine.
Q. When was it to be taken?
A. Friday night and Saturday.
Q. Do you say it was to be taken on Saturday?
A. Yes sir.
Q. In the same quantity?
A. No sir, I doubled the dose.
Q. Do you remember when you were summoned as a witness at the inquest?
A. I do not.
Q. Wasn't it in the early part of the week following the tragedy?
A. I think it was.
Q. Do you remember that Lizzie was called before you were?
A. Yes sir.
Q. You know when she was arrested, don't you?
A. I do not know as I know the day.
Q. Wasn't she arrested a week from the day of the tragedy?
A. I don't remember.
Q. I have asked you about this morphine you were giving her. You have told me that on Friday you gave her an eighth of a grain and that on Saturday you doubled the dose, and that she had it on Sunday and Monday. How long did she have it?
A. She had it all the time she was at the station.
Q. She had it up to the time of her arrest and when she was at the station?
A. Yes sir.
Q. After her arrest she was there at the station when she had taken for several days this double dose of morphine?
A. Yes sir.
Q. I suppose physicians understand that when morphine is given to allay mental distress and mental excitement it affects the memory—changes the views of things and gives people hallucinations?
A. Yes sir.
Q. There is no doubt about it, is there?
A. No sir.
In redirect.
Q. How many times, doctor, did you see her personally take the medicine? asked Mr. Moody.
A. Twice
Q. And when were these two times?
A. On the evening of Thursday.
Q. And that was bromo-caffeine?
A. Yes sir.
Q. Is bromo-caffeine a medicine which has a tendency to create hallucinations?
A. Yes sir.
Q. You have said that the time you sent your telegram was 11 32?
A. Yes sir.
Q. How did you ascertain that time, by your memory?
A. No sir, I went to the telegraph office and got a copy of the telegram that I sent.
Q. You had then the time which they had at the telegraph office?
A. I had a copy of the message.
Q. Do you know whether that contained the time of sending the message from the telegraph office or the time when they received it from you?
A. The telegram was marked 11 32.
Q. That is all you know about it?
A. Yes sir.
Q. And that is the only means you have of fixing the time at 11 32?
A. Yes sir.
Q. What that 11 32 means, whether it means the time received from the sender or the time it leaves the office you do not know?
A. I do not know.
Q. When Dr. Dolan came and inspected the two bodies they were in substantially the same condition as they were when you first saw them?
A. They were.
Q. Is there any difference between the two positions that you can point out?

A. Only those that I have pointed out.
Mr. Adams asked the witness if he did not say that on Wednesday, the day before the tragedy, he saw Miss Lizzie on the street about 6 o'clock. He wanted to know if that was 6 o'clock in the morning or in the evening. And the witness replied in the evening.

BRIDGET RECALLED.

Denial That She Said She Saw Lizzie in Tears.

Bridget Sullivan was recalled, and ex-Governor Robinson began a cross-examination of the witness.
Q. You said yesterday that you went down cellar with the officers after it was found that Mr. Borden was dead?
A. Yes sir, I did.
Q. How many officers went down with you?
A. Three, I think.
Q. Do you know who they were?
A. Mr. Dougherty, the assistant marshal, and Mr. Medley.
Q. Do you know whether any one else went down?
A. I do not know.
Q. Did they go and look about the cellar?
A. Yes sir.
Q. Did you show them anything?
A. No sir, I went down into the cellar with them, and that's all I did.
Q. Where were the hatchets?
A. They were in the cellar in the washroom.
Q. These three men, Mr. Dougherty, Mr. Fleet and Mr. Medley, were the ones who went down with you?
A. I think they were.
Q. You have seen the same men again several times?
A. Yes sir. I didn't know the names then, but I found out afterwards who they were.
Q. You subsequently found out who they were?
A. Yes sir.
Q. Did you show them where the hatchets were?
A. Yes sir.
Q. Did you take them out?
A. No sir.
Q. Are you sure about that?
A. No sir, I didn't put my hand upon them.
Q. Are you sure about that?
A. Yes sir, I am. I did not take them out.
Q. Did you have them in your hands at all?
A. No sir, I did not.
Q. These three men were there all the time?
A. Yes sir.
Q. What was done with the hatchets?
A. I do not know.
Q. You do not know?
A. No sir, I do not.
Q. Didn't you stay there with them?
A. No sir, I didn't stay there all the afternoon.
Q. What time was it?
A. I don't know what time it was.
Q. Was it before 12 o'clock?
A. I can't tell anything about the clock at all.
Q. Was it after Dr. Bowen got back the second time?
A. I do not know.
Q. Did Dr. Bowen come after that?
A. I cannot tell you anything about it.
Q. And you do not know what the officers did with those axes or hatchets?
A. No sir; I don't.
Q. Where did they carry them to that you saw?
A. I think they took them up stairs.
Q. Did you see them on the floor of the wash room?
A. No sir; I didn't stay down there.
Q. What dress did you have on that morning?
A. A calico dress.
Q. What color?
A. Blue calico.
Q. Did it have any figure on it?
A. Yes sir.
Q. What kind of a figure?
A. It had a clover leaf.
Q. Do you call it light blue or dark blue?
A. Dark blue.
Q. Was the clover leaf of white or dark color?
A. White.
Q. Was it dark blue ground or light blue?
A. It was an indigo blue calico.
Q. Was the waist the same as the skirt?
A. Yes sir.
Q. Did you keep it on all day?
A. Yes sir, until the afternoon.
Q. Well, that isn't all day.
A. Well, I kept it on until I had a chance to change it.
Q. What dress did you put on then?
A. A gingham, I think.
Q. What color was that?
A. A blue gingham.
Q. Was it a darker or a lighter blue than you had on in the morning?
A. Lighter.
Q. And did you keep that on the rest of the day after that?
A. Yes sir.
Q. Did you stay all the afternoon in the house?
A. Yes sir.
Q. Didn't you go out of the house at all?
A. I went out on an errand in the afternoon.
Q. At this time you had on this light blue dress?

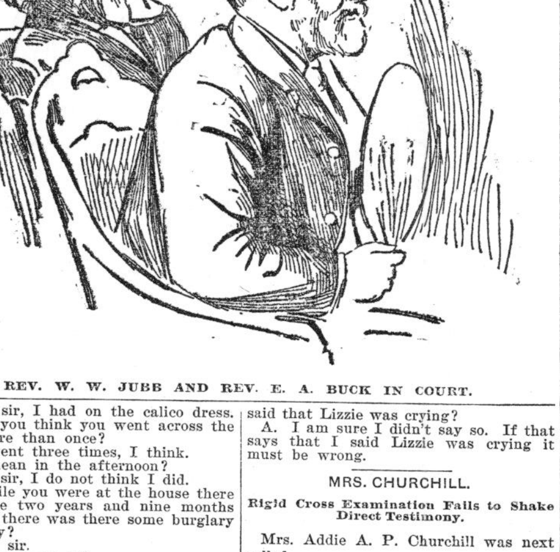

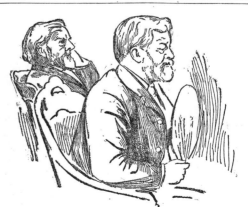

REV. W. W. JUBB AND REV. E. A. BUCK IN COURT.

A. No sir, I had on the calico dress.
Q. Do you think you went across the street more than once?
A. I went three times, I think.
Q. I mean in the afternoon?
A. No sir, I do not think I did.
Q. While you were at the house there during the two years and nine months you were there was there some burglary or robbery?
A. Yes sir.
Q. When was it?
Mr. Knowlton objected to the question, but the witness was allowed to answer.
It was about a month before the time of the tragedy, said Bridget.
Q. Did it occur in the day time?
Mr. Knowlton again objected.
Judge Mason said this was too long before the time of the tragedy. If it had occurred within a few days it would be a very material matter, but he could not allow the question to be admitted.
Mr. Robinson—Your honor will kindly save my rights to the point.
Q. Can you tell us at what time the breaking into the barn occurred?
A. I can't say what time it was.
Q. How long before Mr. and Mrs. Borden were killed?
A. I don't know.
Q. Did it occur in the day time or by night?
Mr. Knowlton—I object.
The question was not urged.
Mr. Robinson showed plans and asked the witness to point out the place where the hatchet was found, but she was unable to do so.
Q. When you came down stairs at the time Lizzie called you, you said you found her at the inside wooden door. What was she doing; was she excited?
A. She was more excited that I ever saw her before.
Q. Was she crying?
A. No sir.
Q. You are quite sure about it; she was not crying?
A. Yes sir.
Q. Have you ever said that she was crying at the time?
A. No sir.
Mr. Robinson read from the stenographic report of Bridget's testimony at the inquest, and then interjected questions in regard to Lizzie's position at the door. Bridget replied that she knew that Lizzie was leaning against the inside or wooden door, and not the screen door.
Q. You know, of course, that the report says that you said that Lizzie was crying when you came down stairs?
A. If it says so, it must be wrong. I never said it.
Q. You want to be right, of course, Miss Sullivan?
A. Yes sir, I do.
Q. Will you swear that you never said that Lizzie was crying?
A. I am sure I didn't say so. If that says that I said Lizzie was crying it must be wrong.

MRS. CHURCHILL.

Rigid Cross Examination Fails to Shake Direct Testimony.

Mrs. Addie A. P. Churchill was next called.
Q. You are unmarried at the present time, I believe?
A. Yes sir.
Q. How long have you resided in Fall River?
A. About 43 years.
Q. You occupy the house just north of the Borden house?
A. Yes sir.
Q. During the past 20 or more years have you known the Borden family?
A. Yes sir.
Q. Been on social and friendly terms with the family?
A. Yes sir.
Q. Was Mr. Borden what we usually call a slender man?
A. He was a tall, thin man.
Q. Describe Mrs. Borden.
A. She was a short, heavy woman.
Q. You, of course, recall the fourth of last August?
A. Yes sir.
Q. During that morning did you see Mr. Borden?
A. Yes sir.
Q. About what time did you see him?
A. At about 9 o'clock in the morning.
Q. In what part of the house were you?
A. In the kitchen.
Q. What did you see him doing?
A. He was standing by the side of the back steps.
Q. How was the screen door?
A. It was shut.
Q. Was he in motion or standing?
A. He was standing.
Q. How far is the kitchen window in your house from the screen door at the Borden house?
A. It is quite near.
Q. Did you leave the house that morning?
A. Yes sir.
Q. At what time?
A. At about 11 o'clock.
Q. Where did you go?
A. I went to the store.
Q. Is the store nearly opposite your house on a parallel street?
A. Yes sir.
Q. For what did you go to the store?
A. To purchase some articles for my dinner.
Q. After you went to the store what did you then do?
A. I returned home.
Q. When you returned you walked south on Second street toward your home?
A. Yes sir.
Q. In taking your return journey you did not pass the Borden house because you reached your home first?
A. No sir, I did not pass the Borden house.
Q. When you reached the front of your house did you notice anything?
A. I saw Bridget coming from Dr. Bowen's house.
Q. Was she going rapidly or slowly?
A. Rapidly.
Q. At what point did you see Bridget?
A. Between Mrs. Burke's house and my own.
Q. What did you do when you reached the house?
A. I went into the kitchen.
Q. Will you describe what occurred?
Witness proceeded at length to describe what occurred after her entry to the house, saying that she found Lizzie sitting upon the stairs; put her right hand on her arm and said, "Where is your father?" She said he was in the sitting room. She did not know where her mother was. She feared that her father must have some enemy for they were all sick the night before. Witness went out and got a man to go for a doctor.
Examination was then resumed.
Q. Did you know Cunningham?
A. No.
Q. When you returned to the house had anyone got there?
A. No.
Q. Who came in next?
A. Bridget.
Q. Who next?
A. Dr. Bowen.
Q. State what occurred when Dr. Bowen came.
A. He passed from the dining room to the kitchen.
Q. Did you see the corpse of Mr. Borden?
A. Yes.
Q. Were the feet covered?
A. Yes.
Q. Did Dr. Bowen ask you for a sheet?
A. I think he did. Bridget and I went upstairs, to Mrs. Borden's room.
Q. How did you find the door?
A. Bridget unlocked it. We brought the sheet down stairs.
Q. What occurred next?
A. Lizzie asked me to send a telegram to Emma.
Q. Was anything further said?
A. After Miss Russell came, Lizzie said she'd like to have Mrs. Borden called. We went up the front stairs, Bridget ahead, and I looked to the left and saw a body through under the bed.
Q. How was the door?
A. It was open.
Q. Did you pursue the journey after seeing the body?
A. I came back to the dining room.
Q. Did anything occur?
A. Lizzie asked if anyone had seen her mother.
Q. Was agitation manifested by Lizzie?
A. No.

Q. Recurring to your first statement, did Lizzie say that she came from the barn because she heard a distressed noise?
A. I don't remember.
Q. Did you suggest a change of dress?
A. No.
Q. When did Lizzie go up stairs?
A. I don't know. She went up after I went away.
Q. Will you describe her dress?
A. It was a light blue and white ground, with a very blue diamond.
Q. Was the skirt and waist alike?
A. Yes.
Q. Counsel produced the dark blue dress shown before and said, "Was that it?"
A. No.
Q. Was there any white in the dress that she wore that morning?
A. It was a light blue and a white ground.
Q. Do you recall whether the color was fresh or faded?
A. Medium.

Mrs. Adelaide R. Churchill.

Q. How long had she had it?
A. I don't know.
Q. How frequently have you seen Lizzie wearing the dress?
A. I can't tell.
Cross-examination was begun by ex-Governor Robinson.
Q. The living side of your house is toward the Borden house, is it?
A. Yes.
Q. Were you engaged in your house on the morning of the murder?
A. Yes.
Q. Did you have a good deal to do?
A. Yes.
Q. While working in the kitchen your attention would not be called to the Borden house, would it?
A. My kitchen is opposite the screen door.
Q. You don't recall anything else except seeing Mr Borden, do you?
A. I saw Bridget.
Q. You saw her washing windows?
A. Yes.
Q. You saw her washing one of the parlor windows.
A. It was a casual glance?
Q. You heard no unusual noise?
A. No.
Q. The street is a traveled one and noisy?
A. Yes.
Q. You might not be able to hear noises in your house which occur outside?
A. That's so.
Q. You didn't notice when Mr. Borden went after seeing him in the yard, and hadn't seen him come from the barn in the early morning?
A. No.
Q. When you saw Lizzie was there anything unusual in her appearance?
A. Yes.
Q. Something startling?
A. Yes.
Q. Was your window open?
A. Yes; I saw her through a window with a screen, and went to another one which had none and opened it.
Q. Without saying a word you passed to the other window?
A. Yes.
Q. Why did you do so?
A. I thought something was the matter.
Q. What attracted your attention?
A. Lizzie was pale and excited. I said, "Wh t is the matter, Lizzie?" She said, "Oh, Mrs. Churchill, come over here; some one has killed father."
Q. She said she wanted the doctor, did she?
A. Yes, and I went and got a man to go.
Q. You were gone a short time?
A. Yes.
Q. When Dr. Bowen got there you and Bridget were both there?
A. Yes.
Q. How long did you remain there?
A. I went home about 12.
Q. Did you go away before Lizzie went up stairs?
A. Yes.
Q. When you saw her standing at the door can you give the time?
A. No, I cannot.
Q. As you recall the dress, was it about the color of that blotter? (Holding up a light blue one.)
A. It was a white and blue groundwork.
Q. Was the ground-work striped?
A. No, blended.
Q. Were the waist and skirt the same color?
A. Yes.
Q. How was the waist made, was it loose?
A. It wasn't tight; it was a blouse waist.
Q. Did you see Lizzie in the afternoon in a pink wrapper?
A. No.
Q. What dress did Bridget have on in the morning?
A. It was a white wrapper, I think.
Q. What kind of a dress did Miss Russell have on?
A. I can't tell.
Q. When you got there was Lizzie on the stairs?
A. Yes. I went away and came back in five minutes and she was still there.
Q. Where then?
A. In the kitchen.
Q. Where then?
A. In the dining room.
Q. Did Miss Russell attend her?
A. Yes, she sat by her side.
Q. Did you participate in the attentions?
A. I might have wet some cloths once.
Q. It was a trying scene, wasn't it?
A. Yes.
Q. After you came down stairs you were round practically most of the time?
A. Yes.
Q. Where was Lizzie?
A. She was in the dining room, and the door closed after Mrs. Borden was discovered.
Q. Did you see blood on Lizzie's dress?
A. No.
Q. If there was blood on a dress as light as that you would have seen it, wouldn't you?
A. If there had been any on the front I should have seen it.
Q. At no time you saw blood on her dress?
A. No.
Q. Did she have on more than one dress?
A. I didn't see that she did.
Q. Was there anything to indicate that she wore a double dress?
A. Nothing.
Q. When you went up stairs Lizzie didn't ?
A. No.
Q. What did Bridget tell you about a note?
A. She said Mrs. Borden received one and was hurried off. She was dusting the dining room then.

Q. It was Bridget who told you this?
A. Yes. She said Mrs. Borden didn't tell where she was as she usually does.
Q. It was Bridget and not Lizzie who told you about the note?
A. Yes.
Q. Did you hear any talk with Miss Lizzie about any farm hands being connected with this crime?
A. I was in the room when the policeman asked Lizzie about the men who worked for her father.
Q. Do you know what policeman it was?
A. I do not.
Q. Do you remember whether there was more than one officer there?
A. No, I do not remember.
Q. Now will you tell us just what the conversation was?
A. They asked about a Portuguese that worked for her father, and Lizzie said he is not a Portuguese, he is a Swede.
Q. She corrected them on the spot, did she?
A. Yes sir.
Q. You are positive about that?
A. Yes sir.
Q. And what more did she say?
A. She said that he was not over to Fall River, that the head man was sick, and he had to work at the farm.
Q. What more did she say?
A. I do not know of anything.
Q. Was there something said about whether or not she would suspect any man?
A. She said who would do something to her.
Q. That was said right out promptly, wasn't it?
A. Yes sir.
Q. Have you any knowledge of any officers coming to the house?
A. The first officer I saw came in after Dr Bowen went out, and his name was Allen. I remember seeing him. He is the first one I remember seeing, and Mr. Sawyer came at the same time.
Q. Mr. Sawyer came about the same time that Mr. Allen did?
A. None that I know of.
Q. Did he come into the house?
A. Mr. Allen told him to come in with him, and to attend to the side door.
Q. And there was no other officer there?
A. None that I know of.
Q. Do you know whether there was anyone outside or not?
A. I didn't go outside, I do not know.
Q. Did other officers come afterwards?
A. Yes sir.
Q. There were several?
A. Yes sir.
Mr. Moody then asked Mrs. Churchill if what she had said with reference to what Bridget told her about the note was given as a substitute for what she had said Lizzie told her about it, and she replied that it was not; Bridget told her about Mrs. Borden receiving the note after Lizzie had told her about it.
Mr. Moody—Mrs. Churchill, was your attention called very soon after this tragedy to the question of the dress Miss Lizzie Borden had on?
A. I was asked at the inquest.
Q. Was the dress called to your attention soon after that?
A. I think so.
Q. When did you see this dress? (producing a dark blue dress.)
A. Mr. Jennings showed it to me the first time that I saw it.
Q. How soon after the homicide?
A. I don't know.
Q. After the inquest?
A. I think so.
Q. Did you have some talk with Mr. Jennings about this dress?
A. Mr. Knowlton—Did you happen to know, Mrs. Churchill, that all the dresses this woman had were taken to the officers?
A. No sir.
Mr. Knowlton to Mr. Robinson—Do you mean to imply that that is so?
Mr. Robinson—I asked the witness if she knew that it was so.
A recess.
At this point a recess of five minutes was announced, and the jury retired.
During the recess Lizzie conversed pleasantly with Mr. Adams, and she was observed to smile pleasantly several times at his remarks, which were evidently of an encouraging and reassuring nature.
Joe Howard seized the opportunity to interview ex-Governor Robinson briefly.

MISS RUSSELL'S STORY.

The New Evidence Pointing to Guilt of the Prisoner.

When the jury returned to the court room Miss Alice M. Russell was called to the witness stand and examined by Mr. Moody.
Q. Where do you reside?
A. Fall River.
Q. How long have you lived in that city?
A. A good many years.
Q. You are unmarried?
A. Yes sir.

Miss Alice M. Russell.

Q. At one time you lived in the house occupied by Dr. Kelly?
A. Yes sir.
Q. How long were you a near neighbor of the Borden family?
A. Eleven years.
Q. During this time you lived in the house just north?
A. Yes sir.
Q. You were well acquainted with all the family, Mr. and Mrs. Borden, Lizzie and Emma?
A. Yes sir.
Q. Where did you live on the 4th day of last August?
A. I lived on Borden street.
Q. Not far from the corner of Second street?
A. Yes sir.
Q. In a small house between Third and Fourth streets on Borden street?
A. Yes sir.
Q. Not far from the bakeshop?
A. Yes sir.
Q. Did you receive calls from the prisoner?
A. Yes sir.
Q. You called at her house oftentimes?
A. Yes sir.
Q. When you called at her house where did she receive you?
A. Up stairs in her own room.
Q. Did she pay you a visit on Wednesday, Aug. 3d, of last year?
A. Yes sir.
Q. When was it?
A. It was in the evening.
Q. Did she come to your house alone?
A. Yes sir.
Q. About how long did she stay?
A. I guess she went away about 9 o'clock, or five minutes past 9.
Q. You talked together?
A. Yes sir.
Q. Was there anything said about Marion?
A. State such conversation as took place that you can recall?
A. Soon after she came in there was something said about her going to Marion. I told her I hoped she would go and have a good time. She said she

didn't know about going, there was something coming over her and that she felt as if something was going to happen. She said her father had much trouble with his tenants; that it worried her. She said they were all awfully sick the night before, except Maggie. She said that she didn't know but that the sickness was caused by baker's bread, and I told her that couldn't be, because if it was the bread she would have heard of others who were made sick by it. She said she sometimes thought it might be the milk and that there might be poison in it. I asked her, about the cans and she said they had two, and the milk man would bring a full one and take an empty one each day. She said the milkman got about at 4 o'clock in the morning, before any of the family were up. She said that she was afraid that her father had an enemy, for a man had come to see him several times. She said that there was a man seen hanging around the house nights and that the barn had been broken into and that the house had been robbed in broad daylight. She said she had to sleep with one eye open half of the time, and that she was afraid that the house would be burned down over their heads.
Q. Is there anything else that occurs to you about any one doing anything to any one of the family?
A. She said that she was afraid sometimes that some one would do something to her father. She said that she told Dr. Bowen that she was afraid they had been poisoned, and that the doctor laughed at her.
Q. On the next morning, Aug. 4th, did you receive a visit from Bridget Sullivan?
A. Yes sir.
Q. At what time was this?
A. Some time about 11 o'clock.
Q. Did you notice whether it was before 11 or the 11 o'clock bell struck?
A. It was after.
Q. Did you go anywhere?
A. Yes sir.
Q. Where did you go?
A. I went over to the Borden house.
Q. When you got to the Borden house do you recall who was there?
A. I only remember Lizzie.

Q. Where was she when you got there?
A. Down stairs.
Q. Did you have any talk with her, or did she say anything to you?
A. No sir.
Q. When you got there, or any time before you went up stairs?
A. Yes sir.
Q. Go on and tell us what it was?
A. I think she was standing in the doorway leaning against the door frame when I saw her. I asked her to sit down, and she did.
Q. Was anything said about her whereabouts when her father was killed?
A. She said she was out in the barn.
Q. What did she say when she told you that?
A. I don't remember, she told us that she came in and saw her father and that he was killed.
Q. Did she say anything about what she went to the barn for?
A. Not until I asked her.
Q. Well, state what you asked her, and what she replied.
A. I said, what did you go to the barn for, and she said, "I went to get a piece of tin and iron to fix my screen."
Q. Was there anything else that was said that you recall, while you were down stairs? Anything about Mrs. Borden that you remember?
A. She asked some one to find Mrs. Borden.
Q. Had she told anything about where Mrs. Borden was?
A. No sir.
Q. Anything about a note?
A. I heard the note talked over.
Q. You do not recall whether she told it or some one else?
A. No sir.
Q. Do you remember of some one asking for a sheet?
A. Yes sir.
Q. Do you remember who went for it?
A. No, I do not.
Q. Do you remember how long you remained down stairs before you went up stairs?
A. No, I don't; I can't remember anything definite.
Q. Are you able to give any description of the dress that Lizzie had on that morning?
A. None whatever; I do not remember.
Q. When she went up stairs did she go up alone?
A. I don't know; I think she did.
Q. Did you go with her?
A. No sir.
Q. Were you with her in the room before she changed her dress?
A. Yes sir.
Q. Was any one else there?
A. No sir.
Q. Was there some conversation there, in consequence of which you left the room?
A. Yes sir.
Q. She said when it was necessary for an undertaker she wanted a certain one. I went down stairs and into the hall and told Dr. Bowen.
Q. After you had had an interview with him did you go up stairs again?
A. Yes sir.
Q. Did you go to her room?
A. Yes sir.
Q. What did you see when you went into the room?
A. I saw Lizzie coming out of Miss Emma's room, tying the ribbons by her wrapper?
Q. What sort of a wrapper?
A. A pink wrapper, I think.
Q. Was it a tight or loose wrapper? Perhaps a wrapper is always loose.
A. I do not know.
Q. At that time see her go with reference to the clothes closet door that is over the front hall?
A. Yes sir.
Q. What did you see her do with reference to that door?
A. I did n't see her do anything just then.
Q. Did you at any time during that day see her go to that room?
A. Yes sir.
Q. When was it?
A. I don't remember.
Q. How many times did you see her go to that room?
A. I guess she went twice.
Q. What did she do when she wanted to get into it?
A. State such conversation as took place that you can recall?
A. Soon after she came in there was something said about her going to Marion. I told her I hoped she would go and have a good time. She said she

JOE HOWARD TAKES DEPUTY SHERIFF BUTMAN'S SEAT.

A. She went into the wash room.
Q. Did you go into the wash room?
A. No sir.
Q. Was there anything in the cellar as you went down there at that time, any clothing?
A. Yes sir.
Q. What clothing?
A. The clothing that came from the bodies.
Q. You say that Lizzie went into the wash room at that time?
A. Yes.
Q. Tell us what she did.
A. She went to the sink and took out a pail.
Q. Did you go down cellar again that night, either alone or with her?
A. No sir.
Q. Do you know where she had been in the meantime?
A. I think she had been in her room.
Q. Was the door open or closed?
A. It was open, I think.
Q. Was the door open all the time?
A. Yes sir, all the time to that time.
Q. After that time was the door open or closed?
A. The door was closed after that.
Q. After the door was closed did you see her again till morning?
A. Yes sir.
Q. How long after you closed the door?
A. I don't know; a few minutes.
Q. How long after you came up stairs was it before you closed the door between the two rooms?
A. I don't know.
Q. Can you give any idea?
A. I don't know; I can't remember.
Q. What were you doing while the door was closed between the rooms?
A. I was getting ready for bed.
Q. How long did you remain at the Borden house after the day of the homicide?
A. I went home Monday morning.
Q. Did you stay the intervening nights?
A. Yes sir.
Q. What room did you occupy?
A. Mr. and Mrs. Borden's room.
Q. Thursday and Friday nights, Saturday and Sunday nights I occupied Miss Emma's.
Q. Do you remember the breakfast on Sunday morning?
A. Yes sir.
Q. Who got the breakfast on Sunday morning?
A. I got the breakfast.
Q. After the breakfast had been got and the dishes had been cleared away did you leave the lower part of the house at all?
A. Yes sir.
Q. Afterwards, did you return?
A. Yes sir.
Q. About what time in the morning was it when you returned, Miss Russell?
A. I don't know.
Q. Was it before noon?
A. Yes sir.
Q. Will you state what you saw when you returned?
A. I went into the kitchen, and I saw Miss Lizzie near the stove. I saw Mrs Emma over by the sink, and Miss Lizzie was at the stove, and she had a skirt in her hand, and her sister came and said, "What are you going to do?" Lizzie said, "I am going to burn this old thing." She said it was all covered with something, and I don't know whether she said it was all covered with paint or all covered with blood.
Q. What did you do then?
A. I think I left the room, I am not sure.
Q. Did you speak to either of them at that time?
A. Yes.
Q. Did you go into the room again?
A. Yes sir.
Q. When did you see taen?
A. Miss Lizzie stood near the cupboard door and was either ripping or

Q. I don't remember.
Q. Did you see her give any key to Mr. Fleet?
A. No sir.
Q. Did you see her unlock the door for Mr. Fleet?
A. No sir, at least, I don't remember.
Q. Now, Miss Russell, did you have any occasion to see the door that leads from Miss Lizzie Borden's room into her father and stepmother's room?
A. Yes sir.
Q. Did you observe the door at any time that morning, or that day on Aug. 4?
A. Yes sir.
Q. Won't you state what you observed with reference to that door?
A. I was in Mr. and Mrs. Borden's room when the officers were searching. They came to the door between that room and Lizzie's, and found it locked, and they pulled it open.
Q. Did you notice how it had been fastened on Miss Lizzie's side?
A. I didn't notice then.
Q. Did you afterwards?
A. Yes sir.
Q. What did you notice about the fastening on Miss Lizzie Borden's side?
A. It had a hook and a screw on it.
Q. Did you notice anything about the hook?
A. It was pulled out.
Q. When the officers pulled this door open what sort of a place was there in the wall when the hook pulled out?
A. I didn't notice, but I saw Lizzie screwing the hook in again after the officers had pulled it out.
Q. Did you remain there all day, Miss Russell?
A. Yes sir. No, I didn't remain there all day; I went home once.
Q. But returned again and remained over Thursday night?
A. Yes sir.
Q. Had you suggested to Miss Lizzie Borden to change her dress?
A. No sir.
Q. Did you hear any one else suggest it?
A. I don't remember.
Q. Upon the Thursday night did you go into the cellar with any one?
A. Yes sir.
Q. Was it after dark?
A. Yes sir.
Q. Who went with you?
A. Lizzie.
Q. Do you remember anything that you saw her do?

tearing a part of the dress. It was a small part. And I said I wouldn't let any one see me do that, Lizzie. She did not make any answer.
Q. Did she do anything when you said that?
A. She stepped just one step farther back.
Q. Did you notice where the waist of the dress was when she was holding the skirt in her hand?
A. I do not know but I saw a piece of this dress on the cupboard shelf.
Q. Inside the cupboard?
A. Yes, the door was wide open.
Q. When you came back the second time and saw her tearing the smaller part did you see the skirt?
A. I am not positive, but I think I did.
Q. Did you have any talk with her that day or did she say anything to you about it?
A. No sir.
Q. At that time were there any police officers in the house?
A. No sir.
Q. Were there officers about the premises?
A. Yes sir.
Q. Do you know whether there was any one else in the house except yourself and Miss Emma and Miss Lizzie Borden?
A. No sir.
Q. When did Bridget Sullivan leave?
A. I do not know.
Q. Do you know whether she had left before Sunday morning?
A. I think she had left before that.
Q. Do you know Mr. Hanscom?
A. Yes sir.
Q. Did you see him at the Borden house on the Monday, that is, the following day?
A. Yes sir.
Q. I do not ask you what he said to you, or you to him, but did you have any conversation?
A. Yes sir.
Q. In what room?
A. The parlor.
Q. In consequence of that conversation what did you do?
A. Nothing that I know of.
Q. Did you see any one after the consultation?
A. I saw Miss Lizzie and Miss Emma.
Q. What talk passed between you in the dining room?
A. I said, "Lizzie, I think the worst thing you could do was to burn that dress."
Q. What did she reply?
A. She said, "O, what made you let me do it?"
Q. Miss Russell, you testified at the inquest, didn't you?
A. Yes sir.
Q. At the preliminary trial?
A. Yes sir.
Q. And you testified once and then again at the grand jury?
A. Yes sir.
Q. At either of the three previous times, the inquest, preliminary, or at the first testimony before the grand jury, did you say anything about the burning of this dress?
This question was objected to by Mr. Robinson and was withdrawn.
Q. On the day of the homicide do you remember a search for a note?
A. Yes. In the dining room. Dr. Bowen said, "Lizzie, do you know about the note? She said, "No." I said, "You must have put it in the fire," and Lizzie said, "Yes."
Q. Can you tell us what kind of a dress she burned Sunday morning?
A. It was a cheap cotton Bedford cord, light blue ground with small figure.
Q. Do you know when she got it?
A. In the early spring.
Q. What spring?
A. The spring of the same year.
Q. Was your attention called to it?
A. Yes.
Q. How?
A. By seeing it on her after the dressmaker had been there.
Q. Between this time you said you saw it on Lizzie, did you not see it again till the Sunday morning after the murder?
A. I don't remember.
Q. Can you give me a description of the blue figure?
A. It was a small dark blue figure.
The cross-examination by ex-Governor Robinson began, and Lizzie, who had been leaning all the time during the direct examination with her head resting on her right hand, looking intently at the witness, now changed her position slightly.
Q. On the Thursday when you got to the house, whom was there?
A. I don't remember.
Q. Did you see Mrs. Churchill and Bridget?
A. Yes.
Q. You certainly saw Lizzie?
A. Yes.
Q. Where was she?
A. In the dining room.
Q. Where the doors to the sitting room and kitchen shut?
A. Yes.
Q. What was done in reference to Lizzie?
A. I think I fanned her.
Q. How soon after?
A. I don't know.
Q. Were her hands and face bathed?
A. I think so.
Q. Was she complaining of feeling badly?
A. I don't know.
Q. Was she faint?
A. I don't know.
Q. I thought you said she was?
A. I said she was sitting down and I thought she might be faint.
Q. Was the talk about the barn in the dining room?
A. No, I think in the kitchen.
Q. Did you see the handkerchiefs?
A. I don't know.
Q. Were you and the others sprinkled.
Q. What was done with them?
A. I asked what I should do with them, and Lizzie said, "Put them in the drawer."
Q. You can't tell anything about the dress Lizzie wore that day?
A. No.
Q. Did you see a speck of blood on her hands, face, hair or clothing?
A. No.
Q. Nothing out of the usual way?
A. Nothing.
Q. How long were you there, all day?
A. Yes.
Q. Were there officers and others about the place?
A. Yes, a good many were there.
Q. Were they searching the house?
A. Yes.
Q. In the afternoon were you in Lizzie's room?
A. Yes.
Q. Were you in the clothes room?
A. Yes.
Q. Will you give an idea of what was there?
A. I don't remember: the room seemed to be full of clothes.
Q. On Thursday night were there officers and other persons about the yard?
A. Yes.
Q. Were the windows open?
A. Yes.
Q. The upper ones were.
Q. When you went up stairs, were you and Lizzie and Emma together?
A. Yes.
Q. After going up did you go down again with Lizzie?
A. Yes.
Q. Which way? down the front?
A. I don't remember.
Q. What did Lizzie have?
A. A pail of slops, which she emptied.
Q. Did you go to sleep immediately after going to bed?
A. I didn't sleep all night.
Q. Did you hear noises outside?
A. Yes.
Q. So far as you know neither of you two (Lizzie and Emma) went down stairs again?
A. No.
Q. On Friday Lizzie and Emma were about the house?
A. Yes sir.
Q. What officers were at the premises on the day of the murder? Was Mr. Fleet there?
A. I am not sure.

Q. You were up-stairs when the officers opened Lizzie's room, were you?
A. Yes.
Q. They pulled open her door?
A. Yes.
Q. Lizzie was not there?
A. No.
Q. What did they do; did you notice?
A. I don't remember.
Q. Was this dress what is called calico?
A. No, sir.
Q. Cambric?
A. No, sir.
Q. This dress is neither calico or cambric?
A. Yes, that is so.
Q. This dress you saw Sunday morning was not calico?
A. I should judge not.
Q. You are very sure it was neither calico or cambric?
A. I didn't take hold of it and examine it.
Q. Any woman ought to know, hadn't she?
A. I don't know.
Q. You got the breakfast Sunday morning?
A. Yes, sir.
Q. Who sat down to the table?
A. There were four of us.
Q. Was Mr. Morse there?
A. Yes, sir.
Q. What time did you get breakfast?
A. I don't know. I suppose it was after eight.
Q. Did you go out of the house after breakfast?
A. No sir.
Q. Did you go out into the kitchen?
A. Yes.
Q. Where did you then go?
A. I went to the room I was occupying.
Q. Emma did; I don't know about Lizzie.
Q. Was it when you came back from the chamber that you saw Lizzie with the dress?
A. Yes sir.
Q. At this time she had the skirt on her arm?
A. Yes sir.
Q. The rest of the dress was somewhere else?
A. It was on the shelf.
Q. In the kitchen?
A. Yes.
Q. Did you see any blood on the dress?
A. No sir.
Q. Not a drop?
A. No sir.
Q. Was the dress soiled?
A. The edge of it was soiled.
Q. You, I believe, did not actually see it put into the stove?
A. No sir.
Q. You made a remark that you wouldn't let any one see it burned if it was you?
A. Yes sir. I said I would let any one see me do it.
Q. Were there officers at the house on Sunday?
A. Yes sir.
Q. As soon as the funeral party left the house?
A. Wasn't the funeral in the forenoon?
A. Yes sir.
Q. You know the location of the cemetery where Mr. and Mrs. Borden were buried?
A. Yes sir.
Q. How far is it from the house?
A. Some considerable distance.
Q. You didn't go to the cemetery?
A. No sir.
Q. You remained at the house?
A. Yes sir.
Q. Didn't the officers come and search every part of the house while Lizzie was gone to the cemetery?
A. No, sir.
Q. They made a search, didn't they?
A. Yes, they searched, but not all of the house. They went into Lizzie's room and searched some, and into Emma's room and looked around.
Q. There was no resistance, the officers had full sway, didn't they?
A. Yes, sir; they went where they pleased.
Q. It was the same at all the searches, there was no resistance, was there?
A. I never heard of any.
Q. Were there other searches Sunday afternoon?
A. Yes sir.
Q. Was the city marshal present?
A. I don't know.
Q. How many officers were present?
A. I don't know. Several.
Q. You talked to Lizzie and Emma about burning the dress?
A. I told her it was the worst thing she could have done, and Lizzie said, "Oh! what made you let me do it, why didn't you stop me?"
Q. Thursday there were many people questioning Lizzie about where she was?
A. Yes sir.
Q. Dr. Bowen searched the wash-basket for the note and said he hadn't burned?
A. Yes sir.
Q. Some one said it must have been burned?
A. Yes sir.
A. Yes sir. I said that.
Redirect by Mr. Moody:
Q. What officers were at the premises on the day of the murder? Was Mr. Fleet there?
A. I am not sure.
Q. Of what material is Bedford cord made?
A. It is cotton.

[Continued on 6th Page, Second Edition.]

FINANCIAL.

SANFORD & KELLEY.

GARDNER T. SANFORD, CHARLES S. KELLEY, } Bankers,
Members Boston Stock Exchange,
47 North Water St., New Bedford.

STOCKS AND BONDS BOUGHT AND SOLD ON COMMISSION
At the New York and Boston Stock Boards.
Local manufacturing stocks a specialty.
Outside investments of a conservative character, paying good rates of interest, on hand and for sale.
Also strictly high class investments for trust funds.
Auction Sale of Stocks and Bonds
WEDNESDAYS AND SATURDAYS, at 10 45 A. M.

ORDERS SOLICITED.

Will be sold at auction SATURDAY, June 10, 1893, at 10 45 a. m., at office—
1 share Wamsutta Mills.
5 shares N. B. Manufacturing Corp.
10 shares City Manufacturing Corp.
10 shares Potomska Mills.
$500 Wamsutta Club 5s.

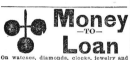

Money —TO— Loan

On watches, diamonds, clocks, jewelry and anything of value; also on pianos, organs, furniture, horses, carriages, merchandise, &c. All business confidential. I have on hand a large assortment of unredeemed pledges for sale; also one Hallett & Davis piano and one Wheeler & Wilson sewing machine; one N. E. Organ. A. L. BRALEY, successor to L. Braley, licensed pawnbroker, 99 Union st. ap20-TTSf

T. E. BOWMAN & CO.,
Topeka, Kansas,
NEGOTIATORS OF
Conservative Mortgage Loans in the Eastern Counties of the State.

WE know every security and give personal attention to every detail. Parties desiring absolute safety and satisfied with six per cent. interest paid promptly by check in their office or home, are invited to investigate our loans.

MONEY TO LOAN!

IN large or small amounts at low rates and easy terms on Real Estate, Pianos, Organs, Horses, Carriages, &c., which can remain in possession of the owners. Loans taken from 30 days to 5 years. ☞ All business strictly confidential. Office Hours 8 to 12 A. M., and 1 to 6 P. M. H. F. DAMON, 34 North Second St., (up one flight) opposite old Post Office. sep17-TTS6ptf

Dividend Notice.

OFFICE OF F. E. BELDEN MICA MINING CO., } 12 Broad Street, Boston, Mass. }
THE regular monthly dividend of this company will be paid June 19, to stockholders of record June 16th.
F. EUGENE BELDEN, Treas.
je6-8-10-13-15

ANNUAL MEETING.

Adjourned Annual Meeting
OF the stockholders of the Morse Twist Drill & Machine Company will be held FRIDAY, June 9, 1893, at 11 o'clock a. m., at the office of Sanford & Kelley. je7-2t

SECOND EDITION.

HOME MATTERS.

PERSONAL.

Harry Vernon Weaver, of this city, was among the graduates from the Boston university yesterday receiving the degree of doctor of medicine; Allen Dexter Hammond of Mattapoisett was a graduate in the same department; Thomas Snowden Thomas of Marion graduated as a bachelor of arts.

William E. Rodenizen, with three associates, all representing the firm of W. A. Greenough & Co., directory publishers of Boston, are in the city compiling a new directory. They are experienced in the work and speak several languages.

Hon. Charles S. Randall left today and will go by Raymond & Whitcomb tomorrow to the World's fair for two weeks, then west, returning about July 15. Letters addressed to him this city will be promptly forwarded.

Paymaster W. W. Barry, U. S. N., having settled his accounts, has been granted a leave of absence for three months, it being one month for each year's duty on a foreign station.

Fred A. Gorham and George T. Sperry were among the successful candidates for admission to the Massachusetts Nautical Training school.

Edward P. Greene, a graduate of the Bangor Theological seminary, has been assigned to preach at North Rochester.

REAL ESTATE AND BUILDING.

Thomas J. Meany has sold to Martin Rogers lots Nos. 12 and 13 on Hemlock street, being a part of the Thompson farm.

John Sylvia has sold to Juan Dutra Pereira a lot of land with buildings thereon on the east side of Belleville road.

Juan Dutra Pereira has sold to John Sylvia lot of land and buildings on Belleville road.

Jireh Swift, Jr., and another have sold to A. H. Covel right and title in the Belleville Wharf association.

Miss J. Cummings has sold for $150 to Thomas Francis land in Westport, a part of the so-called Peckham farm of two acres.

Henry L. Baker has sold to Eli W. Plumpton land at Horse Neck in Westport. The sale includes 5,000 square feet.

Abbott P. Smith and another have sold to Sarah L. Lynch on the south side of Thompson street lot of land containing 15.37 rods.

Abbott P. Smith and another have sold to Maurice Donney a lot of land at the intersection of Rivet and Orchard streets, containing 16.19 rods.

George P. Macomber has sold to William Buckley and one other a lot of land on the west side of a contemplated street running between Elm and Kempton streets, containing 33.96 rods.

Henry T. Weeks asks permission to erect a wooden building 26 by 45 feet on Palmer street.

FAIRHAVEN.

A team belonging to George L. Bauldry at work at the stone crusher became frightened Wednesday noon while being fed to hay and ran out of the lot to Main street and then down to a little south of Cox lane, where they brought up against a telephone pole, breaking the pole of the cart and the cross-bar. No other damaage was done, as the horses were caught when they struck the pole.

A carload of bricks to finish the sidewalk on the William street side of the library has arrived, and will be laid immediately. The slope from the outside curbing to the gutters has been sodded.

When the Oxford extension was built many complaints were heard in the north part of the town on account of the grade established, the people thinking it was too high, but since the street has been graded up to it every one is satisfied that it is a better thoroughfare than before.

CONDENSED LOCALS.

All fire department pay rolls, and pay of special police will be paid on Friday, and monthly bills on Monday the 12th, as the 11th falls on Sunday.

The exports from New York the past week include 4,473 pounds whalebone.

NEW FACTS.

(Continued from Fourth Page.)

Witness was shown the dress and described the waist as satteen.

Q. Is Bedford cord an expensive or a cheap dress?

Mr. Robinson objected and the question was not pressed.

Q. Is this dress an expensive or a cheap one?
A. It is a cheap one.
Q. Which edge of the dress did you see was soiled?
A. The bottom.
Q. The part which touches the ground?
A. Yes sir.
Q. Did you see a soil on any other part?
A. No, sir.
Q. Did it rest so that you could see sufficiently well to tell whether it was soiled or not?
A. No, sir.

Witness was shown a plan of the room and pointed out the place where the dress laid, the position of the stove, and the place where she stood.

John Cunningham, a newsdealer, recalled the 4th day of August. He was on Second street and his attention was attracted to Mrs. Churchill running up Second street toward Hall's stable. He was at the store which is the building next above the Kelly house to collect a bill and from there he went to a piant shop on the opposite side of the street to collect a bill. He saw Mrs. Churchill at Hall's stable and when he came back she had not left. In consequence of what was told him he went to the paint shop at the corner of Second street and telephoned to the city marshal regarding the occurrence at the Borden house. He knows the marshal's voice and it was he who replied to the telephone to the Central police station. He looked at the clock over the telephone at the paint shop and it was just 10 minutes to 11. He knew nothing about the clock. After telephoning he went to dinner.

At this point the court adjourned to come in at 2 15.

Rev. Messrs. Jubb and Buck were not in attendance at court this forenoon, having to attend a funeral in Fall River.

Afternoon Session.

The afternoon session opened promptly at 2 15, the court room being crowded.

John Cunningham took the stand to finish up his testimony.

The testimony of the morning is considered very important, and Assistant Marshal Fleet, in conversation with a Standard man, said he was at loss to understand where that dress which Lizzie is alleged to have burned was when the police went through the house. Certainly they saw nothing of it.

Mr. Cunningham testified that after the murder was discovered he tried the cellar door and found it was locked.

This is considered important for the prosecution, as showing that there was no way to get in the house by the cellar.

THIRD DISTRICT COURT.

Borden, J.

Thursday, June 8.

In the third district court this morning before commencing criminal business, at the request of counsel, in the civil case of Flores vs. Olivera, tried yesterday, Judge Borden announced his decision of the case and gave his reasons therefor. The judgment was for the defendant and is to be entered of record on Monday next, at which time the plaintiff stated he should enter an appeal to the superior court.

In the way of criminal business the first done was the placing of two cases of drunkenness on probation until July 29th next.

Patrick D. Shields and Thomas Moughan for drunkenness were sentenced to 60 days each. Shields appealed.

James Blake, for vagrancy, got three months on the hill. The officers said Blake had been sleeping for some time in a boat on Willis point, and had begged what he had to eat. The people about the point made complaint of his coming to their houses at all times begging for food.

John Moore and Michael J. Shea withdrew their appeals from sentences of three months each for drunkenness and the sentences were affirmed.

Henry Hyland doesn't love the officers a little bit and whenever he is around when an arrest is being made he sets himself up as the special champion of the party under arrest, and proceeds at once to harangue the crowd present as to the general cussedness of the officers. It makes no difference to him whether he knows the circumstances under which the arrest was made or not, his conduct towards the officers is the same. Last night Officers Ivey and Lee arrested John Quill for drunkenness and an assault on his wife at Quill's house, to which they were called by a member of the Quill family, and had him at the box waiting for the "hurry up" wagon to come for him when Hyland came along and at once commenced to condemn the officers and excite the crowd. He went a little too far and created such a row the officers took him into custody for disturbing the peace. Officer Raymond's attention was attracted by Hyland's talk and in court this morning he confirmed the testimony of the other officers. Hyland paid $10 to the city for attending to a matter last night which was none of his business. He admitted to the court that he did not see the arrest; that as he was passing along another party told him about it; that he could not say that the other party saw the arrest.

Timothy Quill pleaded guilty of being drunk last night and not guilty of assaulting his wife. As before stated the officers were called to Quill's house in great haste by one of his children, and when they arrived they found Quill drunk and beating his wife. One of their sons was trying to prevent his father from injuring his mother, and the contents of the room had the appearance of having been struck by lightning. The officers attempted to quell the disturbance, when they were set upon by father, mother and son, and to protect themselves it became necessary to use a club. After a time they got Quill under subjection and took him to the box, when the Hyland affair took place. Quill was sentenced to 30 days on each complaint and appealed.

Mrs. Quill seems to be a rather queer combination, for although she sent out for the officers last night and has often made complaint to them before of her husband's beating her, when they arrived on the scene of action she took sides against them and did all she could to hinder her husband's arrest, and in court this morning told the Judge he did not assault her and she wanted him let off. She did, however, admit he was crazy drunk and did not know where he was or what he was doing.

Murder and manslaughter cases are made up quite frequently of just such a condition of things as the above, and if in this case the wife does not take a more decided stand and the husband drink less rum it is not impossible to foretell the future.

Edward Smith of Fall River, committed to the house of correction March 6th for assault and battery, was released today on recommendation of the probation officer concurred in by the justice of the second district court.

THE COGGESHALL STREET BRIDGE.

Special Commissioners Sitting to Apportion Its Cost Among County Towns.

A hearing was held in City hall this morning before Erastus Worthington of Dedham, Horatio G. Herrick and Samuel P. Snow of Boston, commissioners appointed by the superior court to apportion the cost of the Coggeshall street bridge among the towns of Bristol county and and the county.

New Bedford was represented by City Solicitor Walter Clifford; Dartmouth by William C. Parker, Esq.; Fairhaven by J. L. Gillingham, Esq.; Acushnet by Daniel T. Devoll, Esq.; Taunton by City Solicitor C. A. Reed and Fall River by George C. Grime. Mr. Reed also represented the County Commissioners. There were also present many prominent citizens of all the towns and cities interested in the matter.

It was 10 minutes past 10 o'clock when Mayor Brock called to order. Mr. Worthington presided.

Charles S. Kelley raised objection to the hall, it being so large that it was difficult to hear anything. He moved that the meeting adjourn to the council chamber. The motion met with general favor and the meeting was transferred.

When the meeting was settled in the council chamber the hearing proceeded. Mr. Reed opened for the county commissioners.

County Treasurer George F. Pratt presented a sworn statement of receipts and expenditures of the bridge. The various items were discussed pro and con, and were certified to by Mr. Pratt. These items have been published in the Standard previously and the discussion was of no particular moment. Messrs. Clifford and Gillingham objected to the items for interest being considered an expense in which the cities and towns should participate, and argued that it should be borne by the county; that it is not an expense of construction, and therefore the special commissioners have no province to act upon it at this time.

Mr. Reed argued that interest is a necessary expense of building the bridge and should enter into the apportionment with the rest of the expenses.

The commissioners admitted the item, but did not pass judgment on it, as to its admissability as an expense of construction.

Mr. Pratt continued his testimony stating that three bills have been paid since the filing of the account Sept. 6, 1892. These items were: One of the city of New Bedford (labor and materials), $700; Bowker & Tripp, $361.26 and Joseph C. Jenney (graveling east approach), $300—a total of $1461.26. These repairs were made necessary for reasons unknown to witness.

George A. Briggs presented a plan he made of the bridge as engineer of the bridge. He testified that the bridge was built in accordance with the plan. After the bridge was built several mills were erected near it. Mr. Briggs testified to his knowledge of land values as a surveyor and that land has increased in a great degree since the bridge was built. It has more than doubled in value in five years. Have made mental estimates as to widening the old bridge but not such as he would care now to make public.

Mr. Grime, for Fall River, objected and argued that the fact that a movement to widen the New Bedford & Fairhaven bridge is started so soon after the Coggeshall street bridge is built is a proof that the Coggeshall street bridge did not fill the place it should as a county bridge. It is not a benefit to the county, but merely a benefit to private enterprise. The New Bedford & Fairhaven bridge is a county thoroughfare and needed.

Mr. Briggs continued, stating where the streets have been laid out on the Fairhaven side on the town farm and his own land, and cut into house lots. The land now belongs to F. W. Oesting and John Bertram; witness has sold most of his.

Mr. Reed presented a deed of the land purchased by the town of Fairhaven for a town farm. It recorded the sale of 90 acres of land in 1846 for $4,000. He also presented a deed by which 20 acres of the same farm were sold last April to John Bertram and F. William Oesting for $15,750; also five acres of cove for $1,000.

Mr. Briggs testified that he purchased 20 acres in 1876 for $2,800 and sold about 16 acres last fall, but witness refused to state for how much, declaring it his private business. The point was argued by counsel at length, it being claimed that it was competent as bearing on the increase of value in land in that vicinity.

The question was ruled in, but Mr. Briggs refused to answer definitely.

The commissioners didn't see how this testimony favored the county of Bristol, but learned that it did his other client, the city of Taunton.

Mr. Briggs, in answer to Mr. Parker, admitted that he was financially interested in having the bridge where it is, and that he helped entertain the committee on their visits. In reply to Mr. Grime he said he made the plan gratis, whereupon Mr. Grime remarked that it was probably the cheapest money Mr. Briggs ever invested. In reply to Mr. Clifford witness said John M. and John H. Howland and himself paid for the committee's entertainment. He testified that the bridge was built in accordance with the specifications, but that "Mr. Drake and his boys" came down and tried to run levels, but made some botch, and got it a foot and a half too low for the plans adopted by the harbor commissioners. Mr. Briggs would not state that land value increased on account of the bridge, but more on account of the mills on the New Bedford side. Didn't know as the mills would have boomed land without the bridge. No repairs were made to the bridge after completion to his knowledge. On this point Mr. Briggs got mad and engaged in a tilt with Mr. Clifford, declaring the latter "sour" on him, because Mr. Briggs beat him once on a law suit. Later he acknowledged that the filling washed out of the wall, and other had to be put in. The trouble was that the backing was insufficient. The west approach also settled on account of the mud, which was deeper than he had anticipated. No girders were sprung. Witness received his pay as engineer, but the county still owes him for a subsequent plan, and "it's got to pay it, too."

In answer to D. T. Devoll, of Acushnet, Mr Briggs admitted that the eastern terminus of the bridge was determined in accordance with his wishes. In traveling to New Bedford he uses which ever bridge is most convenient.

At 12 45 a recess was taken till 2 o'clock.

The Allen street Junior Base Ball club has organized with the following players: C. Moody, catch; J. Scules, pitch; C, Wallace, 1st base; R. Morrison, 2d base; W. Robinson, 3d base; O. Booth, s.s.; B. Francis, c.f.; E. Clark, l.f.; Frank Negus, r.f. They would like to hear from nines whose average age is 13 years. Address all communications to J. Scales, 121 Allen street, city.

The Industrial Co-operative Association

Requests the public and members to know that besides the

FULL LINE OF GROCERIES,

THEY CARRY

A Large Assortment of Tin and Woodenware,

INCLUDING

WINDOW BRUSHES AND SCREENS,

For which they would be pleased to take your order.

mh29-TFS6p TELEPHONE 32-2.

CITY HALL NOTES.

Several Financial Orders to be Introduced This Evening.

There will be a regular meeting of the city council this evening for the transaction of routine business. Several financial orders will be introduced.

The superintendent of burial grounds will present a communication asking for an additional appropriation and urging that the government allow him $2,000 to carry forward the work.

The following order will be presented as coming from the finance committee:

That a joint special committee be appointed to examine into the administration, financial and otherwise, of the department of cemeteries.

The city auditor will present a communication to the government recommending various transfers, which are contained in the following orders:

An order calling for the transfer of $64.72 from incidental account to the credit of board of health incidentals.

An order calling for the transfer of $83.33 from fire department, printing and incidentals, and placed to the credit of fire department, fire alarm, labor and supplies.

An order calling for the transfer of $163.11 from public schools' fuel and placed to the credit of public schools, printing and incidentals.

An order calling for the transfer of $51.58 from incidental account and placed to the credit of police station and ward room, Blackmer and South Water streets.

City Treasurer Hathaway will, by vote of the city council, present a statement of the financial standing of the city, giving the amount standing to the credit of unappropriated funds, the anticipated receipts from corporation and other taxes, etc. It might be stated that the amount now standing to the credit of unappropriated funds is about $68,000.

Among the measures laid over was an ordinance in relation to appointment of permanent men in the fire department.

Other orders laid over in the lower branch are as follows: One calling for $400 for construction of a pipe sewer in South Second street, one for $800 for the construction of a pipe sewer in Field street, from Stowell to Babbitt street.

The order fixing the salary of city land surveyor at $2,500, laid over at the last meeting, will be again taken up, and the order instructing the city property committee to make a settlement with Edgar B. Hammond for services as an architect will also be discussed.

In the upper branch the application of T. S. Corson for leave to set up and maintain a steam engine and boiler will be acted on, as also a large number of minor petitions for license to do business as common victualers, and to keep for hire pool tables, while the usual number of applications for leave to keep stores open on Sunday and the transfer of burial lots are on the desk of the city clerk.

ASKED TO RESIGN.

Mayor Brock Sends a Letter to Officer Henry C. Russell.

The following letter was sent this morning to Police Officer Henry C. Russell:

The City of New Bedford,
Mayor's Office, June 6, 1893.
Henry C. Russell, Special Police Officer:

Dear Sir—Charges have been preferred against you by Chief of Police George Douglass, of which the following is a copy:

First—In neglect of duty, in not notifying an officer or arresting a person, knowing said person to be an escaped prisoner, April 29, 1893.

Second—In assisting said prisoner to escape on said date, thus interfering with and preventing Henry Arnett in the discharge of his duty, the said Henry Arnett being then and there a regular police officer of the city of New Bedford.

I hereby request your immediate resignation as special police officer, and the return of the badge held by you, otherwise I will appoint a time and place for a hearing on the above charges.

Yours respectfully,
J. C. BROCK, Mayor.

Mr. Russell is one of the assistant assessors. He was appointed on the police force Feb. 5, 1885, to serve as a special without pay. Previous to the time of the charge made in the mayor's letter there have been no complaints against him.

In the latter part of April Officer Henry Arnett was assaulted by a man named Tripp. Henry C. Russell was a spectator at the time, but the police officials believe from investigation that he did not attempt to assist Officer Arnett and that he did subsequently assist the man in eluding the officer. Tripp was a relative by marriage to Officer Russell, and it is believed that the offender was hidden in Russell's house on the night of the assault, and that he left the city the morning after with a horse and carriage hired by Russell.

Russell was not on duty at the time of the assault, but it did not exempt him from his obligation to assist Officer Arnett or arrest Tripp.

Chief Douglass sent a communication to the mayor yesterday recommending that the resignation be called for. It is not known whether Russell will refuse and be dropped from the force, or whether he will exercise his right and call for a hearing.

DARTMOUTH.

A special town meeting has been called for Friday morning, June 16th, at 10 o'clock to act on an article proposee by Paul Barker and 79 others, mostly residents of Padanaran, to recind all previous action with relation to the new town hall. It is understood that the petitioners desire to have the new building erected nearer the south end of the town. The Hawes lot, however, has already been purchased at Smith Mills in accordance with the vote of the last town meeting and the deeds have been passed. A lively time is anticipated as many think the town cannot afford to hold the Hawes lot unless it is used.

MARINE INTELLIGENCE.

Sch Leader, at Provincetown from St Martins, WI, reports saw whales when crossing Hatteras grounds, and also saw two whalers.

Ar at New York 7th, sch Rhode Island, Soule, Darien; schs George & Albert, Powers, hence; Fred Snow, Tate, do; S Washburn, Keefe, Taunton; Mary A Fisher, Cost, Fall River. Cld, steamer Nacoochee, Smith, Savannah.

Passed through Hell Gate 7th, schs A M Dickinson, Hart, New York for Kettery; Ada Herbert, Harding, do for Wareham; Silvester Hale, Coleman, do for Taunton.

Cld at Philadelphia 7th sch Allen Green, Nickerson, Boston.

Sid from Newport News, 7th, sch Stella B Kaplan, Potter, Portsmouth.

Cld at West Washington 7th, sch Jeanie Lippitt, Chase, Boston.

SPOKEN.

June 5th, lat 36 10 lon 74 20, sch Sarah W Hunt, Gibbons, NB, all well.

June 5th, lat 34 N, lon 74 39 W, sch Chas H Hodgdon, Smith, NB, clean, all well.

June 5th, lat 37 N, lon 74 W, bark Sunbeam, Moulton, NB, All well.

WEATHER INDICATIONS.

Fair and Warmer.

New York, June 8.—At 8 30 a. m., the weather was clear, wind east, temperature 67. The Herald says: In the Middle States and New England on Friday is fair, still warmer weather and fresh to brisk southerly winds, with an increase of actual humidity until Saturday, when probably cloudy weather will prevail, with no decided abatement of the heat until the afternoon.

A SERIOUS RIOT.

Greek Sailors and the People of an Italian Town Quarrel About a Woman.

Taranto, Italy, June 8.—A serious riot occurred here yesterday between the inhabitants of the city and the sailors of the Greek men-of-war Spara and Spexie, lying at anchor in the harbor. The cause of the conflict was the allegation that some of the sailors had assaulted a Taranto woman. Several persons on both sides were seriously injured in the affray and 46 arrests were made. The feeling in the city is one of continued disquietude, and the people of Taranto threaten to take vengeance on the sailors.

Argentine Cabinet Crisis.

London, June 8.—Dispatches received last night from Buenos Ayres states that the Argentine Republic cabinet has resigned.

A TORN COAT.

Another Link in Evidence Against Correiro.

Asked a Woman to Mend It on the Day of the Murder.

Fall River Police Confident They Can Prove Prisoner's Guilt.

(Special Dispatch.)

Fall River, June 8.—The chain of circumstantial evidence which holds Jose Correiro a prisoner for the murder of Bertha Manchester is strengthening daily. The links are being forged stronger and stronger by the police officials and others who have volunteered to assist in ferreting out this mystery.

Yesterday afternoon a Standard reporter made an investigation on his own responsibility. He wanted to learn so far as possible the movements of Correiro on the day of the murder. It was no easy task to trace the man, but with the assistance of a very good interpreter some new light was thrown on the evidence which holds the prisoner.

Correiro met Mr. Manchester on Crab Pond bridge, as before reported, and took the 1 29 train for Taunton. He also bought a pair of shoes from a French dealer at 11 40. It was after this that he saw Mr. Manchester, and went to his former boarding house on Eagle street. Next he took the train for Taunton.

But the most startling discovery made in the north part of the city by the Standard man and his interpreter was, more than any of these facts, evidence which the police may find of great importance.

Before purchasing the shoes Correiro called at the house of an acquaintance and told a story to a woman there which may greatly effect his future career.

He said that he had been in the woods and had torn his coat. He asked the woman to sew it for him and she did so.

This appears to be of the most vital importance to the state, as the contention has always been that Bertha Manchester fought desperately for her life, and her murderer would certainly bear the marks of the struggle.

Correiro's coat was torn, and he gave the lame excuse before mentioned in order to get the woman to sew it for him.

The police have a knowledge of this fact, and think it of great import to the case. They regard it as strange that a man should enter a house unknown and make the request of a woman, more especially where he was of the same nationality as herself.

The officers refuse to answer any questions in regard to the case, but the facts noticed have been well substantiated by the reporter. When the police officers were asked at noon today what they had to say in regard to the new developments they replied: "There is nothing to say. Correiro is guilty, and we will prove it at the time of the trial."

FINANCIAL.

Atchison the Soft Spot—Rallies in Noon Trading However to 24 1-2—General Electric Rises—Money Firm—Bank of England Rate of Discount Reduced—Handsome Flint and Pere Marquette Earnings—During Month of May Gross Increase Over $37,500—New York Central Dividend—In General.

Thursday, June 8.

The stocks will be irregular for a space of time of some length yet was proven in yesterday's trading by the steady decline in the price of Atchison in the face of otherwise firm market, particularly for stocks of the Atchison class. In the forenoon the price was firm near 25, but later trading carried the price to 23¾, within ¼ of the lowest quotation ever made on the stock. Gossip was not bearish on it and its decline was in fact not accounted for by any adequate reason other than liquidation. It has been reported that the system was cutting rates fiercely in the west, but there has been nothing done in this direction since the famous Colorado rate war of three weeks ago. There is no doubt that rates have been reduced on the Atchison's lines, but so they have on all the western roads, and a gentleman generally well informed on Atchison matters says the road is adopting a policy merely necessary to the realizing of its opportunities and consistent with the plan upon which its Chicago line was built. As to the Atchison stock, London is reported daily to be steadily absorbing large quantities of it, and the statement is made from Boston that within five days over 5,000 shares of the stock has been purchased by two leading London houses and the stock transferred to their names. The general list shows signs of an undercurrent of strength, despite the weakness in Atchison, although a sympathetic movement is of course likely to start at any moment. The bears today are in the ascendency and make the market, not only the downward movements but the upward as well, for there has been no rally in the market during the last two months but what has originated with the short interest.

The local money market is firm with a good demand for money ruling. The going rate is 6 per cent.

There is little change to note today in the Boston money market. Call money holds 6 to 7 per cent. Time money 6 per cent. Commercial paper dull. At clearing today loans were made at 7 per cent. New York funds sold at 25 and 30 cents discount.

Money on call is firmer in New York. Loans are making today at 2½ to 7 per cent. Time money is in lighter supply.

Sterling exchange is weaker and no more gold will probably go out this week.

Bonds are dull and prices soft.

The New York market opens higher this morning. Western Union up ⅝ at 82⅝, St. Paul up ¼ to ⅜, General Electric 70, Cordage 12½, and Lake Shore up a point at 123. Atchison a soft spot at 23¾. This stock is very active. At 11 o'clock the market was irregular and quiet. Western Union sunk to 81¼. General Electric rose to 71. Cordage advanced to 13⅜.

At noon the market was firmer under lead of Atchison, which hardened to 24⅛. Rock Island advanced to 72¾, St Paul 68¾.

The following table shows the fluctuations of the leading active stocks during the forenoon:

Stocks.	Opening.	11 a. m.	12 m.
Atchison,	23¾	23⅞	24½
Erie,	17⅝	17½	18
New England,	21⅝	21⅞	22¾
St. Paul,	68⅛	68¼	68¾
Western Union,	82⅝	81¼	82¼
General Electric,	70	71	71½
Cordage,	[illegible]	13⅛	13½

At 1 o'clock the market was a trifle weaker. C. B. & Q. lost ground from 87 to 86⅜. Western Union firm at 83. Lackawanna 140½, Sugar 89 to 88⅛.

At 2 o'clock the market was strong. Union Pacific 29¼, Nashville 66.

The Boston market opened quiet and steady, generally up from close. Calumet sold at 289. Atchison lively, just under 24. C. B. & Q. 86⅛. Flint preferred offered at 59, despite the favorable earnings report for May. At 11 o'clock New England and Atchison were the features. Former sold off to 21⅞. Latter firmer at 24. Sugar 88. Trading light.

Sales to noon in Boston today were: Bonds $33,000; 8,600 shares of stock.

At noon the market was steady, with Atchison stronger at 24⅜.

The following table shows the fluctuations of the leading active stocks during the forenoon:

Stocks.	Opening.	11 a. m.	12 m.
Atchison,	23¾	24	24½
C. B. & Q.,	86	86⅛	87
New England,	21⅞	21¾	22¾
General Electric,	70¼	71	71½

At 1 o'clock stocks were quiet and steady.

At 2 o'clock the market was firm. C. B. & Q. 87.

The slump in Cordage has been accompanied by rumors of a line of 5,000 shares of the stock which has got to be closed out regardless of price, and an assessment on the stock as part of the plan of reorganization. Neither of these rumors are confirmed.

The London copper market is firmer.

Baring, Magoun & Co. will not ship the $300,000 gold engaged by them owing to the weakness in sterling rates.

The surplus of the Rock Island after paying dividends for the year ended March 31st was $201,821. Last year this surplus was $548,557.

New York Central has declared its usual quarterly dividend of 1¼ per cent., payable July 15 to stock of June 15.

Shipments of currency west will probably not be over $500,000 today.

Silver offered the government yesterday amounted to 966,000 ounces. The amount purchased was 360,000 ounces. Prices 83.55 to 83.60.

At the annual meeting of the Rock Island and the old board of directors was re-elected without change.

J. Pierpont Morgan is back on the street again.

Edmund Sweet & Co. say: "Exchange is weak. Runs on Western banks seem to be subsiding but heavy demands on New York continue and money liable to be active here. Market ought to show strength but it is narrow and prices were easily depressed by Cammach party late yesterday."

Early London prices today were ¼ to ⅝ higher.

Sterling rates at $10.15 were lowered to $4.86½ and $4 88½.

At a meeting of the governors of the Bank of England this morning the rate of discount was reduced to 3 per cent.

Taintor & Holt say:

"We look for nothing but a narrow and professional market."

The Wall Street News says: "On May 5, the day of the panic, the lowest price for Missouri Pacific was 38¼. Yesterday this gilt edged chromo sold down to 33½, on transactions of less than 4,000 shares. People who bought it on the 'tip' 'that it was like finding money' to do so, now wish they hadn't."

The Old Colony Trust company has been made transfer agents of the New York, New Haven & Hartford.

Cammack is the biggest kind of a bear on Western Union and predicts very low figures for it.

A banker in a position to know, estimates the westward movement of currency since Monday at about five millions. Up to 1 30 p. m. today the shipments are half a million. Wales & Co., Herrick, and Philadelphia houses sold Reading down. No news in the crowd that can be learned.

"Jim" Keene has been a heavy seller of both Sugar and General Electric.

Flint & Pere Marquette earnings for the fourth week of May compare as below:

Fourth week May,	1893.	1892.	Inc.
Freight,	$53,457	$45,823	$7,634
Passenger,	26,500	21,498	5,002
Total,	$79,957	$67,321	$12,636
Month of May,	$255,615	$217,749	$37,866
Since Jan. 1st,	$1,226,140	$1,245,331	*$19,191
Mileage,	625	625	

*Decrease.

STOCK AND BOND MARKETS.

Bid Prices at 12 o'clock Today.

NEW YORK, June 8.

GOVERNMENT BONDS	
U. S. 2s	98½
" 4s, registered	110½
" 4s, coupons	111½
" currency 6s, 1895	102½
RAILROADS	
Atchison	24½
Clev., Cin., Col. & St. Louis	41
Chicago & Eastern Illinois pref	94¼
Chicago, Burlington & Quincy	87
Delaware & Hudson	121
Delaware & Lackawana	139
Erie	18
Illinois Central	91
Lake Shore	123
Louisville & Nashville	58¼
Manhattan	124⅛
Michigan Central	99
Missouri Pacific	31¾
New Jersey Central	106⅛
New York Central	102
New York & New England	22¾
Northern Pacific pref	33¾
Northwest	105
Philadelphia & Reading	17¾
Rock Island	72¾
St. Paul	68¾
St. Paul pref	115⅛
Richmond Terminal	1¾
St. Paul & Omaha	38¾
Union Pacific	29¼
Wabash pref	
MISCELLANEOUS	
Chicago Gas	69
National Cordage	13¼
Ontario Silver	15
Pacific Mail	18⅞
Pullman	170
Sugar	88⅜
Sugar, pref	87¾
Silver Certificates	83
Western Union Telegraph	82¼

BOSTON, June 8.

BONDS	
Atchison 4s	79
Atchison 2ds	*47½
Bell Telephone 7s	109
Chicago, Burlington & Northern 5s	100
C. B. & Q. Cons. Mort. 7s	116½
C. B. & Q. Conv. 5s	103½
Chicago & West Michigan 5s	*93
Mexican Central 4s	56½
Illinois Steel Co. 5s	*90
RAILROADS	
Atchison	24¾
Boston & Albany	210
Boston & Lowell	185
Boston & Maine	163
Boston & Providence	250
Central Mass. pref	49½
Chicago, Burlington & Quincy	86⅛
Chicago Jun. & Un. Stk. Yds	79
Chicago Jun. & Un. Stk. Yds. pref	*90
Chicago & West Michigan	29
Cleveland & Canton & Southern	5
Cleveland, Canton & Southern pref	14
Fitchburg	*84
Flint & Pere Marquette pref	*59
Mexican Central	7⅞
New York & New England	22
New York & New England pref	63½
Old Colony	186
Oregon Short Line	13
Pullman Palace Car	170
Union Pacific	28¾
Wisconsin Central	8
West End	*56¼
West End pref	79
MINING	
Butte & Boston	6
Calumet & Hecla	288
Centennial	6
Franklin	12
Kearsarge	6
Montana	20
Osceola	*27
Quincy	112
Tamarack	138
MISCELLANEOUS	
American Bell Telephone	*191
Erie Telephone	45½
New England Telephone	*58
Boston Land	8¾
West End Land	13
Topeka Land	.25
Lamson Store Service	*18
Illinois Steel Co	*60
Sugar common	88
Sugar pref	87
Gen'l Electric	71
Westinghouse	25¾
Bay State Gas	8
National Lead	29¾

*Asked.

PROVISIONS AND GRAIN.

Chicago, June 8.

	Wheat.	Pork.	Corn.
Opening.			
July,	66¾	——	39¾
September,	71⅛	20.80	41
Twelve o'clock.			
July,	65⅛	——	38½
September,	70½	20.70	40½

PERSONAL.

The Empress Frederick is expected to visit the Greek royal family at Dekelia toward the end of June.

Rev. Ralph Swinburne, who lives near Charleston, W. Va., is the oldest railroad man living in this country. He was born near Newcastle-on-Tyne, in the county of Durham, Eng., Aug. 4, 1805, and began to work on railroads in the year 1818.

An old married couple from Ardeche, in the diocese of Tours, were admitted to the pope's presence last week. The man, whose name is Charles Pibaleau, is 80 years of age and his wife is 71, and this is their 21st pilgrimage to Rome, the journey being always performed on foot. They have also been to Jerusalem twice in the same manner. The pope spoke with them for some time, questioning them about their journeys, and in the end he bestowed upon them a specially hearty benediction.

London will soon receive a visit from Mascagni, the young Italian composer, some of whose works will form a part of the repertory of the operatic season now under way in that city. Like most Italians, Signor Mascagni has always a pocket full of charms against the jettatura, or "evil eye," without which he would never travel—mostly horns of coral, mother-of-pearl, ebony, and ivory, which are supposed to protect their owner. But though a trifle superstitious, Signor Mascagni is described as exceedingly agreeable. He has known much poverty, and does not presume on his success. In his picturesquely situated villa at Leghorn, he lives a quiet life surrounded by works of art and curios selected with great taste and judgment.

WANTS.

LAUNDRESS—Apply between 7 30 and 9 p. m., at Dr. BULLARD'S, 446 County st. je8-tf

AUCTION SALES.

By STANDISH BOURNE,
(Successor to Geo. A. Bourne & Son,)
Auctioneer, Commission Merchant, Real Estate Dealer and Appraiser.

Cash advanced on goods consigned for auction. Ready buyer for personal property of every description.
Office and Salesrooms 47, 49 and 51 North Second Street, near the Post Office.

Carriages, Harnesses, Etc.
On SATURDAY, June 10th, at 10½ o'clock, at salesrooms, will be sold a variety of new and second hand carriages, harnesses, etc. Also a variety of merchandise usually consigned for our Saturday sales.

Mortgagee's Sale.
On SATURDAY, June 10th, at 2 30 o'clock on the premises, will be sold by order of the mortgagee house and lot of about 15 rods on Rounds street, south of Kempton street. For legal advertisement see N. B. Evening Standard of May 15, 22 and 29.

Cottage House and Lot on Purchase Street.
On SATURDAY, June 10th, at 3½ o'clock, on the premises, will be sold the cottage house together with about 17 rods of land situated on the west side of Purchase street, just north of the Common, numbered 527. The cottage is in first class order, has modern conveniences, and is ready for the purchaser to move into. Terms, 10 per cent. at sale, balance on delivery of deed within 10 days.

Desirable House and Lot.
On MONDAY, June 12th, at 3 o'clock, on the premises will be sold the 2½-story house, together with lot of about 13 rods, situated on the southeast corner of Acushnet avenue and Madison street. The house is in excellent order throughout, roof slated, and ready for the purchaser to move in without any extra expense. Terms 10 per cent. at sale, balance within 10 days.

For Rent.
A furnished house from June 1st to Oct. 1st. Location first class.
Also north half of the double house corner of Orchard and Clinton streets.
A very desirable residence, centrally located, containing all the modern conveniences. Apply to STANDISH BOURNE'S office.

To Let in Our Storage Warerooms.
We constantly have on hand first-class rooms for the storage of household goods, to be rented by the month or year.
Good dry storage room for stoves.

By JOHN B. BAYLIES,
121 and 123 Union Street,
Commission Merchant, Appraiser, and Auctioneer for the sale of Real Estate and every description of Personal Property. Furniture Bought.

H. C. HATHAWAY,
Auctioneer, Real Estate Agent and Appraiser,
Corner Acushnet Ave. and Elm St.
☞ One of the best auction marts in the State for the sale of horses and carriages. Keeps constantly on hand carriages of every description, carriages made to order and repairing in all its branches attended to under the superintendency of J. R. Forbes. Consignments of every description solicited. Cash advanced on goods for auction. Personal property of every description bought at short notice for cash. Negotiable notes bought and sold.

House and Lot.
On SATURDAY, June 10th, at 3 o'clock p. m., on the premises, will be sold the very desirable house and lot of 10 rods situated on the southwest corner of West Middle and Emerson streets. Said house is in good repair and affords a rare opportunity to secure a good home at your own price, as the owner says sell. Terms, 10 per cent. at sale, balance delivery of deed.

ALFRED WILSON,
Auctioneer and Real Estate Agent,
Room 22, - - - Robeson Building.
☞ Houses and land in all parts of the city for sale; tenements for rent; rents collected.

House Lots.
The best location in the city for homes. The land bounded by Union, Court, Tremont and Ocean streets, has been laid out in lots, and offers a rare chance to get a home in a good neighborhood. Sewers, water, and prospective electric cars to the new park makes it the most desirable to be had. Call at room 21 Robeson building and see plan.
ALFRED WILSON.

HEALEY & JENNEY,
Real Estate Brokers,
Successors to T. F. Healey.
Real estate bought and sold on commission at lowest rates.
Farms, houses, house lots and strips of every description always on hand and offered for sale on easy terms at lowest prices.
Any and all parties desiring of buying or selling will do well to call at our office, which will be open day and evening.
Office, 555 Purchase St., Cor. Franklin.
T. F. HEALEY. Telephone 28-5. N. H. JENNEY

BY D. H. HOWLAND, Auctioneer.
WILL be sold at public auction FRIDAY, June 9th, at 3 o'clock p. m., on the premises, a nice farm known as the late Lorenzo D. Wood farm, situated on
Smith's Neck, South Dartmouth, near Nonquitt and Round Hills,
6½ miles from city, one-half mile from meeting and school houses, with macadamized road. Cuts 50 tons hay, has plenty of wood, contains two houses, two barns, carriage houses, etc. Remember that land in this locality is increasing in value rapidly.
je2-6t

REAL ESTATE.

FRANCIS W. TAPPAN,
Agent for Purchase, Sale, and Lease of REAL ESTATE.
Office, 15 North Water St., New Bedford. d&w

H. A. LEONARD,
REAL ESTATE AGENT,
126 UNION STREET.
Houses and house lots in all parts of the city for sale. Three fine residences. Good bargains. Call and examine tenements to let.

FRANK C. SMITH,
BROKER & AUCTIONEER. Office, 47 William St.

M. E. SMITH,
REAL ESTATE BROKER,
Real Estate bought, sold, mortgaged or auctioned. Facilities unsurpassed. Call at
M. E. SMITH'S,
REAL ESTATE EXCHANGE.
619 Purchase Street. Telephone 16-11.

NEW HOUSE — On Morgan st., No. 18, arranged for two families, bath-rooms, hot and cold water, furnace, first-class in every particular, all ready for occupancy, unexceptionable neighborhood. A rare opportunity to secure a beautiful home. Enquire of F. A. SOWLE. je3-6t

FOR SALE—Residence of the late Charles Briggs, 175 Acushnet ave.; cottage house, 10 rooms, steam heat, set bowls, marble mantles, four fireplaces; large barn; laundry, containing set tubs, etc. All buildings in A order; 20 rods land. Apply on premises. my27-12t

FOR SALE.

House and Lot, 86 Walden St.,
Inquire
J. M. WILLIS, 43 Purchase St. my11-tf

VERY DESIRABLE COTTAGE HOUSE—Stable and about 4 acres land on the Old County road, north of Acushnet Village. Practically new buildings, orchard, hennery, carriage house, etc. Will be sold cheap if applied for at once. May be seen at any time. Keys at Mrs. Ashley's opposite. Address J. W. LEONARD, 59 Commercial st., Boston. ap27-tf

D. W. WILSON,
Steam Piping & General Machine Work
PIPE AND FITTINGS
Constantly on Hand.
21 Commercial Street, New Bedford, Mass.
☞ All orders promptly attended to. Satisfaction guaranteed. Telephone No. 344—3.

CALIFORNIA MINING STOCKS.

San Francisco, June 7.

The following are the official closing prices of mining stocks to-day:

Best & Belcher	1 00	Mexican	1 15
Bulwer	[illegible]	Mount Diablo	[illegible]
Chollar	1 00	Ophir	1 70
Con. Cal. & Va.	[illegible]	Potosi	2 80
Crown Point	[illegible]	Savage	[illegible]
Eureka Con	[illegible]	Sierra Nevada	[illegible]
Gould & Curry	[illegible]	Belcher	[illegible]
Hale & Norcross	[illegible]	Yellow Jacket	1 25

AMUSEMENTS.

Bert Poole,

The Boston Globe Artist, will give a

CHALK TALK } ENTERTAINMENT

IN THE Y. M. C. A. HALL,

On MONDAY NIGHT, June 12th,

AT 8 O'CLOCK.

RESERVED SEATS..........25c. and 35c.

je8-3t

ENTERTAINMENT DIRECTORY.

THURSDAY.

China Hall—Friends' union supper.
Fourth Street Church—Strawberry festival and entertainment.
St. Martin's Parish Rooms—Festival and sale.

FUTURE EVENTS.

Guards' Armory—4th, Cadets' prize drill and dance.
Y. M. C. A. Hall—12th, Chalk Talk.

AMUSEMENTS.

In the races at Manchester, N. H., yesterday, bay stallion Jubilee Wilkes, driven by N. J. Stone, came in first in the 2 35 race. The race was won in three straight heats.

Bert Poole, who is here in the interest of the Boston Globe making sketches at the Borden trial, will give his famous chalk talk entertainment in Y. M. C. A. hall next Monday evening. This artist possesses a good voice and delivery, and sketches with wonderful rapidity while he is speaking.

ON THE TENTED FIELD.

How the Boys of the First Infantry are Enjoying Themselves.

Framingham, June 7.

The weather was so hot yesterday that not much work was done, except guard mounting.

The First infantry came out at 6 p. m., and for a first parade did well. It has very often done better before.

We had a very heavy rain storm here in the evening, consequently the boys are confined to their quarters, much against their will.

Captain Perry arrived in camp just as parade was ended.

The camp was fine and all the commands were out for drill, and put in some good work.

The executive committee having in hand the reception to the Army of the Potomac held a meeting at the quarters of Colonel Mathews, First infantry, this afternoon.

Captain N. O. Danforth of Company F, First infantry, was officer of the day. The First infantry today numbered 735, total present for duty. H. S. S.

"A TEMPERANCE TOWN."

Last evening was the closing one of the season at the Opera House, and it was characterized by the presentation of Charlie Hoyt's latest comedy-drama of "A Temperance Town," which had been heralded with loud acclaim from its successful season in Boston. The audience was one of the largest of the season—the largest, it would seem, but Mr. Cross said it has been exceeded once at least. Anyway, standing room was at a premium, and the size of the house caused the lessee's heart to feel glad and his pockets heavier. The play is as is well known a satire on the workings of the prohibitory law in Vermont, but the parallel holds good in many other states. The characters are as a whole well drawn and human nature is fairly depicted. Several character sketches could be duplicated in almost any place in the United States, but while the motive of the play may be all right it is not a faithful representation of a cause. Prohibitionists in Massachusetts are not all either "cranks" or men who "have an axe to grind," and while undoubtedly there is a leaven of personal motives in the constitution of some the work of the majority is one of pure desire to benefit their fellow men. On the other hand, while all liquor sellers are not vile and animated by a desire to ruin their fellow men, but few of them are ex-union soldiers, who were disabled in their country's service and were compelled to sell rum to keep their families from starving. In fact, the average barroom that the writer is acquainted with at least, with its chances for disturbances is a poor place in which to place a disabled man in charge. The rule in real life is that the rumseller is not so very poor. At least his finances are generally on a par with those of the average of the patrons. So much for the plot itself. It is a play with characters strongly marked, and as a campaign work a tour through New England with it just previous to election will do more to create an anti-prohibition sentiment in the community than all the speakers that can be sent out or the tracks that Brothers Faxnor Minor can circulate. There are many bright things in the text. The dialogue is sharp, the scenes clearly defined, and the situations very funny. There is not so much of horse play as in Hoyt's earlier productions, and there is enough of pathos commingled to relieve the monotony of the broader parts. The funniest character is that of Launcelot Jones, commonly known as "Mink," which in the hands of George Richards was made the most of. Eugene Canfield as St. Julien Jones, or "Bingo," was also a well-drawn comic character, and Richard J. Dillon as Ernest Hardman was a carefully conceived and well acted part. Other parts were well taken, and the company as a whole was well balanced, and all did earnest, faithful work. The audience was sympathetic and the applause commensurate with the merits of the production. It is a pity that it was so late in the season when "A Temperance Town" was put on the circuit, for an early reappearance would be heartily welcomed.

COMMUNICATION.

The Power of Music.

To the Editor of the Standard:

I should not wonder if, in the day of judgment, it should be found out that more souls have been saved by music than by preaching. I should not wonder if, out of the one hundred and forty and four thousand ransomed souls that John foresaw before the throne of God, at least 100,000 had been saved by sweet song. Why does not the church on earth rise up and utilize its great musical center of the universe, the place of doxologies and trumpets and harps, and in preparation for that place we ought to make more of music on earth. The band of music at Waterloo played the retreat of the 42d Highlanders back to their places, and sacred music has returned many a faltering host of God into the Christian conflict with as much determination and dash as Tennyson's "Six Hundred." Who can tell what has been accomplished by Charles Wesley's 7,000 hymns, or by the congregational singing of his time, which could be heard two miles off!

When my dear friend, Dio Lewis (gone to rest all too soon), conducted a campaign against drunkenness at the west, marshaled thousands of the noblest women and whole neighborhoods and villages and cities shut up their groghops, do you know the chief weapon used? It was the song

Nearer, my God, to thee,
Nearer to thee.

They sang it at the door of hundreds of liquor saloons which had been open for years, and either at the first charge of the campaign or the second the saloon shut up. At the first verse of "Nearer, my God, to Thee," the liquor dealers laughed; at the third verse they began to cry, and at the fourth they got down on their knees. You say they opened their saloons again. Yes, some of them did. But it is a great thing to have hell shut up if only for a week. Give full swing to a good gospel hymn and it would take the whole world for God!—Rev. T. De Witt Talmage, D.D.

—W. C. T. U.

BROWN OUTPLAYED.

Even Sexton's Pitching Could Not Defeat Amherst.

Amherst, June 8.—For the first time in four years Amherst and Brown met on the ball field yesterday afternoon. Both teams fielded and batted well, but Amherst's work was superior. Gregory pitched a superb game, but retired in favor of Colby in the eighth inning. The score:

AMHERST.

	ab	r	1b	po	a	e
Hunt, 1b.	5	1	1	6	0	0
Cheney, c.f.	5	1	1	3	0	1
Allen, c.	5	3	1	10	2	1
Stearns, 2b.	3	1	1	2	2	1
Smith, l.f.	4	0	1	2	0	0
Landis, s.s.	4	0	1	1	0	1
Millis, 3b.	4	0	2	3	1	
Jackson, r.f.	4	0	0	0	0	0
Gregory, p.	3	0	1	0	3	0
Caley, p.	1	0	0	1	3	0
Totals,	37	6	7	27	18	6

BROWN.

	ab	r	1b	po	a	e
Weeks, 1b.	5	0	1	10	0	0
Sexton, p.	5	0	0	10	2	
Steere, s.s.	4	0	1	3	2	3
Jones, 2b.	3	0	0	3	2	0
Magill, 3b.	4	1	1	1	3	0
George, c.f.	4	0	1	2	0	0
McLane, l.f.	3	0	0	0	0	0
Green, r.f.	3	1	1	2	0	0
Lang, c.	4	0	2	5	2	0
Totals,	34	2	5	27	20	5

Innings,	1	2	3	4	5	6	7	8	9
Amherst,	0	0	0	3	0	0	2	0	1—6
Brown,	0	0	0	0	0	1	1	0—2

Earned runs—Amherst 2. Two-base hits—Smith, Weeks. Stolen bases—Allen, Landis, Sexton, Steere, Magill, Green. First base on balls—Stearns 2, Smith 2, Jones 2, McLane, Green. First base on errors—Amherst 5, Brown 4. Left on bases—Amherst 7, Brown 5. Struck out—Cheney 2, Smith, Landis, Ellis 2, Jackson 2, Sexton, Jones, George 2, Lang 2, Green 2. Passed balls—Lang 3. Wild pitches—Sexton 2. Time—2 hours 15 minutes. Umpire—J. J. Brady of Hartford.

FAVORED BY THE UMPIRE.

Cincinnati Pulls a Game Away From Boston in the Eighth Inning.

Boston, June 8.—The monotony of the contest yesterday was something remarkable up to the eighth inning, the score at that time being 1 to 0 in favor of Boston—Long making a "homer."

Five innings in succession the Cincinnati players were retired in one, two, three order, and it looked like a sleepy game. Comiskey opened the eighth with a hit to center, and a moment later was caught napping by Nichols and was clearly out, but the umpire said nay. Then Smith flew out to Duffy, and Murphy hit safe, while Dwyer put the sphere over the left field fence for a "homer." Six singles and a double followed in quick succession, making 11 in all and earning nine runs.

Prettier hitting was never seen, and the Bostons did not make an error. In the ninth a "homer" by Duffy and two singles, with a wild throw by Latham, gave the Bostons two runs. The spectators thoroughly appreciated the fine hitting of the Cincinnata.

CINCINNATI.

	AB	R	BH	TB	PO	A	E
Latham, 3b.	5	1	1	1	1	4	0
McPhee, 2b.	5	1	1	1	5	1	0
Holliday, c.f.	5	1	3	7	2	0	
Vaughn, r.f.	4	1	1	1	1	0	0
Canavan, l.f.	4	1	1	1	3	0	0
Comiskey, 1b.	4	1	1	1	9	0	0
Smith, s.s.	4	0	1	1	2	4	1
Murphy, c.	4	1	1	2	4	2	1
Dwyer, p.	4	2	3	6	0	3	1
Totals,	39	9	14	21	27	9	3

BOSTON.

	AB	R	BH	TB	PO	A	E
Long, s.s.	4	1	1	4	1	5	0
Carroll, r.f.	4	0	0	0	4	0	0
Duffy, c.f.	4	1	4	6	0	0	0
McCarthy, 2b.	4	0	1	1	4	1	1
Nash, 3b.	4	0	1	1	1	3	2
Quinn, 2b.	4	0	1	1	1	2	0
Tucker, 1b.	4	0	1	1	10	0	0
Rivetts, l.f.	4	0	0	0	0	0	0
Bennett, c.	2	1	1	1	6	2	0
Nichols, p.	2	0	0	0	0	2	1
Totals,	34	3	13	13	27	12	0

Cincinnati	0	0	0	0	0	0	0	9	0—9
Boston	0	0	0	0	0	0	0	0	2—2

Earned runs—Cincinnati, 9; Boston, 1. Two-base hits—Holliday, 2. Three-base hit—Holliday. Home runs—Dwyer, Long, Duffy. Sacrifice hit—Nash. First base on balls—Canavan, Smith. First base on errors—Boston, 3. Struck out—Long, Bennett, Nichols. Double plays—Long, McCarthy and Tucker. Umpire—Emslie.

Other Games.

At New York:

Pittsburg	9	1	0	1	0	2	0	0	3—7
New York	2	0	0	0	1	0	1	0—4

Base hits—Pittsburg, 13; New York, 8. Errors—Pittsburg, 4; New York, 5. Batteries—Killean and Miller; Baldwin and Doyle.

At Brooklyn:

Brooklyn	2	0	0	1	5	0	3	3—14
St. Louis	0	0	1	0	0	0	0	0—1

Base hits—Brooklyn, 14; St. Louis, 6. Errors—Brooklyn, 2; St. Louis, 9. Batteries—Stein and Kinslow; Breitenstein, Clarkson and Gunson.

At Philadelphia:

Philadelphia	1	0	2	1	0	0	0	3	2—9
Louisville	1	0	3	1	0	0	0	2—7

Base hits—Philadelphia, 12; Louisville, 13. Errors—Philadelphia, 3; Louisville, 4. Batteries—Weyhing and Clements; Hemming and Grim.

At Washington:

Washington	0	0	1	3	1	0	1	0—6
Cleveland	0	1	1	0	1	0	0	0—3

Base hits—Washington, 10; Cleveland, 8. Errors—Washington, 1; Cleveland, 5. Batteries—Meekin and McGuire; Cuppy and O'Connor.

At Baltimore:

Baltimore	4	1	4	0	0	0	0	0—9
Chicago	1	0	3	1	0	0	0	0—5

Base hits—Chicago, 14; Baltimore, 8. Errors—Chicago, 6; Baltimore, 5. Batteries—McGill and Robinson; McMahon, McNabb and Robinson.

New England League.

At Fall River—Portland, 4; Fall River, 3.
At Dover—Lewiston, 5; Dover, 4.
At Lowell—Lowell, 11; Brockton, 9.

Eastern League Games.

At Wilkesbarre—Wilkesbarre, 27; Springfield, 22.
At Binghamton—Binghamton, 13; Providence, 12.

National League Standing.

Clubs	Won	Lost	ct.	Clubs	Won	Lost	ct.
Pittsburg	24	13	65.7	Baltimore	17	17	50.0
Boston	24	14	63.1	New York	18	18	47.1
Phila.	19	13	59.3	Cleveland	16	20	44.1
Brooklyn	19	14	57.6	Chicago	14	18	43.0
Cincinnati	19	15	55.9	St. Louis	13	18	41.9
Cleveland	16	15	51.6	Louisville	4	29	12.1

New England League Standing.

Clubs	Won	Lost	ct.	Clubs	Won	Lost	ct.
Fall River	17	7	70.8	Lowell	9	14	39.1
Lewiston	18	8	63.2	Brockton	6	14	30.0
Dover	14	10	58.3	Portland	3	19	22.1

BICYCLING ABROAD.

Zimmerman Wins a Mile Race and Afterward Painfully Injured.

Dublin, June 8.—A. A. Zimmerman, the American champion bicyclist, in a mile invitation scratch race yesterday participated in by bicyclists of the various races of Ireland, won easily by two wheel lengths in 2m. 47 2-5s.

Later in the afternoon was a race for the 25-mile championship. Of the 20 wheelmen who started three fell in the first yard of the first lap. Zimmerman, at an early stage of the race, came in violent collision with another contestant and was thrown with great violence against the railing which encloses the track. Three of his teeth were crushed out, and he was otherwise injured to such an extent that he was compelled to retire from the race. His injuries, although necessarily painful, are not serious.

The Pope and the Schools.

New York, June 8.—The correspondent of The Catholic News has cabled that the pope reached an important official document to the bishops of the United States. This document deals with the school question and upholds the opinion of the majority of the episcopate.

Richmond Terminal Securities.

Richmond, June 8.—The Consolidated Stock Exchange clearing house has given notice that hereafter only Richmond Terminal trust receipts will be considered a good delivery. The old stock will not be cleared.

SEEKING DIVORCE.

A Wealthy Salem (Mass.) Manufacturer Charges His Wife with Infidelity.

White Plains, N. Y., June 8.—Charles P. Vaughan, a millionaire shoe manufacturer of Salem, Mass., brought suit before Judge Brown and a jury in the supreme court here yesterday for divorce from his wife, Annie Lillian Vaughan. The ground for the suit is infidelity, Vaughan naming William F. Kennedy, an iron merchant of St. Louis, as correspondent. The acts of infidelity charged are alleged to have taken place at Salem at the house of Melvin Woodbury, who is a brother-in-law of Vaughan. Mrs. Vaughan was not present at the trial, but through counsel alleged that her husband had conspired with his brother-in-law to ruin her character. The jury was directed to hand in a sealed verdict.

Mrs. Vaughan was formerly Miss Annie L. Todd of Peabody, Mass. She and Vaughan were married in 1887. They formerly lived at Mount Vernon, where they moved in what is known as the "Chester hill circle."

CLAIM TO BE MERCHANTS.

New England Agent Looking After Chinese in Canada.

Boston, June 8.—Special Agent Smith, who is in charge of the New England office, stationed here, received 40 Chinese identification certificates this week from U. S. Collector Benedict of the district of Vermont. The Chinamen are now in Montreal, and claim to be Boston merchants. There are about 100 Chinamen now in that city awaiting the decision of the special agents in Boston and New York. Special Agent Smith will make an examination of the certificates in a few days, to determine whether or not it is true that the 40 Chinamen are Boston merchants as they claim to be. After his investigation he will immediately report the result to Collector Benedict, and if the papers are correct, the men will be admitted into the country.

The department is taking every means to prevent the Chinamen from entering the country who are not merchants, as a great many have made attempts to enter on spurious papers.

BOSTON MERCHANTS.

Discuss Questions of National Importance and Adopt Resolutions.

Boston, June 8.—The board of directors of the Boston Merchants' association held a monthly meeting at which current national questions were discussed. The meeting was presided over by President Lane and important resolutions were adopted, manifesting the desire of the association for better highways throughout the country. The silver question and the financial condition of the country also shared in the discussions. The board instructed its banking committee to give these matters careful attention and make a report at the next meeting, containing suggestions for the repeal of the Sherman silver act and a safe financial policy.

The secretary was instructed to ask trade organizations throughout the country to co-operate in bringing all possible influence to secure such legislation regarding all financial matters as will inure to the benefit of the whole country.

FOUND TRUE BILLS.

General Electric Company Officials Charged With Conspiracy.

Pittsburg, June 8.—True bills charging conspiracy were found by the grand jury against C. A. Coffin of Boston, president of the General Electric company; W. J. Clarke of Lynn, Mass., manager of the railroad department; Milton H. Hamilton of New York, H. W. Rice of Lynn and H. W. Knight of Boston. All these are officials of the General Electric company.

True bills were also found against Morris W. Mead, superintendent of the bureau of elections in this city, for conspiracy, and against C. E. Christian, John Butler and Frank Carey, former employes of the Westinghouse company, for conspiracy and bribery. It is alleged that the defendants conspired to secure blue prints and tracings showing the design and construction of certain machinery owned by the Westinghouse Electric company.

MURDER AND SUICIDE.

The Bodies of a Man and Woman Found Dead in a Room.

Grand Rapids, Mich., June 8.—Yesterday the dreadful evidences of a murder and suicide were discovered in a room in the lodgings over O'Brien's undertaking establishment in this city. On the bed was found the corpse of William G. Grey, O'Brien's bookkeeper, and on the floor was found that of Miss Dora A. Vetzey of Allendale, Ottawa county.

Grey had evidently been shot while asleep, the body of the woman was partly dressed, and near her was found a bulldog revolver with two empty chambers. Both shots had been fired through the head. Nothing is known of the relations of the two persons. Miss Vetzey was about 22 years of age and Grey was 38.

Four Men Seriously Burned.

Hazleton, Pa., June 8.—An explosion occurred in No. 2 Stockton colliery, operated by Linderman & Skeer, and in which Martin Kosack, Michael Lensko, George Palcko and John Morenzi were horribly burned. The explosion was caused by a naked lamp coming in contact with a body of gas, which had collected in a heading. There are in a critical condition.

A Philanthropist's Will.

Cambridge, Mass., June 8.—The will of Henry H. Glover was offered for probate yesterday in the Middlesex probate court at East Cambridge. The property is estimated at about $400,000. About $100,000 is left to public institutions. His widow, Elizabeth F. Glover, and his daughter, Josephine B. Baker, are named as executors, with every authority to dispose of and manage the estate.

Had Their Cases Continued.

Cambridge, Mass., June 8.—Daniel Haley and Charles E. Dumphrey, the motorman and conductor of the electric car which ran over and killed the 4-year-old child of Terrence F. Quinn in East Cambridge Tuesday evening, were before Judge Almy yesterday in the district court charged with manslaughter. Both pleaded not guilty, and the case was continued to June 13.

Severely Beaten by Italians.

Boston, June 8.—James Murphy, 32 years of age, a resident of Cordaville, was at work at the waterworks at that place yesterday when he became involved in a quarrel with a gang of Italian laborers. He was so severely beaten that it was necessary to remove him to the Massachusetts general hospital, where it was found that he had sustained two severe scalp wounds and a broken arm.

Serious Charges Against a Policeman.

Malden, Mass., June 8.—Mayor Winn and the local police committee will investigate the conduct of Patrolman Goode on the occasion of the attempted safe burglary at Faulkner last Saturday morning. It is claimed that the officer allowed the burglars, two in number, to escape. He has been suspended pending the investigation.

[From Yesterday's Extra Edition.]

SERVANT'S STORY

The following is the evidence of Bridget Sullivan late yesterday afternoon, printed in the Standard's extra edition:

Q. When you returned from your unsuccessful hunt for Dr. Bowen had there been any outcry or any alarm of the neighbors?

A. No sir.

Q. Did you find Dr. Bowen?

A. No sir. When I didn't succeed in finding Dr. Bowen, Lizzie told me to get Mrs. Borden as soon as I could.

Q. Where did you first go to look for Mrs. Borden?

A. I went to Miss Russell's at the corner of Second and Borden streets.

Q. You of course learned that Mrs. Borden was not there?

A. No sir.

Q. How far is it from the first house to which you went to: where you afterwards looked for her?

A. I don't know; it is some ways.

Q. When you were going to Dr. Bowen's did you go rapidly or slowly?

A. I don't know, but I guess I ran.

Q. When you returned how did you enter the house?

A. By the screen door. When I returned I found Mrs. Churchill and Dr. Bowen at the house. Mrs. Churchill and I went into the dining room, and Dr. Bowen went into the sitting room. I heard Lizzie say Mrs. Borden may be at Mrs. Whitehead's. She afterwards said that she had heard Mrs. Borden go upstairs, and asked me to go upstairs and see if I could find her, and I told her that I was not going alone.

Q. Before that had you been upstairs?

A. No sir.

Q. What led you to go up stairs in Mrs. Borden's room?

A. Lizzie wanted me to go up, and Mrs. Churchill went up, and I led the way. Dr. Bowen found the key to Mrs. Borden's room for me.

Q. You went up stairs to Mrs. Borden's room after getting the key from Dr. Bowen?

A. Yes sir.

Q. How did you find the door?

A. It was locked.

Q. What was said or done by any one that you can recall?

A. I went into the dining room, from there to the kitchen and up stairs. When I went up stairs I saw the body of Mrs. Borden lying partly under the bed on the floor.

Q. How far did you go before you discovered the body?

A. I can't tell; I don't remember, but I went not very far around to see it. I was the bed high enough so you could see under it clearly?

A. Yes sir, it was high enough for me to see under it easily.

Q. Was the door of Mrs. Borden's room open or closed?

A. It was closed.

Q. Can you tell how light it was in the room?

A. No sir, I cannot; but it was light enough so I could see.

Q. Do you know whether the shutters were shut or not?

A. No sir; I do not.

Q. Did you stop to make examination of Mrs. Borden's body?

A. No sir; I came right down stairs.

Q. Did Mrs. Churchill go into the room with you?

A. No sir, she did not.

Q. While speaking with Mrs. Bowen the second time you went to the house, did anybody say anything to you?

A. Yes sir, Mr. Miller spoke to me.

Q. Do you recall anything else that Miss Borden said about Mrs. Borden's whereabouts?

A. No sir.

Q. I don't recall clearly what you said Lizzie Borden was doing when you went up stairs?

A. She was ironing.

Q. Up to the time Lizzie Borden told her father about the note and told you, had you heard anything about it from any one else?

A. No sir.

Q. Let me ask you, had any one to your knowledge brought a note or a message of any kind to the house for Mrs. Borden?

A. No sir, no one that I know of.

Q. Have you stated all that was said to Mr. Borden about a note?

A. Yes sir.

Q. Was anything said in your conversation with her father about a sick person?

A. I don't know.

Q. At this time Emma Borden was absent from the house?

A. Yes sir.

Q. Did you show the officers about the house?

A. Yes sir.

Q. Did you go into the front part of the house with any of the officers?

A. No sir, not with any of the officers.

Q. Had you ever seen a hatchet with a broken handle about the place—with a handle broken off close to the hatchet?

A. No sir.

Q. Who did the cutting of the wood about the place?

A. The man from the farm they called Alfred.

Q. Did you do any of the chopping or splitting of the wood?

A. No sir.

Q. On Wednesday did you see Lizzie Borden during the day?

A. I saw her down stairs to break-fast and dinner.

Q. Do you usually tend the bell calls at the front door?

A. Yes sir.

Q. At any time did you find the front door locked as you found it this morning?

A. Yes sir.

Mr. Robinson objected, and the question was excluded.

The court directed a chair be brought for Miss Sullivan, but she expressed a preference to remain standing.

The Cross-examination.

Governor Robinson began the cross-examination with a few explanatory remarks to the witness.

Q. How long had you been in the family of Mr. Borden?

A. Two years and nine months.

Q. Did you ever have any trouble with the family?

A. I never have, sir.

Q. Have they always treated you well?

A. Yes sir.

Q. Did you ever see any conflict between the members of the family?

A. Never in the least.

Q. Never saw any quarreling?

A. Yes sir.

Q. Or at all the time that you were at Mr. Borden's house then you never saw any quarreling?

A. I never did.

Q. Did Miss Lizzie and Miss Emma eat at the table with the family?

A. Not all of the time; sometimes they did; most of the time they did not.

Q. Did they get up as early as their father and mother?

A. No sir.

Q. Were they at the table at dinners?

A. Sometimes they were and sometimes they were not. Sometimes one was at the table and the other not.

Q. Their conversation with Mrs. Borden was pleasant?

A. Yes sir.

Q. Did you hear them talking in the house, weren't there?

A. Yes sir.

Q. Will you tell me again what you had for breakfast that morning?

A. Mutton, johnny cakes, coffee and bananas.

Q. Can you tell me just where Miss Borden did the Tuesday before when she came down stairs?

A. She did what she usually did.

Q. Not what she usually did. I want to know what you remember.

A. I heard none.

Q. Where was Mr. Borden?

A. He had gone out.

Q. When Mrs. Borden was feeling ill didn't Lizzie treat her well?

A. So far as I know. I always heard them talking pleasantly.

BRIDGET SULLIVAN ON THE WITNESS STAND.
[From a Sketch by an Evening Standard Artist.]

Q. Talked with anybody?

A. Yes sir.

Q. Have you told today what you did before?

A. I have told all that I know.

Q. After you went out into the yard to vomit what did you do to the screen door?

A. I hooked it.

Q. Did you not say at the preliminary hearing that you could not tell whether you did or not?

A. I don't know, sir.

Q. You say now that you can positively recollect?

A. I don't know, sir.

Q. You said a few minutes ago that you hooked the door, and now you don't know; isn't that right?

A. I don't know whether you are right or not.

Q. Did you hook the door at that time?

A. I don't know whether I did or did not.

Q. Is Second street a quiet thoroughfare?

A. I never knew of any trouble there.

Q. No, no; I mean is it a quiet street as to passing carriages, etc.

A. There are quite a lot of teams and hacks on it.

Q. Who did Dr. Bowen come to see on Wednesday?

A. Mr. Borden.

Q. Was Miss Lizzie complaining?

A. She was complaining some.

Q. Will you tell us again, please, what time they had dinner on Thursday?

A. It was at the usual hour.

Q. You say there was a key to the side wooden door?

A. Yes, Mrs. Borden had a key to it.

Q. You say you did some work in the diningroom?

A. No sir.

Q. You had nothing to do in the parlor, and nothing to do in the spare room upstairs?

A. No sir, nothing.

Q. Did you take care of Mr. and Mrs. Borden's room?

A. No sir.

Q. And you had nothing at all to do with the front part of the house?

A. No, I seldom went in there.

Q. On Wednesday did you see Lizzie in the house and the door bell rang they attended to the door, and you did not go?

A. Yes sir.

Q. Even the little care of the rooms, such as taking care of the toilet slops in the rooms of the daughters, you had nothing to do with this?

A. I had nothing to do with that.

Q. You could easily get to Mr. and Mrs. Borden's room?

A. Yes, if I had the key.

Q. Did they have more than one key to that room?

A. I do not know.

Q. The key was kept on the mantel of the sitting room when it was not in use?

A. Yes sir.

Q. There is a bell that hangs in Mrs. Borden's room, I suppose you know?

A. Yes sir, I do not.

Q. That is not connected with the front door, is it?

A. No sir.

Q. While you were there was that bell ever in use?

A. All the bell that I ever heard was on the lower floor.

Q. Did anybody occupy the other room on the third floor Wednesday night?

A. No sir.

Q. You say if anybody was careless and unhanded the screen door you could hear it in your room, it was easy enough for anybody to go in quietly and you not hear them, wasn't it?

A. Yes sir.

Q. Now you speak about the time you got up as 6 15 o'clock in the morning. How many clocks were there in the house?

A. There was one in the sitting room, one in the kitchen, one in my bedroom and I think there was one in Mr. Borden's room?

A. No sir, I do not know.

Q. Did you ever see a clock in the parlor?

A. I think there was a clock in the parlor; I am not sure.

Q. There were clocks enough in the house, weren't there?

A. Yes sir.

Q. Did you hear them talking in the house on the day of the murder?

A. Yes sir.

Q. Did Miss Lizzie answer her mother properly?

A. She answered her properly.

Q. When you heard them conversing they were talking calmly were they not?

A. No, no loud talking.

Q. Now, while Mr. Borden was out in the back yard do you know whether the door was hooked or not?

A. No, I do not.

Q. What time did you begin to wash windows?

A. I think it was about half past 9.

Q. Mr. Borden had gone down street.

Q. And until you finished washing the windows just before 11 o'clock that door was unhooked all the time?

A. Yes sir.

Q. You told Lizzie she needn't hook it because you would look out for it, did you?

A. Yes sir.

Q. When you first went out you saw Mrs. Kelly's girl and went over to the fence and talked with her?

A. Yes sir.

Q. The screen door was unlocked all that time, and you had left it so?

A. Yes sir.

Q. Can you tell me any reason why a person could not have walked into that house and you not have seen him?

A. No, I cannot. A person could have gone in.

Q. When you talked with Mrs. Kelly's girl the field was pretty clear, wasn't it? You stood back to the Borden house talking with the Kelly girl over the fence?

A. Yes sir.

Q. You couldn't see as you stood by the front gate or the side gate, could you?

A. I could see the front gate.

Q. You could if you looked, but you were talking with that girl, weren't you?

A. Yes sir, I was.

Q. When Mr. Borden let Mr. Morse out you do not know how that door was left, do you?

A. No sir.

Q. You had nothing to do in the parlor or the hall?

A. No sir, I did not.

Q. You certainly did not go up the front stairs?

A. No sir.

Q. And the last time you saw Mr. Borden before he came in at the front door was when he was going up stairs with his pitcher and his key?

A. Yes sir.

Q. When Mr. Borden went to the barn to get water you had to get it at a faucet under the stairs, didn't you?

A. Yes sir.

Q. Could you see much of the yard while you were in there?

A. Yes, I could see the yard.

Q. But you were not on the watch to look out for people, were you?

A. No sir.

Q. How many pails of water did you get, did you say, something like six or seven?

A. Yes sir.

Q. On the front side of the parlor you say the blinds were closed when you went around there?

A. They were closed in the front part of the house?

Q. And you couldn't see whether anybody was in that room?

A. No sir.

Q. When you walk along on the north side of the house on the walk coming from the street how high is the window seat of the dining room?

A. It is quite high I think.

Q. You cannot see in, can you?

A. No sir.

Q. Could you see a person in the room?

A. I think I could not, unless a person was right up to the window.

Q. You say you went into the kitchen to get a dipper to rinse the window off, and when you went into the kitchen you did not see anyone?

A. No sir, I did not see anyone.

Q. Whether there was anyone in the dining room or sitting room or elsewhere you did not know?

A. No sir, I do not know.

Q. Then when you came in you hooked the door?

A. Yes sir.

Q. From the sitting room into the parlor was closed, wasn't it, all the time?

A. Yes sir.

Q. The door from the hall to the parlor was closed?

A. Yes sir.

Q. Are you very certain you had no occasion to go into that part of the house that morning?

A. Yes sir.

Q. After you let Mr. Borden in you say you heard Miss Lizzie laugh and you say she was up stairs?

A. Yes sir.

Q. You heard the sound of the laugh, that was all?

A. Yes sir.

Q. Then you say you next saw her get out of the front hall?

A. I cannot remember about that.

Q. Either side when Mr. Borden came in?

A. No sir.

Q. You say you remember what he said to her, but that you didn't hear any reply?

A. Yes sir.

Q. You say that you saw Lizzie ironing handkerchiefs?

A. Yes sir.

Q. There was nothing unusual in the fact that she was ironing her own handkerchiefs, was there?

A. No sir; Lizzie always washed and ironed her own handkerchiefs.

Q. You didn't even know anything about the condition of the fire at this time, did you?

A. No sir, I didn't.

Q. Didn't even look into the stove?

A. No sir.

Q. What did Lizzie have for breakfast that morning?

A. A cup of coffee and some cookies.

Q. Didn't stop to see her eat, did you?

A. No sir.

Q. What time did you first see flats on the stove?

A. I don't remember.

Q. You haven't the least idea what Lizzie was doing while you were out, whether she was reading or not?

A. No sir.

Q. When you went up stairs she was ironing?

A. Yes sir.

Q. Did you surely notice when you went up stairs that she was ironing?

A. Yes sir.

Q. Then you went up stairs between three and four minutes of 11, and hadn't heard any signs of trouble about the house?

A. Yes sir.

Q. Then you heard Lizzie calling, "Maggie, come down, father is dead. Some one has killed him."

A. Yes sir.

Q. Then you went over to Dr. Bowen's yet left Miss Lizzie at the bottom of the stairs, and as far as you know the screen door was locked. Is that not so?

A. Yes sir.

Q. You went as fast as you could to Dr. Bowen's, did you not?

A. Yes sir.

Q. Then you came back and was asked to go to Miss Russell's, was you not?

A. Yes sir.

Q. Who did you find at the house when you came back?

A. Dr. Bowen and Mr. Churchill.

Q. Who else then you and Churchill?

A. When I got to the house they were both there. I did not see Mrs. Churchill enter, but I saw Dr. Bowen get out of his carriage.

Q. Where was Miss Lizzie when you came back?

A. She was in the kitchen.

Q. Did you see any blood on her?

A. No sir.

Q. None whatever?

A. I saw none.

Q. And saw no blood on her?

A. None sir.

Q. None on her hands or face?

A. None sir.

Q. Was her hair in order?

A. So far as I could tell.

Q. Did you see anybody come with a note?

A. No sir.

Q. They could have come and gone and you would not know it. Is that not so?

A. Yes sir.

Q. Then you don't know any more about it than if you hadn't been in the house?

A. Yes sir.

Q. Can you tell who you first met after the tragedy?

A. I cannot.

Q. There are a good many things which occurred that day not clear in your mind. Is that not correct?

A. Yes sir.

Q. Did you see anybody on Second street when you went after Dr. Bowen?

A. No, I mean when you first went out?

A. No sir, I saw no one.

Q. How did you go out into the room where Mrs. Borden's body was found?

A. Mrs. Churchill and I crossed the sitting room and then went up stairs.

Q. Had you been in the room before that?

A. No sir.

Q. Where was Miss Lizzie when you went up?

A. In the kitchen.

Q. When she passed through the dining room she had no more chance to see him than you had, had she?

A. No sir.

Q. Now, after getting through washing windows what did you do next?

A. I washed the floor and then went up stairs.

Q. Have you any idea of what time it was when Mr. Borden came into the house?

A. I can't tell, but think it was about 10 30.

Q. You think it was about three or four minutes before 11 when you got up stairs, do you?

A. Yes sir.

Q. Did you see Miss Lizzie down stairs before breakfast time?

A. Yes sir.

Q. Do you remember seeing her later in the day?

A. I don't quite remember.

This closed Mr. Robinson's cross-examination, and Mr. Moody started in taking redirect testimony.

Q. Between breakfast time and dinner on Wednesday did you see her?

A. I did not.

Q. You don't know where she was?

A. No, sir.

Q. As to your present occupation; you understand that you are held now as a government witness, do you not?

A. Yes.

Q. You go and come as you choose, and live in the keeper's family, do you not?

A. Not very long; only a day or two.

Q. Was Mrs. Borden in the habit of saying the blinds were closed when you went around there?

Mr. Robinson—I object.

Mr. Moody—Let me modify my question.

Mr. Robinson—I still object, nevertheless.

Mr. Moody—Then this closes the government's examination of this witness.

It was 4 54 when Dr. Bowen was called, but the court deemed it too late to commence the examination of a new witness.

Court adjourned at 5 o'clock until tomorrow at 9 o'clock.

A crowd of several hundred had gathered around the rear entrance, and a long line of teams was stopped on Court street, filled with persons anxious to catch a glimpse of the prisoner as she came out. Getting a glimpse of the crowd through the screen door, Lizzie refused to gratify them and glided quickly through the open door of the van. She made a request of Deputy Sheriff Kirby that she be driven to the jail with haste.

WEAVING WEB

Of Guilt Around Lizzie Borden.

Prosecution Pushing Their Case Ahead.

Fall River Officers Tell Their Story.

Influence of Today's Crime Felt in Court.

Full Report of Evidence of the Forenoon.

This morning there was not so large a crowd as on other days to be seen surrounding the court house, and that was largely composed of men, at least, five minutes before the opening of the court, and it suggested the mental inquiry if popular interest is not subsiding in the trial of the cause celebre which is now progressing within the walls of the building. The inquiry was settled, however, a moment or two later, when the questioner found himself in the court room, where nearly every available seat was found occupied. The spectators were admitted a little earlier than usual, and so the jam and crowd about the entrance was much lessened. Since yesterday an arrangement has been perfected, which renders it much easier to handle the crowd at the main entrance. A barricade of planks has been raised at the steps, and through this portal but one or two persons can pass at a time, and this makes the duty of the officers much easier. On guard at the entrance were Officers Eldridge and Gendron and Special Officer A. J. Smith.

In the Court Room.

In the court room it was noticeable that the front rows of seats were occupied almost entirely by young women, and on their flushed faces there was an air of triumph as if they were rejoicing that for once the victory in the race for place rested with the young. Nearly every seat within the bar was occupied by members of the bar or other favored mortals, who by reason of influence or more than ordinary assurance, had availed themselves of its privileges. The south jury box was with a single exception filled by women, and the solitary male was relegated to a back corner seat. Lizzie was in her seat nearly ten minutes before the court came in, and passed the time in conversation with one or another of her counsel. Her personal escort, or guard, today was Deputy Sheriff Butman, who performed the offices devolving on him with dignity and ease.

Influence of the Home Tragedy.

There was a subdued air noticed amongst the spectators in the room, as if the shadow of the awful tragedy which hovers over the city had exerted its influence on their minds. The news was whispered from one to another and soon became common property. Once in a while a person inclined to levity would be heard to say in a low tone, "It is hard work to beat New Bedford when she gets waked up," the remark, of course, having reference to paralleling the Fall River tragedies, but as a whole the news of the home tragedy of the morning was received with expressions of horror. Whether Lizzie Borden was informed of the affair could not be determined from her demeanor, which was as calm and unruffled as has been usual for most of the time since the commencement of the trial.

Among the interested spectators inside the bar was Egbert C. Smythe, the Andover theologian, whose doctrine of future probation has created considerable discussion.

Editor Strahan of the Marthas Vineyard Herald was present for quite a while today in court.

When the court came in at 9 o'clock, District Attorney Knowlton was given permission to read a letter from Edward M. Cook of Fall River correcting his testimony given at the trial day before yesterday. He said at the time he was on the stand that he did not think Mrs. Borden had any money on deposit with the Trust company But he now finds that Mrs. Borden had deposited $172.75 with the company, and so stated in the letter.

Assistant Marshal Fleet.

The cross-examination of Assistant Marshal Fleet was resumed this morning by Mr. Robinson.

Q. You recall that yesterday I asked you about your testimony given on a former occasion, before the preliminary hearing when Miss Borden was committed to stand for trial? A. I do.

Q. You remember this occasion? A. I do.

Q. That was an open hearing in the district court, wasn't it? A. Yes sir.

Q. Have you since that time looked over your testimony that you gave at that examination? A. No sir.

Q. I ask you if in that hearing you stated that Miss Lizzie Borden said to you that when her father came in she advised him to lie down on the sofa and assisted him in doing it? A. I did.

Q. You say that you did testify so? A. I do.

Q. And you now testify so? A. Yes sir.

Q. I want you to outline your movements on the day of Aug. 4. Did you arrive at the house before 12 o'clock? A. Yes sir.

Q. And went there alone? A. I went in company with another man.

Q. Was there any officer with you? A. No sir.

Q. I want to know just where you went, not what you did, but where you went at the time you went into the house? A. I went to the front door and tried it.

Q. Did you go to the front door first? A. No, I went to the back door and went in the house, through the back entrance and into the kitchen, from the kitchen to the sitting room, looked in the dining room, went up stairs, looked into the room where Mrs. Borden was dead, from there turned to the door at the right, the door which I afterwards found was the clothes press door, and then went to the door of Miss Lizzie's room.

Q. Was the door open? A. The door was closed.

Q. Was it locked? A. I cannot say whether it was locked or not.

Q. You had your first talk with Lizzie there? A. Yes.

Q. And no officer was present with you then? A. No.

Q. From that room where did you go? A. I went from that room back down stairs. Then I went up to Mr. and Mrs. Borden's room and then into the attic.

Q. Was the door to Mr. and Mrs. Borden's room locked? A. It was.

Q. Who went up stairs with you? A. No one.

Q. Did you find any other doors that you tried? A. I tried the doors in the attic and found them locked.

Q. All of them? A. All but the door to Bridget's room.

Q. You are very certain about Bridget's room that that was not locked? A. I feel very certain about that.

Q. Where then did you go? A. I then came down and went into the cellar.

Q. And all the time were you alone? A. Up to this time I was.

Q. When you went into the cellar whom did you find in the cellar? A. Officers Mullaly and Devine.

Q. Any other officer? A. There might have been; I do not recollect.

Q. Was Officer Dougherty there at that time? A. I cannot say.

Q. You did say so before, did you not? A. When?

Q. At the district court. A. If I said that he was there then I think that was about right.

Q. If you said in the district court that he was there he was there, was he? A. Yes sir.

Q. There were two such hatchets taken from there? A. Yes sir.

Q. Where were the axes found? A. I couldn't say. I think they were taken from the same place.

Q. Two hatchets were found in the same room as the one without a handle? A. Yes sir.

Q. There was no fire in the room? A. No sir.

Q. Was there coal there? A. Yes.

Q. Any ashes there? A. Yes.

Q. In the same room where you found the box? A. Yes.

Q. How many ashes? A. Quite a pile.

Q. In what part of the room were the ashes. Near the chimney where the box was in which you found the hatchet? A. Yes sir.

Q. Were the ashes dry, or had they the appearance of the accumulation of months or days? A. I couldn't say about the months or days, but I should think it was some accumulation.

Q. Were they coal or wood ashes? A. Can't say. Should think they were coal ashes.

Q. Can you say as to whether there were two piles of ashes there? A. I should say there were.

Q. Can you tell the place? A. I should say near the coal bin.

Q. Does the opening of the furnace face the north wall? A. Can't say whether it does or not.

Q. You saw the radiators in the various rooms? A. Can't say I did. I don't think I did.

Q. You say you took one of the hatchets away? A. Yes sir.

Q. The one with the claw on the head? A. Yes sir.

Q. Where did you put it? A. In the room where the boxes and kegs were in the southeast side of the cellar.

Q. That's the corner nearer the barn? A. The room is next to the barn.

Q. The first time you went down stairs no other officer went with you? A. No sir.

Q. Who did you find there? A. Officer Mullaly.

Q. Did you find Officer Harrington there? A. No sir.

Q. Did you move the hatchet that time? A. No sir.

Q. You found this with the handle gone at that time? A. No sir.

Q. Was the barn door unlocked then? A. Yes.

Q. Were there others not officers in the yard? A. Yes, but I can't recall them.

Q. Do you recall Mr. Sawyer? A. Yes.

Q. A man named Manning? A. Yes, he was at the front door.

Q. I mean who were in the yard? A. Mr. Porter of the Globe was there.

Q. Porter and a reporter. A. Yes.

Q. Mr. Stevens? A. Yes.

Q. Did you see Mr. Stevens at that time? A. I'm not positive at what time I saw him.

Q. Did you see Clarkson, the hack driver? A. He was there.

Q. Have you given substantially all to the conclusion of your tour in the barn? A. Yes.

Tell what you did the second time in the house, said counsel.

Witness related a trip he and Officers Minnehan (since dead) and Wilson made to Lizzie's room, to the attic, to the storeroom on the west side of the house and to Bridget's room. Then questions were resumed.

Q. Was there a trunk in the room? A. Yes.

Q. Was it locked? A. Yes.

Q. Did you ask her (Bridget) to unlock it? A. Yes.

Q. Did you take out the contents? A. Yes.

Q. Did you find anything? A. No.

Q. There were other trunks there? A. Yes.

Q. Did you examine them closely? A. Not very.

Q. You didn't stay many minutes? A. No.

Q. Was there clothing in the room? A. Yes.

Q. Did you take it down? A. No.

Q. Then you didn't make a search? A. Yes.

Q. Was there any blood on Bridget's dresses? A. No.

Q. Did you look for it? A. Yes.

Q. How did you look at the dresses? A. Took them down.

Q. Where there any grease spots on them? A. I can't say.

Q. You wouldn't tell the jury there were none? A. No.

Q. You say you didn't make a thorough examination? A. Not very.

Q. How many dresses did she have? A. Who?

Q. Bridget. A. I don't know.

Q. Half a dozen? A. Two or three, I think.

"Now," said counsel, "we will go down stairs."

Q. Did you go into Mr. and Mrs. Borden's room? A. Yes sir.

Q. Tell me what you did in there. A. We went in there and looked around the room.

Q. What did you find? A. We did not find anything.

Q. Did you examine the bed? A. Some.

Q. Tell us what that some was? A. Well, we looked on the bed.

Q. On the top of the bed? A. Yes.

Q. You didn't see anything on top of the bed? A. No.

Q. Is that all that you did? A. That is all.

Q. You three officers were making a search, and all you did on going into the room was to look on top of the bed, was it. A. That is all we did just then.

Q. What other active efforts did you make in the search of that room? A. We looked under the bed.

Q. I suppose you did not find any man there? A. No sir.

Q. Did you find any implements that could murder anybody? A. No sir.

Q. Is that all you did? A. Yes sir.

Q. You looked on the top of the bed and looked under the bed? A. Yes sir, we looked on top of the bed and under the bed.

Q. Did all three of you look? A. I presume we did.

Q. What then did you do? A. We looked around the room.

Q. Was there a bureau in the room? A. I do not recollect.

Q. You do not recollect whether you opened any drawers or not? A. If there was one we did.

Q. Can you tell us whether you did or not? A. I tell you that I cannot recollect whether there was one there or not.

Q. Was there a closet there? A. There was.

Q. Did you go into the closet? A. We did.

Q. What was there in the closet? A. I do not recollect.

Q. Was there some clothes in the closet? A. I'm not sure; think there was a row of dresses on the wall.

Q. Then you went into the little room that opens out where the safe is? A. Yes.

Q. What did you find in there, anything but the safe? A. No sir.

Q. The safe was locked? A. I think it was.

Q. Did you try it? A. I think we did.

Q. Did you look at the row of dresses on the wall? A. We did.

Q. Did Bridget stay up stairs? A. She was somewhere around on that floor.

Q. She had keys and let you into the attic rooms? A. Yes.

Q. She had the key that let you into Mr. and Mrs. Borden's room? A. Yes.

Q. And did she lock the door when she came down? A. Yes.

Q. You say you went down stairs after that; where did you next go? A. Into the cellar.

Q. Now before we stop in the cellar I want to ask you to tell me if you didn't find the doors through the house very generally provided with locks? A. Yes sir.

Q. In all parts of the house? A. Yes sir.

Q. Things were more than usually locked up? A. Yes.

Q. Was there anything extraordinary that Lizzie's door leading into the hall had a lock on it? A. No sir.

Q. Or that the door leading into the guest chamber from her room was locked? A. No sir.

Q. And nothing about the fact that the door leading from her room to her father's room was locked? A. No sir.

Q. And Mr. Borden's door had a lock on it? A. Yes sir.

Q. All the doors then were very generally provided with locks? A. Yes sir.

Q. That was the character of the house, was it? A. It was. It even went up to Bridget's room and touched the rooms in the attic.

Q. Now we will go down cellar please. You three officers went together? A. Yes sir.

Q. Tell us what you found down there, this second time, whom did you see and what? A. Officer Mullaly and Officer Devine and Dr. Dolan.

Q. What were they doing when you got there the second time? A. Looking around the cellar.

Q. Did you see the axes and the hatchets then? A. I did.

Q. Were they doing anything with them? A. No sir, I think they were on the cellar floor.

Q. And there were these four—two axes and two hatchets? (pointing to the hatchets on the table.) A. Yes sir.

Q. Anything there at that time of this character that you saw? A. That was all.

Q. Then what did you do? A. Stayed down there a little while, looked around and talked.

Q. What then did you do? A. I went out into the yard.

Q. What, the second time? A. Yes sir.

Q. To again give directions to the officers? A. No sir, to hear reports from them.

Q. After that did you go into the cellar again? A. I did.

Q. What time? A. I should say about 4 o'clock.

Q. Who went with you the third time? A. I do not recollect that anybody went with me.

Q. Was anybody in the cellar when you went the third time? A. Yes sir.

Q. Who? A. There were officers there, but I cannot remember who the officers were.

Q. Were there so many officers there that you cannot remember? A. I did not say there were many officers in the cellar, but I say that there were so many officers in and about the place on that day that I cannot recollect just who the officers were at that particular time. The witness stopped to think and said, I do recollect, now, though; Officer Mullaly and Officer Harrington were there.

Q. Now what did you do then the third time? A. We looked about the rooms to see if we could find any trace of any other axes.

Q. Did you find any? A. We did not.

Q. Did you make a thorough search then? A. We searched to satisfy ourselves.

Q. Did you find any? A. No sir.

Q. Did you go into the cellar again? A. Yes.

Q. Did you find anything else there? A. Yes.

Q. Which time did you find that something else? A. In the afternoon of the second visit.

Q. Why didn't you tell me this before? A. You didn't ask me.

Q. I didn't ask you? Didn't you understand that I asked you what happened on each visit? A. I didn't understand it so.

Q. This was found in that same middle room, in the same box near the chimney from which you, through Mullaly had taken two others? A. Yes sir.

Q. In with the other tools? A. Yes.

Q. Who took it out of the box? A. I did.

Q. Mullaly was standing by at the time? A. He was there. I don't know that he saw me or not.

Q. The room was an ashy, dusty room? A. There were ashes there, but they were confined to a space of four or five feet.

Q. Wasn't the brickwork and box and things covered with ashes? A. They were.

Q. It was an ashy, old place, wasn't it? A. Perhaps so.

Q. It is nothing strange that everything should be covered with ashes when ashes were dumped there. A. No sir.

Q. Did you see that the other two hatchets were covered with ashes? A. No.

Q. How about the claw-headed hatchet? A. It had apparently been wiped.

Q. Does it appear so now? A. There was a spot on the handle that is not there now.

Q. Was it a large or small spot? A. A good sized one.

Q. Dirt or blood? A. I didn't say.

Q. Blood or paint, can you say? A. It might be blood or paint.

Q. How large? A. It might be half an inch across.

Q. On what side of the handle? A. It was one side of the handle.

Q. How else did it look differently than it does now? A. (Examining it.) It looked wet and damp, bluer than now and the rust is deeper now than then.

Q. This is the same hatchet. You can tell it by some mark? A. Yes, (looking it over carefully and finding a bright scratch,) I think this is the same hatchet.

Mr. Robinson at this point showed the jury the mark of identification.

Q. As you picked up the hatchet did you get the dust on your hands? A. No sir.

Q. How about the handles? A. They were clean.

Q. The other tools in the box? A. They might have been dusty. I didn't notice particularly.

Q. There were no ashes on them? A. No sir.

Q. Did you take out the tools? A. Yes.

Q. Were any dusty? A. There were perhaps.

Q. Was there any dirt on this handle? A. There was.

Q. Was there ash dust on both sides or what appeared to be dust? A. Yes.

Q. It looked as if this old hatchet without a handle had got into the ash pile? A. Yes.

Q. The broken end had ashes on it? A. It was a new break. I don't think there were ashes on it.

Q. Did it look as though the whole had been in the ash pile? A. Yes.

Q. Who has changed it? A. I don't know.

Q. Are there any ashes there now? A. No sir.

Q. This was on the 4th day of August? A. Yes.

Q. As far as you know of your information the broken piece stayed in the head? A. Yes.

Q. You don't know who knocked it out? A. No sir.

Q. You don't see any ashes on the end now? A. No sir; I don't see any.

Q. What did you do with that after bringing it out of the box; did you show it to Mullaly? A. I wouldn't say but I did.

Q. Did he see you put it back into the box? A. I think he did.

Q. You went off and left it in that old ashy box where you found it? A. Yes sir.

Q. You didn't do anything to it? A. No.

Q. You say the claw-headed hatchet looked as if it was wet and had been scraped? A. Yes it looked damp, as if it had been wiped or scraped.

Q. You are willing to swear that there was no sign of blood? A. None.

Q. Nor of scraping? A. No.

Q. Now this morning you swear that there were no ashes on this blade at that time? A. Yes.

Q. What of yesterday? A. I said it was all covered with dust.

Counsel read from the testimony of witness yesterday in which he stated that there seemed to be ashes and inquired, "Did you say that?" A. I might have done so.

Q. I want things right. Were you telling right yesterday? A. I was.

Q. At that time did you observe ashes on the point of the handle where there was a break in the wood? A. There were ashes at the point I thought, but it might have been dust.

Q. Can you tell me why you stated this in two different ways? A. I can't.

Q. Are both true? A. They can't both be.

Q. Will you take your choice as to which is the correct statement? A. It was a new break; there might have been ashes there.

Q. Which one of the statements will you take, or do you desire to make another one? A. I didn't notice any ashes on the break.

Q. Now, will you tell me about the ashes? A. I don't remember about them.

Q. Did you put the hatchet in the box? A. Yes.

Q. When did you next see it? A. In Taunton.

Q. Was it never at the marshal's office? A. Not to my knowledge.

Q. Who had charge of the hatchets? A. Officer Medley.

Q. He is specially detailed to look up proofs in cases? A. Yes.

Q. Did he testify in the preliminary hearing in Fall River? A. I think not.

Q. Was this hatchet and broken piece produced there? A. No.

Q. Did Mr. Medley have it? A. I do not know.

Q. Don't you know who had it? A. I don't know.

Q. Do you know if it was turned over to Mr. Wood? A. I do not.

Q. You looked out for this hatchet with the claw, did you? A. I did.

Q. When you examined this blade with the stub on August 4th you didn't lay it aside, did you? A. No sir.

Q. You put it right back in the box? A. Yes sir.

Q. Did you testify at the preliminary examination? A. Yes sir.

Q. Did you in your testimony at that time say a word about this handleless hatchet? A. No.

Q. Any one tell you not to? A. No sir.

Q. And when asked if you found anything didn't you say, "Nothing"? A. No sir.

Q. Didn't you say you didn't find anything else? A. I said I failed to find anything.

Q. Why did you say so? A. Because I didn't take that away.

Mr. Robinson began to read the testimony of witness at the hearing in Fall River, and came to the point where he stated that he searched the cellar, but failed to find anything; except that on the floor were two hatchets and two axes.

Counsel then asked: "Why did you not tell that court about this hatchet?" A. For no other reason than because I failed to take it away.

Q. Do you know whether you went in the front door or not at the Borden house? A. I don't.

Q. Do you remember any one else doing so? A. Yes.

Q. Who was it? A. Emma Borden and a trunk.

Q. Yes, but that was at night; I mean during the day. A. I don't know of any one.

Q. Did you examine the door? A. Yes; about noon.

Witness was then questioned for the purpose of more definitely fixing the time at which he was notified of the homicides and of his arrival at the Borden house.

Re-direct by Mr. Moody.

Q. When did you examine the front door? A. After I came down stairs the first time.

Q. Now will you state how it was locked? A. It was bolted and locked.

Q. What was there about the claw-hammer hatchet which made you separate it from the others? A. There was a spot upon the blade which looked as though it might be blood. There was also a red spot on the handle that looked like blood.

Q. Did you show it to Medical Examin Dolan at that time? A. I did.

Mr. Robinson—How did you say the front door was locked? A. It was bolted and locked.

Q. Did you find out about the locking by trying the knob, or do you recollect that the bolt was set? A. The spring lock was locked and the bolt was set.

Q. Did you testify about this bolting of the front door at the preliminary hearing? A. I don't know whether I did or not.

Officer Philip Harrington of Fall River was next called to the stand. He was examined by Mr. Moody.

Q. Your name is Philip Harrington, I believe? A. Yes sir.

Q. You are a police officer in Fall River? A. Yes sir.

Q. Do you hold any rank? A. Captain.

Q. What was your position in August last year? A. I was a patrolman.

Q. On the 4th day of August was your attention called to anything on Second street? A. It was sir.

Q. Can you tell me about what time it was when your attention was called to Second street? A. About 12 o'clock.

Q. By whom was it called? A. A young man named Turner.

Q. After that what did you do? A. I immediately took a horse car.

Q. How long by horse car were you from Second street? A. I should judge a little over half a mile.

Q. Do you know what time you got there? A. Between 15 minutes and 20 minutes past 12.

Q. Is that your recollection, or did you consult a time piece? A. That is to the best of my judgment.

Q. When you got there had any crowd collected about the premises? A. Yes sir.

Q. Where did you go first? A. I went in the front gate, walked around the yard in front of the house on the north side, along the north side to the north door.

Q. Whom did you see at the north door? A. Mr. Sawyer.

Q. Did you go into the house? A. Yes sir, I went into the house.

Q. Before going anywhere else? A. Yes sir.

Q. Whom did you see in the house on the ground floor? Did you see Miss Lizzie Borden there? A. No sir.

Q. Did you see any of the ladies there? A. I saw some ladies, but I didn't know who they were.

Q. Where did you go after you first entered the house? A. I went to the door on the west side of the kitchen, and it was closed. I opened it and went into the room called the sitting room.

Q. And you discovered Mr. Borden's body there? A. Yes sir, partially covered with a sheet.

Q. Did you do anything but simply notice the body? A. I raised the sheet from the face.

Q. From the appearance could you recognize the person who was there? A. I could not.

Q. Did you know Mr. Borden? A. Yes sir.

Q. How long had you known him? A. For 25 years.

Q. Can you give any other description of the body? A. The face was cut and covered with blood, the blood had stained the shirt front and part of the clothing.

Q. Did you notice anything with reference to the blood? A. Some of it was very bright.

Q. Can you tell anything with reference to the blood on the face? A. Yes sir, just after I got there a small drop of blood trickled down on the face.

Q. Did you notice the temperature of the body? A. I did not.

Q. Did you notice any one else in the room? A. Not in particular.

Q. Then what did you do? A. I went up stairs, went up about half way. I saw under the bed in the front room the form of a woman lying on the floor.

Q. Then where did you go? A. I went into the room and round to the foot of the bed and saw the woman. There was blood on the dress, on the spread and on the sham nearest to it.

Q. Did you notice the condition of the blood? A. Nothing only that it seemed quite dark.

Q. Then what did you do? A. I turned around and came out.

Q. Did you notice anything? A. The door at the end of the room was ajar. I saw Miss Borden and Miss Russell in there.

Q. What did you do next? A. I stepped in and closed the door.

Q. Did you have any conversation with Miss Borden. A. Yes.

Q. What did she say? A. She said, "I can tell you nothing." I asked her when she last saw her father, and she said, "When he came home from the post office. He had a package in his hand. He sat down and read the paper and I went out into the barn." I asked her if she saw anybody while she was in the barn or heard any noise, as of walking, or any one opening or closing the the screen door? She said, "No, I was up in the loft."

Q. And was there anything else said? A. Yes. I asked if she had any idea of a motive. She said she didn't know of any. I asked her if robbery would have been the cause, she said "No, everything is all right, even to his watch and the ring on his finger."

Q. That was her answer? A. That was her answer. I asked her if she had missed anything else from the house. She said, "No; everything is all right." I asked her if she had any reason to suspect any one. No matter how insignificant it might appear to her, it might have some bearings in the case. She said, "No, I havn't any. A few weeks ago father had some angry words with a man, but about what I don't know." I asked her if she heard it. She said, "No, she was in another room." I asked her if her father had said anything about it. She said, "No." "About three weeks later he came again, and they had some more angry words, when father went away, and he said to the man if he came in town again to call on him, and he might tell him something more definite about the store." I suggested that she might not be in a frame of mind to give a clear statement of the facts, on account of it being so soon after the murder, and perhaps tomorrow might be a better time to talk with her, and that she might give me the name of the man who wanted the store. She answered, "No, I can tell all I know about it now just as well as at any other time."

Q. Without characterizing, can you describe her manner and appearance during this conversation?

Mr. Robinson objected. After considering it a moment, the court admitted the question.

Mr. Moody, however, modified this question.

Q. During any part of this conversation was she in tears? A. No.

Q. Was she sitting or standing during this conversation? A. Standing.

Q. During the interview was there any breaking of the voice? A. No.

Q. Did she say anything about the time she was in the barn? A. Yes; she said she was there about 20 minutes. I asked if she might not be mistaken; that it might be 15 minutes or half an hour? She said no, she was sure.

Q Did you notice the dress she had on at that time? A. Yes; it was a house wrap; light drab, and light brown stripes, shirred in front, with bell skirt. (Witness quite surprised the counsel by his minute description of Miss Borden's dress.)

Q. Then where did you go? A. I went down stairs and into the kitchen.

Q. In the kitchen did you notice anything in relation to the stove? A. Yes; I saw Dr. Bowen with some scraps of note paper in his hand, standing to the west of the door leading to the rear hall. I asked him what they were and he said he guessed they had nothing to do with this case. He started to arrange them in some order, as though to read them, and I noticed in the upper left hand corner of one sheet the word Emma, the rest was written in lead pencil. I asked him again what they were and he said they were from his daughter; then he lifted the lid of the stove and put them in.

Q. Did you notice anything? A. I noticed in the south end of the firebox there was a small fire; I should think a coal fire. Some paper had been burned there before, and it had been charred, but still held a cylindrical form. It was about a foot long, two inches in diameter.

A recess of five minutes was taken at this point, and when the court came in Captain Harrington was on the stand.

Q. Can you tell me about the size of the paper bundle? A. I can't.

Q. What did you do then? A. Called Dr. Dolan.

Q. Have any talk with him? A. I had some talk. He had two cans, and I think three hatchets with him.

Q. What did you do then? A. I stood guard over them.

Q. How long? A. Five to seven minutes.

Q. Did you return to the house again that day? A. Yes, in the afternoon.

Q What did you do then? A. The marshal and I went into the barn. By orders I and others went up and searched the loft. I was just ahead of the marshal. Officers Connors, Riley and Dougherty were in the barn.

Witness testified the same as others about the hay in the loft, it being hot and close there; to seeing a basket on a table up there; and to noticing that the west window apparently had a screen over it; a curtain was at one window and it was raised.

Q. How long was you in the loft? A. Twenty minutes or half an hour.

Q. What did the basket contain? A. I don't know.

Q. Did you bring it away? A. No.

Q. Where did you go then? A. Into the house, to the kitchen, opened the dining room door, went down cellar.

Q. Did you search there? A. Yes.

Q. What did you find? A. With Assistant Marshal Fleet I found in the wash room on the floor two axes and two hatchets.

Q. Take them away? A. No. One hatchet was missing. I think I had seen it in the hands of Dr. Dolan. Later saw a hatchet in another part of the cellar and brought it back to the wash room.

Q. Were any axes or hatchets taken away? A. No.

(Continued on Fourth Page.)

True economy doesn't buy what it doesn't need. Indigestion, Biliousness, Sick-Headache, do not need a dollar's worth of doctor, but a quarter's worth of

Beecham's Pills

(Worth a Guinea a Box.) (Tasteless)

Price 25 cents.

33

INSURANCE.

FIRE & LIGHTNING, TORNADO, PLATE GLASS and ACCIDENT INSURANCE.

No. 48 North Water Street.

Etna Ins. Co. .... Hartford
Hartford Fire Ins. Co. .... Hartford
Connecticut Fire Ins. Co. .... Hartford
Merchants Ins. Co. .... Providence
Equitable F. & M. Ins. Co. .... Providence
Springfield F. & M. Ins. Co. .... Springfield
Ins. Co. of North America .... Philadelphia
Ins. Co. of State of Penn. .... Philadelphia
Fire Association .... Philadelphia
Home Ins. Co. .... New York
Continental Ins. Co. .... New York
German Am. Ins. Co. .... New York
Niagara Fire Ins. Co. .... New York
Williamsburgh City Fire Ins. Co. .... New York
Hanover Fire Ins. Co. .... New York
Phenix Assurance Co. .... London
Guardian Assurance Co. .... London
No. British & Mer. Ins. Co. .... London
Imperial Fire Ins. Co. .... London
Fitchburg Mut. Fire Ins. Co. .... Fitchburg
Dorchester Mut. Fire Ins. Co. .... Neponset
New York Plate Glass Ins. Co. .... New York
U. S. Mutual Accident Asso. .... New York

GEO. N. ALDEN.

(Successor to Tillinghast & Alden.) d&w

SAMUEL H. COOK. FREDERIC A. BROWNELL.

SAMUEL H. COOK & CO., Marine & Fire Insurance

AGENT AND BROKER,

No. 37 North Water Street.

(In National Bank of Commerce Building.) Whaling Risks and their Catchings a Specialty at This Agency.

The following First Class Fire Insurance Companies are represented, viz:

Hingham Mutual Fire Ins. Co. .... Hingham
Phenix Ins. Co. .... Hartford
National Fire Ins. Co. .... Hartford
Phenix Ins. Co. .... New York
Westchester Fire Ins. Co. .... New York
Commerce Ins. Co. .... Albany
Pennsylvania Fire Ins. Co. .... Philadelphia
American Fire Ins. Co. .... Philadelphia
Royal Ins. Co. .... England
Queen Ins. Co. .... London
London Assurance Corp. .... London
Norwich Union F. Ins. Society .... London
Northern Assurance Co. .... London
Providence Washington Ins. Co. .... Providence
Firemen's Fire Ins. Co. .... Boston
The Metropolitan Plate Glass Ins. Co. .... New York
Hartford Steam Boiler Inspection and Ins. Co. .... Hartford

EDWIN EMERY. JOHN H. PEDRO

LAWRENCE GRINNELL & CO.,

Fire and Marine, Life and Plate Glass

Insurance

60 No. Water St., foot of William.

(Over Mechanics' National Bank)

Liverpool & London & Globe Ins. Co. .... Liverpool
American Fire Ins. Co. .... New York
London & Lancashire Ins. Co. .... Liverpool
Commercial Union Assurance Co. .... London
Merchants' Ins. Co .... Newark
Boylston Ins. Co. .... Boston
United States Ins. Co. .... New York
Caledonian Ins. Co. .... Scotland
Hamburg-Bremen Fire Ins. Co. .... Bremen
American Ins. Co. .... Boston
Spring Garden Ins. Co. .... Philadelphia
Lowell Mutual Fire Ins. Co. .... Lowell
Wachusett Mutual Fire Ins. Co. .... Fitchburg
Mutual Life Ins. Co. .... New York
Lloyd's Plate Glass Ins. Co. .... New York

HIRAM VAN CAMPEN. JOHN W. PAUL.

HIRAM VAN CAMPEN & CO., FIRE, LIFE AND ACCIDENT Insurance Agency,

No. 15 North Water Street.

Telephone Call .... 241-2.
(Established A. D. 1852.)

The following First Class Companies are represented:

Sun Fire Office .... London, Eng.
Organized A. D. 1710.
The Reliance Ins. Co. .... Philadelphia
Girard Fire & Marine Ins. Co. "
United Firemen's Ins. Co. "
Granite State Fire Ins. Co., Portsmouth, N.H.
Firemen's Ins. Co. .... Newark, N. J.
Newark Fire Ins Co. .... "
New Jersey Plate Glass Ins. Co. "
First National Fire Ins. Co., Worcester, Mass.
Quincy Mut. Fire Ins. Co. Quincy, Mass.
Holyoke Mut. Fire Ins. Co. Salem, Mass.
Traders' & Mechanics' Ins. Co. Lowell, Mass.
Dorchester Mut. Fire Ins. Co. Boston
Cambridge Mut. Fire Ins. Co. Cambridgeport, Mass.
Standard Life and Accident Ins. Co. .... Detroit, Mich.
(Employes Liability Dept.)
Travellers' Ins. Co., Hartford Life & Accident.

All losses equitably adjusted and promptly paid.

New Bedford, November, 1892.

IVORY S. CORNISH. CLIFTON H. CORNISH

I. S. CORNISH & SON, Life, Fire, Accident and Plate Glass —INSURANCE—

Agents and Brokers. 50 North Second St.

NEW BEDFORD, MASS. tf

C. W. HASKINS

No. 20 PURCHASE STREET,

Has replenished his stock since the holidays, and now offers at very low prices a good variety of Diamond Rings, Fine Jewelry, Gold and Silver Watches, Chains, &c.

His stock of Sterling Silver Spoons, Forks, Fancy Table Ware and Novelties is very extensive; these goods are lower in price than ever before.

18 KARAT WEDDING RINGS A SPECIALTY.

You can save money buying of him your Spectacles and Eye Glasses, fit and quality guaranteed.

Watch, Clock and Jewelry repairing by experienced workmen.

HARDY HITCH, JR.,

Awning, Carpet and Shade Upholsterer,

195 UNION STREET.

(Masonic Building.)

Telephone - - - - 153-12

PROFESSIONAL CARDS.

C. L. SEIP, M. D.
Office and Residence—Cor. County and Union streets. Telephone 127—1.
Office Hours—8 to 10 a.m., 2 to 4 and 7 to 8 p.m.

DR. B. C. HOWLAND,
Physician and Surgeon.
Office and Residence—31 Eighth st., northwest corner of William and Eighth streets.
Office Hours—8 to 9 a. m., 2 to 4 and 7 to 8 p. m.
Telephone 135—1.

J. F. SULLIVAN, M. D,
Physician and Surgeon.
Office and Residence—158 Middle street.
Office Hours—8 to 11 a. m., 2 to 4 and 7 to 3 p. m.
Telephone 244—6.

DR. WILLIAM LILLEY.
Office and Residence—77 Thomas street.
Office Hours—From 8 to 12 a. m., 3 to 8 p. m.
Cancers, Tumors and Female Weaknesses a specialty.

DR. A. F. WYMAN,
Dental Rooms,
13 Purchase Street.
Dinner Hour—1 p. m. to 2 p. m.

A. MARTIN PIERCE, M. D.
Physician and Surgeon.
Office and Residence—26 South Sixth street.
Office Hours—2 to 5 and 7 to 8 p. m.

CHAS. R. HUNT, M. D.,
Physician and Surgeon.
Office and Residence—Cor. Union and Seventh streets.
Office Hours—8 to 9 a. m., 2 to 4 and 7 to 8 p. m.
Telephone 64—3.

E. EVERETT WAITE, M. D.
OFFICE AND RESIDENCE, 17 Seventh, corner Spring Street.
Consulting hours, 1 to 3 and 7 to 8 P. M.
Telephone, 105-3.

AMOS P. WEBBER, M. D.,
Office Hours—2 to 4 and 7 to 8 30 p. m.

WILLIAM H. WEBBER, Dentist,
Office Hours—9 a. m. to 5 p. m.
250 Union st., opp. Opera House. Tel. 251—6.

W. J. NICKERSON, M. D.,
Physician and Surgeon.
Office and Residence—164 Middle street.
Office Hours—8 to 9 a. m., 2 to 4 and 7 to 8 p. m.
Brinkerhoff System for Rectal Diseases.
Telephone No. 233—1.

A. M. BIGELOW, M. D. V.,
Veterinary Surgeon.
Office and Residence cor. Fourth and Walnut Sts., at Mr. Alfred Wilson's.
Telephone 104-13
Office hours until 9 A. M. 1 to 2 and 6 to 7 30 P.M.

Dr. EDWARD PEIRCE.
44 FIFTH STREET,
Physician and Surgeon.
Office Hours 9 A. M. 2 to 4 and 7 to 8 P. M.
Telephone—41-4.

DR. EDW. M. WHITNEY.
Office 31 Fifth street.
Office Hours—From 9 a. m. to 2 p. m.
Telephone 278—6.

JOHN T. BULLARD, M. D.
Office and Residence—446 County street, opposite the Court House.
Office Hours—9 a. m., 2 to 4 and 7 to 8 p. m.
Telephone 331—12.

WM. CLINTON SHEEHY, M. D.
Physician & Surgeon,
Office and Residence, 174 Purchase Street.
Office Hours—Until 8 A. M., 2 to 4 and 7 to 8 P. M. Telephone 285—6.

DR. G. DeN. HOUGH.
Office and Residence—542 County street.
Office Hours—at 2 and at 7 P. M.
Telephone 1—5.

REMOVAL.

WILLIAM G. POTTER, M. D.
Office and Residence removed to No. 8 Fifth street, between Union and Spring sts.
Office Hours—8 to 9 A. M., 2 to 4 and 7 to 8 P. M.
Telephone—151-3.

DR. WILLIAM E. BROWNELL,
Physician and Surgeon.
Office and Residence—271 Union street.
Office Hours—8 a. m., 2 to 4 and 7 to 8 30 p. m.
Telephone 310—4.

DR. VERMYNE.
Office and Residence—No. 2 Orchard street, corner of Arnold street.
Office Hours—10 30 a. m. to 1 p. m., and 2 to 4 p. m.; Sunday, 12 to 1.

DR. E. H. NOBLE,
Physician and Surgeon.
(Formerly Dr. Spencer's Office.) Opposite City Clock. Residence 129 Williams st.
Office hours: 8 to 9 A. M., 1 to 3 and 7 to 9 P. M.
Telephone connection.

J. F. BENNETT DRUMMOND, M. D.
Office—174 Purchase street, Lewis building, Room 2.
Office Hours—9 to 10 a. m.; 2 to 4, 6 to 8 p. m.
Residence—36 South Second street.

J. C. SHAW, M. D.
Office and Residence—Cor. Sixth and School streets.
Office Hours—2 to 4 and 7 to 8 p. m. Sunday, 2 and 7 p. m. Telephone 334-1.

MILTON H. LEONARD, M. D.
Office and Residence .... No. 62 Fifth St.
Office Hours—2 to 4 and 7 to 8 P. M.
Telephone 67—12.

CHAS. A. B. PETERSON, M. D.,
Physician and Surgeon.
Office—74 Purchase street.
Residence—90 Hillman street.
Office Hours—9 a. m., 2 to 4 and 7 to 8 p. m.
Telephone 2—3.

H. H. DEWS, D. V. S.
Veterinary Surgeon.
Office—I. L. Ashley's Stable, No. 20 Fourth St
Office Hours—9 to 10; 2 to 4; 7 to 8.
Telephone, 282—1.

Dr. W. W. MANN,
Dental Parlors, ... 174 Purchase St.
Lewis Building. Rooms 3 and 4.
Office Hours—9 to 12 A. M. and 1 to 5 P. M.

DR. CHAS. D. PRESCOTT.
Office and Residence—Cor. Eighth and William streets.
Office Hours—From 2 to 4 and 7 to 8 p. m.

E. J. WEEKS, D.D. S.
Dental Rooms—74 Purchase street.
Office Hours—9 to 12 m., 2 to 4 p. m.

UNDERTAKERS.

E. T. WILSON, Undertaker & Embalmer,
80 PLEASANT STREET.
(Odd Fellows' Building.)

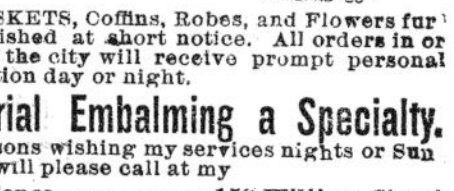

CASKETS, Coffins, Robes, and Flowers furnished at short notice. All orders in or out of the city will receive prompt personal attention day or night.

Arterial Embalming a Specialty.

Persons wishing my services nights or Sundays will please call at my
Residence .... 152 William Street
Telephone number 179—3. d&w

R. G. BENNETT, UNDERTAKER and EMBALMER,
356 Acushnet Avenue,
(Third door South of New Post Office.)

A choice stock of Caskets, Robes and Funeral Supplies. All orders in or out of the city receive prompt attention. Office Telephone, 151—5. Residence Telephone, 346—4. Residence, 47 Chestnut Street, corner Hillman. Orders nights and Sundays received at residence or at Kirby & Hicks' Stable, 60 Elm street, corner Pleasant. d19-d&wtf

WESTON C. VAUGHAN, JR.,
Undertaker and Embalmer,
321 AND 323 PURCHASE STREET.

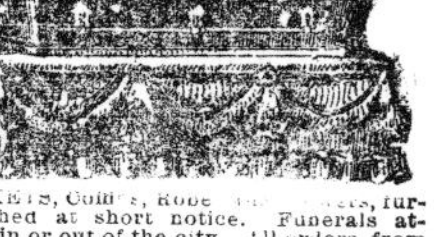

CASKETS, Coffins, Robes ... furnished at short notice. Funerals attended in or out of the city. All orders from neighboring towns by express or otherwise promptly attended to. Telephone connection day or night. Residence, 323 Purchase street. Night bell promptly answered. Telephone number 201—7.

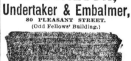

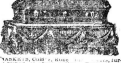

SHOT DOWN.

(Continued from First Page.)

her whose smile was sweeter to him than life itself was what others said.

A few minutes later the assassin himself, half walking and half dragged by Inspector Hathaway, made his way into "The Gazette" on Second street, kept by James F. Moore, and the Standard man followed.

He appeared not only willing, but very anxious, to tell his story, and the Standard man listened as the words fell from the lips of a man, from whose wounds blood was pouring, and whose only regret was, as he often repeated, that he had not died upon the spot with her whom he loved so well. He often stopped to remark that death was sweeter to him than life if the weary round of existence must be dragged out without her.

"Yes," he said in reply to Inspector Hathaway,

"I want to Kill Her! Kill Her! Kill Her!"

"Yes, I couldn't bear to live any longer and know that she loved some one else better than she did me. 'Where did I get the revolver? I got it in a store in

SCENE OF THE MURDER IN THIS CITY.
Southeast Corner of Howland and South Second Streets. Cross Shows Where the Girl Was Killed.

New Bedford, ahd got it not only to kill her but to kill myself, too. I am not a common criminal. I came from a good family. Yes, I told her last Christmas I would kill her. She kept company with me, accepted rings and other things that I gave her. I was her accepted lover, and I loved her better that I did my life. Another fellow gave her his picture. She kept it, looked at it, and I know she liked to look at it. You want to know her name?

It was Mary Francis. Mary was a good girl, but she liked to look at the picture of the other fellow better than she did at mine. No, this is nothing new; way back last Christmas she had the picture of that fellow, and I couldn't bear to think of it. I saw her then, and I asked her to please carry it back. 'Give it to him,' I said; 'please give it to him,' and I pleaded with her to carry it back. She told me she wouldn't, and I was angered. I threatened her then, and told her to give it back or I would kill her. I meant it, I meant it, but I didn't mean to kill her alone; I meant to kill myself, too; I wanted to die with her. I couldn't bear to live and see her smile upon another and frown upon me, and I meant to kill her and kill myself. I saw her again this morning and asked her again if she would carry that picture back. She said she wouldn't. If you won't give back to me the things I gave you I will kill you,' I said to her. She said she wouldn't give them back. I told her I would kill her, and I intended when I did it to kill myself. I am sorry I didn't succeed. I can't tell you when I bought the revolver, but I got it a good while ago, before I thought it would come to this, and when I have thought of carrying out the threat I have often made my mind was on the revolver. It came to me that it would be a good thing to do it with, and I have often thought of it when I have thought of doing this thing and how good it would be for us to die together if we could not live together. She told me she was going to have me arrested, and I couldn't stand that. I made up my mind then and there that it was time that I carried out my threat, and that

BLOODSTAINED SIDEWALK WHERE THE GIRL FELL

the best thing I could do was to kill her now."

At this time the patrol wagon dashed up and Paull was taken bleeding, pale and dejected through the door of the saloon and placed in the wagon and hurried to the station.

While Paull had been talking with Inspector Hathaway his handsome, buxom victim had lain just where she fell on the sidewalk at the southeast corner of Second and Howland streets, surrounded by an excited throng of spectators, which was constantly augmented by newcomers as the news of the terrible tragedy had spread through the city like wildfire.

An intelligent looking Portuguese woman who had witnessed the fearful tragedy gave the reporter the following story:

I was looking out of the window and saw a bright, active and handsome

young Portuguese woman, whom I have known as Mary Francis, walking at a good pace up Second street. Right behind her was the fellow I have heard called John Paull. I thought he accosted her, and an instant later I heard the sharp report of a pistol, and saw blood bleeding to the sidewalk mortally wounded. I can't understand why it was done. It was a thousand times a pity that so bright and handsome a girl should be so cruelly murdered on the street. I saw the man Paull, who had killed her, put the muzzle of the pistol to his own head, pull the trigger, and without any exclamation, stagger, dazed, and, complete- ly unmindful of his surroundings, make an attempt to pass along the street. He went a little ways, faltered, and fell to the ground. After he had fallen he made an attempt to get up, and reached for the pistol, but strong men were around him, and he didn't succeed. I know by his actions that he meant to kill himself, and was sorry that he didn't do it the first time he fired.

James E. Abrams, the fish dealer, who keeps a market on the north side of Howland street, just east of Second street, heard the shot when it was fired and rushed out of his place of business. He had seen the murderer staggering across Second street, and when he fell on the street just at the sandcatcher at the northwest corner of Second and Howland streets, he was at his side. As Paull fell to the ground the pistol with which he had slain the woman whom he claimed to love beyond all else in this world, fell from his grasp. In

an instant he recovered and reached for it, absolutely frenzied and determined to make a second attempt to close his earthly career. Mr. Abrams grabbed the pistol, and then occurred a terrible struggle for the possession of the weapon. Paull said nothing, but from his every action was willing to sacrifice another victim, if necessary, to succeed in his determination to dispatch himself. He fought with all the determination of a tiger at bay, and in his frenzy tore the flesh off the arm of the man who was hindering him from accomplishing his purpose.

While these scenes were being enacted hundreds had rushed to the place. Abrams got possession of the weapon and retained it. The murderer then made a dash to go somewhere, anywhere, to evade the crowd and put an end to an existence that was worse than death.

"Catch the Murderer"

was the word that passed through the crowd quickly, and many made the attempt to detain him.

Thomas Cunniff caught hold of Paull for a moment, and was cast aside by the murderer like a straw in his path.

Philip Scoggle, a young man who was near the scene at the time of the killing, was kicked in the stomach and forced to relinquish his hold upon the frenzied man.

Antone Marshall threw him to the ground, and despite the stream of crimson blood that was flowing from the wound and covering his face and clothing, he made a terrible struggle and got away.

Thomas Connors saw Paull and grasped him as he made the effort to escape. The gathering of the multitude only seemed to aggravate Paull, and he made desperate efforts to break through the crowd, but when he was finally captured and thrown to the ground he accepted the inevitable with good grace and said he wished no one in the crowd any harm; all he wanted to do was to watch his victim die, and be part of his misery. Shortly after Paull was taken into custody by Captain Allen and Inspector Hathaway, and gave the statements printed above.

The Assassin's Story

The murderer and would-be suicide was seen by a Standard man soon after his arrest. He was in a cell at the Central station. The particular cell was one of those provided with a full bed and located in the northeast corner of the lockup. When seen by the Standard man he was being attended by Dr. M. H. Leonard, who had already located the ball. Through the kindness of Chief Douglass an interview was granted and the fellow, after being warned to tell the truth, as his death might come at any moment, told his story.

The name given was Jose Viera Cimento, though his knowledge of English was not sufficient to allow of his telling just how to spell it. The girl's name he could not tell in English, but as near as it could be arrived at it was Mary Conde.

He said he was born in Pico, Western Islands, 25 years ago, and came to this country seven years ago. Three years ago he went back there and remained two years, but returned on the last trip of barkentine Moses B. Tower, about a year ago. He has a sister in Fall River and a brother, Manuel Paull in Dartmouth.

Saramento said he courted Mary in the islands a long time ago, and she came to this country with him on his return. They were not married. After she came here she got too familiar with other Portuguese fellows to suit Saramento, and he expostulated with her. One fellow named Antone in Taunton she exchanged photographs with, and Saramento didn't like it at all. As far back as last Christmas he told her she must do differently and send the picture back or he would shoot her. A week before he had bought a pistol at a store on William street, (probably Selnar Eggers.) Mary didn't pay much attention to his threats, but continued her intimacy with various Portuguese fellows.

Mary worked in the Howland mills and Saramento in another mill, the name and location of which he could not say. He has repeatedly tried to make Mary leave Antone, but she refused to give him any satisfaction. Last night he went to see his cousin Annie Brown on Griffin street, and there he became aware he met Mary, who still refused to give him any promise, but told him that if he must send Antone's picture back to him he would give it to him. Mary didn't pay much attention to his threats, but continued her intimacy with various Portuguese fellows.

He was wholly out of his head when dreadful deed was done, and he does not remember much of what occurred afterward until he reached the hospital, but was unconscious from the instant she was stricken down until the end. Owing to the absence of Medical Examiner Garry de N. Hough, who has gone to the World's fair, Medical Examiner Presbrey of Taunton was summoned and performed an autopsy. He was assisted by Drs. Hayes, Webber and Prescott. At the request of Inspector Parker, O'Neil, the photographer, took three views of the scene. One shows the sandcatcher on the opposite corner where the assassin endeavored to kill himself, and the other two show the blood stained concrete sidewalk from different directions.

The officers made several measurements at the scene of the tragedy. It was found that the first spot of blood is about two inches in width and two feet in length, and seven feet further north where the girl fell is another small pool of blood. This is 15¾ feet from the north end of the fence. Both pools of blood are about two feet from the crowd thrown. The victim survived until she reached the hospital, but was unconscious from the instant she was stricken down until the end.

While Paull was lying on the ground under restraint, before the arrival of the officers, he was accosted by Joseph Frasier, a young Portuguese, who said to him, "What have you done, there is blood all over your head." He replied, "I am only sorry that it didn't go through; I want to die."

Almost at the same minute the patrol wagon put in an appearance the ambulance arrived. The young woman was lifted tenderly into it, while the eyes of many of those standing around were suffused with tears, as it seemed scarcely possible that she would survive the journey to St. Lukes hospital, to which institution she was taken. There was no remorse displayed by the murderer as he gazed through the window of "The Gazette" at the vehicle which was to take his victim to the hospital where her last. He was not unmindful of the seriousness of her condition. He seemed to be glad that she was hurt for this world but terribly dejected as he was told by those in custody of him that he was not seriously wounded and would recover. He was wholly out of his head when dreadful deed was done, and he does not remember much of what occurred afterward until he reached the hospital, but was unconscious from the instant she was stricken down until the end.

in the store to arrest her. Saramento then pulled the revolver from his right hand coat pocket and fired the fatal shot. She fell to the ground. Jose turned the muzzle to his own head and fired as stated above. As he told the tale he expressed regret that he had not succeeded in killing himself. He was warned by the chief to tell the truth as he might die at any moment, whereupon he declared that he hoped he would, and the sooner the better.

Dr. Hayes arrived as Saramento finished his story, and with Dr. Leonard managed to extract the ball. It had entered behind the right ear and glanced on the skull, passing upward. It went only about four inches and lodged beneath the scalp. It was removed without much difficulty, and the wound was dressed. In the opinion of the physicians the wound is not serious.

WEAVING WEB.

(Continued from Third Page.)

Q. Discover anything else? A. No.
Q. Where did you go then? A. Came up stairs and out in the yard. Searched it, and went over the fence and into Chagnon's house; had some talk there and searched the yard. I then went to Dr. Kelly's, to Mrs. Crapo's and to the yard of the Fall River Ice company; searched and spoke to some men. Then went to the corner of Borden and Rodman streets, back to Second street and back to the Borden house.
Q. In all your search did you find any weapon or any sign of blood? A. I did not.

The cross-examination was then begun by Mr. Robinson.
Q. Did you go there more than once in the day? A. Yes sir, I went again in the afternoon.
Q. How long did you stay the first time? A. I cannot say how long.
Q. Give the jury some idea. A. Possibly 20 minutes or half an hour.
Q. And during that time did you have a talk with Lizzie? A. Yes.
Q. How long, did you stay in the afternoon? A. I stayed until close after 6 o'clock.
Q. All your talk with Lizzie was right after 12 o'clock? A. Yes.
Q. And many people were there at that time? A. Yes sir.
Q. Do you recall your asking her at that interview whether she had any suspicions of any of the farm help? A. I do not.
Q. Have you testified in the district court? A. Yes sir.
Q. Do you recall this? (Reading from testimony.) "Then asked her if she had any suspicion of the farm help. That was owing to what I had heard, the reason I asked her. She said, 'No, they are reliable on and have been in our employ for several years.'" Q. Do you recall that? A. Yes sir; I do now.
Q. That is correct as it was at that time? A. Yes sir.
Q. This interview was held between 12 and 1 o'clock? A. Yes sir.
Q. When you met Mr. Fleet about the premises at that time? A. Not at that time, after that I did.
Q. Did you see him before? A. No.
Q. Do you know whether he had been in the room? A. No sir.
Q. Do you know whether any one had? A. No sir.
Q. You advised her not to be interviewed any more that day, did you not? A. Yes sir.
Q. Did she know that you were on the police force? A. I should think so, yes sir.
Q. I was dressed in uniform.
Q. You told her that she had better not be interviewed by anybody any more that day? A. Yes sir.
Q. Do you know whether she was interviewed by Mr. Fleet? A. No sir.
Q. You were then a patrolman? A. I was sir.
Q. And promoted when? A. On the 10th day of February last.
Q. And now captain? A. Yes sir.
Q. Speaking of Mr. Borden as he lay upon the sofa, did he have slippers on? A. No.
Q. What kind of shoes did he have on? A. High laced shoes.
Q. Congress shoes? A. No sir, laced shoes.
Q. Are you certain of that? A. Yes sir.
Q. Have you seen a photograph of the body as he lay there? A. No sir.
Witness was here shown a photograph and after looking at it said to the best of his recollection Mr. Borden did not have on Congress shoes as shown in the picture, but laced shoes, as he had already stated.
Q. Were you much excited at that time? A. I do not think I was.
Q. You had full possession of all your faculties? A. I thought so.
Q. All the time you were there, notwithstanding these horrible sights? A. Yes sir.
Q. Did you ever see worse ones in all your life? A. No sir.
Q. Do you think that you got that those Miss Lizzie had on all right? A. Yes sir.
Q. Did you make any memorandum at that time? A. I think I did sir.
Q. Have you got it with you? A. No sir.
Q. Begin at the beginning and give me all the details; have you seen it since? A. Yes sir; I have.
Q. You would not have remembered it if you had not seen it again? A. I think I would sir.
Q. Did you write the description yourself, or did some woman do it for you? A. I wrote it myself sir.
Q. Now you are going to give me to the very best of your recollection now the dress looked on Thursday? A. I'm going to give it to you from my recollection, with the assistance of the notes I took.
Q. The notes you took on that day? A. I think it was the Sunday following.
Q. Did you see the dress between the 4th and Sunday? A. No sir.
Q. Well, let me hear the description. A. She was dressed in a house dress, pink, with a pink and light brown stripe going over the garment. On the light stripe was a diamond figure. The dress fitted closely to the form and was shirred at the neck.
Q. Was what? A. Shirred, shirred, gathered at the neck. It had a number of bows and on either side was a red ribbon about an inch wide, which was brought around and tied in a bow at the front. It was cut en traine, or what is called bell skirt.
Q. You usually call that kind of a dress a bell skirt, do you? A. The cut of it.
Q. That was your description of it as you spoke in conversation of it? A. Yes sir.
Q. Nobody told you of it? A. No sir.
Q. What was it? A. No sir. I notified the doctor.
Q. Go to the station? A. No, I telephoned.
Q. Who was at the house when you got there, besides Dr. Bowen? A. Bridget Sullivan.
Q. Did you see Lizzie, Miss Russell or Mrs. Churchill? A. No.
Q. When you returned the second day who were you anybody else? A. Yes, Miss Borden in the kitchen, I think.
Q. Was anybody with her? A. Miss Russell.
Q. Have any talk with her? A. No.
Q. What was it? A. I said, "Miss Borden, where were you when this was done?" She said, "I must have been in the barn." I said, "Does a Portuguese work for your father?" She said, "No, Mr. Eddy." I asked her if she heard no outcry or screams. She said she heard no outcry, but a noise. I said, "What kind?" She said a sort of scraping noise.
Q. And no further talk with her at this time.
Q. After your talk with Mr. Mullaly, what did you do? A. I went through the house; up the back stairs, through the attic, into the spare and a couple of other rooms, and then worked our way down stairs and went to the cellar.
Q. What did you find there? A. Near the sink I noticed a pail and towel. Mr. Mullaly with a hatchet.
Q. Any one of these? (Showing several.) A. The smaller one looks like it.
Q. See any others? A. No.
Q. Where did you go there? A. Came up stairs and out in the yard.
Q. Was the west window of the

[Continued on Sixth Page, Second Edition.]

CORREIRO CONFESSES.

Fall River News Authority for the Statement.

The Fall River News has a statement to the effect that Jose Correiro, who has been under arrest for a week or more for the murder of Bertha May Manchester of Fall River in that city on Memorial day has confessed the crime.

A reporter of the Standard called on City Marshal Hilliard of Fall River, while at his dinner in this city today and said:

"Marshal, will you tell me if it is true that Correiro has confessed to the murder of Miss Manchester?"

"Where did you get that information?" asked the reporter.

"It came from Fall River, straight," said the reporter.

"I am only in Fall River at night, and I don't know much of what is going on there," said the marshal, "but I don't believe this story."

"Will you say the story is not true?" asked the reporter.

The marshal avoided a direct answer to the question, and said he wanted to know from a more direct source about the matter than a second-hand story before he believed it.

Capt. Harrington of Fall River was next seen. He was asked whether it was true that a confession has been made by Correiro. He answered, "I have nothing to say on the subject."

"Will you either say it is so or not?" was asked.

"I will not," said he. "You have seen the marshal, and he will not tell. All communications from the police go through his channels."

Fall River reporters in the city stated that the report was current in that city yesterday that Correiro had confessed to the crime the night previous, but they could not get a confirmation of it.

DROWNED.

Dr. Randau of this city was drowned in Long pond today by the capsizing of his boat.

A New Jury.

Rev. Dr. Edward Everett Hale and ex-Governor Ames are on a new jury for the Borden trial. The New York Recorder has asked these two gentlemen and John F. Andrew, George Fred Williams, Colonel A. A. Pope and Mrs. Lucy Stone, all of Massachusetts, and General Thomas L. James, Hon. J. Edward Simmons, Hon. William Sulzer, Hon. De Lancey Nicoll, Mr. Samuel Gompers and T. S. Robertson, all of New York, to say, after the trial, whether the case against Lizzie Borden is "proven" or "not proven," and the twelve have consented.

Briggs & Lawrence are displaying in one of their big show windows today a summer garden tent of wood and inviting construction. The frame is octagonal, with a canopy-shaped top covered with canvas. The best feature is the slat curtains, which may be rolled up or lowered so that the interior will be completely screened. Briggs & Lawrence are the local agents for this seasonable piece of lawn furniture.

FINANCIAL.

SANFORD & KELLEY.

GARDNER T. SANFORD,
CHARLES S. KELLEY, | **Bankers,**

Members Boston Stock Exchange,

47 North Water St., New Bedford.

STOCKS AND BONDS BOUGHT AND SOLD
ON COMMISSION

At the New York and Boston Stock Boards.
Local manufacturing stocks a specialty.
Outside investments of a conservative
character, paying good rates of interest, on
hand and for sale.
Also strictly high class investments for
trust funds.

Auction Sale of Stocks and Bonds
WEDNESDAYS and SATURDAYS, at 10 45 A. M.

ORDERS SOLICITED.

Will be sold at auction SATURDAY, June
10, 1893, at 10 45 a. m., at office—
11 shares Wamsutta Mills.
5 shares N. B. Manufacturing Corp.
10 shares City Manufacturing Corp.
10 shares Potomska Mills.
$500 Wamsutta Club 5s.

T. E. BOWMAN & CO.,

Topeka, Kansas,

NEGOTIATORS OF

Conservative Mortgage Loans in the
Eastern Counties of the State.

WE offer every security and give personal attention to every detail. Parties
desiring absolute safety and satisfied with
six per cent. interest paid promptly by check
in their office or home, are invited to investigate our loans.

SECOND EDITION.

HOME MATTERS.

FATAL FISHING TRIP.

**French Physician Drowned in Long Pond
This Morning.**

A party of eight gentlemen, all Frenchmen, went on a fishing excursion from
this city this morning, and before noon
one of the number, Dr. Rondeau, lay a
corpse in the bottom of Long pond.

The party consisted of Dr. J. E. For-
tin, Dr. Boulanger, Dr. Rondeau, Dr. J.
V. Thuot and his father, Joseph Pinsou,
E. Noel and Gedeon Therien.

The latter gentlemen drove back to
the city, arriving shortly after noon, and
reported that while Drs. Fortin, Boulanger and Rondeau were fishing in the
middle of the pond the boat capsized,
and all the occupants were thrown into
the water. The rest of the party which
were on the bank were attracted by
cries for help and went in a rowboat to
the rescue. Drs. Fortin and Boulanger
had caught hold of the over-turned boat
and were able to keep above water.
Their companion, however, was not
so fortunate. He could not reach the
boat or swim and before the rescuers
had arrived at the spot he had gone
down.

It took some moments to put the men
who were hanging on the boat out of
peril and then there was small hope of
saving Dr. Rondeau.

The accident occurred at 10 45 o'clock,
and the place was in front of Charles
S. Ashley's summer cottage.

Dr. Rondeau was about 28 years old.
He resided at 63 Hicks street, where he
was in practice. He had been in the
city less than three months, and was unmarried.

As soon as the news reached this city
Albert Dunlap, who has been successful in dragging for bodies, was sent with
his apparatus to Long Pond, and a vigorous search for the body of Dr. Rondeau will be made.

PERSONAL.

John McAlpine, wife and child, Christina Shaw, Mrs. George Sneddon and
her two daughters, Mrs. Mary Steen,
Robert McFarlane and wife, all of this
city, sailed from New York Wednesday
on steamer California bound on a trip
through Scotland.

Commander George Laws of Post 146,
G. A. R., Sergeant Charles Gill of Fort
Taber and Chief of Police Douglass will
be among the invited guests at the Sons
of Veterans' banquet next Wednesday
evening.

James E. Dixon, who for over four years
has had charge of the Western Union
branch office at the Parker House, has resigned to accept a position in the employ
of the New York, New Haven & Hartford
Railroad Co., at Providence, R. I.

Rev. B. S. Batcheler has started for a
two weeks' business trip to the World's
fair.

Garry de N. Hough, M. D., and Rufus
A. Soule have gone to the World's 'fair.

THE TEAMERS.

The teamers met again last evening,
and after accepting the resignation of
Henry Shepard as president, elected William Hicks, Jr., in his stead. The idea
of asking for shorter hours was abandoned, and it was voted to ask for $2 a
day. Another meeting will be held on
Saturday evening to hear reports from
the last request.

CONDENSED LOCALS.

The following statistics from the
Banker and Tradesman show the amount
of business transacted at the three regis-
tries in this county, for the week ending
June 8:

	New Bedford.	Fall River.	Taunton.
Conveyances,	69	42	35
Mortgages,	33	25	20
Attachments,	2	3	0
Liens,	0	2	0
	95	72	55

Samuel Nelson, a boy 14 years old,
and another boy of about the same age,
named Desmond, found two cartridges
wrapped in a piece of paper on Hillman
street Wednesday afternoon. The Nelson boy, by means of a stone, exploded
one of the cartridges, and was severely
cut about the face, eyes and breast. He
was taken into a neighboring house and
then to his home, where Dr. Pierce
dressed the wounds.

Commencement week at Howard seminary, West Bridgewater, will be observed as follows: Sunday, June 11,
President E. Benjamin Andrews of
Brown university, Providence, will
preach to the school; Monday evening,
Rev. Charles G. Ames will address the
graduating class; Tuesday evening there
will be an entertainment; Wednesday
the commencement exercises will be held
at 2 p. m., the class exercises at 4 p m.

Members of Engine company No. 1
were called on a still alarm Wednesday
afternoon to the dye house on Purchase
street, just north of Merrimac, where a
considerable quantity of naphtha, used
to clean clothes, had become ignited.
The fire spread quickly about the little
store and a quantity of clothes were
destroyed and the woodwork charred.

The funeral of Peter E. Harrington,
the well-known labor leader, took place
from St. Lawrence church this morning. Rev. Fr. Mahon officiated. There
was a large attendance of friends of
deceased and many elaborate tributes.
The interment was at St. Mary's cemetery.

The neighborhood convention for Friday, June 16th, will be held in the
Baptist church at North Middleboro.

The Citizens Savings bank of Fall
River will pay a dividend of 2¼ per cent.

Good Clean Coal.
Denison Bros. Co.

WEAVING WEB

(Continued from Fourth Page.)

Q. Did you see Miss Borden again?
A. Yes.
Q. Go to her room again? A. I did.
Q. Before you went for the marshal?
A. Yes.
Q. Do you know when she went to
her room? A. I don't know.
Q. When you saw her in her room,
what occurred? A. I went to the door
and when it was opened I and Mullaly
went in. Miss Borden, and I think, Miss
Russell were there.
Q. Have any talk with her (Miss Bor-
den)? A. No, we just glanced around.
Q. Can you give a description of Liz-
zie's dress when she was down in the
kitchen? A. I thought she had on a
light blue dress with a bosom of lace.
Q. Do you remember anything else?
A. I don't.
Q. Did you make a search in the barn
that afternoon? A. Yes sir.
Q. What was the temperature in the
loft of the barn? A. Very warm.
Q. How was the air to breathe? A.
Very bad indeed, it was stifling hot.
Q. Did you notice anything about the
barn, whether dusty or otherwise? A. I
cannot say.
Q. How long did you stay in the barn?
A. I think I stayed in fully an hour.
Q. Did yo: go into the house again on
Thursday after you left the first time—
A. I did not leave until 9 o'clock.
Q. Did you have some part in some
searches on Saturday? A. No sir.
Q. Did you search there at all after
that? A. No sir.
Q. The cross-examination of the witness
elicited nothing new. He said in reply
to questions by Mr. Robinson that it was
11 35 when he arrived at the house. Dr.
Bowen, Bridget Sullivan and Mr. Sawyer
were there. He did not think Dr. Dolan
was there. He did not see Mr. Harrington there until 4 o'clock in the afternoon.
He saw Mr. Medley there about 12
o'clock. He said he went up stairs to the
attic. He was asked if Mr. Borden's room
was not unlocked by the officers, and he
said he could not remember. He did not
make any examination of any dresses. He
did not see the door between Miss Lizzie's
room and Mr. and Mrs. Borden's room
pulled open, if it was pulled open. Mr.
Sawyer was standing inside the screen
door and Mr. Manning outside. He did
not see Officer Allen there. He saw Miss
Russell fanning Miss Borden. He had a
faint recollection that the dress she wore
was light blue. He was quite positive it
was not dark blue. He saw Miss Borden
again Friday morning and thought she
had on the same dress. He did not go in
the cellar with Mr. Fleet. He saw two
men and two hatchets. They were shown
him by the marshal when he was standing near the front gate of the Borden house.
There were persons about the house that
night. Four officers were on duty inside
the yard and others outside.
Q. What kind of a dress did Bridget
have on that day? A. I don't know,
but I think it was brown.
Q. Officer Mullaly was the next witness
called.
Q. Your name is Michael Mullaly?
A. Yes sir.
Q. You are a police officer of Fall
River? A. Yes sir.
Q. How long have you been such?
A. About 15 years.
Q. Your position? A. A patrolman.
Q. Did you go alone? A. No sir, Of-
ficer Hyde went with me.
Q. Who did you see on the premises
on the outside? A. Quite a number on
the outside of the fence.
Q. Was any one on the outside? A.
I didn't notice.
Q. Did you find any one at the door?
A. I didn't notice any one.
Q. It was unlocked at that time was
it? A. Yes sir.
Q. You came in the back door? A. Yes,
the south door.
Q. When you went in who did you
first see? A. Mrs. Churchill and Miss
Borden.
Q. And immediately afterwards did
you see any one else? A. Miss Russell
and Dr. Bowen.
Q. Where? A. On the first floor. Miss
Borden was in the room north of where
her father was.
Q. What did you do? A. I told Mrs.
Churchill I came there for a report.
Q. You talked with Miss Borden?
A. Yes, I told her the marshal sent me
there to find out all that happened. She
told me she was out in the yard, and
came in and found her father dead on
the sofa. I asked her if she knew what
he had on his person, and she said a
watch and chain, a pocketbook with some
money in it, and a ring on his finger. I
asked her if there was a hatchet and an
axe there, and she told me there was.
Q. Did you tell any one? A. Yes, I
told Officer Dougherty and he said the
watch and chain were all right.
Q. Was there any talk about the
pocketbook? A. No.
Q. Any other talk? A. Yes.
Q. What did you do after talking
about the axe? A. I went to the room
in which Mrs. Borden was found. She
laid in a pool of blood.
Q. Did you notice anything about the
blood? A. It looked rather dark.
Q. Did you notice anything about the
blood of Mr. Borden? A. He was pretty well cut up about the head. I didn't
notice much about the blood.
Q. What did you do there? A. I
went to the west end of the house and
up in the attic to Bridget Sullivan's
room. Bridget and Officer Dougherty
went too. We searched the rooms.
Q. Did you find anything or anybody
there? A. We found nothing and nobody.
Q. Where did you go there? A. We
went down cellar. Bridget went too.
And we took two hatchets from a box
in the coal shed. A
Q. How high was the shelf? A. I
don't know. Bridget reached up and
gave them to me.
Q. It was so high then that she had to
reach up? A. Yes.
Q. Could you tell the hatchet if you
saw it again? A. I think so. (Witness was shown hatchets, identified one,
but noticed that the spot was gone from
the claw hatchet.)
Q. What did you do then? A. I took
them to the wash room and put them on
the floor.
Q. And were the axe handles covered
with ashes? A. I should think there
were ashes on them.
Q. Mr. Fleet came there? A. Yes sir.
Q. What was done? A. I called his
attention to the hatchets.
Q. What else did you do? A. I went
upstairs—no, into the yard and into the
barn. I examined everything about the
premises, fences and everything.
Q. Did you notice any blood on the
outside of the house? A. No, I did not.
Q. What did you there? A. I went

---

to the west end of the house into the
room where Mrs. Borden was found.
Q. Was any furniture disturbed there?
A. No.
Q. Well, what did you do next? A.
Came from there and went into the cellar
again.
Q. Did you go alone? A. No, I took
Officer Hyde with me.
Q. Did you find any one there? A. No.
Q. What did you do? A. We searched
around.
Q. Did you find anything? A. Noth-
ing.
Q. What did Mr. Fleet do? A. He
said something to you.
Q. When you saw her in her room,
him? A. I showed him a box.
Q. Did you observe anything that he
did? A. He took a hatchet out of the
box.
Q. Did it look like any of these here?
(Pointing to those on the table.) A. It
looked to me smaller than any there are
here.
Q. What did he do with the hatchet?
A. The handle was broken and he put it
back.
Q. Does this appear to be the hatchet
(passing witness the handleless hatchet)
that Mr. Fleet took from the box? A. It
looks very much like it.
Q. I wish you would describe more
particularly the ashes or dust that was observed on the hatchet.
The witness took the blade, and turning first on one side and then the other
said that the ashes were on both sides of
the hatchet.
Q. Did you observe anything with
reference to the break in the wood? A.
Nothing more than that it was apparently
a fresh break.
At this point, 1 o'clock, the court adjourned for dinner.

MR. ROTCH TALKS.

**Private Sewers He Says Are a Benefit to the
City.**

At a meeting of the finance committee
on Wednesday evening, Samuel C. Hart,
president of the common council, made
some allusion to the construction of sewers, in which the names of Messrs. Rotch
and Drake of the board of public works
were mentioned. Mr. Hart said that
these gentlemen "ordered work without
consulting, and without authority from
the board."

Again at the meeting of the city council last evening, there was more talk on
this subject, during which Lemuel Le
Baron Holmes had full as much to say
as Mr. Hart. The same ground as referred to, only in more detail, was discussed, and this forenoon a Standard reporter called upon Hon. Morgan Rotch,
a member of the board of public works,
to learn from him what all this talk
means about private sewer work.

After calling Mr. Rotch's attention to
the newspaper articles in question, that
gentleman appeared quite indignant at
what had been printed, and seemed perfectly willing to grant an interview on
the subject.

Said he: "In the first place I have
never ordered or asked Mr. Drake to do
any work whatever that had not been
ordered by the board, and I characterize
Mr. Hart's statement before the finance
committee and repeated at the meeting
of the city government last evening as
untrue."

Referring to the Dunbar street sewer
Mr. Rotch said "that it is being built
in accordance with a vote of the board
which was that the superintendent
should be allowed to build private sewers whenever such work did not conflict with public work ordered by the
board."

"Why," said Mr. Rotch, "the building
of such sewers as the one mentioned by
Mr. Hart is a great benefit to the city
because of the fact that it is constructed in accordance with the plans of the
board and does not cost the city a single cent, while at the same time upon
the acceptance of the street the sewer
is turned over to the city, and is from
that time on the property of New Bedford. It is such work as this that Mr.
Holmes says should be stopped. I differ with Mr. Holmes, and I wish we
had more such enterprising citizens who
are far-sighted enough to look after the
city's interest, and for my part I shall
do everything in my power to encourage
such improvements."

In relation to money being taken from
the city treasurer to pay the laborers Mr.
Rotch said "such talk was absurd, as he
could state on authority that the Howland calls were perfectly willing and
ready to pay the bills weekly, or daily
if the board so desires."

Referring to the statement made by
Mr. Hart that Dr. Brownell had been
ordered to get a sewer in Bowditch street
Mr. Rotch said that that matter was
never brought before the board until yesterday afternoon, when every member
present voted to construct this sewer.

EXPENDITURES.

We are indebted to City Auditor George
W. Parker for the following list of expenditures in the various departments of the
city for the week ending June 3:

Cemeteries,	$313.22
Engineering department,	31.50
Fire department:	
Pay rolls and Protecting society,	1,939.63
Salaries,	187.49
Free public library:	
Dog fund,	16.50
Highways and streets:	
Block paving,	72.33
Cinder sidewalks and repairs,	35.88
City ashbin,	79.61
City tool house,	90.39
Cobble paving and repairs,	56.65
Collecting ashes,	93.20
Concrete sidewalks and repairs,	65.03
Crosswalks and repairs,	30.11
Curbing and repairs,	151.43
Filling and grading,	585.71
Flagging and repairs,	67.82
Gutters and repairs,	116.81
Macadam,	386.01
Main office expenses and salaries,	96.69
Miscellaneous,	52.39
Private work and trimming trees,	771.05
Sweeping and cleaning streets,	154.07
Indentals,	156.46
New Bedford & Fairhaven bridge,	21.45
New Bedford water works,	913.75
Parks and squares,	19.83
Police department,	1,540.58
Public schools:	
Pay of teachers,	2,291.57
Janitors, day and evening,	206.15
Office salaries,	104.79
Sewers, general account,	33.45
Sewers, Nye street,	444.35
Pleasant street land damages,	1,925.00
	$13,031.80

COLLAPSED.

[Continued from First Page.]

Connected accounts as to the cause
of the accident are hardly obtainable.
The excavations which were the cause
of the collapse were being made at the
instance of the war department for the
purpose of putting in an electric light
plant.

The insecurity of the building has
been reported. For a long time past
whenever a heavily loaded wagon has
gone by the building seemed to sway.

When the first rumbling warning of
the approaching collapse came the clerks
on the third floor to the number of 80
or 100 rushed to the windows and
jumped for the iron rail of a small building on the northwest side. Many of
them escaped in this way.

George W. Arnold, a colored clerk from
Virginia, was sent at a third story window. He was warned not to jump, but
despite the protestation of numbers of
people he climbed out, and, lowering
himself from the sill, let go. He fell
upon a covering at a lower door and
slid off onto the cornerstone of the alley,
striking on his head and killing him.
His head was mashed to a jelly, and
the cobbles far a distance of several
yards were bespattered with blood.

One of the bravest and most daring
incidents connected with the calamity
was performed by a colored boy 19
years old named Basil Lockwood.

As soon as the floors collapsed and
the dust cleared, realizing the danger of
those at the rear windows who were
wildly climbing out and calling for aid,
he climbed up a large telegraph pole to
the third story and lashed a ladder to
the pole, pulling the other end in the window. By this means 10 or 15 were
aided down the ladder in safety. There
were 47 clerks in the bureau. A portion of them were employed in the addition and in the printing office. These
escaped.

The question of the responsibility is,
of course, already being earnestly discussed. Assistant Secretary Grant was
one of the officials to go to the scene and
get orders by telephone and mounted
messengers to the offices of the department to render all aid.

12 40 P. M.—The following named are
seriously but not fatally hurt and have
been taken to the hospital: J. H.
Thomps, F. J. Smith, N. Gerault and
——Esterling of Fort Scott, Kan. A
colored man named Shadbett of Missouri
is dangerously hurt. Officer Pody of the
police force was also badly injured in the
accident.

The dead bodies of H. S. Wood and
——Jarvis have been taken from the
ruins.

Up to 1 30 p. m. 16 dead bodies had
reached the morgue.

2 p. m.—It will probably be two or
three hours before the mass of debris
can all be cleared away and the exact
number of those who went down in the
crash known. Near the front of the
building still remains a mass of wreckage
which has not been explored.

It is now known that when the crash
came there were in the building 534 persons. A tour of the city hospitals, just
completed, resulted in obtaining the following details of the injured:

Emergency Hospital—Twenty-two injured, four dead; names not taken.

Providence Hospital—E. Eager of Mississippi, head cut and injured internally;
W. S. Gustin, left arm broken.

National Hospital—Clifton Low of
Iowa, scalp injured.

Freedmens Hospital—Dr. J. H. Howard (colored) Maryland, scalp cut and
internal injuries.

Garfield Hospital—J. H. Thomas of
Missouri, arm broken.

REAL ESTATE AND BUILDING.

John B. Whitehead has sold to a syndicate to Albert Cassidy, William Whittaker, William Brown, William J. Thorn-
ley and himself a strip of land, containing
about 80 rods, on Hemlock and Kane
streets.

William Greenwood has sold for James
Powers to Bernard and Jane Gallagher a
lot of land on Ashley street, Dartmouth.

John Crompton has sold to George
Graham a lot of land on Potter street,
containing 39.56 rods.

D. J. Sullivan has sold to Joseph P. St.
Germain a lot of land on Dudley street,
containing about 78.36 rods.

H. A. Leonard has sold for Josiah
Mathews of Dartmouth to Susan K. Snow
of New Bedford a seashore farm, consisting of cottage house, barn and eight acres
of cleared land.

Wenzel Kalos and others have sold to
Mary E. Harrington a lot of land, containing 16.45 rods, with buildings on south
side of Coggeshall street.

A building about 20 feet square has been
erected inside the barge wall on the site
of the Merchants Bank building, which
is occupied as an office by Norcross
Brothers. It is so constructed that it can
be slid out onto the floor of the building
when there is one.

NEW ART STORE.

The new store of Leonard B. Ellis will
be opened with an exhibition of fine
paintings tomorrow night. This is situated just west of the Cummings building, numbered 106 William street. The
store is as well designed as any in the
city for the display of pictures. It is 60
feet long. Two skylights and the long
plate glass windows in front and rear
admit a strong and even light. The walls
are sheathed in natural wood, and,
adorned as they are with artistic
bric-a-brac, the place is a veritable treasure house.

ANNUAL MEETING.

The postponed annual meeting of the
stockholders of the Morse Twist Drill and
Machine company was held at the bank-
ing-house of Sanford & Kelley, 47 North
Water street, this forenoon. Nothing but
routine business was transacted. The following directors were re-elected: Frederick
S. Allen, Thomas N. Stetson, Andrew G.
Pierce, Gilbert Allen, Edward S. Taber.
Gilbert Allen was re-elected clerk of
the corporation.

FAIRHAVEN.

A horse belonging to Amos D. Mitchell
while standing in front of a new house
being built at the corner of Bridge and
Mulberry streets, yesterday morning, took
fright from some cause and ran through
Mulberry and Spring streets, where he
was caught at the foot of Spring street.

Fire was discovered at 5 o'clock this
morning in one of the bathing houses of
the Improvement society. The flames
were confined to the second house from
the office, and was easily extinguished
with buckets of water. It was probably
of incendiary origin, as the window to
the house was found open and an oil can
found in the house.

Edward Smith of Fall River, committed to the house of correction March 6th
for assault and battery, has been released.

MARINE INTELLIGENCE.

Ar at New York 8th, schs R S Dean, Coleman,
Taunton; Clarissa Allen, Tisdale, do; Hast-
ings, Corey, henoc; As R Bryles, Chase,
Newport; G B Reynolds, Raynor, Port Jeffer-
son.
Passed through Hell Gate 8th, schs Han-
nah E Brown, Engle, Trenton for Fall River;
H B Dverty, Taylor, Camden for Fairhaven.
Sld from North Amboy 8th, sch J S Terry,
Terry, New Bedford.
Ar at Philadelphia 8th, schs Maria O Teel,
Johnson, Portland, and old for Badger; D B
Fearing, Clifford, Belfast; King Phillip, Powle,
Salem, and cld to return. Cld 8th C L Mitch-
ell.
Sld from San Francisco 8th, ship Invincible,
Howland, Port Blakely.

Sld from Barbadoes May 17th, bark George
& Mary, Costa, NB, to cruise.

FINANCIAL.

**Stocks Strong and Gossip Bullish—No Wide
Advances but a Gradual Improvement—
Few Stocks Pressing for Sale—Money
Firm—Loans at 6 and 7 Per Cent. This
Noon—Sterling Exchange Weak—Bills
Selling Below $4.87 During the Fore-
noon—General Matters.**

Friday, June 9.

The lower rates for sterling exchange is
one of the most encouraging things at the
moment. To this probably more than anything else is due the small rally in prices, or
rather this is what set the weaker shorts
to covering, thereby raising the level of
prices on money in this country and an increased supply of grain and cotton bills.
At the present quotations gold cannot be
shipped at a profit, and as remarked on
Tuesday there will be no more shipments
of the metal in volume now for some time.
Isolated exports will be made from time to
time, but these have a meaningless import
on the situation. One shipment arranged to
go this week has been canceled, owing to
the decline. Other factors in making up the
stock situation are also improving. The
western bank troubles are drawing to an
end, crop reports are more encouraging and
conservatism is taking precedence, a needful
and obligatory condition in times like the
present. As to railroad earnings the stated
statistics a few days ago showing the remarkable increases all along the line, and
prospects today are that these gains will
be larger in future weeks. The general attention is in fact slowly and legitimately on
the mend.

Money continues steady at 6 per cent. in
the local market. There is no new feature.
Rates for money both on call and on time
are firmer in the Boston money market.
New call loans are not being made at a
lower rate than 7 per cent. and some loans
outstanding at lower prices have been
called in. Time money is less active at 6
point all around. The weakness in sterling
is caused by several reasons, chief among
which are the lower rates for money in the
foreign markets, the reduction in the Bank
of England rate of discount, the higher
prices bar silver and the belief that grain
made at 7 per cent. New York funds sold
at 25 and 30 cents discount.

In New York money on call ranges from
6 to 6 per cent., but loans in certain instances have been made as high as 15 per
cent. Stock houses are large borrowers.
Time money ranges from 5 to 6 per cent.
Commercial paper finds a slow market.
Sterling is decidedly weak, and it is expected that a further decline will take place
daily.

Bonds are fractionally better, but owing
to firmer money it is doubtful if there will
be a marked improvement in prices directly.

The New York opened strong this
morning, St. Paul and Cordage features.
Trading high with more stocks pressing for
sale. Room traders generally bullish. At 11
o'clock the market was firm. Sugar and St.
Paul features. Union, C. B. & Q., St. Paul
and Cordage. Later moved up to 14.

At noon the market weakened somewhat.
More stocks were offered. Philadelphia
sold reading down to 15. Wales, a New York
operator, also sold; New England runs down
to 21½.

The following table shows the fluctuations
of the leading active stocks during the forenoon:

Stock,	Opening,	11 a. m.	12 m.
Atchison,	24¼	24¼	24¼
C. B. & Q.,	87⅞	87⅞	87⅞
Reading,	18¼	16⅞	16⅞
St. Paul,	68½	69½	69½
Sugar,	88⅞	89⅞	89⅝
Cordage,	12¼	14	13¼

At 1 o'clock the market was soft for New
England and Reading. Strong for balances
of the list.
At 2 o'clock the market was strong.
Atchison 25.

The Boston market quiet with prices well
up and the tendency upward. At 11 30 A M
Telephone, which sagged off to 189. At 11
40 o'clock the market was fairly steady except
for Flint preferred, off to 5½ %. Sugar sold as
high as 89¼. A sale of Cleveland & Canton
Equipment 5s sold as reported at 72½.
Sales of bonds in the Boston market have
been heavy today. Up to noon 8 onds to the
amount of $108,000 had been dealt in on the
exchange. Un to noon 6630 shares of stock
had been traded in.
At noon the market was off a fraction.
Atchison 21½, Bell 189, Sugar 89¼, New England 22½ to 22.

The following table shows the fluctuations
of the leading active stocks during the forenoon:

Stock,	Opening,	11 a. m.	12 m.
Atchison,	24¼	24¼	24¼
C. B. & Q.,	87½	87½	87½
Bell Telephone,	190	189	18½
Sugar,	89¼	89⅜	89½
Cordage,	12¾		

At 1 o'clock the market was soft for New
England. Price 15.
12 o'clock Pullman sold at 170. C. B. & Q.
87⅛. Sugar 87 ex-dividend.
C. B. & Northern 5s are quoted at 103 bid
and 101 asked; Steel 5s 70 bid; C. B. & Q.
convertible 5s 109 bid and 109 sales.

Taintor & Holt say: "London prices a
fraction higher, and this will help our market. Gener-l feeling is more cheerful, but
there is no reason why prices should advance much. We do
not look for much change."

Edward Sweet & Co. say: "Early London
prices practically unchanged from our closing. Some hopeiul gossip in connection with
the movement of wheat about and drop in
exchange, but trading is narrow and there is
no indication of a combine of the bulls to put
up prices. Short interest is becoming gradually reduced."

A dispatch at 11 15 says: "Sterling exchange is weak at rates under $4.87."

There were transfers of over the Cleveland
Bank & Terminal railroad during May 1,007
loaded cars despite the fact that business
during two weeks of the month was broken
up by floods and coal miners' strikes.

A dividend of 2 per cent. has been declared on General Electric preferred stock,
payable July 1st to stock of record June
15th.

Directors of Chicago Junction meet next
Monday to declare the usual dividend of $4
per share, payable July 1st. Hereafter dividends on the stock will be at the rate of 2 per cent.
quarterly.

May product of the Franklin mine was
151 tons. The mine was idle twelve days
during the month, owing to the breaking of
a shaft.

STOCK AND BOND MARKETS.

Bid Prices at 12 o'clock Today.
New York, June 9.

GOVERNMENT BONDS	
U. S. 2s,	98½
4s, regi tered,	110¾
4s, coupon,	110½
currency 6s, 1895,	102½

RAILROADS	
Atchison,	24½
Clev., Cin., Col. & St. Louis,	40½
Chicago & Eastern Illinois pref.,	94½
Chesapeake & Ohio,	18½
Delaware & Hudson,	121⅞
Delaware & Lackawanna,	150½
Erie,	17½
Illinois Central,	94
Lake Shore,	124½
Louisville & Nashville,	63½
Manhattan,	125
Michigan Central,	96
Missouri Pacific,	26¾
New York Central,	107¾
New York & New England,	22½
New York & N w England pref.,	84½
Northern Pacific pref.,	100½
Northwestern,	105½
Philadelphia & Reading,	16¾
Rock Island,	77½
St. Paul,	69½
St. Paul & Omaha,	41½
Union Pacific,	18½
Wabash pref.,	16½
MISCELLANEOUS	
Chicago Gas,	66½
National Cordage,	13½
National Cordage pref.,	26½
Pacific Mail,	15½
Silver Certificates,	85
Sugar,	89
Sugar pref.,	99
Silver Certificates,	90
Western Union Telegraph,	82

		BONDS	BOSTON, June 9.
Atchison 4s,			79
Bell Telephone 7s,			46
Chicago, Burlington & Northern 5s,			109
C. B. & Q., Cons. Mort. 7s,			116½
C. B. & Q. 5s,			101
Chicago & West Michigan 5s,			101
Mexican Central 4s,			57
Illinois Steel Co. 5s,			*90

		RAILROADS	
Atchison			24¾
Boston & Albany			210
Boston & Lowell			185
Boston & Maine			163
Boston & Providence			290
Central Mass. pref.			*32
Chicago, Burlington & Quincy			86¾
Chicago Jun. & Un. Stk. Yds			80
Chicago Jun. & Un. Stk. Yds pref.			90
Chicago & West Michigan			29
Cleveland & Canton & Southern			14
Cleveland, Canton & Southern pref.			14
Fitchburg			83
Flint & Pere Marquette pref.			*89
Mexican Central			9
New York & New England			22
New York & New England pref.			64
Old Colony,			183½
Oregon Short Line			13
Pullman Palace Car			168
Union Pacific			29
Wisconsin Central			8
West End			56¾
West End pref.			79

		MINING	
Butte & Boston			4¾
Calumet & Hecla			285
Centennial			6
Franklin			7½
Kearsarge			6½
Montana			21
Osceola			22
Quincy			132
Tamarack			138

		MISCELLANEOUS	
American Bell Telephone			189
Erie Telephone			44½
New England Telephone			*38
Boston Land			5¼
West End Land			21
Topeka Land			1½
Lamson Store Service			17½
Illinois Steel Co.			70
Sugar common			89¼
Sugar pref			99
Gen'l Electric			57¼
Gen'l Electric pref			87½
Westinghouse			23½
Bay State Gas.			9⅝
National Lead			29
*Asked.			

PROVISIONS AND GRAIN.

Chicago, June 9.

	Opening.	
	Wheat.	Pork.	Corn.
July,	45⅜		39¼
September,	48⅝	21.20	39⅞
	Twelve o'clock.		
July,	66⅛		39¼
September,	71⅞	21.60	41½

WEATHER INDICATIONS.

Partly Cloudy.

New York, June 9.—At 8 30 a. m., the
weather was clear, wind southwest; temperature 65. The Herald says for the
Middle States and New England on
Saturday fair to partly cloudy weather
will prevail, with slightly higher
temperature and local rain, followed generally
by falling barometer, to be followed by
colder weather in this section by clearing; and on Friday, fair, slightly cooler weather, preceded by light coast rain north of this
latitude.

GREAT TRAGEDIAN'S FUNERAL.

**Edwin Booth's Remain's Taken to Mt.
Auburn for Interment.**

New York, June 9.—At 10 o'clock this
morning funeral services were performed
over the remains of the late Edwin
Booth at the Little Church Around the
Corner. Bishop Potter officiated, assisted by Dr. Houghton, the rector of the
church, and Dr. Bispham, a friend of
the great actor. The ceremony was simple and the attendance was large. After
the ceremonies carriages were taken to
the Grand Central station, and a special
train took the party to Boston. Interment will be at Mt. Auburn.

COLORED METHODISTS.

New England African M. E. Conference at
Springfield, Mass.

Springfield, June 9.—The annual conference of the African Methodist churches of New England began in this city
yesterday. Bishop Tanner presiding. Conference officers and committees were
elected, but little else of importance was
done. Among the 30 or 40 ministers
present, was Rev. F. T. M. Webster, of
Boston, the presiding elder of the district. The session will continue until
next Monday, when the attendance appointments will be made, including the
settlement of Rev. D. P. Roberts, for the
past four years rector of deeds at
Washington, D. C.

FELL FROM A COACH.

**James Gordon Bennett in a Critical Con-
dition in Paris.**

Paris, June 9.—James Gordon Bennett,
proprietor of the Herald, fell from a
coach on which he was riding last
Wednesday, and was so severely hurt
that medical attendance was at once required. His condition grew worse, and
doctors performed an operation yesterday, with a view of relieving him. The
doctors now declare Mr. Bennett is in a
critical condition.

Sunday Opening of Wor d's Fair.

Chicago, June 9.—The United States
court decided this morning to allow the
World's Columbian exposition an appeal
from the decision granting an injunction
against Sunday opening of the fair. The
time and place of hearing the appeal
will be fixed by Chief Justice Fuller.
Application for a supercedeas, which
would suspend the effect of the injunction
pending a hearing on the appeal,
was refused, leaving yesterday's decision in force. Attorney Walker, representing the exposition directors, moved
in support of the motion. After
hearing Mr. Walker's arguments Judge
Woods announced that the order for injunction was entered in accordance with
the decision of yesterday.

AUCTION SALES.

By STANDISH BOURNE.

(Successor to Geo. A. Bourne & Son,)
Auctioneer, Commission Merchant, Real Estate Dealer and Appraiser.

Cash advances on goods consigned for auction. Ready buyer for personal property of
every description.

Office and Salesrooms 47, 49 and 51 North Second street, near the Post Office.

Carriages, Harnesses, Etc.
On SATURDAY, June 10th, at 10½ o'clock,
at salesrooms, will be sold a variety of new
and second hand carriages, harnesses, etc.
Also a variety of merchandise usually consigned for our Saturday sales.

Mortgagee's Sale.
On SATURDAY, June 10th, at 3 30 o'clock
on the premises, will be sold by order of the
mortgagee houses and lot of about 15 rods on
Rounds street, south of Kempton street. For
legal advertisement see N. B. Evening
Standard of May 13, 22 and 29.

Cottage House and Lot on Purchase Street.
On SATURDAY, June 10th, at 3 o'clock,
on the premises, will be sold the cottage
house together with about 17 rods of land
situated on the west side of Purchase street,
just north of the Common, numbered 527. The
cottage is in first class order, has modern
conveniences, and is ready for the purchaser
to move into. Terms, 10 per cent. at sale,
balance on delivery of deed within 10 days.

Desirable House and Lot.
On MONDAY, June 12th. at 3 o'clock, on
the premises will be sold the 2¾-story
house, together with lot of about 15 rods,
situated on the northeast corner of Acushnet avenue and Madison street. The house
is in excellent order throughout, roof
slated, and ready for the purchaser to move
in without any extra expense. Terms 10
per cent. at sale, balance within 10 days.

For Rent.
A furnished house from June 1st to Oct. 1st.
Location first class.
Also north half of the double house corner
of Orchard and Chnton streets.
A very desirable residence, centrally located, containing all the modern conveniences. Apply to STANDISH BOURNE'S office.

To Let to Our Storage Warerooms.
We constantly have on hand first-class
rooms for the storage of household goods, to
be rented by the month or year.
Goods dry storage room for stoves.

By JOHN B. BAYLIES,

Commission Merchant, Appraiser, and Auctioneer for the sale of Real Estate and every
description of Personal Prop-
erty. Furniture Bought.

131 and 123 Union Street.

H. C. HATHAWAY,

Auctioneer, Real Estate Agent and Appraiser,
Corner Acushnet Ave. and Elm St.

One of the best auction marts in the
State for the sale of horses and carriages.
Keeps constantly on hand carriages of every
description, carriages made to order and repairing is all its branches attended to under
the superintendency of J. R. Forbes. Consignments of every description solicited.
Cash advanced on goods for auction. Personal property of every description bought
at short notice for cash. Negotiable notes
bought and sold.

House and Lot.
On SATURDAY, June 10th, at 3 o'clock p
m., on the premises, will be sold the very desirable house and lot of 10 rods, situated on the
south west corner of West Middle and Emerson streets. Said house is in good repair and
affords a rare opportunity to secure a good
home at your own price, as the owner says
sell. Terms, 10 per cent. at sale, balance delivery of deed.

Administrator's Sale of Real Estate.
By virtue of a license from the Probate
Court will be sold by auction on the premises
on SATURDAY, the 17th day of June instant,
at 3 o'clock p. m., the real estate situate on
Mill street, New Bedford, and numbered
69, bounded and described as follows; on
On the north by other land belonging to the
estate of Mary W. Fales; on the east by land
of Roland T. G. Russell; on the south by land
formerly belonging to the estate of Ez'a W.
Lee, deceased. Contained about eight rods.
Terms. Ten per cent. at sale, balance on
delivery of deed within ten days after.
WENDELL H. COBB, Administrator estate
Mary W. Fales.
June 2d, 1893.

ALFRED WILSON,

Auctioneer and Real Estate Agent.

Room 22, Masonic Bui ding.

Houses and land in all parts of the city
for sale; tenements for rent; rents collected.

House Lots.
The best location in the city for homes.
The land bounded by Union, Court, Tremont
and Ocean streets, has been laid out into lots,
and offers a rare chance to get a home in a
go d neighborhood. Sewers, water, and
prospective electric cars to the new park
makes it the most desirable to be had. Call
at room 21 Robeson building and see plan.
ALFRED WILSON.

HEALEY & JENNEY,

Real Estate Brokers.

Successors to T. F. Healey.

Real estate bought and sold on commission
at lowest rates.
Farms, houses, house lots and strips of
land for sale. Special inducements now
offered for sale on easy terms at lowest
prices.
Any and all parties desiring of buying or
selling will do well to call at our office, which
will be open day and evening.
Office, 555 Purchase St., Cor. Franklin.
T. F. HEALEY. Telephone 28-5. N. H. JENNEY

REAL ESTATE.

FRANCIS W. TAPPAN,

Agent for Purchase, Sale, and Lease of

REAL ESTATE.

Office, 15 North Water St., New Bedford. d&w

FRANK C. SMITH,

BROKER & AUCTIONEER. Office, 47 William St.

M. E. SMITH,

REAL ESTATE BROKER.

Real Estate bought, sold, mortgaged or
auctioned. Facilities unsurpassed. Call at

M. E. SMITH'S,

REAL ESTATE EXCHANGE.

619 Purchase Street. Telephone 16-11.

H. A. LEONARD,

REAL ESTATE AGENT,

126 UNION STREET.

Houses and house lots in all parts of the
city for sale. Three fine residences. Good
bargains. Call and examine tenements to let.

NEW HOUSE—On Morgan st., No. 18
arranged for two families, bath rooms,
hot and cold water, furnace, first-class in
every particular, all ready for occupancy,
unexceptionable neighborhood. A rare opportunity to secure a beautiful home. Enquire of A. J. SOWLE. je3-4t

FOR SALE—Residence of the late Charles
Briggs, 175 Acushnet ave.; cottage house,
10 rooms, steam heat, set bowls, marble mantles, four fireplaces; large barn; laundry, containing set tubs,etc. All buildings in A 1 order,
20 rods land. Apply on premises. my27-12f

FOR SALE.

House and Lot, 86 Walden St.,

Inquire
J. M. WILLIS, 18 Purchase St. my11-tf

VERY DESIRABLE COTTAGE HOUSE—Stable
and about 4 acres land on the Old County
road, north of Acushnet Village. Practically
new buildings, orchard, henery, carriage
house, etc. Will be sold cheap if applied for
at once. May be seen at any time. Keys at
Mrs. Ashley's opposite. Address, J. W. LEON-
ARD, 59 Commercial st., Boston. ap27-tf

HATCH & COMPANY'S

EXPRESS,

No. 5 Ricketson Block, New Bedford,

DAILY,

By Passenger Trains, to all Points
on the Old Colony Railroad and
its Connections.

The Industrial Co-operative Association

Requests the public and members to know that besides the

FULL LINE OF GROCERIES,

THEY CARRY

A Large Assortment of Tin and Woodenware,

INCLUDING

WINDOW BRUSHES AND SCREENS,

For which they would be pleased to take your order.

TELEPHONE 82-2.

mh20-TF56p

WANTS.

MAN TO WORK ON FARM—And take
care of horses; one who can handle a
boat. Apply 84 Allea st., after 2 p m. te9-3t

FACE FLUSHED.

[From Yesterday's Extra Edition.]

The following is the continuation of the testimony of Assistant Marshal Fleet from Thursday's extra edition.

A. At 25 minutes of 12.
Q. Who brought the news?
A. The driver for Mrs. Stone.
Q. What did you do?
A. I put on my coat and hat and went to the Borden house.
Q. What time did you arrive?
A. At 15 minutes to 12.
Q. Who did you first see?
A. Mr. Manning, reporter of the Globe.
Q. Who next?
A. Mr. Medley.
Q. Was he inside or out?
A. Outside.
Q. Where?
A. In the yard, about half way between the fence and door.
Q. Have any words with him?
A. I did.
Q. Where did you then go?
A. In the house.
Q. Who did you then go down stairs?
A. In the kitchen, Mr. Morse and Bridget Sullivan.
Q. Who else was there?
A. I saw Dr. Bowen leaning over the body of Mr. Borden in the sitting room.
Q. Where did you go then?
A. Up stairs to the front bedroom or spare room. I saw Mrs. Borden lying between the bed and dressing case.
Q. Where then did you go?
A. Out and tried the door leading to another room.
Q. Then where?
A. Down stairs to the room where I saw Lizzie sitting on the lounge.
Q. Did you talk to her?
A. Yes.
Q. State what the conversation was?
A. I made known to her who I was, and asked her if she knew anything about how it was done. She said she did not. All she knew was her father got home about quarter to 11 and sat down in the sitting room and took out some papers. She saw he was feeble and went to him and advised and assisted him to lie down on the sofa. She went to the dining room to ironing, and then went to the barn and up in it. I asked her how long she was there. She said about half an hour. I said, "I mean up in the barn." She said about half an hour. When she came down and went in she found her father was killed. I asked what she did when she found what had been done. She said she went to the back stairs and called Maggie. I asked, "Who is Maggie?" She said, "She is our servant girl." She told Maggie to go for Dr. Bowen, and when she came back and said he was not at home, she (Lizzie) told her to go for Miss Russell. I asked, "Who was in the house last night or this morning," Lizzie said, "No one but Mr. Morse, Maggie, father, Mrs. Borden and myself." I asked who Mr. Morse was. She said, "He is my uncle. He came here yesterday and slept upstairs last night." She also said Mr. Morse left the house before 9 o'clock in the morning and did not return till after the murder. I asked her if Bridget Sullivan knew anything about the murder. She said Maggie had gone up stairs before her father laid down and she called her down. I then asked her who could have killed her father and mother. She said, "Not my mother—my stepmother. My

Assistant Marshal Fleet.

mother is dead. I asked her who could have done it. She said it might have been done by a man who called. Miss Russell said, "Tell him all, Lizzie." Lizzie then said about two weeks ago a man came to the front door and talked as if he was angry. I asked her what they were talking about. She said, "Father said, 'I can't let you have the store for that purpose.'"
Q. Was anything said about a note at that time?
A. I think not.
Q. Were any of the officers present at the time of this interview?
A. No sir.
Q. Where did you then go?
A. I went up stairs to Bridget's room and from there I went down stairs to Mrs. Borden's room. I then went back. It was locked, but when I went to Bridget's room the door was unlocked. I then went down into the cellar and found Officer Mullaly there.
Q. Did you make any search of the cellar at that time?
A. I did not personally, but Officer Mullaly had found two hatchets and two axes there.
Q. Where he got them you don't know except by what was told you?
A. No sir.
Q. What did you discover in addition at that time which was of interest?
A. Not anything in the cellar, personally.
Q. What was done with the two axes and the two hatchets?
A. We left them there that day. The largest hatchet had some spots on it that were dark, and upon the handle was some red spots. This one we placed behind some boxes in the cellar adjoining the wash cellar and left it there.
Q. Did you say you put the hatchet there or found it there?
A. Found it there.
Q. You put it there separate and apart from the others?
A. Yes sir.
(The witness was shown two axes and two hatchets, and asked if he identified them as the ones seen in the cellar and he replied that they seemed to be. When asked to designate the one that was placed behind the boxes he designated the larger one.)
Q. You said that you saw red stains on the handle at that time? are they there now?
A. I don't see them.
Q. After separating that hatchet from the others and placing it away, what did you then do?
A. I went up stairs and out of the yard.
Q. At that time did you see Officer Medley?
A. Yes.
Q. Is there a train which leaves Fall River for Providence at 12 30?
A. There is one at 12 29.
Q. Did you have any talk with Officer Medley?
A. Yes, I told him that if he hurried up I thought he could catch that train.
Q. What did he say?
A. All I know is that he went away.
Q. What is the next thing that you did?
A. I took two officers into the dining room; one of them, Officer Minnehan, is now dead.
Q. When you left the house which way did you go out?
A. I went out the front way.
Q. Describe what took place the second time you went to the house.
A. Mr. Morse opened a door about 6 or 8 inches and asked me what was wanted. This was the door of Lizzie's room. He then said, "Lizzie wanted to know if it was absolutely necessary

for me to search that room?" I told them, "Yes," the door was opened and I went in.
Q. What did you do when you got in?
A. I saw Lizzie and told her I had come to make another search. I said to her, "You said this morning that you were up in the barn half an hour. Do you say so now?" She replied that she didn't say half an hour; what she did say was from 20 minutes to half an hour. I then asked her when was the last time she saw her stepmother, and she said it was about 9, and she was in the room where she found her making the bed. Lizzie said that some one had brought a note and she thought that she had gone out, and no one had heard her return. I searched through some parts of the house, and when I came to Lizzie's room, I found the door locked, and Lizzie said that we couldn't go through that way.
Q. Was the bed in the room parallel to the wall?
A. Yes sir.
Q. Did you see anything with reference to the door leading from the guest chamber to Miss Lizzie's room?
A. I saw a door which would lead into Lizzie Borden's room, and on Lizzie Borden's side was a book case, I think.
Q. How was it with reference to the door?
A. It was directly in front of the door or against the door.
Q. Did you notice anything with reference to the fastening of that door?
A. The door was locked.
Q. How and on which side?
A. I am not sure, but I think it was on Lizzie Borden's side.
Q. Did you observe anything else in the guest chamber?
A. I noticed the blood spots on the pillow cases.
Q. After you had completed observation in that room where did you go?
A. I went to the door directly in front of Lizzie's room, the door to the room directly over the stairs.
Q. Is that the door you referred to as having found locked?
A. Yes.
Q. Now go on and say what you did there.
A. Lizzie unlocked the door.
Q. Do you know where she got the key from?
A. She brought it from her room.
Q. How much of an inspection or search did you make in that room?
A. I looked around the floor and on the shelf. We did not search very closely.
Q. Then where did you go?
A. Then I asked how we could get into Mr. Borden's room, and she said we must get the key. Maggie would give me the key, she said.
Q. I went down stairs and saw Maggie; she showed me to the room and unlocked the door.
Q. When you got to that room did you make any inspection of the door which you had seen hooked on Miss Lizzie's side?
A. Yes sir.
Q. What did you discover with reference to the fastening on Mr. and Mrs. Borden's side?
A. I found it to be bolted and locked.
Q. Did you unfasten these locks?
A. I did not.
Q. At any time did you open that passageway yourself?
A. I did not open it.
Q. Now, after you had done that, what did you do?
A. We went up in the attic and searched Bridget's room and the room adjoining and the other rooms at the west end of the attic.
Q. Then what did you do?
A. I came down stairs and went down cellar and saw Dr. Dolan and the officers still there.
Q. What did you do there?
A. I found in what I call the middle cellar on a shelf or jog of an old chimney the head of a hatchet.
Q. What sort of a box was it in which this head of a hatchet was found?
A. Well, it was a box I should say 14 inches long, 7 or 8 wide and 4 or 5 inches deep.
Q. Was there any thing else in the box beside the head of the hatchet?
A. Yes, there were some tools.
Q. Will you tell me what you mean by the middle cellar?
The witness here pointed out on a plan what he meant, and it was shown to the jury.
Q. At the time you found the hatchet was the wood and steel separate?
A. The witness identified the head of the hatchet as one found by him, and also a small piece of wood that fitted into the head of the hatchet. The witness said the piece of wood was in the hatchet when it was found.
Q. Describe everything in respect to the appearance of the hatchet that you can.
A. The hatchet was covered with a heavy dust or ashes.
Q. Describe as well as you can the ashes that was on the hatchet?
A. There were white ashes upon the blade of the hatchet not only upon one side but upon both sides.
Describe further.
A. I should say that upon this hatchet there was dust or ashes, and that the hatchet was covered with the dust or ashes.
Q. Was it fine dust?
A. Mr. Robinson objected, and Mr. Moody asked the witness to describe the dust further.
Q. What did the dust look like?
Judge Mason said the witness may describe it. If he recognized it to be ashes let him say so.
A. It looked like ashes.
Q. Can you tell me how fine or coarse the ashes were?
Q. Did you notice anything with reference to the other tools in the box at that time?
A. Yes sir.

Officer Allen.

Q. Did you notice anything with reference to their condition, whether there was ashes upon them the same as upon this?
A. Yes sir.
Q. How in appearance did it differ from that covering this hatchet?
Mr. Robinson objected to the question.
The witness was allowed to describe it.
A. The dust was finer than on the hatchet.
Q. At that time did you observe anything with reference to the point of breaking of the hatchet.
A. The only thing I recognized at the time was that it was a new hatchet.
Q. What did you do with the hatchet?
A. I put it back in the box.
Q. Where did you go then?
A. I went around the cellar and then went outside.
Q. At any time while you were there did you pay any attention to the door leading from the cellar out into the back yard?
A. I did.
Q. Let me ask you in what condition you found that door at that time? did she wind it. Mr. Borden when he came into the house to lie down on the lounge?
A. I found that the outer door was fastened.
Q. What do you mean by the outer door?
A. The one that leads into the back yard.
Q. Will you swear to that?
A. Yes sir.

Q. By a bolt.
Q. And the bolt was on which side?
A. On the inside.
Q. How long did you stay about the premises, Mr. Fleet, on Thursday?
A. I was there until 6 o'clock. I left, however, in the mean time, going back again.
Q. Will you state what you saw in reference to the blood on the two bodies, beginning first with Mr. Borden.
A. I saw blood on his face and shirt and clothing and on the floor. There was quite a little pool on the floor.
Q. At what time did you make this observation?
A. As soon as I went in I noticed the body, and afterwards I noticed it more closely.
Q. Will you describe the blood about Mr. Borden's head?
A. There was considerable blood under her head, and the blood was dark colored.
Q. Was the color of the blood on Mr. Borden's head?
A. It was more of reddish color.
Q. Now, Mr. Fleet, did you take part in any search on the premises on some day later than Thursday?
A. I did.
Q. When was it?
A. On Saturday.
Q. What time was that?
A. It was just after the funeral.
Q. How long was the search kept up?
A. I cannot say how long.
Q. Upon the Saturday did you go into the clothes closet at the head of the stairs in the front hall?
A. We did.
Q. Did you examine all the dresses that you found there?
A. We did.
Q. Did you see there in that closet or in any other closet in the house or anywhere in the house a dress with marks

of paint on it?
A. No sir.
Q. How carefully were you examining the dresses at that time?
A. Not very.
Q. Did you find anything that looked like blood on any dress?
A. No sir.
Q. Did you assist in another search on Monday after the murder.
A. I did not.
Q. Did you take a hatchet from the box?
A. I did.
Q. Have you had anything to do with custody of the hatchet?
A. With all of them.
Q. Did you go into the barn on Thursday?
A. Yes.
Q. At what time?
A. After 12 o'clock.
Q. How much after?
A. I couldn't say.
Q. Did you go into the loft?
A. Yes.
Q. Any one go with you?
A. Yes.
Q. How long did you stay in the loft?
A. A few minutes.
Q. What was the temperature in there?
A. It was very hot and close.
Q. Did you go there alone?
A. Yes.
Q. What time?
A. It might be 1 or 2 o'clock.
Q. Did others go with you?
A. Yes.
Q. What was the condition of things up there?
A. There were some old boards and rubbish and considerable hay, which filled nearly the north side of the barn.
Q. How was the temperature in the afternoon?
A. It was very hot.
Q. What sort of a day was that generally in Fall River?
A. It was very hot.
Q. How long did you stay in the barn in the afternoon?
A. Long enough to look over the hay.
Q. Did you notice anything in particular about the hay the first time you were in the barn?
A. Nothing, but that it was piled up as it should be.
Q. Did you see anything about a basket or box?
A. Yes.
Q. Did you take it away?
A. No.
Q. Did you notice what was in the box?
A. I noticed iron.
Q. Did you receive any dress, stockings or shoes from any person?
A. No, I think not.
Cross-examined by ex-Governor Robinson.
Q. Did you tell the same story at the hearing at Fall River as you have now?
A. I think about the same. I may have used different words.
Q. Do you think you have testified to more now than then?
A. I may have.
Q. Haven't you?
A. I may have done so.
Q. Do you mean to tell me you haven't?
A. I don't know.
Q. Wasn't your testimony at the district court taken by Miss White?
A. Yes.
Q. Were you given a chance to read it over?
A: No.
Q. Were you furnished a copy of it?
A. No; I have refreshed my memory from notes.
Q. Have you now added to your testimony?
A. I may have.
Q. Do you mean to say you haven't?
A. I think I have.
Q. Haven't you given some names of persons you say were at the Borden house that you didn't give at the district court?
A. I don't think I have given so many.
Q. Will you give some of the names you now say were there?
A. Manning of the Globe, Medley, Sawyer, Allen, Dougherty, Morse, Bridget Sullivan. Some other officers who came after I got there."
Q. Did you give any such statement at the other hearing?
A. I think so.
Q. Have you looked at your notes lately?
A. Yes.
Q. Witness made a statement by leave that he has made no material change in his testimony from that given at Fall River, but said in his direct testimony today he did not give some names he now has.
Q. Did you intend to leave them out?
A. Yes.
Q. Did you see Lizzie Borden when you got into the house?
A. No sir.
Q. Where did you first see Lizzie?
A. In her room up stairs.
Q. You told me that Lizzie said that she asked Mr. Borden when he came into the house to lie down on the lounge?
A. Yes.
Q. Are you testifying just the same as I did before?
A. Yes.
Q. Did you testify about this fact at the other hearing?
A. I think I did.
Q. Will you swear to that?
A. Yes sir.

Q. Did you go out to the barn at this time?
A. No sir, not at that time.
Q. Did she make the remark that Miss Sullivan and Mr. Morse had nothing to do with the murder?
A. Yes, sir.
Q. When did you first go down stairs the day?
A. After I had been into the sitting room, spare bedroom and Lizzie Borden's room.
Q. Do you know how the hook of Lizzie's room came to be pulled out?
A. It wasn't pulled out.
Q. When you got there the door was hooked?
A. Yes, sir.
Q. Did she say anything about a conversation that took place two weeks before?
A. She said a man tried to hire a store from her father. He told her the man that he wouldn't let him have the store for that purpose, and the man seemed to be angry.
Q. Do you remember that she said the man asked for Mr. Borden, "You like money so well I thought you were ready to do anything?"
A. No sir. I remember of her saying nothing of that kind.
Q. Who were at the house at the time of the search?
A. Dr. Bowen, Mrs. Holmes and Lizzie Borden.
Q. What did you look at in the room?
A. The bed. I also looked into Emma's bedroom, but didn't look as closely as I ought to have done.
Q. Didn't look into the bed did you?
A. I did not.
Q. You had liberty to look where you choose, didn't you?
A. Yes sir, but I didn't search as thoroughly as I ought to have done.
Q. What were you looking for?
A. I was looking for an instrument or anything that would give me any light on the matter.
Q. Didn't expect to find the murderer in there did you?
A. No sir.
Q. When you got there no one was doing anything more than to keep a hand on the door, were they?
A. Yes, they held the door open about eight inches. I didn't know but Lizzie was in there sick, they were so private.
Q. Did Lizzie say anything to get through soon or it would make her sick?
A. Yes sir.
Q. You examined the drawers and also the drawers in Emma's room and the beds, didn't you?
A. I searched the rooms, but not carefully.
Q. Did you ask at that time to have the clothes closets opened?
A. Yes sir.
Q. Who let you in at that time?
A. Lizzie Borden.
Q. What was found?
A. Several dresses, 12 or more, hat boxes and other things.
Q. Hung on both sides of the room?
A. I think only on one side.

FINE CARRIAGES

GEO. L. BROWNELL

OFFERS FOR SALE AT HIS
Carriage Manufactory and Repository,
Cor. Acushnet Ave. and Cannon St.,
NEW BEDFORD,............MASS.

A FINE assortment of Carriages, among them Landaus, Coaches, Coupe Victorias, Coupe Rockaways, Extension and Standing Top Family Carryalls, Phaetons, Goddard Box Top Buggies, Open Road and Business Wagons. Also a very large assortment of SECOND-HAND CARRIAGES of all descriptions, which will be sold low.

GILES G. BARKER, Supt.

PUBLIC WORKS.

A Short Session and Considerable Business Transacted.

Mr. Rotch Wants an Explanation from Mr. Hart,

Who Will be Ready At a Meeting to be Held Later,

There was a special meeting of the board of public works this afternoon, when Mayor Brock, President Hart, and Messrs. Rotch and Hathaway were present. Mayor Brock presided.

Bills for the month of May were examined, amounting as follows for the different departments: Highways and streets, $4,625.23; general sewers, $178.23; parks and squares, $7.49; N. B. & F. bridge, $12.76; Myrtle street sewer, $7.81; Myrtle street sewer, No. 1, 14 cents.

The following pay-rolls were read and approved:

For week ending May 20:
Highways and streets	$2,706.92
General sewers	122.89
N. B. & F. bridge	29.11
Parks and squares	21.83
Wamsutta mills village drains,	320.00

For week ending May 27:
Highways and streets	$3643.47
General sewers	62.96
Parks and squares	22.70
N. B. & F. bridge,	21.29

For week ending June 3:
Highways and streets,	$2,886.08
Nye street sewer,	144.35
General sewers,	33.45
N. B. & F. bridge,	21.45
Parks and squares,	19.83
	$3,405.16

Andrew G. Hathaway appeared and asked permission to paint signs on the fence surrounding the basement of the new building in process of construction at the northwest corner of William and Purchase streets. Mr. Hathaway also desired the same privilege for the fence at the northeast corner of Union and Pleasant streets. He said he had an option on the fences, and he wanted to know the sentiment of the board before closing the contract. He said such things were done in other cities.

Mr. Rotch asked at what time the painting would be done, to which Mr. Hathaway said any time to suit the board, and on Mr. Rotch's motion he was relieved from the cost of construction, the rest of the county is burdened with the maintenance. A long legal argument ensued on this point without any definite conclusion.

The application of Herbert E. Blanchard for leave to put up two grates across Coggeshall street at the Bristol mill, ten feet high, caused some discussion. It was thought that they were altogether too low, and on motion of Mr. Hathaway the application was granted provided the grate are placed 14 feet high over the north gutter.

Then came up the question of acceptance of Beech street, north of Kempton street, to Maxfield, and it was decided to give a formal notice of visitation for June 27.

An order was adopted instructing the city land surveyor to define the bounds of Thompson street from Crapo to Bonney street. A hearing was also ordered for June 27th at 4 30 o'clock on the line of this layout.

Mayor Brock brought up the matter of acceptance of Shore street. Placed on the visiting list.

Patrick O'Leary complains that when Dean street was dug out the board took up his fence.

Mr. Drake said that nine-tenths of the fence was in the street.

Mr. O'Leary, it was stated wanted his fence put up, of the matter was laid on the table.

The petition of Dr. Brownell for a sewer in Bowditch street came up, and on motion of Mr. Hart it was voted to recommend that a sewer of suitable size be constructed.

Mr. Hart offered an order asking for an appropriation of $200 to construct a sewer in Thompson street between Crapo and Orchard streets.

But that street hasn't been accepted said Mr. Rotch.

Mr. Hart—I offered it in anticipation of the acceptance of the street.

The order was tabled.

Voted, to request the city council this evening to appropriate $1,071 for a sewer in Bowditch street.

The abatement of sewer assessment made on Rebecca W. Wilcox and Nancy Pickering for construction of a sewer in Beetle and Howard streets was then informally discussed, but no action was taken.

Mayor Brock called the board's attention in very bad shape, and then followed a general discussion on the street work, after which it was decided to visit several locations in need of repair.

Mr. Hart thought it would be well to establish districts and not bob around from one end of the city to the other.

The subject of a sewer in Bullard street again came up and it was decided to request the city government to appropriate $2,200 for such a purpose.

At this point Mr. Rotch took from his pocket a newspaper clipping which Mr. Hart recognized at a glance (it was a report of the proceedings of the finance committee last evening), and as Mr. Rotch started to read it Mr. Hart broke in by saying: "I haven't time to devote to a discussion of that matter now."

But, sir, this is the proper place to have this matter looked into," said Mr. Rotch.

"I agree with you," replied Mr. Hart, "but I haven't time to explain now."

Mr. Rotch. If the board wants to adjourn without an explanation at this time I am agreeable. There are statements in this article, which if made by you are untrue. They concern every member of this board, and if you have made them some explanation is due this board.

Mr. Hart. I will make an explanation at the proper time.

Adjourned to Friday evening.

COGGESHALL STREET BRIDGE.

Afternoon Session of the Hearing in City Hall.

The commissioners appointed to apportion the cost of the Coggeshall street bridge continued their session at 2 o'clock this afternoon in the council chambers.

George A. Briggs was cross-examined by Mr. Gillingham and stated that within a radius of half a mile from the Fairhaven end of the bridge there are 11 houses, and 19 within a radius of a mile. Did not know of any particular enterprise likely to occur near the bridge, though land values have increased materially. Within 10 years about seven houses have been built in the north end of Fairhaven, while 300 or 400 have been built in New Bedford in a similar time. In the opinion of witness as much travel goes by the way of the Coggeshall street bridge today as there did over the New Bedford and Fairhaven bridge in 1860. In opinion of witness the benefits by the building of the bridge did not extend to Fall River, but affected only New Bedford, Fairhaven and Acushnet.

Mr. Grime submitted the original petition of 500 citizens for the bridge. It was finally decided to resume the hearing on next Tuesday at 10 o'clock.

William C. Parker opened his case for Dartmouth.

Luthan T. Davis, chairman of the selectmen, testified that the new bridge is of no use to Dartmouth. A resident of the south part of the town would come into town by way of Dartmouth or Kempton street and then across the old bridge to take a train in Fairhaven or to reach Mattapoisett or Marion, while if he chose to go to the northeast and reach Rochester or Acushnet he would pass up the Chace road and cross at the Head-of-the-River. He would find no occasion to cross the Coggeshall street bridge.

Mr. Parker read a newspaper report of the town meeting, when the town voted to accept the bridge movement.

Selectman Albert S. Sherman of Westport declared that his town is "not in it." The town is willing to pay for what it receives advantages for, but the bridge is of no advantage whatever. The nearest point of the town is 6 1-2 miles from the bridge, and the farthest 18. He had the bridge, call the matter to the attention of the town at its annual town meeting, when an expression of opinion was taken. Only 11 had crossed the bridge for pleasure, three on business and one of those could have saved the toll, and 135 had never been near it.

Daniel T. Devoll opened for Acushnet. Selectman Moses S. Douglass said there are three main roads north and south through the town and from all of them the nearest and the best way into New Bedford is by Lund's Corner and Acushnet avenue. That is invariably the way used. There are only 16 houses, and those farm houses, on the Fairhaven road between Parting Ways and the Coggeshall street bridge. In cross examination Mr. Douglass thought indirectly the bridge has caused the land to be sold at advanced prices. Did not think the enhancement would extend over half a mile from the bridge.

Noah F. Mendall, a selectman, reviewed the situation but did not think the bridge any advantage to the town.

Captain Franklyn Howland has for 20 years lived within three-quarters of a mile from the Fairhaven end of the bridge and in his opinion it has resulted in no advantage to the town of Acushnet. Of the 16 residents between the Fairhaven end of the bridge and Parting Ways, three go by way of Lund's corner, two by the way of the old bridge, one by the new bridge, three own no horses and seven only visit the city occasionally. In his opinion the old bridge is the preferable way of going to New Bedford.

Captain Howland declared that about 5,000 house lots have been laid out in Fairhaven within the vicinity of the bridge, and in his opinion this will preclude the land boom from crossing much into Acushnet. He should prefer to cross the bridge by daylight at any rate, on account of defects resulting from faulty construction.

Mr. Clifford wanted to make a point of this latter bit of testimony, claiming the bridge is faultily constructed and that if New Bedford and Fairhaven are to keep it in repair, their share of the cost of construction should be equally lessened. Messrs. Clifford and Gillingham both stated that they should make this matter an objection to the apportionment of this expense.

Mr. Reed thought the time for this objection has passed, and that just so much as New Bedford and Fairhaven are relieved from the cost of construction, the rest of the county is burdened with the maintenance. A long legal argument ensued on this point without any definite conclusion.

The hearing was closed at 5 15, to be resumed next Tuesday at 10 o'clock.

Officer Wixon.

Knowles & Co.

Now is the time for you to make a call at our store, as we have a full and complete line of warm weather goods.

The largest line of Parasols and Sun Umbrellas to be found in the city.

A bargain in Red and Blue Sun Umbrellas, at $1.75.

Parasols from 89c. to $5.50. Some rare bargains among them. Children's shades 39c. to $1.49.

We have made a cut in Silk Laces, and will sell you all the new and choice effects at 25 per cent. less than you will find them elsewhere.

A splendid line of Cotton Laces from 5 to 45c. per yard.

Our Hosiery Department is full of bargains. An elegant line of fine dropped stitch hose, in blacks, tans, white and almost any color you could wish, at 50c. Also some bargains at 25 and 37 1-2c.

We have secured one case of Ladies' Jersey Vests, worth 12 1-2c., which we shall sell three for 25c. as long as they last.

We are showing the best Ladies' and Gents' 25c. Vest to be found anywhere.

All sizes in Gents' Negligee Shirts, worth from $1.25 to $1.50, for ONE EVEN DOLLAR.

A new and elegant Line of Pampas Cloths, 25 or 30 pieces to select from, at 15c.

Twenty-five new styles of the celebrated Puritan Cloths at 12 1-2c. These goods are selling fast. Come while the selection is good.

A new line of Llama Cloths, just what you want for a summer dress, at 12 1-2c.

A good line of Sateens, fine as silk, at 15c.

Knowles & Co.

UNION and FOURTH STS.

SPECIAL NOTICE.

The demand for the famous "J. H. CUTTER" WHISKIES, (for which we are the sole agents in this city) having become so great, many houses out of the State are sending their travelers in here, with the hope of inducing our trade to buy the "Cutter" whiskies from them, by underselling us, or rather trying to. We therefore beg to say to our friends and the public generally, we will NOT allow ourselves to be undersold by any house dealing in the genuine "J. H. CUTTER" WHISKIES, and we are prepared to protect our trade, not only in QUALITY but in PRICES as well.

Very Respectfully,

BENJAMIN DAWSON,
597 Purchase Street.

Sole agent for New Bedford, Mass., for the famous J. H. Cutter Whiskies. 8p

DRINK
ROXBURY RYE
WHISKEY.
Equaled by few, Excelled by None.
je6-6t8p

MARION.

Among the recent arrivals of summer people are Mrs. Oleys and daughter of Boston, Mr. Wisner and family of Philadelphia, Miss Millicent Sturtevant of Boston, Rev. Mr. Tompkins and family of Chicago, and Mrs. Rebecca Harding Davis and daughter of Philadelphia.

Mrs. Townsend Davis of Buffalo, who has occupied Miss Mary Allen's cottage for several summers, has engaged it for this season, but will be in town only a small part of the summer.

Mrs. Campbell and daughter of Philadelphia will occupy Mrs. Ruth Church's cottage on Main street for a month during the summer.

The following is a list of letters uncalled for at the post office: J. W. Burton, Chas. W. Pierce, Geo. E. Sleeper, Kirby & Hicks, H. Morris, Jr.

Mr. Jacob B. Savory, late in the employ of A. W. Nickerson, has removed his family to North Marion.

Z. W. Kemp has leased his cottage for the season to George B. Chamberlin of Boston.

The new house recently built by Charles B. Blankinship and the tearing down of the porch on the Kelley house are village improvements.

The baseball team at the Tabor Academy expect to play two games in New Bedford Saturday, one with the Y. M. C. A. nine and the other with the New Bedford Blues.

The Tabor academy junior baseball team will play with the South Wareham and Wareham boys on Saturday. The games are called at 9 a. m. and 3 p. m.

Fire in Fall River.

Fall River, June 9.—Two hundred bales of cotton stored in the shed of the Stevens Manufacturing company caught fire last night, causing a damage of about $2,000. The mill is not yet running at its full capacity.

AT THE MUSTER.

City Guards' Tour of Duty on the Tented Field.

South Framingham, June 8.

Last night was very quiet in camp, and lights were extinguished promptly at 11 o'clock. Our boys were quite willing to retire, as it was too wet to do much hazing.

One of the heavyweights who came up in advance of the company met with a slight mishap, so that he appears in citizens' trousers today.

We are having a splendid cool breeze today, and the boys are all willing to drill.

Corporal Gibbs and Privates Duffy, A. E. and J. L. Duffy, W. A. Clarke, S. R. Clarke, J. Crowley and C. Dewhurst are the detail for brigade and regimental guards.

There is a bicycle corps connected with the Sixth regiment consisting of 20 men. They were out this morning going through the intended order drill, and their maneuvers were very interesting.

The following scores were made today at the range:

Serg. Baudoin,	4 4 4 4 3 4 4 4 4 4—39
Sergt. Churchill,	3 0 3 3 0 4 3 0 5 2—23
Corp. Slocum,	3 3 3 5 2 4 5 5 4 5—39
	4 4 5 4 4 4 4 4 4 5—42
Priv. Peck,	4 5 3 4 4 4 4 4 4 3—39
	4 5 5 5 4 3 3 3 4 5—41
Priv. C. H. James,	3 0 5 3 4 4 3 4 4 3—33
Priv. W. E. James,	4 4 4 4 4 4 3 4 3 3—37
Priv. Hall,	4 4 4 4 4 3 4 0 0 4—31
Priv. Mosher,	3 4 4 0 2 3 3 4 4 3—31
Priv. Brownell,	4 3 4 4 0 4 3 4 4 4—34
Priv. Matthews,	4 4 4 2 4 2 3 3 3 2—31
Lieut. Hathaway,	4 2 3 0 4 5 2 3 3 2—28
Corp. Fuller,	5 5 4 4 4 5 5 3 4 4—43
Priv. Tripp,	3 3 2 3 3 2 4 4 3 4—31
Priv. Morse,	0 2 4 0 2 0 4 3 3 0—18
Priv. Hathaway, W. D.,	0 3 0 2 3 3 3 0 2 0—16
Priv. Akin,	3 3 2 4 3—15

Thursday, June 9.

Yesterday was one of the best days we ever had in camp. The weather was just cool enough for all to enjoy it, and the boys were all very anxious to drill. There were only two who were missing, and they were detailed for police duty, which was very distasteful to them.

The governor arrived in camp officially yesterday afternoon, and has been out this morning viewing the guard mounts of the different commands.

The guard mount of the First regiment was an improvement upon yesterday's, but not what the First is capable of.

Major Morgan had command of the regiment on drill this morning and showed skill and a knowledge of drill regulations.

Corporal Fuller of E and Corporal Pope of I had a shooting contest yesterday, which was won by the former, each making a score of 43, but Fuller outranked his opponent.

Corporal Anthony and Privates Gifford and McConvill were detailed on heavy gun drill.

One member of the company was ordered by Major Morgan to appear at his quarters. After quizzing the private about 15 or 20 minutes he discovered a mistake—that is—the private who appeared before him had not been recommended for promotion, but another one, commonly called Lance, Corporal Rogers, who is now junior corporal of the company.

Instead of leaving the headquarters' tents arranged as in former years a new form has been adopted. This is caused by the new regulation. H. S. S.

NANTUCKET.

A special town meeting was held in the selectmen's room evening of 7th. A. H. Gardner, Esq., was chosen moderator. A jury list prepared by the selectmen was accepted, and a by-law prohibiting the pasturing of cattle upon any street or way within the limits of the town was adopted after considerable discussion.

Mr. Tibbets of Dover, N. H., has been in Nantucket for several days looking up data for the genealogy of the Hussey family. He finds abundant material for his work in Obed Macy's diary, now in the possession of his grandson, Mr. Philip Macy, and in the old public records. It was a source of regret to him, as it will be to most Nantucket people, to learn that the entire records of the Society of Friends, covering about two centuries, have been taken from the island because there was no surviving Friend in Nantucket to properly care for them. The Friends' records always supplemented town history, and contained much material nowhere else recorded.

The Methodist church organ is undergoing a change of location from the rear of the gallery to a prominent place behind the pulpit in accord with modern church construction. Rev. Mr. Kellogg, the pastor, is doing the work himself without expense to the church. The pulpit and altar rail will be changed and improved, the latter being in a semicircle.

Mrs. Eliza Corey, a native of Nantucket, but who has resided upon the Pacific coast for many years, made a temperance address in the Baptist church Wednesday evening to a select audience. The address is highly commended by those who were privileged to hear it.

A tract of land on Lily street, taken on execution in an action of C. Hadwen Crowley vs. Thomas B. Field, was sold by the sheriff on Wednesday, for the sum of $171, to Edward H. Wing.

An experiment with dynamite upon a sunken wreck in the channel over the bar was attended with success last week.

Mr. B. A. Blundon of the signal station has leave of absence and will spend his vacation with his mother at Washington, D. C.

An ancient picture of the ship "Boston Packet of Havre de Grace, Captain Joy, bound for the South seas," has been placed in the Pacific club by Mr. Moses Joy, Sr. The ship was comanded by Captain David Joy in 1812. She was engaged in the whaling business as early as 1794, and is supposed to be the same vessel subsequently known as the "Boston," which was broken up in Nantucket harbor some time after 1825, that being the last year that her name appears in the shipping list.

The annual cruise of the New Bedford Yacht club will be to Quisset on Saturday afternoon, June 17th. The run will last until Sunday. A committee from the Dartmouth club has been appointed to confer with the Yacht club members and make the cruise open to members of the Dartmouth club. In case arrangements are made between the clubs, a tugboat will be hired for the accommodation of the Dartmouth club members. The hotel at Quisset will open on the 17th.

[From Yesterday's Third Edition.]

ORDER OF DRUIDS.

An Important Meeting Held in Fall River Yesterday.

(Special Dispatch.)

Fall River, June 8.—At the annual meeting of the Supreme Council of the American Order of Druids, held in the parlor of the Mellen House yesterday, the following were elected permanent members of the order: Dr. Dwight Cone, Rev. John B. Gammons, John M. Young, Charles Earby, John B. Lock, James Bagle of Fall River; Frank Harrop of Centre Falls, R. I.; George Snedden of New Bedford, Joseph Whyatt of Taunton, John L. Schroder of Providence, William J. Pepper of Brockton, Mary I. Bumpus of Campello and Robert McLeod of New Bedford.

The following officers were elected for one year:

S. P.—William Clark.
S. V. P.—Rev. J. G. Gammons.
S. A.—Frank Harrop.
S. N.—William Pierson.
S. P.—J. J. Haywood.
S. W.—George Snedden.
S. G.—Joseph Whyatt.
S. N. D.—Dr. J. H. Jackson.

Board of Directors—William Clark, J. G. Gammons, Frank Harrop, William Pierson, George Snedden, J. J. Haywood, Joseph Whyatt, Dr. J. H. Jackson, Dr. Dwight E. Cone and John L. Schroder

The meeting was a very interesting one. Nearly every officer received a unanimous vote, and the election of additional members to the supreme council is not only satisfactory to the subordinate council but is the watchword of peace and success and growth of the order.

Resolutions were passed unanimously giving direct representation from each subordinate council to the supreme council in addition to the permanent members elected.

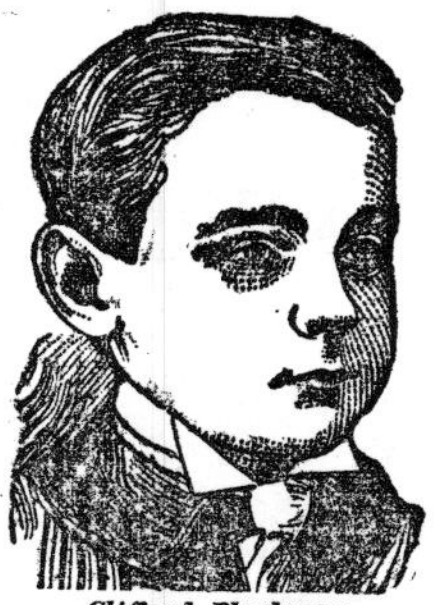

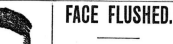

Clifford Blackman

A Boston Boy's Eyesight Saved—Perhaps His Life

By Hood's Sarsaparilla—Blood Poisoned by Canker.

Read the following from a grateful mother: "My little boy had Scarlet Fever when 4 years old, and it left him very weak and with blood **poisoned with canker.** His eyes became so inflamed that his sufferings were intense, and for seven weeks he

Could Not Open His Eyes.

I took him twice during that time to the Eye and Ear Infirmary on Charles street, but their remedies failed to do him the faintest shadow of good. I commenced giving him Hood's Sarsaparilla and it soon cured him. I have never doubted that it **saved his sight, even if not his very life.** You may use this testimonial in any way you choose. I am always ready to sound the praise of

Hood's Sarsaparilla

because of the wonderful good it did my son." ABBIE F. BLACKMAN, 2898 Washington St., Boston, Mass. Get HOOD'S.

HOOD'S PILLS are hand made, and are perfect in composition, proportion and appearance.

HIBERNIANS.

At a meeting of Division 7, A. O. H., Wednesday evening the following officers were elected:

President—Thomas J. Hart.
Vice President—James J. Meade.
Recording Secretary—Patrick Mc Quade.
Financial Secretary—Thomas Norton.
Treasurer—Miles McSweeney.
Sentinel-at-Arms—Peter Tresham.
Doorkeeper—William J. Ryan.
Marshal—John H. Murphy.

This division will hold an excursion June 18.

WESLEY LEAGUE.

The Wesley League connected with the South Primitive Methodist church held its semi-annual meeting last evening when the following officers were chosen:

President—Miss Mahala Evans.
Vice President—Miss Ada Laycock.
General Secretary—Richard G. Smith.
Treasurer—Miss Ellen Fenton.

The officers were chosen a committee of arrangements for the Wesley League convention in this city July 13th.

WAREHAM.

The funeral services of the late Captain William P. Gibbs were held in the chapel at East Wareham on 7th inst., Rev. Noble W. Everett officiating. Captain Gibbs was a native of Wareham, and commenced a seafaring life at an early age. After being employed for a few years in the coasting trade, he went one or more whaling voyages in brig Inga, one of the most successful crafts ever engaged in the whale fishery. He subsequently entered the merchant service, and rose to the rank of captain, commanding the barks Voyager, Moneyick, Lyra, Edward McDowell, Mary S. Ames, and several others. During the civil war he was an officer on board the steamer Pinola. At the close of the war he served as second officer for several years on the steamers of the Pacific Mail Steamship company. At one time he commanded the steamer Bogota. For the last six years he has served as keeper of the lighthouse at Sag harbor, Long Island. In accordance with his wish his remains were interred in the ancient cemetery at East Wareham, not far from his birthplace. He leaves a widow and several children. He was in his 68th year.

GATES MUST CLOSE SUNDAY.

Judges Woods and Jenkins Agree on World's Fair Injunction.

Chicago, June 8.—In the injunction suit brought by the United States to restrain the local directory from opening the fair gates on Sunday Judge Woods announced this morning that he and his associates failed to agree on certain points, and that each would formulate his ideas in an individual opinion. Judge Woods then in a lengthy opinion gave his views of the case, and decided that the prayer for an injunction was well grounded and that the exposition should be enjoined from opening its gates on Sunday. Judge Jenkins agrees with Judge Woods on the main point on the World's fair injunction proceedings, and he also decides that the injunction must issue and the fair be closed on Sunday.

This decides the question as Judge Grosscup, who favors opening, is in a minority, and the court declares with the government for the latter's right to insist on the contract made by the acceptance of the souvenir coin and that the gates of the fair remain closed on Sunday.

BABY ONE SOLID SORE

Tried Everything without Relief. No Rest Night or Day. Cured by Cuticura Remedies.

My baby, when two months old, had a breaking out with what the doctor called eczema. Her head, arms, feet, and hands were each one solid sore. I tried everything, but neither the doctors nor anything else did her any good. We could get no rest day or night with her. In my extremity I tried the CUTICURA REMEDIES, but I confess I had no faith in them, for I had never seen them tried. To my great surprise, in one week's time after beginning to use the CUTICURA REMEDIES, the sores were well, but I continued to use the RESOLVENT for a little while, and now she is as fat a baby as you would like to

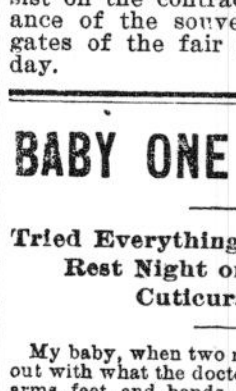

see, and as sound as a dollar. I believe my baby would have died if I had not tried CUTICURA REMEDIES. I write this that every mother with a baby like mine can feel confident that there is a medicine that will cure the worst eczema, and that medicine is the CUTICURA REMEDIES.

MRS. BETTIE BIRKNER, Lockhart, Texas.

Cuticura Remedies

Cure every humor of the skin and scalp of infancy and childhood, whether torturing, disfiguring, itching, burning, scaly, crusted, pimply, or blotchy, with loss of hair, and every impurity of the blood, whether simple, scrofulous, or hereditary, when the best physicians and all other remedies fail. Parents, save your children years of mental and physical suffering. Begin now. Cures made in childhood are permanent.

CUTICURA REMEDIES are the greatest skin cures, blood purifiers, and humor remedies of modern times, are absolutely pure, and may be used on the youngest infant with the most gratifying success.

Sold everywhere. Price, CUTICURA, 50c.; SOAP, 25c.; RESOLVENT, $1. Prepared by the POTTER DRUG AND CHEMICAL CORPORATION, Boston.

☞ Send for "How to Cure Skin Diseases," 64 pages, 50 illustrations, and 100 testimonials.

PIMPLES, black-heads, chapped and oily skin cured by CUTICURA MEDICATED SOAP.

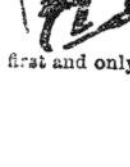

FREE FROM RHEUMATISM

In one minute the Cuticura Anti-Pain Plaster relieves rheumatic, sciatic, hip, kidney, chest, and muscular pains and weaknesses. The first and only instantaneous pain-killing plaster.

FACE FLUSHED.

Miss Borden Seems Agitated

At Opening of Court in the Afternoon.

Discovery of Murders Rehearsed.

Police First Upon the Scene.

Repeat Ghastly Details of That Day.

Evidence Followed With Intense Interest.

The court came in promptly this afternoon at 2 15. Miss Borden was in the dock as early as five minutes past 2. Her face was somewhat flushed, and she seemed a little agitated. She was given a seat inside the bar, as has been the custom for the past two days.

John Cunningham, whose examination was not finished when the court took a recess for dinner, was called to the stand, and testified that after telephoning he went across the street toward the Borden house. He saw Dr. Bowen go up Second street. He also saw Miss Russell and Miss Sullivan. He said he saw Officer Allen going up Second street, and had conversation with him. The officer went to the Borden house. The witness said he followed the officer to the Borden house a couple of minutes later. He was accompanied by John Manning and Walter P. Stevens, Fall River reporters. He said they walked up to the front of the house and jumped over the front fence, and walked around to the side of the house, between the Borden house and Dr. Bowen's house. He said they did not notice any footprints in the grass on that side of the house. They were looking to see if they might not find one. Then they went around to the back part of the house. They tried the cellar door and found it locked. The witness said he did not go into the house at all. He saw officers there while he was there. He could not tell what time it was. He did not try any door but the cellar door.

Cross-examined by Governor Robinson.

Q. When you saw Dr. Bowen where were you?
A. At the corner of Borden and Second streets.
Q. Dr. Bowen and Bridget Sullivan and Miss Russell were together, were they?
A. Yes.
Q. Where did you find Manning and Stevens?
A. They joined me on Second street.
Q. Did you go by the Borden gate?
A. Yes.
Q. Why did you jump the fence?
A. So if any one were standing by the side of the house they couldn't see me.
Q. Did the other men follow?
A. I couldn't say.
Q. When did you next see them?
A. I saw them in the yard.
Q. How high is the fence?
A. I can't tell.
Q. There was a grass plot there, was there?
A. Yes.
Q. You didn't see any marks of travel there?
A. No.
Q. Did you look along near the Kelly fence?
A. Yes.
Q. You saw no marks there?
A. No.
Q. You didn't know about Bridget Sullivan or Mr. Morse being out on the grass, did you?
A. No.
Q. You were really hunting the criminal, were you?
A. Yes.
Q. Who did you see in the yard?
A. Officers Allen, Mullaly, Dougherty and Fleet.
Q. Anybody else.
A. Officer Wixon.
Q. Anybody else?
A. No sir.
Q. Did you go in the barn?
A. No.
Q. Was the barn open?
A. I didn't notice.
Q. See anybody go in?
A. No.
Q. Was Mr. Sawyer at the door?
A. Yes.

Officer Allen.

Officer George W. Allen was the next witness.

Q. You are a police officer?
A. Yes.
Q. In 1892 you were committing officer?
A. Yes.
Q. Do you remember Aug. 4th, 1892?
A. Yes.
Q. Do you remember the hour of 11 and a quarter o'clock?
A. Yes.
Q. What do you remember about it?
A. The marshall came in and said there was a row.
Q. Why did you have occasion to note the time?
A. It being a quarter past 11, I looked to see if it was time to take the prisoners.
Q. In consequence of what was said to you where did you go?
A. To the Borden house.
Q. How many minutes' walk is it?
A. About four minutes.
Q. Did you walk?
A. Walked partly, and ran partly.
Q. Did you see any one?
A. I took Sawyer along with me, and told him to stand at the door and not to allow any one to pass.
Q. What door?
A. The south one.
Q. Who did you see at the house?
A. Mrs. Churchill.
Q. Anybody else?
A. There was not.
Q. Did you see any one else?
A. After going into the room where Mr. Borden lay two ladies came in.
Q. Who were they?
A. I think Mrs. Churchill and Miss Russell.
Q. See anybody else?
A. At the time I went out I saw Lizzie.
Q. Did you see Dr. Bowen?
A. I did.
Q. Where was he?
A. He met me at the door.
Q. Did you go anywhere before you went to the office?
A. I went to the front entry.
Q. Did you see Mr. Borden?
A. Yes, in the sitting room.
Q. Was there a sheet over him?
A. No, but Dr. Bowen said he had sent for one.
Q. Did you notice the front door?
A. Yes, and night lock and bolt were shut.
Q. Did you interfere with the door?
A. No.
Q. After examining the door what did you do?
A. I looked behind it and told Dr. Bowen I'd go down and report.
Q. Did you do anything else?
A. I looked in the closet and kitchen.
Q. Did you make any other investigation?
A. No.
Q. At that time did you know about Mrs. Borden?
A. I did
Q. Where did you then go?
A. To the station.
Q. Where then?
A. To the patrol barn for Officer Mullaly.
Q. How far is that?
A. About 800 feet.
Q. Where did you then go?
A. To the Borden house.
Q. Who was there?
A. Officer Dougherty and Mr. Wixon.
Q. Any one else?
A. No sir.
Q. Where did you go then?
A. Direct to the room where Mrs. Borden lay.
Q. Anywhere else first?
A. Through the dining room and sitting room and up the stairs.
Q. How far up the stairs were you when you caught sight of Mrs. Borden?
A. As soon as my head got above the level of the floor.
Q. What occurred when you went up?
A. Mr. Morse, Dr. Bowen, Officer Mullaly and Mr. Wixon came up.
Q. Was anything said by the doctor?
A. I think not.
Q. Did you observe Mrs. Borden?
A. No sir.
Q. Where did you go then?
A. I started out and met Mr. Morse at the head of the stairs, and he said—

(Objection was made and the question was ruled out.)

Q. Did you go anywhere else in the house?
A. I went down cellar.
Q. What observation did you make there?
A. The door was closed.
Q. What door do you mean?
A. The door leading from the cellar to the yard.
Q. How was this door?
A. It was bolted.
Q. Did you see Lizzie Borden in the house?
A. Yes.
Q. What was her appearance, any tears?

(Objected to and was not pressed.)

A photograph of the room was shown to the witness and he was asked if it showed the condition of the room correctly. He said that it did, with the exception that he noticed a table with books on it in the room when he went in.

Q. Where was this table?
A. It was about three feet from Mr. Borden's head.
Q. Can you tell the color of the covers of the books?
A. No sir.
Q. Were there any marks of any kind on the table?
A. No sir.
Q. I will ask you directly; did you see a spattering of blood on the books or the table?
A. No sir.
Q. Did you notice any article of woman's wearing apparel near Mrs. Borden's body when you saw it?
A. Yes, a handkerchief covered with blood lying near Mrs. Borden's feet.

Here a colored handkerchief was identified by the witness as the one seen near Mrs. Borden's body.

Q. Where was this handkerchief lying when you first saw it?
A. It was about the same distance from Mrs. Borden's body as from the window.

Cross-examined by Mr. Robinson.

Q. You received the message at 11 15?
A. Yes sir.
Q. How far is it from the police station to where you started for, some distance?
A. Yes sir.
Q. Any one outside or around the house when you arrived?
A. No sir.
Q. You and Sawyer were together?
A. I went in and saw Mr. Borden and Mr. Sawyer was put on guard.
Q. Did you see anybody on the south side of the Borden house?
A. No sir.
Q. Did you see Mr. Manning and Mr. Stevens at the house?
A. Yes sir.
Q. Were they together?
A. Yes sir.
Q. This table you speak of was a small stand?
A. Yes sir.
Q. The picture does not show the table in its proper place?
A. No sir.
Q. Where did you go when you left the house?
A. To the station.
Q. How much time did you use up at the house?
A. I couldn't have been at the house more than six or seven minutes.
Q. When did you see the two ladies there?
A. When I went in to see Mr. Borden's body.
Q. Did you see Miss Sullivan at that time?
A. No sir.
Q. Was there any one in the yard when you got there the second time?
A. No one.
Q. What time was it when you went away from the house?
A. It must have been in the neighborhood of 15 minutes to 12.

Deputy Sheriff Wixon.

Deputy Sheriff Frank H. Wixon of Fall River was next called to the stand and questioned by Mr. Moody.

Q. Are you a deputy sheriff of this county?
A. Yes sir.
Q. Have been for some time?
A. Yes sir.
Q. Do you recall Aug. 4th, 1892, the day of the homicide?
A. Yes sir.
Q. On that day were you at the Central police station?
A. I was.
Q. Can you tell me about what time you got to the station that day?
A. Very near it.
Q. Well state about what time you got to the station.
A. About 1 minute past 11 o'clock.
Q. Had you had to consult a timepiece?
A. No, I heard the bell on the city building ring just before I reached the station.
Q. When you got to the marshal's office did you go to doing anything?
A. I merely went there to make a friendly call.
Q. Do you recall his being called to the telephone?
A. I do.
Q. Could you give me an estimate of how long it was after you reached the station?
A. I do not think it was more that 10 or 15 minutes.
Q. Did he go to the telephone?
A. I think he did, he went somewhere and went to talking.
Q. After he had been to the telephone what did you see him do?
A. He came out and went by me and gave some order to some one.
Q. Do you know who it was?
A. No sir, I do not.
Q. Did you talk with him?
A. Yes sir.
Q. How long did you remain at the station?
A. I remained until Officer Allen came in.
Q. Was there any conversation between Officer Allen and the marshal in your presence?
A. I didn't hear any.
Q. How long after that did you remain at the station?
A. Long enough to learn what had taken place?
Q. Where did you go then?
A. I went out and stopped into an office for a minute and then went to the Borden house.
Q. Where did Officer Allen go as you went toward the Borden house?
A. I left him in the marshal's office.
Q. You do not know where he went?
A. No sir.
Q. Did you walk to the Borden house?
A. I did.
Q. Alone, or with some one?
A. I walked part of the way alone, and was overtaken by Officer Dougherty.
Q. Did you mark the time when you left there?
A. I did not, only as my memory serves.
A. As your memory best serves what time do you think it was?
A. It was about 25 minutes of 12.
Q. What did you do after you got at the Borden premises?
A. I went into the house.
Q. Which door?
A. The back door.
Q. Was there any one at the back door?
A. Mr. Sawyer.
Q. What did you do then?
A. I went into the sitting room.
Q. At that time was there any covering over Mr. Borden?
A. There was what I took to be a sheet.
Q. Now go on and tell us what you observed with reference to Mr. Borden's body. Before that I want to ask you if you have had occasion to see wounds fresh or otherwise?
A. I have.
Q. Where did you see them?
A. Most of them I saw at Roanoke Island after an engagement.
Q. Describe Mr. Borden's body.
A. I saw him lying on the sofa with several wounds on his face.
Q. Can you give any other description of his appearance, or of the blood?
A. The wounds looked to me like quite fresh ones.
Q. Can you give any description of the blood?
A. It was bright colored.
Q. How was it with reference to thickness?
A. It did not seem to be thick at all.
Q. Did it look dark, or had it coagulated at all?
A. I did not see any.
Q. After you had observed Mr. Borden, and the blood upon his face, where did you go?
A. I went upstairs.
Q. What examination did you make, if any, of the wounds of Mrs. Borden?
A. Very slight.
Q. Did you notice anything with reference to the blood?
A. I did.
Q. If you examined that state what the appearance was?
A. The blood was very dark and coagulated.
Q. How did its color in darkness or brightness compare with that of Mr. Borden?
A. It was very dark.
Q. How did its thickness and clotting compare with that of Mr. Borden?
A. The blood on the floor looked very thick.
Q. Did you form any opinion at the time as to which of the two had come to their death first?

Mr. Robinson objected to the question.

The judge said the question was excluded.

Mr. Robinson withdrew his objection, and Judge Mason said the witness might answer.

He said he had not formed any opinion.

Q. I forgot to ask you, Mr. Wixon, about going into the Borden yard.
A. I went from the house out into the yard toward Dr. Chagnon's fence. I went east and got up on a pile of lumber. I stepped on the stringer of the fence and worked myself along to the fence dividing the Crow lot and the Borden lot, then I saw a man sawing wood.
Q. Was he a Frenchman?
A. I should judge that he was.
Q. Did you see any one else over in that Crow yard at that time?
A. Over to the east of the yard there were two men.
Q. What were they doing?
A. They were evidently at work. Finally one of the two men came over and had some talk with me.
Q. Did you know who the man was?
A. I did not.

Mr. Wixon pointed on the plan where the man was who was sawing wood and the spot was shown to the jury.

The cross-examination of the witness was then undertaken by Mr. Robinson.

Q. Will you tell me again if Mr. Sawyer was at the house?
A. He was in the entry.
Q. What other persons did you see in the house?
A. I saw Dr. Bowen, and he was the only person I saw.
Q. Then you went up stairs?
A. Yes sir.
Q. Did you see any of the ladies at all?
A. I did when I came down.
Q. Whom did you see then?
A. I saw Miss Bridget Sullivan and Mrs. Churchill.
Q. Did you see Miss Lizzie?
A. I did not.
Q. Did you see Mrs. Bowen?
A. I do not remember whether I did or not.
Q. And Miss Russell?
A. I think I did.
Q. Did you see any other officers in the house?
A. After I came down from up stairs I did.
Q. Who were they?
A. I am sure that I saw Officer Mullaly and another officer. I am not positive who he was, but I think he was Officer Harrington.

Mr. Robinson then read to the witness a part of his testimony given at the preliminary hearing at Fall River.

The witness then said he did not remember giving any testimony in regard to stating positively that Officer Harrington was there.

The rest of Mr. Wixon's cross-examination was confined to statements concerning locality of surrounding yards.

MARSHAL FLEET.

His Evidence of Intense Interest and Closely Followed.

Assistant Marshal John Fleet was the next witness, and his evidence was of intense interest, and was listened to with the closest attention. After stating how long he has been connected with the police force, the first question asked was: "Where were you August 4, 1892."

A. At my house.
Q. What time were you informed of the murder?

(Continued on Seventh Page.)

TELEGRAPHIC BREVITIES.

C. L. Nyehoff & Co's private bank, Chicago, is in the custody of a sheriff.

The Bank of Washburn, a private one, at Ashland, Wis., has closed its doors.

Greenwood C. Pray of Guilford, Me., a young man of 28, shot and killed his wife, then shot himself, at Shirley this morning.

D. B. Loveman of Chatanooga, Tenn., one of the leading dry goods merchants of the south, has filed a deed of trust for the benefit of preferred creditors.

T. H. Brown & Co., of Milwaukee, carriage manufacturers, have assigned.

Bellah & Co., wholesale dealers in iron and steel, Wilmington, Del., have failed.

Highest of all in Leavening Power.—Latest U. S. Gov't Report.

Royal Baking Powder

ABSOLUTELY PURE

THE GREAT FARGO FIRE.

Three Thousand People are Without Homes.

Conservative Figures Make Loss $3,000,000.

One Half of the City Has Been Wiped Out by the Flames.

Minneapolis, June 8.—At 10 last night the fire at Fargo was still burning fiercely in a dozen places. A section in the middle of the city from Robert street and Front street south, four blocks wide and 10 blocks long, is a blackened plain of ashes with not a dozen buildings left standing. Brick buildings seemed to melt away into heaps of crumbling sand, and it was impossible to force enough water through the mains to fight the fire.

A conservative estimate of the loss is $3,000,000, with not over one quarter insurance. Plenty of help is now here. Over 3,000 people are homeless. Practically only one hotel is left, the Headquarters. The fire has burned all around it, but so far it has been saved. Only one restaurant is left. Moorhead hotels are full.

The fire started by hot ashes from the Gem restaurant, thrown out behind, igniting some loose paper back of Houseman's dry goods store. Somebody left the front door open, and inside of three minutes the wind had driven the flames through the buildings to the roof. During the next 15 minutes the flames ran two blocks then jumped across the street to Magill's machinery warehouse. North and east of this for two blocks each way are big machinery depots, mostly two story wooden buildings, and at this time they were filled to the roof with a supply of farm machinery for North Dakota.

At midnight the firemen were still working as hard as ever to stop the mad rush of flames. One-half of Fargo is wiped out, only one-half of the business houses being left. The trestle was burned on the great Northern, so no trains can pass. The firemen are now trying to extinguish the flames along the line of the Northern Pacific to allow the section crew to re-lay the rails and let trains through. Only one telegraph wire was available during the progress of the fire. The Fargo wire was burned and messages have to be sent from Moorehead. Every insurance office was burned. It is impossible to get accurate statements of risks, as the books are all in the safes among the ruins. It will likely be over $3,000,000. Only one bank was saved—the First National. Several firemen were injured by falling bricks.

FRIENDS' YEARLY MEETING.

Rather Smaller Attendance Than Usual at Portland.

Portland, Me., June 8.—The New England yearly meeting of Friends began here today with a rather smaller attendance than usual. The forenoon was devoted to a meeting of the ministry and oversight, Rufus M. Jones and Susan Peckham at the clerk's table. Among those present are: Isaac Sharpe of London, aged 87, who has just returned from a trip to China and Japan, and is now commencing a journey of the United States; Owen Dame of Lynn, W. O. Newhall of Lynn, Joseph Courtland and wife of Newburyport, Samuel R. Buffinton and wife of Fall River, Robert P. Gifford and wife of Providence, W. Thompson and wife of New Bedford, Olney T. Meader and wife of Boston, Dr. Green and wife of Newport. Tonight a representative meeting will be held, and meetings of the regular session will be begun tomorrow with Timothy B. Hussey of North Berwick presiding.

M'KINLEY RENOMINATED.

Scene of Wild Enthusiasm at Ohio Republican Convention.

Columbus, O., June 8.—A few minutes after 10 General Grosvenor called the Republican state convention to order, and Rev. H. E. Holmes implored the divine blessing. A hearty greeting was accorded Hon. H. M. Daugherty when he was introduced as permanent chairman. He made a brief address, after which the report of the committee on resolutions was read by Congressman G. W. Hulick. The planks were loudly applauded. The decks were now cleared for nominations. Governor McKinley's name was presented by Colonel Bob Nevins of Dayton and seconded by J. W. Nichols of Belmost. There were no other names and the governor was declared the nominee amid a wild scene of enthusiasm. The committee was appointed to conduct him into the hall, and a few minutes later he made his appearance. He was greeted with loud and prolonged cheers.

A Mother's Letter:—

"Dear Mrs. Pinkham:—

"Last winter I did not think my little ones would have a mother long. I suffered terribly with female troubles.

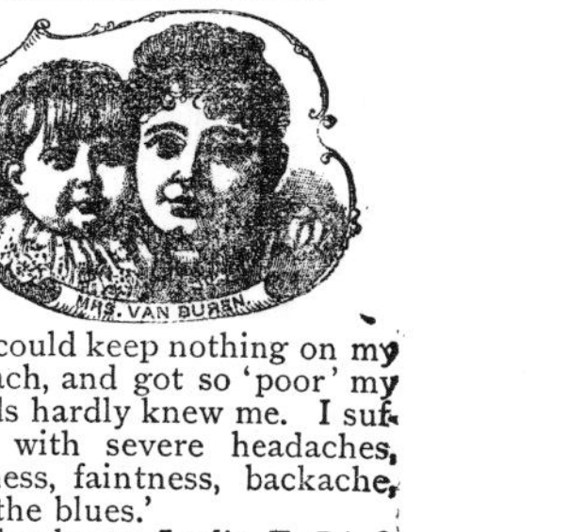

"I could keep nothing on my stomach, and got so 'poor' my friends hardly knew me. I suffered with severe headaches, dizziness, faintness, backache, and 'the blues.'

"Thanks to *Lydia E. Pinkham's Vegetable Compound,* I am now as fat as ever, and have no female troubles.

"If you use my letter I hope it may be the means of saving some other poor mother's life as it did mine."—Mrs. Ella Van Buren, Brazil, Ind.

All druggists sell it. Address in confidence, LYDIA E. PINKHAM MED. Co., LYNN, MASS. *Liver Pills, 25 cents.*

HATCHETS.

(Continued from First Page.)

Q. On the day of the homicide did you go to the Borden house? A. Not in the day time, but I did at night.

Q. At any time did you take any axes or hatchets away from there? A. I did.

Q. When? A. On the morning of the 5th of August.

Q. What did you take? A. Two wood axes, a hand axe and a small sheathing hatchet.

Q. Where did you take them? A. From the cellar.

Q. Where were they in the cellar? A. Three of them were in the washroom on the floor.

Q. Where was the other one? A. In the vegetable cellar on a scaffold or shelf.

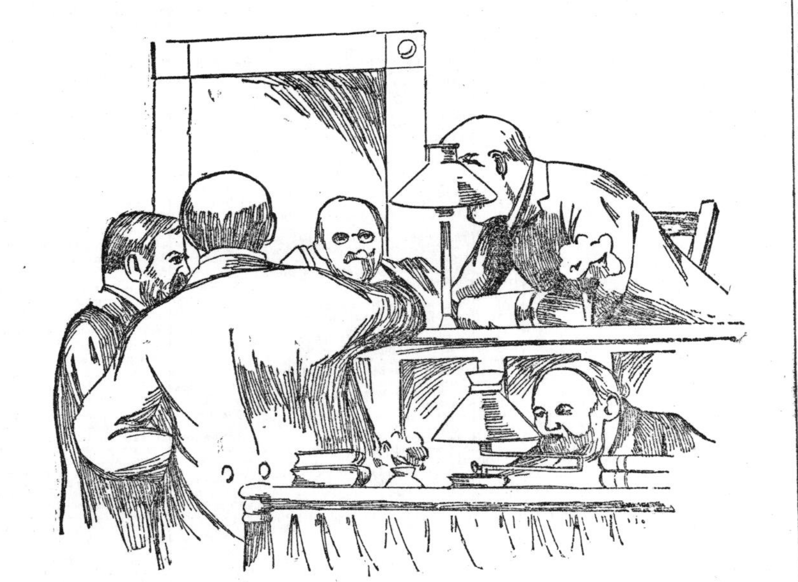

CONSULTATION OF COURT AND COUNSEL OVER ADMISSION OF LIZZIE'S TESTIMONY AT THE INQUEST.

Q. What did you do with these axes and hatchets? A. Carried them to the Central police station.

Q. Into whose custody did you give them? A. Marshal Hilliard's.

Q. Have you had any possession of them since that time? A. I have not.

Q. Did you hear anything about a conversation between Miss Lizzie Borden and Bridget Sullivan in reference to the cellar door? A. I did.

Q. You may state it. A. On the morning of the 5th of August at a quarter past seven I was at the Borden house. I heard Lizzie Borden ask the servant girl, "Are you sure the cellar door was fastened?" And her answer was, "Yes."

Q. Can you tell me whether these are the axes to which you refer? (handing witness two axes.) A. They resemble them sir.

Q. What do you call that? (passing the witness a smaller axe.) A. A hand axe.

Q. And that you call a sheathing hatchet? (holding up a hatchet.) A. Yes sir.

Q. And the claw hammer hatchet?—A. Was in the vegetable cellar on the shelf.

Q. Did you take any part in a search of the premises at any time? A. I did.

Q. When was it? A. Monday, the eighth day of August.

Q. What officers were present? A. Captain Desmond, Mr. Connors, Mr. Medley, myself and an outsider.

Q. Was any one else present during the search except yourselves? A. Yes sir, Andrew J. Jennings and Detective Hanscom. They came after we had been there a few minutes.

Q. Was Mr. Hanscom or Mr. Jennings associated with you? A. No sir.

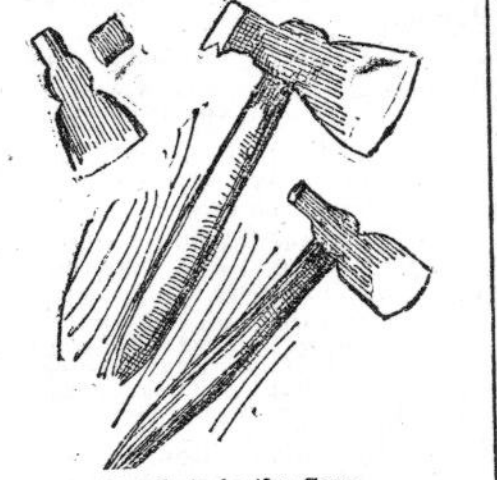

Hatchets in the Case.

[The width of the blade with the fragment of handle corresponds to the wounds on Andrew J. Borden's head.]

Q. So far as you know, was the detective at any time associated with the police? A. Not to my knowledge.

Cross-examined.

Q. What time did you arrive at the house? A. About 10 o'clock.

Q. Be kind enough to tell us just what you did. A. Captain Desmond was in charge of the party, we went into the house, he asked permission of some one, who I do not know, the permission was granted and then we went into the cellar and searched the cellar.

Q. Be very careful of details as to the manner and thoroughness of your search. A. Each one was assigned a certain thing to do and searched for himself.

Q. Perhaps you can go a little more in detail than that? A. As far as I went I searched the vegetable cellar, and moved all the barrels and boxes and tables under the stairs. I also searched the coal pile and in the wood cellar around the furnace.

Q. Which do you call the wood cellar? A. The cellar in the southwest corner of the house.

Q. Is there a steam heater in the room? A. Near by.

Q. Did you notice anything about any boxes in there? A. I do not remember particularly in that room, but there were in the cellar adjoining some boxes.

Q. There were boxes there? A. Yes sir.

Q. Where were they? A. They sat on the ground of the cellar.

Q. Did you see any up on the shelf? A. Not to my recollection, no sir.

Q. Was there a chimney in that cellar? A. Yes sir.

Q. Were there any boxes around that chimney? A. Yes sir.

Q. Did you examine those? A. Only those that had cinders in them. Those containing the cinders or ashes I examined.

Q. Where did these stand? A. One of them or two stood against the wall on the south side of the cellar or room.

Q. Did you notice any box around the chimney up high from the floor? A. I did not, no sir.

Q. Were the things in there very carefully examined? A. Well, what I examined was examined carefully.

Q. And you were very thorough in your search? A. Yes sir.

Q. Did anything escape you? A. There might have done.

Q. You were there to look, that was your business was it not? A. Yes sir.

Q. These other gentlemen of the police are pretty competent men, are they not? A. Yes sir.

Q. All of them? A. Yes sir.

Q. And somewhat experienced in police work? A. Yes sir.

Q. Did you see any slighting of the work by any of them? A. None that came to my knowledge, of course I did not watch them all the time.

Q. You searched in these boxes of cinders and did not find anything there? A. No sir.

Q. Did you find anything there anywhere during your search in the cellar? A. No sir.

Q. Nothing? A. No sir.

Q. You saw these two axes and a small hatchet in the wash cellar on the morning of the 5th? A. Yes sir.

Q. On the morning of the 5th, did you or any of the party take away any of the things? A. Officer Medley had a hatchet in his pocket.

Q. Did you examine it? A. No.

Q. Did you go away first? A. Yes.

Q. The small hatchet with no handle? A. Yes.

Q. Did you see the handle? A. No.

Q. Did you find a handle? A. No.

Q. Did you go to the northeast corner room? A. Yes.

Q. Search there? A. Yes.

Q. Did you find anything that will help us in our investigation? A. No sir.

Q. Did you have a mason to open a chimney? A. Yes.

Q. Where was the chimney? A. Nearly opposite the furnace.

Q. See anything taken out? A. No.

Q. Or learn that anything had been? A. No.

Q. Who was the mason? A. Charles H. Bryant.

Q. Seen him since? A. Yes, in Fall River this morning.

Q. Did he open any other chimney? A. Not to my knowledge.

The rest of the cross-examination about the search of the cellar developed nothing different from the direct examination, except that witness said the hatchets and axes were not taken to the station in a bag, but that witness carried them openly in his hands from the house. A plan of the cellar was shown witness, and he pointed out the location of the rooms in which he took a part in the search, and made a statement about a shelf or shelves which he had an impression he had seen.

One question put was: "Where was the claw-hammer?" A. On the shelf.

Q. Who called your attention to it? A. Captain Harrington; this was on the morning of August 5.

Q. Have you finished all you care to say about the cellar? A. Yes.

"Well," said Mr. Robinson, pleasantly, "Where shall we go now?"

"To the barn," said witness, and the audience was taken to it in imagination.

Q. Will you proceed with what was done in the barn? A. I searched the lower part.

Q. Who was in there? A. Several officers.

Q. Were they searching? A. Yes.

Q. Find anything? A. They took away some lead or were looking at it.

Q. Where was it? A. Some was in the box on the first floor.

Q. While looking in the carriage shed who came? A. Mr. Seaver and Mr. Mc Henry.

Q. Who's Mr. Seaver? A. A state officer.

Q. Who is McHenry? A. A private detective.

Q. Who got him there? A. I don't know.

Q. Where did he hail from? A. Providence, then.

Q. Where is he now? A. I don't know; New York, as far as I know.

Q. Have you seen him since that day? A. Yes sir.

Q. Has he been around police headquarters since that day? A. Yes sir.

Mr. Knowlton—I pray your honors' judgment.

Some little discussion followed, Mr. Robinson claiming if McHenry was investigating and working upon the case the defense is entitled to know it. Mr. Knowlton objected to this line of investigation.

Q. How long was he there since the day of the investigation? A. I don't know.

Q. Have you since the search in the barn seen him around the police headquarters? A. I might or I might not have seen him.

Q. Was he around there before the crime? A. I don't recall whether he was or not.

Q. Do you know whether he was paid by the city for his services or not? A. I do not, of my own knowledge.

Q. Is his name on the police roll for pay? A. I don't know, I don't make up the roll.

Q. Who does? A. The clerk of the police department.

Q. Did you see any basket or box when you went up stairs in the barn? A. I have the impression that there were a willow basket or a box in the barn.

Q. After searching the barn what did you next do? A. Searched the lumber pile in the yard.

Q. How did you search? A. Pulled down a foot or more of the lumber on top and satisfied myself that there was nothing there.

Q. Did you next go into the yard? A. Yes sir, and up to the old well.

Q. Nothing there? A. Nothing but dirt.

Q. What next? A. We searched around the yard to see if the turf had been disturbed.

Q. Did you find it disturbed? A. Nowhere except where the clothes had been buried.

Q. What next? A. I scaled the fence and went into the next yard.

Q. How did you get over? A. I stepped on the lumber pile and went over.

Q. Wasn't there barbed wire on the top of the fence? A. Yes sir.

Q. And you went over the barbed wire? A. Yes sir.

Q. Didn't you tear your clothes? A. No sir, I was careful.

Q. How did the others get over? A. In the same way.

Q. What did you find there, anything but rubbish? A. Nothing but rubbish.

Q. What did you next do? A. Went back to the Borden yard and to the station house.

Here an officer appeared with a box and basket which the witness identified as those taken from the barn, and the cross-examination proceeded.

In answer to questions the witness told of several promotions made in the police force since last February. He said that the box and basket looked the same in a general way as when he had last seen them. A stick of wood found in the basket he didn't remember of ever seeing before and didn't remember anything in addition to what he had just testified to that was of importance.

In redirect.

Q. Where was the box filled with lead found? A. It was found in the carriage room, about three feet from the door leading to the street.

Q. Where was the box containing nails found? A. On the carpenter's bench in the loft of the barn.

Here the contents of the box containing the lead pipe, sheet lead, etc., were shown to the jury.

In answer to further questions by Mr. Robinson, witness replied that he couldn't recall who were present when the wood room was searched, there was so much running around, but Mr. Desmond was superintending matters at the time.

Officer Mahoney.

Benjamin F. Mahoney was next called.

Q. You are a police officer in Fall River? A. Yes sir.

Q. Did you go yesterday afternoon anywhere with Mr. Edson? A. Yes sir.

Q. Where? A. I went to the Borden house on Second street.

Q. About what time? A. About quarter to four.

Q. Did you make any effort to get in? A. Yes sir.

Q. Did you succeed in so doing? A. No sir.

Q. Did any one come to the door? A. Yes sir, a servant.

Q. At any time did you take a dress from the custody of Professor Wood? A. I did.

Q. Can you tell us the day and date? A. It was the 30th of May this year.

Q. Acting under whose instructions? A. The district attorney's.

Q. Would you know the dress? A. I think that is the dress; it was a skirt and waist, (pointing to a dark blue dress which Mr. Moody held in his hand.)

Q. And that was delivered to you by whom? A. Professor Wood.

Q. Did you at any time return it? A. I did.

Q. And returned it to whom? A. Professor Wood.

Q. Between the time you took it from Professor Wood and the time you returned it had there been any change in its possession? A. No sir.

Q. You kept it yourself all the time? A. Yes sir.

The witness was not cross-examined.

Officer Medley.

Officer Medley was the next witness.

Q. Your name is William Medley? A. Yes sir.

Q. You are at present doing special work on the police force? A. Yes sir.

Q. Under the title of inspector? A. Yes sir.

Q. And last year you were a patrolman? A. A patrolman.

Q. Did you act in any special capacity last year? A. On the 4th day of August and afterwards I did.

Q. On the 4th day of August did you obtain any knowledge of a homicide at the Borden house? A. Yes sir.

Q. Where were you when you obtained it? A. Near the North police station or rather in the police station.

Q. From whom did you obtain the information? A. The city marshal.

Q. What time was it at that time? A. About 25 minutes after 11 o'clock.

Q. How did you fix that time? A. I went from the Old Colony depot, where I saw the train for Boston leave, and went part of the way down to the police station with a friend; I left him and met another man, and we went to the police station. While in the police station this friend of mine got up to go, and I started to go with him. I started in the direction of my house. As soon as I got perhaps 50 yards or so the janitor called me back to the telephone.

Q. And is it at that time you got the information? A. Yes sir.

Q. That you say was 25 minutes past 11 or thereabouts? A. Yes sir.

Q. What time did the Boston train leave that you have spoken of as having seen? A. About four minutes past 11.

Q. What depot were you at? A. The Fall River depot in the northern part of the city.

Q. How far is it from that depot to the northern police station? A. Well, I cannot tell by measurement, I can tell better by the length of time it required to walk there.

Q. I should prefer that; give us that. A. About 5 minutes.

Q. Did you delay on your way to the station, or did you go directly there? A. I delayed some.

Q. How long had you been at the station before you started to go away with the friend that you spoke of? A. Perhaps 5 minutes.

Q. Did you consult any timepiece at or about the time you received a message at the telephone? A. Not then.

Q. How soon after? A. I didn't for some time.

Q. When last before had you seen a timepiece? A. When my friend got up to go I looked at the clock.

Q. And what time was it by the station clock at that time? A. Twenty-two minutes past 11.

Q. Do you know whether your friend looked at anything? A. He did

Q. What did he look at? A. He looked at the clock.

Q. Who is it that was there? A. Thomas King.

Q. After getting this message where did you go, Mr. Medley? A. To the city marshal's office.

Q. How did you get there? A. I stopped a team that was going by the police station and got in.

Q. At what pace did you go from the Central police station to the northern police station? A. As fast as we could drive the horse.

Q. How long did it take you to get there? A. About seven minutes.

Q. What was the gait of the horse? A. I could not say as to that; it was quite fast.

Q. How long did you delay at the station? A. Long enough to get a message.

Q. Then where did you go? A. I went to the Borden house.

Q. How did you go? A. I walked.

Q. Do you know what time you arrived there? A. About 20 or 19 minutes of 12.

Q. Did you look at any timepiece? A. Later than the stop in the northern police station? Yes sir.

Q. When was it? A. When I was passing the City hall.

Q. What time was it when you passed the City hall? A. I say 19 or 20 minutes of 12.

Q. Did you go directly to the Borden house? A. Yes sir.

Q. Whom did you see there when you first got there? A. Mr. Sawyer was the first one, the man at the door.

Q. What did you do after you got there? A. Inquired for Mr. Fleet.

Q. Did you see Mr. Fleet when you got there? A. No sir.

Q. Did you see him at any time later than that? A. Yes sir.

Q. Can you tell us about how long after you got there it was when Mr. Fleet got there? A. I cannot.

Q. Had you been into the house before Mr. Fleet came? A. No sir.

Q. Which way did you go? A. I went to the rear and tried the cellar door.

Q. Who did you see in the house? A. Captain Fleet, Mrs. Churchill, Miss Russell, one or two doctors and Lizzie.

Q. Have any talk with Lizzie? A. Yes sir.

Q. What was the talk? A. I asked

(Continued on Fourth Page.)

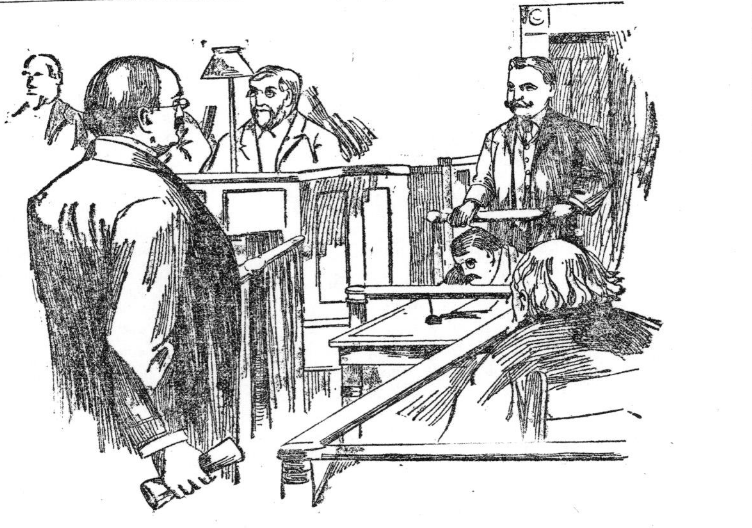

EX-GOV. ROBINSON CROSS-EXAMINING CAPTAIN PHIL HARRINGTON.

WILL LIZZIE TESTIFY?

She May Go on the Stand—She Feels Confident of Acquittal.

Lizzie Borden will tell her story to the judges and jurors in a few days when her turn comes. This has been decided upon by her attorneys, in view of the case thus far presented by the government, and will be carried out unless some startlingly surprising evidence is offered between now and the time when it will be the duty of the defense to put in its case. In all murder cases the nature of the evidence offered against the prisoner has great weight in deciding whether the accused shall testify or not, and, of course, the character and ability of the witness are also taken into consideration. When the trial began it was the intention to have her appear, but the matter could not be definitely decided, of course, until Robinson, Jennings and Adams made up their minds as to how things were going. They felt confident as to Lizzie's behavior on the stand. That she would acquit herself well, and, even under the trying ordeal of District Attorney Knowlton's sharp cross-examination, maintain her composure sufficiently to give clear, concise, direct and unbroken answers to questions. Unexpected developments in the strength of the prosecution would, of course, lead to a change in the programme, but if matters remain as they are now Lizzie Borden will go on the stand and testify when the proper time comes, and her story will not be materially different from that told by the government witnesses, although she will say she did not kill her father and stepmother. There is no question that Lizzie A. Borden is confident of an acquittal at the hands of the jury. She has unreservedly announced that to her friends, and has no doubt that her lawyers will bring her through all right. All her attorneys are also confident, and feel that they have weakened the government's case materially in the cross-examinations. There is, however, an undercurrent of feeling that the government is yet to do something to establish confidence in its case, and that it has the evidence which will do this.

MISS WHITE'S TESTIMONY.

Strong Objection to Reading Lizzie's Evidence at the Inquest.

The arguments on the points raised about Miss White's testimony will be made at the opening of court Monday morning, and will occupy several hours. Of course the discusson desired by Governor Robinson will be upon the admissibility of the evidence given by Lizzie Borden at Fall River during the inquest. It will be recalled that Mr. Knowlton read this evidence, under protest from Mr. Jennings, from a stenographic report at the Fall River hearing. The reasons for the objection will be that Lizzie Borden was compelled to attend the inquest under a subpoena and was not permitted to have counsel present, being therefore forced to testify under compulsion, with no one to instruct her as to her legal rights. There is no statute law in the state bearing on this point, and under common law there have been decisions apparently opposite on cases considered somewhat analogous. New York has such a statute, and in the case against the famous Jacob Sharp a decision was made in his favor.

"Joe" Howard says the objection raised to admitting Lizzie's story at the inquest is a very interesting point, and is analogous to that raised by the counsel for Jake Sharp, when the counsel for the prosecution received permission from Judge Barrett to produce before the petit jury the testimony given under protest by Jake Sharp before the state senate committee. Sharp was convicted, but the court of appeals overruled Judge Barrett's decision, and the old man was permitted to die in his home, as free as air, so far as his illegal conviction was concerned. It is contended that Miss Borden, who was under arrest, virtually charged with the murder of her father and stepmother, should not have been compelled to testify at all, and that to utilize now what she said under those trying circumstances would be not only an insult and an indignity upon a citizen of the commonwealth but an outrage upon decency and a traverse of equity. God save the commonwealth of Massachusetts.

TO TRACE THE STOMACHS.

Blunder That Causes Several Boston Witnesses to be Needed.

Boston, June 10.—By the first of the week probably several witnesses will be summoned from Boston to testify in the Borden case. Feeling not entirely secure as to their evidence on a certain point in regard to the stomachs of the two victims of the alleged daughter-murderer, Detective Medley of Fall River came to Boston yesterday afternoon. At the Park square station he was met by Special Officer Tryder of Division 1. It appears that when Medical Examiner Dolan of Fall River sent the stomachs of the two Bordens to Boston on Aug. 5, he did so by means of express, instead of having them delivered to Professor Wood in person by some one interested in the case. Recently it was realized that possibly when testimony is put in, relative to the stomachs, it would be hard to prove that the stomachs which were examined by Professor Wood were really those of Mr. and Mrs. Borden. With the assistance of Special Officer Tryder it is said that he secured four additional witnesses, an expressman, clerk at the express office, messenger and Janitor Skillers of the Harvard Medical school, who receipted for the package, which was addressed to Professor Wood. Detective Medley left for Fall River on the 5 o'clock train.

A considerable hole was punched in the government's case in the Borden trial by the testimony of the Sullivan girl that the side door was unfastened during a considerable period while she was washing windows out of sight of the door. This was very damaging to the charge of exclusive opportunity.—Lowell Courier.

NOT ALLOWED TO SEARCH.

Lawyer Jennings Prevents Police Entering Borden House.

Fall River, June 10.—Officer Mullaly testified in the Borden case yesterday that he saw the missing piece of the handle which is in the head of the axe that Assistant Marshal Fleet swore to discovering in the box where the ash-stained instrument lay. Officers were sent to search for it. Last night Hon. Andrew J. Jennings telephoned to the Central station that no one would be allowed in the Borden house. Counsel for Lizzie and Charles J. Holmes arrived at the house from the train and refused to let the detail of two men search. The lawyer and banker made a tour of the cellar, but did not find the missing portion of the helve.

The Bristol County Epidemic.

Another murder, this time in New Bedford, adds to the list which is rapidly making Bristol county distinguished. It is a tragedy in low life this time, the outcome of the jealousy of a Portuguese toward his sweetheart. There are some fortunate circumstances attending this incident. The murderer considerately attempted to shoot himself and thus set at rest all doubt as to the criminal and relieved the detective force of a great burden. Also, he will undoubtedly be brought to trial without a delay of ten months. But the epidemic of murder in that corner of the state is becoming unpleasantly prevalent.—Boston Post.

None SO GOOD
None GOES SO FAR
Knapp's ROOTBEER EXTRACT
when tested with others shows its superiority.
Being Stronger, it goes farther.
Being Purer, it is wholesome.
Being Delicious, it is fascinating.
One bottle makes 6 gallons.
How the little ones love it, and how much good it does them in warm weather.
All Grocers and Druggists.
25 cents a bottle.

It is an old theory that new wood is entitled to three coats of paint, but many new houses have but two coats of Chilton paint, and are then allowed to stand two and three years before they are painted again, and then only one coat. Can you not profit by this suggestion? In painting your house this year get estimates on one, two and three coats. If the house is in fair condition and there is not too much difference between the shade you are to put on and the one on the house, probably one coat will suffice. If not one, two coats will surely answer. What is the use then of putting on three? We have had painters tell us that they had painted houses with Chilton Paint where the house looked better after two coats than three. Upon being asked why, then, they put on three they answered that they were obliged to, as the contract called for three. Word your contracts so you can stop when you have gone far enough. Put Chilton Paint over a dry surface only.
DeWOLF & VINCENT, Agents.

Town Talk,
The new High Grade Flour.
Makes
MOST,
BEST,
WHITEST,
SWEETEST
BREAD.
DENISON BROS. CO.,
Wholesale Agents.

HATCH & COMPANY'S EXPRESS,
No. 5 Ricketson Block, New Bedford,
DAILY,
By Passenger Trains, to all Points on the Old Colony Railroad and its Connections.

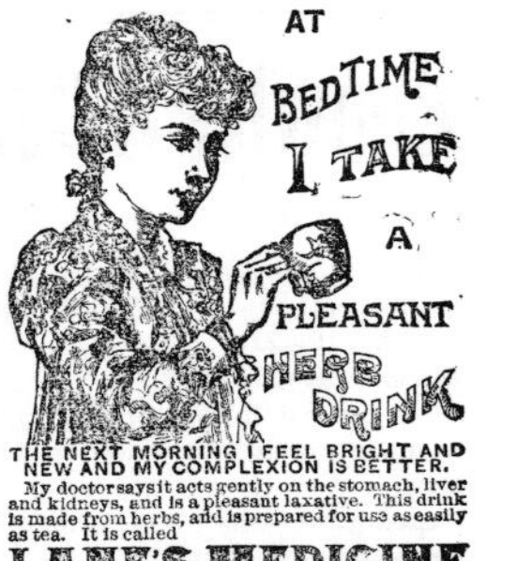

THE NEXT MORNING I FEEL BRIGHT AND NEW AND MY COMPLEXION IS BETTER.
My doctor says it acts gently on the stomach, liver and kidneys, and is a pleasant laxative. This drink is made from herbs, and is prepared for use as easily as tea. It is called
LANE'S MEDICINE
All druggists sell it at 50c. and $1 a package. If you cannot get it, send your address for a free sample. Lane's Family Medicine moves the bowels each day. In order to be healthy this is necessary. Address ORATOR F. WOODWARD, LE ROY, N. Y.

Not how much, but how good.
Williams' Root Beer.
Greatest temperance drink on earth. Has the best flavor and body, combining elements that quench the thirst and strengthen the system. One bottle extract makes 5 gallons of "the kind that suits."
This is not only "just as good" as others, but far better. One trial will support this claim.
SOLD EVERYWHERE.
Williams & Carleton, Hartford, Ct.

Everybody is Drinking
Home-Made Beer
THIS SUMMER.
MASON'S ROOT BEER
Is imported from England, and is incomparably the Best. A Variety of Flavors. Not Alcoholic.
U. S. AGENCY,
408 Chamber of Commerce, Boston.

C. W. HASKINS
No. 20 PURCHASE STREET,
Has replenished his stock since the holidays, and now offers at very low prices a good variety of Diamond Rings, Fine Jewelry, Gold and Silver Watches, Chains, &c.
His stock of Sterling Silver Spoons, Forks, Fancy Table Ware and Novelties is very extensive; these goods are lower in price than ever before.
18 KARAT WEDDING RINGS
A SPECIALTY.
You can save money buying of him your Spectacles and Eye Glasses, fit and quality guaranteed.
Watch, Clock and Jewelry repairing by experienced workmen.

We Must Have Room
SECOND HAND
CARRIAGES
Must Go.
Brownell, Ashley & Co.,
24 to 38 FOURTH ST.

NOTICE.
THE LARGEST STOCK OF
HARNESSES.
Trunks and Bags
IN THE CITY, AT
WILLIAM CRONIN & CO'S.,
Corner Elm and Pleasant Streets.

Madam,
your child needs up-building food generally—
H-O Hornby's Oatmeal
contains all the elements that go to make perfect development.

No MORPHINE CHLORAL ANTI-PYRINE IN Bromo-Seltzer.
It is an Effective, Effervescing Preparation which corrects
Disordered Stomach and Nervous Troubles.

Lawn Mowers!
We carry the Philadelphia, Magic, New Departure, Union, Diamond and New England High Wheel.
You must be suited with some one of these makes. We are selling a warranted mower, parts for which can be supplied at any time, for $3.50.

F. L. SOWLE & CO.,
OPPOSITE CITY CLOCK.

DAZED.

Murderer Sarmento's Arraignment.

Presents Sorry Appearance in Court Room.

Apparently Oblivious of His Surroundings.

Plea of Not Guilty Ordered by Judge Borden.

Ordered Committed Until October Term.

Bradley and Weston the Two Suspects Released.

The arraignment of Jose Sarmento, the assassin of his sweetheart, before Judge Borden, was a rival attraction to the Borden trial in the eyes of the sensation seekers this forenoon. A big crowd early gathered about the Central police station, and pushed into the court room. When Judge Borden entered he found a well filled dock.

Only those spectators who could be accommodated with seats were allowed in the room, and hundreds who had gathered in front of police headquarters for the purpose of being on hand early were not early enough, and remained on the outside, very much disappointed. The interest centered on the preliminary examination of Jose Sarmento, charged with the willful murder of Jose Maria das Candeias.

It was just one minute past 9 o'clock when the prisoner was escorted up stairs by Lieutenant Adams. His head was tied up in bandages, and he presented a sorry appearance. He was given a seat beside Hon. Walter Clifford, his counsel.

Sarmento seemed dazed, he didn't appear to realize where he was, and those who saw and talked with him yesterday were surprised at the change.

Clerk Cobb arose and read the indictment printed in the Standard yesterday, the prisoner being allowed to sit during its reading.

"What say you, Are you guilty or not guilty?" asked the clerk.

To this Mr. Clifford arose and said:

"Your honor I appear in behalf of defendant. I am satisfied that he is not in a condition to plead intelligently to this charge, and I enter a plea of not guilty and waive examination.

Can the prisoner speak sufficient English to plead himself.

"He can," replied Mr. Clifford, "but he's in no condition to plead intelligently."

"Let him plead to the charge," was the instruction given to the clerk, and again Mr. Cobb asked the question.

To this Sarmento made answer by saying, "I can't tell very well."

"Are you guilty or not guilty?" again asked the clerk.

"I don't know as I am," was the reply made in a slow and deliberate manner.

"Enter a plea of not guilty," was the order of the court, and Judge Borden adjudged Sarmento guilty, and he was ordered committed to jail to await the action of the grand jury next October.

Manuel Paull of Dartmouth, brother of the murderer, visited his brother in his cell at the Central station this morning. He stood at the cell door, gave one look at his brother, and with one heartrending shriek dropped to the floor in a faint, and had to be removed from the room.

George E. Bradley, held on suspicion of being an instrument in the drowning of Duncan O'Neil, was called, and had his case nol prossed without comment.

Fred Weston, who was in a similar predicament, held on supicion of being in some way the cause of his wife's death on Tuesday, was also allowed to depart in peace, the case against him being also nol prossed.

Liquors seized from Joseph D. Roberts, James Drew and Michael Tracey were condemned by order of the court.

James W. Welsh, for drunkenness, was sentenced to the house of correction for three months.

Patrick Trainor and Charles W. Bresler, for drunkenness, were each sent to the house of correction for 60 days.

Henry Connelly, who came to the city yesterday for the first time in six months, but was arrested for drunkenness, although William Henry Johnson made an earnest plea for him, was sent to the house of correction for 60 days.

A man who had never before been in court pleaded guilty of drunkenness and had his case continued until Monday.

John Terrien and Michael J. Burke pleaded guilty to being drunk, and each were sentenced to 60 days in the house of correction.

Then Terrien and Burke severally pleaded not guilty to an unnatural and lascivious crime with each other. Officers Brownell and McCarthy testified, and Judge Borden read the statute enacted in 1887. He said the offense was so disgusting that he did not care to comment upon it in the court room. They were adjudged probably guilty, and ordered to recognize in $2,000 to appear at the superior court in October next.

At first Burke was charged with committing a crime against nature, but upon hearing the testimony the court ordered the case nol prossed and the charges above were substituted.

John Fallon, for drunkenness, was defaulted for nonappearance. His case was continued yesterday in order to give him an opportunity to get out of town.

Merrill A. Smead pleaded guilty of larceny of a pistol, the property of Frank B. Carr. Mr. Carr and two pawnbrokers testified. The boy is but 17 years old, and in the course of cross-examination the fact developed that he was unruly and had left home. He, however, promised to return home and do better if allowed to do so. A fine of $15 was imposed.

HATCHETS.

(Continued from Third Page.)

her if she had any idea who committed the crime, and she said she had none. I asked her where she was and she said in the barn. I asked her where Bridget was and she said in her room.

Q. Where was Lizzie then? A. Up stairs in her room.

Q. Did you search the house any before going out? A. No.

Q. How did you find the barn door? A. Closed with hasp fastened.

Q. When you went into the barn what did you do? A. I went up stairs and when part of my head was above the floor I looked to see if anything had been disturbed, and didn't notice that it had. I stooped to see if there was any impression on the floor and didn't see any. I tried the floor with my hands and then stepped four or five times on the floor and looked to see if I could discover any steps and I could.

Q. Did you see any other steps in the dust but those you made? A. I did not.

Q. Did you notice the temperature of the loft when you went up? A. It was very hot.

Q. Did you notice if the windows or hay door were open or closed? A. They were closed at that time.

Q. Which of the three (door and two windows) were closed? A. They were all closed.

Q. You told us you searched about the yard, did you find anything? A. No.

Q. Did you receive instructions in the yard? A. Yes.

Q. How long after you came on the premises before you went up in the barn? A. About 10 minutes.

Q. Where did you go when you went from the place? A. To the Bowenville station.

Q. How did you go? A. By street car.

Q. How soon did you arrive there? A. About half past 12.

Q. In reference to the train for Providence, at what time did you arrive? A. Just as the train was leaving.

Q. Did you go back to the house? A. Yes.

Q. Stay about there a while? A. Yes.

Q. Anything important happen? A. No.

Q. When did you go there again? A. That evening.

Q. Did you take any part in the search of the house? A. The following Monday.

Q. Were any other officers with you? A. Yes.

Q. Was Captain Desmond one? A. Yes.

Q. Where did you first go? A. Down cellar.

Q. What did you do? A. I examined the cellar, looked over a large pile of wood, then went to the room next to the wash room, and there I found the small hatchet.

Q. Where was it? A. In a box.

Q. What was around the box but the handleless hatchet? A. Some old iron and nails.

Q. Were any other officers in the cellar when you found the handleless hatchet? A. Captain Desmond.

Q. What did you do with the hatchet? A. Gave it to Desmond.

Q. Have any talk with him about it? A. Yes.

Q. What was done with the hatchet? A. It was wrapped in a paper, and I took it to the marshal's office.

Q. To whom did you deliver it? A. The marshal.

Q. Have you had possession of it since? A. No.

Q. Was there any difference between this piece of wood in the blade (showing it) then and now? A. Yes.

Q. Can you describe the hatchet? A. I found it in the box covered with dust. There were dark spots that resembled blood on the blade. The places about the edge were more bright then than now. (The blade was on exhibition at this time.)

Q. Describe the dust and its appearance. A. It was coarse, and seemed like ashes.

Q. Did you notice anything with reference to the wood? A. It was a fresh break.

Q. What did you notice in respect to ashes and dust at the point of breaking? A. I don't know that I observed anything. I didn't see any ashes on the break.

Q. Did you notice whether the dust had adhered or was new? A. It looked new.

Cross-examined by Mr. Robinson.

Q. Did you go up to the Borden house with anybody? A. No sir.

Q. You saw Mr. Sawyer there I suppose? A. Yes sir.

Q. Any one else? A. Yes, but I can't recall who they were, all of them. There were several officers there in uniform and one, Mr. Dougherty, was in citizen's clothing.

Q. How many do you think you saw that were not policemen? A. I don't recall all of them, three or four surely.

Q. You know all the policemen that were there? A. Yes sir.

Q. Mr. Sawyer was on the outside steps? A. I don't know whether he was on the steps or not, but he was near the screen door.

Q. Did you remain near the street till Mr. Fleet came? A. Yes sir.

Q. Do you attempt to fix the time? A. It was between 11 40 and 11 45, I think.

Q. Do you think it might have been quarter of 12? A. Yes sir.

Q. That wouldn't be unreasonable at all, considering the distance you had to go? A. No sir.

Q. You passed around the house? A. Yes sir.

Q. When you went in Lizzie's room was Mr. Fleet with you? A. No sir.

Q. This was the time you had the conversation with Lizzie? A. Yes sir.

Q. This was the time you asked where she was at the time of the killing? A. Yes sir.

Q. And she said she was up in the barn? A. Yes.

Q. You had seen both of the bodies before this? A. Yes sir.

Q. Where did you then go? A. Came down stairs.

Q. How many people were there around there then? A. There were more people than when I came the first time, but I can't say how many.

Q. How about the yard to the south, were there a dozen or more people there? A. There were some people there.

Q. When you went into the barn what time was that? A. I only know by the length of time that I was in the house.

Q. You can't really tell us any more than we can infer about the time? A. No sir.

Q. When you went into the barn did you look about? A. Yes sir.

Q. Do you know whether there was a curtain at the west window or not? A. I can't say; I don't know.

Q. Was there a curtain at the window at the east side? A. I can't say. There was a curtain at one side or the other; I can't tell which one.

Q. How long were [illegible] in the barn? A. A while.

Q. What were you doing? A. Looking around.

Q. Didn't you first go up stairs? A. No sir.

Q. Stood on the stairs looking about? A. Yes.

Q. For two or three minutes? A. Yes.

Q. Then you came down and went out into the yard A. Yes.

Q. Where did you go when you went into the house? A. Into the back entry and down cellar.

Q. While you were out in the yard you got instructions? A. Yes sir.

Q. And went to the 12 29 train? A. Yes.

Q. Did you get there in time to catch the train? A. Didn't get there, no sir.

Q. You didn't get back to the Borden premises until 3 o'clock in the afternoon? A. No sir.

Q. And then stayed around till about 5? A. Yes sir.

Q. There were a great many officers about the yard, street, etc., and a great many people had been attracted to the scene? A. Yes sir.

Q. How long were you in the cellar before you left with a hatchet wrapped up in paper? A. Half an hour.

Q. The hatchet looked about the same then as it does now, only the wood was in the eye? A. Yes sir.

Here the witness at the request of Mr. Robinson showed the jury how the wood was in the hatchet.

Q. Did you take the wood out of the eye of the hatchet? A. No sir.

Q. Were there any slivers of the wood broken off? A. I didn't notice any.

Q. Did you have any one with you when you put your hand in the box? A. No sir.

Q. This box, if I understand it correctly, was about a foot and a half above the ground? A. I should think so.

Q. You had no difficulty in looking into the box while standing? A. No sir.

Q. Where were you standing? A. About three feet from the entrance to the cellar.

Q. Where were you standing with reference to the chimney? A. I can't just say, there was a man at work there, taking out brick.

Q. Was the hatchet lying on top of other things? A. Yes sir.

Q. What were the things underneath it? A. I don't know as I can tell all of them; there were umbrellas, old clothing and other articles.

Q. You put all your old broken hatchets in such a place as that, don't you?

Mr. Knowlton objected.

Mr. Robinson—I withdraw the question.

Q. You say the hatchet was all covered with dust? A. Yes sir.

Q. It looks about the same as if it stood where ashes had been dumped and dust had blown all over it? A. Yes sir.

Q. Were they wood or coal ashes? A. I don't know.

Q. Did they look as if they might be coal ashes; you know what coal ashes are, don't you? A. I couldn't tell, I'm not familiar enough with ashes to express an opinion about them.

Officer Medley illustrated to the jury the manner in which he removed the handleless hatchet from the box in which he found it, and being given a piece of paper by Governor Robinson showed as near as he could remember how he wrapped it up to put in his pocket. The witness said he did not do it with much style, and Governor Robinson said he was glad to find a man that was not on the style.

Q. After you carried it to the police station you did not have any charge of it? A. No sir.

Q. Did you state that you were a patrolman last year? A. Yes sir.

Q. And are you now? A. No sir.

Q. You have been promoted? A. Yes sir.

Q. When? A. In December.

Q. Do you know a man by the name of McHenry? A. Yes sir.

Q. Did you see him about these premises after the tragedy? A. I do not remember seeing McHenry there for some days.

Q. Was he ever connected with you upon this case? A. Yes.

Q. When? A. I cannot say as to the date, it was after the finding of the hatchet.

Q. You and he went together to measure distances? A. Yes sir.

Q. Was he working with you? A. Yes sir.

Q. Under whose direction did you go at that time? A. I went at his suggestion. He wanted to go and measure distances about the house.

Q. Were you under his control? A. No sir.

Q. Was he an associate officer on the force? A. O, no sir.

Q. Do you know whether he was engaged to assist in the police service? A. I do not know as to that, but I presume he was.

Q. Did you have any consultation with the marshal in regard to this case when McHenry was present? A. I do not know. I cannot remember. I think it is more than likely that I did.

Q. When you came out of the barn at the time of the investigation about noon on Thursday, August 4, do you know how you left the door? A. Yes.

Q. And will you tell us? A. I closed the door and left it just as I found it.

Q. You put the staple in? A. Yes sir.

Q. Did you testify at the preliminary examination? A. No sir.

Redirect.

Q. Mr. Medley, was this box in which you found the hatchet attached to anything, or was it a removable box? A. A removable one.

The usual recess was given the jury at this point, and during the interval Rev. Mr. Buck engaged in earnest conversation with the defendant.

Officer Desmond.

When the court came in again Officer Desmond of Fall River was called to the witness stand.

Q. What is your full name, sir? A. Dennis Desmond.

Q. You are a member of the police force of Fall River? A. Yes sir.

Q. Upon Saturday following Aug. 4 did you take part in any search in the Borden house? A. Yes sir.

Q. The only thing I desire to call your attention to is the dresses. Did you make any examination of the dresses in the house? A. Yes sir, I think I handled most of those articles.

Q. Did you see any dress that was soiled with paint or with spots of any sort?

Mr. Robinson—Wait a minute, I object.

Mr. Moody—Well, did you see anything that attracted your attention with reference to any dress? A. No sir.

Q. Now I will ask the preceding question. Did you see any dress that was soiled with paint or with spots of any sort? A. I will answer that the same way, No sir.

Q. On the Monday following did you take part in the search? A. Yes.

Q. Were you in command of the squad? A. Yes.

Q. I call your attention to anything that Officer Medley showed you? A. He showed me a small hatchet he brought from the cellar.

Q. Where were you when he brought it to you? A. I can't tell you.

Q. Did it have a handle? A. It had a small piece of wood in the back.

Q. What did you do when he gave it to you? A. I took it for examination.

Q. Describe everything about the hatchet? A. It was covered by dust, which was not of a fine nature, not as if it might have collected from standing, but coarse. There were more spots on it then than now. The broken part looked more fresh than it does now.

Q. Did you examine the box in which it was found? Was it moveable? A. Yes the box was an old one; larger than a small salt box.

Q. Could you tell what the box was used for? A. It had old iron, mostly bolts and nails in it.

Q. What did you observe in respect to the dust on the box you handled? A. I can't say I handled it.

Q. Did you look at it? A. I examined it.

Q. Did you notice dust on the box? A. Yes.

Q. How about the fineness of the dust on the articles in the box? A. The dust on the articles was fine, not like that on the hatchet blade.

Q. Who carried the hatchet away? A. Officer Medley. I gave it to him wrapped up.

Cross-examined by Mr. Robinson.

Q. When at the house on Friday what did you do? A. We commenced in the attic and examined it thoroughly.

Q. Did you examine Bridget's dresses. A. Yes.

Q. Did you find any spots on them? A. Yes.

Q. Were you looking for anything but blood spots? A. That was important.

Q. That was all you attached importance to? A. We were looking for what might appear.

Q. You were looking for the criminal also, weren't you? A. Yes.

Q. Did you find any blood on the dresses? A. I cannot tell.

Q. Were you looking for it? A. Yes.

Q. What did you find? A. Nothing in my opinion that we were after.

Q. Did you search all the things in the attic? A. Yes.

Q. You were given every facility for search, weren't you? A. Yes.

Q. Not the slightest obstacle was placed in your way? A. Not to mine.

Q. You found a box in the attic that you had to send down stairs for some one to open, didn't you? A. I found one I couldn't open.

Q. Didn't some one come up to show you how to open it? A. Yes.

Q. Was her sister there? A. I didn't see her.

Q. You couldn't get it open until one of the sisters came and showed you how, could you? A. I couldn't get it open until some one showed us how. I don't know who it was.

Q. It was a woman, wasn't it, who showed you? A. I don't know who it was?

Q. You searched the attic and the whole top of the house thoroughly didn't you? A. Yes sir.

Q. Did you go out onto the roof? A. No, I didn't go out on the roof, but it seems to me that the assistant marshal looked out onto the roof.

Q. After you looked over the whole top of the house, where did you next go? A. I went down to Mr. and Mrs. Borden's room.

Q. How thorough a search did you give this room? A. I considered that we gave it a good thorough search.

Q. In the room where the safe was did you see any clothes? A. It seems to me there were both ladies' and gentlemen's clothes hung there, covered with a sheet.

Q. Were the dresses or any of them turned inside out? A. I can't tell.

Q. You didn't find any blood on any of the dresses did you? A. No sir, I did not.

Q. Did anybody find any blood on any of the dresses? A. Not that I know of.

Q. Did you find any grease or paint spots on any of the dresses? A. Not that I'm aware of.

Q. And you looked them over thoroughly? A. Yes sir.

Q. You gave things a good, careful, thorough search? You went into Emma's room and went through the same process? A. Yes.

Q. Went through the spare room in exactly the same way? A. Yes.

Q. You made an absolute, complete and unrestrained search of everything about the house? A. I tried to.

Q. When was it that Officer Medley handed you the hatchet head? A. The following Monday.

Q. Did you go down cellar when you made your thorough search before? A. No sir, but instructions had been given to others to do it.

Q. Where were you standing when he brought the hatchet to you? He passed it to you out of his hand? A. Yes sir.

Q. You took it into your hand? A. Yes, and wrapped it up in a newspaper and passed it back again.

Q. Did you look into this box? A. Yes.

Q. What was in it? A. There was nothing but iron in that box.

Q. What became of the hatchet head after it left there? A. I don't know. I supposed it had been with the city marshal.

Q. And been in the custody of the government from that time down to the present? A. Yes sir.

Q. When you took the hatchet head in your hand it was covered with dust? A. I should say it was covered with dirt rather than dust.

Mr. Robinson—There are various kinds of dirt.

Witness—What I mean is it was a coarse substance rather than fine dust.

Q. Whether there was the same kind of dirt on the things in that box you don't know? A. It was coarser on the hatchet than on the other articles in that box.

Q. You saw the pile of ashes, of course? A. Yes, and shoveled them over.

Q. You shoveled bushels of ashes, I suppose? A. Yes sir.

Q. And kicked up considerable dust, too, quite likely? A. I suppose I did.

Q. Were they wood or coal ashes? A. I should call them coal ashes.

Q. Did you testify at the hearing? A. No sir.

Q. Have you been to the trial before today? A. No sir.

Q. You've read the newspaper reports of it? A. No sir, not a word.

Q. The papers are supplied at the police headquarters, of course? A. Yes.

Q. All written out with the questions and answers? A. I suppose so.

The witness showed the jury how he wrapped the hatchet up in a newspaper.

DETECTIVE SEAVER

Testifies to the Finding of the Handleless Hatchet.

State Detective Seaver was the next witness who testified.

Q. George F. Seaver is it? A. Yes sir.

Q. You are a member of the state district police force? A. I am.

Q. Living where? A. In Taunton.

Q. How long have you been a member of the force? A. Fifteen years, about that time.

Q. Did you go to Fall River at any time in reference to the homicide? A. I did.

Q. When did you go? A. I went August 4 in the afternoon about 5 o'clock.

Q. Did you go to the house on that day? A. I did.

Q. Make any observations of any sort upon that day? A. I went over the house and was about the premises that day.

Q. Did you make some observation and take measurements with reference to blood spots? A. I did.

Q. When was that? A. My impression is that it was the 13th.

Q. On the Saturday were you at the Borden house? A. I was.

Q. Were you there during a search that was being made by Captain Desmond and other officers under his control? A. I was.

Q. At any time on the Saturday did you see a hatchet without a handle? A. I did.

Q. Who was present when you saw it? A. Captain Fleet.

Q. Did any one point it out to you, or did you see it without having it pointed out? A. Captain Fleet pointed it out.

Q. Where was the hatchet then? A. It was in a box in the cellar.

Q. Could you tell anything about where the box was? A. It was lying on some wood within perhaps a foot of the floor.

Q. Did Mr. Fleet point out any shelf to you at that time? A. He pointed to a shelf up side the wall.

Q. Did he point out where it was when he first saw the box?

Mr. Robinson—"Wait a minute, I object to the question."

Mr. Moody—I waive the question then.

Q. Will you tell me where the shelf was that he pointed to? Do you recall in which cellar the shelf was? A I do not.

Q. What did you do when you saw this hatchet? A. I took hold of it and laid it back in the box and looked in the box to see if there was any handle to it.

Q. Did you find any handle? A. I did not.

Q. Can you describe the appearance of the hatchet at the time you saw it on Saturday? A. It appeared to be covered with a coarse dust or ashes. I should call it more ashes than dust. It was coarser than the dust on the box.

Q. There were other things in the box? A. There were.

Q. What parts of the hatchet were covered with the coarse dust? A. The sides of the hatchets were covered with the dust.

Q. Did you notice anything with reference to whether there was anything in the eye of the hatchet? A. There was dust in the eye of the hatchet.

Q. Can you give any description of the break in the wood? A. It was apparently a new break.

Q. How does its appearance in respect to color compare with its present appearance? A. It looks darker now.

Q. After you took up the hatchet and looked at it what did you do with it? A. Laid it back in the box.

Q. Now, Mr. Seaver, on the Saturday you made a search with reference to dresses, or an examination, rather? A. Yes sir.

Q. You were with Mr. Desmond's party at that time? A. Captain Desmond and I were up stairs a part of the time.

Q. Where were the dresses that you examined? A. They were in the large closet over the front hall.

Q. Won't you describe the character of your examination of these dresses on Saturday? A. I looked at all the dresses except two or three in the corner and passed them to Captain Fleet and he examined them. The dresses in the corner I am very sure were silk and I did not touch them at all.

Q. Did you discover anything upon any of these dresses? A. I did not.

Q. Did you see a light blue dress with diamond spots upon it and paint around the bottom of the dress and on its front? A. I did not.

Q. Did you make a sufficiently careful examination of them to have discovered such a dress so marked with paint if it had been there? A. I did.

Mr. Robinson—Wait a minute, wait a minute; I do not think that is a proper question. I ask that the question be excluded and the answer with it.

Mr. Moody—I suppose you do not object to the form of it?

Mr. Robinson—I object to the substance of it.

The Court—The question stands.

Mr. Moody—Did you examine any other dresses in any other part of the house except in the front clothes closet? A. No sir.

Q. At some time you have told us you made some examinations of blood spots? A. Yes sir.

Q. When was that? A. My impression is that it was the 13th.

Q. Have you a memorandum of the result of your observation? A. Yes sir.

Q. When was it made, sir? A. It was made at that time. I put it on paper that day and copied it afterwards.

Q. Would the memorandum assist you in your description? A. Yes sir.

Q. Won't you please consult it then, and state in your own way what you found with reference to blood spots? A. There were on the mopboard behind the head of the lounge five small spots of blood. On the wall above the lounge were a cluster of small spots in a radius 18 inches long by 10 wide. On the frame of the glass and picture were 40 spots; the highest four feet 10 inches.

Q. Where was the highest spot in the room? A. On the wall one foot from the kitchen door.

Q. Did you find blood on the door leading from the sitting room to the parlor? A. Yes.

Q. How far was it from the door jamb or head of the lounge to the kitchen door? A. Nine feet 7½ inches.

Q. How much blood was there on the kitchen door frame? A. One spot, three feet and one inch from the floor.

Q. How far was it from the head of the lounge to the dining room table? A. Twenty-five feet.

Q. Did you find any further blood spots in the room on the day of the murder? A. One spot on the door leading to the kitchen.

Q. Did you make any observations up stairs? A. Yes.

Q. Will you state what measurements you made? A. I found seven blood spots on the mopboard on the east side of the room in a radius of two feet five inches.

Q. Did you find any on the marble slab? A. On the slab of the dressing case were 15, on the upper drawer of the dressing case were four, and on the lower 13; on the face board of the dressing case were so many I couldn't count them; on the lower face board of the case were blood and matted hair; on the corner of the dressing case and running east was a smear of blood.

Q. Did you notice on the glass of the dressing case? A. Yes, 15 spots.

Q. What did they look like? A. They were not round; the heaviest parts were at the bottom.

Q. Did you see the spots on the north side of the wall next the dressing case? A. Yes.

Q. It was where a piece was cut out? A. Yes.

Q. You were there when the piece was cut out? A. Yes.

Q. Tell us the distance of that spot on the north side next to the dressing case to the window case. A. It is 9 inches.

Q. Did you notice any other spots? A. There were two blood spots between the dressing case and the window. One of them was cut out and the other was very small.

Q. Have you had any of the axes or hatchets in your possession at any time? A. Yes, I had the two hatchets and took them to the grand jury.

Q. Did you make any change in the hatchets or the loose piece of wood? A. I did not touch it at all.

The witness was cross-examined by Mr. Robinson and got badly "rattled," furnishing much amusement to the spectators.

Q. When you looked in the box down cellar did you see the hatchets in the box? A. I think when I first saw it it was out of the box.

Q. When you first saw it was the piece of wood in the hatchet? A. Yes sir.

[Continued on 6th Page, Second Edition.]

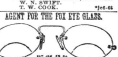

Column 1

Column 2

SECOND EDITION.

HATCHETS.

(Continued from Fourth Page.)

Q. Do you know when those slivers
were taken off?   A. No sir.
Q. Where is it now?   A. I mislaid
it.
Q. Do you know Mr. McHenry?   A.
I have seen the gentleman.
Q. That doesn't exactly answer the
question. Do not know him very
much; no sir.
Q. Has he been in service with you
at all?   A. He was at Fall River, but
he wasn't with me at all.
Q. Where does he belong?   A. I can-
not tell; he came from Providence there.
Q. What did he do while there?   A.
I do not know, sir.
Q. Did you go to the house with
him?   A. No sir, I did not.
Q. Did you see him afterwards?   A.
Yes sir, I saw him at the station several
times.
Q. Do you know where he is now?
A. No sir.
Q. Did you discover in the dining
room a large spot of blood on the inside
of the door post near the bottom?   A.
Yes sir.
Q. Have you got a memorandum of
that?   A. No sir.
Q. Didn't you make a memorandum
of it at that time?   A. I think I did.
Q. Where is it now?   A. I do not
know, I lost it.
Q. When did you lose it?   A. I lost
it, I suppose, at the time of the hearing
at Fall River.
Q. In the original memorandum did
you have a note of the blood on the inside of that jam to the door?   A. I
think not, because the piece of the door
with the blood on it was taken out by
a carpenter and carried to the station.
Q. Didn't you examine it and measure distances from it?   A. I would not
swear that I did not.
Q. Is it not a fact that you did not
make a memorandum because it was not
blood?   A. No sir.
Q. Did you know anything else out of
your memorandum?   A. I do not know.
Q. Where did you say you saw that
box that had the hatchet in it?   A. In
the cellar, sir, near the chimney. The
box was six or eight inches from the
floor.
Q. Was it in the same room as the
furnace?   A. My impression is that it
was in the next room.
Q. That is where the pile of ashes
was?   A. Yes sir.
Q. Didn't you see a blue dress hanging on the second hook from the window

Officer Medley.

the piece of that handle is?   A. No sir,
I cannot.
Q. Let me ask you again as a carpenter, can you tell us what kind of a
piece of wood that is?   A. No sir.
Q. Not with your experience as a carpenter?   A. No sir.
Q. Was the wood sound or rotten?
A. It looked somewhat rotten.
Q. As a carpenter can you tell us
whether it is rotten or not?   A. No sir.
Q. Did the piece of wood in the han-
dle look as if it had been in the water
at that time?   A. No sir, not at that
time, but I thought afterwards that it
had been in the water.
Q. Now, upon your judgment as a carpenter, how long would you say those
slivers had been taken off?   A. I can't
tell.
Q. When was the grand jury held?
A. In November.
Q. Had those slivers been taken off
at that time?   A. I can't say.
Q. Had they been taken off within six
months?   A. I can't say.
Q. Three months?   A. I can't say.
Q. With your best judgment it was a
fresh break?   A. I wouldn't say, it was
within three months of when I first saw
the hatchet.
Q. At the examination of the dresses
on that Saturday you and Officer Fleet
were the only ones there?   A. Yes sir,
at that time.
Q. In the clothes room there was no
piece of furniture with drawers?   A.
No sir.
Q. You wasn't looking for any particular dress with a bold skirt or slivers
with a loose fitting blouse, or a dress
waist, or any particular kind of a dress
were you?   A. No sir.
Q. You wasn't looking for any particular dress of alpaca, delaine, challie, or Bedford cord, were you?   A. No
sir.
Q. You're not in that business are
you?   A. No sir.
Q. You wasn't looking for any blue
dresses were you?   A. No sir.
Q. Will you swear on your oath before this jury whether the dress was
light or dark blue?   A. No sir.
Q. Now on your oath what dress did
she have on that afternoon?   A. I can't
tell.
Q. What was the first dress that you
examined?   A. My impression is that it
was a silk dress.
Q. Did you turn it wrong side out?
A. No sir.
Q. You handed it to Mr. Fleet and
he examined it carefully, didn't he?   A.
Yes sir, I handed them all to Mr. Fleet.
Q. Dr. Dolan was there when you
were making your searches, wasn't he?
A. I don't remember seeing him.
Q. Dr. Dolan examined the blue
dress, didn't he?   A. Not while I was
there.
Q. Were there any other blue dresses
there?   A. I don't know.
Q. Did you see any blue dresses
there?   A. I won't swear to it.
Q. If there was any blue dress there
you didn't discover any paint on it?   A.
No sir.
Q. Do you remember whether there
were any umbrellas, parasols or anything

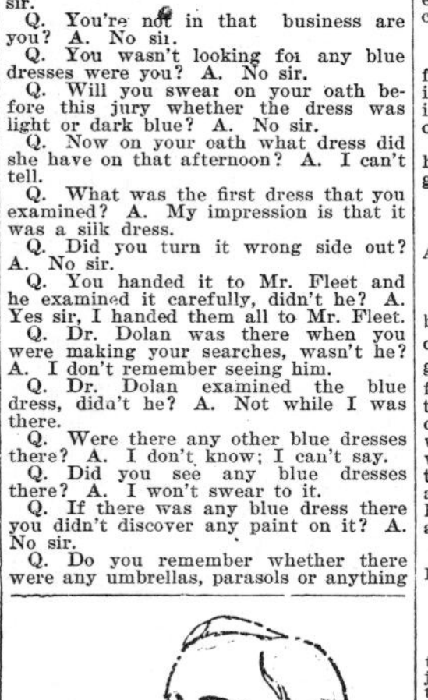

Officer Edson.

in the clothes closet?   A. I do not recall it.
Q. Were you present when Dr. Dolan
examined it?   A. No sir, I do not recall it.

Adjourned Until Monday.

After this testimony the court was
formally adjourned till Monday morning at 9 o'clock. The jurors were placed
in charge of the deputy sheriffs and filed
out of the room.
Miss Borden, before leaving the room,
held an informal levee, and was very
greeted by quite a number of friends.

AGREEMENT OF COUNSEL

As to Circumstances Under Which Lizzie
Testified.

The following is the written agreement
between counsel with regard to the circumstances under which Lizzie Borden
gave her testimony at the inquest last
fall, counsel agreeing upon the state of
the facts, on Monday next the question
of the admissibility of this testimony
will be argued by counsel. The agreement
was submitted to the court just previous
to the adjournment this forenoon. The
agreement was signed by Miss Borden
herself and by counsel for government
and defense respectively:

Commonwealth of Massachusetts.
Bristol ss.
Superior Court, June, 1893.
Commonwealth vs. Lizzie A. Borden.
Agreed Statement.

1. The declarations offered are the testimony under oath of the accused in a
judicial proceeding, namely, an inquest as
to the cause of death of the two persons
named in the indictment now on trial, duly
notified and held by and before the district court in Fall River, in accordance
with the provisions of the public statutes.
2. The defendant was not then under arrest, but three days before the time of
giving such testimony was notified by the
city marshal and mayor of Fall River that
she was suspected of committing the crimes
charged in the indictment on trial; and the
house, and the inmates, including the defendant, were thereafter until her arrest under the constant observation of police officers of Fall River specially detailed for
that purpose and stationed around the
house.
3. That before she so testified she was
duly summoned by a subpoena to attend
said inquest and testify thereat.
4. That before she so testified she requested, through her counsel, A. J. Jennings, of the district attorney and the
judge to preside and presiding at said inquest, the privilege to have her said counsel there present, which request was refused by both the district attorney and the
judge, and said counsel was not present.
5. That when her testimony so given was
concluded she was not allowed to leave the
court house, and was about two hours afterward placed under arrest upon a warrant issued upon the charge and accusation of having committed the crimes set
forth in this indictment. Said warrant was
issued upon a complaint sworn to before
the clerk of said district court acting as
justice of peace under the statute, which
was returnable to said district court but
said city marshal after the conclusion of
the testimony of the defendant at the inquest, being the same complaint upon
which the defendant was tried before and
district court and held to answer before
the grand jury. Said city marshal was present at the inquest when the defendant testified.
6. Prior to said inquest, to wit, on the

Officer Mahoney.

of that sort?   A. My impression is that
there was, but I don't know.
Q. Your impression, don't you know?
A. I won't swear to it.
Q. Did you discover any waterproof?
A. In that closet?
Q. Anywhere.   A. I cannot say that
I did.
Q. You know what I mean by water-
proof?   A. Yes sir.
Q. Wouldn't you remember if you
saw one?   A. I do not know.

The Navahoe's Time of Sailing.

(continued at foot of column 1)

Column 3

FINANCIAL.

**Strong and Active Closing Today—Mar-
kets Advance Under Lead of Sugar—Gen-
eral Electric and the Grangers—Sugar
Touches 93—Money Firm—The New York
Bank Statement Shows Heavy Reserve
Decrease—Has No Effect on the Course of
Stocks—In General.**

Saturday, June 10.

Market values show a slight improvement
over those of a week ago, and the tone of
gossip is much more cheerful. The change
is due to covering by shorts and a freer
movement of grain to European points,
thereby causing a weakening in sterling
exchange and removing for the time being
at least the danger of gold exports. Gold
shipments can only be stopped by natural
means, and the exportation of grain is one
of these natural factors. Special stocks
show considerable activity in the trading,
but the greater part of the list is rather
quiet, one of the favorite points being
that there is just now little pressure to sell.
That liquidation is entirely over is not
thought possible by any means, but a temporary cessation of it is a relief and allows
prices to harden.
The local money market is firm with most
loans at 6 per cent.
Local bank clearances for the week ending
today compare as below:

	1893.	1892.	Dec.
	$479,012	$502,554	$22,583

In Boston the market for money is unchanged. Call loans rule at 5 to 7 per cent.,
though the average rate of call money is 6
per cent. Time money shows no change.
Commercial paper is finding a slightly better market. At clearing today loans were
made at 7 per cent. New York funds sold
at 30 and 40 cents discount.
Call money in New York ranges from 4
to 6 per cent. Time money is not altered.
There is a fair supply offering where the
conditions are favorable at 4½ to 6 per
cent.
Heavy offerings of grain bills have de-
moralized the sterling exchange market.
Rates are soft.
Bonds more active, but hardly steady as
regards prices.
The New York bank opened firm this
morning with prices well up to closings.
Northern Pacific preferred strong at 35%,
Reading at 16. National Lead 31%, General
Electric 72½.
At 11 o'clock the market was strong. Su-
gar-chief active stock, at 90%, dividend on.
Chicago Gas sold at 71¼. C. B. & Q. and
Omaha strong.
At the close stocks were very active and
prices the last seen for some time. C. B. &
Q. 88½, Sugar 90, do. preferred 92, St. Paul
79%, General Electric 73. Finals were at
large gains over the opening. Poor bank
statement had no effect.
The following table shows the fluctuations
of the leading active stocks during the day:

Stocks.	Opening.	11 a.m.	Close.
Atchison,	24%	25%	25%
C. B. & Q.	87½	87%	88½
Omaha,	39%	40	41
Reading,	16¼	16¼	16¼
Sugar,	83%	90%	90
St. Paul,	69%	69%	70%
Western Union,	83%	84	84%

Today's New York bank statement shows
the following changes:

Reserve decreased	$6,566,600
Loans decreased	2,290,000
Specie decreased	677,100
Legals decreased	9,060,900
Deposits decreased	12,485,600
Circulation increased	43,000

The Boston market opened dull and firm.
General Electric 72, Atchison 25, C. B. &
Q. 87%.
At 11 o'clock the market was stronger under the lead of Sugar, which moved up to
87%, ex-dividend. Calumet & Hecla 285 and
288, sales. Bay State Gas 6%.
At the close the market was buoyant at top
prices. Activity was a feature of the last 15
minutes. Sugar a leader, General Electric
advanced to 73.
The following table shows the fluctuations
of the leading active stocks during the day:

Stocks.	Opening.	11 a.m.	Close.
Atchison,	24%	25%	25%
C. B. & Q.	87%	87½	88%
Sugar,	87%	87½	88½
Gen'l Electric,	72	72½	73
Westinghouse,	87	87½	88½
Bay State Gas,			6%
National Lead			

*Asked.   Ex dividend.

REAL ESTATE SALES.

Healy & Jenney have sold for W. H.
Coffin, to Theophile Lebeau, lot on south
side Coggeshall street, containing 10.27
rods; also sold for James Brown, to
Hermine Boucher, lot on north side of
Phillips avenue, containing 14.88 rods.
Elizabeth C. Wood has sold to Rebecca
E. Wood a lot of land with buildings
thereon situated on County street, the
lot containing 24.62 rods.
Josiah Matthews, 2d, of Dartmouth,
has sold to Susan G. H. Snow of this city
a lot of land in Dartmouth, on the west
side of the road leading from the head of
Apponegansett river to the village of
Apponegansett.
H. A. Leonard has sold to Mrs. Carroll
B. Mendell the residence belonging to
George W. Gay, consisting of two story
cottage and 12 rods of land on the west
side of Summer street north of Hillman
street.
Dr. J. P. St. Germain has sold to Walter
G. Card and Ezra G. Farnham 53.45 rods
of land on the Apponegansett road.
Daniel H. Howland sold at auction to-
day an undivided part of a lot of land
numbered eight, near Biles' Corner in
Dartmouth, to Charles W. Howland of
Dartmouth for $334.
George S. Wordell has sold for $2,500
to Benjamin Querripel et al. two lots
of land in Dartmouth.
John Stachman has sold to John Balt-
hazar a lot of land on the north side of
Coggeshall street, containing 13.3 rods.

FAIRHAVEN.

The load of castings for the water works
has arrived and is being stored at Union
wharf. The pumping station will be built
of brick, 72x30, with engine, boiler and
coal room. The foundation is being put
in.
One of William C. Grimshaw's children
was bitten severely the other day by a dog
belonging to Ira A. Reed. The animal was
shot.
Job Parris keeps a small stable on Laurel
street. The other day he let a horse and
buggy to some Mosher children. They got
into a frolic and the one who was driving
let the reins drop. Finding he had things
all his own way the horse ran into a post
and the wagon was badly smashed. Clearly himself he ran from "Madison square"
to the stable. The children were unhurt.
W. H. Fletcher, clerk in Goodnow's store,
is so well pleased with Fairhaven that he
will bring his family here Monday, and occupy one of F. W. Andrew's houses on
Cottage street.
Captain Charles Martin of East Gloucester is visiting Selectman John I. Bryant.
The bathing houses will open Thursday,
June 22. H. H. Rogers has purchased the handsome 28-foot catboat Greilel of Wareham.
She was brought here Memorial Day by J.
K. Nye.
There are now 8,500 books at the Millicent library. The income will permit the
addition of 700 books a year. By putting
in addition stacks accommodations can be
made for 45,000 volumes. No more books
will be added until those already on hand
are catalogued. A room will be prepared
in the basement for books not either referred to.
A recep-ion was given to Rev. W. L.
Mead at the residence of E. F. Williams
Thursday evening. Music was furnished
by A. B. Hmill and Miss Alice G. Anthony
of New Bedford.
The curbing for the town hall is ready to
be shipped from Blue Hill, Me.
Contractor Willcott was in town today.

A FISHERMAN'S PARADISE.

The Hotel Westport, at Westport point,
will open for the season July 1. The hotel
will be this season, as for the past five,
under the efficient management of Mr. H.
A. Brown of Saxonville, which is of itself
a sufficient guarantee as to the quality of
service and comfort offered to guests. To
those in search of health and invigorating
sea air, as well as to lovers of boating and
fishing, and, in fact, all aquatic pleasures,
the Atlantic coast does not offer a superior
retreat.—Boston Journal.

MARRIED.

—Plymouth June 7th, Lewis J. Bridgeman
of Melrose to Annie Page Campbell of Ply-
mouth.
In Kingston, June 3d, Harry E. Littlefield
to Priscilla M. Hunt, both of Duxbury.
In Chicago, May 10th, Herbert Swift of
Jackson, Miss., formerly of Middleboro, to
Mrs. Lizzie Simmons of Vicksburg.

DEATHS.

In Marion, June 9th, Elizabeth C., widow of
James Wettel, aged 79.
In Middleboro, June 5th, John C. Vaughan,
56; 7th, Nathaniel Wing, 81; Charlotte A.,
widow of Edmund Pope, 72; Lydia F., daughter of Abiathar B. Cobb, 10 months.
In Plymouth, June 7th, Henry W. Yeadon,
47.

MARINE INTELLIGENCE.

Sld from Portland 9th, sch John Twohy,
Thatcher, Norfolk.
Sld from New London 9th, sch Luella Nick-
erson, Nickerson, this port.
Ar at New York 9th, steamer Donna Maria,
Marrieuis, Oporto, St. Michaels, Fayal, etc;
City of Columbia, James, West Point; sch
Horace W Macomber, Bray, Boston, and for
for Philadelphia.
Passed through Hell Gate 9th, sch Donna T
Briggs, Garvey, New York for Bath.
Ar at Philadelphia 9th, schs Edw F Mans-
field, Chase, hence. Old,sch Chas L Sprague,
Nickerson, Wareham.
Ar at Newport 9th, sch Robert I Carter,
Peak, Bath. Sld, sch Wm B Herrick, Boston.
Ar at Brunswick, Ga, 9th, sch Maggie An-
drews, Snow, New York.
Ar at Savannah 9th, bark Mary S Ames,
Knowles, New York. Sld, steamer Kansas
City, Fisher, New York.
Old at West Washington 8th, sch A J Par-
dee, Crosby, Boston.
Old at Havana 9th, sch Richmond S Spof-
ford, Nickerson, Mobile.

WEATHER INDICATIONS.

Slightly Cooler.

New York, June 10.—At 8 30 a. m. the
weather was clear, wind south, temperature 63. The Herald says: In the middle states and in New England on Monday partly cloudy to fair, slightly cooler weather and fresh westerly winds will
prevail, preceded by light local coast
rains; and on Monday warmer, fair
weather. Wednesday fair weather, and
in the South on Sunday and Monday fair
will have mostly southwesterly breeze
to the banks.

Fall River Print Cloth Market.

Fall River, June 10.—
The local cloth market has been dull during
the week and there has been only a moderate
inquiry for goods. Prices are still quoted at
3 7-16 cents for regulars, because manufacturers are so well informed on the prospect
that they will not shade that figure, though
brokers report that they could purchase freely at it if there were orders for them. The mills
trade is altogether tight of money. There is
no stock in sight in the country, and the contracts which call for deliveries in the future
show that printers are not heavily supplied.
If confidence in the financial situation could
be restored it is thought that the mills could
dispose of their output up to next fall, but as
things now stand there is a disposition to
buy in a hand-to-mouth fashion.

Column 4

**LOCAL STOCK SALES AT AUCTION
TODAY.**

Sanford & Kelley sold the following shares
of local stocks at auction today:
$500 Wamsutta Club 5's.....95% and interest.

STOCK AND BOND MARKETS.

Bids at close of the Stock Boards today.
New York, June 10.

GOVERNMENT BONDS

U. S. 2s,	98
4s, reg'd,	112%
4s, coupons,	113%
currency 6s,	102%

RAILROADS

Atchison	25%
Clev., Cin., Chi. & St. Louis	48
Chicago & Eastern Illinois pref.	95
Chicago, Burlington & Quincy	88½
Delaware & Hudson	132%
Delaware & Lackawanna	141%
Erie	13%
Illinois Central	98
Lake Shore	125
Louisville & Nashville	67%
Manhattan	132
Michigan Central	98
Missouri Pacific	27%
New Jersey Central	111
New York Central	104%
New York & New England	22%
Northern Pacific pref.	36%
Northwest	107
Philadelphia & Reading	17%
Rock Island	71%
St. Paul	79%
St. Paul pref.	118
Union Pacific	20%
Wabash pref.	17½

MISCELLANEOUS

Chicago Gas	73%
National Cordage	13%
Ontario Silver	14%
Oregon Nav.	44
Pullman	172
Silver	82
Sugar	90
Sugar, pref.	183%
Tennessee Coal	83
Western Union	84%

BONDS

Atchison 4s	78
Atchison 2ds	42
Bell Telephone 7s	109
Chicago, Burlington & Northern 5s	100
C. B. & Q. Cons. Mort. 7s	*115
C. B. & Q. Conv. 5s	110
Chicago & West Michigan 5s	*94
Mexican Central 4s	67
Illinois Steel Co. 5s	*90

RAILROADS

Atchison	25%
Boston & Albany	*208
Boston & Lowell	193
Boston & Maine	163%
Boston & Providence	255
Central Mass. pref.	45
Chicago, Burlington & Quincy	88%
Chicago Jun. & Un. Stk. Yds.	86
Chicago Jun. & Un. Stk. Yds. pref.	89%
Chicago & West Michigan	28%
Cleveland & Canton & Southern	4
Cleveland, Canton & Southern pref.	14%
Fitchburg	85%
Flint & Pere Marquette pref.	59
Mexican Central	13%
New York & New England	14½
New York & New England pref.	66
Old Colony	185
Oregon Short Line	15%
Pullman Palace Car	171
Union Pacific	20%
Wisconsin Central	14½
West End	56%
West End pref.	79%

MINING

Butte & Boston	6%
Calumet & Hecla	285
Catalpa	1
Franklin	14%
Kearsarge	6%
Osceola	25%
Quincy	110
Tamarack	128

MISCELLANEOUS

American Bell Telephone	190
Erie Telephone	64
New England Telephone	55
West End Land	.25
Lamson Store Service	*17%
Illinois Steel Co.	*69
Sugar common	90
Sugar pref.	*93%
Gen'l Electric	73
Westinghouse	37
Bay State Gas	6%
National Lead	31%

*Asked.   Ex dividend.

FOUND.

CHAIRS RESEATED—At 38 Mill st. Send
postal. je10-7t

WANTS.

GIRL—To cane chairs. Call after 6 p. m.,
38 Mill st. je10-7t

FOR SALE.

FIVE NEW BABY CARRIAGES—Cheap.
38 Mill st. je10-7t

F. A. F. ADAMS,

North Second Street (Opposite Post Office,)

Real Estate Agency.

House in good order; nice carriage sheds;
good location; center of village. Cost over
$10,000, will sell for $6,500. A beautiful place;
fine views; a bargain.

FINE 2 1-2 STORY HOUSE on a corner.
New; best of repairs; rents well. Price
$4,000; easy terms.

FIFTH STREET property in the heart of the
city, within 10 rods of land. New.
Price $4,000; easy terms.

COTTAGE HOUSE stable and 1 rod of
1 mile to horse cars. Price $600 if sold at
once; easy terms.

FURNISHED TENEMENT to rent for the
summer. Fifth
thing in first class order.

NEAR WILLIS STREET cottage house,
stable, three fire rooms; large lot of land.
Price $1,600. Very easy terms to right party.

COTTAGE HOUSE stable and 14 rods of
land. Good location. All improvements. Price
$4,000. Easy terms.

COTTAGE HOUSE stable and 42 rods of land.
Near. Modern improvements. First class repair. Price low. Easy terms.

HOUSE LOTS

HOUSE LOTS and houses in Fairhaven.
Some good bargains in house

WE HAVE a very large list of houses, house
lots, land and farms for sale that are
not advertised. Call and see them.

F. A. F. ADAMS,
No. 38 North Second St.

Column 5

CONFERENCE AT SPRINGFIELD.

New England African M. E. Churches Enjoy a Slight Sensation.

Springfield, June 10.—The session of the New England conference of the African Methodist Episcopal church was slighty flavored yesterday by a tiff between Presiding Elder F. I. M. Webster and Rev. W. H. Thomas, pastor of the First church of Providence. The conference was called to order by Bishop Tanner and the religious services were conducted by Rev. Henderson Davis of the Nova Scotia conference. Rev. A. W. Hawley and W. H. Thomas were made trustees for four years. It was voted to appropriate $25 to add to the $125 appropriated by the Philadelphia and New York conference for the election of Bishop Tanner to the directorship of the American Bible society. It was voted to hold the Sunday school convention at Fall River the first week in September. Rev. Dr. Coppin, editor of the Review, was present, and spoke in the interest of his work. The conference presented Bishop Tanner with a copy of discipline and hymn book combined as a token of esteem in which he is held.

LITTLE COMPTON.

At the annual town meeting held Tuesday William S. Briggs was chosen moderator, and the officers chosen for the ensuing year were:

Councilmen—Pardon C. Brownell, George A. Gray, Samuel E. Gray, Philip Wilbour, Frank E. Simmons.

Town Treasurer and Collector—William S. Almy.

Assessors—Philip W. Almy, John H. Tompkins, George H. Peckham.

THE CADETS' DRILL.

Contest for Sanders & Barrows and Company Medals.

Corporal Butterfield and Sergeant Lee Winners.

Company and Battalion Drills Precede Contest for Trophies.

Commencements and graduating exercises may be the red-letter days in the average student life, but to the High School Cadet of New Bedford the semiannual prize drill is the event that marks a culminating point more notably than anything else in his scholastic career.

The semiannual prize drill of the High School Cadets took place in Guards Armory last evening, and about 250 of the friends of the command were present.

It was 8 15 when Bugler Fred C. Graves stepped into the center of the surface and sounded the assembly. The command formed in double rank at the west end of the hall, numbering three officers and 35 men. After a salute to the special guests on the platform Captain John M. Kelleher put his command through an excellent company drill for 20 minutes. The movements which were performed with a creditable degree of accuracy embraced movements in fours and twos, in column and line, single and double rank, platoons, wheeling, fours in circle, opening ranks and the manual of arms. The lines were well preserved and the distances accurate and even.

The next feature was the battalion drill. The command was divided into three companies, commanded by Lieutenant William B. Smith, Jr., Lieutenant Ernest C. Reed and Sergeant John A. Lee, Jr., with Captain John M. Kelleher as major. The various evolutions, intricate in their appearance, were performed in a way that reflected much credit on the officers and men alike, while the general effect was a fitting testimonial to the excellent instruction of Captain John K. McAfee.

The great event of the evening, however, was the competition for the Sanders & Barrows' medal and the company medal, held respectively by Sergeants John A. Lee, Jr., and Arthur R. Magee.

The prize squad consisted of 21 men: Sergeants Arthur R. Magee, John A. Lee, Jr., Bowie and Gammons, Corporals Butterfield and Tripp and Privates Stetson, Weeden, Humphrey, Hunt, White, Keene, Gainswell, McAfee, Arnett, Hillman, Potter, Jenney, Tripp, Chase and Allen.

They were marched out before the judges, ex-Captains Ellis L. Howland and John H. Holt and ex-Sergeant George E. Noble, and were put through a searching drill in the manual of arms for several minutes. Their work was very creditable, but the judges found enough flaws to melt them down to a dozen, who composed the second squad.

These were Sergeants Lee and Magee, Corporals Bowie, Tripp and Butterfield and Privates McAfee, Stetson, Humphrey, Hunt, Arnett, Hillman and Chase. This squad was commanded by Lieutenant Smith and were drilled till seven had displayed points of weakness sufficient to lead the judges to deem them the victims of their weeding process. Consequently all were dropped out after a few moments, except Sergeants Lee and Magee, Corporal Butterfield and Privates Stetson and Hillman, who remained.

This squad was commanded by Lieutenant Ernest C. Reed, and in a few minutes two faded away, Privates Stetson and Hillman, leaving Sergeants Lee and Magee and Corporal Butterfield to compete for the medals.

There was some question about a movement in firing kneeling, in which Sergeant Magee acted entirely different from the other four and stuck to it, but there being a difference of opinion on the matter no account was made of it by the judges.

The three members of the last squad were evenly matched in points, and the judges found it no easy task to decide which were the two best. It was not till a long and tedious contest that they finally made a choice. They unanimously decided that Corporal Butterfield was generally the best man, and Sergeant Lee the next best. Sergeant Magee was deficient in several points, and in his general work was the least steady and precise of the squad. Consequently they rendered their decision accordingly.

The command was then marched upon the floor, and after calling Sergeants Lee and Magee and Corporal Butterfield to the front and center, Principal Ray Greene Huling was introduced to present the medals.

Mr. Huling congratulated the command on its excellent work, and spoke of the prize drill as an event mingling happiness and sadness. As this was a result or culmination of a year's work, he hoped their life work would be crowned with as bright laurels and honors as does this lesser career.

Mr. Huling then pinned the Sanders & Barrows medal on the breast of Corporal Butterfield, and the company medal on the coat of Sergeant Lee. To Sergeant Magee was awarded the second substitute medal, and to Sergeant Lee the first substitute, while the friends and comrades of the winners shouted themselves hoarse and wore out the palms of their hands in their enthusiasm.

Dancing followed to the music of the Germania orchestra, with Thomas Thompson as prompter. The order embraced 14 numbers and the floor was ably managed by the following:

Floor Director—Captain John M. Kelleher.

Aids—Sergeant Arthur R. Magee, Sergeant John N. Gammons, Corporal John M. Hathaway, Private Harry E. Boomer.

Reception Committee—Lieutenant William B. Smith, Jr., Lieutenant Ernest C. Read, Sergeant John A. Lee, Jr., Private Joseph H. Allen.

Among the guests from out of town were noticed Captain Sheldon L. Howard, and Private William L. Galvin of the Taunton High School cadets, Captain William G. Allen of Brockton, Adjutant John Fleet, Lieutenants G. C. Hathaway and H. F. Nickerson, and Privates Dana Everett and H. N. G. Terry of Fall River, and Sergeant Cyrus C. Howland of the Massachusetts Institute of Technology.

[From Yesterday's Third Edition.]

REMAINS RECOVERED.

Word was received at the Central police station this afternoon that the body of Dr. Rondeau had been recovered, and Undertaker Jean has been instructed to proceed to Long Pond and take charge of the body.

PERSONAL.

Thomas F. Glennon, who has charge of the spinning departments of the New Bedford Manufacturing company's mills, is spending a two weeks' vacation at the World's fair.

DISPUTE

Causes Court to Adjourn Early

Over Admission of Short Hand Notes.

Police Tell of Searching the House.

Lizzie Objected to Having Her Room Opened.

Officers Were Asked to Wait a Minute.

"What is the matter with the women? Have they lost their interest in the case, or are they incapable of sustained effort even in such an important affair as this trial?" asked a man as he entered the court room just before the hour for opening this afternoon, and saw that nine tenths of the spectators were of the sterner sex. "That is not the case, my boy," was the answer, but you must remember that they are the weaker sex, and without especial privileges they are sure to go to the wall in the struggle for place." It was noticed that the ladies who were present, however, were in good part provided with the choicest places, and the jury box on the south side of the room held its full quota of them.

The jury and Miss Borden were in their places for full five minutes before the "court" was called.

Despite the exciting occurrences about the city during the day, and the generally uninteresting character of the evidence during the forenoon the seats were all filled at the opening.

The desks of the judges were ornamented by bouquets of red and pink carnations and heliotrope, which considerably brightened the heaviness of the oak paneling.

There was an improvement during the afternoon in the sound of the voices of witnesses. They were prompted to speak up louder by District Attorney Moody, who graciously interposed in behalf of reporters, who have been unable to hear all the proceedings heretofore. The difficulty has not been all with witnesses, but with newspaper men and others occupying desks, and not having to make long reports, have, perhaps unconsciously, at times seriously interfered with others who have all their time occupied.

When the court came in Officer Mullaly was on the stand.

Q. When the court adjourned you were describing the dust on the hatchet. Can you give any further description of how the hatchet was covered? A. It looked as though the ashes were kind of rubbed on.

Q. What did Mr. Fleet do with it after you observed it? A. He put it back.

Q. Did you see that hatchet again afterward? A. Not in the house.

Q. If you saw it at all you saw it after it was taken away? A. Yes sir.

Q. Where did you go then? A. I remained in the cellar a while longer.

Q. Did you discover anything else? A. No sir.

Q. After you had completed what you did in the cellar where did you go? A. We then went up on the first floor.

Q. What did you do on the first floor, if anything? A. Stayed around there awhile.

Q. Did you go anywhere else? A. We then went up stairs to the room where Mrs. Borden lay, and Officer Hyde and myself searched it. I saw Lizzie, and asked her if she saw anybody about the premises. She said yes, she saw a man with dark clothes on. She said he was a man about the size of Officer Hyde.

Q. Anything else that you recall? A. After that I had a search with Mr. Fleet. We went back to the east end of the house and searched the attics over again and some place on the first floor that I called a cupboard.

Q. Did you go into the yard? A. I did.

Q. What did you do in the yard? A. I looked all round there.

Q. Did you go to any of the adjoining premises? A. I got over the fence on the south.

Q. That is over into Mrs. Churchill's yard? A. Mrs. Churchill's I call on the north side. Dr. Kelly's is on the south side.

Q. Did you find any weapon or notice any stain or appearance of blood on these premises? A. I did not.

Q. Did you at any time, Mr. Mullaly, on your search outside of the house either on the Borden land and buildings or on any of the adjoining fences find any weapon or any appearance of blood? A. I did not.

Cross-examined.

Q. I understand that you went there with a Mr. Allen? A. Yes sir.

Q. Did you learn whether that was the first or second time that he was there? A. I think he told me that he had been there before.

Q. You asked Miss Lizzie what her father had on his person? A. Yes sir; she said a silver watch and chain, a pocketbook with some money in it and a gold ring on his little finger.

Q. Did you find these articles? A. I did not.

Q. Did you see any one else find them? Officer Dougherty reported to me that the watch and chain were on him.

Q. Did he say anything about the other things? A. He did not.

Q. On the whole, Mr. Mullaly, you made what you consider a pretty thorough search of that house? A. So far as I know I did.

Q. You went up in the attic? A. I went into the attic.

Q. Who went with you? A. Officer Dougherty went with me and Bridget Sullivan.

Q. Anybody else? A. Not at that time.

Q. You went to her room? A. Whose room?

Q. Bridget's? A. Yes.

Q. Did she have a closet? A. Yes.

Q. Do you remember examining the dresses? A. Not at that time.

Q. Did you later? A. I did not.

Q. Where did you go then? A. To Miss Borden's room.

Q. Is it the one over the kitchen? A. Yes.

Q. Did Officer Dougherty continue with you? A. I think he went to the room where Mrs. Borden lay and then to the cellar.

Q. Did you go to Lizzie's room? A. I went to the room where she was and had conversation with her.

Q. Who went to the cellar with you the first time? A. Officer Dougherty and Bridget Sullivan.

Q. What did Bridget do? A. She went to show us where the hatchets were.

Q. What made her do this? A. Miss Borden said she'd show us where the hatchets were.

Q. Did she call Bridget or did you ask her? A. When we got through the attic we went to the cellar direct.

Q. You had told Bridget what you wanted? A. Yes.

Q. And she led the way to the little room on the south side of the house? A. Yes.

Q. What did she do? A. She went where the hatchets were and took them out of the box.

Q. Did she look around the room? A. I don't know about looking around. She didn't stop around.

Q. They were in the box? A. Yes.

Q. Describe it. A. It was from 14 to 16 inches long.

Q. Did it have a cover? A. None that I saw.

Q. Were things pretty well covered with ashes and dust? A. The axe handles were pretty well covered.

Q. How many things did she take out? A. Two hatchets.

Q. Did she hand them to you? A. She did.

Q. Was one larger than the other? A. Yes.

Q. Did they look about the same as now? A. There was a rust spot on one of them which I don't see now, (looking at one which he held in his hand.)

Q. You said that the handle of this hatchet was covered with ashes? A. I don't say it of that.

Q. Was there any dust or ashes on the other? (Showing it.) A. I think this one looked about the same as now.

Q. Then they were not at that time covered with dust or ashes? A. No; the axes had their handles covered with dust.

Q. Did you find them? A. I won't say if I did or Bridget handed them to me.

Q. You discovered nothing else on them? A. I believe the handle of the big hatchet was cleaner than the other.

Q. When did you see the one with no handle? A. I saw it later when Mr. Fleet called my attention to it.

Q. How did the metal look as compared with today? A. It looked different.

Q. How? A. It was covered with ashes.

Q. Do you know where it's been since? A. I don't.

Q. That piece out of the eye doesn't look so bright as it did then, does it? A. It doesn't.

Q. Did he think that hatchet had been seen by any one? A. No sir.

Q. Are you given to investigating things? A. Sometimes.

Q. Mr Fleet asked you where you got the hatchets? A. I told him and he went to the box, looked in, and took out the axe and the piece of handle.

Q. Do you know what became of the box? A. No sir.

Q. Nothing was taken out while you were there? A. Nothing but the hatchet and piece of freshly broken handle.

Q. Where is the piece? A. I don't know.

Q. Did you see it after that? A. No.

Q. How long was it? A. Shorter than that one you have in your hand.

Q. Who took it out? A. Mr Fleet.

Q. You were there? A. Yes sir.

Q. Mr. Fleet put it back? A. He did.

Q. Did you ever tell this to any one before? A. No sir, I never did.

Q. Do you know where Mr. Fleet is at the present time? A. No sir.

Q. Is he below? A. I don't know. I have seen him there this morning.

Q. Did you see him before this examination? A. No sir.

Re-direct.

Q. This handle, you say, fitted in the breaks? A. I didn't try to fit it in.

Q. Did you notice anything with relation to the handle? A. It was freshly broken.

Q. With respect to the ashes? A. Both sides were covered. I did not notice as there were ashes on the handle.

Mr. Fleet was recalled.

Mr. Moody started to question him in re-direct and Mr. Robinson wanted to proceed with the cross-examination, and claimed the witness. The question was discussed by counsel and the court sustained Mr. Robinson, who proceeded in cross-examination.

Q. Will you state what you found in the box? A. There were some other tools and some iron, I don't know just what it was.

Q. Was this what you found? (holding the hatchet without a handle.) A. Yes sir.

Q. Who was you with? A. Mr. Mullaly.

Q. This small piece was in the eye. It has been driven out since, has it not? A. Yes sir.

Q. That's all there was in the box except the tools, which you did not take out? A. Yes sir.

Q. You have no doubt about this? A. No sir.

The next witness was Officer Charles H. Wilson.

Q. Your name is Charles H. Wilson? A. Yes sir.

Q. You are a member of the police force in Fall River? A. Yes sir.

Q. You were last year? A. Yes sir.

Q. On the fourth of August did you go to the Borden house? A. Yes sir.

Q. What time did you get there? A. About 1 o'clock.

Q. Did you meet Mr. Fleet and Minnehan there? A. Yes sir.

Q. Minnehan is now dead? A. Yes sir.

Q. I only want to call your attention to whether you saw or heard anything while you was in Lizzie Borden's room, any talk between she and Mr. Fleet? A. Yes sir.

Q. Please tell us what it was. A. We went into the room to search it, and asked her when she saw her mother last; she said about 9 o'clock in the morning in the bedchamber making beds. She had received a note and gone out. He asked her how long she had been in the barn. She had replied half an hour in the morning, and he asked her what she had to say now. She said 20 minutes to half an hour. When we went into her room she said we needn't go in there; it was locked, and had been all the morning. She always locked the door when she went out. Mr. Fleet said it was absolutely necessary.

Q. Will you describe what occurred at the door? A. Mr. Fleet knocked and Dr. Bowen came to the door. He was told that the officers wished to search the room. He asked if it was absolutely necessary to search the room, and Mr. Fleet told him it was. He asked us to wait a moment. Lizzie said if they searched the room she hoped they would be as quick as they could about it, she could not stand it much longer, she was sick.

Q. Did you notice anything at that time with reference to the closet over the front door? A. I went into that room to search it.

Q. How did you get in? A. Lizzie opened it with a key.

Cross-examined.

Q. Was there any objection to your search, except that you were asked to wait a moment? A. At first Lizzie seemed to object.

Q. Dr. Bowen came to the door and politely enough said, wait a moment, didn't he? A. Yes sir.

Q. There was nothing about his behavior that was impolite or discourteous was there? A. I do not think so.

Q. Lizzie said, did she, that she hoped you would get through soon, because it was making her sick? A. Yes, she said she couldn't stand it much longer.

Q. Did any one interfere with you or try to keep you out of the room? A. No sir.

Q. Was there anything done that was not just right in treatment towards the officers? A. No sir.

Q. Did you go with Mr. Minnehan and Mr. Fleet into other parts of the house? A. Yes sir.

Q. Please tell the jury where you went? A. We went into the closet at the head of the stairs and we went into the guest chamber and from there to the rear of the house up into Mr. Borden's room and in to the attic.

Q. Wherever you wanted to go you went? A. Yes sir.

Q. You found locks on almost all the doors? A. Yes sir.

Mr. Knowlton suggested when the cross-examination was finished that the court appoint an officer to go to Fall River to ascertain if the missing handle of the hatchet which had been testified about was in the box where the hatchet was found. He said he had no interest in the matter, except the interest of justice.

"Justice is what we want," said Mr. Robinson.

The court said that it could not interfere with anything in regard to the preparation of the case and the matter was dropped.

Miss Annie White was next called to the stand.

Q. (Mr. Moody.) What is your full name? A. Annie M. White.

Q. And you are the official stenographer for Bristol county, are you? A. Yes sir.

Q. Were you present at a proceeding at Fall River some time in August last year? A. Yes sir.

Q. Do you recall the date of it? A. The inquest was Aug. 9th, and the preliminary hearing I think was Aug. 25th.

Q. I am referring to Aug. 9th. Did you see Miss Lizzie Borden at the time? A. I did.

Q. And Mr. Knowlton? A. Yes.

Q. In what room were you present? A. In the district court room in Fall River.

Q. Who was there beside yourself and those whom you have named? A. Judge Blaisdell, Mr. Leonard, clerk of the court, Mr. Seaver was there a part of the time, and there were one or two other persons came in whom I did not know.

Q. Now was there some conversation between Mr. Knowlton and Miss Borden at that time?

Mr. Robinson interrupted, and asked that the examination of Miss White, in consequence of what was to follow her testimony, be postponed until tomorrow morning.

After consultation it was decided not to continue the examination of Miss White today.

George A. Petty was the next witness, and he said he was a grocer, and before the Borden occupancy lived in the upper tenement of that house.

Q. On the 4th of August did you pass the Borden house in the forenoon? A. Yes.

Q. About what time? A. Between 9 and 10 o'clock, I think.

Q. Did you see any one outside? A. Not when I went by the first time.

Q. Did you see Bridget Sullivan at any time? A. Yes.

Q. At what time? A. Between 10 and 11.

Q. What was she doing? A. She had a pail and dipper.

Q. Where did you first learn of trouble at the Borden house? A. In Mr. Waite's store.

Q. About what time? A. After 11.

Q. When you got there who was there? A. Dr. Bowen and Mrs. Churchill, and there may have been others.

Q. Had a crowd collected? A. No.

Q. What did you do? A. I passed into the room where Mr. Borden was lying, and Dr. Bowen was covering him with a sheet. He let me look at him; I stepped back and the doctor then covered him up.

Q. Tell me about the body or blood, if you can? A. He was lying on his back, and his feet were crossed and one was on the floor. I noticed the condition of the head. The cuts seemed to me to be quite fresh.

Q. Where did you go then? A. Then I asked if Mrs. Borden was dead. Dr. Bowen said, "Yes," and I went up the stairs with him. It was quite dark in the room. I passed in and around and knelt down so as to feel the condition of her head. As soon as I touched her hair, I found it to be dry, matted, and rough on the back. There seemed to be no moisture.

Q. Was the dry hair covered with blood? A. I should judge so.

Q. Well, go on, what next? A. I noticed the condition of the blood. It was sort of shiny and skimmed over.

Q. About Mrs. Borden's head or on the floor, did you see any fresh blood or any in motion? A. No, I did not.

Q. Did you notice the condition of the body, as to warmth? A. I don't think I did.

Q. Did you form any opinion as to priority of death in Mr. or Mrs. Borden? A. Yes.

Mr. Moody had charged witness not to give his opinion, and to the court the counsel said, "We offer to show what that opinion was."

A consultation was had and then the opinion was not admitted.

Q. Did you leave the house? A. Yes sir.

Q. How far did you go before you heard the bell? A. Some little distance.

Q. What did it strike? A. It struck eleven.

Augustus P. Gorman was recalled and examined in redirect.

Q. Your business is what? A. I am proprietor of a paint shop at the corner of Second and Borden streets.

Q. What kind of a clock was the one you heard strike? A. A round one, with the box below.

Q. Is it a clock to be depended on? A. No sir.

Mrs. Churchill was recalled and asked relative to the material of Miss Borden's dress.

Q. Do you know what kind of a dress it was? A. I can't say what the material was.

Mr. Robinson—Was it a light calico or gingham, faded somewhat? A. I should think it might be.

Q. Was it much lighter than this one we have here? A. Yes, considerably lighter.

Mr. Moody—Was there any blue in it at all? A. No sir.

At this point Mr. Moody wanted to discuss the question of admitting the stenographic report of Miss White of the inquest, and the jury was excused till tomorrow morning at 9 o'clock. Before they left the room the court cautioned them from discussing the trial, forming any opinion or reaching any conclusions till all the evidence was before them.

The jury retired under the charge of the deputies and the counsel clustered about the bench to discuss the admission of Miss White's testimony. They were unable to reach any conclusions or were not ready to discuss the matter fully, for in less than five minutes the court was adjourned till morning.

The court decided to hear the arguments on the admission of Miss White's stenographic report Monday morning. The prisoner's testimony at the inquest is filled with contradictions and contains, as well, a confession of unfriendly relations between her stepmother and herself.

Officer Daniel J Humphrey, who has been on duty at the rear entrance all through the trial has been very kind, and people having business in the court have found him unfailing in courtesy. He has many applications for admission from people living at a distance. Yesterday he admitted a lawyer and clergyman from Georgia, and today an applicant who blessed him for admission was a Spanish merchant from New York, who made the trip especially to attend.

MURDER IN FIRST DEGREE.

Full Text of Warrant Against Sarmento.

Walter Clifford Will Probably Defend Assassin.

Prisoner Breaks Down with Grief in His Cell.

Jose Vieira Sarmento (Joseph Paull) the slayer of Maria das Candeias (Mary Francis) will be arraigned in the district court tomorrow morning on the following warrant, sworn out by the chief of police:

Commonwealth of Massachusetts.

To Thomas J. Cobb, Esquire, Clerk of the Third District Court of Bristol, in the County of Bristol, and Justice of the Peace within and for said County of Bristol:

George Douglass of New Bedford, in said county, in behalf of said commonwealth, on oath, complains that Jose Vieira Sarmento of New Bedford, in the county of Bristol, at New Bedford aforesaid, in the county aforesaid, on the ninth day of June, in the year of our Lord eighteen hundred and ninety-three, in and upon one Maria das Candeias feloniously, willfully and of his malice aforethought did make an assault, and that the said Jose Vieira Sarmento a certain pistol then and there charged with gunpowder and leaden bullets, which said pistol he the said Jose Vieira Sarmento then and there had and held, then and there feloniously, willfully and of his malice aforethought, did discharge and shoot off, to, against and upon the said Maria das Candeias, and that the said Jose Vieira Sarmento with one of the leaden bullets aforesaid, out of the pistol aforesaid, then and there, by the force of the gunpowder aforesaid, by the said Jose Vieira Sarmento discharged and shot off as aforesaid, then and there feloniously, willfully and of his malice aforethought did strike, penetrate and wound the said Maria das Candeias in and upon the left side of the face of her the said Maria das Candeias, giving to her the said Maria das Candeias then and there with the leaden bullet aforesaid, so as aforesaid discharged and shot out of the pistol aforesaid, by the said Jose Vieira Sarmento, in and upon the left side of the face of her the said Maria das Candeias one mortal wound, of which said mortal wound she the said Maria das Candeias then and there died. And so the complainant aforesaid, on his oath aforesaid, that the said Jose Vieira Sarmento her the said Maria das Candeias in the manner and by the means aforesaid feloniously, willfully and of his malice aforethought did kill and murder, against the peace of said commonwealth and contrary to the form of the statute in such case made and provided.

GEORGE DOUGLASS.

Bristol ss.

Received and sworn to this ninth day of June, in the year of our Lord eighteen hundred and ninety-three.

Before me,

THOMAS J. COBB,
Justice of the peace and clerk of the third district court of Bristol.

Soon after the murder this morning Captain Allen procured a buggy and drove to the Howland mills to apprise a sister of the murdered young woman of the tragedy. She was completely prostrated by the terrible news and soon after reaching her boarding house became violently hysterical. Nothing that could be done for her afforded any relief, and this afternoon her condition is unimproved.

Jose Sarmento, the slayer of Mary Candeias, broke down with grief this afternoon soon after a visit from A. L. Sylvia, with whom he held quite a lengthy conversation. His only desire is that he might die.

Soon after talking with Mr. Sylvia, Hon. Walter Clifford entered the station and at once proceeded to the cell where lays Sarmento and the three conversed together. Afterwards Mr. Sylvia, Mr. Clifford and Dr. Hayes were in conversation. Mr. Clifford will probably be retained to defend Sarmento, who has a brother living in this city.

FRIENDS' YEARLY MEETING.

Proceedings of the Morning Session at Portland.

At the morning session of the Friends yearly meeting in Portland, Me., today, minutes from all quarterly meetings were read. Nineteen ministers and elders have died, whose average age was 77 4-10 years. The credentials of Isaac Sharpe of London yearly meeting, E. C. Silver of the western yearly meeting, Jesse W. Wilmore of Kansas, George N. Hartley and wife of Oregon, Firnando Cortland of New York and William G. Hubbard of Ohio, were received and the delegates welcomed. Epistles were read from all the yearly meetings except London. The balance of the meeting was devoted to the appointment of various committees.

FOUND HANGING BY THE NECK.

Suicide of a Mrs. Edwin F. Pope of Middleboro.

Middleboro, June 9.—Mrs. Edwin F. Pope, a widow residing on Courtland street, was found by her son this morning dead, hanging with a small cord about her neck to a tall bed post. She had recently removed from another house and it is thought that homesickness unbalanced her mind.

Another Bank Failed.

Hudson, Wis., June 9.—The Hudson savings bank closed its doors today. The bank has assets enough to cover all deposits, which amount to nearly $700,000.

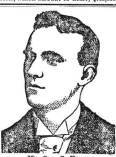

The Evening Standard.

NEW BEDFORD, SATURDAY, JUNE 10, 1893.---TWELVE PAGES.

TWO CENTS.

3

A CREDITABLE EXHIBIT.

Annual Display of Work by the Art Department of the Swain Free School.

The annual exhibition of work by students in the art department of the Swain Free school will open tomorrow morning for public inspection.

The exhibition this year embraces a most creditable collection of work that reflects not only on the ability of the student artists, but upon the careful and painstaking instruction of Mr. Arthur Cumming. The display is made in five rooms, and includes in all something like 300 individual specimens.

The work of the department is divided into four classes, A, B, C and E. The former embodies stump drawing, pen and ink sketches, pencil drawings and sketching from nature in pen and ink. Course B is an industrial designing course of outline and color work. In class C the scope is in water color and oil, while course E, an optional one, provides a line of work advanced beyond the other three courses, but elective to the pupil in its character, under the approval of the instructor.

The pupils this year have been as follows:

Course A—Charles F. Gifford, Abbie J. Gifford, Annie B. Gifford, John M. Hillman, George B. Atwood, Nellie B. Tillson, Henry V. Bisbee, Annie H. Wing, Susie E. Davis, Annie E. Davis, Edward P. Borden (Fall River), Margaret Ingraham, Eunice B. Feltch, George T. Sperry, Mabel B. Lewis, Annie L. Edwards, Abbie Whitney, Frederick G. Hodcliff, Benjamin H. Price, Mary Marshall, Otto Uhlman, Annie Macreading, Lewis W. Uhlman, Octavie La Rose, James H. Francis, Lillian E. Bryant, John P. Rooney and Martha R. Eldred.

Course B—Of the above pupils of course A, Charles F Gifford, John M. Hillman and George H. Atwood have completed course A, and have commenced the work of course B. Abbie J. Gifford and Henry V. Bisbee have also completed course A, but have not yet entered the next course.

Course C—Patty Wilcox, Evelyn C. Kelley, Edna C. Lawton, Edith Hastings and Mary B. Sanford.

Course E—Adolph Frederick, Frank Bradshaw, Mary L. Barstow, Annie H. Barstow and Nathan R. Gifford.

Perhaps the most comprehensive exhibit of the work of the course A class is made in the southwest room of the second floor. All the exhibit is on the second floor. Here are shown drawings in stump work by all the pupils, the various pictures being arranged in a progression of subjects—a cube, a cylinder, a sphere, a skeleton cube and skeleton ring, a flight of steps and double cross, two vases, one glazed and the other plain, a Portland vase, a Grecian vase with pentagonal frame, a panel of apples and a panel of egg plant. While all this work is creditably done, the most pleasing specimens are shown by John M. Hillman, Eunice B. Feltch, Abbie J. Gifford, Jennie B. Gifford, George A. Fox, Edward P. Borden, Abbie D. Whitney, Annie E. Davis and Annie L. Edwards. Aside from this class progression, several pupils have treated busts and statuary in a very creditable way. Charles F. Gifford, Frank Bradshaw, Abbie J. Gifford, Edward P. Borden, George H. Atwood, Henry V. Bisbee, John M. Hillman have some very fine stump drawings of Venus de Milo and Ajax from plaster busts, while Mr. Bradshaw shows two very creditable point drawings of Ajax and a Nubian head.

A number of very fine pen and ink drawings are exhibited by the pupils. John M. Hillman has a splendid drawing of the statuette "The Fisher Boy," while Edward P. Borden and George H. Atwood have treated a violin and bow in a most intelligent manner. A placque and ink stand, by Abbie J. Gifford, displays a marked degree of care, while Henry V. Bisbee's vases are noticeably well drawn.

The north room is filled with pencil drawings of foliage and sketches from nature. The work is all very well done, but it would be difficult to mention any in the way of superiority.

The studio, in the northwest corner of the building, has several fine displays in water color sketchings from out of door subjects. Adolph Frederick has a fine sketch in color of a cabinet and bric-a-brac, besides a water color of Clyte from a bust, and several smaller, though none the less artistic color sketches of the subjects. Otto Uhlman shows several nice specimens of out door work, while Nathan R. Gifford and Frank Bradshaw have a number of sketches of birds and flowers. Miss Evelyn C. Kelley and Edna C. Lawton are also prominent in this room for their excellent specimens.

The exhibition as a whole is probably one of the finest the institution has yet held. It demonstrates the existence of a notable amount of artistic ability resident in our midst, and speaks eloquently of the utility and value of such an institution as the Swain Free school as a developing medium. Mr. Cumming and the faculty may well feel proud of the progress shown by the art department.

The exhibition will be open daily for inspection during this week between the hours of 9 a. m. and 9 p. m.

MAY BREAK UP THE CHURCH.

Rev. C. C. Felts Hotly Attacked by Presiding Elder.

The meeting of the African M. E. conference in Springfield Saturday was one of the stormiest in its history. At the session there was a lively tilt between the presiding elder, P. F. M. Webster, and C. C. Felts, pastor of the New Bedford church. The trouble arose from the fact that Mr. Felts allows his son to sing in the Episcopal choir and attend the Episcopal Sunday school. The presiding elder in making his report said regarding Mr. Felt's church: "There is peace in the church because there is peace in a graveyard. What is needed there is a live pastor with a Methodist affinity."

Mr. Felts, in replying, denied the statement regarding the condition of his church, and asked that a committee of investigation be appointed.

Bishop Tanner took a hand in the discussion, asking the presiding elder to withdraw his statements. This the latter refused to do, repeating the allegations for the second time. The wrangle may have the effect of breaking up the New Bedford church.

WEDDING.

A pretty wedding took place this morning in St. James (Catholic) church, when Miss Mary Goley and Mr. James Byrne were united in the holy bonds of matrimony. The bride and bridesmaid were attired in very pretty dresses of white delaine, with wreaths of white roses, and white tulle veils. The bride wore a gold necklace with a pearl pin, the gift of the groom. Miss M. J. McGladdry acted as bridesmaid and John Rowan was best man. The happy couple received numerous and costly presents from their friends and well wishers.

At the Friends' yearly meeting in Portland, Me., Saturday afternoon, a petition was sent to the president and senate, protesting against the opening of the World's Fair on Sunday and against the outrages on the colored people in the South.

EXCLUDED.

(Continued from First Page.)

missible? The other rule of law which comes into play in this case is a rule which in our government has been sanctified by a position in our constitution, and that is that no person shall be compelled to furnish evidence against himself. The proposition that I desire to submit to your honor is this, that the true rule is that declarations voluntarily given, no matter how or under what circumstances, are competent. Declarations obtained by compulsion are never competent. I think I might very well leave this question entirely upon the authority that we find in the reports of our own state law, and yet I feel that I should not be doing my duty unless I went somewhat farther. I begin as we always do with the English cases, and I dismiss them very briefly. The discussion of English cases I do not consider to be my duty here. I simply say that we cannot obtain any aid upon this question from the consideration of the decisions of the authorities in England. There is only one state so far as my investigation informs me in which this question has been clearly discussed and in which the line has been clearly drawn, and that is the state of New York. We have a steady line of decisions in that state to which I shall call your honors' attention.

This matter was passed upon for the first time in the case of People vs. Hendrickson in the year 1854. This was an indictment for murder. There was an examination of the prisoner before a coroner's jury. This testimony was offered by the state, and was admitted, and the admission was sustained by the court of appeals. In the case it appeared that the testimony was a denial and not a confession. In this case the accused was not under arrest at the time of giving testimony. There was a valuable

discussion by the court, and a discussion that was one of the most valuable in my opinion that has been made.

The same question arose in 1857, when another case was considered. This case may as well be dismissed, for the grounds upon which the testimony was excluded have been exploded, in this commonwealth surely, and I think in that state. The next case is found in 41 N. Y. p. 47. The defendant in that case was informed that he was under suspicion, and was cautioned by the justice of that fact. It was held by the court of appeals that the evidence could be used in the trial.

The last New York case which I shall cite is that of the People vs. Mendrum. In that case the court of appeals held that when the prisoner was arrested without warrant and was actually in custody, and was not cautioned as to his rights, his declarations were not competent against him. The summing up of this case is valuable, for the discussion deals with all the previous cases. The summing up may be reduced to this, the fact that a person is aware that he is suspected and gives testimony does not prevent that evidence from being used against himself. This decision was made in 1886.

This line of argument can be stated in a single word. The question is simply whether the prisoner is under arrest or not when the declaration is made.

There is no doubt if this same question arose in New York the testimony offered here would be admissible. The question has arisen in other states.

At this point Mr. Robinson held a brief consultation with the justices, and a minute later Lizzie left the court room under charge of Deputy Sheriff Kirby.

Mr. Moody resumed: This question was considered in the state of Maine in the case 51 Maine. In this case the prisoner resided in the home of the deceased and was accused by a daughter of deceased as being the murderer. The prisoner was instructed as to his rights by the coroner who held an inquest the same day. The court in considering the case pointed out that the English cases were of no importance. It decided that if the statements of the accused are voluntary then they are admissible, but if obtained by force are then not to be admitted.

The question arose in a recent case in Wisconsin and the court goes farther than in any other case I have seen. Here it is held that the only question is whether the statements are made voluntarily or not. The defendant in that case was at the time under arrest. He testified against A, who was accused of the crime. It was held that his evidence against A was afterwards admissible against himself. This case is Dickinson vs. Wisconsin, and all previous cases were under discussion by the court. This case was decided in 1880, and is very valuable in this connection.

It is very clear, said Mr. Moody, by the authorities that I have quoted, that on an inquiry into the cause of death, if the one under suspicion responds voluntarily, is subsequently arrested, what he testifies to at that time may be admissible. Whether this defendant in question was cautioned or not at the time of the inquest is not necessary. The common practice within this commonwealth, as your honors know, is that hardly a term passes without precisely the same kind of testimony as this being used. One case occurred where a man was tried at one term for perjury, and what he then said was used at another term as the foundation of a complaint. And that person was convicted and is now serving a term in the state prison. In view of the authority quoted from outside states, in view of the common practice in this commonwealth, and in view of the fact that if error is committed this defendant's rights are secured by your honors, I submit, said Mr. Moody, that this testimony is admissible.

WERE NOT VOLUNTARY.

Robinson Protests Against Admitting Lizzie's Words.

Ex-Governor Robinson argued in behalf of the defense. He said the question isn't whether in this court your honors are required to consider rules in force in other states. Your honors are to inquire whether this evidence is admissible. In view of the gravity of the case, where the life of this prisoner is at stake, the matter should be given the most careful consideration. No matter what is the practice elsewhere, we stand

on the rights of this defendant. I would be unjust if I did not know whatever is done here would have no effect without the sanction of the highest authorities. We must not lose sight of the exact facts in this case. These homicides were committed on August 4th, and the evidence shows that Dr. Dolan took possession of the bodies and an autopsy was held to ascertain the cause of death.

Second—An inquest was begun on the 9th and continued through the 10th and 11th.

Third—An accusation was made by the mayor and city marshal on August 6th.

Fourth—This defendant was kept under police surveillance after the 4th. The house was surrounded by policemen and was no time, day or night, but when the eye of the police was upon this defendant.

Fifth—The defendant was summoned on or before August 9th to appear at the inquest.

Sixth—The defendant asked for counsel, but was not permitted to have it.

Seventh—The attorney for the commonwealth conducted the examination, and this woman stood alone for three days with no guidance, under suspicion, and surrounded by the officers of the law.

Eighth—The defendant before testifying was not properly cautioned.

Ninth—The defendant was summoned on or before Aug. 9th, and a complaint, duly made out, charging her with murder, was issued on the 8th. On that complaint a warrant was issued for her arrest and put in the keeping of the city marshal. You have the entire power of the commonwealth exerted over this defendant.

Tenth—And the city marshal held that warrant during all the time she testified. Can any one say she held herself as free and was not being formally proceeded against? We must assume in common sense that what was done was under the direction of the district attorney. Some one in authority certainly did the act.

Eleventh—She was held under surveillance, was never free, and was arrested two hours later on a similar warrant.

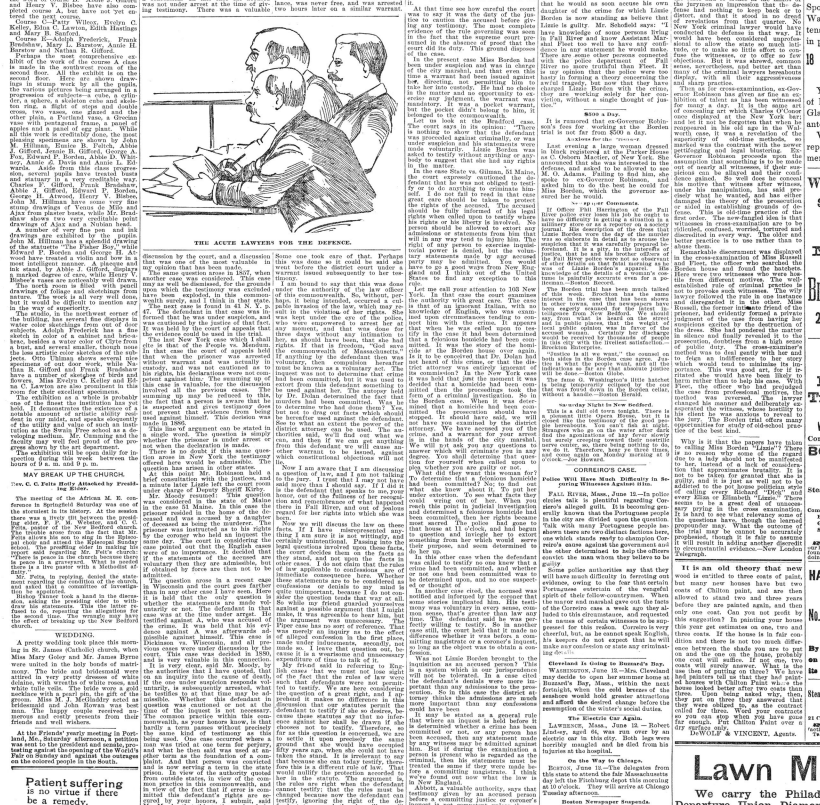

THE ACUTE LAWYERS FOR THE DEFENCE.

Some one took care of that. Perhaps this was done so it could be said she went before the district court under a warrant issued subsequently to her testimony.

I am bound to say that this was done under the authority of the law officer of this commonwealth. So, without, perhaps, it being intended, occurred a culpable invasion of the law, which may result in the violation of her rights. She was kept under the eye of the police, who were empowered to arrest her at any moment, and that was done for three days without any intimation to her, as should have been, that she had rights. If that is freedom, "God save the commonwealth of Massachusetts." If anything by the defendant then was voluntary, then compulsion hereafter must be known as a voluntary act. The inquest was not to determine that crime had been committed, but it was used to extort from this defendant something to be used against her. The autopsy held by Dr. Dolan determined the fact that murders had been committed. Was he to determine who had done them? Yes, but not to drag out facts which should be hereafter used against the defendant. See to what an extent the power of the district attorney can be used. The authorities said, we'll find out what we can, and then if we can get anything from this defendant we will cause another warrant to be issued, against which constitutional objections will not lie.

Now I am aware that I am discussing a question of law, and I am not talking to the jury. I trust that I may not have said more than I should say. If I did it is the defendant that speaks to me, your honor, out of the fullness of her recapitulation and remembrance of what happened there in Fall River, and out of jealous regard for her rights into which she was born.

Now we will discuss the law on these facts. If I have misrepresented anything I am sure it is not wittingly, and certainly unintentional. Passing into the legal questions involved upon these facts, the court decides them on the facts as they stand, and not upon the facts in other cases. I do not claim that the rules of law applicable to confessions are of immediate consequence here. Whether these statements are to be considered as confessions or denials to my mind is quite unimportant, because I do not consider the question tends that way at all. So while my friend guarded yourselves against a possible argument that I might make, it was agreeable to hear him, but the argument was unnecessary. The Piper case has no sort of reference. That was merely an inquiry as to the effect of alleged confession in the first place, made under inducements, secondly, not made so. I leave that question out, because it is a wearisome and unnecessary expenditure of time to talk of it.

My friend said in referring to English cases that we must not lose sight of the fact that the rules of law were such that defendants were not permitted to testify. We are here considering the question of a great right, and I apprehend it makes no difference in this discussion that our statutes permit the defendant to testify if she so desires, because these statutes say that no inference against her shall be drawn if she chooses not to testify. Therefore, so far as this question is concerned, we are to settle it upon precisely the same ground that she would have occupied fifty years ago, when she could not have taken the stand. It is irrelevant to say that because she can today testify, therefore this is a different rule of law. That would nullify the protection accorded to her in the statute. The argument is, the rules are right when the defendant cannot testify; that the rules must be changed because the defendant can testify, ignoring the right of the defendant to say whether he will or will not testify. Therefore all the light that comes down from England, all the illumination that comes from anywhere upon this great question, is as nothing. We bear the constitution of Massachusetts read, and it possess alright over the tongue and in and out the ear. She stands upon that venerable instrument that day and she reads in it, in the bill of rights, that no person shall be compelled to furnish evidence against himself. That was written when Massachusetts was born; that was the instinct of the hour; that has been the spirit of our commonwealth's liberty ever since. When the constitution of the United States was drawn it ran in similar phrase upon this point: "No person shall be compelled to

any criminal case to be a witness against himself." The shield of the state and the shield of the nation are her protection in this hour.

I shall have occasion to state so far as it as it may be important the meaning of the words "in any criminal case." Looking at the report of Massachusetts made by our Supreme Judicial court we find there are but two cases that may be compared with this one. One was an indictment for murder in a barn. There was offered in evidence the testimony of the defendant taken in writing on oath before said fire inquest; it appeared that this inquest was held prior to the institution of any proceeding against the defendant; that he was duly summoned and testified with other witnesses before said inquest on oath and said testimony was reduced to writing and signed by the defendant. In this case the defendant did appear that the defendant was cautioned that he need not criminate himself. Now see how near the facts in the King case. See how they differ from the present. It appeared that the inquest was held prior to any proceedings against the defendant. In this case the proceedings had been commenced and fruited in a warrant before she was present at the inquest. In the King case, the testimony was reduced to writing and signed by the defendant. In this case the testimony, though reduced to writing, was not signed by the defendant, and so far as anything is shown here was never submitted to her for examination or correction. In the King case it did not appear that the defendant was cautioned that he need not criminate himself. In this case it does appear that she was not cautioned. Now we should be surprised indeed if the supreme court of Massachusetts should decide the question in such a manner upon the present facts. Justice Thomas proceeds to say that the only objection ruled upon was that the witness was not cautioned that he need not criminate himself. This objection is not sustained as a matter of fact.

Full opportunity was given to the defendant to object, but he declined to use it.

In that time see how careful the court was to say it was the duty of the justice to caution the accused before giving any testimony. The most complete evidence of the rule governing was seen in the fact that the supreme court presumed in the absence of proof that the court did its duty. This ground disposes of the case.

In the present case Miss Borden had been under suspicion and was in charge of the city marshal, and that even this time a warrant had been issued against her, directing, not permitting him to take her into custody. He had no choice in the matter and no opportunity to exercise any judgment, the warrant was mandatory. It was a pocket warrant, but the pocket didn't belong to him, it belonged to the commonwealth.

Let us look at the Bradford case. The court says in its opinion: "There is nothing to show that the defendant was proceeded against criminally, or was under suspicion and his statements were made voluntarily. Lizzie Borden was asked to testify without anything or anybody to suggest that she had any rights in the matter.

In the case State vs. Gilman, 51 Maine, the court expressly cautioned the defendant that he was not obliged to testify or to do anything to criminate himself. I do not fail to bend in that case great care should be taken to protect the rights of the accused. The accused should be fully informed of his legal rights when called upon to testify where his rights or his liberty is involved. No person should be allowed to extort any admissions or statements from him that will in any way tend to injure him. The right of any person to exercise his total power is denied, but the voluntary statements made by an accused party may be admitted. You would have to go a good ways from New England and I think out of the United States to find any exception to this rule.

Let me call your attention to 103 New York. In that case the court examine the authority with great care. The case is that of an ignorant Italian, with no knowledge of English, who was examined upon circumstances tending to connect him with the crime. It appears that when he was called upon to testify in the case it had been determined that a felonious homicide had been committed. It was the story of the homicide at the Borden house over again. Is it to be conceived that Dr. Dolan had not heard of this crime, or that the district attorney was entirely ignorant of its commission? In the New York case it was held that just the moment it was decided that a homicide had been committed then the proceedings took the form of a criminal investigation. So in the Borden case. When it was determined that a homicide had been committed the prosecution should have stopped. It should have said, we will not have you examined by the district attorney. We have accused you of this crime, and a warrant for your arrest is in the hands of the city marshal. We will not ask you any questions to answer which will criminate you in any way. You shall determine that question for yourself when called upon to plead whether you are guilty or not. What did they want this woman for? To determine that a felonious homicide had been committed? No; to find out what she knew about it. To put her under extortion. To see what facts they could wring out of her. When you reach this point in judicial investigation and determine a felonious homicide had been committed, then her rights became most sacred. The police had gone to that house at 11 o'clock, and had begun to question and inveigle her to extort something from her which would serve their purpose, and seem determined to do her up.

In this other case when the defendant was called to testify no one knew that a crime had been committed, and whether or not one had been committed was to be determined upon, and no one suspected or thought of it.

In another case cited, the accused was notified and informed by the coroner that some stories implicated him. His testimony was voluntary in every sense, common sense, that's greater than law any time. The defendant said he was perfectly willing to testify. So in another case still, the court held that it made no difference whether it was before a committing magistrate or a coroner's inquest, so long as the object was to obtain a confession.

Was not Lizzie Borden brought to the inquisition as an accused person? This is a system which in our jurisprudence will not be tolerated. In a case cited the defendant's denials were given important than any admissions to the prosecution. So in this case the district attorney thinks the admissions are much more important than any confessions could have been.

It may be stated as a general rule that where an inquest is held before it is determined whether a crime has been committed or not, or any person has been accused, then any statement made by any witness may be admitted against him. But if during the examination a person is present who is regarded as the criminal, then his statements must be treated the same if they were made before a committing magistrate. I think we've found out now what the law is in New England.

Abbott, a valuable authority, says that testimony given by an accused person before a committing justice or coroner's inquest is not competent unless the accused has been duly cautioned that it might be used against him, and many cases are cited in support of this.

(Continued on Fourth Page.)

STAR CHAMBER EVIDENCE.

Application of Moral Torture to Miss Borden at the Inquest.

(Boston Post.)

It is expected that the court will decide today the question of the admissibility of the notes of the testimony given by Lizzie Borden at the inquest in Fall River. This is a question involving not only the interests of the accused in this trial, but those of every citizen of Massachusetts.

The circumstances under which this evidence was procured are fresh in mind; they constituted an outrage upon individual rights which aroused widespread indignation at the time. The inquest was in fact an inquisition—the application of moral torture and force to a woman in distress, who was refused the help and the protection of counsel.

If the expressions extorted from Lizzie Borden under the brow-beating examination of the district attorney at this star-chamber inquest are admitted as competent evidence on this trial, it will shake the faith of many in the sufficiency of the laws of Massachusetts for the protection of our citizens.

We do not think it will make any difference as to the outcome of the trial, whether the evidence is admitted or not, but it is high time that there was some official rebuke of the high-handed and suspicious methods adopted in the attempt to convict this woman.

DENOUNCED THE POLICE.

Rev. Mr. Schofield Knew Lizzie Borden and Thinks Her Innocent.

Pittsburg, June 12.—The Rev. John Schofield of Braddocks, a former resident of Fall River, who has known Lizzie Borden ever since she was 9 years of age, stated yesterday to a reporter that he would as soon accuse his own daughter of the crime for which Lizzie Borden is now standing as believe that Lizzie is guilty. Mr. Schofield says: "I have knowledge of some persons living in Fall River and know Assistant Marshal Fleet too well to have any confidence in any statement he would make. There are some other persons connected with the police department of Fall River no more truthful than Fleet. It is my opinion that the police were too hasty in forming a theory concerning the awful tragedy, but now that they have charged Lizzie Borden with the crime, they are working solely for her conviction, without a single thought of justice."

$500 a Day.

It is rumored that ex-Governor Robinson's fees for working at the Borden trial is not far from $500 a day.

Anxious for the 'Prisoner.

Last evening a large woman dressed in black registered at the Parker House as C. Osborn Mactier, of New York. She announced that she was interested in the defense, and asked to be allowed to see M. O. Adams. Failing to find him, she spoke to ex-Governor Robinson, and asked him to do the best he could for Miss Borden, which the governor assured her he would.

No Superfluous Comments.

If Officer Phil Harrington of the Fall River police ever loses his job he ought to have no difficulty in getting a situation in a millinery store or as a reporter on a society journal. His description of the dress that Lizzie Borden wore the day of the murder was so elaborate in detail as to arouse the suspicion that it was carefully prepared beforehand. It is a pity, in the interests of justice, that he and his brother officers of the Fall River police were not so observant of other details on that fatal morning as he was of Lizzie Borden's apparel. His knowledge of the details of a woman's costume is certainly accurate even for a policeman.—Boston Record.

Saturday Night in New Bedford.

This is a dull old town tonight. There is a pleasant little Opera House, but it is closed like the testimony of the good people hereabouts. You can't fail at night. Strangers who go on the street after 9 o'clock may be heard on the street and in public places, that the weight of local public opinion was in favor of the accused woman. Certainly her discharge would be received by thousands of people in this city with the liveliest satisfaction.—Brockton Enterprise.

"Justice is all we want," the counsel on both sides in the Borden case agree. Justice is what the people want, and all the indications so far are that absolute justice will be done.—Boston Globe.

The fame of G. Washington's little hatchet is being temporarily eclipsed by the one that was found down in the Borden cellar, without a handle.—Boston Herald.

CORREIRO'S CASE.

Police Will Have Much Difficulty in Securing Witnesses Against Him.

FALL RIVER, Mass., June 12.—In police circles talk is plentiful regarding Correiro's alleged guilt. It is becoming generally known that the Portuguese people in the city are divided upon the question. Talk with many Portuguese people here shown there are two distinct factions here, one which stands ready to champion Correiro's cause against the government and the other determined to help the officers convict the man whom they believe to be guilty.

Some police authorities say that they will have much difficulty in ferreting out evidence, owing to the fear that certain Portuguese entertain of the vengeful spirit of their fellow-countrymen. When the mayor and marshal gave out the facts of the Correiro case a week ago they allowed much of the circumstance, and requested the names of certain witnesses to be suppressed for this reason. Correiro is very cheerful, but, as he cannot speak English, his keepers do not expect that he will make any confession or state any criminating details.

Cleveland Is Going to Buzzard's Bay.

WASHINGTON, June 12.—Mrs. Cleveland may decide to open her summer home at Buzzard's Bay, Mass., within the next fortnight, when the cold breezes of the seashore would hold greater attractions and afford the desired change before the resumption of the winter's social duties.

The Electric Car Again.

LAWRENCE, Mass., June 12.—Robert Lindsey, aged 66, was run over by an electric car in this city. Both legs were horribly mangled and he died from his injuries at the hospital.

On the Way to Chicago.

BOSTON, June 12.—The delegates from this state to attend the fair Massachusetts day left the Fitchburg depot this morning at 10 o'clock. They will arrive at Chicago Tuesday afternoon.

Boston Newspaper Suspends.

BOSTON, June 12.—The Boston News suspended publication this morning in its 1-cent four-page form. Promise is made that later on it will be resumed in a 2-cent eight-page form.

OLD TIME CRIMINAL PRACTICE.

Borden Murder Trial in Some Respects a Striking Example.

(New York Tribune.)

The Borden murder trial is in some respects a striking example of old-fashioned criminal practice. There are no bickerings between opposing counsel; each side is allowed great latitude in examining witnesses; there are few objections and technical arguments; and the court is seldom asked for a ruling. The trial offers a marked contrast to criminal proceedings in this town, in which the lawyers on each side are constantly in conflict over trivialities of procedure and splitting hairs over technical objections. Each side exhausts its energies in embarrassing the opposing counsel and in badgering and confusing witnesses. While a foundation may be laid in this way for an appeal to higher courts and motions for a new trial, there is seldom any direct benefit so far as influence with the jury is concerned; and not infrequently the client's cause is prejudiced by these legal tactics. In Massachusetts these matters are managed in accordance with the older and better traditions of the bar.

It is for the interest of the defense in the Borden trial to impress the jury with the fact that it has a strong case, and has little to fear from the evidence for the state. At the outset it had few misgivings respecting the character and fair-mindedness of jurors. As the evidence for the state was produced, it allowed the witnesses to tell their stories naturally on the direct examination. Opposing counsel were not warned when they openly coached witnesses by their leading questions. Few exceptions were taken; no anxiety was displayed over trivial points; witnesses were seldom interrupted. The general effect of this method of procedure would naturally be to inspire confidence. It tended to minimize the importance of the evidence for the state and to create in the minds of the jurymen an impression that the defense had nothing to keep back or to distort, and that it stood in no dread of revelations from that quarter. No New York criminal lawyer would have conducted the defense in that way. It would have been considered unprofessional to allow the state so much latitude, or to make so little effort to confuse the witnesses, or to offer so few objections. But it was shrewd, common sense, nevertheless, and better art than many of the criminal lawyers hereabouts display, with all their aggressiveness and sharp practice.

Then as for cross-examination, ex-Governor Robinson has given as fine an exhibition of talent as has been witnessed for many a day. It is the same art of concealing art which Charles O'Conor once displayed at the New York bar; and let it not be forgotten that when he reappeared in his old age in the Walworth case, it was a revelation of the superiority of old-time methods, so marked was the contrast with the newer pettifogging and legal blustering. Ex-Governor Robinson proceeds upon the assumption that something is to be made out of nearly all witnesses, if their suspicious can be allayed and their confidence gained. So well does he conceal his motive that witness after witness, under his manipulation, has said precisely what he wanted, and has either damaged the theory of the prosecution or aided in establishing grounds of defense. This is old-time practice of the first order. The new-fangled idea is that witnesses in cross-examination are to be ridiculed, confused, worried, tortured and discredited in every way. The older and better practice is to use rather than to abuse them.

Remarkable discernment was displayed in the cross-examination of Miss Russell and Fleet, the officer who searched the Borden house and found the hatchets. Here were two witnesses who were hostile from different motives. The well-established rule of criminal practice is not to provoke such witnesses. The wily lawyer followed the rule in one instance and disregarded it in the other. Miss Russell, the former intimate friend of the prisoner, had evidently formed a private judgment of the case from having her suspicions excited by the destruction of the dress. She had pondered the matter in silence and finally revealed it to the prosecution, doubtless from a high sense of public duty. The cross-examiner's method was to deal gently with her and to feign an indifference to her story which would tend to minimize its importance. This was good art, for if irritated she would have been likely to harm rather than to help his case. With Fleet, the officer who had produced the case from professional motives, the method was reversed. The lawyer changed his manner and deliberately exasperated the witness, whose hostility to his client he was anxious to reveal to the jury. The Borden trial offers many opportunities for study of old-school practice of the best kind.

Why is it that the papers have taken to calling Miss Borden "Lizzie"? There is no reason why the name of the regard due to a lady should not be manifested to her, instead of a lack of consideration that approximates brutality. It is not to be taken for granted that she is guilty, and it is just as well not to be addicted to the pot house politician style of calling every Richard "Dick" and every Eliza or Elizabeth "Lizzie." There seems to be a great deal of unnecessary prying in the cross-examination. It is hard to see what relevancy some of the questions have, though the learned propounder may. What the outcome of the trial may be cannot be accurately prophesied, though it is fair to assume it will result in adding another discredit to circumstantial evidence.—New London Telegraph.

It is an old theory that new wood is entitled to three coats of paint, but many new houses have but two coats of Chilton paint, and are then allowed to stand two and three years before they are painted again, and then only one coat. Can you not profit by this suggestion? In painting your house this year get estimates on one, two and three coats. If the house is in fair condition and there is not too much difference between the shade you are to put on and the one on the house, probably one coat will suffice. If not, two coats will surely answer. What is the use then of putting on three? We have had painters tell us that they had painted houses with Chilton Paint who's the house looked better after two coats than three. Upon being asked why, then, they put on three they answered that they were obliged to, as the contract called for three. Word your contracts so you can stop when you have gone far enough. Put Chilton Paint over a dry surface only.

DeWOLF & VINCENT, Agents.

The Evening Standard.

NEW BEDFORD, MASS.

MONDAY EVENING, JUNE 12.

THREE EDITIONS DAILY.

No. 87 Union Street.

PUBLISHED BY

E. ANTHONY & SONS.

INCORPORATED.

—TERMS—

Six Dollars a Year; Three Dollars for Six Months, in advance; Single Copies Two Cents.

ORDER THE EVENING STANDARD TO YOUR VACATION ADDRESS.

Mailed direct from this office for any length of time desired; 50 cents a month, including postage.

Best Family Newspaper in Southern Massachusetts is the REPUBLICAN STANDARD. Our Weekly Edition—a large twelve-page paper of 84 columns, containing more reading matter than any other weekly paper in southern Massachusetts. It is published Thursday mornings. Subscription price only $1.50 a year, in advance.

TWELVE PAGES.

This Evening's Issue Consists of Twelve Pages and Every Patron is Entitled to that Number.

The Boston Traveller defends Attorney General Pillsbury from the insinuations which have been made that political considerations prevented his taking part in the Borden trial. It says there is reason to fear that his health, not yet fully restored, would not stand the strain, and that his physicians advised against his attempting it. In his last report to the legislature he proposed that district attorneys be given the prosecution of capital cases, and that the attorney general might be relieved of that duty except if in his own opinion he might deem it wise or necessary. The district attorneys of Massachusetts are all able lawyers, and are as competent to conduct a murder trial as any other criminal case. The judiciary committee, the legislature and Governor Russell all took the same view of the matter as did Mr. Pillsbury and, acting on the suggestion contained in his report, enacted the law relieving the attorney general from taking part in murder trials.

District Attorney Knowlton has had charge of the Borden case from the start, and the only connection which Mr. Pillsbury has had with it was to give advice and go before the grand jury as the law then required him to do. He took no part in the preliminary examination, but has been consulted frequently by Mr. Knowlton, and is consulted by him now.

The outside reporters are getting some harmless and good natured fun out of the proceedings at the Borden trial, especially the blue coat and brass buttons of the sheriff and his deputies, and the old fashioned formality at the opening of the sessions. The statutes provide that the clerk or the sheriff and his deputies, as the court shall direct, shall perform the duties of crier, and without additional compensation. But had our visitors from abroad witnessed the manner in which Henry F. Cobb, of Taunton, who performed the duties of crier for many years, discharged the important functions of his position, they would have been much more impressed and probably much more amused than they are now.

But all our visitors are strongly impressed with the dignity and order of the court, the decorum which prevails, and the absence of unseemly wrangling among the counsel. In these respects the court sets an example to those of New York, from which the papers of the metropolis admit that it might profit. It has been thus far, and seems likely to be to the end, a model court and a model trial.

Ex-Governor Ames, who is one of the outside jury which is to give an opinion on the evidence in the Borden case, says: I intend to read every word of the evidence, certainly. Whether we can give a correct verdict or not I cannot undertake to say. All we are asked to do is to say whether in our opinion the case against Miss Borden is proven or not by the evidence. We are not to decide whether she is guilty or not, but to give our opinion of the evidence in the case. It is no reflection at all on the jury or on the court. The jury may be much more capable of giving an intelligent verdict on the case than we are, and then again they may not. Our verdict is not to be made known until the trial is finished and the verdict of the jury announced.

We thought the puddle in front of the town clock was to be done away with when the new water pipe was laid. But it is there yet after every shower. We believe the excuse for the delay now is that a sand-catcher is to be dug there. When this is done the pleasure of the street railway company is leveling up their track will have to be awaited; and then there will be a rest till the board of public works can suspend wrangling long enough to order it done. On the whole ladies are likely to have to avoid that crossing all summer long.

The tests at the Watertown arsenal have resulted in the conclusion that cut nails hold better than wire nails, the superiority varying in spruce wood from 47 to 80 per cent., and in pine wood from 64 to 135 per cent., the average of all the tests being 72.74 per cent.

A Frenchman says citric acid destroys microbes, and therefore recommends lemonade as a drink and to neutralize the acidity of the lemon a little board of soda is to be added. But if the acid is neutralized how is it going to hurt the microbes?

The Connecticut assembly has adopted the proposed constitutional amendment, providing for plurality elections of state officers, with only four dissenting votes.

LIZZIE'S STORY.

The following is the verbatim report of the testimony of Lizzie Borden at the inquest on the deaths of her father and stepmother, now printed for the first time:

Q. (Mr. Knowlton.) Give me your full name.
A. Lizzie Andrew Borden.
Q. Is it Lizzie or Elizabeth?
A. Lizzie.
Q. You were so christened?
A. I was so christened.
Q. What is your age, please?
A. Thirty-two.
Q. Your mother is not living?
A. No sir.
Q. When did she die?
A. She died when I was two and a half years old.
Q. You do not remember her, then?
A. No sir.
Q. What was your father's age?
A. He was seventy next month.
Q. What was his whole name?
A. Andrew Jackson Borden.
Q. And your stepmother, what is her whole name?
A. Abby Durfee Borden.
Q. How long had your father been married to your stepmother?
A. I think about twenty-seven years.
Q. How much of that time have they lived in that house on Second street?
A. I think, I am not sure, but I think about twenty years last May.
Q. Always occupied the whole house?
A. Yes sir.
Q. Somebody told me it was once fitted up for two tenements.
A. When we bought it it was for two tenements, and the men who bought it of stayed there a few months until he finished his own house. After he finished his own house and moved into it there was no one else ever moved in; we always had the whole.
Q. Did you ever deed him any property?
A. No sir.
Q. He gave us some years ago, Grandfather Borden's house on Ferry street, and he bought that back from us some weeks ago, I don't know just how many.
Q. As near as you can tell.
A. Well, I should say in June, but I am not sure.
Q. What do you mean by bought it back?
A. He bought it of us, and gave us the money for it.
Q. How much was it?
A. How much money? He gave us $5,000 for it.
Q. Did you pay him anything when you took a deed from him?
A. Pay him anything? No sir.
Q. How long ago was it you took a deed from him?
A. When he gave it to us?
Q. Yes.
A. I can't tell you; I should think five years.
Q. Did you have any other business transactions with him besides that?
A. No sir.
Q. In real estate?
A. No sir.
Q. Or in personal property?
A. No sir.
Q. Never?
A. Never.
Q. No transfer of property one way or the other?
A. No sir.
Q. At no time?
A. No sir.
Q. And I understand he paid you the cash for this property?
A. Yes sir.
Q. You and Emma equally?
A. Yes sir.
Q. How many children has your father?
A. Only two.
Q. Only you two?
A. Yes sir.
Q. Any others ever?
A. One that died.
Q. Did you ever know of your father making a will?
A. No sir, except I heard somebody say once that there was one several years ago; that is all I ever heard.
Q. Who did you hear say so?
A. I think it was Mr. Morse.
Q. What Morse?
A. Uncle John V. Morse.
Q. How long ago?
A. How long ago I heard him say it? I have not any idea.
Q. What did he say about it?
A. Nothing, except just that.
Q. What?
A. That Mr. Borden had a will.
Q. Did you ask your father?
A. I did not.
Q. Did he ever mention the subject of will to you?
A. He did not.
Q. He never told you that he had made a will, or had not?
A. No sir.
Q. Did he have a marriage settlement with your stepmother that you knew of?
A. I never knew of any.
Q. Had you heard anything of his proposing to make a will?
A. No sir.
Q. Do you know of anybody that your father was on bad terms with?
A. There was a man that came there for he had trouble with, I don't know who the man was.
Q. When?
A. I cannot locate the time exactly. It was within two weeks. That is I don't know the date or day of the month.
Q. Tell all you saw and heard.
A. I did not see anything. I heard the bell ring, and father went to the door and let him in. I did not hear anything for some time, except just the voices; then I heard the man say, "I would like to have that place, I would not am not willing to let your business go in there." And the man said, "I thought with your reputation for liking money, you would let your store for anything." Father said, "You are mistaken." Then they talked a while, and then their voices were louder, and I heard father order him out, and went to the front door with him.
Q. What did he say?
A. He said that he had stayed long enough, and he would thank him to go.
Q. Did he say anything about coming again?
A. No sir.
Q. Did your father say anything about coming again, or did he?
A. No sir.
Q. Have you any idea who that was?
A. No sir.
Q. Was he a man from out of town, because he said he was going home to see his partner.
Q. Have you had any efforts made to find him?
A. We have had a detective; that is all I know.
Q. You have not found him?
A. Not that I know of.
Q. You can't give us any other idea about it?
A. Nothing but what I have told you.
Q. Beside that do you know of anybody that your father has had feelings toward, or who had bad feelings toward your father?
A. I know of one man that has not been friendly with him; they have not been friendly for years.

(Continued on Supplement Page.)

EXCLUDED.

(Continued from Third Page.)

The weight of the Wisconsin case is reduced to a minimum, because many essential points do not appear to have entered into it or to have been discussed.

A line of cases, not referred to in the brief was cited, and counsel laid stress upon that of Emery in this state, which the principle laid down that no person shall be bound to testify to his own prejudice. I stand, said counsel, for the defendant on her rights under the constitution, and if they are departed from it will imperil all those who stand in a similar position.

Mr. Moody followed briefly. He said the learned counsel's speech reminded him to apply in different words the statement of a French general on the "charge of the six hundred." "It is magnificent, but it is not law." Governor Robinson says that the testimony is not admissible because it is not, and that is all there is to it, except a few vocal gymnastics and fireworks. There is not a single case cited in the United States or England where such evidence is shown not to be admissible, except when the defendant was under arrest. In the first place, although no case which decides the absence of caution is enough to exclude evidence, yet much stress is laid on that point by the other side. Let us go back to the inquest and see what was the condition of affairs. Mr. and Mrs. Borden had been murdered. Our statutes require a view of the body in such cases by a medical examiner, and if he is of the opinion that death

was caused by violence then he has done his duty, and the matter is to be referred to the district attorney or the justice of the district court. It was the duty of the court to inquire what caused the deaths. At the time of the death of one of the parties but two persons, so far as known, were present in the house, and at the time of the death of the other but one person was in the house; it is to be supposed that Lizzie Andrew Borden was to be exempt from inquiry? She was summoned, and she asked for counsel to be present at the inquest. It was declined, as almost an unbroken line of precedent has established and as the law gives power. She was not cautioned, but was allowed to see her counsel in regard to testifying. Your honors can have no reason to doubt she was not cautioned by so able a lawyer as Mr. Jennings, and received full advice as to her rights. She could only be excused from testifying on the single ground of criminating herself. (She went in, and who can doubt that she did it voluntarily? Why cannot it be assumed that those who had the inquest in charge thought defendant could clear herself from suspicion instead of increasing it. I say that it is not true that she was not cautioned, but that it was done, and most considerately. It has been said that she was constantly under watch, that officers were on the watch in and about the house all the time. So was her sister and Bridget Sullivan and John V. Morse, and the police were only doing their duty in keeping up this guard. The law is no respecter of persons. There was a warrant out for the arrest of this defendant when she testified, but if she was not aware of it how can that be said to be a bar to her testifying willingly. It is assumed that the district attorney knew of this warrant. I deny it, and the assumption of this is not supported by a particle of evidence. No case is to be found or cited that will sustain the exclusion of this evidence.

Consultation of the Court.

After Mr. Moody concluded his evidence Chief Justice Mason said: "We will retire for consultation." The judges departed from the room, and the buzz of conversation was heard on every hand.

Neither Miss Borden nor the jury were present during the arguments, they having retired to adjoining rooms at the commencement.

THE DEFENDANT'S BRIEF.

Points of Miss Borden's Counsel Clearly and Concisely Given.

The following is the defendant's brief:
Commonwealth of Massachusetts, Bristol ss.   Superior Court, June, 1893.

Commonwealth vs. Lizzie A. Borden. Defendant's points on admissibility of defendant's testimony before inquest. The defendant contends that the following facts appear:

1. Homicides committed August 4, 1892.
2. Testimony of defendant begins August 9, 1892, continued during August 10 and 11, 1892.
3. Accusation of these crimes by mayor and city marshal August 6, 1892.
4. Defendant kept under constant observation of police August 6, 1892, and all days following until conclusion of defendant's testimony and arrest.
5. Defendant summoned on or before August 9, 1892, by subpoena to attend and testify before inquest.
6. Before testifying defendant makes request for counsel at inquest, and such request is denied and counsel not present.
7. Counsel for the commonwealth, the district attorney, conducted her examination before the inquest.
8. Defendant before testifying not properly cautioned.
9. Complaint made and warrant placed in the hands of city marshal on or before August 8, 1892.
10. City marshal holding warrant present during defendant's testimony.
11. Upon conclusion of testimony defendant held and arrested two hours later on similar warrant.
12. Before defendant testified it had been duly determined by complaint made and warrant issued that defendant had committed the crime of killing the two persons, the cause of whose death said inquest was held to ascertain.

Testimony so given was not free and voluntary, but was compulsory and is not admissible against defendant.

"No subject shall .... be compelled to accuse or furnish evidence against himself."

Article XII. Bill of Rights, Constitution of Massachusetts.

"No person shall .... be compelled in any criminal case to be a witness against himself."

Article V. Amendments U. S. Constitution.

The only two cases in Massachusetts bearing upon the question here raised are
Com. vs. King, 8 Gray, 501.
Com. vs. Bradford, 126, Mass. 42.
In King's case testimony given before a fire inquest was subsequently admitted against defendant, but no suspicion then

attached to King, and he had not then been implicated; no prosecution had then been instituted.

In Bradford's case, like testimony before a fire inquest was subsequently admitted, but he, at the time his testimony was given, was not proceeded against criminally and was not then under suspicion of crime. His testimony was voluntary.

"It thus appears that when the prisoner was called upon to make his statement on oath before the coroner he stood in the attitude of an accused person and was required to answer for himself as a party and not as a mere witness to aid the coroner in investigating the cause of the death of the deceased. The cause of death was evident. The body had been examined with the marks of violence plainly apparent; the bruised head, the fractured skull and the broken club lying near it with hair still adhering to it. It was evident that a crime had been committed. From the time that a felonious homicide was established the proceedings assumed the form of a criminal investigation."

People vs. Mondon 103, N. Y. 216.

Arrest on charge of murder without warrant and before complaint and defendant taken before coroner as a witness.

In State vs. Coffee, 56 Conn., 399, it was held that evidence voluntarily given after caution that he was not obliged to testify to anything that would criminate himself was admissible.

Testimony given by the accused on a judicial investigation, either when charged before the examining magistrate or under arrest under suspicion at a coroner's inquest, is not competent against him at the trial, unless it appears that before it was given he was duly cautioned that it might be used against him and that it was voluntarily taken according to law.

Abbott's trial brief, Criminal Causes, page 398, section 659, and cases there cited.

The Consultation Ended.

It was 12.25 when the justices emerged from their room and took their places upon the bench. During the long interim while they were considering the points advanced by the counsel Lizzie was in earnest conversation with Mr. Robinson, and leaned forward, so that nothing he said could escape her. She was completely absorbed, and it was plainly to be seen that matters of the greatest importance were being considered. Mr. Jennings showed her numerous photographs taken about the Borden house, and asked her as to how accurately the subjects were reproduced. Judge Borden came in, and soon engaged in conversation with several persons within the rail.

When the judges entered the court room there was a hush of expectancy, and as Chief Justice Mason commenced to read the decision of the judges it was possible to have heard the dropping of a pin, so anxiously were all listening to his words.

THE EVIDENCE EXCLUDED.

Justices Were All Agreed in Not Admitting It.

Chief Justice Mason said: The propriety of examining the prisoner at the inquest and of all that occurred in connection therewith is entirely distinct from the question of the admissibility of her statements in that examination. It is with the latter question only that this court has to deal. The common law regards this species of evidence with distrust. The statements by one accused of crime are admissible against him only when it is affirmatively established that they were voluntarily made. It has been held that the statements of the accused as a witness under oath at the inquest before he had been arrested or charged with the crime given in this connection may be voluntary and admissible against him at his subsequent trial, and the mere fact that at the time of his testimony at the inquest he was aware that he was suspected of the crime does not make them otherwise, but we are of opinion both upon principle and authority that if he be cused was at the time of such testimony under arrest charged with the crime in question the statements she made are not voluntary and are inadmissible at the time. The common law regards substance more than form. The principle involved can not be evaded by reviewing the form of arrest if the witness at the time such testimony is given is practically in custody. From the agreed facts and the facts otherwise in evidence it is plain that the prisoner at the time of her testimony at the inquest was, so far as related to this question, as effectually in custody as if the formal precept had been served. And without delaying on other circumstance we are all of opinion that this consideration is decisive and the evidence is excluded.

Friends of Miss Borden Exultant Over Decision.

When the chief justice finished and the pent-up feelings of those who had been listening so earnestly found vent and the sheriff was obliged to rap vigorously for order. Mr. Jennings' face fairly beamed and he could hardly restrain himself. Lizzie gave one glance in which was pictured all the exultation that is possible to be portrayed upon a human countenance, and immediately buried her face in her fan while the tears trickled down her face like rain. Mr. Adams smiled in a pleased manner, while the expression on Mr. Robinson's face was a sort of "I told you so." Certain it is, that this decision has materially weakened the government's case, but if the exclusion of the damaging evidence was any disappointment to Mr. Knowlton, he gave no evidence of it. He sat as immovable as marble and apparently was the least concerned of any one of the listeners. Upon Mr. Moody's countenance was a disappointed expression. The faces of the spectators were a study. On some were depicted the greatest pleasure, while others tried in vain to hide their disappointment. It is commonly heard about the court house that the failure to get an opportunity to put in the testimony will be extremely damaging if not irreparable to the case against the government.

Dr. Dedrich.

Dr. Dedrich, of Fall River, was called to the stand and sworn.
Q. (Mr. Moody) Albert C. Dedrich?
A. Yes sir.
Q. You are a physician practicing in Fall River? A. Yes sir.
Q. How long have you been there, doctor? A. Five years.
Q. Prior to that time had you had some hospital experience? A. Yes sir.
Q. How long? A. Two years.
Q. On the 4th day of August last did you go to the Borden house at any time? A. Yes sir.
Q. What time did you go? A. After 2 o'clock.
Q. How long after 2 o'clock, can you tell me? A. No sir, I cannot.
Q. When you got there who was there, Dr. Bowen, a number of officers, Dr. Dolan, Dr. Tourtellot, and a number of others.
Q. Did you make an examination of the two bodies? A. Yes.
Q. What did you find? A. I noticed a cut on Mr. Borden's face and one on Mr. Borden's head. I would also state that Mrs. Borden's blood was more copy and Mr. Borden's more free.
Q. Did you notice anything relative to the warmth of the bodies? A. Mrs. Borden's was colder and stiffer.
Q. Did you form an opinion as to the priority of the deaths? A. Yes; Mrs. Borden's occurred first.
Q. Form an opinion as to the time? A. Several hours.
Joseph Hyde was the next witness.
Q. What is your occupation? A. I am a policeman.

Q. What was you last year? A. A patrolman.
Q. Were you at the Borden house on the night of the homicide? A. Yes.
Q. At what time? A. From 1 till 11 o'clock.
Q. See anything at any time of Miss Russell? A. Yes.
Q. Was any one with her? A. Miss Lizzie Borden.
Q. Where was you standing? A. On the east side.
Q. What did you see them do? A. Miss Russell came down stairs through the entry and down the cellar stairs. Miss Russell had a lamp and Miss Borden a slop pail. Miss Borden went to the water closet, and then through the wash room to the sink, and I heard a sound like water. Then they went up stairs.
Q. What time was this? A. Fifteen minutes of 9.
Q. What then? A. Ten or 15 minutes later Miss Borden came out of the sitting room and down cellar to the wash room, put down the lamp, came over to the other side and stooped down.
Q. What did she do then? A. I don't know.
Q. Was she alone? A. Yes.
Q. How long was she there? A. Perhaps two minutes.
Q. Was there anything in the cellar? A. Yes, the clothes taken from Mr. and Mrs. Borden.
Q. How long was this after the first time? A. I'd say ten or fifteen minutes.
Cross-examined by ex-Governor Robinson.
Q. How long had you been about the premises? A. From 1 o'clock till about 11 p. m.
Q. Were you there all that time? A. All but when I went to supper.
Q. Were you gone an hour or so? A. Yes.
Q. Any other officers in the yard? A. Officers Ferguson and Minnehan.
Q. Any one with you when Lizzie came down stairs? A. No.
Q. Could Minnehan have seen them? A. So far as I know he couldn't.
Q. How could you see? A. In the window.
Q. Was the window open? A. Yes.
Q. You had your eyes open? A. I thought I did.
Q. You didn't cover anything up; not trying to shield any one? A. No.
Q. Could you see the light? A. Yes, when they came out of the sitting room.
Q. They had a good sized light, didn't they? A. Yes.
Q. And came right along? A. Yes.
Q. Which came first? A. Miss Russell.
Q. Lizzie had a slop pail? A. Yes.
Q. Nothing suspicious about that was there? A. No.
Q. How did they seem? A. Miss Russell was very nervous.
Q. Won't you tell us about that? A. When Lizzie was in the wash cellar Miss Russell hung back.
Q. Won't you please tell now? A. She looked nervous and acted so.
Q. Well, let us have the looks first? Witness was about to describe them when the court took a recess till 2 15 p. m.

Before going from the court room Miss Borden spoke to Mr. Robinson and shook hands with Rev. Mr. Jubb.

MISS BORDEN'S EVIDENCE.

Her Story at the Inquest Which Has Been Excluded.

Miss Borden's evidence at the inquest, which was excluded by the court today, is printed complete for the first time this afternoon. It has never before been printed.

CONDENSED LOCALS.

A mass meeting is to be held in the Opera House next Sunday evening in the interest of the movement looking toward securing an amnesty for the Irish-American prisoners in British jails who are confined for political crimes. Mayor Brock will preside, and among the speakers will be Father Fox Tucker, John W. Cummings, William M. Butler and Lemuel T. Wilcox. An invitation will also be extended to Rev. P. R. Frothingham and Rev. M. C. Cullen, Captain George S. Anthony and the representatives in the legislature from this city to be present.

Samuel Gibson, a bricklayer, employed on the new building in process of erection on Purchase street, south of Weld street, was assisting in unloading stone this morning when a skid broke and let the heavy stone down onto his hand. Four fingers were badly crushed, and he was removed to his home on the County road.

The New Bedford Baseball association will meet tomorrow night to complete the details of incorporation and to choose a name for the new park.

UNCALLED FOR LETTERS.

The following is the list of advertised letters in the post office June 12:

FAIRHAVEN.

Schooner Harry B. Diverty of Camden, New Jersey, Captain William Taylor, arrived yesterday with 301 tons 150 pounds of pipe for the water works. It consists of 255 pieces of 12-inch pipe and 1,120 pieces of 6-inch pipe from the McNeil Pipe company of Burlington, N. J. There will be two more cargoes of this same size. Work in laying pipe will not be commenced until another cargo comes.

THE VINEYARD.

Trains on the Martha's Vineyard railroad began running regular summer trips this morning. Passengers will be landed from the trains and take the same at a point just beyond the bathing houses, and be transferred to and from the Highland wharf by horse cars, until the Oak Bluffs wharf is far enough along to enable the building of a track upon it. All freight to and from Edgartown will also necessarily be hauled this way for the time being. It is thought the new wharf will be far enough advanced towards completion in a week to allow the boats to make landings there.

OSMOND ELECTROCUTED.

Pays the Penalty of His Crime in the Sing Sing Death Chair.

Sing Sing, June 12—John L. Osmond, who shot and killed his wife, Marie, and John C. Burchell on Oct. 3, 1891, was electrocuted this morning. At 10.41 the current was turned on. The handful figure in the chair straightened up until the straps creaked. For three seconds 1,750 volts surged through Osmond's body, then the current was reduced to 150 volts and at the end of 40 seconds was shut off altogether. The body dropped back limp in the chair and Drs. Irvine and Sheehan listened at the heart for a moment and then pronounced the man dead. There were no signs of burning or scorching and the physicians declared the electrocution a successful one.

BIDDEFORD OPERATIVES STRIKE.

The Long Threatened Trouble Precipitated and Half the Force Out.

Biddeford, June 12—The threatened general strike at the Pepperell and Laconia mills took place this morning. Fully half the employes of the two corporations are out, most of them striking. A big crowd gathered at the mill gates this morning, but aside from yelling and hissing at those who went to work there was no lawless demonstrations.

Dynamiter Gilbert's Plans.

LONDON, June 12—James Gilbert, the dynamiter recently released from Portland prison, because he was thought to be near death, sailed on the steamship Chester from Southampton. Gilbert said that he intended to direct the government's attention to the pitiable cases of Americans imprisoned in Portland. Gallagher, he said, had become hopelessly insane, and Daly was dying slowly. Other political prisoners were threatened with insanity.

Mexican Town Wiped Out.

PUEBLA, Mex., June 12—The most disastrous storm that has ever visited this part of Mexico, has reported from the town of Paradomata. Every house in the place was swept away by the terrific wind. The town had a population of about 2000 persons, all of whom were made homeless.

Shoe Factory Burned.

HAVERHILL, Mass., June 12—Walter Edelstein & Co.'s shoe factory at West Newbury, with its contents, was totally destroyed by fire. The loss on stock and machinery is reported at $8000, and on building $2000.

Strike at Haverhill.

HAVERHILL, Mass., June 12—Fifty hands employed by George W. Gilvert & Co., dealers in cut soles and tops, have struck because the firm would not grant a half holiday without deduction of pay.

Horseshoers Get Nine Hours.

BOSTON, June 12—The Boston Master Horseshoers'association held a large meeting yesterday. It was reported that the nine hours a day demand of the men had been acceded to at the regular salary.

Depositors Lose Half Their Money.

LAWTON, Mich., June 12—The American bank of Dwiggins, Starbuck & Co., has been placed in charge of receivers. The institution will not be reopened. It is expected that the depositors will realize about 50 cents on the dollar.

New Weekly at Washington.

WASHINGTON, June 12—The Capital, a weekly newspaper published by a company of which Marshall Cushing is president and Charles T. Grandy treasurer, has made its appearance here.

Satolli Going West.

WASHINGTON, June 12—Mgr. Satolli, the papal legate, has arranged an extensive trip to the Pacific coast which will begin this week.

Mystery Deep as Ever.

DEDHAM, Mass., June 12—No new developments are reported in the Jacob Littig murder case. The story of two suspects turns out to be without foundation.

Brief Mention.

Ex-Congressman Frederick T. Greenhalge will be the commencement orator at Pinkerton academy, Derry, N. H.

An Italian employed in a quarry at Georgetown, Conn., was drowned in a pond at Cannon's Station while in bathing.

At a reunion of the First Connecticut heavy artillery at Putnam, S. H. Cole was chosen president and E. C. Dow secretary-treasurer.

Austin Lavalley, aged 66, was killed by an east-bound Boston and Albany express in Worcester, Mass. He was deaf and did not hear the train.

Michael Carney, aged 50 years, was drowned at High Bridge, Danversport, Mass. He was alive when taken from the water, but died in an hour.

State Secretary J. B. Cook of the Connecticut Young Men's Christian association has accepted the call to become secretary of Bridgeport's association.

Mrs. Frank Leslie is freed from William C. K. Wilde, her recently acquired English husband. Judge Brown granted her an absolute divorce.

At Middletown, Conn., Alfred and Emil Bergstan, aged 14 and 11 years, were bathing in the Connecticut river. The younger was unable to swim, and the elder, trying to save him, was himself drowned.

The burning of the Bay State House at Worcester, Mass., will not affect the proceedings of the New England waterworks convention, to be held in that city, beginning Wednesday.

At Mittineague, Mass., thieves was broken into and the safe cracked and robbed of between $18 and $19 together with $2 worth of stamps. The burglars overlooked about $300 worth of postage stamps.

Column 1

UNBURIED FOR FIVE DAYS.

Charles Vanslet Found Dead in a Fall River House.

At 3 40 Sunday afternoon John F. Doherty informed Officers Welsh and Douty that there was a dead man in one of the rooms of a house at 270 Bedford street, Fall River. The policemen investigated, and in a small apartment of the attic found the body of a Frenchman lying on a bed. The surroundings were anything but attractive. The flesh of the corpse was black, and the remains so offensive that it was next to impossible to stand guard at the door. Medical Examiner Dolan was notified, and the usual crowd assembled on the premises. Nobody appeared to know much about the dead man. His name was Charles Vanslet, and he was 50 years of age. He lived alone in a room under the eaves, and was employed by the Mr. Doherty who gave the alarm. As nearly as can be ascertained, he had not been seen since a week ago yesterday, and a lodger on the same floor had not seen him for a fortnight. Vanslet called on an acquaintance of his on Monday night, June 5th, and remained about two hours. A woman who resides in the same house, thinks that she saw Vanslet pass through the yard last Wednesday, but others in the neighborhood dispute her. He was mistaken. There were no marks of violence on the body, and it is believed that the man died a natural death five or six days ago. He was dressed in a shirt and trousers of a laborer, and had removed his shoes before lying down. As acquaintance of the deceased stated that he had no relatives in Fall River. He had been married two or three times, it was said, but it was impossible to learn whether he left a widow or not.

Column 2

PUBLICLY REPRIMANDED.

Members of Company E, First Infantry Censured in Front of the Line

Company E, First Infantry, arrived home from its tour of camp duty Saturday afternoon, and was met at the station by Meyrelles band, which volunteered its services, and escorted to the armory. The men showed the good results of their week in camp by their set-up and precision of movements.

An unpleasant thing happened on Friday, which has created indignation in the company. Corporal Slocum and Privates Ellis, Davis, Dewhurst and Folsom, who were on guard Thursday, by the ordinary rules of military life were exempted from duty the next day, and on Friday they were absent from review, and dress parade. For this the men were summoned to the tent of Major R. H. Morgan in the evening and reprimanded, and next morning when battalion line was formed the men were called to the front and publicly censured for neglect of duty. The men are very bitter over the matter and some of their comrades, who side with them, threaten to apply for their discharges.

Major Morgan says special orders were issued on Friday morning for every man in each company not on guard or sick to turn out for review and dress parade, and the men who did not turn out ought to have known better. The reprimand in front of the battalion line was delivered in front of the battalion to which Company E belongs, and was given in accordance with orders from Colonel Mathews.

As a long-time member of the militia, the writer would suggest to the aggrieved men that they let the matter drop right where it is. When they were mustered into the service they swore, among other things, to obey the commands of their commanding officers, and when they are in camp they are theoretically at least under the same discipline as if they were in the regular service. If orders were issued for every man to turn out at review and dress parade they had no option but to obey orders, no matter how disagreeable personally those orders were, and they would have been doing nothing more than thousands of others have done. If they were not notified of the orders the onus of the reprimand does not rest upon them, but upon those who failed to transmit the orders. If they should apply for their discharges in all probability they would not be granted, and the only way they could quit the service would be by dishonorable discharge. They cannot expect their superior officer to apologize to them or to the company for doing what he was ordered to do and which he could only have prevented by resigning. They are fortunate they were not in actual service, for if they had been in addition to a reprimand they would probably have been given extra duty. These statements are made in the kindliest spirit, and as good soldiers and sensible men it is to be hoped that the men concerned will accept the situation and forget the unpleasant affair as quickly as they can.

— Steven to the Steven Beguile

The Fall River correspondent of the Providence Journal states that F company of the naval brigade turned out in Fall River Saturday afternoon and escorted company M, first infantry, to its armory on return from muster, and made a very creditable appearance. The time was when company M had to do its own escorting, and its return from a tour of duty was not particularly imposing. Since company F has been organized, the sailors have turned out cheerfully, and unlike G company of New Bedford they have been on the best of terms with the soldiers. It is said that the latter will escort F company to the Enterprise when that vessel makes her appearance in this harbor.

FIREMEN'S MEMORIAL DAY.

They Attend Services at Universalist Church and Decorate Comrades' Graves.

Yesterday was observed by the active and veteran firemen as their memorial day, and they attended services at the Universalist church, where the pastor, Rev. William F. Potter, delivered an appropriate sermon.

He chose as his subject "Memorials," and his thoughts were suggested by the text, "He being lead, yet speaketh." The services were closed by the singing of "America" and the benediction.

Early in the morning squads of veteran firemen decorated the graves of the following: Fairhaven, Riverside, A. M. Charry; East Freetown, William Hammersville; Acushnet, O. C. Spooner; Oak Grove, Isaac W. Benjamin; Rural, Rural M. Snow, Jethro Hillman, A. K. Dennison.

Ladder company No. 3 placed an elaborate floral piece on the grave of John P. Kelley, who was run over by the truck while responding to an alarm a year ago.

The H. & L. Co. No. 1 decorated the graves of the following deceased members: Oak Grove cemetery, Thomas T. Manley, George Manley, Asa R. Sherman; Rural cemetery, Eben A. Butts, William Clymouns, Robert A. Dilling-ham, Charles Ludberg; Catholic cemetery, James Conway.

PRISON REPORTS.

Josiah A. Hunt, Esq., keeper of the jail and house of correction, reports 32 prisoners in the jail a week ago; since committed, 8; sent to court and not returned, 0; sent to court and returned to house of correction, 2; recognized, 4; remaining, 34, now in confinement.

In the house of correction a week ago there were 257 prisoners; since committed, 15 for being drunk, 3 for assault and battery, 7 for larceny, 2 for vagrancy, 6 for disturbing the peace; discharged as poor convicts, 1; on payment of fine, 3; at expiration of term of sentence, 18; conditionally released by commissioners, 3; remaining, 265.

The commitments to the house of correction include 17 sentences from New Bedford, aggregate 41 2-3 months; 18 from Fall River, aggregate 35 1-3 months. The number of commitments of prisoners of temperate habits is 2; intemperate, 31.

CUTTYHUNK.

Mrs. Benjamin Eisener, an old lady, 86 years of age, met with quite a serious accident last week. She went out in the back yard to empty a pitcher of herbs and in leaning over the embankment lost her balance and fell, striking her head upon the stones, making a deep cut upon the forehead and bruising both eyes. The pitcher was broken in the fall and in trying to help herself the old lady cut her hands in several places upon the fragments. It was quite a severe accident for such an old person, but she is recovering quite rapidly from the effects of the fall.

Steamer Annie with Lieutenant Commander George Colby inspected the light station last Monday afternoon. The steamer anchored in Cuttyhunk harbor over night.

Samuel Baron of Fitchburg is visiting friends on the island.

The club workmen are building a new dock at the head of Lake Gosnold, to take the place of the one destroyed by the ice during the winter.

James Murchison and wife of Fitchburg are boarding with Mrs. Frank Peters.

A florist from New Bedford came on the island Thursday to arrange the gardens for the club. The words "Cuttyhunk Club," which were cut on the front lawn last year, will be changed and planted on the hill where the flagstaff is erected. The cook, second waiter and other help came Saturday. The club will open the 17th this year, instead of the 15th as formerly.

Mrs. Henry Allen has been on a short visit to New Bedford.

Walter Allen has been quite ill.

The school children have been raising a subscription for a school flag. They were successful in their attempt, and there will be a flag-raising this week.

The Newport fishing boats have arrived for the season's fishing.

Column 3

[From Saturday's Third Edition.]

THE BORDEN JURY DISAGREE.

A Drive Saturday Afternoon and a Sermon from Mr. Julien Sunday.

The Borden jury was taken this afternoon for a drive around the Point road in barge Pilgrim. Deputy Sheriff A. C. Kirby handled the reins and Deputy Sheriffs Nickerson and Arnold had the party in charge.

Before leaving the city Chief Justice Mason made arrangements with Rev. M. C. Julien to preach a sermon to-morrow free from all reference to the Borden case, and to guard his prayer and the singing from any possible bearing on the subject. He then gave orders to the deputy sheriffs in charge of the Borden jury to conduct them there to the morning service tomorrow and special seats were assigned them in the center of the church. But after the jury had returned to their stockade in the north end of the third floor of the Parker House there developed a little hitch in the proceedings. It is stated that Augustus Swift, the New Bedford member of the jury, objected to the arrangement, and wanted to go to the North Congregational church and listen to Rev. John A. MacColl. The matter was reported to the deputies, who after a consultation decided that they were not desirous of asking Justice Blodget, who alone of the three remains in the city over Sunday, to make any change in the plans. Therefore, if the difference of opinion still continue among the jurors tomorrow morning they will spend the day in their rooms in sweltering.

COMMENTS ON THE BORDEN TRIAL.

Local interest in the trial is intense. The sessions are attended by as many people as are permitted to enter by the extremely magnificent high sheriff of Bristol county, who goes around in a Websterian blue swallow-tailed coat, with enough gilt buttons on it to fit out a regiment of Haytian generals, and a high silk hat, the sight of which would fill Mr. Morris's with admiration and envy. All the sheriffs of Bristol county are not as high as the high sheriff. The silk hat is his peculiar distinction, and with an irate temper and a stout figure it renders him formidable to look upon. But all the sheriffs have sky-blue swallow-tailed coats and a gross or two of gilt buttons, and when they all stand up to salute the court, and the court stands up to salute them, one is profoundly impressed with the majesty of the commonwealth of Massachusetts.—New York Tribune.

The prosecution in the Borden case has not yet developed any evidence of importance not previously known to the public, while one or two strong points in favor of the defense have been admitted by government witnesses, as, for instance, that the front door may not have been fastened on the fatal morning. The destruction of the dress by Lizzie Borden is somewhat weakened as a piece of evidence by the fact that she destroyed the dress apparently without any effort at concealing what she was about. Nevertheless it is far too early in the trial to pass an opinion as to the strength or weakness of the case against the defendant. If she is guilty it is impossible to believe that she is in a normal condition mentally, and if innocent she is enduring an ordeal the painfulness of which it would be difficult to exaggerate.—New York Press.

Ex-Governor Robinson is certainly without an equal in New York city as a cross-examiner. Hamlet, in the play, is no more

Column 4

(Sheriff Wright.)

Column 5

WIDENING KEMPTON STREET.

Conference of Dartmouth Selectmen and Board of Public Works.

A conference was held this afternoon of the selectmen of Dartmouth and the members of the board of public works, in relation to the widening of Kempton street. It is proposed to widen Kempton street on the south side from the Dartmouth line to Westport Factory. There was present on the part of Dartmouth Lothan T. Davis and Charles W. Howland, 2d, selectmen, and Sylvanus T. Hawes and James T. Howland, road surveyors. On the part of New Bedford were present J. C. Rotch and Hathaway of the board were also present. The conference was held in the rooms of the board, and Mayor Brock presided. Superintendent Drake was sworn in as clerk.

Mayor Brock stated the object of the conference. He said that the city authorities were talking of widening Kempton street from Rockdale avenue to the Dartmouth line, and it was desirable to get at the sentiment of the authorities of Dartmouth. It was proposed to widen to make the thoroughfare 60 feet.

Mr. Hathaway thought the two places were fast being populated and he believed the street should be 80 feet wide.

Mr. Davis, in answer to a query, said the least obstruction would be met on the north side.

Charles Howland thought if the road was to be widened 66 feet, it would be a happy medium. He referred to the King's highway, which comes out at the Hathaway road, and that, he says, is 66 feet wide.

Mr. Hathaway believed in an 80-foot road. He believed that Kempton street kept up as narrow as now, means a new through road to the Slocum road.

Mr. Rotch said he believed New Bedford would be willing to do as much as Dartmouth in this matter, and he thought it would be a great blessing to both places.

Mr. Davis thought if this matter could be delayed for a couple of months until some people cool off, it might be better for the measure.

Charles Howland believed in striking while the iron is hot.

And go in for an 80-foot road, said Mr. Hathaway.

Mr. Hawes favored widening on the north side. It would be the least expense to the town.

Mr. Rotch thought it would be all right for New Bedford on the north side if it wasn't for the cemetery on that side of the street. New Bedford could take off from the south side, and where Dartmouth joins on have a very broad road. He continued by saying that the sooner the town of Dartmouth acts the better. It should at least be done before the street railway company begins laying its tracks.

Mr. Davis said a widening of 20 feet on the south side could be carried out from New Bedford to the Saratoga House.

Mr. Rotch thought Dartmouth ought to act first.

Mr. Hawes thought New Bedford ought to act first. He believed if New Bedford acted first it would be a great help to the authorities of Dartmouth, as the voters would be more likely to vote for widening if New Bedford is known to have started in on the work.

Charles Howland agreed with Mr. Hawes. When asked, he said the road from Smith Mills village to Westport Factory was 50 feet in width.

Mr. Hawes suggested that it be made a county affair.

Mr. Hathaway moved as a sense of the conference that Kempton street be widened from Rockdale avenue to the intersection of Hathaway road 80 feet.

Mr. Davis favored making it 66 feet, and so did Mr. Rotch, who thought the town would be more likely to vote for 66 feet.

Mr. Hawes didn't believe the town would vote for more.

Mr. Hathaway thought if our grandfathers could lay out a 66-foot road, it seemed as though the present generation could afford to improve on that some.

Mr. Hathaway's motion then prevailed unanimously.

Mayor Brock believed that the next thing was to push right along with the work. He also said that if the street railway company was successful in its proposed undertaking it would not be long before a double track would be asked for, and that would bring the street down again to a narrow space. He thought it advisable to ask for the full 80 feet.

At this point the conference came to a close, and the board of public works then assembled and made arrangements for the widening of Kempton street as suggested in the motion of Mr. Hathaway.

A number of catch basins were ordered constructed.

MR. RUSSELL'S DEFENSE.

Special Police Officer Employs Counsel and Demands a Public Hearing.

Special Police Officer Henry C. Russell, against whom charges have been preferred by Chief of Police Douglass, of having obstructed an officer in the discharge of his duty, has demanded a hearing on the same. Mr. Russell in an interview with a Standard man this morning said that he means to fight this matter to the end, and has retained Thomas F. Desmond, Esq., as counsel. He doesn't contest on account of any value he attaches to the position of special police officer, but in order to place himself right in the public eye. He says he was not even present on the occasion when the shielding of the prisoner is alleged. He tells his version of the story, saying that on April 28, George F. Tripp, who he brought up from boyhood, and who is dissolute in his habits, was absent from home and had been for two or three days. He had heard that Tripp was drinking hard, and as he was on probation, he asked William Russell 'to bring Tripp home if he met him. William did meet Tripp, and persuaded him to go home, but on the way passed Officer Arnett, who was standing at the patrol box, corner of Kempton and County streets. Mr. Russell says Tripp was quietly going home with William when Arnett, who he claims bore him an old grudge, grabbed him and against Tripp's protestations pulled in a call. A tussle ensued, in which Tripp was clubbed, but managed to get away. William Russell was so frightened that the hurried away. Henry C. Russell says he knew nothing about it till later in the evening he met Tripp on Summer street, bleeding freely from the wounds on his head. As an act of human kindness and kinship decency he persuaded him to accompany him home, where his wounds were dressed. Later, thinking the publicity of a police visit undesirable, he had Tripp removed from the house, but he says he did not know where. Now the ground of the charges assume that Henry C. Russell should have, as a special officer, turned his wayward nephew over to the police, but this view, Mr. Russell thinks, is far subordinate to blood sympathy. He declares that no other officer would have arrested Tripp, and that the whole affair was born of spite. The hearing in the case will take place in room 4, Library building, next Thursday evening, at 8 o'clock.

REAL ESTATE SALES.

Standish Bourne sold at auction this afternoon the house and 15 rods of land on Rounds street, south of Kempton, to John G. Tabor for $1,255.

Standish Bourne sold at auction this afternoon a cottage house and lot on Purchase street just north of the cotton mill to John Smith for $3,005 and taxes of this year.

Patrick McDermott of Fall River, committed to the house of correction March 20th for drunkenness, was released today by the county commissioners, upon the recommendation of probation officer, concurred in by the justice of the second district court.

Column 6

EXPENDITURES.

We are indebted to City Auditor George W. Parker for the following list of expenditures in the various departments of the city for the month of May:

Board of health.	
Garbage,	$500.00
Incidentals,	64.72
Cemeteries,	235.00
Com. of Mass., Chap. 270,	737.34
Com. of Mass., Chap. 301,	596.00
Com. of Mass., Chap. 447,	724.75
Court judgments,	751.00
Engineering department,	250.00
Fire department,	22.34
Engine, hose wagon repairs, etc.,	6.65
Fire alarm, labor, etc.,	413.11
Harnesses and repairs,	32.40
Horse keeping, feeding, etc.,	210.89
Printing and incidentals,	61.13
Repairs of buildings,	102.65
Wood, coal and lights,	93.31
Free public library.	
Dog fund,	46.22
Trustees of,	777.91
Salaries,	447.50
Highways and streets.	
Block paving,	932.62
City stables,	800.42
City tool house,	193.08
Cobble paving and repairs,	6.89
Collecting sales,	15.15
Concrete sidewalks and repairs,	255.12
Curbing and repairs,	6.39
Filling and grading,	15.15
Flagging and repairs,	7.40
Gutters and repairs,	373.47
Macadam,	1,215.79
Main office expenses and salaries,	173.47
Miscellaneous,	209.40
Private work and trimming trees,	398.44
Sweeping and cleaning streets,	.60
Incidentals,	491.90
Lighting the streets.	
Dog fund,	1,524.42
Gas lights,	807.71
Globe lights,	1,089.18
Incandescent lights,	39.20
Sundries,	24.00
New Bedford & Fairhaven bridge,	12.76
New Bedford school committee,	497.67
New Bedford water works,	3,914.36
Parks and squares,	7.40
Permanent debt,	3,000.00
Police department,	490.87
Poor department, outside relief.	
Burials,	162.00
Clothing and supplies,	8.25
Fuel,	118.47
Groceries,	627.85
Incidentals,	146.96
Salaries,	529.83
State hospitals,	73.11
Poor department, almshouse,	
Furnishing and supplies,	144.52
Grain and provisions,	314.84
Incidentals and pay rolls,	316.19
Printing, binding and stationery,	925.82
Public schools.	
Books, stationery and supplies,	155.21
Fuel, schools,	300.76
Office coal and rent,	41.06
Printing and incidentals,	183.11
Repairs of buildings and furniture	25.26
Repairs of heating apparatus,	6.06
Dog fund,	339.96
Repairs of city property,	122.58
Salaries,	4,154.55
Sewers, general account,	178.22
Myrtle street No. 1,	7.54
Myrtle street No. 2,	7.81
Real estate tax account,	246.24
Cedar Grove schoolhouse addition,	51.50
Engine house No. 5 addition,	45.00
Kempton street schoolhouse lot,	677.92
Cemeteries, Oak Grove tomb,	1,015.00
Police station and wood room, Black	.50
mer and South Water streets,	133.53
Pleasant street land damages,	1,840.00
	$44,435.35

FRIENDS' YEARLY MEETING.

Epistles from Other Gatherings Read at the Portland Meeting.

Portland, Me., June 10.—At the forenoon meeting of the Friends today an epistle was read from the new yearly meeting at Wilmington, O., also an epistle from the yearly meeting at Damascus. Rev. David J. Douglas read the report of the committee on gospel work and the morning was spent in discussing it. A collection amounting to $545 was taken up.

SPINNERS' MEETING.

Call of Secretary Howard for the Semi-Annual Gathering.

Fall River, June 10.—Secretary Howard has issued the following circular for the monthly meeting of the Spinners' association to be held on Wednesday evening, June 14th:

Fellow Workmen—This being the semi-annual meeting the following officers will be elected: President, vice president, treasurer, auditor and two committeemen. There will be recommendations submitted from the committee that contribution books be sent round by the collectors for members' inspection at intervals not exceeding one month, and that the secretary and treasurer be at the association headquarters on the last Saturday night of each month in addition to Friday night, for the purpose of collecting men's contributions.

During the last six months the names of fifty new members have been added to our rolls on account of additional spinning mules being erected in the Keer Thread mill, the Hargraves mills, the King Phillips mills and the Sanford Spinning company, and the association's funds have increased $3,031 in the same time.

There has been paid out in benefits during the same time as follows: For stoppage pay, $400.30; for accident pay, $295.85; for deaths of members and members' wives, $375.00; or a total of $873.15. The committee also have decided to recommend an increase of salary for the president and treasurer.

Trade prospects at the present time are very bright and encouraging. The stock of goods on hand in this city at the last return did not amount to three hours' production, while the margins of profit between cotton and cloth is such that will pay good dividends to stockholders.

Trusting members will continue to work in harmony together, on behalf of the committee.

Robert Howard, Secretary.

TERRIBLE ABUSE OF CONVICTS.

Men Mutilated Themselves to Escape Barbarities of Their Keeper.

St. Petersburg, June 10.—A newspaper in Vladicostock publishes an account of terrible abuse of convicts on the island of Onoro. The man in charge is a convict who was promoted for good behavior. He subjects the convicts to such barbarous practises that 20 of them mutilated themselves in order to escape his cruelties. Others have fled into the wilderness of Taiga, where they have suffered cold and hunger. Of those who have fled few are now alive, and they have sustained themselves only by eating their former companions.

Final Adjournment.

Boston, June 10.—The legislature adjourned at about daylight this morning. The rapid transit bill as amended was passed. It is the same as originally passed by the house, with the exception that the bill must be submitted to the voters of Boston. Speaker Barrett was presented with a gold watch and President Pinkerton of the senate with a mantel clock.

Body Washed Ashore.

Lynn, June 10.—The body of an unknown man, 50 years old, dressed in black clothing, was washed ashore at Ubbuss Point, Nahant, today, and is now at the town hall, The body has been in the water about a week, as part of the fingers are gone, the body badly bloated, the face disfigured by fish and the hair gone.

Small Pox.

New York, June 10.—Two cases of small pox were sent this morning to Riverside hospital from 31 Park street. The patients were Marie Carboni, 22 years old and her eight months' child.

The Worcester Fire.

Worcester, June 10.—Total loss on the Bay State House is $25,000; insured, $7. P. Douglass is the proprietor of the hotel. The stores under the hotel were not damaged.

Petition in Insolvency.

Boston, June 10.—Counsel for Mrs. Sarah H. Cohen today filed a petition in insolvency against Moody Morrill, based upon a debt of $13,000 claimed by Mrs. Cohen.

Column 7

IMPROVED TRAIN SERVICE.

In Keeping with the Growing Importance of Our City.

A new time table on the Old Colony railroad takes effect on Monday next, by which additional facilities are given to this city for communication with all its connecting points.

The 5 25 a. m. train is taken off and connection with the northern division is made by the 7 25 a. m. express. A new train at 12 15 p. m. makes close connection at Providence with the Shore line for New York, and at Mansfield for points on northern division. The train heretofore leaving Park Square station, Boston, for New Bedford at 2 30 p. m. will leave at 3 p. m., and will connect at Taunton with the train leaving New York via Shore line at 10 a. m. and Providence at 3 25 p. m., arriving in New Bedford at 4 50 p. m. Two new trains are put on the Fall River branch, leaving New Bedford at 3 and 9 30 p. m., and returning leave Fall River at 1 and 10 15 p. m. Some slight changes are also made in the time of the other branch trains.

The summer connections with the Vineyard and Nantucket boats also continue on Monday, both for week days and Sundays.

Altogether New Bedford now has 15 passenger trains each way week days and four trains each way on Sundays, a service quite in keeping with the growing importance of our city.

CONDENSED LOCALS.

The whole number of deaths as reported at the office of the board of health for the week ending today at noon is 16, of which five were children under five years. There was one stillborn. Of the deaths there were three from phthisis, two each from typhoid fever, and infantile debility and one each from pneumonia, convulsions, myelitis, angina pectoris, Bright's disease, cap bronchitis, gastro enteritis, diabetes and bullet wound of the head.

The county commissioners will report their decision as to a location for the proposed bridge across the east branch of the Westport river some time next week, probably Tuesday.

CORREIRO'S CONFESSION.

Belief That He Has Made Damaging Admissions to the Police.

Fall River, June 10.—The police refuse to deny or confirm the report that Correiro has confessed. Marshal Hilliard in New Bedford, and Assistant Marshal Fleet says he has nothing to say upon this subject. Mayor Coughlin is also reticent and refuses to talk. The refusal of the authorities to affirm or deny is deemed by many to be sufficient proof that either the report is true or that the prisoner had made certain admissions, which equal a confession. The police are still actively at work upon the case, which would indicate that a full confession had not been made.

FORD THEATER HORROR.

Clerks Tell the Story of Disaster; 23 Deaths Reported.

Washington, June 10.—The death of A. N. Gerault of New Jersey is reported this morning, making the 23d in the list of dead in the Ford theater disaster. Until late last night workmen had been employed in removing the bricks and broken timbers from the building, and today the old hulk looks less hideous than when the scores of dead bodies were being carried from it. A hundred or more broken desks and tables were piled in the rear on each floor and the litter of papers and books had been gathered up and such as were of any value were taken to a place of safe keeping. Broken and twisted gas pipes protruded from every part of the wreck. By 8 o'clock, an hour earlier than usual, the old clerks began to arrive at the building and every new comer was greeted with effusive welcomes by his comrades. And then they told marvelous escapes and each was again and again questioned as to where he was at the time. Tears filled many eyes as each told of his experience, and how he had seen one whom they all knew dashed down to death. Many of the clerks, with a view to not losing any time, knocked on the doors of the annex adjoining the ruined theater and to the officials within reported for duty. But no suitable building had been secured and it will be some days before the force is at work. The coroners' inquiry will commence Monday.

Only 22 Dead.

Lewis W. Boody of New York, reported in the list of dead, escaped uninjured. This reduces the number of deaths to 22. There is also doubt about the death of M. M. Jarvis of Michigan. The report made by the superintendent of the emergency hospital this morning concerning the injured men at that hospital is encouraging. Most of the patients show improvement in their condition. This morning Colonel Ainsworth asked for a court or inquiry to determine the cause of the calamity and fix the responsibility where it belongs. The request was laid before General Lewis A. Grant, the acting secretary of war, this morning. About the same time a telegram was received from the secretary of war, Mr. Lamont, now in Chicago, stating that he was in Washington this afternoon, and in view of this information General Grant did not give consideration to the request. The request will undoubtedly be granted. The president is said to be much perturbed over the calamity, and will give his attention to the matter of securing a full investigation.

Amherst Wins.

Hanover, N. H., June 10.—In the intercollegiate tennis today, in doubles, Reed and Ware of Amherst beat Thursby and Rice of Dartmouth, 6–4, 6–2, 6–10.

Ocean Steamers.

Arrived—At New York, Suevia, Hamburg; New York, Southampton.

Woman's Influence.

Delicate women may exert much influence, but little in comparison with what it would be with abundant health.

The wife wants health that she may be the companion of her husband and her family.

Beware of dizziness, sudden faintness, irritability, backache, nervousness, extreme lassitude, depression, exhaustion, excitability, and sick headache.

These are sure indications of female weakness, some derangement of the uterus or womb; they are danger signals which warn you to avoid a life of misery. *Lydia E. Pinkham's Vegetable Compound* goes to the root of the trouble, and drives disease from your body.

All druggists sell it. In addition to endorses.
LYDIA E. PINKHAM MED. CO., LYNN, Mass.
Lydia E. Pinkham's Liver Pills, 25 cents.

LIZZIE'S STORY.

(Continued from 1st page.)

Q. Who?
A. Mr. Hiram C. Harrington.
Q. What relation is he to him?
A. He is my father's brother-in-law.
Q. Your mother's brother?
A. My father's only sister married Mr. Harrington.
Q. Anybody else that was on bad terms with your father, or that your father was on bad terms with?
A. Not that I know of.
Q. You have no reason to suppose that man you speak of a week or two ago, had ever seen your father before, or has since?
A. No sir.
Q. Do you know of anybody that was on bad terms with your stepmother?
A. No sir.
Q. Or that your stepmother was on bad terms with?
A. No sir.
Q. Had your stepmother any property?
A. I don't know, only that she had half the house that belonged to her father.
Q. Where was that?
A. On Fourth street.
Q. Who lives in it?
A. Her half-sister.
Q. Any other property beside that that you know of?
A. I don't know.
Q. Did you ever know of any?
A. No sir.
Q. Do you understand that she was worth anything more than that?
A. I never knew.
Q. Did you ever have any trouble with your stepmother?
A. No sir.
Q. Have you, within six months, had any words with her?
A. No sir.
Q. Within a year?
A. No sir.
Q. Within two years?
A. I think not.
Q. When last that you know of?
A. About five years ago.
Q. What about?
A. Her stepsister, half-sister.
Q. What name?
A. Her name now is Mrs. George W. Whitehead.
Q. Nothing more than hard words?
A. No sir, they were not hard words; it was simply a difference of opinion.
Q. You have been on pleasant terms with your stepmother since then?
A. Yes sir.
Q. Cordial?
A. It depends upon one's idea of cordiality, perhaps.
Q. According to your idea of cordiality?
A. We were friendly, very friendly.
Q. Cordial, according to your idea of cordiality?
A. Quite so.
Q. What do you mean by "quite so"?
A. Quite cordial. I do not mean the dearest of friends in the world, but very kindly feelings and pleasant. I do not know to answer you any better than that.
Q. You did not regard her as your mother?
A. Not exactly, no; although she came there when I was very young.
Q. Were your relations towards her that of daughter and mother?
A. In some ways it was, and in some it was not.
Q. In what ways was it?
A. I decline to answer.
Q. Why?
A. Because I don't know how to answer it.
Q. In what ways was it not?
A. I did not call her mother.
Q. What name did she go by?
A. Mrs. Borden.
Q. When did you begin to call her Mrs. Borden?
A. I should think five or six years ago.
Q. Before that time you had called her mother?
A. Yes sir.
Q. What led to the change?
A. The affair with her stepsister.
Q. So that the affair was serious enough to have you change from calling her mother, do you mean?
A. I did not choose to call her mother.
Q. Have you ever called her mother since?
A. Yes, occasionally.
Q. To her face, I mean?
A. Yes.
Q. Often?
A. No sir.
Q. Seldom?
A. Seldom.
Q. Your usual address was Mrs. Borden?
A. Yes.
Q. Did your sister Emma call her mother?
A. She always called her Abby from the time she came into the family.
Q. Is your sister Emma older than you?
A. Yes sir.
Q. What is her age?
A. She is ten years older than I am. She was somewhere about fourteen when she came there.
Q. What was your stepmother's age?
A. I don't know. I asked her sister Saturday, and she said sixty-four. I told them sixty-seven; I did not know. I told us nearly as I knew. I did not know there was so much difference between she and father.
Q. Why did you leave off calling her mother?
A. Because I wanted to.
Q. Is that all the reason you have to give me?
A. I have not any other answer.
Q. Can't you give me any better reason than that?
A. I have not any reason to give, except that I did not want to.
Q. In what other respect were the relations between you and her not that of mother and daughter, besides not calling her mother?
A. I don't know that any of the relations were changed. I had never been to her as a mother in many things. I always went to my sister, because she was older and had the care of me after my mother died.
Q. In what respects were the relations between you and her that of mother and daughter?
A. That is the same question you asked before; I can't answer any any better now than I did before.
Q. You did not say before you could not answer, but that you declined to answer.
A. I decline to answer because I do not know what to say.
Q. That is the only reason?
A. Yes sir.
Q. You called your father father?
A. Always.
Q. Were your father and mother happily united?
(Witness pauses a little before answering.)
A. Why, I don't know but that they were.
Q. Why do you hesitate?
A. Because I don't know but that they were, and I am telling the truth as nearly as I know it.
Q. Do you mean to understand that they were happy entirely, or not?
A. So far as I know they were.
Q. Why did you hesitate then?
A. Because I did not know how to answer you any better than what came into my mind. I was trying to think if I was telling it as I should; that is all.
Q. Do you have any difficulty in telling it as you should, any difficulty in answering my questions?
A. Some of your questions I have difficulty in answering, because I don't know just how you mean them.
Q. Did you ever know of any difficulty between her and your father?
A. No sir.
Q. Did he seem to be affectionate?
A. I think so.
Q. As man and woman who are married ought to be?
A. So far as I have ever had any chance of judging.
Q. They were?
A. Yes.
Q. What dress did you wear the day they were killed?

A. I had on a navy blue, sort of a bengaline or India silk skirt, with a navy blue blouse. In the afternoon they thought I had better change it. I put on a pink wrapper.
Q. Did you change your clothing before the afternoon?
A. No sir.
Q. You dressed in the morning, as you have described, and kept that clothing on until afternoon?
A. Yes, sir.
Q. When did Morse come there first, I don't mean this visit, I mean as a visitor, John V. Morse?
A. Do you mean this day that he came and stayed all night?
Q. No. Was this visit his first to your house?
A. He has been in the east a year or more.
Q. Since he has been in the east has he been in the habit of coming to your house?
A. Yes; came in any time he wanted to.
Q. Before that he had been at your house, before he came east?
A. Yes, he has been here, if you remember the winter that the river was frozen over and they went across, he was here that winter, some 14 years ago, was it not?
Q. I am not answering questions, but asking them.
A. I don't remember the date. He was here that winter.
Q. Has he been here since?
A. He has been here once since; I don't know whether he has or not since.
Q. How many times this last year has he been at your house?
A. None at all to speak of; nothing more than a night or two at a time.
Q. How often did he come to spend a night or two?
A. Really I don't know; I am away so much myself.
Q. Your last answer is that you don't know how much he had been here, because you had been away yourself so much?
A. Yes.
Q. That is true the last year, or since he has been east?
A. I have not been away the last year so much, but other times I have been away when he has been here.
Q. Do I understand you to say that his last visit before this one was 14 years ago?
A. No, he has been here once between the two.
Q. How long did he stay then?
A. I don't know.
Q. How long was that?
A. I don't know.
Q. Give me your best remembrance.
A. Five or six years, perhaps six.
Q. How long has he been east this time?
A. I think over a year; I am not sure.
Q. During the last year how much of the time has he been at your house?
A. Very little that I know of.
Q. Your answer to that question before was, I don't know because I have been away so much myself.
A. I did not mean I had been away very much myself the last year.
Q. How much have you been away the last year?
A. I have been away a great deal in the daytime, occasionally at night.
Q. Where in the daytime, any particular place?
A. No, around town.
Q. When you go off nights, where?
A. Never unless I have been off on a visit.
Q. When was the last time when you have been away for more than a night or two before this affair?
A. I don't think I have been away to stay more than a night or two since I came from abroad, except about three or four weeks ago I was in New Bedford for three or four days.
Q. Where at New Bedford?
A. At 20 Madison street.
Q. How long ago were you abroad?
A. I was abroad in 1890.
Q. When did he come to the house the last time before your father and mother were killed?
A. He stayed there all night Wednesday night.
Q. My question is when he came there.
A. I don't know; I was not at home when he came; I was out.
Q. When did you first see him there?
A. I did not see him at all.
Q. How did you know he was there?
A. I heard his voice.
Q. You did not see him Wednesday evening?
A. I did not; I was out Wednesday evening.
Q. You did not see him Thursday morning?
A. I did not; he was out when I came down stairs.
Q. When was the first time you saw him?
A. Thursday noon.
Q. You had never seen him before that?
A. No sir.
Q. Where were you Wednesday evening?
A. I spent the evening with Miss Russell.
Q. As near as you can remember, when did you return?
A. About nine o'clock at night.
Q. The family had then retired?
A. I don't know whether they had or not. I went right to my room; I don't remember.
Q. You did not look to see?
A. No sir.
Q. Which door did you come in at?
A. The front door.
Q. Did you lock it?
A. Yes sir.
Q. For the night?
A. Yes sir.
Q. And went right up stairs to your room?
A. Yes sir.
Q. Was it that you heard the voice of Mr. Morse?
A. I heard him down there about supper time—no, it was earlier than that. I heard him down there somewhere about three o'clock, I think. I was in my room Wednesday, not feeling well, all day.
Q. Did you eat supper at home Wednesday night?
A. I was at home; I did not eat any supper, because I did not feel able to eat supper; I had been sick.
Q. You did not come down to supper?
A. No sir.
Q. Did you hear him eating supper?
A. No sir. I did not know whether he was there or not.
Q. You heard him in the afternoon?
A. I did not.
Q. Did you hear him go about?
A. No sir.
Q. Was in in bed?
A. No sir, I was on the lounge.
Q. Why did you not go down?
A. I did not care to go down, and I was not feeling well, and kept my room all day.
Q. You felt better in the evening?
A. Not very much better. I thought I would go out, and see if the air would make me feel any better.
Q. When you came back at nine o'clock, you did not look in to see if the family were up?
A. No sir.
Q. Why not?
A. I very rarely do when I come in.
Q. You go right to your room?
A. Yes sir.
Q. Did you have a night key?
A. Yes sir.
Q. How did you know it was right to lock the front door?
A. That was always my business.
Q. How many locks did you fasten?
A. The spring locks itself, and there is a key to turn, and you manipulate the bolt.
Q. You manipulated all those?
A. Yes sir.
Q. Then you went to bed?
A. Yes, directly.
Q. When you got up the next morning, did you see Mr. Morse?
A. I did not.
Q. Had the family breakfasted when you came down?
A. Yes sir.

Q. What time did you come down stairs?
A. As near as I can remember, it was a few minutes before nine.
Q. Who did you find down stairs when you came down?
A. Maggie and Mrs. Borden.
Q. Did you inquire for Mr. Morse?
A. No sir.
Q. Did you suppose he had gone?
A. I did not know whether he had or not; he was not there.
Q. Your father was there?
A. Yes sir.
Q. Then you found him?
A. Yes sir.
Q. Did you speak to either your father or Mrs. Borden?
A. I spoke to them all.
Q. About Mr. Morse?
A. I did not mention him.
Q. Did not inquire anything about him?
A. No sir.
Q. How long before that time had he been at the house?
A. I don't know.
Q. As near as you can tell?
A. Yes, he has been there in June sometime, I don't know whether he was there after that or not.
Q. Why did you not go to Marion with the party that went?
A. Because they went sooner than I could, and I was going Monday.
Q. Why did they go sooner than you could; what was there to keep you?
A. I had taken the secretaryship and treasurer of our C. E. society, had the charge, and the roll call was the first Sunday in August, and I felt I must be there and attend to that part of the business.
Q. Where was your sister Emma that day?
A. What day?
Q. The day your father and Mrs. Borden were killed?
A. She had been in Fairhaven.
Q. Had you written to her?
A. Yes sir.
Q. When was the last time you wrote to her?
A. Thursday morning, and my father mailed the letter for me.
Q. Did she get it at Fairhaven?
A. No sir, it was sent back. She did not get it at Fairhaven, for we telegraphed for her, and she got home here Thursday afternoon, and the letter was sent back to this post office.
Q. How long had she been in Fairhaven?
A. Just two weeks to a day.
Q. You did not visit in Fairhaven?
A. No sir.
Q. Had there been anybody else around the house that week, or premises?
A. No one that I know of, except the man that called to see him on this business about the stove.
Q. Was that that week?
A. Yes sir.
Q. I misunderstood you probably, I thought you said a week or two before.
A. No, I said that week. There was a man came the week before and gave up some keys, and I took them.
Q. Do you remember of anybody else being then around the premises that week?
A. Nobody that I know of or saw.
Q. Nobody at work there?
A. Nobody doing any chores there?
A. No sir, not that I know of.
Q. Nobody had access to the house, so far as you know, during that week?
A. No sir.
Q. I ask you once more how it happened, that, knowing Mr. Morse was at your house, you did not step in and greet him before you retired?
A. I have no reason, except that I was not feeling well Wednesday, and so did not come down.
Q. No, you were down. When you came in then out.
A. Do you mean Wednesday night?
Q. Yes.
A. Because I hardly ever do go in. I generally went right up to my room, and I did that night.
Q. Could you then get to your room from the back hall?
A. No sir.
Q. From the back stairs?
A. No sir.
Q. Why not? What would hinder?
A. Father's bedroom door was kept locked, and his door into my room was locked and hooked too I think, and I had no keys.
Q. That was the custom of the establishment?
A. It had always been so.
Q. It was so Wednesday, and so Thursday?
A. It was so Wednesday, but Thursday they broke the door open.
Q. That was after the crowd came; before the crowd came?
A. It was so.
Q. There was no access, except one had a key, and one would have to have two keys?
A. They would have to have two keys if they went up the back way to get into my room. If they were in my room, they would have to have a key to get into my room, and another to get into the back stairs.
Q. Where did Mr. Morse sleep?
A. In the next room over the parlor in front of the stairs.
Q. Right up the same stairs that your room was?
A. Yes sir.
Q. How far from your room?
A. A door opened into it.
Q. The two rooms connected directly?
A. By one door, that is all.
Q. Not through the hall?
A. No sir.
Q. Was the door locked?
A. It has been locked and bolted, and a large writing desk in my room kept up against it.
Q. Then it was not a practical opening?
A. No sir.
Q. How otherwise do you get from your room to the next room?
A. Out into the front hall.
Q. How far apart are the two doors?
A. Very near, I don't think more than so far (measuring.)
Q. Was it your habit when you were in your room to keep your door shut?
A. Yes sir.
Q. That time, that Wednesday afternoon?
A. My door was open part of the time, and part of the time I tried to get a nap and their voices annoyed me, and I shut it. I kept it open in summer more or less, and closed in winter.
Q. Then, unless for some special reason, your kept your door open in the summer?
A. Yes sir, if it was a warm day. If it was a cool day, I should have closed it.
Q. Where was your mother? Do you prefer me to call her Mrs. Borden?
A. I had as soon you called her Mrs. Borden. She was in the dining room with a feather duster dusting.
Q. When she dusted did she wear something over her head?
A. Sometimes when she swept, but not when dusting.
Q. Where was Maggie?
A. Just come in the back door with the long pole, brush, and put the brush on the handle, and getting her pail of water; she was going to wash the windows around the house. She said Mrs. Borden wanted her to.
Q. Did you get your breakfast that morning?
A. I did not eat any breakfast; I did not feel as though I wanted any.
Q. Did you get any breakfast that morning?
A. I don't know whether I ate half a banana; I don't think I did.
Q. You drank no tea or coffee that morning?
A. No sir.
Q. Ate no cookies?
A. I don't know whether I did or not. We had some molasses cookies; I don't know whether I ate any that morning or not.
Q. Were the breakfast things put away when you got down?
A. Everything except the coffee pot; I am not sure whether that was on the stove or not.

Q. You said nothing about Mr. Morse to your father or mother?
A. No sir.
Q. What was the next thing that happened after you got down?
A. Maggie went out of doors to wash the windows and father came out into the kitchen and said he did not know whether he would go down to the post office or not. And then I sprinkled some handkerchiefs to iron.
Q. Tell me again what time you came down stairs.
A. It was a little before nine, I should say about quarter; I don't know sure.
Q. Did your father go down town?
A. He went down later.
Q. What time did he start away?
A. I don't know.
Q. What were you doing when he started away?
A. I was in the dining room I think, yes, I had just commenced, I think, to iron.
Q. It may seem a foolish question. How much of an ironing did you have?
A. I only had about eight or ten of my best handkerchiefs.
Q. Did you let your father out?
A. No sir; he went out himself.
Q. Did you fasten the door after him?
A. No sir.
Q. Did Maggie?
A. I don't know. When she went up stairs she always locked the door; she had charge of the back door.
Q. Did she go out after a brush before your father went away?
A. I think not.
Q. Did you say anything to Maggie?
A. I did not.
Q. Did you say anything about washing the windows?
A. No sir.
Q. Did you speak to her?
A. I think I told her I did not want any breakfast.
Q. You do not remember of talking about washing the windows?
A. I don't remember whether I did or not; I don't remember it. Yes, I remember; yes, I asked her to shut the parlor blinds when she got through, because the sun was so hot.
Q. About what time do you think your father went down town?
A. I don't know; it must have been after nine o'clock. I don't know what time it was.
Q. You think at that time you had begun to iron your handkerchiefs?
A. Yes sir.
Q. How long a job was that?
A. I did not finish them; my flats were not hot enough.
Q. How long a job was it you had been at work?
A. If they had been hot, not more than 20 minutes, perhaps.
Q. How long did you work on the job?
A. I don't know, sir.
Q. How long was your father gone?
A. I don't know that.
Q. Where were you when he returned?
A. I was down in the kitchen.
Q. What doing?
A. Reading an old magazine that had been left in the cupboard, an old Harper's Magazine.
Q. Had you got through ironing?
A. No sir.
Q. Had you stopped ironing?
A. Stopped for the flats.
Q. Were you waiting for your flats to be hot?
A. Yes sir.
Q. Was there a fire in the stove?
A. Yes sir.
Q. When your father went away, you were ironing then?
A. I had not commenced, but I was getting the little ironing board and the flannel.
Q. Are you sure you were in the kitchen when your father returned?
A. I am not sure whether I was there or in the dining room.
Q. Did you go back to your room before your father returned?
A. I think I did carry up some clean clothes.
Q. Did you stay there?
A. No sir.
Q. Did you spend any time up the front stairs before your father returned?
A. No, sir.
Q. Or after he returned?
A. No, sir. I did stay in my room long enough when I went up to sew a little piece of tape on a garment.
Q. Was that the time when your father came home?
A. He came home after I came down stairs.
Q. You were not up stairs when he came home?
A. I was not up stairs when he came home; no, sir.
Q. What was Maggie doing when your father came home?
A. I don't know whether she was there or whether she had gone up stairs; I can't remember.
Q. Who let your father in?
A. I think he came to the front door and rang the bell, and I think Maggie let him in, and he said he had forgotten his key; so I think she must have been down stairs.
Q. His key would have done him no good if the locks were left as you left them?
A. But they were always unbolted in the morning.
Q. Who unbolted them that morning?
A. I don't think they had been unbolted; Maggie can tell you.
Q. If he had not forgotten his key it would have been no good?
A. No, he had his key and could not get in. I understood Maggie to say he said he had forgotten his key.
Q. You did not hear him say anything about it?
A. I heard his voice, but I don't know what he said.
Q. I understood you to say he said he had forgotten his key?
A. I think Maggie said he said he had forgotten the key.
Q. Where was Maggie when the bell rang?
A. I don't know, sir.
Q. Where were you when the bell rang?
A. I think in my room up stairs.
Q. Then you were up stairs when your father came home?
A. I don't know sure, but I think I was.
Q. What were you doing?
A. As I say, I took up these clean clothes, and stopped and basted a little piece of tape on a garment.
Q. Did you come down before your father was let in?
A. I was on the stairs coming down when she let him in.
Q. Then you were up stairs when your father came to the house on his return?
A. I think I was.
Q. How long had you been there?
A. I had only been up stairs just long enough to take the clothes up and baste the little loop on the sleeve. I don't think I had been up there over five minutes.
Q. Was Maggie still engaged in washing windows when your father came back?
A. I don't know.
Q. You remember, Miss Borden, I will call your attention to it so as to see if I have any misunderstanding, not for the purpose of confusing you; you remember that you told me several times that you were down stairs, and not up stairs when your father came home? You have forgotten, perhaps?
A. I don't know what I have said. I have answered so many questions and I am so confused I don't know one thing from another. I am telling you just as nearly as I know.
Q. Calling your attention to what you said about that a few minutes ago, and now again to the circumstance you have said you were up stairs when the bell rang and were on the stairs when Maggie let your father in; which now is your recollection of the true statement of the matter, that you were down stairs when the bell rang and your father came home?
A. I think I was down stairs in the kitchen.
Q. And then you were not up stairs when the bell rang?
A. I think I was not; because I went right down stairs as soon as I took the clothes up, and I stayed down.
Q. What makes you think so?
A. Because I usually went right down stairs.
Q. How can you remember back on the morning when your father came home?
A. I don't know, sir.
Q. Do you remember?
A. I don't remember.
Q. What explanation can you suggest as to the whereabouts of your mother when

A. They could have gone from the kitchen into the sitting room while I was in the dining room, if there was anybody to go.
Q. Then into the front hall?
A. Yes sir.
Q. You were in the dining room ironing?
A. Yes sir, part of the time.
Q. You were in all of the three rooms?
A. Yes sir.
Q. A large portion of that time, the girl was out of doors?
A. I don't know where she was; I did not see her. I supposed she was out of doors, as she had the pail and brush.
Q. You knew she was washing windows?
A. She told me she was going to. I did not see her do it.
Q. For a large portion of the time you did not see the girl?
A. No sir.
Q. So far as you know you were alone in the lower part of the house, a large portion of the time, after your father went away, and before he came back?
A. My father did not go away I think until somewhere about 10, as near as I can remember; he was with me down stairs.
Q. After that time she must have remained in the guest chamber?
A. I don't know.
Q. So far as you can judge?
A. So far as I can judge she might have been out of the house, or in the house.
Q. Had you any knowledge of her going out of the house?
A. No sir.
Q. Had you any knowledge of her going out of the house?
A. She told me she had a note, somebody was sick, and said "I am going to get the dinner on the way," and asked me what I wanted for dinner.
Q. Did you tell her?
A. Yes, I told her I did not want anything.
Q. Then why did you not suppose she had gone?
A. I supposed she had gone.
Q. Did you hear her come back?
A. I did not hear her go or come back, but I supposed she was gone.
Q. When you found your father dead you supposed your mother had gone?
A. I did not know. I said to the people who came in "I don't know whether Mrs. Borden is out or in; I wish you would see if she is in her room."
Q. You supposed she went out in the time?
A. I understood so; I did not suppose anything about it.
Q. Did she tell you where she was going?
A. No sir.
Q. She did tell you who the note was from?
A. No sir.
Q. Did you ever see the note?
A. No sir.
Q. Do you know where it is now?
A. No sir.
Q. She said she was going out that morning?
A. Yes sir.

(Hearing continued Aug. 10, 1892.)

Q. I should like to ask you once more about that morning. Do you know what the family ate for breakfast?
A. No sir, I don't remember whether I ate a molasses cookie or not. I did not eat any regularly prepared breakfast.
Q. Was it usual for your mother to go out?
A. Yes sir, she went out every morning nearly, and did the marketing.
Q. Was it usual for her to be gone away from dinner?
A. Yes sir, sometimes, not very often.
Q. How often, say?
A. O, I should not think more than—well I don't know, more than once in three months, perhaps.
Q. Now I call your attention to the fact that twice yesterday you told me, with some explicitness, that when your father came in, you were just coming down stairs?
A. No, I did not, I beg your pardon.
Q. That you were on the stairs at the time your father was let in, you said with some explicitness. Do you now say you did not say so?
A. I said I thought first I was on the stairs; then I remembered I was in the kitchen when she came in.
Q. First you thought you were in the kitchen; afterwards you remembered you were on the stairs?
A. I said I thought I was on the stairs; then I said I knew I was in the kitchen.
Q. Did you go into the front part of the house after your father came in?
A. I was in the room from where street I was in the sitting room with him.
Q. Did you go into the front hall afterwards?
A. No sir.
Q. At no time?
A. No sir.
Q. Excepting the two or three minutes you were down cellar, were you away from the house until your father came in?
A. No sir.
Q. When do you mean by that?
A. I mean the door was closed. She said she wanted it kept closed to keep the dust and everything out.
Q. Was it a room with a window?
A. It has three windows.
Q. A large room?
A. The size of the parlor; a pretty fair sized room.
Q. It is the guest room?
A. Yes, the spare room.
Q. Where the sewing machine was the guest room?
A. Yes sir.
Q. Was again, perhaps you have answered all you care to, what explanation can you give, can you suggest, as to what she was doing from nine o'clock until eleven, with the clean clothes.
Q. You now say after your father went out, you did not go up stairs at all?
A. No sir, I did not.
Q. Was Maggie in then when washing the windows, you did not appear from the front part of the house?
A. No sir.
Q. When your father was let in, you did not appear from up stairs?
A. No sir, I was in the kitchen.
Q. That is so?
A. Yes, to the best of my knowledge.
Q. After your father went out, you remained there either in the kitchen or dining room all the time?
A. I went in the sitting room long enough to direct some paper wrappers.
Q. One of the three rooms?
A. Yes sir.
Q. So it would have been extremely difficult for anybody to have come through the kitchen and dining room and front hall, without your seeing them?

from the time you saw her in the dining room, and she said her work in the spare room was all done, until 11 o'clock?
A. I don't know. I think she went back into the spare room, and whether she came back again or not I don't know; that has always been a mystery.
Q. Can you think of anything she could be doing in the spare room?
A. As I see I know what she came to do sometimes. She kept her best cape she wore on the street in there, and she used occasionally to go up there to get it and to take it into her room. She kept a great deal in the guest room drawers; she used to go up there and get things and put things; she used those drawers for her own use.
Q. That connects her with her own room again, to reach which she had to go down stairs and come up again?
A. Yes.
Q. Now how will you have it?
A. I think, as nearly as I know, I think I was in the kitchen.
Q. How long was your father gone?
A. I don't know, sir; not very long.
Q. An hour?
A. I should not think so.
Q. Will you give me the best story you can, so far as your recollection serves you, of your time while he was gone?
A. I sprinkled my handkerchiefs, and got my ironing board and took them in the dining room. I took the ironing board in the dining room and left the handkerchiefs in the kitchen on the table and whether I ate any cookies or not I don't remember. Then I sat down looking at the magazine, waiting for the flats to heat. Then I went in the sitting room and got the Providence Journal, and took that into the kitchen. I don't recollect of doing anything else.
Q. Which did you read first, the Journal or the magazine?
A. The magazine.
Q. You told me you were reading the magazine when your father came back?
A. I said in the kitchen, yes.
Q. Was that so?
A. Yes, I took the Journal not to read, and had not read it. I had it near me.
Q. You said a minute or two ago you read the magazine awhile, and then went and got the Journal and took it out to read?
A. I did, but I did not read it; I tried my flats then.
Q. And went back to reading the magazine?
A. I took the magazine up again, yes.
Q. When did you see your mother?
A. I did not see her after when I went down in the morning and she was dusting the dining room.
Q. Where did you or she go then?
A. I don't know where she went. I know where I was.
Q. Did you or she leave the dining room first?
A. I think I did. I left her in the dining room.
Q. You never saw or heard her afterwards?
A. No sir.
Q. Did she say anything about making the bed?
A. She said she had been up and made the bed up fresh, and had dusted the room and left it all in order. She was going to put some fresh pillow slips on the small pillows at the foot of the bed, and was going to close the room, because she was going to have company Monday and she wanted everything in order.
Q. How long would it take to put on the pillow slips?
A. About two minutes.
Q. How long to do the rest of the things?
A. She had done that when I came down.
Q. All that was left was what?
A. To put on the pillow slips.
Q. Can you give me any suggestion as to what occupied her when she was up there, when she was struck dead?
A. I don't know of anything except she had some cotton cloth pillow cases up there, and she said she was going to commence to work on them. That is all I know. And the sewing machine was up there.
Q. Whereabouts was the sewing machine?
A. In the corner between the north and west side.
Q. Did you hear the sewing machine going?
A. I did not.
Q. Did you see anything to indicate that the sewing machine had been used that morning?
A. When you came back did you see your mother?
A. I did not; I supposed she had gone out.
Q. She did not tell you where she was going?
A. No sir.
Q. When you came back was your father there?
A. Yes sir.
Q. What was he doing?
A. Reading the paper.
Q. Did you eat any breakfast?
A. No sir, I don't remember whether I ate a molasses cookie or not. I did not eat any regularly prepared breakfast.
Q. Was it usual for your mother to go out?
A. Yes sir, she went out every morning nearly, and did the marketing.
Q. Was it usual for her to be gone away from dinner?
A. Yes sir, sometimes, not very often.
Q. How often, say?
A. O, I should not think more than—well I don't know, more than once in three months, perhaps.
Q. Now what did you say to her?
A. I asked him if he wanted the window left that way, when he went to the barn, and whether he wanted the window left that way.
Q. Where did you leave him?
A. On the sofa.
Q. Was he asleep?
A. No sir.
Q. Was he reading?
A. No sir.
Q. What was the last thing you said to him?
A. I asked him if he wanted the window left that way. Then I went into the kitchen, and from there to the barn.
Q. Whereabouts in the barn did you go?
A. Up stairs.
Q. To the second story of the barn?
A. Yes sir.
Q. How long did you remain there?
A. I don't know, fifteen or twenty minutes.
Q. What doing?
A. Trying to find lead for a sinker.
Q. What made you think there would be lead for a sinker up there?
A. Because there was some by the door.
Q. Some pieces of lead by the open door?
A. Yes, some pieces of lead that had been—well there, more than once in three months, perhaps.
Q. Did you bring any sinker back from the barn?
A. I found no sinker.
Q. Did you bring any sinker back from the barn?
A. Nothing but a piece of a chip I picked up on the floor.
Q. Where was that box you say was up stairs, containing lead?
A. There was a kind of a work bench.
Q. Is it there now?
A. I don't know, sir.
Q. How long since have you seen it there?
A. I have not been out there since that day.
Q. Had you been in the barn before that day, say?
A. That day, no sir.
Q. How long since you had been to the barn before?
A. I don't know as I had in three months.
Q. When you went out did you unfasten the screen door?
A. I unhooked it to get out.
Q. It was hooked?
A. Yes.
Q. It had been left hooked by Bridget, if she was the last one in?
A. I suppose so; I don't know.
Q. Do you know when she did get through washing the outside?
A. No sir.
Q. Did you know she washed the windows inside?
A. I don't know.
Q. You don't know whether she washed the dining room and sitting room windows inside?
A. I did not see her.
Q. If she did would you not have seen her?
A. I don't know. She might be in one room and I in another.
Q. Do you think she might have gone to work and washed all the windows in the dining room and sitting room and you not know it?
A. I don't know, I am sure, whether I should or not. I might have seen her, and not know it.
Q. Miss Borden, I am trying in good faith to get all the doings that morning of yourself and Miss Sullivan, and I have not succeeded in doing it.

you desire to give me any information or not?

A. I don't know it— I don't know what your name is.

Q. It is certain beyond reasonable doubt she was engaged in washing the windows in the dining room or sitting room when your father came home. Do you mean to say you know nothing of either of those operations?

A. I knew she washed the windows outside; that is, she told me so. She did not wash the windows in the kitchen, because I was in the kitchen most of the time.

Q. The dining room and sitting room, I said.

A. I don't know.

Q. It is reasonably certain she washed the windows in the dining room and sitting room inside while your father was out, and was engaged in that operation when your father came home; do you mean to say you know nothing of it?

A. I don't know whether she washed the windows in the sitting room and dining room or not.

Q. Can you give me any information how it happened at that particular time you should go into the chamber of the barn to find a sinker to go to Marion with to fish the next Monday?

A. I was going to finish my ironing; my flats were not hot; I said to myself "I will go and try and find that sinker; perhaps by the time I get back the flats will be hot." That is the only reason.

Q. How long had you been reading an old magazine before you went to the barn at all?

A. Perhaps half an hour.

Q. Had you got a fish line?

A. Not here; we had some at the farm.

Q. Had you got a fish hook?

A. No sir.

Q. Had you got any apparatus for fishing at all?

A. Yes, over there.

Q. Had you any sinkers over there?

A. I think there were some. It is so long since I have been there; I think there were some.

Q. You had no reason to suppose you were lacking sinkers?

A. I don't think there were any on my lines.

Q. Where were your lines?

A. My fish lines were at the farm here.

Q. What made you think there were no sinkers at the farm on your lines?

A. Because some time ago when I was there I had none.

Q. How long since you used the fish lines?

A. Five years, perhaps.

Q. You left them at the farm then?

A. Yes, sir.

Q. And you have not seen them since?

A. Yes, sir.

Q. It occurred to you after your father came in it would be a good time to go to the barn after sinkers, and you had no reason to suppose there was not abundance of sinkers at the farm and abundance of lines?

A. The last time I was there there were some lines.

Q. Did you not say before you presumed there were sinkers at the farm?

A. I don't think I said so.

Q. You did say so exactly. Do you now say you presume there were not sinkers at the farm?

A. I don't think there were any fish lines suitable to use at the farm; I don't think there were any sinkers on any line that had been mine.

Q. Do you remember telling me you presumed there were lines, and sinkers and hooks at the farm?

A. I said there were lines I thought, and perhaps hooks. I did not say I thought there were sinkers on my lines. There was another box of lines over there beside mine.

Q. You thought there were not sinkers?

A. Not on my lines.

Q. Not sinkers at the farm?

A. I don't think there were any sinkers at the farm. I don't know whether there were or not.

Q. Did you then think there were no sinkers at the farm?

A. I thought there were no sinkers anywhere, or I should not have been trying to find some.

Q. You thought there were no sinkers at the farm to be had?

A. I thought there were no sinkers at the farm to be had.

Q. That is the reason you went into the second story of the barn to look for a sinker?

A. Yes, sir.

Q. What made you think you would find sinkers there?

A. I heard father say, and I knew there was lead there.

Q. What made you think you would find sinkers there?

A. I went to see, because there was lead there.

Q. You thought there might be lead there made into sinkers?

A. I thought there might be lead with a hole in it.

Q. Did you examine the lead that was down stairs near the door?

A. No sir.

Q. Why not?

A. I don't know.

Q. You went straight to the upper story of the barn?

A. No, I went under the pear tree and got some pears first.

Q. Then went to the second story of the barn to look for sinkers for lines you had at the farm, as you supposed, as you had seen them there five years before that time?

A. I went up to get some sinkers, if I could find them. I did not intend to go to the farm for lines; I was going to buy some lines here.

Q. You then had no intention of using your own lines at Marion?

A. I could not get them.

Q. You had no intention of using your own line and hooks at the farm?

A. No sir.

Q. What was the use of telling me a little while ago you had no sinkers on your line at the farm?

A. I thought I made you understand that those lines at the farm were no good to use.

Q. Did you not mean for me to understand one of the reasons you were searching for sinkers was that the lines you had at the farm, as you remembered then, had no sinkers on them?

A. I said the lines at the farm had no sinkers.

Q. I did not ask you what you said. Did you not mean for me to understand that?

A. I meant for you to understand I wanted the sinkers, and was going to have new lines.

Q. You had not then bought your lines?

A. No sir, I was going out Thursday noon.

Q. You had not bought any apparatus for fishing?

A. No hooks.

Q. Had bought nothing connected with your fishing trip?

A. No sir.

Q. Was going to go fishing the next Monday, were you?

A. I don't know that we should go fishing Monday.

Q. Going to the place to go fishing Monday?

A. Yes sir.

Q. This was Thursday, and you had no idea of using any fishing apparatus before the next Monday?

A. No sir.

Q. You had no fishing apparatus you were proposing to use the next Monday until then?

A. No sir, not until I bought it.

Q. You had not bought anything?

A. No sir.

Q. Had not started to buy anything?

A. No sir.

Q. The first thing in preparation for your fishing trip the next Monday was to go to the loft of that barn to find some old sinkers to put on some hooks and lines that you had not then bought?

A. I thought if I found no sinkers I would have to buy the sinkers when I bought the lines.

Q. You thought you would be saving something by hunting in the loft of the barn before you went to see whether you should need them or not?

A. I thought I would find out whether there were any sinkers before I bought the lines; and if there was, I should not have to buy any sinkers. If there were some, I should only have to buy the lines and the hooks.

Q. You began the collection of your fishing apparatus by searching for the sinkers in the barn?

A. Yes sir.

Q. You were searching in a box of old stuff in the loft of the barn?

A. Yes sir, up stairs.

Q. That you had never looked at before?

A. I had seen them.

Q. Never examined them before?

A. No sir.

Q. All the reason you supposed there was sinkers there was your father had told you there was lead in the barn?

A. Yes, lead; and one day I wanted some old nails; he said there was some in the barn.

Q. All the reason that gave you to think there was sinkers was your father said there was old lead in the barn?

A. Yes sir.

Q. Did he mention the place in the barn?

A. I think he said up stairs; I am not sure.

Q. Where did you look up stairs?

A. On that work bench, like.

Q. In anything?

A. Yes; it was a box, sort of a box, and then some things lying right on the side that was not in the box.

Q. How large a box was it?

A. I could not tell you. It was probably covered up with lumber, I think.

Q. Give me the best idea of the size of the box you can.

A. Well, I should say, I don't know, I have not any idea.

Q. Give me the best idea you have.

A. I have given you the best idea I have.

Q. What is the best idea you have?

A. About that large, (measuring with hands.)

Q. That long?

A. Yes.

Q. How wide?

A. I don't know.

Q. Give me the best idea you have.

A. Perhaps about as wide as it was long.

Q. How high?

A. It was not very high.

Q. About how high?

(Witness measures with her hands.)

Q. About twice the length of your forefinger?

A. I should think so. Not quite.

Q. What was in the box?

A. Nails, and some old locks, and I don't know but there was a door knob.

Q. Anything else?

A. I don't remember anything else.

Q. Any lead?

A. Yes, some pieces of tea lead, like.

Q. Foil, what we call tin foil, the same as you use on tea chests?

A. I don't remember seeing any tin foil; not as thin as that.

Q. Tea chest lead?

A. No, sir.

Q. What did you see in shape of lead?

A. Flat pieces of lead, a little bigger than that; some of them were doubled together.

Q. How many?

A. I could not tell you.

Q. Where else did you look beside in the box?

A. I did not look anywhere for lead except on the work bench.

Q. How full was the box?

A. It was not nearly as full as it could have been.

Q. You looked on the bench, beside that where else?

A. Nowhere except on the bench.

Q. Did you look for anything else beside lead?

A. No, sir.

Q. When you got through looking for lead did you come down?

A. No, sir, I went to the west window over the hay, to the west window, and the curtain was slanted a little. I pulled it down.

Q. What else?

A. Nothing.

Q. That is all you did?

A. Yes, sir.

Q. That is the second story of the barn?

A. Yes, sir.

Q. Was the window open?

A. I think not.

Q. Hot?

A. Very hot.

Q. How long do you think you were up there?

A. Not more than fifteen or twenty minutes, I should not think.

Q. Should you think what you have told me would occupy four minutes?

A. Yes, because I ate some pears up there.

Q. Do you think all you have told me would take you four minutes?

A. I ate some pears up there.

Q. I asked you to tell me all you did.

A. I told you all I did.

Q. Do you mean to say you stopped your work, and then, additional to that, sat still and ate some pears?

A. While I was looking out of the window, yes sir.

Q. Will you tell me all you did in the second story of the barn?

A. I think I told you all I did that I can remember.

Q. Is there anything else?

A. I told you I took some pears up from the ground when I went up; I stopped under the pear tree and took some pears up when I went up.

Q. Have you now told me everything you did up in the second story of the barn?

A. Yes sir.

Q. I now call your attention, and ask you to say whether all you have told me— I don't suppose you stayed there any longer than necessary?

A. No sir, because it was close.

Q. I suppose that was the hottest place there was on the premises?

A. I should think so.

Q. Can you give me any explanation why all you have told me would occupy more than three minutes?

A. Yes, it would take me more than three minutes.

Q. To look in that box that you have described the size of on the bench and put down the curtain and then get out as soon as you conveniently could; would you say you were occupied in that business twenty minutes?

A. I think so, because I did not look at the box when I first went up.

Q. What did you do?

A. I ate my pears.

Q. Stood there eating the pears, doing nothing?

A. I was looking out of the window.

Q. Stood there, looking out of the window, eating the pears?

A. I should think so.

Q. How many did you eat?

A. Three, I think.

Q. You were feeling better than you did in the morning?

A. Better than I did the night before.

Q. You were feeling better than you were in the morning?

A. I felt better in the morning than I did the night before.

Q. That is not what I asked you. You were then, when you were in that hot loft, looking out of the window and eating three pears, feeling better, were you not, than you were in the morning when you could not eat any breakfast?

A. I never eat any breakfast.

Q. You did not answer my question, and you will, if I have to put it all day. Were you then when you were eating those three pears in that hot loft, looking out of that closed window, feeling better than you were in the morning when you ate no breakfast?

A. I was feeling well enough to eat the pears.

Q. Were you feeling better than you were in the morning?

A. I don't think I felt very sick in the morning, only— Yes, I don't know but I did feel better. As I say, I don't know whether I ate any breakfast or not, or whether I ate a cookie.

Q. Were you then feeling better than you did in the morning?

A. I don't know how to answer you, because I told you I felt better in the morning anyway.

Q. Do you understand my question? My question is whether, when you were in the loft of that barn, you were feeling better than you were in the morning when you got up?

A. No, I felt about the same.

Q. Were you feeling better than you were when you told your mother you did not care for any dinner?

A. No sir, I felt about the same.

Q. Well enough to eat pears, but not well enough to eat anything for dinner?

A. She asked me if I wanted any meat.

Q. I ask you why you should select that place, which was the only place which would put you out of sight of the house, to eat those three pears in?

A. I cannot tell you any reason.

Q. You observe that fact, do you not? You have put yourself in the only place perhaps, where it would be impossible for you to see a person going into the house?

A. Yes sir, I should have seen them from the front window.

Q. From anywhere in the yard?

A. No sir, not unless from the end of the barn.

Q. Ordinarily in the yard you could see them, and in the kitchen where you had been, you could have seen them?

A. I don't think I understand.

Q. When you were in the kitchen, you could see persons who came in at the back door?

A. Yes sir.

Q. When you were in the yard, unless you were around the corner of the house, you could see them come in at the back door?

A. No sir, not unless I was at the corner of the barn; the minute I turned I could not.

Q. What was there?

A. A little jog like, the walk turns.

Q. I ask you again to explain to me why you took those pears from the pear tree?

A. I did not take them from the pear tree.

Q. From the ground, wherever you took them from. I thank you for correcting me; going into the barn, going up stairs into the hottest place in the barn, in the rear of the barn, the hottest place, and there standing and eating those pears that morning?

A. I beg your pardon, I was not in the rear of the barn. I was in the other end of the barn that faced the street.

Q. Where you could see anybody coming into the house?

A. Yes sir.

Q. Did you not tell me you could not?

A. Before I went into the barn, at the jog on the outside.

Q. You now say when you were eating the pears, you could see the back door?

A. Yes sir.

Q. So nobody could come in at that time without your seeing them?

A. I don't see how they could.

Q. After you got through eating your pears you began your search?

A. Yes sir.

Q. Then you did not see into the house?

A. No sir, because the bench is at the other end.

Q. Now I have asked you over and over again, and will continue the inquiry, whether anything you did at the bench would occupy more than three minutes?

A. Yes, I think it would, because I pulled over quite a lot of boards in looking.

Q. To get at the box?

A. Yes sir.

Q. Taking all that, what is the amount of time you think you occupied in looking for that piece of lead which you did not find?

A. Well, I should think perhaps I was ten minutes.

Q. Looking over those old things?

A. Yes sir, on the bench.

Q. Now can you explain why you were ten minutes doing it?

A. No, only that I can't do anything in a minute.

Q. When you came down from the barn, what did you do then?

A. Came into the kitchen.

Q. What did you do then?

A. I went into the dining room and laid down my hat.

Q. What did you do then?

A. Opened the sitting room door, and went into the sitting room, or pushed it open; it was not latched.

Q. What did you do then?

A. I found my father, and rushed to the foot of the stairs.

Q. What were you going into the sitting room for?

A. To go up stairs.

Q. What for?

A. To sit down.

Q. What had become of the ironing?

A. The fire had gone out.

Q. I thought you went out because the fire was not hot enough to heat the flats.

A. I thought it would burn, but the fire had not caught from the few sparks.

Q. So you gave up the ironing and was going up stairs?

A. Yes, sir, I thought I would wait till Maggie got dinner and heat the flats again.

Q. When you saw your father where was he?

A. On the sofa.

Q. What was his position?

A. Lying down.

Q. Describe anything else you noticed at that time.

A. I did not notice anything else, I was so frightened and horrified. I ran to the foot of the stairs and called Maggie.

Q. Did you notice that he had been cut?

A. Yes; that is what made me afraid.

Q. Did you notice that he was dead?

A. I did not know whether he was or not.

Q. Did you make any search for your mother?

A. No, sir.

Q. Why not?

A. I thought she was out of the house; I thought she had gone out. I called Maggie to go to Dr. Bowen's. When they came I said, "I don't know where Mrs. Borden is." I thought she had gone out.

Q. Did you tell Maggie you thought your mother had come in?

A. No, sir.

Q. That you thought you heard her come in?

A. No, sir.

Q. Did you say to anybody that you thought she was killed up stairs?

A. No, sir.

Q. To anybody?

A. No, sir.

Q. You made no effort to find your mother at all?

A. No, sir.

Q. Who did you send Maggie for?

A. Dr. Bowen. She came back and said Dr. Bowen was not there.

Q. What did you tell Maggie?

A. I told her he was hurt.

Q. When you first told her?

A. I says "Go for Dr. Bowen as soon as you can, I think father is hurt."

Q. Did you then know that he was dead?

A. No, sir.

Q. You saw him?

A. Yes sir.

Q. You went into the room?

A. No sir.

Q. Looked in at the door?

A. I opened the door and rushed back.

Q. Saw his face?

A. No, I did not see his face, because he was all covered with blood.

Q. You saw where the face was bleeding?

A. Yes sir.

Q. Did you see the blood on the floor?

A. No sir.

Q. You saw his face covered with blood?

A. Yes sir.

Q. Did you see his eye ball hanging out?

A. No sir.

Q. See the gashes where his face was laid open?

A. No sir.

Q. Nothing of that kind?

A. No sir. (Witness covers her face with her hand for a minute or two; then examination is resumed.)

Q. Do you know of any employment that would occupy your mother for the two hours between nine and eleven in the front room?

A. Not unless she was sewing.

Q. If she had been sewing you would have heard the machine?

A. She did not always use the machine.

Q. Did you see, or were there found, anything to indicate that she was sewing up there?

A. I don't know. She had given me a few weeks before some pillow cases to make.

Q. My question is not that. Did you see, or were there found, anything to indicate that she had done any sewing in that room that morning?

A. I don't know. I was not allowed in that room; I did not see it.

Q. Was that the room where she usually sewed?

A. No sir.

Q. Did you ever know her to use that room for sewing?

A. Yes sir.

Q. When?

A. Whenever she wanted to use the machine.

Q. When she did not want to use the machine, did you know she used that room for sewing?

A. Not unless she went up to sew a button on, or something.

Q. She did not use it as a sitting room?

A. No sir.

Q. Leaving out the sewing, do you know of anything else that would occupy her for two hours in that room?

A. No, not if she had made the bed up, and she said she had when I went down.

Q. Assuming the bed was made?

A. I don't know anything.

Q. Did she say she had done the work?

A. She said she had made the bed, and was going to put on the pillow cases, about 9 o'clock.

Q. I ask you now again, remembering that—

A. I told you that yesterday.

Q. Never mind about yesterday. Tell me all the talk you had with your mother when you came down in the morning?

A. She asked me how I felt. I said I felt better, but did not want any breakfast. She said what kind of meat did I want for dinner. I said I did not want any. She said she was going out, somebody was sick, and she would get the dinner, get the meat, order the meat. And I think she said something about the weather being hotter, or something; and I don't remember that she said anything else. I said to her: "Won't you change your dress before you go out?" She had on an old one. She said: "No, this is good enough." That is all I can remember

Q. In this narrative you have not again said anything about her having said that she had made the bed?

A. I told you that she said she made the bed.

Q. In this time saying, you did not put that in. I want that conversation that you had with her that morning. I beg your pardon again, in this time of telling me, you did not say anything about her having received a note.

A. I told you that before.

Q. Miss Borden, I want you now to tell me all the talk you had with your mother, when you came down, and all the talk she had with you. Please begin again.

A. She asked me how I felt. I told her. She asked me what I wanted for dinner. I told her not anything, what kind of meat I wanted for dinner. I told her not any. She said she had been up and made the spare bed, and was going to take up some linen pillow cases for the small pillows at the foot, and then the room was done. She says: "I have had a note from somebody that is sick, and I am going out, and I will get the dinner at the same time." I think she said something about the weather, I don't know. She also asked me if I would direct some paper wrappers for her, which I did.

Q. She said she had had a note?

A. Yes sir.

Q. You told me yesterday you never saw the note?

A. No sir, I never did.

Q. You looked for it?

A. No sir, but the rest have.

Q. She did not say where she was going?

A. No sir.

Q. Does she usually tell you where she is going?

A. She does not generally tell me.

Q. Did she say when she was coming back?

A. No sir.

Q. Did you know that Mr. Morse was coming to dinner?

A. No sir, I knew nothing about him.

Q. Was he at dinner the day before?

A. Wednesday noon? I don't know, I had not seen him; I don't think he was.

Q. Were you at dinner?

A. I was in the house. I don't know whether I went down to dinner or not. I was not feeling well.

Q. Whether you ate dinner or not?

A. I don't remember.

Q. Do you remember who was at dinner the day before?

A. No sir, I don't remember, because I don't know whether I was down myself or not.

Q. Were you at tea Wednesday night?

A. I went down, but I think, I don't know, whether I had any tea or not.

Q. Did you sit down with the family?

A. I think I did, but I am not sure.

Q. Was Mr. Morse there?

A. No sir, I did not see him.

Q. Who were there to tea?

A. Nobody.

Q. The family were there, I suppose?

A. Yes sir; I mean nobody but the family.

Q. Did you have an apron on Thursday?

A. Did I what?

Q. Have an apron on Thursday?

A. No sir, I don't think I did.

Q. Do you remember whether you did or not?

A. I don't remember sure, but I don't think I did.

Q. You had aprons, of course?

A. I had aprons, yes sir.

Q. Will you try and think whether you did or not?

A. I don't think I did.

Q. Will you try and remember?

A. I had no occasion for an apron on that morning.

Q. If you can remember I wish you would.

A. I don't remember.

Q. That is all the answer you can give me about that?

A. Yes sir.

Q. Did you have any occasion to use the axe or hatchet?

A. No sir.

Q. Did you know where they were?

A. I knew there was an old axe down cellar; that is all I knew.

Q. Did you know anything about a hatchet down cellar?

A. No sir.

Q. Where was the old axe down cellar?

A. The last time I saw it it was stuck in the old chopping block.

Q. Was that the only axe or hatchet down cellar?

A. It was all I knew about.

Q. When was the last you knew of it?

A. When our farmer came to chop wood.

Q. When was that?

A. I think a year ago last winter; I think there was so much wood on hand he did not come last winter.

Q. Do you know of anything that would occasion the use of an axe or hatchet?

A. No sir.

Q. Do you know of anything that would occasion the getting of blood on an axe or hatchet down cellar?

A. No sir.

Q. I do not say there was, but assuming an axe or hatchet was found down cellar with blood on it?

A. No sir.

Q. Do you know whether there was a hatchet down there before this murder?

A. I don't know.

Q. You are not able to say your father did not own a hatchet?

A. I don't know whether he did or not.

Q. Did you know there was found at the foot of the stairs a hatchet and axe?

A. No sir, I did not.

Q. Assume that is so, can you give me any explanation of how they came there?

A. No sir.

Q. Assume they had blood on them, can you give any occasion for there being blood on them?

A. No sir.

Q. Can you tell of any killing of an animal? or any other operation that would lead to their being cast there, with blood on them?

A. No sir, he killed some pigeons in the barn last May or June.

Q. What with?

A. I don't know, but I thought he wrung their necks.

Q. What made you think so?

A. I think he said so.

Q. Did anything else make you think so?

A. All but three or four had their heads on, that is what made me think so.

Q. Did all of them come into the house?

A. I think so.

Q. Those that came into the house were all headless?

A. Two or three had them on.

Q. Were any with their heads off?

A. Yes sir.

Q. Cut off or twisted off?

A. I don't know which.

Q. How did they look?

A. I don't know, their heads were gone, that is all.

Q. Did you tell anybody they looked as though they were twisted off?

A. I don't remember whether I did or not. The skin I think was very tender, I said why are these heads off? I think I remember of telling somebody that he said they twisted off.

Q. Did they look as if they were cut off?

A. I don't know, I did not look at that particularly.

Q. Is there anything else besides that that would lead, in your opinion so far as you can remember, to the finding of instruments in the cellar with blood on them?

A. I know of nothing else that was done.

(Judge Blaisdell)—Was there any effort made by the witness to notify Mrs Borden of the fact that Mr. Borden was found?

Q. Did you make any effort to notify Mrs. Borden of your father being killed?

A. No sir, when I found him I rushed right to the foot of the stairs for Maggie. I supposed Mrs. Borden was out. I did not think anything about her at the time, I was so—

Q. At any time did you say anything about her to anybody?

A. No sir.

Q. To the effect that she was out?

A. I told father when he came in.

Q. After your father was killed?

A. No sir.

Q. Did you say you thought she was up stairs?

A. No sir.

Q. Did you ask them to look up stairs?

A. No sir.

Q. Did you suggest to anybody to search up stairs?

A. I said, "I don't know where Mrs. Borden is;" that is all I said.

Q. You did not suggest that any search be made for her?

A. No sir.

Q. You did not make any yourself?

A. No sir.

Q. I want you to give me all that you did, by way of word or deed, to see whether your mother was dead or not, when you found your father was dead.

A. I did not do anything, except what I said to Mrs. Churchill. I said to her: "I don't know where Mrs. Borden is. I think she is out, but I wish you would look."

Q. You did ask her to look?

A. I said that to Mrs. Churchill.

Q. Where did you intend for her to look?

A. In Mrs. Borden's room.

Q. When you went out to the barn did you leave the door shut, the screen door?

A. I left it shut.

Q. When you came back did you find it shut or open?

A. No, sir; I found it open.

Q. Can you tell me anything else that you did, that you have not told me, during your absence from the house?

A. No, sir.

Q. Can you tell me when it was that you came back from the barn, what time it was?

A. I don't know what time it was.

Q. Have you any idea when it was that your father came home?

A. I am not sure, but I think it must have been after 10, because I think he told me he did not think he should go out until about 10. When he went out I did not look at the clock to see what time it was. I think he did not go out until 10, or a little after. He was not gone so very long.

Q. Will you give me the best judgment you can as to the time your father got back? If you have not any, it is sufficient to say so.

A. No, sir, I have not any.

Q. Can you give me any judgment as to the length of time that elapsed after he came back, and before you went to the barn?

A. I went right out to the barn.

Q. How soon after he came back?

A. I should think not less than five minutes; I saw him taking off his shoes and lying down; it only took him two or three minutes to do it. I went right out.

Q. When he came into the house did he not go into the dining room first?

A. I don't know.

Q. And there sit down?

A. I don't know.

Q. Why don't you know?

A. Because I was in the kitchen.

Q. It might have happened, and you not have known it?

A. Yes sir.

Q. You heard the bell ring?

A. Yes sir.

Q. And you knew when he came in?

A. Yes sir.

Q. You did not see him?

A. No sir.

Q. When did you first see him?

A. I went into the sitting room, and he was there; I don't know whether he had been in the dining room before or not.

Q. What made you go into the sitting room?

A. Because I wanted to ask him a question.

Q. What question?

A. Whether there was any mail for me.

Q. Did you not ask him that question in the dining room?

A. No sir, I think not.

Q. Was he not in the dining room sitting down?

A. I don't remember his being in the dining room sitting down.

Q. At that time was not Maggie washing the windows in the sitting room?

A. I thought I asked him for the mail in the sitting room; I am not sure.

Q. Was not the reason he went in the dining room because she was in the sitting room washing windows?

A. I don't know.

Q. Did he not go up stairs to his own room before he sat down in the sitting room?

A. I did not see him go.

Q. He had the key to his room down there?

A. I don't know whether he had it; it was kept on the shelf.

Q. Don't you remember he took the key and went into his own room and then came back?

A. No, sir.

Q. You don't remember anything of that kind?

A. No, sir; I do not think he did go up stairs either.

Q. You will swear he did not?

A. I did not see him.

Q. You swear you did not see him?

A. Yes, sir.

Q. You were either in the kitchen or sitting room all the time?

A. Yes, sir.

Q. He could not have gone up without he had gone through the kitchen?

A. No, sir.

Q. When you did go into the sitting room to ask him a question, if it was the sitting room, what took place then?

A. I asked him if he had any mail. He said "none for you." He had a letter in his hand. I supposed it was for himself. I asked him how he felt. He said "About the same." He said he should lie down I asked him if he thought he should have a nap. He said he should try to. I asked him if he wanted the window left the way it was or if he felt a draught. He said "No." That is all.

Q. Did you help him about lying down?

A. No, sir.

Q. Fix his pillows or head?

A. No, sir; I did not touch the sofa.

Q. Did he lie down before you left the room?

A. Yes, sir.

Q. Did anything else take place?

A. Not that I remember of.

Q. Was he then under medical treatment?

A. No, sir.

Q. The doctor had not given him any medicine that you know of?

A. No, sir; he took some medicine; it was not doctor's medicine; it was what we gave him.

Q. What was it?

A. We gave him castor oil first and then Garfield tea.

Q. When was that?

A. He took the castor oil some time Wednesday. I think some time Wednesday noon, and I think the tea Wednesday night; Mrs. Borden gave it to him. She went over to see the doctor.

Q. When did you first consult Mr. Jennings?

A. I can't tell you that; I think my sister sent for him; I don't know.

Q. Was it you or your sister?

A. My sister.

Q. You did not send for him?

A. I did not send for him. She said did we think we ought to have him. I said do as she thought best. I don't know when he came first.

Q. Now, tell me once more, if you please, the particulars of that trouble that you had with your mother four or five years ago.

A. Her father's house on Fourth street was for sale——

Q. Whose father's house?

A. Mrs. Borden's father's house. She had a stepmother and a half sister, Mrs. Borden did, and this house was left to the stepmother and a half sister, if I understood it right, and the house was for sale. The stepmother, Mrs. Oliver Gray, wanted to sell it, and my father brought out the Widow Gray's share. She did not tell me, and he did not tell me, but some outsiders said that he gave it to her. Put it in her name. I said if he gave that to her, he ought to give us something. Told Mrs. Borden so. She did not care anything about the house herself. She wanted it so this half sister could have a home, because she had married a man that was not doing the best he could, and she thought her sister was having a very hard time and wanted her to have a home. And we always thought she persuaded father to buy it. At any rate he did buy it, and I am quite sure she did persuade him. I said what he did for her people he ought to do for his own children. So he gave us grandfather's house. That was all the trouble we ever had.

Q. You have not stated any trouble yet between you and her?

A. I said there was feeling four or five years ago when I stopped calling her mother. I told you that yesterday.

Q. That is all there is to it then?

A. Yes, sir.

Q. You had no words with your stepmother then?

A. I talked with her about it and said what he did for her he ought to do for us; that is all the words we had.

Q. That is the occasion of his giving you the house that you sold back to him?

A. Yes, sir.

Q. Did your mother leave any property?

A. I don't know.

Q. Your own mother?

A. No, sir; not that I ever knew of.

Q. Did you ever see that thing? (Wooden club.)

A. Yes, sir; I think I have.

Q. What is it?

A. My father used to keep something similar to this, that looked very much like it under his bed. He whittled it out himself at the farm one time.

Q. How long since you have seen it?

A. I have not seen it in years.

Q. How many years?

A. I could not tell you. I should think 10 or 15 years; not since I was quite a little girl, if that is the one. I can't swear that it is the one; it was about that size. (Marks it with a cross.)

Q. How many years, 10 or 15?

A. I was a little girl, it must be as much as that.

Q. When was the last time the windows were washed before that day?

A. I don't know.

Q. Why don't you know?

A. Because I had nothing to do with the work down stairs.

Q. When was the last time that you ate with the family, that you can swear to, before your mother was killed?

A. Well, I ate with them all day Tuesday, that is, what little we ate we sat down to the table; and I think I sat down to the table with them Wednesday night, but I am not sure.

Q. All day Tuesday?

A. I was down at the table.

Q. I understand you to say you did not come down to breakfast?

A. That was Wednesday morning.

Q. I understood you to say that you did not come down to breakfast?

A. I came down, but I did not eat breakfast with them, I did not eat any breakfast. Frequently I would go into the dining room and sit down to the table with them and not eat any breakfast.

Q. Did you give to the officer the same skirt you had on the day of the tragedy?

A. Yes, sir.

Q. Do you know whether there was any blood on the skirt?

A. No, sir.

Q. Assume that there was, do you know how it came there?

A. No, sir.

Q. Have you any explanation of how it might come there?

A. No, sir.

Q. Did you know there was any blood on the skirt you gave them?

A. No, sir.

Q. Assume that there was, can you give any explanation of how it came there, on the dress skirt?

A. No, sir.

Q. Assume that there was, can you suggest any reason how it came there?

A. No, sir.

Q. Have you offered any?

A. No, sir.

Q. Have you ever offered any?

A. No, sir.

Q. Have you said it came from flea bites?

A. On the petticoats I said there was a flea bite. I said it might have been. You siad you meant the dress skirt.

Q. I did. Have you offered any explanation how that came there?

A. I told those men that were at the house that I had had fleas; that is all.

Q. Did you offer that as an explanation?

A. I said that was the only explanation that I knew of.

Q. Assuming that the blood came from the outside, can you give any explanation of how it came there?

A. No, sir.

Q. You cannot now?

A. No, sir.

Q. What shoes did you have on that day?

A. A pair of ties.

Q. What color?

A. Black.

Q. Will you give them to the officer?

A. Yes.

Q. Where are they?

A. At home.

Q. What stockings did you have on that day?

A. Black.

Q. Where are they?

A. At home.

Q. Have they been washed?

A. I don't know.

Q. Will you give them to the officer?

A. Yes, sir.

Q. The window you was at is the window that is nearest the street in the barn?

A. Yes, sir; the west window.

Q. The pears you ate you got from under the tree in the yard?

A. Yes, sir.

Q. How long were you under the pear tree?

A. I think I was under there very nearly four or five minutes. I stood looking around. I looked up at the pigeon house that they have closed up. It was no more than five minutes, perhaps not as long. I can't say sure.

(Judge Blaisdell.) Was this witness on Thursday morning in the front hall or front stairs or front chamber, any part of the front part of the house at all?

Q. What do you say to that?

A. I had to come down the front stairs to get into the kitchen.

Q. When you came down first?

A. Yes, sir.

Q. Were you afterwards?

A. No, sir.

Q. Not at all?

A. Except the few minutes I went up with the clean clothes, and I had to come back again.

Q. That you now say was before Mr. Borden went away?

A. Yes, sir.

(Miss Borden recalled Aug. 11, 1892.)

Q. (Mr. Knowlton.) Is there anything you would like to correct in your previous testimony?

A. No, sir.

Q. Did you buy a dress pattern in New Bedford?

A. A dress pattern?

Q. Yes.

A. I think I did.

Q. Where is it?

A. It is at home.

Q. Where?

A. Where at home?

Q. Please.

A. It is in a trunk.

Q. In your room?

A. No, sir; in the attic.

Q. Not made up?

A. O, no, sir.

Q. Where did you buy it?

A. I don't know the name of the store.

Q. On the principal street there?

A. I think it was on the street that Hutchinson's book store is on. I am not positive.

Q. What kind of a one was it, please?

A. It was a pink stripe and a white stripe, and a blue stripe corded gingham.

Q. Your attention has already been called to the circumstance of going into the drug store of Smith's, on the corner of Columbia and Main streets, by some officer, has it not, on the day before the tragedy?

A. I don't know whether some officer has asked me, somebody has spoken of it to me; I don't know who it was.

Q. Did that take place?

A. I did not.

Q. Do you know where the drug store is?

A. I don't.

Q. Did you go into any drug store and inquire for prussic acid?

A. I did not.

Q. Where were you on Wednesday morning that you remember?

A. At home.

Q. All the time?

A. All day, until Wednesday night.

Q. Nobody there but your parents and yourself and the servant?

A. Why, Mr. Morse came sometime in the afternoon, or at noon time, I suppose, I did not see him.

Q. He did not come so to see you?

A. No, sir, I did not see him.

Q. He did not come until afternoon anyway, did he?

A. I don't think he did; I am not sure.

Q. Did you dine with the family that day?

A. I was down stairs, yes, sir. I did not eat any breakfast with them.

Q. Did you go into the drug store for any purpose whatever?

A. I did not.

Q. I think you said yesterday that you did not go into the room where your father lay, after he was killed, on the sofa, but only looked in at the door?

A. I looked in; I did not go in.

Q. You did not step into the room at all?

A. I did not.

Q. Did you ever, after your mother was found killed, go into that room?

A. No, sir.

Q. Did you afterwards go into the room where your father was found killed, any more than to go through it to go up stairs?

A. When they took me up stairs they took me through that room.

Q. Otherwise than that did you go into it?

A. No, sir.

Q. Let me refresh your memory. You came down in the night to get some water with Miss Russell, along towards night, or in the evening, to get some water with Miss Russell?

A. Thursday night? I don't remember it.

Q. Don't you remember coming down sometime to get some toilet water?

A. No, sir; there was no toilet water down stairs.

Q. Or to empty the slops?

A. I don't know whether I did Thursday evening or not. I am not sure.

Q. You think it may have been some other evening?

A. I don't remember coming down with her to do such a thing. I may have, I can't tell whether it was Thursday evening or any other evening.

Q. Other than that, if that did take place, you don't recollect going into that room for any purpose at any time?

A. No, sir.

Q. Was the dress that was given to the officers the same dress that you wore that morning?

A. Yes, sir.

Q. The India silk?

A. No, it is not an India silk, it is silk and linen; some call it bengaline silk.

Q. Something like that dress there? (Pongee.)

A. No, it was not like that.

Q. Did you give to the officer the same shoes and stockings that you wore?

A. I did, sir.

Q. Do you remember where you took them off?

A. I wore the shoes ever after that, all around the house Friday, and all day Thursday, and all day Friday and Saturday until I put on my shoes for the street.

Q. That is to say you wore them all that day, Thursday, until you took them off for the night?

A. Yes, sir.

Q. Did you tell us yesterday all the errand that you had at the barn?

A. Yes, sir.

Q. You have nothing to add to what you said?

A. No, sir.

Q. You had no other errand than what you have spoken of?

A. No, sir.

Q. Miss Borden, of course you appreciate the anxiety that everybody has to find the author of this tragedy, and the questions that I put to you have been in that direction; I now ask you if you can furnish any other fact, or give any other, even suspicion, that will assist the officers in any way in this matter?

A. About two weeks ago——

Q. Was you going to tell the occurrence about the man that called at the house?

A. No, sir. It was after my sister went away. I came home from Miss Russell's one night, and as I came up, I always glanced towards the side door as I came along by the carriage way, I saw a shadow on the side steps. I did not stop walking, but I walked slower. Somebody ran down the steps, around the east end of the house. I thought it was a man, because I saw no skirts, and I was frightened, and of course I did not go around to see. I hurried in the front door as fast as I could and locked it.

Q. What time of night was that?

A. I think about quarter of 9; it was not after 9 o'clock, anyway.

Q. Do you remember what night that was?

A. No, sir; I don't. I saw somebody run around the house once before last winter.

Q. One thing at a time. Do you recollect about how long ago that last occurrence was?

A. It was after my sister went away. She has been away two weeks today, so it must have been within two weeks.

Q. Two weeks today? Or two weeks at the time of the murder?

A. Is not today Thursday?

Q. Yes, but I thought you said she was gone two weeks the day of the murder?

A. Is not today Thursday?

Q. Yes, but that would be three weeks. I thought you said the day your father was murdered she had been away just two weeks?

A. Yes, she had.

Q. Then it would be three weeks today your sister went away, a week has elapsed?

A. Yes, it would be three weeks.

Q. You mean it was sometime within the two weeks that your sister was away?

A. Yes. I had forgotten that a whole week had passed since the affair.

Q. Different from that you cannot state?

A. No, sir; I don't know what the date was.

Q. This form when you first saw it was on the steps of the backdoor?

A. Yes, sir.

Q. Went down the rear steps?

A. Went down towards the barn.

Q. Around the back side of the house?

A. Disappeared in the dark; I don't know where they went.

Q. Have you ever mentioned that before?

A. Yes, sir; I told Mr. Jennings.

Q. To any officer?

A. I don't think I have, unless I told Mr. Hanscomb.

Q. What was you going to say about last winter?

A. Last winter when I was coming home from church one Thursday evening I saw somebody run around the house again. I told my father of that.

Q. Did you tell your father of this last one?

A. No, sir.

Q. Of course you could not identify who it was either time?

A. No, I could not identify who it was, but it was not a very tall person.

Q. Have you sealskin sacks?

A. Yes, sir.

Q. Where are they?

A. Hanging in a large white bag in the attic, each one separate.

Q. Put away for the summer?

A. Yes, sir.

Q. Do you ever use prussic acid on your sacks?

A. Acid? No, sir; I don't use anything on them.

Q. Is there anything else that you can suggest that even amounts to anything whatever?

A. I know of nothing else, except the man who came, and father ordered him out, that is all I know.

Q. That you told about the other day?

A. I think I did; yes, sir.

Q. You have not been able to find that man?

A. I have not; I don't know whether anybody else has or not.

Q. Have you caused search to be made for him?

A. Yes, sir.

Q. When was the offer of reward made for the detection of the criminals?

A. I think it was made Friday.

Q. Who suggested that?

A. We suggested it ourselves, and asked Mr. Buck if he did not think it was a good plan.

Q. Whose suggestion was it, yours or Emma's?

A. I don't remember. I think it was mine.

Pages 1-8.

The Evening Standard.

Pages 1-8.

ESTABLISHED FEBRUARY, 1850.

NEW BEDFORD, TUESDAY, JUNE 13, 1893.---TEN PAGES.

TWO CENTS.

HASKELL & TRIPP.

If the fact of our selling most excellent quality Jersey ribbed undervests for women, at 29c. apiece, possesses any interest for you come quickly.

The undervests in question are not such as you expect from the price quoted. They were made to retail for half a dollar and *are worth that much.* They are fine, high-grade goods, with deep, lace-trimmed neck and sleeves. Twenty-nine cents does not pay the cost of manufacture.

Men's negligee shirts for 50c. apiece are common enough. But where can you see so many sorts, and such good ones for the price, as here?

We have quadrupled our assortment during the past week and can offer really good, well-made shirts for 50c. each.

Plenty at 75c. and $1 for those who want them. Best we can get at these prices. That means they are *better* than some stores can show you.

Parasols and shade hats—The kinds that you want are here in great quantities. Those white sailor hats, trimmed with white ribbon, sell at 75c. and are fine quality and in great demand. Navy blue and black trimmed sailors from 50c. to $1.25.

Choose from a dozen sorts of handsome silk parasols. Pay us $1.89 each. You may get one worth $3.50. None of them are worth under $2.50.

Elegant parasols from $3.50 to $6 in all the novelties of the season.

Navy blue umbrellas for rain or sun, $2 and $2.50.

Dress Goods Specialties.

Printed Oriental cords and dimities, 8c.

Cotton pongees, choice printings, 12½c.

Cream cashmeres, 25c., 37c., 50c.

Navy blue storm serge, 25c.; double width.

Fancy weaves in fine French black dress fabrics, 59c.; worth 87c. a yard.

Ribbons and Laces.

The half-price lots are still in good supply.

Fancy ribbons for any purpose you can use wide, rich silk ribbon for. } 19c. and 29c. a yd. *Not half value.*

"Point de Gene" laces—the heavy sorts for fashionable dress trimming—29c. a yard, worth 50c.; and 39c. a yard, worth 75c.

Visit our cool, comfortable basement, and try a glass of delicious soda water from our new Arctic fountain.

Bonbons and chocolates sold at our candy counter are *first class* in every way.

HASKELL & TRIPP,

Department Stores,

Purchase and William Streets.

TAKEN SICK.

Juror Hodges Had Alarming Attack.

Court Compelled to Take a Recess.

Now Back in His Seat in Apparent Health.

Dr. Dolan's Cold Blooded Words Cut Deep.

Lizzie Hides Her Face and Sheds Tears.

Dr. Wood of Harvard Gives Important Evidence.

Counsel for Defense Saves Exceptions.

Dust Like Ashes on Handleless Hatchet.

Weapon Might Have Been Cleaned of Blood.

Mr. Adams' Cross Examination of Eminent Expert.

The outside scenes about the court house in the morning are as funny as a farce. At the front portal a guard of three stalwart officers was stationed this morning, Messrs. Charles H. Gifford, Mather and Smith, and they kept the crowd of about 100 well in check till the signal was given from the court house to let them come. The guard at the gate was then increased by a deputy sheriff, and the united strength of four men was needed to sway the crowd back and admit but a few at a time. Men and women surged like living waves and pushed and elbowed for a place in front, and when they got through, a few at a time, they rushed up the walk and into the court house like street gamins in a mad rush for the front seats in the Opera House when a play from the wild wooly west, with lots of Indians and cowboys occupies the boards. Women old and young came out of the crush rumpled and disheveled, but triumphant, and made their way as fast as their male competitors up the steps, regardless of decorum or hosiery. At the rear entrance more decorum was shown and people came up slowly and in order and passed the officers with dignity and grace. The offices where reporters, telegraph operators and typewriters work, under the superintendence of Mr. Piper, the janitor, are kept as neat as can be. He has been hardly noticed in these busy times, but he deserves much credit for his industry and unfailing courtesy.

A Grand Rush for Seats.

When the doors were opened at quarter of nine this morning there was a grand rush for seats and in a trice every one was occupied. Ten minutes later Lizzie appeared carrying in her hand a bunch of pink and white peonies. Her manner and bearing betokened the utmost confidence and a kind of care-worn look that has been seen upon her features much of the time since the trial opened was entirely absent.

A Consultation.

The judges entered their room at five minutes of nine and a minute later the door was opened and Messrs. Robinson, Adams, Jennings and District Attorneys Moody and Knowlton entered the room, though for consultation upon what point could not be learned.

It was nearly ten minutes past nine when the counsel and the justices emerged and entered the court room. After the usual formalities, the cross-examination of Dr. Dolan was resumed.

Dr. Dolan's Cross Examination.

Mr. Adams said that the casts that were used yesterday appear to have certain marks upon them, and asked Dr. Dolan if he knew who made them, and the witness answered that he did.

Q. Who did? A. Dr. Draper.

Q. When was that done? A. Last Friday, I think.

Q. Here in New Bedford? A. Yes sir.

Q. I think I left you last night substantially in the sitting room after you had been up stairs to see Mrs. Borden, and did you then make an extended examination of Mr. Borden's body? A. Yes sir.

Q. And that was shortly after 12 o'clock? A. I hardly think it was 12 o'clock.

Q. About 12 o'clock? A. Yes sir.

Q. Is this photographic representation a correct one of Mr. Borden's body as you saw him? (showing the witness a photograph.) A. Yes sir.

Q. In this photograph there appears to be on the arm of the sofa near the dining room door something folded up.

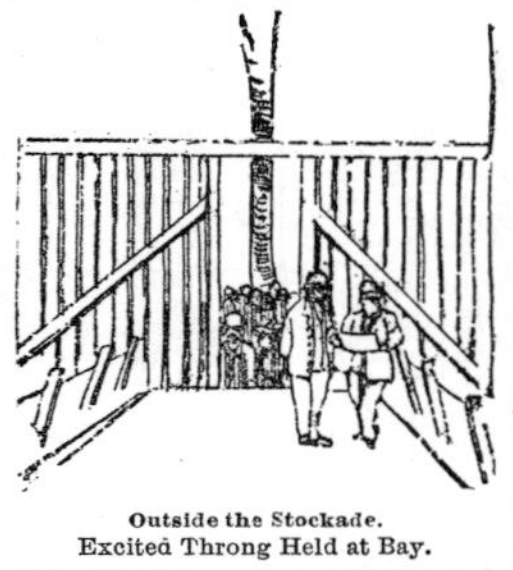

Outside the Stockade.
Excited Throng Held at Bay.

Was that a coat? A. That is a coat, yes sir, a Prince Albert coat.

Q. When you saw him was his head upon that? A. No sir.

Q. How much did he settle in your opinion? A. I cannot say that he settled at all.

Q. Have you any opinion as to the effect that these blows would have with reference to settlement on the arm of the sofa? A. I should think possibly the blows would cause the head to sink some.

Q. So that when Mr. Borden first lay down on the sofa you would judge that his head might have been about touching the Prince Albert coat? A. I would not say that.

Q. This larger cast, (pointing to one of the plaster casts) I believe, is a representation of Mr. Borden? A. Yes sir.

Q. Did you take or cause to be taken any measurement of the height of the sofa from the floor? A. Yes sir.

Q. Do you remember what it was? A. I think it was three feet one at the back.

Q. How high was the seat from the floor? A. I do not think I measured.

At this point a chair was brought into the court room, and Mr. Adams asked Dr. Dolan to measure the height of the chair at the back. He did so, and also measured the height of the seat. The chair with the cushion in it, he said, was about the same height as the sofa seat. The witness then illustrated with a plaster cast the attitude in which he found Mr. Borden on the sofa, and at the request of Mr. Adams folded a coat and placed it in the position he saw it with reference to Mr. Borden's head. Dr. Dolan moved the chair so that the distance of the chair from the wall of the court room was as near as he could remember the same distance that Mr. Borden's head was from the wall of the sitting room. He also explained the relative position of the chair in the court room to the doors in the Borden house.

MISS BORDEN LEAVING THE COURT HOUSE.
Crowd Eager to Catch a Glimpse of the Prisoner.

Dr. Dolan Being Cross-Examined.

Q. I think you told me that there were in all ten blows? A. Yes sir.

Q. And that these ten blows appeared between the line of the opening in the tril? A. Yes sir.

Q. And all upon the left side of the head? A. Yes sir.

Q. How many of these blows went through the bone of the skull? A. Four.

The witness here pointed out on the cast the line representing the cut, which was 4½ inches long.

Q. Did that penetrate into the cavity of the skull? A. No sir.

(Continued on Third Page.)

KILLED IN THE MAD RUSH.

Fatal Fire Among the New York Sweaters' Shops.

Unidentified Bodies Horribly Mangled Lying in the Street.

Others Fatally Injured in the Hospitals--Occupants Were Polish Jews.

New York, June 13.—The six story building filled with "sweaters' shops" at Nos. 10 and 12 Montgomery street, caught fire at 8 30 this morning, and in the mad rush to the street of the 250 people working there at the time, three were killed and several injured. The firemen are now searching the different floors of the burned building, and it is probable that their search will result in adding to the death list.

After the fire had been extinguished it was impossible to identify any one of the three bodies that lay horribly mangled in the street. They are those of a woman and two men.

The injured are: Gussie Augustovsky, 20 years old. She jumped from the first story fire escape. Her legs are fractured. An unknown man has scalp wounds and is so dazed that he does not know his name or what happened to him. They were sent to Governor hospital. Besides these, many others suffered slight injuries.

All the occupants of the building were Polish Jews. The fire started on the first floor of the building, it is supposed from a stove used for heating the irons.

At the nearby hospitals 12 people were treated for injuries received at the fire. It was reported at 11 o'clock that two more bodies had been found.

WEATHER INDICATIONS.

Showers.

Washington, June 13.— For Massachusetts, Rhode Island and Connecticut, fair, preceded by showers on the Massachusetts coast; north to east winds.

OPPOSED TO SUNDAY OPENING.

Ex-President Harrison Talks of the Fair and of Himself.

New York, June 13.—A special from Chicago says, speaking of the Sunday opening of the fair, ex-President Harrison said last night: "All questions in which the public is so deeply interested and which affect an enterprise like the fair should, in my opinion, be settled as quickly as possible. What I think privately about it, it seems to me that when congress made the law and gave an appropriation to the fair, that settled the question." Further than this he preferred not to say anything.

Mr. Harrison said that immediately after his visit to the fair he would go east, spending a short time in New York. He will then go to his summer home at Cape May, where he will remain two months resting and doing a little literary work. He will return to Chicago.

A friend asked the ex-president whether he would resume the practice of law. In reply he said: "I have taken a few retainers, but have not opened an office. I do not know that I shall ever have an office again."

STRUCTURE DECLARED UNSAFE.

Supervising Architect Condemns the Buch Building.

Washington, June 13.—The supervising architect, O'Rourke, of the treasury department, yesterday made an examination of the Buch building, which is occupied by the sixth auditors' office. This is the building which was declared unsafe several months ago by the clerks and on examination it was decided to relieve the floors of the heavy cast iron files of books of record and other weighty matter. During the removal all the clerks were excused. Mr. O'Rourke said that at present the building is entirely unsuited for the purpose for which it is now being used, that it is being weighted down more and more every day, and to stand the strain it would have to be strengthened greatly. "I will give the building one year to stand," continued Mr. O'Rourke. The Windew building, now occupied by the second auditor's office, will undergo a like inspection today.

SMASHED SEATS AND TABLES.

Police Charge Riotous Socialists Injuring Many of Them.

Berlin, June 13.—A mob of 200 Social Democrats broke into a hall near Elbing last evening and attacked the Conservatives, who were meeting there. The Conservatives made little resistance. Upon the advice of Herr Von Putkammer, who was conducting the meeting, they withdrew as quickly as possible, leaving the Socialists to smash seats and tables. The police were called and cleared the hall. Eventually the police charged upon the Socialists before the hall and slashed right and left until the crowd dispersed. Many rioters were injured.

Mitchell Held For the Grand Jury.

BOSTON, June 13.—William E. Mitchell, who is charged with assaulting his wife with a pistol at South Boston Sunday night, was held yesterday in the sum of $5000 for the grand jury.

Revolution is Suppressed.

New York, June 13.—The Herald's Managua, Nicaragua, correspondent cables that a revolution in Leon against the provincial government of Nicaragua has been suppressed and the leaders are now in prison.

Painters Gain Nine Hour Day.

Louisville, Ky., June 13.—Two hundred local painters struck last night for a nine-hour day with 10 hours pay. The demand was granted by nearly all contractors today.

HOME MATTERS.

PERSONAL.

Fred Tenney, catcher of the New Bedford baseball club, has arrived for the summer. He, with several of the other players, will report on Monday morning, and will begin practice that afternoon on the new field.

Special Police Officer Henry C. Russell has retained Thomas F. Desmond, Esq., as counsel at the hearing on Thursday evening.

Mr. and Mrs. Otis N. Pierce and Miss Elizabeth B. Hathaway have gone to the World's fair.

Thursday, June 15th, will be observed as Visitors' day at the Fifth Street Grammar school. All parents of the pupils and friends of education are cordially invited to be present as much of the day as they may be able to devote to this purpose. The work in drawing will be on exhibition, either in the several rooms, or in the hall on the third floor, and visitors are requested to inspect it before leaving the building. The work in sewing will be on exhibition in the hall and visitors are cordially invited to pass to the hall and inspect it without a special invitation at the time to do so.

The Bristol County association of cycle clubs met last evening in Taunton. John L. Coggeshall and Allen W. Swan of this city were in attendance.

THE STANDARD APPRECIATED.

The Standard is the only evening paper in the country to give a nearly verbatim report of the Borden trial, and the public has appreciated the effort as the following figures show:

Monday,	10,615
Tuesday,	9,275
Wednesday,	10,589
Thursday,	10,705
Friday,	11,206
Saturday,	10,777

The city newsdealers and newsboys are enthusiastic in their reports of sales, and say everybody wants the Standard. Out of town newsdealers send orders for increased numbers by every mail, while the number of subscribers was never so large before, and is constantly increasing.

Some of our contemporaries frankly acknowledge that they are using the Standard for copy and ask us to mail them extras as soon as issued. The Standard does not begrudge them, as it gives the news for the public and it is then at their service. The expense is great, but the Standard does not count expense in making a great newspaper.

FOREST FIRES.

Extensive Woodland Burning North of Tarkiln Hill Road.

Since Sunday a big forest fire has been burning in the tract north of the Tarkiln hill road and west of the railroad track. This is the land recently purchased by the new Lambeth Cordage company on which to erect their factory. The tract was covered with a good growth of oak and in preparation for building it had been cut and corded. Upwards of 600 or 700 cords were piled up awaiting transportation to this city.

The cordage company was on the point of starting work on its factory and sent a force of men to the site to burn a quantity of brush that had collected. By some carelessness the fire got beyond control and spread over the tract with lightning rapidity. The corded oak was well seasoned and burned like tinder. All fighting was of little avail, so quickly did the flames spread, and very little water was available to put it out. The force turned to, to cover a surrounding belt with dirt and thus stop the spread. It was hard to approach the burning wood, but after a hard fight the spread was stopped last night. Hancock Engine company was out during the evening, but was unable to do much on account of a lack of water.

The tract burned over embraces eight or 10 acres, and the oak wood stacked up in cords there and destroyed by the fire was about 200 cords. At an average of $3 a cord, which is claimed a fair average, the loss is not far from $600.

MONEY MARKET VERY TIGHT.

The money market has not been so close for a long time as now. But to make things easy for you just read what is going on at the White Cash store. Best Haxall flour 67c. a bag. Best St. Louis flour 57c. bag. Little Duke flour 49c. bag. Best, new June butter 25c. lb. Good, new, sweet butter 23c. lb. Fresh eggs 19c. doz. New Bermuda potatoes 39c. pk. Golden wax stringbeans 8c. lb.. Green stringbeans 6c. lb. New cabbage 3c. lb. Another lot of that canned quince, 17c. a can. Another lot of those elegant California Crawford peaches, all prepared for your table, 20c. a can. One lot of clean, package currants 9c. Great trade on white wine vinegar, 15c. gal. Long Island cucumbers 3c. apiece or 30c. doz. We have just received another lot of those fine mixed pickles for the summer trade, just right for your table or lunch basket; never sold for less than 10c. bottle, our price only 6c. Now then, kind patrons, here are dollars and cents for your own pockets and you cannot afford to be without us. White Cash Store, 134 Purchase street.

ROLL TOP DESKS

Are indispensable to business men.

F. R. Slocum's store is headquarters for these. The leading desk is of paneled oak, finished inside and out with every improvement which ingenuity can suggest. It as nearly perfect and as handsome as a desk can be. There are other styles and sizes more or less ornamental. Slocum makes a specialty of office chairs.

CONDENSED LOCALS.

William Driscoll and John Stringer recently got into a discussion over a statement that Governor Russell released two murderers on Thanksgiving day of 1891. The matter was finally left to Thomas Gardner, and a stake of $5 a side was deposited with Sidney Fisher. The referee looked into the matter and found that the prisoners were thus released and awarded the stake to Driscoll. Cigars have been plenty there since.

The 80th anniversary of the formation of the William Street Baptist church is to be celebrated on Thursday, June 22. In the afternoon there will be a session in the vestry when papers and speeches appropriate to the occasion will be read and delivered. In the evening the Rev. Dr. King of the First Baptist church of Providence will deliver an address in the church on "The Relation of Baptists to Religious Liberty."

There was never a time when there was more harmony at the armory of the City Guards than last evening, and there was no demanding of discharges that was predicted in yesterday's morning paper. The meeting was in no way different than any other company meeting, and the attempt at the disruption of the organization so much talked about failed to materialize.

The Zachariah Hillman engine company decorated graves on Sunday as follows: Zachariah Hillman, Henry Stubbs, Joseph H. Hafford, George Howland, Charles A. Gifford, Martin Murphy Joseph G. Hafford and Jethro Hilllman.

It will pay all who intend papering this season to see the fine line of paper hanging shown by Bliss & Nye. They carry the largest stock of the best selected patterns at the lowest prices in the city.

Dr. Lockhart of Boston says he uses Ayer's Hygienic Coffee in his own family and recommends it to all as a healthful drink. Grocers generally sell it.

"It takes all sorts of folks to make a world," but the Mellin's Food babies are all of one and the same sort,—healthy, happy and good.

Taunton council R. & S. masters of this city will hold its regular assembly in Masonic hall this evening. Read special notice.

Gentlemen, the finest line of Russia leather shoes found at Buchell's. See our $4 shoe.

First clambake of the season at Manhattan House Thursday, June 15.

Sir Knights of Sutton commandery are referred to special notice.

Cutter Whiskey is old, mellow and delicious.

Bake opens at 12 o'clock next Thursday at Manhattan House.

Purify your blood; Hood's Sarsaparilla.

HASN'T YOUR TIME COME TO RE-FURNISH?

Those Old Chairs are Shabby.

Your Dining Table is too Small.

A New Chamber Suite

is needed for the spare room and NEW CARPETS in parlors and hall.

Your Range is Worn Out

and should be replaced by a new one, and the new one should be one of our famous

GLENWOODS.

How About Those Draperies?

In our Drapery Department ideas are multiplied as the possibilities of each lovely fabric unfold themselves. You have long since discovered that it is a department where novelty is conspicuous, and to which it is a pleasure to turn when your mind begins to run on window decorations.

For all Your Household Needs

we will show you greater variety and make you the

LOWEST PRICES.

It will be to your advantage to deal with us.

C. F. WING,

34 to 40 Purchase Street.

WHITING & CO.

Call Especial Attention to Housekeepers, Summer Hotels, Boarding Houses, Yachts and Seashore Places.

Open today 100 pairs of 11-4 White Blankets, at $1.10 a pair.

100 pairs of 11-4 White Blankets at $1.40 per pair.

50 pairs of Red and Gray Blankets, for summer use.

200 cheap White Spreads, for summer use.

200 9-4 and 10-4 White Sheets, made of Fruit of the Loom Cotton.

200 Pillow Cases, made of Fruit of the Loom Cotton.

300 dozen Towels, of all grades, we want you to see what we sell at 12 1-2 and 25c. apiece.

500 pairs of Lace Curtains, from $1.00 to $7.50 per pair. A few odd pairs to be sold very cheap.

25 pairs of those Chenille Portieres left, we have had such large sales on, at $2.95 and $3.95 per pair. This is just half price, do not fail to see them.

100 Rugs, all sizes, for dining room, hall, parlor or chamber, all marked down to prices that will pay you to call and see what a nice rug you can get for a little money.

WHITING & CO.

J. V. SPARE,

41 Purchase St.

HOSIERY.

A fresh assortment of Children's Tan and Red Hose, at

25 CENTS PAIR.

HAMMOCKS.

A close weave Cotton Hammock, with pillow and spreader attacted,

FOR $1.37.

Hammock CHAIRS or SWINGS,

50 CENTS EACH.

Cocoa Door Mats, closely woven, with long thick nap,

ONLY 42 CENTS EACH.

Carriage Lap Dusters, Momie Cloth, PLAIN, 50c., WITH EMBROIDERY, 75c.

Lawn Cushions, Chinese Lanterns, Adjustable Window Screens, fit any window. Fly Netting, in all colors.

9 inch Fry Pans, with long handles, 10c. Agate Stove Mat, keeps food from burning, 10c. Tin Tea Kettles, 17c. Dust Pans, 10c. Lunch Baskets, with cover, 25c. Tar Camphor Balls, 5c. per box. Flower Seeds, 3c. paper.

CORSETS.

A decided bargain in Corsets. 31 doz. Drab and Fawn, made of best quality Satine Jean and extra strong stayed,

AT 39 CENTS PAIR.

UNDERWEAR,

For Ladies. A Genuine Swiss Jersey Vest, low neck and sleeveless, in Pink, Blue, Ecru or White, silk trimmed.

39 CENTS EACH.

Ladies' Jersey Vests, with high or low neck and short sleeves,

15 CENTS EACH.

For Children. A very pretty Cotton and Wool Wrapper, silk stitched, and trimmed, with pearl buttons,

25 CENTS EACH.

For Men. Light weight, Blue Mixed, shirts and drawers,

39 CENTS EACH, 75 CENTS PER SUIT.

GLOVES.

Ladies' Black and Colored Taffeta Silk Gloves,

AT 25 CENTS PAIR.

Ladies' Black and Colored Taffeta Silk Gauntlet Gloves,

50 CENTS PAIR.

J. V. Spare.

BLUE SERGE SUITS $15.00.

The Coolest and Best Fabrics for Summer Wear.

In double and single breasted sacks, made up in first class shape---color and quality guaranteed.

Gentlemen in search of neat, stylish, comfortable and inexpensive rig will find these suits just what they want for the Summer outing.

J. & W. R. WING & CO.,

Clothiers and Hatters,

133 UNION ST.

TAKEN SICK.

(Continued from First Page.)

Q. Did it cut through any of the bony formation of the head? A. Yes sir.
Q. What portion of the bony formation? A. It cut through the bone beneath the eye.
Q. Any other bone? A. Through the upper and lower jaw bones very slightly.
Q. Are the bones at this blow encountered hard and strong bones? A. No sir, they are not so hard comparatively or as strong as the skull.
Q. This portion of the skull immediately in front of the ear is not so strong as some other parts, is it? A. No sir.
Q. This 4½-inch cut bisected the eye, didn't it? A. No sir, not that one.
Q. Which one was it that cut the eye? A. (Witness pointed out the mark on the cast which represented the cut that bisected the eye.)
Q. What is the character of that cut?

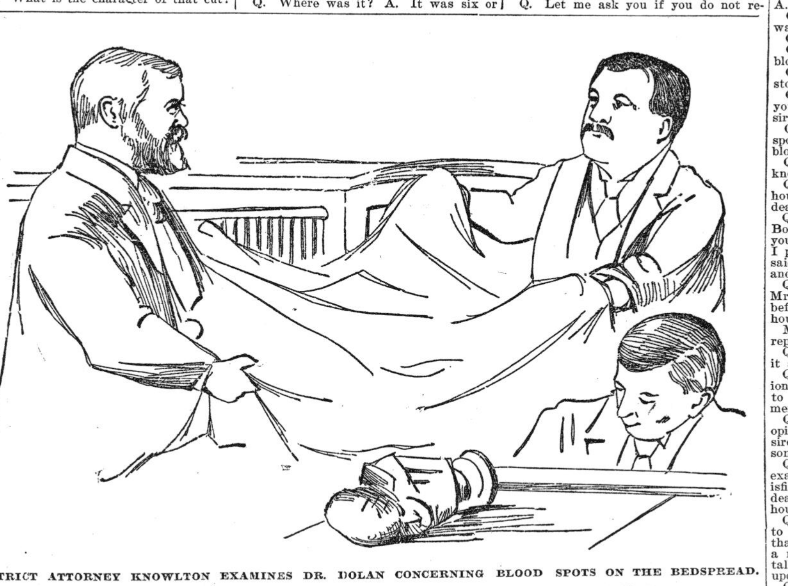

DISTRICT ATTORNEY KNOWLTON EXAMINES DR. DOLAN CONCERNING BLOOD SPOTS ON THE BEDSPREAD.
On the Table is the Plaster Cast Showing the Location of Cuts on Mr. Borden's Head.

A. Clean.
Q. Indicating what kind of an edge? A. A sharp edge.
Q. In your opinion could this claw-hammer hatchet accomplish that? A. I should like to see the hatchet.
Q. Haven't you seen it and expressed an opinion? A. Yes sir.
Q. Is this any new subject to you? A. No sir, but I didn't give any opinion with regard to the eye.
Witness answered, after examining the hatchet, that the cut through the eye could have been made by the hatchet.
The witness then illustrated to the jury the angle at which the instrument might have been held to make the different cuts on Mr. Borden's head.
Q. Was it a glancing blow that shaved off a piece of the eye ball? A. Yes sir.
Q. Have you ever seen this handleless hatchet? A. Yes sir.
Q. When did you see it? A. At the court house in Fall River.
Q. And when in the court house at Fall River? A. I cannot tell you, sir.
Q. Was it the day of the trial? A. I saw it before the trial.
Q. Before you testified? A. Yes sir.
Q. You knew about it when you testified? A. Yes sir.
Q. Were you asked any question about it? A. I do not think so.
Q. Where did it lay when you first saw it? A. In the marshal's office.
Q. Who examined it? A. Marshal Hilliard and myself.
Q. Was there a newspaper around it? A. I do not know.
Q. Was something said about this. A. I cannot tell you.
Q. When you were looking at it do you remember whether there was any conversation? A. Certainly, there was some conversation.
Q. Do you remember what it was? A. I do not.
Q. Did you see the district attorney examine it? A. I did not.
Q. Do you remember whether the district attorney was in the marshal's room when you saw the hatchet? A. I don't remember whether he was there or not.
Q. Since the day you saw the hatchet in the city marshal's room have you seen it again? A. Yes sir.
Q. When did you next see it? A. At Taunton.
Q. Did you see it between the time of the trial at Fall River and the time the grand jury met? A. I don't remember.

ELIZABETH G. JORDAN AND ANNA PAGE SCOTT OF THE N. Y. WORLD.

Q. Did you see the edge? was it a good cutting edge?
Mr. Knowlton—I object.
Q. Does it appear now as it did then? A. Yes sir.
Q. How is it as to sharpness?
Mr. Knowlton—I object.
Chief Justice—The witness may answer.
A. It has a keen, sharp edge.
Q. How did it appear when you first saw it? A. It had small particles of acid upon it.
In answer to various questions by Mr. Adams witness pointed out the relative location of the various spots of blood found in the sitting room of Mr. Borden's house.
Q. Where were the greater part of the spots? A. On the wall paper near the head of Mr. Borden. There were 86 spots within the radius of a foot.
Q. Was the picture hanging upon the wall? A. Yes sir.
Witness pointed out the relative position of the picture, by marking a spot on the wall of the court room, and in answer to further questions designated the relative positions of blood spots in the same manner.
Q. Where were the spots upon the kitchen door? A. On the right hand.
Q. How high was the spot on the jamb in feet and inches? A. Three feet and seven inches.
Q. How high was the spot on the door? A. Thirteen inches.
Q. What other objects were there in the sitting room? A. There was movable furniture.
Q. Chairs? A. Yes sir, and a mirror, table, two pictures, and there was a small center table near the sofa.
Witness pointed out the distance of the small table from the sofa.
Q. Was there something upon the small table? A. Yes sir, books.
Q. You saw no spots on the books that were upon the table? A. No sir.
Q. Was there a spot upon the ceiling? A. Yes sir.
Q. Where was it? A. It was six or seven inches from a line drawn straight upward from the head of Mr. Borden. It was practically overhead.
Q. Examine the piece of wood with a smear; did it appear on the jamb of the dining room door? A. Yes.
Q. Was it on the dining room side? A. Yes.
Q. Did you express an opinion as to the position of the assailant? A. Yes.
Q. Don't you know that the spot isn't blood? A. I have been told so.
Q. If the stringy spot is out of the way, there was no blood in the dining room? A. Not that I saw.
Q. Then you will change your statement so that there was no blood? A. Yes.
Q. Didn't you say that it was caused by the assailant of Mr. Borden standing inside the dining room door and reaching around? A. No sir.
Q. Did you observe the position of things in the dining room behind the sofa? A. Yes.
Q. Did you see any blood on the carpet behind the sofa? A. No sir.
Q. There was no blood on the jamb of the dining room door, was there? A. Yes.
Q. None only on the parlor door? A. Yes.
Q. On what part of the parlor door was there blood? A. Both on the division and panels.
Q. How high? A. Some as high as six feet.
Q. Taking all the spots in the room, from what direction did they come? A. From different ones.
Q. What was the direction of the pear ends of the spots on the parlor door? A. Down.
Q. Have you expressed an opinion where the assassin of Mr. Borden stood? A. I have.
Q. Where? A. Behind the head of the lounge, between the parlor door and the head of the lounge.
Q. You no longer locate the assassin in the dining room? A. I never have.
Q. Have you ever expressed an opinion that the assassin might have reached round from the dining room? A. I never have.
Q. How do you account for there being no spots on the small table? A. In the first place I don't think the blows were swung from that direction.
Q. Do you think they were all swung from left to right? A. To some extent.
Q. Do you think they were fairly strong blows? A. Yes.
Q. Two handed ones? A. They might have been.
Q. If the assassin using the instrument cut the neck wouldn't he have been covered with blood? A. Not necessarily.
Q. Why not? A. The blood would not necessarily come on the assailant.
Q. Wouldn't the assailant's hands be liable to get spotted? A. It is likely.
The cross-exaination was then taken up on the question of Mrs. Borden's position when she was struck, the keenness of the blows inflicted, the amount of hair she had, the thickness of the skull at the point where the wounds were found, and the spots on the pillow shams and bedspread. Nothing was elicited in this examination in addition to what was brought out in the direct.

While this part of the examination was going on Miss Borden's face was concealed in her fan.
Q. Upon the bureau and near the north window in the parlor chamber were there some blood spots on the moulding and base board? A. Yes sir.
Q. On which? A. On both.
Q. How many on the moulding? A. One, and one on the floor.
Q. Were there spots on the plastering? A. Yes sir.
Q. Were there any spots on the window glass? A. No sir.
Q. Taking into account the position of Mrs. Borden, the pillow shams and the bedspread, the spots upon the bureau and on the base board, where in your opinion did her assailant stand when these injuries were given? A. Astride the body.
Q. Astride the body and over it? A. Yes sir.
Q. How did the assailant face? A. The east wall.
Q. And these blows, you say, were generally from a left to right direction? A. Yes sir.
Q. Was the blow in the back a left to right blow? A. I cannot tell you.
Q. Let me ask you if you do not recall that you said yesterday that the assailant stood behind and faced the back of Mrs. Borden? A. Yes sir.
Q. I did not see my coat yesterday when you marked it, but was not one end of the chalk mark higher than the other? A. Yes sir.
Q. Wasn't the left hand end higher than the right hand? A. Yes sir.
Q. Doesn't that indicate to you that the blow must have been a left to right blow? A. No sir, not necessarily.
Q. Will you tell me how the assailant could have struck anything but a left to right blow? A. The blow might have been struck straight.
The witness here took the hatchet and illustrated to Mr. Adams what he meant by saying that the blow might have been delivered straight, or without being struck from right to left, and said that it would be the same whether the person struck was below the assailant or standing.
Q. Were there any physicians present when you discovered the injury in the back of Mrs. Borden? A. Dr. Draper, Dr. Leary and Dr. Cone.
Q. Any other persons? A. No sir.
Q. Were you present at any time with Dr. Dwelley? A. No sir.
Q. When these gentlemen were present with you was there any discussion as to the character of the instrument that must have caused the injury in the back? A. No sir.
Q. Wasn't there a discussion at the Oak Grove autopsy? A. As to the instrument?
Q. The kind of instrument? A. I think we said it must have been a sharp instrument.
Q. You remember that the wound appeared very deep in the center and shallow at the ends? A. Yes sir.
Q. Do you recall a discussion that the instrument must have been one having three edges or triangular in shape? A. No sir.
Q. You do not recall any such discussion? A. No sir.
Q. This was on Thursday? On Friday did you go to the house? A. I cannot tell you.
Q. Were you present there at some time during a search? A. I was.
Q. Do you remember when that was? A. Saturday.
Q. And was that when the other officers were there? A. Yes, Captain Desmond, Marshal Fleet and other officers were there at that time.
Q. Were you there on Friday? A. No sir, I do not remember.
Q. Now, you say that on Saturday a dress was given you by Mr. Jennings? A. It was.
Q. Where did he go to get it? A. He went out of the sitting room, I do not know where.
Q. Did he go down stairs? A. I cannot tell you.
Q. Was this dress given you at the time? (Witness identified the dress.)
Q. Did you express an opinion as to something you saw about the pocket? Won't you find the pocket?
Witness took the dress and showed Mr. Adams the pocket.
Q. Did you point out a place on the pocket that you said looked like blood? A. I do not know that I said it.
A five minute recess was declared at this point.

LIZZIE VISIBLY AFFECTED.

Dr. Dolan's Cold Blooded Words Bring Tears to Her Eyes.

During Dr. Dolan's recital in a cold-blooded, matter-of-fact and straightforward way of the number and character of the wounds on Mr. Borden in reply to Mr. Adams' questions he gave an opinion as to where the assailant stood when the fatal blows were struck; Lizzie was visibly affected, and the tears coursed down her cheeks, while she held her fan to her face to hide her agitation.

Juryman Hodges Ill.

At 10 20 Juryman Hodges, of Taunton, was seen to grow pale, and a deputy sheriff hastened to him with a glass of water, while Juryman Finn, who sits just at his right, fanned him vigorously. The court directed Mr. Adams to desist from his cross-examination of the witness, and after waiting a few minutes, and observing no improvement in Mr. Hodges' condition, granted the jury a recess of five minutes.

District Attorney Knowlton arose and called for Dr. Prescott, but he was not in the court room.

During the intermission Lizzie retired from the room in the company of Mr. Robinson.

The jury returned to the court room at 10 30, and Juryman Hodges had evidently recovered from his slight indisposition.

Bouquet Given the Prisoner.

Lizzie came into the room at 25 minutes of 11 with a handsome bouquet, which had been given her during her absence, and Mr. Adams resumed the cross-examination of the witness.

Cross Examination Resumed.

After the jury returned to the court room the cross-examination of Dr. Dolan was resumed.
Q. Did he bring them to you? A. Yes something upon the pocket had the appearance of blood and call the attention of Mr. Jennings and others to it? A. Yes sir.
Q. You now understand it is not blood? A. I did not really think it was blood at that time.
Q. You do not think it is blood now, do you? A. No sir, I do not.
Q. This was on Saturday? A. Yes sir.
Q. Subsequently, in the early part of the following week did you send for anything else of Miss Borden's wearing apparel? A. Yes sir.
Q. What? A. Shoes and stockings.
Q. By whom did you send? A. The marshal.
Q. Did he bring them to do? A. Yes sir.
Q. What did he bring? A. Shoes and stockings.
Q. More than one pair of shoes? A. No sir.
Q. What sort of shoes? A. Low cut shoes.
Q. Did you examine them at the time? A. Yes sir.
Q. Did you find what you thought was blood? A. Yes sir.
Q. Where abouts? A. On the soles.
Q. Did you claim at that time it was blood? A. Yes sir.
Q. Did you find anything upon the stockings? A. No sir.
Q. At the time this dress was given you did you see a white skirt? A. Yes sir.
Q. And you found upon it a pin head spot on the front which looked like blood, did you? A. Yes sir.
Q. Was it human blood? A. I don't know, it was blood.
Q. Did you say when you got to the house how long Mrs. Borden had been dead? A. Yes sir.
Q. Did you say that in your opinion Mrs. Borden died an hour and a half before you saw her? A. I don't know whether I put it that way or not; or whether I said that Mrs. Borden died an hour and a half before her husband.
Q. Did you testify at Fall River that Mrs. Borden died an hour and a half before the time you saw the body at the house? A. I don't recall it.
Mr. Adams read from the stenographic report of the hearing at Fall River.
Q. Did you say that? A. Yes sir, if it appears there I said it.
Q. Did you not state it was your opinion that Mrs. Borden died at from 10 30 to 11 o'clock? A. According to that statement I said so.
Q. Do you now desire to change your opinion? A. I do not know that I desire to change it, only to explain it in some respects.
Q. What do you now say? A. Upon examination of the two bodies I am satisfied that the difference between the deaths was from one and a half to two hours.
Q. What have you seen that has led you to this view of the matter? A. Since that time I have made the autopsies and a more complete examination, and have talked the matter over and have studied upon it.
Q. Did the coagulation of the blood have any bearing upon your forming an opinion? A. Yes sir.
Q. How soon would coagulation of the blood commence in warm weather? A. Almost immediately.
Q. Would it be safe after 15 minutes to express an opinion based upon the coagulation of the blood. A. No sir, that alone might not indicate correctly.

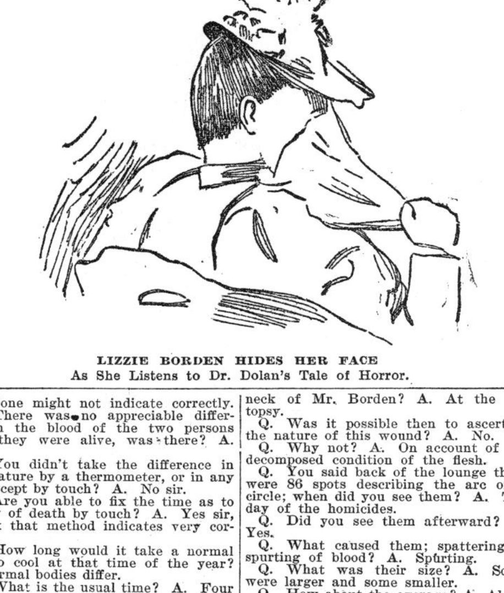

LIZZIE BORDEN HIDES HER FACE
As She Listens to Dr. Dolan's Tale of Horror.

Q. There was no appreciable difference in the blood of the two persons when they were alive, was there? A. No sir.
Q. You didn't take the difference in temperature by a thermometer, or in any way except by touch? A. No sir.
Q. Are you able to fix the time as to priority of death by touch? A. Yes sir, I think that method indicates very correctly.
Q. How long would it take a normal body to cool at that time of the year? A. Normal bodies differ.
Q. What is the usual time? A. Four hours.
Q. How long would it take the body of Mrs. Borden to cool compared with that of Mr. Borden, I mean relatively, Mrs. Borden being a woman weighing about 200 pounds? A. It would take her body longer than that of Mr. Borden.
Q. Did the difference in the state of digestion enter into your opinion? A. No sir, I knew nothing about the condition of the stomachs.
Q. All you know about the priority of death is founded on the coagulation of the blood and the temperature of the bodies? A. And the intestines, yes sir.
Q. The stomach is a very rebellious member, isn't it? A. Yes sir.
Q. Food sometimes passes out of the stomach undigested, doesn't it? A. Not out of a normal stomach.
Q. If a person is ill, this is sometimes the case? A. Yes sir.
Q. If a person had been ill you couldn't tell accurately the time of the death by the condition of the stomach? A. Not always, accurately.
Q. If a person had been sick two days before death and had vomited up food, etc., could you tell within half an hour or an hour the time of death by the condition of the stomach? A. No sir.
Q. Your opinion in regard to the priority of death is largely speculative isn't it? A. No sir; I don't think so.
Q. Assuming that one had been more ill than the other, would it affect the digestion? A. Yes.
Q. You won't fix the time of the death within half an hour? A. No.
Q. Then there is nothing left but the temperature of the body? A. No.
Q. You have spoken of the position of the assassin of Mrs. Borden as being astride her; in that position would there be a general smattering of blood? A. I don't know about a general smattering, there would be some.
Q. If the assassin stood so, where would the smatters be? A. On the lower part of the body.
Q. In reference to Mr. Borden's body, would the assassin be smattered on the top? A. Yes.

Redirect Examination.

Re-direct examination was begun by Mr. Knowlton.
Q. Did you take away any portion of Mrs. Borden's hair? A. Some of the artificial.
Q. In your testimony concerning the thickness of the hair, do you refer to the false or natural? A. To the natural.
Q. You have testified that the wounds varied in length from one quarter to four inches have you? A. Yes.
Q. Would the size give you any idea of the weapon used? A. I don't think so.
Q. If the blow was struck at an angle would that make a slash? A. Yes.
Q. Is there anything in the length of the wounds inconsistent with their having been inflicted by a weapon 3½ inches long? A. No.
Q. How could the wounds be made shorter or longer? A. By an angling blow.
Q. Where were the bodies when the skulls were removed? A. In the cemetery.
Q. They had not been interred? A. No.

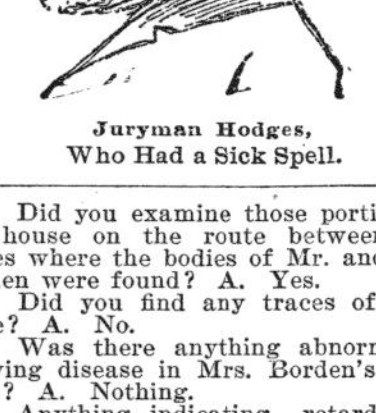

Juryman Hodges,
Who Had a Sick Spell.

Q. Did you examine those portions of the house on the route between the places where the bodies of Mr. and Mrs. Borden were found? A. Yes.
Q. Did you find any traces of blood there? A. No.
Q. Was there anything abnormal or showing disease in Mrs. Borden's intestines? A. Nothing.
Q. Anything indicating retarded digestion? A. Nothing of an abnormal nature in them.
Q. Have you said of the wounds on Mrs. Borden's body that the blows were from right to left or from left to right? A. I have not.
Q. Did you come to a determination if the blows on the body were from right to left, left to right, or vertically? A. My impression is they were mostly vertical.
Q. When did you see the blow on the neck of Mr. Borden? A. At the autopsy.
Q. Was it possible then to ascertain the nature of this wound? A. No.
Q. Why not? A. On account of the decomposed condition of the flesh.
Q. You said back of the lounge there were 86 spots describing the arc of a circle; when did you see them? A. The day of the homicides.
Q. Did you see them afterward? A. Yes.
Q. What caused them; spattering or spurting of blood? A. Spurting.
Q. What was their size? A. Some were larger and some smaller.
Q. How about the average? A. About the same.
Witness then testified concerning the size and direction of blood spots in the guest room, where the body of Mrs. Borden was found.

Annie O'Neill.

Miss Annie O'Neill, best known for her connection with William H. Crane's company, and long a protege of Joe Howard, occupied a seat behind that highly laundered correspondent all day and attracted general attention by her long, wavy hair and girlish appearance.—Boston Post.

Cross-examination.
Q. Can you fix the time that the blood spots were removed from the parlor door? A. I cannot.
Q. There was plenty of opportunity for the house to be examined before the blood spots were removed? A. Yes sir.
Q. You do not think anybody intentionally removed them do you, so as to prevent an examination being made of them? A. I do not.
Mr. Knowlton—I object to the question and answer.
The question was allowed to stand.
Q. From the appearance of the injuries having various length, like one, two, three, four and five inches, you are hardly able to determine the length of the cutting edge of the instrument are you? A. No sir.
Q. I want to ask you one question as to the structure or anatomy of the hu-

(Continued on Fourth Page.)

NEWSPAPER COMMENTS.

Lizzie Borden, if confronted by her evidence at the inquest, would apparently have difficulty in reconciling it with facts now proven by undoubted veracity. In the light of what is now known, the worst phase in Lizzie Borden's defense was this testimony given before her arrest. If it could be introduced she must go on the stand and explain it. With it excluded, she may still confidently hope that not enough proof has been introduced by the government to justify her conviction, and she may easily relieve herself of the ordeal of the witness box. Yet few people who have watched this trial, or who know the respondent, apprehend that in August, when she gave this evidence, she was frightened out of her wits, or had lost mental control. Whatever she swore to then was in general the story she meant to tell, whether true or not. If it was false, she knew it perfectly at the time; if true, why not let it go in now as part of the case? Up to this point the government has distinctly failed to convict Lizzie Borden. The opinion deepens that it will not fasten the guilt upon her. No other person is now or in any reasonable way ever has been suspected. If she is not the one, then the mystery will remain unsolved, for about the only thing that the government has tried to demonstrate is to prove, beyond reasonable doubt, that the parents could not have been murdered by any one else. The duty of the government is to prove absolutely that Lizzie Borden committed these murders, or she ought to, and will, go free. She is entitled to every legal expedient to prevent her guilt being shown, but it is unfortunate for those who would be happiest at her complete exoneration that the exclusion of any sworn statement deliberately made by her should be advantageous to her defense.—Boston Advertiser.

Although the Lizzie Borden case is yet in its early stages, it is already apparent that the prisoner stands in no danger of conviction. The web of circumstantial evidence which the state has been weaving for 10 months, has been rent in various places by the skillful cross-examination of ex-Governor Robinson. That Miss Borden appreciates the hopeful change in her condition is shown by her altered demeanor. When the trial began she assumed an air of stoical endurance, but now her apathy has disappeared and she watches the proceedings with alert interest, and seems to share the confidence of her counsel that the prosecution has done its best and failed. But as the situation of the prisoner improves, the mystery that surrounds the case deepens. If Miss Borden, who had the opportunity and a possible motive, is acquitted there is no likelihood of fastening the guilt on any one else. The state's case begins and ends with the accused in this trial, and there is no clew or suggestion to any other line of investigation than that which the authorities have already followed up and exhausted.—New London Day.

If the government's case against Miss Borden is to break down, then the question as to the identity of the murderer will become a more pressing one than ever. Who, under such circumstances, could have had either the inclination or the opportunity to commit such a crime? A double murder, and one of a woman against whom no outside enemy of Mr. Borden could have any grudge whatever. That is the most mysterious feature of the case, especially if Miss Borden's innocence should be demonstrated, as it hardly seems likely to be, absence of convincing proof being all that those who have followed the trial with a presumption in her favor appear to expect. —Providence Journal.

After a week's testimony on the part of the prosecution in the Borden murder trial, the indications are that the accused young woman will never be convicted. The defense, if the layman can judge, has much the best of the case thus far, for there has been no direct evidence fastening the atrocious crime upon the prisoner, and leading witnesses have, in several important particulars, been flatly contradictory. As the case now stands, a disagreement is the most that the government can expect, while public sentiment already clamors for an acquittal.—Woonsocket Reporter.

It must be with sorrow that the people of New Bedford have read this description, by Joe Howard, of the women who attend the trial of Lizzie Borden: "There were a few who looked like ordinary human beings, intelligent, well-informed, nicely garbed, and there for an obvious purpose, but a large majority are unkempt looking, unintelligent and exceedingly unattractive." Women who are the salt of the earth, or who decorate the land like the floral beauties of June do not become habitual attendants in court rooms.—Brockton Enterprise.

The decision of the judges in the Borden murder case not to admit the defendant's testimony as given at the coroner's inquest seems under the circumstances not only good law but common sense. It also shows that the defendant is being given one of the fairest trials known in the history of criminal jurisprudence. The effect of the decision is, of course, to render it harder for the state to prove the defendant's guilt, but the people, whose cause the district attorney represents, will be content to have it so. The commonwealth of Massachusetts seeks only the murderer. Let not the guilty one escape; but let not the innocent be punished.—Springfield Republican.

The occasion for the exhibition of all the government's ghastly trophies was the appearance on the witness' stand of Dr. Dolan, the medical examiner of Fall River, custodian of the skulls of the dead couple, performer of the autopsy, measurer of the blood spots in the house and analyst of the contents of the stomachs of the deceased couple. The doctor in private life may be a pleasant man for a ladies' tea party, but on the witness stand shows himself competent to add new horrors to the most bloody murder case in New England's history.—Julian Ralph.

Lizzie Borden has not yet been acquitted, but it certainly looks as if the Fall River police were going to be disappointed in their hunger for a "pound of flesh." That warrant for arrest, sworn out before the inquest, but not served till after the girl had given her testimony, was a stroke of forehandedness that quite overreached itself.—Worcester Spy.

The exclusion of Lizzie Borden's testimony taken at the inquest, when she was without counsel, is another important point for the defense, and relieves her lawyers of placing Lizzie upon the witness stand. If the government can show that it was justified in arresting the girl, it had better be about it.—Worcester Telegram.

ANOTHER SURPRISE COMING.

Two Girl Friends Will Testify Against Lizzie Borden.

Fall River, June 13.—That a large hole has been knocked in the bottom of the government case against Lizzie A. Borden is the opinion of a great many people in this city last night.

The failure to secure the admission of the inquest testimony is conceded to be fair and just, when judged from a legal standpoint, but it was wholly unexpected by the best known lawyers and prominent citizens. In their opinion it gave a possible cause for the murders by the prisoner that could not be shown in any other known means.

It was generally admitted by Miss Borden's friends that they had little hope that the evidence would be excluded by the present court, although some few believed that counsel might win before the supreme court.

The police of this city who have worked on the case think the government attorneys have lost a great point, and some of them last night went so far as to declare that there was now no possible chance of convicting the defendant.

Andrew J. Jennings said last evening that he had little doubt of the ultimate acquittal of his client. He did not think the trial would last longer than this week. When asked whether the defense would put on many witnesses, he said he thought it was very probable that he would put on a very few, if any.

Perhaps the hardest and most contemptible treatment accorded to any person connected with the famous trial thus far has been given Miss Alice Russell. Correspondents, manifestly knowing little or nothing about her relations with Lizzie Borden, have called Miss Russell all sorts of cowardly names, such as false friend and informer, ignoring almost wholly how this now distracted woman has suffered because of the disagreeable case.

Although she knew the things to which she testified on the stand, she did not disclose them until she consulted Lawyer Swift concerning her rights and duties in the matter before appearing the second time before the grand jury to tell all she knew.

In this connection it may be said that the prosecution has summoned two young ladies who were to have spent last summer with the prisoner, and it is said that their testimony will surprise the defense quite as much as the prosecution was surprised yesterday. Their testimony will no doubt be in regard to Miss Borden's statements as to her family relations, etc. At least two summoned witnesses are members of the same church as the prisoner.

Professional Witnesses.

Persons who have followed the evidence in the Borden case—and who has not?—cannot have failed to notice that the testimony which stands the weakest against the assault of cross-examination is that given by those who may be called professional witnesses—the police officers engaged on the case. The nonprofessionals, on the witness stand now probably for the first time in their lives, tell a straight story, as far as they have anything to tell. But the police officers, whose business takes them on the witness stand perhaps every day, tell stories which contradict each other at more points than they agree upon. Trained to acute and accurate observation, they see things in exactly opposite and conflicting relations. This is not natural or reasonable. It seems to point to the inference that the professional memory has been distorted by too much theory and the professional acuteness weakened by the strain which in this case imagination has put upon it.—Boston Post.

It is very evident to any clear-headed observer that the case of the prosecution in the Borden trial is weakening at almost every point. The decision yesterday, to exclude the star chamber testimony of the defendant, was a blow at a vital part of the government's structure of theory. Up to date, it has singularly failed to establish its claims in important points. Its witnesses have largely contradicted and discredited themselves. It has utterly failed, as thus far developed, to establish the theory of exclusive opportunity. And on this point, apparently, hinges the entire case. Without absolute exclusive opportunity, one of the most difficult of all propositions to establish, there must exist "reasonable doubt" as to the guilt of the defendant. Where there is reasonable doubt, there can be no conviction. Barring entirely unforeseen and unexpected disclosures, the verdict in the Borden trial is a foregone conclusion.—Boston Post.

The Church is All Right.

To the Editor of the Standard:

Please allow me to contradict the statement in last evening's issue of the Standard, that the "Wrangle may have the effect of breaking up the church." I wish to say that there is no trouble in the A. M. E. Bethel church of New Bedford, much less a danger of "breaking up." What may have occurred between the presiding elder and Rev. Mr. Felts at conference must be of a personal matter, as nothing was known of it here previous to Mr. Felts' departure for conference. As for classing the church as a graveyard, I think that certain people will find some very lively corpses in it if they stir us up.

PROF. T. WMS. JACKSON,
Trustee.

The Evening Standard.

NEW BEDFORD, MASS.

TUESDAY EVENING, JUNE 13.

ORDER THE EVENING STANDARD TO YOUR VACATION ADDRESS.

Mailed direct from this office for any length of time desired; 50 cents a month, including postage.

TEN PAGES.

This Evening's Issue Consists of Ten Pages, and Every Patron is Entitled to that Number.

The collapse of Ford's theater, kept full of documents and clerks long after it had been known to be insecure, is a reproach to those who might have prevented the calamity. It is said there are other unsafe buildings in Washington. Perhaps the loss of 60 lives will lead the present administration to reconsider its notions of petty economy, and to provide structures in which human life will not be in danger.

It came out at the inquest yesterday that the occupants of the old theater had been warned to go up and down stairs lightly, that the clerks were afraid to make suggestions about its dangerous condition, lest they should lose their places, and that one of them who was killed had said to another, pointing to the excavation: "Carter, they are digging your grave." The clerks stood in great fear of Ainsworth, chief of their division, and one of them said to him at the inquest, in a loud voice, "You murdered my brother, and I'd like to know what right you have to sit here and intimidate witnesses;" which was followed by shouts of approval. Ainsworth refused to withdraw when requested, and it looked at one time as though he would be mobbed. The inquest was quickly adjourned, and the clerks held an indignation meeting, at which Ainsworth was vigorously denounced.

The state dispensary, alias liquor store, at Columbia, South Carolina, is getting along swimmingly so far as the preliminaries for action are concerned. It has a big three story building close to the Capitol, and the agent has laid in 60,000 gallons of whiskey, with plenty of wine and beer, apparatus for bottling, etc., and a lot of pretty women to do the work neatly. From this headquarters the supplies are to be distributed throughout the state at the rate of $3 a bottle for common whiskey, and 15 cents for lager, as to which the Hartford Courant observes that with as good a quality of whiskey selling just across the line in Georgia at one half the price a brisk contraband jug trade seems a certainty. Some doubts are expressed as to the constitutionality of some of the provisions of the law affecting railroad companies. Nobody can buy less than half a pint of whiskey in a sealed package, not to be opened on the premises. The progress and result of this experiment will be watched with interest.

The venerable New York Journal of Commerce comes to us as the Journal of Commerce and Commercial Bulletin, the two papers having been merged in one corporation. The blanket form to which the first named adhered to the last is given up for the much more convenient octavo form of 12 pages, and with new type the sheet presents a very handsome appearance. For thirty years the Journal of Commerce has been a leading commercial paper in New York, and had a deserved reputation for fullness and correctness. The senior editor, David M. Stone, who now retires, was rather too conservative in his views to suit the more progressive and radical politicians of his day, and equally conservative in his theological views. But he was honest in his expression of them, and he deserves the good wishes of all his fellow editors. The new paper will be absolutely nonpartisan, and we doubt not that it will be as nearly a perfect commercial paper as it is possible to make it.

On September 18 will be commemorated the centennial of the laying of the corner stone of the Capitol at Washington by George Washington. The exercises, so far as they have been settled, are to include a parade, in which the president and his cabinet, the senate and house of representatives, the supreme court, Masonic orders, societies and civic organizations and detachments of the army, navy and marine corps will take part, and an opening address by President Cleveland from the spot where, 100 years ago, the first president laid the corner stone. Other orations concerning the laying of the original corner stone, the history of the construction of the Capitol, its cost and important events that have occurred within it and their effect will be delivered.

The Boston Globe is a little behind the times in remarking that "it seems somewhat surprising that some Massachusetts man or organization did not exhibit some of the old floating relics of whaling days at the World's fair, for these old whalers are full of romance and valuable history from stem to stern." Bark Progress was sent from this city to Chicago several months ago by way of the St. Lawrence river, and the papers at the time had full accounts of her and her voyage.

Ex-Congressman Poindexter Dunn denied having said on hearing of the collapse of Fords theater: "It's too bad. I wouldn't care so much if they had been pensioners instead of the poor clerks." But two persons have made affidavit that those were his exact words.

The New York Sun reporter sees a good many women of the Lizzie Borden physiognomy in this city, referring especially to the high cheek bones. But he does not seem to stand in any special fear of his life.

TAKEN SICK.

(Continued from Third Page.)

man eye; won't you tell us about that? A. There are three outside coats.

Q. How is the water held? A. In sacks.

Q. Now when you saw Mr. Borden on the day of the tragedy wasn't the left eye ball cut entirely through? A. Yes sir.

Q. Clean through these outer sections? A. Yes sir.

Q. Just as if it had been cut with a razor? A. Yes sir.

Q. Do you think that a hatchet could have made such a blow as that A. Yes sir.

DR. WOOD OF HARVARD.

The Eminent Expert Gives His Testimony.

Professor Edward S. Wood was the next witness called to the stand.

Q. Edward S. Wood is your name? A. Yes sir.

Q. And you live in Boston? A. Yes sir.

Q. At present what is your occupation? A. I am a chemist and professor of chemistry in Harvard Medical school.

Q. What was your medical education? A. It was obtained in the Harvard Medical school and the hospital.

Q. How long were you in the hospital? A. One year.

Q. Did you engage in general practice? A. No, except in the hospital.

Q. Have you given special attention to any branch of science? A. Yes, to medical chemistry.

Q. Is that also sometimes called physiological chemistry? A. Yes sir.

Q. Have you had experience in that sort of work? A. Yes sir.

Q. Have you been called upon as to that branch of science in th trial of causes? A. Yes sir.

Q. How many times? A. I have been called in several hundred cases, I think.

Q. Including capiatl cases? A. Yes sir.

Q. A large number of capital cases? A. Yes sir.

Q. You are a member of the Massachusetts Medical society? A. Yes sir.

Q. When was your attention first called to this matter? A. On the 5th of Aug. I received four preserve jars sealed and marked, one, "Milk of Aug. 3," another, "Milk of August 4th," the third, "Stomach of Andrew J. Borden," and the fourth, "Stomach of Mrs. Andrew J. Borden." The box was tied closely with strings, the strings being sealed.

Q. The seals were unbroken? A. The seals were intact when I got them.

Q. Were the labels stomach on the jars containing stomachs? A. Yes sir.

Q. And were the labels milk upon the milk? A. Yes sir. I first examined the jars containing stomachs; first the stomach of Mrs. Andrew J. Borden. The jar was opened and the stomach removed. The stomach so far as the external appearance was concerned had a perfectly normal appearance; it had not been opened, the ligatures or cords being tied at the upper end and lower end of the stomach.

Q. Surgically unopened? A. Yes sir. I cut these ligatures and opened the stomach myself shortly after I had received it, and removed the contents into separate vessels and thoroughly examined the contents of the stomach. There was no evidence of the action of any irritant whatever. The contents of the stomach was then examined and its quantity noted to be about 11 ounces. It was of somewhat solid constituency, consisting of at least four-fifths of solid food and not more than one-fifth and I should say probably not more than one-tenth of liquid or water. Upon examination of the contents of the stomach I found it to consist of partially digested starch, like wheat starch, such as would be found in any bread or cake or any food in the making of which flour starch is used. There was also a large quantity of partially digested meat, muscular fibres, with the fat, and a considerable quantity of water. And some of the pieces of bread or cake, and some of the pieces of meat were quite sizeable, pieces as large for instance as a whole pea, and some pieces were larger than that, as large as the end of my finger. So that their nature was very readily determined. In addition to this there was a large number of vegetable pulp cells, which resemble those of some sort of a pulp vegetable, or an apple or pear. And there was also the skin of a vegetable or a fruit, one piece of which I removed and have here. It looks like the red skin of an apple or pear. It came from the stomach of Mrs. Borden. I have also under preparation a piece of the skin sealed between two pieces of glass, which shows the color much more distinctly.

These were here exhibited, and the witness continued: From the appearance of the food in the stomach of Mrs. Borden and the quantity of food, it would indicate that the process of digestion had been going on for two or three hours. The stomach of Mr. Borden I removed and examined in precisely the same way, and so far as the external or internal surface is concerned there was the same result, that is, there was no evidence whatever of any diseased condition, or of the action of any irritant, so far as I could determine by inspection. The character of the food contained in the stomach of Mr. Borden differed from that in the stomach of Mrs. Borden in that there was much less of it, and that it consisted mostly of water and only a very small quantity of solid food. The quantity in the stomach was about six fluid ounces, consisting of about nine tenths of water and one tenth of solid food, which contained the same constituents in kind that were found in the stomach of Mrs. Borden, that is some starch, muscular fibres, a little oil, and a good deal of the comparatively small bulk of solid food consisting of vegetable food. I think I mentioned the quantity as about six ounces. This would indicate that the digestion, had it gone on normally in the stomach of Mr. Borden, was much farther advanced than in the case of Mrs. Borden, since nearly all of the solid food had been expelled from the stomach into the intestines, and the stomach digestion was almost completed. And it would make it, therefore, somewhere in the neighborhood of four hours, from 3½ to 4½ hours of digestion, provided it took place in the ordinary way.

Q. That stomach had not been opened? A. That stomach had not been opened; it was in the same external condition as the stomach of Mrs. Borden. The contents were immediately tested for prussic acid, because almost immediately upon being exposed to the air the acid escapes. They were tested for prussic acid with a negative result. I found no evidence of poison of any kind whatever in either case. Both jars of milk were also tested in the same way and without obtaining any evidence of any poison, either in the milk of August 3 or the milk of August 4. The milk apparently I should say was in good condition.

Q. You found nothing abnormal or irregular about the process of digestion either in the case of Mr. or Mrs. Borden? A. No sir, I did not.

Q. Now, professor, assuming that they ate breakfast at the same table and at the same time, what from the indications was the difference in the time of their deaths? A. About one and one half hours, if the process of digestion had gone on regularly.

Q. You cannot say definitely and absolutely? A. Not within half an hour one way or the other.

Q. You have heard the various witnesses and have made examinations, what do you consider important as showing the relative times of the deaths? A. The difference in the state of digestion, the condition of the intestines, and the state of coagulation of the blood.

Q. Do you desire to modify in any way the conclusions you have stated? A. No sir.

Q. Please state them again? A. They are that Mrs. Borden died one and a half hours more or less before her husband.

Q. You received something from the medical examiner? A. On the 10th day of August I received a trunk from Dr. Dolan, in which were two axes, a blue dress skirt, the hatchet that has appeared in this case as the claw-hammer hatchet, a blue dress waist, white skirt, a piece of the sitting room carpet, a piece of the bedroom carpet, a false braid or switch of hair, a lounge cover and a large envelope containing three small envelopes. In one of the small envelopes was hair taken from the head of Mrs. Andrew J. Borden; in another hair taken from the head of Andrew J. Borden, and the third was marked hair taken from a hatchet. Upon the claw-hammer hatchet several stains appeared, which from all exterior appearances might have been blood stains. They were to be seen on the handle along the edge of the hatchet and on the cutting edge. There were two oval stains, and near the edge was an accumulation of dirt. Upon the handle were several large stains, which might or might not from appearances be blood. All the stains upon the head of the hatchet were carefully tested by me. I made careful chemical tests for blood with absolutely negative results.

Mr. Wood continued. The two axes I marked. On axe A were stains which might and might not have been blood. This one also had suspicious marks, but the tests showed no blood. On the hatchet with the claw there was no blood on handle or claw.

Q. On the hatchet did you make such an examination as to be able to determine if it could be used for producing wounds and then be washed so that blood could be detected? A. Not if it was washed quickly, on account of the cavities in the handle and the roughness of the handle.

Mr. Knowlton—"Please proceed in your own way."

Mr. Wood—In the envelope marked "Hair" were two papers. One had hair an inch long, the root and point. Under the microscope it looked like a cow's hair. It was an animal's hair. The envelope had another paper, but I was unable to find any hair in it—nothing but the mucilage to which it was stuck. The one hair was all I had. If any other was put in it was lost. In the examination of the stain on the cutting edge of the hatchet it proved to be not blood.

Mr. Knowlton here exhibited the dark blue dress which has been shown in court, and inquired what was found on it.

Mr. Wood said: The dress skirt had a brown smooch near the pocket which I cut out. It might by the color have been blood, but by testing was found not to be. Another spot lower down was not blood. These were all the spots.

Q. What were they? A. I don't know, I only looked for blood. There was no blood on the waist. The white skirt contains a small spot on a line 16 inches from the plaquet hole to the bottom. This was one sixteenth of an inch in diameter and appeared to be plainer on the outside than on the inside. That spot I examined and found the globules of blood to be one 3,200-43d of an inch in diameter. It was like human blood, and could be consistently called so. Some animals have blood like human beings.

Q. What animals? A. The seal, opossum and some kinds of guinea pigs. The blood of rabbits and dogs are something like.

Q. Any other articles you examined? A. This piece of the sitting room carpet contains two large, dry pools of blood. The carpet was near the head of the sofa. The average of the blood globules is one 3,200 of an inch. This carpet was stained through, as was also this other taken from the bedroom.

Q. Did you experiment on those? A. Yes, to see if they would dry with equal rapidity. I opened an artery in the leg of a dog and allowed about an ounce of blood to flow on each. They absorbed and dried with equal facility.

Q. (By Knowlton, holding up a striped skirt.) What is this? A. That is blood, (pointing to a place.)

Q. What next? A. Then I received an envelope with gray hair marked, "Andrew J. Borden," and dark hair from Mrs. Borden, matted with blood. That was all I received at this time from Dr. Dolan.

Q. Did you examine the sitting room floor for blood? A. Yes; on the morning of August 10 I examined all in front of the sofa in a good light, and found no traces of blood there. Dr. Dolan was with me.

Q. What next? A. On August 16th I received from City Marshal Hilliard a box.

Mr. Knowlton said Marshal Hilliard has not yet been called, but he will connect him with the case.

Mr. Wood said: This pair of low ties and these stockings were in the box. The bottom of one shoe showed a stain of what might be blood, but was not. On the stockings were no suspicion of blood.

Q. What next? A. On August 30 in the court room at Fall River I received some hatchets. One has a cutting edge of 3½ inches and had what, so far as could be seen with the eye or microscope, what might have been blood.

Q. State whether in your opinion this hatchet could have been used and cleaned so that you could not tell if it had blood on it. A. Not by a quick washing.

Q. What next? A. On a piece of moulding I received August 30th I saw what I thought to be blood, but which on being tested proved not to be.

Q. What next? A. This piece of mop-board was taken from near the bureau. It has two small spots of blood which are peculiar. The pear or pointed ends are down, but show that the blow in one case came from an angle and in the other direct.

Q. You received a handleless hatchet? A. After leaving the court room after testifying at Fall River I received it on the 13th of August. The city marshal gave it to me in his office. When I received it the piece of wood that is now detached was in its place in the head. There was a fracture of the end of the handle close up to the iron, and the end of the wood was flush with the lower end of the eye. Both sides of the hatchet were uniformly rusty, and now will be observed on the cutting edge two smooth spots which were made by me when scraping off some of the rust for chemical testing. The chips which are now missing had not then been removed. Upon examination with a magnifying glass I found the break to be perfectly clean, with no dust or dirt to be observed upon it. To determine whether there was blood upon the piece of handle or not I soaked it in a preparation and then tested the solution in which it had been soaked by a chemical process, but found no blood had been derived from the handle. This soaking darkened the fractured end of the piece of wood. When I received the hatchet more white film appeared upon it than does now. By the aid of a magnifying glass a portion of the film may still be seen adherent upon it. The coating looked as if it might be ashes. I did not examine it, and it may be any white dirt so far as I can see. In Nov. 15th I testified before the grand jury, and on the evening of that day, by order of District Attorney Knowlton, I delivered it to Mr. Seaver. It was returned to me Dec. 3d. When it was returned the chips had been removed. The difference in the color between the soaked and unsoaked wood can readily be seen. The blue dress skirt and waist I delivered to Officer Mahoney by order of the district attorney, but I received them again June 3d, and since that time they have been in my possession.

Q. Did you say that the white substance upon the hatchet was adherent? A. Yes sir.

Q. What caused it to adhere? A. It is still to be seen in the crevices, and if the hatchet had been in the water it would present the appearance it does now.

Q. What did you notice in the appearance of the white film? A. It is upon both sides.

Q. Did it appear to be the sort of a covering which would result from exposure to white dust floating in the air?

Mr. Adams—I object to that question.

Q. Is it your opinion that the hatchet was used to inflict the wounds and afterwards subjected to a process to remove the trace of blood?

Mr. Adams—I pray your honors' judgment.

Q. Assuming that a hatchet had been used to inflict the wounds and afterwards subjected to a cleaning process, whether you consider it reasonable or possible for this hatchet to have been the one used?

Mr. Adams—I object.

Chief Justice—The witness may answer.

A. Yes, before the handle was broken off.

Q. Was there any difference in the way in which that handle occupied the head of that hatchet from the claw hammer hatchet you examined? A. Yes sir, it fitted very tightly.

Q. What is the nature of prussic acid with relation to its poisonous effects? A. It is one of the most deadly poisons known.

Q. And how instantaneous or otherwise is it? A. Death would be caused anywhere from a few seconds to a few minutes.

Q. What quantity would be fatal? A. Any solution of prussic acid which contains one grain of acid.

Q. Are there any other points of your investigation that I have not inquired about? A. I do not think of any.

The cross-examination was then begun by Mr. Adams.

Q. The white skirt to which your attention was called had upon it you have stated, I believe, a spot of blood nearly as large as the size of the head of a small pin? A. Yes sir, in diameter.

Q. Where was that spot? A. Sixteen inches from a line drawn from the plaquet hole of the skirt.

Q. Assume that the plaquet hole of the skirt had been worn behind, where would that bring the spot of blood? A. A little to the left of the back.

Q. When you saw it it was dry blood, and was the examination of the corpuscles of dry blood satisfactory in determining whether it was human blood or the blood of some other animal? A. If it was satisfactory at all it was.

The witness was shown two pins, and said that the spot of blood was a trifle smaller than the head of the smaller pin, which was shown to the jury.

Q. Are you able to say that that was a spot of blood which might have gotten on there from the menstural flow of the woman? A. I think it might have gotten on there so.

Q. Did you determine from the appearance of the stomachs, assuming that the two persons had eaten their meal at the same time, who had eaten the larger meal? A. I could not.

Q. All the opinions that you have given in regard to digestion have been based on the digestion being normal, have they not? A. Yes sir.

Q. And had the digestion been deferred in either of these persons that would interfere with your opinion, would it not? A. Yes, it would.

Q. I understand you are unwilling, then, to fix the limit between the times digestion stopped in the stomachs absolutely beyond an hour? A. Yes sir.

Q. So that, if one died about 11 o'clock the other, taking everything into account, might clearly have died at 10 o'clock? A. I think so, at 10 or 9 o'clock.

Q. Is there anything definite that can be determined within half an hour or so from your examination of the stomachs? A. No sir.

Q. This handleless hatchet I understand you say you first saw after you had testified at the trial at Fall River? A. Yes sir.

Q. Was it produced in court then, so far as you know? A. It was not, no sir.

Q. You saw it for the first time after you were at the marshal's office? A. Yes sir.

Q. Did he show it to you or did you see it? A. It was shown to me.

Q. Where did you see it? A. In the marshal's hands.

Q. He handed it to you? A. He gave it to me with other things.

Q. Was it done up? A. No sir.

Q. You had some talk with him at the time? A. There was some conversation about it; yes sir.

Q. When rust gathers upon any iron is it not somewhat moist when it first begins to gather? A. I do not know that it is.

Q. When rust first appears is it not a trifle damp? A. I do not think it always is.

Q. Is it not more likely to be rubbed off when it first begins than when it has been there some time? A. Yes sir.

Q. And when it first begins would dust readily adhere to it? A. I should think so.

Q. Assume that a hatchet like this handleless one fell into a pile of ashes that were lying upon the floor in a place where it was somewhat damp, would the appearance which you would see afterwards be consistent with what you saw in the appearance of this hatchet? A. Yes sir.

Q. Assume that the head of a hatchet like this lies upon a shelf in a cellar where it is somewhat damp and dust from the ashes of the furnace gathers upon it, would not the appearance you saw on this be consistent with an accumulation of dust and rust on a hatchet under these circumstances? A. In the rough places I cannot say whether dust would do that or not.

Q. Have you formed any opinion of the kind of wood the handle was made of? A. It was oak.

Q. You have never seen any piece of the handle that corresponded to this piece? A. No sir.

Q. Therefore, you do not know whether it was a hatchet having a handle? A. I know it must have had a handle, sir.

Q. I understand you have already said that the appearance of the fibres of the wood where the break is at the time you received it was like the place where it is chipped off on the side? A. Yes sir, even lighter.

Q Do you care to express an opinion as to the time that break was made? A. I cannot say how long, it might have been broken a number of months.

Q. Can you form any opinion upon seeing this piece of wood (passing witness a piece of wood) whether it was broken within six months or six years. A. I should want to know where it was kept.

Q. You would not dare to say without you knew? A. No sir, I would not dare to form any opinion.

Q. Upon reflection do you think you will stick to your opinion as to the time of the breaking of this handle being within a few months of the time you saw it? A. If kept in a dirty cellar.

Q. If kept in a fairly clean place? A. I should think it would be darker after several months.

In redirect. Q. Have you had occasion to consider the subject of the spurting or spattering of blood? A. Yes sir.

Q. What can you say of that? A. It might spurt in any direction.

Q. Then there is no rule at all? A. No sir.

Q. How about the spattering? A. It spatters in a direction varying according to the circumstances.

Q. Is there any way in which you could determine whether any surface near the wounds would receive spattering or how much? A. No sir.

Cross-examination.

Q. Assuming that the assailant stood behind Mr. Borden when he was struck, have you formed an opinion as to whether he would be spattered with blood. A. I think he must have been spattered. It would not be absolutely necessary.

Q. Do you give that opinion taking into consideration the blood spots on the wall? A. I wish to change my statement. I do not see how he could avoid being spattered from the waist up.

Q. Assuming that the assailant of Mrs. Borden stood over when she was down on the floor, and taking into account the spatters of blood, can you form an opinion as to whether her assailant would be spattered? A. I don't see how the assailant could avoid being spattered in that case.

Q. What portion of the body? A. The lower portion.

Redirect. Is there any way of determining or forming an opinion as to the number of spatters, whether there are few or many? A. No sir.

PROF. WOOD WITH THE BLOODSTAINED CARPET.

[Sketched from Life by Mr. Ashley of the Standard Staff.]

MEDICAL EXAMINER DRAPER.

Second Eminent Expert Called by Prosecution.

Dr. Draper was next called.

Q. Francis W. Draper? A. Frank W. Draper.

Q. You are by profession a physician? A. Yes sir.

Q. And where were you educated, doctor? A. In the Harvard Medical school.

Q. How long have you been in practice? A. Since 1869; about 24 years.

Q. Have you been in practice in any department of medicine specially? A. I have been in general practice.

Q. And you are also medical examiner for the city of Boston? A. I am one of those for Suffolk county.

Q. How long have you been in office? A. Since the office was created in 1877.

Q. And have of course been called upon in a great many cases? A. Yes sir.

Q. A good many cases of homicide? A. Yes sir.

Q. Have you also been called upon to examine patients and give evidence in court in relation thereto? A. Yes sir.

Q. How extensively in that department? A. I have been called several times each year in cases of homicide.

Q. You are a professor in an institution? A. Yes sir. I am professor of materia medica in Harvard college.

Q. When did you receive your first knowledge of the crime? A. When I received a dispatch summoning me to Fall River.

Q. You saw the bodies? A. Yes sir.

Q. And assisted at the autopsies? A. Yes sir.

Q. Did you make an examination of the wounds? A. Yes sir.

Q. Did you draw the marks upon the plaster cast? A. Yes sir.

In answer to questions witness described the various wounds upon the head of Mr. Borden using the maniken for illustration. His description was the same as that of Dr. Dolan.

Q. How many of the wounds penetrated the skull? A. Four.

Q. How deep was the one that went through the eye? A. I don't know. It went through the eye and went into the bone behind it.

At this time the hour of adjournment arrived.

The Prisoner's Sister Here.

Emma Borden came over from Fall River this afternoon and was driven quietly in a close carriage to the Parker House. It is said that her errand is to consult with the counsel for the defense.

Attorney-General in Town.

Attorney General Pillsbury was in the city last evening, arriving on the 6 40 train from Boston. He took tea with District Attorney Knowlton and District Attorney Moody and returned on the 9 40 train. His errand, no doubt, was to confer with them in regard to several points of the government's case.

RELEASED.

Richard Gero of this city, sentenced to the house of correction yesterday for 60 days for drunkenness, was released today by the county commissioners, on recommendation of the probation officer.

THE COGGESHALL STREET BRIDGE.

Proceedings Before the Commission at This Morning's Session.

The sitting of the commission appointed by the superior court to apportion the cost of the Coggeshall street bridge, adjourned from last week, was continued this morning in the common council chamber in City hall. The full commission was present and about 75 citizens of the various towns and cities were on hand, looking into their several interests. Counsel were present as at the previous session, and Mr. Worthington acted as chairman.

The chairman called up the question that arose at the last sitting, about the admission of testimony relative to the tax for the highway, and which later developed into a request of New Bedford and Fairhaven that the commissioners consider the poor construction of the bridge, and the consequent increased load of maintenance imposed upon these towns by reason of such poor construction, in the apportionment of the cost.

Messrs. Clifford and Reed discussed the point at length, the former urging the consideration and the latter opposing it on behalf of the county.

Chairman Worthington reviewed the matter, stating decisions, and claiming that the consideration of the construction of the bridge, whether bad or good, is not in the province of the commissioners. He therefore ruled the matter out of consideration.

Mr. Clifford asked that an exception to the ruling be recorded.

Captain Franklyn Howland was recalled, and was cross-examined by Mr. Gillingham, of Fairhaven. He stated that he has lived within half a mile of the bridge for 20 years, and does not know of any increase in land values near his house on account of the building of the bridge. There has been an increase near the bridge. Captain Howland presented the following distances, which he has prepared by actual measurement:

From Main street, Fairhaven, to Acushnet avenue across new bridge, 5,100 feet.

From Main street to Acushnet avenue across old bridge, 5,939 feet.

From corner Howland road to corner Middle street and Acushnet avenue via old bridge, 12,400 feet.

From corner Howland road to corner Middle street and Acushnet avenue via new bridge, 12,050 feet.

From Howland road to Acushnet town line, 3,569 feet.

From Howland road to old bridge, 6,460 feet.

Captain George T. Russell stated that he has been a resident of Acushnet 82 years, and has had a wide experience in real estate in that vicinity. There has been very little, if any, increase of value in real estate in Acushnet on account of the bridge, and teaming uses Acushnet avenue almost exclusively for travel into the city. In his opinion the bridge has been of no value to the town of Acushnet.

The following agreement was presented:

New Bedford, June 12, 1893.
Bridge Commissioners Hearing.

Agreement.

It is agreed that William Sanders, the county commissioner residing in New Bedford, did not act with the board in laying out the bridge and highway approaches for the reason that he lived in New Bedford; that Henry A. Slocum of Dartmouth, special county commissioner, acted in the place of Mr. Sanders, and that there was another special county commissioner residing in Attleboro, but he did not act with the board.

(Signed)
W. C. Parker for Dartmouth,
Daniel T. Devoll, for Acushnet,
Walter Clifford for New Bedford,
James L. Gillingham for Fairhaven,
Charles A. Reed for Taunton,
George C. Grimes for Fall River.

Levi Wing testified that as a citizen of Acushnet he objected to the bridge at the preliminary hearing, as he didn't think it would be any great advantage to the town and would be a great expense. Now that the bridge has been built he thinks it is of little value and that the majority of the teaming goes down by way of Acushnet avenue.

At 12 45 the hearing adjourned till 2 o'clock.

SCHOOL CENSUS.

Interesting Figures Gathered by School Committee for 1893.

The folllowing statistics are contained in the school census for 1893:

	Total.	Between 5 and 8 years.	Between 8 and 14 years.	Between 14 and 15 years.
Ward 1,	3,280	1,082	1,905	293
" 2,	784	248	421	115
" 3,	741	203	448	90
" 4,	499	139	313	47
" 5,	827	271	470	86
" 6,	3,335	1,200	1,777	358
	9,466	3,143	5,334	989

The increase for the year is 861, divided as follows: Ward 1, 398; ward 2, 57; ward 3, 43; ward 4, 10; ward 5, 37; ward 6, 316.

The following table shows the number of pupils attending public schools as compared with private schools, together with the number attending no schools.

	Attending Pub. School.	Attending Priv. School.	Attending No School.
Ward 1,	1,166	1,525	589
" 2,	475	170	139
" 3,	614	49	78
" 4,	386	47	66
" 5,	563	164	100
" 6,	1,988	723	624
	5,192	2 678	1,596

ARREST OF "DR." TRAVERS.

"Dr." Matthew Travers, who is resident at the corner of Union and First streets, was arrested today by a Newton, Mass., officer, charged with obtaining money under false pretenses, and will be taken to that city this afternoon.

FINANCIAL.

SANFORD & KELLEY.

GARDNER T. SANFORD, CHARLES S. KELLEY, } Bankers,
Members Boston Stock Exchange,
47 North Water St., New Bedford.

STOCKS AND BONDS BOUGHT AND SOLD ON COMMISSION
At the New York and Boston Stock Boards.
Local manufacturing stocks a specialty.
Outside investments of a conservative character, paying good rates of interest, on hand and for sale.
Also strictly high class investments for trust funds.
Auction Sale of Stocks and Bonds
WEDNESDAYS AND SATURDAYS, at 10 45 A. M.
ORDERS SOLICITED.

Money —TO— Loan

On watches, diamonds, clocks, jewelry and anything of value; also on pianos, organs, furniture, horses, carriages, merchandise, &c. All business confidential. I have on hand a large assortment of unredeemed pledges for sale; also one Hallett & Davis piano and one Wheeler & Wilson sewing machine; one N. E. Organ. A. L. BRALEY, successor to L. Braley, licensed pawnbroker, 99 Union st. ap20-TTStf

T. E. BOWMAN & CO.,
Topeka, Kansas,
NEGOTIATORS OF
Conservative Mortgage Loans in the Eastern Counties of the State.

WE know every security and give personal attention to every detail. Parties desiring absolute safety and satisfied with six per cent. interest paid promptly by check in their office or home, are invited to investigate our loans.

MONEY TO LOAN!

IN large or small amounts at low rates and easy terms on Real Estate, Pianos, Organs, Horses, Carriages, &c., which can remain in possession of the owners. Loans taken from 30 days to 5 years. All business strictly confidential. Office Hours 8 to 12 A. M., and 1 to 6 P. M. H. F. DAMON, 34 North Second St., (up one flight) opposite old Post Office. sep17-TTS6ptf

Dividend Notice.
OFFICE OF F. E. BELDEN MICA MINING CO., 12 Broad Street, Boston, Mass.
THE regular monthly dividend of this company will be paid June 19, to stockholders of record June 16th.
F. EUGENE BELDEN, Treas.
je6-8-10-13-15

SECOND EDITION.

HOME MATTERS.

THIRD DISTRICT COURT.
Borden, J.

Tuesday, June 13.

Maggie S. Campbell was sentenced yesterday for drunkenness to 30 days in the house of correction and appealed. This morning she withdrew her appeal and took sentence.

William W. Reynolds was defaulted for not appearing to answer to a continued case for drunkenness.

Thomas Higgins and J. William Powers, for drunkenness, were each sentenced to 10 days.

Mary Carney, for drunkenness, was sentenced to the workhouse for six months.

One case of drunkenness was placed on probation until July 29th next.

Louis Tessier pleaded guilty of being drunk yesterday. He told the court he came to this city about six weeks ago from Montreal to peddle "physicking medicine" which he manufactured, and for which he has a large number of patrons in this city and the surrounding country. He was fearful for his patrons if they did not have their regular physic, and on this account desired a continuance. The court was also a little solicitous for the health of Tessier's customers and continued his case until tomorrow on his personal recognizance.

John Lannahan pleaded not guilty of interfering with Officer Paige last night while he was making an arrest. At the request of his counsel, B. B. Barney, the case was continued until tomorrow morning.

Charles W. Johnson and George T. Cogey pleaded not guilty of the larceny of 75 cents yesterday, the property of Edward Laws. The testimony showed that these men entered Laws' shop during his temporary absence and took the money from his trunk. Both defendants took the stand and testified, and if the commonwealth case had any weak spots before they were fully strengthened by their testimony. Their stories did not agree in hardly any particular and it was evident to all that they were lying. They were each sentenced to three months in the house of correction and appealed.

At the conclusion of criminal business the inquest on the death of Maria Das Candelas was resumed by the court.

Some 12 or 15 witnesses were examined yesterday and an equal number will testify in the case today. The testimony taken touches on the case in every particular, and includes Sarmento's record from the time he returned to this country with the woman he shot.

ASSOCIATED CYCLISTS.

At the meeting of Associated Cyclists in Taunton last evening an organization was effected with the following officers:

President—Ed. Brown of Fall River.

Vice President—Allen W. Swan of New Bedford.

Secretary—George A. Closson of Taunton.

Treasurer—John L. Coggeshall of New Bedford.

The next meeting will be held on the second Monday in July.

The clubs represented in the association are wheelmen from Taunton, New Bedford, Fall River and Mansfield.

REAL ESTATE AND BUILDING.

John K. Cushing has sold to Bradford and Emerson Smith a lot of land east side of Mt. Pleasant street.

Frederick A. Sowle has sold to Michael E. Smith 48.82 rods land north side of Phillips avenue.

Phebe Harrison has sold to George G. Phillips 36 acres land in Dartmouth.

The work of putting in the foundation of the Merchants bank building has been commenced. The stones are heavy, and come from Jenney & Buffington's ledge, on the Hathaway road.

M. F. Kane, proprietor of the Manhattan House, reports such a demand for hotel accommodations, on account of the Borden trial, that he has leased Greenwood's billiard hall and fitted it with 75 cots to furnish sleeping accommodations for his numerous guests.

The yacht Alva case was resumed in the United States district court in Boston yesterday. The testimony submitted is virtually that given before the inspectors of steam vessels some time ago.

The Iron Spoon club will make a cruise down the bay on Thursday.

Good Clean Coal.
Denison Bros. Co.

MATTHEW TRAVERS' ARREST.

Wanted on a Charge of Swindling a Newton Expressman.

Inspector James D. Henthorn of the Newton police force arrested "Dr." Matthew Travers, whose operations are well known to New Bedford people, in this city this noon. Travers is wanted there on a charge of obtaining $54 from a Newton expressman named W. J. Holmes. Travers, it is charged, represented that he had just returned from the Barbadoes, and that a man named Simmons, a relative of Holmes, had died, leaving the latter a considerable fortune. He agreed that if the expressman would give him $54 to defray expenses he would proceed with the necessary legal steps to secure the fortune. Holmes paid the money, but has seen neither Travers or the fortune since. It is said that Travers is wanted in Cambridge and in several other places near Boston for similar acts. He was taken to Newton this afternoon.

NEW SCHOOLHOUSES.

There was a meeting of the city council committee on city property last evening, when every member was present. Matters of considerable importance were acted on.

It was voted to employ Samuel C. Hunt as architect for the proposed addition to the Acushnet avenue schoolhouse. The addition will front on Fourth street, and it is probable that that end of the building will be made the main entrance to the structure.

It was voted to employ Nat C. Smith as architect for the proposed new schoolhouse at the corner of Madison and Fourth streets.

It was also voted to employ C. Hammond & Son as architects for the new fire station to be erected at the corner of Acushnet avenue and Davis street at the north end of the city.

The above named buildings will be constructed of brick and stone.

Alderman Brightman and Councilman Reynolds were appointed to get prices for two lots to be used for school purposes, one to be located in the vicinity of Rivet and Dartmouth streets, and the other at Mt. Pleasant in neighborhood of Durfee street.

PERSONAL.

Among those who went to Chicago by the Hatch and Abbott excursion, which started from Boston today via. White mountains and Niagara falls, were: Mr. and Mrs. William Kirby, Miss Amy Kirby, Mr. and Mrs. Walter Myrick, Mrs. O. H. Abbott, of this city, and Mrs. Flora Fisher of Edgartown. While in Chicago the party will stop at Hotel Ingram.

Adolph Bonniol of Attleboro registered at the New York Herald bureau in Paris Monday.

NANTUCKET.

William Parsons, said to be a relative of the late Theophilus Parsons, jurist, under an aberation of mind which has developed since the recent death of his wife, attempted suicide Sunday evening by cutting his throat. While inflicting a serious wound, it is not necessarily fatal. It makes the sixth unsuccessful attempt at suicide in Nantucket within a few months.

Captain Benjamin F. Morris has just brought to Nantucket a new cat-rigged boat, 37 feet long, for use during the summer in carrying pleasure parties fishing and elsewhere. She is the largest of the mosquito fleet.

Large fares of bluefish were taken in the seines at Madaket on Monday.

A vessel arrived Sunday with 1,000 ties for the Nantucket railroad.

Owing to the inability to obtain mechanics the additions to the Sea Cliff inn cannot be completed in time for the accommodation of this season's guests. When completed the Sea Cliff is intended to be second to no hotel in the island. It will contain a large hall for dancing and dramatic entertainments.

Mrs. Mary, relict of the late Wm. C. Swain, died at her residence on Main street Sunday morning, in the 90th year of her age. She had never been sick during her entire life, until her last sickness, which terminated her life in a few weeks.

At a trial justice court on Monday evening, on complaint of Mr. C. F. Swain against Everett C. Folger, a minor, for entering his dwelling in the night time with intent to commit larceny, all the parties were present, including the visiting agent, except the boy, who was defaulted, and a warrant issued for his arrest.

MARRIED.

In Cotuit, June 7th, William F. Swift, of Bourne, to Bessie F. Lumbert, of Cotuit.

MARINE INTELLIGENCE.

Sch Beaver, from St. John for Vineyard Haven with cargo of lumber, ran ashore on Stonehorse Shoals yesterday, but was floated by wreckers from Monomy and proceeded.

Ar at New York 12th, schs Royal Arch, Wentworth, Baltimore, and sld for New Haven; Harry Prescott, Dobbin, hence; Mary A Rice, Wentworth, do; S C Tryon, Crowell, Prospect.

Sld from Perth Amboy 12th, sch Francis Goodnow, Coleman, New York.

Ar at Philadelphia 12th, schs Rose Esterbrook, Hammett, Salem; Golden Ball, Gibbs, Hyannis; B B Church, Allen, Kennebec; Anna B Mitchell, Burdick, hence. Cld, schs Marjorie. Edwards, this port; S S Thorp, Bearse, Fall River.

Cld at Baltimore 12th, sch Carrie S Hart, Southard, Allyns Point.

Ar at Norfolk 12th, sch James H Hoyt, Ellis, hence.

Ar at Newport News 12th, sch Job H Jackson, Chase, Boston.

FINANCIAL.

Stocks Sell Off—Atchison Develops into a Weak Spot—General Electric Runs Down—Money Growing Firmer—Predictions are that Tight Money will Rule During the Coming Weeks—Large Deposits of Richmond Terminal Securities—In General.

Tuesday, June 13.

The higher range to which prices had attained invited many sales to realize as well as considerable additional liquidation, thereby forcing the level down a point or two. It is gossip, however, that a downward movement cannot last long. Sentiment is bullish at present, and it is sentiment that always has and always will make Wall street values. In the general trading there is little snap or life. Prices are made constantly in many stocks during the day, but these prices do not vary more than an eighth or a quarter at a time, and hence lack the interest that fluctuations of a point or two points cause. It is rather a trader's market, with chances for profits about even on both sides of the market. As the summer season is now with us it is doubtful if trading receives added activity until the latter part of August, when we generally have a boiling market, lasting through the month of September.

Local money is in sharp demand at 6 per cent. The demand for money in this market from outside points is also heavy.

The Boston money market is very quiet again, and rates today are unchanged. On call loans are made at 5 to 6 per cent., though only private lenders are putting out money at 5 per cent. National banks in most instances are getting 7 per cent. Time money is steady. At clearing today loans were made at 7 per cent. New York funds sold at 30 and 33 cents discount.

In New York money on call is fairly active today, and the tendency is toward higher prices. Loans at 5 to 7 per cent. are common today. Time money is active and firm in this market.

Sterling is quiet and the demand for bills, now that offerings are heavy, is light.

The bond market is without new feature.

The New York market opened irregular this morning, generally a shade weaker. Leading stocks were Nashville 66½, Reading 16¼, Sugar 87¼, St. Paul 69½, Chicago Gas 71½ and General Electric 71½ to 71.

At 11 o'clock the market was dull and prices soft. General Electric 70⅝.

At noon the market was weaker. Atchison sold off to 23⅞ and 23¾. General Electric 70¾. St. Paul 69.

The following table shows the fluctuations of the leading active stocks during the forenoon:

Stocks.	Opening.	11 a. m.	12 m.
Atchison,	24½	24¼	23¾
Nashville,	66¾	66⅝	66
New England,	21	21	20⅞
Reading,	16½	16⅜	16¼
St. Paul,	69½	69⅛	69
Sugar,	87½	86⅞	87
General Electric,	71½	70⅝	70¾
Chicago Gas,	71⅝	71¾	71½

At 1 o'clock stocks were still weak. General Electric 70½, Atchison 23⅝.

The Boston market opened quiet and weak. General Electric sold off to 71, Sugar to 87¼. Atchison active at 24¼. C. B. & Q. 86⅞, and dull. Bell Telephone held 190 for two sales.

At 11 o'clock the market was steady without much activity. West End common 56.

At noon the market was barely steady. Atchison 23⅞. Sugar 87¼.

The following table shows the fluctuations of the leading active stocks during the forenoon:

Stocks.	Opening.	11 a. m.	12 m.
Atchison,	24¼	24½	23¾
C. B. & Q.,	86⅞	86⅝	86⅞
General Electric,	71	71½	70¾
Sugar,	87¼	87⅜	87¼

Sales to noon in Boston today were, bonds $51,000 and 12,100 shares of stock.

At 1 o'clock the market was dull and prices soft. Atchison 23¾, C. B. & Q. 86½ Mexican Central 7⅞.

United States treasury officials expect a demand for currency from western points for some time yet.

The London copper market continues firm without change in the general situation since last described.

Texas advices indicate an increase in the cotton crop of from 13 to 18 per cent., and it is held that these estimates are very conservative.

It is street gossip again that Villard will leave Northern Pacific at the next meeting of the directors.

Eastbound shipments of freight last week were 61,647 tons, as against 52,559 tons the previous week.

Western Union executive committee will recommend the usual dividend.

The Pullman company has practically reached the limit of its ability to supply cars. Passenger traffic is growing rapidly, and western roads expect to reach the limit of their capacity next month.

The Boston News Bureau says that during 1892 the Union Pacific purchased $500,175 stock and $264,325 bonds of the Kearney & Black Hills Railway company, covering the road from Kearney to Calloway, Neb., 65.27 miles, so that the Union Pacific now owns or holds as collateral for Wood River Improvement company notes $836,325 out of $887,000 Kearney & Black Hills first mortgage bonds, and owns $838,142 out of $931,607 capital stock. The Kearney & Black Hills was originally started as a local Nebraska enterprise, to which the Union Pacific lent its assistance, but did not until recently control. It is understood that C. B. & Q. was in negotiation for control when the Union Pacific forestalled it.

The West End Railway company has begun an extension of about two miles from Arlington to Arlington heights. The estimated cost is $60,000.

Edward Sweet & Co. say: "The gossip is meagre. The demand for currency at the west is still large. Money in consequence is stiffer here, and it is predicted it will be higher still before the week is over. On the other hand sterling continues weak, and it is announced that 95 per cent. of the Richmond Terminal securities have been deposited with Drexel, Morgan & Co."

Taintor & Holt say: "London prices are ¼ to ⅜ higher. The bears will do their best to depress the market at the opening on tight money in order to cover. We look for weakness in the morning and a rally in the afternoon."

London bought a little St. Paul this morning.

Coombs hammered the market down shortly after the opening. His views were that tight money will cause further liquidation.

STOCK AND BOND MARKETS.

Bid Prices at 12 o'clock Today.

NEW YORK, June 13.

GOVERNMENT BONDS

U. S. 2s,	98
" 4s, registered	110¾
" 4s, coupons	111
" currency 6s, 1895	102½

RAILROADS

Atchison	23⅞
Clev., Cin., Col. & St. Louis	41⅛
Chicago & Eastern Illinois pref	95
Chicago, Burlington & Quincy	86⅞
Delaware & Hudson	122
Delaware & Lackawana	141
Erie	17⅞
Illinois Central	92¾
Lake Shore	123⅜
Louisville & Nashville	66⅛
Manhattan	129½
Michigan Central	97⅜
Missouri Pacific	35⅛
New Jersey Central	109
New York Central	104½
New York & New England	21⅛
Northern Pacific pref	34⅞
Northwest	105⅝
Philadelphia & Reading	16⅛
Rock Island	72½
St. Paul	69⅛
St. Paul pref	117¾
Richmond Terminal	1⅞
St. Paul & Omaha	39⅜
Union Pacific	29½
Wabash pref	17¾

MISCELLANEOUS

Chicago Gas	71½
National Cordage	13
Ontario Silver	16
Pacific Mail	19
Pullman	171½
Sugar	87
Sugar, pref	86
Silver Certificates	*83
Western Union Telegraph	82⅞

BOSTON, June 13.

BONDS

Atchison 4s	79
Atchison 2ds	47½
Bell Telephone 7s	109
Chicago, Burlington & Northern 5s	100
C. B. & Q. Cons. Mort. 7s	116½
C. B. & Q. Conv. 5s	100
Chicago & West Michigan 5s	*94
Mexican Central 4s	58¼
Illinois Steel Co. 5s	*90

RAILROADS

Atchison	24¼
Boston & Albany	206
Boston & Lowell	186
Boston & Maine	163
Boston & Providence	250
Central Mass. pref	*52
Chicago, Burlington & Quincy	86⅞
Chicago Jun. & Un. Stk. Yds	*87¾
Chicago Jun. & Un. Stk. Yds. pref	*90
Chicago & West Michigan	29
Cleveland & Canton & Southern	*5
Cleveland, Canton & Southern pref	13½
Fitchburg	83⅜
Flint & Pere Marquette pref	58
Mexican Central	7¾
New York & New England	21
New York & New England pref	63
Old Colony	*185½
Oregon Short Line	12½
Pullman Palace Car	170
Union Pacific	29¼
Wisconsin Central	8
West End	56
West End pref	79

MINING

Butte & Boston	6⅝
Calumet & Hecla	285
Centennial	6¼
Franklin	12⅜
Kearsarge	6
Montana	21¾
Osceola	26⅜
Quincy	110
Tamarack	139

MISCELLANEOUS

American Bell Telephone	*190
Erie Telephone	45
New England Telephone	*57
Boston Land	4⅛
West End Land	*13½
Topeka Land	.25
Lamson Store Service	16½
Illinois Steel Co	*60
Sugar common	87⅞
Sugar pref	86¼
Gen'l Electric	70⅛
Westinghouse	25⅛
Bay State Gas	5½
National Lead	31

*Asked.

FALL RIVER STOCK QUOTATIONS.

The following are the quotations of Fall River stocks to-day as reported by Sanford & Kelley, bankers and brokers and stock auctioneers:

	Par.	Bid.	Asked.	Last Sale.
American Linen Co.	$100	104	106	105
Barnaby Mfg. Co.	100	—	130	—
Barnard Mfg. Co.	100	85	89	87
Border City Mfg. Co.	100	140	145	144½
Bourne Mills	100	—	160	156
Chace Mills	100	107	110	108
Cornell Mills	100	—	98	95
Crescent Mills	100	—	—	†36
C. Spring Bleachery	100	—	—	31
Davol Mills	100	92	95	96½
Edison Illuminating	100	—	—	—
Fall River Bleachery	100	—	90	78
Flint Mills	100	—	106	107
Globe Yarn Mills	100	110½	114	114
Granite Mills	100	—	120	121
Hargraves Mills	100	—	96	95
King Philip Mills	100	121	122	121
Kerr Thread Co.	100	—	—	105
Laurel Lake Mills	100	—	103	100
Massasoit Nat'l Bank	100	—	—	185
Mechanics' Mills	100	—	86	87½
Merchants' Mfg. Co.	100	—	119	114
Metacomet Mills	100	—	—	60
Metacomet National Bank	100	—	—	130
National Union Bank	100	—	—	104½
Narragansett Mills	100	—	100	100
Osborn Mills	100	—	112	111
Pocasset Mfg. Co.	100	—	118	118
Pocasset Nat'l Bank	100	—	—	—
Richard Borden Mfg.	100	102	106	102½
Robeson Mill	100	—	70	78
Sanford Spinning Co.	100	—	103	103
Sagamore Mfg. Co.	100	—	116	115
Seaconnet Mills	100	—	113	110
Shove Mills	100	—	106	105
Slade Mills	100	—	59	59
Stafford Mills	100	110	114	115
Tecumseh Mills	100	—	107	107½
Troy C. & W. Manufactory	500	—	1015	1010
Union Mfg. Co.	100	—	*187	185
Wampanoag Mills	100	—	107	107
Weetamoe Mills	100	45	47	45

†Old Stock.

PROVISIONS AND GRAIN.

Chicago, June 13.

	Wheat.	Pork.	Corn.
Opening.			
July,	65½	20.20	39
September,	69¾	—	40¾
December,	75	—	—
Twelve o'clock.			
July,	66⅜	20.20	39⅜
September,	70½	—	41¼
December,	75⅜	—	—

WEATHER INDICATIONS.
Clear and Warmer.

New York, June 13.—At 8 30 a. m. the weather was cloudy, wind east, temperature 62. The Herald says: In the Middle States and New England on Wednesday, the weather will be mostly clear and warmer, with southerly winds and an increase of actual humidity; and on Thursday fair, warmer and more sultry weather and fresh southerly winds.

FRIENDS' YEARLY MEETING.

Business Transacted at Portland Tuesday Forenoon.

Portland, June 13.—At the morning session of the Friends meeting today answers to questions addressed to the quarterly meetings were read. Elwood Giles spoke on the quarterly meeting report. The report of the auditing committee showed $4,643 receipts and $3,509 expenditures. Samuel R. Buffinton was appointed treasurer of the yearly meeting; James H. Chase treasurer of the Providence boarding school fund, and Joseph E. Briggs treasurer of the Oak Grove seminary fund.

BERTHA'S MISSING WATCH.

Report That It Was Found in a Second Hand Store Not Believed.

Fall River, June 13.—It was currently reported here last night that the police had found Bertha Manchester's missing watch in a Bowenville secondhand store, where it had been sold by the suspect Correiro. Marshal Hilliard is in New Bedford and knows nothing of the circumstances, and Assistant Marshal Fleet refuses to either affirm or deny the report. The story of the watch being found is not generally believed.

WEAVERS STRIKE.

Alleged Cut Down at Richard Borden Manufacturing Co.

Fall River, June 13.—Sixty weavers of the Richard Borden Manufacturing Co. struck work and left the mill this morning. The cause of the strike is an alleged cut down in wages from 21 to 17 cents per cut. The case has been placed with the Weavers' Protective association.

FINANCIAL CRASH.

Banks Suspend and Firms Fail in the West.

Mankato, Kan., June 13.—The bank of Burr Oak, Jewell county, closed its doors yesterday. Liabilities, $35,000; assets practically nothing. E. D. Hurlbut, one of the proprietors, has fled.

Salt Lake, Utah, June 13.—The Park City bank suspended yesterday. Liabilities $130,000. The assignee states that the depositors will receive 80 cents on the dollar.

Little Rock, Ark., June 13.—M. Pollock & Bro., the oldest clothing house in the state, assigned yesterday. Liabilities $52,000, assets $55,000.

Kansas City, June 13.—The Peoples Guarantee Savings bank assigned yesterday. Liabilities $70,000; assets between $50,000 and $60,000.

Cholera is Spreading.

Paris, June 13.—Cholera has broken out in Frontinag, department of Herault. In Cette there were three fresh cases and one death yesterday. One suspicious case is reported from Lyons. A dispatch from St. Petersburg says the authorities of Saratoff have sent out an appeal for 60 doctors and 200 assistant nurses. The cholera is spreading so rapidly the authorities say that the local physicians are unable to cope with it.

Invoice of Russian Jews Coming.

Hamburg, June 13.—The embarkation of Russian emigrants from this port to the United States being forbidden, Scharach & Co., who are the agents of several Liverpool steamship lines, have chartered the steamer Red Sea, on which they will send from Bremen to New York 800 steerage passengers, most of whom are Russian Jews.

As a whole, the house has been the most efficient body that has sat in representatives' hall for many a year. It has attended to business, has played politics with much less than customary zeal, has given less than usual cause for scandal, and has passed many useful or promising measures. Not so much can be said in praise of the senate. More than ever has it proved the graveyard of reform and more than ever has its conduct given cause for suspicion as the tool of corporations. From a partisan standpoint, as well as on grounds of justice and right, the senate is to be congratulated that it finally acquired the strength to throttle the Bay State Gas octopus and to bend it to the will of the people. Considered as a whole the legislature of 1892-93 reflects the influence of that public opinion which for several years has criticised the general court, but more particularly the house, for want of dignity, waste of time, lack of energy and absence of good sense if not of ability.—Worcester Spy.

FIELD DAY IN THE BORDEN TRIAL.

Widespread Influence of the Court's Decision Yesterday.

(Editorial in N. Y. Herald Today.)

Yesterday was a field day in the Borden trial, and the result was a substantial victory for the prisoner.

The question was whether the testimony given by Lizzie Borden at the inquest last August should now be admitted against her or excluded. Each side realized the importance of a favorable ruling and earnestly argued for it. The decision of the court was against the admission of the testimony.

The point of contention was whether the evidence had been given voluntarily or involuntarily by Miss Borden at the inquest. If the latter it could not now be produced against her, for the reason that this would be compelling her to be a witness against herself, in violation of a right guaranteed by the constitution to every accused person.

Counsel for the government argued that when Miss Borden testified at the inquest she had not been arrested or formally charged with the crime; that she had been permitted to confer with her counsel before obeying the summons as a witness and that she was free to refuse to give her evidence.

On the other hand it was maintained in her behalf that, though not formally accused, she was openly suspected and under surveillance, and though not actually arrested a warrant for her arrest was in the hands of an officer, who took her into custody as soon as she had given her testimony. In the star chamber proceeding she was not permitted to be represented by counsel and was not cautioned by the magistrate or district attorney that she need not testify to anything that might tend to incriminate her.

It must be obvious to any one having a knowledge of the facts that when she testified at the inquest she was virtually accused, virtually a prisoner and virtually an involuntary witness against herself. This is the view which Chief Justice Mason and his two colleagues take, and accordingly they hold that the evidence cannot now be legally reproduced against her. We venture to say that this exposition of the rights of the prisoner will meet the general approval of lawyers as well as the community at large.

For Miss Borden the result must prove a twofold advantage. It will keep from the jury any contradictions or damaging admissions she may have made when in the hands of secret inquisitors, and it will save her from the necessity of taking the witness stand to break the force of such testimony—a step which would subject her to a searching cross-examination, which might perhaps hurt her case more than help it.

But broader than the fate or fortune of this unfortunate woman is the general principle involved and affirmed. This affects the criminal procedure of the entire commonwealth of Massachusetts on similar points, and must influence even that of other states. It is well known to those conversant with the subject that there has been a marked tendency in criminal courts to undermine the constitutional guaranty that no accused person shall be compelled to be a witness against himself. This is shown by the various pretexts which have been sanctioned or countenanced to extort testimony from persons accused of crime—in violation of the spirit, if not the strict letter, of the constitutional guaranty.

No more forcible or timely illustration of this tendency is needed than the array of authorities cited by the government counsel yesterday in support of their contention and the apt reply of ex-Governor Robinson that it was high time that the vital questions involved be determined on principle rather than precedent. The court did this, and its decision is well calculated to have a wholesome effect and become an oft cited authority.

Law in the Borden Case.
(Editorial in New York World.)

At the time of the Borden inquest Lizzie Borden was called upon to testify. She asked to have her counsel with her, but the request was refused. The marshal stood by with a warrant ready to arrest her. The officers of the law gave her no warning of their purpose to use any testimony she might give in prosecuting her. She was not informed of her right to refuse to testify or permitted to get such information from others.

Yesterday the prosecution tried to use the testimony thus taken in prosecuting her for murder. Her counsel, ex-Governor Robinson, protested in the name of right, justice and law. He insisted that the woman had been virtually under arrest at the time of the inquest, and that her testimony was therefore not voluntary but compelled. He made a splendid plea and invoked the constitution and bill of rights for the protection of his client against the great wrong of thus compelling her to testify against herself.

When he had finished, the prosecutor, Mr. Moody, characterized his argument, as "magnificent, but not law." The court, however, decided that it was law, and excluded the testimony as that exacted of a prisoner under duress and therefore not voluntary.

Certainly all this is good common sense, square with sound ideas of right and justice. If it were not also good law there would be full occasion for Governor Robinson's fervent exclamation, "Then God save the commonwealth of Massachusetts!"

The old commonwealth has, as this trial is proving, not only just laws but model courts and remarkably able and high-minded lawyers.

Lizzie Borden's chances for acquittal seem to grow brighter with every day of the trial. Her latest and probably greatest advantage was gained yesterday, when the judge decided that her evidence at the private hearing last summer is inadmissible at the trial. The responsibility resting on the jury in this case is weighty, but unless some much clearer evidence is brought forward than has yet been produced we do not believe that any twelve men of ordinary intelligence could bring in a verdict of guilty.—Newport Herald.

Mrs. Donahue's Body Recovered.

NEWBURYPORT, Mass., June 13.—The body of Mrs. Annie Donahue, who mysteriously disappeared a few days ago, was found on the Salisbury flats, where it had been washed ashore. Medical Examiner Root of Georgetown made an examination of the body and found no marks of violence. This disposes of the murder theory. The woman undoubtedly committed suicide.

Strike of Brickmakers.

BIDDEFORD, Me., June 13.—Thirteen of the 26 men employed at Marston & Durgin's brickyard struck yesterday. They have been receiving $1.75 a day, and want $2. The firm will not accede to the demands, as they claim to have enough bricks on hand to meet all contracts.

Ate Poisoned Cheese.

PITTSBURG, June 13.—The members of the family of John Davis, seven in number, residing in Allegheny City, are suffering from some kind of poisoning believed to have been contained in some cheese purchased Saturday evening at a grocery store and eaten Sunday at dinner. All are in a fair way to recover, except Lizzie, aged 20, and Edward, aged 7, who are seriously ill.

A Serious Explosion.

MADRID, June 13.—A large petard was exploded last night on the Plaza Oriental, which is directly in front of the left wing of the palace. All the buildings in the neighborhood were shaken by the shock. The explosion was heard throughout the city and at many points in the suburbs.

Foul Play Feared.

HAVERHILL, Mass, June 13.—Horatio Maxwell of this city was found dead in Lloyd Woods, in Plaistow, by James Day. He had been dead about four days. He had been employed as a painter by M. B. Dow, the carriage manufacturer, and had been off on a spree. It is thought that he may have met foul play at one of the road houses. The coroner is investigating.

LANGUAGE OF THE HAND.

Short nails indicate combativeness.

A headline very long and slender shows utter faithlessness.

Fingers whose tips are as thick as their roots belong to the uneducated laborer and indicate a coarse, brutal organization.

The rascettes, or bracelets, indicate length of life and great happiness. One line indicates 30 years, two 60, three 90.

The line of Apollo, or fortune, begins at the mountain of the moon and runs straight up the palm to the base of the third finger.

If the headline branches toward the mount of the moon, it indicates a man who will make any sacrifice to gratify his desires.

A large lunar mount gives a melancholy tinge to the imagination. The individual will be greatly troubled about imaginary evils.

The fourth finger is consecrated to Mercury, and a prominent mount at its base indicates a love of money and skill in getting it.

The hands of George Sand, Victor Hugo, Lamartine and Walter Scott were all of moderate size, with fingers slim and conical tips.

A headline divided at the extremity, with one branch descending to the mount of the moon, is the sign of a hypocrite and deceiver.

The head or thought line begins at a point midway between the thumb and the first finger and runs almost straight across the hand.

The impulse or heart line begins near the base of the first finger and runs across the palm in a semicircle to the outside of the hand.

The psychic hand is of moderate breadth, with very long fingers, smooth and tapering, and with oval nails, the thumb long and narrow.

Large spatulated hands are more common in England than in France, and in France than in Italy, where the artistic hand predominates.

If the mount at the base of a finger is high and well formed, it intensifies the quality indicated by the finger. If low, badly formed or altogether absent, it shows that the quality is weak or lacking in the organization.—St. Louis Globe-Democrat.

THE JEWELERS' ART.

Gold and jeweled side combs are still greatly worn.

After dinner coffees of colored enamel are as lovely as jewels.

Old fashioned, long, square net purses of silver and silver gilt are carried.

Tiny leaves of enamel with pearls make the pretty circular wreath brooches.

Plain enameled sleeve buttons with incrusted edges are more and more popular.

An inkstand in lusterless silver is a large English walnut set in the heart of a walnut leaf.

Candlesticks are built out of twisted silver wire with coiled bases and rising like an engineering structure to support the bowl.

Button hooks and glove buttoners have flat handles with one edge broken. These have an enamel surface and are overlaid with silver ornaments.

An inkstand of silver gilt, evidently intended for a boudoir, has a spray of forget-menots in enamel clinging to its bowl, and poised on this is an enameled butterfly.

The after dinner coffee cups have fallen into the hands of the jewelers, who cover them with garlands and fantastic designs of silver. A set of cups are of different tints, but similarly overlaid.—Jewelers' Circular.

THRIFTY PHILADELPHIANS.

The head waiter in a Market street eating house is worth $30,000.

A car driver yearly receives $2,000 from real estate investments in the Tenth ward.

A cook in one of the city's hotels owns $60,000 in bank stock and $25,000 in real estate.

A letter carrier appointed by Postmaster Huidekoper and still doing duty is worth $20,000.

A man who serves newspapers from door to door has money at interest to the amount of $60,000.

On the city police force is a man worth $150,000, whose income is about $15,000 yearly outside of his $20 a week pay.

The sexton of one of the poorest churches in the city has a yearly income of $7,500 derived from government bonds.—Philadelphia Press.

EXPOSITION ECHOES.

Congress will spend $50,000 at the World's fair to show the progress of the colored race.

The American Bible society has arranged to distribute 250,000 copies of the New Testament at the World's fair.

The mikado of Japan will send his eldest son, Yoshi Hoti, to see the Chicago exposition. The prince is only 14 years old, but he knows how to take care of himself.

Governor Pattison appointed Mrs. E. D. Gillespie as a commissioner to collect colonial records of Pennsylvania for exhibition in the United States building at the World's fair.

The women of Des Moines will build their city in flowers at the World's fair, Dubuque's women will reproduce a mineral cave, while the women of Sioux City will contribute a replica of their last corn palace.

POWDER AND BALL.

The largest single fortification in the world is Fort Monroe. It has already cost over $3,000,000.

At a recent trial off Portsmouth the British cruiser Repulse attained a speed of 18.2 knots per hour.

A type of firearm has been invented in England by which compressed gas is utilized instead of powder as a propelling force.

FOR RENT.

FURNISHED ROOM—106 Cedar st. je13-5t

REAL ESTATE.

H. A. LEONARD, REAL ESTATE AGENT,
126 UNION STREET.
Houses and house lots in all parts of the city for sale. Three fine residences. Good bargains. Call and examine tenements to let.

Shawmut Heights Real Estate Agency,
Z. T. PIERCE, 175 Shawmut Avenue.
I HAVE some very good bargains in Farms, House Lots and Houses. INVESTIGATE.

FOR SALE—Residence of the late Charles Briggs, 175 Acushnet ave.; cottage house, 10 rooms, steam heat, set bowls, marble mantles, four fireplaces; large barn; laundry, containing set tubs, etc. All buildings in A1 order; 20 rods land. Apply on premises. my27-24t

FOR SALE.
House and Lot, 86 Walden St.,
Inquire
J. M. WILLIS, 43 Purchase St. my11-tf

VERY DESIRABLE COTTAGE HOUSE—Stable and about 4 acres land on the Old County road, north of Acushnet Village. Practically new buildings, orchard, henery, carriage house, etc. Will be sold cheap if applied for at once. May be seen at any time. Keys at Mrs. Ashley's opposite. Address, J. W. LEONARD, 59 Commercial st., Boston. ap27-tf

AUCTION SALES.

By STANDISH BOURNE,
(Successor to Geo. A. Bourne & Son,)
Auctioneer, Commission Merchant, Real Estate Dealer and Appraiser.
Cash advanced on goods consigned for auction. Ready buyer for personal property of every description.
Office and Salesrooms 47, 49 and 51 North Second Street, near the Post Office.

New and Second Hand Household Furniture.
On FRIDAY AFTERNOON, June 16th, at 2½ o'clock, at salesroom, will be sold quite a variety of new and second hand household furniture, consisting in part of chamber and parlor suits, tables, chairs, bed lounges, couches, cribs, mattresses, curtains, divans, etc., etc.; also one-half dozen second hand tapestry and ingrain carpets.

Mortgagee's Sale.
On THURSDAY, June 15th, at 3 o'clock, p. m., on the premises will be sold by order of the mortgagee, house and lot of about eight rods on the west side of Chancery street, near Hillman street. For legal advertisement see N. B. Evening Standard of May 23 and 29, and June 6 and 13.

Mortgagee's Sale.
By virtue of a power of sale contained in a mortgage deed from Mary F. Johnston and William E. Johnston to Thomas B. Tripp, dated April 3, 1885, and recorded with the Bristol County, (S. D.) Deeds Book, 112 folio, 25, 26 and 27, and for breach of this condition contained therein will be sold at public auction on the premises on THURSDAY, June 15, at 3 o'clock, p. m., the following described property, viz:
A certain tract or parcel of land with the buildings thereon standing, situated in New Bedford, in the county of Bristol, and bounded as follows: Beginning at the northeast corner of said lot in the west line of Chancery street at a stone monument in the line of land formerly sold to Mary A. Goings; thence westerly in the line of the last named land sixty-one and two-tenths (61.2) feet to land formerly of Paul Howland; thence southerly in the line of the last named land thirty-five and forty-two one hundredths (35.42) feet to land of Patience Wainrood; thence easterly in the line of the last named land sixty and thirty one hundredths (60.30) feet to Chancery street; thence northerly in the line of Chancery street to the place of beginning and containing eight (8) rods more or less and is the same premises conveyed to Atwell Taylor by Mary W. Harlow and Alonzo H. Harlow, of the State of Maine, by deed dated the 12th of January, 1836, and recorded with the Bristol County (S. D.) Land Record, book 57, pages 537, 538, to which reference may be had.
THOMAS B. TRIPP, Mortgagee.
my23-29je6-13

Desirable House and Lot.
On WEDNESDAY, June 28th, at 3 o'clock on the premises, 15 Morgan street, the 2½ story house and lot of 16 rods. The house is arranged for two families, but could be converted easily into one, has three firerooms and two bedrooms on a floor; heated with hot water, has bath and water closet, and both hot and cold water in sink. Can be viewed at any time by calling on auctioneer. A large part of the purchase money can remain on mortgage if desired.

For Rent.
A furnished house from June 1st to Oct. 1st. Location first class.
Also north half of the double house corner of Orchard and Clinton streets.
A very desirable residence, centrally located, containing all the modern conveniences. Apply to STANDISH BOURNE'S office.

To Let in Our Storage Warerooms.
We constantly have on hand first-class rooms for the storage of household goods, to be rented by the month or year.
Good dry storage room for stoves.

By JOHN B. BAYLIES,
121 and 123 Union Street,
Commission Merchant, Appraiser, and Auctioneer for the sale of Real Estate and every description of Personal Property. Furniture Bought.

H. C. HATHAWAY,
Auctioneer, Real Estate Agent and Appraiser,
Corner Acushnet Ave. and Elm St.
One of the best auction marts in the State for the sale of horses and carriages. Keeps constantly on hand carriages of every description, carriages made to order and repairing in all its branches attended to under the superintendency of J. R. Forbes. Consignments of every description solicited. Cash advanced on goods for auction. Personal property of every description bought at short notice for cash. Negotiable notes bought and sold.

Fifty Horses.
On THURSDAY, June 15th, at 10 o'clock, a. m., at mart, will be sold 50 horses adapted for general purposes, these horses were selected for this sale and will arrive from Vermont, Maine, Canada and New York state. Mr. James Chad will also be here with a car load of heavy draught, farm and drivers, from Indiana, this is an extra good chance to secure a good horse.

Furniture, Carpets, Stoves, Plants, etc.
At 2 o'clock, p. m., at salesroom will be sold a good assortment of furniture of the usual variety, consisting in part of parlor suites, chamber sets, rockers, lounges, table, chairs, etc., also carpets, oil cloths, mattresses, crockery, stoves, etc.
Also from A. P. Lawton, Newport, a large assortment of planks of all kinds and will be sold in lots to suit. je12

ALFRED WILSON,
Auctioneer and Real Estate Agent,
Room 22, - - - Robeson Building.
Houses and land in all parts of the city for sale: tenements for rent: rents collected

House Lots.
The best location in the city for homes. The land bounded by Union, Court, Tremont and Ocean streets, has been laid out in lots, and offers a rare chance to get a home in a good neighborhood. Sewers, water, and prospective electric cars to the new park makes it the most desirable to be had. Call at room 21 Robeson building and see plan.
ALFRED WILSON.

HEALEY & JENNEY,
Real Estate Brokers,
Successors to T. F. Healey.
Real estate bought and sold on commission at lowest rates.
Farms, houses, house lots and strips of every description always on hand and offered for sale on easy terms at lowest prices.
Any and all parties desiring of buying or selling will do well to call at our office, which will be open day and evening.
Office, 555 Purchase St., Cor. Franklin.
T. F. HEALEY. Telephone 28-5. N. H. JENNEY

By J. O. DOUGLASS.

REGULAR AUCTION SALE,
Thursday, June 15th, 1893, at 10 a. m.,
OF 30 horses of all grades suitable for any kind of business or any spot or place. In this lot are some very good horses, some quite speedy ones, with trotting gait and well bred from Maine. Also a lot of second-hand horses. Some very good ones sold, as the parties have changed their business. A lot of harness, top buggy, second-hand wagons, etc.

REAL ESTATE.

FRANCIS W. TAPPAN,
Agent for Purchase, Sale, and Lease of REAL ESTATE.
Office, 15 North Water St., New Bedford. d&w

FRANK C. SMITH,
BROKER & AUCTIONEER. Office, 47 William St.

M. E. SMITH,
REAL ESTATE BROKER,
Real Estate bought, sold, mortgaged or auctioned. Facilities unsurpassed. Call at
M. E. SMITH'S, REAL ESTATE EXCHANGE.
619 Purchase Street. Telephone 16-11.

The Industrial Co-operative Association
Requests the public and members to know that besides the
FULL LINE OF GROCERIES,
THEY CARRY
A Large Assortment of Tin and Woodenware,
INCLUDING
WINDOW BRUSHES AND SCREENS,
For which they would be pleased to take your order.
mh29-TFS6p TELEPHONE 32-2.

AMUSEMENTS.

SECOND DEMOREST
Prize Medal Contest in Declamation
—IN—
Y. M. C. A. HALL,
Tuesday Evening, June 13th,
At 8 O'clock.

Music by Y. M. C. A. Orchestra.
Xylophone solos.
Singing by High School Quartet.
Trip to the World's Fair by a crayon artist.
Rev. J. S. Swaim will preside.

ADMISSION......................15 CENTS.
je12-2t

NINTH ANNUAL RECITAL
BY PUPILS OF
Miss Mary Otheman's Violin School,
ASSISTED BY
Mr. Wulf Fries, Violoncellist,
At Y. M. C. A. HALL,
Thursday Evening, June 15th,
At 7 45 O'clock.

A limited number of tickets at 25 cents each for sale at B. Otheman's, Room 1, 52 Pleasant street, Bates & Kirby's new block, and at the hall the evening of the entertainment. je10-13-15

ENTERTAINMENT DIRECTORY.

TUESDAY.

Y. M. C. A. Hall—Demorest Medal Contest.

FUTURE EVENTS.

Y. M. C. A. Hall—15th, Miss Otheman's pupils recital.

AMUSEMENTS.

The annual recital of the pupils of Miss Otheman's violin school will be held in Y. M. C. A. hall Thursday evening. The event is one that is always looked forward to with pleasure.

The second Demorest prize medal declamation contest will be held in Y. M. C. A. Hall this evening. Rev. J. S. Swaim will preside and aside from declamation there will be music by the Y. M. C. A. orchestra, the High school quartet, xylophone solos and a crayon lecture on the World's Fair. The entertainment cannot fail to be interesting and the low rate of admission should call a big attendance.

BERT POOLE'S CHALK TALK.

Bert Poole, staff artist for the Boston Globe, demonstrated last evening that he could make a chalk talk entertaining, a thing which few chalk talkers can do. Mr. Poole caught the audience in the selection of his subjects. He started out by representing a water vase used by the primitive races and ended up with a colored crayon picture of an abandoned whaler in mid-ocean. His most interesting sketches were on the Borden trial. Without any attempt at portraiture, he made some pictures of humorous incidents of the trial which were highly relished. He struck off a few rough sketches of New Bedford scenery as well. The audience was small, so much so that the talk was given in the parlors in the Y. M. C. A. building and not in the large hall.

Cape Cod Yacht Club.

Orleans, June 13.—The first of the Cape Cod Yacht club's series of bay races was held Saturday in a good breeze. Summary:

First Class.

Name and owner.	Water line. ft.in	Elapsed time. h.m.s.	Corrected time. h.m.s.
Eclipse, H. H. Sears,	25 04	2 44 05	2 06 03
Nobscussett, L. Hall,	24 06	2 42 42	2 03 32
City of Chicago, I. F. Crosby,	25 05	2 37 03	1 59 07
Addie, R. H. Nickerson,	25 00	2 27 03	1 48 34
Second Class.			
Iris,	17 09	3 34 47	2 44 23
Attempt, R. H. Shiverick,	18 05	3 11 24	2 22 20

Disgusted Cyclists.

MANASQUAN, N. J., June 13.—Thomas A. Zimmerman, the father of the crack bicycle rider, received a cablegram yesterday announcing that the champion rider would leave England for this country on Saturday. Walter Sanger, the champion Milwaukee rider, who is in England with Zimmerman, leaves on the same steamer. Both leave because the English bicyclists refused them a license to enter races as amateurs.

An Italian Spy Arrested.

NICE, June 13.—Arthur Cipriani, a relative of the notorious socialist of the same name, was arrested as a spy in this city yesterday. He had been surveying the roads on the Italian frontier, and his work was almost completed when he was taken into custody. In his baggage were found plans of several French forts on the Italian frontier. These he acknowledged were intended for the use of the Italian government.

Sues Her Father-in-Law.

PITTSBURG, June 13.—Mrs. Eva Buffun, wife of Dr. Frank Buffun, having won the first round before the grand jury in the litigation between herself and her husband and father-in-law yesterday, followed up her victory by entering suit to recover $10,000 from her father-in-law, J. C. Buffun, for false imprisonment and arrest.

Decided to Go Out of Business.

STAMFORD, Conn., June 13.—T. B. Smart & Co., straw hat makers, employing 300 persons, announced yesterday their intention of going out of business this week. The illness of Mr. Smart is the principal reason for this action, there being no financial difficulty. The firm will try to lease the factory to another firm before autumn.

Attacked by an Elephant.

BOSTON, June 13.—Edwin Goss, employed by Barnum & Bailey's circus, met with a bad accident yesterday morning. One of the large elephants broke loose and knocked Goss over with his trunk and stepped upon him. Goss was rescued by one of the keepers and is now at the City hospital.

Body Recovered After Many Days.

MONTPELIER, Vt., June 13.—The body of Robert, a young son of C. A. Best, drowned last March, was found near Middlesex Village yesterday.

Brief Mention.

Mary Shaw, a servant employed in the family of Ellis Hollingsworth at South Braintree, Mass., disappeared Saturday night, and yesterday her body was found in a pond back of the house. It was clearly a case of suicide, and she is supposed to have been deranged.

A runaway horse in Seymour, Conn., dashed upon three children who were playing on some steps. All of the children were injured, and one of them is in a critical condition.

The body of Patrick Burns, who disappeared from Portland, Me., last winter, was found floating in the harbor at that place. He was 45 years old and leaves a daughter.

The report circulated throughout Vermont that Asa Harrington and wife of Barre had been suffocated in a Chicago hotel is false.

Charles S. Lake of Chelsea, Mass., charged with murdering Henry Kennison, was discharged for lack of evidence.

James Fitzgibbon was held in $16,000 bail at Boston for indecent assault upon Mary Doherty, a child of 7 years.

IN SECOND PLACE.

Stivetts Puzzled Pittsburg and Boston Won by Good Batting and Fielding.

BOSTON, June 13.—The game yesterday was an interesting one, yet the Pittsburgs found Stivetts an enigma, while Ehret was batted freely. The fielding was good until the latter part of the game, when both teams weakened somewhat. Long, Duffy and Donovan hit the ball in great shape, and the fielding of the two former players, with that of Stivetts, Shugart and Lyons, was fine. Duffy caught Ehret at the home plate on a great throw from center field. The umpiring was good.

BOSTON.	AB	R	BH	TB	PO	A	E
Long, ss	4	2	3	3	4	3	0
Carroll, rf	3	0	1	1	2	0	1
Duffy, cf	5	1	3	6	0	1	0
McCarthy, lf	5	1	1	2	0	0	0
Nash, 3b	4	1	1	1	0	3	0
Tucker, 1b	3	1	1	3	12	0	0
Lowe, 2b	2	0	1	3	1	4	2
Ganzel, c	3	0	0	0	6	0	0
Stivetts, p	4	1	1	1	0	4	0
Totals	33	7	12	19	27	15	3

PITTSBURG.	AB	R	BH	TB	PO	A	E
Donovan, rf	5	1	2	2	1	0	0
Van Haltren, cf	4	0	0	0	1	0	0
Shugart, ss	4	1	1	4	2	3	0
Smith, lf	3	0	0	0	3	0	2
D. Lyons, 3b	4	0	1	1	0	3	0
Bierbauer, 2b	3	1	0	0	2	1	0
Beckley, 1b	3	1	1	4	12	0	0
Miller, c	3	0	0	0	3	0	1
Ehret, p	3	0	0	0	0	5	1
Totals	32	4	5	11	24	12	4

Boston.......... 0 0 2 0 0 0 4 1 —7
Pittsburg....... 0 0 0 0 1 0 0 2 1—4

Earned runs—Boston, 3; Pittsburg, 3. Home runs—Duffy, Shugart, Beckley. Three-base hits—Tucker, Lowe. Sacrifice hits—Lowe, Carroll, Long, Miller. Stolen bases—Long, Smith, Beckley, Donovan. First base on balls—Boston, 3. Pittsburg, 3. First base on errors—Boston, 1; Pittsburg, 3. Hit by pitched ball—Tucker. Struck out—Nash, Shugart, D. Lyons, Beckley. Umpire—McQuaid.

Other Games.

At Washington:

Washington........ 2 0 2 0 0 2 0 0 1—7
Chicago........... 0 1 0 4 0 0 0 1 0—6

Base hits—Washington, 10; Chicago, 7; Errors—Washington, 2; Chicago, 2. Batteries—Kost and Schriver; Maul and Farrell.

At New York:

New York.......... 0 0 1 3 2 1 4 2 —13
Louisville........ 0 0 0 0 0 1 2 0 0—3

Base hits—New York, 14; Louisville, 5. Errors—New York, 1; Louisville, 7. Batteries—Harrington and Manning; Baldwin and McMahon.

At Brooklyn:

Brooklyn.......... 0 7 0 0 0 0 0 5 2—14
Cincinnati........ 3 0 1 2 0 0 5 0 2—13

Base hits—Brooklyn, 15; Cincinnati, 12. Errors—Brooklyn, 4; Cincinnati, 1. Batteries—Murphy, Sullivan and Mullane; Haddock, Kennedy and Kinslow.

At Baltimore:

Cleveland......... 4 0 0 1 4 0 1 0 3—13
Baltimore......... 4 0 1 0 0 5 0 0 2—12

Base hits—Cleveland, 14; Baltimore, 19. Errors—Cleveland, 4; Baltimore, 2. Batteries—Cuppy, Young and O'Conner; McMahon and Robinson.

At Philadelphia:

St. Louis......... 0 0 0 3 0 0 0 0 0—3
Philadelphia...... 1 0 0 0 0 0 0 0 1—2

Base hits—St. Louis, 6; Philadelphia, 3. Errors—St. Louis, 2. Batteries—Breitenstein and Gunsol; Vickery and Clements.

New England League.

At Lewiston—Lewiston, 7; Fall River, 2.
At Dover—Lowell, 10; Dover, 9.
At Portland—Portland, 13; Brockton, 11.

Eastern League Games.

At Buffalo—Buffalo, 9, Providence, 8.

National League Standing.

Clubs	Won	Lost	Avg	Clubs	Won	Lost	Avg
Brooklyn..	23	14	62.2	New York.	20	18	52.6
Boston....	24	15	61.5	Wash......	18	19	48.6
Pittsburg..	22	15	59.5	St. Louis..	15	20	42.9
Phila.....	21	15	58.3	Cincinnati	16	22	42.1
Cleveland.	17	14	54.8	Chicago....	15	21	41.7
Baltimore.	20	18	52.6	Louisville.	4	24	14.3

New England League Standing.

Clubs	Won	Lost	Avg	Clubs	Won	Lost	Avg
Fall River.	19	9	67.8	Lowell.....	11	16	40.7
Lewiston..	20	10	66.6	Dover.....	9	19	32.1
Portland...	16	11	59.2	Brockton..	7	17	29.1

A Cup Defender Launched.

PHILADELPHIA, June 13.—The Pilgrim, the Boston syndicate cup defender of Stewart & Binney design, was launched from the yard of Pusey & Jones yesterday morning at Wilmington, Del. There were 500 spectators present. The vessel was christened by Mrs. G. E. Bullard of Boston. The new yacht left under tow for Brooklyn yesterday afternoon, where she will have her fin put on at the Erie basin dock, thence she will go to Boston to be rigged. She floats splendidly.

Land Purchase Rumors.

NEW YORK, June 13.—The report is again revived that John D. Rockefeller is the purchaser of the site of St. Luke's hospital on Fifth avenue, recently sold for nearly $2,500,000. Mr. Rockefeller is amply able to make so large a purchase by himself, but according to some, Mr. Flagler, likewise of the Standard Oil company, is associated with him in the deal. With Mr. Rockefeller out of town it is impossible to confirm or deny the story.

The Graves' Case Continued.

DENVER, June 13.—The case of Dr. Graves came up yesterday on the motion for a continuance to September. District Attorney Steele filed an application, in which he stated that $3000 is ample to cover the expense of securing the attendance of the witnesses in the case who live beyond the borders of the state. On this showing the motion for continuance was granted. Dr. Graves remains out on bail until that time.

Lassell's Commencement.

NEWTON, Mass., June 13.—There was no talk of unlucky numbers at Lassell last evening, although the graduating class numbered 13. The commencement week was ushered in by the seniors of the seminary with the annual observance of class day, or class night, as the program announced, and the 13 bright and pretty maidens of the senior class took possession of the seminary, and during the evening held sovereign sway.

The Machias Arrives at Bath.

BATH, Me., June 13.—At 4:30 yesterday afternoon the ringing of the city bells announced the appearance of the gunboat Machias returning from her triumphal trial trip. Having passed the front of the city, she returned to the Bath iron works wharf, where General Hyde held an informal quarter-deck reception with many citizens, who crowded on board to congratulate him. The Castine will be tried next month.

Italian Warships Coming.

ROME, June 13.—Three Italian warships will sail for New York on June 22 to make a friendly demonstration. The new battleship Re Umbarto will sail for New York in July.

Quarryman Killed.

PORTLAND, Conn., June 13. — Daniel Hickey, aged 65 years, was killed yesterday by a falling rock in the Shaler & Hall quarry.

Destruction of a Sawmill.

BELLEVILLE, Ont., June 13.—Holton's sawmill was struck by lightning yesterday and totally destroyed. Loss $10,000.

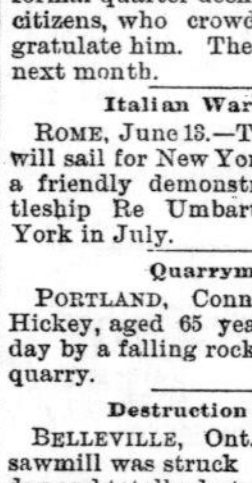

HAS WORKED ITS WAY

Into nearly every house.

DR. HOUGH'S
COUGH AND LUNG BALSAM.

The best remedy for Coughs and Colds. Price 35 cents. Sold by all druggists and medicine dealers.

NOTE AND COMMENT.

THE OHIO REPUBLICANS have done their full duty in renominating Governor McKinley. Now if the Democrats will make the issue a square one let them nominate some well known "tariff reformer" like Frank Hurd and we shall see whether the Buckeye state is for protection or against it. Just for a guess we desire to say that in that event McKinley will be triumphantly re-elected.

CHICAGO NARROWLY ESCAPED offending the charming infanta. The populace crossed the carpet stretched under the canopy in front of Mrs. Potter Palmer's residence and left mud on the same. The infanta had to walk on this carpet, and she was mad; apparently, clear through. What a terrible thing it was for an American citizen to step upon a carpet that the royal visitor was to tread. If the dear infanta cannot conceal her vexation she should go back to Spain. We don't believe, however, that a little contact with American soil would injure her.

WHAT OTHERS ARE SAYING.

It turns out that one mugwump does not want an office. Moses Williams takes the trouble to say that he does not desire it; it may be that there is none to give him for are not the Democrats down on millionaires?—[Taunton Gazette.

If reports can be relied upon, the world's fair is not going to deplete the country boarding places to any great extent. City people who go the fair will need more than ever the country sojourn for rest and recuperation. [Haverhill Bulletin.

Let McKinley be relected governor of Ohio by a rousing majority, and our manufacturers would take heart of grace that another democratic administration might be impossible. But even with that we might look forward to the dullest time our manufacturing centers have known since 1857.—[Lowell Courier.

As Minister Blount hedges on the Hawaiian question until he occupies the same ground and advocates the same policy as did ex-Minister Stevens, it will be interesting to watch the scramble of the mugwump and democratic papers in their efforts to follow him and not make fools of themselves.—[Lawrence American.

A Washington dispatch says the president and his cabinet have finally decided to adopt a waiting policy. This is indeed a bold and radical decision. After doing absolutely nothing for three months, they have now concluded to wait. After having thought they were thinking for 90 days, they now think they will stop and consider. This is statesmanship.—[Concord Monitor.

Now it is the sugar and rice planters of Louisiana who demand the protection which the Democratic party has declared unconstitutional. They are preparing statistics for the information of congress, and Representative Blanchard (Dem.) has pledged them his aid. Instead of sending their statistics to congress the planters should send them to Messrs. Cleveland, Carlisle & Co., who are constructing the administration tariff bill in secret session. —[N. Y. Press.

ANYTHING AND EVERYTHING.

Rapid growth of the finger nails is considered to indicate good health.

The world contains about 7,000,000 Hebrews, about 3,400,000 of whom dwell in Russia and 1,700,000 in Austria.

The shark manifests a distinct liking for certain races, and will eat an Asiatic in preference to a negro and a European rather than either.

The New England states have more savings bank depositors and deposits than all the rest of the country leaving out the state of New York.

The largest private yacht afloat is young Mr. Laycock's Valhalla, lately built upon the Clyde. She is about 1700 tons, is built of steel, and will be shiprigged with an auxiliary crew.

The tomb of Noah is supposed to lie in the small town of Naktchhevan, on the plain of Ararat. The burial place is at the side of the broken walls of an abandoned fortress in the midst of a vast plain, which is literally covered with the remains of bygone glories.

Insects do not breathe through the nose and mouth. Down the body run two main pipes. These pipes send out branches to right and left like a network, extending to the extremities of the body, even to the ends of the antenne and to the claws. Each main tube receives the external air through 9 or 10 spiracles or breathing holes, placed at intervals along the sides of the body. The spiracles are made water tight and dust tight by a strong fringe of hair, which completely guards the entrance.

PERSONAL.

John W. Alexander, the American portrait painter, has just been elected an associate of the Champ de Mars Salon, on his first exhibit. Mr. Alexander has now returned to New York from Paris, where his pictures have been received with much commendation. Several of them obtained high distinction at the last Salon.

Ex-Senator Wade Hampton, now United States Railroad commissioner, is in San Francisco, whither he has gone on a journey of inspection of the Pacific roads. He has with him a party of about a dozen people, including his two daughters. He will go from San Francisco to Tacoma, and from there begin an examination eastward of the northern Pacific.

M. Francisque Sarcey, the celebrated Parasian dramatic critic and chronicler, it is said, is thinking of trying his luck again as a lecturer on the French dramatic art in London during the performances of the Comedie Francaise at Drury Lane. M. Sarcey, it will be remembered, lectured on a similar occasion at the Gaiety theater during the previous visit of the company London.

Edward Greig, the Norwegian composer, is too ill to go to England to receive the honorary degree of doctor of music at Cambridge, and consequently the compliment intended for him will have to be postponed. Saint Saens, Tschaikowsky, Boito and Bruch are expected, however, and all four will receive the degree of Mus. Doc. next week, when they will take part at Cambridge in a concert of their own compositions.

WHAT A POWER for good a great newspaper may be in a practical way is illustrated by the New York Herald when it devotes its efforts to furnishing ice for the poor of that great city. Last year through this dispensary over 1600 families were supplied with free ice who otherwise would have been obliged to do without. Charitable people everywhere can do no better than contribute to some such a fund.

[From Yesterday's Extra Edition.]

BLOODSTAINED.

The following is Medical Examiner Dolan's testimony late yesterday afternoon, printed in the Standard's extra edition:

Q. Do you remember what you said on the markers?A. Sample of milk, August 3. Sample of milk, August 4.

Q. Are these the marks you put on the milk? (Witness here identified the labels.)

Q. You also sealed them? A. Yes sir.

Q. Then what did you do doctor? A. I think then I went with the officers over the lower floor and into the cellar.

Q. Did you take notice of anything on the lower floor or in the cellar? A. In the cellar I saw some axes and hatchets.

Q. How many axes and how many hatchets? A. I think there were two axes and two hatchets.

Q. Did you do anything with them? A. I took one of them upstairs.

Q. Did you make at that time any examination of either of them? A. I did.

Q. Who had the hatchet that you looked at? A. I think Officer Mullaly handed me the hatchet.

Q. Who had the others? A. They were lying on the floor down cellar.

Q. Do you know whether these axes and hatchets are the ones you saw at that time? (Witness identified the hatchets with the exception of one which he was not quite sure about.)

Q. Does that resemble the one you saw? A. Yes sir.

Q. Have you any reason to suppose it is not the one? A. No sir, none at all.

Q. What time of day was it when you saw these first? A. About half-past 12.

Q. What did you next do? A. I do not think of anything else just then.

Q. You went off? A. I went out about half-past 1.

Q. Did you return that day? A. Yes sir.

Q. What time did you get back to the house that day? A. Somewhere between 3 and half-past.

Q. Did you go into the house again? A. Yes sir.

Q. Did you further examine the bodies of Mr. and Mrs. Borden? A. I did after I had the rooms photographed.

Q. Before you had the photograph of Andrew J. Borden taken had any change been made in the position of the body so that you had to restore it? A. No sir.

Q. The body had not been changed since you first saw it? A. No sir.

Q. Did you have a photograph taken of the body of Mrs. Borden? A. I did.

Q. Meanwhile had the body of Mrs. Borden been disturbed? A. Not that I am aware of.

Q. What do you say as to whether the body of Mrs. Borden was in the same position as it was when you first saw it, when the photographs were taken? A. I think the hands had been changed by some one.

Q. Otherwise than that it was in the same position? A. Yes sir.

Q. Will you look at that photograph and see whether that indicates the position of the body as you first saw it? (handing the witness a photograph.) A. It does, yes sir, with the exception of the hands. The hands here rest on the chest and then the hands were around the head.

Q. Will you look at this photograph and see if it correctly indicates the position of the bed as you first saw it? A. No sir, it does not.

Q. The bed had been disturbed? A. Yes sir, this picture shows that it had been moved.

Q. Was the bed made when you first saw it? A. Yes ir.

Q. What was on the bed? A. White spread and shams.

Q. Did you see the bed moved? A. No sir.

Q. Was the position of the bed as indicated in that picture the same as it was when you first saw it?

(Witness examined a photograph and said it was.)

Q. In that case the bed had been moved? (Handing witness another photograph.) A. Yes sir.

Q. Did you have it done? A. No sir.

Q. Were these photographs taken at the same time? A. Yes sir; I think I know how it happened, some one called me down stairs

Q. The body is the same as before the bed was moved? A. Yes.

Q. Did you at that time do anything with the bed clothing or any part of it? A. No sir.

Q. Did you make or have made any measurements? A. I did not make any accurate measurements myself that day; I did afterwards.

Q. Can you tell us the distance of the head of Mrs. Borden from the east wall? A. I cannot accurately.

Q. Do so to the best of your estimation. A. I think it is between two and three feet.

Q. What did you do then? A. I then examine the body of Mr. Borden.

Q. While lying on the sofa? A. No sir.

Q. What did you do with the body? A. I undressed it and laid it on the undertaker's board.

Q. In the same room? A. Yes sir.

Q. Tell in detail what you did at that time. A. I opened the body and removed the stomach, tying it at both ends, and put it in a clean jar and sealed it up.

Q. Did you do anything else at that time? A. No sir.

Q. Did you make any further examination of the wounds at that time? A. No sir.

Q. Did you do anything to the body of Mrs. Borden? A. Yes, I did the same with her's that I did with Mr. Borden's.

Q. What did you do with the body of Mrs. Borden? A. I opened the body, removed the stomach, tying it at both ends, put it in a jar and sealed it.

Q. Did you mark these jars in any way? A. Yes sir.

Q. Did you put labels on them? A. Yes sir

Q. See if these are the labels, (handing witness two tags.) A. Yes sir.

Q. One marked "Stomach of Andrew J. Borden" and one "Stomach of Mrs. Borden?" A. Yes sir.

Q. Which one did you put on the jar containing the stomach of Andrew J. Borden, the one marked Andrew J. Borden? A. Yes sir.

Q. And the one marked Mrs. Borden you put on the jar containing that of Mrs. Borden? A. Yes sir.

Q. Did you further seal the jars? A. Yes sir.

Q. And are these the seals? (Witness identified the seals.)

Q. What did you then do with the jars? A. I packed them.

Q. What did you do with the package? A. I put it in a box and sent it to Professor Wood by express.

Mr. Knowlton stated at this point that the expressmen who handled the package were under subpoena to appear and testify, but the defense would not require them to do so, as Mr. Knowlton said Professor Wood would testify that he had received the jars marked with these labels untouched.

Q. Did you at that time take anything else away from the house? A. No sir.

Q. Did you do anything further or make any further examination of the bodies at that time? A. No sir, I did not.

Q. Is there any other event of that day that I have not called your attention to that you can testify to concerning this matter? A. I do not remember any, sir.

Q. When did you go to the house again? A. I went that evening.

Q. What did you do then? A. The only thing I did that evening was to look at the head of Mrs. Borden.

Q. Did you make any further observation? A. I looked at one of the wounds on her head, that was all.

Q. Did anything else happen that night? A. Not that I can think of.

Q. When did you go to the house again? A. I think I went the next day.

Q. What did you do with the hatchet that you took up stairs and put with the milk jars? A. I think I told an officer to ——

Q. You gave some direction, did you? A. Yes sir.

Q. Do you remember what officer? A. No sir.

Q. You did not take it away at that time? A. No sir.

Q. Did you see the hatchet again the next day? A. Yes sir.

Q. Where? A. At the city marshal's office.

Q. The same hatchet you had seen the day before? A. Yes sir.

Q. Did you examine the hatchets? A. I cannot tell you whether it was that day or the next, but I examined them with a magnifying glass.

Q. But you did on one of the two days? A. Yes sir.

Q. Taking first the claw-hammer hatchet, what did you find with your magnifying glass? A. I found two hairs, one on the blade of the hatchet and one in the fibre of the wood.

Q. What did you do with these hairs? A. I removed them, put them on a piece of paper, put them in an envelope and sent them to Professor Wood.

Q. Did you make any further observation of the hatchet at that time? A. Yes sir, there were several spots on it that looked like blood.

Q. Under the magnifying glass did it look like blood? A. I could not tell whether it looked like blood or rust.

Q. Were there any spots on the handle? A. I think there were, yes sir.

Q. Did you do anything with the hatchets? A. I looked at the other one the same way.

Q. Did you notice anything about the axes? A. There was one that had a knot in it that appeared to be blood.

Q. Did you do anything with the hatchets? A. I gave them to Professor Wood.

Q. Personally? A. Yes sir.

Q. Do you recall the date? A. It was the 9th of August.

Q. Was it Tuesday? A. Yes sir.

Q. And the hairs at the same time? A. Yes sir.

Q. Did you at any time see the hatchet that has been spoken of as the handleless hatchet? A. Yes sir.

Q. Where did you first see that? A. I saw it at the marshal's office.

Q. Did you have anything to do with it yourself? A. No sir.

Q. When did you see it at the marshal's office, can you tell me the date? A. I do not recall the date.

Q. Was it that week? A. I will not be certain.

Q. You had nothing to do with delivering it to anybody? A. No sir.

Q. Did you at any time remove the bed clothing from the bed of the guest chamber? A. No sir, some officers removed it.

Q. You saw them? A. Yes sir.

Q. Do you recall anything else that has been taken from the house? A. The two pieces of carpet, that is all I think I took personally.

Q. Was any part of the mopboards or casing taken away under your direction? A. Yes sir, but they are not in my possession now.

Q. What did you do with them? A. I gave them to Professor Wood.

Q. Where did you take the piece from? A. There was a blood spot on the west side of the dressing case in the guest chamber, which was removed with a piece of plastering.

Mr. Knowlton said some one under the direction of Mr. Jennings had had a number of photographs taken which he had shown to him, and he called the witness' attention to them.

Witness identified the pillow shams and counterpane taken from the bed in the room where Mrs. Borden's body lay, and also the piece of marble taken from the dressing case. All these were taken because they had blood on them. He also identified a piece of the door casing taken from the door leading from the sitting room to the dining room, taken because of a smear of blood on it. There were some blood spots to be seen on the articles at the present time. Witness testified that he had had in his possession at some time the cover to the lounge on which Mr. Borden's body laid, and clothing taken from the bodies. Witness testified that the blood on the counterpane was nearer the head than the foot, and on the side of the bed where Mrs. Borden's body was lying.

Q. Have you had any other clothing? A. Yes; a dress, waist and white skirt.

Q. Where were they taken? A. From the guest room.

Q. Who gave them to you? A. Mr. Jennings.

Q. When was it? A. During the search.

Q. Was defendant present at the time? A. She was.

Q. Did you have anything else? A. Yes; I have the lounge cover, and also shoes and stockings. These were sent to Mr. Wood.

District Attorney Knowlton said he did not want the lounge cover. If defense wishes it, it can be produced.

Witness examined the dress and skirt and identified them.

Q. Did you further see the bodies? A. Yes sir.

Q. And made a further examination? A. Yes sir.

Q. Where was this? A. At the cemetery.

Q. Who was present? A. Dr. Draper of Boston and two physicians belonging in Fall River.

Q. Which was the first body examined? A. That of Andrew J. Borden.

Q. What did you do with the dress waist and skirt? A. I sent them to Professor Wood.

Q. Assuming that this is the skirt (showing it) did it have a hole in it at that time? A. No sir.

Q. You, I believe, found a small spot of blood on it? A. Yes sir, about the size of a pin head.

Q. State what you did to the body of Andrew J. Borden? A. I made an autopsy, and I also copied accurately the number of wounds upon the head.

Q. Did you find anything that could be the cause of death except upon the head? A. No sir.

Q. What was the apparent size and weight of Andrew J. Borden? A. His height was 5 feet and 11 inches. His weight I don't know.

Q. Was he stout or thin? A. Thin.

Q. Did you measure Mrs. Borden's body? A. Yes sir.

Q. What was her height? A. Five feet and three inches.

Q. Do you know her weight? A. She was quite a heavy woman. I should judge she would weigh 200 pounds.

Q. Did you examine the wounds on the head of Mr. Borden? A. Yes sir.

Q. Have you made an attempt to describe the wounds by means of plaster casts? A. Yes sir.

Here an officer was instructed to bring in the casts. They showed simply the head and neck, and the wounds were indicated by blue pencil marks corresponding to the cuts upon the heads of the victims.

Q. How many wounds had Mr. Borden? A. Ten.

Here the witness pointed out each upon the plaster cast and described it. One of them was shown to be four inches in length, and had cut the nasal bone, cut through the fleshy part of the upper side of the face and cut the two lips. Another wound was four and a half inches long. Over the left eye was a cut two inches long. This was a glancing wound and passed through the left eyebrow. The next wound ran into it and came down, cutting the eye in half and cut through the cheek bone. This was four and a half inches long. An inch to the left was another cut about a half inch long. The last four wounds to be described crashed through the skull and went into the brain. Not counting cuts where the hatchet may have gone into the same wound twice, there were 10 wounds.

Q. Did you find any other wounds except what were upon the head? A. No sir.

Q. Could you determine the direction of the wounds, that is, the direction from which they were inflicted? A. Yes sir. They were struck from left to right, and were direct.

Here the witness was handed a hatchet and indicated by means of the plaster cast the manner in which the blows were delivered.

Q. Which of the wounds crushed the skull?

The witness indicated them.

Q. Did you afterwards remove the skulls? A. Yes sir.

Q. Did you remove the flesh from the bones? A. Yes sir.

Q. Does the process of removing the flesh in any way affect the integrity of the bones? A. No sir.

Q. What did you find to be the condition of Mrs. Borden's intestines? A. The lower part of her intestines were empty; in the upper part was some undigested food.

Q. Were there any wounds on Mrs. Borden's body except on the head? A. Yes sir, on her back.

Q. Where? A. At the junction of her head and neck and body was a wound two and a half inches in length.

Here the witness illustrated on Mr. Knowlton's back the exact location of the wound.

Q. All the other wounds were on the head? A. Yes sir.

Q. Were there any other wounds except the cuts? A. Yes sir, there were two contusions.

Q. There was no cutting to be observed about them? A. No sir.

Q. Were they what we commonly call black and blue marks? A. They were rather bruises.

Q. Were the bruises where one would strike if they received a fall in life? A. Yes.

Q. How severe were they? A. Very.

Q. Describe Mrs. Borden's wounds; was any part of the skull crushed in? A. Yes.

Q. What part? A. The right side.

Q. Describe it? A. There was a place crushed in 4½ inches by 5 on the right side.

Q. Describe the wounds in detail? A. On the left side of the head there was a scalp wound, and the flesh was cut off, but not separated, for a distance of two and a half inches in length by 1½ in width. On the left side of the middle line of the head were four wounds, two of which went into the skull and the others left their imprint. On the right side were a number of wounds and the skull was crushed in. In relation to Mr. Borden there were some marks on the skull. The autopsy was performed some time after the death and the possibility of the instrument going in so many time may have sent it several times into the same cut, making a mark in the skull where there was none in the flesh.

Q. Did you make an examination of the blood spots at any time? A. Yes.

Q. Was Mr. Seaver with you? A. Yes.

Q. Did he act under your directions? A. Yes.

Q. Did you and he make a record separately? A. Yes.

Mr. Knowlton said he would not go into the tedious reiteration unless defense wished him to. Defense so desired, and Dr. Dolan testified at length of the blood spots found in various places, his evidence being about the same as that of Officer Seaver on Saturday.

Q. What was the position of Mr. Borden's head as to being on the front or back part of the sofa? A. It was about midway.

Q. What as to being up to the top or half way down the arm? A. About midway.

Q. And that exposed the side of the skull that was crushed in? A. Yes.

Q. Can you give me the direction of the blows on Mrs. Borden's head, whether they went in direct or went in at an angle? A. They were all at an angle.

Q. Assuming that they were blows, were they directed at the right or left? A. More were from the left than the right, and some were direct.

Q. Did you prepare the skull of Mrs. Borden and have it in your possession? A. I did.

Q. What was the thickness of Mrs. Borden's skull where the blows went in? A. I cannot tell.

Q. What was the relative thickness of Mrs. Borden's skull where the blows went in? A. The thinnest.

Q. Was it the thinnest part that was crushed in? A. Yes.

Q. In your opinion, what caused those wounds? A. Some sharp cutting instrument.

Q. Were those blows on the skull of Mr. Borden such as could have been inflicted by an ordinary woman with a hatchet? A. Yes sir.

Q. In your opinion were the wounds on Mrs. Borden such as could have been inflicted by a woman of ordinary strength? A. Yes.

Q. Did you form an opinion which one of them died first? A. Yes.

Q. Which? A. Mrs. Borden.

Q. How long first? A. From one to one and a half hours.

Q. Take all the conditions, such as the condition of the intestines, etc., would they help you in coming to a decision as to the priority of death? A. Yes.

Q. What do they point to, as to which died first? A. They indicate that digestion was going on in Mr. Borden and had ceased in Mrs. Borden.

The direct examination of Dr. Dolan was conducted by District Attorney Knowlton and the cross-examination was conducted by M. O. Adams, Esq.

Q. Was it not nearly 12 when you got to the Borden house? A. It was not so late as that.

Q. Are you especially sure of the time when you got there? A. I don't think it was so late as ten minutes of 12.

Q. Don't you recall that when you went up stairs Dr. Bowen was with you? A. Yes.

Q. Are you able to give an account whether it was light or not? A. I think one curtain was up.

Q. Did Dr. Bowen tell you he had pulled out one of Mrs. Borden's arms? A. I don't recall that he did.

Q. You now know that others had seen and touched her before you got there? A. I do.

Q. Did you know that Captain Desmond had moved the bed? A. I did not.

Q. When you first saw Mrs. Borden did she fill up the space between the bureau and bed? A. She did not.

Q. What you did then was merely to take a general view? A. Yes.

Q. The examination was made later? A. Yes.

Q. After you had seen her you went to the cellar? A. Yes.

Q. You received some axes or hatchets? A. Yes.

Q. You have expressed your opinion freely on the witness stand? A. Yes.

Q. Is your opinion the same now as then? A. Yes.

Q. Did you express the opinion that the small hatchet could adequately cause the injuries which you found on the heads of Mr. and Mrs. Borden? A. I said so then.

Q. Did you have in view the hatchet with the small head? A. Yes.

Q. Do you desire to change the opinion now? A. I hadn't measured it then.

Q. Were there any injuries upon the head of these people that were any more than 4½ inches long? A. Yes sir.

Q. On Mr. Borden there was one 4½ plus, wasn't there? A. Yes sir.

Q. Do you remember that at the former trial I presented to your inspection the head of a china doll, and that you marked upon it the location of the injuries upon Mr. Borden's head? A. Yes sir.

Q. Do you recall the striking upon the left side of Mr. Borden's head above the ear, the crushed place? A. Yes sir.

Q. Do you remember the measurement you gave? A. I think it was something like 4 by 2 inches.

Q. Didn't you call attention to the claw-head of this hatchet and say that it was a rectangular injury that could have been caused by that? A. Yes, but I do not say so now.

Q. You desire to change that opinion? A. Yes sir.

Q. You had performed an autopsy then? A. I had not prepared the skulls.

Q. When were they prepared? A. I do not know. I do not think I had them prepared before a week or two afterward.

Q. Was not the hearing in August? Wasn't it very hot? A. Yes sir, it was very hot.

Q. Didn't you have them at that time? A. I won't say that I didn't.

Q. Hadn't you examined them? A. No sir, I hadn't examined them.

Q. Hadn't they been prepared then? A. If I said so then they certainly had been.

Q. Were not these skulls in your possession? A. Yes sir, they were in my possession. Whether I had them prepared I cannot say. I will say positively that I had not examined them.

Q. And therefore you have since changed your opinion? A. Yes sir.

Q. There were two views or two autopsies? A. Yes sir.

Q. There was one that you made an original report of wasn't there? A. Yes sir.

Q. Did you have authority to make that? A. Yes sir.

Q. And did you subsequently have authority from the law officers to make the second view? A. Yes sir.

Q. That autopsy was at Oak Grove cemetery? A. Yes sir.

Q. Was it the 11th day of August, the day the defendant was arrested? A. I cannot say as to the arrest.

Q. It was on August 11? A. Yes sir.

Q. At that time did you remove something from the bodies? A. Yes sir.

Q. You removed the skulls, did you not? A. Yes sir.

Q. Did you notify these daughters or either of them that you were about to do it? A. No sir.

Q. Did you notify them after you had done it or cause them to be notified? A. No sir.

Q. And when they were interred did you cause any information to be sent them that the interment took place under such circumstances? A. I did not.

Q. This second or Oak Grove autopsy revealed to you some other appearances that you had not discovered, didn't it? A. Yes sir.

Q. It revealed among other things a blow in the back of Mrs. Borden? A. Yes sir.

Q. How long did you say it was? A. Two and one half inches.

Mr. Adams requested the witness to illustrate the location of the cut to the jury, and Dr. Dolan marked counsel's coat just below the collar, nearly in the middle of the back, with a piece of chalk, and he exhibited it to the jury.

Q. Where was the assailant standing in your opinion when that blow was given? A. At the rear.

Q. And how was the assailant's face, toward the rear of the person assaulted? A. Yes sir.

Q. Was there any other injury that you discovered at the Oak Grove view that you did not find at the house? A. I do not think there was, sir.

Q. Didn't you tell us about an injury upon the left temple of Mr. Borden? A. Yes sir; a scalp wound.

Q. There was a cut on the left side of the head, wasn't there? A. Yes sir.

Q. It was cut from the front toward the rear? A. Yes sir.

Q. With a hinge on the back side of the cut? A. Yes sir.

Q. When that blow was given where, in your opinion, did the assailant stand? A. In front.

Q. That is, the assailant and the assaulted stood facing each other? A. Yes sir.

Q. Do you entertain the opinion that the bruises upon the hands and forehead of Mrs. Borden were caused in any other manner than by her falling? A. No sir.

Q. They could adequately and probably be so caused? A. Yes sir.

Q. How many different marks indicating separate blows did you find upon the head of Mrs. Borden? A. Eighteen.

Q. Did Dr. Draper assist you in this Oak Grove autopsy? A. Yes sir.

Q. And did he take notes? A. Yes sir.

Q. You do not recall that there were but 18 blows on the head? A. You do not mean contusions?

Q. No sir. A. And not including the one on the back?

Q. No sir. A. There were 18 without the one on the back.

Q. Upon the head of Mr. Borden there were how many? A. Ten on the face and head.

Q. Ten in all? A. Yes sir.

Q. When the hatchet was seen by you in the cellar did you examine it for traces of blood? A. No sir.

Q. Did you examine the blade? A. No sir.

Q. The handle? A. No sir.

Q. Did you at that time, in the cellar, have the opinion that there was human hair on it or any portion of it? A. No sir.

Q. At anywhere else? A. Yes sir.

Q. Where? A. At the city marshal's office.

Witness—I would like to make an explanation.

Mr. Knowlton—I object.

Mr. Adams—He is your own witness.

Mr. Knowlton—I object.

Q. Did you at any time form an opinion as to the milk, that is as to its containing foreign or poisonous substances? A. I formed no opinion in regard to it?

The cross-examination of the witness was not completed when the hour of adjournment arrived.

Mrs. William H. Faulkner of New Bedford fainted at 4 15 and was attended by Dr. Sullivan and conveyed home in a carriage.

STEAMSHIP LINES.

ANCHOR LINE.
United States Mail Steamships
Sail from New York every Saturday for
GLASGOW VIA LONDONDERRY
Rates for Saloon Passage
By S. S. CITY OF ROME, $50 and upward.
OTHER STEAMERS, Cabin, $45 and upward, according to accommodation and location of Room. Excursion Tickets at reduced rates. Second Cabin, $30. Steerage, Outward, $23. Prepaid, $24. Second Cabin from Glasgow or Derry, $35.
Drafts at lowest Current Rates.
For Book of tours and other information apply to HENDERSON BROTHERS, 7 Bowling Green, N. Y., Thomas Donaghy, Corner Union and Water sts. or Edwin Whittaker 884 Purchase st., or David Waugh, 773 South Water street, New Bedford.

A Refreshing Drink
of our delicious Teas can be enjoyed by the poor as well as rich. We are satisfied with a small profit and will give you full value for your money every time.

Health and Energy
are necessary for the performance of your daily duties. A cup of our delicious Coffee is always invigorating.

China Tea Co.
132 PURCHASE STREET.
Goods delivered to any part of the city without charge. TS

GEORGE C. BLISS,
FLORIST.
34 Arnold Street,
CORNER COTTAGE.
TELEPHONE, DAY OR NIGHT.

Baggage Tags
ALWAYS IN STOCK AT
STANDARD OFFICE.

Knowles & Co.

Now is the time for you to make a call at our store, as we have a full and complete line of warm weather goods.

The largest line of Parasols and Sun Umbrellas to be found in the city.

A bargain in Red and Blue Sun Umbrellas, at $1.75.

Parasols from 89c. to $5.50. Some rare bargains among them. Children's shades 39c. to $1.49.

We have made a cut in Silk Laces, and will sell you all the new and choice effects at 25 per cent. less than you will find them elsewhere.

A splendid line of Cotton Laces from 5 to 45c. per yard.

Our Hosiery Department is full of bargains. An elegant line of fine dropped stitch hose, in blacks, tans, white and almost any color you could wish, at 50c. Also some bargains at 25 and 37 1-2c.

We have secured one case of Ladies' Jersey Vests, worth 12 1-2c., which we shall sell three for 25c. as long as they last.

We are showing the best Ladies' and Gents' 25c. Vest to be found anywhere.

All sizes in Gents' Negligee Shirts, worth from $1.25 to $1.50, for ONE EVEN DOLLAR.

A new and elegant Line of Pampas Cloths, 25 or 30 pieces to select from, at 15c.

Twenty-five new styles of the celebrated Puritan Cloths at 12 1-2c. These goods are selling fast. Come while the selection is good.

A new line of Llama Cloths, just what you want for a summer dress, at 12 1-2c.

A good line of Sateens, fine as silk, at 15c.

Knowles & Co.

UNION and FOURTH STS.

SPECIAL NOTICE.

The demand for the famous "J. H. CUTTER" WHISKIES, (for which we are the sole agents in this city) having become so great, many houses out of the State are sending their travelers in here, with the hope of inducing our trade to buy the "Cutter" whiskies from them, by underselling us, or rather trying to. We therefore beg to say to our friends and the public generally, we will NOT allow ourselves to be undersold by any house dealing in the genuine "J. H. CUTTER" WHISKIES, and we are prepared to protect our trade, not only in QUALITY but in PRICES as well.

Very Respectfully,

BENJAMIN DAWSON,
597 Purchase Street.

Sole agent for New Bedford, Mass., for the famous J. H. Cutter Whiskies. 8p

DRINK
ROXBURY RYE
WHISKEY.
Equaled by few, Excelled by None.
je6-12t8p

LOOKS LIKE BLACKMAIL.

The Suit of Susie Hall Against Dr. Webster Continued Until July 19.

GREAT BARRINGTON, Mass., June 13.—The suit of Susie B. Hall vs. Dr. Webster, a prominent young doctor in Stockbridge, charging him with being the father of her unborn child, came before Judge Sanford yesterday and was continued until July 19. The girl is now in the child's nursery and hospital in New York. It is alleged that Charles Evans, a prominent young attorney in Stockbridge, was approached by agents of the woman who demanded $200 or he would be charged with the paternity of the child. They threatened to tell his invalid wife, and he, though innocent, paid $25. They also, it is claimed, approached Robert Dean in the same way and got $10 from him. Others are said to have been approached, and Stockbridge is much wrought up over the affair.

An Infringement Claimed.

BRIDGEPORT, Conn., June 13.—The Edison Phonograph company has brought suit against the American Graphone company of Bridgeport, claiming an infringement on the patents of Mr. Edison. Superintendent T. E. McDonald said yesterday that the case is in reality a counter suit to the action brought by his company at Washington a short time ago over the patent for a recording point and cutter and their attachments.

Died From Starvation.

SALEM, Mass., June 13.—The body of an unknown man was found in a cellar on Rice street yesterday afternoon. It is understood that he died of starvation.

HANG HIM, HANG HIM!

Exciting Scene at the Fords Theater Inquest.

Colonel Ainsworth Accused of Murder by a Witness.

Bitter Feeling Shown by Frenzied Department Clerks.

WASHINGTON, June 13.—Dr. Shaffer, the deputy coroner of the district, conducted the inquest into the Ford theatre disaster which began yesterday. The jury included architects and builders.

A letter from Secretary Lamont was read, giving assurance that no clerk need fear dismissal on account of his testimony.

The deputy coroner called the jury to order and prefaced the investigation by a statement that holding an investigation in a public hall was something of an experiment, and he admonished the public present to keep perfectly quiet.

There Was Nobody on Trial,

he said. The jury would simply endeavor to get at the facts in the case. He stated that the inquest was to be held over the remains of J. A. Chapin, whose body had been selected for that purpose.

Benjamin Reiss, a clerk of the record and pension division, employed in the old theater building, was the first witness called.

He had been excused, he said, at 9 o'clock on the morning of the disaster and was not present at the building's collapse. He had heard it rumored for several years that the building was unsafe. A day or two before the accident he had seen Colonel Ainsworth at the building. He was there while the excavation was going on.

Smith Thompson, a clerk in the theatre building, who made a bitter speech denouncing Colonel Ainsworth at the relief meeting on Friday, testified that when the accident occurred he was at his desk at work on the second floor, to the rear of the light wall, the part of the building which did not fall.

In describing his experience he said that there was

No Fire Escape

on the building and only one door for entrance and exit. He had hooked an umbrella to a window sill and lowered himself by it to a ladder, which some one below him held, and thus escaped from the building.

After two other witnesses had testified there was a strange scene, illustrating a bitter feeling against Colonel Ainsworth. A majority of the spectators present at the inquest were clerks who were employed in the old theater building. Mr. Warner, one of the jurors, asked the witness what was the feeling of the clerks in the theater building toward their superior officer, Colonel Ainsworth.

"That of abject fear," answered Mr. Thompson, impressively. A slight buzz and shifting of chairs followed, then a slight clapping of hands. Dr. Shaffer looked astonished, and Colonel Ainsworth grew red. Dr. Shaffer arose and delivered a lecture to the offenders.

At the afternoon session of the inquest a well-dressed man walked forward, and with a voice trembling with passion, shaking his fist in Colonel Ainsworth's face, shouted:

"You Murdered My Brother,

and you shan't sit there intimidating these witnesses." The man was Charles Barnes, whose brother was a victim of the disaster. After the uproar had subsided, Mr. Davis, representing Colonel Ainsworth, began to speak, when a dozen excited department clerks rose to their feet and shouted for him to sit down. The excitement grew in intensity. Nearly every clerk present, who was employed in the old building, was on his feet shouting. At first they only called "Sit down," "Shut your mouth," but finally cried "Hang him; hang him!"

Among Other Statements

made by Charles Thompson in the clerks' indignation meeting was the assertion that The New York Times was "the mouthpiece of Daniel S. Lamont and his coajutor, F. C. Ainsworth," and that it "was the only newspaper that did not hold Ainsworth responsible for the disaster on Friday". He also denounced Jacob Frech, whom he called "an unnaturalized Dutchman." Much more intemperate language of a similar kind was used. It was proposed to appoint a committee to secure counsel to represent the clerks at the next session of the inquest, but this was rendered unnecessary by Judge Jere Wilson volunteering his services.

SENSATION IN CANADA.

A Quarrel Between Two of Windsor's Citizens Results In Murder.

WINDSOR, Ont., June 13.—A sensational murder was committed early last evening, which has caused considerable excitement, as the principals are well known citizens. Captain James Hickey, the victim, and John Vrooman were driving along one of the main streets, when apparently without warning Vrooman drew a revolver and shot Hickey in the left breast, pushed him out of the buggy and drove off. Hickey died instantly.

Vrooman's face was covered with blood when arrested, which would indicate that he received a blow from Hickey before doing the shooting. It is said that Vrooman has been intimate with Hickey's wife for some time, and about a week ago she mysteriously disappeared. Vrooman, after being arrested, said that he was driving along Sandwich street, when Hickey appeared and insisted upon getting into the buggy to talk over his domestic troubles. The conversation soon developed into a quarrel, during which Hickey hit him in the face, and, believing that Hickey intended to do him further injury, he shot him. Hickey had a revolver in his possession when found.

QUEEN MARGHERITA'S LACES.

They Arrived at New York All Right, but Were Lost In Transportation.

NEW YORK, June 13.—Inquiry regarding the laces belonging to Queen Margherita of Italy develops the fact that they arrived here on April 2 on the steamship Kaiser William II. The goods were taken in charge by the Italian chamber of commerce in this city, who had them insured for $80,000 and turned over to the Adams express for transportation to the fair at Chicago. The laces were securely packed and sealed with a great number of seals marked with a peculiar stamp not easily counterfeited. The laces were sent to Chicago over the Pennsylvania railroad, and the officials are positive that the seals were not broken or any laces taken from the package while in their charge. The customs authorities here had nothing to do with the laces, as being exhibits for the fair they were not dutiable.

Guests at a Hotel Robbed.

GLENWOOD SPRINGS, Colo., June 13.—A daring robber relieved a number of the guests at the Hotel Colorado Sunday of money and jewelry to the amount of probably $2000. With a six-shooter prominently displayed, the fellow walked through the hotel, collected all he could lay his hands on, and managed to escape.

Highest of all in Leavening Power.—Latest U. S. Gov't Report.

Royal Baking Powder

ABSOLUTELY PURE

THIS IS FETE WEEK.

States and Nations Getting Ready for Their Jubilees at the Fair.

CHICAGO, June 13.—This is to be a week of fetes at the fair. There will be six altogether, three of them being on Thursday, when more people are expected to visit the fair than on any day since the opening. The German Turners and singing societies will easily be in the majority on that day, both in numbers and in merrymaking. At least 50,000 Germans are expected, and there will be half as many more if the day be clear.

Indiana folks are going to have great times with music, speechmaking, school children's exercises and flowers. All the notable men in Indiana are coming up with 15,000 or 20,000 other enthusiastic Hoosiers.

Arkansas people to the number of 2000 or 3000 are also coming to startle the world with the wonders of their exhibits. All these events occur on Thursday.

The Infanta

started the ball of fete days today by helping Senor Puy de Lome dedicate the Spanish pavilion and the exhibits in the Manufactures and Agricultural and Machinery halls.

PEEPING THROUGH THE BIG GUN.

Tomorrow France will have a fete day. The whole of the French pavilion, which is the handsomest foreign building at the fair, will be thrown open, and the exhibit in the Manufactures building will be opened, although it has already been free for inspection for some time. The exercises will be purely informal.

Saturday afternoon, Bunker Hill day, will be celebrated by the Massachusetts folks by an informal reception. At the building of that state Governor Russell will probably receive the guests. As the building has already been dedicated there will be no formal exercises. Friday night Governor Russell will entertain the officials of the fair and foreign representatives at a banquet at the Auditorium hotel, and on Saturday night the Massachusetts society will spread a feast in his honor at the same hostelry.

Ex-President Harrison

was a visitor at the World's fair yesterday. He came out to the grounds about 11:30 o'clock, and was the guest of President Palmer of the national committee.

Upon arriving at the grounds President Harrison was taken for a drive through the winding ways of the White City and shown the beautiful buildings. Shortly after noon President Palmer took his distinguished guest to the Administration building, where he was presented to a number of World's fair officials, after which all sat down to an elaborate luncheon.

William Mayer, the contractor who had the contract for building the spectatorium, filed a sensational intervening petition yesterday in the circuit court in the suit of Steele Mackaye against the Columbian Celebration company. Mayer claims that the company owes him $120,000, and he asks to have all the stockholders decreed to be partners and liable for all of the debts against the company. Mayer charges fraud and corrupt management against the incorporators of the company, Steele Mackaye, Jr., and Howard O. Edmonds.

TRIED TO KILL HER CHILD.

A Crazy Woman Creates a Sensational Scene In a Church.

HANCOCK, N. Y., June 13.—Mary, the wife of Matthew McKenna of Kerryville walked into town yesterday wheeling a 3-months' old baby in its carriage. She went to St. Paul's Catholic church and laid the baby on the altar. Then she knelt before a picture of the virgin and prayed aloud, offering to God the baby as a living sacrifice.

A number of village women and three men entered the church before she finished her prayer, and they were startled to see her rise, run to the altar, leap over the rail and throw herself on the cooing baby. She would have strangled it but for the interference of the men. It required their combined strength to hold her. The baby was taken to a neighbor's house and Dr. Drake was summoned. Mrs. McKenna grew quiet and rational in an hour or two. Her husband arrived from Kerryville and took her and the child home. This is the first time she has shown evidence of insanity. She has a brother in a Pennsylvania insane asylum.

Died From His Injuries.

BOSTON, June 13.—William Tonzalin, 8 years old, while at play on a wagon, fell beneath the heavy wheels, which passed over him. He was carried to the City hospital, where he died from his injuries a short time after being admitted.

A SAD CASE.

An Aged Widow Left Penniless by Moody Merrill's Misdeeds.

DEDHAM, Mass., June 13.—An attachment was filed here yesterday by Otis E. Weld of Boston, doing business under the name of John D. & M. Williams, against Moody Merrill, for $1500. It is stated that Mrs. Sarah P. Bogardus of Newburyport is another loser by Merrill's business methods. She is a widow nearly 86 years old, and her relations with Merrill's family have been intimate. Some years ago she intrusted to Merrill an iron box containing stocks, bonds and money to the value of $50,000. Merrill has always represented, it is said, that the amount had been invested in first-class securities. The interest was paid regularly until a few months ago. Recently a representative of Mrs. Bogardus opened the box and, it is stated, found nothing there except some worthless electric stock and Merrill's note for $10,000, which is not indorsed. Mrs. Bogardus is left almost penniless.

BIDDEFORD'S MILL STRIKE.

Strikers' Ranks Strengthened by Laconia Yard Hands—No Settlement Yet.

BIDDEFORD, Me., June 13.—The strike of the Pepperell and Laconia mill operatives was strengthened yesterday afternoon by the accession of a nnmber of Laconia employes, who have not heretofore been in sympathy with the movement. Among the latter was a full crew of yard hands. The strikers held a mass meeting in the Opera house and listened to a report of the committee appointed to confer with Agent McArthur. The committee reported that the corporation was not ready to accede to a 10 per cent. increase, but if the strikers would return to work the company's managers would investigate, and, if possible, grant the operatives an increase in wages. No action was taken by the meeting, and another will be held tomorrow. McArthur says the mills will be kept running as long as possible with short hands.

Thrown From His Wheel.

HUDSON, N. Y., June 13.—Tom Roe, in his bicycle trip against time from New York to San Francisco, met with an accident yesterday at Union Corners by being thrown from his wheel. He remained unconscious for an hour. He rallied, however, and started for Albany.

New Railroad Line Opened.

WOONSOCKET, R. I., June 13.—Trains began running regularly yesterday between Providence and Southbridge, Mass., via the New York and New England's seven-mile line connecting its Pascoag branch with its main line at Douglass junction.

[From Yesterday's Third Edition.]

THE NEW BEDFORD MURDER.

Inquest on the Death of the Victim of Sarmento's Jealousy.

The police authorities held a star chamber session in the third district court room this afternoon. It was an inquest as to the cause of death of Maria das Candeias, That she was killed by a bullet from a revolver in the hands of Jose Sarmento, nobody will attempt to deny. However, an inquest is being held on the cause of death of the unfortunate victim of that fatal Friday, and great pains are being taken to note the evidence. It is essentially a gathering together of witnesses who may be serviceable in the looked for trial of Sarmento, who is held for willful murder. A stenographer is in attendance and the court room is filled with Portuguese and others, who may prove valuable in the near future. An interpreter is also in attendance. No others are allowed to be present.

INDIGNANT CITIZENS.

Is the Color Line Drawn at the Borden Murder Trial?

Is the color line drawn at the Borden murder trial? It is said that it is, and a number of citizens are indignant in consequence. This afternoon Miss Mary Jackson, a daughter of Rev. William Jackson, called at the court house for admission during the Borden murder trial. She was informed that the court room was filled and that there was no room, but that she might sit on the stairs. She took a seat on the stairs to await an opportunity to sit with the people. While she sat there eight white women presented themselves for admission, and were given seats. Gilman A. King, a well known colored citizen, who saw Miss Jackson sitting on the stairs, then got up from his own seat and gave her his, and while he stood in the aisle to see that she was seated he was informed he could not stand. To this he said: "I can go out, I suppose," and out he went. Mr. King informed Mr. Sullavou of the facts in this case and also stated that when Miss Jackson was refused a seat there was room in the court house for a number of people.

PERSONAL.

Secretary William Alexander Andrew of the Young Men's Christian association of Chicopee Center will be married to Miss Maria Bourne Kelley, daughter of Captain John A. Kelley, of Marion. The ceremony will take place at the home of the bride in Marion next Wednesday, and Rev. Dr. Henry C. Graves, of New Bedford, will officiate. After a trip to Boston and through Vermont, the bride and groom will make their home with Dr. S. E. Fletcher, 96 Grape street, Chicopee.

REAL ESTATE SALE.

Roberts & Thomas have sold for Joseph C. Noria a cottage house and 17 rods of land on South Water street to William A. Pease.

"My Trade will take anything I give them; they believe what I tell them; and I mean to sell them what I make the most on." That is what one grocer actually gives as a reason for selling washing-powders—imitations—instead of the original and best washing-compound—Pearline. If grocers and customers were all like these, the millions of women who are now blessing Pearline would still be doing useless hard work. But when you come across such a dealer, don't let him put you off with anything except Pearline. 397 JAMES PYLE, New York.

BLOODSTAINED.

Grewsome Exhibit in Court Room

Taken from House of Murdered Couple.

Medical Examiner Dolan on Witness Stand.

Description of the Condition of the Two Bodies.

Testimony Terrible for the Prisoner to Hear.

The usual crowd put in its appearance this afternoon, but the masculine element was in the ascendency. The household cares of the staid matrons, and the little attentions to personal appearance that the maidens find so necessary may account for it, but at any rate the "horrid" men had monopolized most of the seats long before the "fair sex" were gathered about the barricade on County street. As usual, the crowd waited for a glimpse of the prisoner, and then wended its way homeward. The crowd was intensely partisan, and there were many expressions of satisfaction that the story "wrung from Lizzie while she was under too much stress to know what she was doing or saying," was not to be given to the jury for consideration.

Lizzie read a paper this forenoon for the first time since the trial commenced. Seeing a paper that was being scanned by a reporter spread wide open she leaned over the rail and eagerly read the headlines. Something in them seemed to possess a fascination for her, and she continued to gaze until Mr. Jennings attracted her attention in another direction.

It was 20 minutes past 2 before the judges were in their seats, and the jury was told off. There were more lawyers and professional men within the rail this afternoon than has been seen at any previous session.

Officer Hyde Cross Examined.

Officer Hyde was cross-examined by Mr. Robinson when the court came in this afternoon. He said that he saw Miss Russell and Miss Lizzie Borden go down into the cellar. He could see them as they went into the wash room. He saw Miss Borden go into the water closet and empty the slops. Miss Russell held a light for her. Miss Borden came out and then went back into the closet again. Miss Russell appeared to be nervous. She had a kerosene lamp in her hand. Her hand shook, but the lamp did not smoke nor the chimney fall. He saw Miss Borden go to the sink and set the light down on the floor. He wouldn't swear whether the window he looked in was open or not. He couldn't see the sink, but could see Miss Borden standing at the sink. He didn't know how he could explain Miss Russell's actions, but she appeared to be very nervous. The clothes he spoke of were on the south side of the wash cellar; they were about five feet back from the sink. He saw Miss Borden stoop down by the sink; he did not see her open any door under the sink. Did not know if there was a door under the sink, but thought there was. She did not remain in the stooping position more than a minute. He did not go into the house that day. Miss Borden afterwards took a light and went up stairs. No one was with him at that time. Officer Minnehan was on the southwest corner of the house right by the front door and another man was on the south side. The other person was George Ferguson. He thought Mr. Ferguson could have seen what was done at the sink. He did not go into the house that night, but continued to patrol around the yard.

In redirect Officer Hyde said his directions were to stay around the north side of the house. When he looked into the sitting room he was looking through the kitchen window on the east end. He could see only when the door was opened.

DOCTOR DOLAN

Medical Examiner Called to the Stand to Tell His Story.

Dr. William A. Dolan was the next witness, and after giving his residence, questions were put.

Q. What sort of practice are you in? A. General.

Q. Does it include surgery? A. Yes.

Q. Have you had anything to do with broken or fractured skulls? A. I have.

Q. Are you one of the medical examiners of the county? A. Yes.

Q. How long have you been? A. Two years.

Q. When did you first go to the Borden house? A. At quarter to 12.

Q. Where were you when you heard of this thing? A. I was passing the house.

Q. How do you fix the time? A. In 10 or 15 minutes I heard the ringing of the bell for 12.

Q. When you first went in who did you see? A. I first saw Charles Sawyer and then Dr. Bowen. In the kitchen I saw Bridget Sullivan and Mr. Morse.

Q. See Mrs. Churchill or Alice Russell? A. Yes.

Q. Where? A. In the dining room.

Q. See any officers? A. Yes; Officers Mullaly, Allen and Dougherty.

Q. Did you have any talk with Lizzie? A. Yes.

Q. When? A. I can't tell the hour; it was when I was there in the forenoon.

Q. What talk? A. I asked about a note said to have been received. She said Mrs. Borden received a note to go to some sick person. I asked where it was. She said she didn't know. Mrs. Borden probably destroyed it.

Q. Where did you first go in the house? A. Into the kitchen and dining room.

Q. Describe what you saw? A. I saw a sofa with a form lying on it.

(A photograph was shown and identified by witness.)

Q. How was the sofa, flush with the dining room door? A. Yes.

Q. You have the sofa here? A. Yes.

Q. Was the body covered? A. Yes, with a sheet.

Q. Any one go in with you? A. Dr. Bowen.

Q. What did you do? A. I looked at the body; took hold of the hand; it was warm; saw blood oozing; it was bright red.

Q. As to the position of the body? (Showing a photograph.) A. It is all right, but perhaps I moved it a little to get at the inside coat pocket.

Q. What was the head resting on? A. The head was on a small sofa cushion, the cushion on a coat, and the coat on an afghan.

Q. Did you examine the body? A. Not at that time.

Q. Then where did you go? A. Up stairs to see Mrs. Borden's body.

Q. Where was it? A. Between the dressing case and bed.

Q. Did you take any measurements? A. Not then.

Q. What examination did you make then? A. I looked at the back of the head and saw the wounds and blood.

Q. Describe the position of the body. A. It was lying with the back of the head and right leg exposed. Her hands were nearer the wall than her head.

Q. Were the hands clasped? A. No.

Q. Did they come together? A. No.

Q. How was the head? A. Turned so that part was exposed.

Medical Examiner Dolan.

Q. Can you tell me how much the head was turned? A. She was lying more on the left side of the head than in any other way.

Q. Did you take anything away? A. Yes sir, a silk handkerchief.

Q. Is it here? A. Yes sir, down stairs.

Q. Where did you find it? A. Near the head.

Q. How was it, knotted or loose? A. Loose.

Q. Was it old or new? A. Old.

Q. Was it cut? A. No.

Q. Was there blood on it? A. Yes.

Q. How far was the head from the wall? A. I can't say.

(The handkerchief was exhibited.)

Q. Is that it? A. Yes.

Q. Did you take it that day? A. No sir, it was buried.

Q. When did it come to you? A. Within ten days.

Q. Do you identify the handkerchief? A. Yes sir.

Q. How long did you occupy in examining Mrs. Borden's body at this time? A. Not over two or three minutes.

Q. Did you examine Mr. Borden's body at this time? A. Yes sir.

Q. How was it with respect to temperature? A. It was warm.

Q. You use the term warm and cold in the medical sense of their meaning? A. Yes sir.

Q. How far apart were the first examinations of the bodies and the second examination of Mr. Borden's body? A. Not over five minutes.

Q. Did you notice in the examination of Mr. Borden's body the condition of the blood on the body and about it? A. It was bright red, and was dripping in two places from Mr. Borden's head and falling upon the carpet. It was not coagulated.

Q. Was there blood under the sofa? A. Yes sir, on the carpet in two places.

Q. How large were those places? A. They were eight or ten inches in diameter.

Q. Where were these spots? A. Right under the head of the sofa.

Q. Was the blood soaked into the carpet? A. Yes sir.

Q. I was going to ask, if I haven't already done so, whether the blood on Mr. Borden, or flowing from him, was coagulated? A. I saw no blood that was coagulated.

Q. Did you make any examination of Mrs. Borden's body? A. Yes sir.

Q. With what result? A. I touched her hands and found that she was much colder than Mr. Borden.

Q. Did you notice the condition of the blood on Mrs. Borden. A. It was coagulated and was of a dark color. The blood on her head was matted and was practically dry.

Q. With reference to coagulation, how did you say it was? A. It was coagulated.

Q. Did you notice anything that I have not asked you about? A. Not that I think of.

Q. Did you remove any of the carpet under either body? A. Yes sir.

Witness was shown a piece of carpet that he identified as the piece taken from under the place where Mr. Borden laid when found and pointed out the location of the two pools of blood referred to.

Q. Does the piece of carpet look the same now as when you first saw it? A. No sir.

Q. In what respect does it differ? A. The blood was then of a bright red color.

Q. How did it appear, did you say? A. It was fresh, bright and shiny.

Q. Did you take the piece of carpet from under Mrs. Borden? A. I did not.

Q. Did some one? A. Yes sir.

Witness identified the piece shown him as the one taken from Mrs. Borden's room.

Q. Does it present the same appearance now? A. No sir.

Q. In what respect does it differ? A. It was smooth when I first saw it.

Q. In speaking of the coagulation you refer to the blood on both the bodies and the carpets? A. Yes sir.

Q. What did you do then? A. After I had seen Mrs. Borden's body for the first time I returned to Mr. Borden and made an examination of the wounds.

Q. What examination did you make? A. At that time I made an examination and found that there were from eight to ten wounds.

Q. You afterwards made a more accurate examination? A. Yes sir.

Q. Did you make any other observation than to count the wounds? A. Yes, I observed the position of the body, the way it was lying.

Q. What did he have on? A. He had on outside a cardigan jacket, he had a black vest, black trousers and a pair of Congress shoes.

Q. Did you at that time notice anything about his valuables? A. Yes sir. He had a watch and pocketbook.

Q. Did you examine the pocketbook? A. Yes sir.

Q. Did you see what there was in the pocketbook? A. Yes sir.

Q. What did you find? A. I found some money; some bills and some specie.

Q. How much money? A. I shall have to refer to my notes.

Q. You may refer to your notes. A. There were $81.65.

Q. The larger portion of that bills? A. Yes sir.

Q. Sixty-five cents only in change or was there some other change? A. Sixty-five cents in change. I can tell you the denomination of the bills.

Q. You may give them, please? A. He had four 10 dollar bills, five fives, two twos, 11 ones, two fifty cent pieces, three twenty-fives, six tens, five fives and five ones.

Q. Did you find anything else in the pocketbook? A. No sir, not in the pocketbook.

Q. The watch and chain were on his person in the usual place? A. Yes sir.

Q. Did you find any other article of jewelry? A. He had a ring, I think.

Q. What kind of a ring? Do you remember whether it was silver or gold? A. I think it was gold.

Q. Then where did you go? A. I went up stairs.

Q. Where did you go up stairs? A. I went into the room where the body of Mrs. Borden was.

Q. Did you make any further observation of the body of Mrs. Borden? A. Yes sir.

Q. Did you observe anything in addition to what you testified to? A. Simply that I examined the wounds and counted them and lifted the body with the assistance of Dr. Bowen to get at the wounds more accurately.

Q. What did you do then? A. Then in consequence of what had been told me I collected samples of the milk.

Q. Of whom did you receive these samples? A. Bridget Sullivan.

Q. What did you do with these samples? A. I sent them to Professor Wood.

Q. In jars or bottles? A. In jars.

Q. In separate jars? A. Yes sir.

Q. Do you remember how you marked them? A. Yes sir.

(Continued on Seventh Page.)

MOODY MERRILL'S RASCALITY.

Entrusted with a Widow's Fortune He Leaves Her Penniless.

Newburyport, June 12.—The mising Moody Merrill, of Boston, has among his victims Mrs. Sarah P. Bogardus, of this city. She is a widow nearly 86 years old, and her relations with the Merrill family have been very intimate. Some years ago she entrusted to Mr. Merrill an iron box containing stocks, bonds and money to the value of $50,000. Mr. Merrill has always represented that the amount had been invested in first class securities, which were absolutely safe in character. The interest has been paid regularly until Mr. Merrill disappeared. A representative of Mrs. Bogardus opened the box and found nothing in it except some worthless electric stock and Mr. Merrill's note for $10,000, which is not endorsed. Mrs. Bogardus is left almost penniless.

A SABBATH BATTLE.

Officers Have an Engagement with Train Robbers in California.

San Francisco, June 12.—A special from Visalia, Cal., says: Another fight between Evans and Sontag, the Colis train robbers, and officers took place Sunday evening. During the conflict an officer was shot in the leg. Evans is probably mortally wounded, if not dead. At the time the wounded officer left the scene Evans was lying on the ground. Sontag had escaped and taken to the hills followed by a heavy fire, which, it is believed, did not injure him, as it was dark and his retreating form could not be seen. H. I. Rapelje, deputy sheriff of Fresno county, and Fred Jackson, an officer from Nevada, have been in the mines for a week, hunting for Evans and Sontag. They were accompanied by Thomas Burns, the man who was with Deputy U. S. Marshal Black when he was shot while in Camp Badger, three weeks ago. Sunday morning they encamped at a vacant house about 18 miles northeast of here and spent the day in sleeping and preparing to continue the search for the bandits. About 20 minutes before sunset Rapelje went to the rear door of the house, and saw two men coming down the hill, who proved to be Evans and Sontag. The officers went out the front door, but as the bandits turned around the rear corner Evans saw Rapelje and, throwing his Winchester to his shoulder, took deliberate aim and fired. Just then Jackson stepped around and both officers opened fire. Evans was seen to throw up both hands and fall backwards. Then the firing became general, Sontag returning the shots with a vengeance. Jackson went around the end of the house to get a better place from which to shoot and received a shot in the left leg, between the knee and the ankle. About 40 shots were exchanged and darkness ended the battle. Later Sontag was seen to crawl behind a pile of rubbish and Rapelje again opened fire on him. Sontag then ran towards the hills, followed by Rapelje, who continued firing. Sontag did not return the fire and was soon out of sight. Sheriff Scott of Fresno has been wired to send out a posse, and officers will go from this city to the scene of the conflict.

BAY STATE AT THE FAIR.

Delegation Leaves Boston for the Columbian Exposition.

Boston, June 12.—The state delegation appointed under the rules of the legislature to represent the state on Massachusetts day, June 17, at the World's fair, left for Chicago at 10 this morning. Of the nine ex-governors invited but two, Messrs. Long and Rice, went with the party. Lieutenant Governor Wolcott, President Pinkerton of the senate, Speaker Barrett and Adjutant General Dalton were with the delegates.

THE SHERMAN LAW.

Attitude of Members of Congress on Its Repeal.

New York, June 12.—In reply to a telegram sent to members of both houses of Congress by the Times as to their attitude in regard to the Sherman law, 122 have been heard from—18 senators and 104 representatives. Of this number 88 are in favor of the repeal, 26 are against the repeal and eight are still undecided.

New Line from Providence to Worcester.

Woonsocket, R. I., June 12.—Trains began running regularly this morning between Providence and Southbridge, Mass., via the New York & New England's new seven mile line, connecting its Pascoag branch at Pascoag, R. I., with its main line at Douglas Junction, Mass. This travel has hitherto gone to Blackstone and thence via the Consolidated road to Providence. A freight service between Providence and Worcester will be inaugurated tonight.

Held for the Grand Jury.

Boston, June 12.—William E. Mitchell, who assaulted his wife and mother-in-law with a pistol last night in St. John's church, South Boston, was held in $5,000 today for the grand jury.

TELEGRAPHIC BREVITIES.

The residence of John McGregor at Nashua, N. H., was burned last night. The buildings were owned by Charles Robbins. Loss about $1,500; partially insured.

Sir:

Your wasted tissues and starved brain need nutriment.

H-O Hornby's Oatmeal

supplies both perfectly and palatably.

Pages 1-8.

The Evening Standard.

Pages 1-8.

ESTABLISHED FEBRUARY, 1850. | NEW BEDFORD, WEDNESDAY, JUNE 14, 1893.---TWELVE PAGES. | TWO CENTS.

HASKELL & TRIPP.

Perhaps the liveliest of the bargains today are these:

Big, handsome rugs, $1.98 each. 2 yds. long by 1 yd. wide.

Women's Jersey undervests, with deep lace finish on neck and sleeves. Price 29c. Made to retail for 50c. and worth that.

Fancy ribbons, 2 inches to 4 inches in width, every color combination, 29c. a yard—less than half the cost to make.

More about shoes.

We know whereof we speak when we say that the kinds of Oxfords we ask you $1.42 a pair for are sold for $2 elsewhere.

Women's white and navy blue canvas Oxfords, trimmed and tipped with white kid, very stylish in appearance, come in four widths. Our price $1.42 a pair. Our stock of the favorite brown Oxfords is immense. No assortment so complete in this vicinity. These were made expressly for us by people who know how to make good-fitting, reliable footwear, and have confidence enough in it to *warrant every* pair. Bring back any that don't give satisfaction and a *new pair will be given for them.*

Just now any sizes and widths can be supplied from our stock in the following varieties:

For $1.25—Women's brown goat Oxfords, opera toe, tipped, common sense heel.

For $1.39—Women's brown Oxfords, "plug cut," machine sewed.

For $1.39—Women's brown blucher, military heel and Piccadilly toe.

For $1.50—Women's brown goat Oxfords, hand turned, pointed toe, tipped.

For $1.50—Women's *genuine Russia* Oxfords, very soft and flexible, both on opera and common sense lasts. A great bargain, as your first glance will decide.

For $1.75—Women's brown Oxfords, extra fine, fancy edges, vamp and quarters.

Extraordinary sale of women's silk waists.

Our offer for the balance of a manufacturer's stock accepted at a low figure, resulting in your favor to the tune of $1.50 or $2 saved on each waist.

Choose from this list, at $5 each, from fine printed Pongee silks. These waists have "leg o'mutton" or "Bishop" sleeves, "cascade" fronts, all newest styles.

- Drab silks, black dot.
- Black silks, red dot.
- Brown silks, gold dot.
- Navy silks, white dot.
- Plain navy surah.

The silks used in above are better than the ordinary. They are genuine Japanese goods, and waists made from this grade have never before sold below $6.50. Some are worth $7.

HASKELL & TRIPP,
Department Stores,
Purchase and William Streets.

HATRED!

A Motive for Borden Murders.

Sensational Story of a Dressmaker.

Government Has Another Set-Back.

Tried to Prove Borden Home Unhappy.

Court Refuses to Admit the Testimony.

Recital of Famous You-Gave Me-Away Story.

Police Matron Tells of the Two Sister' Quarrel.

Prisoner and Her Lawyers Look Triumphant.

Day of Interesting Developments in Great Trial.

The Ejected Artist, de Lipman, Seeks Legal Advice.

This has been a day of surprises, sensations and interesting incidents in the Borden trial. The government receives another severe blow by the court's refusal to allow a friend of the prisoner to repeat a conversation with Lizzie on an ocean steamer, while returning from Europe. The prosecution has shown hatred to be the motive for the crime by the sensational story of a dressmaker, who testified to Lizzie's words about her stepmother. The recital of the quarrel between the two sisters and the famous "You gave me away" story by Police Matron Reagan was another feature of this forenoon's session.

The Ninth Day.

The morning of the ninth day of the trial of the cause of Commonwealth vs. Lizzie Andrew Borden opened with cloud, rain and mugginess, which had the effect of diminishing the size of the crowd in waiting, but the number was large enough to nearly fill the seats. They came in quietly enough and took seats assigned without noise or confusion. The "eccentrics" from abroad are not diminished, but were even added to this morning by the arrival of another woman, an elderly one, who greeted a Standard reporter on the stairs with the remark that she believed they had met earlier at the Parker House table. The scribe gently denied the impeachment and intimated that the while the delights of the aforesaid table would attract the contents of the pocketbook repelled the attendance. Then the lady launched out into a short dissertation on the excellent manner in which she had been treated here.

In the Court Room.

In the court room Lizzie and the jury were in their seats several minutes before the court arrived. Lizzie does not look well, and she walked slowly and alone into the room and sank—hardly another term will answer—into her seat. Deputy Sheriff Kirby, however, is authority for the statement that Lizzie is feeling well this morning, and that her absence from the court room yesterday afternoon did her good.

The Handleless Hatchet.

The handleless hatchet which has been introduced by the government excites much interest, and everybody is interested to know when it will be formally connected with the case. Defense does not know precisely at what point the connection will be established, and is waiting for the government to show its hand.

After the opening of the court there was a very short consultation between Mr. Knowlton, Mr. Adams and the judges.

CITY MARSHAL HILLIARD

Head of the Fall River Police on the Witness Stand.

City Marshal Hilliard of Fall River was the first witness called to the stand. He was examined by Mr. Moody.

Q. What is your full name? A. Rufus B. Hilliard.

Q. And you are city marshal of Fall River? A. Yes sir.

Q. How long have you been on the police force of Fall River? A. A little over 14 years.

Q. How long city marshal? A. A little over seven years.

Q. Prior to that time did you hold any office on the force? A. Yes sir.

Q. What? A. Assistant city marshal.

Q. On the 4th of August last year in what manner was your attention first called to trouble at the Borden house? A. By a telephone message.

Q. Could you recognize the voice of the person at the telephone? A. Yes sir, after he told me his name.

Q. Did the person who telephoned to you tell you his name? A. Yes sir.

Q. What name did he tell you? A. John Cunningham, newsdealer.

Q. After you had received the telephone what did you do? A. I left the telephone and went into the guard room and sent an officer.

Q. What officer? A. Georg. W. Allen.

Q. Where is the guard room situated with reference to the room where the telephone is? A. It adjoins.

Q. Did you yourself at that time notice the time accurately? A. No sir, I did not.

Q. When did you first go to the house yourself? A. About 3 o'clock in the afternoon.

Q. In the meantime had you sent other officers there? A. Yes sir.

Q. Can you tell me anything with reference to the order in which they were sent, either by message or oral communication? A. Yes sir.

Q. You may tell me. A. I sent Officer Allen, Officer Dougherty, Officer Medley, Officer Gillan, Officer Wilson, and the assistant marshal.

Q. Upon the premises on Second street when you went there, what did you do? Tell us generally what you did, not in detail. A. I looked at the yard, around the yard, around the pile of lumber I saw at the east end of the yard.

Q. Do you recall how the door of the barn and the windows in the loft of the barn were? A. Yes sir. The side door, when we went up from the yard to the barn, was open, the side door in the loft was closed; the window at the west end, I am not positive whether that was open or shut.

Q. The other window, do you recall that, the window at the east end? A. That, I think, was shut.

Q. What sort of a day was it with reference to heat on the 4th day of August last? A. Very hot.

Q. How was the heat in this loft? A. Well, it was extremely warm there, almost suffocating heat.

Q. Did you do anything in the house, Mr. Hilliard, on that afternoon? A. No sir, no more than to look at one or two of the rooms.

Q. Did you have any conversation with the prisoner? A. No sir, I did not.

Q. When next did you go to the Borden house? A. The next time I went to go into the house was on Saturday forenoon.

Q. Before or after the funeral service? A. After the funeral service.

Q. Speaking generally, what did you do on the Saturday forenoon? A. I looked into what is called Mr. and Mrs. Borden's room; I also looked into the room at the west of that which is said

Rufus B. Hilliard,
City Marshal of Fall River.

to be Miss Lizzie's room; I looked into the room that was on the north side of the house from that that was said to be Miss Emma's room.

Q. Were there other officers there at that time? A. Yes sir.

Q. Speaking generally, with what duty were they engaged? A. They were looking for anything that could be found in the shape of a weapon or clothing.

Q. Did you personally on that morning make any examination of dresses? A. No sir; I did not.

Q. How long were you at the house on Saturday morning? A. I should say that I was there some half hour.

Q. When did you next go, Mr. Hilliard? A. I went there Saturday afternoon, about 3 o'clock.

Q. In a general way what did you do on Saturday afternoon? A. Searched the house and cellar.

Q. Did you take personal part in that search yourself? A. Yes sir.

Q. There were a number of other officers there? A. Yes sir.

Q. Did you yourself make a personal examination of dresses? A. No sir, I cannot say that I did of dresses, with the exception of one that I took away.

Q. What did you spend your time in doing? A. I went through the drawers of the dressing cases, looked at the bed and bed clothing, and looked into the closet.

Q. You referred to a dress that you took away, will you state all that occurred with reference to that, excluding conversation, except with Mr. Jennings or Miss Borden? A. I asked Mr. Jennings where the dress was that she wore that day. He went out, and when he came back he brought a dress.

Q. Where did he go to? A. I was then in the room where Mrs. Borden was found, up stairs, he went into the hallway and came back into that room; I do not know where he went when he went into the hall. He came back into the room with the dress.

Q. Did you see the prisoner at that time? A. I saw her soon after that in what is called Miss Emma's room.

Q. What had you done with the dress at that time? A. I passed it to Dr. Dolan after it was handed to me.

Q. Did you have possession of the dress at any time when the prisoner was present? A. No sir; not immediately present, that is to say, not in the same room.

Q. Is this the dress skirt and waist which was presented to you by Mr. Jennings?

(Witness identified the dress.) A. I should say that that looks like it; yes, I should say that was the dress.

Q. What did you do with the dress? A. The dress was rolled up and a white skirt—

Q. Excuse me, you spoke of a white skirt. Did you get that at the same time? A. Yes sir.

Q. And from the same person—Mr. Jennings? Did he bring it with the dress or some other trip? A. I won't be sure. I think he brought them in together. He may have possibly gone back and got the white skirt; that I won't be positive of.

Q. What do you say as to that skirt? (Witness was handed the white skirt. A. I should say that this was the skirt.

Q. Now you may go on and tell us what you did with the skirt, under skirt and dress waist. A. I rolled them up with what I called a lounge cover that was taken from the dining room. (Witness identified the lounge cover.) I rolled them up in a paper. Mr. Jennings brought them down on to Main street. I met him at the corner of the granite block, and he passed them over to me.

Q. After Mr. Jennings had first handed them to you, and you rolled them up, do I understand that they were returned into his possession again? A. Yes sir, I turned them over to him, and told him to bring them to me, that I would meet him down street.

Q. And he gave you the same bundle that you gave him? A. Yes sir.

Q. After you got possession of them again what did you do? A. I carried them into my office.

(Continued on Third Page.)

WEATHER INDICATIONS.

Showers.

Washington, June 14.—For Massachusetts, Rhode Island and Connecticut, fair, except probable showers on the coast, variable winds.

"DR." TRAVERS IN JAIL.

Case Continued and He Could Not Procure $500 Bail.

(Special Dispatch.)

Boston, June 14.—"Dr." Matthew Travers, who was arrested in New Bedford yesterday on a charge of obtaining money under false pretenses, was arraigned this morning. The case was continued until Thursday, Travers being held in $500. He was unable to find surety.

Is Unconstitutional.

INDIANAPOLIS, June 14.—Judge Brown, in the county court here, decided that the fee and salary law passed by the legislature of 1891 and affecting every county and state officer in Indiana, except coroners and prosecuting attorneys, and which has recently become operative upon all the county sheriffs of the state, was unconstitutional. The law attempted to grade the aggregate of fees according to the necessities of each county, but the court holds that this graduation is defective.

Break in a Levee.

New Orleans, June 14.—A break in the levee occurred at 10 30 last night just below the oil mill in Baton Rouge and at midnight it was 20 feet wide and increasing fast.

It may be impossible to close the break. It is on the left bank of the river and if allowed to widen will cause great damage as the water will fill the track of the famous Bennett Carre crevasses.

HOME MATTERS.

THE DEMOREST CONTEST.

Second Competition for a Silver Medal in This City.

The second local contest for the Demorest silver medal took place in Y. M. C. A. hall last evening and about 100 were present. These contests are for medals offered by Mr. Demorest of New York, who in order to encourage public speaking on the temperance question, has arranged a system of competition in every place that desires to inaugurate them. After six silver medal contests the winners' contest for a gold medal, and after four such gold medal contests the winners compete for a grand gold medal. After eight of the latter a diamond medal is offered for a prize. The system has been carried on in various cities, but last evening's was the second in this city.

Rev. J. S. Swaim was chairman and the programme was as follows:

Piano solo. Miss M. C. Sylvester
Address by the chairman. Rev. J. S. Swaim
Singing. High School Quartet
Rumselling, the Country's Scourge. Mr. F. L. Thompson
Our National Curse. Mr. Eli Slater
Looking Forward. Mr. Chas. Billington
Brave for the Right. Mr. L. F. DeMoranville
Singing. High School Quartet
Who is to Blame. Mr. J. W. Buchanan
The Deacon's Sunday School Sermon. Mr. C. P. Emery
Reading. Mr. Benj. Drummond
A Trip to the World's Fair in Crayon. Mr. F. L. Thompson
Distribution of prizes.
America. Audience

The judges were A. McLellan Goodspeed, Esq., Rev. W. J. Reynolds and R. F. Raymond, Esq.

All the competitors were good, but the judges decided that Clarence P. Emery's was the most worthy, and accordingly awarded him the silver medal. The second prize, a $6 knife, was awarded to Mr. Buchanan. The winner on the first contest was Miss Mabel Hathaway.

EXAMINED BY AN EXPERT.

The Question of the Sanity of Assassin Sarmento.

Dr. Brown, resident physician at the hospital for lunatics at Taunton, who is an eminent authority on insanity, was in the city on Monday and examined Jose Vieira Sarmento at the house of correction, in company with Dr. Hayes, for the purpose of determining his sanity.

It is understood that Sarmento's counsel is very much pleased with the result of Dr. Brown's examination.

It is also stated that the government will soon begin an examination of the prisoner for the same purpose, and it is probable that Dr. Jelley of Boston, another expert, will be called in the case.

CONDENSED LOCALS.

In the Superior Court at Plymouth yesterday the divorce case of Alice M. Randall vs. Jeremiah L. Randall, both of Mattapoisett, was tried and a decree nisi was ordered by Judge Sherman for cruel and abusive treatment and alimony was also ordered for the libellant for one hundred dollars. Edwin A. Douglass, Esq., for libellant; Hon. E. L. Barnay for libellee.

Freight steamer City of New Bedford arrived at Newport from Fall River Saturday afternoon and laid up under the shears for repairs. It is expected that steamer City of Fall River which has been laid up for some time at Newport will come to this port this week, replacing one of the propellers now running to this port.

Patrick Smith of 23 Newton street was pleasantly surprised last evening. He was escorted by friends to Allen's Hall, where he found about 70 young people awaiting his arrival. He was presented with a handsome silver watch and chain, after which a fine collation and dancing made the event one to be remembered by those present.

There was a meeting of the Fourth of July committe of the Veteran Firemen last evening, when the subject of a celebration was further discussed, and it was decided to adjourn until Tuesday evening, 20th, to await additional replies from other associations.

Ten thousand pounds of Arctic whalebone have recently been sold in New York for export, and on Monday 2,200 pounds were sold at the same place for similar purpose. Both transactions were on private terms.

Persons wishing a cheap house should attend the mortgagee's sale of cottage honse and lot to be sold at auction tomorrow afternoon by Standish Bourne. See advertisement.

The inquest on the death of Maria das Candeias was concluded yesterday. Twenty-three witnesses were examined, Judge Borden conducting the examination.

See H. C. Hathaway's advertisement on page six for Horses, Furniture, Plants, etc. Will also sell Dr. Fortin's pair of Bay Trotters tomorrow morning at 10 o'clock.

The New Bedford Veteran Firemen's Association has voted to purchase 300 feet of hose, and Callahan & Co. of Boston has been given the order.

The city council committee on audit and the finance committee will be in session this evening.

Gentlemen, the finest line of Russia leather shoes found at Buchell's. See our $4 shoe.

Catboat Turk, belonging to Edmund D. Ashley, sunk at her moorings at Pope's Island, this morning.

SONS OF VETERANS.

Convention of the Massachusetts Division in This City.

The eleventh annual convention of the Massachusetts divisions, Sons of Veterans, will meet in Odd Fellows hall in this city this afternoon, and members of the order look forward to a very pleasant session, which will continue over

Arthur W. Forbes,
Chairman of the Local Committee.

through tomorrow. Headquarters have been established at the Parker House parlors, and there the visiting members are properly received as they arrive, and later are assigned rooms in the different hotels in town. Already about 50 delegates have reported, and by night this number will be increased to 100. The division council will meet at headquarters at 3 p. m., and the convention will be rapped to order at 4 o'clock, as stated above. E. B. Estes is mustering officer and Past Captain George N. Gardiner is officer of the guard.

Arrangements for the convention have been in charge of a local committee, made up as follows: A. W. Forbes, chairman; William E. James, secretary; William H. Jennings, George Duckworth, George T. Carpenter and R. E. Washburn. Mr. Forbes as chairman has had a busy time of it today assigning visitors to their rooms.

George N. Gardiner,
Officer of the Guard.

This evening there will be a banquet in Odd Fellows hall, to which delegates and prominent citizens have been invited.

Conventions have been held since 1881 as follows: At Lynn in 82, 83 and 89; at Boston in 84 and 85; at Worcester in 86; at Gardner in 90; at Lowell in 91 and at Milford in 92.

CRANBERRY GROWERS.

A delegation of cranberry growers from Massachusetts have finished an inspection of the cranberry bogs in Burlington and Ocean counties, New Jersey. They were A. D. Makepeace, of Cape Cod, the largest cranberry grower in the country; Emulus Small, a grower, and G. F. Baker, who handles most of the berries grown in Massachusetts. There are several thousand acres of cranberry bogs here, all in the best of condition. Mr. Small says that it costs a great deal more in Massachusetts than in New Jersey to get the bogs into condition. In New Jersey the cost ranges per acre from $30 to $100; in Massachusetts it costs from $500 to $1,000.

DECORATED THE GRAVES.

Yesterday was the annual memorial day for the Knights of Pythias. A committee from Union lodge, No. 7, of this city, decorated the graves of the following deceased members: In Rural cemetery, Harry W. Fisher, Jethro Hillman, Thomas E. Sherman, Thomas P. Lowes, James H. Walmsley; in Oak Grove cemetry, James T. Ashley, Eugene F. Brown, Herbert F. Gooding, John B. Habicht, Thomas M. James, William O. Lawton, Morrill B. Rodgers, William T. Soule, Robert Woolfenden. The grave of Milton B. Crowell of Damocles lodge, No. 16, of Brockton, at Riverside cemetery, Fairhaven, was also decorated.

COUNTY COMMISSIONERS.

The County Commissioners will meet in Fall River when Thomas Kieran, an engineer who has figured in the Borden trial, will present drawings for a bridge across the East Branch of Westport river at two locations. The commissioners will decide on a location. Afterwards the commissioners will confer with Engineer Edward Shaw of Boston in relation to the new bridge across the Acushnet river to take the place of the New Bedford and Fairhaven bridge.

SACRIFICED.

Prices have been cut down on all the piazza chairs in F. R. Slocum's store.

The stock was too large.

These chairs are handsome, durable and absolutely indispensable to a summer cottage. They are useful anywhere on lawns or piazzas.

The prices have been reduced about one third.

Sutton commandery will hold a drill at the armory this evening. Read special notice.

Chiropodist.—Mrs. Williams, 190 Purchase st., Webster block, every Friday.

First clambake of the season at Manhattan House Thursday, June 15.

The reputation of Cutter Whiskey for general excellence is world wide.

Bake opens at 12 o'clock tomorrow at Manhattan House.

Be made strong by Hood's Sarsaparilla.

HASN'T YOUR TIME COME TO RE-FURNISH?

Those Old Chairs are Shabby.

Your Dining Table is too Small.

A New Chamber Suite

is needed for the spare room and NEW CARPETS in parlors and hall.

Your Range is Worn Out

and should be replaced by a new one, and the new one should be one of our famous

GLENWOODS.

How About Those Draperies?

In our Drapery Department ideas are multiplied as the possibilities of each lovely fabric unfold themselves. You have long since discovered that it is a department where novelty is conspicuous, and to which it is a pleasure to turn when your mind begins to run on window decorations.

For all Your Household Needs

we will show you greater variety and make you the

LOWEST PRICES.

It will be to your advantage to deal with us.

C. F. WING,
34 to 40 Purchase Street.

WHITING & CO.

Call Especial Attention to Housekeepers, Summer Hotels, Boarding Houses, Yachts and Seashore Places.

Open today 100 pairs of 11-4 White Blankets, at $1.10 a pair.

100 pairs of 11-4 White Blankets at $1.40 per pair.

50 pairs of Red and Gray Blankets, for summer use.

200 cheap White Spreads, for summer use.

200 9-4 and 10-4 White Sheets, made of Fruit of the Loom Cotton.

200 Pillow Cases, made of Fruit of the Loom Cotton.

300 dozen Towels, of all grades, we want you to see what we sell at 12 1-2 and 25c. apiece.

500 pairs of Lace Curtains, from $1.00 to $7.50 per pair. A few odd pairs to be sold very cheap.

25 pairs of those Chenille Portieres left, we have had such large sales on, at $2.95 and $3.95 per pair. This is just half price, do not fail to see them.

100 Rugs, all sizes, for dining room, hall, parlor or chamber, all marked down to prices that will pay you to call and see what a nice rug you can get for a little money.

WHITING & CO.

BLUE SERGE SUITS $15.00.

The Coolest and Best Fabrics for Summer Wear.

In double and single breasted sacks, made up in first class shape---color and quality guaranteed.

Gentlemen in search of neat, stylish, comfortable and inexpensive rig will find these suits just what they want for the Summer outing.

J. & W. R. WING & CO.,
Clothiers and Hatters,
133 UNION ST.

THE CRESCENT!
22 Purchase St.

ONLY 19c. PER YARD.
VERY WIDE HAMBURGS.
Just right for Skirts.

Excellent Hamburgs at 12 1-2c. A good assortment at 5c.

To close at 19c. per yard.

A Lot of Silk Gloves,
Black and Colors, regular 25 and 29c. quality.

Mitts, good quality, 25c., a better grade at 50c.

Shirt Waists, at 29, 50, 75c.

Better quality at $1.00 $1.25, and $1.50, etc.

An entire new lot of belts, all styles.

Try THE LATEST, Empire styles, in tan and black, at 50c.

GUIMPES.

Guimpes at 39, 50, 58c.
Guimpes at 62, 75, 83c., $1.

Children's Dresses!

Gingham dresses from 50c. to $1.75.

White dresses, all styles and prices.

MARKED DOWN—Children's Short Cloaks.

TAN COLORED HOSIERY.

Children's Tan Hose, 25 and 37c. Ladies' Tan Hose, 25, 33 and 50c. Black Hosiery in all grades.

SUMMER CORSETS.

Good ones at 50c. Better grades at 75c., $1, $1.25 and $2. Corsets of all kinds. Equipoise Waists, Double Ve Waists, Ferris Ventilating Waists. Misses' and Ladies' Summer Vests of all kinds. Gingham aprons, two widths, 25c.

THE CRESCENT!
22 Purchase St.

HATRED !

(Continued from First Page.)

THE HANDLELESS HATCHET FITTED IN THE SKULL.

Q. Have you had possession of them since that time at all? A. No sir; not after they were turned over to Dr. Dolan.

Q. I understand you to say you brought this lounge cover from the dining room? A. Yes sir.

Q. You do not know whether it belonged to that sofa or the sofa in the sitting room? A. No sir.

Q. How long were you there Saturday afternoon? A. I should say about three hours and a half.

Q. Did you go to the Borden house again on the same day? A. Yes sir.

Q. When and with whom? A. I went to the Borden house about quarter to 8 that night in company with the mayor.

Q. When you reached the neighborhood of the Borden house what was there about the house? A. A large crowd of people.

Q. Give us a little more definite description. A. I should say that possibly there may have been between 200 and 300 people; perhaps more than that.

Q. Did you do anything with reference to that crowd? A. Yes sir.

Q. What did you do? A. I sent for officers and roped off the street.

Q. You then went into the house? A. Yes sir.

Q. Did you see after you went in the prisoner, her sister and Mr. Morse? A. Yes sir.

Q. Any one else? A. I think there was somebody that was in the sitting room, I won't be sure about that.

Q. In which room did you go? A. I went in the side door and passed into the kitchen and from there into the sitting room. There we waited perhaps four or five minutes before going into the parlor.

Q. Was there some conversation? A. Yes sir.

Q. Did you take part in it to any extent? A. No sir.

Q. Who were the ones who did the talking? A. The mayor, Mr. Morse, Miss Lizzie and Miss Emma.

Q. Will you state what the talk was? A. Yes sir. After we entered the parlor and sat down the mayor said that he had a request to make of the family and that was that they remain in the house for a few days; that there was a great deal of excitement and he thought it would be better for all concerned if they should remain there and not go out on the street; that if they were annoyed by the people around the house to send to the city marshal or himself and he would see that the crowd was dispersed. I think Mr. Morse spoke up and wanted to know how they were going to get their mail from the post office and the mayor told them it would be better to send some one for it, on account of so much excitement as there was at the time there around the house. I think Miss Lizzie spoke up next and said, "What, is there any one suspected in this house?" The mayor said, "Well, perhaps Mr. Morse can answer that question after what occurred last night." Miss Lizzie spoke up and said, "I want to know the truth." I think she repeated that twice. The mayor said, "I regret very much to say, Miss Borden, that you are suspected." At that Miss Emma spoke up and said, "We have tried to keep it from her as long as we could." That was all the conversation that I remember of.

Q. Do you recall any other subject that was talked of? A. Yes, I do. The mayor asked Miss Lizzie where she was at the time her father was killed. She said she was out in the barn and he asked her what she was out there for. She said that she went out there to get some lead to make some sinkers with. He asked her how long she remained there. She said about twenty minutes.

Q. Do you recall anything else? A. No sir, I do not.

Q. Let me ask you whether Lizzie, when told she was suspected, said anything? A. Yes sir. When she made the remark that she wanted to know the truth, and the mayor told her she was suspected, she then made the remark: "I am ready to go at anytime."

Q. Is there any further conversation that occurred that you can think of? A. No sir, that's all I think of now.

Q. How long a time did this visit occupy? A. Ten or 12 minutes, I should think.

Q. Later did you receive some clothing? A. Yes sir.

Q. Do you recall when? A. It was the 10th of August.

Q. From whom did you receive it? A. From Mrs. Holmes I received some, from another lady some, and some I took myself.

Q. Please state what the articles were? A. A pair of shoes and stockings I asked Lizzie for. She went up the front stairs, and Mrs. Brigham brought them down. From Mrs. Holmes I received the bedspread and two pillow shams. I took away a piece of the moulding from the mopboard of the room where Mrs. Borden was found. I took away a piece of plastering taken from the wall and a marble slab from the dressing case. I also took away a piece of the door jamb between the sitting room and dining room. I took a basket from the barn which contained lead and a box from the barn.

Q. What did you do with the shoes and stockings? A. I carried them to my office and that night turned them over to Dr. Dolan.

Q. What did you do with the piece of the door jamb? A. I took it to the station and afterwards delivered it to the court at the hearing in Fall River.

Q. Where did you say the shorter piece of wood came from? A. It was taken from Mrs. Borden's room.

Q. You said the basket was found in the loft of the barn? A. Yes sir.

Q. Where? A. It was on top of a bench.

Q. How was the loft of the barn Thursday afternoon with respect to dust? A. There was considerable dust there.

Q. Where did you find the box. A. Down stairs in the barn near a door.

Q. Do you know whether the basket and box were in substantially the same position on Thursday as they were the day they were taken away? A. I cannot say.

Q. After delivering over the articles, when did you get them back? A. On the 16th of August, and afterwards turned them over to Professor Wood.

Q. What did you do with the piece of plastering? A. I put it in a trunk at the station house.

Q. How long did you retain it in your custody? A. Until the trial.

Witness identified the piece of plastering.

Q. Did you have other property in your possession? A. Yes sir.

Q. What? A. Hatchets and axes.

Q. When did you receive the two hatchets with handles? A. The 5th of August they were given to me by Mr. Edson.

Q. Who did you then deliver them to? A. Dr. Dolan.

Q. By whom were the two axes delivered to you? A. Mr. Edson.

Q. How long did you retain the custody of them? A. Until the 9th of August.

Q. What did you then do with them? A. Delivered them to Dr. Dolan.

Q. Did you receive any other weapons? A. On August 8th a hatchet.

Q. Describe it. A. The handle was broken off, and only a short piece remained. There was a white substance on the iron part.

Q. Is this the hatchet? A. Yes.

Q. Can you tell what the white substance was? A. I can't.

Q. Where was the wood when you got it? A. In the head.

Q. Where was it broken off? A. Close up.

Q. Anything else? A. Yes sir, the wood part was bright.

Q. Anything in the shape of fragments? A. No sir.

Q. Who gave you the hatchet? A. Officer Medley.

Q. What did you do with it? A. I put it in the trunk.

Q. Is the trunk here? A. Yes.

Q. What was done when it was put in? A. The trunk was locked.

Q. Who had the key? A. I did.

Q. Has the key passed out of your possession until taken by the court? A. I've had control of it.

Q. How long did you have the hatchet head? A. It was delivered to Professor Wood August 30th.

Q. Anything else in your possession? A. I don't remember.

Q. A marble slab? A. Yes.

Q. Anything else? A. The clothing now here.

Q. Do you recall anything else—a handkerchief? A. That was in the box.

Q. Have you made any effort to find a person who sent or carried a note to the Borden house Aug. 4th? A. No further than that I instructed my officers to do so.

Q. Have you been able to find any person who did send one?

Mr. Robinson objected, saying, "It does not appear that he (Hilliard) has done anything himself."

The answer was ruled out.

Q. On Saturday afternoon before the search began, did the prisoner make any request? A. I spoke to her about 4 p. m.

Cross-examined by ex-Governor Robinson.

Q. Mr. Allen was the first officer you sent to the house? A. Yes.

Q. Did you meet him or telephone? A. I sat in my office and telephoned.

Q. Was he in uniform or citizen's clothes? A. He was in citizen's dress.

Q. What time was that? A. About quarter after 11.

Q. You had not been there? A. No.

Q. When you arrived there the first time where did you go? A. I went into the yard, but I am not sure if I went to the barn or to a pile of lumber.

Q. Other officers were with you? A. Yes.

Q. Were you all together? A. No, I think some were in the barn while others went to the pile of lumber with me.

Q. You saw nothing about the lumber? A. No.

Q. Was the lower door of the barn open? A. Yes.

Q. And the loft door open? A. Yes.

Q. Was one of the windows open? A. I can't say.

Q. When did you go into the house? A. From 4½ to quarter of 5 o'clock.

Q. Who did you see there? A. Doctors and the bodies of Mr. and Mrs. Borden.

Q. Go up stairs? A. Yes.

Q. See anybody there? A. Only the doctors who went up with me.

Q. Was there any objection from anybody to your going in? A. No sir.

Q. Did you ask to have any doors unfastened? A. No, I only looked at one door.

Q. What one? A. The front.

Q. Did you go there on Friday? A. No.

Q. By your instructions was there any search on Friday? A. I instructed no one.

Q. When did you next go there? A. At 1 or 1½ o'clock that night—to the yard.

Q. What was the next time to the house? A. I should say about 12¼ o'clock on Saturday.

Q. Were you in the yard before that day? A. Yes.

Q. What did you do in the house? A. I went up the back stairs into what I term Mr. and Mrs. Borden's room.

Q. Were you alone? A. No.

Q. What did you do? A. Looked at the bed and then went to Lizzie's room.

Q. Who showed you up? A. Miss Russell.

Q. Was the door opened with a key? A. I won't say.

Q. You looked at the bed, you say; how fully? A. I looked at the bed and under the head, where something was handed to me.

Q. That was a stick, wasn't it? A. Yes.

Q. You attach no importance to that? A. No.

Q. Did you do anything else with the bed? A. Not at that time.

Dr. David W. Cheever,
Government's Medical Expert.

Q. There was no more search in that room? A. Not on that day.

Q. I mean at that time? A. At 3 o'clock I searched the whole house.

Q. Where did you next go? A. Into the room I called Lizzie's.

Q. How did you go? A. Miss Russell went ahead and we followed.

Q. Was the door locked? A. I won't be sure.

Q. Was that the time when the bolt was pulled off? A. No.

Q. When was that done? A. I don't know.

Q What did you do there? A. I looked at the bed and mattress and went to the west side of the room.

Q. Was the family gone to the funeral? A. Yes.

Q. Who was there? A. Miss Russell and Mrs. Holmes.

Q. Did you do anything else? A. Went into the room called Miss Emma's at the north.

Q. Find anything? A. No.

Q. Nor in Lizzie's room? A. No.

Q. What did you do then? A. Came down stairs and went away.

Q. When did you next go there? A. About 3 p. m.

Q. At that time you said you were there 3½ hours? A. Yes.

Q. Searched thoroughly? A. Yes.

Q. In the presence of Mr. Jennings? A. Yes.

Q. He didn't object? A. No.

Q. In the afternoon did you see any of the family? A. Miss Emma.

Q. She wanted you to search thoroughly? A. Yes.

Q. Have any talk with Lizzie? A. I had no talk with her, but heard her speak.

Q. Anything said about taking the bottom out of the chimneys? A. Yes.

Q. What was said? A. I said I wanted the bottom cut open to see that nothing had been thrown down.

Q. Was Lizzie there? A. No, but Mr. Jennings was.

Q. Describe to the jury the thoroughness of your search; take each room. A. I didn't search every room; we divided up.

Q. You were at the head? A. I was at the head of the forces of my department.

Q. Now go ahead. A. We went from the kitchen to the northeast room in the attic and searched the bed and clothing.

Q. Whose room was this? A. I was told Mr. Morse was occupying it.

Q. Well, go on. A. Mr. Fleet and Officer Desmond were searching Bridget's room, and I went in. We searched the bed and clothing. We also searched what I called the water tank there. Then I went to a room on the south side of the attic. Mr. Jennings, Officer Seaver and Dr. Dolan were there. We searched everything there.

Q. Are you certain of that? A. Yes; I saw some trunks there that the others opened.

Q. Did you have trouble with any of them? A. Yes, with one.

Q. How did you get it open? A. Emma or Lizzie came up. Lizzie, I think, but am not positive, told us how to open it.

Q. There was no trouble about a key? A. No.

Q. Didn't one of them say that trouble would have been avoided if you had sent for them? A. I heard no such remark. The trunk that we had trouble with had a key on it.

Q. Didn't Emma say she wanted a thorough search, and if there was any trunk or box that you couldn't open to ask for the key; or words to that effect? A. Yes.

Q. Where did you next go after you searched the attic? A. I came down into Mr. and Mrs. Borden's room and searched it thoroughly, looked into the closets over the shelves, into the drawers, and examined the cupboard by the chimney. From that room we went into Lizzie's room, and Mr. Desmond and myself searched it thoroughly. Mr. Jennings was there. Mr. Seaver was in the room west, which is Miss Emma's room. That is as far as I searched until I got into the cellar.

Q. Was the clothes room searched? A. By Mr. Fleet and Mr. Seaver, and I am not sure whether by Mr. Desmond or not.

Q. Where were you when you asked for the skirt? A. I was in the hall.

Q. Mr. Jennings brought it right in, didn't he? A. Yes sir, pretty soon.

Q. With no unnecessary delay? A. No sir.

Q. For the time being you handed it back to Mr. Jennings, didn't you? A. Yes sir.

Q. And he afterwards brought it down to you? A. Yes sir.

Q. You have no doubt but what it is the same one? A. No sir.

Q. The whole search, as the doctors would call it, was with negative result? A. Yes, you might so call it, but it was a thorough search.

Q. You went home with Miss Lizzie after the inquest on Wednesday? A. Yes sir.

Q. You went home with her right along, didn't you? A. Yes sir; some of the time.

Q. Rode back and forth in a carriage together? A. Yes sir.

Q. It was Wednesday noon when you asked for shoes and stockings? A. Yes sir; I asked her to hand me the shoes and stockings which she promised the district attorney.

Q. There was no objection made, was there? A. No sir.

Q. What did she do? A. She went up stairs and I think it was Mrs. Brigham who brought them down.

Q. Did you call for a dress pattern? A. No sir, I did not.

Q. Did anybody? A. No; not that I have any knowledge of.

Q. Was the dress pattern given over? A. A dress pattern was brought from the house.

Q. Was it examined by you? A. No sir, but it was in the court room.

Mr. Knowlton—We attach no significance to it.

Mr. Robinson—I drop the matter right there.

Q. You went on Saturday night and had a conversation with the two sisters and Mr. Morse? A. Yes sir.

Q. Whatever was said was heard by all present? A. Yes sir.

Q. You told Mr. Jennings prior to that evening that you suspected Lizzie?

Mr. Knowlton—I pray your honors' judgment.

Chief Justice—The question may be answered.

A. I did not tell him.

Q. Did any one tell Mr. Jennings?

Mr. Knowlton—I pray your honors' judgment.

Chief Justice—The witness may answer.

A. I think so.

Q. You told Miss Lizzie she had better stay in the house? A. Yes sir.

Q. You had a warrant in your possession at this time? A. No sir, the first time I had a warrant was on Monday morning.

Q. The mayor said if the people about the house annoyed them he'd have them dispersed? A. Yes sir.

Q. In this conversation you advised Lizzie not to go out doors? A. The mayor did the talking.

Q. Now in the course of conversation Lizzie asked if any one was suspected? A. Yes sir.

Q. You knew that Mr Morse was about the premises? A. Yes sir.

Q. You knew that Bridget was about the premises? A. Yes sir.

Q. And you knew that the defendant was about the premises? A. Yes sir.

Q. There has been a great deal of comment in the public press, a good deal of street talk, and a good deal of advice had been given to the officers, hadn't there, in that way? A. There was some street talk, but I didn't hear it.

Q. What did Lizzie say in answer to the mayor's question? A. She replied, "I think Mr. Morse can answer that question better than I can, from what occurred last night."

Q. Thereupon Lizzie said, "I want to know the truth"? A. Yes sir.

Q. She spoke earnestly? A. Yes sir.

Q. What reply did the mayor make? A. "I regret very much, Miss Borden, that you are suspected."

Q. What did Emma say? A. "We have tried to keep it from her as long as we could."

Q. Now what did she say? A. Lizzie said, "Well, I am ready to go now," or words to that effect.

Q. She spoke right up openly, earnestly and frankly? A. Yes sir.

Q. Sure about that? A. Yes sir.

Q. That was about what time Saturday evening? A. Well, I should say that was probably somewhere in the vicinity of four or five minutes to 8.

Q. And now to make sure the same five persons were present at that time? A. Yes sir.

Q. And were the doors to the other rooms closed at that time into the hall and the sitting room? A. I think the door that leads into the front hall stood ajar; I won't say it was closed.

Q. Then she was asked where she was at the time her father was killed and she said she was in the barn, looking for some lead to make sinkers of? A. As I understood it, she said she was in the barn, looking for some lead to make some sinkers.

Q. About 20 minutes altogether? A. Yes sir.

Q. Then you gentlemen departed and left the family to themselves? A. Yes sir.

Q. Nothing more that you recall? A. Nothing that I recall, no sir.

Q. Do you recall at that time that you said to them you had finished the search of the house except the cellar? A. No sir, I do not remember making that remark at that time.

Q. But you did make it? A. I think I made that remark to Mr. Jennings on Saturday.

Q. You told Mr. Jennings that except the cellar you had completed the search? A. Yes sir, I told him something like this, that I wanted to have a mason come and take the bricks out of the chimney, but I would not do it the next day, it being Sunday, but I wanted to have it done the first thing Monday morning.

Q. Did you look into the house to see where the running water was supplied? A. No sir, I don't remember.

Q. Did you discover anything in the upper part of the house? A. There was a tank of water where Bridget Sullivan's room was; I cannot say where it went to.

Q. Did you notice on the second floor whether the rooms were supplied with faucets or bowls and pitchers? A. I did not see any faucets there.

Q. You have said that Mr. Allen was not in uniform, are you able to make a statement in regard to the others that went up there? A. I am in regard to Officer Mullaly.

Q. What was it in regard to him? A. I know that he had a uniform on.

Q. What about Mr. Dougherty? A. That I am not able to state.

Q. Or Mr. Medley? A. I cannot say because I did not see him.

Q. Mr. Wilson? A. I saw Mr. Wilson, and gave him orders.

Q. Mr. Fleet? A. I did not see him.

Q. When did you receive the two axes and the two hatchets? A. I received them Friday morning.

Q. Who brought them? A. Officer Edson.

Q. How were they brought? A. I don't know, they were in my office when I came.

Q. You did not see them come? A. No sir.

Q. You got the one without a handle on that day? A. The following Monday.

Q. Who brought it? A. Officer Medley.

Q. What did you do with it? A. I finally locked it up in my trunk.

Q. Yes finally, but what did you do with it that minute? A. Had it there in my private office.

Q. Did you put it with the other four? A. No sir, I did not.

Q. When did it go to either Dr. Dolan or Professor Wood? A. It went to Professor Wood on the 30th of August.

Q. It was not produced at the preliminary hearing at all? A. No sir, not that I know of.

Q. You were present at the preliminary hearing? A. Yes sir.

Q. And saw the two axes and the two hatchets there? A. Yes sir.

Q. And heard the testimony about these? A. Yes sir.

Q. And you didn't bring down the other one at all? A. No sir.

Q. Did you give it to Professor Wood yourself? A. Yes sir.

Q. Where? A. Down at my office.

Q. Was it your own thought or at his request? A. I was ordered to deliver anything that I had in my possession to Professor Wood.

Q. When you got it the little piece of wood was in the eye of the hatchet, apparently in its proper position? A. Yes sir.

Q. There was a whitish substance on the blade? A. All over the iron part of it.

Q. Looked like ashes? A. Looked like ashes to me, I do not know what it was.

Q. You didn't examine it closely then, at all? A. Yes, I looked the hatchet over thoroughly.

Q. Anything more than that? A. No sir.

Q. When you got it was it wrapped up in anything? A. It was in paper.

Q. Do you recall what kind of paper? A. No sir, I cannot tell.

Q. Was it kept wrapped up in paper? A. Yes sir, it was wrapped up in a paper until it was taken out of the paper and handed to Professor Wood.

Q. Was it seen or handled by any one from the time you got it on the 10th of August until the 30th? A. I won't be positive whether Dr. Dolan saw it or not.

Q. Did Mr. Knowlton? A. No sir, I do not think Mr. Knowlton saw it until the 30th of August.

Q. Had Professor Wood testified at that time? A. Yes sir.

Q. You heard his testimony? A. I heard part of it.

Q. It was in substance in regard to stains? A. Yes sir.

Q. You have heard his testimony that there was no blood? A. If I remember it correctly, I think that was what he testified to in the lower court.

Re-direct.

Q. What was this occurrence that was referred to as having occurred to Mr. Morse that night?

Mr. Robinson objected and the question was excluded by the court.

DR. COUGHLIN,

Mayor of Fall River, Tells What He Knows of the Case.

Dr. Coughlin of Fall River was the next witness called to the stand.

Q. Your name? A. John W. Coughlin.

Dr. John W. Coughlin,
Mayor of Fall River.

Q. You are a physician in Fall River? A. Yes sir.

Q. In 1892 and at the present time you are mayor of that city? A. Yes sir.

Q. On the Saturday afternoon following the homicide did you go to the Borden house? A. I did.

Q. With whom? A. City Marshal Hilliard.

Q. As you approached the house did you see any persons on the street? A.

(Continued on Fourth Page.)

THE STANDARD'S ENTERPRISE.

Borden Trial Reports Not Surpassed by Any Paper in the Country.

(Fall River News, June 13.)

The News presents today the full story of Lizzie Borden's testimony at the inquest held in this city last August, and which was yesterday excluded from the present trial by the court. It will be read with interest.

We desire to thank the proprietors of the New Bedford Standard for courtesies and assistance in presenting this supplement, and while so doing to compliment them upon the very full, accurate and nearly verbatim reports which they are giving of the trial. The Standard's enterprise in this is not surpassed by any paper in the country.

We are pleased to add also, at this time, the acknowledgments of our own reporters at the trial of many courtesies shown by the New Bedford press, particularly by Manager Hough, of the Standard.

THE EJECTED ARTIST

Leads Joe Howard to Comment on Newspaper Workers at Trials.

(Joe Howard in Boston Globe.)

Just at this time an incident not set down on the programme occurred, which both attracted and distracted attention. Mr. de Lipman, a competent young artist who came here in the early days of the trial, is a sort of free lance. He has done some excellent work for New York and Boston papers, and, provided with an order from the chief justice, he was in the court room making sketches. Having no regular seat assigned to him, he went from place to place, according to the convenience or courtesy of press men who knew him. This he did rather frequently, to the annoyance of Sheriff Wright, who, after a change of seat made at this moment, went to him and touched him on the shoulder, presumably intending to warn him. Mr. de Lipman, who busily engaged in making a sketch of Dr. Draper, instead of turning to recognize the sheriff, impatiently waved him off with his pencil, as much as to say, "Don't interrupt me now; I am busy." Instantly the sheriff summoned Deputies Favey and Hodges, and another, and ordered them to remove him. This they did with great force and violence, without giving him time to rise, or, so far as I could see, ordering him to leave. The stories are somewhat conflicting tonight, and I have been unable to see either of the parties, both of whom I consider to be in the wrong, Mr. de Lipman in so often changing his seat, and the sheriffs in putting him out of the room with unnecessary violence.

Officials ought to understand that newspaper workers don't attend trials for fun, nor are they drawn to court rooms by the idle curiosity manifested by the people of this region.

They are present for the transaction of mind-straining, muscle-wearing business, in the interests of thousands of individuals who are following intelligently the government and outcome of the celebrated case.

The chief justice has manifested a keen appreciation of the onerous duties of newspaper writers and artists, as have his associates, and, with their approval, the local authorities, Sheriff Wright and his deputies, have done much to make the performance of these duties lighter, so that I regret exceedingly this incident, which I am quite sure must have been born of a misunderstanding, first, on the part of Mr. de Lipman as to his rights in court, and, second, on the part of the deputies as to the manner in which the sheriff's order was to be executed.

NEWSPAPER COMMENTS.

The sentimental interest inspired by Lizzie Borden is not a healthy sign. It may be natural for persons who have known the young woman to sympathize with her and allow their sympathy to take the form of expressions of confidence in her innocence. But for absolute strangers to flock to her defense indicates that there is an abnormal state of feeling existing and that there are many persons ready to encourage crime by placing obstacles in the way of punishing criminals. If the state succeeds in proving that Lizzie Borden is a murderess it will give a wholesome check to the bad fashion of trying to impair the efficacy of the law by clamorous expressions of confidence in the purity and innocence of persons accused of crime.—San Francisco Chronicle.

The Fall River police are bound to be criticised, any way. Now they are catching it from some of their own townspeople because of the contrast between their treatment of Lizzie Borden at the time of her arrest, and their present treatment of Correiro. The former, it is averred, was treated "tenderly," and the unfortunate suspect of today is undergoing what would be severe punishment for the average convict. At least, this is the charge. These are unhappy times for the guardians of the peace in the Spindle City.—New Bedford Mercury.

The Evening Standard.

NEW BEDFORD, MASS.

WEDNESDAY EVENING, JUNE 14.

THREE EDITIONS DAILY.

No. 87 Union Street.

PUBLISHED BY

E. ANTHONY & SONS.

INCORPORATED.

—TERMS—

Six Dollars a Year; Three Dollars for Six Months, in advance; Single Copies Two Cents.

ORDER THE EVENING STANDARD TO YOUR VACATION ADDRESS.

Mailed direct from this office to any address, for one day or any length of time desired, at the rate of 50 cents per month, including postage.

TWELVE PAGES.

This Evening's Issue Consists of Twelve Pages and Every Patron is Entitled to that Number.

The Lowell Courier is a good deal disgruntled with several things connected with the newspaper reports of the Borden trial, one of which is the verbatim reports, which it declares to be stupid and absurd. It says that the papers which do this give fairly intelligent and intelligible summaries of the testimony; but it has to admit that the summaries are in the main absurdly biased and betray the prejudices of the writers. It does not seem to have occurred to the Courier that it is this very fact that gives the verbatim reports their value. How can the Courier know the summaries are biased unless it has compared them with the evidence itself? How can any one who wishes to be able to form a fair and intelligent opinion of the guilt or innocence of Miss Borden do so without reading the evidence as it comes from the lips of the witnesses and everything in connection with it? It may be tedious and repetitious, as is the case in all legal proceedings, but an intelligent person would rather draw his own inferences than have some one else do it for him. The verbatim reports in the Standard are intended for this class of readers, and it would be singular indeed for a newspaper so near the scene of this terrible tragedy not to give the fullest possible account of everything connected with it. If a similar tragedy should occur in Lowell or within a dozen miles of it, we are inclined to think the Courier would perform its functions as a newspaper in the same way the Standard has. If it did not, it would have to march to the rear. Of course it is not so much to be expected that papers at a distance will go into details to the extent the local papers do. But they should not cast any reproaches on the latter for discharging the chief function for which they exist, that of giving the fullest accounts possible of all matters of local interest. The Standard reports of this trial will always be the chief source of information with regard to it, and that they are appreciated by those for whom they are specially intended, its own readers within the limits of its circulation, is shown by the immense sale of its daily issues, and by the use that has been made of them by its contemporaries far and wide.

Another special feature of the Standard in connection with the trial is that while refraining, in accordance with its views of propriety, from editorial comment on the evidence, it has given full extracts from other papers showing the general impression produced on their editors and reporters by the events of each day.

Commencement exercises at Wesleyan university will take place on Wednesday, June 28th, at 10 a. m. The Baccalaureate sermon will be delivered by Rev. B. P. Raymond, D. D., LL. D. on Sunday, June 25th, at 10 30 a. m., and the university sermon will be given by Rev. J. A. M. Chapman, D. D., at 7 30 p. m. same day. Commencement dinner will be on Wednesday afternoon, June 28th, Rev. E. M. Mills, D. D., toastmaster, and the reception by President and Mrs. Raymond will take place on the evening of the 28th.

Ex-President Harrison has not been bored to death with reception committees and hand shakings at Chicago, although he has been received with due honor by the officials of the exhibition. We should think that he would be highly gratified at being left to himself, and would be inclined to agree that "the post of honor is a private station."

The elections for the German reichstag begin tomorrow. There are about 400 members to elect, and it may be some time before it is known whether the emperor or the people have triumphed.

The outside papers are saying that the Borden jury was driven on Sunday to the "heart" of Acushnet. They were slightly mistaken. We know the Head of Acushnet here, but nothing about the heart.

MATTAPOISETT.

Miss Annie M. Almy left Tuesday morning for the Mountain House, Blandford, near Springfield, for the benefit of her health.

William H. Forbes has removed his family from Marion to this place.

Hiram E. Ames has secured a position at this station as station baggage master, and entered upon his duties Tuesday.

Charles L. Keith has been promoted from brakeman to train baggage master on Conductor Bennett's train on the Fairhaven branch.

Mrs Mary L. Seavey and her sister, Miss Munroe, and Eugene Battelle and family of Boston have arrived.

Edmund Merrithew and family of Middleboro are in town.

Rev. H. C. Cunningham and family of Boston have arrived and will summer at Mrs. F. E. Oliver's cottage near Oakland street. He will preach at the Episcopal church this summer.

Schooner Kate Scranton, Kelley, was in last week with a cargo of coal for Captain Keene.

Yesterday there was a general change in the train service. The limited express, for subscribers only, was resumed here as were also the mid-day Boston trains to and from this place.

Hon. George O. Shattuck and family have arrived at their house on Ned's point, and Samuel D. Warren and family and Mr. H. R. Dalton and family, all of Boston, have also arrived at their homes at Ned's point.

Robert C. H. Brock and family of Philadelphia have the Dickerman house.

HATRED!

(Continued from Third Page.)

I saw a large crowd congregated about the Borden house.

Q. What was done with reference to these people? A. I instructed the marshal to have them removed.

Q. Were they removed? A. They were.

Q. Can you give us an idea of how large a crowd there was on the street? A. The sidewalk on the east side for some little distance both north and south was covered with people. And in the middle of the street there were a large number of people; in fact, it was a difficult thing to drive through the street without running some one down. I instructed the marshal to have them removed, and officers were called.

Q. Did you go into the house, doctor? A. I went into the house.

Q. And there did you have an interview with any of the inmates of the house? A. After we had been in the house several moments.

Q. With whom had you the interview? A. The first person whom I saw was Miss Emma Borden.

Q. Then did you see other persons? A. I did.

Q. Whom? A. I saw Miss Lizzie, Miss Emma and Mr. Morse; the three were together.

Q. In what room did you have your talk? A. In the parlor.

Q. Doctor, I wish you would recall that conversation? A. Upon taking my seat, as near as I can recall, I said to the family I have a request to make of the family, and that is that you remain in the house for a few days, as I believe it would be better for all concerned if you do so. There was a question arose; I think Miss Lizzie asked me and said, "Why is there anybody in this house suspected?" I said, well, perhaps Mr. Morse can answer that question better than I, as his experience last night perhaps would justify him in the inference that somebody in this house was suspected. Miss Lizzie said, "I want to know the truth," and I believe she repeated the statement. I said "Miss Borden, I regret to answer, but I must answer yes, you are suspected." And if I remember rightly at that time Miss Borden spoke up and said, "I am ready to go now."

Q. Do you recall whether any one else said anything? A. Yes, Miss Emma Borden said: "Well, we have tried to keep it from her as long as we could."

Q. You may go on. A. I asked Miss Lizzie Borden where she went to after leaving her father. She said she went to the barn for some lead for sinkers. I asked her how long she remained in the barn. She said about 20 minutes. I then said if you are disturbed in any way, or if you are annoyed by crowds in the street, I would like to have you notify the officer in the yard and instruct him to tell the marshal. Or if you will notify me I will see that you have all the protection the law affords. I think Miss Emma Borden made the statement: "We want you to do everything you can in this matter," and on leaving I stated that I would return on Sunday, but I did not on account of my mother being taken ill and I was summoned to see her early in the morning, and I did not get back till late at night.

Cross-examined.

Q. You advised them to remain in the house, or on the premises? A. Yes sir.

Q. And thereupon Miss Lizzie said, "Is there any one in this house suspected?" A. To the best of my knowledge.

Q. She said it promptly? A. She made that statement.

Q. Answer my question.

Mr. Moody objected.

The court said he may answer the question.

A. She said it somewhat hesitatingly, I should say.

Q. What did you say to her? A. I replied by stating that Mr. Morse could best answer that question, as his experience last night would justify him in the inference that some one was suspected.

Q. What was the next thing? A. Lizzie said, "I want to know the truth," and she repeated it, if I remember rightly.

Q. Did you answer? A. Yes sir.

Q. What did you say? A. I regret, Miss Borden, but I must answer, yes, you are suspected.

Q. What did she say? A. She said as I now recall it: "I am ready to go now."

Q. Or any time, didn't she say? A. I cannot recall.

Q. Spoke up promptly then, didn't she? A. Well, it depended altogether by what you mean by earnestly and promptly.

Q. I mean what you know the words mean. Did she speak earnestly? A. I would not say that she did not speak earnestly.

Q. Did she speak earnestly? A. Yes, I should say she spoke earnestly, so far as promptness is concerned.

Q. You do not know any difference between promptness and earnestness? A. Yes sir.

Q. Then keeping that distinction in your mind did she answer earnestly? A. She did so far as I was able to determine by her actions.

Q. What was then said? A. I believe I said if the family were annoyed in any way that they notify the officer in the yard and instruct him to tell the marshal.

Q. When was it that Miss Emma told you that she wanted you to do everything you could? A. When I was about ready to go.

Q. After you had told her that her sister was suspected? A. Yes sir.

Q. That is all, is it? A. That is all I can now recall.

Mr. Robinson—That is all I want, then.

A MEAN OLD THING.

Lizzie's Expression of Hatred Against Her Step-Mother.

Anna H. Gifford was the next witness called, and was examined by Mr. Moody.

Q. Where do you live? A. Fall River.

Q. How long have you lived in Fall River? A. A long time.

Q. Where? A. On Franklin street.

Q. What is your occupation? A. I am a cloak maker.

Q. Have you made cloaks and garments for the Borden family? A. Yes sir, for seven or eight years.

Q. Did you do any work for Lizzie in the spring of 1892? A. Yes sir.

Q. What did you make? A. A Dolman sacque.

Q. Did you have any talk with Lizzie at that time about her stepmother?

Mr. Robinson objected on the ground that the time of the conversation had not been sufficiently defined.

Q. At what part of the spring of 1892 did the talk occur? A. I think it was in March.

Q. Will you state what the talk was?

Mr. Robinson objected, claiming that the time was remote, and could not be connected with the homicide.

Chief Justice—The witness may answer.

A. I was talking with Lizzie, and referred to her mother. She said: "Don't call her my mother; she is a mean old thing, and I don't have much to do with her. I stay in my own room most of the time." I asked her if she didn't go down stairs to her meals, and she said she didn't eat with them any more than she could help.

The prisoner's color rose as she listened to the words of the witness.

Cross-examined by Mr. Robinson.

Q. You have made cloaks for the family during six or seven years? A. Yes sir.

Q. Made garments for all three? A. Yes sir.

Q. Every year? A. Not every year.

Q. Do you recall when prior to March you made garments for them? A. I made a garment for Mrs. Borden within a year; I can't tell just the time.

Q. And for Lizzie? A. Some time before; I don't think I did that year.

Q. You were frequently called upon by the members of the family? A. Yes sir.

ANOTHER SETBACK.

Prosecution Attempts in Vain to Put in Evidence.

The next witness called was Anna H. Borden, a slight built, gray-haired woman, and in her introduction the cause of the government received another setback, to the open and apparent satisfaction of both counsel for defense and Lizzie herself.

After giving her name and residence Mr. Moody asked "How long have you known Lizzie Borden?"

"All her life," was the answer.

Q. Did you and she make a trip abroad together? A. Yes sir.

Q. In what year was that? A. In 1890.

Q. Did you occupy the same stateroom with her? A. Yes.

Q. What time did you return? A. In November.

Q. During the voyage home, previous to the last week, did you have a conversation with Lizzie in regard to her home?

Mr. Robinson immediately objected.

Mr. Moody said it is proposed to show statements on the part of prisoner which indicated a settled purpose, and these statements he contended are admissible.

Chief Justice Mason said: "The witness may step down and the jury will retire."

Mr. Moody, after the jury went out, said we offer to show that on the return voyage there was a conversation, in which prisoner said after such a happy summer abroad she regretted to return to a home where such an unhappy condition of affairs existed. This statement was several times repeated. If it was but a passing expression of resentment, counsel said he would agree that the conversation would not be admissible. But nothing could be introduced that would so well express the condition of affairs at this home, and in this view it is admissible, although the expressions were uttered two years before the homicide. The expressions were not casual expressions to a stranger, but words to one whom she knew well, and with whom she had passed six happy months, and it is to be remembered that this prisoner was then coming to her home, towards which the hearts of all are generally turned after such an absence, no matter what pleasure they have been enjoying. It is to be taken into account also with what we know of her home relations, and it is a hostile expression.

While Mr. Moody had been speaking Lizzie Borden was leaning forward whispering energetically to ex-Governor Robinson. He then arose and made his objection to this conversation being admitted. It was only what is alleged to have occurred between two ladies who had spent a happy summer abroad, and in coming back it was only natural that however happy the home regret would be felt at leaving the scenes of pleasure behind. Suppose this defendant had said she hated to go home, what then? Everything was right after she did get home. In the case of Commonwealth vs. Abbott, it will be remembered defendant used stronger language than this, and it was shown that he even wanted to commit the act against his wife, but as the parties lived together again the court would not admit his alleged expressions.

After Mr. Robinson sat down Lizzie, whose face was flushed, again whispered energetically to him.

Evidence Excluded.

After a consultation of the justices, Chief Justice Mason said: The court are of opinion that the character of the testimony as to the expressions used is so susceptible of other explanations that it is incompetent and cannot be admitted.

Counsel for defense looked triumphant and Lizzie's face flushed and her eyes gleamed, and she used her fan with more than usual energy.

Mr. Moody said: I'd like to reserve the right to present the testimony later.

Mr. Robinson objected, and the court said it would meet the renewed objection at the proper time.

Lucy Collet.

The jury was summoned, and Lucy Collet was called and sworn.

Q. Where do you live? A. On Borden street, Fall River.

Q. With whom? A. With my father.

Q. On the 4th of August did you receive a telephone message? A. Yes.

Q. What time was it? A. At seven minutes after 11.

Q. Did you look at the time? A. At the City hall clock.

Q. What did you do? A. Put on my hat and went over to Dr. Chagnon's.

Q. What time did you get there? A. At quarter past 11.

Q. Have you testified before? A. Yes.

Q. What time did you then say it was? A. Quarter of 11. I made a mistake.

Q. When? A. Today.

Q. Did anything else call your attention to the clock? A. I wanted to see what time Dr. Chagnon took the train.

Q. Where did you go then? A. To Dr. Chagnon's.

Q. Do you know who telephoned? A. Dr. Chagnon's clerk.

Q. What is his name? A. Mr. Norman.

Q. After you tried the door where did you sit? A. On the steps.

Q. Where were you facing? A. I was on the left side of the fence, facing the yard.

Witness pointed out upon a plan where she was sitting.

Q. How much of the yard could you see? A. I could see one half of the yard on one end and the whole of the yard on the other end.

Witness explained that she had difficulty in expressing herself in English and pointed out on the plan the end of the yard of which she could see the whole.

Q. How long did you remain in that position? A. Until quarter of 12.

Q. What were you doing while you were there? A. Nothing.

Q. You had nothing to read and no work of any kind? A. No sir.

Q. What were you doing there? A. I was tending the telephone and the door.

Q. Could you get in? A. No sir; the door was locked.

Q. During the time you were there did any one cross the yard? A. No sir.

Q. Did any one pass in or out of the Chagnon yard? A. No sir.

Cross-examined by Mr. Robinson.

Q. Did you tell us what you went to the house for? A. To keep the door and the telephone.

Q. Wasn't the door locked? A. Yes sir.

Q. Did you have the key? A. No sir.

Q. You said the door was locked, and of course the telephone was inside, you didn't keep it much? A. No sir.

Q. You don't know whether the telephone bell rang or not? A. No sir.

Q. You were sitting there so you could tell any one who called that the doctor was out? A. Yes sir.

Q. Did any one call? A. Yes sir.

Q. Who was he? A. Mr. Robinson.

Q. You could see him as he came along up the street? A. Yes sir.

Q. Who lives in the house next to the Chagnon house? A. I don't know.

Q. As you was sitting on the piazza could you see by that house? A. Yes sir.

Q. Upon which side were the steps upon you were sitting? A. The north side.

Q. Is the driveway between there and the next house? A. Yes sir.

Q. You didn't watch the Chagnon lot very carefully, did you? A. I had no reason to do so.

Q. Do you know whether a man went through that lot or not? A. I didn't see any.

Q. You might not have seen a man if he did go through? A. I would have seen a man if he had gone through.

Q. What time was it when you went there? A. Quarter to 11.

Q. You told Mr. Moody it was ten minutes of 11. A. I will change that.

Q. How did you know the time? A. I looked at the city hall clock before I went there.

Q. Did you see any man getting up on the fence and walking along? A. No sir.

Q. How long did you stay there? A. Until quarter to 12.

Q. Do you know Mr. Wixon? A. No sir.

Q. Did you see a man with whiskers? A. No sir, I didn't see any man.

Q. You didn't go to sleep while there? A. No sir.

Q. You, didn't see any young man going along? A. I didn't see any.

Thomas Boulds.

Thomas Boulds was the next witness.

Q. Resident of Fall River? A. Yes sir.

Q. What is your occupation? A. Hostler.

Q. Where were you on the morning of the murder? A. I was washing carriages in the yard.

Q. What yard do you mean? A. Mrs. Churchill's yard.

Q. Do you work for Mrs. Churchill? A. Yes sir.

Witness was shown a plan, and pointed out where he was at work.

Q. Were you where you could see between Mrs. Churchill's house and the house next north? A. Yes sir, and I could see the well house.

Q. Do you remember when you commenced washing carriages? A. No sir.

Q. How long were you washing the carriage? A. Not over 15 minutes.

Q. Was there anything else in the yard except the carriage? A. No sir.

Q. What did you do after you finished washing the carriage? A. I took it over to Mr. Hall's barn.

Q. Did you see Mrs. Churchill? A. Yes sir.

Q. Where? A. At Hall's barn.

Q. How long did it require to take the carriage from the Churchill yard to the Hall barn? A. Not over two minutes.

Q. While at work did you see anybody come out of or go into the Borden yard? A. No sir, I didn't.

Cross-examined by Mr. Robinson.

Q. What time did you begin washing the carriage? A. Don't know, I didn't have a watch on me.

Q. How soon after breakfast? A. How soon after breakfast, it was nearer dinner time.

Q. Had you got through washing the carriage before you took it to Hall's stable? A. Yes sir.

Q. You think it was half past 11 when Mrs. Churchill came for you? A. Yes sir.

Q. When you were washing the carriage were you pretty close to the Borden barn? A. Yes sir.

Q. How far from the well house? A. Fourteen yards.

Q The Borden barn comes right up to the Churchill yard. There was lattice work around the well house. There wasn't much space that you could see anyway, was there? A. No sir.

Q. You couldn't see through the lattice around the well house, or through the barn or through the house? A. No sir; I couldn't see through them.

Patrick McGowan.

Patrick McGowan was the next witness.

Q. Your name is Patrick McGowan? A. Yes sir.

Q. You live in Fall River? A. Yes sir.

Q. Do you remember the day there was some one killed at the Borden house? A. Yes sir.

Q. On that morning did you go anywhere near the Borden house? A. I went in the yard.

Q. What time did you get to the yard? A. About eight minutes past 10 o'clock, as near as I can remember.

Q. How long did you remain about the yard? A. I was there about 20 minutes.

Q. So that you were there until about half past ten? A. Yes sir.

Q. Now what yard do you mean that you were in? A. The Crow yard.

Q. Was there any one working in that yard? A. Yes sir.

Q. Who was working there, did you know them? A. Yes, I knew a Frenchman named Joseph Derosieur, who was sawing wood, and there was a stone mason there.

Q. What was the name of the mason? A. John Jenney.

Q. What did you do while there? A. I went back into the yard and there was a pear tree there and I wanted to get a few pears from the tree.

Q. Did you go anywhere near the Borden yard at that time? A. Yes sir; I went as far as the fence.

Q. What did you do there? A. I got up on a wooden horse and got a few pears off the tree.

Q. From whose tree? A. The Borden tree.

Q. How long had you been there when this happened? A. About two or three minutes.

Cross-examined.

Q. You were not around there after this affair happened? A. No sir.

Q. How near was your home to that place? A. About three quarters of a mile.

Q. Were you working in the Crow yard? A. No sir; I just happened to be in the Crow yard. I was waiting for orders from Mr. Crow to go to another job.

Q. You were working for him? A. Yes sir.

Q. And you got your orders and went away? A. Yes sir.

Q. While you were there waiting this Frenchman was sawing wood in the Crow yard? A. Yes sir.

Q. Did you have any talk with him? A. Well, just a few words. He can't understand much English.

Q. The stone mason, Mr. Jenney, was there? A. Yes sir.

Q. What part of the yard was he in? A. Out on the front, or Third street.

Q. He was quite a good way off from where the wood sawyer was? A. Yes sir.

Q. Was any man with him? A. No sir.

Q. You tried to get pears off the Crow trees and that didn't go? A. Yes sir.

Q. You found a wooden horse, got upon it and got some pears off the Borden trees? A. Yes sir.

Q. And those went? A. Yes sir.

Q. You didn't see anything around the house, did you? A. No sir.

Q. You didn't look, did you? A. No sir.

Mr. Robinson—Then I will not trouble you any further.

Mrs. Kirby, a neighbor of the Bordens, was the next witness.

Q. What is your name? A. Aruba B. Kirby.

Q. Do you live in the house next north of the Chagnon house? A. Yes sir.

Q. It is a house that faces Third street? A. Yes sir.

(Witness identified a picture of her house.)

Q. Between your house and the passageway leading to Dr. Chagnon's yard is your yard? A. Yes sir.

Q. What sort of a fence is there between your yard and the passageway into Dr. Chagnon's barn? A. There is a slat fence.

Q. Can you see through it, or is it a close board fence? A. You can see through; there is a space between the slats.

Q. How high is the fence? A. I do not know.

Q. Look at the fence in this picture. Is the fence between your yard and the south passageway like that front fence in your yard?

(Witness examined the picture and said that it was.)

Q. Can you not see over the fence as well as through it? A. Yes sir.

Q. And in case a person passes up or down there, are you able to see them from the windows of your house? A. Yes, I can see them.

Q. On the morning of August 4th, last year, the morning Mr. Borden was killed, where were you at 11 o'clock? A. In my kitchen.

Q. How long had you been in the kitchen? A. Since 6 o'clock.

Q. Where were you at 9 o'clock? A. In the kitchen.

Q. Between 11 and 12 o'clock what were you doing in your kitchen? A. Preparing my dinner.

Q. Were you at any time at the window? A. Yes sir.

Q. When? A. I was looking out of the window at half past 11.

Q. Can you tell where you were earlier than that? A. I was in the sink room part of the time.

Q. How much of the time were you in view of the passageway that leads into Dr. Chagnon's barn? A. When I was at the window.

Q. During any time that you could see it did you see any one pass in or out of that passage? A. No sir.

Cross-examined.

Q. The window towards the passageway is on the south side of your kitchen? A. Yes sir.

Q. And your sink room is on the north side? A. Yes sir.

Q. When you were in the sink room you could not see the passageway? A. No sir.

Q. Were you alone in your house that day? A. Yes sir; in the forenoon.

Q. At half past 11 had you heard of the tragedy over at the Borden house? A. No sir.

Q. You spoke of looking out at half past 11; before half past 11 whether you looked out you can't remember? A. No sir.

Q. Where does your stove stand? A. On the north side

Q. You were cooking something for dinner? A. Yes sir.

Q. So that you were working around the stove? A Yes sir.

Q. And your back would be towards this window? A. Yes sir.

Q. I do not think you can tell us whether any one went in or out? A. Not when I was at the stove, no sir.

Joseph Derosier was the next witness. As he cannot speak English, Inspector Perron interpreted.

Q. Do you remember the day the Bordens were killed? A. On Wednesday I think.

Q. Where were you when you heard of it? A. In John Crowe's yard.

Q. What time did you begin? A. At 7 30 o'clock.

Q. When did you first hear of the murder? A. A man came and told us about 10 o'clock.

Q. Up to the time you were told did you see any one go through your yard to Mr. Borden's yard or come from his yard? A. No.

Cross-examined by Mr. Robinson.

Q. How much wood did you have to saw? A. I don't know. I sawed about a cord.

Mr. Robinson tried to entrap witness into speaking English, but couldn't do it.

Q. Did you see anybody in Crowe's yard beside yourself? A. The men working with me.

Q. Who were they? A. One was named Pat. He is an Irishman. I don't know his name.

Q. What did you see him do? A. I saw him go for pears to the Borden tree.

Q. Did you see any officer come into the yard? A. No.

Q. What were you doing? A. Sawing wood all the time.

Q. By the job or day? A. By the day.

Q. Your back was to the pear tree? A. Yes.

Q. Where did the man come from who told you of the murder? A. Through the gate.

Q. Did any one get over the gate and tell you of the murder? A. No.

Q. Was any one sawing wood with you? A. No.

The next witness was John Dinnie.

Q. Do you remember the Borden murder? A. Yes.

Q. Where were you working that day? A. In the Crow yard.

Q. Working alone? A. Yes.

Q. Do you know Derosier? A. Yes.

Q. Where was he working? A. Near me.

Q. What time did you go to work? A. At seven o'clock.

Q. What time did you knock off? A. At 12 o'clock.

Q. Were you working the whole time you were there? A. Yes.

Q. Derosier also? A. Yes.

Q. What time did you hear of the murders? A. About quarter to 12.

Q. Had you seen anyone go through the Crow yard to the Borden premises? A. No.

Q. Or come from there? A. No.

Q. You couldn't see the rear of the barn? A. No.

Cross-examined by Mr. Robinson.

Q. What were you engaged in? A. Cutting stone.

Q. Anyone else? A. No; they were drawing.

Q. You were working near Third street beyond the barn? A. Yes.

Q. If a person got over the Borden fence to the Crow yard could they get out to the street? A. Yes; there's a gap in the fence.

Q. If he wanted to get out could he do so without difficulty on to Second street? A. Yes.

Q. If he had passed you would you have seen him? A. I might.

Q. There would be no difficulty in getting over the Borden fence, across the Crow yard, up on the lumber, to the Crapo yard? A. No.

Q. If the Frenchman looked up he'd see such a man? A. Yes.

Q. Did you see Mr. Wixon? A. Yes.

Q. Before he got to you? A. No.

Q. You hadn't seen any one go by you? A. No.

Q. Were you there all the morning? A. Yes.

Q. Do you know any one there that morning named Pat? A. Yes, Patrick McDonald.

Q. Any one else? A. Yes, Patrick Kavanaugh.

Q. See any Pat go and get pears from the Borden tree? A. No.

At the request of Ex-Governor Robinson Derosier was recalled and identified Patrick McDonald as the "Pat" he referred to in his testimony. He stated that he didn't see McDonald get the pears from the Borden tree.

THE "YOU GAVE ME AWAY" STORY.

Police Matron Reagan Tells of the Sisters' Quarrel.

Mrs. Hannah Reagan was the next witness.

Q. Are you a married or a single woman? A. Married.

Q. You are the matron of the police station at Fall River? A. Yes sir.

Q. And have occupied the position some time? A. Yes sir.

Q. What are the duties of the position? Do you have charge of the women taken into custody? A. Yes sir.

Q. The prisoner was at one time in your custody? A. Yes sir.

Q. What room did she occupy at that time? A. The matron's room.

Q. Your room? A. Yes sir.

Q. Were you with her during the daytime? A. Yes sir.

Q. All day? A. Yes sir.

Q. On the 24th of August did Emma Borden come into that room? A. Yes sir.

Q. At what time? A. At 20 minutes of 9 in the forenoon.

Q. Were you in the same room with them? A. Yes sir.

Q. Tell what occured in your own way? A. Emma came into the room at 20 minutes of nine on the 24th of August and spoke to Lizzie and I heard them talking together. There talk was loud. Lizzie was lying on the lounge and Emma was talking to her. I heard Lizzie say, "You gave me away Emma." Emma said, "No Lizzie, I did not give you away." Lizzie replied, "You did give me away, but I won't give in an inch."

Q. Were they talking in loud tones? A. Yes sir.

Q. And Lizzie's voice was louder than Emma's? A. Yes sir.

Q. Where were they? A. Lizzie laid on her left side and Emma was sitting in a chair beside her.

Q. How long did Emma stay there? A. She sat there until 11 o'clock.

Q. During this time, did they speak again? A. No sir.

Q. Did Lizzie turn her face toward Emma. A. No sir.

[Continued on 6th Page, Second Edition.]

AMUSEMENTS.

SELECT SOCIAL

To be given by the

BAY VIEW ATHLETIC CLUB,

At their rooms,

Foot of County Street,

Friday Evening, June 16th.

TICKETS { Gentlemen............25 Cents. Lady...................15 Cents.
je14-3t

The Ladies' Benevolent Society

Connected with the
MIDDLE STREET CHRISTIAN CHURCH
Will hold a

SALE

In the vestry of the church, THURSDAY, June 15th. ENTERTAINMENT at 7 45. Cake and ice cream will be on sale. je14-2t

ENTERTAINMENT DIRECTORY.

THURSDAY.

Middle Street Christian Church—Sale and Entertainment.
Y. M. C. A. Hall—Miss Otheman's pupils' recital.

FUTURE EVENTS.

Bay View Club Room—16th, Select Social.

AMUSEMENTS.

The Tobin bronze Iselin cup defender, to be commanded by Captain Hansen, of this city, will be launched at Bristol today at 7 30 p. m.

A select social will be given by the Bay View Athletic club in its rooms foot of County street, Friday evening, when a jolly time by the sea will be had.

The Ladies' Benevolent society of the Middle Street Christian church will hold a sale tomorrow evening. It will be one of those pleasant affairs where a man can profitably spend his loose change and be fed on the delicacies of the season.

COMMUNICATION.

Two Much Discrimination.

To the Editor of the Standard:

I was glad on perusing your Monday's paper that some one had taken up the matter of discriminating in admitting persons into the court room at the Borden trial. Discrimination has been used by the sheriffs and officers all through the trial, and I, for one, think that such shabby business ought to be put a stop to.

An Eye Witness.

COLLIDED WITH A FERRYBOAT.

The Garden City and Tugboat William Walker Badly Damaged.

NEW YORK, June 14.—Shortly before 6 o'clock last evening the ferryboat Garden City was making her way to her berth at James slip on her trip from Long Island City. She reached a point near Grand street, when the tide, which was strong, caught the tugboat William Walker, also going down stream.

The tug was a short distance from the ferryboat, and the tide drove her against the side of the ferryboat, just forward of the paddlebox.

Before there was time to sheer off the tug careened so that she almost capsized and her pilot house was held firmly against the side of the larger craft. Both the tug and ferryboat drifted helplessly while pinned together for some distance. On the Walker were five men—the captain, engineer, fireman, cook and a deckhand. The engineer, John Rice, and the fireman, known only as Martin, were thrown into the river.

The tugboat William B. Elbers hastened to the scene of the accident to render assistance. Boats from the Brooklyn navy yard also put out. Men on the Elbers succeeded in rescuing Rice, the engineer, but the fireman went down before he could be reached.

In the meantime the ferryboat and the tug had succeeded in disentangling themselves. The tug was badly battered. The Garden City continued her trip to James slip and returned to Long Island City, where she laid up for the night, little damaged. Rice, the half drowned engineer, was taken to Gouverneur hospital, where he was cared for until he had recovered.

Probable Fatal Assault.

CONCORD, N. H., June 14.—Captain Augustus B. Farmer, a well-known citizen and police officer of Bow, while attempting to arrest James Jameson, was struck on the head by a heavy billet of wood by his brother, Albert Jameson, since which time he has been unconscious, and fears are entertained that he will die. A warrant has been issued for the arrest of both Jamesons. Albert has disappeared.

Missing For Two Weeks.

HAVERHILL, Mass., June 14.—Mamie Fisher, an attractive blonde, aged 19 years, employed at housework for the past 15 months at the home of O. G. Lafore, has been missing for two weeks, and the family are greatly disturbed. It is not known that she had been keeping company with anyone. No trace of the missing girl can be found, and the police are working on the case.

SOOTHING
HEALING
PENETRATING
UNLIKE ANY OTHER.
ORIGINATED
For INTERNAL as much as EXTERNAL use.

JOHNSON'S
Anodyne Liniment

Dropped on Sugar, Children Love It.

Every Traveler should have a bottle of it in his satchel. Acts promptly. Always ready to use, for Coughs, Colds, Sore Throat, Tonsilitis, Colic, Cramps and Pains. Relieves Summer Complaints, Cuts and Bruises like magic. Cures Croup, Asthma, Catarrh, Bronchitis, Cholera Morbus, Chilblains, Chaps, Soreness in Body or Limbs, Stiff Muscles or Strains. Inhale for Nervous Headache. Ill'st'd Pamphlet free. Sold everywhere. Price 35 cts. Six bottles, $2.00. I. S. JOHNSON & CO., Boston, Mass.

AN OLD REMEDY.

A remedy that has been before the public for many years and well earned the enviable reputation it has attained is Hill's Rheumatic Pills. If you want a reliable remedy, call for them. For sale everywhere and by Wright Drug Co. O. A. Hill, Proprietor, Portland, Me. MWS

Indigestion.

HORSFORD'S Acid Phosphate.

Promotes digestion without injury and thereby relieves diseases caused by indigestion of the food. The best remedy for headache proceeding from a disordered stomach.

Trial bottle mailed on receipt of 25 cents in stamps. Rumford Chemical Works, Providence, R. I.

BASEBALL.

Smoky City Boys Down the Champions With Nichols In the Box.

BOSTON, June 14.—Yesterday's game with Pittsburg was played under very unfavorable conditions. Commenciug with the sixth inning, the rain fell thereafter, and it gave the Bostons a defeat, as Nichols could not handle the ball effectively from that time on. Staley succeeded him in the eighth and ninth, while Terry retired at the end of the first in favor of Killen. Fine batting was done by Long, Duffy, McCarthy, Lowe, Bennett, Smith and Bierbauer, while the fielding of the first two, Lyons, Shugart and Bierbauer was very good.

PITTSBURG.	AB	R	BH	TB	PO	A	E
Donovan, rf	4	1	1	2	3	0	0
Van Haltren, cf	4	2	1	0	6	1	0
Smith, lf	4	2	3	0	3	0	0
Lyons, 3b	4	2	1	1	2	2	0
Shugart, ss	4	0	0	4	1	2	0
Bierbauer, 2b	5	1	3	0	1	2	0
Beckley, 1b	5	1	1	4	5	0	1
Mack, c	0	0	0	1	0	0	1
Terry, p	1	0	0	0	0	0	1
Miller, c	4	0	1	0	6	0	0
Killen, p	3	0	0	0	0	0	0
Totals	38	9	14	11	27	9	3

BOSTON.	AB	R	BH	TB	PO	A	E
Long, ss	5	2	3	3	2	3	0
Carroll, rf	4	1	0	0	0	1	2
Duffy, cf	5	1	3	6	3	1	0
McCarthy, lf	3	2	2	1	1	0	0
Nash, 3b	3	0	0	1	3	3	0
Tucker, 1b	5	0	1	3	6	0	0
Lowe, 2b	4	0	2	3	7	4	2
Bennett, c	5	1	2	0	5	0	2
Nichols, p	3	0	1	1	0	1	0
Staley, p	1	0	0	0	0	0	0
Totals	38	7	14	19	27	13	6

Pittsburg	2	0	0	0	0	3	3	0	1	—9
Boston	3	0	1	0	0	2	0	1	0	—7

Earned runs—Pittsburg, 3; Boston, 3. Two-base hits—Beckley, McCarthy. Three-base hit—Miller. Sacrifice hits—McCarthy, Nichols. Stolen bases—Duffy, Nash. First base on balls—Pittsburg, 6; Boston, 4. First base on errors—Pittsburg, 4. Struck out—Pittsburg, 5; Boston, 3. Double plays—Lowe, Long and Nash. Umpire—McQaaid.

Other Games.

At New York:

New York	0	0	4	0	5	3	1	0		—13
Louisville	0	2	1	0	0	2	1	0	0	—6

Base hits—New York, 8; Louisville, 7. Errors—New York, 2; Louisville, 4. Batteries—Rusie and McMahon; Stratton and Grim.

At Brooklyn:

Cincinnati	3	0	0	2	1	1	1	0	1	—9
Brooklyn	0	0	0	0	0	0	1	0	0	—1

Base hits—Cincinnati, 14; Brooklyn, 3. Errors—Cincinnati, 3; Brooklyn, 3. Batteries—Chamberlain and Murphy; Lovett and Dailey.

At Baltimore:

Cleveland	1	1	1	0	2	0	3	0		—8
Baltimore	0	0	0	0	0	0	1	0	1	—2

Base hits—Cleveland, 10; Baltimore, 3. Errors—Baltimore, 2; Batteries—Clarkson and Zimmer; McNabb and Robinson.

At Philadelphia:

Philadelphia	0	5	0	0	0	0	4	1	0	—10
St. Louis	3	0	0	0	0	1	1	0	0	—5

Base hits—Philadelphia, 13; St. Louis, 9. Errors—St. Louis, 3. Batteries—[illegible]y and Clements; Dolan and Gunson.

At Washington:

Chicago	1	2	1	1	0	5	0	0		—10
Washington	0	0	2	1	0	0	0	1	2	—6

Base hits—Chicago, 15; Washington, 5. Errors—Chicago, 4; Washington, 5. Batteries—Shaw and Kittredge; Duryea and Farrell.

New England League.

At Lowell—Dover, 5; Lowell, 1.

At Lewiston—Lewiston, 8; Fall River, 7.

Eastern League Games.

At Buffalo—Buffalo, 8, Providence, 3.

At Wilkesbarre—Wilkesbarre, 13; Albany, 11.

At Binghamton—Troy, 9; Binghamton, 6.

National League Standing.

Clubs	Won	Lost	Avg	Clubs	Won	Lost	Avg
Brooklyn	23	15	60.5	Baltimore	20	19	51.3
Pittsburg	23	15	60.5	Wash	18	20	47.4
Boston	24	16	60.0	Cincinnati	17	22	43.6
Phila	22	15	59.5	Chicago	16	21	43.2
Cleveland	18	14	56.3	St. Louis	15	21	41.7
New York	22	18	53.8	Louisville	4	25	13.8

New England League Standing.

Clubs	Won	Lost	Avg	Clubs	Won	Lost	Avg
Lewiston	21	10	67.7	Lowell	11	17	39.2
Fall River	19	10	65.5	Dover	10	19	34.4
Portland	16	11	59.2	Brockton	7	17	29.1

Local Notes.

The Rogers High School nine easily defeated the Providence High School boys at Newport yesterday, 24 to 7, in the Interscholastic league series. Play was continued for six innings, and improved at the close, the home team not scoring after the forth. Rogers has now completed her series, having lost but one game. New Bedford has played fewer games, but has also lost but one, each having defeated the other. New Bedford failed to appear for the game scheduled at Providence last Saturday, and should this be forfeited the championship would go to the Rogers.

The New Bedfords will open their season next Wednesday with a game with the Newports. Sexton and Tenney will do the battery work for the home team.

At a meeting of the directors held last evening it was decided to adopt a uniform of Yale gray, with blue stockings and trimmings. A name for the new park was discussed but not decided upon.

Accused of Poisoning Her Son.

TRENTON, June 14.—Counsellor Horatio Barton applied to Judge Abbett yesterday for a further bill of pleas in the case of Hattie Shann of Princeton, who is accused of poisoning her son, John C. Shann. He said that the bill provided by the state was not explicit enough. He said there were 38 kinds of mercurial poisons. The application was denied. The case will come up for trial on July 10.

Run on a Kansas City Bank.

KANSAS CITY, June 14.—As a result of the suspension of the People's Savings bank a run was started on the Kansas Safe Deposit and Savings bank. The bank took advantage of that clause of its by-laws requiring depositors to give 30 days' notice of the withdrawal of deposits.

Gherardi's Loving Cup.

NEW YORK, June 14.—The officers of the Russian squadron presented Rear Admiral Gherardi, commandant of the Brooklyn navy yard, with a silver loving cup. The presentation was made aboard the Russian cruiser Dimitri Donskoi.

THE $110 RELAY. The Keating, $150. The McCune, $140. Relay Racer, $125.

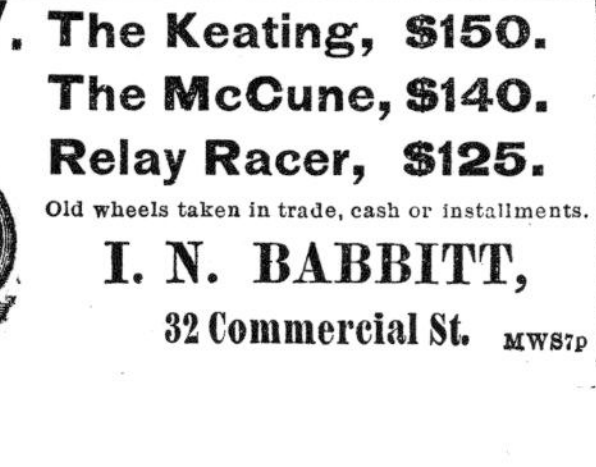

Old wheels taken in trade, cash or installments.

I. N. BABBITT,
32 Commercial St. MWS7p

[From Yesterday's Extra Edition.]

COGGESHALL STREET BRIDGE.

Hearing Continued Until Thursday, July 6, at 9 A. M.

The hearing on the apportionment of the Coggeshall street bridge expense was resumed at 2 o'clock this afternoon.

The first business was that of fixing a date for the continuance of the hearing at the conclusion of the conclusion of the afternoon's session and it was decided to adjourn to July 6 at 9 o'clock.

Samuel Corey resided in Acushnet. Had lived there 26 years. He reached New Bedford by four different ways. Used the Coggeshall street bridge but very little. There had been no sales of real estate since the bridge was constructed.

To Mr. Gillingham he said if avenues were opened leading from the bridge to his property its value might be enhanced. He could not see how Acushnet was benefited by the bridge. Parties in Fairhaven were benefited and the town in a measure was benefited. Howland and others had sold land in consequence of the bridge.

To Mr. Clifford he said the north part of Acushnet might be benefited.

George A. Macomber resided at Long Plain. He lived on the stage road to Boston. There has been no increase in the value of land at the north end of Acushnet. He had tried to sell land and had been unable to dispose of any at any price.

To Mr. Gillingham witness said he could see no benefit to the south part of Acushnet until after new avenues were opened up leading to the bridge. He thought land in Fairhaven within a mile of the bridge would receive the greatest benefit.

To Mr. Clifford his reply was similar to that made by Mr. Corey.

To Mr. Herrick he said he thought the building of the bridge would lead up to the opening up of streets in Fairhaven.

Lawyer Devoll offered a plan of Acushnet drawn by one of the surveyors of that town, and also a letter from the county treasurer to the selectmen of the town. He closed for the town, reserving the right to submit other testimony in rebuttal.

Fairhaven was the next town heard from. Mr. Gillingham presented a certified copy of the report of the commission on the New Bedford & Fairhaven bridge; also the names of petitioners for the Coggeshall street bridge.

Levi M. Snow was the first to come to the front from the town across the river. Had never seen the bridge; had heard of it. There had been an increase in the sales of real estate, but not attributable to the bridge. He thought it was due to the introduction of water, establishment of a free public library, building of a town hall, etc.

To Mr. Clifford he said Fairhaven had taken a start within two or three years; saw no special benefit because of the bridge.

To Mr. Reed he made the same answer, and also that the town farm sale was not due from the fact that the bridge had been built, although it might have been a slight factor in the transaction. He admitted that he had seen the new bridge from the old bridge.

To Mr. Parker he said land had increased in value 50 per cent. within the last five years.

Again to Mr. Clifford he thought Bristol county had received special benefits by the bridge.

To Mr. Parker he said he didn't know as he could define the special benefit, except that there must be a benefit because of the travel over it.

To Mr. Reed he admitted signing a petition for the construction of the Coggeshall street bridge.

Ira D. Packard, keeper of the town farm, said it was a benefit to the north part of the town; had seen loaded teams use the bridge daily.

Captain George H. Taber, well known resident of Fairhaven, said he had lived there for over 40 years. Was a land owner and cited several recent land sales in the town. The values in the north part of the town had increased very materially since the bridge was built. Witness proved an interesting one historically, and he came very near having his own way in the matter of explaining. He did not think the south part of the town had been very much benefited. Witness signed a petition for the bridge. He said land on the New Bedford side had increased in value.

To the query: What is the general benefit to the county by the building of this branch.

After discussing the admissibility of the question it was allowed, and witness said the same benefit as derived by building other bridges.

To Mr. Devoll he stated that farming land north of the bridge was worth $200 an acre. From the Acushnet line south to the bridge the land had doubled in price.

To Mr. Reed he said within six months he had sold farm land in the town for $300 an acre.

To Mr. Parker he reiterated his former statement that the bridge had been a general benefit to the county, the same as other bridges.

Captain Taber caused quite a laugh when, in reply to a question, he said a man would be a "bloody" fool to erect a mill at the north end of Fairhaven if it was not for the bridge.

Joseph K. Capella, another resident of Fairhaven living with Captain James Dahl, formerly lived with Moses Douglass of Acushnet. He named several Acushnet people who used the bridge. He said the bridge was used a great deal on Sundays.

Captain Charles H. Morton, a bank official in Fairhaven. He believed land had increased in value principally because of the fact that Fairhaven had developed as a summer resort, together with the numerous gifts made by Henry H. Rogers. The agitation of the introduction of water was another factor which has improved the land even as far north as Oxford. Five years ago land near the Riverside cemetery was sold at $1,000 an acre. This was George A. Briggs' land. The witness was questioned at length by Mr. Gillingham, and some ancient history was revealed. He also thought Fairhaven's increase of value as to land was in a measure affected by the growth of New Bedford. He thought Fairhaven had received no special benefit by the construction of the bridge, although it had increased the value of land somewhat at the north end of the town.

Witness was examined by counsel from neighboring towns, but nothing new was developed. He proved a witness well informed on the affairs of Fairhaven.

Cyrus D. Hunt resided in Fairhaven. Was engaged in manufacturing; had lived in Fairhaven 28 years. Was one of the remonstrants to the Coggeshall street bridge. He stated that he looked upon the building of the Coggeshall street bridge as an obstruction to the necessary improvements on the old bridge; that, said he, was one of the principal reasons why he remonstrated against the new structure. Like the previous witness he said there had been an increase in the value of lands, undoubtedly due from the causes enumerated by Captain Morton. The special benefit derived by the construction of the Coggeshall street rested alone in the sale of farm land adjacent to the structure.

At 5 30 o'clock the hearing adjourned.

A Peculiar Industry at the Fair.

The facility and frequency with which the Columbian guards pick up officials of the fair and dump them into patrol wagons for rides to the police station is growing to be one of the most extraordinary features of the great exposition. Scarcely a day passes that some prominent official is not bundled into the wagon for some imaginary offense by over officious guards and exhibited en route to the station to the wondering populace. As large numbers of the visitors are from the country and unacquainted with the officials it is not at all unlikely the latter are mistaken for thieves, pick-pockets, or something worse.—Chicago Tribune.

THROWN OUT

The following is the testimony in the Borden murder trial late yesterday afternoon from the Standard's extra edition:

Q. Suppose that the assailant stood behind Mr. Borden using an instrument like the handleless hatchet, but having a handle, what portion of his body would have received spattering? A. Assuming that he used the right hand, I should think that the upper part of his body and clothing on the right side.

Q. Assuming that he used his left hand? A. The left side.

Q. There were no spots upon the carpet in front of the sofa, and it is a fact that there were found no spots upon the books upon the table in front of the sofa. Is there anything in other circumstances that might help you further in forming an opinion? A. In a measure.

Q. If the blows were from right to left the carpet and table would have been spattered, would they not? A. I don't know that they would.

Q. The appearances all indicate that there was a spattering of blood with each blow, do they not? A. In many of them, I should say.

Here Mr. Adams produced a brand new hatchet and asked the witness to place it in the hole upon the skull of Mr. Borden. He did so and Mr. Adams asked him what was the result. He replied that the lower corner would not fit in the hole as the handleless hatchet did. This evidently surprised the counsel, as this was a result that was apparently not expected.

Q. It is not ground enough to fit is it? A. No sir.

Mr. Adams—Will you please compare the hatchet with the handleless one.

This was done, and while the measurements appeared to be about the same the witness showed the jury that while the new hatchet would not fit into the wound the handleless hatchet fitted perfectly.

Mr. Knowlton—Have you another hatchet Mr. Adams?

Mr. Adams—I have disclosed but this one.

Mr. Knowlton—My object in asking was that it might be marked for the purpose of indentification, that's all.

Q. Did you observe when you put the hatchet into the hole that beyond it there was a smooth and polished surface indicating a continuation of the mound? A. I did not notice anything giving that impression.

Q. In preparing the skull was there anything lost in tissue or cartilage? A. There is a thin layer, about 1-16 of an inch of cartilage where the jaw joins the skull, and this cartilage is found on each side.

Q. Upon the head of Mrs. Borden there was how many wounds or injuries? A. Twenty-two.

Q. Were they all cutting wounds? A. No sir, there were three bruises upon the forehead and a wound in the back.

Q. Where was the wound in the back? A. Just where the neck joins the shoulder.

Q. In your opinion was the wound received while sitting or lying? A. Possibly, or may have been given while she was standing.

At the request of Mr. Adams witness took a piece of chalk and marked upon his back the size, direction and location of the wound, whereupon counsel turned his back to the jury and allowed them to see the illustration.

Q. Have you any opinion as to the kind of blow, or whether it was from left to right, or from right to left? A. From left to right, probably.

Q. The head of Mrs. Borden had hair to what extent? A. There was an ordinary growth of hair.

Q. Would it not act as a cushion to a blow? A. To some extent.

Q. Was there anything in the character of the triangular wound on the back to indicate to you that scissors, or a razor, were used? A. No sir.

Q. When a blow is given on a skull does it scarf up the bone? A. There is a chipping up of the bone, and the cut has a beveled edge.

At this point counsel produced a round piece of wood in which cuts had been made by a sharp edged tool held at various angles when the blows were struck, and asked if a very similar effect was produced when blows were struck upon a human skull. Witness answered affirmatively, and the block of wood was shown to the jury.

Q. Did you observe any indications on the skull of Mrs. Borden? A. Yes sir.

Q. Were there not on the head blows as though from both directions, as though from this way and that way? A. Exactly.

Q. In other words it was used in the right hand and then in the left hand? A. There is nothing inconsistent to that.

Q. Now take the injuries on the top of the head. Were there any? A. There were.

Q. Will you indicate on the statuette? Witness at this point indicated the various wounds on the statuette.

Q. Taking all together, did they show that some wounds were from right to left and some from left to right? A. It is my opinion it showed them all from the right to left.

Q. About the blood spots. Were there many upon the drawers to the left, a few upon the shams upon the right and upon the spread and mirror? A. Yes sir.

Q. Taking into account that these points and the number she received, those on the glass, etc., would an assailant standing in front of her have received some of the spatters? A. Yes; I think so.

Q. On what portion of the body? A. The front.

Q. If the injuries had been made with an instrument like this, with a handle a foot long, the assailant would have been near the head? A. I should think so.

Q. Do you think the head, hair and face of the assailant would have been spattered? A. I think so.

Q. When the blood leaves a body in August, let us say, in our climate how long will it be before it will dry? A. It would dry quickly if in a small quantity, if of considerable size it would require over an hour.

Q. If the blood was on the head of a hatchet in August would it be likely to dry quickly? A. If in a small quantity it would dry quickly, but if any considerable amount it would require some time.

Q. Does blood mingle quickly with clothing or with rust? A. With cotton very quickly, but not so quickly with wool.

Q. As to rust, does it mingle quickly? A. I think it would.

Q. If it was washed off would it mingle easily or not? A. Not so easily.

Q. If a hatchet covered with rust were to be smeared with blood, say at 10 o'clock in the morning, and then exposed an hour, it would be well dried in? A. I think it would be.

Q. Under the circumstances it could not be readily washed off? A. Not so readily as if it were a clean, bright surface.

Q. Your opinion seems to be more extensive than some of the others, please inform me if you would expect to get the blood off without the rust? A. I think the blood would come off before the rust.

Q. Could it be removed so as not to show on a subsequent test? A. I think so.

Q. But it could not easily be done? A. No sir.

Q. Your testimony on the intestines and stomach were based on a normal condition? A. Yes sir.

Q. Could you fix the interval of time between the two at about one hour? A. Yes sir.

Q. Was there anything about the coagulation within 15 minutes of death which would lead you to determine the time of death? A. Nothing more in coagulation, but in the drying.

Mr. Knowlton—Did it appear in both cases that digestion had begun? A. O, yes sir.

Q. Suppose the hatchet was used at 10 o'clock and then washed and used again would there be any trouble about removing the blood so that it could not be discovered on a chemical test? A. I think not.

Q. What did this bevel from the right to the left indicate as to direction? A. It was a clear indication of the direction from which the blow came.

Q. A blow from the right to the left would indicate that it came from which direction? A. That it came from the right.

Q. Did the blood on the carpet in front of Mr. Borden tell anything about the direction? A. No sir.

Q. I meant to have called your attention to three contusions. Were they of such a nature as to show what they were? A. I think they were caused by a fall onto the floor.

Q. Could you have formed an opinion any better if you had seen them before they were disturbed? A. I think I could.

Q. Did you attempt to fit the wounds with the hatchet? A. I did.

Q. Why did they not fit? A. Not all cutting edges of 3½ inches will fit the same wounds.

Q. You were asked about the spatters from a carotid artery? Would it increase the blood spatters in that vicinity? A. It would not go far outside. The blow would be inside the skull.

Q. In your opinion were those wounds inflicted with that hatchet?

Mr. Adams objected, and the question was excluded, Mr. Knowlton not pressing it.

Dr. Cheever.

David W. Cheever, of Boston, was the next witness called and asked relative to his medical education. He replied that he was educated at Harvard and in Europe.

Q. Where in Europe? A. Paris.

Q. How long have you been in practice? A. About 25 years.

Q. Any special practice? A. A good deal in surgery.

Q. In what position? A. As demonstrator of anatomy and assistant in surgery. I am now professor of surgery.

Q. How long have you been professor of surgery? A. Since 1880.

Q. How long have you been at Harvard? A. Since 1870.

Q. You are called upon often to give your opinion in surgical matters? A. Yes sir.

Q. You first had an opportunity on this case when? A. About the 31st of last May.

Q. What did you have a consultation on then? A. I was shown the skulls.

Q. Since then have you made a study of them? A. Yes sir.

Q. With reference to the blows and the instruments which caused them? A. I have.

Q. You have also attended the trial of this cause? A. Yes sir.

Q. You heard the evidence? A. Yes sir.

Q. When did you arrive here? A. Thursday.

Q. You heard what was said about the wounds and the character of the blood of the body? A. Yes sir.

Q. Were there any of the facts you have listened to important in showing the priority of death? A. Yes sir.

Q. The time of priority? A. Yes sir.

Q. Will you state the facts and what you have derived from them? A. The fact that Mrs. Borden's body was cooler than Mr. Borden's; that the blood of Mrs. Borden was coagulated and that of Mr. Borden liquid; and the fact that with Mrs. Borden digestion was still going on, while in Mr. Borden it was almost completed, would lead me to infer that Mrs. Borden died first; probably died a considerable interval first.

Q. What interval, doctor, the minimum and maximum? A. The minimum I should say one hour, the maximum two hours.

Q. You understood that both ate at the same time? A. I so understood it in my mind.

Q. In your opinion what caused these wounds, how were they inflicted? A. As far as my own observation confirmed me as to the injury on the bones they indicated that they were made by a heavy metallic weapon with a cutting edge bevelled with a sharp angle, the cutting edge not exceeding three and one-half inches, and attached to a handle like that of a hatchet.

Q. Have you also examined this hatchet head, (passing the witness the handleless hatchet.) A. Yes sir.

Q. Assuming that to have been provided with a handle of ordinary length, what is your opinion as to whether that instrument could have caused the wounds you found? A. I think it could.

Q. You have stated that your opinion was that the cutting edge was not more than 3½ inches. Could the cutting edge be any less than that? A. Yes, it might be.

Q. In your opinion you do not take into account anything of the external appearance of the wounds? A. I have not in my answers so far.

Q. Have you heard the wounds described so that you understand the position and location sufficiently to add that factor to your opinion? A. I think I understand them fairly well.

Q. Adding these facts what is your opinion as to the length of the cutting edge? A. The wounds do not require that the edge should be any longer than 3½ inches, because the wounds could be made by smashing through the flesh, and most of the cuts would seem to show that the hatchet must have been nearly that length.

Q. Why do you say that the cutting edge was not more than 3½ inches? A. Because on examining the skull of Mr. Borden I find that no wider edge than that could have made the wound in the lower jaw.

Q. Can you tell whether that shape of hatchet (the handleless one) would fit these wounds? A. I have tried it and the hatchet fits the wounds.

The witness then stepped in front of the jury and taking the skull and the hatchet head, fitted the blade into the hole in the skull.

Q. Did you form any opinion as to the position of Mrs. Borden? A. I formed an opinion.

Q. You may give it? A. I think that all the wounds except three were inflicted when she was flat upon her face on the floor.

Q. Which three? A. The scalp wound on the side and the two wounds on the top of the head.

Q. Did you form any opinion as to the position of Mrs. Borden when these three wounds were inflicted? A. I think the scalp wound was inflicted when the assailant was face to face with the victim, because it was a glancing blow, and struck toward the back.

Q. Do you desire to express any opinion as to the other two? A. They could have been easily given by a person standing behind the victim.

Q. In your opinion could these wounds have been inflicted with a hatchet of ordinary size, I now refer to all the wounds on both Mr. and Mrs. Borden, wielded by a woman of ordinary strength? A. Judging by the nature of the wounds on the skull, the sharpness and weight of the instrument, I think that they could.

Q. Whether or not these could wounds have been inflicted by a woman of ordinary strength with a hatchet of that size (holding up the hatchet head) provided with a handle? A. If the handle was sufficiently long I think she could.

Q. What do you mean by sufficiently long? A. Not less than 12 or 14 inches.

Q. After listening to the description of the nature of the wounds what is your opinion as to the scattering of the blood, with more particular reference to Mr. Borden? A. I don't think that the matter can be decided upon or that it can be told with any accuracy.

Q. Is there any general rule by which a circumference can be drawn around the point of attack and the amount of blood that would spatter, told? A. I don't think there is.

Q. Did Mrs. Borden's wounds indicate the direction in which her assailant stood? A. Yes sir.

Witness with a hatchet and the skull indicated that the blows were right handed.

Q. The injury to the neck you did not see, but heard described? A. Yes sir.

Q. Did the position of the assailed party make a difference in the direction of the blow? A. I should say that the assailant might have stood directly behind or a little to the right.

The witness, at the request of Mr. Knowlton, pointed out the upper edge of the wound on Mr. Borden's skull, and said that he was able to determine where the weapon entered and left the head by the chip.

Cross-examined by Mr. Adams.

Q. It is your opinion that the wound upon the head of Mr. Borden might have been inflicted prior to that which fractured the skull? A. Yes sir.

Q. In that event a hatchet less than three and one half inches would not adequately account for the wound that went through the skull? A. No sir.

Q. Could not an instrument less than three and one half inches get in? A. Yes sir.

Q. Don't you think upon consideration that a hatchet less than three and one-half inches in width, say three inches, might have been used? A. Yes sir.

Q. Possibly two and three-quarters inches? A. Possibly, but I think not.

Q. Wouldn't there be a large diffusion of blood? A. That would depend upon circumstances. If the wound severing the eye was among the last to be given the victim would have been almost dead, and the circulation would have been very much reduced, in which case there would not be a very great diffusion of blood.

Q. You perform a great many operations during the year? A. Yes sir.

Q. In the performance of your operations do you not put on outer clothing? A. Yes sir, sometimes a white linen coat and sometimes a white linen gown.

Q. And what is this for? A. Partly for absolute cleanliness and partly to protect my clothing.

Q. Protect your clothing from what, blood? A. Yes sir.

Q. You sometimes get blood over your face, hands, beard, etc.? A. Yes sir.

Q. The arteries in the head sometimes spurt during an operation? A. Yes, when cut.

Q. How far will they sometimes spurt? A. From four to six feet.

Q. Is there in the head an artery or arteries where Mr. Borden was wounded? A. Yes.

Q. You expect spurting? A. Yes sir.

Q. How far in your opinion would the blood of Mr. Borden have spurted if the artery was cut when he was first wounded? A. Several feet.

Q. The drops would be in the nature of a spray of drops? A. Yes sir.

Q. Presuming that he was lying on the lounge when the temporal artery was cut, what would be the direction of the spurting of blood? A. It would be out into the room.

Q. In what other direction might there have been spurting of blood? A branch artery was cut which might have spurted in a direction parallel with the body.

MEDICAL EXAMINER DRAPER.
[Sketched from Life by Mr. Ashley of the Standard.]

Assuming that the person who struck the blows was standing behind Mr. Borden, wouldn't the blood naturally have spurted upon him? A. Yes sir.

Q. When the temporal artery is cut blood spurts how far? A. Two or three feet.

Q. Assuming that there was blood on the wall on the kitchen door, and assuming that the assailant stood behind would he not of necessity be spattered with blood? A. Yes.

Q. Upon what part of his body would the blood appear? A. The upper part.

Q. Is it unreasonable to suppose that there would be blood on his face, beard, hair, hands, etc.? A. If he was stooping over he would probably be covered with blood.

Q. The assailant was in all probability stooping over? A. He would have to be stooping over to strike the blows with a common hatchet.

Q. You observed the beveled cut over the eye as you were shown the skull? A. Yes sir.

Q. What was the direction of this cut? A. From left to right.

When witness was shown the manikin and illustrated the blow that cut the artery he modified his statement made in direct examination, and said that he would now say that it was a vertical blow.

Q. In observing the two blows upon the crown of Mrs. Borden's head, if we assume that Mrs. Borden was standing up when struck, her assailant must have been a person taller than herself? A. Yes sir.

Witness continued, and said that he was uncertain whether Mrs. Borden was standing up or lying down when she received the blows on the crown of her head. The other wounds were given when she lay prostrate on the floor on her face. The wounds indicate that the easiest position in which her assailant could have stood was astride of her body. In all probability her assailant would have had to bend over. The witness had learned that there was considerable blood around Mrs. Borden's body on the floor. He would not have expected to find blood on the shoes of her assailant, because they might have been protected by the clothing of the victim.

He could not base any opinion on the coagulation of the blood as to the time of death after 15 or 20 minutes, until the shrinking of the blood which would come later.

In answer to questions by Mr. Knowlton, witness said there would be no spurting of the blood after the action of the heart had stopped.

The various articles of clothing, hatchets and axes and skulls which have been introduced in the case were given into the custody of the clerk. Mr. Knowlton asked that the hatchet used by Mr. Adams might go into the case and be given to the jury.

At this point the hour of adjournment arrived.

T Borden Skulls.

The consultation in court early this morning was in reference to the introduction of Mr. and Mrs. Borden's skulls.

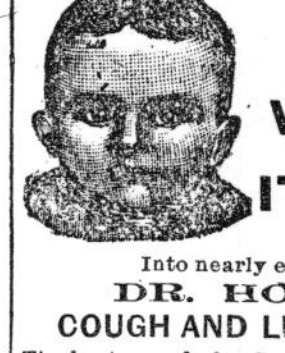

HAS WORKED ITS WAY

Into nearly every house.

DR. HOUGH'S
COUGH AND LUNG BALSAM.

The best remedy for Coughs and Colds. Price 35 cents. Sold by all druggists and medicine dealers.

STEAMSHIP LINES.

ANCHOR LINE.

United States Mail Steamships
Sail from New York every Saturday for
GLASGOW VIA LONDONDERRY
Rates for Saloon Passage

By S. S. CITY OF ROME, $50 and upward. OTHER STEAMERS, Cabin, $45 and upward, according to accommodation and location of Room. Excursion Tickets at reduced rates. Second Cabin, $30. Steerage, Outward, $23. Prepaid, $24. Second Cabin from Glasgow or Derry, $35.

Drafts at lowest Current Rates.

For Book of tours and other information apply to HENDERSON BROTHERS, 7 Bowling Green, N. Y., Thomas Donaghy, Corner Union and Water sts. or Edwin Whittaker 334 Purchase st., or David Waugh, 773 South Water street, New Bedford.

CALIFORNIA EXCURSIONS
VIA
SOUTHERN PACIFIC CO.
Apply to E. E. CURRIER, N. E. Agent.
192 Washington St., Boston, Mass

THE
Hot Weather
IS UPON US.

This is especially the season for

GAS STOVES.

CALL EARLY.

N. B. GAS & EDISON LIGHT CO.

GEORGE C. BLISS,
FLORIST.

34 Arnold Street,
CORNER COTTAGE.
TELEPHONE, DAY OR NIGHT.

Baggage Tags
ALWAYS IN STOCK AT
STANDARD OFFICE.

FINANCIAL.

SANFORD & KELLEY.

GARDNER T. SANFORD,
CHARLES S. KELLEY, } **Bankers,**

Members Boston Stock Exchange,

47 North Water St., New Bedford.

STOCKS AND BONDS BOUGHT AND SOLD
ON COMMISSION

At the New York and Boston Stock Boards.

Local manufacturing stocks a specialty.

Outside investments of a conservative character, paying good rates of interest, on hand and for sale.

Also strictly high class investments for trust funds.

Auction Sale of Stocks and Bonds
WEDNESDAYS AND SATURDAYS, at 10 45 A. M.

ORDERS SOLICITED.

T. E. BOWMAN & CO.,
Topeka, Kansas,

NEGOTIATORS OF

Conservative Mortgage Loans in the
Eastern Counties of the State.

WE know every security and give personal attention to every detail. Parties desiring absolute safety and satisfied with six per cent. interest paid promptly by check in their office or home, are invited to investigate our loans.

SECOND EDITION.

HOME MATTERS.

REAL ESTATE AND BUILDING.

Standish Bourne has sold the 2 1-2 story house, with lot, on the corner of Madison street and Acushnet avenue to Charles H. Pierce for $3,490.

John Knott has sold to Richard Schofield 13.63 rods land at the northwest corner of Reynolds and Peckham streets. Mr. Schofield will erect a dwelling house on the lot.

John Whitehead has sold for Daniel Cavanagh to Bridget Mary Dowd 18 rods of land on the east side of River avenue. Henry M. Mosher has sold to Sylvester F. Lawton a lot of land on Woodlawn avenue containing 13.77 rods.

Daniel Cavanaugh has sold to Bridget M. Dowd a lot of land on Oxford heights, Fairhaven.

Work on the new Columbia mill is being pushed ahead rapidly. The roof of the engine house is nearly completed and the picker house is up one story. The floor timbers have arrived and those of the second story will be placed in position in a few days.

Frank Gay is building for James McFarlin on the west side of Spruce street between Sycamore and Smith streets a dwelling house 24 by 40 feet, 16 feet posts.

ACCIDENT.

John W. Taylor, machinist, employed at the works of the Morse Twist Drill & Machine Company, fell his little finger becoming down a brow into the blacksmiths' shop, and dislocated his left shoulder. Drs. Pothier and Leonard attended him.

MARION.

A Children's Day concert was given by the Sunday school in the M. E. church Sunday evening at North Marion. The programme carried out was appropriate for the year, it being entitled "Columbia's Defenses." Maria Hathaway of Wareham took the part of Columbia, and was supported by three boys and three girls. The church was prettily trimmed and a large audience was present.

Robert H. Luce, formerly in the employ of the Old Dominion Steamship company of New York, has recently entered the employ of the Mathison Alkali company at Saltville, Va.

Dr. George E. Richards has been appointed a special agent on the board of health.

The residence of Henry F. Weeks on Front street has been sold to H. B. Worth of New Bedford.

Fred T. Hathaway of West Troy, N. Y., has sold the house now occupied by Mrs. William J. Robinson to Ward P. Delano of Worcester.

WEST TISBURY.

Mrs. Mary C. Luce's house is open again. Mrs. Wm. Lewis and two daughters, who have been the guests of Mrs. Matilda Campbell, left for their homes in New Bedford last Wednesday accompanied by Miss Medora Pool.

Mr. Herman Straiter arrived last Saturday, and is stopping at Sunnyside farm. Children's Day was observed in the Congregational church.

Professor H. L. Whiting and Lawyer E. A. Davis spent a few days at home recently.

Miss Bessie L. Luce of Falmouth arrived last week.

Dr. Daniel A. Cleveland of Middletown, Conn., is here for the summer.

DEATHS.

In Marion, June 13th, Caleb W. Macomber, aged 85 years 7 months. Burial at Hixville.

MARINE INTELLIGENCE.

Sld from Wareham 14th, schs A H Terry, Terry, New York; Hannah Blackmer, Chadwick, do.

Sld from Tarpaulin cove 13th, schs Samuel C Hart and Thomas H Lawrence.

At Newburyport 13th, sch R R Nickerson, Nickerson, Philadelphia.

At at New York 13th, sch Royal Arch, Wentworth, Baltimore.

At at New York 13th, steamer Vega, Ross, Lisbon, 35 Minds, Tolosia, Fayal, etc., with 53 cabin and 273 steerage passengers; sch James Rothwell, Fisher, Boston.

At at Perth Amboy 13th, sch Rebecca F Lamdin, New York.

At at Philadelphia 13th, schs G B Reynolds, Raynor, Newport. Cid, sch Rose Esterbrook, Hammett, Boston.

At at Norfolk 13th, sch O D Witherell, Chase, Clark's cove. Sld, sch James H Hoyt, Ellis port.

Sld from Newport News 13th, sch J H Jackson, Chase, Fall River.

Sld from Fernandina 13th, sch Rebecca P Lamdin, Raye, Fall River.

Passed Anjier May 9th, ships Earnock, Parsons, Manila for Boston; Parthena, Federsen, do for do.

Ocean Steamers.

Arrived—At New York, Pocahontas, Messina; Hermann, Antwerp; Saardam, Rotterdam.

Passed Brow Head—Servia, New York.

HATRED !

(Continued from Fourth Page.)

Q. Then Mr. Jennings' came? A. He came at 11 o'clock.

Q. After he came you didn't remain in the room. A. No sir.

Q. Where were you standing when the conversation between Emma and Lizzie commenced? A. I was right at the door.

Q. Where did you see them, in what position? A. Emma was pending over Lizzie.

Q. Did you see them, that is, Lizzie and, Emma when they parted? A. Yes

Q. Was there any good by on either side. A. No sir.

Q. Did you see either of them looking at you when this conversation took place? A. Yes sir, they saw me.

Q. How long did Emma remain? A. She came at 20 minutes of 9.

Q. Where did she go when she went out? A. Home, I suppose.

Q. What happened after Emma came out? A. Mr. Jennings went in and stayed until half-past 12.

Q. Did Emma come again that day? A. Yes sir.

Q. What time did she come that afternoon? A. I don't know, she came in and out so many times during Lizzie's stay that I can't recall the time she came that afternoon.

Q. Can you give us any idea what time she came in the afternoon? A. No sir, I cannot.

Q. Did anybody else come in the afternoon? A. Yes.

Q. Who came? A. Mr. Buck came in the afternoon.

Q. Are you sure he came that afternoon? A. I think he did; yes, he came every afternoon.

Q. Are you sure that he came in the afternoon? A. I cannot say.

Q. You were so taken up by this trouble that happened in the morning that you cannot recollect what took place in the afternoon? A. Yes sir.

At this point a recess was given for dinner.

During the cross-examination of Miss Collette and of Mrs. Churchill's coachman Sheriff Wright found difficulty in preserving order. Mr. Robinson's quaint humor and inimitable manner of putting questions amused the crowd greatly, and there were several bursts of laughter that were gunned throughout the court-room.

THE EJECTED ARTIST.

Action to be Taken Against the Sheriff for Having Him Thrown Out.

Max de Lipman, the New York artist, who was hustled from the court room yesterday afternoon by order of Sheriff Wright, came into the Standard headquarters near the court house this afternoon just as the court adjourned. He greeted a Standard reporter cordially, and said, "Much obliged, old man, for what you wrote about that affair yesterday."

The reporter expressed regret that Mr. de Lipman should have passed through such an experience as he did.

"I am more sorry for the sheriff," said Mr. de Lipman, "but the affair has gone beyond my hands."

"Have you taken action for assault?" asked the reporter.

"I don't care to say much about it just now," was the answer.

"Will you tell me if you are going to bring a criminal or civil action?" asked the reporter.

"I am acting under legal advice," said Mr. Lipman in conclusion.

SAID HE KILLED THE BORDENS.

Curious Story Told by a Barber of Newark, N. J.

Newark, N. J., June 14.—William M. Devere, a barber, yesterday said to Police Captain McManus: "One day last fall a man entered my shop. He was about 5 feet 6 inches tall and weighed about 150 pounds. He wore a heavy black beard and moustache. His hair was black. He was about 45 years of age. His clothes were neat. He wore a black Derby hat and no coat. He said he wanted me to shave off his hair, beard and moustache. I did so. He offered me a shave of opium, which I refused. When I finished shaving the man he asked for writing paper. He wrote three letters. They did not seem to suit him, so he rewrote them. He wrote a fine hand, and appeared to be trying to disguise his handwriting. He acted strangely. Before the man went away he looked at himself in the glass and said, 'You wouldn't know me, would you?' I told him 'No, I would not.' He left behind two spoiled sheets of paper on the floor. One of them was addressed to Mayor Coughlin of Fall River. It read: 'I murdered Mrs. Borden. I did it out of revenge. It is no use trying to catch me, because I am so disguised you would not know me.' Devere had not heard of the Borden murder, and he burned the sheet. The police don't know what to make of it.

JUSTICE THAT IS OVER ZEALOUS.

Sensible Judicial Decision Rendered in the Borden Case.

(Editorial in Providence Journal.)

The greatest and best safeguard of American liberties and life has always been the proper administration of justice. Different gradations of authority in that sphere of government have contributed to the careful sifting of evidence in court cases and given to the higher branches of the judiciary an opportunity to administer laws with calmness and equity. As in the Borden case on the question of admitting the prisoner's testimony at the inquest, and in the first trial of the suspected murderer of Mrs. Barnaby, the officers of the law and justice who first pass justice on evidence and involve prisoners in critical surroundings are very liable to go wrong. They rush into errors which might lead to the irremediable mistakes of hands of lynchers were it not for the supervising and final attention bestowed by competent superiors. It is true there is a popular feeling in almost all great crimes that justice is slow-footed, but it is a maxim of law as well as of practical life that haste makes waste. A person suspected of great crime should have the protection of that knowledge and the form of law which, when set to rights through knowledge of Atchison's affairs there is no question whatever. Atchison has not been slow in showing weakness in the trading. Nearly all the other shares of its class have fallen off. St Paul has retired below 70. C. B. & Q. below 87, while such stocks as Rock Island, Missouri Pacific and Northwest show losses varying from ⅜ to 2 per cent. Industrials continue feverish, generally soft. The reactions are due chiefly to fears of tight money. Probably money will work rather close between now and the 1st of July, owing to the tremendous demand for funds from western points and the constant shipment west of currency, but it is not believed that after the 1st of July this firmness will be maintained.

The local money market is firm and rates hold near 6 per cent.

The money market is undervalued today. Sentiment favors an advancing range of rates, and probably rates will be raised somewhat before the week closes. Time money is in steady demand, at clearing house loans were made at 7 per cent. New York funds sold at 30 and 20 cents discount.

Money on call is loaning in New York today at 4 to 7 per cent. Time money shows little if any change.

Sterling exchange is quiet. Rates $4.86 and $4.85½.

Bonds are barely steady.

The New York market opened fairly active this morning with prices, except the Louisville & Nashville, which opened at 67½ to 70, a shade weaker.

---

pretation of his rights by officers who are over-zealous. The court has also learned by experience how far wrong one man's decision may be in the plans necessary to ferreting out or convicting a guilty or innocent person.

Miss Borden has a right to that zealous protection which a state is supposed to afford every prisoner until he or she is proved guilty. Every other prisoner has an equally powerful friend in the law. He has an enemy in it, too, but there is never reason to fear the movements of such an enemy unless it escapes from the region of reason to the abode of prejudice. Our higher courts secure the temperate activity of this spirit of justice. It is within bounds where all men may respect it. "Justice" without such respect springs from a lawlessness as culpable as lynching. The preservation of custom and precedent to assist in executing the laws is absolutely necessary. There should as a rule be as few additions to the list of precedents as possible. For the judges at New Bedford to have admitted as evidence the testimony of Miss Borden before the inquest would have been to establish a most dangerous precedent. It is true the exclusion of evidence takes away from the state the power to deny the prisoner's claim that she was not in the house at the time of the murder of her father. That leads to no extraordinary change in the looks of the affair to the state. But it was a sensible judicial decision which left the matter out, and it increases the general belief in the desire of our higher courts to guard the laws for the better protection of every citizen.

A WISE COURTESY.

District Attorney Knowlton's Favor Granted the Prisoner.

(Joe Howard in Boston Globe.)

Miss Lizzie, escorted by an attentive deputy sheriff, clad in a mode, but very pale and nervously anticipating the horrors of the day, took her seat near Governor Robinson, where she was pleasantly greeted by her clerical friend and her counsel, but not by any one of the wild-eyed, haggard-featured, thick-skinned women who stared at her through their spectacles and opera glasses as though she were a beast. The counsel for the defense, forewarned by her collapse of last week, and distressed by her hysterics of yesterday, interviewed District Attorney Knowlton and his associate as to the necessity of bringing the literal skulls into court.

Yesterday's examinations were all made by the aid of plaster casts, not representing these skulls, but ordinary baldheaded casts of monks. District Attorney Knowlton, in spite of his forceful manner, has a very tender heart, is a good husband and a considerate father, and the appeal made by Governor Robinson fell in fallow ground, bringing forth not precisely the kind of fruit desired, but a consent born of thoughtful courtesy and manly consideration, tinctured possibly with a desire that the case should be continued, and not come to grief by reason of nervous prostration, to the effect that when the skulls were exhibited the prisoner need not be present in the court room, but might remain in the little adjacency, where, although she could neither see nor be seen, she could hear all she chose and avoid beating that which was unpleasant.

It was a wise courtesy on the part of the prosecution, for no one doubts what she been compelled to confront those ghastly evidences of the assassin's brutality, and the equally offensive illustrations of the carelessness of the prosecuting experts, who deliberately severed the heads from the bodies of her father and stepmother, she believing that they had been decently interred in the family plot in the Fall River cemetery.

Mr. Jennings' Pictures.

"If I were attorney J Jennings, when I had leisure I would sit for some pictures and distribute copies among the artists, that they might at least do me partial justice and give me in the pictures they draw credit at least for what hair I possess," said one of the newspaper men in court this forenoon. In a number of cases Mr. Jennings has been represented as being bald from the crown of his head to the height of his ears, whereas he is favored with a complete head covering except about the temples, where it is worn a little thin.

The latest news from New Bedford indicates that the law passed by the late legislature prohibiting discrimination against the colored folks in barber shops will have to be amended so as to make it operative at murder trials.—Boston Herald.

It does not begin to look so much like a trial of Lizzie Borden as it does like an exposition of the incompetency of the Fall River—Providence Journal.

It rather looks as if Lizzie Borden would get off on the Scotch verdict "not proven." She is not being defended like an innocent party, but as one who could not be convicted.—Boston Record.

FINANCIAL.

Bad Break in Atchison—Prices Run Off to Lowest Point Ever Touched—London a Heavy Seller of the Stock—Other Shares Soft—Money Firm and Rates Expected to Work Higher—London Houses Buy Nashville and St. Paul—Numerous Dividends Just Declared—Matters in General.

Wednesday, June 14.

Atchison has once more proven a soft spot in the markets, though there is nothing new to account for the drop in price. It is true that fears are expressed in current gossip that the road lacks ready money and that net earnings are by no means as good as gross, but this is mere gossip and not entitled to weight. In fact President Reinhart says the company has all the money necessary to meet its July interest charges already in hand and an ample supply besides for general purposes. The floating debt is less than it was a year ago. So far as earnings are concerned they are excellent both gross and net and the condition of the crops could not be better for the company. Taken as whole the financial and physical conditions of the Atchison company and the promises for revenue in the future were never better than today.

(For Other Markets See Second Page.)

NEW YORK PRODUCE MARKET.

Flour sales 2,975 packages; quiet.

Wheat sales 5,200,000 bushels; active and steady.

Corn sales 675,000 bushels; higher on better cables;

Oats sales 65,000 bushels; firmer and quiet.

Beef limited demand and unchanged.

Pork more demand and easy.

Lard quiet.

Butter firm.

Sugar (raw) firm and active.

Petroleum quiet and firm.

Turpentine quiet firm.

Rice quiet and firm.

Freights quiet and firm.

Rosin dull and weak.

Tallow inactive and steady.

PROVISIONS AND GRAIN.

Chicago, June 14.

Opening.
	Wheat.	Pork.	Corn.
July,	66⅞	20.00	44¾
September,	71	20.40	42½

Twelve o'clock.
July,	66⅞	20.00	40⅝
September,	71⅛	20.40	42½
December,	75¾		

WEATHER INDICATIONS.

"Warm Wave."

New York, June 14.—At 8 30 a. m. the weather was cloudy, wind east, temperature 67. The Herald says: In the Middle states and New England on Thursday, warmer, clear weather and fresh southwesterly to southerly winds will prevail, with the "warm wave" lasting through Friday, and followed in the western portions of this section by thunder storms.

Fair and Warmer.

Washington, June 14.—Local forecast for New England until Thursday night: Fair, preceded by rain today near the eastern coast; fair Thursday, warmer; variable winds, becoming northwest.

TO CUT EXPENSES.

Financiers of the World's Fair Becoming Alarmed.

Chicago, June 14.—Auditor Ackerman made a statement to financiers of the World's fair yesterday that alarmed them. He told them that the salary list for May reached the enormous total of $360,000, and that more than 6,000 employes were on the pay roll during that period. There was a general exclamation that the running expenses were at least $400,000 a month too high, and the announcement was made that Director of Work Burnham had decided to drop 3,000 men from the rolls this week.

COL. AINSWORTH'S PETITION

Dismissed by Supreme Court of District of Columbia.

Washington, June 14.—The supreme court of the district this morning dismissed Colonel Ainsworth's petition for a mandamus on two grounds; First—Holding that a deputy coroner is not a legal officer. The invalidates the inquest into the Fords theater disaster as far as held. Second—That the right of a person to be present at an inquest in person or by counsel is discretionary with a coroner, and therefore not a subject for mandamus.

RUN ON A SAVINGS BANK.

Paying Teller in York City Met Every Demand.

New York, June 14.—A run was started on the Irving Savings Bank institution this morning almost as soon as the doors were opened. By 10 20 the paying teller had paid out $75,000. A speculator was on hand offering to buy up all the books he could get for 10 per cent. commission. Treasurer G. B. Latimer said the bank had on hand a million dollars, and could get that much more. This is the bank in which Superintendent of Banks Preston of the state of New York discovered a deficiency of $70,800.

China Preparing to Retaliate.

New York, June 14.—The Herald's Victoria (B. C.) special says: "The North China News, received by the steamship Empress of Japan, which has just arrived, states that the recent proclamation by Hsu Tsotai of Amoy against the sale or use of American kerosene in his jurisdiction is the first step toward retaliatory measures against everything American in the event of the Geary act being enforced. Canton and Swatow will follow the examples set by Amoy."

The United States marshal at Nagasaki who was arrested on a charge of assisting to export Japanese women for immoral purposes has been honorably acquitted.

Dr. Walker's Situation a Mystery.

Minneapolis, Minn., June 14.—Nothing whatever has known at a late hour last night regarding Dr. Walker's position at Leach lake, who is held a prisoner by the Indians. No news can be had from the agency, on account of the Indians having doubled pickets. The Indians concerned in the uprising are the Leach lake Chippewas, a friendly and peaceable tribe. Colonel Barber stated last night that he hardly expected the matter to end fatally for the doctor.

A Village Wiped Out.

Grand Rapids, Mich., June 14.—Alba, a village of 800 population in Antrim county, was destroyed by fire yesterday. The wires are down and no communication can be had with the town.

Pages 1-8.

The Evening Standard.

Pages 1-8.

ESTABLISHED FEBRUARY, 1850.

NEW BEDFORD, THURSDAY, JUNE 15, 1893.---TEN PAGES.

TWO CENTS.

DEFENSE!

A Bright Day for Lizzie Borden.

Collapse of Commonwealth's Case.

The Prussic Acid Story Not Allowed.

That Ended Evidence for Prosecution.

Defense Outlined by Mr. Jennings.

Exclusive Opportunity to be Negatived.

No Motive for Murder of Andrew J. Borden.

Burning of the Dress Satisfactorily Explained.

First Witnesses Put on This Forenoon.

Most Interesting Evidence of the Trial to Come.

This, in many ways, has been one of the most interesting days of the famous trial. The government received another set-back in the refusal of the justices to allow the evidence of the attempt to purchase prussic acid to go to the jury for their consideration. A prediction that has been made that the government would directly connect the prisoner with the famous handleless hatchet was unfulfilled. The government rested its case, much to the surprise of many, but those who have followed the trial closely were expecting it. Mr. Jennings presented the outline of the defense, and his effort compared favorably with the splendid opening by Mr. Moody.

STRUGGLING FOR SEATS.

Another Surging Crowd at the Court House Stockade.

At no time since the trial opened has there been any such rush for seats as there was this morning. At the stockade the officers in charge found it almost impossible to restrain the surging crowd, and several women who had taken up their positions near the entrance, so as to be on hand when the spectators were admitted, were crushed until they screamed with pain. The crowd had a martial appearance and many of the Sons of Veterans were the first to arrive. At the rear entrance a long line of the Sons of Veterans were standing shoulder to shoulder, as if on dress parade, and one would almost think they were making preparations to salute the prisoner when she arrived.

The expedients resorted to by many to pass the alert officers are amusing. Two women, each having a document in their hand asked the deputy sheriff at the rear door to direct them to the register of deeds' office, a request that was promptly complied with. The reporter afterwards saw the deeds and they were dated over five years back.

Miss Borden's Arrival.

When the cab containing Miss Borden arrived the rush for positions to gain a view of her when alighting was tremendous, and when the court house walls hid her from sight the crowd quickly melted away. She gave a quick comprehensive glance at the people over Deputy Sheriff Kirby's shoulder as she stepped from the carriage, but met so far as could be seen nothing but looks of curiosity—not a glance of sympathy, and she hurriedly withdrew her gaze. What must her thoughts have been as she gazed on the care-free people, standing about in the bright sunlight of a perfect June morning, with no let or hindrance to their movements, and then contrasted their condition with her own, cribbed, cabined and confined. Surely her reflections could not have been pleasant ones.

WOMEN ALL TURN FOR A LOOK AT LIZZIE AS THEY GO OUT.

PRUSSIC ACID.

Charles H. Lawton Called as a Government Expert.

Charles H. Lawton of this city was the first witness this morning. He was examined by Mr. Knowlton.

Q. Charles H. Lawton is your name? A. Charles Henry Lawton.

Q. Do you live in New Bedford? A. I do.

Q. How long have you lived in New Bedford? A. Forty years.

Q. What is your business?

At this point there was an interruption by Mr. Robinson, who objected to the admission of the evidence in regard to prussic acid on any other grounds than those agreed upon yesterday.

The court directed that no evidence be offered upon the direct proposition until after the preliminary evidence had been heard.

Mr. Knowlton resumed.

Q. What is your business, Mr. Lawton? A. I am a druggist.

Q. Do you carry on the drug business? A. I carry on the business with my brother.

Q. How long have you carried on the drug business? A. Twenty years.

Q. Where is your store? A. We have two stores, one corner of Union and Purchase streets and one corner of Union and Second streets.

Q. In New Bedford? A. Yes sir.

Q. Purchase street and Union street are perhaps the principal streets of this city? A. Yes sir, they are supposed to be.

Q. Do you carry on both wholesale and retail business? A. Yes.

Q. How large a retail business do you carry on? A. The heaviest retail business of any one in this city.

Q. Before you went into business yourself were you also engaged in any one's employ? A. I was.

Q. Including your services as retail clerk and all your connection with the business, what time does it cover? A. My previous answer will cover that, 40 years.

Q. You are acquainted with the drug called prussic acid? A. Yes sir.

Q. Always? A. Yes sir.

Q. Is the drug kept in the pure form? A. We never have had it.

Q. What is your experience in the matter as to how it is kept?

Mr. Robinson—I object.

Mr. Knowlton—I will not press the question.

Q. What is the proper name of the acid? A. Prussic acid or hydrocyanic acid.

Q. Is prussic acid the proper name, or hydrocyanic? A. It is called both.

Q. In the time that you have been in business for what purpose have you sold it other than a medicine?

Mr. Robinson—I object.

Q. Have you sold it during that time for any other purpose than upon the prescription of a physician?

I object said Mr. Robinson.

Q. Mr. Lawton, is the drug called prussic acid sold commercially for any other purpose than upon the prescription of a physician?

Mr. Robinson again objected.

Mr. Knowlton—I will add "for medicinal purposes."

Mr. Robinson—I object.

The question was excluded.

Q. Have you ever had in your experience a call for prussic acid for any other than upon the prescription of a physician?

Mr. Robinson—I object.

The question was excluded.

Q. Do you know of any use to which prussic acid is put other than for the purpose of a medicine?

Mr. Robinson—I object to that.

The court—The question may be answered.

Mr. Robinson—Please save my rights of acception.

A. Not that I know of.

The witness was not cross-examined.

Mr. H. H. Tillson was called.

NOT USED ON FURS.

Henry H. Tillson's Evidence Regarding Hydrocyanic Acid.

Q. Henry H. Tillson is your name? A. That is my name, yes sir.

Q. Do you live in New Bedford? A. New Bedford.

Q. How long have you lived here? A. Sixty years.

Q. What is your business? A. I am in the fur business and gentlemen's furnishing business.

Q. What have you had to do with furs? A. I have always had the care of furs since I have been in the business, packing them and preserving them from moths.

Q. That is you mean simply those furs that you have in stock? A. No, not altogether. I have had the care of furs belonging to others.

Q. Does that include the cleaning of furs?

Mr. Robinson—I object.

The question was not pressed.

Q. Does your business have anything to do with the cleaning of furs? A. Nothing more than the preserving of furs.

Q. Mr. Tillson, is prussic acid used in any connection with the care of furs? A. I never heard of it.

(Continued on Third Page.)

SONS OF VETERANS.

Albert C. Blaisdell Elected Division Commander.

Presentation of an Elegant Watch to Commander Delano.

Proceedings of To-day's Session of the Mass. Division Convention.

This morning's session of the 11th annual convention of the Massachusetts Division, Sons of Veterans, convened at 9 o'clock, and was called to order by Commander W. H. Delano.

At the roll call of officers Charles H. Darling, of the division council, Inspector C. F. Cook and Judge Advocate C. F. O'Brien were reported absent.

The records of the session of yesterday were read and approved.

Brother Quigley of Camp 33 was voted a seat in the convention.

The members present and entitled to vote was reported as 180.

It was voted to attend the June 17th celebration on invitation of Abraham Lincoln Camp 106 of Charlestown.

Brother C. D. Rooney explained that at the session of the commandery in chief a recommendation that the quorum be reduced from 7 to 5 was referred to a committee, and as that committee did not report no action had been taken.

A communication of greeting from Women's Relief No. 53 was received and filed.

Albert C. Blaisdell,
The New Division Commander, Sons of Veterans.

The committee on officers' reports reported through its chairman, Past Colonel Hinckley, as follows:

On recommendation No. 1 of the commander's report, recommending that a sum not exceeding $100 be appropriated for extra clerical help, the committee reported "ought not to pass." The report was voted affirmatively.

On recommendation No. 2 of the commander, that the sum of $200 be appropriated for the inspectors' department, $50 of which to be paid to the inspector, the committee reported that $175 be appropriated. Past Colonel Upham made a substitute motion that the matter be left to the discretion of the incoming commander, and it was carried.

On recommendation No. 3 of the commander, that the delegates to the National encampment be instructed to recommend a change in the time of inspection from "between April 15 and May 15" to "between Sept. 15 and Oct. 15," the committee recommended that it be referred to the committee on constitution, rules and regulations.

On recommendation No. 4, that the per capita tax be raised from 50 to 60 cents, and that the Andersonville fund be taken from the division fund, the committee asked for information, and on motion of Past Captain Campbell the quartermaster's report was referred to the committee for information.

On the recommendation of the division chaplain the committee reported "ought not to pass."

The committee on credentials reported having received 180 credentials. The report was accepted.

The committee on ritual was not ready to report and consequently did not do so.

The committee on constitution, rules and ritual, to whom was referred recommendation three, reported "ought not to pass."

The same committee reported with regard to changing the quorum, "ought not to pass." Also that the date of the annual inspection be changed to "between Sept. 15 and Oct. 15," and that it be referred to the commander-in-chief. Remarks were made by Past Colonel Burbeck, Past Captain Bolton and Brother Couch, and a vote was taken, resulting 76 in favor and 71 in opposition. It was doubted and a rising vote resulted 98 to 92.

Recommendation four was reported upon adversely and the committee reported against any change in the age limit. Remarks followed by Past Colonel Hinckley, and a substitute motion, "ought to pass" was made by him. Other remarks followed by Past Colonel Stevens and Brothers Bruce, Messenger, Davis, Merriam, Coolidge, O'Brien, Hargraves and Wellington. The substitute motion was lost.

At this point the convention engaged in a happy ceremony, Senior Vice Commander Blaisdell stepping forward and on behalf of the Massachusetts division presenting Commander Delano an elegant 14-karet gold Waltham watch. The exchange of sentiment was most pleasing.

The committee on resolutions reported, recommending that its recommendations be referred to the next division encampment. The committee recommended "ought not to pass" with regard to the change of date of the encampment.

Past Colonel Upham moved that so much of the resolution as refers to changing the date from June to February be adopted.

Brother Rooney moved as a substitute that it be laid on the table.

On reading the first and last articles of the division bylaws the resolution was declared out of order.

The committee recommended that the invitation to hold the 1894 convention at Pittsfield be accepted. On motion of Past Colonel Stevens, it was unanimously voted to accept.

Resolution four was adversely reported upon, and resolution five was reported favorably upon by a majority of the committee. Upon a rising vote is was voted to concur in the recommendation.

The committee on ritual reported that recommendation one should not pass.

On motion of Past Colonel Stevens a recess was taken until 1 30 o'clock.

The afternoon session opened with the annual election and by nearly a unanimous vote Senior Vice Commander Blaisdell was chosen commander. The other officers will be found in a later edition.

Past Colonel Fisher of New Hampshire is in attendance at the convention.

[Continued on Fourth Page.]

A VALUABLE PAPER.

The Republican Standard issued this morning is the largest weekly paper ever printed in southern Massachusetts, and a valuable one to send away to distant friends or preserve for reference. Twenty pages are crowded with interesting news matter. The great feature, of course, is the magnificent report of the Borden murder trial, more complete than can be found elsewhere. The Republican Standard is now on sale in wrappers for mailing.

WEATHER INDICATIONS.

Showers.

Washington, June 15.—For the 24 hours from 8 a. m. today for New England, generally fair, with increasing cloudiness and probably showers on the Massachusetts and western Maine coasts this afternoon or evening; cooler in the interior; variable winds.

HOME MATTERS.

THIRD DISTRICT COURT.

Borden, J.

Thursday, June 15.

Frederick P. Jennings pleaded guilty of being drunk and not guilty of disturbing the peace on the 14th inst. Walter H. Braley said Jennings came to his house last night and threatened to whip him, and he was compelled to put him out of the house. He made so much noise he called Officer Weston, who arrested him. For drunkenness he was sentenced to the house of correction for 30 days and for disturbing the peace 60 days.

James Quigley for drunkenness was sent up for three months.

Peter McKenna was before the court yesterday for drunkenness and was put on probation until July 29th next; this morning he was before the court again for drunkenness, and was sent up for 60 days.

Charles W. Johnson and George T. Cogey withdrew their appeals from sentences of three months each for the larceny of 75 cents, the property of Edward Laws on the 12th inst., and sentence was reaffirmed.

Thomas Williams for drunkenness was sentenced to 30 days and appealed.

One case of drunkenness was placed on probation until July 29th next.

John Perry was defaulted on a continued case for drunkenness.

George E. Baldwin of Fairhaven pleaded not guilty of drunkenness. After hearing the testimony the case was continued to July 29th next.

Thomas B. Rowe for keeping a disorderly house and for disturbing the peace and Robert Gillespie for disturbing the peace on the 9th inst. were the next cases called, and they were all tried together. Several officers and a number of neighbors testified to hearing loud noises in the house and to cursing and swearing. No evidence was offered for the defense. Hon. E. L. Barney for the defense. Upon the promise of Rowe to have things different at his home in future the complaint for keeping a disorderly house was with the consent of the chief of police nol prossed, and the case against him for disturbing the peace was continued to June 24th, with the understanding that a fine of $20 would then be imposed. Gillespie was adjudged guilty and paid a fine of $10.

A woman, another of the parties at Rowe's house on the 9th inst., whose daughter is ashamed of her conduct, was fined $5.

Certain liquors seized from Louis H. Lanneau and Condit Patneaude on the 27th day of May last were declared forfeited.

At a juvenile session Augustine Lagasse pleaded not guilty of the larceny of a watch valued at $6, the property of John Fortier, this morning. The case was continued until tomorrow.

Manuel J. Fernandez and Adam R. Gonsalves pleaded guilty of the larceny of 25 cigars from John Enos and $6 in money from Samuel P. Richmond on the 13th inst. This case was also continued until tomorrow, when the state agent will be present.

STOVES.

F. R. Slocum will make a run on Kitchen Ranges for the next few weeks. One side of the store is crowded with new stoves which must be sold. Most of these are the celebrated "Hub Goods" manufactured by Smith & Anthony of Boston. These have the famous patent gaulge doors which ventilate the oven and are made on no other stove. F. R. Slocum keeps all of the standard makes of Ranges. Don't neglect buying in the summer when Ranges are cheap, and don't forget Slocum has the best assortment.

CONDENSED LOCALS.

—F. E. Tinkham's bulletin for to-morrow: Fresh salmon, 20 cents per pound; Nantucket bluefish, halibut, scup, tautog, fresh mackerel, perch, flounder, cod, haddock, rock bass, lobsters, oysters, clams, quahogs, &c. 9 North Sixth street. Telephone 252-1.

"Worth its weight in gold" Mellin's Food would be to the frail little creature you scarcely dare hope to keep from slipping away from your love and care. The use of Mellin's Food will make the pale, pinched face grow rosy and round, and the feeble limbs active and strong.

—Nooning's flower sale was such a success the past week that we give you another chance to secure one of the great bargains. Handsome bunches for 49c. and 69c. per bunch.

—Sanders & Barrows have erected on the big derrick on Liberty Hall corner a large sign, 24 by 15 feet, which announces the fact that that particular site will be occupied about March 1, 1894, by them.

—When you can purchase at Whiting & Co's the best 12 1-2 ct. Ginghams at 7 1-2 cts. do not fail to lay in a year's supply.

Over 20,000 families in Boston are using Ayer's Hygienic Coffee. Principal grocers sell it. Try a package.

—The letter carriers have all been furnished with straw hats this week at Gifford & Co's.

—Great drive at Nooning's on the flower sale. Elegant sprays for 49c. and 69c. per bunch.

—There will be a special communication of Eureka lodge in Masonic hall tomorrow evening.

—The best blue flannel suits to be found in the city for $8, $12, and $13, at Gifford & Co's.

Gentlemen, the finest line of Russia leather shoes found at Buchell's. See our $4 shoe.

—The best stock of Shirt Waists can be seen at Whiting & Co's—all choice styles.

—Headquarters for straw hats is at Gifford & Co's, 139 Union street.

Cutter Whiskey is the leading fine whiskey in Boston.

—Go to Whiting & Co's for Gingham and Cambric Wrappers—all styles and prices.

—Large line of new neckwear just arrived at Gifford & Co's.

—Fancy straw hats at Nooning's marked down to 25c., 50c. and 75c.

—Whiting & Co. are selling Ladies' 75 cent Shirt Waists at 50 cents each.

—Children's sailor hats at Nooning's, very cheap.

—Bicycle goods of all descriptions at Gifford & Co's.

Scrofula cured by Hood's Sarsaparilla.

DEFENSE!

(Continued from First Page.)

Mr. Robinson—I object.

The question and answer were allowed to stand.

Q. Mr. Tillson, have you any knowledge of the effect of prussic acid upon furs; have you any knowledge of that subject? A. Not at all, sir.

The witness was not cross-examined.

NATHANIEL HATHAWAY.

Expert Testimony of Well Known New Bedford Chemist.

Nathaniel Hathaway, the well-known New Bedford chemist, was the next witness called.

Q. Nathaniel Hathaway is your name? A. Yes sir.

Q. Your residence? A. New Bedford.

Q. You are an analytical chemist? A. Yes sir.

Q. Where were you graduated? A. School of Mines, Columbia college.

Q. You are often called upon to give information in matters connected with

MATRON REAGAN CROSS-EXAMINED BY ATTORNEY JENNINGS.

your profession? A. Yes sir.

Q. You are acquainted with the nature of drugs? A. Yes sir.

Q. Are you acquainted with hydrocyanic, or, as it is sometimes called, prussic acid? A. Yes sir.

Q. How is it sold commercially? A. It is sold in a two per cent. solution.

Q. What is its adaptability or suitability for use in connection with furs?

Mr. Robinson—I object.

Chief Justice—The qualification of the witness is deemed sufficient by the court, but the question as put is thought to be incompetent.

Mr. Knowlton—It is precisely in line with what I offer to prove.

Q. Has prussic acid a suitability or adaptability for use in connection with seal skin furs?

Mr. Robinson—I renew my objection.

Chief Justice—The witness may answer.

Mr. Robinson—Your honors will save my rights to the point.

A. I think it is unsuited.

Q. Has it any suitability for use in cleaning furs? A. None.

Q. What is its nature as to volatility? A. Are you speaking of commercial prussic acid? Yes; it is very volatile.

Q. Has it any effect when it is distributed in the air in its volatile form upon any person in the vicinity?

Mr. Robinson—I object to the question.

Chief Justice—The witness may answer.

A. No sir.

Q. Is prussic acid used for cleaning furs? A. Not to my knowledge.

Mr. Robinson—We desire your honors to note my general objection to the testimony of the witness.

Chief Justice—Your exceptions will be saved.

Cross-examined by Mr. Robinson:

Q. Prussic acid is very volatile, you say? A. Yes sir.

Q. By that you mean that it passes off in the air? A. Yes sir.

Q. There are a number of substances that are very volatile, are there not?

Witness enumerated a number of volatile substances.

Q. How about ether? A. It is very volatile.

Q. In any very great quantity is deadly? A. Yes sir.

Q. Ether, chloroform and benzine are volatile, and are in common use? A. I don't know in how common use.

Q. Naphtha is a common article of use and is very volatile? A. Yes sir.

Q. Benzine is on sale in all the drug stores labeled benzine? A. I don't know.

Q. Are you a family man? A. Yes sir.

Q. Don't you know that benzine is commonly used in cleaning spots off of clothing and all such things? A. Yes sir.

Q. It is destructive to animal life, such as bugs, flies and small animals. They have either got to emigrate or die?

THE NEW YORK NEWSPAPER MEN.

A. Yes sir.

Q. Ether, naphtha and chloroform are all volatile. There is no objection to their use for this purpose because of their voltility, is there? A. I think they are unsuitable for use for these purposes.

Q. It is because they are liable to take fire that you object to their use? A. They are very dangerous compounds to have about.

Q. You use gas in your house. That can be used so as to be dangerous? A. Undoubtedly.

Q. Some kinds of illuminating gas are not susceptible to the smell? A. I have heard of it, but never saw it.

Q. What is the effect of illuminating gas on human life. That is, if turned on unlighted, I mean? A. To suffocate or poison.

Q. Am I right, because an article is volatile in its character, there is no objection to its use for a legitimate purpose? A. I think not, if carefully used.

Q. Arsenic is poisonous, isn't it? A. Yes sir.

Q. It is an ingredient of the article commonly sold, known as Rough on Rats, isn't it? A. I believe it is.

Q. It is commonly used to rid houses of rats, and very properly, too, isn't it? A. I think not.

Q. Would you rather have the rats than use it? A. Yes sir.

Q. Do you know anything about the use of arsenic to beautify the complexion? A. No sir.

Q. You probably never used it yourself, but you have heard of its use in cosmetics? A. Yes sir.

Q. How would you kill cats if you didn't want to whack them in the head, shoot them or tie them up in a bag and take them down to the river? A. I don't know.

Q. You never had much experience in that line, I take it? A. No sir.

Q. Take prussic acid as commonly sold, it can be diluted still more. What would you use? A. Water or alcohol.

Q. Suppose you dilute it 100 times more, would you say that such a solution as that wouldn't kill animal life on fur? A. I haven't tried that.

Q. Have you had experience in killing animal life with prussic acid? A. With a 2 per cent. solution.

Q. Would that kill? A. Yes sir.

Q. When were your experiments in regard to killing animal life with prussic acid made? A. Between last night and this morning.

Q. When did you begin to experiment last night? A. At 10 o'clock.

Q. Did you keep it up all night? A. Until about 12 o'clock, and commenced again early this morning.

Q. What insects did you kill with the acid? A. I don't know all of them, I am not a naturalist. I killed some spiders.

Q. You can't tell what the effects would be if more than 2 per cent. was used? A. No.

Q. Because it will kill insects is no objection to its use, is it? A. Not that in particular.

Q. Have you any other objection? A. Being a poison is an objection.

Q. Suppose that a person was careful in its use, you don't see any harm in using it to kill insects on a cape, do you? A. No.

Q. There is nothing in the acid which makes it unsuitable to use on moths in furs is there? A. No objection that I know of.

Q. The effect of the poison would depend upon its strength, would it not? A. Yes.

Dr. Dolan as an Expert.

Dr. Dolan was the next witness.

Q. Are you acquainted with the qualities of prussic acid? A. Yes.

Q. Of its use and properties? A. Yes.

Q. What do you say as to its volatileness? A. It is the most voatile drug to be had.

Q. As to its poisonousness? A. It is most poisonous.

Q. Has it any adaptability to its use in cleaning furs?

The question was objected to and ruled out.

Q. What study have you made of the acid? A. None, except as it came to my knowledge as a physician and as a medical examiner.

Q. Have you attended lectures in the course of your education on materia medica? A. Yes.

Q. And that included the properties of prussic acid?

An objection was made and after consultation the answer was ruled out as incompetent when coming from the witness.

A long wait then ensued, pending the arrival of Professor Wood, and the jury left their seats and retired.

Mrs. Livermore Appears.

Mrs. Mary Livermore appeared during the recess which followed the resting of the government and held a moment's conversation with Lizzie Borden. While she was so engaged the great exponent of women's rights was closely watched by the audience.

THE DEFENSE SURPRISE.

Unprepared for the Government's Sudden Closing.

The close of the government's case was a complete surprise to the defense, and found counsel unprepared to go on for the moment. The quick closing (I had almost written collapse) was due to the exclusion of the evidence in regard to the effects of prussic acid, on which the government had confidently relied—connected with alleged attempt to purchase by Miss Borden—to produce a strong effect on its behalf.

The counsel for defense held a consultation as to the best method of procedure, and after it, Attorney Adams was seen by a reporter, who said if he was one of counsel for defense he would be willing to give the case to the jury without argument or putting in any evidence. Said Mr. Adams, "If it was a case of larceny, I would be perfectly willing to do so, but where a human life is at stake, all precautions must be taken."

"You must be aware of the general feeling that the government has not made out a case, and that an acquittal will follow," said the reporter.

"While we have organs that lead to pleasurable emotions, you can imagine what our feelings must be," said Mr. Adams, smiling pleasantly.

Miss Borden Looks Relieved.

Ex-Governor Robinson, who sat near, smiled approvingly at the turn of the conversation, or at his thoughts mayhap, and Miss Borden, who also sat listening showed her pleasure, and her face lit up with one of those smiles so rarely to be seen upon it of late, and she looked gratefully at her counsel, as if she fully appreciated the encouraging nature of their words.

ALL EVIDENCE EXCLUDED.

Judges Will Not Permit Jury to Hear Drug Clerk Bence.

The jury returned to the court room at 10 20, and Mr. Tillson was recalled. He was asked two questions in regard to the preparation of seal skins for commerce, and they were objected to and

LIZZIE AND HER COUNSEL IN CONSULTATION.

excluded.

Mr. Knowlton said: "I now offer the testimony of Eli Bence."

Chief Justice Mason said the court did not care to judge upon the matter by piecemeal, and the evidence would be excluded.

The Charnel House Display.

Mr. Knowlton said the government now formally offered all the plans and photographs introduced, the various exhibits which have been produced and identified by the various witnesses, the hatchets, skulls, dress and skirt, the various pieces of the house, the marble slab, bedspread and other bed clothing, the pieces of carpet and also the things that were produced by Professor Wood.

COMMONWEALTH RESTS.

Recess Granted Defense to Arrange Their Matters.

The commonwealth rests, said Mr. Knowlton.

Mr. Robinson then requested that counsel for defense be given ten minutes to arrange their matters, and the court granted a recess of ten minutes, and the jury and counsel retired.

PLEADING OF THE PRISONER.

Lizzie Deeply Agitated by Mr. Jennings' Words.

The jury returned to the court room at 10 minutes to 11, and Mr. Jennings immediately began outlining the defense. Before he had fairly commenced, Lizzie placed her handkerchief to her eyes, her face paled and she was deeply agitated. Her bosom heaved and it was only with considerable effort that she was able to restrain herself.

To Mr. Jennings the utmost attention was given and the deep hush of the court room was broken only by the words of the counsel. His eloquence was masterly and captivated all within the range of his voice. As he proceeded all eyes were fastened upon him, and all ears were strained to catch the words as they fell from his lips. At the outset his manner was somewhat subdued and deliberate and he appeared to feel the full weight of the situation, but as he proceeded his manner became more earnest and his lips seemed to be unable to keep pace with the thoughts that rushed through his mind and sought utterance.

Mr. Jennings' Address.

Mr. Foreman and Gentlemen of the Jury—One of the victims of the murder charged in this indictment was for many years my client and my personal friend. I have known him since my boyhood. I had known his eldest daughter for the same length of time, and I want to say right here and now if I manifest more feeling than perhaps you may think necessary in making an opening for the defense in this case you will ascribe it to that cause.

Facts and fiction have furnished many extraordinary examples of crime that have shocked and staggered men. I think not one of them has ever surpassed in its mystery the case that you are now considering. The brutal character of the wounds, as well as the audacity of the time and place chosen, would make this the act of an insane person or a fiend.

I do not propose to go into detail about the character of these wounds or their appearance. I think you have heard sufficient about that already. But, Mr. Foreman and gentlemen, knowing what they were, the person who is arrested for doing the deed, which I have characterized as I have, was the youngest daughter of one of the victims, a young woman 32 years of age, up to that time of spotless character and reputation. She had spent her life in that immediate neighborhood, she had moved in and out of that old house for 20 or 21 years, living there with her father and with her stepmother and with her sister. This crime that shocked the whole civilized world, Mr. Foreman and gentlemen, seemed from the very first to be laid at her door by those who represented the government in the investigation of the case. We shall show you that this young woman, as I have said, had apparently lead a spotless life; she was a member of the church; she was interested in church matters; she was connected with various organizations for charitable work; she was ever ready to help in any good thing and in any good deed. And yet for some reason or other the government in its investigation seemed to fasten the crime upon her.

Now, a crime like this naturally awakens as its first result a sort of selfish fear; there is an outcry of human hearts to have somebody punished for the crime. But, Mr. Foreman and gentlemen, no matter how much you may want somebody punished for the crime, it is the guilty, and not the innocent, that you want. The old law of blood for blood and life for life, Mr. Foreman and gentlemen, even in its strongest form in the past, never, except in barbarous and uncivilized nations, called for the blood of the innocent in return for the blood or life of the murdered. I am told there is one country, at least, one of the great countries of the world, where it has been the practice in case there is no direct evidence of who the murderer is, to measure the distance to the nearest person at the time the murder was committed, and if he cannot prove his innocence or make known the guilty party he is executed, the rules of that country requiring that some one shall be punished for the crime. But, Mr. Foreman and gentlemen, that is not the law of Massachusetts today. That is not the law of this Christian civilization of today. Our law, and it is the law that you have sworn to apply to the evidence in this case, presumes every man innocent until he is proved guilty, not guilty until he is proved innocent. I know you may say it is the duty of the state to vindicate the death of one of its citizens. Mr. Foreman and gentlemen, it is a higher duty, and one recognized by the law of this state, that it shall protect the lives of its living citizens.

Mr. Foreman and gentlemen, I say this is a mysterious case, everbody, every thinking man must say the same. But you are not sitting there, Mr. Foreman and gentlemen, to answer the question how this deed could have been committed or who committed it, that is not the issue at all. The issue is very simple. The commonwealth here has charged that Lizzie Borden, Lizzie Andrew Borden, in a certain way, at a certain time, killed Andrew Jackson Borden and Abby Durfee Borden with malice aforethought. And that alone is the question that you are to answer. Did she on that day commit that deed? Did she commit it in the way alleged? To put it in its other form have they satisfied you beyond a reasonable doubt that she did it?

And what is a reasonable doubt? I saw a definition and it struck me as a very good one: "A reasonable doubt is a doubt for which you can give a reason." If you can conceive of any other hypothesis that will exclude the guilt of this prisoner and make it possible or probable that somebody else might have done this deed, then you have a reasonable doubt in your mind.

Now, Mr. Foreman and gentlemen, I want to say a word about the kinds of evidence. There are two kinds of evidence, direct evidence and circumstantial evidence. Direct evidence is the testimony of persons who have seen, heard or felt the thing or things about which they are testifying. They are telling you something which they have observed or perceived by their senses. In this instance if this was a case of murder by stabbing, and a man should come before you and testify that he saw the prisoner strike the murdered person with a knife, that is direct evidence; that tends directly to connect the prisoner with the crime itself.

Circumstantial evidence is entirely different, and I want to say right here, Mr. Foreman and gentlemen, call your attention to it now, and I do not think that the commonwealth would question the statement when I make it, that there is not one particle of direct evidence in this case from beginning to end against Lizzie A. Borden. There is not a spot of blood, there is not a weapon that they have connected with her in any way, shape or fashion. They have not had her hand touch it, or her eye see it, or her ear hear of it. There is not, I say, a particle of testimony in this case, direct testimony, connecting her with this crime. It is wholly and absolutely circumstantial.

Now, what do we mean by that? We know, of course, that almost everything occurs under regular and general laws, and we know that if certain things exist certain other things will exist, that is, they follow as a consequence. We know, for instance, that water, if the temperature of the atmosphere falls below a certain degree, will transform itself into ice. And so other things in the same way. Now, circumstantial evidence consists of certain facts, which, if proved true, necessarily cause you to infer that a certain other fact must have followed or existed. And in proving a murder it is necessary for the government to prove that all of the facts existed which to your minds make you certain, make you morally certain, that the murder must have followed from it. In other words, in circumstantial evidence it is simply an opinion on your part, it is simply an inference drawn by you from the facts that were proved as to whether the essential issue has been proven or not.

Now, in certain cases, Mr. Foreman and gentlemen, circumstantial evidence

(Continued on Fourth Page.)

NEWSPAPER COMMENTS.

Marshal Hilliard's testimony that the bloody shams, bedspreads and other things, apparent to everybody as necessary in evidence in the Borden murders, were not taken possession of until the Saturday after the tragedy, is the most striking statement of police bungling in the management of this case. When the full story comes out of how these articles were finally secured, the wonder will be that some damaging blood spots were not found about the house or the clothing of its inmates. Some good luck, as well as bad, has attended the unfortunate defendant in this case.—Fall River News.

I know of at least one woman in Lowell who is reading all the testimony in the Borden case. She was an old schoolmate of Lizzie, and for several years lived on the opposite side of the street from her. She says that as a girl Miss Borden was quiet and she never knew of her having any trouble with the other girls. Mr. Borden she remembers as a man to whom she never felt favorably attracted.—Lowell Courier.

That pin-head blood spot on Lizzie Borden's white skirt will not go a great way toward convicting the defendant, situated as it is on the back side of the skirt. The commonwealth of Massachusetts is having pretty hard sledding, it appears to us, trying to prove that Mr. and Mrs. Andrew Borden were murdered by their daughter. We say this with no intention of prejudging the case now on trial.—Springfield Republican.

TREATMENT CHANGED.

Miss Jackson Before the Union League of Colored Citizens.

At a meeting of the Union league of colored citizens last evening, which, by the way, was fully attended, the subject of Miss Jackson's episode at the court house on Monday last was discussed. Miss Jackson appeared before the league and told her story as stated in the Standard.

The league finding, upon subsequent visits to the court house by Miss Jackson and other colored persons, that the treatment had changed, it was decided not to take action in the premises. Emanuel Sullavou, Esq., presided over the deliberations.

EXPENDITURES.

We are indebted to City Auditor George W. Parker for the following list of expenditures in the various departments of the city for the week ending June 10:

Cemeteries,	$329.63
Engineering department,	409.23
Fire department.	
Pay rolls and Protecting society,	473.05
Free public library,	
Dog fund,	16.50
Highways and streets.	
Block paving,	104.23
Cinder sidewalks and repairs,	37.60
City stables,	80.96
City tool house,	117.89
Cobble paving and repairs,	151.02
Collecting ashes,	89.20
Concrete sidewalks and repairs,	79.72
Crosswalks and repairs,	70.22
Curbing and repairs,	130.31
Filling and grading,	647.22
Flagging and repars,	94.98
Gutters and repairs,	16.42
Labor, stable yard,	10.60
Macadam,	413.06
Main office expenses and salaries,	98.31
Miscellaneous,	80.45
Private work and trimming trees,	953.79
Sweeping and cleaning streets,	228.91
Incidentals,	172.46
New Bedford & Fairhaven bridge,	21.67
New Bedford water works,	918.91
Parks and squares,	44.72
Permanent debt,	105.00
Police department,	1,342.32
Public schools.	
Pay of teachers,	2,303.27
Janitors, day and evening,	202.95
Office salaries,	104.79
Sewers, general account,	51.03
Sewers, Nye street,	420.92
Kempton street schoolhouse and lot,	690.66
	$11,012.00

Mrs. Lamont Fainted at the Fair.

Chicago, June 15.—At about 5 o'clock yesterday afternoon Mrs. Daniel Lamont, wife of the secretary of war, was overcome by heat and exhaustion while in Midway plaisance and without warning fell in a faint. The party had been at the Jackson park all day and had made an extended tour of the grounds. Mrs. Lamont was taken to Columbian Emergency hospital, where restoratives speedily restored consciousness. The physicians do not anticipate any serious results.

Orangemen Elect Officers.

Minneapolis, June 15.—At the election of officers of the Orangemen yesterday, the following were chosen: Most worshipful grand master, Francis C. Campbell, Minneapolis; deputy grand master, William Gillan, Philadelphia; grand chaplain, M. L. Seook, Omaha; grand secretary, Thomas Mulligan, Everett, Mass.; grand treasurer, James Caldwell, Philadelphia; grand lecturer, L. McLeod, Boston; grand director of ceremonies, William McCullough, Pittsburg; assistant grand secretary, William Dawson, Everett, Mass.

To Keep Out Russian Emigrants.

Hamburg, June 15.—The senate, in order to prevent the introduction of cholera has issued a notice to the police to strictly enforce the ordinance prohibiting the entry of Russian emigrants either by land or water, even though they are duly furnished with money. First class saloon passengers with tickets for the United States are not affected by the ordinance.

To Resume Business.

Chicago, June 15.—At a meeting of the stockholders of the Chemical National bank yesterday it was decided by a practically unanimous vote to resume business. The conditions laid down by Comptroller Eckles as necessary to be agreed to before the bank will be allowed to open its doors was accepted, and steps were taken.

ANOTHER BORDEN HATCHET.

This Just Discovered on the Top of Crowe's Barn.

(By Associated Press.)

Fall River, June 15.—Another Borden hatchet has been discovered. Last night a boy named Potter, son of C. C. Potter, clerk in the Fall River water works office, while looking for a ball found a hatchet on the top of John Crowe's barn, which is located just in the rear of the Borden property. Mr. Potter this morning reported his find to the police, and also sought an interview with the counsel for defense, but was unable to find Mr. Jennings. He still has the hatchet in his possession, and describes it as an ordinary implement with hammer head. The handle was weather beaten and the blade covered with rust. Some of the particles of rust being removed a slight coloring of gilt was disclosed, which would either indicate that the hatchet was at one time used as an ornament or was quite new when lost or discarded.

SUICIDE IN FALL RIVER.

Thomas Cox Cuts His Throat in a Fit of Delirium.

(Special Dispatch.)

Fall River, June 15.—The already excited people of this city were further alarmed about 7 o'clock this morning by rumors of another murder. Upon investigation it was found that Thomas Cox, a laborer, aged 35 years, had cut his throat with a razor and died immediately at his home, 56 Rodman street. It is reported that he has been drinking heavily of late, and was no doubt suffering from delirium. John Lahey, who lives in the same building, discovered the suicide a few minutes after the deed was done. The bloody razor was picked up beside the body, which lay stretched on the kitchen floor in a pool of blood. It is also reported, though it cannot be ascertained, that Cox imagined himself in danger of arrest for the larceny of a watch, but owing to his condition this may have arisen from his wild talk.

INSPECTING THE ROAD.

Consolidated Officials Travel Over the Old Colony System.

President C. P. Clark of the New York, New Haven & Hartford railroad, Charles F. Choate, president of the Old Colony railroad, J. R. Kendrick, general manager of the Old Colony system, and about 25 or 30 other officials and directors of the Consolidated road, are making a tour of inspection over the newly acquired Old Colony system in a special train, consisting of two drawing room and one observation cars, and visited this city Tuesday for a few minutes.

The officials started on their inspection Tuesday at Fall River, and proceeded first to this city by the Fall River branch. Then they went over the Central division to Taunton, and proceeded to Boston by way of the Plymouth and Nantasket Beach branches. On Wednesday they inspected the Dedham, Walpole and Plainville branches and the Northern division to Providence. Today the party proceeded over the Providence, Warren & Bristol road to Fall River, and thence to Newport, and will return after a brief stop to Fall River and Boston. Tomorrow the Cape division will be visited to Provincetown and Saturday the time will be spent in riding over the various Boston suburban branches.

CONSIDERATE TO AMERICAN CLERGY.

Reason for Suppressing the Encyclical on the School Question.

Rome, June 15.—The newspaper organs of the Vatican are silent in regard to the alleged encyclical on the school question, ordered to be sent to the American bishops. The Corriere Di Napoli says that the publication of the text of the encyclical has been delayed, owing to the fact that the Vatican has received a notification that it will be coldly received by a majority of the clergymen in the United States. The Corriere di Napoli adds that the rebellion among the American clergymen has deeply impressed the Vatican officials with the necessity of pursuing a conciliatory policy. The pope will instruct Mgr. Satolli to confer with Cardinal Gibbons for the purpose of devising some method of effecting a compromise between the two elements.

Condition of the Capital National Bank.

Indianapolis, June 15.—The comptroller of the currency has extended the time for opening the Capital National bank until Monday next, at which time it will resume. The bank has now $500,000 in its vaults, and the directors announce that it will have $750,000 with which to open its doors, sufficient to pay every depositor on sight.

President Carnot's Condition Serious.

Paris, June 15.—It is believed that the condition of President Carnot, who is said to be suffering from a liver trouble, is much more serious than is stated in the official reports regarding his illness. The Siecle, a Republican newspaper, says today that M. Carnot is suffering with intestinal stoppage.

Lightning Struck Six Brothers—Four Dead.

Adrian, Mo., June 15.—The six Wright brothers were standing under a tree near their home yesterday when lightning killed four of them and injured the other two so that they may die.

Ocean Steamer.

Passed Lizard—Columbia, New York.

SAILORS COULD NOT SEE OR HEAR.

Details of the McCallum Sinking Told by Second Mate.

Liverpool, June 15.—James White, second mate of the American ship A. Mc Callum of Thomaston, Me., which was sunk by the Servia, says that the Mc Callum entered a fog bank at midnight, June 7. The fog horn of the ship was kept going at regular intervals. About 3 o'clock in the morning, when the ship was in lat. 40 N., lon. 69 W., or about two hundred and forty miles from Sandy Hook, the Servia emerged from the fog bank and came, bow on, to the McCallum, smashing her planking as if they were mere match sticks. White learned, after reaching the steamer, that no one on the Servia heard his fog horn or saw anything of her. A few seconds before she was sighted lying directly across the steamer's bow. Even the sailing vessel could not be seen distinctly, though some of her lights were visible. It was too late to stop the momentum of the steamer.

White was asleep in his room aft when the collision occurred. He was awakened by the shrieks and rushed on deck. The McCallum was even then settling and he did not have time to run to the bows of the Servia, which were more than three quarters of the way through the hull of the McCallum. As the ship foundered White was thrown into the water, where he swam around for about 20 minutes, when he was picked up by a boat from the Servia. Mr. Hedley, a saloon passenger, states that the pasengers were aroused by the shock and ran on deck without taking time to dress. There was some little excitement, but no symptom of a panic. The crew obeyed orders rapidly and the boats were lowered in the promptest manner. The sailing vessel went down shortly after she was struck.

HUNGARIAN STRIKERS CAUSE A RIOT.

Two Received Crushed Skulls in a Battle with Police.

Reading, Pa., June 15.—About 30 Hungarian laborers, who struck at the Henry Clay furnace in this city, engaged in a riot yesterday, taking forcible possession of the stack and stationing themselves on the top platform. The police were summoned to the scene, and a desperate battle ensued in which two of the foreigners received crushed skulls, and are likely to die. The rioting continued for nearly an hour. Four Hungarians were arrested and sent to jail, and warrants have been sworn out for eight more who are supposed to be hiding in the hills.

Everything Quiet at Leon.

New York, June 15.—The Herald's Managua, Nicaragua, correspondent cables: United States Minister Baker and Senor Castillo, the Nicaraguan minister of war, deny the report that marines have been landed from the Atlanta at Greytown to protect the interest of citizens of the United States. Each said there was absolutely no foundation for the story. Everything is now quiet at Leon. The government is returning to the owners the property confiscated by Sacasa.

Divorces at Plymouth.

Plymouth, June 15.—Divorce cases were in order yesterday in the superior court. Decrees nisi were granted in the following cases: Emily W. Leavitt, Brockton, against Frederick A. Leavitt, desertion; Flora L. Davis, Brockton, against John G. Davis, desertion; Hannah T. Shaw, Middleboro, against Elmer E. Shaw, cruel and abusive treatment and gross and confirmed habits of intoxication; Arthur H. Baker, Brockton, against Lillian M. Baker, desertion.

The Evening Standard.

NEW BEDFORD, MASS.

THURSDAY EVENING, JUNE 15.

THREE EDITIONS DAILY.

No. 87 Union Street.

PUBLISHED BY

E. ANTHONY & SONS.

INCORPORATED.

—TERMS—

Six Dollars a Year; Three Dollars for Six Months, in advance; Single Copies Two Cents.

ORDER THE EVENING STANDARD TO YOUR VACATION ADDRESS.

Mailed direct from this office to any address, for one day or any length of time desired, at the rate of 50 cents per month, including postage.

BRANCH OFFICE AT NORTH END.

For the Convenience of the patrons of the EVENING STANDARD at the North End of the City, a branch office has been established at the stores of A. F. Wilde, Nos. 842 and 844 Purchase street, where advertisements will be received at office rates. Telephone number 32—4.

Best Family Newspaper in Southern Massachusetts is the REPUBLICAN STANDARD.

Our Weekly Edition—a large twelve-page paper of 84 columns, containing more reading matter than any other weekly paper in southern Massachusetts. It is published Thursday mornings. Subscription price only $1.50 a year, in advance.

TELEPHONE CALLS.

Counting Room,	308-2
Editorial Room,	308-3

TEN PAGES.

This Evening's Issue Consists of Ten Pages, and Every Patron is Entitled to that Number.

The Boston Herald having predicted calamity to the regular ticket of the Democratic party in New York this year under the auspices of Hill-Tammany, the New York Sun takes occasion to say that the business office of the Boston Herald is more than large enough to hold a full meeting of the Anti-snapper Democracy, the unsatisfied remnant that kicks vainly against the regulars. The Hill Democracy is the regular Democracy, and under his leadership it hasn't failed of a plurality in recent years. There is a slight soreness in Buffalo, but in a body as large as the New York Democracy a few abrasions and solutions of continuity here and there are of small account. There is no evidence as yet of dissatisfaction with the administration. There is no evidence, save the dying echoes of a teapot tempest in Erie county, of dissatisfaction with the state administration. Now, as long as the regular Democracy of New York is satisfied, New York will remain a Democratic state, and Mugwumps, Maybugs, and Republicans, all together, can't prevent it.

The flukes of the Anti-snappers in the past would seem to lend considerable force to this view of the position in the Empire state.

Yesterday was the centennial anniversary of the adoption of the stars and stripes as a flag of the 13 United States. It was to be 13 stripes alternately red and white, with 13 stars white in a blue field, representing a new constitution, for the union. The 13 stars were arrayed in a circle. The flag raised by Washington at Cambridge, Jan. 2, 1776, had 13 stripes, but the union was a blended St. George and St. Andrew cross. In 1815 on the admission of Kentucky and Vermont the number of stars and stripes was increased to 15, but the inconvenience of a large number of stripes led to legislation, by which the number of stripes was fixed permanently at 13, and it was provided that the number of stars should be equal to the number of states, so that their number is now 44. May they never be less. Those who fought against the nine stars of the confederate banner will see to it that they are not.

A new law authorizes innkeepers to sell abandoned baggage of guests or that held for charges after retaining it one year by auction on putting a notice of the sale in a conspicuous place in the office of the inn for four weeks prior to the date of such sale, and by publishing the same once a week for three successive weeks in some newspaper. The proceeds, after discharging the lien and expenses, are to be paid into the treasury of the commonwealth.

At this season of the year it is important that all offensive matters should be removed as soon as possible. If the board of health hasn't sufficient facilities for doing this promptly, at least it shouldn't stand in the way of individuals doing it nor compel them to maintain nuisances on their own premises against their will.

The latest Populist fad in Kansas is to have the state own all the flouring mills, and fix the rates for grinding, just as in South Carolina it owns the liquor business and controls the price of whiskey. The Nationalists ought to be delighted at this prospect.

There is to be an inspection of the condition of some of the government buildings in Boston. We guess none is needed of the custom house and post office in this city.

The exclusion of Miss Borden's testimony at the inquest has probably shortened the trial several days, for which let us be duly thankful.

The American Israelites in Jerusalem have made an appeal to their co-religionists in this country for funds to build an asylum in the sacred city.

How many girls there are among us who call one another "You hateful thing," without being suspected of murderous intentions!

DEFENSE!

(Continued from Third Page.)

may be as sure and as certain as direct evidence. In some cases it may be more so, because the eye and ear deceive as well as circumstantial evidence. But, Mr. Foreman and gentlemen, there is no class of evidence known that under certain circumstances is so dangerous and uncertain as circumstantial evidence. Our books are filled with cases where a party has evidently been proven by circumstantial evidence to have committed a crime and subsequent investigations or confessions have shown that he did not.

Now to illustrate how certain circumstantial evidence may be and at the same time how uncertain. A man is shot. No evidence whatever connected the accused party of the crime, no direct evidence, but in extracting the ball there was drawn from the wound a roll of paper which turned out to be the wadding of the pistol or the gun which fired the bullet. Upon unrolling that roll of paper, Mr. Foreman and gentlemen, it was found to be a portion of a piece of paper upon which was printed a song and in the pocket of the arrested man at the time that he was arrested was found a piece of paper which fitted to that part. That made it pretty certain that that man fired the shot.

But on the other hand, take this case of circumstantial evidence which was brought to my notice last August. A man was found dead in the car in Jersey City. I think it was in the morning. Upon the floor of that car was found a piece of cotton cloth stained with blood, evidence of a struggle. The man was stabbed to the heart. The police investigated. A woman was found who had seen a man run through the car about 4 o'clock in the morning. A man was found who saw two tramps come into town on the edge of the evening before, and that was all the evidence they had.

For some time searching parties were organized, and they searched the woods where the woman saw the man disappear, and a man was found there. He was identified by the person who had seen the two tramps the evening before as one of them. The woman thought he was about the same height and general appearance of the man she had seen run through the car in the morning. Mr. Foreman and gentlemen, this piece of cotton cloth fittted right into the tear in that man's sleeve. He was arrested, charged with murder. They tried him and convicted him, but as there was evidence of a struggle he was imprisoned for life, convicted, I think, of manslaughter or murder in the second degree, or something, I don't know what it was. He remained in prison seven years and was pardoned out last August on a confession of a man who did the deed.

Here was a case where a man told a story that no one believed. He said that he went into a car to sleep and found a man there as he supposed asleep. In the morning he awoke and saw that the man was dead. He became frightened, tore the stain from off his sleeve and fled. This was the literal truth and as the dying man told his story of how the murder happened that story just exactly fitted with that of the man told upon the stand. The dying man said that he also sought the car as a place to sleep. When he went into the car that night he stepped upon the head of a man who had preceded him. The man rose up, there was a terrible struggle, and he drew his knife and stabbed him with no idea of killing him. He immediately fled.

It seemed absolutely certain that the accused man was the guilty party, and yet how simple the explanation.

You remember what was said when Columbus returned from his great voyage of discovery. All these things are simple when explained, but how deep the mystery before the explanation. They said to Columbus, all you had to do was to head westward and keep on sailing to the west. You remember the reply of Columbus, when he asked them to stand an egg on end. You remember how they tried, and tried, and were unsuccessful, and how he showed them it was a simple matter by just striking it down hard enough to crush the shell.

It is just the same in circumstantial evidence. The mystery that seems to be almost impenetrable, and that which seems to be impossible at the time, is plain when the full story is told, and the person who is accused accounts for what seems almost impossible at the time.

It isn't for you to unravel the mystery of how he died, not for you to satisfy yourself how the deed was done, it is simply for you to satisfy yourselves that no one else than Lizzie Andrew Borden could have done it.

Circumstantial evidence is often likened to a chain; and every essential fact in the chain must be proved beyond a reasonable doubt. You must throw aside everything about which you have a reasonable doubt, and after having thrown aside all such, the chain must still be complete.

Now the facts from which you are to draw your inferences are four in number —motive, weapon, exclusive opportunity, and the conduct and appearance of the prisoner. We contend that there is no object, no motive for these murders on the part of defendant. The government haven't a scrap of evidence showing a motive. It may be said no motive is necessary. This murdered person, or one of them, was defendant's own father. Where there is direct evidence of a crime no motive is necessary. Where you want a motive as a link in the chain of evidence it becomes of tremendous importance. We shall show you that this defendant lived with her father in ordinary pleasant relations, and that there was nothing which should cause her to do such a wicked deed. The government's theory is that whoever killed Andrew J. Borden also killed Abbie Durfee Borden. If they have shown a motive to kill her they have shown none to kill him. In measuring the question of a motive you have got to measure in it the question that she killed her father. As to the weapon it is not necessary for me to say much. The blood on the one shown has disappeared like the dew before the morning sun. The hatchet that Dr. Dolan was so certain the deed was done with has disappeared. When Professor Wood testified before the district court in Fall River that blood could not have been removed from it quickly by washing, it was found necessary to provide a new weapon. An attempt has been made to close the Borden house quickly. You have heard the evidence of Lucy Collette, the Frenchman, and others, that they could see no one about the house at the time of the murder. We shall show you that they could have seen into the Borden yard. If it were not for the gravity of the occasion what I should be tempted to call the "cake walk" of Officer Medley in the barn, when he testified that he could see no footsteps in the loft, existed only in his own imagination. There has not been a living soul on the stand to testify that they saw Andrew J. Borden go from his house down street on the morning of the 4th of August. From his house to the Union Savings bank he was seen by no one. We shall show you that there were others and strange people about that house. We shall show you that the government statement that this defendant was not in the barn that morning is false. We shall show you that she did go there and was there when the deed was done, so far as Mr. Borden was concerned. We shall show you that the dress which was burned did have paint on it, and that it was burned in the broad light of day, with no attempt at concealment, when there were officers about the house. We will introduce evidence to show you that defendant did not have this dress on the day of the murders, and that the one she did have on was the one which I gave to the officers. So, Mr. Foreman, we shall ask in view of the presumptions of human nature, in view of the relations between the father and daughter, from the fact that there was no blood on her dress, or her head, or on any part of her body, from the fact that there was no motive, from the fact that there were others around and that Lizzie was in the barn, we shall ask you to say if you believe that she killed not only Abbie Durfee Borden, but her own loving father, on the 4th of August.

THE FIRST WITNESS.

Martha Chagnon Tells of the Noise She Heard.

The first witness summoned was Mary A. Durfee. She did not respond, and then Martha Chagnon, a dark haired, pretty young lady, dressed in dark blue, with a pink shirt waist, and wearing a broad brimmed sailor hat, responded to the call.

Q. Are you Dr. Chagnon's daughter? A. Yes.

Q. Is your yard near that of the Bordens? A. Yes.

Q. Is there a fence between the yards in the rear? A. Yes.

Q. Is that in the corner where the dog house is? A. Yes.

Q. Does that fairly show where it is? (showing a photograph,) A. Yes.

Q. Did you hear a noise that disturbed you the night preceding the murder? A. Yes.

Q. When was it? A. About 11 o'clock.

Q. Tell me what the noise was?

Objected to and withdrawn.

Q. Describe the noise? A. It frightened me.

Q. How did it sound? A. It sounded like pounding.

Q. Pounding on what? A. On wood.

Q. In what direction, on what part; somewhere on that fence? A. Yes.

Q. What was the effect on you?

Objected to and ruled out.

Q. What did you do?

Objected to and withdrawn.

Q. Did you go out to look? A. No.

Q. Did you investigate? A. No sir.

Q. Where were you sitting? A. In the dining room.

Q. Is it down or up stairs? A. Down stairs.

Witness showed the location of a fence, dog house, etc., upon the premises, and pointed them out on a photograph.

Q. Where were you when you heard the noise? A. On the sofa in the sitting room.

Q. On which side of the house? A. On the south side.

Q. What is directly in the rear of the sitting room? A. The dining room.

Q. What is the direction of the dog house from the dining room window? A. It is near the fence.

Q. What fence? A. The Borden fence.

Q. From what direction did the sound seem to come? A. From the back yard.

Q. Can you tell whether it was from the direction of the doghouse? A. I couldn't tell; the noise came from the back yard.

After considerable difficulty, owing to the witness not understanding English, the portion of the yard which she called the back yard was discovered.

Q. Is there a barn near the doghouse? A. Yes sir.

Q. Was there a fence between the orchard and the back yard? A. Yes sir.

Q. Is there a little fence from the corner of the Borden yard toward your house? A. Yes sir.

Q. As you look out of your dining room window, which part of the yard do you call the back yard? A. Behind the house, and there is where I heard the noise.

Cross-examined by Mr. Knowlton.

Q. You didn't go out when you heard the noise? A. No sir; I went into the dining room.

Q. You said you heard two noises; how much time was there between them? A. Two or three minutes.

Q. Did you think it was the sound of a dog?

Objection was made, but the witness was directed to answer.

A. No sir, not at the beginning.

Q. Dogs sometimes come into your backyard? A. Yes sir.

Q. Is there an ash barrel in your back yard? A. Yes sir.

MR. JENNINGS OPENING FOR DEFENSE.
[Sketched from life by Mr. Ashley of the Standard Staff.]

Q. The dining room was between you and the noise? A. Yes.

Q. Where was the fence and dog house; in what direction from the dining room window? A. West.

Q. Did you keep a horse at that time? A. Yes sir.

Q. Was anybody present at that time besides yourself? A. Yes sir.

Q. Who? A. My stepmother.

Q. Did any one hear the noise besides you?

Mr. Knowlton—I object.

Q. Where was the piazza relative to the room? A. East.

Q. At the southeast corner? A. Yes sir.

Q. Can you describe the noise any more accurately than that it sounded like pounding on boards? A. No sir.

Q. Could you see out into the back part of the yard? A. No sir.

Q. Is there a door between that room and the dining room? A. Yes sir.

Q. Are there windows in the dining room? A. I couldn't see out.

Q. Is there a piazza at the front part of the house and steps and a concrete walk? A. Yes sir.

Q. Is there a settee usually kept there for people to sit on? A. Yes sir.

Q. Was you at your house on the day of the murder? A. Yes sir.

Q. Did you go away on the day of the murder? A. Yes sir.

Q. Where was the settee when you went away? A. I don't know.

Q. Was it on the concrete? A. Yes sir.

Cross-examined by Mr. Knowlton:

Q. Were you away all day? A. Yes sir.

Q. What time did you get home? A. Six o'clock.

Q. Who else in the room heard the noise? A. My stepmother.

Q. What is her name? A. Mary A. Chagnon.

Q. Was she in the room when you were? A. Yes sir.

Q. There was no window open? A. No sir.

Q. Is there one window which opens out on to the piazza? A. Yes sir.

Q. How many windows open toward the south? A. I think one.

Q. Were the windows all closed? A. Yes sir.

Q. How could you tell the direction of the sound?

The witness hesitated for a considerable time, and the question was not pressed.

Q. Did you have anything more than an impression of the direction from which it came? A. No sir.

Q. You wouldn't say positively that it was in that direction? A. I would say that it was in that direction.

Q. You made no other examination except listening, did you? A. I don't understand.

Q. You simply heard the noise? A. Yes sir.

Q. For aught you know it may have come from further south? A. Yes sir.

Q. For aught you know it may have come from somewhere else? A. Yes sir.

Q. Do you know that there is an ice house near? A. Yes sir.

Q. Do you know that there is a plank floor there upon which ice carts are sometimes driven? A. No sir.

Q. Could you say positively that it was not from the ice house? A. I don't think it came from there.

Q. Have you testified before in this case? A. Yes sir.

Mr. Knowlton read from testimony given at the hearing in regard to the sound coming from the ice house and asked witness if she made statements reported there. Witness hesitated a long time and the answer was not demanded.

Q. Is there a dog on your premises? A. Yes sir.

Q. What kind of a dog? A. Newfoundland.

Q. Did the dog leave the piazza? A. No sir.

Q. At no time during the time the noise was going on? A. No sir.

Mrs. Mary A. Chagnon.

Mary A. Chagnon, wife of Dr. Chagnon, was the next witness called.

Q. You live on Third street in Fall River? A. Yes sir.

Q. In the rear of the Borden house? A. Yes sir.

Q. Do you remember the murder last August? A. Yes sir.

Q. Did anything happen the night before the murder? A. Yes sir. I heard a noise.

Q. Describe the noise? A. It sounded like pounding on a board fence or the sidewalk.

Q. Did the dogs sometimes go to the ash barrel in the backyard? A. Yes sir.

Q. And make a noise that sounded like pounding? A. I don't know the word.

Counsel described the meaning of the word as well as he could, and witness answered affirmatively.

Q. Do you remember of your husband moving the ash barrel any time? A. Yes sir.

Q. Do you remember Mr. Harrington an officer being there one day. A. Yes sir.

Q. And your husband made a noise with that barrel? A. Yes sir.

Q. And didn't you say that that noise sounded like the noise you heard? A. It wasn't in the same direction.

Q. Don't you remember that you said the noise you heard was the same noise? A. Yes sir.

Q. Where was that barrel that night? A. In the barn.

Q. That is right out of the back yard? A. Yes sir.

Q. Was the ash barrel in the yard or in the barn? A. In the barn.

Q. You said that was the noise you heard when your husband did something to the ash barrel? A. I don't remember.

Q. What was it your husband did to the ash barrel. A. He struck the barrel.

Q. Did he strike the barrel with his hands? A. Yes sir.

Q. And when he struck the barrel with his hand it seemed like the same noise you heard? A. Yes.

Q. But it didn't seem to come from the direction from which you heard it? A. No sir.

Re-direct—Mr. Jennings asked the witness if her barn was next to the Kirby yard. She answered that it was, and pointed out on the plan to the jury where the barn and the dog house were situated.

John W. Grouard was the next witness. He had been seated within the rail, among the members of the bar and other spectators.

Mr. Knowlton said that the commonwealth had been very careful to keep its witnesses out of the court room, and supposed the defense would do the same.

Mr. Robinson said they had no desire to have their witnesses in the court room, and Clerk Borden ordered all witnesses who had been called or summoned for the defense to retire from the room and remain out of the room until they should testify.

Mr. Jennings then proceeded with the examination of witness.

Q. What is your name? A. John W. Grouard.

Q. What is your occupation? A. A painter.

Q. Did you paint the house of Andrew J. Borden on Second street at any time? A. Yes sir.

Q. When did you paint it? A. In May a year ago.

Q. 1892? A. Yes sir.

Q. Can you tell when you carried the paint there? A. The 9th of May.

Q. And did you see Miss Lizzie Borden at that time? A. Not that day.

Q. When did you see her? A. I saw her the next morning early.

Q. Where was that? A. In the back yard.

Q. Where was your paint? A. In the barn.

Q. What was it in? A. In tubs.

Q. Now won't you tell us what was done by you and her at that time? A. The color was not satisfactory to her and I mixed the color to suit.

Q. What did she do, was she out and in where the paint was? A. Yes sir, she was.

Q. Will you state what part of the barn the tubs were in? A. Near the door.

Q. The front door or the side door? A. Side door.

Q. Was she during any portion of that time in the immediate vicinity of those tubs of paint? A. I think she was.

Q. Did you paint the house? A. We did.

Q. How soon after that? A. On the morning of the 10th.

Q. Outside or inside? A. Outside.

Q. What was the color of the paint? A. Drab.

Q. The same as is now upon it? A. Yes sir.

Q. Was that the last time it was painted so far as you know? A. Yes sir.

Q. What were the trimmings? A. A little darker.

Q. Do you remember or not whether any test was made from time to time by you and her? A. The paint was carried there on the afternoon of the 9th. Her father said that she was to select the color and that the paint could not be put on until it had been determined. That evening she came to my house and said the color was not what she wanted.

Q. She came to your house and in consequence of what she said to you, there was an appointment made for the next morning early? A. Before the men came to work—about 6 o'clock in the morning.

Q. And that is the time your have told us about? A. Yes. I mixed the colors then satisfactorily.

Q. She was there at that time? A. Yes sir.

Cross-examined — Q. Where was the paint? A. In the barn near the door.

Q. Not in the stall? A. One of the tubs may have been.

Q. Did you do all the mixing? A. Yes sir, I directed the mixing of it.

Re-direct. After the paint was ready did you take it and try it on the house in consultation with her? A. Yes sir.

Mary A. Durfee was the next witness called.

Q. What is your name? A. Mary A. Durfee.

Q. Where do you live, Mrs. Durfee? A. At 21 Second street, Fall River.

Q. Did you know Andrew J. Borden when he was alive? A. Yes sir.

Q. Did you know where his house was on Second street? A. Yes sir.

Q. Familiar with the premises? A. Yes sir.

Q. Do you recall a time when you saw a man there on the steps talking with him? A. Yes sir.

Q. When was it? A. It was some time before the murder.

Mr. Knowlton objected that that did not fix the time.

Q. Can you tell any nearer than that? A. No, I can not, it was before Thanksgiving.

Mr. Knowlton objected to the evidence and the judges consulted in regard to the admission of it.

The court said the question as to time might be put.

Q. How near Thanksgiving was it? A. I can't tell.

Q. How do you locate the time? A. It was before my sister died, and that was Oct. 27th.

Q. How long before that? A. I don't know. I was going for medicine for my sister, and I heard a noise.

Mr. Knowlton—"That's enough. Didn't you tell me it was two months before your sister died?" Witness replied: "I don't know."

Q. Should you judge it was as much as that? A. I think as much as that; I didn't put the date down.

Chief Justice Mason—It seems to the court that the time is too remote.

Charles M. Gifford testified that he lives next door to Dr. Chagnon. About 11 o'clock on the night of August 3d he saw a man lying on the steps leading to the yard of Uriah R. Kirby's house. He was a man of about 180 to 190 pounds weight. Witness lighted a match to see the man's face, his straw hat having fallen off. The man was apparently asleep, and there was no smell of liquor on him.

Uriah R. Kirby testified that he lives next door to Dr. Chagnon. About 11 o'clock night of August 3d witness went home and found a man lying or sitting on his steps. He spoke to the man, but got no answer and the man paid no attention to his voice. The man's hat—a dark one—was taken hold of by witness. He went into the house and left the man on the steps; found no signs of liquor on the man. The steps are 15 or 17 feet away from the driveway to Dr. Chagnon's yard.

Mark Chase, a hostler at a barn just opposite Mr. Kelley's house, said he was at the barn all the day of the murder. About 11 o'clock he saw a horse attached to an open box buggy standing under a tree in front of Andrew J. Borden's house. In the buggy was a man wearing a brown hat and having on a black coat. He had never seen the turnout or the man before.

"Did you inform the police of this about the time of the murder?" asked Mr. Jennings.

"Hold on a minute," said Mr. Knowlton.

The question was ruled out, and the court took a recess till 2 15 p. m.

Deserved to Get In.

Among the spectators, or rather would-be ones, who gained admission to the lower corridor this forenoon, and there patiently awaited a chance to gain entrance to the court room, was Edward Tilton, hailing from Plymouth. He is a countryfied youth, with an open, frank countenance, and was dressed in an old-fashioned manner, and did not seem to care in the least for the gibes and jeers of the crowd. He came here from Plymouth, and was at the court house at 3 o'clock this morning, and said he intended to gain admission if possible.

NEW ENTRANCES;

Say the Aldermanic Committee on Burial Grounds.

Yesterday afternoon members of the board of public works and the aldermanic committee on burial grounds paid a visit to Rural cemetery, where the avenues near the pond were examined with a view of fitting the same as an open way from Field street to Allen street. The plan was looked upon with much favor, and it was decided to recommend that new entrances be put in at these points. This done, streets will at once be laid out and fitted so that carriage travel in the cemetery can avail itself of both entrances. It is also suggested that such a way will be of great benefit to carriage travel to and from South Dartmouth during the day time.

WANT DETAILED STATEMENTS.

The Committee on Audit Wish to Know Concerning Private Work.

The city council committee on audit held a very interesting meeting last evening, when weekly bills were audited by Alderman Barrows and Councilmen Shurtleff and Vinal, who were present.

The bill from the board of public works for private work, amounting to something like $900, was discussed, and it was voted to request the board of public works to furnish in the future a detailed statement and separate pay roll for all work done for private individuals.

It is also said that at the next meeting of the government an effort will be made to have the board furnish a similar statement to the city treasurer.

VINEYARD HAVEN.

Professor F. E. Bristol with a large crowd of students arrived yesterday and will at once take possession of their summer hotel at Oklahoma springs. They brought with them a handsome new naphtha launch named Musurgia, which will make trips this summer between Oklahoma, Lagoon heights and the pier at this place.

Mrs. L. R. Lee of Washington, D. C., arrived last evening, and will occupy her summer residence here during the summer. Mrs. Lee has just returned from a trip to the World's fair.

MARION.

Rev. A. H. Quint will be a guest of Rev. R. P. Gardner during his stay in Marion.

Mr. Arthur Tuffts of Boston has leased the new Waters cottage for the season.

Mr. and Mrs J. E. Hadley of St. Paul, Minn., are visiting relatives in town.

—The finance committee met last evening and voted to make one transfer from private work and trimming trees to city toolhouse and workshop. The amount was $117.89.

—The assessors have completed their work in wards 1, 3 and 4.

Cholera Raging in Mecca.

London, June 15.—The latest advices from Mecca, where the cholera is raging, show that there been 350 deaths from the disease during the last five days.

TELEGRAPHIC BREVITIES.

A marked improvement in winter wheat is shown.

The home rule bill may be passed by the last of July.

The village of Alba, Mich., has been destroyed by fire.

There is a dangerous break in the levee at Baton Rouge, La.

A new Japanese-Australian steamer line has been established.

China retaliates for the Geary exclusion act by an embargo on American oil.

SONS OF VETERANS.

[Continued from First Page.]

A large number of members from both of the local camps have been assigned to guard duty, and two members were kept at the Old Colony station to give new arrivals instructions as to locations.

ALBERT C. BLAISDELL.

Sketch of the Career of the New Division Commander.

Albert C. Blaisdell is a native of Lowell, and deserves his right of membership from his father, Charles R. Blaisdell, Esq., an old and respected member of the Middlesex bar, who served nearly three years during the war of the rebellion in company I, 38th Massachusetts volunteers, and was discharged from the service by reason of a gunshot wound. Among the many well known members of the 38th Massachusetts are Chief Justice Mason of the superior court, and General Charles H. Taylor, of Boston. Albert C. Blaisdell was educated in the public schools of Lowell, and prepared for a legal profession in the office of his father, but an unexpected vacancy occuring in a grammar school in Dracut changed the course of his life, and he took up a teacher's profession. After teaching in the public schools for several years, he accepted a call to become teacher of mathematics, etc., in the Lowell Commercial college, and continued in this position until August, 1885, when he purchased the school and immediately thereafter sold an equal interest to L. E. Kimball, of Lowell, and a partnership was formed known as the Lowell Commercial college, which has continued until the present time. In the Sons of Veterans' order he has always taken a high rank, both in camp and division work. He joined Admiral Farragut camp in 1888; was elected captain and installed in January following. The affairs of the camp were in a bad financial condition, and during his term as captain the affairs were straightened, and he placed the camp on a good financial basis. In division work he has established a strong reputation for good faithful work, not simply doing his work, but assisting all associates wherever he could. The camps at Milford, Haverhill and Littleton were mustered by him. In installation work his services are in special demand, as he is a popular officer. One camp in every eleven invited him to install their officers in Massachusetts division in January, 1893. In 1890-1 he served as division inspector, and his work in this department received high praise from national headquarters, and his system of inspection was recommended for adoption by Inspector General Hall, now commander-in-chief of the order. In 1891 he was elected major of the Massachusetts division, receiving 106 votes, to 32 for his nearest competitor. In 1892, at Milford, he was elected senior vice division commander without serious opposition, receiving 194 votes, to one against. In the division encampment he has been an influential member. At Lynn he acted as chairman of the committee on resolutions, and in the absence of the chairman, made the committee's report. At Gardner in the following year he was chairman of committee on ritual, and his work there was of a high order. He will bring to the position a good business and legal training, which will enable him to give the division a careful administration. In other orders he is also prominent. He is a member of William North lodge, F. and A. M.; trustee of Spindle City Council of United Friends; auditor and executive committee of company D, second corps cadets, M. V. M., and noble grand of Integrity lodge, I. O. O. F.

Mr. Bennett Gradually Rallying.

PARIS, June 15.—James Gordon Bennett continues to improve. He sleeps fairly well and was able to pay some attention to his correspondence yesterday. The physicians hope that the patient will not be compelled to keep his bed more than a month longer.

Good Templars In Session.

DES MOINES, June 15.—The Good Templars, in session here, changed the name of the head of the body to the international supreme lodge by a vote of 121 to 36. A heated discussion is now general as to the striking out of the word "race" from section 8 of the constitution.

Reception For Captain Anderson.

NEW YORK, June 15.—At the suggestion of Professor H. H. Boyesen of the New York committee for the reception of the Viking ship, Mayor Gilroy and the heads of the city departments will give a reception to Captain Anderson in the governor's room next Monday morning.

Anent the Squires Murder.

BOSTON, June 15.—Alexandro Brioll, alias Prola, an Italian, who was arrested as one of the murderers of James Squires at the North End some weeks ago, was discharged from custody. Antonio Sacco, who is supposed to be the murderer, is still at large.

Cholera Reports.

LONDON, June 15.—There have been four deaths from choleraic causes at Cette, in France, since Friday. At Mecca, in Arabia, during the same period, there were 155 deaths from cholera.

Movements of Currency.

NEW YORK, June 15.—The shipment yesterday of currency from New York to the interior aggregated nearly $2,000,000, of which $1,000,000 was obtained at the sub-treasury.

AMUSEMENTS.

NINTH ANNUAL RECITAL

BY PUPILS OF

Miss Mary Otheman's Violin School,

ASSISTED BY

Mr. Wulf Fries, Violoncellist,

At Y. M. C. A. HALL,

Thursday Evening, June 15th,

At 7 45 O'clock.

A limited number of tickets at 25 cents each for sale at B. Otheman's, Room 1, 25 Pleasant street, Bates & Kirby's new block, and at the ha l the evening of the entertainment. je10-13-15

SELECT SOCIAL

To be given by the

BAY VIEW ATHLETIC CLUB,

At their rooms,

Foot of County Street,

Friday Evening, June 16th.

TICKETS { Gentlemen............25 Cents. Lady..................15 Cents.
je14-3t

The Ladies' Benevolent Society

Connected with the

MIDDLE STREET CHRISTIAN CHURCH

Will hold a

SALE

In the vestry of the church, THURSDAY, June 15th. ENTERTAINMENT at 7 45. Cake and ice cream will be on sale. je14-2t

Strawberry Festival.

Sylvia H. Delano Circle No. 1, Ladies of the G. A. R., will give a Strawberry Festival at

CHINA HALL,

FRIDAY, JUNE 16th, from 6 to 9 o'clock.

The public is invited. je15-2t

RAYMOND'S VACATION EXCURSIONS.

All Traveling Expenses Included.

Parties will leave BOSTON, July 8 and 22 for Two Grand Excursions of Fifty-six Days to

ALASKA.

The outward route is to be over the Picturesque Canadian Pacific Railway, through Montreal, Winnipeg, Bamff Hot Springs, the grand scenery of the Selkirks and Victoria; the homeward route, after the Alaska Voyage, of Twelve Days, via Tacoma, Portland, etc., and the Northern Pacific Railroad, with a week in the Yellowstone National Park and a week at the World's Columbian Exposition.

Magnificent Trains of Palace Sleeping and Dining Cars, with every first-class appointment, are to be used in crossing the continent. The Alaska trip will be on the favorite steamer "Queen."

Colorado and the Yellowstone National Park: Two 39-Day Excursions, leaving Boston July 10 and August 7.

Colorado Tours: Four Excursions to the most famous Rocky Mountain Resorts, leaving Boston July 17, August 28, September 11 and October 9.

The Yellowstone Park and California: A 72-Days' Excursion, leaving Boston August 30; also a 27-Days' Excursion to the Yellowstone Park and return.

Each of the above parties will have a week at the World's Fair.

The World's Columbian Exposition: Special Pullman Vestibuled Trains with Dining-Cars will leave Boston for Chicago daily. A week at the Raymond & Whitcomb Grand Hotel, opposite the Fair Grounds, is included in the tickets.

☞ Send for descriptive book, mentioning the particular tour desired.

RAYMOND & WHITCOMB,
296 WASHINGTON ST., (Opposite School St.,)
BOSTON, MASS. je15-3t

STEAMSHIP LINES.

ANCHOR LINE.

United States Mail Steamships
Sail from New York every Saturday for
GLASGOW VIA LONDONDERRY
Rates for Saloon Passage

By S. S. CITY OF ROME, $50 and upward. OTHER STEAMERS, Cabin, $45 and upward, according to accommodation and location of Room. Excursion Tickets at reduced rates. Second Cabin, $30. Steerage, Outward, $23. Prepaid, $24. Second Cabin from Glasgow or Derry, $35.

Drafts at lowest Current Rates.

For Book of tours and other information apply to HENDERSON BROTHERS, 7 Bowling Green, N. Y., Thomas Donaghy, Corner Union and Water sts. or Edwin Whittaker 884 Purchase st., or David Waugh, 773 South Water street, New Bedford.

ENTERTAINMENT DIRECTORY.

THURSDAY.

Middle Street Christian Church—Sale and Entertainment.
Y. M. C. A. Hall — Miss Otheman's pupils' recital.

FUTURE EVENTS.

China Hall—16th, Strawberry festival.
Bay View Club Room—16th, Select Social.

AMUSEMENTS.

Sylvia H. Delano Circle, No. 1, will hold a strawberry festival in China hall tomorrow evening, from 6 to 9 o'clock.

The Bay View Athletic club will hold a social in the club rooms at the foot of County street tomorrow evening. The place is always cool.

The sale and entertainment by the Ladies' Benevolent society of the Middle Street Christian church this evening will be well worth going to. The proceeds will be devoted to the church charities. Entertainment begins at 7 45.

The annual violin recital of Miss Otheman's violin school will take place this evening in Y. M. C. A. hall. One of the features of the occasion will be the appearance of Wulf Fries, the veteran violoncellist, who will play several selections. The class work is always entertaining.

Alaska and the Yellowstone Park.—The geysers and canyons of the Yellowstone National park, the Canadian Rocky mountains, and the glaciers of Alaska are among the foremost natural wonders of the continent. These three regions are included in the itinerary of two Raymond & Whitcomb excursions which are to leave Boston July 8 and 22. The outward journey will be over the Canadian Pacific route, with stops at the most interesting points; and the return, after the Alaska voyage of twelve days, by the Northern Pacific road, with a week's detour through the Yellowstone park. A week will also be passed at the Columbian Exposition. Particulars about these trips are given in a book which may be had free of Raymond & Whitcomb, 296 Washington street, Boston.

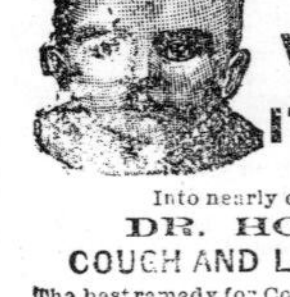

HAS WORKED ITS WAY

Into nearly every house.

DR. HOUGH'S
COUGH AND LUNG BALSAM.

The best remedy for Coughs and Colds. Price 25 cents. Sold by all druggists and Medicine dealers.

JUBILEE WILKES PACES IN 2.22.

N. J. Stone Handled the Reins and a Record Was Lowered.

Milford, June 15.—The 2 37 and 2 32 races at Charles River Driving park yesterday were full of close finishes. In the 2 37 Jubilee Wilkes, the green pacer that jumped into the 2 25 record at Manchester, lowered the track race record to 2 22, and he should have taken first money. Tuesday's new track record was also beaten by Duex.

For pulling Whisper in the second and third heats of the 2 37, that horse's driver was taken off and Bard Palmer substituted. The judges gave Whisper's fourth money to Palmer for his work.

The events today are the 2 40 trot and pace, 17 entries, and the 2 27 trot and pace, seven entries. Yesterday's summary:

2 37 class, trot and pace; purse $250.

Henry Titer's b. s. Little Chief,	2	4	1	2	1	1
N. J. Stone's br. s. Jubilee Wilkes,	1	3	5	1	4	3
G. J. Mongeon's b. s. Duex,	4	1	2	3	3	2
Sam Hyde's ch. h. Whisper,	3	2	3	4	2r. o.	
Harlow & Mathewson's ch. g. Charles J,	5	5	4	dis.		

Time—2 22, 2 24¼, 2 30, 2 24¼, 2 27½, 2 28½.

A CLOSE GAME.

Boston Victorious Over St. Louis—McCarthy's Batting the Feature.

BOSTON, June 15.—The first game with the St. Louis team was an intensely interesting one, full of fight, and won in the last half of the ninth. Long did not play, having met with an injury the day before, and this handicapped the home team very much. Four pitchers were used, and Stivetts was very effective. McCarthy's batting won the game. The St. Louis team fielded elegantly, but were rather weak with the stick. Quinn was received handsomely and he played well.

BOSTON.	AB	R	BH	PO	A	E
McCarthy, ss	5	2	4	2	2	0
Lowe, 2b	2	1	0	2	5	1
Duffy, cf	4	1	2	4	0	0
Ganzel, rf	4	1	1	4	0	0
Nash, 3b	2	3	1	1	1	1
Tucker, 1b	4	1	3	10	0	0
Carroll, lf	5	2	2	2	0	0
Merritt, c	5	0	2	2	1	0
Staley, p	2	0	0	0	1	0
Stivetts, p	2	0	0	0	0	0
Totals	35	11	15	27	10	2

ST. LOUIS.	AB	R	BH	PO	A	E
Crooks, 3b	4	1	1	1	3	0
Brodie, cf	4	1	1	3	0	0
Glasscock, ss	4	0	0	1	4	0
Werden, 1b	5	0	1	7	0	0
Whistler, rf	4	0	0	0	0	0
Dowd, lf	5	2	2	1	1	0
Quinn, 2b	3	3	1	5	2	0
Peitz, c	2	3	1	7	1	0
Gleason, p	3	0	1	0	0	0
Breitenstein, p	1	0	0	0	0	0
Totals	35	10	8	25	11	0

Boston	1	2	1	0	4	0	0	0	3	—11
St. Louis	0	2	0	3	0	3	0	0	2	—10

Earned runs—Boston, 5; St. Louis, 2. Home run—Peitz. Two-base hits—Nash, Carroll, Werden. Sacrifice hits—Lowe (2). Stolen bases—McCarthy, Carroll, Crooks, Brodie (2). First base on balls—Boston, 6; St. Louis, 5. First base on errors—St. Louis, 2. Struck out —Dowd, Merritt, Lowe, Ganzel, Stivetts. Double plays—McCarthy, Lowe and Tucker; Glasscock, Quinn and Werden. Umpire—McQuaid.

Other Games.

At New York:

New York	0	1	0	10	2	2	0	0		—15
Chicago	2	0	0	0	2	0	3	1	3	—11

Base hits—New York, 16; Chicago, 14. Errors—New York, 1; Chicago, 9. Batteries—Crane and McMahon; McGill and Schriner.

At Brooklyn:

Brooklyn	2	0	0	2	0	0	0	0		—4
Cleveland	0	0	0	1	0	1	0	0	0	—2

Base hits—Brooklyn, 5; Cleveland, 6. Errors —Brooklyn, 2; Cleveland, 4. Batteries—Stein and Kinslow; Young and Zimmer.

At Baltimore:

Cincinnati	0	0	3	0	0	0	0	0	4	—7
Baltimore	0	2	3	0	0	0	0	1	0	—6

Base hits—Cincinnati, 12; Baltimore, 5. Errors—Cincinnati, 4; Baltimore, 5. Batteries—Sullivan and Murphy; Hawkes and Robinson.

At Philadelphia:

Philadelphia	4	1	0	1	0	0	0	0	0	—6
Pittsburg	0	1	1	0	0	0	0	1	0	—3

Base hits—Philadelphia, 6; Pittsburg, 8. Errors—Philadelphia, 1; Pittsburg, 3. Batteries —Keefe and Cross; Terry and Miller.

At Washington:

Louisville	0	2	2	0	0	2	1	2		—9
Washington	3	1	0	1	0	0	0	0	0	—5

Base hits—Louisville, 11; Washington, 11. Errors—Louisville, 3; Washington, 6. Batteries—Rhodes and Grim; Duryea and Farrell.

New England League.

At Portland—Portland, 10; Fall River, 8.
At Lewiston—Brockton, 13; Lewiston, 12.
At Dover—Dover, 9; Lowell 6.

Eastern League Games.

At Buffalo—Providence, 11; Buffalo, 10.
At Erie—Springfield, 10; Erie, 4.
At Binghamton—Binghamton, 9; Troy, 2
At Wilkesbarre—Wilkesbarre, 5; Albany, 2.

National League Standing.

Clubs	Won	Lost	Avg	Clubs	Won	Lost	Avg
Brooklyn	24	15	61.5	Baltimore	20	20	50.0
Boston	25	16	61.0	Wash	18	21	46.2
Phila	23	15	60.5	Cincinnati	18	22	45.0
Pittsburg	23	16	59.0	Chicago	16	22	42.1
New York	22	18	55.0	St. Louis	15	22	40.5
Cleveland	18	15	54.5	Louisville	5	25	16.7

New England League Standing.

Clubs	Won	Lost	Avg	Clubs	Won	Lost	Avg
Lewiston	21	11	65.6	Lowell	11	18	37.9
Fall River	19	11	63.3	Dover	11	19	36.6
Portland	17	11	60.7	Brockton	8	17	32.0

Brown defeated Amherst 10 to 1 yesterday.

EVADING THE 58-HOUR LAW.

Factory Inspector Tierney Stirring Up Mill Managers.

Fall River, June 15.—Factory Inspector Tierney reports that he has been stirring up the managers of the mills on the stream, particularly the Pocasset Manufacturing Co. and the Fall River Manufactory. He alleges that these concerns have been running over time, and that when a protest was entered they had an explanation ready. They had been starting at an irregular hour since the beginning of things, because they were obliged to wait for water from the Troy mill, and there was no help for it. The inspector insists that this was merely an excuse to enable the companies to evade the 58-hour law, and consequently he threatened to proceed against them. Yesterday he stated that they had agreed to come to terms. The Pocasset will start at 6 02 a. m., and the Fall River Manufactory at 6 35 a. m., and they will stop for the day at the proper hour.

COLONEL CHARLES R. CODMAN.

Latest Name Proposed for Collector of Customs at Boston.

Washington, D. C., June 15.—"Charles R. Codman of Boston for collector of customs, by a friend," is the latest Massachusetts entry in the book of applications kept at the treasury department. Colonel Codman has made no application for himself, and the name of the friend who has set forth his qualifications is not disclosed at the department. He and Mr. Winslow Warren are the only men who have been left in the field, since the refusal of Moses Williams to be considered.

Grand Lodge of Masons.

Boston, June 15.—The quarterly communication of the grand lodge of Massachusetts, F. & A. M., was held yesterday at Masonic temple, with a fair attendance of members. Only routine business was transacted. The proposed amendment regarding the publication of the names of candidates was defeated by a decisive vote.

War Threatens Samoa.

Auckland, N. Z., June 15.—Advices received from Samoa announce that Maleito, still refusing to compromise with his rival, has directed the government forces to advance and enforce Mataafa's submission to him. War is believed to be inevitable. Mataafa is very popular and has numerous devoted adherents.

ANOTHER BIG DAY.

Governor Russell and Party Enjoying the World's Fair.

CHICAGO, June 15.—Yesterday was a perfect day for World's fair visitors, and every hour enormous crowds entered the grounds. The weather was delightful, and every condition favored the comfort and happiness of the people. The state buildings drew an unusually large number of guests, and the people from Indiana and Arkansas came in flocks to look over the grounds prior to the opening of their buildings today.

The official number of paid admissions to the gate yesterday was 83,452.

Representatives From Massachusetts.

The Massachusetts state's officials left Auditorium hotel in a body yesterday with Governor Russell and spent the day in the exposition. Today and Friday the visitors will follow their own inclinations. Friday night they will be banquetted at the Auditorium by Governor Russell and on Saturday night by the Massachusetts society of Chicago.

A Fire Nipped In the Bud.

What might have been a disastrous fire was extinguished by the firemen last evening. A guard in the employ of the Intramaral elevated road at the station on the roof of the transportation building annex saw fire climbing up a draped post in the exhibit of the transatlantic French mail line steamers in the gallery and turned in an alarm, at the same time trying to extinguish the blaze. When the firemen arrived the blaze had reached the overhanging streamers and was rapidly approaching the adjoining sections. The fire was extinguished, however, in a few minutes, but it necessitated the throwing of water, which did considerable damage. The exhibition contained many handsome paintings of steamships and some books. The display was opened a few days ago, and the fire, it is thought, has ruined two of the big pictures. The guard was badly burned about the neck and was taken to the hospital.

ANXIOUS TO SELL.

Producers of Silver Want the Government to Buy Stock.

WASHINGTON, June 15.—The practice of making counter bids for silver bullion was continued yesterday by Mr. Preston, the acting director of the mint, and only a small portion of the silver offered by the New York brokers was accepted.

The offer which was accepted—150,000 ounces at $0.838—was more than 6 mills below the London price, or 1 mill more below London than the usual allowance for freight purposes.

Secretary Carlisle was so well pleased with the result of Mr. Preston's experiments in the way of counter offers on Monday that when they were reported to him he authorized the continuation of the system.

The price of silver yesterday was 4 mills higher than on Monday, but the acting director does not believe that the increase is an indication of any scarcity of the metal in the market.

The smelting works are now working at high pressure for the benefit of the owners of silver, with a view to getting their silver upon the market and having it purchased by the government before the Sherman law is repealed.

This remarkable activity of the silver workers was shown when Mr. Preston recently attempted to dispose of some 200 barrels of sweepings from the mints, which are usually eagerly taken for the purpose of extracting the silver. He found himself unable to dispose of the accumulation, because the works were running at full time extracting the metal from the ore.

RAILROAD SENSATION.

Report That An American-Canadian Syndicate Will Purchase the Grand Trunk.

MONTREAL, June 15.—The greatest sensation ever caused in Canadian railway circles was that made yesterday. Through a cable from Duncan McIntyre, one of Montreal's railway kings, at present in London, the fact became public that a great American-Canadian syndicate had been formed to purchase the Grand Trunk railway with the avowed intention of transferring the directorate and head offices of the company from London to Montreal. An idea of the magnitude of the deal and the capital necessary to carry it through may be had from the fact that the company's bonds and stocks, a controlling interest of which the syndicate will secure, reach the total of $275,000,000. The report spread rapidly and Grand Trunk went bounding upward in consequence.

THE GERMAN ARMY.

Bismarck Says the Battles of the Future Will Be Decided by Artillery Forces.

BERLIN, June 15.—Prince Bismarck has come out in favor of an increase of the defensive strength of the empire, but not on the lines laid down by the government in the army bill. Conversing with Professor Kahl, who was visiting the ex-chancellor at Friedrichsruhe, Prince Bismarck declared that an increase of the army was necessary. He differed with the government, however, as to how the increase should be made. He did not approve of adding to the infantry or cavalry strength of the army, but maintained that the increase should be made in the artillery forces, which, he declared, would decide the battles of the future.

Indignant British Workmen.

LONDON, June 15.—The recent agitation of the Radicals against practically taxing workingmen by the loss of a day's work and the contributions for wedding presents for the Duke of York and Princess May, is beginning to be felt. Meetings have been held at Oldham, Bristol and other places throughout England. At these meetings there was much enthusiasm, and the names of royalty were vigorously hissed. Resolutions were also passed in favor of ignoring the event altogether.

A Place For Rear Admiral Walker.

WASHINGTON, June 15.—The long standing question as to what place was to be found for Rear Admiral John Walker has been settled by the assignment of the admiral to a place on the board charged with the trial and inspection of the new ships added to the navy. There was no vacancy on the board, but the admiral was made an additional member and will so serve until next January, when Admiral Belknap retires, when he will become president of the board.

Excitement Dying Out.

DETROIT, June 15.—A better feeling prevailed on Griswold street yesterday, but there was still a large crowd waiting for admission to the People's Savings bank when the doors were thrown open for business. Many Detroit business men aided in the work of restoring confidence by personally talking with depositors in the bank corridors, and advising them to go quietly home and allow matters to assume their normal condition.

An Alleged Forger Arrested

JERSEY CITY, June 15.—Dominco Finnimore, charged with forgery, was arrested at the Red Star dock last evening just as he was about to sail for Antwerp on the steamer Noordland. The amount and nature of the forgery are not known, as the arrest was made on a telegram from Chief Linden. Finnimore was accompanied by a good looking young woman, who says she is his wife.

Doings of the Printers.

CHICAGO, June 15.—The convention of the International Typographical union yesterday sat down on innovations regarding apprentices and foremen and defeated any change in the basis of representation for allied crafts—stereotypers, mailers and pressmen. The plan for the institution of a loan association for the relief of travelling printers was also voted down. The question of creating an international fund was referred to subordinate unions. Similar action was taken regarding the question of paying death benefits.

To Come Before the Grand Jury.

NEW YORK, June 15.—District Attorney Nicolls said yesterday that the Gueterbock case would be placed before the grand jury some day next week. Barnard H. Gueterbock, city editor of The Staats Zeitung, was found dead at his home on the night of May 27. A coroner's jury found that he had committed suicide, but his widow, C. Otto Baess, a broker, and the servant, who were in the house at the time, are on bail pending the action of the grand jury.

A Salem Man In Trouble.

SALEM, Mass., June 15.—Alfred A. McCurdy, a deserter from the United States army, who was arrested in New Orleans Monday for killing a guard, was a former resident of this city. He was a professional bicycle rider of some distinction, holding the record for 24 hours for some time. He was sent west by the Star Bicycle company as a racer and was matched for $10,000 in a race to take place in St. Louis in the spring of 1888. The race proved a farce, and McCurdy joined the army two days later.

Mill Company Assigns.

CLEVELAND, June 15.—T. Raacks Wire Nail company has made an assignment. The inability to raise money to meet maturing paper was the sole cause of the failure, for the liabilities of the company are only $225,000. C. R. Lockwood, the president of the company, said: "We simply got under cover to keep creditors from slaughtering us. We could not get money, and were afraid of slaughter with attachments."

Clever Check Raiser In San Francisco.

SAN FRANCISCO, June 15.—The fact became known yesterday that two local banks had been swindled by cleverly raised checks. One for $3800 on the Farmers' Bank of Fresno was cashed by the London, Paris and American bank, and another for $5500 on the Bank of Butte County of Chico was cashed by the London and San Francisco bank. The checks had been raised from $38 and $55 respectively.

Four Holes In Her Hull.

LONG ISLAND CITY, L. I., June 15.—The iron steamboat Cepheus, with 500 passengers on board, struck a rock in Flushing bay yesterday and four holes were made in the hull. The passengers were landed, and the vessel, with her pumps working, started for New York, but began to fill rapidly and was run ashore on the mud flats near College Point.

Verdict Set Aside.

BOSTON, June 15.—A verdict of $10,275 in favor of Labius H. Hyde, a client of the late General Butler, against the New York and New England railroad, was set aside by the circuit court of appeals in a decision sent down upon an appeal taken by the railroad.

Sad Poisoning Case.

SPOKANE, Wash., June 15. — James Kirandall, a farmer of Paradise Prarie, found his wife and her little daughter dead in the woods half a mile from the house. Her little son said his mother had given him and his sister "some stuff" to drink and had taken some herself. He spit it out. It was undoubtedly poison. No motive can be given for the woman's act.

Malietoa Refuses to Compromise.

AUCKLAND, N. Z., June 15.—Advices received from Samoa yesterday announce that Malietoa, still refusing to compromise with his rival, has directed the government forces to advance and enforce Mataafa's submission to him. War is believed to be inevitable. Mataafa is personally very popular and has numerous devoted adherents.

Schaffner's Body Found.

CHICAGO, June 15.—The body of Hermann Schaffner, the banker who has been missing since the day his bank collapsed two weeks ago, was found floating in the lake yesterday. The body was at once brought to the shore and fully identified by papers found upon it and by the relatives of Mr. Schaffner.

To Succeed Dr. Maban

ASBURY PARK, N. J., June 15.—After two days' balloting the members of the general synod of the Reformed church in America elected a professor of theology in Rutgers Theology college to succeed the late Dr. Maban. The successful candidate is Rev. J. P. Searle of Somerville.

Dr. McGlynn Heard From.

LONDON, June 15.—A correspondent in Rome telegraphs that his holiness has given a long audience to Dr. McGlynn. It was very cordial, Cardinal Rampolla and Cardinal Ledochowski being extremely courteous to the doctor. Dr. McGlynn was enchanted with his reception and is completely reconciled to the pope, and left last night after a five days' sojourn at Rome.

Corinthian Yacht Club Races.

MARBLEHEAD, Mass., June 15.—In the Corinthian Yacht club race June 17, there will be two special classes: Special class A, 21 feet and not over 35 feet water line; first prize $25, second prize $15, third prize $10. Special class B, 16 feet and not over 21 feet water line; first prize $15, second prize $10, third prize $5. The yachts will be restricted to low working sails.

Had Their Cases Continued.

CONCORD, N. H., June 15.—James and Albert Jameson were arraigned yesterday, charged with making an assault with intent to kill upon Augustus B. Farmer at Bow Monday afternoon. They pleaded "not guilty." The case was continued until a week from Monday, and the prisoners were committed. Farmer died last night.

Minnie Webb Sent to Prison.

FITCHBURG, Mass., June 15.—In the police court yesterday Minnie Webb was sentenced to six months' imprisonment for concealing the death of her illegitimate child on May 17. Arthur B. Rockwell was sentenced to nine months' imprisonment as an accessory. He appealed, and was held in $1500 for the grand jury.

Graduation of Deaf Mutes.

NORTHAMPTON, Mass., June 15.—Clarke Institution for Deaf Mutes, the first school in America to teach mutes, orally, graduated four yesterday, Bertha H. Dutton, Boston; Heber N. Haynes, Lawrence; Mary K. Trainor, Pittsfield; Alice L. Ware, Worcester.

Brief Mention.

A boy was dragged to death by a horse at Bethel, Me.

E. G. West of Bradford, Mass., was probably fatally injured.

Daniel Leach of Brockton, Mass., attempted suicide at Lowell, Mass.

An evening Democratic 1 cent news paper is to be issued at Boston about July 1.

One of three Italians who murderer a compatriot in South Lyme, Conn, has been captured in Italy.

NOTE AND COMMENT.

IT APPEARS FROM REPORTS and investigations that there are other structures in Washington occupied by the government that are unfit for human habitation. The government printing office is one of them. It was condemned some years ago as unsafe, but is still being occupied, to the great peril of the army of employes within its walls. All these shaky structures should be torn down and replaced by strong and safe ones. "Economy," as Holman terms it, is in this direction criminal.

CITIZENS OF THE UNITED STATES instinctively hope that the German emperor will be rebuffed in his war aspirations at the elections Thursday. William's request is really for 4,000,000 soldiers, though in 1868 an army of 202,728 men sufficed. Taxation to meet this enormous expansion has of course increased proportionately—from $113,050,000 to $238,000,000 annually. It is time the emperor's ambition in this direction is checked for it not only burdens his own people but causes other governments to put themselves upon a war footing and this increases the general burden of Europe.

WHAT OTHERS ARE SAYING.

The czar has sent to the Sultan of Turkey an album of paintings of the warships in the Russian Black sea fleet. Considering the ravenous desire of the northern bear to feed on turkey, the above is certainly a significant present.—[Fall River News.

Governor Flower remarks that there is no reason why Cleveland should not be renominated in 1896. There is certainly none apparent now. The Republicans are all in favor of it, and there is no other Democrat who wants the position under present circumstances.—Manchester Mirror.

Of course the sugar and rice planters of Louisiana and other sections believe in protection for their especial interests, and are preparing to oppose any free trrde in their sections except for other people. They vote for free trade as Democrats and then whine when the medicine is seriously applied.—[Taunton Gazette.

All over America the question has been asked "Who will follow Edwin Booth?" And only the melancholy answer has been returned tnat America has now not one great serious actor. This condition seems to be more than the result of chance; it is rather due to the tendencies of the modern drama.—[Portland Press.

The Salem News very pertinently queries if Henry B. Sayles is the proper person for a bank commissioner which Governor Russell and the Democratic party so vociferously claimed him to be, why is it that in a similar position under the general government he must be sent to Pennsylvania to be schooled in his duties?—[Waltham Free Press.

ANYTHING AND EVERYTHING.

An English firm that has been selling manuscript sermons to indolent clergymen has decided hereafter to have them typewritten.

The Congregationalist says that this is the season in which some churches examine the building for sufficient justification to announce: "Church closed during the summer for repairs."

The origin of "feather in his cap" is thus explained: In Hungary, in 1599, it was decreed that only he who had killed a Turk should wear a feather, and he was permitted to add a fresh feather to his cap for each Turk whom he had slain.

The royal crown of Roumania is made of bronz, the metal having once done service in the shape of cannons. Samples from 62 war tested guns, each of whom was captured from some enemy, are included in the make-up of this royal insignia.

Excavations are now being made in the famous two-headed hill mentioned by Virgil, about eight miles from Tunis. Many interesting remains have already been unearthed, the largest being the famous temple of Baal Saturn, in which the Carthagenians worshipped.

While the western movement of population in the United States for the century aggregates 505 miles, the extreme northern and southern variation is a little under 22 miles, and the finishing point of the line is only some six miles south of the starting point.

PERSONAL.

Eugene Field has received the honorary degree of master of arts from Knox college, Galesburg, Ills.

Count Reventlow, Danish secretary of legation in St. Petersburg, has been appointed minister to the United States.

Dr. William C. Prime of New York is at his summer villa at Franconia, N. H., accompanied by his sister, Mrs. Slawson.

Ensign Lloyd H. Chandler, United States navy, a son of Senator William E. Chandler, has been ordered to duty on the coast survey.

Lord Lorne receives $6000 a year as governor and constable of Windsor castle. Absolutely his only duty in this sinecure is to sign a receipt for his salary every quarter.

Lieutenant Harry H. Hosley, United States navy, of Lebanon, N. H., has been detached from the United States steamship Philadelphia, and granted three months' leave of absence.

Charles Ladd Norton, son of Tax Collector Norton of Springfield, Mass., has been chosen an instructor in the department of physics in the Massachusetts Institute of Technology. The appointment is for two years. Mr. Norton is 23 years old, and was graduated from the school last May.

Ex-Postmaster General Wanamaker has telegraphed ex-President Harrison asking him to accept the invitation of the Philadelphia city council to deliver an oration at the Fourth of July demonstration in Fairmount park. The ex-president has not yet reached a determination in the matter.

The Emperor William will command in person the Sixteenth army corps at the autumn maneuvers. A novelty in the maneuvers will be the appearance behind the cavalry of a corps of sharpshooters, armed with the new small caliber rifles, provided with smokeless powder and riding in steel clad, bullet-proof vehicles.

Artist J. G. Brown, who makes newsboy and bootblack studies for pictures, is of medium height, white bearded and ruddy. He is upward of 60 years old and is the father of 19 children.

William Ordway Partridge, the Boston sculptor, is a young man of 31 years of age, but has already established such a reputation that his price of $27,000 for the equestrian statue of Garfield is considered a very reasonable one.

[From Yesterday's Extra Edition.]

POISON!

The following is the proceedings of the Borden trial late yesterday afternoon printed in the Standard's extra edition:

Mr. Robinson replied to Mr. Moody, saying that before August 3d there was no evidence given which implicates the defendant, except that at a time prior, in March, 1892, she spoke of Mrs. Borden in the language given by Mrs. Gifford. But surely there is nothing whatever in that that anyone can say manifests a murderous intent or an intent to injure or harm any one physically. Subsequent to the murder upon the defendant being talked with by the police, she said of Mrs. Borden that she was not her mother, but her stepmother. She had said to Mrs. Gifford, "She is not my mother, my mother is dead." That statement was true in either case. Now can that statement made to the policeman which was subsequent to the crimes or the statement to Mrs. Gifford be raised into the force of a declaration indicating any personal violence to Mrs. Borden? I do not discover anything of that kind. If there is anything else in the evidence that has gone in thus far I should be very glad to have it suggested to me. But these are all that I recall now.

Now on the 3d of August nothing has been said more than I quoted, nothing has been shown other than I have said. A previous sickness of Mrs. Borden has been alluded to, but the evidence of the examining physician, Dr. Wood, disposes of any possible connection between the defendant and these two persons. And the evidence clearly shows that the defendant herself was ill, and in the same way. So that there is nothing in the fact of sickness that gives any force to the argument. On Wednesday night, the 3d, the defendant in narrating the experience of the family on the prior day, Tuesday, said that Mrs. Borden and Mr. Borden had been ill, as she had on Tuesday the day before. And talking of the trouble it appears that Mrs. Borden on Tuesday had visited her family physician, with her statement of her suspicion that they were all poisoned. Now is there anything whatever up to the time of Wednesday morning that indicates or involves or implicates this defendant in a murderous intent? I fail to see it.

If we are bound to consider this act of the defendant, assuming it to be an act for the purpose of this discussion, as my friend said, "was she in a murderous state of mind?" That is the inquiry. Is there the slightest evidence that rises to the dignity of truth? It is not as if she had said, as cited in another case, "I intend to kill somebody before the end of this week. I have murder in my heart." There is the absolute plain declaration of a criminal. But there is nothing of that, it is entirely absent. Now, of course, as has been said, this evidence ought not to go in so as to operate to the prejudice of this defendant before the jury, unless it is legal, logical and fairly competent to prove the act with which she stands charged.

My friend said in his argument that there is nothing in this evidence to show to whom she meditated the malice. The commonwealth admits that up to this time there is nothing in the evidence to show to whom she meditated the malice. Therefore, can it any more be said that that act of August 3 is at all indicative of an intent to injure these two persons? Suppose for the purpose of a violent assumption it had been claimed that she bought this poison to poison some other person. I do not quite dare to take it, but I assume Miss Sullivan. Suppose that had been her intent? Would it be competent to use that intent to prove the tragedy for which she is now on trial? That would be a distinct crime. There is nothing to show upon whom she had meditated the malice. Would this court sit for a minute and listen to a proposition that she undertook on a former day to shoot Dr. Bowen, for instance, to show that she had murderous intent toward Mr. and Mrs. Borden. It would be said to be a distinct and separate crime. Nothing in this case has a tendency to show that she intended malice to those two persons. People buy prussic acid to kill animals; that is innocent of crime at any rate. I can not see any difference.

My friend argued that if there is a link in the chain, although that link may be in itself a crime, if there is a link that connects the two pieces of chain together, then that link may be brought forward. Yes, but you must have your chain with two ends or else there is not a link. Now, said the government, we do not know anything about this; we do not claim that it points to these two persons, but we want to show that she had something in her possession, not that she intended to use it, but something she might have used, although there is no evidence to sustain it.

There are cases reported in which a man is upon trial for firing his own buildings to get the insurance money. It is clearly competent to show that he had previously burned one building, but I do not suppose that my learned friend would offer to put in evidence of his attempt to tear it down as showing that it was his intent to burn it.

My friend cites the case of a man found in a building with a jimmy on him, that is evidence of his guilt. Supposing he did have a jimmy, what is a jimmy used for? The man says he had it for an innocent purpose. What is its innocent purpose? I don't know what it is, it surely has a bad name.

Take another case, that of a man arrested in the City hall of Charlestown years ago. He was charged with having committed a burglary. On his person was a key fitted to the Lancaster bank. This was offered in evidence for the purpose of showing that he went into the building with burglarious intent. It is different in this case, in which is an article entirely innocent in itself.

If an intermediate act connects the two acts it is proper to be shown, but if they do not so connect, the evidence is incompetent.

The Justices Retire.

At 4 o'clock the justices retired to their room for a conference.

The judges returned to the court room at 4 32.

Chief Justice Mason said he desired a restatement of the limitations and of the purposes for which it was desired to put in the testimony.

Mr. Moody—There is no purpose in offering the testimony for any other use, or for using it for any other purpose, than as bearing upon the state of mind of the defendant prior to the homicides. We intend to show intent, deliberation and determination.

Evidence Admitted.

Justice Mason said: "We are of opinion that for that purpose it would be competent. You will be allowed to open, and if the preliminary is satisfactory you will be allowed to continue."

There was a conference between the justices and District Attorneys Knowlton and Moody and Messrs. Robinson and Adams. It continued until 4 50, when the jury was summoned into the court room and delivered into the charge of the deputy sheriffs. The court then adjourned.

District Attorney Moody, in answer to a question after the adjournment, stated that the consultation between court and counsel related solely to the nature of the evidence to be offered concerning the attempted purchase of prussic acid, and that nothing of any interest transpired beyond what occurred in open court.

It was pretty generally expressed that the ruling in regard to admitting the evidence relating to the poison was the most substantial government triumph of the day.

PROSECUTION ALMOST FINISHED.

What It Has Made Out and What It Has Failed to Prove.

The case for the prosecution is substantially closed, says the New York Tribune. It has been well put in. The state has made all the case possesses. It is not responsible for the fact that most of its witnesses are unfriendly, nor that some of them have been indiscreet and overzealous. Almost without exception they have either weakened on the cross-examination or have been induced so far to modify what they had previously said as to produce the effect of a weakening. But the case, as it stands with these modifications and qualifications, is the state's real case—all it is entitled to on what it really knows. So as it has information it has proved.

The state has made it appear that Lizzie Borden is probably guilty. There are so many little facts accusing her as to make her guilt certainly probable. But it seems safe to say that in the minds of most rational men, supposing them to be sitting here listening to all the evidence and watching every detail of the trial, there would be, as the case now stands, without a word yet said in her defense, a reasonable doubt of her guilt. When the state sets out to prove that a young woman against whose life there has hitherto been no breath of suspicion crushed with the blade of a hatchet ten times into the skull of her stepmother, and having removed all traces of that crime, after the interval of an hour or more, during which she laughs and works and chatters with her father, resumes the garb of murder and crushes 18 times into his skull—when the state sets out to prove this it ought to be required to prove it with even more than ordinary certainty before it asks that woman's life.

I have not listened to this evidence as a partisan of the prisoner. I came here, supposing on the state's theory that she must be guilty, because there was no one else at hand who could be. But it is a serious matter to take away a human life, and I do not see the justification of that in the facts as the state knows them. It has no need to accuse itself for not knowing more or better. The officers of the law have done the best they could. They have been too smart and zealous, rather than too little so. The person who killed Andrew J. Borden and his wife had the gifts of a maniac.

MISS BORDEN BREAKING DOWN.

Condition Pitiful as viewed by Those in Court Room.

(New York Tribune.)

Miss Borden is breaking down. Her condition today is pitiful. There is no longer room for the feminine prejudice which has arrayed itself so strongly against her because she has been so firm and unmoved. What the repression and suppression of her emotions during these months of confinement must have cost her can be somewhat, if inadequately, guessed from her agitation and anguish today. Throughout the morning session, while the doctors with their plaster casts, marked in red to show where the wounds had been made in the faces, heads and necks of Mr. and Mrs. Borden, were testifying, she sat with red eyes and trembling lips and with deep marks in her pale face, looking as long as she could, listening as much as she could, and finally retreating in grief and tears behind her fan. At one time she had to leave the room; the recital was more than she could bear. Finally, at the afternoon session, when the skulls of her murdered father and stepmother were brought into the room, the court conferred a moment, and then the chief justice said in a quiet, kindly voice that the prisoner would be allowed to remain in the custody of the sheriff in another part of the building while this portion of the examination proceeded. It was an act of genuine mercy. She could not possibly have endured the scenes which followed. Even to the ordinary spectator they were terrible. To a woman, the daughter and stepdaughter of those to whom these ghastly relics belonged, and who was there accused of having with her own hands made the long rents and great holes exposed in them, their exhibition must have been worse than the tortures of the Spanish Inquisition. Her departure from the room was a great relief to her counsel, and operated clearly in the interest of justice.

THEY ATTACK THE SHERIFF.

New York Newspapermen Resent the Artist's Expulsion.

(Julian Ralph in New York Sun.)

The Sun has had too much that was more important to be able to devote adequate space to the extraordinary high sheriff of Bristol county, who acts as executive officer of the court in which Miss Lizzie Borden is on trial for her life, but today he has forced himself into the front rank as an object of interest. He hates the sight of a New Yorker, and has allowed none from that city to enter the court room except when the chief justice has ordered them in. Today an artist employed by the New York Herald was invited to occupy the seat of the reporter of that paper in order to make a sketch of an important witness. The sheriff saw the artist out of his place, as he supposed, and without warning had him forcibly removed from the court room. Thrown out is the only phrase that describes the manner in which he was expelled.

The extraordinary little creature, in his shad-bellied coat of blue, pointed out the artist to a deputy. The deputy was about to throw out the reporter of the Evening Sun when the sheriff corrected him, and again pointed to the artist.

The deputy then, without a word in advance, tore the artist from his seat and desk and dragged him with violence through the crowd in the court room. The people started from their seats with fright, and for a time the impression was that the man was suddenly stricken with an illness, there was such a crashing of timber and other noise.

The artist is said to have been advised by the lawyers on both sides to bring suit in the federal courts for damages. All who saw the assault speak of it as brutal. Thus the sheriff, who at first seemed only a ridiculous coxcomb, has developed into a dangerous character, who is the first to mar the dignity and decorum of this otherwise model court.

In the Borden case, conviction is unlikely from the character of the evidence that has been offered, but though the prisoner will be pronounced legally free there will always remain a stain upon her unless she takes the stand in her own defense. Many people will think that she ought to be anxious to do so if she were innocent. It is a curious fact about this trial that there has not been offered a single statement or suggestion that would afford a clew to another person. Everything that Miss Borden's friends hope to prove is comprised in demonstrating the instability of circumstantial evidence, thereby saving her life. Yet though with success, there will come no clearing up of the mystery, there should be no effort left unexerted by the Bordens to discover the murderer. Otherwise one of them is doomed to have a horrible suspicion hang over her all the rest of her life.—New London Telegraph.

REAL ESTATE SALES.

Elizabeth B. Russell et als. have sold to Matthew Russell four lots of land in Dartmouth for $1,670; the first three lots contain 27½ acres.

Elizabeth B. Russell has sold to Matthew Russell a lot of woodland in Dartmouth containing 15 acres.

Humphrey Howland has sold to John H. Nickerson land and buildings in Apponegansett, on the west side of Elm street, containing 3 acres and 13 rods.

Willard Nye, Jr., has sold to Andrew J. Pierce, Jr., et als. a lot of land on the north side of contemplated Tallman street, containing 126.58 rods.

James Brindley, Sr., has sold to George P. Booth land in Dartmouth on the road leading from the residence of Andrew H. King to the old road, containing 7 square rods for $18.

George K. Russell has sold to Daniel W. Dean a lot of salt meadow on Sconticut Neck, containing 4 acres for $100.

The Evening Standard.

ESTABLISHED FEBRUARY, 1850. | NEW BEDFORD, FRIDAY, JUNE 16, 1893. | TWO CENTS.

HASKELL & TRIPP.

A third off the price.

Sixty pieces, about 3,000 yds., of very choice printed muslins for hot weather dresses went on sale yesterday at a reduction of one-third from recent selling price.

Choose for 8c. a yard from a beautiful line of muslins regularly sold at 12½c. — In these grounds: Pink, Old rose, Heliotrope, Light blue, Nile green, Cream, Ecru.

We are reminded to say right here that we have just the ribbons to use with above muslins, in that collection of rich, fancy silk and satin ribbons at 29c. a yard, worth more than double the price. Surely *you can buy your dress and trimmings for less than either would have cost ten days ago.*

For children.

Cotton kilts for small boys are now made from ginghams, prettily trimmed, combined with matching shade in chambray. Sizes 2, 3, 4 and 5. Price 50c. for either. Will wash perfectly.

Girls' dresses, made from fast color Turkey red, are trimmed with white featherstitch braid on yoke and sleeves. Sizes 2 to 5. Price 50c.

A few gingham dresses remain from the big lot recently advertised, 98c. each, worth $1.50. Sizes fit girls from 6 to 14 years.

Cotton underclothing.

Nightgowns for girls begin at 50c. for size 1 and advance 5c. with each larger size. These gowns are in the "Mother Hubbard" style, tucked and ruffled yokes.

Drawers for girls:

Sizes,	1	2	3	4	5 6 7
Prices,	12½c	15c	17c	20c	25c

We're having large sales for our specialties in women's cotton underclothing.

Special gowns, 50c., 69c., 89c.

Special skirts $1.

Special corset covers, 25c. (seven styles.)

Cambric underwear for the warm weather is here in immense variety. Perfect in all details. The new *full* skirts are ready.

Keepers of summer hotels and boarding houses at our neighboring shore resorts can buy here—

Good white blankets, 75c. a pair.

Good white bedspreads, 75c. each.

Copies of India rugs, $1.98 each. Size 2 yards long by 1 yard wide.

☞ Refreshing soda from our new Arctic fountain in the basement.

HASKELL & TRIPP,
Department Stores,
Purchase and William Streets.

HER SISTER.

Lizzie's Foster Parent Called.

Miss Emma L. Borden a Witness.

Most Interesting One of the Whole Trial.

No Lack of Cordiality with Stepmother.

No Truth in Police Station Quarrel.

Mr. Knowlton's Cross Examination.

Obtained Admissions Valuable to Him.

Evidence About Wild Man Not Admitted.

Day of Denials in the Great Murder Trial.

The day of denials is perhaps a good characterization of this, the eleventh, in the great murder trial. On the opening of the court the justices refused to allow the defense to produce a witness who was to tell of a man with a hatchet in the woods muttering "Poor Mrs. Borden." The defense is bringing forward a formidable array of witnesses to contradict those of the prosecution. Police Matron Reagan's story has occupied considerable attention. The most interesting witness of the day and perhaps of the whole trial was Miss Emma Borden, the prisoner's sister.

THE ELEVENTH DAY.

Sad and Careworn Sister of the Prisoner in Court.

The morning of the eleventh day of the Borden trial proved to be the second unpleasant one during the course of proceedings. It did not rain, but it was cloudy and cheerless, with a wind that searched one's marrow and made the unfortunae wight who has trusted to the fickleness of a New England climate and removed his flannels to mentally berate himself for his shortsightedness. The crowd about the barricade before the opening was smaller than for several days, and composed in about equal proportions of men and women, all of whom succeeded in getting seats.

Just before the time for opening the court Emma Borden, accompanied by another lady, drove to the rear entrance and alighted. Emma has a sad and careworn appearance, and the troubles which have fallen upon the younger sister whom she nurtured and cared for with a mother's love in her infantile years have left a deep impress upon her appearance.

Lizzie Looks Happy.

Lizzie looks quite happy today. Some of the lines about her mouth, which seemed at one time as though they might become permanent, are gradually being erased, and if, as now seems to be generally considered probable, the trial will result in an acquittal, there is no doubt but she will assume much more of a youthful appearance.

The court was promptly called at 9 o'clock, and the justices were received at the call by a general uprising of the men in the audience, while it was equally noticeable that the women, with a few exceptions, kept their seats. Why is it? Do the ladies as a class have less reverence in their compositions, or is it the result of ignorance of customs appertaining to court rooms?

When the jurors had been polled and answered to their names business at once began.

NOT COMPETENT.

Story of the Man with the Hatchet in the Woods Excluded.

After the opening of the court there was whispered consultation for ten minutes between counsel for government and defense and the judges, at the close of which Chief Justice Mason announced that the evidence of Joseph Lemais was not competent, and would be excluded.

SARAH R. HART

Saw a Man at the Borden Gate at Time of the Murders.

The first witness called was Sarah Hart, who was examined by Mr. Jennings.

Q. What is your name? A. Sarah R. Hart.

Q. You used to live in Fall River? A. Yes sir.

Q. How long ago was it? A. About a year ago.

(Continued on Third Page.)

WEATHER INDICATIONS.

Cool and Rainy.

Boston, June 16.—Local forecast for New England until Saturday night: Rain Saturday, probably beginning tonight in southern sections; continued cool, high northeast winds.

Cloudy and Rainy.

Washington, June 16.—For New England and eastern New York: Increasing cloudiness and rain; cooler in western Massachusetts, New York, Vermont and northern New York; northwest winds increasing in force.

STARVING TO DEATH.

A Rich Man's Wife Denied Food and Medical Attendance.

BROOKLYN, June 16.—Eliphalet Stratton is the owner and occupant of the three-story and basement brick dwelling 124 Gates avenue, near Cambridge place. The house is a handsome one, and is worth $15,000. Mr. Stratton owns other property in this city and in New York. He lives on the income derived from his real estate. It is said that he is the owner of property in the two cities worth between $200,000 and $400,000. He is 83 years old. His oldest son is about 55 years old.

Five or six years ago Mr. Stratton's wife died. Three years ago the colonel, as he is familiarly called, married again. His wife was a woman only 35 years of age. In January last Mrs. Stratton was taken sick with peritonitis. Dr. Cooper was called in to attend her. About a month ago he stopped calling at the house, and Dr. Rushmore of Montague and Henry streets has since been attending her. The reason why Dr. Cooper ceased his professional calls was explained by him during a short conference he held with Superintendent Campbell at police headquarters.

The Story Told by Dr. Cooper

to Superintendent Campbell was to the effect that Mrs. Stratton was not only suffering from peritonitis, but also from lack of proper food and clothing. He said that he found her alone in the house with no servants. Her sole attendant was her husband, and Dr. Cooper said he was by no means careful in administering to her. The reason why the doctor ceased attending the sick woman was because Mr. Stratton had asked him what was the best way he could get rid of her. He thought then it was a case for police investigation.

Superintendent Campbell lost no time in notifying Captain McKelvey of the fourth precinct of the case, and he detailed Detective Sergeant Delahanty to investigate. Delahanty went to the house. In answer to his question the sick woman told the detective that she and her husband were the only occupants of the house; that there was no servant or nurse to wait upon her and that she was compelled to wait upon herself as best she could.

Mrs. Stratton said that shortly after their marriage her husband refused to furnish her with any money, although he was well able to do so. He even refused to give her enough to provide necessary household supplies, and for that reason they could not keep any servants. She had been compelled to do dressmaking with her sister, who had come to live with her, in order to get money enough for her own personal needs. When she was taken sick her husband ordered the sister to leave the house, although there were no servants there and

She Needed Help.

She told her husband that she required the services of a nurse to wait upon her, but he replied that he would get a servant, who would do this as well as the household work. He did not do this, however. Mrs. Stratton showed Detective Delahanty her arm. He said it was merely skin and bone and proved the truth of the woman's words that she was starving. Mrs. Stratton said she would have starved had it not been for the kindness of the neighbors, especially Mrs. Jedwin, who lives in the adjoining house.

Mrs. Stratton managed to crawl to one of the rear windows last week and called to one of Mrs. Jedwin's children, saying that she was starving and asking that the neighbors get food to her in some way. Mrs. Jedwin, finding that she could not get into the house, tied up some food in a napkin which she managed to get into Mr. Stratton's room by means of a long pole. When Stratton discovered this he

Barricaded the Windows.

Afterward this neighbor secured keys to the house, and for the last three or four days has visited the house during the absence of Mr. Stratton and given food to his wife and in other ways cared for her. This was the story told by Mrs. Stratton, and Delahanty asked her husband, who was in the room at the time, why he did not provide a nurse and servant for his wife. He said that he had been trying to secure some woman, but had not been able to find one.

"If you want me on any charge you had better take me now," he said. He professed to believe that his wife was not as ill as she tried to make out.

In compliance with an agreement made with Detective Dolahanty, Mrs. Jedwin accompanied by another neighbor of Mrs. Stratton, visited the Myrtle avenue police court yesterday and made complaint to the effect that they believe Mr. Stratton was trying to starve his wife to death. Clerk Steinworth, who listened to the complaint, advised the two women to bring the matter before the commission of charities.

By Justice Haggerty's decision Delahanty swore a warrant charging Stratton with attempt at homicide. The justice signed it.

HOME MATTERS.

—There will be a meeting of the special committee on cemeteries tonight in room 8, Library building, to investigate into the matter of laying out lots and introducing water.

—Steamer Haytien Republic, libeled some little time ago at Seattle on a charge of smuggling opium and Chinese, was released on $30,000 bonds June 9th.

—N. S. Greet of Somerville will give his Chalk Talk on the Sunday school lesson this evening at 7 30 o'clock in the Y. M. C. A. hall.

—The bathing houses in Fairhaven opened Thursday, and a large number of persons enjoyed the first dip of the season.

—Large line of new neckwear just arrived at Gifford & Co's.

—Above criticism. Colby's Baking Powder.

—Red, White, Blue, White and Blue, White and Red Hat Ribbons. Phinney's.

—Children's sailor hats at Nooning's, very cheap.

—Great rush at Nooning's on 79 cent Sailors.

—Sure results from Colby's Baking Powder.

—Bicycle goods of all descriptions at Gifford & Co's.

—You need it. Favorite Baking Powder.

—Summer Underwear at Phinney's.

Hood's Sarsaparilla sharpens the appetite.

DARTMOUTH TOWN MEETING.

One of the Largest Ever Known by Citizens.

Hot Fight Over the Town House Location.

Test Vote Shows 164 in Favor and 149 Against a Change.

It wasn't exactly town meeting day as the term applies to the annual gathering in the various towns throughout the state, but a stranger, had he been in the neighborhood of the town house in Dartmouth today would have thought it was, so large was the crowd. The "annual" wasn't in it as compared with today's meeting. It seemed as though both ends of the town had turned out, and for half an hour prior to calling to order the subject of new town house was discussed in groups here and there.

It will be remembered that a few weeks ago the town voted to build a new town house, and after much backing and filling it was decided to locate the structure at Smith Mills. Since then a change has come about with some, and Smith Mills is not looked upon as a suitable location, inasmuch as it cannot be reached readily by the great majority. Hence the special meeting today. It is needless to add to the cold northeast wind did not in the least cool the ardor of the townspeople, and when the hour arrived for assembling the town house at the head of Apponegansett river was filled to its utmost capacity.

It was evident from the talk heard in the groups gathered about the premises that the change of location asked for is due to the expense to be incurred, rather than from a desire to locate farther south. A prominent north ender remarked to the Standard man that this meeting would never have been called if the appropriation made had been $5,000 instead of $10,000.

The meeting was called to order by the town clerk, Benjamin J. Potter, who read the two principal articles in the warrant, which follow:

To see if the town will vote to rescind a vote passed by the town April 8th, 1893, which is as follows: "To purchase a lot and build a new town hall as near Smith Mills village as practical." Also to rescind a vote passed by the town May 27th, 1893, which was to purchase a lot known as the Hawes lot and build a town hall at Smith Mills and appropriate a sum not exceeding ten thousand ($10,000) dollars, and choose a committee to carry the vote into effect.

To see if the town will vote to purchase a lot and build a new town hall at or near Macomber corner so called, and if so, to appropriate a sum of money and choose a committee to carry the vote into effect agreeable to the petition of Paul Barker and sixty-seven (67) others.

Joshua V. Davis was nominated for moderator by Elbridge Faunce. The ballot resulted as follows:

Whole number of votes,	249
Necessary for choice,	125
Joshua V. Davis had	114
Job S. Gidley,	135

The vote for moderator was the largest ever cast in the town, and over half an hour was consumed in voting and counting ballots cast.

Before taking his position Mr. Gidley said he was in hopes to have met with defeat. He asked as a favor that the meeting assist him in maintaining order. He believed in settling difficulties by arbitration, and there is an apparent difference of opinion between those at the north end and the south end. Had the civil war been settled by arbitration how much better it would have been for the country. He urged the people in discussing the question of the hour to keep to the question. He then referred to the previous action of the town, and in speaking of the necessity of a new town hall he said it was his opinion that a village was the proper place for a town house, and when he mentioned Smith Mills as a suitable place the cry of question brought him up with a short turn, and he proceeded to business.

John W. Howland moved to rescind the vote contained in the first article.

On the question being presented Mr. Howland said as two thirds of the people live south of Smith Mills, he did not favor such a location. It is not the question of village. It is the question of public convenience. Macomber's corner was his ideal of a place.

Otis F. Thatcher had hoped that this meeting would have been held in the new town house. He referred to votes of previous meetings on this question. The sentiment of the town was then in favor of Smith Mills, after several other locations had been voted down. By the vote of the town May 27th $10,000 were appropriated. It is not necessary that the committee should expend the whole amount. The lot has been purchased and the contract sealed and delivered. The vote, whatever it is today, will have no effect. Counsel say that the town will have the bill to pay. Do we want two houses?

"Yes," cried several.

If this vote is rescinded it will not be a benefit to the town. The contractor has sub-let the contract.

Wm. H. Potter thought it was essential to do business on business principles. He didn't believe in gagging people. Justice should prevail. It was the sentiment of previous meetings that the town-house should be centrally located. A lot had been selected, but is it as defined to the meeting when the town appropriated the money? I claim that the town is not bound to purchase the Hawes lot. Mr. Hawes tells me it has not been bought. It has not been paid for. Two selectmen say that no paper has been presented them for the payment of such money. Mr. Thatcher says there was no opposition to the appropriation of $10,000. "I think there was," he said, "for $5000 would have been sufficient." It has been talked if you don't do this we will take $7000 of the road money. He didn't like that sort of talk. If we have made a mistake let's correct it. He was down on appropriating money at special meetings.

William B. Bennett said that the meeting was held for a purpose. That purpose should be carried out for the benefit of every taxpayer. Mr. Thatcher says the lot has been purchased and paid for. The committee has, he said, made a contract for that building. The selectmen it is said have indorsed no order for the payment of money. He should like to know whether the money has been drawn from the treasury or not. He also wanted to know if a contract had been signed.

Joshua V. Davis thought the talk was foreign to the subject. He was of the opinion that it was necessary to know whether the declarations made by Mr. Thatcher are true or not.

Henry Plummer wanted to know whether bills audited by the selectmen require the majority of the board, or not. He also wanted to know whether the bill had ever been presented to the board.

Otis F. Thatcher said he was neither one of the committee to build nor on the selectmen, but he understands that the bill has been paid.

William H. Potter thought the committee or selectmen should give the information. He asked the town treasurer to make an explanation.

Benjamin J. Potter, town treasurer, then read from the records. The committee, he said bought the lot and the

[Continued in a Later Edition.]

SATURDAY'S STANDARD.

Tomorrow evening's Standard will consist of 12 pages, crowded with important news matter, the elaborate and full report of the great murder trial and all local happenings, the full Associated Press telegraphic service and special dispatches, with much valuable, entertaining and instructive literary matter. As tomorrow is Bunker Hill Day there will be no Boston evening papers, but the Standard will be printed as usual.

A PLEASANT OCCASION.

A very pleasant occasion last evening was a recital given by 18 of Miss Ella Bassett's pupils. The programme was as follows:

Grand March.		
Duet—Fairy Queen Galop.	Edith and Lydia Devoll.	Smith
The Storm.	Gertrude Spooner.	Weber
Old Oaken Bucket.	Jennie Richardson.	Durkee
Florie Waltz.	Adela Young.	Rosewig
Perles et Dentelle.	Annie Ryder.	Ludovic op. 50
Song and Whistling Solo.	Lila Cameron.	
Feast of Roses Nocturne.	Susie Bradley.	Hevery op 3
Recreation March.	Hattie Perry.	Mack
Violin Solo.	Edith Hawes	
Auld Lang Syne.	Lydia Devoll.	Bellak
Little Fairy Galop.	Etta Johnson.	Streabbog
Blackhawk Waltz.	Lizzie Murphy.	Walsh
Mountain Zephyrs.	Maud Tabor.	Clay
Little Fairy Schottische.	Mamie Niles.	Streabbog
Cleveland's Luck and Love March.	Emma Spooner.	Miss Ida
Violin Solo	Edith Hawes.	
Mayflower Galop.	Hattie Perry.	Streabbog
Sylvan Stream Waltz.	Edith Devoll.	Freeman
Duet—One Heart, One Mind.	Emma and Gertrude Spooner.	Waternberg
Serenade March.	Miss Mamie Warren.	Aubert
Cascade of Roses.	Essie Parker.	Snow
Les Etincelles.	Maud Tabor.	Hammerel op. 11
Grande Valse de Concert.	Susie Bradley.	Mattei
Juvenile Melody.	Lizzie Nickerson.	Kohler
Piano Solo.	Miss Bassett.	
Home, Sweet Home.	Everet Tinkham.	Rienbault

SUMMER SERVICE VIA FALL RIVER LINE.

The Double Service of the Fall River Line became effective for the Summer season on Monday, June 12th, when the great steamboats the Puritan, Pilgrim, Plymouth and Providence were placed in commission and will be operated together, two boats being run in each direction daily. Pullman Vestibuled trains will leave Park Square Station, Boston, week days and Sundays at 6 00 and 7 00 p. m., connecting at Fall River with steamers leaving week days at 7 30 and 8 25 p. m., Sundays 7 40 and 8 30 p. m. The first boat from Fall River touches at Newport 9 15 p. m., the second running express to New York.

The Summer arrangement of trains on the Old Colony System became effective on the same date, trains being run to the steamboat wharf, Fall River, from all divisions of the Road on schedules differing somewhat from those heretofore in effect.

AT THE WHITE CASH.

Thick rib Corned Beef, Spinach, Beet Greens, new Cabbage, green Beans, Cucumbers, Strawberries, Asparagus, Rhubarb, Lettuce, green Onions, legs of Mutton, roasts of Beef, loins and forequarters of Lamb, Green Peas, new Potatoes, Bananas, Lemons, Oranges, Eggs, Butter, Cheese, Lard, Cottolene, Salt Pork, Beans, Flour, Tea, Coffee, Sugar, Rice, Tapioca, Corn Starch, Baking Powder, fine bottle Pickles, fine Currant Jelly, pure Leaf Lard in 5 lb. pails. These are all on sale at the White Cash Store, 134 Purchase street.

SECRETARIES.

These useful articles of house furnishing are economical from three standpoints—money, room and labor.

See F. R. Slocum's line of oak secretaries. They are a handsome combination of bookcase, writing desk and cheffonier. Each appartment is commodious, and yet the whole occupies but little room. One very neat secretary sells for $22.50 now, though it is worth more money.

CONDENSED LOCALS.

—For Saturday at B. H. Waite & Co's, 71 Wm. st., the best bargain you ever saw in straw mattings, 18 rolls of 35, 40 and 50-cent quality, your choice for 25 cents a yard. Remnants of all-wool carpets from 25 cents a yard upwards, according to their length. Oil Cloths again, 2-yards wide, 75-cent quality for 50 cents. The best goods made and always sold for $1.20, today for 94 cents. Holland window shades, all ready to hang, for 25 cents.

—H. C. Hathaway's Auction Bulletin for tomorrow at 9 o'clock a. m., at salesroom: Furniture, Oil Cloths, Cigars, Jewelry, etc., etc. 10 o'clock at mart: Horses, Carriages, etc. 3 o'clock p. m.: House and Lot on Mill street.

—Nooning's flower sale was such a success the past week that we give you another chance to secure one of the great bargains. Handsome bunches for 49c. and 69c. per bunch.

—Ladies' Muslin Underwear at bargain prices for Saturday. White skirts tucked with hemstitched ruffle 65c. Gowns and drawers low prices. Moynan & Co.

—The letter carriers have all been furnished with straw hats this week at Gifford & Co's.

—Saturday will be a busy day at Whiting & Co's. They are selling all kinds of Dry Goods very cheap.

—Great drive at Nooning's on the flower sale. Elegant sprays for 49c. and 69c. per bunch.

—Moynan & Co. offer for Saturday a special odd lot of Ladies' gloves, former prices were $1,00, $1.25 and $1.50 now, 50c. a pair.

—The best blue flannel suits to be found in the city for $8, $12, and $13, at Gifford & Co's.

Gentlemen, the finest line of Russia leather shoes found at Buchell's. See our $4 shoe.

—See our Boys' "Hard Wear" Suits with pants extra at $1.39. Waists in abundance low prices. Moynan & Co.

Good, pure whiskey is good for lung troubles. Be careful and buy the Cutter Whiskey.

—Boys' Laundered Cheviot and Madras Shirts at Phinney's.

—Headquarters for straw hats is at Gifford & Co's, 139 Union street.

—Great Glove, Hosiery and Underwear day tomorrow at Whiting & Co's.

—Sold by Grocers—Favorite Baking Powder.

—Fancy straw hats at Nooning's marked down to 25c., 50c. and 75c.

—Straw Hats, extra wide brims, at Phinney's.

—Call and see Nooning's trimmed Sailors, fine straw, for 79 cents.

—Negligee Shirts at Phinney's.

Our Semi-Annual

STOCK TAKING

IS CLOSE AT HAND.

We wish to reduce stock all around. Instead of our regular

SATURDAY SALE

We shall inaugurate

Saturday, June 17, — A Special Clean Up Sale!

Of goods in each department, changing our programme every two days.

WATCH THIS COLUMN FOR CHANGES!

We advertise today and Friday bargains for SATURDAY and MONDAY as follows:

FIRST.

The balance of the EXTRA SUPER

INGRAIN REMNANTS,

4 to 16 yds. Regular price 85c. yd.

CLEAN UP PRICE 55 CENTS PER YARD.

SECOND.

A lot of

OIL CLOTH REMNANTS

Of all grades at 1-3 off the regular retail price, viz:

60c. Oil Cloth for	40 cents per yard
50c. " " "	33 " " "
42c. " " "	28 " " "
30c. " " "	20 " " "

THIRD.

We have BROKEN THE RECORD on

CHENILLE CURTAINS,

This spring's sales leading all previous seasons over one-half. We want to sell 75 pairs of Portieres in the next two weeks, and we know the prices we shall make will do it. We are by far the largest handlers of these goods in Southern Massachusetts and our fall purchases will be very much larger than ever before. Therefore we shall clean up the stock now on hand, in many instances at less than cost.

WE SHALL SELL

A $15.00 Portiere for	$11.50
A $12.00 " "	$9.25
A $9.00 " "	$6.50
A $8.00 " "	$5.50

The same proportion of reduction runs through the entire line.

FOURTH.

A LOT OF STAIR CARPETS

For summer cottage use.

1-2 yard wide,	10c. per yard
5-8 " "	12c. " "

FIFTH.

A LOT OF WALL PAPERS.

Regular 20, 25, 35 and 45c. goods will go for 12c. per Roll.

This column will be changed Saturday, watch for further bargains.

C. F. WING,

34 to 40 Purchase Street.

WHITING & CO.

We have prepared for the Warm season before us, and have had made to our own order the largest and finest stock of Ladies' Shirt Waists and Wrappers ever shown in this city.

3,000 Shirt Waists, in Silk, Satine, Cambric and Lawn, in all sizes and prices.

See the 75c. Shirt Waists, we are selling at 50c. apiece, they are fine.

500 Ladies' House Wrappers in Gingham, Cambric, and Print. We have styles to be found only at our store, prices from $1.25 to $2.50 each, 34 to 44 bust measure.

100 Children's Gingham Dresses to be closed out at 50c. on the dollar, 95c. and $1.50, former price $2.00 to $3.00.

We shall make some very low prices tomorrow on

CAPES and JACKETS.

8.00 Capes, $4.95.

$7.50 Jackets, $2.95.

$10 and $12 Jackets, $4.95.

4 Blazer Jackets, $7 and $8 ones, to close, $3.95 apiece.

8 Children's Reefers, $5 quality, all to be closed out at $2.95 apiece, all 8 and 10 years sizes.

If you want a good Jacket at less than half price you can find it at our store.

WHITING & CO.

A—— Ten Dollar Cheviot Suit

THAT BEATS THEM ALL.

Made from a handsome smooth faced, all wool black Cheviot, cut single breasted style, make up and fit equal to a $16 suit. In fact, these suits were made up to retail at $16, but the manufacturer needed money and we secured this lot of suits at our own figures. This is the BIGGEST BARGAIN in Cheviot Suits you ever saw. A genuine $16 suit for only

$10!

J. & W. R. WING & CO.,

133 UNION ST.

THE CRESCENT

22 Purchase St.

FOR SATURDAY, June 17.

Children's Corded Waists,	19c.
Very Wide Hamburgs,	19c.
Gingham Aprons,	19c.
Muslin Hats,	19c.
Muslin Bonnets,	19c.
Silk Gloves,	19c.
White Jersey Vests,	19c.
Ecru Jersey Vests,	19c.
Blue Jersey Vests,	19c.
Salmon Jersey Vests,	19c.
Boys' Blouse Waists,	19c.
Child's White Apron,	19c.

CORSETS.

Summer Corsets,	39c.
Summer Corsets,	50c.
Summer Corsets,	75c.
Summer Corsets,	$1.00
Summer Corsets,	$1.25
Summer Corsets,	$2.00

Ferris Ventilating Waists for ladies and misses.

THE CRESCENT!

22 Purchase St.

HER SISTER.

(Continued from First Page.)

Q. How long did you live in Fall River? A. Fifteen or twenty years.
Q. Where did you live? A. On Second street.
Q. So that you are very familiar with Second street? A. Yes sir.
Q. Did you know Andrew J. Borden when he was alive? A. I knew him by sight.
Q. Did you know where his house was on Second street? A. Yes sir.
Q. Did you have a sister who lived near by that house? A. My sister lived in the house now occupied by Dr. Kelly.
Q. How long did she live there? A. Two or three years.
Q. Were you in the habit of frequently going there while she was there? A. Yes sir, quite often.
Q. Were you on Second street the day of the murder? A. I was.
Q. Did you pass by Andrew J. Borden's house? A. I did.
Q. What time was it? A. I think near 10 o'clock, somewhere from ten minutes of to 10.
Q. Was anybody with you at the time? A. Yes sir.
Q. Who? A. My sister-in-law, Mrs. Manley.
Q. Did you have occasion to stop near the gate of the Borden house? A. I did.
Q. Which gate do you refer to? A. The north gate.
Q. What caused you to stop there? A. I stopped to speak to my nephew.
Q. Where was he? A. In a carriage.
Q. What did you do? A. I stepped from the sidewalk to the back of the carriage to see some pond lilies.
Q. Where were the pond lilies? A. In a tub in the back of the carriage.
Q. Did you notice anybody on the Borden premises at that time? A. I noticed some one in the gate way.
Q. Did you know who it was? A. No sir.
Q. Was it a young man or an old man? A. I should judge it was an elderly man.
Q. Was it Mr. Borden? A. No sir.
Q. What was he doing? A. He was standing resting his head on his left elbow, and his elbow was on the south post of the gate way.
Q. Was he doing anything more than that? A. He was looking at me, and then looked up the street. He looked as if he was trying to pry into my business.
Q. Did you notice him go up the street? A. I did not.
Q. How long did you stay there? A. Five minutes.
Q. Was he there when you went away? A. He was, sir.
Q. Which way did you go from there? A. I went down to Borden street.
Q. And from there? A. On to Main street. I went down just in time to catch the 10 o'clock car from the north.
Q. Where does that 10 o'clock car start from at 10 o'clock? A. It comes down Main street and stops at the City hall. It left the City hall when the clock was striking 10.
Q. Were you walking? A. I was.
Q. Is it by the fact that you took a horse car there at 10 o'clock that you fix the time at 10 minutes of 10? A. It was sir.
Q. See if you can point out on that picture where you saw the man? (Witness took the photograph and pointed out the gatepost where the man was leaning, and the spot was pointed out to the jury.)
Cross-examined.
Q. Where was the carriage at that time, Mrs. Hart? A. A little to the north of the gateway.
Q. You say you didn't notice this man as you passed by the gate? A. I did not.
Q. The next house north is Mrs. Churchill's house? A. Yes sir.
Q. And the carriage in which your nephew was, with whom you talked, was somewhere in front of the Churchill house? A. It was between the houses.
Q. That is partly abutting the premises of Mr. Borden and partly the premises of Mrs. Churchill? A. The horse stood with his head near that tree near the gateway. (Witness pointed out the tree in the photograph.)
Q. What is your nephew's name? A. (With some hesitation.) Ezra, Ezra P. B. Manley.
Q. Was he facing towards you? A. He was.
Q. And the team was right close to the sidewalk? A. Yes sir.
Q. Of course you knew him? A. Yes sir.
Q. Knew him well, I suppose? A. Yes sir.
Q. Had you seen him before he spoke to you? A. No sir.
Q. There was nothing to obstruct your view of him as you came down the street? A. Of my nephew?
Q. Yes. A. No sir.
Q. But you didn't see him until he spoke to you? A. I was talking with my sister-in-law.
Q. So that you were so absorbed in talking with your sister that you did not see your nephew? A. Yes sir.
Q. You do not mean to say that the man was not standing there when you went by? A. I didn't notice.
Q. You didn't either notice your nephew, did you? A. No sir, not until he spoke.
Q. So that you wouldn't be quite sure that he was not standing there when you went down? A. No sir.
Q. For aught you know the man might have been there before you turned around? A. Yes sir.
Q. What was he doing? A. He was resting against the post.
Q. That was the nearest to the Borden house, or nearest to the Churchill house? A. His hand rested on the south post.
Q. That is the one nearest to the house? A. It was.
Q. Did he change his position while you saw him? A. Simply his head.
Q. Did he turn to look at you? A. He was looking at me and turned to look up the street.
Q. He didn't move except to turn his head to look up the street? A. No sir.
Q. He didn't say anything to you? A. No sir.
Q. And remained in that position all the time that you saw him? A. Yes sir.
Q. And was in that position when you went away? A. Yes sir.
Q. You didn't know the man? A. No sir.

CHARLES S. SAWYER.

Tells How Lizzie Appeared After Discovery of the Crime.

Charles S. Sawyer was next called.
Q. What is your business? A. Painter.
Q. Do you recall the day of the Borden murder? A. I do.
Q. When was it that you first heard of the murder? A. I first heard a man was stabbed while I was in a shop at 81 Second street.
Q. Is this near the Borden house? A. Yes sir.
Q. On the same side of the street as the Borden house? A. No sir.
Q. Is it on the same side of the street as the Dr. Bowen house? A. Yes sir.
Q. How many houses is there between the Rich shop where you were and the Borden house? A. One.
Q. Is there other buildings, stables, etc., between? A. Yes sir.
Q. House lots also? A. Yes sir.
Q. What did you do after you heard of the stabbing? A. I went out and asked a man who was outside what he knew about it.
Q. Who else did you see? A. Miss Alice Russell.
Q. What did you do then? A. I crossed the street and had a talk with her.
Q. Did you walk along with her? A. Yes sir.
Q. What did you do when you got to the house? A. I said I wouldn't go in, and turned and walked away.
Q. Did you afterwards return? A. Yes sir.
Q. Did you see Officer Allen there? A. Yes sir.
Q. Where were you when you saw him? A. Near Mrs. Churchill's gate.
Q. Did you go to the house with him? A. Yes sir.
Q. Officer Allen was stationed there keeping people out? A. Yes sir.
Q. How long did you remain at the house? A. Until 6 o'clock.
Q. Who did you see inside the house? A. Miss Russell, Mrs. Churchill, Miss Lizzie and Bridget.
Q. Where were they? A. In the kitchen.
Q. Tell what Miss Lizzie was doing? A. She was sitting in a rocking chair, near the center of the room.
Q. Tell what the others were doing? A. Lizzie was sitting in the chair, and the others were administering to her, fanning her, etc.
Q. Were they rubbing her hands and doing what they could for her? A. Yes sir.
Q. Did you go near her? A. Within about three feet, I think.
Q. Was there anything about her that attracted your attention? A. Yes sir, she appeared distressed.
Q. Anything else? Anything about her dress, face, hands or hair? A. No sir.
Q. Were there any signs of blood on her dress, face, hands or hair? A. No sir.
Q. Can you tell what dress she had on? A. No sir.
Q. Can you tell whether her dress was light or dark? A. No sir.
Q. Where did you go after you left the kitchen? A. I went back into the entry leading from the front door.
Q. How long is this entry? A. Eight or 10 feet.
Q. Were you at any time out on the steps? A. Yes sir.
Q. Who was the first officer you saw after Mr. Allen left? A. The first one I recollect is Officer Dougherty.
Q. Have you an idea how long it was after Officer Allen left before Officer Dougherty came? A. About 15 minutes, I think.
Q. Did any one come with Mr. Dougherty? A. Yes sir.
Q. Do you know who it was? A. Mr. Wixon.
Q. Frank Wixon? A. Yes sir.
Q. Did they both go into the house? A. Yes sir.
Q. Who came next? A. I am not quite sure; I think Officer Mullaly followed right in with them.
Q. Who came next? A. I don't really know; Officer Harrington, I think.
Q. And where did you go to? A. All around the building.
Q. What do you mean by that? A. All around the front of the barn and of the door.
Q. You couldn't see the side door, could you? A. I didn't know there was one.
Q. You mean the front door of the barn? A. I mean the door facing the street.
Q. Do you remember seeing Albert Clarkson? A. Yes.
Q. Do you know if you came before or after Officer Fleet? A. Before.
Q. Were there any boys in the yard? A. Yes.
Q. Did you know any of them? A. I knew the Rich boy; I saw a great many I didn't know.
Q. How often did people come to the door? A. Every few minutes.
Q. Do you remember all who came? A. No.
Q. Did anybody go in while you were in the house? A. Dr. Bowen and Officers Dougherty and Mullaly.
Q. How long did you stop up stairs? A. Five minutes perhaps.
Q. What did you do then? A. I came down stairs and left.
Q. Did you see Officer Medley there? A. Not very early in the day.
Cross-examined.
Q. How soon did you know there had been a murder? A. Some time after it was committed.
Q. Before you went up stairs you knew of both murders? A. Yes.
Q. Did you shut or lock the door, the one that goes down cellar? A. I pushed the bolt.
Q. You mean the door inside the house? A. Yes.
Q. Why did you do it? A. I did it so that if there was anybody concealed there they couldn't get away.
Q. Were you afraid of an assassin coming down on you? A. I didn't feel just right.
Q. You were nervous weren't you? A. I didn't know what might come.

JOHN H. MANNING.

Newspaper Man Who Was Early at the Scene.

John H. Manning, a reporter of the Fall River Herald was the next witness.
Q. Were you a reporter last August? A. Yes.
Q. In Fall River? A. Yes.
Q. At what time did you hear of the murder? A. Some time after 11.
Q. How did you hear of it? A. Mr. O'Neil told me there had been a stabbing case.
Q. What time did you get the information? A. Between 25 minutes past and half past 11.
Q. How long were you going to the house? A. I don't know, I ran part of the way and walked part.
Q. Who did you see? A. At the stable I saw Mr. Cunningham.
Q. When you got to the house what did you do? A. I wasn't allowed to go in and waited around. Dr. Bowen went in and then Officer Dougherty, and I went in with him.
Q. When you got in who did you see? A. I saw Miss Borden on the lounge and Mrs. Churchill was with her; I went to the sitting room and saw the body of Mr. Borden on the lounge covered with a sheet. Dr. Bowen uncovered it, and with his fingers described the wounds. I saw blood on the walls. I went upstairs through a dark hallway into a bed chamber. Dr. Bowen went round the foot of the bed and between that and the dressing case.
Q. Do you recollect if it was dark? A. My impression is that it was not very light; some of the shutters were closed.
Q. Do you recollect the position of the body? A. Yes.
Q. How was it? A. The right arm was under the body.
Q. How about the left one? A. I don't recall.
Q. What else about the position of the body? A. Dr. Bowen and Officer Dougherty went around by it and bent down so they could see more clearly.
Q. What then? A. Then some one went down stairs and I followed.
Q. Who was it? A. I didn't know, but thought it was Mr. Morse.
Q. It was not Mr. Pettey? A. I don't know.
Q. What did you do down stairs? A. I saw Bridget Sullivan, had a talk with her and went to the yard.
Q. How long had you been in the house? A. Not over ten minutes.
Q. Did you see any officers on the north side of the house when you came out? A. I think I saw Assistant Marshal Fleet.
Q. Are you sure there was no one else? A. I am pretty sure.
Q. What did you then do? A. I went to the south side of the house, then examined a pile of lumber near the Kelly fence, and then went to the barn.
Q. Was there anybody there? A. Two or three persons.
Q. Was there anybody upstairs? A. I don't remember anybody.
Q. Did you see any boys there? A. I didn't.
Q. See any men? A. I saw Mr. Clarkson.
Q. What did you do after you came out of the barn? A. Walter Stevens and I looked around for footsteps in the yard, and tried the cellar door; it was fast.
Q. See Officer Medley there? A. No.
Q. Did you see him before you came away? A. I don't remember.
Q. Do you recall the story of Mrs. Reagan of the quarrel between the two sisters? A. Yes.
Q. Did you see her about it? A. Yes, the same night.
Q. Do you recall what was said? A. In answer to a question she said there was nothing in it.
Cross-examined.
Q. Where did you see her? A. I went to her house.
Q. You had no part in the affidavit? A. I was there.
Q. Did you read the report of the interview to her? A. Yes.
Q. Did she say anything about what she had to tell would be said on the stand? A. I don't recall.
Q. You don't undertake to say Officer Medley wasn't in the house when you were there? A. No.
Q. How near the body of Mrs. Borden was the bed when Mr. Dougherty moved it? A. There was room enough for Dr. Bowen to put his foot in the space between it.
Q. Do you remember that the shutters were partly shut or opened? A. My impression is that Dr. Bowen opened some of them.
Q. Who went to the barn with you? A. Mr. Stevens of the News.
Q. Did he search the yard with you? A. Yes.
Q. How long did you remain in the barn? A. A few minutes.
Q. Did you try the front door? A. No, I went to the front steps and looked them over.
Q. What were you looking for? A. Blood.
Q. Did you see any blood about Mr. Borden's body? A. Yes, on the parlor door and back of the sofa.
Q. The spots were not easily visible? A. Not unless you looked for them.
Q. Notice any other blood spots? A. I don't recall any.
Q. You were looking for blood spots? A. Yes.
Q. The door leading from the parlor to the hall was white, wasn't it? A. Yes.
Redirect.
Q. At the time you went to interview Mrs. Reagan you were also local agent for the Associated Press, weren't you? A. Yes.
Q. Was it or was it not in that capacity that you went to learn the truth or falsity of the reported interview? A. Partly in that capacity and partly in a local one.
Q. Mrs. Reagan understood you were a reporter? A. Yes.
Q. Reporters were numerous at that time, weren't they? A. Yes.
Q. And very persistent? A. You can answer that question yourself.

THOMAS HICKEY.

Mrs. Reagan Told Him the Gave Me Away Story Was False.

Thomas Hickey, a Fall River Globe reporter, was the next witness.
Q. Is your name Thomas H. Hickey? A. Yes sir.
Q. You are a reporter on the Fall River Globe? A. Yes sir.
Q. Were you reporter for the Fall River Globe last August? A. Yes sir.
Q. Also for the Boston Herald? A. Yes sir.
Q. In your capacity as a reporter did you see Mrs. Reagan in relation to the story published about a quarrel between Emma and her sister? A. Yes sir.
Q. Can you tell us when it was, i. e., after the publication? A. I think the publication was Thursday morning, and I think I saw Mrs. Reagan Friday morning.
Q. Now tell us what you said to her and what she said to you. A. I think I was sent to Mrs. Reagan's room by Mr. Billings, who was then in charge of the Boston Herald work in Fall River.
Q. What did you do? A. I remember going into Mrs. Reagan's room and making a remark something like this, "I see you are getting yourself in the paper, Mrs. Reagan." She laughed and said, "Yes, but I have got to take that all back." After some other questions which I have forgotten now, I remember I asked her about the alleged quarrel between Lizzie and Emma. I asked her if there had been a quarrel and she said "No." I asked her if she had repeated any words which had appeared in the paper, "You gave me away," and she said that she did not. Then I said, "Mrs. Reagan, there is absolutely no truth in the story that was printed?" and she said, "No sir, no truth at all."
Cross-examined.
Q. You were a representative of the Boston Herald? A. Yes sir.
Q. And whatever was published was in the Boston Globe? A. Yes sir.
Q. And the Boston Globe and the Boston Herald are papers of considerable prominence in the city of Boston? A. Yes sir.
Q. And in one sense they are sort of rivals?
Mr. Jennings—Wait a minute; how do we know anything about that?
The court will not interfere, said Chief Justice Mason.
Mr. Knowlton—I thought not. They are pretty active competitors, aren't they? A. Yes sir.
Q. When one gets an item of news that the other don't that comprises what they call a scoop, doesn't it? A. Yes sir.
Q. And in this particular instance the Boston Globe had got what was called a scoop, hadn't it? A. Yes sir.
Q. And your office was to say that the scoop was good for nothing wasn't it? A. I understood that the Herald had published the story.
Q. They hadn't had they? A. I did not see it.
Q. And you went into her room where she was on duty? A. Yes sir.
Q. Did anybody go with you? A. No sir.
Q. You went and introduced yourself as a reporter? A. Mrs. Reagan knew me.
Q. That was Friday morning and the publication was Thursday morning? A. Yes sir.
Q. And you were sent by Mr. Billings? A. Yes sir.
Q. Mr. Billings represented the Herald, that is, he was your superior officer? A. Yes sir.
Q. You published it in the Herald as soon as you got it from her? A. Yes sir.
Q. To show that the Globe scoop wasn't good for anything, that was what you were sent for, wasn't it? A. I sent the Herald Mrs. Reagan's story.
Q. That was what you were sent for, wasn't it? A. Yes sir.

Unimportant Evidence.

Isaac B. White was called, but could not be found.
James Renwick was the next witness.
Q. Your name? A. James C. Renwick.
Q. Are you an undertaker? A. Yes sir.
Q. Did you have charge of the funeral of Andrew J. Borden and his wife? A. Yes sir.
Q. When you prepared the body for the grave did you observe whether he had any ring on his finger? A. I do not remember.
Q. Did you see him have any ring upon his finger while you were having anything to do with the body? A. I don't remember, it was so long ago.
Charles J. Holmes was called, but he was not in the court house.

MARY R. HOLMES.

One of the Most Interesting Witnesses of the Forenoon.

Mrs. Mary R. Holmes was next called, and her testimony was listened to with a marked degree of attention by all in the court room.
Q. Are you the wife of Charles J. Holmes? A. Yes sir.
Q. Do you live in Fall River? A. Yes sir.
Q. Do you know Lizzie Borden? A. Yes sir.
Q. How long? A. I have known who she was from her childhood, and she went to school with my daughters.
Q. Is she a member of the same church as yourself? A. Yes sir.
Q. What church is it? A. The Central Congregational church of Fall River.
Q. Did she take part in the various church enterprises and benevolent work? A. Yes, same as all the young people.
Q. What? Witness started to answer, but Mr. Knowlton interposed an objection.
Chief Justice—I think this line of examination is competent.
Q. You were engaged with her in some church enterprises? A. I am somewhat older than she is, and while I know she is identified with church work of various kinds, I could not say that I was particularly associated with her.
Q. You were connected with her in regard to some hospital? A. Yes sir.
Q. What hospital is it? A. It is the Fall River hospital, sometimes known as the House of the Good Samaritan.
Q. It's a charitable institution isn't it? A. Yes sir.
Q. Are you a member of some board with her connected with the hospital? A. Yes sir, the woman's board.
Q. How long have you known her personally and been connected with her in this work? A. We have been on the same board between two and three years.
Q. Did you know Mrs. Abby Durfee Borden? A. I was very little acquainted with her personally, but I have known who she was for a great many years.
Q. Did they come to church together? A. They did.
Q. And go away together? A. They did.
Q. When did you first hear of the murder? A. At quarter of 12 on the day it occurred.
Q. What did you do? A. I went first to a neighbor's house.
Q. Did you go to the Borden house? A. I did at 1 o'clock. I first went to Dr. Bowen's and he went there with me.
Q. What did you do after you arrived there? A. Sat down in the kitchen.
Q. What then occurred? A. Some one told me that Lizzie would like to see me, and I went up stairs to her room.
Q. Who was there? A. I can't tell; there were a great many up there. Some of them were talking with her.
Q. Were they officers? A. I think they were.
Q. Were you there at any time when Dr. Bowen was there and Mr. Fleet came in? A. I was.
Q. Who came first? A. The house was full of men. My impression is that Dr. Bowen—
Mr. Knowlton objected, and said: "I beg your pardon, madam, but you go beyond the questions." Witness replied: "I'm not surprised; I'm not much used to this business."
Q. When the officers wanted to search did any one hold the door? A. Yes sir.
Q. Was there any resistance to the officers in opening the door? A. I hardly know how to answer. The door was held until we were asked whether they should be allowed to enter the room.
Q. After Mr. Fleet came in what was done and said? A. Mr. Fleet said he wanted to ask some questions, and Lizzie said, "Please be brief, I am weary; I have answered so many questions."
Q. Anything else? A. When Lizzie was asked where she was, she said she went to the barn for a piece of lead or iron or tin to fix the screens. I don't know which one of these things it was she said, for she has said that she went for all these things, at different times.
Q. Was a search made? A. Yes, the officers wanted to search her room, and they made a thorough search, as I called it.
Q. Who told them they could make the search? A. Miss Lizzie.
Q. Where was she at this time? A. She was lying on the lounge, paying no attention to what was going on, and scarcely opened her eyes.
Q. Tell us about this search? A. The officers looked thoroughly about the room; they looked back of the portieres; over, under and about the bed; looked into the closet that was used as a toilet room; looked over the shelves and all around, and made what I call a very thorough search. Then they went into Emma's room and came back.
Q. What was Lizzie doing all this time? A. She was lying on the lounge.
Q. What time did you go away? A. Half past 8.
Q. Will you tell us anything about Lizzie's conduct at the funeral, more particularly as to her conduct with reference to the dead body of her father?
Mr. Knowlton objected and the question was not pressed.
Q. Tell us about her conduct on the day of the funeral? A. Did Miss Lizzie go down to see her father's remains before the funeral?
Mr. Knowlton—Wait a minute, wait a minute. I pray your honors' judgment.
A long consultation followed, during which the counsel were called to the desk by the chief justice in order that the jury might not hear what was said. After the matter had been discussed it was decided that the answer might be given as preliminary and witness replied, "She did."
Q. Where were the bodies? A. In the sitting room.
Q. Were both bodies in that room? A. They were.
Q. What did Miss Lizzie do after she went down into the room?
Mr. Knowlton again objected, and after a tedious wait, during which the judges and counsel were in consultation the examination proceeded without the witness being required to answer.
Q. When viewing her father did Lizzie shed tears? A. Yes.
(At this time Lizzie sat immovable, with her handkerchief pressed closely to her eyes.)
Q. Did you see any handkerchiefs on the day of the murder? A. I can't say if it was that day or the day after.
Q. In what condition were they? A. Part were ironed and part were rough dried.
Q. What was done with them. A. The ironed ones were put in the bureau; I don't know what was done with the others.
Q. What dress did Lizzie have on the morning of the murder? A. A wrapper striped pink and white.
Q. How many days were you there? A. I went there on the morning of the 4th of August, and was there parts of every day till Lizzie was arrested.
Q. See this dress, (showing the dark blue one with the figure that has been in court all the time of the trial); what do you say to it? A. Lizzie had it on that morning and I think on Friday morning.
Q. What did she wear at the funeral? A. I don't know the material; it was a black dress.
Q. Was Lizzie a member of the party that went to Marion? A. She was to be, but didn't go.
Q. Do you remember the published story of the quarrel between the two sisters? A. I do.
Q. Do you remember having a talk with Mrs. Reagan subsequently? A. Yes, why, yes; I don't know exactly how to answer.
Q. What did Mrs. Reagan say? A. She said, "You know, Mrs. Holmes, that wasn't so; we were talking about an egg.
Q. Where was the talk? A. In the matron's room.
Q. What time was it? A. Some time on Friday, Aug. 6th.
Q. Do you remember that some time after this conversation there was some talk about Mrs. Reagan's signing a paper? A. It was the same night.
Q. Where were you? A. I was sitting in the room. A gentleman came in and talked with her. She came back and seemed excited. She sat down and had some conversation, but not with me.
Q. Did you hear any part of it? A. Not distinctly enough to repeat it.
Q. Did you hear anything else about the interview? A. She didn't talk to me.
Q. Can you state any portion of that conversation? A. No.
Q. Who was she talking to? A. I don't know. She seemed to be speaking generally.
Q. Was Emma there? A. I think not.
Q. Was Miss Lizzie there? A. I don't remember.
Q. Have you now stated all the conversation between you and Mrs. Reagan relating to the quarrel? A. All that took place after it.
Q. Did you hear her say anything about signing a paper? A. I heard her say she would if Marshal Hilliard agreed.
Q. When was that? A. Just after talking with the gentleman before going out of the room.
Cross-examination.
Q. Did Lizzie occupy the matron's room? A. She did.
Q. She received her friends in that room? A. Certain friends.
Q. Those that she wanted? A. No sir, I think there were exceptions made.
Q. You went when you pleased? A. Yes sir.
Q. You do not know of anybody who was refused? A. I do not think of any.
Q. Her counsel, of course, went when they pleased? A. Yes sir.
Q. And the pastors when they pleased? A. Yes sir.
Q. And her sister? A. Yes sir.
Q. She was there quite a while after this episode? A. Yes; until she went to Taunton.
Q. That was some weeks afterwards? A. I am sure I cannot remember.
At this point the usual forenoon recess of five minutes was given the jury.

CHARLES J. HOLMES

Reads Mrs. Reagan's Denial of the Sisters' Quarrel.

Charles J. Holmes was the first witness after the recess.
Q. What is your name? A. Charles J. Holmes.
Q. What is your occupation? A. I am a banker.
Q. Are you treasurer of the Five Cent Savings bank of Fall River? A. I am.
Q. How long have you lived in Fall River? A. Forty years.
Q. Did you know Andrew J. Borden? A. I did.
Q. Do you know Miss Lizzie Borden? A. I do.
Q. Were you present at the district court at Fall River the first day of the hearing there? A. I was.
Q. Do you know anything about any paper that was prepared for Mrs. Reagan to sign? A. I do.
Q. Do you know anything about the nature of the paper, what was the substance of it? A. I do.
Q. Well, what was it? A. That the statements that had been previously made in a paper were not true.
Mr. Knowlton objected to the question and answer and the court ruled that they be stricken out.
Q. What was said to her in the reading of that paper?
Mr. Knowlton—I object.
The court—The question should be made clearer.
Q. Was the paper read aloud to Mrs. Reagan? A. It was.
Q. Did you hear it read to her? A. I did.
Q. Won't you state the substance of what you heard read to her?
Mr. Knowlton—I object.
The witness said that he had a copy of the paper in his pocket, and Mr. Knowlton said that Mr. Jennings might look at the paper, and if he recognized it as being a copy of the original he had no objection to the witness reading it.
Mr. Jennings said it was a copy of the original, and the witness read as follows:
"This is to certify that my attention has been called to a report said to have been made by me in regard to a quarrel between Lizzie and her sister Emma, in which Lizzie said to Emma, you have given me away; and that I expressly and positively deny that any such conversation took place. And I further deny that I ever saw anything that could be construed as a quarrel between the sisters."
Q. After that was read to Mrs. Reagan, did Mrs. Reagan say anything about it? A. She said it was true.
Q. Anything else? A. Do you mean what was done?
Q. Yes. A. Mr. Buck read the statement to her; she said it was true and she was asked if she was willing to sign the document. She said she was willing if the marshal didn't object.
Q. What took place then? A. Then

(Continued on Fourth Page.)

A world of misery is implied in the words "Sick Headache" A world of relief is wrapped up in a twenty-five cent box of

Beecham's Pills

(Tasteless)

35

CARRIAGES!

—AT—

A. DAVIS ASHLEY'S,

947 Acushnet Avenue,

IN ENDLESS VARIETY.

New and Secondhand for sale and exchanged. We trade quick and often and give you an equivalent for your money.

—ALSO—

Several Horses!

For sale LOW to clean out the lot. Call early and get your money's worth at

A. DAVIS ASHLEY'S,

947 Acushnet Avenue,

Cor. Coggeshall Street.

HATCH & COMPANY'S EXPRESS,

No. 5 Ricketson Block, New Bedford,

DAILY,

By Passenger Trains, to all Points on the Old Colony Railroad and its Connections.

PROFESSIONAL CARDS.

DR. B. C. HOWLAND,
Physician and Surgeon.
Office and Residence—31 Eighth st., northwest corner of William and Eighth streets.
Office Hours—8 to 9 a. m., 2 to 4 and 7 to 8 p. m.
Telephone 135—1.

J. F. SULLIVAN, M. D,
Physician and Surgeon.
Office and Residence—158 Middle street.
Office Hours—8 to 11 a. m., 2 to 4 and 7 to 3 p. m.
Telephone 244—6.

DR. WILLIAM LILLEY.
Office and Residence—77 Thomas street.
Office Hours—From 8 to 12 a. m., 3 to 8 p. m.
Cancers, Tumors and Female Weaknesses a specialty.

DR. A. F. WYMAN,
Dental Rooms,
13 Purchase Street.
Dinner Hour—1 p. m. to 2 p. m.

A. MARTIN PIERCE, M. D.
Physician and Surgeon.
Office and Residence—26 South Sixth street.
Office Hours—2 to 5 and 7 to 8 p. m.

CHAS. R. HUNT, M. D.,
Physician and Surgeon.
Office and Residence—Cor. Union and Seventh streets.
Office Hours—8 to 9 a. m., 2 to 4 and 7 to 8 p. m.
Telephone 64—3.

E. EVERETT WAITE, M. D.
OFFICE AND RESIDENCE, 17 Seventh, corner Spring Street.
Consulting hours, 1 to 3 and 7 to 8 P. M.
Telephone, 105-3.

AMOS P. WEBBER, M. D.,
Office Hours—2 to 4 and 7 to 8 30 p. m.

WILLIAM H. WEBBER, Dentist.
Office Hours—9 a. m. to 5 p. m.
250 Union st., opp. Opera House. Tel. 251—6.

W. J. NICKERSON, M. D.,
Physician and Surgeon.
Office and Residence—164 Middle street.
Office Hours—8 to 9 a. m., 2 to 4 and 7 to 8 p. m.
Brinkerhoff System for Rectal Diseases.
Telephone No. 238—1.

A. M. BIGELOW, M. D. V.,
Veterinary Surgeon.
Office and Residence cor. Fourth and Walnut Sts., at Mr. Alfred Wilson's.
Telephone..........104-13
Office hours until 9 A. M. 1 to 2 and 6 to 7 30 P. M.

Dr. EDWARD PEIRCE.
44 FIFTH STREET,
Physician and Surgeon.
Office Hours 9 A. M. 2 to 4 and 7 to 8 P. M.
Telephone—41-4.

DR. EDW. M. WHITNEY.
Office 31 Fifth street.
Office Hours—From 9 a. m. to 2 p. m.
Telephone 278—6.

JOHN T. BULLARD, M. D.
Office and Residence—446 County street, opposite the Court House.
Office Hours—9 a. m., 2 to 4 and 7 to 8 p. m.
Telephone 331—12.

WM. CLINTON SHEEHY, M. D.
Physician & Surgeon,
Office and Residence, 174 Purchase Street.
Office Hours—Until 8 A. M., 2 to 4 and 7 to 8 P. M. Telephone 285—6.

DR. G. DeN. HOUGH.
Office and Residence—542 County street.
Office Hours—at 2 and at 7 P. M.
Telephone 1—5.

REMOVAL.
WILLIAM G. POTTER, M. D.
Office and Residence removed to No. 8 Fifth street, between Union and Spring sts.
Office Hours—8 to 9 A. M., 2 to 4 and 7 to 8 P. M.
Telephone—151-3.

DR. WILLIAM E. BROWNELL,
Physician and Surgeon.
Office and Residence—271 Union street.
Office Hours—8 a. m., 2 to 4 and 7 to 8 36 p. m.
Telephone 310—4.

DR. VERMYNE.
Office and Residence—No. 2 Orchard street, corner of Arnold street.
Office Hours—10 30 a. m. to 1 p. m., and 2 to 4 p. m.; Sunday, 12 to 1.

DR. E. H. NOBLE,
Physician and Surgeon.
(Formerly Dr. Spencer's Office.) Opposite City Clock. Residence 129 Will s st.
Office hours: 8 to 9 A. M., 1 to 3 and 7 to 9 P. M.
Telephone connection.

J. F. BENNETT DRUMMOND, M. D
Office—174 Purchase street, Lewis building, Room 2.
Office Hours—9 to 10 a. m.; 2 to 4, 6 to 8 p. m.
Residence—36 South Second street.

J. C. SHAW, M. D.
Office and Residence—Cor. Sixth and School streets
Office Hours—2 to 4 and 7 to 8 p. m. Sunday, 2 and 7 p. m. Telephone 334-1.

MILTON H. LEONARD, M. D.
Office and Residence..........No. 62 Fifth St.
Office Hours—2 to 4 and 7 to 8 P. M.
Telephone 67—12.

CHAS. A. B. PETERSON, M. D.,
Physician and Surgeon.
Office—74 Purchase street.
Residence—90 Hillman street.
Office Hours—9 a. m., 2 to 4 and 7 to 8 p. m.
Telephone 2—3.

H. H. DEWS, D. V. S.
Veterinary Surgeon.
Office—I. L. Ashley's Stable, No. 20 Fourth St
Office Hours—9 to 10; 2 to 4; 7 to 8.
Telephone, 282—1.

Dr. W. W. MANN,
Dental Parlors,........174 Purchase St.
Lewis Building. Rooms 3 and 4.
Office Hours—9 to 12 A. M. and 1 to 5 P. M.

DR. CHAS. D. PRESCOTT.
Office and Residence—Cor. Eighth and William streets.
Office Hours—From 2 to 4 and 7 to 8 p. m.

E. J. WEEKS, D.D.S.
Dental Rooms—74 Purchase street.
Office Hours—9 to 12 m., 2 to 4 p. m.

C. L. SEIP, M. D.
Office and Residence—Cor. County and Union streets. Telephone 127—1.
Office Hours—8 to 10 a.m., 2 to 4 and 7 to 8 p.m.

UNDERTAKERS.

E. T. WILSON,
Undertaker & Embalmer,
80 PLEASANT STREET.
(Odd Fellows' Building.)

CASKETS, Coffins, Robes, and Flowers furnished at short notice. All orders in or out of the city will receive prompt personal attention day or night.

Arterial Embalming a Specialty.

Persons wishing my services nights or Sundays will please call at my
Residence.............. 152 William Street
Telephone number 179—3. d&w

R. G. BENNETT,
UNDERTAKER and EMBALMER,
356 Acushnet Avenue,
(Third door South of New Post Office.)
A choice stock of Caskets, Robes and Funeral Supplies. All orders in or out of the city receive prompt attention. Office Telephone, 151—5. Residence Telephone, 346—4. Residence, 47 Chestnut Street, corner Hillman. Orders nights and Sundays received at residence or at Kirby & Hicks' Stable, 60 Elm street, corner Pleasant. d19-d&wtf

WESTON C. VAUGHAN, JR.,
Undertaker and Embalmer,
331 AND 323 PURCHASE STREET.

CASKETS, Coffins, Robes and Flowers, furnished at short notice. Funerals attended in or out of the city. All orders from neighboring towns by express or otherwise promptly attended to. Telephone connection day or night. Residence, 323 Purchase street. Night bell promptly answered. Telephone number 201—7.

INSURANCE.

FIRE & LIGHTNING,
TORNADO,
PLATE GLASS and ACCIDENT
INSURANCE.

No. 48 North Water Street.

Etna Ins. Co.	Hartford
Hartford Fire Ins. Co.	Hartford
Connecticut Fire Ins. Co.	Hartford
Merchants Ins. Co.	Providence
Equitable F. & M. Ins. Co.	Providence
Springfield F. & M. Ins. Co.	Springfield
Ins. Co. of North America	Philadelphia
Ins. Co. of State of Penn.	Philadelphia
Fire Association	Philadelphia
Home Ins. Co.	New York
Continental Ins. Co.	New York
German Am. Ins. Co.	New York
Niagara Fire Ins. Co.	New York
Williamsburgh City Fire Ins. Co.	New York
Hanover Fire Ins. Co.	New York
Phenix Assurance Co.	London
Guardian Assurance Co.	London
No. British & Mer. Ins. Co.	London
Imperial Fire Ins. Co.	London
Fitchburg Mut. Fire Ins. Co.	Fitchburg
Dorchester Mut. Fire Ins. Co.	Neponset
New York Plate Glass Ins. Co.	New York
U. S. Mutual Accident Asso.	New York

GEO. N. ALDEN.
(Successor to Tillinghast & Alden.) d&w

SAMUEL H. COOK. FREDERIC A. BROWNELL.

SAMUEL H. COOK & CO.,
Marine & Fire Insurance
AGENT AND BROKER,
No. 37 North Water Street.
(In National Bank of Commerce Building.)
Whaling Risks and their Catchings a Specialty at This Agency.
The following First Class Fire Insurance Companies are represented, viz:

Hingham Mutual Fire Ins. Co.	Hingham
Phenix Ins. Co.	Hartford
National Fire Ins. Co.	Hartford
Phenix Ins. Co.	New York
Westchester Fire Ins. Co.	New York
Commerce Ins. Co.	Albany
Pennsylvania Fire Ins. Co.	Philadelphia
American Fire Ins. Co.	Philadelphia
Royal Ins. Co.	England
Queen Ins. Co.	London
London Assurance Corp.	London
Norwich Union F. Ins. Society	London
Northern Assurance Co.	London
Providence Washington Ins. Co.	Providence
Firemen's Fire Ins. Co.	Boston
The Metropolitan Plate Glass Ins. Co.	New York
Hartford Steam Boiler Inspection and Ins. Co.	Hartford

EDWIN EMERY. JOHN H. PEDRO

LAWRENCE GRINNELL & CO.,
Fire and Marine, Life and Plate Glass
Insurance
60 No. Water St., foot of William,
(Over Mechanics' National Bank)

Liverpool & London & Globe Ins. Co.	Liverpool
American Fire Ins. Co.	New York
London & Lancashire Ins. Co.	Liverpool
Commercial Union Assurance Co.	London
Merchants' Ins. Co	Newark
Boylston Ins. Co.	Boston
United States Ins. Co.	New York
Caledonian Ins. Co.	Scotland
Hamburg-Bremen Fire Ins. Co.	Bremen
American Ins. Co.	Boston
Spring Garden Ins. Co.	Philadelphia
Lowell Mutual Fire Ins. Co.	Lowell
Wachusett Mutual Fire Ins. Co.	Fitchburg
Mutual Life Ins. Co.	New York
Lloyd's Plate Glass Ins. Co.	New York

HIRAM VAN CAMPEN. JOHN W. PAUL.

HIRAM VAN CAMPEN & CO.,
FIRE, LIFE AND ACCIDENT
Insurance Agency,
No. 15 North Water Street.
Telephone Call .... 241-2.
(Established A. D. 1852.)
The following First Class Companies are represented:

Sun Fire Office. Organized A. D. 1710.	London, Eng.
The Reliance Ins. Co.	Philadelphia
Girard Fire & Marine Ins. Co.	"
United Firemen's Ins. Co.	"
Granite State Fire Ins. Co.,	Portsmouth, N.H.
Firemen's Ins. Co.	Newark, N. J.
Newark Fire Ins Co.	"
New Jersey Plate Glass Ins. Co.	"
First National Fire Ins. Co.,	Worcester, Mass.
Quincy Mut. Fire Ins. Co.	Quincy, Mass.
Holyoke Mut. Fire Ins. Co.	Salem, Mass.
Traders' & Mechanics' Ins. Co.	Lowell, Mass.
Dorchester Mut. Fire Ins. Co.	Boston
Cambridge Mut. Fire Ins. Co.	Cambridgeport, Mass.
Standard Life and Accident Ins. Co. (Employes Liability Dept.)	Detroit, Mich.
Travellers' Ins. Co., Hartford Life & Accident.	

All losses equitably adjusted and promptly paid.
New Bedford, November, 1892.

IVORY S. CORNISH. CLIFTON H. CORNISH

I. S. CORNISH & SON,
Life, Fire, Accident and Plate Glass
—INSURANCE—
Agents and Brokers. 50 North Second St.
NEW BEDFORD, MASS. tf

C. W. HASKINS
No. 20 PURCHASE STREET,
Has replenished his stock since the holidays, and now offers at very low prices a good variety of Diamond Rings, Fine Jewelry, Gold and Silver Watches, Chains, &c.
His stock of Sterling Silver Spoons, Forks, Fancy Table Ware and Novelties is very extensive; these goods are lower in price than ever before.
18 KARAT WEDDING RINGS
A SPECIALTY.
You can save money buying of him your Spectacles and Eye Glasses, fit and quality guaranteed.
Watch, Clock and Jewelry repairing by experienced workmen.

HARDY HITCH, JR.,
Awning, Carpet and Shade Upholsterer,
195 UNION STREET.
(Masonic Building.)
Telephone - - - - 153-12

HER SISTER.

(Continued from Third Page.)

Mr. Buck and Mrs. Reagan went down stairs.

Q. Do you know what happened after that? Did you see her again? A. Yes, after some interval of time she came back with several other parties, and they went into the matron's room.

Q. Did you go in with them? A. I did not.

Q. Did you hear anything that took place afterwards in regard to this matter? A. Personally I did not hear the conversation that took place in there.

Q. Is that all you know about the matter? A. I heard part of an altercation down stairs after the refusal of the marshal to have it signed.

Q. That was nothing that Mrs. Reagan said? A. Nothing that Mrs. Reagan said.

Cross-examined.

Q. Who was the altercation between, Mr. Holmes? A. I do not know the names of the parties; there were 20 or 30 in the corridor. I was up stairs near the matron's room and the altercation was down below in the corridor.

Q. Was there the voice of any one that you knew? A. I heard Mr. Jennings' voice.

Q. Whose else did you hear? A. A reporter whose name I do not know, but I think I've heard him spoken of as Mr. Porter.

Q. Was he a reporter of the Boston Globe? A. I can hardly say what paper. There was a very heated conversation between the parties, and I had the idea he was connected with a Fall River paper in some way.

Q. Who had this affidavit when it was read? A. Mr. Buck.

Q. Who was present besides Mr. Buck? A. Dr. Bowen and several parties came while it was being read. When Mr. Buck came out of the room with the matron Dr. Bowen and myself were standing by the window talking, and no one else was present. But before the thing was concluded there were six or seven present.

Q. Where were they? A. I do not know. I only knew that Dr. Bowen was there. While I was talking some policemen came up.

Q. Was Mr. Jennings there? A. No sir.

Q. Do you know the name of the policeman? A. There was no policeman there that I recognized.

Q. Did you know Mrs. Reagan? A. Yes.

Q. Was there anybody in the corridor? A. Dr. Bowen and myself.

Q. How long had the court been adjourned? A. Not over 15 minutes.

Q. Had the crowd gone out? A. Not many were there.

Q. Had you been present every day in court? A. Yes.

Q. You attended as a friend of Miss Borden? A. Yes.

Q. And accompanied her to and from the court room? A. Yes.

Q. The same is true of Mr. Buck, isn't it? A. Yes.

Q. Had Mrs. Reagan been summoned as a witness at that hearing? A. I don't know.

Q. Nothing had appeared but a publication in a paper? A. That's all.

Q. Was that was wanted to do was to deny a newspaper report, was it? A. Yes.

Q. What did she say about the affidavit? A. She said it was true.

Q. Did she say she must see Marshal Hilliard? A. No.

Q. Wasn't it an exciting day? A. No.

Q. And everybody was strained up? A. Not more than on other days.

Q. And very few were calm? A. I can hardly answer that yes or no.

Q. You were trying to get a denial of a newspaper story? A. I was.

Q. For what purpose? A. For publication.

Q. For what purpose? A. To get a contradiction of the story.

Q. What for? A. Because I thought it ought to be done.

Q. It was not to have an effect in court, was it? A. No.

Q. It was only to correct one story, was it? A. That's all.

Q. There were all kinds of stories then being published, weren't there? A. Yes.

Q. And you only wanted one corrected? A. Yes. For a particular purpose.

Q. She didn't sign the affidavit, did she? A. No.

Q. Did you hear her say that what she had to say would be in court? A. I did not.

John R. Caldwell.

John R. Caldwell was the next witness.

Q. What is your business? A. A reporter.

Q. Do you recall the time Mrs. Reagan was asked to sign a paper? A. I recall the day.

Q. Where was anything done? A. In the corridor outside the matron's room.

Q. Did you see or hear what the paper contained? A. I saw it read, but did not hear.

Q. What was done afterwards? A. Mrs. Reagan took the paper and went down stairs. She said something I could not hear, and I heard the marshal say, "If you sign it, it will be against my orders." Then he saw me and ordered me out of the room.

Cross-examined by Mr. Knowlton.

Q. Did you go out pretty quick? A. I went after remonstrating with the marshal.

Q. Did you hear him say, "Whatever you say, you'll say in court"? A. I did not.

Q. Were there many about the corridor? A. Yes.

Q. Were there many reporters there? A. Yes.

Q. When Mrs. Reagan went down stairs did the crowd follow her? A. Some did.

Q. Who else went to the guard room with you? A. Mrs Percy.

Q. Where is she now? A. In Europe.

Mrs. Brigham was called.

Q. Your name? A. Mary E. Brigham.

Q. Your residence? A. Fall River.

Q. Do you know Lizzie Borden? A. Yes sir.

Q. How long have you known her? A. All her life.

Q. Went to school with her? A. Yes sir.

Q. Do you attend the same church? A. Yes sir.

Q. Are you in the habit of visiting each other? A. Yes sir.

Q. How frequently? A. Quite frequently.

Q. Do you remember what was said by Mrs. Reagan about the quarrel of the sisters? A. Yes sir.

Q. Where did it occur? A. In the matron's room, at the time a paper was brought to her to sign.

Q. Tell what was said and done? A. I saw Mr. Buck with a paper in his hand.

Q. Did Mrs. Reagan leave the room? Yes sir.

Q. And afterwards came back? A. Yes sir.

Q. After she came back tell how she appeared. A. She acted mad.

Q. Mad? A. Yes sir.

Q. What did she do and say? A. She

sat down beside me just as near to me as she could sit and commenced to talk. She said she would have signed the paper if the marshal would let her, and that she would rather leave the place than be lied about so.

Cross-examined by Mr. Knowlton.

Q. Did you hear the paper read in the corridor? A. No sir.

THE PRISONER'S SISTER.

Miss Emma L. Borden the Most Interesting Witness of the Trial.

As the next witness was called every eye was turned toward the door to catch a glimpse of her as she entered. It was the prisoner's sister, and as she came in she appeared greatly embarrassed. She quickly recovered herself, however, and answered the questions put to her promptly.

Q. Your name? A. Emma L. Borden.

Q. You are a sister of Lizzie Borden? A. Yes.

Q. How long have you lived in the home where you were living at the time of the tragedy? A. I think about 21 years.

Q. Lizzie, yourself, your father and Mrs. Borden had lived there during this time? A. Yes sir.

Q. Do you know what property Lizzie had at the time of the murder? A. Yes sir.

Q. Can you produce evidence of it? Yes sir.

Witness handed envelopes and documents to Mr. Jennings, who proceeded to enumerate them. The effects comprised $107 subject to check on deposit with the B. M. C. Durfee Safe Deposit & Trust company; a deposit of $2,000 in the Massasoit National bank, subject to check; a deposit of $500 in the Union Savings bank; $141 in the Fall River Five Cents Savings bank; four shares of the Merchants Manufacturing company of one issue, and five shares of the Merchants Manufacturing company of another issue.

MISS EMMA L. BORDEN.

[From a Sketch by Mr. Ashley, of the Standard.]

Q. Did your father wear a ring on his finger? A. Yes sir.

Q. Was that the only article of jewelry he wore? A. Yes sir.

Q. How long had he worn it before his death? A. Ten or 15 years.

Q. Did he wear it constantly? A. Yes sir.

Q. Was it upon his finger when he was buried? A. Yes sir.

Q. Have you an inventory of the clothes which were in the clothes closet on the Saturday afternoon of the search? A. Yes sir.

Q. Can you produce it? A. Yes sir. (Witness held it up in her hand.)

Q. When was it made up? A. About a week ago.

Q. Was it compiled from your recollection? A. Yes sir.

Q. Were you there on the afternoon of the search? A. Yes sir.

Q. Do you know what dresses there were there? A. Yes sir.

Q. How many dresses were there in the closet? A. About 18 or 19.

Q. Whose were they? A. They all belonged to my sister and I except one that belonged to Mrs. Borden.

Q. How many of them were blue? A. Ten.

Q. To whom did the blue dresses belong? A. Two to me and eight to my sister.

Q. You were there the Saturday afternoon that the search was going on what was said? A. I heard you say——

Mr. Jennings—You can't tell what I said.

Q. Did you hear Dr. Dolan say anything? A. I heard Dr. Dolan say——

Mr. Knowlton—I object.

Chief Justice—If you propose to show that Dr. Dolan has made any statement different than he made on the stand you may put the question.

Mr. Jennings—I desire to make it a base of subsequent acts.

Mr. Knowlton—On that ground I certainly object.

The question was not insisted upon.

Q. What, if anything, did Dr. Dolan say to you as to the character of the search?

Mr. Knowlton—I object.

Chief Justice—You may show it.

A. He told me that it was as thorough a search as could be made unless the paper was torn from the wall and the carpets taken from the floor.

Q. Now without telling me what I said, I communicate to you what Marshal Hilliard said in regard to the search of the upper portions of the house?

Mr. Knowlton—Wait a minute, I object.

Mr. Jennings—I will add "as to whether it was completed or not."

Mr. Knowlton—I object.

The Court—The counsel should state a little more fully.

Mr. Knowlton—I object to the substance of the question.

Then followed a consultation between Mr. Jennings, Mr. Knowlton and the judges, and Mr. Jennings further modified his question by adding, "Did I communicate to you what your sister Miss Lizzie?"

A. You did.

Q. And when was that? A. Saturday afternoon.

Q. Was that after they had taken a dress away; after a dress had been given them? A. Yes sir.

Q. Was that after they had received the other things they took that afternoon? A. I think so.

Q. Can you tell what time in the evening it was? A. I think about 6 o'clock.

Q. They had been searching all the afternoon, had they? A. Yes sir.

Q. Was that at the time they were going away? A. Yes sir.

Q. I ask you, Miss Emma, to state what I said to you Marshal Hilliard in regard to the search of the upper portions of the house. A. You said everything had been examined, every box and bag.

Q. Was anything said about the cellar? A. Yes, I think there was.

Q. What was it? A. I think he said there would be a search in some portion of the cellar Monday.

Q. Whether or not you or Lizzie furnished assistance to the search? A. We both went to the attic to assist.

Q. Did both of you assist them? A. All we could.

Q. Do you know of a Bedford cord dress that Lizzie wore? A. Yes sir.

Q. Will you describe it? A. It was a light blue ground.

Q. Do you know when it was made? A. Yes, in the spring.

Q. Where was it made. A. At our house.

Q. What was the material as to cost? A. It was very cheap; either 12 1-2 or 15 cents a yard.

Q. How was it trimmed? A. With a ruffle around the bottom.

Q. Did you or Lizzie assist in making it? A. Yes.

Q. Was the work carried on? A. In the guest chamber.

Q. When was this dress-maker many years? A. Yes, a number.

Q. Did she make more than one dress for your sister at that time? A. Yes, several.

Q. Which one was made first? A. The Bedford cord.

Q. Do you remember Lizzie getting paint on this dress? A. Yes.

Q. When was the paint? A. Some on the front and some on the wrong side.

Q. When was the dress put on after it was done? A. I think the next morning.

Q. Where was the dress on the Saturday of the search? A. I saw it hanging in the clothes press.

Q. What time was this? A. I think about 3 o'clock.

Q. Did you say anything about seeing it in consequence of not doing a nail on which to hang your dress? A. I did.

Q. What did you say?

Mr. Knowlton objected, but the question was admitted.

Q. What did you say? A. I said, "Why haven't you destroyed that old dress yet?"

Q. Did Lizzie say anything? A. I don't remember.

Q. Where was the dress prior to the murder? A. I don't know.

Q. Was the material in condition to be made over? A. No.

Q. Was it soiled, but faded.

Q. How long was the dress? A. So long that in the back it trailed an inch.

Q. How long was it as compared with other dresses that she had? A. Longer than others, except trained dresses.

Q. How was it as to the waist? A. Full in front.

Q. Did she have any dress on over that one? A. No.

Q. How do you know? A. Because that one was too full.

Q. What dress did Lizzie have on at the funeral? A. A black net.

Q. Did she have the blue wrapper on under? A. No.

Q. Was she lying down with the pink wrapper on? A. Yes.

Q. When did you next see the Bedford cord dress? A. Sunday morning.

Q. Tell the court and the jury about that Sunday morning? A. I heard Lizzie's voice and saw that she was standing in the room. She said, "I think I'll burn this old dress." I said, "Why do you" or "I wouldn't," or something of that sort. Then I turned away to wash the dishes.

Q. Were the windows open? A. Yes.

Q. Were there officers around? A. Yes.

Q. What time was this? A. I think about 9 o'clock. Q. Had you been to breakfast? A. Yes.

Q. Was Miss Russell there? A. Yes.

Q. What was your or your sister's custom with regard to old rags?

Objection was made by Mr. Knowlton. "I withdraw the question for the moment with your honors' permission," said Mr. Jennings.

Q. Did you or your sister keep a rag bag?

Objection was made and the question was excluded.

Q. What was done with pieces of cloth or pieces of old dresses that you had to dispose of?

Mr. Knowlton—I object.

Q. Or that your sister had to dispose of?

Mr. Knowlton—I object.

The question was excluded.

Q. Do you know of your sister's habit of burning old dresses previous to this time?

Mr. Knowlton—I object.

The court—That is excluded.

Mr. Jennings—Save my exceptions to that, your honor.

Q. What happened next Miss Emma? Do you recall any reference to this dress, anything being said about it after the burning; was anything said by Miss Russell in the presence of Miss Lizzie and yourself in regard to this dress? A. Sunday.

Q. No Monday? A. Yes sir.

Q. Was there anything said Sunday? A. Not that I know of.

Q. What was said Monday? A. Miss Russell came from the dining room and said that Mr. Hanscom had asked her if all the dresses were there that were there on the day of the tragedy, and she had told him yes, and that she had told him a falsehood. It was decided by my sister and myself that she should go and tell him that she had told a falsehood and tell him that a dress had been burned.

Q. What was the time Miss Russell said it was the worst thing that could be done? A. Yes, she said that Monday morning, and my sister said "Why did you let me do it?"

Q. Do you recall a story that was told by Mrs. Reagan about a quarrel between yourself and your sister? A. I did not hear Mrs. Reagan say anything about it.

Q. But do you remember there was a story at that time? A. Yes sir.

Q. Was your attention called to the fact by me? A. Yes sir.

Q. How soon after, do you know? A. The morning following.

Q. Is this the morning the story was published in the paper? A. Yes sir, yes sir.

(Mr. Jennings attempted to read some of the testimony given by Mrs. Reagan, and Mr. Knowlton asked that he be not allowed to do it.)

The court said that Mr. Jennings could call the attention of the witness to statements made by Mrs. Reagan and question her in regard to them, and Mr. Jennings proceeded.

Q. When Miss Emma, on that morning did you have any conversation with Miss Lizzie in which she said, "Emma you have given me away, haven't you"? A. I did not.

Q. Or did your say in reply, "No Lizzie I haven't"? "You have," she said,

"and I will let you see I won't give in one inch"? Was there any such talk as that? A. There was not.

Q. Anything like it? A. No sir.

Q. Was that morning or at any time? A. No sir.

Q. Was there ever any trouble between you and your sister in the matron's room? A. No sir.

Q. Anything that could be construed as a quarrel? A. No sir.

Q. Did Lizzie put up her finger and say anything about not giving in? A. No sir.

Q. Did I go there that morning before you went away? A. The morning before the hearing began, yes sir.

Q. Now when you went out did I say to you, "Have you told her all," and you said "Everything?" A. No sir, you did not.

Q. Either that morning or any other morning? A. No sir.

Q. Were you there at the time that there was some talk in the matron's room about a paper being signed? A. I don't remember.

Q. Do you think you were there? A. I cannot tell you; I do not know; I do not remember.

Q. Now, so that there may be no mistake, I would like to ask you again who it was that said she told a falsehood to Mr. Hanscom? A. Miss Russell said she had told a falsehood.

Cross-examined.

Q. On the day that this happened you were in Fairhaven? A. Yes sir.

Q. How long had you been in Fairhaven? A. Just two weeks.

Q. At whose house? A. At Moses Delano's, Spring street.

Q. You received a telegram from Dr. Bowen? A. Yes sir.

Q. And came of course as soon as you could? A. Yes sir.

Q. Where were you when you received the telegram? A. I was at the house.

Q. What time did you arrive at your house? A. About 5 o'clock.

Q. That same afternoon? A. Yes sir.

Q. Had you seen Miss Lizzie during the two weeks? A. Yes sir.

Q. When? A. I cannot tell you what day it was; a few days before.

Q. Was it Saturday? A. No sir.

Q. Did you see her on the way to or from Marion? A. No sir.

Q. She told you that she simply spent the day there? A. Yes sir.

Q. How long have you lived in the house; have you lived there all your life? A. No sir; I think about 21 years.

Q. Had your father always occupied the whole house? A. Yes; excepting the first few months that we lived there.

Q. Was any change made in the house when you began to occupy the whole house? A. Two of the sleeping rooms down stairs were made into a dining room.

Q. You have lived there ever since? A. Yes.

Q. Live there now? A. Yes.

Q. Do you live alone now? A. All except a servant.

Q. Had you seen Mr. Morse that week? A. No sir.

Q. When had you last seen him? A. I can't tell I don't know.

Q. How long before had you seen him? A. I don't know, I think about three or four years.

Q. Did he come to the house? A. Yes sir.

Q. Were both of you girls at home? A. Yes sir.

Q. Did he stay over night? A. I don't know.

Q. Where did he sleep at his last visit that you remember of? A. I think in the attic.

Q. Did you then have company? A. I think so.

Q. Did he usually sleep in the attic or in the guest chamber? A. Sometimes he slept in the attic, it was just as it happened.

Q. Did he come to the house often after the last time you remember of his being there? A. It was just as it happened.

Q. How many times did he come that year? A. I don't know, several.

Q. How many times did he stay over night? A. I don't know, two or three times perhaps.

Q. Mr. Morse was your own uncle? A. Yes.

Q. Have you other kin? A. Yes sir.

Q. Who are they? A. My uncles all but one are now dead, I have an aunt in Fall River.

Q. Where does your aunt in Fall River live? A. I don't know.

Q. Do you go there? A. Not very often.

Q. Has your stepmother relatives in Fall River? A. Yes sir.

Q. Who? A. A half sister.

Q. How did your stepmother's sister come into possession of the property she occupies, by inheritance? A. No sir.

Q. How then? A. My father purchased it and gave it to her.

Q. Did this make trouble in the family? A. Yes.

Q. Did it make trouble between your stepmother, Lizzie and you? A. Yes sir.

Q. Did you find fault with it? A. Yes sir.

Q. Did Lizzie find fault with it? A. Yes sir.

Q. In consequence of that did your father give you money? A. I don't think it was in consequence of this.

Q. Did he give you any property? A. About that time he did—grandfather's house.

Q. Was this as remunerative as the other property in the way of rents? A. No sir.

Q. Were the relations entirely cordial between Lizzie and your stepmother since that time? A. Yes sir.

Q. Did not Lizzie cease to call her mother? A. Yes sir.

Q. Wasn't it at that time? A. I don't know.

Q. What did she call her? A. Mrs. Borden.

Q. And she had previously called her mother? A. Yes sir.

Q. Do you recall what you testified to before regarding this matter? A. I don't know.

Q. Did you say that it was about the time of this transaction that Lizzie ceased to call her mother? A. I don't remember.

Mr. Knowlton read from the inquest, and asked witness if she made certain statements, and she said that she recalled that she did.

Q. Did you answer truly? A. I tried to.

Q. Do you still say that the relations between them were cordial? A. They were cordial. The thing is that they were cordial.

Q. For how many years before were they not cordial? A. I don't know; I know they were.

Counsel then quoted at some length from Emma's testimony at the inquest with regard to the relations of Lizzie and her stepmother not being as cordial as they might be, and asked her what she now says about it. Emma answered that in some cases she could not remember what answers she gave. She remembered giving as a cause of want of cordiality between them the giving of property by Mr. Borden to his wife, and that the daughters saying they ought to have something done for them, and that their father did give them some money.

The cross-examination then concluded.

Q. Do you know of anybody who bore ill-will toward your stepmother? A. No.

Q. Do you know of any enemy your stepmother had in the world? A. No.

Fatal Accident in Taunton.

Taunton, June 16.—John Ryan, aged 46, fell down stairs last night and broke his neck, dying instantly.

SISSON & RING.

WINDOW SHADES.

37 PURCHASE ST.

New Bank Building.

UPSTAIRS. TAKE ELEVATOR.

MWF

TRAVELING SUITS

Are now in demand, and our store is the place to get them. A brisk trade has set the stock traveling very fast, and crowds of buyers are eager to secure first choices. They are here in every variety of style and material. Travel in good form while you're about it; to do that you must make a

Short Trip to Our Store

before you make a long journey. You can't fail to be suited, because our stock includes $12.00 suits for $10.00 and $10.00 suits for $7.95. These suits are all the go, and just the things for travelers to wear, because they're neat, easy, comfortable and perfectly suited for summer. We have a choice assortment of trousers at $2.00, $2.50 and $3.00.

M. C. SWIFT & SON,

153, 157 and 159 Union St.

NEW BEDFORD, MASS.

SPEAK HIGHLY OF IT.

Sanford & Kelley's Handbook on New Bedford Appreciated.

In our article yesterday we should have stated that the banks and others of our city accepted that firm's generous offer to furnish them with copies of the book at the mere cost of printing and binding, so that all the savings banks, the two savings banks, the New Bedford Safe Deposit & Trust company, the New Bedford Co-operative bank, the New Bedford Board of Trade, Abbott F. Smith, F. A. F. Adams, Charles S. Paisler, George S. Homer, George Delano's Sons, Charles O. Brightman, Thomas B. Tripp, Isaac B. Tompkins, Jr., Steven A. Brownell and others have the books on hand for distribution so long as the supply lasts among their customers and friends, thus helping to advertise New Bedford and increase its growth.

The book contains 74 pages instead of 60, as stated.

Some of the books were yesterday sent to Europe, and others will follow on receipt of letters requesting them.

Our citizens who have already received copies of the books speak very highly of them.

DR. TRAVERS' CASE.

He is Held for the Grand Jury Without Bail.

(Special Dispatch.)

Boston, June 16.—Dr. Matthew Travers charged with obtaining money under false pretences was today held in the sum of $1,000 for the grand jury. No bail.

STORY UNFOUNDED

Yankee Capital Not Trying to Secure the Grand Trunk Road.

New York, June 16.—It was reported from Montreal that George J. Gould and Russell Sage were at the head of a movement to bring within the control of American capital the management of the Grand Trunk railway system, which is now directed by Englishmen in London. The story seems to be a greatly exaggerated growth out of a movement to get possession of a branch of the Grand Trunk, the Great Western railroad, in order to form a distinct and continuous line with the Wabash.

It is believed, now that the original plan which came from Canadian interests was to parallel the Canadian Pacific, but that the New York capitalists entered only so much of the scheme as was to the advantage of their existing roads. The lease of the Great Western may, however, be only the first step toward the execution of those larger schemes. George J. Gould is preparing to leave for London soon, and this was part of the program telegraphed from Montreal.

Mr. Sage, in speaking of the deal, spoke of the state of the money market as being a limiting condition on any large transaction, especially of one contemplating the investment of such enormous sums as the acquisition of the control of the Grand Trunk. The value of the stock and bonds of the Grand Trunk is about $300,000,000.

Hunting for a Hidden Fortune.

Salem, Mass., June 16.—The relatives of Henry Morgan, whose body was not found until two weeks after his death, are looking for a small fortune hidden about the house. It is claimed that there is $3000 secreted there.

Successful Burglars.

Biddeford, Me., June 16.—Burglars entered Polakewich Bros.' store near mid-night and carried off about $400 worth of jewelry, clothing and furnishing goods. The break was made by forcing a shutter of the rear window.

AMUSEMENTS.

SELECT SOCIAL

To be given by the

BAY VIEW ATHLETIC CLUB,

At their rooms,

Foot of County Street,

Friday Evening, June 16th.

TICKETS { Gentlemen.........25 Cents. Lady.........15 Cents.

je14-3t

Strawberry Festival.

Sylvia H. Delano Circle No. 1, Ladies of the G. A. R., will give a Strawberry Festival at

CHINA HALL,

FRIDAY, JUNE 16th, from 6 to 9 o'clock.

The public is invited. je15-2t

PUBLIC CLAM BAKE!

WILL BE GIVEN AT

SYLVAN GROVE,

Sunday, June 18th.

No postponement on account of weather, as dinner will be served in hall if stormy. Bake open at 2 o'clock.

je16-2t OTIS A. SISSON.

GRAND MASS MEETING!

SUNDAY, June 18, 1893,

—AT THE—

OPERA HOUSE,

To adopt resolutions in favor of the amnesty of the Irish-American political prisoners now confined in English prisons.

Hon. J. C. Brock will preside.

Rev. James F. Clark will open the meeting.

Judge John J. McDonough of Fall River will be the principal speaker of the evening. Addresses will also be made by George Fox Tucker, Hon. William M. Butler, Lemuel T. Willcox and others. There will be a recitation by John J. McCullough, Jr. Music, Sullivan's Orchestra. Doors open at 7 o'clock; meeting at 7 30. Admission FREE.

je16-2t

RAYMOND'S VACATION EXCURSIONS.

All Traveling Expenses Included.

Parties will leave BOSTON, July 8 and 22 for Two Grand Excursions of Fifty-six Days to

ALASKA.

The outward route is to be over the Picturesque Canadian Pacific Railway, through Montreal, Winnipeg, Bamff Hot Springs, the grand scenery of the Selkirks and Victoria; the homeward route, after the Alaska Voyage, of Twelve Days, via Tacoma, Portland, etc., and the Northern Pacific Railroad, with a week in the Yellowstone National Park and a week at the World's Columbian Exposition.

Magnificent Trains of Palace Sleeping and Dining Cars, with every first-class appointment, are to be used in crossing the continent. The Alaska trip will be on the favorite steamer "Queen."

Colorado and the Yellowstone National Park: Two 39-Day Excursions, leaving Boston July 10 and August 7.

Colorado Tours: Four Excursions to the most famous Rocky Mountain Resorts, leaving Boston July 17, August 28, September 11 and October 9.

The Yellowstone Park and California: A 72-Days' Excursion, leaving Boston August 30; also a 27-Days' Excursion to the Yellowstone Park and return.

Each of the above parties will have a week at the World's Fair.

The World's Columbian Exposition: Special Pullman Vestibuled Trains with Dining-Cars will leave Boston for Chicago daily. A week at the Raymond & Whitcomb Grand Hotel, opposite the Fair Grounds, is included in the tickets.

☞ Send for descriptive book, mentioning the particular tour desired.

RAYMOND & WHITCOMB,

296 WASHINGTON ST., (Opposite School St.,)

BOSTON, MASS. je15-3t

RAYMOND'S VACATION EXCURSIONS.

ALL TRAVELING EXPENSES INCLUDED

THE WORLD'S Columbian Exposition.

The greatest Exposition the world has ever seen is now complete in every department. Nothing remains unfinished.

The Raymond & Whitcomb Grand Hotel (Mr. Oscar G. Barron, Manager,) at which our parties sojourn, is a permanent brick structure of the best class, only four stories in height, splendidly arranged, provided with every luxurious appointment of the best modern hotels, and elegantly furnished. Its situation, in a fashionable residence section of city, near the Exposition grounds and exposed to the lake breezes, is unexcelled. Passengers are landed at a special station only a single block distant, and an entrance to the Exposition grounds is directly opposite the hotel, while others are near at hand. All water used for drinking and cooking purposes is distilled and absolutely pure, and the purest Wisconsin ice is also supplied.

Daily special trains from the East, made up wholly of elegant vestibuled Pullman palace sleeping cars with dining cars, run through to the hotel without change.

While many parties for the coming months were long since filled, the following dates are still open to the public, an early registration, however, being in all cases advisable:

June 28 and 29.

July 5, 6, 8, 11, 12*, 14, 15, 17, 18, 21, 22, 25, 26*, 27, and 29.

August 1, 4, 5, 7, 8, 9, 11*, 12, 15, 16, 17, 19, 23, 25, 26 and 29.

*July 12 and 26 and August 11 give two weeks' sojourn in Chicago.

Colorado Tours: Four remaining Excursions to the most famous Rocky Mountain Resorts, July 17, August 28, September 11, and October 9.

Summer Alaska Trips: Two 56-day Excursions, July 8 and 22.

Colorado and the Yellowstone National Park; Two 39-day Excursions, July 10 and August 7.

Yellowstone National Park: A 27-day Tour August 30.

Yellowstone National Park and California: Tour of 72 days, August 30.

Each of the above parties will have a week at the World's Fair.

Ten Summer and Autumn Tours to Eastern Resorts in July, August, and September.

☞ Send for descriptive book, mentioning the particular tour desired.

RAYMOND & WHITCOMB,

296 Washington Street (opposite School St.,)

Boston, Mass. je16-3t

ENTERTAINMENT DIRECTORY.

FRIDAY.

China Hall—Sylvia H. Delano Circle strawberry festival.

Bay View Club Room—Select social.

FUTURE EVENTS.

Opera House—18th, Irish mass meeting.

Sylvan Grove—18th, Clambake.

AMUSEMENTS.

The Bay View Athletic club will give a select social this evening at the club room at the foot of County street.

A public clambake will be given at Sylvan Grove Sunday, opening at 2 p. m. A dinner will be served in the hall if stormy.

If you want an enjoyable time and a nice dish of strawberries and cream, drop in at China hall this evening between 6 and 9 o'clock. Ladies of the Sylvia H. Delano circle have arranged for a strawberry festival.

Sunday evening a mass meeting to adopt resolutions in favor of the amnesty of the Irish-American prisoners now confined in English prisons will be held in the Opera House. Mayor Brock will preside. Judge McDonough, George Fox Tucker and William M. Butler are among the speakers.

Messrs. Raymond & Whitcomb's World's Fair Tours.—Messrs. Raymond & Whitcomb are meeting with wonderful success in their exposition tours. With daily special trains of elegant Pullman vestibuled palace cars, a complete dining car service, and a magnificent first class hotel contiguous to the grounds, nothing is left to be desired, and it is not surprising that their passenger lists are made up of the best people in New England. While the hotel is situated in a quiet and fashionable section, its guests have only to step across the street to enter the exposition grounds. Passengers are provided with tickets of admission in sufficient numbers to enable them to return to the hotel for lunch, and it speaks volumes in behalf of the hotel management that few choose to do otherwise. As these admission tickets are redeemed if not used the holder is not compelled to lose them by remaining inside the grounds for meals. The guests at the Raymond & Whitcomb Grand are fortunate in the possession of absolutely pure water to drink. Every drop of water used for drinking purposes is distilled, and thus rendered thoroughly harmless and healthful. There are vacancies in some of the parties in July and August, as will be seen by an advertisement elsewhere. An early registration is advisable.

BASEBALL.

Yesterday afternoon the Freshman team of the High school defeated the Juniors by a score of 16 to 8. The fourth class played a stiff game. Brady, '93, and Kirby, '93, were umpires.

The Y. M. C. A. nine will go to Marion tomorrow afternoon and play a return game with the Tabor Academy team.

The Boston Herald says that Steere is "a brilliant and plucky youngster and any club under him ought to be a winner."

After a few more games the Holy Cross team will disband. Stafford has joined the Clevelands and will be with them the rest of the season. Cotter and Lowney have received various offers, but will probably play in this city. Several clubs want Bannon, but he has signed with no one as yet.

TRAVELLERS' GUIDE.

THE NEW YORK, NEW HAVEN AND HARTFORD RAILROAD COMPANY, LESSEE.

OLD COLONY RAILROAD.

TIME tables showing local and through train service between all stations may be obtained at all ticket offices of this company.

Week day passenger trains Leave New Bedford for Boston (Park Square Station) at 7 25, 8 45, 10 55 A. M., 1 25, 3 40, 5 50, 9 40 P. M. Return, 8 00, 9 30 A. M., 12 M., 3 00, 5 10, 7 00, 11 00 P. M. Boston (Kneeland Street Station) at 5 50 P. M. Return, 5 45 A. M. Providence at 7 25, 8 45, †10 55 A. M., 12 15, †1 25, 3 40, †5 50, †9 40 P. M. Return, †6 00, 8 15, †9 00 A. M., 12 10, 3 25, 5 05, †6 22, †10 05 P. M. Lowell at 7 25, 8 45 A. M., 3 40 P. M. Fitchburg at 8 45 A. M., 12 15, 3 40 P. M. Mansfield at 7 25, 8 45, 10 55 A. M., 12 15, 1 25, 3 40, 5 50, 9 40 P. M. Taunton at 7 25, 8 45, 10 55 A. M., 12 15, 1 25, 3 40, 5 50, 9 40 P. M. Return 12 08, 7 18, 9 12, 10 31 A. M., 1 05, 4 15, 6 03, 7 58 P. M. Newport at 8 45 A. M., 12 15, 3 40 P. M. Fall River at 8 45 A. M., 9 40 P. M. New York, via Fall River Line, at 6 15 P. M. New York, via Shore Line, at 7 25, 8 45, A. M., 12 15, 3 40, 9 40 P. M. Myricks at 8 45, 10 55 A. M., 12 15, 1 25, 3 40, 5 50, 9 40 P. M. East Freetown and Braley's, 8 45 A. M., 1 25, 5 50, 9 40 P. M. Fall River and Way Stations, via Fall River Branch, at 7 05, 10 00 A. M., 12 20, 3 00, 5 45, 9 30 P. M. Return, 8 15, 11 15 A. M., 1 00, 4 00, 6 30, 10 15 P. M.

†Via Mansfield.

SUNDAY TRAINS.

Leave New Bedford for Fall River and New York, via Fall River Line, at 7 20 P. M. Providence, Taunton and Boston at 7 25 A. M., 12 50, 7 30 P. M. Return — Boston, Park Square Station, 4 15 A. M., 6 00 P. M. Providence 6 45 A. M., 7 15 P. M. Fall River, 7 35 A. M., 7 25 P. M.

FAIRHAVEN BRANCH.

Leave Fairhaven (week days) for Boston, Brockton, Bridgewater and Middleboro, at 7 57, 11 15 A. M., 4 35 P. M.; Sundays, 5 55 P. M. Tremont, Marion, Mattapoisett, Sandwich, Hyannis and points on Cape Cod at 7 57, 9 28, 11 15 A. M., 4 35 P. M.; Sundays at 8 00 A. M.

Horse cars will leave William street at 7 30, 8 50, 10 50 A. M. and 4 00 P. M., week days, to connect with trains at Fairhaven.

J. R. KENDRICK, Third Vice-Pres., Boston.
GEO. L. CONNOR, Gen'l Pass. Agent, Boston.
WILLIAM B. FISHER, Agent, New Bedford.
June 12, 1893.

NEW BEDFORD, MARTHAS VINEYARD & NANTUCKET STEAMBOAT CO

SUMMER ARRANGEMENT,

Commencing Monday, June 12, 1893

Nantucket and Marthas Vineyard, Cottage City, Oak Bluffs, Vineyard Highlands, Edgartown, Vineyard Haven, Woods Holl, Katama.

Steamers Gay Head, Nantucket, Monohansett, will leave daily, on and after MONDAY, June 12, Sundays excepted.

Leave New Bedford for Cottage City, 7 05, 10 00 a. m., 1 50, 5 p. m. RETURN—Leave Cottage City, 6 15, 9 30 a. m., 1 00 and 3 15 p. m.

Leave New Bedford for Nantucket, 7 05 a. m., 1 50 p. m. RETURN—Leave Nantucket 7 a. m., 12 45 p. m.

Leave New Bedford for Woods Holl, 10 00 a. m., 1 50 5 00 p. m. RETURN—Leave Woods Holl, 7 00 and 10 10 a. m., 4 00 p. m.

Leave Woods Holl for Cottage City, 11 35 a. m., 3 20, 6 45 p. m. RETURN—Leave Cottage City, 6 15, 9 30 a. m., 3 15 p. m.

Leave Cottage City for Nantucket, 9 00 a. m., 4 00 p. m. RETURN—Leave Nantucket, 7 00 a. m., 12 45 p. m.

Leave New Bedford for Vineyard Haven, 5 00 p. m. RETURN—5 45 a. m.

SUNDAYS.

Commencing June 18th, leave New Bedford for Woods Holl, Cottage City and Nantucket, 9 00 a. m. RETURN—Leave Nantucket 2 00 p. m., Cottage City, 4 30 p. m., Woods Holl 5 10 p. m.

EXCURSION TICKETS.

New Bedford to Cottage City and Return, good until October 31, 1893, $1.00

New Bedford to Nantucket and Return, good until September 16, 1893, $2.00

EDWARD T. PIERCE, Agent.

New Bedford, June 8, 1893.

Mattapoisett Stage.

On and after MONDAY, May 8th, and until further notice, the Mattapoisett and New Bedford stage will run twice daily leaving Mattapoisett, from H. A. Shurtleff's store, at 8 00 a. m., and 1 15 p. m. Returning, leave New Bedford at 11 a. m., and 5 00 p. m., from Nichols & Damon's shoe store, 71 Purchase street. All express business promptly attended to.

C. E. FULLER, Proprietor.

South Dartmouth Stage.

Will leave South Dartmouth on and after MONDAY, Oct. 10, at 7 45 A. M. and 1 30 P. M. Returning, leave New Bedford at 11 00 A. M. and 5 P. M. Office at Hatch & Co's express office, No. 5 Ricketson Block, New Bedford, and at Post Office in South Dartmouth. Passengers to be called for must book their names 30 minutes before starting.

FREDERICK C. SWAIN, Prop'r.

Little Compton Stage.

On and after this date the stage will leave Little Compton at 6 30 A. M., passing through Adamsville, Central Village, South Westport, Russell's Mills, Apponegansett. Returning, leaves office 104 North Second street, New Bedford, at 3 P. M. Order slate at Nichols & Damon's shoe store, 68 Purchase street.

A. RICHARDS, Proprietor.

Westport Point and New Bedford Stage.

Leaves Westport Point at 7 A. M., passing through Central Village, Head of Westport, Westport Factory and Smith Mills. Returning, leaves No. 104 North Second street, New Bedford, at 3 P. M. Order slate at Nichols & Damon's shoe store, 63 Purchase st.

A. RICHARDS, Proprietor.

Long Plain Stage.

Leaves Long Plain at 7 A. M. Return, leaves Hatch & Co's Express Office, Union street, at 3 45 P. M., Post Office at 4 P. M. Express and errands attended to carefully and promptly. A. C. SHATTUCK.

Rochester and New Bedford Stage.

On and after MONDAY, April 24th, the stage will run daily, leaving Rochester at 7 30 a. m., returning leave Douglass' stable, Mechanics lane at 4 30 p. m. Express business and errands promptly attended to.

ap22-tf A. D. WATSON, Driver.

[From Yesterday's Extra Edition.]

THE ASSASSIN!

The following is the report of the Borden trial proceedings late yesterday afternoon from the Standard's extra edition:

Q. What is your business? A. Teamer.

Q. Were you at the Borden house on the day of the murder? A. Yes sir.

Q. What time did you get there? A. At half past 11.

Q. Did you go to the upper part of the barn? A. Yes sir.

Q. What did you do? A. I looked around.

Q. Was there anybody up there? A. Yes sir.

Q. Who were they? A. I didn't know them.

Q. How many were there? A. Three.

Q. Were they men or boys? A. I should say that they were young men.

Q. Do you know Officer Medley? A. Yes sir.

Q. Was he there? A. No sir.

Q. Was Mr. Fleet there? A. No sir.

Q. Where were you when Mr. Fleet came? A. Out in the yard.

Q. How long were you up in the barn? A. Seven or eight minutes.

Cross-examined by Mr. Knowlton.

Q. Did you see Mr. Medley at all while you were there? A. No sir.

Q. When was the first time you saw Officer Medley? A. In the afternoon.

Q. At any time you didn't see Mr. Medley in the barn? A. No sir.

Q. You didn't see him come? A. No sir.

Q. If he didn't come you didn't see his movements? A. No sir.

Q. Did you go to the barn alone? No sir.

Q. Who went with you? A. Mr. Wixon.

Q. Nobody but you and Mr. Wixon went at that time? A. No.

Q. Did Mr. Wixon come to the house with you? A. No sir.

Q. You saw him after you got there? A. Yes sir.

Q. You said it was seven or eight minutes after you got there you went into the barn; did you look at your watch? A. No sir.

Q. You talked with people when you got to the house? A. Yes sir.

Q. Will you swear it wasn't nine minutes after you got there before you went to the barn? A. No.

Q. Will you swear it wasn't 10 minutes? A. Yes sir.

Q. Was there any excitement about the house? A. Yes sir.

Q. You knew a murder had been committed? A. Yes sir.

Q. But there was no excitement so but that you could fix the time accurately by estimating it? A. No sir.

Q. You said you got there about half past 11? Yes sir.

Q. Have you ever said different than that? A. I don't know that I have.

Q. Under oath have you said different than that? A. Not that I know of.

Mr. Knowlton read from testimony given at the hearing, in which witness placed the time of his arrival at the house at 11 40.

Q. Will you now swear that you didn't say 11 40 at another time? A. No sir.

Q. Was your recollection full as good then, two weeks after the murder, as it is now? A. I don't know.

Q. Have you had anything to refresh your memory since that time? A. No sir.

Q. Will you now swear that it was any earlier than 11 40 when you got there? A. I have testified to the best of my belief.

Q. Was the barn door open when you got there? A. Yes.

Q. Did you find anybody up in the barn when you got there? A. Yes sir.

Q. Did you see anything of Mr. Stevens, the reporter, there? A. I saw him on the steps.

Q. When? A. Before I went into the barn.

Q. Did you see Mr. Manning there? A. No.

Q. Did you see any more than three there? A. I saw another man.

Q. When? A. I don't know whether I was going up or coming down when I saw him.

Hyman Rubinsky.

Hyman Rubinsky was the next witness.

Q. What is your profession? A. I am a peddler.

Q. Run a team? A. Yes.

Q. Do you remember the time of the Borden murder? A. Yes.

Q. Do you know where the Borden house is? A. I didn't then.

Q. Do you know now? A. Yes.

Q. Where do you keep your team? A. On Second street.

Q. Near the Borden house? A. Between Rodman and Borden streets.

Q. Did you go by the Borden house on the day of the murder in your team? A. Yes.

Q. Can you tell the time when you left the stable? A. It was after 11.

Q. How much after? A. Perhaps 15 minutes.

Q. Anybody there when you left? A. Yes.

Q. Did you drive by the Borden house? A. Yes.

Q. Did you see anybody there? A. I saw a lady coming away from the barn.

Q. How was she dressed? A. I can't tell.

Q. Have anything on her head? A. No sir.

Q. What was she doing? A. Walking.

Q. Towards the steps or away? A. Towards the house.

Hyman Rubinsky.

Q. See her go in? A. No.

Q. Stop the team? A. No.

Q. Ever seen the servant who works in the house? A. Yes.

Q. Ever deliver ice cream to her? A. Yes.

Q. Was the woman you saw that day the servant? A. No.

Cross-examined by Mr. Knowlton.

Q. Where did you go after leaving the Borden house? A. To the store.

Q. What did you do after leaving that? A. Went to June street.

Q. Where then? A. Peddling on Rock and other streets.

Q. Did you "halloo" ice cream? A. No.

Q. How do you peddle? A. I ring the bell and look at the windows.

Q. What did you do then? A. I went back to the stable.

Q. Did you peddle before 1 o'clock? A. I peddle all the time.

Q. How long did you peddle before dinner? A. I didn't eat any dinner that day.

Q. Did you put up the horse for dinner or not? A. Yes.

Q. What time was this? A. This was from 1 to half past 1.

Q. How long did you peddle before this? A. Perhaps two hours.

Q. Weren't you peddling three hours? A. I don't know, I might have been.

Q. Are you sure you didn't peddle four hours? A. About two hours, I think.

Q. Did you look at your watch that day? A. Yes, a little after 11.

Q. How much after 11? A. I can't tell.

Q. Did you look at any yard besides the Borden yard? A. Yes.

Q. Were you trotting when you went by the Borden house? A. Yes.

Q. Where were you when you saw the woman? A. In the street.

Q. Where was your team? A. In the street.

Q. What part of the street? A. Between the Borden house and the next one.

Q. Did you know the woman? A. No sir.

Q. Had you got by the house when you saw her? A. I don't know what you mean.

Q. Had you passed the house? A. Yes.

Q. Where was she coming from, the barn, or had she got as far as the house? A. No.

Q. Was she nearest to the house? A. Yes.

Q. How near to it? A. Four or five feet.

Q. Was she walking? A. Yes.

Q. Towards the stairs? A. Yes.

Q. How near was she to them? A. I don't know.

Q. Give me an idea? A. Three or four feet.

Q. Was she on the side of the house? A. On the side.

Q. Was she on the walk, or don't you know where the walk is? A. I don't know.

Q. Did she go up the steps? A. I don't know.

Q. Where she came from you don't know? A. She came away from towards the barn.

Q. You don't know if she'd been in the barn? A. No.

Q. Was she on the steps nearest the street? A. On the side away from the street.

Q. Why did you look at your watch? A. Because I was late that day.

Q. What hand did you notice? A. The little hand.

Q. Who have you told about this? A. Officer Mullaly.

Q. When did you tell him? A. A few days after it happened.

Q. Why did you tell him? A. Because I wanted to.

Q. Who else have you told about it? A. A reporter.

Q. Did you see anybody in the Kelley or Churchill yards that day? A. I don't know.

Q. When did you hear of the murder? A. About 12½ o'clock.

Q. Do you remember what you told Mr. Mullaly? A. Yes.

Q. Was anybody else present at the time? A. Yes.

Q. Did you tell anybody else? A. Mr. Phillips.

Q. Was that before the trial in the district court? A. I don't know when that trial was.

Q. Did you hear that one question was whether Lizzie went in the barn or not? A. I didn't hear that.

Q. Did you go to the district court trial? A. I don't know what you mean.

Q. I mean to the court in Fall River. A. No.

Q. Have you talked with Mr. Phillips since that time? A. Yes.

Q. When? A. Before this trial began.

Q. Did you go before the grand jury? A. I don't know what you mean.

Q. When did you tell Phillips? A. Two weeks after the murder.

Q. What makes you remember the day of the murder? A. Because it was called to my attention.

Q. Ever see any one in the Borden yard before? A. No.

Q. What made you look out that day? A. What have I got eyes for?

Charles E. Gardner.

Charles E. Gardner of Fall River was the next witness.

Q. Your name is Charles E. Gardner? A. Yes sir.

Q. Last August did you keep a stable on Second street in Fall River? A. Yes sir.

Q. Did Mr. Wilkinson, the ice cream man, put up his horse and carriage there? A. Yes sir.

Q. Did you know the man who drove that carriage? A. Yes sir.

Q. The man who just testified? A. Yes sir.

Q. Do you remember the day of the Borden murder? A. Yes sir.

Q. Do you remember anything about what time it was that day when Mr. Rubinsky took his cart away? A. I do.

Q. Won't you tell us about what time it was that day? A. It was between five and ten minutes past 11.

Q. How do you fix the time? A. My man used to feed at 11 o'clock and that day when Rubinsky came in and ordered his horse the horse was eating.

Q. Did he have to wait at all to get his horse? A. Yes sir.

Q. For what reason? A. There were a number of teams ahead of him.

Q. Do you know whether either one of those went out while he was waiting? A. Yes sir, one or two went out ahead of him.

Q. Do you know who? A. Yes, I remember one of them was George Douglass.

Q. Did you drive down Second street yourself? A. Yes sir.

Q. Did you go alone? A. I had Mr. Newhall of Worcester, a drummer, with me.

Q. Where did you go? A. To the Massasoit bank, corner of Bedford and Second streets.

Q. What did you do then? A. We went to get a bill changed.

Q. Where did you go after that? A. We went back up Second street, and I took Mr. Newhall to the train.

Q. What train? A. The 11 50 train.

Q. Did you hear anything about any trouble as you were driving down Second street? A. Yes sir, a young lad told me that there had been a fight. I did not know at the time where.

Q. About how long was it, do you think, after Rubinsky left before you went? A. I should judge from 10 to 15 minutes.

Q. Did you see Mr. Manning at any time while you were driving? A. Yes sir, when we left the bank we went up Second street, and as we turned to go up Pleasant street I saw Manning going up Second street.

(Mr. Manning, who occupied a seat among the reporters, was asked to stand, and the witness was asked if he was the gentleman. His answer was "Yes sir, sure.")

Cross-examined.

Q. Where were you when you saw Mr. Manning? A. I was turning the corner of Second onto Pleasant.

Q. Going south on Second street? A. Yes sir, I was going from the bank.

Q. Did you hear about the fight then? A. Yes sir.

Q. Did you go to the Borden house? A. No sir.

Q. Did you look into the yard? A. No sir.

Q. Although you had heard that there was a fight there? A. No, I did not hear it was there, I didn't know where it was.

Q. That was ten or fifteen minutes, you think, after Rubinsky went down? A. Yes sir.

Q. What time of day was that do you think? A. Quarter past 11. I cannot say what time it was I went by the house.

Q. If it was fifteen minutes after then it was 11 o'clock when Rubinsky started? A. He didn't leave at 11.

Q. What time do you think he left the stable? A. I think about ten minutes past.

Q. So that if you fix the time when he left the stable at ten minutes past 11, your time must have been 20 or 25 minutes? A. Possibly.

Q. And at that time you were not attracted to the Borden house so as to notice anything at all? A. No sir.

Q. You didn't see any commotion on the street? A. No sir.

Q. What makes you think it was 10 minutes past 11 when he left? A. Because I always feed at 11 o'clock. And when he came in and ordered his horse the feed cart was on the floor. I told him to wait until the horse ate.

Q. That is how you know that it was 11 o'clock? A. Yes.

Q. For aught you know it was quarter past 11 when he left, wasn't it? A. I don't think it was more than 10 minutes past.

Q. But it is only estimation, isn't it, for aught you can say now it was quarter past 11? A. Possibly.

Q. I don't suppose you took any particular notice of how long you left afterwards? A. Several other teams left before I did. There was some one else who left before he did beside George Douglass, but I don't remember who it was.

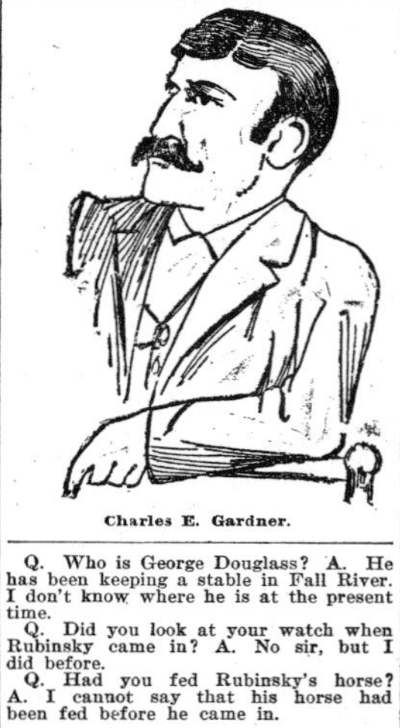

Charles E. Gardner.

Q. Who is George Douglass? A. He has been keeping a stable in Fall River. I don't know where he is at the present time.

Q. Did you look at your watch when Rubinsky came in? A. No sir, but I did before.

Q. Had you fed Rubinsky's horse? A. I cannot say that his horse had been fed before he came in.

Charles B. Newhall.

Charles B. Newhall of Worcester was called to the stand.

Q. What is your name? A. Charles B. Newhall.

Q. Where do you live? A. In Worcester.

Q. What do you do? A. I am in the hardware business.

Q. Were you in Fall River on the day of the murder? A. I was.

Q. Were you at Charles E. Gardner's stable on Second street? A. Yes sir.

Q. What time did you arrive in Fall River? A. At 10 25.

Q. How long did you stay at the stable? A. Until after 11 o'clock.

Q. Where did you go from there? A. Went down to the bank.

Q. Did you walk? A. No sir; I rode with Mr. Gardner.

Q. Going down there did you hear about any trouble? A. Yes sir.

Q. What was it? A. Some one said that a man stabbed another man.

Q. Did he say who? A. I didn't understand that he did.

Q. Did you go to the station? A. Yes sir.

Q. Did you know what time the train left? A. Yes sir, 7 50.

Q. Was your attention called to anything by Mr. Gardner while on the route? A. Yes sir, to a man running.

Q. Do you remember where this was? A. We were turning the corner of Second and Pleasant streets.

Q. Where was the man? A. He was crossing the street.

Q. There you heard some one had been stabbed? A. Yes sir.

Witness was not cross-examined.

Everett Brown.

Everett Brown was the next witness, and the sheriff was continually rapping for order while he was on the stand. His answers proved very amusing.

Q. Your name? A. Everett Brown.

Q. Where do you live? A. At 117 Third street in Fall River.

Q. You were there in Fall River on the day of the Borden murder? A. Yes sir.

Q. You went down there to the Borden house? A. Yes sir.

Q. Alone or with somebody? A. With somebody.

Q. What time was it when you left your house to go to the Borden house? A. I was to leave my house at 11 o'clock. That was the arrangement with the other party.

Q. Who was the other party? A. Thomas C. Barlow.

Q. Should you say it was nearer 11 or 12 when you left the house? A. I wouldn't say, I don't know the time.

Q. Did you see anybody come out of the Borden yard when you got there? A. Yes sir.

Q. Who? A. Officer Dougherty.

Q. Where did you go when you got to the Borden yard? A. We went into the yard and tried to get into the house, and "Charlie" Sawyer wouldn't let us.

Q. Was Officer Medley there? A. No sir.

Q. Was he on the steps? A. No sir.

Q. Or in the yard? A. No sir.

Q. Where did you then go? A. To the barn.

Q. Where? A. We went into the barn and stayed there to see which would go up first.

Q. He dared you? A. He said he wouldn't go up, because some one might drop an axe down on us.

Q. Go ahead. A. We went up and stayed about five minutes, and then went around the yard and tried to look into the windows of the house, but they wouldn't let us.

Q. Did you see Mr. Fleet? A. Yes, when he was coming up the concrete walk.

Q. Did you see him come in through the gate? A. I saw him when he was coming up the walk.

Q. What did he do? A. I think he stopped to talk with some one.

Q. What happened next? A. Everybody was put out of the yard.

Cross-examined by Mr. Knowlton.

Q. What time was this? A. I don't know.

Q. Was it near 11 or 12? A. I don't know anything about the time.

Q. Was Mr. Morse there? A. He might have been; I don't know.

Q. Did you see Mr. Medley there? A. No sir.

Q. Do you know him? A. No sir.

Q. After this you hung around the yard? A. Yes sir.

Q. Do you remember seeing Mr. Medley about the yard anywhere? A. No sir.

Q. Do you know when he was there? A. No sir.

Q. Do you know when he came? A. No sir.

Q. Do you know when he went away? A. No sir; I don't.

Q. Do you know what he did while he was there? A. No sir.

Q. You don't know anything about his movements? A. I don't remember of seeing him.

Q. Was the door of the barn fastened? A. I don't know, I didn't open the door to the barn.

Q. Who did? A. Thomas C. Barlow.

Thomas C. Barlow.

Thomas C. Barlow was the next witness.

Q. Do you live in Fall River? A. Yes sir.

Q. On the premises that day? A. Yes sir.

Q. What place did you come from? A. Home.

Q. Where did you go to from home? A. To Everett Brown's house.

Q. What time did you leave home? A. Eleven o'clock.

Q. How long did you stay at Brown's house? A. Eight minutes.

Q. When you got to the Borden place did you see anybody come out? A. Yes, Officer Dougherty.

Q. You went into the barn? A. Yes.

Q. You know Officer Medley? A. No.

Q. Tell us what you did in the barn? A. Went into the barn, up into the hay loft, and looked out of the window at the west end and looked over the hay.

Q. How was the heat in the barn compared to that outdoors? A. It was cooler in the barn that it was out doors.

Q. What did you do next? A. Came out and tried to look into the windows of the house.

Q. How many was there out around there? A. I can't say, there were several.

Q. Do you know Officer Fleet? A. Yes.

Q. Did you see him when he came? A. Yes.

Q. Do you know which way he came? A. I think through the front gate.

Q. What did you do after that? A. I hung around the house that afternoon.

Q. Did you get any supper? A. Yes.

Q. What did you do then? A. I came back.

Q. What did you do then? A. I staid around there till 12 o'clock.

Cross-examined by Mr. Knowlton.

Q. Where are you employed? A. Shannon's pool room.

Q. How long have you been there? A. About a month.

Q. What was you doing at that time? A. Nothing.

Q. Is your father living? A. No sir.

Q. Mother living? A. No.

Q. Who do you live with? A. My grandmother.

Q. Grandfather living? A. Yes sir.

Q. What time does he go to work in the morning? A. Seven o'clock.

Q. So you got your dinner pretty early that day? A. Half-past 10.

Q. Is it your general habit to get your dinner at half-past 10? A. Yes sir.

Q. What did you have for dinner that day? A. I don't know.

Q. Did your grandmother set the table for you? A. Yes sir.

Q. And cooked you the dinner? A. Yes sir.

Q. What time did you get your breakfast? A. About 7.

Q. And you got your dinner before 11? A. Yes sir.

Q. So you want the jury to understand that your grandmother gets your dinner for you before 11 o'clock—a common habit? A. Yes sir.

Q. You get your supper what time? A. About 5.

Q. How do you know you got your dinner at quarter of 11 that day? A. Because I looked at the clock.

Q. You said it was cooler in the barn than it was out doors? A. Yes sir.

Q. Do you recall that that was a sloping roof? A. Yes sir.

Q. Does the roof run right down to the plates, and do you know the sun was beating right down there? A. Yes sir.

Q. Now what made you think it was cooler in there? A. Its always cooler in the house than it is out doors.

Q. Have you talked with any one about this case? A. Nobody but Mr. Jennings.

Q. And you want the jury to understand that the barn was a cooler place than anywhere else? A. Yes sir.

Q. How long did you stay there? A. A half an hour.

Q. How do you know? A. I looked at the clock.

Q. What time did you arrive? A. Eight minutes after 11.

Q. How far is it? A. About three squares.

Q. What made it take you so long? A. I was just loafing along.

Q. Delay was caused by what? A. I stopped to push a boy off the sidewalk.

Q. Where were you fooling? A. All the way to the Borden house.

Q. That delayed you 10 or 15 minutes? A. Yes.

Q. Couldn't it have been 20 minutes? A. I don't think so.

Q. Then you can't remember? A. I don't think it was 20.

Q. Did you see anybody in the yard? A. No.

Q. After you came from the barn? A. Yes.

Q. Who did you see? A. I didn't know them.

Q. Was the barn fastened when you went in? A. Yes.

Q. How? A. The door was hooked.

Q. Did you shut the door when you came out? A. Yes.

Q. Fasten the door? A. Yes.

Q. When you went in you went right up to the loft? A. Yes.

Q. Walk around up there? A. Yes.

Q. Turn the hay over? A. Yes.

Q. Stay up there some time? A. Yes.

"That will do," said Mr. Knowlton, and the boy went out.

The next witness was Joseph Lemay, a Frenchman, who cannot understand English, and Officer George Gendron of this city was engaged as interpreter.

Q. Where do you live? A. On the Wilson road, Fall River.

Q. What is your business? A. A farmer.

Q. How many acres in your farm? A. Fifty-six.

Q. Are there woods there? A. On each side of my farm.

Q. On August 16th—

Mr. Knowlton objected at this point, and after he and Mr. Jennings had had a conference with the judges the jury was dismissed till 9 o'clock tomorrow morning.

Mr. Knowton addressed the court and said the evidence which Lemay was expected to give has no relation to the time of the homicides, and no connection to them, except in so far as witness is alleged to have had some talk with somebody. How far do your honors think this evidence should go? Suppose that a man living four miles from the city should say that 12 days afterward he had seen a man and claimed to know something about the matter, but whose statement was wild and imaginative. Should such evidence as this be allowed to go in.

Mr. Jennings said Lemay lives at a place which is not more than half an hour's travel from the City hall by electric cars, which go to a point within a mile of his house. His evidence isn't in the nature of conversation or declaration. He was not aware of the presence of the man until late. There was blood on the person of the man, and he had a hatchet similar to that which the government has put in. The commonwealth was notified of the presence of this man and had an opportunity to go and see him. The evidence of this witness is important and should be allowed to go in. We do not connect the man with the murders.

Chief Justice Mason said: "We will reserve the decision as to admitting the evidence till tomorrow morning.

After a short consultation between the judges and counsel the court adjourned.

Marked for Life.

But it is a strange case. The wildest intellect among the French romantists never produced a stranger. If she is guilty, she is a monster of surpassing malignity and surpassing genius for evil. If she is innocent, she is the most cruelly used of unhappy women. Guilty or innocent she is marked for life. She has nothing now at stake but existence; and what will that be? The crier of the court, as he opens it in the morning and adjourns it at night, pronounces in solemn accents: "God save the commonwealth of Massachusetts!" So may we all now pray, God save it from an act of irremediable wrong.—New York Tribune.

A STUDY OF MOTIVE.

The Slaughter of Andrew J. Borden Utterly Unintelligible.

(New York Tribune Editorial.)

One of the many inexplicable things which the prosecution in the Borden case has failed to unravel is the prisoner's motive for killing her father. An attempt has been made to show that her relations with her stepmother were unfriendly, that she was unhappy in her home and that there had been a quarrel over the disposition of her father's property. In the opening address for the state Mr. Moody referred to this branch of the case, and in anticipation of the admission of the prisoner's statement at the inquest affirmed that there was a mercenary motive for the crimes. This motive has not been clearly established by evidence; but whatever bearing it may have upon the case is derived from the commission of the first crime. Let it be assumed for the sake of the argument that the prisoner disliked or even detested her stepmother, and that she apprehended a diversion of her father's fortune from the future use of herself and her sister. Let it be granted, furthermore, that either in consequence of a deliberate, premeditated plot or of a sudden outbreak of passion, the prisoner may have murdered her stepmother. What motive could she have had for killing her father also? There is no evidence indicating that she hated him. With her stepmother out of the way, her father's property upon his death would naturally have been shared by the sisters; and he was an old and feeble man.

Lizzie Borden, if guilty, must at least be credited with coolness of judgment and quickness of wit. Her success in removing twice in the course of two hours all evidence of guilt from her person and her clothing indicates that she retained her self-possession. The fact that she was ironing on the first floor and laughing and chatting with her father when they were last seen together, betokens on the theory of the state, both presence of mind and powers of dissimulation. If she had killed her stepmother, she was acting with extraordinary coolness, and was evidently in full possession of her mental faculties. It would have been easy for her to leave the house soon after the first murder and to divert suspicion from herself by spending an hour or two with a friend or neighbor. Why should she have remained behind to lie in wait for her father, to put on anew the murderer's gown and to take away a second life? She had nothing to gain by killing her father. The chief object of her dislike and the main source of family discord, if any there were, had been removed. There was no apparent motive for the second murder, by which suspicion was riveted upon her. Indeed if she had left the house promptly after the first crime, she could have cleared herself, and the police would subsequently have been forced by their process of exclusive opportunity to make out a case against the servant in the kitchen.

In every murder case grounded upon circumstantial evidence the motive must be set forth with clearness and positiveness before reasonable doubt of guilt can be removed. This was done in the Harris case which recently occupied public attention. While the evidence was indirect the motive was adequate to account for the crime. When there is direct evidence of a murderer's guilt the motive is less important; but it would seem to be absolutely essential to a successful prosecution in the Borden case. While something vaguely resembling a motive can be supplied for the commission of the first crime, the second murder is absolutely inexplicable on the theory of the state. The slaughter of the helpless old man was not required for the protection of the murderer. It increased immeasurably the murderer's difficulty and danger. As a crime committed by Lizzie Borden it is utterly unintelligible.

SONS OF VETERANS.

Annual Election and Close of the Convention.

The afternoon and closing session of the 11th annual convention of the Massachusetts Division Sons of Veterans was called to order at 3 o'clock by Commander Delano.

The first business was the choice of officers for the ensuing year, and the following were elected:

Commander—A. C. Blaisdell of Lowell.

Senior Vice Commander—J. D. Seymour of Whately.

Junior Vice Commander—C. F. Cook of Whitman.

Division Council—Charles K. Darling of Fitchburg, O. H. Cook of Melrose and Walter H. Delano of Sharon.

Delegates to the National Encampment—At large, G. N. Howard of Lowell, George W. Penniman of Brockton, C. D. Rooney of Winchester, F. W. Eager of Fitchburg, F. C. Bruce of East Hampton, D. F. Goulding of Somerville.

Alternates were chosen as follows:

William J. Moseley of Needham, at large.

William B. Davis of Cambridge.

G. W. Gregg of Everett.

William R. Waterman of Hanover.

Ralph S. Wentworth of Canton.

William E. James of New Bedford.

The installing officer was F. T. Merrill of Maine, past commander-in-chief.

Immediately after the election the new officers were installed, and about 5 30 the convention dissolved.

STEAMSHIP LINES.

ANCHOR LINE.

United States Mail Steamships

Sail from New York every Saturday for GLASGOW VIA LONDONDERRY

Rates for Saloon Passage

By S. S. CITY OF ROME, $50 and upward. OTHER STEAMERS, Cabin, $45 and upward, according to accommodation and location of Room. Excursion Tickets at reduced rates. Second Cabin, $30. Steerage, Outward, $23. Prepaid, $24. Second Cabin from Glasgow or Derry, $35.

Drafts at lowest Current Rates.

For Book of tours and other information apply to HENDERSON BROTHERS, 7 Bowling Green, N. Y., Thomas Donaghy, Corner Union and Water sts. or Edwin Whittaker 884 Purchase st., or David Waugh, 773 South Water street, New Bedford.

THE Hot Weather IS UPON US.

This is especially the season for

GAS STOVES.

CALL EARLY.

N. B. GAS & EDISON LIGHT CO.

NOTICE.

THE LARGEST STOCK OF

HARNESSES. Trunks and Bags

IN THE CITY, AT

WILLIAM CRONIN & CO'S.,

Corner Elm and Pleasant Streets.

Knowles & Co.

Now is the time for you to make a call at our store, as we have a full and complete line of warm weather goods.

The largest line of Parasols and Sun Umbrellas to be found in the city.

A bargain in Red and Blue Sun Umbrellas, at $1.75.

Parasols from 89c. to $5.50. Some rare bargains among them. Children's shades 39c. to $1.49.

We have made a cut in Silk Laces, and will sell you all the new and choice effects at 25 per cent. less than you will find them elsewhere.

A splendid line of Cotton Laces from 5 to 45c. per yard.

Our Hosiery Department is full of bargains. An elegant line of fine dropped stitch hose, in blacks, tans, white and almost any color you could wish, at 50c. Also some bargains at 25 and 37 1-2c.

We have secured one case of Ladies' Jersey Vests, worth 12 1-2c., which we shall sell three for 25c. as long as they last.

We are showing the best Ladies' and Gents' 25c. Vest to be found anywhere.

All sizes in Gents' Negligee Shirts, worth from $1.25 to $1.50, for ONE EVEN DOLLAR.

A new and elegant Line of Pampas Cloths, 25 or 30 pieces to select from, at 15c.

Twenty-five new styles of the celebrated Puritan Cloths at 12 1-2c. These goods are selling fast. Come while the selection is good.

A new line of Llama Cloths, just what you want for a summer dress, at 12 1-2c.

A good line of Sateens, fine as silk, at 15c.

Knowles & Co.,

UNION and FOURTH STS.

SPECIAL NOTICE.

The demand for the famous "J. H. CUTTER" WHISKIES, (for which we are the sole agents in this city) having become so great, many houses out of the State are sending their travelers in here, with the hope of inducing our trade to buy the "Cutter" whiskies from them, by underselling us, or rather trying to. We therefore beg to say to our friends and the public generally, we will NOT allow ourselves to be undersold by any house dealing in the genuine "J. H. CUTTER" WHISKIES, and we are prepared to protect our trade, not only in QUALITY but in PRICES as well.

Very Respectfully,

BENJAMIN DAWSON,
597 Purchase Street.

Sole agent for New Bedford, Mass., for the famous J. H. Cutter Whiskies. 8p

DRINK
ROXBURY RYE
WHISKEY.
Equaled by few, Excelled by None.
je6-12t8p

THE BIDDEFORD STRIKE.

No Change in Number of Men at Work in the Mills.

Biddeford, Me., June 15.—No demonstration occurred here today in connection with the mill strike. There is no change in the number of men at work in the mills. The executive committee will meet Agent McArthur this afternoon, and probably a mass meeting will be held then. The strikers will be asked to resume work pending a settlement by arbitration.

EAT H-O
HORNBY'S OATMEAL
EAT H-O
FOR BREAKFAST.
EAT H-O
HORNBY'S OATMEAL
EAT H-O
FOR BREAKFAST.
EAT H-O

[From Yesterday's Third Edition.]

THE ASSASSIN!

Seen on the Day of the Murders.

Mysterious Stranger Near the House.

Dr. Handy Again Tells of Wild Eyed Man.

Visitors to the Barn Before the Police.

Government Points Being Flatly Contradicted.

As the end of the trial appears in sight, the interest, which has been absorbing throughout, seems if possible to be growing in intensity. The crowds which seek admittance are growing much larger and correspondingly importunate. Throughout the dinner recess the number who were on hand waiting for seats remained undiminished and was constantly augmented as the time for the afternoon session arrived, until when the doors were opened there were more than twice as many on the outside as could be admitted. Emma Borden was at the court this afternoon for the first time since the trial commenced, and arrived at about 2 o'clock. There were many who desired to see her, and a grand rush was made for the rear entrance when the carriage in which she rode drove up. There is a marked change in Lizzie's manner and appearance. She came into the court room with a sprightly step and manifests a deep interest in the evidence that is being offered. She plainly shows that she believes the witnesses now testifying are her friends, and she appears anxious to hear all they have to say. There was an unusually large attendance of the members of the Bristol county bar and every seat within the rail was occupied.

THE EVIDENCE.

Cross-Examination of Mark Chase by Mr. Knowlton Resumed.

When the court opened this afternoon the cross-examination of Mark Chase was begun by Mr. Knowlton.

Q. You say the place where you were standing was north or south of the Borden house, which? A. South.

Q. Pretty near the corner of Spring street? A. Very near it.

Q. On the same side of the street, or the opposite side? A. On the opposite side.

Q. When was your attention attracted to the team? A. About ten minutes of 11.

Q. The team was facing to the north? A. Yes sir.

Q. How many times did you see the team? A. I saw it once.

Q. Did you stop to look at it? A. I didn't.

Q. Just glanced at it? A. Yes.

Q. Could you tell what position the team was with reference to Dr. Kelly's house? A. It was below, next to a tree.

Q. Next to a tree that stood near the fence? A. Near the Borden fence. (Witness pointed out the tree in a photograph.)

Q. Was the head of the horse toward that tree? A. Yes sir.

Q. That is, the body of the wagon was nearer you than the tree? A. Yes sir.

Q. Was any part of the horse by that tree? A. No sir.

Q. The horse was facing down hill? A. Yes sir.

Q. Was any part of the team in front of the Borden property? A. That I cannot say.

Q. Was the horse hitched? A. I did not notice.

Q. Is there a place on that tree to hitch a horse? A. I do not know.

Q. Was it a top buggy? A. No sir.

Q. Was it a buggy with a high back? A. Yes sir.

Q. A padded cushion back? A. I could not say.

Q. How much of the man did you see? A. From his shoulders up.

Q. You saw the back of his head, his shoulders and his hat? A. Yes.

Q. Did you see any part of his face? A. Just the side of his face.

Q. I suppose you would not undertake to say whether it was anybody you knew? A. No sir.

Q. How far was the rear of the team from Dr. Kelly's front door? A. I didn't measure, I should say about 25 feet.

Q. Further north or south? A. Further down hill.

Q. Did the man turn around? A. No sir.

Q. Did you see anything in the team? A. No sir.

(Mr. Knowlton here consulted a plan and asked witness if the whole distance between Dr. Kelly's front steps and the Borden fence was not less than 25 feet? Witness said he didn't know.)

Mr. Knowlton—If that is so, then it could not have been 25 feet away? A. No sir.

Q. Was there anything except that it was a little further down hill to show you it wasn't somebody who was waiting for a call on the doctor? A. No sir.

Q. Nothing to indicate to the contrary that you saw? A. No sir.

"DR. HANDY'S WILD EYED MAN."

Fall River Physician Testifies About a Mysterious Stranger.

Dr. Benjamin J. Handy was next called.

Q. You are a physician? A. Yes sir.

Q. Where do you practice? A. In Fall River.

Q. Did you go by the house on the morning of the murder? A. Yes sir.

Q. At what time? A. At half past 10.

Q. You saw a man who attracted your attention? A. Yes sir.

Q. Will you describe his appearance? A. He was a medium-sized young man, pale in complexion. He kept his eyes fixed on the sidewalk, and he was going south.

Q. Where did you see him? A. In the open space between the Kelly house and the next one.

Q. What in his appearance most strongly attracted your attention? A. He was paler than it is usual to see persons.

Q. In consequence of his appearance did you do anything? A. I turned in my carriage to watch him as I drove by.

Q. Had you ever seen him before? A. I have a faint idea that I had seen him on Second street some days before.

Q. Do you know Thomas Boulds? A. Yes sir, he used to work for me.

Q. Do you know George L. Douglass? A. Yes sir.

Q. Was it he? A. No sir.

Q. Can you describe him any further? A. He was dressed in a light suit of clothes.

Q. Have you searched or made any attempt to find him since. A. Yes sir.

Q. Have you helped the police to search for him? A. Yes sir.

Q. So far as you know he has never been seen since? A. No sir.

Cross-examined by Mr. Knowlton.

Q. What time did you say you saw him? A. Somewhere between 20 minutes past 10 and 20 minutes to 11.

Q. Which way was he progressing? A. Toward the south.

Q. Away from the Borden house? A. Yes sir.

Q. And walking very slowly? A. Yes sir.

Q. Describe what you meant by acting strangely? A. I can't put it in words. He was acting differently than I have ever seen a man acting on the street.

Q. Did he turn around? A. No sir.

Q. Did he look back? A. No sir.

Q. Did he appear like a man who was intoxicated? A. No sir.

Q. Did he turn like a man hesitating where to go? A. He appeared mentally agitated.

Q. Was there anything in his movements which showed mental agitation? A. Not that I can describe.

Q. Did he half stop and then go on? A. No sir.

Q. You say he had his eyes on the sidewalk? A. Yes sir.

Q. And didn't look up? A. No sir.

Q. He walked very slowly? A. Yes sir.

Q. All you tell us about his appearance that attracted your attention to him was that he was pale, walked slowly and kept his eyes on the sidewalk? A. Yes sir.

Q. There was nothing about his clothing that attracted your attention? A. No sir.

Q. How long before that time had you seen him? A. Several days.

Q. This was the only time you had seen him that day? A. Yes sir.

Q. He was alone? A. Yes sir.

Q. Was there any one else on the sidewalk? A. No sir.

Q. Which way did you say he was going? A. North.

Q. He was on the sidewalk? A. Yes sir.

Q. He was looking down toward the sidewalk and walking very slowly? A. Yes sir.

Q. Did he stagger? A. No sir.

Q. Was there any movement that was any different from that of a man walking slowly and lost in thought? A. I thought there was.

Q. What was it? A. A swaying, rolling movement.

Q. Anything more than that of a man hesitating about turning around? A. I thought it was.

Q. Did his feet oscillate? A. No sir.

Q. All the oscillation was in his body? A. Yes sir.

Q. Was the time you saw him nearer 20 minutes past 10 or 20 minutes of 11? A. I couldn't tell.

Q. Do you own a cottage in Marion? A. Yes sir.

Q. Had the defendant been down there? A. No sir.

Q. You expected her? A. Yes sir.

DELIA S. MANLEY

Sawa Mysterious Man on the Day of the Murder.

Mrs. Delia S. Manley.

Q. Where do you live? A. 206 Second street, Fall River.

Q. Were you acquainted with Andrew J. Borden when alive? A. Yes.

Q. Do you know the Kelley house? A. Yes.

Q. Did you have relatives occupy it? A. Yes.

Q. Did you pass the Borden house on the morning of the murder? A. I did.

Q. Did you stop in the vicinity? A. Yes.

Q. See anybody on the premises? A. Yes.

Q. What time? A. About a quarter of 10.

Q. Describe who it was that you saw? A. I saw a man dressed in light clothes, (I should say he was a young man,) standing there.

Q. What was he doing? A. Standing in the gateway, leaning on the gate post.

Q. Was it Andrew J. Borden? A. No.

Q. Was it Mr. Morse? A. No.

Q. Was it anybody you had seen before? A. No.

Q. What were you doing at the time? A. I was looking at a horse and carriage standing there.

Q. Was anybody with you? A. Yes.

Q. Where was the horse and carriage? A. Under the tree between the two houses.

Q. When you first saw the man where were you? A. It was when I was coming back up onto the sidewalk.

Q. Had you seen him the first time you passed? A. No.

Q. Is there any other similar gateway in that vicinity? A. There are others like it, but none with a tree in front.

Q. Do you know what became of the man? A. No, he was standing there when I came away.

Q. What were the people in the team doing? A. They were looking the other way.

Q. Did they come away when you did? A. Yes.

Cross-examined by Mr. Knowlton.

Q. Were you where you could see the man plainly? A. Yes.

Q. You say he was there when you came away? A. Yes.

Q. What was he doing? A. Nothing only just standing there.

Q. Did he have anything in his hand? A. No.

Q. Any one else could have seen him, could they? A. Yes.

JEROME T. BORDEN

Cousin of the Prisoner Gives Some Facts That Help Her.

Jerome T. Borden was the next witness.

Q. What is your business? A. Lumber.

Q. You live in Fall River? A. Yes.

Q. Are you a cousin—relative of the defendant? A. I am.

Q. Did you go to the Borden house soon after the murder? A. I did, the same day.

Q. What time did you arrive there? A. Soon after 2 o'clock.

Q. What door did you go in by? A. The front door.

Q. Was it opened or unlocked? A. I opened it.

Q. How close to was it, shut? A. Close to.

Q. Did you observe the spring lock? A. I didn't examine it.

Q. Was or was not there a manifestation by the inmates of the house of surprise at your coming in the door without it being opened for you?

Objection was made, and the question was ruled out.

Q. Did you ring? A. I did not.

Q. Tell what you did do. A. I went up the steps, opened the door and went in.

Q. Were there any officers present? A. One was leaning over the front fence.

WALTER B. STEVENS,

A Wideawake Newspaper Man Testifies for the Defense.

Walter B. Stevens, reporter for the Fall River News, was the next witness.

Q. What is your name? A. Walter B. Stevens.

Q. Were you a reporter for the Daily News of Fall River at the time of the Borden murder? A. Yes sir.

Q. Did you go there that morning? A. I did.

Q. What time did you first hear of the trouble up there? A. I don't know just what time it was.

Q. Can you tell us what time it was when you arrived there? A. I arrived there with Officer Mullaly.

Q. Whom did you see there when you arrived? A. There were several people about the house.

Q. Was Officer Medley there? A. I didn't see him then.

Q. How soon did you go into the yard? A. Very soon after.

Q. Where did you go first when you went into the yard? A. In the yard between the Kelley yard and the Borden house and looked at the grass.

Q. What did you do next? A. I then went to the rear fence and looked over the fence into the Chagnon yard, then I went into the barn.

Q. Did you go into the house? A. Yes sir.

Q. Did you see Officer Medley in the house? A. Yes.

Q. Where was he? A. He was going in.

Q. Did he come out after you went in? A. No, I think not.

Q. When you went into the barn was anybody in there? A. No sir.

Q. Did anybody come in there while you were in there? A. Yes.

Q. Who? A. I don't know.

Q. Did you go up stairs? A. No, I did not.

Q. Did you see anybody go up stairs? A. I heard somebody going up stairs.

Q. How many people did you hear go up stairs? A. At least three.

Q. Did you go up stairs at all in the barn? A. No.

Q. What time did you go away? A. I don't know just what time, when I turned into Second street the clock struck 12.

Cross-examined.

Q. Did you say what time you got there? A. No sir.

Q. Can you give me an approximate of the time? A. No sir.

Q. After you got there did you see Mr. Medley? A. I was standing in the hallway and he came in the door.

Q. Did you see him come on to the premises? A. No sir.

Q. Nor when he came you do not know? A. No sir.

Q. Where was Mr. Medley when you first saw him? A. In the entry.

Q. Did you see him again after that? A. I don't recall that I saw him again.

Q. When he went into the barn you don't know? Nor whether he was one of the three that went into the barn you don't know? A. He was not.

Q. Do you know who they were? A. I am not sure who they were. I think one was John Donovan.

Q. When you first got there where did you go? A. I went into the yard between the Borden house and the Kelly yard.

Q. Where did you get your information of the murder? A. From the police station.

What were you doing in the yard? A. Looking around.

Q. Looking around where? A. Looking in the grass.

Q. Which side of the house was that on? A. On the south side.

Q. Next to Dr. Kelly's? A. Yes sir.

Q. Did you find the tracks of a person there? A. Yes sir.

Q. Were there tracks next to the Kelley fence? A. I do not remember that the grass was trampled next to the fence.

Q. Do you not know but that these tracks were made by people who were there before you were? A. No sir.

Q. Where did you go then? A. To the back of the yard by the Chagnon fence.

Q. What were you looking for there? A. Tracks.

Q. Did you find any tracks over there? A. No sir.

Q. Did you look over the fence? A. I stood on the stringer.

Q. You did not get up on the lumber pile? A. I do not remember.

Q. What did you do then? A. I followed the fence way along to the barn.

Q. Doing what? A. Looking on the other side.

Q. Did you look over the fence without climbing on the stringer? A. I was on the stringer.

Q. You mean you walked on the stringer? A. Yes sir.

Q. You went clear to the corner? A. Yes sir.

Q. Were you looking for anything else? A. Looking for anything I could find.

Q. Were there blood stains on the fence? A. I do not recall that I found blood stains.

Q. Did you look over into the Crow yard? A. I didn't look over there then.

Q. Did you afterwards? A. Not that day.

Q. After you got to the corner what did you do then? A. I stepped down and walked by the barn.

Q. You did not go into the barn at that time? A. No sir, I was looking at a filled-in well.

Q. Did you look in the vault behind the barn? A. Yes sir.

Q. You had to take off the boards? A. The boards were removed.

Q. After you looked into the well where did you go then? A. I do not recall at that time whether I went to the rear cellar door or not.

Q. Did you go to the rear cellar door? A. I went there at one time.

Q. How did you find it? A. It didn't open.

Q. Did you try to open it? A. Yes sir.

Q. And you failed to open it? A. Yes sir.

Q. How was it fastened, you don't know? A. I don't know whether it was fastened.

Q. Did it appear to you to be fastened? A. It didn't open when I tried it.

Q. Did it appear to you to be fastened? A. My impression is that it was fastened.

Q. Then what did you do? A. I went into the house.

Q. When did you see Donavan first? A. I do not recall whether it was before or after.

Q. When did you first see the other men that you saw going up into the barn? A. I never saw them before that I know of.

Q. Did you talk with anybody in the house? A. Mrs. Churchill.

Q. Did you make notes of the talk? A. No sir.

Q. Did you talk with anybody else? A. Not at that time.

Q. Where did you go then? A. I went into the barn.

Q. Was the door shut when you went into the barn? A. It was not.

Q. How long did you stay in the barn? A. I came right out.

Q. Then you went right away? A. I won't be certain whether I went right away or not.

Q. Why won't you be certain? A. Because I don't recall whether I did or not.

Q. Do you recall any of your movements in the order of them? A. Yes, I remember the first part.

Q. Do you remember of doing anything else before you left the premises? A. Not in particular.

Q. Have you any remembrance in general? A. I think I started away shortly afterwards.

ALFRED CLARKSON

Says He Visited the Borden Barn Before the Police.

Alfred Clarkson was the next witness called.

(Continued on Seventh Page.)

Highest of all in Leavening Power.—Latest U. S. Gov't Report.

Royal Baking Powder

ABSOLUTELY PURE

THE MYSTERY NOT SOLVED.

Opinion of the Government's Case Against Lizzie Borden.

(Editorial in N. Y. Herald of June 15.)

The government is expected to close its case in the Borden trial today, when evidence will be offered to show that Lizzie Borden tried to buy poison on the day before the tragedy. Its evidence is substantially all in now, and hence may be reviewed and judged by the public.

In the mind of every one who has taken an interest in this absorbing trial the uppermost question now is, has the commonwealth of Massachusetts solved the mystery of the most remarkable tragedy of this generation? Has it revealed in the unfortunate woman at the bar the heartless criminal who struck down the aged couple in their Fall River home last August with such fiendish ferocity?

Whether the jury will convict, acquit or disagree no one can tell. But it is safe to say that while opinions may differ as to whether Lizzie Borden committed that ghastly crime, the great popular verdict is likely to be that the government has failed to prove her guilt and leaves the mystery as unfathomable as ever.

The corner stone of its case in that no one else could have been the perpetrator and escape detection. But that is merely negative proof, and while it has its force it still leaves guilt to be shown by affirmative evidence.

In the affirmative evidence produced by the government there is much that bears against Lizzie Borden's innocence. It was shown that she was up stairs when her stepmother lay murdered on the floor, and must have seen her mangled body. The young woman declared she was in the barn when her father was murdered. Yet no one saw her go or come from there, and the government witnesses swear they found the barn locked and no footprints in the dust that covered the loft floor. She explained that her stepmother had been summoned by note to a sick friend. Yet no trace of any such note could be found, and the sick friend appears to have been a myth. Moreover, it is significant that after the alarm of the father's murder had been given, Miss Borden suggested that some one go up stairs and look for Mrs. Borden, saying that she thought she heard her come in. Then there was the extraordinary composure shown by the daughter in a crisis that would have overcome any ordinary woman with shock and uncontrollable emotion.

But is all this sufficient to prove guilt? In every capital trial it is all important to prove the motive and produce the weapon. In this trial it was further imperative to produce the blood-bespattered garments worn by the murderer or account for their nonproduction. No one of these vitally essential points has been established by the government.

To supply a motive it was charged that Miss Borden's home life was not happy, and, furthermore, that she dispatched the couple that she might inherit her father's wealth. The evidence offered in support of this theory is vague and weak, and even if the motive were proved it would hardly account for a double murder characterized by such atrocity. As for the weapon, the prosecution has produced a varied assortment of axes and hatchets, but has failed to show that any one of them was even probably the instrument of death.

But the weakest feature of the government's case is its failure to produce any blood-stained garments of the accused, to account for their nonproduction, or to prove any stain on either her apparel or person. Even its own experts have testified that the murderer must have been bespattered with crimson. Yet all the witnesses who saw Lizzie Borden immediately after the alarm was given observed no trace of guilt on her, and science itself has not since been able to reveal any on the clothing she then wore.

The government has offered evidence to show that on Sunday, three days after the tragedy, Miss Borden burned a dress in the presence of two witnesses because it was "all covered with paint." But would any criminal of intelligence keep for three days such damning proof of guilt and then seek to destroy it in the face of others? Even the witness who gave this testimony saw on the garment no trace of either blood or paint. Moreover, according to the government's witnesses, it was the same dress worn by Lizzie Borden when the alarm was given and no stain on it was then seen by any one.

While the government has shown much which is hard to account for on any theory of her innocence, its failure to establish a motive, produce the weapon, or fix any blood stain on the person or the apparel of Lizzie Borden must be taken as a failure to prove guilt beyond a reasonable doubt. The trial bids fair to leave the mystery as much a matter of speculation as ever.

Diamond Dealers Assigned.

New York, June 15.—Charles Cottier and Jean Cottier, composing the firm of Cottier & Son, dealers in diamonds at 171 Broadway, assigned today without preferences. Liabilities exceed $100,000.

Two Women Speak

For the benefit of others.

Miss Helen Smith,

43 22d Place, Chicago, Ill., says:—

"I was troubled with irregularity and leucorrhœa. I followed Mrs. Pinkham's advice, took her *Vegetable Compound*, and used her Sanative Wash. I now feel like a new woman, and am perfectly healthy."

Mrs. E. Fox,

Woodstown, N. J., writes:—

"I had been sick 10 years with womb trouble and leucorrhœa. I could do no work. Doctors could not help me. *Lydia E. Pinkham's Vegetable Compound* did. Now I can do all my work, and stand nearly all day, and not feel tired. I cannot thank you enough. I recommend it to every woman who has any weakness."

Yours for Health
Lydia E. Pinkham

All druggists sell it.
Address in confidence,
LYDIA E. PINKHAM MED. CO., LYNN, MASS.
Liver Pills, 25 cents.

THE NEW SENSATION.

"I Have Found Lizzie Borden's Hatchet,"

Cried a Boy in John Crowe's Barn in Fall River.

Discovery Made in Rear of the Borden Estate.

Fall River, June 15.—The Daily News Bulletin this afternoon has the following:

About 7 o'clock last evening a number of boys were engaged in playing ball on Third street, in front of John Crowe's barn, which is nearly in the rear of the Borden estate, the north side of the barn serving as a fence between Dr. Chagnon's orchard, which is directly in the rear of the Borden house, and the Kelly lot, on which the barn stands.

The barn is a flat roof structure about 18 feet high. In the rear is an ell, the full width of the main building, but not more than 12 feet high. Still extending to the west and toward the Borden estate is a narrow flat roofed ell, about nine feet high. A six-foot fence runs diagonally and south-easterly from the north line of the first ell to the second ell, so that it is very easy to scale the roof.

During the game of the boys, the ball was knocked, or thrown, upon the roof of the main barn, and Master Arthur Potter, 14 years old, son of Caleb C. Potter, of the water works office, scaled the building in quest of it.

Near the northwest corner of the main building—about six feet from the west and four feet from the north line of the structure—on the northeast corner of the roof, he found a hatchet of ordinary size, lying with the head toward the southeast, the handle towards the northwest corner.

He forgot the ball and he rushed for the hatchet, and then rang out his salute to the boys below:

I've Found Lizzie Borden's Hatchet.

The hatchet is an ordinary shingle hatchet with a blade 3¾ inches in length. It was covered in rust and part of this was scraped off by the boy when found. It has the appearance of having been comparatively new and but little used.

The handle, which is 13½ inches long, looked weather-worn as if it had been long exposed to air, sun and storm. The under side of the handle had a few slight stains, but nothing that resembled spots. Near the head of the hatchet, these stains were more pronounced.

The boys were much excited over the find, and it was given to Mr. Potter, the father of the finder, who now has it in his possession. He at once notified the police and tried to find Mr. Jennings, but in this was unsuccessful.

If the murderer of Andrew J. Borden and his wife escaped from the Borden premises by the rear, and it was a very easy way for him to so escape, he could easily have thrown the hatchet to the place where it was found.

So far as is known no man has been on the roof within two years. Mr. Crowe knows of none; all telegraph, telephone, electric light wiremen, roofers and several photographers agree on this. The police did not visit it in their thorough search.

The police have been carefully examining the hatchet this morning. They thought they could tell whether there had been blood on it or not. They confess that they are baffled.

But one of them, who has been an important witness in the Borden case, admits that with the new find and the exclusion of the Bence story everything has gone up for the government so far as a possible conviction of Lizzie Borden is concerned.

The defense has opened its case. Now look for important and vital contradictions of government testimony.

Mamie Adams
Waterbury, Vermont.

Wonderful and True

Totally Blind with Scrofulous Sore Eyes

Hood's Sarsaparilla Gave Back Her Sight, and Joy to Her Father's Heart.

"Waterbury, Vt., Nov. 19, 1892.

"C. I. Hood & Co., Lowell, Mass.:

"In April, 1889, my little girl Mamie, who was then 3 years old, commenced having ulcerated eyes, also had sores back of her ears. Her sight began to grow dim, and I feared she

Might be Blind.

I then lived in Jericho, Vt. In the early days of June I went with her to the Mary Fletcher hospital in Burlington, and there she was treated four different times—a surgical operation each time, one of which left the scars now visible on the eye balls. She recovered from this treatment each time, a slight improvement for a few days, was soon **worse than ever.** She could discern daylight from darkness, but **could not see to walk across the room.**

"I next went to a large hospital in Hartford, Conn. At this hospital no surgical operations were performed, but medicine was dropped into her eyes and given her to take. She was at this hospital about ten weeks, **continually growing worse,** and when I took her in November

Was Totally Blind.

"I arrived at my station in Jericho with the child, sad in spirit and impoverished in pocket **completely discouraged.** On our way to the house from the station, we stopped at the store of Capt. McKinnan, who was an old sea captain, to warm ourselves. The captain had known the child before we went away. While we were warming ourselves Mamie said:

"'Papa, it's dark, where are you? I can't see you, come to me.'

"The captain's heart was touched, and with tears in his eyes he said:

"'Charley, you go and get a bottle of Hood's Sarsaparilla and give it to her, and if it don't help her I will pay for it.'

"That very afternoon I got Hood's Sarsaparilla and commenced giving it to her according to directions. The first beneficial result was a brightening of the eyes, which continued steadily improving until, under the treatment of Hood's Sarsaparilla, on the ninth day she **could see to pick up a pin** on the floor without its being pointed out to her, and before the first bottle was all used

Her Sight was Entirely Restored.

I keep Hood's Sarsaparilla in the house always, and when the child gets a little cold, if her eyes appear inflamed, a few doses settles it. I thank God first, Hood's Sarsaparilla second,

Hood's Sarsaparilla Cures

and Capt. McKinnan third. Many of the first families in Jericho can vouch for the facts given above. I am glad to give this testimonial of what Hood's Sarsaparilla has done for me, which is good and lots of it." CHAS. A. ADAMS.

C. L. SMITH, C. M. GRIFFITH,
Witnesses to above signature.

HOOD'S PILLS cure all Liver Ills, Biliousness, Jaundice, Indigestion, Sick Headache.

THE FOXY TRAVERS.

Bound Over for Sentence in Newton Friday.

Police Have Still Another Warrant Against Him.

Interesting Story Told by Prisoner in His Own Behalf.

(Special Dispatch.)

Newton, June 15.—The case of Dr. Matthew Travers of New Bedford, charged with obtaining money under false pretenses from William J. Holmes, a colored expressman of this city, came up in the police court this morning before Judge John C. Kennedy.

The story of Holmes' claim is that Travers on April 29, under the name of Shorter, obtained $49 from him under the pretense of collecting a legacy left by a friend in Barbadoes, has already been told in the Standard. Mrs. Caroline Holmes, wife of the plaintiff, told how the defendant came to the house, told the same story, and how her son copied the English portion of the letter claiming to come from the Barbadoes.

William Holmes, employed in Boston, told how the defendant and plaintiff called upon him, went through the same story, and his father borrowed $25 to help make up the $49. Recently the defendant called at his boarding house to see the landlady. He recognized him, learned his correct name and address, and the warrant was obtained.

Joseph, another son, was at home when prisoner called, and testified to copying the letter from Barbadoes.

Katie V. Kehoe, clerk in a Boston lawyer's office, testified to writing out a power of attorney, and hearing defendant saying he would give a receipt.

Inspector Henthorn said the man was known as Matthew Travers in New Bedford.

The defendant then took the stand. He said he had such a letter from Barbadoes in which Mr. Holmes' name was mentioned. Mr. Holmes said he knew the person who had left the legacy, and he gave the witness a power of attorney, but did not pay the money. The receipt was forged from some other paper. Shorter was his name in Spanish. He was a practicing physician. Had been in New Bedford five years. Was a graduate of Bishop university and had a diploma.

Judge Kennedy finally bound the prisoner over for sentence to Friday morning in the sum of $800. Bail was not furnished.

The Newton officials have another warrant against Dr. Travers for obtaining $80 from another Newton party on a similar story. Among the uncalled witnesses this morning was a lady who claims the doctor was unsuccessful in getting her to advance quite a neat sum for a like purpose.

A FAST YOUNG CLERK.

Drove a Horse to Death, Stole Jewelry, was Arrested and Escaped.

Fall River, June 16.—William A. Harpin, 16 years of age, was arrested Thursday on complaint charging him with stealing jewelry from the store of A. B. Bruneau. The prisoner was employed as a clerk, and first attracted attention a few weeks ago by driving a horse to death. That splurge took him into the district court, and there were suspicions that he was following the pace which he had set with the animal. At all events he was watched and taken into custody once more. His employer declines to give any information regarding the extent of the alleged stealing. Harpin did not remain a great while in the cell room after his arrest by Inspector Medley. The police discovered that he was missing last evening, and up to a late hour no trace of him had been obtained. There is a narrow space between the top of the iron grating and the arch of the door, and it is supposed that the prisoner climbed over into the corridor. The door leading into the guard room must have been unlocked, and it was an easy matter to get to Court square if that were the case. The windows behind the cells are covered with a heavy grating and Harpin could not have forced his way through them.

DARBY O'BRIEN DEAD.

A Star Ball Player and Left Fielder of the Brooklyns.

New York, June 16.—A special telegram from Peoria, Ill., announces the death of "Darby" O'Brien, the well known left fielder of the Brooklyn Base-ball club. O'Brien has been dying with consumption for some time, and a month or so ago the members of the New York and Brooklyn clubs got up a benefit which yielded $3,000.

W. D. O'Brien, best known as "Darby," was born in Peoria, Ill., Sept. 1st,

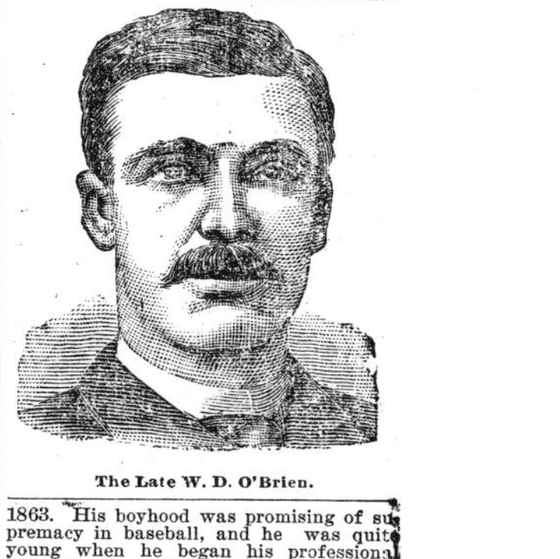

The Late W. D. O'Brien.

1863. His boyhood was promising of supremacy in baseball, and he was quite young when he began his professional career as a member of the Peoria Reds, with whom he played in 1882. He rested the next season, but was the successful captain of the Keokuk (Ia.) club in 1884. The ensuing two years he played ball for the Denver (Col.) club, and was captain both seasons. In 1887 he was engaged for the Metropolitans of New York. Before long he was one of the star players of the American association. When Brooklyn bought the Metropolitans, O'Brien was transferred to the purchasers. His cleverest work was in the left field, but he was also a fine batter and base runner.

AN UNLUCKY START.

The Navahoe Runs Into a Pilot Boat and Is Laid Up For Repairs.

BOSTON, June 16.—The steel sloop Navahoe was picked up during a dense fog, near Minot's light, in a disabled condition by the tugboat Peter B. Bradly, which assisted her to an anchorage below Boston light. She was afterward towed to this city and anchored off the Atlantic works. She will be repaired there. She left Newport, R. I., on Sunday last at 3:30 p. m., bound to Southampton, Eng., where she was to race with the English yachts. At 2:30 a. m. on Monday, when in the vicinity of the southe[illegible] edge of Georges bank, she came in col[illegible]on with New York pilot boat No. 5 in [illegible] thick fog. She had her starboard bow stove above the water line; also had topmast carried away and sprung bowsprit. The damage to the pilot boat was not ascertained, as she disappeared in the fog immediately after the accident.

The six Wright brothers were standing under a tree at Adrian, Mo., when lightning killed four of them and injured the other two so they may die.

HASKELL & TRIPP.

The laziest, dreamiest resti s in an easy hammock. Have you one? The price needn't stand in the way.

White or fancy colored, improved Mexican hammocks, 14 feet long, are $1.25 each. Very handsome, colored hammocks with fancy tassel trimming, are $2.39 each.

The cottage furnisher will find economy and good style combined in those big rugs we are making a "run" at at $1.98. Colors and designs copy India rugs, 2 yards long by 1 yard wide.

Summer blankets, 75c. and $1 a pair. Summer crochet bedspreads, 75c. and $1 apiece. Hard wood, nicely finished small tables, 89c.

Best adjustable fly screens in the market, openwork at sides to admit all the air possible. Price only 25c. each.

White Mountain ice cream freezers.

Galvanized iron drip pans for the refrigerator.

Let us help you to save part of the purchase money if you are thinking of buying a refrigerator of any size. See *ours.*

White Goods Department. We found an importer with a lot of English Batistes that he was anxious to turn into money. *We took 'em for less than half cost.* That's the reason we can offer those who come soon beautiful cream white Batistes, 32 inches wide, for 12½c. instead of 25c. a yard. Right for hot weather dresses or for shade hat trimmings, very soft thin material that will drape nicely.

Irish lawns, 38 inches wide, 12½c. a yard, neat designs printed on white grounds. The correct fabric for shirt waists.

Polka dots, white or navy blue ground sateen, only 12½c. a yard.

Black ground printed Organdies, 15c. Solid black cotton goods that look just like wool grenadines, 15c. a yard. Both new and very desirable for immediate use.

Corded ginghams, twenty choice styles, 10c. a yard.

Fully thirty styles of the 8c. per yard printed muslins. *Nothing we ever had in such goods could compare in value with these.* The cloth is right — thoroughly right. But the printing! There is where this bargain lot excels. Notice the roses, the pansies, the vines and blossoms, natural as if a careless hand had dropped them, on grounds of soft tints of heliotrope, nile green, ecru, cream or pink.

Special counter, middle aisle, for this great sale of choice summer muslins, 8c. a yard.

Visit our Candy Department and try a ride of soda water from our new Arctic fountain —basement.

HASKELL & TRIPP,
Department Stores,
Purchase and William Streets.

FOR HER LIFE

Miss Borden's Counsel Speaks.

Urging Her Innocence Upon Jury.

Ex-Gov. Robinson's Masterly Argument

Occupied Whole of Forenoon Session.

Not Concluded When Court Adjourned.

Lizzie's, Statements are Reconcilable.

Burning of the Dress Covered With Paint.

Police Matron Reagan's Story Was False.

Careful Analysis of Evidence Presented.

In the trial of the most celebrated cause in the history of criminal annals in Massachusetts, if not in the country, today will be big with events. All that can be offered by government to convict Lizzie A. Borden of murdering her father and stepmother and all that defense can

offer to show that she could not and did not commit these crimes has been submitted and now the time has arrived for eminent counsel to offer arguments. That these arguments will be masterpieces is a foregone conclusion, and they will be delivered by ex-Governor Robinson, whose clearness and incisiveness has created universal admiration, and by Hon. H. M. Knowlton, whose eloquence and force are well known, and who will make the effort of his life in his attempt to convince the jury that the government has made out its case.

The jury in the Borden case remained in its rooms at the Parker House on Saturday on account of the storm, and passed the time in card playing and letter writing. Yesterday forenoon the members attended the Trinitarian church, where Rev. M. C. Julien preached from I Corinthians 1, 17, "For Christ sent me not to baptize, but to preach the gospel; not with wisdom of words, lest the gospel of Christ should be made of none effect." Mrs. William P. Covell finely rendered a solo. In the afternoon the jurymen were given a ride in a drive to South Dartmouth.

The arguments will occupy all the day and the case will go to the jury tomorrow. Defense will have the opening, and it is impossible to find any one who thinks a verdict of guilty will be rendered by the jury. A good many think the delibera-

---

AN IMMENSE CROWD.

Biggest Ever Gathered Within Walls of Court House.

tions will result in a disagreement, but it is still larger number predict an acquittal of the prisoner.

I thought there had been crowds present in the court house at other times during the trial, but I never realized that so many people could be gathered within the walls as was done. The regular seats were all filled, extra ones placed in the aisles were occupied, the anterooms were packed, women sat upon the stairs, and the lower corridor was beset by anxious and eager people. The seats inside the rail were occupied by notables, including among them ex-Governor Davis of Rhode Island, ex-mayors of this city, and even two ladies were present. Members of the bar who were unable to get seats stood up in corners or any possible place.

Lizzie Borden came in just before the opening of the court, and instead of taking a seat within the rail occupied her usual one in the dock, with Deputy Sheriff Kirby beside her.

Some preliminaries after the jury was polled, but ex-Governor Robinson proceeded, while a hush fell on the audience.

GOV. ROBINSON'S ADDRESS.

His Masterly Plea to the Jury in Lizzie Borden's Behalf.

Mr. Foreman and Gentlemen:—One of the most dastardly and diabolical crimes that was ever committed in Massachusetts was perpetrated in August, 1892, in the city of Fall River. The enormity and outrage startled everybody, and set all into the most vigilant inquiry as to the perpetrator of the terrible acts. Our society is so constituted, gentlemen, that every man feels that the right must be done, the wrong punished, and the wicked doer brought to his accounts as promptly as due procedure of law will permit.

Here then was a crime with all its horrors, and well may those who stood first to look at the victims have felt sickened and distressed at heart and human nature be broken.

Who could have done such an act, says everybody. In the quiet of the home, in the broad daylight of an August day, on a street of a popular city, with houses within a stone's throw away, almost within touch, who could have done it? An inspection of the victims disclosed that Mrs. Borden had been slain by the use of some sharp and terrible instrument inflicting upon her head 18 blows, 13 of them crushing through the skull. And below stairs, lying upon the sofa, was Mr. Borden's dead and mutilated body with 11 strokes upon the head, four of them crushing the skull. The terrors of these scenes no one can portray, the horrors of that moment we can all fail to describe, and so we are challenged at once at the outset to bind somebody that is equal to that execution, whose heart is blackened with depravity, whose whole life is a reign of crime, whose past is a prodigacy of that awful deed. A maniac or a fiend you say, not a man in his senses, and with his heart, but one of those abnormal productions that Deity creates or suffers, a lunatic or a devil. So do we measure by degree of character or want of it, that could possibly prompt a human being to such acts. They were well directed blows, they were not the result of blundering, they

the county is called together, sits by itself under the direction of the district attorney to investigate and say whether it ought to come before a jury like yourselves. Now remember that the time when this indictment of last December was framed this defendant had no voice, it was purely one-sided. It said we make this charge, serious as it is, against this defendant, and we will ask her to go to the Bristol county court house, and if we cannot prove it against her in the ordinary way

She Shall Go Free, She is Not Guilty.

Now that is all one-sided up to that point, practically. And so you are to draw no inference whatever, and I know you will not; will draw no inference whatever as against this defendant, until you have heard the evidence in this case, in this court room, at this time. You have nothing to do with what was done in Fall River any more than you have in what is proceeding now in Australia. It is of no consequence that Judge Blaisdell of the district court of Fall River, worthy man as he may be, has any sort of influence or obligation over you. He is free, here is free, here are you gentlemen.

I say then at the outset, as you begin to contemplate this crime, and the possible perpetration by this defendant, we must conclude at the outset that such acts as these are morally and physically impossible for this young woman defendant. To foully murder her stepmother, then go straightway and brutally slay her own father is a wreck of human morals, is a

Contradiction of Her Physical Capacity.

Now, before I pass let me say that this defendant complains of no persecution on the part of the district attorney. He has only one duty, that is, as a gentleman and a lawyer, to conduct this investigation so that the truth as to her may be illustrated. With his well earned fame and his high standing at the bar, he would have no need to search for laurels for his fame, and he is one of the last men that would demean himself so as to even think of it. He stands above the miserable assertions that unthinking people will make; he walks into this court room only as the representative of the commonwealth of Massachusetts—that is yours, and mine, and his. He says, gentlemen, all I have to show you is the case we have against this woman, and if the case I have had brought to me by the Fall River police is not sufficient, or you have any doubt about it, he will say, if he speaks what for God's sake, say so like men, and Bristol county will be the purer and the securer afterwards. He is not here for blood, neither is he helped to such dishonorable work if it were attempted by our counsel's friend, the district attoney from the great county of Essex, one of the best and most reliable lawyers. Here is only the presentation, but you see not merely play, you will see no mean tactics on the part of the commonwealth. Here is only the presentation, and not over-strained in one jot or one tittle, only the presentation of what has been proved here, and only that.

So merciful is our provisions of the law that a defendant shall have a decent chance that she becomes convinced how thoughtfully that is carried out when she recalls the numerous kindnesses and considerations on the part of the sheriff of this county he has done her, not as a convicted criminal, but as a woman of this county entitled to her rights guaranteed to her under the constitution and laws.

So she comes into this court, presided over by our best of the judiciary, clean, able, honorable gentlemen, who sit vigilantly by on the bench to guard against any possible wrong, who wants the commonwealth's case tried, but the defendant to pass without abuse or wrong.

I said the case was brought to the district attorney by the Fall River police. I have not time to go into any sarcasm or denunciation of these gentlemen, they are like a great many bodies of police that you find in all communities. Policemen are human, made out of men and nothing else, and **The Blue Coat and the Brass Buttons Only Cover the Kind of a Man That is Inside.** You do not get the greatest ability in the world inside of a policeman's coat, you may perhaps get what you want, what is sufficient, but you must only call for him for such service as he can render. Now, when a police officer undertakes to investigate a crime he is bent on the detection of the criminal. He is blamed if he does not get somebody into the lockup. The newspapers are not always right mostly. The marshal says these murders were committed yesterday. Haven't you got anybody yet? Get somebody into the lockup. They are sensitive to all this. But when they go upon the witness stand they reveal their weakness.

They knock their own heads together and make themselves ridiculous asking the defendant to tell over and over again where she was at various times of the day and telling it always the same. They are but human, and don't ask of them anything impossible, but don't wonder they do not always come up to the standard that they would like to set for every one else.

An eminent counsel once said in a case, and I am impressed with it in this case, that the most refreshing thing that ever came to the sight of an accused party is the jury. Who are you, men? You are Bristol county men. Men of heads and hearts and souls—honest men selected out of 150 who were summoned here. You came here because you were men loyal to the commonwealth. You are not of families where there are daughters, wives and sisters, and recognize the bonds which unite households. Let us talk together as men, honest, and not mean men.

You remember your oath, and that oath deeply impressed me. "You shall well and truly try and true deliverance make between the commonwealth and the defendant." Lizzie Andrew Borden from the time the trial opened to this hour has been in your charge. Now has come the time, not for her lawyers to speak for her, not for the judges to protect her, not for the district attorney no longer proceed against her, but for 12 men to take their fingers in charge and the commonwealth says we can trust her to you. She isn't a horse, a house or a parcel of land, but is a

Free, Thinking Innocent Woman in your charge.

I noticed a little scene during this trial that made its imprint upon my mind, you will remember it. When you were coming in and the judges were about to take their places upon the bench the defendant asked to pass around so that she could sit with her counsel. There she stood waiting, calmly waiting, between the judges and the jury, and the thought flashed through my mind, there she stands waiting over and cared for. If it be true that the sparrow's fall is known to the great ruler and controller of all things, then that woman stood there not alone in the court room, but was the object of the sympathy and watchful care of more than man.

This is a capital case and involves her life. It calls for only one penalty, and that is death. You understand that, I will consider this case critically and to the best of my judgment, and then no power on earth or in heaven can accuse me." You came here, I believe, as you

(Continued on Third Page.)

Ex-Governor George D. Robinson.

This picture is taken from ex-Gov. Robinson's latest photograph, and is the most accurate of any published during the trial. To the public who followed him through the gubernatorial campaign he is remembered with an entirely different dress of beard—an extended fine reaching down the cheeks and under the chin. To the public who saw him afterward he is pictured with the short side whiskers alone—the most becoming dress of beard he has assumed. Of late, however, Gov. Robinson has worn only a moustache, thus changing the appearance of his face considerably.

were aimed steadily and constantly for a purpose, each one finding its place where it was aimed, and none going amiss on the one side or the other.

Surely we are prompted to say at the outset the perpetrator of that act knew how to handle the instrument, was experienced in its control, had directed it before or others like it. And it was not the careless, sudden, untrained doing of somebody who had been unfamiliar with such an instrument. Now suspicions begin to fall here and there, everybody about there is called to give an account. That is proper, that is right and necessary. Investigation proceeds, the police intervene. They form their theories, they proceed to act; they follow out this and that one. They are human only. When once a theory possesses the mind how firmly we stick to it until we are driven out, perhaps against our own preference to find lodgement in something else. Now no honest man complains of investigation, no one says there ought not to have been anything done, everything ought to have been done, any more, we say that everything was not done and that the proper procedure was not taken.

Now proceed with this matter a little, let us see how we stand. A person is charged with the crime like this this defendant, suspicion surrounded her, and the investigation in regard to her proceeded and she is brought before the district court, in this instance, to have an investigation preliminarily into the probabilities of the crime. Let us remember that that that occurred, she having nothing to do with it, having no control of it, having no part except to answer some." You came here, I believe, as you

---

WEATHER INDICATIONS.
Slightly Warmer.

Washington, June 19.—For the 24 hours from 8 a. m. today: For New England warmer and fair weather; slightly warmer in New Hampshire; northerly winds, becoming variable.
Fair.

Boston, June 19.—Local forecast for New England until Tuesday night: Fair weather; slightly warmer; variable winds.

HOME MATTERS.

THIRD DISTRICT COURT.
Borden, J.
Monday, June 19.

George Seddons was brought into court by Keeper Hunt from the jail and withdrew his appeals from sentences imposed on Saturday of $100 for liquor keeping and $100 for keeping a liquor nuisance and the sentences were reaffirmed.

The appeals of Richard Friday who appealed last Friday from a sentence of three months for keeping a disorderly house. Richard had changed his mind and did not care to have a jury pass on his case. He was sent up for three months.

Eleven cases of drunkenness were disposed of as follows: John R. Collins, 30 days; John McGarr, ten days; John Couza, 10 days; John Conway, 10 days; John Parks, 10 days; Fred Limore, 10 days; Charles Perry, 10 days, and four cases on probation until July 29.

William McCutoking and John Sharp got into a row Saturday night and this morning were each fined $5 for disturbing the peace.

OBITUARY.

Warren Sears, a commercial traveler for Saville, Somes & Co., wholesale grocers, Commercial street, of Boston, died at his home at East Dennis, Tuesday, of consumption. He was a member of the Cape Cod Commercial Travelers association, formed six years ago, and his was the first death that has occurred in the association. Mr. Sears was 45 years of age and leaves a widow.

J. Frank Winslow, next to the youngest son of John T. and the late Mary K. Winslow of Deering, died in Portland, Me., 16th, aged 44 years. Mr. Winslow underwent an operation at the Eye and Ear infirmary a few days ago, and it was thought he would pass through the ordeal all right. But late Thursday afternoon a change for the worse set in and he continued to fail until the end came Friday evening. Deceased, with his family, removed from Portland, Me., to New Bedford several years ago, where he has had charge of the freight department of the Old Colony road. His immediate family consisted of a wife, three sons and a daughter. Besides his father, he had many relatives in Portland and Deering, including E. B. Winslow, Esq., president of the Portland board of trade, his brother. The Winslow had many friends here who will be pained to learn of his death, and whose sympathy will be extended the bereaved relatives.

CIVIL SERVICE EXAMINATION.

In pursuance of the presidential order of Jan. 5, 1893, extending the civil service law to all free delivery post offices, the civil service commission at Washington has ordered that an examination be held in this city on Saturday, July 8, 1893, commencing at 9 o'clock a. m., for the grades of clerk in the city post office. Only citizens of the United States 18 years old or over, can be examined. No application will be accepted for this examination unless filed with the undersigned, on the proper blank, before 12 o'clock, noon, on July 5, 1893. The civil service commission takes this opportunity of stating that the examinations are open to all reputable citizens who may desire to enter the postal service, without regard to their political affiliations. All such citizens, whether Democrats or Republicans, or neither, are invited to apply. They shall be examined, graded, and certified with entire impartiality, and wholly without regard to their political views, or to any consideration save their efficiency, as shown by the grades they obtain in the examination. For application blanks full instructions, and information relative to the duties and salaries of the different positions, apply at the post office to S. S. Tabor, secretary board of examiners.

TURKISH CHAIRS.

These are often looked upon as luxuries which are far too expensive for a poor man's home.

Whether they are or not depends much on who your furnisher is.

F. R. Slocum has a line of chairs which will suit the popular trade. They are made on iron frames, upholstered in a variety of materials from leather to brocatelle. They are big, soft and elegant, and purchasers are surprised at the prices.

CONDENSED LOCALS.

—Barnum's circus, with its menagerie, is very instructive to the young folks' minds. We give free tickets to the whole show to those selling tea for us this week. See advertisement in miscellaneous wants. C. Y. Wilcox, 28 Pearl street.

—Attention is called to the special notice in another column announcing a trial that woman stood there not alone in the court room, but was the object of the New Bedford Veteran Firemen's association tomorrow evening, when Foreman Lewis requests every member to take a position on the brakes.

—Hedley's National band of Providence will accompany Bristol commandery of Attleboro on its pilgrimage to this city Thursday.

—Remnants of Cheney's figured silks for vests to dress waists, also for trimmings, regular $1 quality, now 39 cents, at Whiting & Co's.

Gentlemen, the finest line of Russia leather shoes found at Buchell's. See our $4 shoe.

—Go to Whiting & Co's for your summer wash goods, as they are closing them out very cheap.

—Kid gloves cleaned in first class manner, ready in 24 hours, at C. T. Johnson's, 7 Pleasant street.

—Chairs caned by John S. Williams, 514 South Water street.

—Go to Whiting & Co's for your waists and wrappers of all those 60cts. French all wool Challies at 41cts. per yard, these are the best quality made.

—Steamer Martha's Vineyard sailed from this port Sunday for Newark, N. J. Hood's Sarsaparilla cures biliousness.

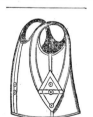

FOR HER LIFE

(Continued from First Page.)

said, without bias. You had, some of you, expressed opinions, as you said. Of course you did. Most people do in this progressive age, but you said, honestly and manfully, when asked those questions by the court, you had formed no opinions but what could be changed by reasonable evidence. Of course you were not without opinion. I hate to see a man like a piece of putty, upon which the last man who sticks his finger into it can make an impression. You are to eliminate from your minds everything that has been said by the press or by the neighbors, except what has been said in this court—every rumor you may have heard, and only to consider the evidence. Every tale you will banish forever. Had we been trying this case on the street we would not now be here. Every man of you is man enough too, when you go to the jury room to say, "That is not in the case" to every point that may be brought to your attention which does not belong there. You have no more right to consider them than you have to take a knife and cut her throat. You have come here day after day to hear this case and to retire and consider it justly. When man is in the balance it is time to hear all and weigh all.

You are not here to consider who created the murder. You are solely to say is this woman guilty, and though the real criminal is never found it is better than that you shall find an unjust verdict. It is not "who did it?" nor "how could it have been done?" but only "did she do it?" That is all, and if you find it is not proven against her you have then done your duty as men. If you say she is guilty you may wish a week later that you had not. The commonwealth says if she did not find the one who did the murder, why, hang her.

For 11 months they have had her in jail under the complete control of the police, where she couldn't go or come as she chose. Now, don't load upon her the burden of doing what she couldn't do. The commonwealth wants no victim either. In the old time we made sacrifices—of lambs, goats, and even human beings—for the expiation of sins and wrongs, but we don't even burn witches in Massachusetts now. She gentlemen, I have tried to show you what limitations are upon you.

What is the call on you? Simply to be true to yourselves. There always goes with any individual a presumption of innocence of crime. It is a presumption which holds true with me and with each one of you; that is your bulwark under the laws of this country. The court will tell you that that presumption started with this defendant on the 4th of August last, has been with her ever since, and will continue with her until the jury decides whether it remains with her or otherwise. This presumption is all the time in the scale. We talk about the scales being even, but it is not so. All the time has the commonwealth to load in facts till the balance is overcome. You will know when his honor has uttered the charge the difference between direct and circumstantial evidence. Direct evidence is that where a person is seen committing an act, but even that may be unreliable, for the person swearing to have seen an act done may be a liar. If you are asked to convict on any evidence bring to it your keenest perception and your strictest honesty. Search it all through and see if it is reliable. Proof must come to your minds with the force of moral certainty; you must be satisfied beyond a reasonable doubt. The rule of law in a case involving a brief imprisonment or fine is the same as in this, but here a human life is in jeopardy, and this constitutes the magnitude of this case. To sit here and have in charge this young woman, to say if she is guilty or not guilty, is what you never had before, and may never have again. Therefore see to it that you make no mistake—or take a step that cannot be rectified. The law says that the failure of a defendant to go on the stand shall not be taken as acting to his or her prejudice, and the learned district attorney will not insult this court by insinuating that the failure of this defendant to do so shall be taken as acting to her prejudice. You must leave out, as I have before said, all rumors, deports and statements that you heard before the trial commenced. But more, you must leave out all that the learned gentleman who opened said he was going to prove, but hasn't. Mr. Moody said he was going to prove that this defendant was preparing a dangerous weapon on August 4th. He hasn't proved it, has he? So, many things, offered in good faith, I have no doubt, have not been proved because the court decided it was not proper to place them before the jury, as it would only complicate the case and create a bias.

You Have No Proof At All Against This Woman.

Mr. Moody said in his opening that evidence was to be introduced about her going out to buy poison. That isn't so. The court said that it would not allow you to consider any such thing, and it isn't in the case. So you see that the prussic acid that you have read about in the paper isn't so. You were told that evidence would be introduced to show you that the defendant had contradicted herself when telling about the crime. That isn't so. You are not to sit back there and say Mr. Moody or Mr. Knowlton wouldn't tell us so unless it was true. If that was the case you might just as well sit right there and find a verdict of "guilty" before you had any trial at all. You might just as well say "Well, we will hang somebody, no matter who it is or whether they are guilty or not." That isn't the way cases are tried; they are tried upon the evidence, and only upon the evidence are you to find facts. Some day you or men like you may sit in the dock, and you will turn toward the twelve honorable men, expecting them to find their verdict upon the evidence, and only the evidence that is presented to them. There is no poison in this case and no statement made by her under oath that you know anything about or have any right to consider.

In this case are many things in which we agree.

This Defendant Wants Nothing but Justice

under the proper administration of justice.

Now as to those facts. Andrew J. Borden went down town on the morning of August 4, Thursday morning, and at about 9 30 o'clock we find him in the savings bank. Later he started toward home, and we find that he talked with Mr. Shortsleeves, another man, and that he arrived home at about 10 45. This time didn't vary more than two or three minutes. It was 10 40 when we find that he was at the store, and two or three or four minutes will account for such little things as occupied his mind, and it is safe to infer that he was home by 10 45. The alarm of the murders reached the police station at 11 15. We have learned several things which he did, and we can say fairly that the murder was between five minutes of 11 and ten minutes past 11. We propose to take that as a fact, and that Mrs. Borden died earlier, as was shown by the state of the blood, stomach and intestines, and from an hour to an hour and a half earlier. According to this, and it agrees with the doctors, Mrs. Borden died at about 10 15. Within that short space of time it is for us to examine whether the defendant did the deed. There is no evidence of an accomplice, and we will not suggest, and you have no right to think that there was any accomplice. I have no personal opinion to put forward in the case. I have an opinion, but it is for me to keep it within myself. I have no right to use any personal influence in this matter, and if I get over the line I trust the court will call me to order. I trust I know my place, and that the district attorney will do the same.

The defendant comes here under the presumption of innocence, and

You Must Tie Her Up to Facts Before You Can Hold Her.

What is the cord that holds her to these terrible criminal acts. It is not in the charge or in the proceedings of the court, but must be in this chain of circumstances to show how she is tied up to this terrible thing. That's what they are bound to meet to make out to hold her to it. If a person commits a murder and we know it, there is no reason for finding his reason. If he did it, there is no need of a motive. Perhaps he did it for pure deviltry, or for insanity, a case in which the government intercedes in another way, but if it is known and proved that he did it there is no need whether you show a motive or not. They say she did it. There's the crime, there sits the defendant. Now to show her guilty you have got to bind her up to it. But they have got no evidence that she did it; they have only some things that make it look as though she did it. Motive is to be shown only by the evidence. How can you explain these acts? If you can't explain them, then she didn't do it. The motive is only to explain the circumstances to you. Suppose the crime was somewhere else and the man was way down in Georgia—even if he swore, profanely, that could he have got to the scene in time he would have killed the victim—that statement has nothing to do with it. The government says Lizzie Borden has these acts to explain. I say the argument is only look at the motive to get at the evidence. Now, there is absolutely, and I think the commonwealth will agree with me in the statement, no direct evidence. No one saw or experienced anything connecting her with the crime. If you had found her with the weapon or with it in her room, that would be direct evidence. It has not been shown that she ever had, touched or owned such an implement as committed these acts. In fact, she did not even know where such ordinary implements of the house were kept. The murder tells no tales on her.

Blood Will Speak Out, Whether It be Dead or Alive.

but no spot was found on her in any way. Yes—there was one spot as small as the head of a pin, perhaps one-sixteenth of an inch in diameter, Professor Wood says, but not where it would be expected to be—not in front where it would be if the wearer had done the deed—but way round in back near the bottom on the "placket," as the women would say. Perhaps the government would like to say that she turned it around hind side before, before she committed the deed. Dr. Dolan does not say—although he did—or the Fall River police do not claim now, that that had anything to do with it. There is nothing to show that it was not menstrual blood.

Now they talk about burnt paper in the stove. Phil. Harrington took off the cover and saw a roll of burnt paper there, and there is some mean insinuation made on this point that Dr. Bowen had something to do with it. I hope they don't claim Dr. Bowen had anything to do with the murder or shielding the murderer. He threw in some pieces of a letter, they say, but that had nothing to do with the case. We thought at first that they had the handle of the hatchet—that the stick of solid oak had been wrapped in newspaper and thrown in the stove—that the handle had burned and that the newspaper remained. What a theory! We were troubled about it, and laid awake nights worrying about it, till Fleet and Mullaly came and showed us the situation. Mr. Fleet denying that he took it out of the stove and Mullaly saying that he saw him do it. Now they run over to Fall River and try to get into our house to get it, but they can't get in and go around complaining about it. Now that handle is still flying around in the air—an orphan handle without a hatchet. For heaven's sake, why don't they get those 125 Fall River policemen to go and chase it up; drive it in somewhere, catch it, capture it, and tie it up to the place where it belongs. Now you are to conceive that the murderer of Mrs. Borden stood astride of her body and chopped the head in pieces. We will say something about that later. They will agree that Mr. Borden was murdered by some one who stood back of his head in the parlor door.

Now what reason is there to say that this defendant is guilty? The commonwealth says if you don't find her guilty it is satisfied. The district attorney will go away, glad to get rid of the case. Or, if you say she is guilty, on the other hand, it relieves me, and puts the responsibility on you.

Now let me show why they claimed she did it. They say because she was in the house. Now, gentlemen, you may say that she was in the wrong place, that she should not have been there, in her own home. Perhaps she ought to be on the streets. Now I don't know whether my daughter should be in the house where her mother, who I am pleased to say is my wife, knows where she is, or running about the streets where no one can keep run of her.

She is shown to have been up to the room, and must have seen the body of Mrs. Borden, says the government. Well, let us see about that. You have been to the house, and you know you can't see into the room when on the landing. Then it is said that on a certain point you could see through under the bed, and therefore Lizzie must have seen the body. If we had marched you up and no one had said anything to you you wouldn't have noticed anything. People don't go around their own houses spying, and if they did you would say they were rascals. If Lizzie Borden had seen that body the commonwealth would have said at once she was a criminal, and raised the cry, "There's the murderess." There is no evidence that the door of this room was open before Mr. Borden came home, and that is very important. The government starts with the theory that the door was wide open, while it was only open a little, if at all. If the body had been lying in front of the bed, or if she had been looking for it, Lizzie might have seen it, but an innocent person wouldn't have been on the lookout for such a thing. It was not her habit to go into that room, and therefore there was no reason why she should have been looking into it. The shutters were partly closed at least, and you know from your observation that this makes the room dark. The government says defendant is guilty because Mr. Fleet said Lizzie said to him about 9 o'clock as she went down or up the stairs she saw Mrs. Borden making the bed in the spare room. Well, what of that? She was up in her own room at a time when an orderly person would be to see if her work was done. Grant that Lizzie did go up and down. The commonwealth said she did. I claim there's no evidence of it, but if she did no one says she stayed up. She told about Mrs. Borden having a note, it is said. There's interest in that. It is said she told Bridget Mrs. Borden had a note and went out. Then Lizzie is said to have told Mrs. Churchill Mrs. Borden had a note. Is this so? Let us see what Mrs. Churchill says in her evidence. She says Bridget said, "She (Mrs. Borden) had a note and hurried off. She didn't tell me where she was going, as she usually does." Now, you see, both Lizzie and Bridget are said to have told this story. That was what Mrs. Churchill says Bridget told her, not what Lizzie said. My friend who opened for the commonwealth said Lizzie told a lie. I submit that this is not so. Bridget tells the story with exact detail, and her story bears the impress of truth.

There isn't anything that qualifies the evidence of Miss Russell that she heard talk about a note, but doesn't know who told her. Miss Russell tells about a conversation, but she says that "I said some one must have put it in the fire." Mark that, it was Miss Russell who said some one must have put it in the fire, not Lizzie. There were several present, and they all assent to it; it is very likely true. Dr. Bowen searched for it, and came to the conclusion that some one must have burned it. We kept nothing from the officers. Officer Fleet was told the same story. Wilson tells the same, and they were told that Lizzie thought her mother had gone out. When we consider that it comes from what Bridget and Lizzie told in the first instance, isn't it to be believed that Mrs. Borden did tell Bridget and Lizzie she had received a note, and that Lizzie thought she had hurried off, without telling either of them where she was going? Is it not likely that the note was tossed away by somebody? It was not a bank note, to be kept, and most likely was nothing more than a scrap of paper. It is natural for people to say, "Where is the note?" No one has come forward to say who sent it." I presume you can find people in this county who don't know this trial is going on. It is a common thing for people to come forward after a trial and say, "Why! I could have given you this or that information if I had known you were seeking it!"

People Have a Horror of Coming Into Court,

especially women, and a perfect dread of giving evidence in a case.

That a note came there on this evidence you cannot question. That Lizzie lied about it is a wrongful assertion born out of the ignorance of the facts. Suppose that Bridget was suspected and Mrs. Churchill came forward and said these very words. How quick some people would say "Oh, Bridget did it, she did it, she told a lie about that note." Now I dismiss it with the remark that nobody thinks that Bridget had anything to do with this crime at all. Lizzie doesn't think so, because she has said so.

Now she told us about her visit out to the barn, they say. She told it to the officers that she went out to the barn, went out in the yard some twenty or thirty minutes. Now, remember that we get this information from the police officers, and others told us that she said she went to the barn. It takes Assistant Marshal Fleet to tell us about 30 minutes. The set of that moustache, and the prominence of those lips, and the distinction that he wrought here in the court room telling that story. And there he was up in this young woman's room in the afternoon with some other officers plying her with questions in a pretty direct and peremptory way. "You said 30 minutes, and now you say twenty minutes; which way will you have it?" Is that the way for an officer of the law to deal with a woman in her own house. What would you do if a man, I do not care if he had blue on, who was talking with your wife or daughter in that way? Recall that this was after the tragedy, that this was when the terrible pall was over that house; recall that the air was full of policemen at that time. They were running all over the house, putting her to every possible strain, asking her questions in her loneliness, her sister gone, following her up in this way, insinuating in that way, talking to her as if she were a liar. I can tell the truth and behave pretty well if a man treats me decent, but I want to get him out if he talks to me as if I were a liar to begin with.

Now she tells about her visit to the barn, and they undertake to tell you that she didn't go out to the barn. Now let us see about it. We know what the small words in the English language mean in the idea of the commonwealth. We can get rid of three letters pretty quick, but we cannot dispose of facts. Did she go to the barn?

They Say She Could Not Have Gone to the Barn.

We will see whether she did or not. If she did go out into the barn then she was there upon her own showing at the time when the murder of her father was committed. That will end the case if you see it. Now, Bridget said, "I went right over to Dr. Bowen's, and when I came back I says Miss Lizzie where was you? I says, didn't I leave the screen door hooked? She says I was out in the back yard and heard a groan and came in, and the screen door was wide open." And that is what Lizzie told Bridget right off.

Now she says she went out in the yard. What did they have in the yard? A pear tree, that is the evidence, and the evidence is that in the digestion of the stomachs pear skins were found. Bridget says Mr. Borden had been out and brought in a basket of pears. Patrick McGowan saw them and got up and helped himself. There is no lie about that. This was an August morning, and it appears that at that time Lizzie had been around the kitchen trying to iron some handkerchiefs. She had been about her work, and she tells us she went out into the yard. Now that was true we will say upon that statement. Dr. Bowen said, "Where were you?" Her reply was, "Out in the barn looking for some iron." Both can be reasonably true. If she was out in the barn she was also in the yard. And she says she stopped there about five or ten minutes. Does that look unreasonable? Do you not see families out in the yard strolling about. Mrs. Churchill said, "I stepped inside the screen door and saw her sitting on the second stair at the right of the door. I said where is your father, and where were you when it happened. She said, I went to the barn to get a piece of iron to fix my screen. Mrs. Churchill said after she told her about going into the barn she said when she came in

She Saw Her Father and He Was Killed.

Mr. Fleet says that she went into the dining room; she said her father lay down, and that she went out into the barn, and he brings in the half hour. He is the only one that does, and he goes on and talks to her about it as to whether she means a half hour or twenty minutes. Recall that he is the same man that said Dr. Bowen was holding the door on him. Mrs. Holmes, Dr. Bowen, Miss Russell and Officer Wilson each comes right here and says that there wasn't the slightest resistance. Now this man Fleet he saw trouble, and he was on a scent for a job. He was ferreting out a crime. He had got a theory. He was a detective and so he says, "You said this morning you were out in the barn for half an hour or so, will you say that now?" I think, I beg pardon, the defendant thinks the man was impertinent. She said, "I did not say half an hour, I said 20 minutes to half an hour." "Well, we will call it 20 minutes." Much obliged to him. He was ready to call it 20 minutes, was he? Now Lizzie had some sense of her own, and she said, "I was there 20 minutes to half an hour." She still breathed, although he was there.

Mr. Harrington, she says to him about 20 minutes, and he asks her whether she would not have heard the opening of the screen door. But Bridget said she did not hear the screen door shut and she says she would not hear it and never heard it when it shut unless somebody was careless and slammed it. There is no inference to be drawn from the fact that Miss Lizzie did not hear it when she was in the barn or in the yard for that matter. If she had been under the pear tree anybody could have passed in and out of the side door without her seeing them, much more if she were in the barn, either up stairs or down stairs.

Wilson, he has told us 20 minutes to half an hour. He was there with Fleet. Medley, he says that she said she was up stairs in the barn. Now is there anything unnatural or improbable in her going to the barn after anything that she wanted? Not at all, she you will see is a person who was allowed to go about as she pleased.

You Have Heard the Talk About Marion.

You know better than I where the place is. But I suspect from what has been said about it here that it is somewhere near the water and where fish swim. It would not be strange if a number of women were going there that they should try to catch something, I mean fish, and when they got there they would want something to catch fish with. If there was lead it was in the barn, and she went there to find some old sinkers. Probably she had both things in her mind. The screen rattled and she wanted to get something to put in it.

If she had set about to be the arch criminal that they try to make her out she would have had it all marked out in her own mind, and she would have told it every time just the same. Honest people are not particular about the punctuation and the prepositions every time.

Did she go the barn? She says she did, and her statement is entitled to credit, as she gave it right on the spur of the moment. When Bridget was up stairs did she go out, did she go to the barn? Well, we find she did. Find it by independent, outside evidence, that is, by somebody who saw. Possibly this life of hers is saved by the observation of a passer on the street. There comes along a man there, this peddler, the ice cream man, known to everybody in Fall River. He is not a distinguished lawyer or a great minister or a successful doctor. He is only an ice cream peddler. But he knows what an oath is and tells the truth about it. He passes along the street and sees a woman, not Bridget Sullivan, whom he knew, coming along walking slowly around the corner near the side door. Now there was no other woman left in that house except Bridget and Lizzie at that time. He knew it was not Bridget, because he had sold her ice cream, and he knew her. And so he said it was the other one to whom I had never sold ice cream. Recall that that was either Lizzie or some stranger in the yard, you will see it was undoubtedly Lizzie, and she was coming back from the barn. They say why did he look in there? I say why does any one look anywhere?

Is that something that he remembers today, or that anybody has bought him to tell? Now let us see. He told it the 8th day of August to the police, and they had it in their possession. Now he is not a man made up for the occasion at all, and the only conflict about it is attempted in this way, not to dispute it, but it is that Mr. Rubinsky is mistaken by about half an hour of time. Mr. Mullaly, he is one of the knights of the handle, he comes here with a book, and it is thrown down here on the table with great display for us to look at. He says that on the 8th of August he had a talk with Rubinsky, and Rubinsky told him it was half past ten. Now if Rubinsky went by there at half past ten then he did not see Miss Lizzie in the yard.

Is Mullaly mistaken or is he busy trying to work up this case? You are going to say whether you believe Rubinsky, who stands uncontradicted or whether you believe a man that is flatly contradicted by the man that is with him in another transaction.

The government knew where Rubinsky worked. That was for Mr. Wilkinson, the ice cream man, they knew that the horse of Wilkinson was kept at Gardner's stable. They could have found out by going over there whether Rubinsky left at 11 o'clock or half past ten. Mr. Gardner, the man who owns the stable, comes here and you have seen him and he tells his own story. Hasn't he convinced you that Rubinsky's story is correct, that he did not leave the stable until after 11 o'clock? He was late that day and he was hurried and he did not get away until some time between 11 and five minutes past.

My friend Mr. Knowlton in the cross-examination was trying to find out how good a watch he had. Perhaps he wanted to swap, I do not know. He wanted to know whether he told the time by long hand or short hand. Gardner says he left the stable and drove down Second street, going right by the house.

And Mr. Newhall who happened to be there comes here and tells us and fixes the time, and you have got these three men. Isn't it fair to say that Mr. Mullaly is mistaken? And if they wanted to find out anything more they learned that Mr. Douglass was there at the time, and they were told about that, and they could have proved it. But they know it was as we said so they did not try to prove it.

As you take cases as they are proven in court wouldn't you consider that question settled, that Rubinsky did go by there at that time, and that he did see Miss Lizzie going into the house? that is true, that the commonwealth must take back the charge that she lied about going to the barn. And if she did not lie about going to the barn she was out of the house at the very time that the slayer murdered Mr. Borden.

At this point a recess of five minutes was taken, in which the court and jury retired and the audience indulged in a general chat. Miss Emma Borden and Lizzie leaned over the rail, and chatted earnestly, while Elder Buck and another old gentleman craned forward and listened intently.

When the court again came to order Mr. Robinson resumed his argument.

The district attorney brought out the fact from Mrs. Bowen that when Lizzie sat there in the kitchen her hands were white. This will indicate, according to his argument, that it was strange that they were not covered with rust or dust. I don't know why you should assume that because she was handling some lead and iron in the barn she should get her hands dirty and rusty. Any woman can handle iron or lead carefully and not get her hands dirty or rusty.

Officer Mullaly tells us that he heard a groan. It is like anything else, if you imagine you hear anything you will hear something, and if you do not then you may not. In the excitement of his zeal, he may have heard something, but he may have got it wrong about its being a groan. Now Lizzie thought she heard a groan. [illegible] this came from Bridget Sullivan. What happened then? Bridget says Mrs. Borden had had a note and gone out; so you see it is perfectly consistent. Mrs. Churchill said if she knew where Mrs. Whitehead was she would go and tell Mrs. Borden that Mr. Borden was very sick. Then Lizzie says, "Maggie, I thought I heard her come in; you had better go up stairs and see if she is not there. And she said, I'm not going alone. Now, she had been upsatirs to get the sheets for Dr. Bowen, but she had gone to the back room and not up the front stairs. Bridget and Mrs. Churchill therefore knew that Mrs. Borden was not in her own room or the back part of the house. It was very plain you see when Lizzie spoke of going upstairs to see if Mrs. Borden was not there, she meant in the front part, because she knew she was not in her own room. She thought she heard a noise, and that she came in, and as she was not in the back part of the house she must be in the front making beds or doing something of that sort. All testified to the same thing. After they came down from the back part of the house there followed the conversation about going to Mrs. Whitehead's, relying on the truth of the note. She went the front way and found Mrs. Borden killed. Now the suggestion of the government will be that Lizzie said for them to go up the front way, knowing that Mrs. Borden was lying there, and that she had killed her. If you understand this explanation then you won't believe that she knew Mrs. Borden was dead.

Her father came in and Mrs. Borden had not appeared in the sitting room, and she knew he was not in the back part of the house, then she must have known if her stepmother had come in she must be in the front part of the house. Then they say that she showed no feeling when her stepmother was lying dead on the guest room floor. Bridget tried to open the door, and when she couldn't she said pshaw! Lizzie was standing where she couldn't see the body, and why shouldn't she laugh Gentlemen, one of you might go to your home, and when you entered some one make a remark that pleased you and you laugh. Perhaps at that instant your son lies dead on one of the floors, are you a heartless, depraved, inhuman wretch if you know nothing of it? They say she knew it, then she would be to blame, but they assume that she knew it, there is no evidence of it.

Their inference is that she had murdered them and then, laughed. They say that she had not seen her dead father. (Lizzie's face at this time was buried in her fan.) Did they ask her to wring her heart before the dead body of her father battered beyond recognition? Others came to that house and didn't want to pass the body, even after it was covered up with a sheet. They say that she showed no fear. Doesn't it sound like a cry for help when she says to Bridget, "Go and get somebody." Bridget goes to Dr. Bowen's and returns, and Dr. Bowen is not there. Then Lizzie says "Go somewhere, anywhere, go to Alice Russell's, I can't be alone." Look at these things in a common sense, every day manner, assuming her innocence and not presuming her guilt. Then they say she killed them because she had no comforts. I hope you all live better than the Bordens. Do you have carpets on all your floors, plenty of furniture in all your rooms, a piano and all that you could desire in your homes? If you do I congratulate you. Then they bring out the bill of fare and tell about the breakfast. What do you have for breakfast? I sometimes think that the homely, simple food that satisfies most families for breakfast is superior to the mixtures of the hotels. Andrew J. Borden was a simple, old-fashioned man; he didn't load himself up with jewelry; he carried a silver watch and, in fact, was a common gentleman of 50 years ago.

This Defendant Was Not Starved Into Crime and Pinched Into Wrong.

She had property in her own right and was worth enough so that she was not pinched into killing her father and mother Does she want anything more than to live in comfort? They are here before you, both the sisters, do they look as if they were starved into the commisssion of such a crime? Do they say that she killed her stepmother because of trouble? She had no trouble with her father. They say she killed Mrs. Borden because she didn't like her, and killed her father because she did like him, but wanted his money. Killed her, cleaned her dress, became an entirely new woman, and then proceeded to the brutal slaying of her father.

They tell us about ill-feelings. The government has made a lamentable failure in this. Then they say that after murdering Mrs. Borden she murdered her father to conceal it. In this they destroy the theory of the family relations. Let us see about these family relations. For five or six years Lizzie did not call Mrs. Borden "mother." How many a man in after years, with the remembrance in his heart of the mother who died in childhood, although he may introduce her as his mother, fails at home to call his stepmother by the sacred name learned in his childhood years. You may talk about a mother as you will, there never goes out of a man's heart the love for that one who his prattling baby lips first learned to call mother. Mr. Fleet, in his policeman-like manner, tells us of Lizzie's saying, "She is not my mother."

Is That Anything on Which to Build a Theory of Murder?

There are many who speak out their minds, but because they do so we never think they are going to murder us. Mrs. Gifford, the cloakmaker, whom you all remember, and to whose evidence we will give all credence, says Lizzie said "Don't 'mother' her to us. She is a mean, good-for-nothing thing." That's all. Mr. Moody in his opening said Mrs. Gifford would say Lizzie said she hated Mrs. Borden, but she didn't say so, and

The District Attorney Will Have to Take That Back.

Sometimes people speak too quickly for their own good. I dare say some of you have spoken more quickly at home than you wish you had, but we don't feel that because you have done so that you are going to kill us. In the same impulsive manner did Lizzie Borden speak when asked about a man on the farm, "He isn't a Portuguese, he's a Swede." Those who speak right out are not the ones who are to be feared as doing dark deeds. But that is only one declaration. Bridget Sullivan, who lived in the Borden household for two years and nine months, says she never heard a word in all that time, and everything seemed kindly. That Thursday morning, when Lizzie is said to have been entertaining a plan to murder, she came down and was talking pleasantly with her mother, and when Mr. Borden came home she greeted him cordially. Well, that's the way my people do at home; that is the ordinary way of most people. You, gentlemen, have come from homes, and your folks are waiting for you to come back, and when you do will probably do the same. The government says that, fiend, villain that she was, this was all put on. Then there is Mrs. Raymond, the dressmaker, who comes here and tells us when she was working at the house that all sat up stairs sewing—a regular dressmaking party. Phil. Harrington ought to have been there and got some points into his head if he could. Now, was that a murderous party? Now Emma comes here and shows us the inside relations of their family. She cannot be charged with anything, but they say that her sympathy with her sister has diverted her from the truth. But out

(Continued on Fourth Page.)

ANYTHING AND EVERYTHING.

Artificial ivory is now manufactured out of condensed skim milk.

Sir Lyon Playfair says that the entire nitrogenous material in the body is changed in six weeks.

One hundred and eighty thousand suicides occur every year among the civilized nations of the world.

The Emperor of China chooses his own successor, whether the person chosen is a member of the royal family or not.

Taking the earth all over into consideration the amount of rain that falls on its surface comes to about five feet annually.

Charles Allard of Missoula has 100 buffalos on the Flathead reservation, the only live herd of such magnitude in the world.

West Virginia has a two headed woman who has two voices entirely different in tone. She talks bass on one side and tenor on the other.

The Chinese, Japanese, Malayans, Siamese, New Zealanders and the North American Indians are recognized as the "beardless races."

The dock at Cardiff is said to be the largest in the world. It is 600 feet long and 80 feet wide, and has 36 feet of water lying immediately in front.

PERSONAL.

The Queen of Greece is president of a sisterhood devoted to the reformation of criminals.

Emperor William is well grounded in classical and current French, and is a great reader of French poems.

William Black, the novelist, is of such a nervous temperament that he lays down his pen at the slightest sound.

Lord Wolseley, the greatest of living English soldiers, is be low medium height and slender and lithe of frame.

Charles Revere Curtis, a great grandson of Paul Revere, resides at Rockland, Me., and is hale and hearty, though fourscore.

Mrs. Increase Sumner of Starke, Fla., raises three crops of tea a year, and claims that it is the same as that raised in China.

Ario Bates, the Boston novelist, has been elected professor of English literature in the Massachusetts Institute of Technology. Mr. Bates is not only a writer of books, but an experienced journalist as well, having been editor of The Boston Courier for several years.

Above the grave in New Bedford, Mass., of William Bradford, the quaker painter who first showed to the world what color was in the Arctic ice and how impressive were the bergs and the skies and the ships, has been placed a granite bowlder. The bowlder had rested for ages on the shore near Fort Phenix, and was a landmark where the painter used to stroll; it lies rough as it was over the grave, with the barnacles still clinging to it, save for the face, where the artist's name is cut, with dates of birth and death, and two lines from Whittier's dedication to him of his poem, "Amy Wentworth."

FLASHES OF WIT.

A private soldier walking arm-in-arm with his sweetheart, met his sergeant when about to enter a cheap restaurant. He respectfully introduced her to him: "Sergeant, my sister!"

"Yes, yes," was the reply, "I know; she was mine once."—[Le Littoral.

Tutter—"Have you ever observed Miss Clara, that sometimes when a thing happens it comes to you as a souvenir of a past age? Sometimes a slight thing—a word, a strain of music—awaken hidden memories and revives a prehistoric age, and you exclaim to yourself involuntarily, 'I have lived before.'"

Miss Slimson—"Oh, yes, indeed, Mr. Tutter; that's the way I felt when I heard that story you told me."—[Truth.

Secretary Gresham draws a pension of $30 a month from the government. He should remember that this will tend to disqualify him for the democratic presidential nomination in 1896, as it is proof that he is a man who has not always been friendly to the south.—[St. Paul Pioneer Press.

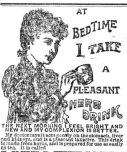

The Evening Standard.

ESTABLISHED FEBRUARY, 1850.
NEW BEDFORD, TUESDAY, JUNE 20, 1893.
TWO CENTS.

HASKELL & TRIPP.

Cool and Comfortable.

Here are two new sorts of white dresses for girls from four to fourteen years old.

First:
This dress costs $1.69. It is made from white, fine quality lawn, waist and sleeves trimmed with wide Hamburg embroidery, has full sash.

Second:
This dress costs $2.50. The material is extra fine lawn, it has shoulder bretelles of wide Hamburg, full sleeves, skirt of embroidered flouncings with deep hemstitched edge.

For boys, new white waists, have box-plaited back, fine tucked front, linen collar and cuffs. Price 48c. Combined with a pair of our fast color blue yacht cloth pants, with double knees, costing $1.25 a pair, you have a neat and comfortable outfit for the lad at trifling expense. Every size in stock today.

TRY OUR SODA WATER.

Fast black, seamless hosiery for children—106 doz. bought below the market value—go on sale today for 12½c. a pair. Never before have stockings of such good quality been offered at the price. *Buy all you will need for the season while you have a chance.*

Our fast black imported hose for women are matchless at 25c. a pair.

Kayser "finger-tipped" silk gloves, every pair warranted, 75c. a pair.

New silk mitts, 25c. and 50c. a pair.

Have you seen the genuine "Liberty silk" squares at $2 and our very choice new patterns in Windsor silk ties for 25c. and 50c. each? Glad to show you.

Novelties in percale collars and cuffs and fancy chemisettes for summer wear now ready.

TRY OUR SODA WATER.

One item from the handkerchief stock. 25 dozen elaborately embroidered, pure white, hemstitched handkerchiefs, usual 25c. quality, our price only 12½c. each. *Worth your while to inspect this offering.*

One item from the towel stock.

Big, spongy, full-bleached towels selling at 12½c. each. Nearly 400 dozens already disposed of, all within a short time, shows what the people think of them.

Dress goods that are quick sellers.

Navy blue storm serge, 25c. a yard.

Heavy twill navy storm serge, 29c. a yard.

All-wool Henriettas, fashionable shades, 39c. a yard.

Printed muslins, copies of India silk, 8c. a yard.

Printed organdies, 15c. a yard.

TRY OUR SODA WATER.

HASKELL & TRIPP,
Department Stores,
Purchase and William Streets.

VERDICT

All That Remains in Great Trial.

Knowlton's Argument a Powerful One.

An Awful Denunciation of Lizzie Borden.

Circumstance Piled Upon Circumstance

Hurled Against the Accused Woman.

Lizzie Listens with Seeming Indifference.

Most Unconcerned of All in Crowded Court Room.

Judge's Charge Given Early This Afternoon.

Last Words Now Said in the Celebrated Case.

While the court room was comfortably filled this morning at the opening of the Borden trial and the quarters reserved for the bar were crowded, there was nothing like the crush of yesterday, and the police guard and deputy sheriffs were able to handle the people easily and without friction.

Lizzie came in early and had an animated conversation with ex-Governor Robinson before the court opened. There was a restless activity about her which betrayed itself in an unusual nervousness, and it is plain to see that despite her wonderful self-control that she is full of internal excitement.

After the jury had been polled, Mr. Knowlton at once resumed his argument.

JURY ROOM WHERE LIZZIE BORDEN'S FATE WILL BE DECIDED.

MR. KNOWLTON'S ARGUMENT.

The District Attorney Resumes His Broken Discourse.

Mr. Foreman and gentlemen of the jury, I congratulate you that the end of this hard season is drawing nigh. I trust that before even another day shall have gone you will be able to return to the home, to the family, to the dear ones around you who have become doubly dear to you by your long and enforced absence. I had hoped before the day closed yesterday to have finished what I had to say to you. But is was felt, and I shared in the feeling, that you were too weary to longer listen to us. My distinguished friend had occupied the greater part of the day, and you had followed his masterly and able presentation of the facts that bore upon his client's case with that fidelity which had marked your course during this whole proceeding. You did the honor also to give me your respectful attention, and it was thought but fair that after a rest I should take up the thread of my broken discourse, and, so far as I could

Proceed with This Unwelcome Task to the Bitter End.

The learned counsel who opened this cause for the defense said that one of the essential facts to be proven in connection with the case was the question of motive. I allude to that for fear that I may not have fully explained, already made you understand, the position of the commonwealth in this respect. I think upon reflection my learned friend will agree with me that that was not so accurate a statement of law as he is accustomed to make upon consideration of the case. It is not so, Mr. Foreman and gentlemen, motive has no part of the case of the commonwealth. We are called upon to prove that the thing was done, and our duty stops there. We are not called upon to prove why it was done, it is no part of the commonwealth evidence, it is no essential link in its chain of proof, and it has happened, nay often will happen, that the whole cause is substantially proved, thoroughly proved, and the jury's minds are made to a degree of satisfaction that is expressed by the term reasonable doubt when no apparent motive is shown for the crime at all. I do not disguise the fact that the consideration of motive has its weight in helping us to elucidate the mystery. I do not either conceal the fact, for I desire to be as frank as frankness can be in discussing the case, that the lack of apparent motive, nay, that the existence of motive not to have done the crime, is a circumstance that must be well weighed before you can arrive at the result that the commonwealth asks. It is a matter of history that motives are not adequate, nor even tolerable, when considered in connection with the crime. It is a matter of public history that a professor in one of our learned institutions, a man whose character was above reproach, whose surroundings were of the best, whose position, if I may be pardoned for doing so, was not less eminent and respectable than the learned judges who preside here themselves, was

Tempted by the Demon of Sin to Commit Foul Murder

for no higher motive than because he was pressed for the payment of a debt less than $1,000 so far as anybody knew in the world. Neither was his character a bulwark against crime. Nor was his motive at all to be compared with the enormity of the crime committed. The motives of mankind, Mr. Foreman and gentlemen, are as inscrutable, though for a different reason, as are the ways of divine providence. It does offer some satisfaction to the conclusions to which we are compelled to be brought in this case; it does offer some satisfaction to our reason, but it is no part of the essential elements of the case to have discovered that there are conditions, that there were conditions, existing in that unfortunate family which we can take our experience of mankind from and suspect the existence of the malice which prompted that deed.

I have referred to that condition, I have called your attention to the circumstances under which they were compelled to live under the same roof. I can only say to you that this must impress you as you find your consciences to respond, and you must answer whether it finds a responsive cord in your hearts. Fathers, if you are fathers, if I were to have my choice whether a daughter of mine should dash me from life instantly to death without my knowledge or should live with me for years and haunt me with ingratitude, deny the title I had earned by years of patient devotion, far would I prefer the unconscious ending of a life that knew not the ingratitude that had marked it. The malice was all before this fact, the wickedness was all before the 4th day of August, the ingratitude, the poisoning, the hatred, the stabbing of the mind, worse than the stabbing of the body, had gone on under that roof for many months, and we cannot tell, it is not necessary that we should be able to tell, what new fuel was added to that fire of discontent. It is only necessary that we can consider what there may have been. There had been a quarrel unworthy of that girl, unworthy of anybody, because the man wanted to make a present to his wife of her homestead. We do not know, the lips of those that know are sealed in death, and we never shall know in this world. We do not know what new propositions this poor man had ventured to make with regard to his own, we do not know what had occurred in that family that

Kept That Young Woman from the Delightful Shores of Marion

where her friends are, and kept her by her father and mother during those hot days of that hot summer. We do not know but that man had talked, as many a man does when he comes to that age of exercising his legal right, of making testamentary disposition of his property. We know nothing if it. It is not necessary that we prove it. It is no part of the commonwealth's case; but we do know that there was a jealousy which was unworthy of that woman. All we know is that, as Emma expressed it herself, they felt that she was not interested in them, and consequently was interested against them with her father. And no step could be taken by that poor man, no suggestion be made by that poor man, that would not fan the embers of that discontent into the active fire of hatred that we have seen alas many times manifested in many an unhappy home.

I speak of these things, Mr. Foreman, at this time because I have left the dead body of that aged woman upon the guest chamber floor in the room where she was last at work, and am now asking you to come down with me to a far sadder tragedy, to the most horrible word that the English language knowsto parricide. I do not undertake, far be it from me, to seek to detract one iota from the terrible significance of the words, and when I am asked to find a proof and declare an explanation, a motive for that act, well may my feeble powers quail before the undertaking. I do see, I do think I see, and I only suggest it as a course of comment upon the conduct of that young woman for your consideration and without endeavoring to prove it, for as I have undertaken to say, mankind's motives are not a part of our case. There may be that in this case which staves us from the idea that Lizzie Andrew Borden planned to kill her father. I should be slow to believe it so; I should be slow to ask you to believe that she did, but Lizzie Andrew Borden never thought of Andrew Jackson Borden as she came down those stairs.

It Was Not Lizzie Andrew Borden, Daughter of Andrew Jackson Borden, that Came Down those Stairs, but a Murderess,

transformed from all her 33 years of an honest life, transformed from a daughter, transformed from the ties of affection, to the most consummate criminal we have read of in all our history. Nay, Mr. Foreman, that was not all; she came down to meet that stern old man, (his picture shows that if nothing more even in death) that just old man of the stern Puritan stock that most of you are from, that man who loved his daughter, but who also loved his wife, as the Bible commanded him to, and above all the one man in all this universe who would know who killed his wife. She did not think of that; she

(Continued on Third Page.)

MINING TOWNS WIPED OUT.

Woods in Meashba Range Still Burning.

A Town's Population Without Shelter Food or Clothing.

Duluth Subscribes Generously and Asks No Outside Aid.

Duluth, Minn., June 20.—The first accurate news of the fire in the Meashba range shows the situation at Virginia as serious as reported. The entire business part of the town is destroyed. About 30 houses are standing, and 340 were burned. Merritts is nearly wiped out, only 16 buildings remaining. It is impossible to reach Merritts, as the woods are still burning all about the village. At Mountain Iron only six buildings were burned.

The situation of the sufferers at Virginia is peculiarly unfortunate. Most of them are without shelter; clothing is scarce, and food is still scanty, despite the supplies that have been sent from Duluth. Everything possible is being done for them. On the whole range about 3,500 people are for the time being entirely dependent on charity. Many of the women and children have been brought to Duluth. At a citizens' meeting yesterday a relief committee was appointed, and it was decided not to apply for outside aid. Between $5,000 and $6,000 has been subscribed, and clothing and provisions are coming in on every hand. Trouble is feared at Virginia, owing to the character of the population, as in all new mining towns many of the men are hard characters, and lawlessness is anticipated. Several citizens have been sworn in as deputy sheriffs, and will be sent to Virginia today.

The loss is estimated at $1,500,000. The insurance is estimated at about $300,000.

MADE A RUSH ON THE JAIL.

Swiss Workmen Fight for the Release of Their Friends.

Berne, June 20.—About 50 Swiss workingmen attacked a gang of Italians who had been employed to work on the streets. The police interfered and arrested 15 of the attacking party, locking them up. Last evening a turbulent crowd gathered near the jail. When the police tried to disperse them the men made a rush for the jail to release the prisoners. The police fired upon the rioters, but were unable to drive them back till ten had been arrested and 14 wounded. During the pause in the hostilities a company of soldiers was brought up to guard the approaches to the jail. By repeated charges the police drove off the crowd. Later a thousand or more workmen gathered near the jail. A detachment of artillery was brought from Thun to hold them back, and up to a late hour last night no fight had occurred.

Smith College Graduates.

NORTHAMPTON, Mass., June 20.—The graduates of Smith female college observed their Ivy day yesterday on the college lawn. The address of welcome was delivered by Laura Melancy Pratt of Kalamazoo, Mich. This was followed by the song "Fair Smith." The ivy song was written by Caroline B. Rourland of Peoria, Ills., and set to music by Grace Constant Smith.

Freshmen to Row Today.

NEW LONDON, Conn., June 20.—The time of the Columbia-Cornell freshmen race has been changed to 5 o'clock this afternoon. This was done in deference to the wishes of people who desire to witness the race, although there is no great interest attached to it outside the college men.

Three Miners Entombed.

PITTSBURG, June 20.—An explosion of firedamp occurred in the coal mines of Hartley & Marshall here yesterday. Three miners are believed to be entombed in the mines. Their names are John R. McLain, William Chappell and John Lagersti. Rescuing parties are at work, but so far they have been unable to reach the imprisoned men.

Convicts Make Their Escape.

JACKSON, Mich., June 20.—James Morrison and William Henson escaped from prison yesterday by scaling the walls. They were employed about the engine room of the electric light plant. At the time of their escape no guards were on the wall. They were not missed until three hours after their escape.

Suicide of a Canadian Lawyer.

MONTREAL, June 20.—Sunday night Louis Prevost, a well known young lawyer of this city and a son of Hon. Wildred Prevost, committed suicide by shooting himself through the head in his rooms in a fashionable boarding house here. No cause can be assigned for the act.

Butchman Discharged.

WELLESLEY, Mass, June 20.—Fritz Butchman, who was arrested charged with the murder of Jacob Littig three weeks ago, was arraigned before Judge Washburn at Wellesley Hills. There being no evidence sufficient to cause his detention, he was discharged.

Their Bodies Recovered.

ANSONIA, Conn., June 20.—In Seymour, Sunday afternoon, a boat, in which were Howard Hawley and four girls, was capsized, and Kate O'Donnell and Mamie McCarthy, each 14 years of age, were drowned. The bodies were recovered.

Satolli In Omaha.

OMAHA, Neb., June 20.—Archbishop Satolli, accompanied by Dr. O'Gorman of Washington, has arrived in the city and is conferring with Bishop Scannell concerning the multitudinous disputes of Bishop Bonacum of the Lincoln see.

Suicide of a Cigar Manufacturer.

NEW YORK, June 20.—Adolph C. Jaeger, 50 years old, the senior partner of the cigar manufacturing concern of Jaeger Bros., committed suicide at his home yesterday by shooting himself in the left breast.

Wood Pulp Mill Destroyed.

BALLSTON, N. Y., June 20.—Fire yesterday wrecked the George West's chemical wood pulp mill. The origin of the fire is supposed to have been spontaneous combustion. Loss $25,000; partly covered by insurance.

Lynched the Wrong Man.

MILAN, Tenn., June 20.—The mob which was supposed to have lynched Lee Bennett, at Gleason, hanged Jim Harris, an innocent man, instead. Bennett is in jail at Dresden heavily guarded.

Rates Advanced July 1.

PHILADELPHIA, June 20.—The Pennsylvania and Reading roads will advance rates to Atlantic City 25 cents, taking effect July 1.

Court Shut Down on It.

Mexico, Mo., June 20.—No more vagrants will be sold off the block in Missouri, as the supreme court decided yesterday that the law was unconstitutional.

THE STANDARD'S SALES.

The demand for the Evening Standard continues to be unprecedented and the sales have been enormous. From every point the compliments pour in upon the masterly manner in which the Borden trial has been handled. These are last week's figures.

Monday,	10,400
Tuesday,	10,403
Wednesday,	10,350
Thursday,	10,304
Friday,	10,013
Saturday,	10,554
Total for one week	62,024

HOME MATTERS.

TABOR ACADEMY.

A Pretty Graduation, Splendid Weather and a Crowded Hall.

Today was graduation day at Tabor academy in Marion. Music hall, where the exercises were held, was crowded to the doors with people, who were willing to endure the oppressive heat in order to catch a glimpse of the graduating gowns and hear the class farewells. The hall was prettily decorated with wild flowers, and the lovely gowns of the girls were a set-off to the otherwise modest little stage.

The programme, which has previously been printed in the Standard, was carried out without a break or mistake. The essays were really bright and interesting papers and showed that the time at Tabor had been well spent. The presentation of diplomas was made by Rev. Frank L. Goodspeed.

The Jadassohn club of this city played several times during the exercises.

The graduation was one of great interest, as it closes Prof. C. P. Howland's connection with the school, where he has been master for nearly ten years.

The following is the graduating class:

Classical Course—Horatio Cushing Allen, Lucy Edith Blake, Eunice Elizabeth Ransom, Delano Richmond Ryder, Grace Wilbur Thomas.

Scientific Course—George Parker Bolles, Jr.

English Course—Lester Winfield Jenney.

THIRD DISTRICT COURT.

Borden, J.

Tuesday, June 20.

Five cases of drunkenness were disposed of as follows: Maxim Dufresne, three months in the house of correction; John J. McGuire, 30 days; Thomas Connor, 30 days; John King, 30 days; and one case against an old man 71 years of age was placed on probation. The old man was so obstinate yesterday that he would not go home when the officers told him to, and they were compelled to arrest him, he made such a nuisance of himself.

William Bussell paid a fine of $7 for disturbing the peace last night. He asked a man to have a glass of beer with him, and because he refused to drink Bussell attempted to "lick him."

Etiene Martin pleaded guilty of keeping an unlicensed dog. A few days since the dog bit a boy, and all the people in Martin's neighborhood are afraid of the dog. When asked by the neighbors to kill him Martin refused to do so, and they made the complaint to the police. He was fined $15, which he paid, and informed the court he would have the dog killed.

FAIRHAVEN.

Three More Breaks at the North En of the Town Last Night.

Some thief entered three barns in the north end of the town last night and secured from all a complete turnout. The first place visited was the Laura Keene farm, on the Acushnet side of the line. The person or persons carried off from there a good horse, which was being boarded on the farm. The thief then worked south and took a new harness from Daniel Kendrick's stable. He needed a wagon to complete the outfit and he found a new open business wagon in Adino Tripp's barn, which he took. This vehicle had yellow wheels and a black body. The turnout thus secured was quite valuable. This breaking and entering business has been altogether too common in the village for the past six months and the constables and selectmen are keeping a lookout for the thief. The party who took the horse and wagon is probably the same one who entered the Lawton house, and he appears to understand the territory thoroughly.

FUNERAL.

The funeral of the late Margaret M. O'Reilly took place at her sister's residence, 412 South First street, this morning. Thence to St. James church, where a requiem high mass was sung by the pastor, Rev. James F. Clark. The floral tributes were very numerous The following are a few of the many pieces presented: Large pillow of white pinks with "Sister" on it from Mr. and Mrs. Enos; standing crescent from Mr. and Mrs. James F. Moore; wreath from C. H. Murphy and family; basket of Jacqueminot roses from Mr. and Mrs. Enos, wreath from Mrs. Charles A. Case; cross from Mr. and Mrs. Thompson and family; basket of flowers from Mr. E. M. Holcomb, and numerous other designs. The pall bearers were Dennis E., John H., Cornelius H. and T. J. Murphy.

200 BY 60.

That is the size in feet of F. R. Slocum's storeroom on the second floor of his store. It is a veritable treasure house of first-class house furnishings, and people who would know what the modes are in furniture are invited to visit this room, even though they may not care to purchase. Consider that there are nearly 150 chamber suits, an endless variety of parlor suits, chairs by the hundred, couches, odd pieces and bric-a-brac in pleasing array, to be seen and purchased if so desired. The room is always open to the public.

CONDENSED LOCALS.

—Edward S. Shaw, an engineer from Boston, is in the city today, and with County Commissioners Babbitt and Sanders viewed the proposed locations for a new bridge across the Acushnet river to relieve the travel on the New Bedford & Fairhaven bridge. There are three proposed approaches on this side of the river—one at the foot of North street, another at the foot of High street and the third at the foot of Middle street.

—Received the Contract.—Charles F. Perry of the White Cash store has received the contract to furnish Barnum & Bailey's great show with groceries and provisions during their stay in this city.

For the sick and delicate, as well as the strong and healthy child, Mellin's Food is unrivalled. It is the best gift that the household has received from modern science.

Avoid all diseases of the liver, kidneys and stomach by drinking Ayer's Hygienic Coffee. Grocers sell it. Try it.

—Ladies will be admitted free to the base ball game tomorrow.

Hood's Sarsaparilla vitalizes the blood.

OUR SPECIAL
Clean Up Sale
Presents the following
BARGAINS
—FOR—
TUESDAY and WEDNESDAY.

Friday we received from New York
138 Rolls of STRAW MATTING,
which is by far the best Matting bargain we have ever offered.

Lot 1: Slightly Wrapper Stained Inlaid, and Fine Weave String Warp Japanese Mattings,
regular 62 1-2 cent goods, you will buy this Matting for
27 Cents per yard, or
$7.50 for a roll!

EXTRA WEIGHT
CANTON MATTINGS
very heavy, weighing from 80 to 100 lbs. to the roll, perfect goods and are considered cheap at 50 to 62 1-2c. per yard. We have marked these goods at
30, 33 and 35c. per yard,
$8, $8.50 and $9 per roll.

For Summer Cottage Furnishing this is an opportunity seldom offered.

OUR PORTIERE SALE
is immensely popular and we are not surprised, for it's not often even in the large cities that such a splendid assortment is shown. There are beautiful designs in high art colorings, with very heavy fringe top and bottom in new effects scrolls and florals, or in the much sought shades in plain goods, capable of the most artistic draping. We have started in to sell 75 pairs of Chenille Curtains between now and July 1st.

Watch this column closely for changes.

C. F. WING,
34 to 40 Purchase Street.

WHITING & CO.
Great Sale
—OF—
SUMMER
Wash Dress Goods
—AT—
ABOUT HALF PRICE

800 yards of Real French Satines, all Black ground with White and Colored Figures, the best 37 1-2cts. quality, our price for this lot until all sold 17cts. per yard.

300 yards more of those 12 1-2 and 15c. Figured Pongees left, to be sold at 9cts. per yard.

100 more pieces of those best 12 1-2cts. Ginghams, to be sold by us at 7 1-2cts. per yard.

1500 yards of Real Scotch Ginghams and best styles, such as we have sold this season at 33 and 37 1-2cts. per yard, all to be sold by us at 17cts. per yard.

200 yards of Figured French Organdie Muslins, such as we sold last season at 37 1-2cts., closing out price 12 1-2cts.

200 yards left of those 60cts. French all wool Challies, that we are closing out at 41cts. per yard, these are the best quality made.

NO SAMPLES GIVEN.

WHITING & CO.

J. V. SPARE,
41 Purchase St.

Magnetic Offerings This Week in Many Departments.

28 dozen Ladies' Jersey Vests,
Ribbon trimmed and made of pure Egyptian yarn, in sleeveless or with short sleeves, at
15c. each

31 1-2 dozen Ladies' Soft Lisle Thread Jersey Vests,
Low neck and sleeveless, with silk ribbon and silk shell trimming at neck and arms, at
25c. each

Children's Gauze Vests,
With long sleeves, sizes 16 to 26, at
13c. each

Have You Seen
That "money saver" in Corsets we are offering at
39c.
Don't wait until your size is all sold.

Men's Seamless Cotton Hose,
In all the shades of tan, slate and fast black, either plain or drop stitch, at
19c. pair

Men's Normal Mixed Balbriggan Shirts and Drawers
To match, with strap back, at
50c. each

Keep your eyes on our windows. It will be time well spent.

25 dozen Pure Silk Windsor Ties,
In stripes, new plaids, new figures and plain colors, either plain or hemstitched ends, at
25c. each

Call for July Fashion Sheets.

Ladies' Cambric Shirt Waists,
In Pink and Blue, with neat spots and stripes and ruffle down front, at
50c. each

Ladies' Navy Blue Satine Waists,
In neat stripes with ruffle front, at
75c. each

These are offerings which must appeal direct to your economical instincts.

J. V. Spare.
41 Purchase St.

A ——
Ten Dollar
Cheviot Suit
THAT BEATS THEM ALL.

Made from a handsome smooth faced, all wool black Cheviot, cut single breasted style, make up and fit equal to a $16 suit. In fact, these suits were made up to retail at $16, but the manufacturer needed money and we secured this lot of suits at our own figures. This is the BIGGEST BARGAIN in Cheviot Suits you ever saw. A genuine $16 suit for only

$10!

J. & W. R. WING & CO.
133 UNION ST.

VERDICT

(Continued from First Page.)

had gone on. There is cunning in crime, but there is blindness in crime, too. She had gone on with stealth and cunning, but she had forgot the hereafter. They always do, and when the deed was done she was going down the stairs to meet Nemesis. There would not be any question but what he would know of the reason that woman lay in death. He knew who disliked her, he knew who could not tolerate her presence under that roof, he knew the discussion which had led up to the pitch of frenzy which resulted in her death, and she did not dare to let him live, father though he was, and bound to him by every tie of affection. Ah, Mr. Foreman, how many a man, if he could only be told before he began to commit a crime, could be told that there is no such thing as stopping with one crime, would hesitate before he crossed the threshold of virtue? He must go on, he cannot go back.

Crime Breeds Crime and is the Mother of Crime.

'And so, when she came down stairs it was her father she met, but it was also the husband of her stepmother. It came to her then as if it had not before that she had become a criminal, and that

In No Way Could She Escape the Consequences of Her Crime

but by completing the bloody work. Don't misunderstand me, Mr. Foreman. I don't say this took place—it is not our duty to do so. It is ours to say that he was killed, and not why he was killed. But it is a consolation to us to think that the murder of Andrew J. Borden was not planned, but was done as a work of necessity, which, could she have seen, would have caused her not to give orders to Bridget to wash the windows or to go up stairs after it was done. And so I leave it there, not as a matter of proof—O no, O no, but to relieve my mind of believing that there was not a parricide at heart living there.

Let us go back and see what happened. Bridget finished washing windows and came in. There was no one below stairs. She took her stepladder and began her work inside. Meanwhile the old gentleman was finishing the last walk of his life. You have followed his movements. It is unnecessary to recapitulate them. We see him leaving the house, we find him at his accustomed place at the bank, which had honored him with its presidency, at his usual hour, 9 30; and then at that other bank, which had also honored him, though later, with a position as trustee. He moved slowly—every one moved slowly that day—out of it—member it, Mr. Foreman and gentlemen, came back by Clegg's store, talked with him, walked by that store he was having repaired on Main street, passed to Spring street, turned down Borden street, and into that house where his wife lay dead, all unknown. He went to the back door as he was accustomed to, but there was no one to open it. He went to the front door and thought to enter it as every man does, by the spring lock. There was the usual noise on the street, but Lizzie heard him put the key in the lock and yet Bridget let him in. He went into the dining room, changed his coat, and sat down to read. In came Lizzie from the place where Mrs. Borden lay dead, and told him what we cannot believe about where his wife was. I believe the circumstances are to be regarded in this case, but

The Falsehood that Goes to the Vitals of the Crime

is not a circumstance—it is a proof. Where was her mother? She knew. She told the falsehood. It would pass for a while—it would keep the old man silent for a time. She took her ironing board in the heat of the day. Why had she not taken it earlier. No—I am ahead of my story. I want to get it all right. The old man goes up stairs to his room, comes down again and sits down. Then she suggests—with the same spirit with which Judas kissed the master—that it would be well for him, tired from his walk, to lie down on the sofa and rest. Then she goes to the dining room again, gets her ironing board, and goes to ironing handkerchiefs. Bridget gets through her work. She tells Bridget to be sure, if she goes out that afternoon, to lock all the doors, as Mrs. Borden has gone out to see some one that is sick—she thinks somewhere in Fall River. And Bridget goes up stairs to rest and leaves this woman ironing handkerchiefs nearer her father on the sofa there than my distinguished friend is to me now.

Again she was alone. O, unfortunate combination of circumstances! Again alone with the man who was found murdered. In what may be safely said to have been less than 20 minutes she called Bridget and tells her her father is dead.

There is another straw, not floating on the surface of the stream of evidence, or in an eddy, but in the broad current, that tells with irresistible distinctness what happened. She had a good fire to iron clothes with. Officer Harrington takes the car that reaches the city hall at quarter past 12, walks up to the house, talks with Lizzie, goes about the house, and last of all looks into the stove. This could not be earlier than half-past 12. I need not say to you that if there was a fire at half-past 12, such as he saw, larger than your hand, in one end of the stove, the remnants of a coal fire of an hour and a half earlier, there was enough for her to have finished her job. It was a little job, there were not over nine handkerchiefs at the outside. When this thing is over four or five are ironed and four or five were sprinkled, ready to iron. Whatever else is true she had commenced the work and was at work when Bridget went up stairs. The work was almost done, the day was growing hotter and the dinner hour was approaching. This, gentlemen, is significant, terribly significant. Why did she stop right at the eve of the work being done?

The officers have been criticised for their catechism of Lizzie. I could never see the force of that. It would be the most natural thing in the world for them to invite the officers of the law to punish the criminal who was guilty of such an awful crime as killing their father and mother. It was commendable that leaped to the lips of all, servant, family doctor and friends, "You were in touch with your father, how did it happen and you didn't know it? Where were you? Didn't you leave the door hooked?" There is that in this case more significant than the questions of the officers. She has said to her friends that she heard a groan and came in. I may be permitted to say that this is not so. Dr. Bowen came and asks first of all, "Where were you, Lizzie?" To him she gives one reply. Then Mrs. Bowen, that honest woman and faithful friend, asks "Where were you, Lizzie?" "I was in the barn after lead." To Miss Russell, her friend, if she ever had a friend, she tells she was after ink or iron to fix the screen. There came among the first a representative of the majesty of the law, as my esteemed friend would call him, the assistant marshal. He had about as much suspicion of her at that time as he did of his own chief. He is a gentleman, with the instincts of a gentleman, and questioned her in

No Spirit of Prying Faultfinding or Inquisition,

but came to her room to get the correct story of all this. And I'm going to give you the story, and it is no doubt true, word for word, and letter for letter. When he went into the room she was not alone. Miss Russell was there, and that Christian gentleman, Mr. Jubb, whose fidelity and interest has been so manifest, who has been by her side all through this trial, giving her such consolation as he can impart, and whom I honor for his course. If Officer Fleet had misrepresented things that friend would have been heard from. And am I not justified by his silence in saying that the officer was truthful. We are met by the suggestion that this woman

could not tell the truth because she had taken drugs. Nay, it was before that, when she was cool, with the coolness which has astonished the world. Fleet came in and talked with her. Let me read what was said for it is vital. He asked her about the murder and she Answered "No."

All that she knew was that her father came home and sat down in a chair and took out some papers. She was ironing in the dining room she saw that he was feeble, and she assisted him to lie down on the sofa. She then went back to her ironing, but left and went out into the yard and up in the barn. "I asked her how long she was there," says Officer Fleet, and she said 'she meant she was up stairs in the barn. I asked her how long she was there, and she said for half an hour, and when she came in she found her father dead. We must treat all these facts as an appeal to your common sense. Tried by that standard it is absurd and not within the bounds of reasonable possibility. There isn't a man of you that doesn't remember that this was within four days of Charles S. Sawyer? He betrayed fear as he stood at that screen door, even after the officers had come, the woman were in the room with the body, and he was secure in the public presence. He—man though he was—did not dare to stand there without first locking the cellar door, and even then going outside once in a while. We laughed at it a little, but put yourself in his place and see what you would do. Lizzie Borden could not know the assassin was not still there—that he might not still be there, but she stayed there. The neighbors say a single cry would have brought aid to her assistance. She did not leave the house. She stood there calmly in the door and quietly summoned her intimate friends. The physician across the street. What on earth did she want a doctor for? I don't know. Her father was dead, and she knew it. She had told Bridget Sullivan so when she called her down stairs. She sent Bridget out to tell the public. Did it ever occur to you before, that the public never knew of this murder till accidentally Mrs. Churchill saw Lizzie at the window and asked—notice, she asked her what was the matter. But for the bright eyes of Mrs. Churchill it would not have been known. There was no cry—no attempt to call her—but she stood there with her calm, peaceful demeanor, although surrounded by her victims. I don't care to refer to the coolness of the defendant when interviewed by the officers, about her going down cellar I have little to say. But at such a time, I think you and I wouldn't care to do it. Her friend

In my desire to tell you every fact, I forbear to ask you to criticise or look unfairly against her behavior. I agree with my learned friend that her absence of tears,

Her Icy Demeanor Due to the Consciousness of Guilt,

or because she was overcome with her emotions. She has ever been cool, self-possessed as she is now, and she had consciousness of guilt—she forced back any tears that might flow. But there are some things here that are pregnant, and if they occur in real life are thoroughly bad. She goes to her friend the evening before and prepares her for something awful. As my associate has said, "She catalogued these offenses." She said she felt that something was hanging over her. All disasters of your life, Mr. Foreman, came upon you like a flash. Today you are happy and tomorrow you are plunged in grief. You don't speak of it before. Look at this as the ship in the current, or in the eddy, as you choose.

But I come to one remarkable fact. Do you remember that great strong man, Charles S. Sawyer? He betrayed fear as he stood at that screen door, even after the officers had come, the woman were in the room with the body, and he was secure in the public presence. He—man though he was—did not dare to stand there without first locking the cellar door, and even then going outside once in a while. We laughed at it a little, but put yourself in his place and see what you would do. Lizzie Borden could not know the assassin was not still there—that he might not still be there, but she stayed there. The neighbors say a single cry would have brought aid to her assistance. She did not leave the house. She stood there calmly in the door and quietly summoned her intimate friends.

That isn't all. The next day, the mayor of the city, whom I believe to be a gentleman, and the city marshal, who in spite of all that is said of him, is a truthful man, went there, and this woman told them she was after lead for a sinker, while to her friend Miss Russell she said she was after ink to mend the screen door. Show us the fish lines those sinkers were to go on.

Show us Something to Establish the Alibi She Has Attempted to Set Up

in view of the terrible event. She got to another point with Officer Harrington. He asked her if she heard no noise; no scream. "No sir," she said, "I was in the loft." Ah, it was necessary to put her there. It was the only place she could be where it could be said she would not hear. Let us be just. We are trying a woman of high station for a high crime. Some of you may have sat on a jury and have heard of alibis. Have you ever heard of a more absurd one? My learned friend fails to tell why she was there. She failed when she was beside her clerical friend to say she was there.

But as to the Second Murder

The question is one more difficult to answer.

I cannot answer it, you cannot answer it. You are neither a murderer or woman and have not the craft of an assassin. After the officers had completed their search and had been throughout the house they demanded a dress and were fooled by the dress given them.

Up to This Time I Have Traveled in the Path of Unchallenged Facts

and now approach the first subject about which there is any contradiction.

That dress has been described to you as a silk dress, a dark blue, evidently a dress with a figure, which is not at all like a diamond, a dress which is not at cheap dress, a dress which would not be worn in ironing by any prudent woman. Of course not, it is an afternoon dress. Do your wives dress in silk when they go down in the kitchen to work and in the morning before dinner? There was one woman in this world who saw Lizzie Borden after these murders; we do not doubt when she had not suspected that murder had been committed. Who was that? She was that clear-eyed, honest daughter of one of Fall River's most honored citizens, Adelaide Churchill. Somebody else saw her when they knew that murder had been done. Mrs. Churchill saw her when she at least thought that somebody was sick in the house. She saw Bridget going to the Borden house, and saw Lizzie in agitation, she thought somebody was sick, and she raised the window to inquire and was summoned to the house. She describes the dress she saw and I will read it from her testimony: "Will you describe the dress she had on while you were ironing?" It looked like light blue and white ground work, and it seemed like calico or cambric, and it had a light blue or white ground work, with a navy blue diamond printed on it. Was the whole dress alike; skirt and waist? Yes. Was that the dress she had on that morning? She looked at the dress shown her and said it does not look like it. Mr. Moody wants a little more positive answer than that and he puts the question again. Was it?

Ah, Adelaide Churchill Must Give an Answer That Will Convict This Woman.

She is no police officer conspiring against her life, she is her next door neighbor and her friend, her friend today, and Mr. Moody yet the question goes to her Was it this dress? she says that is not the dress I described. My learned friend wants it exactly. Was it the

take the cloth it shook like an aspen leaf. She knew that she hadn't described that dress, and I pitied her from the bottom of my heart. I turn back from Mrs. Bowen eager for the defense of this girl to Mrs. Bowen before it was known that there was to be any controversy in regard to this dress. "What dress did she have on? A dress with a white spray." That does not mean much to you or me. But if a carpenter calls a cornice a pilaster it means much. If a lawyer calls a deed a lease it means much. If a woman calls a circle a spray she is not a woman.

She goes further. "What was the body of the dress? I did not notice particularly. The ground you say had a white spray?. O, it was blue. Light or dark blue? I should say quite a dark shade, I cannot tell. I was not looking for fashions then. Do you know the skirt she had on? I do not. It was nothing more than an ordinary morning dress, such as I have seen her wear before. Something you had seen her wear frequently? Yes sir. When, in the morning? Yes sir."

A morning dress she had on that morning by the testimony of everybody in this case, and there is not a human being brought forward to say that up to the time her father and mother were killed they saw her wearing that silk dress before dinner. Mrs. Bowen, all at sea, but voluntarily described it as a dress which was a cheap morning dress. Dr. Bowen, strained to the utmost, he could not describe it, other than as a drab which looked like a light blue, as Mrs. Raymond well put it, and Mrs. Churchill, calm, self-reliant, friendly to the uttermost point of human interest for this poor girl, accurately telling us that that was the dress. Do you believe it? Do you believe that that hot morning in August, the hottest of that year, that girl would be found in the hottest occupation that a girl can be engaged in in the morning, ironing in a silk dress? That is not all the morning dress she had worn, she had worn for many years, as Miss Emma is obliged to say. She put it in the testimony, she wanted to help her sister, "I was very early in the morning." O, unfortunate expression. Did you ever know of a girl to change a dress twice in a morning? On the day of the tragedy Bridget Sullivan tells us that that cheap morning dress, light blue with a dark blue figure, was worn. Wednesday morning the dress she had on was that description. She never wears it afterwards. Friday, Saturday she has on this blue dress mornings and afternoons.

But I pass rapidly on to one other fact which has not been explained. We have contradiction in the character of the search that was made in that house. It cannot, perhaps, be denied that the search of Thursday was perfunctory, insufficient and undecisive. It was with no particular definite aim in view; it was absolutely without any idea that the inmates of the house knew of this crime; it was that sort of a search which goes through and doesn't see what it ought to see. But it was enough to put them on their guard; there was in that house somewhere a Bedford cord dress; that Bedford cord dress had been stained with paint. My learned associate never said it had not been stained with paint; there is no assertion nor pretense that it had not been stained with paint. It had not stopped the wearing of it, however. It was good enough for a morning dress, good enough for a ironing dress, good enough for a chore dress around the house in the morning before the Thursday search had put them on their guard, and when Saturday afternoon the officers came there they were prepared for the most absolute and thorough search that could be made in that house. Where was that paint-stained Bedford cord?

Where Was That Dress with Paint Spots on Its so Thickly Covering It

that it was not fit to wear any more? Where was it that the officers did not see it? Emma alone can tell us, and Emma tries to tell us that it was in that closet.

Mr. Knowlton read from the testimony the statement of Officer Fleet that he looked in the closet in the front hall up stairs, and examined the dresses, but didn't see any with marks of paint upon them, or anything that looked like paint. My distinguished friend may say that he could not help it, he was in the conspiracy, but his partner in that search was State Detective Seaver of Taunton, a man who holds commission from the executive of this commonwealth many times repeated for 13 or 15 years, a man out of the reach of the attaches of suspicion, if there was any attached to the Fall River police. He says he did not see any light blue dress with diamond spots with paint around the bottom, or upon the side. Men are not credited by servers generally, but Officers Fleet and Seaver could see a dress that was so dirty that it had got to be destroyed.

It was not found, it was concealed. It was the dress that Mrs. Raymond made in the spring, it was a cheap morning dress that had been soiled with paint. It had, however, been good enough to wear for mornings. It was even worn by her on Wednesday morning before the tragedy, it corresponds to the dress Mrs. Churchill saw her have on that morning. It corresponds from the description that is received from Dr. Bowen. It was not seen there that time until Sunday, it was not where the officers could find it on Saturday night, it was concealed.

I mean to be courteous and fair, but I am forced to assert that the dress was concealed. I can't answer how it didn't get covered with blood. There is a cruel deftness that I cannot and you cannot explain or understand. Burnt paper was found in the stove. Is that a solution? That is for you to determine. My learned friend raises the point that in it was wrapped the handle of the hatchet. He raises that point, not I. It isn't our place to prove concealment of the crime.

Concealment is Part of the Business of Defense.

It is possible that very few spots of blood got upon that dress. Mr. Manning went into the room to see what he could see. What a reporter can't see no one can see. All he saw was one spot of blood on the white door. The books upon the small table were unspotted and there were no spots on the carpet.

She had had one experience, she knew how blood spurted from hatchet wounds. Thereupon been one search on Saturday and the dress and skirt had been demanded. Upon the skirt was found a drop of blood that came there from without and came by spattering. Upon that dress of Bedford cord there might have been drops, microscopic drops, to tell the tale, and while the bells were ringing the people to come to divine worship that dress was burned. This was the morning after the search, the dress hadn't been found; now was the time to burn it. There are two versions of that story, it is for you to search the truth. Emma says that on Saturday night she saw the dress on the hook, and told Lizzie said she would. We can't contradict that except by what followed. Alice Russell

I should judge this a pretty good description for a man, not exactly correct as to color, but he hit so near the mark that Mrs. Raymond, a witness called by them, said when she read Dr. Bowen's testimony she thought that the Bedford cord was undoubtedly the dress he had in mind. Dr. Bowen when asked "what do you call this?" (the dress in the case) said, "I call that dark blue."

On the Significance of Unwilling Testimony

as to the character of that dress. Unwilling testimony, not necessarily or even remotely tending to perjury, but the evidence of one who does not want to hurt his friend, but whose very words have injured her, because he has described the dress.

In this case the only person who comes forward to contradict that is Mrs. Bowen herself, and when her testimony is considered with reference to all the facts in this case it is a most significant corroboration of it. She says today that it is a dark blue. Witnesses are put on the stand, his learned friend after the search, the dress shown her as to testify. It may be you observed when Mrs. Raymond raised her hand to

she were not convicted.

Some little point was made as to whether it was a Bedford cord or not. Mrs. Churchill didn't know a Bedford cord. She knew it was a cheap cotton or calico dress. Officer Dougherty, who I do not attach great importance to, but he is in the case, said, I think, it was a light blue dress, with a bosom in the waist. Whatever that means I do not know. On being shown the dress in the case when the question was put "I will ask you—if that was the dress?" he said "No, I do not think it was." My distinguished friend tries to turn it into a faint recollection. Dougherty says I have a faint recollection that it was a light blue. The ex-governor says but it is only a faint recollection. Dougherty replies, but I am confident it is not a dark one, not as full blue as that.

Now comes another witness, who I believe would break his heart strings before he would say a word against that girl if he could help it, and I do not blame him for it, I honor him for it, and that is her physician friend, Dr. Seabury W Bowen. And the testimony in all the more feasible because it comes from her intimate friend, and comes in advance of the suggestion that there was ever going to be discussion about it. He undertakes to describe that dress, and these are the words which he does not dare to take back. "I saw her dress that day, it is pretty hard work for me to describe it; perhaps if I could see a dress something like it I could guess; it was sort of a drab, a sort of morning dress."

DISTRICT ATTORNEY KNOWLTON ASKING FOR LIZZIE BORDEN'S CONVICTION.

That alibi will not stand. We leave her by the murdered woman and by her father's side, and we come back to find her with a story which is absolutely untrue. I will now devote a word to Rubinsky. He is a discarded witness. He has been to Wilson and Mullaly and Phillips. He told Mullaly on the 8th of August that it was about 1030 when he went by the house, and he told another story to Phillips. At the district court in Fall River he was called by defense. It has been shown that it was ten minutes to 11 when Rubinsky went for his horse, and he had to wait to have him fed before going out. He was late, and he drove fast. He was not looking for customers, for he had no ice cream in his cart. It may have been Mrs. Churchill, Miss Russell or Bridget Sullivan he saw in the yard, for it was probably after the crime was committed when he went by the Borden house. Is it changed that Lizzie didn't go into the barn. What is charged is that her statement that she was in the barn for 20 minutes is absolutely beyond human power to believe. The barn had ceased to be used. It was a repository for rubbish. The learned eyed Officer Medley was present, and he heard her story. It was a day of excitement in Fall River. and this woman was about the only one who kept her head. Hard-headed police officers forgot their duty. Mr. Medley heard her story, and went to the barn and found it closed. He went in and up the stairs, and then he got in the right position he looked at the door and found it covered by hay-seed and dust. He tried it with his fingers, and he went up and took a few steps, and found when he came down that he could see the impression. Gentleman, that thing occurred. There isn't a man on this panel who believes that officer would stand up and take the oath of God on his lips and deliberately perjure himself.

Mr. Manning and Mr. Stevens went up there. They didn't see Mr. Medley and can't "say they went there. They looked at the front door and found it open. Mr. Clarkson went there and tries to tell us that he went first, but can't. He said to the court that he didn't go till 11 40 o'clock, and that is as near as he could fix the time. He found the door open. I dismiss this. O, did my learned friend expect when he asked those boys as to whether it was a hot or a cool place to offer evidence which should control your very own senses, by trying to say it was a cool and comfortable place. Medley was there first. He got a team and drove to the Borden house—drove as fast as he could—wear by the City hall clock at just 19 minutes past 11—went to the barn, went through it, went to the house—all the time, 11½ minutes. All the contradiction there is to Officer Medley is regarding time.

You visited that barn, gentlemen, cool, deliberate and with a purpose of taking all the time you wanted to. Are there two men on this panel who can say how long—whether half an hour, or 10 minutes—how long you were in that house, or the cellar, or the barn, or how long you were in all? People are not accustomed to notice particularly the flight of time. And here we have the occurrence of a century, when every face paled, every heart stood still at its enormity, and yet she knew she was there just 20 minutes.

didn't dare to go into the room where

the clothes were, but she went into the room quietly and calmly. When a woman dares she dares, and when she will she will. Given, a woman, absolute in her confidence, who told Mrs. Reagan that she failed to break eggs it was the first time she ever failed to do anything. These are trifles, little chips, that may or may not indicate which way the current goes.

But there is more in this case than that. Of course the question arises, "How did she avoid the spatters on the dress if she was the author of these awful crimes?"

As to the first of these, I scarcely think it necessary to answer. In the solitude of that house, with ample fire in the stove, with the ample wit of woman, nobody has suggested that there was not ample opportunity and there is nothing in it to show she had no reason. I will dwell no more on that.

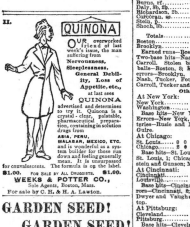
CALISTHENIC EXHIBITION.

A very unique entertainment was the
Calisthenic Exhibition given in Y. M.
C. A. hall last evening under the management of Miss Walker. About 40 performers, most of them young ladies,
were on the stage. The programme was
as follows:

March.
Dumb Bell Drill.
Solo.　　Mr. H. Winfred Goff
Wand Drill.
Autoharp Solo.　Miss Alice Bertram
March.
Hoop Drill.
Solo.　　Mr. Goff
Indian Club Exercises.
Autoharp Solo.　Miss Walker
Little Patriots Drill.

The various drills were performed by
Miss Walker's gymnasium class, which
was formed last winter. Miss Walker's
Indian club swinging was a marvel of
grace and beauty. She has no superior
in this branch of athletics. The lady
was formerly an instructor in gymnastics in the Mount Holyoke seminary.
The musical features of the programme
were well carried out. Mr. Goff especially pleased with his solos. Miss Laura
McCabe was the pianist.

FASHIONABLY BRED HORSES.

At the foot of Middle street in this
city Mr. C. A. Sisson has two stallions,
Policy and Locksley. Policy is by Albert
W, 2 20, a game race horse, and the
most prominent race horse sire of the
Electioneer family. Policy's dam is by
Echo, a superbly bred and successful son
of Hambletonian, one of whose daughters is the dam of the famous trotter and
pacer Direct, while the indications are
from the success of several others as
brood mares that Echo is to take a very
high rank as a brood mare sire. Policy's
second dam is Lightfoot (dam of El
Monte, 2 29,) by Hubbard, son of Planet;
third dam by Rifleman (sire of Colonel
Lewis, 2 18¾,) a thoroughbred son of
imported Glencoe. Policy is a seal
brown, now three years old, 15¼
hands high, and weighs 1,000 pounds.
He is richly bred, and is a typical Electioneer in gait, form and action, with
superior style and action.

Locksley, his stable companion, belongs
to the popular Wilkes family, the only
real rival to the Electioneers, being by
Lumps, 2 21, a very successful sire, with
sixteen 2 30 performers to his credit,
several of which have proven remarkably
game race horses, four having already
beaten 2 20. Locksley's dam is May Bee,
by Matt Duffy, 1,564, an inbred Morgan,
his dam being by Western Fearnaught,
grandam by Ethan Allen. Locksley's
second dam is by Roebuck's Abdallah;
third dam by Billy Boston, a thoroughbred son of Boston. He is also a handsome seal brown, with white markings,
15 hands high, weighs about 1,000
pounds, has a quick, nervy way of moving, and is certainly fast. Mr. Sisson
purchased Locksley about the middle of
last March from George Leavett, who
has owned so many good ones by sons of
George Wilkes.

Policy will be sent to Boston in a few
days, and placed in the hands of Jerry
O'Neil at Mystic Park.

BOSTON VICTORIOUS.

**Stivetts Proved Effective In Puzzling the
Men From the City of Churches.**

BOSTON, June 20.—The first Brooklyn
game was played yesterday under very
favorable circumstances, and a crowd of
over 4100 attended. Stivetts and Stein
were the pitchers, and the former was
very effective indeed, but six hits being
made off his delivery. Lowe was injured
and Richardson was ill, so both retired
from the game, Merritt and Shoch taking
their places. Tucker, Long and Stein
batted finely. Carroll made one of the
most wonderful catches ever seen on a ball
field, while the fielding of both teams was
excellent as a whole. The umpiring was a
trifle unsteady on balls and strikes.

	AB	R	BH	PO	A	E
Long, s s	4	0	1	3	3	0
Lowe, 2b	1	0	0	1	2	1
Duffy, cf	4	1	1	3	0	0
McCarthy, lf	3	2	1	4	0	0
Nash, 3b	4	1	1	1	1	1
Tucker, 1b	4	1	2	9	0	0
Carroll, rf	4	0	1	2	0	0
Ganzel, c	4	0	0	4	1	0
Stivetts, p	3	0	0	0	3	0
Merritt, c	0	0	0	0	0	0
Totals	31	6	7	27	13	4

BROOKLYN.	AB	R	BH	PO	A	E
Foutz, 1b	4	0	1	13	0	0
Griffin, cf	3	0	0	1	0	0
Stovey, lf	3	1	1	1	0	0
Brouthers, rf	4	0	1	0	0	0
Kinslow, c	3	0	0	3	0	0
Burns, rf	4	0	2	1	0	0
Daly, 2b	4	0	0	5	3	0
Corcoran, ss	3	0	0	2	3	0
Stein, p	3	0	0	0	3	0
Shoch, 3b	2	0	0	0	0	0
Totals	33	1	6	24	9	0

Boston . . . . 0 1 0 0 1 0 0 0 x—6
Brooklyn . . 0 0 0 0 0 1 0 0 0—1

Earned runs—Boston, 2. Home run—Burns.
Two-base hits—Nash, Tucker. Sacrifice hit—
Carroll. Stolen base—Long. First base on
balls—Boston, 8; Brooklyn, 2. First base on
errors—Brooklyn, 3. Struck out—Merritt,
Nash, Tucker, Foutz, Daly. Double play—
Carroll, Tucker and Lowe. Umpire—Hurst.

Other Games.

At New York:
New York . . . 2 0 1 1 8 1 1 0 —14
Washington . . 2 0 0 0 0 0 0 1 3— 6
Base hits—New York, 13; Washington, 8. Bat-
teries—Rusie and McMahon; Maul and A.
Gumbert.

At Chicago:
St. Louis . . . 0 0 0 0 2 5 0 1 0— 8
Chicago . . . . 0 0 0 0 0 0 1 0 1— 2
Base hits—St. Louis, 9; Chicago, 12. Errors—
St. Louis, 1; Chicago, 5. Batteries—Breiten-
stein and Gunson; McGill and Schriver.

At Cincinnati:
Cincinnati . . 4 0 0 0 2 3 2 0 —11
Louisville . . . 0 0 0 0 1 1 0 0 — 2
Base hits—Cincinnati, 13; Louisville, 14. Er-
rors—Cincinnati, 3; Louisville, 4. Batteries—
Dwyer and Vaughan; Stratton and Harring-
ton.

At Pittsburg:
Cleveland . . . 6 0 0 4 3 0 4 0 —17
Pittsburg . . . 0 0 1 0 0 0 0 0 — 1
Base hits—Cleveland, 20; Pittsburg, 6. Er-
rors—Cleveland, 3. Batteries—Cuppy and
Zimmer; Terry and Miller.

At Philadelphia:
Philadelphia . 0 0 0 0 0 0 1 0 0— 1
Baltimore . . . 0 0 0 2 2 0 0 0 x— 4
Base hits—Philadelphia, 13; Baltimore, 4.
Errors—Philadelphia, 1; Baltimore, 5. Bat-
teries—Keefe and Clements; Mullane and
Robinson.

New England League.
At Fall River—Fall River, 23; Portland, 5.
At Dover—Dover, 6; Lewiston, 4.

Eastern League Games.
At Providence—Albany 7; Providence, 4.
At Springfield—Troy, 16; Springfield, 9.
At Buffalo—Buffalo, 14; Binghamton, 13.

National League Standing.

Clubs	Won	Lost	Avg
Boston	35	13	.729
Brooklyn	29	16	.644
Philadelphia	25	19	.568
Cleveland	23	19	.547

Clubs	Won	Lost	Avg
Pittsburg	24	21	.533
New York	22	23	.489
Cincinnati	22	23	.489
Chicago	20	23	.465

Clubs	Won	Lost	Avg
St. Louis	18	26	.409
Baltimore	17	26	.395
Louisville	13	29	.309
Washington	12	31	.279

[From Yesterday's Extra Edition.]

TO CONDEMN

In the midst of the largest city in this
county, in the midst of their household,
surrounded by houses and people and
teams and civilization, in the midst of
the day, right in their household, while
they were attending to their household
duties, in the midst of the forenoon, an
aged man and an aged woman are suddenly and brutally assassinated. It was
a terrible crime, it was an impossible
crime it seems, and very much, Mr. Foreman, of the difficulties of solving this awful tragedy start from the very impossibility of its thing itself. But any human being you think of, put any degraded man or woman you ever heard
of at the bar and say to them you did
this thing, and it would seem incredible.
And I am bound to say, Mr. Foreman,
and I say it out of a full heart that it
is scarcely more credible to place the
charge for the awful crime. I would
not for one moment lose sight of the incredibility of that charge nor ask you to
believe it, unless you found it supported
by facts that you cannot explain.

The prisoner at the bar is a woman
and a Christian woman, as the expression is usual.

It is No Ordinary Criminal.

it is one of the rank of lady, the equal
of your wife and mine, and your friend
and mine, of whom such things have
never been suspected or dreamed of. I
hope I may never forget nor in anything that I say here today lose sight of
the terrible significance of that fact.

We are trying a crime that would have
been deemed impossible but for the fact
that it was. We are charging with the
commission of it a woman whom we
would have believed incapable of doing
it but for the evidence that it is my duty,
my painful duty today, to present to you.
But I beg you to observe, Mr. Foreman,
and gentlemen, that we cannot dispose
of the case upon that consideration alone,
that it is so. No situation in life is a
pledge or a security against the commission of crime, and we all know those who

are entrusted with the most precious savings of the widow and the orphan, who
stand in the community towers of
strength and fidelity, suddenly fall and
their wreck involves the ruin of many
happy homes. They were Christian men.
They were devout men. They were members of some Christian church. They had
every inducement around them to preserve the lives that were placed in their
care, and yet when the crash came it
was found that they were not equal to it.
Nay, Mr. Foreman, those who are installed in the sacred duties of the church
are not exempt from the law of humanity. Time and again we have been
grieved to learn, pained to find that those
who are set up to teach us the way of
correct life have been found to be
foul as hell.

Nobody is Beyond Temptation

else would it not have been said even by
the disciples themselves "Lead not thy
servant into presumptuous sins." It was
not considered by the Savior that the
wicked should pray the prayer "Lead us
not into temptation."

We are none of us secure. If you
have led, sir, an honorable and upright
life, thank your heavenly father that the
temptations have not been too strong
for you. If you, sir, have never been
guilty of heinous crimes, is it your
strength of character or is it your fortune that you have been able to resist
the charges brought against you?

Of course, let me be understood. Not
for one moment would I urge that because a man or a woman has led an
upright and devout life that therefore
there should be no reason for suspecting
him or her of a crime.

I am obliged to tread now upon very
delicate ground. The prisoner is a
woman, one of that sex that all high-
minded men revere, that all generous
men love, that all wise men acknowledge
their indebtedness to. It is hard, it is
hard, Mr. Foreman and gentlemen, to
conceive that woman can be guilty of
crime. It is not a pleasant thing to say,
but while we revere the sex they are human like us. They are no better than we.
They are no worse than we. If they
lack in strength and coarseness and
vigor they make up for it in cunning,
in dispatch, in subtlety. There are those
If their lives are stronger and more enduring their hates are undying and more
unyielding. I read in my library in history and fiction that the most famous
criminals, weighing crime by its iniquity,
have been women. We must face the
case as men, not as philanthropists. We
will be slow to believe that it could be
possible for a man to have done it, we
will be slow to believe that it was within
the capacity of a woman to do it, but
it was done—done for a purpose—done

DISTRICT ATTORNEY KNOWLTON ADDRESSING THE JURY.

seen fit to criticise as interested in this
case. He put a question—the other day
that illustrates what I mean. You heard
it all. Police officers are but men, too,
trying to find out all they can. They
may have made lots of mistakes. What
wonder that they did. This crime is beyond the scope of any man. But honestly, as far as God as given them the
ability, they have pursued the various
avenues leading to the detection of the
criminal. It is untrue that they have
been unfair in it. Clew after clew has
been followed without avail. I am unable to tell you how many clews have
been followed, of the number of cities
visited or of the people watched. Don't
you suppose these men would be glad if
they could find some one else who did
this? Is there is a man so base as to
wish that she did it?

Nay. Every evidence that has come
before them has pointed toward her, and
not till they had got all these facts before them did conviction force itself
upon their minds, as it may on yours before we are through, that she was the
guilty person. A blue coat does not
make a man any better. Marshal Fleet,
Mr. Mullaly and Mr. Harrington are all
men. There is no presumption that any
one class does not tell the truth; thieves
may tell the truth, carpenters, police,
lawyers,—there is no presumption that
they don't tell the truth. And now, because they tell the truth, they are branded as not telling it, and as being interested. Mark them as they appear before
you. Now as to those who gave their
opinions, the experts, who may often disagree, their testimony has been such as
meets no denial. It is the privilege of
the defense to select such men as they
see fit, also capable of judging on these
facts. These points of evidence have
been put in no less capable hands than
those of Dr. Draper, and for the defense
have been examined by Dr. Richardson
to his heart's content; and it is not the
business of my learned friend to dispute
their own experts; their testimony does
not find denial; when one expert says one
thing and another another you cannot
place much dependence on their testimony, but when all agree, their testimony is beyond doubt.

There is another thing which troubles
my learned brother, and which may
have troubled you. I have heard many
honest men say that they cannot believe
circumstantial evidence.

**It is the Mark of an Assassin We are
Trying to Discover,**

one who does his work beyond the eyes
of men. Direct evidence is the work
of witnesses who sees and hears a crime
committed. Circumstantial evidence is
that of all other kinds. What follows
if you don't believe such evidence? Did
you ever hear of a murderer getting a
witness to his crime? Murder is the
work of assassination when without seeing the crime you are able to tell it. "I
stay in my room all the time." John
Morse comes there and stays over night
several days, and yet he says he did not
see her but seldom. She said, "We don't
eat with her if we can help it." I don't
blame Emma for her uneasy yesterday;
she was in a terrible strait, and hated
to tell us what she did. This separation
of the family was like a cancer in the
family, and all arose about property.
Now the old gentleman had a right to do
as he chose about his property. He does
not give up his right to dispose of it till
he is dead, and not even then unless he
chooses. She had repudiated her mother,
and this hatred continued till we don't
know how far it had gone. Now
to come back to that poor
murdered woman. Had she an enemy
in all the world? Was there any one that
could be benefited by her being taken
away. There was, there was. It is hard
to believe that property should cause this
terrible crime. But one woman in the
world believed that this dead woman
stood between her and her friend—that is
an enemy to her and a friend to that
father and had prevented him from giving
her what belonged to her. We are able
to try this case, this horrid case, and I
am glad my distinguished friend does not
criticise us for producing these bones in
court. It is necessary for the purpose of
evidence, and if others had taken another turn they might have been her
friends in the scale. It is usual to use
such evidence in criminal cases. The
last capital case tried in this room that
were used.

So we have looked at these skulls and
the wounds in them and what have we
found there? They were nothing in the
blows but hatred. What sort of blows

---

case, but in this sacred presence there is
no room for prejudice. You have been
educated to have loyalty and fealty to
the sex, and I am glad that this is so.

I am said to be impervious to criticism; to all that think me so. I tell them
they may have the satisfaction of knowing their shafts struck home. If I have
approached this case in any spirit of revenge, to satisfy any ambition or for any
unworthy glory, those slanderous tongues
would have framed the word. I have
shrunk from the duty and would have
withdrawn if I could have done so honorably. If I have thought or sought to
do injustice in this case I would that my
right hand should wither and my tongue
cleave to my mouth. With due regard to
the consequences of your action you
stand not only to deliver this woman
but to deliver the commonwealth as well.
This is a crime which may well challenge your consideration. This old man
and this old woman had gone by the
noon time of their life, and were beyond
of a competence would have been enjoying this beautiful day together and
would have gone down together to a
serene old age earned by a lifetime of
toil but for the terrible crime. Over
their bodies we stand today. You are
standing in the presence of death itself.
This is a place where no personal ani-
mosities of any kind have any place, and
in a fitting spirit I adjure you to take
consideration of this case.

Before passing to a consideration of
the evidence in this case, which I propose to state exactly as it is, let me say
something as to its nature. We have
brought before you as fairly and frankly as we could every witness who had
any knowledge of this case whatever.
I do not know a single one that has been
kept away. The domestic of the establishment, the tried and faithful servant
of the household; the family physician,
who was the first called on the discovery
of the murder; the faithful friends and
companions of the defendant; all were
summoned and called upon to come before you and tell you what they knew.
Nay, we called the relative himself, and
you heard him. We have called every
one we could to hear what they had to
say.

When the crime became known it is
our duty to find out what we can. When
you go home to your family after this
agony is over and any crime happens, on
whom will you rely? Upon these very
men whom my distinguished friend has

know better. The remark made to
that dressmaker was not a petulant remark. That giggle when the woman's
dead body was within ten feet of her
goes down deep in the springs of human
nature. She had no remembrance of the
tender lips of any other mother, she had
no remembrance of her mother. Yet she
had a mother. Before she was old
enough to go to school or to reach the
years of understanding her father had
loved and lost, mourned and loved again.
Her father's choice had come into her
home and it was

The Only Mother She Had Ever Known

Through all her childhood's sicknesses
she had nursed her and it was upon her
breast that her head had rested when
the cancer in weary of her games and play.
It was by her that she had been brought
up to an honorable and worthy woman
in appearance and manner. It was not
like a case where another mother comes
into a home when a child has reached
10 or 15 years. It was the only mother
she had ever known. She had given to
Lizzie a mother's love, given it to a child
that was not her own, because she was
her husband's daughter. Just think of
it, a man worth a quarter of a million
dollars wants to give to his faithful wife,
who has done his work and reared his
children, the right in a homestead occupied by her sister. How petty and despicable the cause of the fault finding.
Nay, if this defendant were a man instead of a woman I would couch it in
more forcible terms. Though it is my
painful duty, I hope I shall never forget this defendant is a woman. This
has been to me the most unnatural of
things, murdering the woman who has
cared for her from childhood. But my
friend says she has grown to be a woman.
That is true, but her victim has meantime grown to be an old woman. Those
wounds were cut deep, but never so
deep into the skull of Abbie Durfee Borden as the refusal of this child to call
her mother. It was an insult. These
two girls say "You have worked around
our father and got out of him a pittance
of $1,500, and you ask my mother no
more." She never showed her feelings
till some one else tried to call her mother.
Then her fury broke forth, and in rage
she denied that she was her mother.
During all her younger days this had
been her mother, as every mother is to
her offspring. They still lived in the
same house, and yet she would not call
her mother. You may have a casual acquaintance or some man may make it
a practice to daily pass your office, and
you may be on speaking terms with
him, and after a time refuse to call him
by name. He goes his way and you go
yours, and that's all there is to it. But
these go on in much the same way; compelled to live in the same house, to eat
the same bread, compelled to meet one
another daily. I don't know, Mr. Foreman and gentlemen, but what some of
you may be connected with families in
which there are two wives and two sets
of children. I am not in my own, but
by connection. In very many cases it
happens that a man dies and his relict
marries again, and the mutual love
causes the relations to go on unimpaired.
Alas you know when the seeds of discord are once sown, no more bitter hatred
can be imagined. It must be so, because
it is festered and brought to mind every
day. Like a jaded horse—he may be
driven day after day, with his collar
chafing, chafing and festering, but at
length it becomes so that he cannot longer endure it. They did not even eat together. Bridget says so. My distinguished
friend tried to make her take it back
and she did—some of it. Any woman
would have if she could. Bridget had
her say, but I put it on Lizzie herself.
She said, "Don't say mother to me."
That woman who had reared her she had
repudiated as a mother, and declared
"She is a mean, good for nothing old
thing." Nay, that is not all. She says,
"I stay in my room all the time." John
Morse came there and stays over night
several days, and yet he says he did not
see her but seldom. She said, "We don't
eat with her if we can help it." I don't
blame Emma for her uneasy yesterday;
she was in a terrible strait, and hated
to tell us what she did. This separation
of the family was like a cancer in the
family, and all arose about property.

---

the old man and woman, but this has
proved to be so entirely not so that it
is hardly necessary to recapitulate the
evidence. The doctors have shown that
the death of the woman must have been
from one to two hours first. There has
never been a word on our side about the
poverty of living of the Borden household. The stomachs were taken out
alone to prove what time these people
sat down to breakfast. Their lives were
prematurely cut off by an assassin. Their
stomachs were examined by that pre-
eminently fair man, Professor Wood,
against whom the other side have not a
word to say, and he says that Mrs.
Borden's death preceded her husband by
an hour and a half perhaps, not more
and possibly half an hour. We
find here the most remarkable
home on record. Everything was locked.
There was barbed wire on the bottom as
well as along the top of the fence. The
most jealously guarded house you ever
heard of. The barn door was locked at
night and opened in the morning, as testified to by Bridget, who no one has accused of telling any thing but the truth.
The door to the attic was locked, and on
that day—mind you that day, the
screen door was secured by a spring lock.
They day before when Dr. Bowen came
in it was held by a spring lock. There
was a spring lock on the front door, and
it was that woman's custom to keep it
locked every time. But on this morning it was
not unlocked, and Mr. Borden when he
came in called her attention to it. And
it was locked, not only by the spring
lock, but with the other locks and a bolt.
This was so the getting in of an assassin who was trying to lock himself
in, but the house was locked as is done
when people retire at night, and it was
not unlocked in the morning. The first one
to go out of the house through the screen
door was Bridget, when she was washing windows. But let us go back for a
moment to the night previous. The doors
were all locked then, and the cellar door
was never unlocked. Bridget came
down in the morning and took in the
milk, opening the inner door and closing
the screen one. Mr. Borden went out
of this door, but he was out of the sight
of Bridget, who was in the kitchen. He
must have fastened it when he came in,
as Mr. Morse testified that after he went
out Mr. Borden locked it. Bridget was
in the kitchen all this time. Lizzie came
down after a time and Bridget being sick
went out into the back yard. When she
got back she found that Mr. Borden had
gone and that Lizzie had finished her
breakfast. Bridget says she must have
locked the screen door when she came
in, but cannot remember. Mr. Borden
must have left the house soon after 9,
as he got to the bank at his accustomed
time of 9 30. Bridget saw Mrs. Borden
dusting the parlor, and soon after got
a pail and went out to wash windows.
At this time no one could spot her
into the house by that door. Lizzie says
she saw her mother up stairs in the front
room, and the next that is seen of Lizzie
she was at the screen door. Up to the
time of the murder there had been no
chance for any one to enter the house,
and after that it was quickly filled with
people. Another thing that the dead body
of Mrs. Borden tells. She was the only
one who would have struck so as to fall with
all her weight and a noise must have been
made that would be heard all over the
house. For Bridget has testified that
she could hear the screen door slam when
in her room. If Lizzie Borden went up
stairs when she said she did she must
have been in the path of the assassin.
Do you believe, Mr. Foreman, that a
woman as heavy as Mrs. Borden, weighing nearly 200 pounds, could have fallen
without Lizzie hearing it? After Bridget had gone out she left in the house
the only enemy this poor woman had in
the world. No one could have gotten
in any more than a man could enter this
room without you or I knowing it.
That is not all. It is provided, as I
humbly and devoutly believe, that no
matter how craftily a murder is planned
it fails to be hidden and it failed her at a
fatal point. She attempted to answer and
utterly failed. She was alone in the house
with the murdered woman. She was out
of sight and Mrs. Borden was out of
sight. There was coming a stern and just
man who knew the feelings between them
and would say to her as the Almighty
said to Cain, "Where is Abel, thy brother?"

He came in and sat down and was told
that Mrs. Borden had received a note and
gone and this quieted any apprehension he
had felt. When Mrs. Borden went to
her room before Lizzie went up stairs
Lizzie said to Bridget "if you go out be
sure and lock the door. Mrs. Borden
has gone out, some one sick it." Bridget
asks the most natural thing in the world,
"who is sick?" and got the reply, "I don't
know; she had a note this morning." These
are not the inquisitorial disclosures
of the police-officers. Mrs. Churchill came
over and was told the same thing. Officer Fleet was told the same story. Bridget says to them some one brought the
letter to Mrs. Borden. Bridget says after she came back, "If I only knew where
Mrs. Whitehead lived I would go for
her."

You are charged with a solemn trust.
As my associate said in the opening of
the case, that is a lie. Conscious as I
am that my conscience would give me no
rest if I tell or argue this matter from
anything but the facts involved in it, I
repeat, no note came, no one was sick.
Mrs. Borden never had a note. Where
the evidence in any way you choose.
There is nothing that any one says about
that note except what is told there but
Lizzie Borden. My friend says I make
my case upon the hatchet. I will stake
it on the note and the note alone.

That story of the note traced through
all its sources finds its origin with Lizzie Borden. Bridget, when asked about
it on the stand, tells us that she never
saw the note, and knew nothing about
it except what she was told by Lizzie.
At the time Lizzie told about this note
no one was suspecting her, no one was
dreaming that there was no truth in
the story then.

There isn't any ground to argue that
Bridget heard anything about a
note from Mrs. Borden.

Almighty providence has directed affairs to bring murderers to justice. If
there was any one among the 50,000
people in that largest city of this county who had any knowledge of the writing of that note he would have been
here long before this telling us "I wrote
that note."

They brought to us the evidence of
drunken men around the house the night
before. They brought to us men standing under the shadow of the trees to get
out of the direct rays of the sun. They
advertised for the writer of that note,
but he was never brought forward.

My learned friend ventures to say that
the note was part of the scheme to get
the woman away, when it was part of
his purpose to go there and assassinate
her. If it was his purpose to murder
Mr. Borden, of what earthly use was it
to him to get Mrs. Borden away with
Bridget and Lizzie still left in the house?
It pains me beyond expression to be obliged to state these things. God forbid that
anyone should kill this woman, but some
one did. They were not the blows of a
man, but of a woman inspired by hatred.
She was left alone with the only enemy
under God's heaven who hated her.

At this point the court declared a recess.

There was some talk about the court
sitting late in order that Mr. Knowlton
might finish his argument this afternoon,
but after a short recess at 5 o'clock, when
a consultation was had, an adjournment
was had till 9 o'clock tomorrow morning.

Mr. Knowlton's argument, so far, he
acknowledged by even the friends of defense to be the ablest one of his life. It is
strong, clear, keen cut and incisive, thoroughly logical, full of strength and viril-
ity, and at times rising to the height of
eloquence. All through the hours that
he spoke he chained the closest attention at
every moment, and even counsel for defense never took their eyes off him. It
was an argument of a man who fully believes in the truth of his cause, and he
threw into it all the energy and vigor of
his fiery, passionate nature. When
he laid bare the exclusive opportunity
which existed he seemed to have
the whole interior of the house in his vision,
and when he said that when Bridget
Sullivan went out into the yard to wash
windows she left behind in the house the

Knowles & Co.

Now is the time for you to make a call at our store, as we have a full and complete line of warm weather goods.

The largest line of Parasols and Sun Umbrellas to be found in the city.

A bargain in Red and Blue Sun Umbrellas, at $1.75.

Parasols from 89c. to $5.50. Some rare bargains among them. Children's shades 39c. to $1.49.

We have made a cut in Silk Laces, and will sell you all the new and choice effects at 25 per cent. less than you will find them elsewhere.

A splendid line of Cotton Laces from 5 to 45c. per yard.

Our Hosiery Department is full of bargains. An elegant line of fine dropped stitch hose, in blacks, tans, white and almost any color you could wish, at 50c. Also some bargains at 25 and 37 1-2c.

We have secured one case of Ladies' Jersey Vests, worth 12 1-2c., which we shall sell three for 25c. as long as they last.

We are showing the best Ladies' and Gents' 25c. Vest to be found anywhere.

All sizes in Gents' Negligee Shirts, worth from $1.25 to $1.50, for ONE EVEN DOLLAR.

A new and elegant Line of Pampas Cloths, 25 or 30 pieces to select from, at 15c.

Twenty-five new styles of the celebrated Puritan Cloths at 12 1-2c. These goods are selling fast. Come while the selection is good.

A new line of Llama Cloths, just what you want for a summer dress, at 12 1-2c.

A good line of Sateens, fine as silk, at 15c.

Knowles & Co.

UNION and FOURTH STS.

SPECIAL NOTICE.

The demand for the famous "J. H. CUTTER" WHISKIES, (for which we are the sole agents in this city) having become so great, many houses out of the State are sending their travelers in here, with the hope of inducing our trade to buy the "Cutter" whiskies from them, by underselling us, or rather trying to. We therefore beg to say to our friends and the public generally, we will NOT allow ourselves to be undersold by any house dealing in the genuine "J. H. CUTTER" WHISKIES, and we are prepared to protect our trade, not only in QUALITY but in PRICES as well.

Very Respectfully,

BENJAMIN DAWSON,
597 Purchase Street.

Sole agent for New Bedford, Mass., for the famous J. H. Cutter Whiskies. 8p

DRINK
ROXBURY RYE
WHISKEY.
Equaled by few, Excelled by None.
je6-12t8p

THE LOWELL MYSTERY.

Leclerc Released From Custody For Implication In the Murder of Chaput.

LOWELL, Mass., June 20.—J. E. Leclerc, arrested on Dr. Chaput's statement that he was the man who stabbed him on Merrimac street, Thursday evening, was released from custody yesterday. Leclerc is the third man arrested on Chaput's statements, and each has been released because of contradictory statements of the doctor. Now, that Dr. Chaput is dead, the case is more mysterious than before. The suicide theory is scouted by some, supported by others. Some incidents point to suicide, others to murder. One of the two men seen to run out of the building shortly after the stabbing, was the man who was attracted by the cries of the wounded doctor and ran down Kirk street to the office of another doctor and returned with him. The body was taken to Montreal last evening by the doctor's brother.

Strikers Confident of Success.

BOSTON, June 20.—There are no indications apparent that the men now on strike at the Sturtevant blower works will fail in their effort to establish the nine-hour work day in the work shops of this concern. The action of the Boston Central Labor union in endorsing the strike has given the men renewed courage and they feel more confident than ever that the struggle will result in their favor.

John Knox Is Dead.

SPRINGFIELD, Mass., June 20.—Blandford's physician, Dr. Dean, has decided that John Knox is dead.

TOOK HER OWN LIFE.

Tragic Death of an Unhappy Young Everett Woman.

EVERETT, Mass., June 20.—By her own hand Laura Mirick of this place ended her life yesterday afternoon at 2 o'clock.

The circumstances which led up to this sad ending of a bright, beautiful and popular young woman, are remarkable. The agent used was poison, the place was her own home; the result death, a distracted family and a shocked community.

This act of self-destruction was undoubtedly committed during a moment of temporary insanity, but when the comprehension of the deed dawned upon the poor girl she begged piteously that her life might be saved.

Laura Mirick loved a young physician of Reading, at present nameless. Her love was returned. She was an ardent Methodist, he a materialist. She hoped for and believed in a future life, he believed that when the soul filled the grave the end of man had come.

"But why need this disturb the course of love?" argued the man of medicine. "Love transcends all obstacles; it makes the poor man rich, it gives a flavor to life unknown before, and above all it is the very substance of all religions—or should be."

But Laura failed to see. She was filled with love for this man, it is said. But then,

Love Is Blind.

Her religion seemed to preclude the possibility of a union with one whose belief was so different as to the future, and yet morally the same.

For some time she kept him company, it is claimed, but, paradoxical as it is, the longer they were close companions, the farther apart these different beliefs drew them, till at last, about five months ago, she formally broke off the engagement.

As she saw it her sense of duty had been made clear. Religion conquered love, while death is cheated not.

Since the breaking off of the ties of love Miss Mirick was at times a very

Strange Young Woman.

Her actions can be accounted for only as the result of some great mental disturbances. These increased of late, so much so that her health was impaired, and for the past six or eight weeks she remained at home helping her mother.

At times she would break forth in a violent fit of profanity, it is claimed, and when her mother would ask why she said such awful things she would reply that she had a little devil in her breast and she couldn't help it.

Yesterday she went up into the attic and there found a bottle containing a preparation of corrosive sublimate, which had been used to kill rats. She drank a part of it and then, when too late, realized her awful fate. With her last breath she said:

"God will forgive me; I could not help it."

Miss Mirick was a very popular young woman. She was 23 years old, a perfect brunette, and possessed of regular and attractive features. She was always a bit odd, and kept very much within herself. Her father is William H. Mirick of 2 Franklin place, and employed at the Corcoran Chemical works. A brother is a civil engineer.

The funeral will take place tomorrow afternoon at 4 o'clock, and will be private.

Navahoe About Ready to Sail.

BOSTON, June 20.—Repairs of the Navahoe at the Atlantic works have progressed so rapidly that it may be possible for her to sail tomorrow, instead of toward the latter part of the week, as was thought. Her new mast is stepped and her bowsprit swung into place. The new plating is all on, and now all that remains is the new topmast to be placed and the rigging and painting to be done.

Recovered For Malicious Prosecution.

BOSTON, June 20.—A verdict of $1869.23 for the plaintiff was returned in the suit for damages for malicious prosecution brought by Charles F. Wheeler against J. W. Hanson in the superior court. The plaintiff said the defendant arrested and prosecuted him on the charge of embezzlement without probable cause, and afterward the grand jury for Suffolk county found no bill against him.

Probably Fatally Burned.

PITTSFIELD, Mass., June 20.—A gasoline stove in Miss Baker's apartments in Pierce's block, North street, exploded yesterday, setting fire to the woman's clothing and burning her terribly about the face and breast and arms. She was taken to the House of Mercy, and it is feared that, owing to the advanced age of the unfortunate woman, she cannot recover.

New Hampshire's Medical Society.

CONCORD, N. H., June 20.—The 102d anniversary meeting of the New Hampshire Medical society began in Grand Army hall yesterday and will continue today. There was a large attendance of members. The morning session was devoted to reports of officers and committees, and the appointment of standing committees by the president, Dr. J. H. Wheeler of Dover.

A Brute In Human Form.

BOSTON, June 20.—Yesterday afternoon an unknown man about 35 years old enticed little Lillie Lock, aged 9 years, into the Catholic church on Rutherford avenue, and there attempted a felonious assault on the child. The child's screams brought assistance, and foiled in his dastardly purpose he escaped, but not until he had severely ill-used the child.

Fatal Runaway Accident.

MILFORD, Mass., June 20.—Patrick Dillon and William P. Brown, while riding in Blackstone Sunday, were thrown from their buggy by the horse running away. Brown was killed and Dillon had two ribs broken and cut about the head. Dillon is a well-known building contractor and Brown a stonemason contractor. Brown leaves a widow.

Story Was False.

BOSTON, June 20.—The report in yesterday's dispatches of the suicide in New York of the unfortunate John J. Mulrennin was confirmed, but the stories first circulated about the man's ill-treatment of his wife were false. It is admitted that the man drank heavily, but the wife's honor is defended by all who knew her.

Marvellous Complexion Restorer and Improver
H-O Hornby's Oatmeal.
A clean healthy skin comes of its use.

Highest of all in Leavening Power.—Latest U. S. Gov't Report.

Royal Baking Powder

ABSOLUTELY PURE

Reported In Favor of the Plaintiff.

BOSTON, June 20.—In the suit of the Blackstone National bank against Charles A. Rogers and others, the jury reported a verdict of $3028.89 for the plaintiff against George E. Rogers in the superior court. The suit was based upon a $4000 note given by C. A. Rogers and endorsed by the firm of Rogers & Co.

Pilgrim Nearing Completion.

BOSTON, June 20.—Messrs. Stewart & Binney are both in New York superintending the fitting of the lead to the fin of the Pilgrim, the Boston syndicate boat. She is expected to arrive at Lawley's South Boston yard tomorrow. Rigger Billman will begin fitting her out at once.

Celebrating the Sinking of the Alabama.

PORTSMOUTH, N. H., June 20.—The 29th anniversary of the sinking of the rebel cruiser Alabama by the United States steamer Kearsarge was observed yesterday by the Kearsarge Naval association of this city, who had as guests the Kearsarge association of Boston.

Unsuccessful This Time.

BOSTON, June 20.—A daring and nearly successful attempt to escape from the Charlestown state prison was made early yesterday morning. An assault was also made on an officer by two of the convicts, and an effort made to relieve him of his pistol.

Seriously Injured by Bicycle and Wagon.

SALEM, Mass., June 20.—Arthur, the 5-year-old son of Arthur G. Frothingham, was knocked down by a bicycle yesterday. The wheels of an express wagon passed over his body, and he was taken to the hospital and is in a critical condition.

Decapitated by an Engine.

LYNN, Mass., June 20.—Richard Martin, 21 years of age, fell from a shifting engine in the local freight yards of the Boston and Maine railroad here yesterday. He fell under the engine and his head was severed from the body.

Brief Mention.

Two old ladies of Rochester, N. H., were left helpless and destitute by an inhuman sister.

Levi Wright of Fitchburg, Mass., is held for trial at Leominster, Mass., for incendiarism.

A special convention to elect a succesors to the late Bishop Bissell of Vermont is to meet Thursday afternoon.

Associate Justice Blatchford was stricken with paralysis at Newport, R. I., and is not expected to recover.

[From Yesterday's Third Edition.]

NANTUCKET.

A bill in equity has been filed in the superior court by Captain John Killen, praying that the officers of the corporation known as the Proprietors of Common Lands of Nantucket be restrained from issuing any deed or other document granting or setting off to William T. Swain any land or rights or ways near and adjoining the Straight wharf. The Proprietors had voted to grant such rights to Swain against the protest of Killen, who claims to have been the prior applicant for the same lands. The real contest is between the owners of two wharves, as to the right to land lying between the same, and involves the Proprietors' right to dispose of the flats under the act of 1866, creating the board of harbor and land commissioners.

The steamer Nantucket had a rough passage on Sunday and landed but few passengers.

Rain came down in copious showers on Saturday night, which will revive the growing crops heretofore suffering from want of moisture.

The hotels are now all open for the summer except the Surfside Hotel, which will soon be opened under the management of James Patterson of the Sherburne House.

The convention of the W. C. T. U., held in Nantucket last Friday, was well attended. Interesting papers were read and addresses made by Mrs. Eldridge, Mrs Bradley and Mrs. Andrews of Marthas Vineyard, and by Mrs. Valentine, Mrs. Mary T. Coffin, Mrs. Dr. Mann and Miss M. Elia Mann, Rev. Louise S. Baker, Anna Gardner, Elizabeth Starbuck and others of Nantucket. Mrs. Susan S. Fessenden, president of the state union, made an able address in the evening. And a reception was afterward tendered Mrs. Fessenden, at which ice cream and cake was served.

SWAMPED BY A FAILURE.

Taunton Lumber Co. Assigns to Lawyer H. W. Chaplin.

Boston, June 19.—On account of the failure of the Kenawha Lumber Co., the firm of Andrew F. Leatherbee, William H. Leatherbee & Sons and the Taunton Lumber Co. have assigned to Lawyer H. W. Chaplin.

THIEVES WITH THE CIRCUS.

Gang Following the Big Show Make a Haul in Providence.

Providence, R. I., June 19.—Last night the gang that came here with the circus worked several places and at J. E. Angells, 138 Rhodes street, stole jewelry and diamonds valued at $1,200.

LACK OF EVIDENCE.

Fritz Butchmann Suspected of the Natick Murder Discharged.

Wellesley, June 19.—Fritz Butchmann, arrested yesterday for the murder of Letig, was discharged today for lack of evidence.

Readville the Transfer Point.

Boston, June 19.—The railroad commissioners decided today that Readville shall be the transfer point between the New York, New Haven & Hartford and the New York & New England roads.

Largest Dredger in the World.

Liverpool, June 19.—The largest dredger in the world, 320 feet long, lifting 24,000 tons daily, had a successful first trial here today.

NEARLY KILLED IN THE STREET.

Providence Detective Beaten in a Crowded Thoroughfare.

(Special Dispatch.)

Providence, R. I., June 19.—Detective Swan, of this city, an officer well known all over the country, was attacked on Exchange place at 10 o'clock this morning by two professional burglars and nearly killed. When one man beat him the other with revolver in hand kept a good sized crowd at bay, and then they escaped. Detective Swan had arrested one man for thieving in John Wood's office in the Wilcox building, and was taking him to City hall. The streets were crowded at the time and Barnum's circus was parading. Swan started through Exchange place, and near the corner of Exchange street two of the prisoner's pals attacked him from behind and beat him seriously, laying open his scalp and face in many places. After rendering the detective unconscious the three burglars escaped, and as they retreated kept the crowd well in the rear, threatening to shoot. A general alarm was sent out, but up to 2 o'clock no arrests had been made. Detective Swan was attended at City hall by Dr. Sheffield Smith, and later was removed to his home in Mount Pleasant. He is dangerously hurt, and as yet the physicians can give no probable result of his many cuts and broken bones.

CAPT. ANDERSON ARRESTED.

Master and Five of Crew of the Viking Ship in Custody.

Brooklyn, N. Y., June 19.—Captain Magnus Anderson of the Viking ship and five of his crew were arrested at 4 o'clock this morning as they were proceeding through Hamilton avenue on their way to New York. They had been to a reception and banquet given in their honor by the Norwegian societies of Brooklyn, and while quietly passing along the street an intoxicated Scandinavian ran up behind the chief mate and struck him. The captain and his men attempted to defend the mate when an officer arrested the party, charging them with being drunk and creating a disturbance. The man who started the row escaped. They were locked up and this morning arraigned and held in $200 bail each for appearance next Monday. Bail was furnished.

VACANT CELLS AT CHARLESTOWN.

Convicts Attempt to Escape and a Yelling Concert Follows.

Boston, June 19.—Last night several vacant cells were discovered in Charlestown state prison. Pettigrew, a 25-year man, was found cutting through the roof, and was locked up. Later, Officer Patten was assaulted by Richie, a 20-year man. The latter was overpowered. A yelling concert followed. Some saws, hooks, and other implements were found.

Dishonest Collectors in Detroit.

Detroit, Mich., June 19.—Yesterday D. H. James, an employe of the water commissioners' office, whose accounts are short $1,500, shot himself and died immediately. Yesterday it was discovered by experts who were looking over the books that almost $7,000 had been taken by A. T. McLogan, H. L. James, M. F. Greuner, A. W. Goodsell and August Kensal, collectors. McLogan, whose stealings amounted to $4,000, is out of the city. It is said the stealing has been going on for several years.

The Biddeford Strike.

Biddeford, Me., June 19.—One thousand mill operatives remained out this forenoon, and the strike is no nearer settlement today than heretofore.

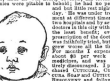

ON FIRE WITH ECZEMA

Terrible Sufferings of Little Baby: Seven Doctors and Two Hospitals Fail. Cured by Cuticura.

My baby boy, 5 months old, broke out with eczema. The itching and burning was intense; the eczema spread to his limbs, breast, face, and head, until he was nearly covered; his torturing agonies were pitable to behold; he had no peace and but little rest night or day. He was under treatment at different times at two hospitals and by seven doctors in this city without the least benefit; every prescription of the doctors was faithfully tried, but he grew worse all the time. For months I expended about $3 per week for medicines, and was entirely discouraged. I purchased CUTICURA, CUTICURA SOAP and CUTICURA RESOLVENT and followed the directions to the letter. Relief was immediate, his sufferings were eased, and rest and sleep permitted. He steadily improved and in nine weeks was entirely cured, and has now as clear a skin and is as fair a boy as any mother could wish to see. I recommend every mother to use it for every Baby Humor.

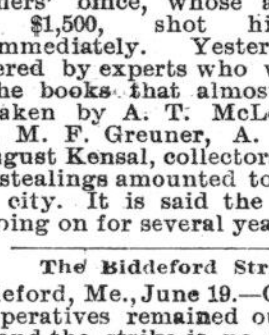

MRS. M. FERGUSON,
86 W. Brookline st., Boston.

Cuticura Remedies

The greatest skin cures, blood purifiers, and humor remedies of modern times, instantly relieve the most agonizing forms of eczema and psoriasis, and speedily, permanently, economically, and infallibly cure every species of torturing, disfiguring, itching, burning, bleeding, scaly, crusted, and pimply diseases and humors of the skin, scalp, and blood, with loss of hair, from infancy to age, whether simple, scrofulous, or hereditary, when all other methods and best physicians fail.

Sold everywhere. Price, CUTICURA, 50c.; SOAP, 25c.; RESOLVENT, $1. Prepared by the POTTER DRUG AND CHEMICAL CORPORATION, Boston.

Send for "How to Cure Skin Diseases," 64 pages, 50 illustrations, and 100 testimonials.

PIMPLES, blackheads, red, rough, chapped, and oily skin cured by CUTICURA SOAP.

OLD FOLKS' PAINS. Full of comfort for all Pains, Inflammation, and Weakness of the Aged is the Cuticura Anti-Pain Plaster, the first and only pain-killing strengthening plaster. New, instantaneous, and infallible.

Lost his Position.

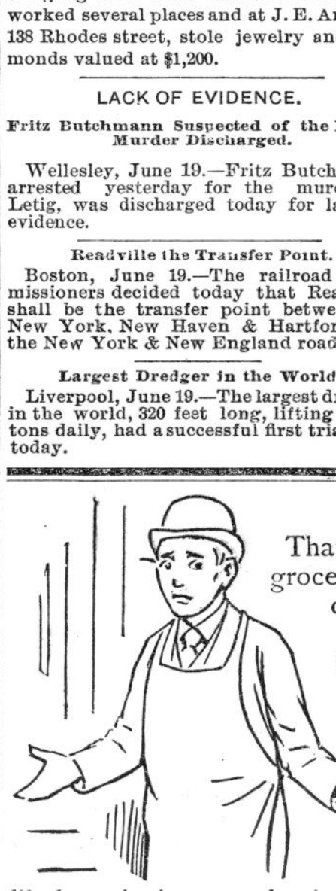

That really happened to a certain grocer's clerk, because he couldn't induce customers to take an inferior brand of washing-powder in place of Pearline. The grocer said, "If you can't sell what I want you to sell, I don't want you."

Now it doesn't take a very wise woman to decide whether this was an honest grocer. And a woman wise enough for that, would be likely to insist upon having nothing but Pearline. There is nothing "as good as" or "the same as" Pearline, the original—in fact, the only—washing-compound. If they send you something else, send it back. 399 JAMES PYLE, New York.

TO CONDEMN

The District Attorney's Argument.

Arraying Damaging Facts Against Prisoner.

Powerful Arrangement of the Evidence.

Gov. Robinson Concluded With Remarkable Peroration.

Mr. Knowlton's Argument the Effort of His Life.

The scenes about the court house on County street this afternoon just preceding the opening of the afternoon session of the court, were by far the most turbulous of the famous trial. As the last few moments of the public's opportunity to see the scenes of this greatest trial of the age diminished in number the fervor and enthusiasm of the people seemed to grow greater, and their regard for conventionality and order less. The jam about the entrances was by far the densest of the trial, and even the press representatives and court officers had difficulty in forcing a passage through. The women were in the majority, as usual, and were noticeably less good natured in the rush than the men. For fully ten minutes before the court came in every seat was full, and the corridors were filled with densely packed crowds.

Miss Borden came in with Deputy Sheriff Kirby at 2 10 and went at once to her seat in the dock, where she at once entered into conversation with her friends.

GOVERNOR ROBINSON.

Conclusion of His Argument in Defense of Miss Borden.

Governor Robinson at once launched out into his argument.

Said he, As I said, if you have found in your opinion that the government has proven its case, as it claimed in its opening, exclusive opportunity, that is all there is to it. We are not bound to furnish you anything. That she went up stairs and stayed there does not prove anything. We do not take the place of finding somebody who did do this murder if you say the prisoner did not. If we knew him, we are not bound to bring him in. The question only is "Did she do it?" If she goes free, clews will probably be followed up and the real criminal will, perhaps, be brought in. It means nothing to us, even if he goes unpunished. It is dangerous ground to say that she murdered these people, because no one else is found who did. Suppose one of you, gentlemen, leaves his home and goes to his business and soon after learns that his wife and daughter have been murdered. You go home and in handling the body may get blood on your clothing. You may have had trouble at the breakfast table, or you may not have been on good terms, but that doesn't make you guilty. So I bring to you the dangers of jumping at conclusions. So it is better that she go free, rather than be punished unjustly.

It is only a short time ago, and probably you are familiar with the circumstance, that there was a murder committed in a house in Philadelphia. A woman was killed, and the doors were fastened on the outside and inside. Nobody could discover how any person could get into that house. It was found out after some time how it was done, when it was discovered that the murderer had climbed up on a block in the vicinity of the building where the crime was committed, had gone along on the roof, had crawled in a window, committed the murder, and returned in the same way. Had there been some other person in that house, a servant, perhaps, or somebody who had been timid when charged with the crimes, who had made contradictory statements, how almost impossible that that person could bring any proof that he or she did not do it. Instances will occur all the time of that kind.

There are two or three things which in the hurry of speaking this morning I omitted. Miss Lizzie was ironing, Bridget says so, and you recall the testimony of Mrs. Russell and Mrs. Holmes that after the murders the handkerchiefs which she had ironed in part were taken up stairs and put away, so that you see that is reality. And little things of that kind go to establish the truth.

Then I omitted in connection with the visit of Lizzie to the barn to speak to you about Mr. Medley's testimony, because the commonwealth relied on Mr. Medley, who made an examination, and said there was dust there to show you that Miss Lizzie could not have walked on the floor. If you were sure about that there would be some test in it, but when you find a detective looking for those things you can suspect that he may be in error, and therefore you are not surprised in this case to find that a half dozen or more people were up in that barn before Mr. Medley got there at all. And the testimony comes from Mr. Medley himself, that when he got there he met Mr. Fleet between the gateway and the back steps, and that they went directly into the house, Mr. Sawyer being at the door. You then have the testimony of Mr. Clarkson, and you have that of Mr. Manning and Mr. Stevens and the two boys who call themselves "Me and Brownie." Now these boys, like all boys, always want to be first, want to stay as long as they can. They were there and they went all around that barn before Mr. Medley came there. He was not there many minutes before he came down and went out to the barn, but when he got there, there had been people about all over that loft. The two boys had been there and described the situation, and told what they did. So you find that by their walking around and in the very place where Mr. Medley went to look shows you that Mr. Medley must have been in error. Medley is mistaken and he lacks confirmation, for there is no one to support him. They speak about a 3½ inch hatchet. The hatchet Mr. Adams had wouldn't fit, as the ends were not ground enough, yet 3½-inch hatchets of some makes would fit the wounds nicely. We regard it as

Significant That There Was No Blood on Miss Lizzie's Hair.

She couldn't have got it out in any brief space of time. It is almost impossible to get it out except by special treatment. Ladies were about her caring for her, doing little acts of kindness for her, and bathing her head, and if there had been blood upon her head, or if it had been wet they would have known it. Assume for a minute that she did do it. We have spoken about blood-stained garments. She did not go out of the house with no one near her. Whatever she had on remained in that house. Assume that she committed the first murder, she would have to change her clothes. A waterproof was not used and she had nothing over her. Every waterproof in the house was accounted for. There is one difficulty she would have to encounter, she would have to go to the cellar, where there was running water, and return so that she could be all right when her father came. The blue dress would have been covered with blood, and this she would have to keep on her until 12 o'clock. No witness speaks of any change in the forenoon. Bridget didn't notice any change of dress. She must have come down in the morning in a blue dress, and got out of it and into it again within 12 or 15 minutes. The notice got to the police station at 11 15. She would have had to get out of the second bloody dress into another. The government says that the blue dress it wanted is burned up. That dress we have shown was as clear and pure and free from blood stains as the blue sky. After killing her father she must have got the dress on again, and no other dress is missing. It is impossible to conceive how the traces of the crime were removed and things were restored. No process of human ingenuity could clean things up in that space of time, and remember that

A Spot of Water Would be as Significant as a Spot of Blood.

She had no dress underneath. The dressmaker has assured you of that. This blue dress was two or three inches longer than any other that she had and do you suppose that no one would have noticed it?

What a blessed Providence it was that Lizzie didn't walk about the house and get blood upon her, not so much as a pinhead spot. Then she would have to clean and secrete everything. The theory of the use of the handleless hatchet was that afterwards the handle was broken off. Says the government, she washed the hatchet after it was used. Isn't it singular that after this carefully planned scheme was carried out she should have assisted all she could. The washing must have been done so successfully that the blood was removed in some way unknown to science, and after it was covered with coarse dust Lizzie must have run up stairs and changed her clothes and called Bridget. I have said it was morally and physically impossible for her to do this deed. So it is. You cannot look pale and faint at will. Tell me if you think any woman could have gone through with what we have heard she did, and come up here and appear as she has done. It is the duty of the government to prove this crime and this they haven't done. There is not a showing on which it would be safe to convict. You will not find her guilty for two reasons. One of these is because is has not been proved beyond a reasonable doubt; a well founded reasonable doubt of a reasonable man. I might have said you would believe the charge if you believed all the stories that have been told and printed, but it is your duty to cast all these aside and be governed solely by the evidence in the case. Another reason is that you may believe affirmatively that she is not guilty. It is rare that a defendant proves his innocence; he is not called on to do so. But what is there to prove to you her innocence? In the first place you should consider the life and standing of the prisoner. A good person may go wrong, but our experience teaches us that one who was engaged in good works, in binding up wounds, and in making others better, is not liable at a moment to come out and change her whole course of life. Then when a person is under suspicion, and knows it, he is always ready to throw suspicion on some one else. Now what has been the course of this defendant? She has shut the doors of suspicion against all outside parties. Yes, you may say, and shut them against herself, but if she has done so it has only been caused by her frank unspokenness.

The Finger of Suspicion Was Pointed at Two Others,

John V. Morse and Bridget Sullivan, but Lizzie spoke out promptly with a denial and said they could not be guilty. Suppose she had been a wicked and designing woman, and Bridget Sullivan, innocent as she is today, she could have led her into the toils. Then I say, although the government says her conduct lays her open to suspicion, that it is such that she is far above of anything like it. The commonwealth says, "See how she shrinks from the compunctions of conscience?" I say how would your wife or mine act encompassed about as Lizzie Borden has been, compelled to stay so long in jail and endure the gaze of the people as she has had to in these last two weeks?

Men of the jury, you would have quailed. You may look a man out of countenance, and it is not considered civil to stare people out of countenance who are going about their business. Yet you put this prisoner to a strain you are not equal to, and because she has nerve enough to stand it, though she knows and says "I am wronged and abused, and am innocent as a child just born, I recognize that I must stand this ordeal, and I'll bear it, and when it is over and I walk again the ground of liberty then will be the time to resume the woman's nature again. What I do now is bound to be misrepresented and misunderstood, and I will behave in the proper way." The time will come, gentlemen, when you shall render your verdict by which she shall be able to retire to the quiet of her own home and give vent to all these pent-up feelings. Gentlemen, you know how run the words of the old song, "And the eyes that cannot weep are the saddest eyes of all." And then, as the tears gush forth and run her heart breaks out with "O, ye tears, O, ye tears, I am thankful that ye run."

Did she ever stand in the way of the officers in their search? No. She did all she could for them. Not at all reluctant, and offering no objection. This is unanimous in the testimony of every one. They say she was cool.

Thank the Lord She Had Enough of a Visitation of Providence to be Cool.

Note her absolute freedom from marks of crime—that scene of Saturday night. There had been this woman shut up virtually under arrest in that house up to Saturday night. Then, in that parlor, in the presence of the city marshal and the mayor, she, her sister and uncle, were called, and the authorities began by advising—notice how it was done—began by advising her that she had better remain in the house. "Why," she asked in unfeigned surprise. And then the mayor answers and says that Mr. Morse will tell her why. Mr. Morse had been down town, and this might indicate that Mr. Morse was suspected. And when they talked of putting officers around the house, she asks, "Why, is any one in this house suspected?" And the mayor says, "You are." And now, mark you, what is her answer? She said, "I am ready to go now, at any time."

Murderers do not talk that way. Gentlemen, as you look upon her you will pass your judgment that she is not insane. To find her guilty you must believe that she is a fiend. Does she look it? As she has sat here during these long and weary days and moved in and out

Have You Seen Anything That Shows a Lack of Womanly Feeling

and womanly bearing?

A word more. There must be no mistake. There can be but one mistake, which nobody can ever righten, for which there can never be any atonement to her. If you make a mistake as against the commonwealth that is something that may be corrected, but if you go wrong as to this woman now, and go to the length that she is guilty, and you have done it upon insufficient grounds and improper finding, the case and the woman have gone beyond your control, so far as you know, beyond the power of humanity. To condemn her as guilty of the diabolical crimes that have been described to you when there remains any reasonable doubt in the mind of any one of you,

The Verdict Would be so Deplorable and Evil

that the tongue could never cease to speak of it. We say, the crier utters it, "God save the commonwealth of Massachusetts," and the prayer is heard in the prosperity of the old Bay state, but little it amounts to if we hear some one pray to God for his guidance of the old commonwealth and we, when we have a prisoner in charge forget that we can do a great deal toward saving the commonwealth. It would be little worth preserving if the innocent are to be executed, and when calamity and wrong step fast upon the heels of each other, and that, too, under the forms of the law, made as well to shield the innocent as to punish the guilty.

Do I plead for her sister? No. Do

I Plead for Lizzie Andrew Borden Herself?

Yes. I ask you to consider, to put her into the scale as a woman, and to say to the commonwealth, whom you represent, "It is unjust to hold her a minute longer." And pleading for her I plead for you and myself and all others that the verdict you shall register in this most important case shall not only commend your approval now, unqualifiedly and beyond a reasonable doubt, but shall stand sanctioned and commended by the people everywhere in the world who are listening to the telegraphic wire to know what is the outcome as to her. She is not without sympathy, are not the people by day and by night thinking that it is not to be found out in Massachusetts that so great a wrong against her can be committed as to condemn her upon the evidence that has been offered.

With abundant patience on your part and intelligence and care you have listened to what I have offered. As far as you are concerned, it is the last word of the defendant to you. Take, take care of her as you have, give us promptly your verdict "not guilty," that she may go home and be Lizzie Andrew Borden of Fall River

In That Blood Stained and Wretched Home

where she has passed her life so many years.

At the conclusion of Mr. Robinson's plea a recess of five minutes was given the jury, after which Mr. Knowlton for the prosecution made the closing argument of the great trial. The district attorney spoke as follows:

THE DISTRICT ATTORNEY'S PLEA.

Mr. Knowlton's Remarkable Arraignment of the Prisoner.

Mr. Foreman and Gentlemen.—Upon one common ground in this case all men stand here. I do not disguise my appreciation of the fact that it is a most heart-rending case. Whether we consider the tragedy that we are trying, and the circumstances that surrounded it, the charge that followed it, the necessary force of the trial that has been had before you, the difficult and painful duty of the counsel upon both sides of the case, or the evidence that shall finally be committed to your charge, there is that in it all, which lacerates the heart strings of humanity. It was an incredible crime. Incredible but for the merciless facts which confront and defeat that incredibility. There is that in the tidings of a

District Attorney Knowlton.

murder that thrills the human heart to its depths. When the word passes from lip to lip, and from mouth to mouth, that a human life has been taken by an assassin, the stoutest hearts stop beating. Lips pale and cheeks blanch, strong men grow pale with the unknown and the mysterious, and if that be so with what I may perhaps call an ordinary assassination, what were the feelings that overpowered the community when the news of this tragedy were spread by the lightning to the end of the world?

Now, gentlemen, I need not ask you to imagine it. You were part of the community. It came to you in your daily avocations, it sent a thrill through your beings, and you felt that life was not secure. Every man turned detective, every act and fact and thought that occurred to the millions of men all over the United States was spread abroad and furnished and given for the identification of the criminal, and still it remained an impenetrable mystery. My distinguished friend says "Who could have done it?" The answer would have been "Nobody could have done it." If you had read an account of these heartless facts in any tale of fiction before this thing had been done you would have said, Mr. Foreman, that will do for a story, but such things never happened.

(Continued on Seventh Page.)

A Tardy Discovery.

The Boston Post is confident that it has at last brought to light the mysterious man whom Samuel Robinsky described in his letter to Miss Emma Borden on August 19, 1892. Captain A. C. Taylor of the United States army, now stationed at Fort Warren, but acting as recruiting officer at Lowell at the time of the murders, was visited by a man on August 6th, who wanted to enlist. Captain Taylor took him into the examining room; he was divested of all his clothing and underwent the required examination. He passed the examination all right, but as he gave evidence of being under the influence of intoxicants, he was, as provided by the laws governing enlistments, rejected.

When the peddler's letter was published the captain compared the description and measurements which he had made of the applicant and found they were identical with the person Robinsky described. The tan shoes, with ill-concealed dark spots, he remembered particularly, and he also recalled that the applicant had, upon being questioned, stated that he had walked from Fall River. The man's face was disfigured by an abrasion which Captain Taylor thought was the result of a collision with a fence, or was consequent from a blow from a club.

No Disagreement.

Ex-Governor Robinson is authority for the statement that no diagreement whatever had taken place between the counsel for Lizzie Borden and that the defense had been conducted with harmony on the part of all, despite the rumors that there had been a disagreement relative to allowing Miss Borden to take the witness stand in her own defense. The rumor, he says, was without foundation.

Not Proven.

The Boston Journal has secured the opinion of prominent people in the largest New England cities as to the guilt of Lizzie A. Borden. The canvass was made after the evidence was all in. Under the head of "Not Proven" appear the names of Mayor Brock and Chief of Police Douglass.

SECOND EDITION.

HOME MATTERS.

REAL ESTATE AND BUILDING.

Daniel W. Baker has sold to Pardon
Cornell an undivided sixth of a lot of land
on the south side of Kempton street, in
Dartmouth, containing about 505.25 square
rods.

Adolph Genhart and others have quitclaimed to Frank P. Genhart a lot of land
with buildings thereon, on Washburn
street.

William W. Crapo, executor, has sold
to James Talbot a lot of land on the west
side of Bourne street, containing about
11.85 rods.

An addition 35 feet 6 inches by 24
feet 4 inches, two stories high, is being
built to the office of the Grinnell mill.
D. H. Cook is the mason, and Sturtevant
Bros. the carpenters.

FUNERAL.

The funeral of Edward Swan occurred
this afternoon from his late residence on
Pleasant street in Fairhaven, and was
largely attended by relatives and friends.
Rev. William Carruthers officiated, and
the Orpheus quartet rendered appropriate selections. At the conclusion of the
service the remains were escorted to
Riverside cemetery by Eureka lodge of
Masons, where the burial was conducted
with Masonic honors. The pall bearers
were members of Eureka lodge, and
among the floral tributes was a square
and compass from that organization.

—The books of the Taunton Lumber
company show a surplus of assets above
liabilities of about $20,000.

Good Clean Coal.
Denison Bros. Co.

VINEYARD HAVEN.

Work has been commenced on Association
hall with a view of raising it up one story.
The lower story will then be used for all
the various offices and town hall, and also
a place for the fire apparatus. This has
been needed for some time, as heretofore
these were scattered all over the village.

MARINE INTELLIGENCE.

TUESDAY, June 20.
ARRIVED.

Bark Sunbeam, Moulton, South Atlantic, St
Helena, March 22d, with 1150 bbls sperm oil
on board, 400 taken on the passage, to J & W
Wing; sent home on the voyage 1670 bbls sp
125 do whale and 650 pounds bone. Reports
had very light weather most of the passage,
was two weeks becalmed on the line. Ar on
Hatteras grounds May 28th, and spoke brig
D A Small and sch Wm A Grozier,of Provincetown, they report, to wit: brig D A Small,
Provincetown, May 31, 950 sp 1100 bbls sp,
this season; sch Wm A Grozier, do, June 9,
with 130 do do, this season; Baltic,do, May 24,
80 do do, this season; Gage H Phillips, do,
May 24, 110 do do, this season; sch Rising Sun
do, June 1, 140 do do, this season; E B Conwell, NB, June 3d, 25 do do, this season;
Golden City, do, May 25,140 do do,this season;
Chas Hodgdon, do, May 25,440 all told, 80 do;
Hattie E Smith, Edgartown, May 25, 300 all
told,30 do do,this season; A'ceone, Provincetown, May 24, with 180, do do, this season;
Mary E Simmons,-'N R, May 15, (clean)
Pedro, Varila, do, May 15, 1,300 all told.

Bark Xi nthea, Edwards, Atlantic ocean,
St Helena April 27th, with 300 barrels sperm
oil on board, 130 barrels taken on the passage
home, to J & W Wing; sent home on the
voyage 1860 barrels sperm oil and 117 do
whale oil. Reports had bad weather all the
passage home.

Sch Edward F Mansfield, Chase, Philadel-
phia.
Sch Eagle Wing, Van Horn, Philadelphia.
Tug Minnie and with light barge.

ARRIVED YESTERDAY.

Sch George & Albert, Powers, Ne w York
via Providence.
Sch Veranda, Pettl, New York.
Sch Annie E Webb, Fishers Island.
The Dudley Pray, New York, with barges
Wyoming, Delaware and Marvis, and tug
sailed with light barge.

Smack Annie D, of New London, went
ashore in Mud Gut creek, Hadley harbor,
Naushon, in the Northeast storm of Saturday night. Captain Canedy, who is also
owner, was in the city when the affair
happened. She is well up on the beach, and
it is very doubtful if she will be floated
again. It is understood there was no Insurance on her and she will be a heavy
loss to the captain.
Sid from Tarpaulin cove 19th, schs J
Kennedy, Campbell, Calais for this port; L
P Wyman, hence for Gloucester.

At ar New Haven 19th, sch Royal Arch,
Wentworth, Baltimore.
Ar at Boston 19th, schs Chas of Co-
lumbia, Jersey, West Point; sch Waterman
A Taft Jr, McKenzie, Darien; Eugenia, stout,
hence.
Passed through Hell Gate 19th, schs Sloop
Brook, Wells,New York for Wareham; Hat-
tie E Russell, Hawkins, Port Johnson for
Fall River.
Cld at Charleston 19th, sch Mary S Brad-
shaw, Farnham, Baltimore.
Ar at Mobile 19th, sch Richard S Spofford,
Nickerson, Havana?

I AM INNOCENT!

Lizzie Borden Speaks for Herself.

Unhappy Woman Denies Her Guilt.

Charge to the Jury Given by Judge Dewey.

Although the court room was crowded
this afternoon there were fewer present
than have been seen since the arguments
were commenced. The fair sex were in
a large majority, and many of them had
remained after the morning adjournment
to be assured of a good seat. Lizzie
came in fully five minutes before the
judges arrived, and occupied the time
until their arrival in conversation with
ex-Governor Robinson. The one thing
that many who have constantly attended
have hoped for, that is, a chance to
hear Lizzie Borden speak in connection
with the case, has taken place, and it
is needless to say that every eye was
riveted on her when she arose to speak.
There was no tremor in her voice and
no embarrassment in her manner.

When the court came in Chief Justice
Mason said, "Lizzie Andrew Borden, it
is your privilege to add any word which
you may desire to say in person to the
jury."

I Am Innocent.

At this Lizzie rose in the dock and
said, "I am innocent, but I leave it to
my counsel to speak for me."

Judge Dewey then delivered the charge
to the jury, who stood during the ceremony. Judge Dewey spoke as follows:

You have listened with attention to
the evidence in the case and to the arguments of the defendant's counsel and
of the district attorney. It now remains
for me, acting in behalf of the court, to
give you such aid in the performance of
your duty as I am able to give within
the limits of judicial action described by
law. It may be well for me to bring
to your attention at the outset that it
is provided by the statutes of this state
that the court shall not charge the jury
with respect to matters of fact. The law
places upon the court the duty and responsibility of furnishing you with a
correct statement of the rules and principles of law that will be applicable to
the case, and places upon you, and you
only, a distinct duty and responsibility
of deciding all questions of fact involved
in the issue between the commonwealth
and the prisoner. And your decision
can properly rest only on the law and the
evidence together with those matters relating to the ordinary affairs of life and
the common qualities of men, which as
jurors you are expected to bring with
you to the court room.

Neither the inquest nor the hearing
on trial in the district court of Fall River
nor the action of the grand jury in finding the indictment can properly influence
your judgment in this case. The case
is brought before you for inquiry and
decision independently of any official
action that has gone before. Neither the
defendant's confinement in prison, nor
her coming here in the custody of an
officer weighs against her in presumption of guilt. They are a part of that
necessary formality which one is called
upon to experience who is regularly
charged with a capital crime.

The defendant is tried on a written accusation termed an indictment, and embodying two counts. The first, couched
in legal language, charges her with the
murder of Abbie Durfe Borden; the second with the murder of Andrew Jackson
Borden, at Fall River, in this county, on
August 4th, 1892. Chapter 202 furnishes
the definition of the two degrees of murder, but leaves the degree of the specific
murder to be determined by the jury.
The government claims that the killing
of Mr. and Mrs. Borden was deliberate
and premeditated, and with malice aforethought, and so is the first degree.

We are to assume that such killing is
an act arising after reflection and deliberation. The law does not assume that
the deliberation must have been for a
long time; it may have been a brief short
time. And so the government claims
that the killing of Mr. and Mrs. Borden was wrongful, wilful, and deliberately premeditated, and after such a consideration carried out. The two counts
are distinct and require separate returns.

The statute tells nowhere a definition
of murder itself and, therefore, we must
refer to the law for one. It is the unlawful killing of a human being. The
words "malice aforethought," as has
been said by one supreme court, mean
the killing from purpose, design and after
a consideration.

The second main proposition is that
the killing was done by the defendant.
In considering the evidence in regard
to this you will need to bear in mind

FINANCIAL.

Sugar Slumps—Touches 85 During Noon
Trading—Manhattan Active in New York
—General List Shows Steadiness—Money
Market Firm—Loans in New York Made
at 20 Per Cent.—Nothing New to Account for Drop in Sugar—Heavy Currency Shipments—In General.

Thursday, June 20.

Stocks in face of summer heat show considerable activity if not remarkable steadiness. The close of yesterday was active
and rather firm, save for a few specialties
which had been weak throughout the day's
trading. Sugar showed a loss of ⅝, but
this was the widest decline, and considering the character of the stock and the
tightness of money it is wonderful that the
loss was not greater. When tight money is
ruling the shares of the industrial group
are usually the first to go down, and fractional declines in these stocks usually give
way as well to wholesale drops, that is
drops by a point or two points at a time.
It must then be taken for granted that the
situation has improved in its various phases
else the decline in this leading industrial
stock would have been greater.

In Boston the money market offers no
change. Money is firm in this market and no
new money is being put out at a less rate
than 6 per cent.

In Boston money on call today is ruling
at 6 to 8 per cent., a bit closer. Time
money is nominally 6 per cent., but it must
be admitted that time loans are rather difficult to effect just at present at any price.
Commercial paper is slow and outside of the
fact that the banks are accommodating
their customers at from 6 to 7½ per cent.,
there are no quotable rates. At clearing to-
day loans were made at 6 and 7 per cent.
New York funds sold at 17 and 25 cents
discount.

In New York the monetary situation is still
of the greatest importance. Call money is
in very sharp demand today at least 10 per
cent., though some loans at lower rates are
reported, as well as some at higher prices.
Shipments of currency are aeavy, over
$750,000 leaving the city yesterday.

Sterling exchange is very weak, and owing to the prevailing high rates for money
in New York is likely to be weaker before
it is firmer. Rates $4.84½ and $4.88.

Bonds are dull and weak.

The New York market opened soft this
morning and fairly active. Sugar shortly after the start fell off quickly to 85⅝. New
England 20⅞, same as close. Manhattan
strong at 131½. St. Paul steady at 85%.
Nashville 67⅝ to 67.

The following table shows the fluctuations
of the leading active stocks during the forenoon.

Stocks.	Opening.	11 a. m.	12 m.
Nashville,	67⅝	67⅝	66½
Reading,	16¼	16½	15⅞
St. Paul,	85	85⅝	85⅝
Sugar,	86¼	34⅛	34⅛
Manhattan,	131	129½	129½

At 1 o'clock stocks were weak and unsettled.

The Boston market opened dull and
steady. Atchison 23½ to 23⅝, C. B. & Q.
87¼.

The following table shows the fluctuations
of the leading active stocks during the forenoon:

Stocks.	Opening.	11 a. m.	12 m.
Atchison,	23¼	23⅞	23¾
C. B. & Q.	87⅛	87⅝	87
Mexican Central,	8	8½	8
Bell Telephone,	192¾	192½	192
Sugar,	86	85½	84%

Sales to noon in Boston today were, bonds
$43,000 and 9,300 shares of stock.

At 1 o'clock the market was featureless.
Money loaned at 20 per cent. at 11 30 this
forenoon.

The shipments of currency to the west
since Friday are estimated by good authorities at from $3,000,000 to $5,000,000.

Eastbound shipments last week were 59,-
670 tons, against 56,122 tons the same week
last year.

Stringent money is making itself effectively felt in our grain market. It costs 1½
cents per bushel to carry wheat to July 1,
giving a profit of nearly $100 on each 10,-
000 bushels, out of which to pay interest.
From July to September differences are 4½
cents, giving a profit of about $100 per
month in addition to 5 per cent. interest.
Within the past few days there have been
sales of Lake copper aggregating some several hundred thousand pounds. Some of
these sales were for export at 10% cents.
The general tendency of the copper market
is toward an improvement.

St. Paul earnings for the second week of
June show a gain of $70,937 gross.

Missouri Pacific gross for the second week
of June show a decrease of $57,000.

Coal shipments over the Philadelphia &
Reading for the week ending Saturday last
were 327,000 tons.

Mexican Central earnings second week of
June increased $11,129.

Nashville gross for second week of June
decreased $8,633. Increase since July 1st,
$1,158,825.

Taintor & Holt say: "London generally
lower. Tightness of money market and general demoralizing we believe will give us
somewhat lower prices and a dull market."

Edward Sweet & Co. say: "Early London prices show fractional losses. Gossip
on street contains little that is new or hopeful and is chiefly confined to money market.
Rates on call run up easily to high figures,
and the drain from the city continues.
Pennsylvania railroad is said to have discharged a thousand men on account of falling off in freight business."

A dividend of $3 has been declared of
Worcester, Nashua & Rochester stock, payable July 3 to stock of record June 20.

The Norwich & Worcester railroad has declared a semi-annual dividend of 4 per
cent., payable July 5 to stock of record
June 21.

The Homestake Mining company has declared its regular monthly dividend, 10
cents per share ($12,500,) $4,006,250 to date.
The statement made by President Reinhart with respect to Atchison floating debt
and the surplus after providing for fixed
charges on July 1, has aroused a good deal
of comment, because of the frankness displayed by the Atchison people in stating
the facts about the company. The statements made reflect a favorable condition of
the company's affairs, and holders of Atchison securities are making the point that at
a time when the company is subjected to
special attacks of hostile people, the management is giving ammunition to friends of
the company to support its credit.

Fall River Print Cloth Market.

Fall River, June 20.

Even the drop to 3¾ cents in the print cloth
market, which took place on Friday night,
has not tempted printers to come in and
place orders. They were not expected to
come in on Saturday, because Boston was
celebrating, and New York rarely does anything on the last day of the week except to
go to the races, but there was no interest
manifested yesterday. Brokers reported
that they had few orders to fill, and that there
was no demand that they had heard of.
There is a feeling, however, that the buying
must begin before long, inasmuch as the sales
of the past fortnight would not furnish a
corner of Delaware with cloth, and nobody
is well supplied beyond the present month.

STOCK AND BOND MARKETS.

Bid Prices at 12 o'clock Today.
New York, June 20.

GOVERNMENT BONDS.

U. S. 2s,	99
" 4s, registered	109
" 4s, coupons,	110
" currency 6s, 1895	103

RAILROADS.

Atchison	23½
Clev.,Cin., Col. & St. Louis	11½
Chicago & Eastern Illinois pref.	95
Chicago, Burlington & Quincy	87
Delaware & Hudson	121½
Delaware & Lackawana	142½
Erie	17½
Illinois Central	98½
Lake Shore	123½
Louisville & Nashville	46½
Manhattan	129½
Michigan Central	102
Missouri Pacific	30½
New York & New England	24%
New York Central	102
Northern Pacific pref.	38½
Pacific Mail	16½
Philadelphia & Reading	15½
Richmond Terminal	7½
St. Paul & Omaha	40%
Union Pacific	17%

MISCELLANEOUS.

Chicago Gas	69½
National Cordage	15
Ontario Silver	16
Pacific Mail	18½
Pullman	165
Sugar	84½
Sugar, pref.	94
Silver Certificates	82
Western Union Telegraph	83

Boston, June 20.

BONDS.

Atchison 4s	77%
Atchison 5s	95
Bell Telephone 7s	109
Chicago, Burlington & Northern 5s	100
C. B. & Q. Cons. Mort. 7s	133
C. B. & Q. Conv. 5s	113
Chicago & West Michigan 5s	*98
Mexican Central 4s	60
Illinois Steel Co. 5s	*90

RAILROADS.

Atchison	23⅝
Boston & Albany	*200
Boston & Lowell	*186
Boston & Maine	162
Boston & Providence	250
Central Mass. pref.	*54
Chicago, Burlington & Quincy	87
Chicago Jun. & Un. Stk. Yds.	90
Chicago Jun. & Un. Stk. Yds. pref.	*87
Chicago & West Michigan	14
Cleveland & Canton & Southern	*5
Cleveland, Canton & Southern pref.	14
Fitchburg	*83
Fitchburg pref.	100
Mexican Central	8
New York & New England	20½
New York & New England pref.	60
Old Colony	170
Oregon Short Line	*13
Pullman Palace Car	165
Union Pacific	17%
Wisconsin Central	18
West End	*35
West End pref.	*78

MINING.

Butte & Boston	6¼
Calumet & Hecla	280
Centennial	14
Franklin	12
Kearsarge	21
Osceola	26%
Quincy	105
Tamarack	140

MISCELLANEOUS.

American Bell Telephone	192
Erie Telephone	*45
New England Telephone	*67
Boston Land	*4
West End Land	*4
General Electric	64
Lamson Store Service	*15½
Illinois Steel Co.	*50
Sugar	86
Sugar common	86
Thomson-Houston	64½
Westinghouse	25
Bay State Gas	6½
National Lead	32

*Asked.

CALIFORNIA MINING STOCKS.

San Francisco, June 19.
The following are the official closing prices
of mining stocks to-day:

Best & Belcher	1 10	Mexican	1 15
Bulwer	—	Mount Diablo	—
Chollar	—	Ophir	1 70
Con. Cal. & Va.	1 80	Potosi	—
Crown Point	—	Savage	—
Eureka Con.	—	Sierra Nevada	—
Gould & Curry	—	Yellow Jacket	1 40
Hale & Norcross	—	Belcher	1 05

FALL RIVER STOCK QUOTATIONS.

The following are the quotations of Fall
River stocks to-day as reported by Sanford &
Kelley, bankers and brokers and stock auc-
tioneers:

	Par.	Bid.	Asked.	Sale.	Last
American Linen Co.	100	102¼	105	105	
Barnaby Mfg. Co.	100			85	
Barnard Mfg. Co.	100	85	89	87	
Border City Mfg. Co.	100		50	50½	
Bourne Mills.	100		160	161	
Chace Mills	100		110	108	
Cornell Mills.	100		97	95	
Crescent Mills.	100		87	97	
Davol Mills.	100	92	95	94	
Durfee Mills	100			100	
Fall River Bleachery	100	90		79	
Flint Mills.	100		108		105%
Globe Yarn Mills.	100	110¼	114	110	
Granite Mills.	100		118	121	
Hargraves Mills.	100		95	94	
King Philip Mills	100	121	122	121	
Kerr Thread Co.	100			95	
Laurel Lake Mills.	100	108		105½	
Massasoit Nat'l Bank	100			100	
Mechanics' Mills.	100	85	87%	87%	
Merchants' Mfg. Co.	100	112½	117	115	
Metacomet Mills.	100		100		
Metacomet National	100			100	
Bank	100			100	
National Union Bank	100			100	
Narragansett Mills	100			102	
Osborn Mills.	100		112	109	
Pocasset Mfg. Co.	100		100		
Pocasset Nat'l Bank.	100		100		
Richard Borden Mfg.	100	115	116	115	
Robeson Mills.	100		79	79	
Sanford Spinning Co.	100		103	102	
Sagamore Mfg. Co.	100		105	115	
Seaconnet Mills.	100		100		
Shove Mills.	100	100	103	103	
Slade Mills.	100		90	90	
Stafford Mills.	100	108	110	107½	
Tecumseh Mills.	100		116		
Troy C. & W. Manufac.	100				
Co.	100		1015	1000	
Union Mfg. Co.	100		108	108	
Wampanoag Mills	100		107	107	
Weetamoe Mills.	100	47	47	47	

*Old Stock.

NEW YORK PRODUCE MARKET.

New York, June 20.

Flour sales 2,350 packages; quiet and
firm.

Wheat sales 1,025,000 bushels; 3-5 lower
Corn sales 725,000 bushels; ⅛ lower and
steady and active.

Oats sales 100,000 bushel; quiet and
firm.

Beef quiet.
Pork dull and steady
Lard quiet.
Butter quiet.
Cheese quiet and easy.
Sugar (raw) quiet and firm.
Petroleum quiet.
Turpentine dull and firm.
Molasses quiet.
Rice dull and firm.
Freights firm and quiet.
Rosin quiet.
Tallow firm and dull.

PROVISIONS AND GRAIN.

Chicago, June 20.

Opening

	Wheat.	Pork.	Corn.
July,	66¼		38½
September,	71½		—
December,	76¾		—

12 o'clock.

	Wheat.	Pork.	Corn.
July,	65⅝		42
September,			43¾
December,	78%		

WEATHER INDICATIONS.

Fair and Sultry.

New York, June 20.—At 8 30 a. m. the
weather was clear, wind south, temperature 79. The Herald says: In the Middle states and New England on Wednes-
day, fair, sultry weather will probably
prevail, with slight temperature changes
and light to fresh variable winds, mostly
southerly, followed by partial cloudiness,
and on Thursday sultry and fair to partly cloudy weather, with slightly lower
temperature.

OFF FOR BUZZARDS BAY.

Mrs. Cleveland and Baby Ruth Leave Washington.

Washington, June 20.—Mrs. Cleveland,
her little daughter and household servants left on a special car at 9 40 a. m.
today for Buzzards Bay. The president
did not accompany her.

CALIFORNIA'S DAY.

Her Building at Chicago Dedicated by Sons
of Golden Gate.

CHICAGO, June 20.—The first visitors to
the fair yesterday were the folks who
came to town over Saturday, and started
in to do the show in a systematic manner.
Monday is strangers' day at the fair, and
75 per cent of the persons who bought
tickets at the gates of the big show were
looked upon its beauties for the first time.

There were no special events except the
dedication of the California building,
which brought 2000 or 3000 native sons and
daughters of the Golden State to the
grounds. The crowd took advantage to
inspect the exhibits in the great buildings, which, with very few exceptions, are
all complete.

Change of Time.

By the action of the council of administration yesterday the fair will hereafter be
kept open for visitors until 11 o'clock every
night instead of Sunday, Tuesday, Thursday and Saturday nights, as heretofore.
The new order of things goes into effect
on Wednesday night, and will be in force
until the end of October. The exposition
buildings are to be kept open until 10
o'clock and the grounds until 11 o'clock.

Keeping Up the Sunday Question.

The Methodist preachers of Chicago do
not like the decision of Chief Justice Fuller, and at their weekly meeting yesterday
decided to keep up the fight against Sunday opening. Rev. P. S. Hanson, although
a Baptist, had been invited to make the
address to the meeting, during which he
administered to the chief justice a palpable
slap: "I can imagine a personal devil
squatting like a black toad at the bar of
justice itself and dictating the decision of
the court, and then after the judgment had
been pronounced slapping the judge on
shoulder and saying, 'Well done; I could
not have written that better myself.'"
These remarks were received with enthusiastic applause by the preachers.

New Cruisers to Be Tested.

BALTIMORE, June 20.—Arrangements
have been completed by the Columbian
iron works for the official trial trip of the
cruiser Montgomery, which will be made
over the same route and under the same
conditions as was the trial of the Detroit.
The trial will be made in less than two
weeks. The board of naval officers will
make a final examination of the Detroit
preparatory to her acceptance by the government next Thursday. The cruiser is
now ready for the reception of her arm-
ament and crew.

Ainsworth Held For Manslaughter.

WASHINGTON, June 20.—Colonel Ainsworth, chief of the record and pension
office, and in charge of the Ford's theater
building, Contractor Dant, Engineer
Sasse and Superintendent Covert were
yesterday found guilty of criminal negli-
gence and responsible for the Ford's
theater disaster by the coroner's jury, and
held by the coroner for indictment for
manslaughter by the grand jury, the
penalty, upon conviction, being 10 years in
the penitentiary.

Must Serve His Term.

DENVER, June 20.—In the petition of
Alfred Packer for a writ of habeas corpus
argument upon his upheld the district
court, inflicting accumulative sentence,
and remanded the petitioner to complete
his sentence. The indictments against
him charge him with the murders of Israel
Swan, Shannon Wilson Bell, Frank Miller, George Noon and James Humphrey.
He was given eight years for each murder,
and will be compelled to serve out the 40
years if he lives.

Fatally Gored by a Bull.

LAMBERTVILLE, N. J., June 20.—George
Emmitt started to town to have a scalp
wound dressed. In cutting across a lot a
bull became enraged at the sight of his
bloody face and charged him. Emmitt
ran for the fence, but he was weak from
the loss of blood, and the beast overtook
him and gored and trampled upon him.
When he was finally rescued he was so seriously injured that physicians say he will
not recover.

Heavy Armor For the Indiana.

WASHINGTON, June 20.—A 17-inch nickel
steel armor plate was received at the navy
yard yesterday and will be sent to the Indian Head proving ground and placed in a
position for test at an early date. The
plate represents the side armor of the Indiana, and is the heaviest plate ever made
for an American vessel.

Sanger Lowered Records.

LONDON, June 20.—Walter Sanger, the
bicyclist, surpassed at Herne Hill yesterday all his previous work. After taking
a flying start he beat his quarter mile
record of Saturday, which was 28 4-5s, by
one second. He did a mile in 10 1-5s,
thus beating Harris' record of 2m. 12 3-5s.
While performing the one mile feat he
also surpassed by.2 1-5s. Scofield's record
of 1m. 38 2-5s. for three-quarters of a mile.

An American Architect Honored.

LONDON, June 20.—Richard M. Hunt
of New York received at the Royal Institute of British Architects the queen's
gold medal. This distinction was conferred on him in view of his work at the
World's fair at Chicago. In presenting
the medal President Paterson of the institute said that he was the first American
whose name had been inscribed on the institute's illustrious roll of honor.

Sawmill Totally Destroyed.

MILFORD, N. H., June 20.—Ware & Co.'s
two-story sawmill was burned yesterday.
Loss, $4000.

TELEGRAPHIC BREVITIES.

Yellow Springs, O., is in danger of destruction by fire.

The French have taken possession of the
Island of Samit, in the Gulf of Siam.

The Kansas state militia is being reor-
ganized to give it a Populist complexion.

A modified form of home rule for the
Antilles has been proposed in the Spanish
cortes.

Berlin correspondents think the next
reichstag will pass the German army bill
by a good majority.

Officials in the Detroit water department have embezzled about $7000; one of
them committed suicide.

The widow of one of the Italians lynched
at New Orleans is being sued as an
alien, but the courts decided that she was
an American.

Three young men were drowned in
Chequamegon bay, near Washburn, Wis.
Their boat was capsized. They were Lyle
Kellogg, John Ford and George Gay.

(Continued in Third Edition, Eighth Page.)

WHERE IS THE ASSASSIN?

There is Mystifying Work Ahead for the Police.

Miss Borden in Fall River Among Her Friends.

Immense Crowd Besieged the Second Street Mansion.

Fall River, June 21.—The verdict which was flashed into this city late yesterday afternoon occasioned considerable surprise, because it found its way into town at an unexpected hour. It was supposed that the jurymen would at least deliberate until morning, and until the text of the charge reached the public their prompt return could not be explained.

Now that it has been proved to the satisfaction of 12 men that a mistake was committed, and that Miss Lizzie Borden did not butcher her father and stepmother, as alleged, the crime is thrown back to the afternoon of Aug. 4, 1892, when the police were scouring the country for a murderer. Nothing remains except the fact that Mr. and Mrs. Borden were slain in cold blood, and the community is still saddled with a tragedy that remains unexplained. Opinions, whether changed or unchanged by the decision reached, no longer count. The accused has been removed from consideration.

It is now necessary to pursue an entirely new line. No member of the family took the lives of the aged couple, and an assassin must be found, or it must be said of Fall River that a fiend can kill there as he pleases and escape punishment. The work of the authorities has just begun. The investigation which has been pursued and the mass of evidence which has been collected are worthless. Every clew which has been pointing in one direction for 10 exciting months must be discarded.

From a legal standpoint, if from no other, it is plain that some monster did just what it has been claimed no monster could do. He sent a note to Mrs. Borden on the morning of August 4th and stole into the house on Second street. He entered by the front door, which was double locked, or through the side door, which was hooked, or by means of the chimney. It matters not how he entered so long as it had been demonstrated that he got in and accomplished his unholy undertaking. He concealed himself somewhere on the premises. The world knows that he was not seen there and that he has not been seen since. Perhaps he secreted himself in the cellar or in a clothes press on the second floor, or in the attic; it doesn't matter where. He finds that his note has not accomplished his purpose, and being discovered strikes down Mrs. Borden.

It is the old story, but a new character is playing the part of the villain, and circumstances must be made to fit his convenience. He is not detected and he waits an hour or an hour and a half until Mr. Borden arrives. It is fair to presume that he does not go to the stable. He follows Miss Lizzie Borden down stairs, if he is hiding in that part of the house, or he waits until she disappears, if he is in the basement or on the first floor, and then wields the axe again. He takes himself off noiselessly north, south, east or west, with the axe and the note in his possession. His motive cannot be imagined. If it were robbery, he lost the nerve which enabled him to endure the strain after the first crime, and fled without helping himself to plunder. If it were revenge, he surely had it.

To track him will be difficult. He has nearly a year's start. He has no name, and no description of him can be furnished. Nothing short of a miracle will ever reveal his identity. But this is an age of miracles, and he may be overtaken. At all events the above is a shadowy picture of the individual who drove a blade into the skulls of Mr. and Mrs. Borden, and who has never been suspected except for a few hours after the discovery of the frightful deed.

It seems inconceivable that with three people about the premises there could have been more than one such individual. It isn't necessary to double the difficulties of the unsolved problem. But there is no denying that as this perplexing slaughter stands now some scoundrel who answers this meagre picture is still at large, and if he keeps his own counsel he is likely to remain at large. It is safe to assert that he cannot be painted in stronger colors. He is a phantom so far as the most brilliant imagination goes. Nobody can set him down as a farm hand, as a sailor, as a tramp or as a business man. Who and what he was cannot be determined. Nevertheless, he must be substituted at this late hour in this marvelous case, and the interest which once centered elsewhere must henceforth center in him.

Judgment has been pronounced, and it is a judgment which cannot fail to bring this unknown, unknowable stranger into prominence. The drama which was laid in the court room in New Bedford is over. Three justices have weighed the evidence, and the charge has been delivered. Twelve men have weighed the evidence and the charge, and have announced for all time that the state was wrong in its conclusions.

There is no appeal, and there can be no new finding. The police must strike another trail.

Miss Lizzie Borden arrived in this city soon after 8 o'clock last evening. An immense crowd, which reminded one of the early days of the horror, surged about the brown house on Second street. They were prompted by the same curiosity which chained them hour after hour when the grim story of what had happened there was still fresh in their minds. Finally a posse of police was sent to disperse the mob. Miss Borden did not go to her home. With Mr. Charles J. Holmes, Miss Annie Holmes and her sister she drove over from New Bedford in a carriage which had been ordered in this city, and was taken at once to the residence of Mr. Holmes on Pine street, where her friends crowded in to congratulate her. Among them were Dr. Bowen and his wife and Mr. and Mrs. B. A. Bowen. Supper was served shortly after the arrival of the party, all of whom were naturally in the best of spirits. Mr. Holmes said that the subject of the trial was tabooed on the journey, but that Miss Borden, who felt greatly relieved now that the ordeal was over, expressed her gratitude for the efforts of her counsel in her behalf. Her faithful attendant, Rev. E. A. Buck, was overjoyed when seen this evening. From the first he had been confident of the innocence of the woman who assisted him in his mission and charitable work, and on whose character he felt qualified to pass. If he entertained fears regarding untoward circumstances, which the accused was powerless to control, they have been dispelled, and his sentiments are shared by all of Miss Borden's friends.

JUDGE DEWEY CHARGING THE JURY IN THE BORDEN TRIAL.

LET MISS BORDEN SPEAK.

What She Owes to the Memory of the Dead and Her Own Reputation.

(Providence Journal Editorial.)

With the proceedings at New Bedford yesterday one of the most celebrated criminal trials of modern times comes to an end. Lizzie Borden has been adjudged not guilty by a jury of her peers, after a careful presentation of evidence, elaborate arguments by distinguished counsel, and a lucid charge by a learned judge. There is no doubt of the fairness of the trial, so far as the prisoner is concerned, or of the honesty of the jury in reaching a verdict upon the facts laid before them. But it would be idle to assert that this outcome of the case is satisfactory. Those who believe Miss Borden to be guilty will hardly be swayed by it, and those who believe her to be innocent will regret that some positive proof was not adduced. No more brutal murders were ever committed, and that the murderer should escape is revolting to the public sense of justice. Now that Miss Borden is free she should lose no time and spare no effort in trying to secure the detection of the real criminal. She owes this much to the memory of her dead father and stepmother, and to her own reputation. Others than the jury are not bound by the rulings of the court, and they cannot help giving weight to that portion of the government's case which was not admitted, but which could not fail in some degree to compromise her.

There has been throughout the trial a disposition in many quarters to criticise with undue severity the conduct of the district attorney and his associates. But surely no fair-minded person, bearing in mind Miss Borden's own statements, to say nothing of all the circumstances of the crime, can deny that there was ample reason for the arrest and prosecution. Nor is it just to say that their theory as to Miss Borden's guilt made them indisposed to follow up other possible subjects of suspicion. On the contrary, the most unpromising clews were diligently followed. That Mr. Knowlton himself believed firmly in the strength of his case, that he reached the conclusions he set forth so eloquently with deep reluctance and with a full sense of his responsibility, there is no reason to doubt. His closing argument was a masterly presentation of that side of the case; and we regret to say that it has carried conviction to many minds, in spite of the verdict. Such an outcome is inevitable in a case so strange, so unparalleled as this. No one has any desire to see Miss Borden proved guilty; every one instinctively shrinks from a conclusion so horrible. But there is no use in shutting our eyes to the fact that she leaves the court room at New Bedford still under a grave cloud of suspicion.

Arguments about the monstrosity of the crime, of the absurdity of imputing it to the daughter of the murdered man, are of little value. The workings of the human heart, like the decrees of fate, are inscrutable. Men and women of apparently blameless lives have many times in the history of the world become of a sudden little less than fiends. It is not so very long since a respectable woman, the last person in the world whom her friends and neighbors would have suspected of such an act, poisoned her children in cold blood for the sake of the money which the insurance on their lives would bring. And it is not inconceivable, however revolting the thought may be, that one situated as Miss Borden was, surrounded by a sordid atmosphere which choked out natural affection and stifled innocent tastes, living after a glimpse of the outer world in the narrow and squalid circle of petty avarice, dowered with the sour and self-concentrated Puritan temperament, should be wrought to a pitch of unnatural frenzy and endeavor to free herself by a deed from which the most hardened criminal might shrink. Moral wrecks enough have been wrought elsewhere by the same conditions, although the usual end is insanity or suicide. The question of motive may be barred out legally, but it cannot be made inoperative ethically.

Then take all the circumstances of the murder. Did Miss Borden have "exclusive opportunity," as the government sought to prove? Perhaps not, and yet it is difficult to see how two such murders could have been committed without her knowledge. It is to be said in her behalf that the assumption of her guilt presupposes an iron will, great cunning, and the most favorable conditions. How far all these things existed every one who has followed the case can judge for himself. It is certainly quite as extraordinary to suppose that any person from outside the house could have gained access undetected at such a time, murdered Mrs. Borden, waited more than an hour for the return of Mr. Borden, murdered him, and then escaped, leaving absolutely no trace. Yet that is what the verdict compels us to suppose. Mr. Borden, to be sure, was not an agreeable man, and he undoubtedly had many enemies. But who had any motive for killing Mrs. Borden? Or is there any reason to believe, from the position of her body, from the absence of any outcry, which must surely have been heard by Miss Borden, who was in the house at the time, that it was detection or fear of interruption by her which led to this first brutal butchery? And why should the outer door have been bolted and locked by one whose only anxiety was to get away from the house unharmed? We have no desire to press the points, to interpret their meaning one way or the other, the question the justice of the legal acquittal of the prisoner. But so long as they remain unsolved, so long will people be found to place the same interpretation upon them which Mr. Knowlton placed.

The inaccuracies and inconsistencies of Miss Borden's testimony at the preliminary hearing, concerning which the jury were not called upon to decide, stand in imminent need of explanation, and Miss Borden owes it to her friends, no less than to herself, to endeavor to explain them. The story about the note which Mrs. Borden received from "a sick friend," who has been strangely silent during all these proceedings, the visit to the barn, the allusions to Mrs. Borden after the murder had been discovered, the burning of the dress, the conversation with Miss Russell—upon all these points some clearer light should be thrown. There is no reason now for Miss Borden's silence: let her speak. And let her also, as we have said, spare no effort to bring this horrible case to a more satisfactory conclusion than it has now reached, after months of investigation by the government and floods of eloquence from the defense, with so much evidence barred out by the court and the presumption of innocence most strenuously insisted upon by the learned judge who delivered the charge.

WHAT IS SAID OF THE VERDICT.

Mrs. Mary A. Livermore Expected That Lizzie Would be Acquitted.

When a reporter called on Mrs. Mary A. Livermore at her home in Melrose last evening she was writing the following telegram to Lizzie A. Borden:

Thank God, dear Lizzie, that you are acquitted. Everybody is rejoicing and the wires are freighted with the good news. I kiss you in my heart.

All the time people kept passing and speaking from the street, or coming up onto the piazza to ask if Mrs. Livermore had heard the news and there was great excitement and rejoicing in the household.

Mrs. Livermore said: "I expected a verdict of acquittal, as every point in the testimony of the prosecution was broken down. I knew from my talks with the Borden girls of Mrs. Reagan's falsehoods and that she only stuck to them fearing she would lose her place, but I was afraid it might not be brought out in the evidence.

"I think Lizzie knows nothing at all about the murder. I have talked with her and with Emma, and they can form no theory about it. They say their father often had differences with his workmen, but not serious enough to cause such a terrible catastrophe.

Lizzie is the soul of honor and truth. Neither of the girls are liars or quarrelsome. If injured, they would say nothing, but be silent and repress all feeling. Lizzie is a most intensely self-poised person, and can control herself beyond description. She has suffered more than language can describe, shut up in jail with common criminals, her name a byword of reproach, not allowed to walk God's green earth, mud thrown at her, some of which must stick, and yet for all this she has no redress.

"If women were allowed to make the laws, there would be a meeting called at once to take steps to reform them so that suspected persons should not be treated worse than murderers.

"I remember a case that happened many years ago of a minister who was accused of murdering a young girl of his parish. He was acquitted, but the man was ruined for life. He could never get another parish; nobody would take him by the hand, and he died not long ago, a ruined man.

"I think Lizzie has friends enough to stand by her and support her, so the effect upon her will not be so terrible. I think Emma will suffer the most and the longest. She will be hurt by it forever. Lizzie will recover from the accusation sooner."

JUDGE DEWEY INTERVIEWED.

One of the Presiding Justices Thinks the Verdict Just.

Justice Dewey said to a Standard reporter last night: "I am perfectly satisfied with the verdict, and as far as I know, my opinion is that of my associates. We talked the matter over at considerable length, and it was our opinion that no other verdict could justly be rendered.

"The trial has been a fair and a just one, and the government has made as much of the case as could have been done. The arguments were both good, but very different. Mr. Knowlton did his work for the state in the best manner possible, while ex-Governor Robinson defended the prisoner in an able way.

"The quiet manner in which Miss Lizzie Borden conducted herself impressed the judges and the jury very much. She was carefully watched, and when she said 'I am innocent,' she excited considerable feeling.

"Every atom of evidence which the government presented was done so strongly, and every point was brought to bear that was worth anything, but it was not sufficient in my mind to convict Miss Borden.

"I was satisfied when I made my charge to the jury that the verdict would be 'not guilty,' although one cannot always tell what a jury will do. They were carefully watched, and had no means of knowing what the outside world thought of the case."

The judge was of the opinion that Miss Borden helped her case by not making a scene as many would have done. Continuing on this point he said:

"It was much better that she did not make a scene. It helped the counsel, the jurors and the judges, and although she did what many would not have done—not break down—it was apparent to all that she was deeply affected.

"To those who watched her carefully throughout the entire trial she appeared different than to those who saw her but once or twice. Tears glistened in her eyes many times. To conduct oneself as she did requires a strong mind.

"The reason why the two indictments were made was because there were two crimes committed, and the government did not want to make one indictment for the two crimes and then find that they could not try her without separate indictments. To overcome this they had an indictment covering both crimes and then one for each crime. In this way they covered both crimes and left no loophole whereby they could be headed off.

"After the court these indictments, which remained, were nol prossed and Miss Borden went from the court a free woman and entirely exonerated from all charges which had been made against her."

DARTMOUTH.

Joseph S. Elkinton of Philadelphia, a minister of the society of Friends, will attend a meeting for divine worship at the Friends meeting house at Smith Mills on Thursday, the 22d inst., at 11 o'clock.

and strong and the very picture of health. We have fed him on lactated food ever since and he has not been sick a single day."

Mrs. L. L. Bartlett, 568 W. Sanborn St., Winona, Minn., writes: "I nursed our baby until he was four months old, and my health was in such a terrible state that it threw him into inflammation of the bowels of a severe type. His life was despaired of. I had heard about lactated food, and by the advice of the attending physician we purchased some. The baby liked it from the first and it agreed with him. He got well and began to grow fat at once. At six months of age he weighed twenty-five pounds. He never had the slightest trouble with teething, his teeth coming without our knowledge until we could see them. On the whole he is one of the happiest, sweetest babies one would care to see."

MARRIAGE BELLS.

A Home Wedding at the Residence of Hon. T. W. Cook.

The residence of Hon. Thomas W. Cook at the corner of Ash and Union streets was the scene this afternoon of a very happy gathering, the occasion being the marriage of John Otheman, of the firm of Otheman & Dunham, to Miss Bessie Hudson Cook, daughter of Mr. Cook, member of the board of health. The house was beautifully decorated with palms, ferns, potted plants, roses and wild flowers in abundance. Florist Haskell did his best in this floral display. At 2 o'clock, the appointed hour, while the guests were enjoying the fragrance of the lovely flowers, of which there was a great abundance, the wedding party made its appearance from the rooms above. The bride wore a pale blue silk, cut en traine, and trimmed with lace. She carried in her right hand a large bouquet of pink roses. Rev. Paul R. Frothingham of the Unitarian church officiated. An informal reception was held after the ceremony, when Mr. and Mrs. Otheman left the city for a brief wedding tour. On their return to the city they will give a reception to friends, and during the coming summer they will take up their abode in Dartmouth.

Warren-Slade.

About 350 invited guests were present at Elmwood Congregational church, Providence, yesterday afternoon to witness the marriage of Helen Manton, second daughter of Mr. and Mrs. Henry Warren of 436 Public street, to Mr. Edward Nichols Slade, formerly of Fall River, now of Providence. Rev. Joseph Lambert, pastor of the church, officiated. Mr. E. S. Roberts presided at the organ, and rendered the following pieces: "Bridal Song from Lohengrin" and "Mendelssohn's Wedding March." The bride was attended by Miss Lucia Hervey Slade of Fall River, sister of the groom, a maid of honor. The following acted as bridesmaids: Miss Helen Curtis Hervey of New Bedford, Miss Lillie Stone Bliss of Fall River, Miss Mary Woodbury Polleys and Miss Mary Madison Horton of Providence. The best man was Mr. George C. Hill of New York, and the ushers were Mr. John H. Lindsey of Fall River, Mr. Charles H. Stanley of North Attleboro, Mr. Eugene A. Cory, Jr., of Providence and Mr. W. Irving Nichols of Fall River. After the c remony a reception was given at the home of the young couple, 16 Mawney street. A large number of valuable presents were received by the bride and bridegroom, who, after the reception, started on an extensive tour, to be at home to receive their friends in September.

—Peter Nelson's new catboat, the Shawnee, was successfully launched at midnight last night from Greene & Wood's wharf. The Shawnee is 22 feet 4 inches over all, 19 feet 6 inches keel, and 9 feet 6 inches beam. She was built from Mr. Nelson's model by George W. Thatcher of Leonard street. It is expected that she will be ready for use tomorrow.

OLD AGE OF INDIANS.

Defying All Rules of Health They Keep Well and Strong.

The Remarkable Longevity of the Indian Race Explained.—For Every Human Ill They Have a Cure—They Know Where to Find the Roots, Herbs and Barks that will keep them in Good Health—The Secret Now Given to the World.

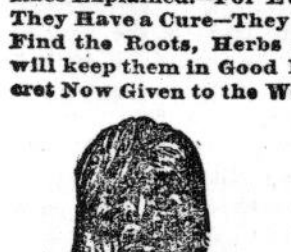

Laughing Dog. Age 106 Yrs.

Indians are long lived.

There are many Kickapoos now living who have trod parts of this vast continent long before white men ever set his foot on the soil of their vast domain. Their lives have been spent with nature.

Born to good health, as the saying goes, they keep it.

Think how they live, eat, sleep, travel about, exposed to climatic changes, poisonous night airs, damp sleeping places, food half cooked, and eaten with utter disregard of all common rules of health.

Yet, look at them! Pictures of health. *Chronic* Rheumatism? Never. Malaria and Chills? Very rarely. Indigestion? Occasional symptoms perhaps, but Chronic Dyspepsia, utterly unheard of. While any of the numerous afflictions of the liver, kidneys or bladder, so frequently found among the whites, is rarely heard of among the Indians.

Why is it?

For centuries these children of nature have studied her ways. For centuries they have known where to look in the forest and field for a certain cure for the ills which arise from the disobedience of nature's laws. At the first sign, the first symptoms of sickness, they resort to their "Sagwa"—the most potent, remedial combination of roots and herbs known to the Indian or any other race.

A combination so valuable that the learned professor of Physiological Chemistry at Yale college commended it, and could offer no suggestions.

Science surpassed by Indian craft! Nature undefiled by mineral poisons.

Indians are subject to ills of the flesh, but they have a remedy for all.

Kickapoo Indian Cough Cure breaks up their colds and stops their coughs. Kickapoo Indian Worm Killer keeps their children free from these troubles; and Kickapoo Indian Oil arrests croup, allays pain, heals bruises, and quickly kills all pains; Kickapoo Indian Salve heals, wounds, cuts, abrasions of the skin, humors, eczema, etc.

Afraid of the Moon. Age 117 Yrs.

These remedies are now sold by every druggist in the land, and their best proof of genuine worth is in the fact that on their merit solely they have achieved this sale within a few short years. Ask for them at the Trading Post on the Frontier, and you'll find them there. Go into the fashionable drug stores of New York City, and these remedies of the Indians are to be bought. Everywhere, high and low, they have made friends by their intrinsic value. Sold by Druggists and Dealers.

Kickapoo Indian Sagwa,

The Incomparable Liver, Stomach and Blood Medicine. $1 per bottle; 6 for $5.

Sold by Druggists and Dealers.

THE BORDEN VERDICT.

Prosecution and Defense Alike Only Did Their Duty.

(Editorial in Boston Advertiser.)

In accordance with its well known and invariable practice, the Advertiser has refrained from editorial comment upon the merits of the question at issue in the trial of Miss Lizzie Borden during the progress of the case. Our practice in that respect is based upon principle. It is a principle often enunciated by the highest judicial authorities and that commends itself to such newspaper men as care more for the dignity of their profession and the interests of public justice than for sensationalism. Our news columns have contained from day to day complete and carefully prepared intelligence regarding every development at the New Bedford court room. This was due to our readers and was strictly within limits sanctioned by law and unquestioned requirements of the general welfare. Beyond this it seems to us no self-respecting journal should go. It is of the utmost importance that while a trial involving the life or death of an accused person is in progress no effort shall be made to create by partisan appeals on the one side or on the other a public sentiment that can in no event tend to aid in securing a fair and impartial trial, and may possibly tend toward defeating that object which ought to be the desire of all good citizens. It is to be regretted extremely that these obviously sound considerations have been so often disregarded in certain newspaper quarters during the past few days.

The time has at length arrived when editorial comment is permissible. In dealing with the subject it shall be our endeavor to avoid everything inconsistent with perfect fairness and with due regard for all the sacred rights concerned.

The verdict of "Not guilty" was generally and with ample reason expected. Even before the trial began it was the prevailing opinion that no conviction was possible. This view rested on the understanding that all important evidence in the possession of the government had already, in substance, been made public. The event showed that this understanding was not far wrong. The chief exception was the proof about the burning of that "Bedford cord" dress. This testimony was a surprise, and certainly bore with considerable weight against the prisoner; but the government was totally unable to show beyond a reasonable doubt that the dress was worn at the time of the murder, or that the so-called "paint spots" were blood spots. The same inconclusiveness attached to every other vital part of the state's evidence. Various suspicious circumstances were established, but no one of them amounted to clear demonstration of guilt. The district attorney declared in his closing argument that the prosecution rested its case upon the note which Miss Borden said her stepmother received on the morning of the tragedy, summoning her to the bedside of a sick friend. Beyond question the failure of the defense to produce any such note, or to offer the slightest proof that it had ever been received, coupled with the enormous improbability that any person in Fall River, particularly any friend of the family, who knew anything of such a note would have withheld that knowledge, was a most significant circumstance. Nevertheless, even this was not conclusive against the defendant. A reasonable doubt remained. Possibly, barely possibly, as ex-Governor Robinson suggested, the note was sent by the murderer or an accomplice. On that hypothesis the question remained unanswered as to why it was not found in the house. But the defense was not legally bound to answer the question. Perhaps Mrs. Borden received the note, read it, told Lizzie about it, then threw it into the fire.

The law gives, and rightly gives, the prisoner the benefit of every reasonable doubt. That is of course an immense advantage for the defense, and is meant to be so. A verdict of guilty can be rendered only when every fact necessary to prove guilt is completely established, and when no one of these facts is susceptible of any explanation consistent with innocence. The question for the jury to decide was not as to the balance of the weight of evidence. In that respect a criminal trial differs totally from the trial of a civil action. The question for the jury to decide was not as to the probabilities, but as to the certainties. The members of the jury were not called upon to declare their personal opinions touching guilt or innocence. In that as in all such cases the instructions of the court were explicit. The prisoner must be acquitted unless the jury found not merely a preponderance of evidence against her but such overwhelming demonstration that no reasonable doubt remained in the mind of any one of the 12 men selected to decide the awful issue. And, whatever individual opinions may have been reached by the people at large who have watched the course of this remarkable trial, there are probably very few if any unprejudiced people who will say that, under the circumstances, the verdict rendered at New Bedford yesterday ought to have been different from what it was.

For some time to come the subject of the Borden murder will continue to be a topic of discussion in the press and in private conversation. This is unavoidable, nor is it objectionable, provided passion be held in check and calm reason hold sway. It is not to be expected that a tragedy so extraordinary, shocking and mysterious will at once drop out of public thought. Probably nobody anticipates with any degree of confidence the throwing of further light upon the dark and bloody crime. It will now take its place in the long list of murders whose victims' blood cries to heaven unavenged. But the known circumstances are too dreadful to be soon forgotten.

It is to be hoped that further violence of language will be avoided by those who see fit to express themselves. Differences of opinion will remain, but they imply no wilful wrong-headedness, wrong-heartedness on one side or the other. Especially is it to be hoped that we shall hear no more railing accusations against those who have been officially engaged in the preparation or management of the case. The prosecution and the defense have alike done their duty, nothing less or other. It is to the last degree absurd to claim that Lizzie Borden ought not to have been tried and that those who brought her to the bar of justice were engaged in "hounding an innocent woman." The more her champions are assured in their own minds of her innocence, so much the more ought they to rejoice that she was brought to a position where a jury of her countrymen could, after hearing the worst and utmost that might legally be presented against her, pronounce the accused to be "not guilty."

COMMENTS OF THE PRESS.

Newspapers Think the Verdict the Only Possible One.

Editorially, papers expressed themselves in the following manner today on the acquittal of Lizzie Borden:

New York World—No other verdict could have been expected. It was the necessary outcome not only of the whole sum of the testimony, but of the testimony offered by the prosecution taken by itself. There was absolutely no case against the accused woman. The case is one of police blundering, after a familiar fashion, but with rather more than ordinary stupidity.

New York Times—The acquittal of this most unfortunate and cruelly persecuted woman was, by its promptness, in effect a condemnation of the police authorities of Fall River and of the legal officers who secured the indictment and have conducted the trial. It was a declaration not only that the prisoner was guiltless, but that there never was any serious reason to suppose that she was guilty. She has escaped the awful fate with which she was threatened, but the long imprisonment she has undergone, the intolerable suspense and anguish inflicted upon her, the outrageous injury to her feelings as a woman and as a daughter, are chargeable directly to the police and legal authorities. That she should have been subjected to these is a shame to Massachusetts, which the good sense of the jury in acquitting her only in part removes.

New York Recorder—No other verdict was possible, in view of the utter destruction of the theory, not at one point but at many, and at all points that were vital on which District Attorney Knowlton sought to convict Miss Borden. There is, we believe, a very general feeling of indignation over the methods of the prosecuting authorities in this case. From first to last it was not a prosecution in the interest of society, but a persecution in the interest of a police conspiracy to fit facts to preconceived theory, and convict an innocent woman by fair means or foul.

New York Herald—It will be the verdict of the great public, which has read the evidence given in the case. Any other result of the trial would have shocked the popular mind as a wrenching of justice. The government made the most of the evidence within its reach, and its side was summed up by its counsel with masterly ability. But the government had no case.

Boston Globe—The verdict of acquittal which was given yesterday by the "twelve good men and true" at New Bedford will find, from that larger jury, the public, general acquiescence and approval. It was, indeed, foreshadowed during the memorable trial. It may almost be said to have been anticipated by the great majority who followed the case, before either of the great final arguments of the counsel on either side. Congratulations upon the outcome of the trial will assuredly be showered in generous measure upon the woman who, after ten months of uncertainty, anxiety and imprisonment, is now to regain the boon of freedom. There may well be congratulations, also, for Massachusetts and her people upon the possession of so excellent and so impartial a judicial system as that under which, without delay as without haste, one of the most celebrated cases of the time has been heard and definitely decided.

Boston Herald—The acquittal of Lizzie Borden cannot have been a surprise to the public, for the tendency of the trial in its later stages was distinctly against a verdict of guilty. People—and there are a good many of them—who have believed from the first that she was not clear of grave suspicion, have been compelled to recognize that the evidence as brought out at the trial fell far short of fixing the crime upon her. The charge of Judge Dewey was practically and logically an instruction to acquit. The judge laid down the sound principles that "the law puts on the government the burden of proving guilt beyond a reasonable doubt," and that, "if not legally proved to be guilty, the defendant must be declared to be not guilty." With this instruction in mind the defectiveness of the evidence made the duty of the jury plain.

Boston Journal—The verdict of the jury at New Bedford, acquitting Miss Lizzie Borden of the charge of murdering her father and stepmother, saves from deadly peril and vindicates from cruel suspicion a true, modest and upright woman. The justness of the verdict will be approved by the almost unbroken sentiment of the community. The swiftness with which it was rendered, especially when the force and ability with which Mr. Knowlton presented the case of the prosecution is considered, is almost as gratifying as the verdict itself, for it attests the completeness with which Miss Borden's innocence was established in the minds of the jury.

It is with no ordinary satisfaction that we record this result of the trial. We make no pretense of having been wholly calm and impartial in our attitude touching this remarkable case. From the outset, when it became apparent that the suspicions of the police were centered upon Miss Borden, our sympathies have been with her. The theory of the government involved such monstrous and incredible wickedness in the prisoner as to make its acceptance revolting to every humane instinct. That the accused person was a woman, that she had led hitherto a blameless and useful life, and that the victims of the tragedy were her own parents were reasons sufficient to enlist sympathy with her; and to these reasons were added the pertinacity savoring of persecution with which the Fall River police, once possessed of their theory, bent all their energies to securing her conviction. The ordinary rules of decorum, which forbid the expression of opinion while a cause is pending, were suspended in this unusual case, and the guidance of popular judgment in right channels became a duty, in view of the flood of malignant calumnies to which the prisoner was subjected. Nothing can efface from her memory these 10 dreadful months of grief, suspicion and imprisonment, and no recompense can be made her for all that she has passed through; but she passes from the New Bedford court room into the light of day a free woman, relieved and vindicated.

Boston Post: The verdict of the Borden jury undoubtedly meets popular approval. It satisfies the judgment which the great public has passed upon the evidence produced at the trial. And now that Lizzie Borden has been pronounced innocent, no man or woman has a right to question her innocence. She has passed through the fiery ordeal and has come out unscathed. The supreme test which the justice of civilized peoples prescribes for those accused of crime has been applied to this woman and the highest authority known to our law has declared her guiltless. This should be the end of it. The mystery may remain. A thousand puzzling things connected with the tragedy may never be explained. But the verdict rendered yesterday must forever stop the mouth of calumny and forbid the utterance of suspicion regarding the woman who has faced her accusers and successfully refuted their charges. Lizzie Borden is innocent in the eyes of the people as she is before the law.

Springfield Republican—Lizzie Borden is legally innocent. A person is presumed to be guiltless until guilt is proved, and in her case guilt was very far from being proved. But this unfortunate woman, even now that she has been acquitted, stands in a terrible position, because so long as the assassin of her father and stepmother remain undiscovered and unpunished there will be many people who will still believe her guilty. Casting aside speculations as to the woman's sanity—and these murders were truly maniacal—the result of this trial leaves no one with any intellectual justification for affirming that Miss Borden is guilty; it leaves every mind suspended in an atmosphere of doubt, and all who fairly consider the problem must now become agnostics as to the identity of the guilty one. But the human mind is not content with negations, and thus in its groping for affirmations a cruel injustice may be done the acquitted person. It is to be sincerely hoped that Miss Borden will not be wronged in this manner. But who killed Abbie and Andrew Borden? We cannot help seeking the solution of the mystery which is now back in the hands of a baffled police, deep and dark as ever.

Worcester Spy—Now that Miss Lizzie Borden is acquitted, it is to be hoped that she will be allowed that seclusion and rest from the popular gaze which she so deeply yearns for and which she so richly merits, as well because of her plucky bearing under terrific strain, as because, at the demand of technical justice, she has been forced to undergo horrible and undeserved torture.

Worcester Telegram—The speedy verdict of not guilty in the Borden case meets popular approval, and no one doubts that from the evidence presented justice is done. It is seldom that a case is discussed with such temper at so great a distance from the scene of the tragedy, as this case has been, considered here in streets and everywhere that men gather. The male residents of this city by a large majority consider the verdict insufficient, because it did not order the entire police force of Fall River to be hanged or imprisoned for life, while the government prosecutors are denounced in fiery language. As a matter of fact, the Fall River police deserve general condemnation. They were inefficient and blundering to begin with, and having blundered they sought to strengthen the insufficient evidence they had stumbled upon by trickery that was uncovered by the skillful cross-questioning of ex-Governor Robinson, thus destroying the case the government had fashioned against the prisoner. She is now guiltless of the murders in the eye of the law, and cannot be tried for that crime again, should she today state that she killed her father and stepmother. Had the Fall River police made no arrests they might have secured evidence in time that would have led to the solution of the mystery and the punishment of the murderer. No one will ever again be arraigned for the murder of Andrew J. Borden and his wife. The object lesson in this case is the danger of democracy. The Fall River police were useless, inefficient, the tools of a rum city government; instead of working they did not hesitate to lie and put up just such tricks to procure the conviction of a prisoner whose life would have paid the penalty that they would upon a prisoner charged with petty larceny or drunkenness, or in getting an office for a Democrat. A Democratic city government and police force is a menace to life and good government. Lizzie Borden should ever remember the good-for-nothing police of Fall River with gratitude.

We have been time and again asked the question why the Chilton Paints have such a high gloss. The Chilton Paint Co. in buying linseed oil, contracts for "prime, well-settled, old-fashioned, raw linseed oil." This is, being interpreted, oil crushed from prime or first quality flaxseed and which has been tanked and allowed to settle. The oil is then drawn from the upper part of the tank, leaving undisturbed the lower part. "Old-fashioned linseed oil" is from seed crushed and pressed instead of a recent method called the naphtha process. Having obtained this oil, the Chilton Co. tank it again, and the oil gradually loses what little moisture it originally possessed and becomes very heavy bodied. It is this cause and the seven mixings and grindings given each shade, crushing and grinding each particle of pigment into each particle of oil that produces the lustre. On well painted houses this gloss alone has been known to last three years; ordinarily the gloss on newly painted houses where common paints are used vanishes in from six months to one year.

DE WOLF & VINCENT, Agents.

THE COUNSEL INTERVIEWED.

Participants in the Famous Trial Express Their Views.

Mr. Robinson was seen after the adjournment of the court by a Standard man. He said: "It was a just and proper verdict, rendered on the evidence, and the jury have freed an innocent woman." Speaking further of the case, he stated that he had received during the past two weeks more than 50 letters from persons alleging that they had committed the crime. He had also received hatchets and other articles, the latest arrival being the handle of a hatchet. The prisoner has received his constant aid and advice, Mr. Robinson having visited her each evening at the jail. Last night she was very nervous, and the intense strain seemed to have completely undone her.

Mr. Jennings said: "I do not see how any other verdict could have been given under the circumstances. There was no evidence to convict her, and I have been confident all long that she would be acquitted."

Mr. Adams expressed the opinion that a verdict of "Not guilty" meant more than that. It meant that the girl's innocence was established. He also stated that there had not been one of the three counsel for the defense who thought her guilty since the commencement of the case.

Mr. Knowlton, when questioned, was silent concerning the verdict, not wishing to express an opinion in his capacity as prosecuting officer of the commonwealth.

Miss Lizzie Borden was unwilling to make any statement in regard to her future plans, and Mr. Robinson stated that she had now been an object of public curiosity for so long that he should desire to have her remain quiet as long as possible.

It is understood that but one vote was taken in the jury room on the guilt of the defendant. The skulls and hatchets were not examined, and there was but little deliberation.

HER RELIGIOUS ADVISERS.

Rev. Messrs. Jubb and Buck Were Confident of Miss Borden's Innocence.

Fall River, June 21.—Rev. W. Walker Jubb, in reply to questions put to him by the newspaper men, said:

"I am thoroughly convinced of Lizzie Borden's innocence. She is no more guilty of the murder of her father and stepmother than I am. I have seen a good deal of Miss Borden prior to her confinement in jail and after it. I held several interviews with her, both in Taunton and while she was in the dock at New Bedford. My theory is that the murders were committed by some one who had spite against Mr. Borden, and who had a double object in view, murder and robbery. Lizzie never was on unpleasant terms with her stepmother. Occasionally Emma and her stepmother had words. Lizzie always attended church in company with her stepmother when the latter was able to attend church. No one can alter my idea as to the fact that some unknown man committed the murders."

Rev. E. H. Buck said the verdict was what he had expected. The government's case would not admit of any different decision at the hands of the jury, he said. "I feel much confidence in Miss Borden, because I have known her in church work for five years previous to the murders. She was a teacher in my Sunday school class, and a constant attendant at prayer meetings. My estimate of her character was based on the conversations I had with her, and from what I know of her church work. I could not believe, and never have believed, that she was guilty. At one time I did expect a disagreement, but I am happy to say that I drove that terrible thought from my mind. Mr. Knowlton's plea was gossip. He placed no credence at all on the testimony of the defense's witnesses. In my opinion the slayer of the murdered couple got into the house unknown to Lizzie or Bridget, and completed his horrible work."

Hon. Charles T. Gallagher.

Hon. Charles T. Gallagher of Boston, who was a boy friend of District Attorney Hosea Knowlton, and in the law school with both Lawyers Adams and Jennings, said: "I am not surprised at the verdict. The evidence was entirely circumstantial, but, to my own mind, it satisfies me that if Lizzie Borden did not commit the crime she certainly must have knowledge of the guilty party, because, on the facts, it would be impossible for her to have been in the house while the murders occurred without her being aware of the fact. From a lawyer's standpoint there was certainly evidence of opportunity on her part coupled with a motive. The motive, of course, is shown in the killing of the stepmother first and the father afterward, as the inheritance of property would thus run to her, and the opportunity is patent. The case will go down to history as one of the famous murder trials of modern times."

Governor Russell.

Governor Russell—"I am not surprised. No other verdict could have been rendered by the jury on evidence not proven. I think that it is also in accord with public opinion. No matter what the suspicions may have been, if not proven in law, of course, they do not hold."

Attorney General Pillsbury.

"Newspapers can take care of their own lies in the Borden case," said Attorney General Pilsbury to a Boston Herald reporter on School street yesterday, shortly after the bulletins had announced the acquittal of Lizzie Borden. He had just finished a sidewalk conversation with two gentlemen in regard to the case, and they appeared to be chaffing him on the turn in affairs. He appeared to the Herald representative to be very much displeased with the verdict, whether it was a disappointment or not, and refused absolutely to comment any further than the remark above quoted, upon which readers can place their own construction.

George Fred Williams.

Hon. George Fred Williams thinks the acquittal was eminently just, and further, taking into consideration the evidence presented by the government, that the verdict not only acquits Miss Borden of the legal charge of murder, but of the crime itself. The government had a very weak case.

He had read all the evidence, and had become convinced of the utter impossibility of Miss Borden committing the crime. It seemed possible to Mr. Williams, although he did not advance the theory as infallible, that the murder might have been committed by some man who knew the house, and had entered it with the premeditated idea of killing both people.

So far as the stain of suspicion was concerned Mr. Williams thought the trial was in one way a kindness to the discharged prisoner, as malicious persons who would naturally be delighted to point her out as the probable murderess could now do her no injury.

The News at Fall River.

FALL RIVER, Mass., June 21.—The news of Lizzie Borden's acquittal was received with the greatest surprise in this city. Even her warmest friends and most ardent supporters dared not hope anything better than a disagreement, after reading the district attorney's forcible argument in behalf of the government.

When it was flashed over the wires that the prisoner had been acquitted, the greatest excitement prevailed. Upon the streets the sole topic of converstaion was the unlooked-for discharge of Lizzie Borden.

A reporter entered the house and was granted an interview with Lizzie, through an introduction by a friend who accompanied him. The party, which included Mr., Mrs. and Miss Holmes, Emma and Lizzie Borden, Joseph A. Bowen and Mrs. Jubb, was seated in the drawing room. Lizzie said, "I am the happiest woman in the world." She did not care to dwell upon the subject of the trial, and said that the whole party had agreed not to discuss that subject.

Lizzie is looking better than ever before. She was dressed in a black silk dress and was smiling pleasantly while conversing with everybody. She said she had a pleasant journey from New Bedford, being on the road a little over an hour.

About the street corners groups gathered, discussing the all-absorbing topic, and the general feeling is surprise, bordering upon indignation.

District Attorney Knowlton.

The compliments that have been paid District Attorney Knowlton's plea are deserved, and they come at a time when they can hardly be otherwise than peculiarly grateful to their recipient. The government has had a hard task in this trial, and it has received small encouragement in comparison with the defense in its prosecution of its work. Yet the lawyers concerned in it have done their full duty, and if the acknowledgment of this does come a trifle tardily, it is better than for it not to come at all.—Boston Herald.

Knowlton has had an uphill task from the beginning, even the judges had to decide against him every time, but he will make a strong candidate for attorney-general just the same.—Boston Record.

"CHIMMY."

He Attended the Borden Trial as the Standard's Prize Hustler.

Jimmy Harlow was a professional bootblack before the exigencies of the Borden trial generated chain lightning in his feet, then he became a copy hustler for the Standard. Of the tireless and devoted army of boys who have rushed copy between the court house and Standard building for the past two weeks Jimmy, or "Chimmy" as he calls himself, was the swiftest. The undeveloped speed which has been going to waste in the bootblacking business was let loose.

Jimmy Harlow.

Jimmy has tawny hair and a tilt on his nose and a twinkle in his left eye, and he likes to be mixed up in big events. When he is very much on the alert he seems to expand and almost fill the regimentals which his tailor cut too large.

Like his famous brother craftsman, Gavroche, in fiction, Jimmie must have been born for great things. The French revolution "discovered" Gavroche, and the Borden trial will make Jimmie famous as a prize hustler.

The Standard is glad to print his picture. If the reader sees a very bright, very dirty, very cute bootblack with a brand new box slung over his arm, who can run like a professional sprinter, talk like a professional scrapper and black boots like a profesional bootblack, why, that's "Chimmy."

Postmaster Arrested.

Yankton, S. D., June 21.—Michael O'Shea, deputy postmaster at Running Water, a small place west of Yankton, is here under arrest, charged with defrauding the government. He is $10,000 short in his accounts. He forged orders upon other officers and cashed them himself.

Death of Pitcher Bayne.

PHILADELPHIA, June 21.—Clarence S. Bayne, the star pitcher and captain of the University of Pennsylvania baseball team, died last evening.

ART AT THE ACADEMY.

Excellent Showing Made by Youthful Pupils in Drawing.

At the art rooms of H. S. Hutchinson & Co. is shown an exhibit of work done by pupils at the Friends academy. This branch of work was opened at the academy in January last, under the supervision of Arthur Cumming, and considering the age of the pupils, ranging from 10 to 15 years, the results are remarkable, and reflect any amount of credit upon this effective and successful teacher, as well as upon the pupils.

The work is divided into two classes, the pupils of which are as follows:

Mechanical Drawing—Charles F. Wing and Atmore Robinson, both of whom are fitting for the Massachusetts Institute of Technology.

Stump Drawing—Roger D. Swaim, Nina Thornton, Leroy Thornton, Charlie Clifford, Stanley Wood, Francis Allen, Tom Knowles, Francis Winslow, Emma F. Dodge, Nat Gifford, C. A. Milliken, Edith Terry, Bertha A. Cook, Helen Freeman, Leroy Howland, Henry White, Ned Pierce, Fred H. Taber, A. B. Sturgis, S. R. Negus, Lillian Swift, Annie Winsor, Tom Tillinghast, Arthur G. Rotch, Harry S. Knowles, Bessie Handy, Charlie S. Kelley, W. P. Winsor, Bessie Hayes, Lizzie Wood, Rachel G. Grinnell, Emerson H. Slade.

The mechanical drawing class shows 24 sheets, excellently performed, and showing much ability, especially in so short a period of development.

The stump work is all done in solid, light and shade, very effective and quite artistic. No outline work is permitted at the school. The drawings, although not always perfect in line and angle and curve, are yet an interesting study, and the results are encouraging to the pupils, who are able with this method to get considerable striking effect with a short season's work. It is the purpose of the trustees to make this branch of the curriculum preliminary to the work at the Swain Free school, and it is believed that when the equipment for the branch is made more complete, a foundation will be laid which will enable academy graduates to accomplish remarkable results in the advanced courses.

NEW FIRE ALARM BOXES.

Two new fire alarm boxes have just been set up: No. 134 at the corner of Belleville avenue and Nye street, and No. 135 at the corner of Belleville avenue and Coggeshall street. Engines will respond as follows: First alarm, engines 1 and 7, ladder 2 and hose 2; second alarm, engines 2 and 5, ladder 1 and hose 1; third alarm, engine 4.

Modern Methods.

New Business Manager, (discussing projects for putting "Daily Relapse" on its feet)—In the first place we want to get out a paper twice the present size; then, reduce expenses by cutting telegraph down two-thirds, discharging all but two or three of the reporters, and—

Managing Editor—But what on earth will we fill the paper with?

New Business Manager—Why, with coupons, of course!—Puck.

DO YOU COUGH DON'T DELAY TAKE KEMP'S BALSAM THE BEST COUGH CURE

It Cures Colds, Coughs, Sore Throat, Croup, Influenza, Whooping Cough, Bronchitis and Asthma. A certain cure for Consumption in first stages, and a sure relief in advanced stages. Use at once. You will see the excellent effect after taking the first dose. Sold by dealers everywhere. Large bottles 50 cents and $1.00.

Town Talk,

The new High Grade Flour.

Makes MOST, BEST, WHITEST, SWEETEST BREAD.

DENISON BROS. CO., Wholesale Agents.

C. W. HASKINS

No. 20 PURCHASE STREET,

Has replenished his stock since the holidays, and now offers at very low prices a good variety of Diamond Rings, Fine Jewelry, Gold and Silver Watches, Chains, &c.

His stock of Sterling Silver Spoons, Forks, Fancy Table Ware and Novelties is very extensive; these goods are lower in price than ever before.

18 KARAT WEDDING RINGS A SPECIALTY.

You can save money buying of him your Spectacles and Eye Glasses, fit and quality guaranteed.

Watch, Clock and Jewelry repairing by experienced workmen.

Pimples, blotches and eruptions completely vanish before a steady use of Beecham's (Worth a Guinea a Box.) Pills (Tasteless) and health again glows in the pure skin and clear complexion.

25 cents a box. 37

GEORGE C. BLISS, FLORIST.

34 Arnold Street,

CORNER COTTAGE.

TELEPHONE, DAY OR NIGHT.

ELLIS'S FINE ART STORE,

106 William Street 106

Telephone Number 64-6.

Now Open with a Splendid Stock of Art Goods, Art Materials, Statuary, &c.

Fine Selection of BRIDAL GIFTS AND SEASON PRESENTS.

COAL —OF— All Kinds and the Best Quality —FOR— DOMESTIC AND FACTORY USE CONSTANTLY IN STOCK.

HAVING purchased the business and good will of Bates & Howard, am prepared to fill orders at either my old office at yard or new office, No. 224 Purchase street.

YARD, ATLANTIC WHARF, FOOT OF CANNON STREET.

ALBERT W. HOLMES.

TELEPHONES;

YARD OFFICE, 92—3.

PURCHASE STREET OFFICE, 92—2.

Lawn Mowers Sharpened, Cleaned, AND Repaired, —AT— P. P. JENNEY & SON'S, 148 PLEASANT ST.

Telephone, 237-3. ws

HATCH & COMPANY'S EXPRESS,

No. 5 Ricketson Block, New Bedford,

DAILY,

By Passenger Trains, to all Points on the Old Colony Railroad and its Connections.

Administrator's Notice.

NOTICE is hereby given that the subscriber has been duly appointed administrator of the estate of MANUEL PHILIP DE SIMAS late of Pico, Western Islands, deceased, intestate, and has taken upon himself that trust by giving bond, as the law directs. All persons having demands upon the estate of said deceased are hereby required to exhibit the same; and all persons indebted to said estate are called upon to make payment to

ANTONE L. SYLVIA, Administrator.

June 20, 1893. je21-28-jy5

Executor's Notice.

NOTICE is hereby given that the subscriber has been duly appointed executrix of the will of JOHN KIRK, late of New Bedford, in the County of Bristol, deceased, and has taken upon herself that trust by giving bond, as the law directs. All persons having demands upon the estate of said deceased are hereby required to exhibit the same; and all persons indebted to said estate are called upon to make payment to

EVELINE KIRK, Executrix,

Or J. Frank Kirk, 374 Purchase street.

June 2d, 1893. je7-14-21

FOR LANGUOR AND LOSS OF APPETITE, USE

BROMO-SELTZER,

IT INVIGORATES PROMPTLY AND SURELY.

Lawn Mowers!

We carry the Philadelphia, Magic, New Departure, Union, Diamond and New England High Wheel.

You must be suited with some one of these makes. We are selling a warranted mower, parts for which can be supplied at any time, for $3.50.

F. L. SOWLE & CO.,

OPPOSITE CITY CLOCK.

NEW BEDFORD, Saturday, June 24.

THE BARNUM & BAILEY

Greatest Show on Earth

AND IN ADDITION THE

Unparalleled Terpsichorean Spectacle

IMRE KIRALFY'S

Columbus

—AND THE—

DISCOVERY OF AMERICA.

The Most Amazing Production Ever Devised.

3 Circus Companies in 3 Rings.
Stupendous Olympia Hippodrome.
2 Menageries of Wild and Trained Beasts.
2 Elevated Stages, 2 Herds of Elephants.
2 Droves of Camels, 2 Open Dens,
80 Daring Circus Acts.
20 Clowns, 30 Animal Clowns,
50 Aerialists, 100 Performers.

Beautiful Supernatural Illusions.
400 Horses, 64 Cars, 4 Trains, 400 Dancers.

ACTUALLY 1,200 PEOPLE EMPLOYED.

Positively Everything as Represented without Exaggeration.

CAPITAL INVESTED, $3,500,000. DAILY EXPENSES, $7,300.

P. T. BARNUM & J. A. BAILEY Equal Owners

Now Presented Truthfully in all its Monster Magnificence of Historical Pageantry and Display, and with all its vast Departments added to and overflowing

With the World's Greatest Attractions.

Thick Animals, Athletic Sports,
Curious Creatures, Spanish Games,
Intrepid Acts, Daring Feats,
Dancing Girls, Moorish Warriors.

Tournaments, Sieges, Battles, Fetes, Dances, Songs

Religious Ceremonies, Premiere Danseuses,
Royal Receptions, Triumphal Pageants,
Living Tableaux, Ancient Combats,
Enchanting Music, Nautical Scenes,
Imperial Splendors, Tremendous Displays.

300 Specially Imported Foreign Dancers.

Columbus Triumphal Entry into Barcelona.

The First Voyage of Discovery.

SPAIN and the SPANIARDS under FERDINAND and ISABELLA.

With all the Splendors of their Brilliant Court.
Moonlight Scenes in Granada's Palaces.
The Famous Palace of the Alhambra.

Entrancing and Delightful Views of Old Spain.

Magnificent Fetes and Triumphs.
Life and Trials of Columbus Illustrated.

Pitched Battles, Desperate Sorties,
Street Fights, Single Encounters,
Elegant Scenery, Costly Costumes,
Wonderful Effects, Ancient Armor.

Forming without doubt the most wonderful and really sublime Historic, Nautical and Dramatic Spectacle ever witnessed.

Giant Horse, 7 1-2 Feet High.

Dwarf Cow, 2¾ feet high; Miniature Zebu, 2¾ feet high; Hairless Horse, without a single hair; Curious Bull, with 3 eyes, 3 nostrils and 2 horns.

2 Monster Performances Daily at 2 and 8 P. M.

Doors open an hour earlier.

Admission to everything, 50 cents.
Children under 9 years, 25 cents.
Reserved numbered seats at the regular price, and admission tickets at usual advance at Wright Drug Co's Store on Purchase St.

GORGEOUS NEW STREET PARADE

With Elegant Floats, Illustrating the History of America, Arabian Nights, Children's Fables and Nursery Rhymes, with Living Representations of Fairies, Historical Persons, &c., at 9 o'clock a. m. on day of show.

Cheap Excursions on all Railroads.

Will Exhibit in Fall River June 23

je17-19-21-23-w15-22

HOLY CROSS 10. BROWNS 5.

Wretched Fielding and Stupid Base Running at Providence.

Providence, R. I., June 21.—The Browns played a wretched fielding game yesterday, and when they got on bases failed to score because of stupid running. The score:

HOLY CROSS.

	ab	r	1b	po	a	e
Bannon, p.	5	2	1	2	9	0
Cotter, 1b.	3	3	1	13	0	0
McCarthy, l.f.	3	3	3	1	0	0
Lowney, 3b.	3	0	0	3	1	0
Igoe, 2b.	4	0	0	1	0	1
Howard, s.s.	4	0	0	3	5	0
Kelley, r.f.	4	0	0	0	0	0
Grady, c.	4	2	1	3	1	0
Johnson, c.f.	4	0	0	1	0	2
Totals,	36	10	6	27	16	3

BROWN.

	ab	r	1b	po	a	e
Weeks, 1b.	4	1	1	9	0	2
Sexton, r.f., p.	3	1	2	1	1	1
Steere, s.s.	5	1	2	1	4	2
Jones, 2b.	3	0	1	0	0	1
Magill, 3b.	3	1	0	2	2	1
George, c.f.	4	0	0	0	0	1
McLane, l.f.	4	0	2	1	0	2
Lang, c.	3	0	0	8	1	1
W. Steere, r.f.	1	0	1	0	0	0
Robinson, p.	2	0	0	0	1	1
Greene, r.f., c.	1	0	0	2	6	1
Totals,	33	5	9	24	9	13

Innings, 1 2 3 4 5 6 7 8 9
Holy Cross, 1 3 0 0 0 1 2 2 x—10
Brown, 4 0 0 0 0 0 1 0 0—5

Earned runs—Holy Cross 2. Brown 1. Two-base hits—McCarthy, Steere. McLane, Weeks. Three-base hit—Cotter. Stolen bases—Bannon, Cotter 2, McCarthy, Lowney 2, Grady, Sexton, Jones, Magill. First base on balls—Off Bannon 4, off Sexton 2. First base on errors—Holy Cross 7, Brown 3. Struck out—Igoe 3, Bannon, Lowney, Kelley, Johnson 2, George, Robinson, Greene. Passed balls—Greene 2, Grady 1. Wild pitch—Bannon. Hit by pitched ball—Lowney, Cotter. Sacrifice hit—Sexton, Jones, Greene, r.f., c. Time—2 hours 15 minutes. Umpire—McMurray.

QUITE DIFFERENT.

The Brooklyns Show the Bostons What They Can Do In Batting.

Boston, June 21.—The second game of the present Brooklyn series was considerably different than the one of Monday, and Boston was not "in it" at all. Kennedy pitched a fine game and was grandly supported, while Nichols was easy to hit, and his fielders were decidedly "off." Ganzel made a wonderful one-hand catch in right field, as did Stovey in left. Long made a phenomenal stop and throw. Foutz, Stovey, Burns, Ganzel, Duffy, McCarthy, Carroll and Corcoran batted very hard.

BROOKLYN.	AB	R	BH	PO	A	E
Foutz, cf.	4	3	3	3	0	0
Stovey, lf.	4	4	3	2	0	0
Brouthers, 1b.	3	1	1	6	0	0
C. Daily, c.	4	0	1	8	0	0
Burns, rf.	4	0	0	2	0	0
T. Daily, 2b.	5	1	0	3	2	0
Shoch, 3b.	3	0	1	0	0	0
Corcoran, ss.	4	2	1	2	1	3
Kennedy, p.	4	1	0	1	0	0
Totals,	38	11	12	27	6	1

BOSTON.	AB	R	BH	PO	A	E
Long, ss.	5	1	0	1	3	1
Ganzel, rf.	5	0	1	2	0	0
Duffy, cf.	4	1	3	3	2	0
McCarthy, 3b.	4	0	4	0	0	0
Nash, 3b.	4	0	0	0	3	0
Tucker, 1b.	3	1	0	8	0	0
Carroll, lf.	3	1	2	1	0	0
Bennett, c.	3	0	0	2	1	2
Nichols, p.	4	0	0	0	4	1
Totals,	35	4	10	27	13	5

Brooklyn 2 0 0 4 4 1 3 1 0—11
Boston 0 0 0 1 1 2 0 1 0—4

Earned runs—Brooklyn, 3; Boston, 4. Home run—Foutz. Three-base hit—Corcoran. Two-base hits—Foutz, Burns, Stovey, Duffy, Ganzel. Sacrifice hits—C. Daily, Carroll. Stolen bases—Stovey, McCarthy. First base on balls—Brooklyn, 4; Boston, 2. First base on errors—Brooklyn, 3. Struck out—C. Daily (2), Nash, Nichols. Umpire—Hurst.

Other Games.

At New York:
Washington, 0 0 0 0 0 5 2 1—16
New York, 0 0 0 1 1 2 0 1—5
Base hits—Washington, 14; New York, 9. Errors—Washington, 8; New York, 7. Batteries—Meekin and Farrell; Baldwin and Milligan.

At Cincinnati:
Louisville, 1 0 1 0 1 0 0 0 0—3
Cincinnati, 0 0 0 0 0 0 0 0 0—0
Base hits—Louisville, 8; Cincinnati, 7. Error—Cincinnati, 1. Batteries—Hemming and Weaver; Sullivan and Vaughan.

At Pittsburg:
Cleveland 3 2 0 0 2 4 0 0—10
Pittsburg 2 2 2 0 0 0 1 0—6
Base hits—Cleveland, 14; Pittsburg, 10. Errors—Cleveland, 6; Pittsburg, 4. Batteries—Clarkson and Zimmer; Ehret and Miller.

At Philadelphia:
Philadelphia 0 2 8 0 0 0 0 0—10
Baltimore 0 0 0 0 1 0 0 2—3
Base hits—Philadelphia, 10; Baltimore, 10. Errors—Philadelphia, 10; Baltimore, 7. Batteries—Weyhing and Cross; McNabb and Clark.

New England League.

At Lowell—Lowell, 12; Lewiston, 10.
At Brockton—Portland, 22; Brockton, 21.

Eastern League Games.
At Providence—Providence, 12; Albany, 9.
At Springfield—Springfield, 19; Troy, 7.

National League Standing.

Clubs	Won	Lost	Avg	Clubs	Won	Lost	Avg
Phila...	27	15	64.3	Baltimore	22	24	47.8
Boston...	27	16	62.8	Wash...	20	23	46.5
Cleve...	29	17	62.3	Cincinnati	19	25	43.2
Pittsburg.	24	20	54.5	Chicago...	18	23	43.9
Brooklyn.	23	19	53.6	St. Louis..	18	24	42.9
New York.	23	22	51.1	Louisville.	7	32	21.2

New England League Standing.

Clubs	Won	Lost	Avg	Clubs	Won	Lost	Avg
Fall River	21	12	63.6	Dover....	14	19	42.4
Lowell	19	14	57.6	Lewiston..	12	20	37.5
Brockton.	20	16	55.6	Portland..	8	24	25.0
Portland..	20	13	60.6	Brockton..	8	24	25.0

NINE PERSONS KILLED.

Dozen Out of One Hundred Injured May Die.

Bad Disaster on Manhattan Beach Railroad.

Train from Sheepshead Bay Wrecked by a Defective Switch.

NEW YORK, June 21.—A Manhattan beach train, loaded with hundreds of passengers on the way from Sheepshead bay track to the Bay Ridge ferry last evening, was wrecked at the Ocean parkway tunnel at Parkville. Over 100 persons were seriously injured, 9 were killed, and a dozen may die from the effects of their injuries. Those killed were:

Patrick Daly, court officer in Third district police court, New York, crushed to death beneath a car in the tunnel.
William Pringle, residence unknown, was beheaded.
Robert Curry, New York policeman, 652 West Fourteenth street, died in half an hour after the accident.
Henry Spink, city marshal, attached to Jefferson market court.
Unknown man.
P. J. McDonegal of Philadelphia died at Seney hospital.
Fred Johnson, West Seventeenth street, this city.
An unknown man also died at Seney hospital.
Bartholomew, died at the same institution.

The Train Was Derailed

at the entrance to the tunnel under the Parkway boulevards, Parkville, by a defective switch. Four cars went off the track. Men who rode upon the steps of the open excursion cars were hurled against the side of the tunnel and ground under the wheels.

All the ambulances of the Brooklyn hospitals were called out to carry the injured to hospitals. The injured were those who were riding upon the steps and those who jumped.

The track is double, but in the tunnel the two tracks come together. To the south of the tunnel about 100 yards is a switch operated from a tower on the west side of the tunnel.

This switch consists of two lengths of rails and was intended to prevent a collision. Should the switchtender see that two trains were likely to collide in the tunnel he could throw the west bound train from the track into the ditch by means of the switch. Switchman Gary, 21 years old, was in charge of the switch when the accident occurred. A youth with a bicycle says that as the train approached the switchtender

Started Up From a Sleep

and pulled a lever, and the rumble and jar of four derailed cars was heard.

There is a ditch on the right hand side of the track, and the embankment rises abruptly at an angle of about 50 degrees. The men who sat upon the steps on the right hand side of the cars were jammed against the earth, and their feet and legs were caught under the steps.

General Superintendent Blood was at the scene within 20 minutes after the accident. He took off his coat and directed his attention to the railroad men.

Switch Operator P. S. McGarry was arrested and taken to Gravesend. He took his arrest in a dazed sort of a way.

The accident delayed trains more or less on all the branches of the Long Island railroad. At Coney Island the story of what had happened was known long before the last train left. This made most of the passengers timid, and as a result when another accident happened to one of the trains running from the race track while it was running into the depot, there was considerable excitement. The train consisted of an engine and eight cars. It was loaded as full as possible with passengers. As it made the last switches in the yard four of the cars left the track. As the cars went bumping over the ties the passengers leaped from their seats. The train was running slowly, however, and no one was injured.

A Courageous Woman.

CHAMPAIGN, Ills., June 21.—A New Orleans limited passenger train bound for Chicago with eight loaded coaches, when near Rantoul, running at a high rate of speed, was flagged by a woman, who informed the crew that a short distance ahead of them a trestle had burned out. The passengers made up a handsome purse of money and presented it to the woman.

Grover's Affliction.

WASHINGTON, June 21.—President Cleveland's illness is caused by gout. His right foot is so swollen that it is difficult for him to get on a shoe in the morning. Within the last week while at work in the office of receiving a caller he has often been unable to suppress a cry of pain at a sudden twinge of spasm.

No Let-Up.

WEST SUPERIOR, Wis., June 31.—The forests fires along South Shore and Northern Pacific railways are still burning and at Sanborn & Lampson's lumber yard, and several dwellings have also been burned. Conditions on the South Shore report Ewen, Mich., entirely devastated.

Appraiser Cooper's Case.

WASHINGTON, June 21.—The preliminary report of the committee on Appraiser Cooper of New York was received yesterday by Secretary Carlisle. He left for Philadelphia before examining the report in detail, and his absence in that city will delay action in the case.

To Help Others.

NEW YORK, June 21.—The national Bank of Commerce has decided to take out $1,000,000 in clearing house certificates. This action was taken not because it needed funds for its own use, but to make it easier for less strong banks to follow the precedent.

Firemen Probably Fatally Injured.

NEW YORK, June 21.—A fire at 887 Ninth avenue yesterday afternoon resulted in the injury of eight firemen. Three of the men will probably die. The fire was in the cellar of the building, which is occupied as a dyeing and cleaning establishment.

Cheap Rates to the Fair.

NEW YORK, June 21.—The general agents of the trunk lines have decided to recommend to the executive committee of the Trunk Line association a special rate of one fare to Chicago and return on special World's fair excursion trains.

(From Yesterday's Latest Edition.)

NOT GUILTY!

Jury Was Out Only an Hour.

Scene of Enthusiasm in Court Room.

Waving of Handkerchiefs and Cheers.

Accused's Iron Composure Fails Her.

She Bursts Into a Torrent of Tears.

Miss Borden Returns to Fall River.

Scenes Following the Return of the Verdict.

The great trial of Lizzie Andrew Borden, charged with the murder of her father, Andrew Jackson Borden, and her stepmother, Abbie Durfee Borden, came to an abrupt end this afternoon, although the closing scenes were of an intensely dramatic nature.

It was 4 30 o'clock when Lizzie sat in her seat in the dock with a box of flowers in her lap, and was leaning forward and conversing with Charles J. Holmes in a desultory manner. All at once there was a stir, and people began to gather in the room, the reporters' seats being the first to fill.

"What is the matter?" was asked a reporter who had just come in, and he answered, "The jury is ready to report." Miss Borden's face for an instant became very pale, and then the red tide surged back, leaving her with more color than she has had since the commencement of the trial.

Justices Mason, Dewey, and Blodgett took their places on the bench, and the jury who has listened with such patient interest during the long and sweltering days in which the trial has progressed, filed in at 4 32 and took their places.

Simeon Borden, Esq., clerk, said: "The jury will answer to their names as the roll is called," and to the tally of Deputy Sheriff Butman every one of the 12 answered, "Here."

"Lizzie Andrew Borden, stand up," said the clerk, and she did so.

"Gentlemen of the jury, have you agreed upon a verdict?" asked the clerk.

"We have," answered the foreman.

"You will hand it to the court," said the clerk, and it was done.

"Mr. Foreman, look upon the prisoner. Prisoner, look at the foreman," said the clerk.

"What say you, is the prisoner at the bar guilty or not guilty?" asked the clerk.

"Not guilty," said the foreman in a clear, strong voice, which was audible in every part of the room.

In a moment the tense nerves were relaxed, and a storm of applause swept through the audience. Men and women clapped their hands, and in one or two instances cheers were given, while handkerchiefs, fans and hands were waved in the air, by the crowd which had arisen to its feet as if by a common impulse. While these demonstrations were in progress it must not be understood that they were participated in by all, even of the spectators, many of whom looked on glum, mute and unsympathizing, while even others were heard to express decided disapproval at the course events had taken.

In vain did Sheriff Wright stand up and pound frantically on his desk. Order could not be produced for several minutes, and together with the handclapping and other applause the crowd started to get out of the room. The efforts of the sheriff were strongly aided by his deputies, who pushed forward crying "Sit down," and enforcing their commands by vigorous pushing. At length some degree of order was obtained, and then attention was bestowed upon Lizzie A. Borden.

On the announcement of the verdict her iron composure again failed her, and

she bowed her head on the rail of the dock, and burst into a very passion of tears. Her friends, including her faithful sister, Emma, gathered around her and counseled her so that she became after a minute or two more composed.

On the faces of District Attorneys Knowlton and Moody during the announcement of the verdict could not be seen any signs of emotion, and if they felt disappointment they were very successful in hiding it. The face of Andrew J. Jennings was radiant with joy at the announcement and Mr. Adams seemed not much less rejoiced.

A moment later Mr. Knowlton moved that two indictments against Lizzie A. Borden for assault on the person be not prossed, and this was done.

The clerk arose again and said, "Lizzie Andrew Borden, the court orders that you be discharged and go without day."

Chief Justice Mason addressed the jury, thanked them for the patience they had exhibited during the days of the trial, spoke of the fidelity with which they have performed their duties, and said they have the satisfaction of having done their work with fidelity.

The court was adjourned in due form till Monday next, and the final scene in the drama closed, and the greatest criminal trial in the history of the old Bay State was over. The court remains—that Andrew J. Borden and his aged wife were brutally murdered on the 4th of August last, and the question which yet remains to be asked is "Who did it?"

Immediately after the adjournment of the court Miss Borden, accompanied by Miss Emma and John V. Morse, her counsel and other friends, took possession of the judges' room. There an informal reception was held.

When a Standard man looked in on the happy party every lady was in tears. At 5 45 o'clock Miss Borden, accompanied by her sister, left the city for Fall River.

She had the best carriage in Kirby & Hicks' stable. It was in that firm's new landau, drawn by a pair of black horses, set off with gold mounted harnesses, that she departed from the building where so much of her time has been passed during the last two weeks.

A BIG SCOOP.

Evening Standard Led from the Start to the Finish.

The Evening Standard from the start to the finish has led the country in its reports of the Borden murder trial. This afternoon the verdict in the great trial was rendered at 4 32. In three minutes from that time the Standard's big perfecting press started, and in five minutes newsboys were rushing through the streets crying "Standard extra, Lizzie Borden adjudged not guilty!" In less than 10 minutes a second extra was issued with more particulars. At this writing (5 p. m.) the demand for the Standard extras have been enormous, and newsboys who have sold out are besieging the counting room for fresh supplies.

A more complete scoop and signal triumph than the Standard's of this afternoon is unknown in the history of newspapers, not of Bristol county or of this state, but of the country. From the

very first day the Standard's reports have excited the admiration of the visiting newspaper men. Its rapidity in announcing the verdict today awakened amazement, and has been the cause of many hearty congratulations already.

BOARD OF ALDERMEN.

A Special Meeting Draws Jurors and Grants Licenses.

At a special meeting of the board of aldermen at 4 o'clock this afternoon, Mayor Brock presiding, and every member present, the Albion Social and Musical association was granted a club license.

In the absence of City Clerk Leonard, George W. Parker was chosen clerk pro tem.

Aldermen Crapo and Brightman were appointed a committee to draw jurors, and accomplished their duty as follows: Grand Jurors—Mason W. Paige and Dennis Murphy.

Petit Jurors—Amos F. Lovejoy, Pardon A. Macomber, William W. Arnold.

A number of minor petitions, such as common victualers, pool and others, were granted.

It was voted to reconsider the license granted to Mrs. Goggin.

LIZZIE BORDEN LEAVES THE COURT HOUSE A FREE WOMAN.

Knowles & Co.

Now is the time for you to make a call at our store, as we have a full and complete line of warm weather goods.

The largest line of Parasols and Sun Umbrellas to be found in the city.

A bargain in Red and Blue Sun Umbrellas, at $1.75.

Parasols from 89c. to $5.50. Some rare bargains among them. Children's shades 39c. to $1.49.

We have made a cut in Silk Laces, and will sell you all the new and choice effects at 25 per cent. less than you will find them elsewhere.

A splendid line of Cotton Laces from 5 to 45c. per yard.

Our Hosiery Department is full of bargains. An elegant line of fine dropped stitch hose, in blacks, tans, white and almost any color you could wish, at 50c. Also some bargains at 25 and 37 1-2c.

We have secured one case of Ladies' Jersey Vests, worth 12 1-2c., which we shall sell three for 25c. as long as they last.

We are showing the best Ladies' and Gents' 25c. Vest to be found anywhere.

All sizes in Gents' Negligee Shirts, worth from $1.25 to $1.50, for ONE EVEN DOLLAR.

A new and elegant line of Pampas Cloths, 25 or 30 pieces to select from, at 15c.

Twenty-five new styles of the celebrated Puritan Cloths at 12 1-2c. These goods are selling fast. Come while the selection is good.

A new line of Llama Cloths, just what you want for a summer dress, at 12 1-2c.

A good line of Sateens, fine as silk, at 15c.

Knowles & Co.

UNION and FOURTH STS.

SPECIAL NOTICE.

The demand for the famous "J. H. CUTTER" WHISKIES (tor which we are the sole agents in this city) having become so great, many houses out of the State are sending their travelers in here, with the hope of inducing our trade to buy the "Cutter" whiskies from them, by underselling us, or rather trying to. We therefore beg to say to our friends and the public generally, we will NOT allow ourselves to be undersold by any house dealing in the genuine "J. H. CUTTER" WHISKIES, and we are prepared to protect our trade, not only in QUALITY but in PRICES as well.

Very Respectfully,

BENJAMIN DAWSON,
597 Purchase Street.

Sole agent for New Bedford, Mass., for the famous J. H. Cutter Whiskies.   8p

---

A WELCOME WINDFALL

Comes to Arcee Booth's Niece Just When She Was In Need of It.

ASBURY PARK, N. J., June 21.—Marion Booth Douglass, niece of the late Edwin Booth, under whose will, filed yesterday, she will receive a bequest of $10,000, yesterday appeared before the overseer of the poor for Neptune township and requested the township's support of herself and child, alleging that her husband, Byron Douglass, the actor, refused it. Douglass, who is living luxuriously in a cottage here, was thereupon arrested and brought before Justice of the Peace Borden, who directed him to either furnish bonds for the support of his wife (or cause her to go to jail). Douglass, after some negotiation, gave his wife $100, and she thereupon withdrew her suit. A few hours after this young woman both at the time of the murder and at the time nearly approaching it.

Won by Lowlander.

NEW YORK, June 21.—The suburban handicap, of a guaranteed value of $25,000, was decided at Sheepshead Bay in the presence of 25,000 persons, and, for the fourth time in the history of this race, it was won by a poor man's horse, Lowlander, the property of Fred Lowa, winning, with W. C. Daly's Terrifier second and the favorite, Pierce Lorillard's Lamplighter, third.

Dr. Graves Dead.

DENVER, June 21.—Dr. T. T. Graves yesterday afternoon surrendered himself to the authorities and his attorneys will go before the supreme court with a motion that he be released from custody on the ground that there is no legal reason for a continuance of the case, as no appropriation has been made by the county commissioners for the trial of the case.

Lucky Son of a Gun.

LONDON, June 21.—The race for the North Derby stakes of 1500 sovereigns was won by Son of a Gun.

I AM INNOCENT!

(Continued from Yesterday's City Edition.)

ill-feeling existing against her stepmother, and the fact that her father had from $250,000 to $300,000, and if he died without making a will this would go to the children. You will be asked to consider all these things as furnishing a motive for the crime. As a noted writer on criminal law asks, Will the desire to come into an inheritance furnish an active motive to taking a parent's life. It is not necessary for the government to prove a motive. Imputing a motive is not proof. The government states that this defendant had a feeling toward her stepmother amounting nearly to hatred. You are, in judging, to give all parts their due weight. You are not to enlarge one or belittle another. Take Mrs.Gifford's testimony and give it due weight, and then consider the manner of speech of young women as to intensity or extravagance. You want the true conception of the state of mind of this young woman both at the time of the murder and at the time nearly approaching it.

To get a true conception you must separate Mrs. Gifford's testimony from all the rest. You must consider whether the members of the family went to church together, sat together and returned together, in fact, you must consider the general tenor of their lives. Weigh all the facts and satisfy yourselves whether there is anything to justify the conception that there was anything amounting to hatred. Recall the evidence and see whether there is anything to justify a true standpoint in taking into your minds the conception that at about that time the defendant had a feeling toward her stepmother that could properly be called hatred. If it is not a correct conception, then it should not be a controlling idea under which the evidence should be judged. Such a question may be many times worse than any mistake in the evidence. If you start out wrong, then your whole consideration of the case is colored by your wrong conception. The government charges in the indictment, malice aforethought. Before the defendant can be found guilty every material fact must be proven beyond a reasonable doubt.

The justice quoted from the authorities defining a reasonable doubt, and instructed the jury that they should be satisfied not beyond an imaginary doubt, but that it should be proved to a moral certainty.

Now you will observe what the government submits you is largely circumstantial. No witnesses have testified to seeing the actual commission of the crime, but the government seeks to prove the facts of this case by the circumstances, on which you are asked to conclude that the defendant killed Mr. and Mrs. Borden. This is common practice and it is competent for a jury to find a verdict of guilty on circumstantial evidence. Direct evidence is where a witness testifies to actual knowledge of the crime, and all there is in question is to see if the witness is worthy of belief. The chief question is whether the witness may be false. In circumstantial evidence the facts are usually various and the testimony given by a large number of witnesses. When by several it is more difficult to arrange it. The principle which underlies circumstantial evidence we are constantly applying in our business. But sometimes the evidence is direct. For instance, a pistol shot is heard and we go to the room whence it issues, and there find a man dead, with a revolver lying by his side, with one barrel discharged. In such a case when no contradictory evidence is brought forth, it is just for us to conclude that he died by being shot with the pistol. Sometimes the facts are not as direct. This illustrates the case on trial. It is a long process to determine the facts and then, after determining them, we must see if we are justified in believing them. Here is a liability for a two-fold error. First to decide the facts, and second to see if they are sufficient to warrant us in the conviction. This is the critical point of a trial. The law requires you to use great judgment and provides that you shall be free from all complications of law. The result to be drawn must be reasonable and morally certain.

In dealing with circumstantial evidence in such a case as this some substantial considerations have to be borne in mind. One of them is that inasmuch as the conclusion of guilty, if reached at all, must be inferred by the jury from facts that are proved, from that which in your judgment is so important and essential that without it the conclusion of guilty could not be reached, must itself be proved beyond reasonable doubt. But in seeking to establish a case of circumstantial evidence it may often happen that many facts are in evidence not because they are thought to be necessary to the conclusions as it is sought to be proved, but to show that they are not inconsistent with other facts. If any facts of this second class should fail to be proved to your satisfaction that would not prevent you from drawing a conclusion from the other facts if they were sufficient to warrant. In other words, failure to prove an act essential to the conclusion of guilt, a fact which that conclusion would not be reached, is fatal to the government's case, but failure to prove a helpful or not an essential fact may not be so.

Now let me illustrate. Take an essential fact. The necessity of establishing the presence of the defendant in the house when, for instance, her father was killed is a necessary fact. The government cannot expect that you would find her guilty of the murder of her father by her own hand unless you are satisfied that she was where he was when he was murdered.

Now take an instance of a helpful fact, the question of the relation of the hatchet, for instance, of this handleless hatchet. It may have an important bearing on the case or your judgment as to the relation of the defendant to these crimes. Whether the crimes were done by that particular hatchet or not cannot be said, is not claimed by the government that it bears the same essential and necessary relation to the case that the matter of her presence in the house does. It is not claimed by the government but what that killing might have been done with some other instrument.

Take another illustration. I understand the government to claim substantially an alleged fact that the defendant made false statements in regard to her stepmother's having received a note or letter that morning. There is an essential relation to the case. It bears to it the relation of an essential fact. The counsel in his opening, referring to that charge, deliberately said of the defendant that she had told a falsehood in regard to that note. In other words, that she made statements about it which she knew at the time of making them were untrue and the learned district attorney in his closing argument reaffirms that charge against her.

Now what are the grounds on which the government claims that that charge is true? There are three, as I understand it, one that the man who wrote it has not been found; second, that the man or party who brought it has not been found; third, that no letter has been found. And substantially, if I understand it, upon these three grounds you are asked to find that an essential fact, a deliberate falsehood on the part of the defendant, has been established.

Now what answer or reply is made to this charge? First, that the defendant had time to think, that she was not put in a position upon the evidence where she was compelled to make that statement without any opportunity for reflection. If, as the government claims, she had killed her stepmother some little time before, she had a period in which she could go over the matter in her mind.

She must naturally anticipate, she knew that the question at no remote period would be asked where Mrs. Borden was, or if she knew where she was. She might reasonably and naturally expect that question would arise. Again, it would be urged in her behalf what motive had she to invent a story like this? Would it not have answered every purpose for her to have said, and been more natural for her to say simply that her stepmother had gone out on an errand, or to make a call? What motive had she to take upon herself the responsibility of giving utterance to this distinct and independent fact of a letter or note received, with which she might afterwards find herself called to explain if she knew that no such thing was true. Was it a natural thing to say? Constituted as they were, living as they did, taking the general tenor of their ordinary life, was it a natural thing for her to invent such a story? Suppose you look at the case for a moment and contemplate the possibility of there being another assassin than herself. Might it not be a part of the plan or scheme of such person that such a document should appear to withdraw Mrs. Borden from the house. If he afterwards came in and there came upon her and killed her, might he not have found the letter with her, if there was one, or in the room? Might he not have a reasonable and natural wish to remove that as one possible link in tracing himself.

Taking the suggestion on the one side and on the other, judging the matter fairly, not assuming beforehand that the defendant is guilty, does the evidence satisfy you as reasonable men beyond a reasonable doubt about this statement of the defendant in regard to that note?

Sometimes people, judges and writers in dealing with circumstantial evidence have made use of illustrations. They have compared the indispensable facts to the several links in the chain. If one link breaks, the chain ceases to serve its purpose. So in the chain of circumstantial evidence if one essential fact fails to be proved the connection is broken and it could not be legally affirmed, and the conclusion established beyond a reasonable doubt.

Judge Dewey proceeded at length to consider the principles of law governing circumstantial evidence, and said: Now, gentlemen, I am not expressing an opinion as to the guilt of this defendant. Suppose you are satisfied she committed these homicides and she couldn't do it without having blood on her, that she had none on her and had had no time to remove it, then you couldn't say she did it beyond a reasonable doubt. So you see, some facts may be controlled by one fact. The evidence must be such as to produce a reasonable certainty that she committed the deed. Whether this is proved is for you to determine. What time was Mrs. Borden killed, what time was Mr. Borden killed, was defendant in the house at the time. You will consider her statements and all the other evidence bearing on it. Was anybody else likely to do it, and was there any motive for them to do it. What was the weapon used, and what degree of force was used in committing the deed.

Medical experts have been brought before you and have made positive assertions. Now, are they correct? Is it credible to think she killed Mrs. Borden and then later killed her father, and then had gone about her affairs with no appearance which would excite suspicion. And if, as has been suggested, the killing of Mr. Borden was not a part of the original plan, but was an incident afterward—that is a fact to be considered as to whether it is reasonable or not. Considerable importance has been attached to her answers when interviewed about her presence at the time of the murder and she said she was in the barn. The government thinks it is not reasonable because of the presence of excessive heat there, and because there was no dust disturbed on the barn floor. What are the facts that establish you to consider this? There is no rule of law to govern you. I may, in way of suggestion, repeat the words of a great writer on law, which I think very applicable now.

The court then read an extract with reference to the admission of verbal evidence—that oral statements are subject to mistakes because ofttimes they are not expressed just as the speaker intended and are not understood; but when the admissions are deliberately made the evidence affords more satisfaction.

This is merely a suggestion, continued the court, but it expresses a reasonable principle, wise, prudent and proper to act on in this instance. Whether or not there is more liability to error when it relates to statements than when it relates to facts. Those statements must be carefully and thoroughly proved. The government has called in certain medical gentlemen, scientists, experts, and you are to consider their testimony. Following the distinction I have put out with regard to expert testimony—the law requires you to weigh it carefully. Sometimes an opinion in an expert may cause his statements to be biased, sometimes to follow it forward with fear. While they are supposed to testify to things not of common knowledge, yet when the jury comes to pass judgment upon it, they have a full right to use their own judgment of it and its weight, and finally acting, to give to the testimony just such value and weight as it seems to deserve. A surveyor may by careful measurements give a distance between two points. So Professor Wood may say after his tests that he found "I find blood" or "I find no blood." This may be regarded as a matter of opinion. On the other hand if he is called on to testify as to the time of death, this is also a matter of opinion, but it may vary according to the vigor or health of the party, etc. It is to be dealt with as to its essential nature and its importance.

So as to the wounds on the skull. Were they caused by any particular hatchet head? You may conclude. I say first—you are not confined to expert testimony, and second, you are to apply it for yourself. So the weight of the experts' opinions lies with you.

In the closing argument. It is a matter of law that I will instruct you upon, the matter of fact is for you to consider, and whether it was the act of her own hand. It is a principle of law that a person may be indicted in just the form that the district attorney sees fit. She may be convicted if she was concerned in the crime, even if the blows were not struck by her personally. If she personally was concerned in it by abetting, aiding, assisting or encouraging some other person, and was present rendering him assistance, or for the purpose of assisting him. Upon these facts being proven she could be found guilty, but she must have given assistance or encouraged him by virtue of an understanding. She must have assisted in some way such as by watching for a person coming, for instance, or by furnishing an opportunity for escape to the one who struck the blows. The central feature is that she must have been present. If there was another party, and she is proved beyond a reasonable doubt to have been present, she can be found guilty, because in such a case in the eyes of the law she would be a principal. Another thing, you must not allow the fact of the defendant not testifying to weigh against her. The bill of rights provides that no one shall be obliged to implicate himself. The common law provided that no one should have a right in a criminal cause to testify in his own behalf.

The statutes provide that the evidence of a defendant is competent only upon his own request. In this case you are to view the evidence of the defendant as incompetent, and consider it just as if she had no right to testify. Any implication based upon her failure to testify must be driven from your minds. Nor is the failure to demand the right to testify to weigh against her in your minds. There is good and sufficient reason which she could give for not testifying. She is guarded by the law which presumes her innocent until guilt is proven. If a defendant takes the stand he is subject to cross-examination, and may be asked questions which are entirely competent, and which he finds himself unable to answer, not because of incriminating himself, but because he has no knowledge to impart. It may be argued that answers honestly given are untrue, and the facts in evidence, if favorable to himself misconstrued, or misunderstood, and so the defendant is left free to avoid all such risks.

Gentlemen, we have given attention to the evidence. The government charges defendant with these murders, and she denies them. The government has the burden of proof. You are not to be captious, to let the evidence have due weight, remembering that upon the government at all times is the burden of proof. If you are convinced that the case is made out you will render a verdict of guilty, and if not of not guilty. You will be inquired of by the clerk as to each count and degree, and you will answer.

Judge Dewey then took up statements concerning defendant's alleged attitude toward the officers, and the jury was requested to turn over the evidence and see if they could recall any evidence where she had found any fault with them for asking questions or making assertions. Something has been said about her assertions the day before the homicides in relation to an impending disaster, and the jury were requested to consider the evidence on this point and see whether a person meditating a great crime would make such a prediction. Is it a reasonable prediction to offer that she would do so? Take the evidence in regard to the dress. Can you extract from the description given anything which will enable you to identify it, or was any given dress accurately described. Take Mrs. Reagan's testimony. It is suggested that there has been no denial of it. It will be reasonable for you to consider whether Mr. Holmes or the clergyman, or those who started out to get a contradiction, did so without first having ascertained whether it was a report that ought to be denied or not.

The jury was told that the matter they have to decide is of the gravest importance, and Judge Dewey said he knows of no other jury before whom other evidence can be put. The press has added to the excitement by its publications, and the statement was made that the jury has undoubtedly read these accounts. The members in considering the case were cautioned to cast out from their minds any impressions formed from what they have read, and were told that they cannot consistently enter upon a discussion of those reports. Judge Dewey closed as follows: "On entering on your deliberations with impartial, thoughtful minds, you will lift the case above the plane of rage and passion into the clear atmosphere of reason and of law, and we hope this trial may express in its decision some of that justice with which Providence governs the universe of men."

Mr. Knowlton asked at 3 25 that the jury retire, and in the meantime the counsel consider what exhibits shall be presented then.

The Jury Retires.

The court acquiesced, and the jury retired.

District Attorney Moody for the government and Mr. Jennings for the defense examined the skulls, photographs, hatchets, documents, plans, dresses, pieces of wood from the mopboards of the Borden house, and other various bits of evidence of a material form, loaded down Deputy Sheriff Arnold with them, and he retired to the jury room, deposited them and came out.

The jury was alone.

At last they were confronted with the final scene in this great case. Now was the time when, after all the excitement and the fluctuations of public opinion as the evidence proceeded and the arguments became known—they were to give the final answer to it all—to pronounce the momentous decision whether Lizzie Andrew Borden shall walk the earth a free woman, clear of the fearful stigma that for a year has hung like a pall over her. They were exiles for the time and till they again issue with that fateful verdict their deliberations and its results will be awaited by thousands of anxious people.

IN THE DARKEST MOMENT.

Lizzie Given a Beautiful Bouquet of Cut Flowers.

Soon after the jury retired, Miss Lizzie Borden was the recipient of a mysterious looking square parcel. She opened it to find it a kindly remembrance from some well wisher to cheer up her spirits in this the darkest, most critical and anxious moment of her life. It was a large bouquet of cut flowers and as their fragrance wafted in sweetness over to Elder Buck with a smile and a casual remark, and then entered into a conversation with him that lasted some minutes.

It was about quarter of four when the judges left the bench and retired to their room, there to await the return of the jurors.

The defense made motions for the release of John V. Morse and Bridget Sullivan from their bonds as witnesses, and they were granted.

Deputy Sheriff Kirby, who through the trial has been the custodian of the prisoner, told a Standard man this afternoon that she remains remarkably self-possessed and cool, and bears up under the excitement with marvelous fortitude.

Not Guilty.

At 4 35 the jury returned a verdict of not guilty.

THE ARGUMENTS.

Julian Ralph's Opinion of Those of Robinson and Knowlton.

(Julian Ralph in New York Sun.)

Ex-Governor Robinson did not rise to the occasion. There is only one Joseph H. Choate within the ken of New Yorkers, and it is fair to presume that great ability as a cross-examiner is not often allied with an equally high grade of eloquence. It is a pity for Miss Lizzie Borden that she ex-Governor was not able to do justice to the situation, but it is of advantage to the world upon which Mr. Robinson has flashed like a star of the first magnitude to know that he is not in all respects a prodigy unparalleled. It would be expecting a great deal of any lawyer to make the most of the Borden case, since it unquestionably offered the grandest opportunity and widest variety of chances that any modern criminal case has held out to a skillful orator. With a jury chosen because every man on it was a father, what a chance was there to touch the tenderest and noblest nerves that led to the heart, with a girl of spotless life and a Christian career trembling in a prisoner's box, and actually facing a scaffold! What a chance there was to win sympathy for her, with a thick volume of evidence that almost directly after the homicides she had been cast off from friends and relatives, hemmed around by spies, and made conscious that a whole police force had combined to twist every breath and motion into proof of her guilt! What a field for invective, for scorn, for denunciation, for ridicule and indignation a lawyer had at hand, with all the chief elements of the case against her displayed, broken down, disproved, and set at naught! What an opportunity there was for triumph, confident, impressive demand for an acquittal!

Ex-Governor Robinson's speech was commonplace. It never reached up to eloquence and it never reached into the heart of a hearer. Worse yet, it seemed to this correspondent that it was conceived in a wrong spirit—a spirit that might be disastrous to his client in a less clear case. There was never a note of triumph in four hours of talking, nor was there loud declaration of the woman's innocence. Instead of adopting this manner, Mr. Robinson took the defensive to such a degree and to such an extent that he actually spent long and impressive minutes on the subjects that the court had excluded to the advantage of the woman. He talked more than once about the private solid story and about the defendant's confusing testimony at the inquest, all of which he had fought to keep out. It is true that he referred to these things only to warn the jury not to think of them, but one word in that respect would have been priceless where hundreds of words were very dangerous.

Mr. Knowlton made an impression as a pleader. A giant of a man, with a physique of a bull and the voice of a soldier in battle, he sprang upon the arena armored and armed as only a man could be who knew the case by heart, and with equal confidence believed in his own side of it. He endeavored to choose moderate language, and to be considerate, gentle, but it was his earnestness that made his speech memorable, and that was the quality which necessarily made it seem relentless and stern and angry. He is a natural born and redoubtable fighter. He probably wished to be gentle in his summing up of the evidence against General Sherman, who said that war should be made as terrible as possible in order to end it quickly.

The Jury Had a Ride.

The jury put in an appearance at the court room this afternoon much earlier than usual, and instead of walking from the hotel in the extreme heat of mid-day, they were conveyed by carriage. The vehicle used on previous excursions to suburban towns was utilized for this purpose, and on the seat with the driver was Deputy Sheriff Arnold, while on the rear step was Deputy Sheriff Nickerson.

ANOTHER HATCHET.

Ex-Governor Robinson Receives an Express Package from the West.

Ex-Governor Robinson today received by express from some unknown party in the west an old hatchet, which showed evidence of being quite ancient. It was similar to the claw hammer hatchet mentioned in the trial, and had in its head a broken handle.

JOE JEFFERSON BETTER.

Passes Through This City on His Way to Buzzards Bay.

Joseph Jefferson has fully recovered from the illness which prostrated him for a few days in Fall River. He left there on the 8 05 train this morning for this city, en route for Buzzards Bay. He was accompanied by his wife, Mrs. Lyman, and the nurse.

REAL ESTATE SALES.

Henry L. Baker has sold to Edwin Borden land at Horse Neck, containing 5,000 square feet.

Patrick W. Andrews has sold to Benjamin Jones Weeks land in Fairhaven on the north side of Washington street. The sale includes 5,842 rods.

Rudolphus Beetle has sold to Ellie Lussier land on the north side of Beetle street, containing 14.69 rods.

Rev. W. R. Puffer, Of Richford, Vt.

I Vote for Hood's

Forty Years in the Ministry

Rheumatism, Dyspepsia and Insomnia—Great Benefit From Hood's Sarsaparilla.

"I have been taking Hood's Sarsaparilla for four or five months, and am satisfied that it is a very excellent remedy. I have been troubled with rheumatism more or less for a number of years. My back and hips, and indeed my whole body at times, have been afflicted. The rheumatism has been especially severe in my right arm between the elbow and shoulder, which has been so lame that I sometimes feared

I Should Lose the Use of It

entirely. I was in this condition when I began to take Hood's Sarsaparilla, but I had not taken more than a bottle or two when I began to feel better, and when I had taken four bottles, my rheumatism had entirely left me. I have been more free from rheumatism this season than for years. Besides the rheumatism, I, like

Hood's Sarsaparilla Cures

many others of sedentary habits—for I have been a minister of the Methodist Episcopal church forty years—have been troubled with dyspepsia, but while taking the medicine my

Appetite has Been Good,

food digested well and I have gained several pounds. I have also been troubled with insomnia, but since taking Hood's Sarsaparilla, sleep much better." REV. W. R. PUFFER, Richford, Vt.

N. F. Be sure to get Hood's Sarsaparilla.

HOOD'S PILLS cure liver ills, constipation, biliousness, jaundice, sick headache, indigestion.

A RELIGIOUS BOYCOTT.

Methodists Advise Withdrawing Support of World's Fair.

Philadelphia, June 20.—The Methodist ministers of Philadelphia yesterday adopted a resolution declaring that inasmuch as the enemies of the Sabbath have secured the opening of the World's fair on the Lord's day we give it as our judgment that it would be consistent for all Christian and loyal Americans to withhold their patronage from an exhibition kept open on the Christian Sabbath in defiance of the law of God. A resolution criticising the action of the United States appellate court was stricken out.

Church Societies Balked.

Chicago, June 20.—The Methodist and other church societies which threaten to remove their exhibits from the liberal arts section because the exposition is to be kept open on Sundays will find themselves balked. Director General Davis will inform them that goods were received for the period of the fair, and that they will remain until the fair is over.

TO KEEP AWAY THE CHOLERA.

Consul General Collins Confers with Ship Owners.

London, June 20.—James A. Collins, American consul general at London, has had a conference with a number of ship owners and rag importers in regard to the measures to be taken to prevent the introduction of cholera into the United States. The shipowners and dealers promised they would take every precaution against the goods carried or shipped by them being infected with cholera germs.

Justice Blatchford's Condition.

Newport, June 20.—Chief Justice Blatchford's physicians are exceedingly reticent when questioned about their patient. There are reasons to believe that his condition is critical, in spite of reports from the house that morning that he would be himself again in a few weeks. Today it has come from the house that he is rapidly failing, and his death is only a matter of a few days.

Eulalie at Newport.

Newport, June 20.—Infanta Eulalie arrived in the harbor on steamer yacht Susquehanna about 3 o'clock this morning. So quiet was the arrival that those upon other yachts did not know of her arrival until this morning when the ship's flags were run up to the peak. The princess preferred not to be interviewed and gave out the statement that she would receive no invitations of any kind.

New Hampshire Town in Flames.

Henniker, N. H., June 20.—Noyes' block, Preston's block, Senator Preston's house, the meat market and blacksmith shop are now burning. A steamer from Concord has arrived.

TELEGRAPHIC BREVITIES.

Charles H. Porter, of Cheney & Porter, Templeton, has filed a petition in insolvency against the firm. He states that his partner has absconded and is out of the state.

The Kansas state bank commissioner yesterday ordered the State bank of Plainville closed. The capital stock is $50,000, but the amount of liabilities is not obtainable.

Gilbert, the dynamiter, recently discharged from an English prison, arrived at New York this morning on the steamer Chester. He declined to talk.

The Pall Mall Gazette says it is the intention of the government to abandon the financial clauses of the Irish home rule bill, and to substitute clauses empowering the Irish legislature to frame its own budget to the amount of £5,000,000, said budget to be submitted to the imperial government for ratification.

J. & G. Butler, wholesale grocers of Columbus, O., assigned yesterday. Liabilities $450,000; assets $80,000 to $100,000.

Found Dead in a Swamp.

Hartford, June 21.—Emer Mills, a colored man aged 45 years old, was found in a swamp at the foot of Water street. It is supposed he died a hemorrhage. Two weeks ago he was an inmate of the town house.

Stole $16,000.

Ellsworth, Me., June 21.—The defalcation of Fred L. Kent, cashier of the First National bank of Ellsworth, is announced. The amount is about $10,000, of which $10,000 is covered by his bond. The bank loses about $9000.

HAD NO FIRE COMPANY.

Several Stores Burned at Henniker, N. H.—Loss Reaches $40,000.

HENNIKER, N. H., June 21.—A fire broke out here on the corner of Depot and Main streets in Noyes' block yesterday. It spread rapidly and was soon beyond control. The block was of wood and three stories high, and it fell in ruins in less than an hour. The loss on the building is $5000; insured.

The next building burned was a two-story wooden block, and the loss was $8000.

The next building burned was a dwelling owned by Hon. George C. Preston. Loss on house, $4000.

Spreading toward the depot the fire extended to the store bridge, burning J. S. Whitney & Co.'s meat market and W. W. Skillen's blacksmith shop.

Several blocks and dwelling houses took fire, but were saved by the efforts of the owners and citizens. Henniker has no fire company, and the works of the Henniker Spring Water company was of great service. The total losses are estimated from $40,000 to $45,000.

More Crookedness Looked For.

BOSTON, June 21.—The office safe of Charles F. Walker, who was arrested recently, charged with forgery, has been opened by the police inspectors, and a number of blank notes bearing the forged indorsements of Henry S. Walker and A. R. Rogers were found. It is believed that Walker intended securing $20,000 or $30,000 on forged paper and then leave the city.

Earthquakes Down South.

AUGUSTA, Ga., June 21.—A slight earthquake shock was felt here last night.

CHARLESTON, June 21.—A very distinct shock of earthquake was felt here at 11:05 last night.

Caught in the Act.

HUNTINGTON, W. Va., June 21.—Fred Miller, about 30 years of age, was arrested while attempting to assault a girl named Powell, 12 years old.